韓日辞典을 兼한

# NEW STANDARD
## KOREAN-ENGLISH DICTIONARY

새 스탠다드

# 韓英辞典

— 韓英辞典의 決定版 —

明文堂

# 머 리 말

사전이란 지도와 같아서 언어의 사용 방법을 알리는 이정표(里程標)다.
— Barnhart —

언어의 중요성은 새삼 언급하지 않더라도 현대인이라면 누구나 절감하고 있는 바이다. 더구나 급변하는 국제 정세에 비추어 보건대 영어를 모르고서는 도저히 국제 생활에 보조를 맞추지 못할 것이다. 한 마디로 말하여 영어는 어느 한정된 나라 안에서만 제1 외국어로 군림하는 것이 아니라 명실상부한 국제어로서 그 용도가 자못 크다.

그러나 외국어를 자국어(自國語)와 같이 구사한다는 것은 결코 쉬운 일이 아니다. 정확히 읽고 듣는 것뿐 아니라 정확히 쓰고 말할 수 있어야 한다.

사전이란 이런 여러 가지 점을 집대성한 책자로서 학습상·일상생활상 없어서는 아니 될 반려자라 할 수 있다. 이에 우리는 사전 편찬인으로서의 의무를 절감하고, 지대한 목표를 향하여 과감히 착수해 보았다.

그 첫 시도로 영한사전의 최신 결정판 「새 스탠다드 한영사전」을 출간하게 되었다. 본 「새 스탠다드 한영사전」은 단순히 영어 단어를 찾아보기 위한 사전이 아니라, 영어의 실용성을 다각적인 견지에서 다루어 놓음으로써 학습인은 물론 실무자에게도 실질적으로 영어 지침서가 될 수 있게 하였다.

시시각각으로 변천을 거듭하는 영어의 동향(動向)을 충실히 뒤쫓고, 시대성에 예민하게 적응한바, 언필칭 살아 있는 한영사전으로서 그 이용도가 한결 높으리라 믿는다.

본 사전을 기획 편찬함에 있어서 특히 주안점을 둔 사항은 아래와 같다.

1. **실용도 높은 사전** : 실용성을 드높이기 위하여 종전의 사전들과는 그 양상을 달리하여 포켓용으로 가장 알맞는 지면을 택하였다.
2. **정선(精選)된 어휘** : 중·고·대학의 학습에는 물론 일반 실무에 도움을 줄 수 있는 7만 어휘를 엄선 수록하는 한편, 파생어는 그 쓰임새가 높은 것들을, 예문은 영작에 실질적으로 도움이 될 수 있는 것들을 간추려 수록하였다. 아울러 실생활에서 거의 쓰이지 않는 사어(死語)는 전혀 싣지 않음으로써 그에 해당되는

지면을 활용도 높은 시사어에 할애하였다.
3. **충실한 역어**: 우리말 중에서도 사용 빈도수가 높은 50여 기본 표제어에 대해서는 따로 별항을 마련하여 말뜻을 세분하고, 그에 따른 역어와 예문을 풍부하게 실었다.
4. **영미어의 차이점 구명**: 영어(英語)와 미어(美語)의 차이점은 그때그때 역어에서 〈영〉·〈미〉의 방식으로 명시하였다.
5. **각 분야의 전문 어휘 수록**: 현대 생활에 긴밀하게 관련을 갖고 있는 정치·경제·문화·과학·군사 방면의 어휘도 지면을 최대한으로 활용하여 채록하였다.
6. **일본어의 수록**: 영어 공부는 물론 제2 외국어인 일본어 공부도 아울러 할 수 있도록 표제어의 기본 뜻에 해당하는 일본어를 표제어 풀이가 끝난 뒤에다 실어 놓았다.
7. **다양성 있는 부록**: 실생활에 유용도가 높은 영문 편지·일기·전보 등과 영작문 실력을 향상시킬 수 있는 기본 문형(文型)을 부록난에 따로 실었다.

이상 열거한 점들에 주력을 하면서, 적은 지면을 최대한 활용하여 항시 영어 생활 속의 반려로서 그 구실을 다 할 수 있도록 심혈을 기울였다. 그러나 능력이 미치지 못하고, 시간도 부족하여 당초에 의도했던 바가 얼마만큼 본 사전에 반영이 되었는지 의문이다. 아무쪼록 여러분의 끊임없는 성원과 지도 편달에 적응, 미흡한 점은 계속하여 보강·수정해 나갈 작정이다.

끝으로, 본 사전의 출간을 위해 시종일관 길잡이가 되어 주시고, 난관에 봉착할 때마다 바쁜 중에도 자문에 기꺼이 응해 주시고 귀중한 자료를 제공해 주신 여러 관공서·군 기관·학계·업계 등의 관계자 제위께 지면으로나마 심심한 감사를 드림과 동시에 본 사전이 빛을 보게 된 오늘의 영광과 보람을 바라고 오랜 세월 동안 단 하루도 빠짐없이 묵묵히 편찬과 교정에 참여해 주신 여러분께 충심으로 감사를 드리는 바이다.

편저자 씀

# 일 러 두 기

## 🞖 표 제 어

1. 표제어는 고딕체 활자로 표시하였으며, 배열 순서는 가나다순으로 하였다.
   (1) 같은 자모로 표기되는 말은 우리말, 한자어, 접두어, 접미어순으로 실었다.
       **가, 가(加), 가(可), 가-(假), -가(哥)**.
   (2) 우리말이나 한자어에서 글자와 음이 같은 말에는 그 쓰이는 빈도에 따라 수록 순위를 정하고, 표제어의 오른 쪽에다 어깨 번호를 달았다.
       **거리, 거리², 거리³**.
2. 표제어가 한자어인 경우에는 그에 상당하는 한자를 달았다. 그리고 한자를 두 가지로 쓸 수 있는 것은 둘을 병기하였다.
   **수호(修好), 만장(輓章, 挽章)**.
3. 표제어 중 접두어·접미어는 그 앞이나 뒤에 하이픈(-)을 넣었다.
   **최-(最), -인(人)**.
4. 표제어 중 센말·거센말은 병행을 잊지 않고 예삿말과 병기하였다.
   **잘랑잘랑, 짤랑짤랑. 달랑거리다, 딸랑거리다**.
5. 표제어 중 일부는 우리말이고 일부가 한자인 경우에는 아래와 같이 표시함으로써 이를 밝혔다.
   **긴사설(-辭説), 소목장이(小木-)**.
6. 표준어 수록을 원칙으로하여 방언은 싣지 않았으며, 비어·속어 따위는 사용도가 높은 것만 엄선 수록하였다.

## 🞖 본    문

1. 어 의(語義)
   (1) 한 표제어가 몇 가지 다른 뜻을 지니고 있는 경우에는 ①②③……등의 번호로 이를 분리하였다.
       **치우다** ①(정리하다)put things in order;…… ②(딸을)give inmarriage;……③(제거하다) take away; remove; get rid of…….
       **부정(不淨)** ① uncleanliness; dirtines; filthiness; ② an unclean event;……
   (2) 그러나 유사한 차이를 보이는 경우에는 번호를 사용하지 않고 ( )로만 구분하였다.
       **일부러**(고의로) on purpose; intentionally; by design; deliberately (짐짓) knowingly; wittingly (특히) specially; expressly…….
       **추(錘)**(저울의) a weight; …… (낚시줄의) a bob; …… (먹줄의) a pendulum〔weight〕; (시계의) a pendulum weight.
   (3) 표제어마다 가능한 대로 동사형이나 형용사형을 다음과 같이 밝혀 두었다.
       **주문(注文)** ①(맞춤)an order / ~하다 order(a thing) from ② (요구) a request/ ~하다 request.
       **사고(思考)** thought; consideration; contemplation / ~하다 think; consider; speculate; conceive; reflect; cogitate.
   (4) 표제어·용례의 뜻을 보충하고, 역어의 올바른 이해를 도모하고자 역어 뒤 ( ) 안에 뉘앙스의 차이를 명기하였다.
       **자국**(흔적)a mark; a track(한 줄기의); a train (지나간).
       **포좌(砲座)**〔군〕a gun platform; a barbette (성의); …….

2. 역   어(譯語)
  (1) 역어는 현대 영어를 표준어로 하되 필요에 따라서는 속어·구어·비어 따위도 실었다.
    **누다** evacuate; pass / 오줌을 ~ urinate; pass water; piss 《비》.
    **높다** (be) high; lofty tall (코 따위가) elevated- prominent / 하늘 높이 high up in the air; way up in the sky 《미·구》.
    **네** (대답) yes; all right; sure; surely; certainly; O. K. 《미·속》.
  (2) 표제어 또는 역어의 용례가 둘 이상 있을 경우에는 (;)로 구분하였고, 둘 이상의 문장일 경우에는 (,)를 사용하였다.
    **덜렁하다** (겁먹다) feel a shock; get a start / 소식을 듣고 마음이 덜렁했다. The news gave me a shock. The news came as a surprise to me.
  (3) 표제어 중 동의어 및 원말·변한 말 따위의 역어를 하나 내지 둘만 싣고 ⇨ 표를 사용하여 해당 표제어를 참조하게 하였다.
    **눈곱자기** a discharge from the eyes; *a billet-doux* (F) ⇨ 눈곱.
    **염문 (艶文)** a love letter ⇨ 염서 (艶書).
  (4) 큰말과 작은말과 경우 표제어의 역어를 원칙적으로 큰말 쪽에 싣고, 작은말 쪽에서는 ⇨ 표를 하여 큰말을 참조토록 하였다. 단 작은말이 큰말보다 많이 쓰이는 경우에는 작은말 쪽에다 역어를 모았다.
    **찰딱거리다** cling (*to*) ⇨ 철떡거리다.
    **철떡거리다** cling (*to*); stick (*to*) / 옷이 젖어서 철떡거린다 My clothes are wet and cling to my body.
  (5) 표제어 자체의 역어가 불필요하다고 생각되는 경우에는 대표를 하고 용례와 그 역어만 실었다.
    **듯** 대 …듯 마는 듯하다 it hardly seems one way or the other.
  (6) 역어가 영어의 입장에서 보아 외래어인 경우에는 완전히 영어화된 말은 그대로 살려 두되 그렇지 않는 것은 이탤릭으로 표기하고 그 뒤에 국명을 밝혔다.
    **출신 (出身)** (태생) a native (졸업) a graduate (가문) origin / ~교 *one's alma mate* (L).
    **술안주 (-按酒)** relishes; a side dish; *hors d'oeuvres* (F).
  (7) 표제어가 형용사이고 그에 대한 역어가 역시 형용사일 때, 한정·서술 양쪽으로 쓰이는 형용사 앞에는 (be)를 달았다. 그리고 형용사가 둘 이상 나열되는 경우에는 맨 앞의 형용사 에만 (be)를 달았으며, 서술적으로만 쓰이는 형용사와 구를 이루는 경우에는 be를 달아 주었다.
    **다감 (多感)** sensibility; susceptibility / ~하다 (be) sensitive; susceptible.
    **다난 (多難)** many difficulties; lots of trouble / ~하다 be full of troubles [difficulties]; be eventful; be fraught with difficulties.
  (8) 역어가 미국·영국의 어느 한쪽에서만 쓰이는 경우에는 〈미〉·〈영〉으로 표시하였다.
    **발송 (發送)** sending; dispatch; shipping 〈미〉 / ~하다 (물품을) send out; post; ship; despatch; mail 〈미〉.
    **되갈다** ① (논밭을) replow; replough 〈영〉 ② (가루 따위를) regrind.
  (9) 역어에 대하여 특정의 연결 관계를 보이는 관계어는 ( )로 싸서 이해를 하는 데 도움이 될 수 있게 하였다.
    **국으로** within keeping (of *one's position*); within ……
3. 관사의 용법
  (1) 역어가 가산 명사(Countable) 일 때는 복수형을 제외하고 관사 "a"를 달았다. 그리고 가산·비가산(Uncountable) 일 때는 공히 사용되는 것은 "a"를 [ ] 안에 넣어 생략할 수 있음을 암시 하였다.
    **알** ① (물고기·새 따위의) an egg ② (달걀) a chicken egg ③ (낱알) a grain; a berry / ~을 낳다 lay eggs; spawn.
    **압수 (押收)** [법] confiscation; [a] seizure; attachment / ~하다 seize.
  (2) 언제나 정관사를 수반하는 말에는 the를 붙였다.

**우두머리** ① (꼭대기) the top ② (사람) the top; the boss.
### 4. 명사의 복수형
명사의 역어로서 그 복수형이 불규칙적 변화를 하는 것, 또는 규칙 변화를 하지만 틀리기 쉬운 것 따위에는 (*pl.*) 안에 변화형을 표시하였고, 단수형은 (*Sing.*) 안에 표시하였다.
**추가**(追加) an addition (추가물) an appendix; an addendum (*pl.*-da).
**낙인**(烙印) a brand [mark]; a stigma (*pl.* ~s.-mata).
**자료**(資料) material; data (*Sing.* datum).
### 5. 전치사와 목적어
역어가 취하는 전치사·목적어는 ( ) 안에 기입하였다. 단 역어가 숙어인 경우에는 전치사에 ( )를 씌우지 않았다.
**추적**(追跡) chase; pursuit; tracing; following (*after*) / ~하다 pursue; follow (*after*); give chase (*to*).
**업히다** ride on (*a person's*) back; be carried on (*a person's*) back.

## ✕ 기　　호

[ ] 학술어(學術語) 기타 전문 용어(專門用語) 임을 나타낸다.
　　**사낭**(砂囊) ① [군] a sandbag ② [조] a gizzard.
( ) (1) 표제어가 한자어일 때 한자를 기입하였다.
　　**순응**(順應) adaptation; accommodation; adjustment.
　(2) 역어의 약자 또는 화학기호를 표시할 때 사용하였다.
　　**질소**(窒素) [화] nitrogen (기호: N).
　　**지능**(智能) intelligence; intellect / ~지수 intelligence quotient (I.Q.).
　(3) 문법상·어법상의 관계를 보이기 위하여 보충어를 기입하였다.
　　**동일시하다**(同一視一) identify (*a thing*) with (*another*); treat (*matters*) without discrimination.
　　**돌관**(突貫) a charge; [a] drush / ~하다 charge (*on*); rush (*at*).
( ) 표제어·복합어·용례의 뜻을 부연하거나, 바꾸어 말하거나, 동의어 따위를 기입하는 데 사용 하였다. 그밖에 역어·역문의 용법상의 주의·보충 사항 따위를 기입하였다.
　　**섯사다** (의심이) be resolved; be dispelled (노여움이) relent; fade.
　　**민가**(民家) ① (개인 집) a private house ② (일반 집) a commoner's house.
[ ] 그 부분을 생략할 수 있을 때를 나타내었다.
　　**선술집** a [stand] bar; a [drinking] tavern; a grogshop 〈영〉.
　　**도급**(都給) a contract [for work]; undertaking.
[ ] 그 부분이 바로 앞의 말과 대체될 수 있음을 나타내었다.
　　**빈고**(貧苦) the hardship [pinch, pressure] of poverty.
　　**빈미주룩하다** (be) slightly showing [protruding].
~ 표제어와 연결되어 표제어를 대신하거나, 복합어 또는 예문을 이룬다.
　　**절개**(切開) incision; operation; removal / ~하다 incise; operate (*on*) / ~수술 an operation / ~하다 ; 종기를 ~하다 incise a tumor.
　　**정상**(正常) normalcy; normality / ~하다 (be) normal / ~화 normalization / ~으로 돌아가다 return to normalcy [normal condition].
／ 용례가 둘 이상일 때 그사이를 구분하였다.
　　**바다** the sea (대양) the ocean / ~건너 beyond [across] the sea / 고요한 ~ a calm [placid] sea / 푸른 ~ the blue expanse of water.

# 약 어 표

## 1. 전문어

| | | | | | |
|---|---|---|---|---|---|
| 〔건〕 | 건축(建築) | 〔상〕 | 상업(商業) | 〔전〕 | 전기(電氣) |
| 〔경〕 | 경제(經濟) | 〔생〕 | 생물(生物), 생리(生理) | 〔정〕 | 정치(政治) |
| 〔고〕 | 고고학(古考學) | | | 〔조〕 | 조류(鳥類) |
| 〔공〕 | 공학(工學) | 〔수〕 | 수학(數學) | 〔종〕 | 종교(宗教) |
| 〔군〕 | 군사(軍事) | 〔식〕 | 식물(植物) | 〔지〕 | 지리(地理), 지질(地質) |
| 〔기〕 | 기계(機械) | 〔심〕 | 심리학(心理學) | | |
| 〔논〕 | 논리학(論理學) | 〔약〕 | 약학(藥學) | 〔천〕 | 천문(天文) |
| 〔농〕 | 농업(農業) | 〔어〕 | 어류(魚類) | 〔철〕 | 철학(哲學) |
| 〔동〕 | 동물(動物) | 〔언〕 | 언어(言語) | 〔체〕 | 체육(體育) |
| 〔문〕 | 문학(文學) | 〔역〕 | 역사(歷史) | 〔충〕 | 곤충(昆蟲) |
| 〔물〕 | 물리(物理) | 〔예〕 | 예술(藝術) | 〔한〕 | 한의학(漢醫學) |
| 〔미〕 | 미술(美術) | 〔윤〕 | 윤리학(倫理學) | 〔항〕 | 항공(航空) |
| 〔민〕 | 민속(民俗) | 〔음〕 | 음악(音樂) | 〔해〕 | 해부(解剖) |
| 〔법〕 | 법률(法律) | 〔의〕 | 의학(醫學) | 〔해양〕 | 해양학(海洋學) |
| 〔사〕 | 사회(社會) | 〔인〕 | 인쇄(印刷) | 〔화〕 | 화학(化學) |

## 2. 외래어

| | | |
|---|---|---|
| (Russ)…Russian | 러시아어 | |
| (Chin)…Chinese | 중국어(中國語) | |
| (Sans)…Sanskrit | 범어(梵語) | |
| (It)…Italian | 이탈리아어 | |
| (Ar)…Arbic | 아라비아어 | |
| (Gk)…Greek | 그리스어 | |
| (G)…German | 도이취어 | |
| (L)…Latin | 라틴어 | |
| (F)…French | 프랑스어 | |
| (J)…Japanese | 일본어(日本語) | |
| (S)…Spanish | 스페인어 | |
| (P)…Portuguese | 포르투갈어 | |

## 3. 기 타

| | | |
|---|---|---|
| 〈영〉영어(英語) | Britishism | |
| 〈미〉미어(美語) | Americanism | |
| 《구》구어(口語) | Colloquialism | |
| 《속》속어(俗語) | Slang | |
| 《고》고어(古語) | Archaic Word | |
| 《문》문어(文語) | Literary Language | |
| 《시》시어(詩語) | Poetic Diction | |
| 《비》비어(卑語) | Vulgarism | |
| 《속담》 俗談 | Proverb | |
| 《아》소아어 Children's Language | | |
| 《영·구》영국 구어(英國口語) Colloquial Britishism | | |
| 《영·속》영국 속어(英國俗語) Slang, Britishism | | |
| 《미·구》미국 구어(美國口語) Colloquial Americanism | | |
| 《미·속》미국 속어(美國俗語) Slang, Americanism | | |

**가** ①《가장자리》an edge; a border; a margin; a brink; a verge 《옆·곁》a side/연못~ the margin of a pond/강~ a riverside/길~ the roadside; the wayside ②《끝》 the end; the limit; [the] bounds. ふち

**가**(加) addition/ ~하다 add; plus. か

**가**(可) 《성적》 C; pass; fair 《좋음》 good; right/~히 짐작할 수 있다 It can readily be imagined that…. よいこと

**가-**(假) 《임시의》 temporary; provisional 《잠시의》 transient 《비공식의》 informal 《가짜의》 false; assumed/~계약 provisional contract/~계정 temporary account. かりー

**가**(家) a man/혁명~ a revolutionist; a revolutionary/문학~ a literary man/자본~ a capitalist. —か

**가**(街) a street; an avenue; St.《고유명사용》/3~ the 3rd St./은행~ the banking area. ちまた. まち

**가**(歌) 《노래》 song/애국~ the national anthem. —か. うた

**가가**(家家) every[each] house; all the houses. いえごと

**가가 대소**(呵呵大笑) a great[a good] laugh; a roar[a burst] of laughter/~하다 have a good laugh; laugh heartily[loudly]. かかたいしょう

**까까머리** a head shaved bald; a close-cropped head. まるぼうず

**가까스로** barely; narrowly; with difficulty; laboriously; with much effort/~ 도망치다 have a narrow escape. やっと

**가까와지다** 《때·거리가》 approach; be at hand 《사이가》 draw near; make friends with/완성에 ~ be near completion/종말에 ~ draw to a close[an end]. ちかくなる

**가까이** [near] at hand; close by; handy/~ 가다 approach; draw[come] near/~하다 make friends with; mix in *one's* company; make up to/나쁜 친구들을 ~하지 말아라 Keep away from bad company. ちかく

**가가 호호**(家家戶戶) each[every] house; all the houses. いえごと

**가각**(苛刻) brutality; cruelty; severity/~하다 (be) cruel; severe; brutal; heartless. むごくきびしいこと

**가간사**(家間事) domestic affairs; *one's* family affairs. うちのできごと

**가감**(加減) 〖수〗addition and subtraction; increase and decrease/ ~하다 add and deduct; moderate 《조절》adjust/~ 승제(乘除) the four species; addition, subtraction, multiplication and division. かげん

**가깝다** ①《거리》 (be) near; be close [near] by; be not far off; be [close] at hand ②《시간》 be near[close] at hand; draw near; be comming on ③ 《관계》 be close to; be intimate with; be related to. ちかい

**가건물**(假建物) a temporary building.

**가게** a shop《영》; a store《미》《노점》a stall/~를 보다 tend the shop/ ~를 내다 open a shop/구멍~ a penny candy store. みせ

**가격**(價格) 《가치》 worth; value 《값》 price/시장~ the market price/ ~표 a price list/일정한 ~으로 at a fixed price/~ 인상 a price advance/ ~ 절하 reduction; discount/~ 표기 declaration of value/공정[협정] ~ the official[stipulated] price. ねだん

**가결**(可決) approval; adoption; passage; decision/~하다 pass; carry; approve; adopt; vote/그 동의는 5표의 차로 ~되었다 The motion was carried by a majority of five. かけつ

**가결의**(假決議) a temporary decision; a provisional resolution. かりけつぎ

**가경**(佳景) fine scenery; a picturesque scene; a wonderful view. かけい

**가경**(佳境) a delightful[an interesting; an exciting] part; a climax; a pleasant[beautiful] spot/얘기는 ~에 들어간다 The plot thickens. かきょう

**가계**(家系) a family line; lineage; pedigree; genealogy; ancestry/~도 a family tree; genealogical. かけい

**가계**(家計) housekeeping; livelihood; family budget/ ~부 a domestic account book; a petty cashbook/ ~비 household expenses/ ~가 넉넉지 못하다 be badly off. かけい

**가계약**(假契約) a provisional[an temporary] contract. かりけいやく

**가고**(家故) an accident in a family; domestic[family] incidents.

**가곡**(歌曲) 《노래》 a song 《곡조》 a melo

dy; a tune/ ~집(集) a collection of songs. かきょく

**가공(加工)** manufacturing; working; treatment 《보석 따위의》cutting/ ~하다 manufacture; work upon/ ~품 processed[finished] goods/보세 ~ bonded processing. かこう

**가공(架空)** ①《공상적》 fiction/ ~의 unreal; imaginary; fictitious ②《공중 가설》 ~의 overhead; aerial/~하다 construct[build] in the air[overhead; aerially]. かくう

**가공사(假工事)** 〖건〗 temporary construction[works]. かりこうじ

**가공적(架空的)** visionary; fictitious; imaginary/ ~ 이상 세계 a Utopia/~ 이론 a theory built on thin air. かくうてき

**가과(假果)** 〖식〗 a pseudo-carp; an accessory[a spurious] fruit. かか

**가관(可觀)** a sight [worth seeing]; a spectacle; an object of interest; an affraction; a highlight(미)/ ~이다 be a sight [worth seeing]/앞으로의 전개가 ~이다 The future development may well be watched with keen interest. みるべきこと

**가교(架橋)** bridge building[construction]/ ~하다 [build a] bridge/ ~ 공사 bridge construction; bridgework/강에 ~하다 bridges a river. かきょう

**가교(假橋)** a temporary[makeshift] bridge. かりばし

**가교사(假校舍)** a makeshift school building. かりこうしゃ

**가구(家口)** a household 《식구》a family 《집》 a house. いえのこうす

**가구(家具)** [a piece of] furniture; upholstery/ ~장이 a cabinet maker; a joiner/ ~점(店) a furniture store [shop]. かぐ

**가꾸다** ①《자라게 하다》grow; cultivate; rear ②《치장하다》decorate. くえだてる

**가꾸러뜨리다** throw down ⇒거꾸러뜨리다. くつがえす

**가꾸러지다** fall head first ⇒거꾸러지다. たおれる

**가꾸로** inversely; conversely; in the wrong way 《안팎이》inside out 《상하가》upside down/ ~ 떨어지다 fall head foremost. さかさまに

**가권(家眷)** one's family ⇒식구. かけん

**가구(佳句)** a beautiful[happy, fine] sentence[phrase, passage]. かく

**가규(家規)** the rules[the customs] of a family.

**가극(歌劇)** 《연》 an opera; a lyric drama/ ~ 여우 an opera-singer/ ~장 an opera house/소녀 ~단 a girl's opera company. かげき

**가끔** occasionally; once in a while/ ~ 들르다 drop in from time to time; make frequent calls (at); frequent (a place). たびたび

**가금(家禽)** domestic fowls; poultry/ ~ 상인 a poulterer. かきん

**가급적(可及的)** as … as possible; as … as one can/ ~이면 if possible; if one can help it. なるべく

**가긍하다(可矜—)** (be) poor; pitiful; touching; miserable. かわいそう

**가기(家忌)** memorial services for one's ancestors. うちのそせんのまつり

**가기(佳期)** 《좋은 철》 a good[favorable] season 《첫 애인을 만날 시기》high time to meet one's first sweetheart 《혼기》 marriageable age. よいじき

**가기(嫁期)** marriageable age for women ⇒혼기(婚期). よめいりどき

**가기(歌妓)** a professional woman singer; an entertainer; a songstress; a singing girl. うたのじょうずなげいぎ

**가나다** 《한글》the Korean alphabet/ ~ 순으로 하다 alphabetize; arrange in alphabetical order.

**가나오나** wherever one may go[be]; always; all the time; constantly/ ~ 그는 말썽을 일으킨다 He is a constant troublemaker. いつも

**가난** poverty; indigence; destitution; want; penury/~하다 poor; destitute; needy; in want/《몹시 ~한 사람 a poverty-stricken man/~해지다 become poor; be impoverished; be reduced to poverty. びんぼう

**가난듣다** want; lack; be in want[need] of; run out of; be deficient in; be short of. まずしくなる

**가난뱅이** a poor man; a pauper 《총칭》the poor/ ~는 쉴 겨를이 없다 Poor men have no leisure. びんぼうにん

**가납(嘉納)** 《물건의》acceptance 《충고의》approval; appreciation/~하다 approve; appreciate; accept. かのう

**가납금(假納金)** a deposit; a cover. かのうきん

**가납사니** a talkative person; a chatterbox; a tattler; a prattler; a rattler 《고자장이》a taleteller. おしゃべりするひと

**가내(家內)** a family; a household/ ~ 공업 domestic[home] industry/ ~ 일동이 다 편안하신지요 Are your family all well? かない

**가냘프다** (be) slender; slim; delicate; fragile; frail; feeble. ひよわい

**까놓다** open[unlock] one's mind; unbosom oneself; disburden oneself (of a secret).

**가누다** control[handle] oneself/그는 몸을 가누지 못할 정도로 취했었다 He was as drunk as dead. よくささえる

**가느다랗다** (be) very thin ⇒가늘다.

**가느스름하다** (be) rather slender[thin, fine]. ややほそい

**가는귀 먹다** be a little deaf; become somewhat hard of hearing. 꾸가少し遠い

**가늘다** 《목소리가》(be) thin 《섬세하다》slender 《실 따위가》fine/가는 목소리 a thin voice/가는 손 a slender hand/

가는 실 a fine thread[line]. ほそい

**가늠** 《헤아림》 guess 《겨냥》 aiming 《대중》 estimate／～보다 guess; aim; estimate／～쇠 the gunsight; the front sight／～자 the backsight; the rear sight [on a gun] ねらい

**가능**(可能) possibility／～하다 (be) possible; feasible; practicable／～하면 if possible; if I can 《형편이 되면》 if convenient／～한 한 빨리 as soon as possible. かのう

**가능성**(可能性) possibility; potentiality／～이 있다 be possible 《실행할》 be feasible. かのうせい

**가다** ⇒별항 참조.

**까다**¹ ①《껍질을》 peel; rind; pare; skin; shell; hull ②《새끼를》 hatch; incubate ③《안다》 sit on eggs. かわをむく

**까다**² 《입으로》 tell; talk; sophisticate／까지다 become sophisticated／뻥을 ～ tell a lie; talk big. しゃべる

**까다**³ 《신문 따위에서》 condemn; criticize severely; attack. うちたおす

**까다**⁴ 《제하다》 deduct; subduct; subduce; recoup／그 비용은 내 월급에서 깠다 The cost was taken away[deducted] from my pay. さしひく

**가다가** 《때때로》 sometimes; once in a while; occasionally; now and then; on occasion. たまには

**가다듬다** ①《전신차리다》 brace oneself [up]; brace[strain, tighten] one's nerves 《안정시키다》 calm[collect] oneself; gather one's scattered wits ②《목소리를》 put one's voice in tune; cultivate one's voice. ととのえる

**가다랭이** 《어》 a bonito; a shipjack.

**까다롭다** ①《성미가》(be) particular, fastidious; hard to please／까다로운 사람 a particular person; a man hard to please／까다롭게 굴다 be particular (about) ②《문제 따위가》 (be) troublesome; complicated; difficult／까다로운 문제 a delicate matter; a ticklish question. ややこしい

**가다리** 《농》 plowing[ploughing《영》]; paddy land forwages paid by the strip.

**가닥** a piece; a strand. かせ、より

**까닥거리다, 까딱거리다** nod repeatedly; bob one's head up and down 「고덕이다. しきりにうなずく

**까딱수**(-手) a speculative[risky] move; a shallow trick; a risky measure.

**까딱없다** (be) safe and sound 「끄떡없다. びくともしない

**까딱하면** very nearly (do)／～ 화를 낸다 get easily excited; get angry on the slightest provocation. ひょっとすれば

**가단성**(可鍛性) malleability.

**까닭** 《이유》 reason; why 《원인》 a cause 《사정》 circumstances; the matter／무슨 ～으로 why／～없이 without any reason／무슨 ～인지 for some reason or other; somehow or other. ため

**가담**(加擔) ①《원조》 help; assistance; aid／～하다 take part in; side; cast in one's lot with ②《가맹》 participation; confederacy 《공모》 conspiracy; complicity／～하다 take part in; be a party to; conspire[fall in] with／～자 a conspirator. かたん

**가당**(可當) 《합당》 being right 《감당》 being adequate／～하다 《온당》 (be) reasonable; proper; right 《감당》 (be) able to cope with. よくまとを得ていること

**가당찮다**(可當—) (be) unreasonable; unjust 《온당찮다》 improper; excessive 《엄청나다》 extravagant 《난감하다》 hard; touch／가당찮은 요구[값] an excessive demand[unreasonable price]. ふごうりだ

**가대**(家垈) a homestead; a home and its site; a house and lot; a residence 《농가의》 a farmstead. いえのしきち

**가대**(假貸) ①《용서》 forgiveness; forbearance; mercy; pardon tolerate ②《대여》 lending generously／～하다 forgive; forbear 《대여》 lend generously; deliver up.

**가대인**(家大人) my father. ちちの謙稱

**가댁질** a game something like tag／～하다 play tag. おにごっこ

**가도**(街道) a highway; a road; a highroad; a thoroughfare／경인 ～ the Kyung-In highway. かいどう

**가도**(家道) ①《가풍》 family customs; family traditions ②《가규》 livelihood; family morality. かどう

**가독**(家督) the headship of a family 《가산》 a family estate; an inheritance; a patrimony／～ 상속인 an heir; an heiress(여자). かとく

**가돈**(家豚) my son. じぶんのこ

**가동**(家僮) a boy servant; a page 《하인》 a servant; a menial. かどう

**가동, 가동성**(可動, 可動性) mobility; movability／～의 movable; mobile／～ 장치 movable equipment. かどうせい

**가동**(稼動) operation; work／～를 the rate of operation; the working ratio／～ 시설 available[working, operative] equipments.

**가두**(街頭) 《모퉁이》 a street corner 《십자로》 a crossing 《가로》 a street／～에서 in[on] the street／～ 연설(선거의) a stump speech／～ 녹음 a street corner transcription. がいとう

**가두다** shut in[up]; confine (one); lock in; keep (one) indoors; hold (one) for a prisoner; imprison in. かこう

**가둥거리다** sway one's hips／가둥가둥 swaying one's hips. しりをゆすりうごかす

**가드락거리다** strut 「거드럭거리다.

**가득, 가뜩**¹ full; crowded／～하다 be full (of); be filled with／～ 차다 be chockfull／한 잔 ～ a glass full; 컵에 ～ 붓다 fill a cup to the brim. たっぷり

**가뜩**² 《그러잖아도》 besides ⇨가뜩이나.

**가득가득, 가뜩가뜩** full [to the brim]; to the full; packed; close[ly]; tight [ly]/~하다 (each one) be full. いっぱい
**가뜩이나** to add to; in addition to; more over/~곤란한데 to add to one's misery; to make matters worse. そのうえ
**가득하다** (be) full (of); filled (with); be filled to the brim; be full up/가득히 full; filled/가득히 담다 stuff full; pack solid. いっぱい. なみなみ
**가든하다** (be) light; nimble; agile/가든히 lightly; nimbly. かるい
**가들거리다** keep strutting
**가등(街燈)** a street light[lamp]. がいとう
**가라말** an all-black horse.
**가라사대** say/공자 ~ Confucius said…/성경에 ~ The Bible says…. いわれるのに
**가라앉다** ①(물속으로) sink; go down; settle down; descend/배는 이물부터 가라앉았다 The ship settled down by the bow. ②(고요해지다) become quiet; calm down《풍파가》go[die] down; subside ③(마음·성질이) recover one's composure; restore the presence of mind; become calm; calm down ④(부기·고통 등이) abate《경감》subside; go down; sink (내리다) fall. しずむ. おちつく
**가라앉히다** ①(침몰) sink; send to the bottom; make dregs settle ②(마음을) calm[compose] oneself; keep cool; gather one's wits ③(조용해지게) calm; quiet down; still/성을 ~ soothe one's ruffled nerves ④(고통 따위를) allay; alleviate; lessen; lighten; mitigate /진통을 ~ allay[relieve] labor pains.
しずめる. おちつかせる
**가락¹** ①(음조) a key; a pitch; a tune; tone ②(박자·장단) time; rhythm/~에 맞춰 to the time of (the music) ③(솜씨) dexterity; skill; effectiveness.
きょくのただしいちょうし
**가락²** ①(방추(紡錘)) a spindle; a distaff ②(갯수) a stick/한 ~ a stick of

## 가 다

①(일반적으로) go; proceed; travel; frequent (a place); attend (school); (a road) lead to (the station); leave for (Mokpo); (I will) come (to see you) /미국으로 가는 비행기 a plane for America 집 쪽으로~make for the house/왼편으로 ~ turn to the left/가는 도중에 on one's [the] way to; enroute to/이 길은 런던으로 가는 길이다. This road goes to London/산책하러 나가다. go for a walk/하루에 10마일을 ~ make [measure, do] ten miles a day/그는 미국에 가 버렸다. He has gone to America/어디 갔다 왔나 —일본에 갔다 왔네 Where have you been? —I have been to the Japan/그가 죽은 다음에 그의 재산은 누구의 손에 가는가? To whom did the property go when he died?/그는 언제나 형에게 가서 도움을 청했다. He always goes to his brother for help/해 지기 전에 다녀오기는 어려울 것이다. It will be difficult for us to be back before sun set./그 친구 집에는 다시 가지 않겠다. I shall never darken his door [visit him]/저리 가라 Get[Go] away!; Away [Be off, Get along] with you!; Be gone!/걸어서 30분이면 갈 수가 있다 It's only 30 minutes walk./내 핸드백이 어디에 갔나 Where is my handbag I wonder?

②(꺼지다) be out; go out/전기불이 갔다 The electric lights are out[have gone out]., Electric light has failed.

③(죽다) die; pass away; depart (from) this life/그는 가고 없다 He is dead and gone., He is no more.

④(시간, 세월이) pass; pass away[by]; go by; elapse; fly/세월 가는 줄도 모르다 be unconscious of the flight[the elapse] of time/시간이 감에 따라서 as time passes/세월은 빠르게도 가는구나 How quickly time flies!

⑤(없어지다, 변하다) spoil; go bad; rot; get stale(생선 따위의 맛이) turn sour(시어지다)/더위에 이 음식도 맛이 갔다 This food was spoiled by the heat.

⑥(보존되다) wear; last; be durable; keep (good); hold; endure《목숨이》 live out; survive/양식은 1주일도 가지 못할 것 같다 The provisions will not last for a week./이 물건은 오래 가지 못할 것 같소 I am afraid this stuff won't wear well./이 환자는 앞으로 1년도 못 갈 것 같다 The patient will not stand another year./그의 저런 상태로는 앞으로 한 시간도 가지 못할 것 같습니다 I fear from his condition that he will not have an hour to live.

⑦(금, 주름 따위) get creased; be wrinkled/주름간 얼굴 a wrinkled face

⑧(필요하다, 들다) be needed[required]/그것은 많은 손이 가야만 한다 It requires a great deal of care.

⑨(무게·값이) cost; be worth; weigh /이것은 5불 정도 갈 것이다 It will cost five dollars/구두 한 켤레에 2,000원 간다. The market price of shoes is 2,000 won a pair/그의 중량은 180 파운드 간다 His weighs 180 pounds.

(gluten candy).　つむ
**가락국수** Korean noodle.　うどん
**가락지** a set of twin rings.　ゆびわ
**가람(伽藍)** 〖종〗 a Buddhist temple; a cathedral.　がらん
**가랑눈** fine[powdery] snow.　こなゆき
**가랑니** a young louse (*pl.* lice); a nit; a baby louse.　ちいさいしらみ
**가랑머리** hair plaited in two pigtails [queues].　ふたまたあみのとうはつ
**가랑무우** a bifurcated radish; a radish having a forked root.
　ふたまたになった大根
**가랑비** a drizzle; light[drizzling] rain ∕ ～가 내리다 It is drizzling.　こさめ
**가랑이** a crotch; a fork∕바짓～ the crotch of a pair of pants.　また
**가랑잎** ① dead[withered] leaves ② 《떡갈잎》 an oak leaf.　おちば
**가래**¹ 〖생〗《담(痰)》phlegm; sputum(*pl.* sputa)∕ ～를 뱉다 spit [out]; expectorate phlegm.　たん
**가래**² 〖식〗 a wild walnut∕ ～나무 the wild walnut tree.　ひさぎ
**가래**³ 《갯수》 a piece; a long round chunk ∕엿 한 ～ a piece of taffy∕～떡 glutinous rice-jelly in the form of rounded sticks.　まるめてほそながくきったもの
**가래**⁴ 《농기구》 a spade; a plough; a plow《미》.　すき
**가래다** distinguish; discriminate; tell∕ 시비를 ～ distinguish right from wrong.　むかいあってせびをあらそう
**가래질** 〖농〗 spading; plowing∕～하다 plow; turn the soil with a three-man plow.　鋤で土を鋤きおこすこと
**가래침** spittle; spit∕～을 뱉다 spit; expectorate∕마루에 ～을 뱉지 말라 No spitting on the floor.　たんつば
**가래톳** an inflammation[a swelling] of the lymphatic glands in the groin; a bubo ∕ ～이 서다 have an inflammation of a lymphatic; a lymphatic is swollen.
**가량(假量)**¹ 《쯤》 about; some; approximately∕30명 ～ some thirty people∕두 시간 ～ 지나면 in about two hours ∕2백원 ～ about 200*won*.　くらい。ばかり
**가량(假量)**² estimate ⋯어림∕～없다 《터무니 없다》 be unreasonable 《짐작할 수 없다》 be beyond measure ∕네 말이 ～없다 Your story is quite absurd.
**가량가량하다** be thin-faced; be thin but look healthy; look[be] some thin and elastic.
**가려잡다** select; pick; take.　えらびとる
**가려하다(佳麗—)** (be) beautiful; fine; lovely; charming; picturesque; (be) nice; is pretty.　きよくつくしい
**가련하다(可憐—)** (be) poor; pitiful; pathetic; sad; miserable∕가련히 여기다 take pity on (*one*)∕가련한 친구로군 What a poor fellow he is!　かわいそうだ
**가렴(苛斂)** exacting; demanding; extorting∕ ～하다 exact; extort∕ ～ 주구(誅求) extortion; exaction.　かれん
**가렵다** 《피부가》 (be) itchy; itching∕온 몸이 ～ I feel itchy all over.　かゆい
**가령(假令)** [even] if; though; although; supposing that; granted that; suppose; for example.　たとえば
**가례(家禮)** a family code of etiquette [decorum]; the costomary formalities [proprieties] of a family.
**가례(嘉禮)** a state ceremony; an august ceremonial; Grand Ceremony.かれい
**가로** 《폭》 width 《부사적》 across; sideways; horizontally; crosswise; transversely∕ ～의 sidelong; horizontal∕ ～ 3피트 three feet in wide∕～쓰다 write sideways.　よこ
**가로(街路)** a street; a road; an avenue 〈미〉; a boulevard∕ ～수 street[road side] trees∕～등 a street lamp[light]∕ ～ 청소부 a street cleaner.　がいろ
**가로놓이다** lie; lie sideways; lie across.
**가로누이다** lay (*a thing*); lay (*a thing*) down[across].　よこにたをす
**가로닫이** a sliding door[window].やりど
**가로되** say∕옛 말에 ～ An old saying has it that….　いうには
**가로막다** interrupt (*one*); obstruct (*the view*); block[bar] (*the way*)∕ 길을 ～ block the way; bar the passage; stand in another's way.　ふさぐ
**가로막히다** get obstructed; get blocked [barred]; cut off.　ふさがる
**가로말다** arrogate; usurp; take over unduly.　ひきつづく
**가로변(街路邊)** the roadside.　みちの道端
**가로새다** drop out of (*ranks*); fall out; escape.　こっそりたちさる
**가로서다** ①《빠져 나서다》 drop out of (*ranks*); fall out ②《옆으로 서다》 stand sideways; stands aside; stand looking aside.　よこむきにたつ
**가로세로** ①《명사적》 breadth and length ②《부사적》 longitudinally and latitudinally; breadthwise and lengthwise; horizontally and vertically 《사방으로》 in all directions; in every direction; to all points.　たてよこ
**가로쓰기** writing in a lateral line; writing from left to right.　よこかき
**가로지르다** 《건너지르다》 put (*a bar*) across 《가로긋다》 draw (*a line*) across 《건너가다》 cross; traverse; go[cut] across; intersect.　よこにおく
**가로차다** seize [on the way]; snatch; usurp; intercept.　よことりする
**가로채다** 《피동-》 snatch away (*a thing*) from (*one*); seize; intercept. ひったくる
**가로퍼지다** grow sideways.よこにひろがる
**가뢰** 〖종〗 a blister-beetle; a Spanish fly; cantharides; a meloid.
**가료(加療)** medical treatment∕～중입니다 be under medical treatment.
　かりょう

**가루** 《분말》 powder; dust 《곡식 가루》 flour; meal／ ∼ 비누 powder soap; soap flakes／ ∼ 우유 powder[ed] milk; evaporated milk／ ∼ 식료 우 food／ ∼약 a [medicinal] powder／옥수수 ∼ corn flour. こな

**가르다** ①《분할》 divide; part; sever; split／다섯으로 ∼ divide into five parts／머리를 한가운데서[오른쪽에서] ∼ part one's hair in the middle[on the right]／부부의 의를 ∼ sever husband and wife; cut a husband from his wife. ②《분배》 distribute; divide; share; portion [out]／음식을 갈라먹다 share food with others／다섯 몫으로 ∼ divide into five shares ③《분류》 sort [out]; group; classify; assort／갈라 두다 keep (things) apart／크게 둘로 ∼ classify into two large groups ④《판단·구별》 discriminate; distinguish; know[tell] (A) from (B); judge／시비를 ∼ discriminate right from wrong. わける

**가르치다** 《지식을》 teach; instruct; give lessons (in)《교육》 educate《지도》 coach《계몽》 enlighten《알아듣게》 show; tell; inform; explain／수학을 ∼ teach mathematics／피아노를 ∼ give lessons in piano／집을 가르쳐 주다 refer (one) to a house. おしえる

**가르친사위** a person too stupid to do anything without first being shown how. 他人のいうなりになる愚者の別名

**가르침** 《교훈》 teaching[s]; an instruction 《교의》 a doctrine 《계율》 a precept 《신조》 a creed／소크라테스의 ∼ the teachings of Socrates. おしえ

**가름** 《쪼갬》 dividing; cutting 《분리》 separating 《분류》 classifying 《분배》 distributing／ ∼하다 divide [up]; separate; discriminate. わけること

**가리**¹ 《고기 잡는》 a weir; a fishweir; a fish trap; a fishpound.

**가리**² 《갈비》 ribs [of beef]／ ∼찜 steamed beef ribs. うしのろっこつ

**가리**³ 《더미》 a stack; a pile; a rick／ ∼를 가리다 make a pile. つみかさねる

**가리가리** in pieces; in fragments 《남루》 in rags[tatters, shreds]／ ∼ 째다 tear [rend] to[in] pieces[ribbons, shreds]. いくつにもやぶけたさま

**가리개** a twohold screen. ついたて

**가리나무** a rick of needles and twigs of pine trees. たばにしたたききぎ

**가리다**¹ ①《선택》 choose; select; make a choice of; prefer; pick out; assort; fix out 《음식을》 be particular[fussy] (about food)／때와 장소를 가리지 않고 disregarding the time and place ②《셈을》 square account with ③《머리를》 do; arrange ④《낯을》 be shy of strangers [persons]. えらぶ

**가리다**² 《쌓다》 heap up; pile up in ricks. かさねる

**가리다**³ 《막다》 shield; shelter; cover; screen 《햇빛을》 shade; hide; conceal／손수건으로 얼굴을 ∼ cover one's face with handkerchief／태양이 구름에 가려졌다 The sun was hidden by the clouds. さえぎる

**가리마** parting of hair／ ∼를 타다 part one's hair. かみのけのわけめ

**가리맛** 《어》 Novaculina constricta《학명》.

**가리비** 《어》 a scallop; Fecten yessoen《학명》.

**가리사니** ①《분별》 discretion; prudence; sense ②《지각》 knowledge; wisdom ③《실마리》 a clue; the drift of an affair／ ∼를 잡을 수 없다 can't get[understand] what it's all about. ぶんべつ

**가리새**¹ 《까닭》 reason; ground; why; cause 《사정·형편》 circumstances; the matter; the case／어찌된 판인지 ∼를 모르겠다 I don't know what all these things are about. りゆう

**가리새**² 《조》 a spoonbill; Platalea leucorodia major《학명》.

**가리우다** 《덮다》 cover; veil; overspread; hang over; brood over 《감추다》 hide; conceal 《가로막다》 screen; shade. さえぎる

**가리이다** be covered; be overspread; be hidden; be concealed. さえぎられる

**가리키다** point to[at, toward]; indicate; show; tell／방향을 ∼ point the direction. さす

**가리틀다** ①《훼방》 counteract; counterwork; frustrate; interfere with; baffle ②《요구》 claim a share in one's accidental profits. むりにじゃまする

**가리스럽다** (be) miserly; stingy; niggardly けちだ

**가린주머니** a miser; a stingy[a closefisted] fellow; a niggard; a stinkard; a pinchpenny けちんぼう

**가마**¹ 《머리의》 the whirl[vortex] of hair on the crown of the head. のうてん

**가마**² ①《화덕》 a furnace ②《기와·질그릇을 굽는》 a kiln; a stove 《빵 굽는》 an oven 《기와 굽는 ∼ tilekiln ③《가마솥》 an iron pot; a kettle. かま

**가마**³ 《타는》 a palanquin 《주로 유럽의》 a sedan chair. かご

**가마**⁴ ①《가마니》 a bag; a sack ②《쌈지 따위》 a group of one hundred pieces (of tarpaulin etc).

**까마귀** 《조》 a crow 《갈가마귀》 a raven; a bird of ill omen 《별명》; 《망까마귀》 a rock. からす

**가마니** a straw-bag[sack]／쌀∼ a rice bag／ ∼쩨기 a worn-out bag. かます

**까마득하다** be far off はるかかなただ

**-가마리** a person who is the butt[the target; the mark; the object] of ridicule[beating, criticizm, scolding]／욕∼ the butt of abuse／뺨∼ the butt of abure／조소∼ the laughingstock. まと

**까마무트롬하다** (be) dark and chubby.

**가마솥** cauldron; an iron pot; a large kettle 《증기》 a boiler. おおかま

**까마아득하다** 《공간》(be) far; distant; faraway; be a long way off; (be) far[distant, remote] 《from》《시간》(be) remote; long past 《과거》 a long time ago 《미래》 many years away. はるかかなただ

**가마우지** 《조》 a cormorant; *Phalacrocorax carbo*《학명》. がらんちょ

**까막까치** a crow and a magpie. からすとかささぎ

**까막눈이** an illiterate; an ignoramus; an unlettered person. むがくもんもうしゃ

**가막사리** 《식》 a kind of cosmos plant; *Bidens tripartita*《학명》.

**까막잡기** blindman's-buff. おにごっこ

**가막조개** a corbicura; a kind of smell shell. くろかい

**가만가만** stealthily; quietly; gently; softly; lightly. しずかに

**가만하다** (be) quiet; soft; gentle; calm. おだやかだ

**가만히** ①《넌지시》 covertly; tacitly; imperceptibly 《몰래》 in secret[private]; privately; secretly／ ~ 남의 얼굴을 살피다 scan one covertly,／ ~ 집을 빠져 나오다 slip out of the house ②《조용히》 still; calmly; quietly; silently; motionlessly 《방관》 look on; stand by idly／~ 있다 keep still; remain quiet／그런 모욕을 받고 ~ 있지는 않겠다 I would not stand such a humiliation. しずかに

**가말다** manage; arrange; dispose of; deal with; give free hand to 《a matter》. かんりする

**가망**《可望》hope; promise 《가능성》 chance; probability; possibility 《전망》 a prospect／~없는 hopefulless／성공할 ~ a hope[chance] of success のぞみ

**가맣다, 까맣다** ①《검다》(be) black; dark ②《멀다》(be) distant; far; remote far off[away]. ひじょうにくろい

**가매**《假寐》 a nap; a doze／ ~ 하다 take a nap; have a short sleep.

**가매장**《假埋葬》 temporary interment[burial]／~하다 bury 《a person》 temporarily. かりまいそう

**가맹**《加盟》joining; participation; accession; alliance; affiliation／ ~하다 join; participate in; take part in; associate *one*self with／ ~국(國) a member nations; a signatory. かめい

**까먹다** ①《음식을》crack[peel, shell] and eat ②《밑천을》 squander; run through ③《잊다》forget. かわをむいてたべる

**가면**《假面》 a mask; disguise／ ~극 a masque／ ~ 무도회 a masked ball; a masquerade／《…의》~하에 under the mask of; under cloak of／~을 쓰다 《탈을 쓰다》 mask *one's* face 《위선을 부리다》 wear a mask dissemble play the hypocrite. かめん

**가면허**《假免許》 a temporary[provisional] license. かりめんきょ

**가멸다**《재산이》(be) rich; wealthy; affluent. ゆたかだ

**가명**《假名》 an alais; an assumed name; a pen-name 《아호》 a pseudonym／ ~으로 under an assumed name; incognito. かめい

**가명**《佳名》fame; reputation; renown／ ~을 떨치다 be famous; enjoy good reputation.

**가명**《家名》 the family name[honour]; the good name of a family／ ~을 더럽히다 disgrace[stain] the family name. かめい

**가모**《家母》《제 어머니》my mother《주부》 the mistress[the lady] of the house; a house wife; a landlady. じぶんのはは

**가묘**《家廟》 a family shrine. しかの祠堂

**가무**《歌舞》 singing and dancing; songs and dances; all musical and other entertainments／ 정부는 ~ 음곡 일체를 중지시켰다 The government order a suspension of all public performances in music and dancing. かぶ

**까무러뜨리다** ①《남을》 deprive 《one》 of *one's* sense; make insensible; cause 《a person》 to lose consciousness 《때려서》 ②《까무러치다》 swoon; faint dead away. しっしんさせる

**가무러지다, 까무러지다** have an indistinct consciousness; faint 《with》; swoon. きがとおくなる

**까무러치다** faint; swoon; lose *one's* senses／놀라 ~ be frightened out of *one's* senses[wits].

**가무스름하다, 까무스름하다** (be) blackish; darkish; swarthy; sunburnt.

**가무잡잡하다, 까무잡잡하다** (be) dark and flat; dusky／까무잡잡한 얼굴 a dark and flat face. ややくろくてばっとしない

**가문**《家門》《가계》 birth; lineage／ ~이 좋은[나쁜] of good[bad] stock; of high[low] descent／ 좋은 ~에 태어나다 come of a good stock[family]. かもん

**가문비**《식》a spruce; a silver fir; *Picea jezoensis*《학명》.

**가물** a drought  가물음／~철 dry season. かんばつ

**가물가물, 까물까물** 《희미하게》 dimly; vaguely; faintly; dreamily; indistinctly 《불빛이》 flickeringly; glimmeringly  가물거리다. ちらちら

**가물거리다, 까물거리다** ①《불빛이》 flicker; glimmer; blink／가물거리는 불빛 a flickering light ② 《희미하다》 (be) dim; misty 《정신이》have an indistinct consciousness[memory]／ 가물거리는 기억 a faint[dreamy] memory; a faint recollection／가물거리는 과거의 추억 misty recollections of the past. しきりにちらつく

**가물다** be droughty; have a spell of dry weather; rainless; arid／날씨가 ~ have a drought. ながくひでりがつづく

**가물들다** ①《날씨가》 become droughty;

**가물음** dry weather; a drought／오랜 ~ a long drought. かんばつ

**가물치** 《어》 a snake fish; a snakehead; a spotted serpent head; *Ophiocephalus argus*(학명). かむるち

**가물타다** be easily affected by dry weather.

**가뭄** ⇨가물음／~에 단비 a rainfall eagerly longed for. かんばつ

**가뭇가뭇, 까뭇까뭇** dotted[spotted] with black／~하다 be dotted[speckled] with black. てんてんとくろい

**가뭇없다** ①(눈이 안 보이다)(be) blurred; dimmed; purblind ②(증적이 없다)(be) gone; be nowhere to be seen; have left no clue behind; lost to sight[view]／그의 소식은 ~ His whereabouts are utterly unknown. きえうせる

**가뭇하다, 까뭇하다** (be) blackish; dark'sh ⇨가무스름하다. ややくろい

**가미**(加味) 《맛》 flavouring; seasoning 《부가》 addition／~하다 season; flavour (with) 《부가》 add. かみ

**가미, 嘉味** a nice[a pleasant] taste; good flavour; deliciousness 《음식》 dainty food. よいあじ

**까바치다** confide (a secret to another); tell[squeal] (on a person). こくはつする

**가발**(假髮) a [peri]wig; false hair／~을 쓰다 wear a wig.

**가방** a bag (멜빵이 있는) a satchel 《큰 가방》 a trunk 《여행용》 a suitcase／손 ~ a handbag; a valise. かばん

**가배**(嘉俳) a game played in *Silla* times on midautumn day; the midautumn festival day.

**가배절**(嘉俳節) ⇨가윗날.

**가백**(家伯) my eldest brother.

**가벌**(家閥) the standing of a family; 《가계》 lineage. もんばつ

**가법**(家法) a family constitution; household regulations; rules of the home; family rules. かほう

**가법**(加法) 《수》 addition. かほう

**가법**(苛法) oppressive laws.

**가벼이, 가볍게** sightly; lightly (경솔하게) rashly／행동을 ~하지 않다 use prudence. かるく

**가변**(可變) variableness 《형용사적》variable／~ 전압 발전기 a variable voltage generator. かへん

**가볍다** ①(무게가)(be) light; not heavy; lacking in weight／가볍디~ be as light as a feather／가벼운 짐 a light load[baggage]／체중이 ~ weigh little; one's weight is light ②(경미)(be) slight; not serious; trifling／가벼운 두통 a slight head ache／가벼운 범죄 minor offense ③(식사 따위) (be) light; not heavy; plain／가벼운 식사 a light meal; a snack／가벼운 기분으로 with a light heart ④(사람이)(be) imprudent; indiscreet; thoughtless; rash. かるい

**가보** 《투전판의》 a lucky nine. かぶ

**가보**(家寶) a family[an ancestral] treasure; an heirloom／역대의 ~ an heirloom of the family handed down for generations. かほう

**가보**(家譜) a .nily tree[record]; a genealogy; a pedigree; a genealogical table. いっかのけいふ

**가본**(假本) a counterfeit copy ; a spurious edition. にせのほん

**가봉**(加俸) an extra[additional] allowance／연공(年功) ~ a long service allowance. かほう

**가봉**(假縫) basting; tacking／~하다 baste; tack 《양복 따위를》 try[fit] (a coat) on. かりぬい

**가부**(可否) 《옳고 그름》 right or wrong; proper or improper 《찬부》 ayes and noes; pros and cons; for and against; yes or no; approval or disapproval／~간 《옳고 그름》 right or wrong 《찬부》 for or against／투표로 ~를 결정하다 decide (a matter) by vote; take a vote. かひ

**가부**(家父) my father. じぶんのちちの謙稱

**가부**(家夫) my husband; my hub 《아내에게》 I your husband.

**까부르다** winnow; fan. みでふりわける

**가분수**(假分數) an improper fraction. かりぶんすう

**가분하다, 가뿐하다** (be) light; not heavy／가분가분[가뿐가뿐] lightly; airily 《동작 따위》 gently. ほどよくかるい

**가불**(假拂) 《미리 주는》 an advance; advance payment 《임시로 주는》 suspense payment／~하다 pay in advance; advance／~받다 receive (money) in advance; obtain an advance (on one's salary); draw (a part of one's salary) in advance. かりばらい

**가불가**(可不可) 《옳고 그름》 right or wrong 《찬부》 yes and no, aye and nay.

**까불거리다** act flippantly; be frivolous; act rashly しきりにあそびさわぐ

**까불다** ①(행동) act frivolously; be flippantly／까불까불 flippantly ②(물건을) jolt; move repeatedly up and down ③⇨까부르다. じょうげにゆれる

**까불리다**¹ (탕진) squander; dissipate; run through. ろうひする

**까불리다**² (키질) be winnowed; let winnow. みでふりわけられる

**까불이** a frivolous[flippant] person; a flibbertigibbet. けいはくにこうどうする

**까붐질** winnowing; fanning／~하다 do winnowing. みで振りわける

**가붓하다, 가뿟하다** (be) rather light; not heavy／가붓가붓[가뿟가뿟] lightly; airily. ほどよくかるい

**가붕대**(假繃帶) field-dressing／~소 a field-dressing station／~을 하다 apply first-aid dressing. かほうたい

**가쁘다** (숨이) be out of breath; breathe with difficulty. あえぐ

**가빈**(家貧) home poverty/ ~하다 (be) poor; be badly off; be in want; be of a poor family. うちがまずしいこと

**가사**(家事) household affairs; domestic duties; housekeeping/ ~ 형편으로 for family reasons; owing to family matters. かじ

**가사**(假死) apparent death; syncope; suspended animation/ ~ 상태에 있다 be in a syncopic state. かし

**가사**(歌詞) the text[words] of a song; poetry. かし

**가사**(袈裟) a surplice; a stole; a cope; a priest's robe. けさ

**가산**(加算) addition; inclusion/ ~하다 add; include/ ~기 a calculating[an adding] machine/이자를 ~하다 include interest. かさん

**가산**(家産) family property[estate]; one's fortune. かさん

**가산**(假山) an artificial[a miniature] hill; a rockery. つきやま

**가산호**(假珊瑚) imitation coral.

**가살** narrow-mindedness; intolerance; lack of magnanimity; a hateful stuck-up attitude/ ~장이 a hateful stuck-up[arrogant] person. なまいき

**가삼**(家蔘) a cultivated ginseng.

**가상**(假像) a ghost; a secondary image 《광석 결정의》 a pseudomorph. かぞう

**가상**(假想) imagination; supposition/ ~하다 assume; imagine; suppose/ ~적인 imaginary; hypothetical/~의 적 (敵) a hypothetical[potential] enemy /~국 a given country. かそう

**가상**(嘉尙) ~하다 approve (one's conduct); approve of (one's servces). かしょう

**가서**(家書) a letter from[to] one's home. うちからのてがみ

**가석방**(假釋放) parole 《가출옥》 (a) release on parole. かりしゃくほう

**가석하다**(可惜—) (be) regrettable; sad; pitiful 《사람이 죽어》 be sorry/그것 참 가석한 일이군 That's pity!; It is a matter for regret. おしい

**가선**(架線) 《공사》 wiring 《선》 a wire/~ 공사 wiring work. かせん

**가설**(架設) construction; building 《전화 따위의》 installation/~하다 construct 《전화를》 instal 《다리를》 span. かせつ

**가설**(假設) ①~의 《임시의》 temporary/ ~ 극장 a temporary theatre/~교(橋) a temporary bridge/~ 정거장 a temporary station ②《상상적》hypothesis; supposition/ 《법》 fiction/~의 hypothetic[al]/~ 연습 a skeleton drill. かせつ

**가설**(假說) 《논》 a hypothesis; assumption 《가정》 supposition/~적인 hypothetical.

**가성**(家聲) the family honour; the good name[reputation] of a family. かせい

**가성**(苛性) 《화》 causticity/ ~소다[알칼리] caustic soda[alkali]/~석회 quicklime. かせい

**가성**(假聲) falsetto(pl. ~s); a feigned voice; a disguised tone. かせい

**가성대**(假聲帶) 《해》 a false vocal cord.

**가세**(加勢) help; aid; assistance/~하다 《조력》 help; aid; assist 《지지》 support; take sides (with); stand by. かせい

**가세**(家勢) a family's financial condition. うちのせいりょく

**가세**(苛稅) a heavy tax; overtaxation / ~에 허덕이다 groan[moan] under the heavy burden of taxation. かぜい

**가소**(可塑) ~의 plastic/~성 plasticity /~품 plastics. かそ

**가소**(假笑) a forced[a feigned] laugh; an affected smile; a simper/~하다 force[affect] a laugh; smile a forced smile; simper. つくりわらい

**가소롭다**(可笑—) (be) laughable; ridiculous; silly; absurd. おかしい

**가속**(家屬) 《가족》 the members of a family[a household]; one's people[folks] 《아내》 one's wife. かぞく

**가속**(加速) 《물》 acceleration/ ~기 an acelerator/~도 (degree of) acceleration. かそく

**가솔**(家率) one's family; members of one's family. かぞく

**가수**(歌手) a singer 《여자 성악가》 a songstress 《성악가》 a vocalist 《독창자》 a soloist/유행~ a crooner《미·속》.かしゅ

**가수**(假睡) a feigned sleep.

**가수**(假數) 《수》 a mantissa. かすう

**가수 분해**(加水分解) 《화》 hydrolysis/ ~하다 hydrolyze; decompose in water.

**가수요**(假需要) disguised demand. かりじゅよう

**가스러지다** become intractable.

**가슬가슬하다** ①《살결이》 (be) rough; chappy; bristly; sharp ②《성질이》 (be) rough; fastidious; peevish; willful; shap; stubborn; intractable.ざらざらする

**가슴** 《가슴팍》 the breast 《흉곽》 the chest 《품》 the bosom 《심장》 heart 《마음》 mind/~의 병 chest troubles/~속 깊이 간직한 생각 an idea cherished deep in one's heart/~이 뭉클해지다 have a lump in one's heart. むね

**가슴걸이** a girth; a cinch; a bellyband.

**가슴둘레** the girth of the chest 《양장의》 bust. むねのまわり

**가슴앓이** 《의》 heartburn; pyrosis; cardialgia; a sour stomach/~를 앓다 have a heartburn. むねやけ

**가슴츠레하다** 《술이 취해》 (one's eyes are) heavy with drinking 《졸려》(one's eyes are) drowsy. うとうとしている

**가슴통** the chest; the breast 《너비》 the breast of the chest/~이 좁다[넓다] have a narrow[broad] chest. むねのまわり

**가슴패기** the chest ·가슴통.

**가시**[1] 《장미 따위의》 a thorn 《풀잎 따위의》 a prickle 《덤불의》 a bramble 《밤송이

**가시** 의)a bur 《나무·대·뼈 따위》a splinter 《물고기의》a spine/~ 많은 thorny; spiny/~ 나무 a thorn [bush]; a bramble/~나무 울타리 a hedge of thorn/~ 덤불[밭] a thorn thicket/~ 밭길 a thorny path. とげ

**가시²** 《구더기》 a worm; a maggot.

**가시나무** ①《가시돋힌 나무》a thorn; a thorn bush; a thorny tree; a bramble; a brier/~ 울타리 a hedge of thorn ② ⇨가시목. いばら

**가시다** ①《씻다》 wash (out); rinse/물로 ~ rinse in clear water ②《고통 따위가》 abate 《덜어지다》lessen/고통이 가셨다 The pain is gone[has left me]., The pain is eased. みずがめをざっとあらう

**가시덤불** a thornbush; a thorn thicket; a bramble/ ~길 a thorny path/~길을 걷다 tread a thorny path. いばらやぶ

**가시랭이** a fragment of splinters; a prikle; a thorn. とげのきれはし

**가시목** 《식》 the white oak; Quercus mysinaefolia《학명》.

**가시밭** a thornbush, a thorn thicket; brambles/ ~길을 걷다 follow a thorny path. いばらのやぶがあるところ

**가시버시** husband and wife; man and wife; a [married] couple. ふうふ

**가시세다** 《완고》(be) stubborn; wilful; obstinate; headstrong; perverse unyielding. きょうせいだ

**가시철**(-鐵) barbed wire/~망 barbed wire entanglements. とげのあるはりがね

**가식**(假飾) affectation; hypocrisy/~하다 affect; play the hypocrite /~적 hypocritical; false; affected. かしょく

**가신**(家信) a message [a letter, tidings] from *one's* home. うちからのてがみ

**가신**(嘉辰) an auspicious [a happy] occasion[day].

**가신**(可信) credibility/ ~하다 (be) believable; credible; trustworthy《근거》 authentic.

**가심** 《부심》 a rinse; a wash[ing]/ ~하다 wash out; rinse.

**가아**(家兒) my son. じぶんのこの謙称

**가악**(歌樂) songs and music. うたとおんがく

**가야금**(伽倻琴) a *kayakum*; a Korean harp/~ 탄주자 a *kayakum*-player.

**가약**(佳約) the pledge of eternal love; a deep pledge ⇨백년 가약/백년 ~을 맺다 get married. ふうふになるやくそく

**가얌** a hazelnut ⇨개암

**가양주**(家醸酒) home-brewed liquor; bathtub liquor. うちでつくったさけ

**가언**(假言) 《논》 a conditional [word]/~적 conditional; hypothetic[al]/ ~ 명제 a hypothetical proposition. かげん

**가업**(家業) *one's* trade[business; occupation]. かぎょう

**가없다** (be) endless; interminable; never-ending; boundless; limitless/가없이 endlessly; eternally/가없이 넓은 바다 a boundless ocean. おわりのない

**가역**(家役) construction of a house; house repairs. うちのこうじ

**가역**(可逆) ~의 reversible/ ~ 반응 reversible reaction/ ~ 변화 reversible change. かぎゃく

**가연물**(可燃物) combustibles; inflammable. かねんぶつ

**가연성**(可燃性) inflammability; combustibility/ ~의 combustible; inflammable. かねんせい

**가열**(加熱) heating/~하다 heat/~분해 decomposition by heating. かねつ

**가엾다** 《불쌍하다》(be) pitiable; pitiful; poor; sad; miserable 《애틋하다》(be) pathetic; touching/가엾이 여기다 feel pity[sorry] for; take pity on; pity (one)/가엾어라 What a pity!, Alas poor thing! かわいそうだ

**가영수증**(假領收證) an interim receipt; a scrip.

**가영업**(假營業) temporary business/ ~소 a temporary office.

**가오리** 《어》 a stingray; a stingaree; *Dasyatis akaci*《학명》. あかえい

**가옥**(家屋) a house; a building 《법》; a messuage/~세 a house tax/~의 매매에 종사하다 deal in real estate/~ 대장 a house register. かおく

**가옥**(假玉) an artificial pearl[gem].

**까옥거리다** keep cawing[croaking]. かあかあする

**가외**(加外) extra; excess; surplus/~의 extra; spare; excessive/가욋일을 하다 do extra work 《시간 외에》work over time. いがい

**가외**(可畏) being to be feared/ ~지사(之事) a matter to be feared. おそれ

**가요**(歌謡) a song; a melody/ ~곡 a popular song. かよう

**가용**(家用) 《집안의 씀씀이》cost of household; house hold expenses 《자가용》 domestic use; family use. かていのひよう

**가용**(可溶) soluble/~물 a soluble [body] /~성 a solubility. かよう

**가용**(可鎔) fusible/~금 a fusible metal /~물 a fusible [body]/~성 fusibility /~성의 fusible. かよう

**가운**(家運) a family fortune. かうん

**가운데** ①《중간》 the middle; the midway 《안쪽》 the interior; the inside; within/~로 들어가십시오 《차창 등의》Step forward, please. ②《일부분》 among (them)/그 서 어느 거나 다섯 개만 골라라 Choose any five from among the number. ③《한가운데》 the middle; the center; the heart the midst/길 ~로 걸어가다 walk in[keep to] the middle of the road.

**가운뎃손가락** the middle finger. なかゆび

**가위¹** scissors; shears 《털 베는》clippers / ~ 한 자루 a pair of scissors/ ~질 scissoring. はさみ

**가위²**(악몽) a nightmare; an incubus/ ～눌리다 have a nightmare. あくむ

**가위**(可謂) literally; exactly; truly; practically; in a sense; so to speak; what is will named. いわゆる

**가위춤** the opening and shutting of scissors.

**가윗날** the fifteenth day of August of the lunar calendar.

**가윗밥** scraps of cloth[paper] [left from scissoring]; cuttings. たちくつ

**가으내** the whole autumn; all the autumn《부사적》through the fall; through out the autumn. ずっとあきの

**가을** autumn; fall〈미〉/ ～의 autumn [al]; fall/ ～바람 autumn wind/～ 보리 autumn-sown barley/～갈이 autumn ploughing / ～ 경치 autumnal scenery. あき

**가인**(佳人) a beautiful woman; a beauty/～ 박명(薄命) Beauty and fortune make bad friends., A beauty is always unlucky. かじん

**가인**(家人) the family; *one's* people; *one's* folks; the inmates[the occupants] of a house. かじん

**가인**(歌人) a poet. かじん

**가일**(佳日) an auspicious day. きちにち

**가일층**(加一層) more and more; increasingly / ～ 노력하다 make still more efforts. よりいっそう

**가입**(加入) entry; entrance 《전화 따위의》admission/ ～하다 enter (*for*); join; associate; affiliate *one*self with; become a member of; subscribe for /～금 an enterance fee. かにゅう

**가입학**(假入學) admission of students on probation.

**가짜**(假一)《모조품》an imitation; a sham; bogus; a spurious article; a fake/ ～ 도장 a forged seal/～ 다이아먼드 an imitation diamond. にせもの

**가자미**《어》a flatfish; a sole.

**가작**(佳作) a fine piece of work; a work of merits/선외 ～ a work to which honorable mention is given; a fine work left out of the selection. かさく

**가작**(假作) ①《거짓 행동》a fraudulent act; fiction ②《일시적 제작》temporary manufacture; make-shift production. いつわりのこうどう

**가장** most 《적을 때》least / ～ 쉬운 방법 the easiest method. さいも

**가장**(假裝) ①《변장》disguise; masquerade/ ～하다 disguise *one*self; dissemble; dress up/ ～ 행렬 a fancy dress parade ②《거짓》pretence; semblance; simulation; camouflage/～하다 feign; affect; assume/양민으로 ～하다 counterfeit[pose as] a good citizen. かそう

**가장**(家長) the head of a family 《남자》a patriarch 《여자》a matriarch/～ 제도 patriarchism. かちょう

**가장**(家藏) family heirlooms; a household possession/～ 집물(什物) all the household articles. かぞう

**가장**(假葬) temporary internment/ ～하다 bury temporarily. かそう

**가장귀** a crotch of a tree. また

**가장이** a branch 《큰 가지》a bough; a limb; a twig. えだ

**가장자리** an edge; a verge; a brink; a margin. ふち. まわり

**가재**《동》a crawfish; a crayfish; *Cambaraides similis*(학명). ざりがに

**가재**(家財) household belongings[goods]; furniture and effects; the family property[estate]. かざい

**가재걸음** crawfishing/ ～치다 crawfish; back out. ざりがにのようなあるき

**가전**(家傳) a family transmission/ ～ 의 hereditary; proprietary/ ～의 보물 a family heirloom. かでん

**가절**(佳節) an auspicious occasion. かせつ

**가정**(家庭) home; a family /～의 home; domestic; family/ ～란 a domestic column/～ 생활 home life/ ～ 경제 household economy/ ～ 교사 a private teacher; a tutor/ ～ 교육 home education/ ～ 부인 a housewife/ ～ 을 갖다 start a home. かてい

**가정**(家政) household management; housekeeping/～부 a housekeeper; a lady help/～과 《학문》[the] domestic economics [course]《학과》the department of domestic science. かせい

**가정**(家丁) a [man] servant; a domestic; a footman. うちでつかう召使

**가정**(苛政) tyrannical government/ ～에 신음하다 groan under tyrannical government. ぎゃくせい

**가정**(假定) supposition; assumption; hypothesis;《법》[legal] fiction/～ 하다 suppose; take for granted/ ～법 《언》the subjunctive mood/～적인 hvpothetic[al]; imaginary; assumptive/…이라 ～하여 supposing that… /～ 상속인 heir presumptive. かてい

**가정거장**(假停車場) a temporary station. かていしゃじょう

**가정부**(假政府) a provisional government. かせいふ

**가제**(家弟) my younger brother. じぶんのおとうとの謙称

**가져가다** take[carry] away; take (with *one*); make off with. もっていく

**가져오다** 《지참》bring; fetch;get; carry take (*a thing*) with[along]《초래》invite; cause; result[end] in; bring about. もってくる

**가조**(佳兆) a good omen; a lucky sign; a happy augury. よいきざし

**가조**(一調)《음》the tone A/ 가단조 A minor/가장조 A major.

**가조약**(假條約) a provisional treaty. かりじょうやく

**가조인**(假調印) a preliminary[provisional] signature/ ～하다 affix a perlim-

**가족**(家族) a family; a household; members of a family/ ~ 계획(計畫) a family planning/ ~ 수당[석] a family allowance[box]/ ~ 동반의 여행 a family trip/~ 제도 the family system /핵~ nuclear family. かぞく

**가죄**(嫁罪) imputation [of a crime]/ ~하다 impute (a crime to one); lay [throw] (the blame on one); shift [stuffle off] (a crime on another's shoulders). つみをてんかすること

**가주**(家主) (집 임자) the owner of a house (主人) a master; the head of a family[a house]. いえのしゅじん

**가주**(假主) a temporary ancestral tablet made of paper. かりのいはい

**가주권**(假株券) a scrip certificate.

**가주소**(假住所) a temporary address[residence abode]. かりじゅうしょ

**가죽** (짐승의) skin (주로 마소의) a hide (무두질한) [tanned] leather; tanned [dressed] skin; buff (양, 사슴의)chamois leather (모피)[a] fur/~ 주머니 a leather bag/~ 표지 a leather cover; leather binding/~ 장수 a leather dealer; a tanner/~ 숫돌 a strap/ ~을 벗기다 skin. かわ

**가죽나무** 〘식〙a tree of heaven; *Ailanthus altissima*(학명).

**가중**(加重) ①~하다 (무게를) weight /~ 평균 weighted average ②~하다 (형벌의) aggravate/형을 ~하다 raise[aggravate] the penaltyx/~ 과세 surcharge ; additional tax. かじゅう

**가중**(家中) the whole family; all the family; inside the house. うちのなか

**가중하다**(苛重-) (be) heavy; severe; burdensome; excessive/가중한 세금 a heavy tax. かこくでふたんのおもいこと

**가중**(加症) a complication of all illness/ ~하다 accompany.

**가중서**(假證書) a scrip;an interim bond.

**가증하다**(可憎-) (be) hateful; abominable; disgusting: detestable. にくいこと

**가지**[1] (나무의) a branch(일반적); a bough(큰); a twig; a spring(작은); a ray(꽃이 있는). えだ

**가지**[2] 〘식〙an eggplant (열매)an egg apple. なす

**가지**[3] (종류)a kind; a class/그것을 하는 데는 두 ~ 방법이 있다 There are two ways of doing it. しゅるい

**까지** ①(때) till; until; [up] to: before; (미래) by/아침부터 저녁 ~ from morning till night/다음 달~ till next month/그때~ till then; up to that time /저녁 식사 때~는 돌아오마 I will be back by supper time. ②(장소) to; up to; as far as/서울~ to[as far as] Seoul/여기서 거기~ from here to there ③(정도) to [the extend of]; so far as; even. まで

**가지가지** various kinds every[all] sorts / ~의 various; diverse; sundry/ ~ 이유로 for various reasons/ ~ 물건 many different things. あらゆるしゅるい

**가지각색**(一各色) (of) every kind and description/ ~의 various; diverse; motley; of all kinds[sorts]. いろいろ

**가지고** ①(…을)ⓠ그 사람 ~ 너무 그러지 마시오 Don't pick on him so! ②(…으로) with; by means of/공을 ~ 놀다 play with a ball.

**가지다** ①(손에 쥐다) have; take; hold (휴대·운반) carry with one; have (a thing) with[about] one ②(소유) have; own; possess; keep (마음에) cherish; bear; hold/큰 재산을 ~ possess an enormous wealth ③(임신) conceive; become pregnant (동물이) be with young. /그 여자는 또 아이를 가졌다 Again she is with child. もつ

**가지런하다** (be) trim; even; equall; uniform /가지런히 trimly; evenly/키가 ~ be of the same height/높이가 ~ be of uniform height. せいぜんとしている

**가지치다**[1] 〘번다〙 spread[put out] branches. えだがひろがる

**가지치다**[2] 〘베다〙 cut off branches; trim a tree. えだをきる

**가직하다** (be) near; not far off; near [close] by /가직하게 within reach; near by. きょりがちかい

**가진급**(假進級) passing on probation; conditional pass (of *a student*).

**가집행**(假執行) 〘법〙 provisional execution; a temporary injunction/~하다 execute provisionally. かりしっこう

**가차압**(假差押) provisional attachment [seizure]/~하다 seize[attach] (*a person's*) property provisionally/ ~당하다 have one's property attached provisionally. かりさしおさえ

**가차없다**(假借-) (be) unadaptable; stiff; stubborn; relentless/가차없이 without reserve; relentlessly. ようしゃしない

**가창**(街娼) a woman of streets; a street girl. しょうじょ

**가책**(呵責) torment; torture 《양심의》 pangs/양심의 ~을 받다 be consciencestricken, feel remorseful.

**가책**(苛責) violent scolding 《고문》 torture; torment; racking. かしゃく

**가처분**(假處分) temporary handling provisional disposition /~하다 make provisional disposition. かりしょぶん

**가철**(假綴) temporary paper binding /~하다 bind temporarily [in paper]/ ~본 a paper-bound book. かりつづり

**가첨**(加添) an addition; a supplement /~하다 supplement; add[append] (*something*) to. つけくわえること

**가청**(可聽) 〘형용사적〙audible; audio/ ~ 음파[주파] audio frequency.

**가축**(家畜) domestic animals; livestock /~ 병원 a veterinary hospital/ ~을 치다 raise livestock. かちく

**가출(家出)** abscondence; leaving home / ~하다 run away from home; leave *one's* house/ ~ 소년[소녀] a runaway boy[girl]. かしゅつ

**가출옥(假出獄)** provisional release; release on parole/ ~하다 be released on parole 《보석》 be out on bail/ ~자 a paroled man; a man on parole; a ticket-of-leave man. かりしゅつごく

**가취(佳趣)** charm; elegance; grace; tastefulness. かしゅ

**까치** 〖조〗 a magpie; ~걸음 a bouncy walk [gait]. かささぎ

**가치(價値)** value; worth; merit/ ~ 판단 valuation; evaluation/~ 있는 valuable; worthy/~ 없는 worthless; of no value. かち

**까치발** ①a bracket; a cross-arm ②〖식〗 *Bidens paviflora*(학명). はりだしだな

**까치선(-扇)** a four-colored fan.

**까치저고리** a multicolored Korean coat worn by children on gala days.

**가친(家親)** my father. じぶんのちちの謙稱

**가칠(加漆)** recoating/~하다 recoat; coat again. うえぬり

**가칠하다, 까칠하다** 《피부가》(be) dry; rough; chappy/까칠한 얼굴 haggard face. やせてひふがざらざらしている

**가칭(假稱)** ①《가정의》a provisional designation; a tentative name ②《사칭》impersonation; misrepresentation; false assumption. かしょう

**가탁(假託)** pretext; pretense; excuse; plea/ ~하다 make an excuse[a pretext]《of》. かたく

**가탄(可歎)** ~하다 (be) lamentable; grievous; deplorable; regrettable/가탄할 일 a matter worthy of grief; a deplorable affair. よろこぶこと

**가탈** ①《방해 조건》a hindrance; an impediment; an obstacle; a hitch 《이유》 reason, cause/~스럽다 be troublesome ②《걸음걸이》rough pace of a horse/ ~걸음 a jogging pace. じゃま

**가탈부리다, 까탈부리다** raise problems; make trouble; put a spoke in another's wheel; throw an obstacle in 《*a person's*》path. じゃまする

**가탈지다, 까탈지다** run into problems [obstacles]; come[be brought] to a standstill; be frustrated; bogdown. じゃまがはいってわるくなる

**가택(家宅)** a house 《법》a domicile; a residence/~ 수색 a domiciliary search[visit]/~ 수색 하다 search a house / ~ 침입 trespass; unlawful entry/~ 침입 하다 trespass. かたく

**가토(加土)** ~하다 《뿌리의》earth up; put on earth 《무덤의》rebuild[recover] a grave. つちをかぶせること

**가통(加痛)** ~하다 (be) deplorable; lamentable; regrettable. なげかわしい

**까투리** a hen pheasant. めすきじ

**가파르다** 《경사가》(be) steep; sheer; precipitous/가파른 언덕[길] a steep hill [path]. ひじょうにけいしゃしている

**까팡이** fragments[broken pieces] of unglazed pottery; potshreds. じきのはへん

**가편(可便)** the consenting party 《토론의》 the affirmative side. さんせいのそく

**가편(加鞭)** whipping apply the whip/ ~하다 apply the whip; whip up/주마 ~하다 exert *one*self to the utmost.
むちうって歩みを速めること

**가평(苛評)** severe[bitter; cutting] criticism/ ~하다 criticize severely; be severe (*upon*); speak bitterly (*of*); say harsh things (*about*). ひどいひひょう

**가표(加票)** plus sign (+).

**가표(可票)** an affirmative vote.
さんせいのしるし

**까풀** skin; film coat; scum; skim/눈 ~ an eyelid 《주름》a wrinkle on the eyelid. こくもつまだはかわのかさなり

**가풀막** a steep slope; a steep ascent [acclivity]; a steep descent[declivity] /~지다 slope up[down] sharply; be precipitous. けわしいこうばい

**가품(家品)** the character[disposition] of a family 《품성》refinement. かひん

**가풍(家風)** the family tradition[custom]; the ways of a family. かふう

**가필(加筆)** revision; correction/ ~하다 correct; retouch; touch up; revise; add some touches to. かひつ

**가하다(可-)** 《옳다》(be) right; rightful; reasonable 《좋다》(be) good; fair; nice; passable. よろしい

**가하다(加-)** ①《가산》add [up]; sum up 《부가》add ②《주다》give; inflict (*on*) /일격을 ~ deal (*one*) a blow/압력을 ~ give pressure (*to*). くわえる

**가해(加害)** ①《손해를》harm; damage; loss/~하다 damage; do damage to; inflict a loss on ②《상해를》an assault; violence 《살해》murder/~하다 commit a violence; assault/~자 an assaulter; an assailant; a person who has caused damage. かがい

**가향(家鄉)** *one's* home; *one's* native place; *one's* native hearth. こきょう

**가헌(家憲)** household regulations; a family tradition.

**가형(家兄)** my elder brother.
じぶんのあにきの謙稱

**가호(加護)** divine protection; special providence; guardianship/신명(神明)의 ~에 의해 by the protection of Heaven. ほごをくわえること

**가혹(苛酷)** 《무참》cruelty 《잔인》brutality 《엄혹》severity; harshness/ ~하다 (be) severe; cruel; hard/ ~하게 cruelly; harshly; relentlessly/ ~한 벌 a severe punishment/~한 처사 harsh treatment. むごたらしいこと

**가화(佳話)** 《미담》a good[fine] story; a beautiful story. おもしろいはなし

**가화(家禍)** family disaster[calamity];

가화(假花) artificial flowers ≒조화(造花). ぞうか
가환(家患) (병) sickness in one's family (걱정) family misfortunes[cares]; domestic cares. うちのわざわい
가효(佳肴·嘉肴) a tasty side dish to go with wine. あじのうまいさかな
가훈(家訓) family precepts. かていのきょうくん
가희(歌姬) a singeress; a songstress; a girl singer. うたひめ
가히(可—) easily; properly; really/~ 짐작할 수 있다 It may easily be perceived[presumed] that….
각(各) every; each/~ 개인 each individual.
각(角) ①(뿔) a horn 《사슴의》 an antler 《촉각》 a feeler ②(모퉁이) a corner; 《돌아가는》 a turn[ing] ③(사각) square ④(각도) an angle; angular measure; degrees of an angle/직~ a right angle/내〔외〕~ an interior[an exterior] angle/~에 a acute angle/~테 안경 a horn-made spectacle frame.
각(刻) (새김) engraving carving 《시간》 a quarter-hour/~하다 carve (out); engrave; sculpture. ちょうこく
각(脚) one of the four or five parts into which a slaughtered animal is cut. あし
각가지(各—) various kinds/~의 various kinds[all sorts] of. いろいろ
깍깍 Caw-Caw!/~ 울다 caw; croak.
각각(各各) (따로따로) separately 《각기》 respectively; each. おのおの
각각으로(刻刻—) every moment; moment by moment ⇨시시각각. こっこくと
각개(各個) each; each one. かこ
각개인(各個人) every one; each; every individual. ひとりひとり
각거(各居) seperation/~하다 live apart[seperately]. べっきょ
각경증(脚硬症) a stiffening of legs.
각계(各界) every field[sphere] of life; various circles[quarters]/~ 각층의 명사[대표]. notables representing various departments of society. かっかい
각고(刻苦) hard work; close application; indefatigable industry/~하다 work hard[laboriously]; apply oneself closely to/~ 면려하여 by dint of industry. こっく
각곡(各穀) all sorts of grains.
각골(刻骨) ~하다 engrave[impress] on one's mind; lay (a fact) to heart/~난망(難忘) remembering forever; cherishing the memory of.
각광(脚光) the footlights/~을 받다《사람이》 make one's appearance before the footlights 《극이》 be performed before the footlights. きゃっこう
각국(各國) 《각 나라》 every country; each nation 《여러 나라》 various countries 《만국》 the world/세계 ~ all countries of the world. かっこく
각군(各郡) each goon; every country; all districts.
각군데(各—) each place 《여러 군데》 various places. ところところ
각근(恪勤) faithful service; hard working; attending faithfully to one's duties/~하다 perform (one's duties) faithfully; make best effort/~ faithfully. まじめにつとめること
각기(各其) (명사) each (one); every one (부사) respectively; severally; in one's own way/제~ respectively; in one's own way おのおの
각기(脚氣) beriberi/~약 specific for beriberi; anti-beriberi. かっけ
각내(閣內) ~의〔에서〕 in[inside] the cabinet.
깎다 ①(값을) beat[knock] down/100원으로 ~ beat down the price 100won ②(머리를) cut 《수염을》 shave 《양털을》 shear/머리를 짧게 ~ cut one's hair short [close] ③(껍질을) peel; pare; skin 《연필 등을》 sharpen/배〔사과〕를 ~ peel a pear[an apple] ④《명예 등을》 injure; hurt; mar; disgrace ⑤《봉급 등을》 reduce; cut. けずる
각다귀 ①《충》《모기의 일종》 a striped mosquito ②《착취자》 an extortioner; a bloodsucker; a vampire; a sponge; a parasite/~판 a state of mutual parasitism. か(蚊)の一種
각도(各道) each province; all the provinces. かくどう
각도(角度) an angle; angular measure; degrees of an angle/~를 재다 take [measure] the angle (of)/모든 ~에서 검토하다 survey (a problem) from an angles[viewpoints]/~기(器) a [graduated] protractor; a graduator/반원 ~기 a semicircular protractor. かくど
각도(角堵) 《수》 a prism. かくとう
각동(各洞) each[every] village.
깍둑거리다 cut in uneven slices/깍둑깍둑 cutting in uneven slices; chop-chop. ずたずたにきる
각뜨다(脚—) cut in several parts; dismember.
깍듯이 politely; courteously; respectfully; civilly. ていねいに
깍듯하다 (be) courteous; polite; civil; respectful. れいぎただしい
각등(角燈) a square hand-lantern 《렌즈가 달린》 a bulls-eye. かくとう
각띠(角—) a sash; cordons [worn by officials].
각령(閣令) a Cabinet ordinance.
각로(脚爐) a foot warmer[pan].
각론(各論) consideration in detail; detailed exposition/해부학 ~ special anatomy. かくろん
각료(閣僚) 《전부》 the Cabinet[Ministerial] colleagues 《개인》 a cabinet member[minister]/한일 ~ 회담 the ROK

Japan ministerial meeting.

**각루**(刻漏) a water clock. かくりょう

**각리**(各里) each *ri*; every village. かくり

**각립**(各立) separating; splitting up/ ～하다 separate (*from*); part (*with*); break up; split (*into*)《집단 퇴》 withdraw in a party; secede collectively.  かくりつ

**각막**(角膜) 『해』 the cornea/ ～염(炎) keratitis. かくまく

**각면**(各面) ①《행정 구역》 each *mycon*; every *mycon* all the townships in a couny ②《각방면》 each side; every direction.

**각모**(角帽) a college[square] cap; a mortarboard; a graduation cap. かくぼう

**각박**(刻薄) inhumanity; cold-[hard-]heartedness; heartlessness; coolness/ ～하다 (be) hard-hearted; unfeeling; heartless; cruel. はくじょう

**각반**(脚絆) leggings; gaiters; spats《감는》 puttees. きゃはん

**각방**(各房) each room; every chamber; all rooms. かくへや

**각방면**(各方面) every direction[quarter] ; all directions/사회 ～ all sorts and conditions of men; all strata of society. かくほうめん

**각배**(各—) ①《짐승의》 different litters from the same mother ②《사람의》 having different mothers. はらちがい

**각벌**(各—) 《옷》 separate garments《서류》 separate copies.

**각별하다**(各別—) ①《특별》 (be) especial; special; particular 《과격적》 exceptional/각별히 especially/각별히 주의하다 pay special attention ②《깍듯하다》 (be) polite; decorous; courteous/각별히 정중히 대우하다 give a warm reception; treat with kindness. かくべつな

**각본**(脚本) a play-book]; a drama《영화의》 a script; *a scenario* (It)/～ 작가 a playwright; a dramatist; *a scenacio* writer. きゃくほん

**각봉하다**(各封—) seal (*a letter*) under separate cover. こべつにとじること

**각부**(各部) ①《각 부내》 each section《정부의》 every department[ministry]/～장관 the minister of each department ②《각부분》 each part; all departments; the departments. かくぶ

**각부**(脚夫) a messenger; a courier. ひきゃく

**각부분**(各部分) each[every] part; all parts《여러 부분》 various parts. かくぶぶん

**각사탕**(角砂糖) cube[lump] sugar; sugar cubes. かくざとう

**각살림**(各—) living separately/ ～하다 live separately; establish[set up] a separate family. べっきょ

**각상**(各床) separates tables[boards]; each dinner table. かくじのおぜん

**각색**(各色) ①《종류》 many kinds; a large variety/각양 ～의 various; diverse ②《빛깔》 various colo[u]r; each colo[u]r. いろいろないろ

**각색**(脚色) dramatization/ ～하다 dramatize; adapt for a play/～가 a dramatizer; an adapter. きゃくしょく

**각서**(覺書) a memorandum; a memo; a note/～의 교환 an exchange of note [memoranda]. おぼえがき

**각선미**(脚線美) the beauty of leg lines; a nice leg line. きゃくせんび

**각설**(却說) now / ～하다 return to the topic[main subject]; resume *one's* story/～하고 now resume our story ; now let us proceed. さて. ところで

**각섬석**(角閃石) 『광』 amphibole.

**각성**(覺醒) awakening; arousal; disillusion/～하다 awake (*from·to*); wake up (*to*)《미몽에서》 be disillusioned/ ～시키다 awaken; open *one's* eye; bring (*one*) to *one's* senses. かくせい

**각성**(各姓) each surname[man]; men of different surname. おのおのの姓

**각세공**(角細工) hornware; horn manufactures; hornwork. つのざいく

**각소**(各所) each place; various places 각군데. かくしょ

**각속도**(角速度) 『물』 angular velocity. かくそくど

**각수**(恪守) adherence/ ～하다 adhere to; stick to; cling to; hold fast to; be loyal to.

**각수**(刻手) an engraver; a carver; a sculptor. ちょうごくか

**각시** (인형) a doll 《새색시》a bride/～놀음하다 play with dolls. にんぎょう

**각양**(各樣) diversity; variety; manifoldness; all sorts/～의 various; diverse; manifold/ ～ 각색(各色) variety; diversity. かよう

**각연증**(脚軟症) debility of legs.

**각오**(覺悟)《알아차림》 readiness; preparedness《결심》 resolution; resolve《대기》 expectation《단념》 resignation/～하다 be ready[prepared] for; resolve; be determined; expect. かくご

**각외**(閣外) ～의[에서] outside the Cabinet

**각운**(脚韻) 『문』 an end rime; a rhyme/～을 맞추다 rhyme きゃくいん

**각원**(各員) every one[man]; [each and] all/ ～은 최선을 다하라 Let everyone do his best. かくいん

**각원**(閣員) a Cabinet minister[member]; a member of the Cabinet. かくいん

**각위**(各位) every one; all 《제군》 gentl-*emen*《편지용》 sirs/관계자 ～《서한에서》 To whom it may concern. かくい

**각의**(閣議) a Cabinet conference[council; meeting]/정례[임시] ～ an ordinary[extraordinary] Cabinet council [meeting]. かくぎ

**각이**(各異) ～하다 (be) each different from another; different from each other. べつべつことなること

**깎이다** ①《사역》 let (one) cut[shave, shear]／들의 풀을 ~ get the grass cut ② 《피동》 have (one's hair) cut; be hurt; be reduced; be trimmed／낯이 ~ loss face. そられる

**각인**(刻印) engraving[carving; cutting] a seal／~하다 engrave a seal. こくいん

**각인**(各人) each person; every one 《모두》 everybody. かくじん

**각자**(各自) each [one]／~의 each; respective. かくじ

**각자**(刻字) engraving characters／~하다 chase[carve, engrave] letters (on a surface). こくじ

**각장**(各葬) a separate burial／~하다 bury (a couple) separately. べつべつにほうむること

**각재**(角材) square timber[lumber]《작은 것》 a scantling. かくざい

**각적**(角笛) a horn; a bugle かくふえ

**깍정이** 《인색한》 a miser; a niggard; a stinkard. けちんぼう

**각조**(各條) each[every] article[item]《조》 article by article. かくじょう

**각종**(各種) every kind; various kinds; all kinds／~의 all sorts of; of all kinds; various／~ 경기 all sorts of sports[games]. かくしゅ

**각주**(角柱) a square pillar[column]《수》 a prism. かくちゅう

**각주**(脚註) footnotes／책에 ~를 달다 give footnotes to a book.

**각죽**(刻竹) a carved bamboo pipe; a carved tobacco pipe of bamboo.

**깍지**¹ 《활 쏠 때의》 an archer's thimble／~끼다 cross one's fingers. ゆみがけ

**깍지**² 《껍질》 an empty pod; a shell. かわ

**각지**(各地) every place 《여러 지방》 various places[quarters] 《전 지방》 all parts of the country／세계 ~로부터 from every corner of the earth. かくち

**각질**(脚疾) disease of the legs; leg ailments. あしのびょうき

**각질**(角質) horniness 《생화학》 keratin 《곤충 등의》 chitin／~층(層) horny layer; stratum corneum. かくしつ

**각처**(各處) each place 《여러 곳》 various place／~에 everywhere. かくしょ

**각체**(各體) 《서체의》 various styles of writing 《인쇄의》 various prints[types]; fonts[founts《영》]. いろいろなていさい

**각촌**(各村) every[each] village; all the villages. いろいろなむら

**각추**(角錐) 《수》 pyramid. かくすい

**각추렴**(各―) collection (of money) from each individual／~하다 collect (money) from each one.

**각축**(角逐) competition; rivalry; contest／~하다 compete (with); contend (with); vie with (for)／~장 the arena of competition. かくちく

**각층**(各層) each class [of society]／각계 ~의 명사 notables in[of] all walks of life. かくそう

**각테**(角―) a rim made of horn／~ 안경 horn-rimmed glasses.

**각파**(各派) each[political] party 《정당》 all the parties 《종파》 all sects[denominations] 《유파, 학파》 all schools／~ 교섭회 a joint conference of all political parties. かくは

**각판**(刻版) 《판목》 a printing block; a woodcut 《판각》 woodcutting／~본 a woodcut; a wood block. はんぽん

**각필**(擱筆) ~하다 lay down one's pen; leave off[stop] writing; conclude (a writing). かくひつ

**각하**(却下) dismissal; rejection／~하다 dismiss; reject; turn down. きゃっか

**각하**(閣下) 《이인칭》 Your Excellency《삼인칭》 His[Her] Excellency《단수》／Their Excellencies《복수》／장관 ~ Your Excellency the Minister. かっか

**각하**(刻下) the urgency of the moment／~의 present; of the day[hour, moment]. こっか

**각항**(各項) each item[paragraph]; every clause[provision]. かくこうもく

**각혈**(咯血) hemoptysis ⇨객혈. かっけつ

**각형**(角形) 《모난 형상》 square shape 《사각형》 a quadrilateral. かくがた

**각희**(脚戯) the spots of wrestling.

**간** 《소금 성분》 the ingredient of salt 《소금 맛》 a salt taste; saltiness／~다 salt down; season／~보다 taste (a thing) to see how it is seasoned; taste the seasoning of. しおのせいぶん

**깐** calculation／제 ~에는 in one's own calculation; to oneself. すいりょう

**간**(艮) 《간쾌》 the trigram(☶). かん

**간**(肝) ①《해》 the liver ②《뱃장》 pluck; courage; spirit; spunk／~이 큰 daring; bold; plucky; spunky; adventurous／~이 콩알만해지다 be terrified／~이 작은 timid. きも

**간**(間) ①《길이》 a kan (about six chuk) ②《가옥의》 a room／세 ~ 집 a three-room[ed] house ③《동안》 duration; for 《장소》 between／1개월 ~ for a month. あいだ

**간간이**(間間―) occasionally; at times; [every] now and then. たまに

**간간하다**¹ 《맛이》 be somewhat salty; have salty flavour.

**간간하다**² 《마음이》 (be) ticklish; exciting; thrilling.

**깐깐하다** ①《성질이》 (be) sticky; pertinacious; tenacious／《깐깐한 사람》 a particular person ②《차지다》 (be) sticky and stiff. ねばりつよい

**간거르다**(間―) skip every other one [time]. あいだをおく

**간검**(看檢) inspection; survey／~하다 inspect; survey; overlook. けんじ

**간격**(間隔) 《공간》 a space; an interval; a distance／3미터의 ~을 두고 at three-meter interval; at intervals of three meters. かんかく

**간결(簡潔)** brevity; conciseness; terseness; pithiness／～하다 brief; concise; terse／～히 briefly; concisely／～한 설명 a brief explanation. かんけつ

**간계(奸計)** a trick; an evil[a dark, a crafty] design; a vicious plan; an artifice. かんけい

**간고(艱苦)** hardships; suffering; privations／～를 겪다 go through[undergo] hardships; suffer privations; taste the bitters of life. かんく

**간곡(懇曲)** kindness; cordiality 《자상》 exhaustiveness／～하다 《정중》 polite; courteous 《친절》 kind; friendly 《극진》 cordially; warmhearted; hospitable／～하게 대접하다 receive (one) cordially; entertain (one) hospitably. こんせつ

**간곤(艱困)** 《빈곤》 poverty; need; penury; want／～하다 (be) poor; needy

**간과(干戈)** arms; weapons [of war]／~를 건네다 go to war (with). かんか

**간과(看過)** overlooking ／ ～하다 pass over; overlook; fail to notice; connive at 《묵인》 wink at (a fault). みすごすこと

**간교(奸巧)** craft; wiliness／～하다 (be) cunning, wily; crafty; artful; slippery. わるくたくみなこと

**간구(懇求)** an earnest request; an entreaty／～하다 entreat; request earnestly. こんせつにもとめること

**간구(艱苟)** poverty; destitution; need; penury want／～하다 (be) poor; needy; destitute. ひんこん

**간국** ①《짠물》 salty liquids; a salt solution; brine ②《기름때》 sweaty grime. しおけのおおいしる

**간국(幹局)** ability; talent; parts.

**간극(間隙)** a gap; an aperture. かんげき

**간기(肝氣)** a child's disease characterized by indigestion and dull appetite. しょうにのきふかりょう

**간기(刊記)** a colophon; an imprint.

**간난(艱難)** hardships; privations; difficulties; trials. かんなん

**간난 신고(艱難辛苦)** hardships; privations; difficulties; trials; afflictions／～하다 undergo[go through] hardships. かんなんしんく

**간녕(奸佞)** craftiness; viciousness; wickedness／～하다 (be) crafty; cunning; wily; vicious; wicked; treacherous. じゃあくにしてへつらうこと

**간능(幹能)** ability; talent; parts; capacity. さいのうのりりょく

**간닥거리다, 깐닥거리다** budge; totter; be shaky; be loose. ゆらゆらする

**간단(間斷)** intermission; interruption; a break／～없는 continual; incessant; continuous. たえず

**간단(簡單)** brevity; conciseness; simplicity／～한 brief; simple 《식사 등이》 right／～히 말하다 speak in plain language. かんたん

**간단 명료(簡單明瞭)** terseness; brevity; simplicity／～하다 (be) simple; brief ／글은 ～함이 생명이다 Brevity is the soul of writing. かんたんめいりょう

**간달** last month; the preceding month; ultimo. せんげつ

**간담(肝膽)** ①《간과 쓸개》 liver and gall ②《마음·심중》 one's innermost heart／~을 서늘케 하다 strike chill into one's heart; curdle one's blood／～ 상조(相照)하다 exchange confidences. かんたん

**간담(懇談)** a chat; a familiar[friendly] talk／～하다 have a familiar talk (with); chat (with)／～회 a round table conference. こんだん

**간당(奸黨)** a group[band] of old foxes; sly dogs. あくとう

**간대로** (not) likely; (not) possibly; (not) so easily; so. そんなにたやすくは

**간댕거리다** dangle; tremble; swing／간댕 간댕 danglingly. ゆらゆらする

**간데족족** everywhere[wherever] one goes; all over. どこも

**간도(間道)** a secret path; a bypath 《지름길》 a short cut. わきみち

**간도(奸徒)** a group of wily characters; villains. あくにん

**간독(奸毒)** viciousness; wickedness／～하다 (be) vicious; wicked.

**간동그리다** bundle [it] up neat.

**간두(竿頭)** the greatest extreme ⇒백척 간두(百尺竿頭)／～지세(之勢) the last extreme; the most critical situation. ひじょうにきけんなじょうたい

**간드랑거리다** swing gently; dangle／간 드랑간드랑 danglingly. ゆらゆらゆれる

**간드러지다** (be) charming; fascinating; radiant; bright; coquettish／간드러진 웃음 a radiant smile.

**간들간들 《태도》** charmingly; in fascinating manners 《바람》 gently; lightly 《물체》 rockingly; unsteadily; shakingly 《소리》 lilting[ly]. そよそよ

**간들거리다** ①《태도》 act in a charming manner; coquet play a fascinating part ②《바람》 blow gently; breeze ③《물체》 shake; rock; totter.

**간략(簡略)** simplicity; brevity／～하다 (be) simple; brief 《약식》 (be) informal ／～하게 하다 simplify. かんりゃく

**간리(奸吏)** a corrupt official.

**간막이(間一)** 《분할》 partition; division 《포장》 screen／～하다 partition[divide] off. あいだのしきり

**간만(干滿)** ebb and flow; flux and reflux; tide; rise and fall／～의 차 the difference between the rise and fall of the tide. かんまん

**간망(懇望)** an entreaty; solicitation／~하다 entreat; desire earnestly／～에 의하여 at one's earnest request. こんもう

**간맞추다** season (food) with salt; salt; flavour (soup) with salt; salt properly ; season well. しおけをよくする

**간명**(簡明) terseness; brevity; conciseness/ ~하다 concise; terse; short and clear/ ~하게 말하다 speak in plain words. かんめい

**간물** salt[y] water; soy water 《간국》 brine. しおけのあるみず

**간물**(奸物) a crafty fellow; a villain; a knave. かんぶつ

**간물**(乾物) dry provisions; dry goods; dried fish[meat] groceries〈미〉/ ~상 (商) a grocer. かんぶつ

**간밤** last night; yesterday evening/ ~의 불 last night's fire. さくや

**간방**(艮方) the northeast; the northeastern quarter.

**간방**(間方) the directions lying midway between each two main points of the compass; northeast, northwest, southeast, and southwest.

**간병**(看病) nursing/ ~하다 nurse; tend; care for; attend on/ ~인(人) a [sick] nurse. かんびょう

**간보다** taste; see how the food is salted[seasoned]. しおかげんをみる

**깐보다** ①《헤아리다》 calculate; observe; wait and see ②⇒깔보다. すいりょうする

**간봉**(桿棒) a club; cudgel; a stick.

**간부**(姦夫) an adulterer; a paramour. かんぷ

**간부**(姦婦) an adulteress. かんぷ

**간부**(間夫) a secret lover. まおとこ

**간부**(幹部) the management; the managing staff; the executive; the leaders /~회의 a meeting of the managing staff; a directorial meeting/ ~ 후보생 a cadet; an officer cadet かんぶ

**간사**(奸詐) craft; guile; artifice; deceit /~하다 (be) crafty; wily; artful; deceitful. いつわり

**간사**(幹事) 《사람》 a manager; a secretary/원내 ~ the whip. かんじ

**간사위** resourcefulness; an elastic[a flexible] means.

**간살**(間一) a space of seven feet square; a space. しきりのめんせき

**간살부리다** flatter; fawn upon; 'curry favour with. おせじをいう

**간상**(奸商) a dishonest merchant; a fraudulent dealer; a profiteer/~배(輩) profiteers. わるいしょうにん

**간색**(看色) 《보기》 sampling 《물건》 a sample. みほん

**간색**(間色) a compound colo[u]r; demitint; halftone. かんしょく

**간석지**(干潟地) a dry beach; a beach at ebb tide. かいすいのていりするところ

**간선**(看一) an interview with the prospective bride[bridegroom]/~보다 see each other with a view to marriage. みあい

**간선**(幹線) a trunk[main] line/ ~ 도로 a principal road; an arterial road 〈영〉; a boulevard〈미〉; a trunk road. かんせん

**간섭**(干涉) interference; intervention; meddling/ ~하다 interfere (in *a matter*) with; (*one*) meddle in (*with*); step in/무력 ~ armed intervention/선거 ~ Government[official] interference in an election. かんしょう

**간성**(干城) a bulwark; a defender; a safeguard/국가의 ~ the bulwark of the state. くにのまもりとなるぶし

**간세**(間稅) an indirect tax ⇒간접세.

**간소**(簡素) simplicity/ ~하다 (be) simple; plain [and simple]/ ~한 식사 a plain meal/~화하다 simplify (*a ceremony*). かんそ

**간솔**(簡率) being honest and direct/ ~하다 (be) straightforward; candid; brief and frank. かんたんなこと

**간수**(一水) 《소금성의》 salt water; brine.

**간수**(看守) ①《형무소의》 a prison guard; a turnkey; a warder; a jailer ②《지킴》 guard; watching. かんしゅ

**간수**(間數) the numbers of *kan* of a house; the floor space of a house. まかず

**간수하다** keep; preserve. よくほかんする

**간식**(間食) eating between meals; a snack/~하다 eat between meals; have a snack. かんしょく

**간신**(奸臣) a villainous retainer; a treacherous subject; a traitor. かんしん

**간신**(諫臣) a remonstrant subject; a faithful retainer. かんしん

**간신**(艱辛) hardships; privations; afflictions/ ~히 with difficulty; narrowly; barely/ ~히 살아가다 eke out a scanty livelihood. かんなんしんく

**간실간실, 깐실깐실** fawningly; in a flattering manner. ぺこぺこ

**간악**(奸惡) wickedness; treachery/ ~하다 (be) wicked; villainous; knavish; treacherous. かんあく

**간약**(簡約) conciseness; brevity; simplification/ ~하다 condense; abridge; simplify; abbreviate; shorten/ ~한 simple; brief; concise.

**간언**(間言) discord-producing speech; alienating words. りかんすることば

**간언**(諫言) remonstrance; advice 《간함》 remonstration; expostulation; admonition/~하다 remonstrate[expostulate] with (*one of his folly*); admonish (*one for his faults*). かんげん

**간요**(肝要) 《중요》 importance 《필요》 necessity/ ~하다《중요》 (be) important; of [vital] importance; vital 《필수》 (be) essential. かんよう

**간웅**(奸雄) a great villain; a Mephistophelian hero; a great traitor; a major traitor. かんちにたけたえいゆう

**간원**(懇願) solicitation; supplication/ ~하다 beg earnestly; solicit; supplicate (*for*); beseech. こんがん

**간위**(奸僞) wile; trickery; trickishness; guile. よこしまないつわり

**간유**(肝油) cod-liver oil/ ~ 드롭스 cod-

**간음(姦淫)** adultery; misconduct; illicit intercourse/ ~하다 commit adualtery; have illicit intercourse with/ ~죄 adultery. かんいん

**간이(簡易)** simplicity; easiness/~하다 (be) simple; easy; plain; elementary; simplified/ ~ 생활 a simple life/ ~ 주택 a simple frame house/ ~ 식당 a quick-lunch room; a chophouse/ ~ 재판소 a summary court. かんい

**간인(奸人)** a knave; a villain; a wicked man; a scoundrel よこしまなひと

**간인(刊印)** ~ print ⇒인쇄.

**간자(間者)** 《염탐군》 a spy; an agent; an emissary; a secret agent. スパイ

**간작(間作)** catch-cropping/~하다 grow (*some vegetable*) between the rows of another crop; intercrop/ ~물 a catch-crop. かんさく

**깐작거리다** stick (*to*); be tenacious ⇒끈적거리다. ひじょうにねばりつよくする

**간잠지런하다** have sleepy eyes[be drowsy] with lack of sleep[drunkenness]; *one's* eyelids are heavy. うとうとする

**간장(一醬)** soy [sauce]; soybean sauce/ ~콩 soy-bean. しょうゆ

**간장(肝腸)** heart; the seat of emotion [sorrow]/ ~을 녹이다 burn with passion (*for*). かんちょう

**간장(肝臟)** 〖해〗 a liver/ ~병 liver trouble/ ~염 hepatitis/ ~디스토마 distoma hepaticum; distomatosis/ ~ 절개(切開) hepatotomy. かんぞう

**간재(奸才)** cunning; trickiness; craftiness. よこしまなさいのう

**간적(奸賊)** 《역적》 a traitor; a reble 《악한》 a knave; a villain; a ruffian; an outlaw. ぎゃくぞく

**간절(懇切)** ①《지성스러움》 earnest; eagerness; ardentness/ ~하다 (be) earnest; eager; fervent; ardent/~한 소원 *one's* fervent desire ②《친절·극진》 kindness; cordiality; hospitality/~하다 (be) kind; cordial/~히 earnestly; eagerly; fervently; ardently. こんせつ

**간접(間接)** indirection; indirectness/~의 indirect; roundabout; second-hand / ~적으로 indirectly; at secondhand / ~ 목적어 an indirect object/ ~ 선거 indirect election; voting for the presidential electors〈미〉/~세 an indirect tax. かんせつ

**간조(干潮)** ebb tide; low water[tide]/ ~시에 at low tide. かんちょう

**간주(看做)** ~하다 consider[regard, look upon] (*as*); take (*for*); deem/해결된 것으로 ~하다 look upon (*a matter*) as settled. みなすこと

**간주곡(間奏曲)** an interlude; an intermezzo. かんそうきょく

**간증(干證)** ①《종교의》 profession; confession/ ~하다 profess; confess ②《증인》 a witness.

**간지(奸智)** cunning; craft; guile; wiles; subtlety. かんち

**간지(簡紙)** letter-paper; stationery; writing paper. よいびんせんじ

**간지(諫止)** dissuasion/ ~하다 dissuade (*one from doing*). いさめとめること

**간지(干支)** the sexagenary cycle. かんし

**간지럽다** tickle; titillation/ ~타다 be keenly sensitive to ticking; be easily tickled. くすぐったいこと

**간지럽히다** ①《몸이》 (be) ticklish/발이 ~ My feet tickle ②《마음이》 be thrilled; feel shameful; be fearful; be nervous; feel insecure. くすぐったい

**간직하다** keep; store; put away (가슴 속에) hoard/가슴 속에 깊이 간직해 두다 keep in *one's* heart. ほかんする

**간질(癎疾)** 〖의〗 epilepsy 《발작》 an epileptic fit. てんかん

**간질 세포(間質細胞)** 〖해〗 interstitial cells;

**간질이다** tickle; titillate/겨드랑 밑을 ~ tickle (*one*) under his arm[s]. くすぐる

**간짓대** a long bamboo pole. ながいたけざお

**간책(奸策)** a sinister scheme; a crafty design; a [shrewd] trick/ ~을 부리다 lay schemes. かんさく

**간척(干拓)** land reclamation by drainage/ ~하다 reclaim (*land*) by drainage/~지 reclaimed land. かんたく

**간첩(間諜)** a spy; an agent; a political [secret] agent/ ~을 색출하다 hunt out spies; dig up spies. かんちょう

**간첩(簡捷)** expedition; promptitude; dispatch/ ~하다 (be) prompt (*in handling*).

**간청(懇請)** entreaty; solicitation; an earnest request/ ~하다 entreat; implore; solicit (*one for*); earnestly request[ask for]/ ~에 의하여 at *a person's* earnest request. こんせい

**간초(艱楚)** hardships; privations/ ~를 견디어 내다 endure hardships; go through privations.

**간촉(懇囑)** an earnest request; supplication/~하다 beseech; earnestly request. こんせつなしょくたく

**간추(看秋)** ~하다 oversee harvesting.

**간출(刊出)** publication/ ~하다 publish; issue; bring out.

**간취(看取)** ~하다《보다》 perceive; notice; divine 《간파하다》 see through/나는 그의 간계를 ~했다 I saw through his wiles. みなすこと

**간치다** salt; season.

**간친(懇親)** friendship; sociability; good fellowship/~하다 (be) friendly (*with*); intimate (*with*)/~회 a social meeting [gathering]; a social〈미〉/ ~ 맺다 make friends hip with. こんしん

**간통(姦通)** adultery; illicit intercourse; criminal connections/~하다 have[illicit] intercourse; commit adultery; have a liaison (*with*)/ ~죄(罪) adu-

간투사(間投詞) 《언》 an interjection ⇨감탄사.

간파(看破) penetration; pierce into／～하다 see through; take in; penetrate [into]／동기를 ～하다 penetrate another's motives.

간판(看板) a sign [board]; a billboard (외관) show; appearance／～을 걸다 hang out a signboard.

간판장이(看板—) a sign maker[painter].

간편(簡便) simplicity; convenience／～하다 (be) easy; handy; convenient／～법(法) an easy[a simple] method; an easy way.

간품(看品) inspection; sampling／～하다 sample; inspect.

간핍(艱乏) utter deistitution／～하다 (be) utterty destitute.

간하다 salt ⇨간.

간하다(諫—) remonstrate with; expostulate with; admonish; advise.

간하다(奸—) (be) treacherous; wily; (be) wicked.

간해 last year.

간행(刊行) publication／～하다 publish; issue; bring out／～물 a publication／정기 ～물 a periodical.

간헐(間歇) intermittence／～하다 intermit／～열(熱) intermittent fever／～천(泉) an intermittent fountain／～적인 intermittent.

간호(看護) nursing; tending; care [of the sick]／～하다 nurse; care for; watch [sit up] with.

간호법(看護法) the art of nursing.

간호병(看護兵) a nurse; a hospital orderly; a medical-corps man.

간호원(看護員) a nurse; a trained nurse; a hospital nurse ⇨간호인.

간호인(看護人) 《여자》 a nurse 《남자》 a male nurse.

간호학(看護學) the science [study] of nursing.

간혹(間或) occasionally; sometimes; once in a while／～ 있는 occasional; infrequent／～ 오는 손님 a casual visitor.

간혼(間婚) ～하다 cause a proposed match to be broken off; undo a match.

간활(奸猾) cunning; slyness; carftiness; wiles／～하다 (be)cunning; sly; crafty.

간흉(奸凶) wickedness; viciousness／～하다 (be) wicked; villainous; utterly wicked.

간힘쓰다, 간힘주다 hold one's breath in an effort to endure[stand] pain.

갇히다 be confined; be shut up; be locked in 《감옥에》 be imprisoned; be kept indoors.

갇힌물 standing[stagnant] water.

갈¹ 〖식〗 a reed ⇨갈대.

갈² 〖학(學)〗 science of; study of;-ology／한글～ the study of the Korean language／소리～ phonology／월～ syntax.

갈가리 in pieces ⇨가리가리.

갈가마귀 〖조〗 a jackdaw; Corvus monedula(학명).

갈가위 a screw; an avaricious man; a rapacious fellow.

갈개 a cushion.

갈갈 avidly; greedily

깔깔 screaming with laughter／～ 웃다 laugh loudly

깔깔하다 ①《성질이》(be) moody; particular; fastidious; fussy; touchy ②《표면이》 (be) rough.

갈강갈강 wheezing ⇨갈그랑갈그랑.

갈개 a ditch; a gutter; a drain.

깔개 a cushion.

갈개발 ①《연의》 a pair of tags hanging from a kite ②《사람》 one who makes use of another's influence; a hanger-on.

갈갯군 one who interferes with another's business; an intruder; a meddler.

갈강갈강하다 (be) thin in the face; slender; slim.

갈거미 〖충〗 a long-legged spider; Tetragnatha praedonia(학명).

갈겨먹다 seize [on the way]; snatch; usurp.

갈겨쓰다 scrawl; scribble [busily].

갈고리쇠 ①《쇠》 a hook; crook; a gaff ②《사람》 a cantankerous person; a crooned stick.

갈고랑이 a hook 《작살》 a gaff.

갈고쟁이 a hook.

갈구(渴求) a craving (for); a longing (for); an ardent wish／～하다 crave [long, yearn] for; hanker after; desire eagerly.

갈구리 a hook ⇨갈고랑이.

갈그랑거리다 gurgle; wheeze.

갈근거리다 《욕심으로》 strive hard after gains 《목에서》 have an itching sensation in throat [caused by a hard obstructive phlegm].

깔끔거리다 prick; stick; irritate ⇨껄끔거리다.

깔끔하다 (be) particular; fastidious／성미가 깔끔한 사람 a man of fastidious character.

갈급(渴急) thirst; impatience／～하다 (be) thirsty (for); athirsty (for); impatient (to do).

갈기 a mane.

갈기갈기 in pieces; [in]to shreds／～ 찢다 tear to pieces; tear into strips; tear piecemeals.

갈기다 《때리다》knock; beat; strike; 《베다》slash; prune.

깔기다 discharge [excrements] indiscr-

**갈다**[1] 《밭을》till; plough; cultivate; put under cultivation. たがやすこと

**갈다**[2] 《바꾸다》change; replace; alter; substitute. とりかえる

**갈다**[3] ①《숫돌에》whet; sharpen 《면도칼을》grind; hone/칼을 ~ sharpen a knife; scour a knife/칼 가는 사람 a grinder; sharpener ②《광내게》polish; burnish 《광석을》cut/다이아몬드를 ~ cut[polish] a diamond ③《먹 따위를》rub; chafe 《줄로》file/먹을 ~ rub [down] an inkstick; rub fine; reduce to powder ④《이를》grind one's teeth/이를 갈며 분해 하다 grind one's teeth with vexation (at). とぐ

**깔다** ①《이불 따위를》spread; cover (with) 《돌 따위를》pave with/요를 ~ make a bed/자갈을 ~ spread gravel ②《깔고 앉다》sit[seat oneself] on/방석을 ~ sit [seat oneself] on a cushion ③《늘어 놓다》spread; lay out 《돈을》invest in; loan. しく

**깔딱거리다** keep gulping; gulp repeatedly. ごくりごくりする

**갈대** 【식】a reed; a rush/ ~가 많은 reedy/~ 피리 a reed[-pipe]. あし

**깔때기** a funnel じょうご

**갈대밭** a reed-blind; a hanging screen made of reeds. あしのはたけ

**갈등**(葛藤) complications; trouble; dissension; discord/ ~을 일으키다 cause 'give rise to] complications; breed discords. かっとう

**갈라내다** sort out. わける

**갈라서다** break with; separate; part from[with] 《이혼》divorce/ 그는 아내와 갈라섰다 He is parted from his wife. わかれる

**갈라지다** ①《쪼개지다》split; divided; cleave; fissure; crack; break/둘로 ~ break in two ②《사람 사이가》break up (with); split; fall out (with); be estranged (from)/여러 파로 ~ split into several factions. わかれる

**갈래** 《분기》a fork; a branch 《구분》a division 《분파》a section; a subdivision/두 ~ 길 a crossroad[s]/세 ~의 three-forked. ぶんり

**갈래다** ①《짐승이》rove; wander ②《길이》break[divide] into several branches; fork. まよう

**갈리다**[1] ①《갈게 하다》have (something) replaced/구두창을 ~ have one's shoes resoled ②《자리가》be replaced; be changed. とりかえられる

**갈리다**[2] 《칼 따위를》have (a knife) sharpened(갈게 하다); be sharpened(갈아지다). みがれる

**갈리다**[3] 《분리》be divided (into); break into; branch off (from); fork/ 두 패로 ~ be divided into two groups/이 지점에서 길이 갈린다 At this point the road branches. わかれる

**갈리다**[4] 《논밭을》have (land) cultivated (갈게 하다); be cultivated(갈아지다); m-ake (a person) till. たがやせる

**깔리다** ①《널리》cover all over/얼음이 ~ be frozen all over ②《밑에》get[be caught; be pinned]under/전차 밑에 ~ be pinned under a tram-car. しかれる

**갈림길** a branchroad; a forked road; a crossroads. わかれみち

**갈림목** a fork of the road; a corner at a juncture of streets. わかれみち

**갈마**(羯磨) karma (Sans).

**갈마들다** take turns; alternate (in); take one's turn. こうたいする

**갈망** ~하다 《감당》cope with; meet; deal successfully with; set (matters) right. しごとをなしとげうること

**갈망**(渴望) a longing (for); a craving (for); an eager[an earnest] desire; an ardent wish (for); thirst (for)/ ~하다 long[yearn, thirst] for; hanker after; desire eagerly/지적 ~ an intellectual thirst(desire). かつぼう

**갈매** ①《색》deep green ②《열매》fruit of the buckthorn. こいくさいろ

**갈매기** 【조】a sea-gull[-mew]. かもめ

**갈모** a rain cover for a hat.

**갈목** a spike[an ear] of a reed. あしの穂

**갈무리** ~하다 keep; preserve. ほぞん

**갈미** 【동】a sea cucumber; a holothurian. なまこ

**깔밋하다** (be) simple and neat; attractive. さっぱりしている

**갈바람** a west wind 《서풍》. にしかぜ

**갈밭** a field of reeds; a reedy marsh. あしはら

**갈범** a real tiger. とら

**갈보** a harlot; a prostitute; a street walker/~집 a brothel; a whorehouse; a house of ill fame/ ~ 노릇을 하다 go [live] on the streets; walk the streets. ばいいんふ

**깔보다** make light of; hold cheap; belittle; depreciate; underrate. けいしする

**갈분**(葛粉) arrowroot starch. くずのこな

**갈붙이다** alienate; estrange; set (people) at variance. なかたがいさせる

**갈비** the ribs; the costae/ 소의 ~ ribs of beef. ろっこつ

**갈빗대** a rib; a rib-bone/~를 분지르다 get a rib broken. あばらぼね

**갈삿갓** a conical reed hat.

**갈새** 【조】the reed warbler.

**갈색**(褐色) brown/ ~의 brown/ ~인종 the brown races. かっしょく

**갈서다** stand in a line; form in line; form a line; line up. ならんでたつ

**갈수**(渴水) a dearth of water/ ~기 a dry season. かっすい

**갈수록** all the more; increasingly; as time goes by. ますます

**갈씬하다** (a skirt) almost touch (the floor); scrape; graze. ふれかする

**갈아내다** remove; replace. とりかえる

갈아들다 supplant; supersede; take the place of. いれかわる
갈아들이다 replace (a person) with (another). いれかわらせる
갈아붙이다 ①(이를) clench (one's teeth); grind (one's teeth) ②(바꾸어 붙임) renew; replace; change (for a new one); attach[fix] a new. くいしばる
갈아입다 change (one's clothes)/젖은 옷을 마른 옷으로 ~ change wet clothes for dry ones. きかえする
갈아주다 buy up (things) from a retailer giving him due profit. かってやる
갈아타다 make change (at); change; transfer (to) (배를) trans-ship/갈아타는 역 a junction [station]; a transfer point/예산до으로 ~ transfer to a Yesan train のりかえる
갈음 《바꿈》substituting; replacing; changing; switching. かわり
갈음질 whetting; sharpening/ ~하다 whet; sharpen ~갈다. みがくこと
갈이¹ ①《논밭의》cultivation; tillage; plowing; farming ②《넓이》the acreage that may be covered by a day's plowing of a man. たがやす
갈이² 《일》turnery; lathing/ ~장이 a turner/ ~칼 a lathing hammer/ ~틀 a lathe/ ~방 세공품 a turnery; lathing. せんばんさいく
갈이³ 《대체》replacement; change; substitution. とりかえ
갈이질 plowing; farming; tillage; cultivation/ ~하다 plow; farm; till; cultivate. たがやすこと
갈잎 leaves of the overcup oak. かしわらのは
깔쭉거리다 《표면이》be rough 《천이》be coarse; be granular; feel rough to the touch. ぎざぎざする
갈쭉하다 (be) thick; heavy; (be) pulpy; mushy. とろりとしている
갈증(渴症) thirst/ ~이 나다 feel thirsty. のどがかわくこと
갈진(竭盡) exhaustion/ ~하다 exhaust; run out. つかいつくすこと
갈짓자걸음(一之字一) staggering; reeling; a tipsy lurch.
갈참나무 《식》an white oak; Quercus aliena(학명).
갈채(喝采) cheers; applause; an ovation / ~하다 applause; acclaim; cheer; give cheers/우뢰 같은 ~ a storm of applause. かっさい
갈청 the membranous layer lining the hollow of the stem of a reed. あしのこ
갈충 보국(竭忠報國) loyalty and patriotism. じんちゅうほうこく
갈치 《어》a hair-tail; Trichiurus japonicus(학명). たちうお
갈퀴 a rake/ ~로 긁다 rake. さでま
갈탄(褐炭) brown coal; lignite; sub-bituminous coal.
갈파(喝破) ~하다 declare; affirm; proclaim; expound; pronounce. かっぱ
갈팡지팡 confusedly; in a flurry; helter-skelter; pell-mell; this way and that / ~하다 run helter-skelter; get flurried; do not know what to do; be at a loss. うろうろ
갈포(葛布) grass cloth; cloth made of the fibre of a kohemp. くずぬの
갈품 an unblown spike of a reed.
갈피 a space; a division/책 ~ 속에 사진을 넣어 두다 keep a picture between the leaves of a book/ ~ 잡을 수 없는 말 a disjointed remark. ようりょう
갈화(葛花) flowers of an arrowroot; a flower of a kohemp.
긁다 《잘게》scratch; scrape 《이 따위로》crunch 《갈퀴로》rake 《험을》peck at; cavil (at, about); carp at; nag 《재물을》squeeze; extort. ほそかくこする
긁아먹다 ①《이로》gnaw (upon); nibble (at); crunch; bite (at) ②《재물을》squeeze; extort. かじってたべる
긁이 an iron piece used for polishing silverwork. けんまき
긁작거리다 scrape; crunch; gnaw; scratch and scratch. しまりにさわく
긁히다 be scratched/얼굴을 ~ be scratched on the face. さわかれる
감¹ 《식》a persimmon/ ~나무 a persimmon[-tree]. かき
감² 《재료》material; matter; stuff/옷 ~ woven materials; textiles/물 ~ dye stuffs; dyes. ざいりょう
감(感) 《느낌》feeling; sense; sentiment 《인상》an impression/제6~ the six senses/…의 ~을 주다 impress (one) as; give an impression of. かん
감(減) 《덞》deduction 《줄임》reduction 《감소》decrease 《할인》reduction (in price) 《감산》subtraction/ ~하다 decrease; diminish; reduce; deduct; cut down; mitigate/값을 ~하다 cut down a price/죄를 ~하다 mitigate[reduce] a punishment. げんずること
감가(減價) reduction of price; depreciation; a discount/ ~하다 reduce the price (of)/ ~ 판매 a discount sale; a bargain sale; slaughter/ ~ 상각(償却) depreciation. げんか
감각(感覺) sense; feeling 《감성》sensation / ~하다 feel/ ~미 sensuous beauty/ ~ 기관 a sense organ; a sensory/ ~력 sensibility/ ~론 《철·심》sensationalism; sensualism/ ~을 잃다 be benumbed/ ~이 날카롭다〔둔하다〕have keen[dull] senses. かんかく
감감하다 ①《소식이》hear nothing of; learn no news of (one)/그 후로 소식이 ~ I have not heard from him ever since. ②《차이·시간 등이》(be) long (before) 《아득하다》be far off[away]/내가 그의 학식을 따라가려면 아직 ~ It will be long before get as much knowledge as he has. しょうそくがない

**깜깜하다** (be) pitch-dark. ひじょうにくらい
**감개**(感慨) deep emotion/~하다 be full of deep emotion. かんがい
**감격**(感激) deep emotion/~하다 be deeply moved (*by*); be deeply impressed (*with, by*); be deeply stirred; be carried away with emotion; strong feeling/~적 연설 an inspiring speech/~시키다 inspire[impress, stir] deeply; move *another's* heart [deeply]/~의 눈물을 흘리다 be moved to tears. かんげき
**감경**(減輕) reduction[mitigation] of penalty; commutation; remission/~하다 reduce (*penalty*); commute (*a sentence*); mitigate (*a punishment*); remit; lower a penalty.
**감고**(甘苦) sweets and bitters; pleasure and pains; joys and sorrows; prosperity and adversity.
**감관**(感官) a sense [organ]/~적 착각 sensory illusion. かんかくきかん
**감광**(感光) 《사진의》 exposure [to light]; sensitization 《감광도》 sensitiveness/~지(紙) sensitive paper/~제(劑) a sensitizer/~판(板) a sensitive plate/~필름 sensitive film/~시키다 expose to light; sensitize. かんこう
**감국**(甘菊) 『식』 a winter chrysanthemum; *Chrysanthemum indicum*(학명).
**감군**(減軍) a cut in the armed forces; a military manpower reduction; arms reduction. くんたいをへらすこと
**감궂다** (be) atrocious; heinous; villainous; fiendish. じゃあくだ
**감금**(監禁) confinement; imprisonment; detention/~하다 confine; imprison; detain; lock in/불법 ~ illegal[unlawful] detention. かんきん
**감기**(感氣) a cold/유행성 ~ influenza; flu/《속》심한 ~ a bad cold/코~ a cold in a nose/ ~약 medicine for a cold; a cold-cure/~에 걸리다 catch [a] cold; have a cold. かぜ
**감기다**[1] ①《덩굴 따위가》 twine[coil] itself round; entwine 《태엽 따위가》 be wound 《거치적거리다》 cling to 《걸리다》 be caught in/나무에 뱀이 감겨 있었다 A snake coild itself around the tree. ②《감게 하다》 let (*one*) wind. まかれる
**감기다**[2] 《눈이》 be closed 《감게 하다》 let (*one*) close (*one's* eyes). めがとじられる
**감기다**[3] 《머을》 subject (*one*) to a wash [bath]. からだをあらわせる
**감내**(堪耐) endurance; patience/ ~하다 bear; endure; stand. にんたい
**감농**(監農) ~하다 oversee farmhands; oversee agriculture. かんのう
**감능**(堪能) ①《능력》 ability skill(감당하는); 《능숙》 mastery/~하다 (be) able; skilled; skillful ②《사람》 a man of ability; a master.
**감다**[1] 《눈을》 shut; close. めをとじる
**감다**[2] 《씻다》 wash; bathe; have a bath. からだをあらう

**감다**[3] 《실 따위를》 wind; coil; twine; bind [tie] round/목에 붕대를 ~ tie a bandage round the neck. まきつける
**감다**[4], **깜다** 《빛이》 (be) black; dark 〔=검다〕. くろい
**감당**(堪當) ~하다 cope with; deal well with / ~해낼 만하다 be equal to; be competent for/적을 ~해내다 cope with the enemy. たんとうする
**감때사납다** (be) very rough[tough]; unbending; coarse. あらあらしい
**감도**(感度) sensitivity; sensitiveness; severity. かんど
**감독**(監督) supervision; control; direction 《감독자》 a supervisor; an inspector 《경기의》 a manager 《영화의》 a director 《승려의》 a bishop/~하다 superintend; supervise; control; over see 《경기자를》 coach/~ 관청 the competent authorities /…의 ~하에 under the supervision of. かんとく
**감독파 교회**(監督派敎會) the Episcopal Church.
**감돌다** 《물이》 eddy; swirl; whirl 《돌아오다》 return; come and go. うずまき
**감돌이** one who returns for a small profit. けちんぼう
**감동**(感動) impression; inspiration; emotion/~하다 be impressed (*with, by*); be moved[touched] (*by*)/~시키다 impress; move; affect; appeal to (*one*)/크게 ~하다 be filled with emotion; be deeply moved. かんどう
**감득**(感得) ~하다 《눈치채다》get conscious (*of*); take hint (*of*) 《깨닫다》 realize; perceive. かんとく
**감등**(減等) 《강등》 demotion 《감형》 commutation/~하다 demote; commute; dogged; unbending. げんとう
**감람**(橄欖) ①『식』 a Chinese olive; a Java almond/~나무 a Java almond/~기름 olive oil ②⇒올리브/~빛 olive color[green]. かんらん
**감로**(甘露) nectar; honeydew. かんろ
**감루**(感淚) tears of gratitude/ ~를 흘리다 shed tears of gratitude. かんるい
**감률**(甘栗) sweet chestnuts. あまぐり
**감리**(監理) supervision; superintendence /~하다 supervise; superintend; have control of[over]. かんり
**감마제**(減摩劑) a lubricant. げんまざい
**감면**(減免) reduction and exemption/ ~하다 exempt; remit. げんめん
**감명**(感銘) [deep] impression/~하다 be impressed with[by]; be moved by; be deeply touched by / ~시키다 impress (*one*); make an impression on (*one's* mind). かんめい
**감미**(甘味) sweetness; a sweet taste/~료(料) sweetenings. かんみ
**깜박, 깜빡** 《잠시》for the moment/~ 잊다 forget for the moment; escape *one's* memory. ひかりのきらめくさま
**깜박깜박, 깜빡깜빡** flickeringly; waver-

깜박거리다, 깜빡거리다 ((눈·별이)) wink; twinkle; blink ((불이)) flicker; waver /눈을 ~ blink *one's* eyes.

감발 feet wraps; coverings of cloth for protecting the feet. きゃはんのひとつ

감빨다 ((입맛)) lick up with a good appetite; enjoy licking up (*a taffy*) ((욕심)) (be) greedy (*for*); bent upon gain. うまそうにすう

감빨리다 ((식욕이)) feel the appetite aroused ((잇속·욕심이)) be tempted by gain. しょくよくをそそられる

감발저뀌 a flatterer; a sycophant; a toady. わるがしこいひと

감방(監房) a cell; a ward. かんぼう

감법(減法) 【수】 subtraction. げんぽう

감별(鑑別) discrimination; discernment /~하다 discriminate; distinguish [between A and B]; judge. かんべつ

감복(感服) admiration; wonder/ ~하다 admire; be struck with admiration; wonder at/ ~할 만한 admirable; laudable; praiseworthy/ ~시키다 excite *one's* admiration; strike (*one*) with admiration. かんぷく

감복숭아 〖식〗 an almond.

감봉(減俸) reduction of *one's* salary [pay] ((벌몰)) downgrading mulct/ ~하다 reduce[cut] *one's* salary. げんぽう

깜부기 ((곡물의)) smut; black. くろほ

감사(監査) ((검사)) inspection ((회계)) audit/ ~하다 inspect ((회계)) audit (*accounts*)/ ~역(役) an auditor. かんさ

감사(監事) ((사람)) an inspector; a supervisor ((회계 따위의)) an auditor. かんさ

감사(感謝) thanks; gratitude; appreciation ((신에의)) thanksgiving/ ~하다 thank; be thankful[grateful] (*for*); feel grateful; express *one's* gratitude./ ~장 a letter of thanks[appreciation]/ [추수] ~절 Thanks giving Day(미). かんしゃ

감사납다 (be) touch; stiff; dogged; unbending. こわい

감싸다 protect; shield; shelter; cover (*a person* from) ((변호)) plead for (*another*); plead in (*a person's*) favor; take (*a person*) under *one's* wing/죄인을 ~ shelter a culprit. かくしてまもる

감삭(減削) reduction; curtailment; retrenchment/ ~하다 curtail; retrench; reduce; cut [down]; slash; pare down; diminish. さくげん

감산(甘酸) ((맛)) the sweets and sours; pleasures and pains; joys and sorrows. あまさとすっぱい

감산(減算) 【수】 subtraction. げんざん

감산(減産) ((자연적)) a decrease in production ((인위적)) a crop reduction. げんさん

감상(鑑賞) appreciation/ ~하다 appreciate; enjoy/ ~력 an appreciative power/영화 ~회 a private show of noted films [for appreciative spectators/ ~적 appreciative. かんしょう

감상(感傷) sentimentality/ ~적 sentimental/~주의 sentimentalism/ ~주의자 a sentimentalist. かんしょう

감상(感想) feelings; thoughts; impression〖s〗/ ~담 comments; expression of *one's* feeling/ ~문 description of *one's* feeling/ ~을 말하다 state[give] *one's* impression (*of*). かんそう

감색(紺色) dark[deep] blue; navy blue. こんいろ

감성(感性) sensitivity; sensibility; the sense ((감수성)) susceptibility. かんせい

감세(減税) reduction of taxes; a tax reduction[cut]/ ~하다 reduce[cut, lower] taxes. げんぜい

감세(減勢) subsidence; abatement/ ~하다 subside (*power, influence, etc.*); abate. せいりょくがへること

감소(減少) diminution; decrease ((저감)) reduction/ ~하다 diminish; decrease; drop ((점차로)) dwindle. げんしょう

감속(減速) speed reduction/~ 장치 reduction gear; a speed reducer/ ~ 운동 deceleration. げんそく

감손(減損) ((줌)) decrease; diminution ((손해)) loss ((마손)) wear/~하다 diminish; decrease; lessen; be impaired ((마손)) wear out. げんそん

감쇄(減殺) diminution; decrease; reduction; attenuation; detraction/ ~하다 lessen; diminish; reduce; attenuate; deaden (*force*). げんさつ

감수(甘受) willing submission/ ~하다 submit (*to*); put up with/모욕을 ~하다 brook[pocket, swallow] an insult; eat dust[dirt]. かんじゅ

감수(減水) the fall[decrease] of water /~하다 decrease; recede; fall; subside. げんすい

감수(減收) a decrease (of *income, production*). げんしゅう

감수(減壽) shortening of *one's* life/~하다 shorten *one's* life. じゅみょうがへること

감수(感受) reception; impression/ ~하다 be impressed with; receive an impression ((무전)) pick up/ ~성(性) sensibility; impressibility; receptivity/ ~성이 강한 sensitive. かんじゅ

감수(監修) [editorial] supervision/~하다 supervise [the compilation of]/ ~자 a chief editor. かんしゅう

감수(監守) custody; keeping/~하다 keep watch; guard; take into custody/ ~인 a keeper ((산림의)) a ranger. かんとくしてまもるひと

감수(減數) 【수】 a subtrahend/ ~ 분열 〖생〗 reduction division; meiosis; reducing division. げんすう

감숭하다 (be) covered with blackish fluff; blackish/감숭감숭 darkly[sprouting] here and there; dotted sparsely. くろみがかっている

감시(監視) ①((파수)) watch; lookout; vi-

**gil; observation 《노동 쟁의 동의》 picketting 《감독》 superintendence; supervision／~하다 watch; observe; keep an eye on; supervise／~원 《감독》 a superintendent; a watchman; a guard 《노동 조합의》 a picket 《세관의》 a tide waiter ②《형법상의》 surveillance; police supervision.　かんし

**감식**(鑑識) judg[e]ment; critical talent; discrimination; appreciation／~하다 judge; discriminate; appreciate／~안 a discerning eye／~가 a judge; a connoisseur／범죄 ~ criminal identification.　かんしき

**감식**(減食) reduction of one's diet; a short allowance of food／~하다 reduce one's diet; underfeed oneself／~ 요법(療法) reduced diet cure.　げんしょく

**감실거리다** flicker; flitter／깜실깜실 flickeringly; flitteringly.　ちらつく

**감심**(感心) admiration; wonder／~하다 admire; be struck with admiration; wonder at.　かんしん

**감아올리다** wind up; heave up／수부들은 닻을 감아올렸다 The sailors heaved the anchor.　まきあげる

**감안**(勘案) ~하다 take into account.

**감액**(減額) a reduction; a curtailment; a cut; diminution／~하다 reduce; curtail; cut down; diminish.　げんかく

**감언**(甘言) honeyed[sweet] words; flattery; cajolory／~으로 속이다 coax (one) to.　かんげん

**감언 이설**(甘言利說) honeyed words; fair speech; fine words／~로 꾀이다 talk [cajole, wheedle] (one) into.

**감역**(監役) supervision; superintendence／~하다 supervise; oversee; superintend.

**감연하다**(欲然—) (be) somewhat regrettable; somewhat disappointing.

**감연히**(敢然一) daringly; boldly; bravely; resolutely.　かんぜんとする

**감염**(感染) 《간접의》 infection 《접촉의》 contagion／~하다 《병이 사람에게》 infect; be infected (with); catch; contract／~성의 infectious; contagious; catching.　かんせい

**감옥**(監獄) a prison; a gaol〈영〉; a jail〈미〉／~살이 imprisonment 《징역》 servitude／~살이하다 be in prison; serve a [prison] term.　かんごく

**감우**(甘雨) a welcome[seasonable] rain.　じう

**감원**(減員) reduction of the staff; a personnal cut／~하다 reduce the personnel (of an office).　げんいん

**감은**(感恩) gratitude; gratefulness／~하다 feel gratitude.　かんおん

**감읍**(感泣) ~하다 be moved to tears; shed tears of gratitude (for).　かんきゅう

**감응**(感應) 《전기 동의》 induction; influence 《공감(共感)》 sympathy 《영감》 inspiration 《신명의》 [divine] response;

answer／~하다 induce; sympathize with; respond to／~ 변색 sympathetic coloration／~ 유전 telegony／~ 전기〔전류〕 induced electrical current／~ 코일 an induction coil.　かんのう

**감자** a [white] potato〈미〉.　じゃがいも

**감자**(甘蔗) 《사탕수수》 sugar cane／~당 (糖) cane sugar; sucrose.　さとうきび

**감자**(減資) reduction of capital; a capital decrease／~하다 reduce capital／~ 차익 gains from stock retirement.　げんし

**감작**(減作) a short[a bad; a poor]crop; the reduction of crop.　げんさく

**깜짝깜짝** 《놀라다》 with repeated starts; 《움직이다》 budging repeatedly 《눈을》 with repeated blinking／~ 놀라다 be startled again and again.　びっくり

**깜짝거리다** 《놀라다》 start repeatedly with fright(in fright) 《눈을》 blink; wink 《몸을》 stir about.　めをぱちぱちする

**깜짝이다** ①《눈을》 blink; wink · 깜박이다 ②《몸을》 budge; stir; make a movement.　まばたきする

**감잡히다** be taken advantage of one's weak point.　じゃくてんをつかれる

**감장, 깜장** black　くろ

**감전**(感電) an electric shock／~하다 receive an electric shock; be struck [affected] by electricity／~하여 죽다 be killed by an electric shock; be electrocuted.　かんでん

**감점**(減點) a demerit mark.

**감접이** a hem; hems at the ends of a bolt of cloth.　へりぬい

**감정**(鑑定) ①《판단》 judg[e]ment 《전문가의》 an expert opinion／~하다 judge; give an [expert] opinion／정신 ~ a psychiatric test／필적을 ~하다 give an expert opinion on handwriting ②《가격의》 appraisal／~하다 appraise; estimate／~ 가격 an appraisal; the estimated value ③《소송의》 legal advice／~하다 give legal advice／소송 ~ legal advice[consultation].　かんてん

**감정**(戡定) suppression／~하다 suppress.　へいてい

**감정**(感情) feeling[s] 《열정》 passion 《충서》 emotion 《정조(情操)》 sentiment 《충동》 impulse／~의 충돌 a collision of feelings／~적인 sentimental; passionate; emotional／한때의 ~으로 driven by a passing emotion; on the impulse of the moment／남의 ~을 해치다 hurt [wound] another's feelings.かんじょう

**감정**(憾情) ill feeling; a grudge; resentment; indignation; ill[bad] blood／~을 내다 get angry.　うらみ

**감쪽같다** 《수선해서》 (be) as good as before; so nicely prepared as not to allow any difference from the former state 《꾸민 일이》 (be) successful／감쪽같이 nicely; artfully／감쪽같이 속다 be nicely taken in; fall an easy victim to

감죄(減罪) commutation/ ~하다 commute. つみをへらすこと
감주(甘酒) a sweet drink made from rice. あまざけ
감지(感知) perception/ ~하다 perceive; sense; become aware (of). かんち
깜찍기실 fine[thin] but durable[strong] thread. きわめてほそくてつよいいと
감지덕지(感之德之) with hearty appreciation; with thanks; gratefully/ ~하다 heartily appreciate; offer cordial gratitude to[for].
깜찍스럽다 (be) precocious ⇨깜찍하다.
깜찍이 exceedingly; surprisingly; shrewdly; selfishly.
깜찍하다 (영리하다) be clever for *one's* age; (be) precocious; too sharp; overly shrewd 《단작스럽다》 cunning; crafty; sly; selfish 《놀랄 만하다》 surprising; unexpected 《비참하다》 pitious; sad; wretched 《아주 작다》 surprisingly small. すごい
감질나다(疳疾—) grow impatient; be irritated; become vexed (at).
감찰(鑑札) a license/영업 ~ a trade license/~료 a license fee. かんさつ
감찰(監察) 《행위》 inspection 《사람》 an inspector; a supervisor/ ~하다 inspect/~부 the supervisory section/~관 a supervisor. かんさつ
감채(減債) partial payment of a debt/ ~기금(基金) a sinking fund; an amortization fund. ふさいをへらすこと
감천(甘泉) a spring of a sweet[fresh] water. かんせん
감청(紺青) deep blue; ultramarine; denavy. あおこん
감초(甘草) 《식》 a liquorice -plant/《나무》 licorice; liquorice[-root] 《뿌리》 licorice. かんぞう
감촉(感觸) the [sense of] touch; feeling; sensation/ ~하다 feel; perceive through the senses. かんしょく
감추다 《숨겨 두다》 hide; conceal; put out of sight; keep secret 《안 드러나게》 cover; veil; cloak; disguise/행방을 ~ disappear; cover *one's* trails 《도망》 abscond/눈물을 ~ stifle *one's* tears. かくす
감축(減縮) reduction; diminution; retrenchment/~하다 reduce; diminish; retrench; cut down. げんしゅく
감축하다(感祝—) be thankful; be full of congratulation.
감취(酣醉) dead drunkenness/ ~하다 get as drunk as a lord. かんすい
감치다¹ 《마음에》 be on *one's* mind; be haunted (by). こころにとどめる
감치다² 《바느질의》 hem; sew up; stitch up; put a hem (in). ひだぬいする
감칠맛 《맛》 sapidity; relish; a pleasant taste 《끄는 힘》 charm; attraction; magnetism. うまみ
감탄(感歎, 感嘆) admiration; wonder; marvel/~하다 admire; be struck with admiration; marvel (at)/~할 만한 솜씨 an admirable performance/ ~사 《언》 an interjection; an exclamation/~문 an exclamative sentence/ ~부호 the exclamation mark[point]. かんたん
감탕 ①《풀》 animal glue mixed with pine resin ②《진흙》 mud; mire.
감퇴(減退) decline; ebb; loss/ ~하다 decline; ebb; recede; fall off/기억력의 ~ failing of memory/정력의 ~ a decline in energy. げんたい
감투 ①《모자》 a cap of horse hair formerly worn by the common people ②《벼슬》 a high office; a distinguished post/ ~를 쓰다 be appointed to a distinguished office; wear a horsehair cap. うまのたてがみでつくったかんむり
감투(敢鬪) fight courageously /~ 정신 a fighting spirit. かんとう
감파르다 (be) dark-blue; blueblack. あおくろい
감표(減票) a minus[subtraction] sign; a minus(—). マイナスの記号
감하다(減—) subtract; reduce; deduct; decrease. へらす
감행(敢行) 《단행》 decisive action/ ~하다 venture; dare; carry through; resolutely carry out. かんとう
감형(減刑) reduction of penalty; commutation of the sentence/~하다 reduce[mitigate] the penalty; commute the sentence. げんけい
감화(感化) influence 《교정》 correction/ ~하다 influence; inspire; reform 《교정하다》 correct/~력 influence/~사업 reformatory work/~원 a reformatory; a workhouse/~를 받다 be influenced (one). かんか
감회(感懷) thoughts; impressions; sentiments; feelings. かんかい
감흥(感興) interest; inspiration; fun; sport/~을 자아내다 stimulate[excite] interest. かんきょう
감히(敢—) boldly; daringly; positively / ~ …하다 dare; venture/~ 묻다 venture to ask *one's*. あえて
갑(甲) 《갑을병의》 the former; the one; A 《성적의》 class "A". こう
갑(匣) a case; a box 《담배 따위의》 a pack /담배 한 ~ a packet[pack《미》] of cigaret[te]s. ちいさいはこ
갑(岬) a cape; a promontory; a headland. みさき
갑각(甲殼) a shell; a crust; a carapace / ~류(類) 《동》 Crustacea. こうかく
갑갑증(一症) ennui; irksomeness; unpleasantness caused by stuffiness; impatience with stodginess. しんぱい
갑갑하다 (be) stodgy; stuffy; irksome; tedious; heavy/가슴이 ~ feel heavy in the chest/좁은 방 속에 있어서 ~ feel stuffy. いきづまる

**갑년**(甲年) the sixty-first year of one's birth.
**갑론 을박**(甲論乙駁) ~하다 argue for and against (*a matter*); argue pro and con. こうろんおつばく
**갑문**(閘門) a lock gate.
**갑부**(甲富) the richest man; the welthiest. いちばんかねもち
**갑사**(甲紗) fine gauze.
**깝살리다** ①《못다》 turn away; refuse to see; be not at home to [a caller]; send away ②《써 없애다》 squander; run through. たずねてきた人を追いだす
**갑상선**(甲狀腺) 〖의〗 thyroid gland/~비대(肥大) dilation of the thyroid gland/~ 호르몬 thyroin[e]. こうじょうせん
**깝신거리다** behave frivolously; behave lightly; act rashly. つまらないことをする
**갑오**(甲午) the 31st binary term of the sexagenary cycle. こうご
**갑옷**(甲一) a suit of an armo[u]r; a suit of mail. よろい
**갑을**(甲乙) 《갑과 을》 (A) and (B) 《성적 표의》 mark (A) and (B); mark Excellent and Good 《우열》 superiority and inferiority. こうおつ
**갑의**(甲衣) a suit of armo[u]r.
**갑이별**(甲離別) sudden parting; unexpected separation/ ~하다 be suddenly separated; be unexpectedly parted with. きゅうなわかれ
**갑일**(甲日) one's sixty-first birthday.
**갑자기** 《별안간》 suddenly; all of a sudden 《뜻밖에》 unexpectedly/~ 병에 걸리다 be suddenly taken ill. きゅうに
**깝짝거리다** behave[act] frivolously ⇒깝죽거리다
**갑작스럽다** (be) sudden; abrupt; unexpected/ 그의 죽음은 갑작스러웠다 His death was unexpected. にわかだ
**갑작스레** suddenly; all of a sudden ⇒ 갑자기. にわかに
**갑절** 《두 배》 double; twice; twofold; as much again / ~의 double; twice; twofold. ばい
**갑제**(甲第) a lordly[a stately] mansion; a fine house[home]. りっぱなやしき
**갑종**(甲種) grade A; first grade/~ 합격자 a first-grade conscript. こうしゅ
**갑주**(甲冑) [helmet and] armo[u]r; panoply. かっちゅう
**깝죽거리다** behave frivolously; act flippantly. けいそつにふるまう
**깝질** skin; bark; shell. かわ
**갑철판**(甲鐵板) 〖군〗 armo[u]r plate[plating]. てっぱん
**갑충**(甲蟲) 〖충〗 a coleopteron. かぶとむし
**갑판**(甲板) a deck/ ~ 사관 a deck officer/~ 수부(水夫) a deck hand/~산인도(引渡) free on board(略: f. o. b.)/~에 나가다 go on deck. かんぱん
**갑피**(甲皮) uppers [of a shoe]. こうひ
**값** 《가격》 price; cost 《가치》 value; worth/엄청난 ~ an unreasonable price./알맞는 ~ a reasonable price/ ~나가는 dear; expensive/ ~없는 valueless /~지다 be valuable/~을 치르다 pay for (*an article*); pay the price for/~을 보다 estimate. ねだん
**값어치** 《가치》 value; worth. かち
**값없다** ①《무가치하다》 (be) cheap; of little value ②《무한하다》 (be) invaluable; priceless. やすすぎる
**값지다** (be) valuable; of much value; expensive. ぜいたくだ
**값치다** name a price for (*an article*); value (*something*) at. ねだんをきめる
**값치르다** pay for (*an article*); pay the price for. たいきんをはらう
**갓**¹ 《쓰는》 a Korean hat; a *kat*/ ~집 a *kat*-case. かんむり
**갓**² 《방금》 fresh from; just/ ~ 구운 빵 bread fresh from the oven/~ 사온 책 a brand-new book. ちょうどいま
**갓나다** be just born; has just seen the light. ちょうどいまうまれる
**갓난아이** a newborn baby; a baby. うまれたばかりのこども
**강-** severe; harsh; forced; rough; trying; unreasonable; straight; pure; unmitigated; dry/ ~더위 a spell of intense heat with no rain at all.
**강**(江) a river/~바닥 a river-bed; the bottom of a river/ ~을 내려가다[거슬러 올라가다] go down[up] the river/ ~을 건너다 cross a river. たいが
**강**(講) 《읽》 recitation 《강의》 a lecture / ~하다 《외다》 recite 《강의하다》 give a lecture. あんしょう
**-강**(強) a little over; and a fraction/ 4할~ a little over 40 percent. きょう
**강가**(江一) a riverside; a river-bank; a water front. かわべ
**강가**(降嫁) 《왕실의》 the marriage of an Imperial princess to a subject 《일반의》 marriage into a family of inferior social standing/~하다 《왕실의》 be married to a subject 《일반적으로》 marry beneath one. こうか
**강간**(強姦) rape; outrage; violation/~하다 rape; outrage; violate;/ ~죄 rape; criminal assault. ごうかん
**깡깡이** a three-stringed fiddle.
**강강하다**(剛剛—) (be) strong; stout; steady; solid. しんしんがつよい
**강개**(慷慨) righteous indignation/ ~하다 be indignant (*at*); bewail; deplor /~가 a deplorer. こうがい
**강건**(強健) sturdiness; robust health/~하다 (be) robust; healthy; strong; hardy. きょうけん
**강건**(剛健) sturdiness; manliness/ ~하다 be sturdy; manly. ごうけん
**강경**(強硬) toughness; firmness; resoluteness; vigour/ ~하다 (be) strong; firm; vigorous; resolute /~히 strongly; firmly; vigorously; resolutely/ ~한 결의문 a strongly-worded resolution.

**강계**(彊界) the frontier; a border; the boundaries [of a country]. こくどのきょうかい

**강고**(强固) firmness; stability; solidity; constancy; soundness; consolidation / ~하다 (be) firm; stable; strong; solid; sound. きょうこ

**강골**(强骨) 《기질》 a (*person of*) sturdy constitution 《사람》 a sturdy fellow. きしつがつよいこと

**강교**(江郊) the suburbs in the vicinity of a river; the neighbo[u]rhood of a river. たいがのあるこうがい

**강구**(江口) ①《강어귀》 a river mouth; an outfall; the issue [of a river] ②나루. たいがのかこう

**강구**(强求) persistent demand / ~하다 demand persistently; force; demand strongly. むりにもとめること

**강구**(講究) consideration; study; research; investigation / ~하다 consider; devise; think out 《채택》 adopt/적당한 수단을 ~하다 take[devise; adopt] a proper step. こうきゅう

**강국**(强國) a great[strong] power/세계의 ~ the power of the world; world powers. きょうこく

**강군**(强軍) a powerful army 《경기단체》 a strong team. きょうくん

**강권**(强權) authority / ~ 발동 invocation of legal authority / ~적 authoritarian / ~을 발동하다 institute vigorous action (*against*); take strong measures; appeal to legal action; invoke legal authority. きょうけん

**강권**(强勸) a persistent[insistent] recommendation / ~하다 press (upon *a person*). むりにすすめる

**깡그리** all; wholly; altogether; utterly; entirely / ~ 자백하다 make a clean breast of. すっきり

**강기**(剛氣) fortitude; firmness of character; sturdiness. ごうき

**강기**(强記) a prodigious memory; tenacity / ~하다 retain well.

**강기**(綱紀) 《기율》 official discipline 《질서》 public order; law and order / ~ 숙정(肅正) enforcement of official discipline. こうき

**강기슭**(江一) a riverside. かわべ

**강남콩**(江南一) 《식》 the common kidney bean; French bean. なんきんまめ

**강녕**(康寧) healthiness / ~하다 (be) healthy; sound. けんこう

**강다리** a brace; a strut. つっぱり

**강다짐하다** ①《먹다》 eat (*cooked rice*) without mixing [it] with water or soup ②《누르다》 oppress; keep down ③《부리다》 force[drive] (*one*) to work. よくせい

**강단**(剛斷) decisiveness; resolution; determination.

**강단**(降壇) ~하다 leave[go down] the platform the rostrum.

**강담**(돌담) a stone wall. いしのかき

**강담**(講談) 《서술》 storytelling; narration 《강화》 a lecture; a discourse / ~사 a [professional] story-teller; a narrator. こうだん

**강당**(講堂) a [lecture] hall; an auditorium. こうどう

**강대**(强大) ~하다 (be) powerful; mighty; strong / ~국 a powerful[big] country. きょうだい

**강도**(强度) intensity; powerfulness / ~의 powerful; intense / ~의 확대경 a powerful magnifying glass. きょうど

**강도**(講道) preaching; a discourse / ~하다 preach; expound the teachings [doctrines]. こうどう

**강도**(强盜) a burglar; a robber 《행위》 burglary / ~질하다 burglar; commit burglary. こうどう

**강독**(講讀) textual exposition; reading / ~하다 read. こうどく

**강동거리다, 깡동거리다** skip; caper / 강동강동[깡동깡동] skippingly.

**강동하다, 깡동하다** (be) rather short.

**강두**(江頭) a landing place; moorings; a pier. ふねのていはくしょ

**강둑**(江一) a river embankment.

**강등**(降等) degradation; demotion / ~하다 demote; reduce[degrade] to a lower rank. こうとう

**강력**(强力) great strength [power]; might / ~하다 (be) strong; powerful; mighty / ~범 a crime of violence / ~지배 control by force. きょうりょく

**강렬**(强烈) ~하다 (be) severe; intense; strong / ~한 색채 a loud[gaudy] colo[u]r / ~한 술 strong liquor / ~한 의지 a strong will. きょうれつ

**강령**(綱領) a compendium; principles; essential points; a summary 《정당의》 a platform / 정당의 ~ a party program《영》; a party platform 《미》《항목》 a plank. こうりょう

**강론**(講論) 《토론》 exposition; discussion 《강의》 preaching; teaching / ~하다 expound; discuss; preach; teach; explain (*a book*). こうろん

**강린**(强隣) a powerful neighbour; a powerful neighbouring country; a formidable rival. つよいとなりくに

**강림**(降臨) descent from Heaven; advent / ~하다 descend from Heaven; [god] come down. こうりん

**강마르다** (be) dried up; parched. やせている

**강매**(强買) forcing a purchase / ~하다 force (*one*) to sell. きょうばい

**강매**(强賣) forcing a sale; high-pressure salesmanship 《미》 / ~하다 force a sale (*on*). きょうばい

**강멱**(降冪) 《數》 a descending series [powers]. こうべき

**강명**(剛明) uprightness and clearness / ~하다 (be) upright and clear; intrepid

**강모** young rice plants planted in a dry paddy.

**강모**(剛毛) a bristle; a seta.

**강목** lost labour; fruitless effort／～치다 waste labour; make fruitless vain effort. むだぼねおり

**강목**(剛目) 《분류》 classification; classes 《요점》 the main points; the gist; an epitome; an outline. こうもく

**강무**(講武) military training／～하다 practise military arts. こうぶ

**강물**(江—) a river; a stream; river water. たいがのみず

**강바람** 《마른 바람》 a dry wind.

**강바람**(江—) a river wind. こうふう

**강박**(强迫) coercion; duress[e]; compulsion／～하다 coerce; compel; force／～ 관념 fear complex; an imperative conception; an obsession／～ 념에 사로잡히다 be obsessed (by, with); suffer from an obsession. きょうはく

**강반**(江畔) a riverside; the shores of a river; bottomlands. こうはん

**강밥** boiled rice eaten without being mixed with soup or water／～을 먹다 eat (cooked rice) without soup or water. おかずなしのめし

**강배**(江—) a river boat. かわぶね

**강변**(江邊) the riverside.

**강변화**(强變化) 《언》《동사의》 strong conjugation／～ 동사 strong verbs.

**강병**(强兵) 《군사》 a strong soldier 《병력》 a powerful army. きょうへい

**강보**(襁褓) swaddling clothes; a diaper／～ 유아 an infant; a baby. おむつ

**강복**(降福) god's blessing; bliss／～하다 bless. こうふく

**강사**(講士) a speaker; a lecturer.

**강사**(講師) a lecturer 《직분》 an instructor lecturership／서울 대학교 ～ a lecturer at [the] Seoul University. こうし

**강산**(江山) 《강과 산》 rivers and mountains 《땅》 a land; the territory／금수 ～ a beautiful land. かわとやま

**강상**(江上) 《물가》 (on) the riverbank 《물》 (on) the surface of the river [water]. かわほとり

**강상**(綱常) moral principles; a code of morals; morality.

**강새암, 강샘** unreasonable[intense] jealousy. やきもち

**강색**(鋼索) a steel[wire] rope; a cable／～ 철도 a cable rail-way.

**강생**(降生) incarnation／～하다 be incarnated. せいけんがうまれること

**강서**(講書) explanation; exposition／～하다 explain a book. こうしょ

**강서리** heavy frost.

**강석**(講席) a chair; a lectured. こうせき

**강석**(講釋) a lecture; exposition／～하다 lecture (on); explain. こうしゃく

**강설**(講說) a lecture; explanation／～하다 lecture (on); explain. こうせつ

**강설**(降雪) snow; [a] snowfall／～량 the amount of snowfall／6센티의 ～이 있었다 Snow fell six centimetres deep. こうせつ

**강성**(强盛) ～하다 (be) strong; powerful; thriving. きょうせい

**강세**(强勢) 《음(音)의》 stress; emphasis 《시세의》 a strong[firm] tone; a bullish tendency. きょうせい

**강세**(降世) incarnation; advent／～하다 be incarnated. こうたん

**강속**(江—) in the river. かわのなか

**강송**(講誦) recitation／～하다 recite. あんしょうすること

**강쇠**(降衰) decline; wane; decadence／～하다 decline; wane; decay; be on the decline. とうきゅをへらすこと

**강쇠바람** the east wind in early autumn. しょしゅうのひがしかぜ

**강술** rice wine accompanied with no dish[food]／～ 마시다 drink rice wine without any dish. さかななしのさけ

**강술**(講述) expounding; exposition; a lecture delivery／～하다 expound; deliver a lecture (on). こうじゅつ

**강습**(强襲) a storm; an assault／～하다 storm; assault／～대 a storming party. きょうしゅう

**강습**(講習) a short [training] course; a class／～하다 take a short course of／～생 a student 《총칭》 a lecture class; a trainee／～소 a training school[course]. こうしゅう

**강시**(僵屍, 殭屍) the body of a person frozen to death; a body dead from cold. とうし

**강신술**(降神術) spiritualism; mediumism; typtology.

**강심**(江心) the very middle[heart] of a river. たいがのまんなか

**강심제**(强心劑) a heart medicine; a medicine stimulating the action of the heart. きょうしんざい

**강아지** a little dog; a pup; a puppy; a whelp. こいぬ

**강아지풀** 《식》 a foxtail; Setaria viridis (학명). いぬあわ

**강안**(江岸) a riverside. かわべ

**강압**(强壓) pressure; coercion; high-handedness／～하다 bring pressure to bear upon; oppress／～설 theory of coercion／～적 high-handed; coercive／～정책 a high-handed policy. きょうあつ

**강약**(强弱) strength and weakness; the strong and the weak／～부동 (不同) the weak cannot beat the strong／～을 다투다 contend for mastery. きょうじゃく

**강어귀**(江—) a river mouth. かわのいりくち

**강역**(疆域) a boundary; a border; a frontier.

**강연**(講演) a lecture; an address; a talk／～하다 give a lecture; address (an audience)／라디오 ～ a radio talk; an address

**강옥(鋼玉)** corundum ⇨강옥석.

**강옥석(鋼玉石)** 〖광〗 corundum 《붉은 것》 ruby 《푸른 것》 sapphire.

**강요(綱要)** 《골자》 elements 《개요》 an outline; essentials; a summary; a synopsis. ようこう

**강요(强要)** enforcement; extortion; exaction / ~하다 exact; demand; force; compel / …에게 …을 ~하다 force[compel] one to (do). きょうよう

**강용(剛勇)** adamantine courage; intrepidity; doughtiness; valour; prowess / ~하다 (be) daring; intrepid; valiant; doughty. ごうゆう

**강우(降雨)** rain; a rainfall / ~기 wet[rainy] season / ~량 the amount of rainfall; a rainfall (of 70 inches a year). こうう

**강울음** make-believe crying / ~울다 shed crocodile tears. むりなくこと

**강유(剛柔)** hardness and softness; resistance and elasticity. ごうじゅう

**강음(强音)** stress; accent; emphasis / ~부 an accent. きょうおん

**강음(强飮)** ~하다 drink against one's will.

**강의(剛毅)** fortitude; sturdiness. ごうき

**강의(講義)** a lecture 《설명》 an explanation 《해설》 an exposition / ~하다 lecture; give a lecture; explain (a book) / ~록(錄) a correspondence course; a lecture magazine / 문법 ~a lecture on grammar / ~방법 the manner of lecturing. こうぎ

**강인(强靭)** toughness; tenacity; perseverance / ~하다 (be) strong; tough; tenacious; stiff; firm / ~성 toughness; solidarity; strength. きょうじん

**강임히(强仍—)** reluctantly; against one's will. やむをえずそのまま

**강짜** jealousy / ~를 부리다 be[feel] jealous. やきもち

**강자(强者)** a strong man 《총칭》 the strong the powerful. きょうしゃ

**강자성(强磁性)** ferromagnetism.

**강장(强壯)** robustness; healthiness / ~하다 (be) strong; robust; sturdy; sound; lusty / ~제(劑) a tonic; a restorative. きょうそう

**강장거리다, 깡장거리다** walk in a leaping manner walk with short steps / 강장강장〔깡짱깡짱〕 at a trot; with short[mincing] steps. ぴょんぴょんとんでいく

**강장 동물(腔腸動物)** a coelenterate; Coelenterata(학명). こうちょうどうぶつ

**강재(鋼材)** steel[material]

**강적(强敵)** a great[powerful] enemy 《경쟁자》 a formidable rival.

**강정** ①《참쌀의》 a kind of cake made from glutinous rice flour ②《일반의》 a gluten and rice(bean, etc.) cake.

**강제(强制)** compulsion; constraint; enforcement / ~하다 force; enforce; compel; coerce / ~가격 compulsory price / ~집행 compulsory execution; distraint / ~노동 forced[compulsory] labour / ~수단 coercive measure /~적 compulsory; forced; coercive / ~로 by force; forcibly; by compulsion. きょうせい

**강조(强調)** ①《고조》 stress; emphasis / ~하다 stress; emphasize; lay stress on /저축의 필요를 ~하다 stress the need of saving ②《시의》 a strong[firm] tone; bullish[strong] feeling / ~요소 a bullish factor きょうちょう

**강조밥** unmixed boiled millet.

**강종거리다, 깡쫑거리다** hop along; walk with hopping steps. かろくはねとぶこと

**강좌(講座)** a [professional] chair; professorship 《강의》 a lecture; a course /라디오 영어 ~ a radio English course / ~를 위촉하다 give (one) a chair. こうざ

**강주정(一酒酊)** an affected drunkenness / ~하다 rave with a semblance of drunkenness; pretend to be drunk.

**강줄기(江—)** a river course. たいがのながれ

**강즙(薑汁)** ginger juice. しょうがのしろ

**강직(剛直)** uprightness; integrity; rectitude; probity / ~하다 (be) upright; incorruptible /~한 사람 a man of integrity. ごうちょく

**강직(强直)** 《굳어짐》 stiffness; rigidity /사후(死後) ~ rigor mortis(L); cadaveric rigidity. きょうちょく

**강진(强震)** a violent earthquake; a severe shock [of earthquake]. きょうしん

**깡창거리다** hop; skip; gambol /깡창깡창 hopping. ぴょんぴょんとぶ

**강철(鋼鐵)** steei / ~판 a steel plate / ~같은 의지 an iron will. こうてつ

**강청(强請)** exaction; persistent demand ~하다 extort(money); blackmail 《강요》 demand forcibly. きょうせい

**강촌(江村)** a riverain[riverside] village. こうそん

**강추위** dry cold weather. きびしいさむち

**강충하다** (be) lanky; tall and slender.

**강타(强打)** a hard [heavy] blow; 〖체〗 a heavy hit; a slug 《속》 / ~하다 deal a heavy blow /~를 퍼붓다 rain hard blows (on). きょうだ

**강탄(降誕)** birth; nativity; advent; incarnation / ~하다 be born; see the light; be incarnated. こうたん

**강탈(强奪)** seizure; extortion; robbery; plunder; plunderage / ~하다 seize; extort (a thing) from (one); rob[plunder](one) of (a thing). ごうだつ

**강태공(姜太公)** an angler; a Waltonian.

**강토(疆土)** a country; a territory; a domain; a realm. きょうど

**깡통** an empty[tin] can 《사람》 an empty-headed fellow / ~차다 be reduced to begging. かんづめのかん

**강파르다** ①《몸뚱이가》(be) gaunt and fiery; have a lean and hungry look ②《가파르다》 (be) steep. やせてもけんこうだ

**강판(薑板)** a ginger-grater.

**깡패** a terroist

**강퍅(剛愎)** perverseness; obduracy; petulance; / ～하다 (be) perverse; obdurate; petulant; cantankerous. ごうふく

**강평(講評)** comment; criticism; review / ～하다 criticize (*essays*); comment on; review. こうひょう

**강포(强暴)** atrocity; ferocity; heinousness / ～하다 (be) atrocious; ferocious; heinous. きょうぼう

**강풀** 《된 풀》 thick paste〔starch〕 こいのり

**강풀치다** paste again; starch once more. のりをつけかさねる

**강풍(江風)** a river wind〔breeze〕 こうふう

**강풍(强風)** a strong〔high〕 wind 《기상 용어》 a moderate gale / ～주의보 a strong wind warning. きょうふう

**강하(江河)** rivers. こうとかわ

**강하(降下)** descent; falling; dropping; 《기압의》 depression 《착륙》 landing / ～하다 descend; fall; drop 《착륙하다》 land / 급～ a nose dive / 기온의 ～ a drop in temperature. こうか

**강하다(强—)** 《강력》(be) strong; powerful; mighty 《기력이》 vigorous 《근력이》 muscular 《강렬》 (be) violent; strong; hard; severe / 강하게 hard; severely; strongly; powerfully / 강해지다 grow strong〔powerful〕 / 강하게 하다 make strong; strengthen. つよい

**강하다(剛—)** (be) stiff; solid; firm; hard; resistant. かたい

**강한(强悍, 剛悍)** fierceness; ferocity; heinousness; savageness / ～하다 (be) fierce; ferocious; savage. ごうかん

**강해(講解)** explanation; explication / ～하다 explain; elucidate; explicate; expound こうかい

**강행(强行)** ①《강제적인》 forcing; enforcement / ～하다 enforce; force / 저물가 정책을 ～하다 enforce a low-price policy ②《하지못해》 doing of perforce / ～하다 do against *one's* will; do of perforce. きょうごう

**강호(江湖)** ①《세상》 the public; the world / ～제현(諸賢) the general public; people at large ②《은둔자의 거주지》 a secluded place where hermits wander ③《강과 호수》 rivers and lakes. ごうこ

**강호(强豪)** a veteran ; a champion ; a hero.

**강화(講和)** peace; peace settlement (negotiation) / ～하다 make peace (*with*) / 단독〔전면〕～ separate〔overall〕 peace / ～조약〔회의〕 a peace treaty〔conference〕 / ～조건 terms of peace. こうわ

**강화(强化)** strengthening; solidification; intensification; tightening / ～하다 strengthen; consolidate; increase; firm up; reinforce / 내각〔국방〕을 ～하다 strengthen the Cabinet〔national defense〕. きょうか

**강화(講話)** a lecture; a talk.

**강회(一蛔)** 《회충》 a roundworm.

**강회(一膾)** 《음식》 a dish of boiled stoneleeks or parsleys.

**강회(剛灰)** limestone; quicklime.

**갖다¹** 《구비》 (be) furnished〔arranged〕 so well as to meet all the necessary requirements; enough to meet various demands. ととのつていろ

**갖다²** hold ⇨가지다

**갖두루마기** a Korean robe lined with fur.

**갖바치** a shoemaker; a maker of leather shoes. くつや

**갖옷** clothing lined with fur. かわごろも

**갖은** all sorts of; every〔possible〕 / ～고생 all sorts of hardship / ～수단을 다 쓰다 try every means available; try every possible means. いろいろな

**갖은 삼거리** decorations of saddle.

**갖은 소리** nonsense; assuming talk.

**갖저고리** a Korean jacket lined with fur.

**갖추** exhaustively; with no omissions; thoroughly; all; inclusively / 세간살이를 ～차리다 get an assortment of household goods. すつかり

**갖추다** 《구비》 possess; complete; assort; have 《준비》 furnish〔prepare〕 in a way to meet every need / 위엄을 ～ have dignity / 상식을 ～ possess common sense / 준비를 ～ prepare for; make full preparation / 상품을 ～ keep various articles in stock. そなえる

**갖추쓰다** write (*a Chinese character*) without omitting any storke; follow each stroke exactly 一畵もかかさずにかく

**갖풀** 〔animal〕 glue / ～로 붙이다 glue.

**같다** ⇨별항 참조 (page 1287).

**같은 값에** at the same cost; for the same price.

**같은 값이면** if … at all; if possible / ～잘해라 If you do it at all, do it well. / ～이것을 가지겠다 I prefer this〔to that〕 どうせおなじならば

**같이** ①《같게》 like; as; likewise; similary; 〔in〕 the same〔way〕; 《동등하게》 equally / 보통 때와 ～ as usual / 말씀하시는 바와 ～ as you say / 이와 ～하여 in this manner〔way〕 / 의견을 ～하다 have the same view ②《함께》 together(*with*); along〔in company〕 with / 자리를 ～하다 sit together / 행동을 ～하다 co-operate with. いっしょに

**같잖다** (be) trival, insignificant; (be) worthless; unseemly / 같잖은 일 a matter of no importance; a trival matter. おなじでない

**갚다** ①《금전을》 repay; pay back; refund / 빚을 ～ pay *one's* debt; pay the money back ②《물어주다》 indemnify; retrieve; compensate (*for*); requite; make reparation. ③《죄를》 atone〔expiate〕 for / 죄를 ～ expiate for an offense ④《은혜 따위를》 return; repay; requite; reward / 은혜를 원수로 ～ return evil for good ⑤《원수를》 revenge; avenge; requite; take vengeance (*upon*). かえす

**갚음하다** repay; pay back; compensate (*for*); make reparation (*for*); atone for. ⇨갚다. かえしてはらう

**개¹** 《강가의》 an inlet; a creek. いりえ
**개²** 〖동〗 dog 《사냥개》 a hound／～의 canine／～새끼 a pup; a puppy／～집 a kennel／～같은 doggish; doglike／～를 기르다 keep a dog. いぬ
**깨** 《참깨》 sesame; *Sesamum orientale*(학명); a gingili [plant] 《들깨》 wild sesame; *Perilla frutescene*(학명). こば
**개(蓋)** a lid; a top; a cover. ふた
**개(個, 箇, 介)** a unitian; an item; a piece／사과 네 ~ four apples／비누 두 ~ two cakes of soap. へん(片)
**개가(凱歌)** a triumphal song／～를 올리다 win a victory (over). がいか
**개가(改嫁)** remarriage／～하다 marry again; remarry. かいか
**개각(改閣)** a cabinet reshuffle; a cabinet shake-up／～을 단행하다 effect a cabinet reshuffle.
**개간(開墾)** cultivation; land reclamation／～하다 bring under cultivation; clear (*the land*); reclaim／～지 reclaimed land. かいこん
**개간(改刊)** revision／～하다 issue a revised edition; rivise. かいかん
**개감스럽다** (be) voracious; ravenous; gluttonous／개감스럽게 먹다 eat voraciously; gormandize; wolf *one's* food; stodge《속》. くいしんぼうでみぐるしい
**개갑(介甲)** ①《게 따위의》 a crust; a carapace; a [crust-like] shell ②《갑옷》 a coat of armor. こう(かめなどの)
**개강(開講)** beginning a series of *one's* lectures／～하다 give *one's* first lecture (*on*); begin a series of *one's* lectures 《수업 개시》 open a course; begin school. かいこう
**깨강정(―羌飣)** sesame-and-gluten cake.
**개개(個個, 箇箇)** an individual／～의 individual; separate. ここ
**개개다** wear away; rub (*off*); abrade; wear (*off*). おたがいにそんする
**개걸(丐乞)** begging／～하다 go (*about*) begging; live as a beggar こじきすること
**개결(介潔)** uprightness; purity; stern integrity／～하다 (be) upright; incorruptible／～한 사람 a man of stern integrity. かいけつ
**개고기** ①《개의 고기》 the flesh of a dog ②《사람》 a wicked[a cruel] person(남자); a minx(여자). いぬのにく
**개골(―골)** rage; anger; wrath／～내다 snap at; snarl at; get angry. げきど
**개골개골** croak／~ 울다 croak. げろげろ
**개골창** a draine; a gutter; a ditch(미); a sewer. どぶ
**개과(改過)** repentance; penitence; contrition／～하다 repent; mend *one*self; turn over a new leaf. かいか
**개관(開館)** the opening／～하다 open (*a hall*)／～식을 하다 inaugurate[open] a hall. かいかん
**개관(槪觀)** a general survey; an outline／～하다 take a bird's-eye view (*of*). がいかん
**개괄(槪括)** a summary／～하다 sum up／～적인 general／～해서 말하면 on the whole; generally; in a word. がいかつ
**개교(開校)** the opening of a school／～하다 open a school／～식 the opening [inauguration] ceremony of a school. かいこう
**개교식(開校式)** the opening ceremony of a new bridge. かいこうしき
**개구리** a frog／～헤엄 the breast stroke [swim]. かえる
**개구리밥** 〖식〗 a great duckweed; *Spirodela polyrhiza*(학명).
**개구리참외** a spotted cantaloupe; *Cucumis microsperma*(학명). しまのあるまつかわうり
**개구멍** a doghole. いぬのていりするあな
**개구멍바지** a child's trousers open at the back.
**개구멍받이** a foundling.
**개국(開國)** ①《건국》 the foundation[the founding] of a country[a state]／～하다 found a state ②《문호 개방》 the opening of a country／～하다 open a country to foreign intercourse[the world]. かいこく
**개근(皆勤)** non absence; perfect attendance; regular attendance／～하다 attend regulary／～상 a reward for regular attendance. かいきん
**개금(開襟)** open-heartedness; unreserve／～하다 open[lay bare] *one's* heart; open up *one's* mind; unbosom *one*self to.
**깨끗이** ①《청결》 clean[ly] ②《정연》 neatly; tidily／～하다 [make] clean; make neat ②《결백》 clean[ly] 《공정》 fairly／~ 지다 be fairly beaten／~ 살다 lead a pure life ③《아주》 clean; completely; thoroughly／~ 청산하다 settle the account in full. きれいに
**깨끗하다** ①《청결》 (be) clean; cleanly; pure (맑다) (be) clear 《정연》(be) tidy neat／깨끗한 물 clear pure water／옷차림이 깨끗한 neatly-dressed ②《결백》 (be) clean; innocent 《고상》 noble; 《순결》 chaste 《공정》 (be) fair; clean／깨끗한 일생 a carrer with a clean record／깨끗한 사랑 Platonic[pure] love ③《심신이》 (be) well; refreshed／몸이 깨끗지 않다 be unwell. さっぱりしている
**개기(開基)** ①《터 닦기》 ground leveling; laying the foundation／～하다 level [smooth] the land ②《정의》 the founding of a temple 《개기승》 the founder／～하다 found. かいき
**개기(皆旣)** 〖천〗 a total eclipse／~ 일[월]식 a total solar[lunar] eclipse. かいき
**개기름** oily excrements of the skin of the face／~ 낀 얼굴 an oily[a greasy] complexion. あぶらあせ
**깨나다** come to *one*self; recover *one's* senses; come round; rivive. めがさめる

**개나리** 〖식〗《들나리》a gold-banded lily; a golden-bell tree; a forsythia; *Forsythia suspensa*(학명). れんぎょう

**개념**(槪念) a general idea; a notion; a concept／~적 conceptional; notional／~ 작용 conception／~론 conceptualism. がいねん

**개다**¹ 《날이》 clear [up] 《비가》 hold up; stop 《안개가》 lift. はれる

**개다**² 《으깨다》 knead (*flour*); mix up. (のりなどを)とかす

**깨다**¹ ①《잠을》 wake up; awake／잠이 ~ awake from *one's* sleep ②《술을》 get sober; sober off[up] ③《각성》 have *one's* eye opened; be aroused; be disillusioned ④《개화》 become civilized／깬 civilized; modernized; enlightened／망상에서 깨어나다 be awakened from *one's* illusions. めがさめる

**깨다**² ①《부수다》 break; crush; smash／주발을 ~ break[smash] a bowel ②《일을》 bring to a repture; break off; baffle／혼담을 ~ break off a proposed marriage. こわす

**깨다**³ 《알이》 be hatched; hatch 《알을》 make hatch; cause (*a chicken*) to hatch (*eggs*). ふかされる

**개다래나무** 〖식〗 a silvervine.

**개다리소반**(一小盤) a small dining table of coarse manufacture.

**깨닫다** see; perceive; realize; understand; be aware of; be convinced of／진리를 ~ perceive a truth／제 잘못을 ~ be convinced of *one's* error／형세가 심상치 않음을 ~ be awake to the gravity of the position. さとる

**깨달은이** a man who has attained the highest state of enlightenment; a philosopher. さとったひと

**개떡** a bran cake; steamed bread of bran.

**깨떡** steamed rice-cake coated with sesame seeds.

**개떡같다** 《가치없다》 (be) worthless; scummy〈미〉; rubbish／개떡같이 여기다 make nothing of. ばかばかしい

**개똥밭** 예 ~에도 이슬 내릴 날이 있다《속담》 Every dog has his day.

**개똥벌레** 〖충〗 a firefly; a glowworm; a lightning bug〈미〉. ほたる

**개똥상놈** a cad; a ribald; a yahoo; a vulgarian.

**개똥지빠귀** 〖조〗 a thrush; a dusky ouzel.

**개똥참외** 〖식〗 a wild musk melon; a wild melon. やせいのまつかうり

**깨뜨리다** break ⇨깨다². こわす

**개략**(槪略) an outline; a summary; a resume; a gist; a skeleton／~을 얘기하면 roughly speaking. がいりゃく

---

# 같 다

①《흡사》 (be) like; similar; be a like／여자와 〖꼭〗 ~ look like a woman; be no better than a woman／아주 ~ 《전혀 다르지 않은 것 같다》 be very much alike／새것 ~ be as good as new.

②《동일》 (be) the same; identical (*with*) 《균일》 equal (*to*); equivalent (*of*)／이와 같은 이유로 on the same reason／똑~ be the very same; be just the same; be all one／같은 말을 되풀이하다 harp on the same string／네 것과 똑같은 책을 가지고 있다 I have the same book as yours／오늘 가나 내일 가나 똑~ It makes little difference whether I go today or tomorrow.／다른 사람들도 똑같은 말을 했다 Other people traveled on the same road.

③《동등》 (be) equal (*to*); uniform; equivalent (*to*)／품질이 같은 재료 material of comparable quality／같은 자격으로 교섭하다 negotiate on equal terms／자네와 나의 키는 거의 ~ You are about as tall as I.／두 책상의 높이가 ~ The two tables are of even height.

④《종류》 (be) a sort of; like／책 같은 것 something like a book／헛간 같은 것 a crude sort of barn

⑤《추측》 appear; seem; look; be likely (*to*)／비가 올 것 ~ It looks like rain.／여간해서 곧 떠날 것 같지가 않다 He doesn't seem to be leaving soon.

⑥《…이라면》 if; in case／옛날 같으면 if these were the old days／나 같으면 그런 짓은 하지 않겠다 If I were you, I would not do so.

⑦《답다》 be worthy of／집 같은 집이 없다 There is no house to speak of[worth mentioning].

⑧《불변》 (be) changeless; immutable permanent／그는 나이는 먹었어도 성벽은 젊었을 때와 ~ Though he is advanced in age, he remains the same in disposition as when he was young.

⑨《공통》 (be) common／기원이 ~ have a common orgin (*with*)／살기를 원하고 죽기를 싫어하는 것은 사람이나 하등 동물이나 똑~ Love of life and fear of death are common to man and the lower animals.／이들은 국적은 다르지만 이해 관계는 ~ Theses men differ in nationality, but their interests are identical[common].

개량(改良) improvement; reform; betterment/ ~하다 improve; reform; better/사회 ~ social reform/~종(種) a select breed/~의 여지가 없다 It can hardly be improved upon. かいりょう

개력하다 shift; change; undergo vicissitude.

개론(槪論) an introduction; an outline; general remarks; a summary. がいろん

개막(開幕) the rising of the curtain/ ~하다 raise the curtain; commence the performance; open. かいまく

개머루 《식》 a wild grape.

개머리 a gunstock/ ~판 the butt [of a rifle]. じゅうしょう

개먹다 wear out; wear[be worn] through.

개명(改名)·changing one's name; rechristening / ~하다 change one's name; rename. かいめいする

개명(開明) civilization; enlightenment /~하다 be[become] civilized; be enlightened. かいめい

개문(開門) the opening of the gate/ ~하다 open the gate. かいもん

깨물다 bite (on); gnaw (at). がりがりかむ

개미 《충》 an ant/ ~집 an ant hill/핥기《동》 an ant-eater/~허리 a small [narrow, wasp] waist. あり

개발(開發) 《개척》development; exploitation/ ~하다 develop; cultivate; exploit; open out. かいはつ

개발코 a short flat nose; a snub nose; a pug nose. みじかくてひらたいはな

개방(開放) opening《문호》leaving open /~하다 leave open/문호 ~주의 the open-door policy/성품이 ~적인 frank; candid; open-hearted.

개백장 a dog killer. いぬころし

개벽(開闢) the creation; the beginning of the world/~ 이래 since the beginning of the world. かいびゃく

개변(改變) innovation; renovation; reformation/~하다 innovate; renovate.

개별(個別) an individual[a particular] case/~적[으로] individual[ly]; separate[ly]. こべつ

개병(皆兵) universal conscription/국민 ~ 제도 a universal conscription system. かいへい

개복 수술(開腹手術) ventrotomy; laparotomy かいふくしゅじゅつ

개봉(開封) unsealing 《영화의》opening; release/~하다 release (a film); open (a little); break a seal/~ 영화 a newly released[first-run] film/ ~관 a first runner. かいふう

개비 a piece of split wood; a stick/성냥 ~ match-sticks. きのきれっぱし

개산(開山) ①《절을 세움》the founding of a temple/ ~하다 found[establish] a temple ②⇒개산 조사(開山祖師). かいざん

개산(槪算) a rough calculation/ ~하다 make a rough estimate (of). がいさん

개산 조사(開山祖師) the founder [of a temple]; the originator; the creator. かいざんそし

개살구 《식》a wild apricot. やせいのあんず

개상(一床) a wooden thrasher with four legs; a log threashing-stand.

개새끼 ①《개의 새끼》pups [of a dog] ②《욕설》a "son-of-a-bitch". わるいやつ

개선(改善) improvement; betterment/ ~하다 improve; ameliorate; reform; better/생활의 ~ the betterment of living. かいぜん

개선(改選) re-election/ ~하다 re-elect (members). かいせん

개선(凱旋) a triumphal return/ ~하다 return in triumph/ ~문 a triumphal arch/ ~군 a victorious army; returning troops. がいせん

개선(疥癬) the itch; scabies. かいせん

개설(開設) opening; establishment; installation/ ~하다 open; establish; set up; install (a telephone). かいせつ

개설(槪說) a summary [account]; an introduction; an outline/ ~하다 treat (a subject) in outline. がいせつ

개성(改姓) a change of one's family name/ ~하다 change one's family name. かいせい

개성(個性) individual character; individuality; personality/ ~을 존중하다 respect one's personality. こせい

개세(蓋世) ~하다 sway the whole world; reign supreme all over the land. いりょくがてんかをおおうこと

개소(個所) 《곳》 a place; a spot 《점》 a point 《부분》 a part; a passage. かしょ

깨소금 powdered sesame mixed with salt. ごばとしおのこな

개소리 stupid talk; nonsense. ばかなはなし

개소리괴소리 stupid talk ⇨개소리.

개수(改修) repair; improvement/ ~하다 repair; improve /도로의 ~ the improvement of roads. かいしゅう

개수(槪數) round numbers. がいすう

개수(箇數) the number (of articles)/~ 불임금 piecework wages. こすう

개수작(一酬酌) silly talk; nonsense; a foolish remark. つまらないこうどう

개수통 a slop-basin. おすいおけ

개술(槪述) a general[a rough] statement/ ~하다 give an outline (of); summarize. がいじゅつ

개숫물 dishwater; refuse water; liquid refuse. さらをあらうみず

개시(開市) ①《시장을 엶》opening up a market/~하다 open up a market ②《처음 팖》the first sale of the day /~하다 make the first sale of the day. しじょうをあける

개시(開始) start; opening; beginning / ~하다 open; start; begin / 교섭을 ~하다 open negotiations. かいし

개시장(開市場) a treaty market; a market place open to foreigners. しじょうをあける

**개식**(開式) the opening of a ceremony/~하다 open a ceremony/ ~사 an opening address. かいしき

**개신**(改新) reformation; renovation/~하다 reform. かいしん

**개실**(個室) a private room. へや

**개심**(改心) reform; amendment/~하다 reform; turn over a new leaf. かいしん

**개악**(改惡) a bad change / ~하다 change for the worse; deteriorate make worse for the change. かいあく

**개암** a hazelnut/ ~나무《식》a hazel; a filbert. はしばみのみ

**개암들다** get sick after childbirth. さんごのわずらいをする

**개어귀** the mouth of a river 《강의》an estuary.

**깨어나다** regain consciousness ⇒깨나다.

**깨어지다** be broken ⇒깨지다. こわれる

**개업**(開業) opening of business《의사·변호사의》commencement of practice/~하다 start a business/ ~의(醫) a medical practitioner/ ~중이다 be in practice/변호사를 ~하다 practice the law. かいぎょう

**개역**(改易) change; alteration/ ~하다 change alter (a play). かいえき

**개역**(改譯) retranslation; revision/ ~하다 retranslate; revise a translation. ほんやくしたのをかきなおすこと

**개연**(開演) the rising of the curtain; the opening of the performance《상연》staging/ ~하다 raise the curtain; perform; stage (a play). かいえん

**개연**(慨然) ~하다《분개》(be) indignant; resentful《강개》(be) deploring/ ~이 in resentment; deploringly. がいぜん-

**개연성**(蓋然性) probability. がいぜんせい

**개염** envy /~나다 grow envious/ ~부리다 show envy. うらやむ

**개오**(開悟) spiritual awakening; philosophy/ ~하다 be spiritually awakened. かいご

**개요**(概要) an outline; a synopsis; a summary/~를 진술하다 give an outline of; outline. がいよう

**깨우다**《잠을》wake up; awake; arouse《아침에》call. めをさます

**깨우치다** awaken; disillusion《계몽》enlighten. さとること

**개운**(開運) betterment of one's; fortune; improvement of one's lot; better fortune/ ~하다 be in luck's way; one's fortune change for the better fortune turns in one's favour. うんがあけること

**개운하다** feel refreshed; be refreshing; fresh. きぶんがさっぱりする

**개울** a brook; a stream. こかわ

**개원**(改元) the change of the era/~하다 change the era. かいげん

**개원**(開院)《하원의》the opening of the House/~하다 open the national assembly/~식 the opening ceremony of the House. かいいん

**개으르다** (be) idle; lazy; indolent ⇒게으르다. なまけている

**개으름** idleness; laziness; indolence/ ~부리다[피우다] be idle; drone/ ~뱅이[장이] an idle fellow. たいまん

**개의**(介意) ~하다 care about; worry about; mind/ ~치 않다 do not care about; pay no attention. かいい

**개의**(改議)《재론》rediscussion《수정·동의》a revised motion; an amendment/~하다 discuss again; propose[move] an amendment. かいぎ

**개인**(改印) the change of one's seal/ ~하다 change one's seal. かいいん

**개인**(個人) an individual《사인(私人)》a private person[individual, citizen]/ ~의 individual; personal; private/ ~ 문제 a private affair; a personal matter/ ~ 소득 an individual income/ ~ 교수 private lessons; individual instruction/ ~전(展) a personal exhibition; a one-man show/ ~주의 individualism/ ~적[으로] individual[ly] personal[ly]/ ~ 자격으로 in one's private capacity/나 ~의 의견으로는 in my personal opinion; individually [speaking]. こじん

**개입**(介入) intervention/ ~하다 intervene[interfere] in (another's affair); meddle in. かいにゅう

**개자**(芥子) mustard ⇒겨자. からし

**개자리**《식》a snail clover; a medick; a trefoil; Medicago minima(학명).

**개자식** a son-of-a-bitch. ばかやろ(いぬのこ)

**개작**(改作) adaptation ~하다 adapt/ ~자 an adapter; an adaptor. かいさく

**개잘량** a strip[a piece] of dressed pelt of the dog used as a cushion or a mat.

**개잠** sleeping curled up as a dog; sleeping with one's limbs drawn in.

**개잠들다**(改—) fall asleep again after waking up once in the morning.

**개잡놈**(—雜—) a vile wretch; an abandoned villain. あさましいやつ

**개장**(改葬) reinterment; reburial/ ~하다 reinter; rebury. かいそう

**개장**(改裝) remodeling; refitment; conversion. かいそう

**개장**(開場) (be) opening/ ~하다 open (a place); open (the door). かいじょう

**개장국**(—醬—) soup of dog's meat. いぬのにくりょうり

**개재**(介在) interposition《개입》intervention/ ~하다 lie[stand] between; interpose (between). かいざい

**개전**(開戰) the outbreak of war/ ~하다 begin war; open hostilities; make war (on). かいせん

**개전**(改悛)《회오》repentance; penitence《개심》reform/ ~하다 repent; be penitent (of); reform oneself; mend one's

개점(開店) the opening[establishment] of a shop/~하다 open a shop. かいてん

개정(改正) 《수정》 revision; amendment 《변경》 change; alteration/~하다 revise; reform; amend; alter; change/~안(案) an amendment. かいせい

개정(改定) a reform; fixing anew/~하다 reform. かいてい

개정(改訂) revision/~하다 revise/~판 a revised edition/~ 증보판 a revised and enlarged edition. かいてい

개정(開廷) the opening of a [law] court/~하다 open[hold] court; give a hearing. かいてい

개제(改題) a change of the title; retitling/~하다 change the title (of a book); retitle. かいだい

개조(改造) reconstruction; reorganization/~하다 reconstruct; reorganize/내각~하다 reorganize[reshuffle] the Cabinet. かいぞう

개조(開祖) the founder (of a sect). かいそ

개조(改組) reorganization/~하다 reorganize; reconstruct.

개종(改宗) conversion/~하다 get[be] converted; change one's religion[sect]/~자 a convert. かいしゅう

개종(開宗) the founding of a religious sect/~하다 found a religious sect/~조 the founder of a sect.

개주(改鑄) 《화폐의》 recoinage 《종·대포 등의》 recasting/~하다 recoin; recast.

개죽음 useless death/~하다 die in vain. いぬじに

개중(個中) among the rest/~에는 among (them)/~에는 반대자도 있었다 Some of them objected it. そのなか

깨지다 ①《부서지다》 break; be broken [smashed]/깨지기 쉬운 be brittle; easily breaking; fragile ②《알이》 fall; come to a rupture; be broken off ③《흥 따위가》 be dampened. やぶれる

개지랄 ①~치다 《투덜거리다》 grumble 《화내다》 be in a huff. つまらないこうどう

개진(開陳) statement/~하다 state; express. かいちん

개짐 a sanitary towel[napkin]; a menstrual cloth. げっけいたい

개차반 a vulgarian; a man of illconduct. ぞくぶつ

개착(開鑿) excavation/~하다 excavate; cut; sink/~ 공사 excavation works/운하를 ~하다 cut a canal. かいさく

개찬(改竄) falsification; alteration/~하다 falsify; tamper with; cook; doctor. かいざん

개찰(改札) the examination of tickets/~하다 examine[punch] tickets; collect tickets/~구 a [platform] wicket; a ticket gate. かいさつ

개찰(開札) opening of the bids[tender]/~하다 open [the bids]. かいさつ

개창(疥瘡) the itch 음. かいせんびょう

개척(開拓) 《토지의》 clearing; cultivation; reclamation of waste land 《척식》 colonization/~하다 (토지를) bring (waste land) under cultivation 《자원을》 exploit 《식민지를》 colonize/ ~자 a pioneer; a colonist/ ~민 a settler/자원을 ~하다 exploit [develop] natural resources/~지 a clearing. かいたく

개천(開川) a creek; a ditch. どぶ

개천절(開天節) the Foundation Day of Korea.

개청(開廳) inauguration; opening /~하다 inaugurate; open [a government office]. かいちょう

개체(個體, 箇體) an individual/~ 발생 《생》 ontogeny. こたい

개초(蓋草) 《이영》 thatch[ing] 《잇기》 thatching/ ~하다 thatch; roof with thatch / ~장이 a house thatcher; a roofer. わらぶきをすること

개최(開催) holding (a meeting)/~하다 hold; open /~지 the site (of a meeting) / ~중이다 be open 《회의가》 be in session. かいさい

개축(改築) rebuilding; reconstruction /~하다 rebuild; reconstruct/ ~ 공사 reconstruction works. かいちく

개춘(開春) the beginning of spring.

깨치다¹ 《해득》 master; learn; understand; comprehend/한글을 ~ learn[master] Korean language. さとる

깨치다² break ⇒깨뜨리다.

개칠(改漆) ~하다 《칠을》 reprint; recoat 《획을》 retouch; add an improving touch to a character. ぬりかえる

개칭(改稱) the change of a name[a title, a designation]/~하다 change the name (of); rename. かいしょう

개키다 fold (up)/옷을 ~ fold one's clothes. たたむ

개탄(慨嘆) deploring; lamentation; regret/~하다 deplore; lament; grieve/ ~할 만한 deplorable; lamentable; grievous. がいたん

개탕 a groove; a quirk.

개통(開通) opening to[for] traffic/ ~하다 be opened to traffic 《불통선이》 be reopened for service / ~식 an opening ceremony (of a railway). かいつう

개판 utter confusion or disorder; a mess; a jumble.

개판(改一) 《씨름의》 a run-off bout.

개판(改版) 《인》 revision 《개정판》 a revised edition / ~하다 revise; issue a revised[new] edition. かいはん

개판(蓋板) a shingle. やねいた

개펄 a marsh; a swamp. なぎさ

개편(改編) reorganization/~하다 reorganize; remodel. かいへん

개평 《노름의》 money given by a winner at play to an onlooker or a loser. ただもらい

개평(概評) a general review[comment]

**개평(開平)** 《수》 evolution; the extraction of a square root／〜하다 extract the square root (of)／〜근(根) the square root. かいへいほう

**개평방(開平方)** evolution ⇨개평(開平).

**개폐(開閉)** opening and[or] shutting; 《전》 make and break／〜기 (전기의) a [break and make] switch 《사진기의》 a shutter. かいへい

**개폐(改廢)** alteration and abolition; a change; reorganization／〜하다 reorganize; alter and abolish. かいはい

**개표(開票)** ballot counting／〜하다 open the ballot boxes; count the votese／〜소 a ballot-counting place. かいひょう

**개피떡** a crescent-shaped rice-cake filled with bean jam.

**개학(開學)** commencement of school; reopening of school; the opening of a new school year[term]／〜하다 commence school; open 《휴가 후의》 reopen／〜식 the opening ceremony [of the school year]. かいがく

**개항(開港)** the opening of a port／〜하다 open a port to foreign trade／〜장 an open port. かいこう

**개헌(改憲)** amendment of a constitution; a constitutional amendment[revision]／〜하다 amend a constitution. かいけん

**개혁(改革)** 《혁신》 reform; reformation; innovation／〜하다 《혁신하다》 reform; innovate／〜자 a reformist; an innovator; a reformer. かいかく

**개호(改號)** changing one's pen name [nom de plume(F)]. かいごう

**개호주** 《동》 a cub tiger. とらのこ

**개화(開化)** civilization; enlightenment／〜하다 be civilized／〜한 civilized; enlightened. かいか

**개화(開花)** ef florescence／〜하다 flower; bloom／〜기 the flowering season; ef florescence. かいか

**개활(開豁)** 〜하다 《트임》(be) open 《마음이》(be) broad-minded; liberal. ひろい

**개황(概況)** a general condition; an outlook／기상 〜 a general weather condition. がいきょう

**개회(開會)** the opening of a meeting 《의회의》 a session／〜하다 open a meeting; go into session／〜사(식) an opening address[ceremony]／〜중이다 be open; be in session. かいかい

**개흘레** 《전》 an alcove.

**개흙** black soil[mud] on the water shores. なぎさ

**깩** shrieking; screaming; shouting; screeching／〜 소리치다 scream; shout; roar; bawl. ぎゃあ

**객(客)** a guest 《덧붙음》 extra／일등〜 a first-class passenger. きゃく

**깩깩** screaming; screeching／〜거리다 scream harshly; screech／원숭이가 〜 운다 A monkey chatters. ぎゃあぎゃあ

**객거(客居)** living away from home; staying away from home／〜하다 live away from home. たきょうですむこと

**객고(客苦)** discomfort suffered in a strange land. たびさきのくるしみ

**객관(客觀)** 《객관성》 objectivity 《대상》 the object／〜적 objective／〜주의 objectivism／〜적으로 보다 look at (a thing) objectively. きゃっかん

**객기(客氣)** youth ardour; rashness; blind daring. からげんき

**객년(客年)** last year. かくねん

**객담(客談)** unnecessary talk; idle talk; nonsense. むだばなし

**객담(喀痰)** expectoration／〜하다 spit; expectorate. かくたん

**객동(客冬)** last winter. さくねんのゆき

**객랍(客臘)** last December; the end of last year. さくねんの12がつ

**객사(客死)** dying while staying away from home／〜하다 die while staying abroad／파리에서 〜하다 pass away during one's stay in Paris. たびさきのし

**객상(客床)** an extra [dinner-]table; a guest table. きゃくのおぜん

**객석(客席)** a seat for a guest. きゃくせき

**객선(客船)** a passenger-boat[-steamer]. きゃくせん

**객설(客說)** an uncalled for remark; unnecessary talk; idle talk／〜하다 talk unnecessary things; make an uncalled for remark. むだばなし

**객소리(客—)** idle talk; windy eloquence／〜하다 talk rot. むだくち

**깩소리 못하다** cannot let out a peep.

**객수(客水)** ①《비》 rain out of season; unwanted rain ②《물》 unwanted water flown in from a source other than needed. たしょからながれこむみず

**객수(客愁)** loneliness in a strange land [town, place] 《여수》 sadness felt while on a journey 《향수》 nostalgia; homesickness. かくしゅう

**객스럽다(客—)** (be) useless; unnecessary; uncalled for. むだらしい

**객승(客僧)** a travelling priest. きゃくそうりょ

**객식구(客食口)** a dependent other than one's own family 《공식객》 a sponge; a parasite. いそうろう

**객실(客室)** a drawing-room; a parlour 〈미〉 《여관의》 a [guest] room.

**객심(客心)** the heart of a stranger; a traveller's feeling. きゃくしん

**객원(客員)** 《회의》 associate[an honorary] member 《신문 잡지의》 an associate editor. こうきなきゃく

**객월(客月)** last month; ultimo(L) 《날짜 뒤에》 ult／〜 5일에 on the fifth of last month; on the fifth ult. せんげつ

**객인(客人)** ①《손님》 a guest ②《객적은 이》

a nobody; a man of no account; a person of no importance. おきゃく

**객적다** (be) unnecessary; useless; of no account. つまらない

**객정**(客情) the heart of a stranger; the feeling of one who is away from home; a traveller's feeling. きゃくじょう

**객주**(客主) an inn run by a broker[a middle-man] for travelling merchants and peddlers; a brokerage house where are offered accomodations for travelling merchants and peddlers; commission agency. ちゅうかいにん

**객중**(客中) one's absence from home; while one is away from home; on a trip. たびにでているあいだ

**객증**(客症) sequela; a disease resulting from a previous disease. ほかのびょうき

**객지**(客地) a place where one is temporarily staying; a strange land. かくち

**객차**(客車) a passenger car[train]; a coach〈영〉. きゃくしゃ

**객체**(客體) 【법·철】 an object/범죄의 ~ the object of a crime. きゃっかん

**객초**(客草) tobacco[cigarettes] for guests. せったいようのたばこ

**객추**(客秋) last autumn. さくねんのあき

**객춘**(客春) last spring. さくねんのはる

**객토**(客土) soil brought from another place. きゃくど

**객하**(客夏) last summer. さくねんのなつ

**객향**(客鄕) a foreign land[town]; a place where one abides as a stranger; a strange land. かくち

**객혈**(喀血) hemoptysis; a hemorrhage of the lungs; blood-spitting/~하다 raise blood; spit[cough out] blood; have hemoptysis. かっけつ

**객회**(客懷) the heart of a stranger[a traveller] (향수)nostalgia. きゃくじょう

**갭직하다** (be) light. すこしかるい

**갯가** the shore; the coast. はまべ

**갯가재** 【동】 a squilla (pl.-s, -lae).

**갯고랑** a ditch on a sea shore.

**깻묵** oil-cake. あぶらかす

**갯물** an inlet; a creek; the water of an inlet[a creek]. うらべをながれるみず

**갱**(坑) a pit; a shaft. ほらあな

**갱갱** yelping/~ 울다 yelp; yap; yip. わんわん

**갱내**(坑內) a pit; a shaft/~ 노동자 a pit worker; an underground worker. こうない

**갱년기**(更年期) the turn[change] of life (부인의) the menopause. こうねんき

**갱도**(坑道) (광산의) a gallery; a drift (가로); a shaft; a pit(세로); (지하의) a mine; a tunnel. こうどう

**갱발**(更發) recurrence/~하다 recur. さいせい

**갱부**(坑夫) a miner; a mine worker; a pitman; a digger. こうふ

**갱생**(更生) rebirth; regeneration; rejuvenation/~하다 make a fresh start in life; start life anew; rejuvenate; be regenerated. こうせい

**갱생사위**(更生—) an opportunity of a narrow escape [for revival]. そせいのきかい

**갱소**(更蘇) revival; resuscitation/~하다 revive; resuscitate; be restored to life. こうせい

**갱신**(更新) renewal; renovation/~하다 renew; renovate. こうしん

**갱신못하다** cannot move about; cannot stir an inch. みうごきができない

**갱정**(更訂) revision ⇒경정(更訂).

**갱지**(更紙) pulp paper; rough [printing] paper. ざらがみ

**갱지미** a brass soup-bowl (for children).

**갱진**(更進) further proceeding/~하다 proceed further. こうしん

**갱충적다** (be) loose[careless and stupid]; slovenly; imprudent/갱충적은 짓 imprudent conduct. だらしがない

**갸기** haughtiness; arrogance/~부리다 assume a haughty attitude ⇒교기(驕氣). ごうまんふそんなたいど

**갸륵하다** (be) praiseworthy; laudable; admirable; commendable/갸륵한 정신 a commendable spirit. すばらしい

**갸름하다** (be) somewhat long; lanky; oval/얼굴이 갸름한 oval[slender]-faced. ややながい

**갸우뚱거리다** shake; rock; jog swing; roll/갸우뚱갸우뚱 shakingly; rockingly. かたむきながらゆらゆれる

**갸우듬하다** (be) somewhat slanting; inclined. ややかたむいている

**갸울다** lean (to, toward); slant; sinking ⇒기울다. ややかたむいている

**갸울어뜨리다** incline; bend; lean; list; tilt; slant かたむける

**갸울이다** incline; lean; tilt; slant; bend ⇒기울이다. ちょっとかたむける

**갸웃거리다** peep; tilt one's head (to see something). しきりにあたまをかしく

**갸웃이** aslant; obliquely; slopewise; askant; on the slant. すこしななめに

**갸웃하다** (be) somewhat slanting[inclined]. ややななめだ

**갹금**(醵金) a subscription; a collection (기부) a contribution/~하다 take up a collection; raise money; get up a subcription; contribute. きょきん

**갈쭉하다** (be) somewhat long and slender; lanky; oval/갈쭉한 얼굴 an oval face. ややながい

**갈쭉막하다** (be) somewhat long and slender; lanky. ちょっとながすぎる

**갈쭘하다** (be) fairly long and slender; rather lanky. かなりながい

**갈찍하다** (be) fairly long. かなりながい

**거**(車) vehicle; carriage; chariot/자전 ~ a bicycle. くるま

**거가**(車駕) ①《수레》 the royal palanquin ②《행차》 going[a visit] (of the emperor); an Imperial visit; a royal trip.

おおさまがのるくるま
거가(擧家) the whole family. ぜんかぞく
거가 대족(巨家大族) a distinguished family; a powerful family.
거간(居間) (일) brokerage/ ~하다 act as [a] broker 《사람》a broker; a middleman. なこうど
거간군(居間軍) a broker; a middleman 《위탁 판매인》 a commission agent/~집 a house agent. なこうど
거개(擧皆) the greater part (of); almost all; the majority[bulk]. ほとんどみんな
거녀년(去去年) the year before last.
おとどし
거거 익심(去去益甚) ~하다 get worse and worse; grow worse increasingly.
ますますはなはだしくなること
거골(距骨) 《해》 the astragalus; the anklebone[ankle]. きょこつ
거괴(巨魁) a ringleader; the chief; the boss. とぞくのおやぶん
거구(巨軀) a big[massive] figure; a big frame. きょく
거꾸러뜨리다 overthrow; throw down; make fall flat; beat. てんとうさせる
거꾸러지다 tumble down; fall prone; be thrown down. さかさにたおれる
거꾸로 reversely; [in] the wrong way; the other way [about] 《안팎을》 inside out 《아래 위를》 upside down; the wrong side[end] up 《곤두박혀》 head over heels/빗자루를 ~ 세우다 stand a broom the wrong end up/~ 떨어지다 fall head over heels. さかさに
거국(擧國) the whole nation/~ 일치 내각 a national government[cabinet]/~ 일치하여 당하다 present a united front; stand together as one man.
きょこく
거금(距今) ago/~ 500년 five hundred years ago. いまから
거금(巨金) big money. たいきん
거금(醵金) collection of funds ~갹금.
거기 ①《장소》 that place; there/~서 기다려라 Wait there ②《그것》 that 《범위》 so far; to that extent/~까지는 좋았으나 … so far so good, but…/~까지는 인정한다 I admit as much.
-거나 if; whether … or/너야 하~ 말~ whether you do it or not.
거나하다 (be) mellow; tipsy.
거납(拒納) refusal of tax payment/ ~하다 refuse to pay taxes.
꺼내다 ①《속에서》 take[put, draw, bring] out/지갑을 ~ draw one's purse from one's bosom ②《얘기를》 bring forward; introduce; broach/문제를 ~ broach a matter. ひきだす
거냉(去冷) warming; heating/ ~하다 warm; heat. あたためる
거년(去年) last year. きょねん
거느리다 have [with one]; lead; head 《지휘·인솔하다》 command/부하를 거느리고 with subordinates/많은 식구를 ~ h-ave a large family to support. ひきいる
거늑하다 (be) satisfying; enough; sufficient; abundant. いごこちがよい
-거늘 much[still] more; much[still]less; while/개조차 사람에 충실하~ 하물며 사람에 있어서야 If a dog is so faithful to its master, how much more should we human beings so!
—たが、—なのに
-거니와 as well as; still[much] more; stll[much]less; yet; while/속이는 것도 좋지 못하~ 도독질하는 것은 더욱 나쁘다 It is bad to cheat, still more to rob. —であるが
거니채다 sense; suspect; perceive; become aware of. それとなくかたる
거닐다 [take a] stroll; ramble about.
ぶらぶらあるく
거대(巨大) ~하다 (be) huge; gigantic; colossal; monstrous; mammoth; enormous. きょだい
거떡거떡, 꺼떡꺼떡 ~하다 (be) damp-dried.
꺼떡거리다 ride the high horse; be puffed up. なまいきにふるまいする
거떡치다, 꺼떡치다 (be) awkward; not becoming well; out of harmoney.
げひんでみかっこうだ
거멀거멀하다 (be) shaky; unsteady; rickety たおれそうだ
거멀나다 collapse; smash; fail 《파산》 go bankrupt[into bankruptcy]. つぶれる
거독(去毒) ~하다 neutralize the poison contained in medicinal herbs; detoxication. とくをのぞくこと
거동(去冬) last winter. さくねんのゆき
거동(擧動) 《행위》 action; movement; doings 《처신》 conduct; manner; behaviour/ ~이 수상하다 act suspiciously / ~을 감시하다 watch one's movement. きょどう
거두(巨頭) a leader; a prominent figure/삼~ the big three/~ 회담 a top level conference きょとう
거두다 ①《모으다》 gather [up]; collect/세금을 ~ collect taxes ②《선과 따위를》 gain; obtain/승리를 ~ gain[win] the victory ③《돌보다》 take care of; care for; look after/아이들을 ~ take care of the children ④《숨을》 die; expire /숨을 ~ breathe one's last. おさめる
꺼두르다 pull about. ひっぱりまわす
거두 절미(去頭截尾) ①《자르기》 cutting off the head and tail/ ~하다 cut off the head and tail ②《얘기의》 summarization/ ~하다 summarize; leave out details. ようてんだけいうこと
꺼둘리다 get grabbed and pulled about; get dragged.
거둠질 harvesting; ingathering/~하다 harvest; collect. とりいれさぎょう
거둥 a royal visit/ ~하다 pay a visit (to). おおさまのじゅんし
거드럭거리다, 꺼드럭거리다 assume an air of importance; swagger.

**거드름** a haughty attitude; an air of importance/~스러운 haughty/ ~부리다(피우다) give oneself airs; act important; mount the high horse; swagger. ごうまんなたいど

**꺼뜨리다** cause to go out; let die out; put out by mistake. けす

**-거든** ①(가정) if; when/그를 만나ー 오라고 전해라 If you meet him, tell him to call on me. ②(이상함) indeed; to one's surprise/비가 오기는 많이 왔ー We had a heavy rain, indeed. ③(더구나) more; still more. ―ならば. ―たら

**거든그리다** wrap up neatly.

**거든하다** (be) light; nimble; feel light (몸이) feel good ⇨가든하다. かるい

**거들거리다** give oneself airs ⇨거드럭거리다.

**거들다** help; give help (to); assist; lend a hand/일을 ~ help (one) with one's work たすける

**꺼들다** take up; pick up; hold up/웃자락을 ~ hold up the edge of one's skirt.

**거들떠보다** pay attention (to); take notice of (one)/거들떠보지도 않다 pay little attention to. ちゅうもく

**거들먹거리다** mount the high horse; put oneself airs; swagger. しきりにえらぶる

**거듬거듬** roughly; skipping about. ざつと

**거듭** again; repeatedly/ ~하다 repeat / ~거듭 over and over again; many times/판(版)을 ~하다 run into several editions. かさねて

**거래**(去來) (상행위) transactions; dealings; business/ ~하다 transact(do) business with; have dealing with; trade/ ~소 an exchange; a stock exchange(market)/현물(현금) ~ direct(cash) transactions/신용 ~ dealings on credit/부정 ~ shady transactions / ~ 관계 business relations/ ~ 은행 one's banker/ …과 거래 [관계]가 있다 deal with; have business relations with. とりひき

**거레** ~하다 dawdle; dally; loiter; linger; loaf.

**거론**(擧論) discussion; a proposal/ ~하다 discuss; propose; suggest.
ことばをれつきょしてろんだいすること

**거룡**(巨龍) (고생물) a megalosaur.

**거루** a single-oar rowboat.

**거룩하다** (be) divine; solemn; sublime; sacred; holy; venerable/거룩하신 가르침 holy teachings; a sacred discourse. しんせいでりっぱだ

**거룻배** a boat (큰) a lighter (중국의) a sampan (짐 푸는) a barge (종선(從船)) a jolly-boat. ほのないみたしぶね

**거류**(居留) residence; residing/~하다 live; reside; dwell/~민 residents/~지 a foreign concession(settlement, quarter). きょりゅう

**거르다**¹ (여과) filter; strain; percolate; put (a thing) through. こす

**거르다**² (차례를) skip; omit; leave out /하루(이틀) 걸러 every other(third) day. (じゅんしょを)とばす

**거름** (비료) manure; muck; a fertilizer (똥·오줌) night soil/~치는 사람 a nightsoil man/ ~주다 spread manure; apply fertilize. ひりょう

**거리**¹ a street; a town/~를 걷다 walk [on] the street. ろじょう

**거리**² (재료) material (대상) an object (원인) cause/국~ materials for soup / 웃음~ an object of ridicule/걱정~ the cause of one's anxiety. ざいりょう

**거리**(巨利) a big profit; a huge gain.

**거리**(距離) a distance (간격) an interval (차이) a difference; a gap/원(근)~ a long(short) distance /100미터의 ~를 두고 at intervals of a hundred meters. きょり

**거리끼다** (물건에) be an obstacle (to); interfere with (마음에) weigh (on); bear down/거리낌없이 without hesitation [reserve]. かかる

**꺼리다** ①(싫어하다) dislike; abhor; loathe; regard with aversion ②(피하다) avoid; shun (두려워하다) be afraid of.
いやがる

**꺼림칙하다** feel somewhat uneasy; be rather unwilling (to). きにかかる

**꺼림하다** be uneasy (about); be unwilling (to); be afraid (of). きにかかる

**거마**(車馬) horses and vehicles/ ~ carriage. くるまとうま

**거만**(巨萬) millions/ ~의 million; myriad; immense/ ~의 부를 쌓다 amass a vast fortune; have millions wealth; become a millionaire. きょまん

**거만**(倨慢) arrogance; haughtiness/ ~하다 (be) arrogant; haughty; insolent / ~을 떼다 give oneself airs; ride the high horse. ごうまん

**거매지다, 꺼매지다** turn black (볕에 타서) get tanned. くろくなる

**거머리** ①(동) a leech ②(사람) a bur.

**거머먹다** (탐식) eat greedily; enjoy the meal; play a good(capital) knife and fork. わしづかみにしてくう

**거머트름하다, 꺼머트름하다** (be) brown and well fleshed; dark and plump.
くろみがかってまるまるふとっている

**거머삼키다** swallow; gulp; bolt. のみこむ

**거머잡다** grab(clutch, take hold of) greedily. ぎゅっとつかむ

**거머쥐다** clasp; grasp; grip; clutch.
ぎゅっとにぎる

**거멀못** a clamp; a cramp; a clincher
かすがい

**거멀장** a clamp; a cramp. かすがい

**거멀장식** an ornamental stud; an ornamental metal reinforcing piece.
とめがねのかざりきぐ

**거멓다, 꺼멓다** (be) deep-black; jet-black/햇볕에 거멓게(꺼멓게) 타다 be tann-

거무데데하다, 꺼무데데하다 (be) dark; black; swarthy; dusky; murky; dark. ややけひんにくろい

거무스름하다, 꺼무스름하다 (be) blackish; darkish. やゝくろい

거무죽죽하다, 꺼무죽죽하다 (be) dark; blackish; dusky. くろくてすんでいない

거문고 a Korean harp.

거물(巨物) 《사람》a leading[prominent] figure; a big wig《속》/정계의 ~ a leading figure in politics. おおもの

거물거리다, 꺼물거리다 《불빛이》flicker; glimmer; blink 《정신이》have an indistinct consciousness/거물거물[꺼물꺼물] flickeringly; faintly; dimly; indistinctly ちらちらする

거뭇거뭇, 꺼뭇꺼뭇 ~하다 (be) dotted with black spots; be blackish. こくてんがてんてんとあるさま

거뭇하다, 꺼뭇하다 (be) blackish; tinged with black. やゝくろい

거미 《동》 a spider/~알 슬듯 propagating vigorously everywhere/~집 a spider's web; a cobweb. くも

거미줄 ①《거미의》 a spider's thread[web]; cobwebs/~치다 weave a web ②《비상선》dragnet; a search apparatus/~치다 cast a close dragnet.

거미치밀다 get covetous; grow envious. よくがおこる

거민(居民) inhabitants; residents; the people きょじゅうみん

거반(居半) over half; the greater part (of); nearly all; almost; nearly ⇒거지반. ほとんど

거방지다 (be) of dignified presence; grand; important; be stately in mine. いげんのあるふうさいだ

거번(去番) 《저번》 the last time; the other day ⇒저번, 지난번. このまい

거벽(巨擘) a leading scholar; a great authority; a shining light (of science). がくしきがばっぐんなひと

거볍다 ①《무게가》(be) light; not heavy ②《가치가》(be) of little value; worthless. かるい

거병(擧兵) raising an army; rising in arms/~하다 rise in arms; raise an army; take up arms. きょへい

꺼벙이 《꿩 새끼》a young[chick] pheasant 《사람》a man of unsightly appearance. きじほ

거보(巨步) ¶ ~를 내디디다 make long strides (in). きじのこ

거봐라 look!; you see!; I told you so! それみろ

거부(巨富) a man of great wealth; a millionaire かねもち

거부(拒否) refusal; rejection; veto/~하다 refuse; turn down/요구를 ~하다 turn down a request. きょひ

거부지 pubic hair. いんもう

거북 《동》 a tortoise 《바다의》a [sea-] turtle. かめ

거북살스럽다 (be) uncomfortable; awkward; ill at ease. ひじょうにこまっている

거북선(―船) a turtle-shaped battleship. かめかたちのふね

거북점(―占) divination by tortoise-shells.

거북하다 (be) inconvenient; uncomfortable; ill at ease; awkward; unwell /입장이 ~ be in an awkward position. きもちがわるい

거분하다, 거뿐하다 (be) light; nimble ⇒가뿐하다. かるい

거불거리다, 꺼불거리다 romp; act rashly ⇒까불거리다. あそびさわる

거붓하다, 거뿟하다 (be) rather light ⇒가뿟하다. ちょうどよくかるい

거비(巨費) an enormous expenditure; a great cost. ばくだいなひよう

거사(居士) ①《불교도》 a Buddhist layman ②《처사》a scholar[a man] out of government service.

거사(擧事) ~하다 set a project on foot 《폭동을》rise in rebellion; start a revolt. おおきなことをおこすこと

거상(巨商) a wealthy merchant; a merchant prince. おおはなしょうにん

거상(居喪) ①《상중》mourning/~하다 be in mourning (for) ②《상복》a mourning dress; sables. とむらいにふくするあいだ

거상(巨像) a colossus; a gigantic statue.

거석(巨石) a huge stone 《고》《기념물》a megalith/~ 문화 megalithic culture. きわめておおきないし

거선(巨船) a big[huge, mighty] ship; a superliner. きょだいなふね

거성(巨星) a giant star 《거물》a great man; a big shot《속》/문단의 ~ a great writer. おおきなほし

거세(去勢) ①《불을 깜》castration; emasculation/ ~하다 castrate; emasculate; geld 《단종(斷種)》sterilize/~한 소 a bullock ②《세력 제거》weakening (약화); exclusion(배제); eradication(근절)/~하다 weaken; exclude; sterilize. きょせい

거세(擧世) the trend of the world; the current movements of the world. せかいぜんたい

거세다 (be) rough; wild; violent/거센 세파 the storms of life/거센 바람 fierce wind. あらっぽくてつよい

거소(居所) a dwelling place; one's abode(address); one's place of residence; one's whereabouts. いどころ

거수(擧手) raising one's hand 《가부의》a show of hands/ ~하다 raise one's hand/~ 표결 voting by show of hands/~ 경례 a hand salute; a military salute. きょしゅ

거스러미 《손톱의》an agnail; a hangnail 《나무의》a splinter. ささくれ

거스러지다 1《선길이》grow[become] wild; get violent 2《털이》fluff; become

거스르다 ①(반대) oppose; go[act] against; run counter to; cross/뜻을 ~ cross another's will/거슬러 올라가다 go against the stream ②(돈을) give [back] the change/거슬러 받다 get the change.

거스름돈 change/~을 주다 give the change. おつりをかへす

거슬거슬하다 (be) rough/성질이 ~ have a rough disposition. ざらざらする

거슬러 올라가다 go upstream; go up (a river); go against the stream (과거로) go back (소급) retroact. さかのぼる

거슬리다 《비위에》 be against the grain with (one). やくになっている

거슴츠레하다 (be) drowsy; heavy; dull; sleepy/거슴츠레한 눈 drowsy[heavy] eyes. うとうとしている

거시적(巨視的) macroscopic/~ 분석 macro-analysis.

거식(擧式) the ceremony; the celebration; the exercises〈미〉/ ~하다 hold a ceremony 《결혼》 celebrate[solemnize] a wedding. しきをきょこうする

거실(居室) 《자기의》 one's own room 《가족의》 a living room. いま

거심(去心) ~하다 remove knotty parts of (a medicinal herb).

거액(巨額) a colossal[an enormous] sum; a large amount/~에 달하다 amount to a colossal sum. きょがく

거야(去夜) last night. さくや

거여목(一木) 《식》 a clover; a trefoil.

거역(巨役) a colossal undertaking. おおきなしごと

거역(拒逆) disobedience; opposition; objection/ ~하다 disobey; object to; oppose/부모에게 ~하다 contradict one's parents. さからうこと

거오(倨傲) insolence; haughtiness; arrogance; pride/ ~스럽다, ~하다 (be) arrogant; proud[-hearted]; haughty.
おごりたかぶること

거우다 provoke; irritate; vex; tease.
おこらせる

거우듬하다 (be) somewhat inclined 〈기우듬하다〉. すこしかたむいている

거우르다 tip; tilt; slant かたむける

거울 ①《모양을 보는》 a mirror; a looking glass/ ~을 보다 look in a glass ②《모범》 a mirror; a pattern; model; a paragon/…을 ~로 삼다 model after; follow the example of (one). かがみ

거웃 pubic hair; pubes. いんもう

거월(去月) last month ultimo 《날짜의 뒤에》 ult; ultimo/ ~ 5일에 on the fifth last month; on the fifth ult. せんげつ

거위¹ 《조》 a goose (pl. geese)/수커위 a gander/~ 새끼 a gosling. がちょう

거위² (회충) a round-worm/ ~약 a worm medicine; a vermifuge/ ~배 stomach trouble caused by roudworms/ ~가 생기다 get roundworms. かいちゅう

거위영장 a lanky person; a beanpole 《속》; a gangling fellow〈미〉.

거유(巨儒) a savant; a great scholar of Confucianism. きょじゅ

거의 (대체로) almost; nearly; practically (부정) little; hardly; scarcely/ ~ 다 almost all; mostly; the greater part (of)/~ 불가능하다 be next to impossible/그것을 믿는 사람은 ~ 없다 Scarcely anybody believes that.
ほとんど

거의거의 almost; nearly 〈거의〉.
もうほとんど

거인(巨人) a giant; a Titan (위인) a great man. きょじん

거일(去日) the days gone by; old days; other days. せんじつ

거장(巨匠) a great master; a great artist; a maestro (It). きょしょう

거재(巨財) a vast fortune; millions/~를 쌓다 amass millions. きょざい

거저 gratis; free [of charge]; for nothing/ ~ 일하다 work for nothing/ ~ 주어도 싫다 I would not have it as a gift. ただ

거저먹기 an easy task; a cinch; a snap /그것은 ~다 That's an easy job., That's nothing. やすいしごと

거적 a coarse straw mat. むしろ

거적눈 eyes with the upper eyelids hanging down loosely.
まぶたがたれさがっているめ

거절(拒絶) [a] refusal; rejection/ ~하다 refuse; reject; decline/ ~하다 give a square refusal; refuse point-blank. きょぜつ

거점(據點) a position; a point/중요 군사 ~ a strategic position.

거조(擧措) manners; behaviour.

거조(擧朝) the whole [Imperial] court.
ちょうていぜんたい

거조 해망(擧措駭妄) irregularities; wrongdoing; misconduct/ ~하다 (be) irregular; outrageous; nefarious.
きょどうをきわめてせっせいがないこと

거족(巨族) a powerful family; a prosperous clan.

거족(擧族) the whole nation/ ~적 nationwide. みんぞくぜんたい

거좌(踞坐) ~하다 sit on (a chair). すわる

거주(居住) residence; dwelling/ ~하다 dwell; reside; inhabit; live/ ~인 a resident; a dweller; an inhabitant/ ~권 the right of residence/ ~ 증명서 a certificate of residence. きょじゅう

거죽 (표면) the face 《외면부》 the exterior (외견) the appearance. おもて

거중 조정(居中調停) mediation; intermediation; intervention; arbitration.
なかほどちょうていすること

거지 (걸인) a beggar; a mendicant/ ~ 근성 a mean spirit. こじき

거지(居地) a place[locality] of residence. きょじゅうち

거지(擧止) behavior ⇨행동거지.

꺼지다¹ ①《불이》 go out; die out 《화재가》 be put out; be extinguished ②《거품이》 break; burst. きえる

꺼지다² 《들어가다》 cave in; sink; subside; be depressed; become dented／눈이 ~ one's eyes become hollow／얼음이 ~ ice breaks. へこむ

거지반(居之半) 《반수 이상》 the [great] majority; the bulk 《태반》 the greater part; the great portion 《대개》 mostly; for the most part. ほとんど

거진 almost ⇨거의.

거짓 fraud; falsehood; untruth 《거짓말》 a lie; ~의 false; untrue; unreal／~ 웃음 a feigned smile／~ 울음 crocodile tears きぎ

거짓말 a lie; falsehood; a story／그럴듯한 ~ a plausible lie／뻔히 들여다뵈는 ~ a transparent falsehood／~장이 a liar; a story-teller／~ 같은 얘기 an incredible story／~ 탐지기 a lie detector／~을 하다 lie; tell a lie. うそ

거짓부렁 a lie ⇨거짓말.

거찰(巨利) a grand temple; a cathedral. きょだつ

거창(巨創) large[huge] scale／~하다 (be) large[grand] scale[d]; ambitious; wholesale. きょだい

거처(居處) one's [place of] residence; one's abode 《행방》 one's whereabouts／~하다 《살다》 reside; live／~을 정하다 take up one's residence (at, in). いどころ

거처(去處) 《목적지》 one's destination 《행방》 one's whereabouts／~하다 reside; live／~를 정하다 take up one's residence (at, in). ゆくえ

거체(巨體) a huge form[body]; a gigantic figure. きょたい

거촉(炬燭) torchs and candles.

거추(去秋) last autumn. さくねんのあき

거추장스럽다 (be) hard to handle; unmanageable; troublesome. めんどうだ

거추하다 look after; care for; help; stand by; see to; use one's good offices. たすけてやる

거춘(去春) last spring. さくしゅん

거춤거춤 cursorily; roughly. たいたい

거춧군 a caretaker; a sponsor. せわやく

거취(去就) 《행동》 one's course of action 《태도》 one's attitude／~를 결정하다 decide on one's attitude. きょしゅう

거치(据置) 《공채·저금 따위의》 deferment／~하다 leave (a loan) unredeemed.

거치(鋸齒) 《톱니》 saw tooth 《잎의 톱니》 serration (on a leaf)／~의 serrated; saw-toothed. のこぎりめ

거치다 ①《통과》 pass through; go by way of／구청을 거쳐 시청에 제출하다 submit to the city hall through the district office ②《걸리다》 hitch; hinder; tangle. すれる

거치적거리다, 꺼치적거리다 cause hindrance to; stand[get] in the way; be an encumbrance to; tangle 《옷 따위가》 cling to しきりにひっかかる

거칠다 (be) coarse; rough 《목소리 따위가》 harsh 《반죽이》 violent／거친 성미 a violent temper／거친 물결 a rough sea／숨지다 breathe hard. あらい

거칠하다, 꺼칠하다 (be) haggard; worn out; emaciated／거칠한[꺼칠한] 얼굴 a haggard[worn] face. ざらざらうる

거침 a hitch; an obstacle; an impediment／~없이 without a hitch 《서슴지 않고》 without hesitation. ひっかかり

거침새 a hitch; an obstacle; an impediment. じゃまもの

거침없다 free from hindrance 《수월한》 without difficulty[hindrance] 《거리낌없음》 unreserved 《술술》 smooth; easily. さしつかえがない

거침거리다, 꺼침거리다 《걸려댐》 (be) tangling 《껄껄함》 rough／거칫거칫[꺼칫꺼칫] tangling; rough しきりにひっかかる

거칫하다, 꺼칫하다 ①《껄껄함》 (be) rough; coarse ②《여윔》 (be) haggard; worn out. やつれている

거쿨지다 (be) grand; manful; commanding. たいかくがおおきくておとこらしい

거탄(巨彈) ①《탄환》 a huge shell ②《비유적》 a hit; a feature (영화의); sensation. きょだん

거통 ①《실권 없는 이》 a figurehead ②a grand appearance; a dignified attitude. なまいきなたいど

거판(擧板) 《탕진》 squandering; dissipation／~하다 squander[dissipate] one's fortune. さいさんをなくすこと

거폐(巨弊) 《폐단》 great difficulties 《나쁜 일》 a great evil; influential abuses. おおきなへいがい

거폐(去弊) ~하다 stamp out evils; sweep away abuses; clear society of its evils. へいがいをとりのぞく

거포(巨砲) a big gun. きょほう

거푸 over again; repeatedly. かさねて

거푸집 ①《주형》 a mould; a cast; a pig ②《몸의》 a figure ③《공간》 an enclosed raised spot caused by irregular pasting; a blister. いがた

거푼거리다 fly in the wind; flap; wave; flutter／거푼거푼 fluttering; waving. ひらひらとぶ

꺼풀 a layer of the outer cover. かわ

거풀거리다 flutter; flap; wave／거풀거풀 fluttering; flapping. ばたばたする

거품 foam; froth; a bubble／맥주 ~ froth[barm] of beer／비누 ~ lather／~이 일다 foam; froth; bubble. あわ

거풍(擧風) airing／~하다 air. さらすこと

거피(去皮) ~하다 skin; rind (mellons); shell (pears); peel (an orange); pare (an apple); bark. かわをむく

거하(去夏) last summer. さくか

거하다 ①《산이》 (be) lofty; steep; sheer ②《나무가》 (be) thick; dense; rampant.

거하다(居一) ①(살다) live; dwell; reside; inhabit ②(머무르다) stay; sojourn (in, at). きょじゅうしている
거한(巨漢) a man of gigantic stature; a giant. たいかくがおおきなおとこ
거함(巨艦) a big[monster] warship; a leviathan. きょかん
거행(擧行) performance; celebration/~하다 (모임을) hold; give; perform (식을) cerebrate; observe/졸업식을하다 hold a graduation ceremony.
きょこう
거향(居鄕) ~하다 live in the country.
거화(炬火) torchlight. たいまつ
꺽꺽 ◉ 장끼가 ~ 운다 A cock-pheasant cries. けんけん
꺽꺽하다 (be) rough; stiff; hard; harshtasting. かたい
꺾다 ①(분지르다) break; snap(딱 하고)/꽃을 ~ pluck[pick] a flower/나뭇가지를 ~ break off a branch ②(접다) fold [up]; double; turn [down] ③(방향을) make a turn ④(기운을) weaken, lower; break; crush/사기를 ~ lower the morale/적의 예봉을 ~ break the brunt of the enemy. おる
꺽둑거리다 cut in uneven slices/꺽독꺽둑 chop! chop! めったぎりにする
꺾쇠 a clamp; a staple. かすがい
걱실거리다 behave agreeably; bear oneself cheerfully. かいかつにこうどうする
꺾어지다 《부러지다》 break; be broken 《접히다》 be doubled; be folded. おれる
꺾이다 ①《부러지다》 be broken; break; snap ②《접히다》 be folded; be doubled ③《방향이》 bend; turn ④《기운이》 break [down]. おられる
꺾자치다(一字) cross out; strike out.
꺽저기 《어》 Coreoperca herzi(학명).
걱정 ①(근심) anxiety; concern; worry; apprehensions/~하다 be anxious; be concerned about; feel uneasy; be worried about/~거리 a cause of anxiety/~돈 pecuniary anxiety; worries about money/~ 말게 Never mind! ②《나무람》 scolding; lecture; reproach/~하다 scold; reprove; reprimand/ ~듣다 receive a reprimand; be reproved しんぱい
걱정꾸러기 ①(걱정 많은) one who is given to worries; one who is loaded with cares ②(나무라는) one who receives reprimand all the time; a constant trouble. つねにしんぱいのおおいひと
꺽지다 (be) stout; firm; tough; bold.
ごうじょうでゆうかんだ
건(巾) a hemp cap worn by a mourner; a hood; a kerchief. ずきん
건(鍵) ①(열쇠) a key ②(음) a key. かぎ
건(件) 《일·사건》 a matter; a case; an affair; a subject (항목) an item/도난 ~수 cases of theft. ことがら
건(腱) 《해》 a tendon/아킬레스의 ~ Achilles' tendon. けん
건-(乾) dried/~대구 a dried cod. かん—
건각(健脚) strong legs. けんきゃく
건갈이(乾一) plowing a rice-field while it is dry.
건강(健康) health/~하다 (be) healthy; sound; well/~체 a healthy body[condition]/~ 진단 a medical examination/ ~에 좋은 good for the health; wholesome/ ~이 나쁘다 be unhealthy; be out of health; be in bad[poor] health/ ~은 재물보다 낫다 Health is above wealth. けんこう
건건 사사(件件事事) every event[matter, affair, case]. もろもろのじけん
건건이 subsidiary articles of diet; salty tidbits. かんたんなおかず
건건찝질하다 (be) unsavoury and salty.
ふうみがなくただしおっぱい
건건하다 (be) salty. すこししおからい
건경(健勁) robustness; sturdiness/ ~하다 (be) robust; sturdy; strong and valiant. つよくげんきなこと
건곡(乾穀) dried grain. ほしたこくもつ
건곤(乾坤) 《천지》 heaven and earth; the universe/ ~ 일척(一擲)하다 stake all upon the cast. けんこん
건공(建功) ~하다 render distinguished services to the State; perform great services. くににこうをたてること
건교자(乾交子) a grand table of relish served at a drinking bout.
건국(建國) the founding of a nation/ ~하다 found a state[nation]/ ~일 National Foundation Day. けんこく
건너 《맞은 쪽》 the opposite side/~편에 on the opposite side. むこうがわ
건너가다 go[pass] over; go across; cross over/다리를 ~ cross a bridge/배 로 강을 ~ get across a river by boat/바다를 ~ sail[go] across the sea.
わたっていく
건너긋다 draw (a line) across.
건너다 cross [over]; go across/나루를 ~ ferry across a stream. わたる
건너다보다 ①(저쪽을) look out over[across] ②(남의 것을) covet; envy; look at covetously. みわたす
건너뛰다 jump across[over]; leap over; clear/개울을 ~ jump across a stream /담을 ~ leaps over a wall; (a horse) clears a wall. とびこえる
건너오다 《사람이》 come over[across] (the sea); cross over (to Korea) 《사물이》 be imported; be brought over[from]; be introduced/이리 건너오게 Come over here. わたってくる
건너지르다 lay[put] it across. よこギス
건너짚다 guess; anticipate. すいていする
건너편 the opposite side; the other side /~에 opposite; on the opposite side.
むこうがわ
건널목 《도로의》 a road crossing 《철도의》 a railway[railroad〈미〉] crossing; a

**건넛방** level[grade(미')] crossing／ ～지기 a gateman; a watchman; a flagman〈미〉. ふみきり

**건넛방(一房)** an opposite room; the room on the opposite side. むかいがわのへや

**건넛집** an opposite house; the house on the opposite[other] side; the house over the way. むかいかたわらのいえ

**건네다** ①《건네게 하다》carry across; take over(배로); lay[place] over(건너 놓다)／나룻배로 사람을 ～ ferry people across a river ②《넘겨 주다》hand over; deliver; transfer. こえさせる

**건네주다** pass (one) over; (a river); carry across 《배로》ferry (one) over[across]. わたしてやる

**건달(乾達)** a libertine; a scamp／～패 a crowd of scamps. やくざもの

**건담(健啖)** strong appetite; gluttony／～가(家) a heavy eater; gluttony.

**건답(乾畓)** a dry rice field; paddle fields easily affected by a short spell of dry weather.

**건땅** rich[fertile] soil. よくと

**-건대** according to／듣～ as I hear; according to what people say／결론을 말하～ to conclude. —に

**건대(巾帶)** the cowl and belt worn by people in mourning.

**건대구(乾大口)** a dried cod. ほしたら

**건더기** solid ingredients of a solid and ·liquid mixture. かす

**건둥하다, 껀둥하다** (be) neat; tidy; in good order. さっぱりしている

**건드러지다** (be) lithe; smart and graceful; charming. ほれぼれするようなすっきりしたようすた

**건드레하다** (be) half tipsy; slightly intoxicated; be a bit high; (be) happy／건드레한 기분이다 be slightly intoxicated; have a drop in one's eye; be tipsy. よつぱらい

**건드리다** ①《대다》touch (a thing) ②《집적이다》provoke; vex. ふれる

**건들거리다** 《바람이》blow gently 《사람이》behave charmingly. ぶらぶらする

**건들바람** a cool[a refreshing] breeze [in early autumn.／～이 선들선들 불어왔다 A refreshing breeze came blowing gently.

**건들장마** capricious autumn rain. きまぐれなしゅうう

**건듯, 건뜻** 《대강》hastily; cursorily; hurriedly《빠르게》quickly／바람이 ～ 불었다 There came a quick puff of wind.／일을 ～ 해치우다 make a quick job of it; get the work out of the way quickly. ちょっと

**건락(乾酪)** cheese／～ 제품 cheese products. かんらく

**건락소(乾酪素)** casein. かんらくそ

**건류(乾溜)** dry distillation 《석탄의》carbonization／～하다 dry [up] by distillation; carbonize. かんりゅう

**건립(建立)** erection; building; construction／～하다 build; erect. こんりゅう

**-건마는** but; though; still／생각은 있～ 돈이 없네 I want it, but I don't have the money to get it. ─が

**건망(健忘)** forgetfulness; a short memory／～증 amnesia. けんぼう

**건면(乾麵)** ①《요리 안 한》uncooked vermicelli ②《말린》dried vermicelli[noodle]. かんめん

**건목(乾木)** seasoned lumber／～치다 season; lumber. かわかしたたき

**건몰(乾沒)** confiscation; seizure／～하다 confiscate; seize. ぼっしゅうすること

**건몸달다** make vain efforts; struggle in vain. むだぼねをおる

**건물** sperm ejaculated involuntarily. むだにてたせいえき

**건물(建物)** an erection; a building; a structure 《큰》an edifice／목조 ～ a wooden building. たてもの

**건물로(一)** promiscuouslike; blindly 《힘 안 들이고》perfunctorily. ただて

**건반(鍵盤)** a key board; a finger board／～ 악기 keyed instruments. けんばん

**건밤** a sleepless night／～[을] 새우다 spend sleepless night. ねむれないよ

**건빵(乾一)** a biscuit. かんぱん

**건방지다** (be) impertinent; saucy; overbearing; haughty; pert／건방진 태도 a haughty bearing／건방지게 굴다 behave oneself haughtily／건방진 소리를 하다 talk big. なまいきである

**건백(建白)** a memorial; a representation; a petition／～하다 memorialize／～서 a written memorial. けんぱく

**건보(健步)** strongness in walking 《사람》a good walker. けんきゃく

**건복(乾鰒)** a dried abalone ≳건전복.

**건사하다** ①《일거리를》provide work (for) ②《수습》manage; deal with ③《간수》keep; preserve. わりあてる

**건삼(乾蔘)** skinned and a dried ginseng with its fibrils cut off. ほしたにんじん

**건선거(乾船渠)** a dry[a graving] dock. けんドック

**건설(建設)** construction; establishment／～하다 construct; establish／～적인 constructive／～부(部) the Ministry of Construction／～ 분과 위원회《국회의》the Construction Committee. けんせつ

**건설방** a libertine; a debauchee; a rake; a reprobate. どうらくもの

**건성** aimlessly; without purpose; halfheartedly 《엉터리로》perfunctorily／너는 내가 여기 ～ 와 있는 줄 아니 Do you think I am here without any purpose? おうざっは

**건성(乾性)** ～의 dry／～유(油) drying oil. かんせい

**건수(乾水)** a temporary spring; water welling out of the ground temporarily in the rainy season

**건수(乾嗽)** a dry cough; a hawk.

건수(件數) the number of cases. からぜき/けんすう
건습(乾濕) dryness and moisture; [degree of] humidity/ ~계(計) a meter for humidity; a psychrometer. かんしつ
건시(乾柿) a dried persimmon. ほしがき
건실(健實) soundness; steadiness; solidness/ ~하다 (be) steady; sound; solid; reliable; safe / ~하게 steadily; soundly/ ~한 사상 sound ideas /~한 사람 a steady person; a reliable person. けんじつ
건아(健兒) a vigorous[stalwart] boy[youth]; a stalwart. けんじ
건어(乾魚) dried fish/ ~로 만들다 dry fish. ほしこ
건언(建言) a memorial; a representation; a petition/ ~하다 memorialize; make a representation to. けんげん
건용(健勇) ~하다 (be) strong and brave; sturdy and manly. きょうけん
건울음 make-believe crying/ ~ 울다 shed crocodile tears. うそなき
건원(建元) establishment of the name of an era/ ~하다 establish the name of an era. くにのねんごうをたてること
건위(健胃) strengthening of the stomach /~제(劑) a stomachic; a peptic; a digestive.
건육(乾肉) dried meat; jerk 《쇠고기의》 pemmican. ほしにく
건으로(乾—) without reason; without purpose. わざと
건의(建議) a proposal; a suggestion/ ~하다 propose; suggest move/ ~안(案) a proposition. けんぎ
건잠머리 general instructions for doing a job/ ~하다 provide the means to do the job.
건장(健壯) good[robust] health/ ~하다 (be) healthy; robust; sound/ ~한 사람 a healthy person; a person in good health. そうけん
건재(乾材) Chinese drugs 《법제 않은》 dried medical plants/~ 약국 a store where Chinese drugs are dealt with; a wholesale drugstore. かんざい
건재(健在) ~하다 be well[in good health]; enjoy good health 《사업 따위가》 be as prosperous as usual. けんざい
건전(健全) sound[good] health; soundness; healthiness/ ~하다 (be) healthy; sound; wholesome/ ~한 사상(思想) wholesome ideas/ ~한 정신은 ~한 신체에 깃든다 A sound mind in a sound body. けんぜい
건전복(乾全鰒) a dried abalone. ほしあわび
건전지(乾電池) a dry cell[battery]. かんでんち
건정건정 hurriedly; cursorily. さっさと
건제(乾製) drying; desiccation; exsiccation/ ~하다 dry up; exsiccate; prepare dry. かんそうする
건조(乾燥) dryness; drying/ ~하다 (be) dry; arid/~기(期) the dry season/ ~실 a drying room. かんそう
건조(建造) building; construction/ ~하다 build; construct/ ~물 a building; a constructure/ ~중이다 be under construction. けんぞう
건조 무미(乾燥無味) dryness; dullness; tastelessness 《글의》 baldness/ ~하다 (be) dry; tasteless; dull; flat; bald/ ~한 문체 a bald style. かんそうみ
건주정(乾酒酊) a show of intoxication; a feigned tipsiness; an affected inebriation/ ~하다 pretend to be drunk. わざとよっぱらったふりをする
건중건중 roughly; cursorily. おうざっぱに
건지 a plumb[a sounding] line.
건지다 ①《꺼내다》 take up; scoop up; dip up; pick up/시체를 ~ bring a dead body to the land ②《구멍·주제》 save (one) from; help (one) out of /목숨을 ~ escape death ③《손해를》 save from; retrieve 《벌충》 cover up. すくいあげる
건책(建策) suggestion; advice/ ~하다 suggest a plan; make suggestion.
건천(乾川) a dry stream; a stream which is easily affected by dry weather. よくかれるかわ
건초(乾草) dry grass; hay. ほしくさ
건축(建築) construction; building; erection/ ,~하다 build; construct; erect / ~물 a building; a structure/ ~술[학] architecture/ ~가(家) an architect/ ~업자 a builder; a constructor / ~ 공사 construction work[s]; building operations/ ~중 under[in course of] construction. けんちく
건투(健鬪) a good fight 《노력》 strenuous efforts/ ~하다 put up a good fight; make strenuous efforts. けんとう
건투(健投) 《야구》 nice pitching; tossing [throwing] nicely/~하다 pitch well.
건판(乾板) a dryplate; a plate; 《인》 a dryer. かんばん
건평(建坪) a floor space. たてつぼ
건폐율(建蔽率) building coverage.
건포(乾脯) slices of dried meat or fish. ほしにく
건포도(乾葡萄) raisins; dried grapes; currants 《과자에 든》 plums. ほしぶどう
건필(健筆) a ready[facile, powerful] pen/ ~가 a prolific writer. けんぴつ
건하다 ①《풍족》 (be) abundant; plentiful ②《거나하다》 (be) tipsy ③《흥건하다》 (be) brimful. ひじょうにゆたかだ
건하다(乾—) 《습기가 없다》 (be) dry; easily affected by dry weather. ほす
건함(建艦) naval construction; building of warship. けんかん
건흔나다 alarm oneself at nothing; start at one's own shadow.
걷다¹ ①《말다》 roll[tuck, turn] up/ 스매를 ~ tuck up one's sleeves ②《치우다》 take down; strike/천막을 ~ strike a tent; break camp. まきあげる

걷다² 《발로》 walk; go on foot／걸어 돌아다니다 walk about／걷기 시작하다 《갓난 애기가》 begin to toddle. あるく
걷몰다 gather[collect] hurriedly; do a passing job. かりたてる
걷어들다 hold up (the skirt). とりあげる
걷어지르다 pull up; roll up; tuck up (one's skirt).
걷어질리다 sink; fall in／그는 앓았기 때문에 눈이 걷어질렸다 He had been sick and his eyes sank. めがへこむ
걷어차다 kick; give (one) a kick／문을 걷어차 열다 kick the open door. けとばす
걷어치우다 《걷어서》 gather up and remove《그만두다》 give up; quit. かたづける
-걷이 a gathering-up; a collection／가을~ harvest; gathering. とりいれ
걷잡다 support; hold; check. ささえる
걷히다 ①《구름 따위가》 clear up; vanish; lift／안개가 걷힌다 The fog lifts. ②《돈이》 be collected 《곡식이》 be taken [gathered] in. はれる
걸객(乞客) a beggar; a hanger-on. こじき
껄껄 ha-ha; haw-haw／~ 웃다 laugh outright[uproariously]; roar with laughter; burst into a roar of laughter; laugh aloud. からから
걸걸거리다 be gluttonous; be greedy; behave greedily. からからわらう
껄껄하다 (be) rough; coarse; harsh. ざらざらする
걸걸하다(傑傑—) (be) cheerful; sprightly; agreeable; candid. かっぱつだ
걸귀 ①《사람》 a glutton／~들린 gluttonous ②《암돼지》 a mother hog[sow]. こをうんだめすぶた
걸귀(傑句) an excellent piece of writing; a fine poem. けっさくのく
껄끄럽다 (be) rough; coarse. ちくちくする
근거리다 ①《욕심내다》 covet; be greedy (for) ②《가래가》 obstruct the throat. ほしくてむずむずする
껄끔거리다 feel prickly; stick; prick; irritate. ちくりちくりする
걸기(傑氣) a heroic temper; a sturdy spirit; a stout heart／~이 있는 of a heroic temper intrepid; gallant.
걸기대(乞期待)《게시》 Coming soon!
낭(一囊) ①《걸어 두는》 a bag not carried but hung on the wall ②《바랑》 a knapsack; a pack. こじきぶくろ
걸다¹ ⇨변항 참조(page 1295).
걸다² ①《땅이》 (be) rich; fertile ②《액체가》 (be) turbid; thick／건죽 thick gruel ③《식성이》 (be) not particular; not fastidious ④《언사가》 (be) foulmouthed; abusive. こえている
걸대 a bamboo pole used in hanging something on the wall. かけざお
걸때 the size of the body／~가 크다 have a huge body. たいかく
껄떡껄떡 with a gulp; cracking／~ 삼키다 gulp down. がぶがぶ
껄떡하다 (one's eyes) be drawn with fatigue[hunger]. めがおちくぼんでいる
걸러 at intervals of; apart／하루[이틀] ~ every other[third] day／6피이트 ~ at intervals of six feet. ぬかって
걸러뛰다 skip; leave out; pass over; bypass; omit. とばす
껄렁껄렁 ~하다 (be) poor; worthless; trashy; good-for-nothing／~한 사내 a good-for-nothing[wretched] fellow／~한 학생 a student lacking discipline. でたらめだ
걸레 a mop; a clout; a rag／~질하다 swab／~ぞうきん
걸레부정(—不淨) 《물건》 rubbish 《사람》 human debris. はいぶつ
걸리다¹ ①《매어 달리다》 be hung; be hooked ②《돈·생명이》 be deposited; be bet ③《전화가》 have a [telephone] call (from) ④《함정 따위에》 be caught; be trapped ⑤《방해되다》 be caught (in, on) ⑥《법 따위에》 be against [a law]; be contrary[contradictory] to ⑦《병에》 be attacked[seized, afflicted] with ⑧《시간이》 take／시간이 ~ It takes time. ⑨《마음에》 worry; weigh／마음에 ~ be concerned. かかる
걸리다² 《걷게 하다》 make (one) walk; walk (one)／야구 walk the batter(4구로). あるかされる
망(一網) a Buddhist monk's knapsack; a pack. あみのリュクサック
걸맞다 be in harmony with; bear proportion to; match with. つりあっている
껄머리 a wig; a false hair; a big false-hair chignon worn by the bride at a wedding. おおきなかもじ
걸말다 assume; take over (another's task). うけもつ
걸잡다 hold; clasp; grab; grip; clutch at. わしづかみにする
걸머지다 ①《등에》 carry (a thing) on one's back; shoulder; bear／한국의 장래를 걸머진 젊은이 young men on whose shoulders rest the destinies of Korea ②《빚을》 be saddled with; shoulder; fall into／빚을 많이 ~ make[be saddled with] a lot of debts. せおう
걸메다 carry on one's shoulder; shoulder (a gun). ものをかたにかける
걸물(傑物) a great man[character]; a master spirit. けつぶつ
걸빵 《멜빵》 braces; suspenders 《질빵》 a back-strap.
걸싸다 (be) quick; nimble. てはやい
걸상(—床) a couch; a lounge; a bench; a seat. こしかけ
걸쌍스럽다 (be) charming[attractive] [in eating]. うっとりするほどよい
걸쇠 a catch; a latch／~를 채우다 fasten [with] a latch. かけがね
걸식(乞食) begging; pauperism／~하다 go begging; beg one's bread. こじき
걸신(乞神) voracity; ravenousness; ed-

걸씬거리다 be close (to); be almost touching. かすめる
걸어앉다 sit (on, in); take a seat/의자에 ~ sit on a chair. こしかける
걸어총(一銃) ⓐ stack[pile] of arms 《구령》 Pile[Stack] arms!
걸우다 manure; fertilize; enrich/밭을 ~ manure a field. とちをこやす
걸음 walking; a step; gait/첫 ~ the first step/ ~이 빠른[느린] swift-[slow-] footed. あゆみ
걸음걸이 gait; pace; a tread; a step/무거운[가벼운] ~로 with heavy[light] steps/이상한 ~로 걷다 walk with an odd gait. あるきぶり
걸음마 《어린애에게》Step firm! よちよち
걸음발타다 find one's feet; toddle one's way; start to toddle; try its feet.
よちよちとあるきはじめる
걸음쇠 [a pair of] compasses. コンパス
-걸이 《거는 제구》a peg; a rack; a hanger/모자 ~ a hat-rack/옷 ~ a clothes-rack. かけるもの
걸인(乞人) a beggar ⇨거지. こじき
걸작(傑作) a masterpiece; a great work / ~집(集) a collection of masterpieces. けっさく
걸쩨거리다 be active; be free hearted and lively. かつどうてきだ
걸쭉하다 (액체가)(be) somewhat thick; somewhat heavy/걸쭉한·국 thick soup.
どろどろする
걸차다 (be) fertile; rich; productive.
걸쳐두다 leave (a matter) in suspense; leave (an affair) unsettled; suspend; hang up. ふたまたをかける
걸출(傑出) 《뛰어남》 excellence; prominence 《사람》a distinguished character; 《걸물》 a master spirit/ ~하다 (be) distinguished; prominent/ ~한 인물 a distinguished character; a master spirit. けっしゅつ
걸치다 ①《미치다》 range; reach; extend; cover; last/화요일에서 토요일에 걸쳐 extending from Tuesday to Saturday; Tuesday through Saturday/여러 해에 ~ extend over so many years ②《양쪽으로》 stretch over; hang over ③《웃을》 throw on; slip on/누더기를 걸치고 있다 be clad in rags. かける
걸태질 screwing and scraping/ ~하다 scrap and screw. こつこつためること
걸터듬다 grope; fumble for; feel about for. てさぐりする
걸터앉다 sit a stride; bestride; stride over. またがる
걸터타다 mount[get up on]; ride astride (a horse). うまなどにのる
걸핏하면 too often; not infrequently/ ~ …하다 be apt to; be liable to; be inclined to. ややもすれば
검(劍) 《도검》 a sword 《군도》a sabre 《총검》 a bayonet. けん

검객(劍客) a [master] swordsman; a fencer. けんきゃく
검거(檢擧) an arrest; a round-up/ ~하다 arrest; round up; apprehend/ ~자 a person in custody. けんきょ
껌껌하다 (마음이)(be) pitch-dark; insidious. ひじょうにくらい
검극(劍戟) 《칼과 창》swords and spears 《무기》 weapons; arms. かたなとやり
검기다 blacken; soil. くろくよごす
검기울다 become dark [with clouds overspreading the sky]; turn down.
ひぐれてくらくなる
검뇨(檢尿) examination of the urine/ ~하다 examine one's urine/ ~기(器) a urinometer. けんにょう
검누렇다 (be) dark yellow; blackish yellow. くろみがかってきいろい
검다¹, 껌다 (be) black; dark/검은 옷 a black robe; [a suit of] black clothes/검디 ~ be jet-black/검게 하다 blacken. くろい
검다² 《그러모으다》rake up; gather up; scrape up/낙엽을 ~ rake up fallen leaves. かきあつめる
검댕 soot/ ~투성이의 sooty; sooted/ ~이 껴다 Soot collects. すす
검덕귀신(一鬼神) a person who is dirty in his appearance.
かおまたはきものがきわめてよごれたひと
검도(劍道) [the art of] fencing; swordsmanship. けんどう
검독(檢督) overseeing/ ~하다 oversee; take charge of.
검둥개 a black dog. くろいぬ
검둥이 《얼굴이 검은 이》a dark-faced person 《흑인》 a negro; a black; a coloured man[woman]. くろんぼう
검뚜다 badger (one to do); tease; press; importune (one for). せがむ
검디검다 (be) jet[coal]-black.
ひじょうにくろい
검류계(檢流計) 《조류(潮流)의》a current indicator 《전류의》a galvanometer.
けんりゅうけい
검무(劍舞) a sword-dance/ ~하다 perform a sword-dance けんぶ
검문(檢問) inspection; examination; check up/ ~하다 inspect; check up; examine/ ~소 a check-point. けんもん
검박(儉朴) simplicity; plainness/ ~하다 (be) simple; frugal. けんそ
검버섯 dark spots [on the skin of an old man]. しみ
검변(檢便) an examination of feces; scatoscopy.
검부나무 dry grass[dead leaves] used for fuel. かれは
검불 dry grass; dead leaves. かれは
검불덤불 confusedly; pell-mell; higgledypiggledy. こんがらかって
검붉다 (be) dark-red; blackish red.
くろみがかってあかい

**검사(檢査)** inspection; examination; test/ ～하다 inspect; examine; test 《회계를》 audit 《상품을》 condition/ ～관 an inspector; an examiner 《회계의》 an auditor. けんさ

**검사(檢事)** a public procurator[prosecutor] 《총칭》 the prosecution/ ～장 a chief public procurator. けんじ

**검산(檢算)** verification of accounts/ ～하다 verify[check] accounts. けんざん

**검색(檢索)** reference; a search; examination/ ～하다 refer to. けんさく

**검세다** (be) stiff; unyielding; dogged; stubborn. せいしつがあらっぽくてつよい

**검소(儉素)** frugality; simplicity; ~lainness/ ～하다 (be) frugal/～한 생활 a frugal life. けんそ

**검속(檢束)** arrest; custody; detention/ ～하다 arrest; detain; take (one) into custody. けんそく

**검수기(檢水器)** a water-gauge.

**검술(劍術)** [the art of] fencing; swordsmanship 《목검 시합》 singlestick/ ～을 하다 practise fencing. けんじゅつ

**검숭검숭** ～하다 (be) blackish; black sparsely. くろみがかっている

**검쓰다** as bitter as gall; (be) very bitter. ひじょうにくるしい

**검시(檢屍)** a coroner's inquest; a post-mortem examination; autopsy; an inquest/ ～하다 examine (a corpse); hold an inquest over (the body)/～관 a coroner. けんし

**검실거리다** flicker ⇨감실거리다. ちらつく

**검실검실** ～하다 (be) sparsely dotted with dark spots.

**검안(檢案)** the written result of an autopsy. けんあん

**검안(檢眼)** an eye examination; optometry/ ～하다 examine one's eyes; test one's vision. けんがん

**검약(儉約)** economy; thrift; frugality / ～하다 be thrifty; be frugal; be economical/ ～한 사람 a thrifty[frugal] person. けんやく

**검역(檢疫)** medical inspection/ ～하다 quarantine; inspect/ ～소[관] a quarantine station[officer]. けんえき

**검열(檢閱)** 《간행물의》 censorship 《점검》 inspection 《군대의》 review/ ～하다 censor; inspect; review/～관 a censor; an examiner. けんえつ

**검온(檢溫)** 《의》 thermometry/ ～하다 take one's temperature [with a thermometer]/ ～기(器) a clinical thermometer. けんおん

**검은깨** black sesame. くろいごま

**검은그루** a field that has been kept

---

# 걸 다 [1]

①《매달다》 hang; suspend; put up; hook; set up/간판을 ～ put up a signboard/못에 ～ hang (a thing) on a peg/그림을 벽에 ～ hang a picture on the wall/모자를 못에 ～ hang one's hat on a hook/벽에는 묵직한 액자에 든 큰 그림이 걸려 있었다 The wall was hung with large paintings in massive frames., Large pictures in massive frames hung[were hung on] the wall.

②《말·시비를》 speak to (a person); address (a person); talk to (a person); pick; fasten; force/농을 ～ play a joke on (a person)/정중하게 말을 ～ speak seriously to (a person)/싸움을 ～ pick a quarrel with (a person).

③《돈·목숨을》 stake; bet (money on); wager; lay a wager (on); risk; pay; advance/계약금을 ～ advance money on a contract; pay earnest money; place money on deposit/목숨을 ～ risk [stake] one's life; take a risk of one's life/경마에 돈을 ～ stake a horse; stake[bet] money on a horse race; bet on a horse race/검은색 말에 천 원을 ～ bet[stake] a thousand won on a black horse/권투 선수는 목숨을 걸고 있다 A boxer carries his life in his hand./그는 목숨을 걸고 강물에 뛰어들었다 He dived to the bottom of the river at [the] risk of his life./그는 사업에 전 재산을 걸었다 He staked all his fortune on business.

④《시동을》 start [a engine] going.

⑤《전화를》 dial the number; telephone (to a person); make a [telephone] call to (a person); ring (a person) up [on the telephone]〈영〉; call (a person)[on the telephone]〈미〉/나에게 전화가 걸려 왔다 I was called up./119번으로 전화를 걸었다 I dialed 119./경찰에 전화를 걸어라 Dial the police station./여자는 쓸데 없는 일로 곧잘 전화를 건다 Women often use the telephone for trifling purposes./거기 도착하는 즉시로 전화를 걸어다오 Phone me[Give me a ring] as soon as you get there.

⑥《문고리·자물쇠 따위를》 fasten; lock; turn a key/문에 자물쇠를 ～ Lock the door/금고에 자물쇠를 ～ Lock the safe. /대문을 ～ fastens the front door.

⑦《올가미를》 lay (a snare); set (a trap)/나는 짐승을 잡으려고 올가미를 걸어 두었다 I set a trap for the animal.

⑧《재판을》 institute court proceedings (againt a person).

검은도요 〖조〗 an oyster-catcher.
검은엿 black rice-jelly. くろいあめ
검은자[위] the iris [and pupil] of the eye. くろいひとみ
검은콩 a black soy bean. くろいまめ
검은팥 a black Indian bean.
검인(檢印) a seal[stamp] [of approval] / ~을 찍다 stamp. けんいん
검인정(檢認定) official approval／문교부~필(畢) 〔표시〕 Approved by the Ministry of Education／~ 교과서 an anthorized textbook. けんていとにんてい
검적검적 ~하다(be) studded with black spots.
검전기(檢電器) 〖물〗 a galvanoscope 《누전의》 a detector. けんでんき
검정, 껌정 black [colour] 〖물감〗 black dye. くろいろ
검정(檢定) 《면허》 official approval[sanction] 《검사》 examination／~하다 give official approval to; authorize; examine; inspect／~ 고시 a qualifying examination; the examination for the license (of). けんてい
검증(檢證) verification; inspection 《유언의》 probate. けんしょう
검진(檢診) medical examination／~하다 examine (one) medically／성병 ~ a V.D. check. けんしん
검질기다 (be) persistent; untiring; indefatigable. ひじょうにじょうぶだ
검찰(檢札) examination of tickets／~하다 examine tickets. けんさつ
검찰(檢察) examination; investigation and prosecution／~관 a public prosecutor／~ 총장 the attorney general／대[고등, 지방]~청 the Supreme[High, District] Public Procurator's[prosecutor's] Office. けんさつ
검출(檢出) 〖화〗 detection [as a result of chemical analysis]／~하다 detect (poison)／~ 장치 a detector.
검측스럽다 (be) tricky; snaky; blackhearted; double-dealing; covetous; treacherous; crafty. はらぐろい
검측측하다 ①《마음이》(be) snaky; covetous ②《색이》(be) black[dark] unevenly. はらぐろい
검치다 attach along a corner at an angle.
검침하다(黔沈一) (be) tricky; snaky; wily; treacherous; insidious／검침한 사람 a snaky person. いんけんだ
검토(檢討) examination; study／~하다 study; examine／재~ reexamination; review. けんとう
검특하다(黔慝一) (be) black-hearted; tricky; treacherous; snaky; insidious. はらぐろい
검파(檢波) detection／~하다 detect／〖광석〗 ~기 a [crystal] detector. けんぱ
검표(檢票) examination of tickets／~하다 clip[examine] tickets; check a person's tickets.
검푸르다 (be) dark-blue. あおくろい
검푸르죽죽하다 (be) blackish tinged with blue. くろみがかっている
검협(劍俠) a chivalrous[a gallant] swordsman. ぎきょうしんのあるけんきゃく
검호(劍豪) a master[a skilled] swordsman.
검화 〖식〗 a dittany; a fraxinella; a gas plant; *Dictamnus albus*(학명).
검흐르다 run over; overflow; flow[spill, run] over. あふれてながれる
겁(怯) 《소심》 cowardice; timidity; fear; awe／~많은 cowardly; timid; weak-kneed; white-livered／~을 집어먹다 be frightened; be scared. きょうふ
겁(劫) a *Kalpa* (Sans); an [a]eon. せつな
겁간(劫姦) outrage; violation; rape／~하다 violate; outrage. ごうかん
겁겁하다(劫劫一) ①《성급하다》(be) impatient; hasty; quick-tempered ②《급급하다》(汲汲一). きゅうきゅうしている
겁결(怯一) the impetus of fear／~에 driven by fear; in one's horror; in the excess of fear. きょうふのはずみ
겁꾸러기(怯一) a coward; a recreant; a pudding heart; a poltroom; a milksop; a funk. おくびょうもの
겁기(劫氣) an evil appearance; an ugly aspect. おそろしいせいき
겁나(怯懦) timidness; poor courage; faint-heartedness／~하다 (be) cowardly; timid; chicken-hearted. きょうふ
겁나다(怯一) be seized with fear; be overcome with fright; be struck with awe; be scared; grow timid; get into funk; become nervous; be daunted (at). きょうふにとりつかれる
겁내다(怯一) fear; dread; apprehend; stand in; fear of; have a horror of; be afraid of; shy at. こわがる
겁년(劫年) an unlucky year.
껍데기 《조개의》 a shell 《곡물의》 hulls.
겁략(劫掠, 劫略) plundery; pillage; robbery.
겁박(劫迫) a threat; a menace; coercion 《강제》 compulsion／~하다 threaten; intimidate; compel. きょうはく
겁성(怯聲) an exclamation of fear／~을 내다 express one's fear.
껍신거리다 behave frivolously[lightly, giddily].
겁심(怯心) fear; fright; awe; timidity; cowardice; funk. こわがるこころ
겁약(怯弱) faint-heartedness; poltroonery; timidness; funk／~하다 faint-hearted; white-livered; timid; coward. きょうじゃく
겁운(劫運) the devil's luck; ill fate; ill luck. ひじょうにおおきなやくうん
겁장이(怯一) a cowardice; a pudding heart; a funk; a dastard; a craven; a pussyfoot[yellow belly]. よわむし
껍적거리다 behave frivolously.

껍죽거리다 behave frivolously. けいそつにふるまう
껍질 (나무의) bark 《과실의》 rind; peel 《깍지》 husk; shell 《얇은 껍질》 film/ ~을 벗기다 bark; skin; rind; peel; shell. かわ
겁탈(劫奪) 《약탈》 plunderage 《강간》 rape/ ~하다 plunder; rape. ごうだつ
겁화(劫火) the cosmos destroying conflagration at the close of a Kalpa.
것¹ ①《사람·물건》 a one; the one/새 ~ a new one ②《소유》 the one of; your's/우리~ ours. もの
것² ①《일·사실》 the fact that…; the act of (doing)/비가 오는 ~을 알다 Knows that it is raining. ②《가능성》 likely[probable] fact/이겼으로 충분할 ~이다 This will be probably be enough. ③《의무·금지》 the thing to do/미성년자는 담배 피우지 말 것 The law prohibits minors from smoking. もの
-껏 as possible; to the best of/힘~ as far[much] as one can; to the best of one's ability[power]/성의~ with utmost sincerity/힘~ 싸우다 fight for all one is worth.
-젓다 ①《사실의 다짐》 be; do; I assume [suppose, think]/너 이 동네 살~ You must live in this village. ②《은근한 협박》 surely[certainly] be[do]/너는 그리 했~ You certainly did do so. ③《원인·조건을 갖춤》 given this and that /돈 있~ 힘 있~ 무슨 걱정이오 You've got money, you've got power so what's your worry? —と。—し
껑 a lie; fabrication; a fake/ ~을 까다 tell a lie. うそ
깅그레 a steamer rack/ ~[를] 놓다 fix a steamer rack at the bottom of the oven.
겅둥거리다, 껑둥거리다 gambol; hop; leap about; jump up and down/경둥경둥 leaping. ぴょんととぶ
겅성드뭇하다 lie scattered about/경성드뭇이 scatteringly. ちらばっている
정정거리다, 껑정거리다 walk with rapid strides. おおまたであるく
껑충이 a lamp-post; a gangling fellow; a lanky and fickle man. のっぽ
겉 《표면》 the face; the surface; 《옷의》 the right side 《외면》 the outside; the exterior 《외관》 outward appearance/~으로는 outwardly; on the surface/ ~을 보고 판단하다 judge by appearance/ ~을 꾸미다 make outward show. おもて
겉가량(一假量) a rough estimate; guess. だいたいのけんとう
겉가루 the first [and tastiest] grindings. ぬか
겉가죽 the outer skin. うわかわ
겉꺼풀 an outer covering; a husk 《곡식의》 a shuck; a crust; a shell 《동식물 체의》 an investment. そとおおい

겉껍질 a soft outer covering; a husk; a hull; a shuck. そとかわ
겉겨 bran; chaff.
겉곡식(一穀食) unhulled grain.
겉꾸리다 make outward show; keep up appearance. そとかざりする
겉꾸림 making outward appearance; saving appearance. そとかざり
겉나깨 bran. ぬか
겉날리다 scamp (one's work); do in a careless manner. ぞんざいにする
겉놀다 《못·나사 따위가》 slip; do not fit 《겉돌다》 do not get along well.
つきあわない
겉눈감다 pretend to have shut one's eyes. めをとじたようにみせかける
겉눈썹 an eyebrow. まゆげ
겉늙다 look old for one's age; be prematurely gray. としがふけてみえる
겉대¹ 《푸성귀의》 the outer stalk of vegetables.
겉대² 《대의》 the outer surface of bamboo. たけのそと
겉대중 a rough estimate 《눈대중》 eye measure. あてすいりょう
겉더께 surface scum. うすかわ
겉돌다 stay out of the party; do not mix well. よくこんごうしない
겉마르다 be dry on the surface; dry out before ripening. そとづらだけほす
겉말 lip service; lip homage. からせじ
겉맞추다 gloss; smooth over; temporize.
겉면(一面) the surface; the exterior; the face. そとづら
겉모양(一貌樣) [outward] appearance; show; look. がいかん
겉물 ①《따로 도는 물》 fluid in a mixture which has no natural affinity with the other ②⇒겉물.
겉바르다 make outward show; put good face on. そとづらだけをうまくかざる
겉밤 an unhulled chestnut.
からをむかないくり
겉보기 the outer appearance; show; look/ ~에는 outwardly; on the surface; apparently. がいけん
겉보리 unhulled barley. からむぎ
겉봉(一封) 《봉투》 an envelope 《겉에 쓴 것》 an address(주소 성명)/ ~을 쓰다 address an envelope. うわふう
겉싸개 a cover; a wrapper; an outer covering; an envelope. 外つつみ
겉살 bare skin. むきだしのはだ
겉수수 unhulled millet.
겉약다 (be) shrewd in mere appearance; be clever in a supperfitial way.
겉어림 a rough estimate; guess 《눈어림》 eye measurement. あてすいりょう
겉언치 a pair of straw pads attached to the both sides of a pack-saddle.
겉옷 an upper garment; overclothes.
겉잎 an outer leaf. がいそくのは
겉잡다 make a rough estimate.
겉잣 pine-nuts with their shells on.

**겉장**(-張) the first[front] page; a title page. ひょうし
**겉저고리** an outer coat.
**겉절이** a dish of salted vegetables prepared with a dressing of oil.
**겉절이다** salts [vegetables] before seasoning elaborately; pickles["wilts"] vegetables right before eating.
**겉조** unhulled millet.
**겉짐작** a rough estimate. おくそく
**겉창**(-窓) an outer window; a shutter. がいそくのまど
**겉치레** cutting a dash; putting on a fair show; making outward show/ ~하다 show off; cut a dash; put on a fair show.
**겉치마** an outer skirt. うえにきるスカート
**겉치장**(-治粧) an outward show/ ~하다 put on a fair outside appearance; cut a dash. うわべのかざり
**겉피** unhulled barnyard millet. から
**겉핥다** just scratch the surface (of a situation); have a superficial knowledge (of).
**게¹** 《거기》 there 《너》 you; you there/~ 누구 있느냐 Is anybody there?/~ 섯거라 Stop! you there. そこ
**게²** 《에게》 for; to/내~ 온 편지 a letter for me. ーに
**게³** 《동》 a crab/ ~딱지 a crust; a carapace/ ~의 집게발 claws/ ~걸음 side-crawl of a crab. かに
**께** 《즈음》 toward; around (天) near/그 믐~ toward the and of the month /정거장~ near the station. あたり
**-게** ①《명령》 ᄋ가끔 놀러 오~ Come to see me now and then ②《내용 한정》 ᄋ 아름답~ beautifully; charmingly/뜻 듯하~ hot; warm.
**게거품** ①《게의》 foam at the mouth of a crab ②《동물의》 foam; froth. かにのくちからでるあわ
**게걸** greed; voracity; gluttony; rapacity. くいしんぼう
**게걸거리다** grumble; groan; mutter; murmur [with discontent]; gripe/《미·속》 /게걸게걸 grumbling; groaning.
**게걸들다** have voracity; be gluttonous. かわきのやまいにかかる
**게걸들리다** become greedy[voracious].
**게걸스럽다** (be) gluttonous; voracious; greedy/게걸스럽게 먹다 guzzle; devour; shovel (food) into one's mouth; eat greedily. くいしんぼうらしい
**게걸음** crawling sidewise; sidling 《게 의》 the side crawl of a crab/ ~치다 sidle along; move[walk] sidewise [sideways]. よこにはっていく
**게걸장이** a grumbler; a malcontent; a grouch. ぐちをよくいうひと
**게검스럽다** (be) gluttonous; voracious.
**께끄름하다** 《사물이 주어》 weigh on one's mind; lie at one's heart; get on one's nerves 《사람이 주어》 be anxious (about); feel uneasy (about); feel a bit unpleasant/뒷맛이 ~ leave an unpleasant taste behind. きにかかる
**께끔하다** (be) uneasy (about) 《《일이 주어》 get[jar] on one's nerves.
**게다가** moreover; besides; what is more; in addition (to that)/ ~ 눈까지 내 렸다 To make the matters worse, snow came on. そこに
**게딱지** the shell[crust] of a crab/ ~ 만하다 be small as a crab shell; (be) tiny. かにのかたい甲
**게두덜거리다** mutter; grumble; groan. きたないぐちをしきりにこぼす
**게발** a crab's claws/글씨를 ~ 그리듯 하 다 scribble; write in poor hand; write a crabbed hand. かにのあし
**게방**(揭榜) posting a notice/ ~하다 post a notice; put up a proclamation.
**께서** ᄋ모친~는 안녕하신가? Is your mother well? が
**게시**(揭示) a notice; a notification; a bulletin/ ~하다 post[put up, write up] a notice; notify/ ~판 a notice [bulletin] board. けいじ
**-게시리** so that indeed/뒷탈 없~ 잘 처 리하시오 Manage the matter carefully so that there will be absolutely no trouble in the future. ーように
**게알젓** pickled spawn of crabs.
**게양**(揭揚) raising/ ~하다 hoist; fly; raise; display/국기를 ~하다 hoist a national flag. けいよう
**게염** covetousness; envy/ ~스러운 covetous/ ~나다 grow covetous/ ~내 다 covet; feel envious. どんよくな
**께옵서** ᄋ상감~ 칙령를 내리셨다 The king issued a proclamation.
ーにおかせられては
**게우다** vomit; throw up; fetch up; bring up. はきだす
**게으르다** (be) idle; lazy; tardy; indolent; slothful. なまける
**게으름** idleness; laziness; indolence / ~부리다 be idle[lazy]; drone. なまけ
**게으름뱅이** an idle person; a lazybone; a sluggard. なまけもの
**게을러빠지다** (be) intolerably lazy; quite in dolent. ひじょうになまけである
**게을리하다** neglect; slight/학업을 ~ neglect one's studies. なまける
**게장**(-醬) ①《장》 soy sauce in which crabs are preserved ②《젓》 pickled crabs. かにをつけたしょうゆ
**게재**(揭載) publication; printing/ ~하 다 publish; print; report (in a paper) / ~ 금지 a press ban. けいさい
**게저분하다** (be) dirty; unclean; soiled. きたない
**께적거리다** do[go at] something halfheartedly ⇒께지럭거리다.
**게적지근하다** (be) nervous (about); feel uneasy. きたならしい
**게접스럽다** (be) filthy; squalid; dirty.

게젓 pickled crabs; crabs preserved in soy.
게정 a grievance; a murmur; a complaint/ ～내다 grumble. なきごと
께죽거리다 《중얼거리다》grumble 《되씹다》chew repeatedly in a sluggish manner. ぶつぶつへいをいう
께지럭거리다 do[go at] something half-heartedly/께지럭거리지 말고 빨리 먹어라 Stop picking at your food eat it up. なまけていやいやながらする
게트림 belching in haughty manner; an arrogant belch/～하다 belch in haughty manner. おくび
-겠다 ①《결심·필연성》 will [do]/그 일을 내일 하～ I will do it tomorrow. ②《추측·판단》 probably do[be] ③《인사》이 처음 뵙겠습니다 How do you do?
겨 chaff 《속의》 bran 《겉의》 husks. ぬか
겨끔내기 doing on a two-shift basis; alternating. こうたいしておこなうこと
겨냥 aim; sight/ ～하다 aim at; level at/ ～이 어긋나다 be faulty at aim; miss the mark. げんとう
겨냥내다 sight; take sight at. はかる
겨냥대다 take aim at. ねらいをきめる
겨냥보다 aim; take aim at. ねらいをつける
겨누다 ①《겨냥하다》 take aim at; level (a gun at)/권총을 가슴에 ～ point a pistol at the breast ②《대보다》 compare (A with B); measure/길이를 ～ compare length. ねらう
겨드랑이 ①《몸의》 the armpit/ ～에 under one's arm/ ～털 hair of the armpit ②《옷의》 the armhole. わきのした
겨들다 《두 팔로》 hold (a thing) between one's hands[arms] 《두 물건을》 hold both at once. いだきあげる
겨레 《혈족》a family; a kinsfolk 《민족》a race; a nation; a people. みんぞく
겨루다 compete; contest; match; measure/힘을 ～ measure oneself against another in strength. にらみあう
겨룸 contest; competition. きょうそう
겨를 leisure; spare moments; time to spare/…할 ～이 없다 have no time to do…. ひま
겨릅 a hemp stalk with its bast peeled off; a skinned hemp stalk. おがら
겨리 a plough pulled by a yoke of oxen/겨릿소 a yoke of oxen.
겨반지기 rice with much bran or chaff. ぬかまじりのこめ
껴안다 embrace; hug; take into one's arms/서로 ～ embrace[hug] each other. いだく
겨우 barely; narrowly; with difficulty / ～ 살아가다 make a bare living; live barely/ ～ 목숨을 건지다 narrowly escape death. やっと
겨우내 all winter through. ゆきのあいだ
겨우살이¹ 《옷》 winter clothes; winter wear. ゆきのきもの
겨우살이² 《식》 a mistletoe; a parasite.
겨울 winter/ ～의 winter; wintry/ ～옷 winter clothes; winter wear/ ～ 방학 the winter vacation[holidays]/ ～철 winter [time]. ゆき
겨워하다 feel unequal to do; find it difficult to do; feel [it] difficult to do ⇒겹다. ちからがたらなくむずかしくおもう
껴입다 wear (a coat) over another; take over another. かさぬてきる
겨자 《양념》 mustard 《풀》 a mustard [plant]; a rape. からし
겨죽 rice-bran gruel.
격(格) ①《지위》 standing; rank 《품위》 dignity; grace 《등급》 class; grade/ ～이 다르다 stand on different levels/ ～이 떨어지다 《사람의》 lower one's dignity ②《자격》 capacity 《인격》 character /～에 안 맞는 짓을 하다 go out of one's character; do something unbecoming to one's standing ③《문법의》 the case 《논리학의》 the figure. かく
격감(激減) a sharp decrease/ ～하다 decrease sharply; decline[fall off] remarkably. げきげん
격검(擊劍) ①《검술》 fencing/ ～하다 practise fencing ②⇒검도(劍道). げっけん
격구(擊毬) a kind of polo played by the military in former days. げききゅう
격나다(隔一) break up with; be alienated[estranged] from. なかがわるくなる
격납고(格納庫) a hangar; an aeroplane [aviation] shed. かくのうこ
격년(隔年) every other year/ ～하다 pass a year. かくねん
격노(激怒) wild rage; violent anger/ ～하다 rage; be enraged; fly into a violent anger; be exasperated. げきど
겪다 ①《경험》 experience; go through/ 가난을 ～ go through hardship ②《치르다》 receive; have a visitor/손님을 ～ receive guests. けいけんする
격단(激湍) rapids; a torrent. はげしくながれるはやせ
격돌(激突) a crash/ ～하다 crash into /열차의 ～ a train crash. げきとつ
격동(激動) 《진동》 violent shaking; a severe shock 《사회 등의》 excitement; agitation; convulsion/ ～하다 be stirred up; be excited; be agitated; be convulsed/정계를 ～시키다 stir up political circles. げきどう
격랑(激浪) raging[stormy] waves; heavy seas. げきろう
격려(激勵) encouragement; urging; incitement/ ～하다 encourage; urge; incite/ ～의 말 words of encouragement; stirring remarks. げきれい
격렬(激烈) violence; severity; vehemence/ ～하다 (be) violent; severe; vehement. げきれつ
격론(激論) a hot argument; a heated

격류(激流) a rapid stream; a swift current; a torrent／ ~에 휩쓸리다 be swept away by a torrent. げきりゅう

격리(隔離) isolation; insulation／ ~하다 isolate; insulate／ ~ 병실[병원] an isolation ward[hospital]. かくり

격막(隔膜)《인체의》the diaphragm《생물의》the septum／ ~염(炎) inflammation of the diaphragm. かくまく

격면(隔面) breaking relations／절교(絕交)

격멸(擊滅) destruction; annihilation／ ~하다 destroy; exterminate; annihilate. げきめつ

격무(激務) a busy office; a severe[toilsome] duty／ ~에 시달리다 be worn to a frazzle by a hard work. げきむ

격문(檄文) a manifesto; an appeal; a declaration／~을 내다 issue a manifesto; appeal (to). げきぶん

격물(格物) study of the principles of nature／ ~ 치지(致知) observation of nature. ものの理をけんきゅうすること

격발(擊發) percussion; outburst.げきはつ

격벽(隔壁) a partition 《동》a septum 《식》a dissepiment 《화》a diaphragm 《배의》a bulkhead／방수 ~ watertight bulkhead.

격변(激變) a violent change《사회의》an upheaval 《감정의》revulsion／~하다 undergo a sudden change; change violently／ 물가의 ~ a wild fluctuation in price. げきへん

격분(激忿) wild rage; violent anger／ ~하다 be enraged; fly into a fury. ひどくこうふんすること

격상(激賞) high praise; a high tribute ／ ~하다 praise highly; speak highly of; pay a high tribute (to).げきしょう

격서(檄書) a written appeal; a manifesto; an urgent declaration. げきしょ

격세(隔世) a distant age; another age; a different world／ ~ 유전 atavism; reversion／ ~의 감이 있다 It seems as if it belonged to another age.かくせい

격식(格式) an established form; social rules; a rule／~을 차리다 stick to formality. かくしき

격실(隔室) a compartment; a bay.

격심(激甚) severity; vehemence; intensity; keenness／ ~하다 (be) extreme; intense; severe; fierce; keen／~한 추위 severe cold／ ~한 경쟁 keen competition. ひどくはなはだしいこと

격앙(激昂) excitement; agitation; flaring up／~하다 get excited; be agitated; fire up. げっこう

격야(隔夜) a night's interval／ ~하다 have a night's interval.

격양가(擊壤歌) a farmer's song celebrating national peace and prosperity. げきじょうのうた

격어(激語) strong[violent] language; high words; bitter remarks／ ~를 발하다 use high words; launch out into strong language.

격언(格言) a proverb; a maxim; a [wise] saying. かくげん

격외(格外) exception; speciality／ ~의 extraordinary; special; exceptional.

격원(隔遠) ~하다 (be) a long way off. とおくはなれていること

격월(隔月) every other[second] month ／~하여 every other month. かくげつ

격의(隔意) reserve; estrangement; standoffishness／ ~없는 unreserved; frank; confidential／ ~없이 얘기하다 have a frank talk. かくい

격일(隔日) a day's interval ／ ~하여 every other day; an alternate days／ ~열(熱) tertian. かくじつ

격자(格子) ①《문의》 a lattice 《창문의》a latticework 《천장의》a coffer ②《갓끈의》beads attached to the strings of a Korean hat. こうし

격전(激戰) hot fighting; a severe fight; a fierce battle／ ~하다 fight hard; have a fierce battle. げきせん

격절(隔絕) isolation; separation; blockade／ ~하다 be separated; be isolated (from). かくぜつ

격정(激情) a violent[strong] emotion; passion; an outburst. げきじょう

격조(隔阻) ~하다 hear nothing (from); have no news (from).

격조(格調) ①《문》 rhythm; swing ②《사람의》personality; character／ ~높은 noble; refined. かくちょう

격주(隔週) a weekly interval／ ~의 fortnightly; biweekly／ ~하여 every other week; fortnightly. かくしゅう

격증(激增) a sudden increase／ ~하다 increase suddenly[markedly].げきぞう

격지 (켜) layers; plies. かさね

격지(隔地) a distant[remote] place [area].

격지(隔紙) a paper inserted between two layers. しおり

격진(激震) a severe earthquake; a severe[violent] shock. げきしん

격차(格差, 隔差) difference in quality. かくさ

격찬(激讚) high praise;a high tribute ／ ~하다 praise highly; speak highly of; pay a high tribute (to). げきさん

격철(擊鐵) a cock; the hammer (of a rifle); a gunlock.

격추(擊墜) shooting down《지상에서》bringing down／ ~하다 shoot[bring] down; down (a plane). げきつい

격침(擊沈) sinking; sending (a ship) to the bottom／ ~하다《attack and》sink (a ship); send (a ship) to the bottom. げきちん

격통(激痛) an acute[intense] pain; a severe[sharp] pain; a pang. げきつう

**격퇴(擊退)** a repulse; dislodgement 《거절》rejection／ ～하다 repulse; repel; drive back;beat off; dislodge. げきたい

**격투(激鬪)** a hot scuffle／ ～하다 scuffle furiously. げきとう

**격투(格鬪)** a grapple;a fight; a scuffle／ ～하다 grapple[scuffle; fight] (*with*). かくとう

**격파(擊破)** defeating; destruction; beating out／ ～하다 defeat; beat out; crush; smash up. げきは

**격하(格下)** degradation; downgrading; demotion⟨미⟩／～하다 lower (*a person*) in rank; demean (*one*self); downgrade.

**격하다(隔—)** 《가르다》part; separate 《사이에 두다》interpose 《막다》screen 《시간을》make intervals between／강을 격하여 across a river／벽 하나를 격하고 on the other side of the wall. へだてる

**격하다(激—)** (be) violent; infuriated.／ …을 격하고 with…between. はげしい

**격화(激化)** intensification; aggravation／ ～하다 intensify; aggravate／～ 일로에 있다 be increasingly intensified. げきか

**격화 소양(隔靴搔痒)** ¶ ～의 감이 있다 feel irritated; feel impatient; be irritating (사물에 주어). かっかそうよう

**견(絹)** silk 《전본》a sheet of silk [used for painting or writing]. きぬ

**견(遣)** dispatching; sending (*to*).

**견갑(肩胛)** the shoulder／ ～끝 the shoulder blade; the scapula. けんこう

**견강(堅剛)** firmness; solidity／ ～하다 (be) firm; steady; stiff; solid. けんごう

**견강(堅強)** sturdiness; solidity; stoutness／～하다 (be) strong; solid; sturdy; stout. けんきょう

**견강 부회(牽強附會)** a far-fetched interpretation; distortion／～하다 force[wrench] the meaning; draw a forced inference. けんきょうふかい

**견경(堅硬)** hardness; solidity／ ～하다 (be) hard; solid; strong; stout.

**견고(堅固)** solidity; stability; firmness／ ～하다 (be) strong; solid; stout; firm／ ～한 진지 a strong position; a stronghold. けんご

**견과(堅果)** 《식》a nut／～상(狀)의 glandiform. けんか

**견디다** ①《참다》bear; endure; put up with; stand／견딜 수 있는 bearable; endurable; tolerable／견딜 수 없다 be unable to bear; cannot stand; be unbearable／시련에 ～ bear a trial ②《일·사용에》last; be good for; be equal to.

**견딜성(—性)** endurance; perseverance; patience. たえる

**견련(牽連, 牽聯)** connection; linking; joining／ ～하다 (be) related; affiliated (*to*). けんれん

**견마(犬馬)** ①《개와 말》dogs and horses ②《자기》my humble self. けんば

**견마지로(犬馬之勞)** 《나라 위한》devoted service 《자기 수고》my bit; my little service. けんばのろう

**견목(樫木)** an overcup oak. かしのき

**견문(見聞)** 《지식》information; knowledge 《경험》experience 《관찰》observation／ ～하다 see and hear; observe; experience／ ～록(錄) a record of personal experiences／ ～을 넓히다 enrich one's stock of information; see more of life; add to one's experience. けんぶん

**견문 발검(見蚊拔劍)** drawing the sword at a mosquito; making a fuss about trifles.

**견물 생심(見物生心)** As we see things so we arises desire.

**견본(絹本)** silk cloth; silk canvas.

**견본(見本)** 《상품의》a sample 《표본》a specimen 《무늬·천의》a pattern 《서적·잡지의》a sample copy. みほん

**견사(絹絲)** silk [thread]／ ～ 방적 silk-reeling; silk-spining. うすぎぬ

**견사(繭絲)** raw silk. まゆといと

**견사(絹紗)** silk and gauze. うすぎぬ

**견성(堅城)** a strong fortress; an impregnable castle. けんごなじょう

**견수(堅守)** strong defense／ ～하다 defend stoutly. かたくまもること

**견습(見習)** apprenticeship; probation／ ～하다 learn; practise／ ～생 an apprentice-student; probationer; a trainee／～ 기간 the period of apprenticeship; the probationary period. けんしゅう

**견식(見識)** 《의견》a view; an opinion 《지식》knowledge; information／～이 풍부한 사람 a man of insight; a discerning man. けんしき

**견실(堅實)** steadiness; solidity; soundness／ ～하다 (be) steady; steadfast; sound; solid; reliable／ ～하게 steadily; reliably; soundly／ ～한 사람 a steady[reliable] person. けんじつ

**견우성(牽牛星)** 《천》Altair. けんぎゅうせい

**견우화(牽牛花)** a morning-glory.

**견원(犬猿)** a dog and a monkey／ ～지간이다 lead a cat-and-dog life; be on bad terms with. いぬとさる

**견유(犬儒)** a Cynic／～학파 the Cynics.

**견인(堅忍)** [dogged, indomitable] perseverance; fortitude; stoicism／～하다 persevere; bear patiently; endure undauntedly／ ～지구(持久) dogged perseverance; untiring patience. けんにん

**견인(牽引)** pulling; hauling; traction／ ～하다 pull; draw; drag; haul／ ～력 pulling[traction] capacity／ ～차 a tractor. けんいん

**견인 불발(堅忍不拔)** perseverance; fortitude; untiring patience／ ～하다 persevere; have untiring patience／ ～한 정신 an iron will; an indomitable spirit. けんにんふばつ

**견장(肩章)** a shoulder strap 《정장(正裝)》

**견적(見積)** an estimate／～하다 estimate; put (*at*)／～서 an estimate. みつもり

**견제(牽制)** check; restraint; curb; constraint／～하다 check; hold in check; restrain／～구(球)《제》 a feint ball／서로 ～하다 hold each other in check. けんせい

**견주다** compare (*with*); measure／길이를 견주어 보다 compare length／견주어 보면 by comparison. なぞらえる

**견지(堅持)** ～하다 hold fast to; stick to; adhere to. けんじする

**견지(見地)** a standpoint; a viewpoint; a point of view; an angle. けんち

**견직물(絹織物)** silk fabrics; silk goods; silks／～ 공장 a silk mill／～ 장수 a silk mercer. きぬおりもの

**견진(堅振)** 《종》 confirmation／～ 성사(聖事) the order of confirmation.

**견칫살** the white meat from under the wings of chicken.

**견책(譴責)** censure; reprimand; reproof／～하다 censure; reprimand／～을 받다 be reprimanded. けんせき

**견척(見斥)** ～하다 be rejected; be excluded.

**견취도(見取圖)** a [rough] sketch／～를 그리다 sketch; make a sketch of (*a scene*)

**견치(犬歯)** a canine; an eyetooth. けんし

**견포(絹布)** silk; silk stuff[cloth fabrics]／～이불 silk beddings／～ 옷을 입고 있다 be dressed in silks. きぬ

**견학(見學)** [study by] inspection; observation／～하다 acquire information [knowledge]; study and observe 《체조 시간 등에》 look on／～ 여행 a tour of study. けんがく

**견해(見解)** an opinion; a view／～의 차이 divergence of opinion／그릇된 ～를 가지다 take a wrong view of (*a matter*)／～를 달리하다 differ in opinion; hold a different view. けんかい

**겯고틀다** struggle with (*one*); dispute.

**겯다¹** ①(기름에) be infiltrated with oil; infiltrate (*something*) with oil ②(일에) get used to; become skilled ③(배게 하다) oils. しみこむ

**겯다²** ①(짜다) weave; interlace ②(걸쳐 세우다) cross; link; join crosswise; stack／총을 ～ stack arms. あむ

**겯지르다** place (*a thing*) crosswise; cross.

**결¹** (나무의) grain 《천의》 texture／～이 고운 close-grained／～이 거친 coarse-grained. はだめ

**결²** ①(언뜻·우연히) incidental (*to*); happening (*to*) in passing ②(…하는 길)(*in*) the course of;`when; while／지나가는 ～에 잠깐 들르다 drop in for a moment on *one's* way (*for*).

**결가 부좌(結跏趺坐)** 《종》 sitting with legs crossed. あぐらをかくこと

**결강(缺講)** ～하다 cut a lecture; absent *oneself* from school.

**결곡하다** (be) firm; spruce; solid; resolute. しょうじきでけっぱくた

**결과(結果)** result; consequence 《원인에 대하여》 effect 《성과》 fruit; outcome 《결말》 issue; end／원인과 ～ cause and effect／～론(論) consequentism／…의 ～ as a result of／…한 ～가 되다 result [end] in／～가 좋다[나쁘다] be successful[unsuccessful]. けっか

**결교(結交)** ～하다 form a friendship with; associate with.

**결구(結構)** 《구조》 structure; construction 《구상》 a plan; a scheme. けっこう

**결국(結局)** in the end; in the long run; finally; eventually; after all ～에 가서는 ultimately. けっきょく

**결궤(決潰)** a rip; a break; cleavage; crevasse 《미》 ～하다 collapse; break (*down*); give way. けっかい

**결귀(結句)** the conclusion; the concluding part. けっく

**결근(缺勤)** absence (*from*)／～하다 be absent[absent *oneself*] (*from*)／～자 an absentee／～계 a report of *one's* absence. けっきん

**결기(一氣)** impetuosity; impetus; strain; vehemence; hot temper. たんき

**결나다** lose *one's* temper; fall into a passion. はらがたつ

**결내다** become indignant; get mad; blow up; flash up. たんきをおこす

**결딴** failure; rupture; ruin／～나다 be spoilt; be ruined／～내다 spoil; mar; ruin; destroy. がかい

**결단(決斷)** decision; determination; resolution／～하다 decide; determine; resolve／～력이 강한 사람 a man of decision／～코 never; by no means; on no account／～성이 있다[없다] be resolute[irresolute]. けつだん

**결당(結黨)** formation of a party／～하다 form a party／～식 the inaugural ceremony of a party. けっとう

**결련(結連)** connection; linking／～하다 be connected; be linked; be joined; be coupled; connect; link; join; couple. むすびつらねること

**결렬(決裂)** rupture; breakdown; failure／～하다 [come to a] rupture; breakdown／협상의 ～ rupture of negotiations／～시키다 break off; rupture. けつれつ

**결례(缺禮)** failure to pay *one's* compliments; want of respect. けつれい

**결론(結論)** a conclusion; a concluding remark／～하다 conclude; close／～으로서 in conclusion; to conclude [by saying that…]／～에 도달하다 reach [come to] a conclusion. けつろん

**결리다** hurt; pain／숨을 쉬면 가슴이 결린다 It pains me to breathe; be daunted. ずきずきいたむ

**결막(結膜)** 《해》 the conjunctiva／～염 conjunctivitis. けつまく

**결말(結末)** 《끝》 an end; conclusion 《낙

착) settlement 《결과》 a result／ ～나다 be settled; come to a conclusion; [be brought to an] end／내다 settle; dispose of／ ～짓다 finish; settle; put an end to.　けつまつ

**결맹**(結盟) ～하다 form a league[a federation].　けつめい

**결박**(結縛) binding; tying／～하다[짓다] bind; tie; pinion／범인을 ～하다 tie a criminal with cords; pinion a criminal.　てをしばること

**결백**(潔白) 《순결》 purity 《무죄》 innocence 《청렴》 integrity／～하다 (be) pure; upright; innocent／～한 사람 a man of integrity.　けっぱく

**결번**(缺番) a missing number／4번은 ～이다 The number four is blank on the roll.

**결벽**(潔癖) excessive love of cleanliness ／～하다 (be) fastidious; dainty; overnice; particular.　けつぺき

**결별**(訣別) 《작별》 parting; separation 《고별》 leave-taking; farewell／～하다 part from; separate from; take leave of; say good-bye (to); bid farewell (to).　けつべつ

**결본**(缺本) a missing volume.　けつぽん

**결부**(結付) connection; tying; linking／～하다 connect; link／양자를 밀접히 ～시키다 link the two into closer relations with each other.　むすびつけること

**결빙**(結氷) freezing／～하다 freeze over; be frozen over; be ice-bound／～기(期) the freezing time.　けつぴよう

**결사**(結社) an association; a society／비밀 ～ a secret society／～의 자유 the freedom of association.　けつしや

**결사**(決死) preparedness for death; "do-or-die" spirit／～적 desperate; death-defying／～대 a forlorn hope; a death band／～ 투쟁하다 struggle desperately.　けつし

**결삭다** soften; become soft; be mollified.

**결산**(決算) settlement of accounts; liquidation／～하다 settle[balance] an account／～기 settlement terms／～일 a settling day／～ 보고 [시류] balance sheets 《일람표》 a statement of accounts.　けつさん

**결석**(結石) 《의》 a calculus (pl -li); a stone／～병 lithia sis.

**결석**(缺席) absence; 《법》 default／～하다 be absent (from); fail to attend．병고 ～ absence on accounts of illness／～자 an absentee．～계 a report of absence／～ 재판 judgement by default.　けつせき

**결선**(決選) a final vote[election]／～투표 a final vote[ballot].　けつせん

**결성**(結成) formation; organization; inauguration／～하다 organize; form; inaugurate／～식 inaugural ceremony.　けつせい

**결속**(結束) union; combination; unity; solidarity／ ～하다 unite; band together; be united／ 당의 ～을 강화하다 strengthen the party unity.　けつそく

**결손**(缺損) 《부족》 shortage; deficit 《손실》 loss／…의 ～을 가져오다 suffer a loss of….　けつそん

**결승**(決勝) the decision／ ～전 a final match, game, 《등점시의》 a play off ／ ～선 the goal line; the finishing line／～전 the semi-finals.けつしよう

**결승 문자**(結繩文字) a quipu; a preliterate notation by rope knots.けつじようもじ

**결식**(缺食) going without a meal／～하다 go without a meal／～ 아동 a pupil without a meal; pupils [going to school] without lunch.　けつしよく

**결실**(結實) fruit-bearing; fructification ／～하다 bear fruit 《비유적으로》 be successful; achieve a success／～기 the fruiting season.　けつじつ

**결심**(決心) determination; resolution／～하다 determine; resolve; make up one's mind／ 확고한 ～ a firm resolution／…할 ～이다 be determined to do….　けつしん

**결심**(結審) the conclusion of an examination[a hearing]／ ～하다 conclude an examination[a trial].　けつしん

**결여**(缺如) lack; want; deficiency／ ～하다 lack; want; be lacking[wanting] (in); be destitute of／신뢰의 ～ want of confidence.　けつじよ

**결연**(結緣) ①《관계를》 forming a connection／ ～하다 form a connection (with) ②《불교외》 becoming a believer in Buddhism／ ～하다 be converted to Buddhism.　けつえん

**결연하다**(決然一) (be) resolute; firm; decisive.　ものたりない

**결원**(缺員) a vacancy; a vacant position; an opening／ ～을 보충하다 fill [up] a vacancy.　けついん

**결의**(決議) a decision; a resolution; a vote／～하다 decide; resolve; vote／ ～ 사항 resolutions／～안[문] a resolution／ ～ 기관 a voting organ.　けつぎ

**결의**(結義) ～하다 swear to be (brothers, sisters, etc.); take an oath of brotherhood／ ～ 형제 sworn brothers.

**결의**(決意) resolution; determination／ ～하다 determine; resolve; make up one's mind.　けつい

**결자**(缺字) an omitted word; a blank type.　けつじ

**결자해지**(結者解之) He who has sown the seed should gather the fruit.

**결장**(結腸) 《해》 the colon／ ～염(炎) colonitis.　けつちよう

**결재**(決裁) sanction; approval／ ～하다 decide (upon); approve; sanction; authorize／～를 맡다 get one's sanction.　けつさい

**결전**(決戰) a decisive battle／ ～하다 fight it out; fight a decisive battle

**결절**(結節) a knot 〖해〗 a tuber; a tubercle 〖식・의〗 a node; a nodule／ ~있는[모양의] knotted; tuberous; nodose. けっせつ

**결점**(缺點) 〖비난할 점〗 a fault; a defect; a flaw; a shortcoming 〖약점〗 a weak point; a weakness／ ~을 찾다 find fault with; pick out *another's* defects. けってん

**결정**(結晶) 〖작용〗 crystallization 〖결정체〗 a crystal／ ~하다 crystallize／ ~한 crystallized／노력의 ~ the fruit of *one's* efforts. けっしょう

**결정**(決定) decision; conclusion; settlement／~하다 decide (*upon*); conclude; agree upon／ ~돈 〖철〗 determinism／ ~권 the right of decision; decisive power／ ~ 투표 the casting-vote／ ~판 a definitive edition／~적[으로] decisive[ly]; conclusive[ly]／날짜를 ~하다 fix the date (*for*). けってい

**결제**(決濟) settlement／ ~하다 settle [square] accounts／대차(貸借) ~ the settlement of accounts／미~의 계정 an outstanding account. けっさい

**결증**(一症) [a fit of] anger.

**결집**(結集) ①〖모음〗 concentration; regimentation／ ~하다 concentrate; collect in mass ②〖종〗 *Samgiti* (Sans).
けっしゅう

**결착**(結著, 決著) end; conclusion; settlement; decision／ ~하다 end; be settled; be decided. けっちゃく

**결책**(決策) settlement of strategy／ ~하다 take a decision of strategy; form a plan[a stratagem].

**결처**(決處) disposition; settlement／~하다 settle; resolve; dispose of (*a matter*).

**결체**(結滯) 〖의〗 acrotism; pause[intermission] in the pulse.

**결체**(結締) tying up／~하다 tie up／ ~조직 〖해〗 connective tissue.
くくってむすぶこと

**결초 보은**(結草報恩) ~하다 requite *another's* kindness even after *one's* death; carry *one's* gratitude beyond the grave.

**결코**(決一) never; by no means; not in the least; on no accounts; under no circumstances. けっして

**결탁**(結託) collusion; conspiracy／ ~하다 conspire with; act in collusion with／…과 ~하여 in conspiracy with; in collusion with. けったく

**결투**(決鬪) a duel; an affair of hono[u]r／ ~하다 fight a duel (*with*); duel／~자 a duelist. けっとう

**결판**(決判)／~내다 settle (a quarrel); bring (*a matter*) to an end.

**결판나다**(決判—) be settled; be brought to an end. ぜひがけっていされる

**결핍**(缺乏) 〖결여〗 want; lack; absence 〖부족〗 shortage; scarcity／~하다 lack; want; be wanting[lacking] (*in*); be [run] short of／종이의 ~ a shortage of paper／ ~증〖비타민 등의〗 a deficiency disease／우리에게는 자금이 ~하다 We are short of money. けつぼう

**결하다**(決—) decide／승부를 ~ 〖경기의〗 decide a contest.

**결하다**(缺—) (be) lacking; deficient; wanting; missing. ふそく

**결함**(缺陷) a defect; a fault／성격의 ~ a defect in *one's* character／~있는 defective; faulty. けっかん

**결합**(結合) union; combination／~하다 unite; combine (*with*); join together.
けつごう

**결항**(缺航) suspension of steamship service. けっこう

**결핵**(結核) 〖의〗 a tubercle 〖병〗 consumption; tuberculosis／ ~성의 tubercular; tuberculous／ ~균 tuberculous bacilli／~ 환자 a tuberculosis patient ／폐~ 〖의〗 pulmonary tuberculosis; phthisis. けっかく

**결행**(決行) decisive action; a resolute step／ ~하다 carry out [resolutely].
けっこう

**결혼**(結婚) marriage; matrimony; wedding／~하다 marry; be married (*to*); wed／ ~적령기 marriageable age; the age for marriage／~ 기념일 a wedding anniversary／사기 ~ a false marriage ／ ~생활 a married life／~식 a marriage ceremony; a wedding; nuptials ／~ 피로연 a wedding reception／연애 ~ a lovematch; a love marriage.
けっこん

**결후**(結喉) 〖해〗 Adam's apple.

**겸**(兼) in addition; and; concurrently; at the same time／수상 ~ 외상 the Premier and Minister of Foreign Affairs／서재 ~ 응접실 a room used as study and parlour／사업도 할 ~ 관광도 할 ~ with a double purpose of business and sightseeing. かねること

**겸공**(謙恭) modesty; humbleness／ ~하다 (be) modest; humble. けんそん

**겸관**(兼官) holding an office concurrently with *one's* main post 〖벼슬〗 an additional office.

**겸근**(謙謹) moderation; discretion; modesty／ ~하다 (be) moderate; discreet; modest.

**겸덕**(謙德) the virtue of modesty.

**겸두겸두**(兼頭兼頭) partly; at the same time; combined with／볼일 유흥 ~ partly on business and partly for pleasure; on business combined with pleasure.
あれこれかねて

**겸무**(兼務) an additional office; another post; a concurrent office／~하다 hold (*a post*) as an additional office; hold (an office) in addition. けんむ

**겸비**(兼備) ~하다 combine (*one thing* with

*another*)／재색(才色)을 ~한 부인 a woman combining wit with beauty. けんび
**겸비**(謙卑) self-abasement; self-depreciation; humility／~하다 depreciate (*oneself*); humble (*oneself*).
**겸사**(謙辭) modesty; humility ⇨겸손. けんじ
**겸사겸사** partly and partly ⇨겸두겸두.
**겸상**(兼床) a table laid for two 「persons」／~하다 dine in a pair; eat[sit down to table] with another.
**겸손**(謙遜) modesty; humility; self-effacement／~하다 (be) modest; humble; unassuming／~하게 with modesty; in a modest way. けんそん
**겸애**(兼愛) universal love／~하다 love all equally. けんあい
**겸양**(謙讓) modesty; humility; diffidence／~하다 be humble; be modest; compliant; self-effacing／~지덕 the virtue of modesty. けんじょう
**겸업**(兼業) a side job; a subsidiary business／~하다 take up a side job; pursue (*some trade*) as a side job. けんぎょう
**겸연쩍다**(慊然) feel ashamed; be abashed; feel small; feel awkward.
もうしわけなくてひじょうにはずかしい
**겸용**(兼用) a combined use／~하다 use (*a thing*) as both… and…; make (*a thing*) serve a double purpose; employ for more than one purpose. けんよう
**겸유**(兼有) ~하다 possess [both] (*A* and *B*). けんゆう
**겸임**(兼任) 「holding」 plural offices／~하다 hold (*an office*) in addition／두 학교를 ~하다 teach in both schools. けんにん
**겸전**(兼全) ~하다 (be) perfect in all; proficient both in (*A* and *B*).
すべてをかねそなえていること
**겸직**(兼職) a concurrent office[position]／~하다 hold (*a position*) concurrently with the principal; hold an additional position. けんしょく
**겸치다**(兼一) combine (*A* and *B*); hold in addition. かねている
**겸퇴**(謙退) a modest declination (of *an offer*); a modest retreat (of *a servant*, of *a subject*)／~하다 decline (*an offer*) with modesty.
**겸하다**(兼一) 《구비하다》combine; possess both; serve both as 《겸직하다》 hold (*a post*) as an additional office／국무총리가 외무장관을 겸하고 있다 The Premier holds the portfolio for Foreign Affairs in addition to the premiership.
かねる
**겸행**(兼行) ❶주야 ~으로 일하다 work day and night. けんこう
**겸허**(謙虛) modesty; humbleness; humility／~하다 (be) humble; *oneself* modest／~하게 in a humble way; with modesty. けんきょ

**겹** a pile; a layer; a ply／세 ~ three-fold／여러 ~ many folds. かさねり
**겹것** 《물건》 things with plural layers of plies 《겹옷》 lined clothes.
にじゅうにかさなっているもの
**겹겹이** ply on ply; in so many folds; one over another／~ 쌓여 있다 be piled thick one over another／~ 둘러싸다 surround (*the enemy*) thick and threefold. かさなりあって
**겹눈** 【충】 compound eyes; an ommateum (*pl.* -tea)／~의 ommateal.
**겹다** (be) beyond *one's* control[*power, ability, etc.*]; too much for／힘에 기운 일 work beyond *one's* power／눈물겨운 노력 pathetically sincere efforts／설움에 겨워 in a passion of grief.
**겹두루마기** a lined overcoat.
**겹말** a pleonasm; a redundant words.
じゅうふくご
**겹문자**(一文字) a pleonasm; a redundant passage. じゅうふくもんじ
**겹사돈**(一查頓) a relative double-conncted by marriage.
**겹살림** maintaining more than one household.
**겹씨** a compound word ⇨복합어.
**겹옷** a lined garment; clothes with a lining. あわせのきもの
**겹저고리** a lined jacket.
**겹질리다** sprain; be sprained; [a joint] be wrenched. ねんざする
**겹집** a house consisting of several rows of partitioning walls.
**겹창**(一窓) a double window; a storm window. にじゅうまど
**겹치다** pile up; heap up; put *one* upon *another*; lay on top of another[the other]／불행에 불행이 ~ have a series of misfortune. かさねる
**겻불** chaff-fire. ぬかをもやすひ
**겻섬** a chaff sack.
**경** punishment imposed on thieves ⇨경치다. どろぼうをちょうかいするけいばつ
**경**(更) a watch of the night／초~ the first watch of the night／삼~ midnight.
**경**(京) 《숫자》a ten-million billion 《서울》 the capital. おくのおくのばい
**경**(經) ❶《불경》 the sutras; the Buddhist scriptures／~을 읽다 chant a sutra ❷《경도》 longitude. きょうもん
**경**(徑) 《직경》 a diameter／반~ a radius. けい
**경**(景) ❶《경치》 a view／관동 팔~ the eight famous beauty spots in Eastern Korea／삼~ the scenic trio ❷《경황》 《景況》. ふうけい
**경**(卿) lord; Sir 《대신》 a minister; a secretary.
**-경**(頃) about; toward[s]; around《미》／세 시~ about three o'clock／월말~에 around the end of this month. ころ
**경가극**(輕歌劇) a light opera; an opere-

**경가 파산**(傾家破産) bankruptcy 《탕진》 squandering of one's fortune/ ~하다 squander one's fortune; run bankrupt. かんぜんにはさんすること

**경각**(頃刻) a moment; an instant/ ~지간에 in a moment[an instant]; in the twinkling of an eye. しばし

**경각**(警覺) warning; awakening; remonstration/ ~하다 awaken; warn; shake up.

**경각**(傾角) 《물》 inclination. けいかく

**경간**(耕墾) clearing; bringing (waste land) under cultivation/ ~하다 bring under cultivation; clear (the land). かいこんすること

**경감**(輕減) reduction; mitigation 《교통 따위의》 alleviation 《죄의》 commutation / ~하다 reduce; lighten; mitigate; alleviate. けいげん

**경감**(警監) a police inspector. けいかん

**경개**(梗概) an outline; a summary; a synopsis. こうがい

**경거**(輕擧) a rash[hasty] action; rashness/ ~「망동」하다 behave rashly/ ~ 망동을 삼가다 behave[proceed] prudently. けいそつなこうどう

**경건**(勁健) robust health/ ~하다 (be) robust; stout.

**경건**(敬虔) piety; devotion; reverence/ ~하다 (be) pious; devout. けいけん

**경겁**(驚怯) awe; alarm; fright; scare/ ~하다 be scared; be frightened; be struck with awe.

**경결**(硬結) solidification; coagulation/ ~하다 solidify; coagulate; congeal. かたくむすぶこと

**경경**(輕輕) ~하다 《경박》(be) light; imprudent; indiscreet; hasty; rash/ ~하게 lightly; hastily; rashly; indiscreetly. けいけい

**경경**(耿耿) ~하다 《불빛이》 flicker; glimmer; blink 《마음이》 feel ill at ease; disturbed. こうこう

**경계**(境界) a boundary; a border 《국경》 a frontier/ ~선 a boundary line/~표 a landmark; a boundary stone; a demarcation post. きょうかい

**경계**(警戒) precaution; caution; watch; guard/ ~하다 watch[look out] for; be on one's guard; take precautions [guard] (against)/ ~망 a police cordon/ ~ 경보 an air-defence preliminary alarm/ ~망을 펴다[뚫다] throw [slip through] a police cordon. けいかい

**경계**(驚悸) 《놀람》 nerves 《가슴이 뜀》 heart acceleration.

**경계색**(警戒色) 《동》 sematic[warning] colouration. けいかいしょく

**경고**(警告) warning; caution; admonition/ ~하다 warn; caution (one of); give warning[notice] to; advise (one) to do. けいこく

**경골**(硬骨) ①《굳은 뼈》 hard-bone/ ~어(魚) a teleost ②《기골참》 inflexibility; a firm character/ ~한(漢) a man of firm character. こうこつ

**경골**(頸骨) 《해》 the neck bone. けいこつ

**경골**(脛骨) 《해》 the shin-bone; the tibia / ~ 동맥 the tibial artery. けいこつ

**경공업**(輕工業) the light industry. けいこうぎょう

**경과**(經過) ①《일의》 progress; development; course/사건의 ~ the development of an affair/수술 후의 ~ the post operation course/~가 양호하다 progress favourably[satisfactorily]; go on well ②《시간의》 lapse; flight 《기한의》 expiration/~하다 lapse; pass; go by. けいか

**경관**(景觀) a scene; a spectacle; a view. けいかん

**경관**(警官) a policeman; a constable 《영》; a cop 《속》; 《총칭》the police/여자~ a policewoman; a woman costable. けいかん

**경교**(景敎) Nestorianism/~의 Nestorian.

**경구**(硬球) 《체》 a hard(regulation) ball. こうきゅう

**경구**(敬具) Sincerely yours; Yours respectfully; Yours truly. けいぐ

**경구**(警句) an aphorism; an epigram. けいく

**경구개**(硬口蓋) 《해》 the hard palate. こうこうがい

**경국**(經國) administration; statemanship/~지책 a state policy/~지재(之才) administrative ability; statecraft; statesmanship. けいこく

**경국**(傾國) decline of a nation/ ~지색 a woman whose eyes are the dooms of a king; a woman of matchless beauty. けいこく

**경근**(敬謹) ~하다 pay modest respect to (one). つつみうやまうこと

**경금속**(輕金屬) light metals. けいきんぞく

**경기**(景氣) business[conditions]; transactions; [the tone of] the market; the times 《호경기》 prosperity /벼락 ~ a boom; a flush/ ~ 변동 industrial fluctuation/ ~ 순환 a business cycle/ ~ 정책 a countercycle policy/~가 좋다[나쁘다] The times are good[bad]. けいき

**경기**(競技) a game; a match; a contest; a competition/ ~ 운동 ~ athletic contests/학교 대항 ~ an interschool match/ ~ 대회 a competition; an athletic meet/~장 a ground; an area; a stadium. きょうぎ

**경기관총**(輕機關銃) a light machine gun. けいきかんじゅう

**경기구**(輕氣球) a hot-air balloon; a dirigible balloon. けいききゅう

**경기병**(輕騎兵) 《부대》 light cavalry 《병사》 a light cavalryman[horseman]. けいきへい

**경내**(境內) the precincts; the inclosures; the premises; the compound. けいだい

**경년**(經年) the elapse of a year / ~하다 pass a year. としをへること
**경노동**(輕勞動) light labo[u]r[work] / ~자 a light worker. けいろうどう
**경농**(經農) ~하다 follow the plow; run a farm. のうぎょうをけいえいすること
**경뇌막**(硬腦膜) 〖해〗 *dura mater* / ~염 pachymeningitis. こうのうまく
**경단**(瓊團) a dumpling; a doughboy.
**경대**(鏡臺) a toilet[mirror] stand; a dresser〈미〉. きょうだい
**경도**(傾度) gradient; inclination. けいど
**경도**(傾倒) ①~하다(쏟다) tip; tilt ②~하다(넘어지다) fall down; turn over; topple ③~하다 《경주하다》devote *one*self to; concentrate on; be wholly devoted to. かたむけてそそぐ
**경도**(經度) ①《지구상의》 longitude / ~를 재다 calculate the longitude ②《월경》 the menses; menstruation. けいど
**경도**(硬度) hardness; solidity / ~계(計) the scale of hardness. こうど
**경도**(驚到) astonishment / ~하다 be astonished; be amazed; be dumfound. おどろいてたおれること
**경동**(驚動) arousal; awakening / ~하다 awaken; stir up; stagger in surprise. ひじょうにおどろいてうごくこと
**경동**(輕動) a rash action; rashness / ~하다 behave rashly. けいそつなこうどう
**경동맥**(頸動脈) 《해》the carotid artery けいどうみゃく
**경락**(經絡) a blood vessel; a vein(정맥) an artery(동맥).
**경량**(輕量) light weight / ~급 권투 선수 a light-weight boxer. けいりょう
**경력**(經歷) a career; a record; personal history / ~의 소개 a biographical introduction. けいれき
**경련**(痙攣) 〖의〗 convulsions; a spasm; a jerk; a fit / ~성의 spasmodic; convulsive / ~이 일어나다 have a convulsive fit; fall[go off] into convulsions. けいれん
**경례**(敬禮) a bow; a salute; a greeting; an obeisance; salutation / ~하다 salute; bow; make a 「respectful」 salutation. けいれい
**경로**(經路) ①《길 순서》a route; a course ②《과정·단계》a channel; a course; a stage; a process / 발달의 ~ the processes of growth. けいろ
**경로**(敬老) respect for the aged. けいろう
**경루**(經漏) 《의》menorrhagia.
**경륜**(經綸) government; administration; statecraft. けいりん
**경륜**(競輪) cycling race; a bike race〈미〉 / ~ 선수 a cycle racer. けいりん
**경리**(經理) 〖회계〗 accounting 《처리》management / ~에 밝다 be expert in accounting. けいり
**경리**(警吏) a man in police service けいり
**경마** a leading rein; a halter / ~잡다 lead a horse.
**경마**(競馬) horse-racing; a horse-race / ~하다 ride a race; race horses / ~말 a race horse / ~장 a race course; the turf / ~광(狂) a turf fan; a racing man. けいば
**경망**(輕妄) imprudence; indiscretion; rashness; lightness / ~스럽다[하다] (be) thoughtless; rash; imprudent / ~한 짓 a rash act.
**경매**(競賣) auction; public sale / ~하다 sell by[at] auction; put to auction; auction off / ~인 an auctioneer / ~장 an auction-room. きょうばい
**경면**(鏡面) the surface of a mirror. きょうめん
**경면지**(鏡面紙) glossy paper; slick paper.
**경멸**(輕蔑) contempt; disdain; scorn / ~하다 despise; scorn; look down upon; hold in contempt / ~할 만한 contemptible; despicable. けいべつ
**경모**(輕侮) contempt / ~하다 despise; scorn; set at naught. けいぶ
**경모**(敬慕) admiration / ~하다 admire; adore; love and respect. けいぼ
**경모**(景慕) worship; admiration / ~하다 look up to; honour; worship; admire. けいぼ
**경묘**(輕妙) ~하다 (be) light; ready; witty; clever.
**경무**(警務) police affairs 《경찰 행정》police administration. けいむ
**경문**(經文) ①《불교 경전》 the Buddhist scriptures; sutras; sacred books ②《도교 서적》 the Taoist scriptures.
**경문학**(輕文學) light literature[reading]. けいぶんがく
**경문학**(硬文學) solid reading; metaphysical literature. こうぶんがく
**경미**(輕微) ~하다 (be) slight; trifling; insignificant. けいび
**경미**(粳米) nonglutinous rice. こうまい
**경박**(輕薄) 《불성실》insincerity; untruthfulness 《부박》frivolity 《변덕》fickleness; in constancy / ~하다 《불성실》(be) insincere; flippant; untruthful 《부박》(be) frivolous; light 《변덕》(be) fickle. けいはく
**경방**(庚方) 〖민〗 west-by-southwest. かのえのほうこう
**경배**(敬拜) bowing respectfully 《절》a respectful bow / ~하다 worship; pay homage (to).
**경백**(敬白) Yours respectfully. けいはく
**경범죄**(輕犯罪) a minor offence / ~법 the Minor Offence Law. けいはんざい
**경보**(警報) an alarm; a warning; a signal / ~기 an alarm signal / ~를 내리다 warn; give[raise] an alarm. けいほう
**경보**(競步) 《경기》 a walking race; a 40 km walk. きょうほう
**경복**(敬服) admiration; respect / ~하다 admire; respect. けいふく

**경복**(敬復, 敬覆) Dear Sir; In reply to your esteemed letter. けいふく

**경봉**(警棒) a truncheon; a cudgel; a club.

**경부**(頸部) 〖해〗 the neck area; the cervical region. けいぶ

**경비**(經費) 《비용》 expenses; cost 《지출》 expenditure; outlay／ ~ 관계로 for financial reasons; owing to the expenses involved／~를 절약하다 cut down the expenses; curtail[retrench] expenditures. けいひ

**경비**(警備) defence; guard／ ~하다 defend; guard／~병[원] a guard／ ~대 a garrison／ ~함 a guard ship. けいび

**경사**(傾斜) inclination; a slant; a slope 《배의》 a list／ ~지다 incline; slant; slope／ ~면 an inclined plane; a slope／ ~도 a gradient／~계(計) a clinometer. けいしゃ

**경사**(經絲) warp.

**경사**(經史) books on Chinese classics and history. けいし

**경사**(京師) the metropolis.

**경사** a happy event; a matter for congratulation; an auspicious occasion. けいしゅくすべきこと

**경사**(警査) a police sergeant.
じゅんさぶちょう

**경상**(經常) ~의 current; ordinary; working／ ~비(費) current[fixed] expenditure／ ~예산 the working[ordinary] budget. けいじょう

**경상**(輕傷) a slight injury[wound]／ ~자 the slightly injured[wounded] person. けいしょう

**경색**(梗塞) stoppage; blocking 《핍박》 tightness; choking; 〖의〗 infarction／금융 ~ tightness of money; tight money market. こうそく

**경서**(經書) Chinese classics. けいしょ

**경석**(輕石) 〖광〗 a pumice-stone. かるいし

**경석고**(硬石膏) 〖광〗 anhydrite.

**경선**(經線) 〖천〗《자오선》 the meridian; circles of longitude 《경도》 longitude. けいせん

**경선**(頸腺) 〖해〗 cervical gland.

**경설**(經說) the theories and principles expressed in the Chinese classics.

**경성**(硬性) hardness; solidity. こうせい

**경성**(警醒) awakening／ ~하다 awake; arouse; warn; bring (one) to his senses. けいせい

**경세**(經世) administration; statsmanship／ ~가 a statesman; an administrator／~지재(之才) a talent for administration [for government]; executive ability. けいせい

**경세**(警世) a warning to the times／ ~하다 warn to the times; awaken the public. けいせい

**경소**(輕少) ~하다 (be) little; slight; trifling.

**경솔**(輕率) rashness; recklessness; hastiness; thoughtlessness; precipitancy; heedlessness／~하다 (be) rash; hasty; careless; thoughtless; imprudent／ ~히 rashly; hastily; thoughtlessly／ ~한 짓(을 하다) commit a rash act.
けいそつ

**경쇠**(磬─) ①〖옛 악기〗 a kind of Korean musical instruments ②〖작은 종〗 a handbell used by fortunetellers or Buddists.

**경수**(硬水) hard water. こうすい

**경수**(鯨鬚) a baleen; whalebone; whale fin.

**경승**(景勝) picturesque scenery／ ~지 a place of scenic beauty; a picturesque place; a beauty spot. けいしょう

**경시**(輕視) contempt; negligence／ ~하다 slight; neglect; make light of; think little of. けいし

**경시**(庚時) 〖민〗 the 18th of the 24 hour periods(＝4：30〜5：30 p. m.).
かのえのとき

**경식**(輕食) a light meal; a lunch; a snack. けいしょく

**경식**(硬式) rigid; hard／~ 탁구 hard-ball tennis. こうしき

**경식당**(輕食堂) a lunchroom; a cafeteria; a snack bar〈미〉. けいしょくどう

**경신**(更新) renewal; renovation／ ~하다 rénew; renovate. こうしん

**경신**(輕信) credulity; ready belief／ ~하다 believe readily; be credulous [easily convinced, gullible].

**경신**(敬神) devoutness; piety; godiness／ ~하다 worship[revere] God. けいしん

**경아**(驚訝) astonishment; surprise; consternation／ ~하다 be astonished; be thrown into consternation.
おどろきうたがうこと

**경악**(驚愕) shock; astonishment／ ~하다 be astonished[shocked] (at); have a surprise; look up to. きょうがく

**경앙**(敬仰) adoration; reverence; admiration／ ~하다 adore; admire; revere ; look up to. けいこう

**경애**(境涯) life; circumstances.

**경애**(敬愛) respect and affection／ ~하다 venerate; love and respect. けいあい

**경야**(經夜) ①《지냄》 passing a night／ ~하다 pass a night ②《새움》 a wake; vigil; lichwake／ ~하다 keep wake; hold a wake; keep vigil.

**경어**(敬語) a term of respect; an honorific [expression, word]. けいご

**경역**(境域) the grounds 《경계》 the boundary; the border. きょういき

**경연**(硬軟) hardness and softness; [the relative] hardness.
かたいものとやわらかいこと

**경연**(慶宴) a feast; banquet; a party／ ~을 베풀다 hold[give] a banquet; give a party. しゅくえん

**경연**(競演) a contest; a match／음악 ~회 a music contest. きょうえん

**경연극**(輕演劇) a light theatrical performance.

**경영**(經營) 《관리》 management; administration 《운영》 operation 《계획》 a program; a project/ ~하다 manage; operate; run; conduct/ ~ 경제학 business economics[management]/ ~자 an operator/~난 financial difficulty. けいえい

**경영**(競泳) a swimming race[match, contest]; a swim/ ~하다 swim [a race]/ ~자 a swimmer/~ 대회 a swimming meet/10마일 ~ a ten-mile swimming race. きょうえい

**경옥**(硬玉) 《광》 jade; jadeite. こうぎょく

**경외**(境外) outside of the boundary. きょうがい

**경우**(境遇) 《형편》 circumstances; a situation 《어떤 때》 a case; an occasion/ 나의 ~에는 in my case/이런 ~에는 in such a case; in such circumstance/ 여하한 ~에나[에도] under all[no] circumstances. きょうぐう

**경운기**(耕耘機) a cultivator. こううんき

**경원**(敬遠) keeping at a distance/ ~하다 keep (one) at a distance; give (one) a wide berth. けいえん

**경위**(經緯) ①《옳고 그름》 good and evil; vice and virtue; right and wrong. ②《판단·식별력》 judgment; discernment; good sense. ものごとのぜひ

**경위**(經緯) ①《경위도》 longitude and latitude ②《피륙의 날과 씨》 warp and woof[weft] ③《일의 전말》 circumstances; details; particulars/ ~선 lines of longitude and latitude. けいい

**경위**(警衛) ①《경관의 계급》 a police lieutenant ②《호위》 guard; patrol; escort / ~하다 guard; patrol; escort; convoy. けいえい

**경유**(經由) ~하다 go by way of; pass through/ …을 ~하여 via; by way of; through. けいゆ

**경유**(輕油) light oil; gasoline. けいゆ

**경유**(鯨油) whale oil; train oil. げいゆ

**경음**(硬音) glottalied sounds. こうおん

**경음**(鯨飮) swig; heavy drinking; drinking like a fish/ ~하다 drink like a fish. げいいん

**경음악**(輕音樂) light music. けいおんがく

**경의**(敬意) respect; regard; homage/~를 표하다 pay one's respects[regards] to; do honour to; do[pay] homage to. けいい

**경이**(輕易) lightness; easiness / ~하다 (be) easy; simple; light. けいい

**경이**(驚異) a wonder; a marvel/ ~하다 wonder[murvel] (at)/ ~적 wonderful; marvellous; phenomenal. きょうい

**경이원지**(敬而遠之) keeping (one) at a respectful distance/ ~하다 keep (one) at a respectful distance; give a wide berth. けいえんすること

**경일**(慶日) a happy day; an auspicious occasion. めでたいひ

**경작**(耕作) cultivation; farming; tillage / ~하다 cultivate; farm; till/ ~물 farm products /~ 면적 the acreage under crops; planted acreage. こうさく

**경장**(輕裝) a light dress; light attire; light equipment/ ~하다 be lightly dressed[outfitted]. けいそう

**경장**(警長) a senior patrolman.

**경장**(更張) 《쇄신》 renovation; innovation; reformation/갑오 ~ the Reformation of Kabo.

**경쟁**(競爭) competition; rivalry; contest / ~하다 compete with (a person for a thing); contest; rival/ 생존 ~ the struggle for existence /~자 a competitor; a rival/ ~심[가격, 률] a competitive spirit[price, rate]/~ 시대 competitive age. きょうそう

**경적**(警笛) an alarm whistle; a [warning] horn/ ~을 울리다 sound the horn. けいてき

**경전**(經典) the scripture; the sacred books 《불교의》 the Sutras 《기독교의》 the Bible 《회교의》 the Koran. けいてん

**경절**(慶節) a fête day; a gala day; a festival. めでたいひ

**경정**(更正) correction; revision; rectification/ ~하다 correct; rectify; alter/ ~ 결정 reassessment. こうせい

**경정**(更訂) revision; rewriting/ ~하다 revise; rewrite. こうてい

**경정**(警正) a superintendent (略: supt.).

**경정맥**(頸靜脈) 《해》 the jugular vein.

**경제**(經濟) ①《일반의》 economy; finance 《재정》 ~(상)의 economic; financial / ~학 economics; political economy / ~학자 an economist/ ~계 the economic world; financial circles/ ~력 economic power[capacity]/ ~력 봉쇄 an economic blockade/~ 원론 the principles of economics/ ~ 문제[정책, 신문] an economic problem [policy, paper]/~ 기사 financial news/ ~ 조직[구조] economic organization[structure]/ ~ 원조 economic aid; financial support/ ~ 관념 a sense of economy / ~ 행위 economical activities. ②《절약》 thrifty; saving; economy/시간[노력]의 ~ saving of time[labour]/ ~적 economical/ ~가 되다 be economical; save (one time). けいざい

**경조**(輕躁) rashness; hastiness; precipitancy/ ~하다 (be) rash; precipitant; indiscreet; imprudent. けいそう

**경조**(競漕) a boat-race; a regatta/ ~하다 have a boat race; row a race/ ~ 대회 a regatta; boat races. きょうそう

**경조 부박**(輕佻浮薄) frivolity; levity/ ~하다 flippant. けいちょうふはく

**경조비**(慶弔費) expenses for congratulations and condolences.

**경종**(警鐘) an alarm[a fire] bell/ ~을 울리다 ring[sound] an alarm bell.

**경죄**(輕罪) a minor offence; a misdemeanour. けいざい

**경주**(輕舟) a light boat; a skiff; a cockleshell[cockleboat].

**경주**(傾注) devotion *one*self to; concentration/〜하다 devote; concentrate/…에 정력을 〜하다 concentrate *one's* energies on. けいちゅう

**경주**(競走) a race; a run 《단거리의》a dash; a sprint /〜하다 have[run] a race with (*one*); race against/ 〜장 the track; the course /〜용의 racing (*cars*)/〜에 이기다[지다] win[lose] a race. きょうそう

**경중**(敬重) respect; reverence/ 〜하다 respect; revere. そんちょう

**경중**(輕重) 《사물의》 relative importance [seriousness] 《물체의》 relative weight. けいちょう

**경증**(輕症) a slight illness; a mild case /〜 환자 a mild case. けいしょう

**경지**(境地) ①《상태》 a state; a condition; a stage; circumstances/…의 〜 에 이르다 reach[attain] the stage of. ②《분야》ground/새로운 〜를 개척하다 break new ground; open up a new path (in *literature*). きょうち

**경지**(耕地) a cultivated field[area]; arable land; land under cultivation ploughed land/〜 면적 acreage under cultivation/〜 정리 readjustment of arable lands. こうち

**경지**(鯨脂) blubber; whale fat.

**경직**(勁直) sturdiness; uprightness; integrity/ 〜하다 (be) sturdy; tough; unbending; upright.

**경진**(輕震) a weak earthquake[tremor].

**경질**(更迭) change 《대이동》shake-up / 〜하다 [make a] change/장관의 〜 a change of ministry; a reshuffle of the Cabinet. こうてつ

**경질**(硬質) hardness/ 〜의 hard/ 〜 유리[고무] hard glass[rubber]. こうしつ

**경차**(經差) 《지》a longitudinal difference.

**경찰**(警察) the police; the police force/ 〜관 a police officer; a policeman; 《총칭》 the police [authorities]/ 〜전 문학교 a police academy/[시] 〜국 the [Metropolitan] Police Bureau/ 〜견 (犬) a police dog/〜 국가 a police state/ 〜권(權) police authority[power]/〜서 a police station; a station house〈미〉/ 〜서장 the chief of a police station; the chief constable〈영〉; the chief of police〈미〉. けいさつ

**경책**(警責) admonition; caution/ 〜하다 admonish; caution.

**경척**(鯨尺) a cloth-measure(14.91 inches). くじらじゃく

**경천**(敬天) reverence of Heaven/ 〜하다 worship[reverse] Heaven. けいてん

**경천 동지**(驚天動地) 〜하다 astound[startle] the world; take the world by surprise.

**경천 위지**(經天緯地) the executive ability enough to govern the whole world/ 〜하다 govern the world; show great statesmanship.

**경첩** a hinge/〜을 달다 hinge/〜이 달 린 문 a hinged door. ちょうつがい

**경첩**(輕捷) agility; nimbleness; alacrity / 〜하다 (be) light; light and easy; free; simple. けいしょう

**경청**(傾聽) listening closely/ 〜하다 listen [with attention]; to; be attentive to; pay attention to; give ear to; be all attention to. けいちょう

**경청**(敬聽) listening courteously/ 〜하 다 listen courteously. つつんできくこと

**경추**(頸椎) 《해》the cervical vertebral.

**경축**(慶祝) congratulation; celebration / 〜하다 congratulate; celebrate/ 〜 일 a national holiday; a festival[red-letter] day. けいしゅく

**경치**(景致) a scene; scenery; a view; a prospect/좋은 〜 fine scenery; a picturesque[a charming, a lovely] scene. けいち

**경치다**《도둑이》 be severely punished [for committing a theft]; be given a good licking 《혼나다》 have a hard time of it; be taught a lesson; pay dearly for. どろぼうがけいばつをうける

**경칭**(敬稱) a title of honour; a term of respect. けいしょう

**경쾌**(輕快) 《몸이》lightness; nimbleness 《마음이》 light-heartedness; cheerfulness. 〜하다 (be) light; nimble; light hearted/ 〜한 복장을 하고 있다 be lightly dressed. けいかい

**경타**(輕打) 《체》 a light hit; pat; a light blow/ 〜하다 pat; hit lightly.

**경탄**(驚歎) wonder; admiration/〜하다 wonder[marvel] at; admire/ 〜할 만 한 wonderful; admirable; marvellous / 〜하여 in wonder. きょうたん

**경토**(耕土) fine[rich, fertile] soil; mold. こうど

**경토**(境土) a realm; a domain.

**경파**(硬派) ①《강경파》the stalwart party [faction]; the tough elements ② 《반대파》the opposing party. こうは

**경파**(鯨波) a billow 《큰 놀》 a big roller; a great wave. げいは

**경편**(輕便) convenience; handiness 《간 편》 simplicity/ 〜하다 (be) convenient; handy; simple 《간이》 light/ 〜 한 복장 a light dress/〜 철도 a narrow gauge railway. けいべん

**경포**(警砲) an alarm gun; a warning gun/ 〜를 놓다 fire an alarm gun.

**경포**(輕砲) a light gun. けいほう

**경표**(警標) a warning post; a danger signal. けいひょう

**경품**(景品) a gift; a premium/〜권 a premium[gift] ticket/ 〜부(付) 대매출 a

**경풍**(輕風) a [light] breeze; a zephyr; a soft wind. かるくふくかぜ
**경풍**(勁風) a gale.
**경풍**(驚風) 〖의〗 convulsion; paroxysm /급성[만성]~ an acute[chronic] convulsion.
**경하**(慶賀) congratulation; felicitation /~하다 congratulate (*one*); offer *one's* congratulations (*on*).
**경하다**(輕一) 《가볍다》(be) light 《경솔》(be) rash; imprudent 《경미》(be) light; slight; trifling. かるい
**경학**(經學) the knowledge[study] of Chinese classics. けいがく
**경한**(勁悍) ~하다 (be) sturdy and fierce. つよくてたけだけしい
**경합**(競合) concurrence; conflict 《경쟁》competition. きょうごう
**경합금**(輕合金) a light alloy. けいごうきん
**경해**(驚駭) surprise; astonishment; amazement / ~하다 be surised[astonished, amazed]; be thrown into consternation. けいがい
**경향**(京鄕) the capital and the country; town and country / ~ 각지에 all over the country. みやこといなか
**경향**(傾向) a tendency; a trend; a drift; an inclinaion / ~ 문학 tendency literature / …한 ~이 있다 have a tendency to; be disposed to; be abt[inclined, liable] to (*do*). けいこう
**경험**(經驗) experience / ~하다 experience; undergo; go through / ~자 an experienced man ~론 empiricism; experimentalism / ~적 empirical 모든 것이 ~에서 나온 것이었다 It was all done by rule of thumb. けいけん
**경호**(警護) guard; escort / ~하다 guard; escort; convoy. けいご
**경홀**(輕忽) ~하다 (be) careless; hasty; imprudent. うかつだ
**경화**(京華) the busy streets of *Seoul* the capital . みやこ
**경화**(硬化) hardening; cementation / ~하다 harden; stiffen; cement. こうか
**경화**(硬貨) hard money; metallic currency; effective money. こうか
**경화학 공업**(輕化學工業) light chemical industry.
**경황**(景況) a joyful state of things / ~ 없다 be too depressed to become enthusiastic; be too dispirited to be interest in. おもしろいじょうきょう
**경희**(驚喜) pleasant surprise / ~하다 be surprised with joy. きょうき
**곁** side; neighborhood / ~에 by the side of; beside. そば
**곁가리** false ribs.
**곁가지** a lateral branch. よこのえだ
**곁간**(一肝) 《소의》the lobe of the liver of cattle.
**곁간**(一間) a side room. わきのへや

**곁군** an assistant; a helper; an extra hand. じょりょくしゃ
**곁노질**(一櫓一) sculling; rowing.
**곁눈** a side glance 《윙크》an amorous glance / ~주다 make a sign with a side glance; wink (*at*) / ~으로 보다 cast a side glance at; glance sidewise at; look out of the corner of *one's* eyes (*at*). よこめ
**곁눈질** a sidelong glance; looking askance (*at*) / ~하다 look askance (at *one*); give (*one*) a sidelong look; glance sideways at; suggest by a side glance. よこめづかい
**곁다리** a secondary thing; someone other than the party concerned.
**곁땀** perspiration[sweat] from the armpit. わきのあせ
**곁두리** snacks for farmhands at work between meals. かんしょく
**곁들다** 《돕다》help; assist. ふきえする
**곁들이다** ①《음식을》put all on one plate; dress; garnish ②《일을》do all at once. かねる
**곁마부**(一馬夫) an assistant groom.
**곁말** a pun; a word play. じぐち
**곁매** blows in assistance of one party in a fighting; an attack by an outsider in an exchange of blows / ~질 dealing blows in assistance.
**곁방**(一房) ①《협방》a small room attached to the main one; a side room ②《셋방》a rented room. まがりのへや
**곁방살이**(一房一) 《생활》living in a rented room / ~하다 live in a rented room. まがりのくらし
**곁방석**(一方席) one who frequents the house of an influential man; one who dances in attendance upon an influential man; a sycophant; a toady. いそうろうやこぶんのひしょう
**곁부축** ①《걸음의》holding one under the arms to help walking / ~하다 hold (*one*) under the arms and help walking ②《일의》help; assistance / ~하다 help; assist (*one in doing*). ふきえ
**곁불이** a distant relative. えんのとおいしんせき
**곁비다** (be) without protection; be not cared for; be not looked after: be unguarded. せわやくがあいている
**곁상** a small dinner-[table set at the side of the main one. わきぜん
**곁쐐기** a side wedge; an additional wedge. わきぞえのくさび
**곁쇠** a pass-key; a dulicate key.
**곁순**(一筍) a lateral bud. わきのめ
**곁자리** a side seat; seats on either side. となりのせき
**곁쪽** a close relative. きんしん
**곁집** an adjoining house. となりのうち
**곁채** a detached building; an outbuilding; an outhouse. となりのいえ
**계**(戒, 誡) ①《계율》a precept ②《중이 지

키는) Buddhist commandments. かい
계(契) a mutual financing association. ; a credit union.
계(階) official rank; a grade. きざはし
계(係) 《담당》 charge; duty; business 《담당자》 a clerk[an official] in charge／~ 일원의 지도에 따라 led by a clerk in charge. かかり
계(計) ①《총계》 the total 《합계해서》in total; in all; all told ②《계기》a meter; a gauge/우량~ a rain-gauge ③《계략》 a plot. けい
-계(系) 《조직》 a system an organ 《혈통》 a family line; lineage 《당파》 a faction; a clique; a party 〖수〗 a corollary. ーけい
-계(界) circles; a community; a world; 《박물》a kingdom／실업~ business circles／동물~ the animal kingdom／문학~ the literary world. ーかい
-계(屆) a report; a notice／결석~ a notice of absence／사망~를 내다 send in a notice of death ⇨신고.
계간(季刊) [a] quarterly publication／~지 a quarterly; a quarterly magazine. きかん
계간(鷄姦) buggery; sodomy; pederasty／~하다 commit sodomy. かいかん
계계승승(繼繼承承) ~하다 be succeeded; from generation to generation; be inherited generation after generation. だいだいあいつぐこと
계고(戒告) a warning; a caution 《서면통고》notification／~하다 give a warning to; caution; warn. かいこく
계고(稽古) consideration; examination; study; inquiry／~하다 consider; examine; study; inquire into; contemplate. むかしのことをべんきょうすること
계곡(溪谷) a valley; a glen; a dale; a ravine; a canyon. けいこく
계관(鷄冠) ①《볏》 a cockscomb; a cock's crest ②⇨맨드라미. けいかん
계관(桂冠) a laurel wreathe／~시인 a poet laureate. げっけいかん
계관(係關) connection; relation ⇨관계. かんけい
계관석(鷄冠石) 〖광〗 realgar; sandarac.
계교(計巧) a design; a scheme; a trick ; an intrigue. こうみょうなたくらみ
계구 우후(鷄口牛後) Better be the head of an ass[a dog] than the tail of a horse[a lion].
계군 일학(鷄群一鶴) a jewel on a dunghill; the only figure among ciphers; a trout[Triton] among the minnows the sun among of inferior lights.
계궁 역진(計窮力盡) ~하다 come to the end of one's tether.
계급(階級) a class; an order 《봉건적》 a caste／상[중,하]류~ the upper[middle, lower] class／유산~ bourgeoisie／무산~ proletariat／~ 투쟁[의식] class strife [consciousness]. かいきゅう

계기(契機) a moment; an opportunity; a chance／이것을 ~로 하여 taking this opportunity; with this as a momentum. けいき
계기(計器) a gauge; a meter. けいき
계단(階段) steps; [a set of] stairs／~ 교실 a [lecture] theatre. かいだん
계대(繼代) succeeding a generation; succeeding (one's father)／~하다 succeed (one's father). だいをつづくる
계도(系圖) genealogy; pedigree; a family-tree. けいず
계도(啓導) enlightenment; illumination; guidance; leading／~하다 enlighten; illuminate; guide; lead.
계란(鷄卵) a hen's egg ⇨달걀. たまご
계란지(鷄卵紙) 〖사〗 albumenized paper
계략(計略) a scheme; a design; a plot／~에 능한 사람 trick a resourceful man; a man of resources／~을 꾸미다 lay a plan; hatch a plot; think out a scheme. けいりゃく
계량(計量) 《무게의》weighing (길이·부피의) measuring／~하다 measure; weigh／~기(器) a meter; a gauge; a scale. けいりょう
계련(係戀) a lingering love／~하다 be ardently attached to; cling to.
계루(係累,繫累) 《처자 따위》dependents; [family] ties; encumbrances 《연루》implication; involvement; complicity／~가 없다 have no dependants; 《독신이다》be single. けいるい
계류(溪流) a mountain torrent[stream]. けいりゅう
계류(繫留) mooring／~하다 moor (at, to)／~탑 a mooring mast／~ 기구(氣球) a captive balloon. けいりゅう
계륵(鷄肋) a superfluity; a redundancy／~집(集) a miscellany. けいろく
계리사(計理士) a public[a certified] accountant. けいりし
계림(鷄林) Korea; the Land of Morning Calm.
계명(戒名) 《생전의》a Buddhist name 《죽은 후의》a posthumous Buddhist name.
계명(誡命) 〖종〗commandments／십~ the Ten Commandments; the Decalogue.
계명성(鷄鳴聲) a crow. とりのなきごえ
계명성(啓明星) Venus; the morning star; Lucifer. あけのみょうじょう
계명워리 a flirt; a minx; a hussy; a flapper. だらしのないおんな
계모(繼母) a stepmother. ままはは
계몽(啓蒙) enlightenment／~하다 enlighten; educate／~적 enlightening 《초보적》elementary／~ 운동 an enlightenment movement. けいもう
계박(繫泊) mooring／~하다 moor (at, to). ふねをつなぐこと
계발(啓發) development; enlightenment／~하다 develop; enlighten. けいはつ
계방(季方) a younger brother／~형

brother your[his] younger brother.
**계방**(癸方) 〖민〗 north-by-northeast.
**계보**(系譜) pedigree; genealogy; lineage／한국 문학의 ~ genealogy of Korean literature. けいふ
**계보**(季報) a quarterly bulletin.
**계부**(季父) the youngest brother of *one's* father. ちちのすえのおとうと
**계부**(繼父) a stepfather. けいふ
**계사**(繫辭) 〖문〗a copula／~적 접속사 a copulative conjunction. けいじ
**계산**(計算) calculation; reckoning; counting; computation; figure work／~하다 calculate; reckon; count; sum up／~서 a bill; an account／~자[척] a slide rule. けいさん
**계상**(計上) ~하다 〖합계〗add up; sum [count] up 《충당》 appropriate for; put in the budget. けいじょう
**계색**(戒色) continence; sexual abstinence. おんなをいましめること
**계선**(繫船) mooring 《매어둔 배》a laid up [an idle] ship／~하다 moor a ship; lay up a ship. けいせん
**계속**(繼續) continuance; continuaion 《경신》renewal／~하다 continue; go on with; last／~범(犯) a continuing crime／~적인 continuous; continual／~하여 in succession. ぞく
**계속**(繫屬) 〖법〗pendency／소송의 ~중에 는 during the pendency of action／when an action is pending. けいぞく
**계수**(季嫂) a sister-in-law. おとうとのつま
**계수**(計數) calculation; computation／~하다 number; count; calculate; compute／~기 a calculating machine.／~적으로 numerically. けいすう
**계수**(溪水) a mountain stream; a rill. けいすい
**계수**(係數) 〖수〗a coefficient. けいすう
**계수나무**(桂樹-) 〖식〗a 〖Chinese〗cinnamon; a cassia [bark] かつらのき
**계수법**(繼受法) 〖법〗an adopted law. けいじゅほう
**계술**(繼述) ~하다 follow; succeed to (*one's fathers profession*); take over (*the work* of). けいじゅつ
**계승**(繼承) succession／~하다 succeed to; accede to; inherit. けいしょう
**계시**(計時) clocking／~ 하다 《경기 따위에서》[check] time; time stay／~원 a time keeper.
**계시**(啓示) 〖종〗revelation; apocalypse／~하다 reveal／신의 ~ a revelation of God. けいじ
**계시**(癸時) 〖민〗the 2nd of the 24 hour periods (=0:30~1:30 a.m.).
**계씨**(季氏) your (*one's*) younger brother.
**계시다** be／아버지는 어디 계신가요? Where is father? いらっしゃる
**계심**(戒心) prudence; caution.
**계약**(契約) a contract; an agreement; a promise／~하다 contract; make a contract [promise]／~자 a contractor／~ 기한 the term of a contract／수의 ~ private contract／~ 위반 a breach of contract. けいやく
**계약서**(契約書) an agreement; a bond; a [written] contract. けいやくしょ
**계엄**(戒嚴) guarding against danger／~ 사령부 the Martial Law Enforcement Headquarters／~ 사령관 the commander of the forces enforcing martial law. かいげん
**계엄령**(戒嚴令) martial law. かいげんれい
**계열**(系列) ①〖생〗order ②〖당파〗a faction; a clique; a party. けいれつ
**계원**(係員) a person in charge; a section man; a clerk. かかりいん
**계원**(契員) a member of a credit union [loan club]. けいいん
**계월**(桂月) ①〖달〗the moon ②〖음력 8월〗August of the lunar year.
**계육**(鷄肉) chicken; fowl. にわとりのにく
**계율**(戒律) commandments; religious law; Buddhist precepts. かいりつ
**계음**(戒飮) temperance; moderation in drinking／~하다 drink with moderation.
**계인**(契印) a tally; a joint seal／~하다 seal the two papers. けいいん
**계일**(計日) ~하다 count the [number of] days. ひをけいさんすること
**계장**(係長) a chief (*pl.* ~s); a chief clerk. かかりちょう
**계쟁**(係爭) dispute; a law suit; controversy／~중의 in dispute; at issue／~점 a point at issue; a disputed point. けいそう
**계전**(契錢) an installment payment [to one's mutual finance association].
**계절**(季節) a season／~의 seasonal／~ 풍의 the monsoon／~을 가리지 않고 in all seasons; all the year [round]; in and out of season. きせつ
**계정**(計定) an account (略:a/c)／당좌[대체] ~ a current[postal transfer] account. かんじょう
**계정**(啓程) departure; starting; setting out (on a *journey*).
**계제**(階梯) ①〖순서〗a step; a stage; the course (of *things*) 《사정》circumstance ②〖기회〗an opportunity; a chance／이 ~에 taking this opportunity; with this as a turning-point. かいて
**계좌**(計座) an account／《은행에》 ~를 트다 open an account [with a bank].
**계주**(契主) the organizer of a mutual financing association.
**계주**(戒酒) moderation in drinking. さけをつつしむこと
**계주 경기**(繼走競技) a relay [race]. けいそきょうぎ
**계집** ①〖여자〗a female; the fair sex／~아이 a girl ②〖아내〗a wife 《정부》a mistress／~ 자식 *one's* wife and children; *one's* dependents. つま, おんな
**계차**(階次) the order of rank.

계책(計策) a stratagem; a design; a scheme; a plot/ ～을 쓰다 adopt[use] a stratagem. けいさく
계천(溪川) a stream; a brook a rivulet a rill. とぶ
계촌(計寸) ～하다 count the degree of relationship. 親等をけいさんすること
계추(季秋) September of the lunar year.
계추(桂秋) August of the lunar year.
계춘(季春) March of the lunar year.
계출(屆出) report; notification/ ～하다 notify; send in a report/ ～인 a notification giver; a notifier/당국에 ～하다 report to authorities/경찰서에 ～하다 report to the police. とどけいで
계측(計測) ～하다 measure 《토지를》 survey. けいそく
계층(階層) a class; a social stratum. かいそう
계통(系統) 《조직》 a system 《제도》 a family line; lineage 《당파》 a party/～적 systematic/ ～으로 systematically; methodically/ ～을 세우다 systematize. けいとう
계통(繼統) ～하다 succeed to the throne.
계피(桂皮) cinnamon; cassia bark/ ～산 cinnamic acid. かつらのかわ
계하(季夏) June of the lunar year. なつのすえ
계하(啓下) ～하다 obtain royal sanction; be sanctioned by the king. おおさまのさいかをうけること
계하(階下) place below the stairs/～에 down the stone steps. かいか
계한(界限) a boundary; a border.
계합(契合) coincidence; agreement; tallying. びったりいっちすること
계행(戒行) religious austerities; penance; ascetic practice. かいぎょう
계화(桂花) cassia flowers.
계획(計劃) a plan; a project; a scheme a program[me] 《의도》intention/ ～하다 plan; project; scheme; intend/도시 ～ town planning;city planning〈미〉/가공적 ～ a castle in the air; a visionary scheme/5개년 ～ a five-year plan/～ 경제 planned economy/ ～적[인] intentional; deliberate; calculated; systematic/ ～적으로 intentionally; deliberately; on purpose. けいかく
곗돈(契—) ①《내는 돈》 an installment/ ～을 내다 pay one's share in a mutual financing association by installments ②《받는 돈》 the loan given to one by the mutual financing association.
고 《끈이나 옷고름 따위의》 a loop (of a string). むすびたま
고² that ·그/ ～것 that [one]/ ～까짓 such. その
-고 ①《잇달》 and also/붉～ 큰 꽃 a huge red flower ②《대등한 연결》 do[ing] and then/문을 열～ 손님을 맞다 open the door and welcome a visitor ③《동작의 진행》 be doing/모자를 쓰～ 있다 be wearing a hat. —なり。—たり

고(高) ①《높이》 height ②《수량》 a mount; volume 《금액》 an amount; a sum/매상～ the amount sold; the sales; the proceeds. たかさ
고(鼓) a drum. たいこ
고(考) ①《선고》 one's deceased father ②《연구》 a study of/《동양 철학 ～》 "A Study on Oriental Philosophy".
고(膏) plaster; paste. しっくい
고(故) the late; the lamented; the deceased/～ 백 영순씨 the late Mr. youngsoon back. むかしの
고(稿) a manuscript. げんこう
고(苦) difficulty; hardship; pain; suffering; affliction. くるしみ
고(庫) 《곳간》 a warehouse; a storehouse 《차고》 a garage. そうこ
고가(古歌) an old song[poem]. こか
고가(古家) an old house[building] 《폐가》 a deserted house; a dilapidated cottage. こか
고가(高價) a high price/ ～의 expensive; costly; dear. たかね
고가(高架) an elevated construction/ ～철도 an elevated railway[railroad] ～도로 an elevated road. こうか
고가(故家) a family of old standing/～ 대족(大族) a family with illustrious[distinguished] history behind it. こか
고가(雇價) wages. ちんぎん
고까옷 children's gala dress. おしゃれ着
고까짓 that much; such/～ 울 게 없냐 It is silly of you to cry over such a trifle/～ 실망해서야 되겠느냐 Don't be disappointed at such a trifle. やっとそのていどに
고까짓 so trifling; so trivial/～ 일로 화내지 말아라 Don't be offended at such a trifle. やっとそのていどの
고각(高閣) a lofty building; a high building. たかいろうかく
고각(高角) an altitude; a high angle/ ～포 a high-angle gun/～ 발사 a vertical [a high] fire. こうかく
고각(鼓角, 鼓角) drums and trumpets. たいことらっぱ
고간(苦諫) earnest admonition[request] / ～하다 earnestly admonish (one not to do). くげんを呈していさめること
고깔 a cowl; a monk's hood; a wimple そうりょのぼうし
고갈(枯渴) ①《물이》 drying up; running dry/ ～하다 be dried up; run dry; be parched ②《결핍》 exhaustion; drain / ～하다 be exhausted; be drained; give out. こかつ
고깝다 (be) disagreeable; unpleasant; offensive; feel bad [about a person's lack of kindness] /고깝게 여기다 be displeased (at). じつにいやだ
고개 ①《목의》 the nape; the scruff [of the neck] ②《산·언덕의》 a ridge; a mountain pass/ ～턱 the head of a

고객 | 고객 pass[slope] ③(절정) the crest; the height; the summit. うなじ
고객(孤客) a solitary[lonely, lone] traveller. ひとりさびしいりょじん
고객(顧客) a customer; a patron; a client. こきゃく
고갯짓 (좌우로) shaking one's head (아래위로) a nod/~하다 shake one's head; nod.
고갱이 the heart; the essence. かくしん
고것 (사물) it; that [one] (사람) that fellow[man]; he. この. あれ
고견(高見) ①(남의 의견) your opinion [views, ideas] ②(뛰어난 의견) an excellent opinion; a fine idea. こうけん
고결(高潔) noble-mindedness; nobility; loftiness; purity/ ~하다 (be) noble; lofty; pure; noble-minded; high-mind. こうしょうでけっぱくなこと
고경(苦境) adverse circumstances; a difficult position; a fix; a sad plight/ ~에 있다 be in a fix; be in great difficulties. くきょう
고계(苦界) the bitter world; the world [of mortals]. くるしいにんげんせかい
꼬꼬 (닭) a chicken (꼬끼오) cock a doodle-doo. にわとり
고고(孤高) a proud loneliness[isolation, aloofness]/ ~하다 stand in lofty solitude/ ~한 생활 a life of proud loneliness. ここう
고고(考古) study of antiquities. こうこ
고고(呱呱) the first cry of a new born infant/~지성(之聲)을 울리다 see first the light of day; be born; come into being[the world]. うぶこえ
고고학(考古學) arch[a]eology/ ~의 arch[a]eological/ ~자(者) an archaeologist. こうこがく
고골(枯骨) a skeleton. ここつ
고공(高空) a high sky; high [up] in the air; high altitude/ ~의[에서] high in the air; at a high altitude/ ~ 비행(飛行) high altitude flying[flight]. こうくう
고공(雇工) (머슴)a servant; a farm hand; a farm laborer (품팔이) an extra hand (경멸적)a hireling/ ~살이 the life of a farm hand; the life of a hireling. ひやとい
고과(考課) consideration of services; evaluation of merits/ ~표(表) an efficiency report. こうか
고관(高官) a high official[officer]; a dignitary (직위) a high office/ ~ 대가 a high; dignitaries. こうかん
고광나무 【식】a mock orange; a syringa; Philadelphus schrenckii(학명).
고굉(股肱) one's right-hand/ ~지신(之臣) one's trusted retainer. ここう
고교(高校) a high school/ ~생 a high school student. こうとうがっこう
고교회파(高教會派) High Church/ ~의 High-Church/ ~의 신도 a High Churchman.

고구(考究) (연구) research; study (숙고) consideration; deliberation/ ~하다 in vestigate; inquire into (연구) study (고려) consider; take (a matter) into consideration; do research.
よくこうさつしげんきゅうすること
고구(故舊) an old acquaintance [friend, crony]. こきょう
고꾸라지다 fall; drop (죽다) die; be off one's feet. たおれる
고구마 a sweet potato. さつまいも
고국(故國) one's native land[country]; one's home; land.
고군(孤軍) a forlorn force; an isolated [alone] force/ ~ 분투하다 fight alone; fight unsupported. こぐん
고궁(古宮) an ancient[old] palace.
ふるいおうきゅう
고귀(高貴) nobility; valuableness/~하다 (be) noble; highborn; exalted/~한 사람 a dignitary. こうき
고규(古規) old[ancient] regulations; an old law. むかしのきそく
고금(古今) ancient and modern ages [times]; all ages/ ~에 유례없는 unprecedented. こさん
고급(告急) an alarm; a warning; an emergency call/ ~하다 send an urgent[emergency] message[call]; raise an alarm; send out an SOS call; give [spread] an alarm[warning]. こきゅう
고급(高級) (계급) high rank (등급) high class[grade]/ ~의 high-class[-grade]; higher; senior/ ~품 goods of superior quality; high-grade articles [goods]/ ~ 관리 higher officials/ ~차 a high-class car. こうきゅう
고급(高給) a high[big] salary/ ~ 사원 high-salaried employees. こうきゅう
고기¹ ①(동물의) meat (소의) beef (돼지의) pork ②(물고기) fish/ ~국 a meat [beef] soup. に
고기² (장소) that place; there; yonder (범위) that; so far; that extent/ ~가 문제다 That's the question. そこ
고기(古記) antique records; ancient documents. こき
고기(古器) an antique; a relic of antiquity. こき
고기깃 plants set in the water to lure fish.
고기다, 꼬기다 crumple; wrinkle; rumple; crease. しわくちゃにする
고기밥 fish food; food given to fish (미끼) bait. えさ
고기붙이 meats [including fish]/ ~를 먹지 않다 abstain from meat[s].
고기압(高氣壓) high atmospheric pressure; barometric maximum/ ~ 구역 a high pressure area/ ~ 대륙성 the continental high pressure. こうきあつ
꼬끼요 cock-a-doodle-doo; cock-a-doodle / ~하고 울다 cry cock-a-doodle.

고기작거리다, 꼬기작거리다 crumple [up]; wrinkle [up]; rumple. しわくちゃにする

고기잡이 《어업》 fishing; fishery 《어부》 a fisher. さかなとり

고김살, 꼬김살 creases; rumples; folds; delve; cockle. しわ

고깃배 a fishing boat[vessel, craft]; a fisher-boat.

고난(苦難) distress; suffering; hardship; affliction/ ～을 겪다 undergo hardships. くなん

고냥 ①(그대로) as it is[stands]; as you find it./ ～ 주십시요 Please hand it over to me as it is. ②(줄곧) all the time; through; throughout/아침부터 ～ all through the morning. そのまま

고녀(雇女) a maid; a woman servant; a hired girl[woman]. 傭われおんな

고녀(敳女) a woman who has under developed genitals.

고녀(䕮女) a hermaphrodite 어지자지. ふぐりのあるおんな

고년(高年) an advanced age. こうねん

고념(顧念) patronage; care/ ～하다 favour; patronize; look after; care for; mind. かえりみておもうこと

고뇌(苦惱) suffering; distress; affliction; agony. くのう

꼬느다 hold (a child, a thing) up right on one's finger[s, or palm; grade; give marks. しんちゅうにねらいをつける

고니 《조》 a swan. はくちょう

고다 ①(끓이다) boil hard; boil to a pulp/쇠고기를 ～ boil beef to a pulp ②《양조하다》brew; distil/소주를 ～ distil sojoo. にる

꼬다 ①(새끼 따위를) twist; twine/새끼를 ～ make a rope with straw ②(몸을) writhe; wriggle. よる

꼬다리 a branch stretched out over the legs of an A-frame.

고다지 so; to that extent; that much /그녀가 ～ 바본 줄은 몰랐다 I didn't know she was so stupid. そんなにまで

고단하다 (be) tired; fatigued; wearied /고단해 보이다 look tired. くたびれる

고달¹ ①(자루에 박힌 두부분) a tang ②(쇠붙이 부리) a ferrule; a metal cap.

고달² ①(거만) arrogance; haughtiness; insolence ②(보챔) fret; petulance (of a baby). よこがら

고달이 a loop [of a string].

고달프다 (be) exhausted; fatigued; tired out; done up. つかれきっている

고담(古談) an old tale; folklore/ 한국의 ～ tales of old Korea. むかしのはなし

고담 준론(高談峻論) 《고상한 언론》a lofty and stern discourse 《과장한 말》high sounding words; tall talk 《자랑하는 말》 a loud boast. こうだんしゅんろん

고답(高踏) transcending the mundane w-orld/～적/transcendent/～주의 transcendentalism/ ～파 the Parnassian school; the transcendentalists. こうとう

고당(高堂) ①(집) a lofty house 《훌륭한》 a fine house ②(남의 집) your esteemed house ③(양친) parents; father and mother. たかいいえ

고대(막) just now; a moment[minute] ago. ちょうどいま

고대(古代) ancient[old] times; antiquity/ ～의 ancient; antique/ ～인 the antiquity. こだい

고대(苦待) waiting with impatience/ ～하다 wait eagerly for; eagerly look forward to. まちこがれること

고대 광실(高臺廣室) a grand[de luxe] house; a lordly mansion.

고도(古都) an ancient city 《구도》 a former capital こと

고도(高度) 《높이》 height; altitude 《전도》 a high power[degree]/ ～의 height; strong; powerful; intense; 《전진된》 advanced/ ～계(計) an altimeter; a height-indicator/ ～의 문명 a high state[standard] of civilization. こうど

고도(孤島) a solitary[desert] island/ 절해의 ～ a solitary island in the far-off sea. ことう

고도(高跳) high jump/주～ running high jump. たかとび

고도리 《어》 a young mackerel. さばのこ

고독(孤獨) solitude; loneliness; isolation/ ～하다 (be) solitary; lonely; isolated. こどく

고동 ①(장치) a handle; a spigot; a faucet; a tap; a switch 《수도 따위의》 a stopcock ②(기적) a steam whistle; a syren; a siren《미》/ ～을 울리다 give a whistle ③(요점) a vital point; a decisive factor. ハンドル

고동(古銅) old copper/ ～색 dark brown; dun. ふるいあかがね

고동(鼓動) beat; pulsation; palpitation / ～하다 beat; palpitate; throb. こどう

고되다 (be) hard [to bear]; painful/ 고된 일 hard work; toil. つらい

고두(叩頭) a kotow; a bow. こうとう

고두리 a blunt tip. とがっていない先端

고두머리 the roller of a flail; the pivot pin of a flail. からさおのくるま

고두밥 hard-boiled rice. むしたごはん

고등(等) gast'e ropods.

꼬드기다 ①(부추기다) incite; instigate ②(연줄을) pull in suddenly. そそのかす

고드러지다, 꼬드러지다 dry up; be parched. かたくなる

고드렛돌 stones attached to the end of each warp to hold it in place in weaving.

고드름 an icile; an ice pillar/～이 처마 끝에 달려 있었다 Icicles hang from the eaves. つらら

고들개¹ ①(방울) a cowbell; a horsebell ②(채찍의 주)a-loaded lash [of a whip] / ～ 채찍 a loaded whip ③(굴레의 턱 밑 가죽) a throatlatch.

고들개² 《천엽의》 honeycomb; reticulum.

**고들고들, 꼬들꼬들** hard / ~하다 (be) hard; dry. ほどよくかたいさま

**고들빼기** 〖식〗 a kind of lettuce. にがな

**꼬등** the first; first and foremost.

**고등**(高等) high class; high grade/~의 high; higher; advanced; high-class [-grade]/ ~학교 a ˈsenior˩ high school; an upper secondary school/ ~교육 higher education/ ~관 a higher official/ ~동물 a higher animal/ ~법원 a high court of justice. こうとう

**고등**(高騰) 《가격의》 a rise[an advance] in price; an increase in value/ ~하다 rise; advance in price/쌀값의 ~ a rise in the price of rice/ ~을 예기하여 in expectation of increased value.

**고등어** 〔어〕 a mackerel. さば

**고라니** 〖동〗 an elk; a moose〈미〉.

**고라말** a chestnut[-horse] with black haired back. せなかがくろいうま

**고락** ①《낙지의 뼈》 a cuttlebone; a pen. ②《낙지의 먹》 cuttlefish ink/ ~을 뿜다 spurt the ink. たこのはら

**고락**(苦樂) pleasure and pain; joys and sorrows/ ~을 같이하다 share *one's* joys and sorrows[*one's* fortunes]. くらく

**꼬락서니** 《상태》 a state; a condition 《외양》 appearance 《광경》 a spectacle/ ~좋다 Serve you right! ざま

**고람**(高覽) your inspection; your perusal. こうらん

**고랑** 《수갑》 a handcuff; manacles; shackles/ ~을 채우다 shackle. てじょう

**고랑** 《두둑 사이》 a furrow.

**꼬랑이** a tail. しっぽ

**꼬랑지** the tail of a bird. とりのお

**고랑창** a narrow deep furrow; a ditch. はばがせまくてふかいみぞ

**고래¹** 〖동〗 a whale/~ 기름 whale oil/ ~ 작살 a harpoon; a gaff/~ 수염 a baleen; whalebone; whale fin. くじら

**고래²** hypocaust[heating system] flues.

**고래**(古來) ~로 from olden[ancient] times/ ~의 old; time-honoured. こらい

**고래고래** loudly; snarlingly/~ 소리지르다 raise a shout. さけぶこえ

**고래둥 같다** (be) very large; (be) grand; magnificent; palatial; be as big as a whale's back/고래둥 같은 집 palatial house. くじらのせのようだ

**고량**(高粱) 〔식〕 *kaoliang*(Chin); the sorghum/ ~주 *kaoliang* wine. おうあわ

**고량 진미**(膏粱珍味) rare delicacies of all descriptions; all sorts of delicacies. うまいしょくぶつ

**고려**(考慮) consideration; deliberation; reflection/~하다 consider; think over; take (*a matter*) into account; deliberate on; reflect upon. こうりょ

**고려**(顧慮) regard; respect; consideration concern; solicitude/~하다 regard; consider; have respect to; take into consideration. こりょ

**고려 자기**(高麗磁器) Korea pottery; porcelain produced in the reign of the Korea dynasty.

**고려장**(高麗葬) burying (*an old man*) alive/ ~하다 bury (*one*) alive.

**고령**(高齡) a great[an advanced] age/ ~자 the aged; a person of advanced age. こうれい

**고령토**(高嶺土) kaolin[e], Kaolinite.

**고례**(古禮) old etiquette[manners, propriety]. これい

**고로**(故—) so; accordingly; therefore.

**고로**(古老) an old man; an elder; the aged/마을의 ~ elders of the village; village seniors. ころう

**고로**(故老) an old man; old folks. ころう

**고로**(高爐) a shaft[blast] furnace.

**고로통거리다** be troubled with a lingering desease. しんぎんしている

**고로 여생**(孤露餘生) a lonely person who has lost the parents at an early age.

**고론**(高論) a lofty opinion; an exalted view 《상대자의 의견》 your ˈvalued˩ opinion. こうろん

**고료**(稿料) fee for a manuscript; compensation for *one's* writing. こうりょう

**고루** equally; 《같게》 evenly 《차별 없이》 indiscriminately. おしなべて

**고루**(固陋) bigotry; narrow-mindedness; conservatism; perversity; obstinacy / ~하다 (be) bigoted; narrow-minded; conservative; obstinate. ころう

**고루**(高樓) a lofty building/ ~ 거각(巨閣) a lofty structure; a noble pile. こうろう

**고르다** (be) even; equal; similar; uniform/고르게 evenly; equally; all alike. へいじゅんだ

**고르다** ①《평평하게》 level; make even; 《둘러로》 roll/땅을 ~ level the ground ②《선택》 choose; select/골라내다 pick out; select. えらぶ

**고름** pus; ˈpurulent˩ matter; discharge / ~이 생기다 form pus; fester. うみ

**고리¹** 《둥근 것》 a ring 《쇠사슬의》 a link / ~를 만들다 form a ring. わ

**고리²** 《고리짝》 a wicker-trunk. こうり

**고리³** 《그렇게》 so; so much; like that/ 왜 ~ 뻔뻔스러우냐? How could you be so impudent? そのように

**꼬리** 《일반의》 a tail 《더우 따위의》 a brush 《토끼 따위의》 a scut 《해선 따위의》 a trail 《물고기의》 a caudal fin/ ~를 물고(연달아) one after another; in rapid succession/ ~치다 wag the tail / ~를 밟히다 give a clue (*to*); be found out. お

**고리**(高利) high interest; usury/ ~로 at a high rate of interest/ ~ 대금업 usury/ ~ 대금업자 a usurer; an extortionate creditor; a loan shark〈미〉/ ~로 at a high rate of interest こうり

**고리눈** an eye with white tint forming; a ring around the iris/ ~이 *one* whose eyes have rings of white tint ar-

고리다 ①(냄새가) (be) rancid; stinking; rank; fetid ②(행동이) (be) illiberal; small; mean. くさい

고리못 a ring-shaped nail[hook]. かんじょうのくぎ

고리버들 【식】 an osier; red osier. こうりをつくるやなぎ

고리삭다 (be) not sprightly; too discreet for *one's* age. としよりくさい

고리짝 a wicker-trunk 《짐》 luggage; baggage《미》. こうり

고리장이 a wicker-trunk maker. こうりや

고리지느러미 the caudal fin.

고리타분하다 ①(냄새가) (be) stinking; rancid; fetid; rank ②(성질이) (be) narrow-minded; small; stingy; 《전부한》 hackneyed /고리타분한 소리 a trite remark. くさい

고리탑탑하다 (be) foul-smelling; mean ⇨고리타분하다. くさい

고리표(一標) a tag; a label. にふだ

고린내 a bad smell; an offensive odour; stench; stink. くさったにおい

고릴라 《동》 a gorilla.

고림보 ①(늘 앓는 이) a valetudinarian; an invalid ②(옹졸한 이) a narrow-minded person; a stingy fellow 《인색한 이》 a niggard. びょうじゃくしゃ

고립(孤立) isolation; helplessness/ ~하다 be isolated; be cut off; stand alone/~된 isolated; solitary; helpless/ ~주의 isolationism/ ~파 the isolationists. こりつ

꼬마 a dwarf; a pigmy; 《소년》 a boy [kid] 《소형》 baby; midget; miniature /~ 자동차 a baby-auto. こども

꼬마동이 a small child; a little darling ; a midget. こびと

고마와하다 be thankful[grateful] to (*a person*) for; appreciate. かんしゃする

고마움 《감사》 gratitude; thankfulness 《가치》 value; blessing (of *health*). ありがたみ

고막 《어》 an ark shell.

고막(鼓膜) the eardrum; the tympanum; the tympanic membrane/ ~염 (炎) myringitis; tympanitis. こまく

고막(痼瘼) irremediable evils[abuses]

고만고만하다 (크기가) (be) of even size; 《능력·정도가》 of even ability; of a sort. まあまあだ

고만하다 《비슷하다》 (be) much the same; similar; of a sort 《같다》 the same equal. それくらいだ

-고말고 it is needless to say that……; it is a matter of course that…/ 가~ Of course I will go. ーとも

고맙다 (be) kind; obliging; welcome; gracious/ 고마와하다 be[feel] thankful; be obliged/고마운 말씀 *one's* kind words. ありがたい

고매(高邁) ~하다 (be) lofty; noble; high-minded. こうまい

고매(故買) fencing/ ~하다 fence; receive[purchase] stolen goods[knowingly]/장물(臟物) ~자(者) a fence; a receiver [of stolen goods].

고명 《양념》 a garnish; a relish; a condiment. あじのもと

고명(古名) an old name. むかしのなまえ

고명(高名) ①(명성) fame; reputation; renown; distinction ②(경어) your[famous] name. こうめい

고명(顧命) the will of a king; orders issued at the death-bed of a king/ ~대신(大臣) ministers entrusted with the last words of the king.

고명(高明) ~하다 《현명》 (be) noble and wise 《밝다》 (be) well-grounded; well-versed. こうめいた

고명딸 the only daughter among many sons. ひとりむすめ

고모(姑母) an aunt; a sister of *one's* father. こぼ

고모부(姑母夫) the husband of *one's* aunt; an uncle. こぼのおっと

고목(古木) an old tree. こぼく

고목(枯木) a dead tree. かれたき

고묘(古廟) an ancient mausoleum; an old shrine. こびょう

고묘(古墓) an old tomb; an ancient mound. ふるいはか

고무 rubber; gum/~ 나무[재배원] a rubber tree[plantation]/ ~줄[끈] an elastic cord[string]/ ~신 rubber shoes gums《속》/ ~풀 gum arabic; mucilage《미》 《사무용》 glue/지우개 ~ a rubber; an eraser/ ~창을 댄 rubber. soled/ ~ 제품 rubber goods/생~ crude rubber/경화(硬化) ~ ebonite; celluloid/인조 ~ synthetic rubber/~를 입힌 rubbered. ゴム

고무(鼓舞) encouragement/ ~하다 cheer up; encourage; inspire; stir up/사기를 ~하다 stir up the morale of the troops. こぶ

고무라기 crumbs of rice-cake. もちの小片

고무라거리다, 꼬무라거리다 move sluggishly/ 고무락고무락[꼬무락꼬무락] tardily; idly; sluggishly. のろのろと

고무래 a rake. レーキ

고문(古文) ancient[archaic] writing/ ~체 an archaic style. こぶん

고문(拷問) torture; the third degree 《미》 ~하다 torture; give *one* the third degree; rack. ごうもん

고문(顧問) an adviser; a counsellor; a consultant/법률 ~ a legal adviser/ ~ 변호사 a consulting lawyer/군사 ~ 단 Military Advisory Group. こもん

고물¹ ground grain used for coating rice-cake and other candies. ふんまつ

고물² 《배의 뒤쪽》the stern/ ~에 astern; aft. せんび

고물(古物) 《골동품》a curio; antique objects 《낡은 것》used articles; an old article 《중고품》 a second-hand article

고물거리다, 꼬물거리다　　　　　73　　　　　고빙

/ ~상 《골동품상》 a dealer in curios 《고물 상인》 a second-hand dealer. ふるもの

고물거리다, 꼬물거리다 move sluggishly; move slowly. うごめく

꼬미 a roof which is at the same time the top covering of a room / ~ 다락 an attic; a garret; a loft.

고미(苦味) a bitter taste / ~ 전기[약] bitter tincture. にがみ

고민(苦悶) agony 《심통》 anguish / ~하다 be in agony; agonize; writhe [with pain]. くもん

꼬바기 whole; full / ~ 하루 a full day / ~ 밤을 새우다 sit up all night; pass a sleepless night. つらぬいて

꼬박, 꼬빡 without sleeping a wink ⇨ 꼬바기. こっくり

고박(古朴) simplicity 《고풍》 antiquity / ~하다 (be) simple and antique.

고발(告發) 《검사의》 prosecution; indictment 《민간의》 complaint / ~하다 prosecute; in dict; charge; inform (against) / ~자 a prosecutor; an accuser; an informant / ~장 a bill of indictment. こくはつ

고방(庫房) a storeroom. そうこ

고배(苦杯) a bitter cup / ~를 마시다 drink a bitter cup; go through the ordeal (of) 《승부에서》 be sadly defeated [beaten]. はい

고배(高排) a heap; a heaped measure / ~하다 heap up. もりあげること

고백(告白) confession; admission 《신앙의》 profession / ~하다 confess; profess; own; admit / 죄상을 ~하다 confess one's guilt[fault]. こくはく

고백반(枯白礬) burnt alum.

고범(故犯) a calculated crime; a deliberate offence. わざとおかしたつみ

고벽(痼癖) an inveterate habit 《나쁜 버릇》 a fatal vice. がんこなくせ

고변(告變) ~하다 inform (the government) of an uprising; report treason. はんぎゃくをつげること

고별(告別) leave-taking; farewell; good-bye / ~하다 take leave (of); say good-bye; bid adieu[farewell] / ~사 a farewell address / ~식 a farewell ceremony. こくべつ

고병(古兵) a veteran; an old-timer; a senior comrade. こへい

고본(稿本) a manuscript; an original draft. したがき

고본(古本) a second-hand book; an old book; a used book / ~ 가게 a second-hand book store[shop]; an old bookseller. ふるほん

고봉(高峯) a lofty peak; an alp. たかい峰

고부(姑婦) a mother-in-law and a daughter-in-law. しゅうとめとよめ

고부(告訃) 《신문의》 an obituary (notice); the announcement of (a person's) death / ~하다 announce one's death; report the death of (one). ふこく

고부라뜨리다, 꼬부라뜨리다 bend; curve; crook / 철사를 ~ bend a wire. おりまげる

고부라지다, 꼬부라지다 bend; curve; be bent; be crooked. まがる

고부랑이, 꼬부랑이 a bent[curved, crooked] object 《사람》 a person whose back is bent. まがったもの

고부랑하다, 꼬부랑하다 《잔등》 (be) bent 《나무 따위》 crooked 《길이》 winding 《개천 따위》 meandering 《진로 따위》 zigzag. まがっている

고부리다, 꼬부리다 bend; curve; crook / 허리를 ~ bend one's back / 철사를 ~ curve a wire. まげる

고부스름하다, 꼬부스름하다 (be) somewhat bent; slightly curved; crooked a little. ややまがっている

고부장하다, 꼬부장하다 (be) bent; curved; crooked 《마음이》 perverse / 고부장고부장[꼬부장꼬부장] crookedly; windingly. すこしまがっている

고부조(高浮彫) high relief.

고부탕이 a crease; a fold. ひだ

고분(古墳) an old mound; an ancient tomb. こふん

고분고분 gently; meekly; obediently; submissively / ~한 gentle; meek; mild; obedient / ~하다 (be) gentle; mild. ことばをていねいにきくこと

고뿔 a cold / ~에 걸리다 catch cold. かぜ

고불거리다, 꼬불거리다 wind; meander; curve. まがりくねっている

고불고불, 꼬불꼬불 windingly; zigzag / ~하다 (be) winding; zigzag; meandering / ~한 산길 a zigzag[winding] mountain path / ~한 냇물 a meandering stream.

고불탕하다, 꼬불탕하다 (be) winding; meandering; zigzag. ゆるくまがっている

고붓하다, 꼬붓하다 (be) somewhat bent; slightly curved; crooked a little. すこしまがっている

고붙치다 crease; fold to make a crease (in). おりめをつける

고비¹ 《절정》 the climax; the crest; the height 《위기》 the crisis; a critical moment 《대목》 a turning point / ~를 넘다 《병 따위》 pass the crisis 《물가 따위》 pass the peak (of). しごとのやま

고비² 《편지 꽂는》 a letter holder; a letter file. てがみさし

고비³ 《식》 a flowering fern. わらび

고삐 reins; a bridle. たづな

고비(考妣) one's deceased parents. なくなったふぼ

고비(高飛) high flight / ~하다 fly high / ~ 원주(遠走) abscondence; decampment. たかとび

고빗사위 a critical moment; a psychological moment. きわどいしゅんかん

고빙(雇聘) employment; engagement; invitation / ~하다 employ; engage; invite. こへい

고사(古史) ancient history. こし
고사(古寺) an old Buddhist temple. こじ
고사(古事) an ancient event[happening]. こじ
고사(考査) consideration; examination; test/ ~하다 consider; examine; test /성적~ an achievement test/인물~ a character test. こうさ
고사(固辭) positive refusal/ ~하다 refuse[decline] positively/그 사람은 그 지위를 ~하였다 He positively declined to receive the chair that was offered. こじ
고사(告辭) (식사) an adress 《고별사》 a farewell adress. こくじ
고사(枯死) death/ ~하다 die; wither; be blighted; be withered. こし
고사(故事) (유래) an origin; a source; a historical fact 《구비(口碑)》 tradition; folklore. こじ
고사(苦辭) ~하다 refuse[decline] cordially/ ~하고 받지 않다 cordially decline to accept an offer; decline with regret. こんせつにえんりょうすること
고사(高士) a noble character; a man of high[lofty] character.
고사(告祀) a religious service. さいし
고사 기관총(高射機關銃) an anti-aircraft machine gun; an A. A.-machine gun. こうしゃきかんじゅう
고사리 【식】a fernbrake; a bracken. ぜんまい
고사포(高射砲) an anti-aircraft gun; an A A. gun; an ack-ack《속》/~탄 an anti-craft shell. こうしゃほう
고사풍 【의】a kind of horse disease. うまのびょうき
고사하고(姑捨—) apart from; setting aside[apart] 《물론》 to say nothing (of); not to mention/이 문제는 ~ apart from this question. —はべつとして
고산(孤山) a solitary hill[mountain].
고산(高山) a high[lofty] mountain/~의 Alpine/~ 식물 an Alpine plant; Alpine flora. こうざん
고산(故山) one's home; one's native place[province]. こきょう
고살(故殺) murder; wilful murder; 《법》 manslaughter/ ~하다 commit manslaughter. わざとひとをころすこと
고상(苦狀) distress; a sad plight; straitened; circumstances/농촌의 ~ the farmers' difficulties[distress]. つらいじょうたい
고상(高尙) ~하다 (be) lofty; noble; sublime; refined; elegant/ ~한 취미 an elegant taste/ ~한 인격 noble character. こうしょう
고상고상 wakefully/ ~하다 remain wakeful; make vain effort to get to sleep. ねむれずに
고샅 《골목길》 an narrow alley 《골짜기》 a gorge. せまいみち
고색(古色) an antique look; a note of antiquity/ ~ 창연한 antique; grey with age; hoary with antiquity hoarylooking. こしょく
고생(苦生) 《곤고・고난》 hardships; difficulties; troubles; trials; afflictions; sufferings; adversity 《수고》 labour; toil; pains/ ~하다 suffer troubles; undergo hardships; have one's trials; struggle with difficulties; take pains / ~살이 hard life; adversity/ ~스러운 hard; painful; toilsome; arduous / ~길에 들어서다 be thrown into adversity. こくろう
고생대(古生代) 【지】 the Pal[a]eozoic era / ~의 Pal[a]eozoic. こせいだい
고생물(古生物) extinct animals and plants 《화석》 fossils. こせいぶつ
고생스럽다(苦生—) (be) hard; tough; trying. くるしい
고서(古書) old books; classics; rare books. こしょ
고석(古昔) ancient times. こせき
고성(古城) an old[ancient] castle. こじょう
고성(孤城) a solitary castle 《포위당한》 a helpless castle. こじょう
고성(高聲) a loud voice/ ~으로 loudly; aloud/~ 전화 a loud[multiple] telephone. こうせい
고성(古聖) an ancient sage; an old saint; a sage of antiquity. むかしの聖人
고성능(高性能) high effectiveness[efficiency]/~ 폭약 a high explosive; TNT. こうせいのう
고소(告訴) accusation; complaint; an action/ ~하다 accuse (one of a crime); bring a charge (against); proceed (against); sue/ ~인 an accuser; a complainant/ ~장(狀) a written complaint; a bill/ ~를 수리[각하, 취하]하다 accept[reject, withdraw] a conmplaint. こくそ
고소(苦笑) a forced[sardonic] smile/ ~하다 smile bitterly[sardonicaly]; force a smile. にがわらい
고소(高所) the high ground; an eminence; an elevation; a height; a high place. たかいどころ
고소하다 ①《맛이》 taste of sesame oil; have a flavour of nut ②《남의 일이》 be pleased to see other's fault/고소하게 여기다 gloat (over); take an unholy pleasure (in). こうばしい
고속(高速) high-speed; rapid transit/ ~으로 at high speed/ ~ 도로 an express high way; a free way. こうそく
고송(古松) an old pine-tree. こしょう
고송(孤松) a solitary pine-tree. こしょう
고수(固守) adhesion; persistence; tenacity/ ~하다 adhere[stick, keep, cling] to. こしゅ
고수(鼓手) a drummer. こしゅ
고수레 mixing hot water in flour to make dough/ ~하다 make dough/

~떡 a kind of steamed rice-cake.
**고수련** nursing; service/ ~하다 give (*a patient*) one's best service; afford (*a sick man*) every facility; take care. かんごすること
**고수머리** (머리) curly hair; naturally wavy hair (사람) a curly pate; a curly-pated person. ちぢれかみ
**고스란하다** (be) untouched; unchanged; as sound[safe] as ever/고스란히 all; altogether; entirely; wholly/고스란히 그대로 있다 remain as it was; remain intact. あいかわらずだ
**고슬고슬하다** (밥이) (rice) be properly boiled. こんがり. ふんわり
**고슴도치** 〖동〗 a hedgehog. はりねずみ
**고승**(高僧) a high priest; a prelate; a bishop. がくとくあるぼうず
**고시**(古詩) an old[ancient] poetry. こし
**고시**(古時) ancient times; antiquity; times of your; old days. むかし
**고시**(告示) a notice; a bulletin; announcement/ ~하다 notify; give notice (*of*)/ ~판 a bulletin board 《공중용》a message board. こくじ
**고시**(顧視) looking back/ ~하다 look back. こし
**고시**(考試) examination/ 고등[보통] ~ the higher[ordinary] civil service examination. こうし
**고식**(古式) an old[ancient] rite/ ~에 따라서 accordance with the time-honored rite. こしき
**고식**(姑息) ①《임시 변통》a mere makeshift/ ~적 temporizing; timeserring; patch-up; makeshift/ ~적 해결 halfway solution ②《처자》one's wife and children; one's family. しゅうととよめ
**고실**(鼓室) 〖해〗 the eardrum; the tympanic cavity; the atrium(*pl.* ·ria). こしつ
**고심**(苦心) 《노력》 pains; hard work 《심로》 care; anxiety/ ~하다 work hard; take pains; be anxious; worry/ ~담 an account of the difficulties experienced/ ~하여 by hard work; with great pains. くしん
**고아**(高雅) elegance; refinement/ ~하다 (be) elegant; refined; graceful; chaste. こうが
**고아**(孤兒) an orphan/ ~원 an orphanage; an orphan asylum/전쟁 ~ a war orphan/ ~가 되다 be orphaned; be left an orphan. こじ
**고아**(古雅) classical grace; classicality; antique beauty/ ~하다 (be) classical; antique and elegant; have a classic beauty. こが
**고악**(古樂) ancient music. がく
**고안**(孤雁) a solitary wild goose; a wiid goose flying all by itself. こがん
**고안**(考案) an idea; a plan; a design; a project; a device/ ~하다 conceive; plan; design; devise/ ~자 a designer; an originator. こうあん
**고압**(高壓) 《증기의》 high pressure 《전기의》 high tension; high voltage/《미》《압제》a high-handed measure/ ~선 a high-tension[-voltage] wire/ ~적으로 high-handedly. こうあつ
**고액**(高額) a large amount[sum] (of *money*)/ ~ 납세자 a high[an upperbracket] taxpayer/ ~소득자 a large income earner.
**고약**(膏藥) a plaster; an ointment; an unguent. こうやく
**고약하다** 《성미가》 (be) ill-natured 《냄새가》 offensive 《용모가》 ugly 《일이》 hard せいしつ・かお・てんきなどがわるい
**고양이** 〖동〗 a cat 《애칭》 a puss[y]/ ~새끼 a kitten. ねこ
**고양이소**(一素) a hypocrite; a wolf in sheep's clothing.
**고양하다**(高揚—) exalt; raise; enhance.
**고어**(古語) 《폐어》 an archaic word. こご
**고언**(古諺) an old saying; an old adage. むかしからのぞくだん
**고언**(苦言) outspoken[unwelcome] advice; a bitter pill. くげん
**고역**(苦役) hard work; a tough job; toil; drudgery. くえき
**고열**(高熱) a high fever[temperature]; a super-heal. こうねつ
**고옥**(古屋) an old house 《폐옥》 a dilapidated cottage. ふるいえ
**고온**(高溫) a high temperature/ ~계 (計) a pyrometer. こうおん
**고와**(古瓦) an ancient tile; antique tiles. ふるいかわら
**고왕 금래**(古往今來) all ages[times]《부사적》 in all ages; at all times; the all ages. むかしからこんにちまで
**고요하다** (be) quiet; silent; still; calm; placid; tranquil/고요히 still; calmly; quietly/고요한 거리 a deserted street /고요한 바다 a calm sea. おだやかだ
**고욤** 〖식〗 a small kind of persimmon/ ~나무 a kind of persimmon-tree; *Diosoyros lotas*(학명). さるがき
**고용**(雇用) employment; hire/ ~하다 employ; hire/ ~주 employer. こよう
**고용**(雇傭) employment; hire/ ~하다 employ; hire; engage/완전 ~ full employment/불완전 ~ under employment/ ~ 계약 an employment contract/ ~주 an employer/ ~인(피고용자) an employee/ ~조건 employment conditions. やとわれること
**고우**(故友) an old friend; a friend of long standing. こゆう
**고운 야학**(孤雲野鶴) a hermit; a recluse; an anchorite/세상을 버리고 ~으로 자처 하다 renounce the world and become a hermit. いんしのたとえ
**고원**(高原) a plateau; a tableland/ ~ 요양소 an alpine sanatorium. こうげん
**고원**(故園) 《옛 뜰》an old garden; *one's* old nest 《고향》*one's* [old] home; *one's*

고원(高遠) loftiness; nobleness/ ~하다 (be) lofty; noble; high. こうえん

고원(雇員) an [a minor] employee; a worker.

고월(孤月) a solitary moon. こいん

고위(高位) a high rank/ ~ 고관들 persons of [high] rank and office; dignitaries. こうい

고위도(高緯度) a high latitude.

고유(固有) 《특유》characteristics; peculiarity 《본질》essence 《천성》inherence/ ~하다 《특유》(be) peculiar (to) 《천성의》 inherent; inborn; innate/ ~ 명사 a proper noun/동양의 ~ 풍습 a custom peculiar to the Orient. こゆう

고육지계(苦肉之計) conspiracy for dissension; alienting; a [deceitful] plot.
くにのけい

고율(高率) a high rate/~의 이자 a high [rate of] interest. こうりつ

고은(高恩) deep kindness; obligations; great favour; indebtedness/ ~을 입다 be deeply indebted to; own (one) great obligations. こうおん

고을 a country; a district. むら. まち

고음(高音) a loud sound; a high key / ~부 《음》 soprano; treble. こうおん

고읍(古邑) an ancient town.

고의(故意) intention; deliberation; purpose/ ~의 intentional; deliberate; will[ful]/ ~로 intentionally; on purpose; deliberately. こい

고의(袴衣) summer shorts[short pants].
おとこのなつの下着

고의(高誼) 《두터운 정》close friendship 《남의 정》 your favo[u]r.
とくべつにあついゆうじょう

고의춤 the space between one's abdomen and the belt of clothing/ ~에 손을 넣다 thrust one's hand into one's abdominal region. したぎのこしまわり

고이 ①《곱게》beautifully; finely; gracefully/~ 차리다 dress oneself beautifully ②《조용히》peacefully 《조심해서》 gently; quietly; carefully/ ~ 잠자다 sleep peacefully/~ 다루다 handle carefully. よくちゅういして

고이다 stagnate. たまる

고이다 ①《실·끈 등이》get[be] twisted ②《일이》suffer a setback; go wrong; miscarry ③《마음이》be offended; become perverse. ひねくれる. ねじられる

고인(古人) ancient people; men of old; the ancients. こじん

고인(故人) the deceased; the lamented / ~이 되다 be no more; die. こじん

고인돌 a dolmen. ドルメン

-고자 [in order] to/하~ 하다 intend (to); plan; be going to.

고자(告者) an informant; ~장이 an informer; a taleteller/ ~질하다 tell[carry] tales (to). つげぐちや

고자(鼓子) a man with underdeveloped genital organs.

고자누룩하다 become quiet; calm down.

고자세(高姿勢) an aggressive attitude/ ~를 취하다 assume a high-handed attitude. こしせい

고작 at [the] most; [the] best. せいぜい

고장(지방)a place; a locality. ちほう

고장(故障) 《장애》a hindrance; an obstacle; an obstruction; an impediment; a hitch 《사고》 an accident; a trouble / ~차 a disabled car/ 기관의 ~ engine trouble/ ~나다 get out of order; break down; (something) go wrong (with)/ ~을 내다 bring about a hitch.
こしょう

고장고장하다 《물건이》(be) straight and strong 《노인이》hale and hearty; vigourous. ほそながいものが硬直だ

고장 난명(孤掌難鳴) It takes two to wrestle; One needs assistance to accomplish anything.

고장물 《흐린 물》used dirty[filthy] water 《진물》 watery discharge from a sore. きたないみず

고장애(高障礙) 《체》a high hurdle/ ~경주 a high hurdle race.

고재(高才) great ability; genius; brilliant talent. こうさい

고쟁이 drawers[panty bloomers] worn by Korean women. おんなのしたき

고저(高低) unevenness; undulations 《시세의》 fluctuations 《높이》height 《음성의》pitch; modulation/~ 있는 undulating; uneven; fluctuating. こうてい

고적(古跡, 古蹟) historic remains; ruins ; a historic spot. こせき

고적(孤寂) solitude; loneliness/ ~하다 (be) solitary; lonely; lonesome.
ひとりぼっちでさびしいこと

고적대(鼓笛隊) a drum and fife band [corps]/ ~장 a drum major[majorette (여자)].

고적운(高積雲) 〖천〗 an alto-cumulus[cloud].

고전(古典) classics/ ~주의 classicism/ ~적 classic[al]/ ~미 classical beauty / ~학파 a classical school. こてん

고전(古錢) an ancient coin/ ~수집가 a collector of old coins. むかしのおかね

고전(苦戰) hard fighting; a desperate fight 《경기의》 a close game; a tight play / ~하다 fight hard; have a close contest. くせん

고전장(古戰場) an old battlefield.

고절(高節) lofty virtues; noble character. こうせつ

고정(固定) fixing; fixation 《자금의》tie up/ ~하다 be fixed; settle; fix/ ~급(給) a regular pay/ ~ 자본 fixed capital. こてい

고정(苦情) a tough[hard] situation; a sorry state. くじょう

고정(故情) old friendship. 昔のゆうじょう

고정(孤亭) a lonely arbo[u]r.
고제(古制) old systems; ancient institutions. こせい
고제(高弟) one's best pupil; a leading disciple. こうてい
고조(高調) ①《높은 곡조》 a high-toned melody ②《의기를 돋움》 elation; exultation; encouragement/ ~된 highly elated; inspired; exulting ③《역설》 emphasis; stress. こうちょう
고조(高潮) the high tide[water] 《극도》 the climax/ ~된 장면 a climax; a thrilling scene/ ~선(線) the high water line. たかしお
고조(枯凋) withering; decay; decline; blight/ ~하다 wither; decay; decline; be blighted. こちょう
고조(高祖) ①the founder of a dynasty [a sect] ②《고조부》 a great-great-grandfather. こうそ
고조(古調) an old tune; an ancient air. ふるめかしいちょうし
고조고(高祖考) one's deceased great-great-grandfather.
고조모(高祖母) one's great-great-grandmother. こうそば
고조부(高祖父) one's great-great-grandfather. こうそふ
고조비(高祖妣) one's deceased great-great-grandmother.
고족 제자(高足弟子) an eminent disciple [pupil]; one's best pupil. ゆうしゅうなでし
고종(古鍾) an ancient bell. ふるいかね
고종(姑從) a cousin by one's father's sister. いとこ
고죄(告罪) a confession/ ~하다 confess one's sins. つみをこくはくすること
고주(孤舟) a solitary boat. こしゅう
고주(雇主) an employer; a master; a hirer. こしゅ
고주(苦酒) a hard[dry] liquor; a strong wine. きついさけ
고주망태 [dead] drunkenness/ ~가 되다 get[be] dead drunk; be boozy.
고주파(高周波) 《물》 high-frequency.
고즈넉하다 (be) quiet and lonely/고즈넉이 quiet[ly] and alone. さびしい
고증(考證) inquiry; research; study/~하다 study; investigate; inquire into / ~학(學) the methodology of historical researches. こうしょう
고지¹ 《호박 따위의》 chopped and dried pumpkins, eggplant, etc.
(かぼちゃ・なすなどの)乾物
고지² 《메주 만드는》 a wooden frame for pressing malt, boiled beans, etc. into a lump. ふね
고지(故地) one's native place; one's former haunts. むかしのえんこのあるどころ
고지(古址) [historic] remains. こし
고지(高地) high ground; a hill 《고원》 a plateau. こうち
고지(告知) a notice; a notification; an information/ ~하다 notify; inform /《납세》 ~서 a notice [for payment of tax]. こくち
고지(固持) ~하다 hold fast to; adhere to; persist in. こじ
고지기(庫一) a warehouse keeper; a store keeper〈영〉. そうこをまもるやくにん
고지새 《조》 a migratory Chinese grosbeak.
고지식하다 (be) simple and honest; simple-minded; unadaptable. ばかしょうじき
고진 감래(苦盡甘來) Sweet after bitter, Pleasure follows pain.
고질(痼疾) an inveterate[a chronic] disease. こしつ
고집(固執) persistence; obstinacy; adherence/ ~하다 persist in; adhere to; hold fast to/ ~장이 an obstinate person/ ~센 stubborn; obstinate; headstrong; self-willed/ 자기 설을 ~하다 hold fast to one's view. こしつ
고집다 ①《손가락으로》 pinch; give a pinch to ②《꼬집어 말하다》 be sarcastic[cynical] (about); say spiteful things; make cynical remarks. つねる
고집 불통(固執不通) extreme obstinacy [stubbornness, perversity, bigotry, persistence]/ ~하다 (be) extremely obstinate[stubborn, perverse, bigoted, persistent].
고집통이 a stubborn[stiff-necked] fellow; an obstinate person; a pigheaded person. いじっぱり
고차 방정식(高次方程式) 《수》 an equation of higher degree.
고착(固着) adherence sticking/ ~하다 adhere[cohere, stick] to/ ~색(色) fast colour. こちゃく
고찰(古刹) an old[ancient] temple. こさつ
고찰(考察) consideration; study/~하다 consider; study; examine/사회 문제 에 관한 ~ a study of the social problem. こうさつ
고참(古參) seniority 《사람》 a senior; a veteran/ ~병 a veteran conscript; a senior comrade. こさん
고창(高唱) ~하다 《노래》 sing loudly 《창도》 advocate; stress. こうしょう
고챙이 a spit; a skewer; a spear; a prod. さきのとがったもの
고천문(告天文) an announcement to Heaven[God].
고철(古鐵) scrap iron; [pieces of] old metal; ferrous scraps. ふるいてつ
고체(古體) orchaic style[form] archaism. こたい
고체(固體) a solid[body]. こたい
고쳐 again; over again/~ 쓰다 rewrite.
고초(苦楚) hardships; sufferings; troubles; trials/ ~를 겪다 suffer [hardships]; have one's trials. しんく
고총(古塚) an old mound[tomb].
고추¹ red pepper; cayenne pepper/ ~가

루 powdered red pepper. とうがらし
**고추²** (곧게) upright; erect; straight; in a straight line; in a beeline. まっすぐに
**고추바람** a biting[piercing, cutting] wind. からいかぜ
**고추박이** a low woman's husband. いやしいおんながおっとをいう卑語
**고추상투** a small topknot.
**고추잠자리** a red dragonfly.
**고추장**(—醬) thick soypaste mixed with red peppers. とうがらしみそ
**고충**(苦衷) a painful position; a dilemma; a predicament; solicitude/~을 알아주다 appreciate *one's* painful position; sympathize with one in a predicament. くちゅう
**고충실도**(高忠實度) 《전축 따위의》 high-fidelity (略: hi-fi).
**고취**(鼓吹) inspiration 《창도》 advocacy /~하다 inspire; instil; stir up; advocate/애국심을 ~하다 instil[infuse] patriotism into the hearts of (*people*).こすい
**고층**(高層) 《건물의》 higher stories; upper floors 《대기의》 the upper layer/~의 high-storied (*building*)/~ 건물 a tall building. こうそう
**고치** a (silk) cocoon. まゆ
**꼬치** food on a skewer; skewered stuff. くしざし
**꼬치꼬치** ①~ 마르다 be nothing but skin and bones; be worn to shadow/~ 캐묻다 be inquisitive (*about*); make a searching inquiry; ask inquisitively. やせこけたようす
**고치다** ①《치료》 cure; heal; remedy/환자의 병을 ~ cure a patient of his illness ②《수리》 mend; repair; fix [up] 〈미〉/기계를 ~ repair a machine ③《교정(矯正)》 remedy; reform; correct /결점을 ~ correct *one's* shortcomings ④《정정》 correct; rectify; amend/틀린 데를 ~ correct errors[mistakes] ⑤《변경》 change; alter; shift/시간표를 ~ change the schedule ⑥《번역》 translate (*into*)/영어를 우리말로 ~ translate English into Korean ⑦《조정》 set right; put in order; adjust/복장을 ~ adjust *one's* dress; tidy *oneself*. なおす
**고침**(高枕) 《높은 베개》 high pillow 《편한 생활》 a peaceful life. たかいまくら
**고칭**(古稱) an old name[designation]; an archaic term. むかしのなまえ
**고탑**(古塔) an old tower; an ancient pagoda.
**고태**(古態) on old state of things; an antique and elegant appearance/ ~의연하다 remain unchanged[as it was]. むかしながらのさま
**고토**(膏土) rich[fertile] soil[land]. ひよくなつち
**고토**(故土) *one's* native land; *one's* native place; *one's* [old] home. こきょう
**고통**(苦痛) 《아픔》 pain; 《괴로움》 suffering; 《마음의》 agony; anguish/심한 ~

pang/ ~을 느끼다 feel a pain; suffer (*pain*); be in pain. くつう
**고투**(古套) an old style; a conventional form.
**꼬투리** ①《깍지》 a pod; a legume; a hull; a shell; a sheath; a shuck ②《사건의 발단》 cause; reason; origin [of an affair]. すいがら
**고판**(古版) an old edition 《책》 old books in block print 《판》 an old printing block.
**고판**(古版) 《책》-old books[editions] 《옛목판》on old printing[engraving] block.
**고패** a pulley/고팻줄 a pulley cord[rope]. かっしゃ
**고팽이** ①《새끼의》 a fold; a coil ②《왕복》 a return trip; a round trip. ひとまき
**고평**(高評) your criticism. こうひょう
**고평**(考評) review; comment; criticism / ~하다 review; comment (*on*); criticize. こうしてひひょうすること
**고푸리다, 꼬푸리다** stoop; lean over (앞으로) bend forward. かがむ
**고풍**(古風) an antique style; old fashion[manner]/ ~에 따르다 follow the old ways. こふう
**고프다** (be) hungry; famished〈미〉/배가 ~ feel hungry. ひもじい
**고하**(高下) 《지위의》 rank 《품질의》 quality 《시세의》 fluctuations; rise and fall/품질이 ~ 여러 가지이다 be various in quality. こうげ
**고하다**(告—) tell; inform; announce/ 종언(終焉)을 ~ come to an end. つげる
**-고 하여** on the ground[s] that…/뇌물을 먹었다고 ~ 실직되었다 He got fired on the ground that he had taken a bribe.
**고학**(苦學) studying under adversity/ ~하다 study under adversity; work *one's* way [through *college*]/ ~생 a self-supporting student.
**고함**(高喊) a shout; an outcry; a yell; a shriek/ ~지르다[치다] shout; cry; make an outcry; shriek; roar; howl. こうせいでしっこうすること
**고해**(苦海) the bitter human world 《불》 this world. くかい
**고해**(告解) 《종》 confession.
**고행**(苦行) asceticism; penance 《종교상의》 religious austerities/ ~하다 practise asceticism; do penance/ ~자 an ascetic. くぎょう
**고향**(故鄕) *one's* home; *one's* native place; *one's* birthplace/제2의 ~ *one's* second home; *one's* land of adoption/~을 그리워하다 long for home; be homesick. こきょう
**고현학**(考現學) study on modern phenomena; modernology. こうげんがく
**고혈**(膏血) sweat and blood/백성의 ~ 빨아먹다[짜내다] exploit[sweat] the people. こうけつ
**고혈압**(高血壓) high blood-pressure/ ~증 hyperpiesia; hypertension/ ~ 환자

고형 (固形) solidity／ ～의 solid／ ～물[체] a solid body; a solid. けい

고호 (古號) an old[ancient] designation; a name[pen name] used in the old days. むかしのな

고혹 (蠱惑) fascination; enchantment (유혹) seduction／ ～적인 fascinating; attractive; alluring. こわく

고혼 (孤魂) a solitary spirit. ひとりさりいくたましい

고화 (古畵) an ancient picture; an old painting. むかしのえ

고환 (睾丸) the testicles ‥불알／ ～염 (炎) orchitis. こうがん

고훈 (古訓) the teachings of the ancients; an old precept. こくん

고휼 (顧恤) compassionate; care and relief／ ～하다 patronage; look after out of compassion. あわれみたすけること

고희 (古稀) three scores and ten／연세가 ～에 이르다 obtain *one's* 70th year of age. こき

꼭 ①(단단히) tightly; fast; firmly; securely／～ 묶다 bind[tie] (*a thing*) tightly; fasten tight／～ 쥐다 grasp; grip; hold (*a thing*) tightly[fast]; take fast hold of ②(빠듯이)tight[ly]; closely／～ 끼는 모자 a tight cap／새 신 받이 ～ 껀다 My new shoes pinch. ③(정확히) just; exactly; right; precisely／ ～ 1시간 just an hour; one hour to the minute ④(반드시) surely; certainly; no doubt; for sure without fail; by all means; at any cost; in any case／～ 오게 Never fail to come., Come without fail[by all means]. ⑤(마치) as if[though]; as it were; just like／ ～ 죽은 사람 같다 look as if dead. きっと. しっかり

곡 (曲) (음악의) a tune; an air; a piece; music; a melody. きょく

곡 (哭) wailing; lamentation; keening／ ～하다 lament about; bewail; weep; keen. おおごえでなくこと

곡가 (穀價) the price of grain. こくもつのねだん

곡간 (谷澗) a mountain stream; a rill. たにのながれ

곡경 (曲境) a difficult[hard] position; a sad plight[predicament]; difficulties／～에 있는 사람을 돕다 help (*a person*) in trouble. くきょう

곡곡 (曲曲) ①(굴곡) curves; turns; twists ②(도처) the whole length and breadth of the land.

곡괭이 a pick; a picker; a pickax[e]. つるはし

곡구 (曲球) a curve [ball]; 《야구》 a bender 《당구》 a fancy shot.

곡기 (穀氣) food／환자는 이틀 간 ～를 입에 못 댔다 The patient was unable to take any food for two days.

곡대기 ①(물건의) the top; the summit; the peak; the crest; the crown ②(사람)a boss; the chief; the head; a top man. ちょうじょう

곡두 《환영》 a phantom 《환상》 a vision 《착각》 an illusion; a delusion／～ 같은 dreamlike. あやつりにんぎょう

곡두새벽 daybreak; dawn; peep of day. はやいよあけ

곡둑각시 a puppet; a marionette／～놀음 a puppet show. おんなのにんぎょう

곡뒤 《뒤통수의》 the back of the head.

곡뒤누르다 oppress; repress; keep[hold, put] down; have (*a person*) under *one's* thumb[control].

곡뒤눌리다 be oppressed; be repressed; be dominated; be under (*a person's*) thumb.

곡뒤지르다 go ahead (*of*); precede; forestall (*a person*); be beforehand with (*a person*); get the start of (*a person*); steal a march upon (*a person*). せんてをうつ

곡뒤질리다 be forestalled (*by*); get beaten to something. せんてをうたれる

곡론 (曲論) sophistry; a biased argument; a distorted[devious] argument; casuistry. きょくろん

곡류 (穀類) cereals; corn; grain〈미〉. こくるい

곡류 (曲流) a meander; a meandering stream; a winding stream. だこう

곡률 (曲率) curvature／～ 중심[반경] the center[radius] of curvature. きょくせんやきょくめんのまがりのていど

곡마 (曲馬) a circus; equestrian feats／ ～단 a circus [troupe]. きょくば

곡면 (曲面) a curved surface. きょくめん

곡목 (曲目) a program[me]; a selection; a musical number. きょくもく

곡물 (穀物) corn; cereals; grain〈미〉／～ 장수 a corn factor. こくもつ

곡보 (曲譜) musical notes; a music; a score. きょくふ

곡복 사신 (穀腹絲身) food and clothing. たべものときもの

곡사 (曲射) high-angle fire／～포 a howitzer. きょくしゃ

곡상 (穀商) a grain dealer[merchant]; a corn factor〈영〉. こくもつしょう

곡선 (曲線) a curve; a curved line／～미 the beauty of contour[line]; curve beauty／ ～미(美)의 너인 a curvaceous woman. きょくせん

곡설 (曲說) a sophistry; a biased argument.

곡성 (哭聲) a cry; a wail. なきさけぶこえ

곡식 (穀食) cereals; corn; grain〈미〉. こくもつ

곡신 (穀神) the God of Cereals; Ceres. こくもつをつかさどるしん

곡예 (曲藝) [acrobatic] feats; stunts; tricks; fancy performances／ ～사 an acrobat／ ～ 비행 stunt flying; airstu-

곡읍(哭泣) lamentation; wailing/〜하다 lament aloud; wail; weep bitterly. こえをたててなくこと

곡장(曲墻) a round mud parapet at the back of grave.

곡절(曲折) ①(우회) meandering; turns and twists (파란) vicissitudes; ups and downs (착종) intricacies; complications of an affair/인생의 파란 〜 the vicissitudes[the ups and downs] of life ②(까닭)reason; the whys and hows (사정) circumstances/무슨 〜인지 for some unknown reason/ 〜을 말하다 explain the reasons. きょくせつ

곡조(曲調) a tune; an air; a melody; strains; music. きょくちょう

꼭지 ①(식물의) the stem; the stalk ②(그릇·뚜껑의)the handle; the knob ③(거지·단군의 두목)a boss; the head ④(도리깨의) the pivot of a flail ⑤(묶음)a bunch (of laundry); a clump. へた

꼭지딴 the head of security officials.

꼭지마리 the handle of a spinning wheel.

꼭지표 a stem-winder watch; a watch. ぜんまいまきのとけい

곡직(曲直) right or[and] wrong; merits (of a case). きょくちょく

꼭짓집 a building where laundry bundles are taken to be counted after washing.

꼭차다 be chockfull; be full up; be filled to the brim; be packed solid; be crowded (with). みちる

곡창(穀倉) ①(창고)a granary; a grain elevator〈미〉; a silo ②[많이 나는 데]a granary. こくそう

곡척(曲尺) 〔목수의〕a metal measure; a carpenter's square ⇒곱자. かねじゃく

곡필(曲筆) perversion[falsification, misrepresentation, distortion] in writing. きょくひつ

곡하다(曲ー) 《바르지 않다》(be) untrue; irrational; unjust; unreasonable 《고깝다》vexing. りくつにあわない

곡학(曲學) prostitution of learning/ 〜아세지도(阿世之徒) literary sycophants. きょくがく

곡해(曲解) distortion; misinterpretation; strained interpretation; perversion/ 〜하다 interpret wrongly; misconstrue; twist. きょっかい

곡향(穀鄕) a granary. こくそう

곤경(困境) an awkward position; a predicament; a fix/〜에 빠지다 be thrown into a fix; be placed in an awkward position. くるしいたちば

곤고(困苦) hardships; sufferings; prevations. こんく

곤곤(滾滾) 〜히 ceaselessly/〜히 흐르다 gush down. こんこん

곤군(困窘) poverty; destitution; needy circumstances/〜하다 (be) very poor; be hard up. ひんこん

곤궁(困窮) poverty; destitution; distress /〜한 poor; needy; destitute; distressed/ 〜한 사람들 the poor; the needy. こんきゅう

곤대 the stem of a taro. たろいものみき

곤맷짓 arrogant[overbearing, haughty] behavior; cocky attitude/〜하다 (be) arrogant. いばらってあたまをふること

곤두박이다 fall upon one's head; fall head over heels/곤두박이치다 fall headlong. まっさかさまにおちる

곤두서다 stand erect[upright, on end] 《털이》bristle up. さかたちする

곤두세우다 set on end. とうりつさせる

곤드라지다 drop off to sleep; sink into a slumber.

곤드레만드레 drunk as a fiddler/ 〜가 되다 be dead drunk. ふらふら

곤란(困難) difficulty 《성가심》trouble 《곤궁》distress; hardships 《낭처》embarrassment; perplexity/ 〜한 difficult; hard; troublesome; awkward; needy; distressed/ 재정 〜 financial difficulty/ 〜을 극복하다 overcome a difficulty/ 〜을 받다 have difficulty (in); feel difficulty. こんなん

곤룡포(袞龍袍) a royal robe; an Imperial robe. おおさまのせいふく

곤봉(棍棒) a club; a cudgel 《체조용》an Indian club 《순경의》a truncheon/ 〜체조 an Indian club exercise. こんぼう

곤쇠아비동갑(一同甲) a wicked[foxy] old man. ずるいおいぼれ

곤액(困厄) trouble; misfortune; suffering; hardships. なんぎ

곤욕(困辱) extreme insult; bitter affront. こんじょく

곤이(鯤鮞) milt (of fish); hard roe.

곤장(棍杖) a long flat wooden implement for flogging criminals/ 〜을 안기다 flog.

곤쟁이 a kind of shrimp/ 〜젓 a kind of shrimp preserved with salt.

곤죽 ①《진창》quagmire ②《뒤범벅》mess; utter confusion. ぬかるみ

곤줄매기 〔조〕a wood-cracker; a titmouse.

곤지 rouge/ 〜 찍다 put rouge on one's forehead. かおにつける·べに

끈질끈질하다 (be) over-meticulous; excessively scrupulous; be too fussy. あまりにもほそかすぎる

곤충(昆蟲) an insect/〜학 entomology; insectology/ 〜학자 an entomologist/ 〜[채집]망(網) an insect net/〜 채집 insect collecting. こんちゅう

곤핍(困乏) fatigue; weariness; exhaustion/ 〜하다 (be) fatigued; tired; exhausted; weary. こんぱい

곤하다(困一) (be) exhausted; weary; fatigued; dog-tired/〜몹시 〜 be ready to drop [with fatigue]; be tired to death/곤히 자다 sleep like a top[a log].

**꿇다** mark; give marks; grade; rate. つかれている　さいてんする

**끈** at once; immediately; directly without delay 《이내》 soon／~ 지금 ~ this very instant; right now／식사가 끝나자 ~ right[immediately] after dinner ～ …하다 lose no time in …ing; do … without delay／ ~ 돌아오겠다 I'll come back soon. すぐ(に)

**끈날대패** a straight-blade plane. かたなを90度にしたかんな

**끈다** ①《물건이》(be) straight; upright／곧은 길 a straight road ②《마음이》(be) honest; upright／곧은 사람 a man of upright character. まっすぐだ

**끈바로** at once; straightly. すぐに

**끈바르다** (be) straight and right. まっすぐだ

**끈은창자** ①【해】 the rectum ②《고지식한 사람》 a naive[tactless] person／ ~의 rectal. ちょくちょう

**끈이끈대로** frankly; plainly; honestly／~ 말하다 tell the truth. しょうじきに

**끈이듣다** take (one's word) seriously; accept (a thing) as truth swallow／남의 말을 ~ take another's words as truth. だまされる

**끈잘** 《꽤 잘》 fairly well; readily; pretty good. ほんとうによく

**끈장** directly; straight／ ~ 집으로 돌아가다 go straight home. いつも

**끈추** straight; in a straight line; upright; perpendicularly; vertically／ ~ 앉다 sit up straight[erect]. ちょくりつ

**끌**[1] 《노여움》 anger; dander; temper／ ~ 나다 get angry. おこり

**끌**[2] 《틀》 a block; a mold; a cast. かた

**끌**[3] 《금》 the crease made when a sheet of cloth, paper, or cardboard is folded into two equal parts 《머리의》 an even hair part down the middle of one's head. おりめ

**끌**[4] 《골수》 the marrow (of bones); the medulla 《머리골》 the brain. こつずい

**꼴**[1] 《모양》 shape; form 《외양》 appearance 《복장》 clothes 《체제》 respectability 《상태》 a state; a condition; a situation 《광경》 a sight; a spectacle; a scene 《경멸적》 face; countenance. かたち

**꼴**[2] 《먹이》 feed; fodder; forage. まぐさ

**-꼴** 《접미어》 at the rate of; per unit／쇠고기는 한 근에 800원~로 판매되고 있다 Beef is sold at the rate of 800 won a keun. ―ねうち

**꼴깍** gulping down ⇒꿀꺽. ごくり

**꼴갱이** ①《단단한 부분》 a core; the heart ②《골자》 the gist; the pith. しん(芯)

**골격(骨格)** frame; build. こっかく

**골계(滑稽)** humour; a joke; a jest; pleasantry／ 문학 humorous literature／ ~화(畵) a caricature. こっけい

**골고래** 《방고래》 a hypocaust system with several flue entries.

**골고루** among all; indiscriminately／~ 나누어 주다 divide among all without discrimination. びょうどう

**꼴꼴** trickling／ ~ 흐르다 trickle; ripple; bubble. ちょろちょろ

**꼴꼴하다** suffer from a chronic disease; suffer constantly from weak health／꼴꼴하는 사람 a confirmed invalid.

**꼴군** a mower (of fodder). まぐさをかるひと

**꼴김** a moment of anger[temper]／ ~ 에 사람을 치다 beat (a person) in a fit of anger. はこったひょうし

**골다** 《코를》 snore／드렁드렁 코를 ~ snore heavily. いびきをかく

**골답(—畓)** a rich[productive] paddy.

**골땅땅이(骨—)** a kind of dominoes. こっぱいあそびのひとつ

**골똘하다** be absorbed in; be devoted to; be given to. むちゅうだ

**골동(骨董)** curios; objects[articles] of virtu／ ~품(品) curios; antiques／ ~ 품상 a curio[sity] shop 《사람》 a curio dealer／ ~품 애호가 a virtuoso; a curioso. こっとう

**꼴뚜기** 【어】 a kind of octopus; Octopus ocellatus《학명》. いいだこ

**꼴뚜기장수** an octopus dealer 《비유적》 a man of broken fortunes. たこしょうばいにん

**골라잡다** select; choose; take one's choice. えらんでもつ

**골락새** 【조】 a woodpecker.

**골마루** a rear veranda[h]. せまいろうか

**골마지** scum. うきかす

**골막(骨膜)** 【해】 the periosteum／ ~염(炎) periostitis. こつまく

**골막이** 【전】 plastering between rafters.

**골머리** the brain; the head／ ~를 앓다 be troubled; be annoyed. のうずい

**골목** an alley; a by-street／막다른 ~ a blind alley／ ~ 대장 the cock of the walk; the boss of youngsters of the neighborhood. うらとおり

**골몰(汨沒)** engrossment; absorption／~ 하다 be absorbed in; be engrossed in; be devoted to／일에 ~하다 be engrossed in one's work. ねっちゅうすること

**골무** a thimble. ゆびぬき

**골무떡** thimble-shaped pieces of rice cake.

**골밀이** 【전】 a groove in the sash of a window[door].

**골박다** limit it (to a fixed sphere); keep it [to its intended shape]. せいげんする

**골반(骨盤)** 【해】 the pelvis. こつばん

**골방(—房)** a back room; a closet; a small room attached to the main room. おしいれ

**골병** a deep-rooted[-seated] illness[injury]; an internal injury 《타격》 a mortal blow.

**골분(骨粉)** powdered bones; bone-dust／ ~ 비료 bone manure. こつぶん

**골불견(—不見)** ugliness; shabbiness; fu-

꼴사납다 / ~이다 look funny; be a sight to see; be an ugly scene; be unsightly; be unbecoming; be shabby.

꼴사납다 (be) ugly; unbecoming; unsightly; disgusting; detestable; shameful; indecent. いまいましい

골산(骨山) a rocky mountain.

골상(骨相) physiognomy; one's features / ~학 phrenology. こっそう

골생원(一生員) 《옹졸한》 a little soul 《허약한》 a weak person. ころうなひと

골속 ①《머리 속》 the brains ②《골풀 속》 the heart of a rush ③《왕골 속》 the heart of a sedge. のうずいのなか

골수(骨髓) the marrow / ~에 사무치다 cut deep into one's heart / ~염 《의》 osteomyelitis. こつずい

골안개 the morning mist in the valley.

골육(骨肉) one's own flesh and blood; kindred; blood relations / ~ 상잔 a strife among fresh and blood. こつにく

골자(骨子) the gist; the essence; the main point / 문제의 ~ the gist of the question. かなめ

골짜기 a valley; a vale 《협곡》 a ravine; a dale; a gorge / 산~ a ravine; a gorge. おくふかいたにま

골저리다(骨—) be chilled to the bone. ほねまでしびれる

골절(骨折) a fracture [of a bone] / ~하다 suffer a fracture. こっせつ

골절(骨節) a joint. ほねぶし

꼴찌 the last; the bottom; the tail end; the last man (in a race). さいごのもの

꼴찌락 ~거리다 splash; splatter; plop. じゃぶじゃぶ

골질(骨質) bony tissue. こっしつ

골창 a ditch; a gutter; a drain.

골초(一草) 《질이 낮은 담배》 tobacco[cigarette] of inferior quality 《사람》 a heavy smoker; a chain smoker. しつのわるいにがいタバコ

골치 the head / ~아픈 문제 a troublesome question / ~앓다 be troubled; be annoyed; be worried / ~가 아프다 have a head-ache. あたま

골치다 put (a thing) on the block [mold, last] for shaping. かたをすえる

골탄(骨炭) animal[bone] charcoal; boneblack. こつたん

골탕(一湯) ①《골국》 a soup made of fried ox-brain or ox-marrow coated with flour ② great injury[insult] / ~먹다 suffer a big loss; be cheated; suffer an injury. むごいそんがい

골통 the head the skull. あたま

골통(骨痛) 《의》 ostalgia; bone pain[aches]. ほねいたみ

골통대 a [tobacco-]pipe.

골틀리다 get angry; be vexed; be offended; be displeased; sulk; become cross; get upset (with a person, at a thing). おこりをふかいにおもう

골파 a variety of leek. ねぎ

골패(骨牌) a domino. こっぱい

골풀 《식》 the common rush. とうしんぐさ

골풀무 a kind of bellows. つちをほってつくったふいご

골풀이 ~하다 vent one's anger[wrath, rage]; give vent to one's anger; work off one's anger an (a person).

골필(骨筆) a stylus; a stencil pen; an iron pen; a horn pen. かくさいのペン

골학(骨學) 《해》 osteology.

골함석 corrugated sheet iron[zinc]. なまこトタン

골혹(骨—) 《의》 a bone tumor. ほねこぶ

골회(骨灰) bone ashes. ほねをやいてつくったこな

곪다 《상처가》 gather; fester; form pus 《일이》 (an affair) come to a head / 종기가 ~ a festers. うむ

곬 《물길》 a waterway; a watercourse 《방향》 a [fixed] direction 《유래》 origin; source; cause / 물~ a channel; a watercourse; a drain.

곯다¹ ①《배를》 go hungry; starve. うえる

곯다² ①《썩이》 rot 《달걀이》 addle / 곯은 달걀 bad eggs ②《엉걸들다》 suffer; sustain damage; receive injuries. くさる

곯리다¹ ①《배를》 leave (someone) still hungry ②《그릇에》 underfill; leave half-empty.

곯리다² spoil[addle, rot] (something) make (it) stale 《해롭게 하다》 do harm to; cause damage to; play trick; vex; embarrass; put in an awkward position. くさらせる

곯아떨어지다 《술에》 lie with liquor; be dead drunk; be helplessly drunk 《잠에》 be dead asleep. しんだようにねむる

곰 ①《동》 a bear / ~ 새끼 a [bear's] cub / ~ 가죽 bearskin ②《사람》 a fat-head; dullard. くま

곰곰 carefully; deeply; deliberately / ~ 생각하다 think (a matter) over [and over]; reflect carefully; muse on ponder over. じっくり

꼼꼼하다 (be) very carefully; scrupulous; elaborate; conscientious; deliberate; attentive; detailed / 꼼꼼히 carefully; minutely; elaborately; in detail. ちゅういふかい

곰국 a thick beef soup.

꼼바르다 (be) niggardly; stingy; (be) illiberal. けちんぼうだ

꼼바리 a meticulous[scrupulous] person; an attentive[a conscientious] person. きちょうめんでせまくけちなひと

곰방대 a short [tobacco-]pipe.

곰방메 a mallet [used for crumbling clods of earth when covering seeds].

곰배팔이 a person with a deformed [mutilated] arm. かたうでのひと

곰보 a pockmarked person. あばた

곰비임비 in [rapid] succession; one after another; upon heels of another;

manifoldly overlapped. かさねて
**곰살갑다** 《너그럽다》(be) generous; broad-minded 《다정스럽다》 delicate; tender; kind; cordial; good; gentle.
**곰살궂다** (be) gentle; meek; kind; good; cordial. ていねいだ
**곰상곰상** ~하다 ①(be) gentle and kind ②(be) meticulous; narrow-minded.
**곰솔** 《식》 a Japanese black pine; *Pinus thunbergii*(학명).
**곰실거리다, 곰실거리다** wriggle; writhe; squirm. しきりにうごめく
**곰작, 곰짝, 곰짝** budging; stirring; moving/~거리다 stir[about]; move[about]/~하다 budge; stir; move/~하면 죽는다 One move and you are a dead man/기계가 ~ 않는다 The machine won't work at all/그는 ~ 않고 서 있다 He is standing motionless. のろのろ. ぐずぐず
**꼼짝 못하다** ①《움직이지 못하다》be unable to move[budge] an inch ②《곤경에 빠지다》be in a fix; be in a [perfect] dilemma; stick in the mud; get into a fix ③《기를 못 펴다》be under (*a person's*) thumb; be cowed; be intimidated. びくともみうごきできない
**꼼짝없다** (be) helpless; inevitable; unavoidable; without resource/꼼짝없이 helplessly; inevitably; with no way out. どうすることもできない
**곰지락, 꼼지락** ~거리다 move suggishly; stir leisurely; get about lazily; make a move. のろのろ
**곰틀, 꼼틀** with a wriggle[wiggle]/~ 하다 give a wiggle; wiggle; twist/뱀이 ~거리다 A snake twists[wriggles] to and fro. からだをひねってうごかすさま
**곰팡** mold; mildew ⇒곰팡이/~나다 grow mouldy/~ 냄새 mustiness/~슬다[피다] mildew; get musty. かび
**곰팡이** mo[u]ld; mildew; must. かび
**곱**[1] double; times/~하다 multiply; (*a number by*); double (*it*)/두 ~ double; twice; twofold; two times/세 ~treble; three times/네~ quadruple. ばい
**곱**[2] 《부스럼 따위의》 a mucous discharge [usually on a skin wound]/~ 똥 mucous feces/눈~ a mucous discharge from the eyes; matter[gum] in an eye; eye wax. かさぶた
**곱꺾이** bending and stretching a joint.
**곱걸다** ①《노름에서》 double (*one's bet*) ②《겹쳐 얽다》 double-bind. ばいにかける
**곱놓다** double (*one's bet*).
**곱다**[1] 《아름답다》 (be) beautiful; lovely; fair; fine; nice; good-looking 《가루가》 fine. うつくしい
**곱다**[2] 《휘다》 (be) bent; stooped/허리가 ~ be stooped. すこしまがっている
**곱다**[3] 《손놀이》 (be) numb[benumbed](*with cold*) /~이가 have *one's* teeth set on edge/추워서 손가락이 ~ *one's* limbs are numb with cold. しびれる

**꼽다** count (on *one's fingers*); number; reckon; take a count (*of*)/손꼽아 세다 count on *one's* fingers/날짜를 ~ [count reckon] the days. ゆびをまげてかぞえる
**곱다랗다** ①《아름답다》(be) very beautiful [pretty, lovely] ②《보존》(be) left intact. ひじょうにうつくしい
**곱돌** 《광》 a kind of alabaster. ろうせき
**곱똥** mucous feces. ねばいだいべん
**곱드러지다** stumble over[upon, against] (*something*); trip over[on]; lose[miss] *one's* footing. たおれる
**곱들다** 《갑절들다》 cost twice as much [as]; take twice as much [as].
**곱들이다** spend[put out] twice as much [as]; consume twice as much [as]/공을 ~ take twice as much trouble.
**곱디디다** take a false step and break *one's* ankle. つまずく
**곱바** a rope attached to an A-frame to tie a load.
**곱배기** ①《술》 a double the ordinary cup of liquor 《요리》 a double-the-ordinary dish a double measure of wine ②《두 번 거듭》 two times. ばいのぶんりょう
**곱사등이** a crookback; a hunchback/~의 hunchbacked. せむし
**곱살끼다** be fretful fret. せがむ
**곱살스럽다** 《얼굴이》(be) pretty beautiful tender. かおだちがよい
**곱새기다** misconstrue; misinterpret; interpret wrong. ごかいする
**곱셈** multiplication. じょうほう
**곱소리** elephant-tail hair.
**곱송그리다** flinch; wince; shrink; crouch. いしゅくする
**곱슬곱슬하다** (be) curled; curly; frizzled; wavy. けがちぢれている
**곱씹다** 《말 따위를》rechew; repeat (*a word*) 《다짐받듯》 harp on (*a question*).
**곱은성**(一城) a circular wall protecting a castle gate.
**곱자** a carpenter's square; a metal footmeasure. かねじゃく
**곱잡다** take[treat, figure] (*it*) double.
**곱장다리** bowlegs 《사람》 a bowlegged person. がにまた
**곱장선**(一扇) a kind of fan.
**곱재기** ①《때》 dirt; filth; grime 《눈곱》 gum ②《아주 작은 물건》 a bit[trifle, mite]. あか
**곱쟁이** double. ばいのすいりょう
**곱절** 《두 배》 times; fold/두 ~ double; twice; twofold/두 ~의 양[수] twice as much[many] as. ばい
**곱창** the small intestines of cattle 《돼지의》 chitterlings. うしのしょうちょう
**곱치다, 꼽치다** double; fold up/값을 ~ double a price. ふたつにおる
**곱하다** double (*it*). かける
**곳** 《장소》 a place 《좁은 곳》 a spot 《현장》 a scene 《지역》 district/안전한 ~ a place of safety/숨을 ~ a hiding place/가는 ~마다 everywhere; wherever

곳간(一間) a storeroom; a repository/ ～차 a boxcar(미). ばしょ そうこ

곳곳 《부사적》 on all sides; in several places; in spots; here and there; everywhere. あちこち

꼿꼿하다 ①(곧다)(be) straight; upright; erect ②(정직하다)(be) honest; upright; straight; straightforward; firm; strong ③(굳다)(be) hard; tough; stiff. こうちょくしている

곳집 a warehouse; a storehouse. そうこ

공 《볼》 a ball; a handball 《원구》 a circle; a sphere/ ～타기 walking on a ball/ ～을 던지다 throw a ball. まり

공(空) 《영(零)》 zero; cipher 《무(無)》 naught 《허사》 nothing 《빔》 emptiness. から

공(功) [meritorious] services; merits; a meritorious deeds/ ～을 세우다 render meritorious services; perform a meritorious deed; serve with distinction/ ～들이다 elaborate; exert oneself; take pains. こう

공(公) ①(공사) public matters; public affairs/ ～과 사를 구별하다 draw the line between public and private matters ②(공작) a prince (영국의)a duke /에딘버러 ～ the Duke of Edinburgh. おおやけ

공(工) 《직공》 a worker; a mechanic; a workman /인쇄～ a pressman. こう

공가(空家) a vacant house. あきや

공가(工價) wages; pay for work ⇒공전.

공간(空間) space 《여지》room/～적 spatial. くうかん

공갈(恐喝) a threat; a blackmail; a menace; intimidation/～하다 threaten blackmail/～ 취재(取材) blackmail; extortion by threats. きょうかつ

공감(共感) sympathy; response/ ～하다 sympathize (with a person). きょうかん

공개(公開) opening to the public/ ～하다 [throw] open to the public 《진열》 exhibit 《영화 따위의》release/～된 open [to the public]/～장 an open letter/ ～회의 an open session. こうかい

공검(恭儉) respectfulness and modesty /～하다 (be) respectful and modest. きょうけん

공것 a thing that can be had for nothing.;an article obtained without cost; a gift. ただのもの

공격(攻擊) an attack; an assault; a drive; a push 《비난》an attack; censure / ～하다 attack; assail; assault; charge 《비난》attack; censure; criticize/ 총～ a general attack/불의의 ～ a surprise attack/～군 an attacking force 《야구》 the team at bat/～ 정신 an offensive spirit/ ～ 개시 시간 H-hour; Zero. こうげき

공겸(恭謙) modesty; humility; courteousness; deference/～하다 (be) modest; humble; courteous; deferential.

공경(公卿) a court noble. くぎょう

공경(恭敬) respect; reverence respect; veneration/～하다 revere; hold (one) in esteem. そんけい

공고(公告) a public[an official] announcement[notice]/ ～하다 notify publicly; announce. こうこく

공고(鞏固) firmness; solidity; strength; constancy; stability; consolidation/ ～하다 (be) firm; stable; strong;sound /～한 유대 strong ties. きょうこ

공골말 a chestnut horse;a bay [horse]; a sorrel [horse]. きいろいうま

공골차다 (be) full; substantial; rich; solid. みちている

꽁꽁¹ 《앓는 소리》moaning; groaning. うんうん

꽁꽁² 《언 모양》 frozen hard 《숨는 모양》hiding oneself "good" getting well hidden. こちんこちん

공공(公共) the public society; the community/ ～의 public; common/ ～심 public spirit/～ 단체 a public body/ ～의 복리 public welfare/～ 사업 public enterprise; public utility /～ 기관 a public institution. こうきょう

공공연하다(公公然一) (be) open; public /공공연히 openly; in public; overtly; avowedly. こうこうぜんだ

공과(公課) public imposts; taxes. こうか

공과(工科) the engineering department /～ 대학 an engineering college. こうか

공과(功過) merits and demerits.

공관(公館) an official residence 《공사관》 a legation 《공공의 집》a public hall /재외 ～ Korean diplomatic and consular offices in foreign countries. こうかん

공관 복음(共觀福音) 《성경》a diatessaron [of the Christian Gospels].

공교롭다(工巧一) 《우연》 (be) accidental; casual 《때가 나쁘다》(be) untimely; unlucky 《의외》(be) unexpected 《때가 좋다》(be) lucky; (be) coincidental/공교롭게도 그날은 비가 왔다 The day happened to be rainy. ぐうぜんのようだ

공구(工具) a tool; an implement/기계 ～ a machine tool.

공구(恐懼) awe; dread; fear. きょうく

공국(公國) a dukedom;a [grand] duchy; a principality. こうこく

공군(空軍) an air force a flying corps /～력 air power;aerial strength/～ 기지 an air base/～ 사관 학교 an air-force academy. くうぐん

공권(公權) civil rights; citizenship/ ～ 정지 suspension of civil rights.

공권(空拳) a bare hand/(도수) ～으로 with one's naked[bare] hands. くうけん

공규(空閨) the bedchamber of a neglected wife/～를 지키다 be a lonely wife (남편 출타중) くうけい

공극(空隙) an opening; a gap. すきま

공근하다(恭勤一) (be) courteous and diligent; polite and industrious.

**공금**(公金) public funds[money]; government funds／ ~유용 misappropriation of public money; peculation／ ~횡령 embezzlement[misappropriate] of public money. こうきん

**공급**(供給) supply; provision／ ~하다 supply[furnish, provide] (one) with／ ~자 a supplier／ ~원(源) a source of supply. きょうきゅう

**공기** (돌) a jackstone 《놀이》jackstones ／ ~놀다 play jackstones. てだま

**공기**(空氣) air 《분위기》atmosphere／ ~전염 infection／ ~총[베개] an air gun [-cushion]／~제동기[압착기] a pneumatic brake[compressor]／탁한 ~ foul air／좌중의 ~ the atmosphere of a meeting／~ 요법 aerotherapy. くうき

**공기**(公器) a public organ[institution, instrument]. こうき

**공기**(空器) ①(빈 그릇) an empty vessel ②(식사용) a (rice-)bowl／밥 한 ~ a bowl of rice. くうき

**공기업**(公企業) public enterprise; a government project. こうきぎょう

**공납**(公納) public imposts; taxes.

**공납**(貢納) a tribute; a tributary payment／ ~하다 pay tribute (to).

**공낭**(空囊) an empty purse. あいたさいふ

**공능**(功能) 《효능》effect; efficacy; use; benefit avail 《공적과 재능》merits and ability. ききめ

**공단**(貢緞) woven silk without patterns; satin.

**공단**(公團) a public corporation.

**공담**(公談) an official talk; a public conversation. こうへいなはなし

**공담**(空談) an idle[empty] talk; an empty prattle; a tittle-tattle; gossip／~하다 talk idly; gossip; prattle; chatter. むだなはなし

**공답**(公畓) state-owned[national] rice field.

**공대**(恭待) an honourable treatment／ ~하다 《대접》receive (one) cordially 《존대》address with respect.

**공대**(工大) an engineering college. こうかだいがく

**공대공**(空對空) air-to-air／ ~ 미사일[유도탄] an air-to-air[guided] missile.

**공대지**(空對地) air-to-surface／ ~ 미사일 an air-to-surface [guided] missile.

**공떡**(空—) a godsend; a windfall.

**공덕**(公德) public morality／~심 public spirit. こうとく

**공덕**(功德) 〖종〗charity; a pious act; a charitable deed／~을 쌓다 accumulate virtuous deeds. こうとく

**공도**(公道) 〈도로〉a highway; a public way; a highroad〈미〉 《정의》justice; equity／~를 밟다 act with[take the path of] justice. こうどう

**공도**(公度) a common factor of measurement.

**공돈** unearned[windfall] income; easy -gotten money; easy money; gravy／~은 오래 못 간다 Lightly come, lightly go. ただもうけのおかね

**공돌다**(空—) (be) ownerless[unattached free-floating]; lack an owner. よりどころなくあちこちころがる

**공동**(共同) co-operation; concert association; union／ ~의 common; joint; public／ ~의 적 a common enemy／ ~경영 joint operation／~ 변소 a public lavatory／~ 묘지 a [public] cemetery ／~ 성명 a joint statement／~으로 jointly; in concert (with). きょうどう

**공동**(空洞) a cave; a cavern. くうどう

**공뜨다**(空—) ①lack an owner ② be free -floating. よりどころなくうかんでいる

**공득**(空得) an unearned income; a windfall[income]／ ~하다 get[gain, obtain] (a thing) for nothing[efforts]. ただでもらうこと

**공들다**(功—) require much labour; cost strenuous effort／공드는 세공 elaborate workmanship. ねんをいれる

**공들이다**(功—) elaborate; take pains; exert oneself; apply oneself to／공들인 elaborate; painstaking. ねんいりにする

**공락**(攻落) surrender／~하다 take (a castle); capture (a fort). こうらく

**공란**(空欄) a blank; a [blank] space; a column／~에 기입하다 fill up the blanks in the sheet. くうらん

**공랭식**(空冷式) air-cooling／ ~ 엔진 an air-cooled engine.

**공략**(攻略) capture 《침략》invasion; attack; occupation. こうりゃく

**공력**(公力) the power of the state; public force; legal authority.

**공력**(功力) effort; labo[u]r; elaboration; 〖종〗Buddhist merit acquired by practicing austerities. はだらき

**공로**(公路) a [public] road; a highroad; a highway. こうろ

**공로**(功勞) [meritorious] services; merits; an exploit／ ~자 a person who has done good service; a person of distinguished service／ ~장(章) a distinguished service medal. こうろう

**공로**(空路) an air route[lane]; a skylane／ ~로 귀국하다 return home by plane[air]. くうろ

**공론**(公論) 《세론》public opinion 《정론》 an impartial view. こうろん

**공론**(空論) an empty theory; an academic argument／ ~가(家) a doctrinaire. くうろん

**공뢰**(空雷) an aerial torpedo. くうらい

**공룡**(恐龍) 《고생물》a dinosaur; a titanosaur.

**공률**(工率) rate of production 〖물〗power; activity.

**공리**(公吏) a public official[servant]; an officeholder. こうり

**공리**(公利) public[common] welfare [interests]. こうり

공리(公理) 〖수〗an axiom; an maxim 《도리》a self-evident truth.

공리(功利) utility/ ~적 utilitarian/~주의 utilitarianism/~주의자 a utilitarian.　・こうり

공리(空理) an empty theory; doctrinarianism/~ 공론에 흐르다 indulge in academic controversies.　くうり

공립(公立) public institution/ ~의 public/~ 학교 a public school. こうりつ

공막(鞏膜) 〖해〗the sclera/~ 절개(切開) 수술 sclerotomy.　きょうまく

공매(公賣) public auction[sale]/ ~하다 sell by auction; sell at auction《미》/~ 처분 disposition by public sale; tax sale.　こうばい

공맹(孔孟) Confucius and Mencius.

공명(公明) fairness; justice; openness/ ~ 정대한 fair; just; open/ ~ 선거 a clean election/ ~ 정대(正大) fairness and justice; fair play.　こうめい

공명(功名) a great exploit; a glorious deed; distinction; fame/~심 aspiration; ambition/~을 세우다 distinguish oneself love of fame.　こうみょう

공명(共鳴) 《동감》sympathy; response; 〖물〗resonance/ ~하다 《마음이》 sympathize[feel] with; respond to 《물체가》 be resonant with; reverberate; echo / ~기(器) a resonator/ ~자 a sympathizer.　きょうめい

공모(公募) public subscription/ ~하다 collect[invite] publicly; raise by subscription.　こうぼ

공모(共謀) conspiracy; collusion/ ~하다 conspire with; plot together/~자 a conspirator; an accomplice/~해서 in collusion with.　きょうぼう

공목(空木, 空目) 〖인〗lead; furniture.

공무(工務) engineering works.　こうむ

공무(公務) official business[duties]/ ~원 《개인》an official; a civil servant/ ~원법 the Public Officials Law/ ~ 집행 방해 interference with a government official in exercising one's public duty/ ~로 on official business/ ~ 다단으로 owing to the pressure of public business.　こうむ

꽁무니 the lower end of backbone 《끝》 the end; the rear; the tail/~빼다 run away; back down.

꽁무니바람 a fair[favorable] wind; a tail wind.

꽁무니뼈 〖해〗the coccyx.　びこつ

공문(公文) 《문서》an official document; archives 《통신》an official despatch/ ~서 위조 forgery of an official documents.　こうぶん

공문(空文) a dead letter/ ~화하다 turn out a dead letter.

공문(孔門) the Confucian school.

공물(公物) government property 《관리품》government issues.　こうぶつ

공물(供物) a votive offering 《제물》acrifice.　くもつ

공물(貢物) a tribute; a tributary payment; tax paid in kind.　みつぎもの

공미(貢米) rice paid as taxes; rice for government taxes.　みつぎこめ

공미리 〖어〗a snipe-fish[-eel].

공민(公民) a citizen/ ~학 civics/~ 교육 civic education; education for citizenship/~권 citizenship; civil[civic] rights.　こうみん

공박(攻駁) attack/~하다 refute; controvert; attack; oppose.

공밥(空-) meals one has not paid[worked] for/~을 먹다 take one's reward without working for it.

공방(攻防) offence[attack] and defence /~전 an offensive and defensive battle.　こうぼう

공방(空房) 《빈방》a vacant room; an unoccupied chamber 《공규(空閨)》the bedchamber of a deserted wife.　あきま

공방(工房) a workshop.

공배수(公倍數) 〖수〗a common multiple /최소 ~ the least common multiple (略：L.C.M.).　こうばいすう

공백(空白) a blank; a space 《비유적》a vacuum; a veid.　くうはい

공벌(攻伐) attack; assault; invasion/~하다 invade; go an expedition.

공범(共犯) complicity; joint commission of an offence; a confederate/~자 an accomplice.　きょうはん

공법(公法) public law/~학자 a publicist/국제~ international law.　こうほう

공변되다 (be) fair; just; impartial; even-handed.　こうへいむしだ

공변 세포(孔邊細胞) 〖식〗guard cells.

공병(工兵) a military engineer; a member of the engineers; a sapper《영》/~대 an engineer corps.　こうへい

공보(公報) an official report; an official bulletin/ ~실 the Office of Public Information.　こうほう

꽁보리밥 boiled barley taken as a meal [instead of rice].　むぎめし

공복(公服) an official uniform[outfit].　こうむいんのふく

공복(公僕) a public servant.　こうぼく

공복(空腹) hunger; an empty stomach /~에[으로] on an empty stomach; before meal.　くうふく

공부(工夫) study/~하다 study; learning /~방 a study; a sanctum.　べんきょう

공부승(工夫僧) a priest learning Buddhist scriptures.

공분(公憤) righteous indignation; public rage[resentment].　こうふん

공분모(公分母) 〖수〗a common denominator.　こうぶんぼ

공비(工費) the cost of construction 《공임》labor costs.　こうひ

공비(公費) public expenses.　くうひ

공비(空費) waste; useless expense.

공비(共匪) red[communist] guerrillas.

공사(工事) works; construction; engineering work/철도 ~ railway construction[work]/수리 ~ repair works/비(費) the cost of construction. こうじ

공사(公司) a firm; a company. こうし

공사(公私) official[public] and private matters[affairs]/~를 구별하다 draw the line between public and private

공상(空想) an idle fancy; fanciful idea; a daydream/ ~하다 fancy; imagine; [day]dream/ ~가 a dreamer; a visionary; a daydreamer/ ~적 fanciful; visionary. くうそう

공상(貢上) a tribute/ ~하다 pay a tribute (to).

공상(工商) (직업) industry and commerce (계급) the classes of artisans and tradesmen.

공생(共生) 《생》 symbiosis; commensalism /~ 동[식]물 a commensal. きょうせい

공생애(公生涯) a public life[career].

공서 양속(公序良俗) good public order and customs. こうじょりょうぞく

공석(公席) ①(공식 석상) a public occasion /~에서 an a public occasion ②(공무보는 자리) on official post. おおやけのせき

공석(空席) a vacant seat; a vacancy/~을 채우다 fill a vacancy. くうせき

공선(公選) (공중의 선거) public[popular] election/ ~하다 elect by popular vote /~ 지사 a publicly-elected [provincial] governor. こうせん

공설(公設) ~의 public (시립)municipal /~ 시장 a public market. こうせつ

공성(攻城) a siege. こうじょう

공세(攻勢) the offensive[aggressive]/~를 취하다 take an offensive. こうせい

공사(公事) public[official] affairs. こうじ

공사(公使) a [diplomatic] minister/~관 a legation/ ~관원 [a member of] the legation staff. こうし

공사(公社) a public corporation/대한조선 ~ the Korea Shipbuilding Corporation. こうしゃ

공산(共産) common property/ ~주의 communism/~당 the Communist party; the Communists/~ 당원[주의자] a Communist/~주의의 communist[ic] /~ 진영 the communist camp/~화 communization. きょうさん

공산(公算) probability/ ~이 크다 There is every probability that…. こうさん

공산 명월(空山明月) the moon shining on a lone mountain (대머리)a bald-head. くうざんめいげつ

공산주의(共産主義) communism; collectivism/~ 동맹 a communist league[alliance]. きょうさんしゅぎ

공상(供上) presentation [of local product to the king]/~하다 present.

공상(公傷) an injury sustained while on duty.

공소(公訴) 《법》 arraignment; prosecution; accusation; public action/ ~ 사실 charge. こうそ

공소(控所) a lobby; a waiting room.

공소(控訴) an appeal (to a higher court) / ~하다 appeal (to a higher tribunal); appeal against (a decision). こうそ

공손(恭遜) politeness; civility; courtesy; courteousness; respectfulness; deference/~하다 (be) polite; civil; courteous; respectful/~히 절하다 salute[bow] politely. ていねい

공수(攻守) offence and defence (야구) batting and fielding/~ 동맹 an offensive and defensive alliance. こうしゅ

공수(空手) an empty[a bare] hand; a bare hand. からて

공수(空輸) air transport; an airlift/ ~하다 transport[carry] by air/ ~ 부대 an air-borne troops. くうゆ

공수(拱手) ①placing one's left hand over the right hand [as a gesture of respect]. ②folding one's arms/~하다 cross one's hands in respect; fold one's arms. きょうしゅ

공수병(恐水病) 《의》 hydrophobia; rabies /~에 걸린 개 a mad dog; a rabid dog. きょうすいびょう

공수표(空手票) a wind bill; a kite; a bad cheque; an accommodation bill/ ~를 떼다 fly a kite (비유) make an empty promise/~로 끝나다 end in an empty pledge. からてがた

공순(恭順) obedience; submission/ ~하다 (be) submissive; gentle; meek.

공술 free liquor; a gratis drink; a free drink. ただでのむさけ

공술(供述) a deposition; affidavit/~하다 depose; make affidavit/ ~서 an affidavit; a written statement/~인 a deponent.

공습(空襲) an air raid[attack]/ ~하다 make an air attack (on)/ ~ 경보 an air-raid alarm. くうしゅう

공시(公示) public announcement[notice] / ~하다 announce publicly. こうじ

공식(公式) 《수》 a formula (정식) formality/ ~의 formal; official; state/ ~으로 formally; officially/~ 방문 a formal visit; an official call (국가 원수의) a state visit. こうしき

공식(空食) ~하다 eat[get] for nothing. ただでくうこと

공신(公信) public confidence.

공신(功臣) a meritorious retainer[subject]. こうしん

공심(空心) an empty stomach. くうふく

공안(公安) public peace [and order]; public security/~ 경찰 the public peace police; the security police/ ~ 위원회 a public safety commission[commissioner]. こうあん

공안(公案) (공문서의 안)the draft of a public document (여론의)a bill dra-

fted in accordance with public opinion. こうあん
공알 【해】(음핵) the clitoris. いんかく
공액(共軛) 【수】 being conjugate/ ～각 [점·호(弧)] a conjugate angle[point, ark]. きょうやく
공약(公約) a [public] pledge; a commitment/～하다 pledge *oneself*. こうやく
공약수(公約數) a common measure/최대 ～ the greatest common measure (略: G.C.M.). こうやくすう
공양(供養) (어른에게의) providing one's elders with food (부처에게의) offering food to Buddha/～하다 make an offering; hold a mass for (*the dead*)/ ～미 rice offered to a deity. くよう
공언(公言) [open] declaration; profession; avowal/ ～하다 declare openly; profess. こうげん
공언(空言) an empty[a vain] word; prattle; idle talk (거짓)a lie. うそ
공얻다(空─) get for nothing[gratis, free of charge]. ただでもらう
공업(工業) industry/ ～의 industrial; technical/ ' ～국 an industrial nation / ～가 an industrialist/ ～계 industrial circles; industrial world/～ 지대 a manufacturing district/ ～ 도시 an industrial[a manufacturing] town/ ～ 학교 a technical school/～화 industrialization. こうぎょう
공업(功業) an achievment; an exploit; services. こうぎょう
공역(公役) public service.
공역(共譯) joint translation. きょうやく
공연(公演) a public performance/ ～하다 perform; play; exhibit. こうえん
공연(共演) co-acting; co-starring/ ～하다 co-act; co-star; play together/ ～자 a co-actor. きょうえん
공연(空然) ～하다 (be) useless; futile; unavailing; needless; unnecessary; fruitless/공연히 to no purpose; needlessly; uselessly; vainly. むだだ
공염불(空念佛) a fair but empty phrase / ～에 그치다 end in an empty talk.
공영(公營) public management/ ～하다 place (*an undertaking*) under public management. こうえい
공영(共營) joint management/ ～하다 operate jointly (*with*). きょうえい
공예(工藝) industrial arts; technology / ～의 industrial; technical/ ～가 a technologist/ ～품 an industrial product/ ～ 학교 a technological school/ ～물 objects for public use. こうげい
공용(公用) public use; official[public] business/～으로 on official business. こうよう
공용(功用) beneficial result; efficacy; use.
공용(共用) public use; official[public] business/ ～으로 on official business. きょうよう

공원(公園) a park/국립 ～ a national park. こうえん
공위(攻圍) siege; investment; envelopment/～하다 (be) siege; invest; lay siege to; envelope. かこんでせめること
공위(空位) ①(빈) vacancy; vacant position ②(실권 없는) a nominal position.
공유(公有) public ownership/ ～의 public; public[ly]-owned/～물[재산] public property. こうゆう
공유(共有) joint[common] ownership/ ～의 for common use/ ～하다 hold in common; own (*a thing*) jointly/ ～물 common property. きょうゆう
공으로 free [of charge]; for nothing; gratis/～ 얻다 get for nothing. ただで
공의(公醫) a government physician; a doctor authorized by a public body.
공의(公議) an unbiased view. こうぎ
공이 a pestle; a pounder/ ～로 찧다 pestle. きね
공이치기 the hammer (of *a rifle*).
공익(公益) the public benefit[good] / ～ 단체[사업] a public corporation[utility]. こうえき
공익(共益) common profit(benefit)/public good. きょうえき
공인(公認) authorization; official approval[recognition]/ ～의 authorized; approved; official/ ～하다 recognize officially; authorize/～ 후보자 a recognized candidate; an officially endorsed candidate. こうにん
공인수(公因數) 【수】a common factor. こういんすう
공일 (거저 하는 일) working for nothing; a job in vain (헛수고) lost labor; labor lost. ただはたらきのしごと
공일(空日) (일요일) Sunday (일반)a holiday; a day off. にちようび
공임(工賃) (임금) a wage; wages; pay; [cost of] labo[u]r.
공짜 a thing got for nothing; free charge. ただでえたもの
공자(公子) a young nobleman; a scion of nobility. こうし
공자(孔子) Confucius/ ～의 Confucian.
공작(工作) work; construction (공작) operation/～ 기계 a machine tool/ ～ 장 a workshop/ ～품 handicrafts/정 치 ～ political maneuvering/준비 ～을 하다 prepare the ground in advance for. こうさく
공작(孔雀) 【조】a peacock (암컷)a peahen/ ～고사리 【식】the maidenhair fern/ ～석 《광》 malachite. くじゃく
공작(公爵) a prince; a duke(영)/～ 부인 a princess; a duchess. こうしゃく
공장(工匠) a mechanic; an artisan; an artificer. こうしょう
공장(工場) a factory; a plant; a works; a mill; a workshop/유리 ～ a glassworks/ ～장[감독] a factory[works] manager/～ 지대 a factory zone/ ～ 노

공저      89      공천

-동자 factory workers. こうじょう
**공저**(共著) collaboration 《책의》a joint work/ ~자 a joint author; a coauthor. きょうちょ
**공저**(公邸) an official residence.
**공적**(公的) (being) open 《일반의》public 《공식의》formal 《관공의》official; governmental/~ 생활 public life. こうてき
**공적**(公敵) a public[common] enemy. おおやけのてき
**공적**(功績) a meritorious deed; merits; distinguished services. こうせき
**공전**(工錢) wages; a wage; pay; [cost of] labour.
**공전**(公轉) 【천】 revolution/~ 하다 revolve [round the sun]; move around the sun. こうてん
**공전**(公電) an official telegram. こうでん
**공전**(空前) unprecedentedness/~의 unprecedented; unheard-of; epoch-making/~ 절후의 the first and probably the last/~의 성황 unprecedented success. くうぜん
**공전**(空電) static; atmospherics/~ 장해 atmospheric disturbance. くうでん
**공전**(空轉) 《자동차 따위의》skidding《엔진의》racing/~하다 skid; race《기계 따위가》run idle. くうてん
**공정**(工程) the amount of work《생산 과정》a process《공률》power.
**공정**(公正) justice; fairness; impartiality/~하다 (be) just; equitable; fair/~ 증서 a notarial deed/ ~한 처치 a fair[square] deal. こうせい
**공정**(公定) official; fixture/~의 official; legal; [officially] fixed/~ 가격 an official price. こうてい
**공정대**(空挺隊) air-borne troops《낙하산 부대》paratroops. くうていたい
**공제**(共濟) mutual aid[relief]/~ 사업 a mutual benefit[aid] project/~ 조합 a mutual benefit society[association]. きょうさい
**공제**(控除) subtraction; deduction/ ~ 하다 subtract; deduct (from). こうじょ
**공조**(共助) mutual assistance; cooperation/ ~하다 mutually assist; cooperate. きょうじょ
**공존**(共存) coexistence/ ~하다 coexist; live together/~ 공영 coexistence and coprosperity/평화적 ~ peaceful coexistence. きょうぞん
**공졸**(工拙) dexterity and clumsiness; relative skill. こうせつ
**공죄**(功罪) services and crimes; merits and demerits. こうざい
**공주**(公主) an Imperial[a Royal] Princess; a princess [of the blood]; a Royal Princessan. こうしゅ
**공준**(公準) 【수】 a postulate.
**공중** uselessly; vainly; to no purpose. むだに
**공중**(公衆) the public/~의 public; common/~ 전화 a public telephone/~ 도덕 public morality/~ 목욕탕 a public bath/~ 위생 public health/~의 이익 the public interest; the general good/~ 변소 a public[street] latrine; a public toilet/~ 앞에서 in public; before company. こうしゅう
**공중**(空中) the air; the sky; space/ ~ 의 aerial; air/ ~에 in the air[sky]; in mid-air/ ~전 an air battle; air fighting/ ~수송 air transport/~ 열병식 an air-review/ ~선(線) an antenna/~ 누각 a castle in the air/~ 방전[질소] atmospheric discharge[nitrogen]/~ 활주 volplane; gliding/~ 광고 advertising by airplane. くうちゅう
**공중제비**(空中—) a somersault; a tumble/ ~를 넘다 turn a somersault; turn head over heels. くうちゅうとび
**공증**(公證) a notarial act; authentication; official endorsement/ ~하다 authenticate; notarize; attest/~인 a notary [public]. こうしょう
**꽁지** a tail《공작 따위의》a train/ ~점 the comma mark. とりのお
**공지**(空地) vacant ground[land]; a vacant lot; an open space. くうち
**공지**(空紙) a blank paper.
**꽁지벌레** 【충】 a maggot.
**꽁지별** 【천】《살별》a comet.
**공직**(公直) justice and honesty; fairness and uprightness/~하다 (be) just and honest; fair and upright; impartial and frank.
**공직**(公職) a public office[duty]/~ 추방 purge from public office/ ~에 있다 hold a public office. こうしょく
**공진**(共振) 【물】 resonance; sympathy. きょうめい
**공진회**(共進會) a competitive exhibition; a prize show; a fair〈미〉/농업 ~ an agricultural show. きょうしんかい
**공차**(公差) 【수】 a common difference《조폐(造幣)》allowance; tolerance. こうさ
**공차**(空車)《무료 승차》a free ride; a stolen ride/~타다 steal a ride on; jump the taxifare. くうしゃ
**공찰**(公札) an official letter.
**공창**(工廠) an arsenal. こうしょう
**공창**(公娼)《사람》a licensed prostitute《제도》licensed prostitution. こうしょう
**공채** a [tennis] racket; a [pingpong] paddle; a [polo] mallet. まりをうつぼう
**공채**(公債) a public loan[debt]《증권》a public loan bond/군사 ~ war loan bonds/정리 ~ consols. こうさい
**공책**(空冊) a notebook. ひっきちょう
**공처**(空處) vacant land; unoccupied ground; an open space; a blank [space].
**공처가**(恐妻家) a hen-pecked[wife-ridden] husband; a man afraid of his wife. きょうさいか
**공천**(公薦) public nomination/ ~하다 nominate publicly/후보자를 ~하다 officially adopt a candidate; nominate

공첩(公牒) a note; a notification.
공청(公廳) a public office. かんちょう
공청회(公聽會) a public[an open] hearing.
꽁초(一草) a cigarette-butt[-end] 《엽궐련의》 a cigar end. すいがら
공출(供出) delivery/ ~하다 deliver; offer/ ~ 할당 allocation of delivery quotas. きょうしゅつ
꽁치 《어》 a saury; *Cololabis saira*《학명》.
공치기 a ball game; playing ball.
공치다¹ ①draw a circle; mark down an 0 ②be fruitless[vain, in vain]; get nothing. まるをつける
공치다² hit the ball. まりをうつ
공치사(功致辭) self-praise; admiration of *one's* own merit/ ~하다 praise *one's* own service; admire *one's* own merit.
공칙하다 (be) unfortunate; unluck; ill timed[chosen, planned]; be amiss/ 공칙하게 unluckily. あいにくわるくなる
공칭(公稱) ~의 nominal/ ~ 자본금 nominal[authorized] capital. こうしょう
공탁(供託) ①《보관》deposit; trust; lodgement/ ~하다 deposit (*a thing*) in [with]; give (*a thing*) in trust; lodge (*with*)/ ~물 a deposit; a deposited article/ ~소 a deposit office/ ~금 deposit money ②《법》consignment/ ~법 the Deposit Law. きょうたく
공탈(攻奪) capture; reduction; occupation/ ~하다 take by storm[assault]; reduce; carry [a fortress]; capture. せめうばうこと
공터(空—) an empty[a vacant] lot.
공통(共通) commonness/ ~의 common; mutual; general; public/ ~의 이해 common interests. きょうつう
공판(公判) a [public] trial; a [public] hearing/ ~정 the court; a public trial court/ ~에 회부하다 bring (*a case*) to trial; put (*a case*) on trial/ ~ 중이다 be on trial. こうはん
공편(共編) co-editorship colloboration.
공평(公平) impartiality; justice/ ~하다 fair; just; impartial/ ~히 impartially; fairly; justly/ ~ 무사 impartiality; fair play. こうへい
공평(公評) a just criticism; a public view[opinion]. こうへいなひひょう
공포(公布) promulgation; proclamation [official] announcement/ ~하다 promulgate; proclaim; make public. こうふ
공포(空砲) a blank shot[cartridge]/ ~ 를 쏘다 fire a blank shot. くうほう
공포(空胞) 《생》vacuoles.
공포(恐怖) fear; dread; terror; fright; scare; horror 《공황》panic/ ~증 phobia; morbid fear/ ~ 관념 a fear complex/ ~ 정치 terrorism/ ~에 사로잡히다 be seized with fear; be struck with horror. きょうふ
공폭(空爆) an air bombardment/ ~하다 bombard from the air. くうばく

공표(公表) 《공포》official[public] announcement; proclamation 《발표》publication/ ~하다 announce officially; publish. こうひょう
공하(恭賀) respectful congratulations/ ~ 신년(新年) I wish you a happy New Year; A happy New Year to you; With New Year's greetings. きょうが
꽁하다 (be) reserved and unsociable; introvert, hide-bound.
공하다(空—) get for nothing; (be) free.
공하다(貢—) 《공물을》pay 《이바지하다》contribute. みつぎものをそなえる
공학(工學) engineering; technology/ ~사 [박사] a bachelor[doctor] of engineering. こうがく
공학(共學) mixed education《영》; co-education/ ~하는 여학생 a co-ed《미》/ ~제 the coeducationalism. きょうがく
공함(公函) an official letter.
공항(空港) an airport; an aviation field /김포 ~ *Gimpo* Airport. くうこう
공해(公海) the open sea; the high seas /~ 어업 high sea fishery. こうかい
공해(公害) a public nuisance; [a] menace[a threat] to public health; public hazard; pollution/ ~병 a public hazard disease.
공허(空虛) vacancy; emptiness/ ~하다 (be) empty; blank; void/ ~감 a sense of emptiness. くうきょ
공헌(貢獻) contribution; service/ ~하다 contribute to; render services to; make a contribution. こうけん
공혈(供血) blood donation/ ~하다 donate[furnish] blood [for transfusion].
공화(共和) ~의 republican/ ~국 a republic/ ~제(制) republicanism/ ~ 정치 republican government/ ~당 the Republican Party. きょうわ
공황(恐慌) a panic; a scare; alarm/ 금융 ~ a financial panic/ ~을 가져오다 bring on a panic. きょうこう
공회(公會) a public meeting/ ~당 a public hall; a city[town] hall. こうかい
공효(功效) effect; use ⇨보람. ききめ
공훈(功勳) merits; an exploit/ ~을 세우다 perform meritorious deeds/ ~이 있는 meritorious. くんこう
공휴일(公休日) 《법정의》a [legal] holiday. 《일반적》a holiday. こうきゅうび
-곶 a cape; a headland; a spit.
곶감 a dried[cured] persimmon.
꽂다 《박다》stick; drive in 《빗장을》bolt; bar. さしこむ. はめる
꽂히다 《박히다》get inserted; be stuck; be driven in. さしこまれる
꽃 ①《초목의》a flower 《과수의》a blossom 《헌화》a floral tribute ②《정수》essence; pride; flower 《사교계의》a belle. はな
꽃가루 pollen; anther-dust. かふん
꽃구경 flower-viewing.
꽃나무 a flowering tree[plant].
꽃놀이 flower viewing; a picnic for

viewing flowers.
꽃눈 a flower bud. はなのめ
꽃다발 a bouquet (F); a bunch of flowers. はなたば
꽃다지 the first fruits [of a plant].
꽃답다 be lovely[pretty, beautiful] as a flower. はなのようにうつくしい
꽃돗자리 a figured mat; fancy matting.
꽃동산 a flower garden; a flowery hill. はなぞの
꽃망울 a young flower-bud. はなのつぼみ
꽃맞이 a shamanistic ceremony to welcome the new blossoms. はなみ
꽃맺이 unripe fruit in its early stage.
꽃무늬 floral design; flowery patterns; flowerings; 《인》 a printer's flower. はなのもん
꽃물 a kind of thick soup.
꽃받침 the calyx [of a flower]. がく
꽃밥 the anther. やく
꽃방(一房) ① a shop which deals in imitation[artificial] flower ② a flower shop; a florist. はなや
꽃방석(一方席) a figured[fancy] cushion. はなもようのあるざぶとん
꽃밭 a flower garden; a flower bed; a field of flowers. はなばたけ
꽃병(一瓶) a flower vase. はながめ
꽃봉오리 a [flower] bud; a budding flower. はなのつぼみ
꽃부리 a corolla. はなかんむり
꽃불 ①(이글이글 타는) a blazing fire ②《화약으로 만든》 fireworks; a fireworks display/〜을 울리다 let[set] off fireworks. あかいはなのようなかえん
꽃샘 a cold[windy] weather in the blooming season. はながさくときのさむさ
꽃송이 an open flower; a blossom; a flower. はなぶさ
꽃수레 a car decorated with flowers; a flower-bedecked car[streetcar]; a float [in a parade]. はなでんしゃ
꽃술 《수술》a stamen 《암술》a pistil.
꽃시계(一時計) a floral[flower] clock.
꽃식물(一植物) a flowering plant; a phanerogam.
꽃잎 a petal [of a flower]. はなべん
꽃자리 a figured[fancy] mat.
꽃재배(一栽培) floriculture; flower gardening.
꽃전(一煎) griddle cake of glutinous rice prepared in the form of a flower griddle cakes made in flower patterns.
꽃주일(一主日) the first Sunday of June. 6がつのだいいちにちようび
꽃차(一車) a car with floral decorations ⇨꽃수레. はなくるま
꽃차례 inflorescence.
과 and; [together] with; against. /김군〜 이군 Mr. Kim and Mr. Lee. ―と
과(科) 《학교의》a course; a faculty; a department 《동식물의》a family 《병과》 an arm/ 영문〜 the English course; the Department of English/고양이〜

the cat family/보병〜 the infantry arm. か
과(課) 《학과》a lesson 《분과》 a section; a division/ 〜장 the head of section; a section chief/ 〜원 the staff of section. か
과감(果敢) 《결단》resolution; decision 《용감》daring/ 〜하다 (be) daring; bold; resolute; determined. かかん
과객(過客) a passer-by; a foot passenger. ほうろうきゃく
과거(科擧) the state examination/ 〜하다 pass the state examination. かきょ
과거(過去) the past [days] 《과거 생활》 one's previous life 《시제의》the past; the preterite/ 〜의 past; bygone/ 〜분사 a past participle/〜 완료 the past perfect tense/ 〜지사 past events; bygones/〜 4년 동안 for[during] the past [last] four years. かこ
과거장(過去帳) 《종》 an obituary; a roster of the dead.
과격(過激) being extreme[radical]/ 〜하다 (be) excessive; violent; radical; extreme/ 〜 분자 a radical element/ 〜파 the Bolshevists[Reds]; the extremists[radicals]/ 〜주의 Bolshevism; radicalism. かげき
과겸(過謙) 〜하다 (be) overmodest.
과공(過恭) 〜하다 be humble; be humble to a fault/ 〜은 비례이다 It is impolite to be too modest.
과공(誇功) 〜하다 boast of one's achievements; be proud of one's merits.
과공(課工) a daily lesson. にっかとしてのべんきょう
과꽃 《식》a [China] aster; Callistephus chinensis(학명).
과긍(誇矜) 〜하다 boast (of); brag (of); be proud (of). じまんすること
과기(瓜期) ①《기한의》expiration ②《임기》 a term ③《여자의》teens
과기(過期) 〜하다 pass a fixed term. きげんがすぎたこと
과남(過濫) 〜하다 be above one's deserts; be too good for one; be more than one deserves. あつかましさ
과녁 a target; a mark. まと
과녁배기 the right opposite side[direction]; a place one faces right ahead.
과년(瓜年) ①《여자의》teens ②《임기가 다 한 해》the last year of one's term of service. こんき
과년(過年) getting past the marriageable age; 《지난해》the past year/〜하다 (be) past the marriageable age/ 〜한 처녀 an old maid. じょしのこんきがすぎたこと
과년도(過年度) the past financial[fiscal] year. さくねんどう
과념(過念) excessive worry/ 〜하다 mind excessively; worry too much; be overcautious. しんぱいしすぎている
과다(過多) excess; superfluity; supera-

bundance/ ~하다 (be) excessive; superfluous; superabundant; too much/ 공급 ~ an excess of supply. かた

과단(果斷) resolution; quick action; decision/ ~한 decisive; resolute; quick / ~성 있는 사람 a man of determined character[quick decision]/~성이 없다 lack decision; be irresolute. かだん

과단(科斷) judg[e]ment; decision/ ~하다 decide; give decision on (*a case*).

과당(果糖) fruit sugar; fructose; levulose.

과당(過當) ~하다 (be) excessive; be more than needed/~ 경쟁 an excessive competition (in *sales*). かとうだ

과대(過大) exaggeration/~하다 exaggerative; excessive/~한[하게] excessively; exorbitant[ly];/~ 평가하다 overestimate; overstate. かだい

과대(誇大) exaggeration/ ~하다 exaggerate; overstate; magnify/ ~ 망상증 megalomania. こだい

-과도 with[and, like] also[either, even] /형~ 의논해 봐라 Talk it over with your elder brother too. —とも

과도(果刀) a fruit knife.

과도(過度) excess; immoderation/~하다 (be) excessive; immoderate; undue; too much/~하게 excessively; immoderately; too much; to[in] excess. かど

과도(過渡) transition/~기(期) a period of transition; a transitional period /~ 정부 an interim government/~ 시대 an age of transition. かと

과동(過冬) wintering/ ~하다 pass the winter; winter. えっとう

과두(裹肚) a cloth used to wrap the trunk of a corpse for burial; a shroud.

과두(裹頭) a cloth used to wrap the head of a corpse for burial.
すくないじんいん

과두 정치(寡頭政治) oligarchy/~의 oligarchic[al]. かとうせいじ

과람(過濫) ~하다 (be) excessive; too much; undeserved; more than one deserves. あつかましさ

과량(過量) an excessive of quantity. かだいなぶんりょう

과려(過慮) overcautiousness; excessive scrupulosity/ ~하다 be overcautious; mind excessively; worry too much. ひじょうにしんぱいすること

과로(過勞) excessive labour; overwork; strain/ ~하다 work too hard; overwork *oneself*; overtax *one's* powers; work under a strain. かろう

과료(科料) a fine/~에 처하다 fine (*one* for *an offence*). かりょう

**파르르** gurgling[ly]; with a gurgle.
どくどく

**꽈리** 【식】 a ground cherry; a strawberry tomato (**물집**) a blister.

과린산(過燐酸)【화】 superphosphate/ ~ '회 superphosphate of lime; superphosphates.

과립(顆粒)【의】 a granule; a rash/~을 형성하다 granulate. かりゅう

과명(科名)【생】 a family name.

과목(果木) a fruit-tree. かじゅ

과목(科目) a subject; a lesson 《과정》 a course 《전과목》 a curriculum/선택 ~ an optional subject; an elective [course]/필수 ~ a compulsory[required] subject. かもく

과묵(寡默) taciturnity; reticence/ ~하다 (be) reserved; taciturn; reticent/ ~한 사람 a taciturn person. かもく

과문(寡聞) limited information; a little knowledge/ ~하다 (be) ill-informed; limited in knowledge. かぶん

과물(果物) fruit. くだもの

과민(過敏) nervousness; over-sensitiveness/ ~하다 (be) too keen; nervous; touchy; over-sensitive/신경 ~ morbid sensitiveness; neurosis. かびん

과밀(過密) 인구의 ~화 overpopulation.

과반(過半) the greater[most] part (*of*); the majority. かはん

과반(過般) last time; some time ago; the other day. かはん

과반수(過半數) a majority 《대부분》 the greater part (*of*). かはんすう

과방(過房) adopting a nephew as *one's* heir.

과병(寡兵) a small force[army]; insufficient strength; a scanty army.

과보(果報)【종】 retribution ⇨인과 응보 (因果應報). かほう

과부(寡婦) a widow; a relict/~ 사정은 ~가 안다 It takes a widow to know widow's difficulties. かふ

과부적중(寡不敵衆) "The few cannot with stand the many".

과부족(過不足) excess or[and] deficiency; overs and shorts. かぶそく

과분(過分) being excessive/ ~하다 (be) excessive immoderate 《과람》 (be) undeserved. かぶん

과불(過拂) overpayment/ ~하다 overpay.

과불급(過不及) excess or[and] deficiency/ ~없이 in proper quantities.
すぎることとおよばないこと

과산화(過酸化) 의 【화】 ~ 작용 peroxidation/~수소 peroxide of hydrogen.

과세(過歲) greeting[celebration] of the New Year/~하다 greet[celebrate] the New Year.

과세(課稅) taxation 《세》 a tax; a duty / ~하다 tax; impose a tax; levy duties (*on*). かぜい

과소(寡少) littleness; fewness/~하다 (be) little; few; scanty. すくなさ

과소(過少) being too little/~하다 (be) too little. かしょう

과소(過小) being too small/~하다 (be) too small. かしょう

과수(果樹) a fruit-tree/ ~원 an orchard/ ~의 재배 fruit-culture. かじゅ

**과수**(過數) excess 《잉여》 surplus／～하다 exceed; be above[over].

**과수댁**(寡守宅) a widow. やもめ

**과시**(誇示) ostentation; display; showing parade／～하다 a parade; show off; make [a] display of. こじ

**과식**(過食) overeating; excessive eating／～하다 overeat oneself; eat too much; eat to excess. たべすぎ

**과신**(過信) excessive confidence／～하다 place too much confidence in (one); be overconfident; be credulous. かしん

**과실**(果實) ①《총칭》fruit[age] 《단칭》a fruit 《견과》a nut 《장과(漿果)》a berry ②〖법〗fruit／법정[천연] ～ legal[natural] fruit. かじつ

**과실**(過失) ①《과오》a fault; a mistake; an error; a blunder／～을 저지르다 commit a fault ②《사고》an accident／～치사 accidental homicide ③《태만》negligence; carelessness／～범(犯) a careless offence. かしつ

**과액**(寡額) a small sum [of money].

**과언**(過言) 《지나치게 말함》saying too much 《과장》exaggeration／…이라고 말해도 ～이 아니나 It is not too much [no exaggeration] to say that…. かごん

**과업**(課業) ①《학업》a lesson; school work; a task ②《업무》a task; a piece of work imposed. かぎょう

**과연**(果然) as[was, had been] expected; as sure enough 《정말》really／～ 그렇다면 one thought; if that is the case; if so／～ 그는 거기 있었다 Sure enough, there he was. かぜん

**과열**(過熱) overheating; superheating／～하다 overheat. かねつ

**과염소산**(過鹽素酸) 〖화〗perchloric acid.

**과오**(過誤) 《과실》a fault; an error; a blunder 《잘못》a mistake; an error 《죄과》blame／～를 깨닫다 see the error of one's ways／～를 저지르다 commit a fault; make a mistake. かご

**과외**(課外) ～의 extra-curricular; extra-curricular／～ 강의 an extra-curriculum lecture; an extra. かがい

**과욕**(寡慾) unselfishness; disinterestedness／～하다 (be) unselfish; content with little disinterested／～한 사람 a man of few wants. かよく

**과용**(過用) extravagance; excessive expenditure／～하다 waste; spend (money) too much. つかいすぎ

**과원**(果園) an orchard. かじゅえん

**과원**(課員) a member of the section staff 《총칭》the staff of a section. かいん

**과유불급**(過猶不及) Too much is as bad as too little.

**과육**(果肉) flesh [of fruit]; sarcocarp. かにく

**과음**(過淫) carnal excess; sexual indulgence[intemperance]／～하다 indulge in sexual pleasure. かいん

**과음**(過飲) excessive drinking／～하다 drink too much; drink to excess; overdrink oneself. のみすぎ

**과일** 《총칭》[edible] fruit[age]. かじつ

**과잉**(過剩) excess; surplus／～의 surplus; superfluous／인구 ～ over-population surplus population／생산 ～ over-production. かじょう

**과자**(菓子) 《총칭》confectionery 《생과자》cake 《당과(糖菓)》sweets; candy〈미〉／과잣집 a confectionery; a sweet shop; a candy store〈미〉. かし

**과장**(誇張) exaggeration; grandiloquence; magnification; overstatement／～하다 exaggerate; magnify; overstate／～법 hyperbole. こちょう

**과장**(科長) the chairman of a department (in a college etc.). かちょう

**과장**(課長) the chief of a section; a section[al] chief／～ 대리 the acting chief a section. かちょう

**과정**(過程) process; course／생산 ～ the process of production. かてい

**과정**(課程) a course; a curriculum／나날의 ～ a daily routine. かてい

**과제**(課題) a subject; a theme 《숙제》home task[work] 《연습 문제》exercises／～를 주다 give a subject; impose a task on (one). かだい

**과죄**(科罪) judgment of a crime; conviction／～하다 convict; condemn／～되다 be convicted of a crime.

**과주**(果酒) [a] fruit wine; fermented fruit drink.

**과줄** 《유밀과》a candy prepared by frying sweetened dough.

**과중**(過重) overweight／～하다 (be) too heavy; burdensome. かじゅう

**과즙**(果汁) fruit juice. かじゅう

**과찬**(過讚) overpraise／～하다 overpraise; give an undeserved reward.

**과채**(果菜) greens and fruits; fruits and vegetables. かじつとやさい

**과태금**(過怠金) a fine for default; a negligence fine. かたいきん

**과판** ① a hairpin in the shape of a China aster ② a mold shaped like a China aster.

**과하다**(課一) 《세금 따위를》impose (a tax); assess; assign (a task to)／세금을 ～ tax; impose tax (on). かする

**과하다**(過一) (be) too much; excessive; undue/과하게 excessively; unduly／술을 과하게 마시다 drink too much; drink to excess. ありすぎだ

**과학**(科學) science／응용 ～ 《자연, 사회》applied[natural, social] science／～자 a scientist／～적[으로] scientific[ally]／～전[병기] scientific warfare[weapon]／～ 연구[지식] scientific research[knowledge]／～ 시대 a scientific age／～화하다 make scientific. かがく

**과히**(過一) too; too much; excessively; to excess; overly; extremely. あまり

**곽** a box; a case ⇨갑. はこ

**꽉** ①(단단히) tighty; firmly; fast; closely/ ~ 쥐다 grasp[grip] with force; hold fast; take fast hold of/ ~ 묶다 bind[tie] fast. ②(가득히) closely; tight[ly]; to the full; to [full] capacity; chock-full (승객 따위) be jam-packed (*with*) ③(참는 모양) patiently; stoically/그는 이가 아픈 것을 ~ 참았다 He bore[stood] the toothache stoically./그녀는 울고 싶은 충동을 ~ 참았다 She resisted an impulse to cry out.

**곽**(槨) an outer coffin. しっかり

**곽공**(郭公) a cuckoo ⇒뻐꾸기. ひつぎ ほととぎす

**꽉꽉** ①(힘을 주어) tight; hard; fast; firm[ly]; securely/밥을 ~ 눌러 담다 stuff [a bowl] full of rice ②(가득) full; chock-full/방안은 모두 사람으로 ~ 들어차 있다 All the rooms are crowded [packed, jammed] with people.

**곽란**(癨亂) 〔醫〕 cholera nostras.

**관**(冠) a crown; a coronet/영광의 ~ a crown of glory. かん

**관**(貫) *one's* ancestral home; family seat ⇒본관(本貫). ほんかん

**관**(棺) a coffin; a casket〈미〉/ ~에 넣다 lay (*one*) to rest in a coffin. かん

**관**(管) a pipe; a tube/소화(消化) ~ a digestive tract/모세 ~ capillary tubes. かん

**관**(館) ①(푸주간) a butcher's shop ②(요정) a restaurant. かん

**관**(款) (조항(條項)) an article; a subsection. かん

**-관**(觀) a view; an outlook/세계~ an outlook on the world/인생 ~ a view [a philosophy] of life; an outlook on life.

**관가**(官家) a government office; a public office; a yamen. かんか

**관개**(灌漑) irrigation/ ~하다 irrigate; water/ ~ 공사 irrigation works/ ~지 (地) an irrigation reservoir. かんがい

**관객**(觀客) a spectator; the audience; a visitor (입장자) an attendant/ ~이 많다 draw a large house. かんきゃく

**관건**(關鍵) ①(문빗장) a bolt; a bar ②(중요한 것) a key/문제의 ~ the key to the question/그것이 문제 해결의 ~이 된다 It furnishes a key for the solution of the problem. かんぬきとかぎ

**관견**(管見) a narrow view. かんけん

**관계**(官界) the official world[life]; official[government] circles; officialdom/ ~에 들어가다 enter government service. かんかい

**관계**(官階) an official rank; a civil service grade. かんのかいきゅう

**관계**(關係) ①(관련) relation; relationship; reference; bearing; respect (연분) connection; connexion〈영〉 (교제 관계) relations (이해 관계) an interest; concern/ ~하다 relate to; bear on[upon]; concern; bear reference to; refer to; get in touch with/정신과 물질의 ~ the relation between matter and mind[spirit]/문장의 전후 ~ the context/외교 ~ diplomatic relations/ ~ 법규 the related laws and regulations/ ~ 대명사 a relative pronoun/ ~ 부사 a relative adverb/ ~하고 있다 do (*with*); be concerned (*with*); be involved in/…과 아무 ~ 가 없다 have nothing to do with ②(관여) participation; concern/ ~하다 participate in; take part in; be concerned in/ ~ 당국 the authorities concerned / ~자 the persons concerned (이해의) an interested party/경영에 ~하다 participate in the management ③(영향) influence; effect/ ~하다 affect; have influence on; matter/ ~가 크다 (일을 좌우로) exert a wide influence (*over*, *upon*); affect deeply ④(성교) connection; [sexual] relations; misconduct; an intrigue/ ~하다 have connection with; keep company with (*a woman*)/…와 불의의 ~를 계속하다 continue illicit connection with…. かんけい

**관곡**(款曲) kindness; cordiality/ ~하다 (be) kind; cordial; warm/ ~히 kind[ly]; cordially. ひじょうにしんせつなこと

**관골**(顴骨) the cheek-bone; the zygoma ⇒광대뼈. ほおぼね

**관공리**(官公吏) government and public officials; public servants. かんこうり

**관공립**(官公立) government and public (*institutions*). かんこうりつ

**관공서**(官公署) government and public offices. かんこうしょ

**관곽**(棺槨) the inner and outer coffins. / ~장이 a coffin maker. ひつぎ

**관광**(觀光) sightseeing/ ~하다 go sightseeing; do[see] the sights (*of*); visit/ ~객 a sightseer; a tourist/ ~단 a sightseeing[a tourist] party/ ~ 여행 a sightseeing tour; touristing〈미〉/ ~차 a scenic train/ ~ 버스 a sightseeing bus/ ~ 사업 the tourist industry. かんこう

**관구**(管區) the district [under jurisdiction]; a jurisdiction[area] (교회의) a parish. かんく

**관군**(官軍) the government forces[troops] (왕국의) the royal army. かんぐん

**관권**(官權) government authority/ ~을 남용하다 abuse government authority; make an improper use of government power. かんけん

**관극**(觀劇) play-going; theatre-going/ ~하다 see a play; enjoy a theatrical performance/ ~회 a theatre-party; a box party〈미〉. かんげき

**관금**(官金) government money. かんきん

**관급**(官給) government supply[issue] / ~품 articles supplied by the government. かんきゅう

**관기**(官紀) official discipline/ ~ 숙청 [strict] enforcement of official discipline; corruption of officialdom／~를 숙청하다 enforce official discipline; maintain rigid discipline among officials.

**관내(管內)** ¶~에 within the jurisdiction (of)／~를 순시하다 make a tour of inspection through one's [area of] jurisdictions.

**관념(觀念)** ①(생각) a sense; a spirit／의무[책임, 정의]의 ~ a sense of duty[responsibility, justice]／도의 ~ a moral sense／시간의 ~이 없다 take no thought of time／책임 ~이 없다 have no sense of responsibility ②(철학·심리학의) an idea; conception; thought; intention／추상적 ~ an abstract idea／고착 ~ a fixed idea／이차적 ~ second intentions／본유 ~ an innate idea／론 idealism／~작용[구성] ideation／~적 실재론(實在論) ideal realism／~소설 an ideological novel／~론자 an ideologist.

**관노(官奴)** a man-servant in government employ.

**관능(官能)** sense (기능) function／~주의 sensualism／~적인 functional(기능); sensuous(육감적).

**관다발(管一)** 【식】 vascular bundle; fibrovascular bundle.

**관담(款談)** a heart-to-heart talk／~하다 have a heart-to-heart talk (with).

**관대(款待)** welcome; a warm reception／~하다 welcome; give a warm reception.

**관대(寬大)** generosity; tolerance; magnanimity; liberality／~(하)다 (be) generous; magnanimous; liberal; broad-minded.

**관대(寬待)** liberal treatment; generous [lenient] reception／~하다 give a liberal treatment; receive[treat] with generosity.

**-관데** such that; so that／요새 무엇을 하~ 한 번도 오지 아니하요 What in the world are you doing these days that you never come to see me?

**관돈** a kwan; ten niang.

**관두(關頭)** a crisis ⇒간두(竿頭) 시곳도의 야마

**관등(官等)** official rank／~이 높다[낮다] be high[be low] in rank／~이 오르다 be elevated to a higher rank; be promoted in rank.

**관등(觀燈)** [celebration of] an anniversary of Buddha's birth／~하다 celebrate the anniversary of Buddha's birth.

**관디** an ancient court dress (신랑의) a bridegroom's attire.

**관디목 지르다** bow to one's superior.

**관람(觀覽)** inspection; viewing／~하다 view; inspect; look at／~객 a spectator; a visitor／~석 a seat; a box; a stand／~료 admission fee／~권 an admission ticket.

**관력(官力)** government authority.

**관련(關聯)** relation; connection; reference／~하다 relate; be relate (to); be connected (with)／…과 ~해서 in connection with／이 사건에 ~해서 여러 가지 시끄러운 일이 생겼다 Many a trouble has started up incidental to this affair.

**관령(官令)** official orders; orders of the government.

**관례(冠禮)** the celebration of one's coming of age.

**관례(慣例)** a custom; a usage; a practice (선례) a precedent (습속) a convention／~의 customary; conventional; time-honoured／사회의 ~ a social code [custom]／~를 깨뜨리다[따르다] break [follow] the custom.

**관록(官祿)** a stipend; a salary／~을 먹다 receive a stipend.

**관록(貫祿)** dignity; importance; weight of character／~ 있는 풍채 a dignified [a commanding] appearance[presence]／~ 있는 사람 a man of weight[importance].

**관료(官僚)** bureaucracy; officialdom (사람) a bureaucrat／~주의 bureaucratism／~적 bureaucratic／다소 ~적인 데가 있다 (사람이) have something of the bureaucrat about one.

**관류(貫流)** ~하다 run[flow] through [a city].

**관리(官吏)** a government official; a public servant／~가 되다 enter the government service.

**관리(管理)** (지배·취체) management; administration; control; supervision (보관) custody; charge; care／~하다 administer; manage; take charge of／~인 a manager; a superintendent; a custodian (집의) a caretaker／~권 right of management.

**관림(官林)** a government forest; a state-owned forest.

**관립(官立)** government institution／~의 government[al]／~ 학교 a government school.

**관망(冠網)** a hat and a head-band.

**관망(觀望)** watching observation／~하다 observe; watch (형세를) wait and see; ／형세를 ~하다 watch the course of events; sit on the fence／~주의(主義) a wait and see policy.

**관머리(棺一)** the head of a coffin.

**관멤(棺一)** filling the coffin space not taken up by the corpse.

**관명(官名)** an official title.

**관명(冠名)** the name given on coming of age.

**관명(官命)** official orders (관용) an official mission[business]／~에 의해서 by order of the government; by offi-

**관모(官帽)** an official hat. かんりのぼうし
**관모(冠毛)** ①【식】an egret; a pappus ②【조】a crest.
**관목(灌木)** a shrub; a bush. かんぼく
**관물(官沒)** confiscation; forfeiture; seizure/~하다 confiscate; forfeit; seize.
**관문(關門)** a barrier; a gateway/시험의 ~을 통과하다 pass the examination/~지기 a barrier-keeper. かんもん
**관문서(官文書)** an official document/~위조(僞造) forgery of an official document. かんのぶんしょ
**관물(官物)** government property; government issues. かんぶつ
**관민(官民)** officials and people; the governing and the governed/~이 협력하여 by the united efforts of government and people. かんみん
**관발(管一)**【동】a tube[ambulacral] foot.
**관변측(官邊側)** (in) official[government] circles[quarters]; government sources. かんぺんがわ
**관병(官兵)** the government forces[troops]. かんぐん
**관병식(觀兵式)** a military review; a parade/~장(場) a parade-ground/~을 거행하다 hold a grand review of the army[troops]. かんぺいしき
**관보(官報)** the official gazette (전보) an official telegram/~로 발표하다 gazette; announce[publish] by[in] the Official Gazette/~에 나다 be published in the Official Gazette. かんぽう
**관복(官服)** an official uniform[outfit, garb, attire]. かんぷく
**관봉(官封)** an official seal.
**관부(官府)** the government; the authorities. せいふまたはやくしょ
**관북(關北)** the *Kwanbuk* districts; the *Hamkyongdo* area.
**관불(灌佛)**【종】celebration of an anniversary of Buddha's birth.
**관비(官婢)** a woman-servant in government employ. かんちょうづかえのおんな
**관비(官費)** expense of the government; government expense/~ 학생 a student at government expense/~로 정부 rnment expense. かんぴ
**관사(官舍)** an official residence/~를 배당받다 be provided with an official residence. かんしゃ
**관사(官事)** government affairs; official business.
**관사(冠詞)**【언】an article; a determiner/정[부정]~ a definite[an indefinite] article. かんし
**관상(冠狀)** ~의 coronary; coronal; coronate/~ 동맥[정맥]《심장의》the coronary arteries[veins]/~ 봉합(縫合)【해】a coronal suture.
**관상(管狀)** ~의 tubular; tubulous; tubiform/~의 물건 a tube.
**관상(觀象)** meteorological observation/~하다 make a meteorological observation/~대 an observatory; an observation station[post]. かんしょう
**관상(觀相)** phrenological interpretation/~술(術) physiognomy; phrenology/~장이 a physiognomist; a phrenologist. かんそう
**관상(觀賞)** admiration; enjoyment/~하다 admire; enjoy/~ 식물【식】an ornamental plant. かんしょう
**관서(官署)** a government office. かんしょ
**관서(寬恕)** forbearance; forgiveness; tolerance/~하다 forbear; forgive; pardon; tolerate. かんじょ
**관선(官線)** a state [railway] line **(총칭)** the government railways. かんせん
**관선(官選)** ~의 chosen[appointed] by the government/~ 변호인 an official counsel. かんせん
**관설(官設)** ~의 established by the government; government.
**관섭(關涉)** interference; intervention; meddling/~하다 interfere (in *a matter*) with (*one*); meddle in[with]; step in; intervene (*in*). かんしょう
**관성(慣性)**【물】inertia/~ 능률 the moment of inertia/~ 기동기 an inertia starter. かんせい
**관세(關稅)** customs; a [customs] tariff **(세율)** tariff rates/긴급 ~ an emergency tariff/협정 ~ conventional customs duties/~ 장벽 a tariff barrier[wall]/~ 자주권 customs autonomy/~국 the Customs Bureau/~ 정책 a tariff policy/보호 ~ a protective[preferential] tariff. かんぜい
**관세(觀勢)** ~하다 watch the situation; watch the development of affairs; wait for a turn of events; sit on the fence.
**관솔** resinous knots of pine tree/~불 a fire set to pine knots. まつやにのこぶ
**관수(貫數)**《무게》weight/~가 나가다 be heavy; weigh much.
**관수 지대(冠水地帶)** a submerged[flooded] zone.
**관숙(慣熟)** ①《눈이나 손에》familiarity/~하다 (be) practised; familiar ②《친숙》familiarity; intimacy/~하다 (be) intimate; familiar; close.
**관습(慣習)** custom; usage; convention; usual practice/~적 customary; usual/~법 a customary law; the common law /사회의 ~ the social code; the mores. かんしゅう
**관심(關心)** concern; interest/~사 a matter of concern/…에 ~을 갖다 be concerned with[about]; be interested in /…에 ~이 없다 be indifferent to/우리들은 선거의 결과에 ~을 갖고 있다 We are interested in the result of the election. /그 여자는 옷차림에 관심이 없다 She is indifferent about her appearance. かんしん

**관아(官衙)** a government office; a yamen. かんが

**관악(管樂)** pipe-music; the wind music.

**관악기(管樂器)** a wind-instrument.

**관약(管籥)** flutes.

**관업(官業)** a government enterprise[undertaking] 《전매》 a government monopoly/~ 노동자 workers in state enterprise. かんぎょう

**관여(關與)** participation/ ~하다 take [have] part in; participate in; be concerned in; play a part in/정치에 ~하다 mix[have a part] in politics/사건에 ~하다 be involved in a case; take part in an affair. かんよ

**관역(官役)** ①《관청의 역사》official[government] [construction] work ②《부역》labour service [requisitioned by local authorities]. かんやく

**관영(官營)** government management/~의 government-managed; government-controlled/~ 사업 a government undertaking[enterprise]/ ~으로 하다 nationalize. かんえい

**관옥(冠玉)** ①《관 꾸미는 옥》jewels or jades attached to the front part of a crown ②《남자 얼굴》a handsome face.

**관외(管外)** ~의 outside the jurisdiction. かんがい

**관용(寬容)** magnanimity; tolerance; leniency/ ~하다 tolerate; bear[put up] with; forgive; pardon; be generous; /~의 정신(精神) the spirit of tolerance. かんよう

**관용(官用)** official[government] business; government service/ ~으로서 for official use/ ~으로 on official business. かんよう

**관용(慣用)** usage; common use 《인습》 convention; tradition; custom/ ~의 common; usual; customary; accustomed; conventional; of common[everyday] use 《어귀의》 idiomatic[al]; colloquial/ ~어 an idiom. カんよう

**관원(官員)** a government official[clerk]; a public official[servant]; a public functionary. かんいん

**관위(官位)** 《관(官)과 위(位)》 office and rank 《관등》 official rank/~도 아무 것도 없는 사람 a plain man holding neither office nor rank. かんい

**관유(官有)** government ownership/ ~의 government-owned/ ~물 government property/~림 government[state] forests/~가 되다 become government[state] property; be nationalized/~지 government land. かんゆう

**관유(寬裕)** ~하다 (be) gracious; tolerant; lenient; magnanimous.

**관이** one who leads [the trumps]. おや

**관인(官人)** a government[a public] official; an official. やくにん

**관인(官印)** an official[a government] seal. かんいん

**관인(寬仁)** generosity; liberality; magnanimity/ ~하다 (be) generous; liberal / ~한 generous; liberal.

**관자(貫子)** head-band buttons.

**관자놀이** the temple [of one's head]. あたまのりょうほうのびんぎわ

**관작(官爵)** office and rank. かんしゃく

**관장(灌腸)** an injection; an enema/ ~하다 clyster; administer[give] an enema to/ ~기 an enema; a clyster pipe. かんちょう

**관장(管掌)** management; administration / ~하다 manage; administer; have (a matter) in charge. かんしょう

**관장(館長)** a superintendent; a director 《도서관의》 a [head] librarian 《박물관의》 a curator. かんちょう

**관재(管財)** 《유산의》 administration 《파산시의》 receivership; property custodianship/~하다 administer; put [property] under one's custody/ ~인 《공공물의》 a trustee 《유산의》 an administrator 《청산시의》 a receiver 《정부 등의》 a property custodian/ ~국 the Property Custodian Bureau. かんざい

**관저(官邸)** an official residence /장관을 ~로 방문했다 I called on the Minister at his official residence. かんてい

**관전(觀戰)** 《전쟁의》 witnessing a battle; observation of military operations 《경기의》 witnessing a game/~하다 witness a battle; observe [a game]. かんせん

**관절(關節)** 【해】 a joint; an articulation 《이어서 이루어지는》 a joint/~의 articular/ ~부 joint region/ ~염 inflammation of a joint/~병 a joint[an articular] disease. かんせつ

**관절(冠絶)** ~하다 be unsurpassed; be matchless; ・be unique; have no peer; rank[stand] foremost; stand[be] peerless[unparalleled]. かんぜつ

**관점(觀點)** a point of view; a viewpoint; a standpoint/이 ~에서 from this viewpoint. かんてん

**관정(寬政)** liberal rule; benevolent government/ ~을 베풀다 govern with generosity.

**관정(灌頂)** 《세례의》 sprinkling of water/ ~하다 sprinkle water.

**관제(官制)** government organization[set up]; official regulations/~ 개혁(改革) reform of government organization/ ~를 정하다 establish a government organization. かんせい

**관제(官製)** ~의 manufactured by the government; of government make/~ 엽서 government post-cards/ ~ 담배 tobacco manufactured by the Office of Monopoly. かんせい

**관제(管制)** control; controlling /~동화 control of light 《소등》 black-out《속》; brown-out 《제한》 dim-out/~ 장치 controlling gear/ ~판(版) a controlling valve/ 보도(報道) ~ news censorship[bl-

관조(觀照) contemplation; meditation; observation 《미학》 intuition. かんせい

관존 민비(官尊民卑) preponderance of official power; putting government above [before] people／ ～의 폐풍 the deplorable custom of making much of the government and little of the people. かんそんみんぴ

관주(貫珠) a small circle marked on the right-hand side of a letter to distinguish it from others.

관중(貫衆) 【식】*Athyrium brevifrons*(학명).

관중(觀衆) spectators; an audience; onlookers／그는 ～의 우뢰 같은 박수를 받으며 등장했다 He appeared on the stage amid a thunderous hand-clapping of the audience. かんしゅう

관직(官職) government service; a government post／ ～에 앉다 enter government service. かんしょく

관찰(觀察) observation; survey／～하다 observe; survey; watch／～력 the power of observation／ ～안(眼) an observing eye／ ～자(者) an observer／그의 ～안은 날카롭다 He is a man of observation／정확한 ～ an accurate observation／～점 a view point. かんさつ

관찰사(觀察使) a [provincial] governor.

관철(貫徹) ①《수행》 accomplishment; consummation; fulfil[l]ment／～하다 accomplish; realize; carry out／목적을 ～하다 realize[carry through] one's purpose; attain one's object ②《투철》 penetration／ ～하다 penetrate; pierce; run through. かんてつ

관청(官廳) a government[public] office ／ 해당 ～ the authorities concerned／ ～식 officialism; red-tapism／～식의 official／ ～에 근무하다 attend[serve in] a government office. かんちょう

관측(觀測) observation; survey／～하다 observe; survey／ ～소 an observatory ／ ～자 an observer／ ～의(儀) an astrolabe／희망적 ～ wishful thinking／기상을 ～하다 makem eteorological observation. かんそく

관통(貫通) penetration／ ～하다 pierce; penetrate; pass through 《탄환 따위가》 shoot through／～총창(銃創) a piercing bullet-wound／흉부에 ～상을 입히다 shoot (one) through the chest. かんつう

관포지교(管鮑之交) a Damon and his as friendship／ ～를 맺다 beco bosom friends; enter into intimate relations with; be as thick as thieves. かんぽうのまじわり

관품(官品) an official rank.

관하(管下) ～의[에] under the jurisdiction[control] of. かんか

관하다(關一) ①《관계》 be connected with; concern; relate to／ …에 관하여 about; as to; regarding; concerning; with respect to／…에 관한 한 as far as (it is) concerned／그 점에 관해서 on that point; in that connection／철학에 관한 책 a book on philosophy ②《영향》 affect; concern; compromise／명예에 관하여 concern one's hono[u]r. かんする

관학(官學) a government school; an academy. かんがく

관한(寬限) gernerous postponement[deferment]／～하다 postpone; put off.

관할(管轄) jurisdiction; control; competence 《영역》 province／ ～하다 exercise jurisdiction (over); control; govern; have competence over (a matter)／ ～ 관청 the competent authorities／ ～권 jurisdiction／…의 ～에 속하다 be within the province (of); fall under the jurisdiction (of). かんかつ

관함(官銜) an official title.

관함식(觀艦式) a naval review. かんかんしき

관항(款項) ①《적요》 a summary 《요점》 the gist; the point; essentials 《요령》 the substance ②《관과 항》 a title and an item. かんこう

관행(慣行) custom; practice. かんこう

관향(貫鄕) the birthplace of one's first ancestor. かんきょう

관허(官許) government permission[licence]／～의 licenced／～를 얻어 under government licence; with government permission. かんきょ

관헌(官憲) the authorities; the official ／지방(地方) ～ the local authorities／ ～의 압박 the pressure of the authorities. かんけん

관현(管絃) wind and string instruments ／ ～악 an orchestra／～악단 an orchestra band. かんげん

관형사(冠形詞) an unconjugating adjective. かんけいし

관혼 상제(冠婚喪祭) ceremonial occasions; the ceremonies of coming of age, marriage, funeral, and ancestral worship, etc. かんこんそうさい

관화(官話) Mandarin [dialect](Chin).

관후(寬厚) generosity; liberality; catholicity; large-heartedness; lenity; leniency／ ～하다 (be) generous; liberal／ ～ 하게 generously; liberally／ ～한 태도 an air of magnanimity／ ～히 하다 be generous; show clemency; deal lenientiy with (one).

괄괄 gurgling; gushing; with a gurgle; with a gush. どくどく

괄괄하다 ①《성질이》 (be) vigorous; brisk; spirited; mettlesome; rough; harsh／ 괄괄한 사람 a man of spirit ②《풀기가》 (be) too stiff; be sticky／이 샤쓰는 풀이 너무 ～ This shirt is starched too stiff. せいしつがあらい

괄다 《화력이》 (be) strong;lively; intense ／화력이 ～ have strong caloric force; ひのせいがつよい

괄대(忽待) inhospitality; a cold treat-

괄목 괄목(刮目) ~하다 watch with keen interest; watch eagerly[closely]/ ~ 상대하다 watch with great expectation [close attention]/~하고 기다리다 wait with keen interest. かつもく

괄선(括線) 〖수〗 a vinculum; a bracket; a ligature. かっせん

괄시(恝視) ~하다 (박대)treat (one) cooly; be inhospitable toward (업수이 여기다) look down on; look on (one) with contempt; disparage; be treated with contempt/너무 ~를 말게 Don't hold me so cheap. いやなたいどでたいすること

괄약(括約) constriction/ ~하다 constrict/~근(筋) 〖해〗 a sphincter; a constrictor; sphincterial muscles.

괄연히(恝然─) coldly; indifferently.

괄하다 be stickly; be spirited ⇒괄괄하다.

괄호(括弧) 《둥근 괄호》 parenthesis 《각 괄호》 brackets 《큰 괄호》 a brace/이중 a double parenthesis/ ~ 안의 부분 a parenthesized[a bracketed] passage/ ~ 속에 넣다 parenthesize; bracket/~로 묶다 put in parentheses. かっこ

광 a store-room (망광)a cellar; a storehouse. そうこ

광 with a bang[boom]; with a thud [bump, thump]/문을 ~ 닫다 bang[slam] a door [shut]/총소리가 ~하고 났다 Bang! went the gun. ずどん

광(光) 《윤》 gloss; luster/ ~내다 polish up; make (a thing) glossy/ ~나다 be glossy. つや

광(廣) 《넓이》 area; extent (너비) width; breadth/ ~이 5피트다 be five feet broad[in breadth]. ひろさ

광(壙) a grave. はかのあな

광(鑛) ore/~철~ an iron ore. こうぎょう

-광(狂) 《광인》 a maniac; an enthusiast; a fan/영화~ a movie[a cinema] fan /살인~ homicidal mania/야구~ a homicidal maniac/야구~ a baseball fan; a mania for baseball. きちがい

광가(狂歌) 《우스운 노래》 a comic poem; a satirical poem 《곡조 안 맞는 노래》a song out of tune.

광각(光覺) sensation of light; the optic sense. こうかく

광각(光角) 〖물〗 an optic angle. しかく

광각(廣角) a wide-angle/~ 렌즈 a wide-angle lens; a pantoscope. こうかく

광갱(鑛坑) a mine [shaft]; a pit.

광견(狂犬) a rabid[a mad] dog/~병(病) rabies; hydrophobia/~병 예방 접종(豫防接種) anti-hydrophobia inoculation. きょうけん

광경(光景) a spectacle; a sight; a view; a scene/참담한 ~ a terrible spectacle; a disastrous scene/그것은 슬픈 ~이었다 It was a sad sight. こうけい

광고(廣告) an advertisement 《선전》 publicity/ ~하다 advertise; announce/ ~탑 an advertisement tower[pillar] / ~ 삐라 a bill; a handbill/ ~란 an advertisement column/신문 ~ a newspaper advertisement/~ 방송 a commercial [broadcast]/ ~술 [the art of] advertising/~ 우편[물] advertisement mail[matter]. こうこく

광공업(鑛工業) the mining and manufacturing industries. こうこうぎょう

광광 bang-bang; boom-boom/ ~하다 go bang bang/대포를 ~ 쏘다 boom a cannon repeatedly. ずどんずどん

광구(匡救) relief; succour/~하다 relieve; give succour (to). ただしくすくうこと

광구(鑛區) a mine-lot; diggings. こうく

광구(光球) 〖천〗 photosphere.

광군(鑛軍) a miner; a mine-worker; a pit man/ ~ 노릇을 하다 work in a mine.

광궤(廣軌) a broad-gauge; the standard gauge/~ 철도 a broad-gauge railway [railroad]. こうき

광기(狂氣) madness; craziness; insanity; lunacy; frenzy; mental derangement/ 그의 영주도는 ~에 가깝다 His zeal verges on madness. きょうき

광나다(光─) become glossy; become lustrous; grow bright/닦아서 ~ admit [take] a good polish/마호가니는 닦으면 아름답게 광난다 Mahogany polishes beautifully. つやがでる

광내다(光─) shine 《닦아서》 polish; make (a thing) shine[bright]. つやをたす

광녀(狂女) a madwoman. きちがいおんな

광년(光年) 〖천〗 a light year. こうねん

광담(狂談) crazy[mad, frantic] talk; nonsense.

광대[1] an actor; an actress(여자); a player 《출연자》 a performer/소인(素人) ~ an amateur actor 《임시의》 an extra/ 익살 ~ a professional jester; a buffon / ~질 the stage[career].

광대[2] 《용모》 a countenance; a face; a look. かお

광대(廣大) ~하다 (be) immense; vast; enormous; stupendous; extensive; boundless/~ 무변한 [vast and] boundless; infinite. こうだいだ

광대나물 〖식〗 a henbit; a dead nettle; Lamium amplexicaule(학명).

광대뼈 the cheekbone; the malar bone / ~의 zygomatic; malar/~가 쑥 나와 있다 have a prominent[high] cheekbone. ほおぼね

광도(光度) intensity of light; illuminating power/ ~계 a photometer. こうど

광도(廣跳) 〖체〗 a broad jump. はばとび

광도(狂濤) the raging waters; a stormy sea. きょうとう

광독(鑛毒) mineral pollution; copper poisoning/ ~의 피해 damage from mine pollution. こうどく

광란(狂亂) madness; craziness; fury;

frenzy/ ～하다 go mad[crazy]; become mad 《비통해서》be[become] frantic; get wild; be beside *oneself*; rage; 《미쳐 날뛰다》rave/ ～한 mad; crazy; insane; wild; raving/ ～하는 파도 raging waves[seas]. きょうらん

**광란**(狂瀾) raging waves[seas]/～ 노도(怒濤) the angry[the violent] waves; the mountainous seas; the boiling[the weltering] seas. きょうらん

**광량자**(光量子) 【물】a photon; light quantum. こうりょうし

**광력**(光力) illuminating power; light; brightness. こうりょく

**광림**(光臨) your visit; your coming; your presence; your call/ ～하다 come; call on/ ～의 영광을 얻고 싶습니다 I will be glad to be honoured with your presence. こうりん

**광막**(廣漠) extent; expanse (of *water*); a stretch/ ～하다 (be) vast; wide; boundleas/ ～한 땅[토지] a wide spread of country; a vast tract of land/～ 한 초원 the vast plains(미). こうばく

**광망**(光芒) light; beam. こうぼう

**광맥**(鑛脈) a vein of ore; a lode; a lead; a deposit; a mineral vein/ 그는 바위 속에서 ～을 발견했다 He discovered the veins of metal in a rock/～층 seam[vein] of ore. こうみゃく

**광면**(廣面) a wide circle of acquaintance/～하다 have large social connections; have a large[wide] circle of acquaintances;. かおがひろいこと

**광명**(光明) ①《빛》light ②《희망》hope; a bright future. こうみょう

**광명두** a wooden lamp holder.

**광명 정대**(光明正大) fairness; justice; openness; [a sense of] fair play/～하다 be fair; just. こうめいせいだい

**광목**(廣木) cotton cloth. もめん

**광무**(鑛務) the Mining Bureau/ ～소 a mining scrivener's office.

**광물**(鑛物) a mineral/～질 mineral matter/ ～학 mineralogy/ ～학자 mineralogist. こうぶつ

**광범위**(廣範圍) a wide scope; a vast range/ ～한 extensive/ ～한 개혁 a far reaching reform. こうはんい

**광복**(光復) revival; rehabilitation; restoration of independence/ ～절 Independence[Liberation] Day of Korea.

**광부**(鑛夫) a miner; a mine worker; a pitman; a digger. こうふ

**광분**(狂奔) ～하다 run wild; busy *oneself* about; run madly about; make desperate efforts. きょうほんする

**광산**(鑛山) a mine; a mine field/ ～ 기사 a mining engineer/～ 노동자 a miner; a mine worker/ ～업 the mining industry; mining/～학 [the study of] mining. こうざん

**광산**(鑛産) a mineral product/ ～지(地) a mineralized area.

**광상**(鑛床) 【광】[mineral] deposits; an ore deposit. こうしょう

**광상곡**(狂想曲) 【음】a rhapsody/～을 짓다 rhapsodize. きょうそうきょく

**광석**(鑛石) a mineral; an ore 《라디오의》a crystal. こうせき

**광선**(光線) light; a ray[beam] of light / ～의 반사 the reflection of light/～ 요법 phototherapy. こうせん

**광세**(曠世) being unparalleled[unprecedented]/ ～하다 be rare; extraordinary; unparalleled/ ～지재 a man of unparalleled talent.

**광속도**(光速度) the velocity of light. こうそくど

**광수**(鑛水) a mineral water.

**광시**(狂詩) a comic[satirical] poem; a parody. きょうし

**광신**(狂信) [religious] fanaticism/～하다 be devoted blindly; fanatically believe/～자 a fanatic. きょうしん

**광심**(光心) 【물】an optical centre. こうしん

**광야**(曠野) a wilderness; a wide plain; a desolate plain. こうや

**광어**(廣魚) a [dried] flatfish.

**광언**(狂言) unreasonable talk; nonsense¹/～ 망설(妄說) absurd nonsense; incoherent ravings. きょうげん

**광업**(鑛業) mining [industry]/ ～가 a mine operator; a mine owner/～ 회사 a mining company. こうぎょう

**광역 경제**(廣域經濟) great-sphere economy.

**광영**(光榮) honor; glory. こうえい

**광우리 장수** a woman carrying a basket load of articles on the head.

**광원**(廣遠) ～하다 extensive; be vast and far-reaching/ ～한 계획 far-reaching designs.

**광원**(光源) 【물】a source of light; a luminescent source.

**광유**(鑛油) mineral oil. こうぶつゆ

**광음**(光陰) time/ ～은 쏜살같이 흐른다 Time flies like an arrow. こういん

**광의**(廣義) a broad sense/ ～로 해석하다 interpret (*it*) in a broad sense. こうぎ

**-광이** a person/느리～ a slowpoke.
—もの

**광인**(狂人) a lunatic; a madman; an insane person. きょうじん

**광자**(光子) 【물】a photon.

**광장**(廣場) an open space; a [public] square. ひろば

**광재**(鑛滓) slag; dross.

**광저기** 【식】the common cowpea. ささげ

**광적**(狂的) mad; insane; lunatic; frantic; wild/ ～으로 madly; frantically; wildly.

**광전**(光電) photoelectricity/ ～자 a photoelectron/ ～ 효과 the photoelectric effect. こうでん

**광점**(光點) a luminous point; a radiant 《태양의》a facula. こうてん

광정(匡正) reform; correction/~하다 reform; remedy. きょうせい

광조(狂躁) frenzy; fury/~하다 be mad; be raving; be frantic; be furious/~한 mad; wild; frantic. きょうそう

광주(鑛主) the owner of a mine; a mineowner. こうざんのしゅじん

광주리 a round basket made of bamboo, wicker, twigs and the like. かご

광중(壙中) the hollow of a grave.

광증(狂症) insanity; frenzy; madness; lunacy. きょうしょう

광채(光彩) lustre; brilliancy; splendor /그녀의 눈은 ~를 잃었다 Her eyes lost their luster. こうさい

광천(鑛泉) a mineral spring 《광수》 mineral water. こうせん

광체(光體) 【물】 a luminous body; a luminary. こうたい

광축(光軸) 【물】 an optical axis.

광층(鑛層) an ore bed. こうそう

광치다 show off; display; make a show of; flaunt. ぴかぴかひかる

광탄(光彈) a flare bomb; a star shell; a light-ball.

광태(狂態) shameful[disgraceful] conduct; crazy; behavior. きょうたい

광택(光澤) lustre; gloss; brilliance; glaze/~ 있는 lustrous; glossy. こうたく

광파(光波) 【물】 a light wave. こうは

광패(狂悖) frenzy; fury/~하다 be furious; frenzied.

광포(廣布) announcement; propagation; diffusion/~하다 propagate; spread.

광포(狂暴) outrage; frenzy; fury; wildness. きょうぼう

광폭(廣幅) ①(넓은 폭) double width; an wide width (of cloth) ②(간섭) interference; meddling. ひろはば

광풍(狂風) a raging wind; a violent gale. きょうふう

광학(光學) optics; optical science/~ 기구 an optical instrument. こうがく

광한(狂漢) a madman; an insane person.

광행차(光行差) 【천】 an aberration/유성 ~ planetary aberration.

광협(廣狹) relative width.

광화학(光化學) 【물】 photochemistry.

광활(廣闊) spaciousness; extensiveness /~하다 (be) spacious; wide; extensive. こうかつ

광휘(光輝) brilliance; splendor; glory; glow. こうき

광희(狂喜) wild joy; a frenzy of joy; exultation; ecstasy. きょうき

꽤 fairly; pretty; quite; tolerably; rather; considerably/~ 많은 돈 a sizable [considerable] sum of money. かなり

괘(卦) divination; prediction; fortunetelling. け

괘경(掛鏡) a hanging mirror; a wall mirror. かけかがみ

괘괘떼다, 괘괘이떼다 refuse flatly; give a flat refusal. きっぱりことわる

괘괘스럽다 be most peculiar.

괘그르다(卦—) have bad luck; go wrong; miscarry. しっぱいする

괘금(掛金) ①(보험료) an insurance premium ②(도박) stakes; a bet. かけきん

괘념(掛念) ~하다 mind; care; be concerned over; worry about. しんぱい

괘다리적다, 괘달머리적다 ①(거칠다) be boorish; unmannerly ②(뻔뻔하다) be impudent orish; brazen; unblushing; cheek brazen. みずくさくあつかましい

괘도(掛圖) a wall map[chart]. かけず

괘력(掛曆) a wall calendar. かけごよみ

괘방(掛榜) a notice; an official list of successful candidates.

괘사 a prank; practical joke; ~떨다 play pranks on; play a practical joke on. おどけたしぐさ

괘씸하다 be insolent; impertinent; outrageous; offensive; detestable/괘씸한 짓 an improper act. けしからん

괘장 a sudden switch[reversal] in attitude/~부치다 suddenly reverse one's attitude. きまぐれ

괘종(掛鍾) a [wall] clock. はしらとけい

괘지(罫紙) ruled[lined] paper. けいし

꽥 with a shout[scream, shriek, yell] /~하다 utter[give] a shriek[shout, yell].

꽥꽥 screaming; screeching; quack-quack/~하다 shout; yell. きゃっきゃっ

꽥 지르다 cry; shout; roar; thunder; bark《속》. きゃっとさけぶ

괜찮다 ①(쓸 만하다) be passable; good ② (상관 없다) don't care[mind]/ 나는 ~ I don't mind. かまわない

괜히 in vain; uselessly; fruitlessly; pointlessly/~ 애쓰다 labor in vain.

꽹과리 a [small] gong/~를 치다 beat a gong.

꽹이¹ a hoe; a pick/~로 파다 dig with a hoe; hoe up the soil. くわ

꽹이² a cat ⇨고양이.

괴 ①(지혜) wise counsel; wit; resources ②(계략) an artifice; a trick; a ruse/ ~가 많은 crafty.

괴까다롭다, 괴까다톱다 ①(문제가) (be) tricky; intricate; be difficult ②(성미가) (be) particular; fastidious; fussy; finicky; be hard to please. きむずかしい

괴걸(怪傑) a mystery man; a person of remarkable qualities/a wonder man 《미》. ふしぎなちからをもつにんげん

괴경(塊莖) 【식】 a tuber; a seed/~ 식물 a tuber plant. かいけい

괴꼬리 a [Korean] nightingale; a bush warbler; an oriole. うぐいす

괴꼬로 taking advantage of odd moments; in one's spare moments.

괴괴망측하다(怪怪罔測—) (be) grotesque; mysterious; queer/괴괴측한 풍설 a wild rumor. ひじょうにおかしい

괴괴하다 (be) quiet; still; silent; deserted. ひじょうにものしずかだ

**괴근(塊根)** 【식】 a tuberous[a tuberose] root. かいこん

**괴금(塊金)** a nugget of gold; gold ingot; gold bullion. かいきん

**괴나리봇짐** a traveler's rucksack[knapsack].

**괴다¹** 《물이》 gather; collect; form a puddle; stay; stagnate. たまる

**괴다²** 《발효하다》 ferment; undergo fermentation; be in a ferment. わく

**괴다³** ①《받치다》 support; prop ②《음식을 상에》 arrange[pile up] food on the table. ささえる

**꾀다¹** swarm; crowd; gather; flock; be infested with／음식에 파리가 꾀지 않도록 하다 keep flies away from the food. むしなどがむれる

**꾀다²** 《유혹하다》 tempt; entice; lure; decoy; seduce. だます

**괴담(怪談)** a ghost[spooky] story; a strange story. かいだん

**괴덕부리다** act in a flippant[frivolous] manner. ふざける

**괴덕스럽다** be flippant; frivolous; (be) frivolous and unfaithful. ふまじめだ

**괴도(怪盜)** a mysterious thief.

**괴란(壞亂)** ①《풍속의》 corruption ②《질서의》 subversion／～하다 demoralize; corrupt; destroy. かいらん

**괴란(愧赧)** blushing with shame／～하다 blush with shame; be ashamed.

**괴란쩍다(愧赧一)** be disgusting[repellent, sickening, disagreeable] [to see]; unpleasant. むかつくようだ

**괴력(怪力)** superhuman[Herculean, hyperphysical] strength. かいりき

**괴로움** 《수고》 trouble; agony; sufferings; distress; hardship／삶의 ～ worries[troubles] of life. くるしみ

**괴롭다** ①《고통스럽다》 be painful; distressing; trying ②《곤란하다》 be hard; difficult ③《귀찮다》 be troublesome／피로운 나머지 driven by pain. くるしい

**괴롭히다** afflict[harass, torment] (a person); worry[annoy, bother] (a person). くるしめる

**괴뢰(傀儡)** a puppet; a marionette; a robot; a tool／～ 노릇을 하다 act as another's tool／～ 정부 a puppet government. かいらい

**괴망하다(怪妄—)** be monstrous; scandalous; eccentric. きいだ

**괴멸(壞滅)** destruction; ruin; annihilation／～하다 《스스로》 be destroyed 《남을》 destory.

**괴문(怪聞)** a strange[wild] rumo[u]r 《추문》 a scandal. あやしいうわさ

**괴문서(怪文書)** reprehensible literature; an irresponsible[slanderous] writing.

**괴물(怪物)** a monster; a ghost; a bogey 《사람》 a mysterious man. かいぶつ

**괴바르다** be crafty; shrewd; cunning; sly. ずるい

**괴발개발** clumsily; write at random; sloppily／～ 그리다 write clumsily; write at random. 走り書きするさま

**괴배** fake stomachache; feigned stomachache／～를 앓다 pretend to have a stomachache. にせふくつう

**괴벽(乖僻)** oddity; eccentricity／～하다 (be) eccentric／그는 ～하기로 유명했다 He was pretty well known for his eccentricity. きいなくせ

**괴변(怪變)** a strange accident; an odd mishap. きかいなじこ

**괴병** feigned[pretended, fake] illness／～부리다 feign[sham] illness. けびょう

**괴병(怪病)** a mysterious disease. きかいなびょうき

**괴보** a man of quick wit; a man of resources; a tricky person; a wily person. りこうもの

**괴부리다** shirk [one's duty]; dodge; evade／꾀부리고 숙제를 않다 shirk one's home works. ずるける

**괴사(怪死)** a mysterious death／～ 사건 a case of mysterious death.

**괴사(怪事)** a mysterious; a wonder; a strange event. かいじ

**괴상(怪常)** ～하다 (be) strange; queer; peculiar; odd／～하게 생각하다 think strange. ひじょうにおかしい

**괴석(怪石)** a oddly shaped stone; a fantastic stone. いしころ

**괴수(怪獸)** a monster. かいじゅう

**괴수(魁首)** a ringleader／폭도의 ～ the ringleader of a mob. かいしゅ

**꾀쓰다** use[play] tricks; resort to wiles [a ruse] 《꾀부리다》 shirk／꾀를 써서 적을 물리치다 employ a stratagem to repulse the enemy. ちえをしぼる

**괴음괴음** with honeyed[fair] words; tempting (a person) with fine words／～하다 seduce; tempt; lure.

**괴이다** get propped; be supported 《음식이 상에》 be piled up. ささえられる

**꾀이다¹** tempt; seduce ⇒꾀다.

**꾀이다²** 《꾐을 당하다》 be lured; be enticed [tempted, seduced]. ゆうわくされる

**괴이쩍다(怪異一)** (be) strange; queer ⇒ 괴이하다. ふしぎだ

**괴이하다(怪異一)** (be) strange; funy; mysterious; grotesque／～한 이야기 a strange[weird] story. かいい

**괴짜(怪一)** an odd person; a mystery man; a crank; an odd fish／그 친구는 ～다 He is a character.

**꾀자기** a crafty[sly, wily] person; an old fox. ずるいやつ

**괴잠** sham[feigned] sleep; fox-sleep／～을 자다 feign to be asleep; sham sleep. たぬきねいり

**괴저(壞疽)** 【의】 gangrene; necrosis.

**괴죄하다** (be) shabby; miserable; untidy; seedy; poor[wretched] looking／옷차림이 ～ be shabbily[poorly] dressed; be ill-clad. だらしなくきたない

**괴질(怪疾)** a mystery disease; a strange

**괴철**(塊鐵) an iron ingot. てつのかたまり
**괴춤** [the area] between abdomen and belt.
**괴탄**(塊炭) lump coal. かいじょうのせきたん
**괴패**(乖敗) absurdity; unreasonableness／~하다 (be) absurd; unreasonable.
**괴팩스럽다** (be) fastidious ⇨괴팍하다. せいしつがへんでひとつきあいがわるい
**괴팍하다**(乖愎―) (be) fastidious; finical; fussy; obstinate／괴팍하게 음식을 가리다 be fastidious about food／괴팍한 사람 fastidious[finical, particular] person.
**꾀피우다** resort to petty tricks; play [use] tricks; frame up (*an ill design*); resort to artifice. ちえをしぼる
**꾀하다** plot; plan; attempt; conspire; design; project／자살을 ~ attempt suicide. くわだてる
**괴하다**(怪―) (be) strange; odd; queer; eccentric. おかしい
**괴한**(怪漢) a strange-looking character; a suspicious-looking fellow. かいかん
**괴혈병**(壞血病) 《의》 scurvy; scorbutus／~ 환자 a scorbutic. かいけつびょう
**괴화**(怪火) a mysterious fire; a fire of unknown origin. かいか
**괴후**(怪候, 乖候) unseasonable[unusual] weather. きみょうなてんこう
**괵수**(馘首) 《참수》 beheading; decapitation／~하다 behead; decapitate.
**괸돌** a dolmen ⇨고인돌. ドルメン
**꾐** temptation; allurement; enticement; seduction／~에 빠지기 쉽다 be easily overcome by temptation; be fragile; be weak. あざむくしゅだん
**굄돌** a stone prop[support].
**굄목**(―木) a wooden prop[support]. つっかいぼう
**굉굉하다**(轟轟―) (be) roaring; thundering rumbling. ごうごうとしている
**굉대**(宏大) ~하다 (be) vast; huge; grand; monstrous. こうだいだ
**굉연하다**(轟然―) (be) roaring; thundering; deafening／굉연히 폭발하다 explode with an ear-rending noise.
**굉원**(宏遠) ~하다 extensive; (be) vast and farreaching.
**굉장**(宏壯) ~하다 (be) grand; magnificent; splendid; stately; imposing／~히 magnificently／~한 미인 a strikingly beautiful woman. こうそう
**굉침**(轟沈) sinking by explosion／~하다 sink by explosion. ごうちん
**굉활**(宏闊) ~하다 extensive; wide; (be) spacious. こうかつ
**교**(敎) a faith; a religion; a teaching／~를 믿다 believe in a religion／불~ Buddhism／유~ Confucianism／그리스도~ Christianity. しゅうきょう
**교**(驕) haughtiness きょまん
**교가**(校歌) a school[college] song; an Alma Mater [song]. こうか
**교각**(橋脚) a bent; a pier.

**교각**(交角) 《수》 an angle of intersection.
**교각 살우**(矯角殺牛) The remedy is worse than the evil.
**교감**(校監) a head teacher; an assistant principal.
**교감**(交感) consensus; rapport; [mutual] sympathy／~ 신경 the sympathetic nerve. こうかん
**교갑**(膠匣) a capsule. カプセル
**교계**(交契) friendship; friendly relations.
**교골**(交骨) 《해》 pubis; the bones of the pelvis.
**교과**(教科) a course of study; the curriculum／《과목》 a subject／~서 a textbook; a schoolbook. きょうか
**교관**(教官) a teacher; an instructor; a professor. きょうかん
**교교하다**(皎皎―) (be) brilliant; bright／교교히 bright[ly]／달빛이 ~ The moon shinesbright[ly]. ひかりがあかるい
**교구**(教區) 《종》 a parish／~ 목사 a parish priest／~민 a parishioner. きょうく
**교구**(教具) teaching tools[aids]; teaching implements. きょうぐ
**교군**(轎軍) 《가맛군》 a palanquin bearer 《가마》 a palanquin. かごかき
**교권**(教權) ①《교회의》 ecclesiastical authority ②《교육상의》 educational authority. きょうけん
**교규**(校規) school regulations. こうき
**교기**(校旗) a school banner[flag]. こうき
**교기**(校紀) school discipline. こうき
**교기**(驕氣) a proud air; haughtiness; arrogance; insolence／~부리다 behave haughtily. きょうき
**교내**(校內) the school ground; the campus〈미〉. こうない
**교단**(教壇) the platform 《목사의》 the pulpit／~에 서다 teach at a school; be a teacher. きょうだん
**교단**(教團) a religious body[association, order, brotherhood]. きょうだん
**교당**(教堂) a church; a temple; a cathedral. きょうどう
**교대**(交代) change; alternation; relief; shift; relay／~하다 take *one's* turn [place]. こうたい
**교도**(教徒) a believer; an adherent／마호멧~ a Mohammedan. きょうと
**교도**(教導) teaching; instruction; training; guidance／~하다 instruct; teach; train. きょうどう
**교도관**(教導官) a prison officer; a warder〈미〉; a person guard.
**교도소**(矯導所) a prison〈미〉; a jail; a penitentiary; a gaol〈영〉.
**교두보**(橋頭堡) a bridgehead; a beachhead／해안에 ~를 확보하다 secure a beachhead on the enemy shore／~를 만들다 establish a bridgehead. きょうとうほ
**교란**(攪亂) disturbance; derangement／~하다 disturb; derange; upset; throw into confusion. かくらん

**교련(敎練)** training; drill; exercises 《군사 훈련》 military exercises; military drill. きょうれん

**교령(敎令)** a king's ordinance. きょうれい

**교료(校了)** finishing proofreading 《부호》 O.K. / ~쇄 a press proof. こうりょう

**교류(交流)** interchange 《전기의》 an alternating current / 인사 ~ interchange of personnel. こうりゅう

**교리(敎理)** a religious doctrine; a tenet / ~론 dogmatics. きょうり

**교린(交隣)** relations of neighbo[u]ring countries.

**교만(驕慢)** pride; elation; haughtiness; arrogance / ~하다 (be) proud; haughty; arrogant. きょうまん

**교모(敎母)** a [Catholic] sister.

**교목(喬木)** a tall tree; a forest tree; an arbor / ~대 the forest tree zone / ~성 arboreal. きょうぼく

**교묘(巧妙)** skill; deftness; cleverness / ~하다 (be) clever; skillful; expert; deft; tactful / ~하게 cleverly; skillfully; expertly / ~한 수단 a subtle trick. こうみょう

**교무(敎務)** ①《학교의》 school affairs / ~과 [주임] [the head of] the instruction department; the chief of school affairs ②《교회의》 religious affairs. きょうむ

**교문(校門)** a school-gate / ~을 나서다 leave school. こうもん

**교미(交尾)** copulation; coition / ~하다 copulate; couple 《새 따위》 tread 《짐승》 cover / ~기 the breeding[mating] season. こうび

**교배(交拜)** exchange of bows between the bride and the bridegroom at a wedding ceremony / ~하다 exchange nuptial bows.

**교배(交配)** crossing; cross-breeding 《식물의》 cross-fertilization / ~하다 cross; crossbreed; cross-fertilize. こうはい

**교번(交番)** alternation; change; [duty] relief; shift / 세대 ~ alternation of generations 《생물의》 digenesis. こうばん

**교범(敎範)** teaching methods; pedagogics; pedagogy. きょうはん

**교법(敎法)** a religious doctrine; a religion; a creed / ~사(師) a Catholic missionary. きょうほう

**교복(校服)** a school uniform. がっこうのせいふく

**교본(敎本)** a textbook. きょうほん

**교부(交付)** delivery; grant / ~하다 deliver; hand over; serve; grant / 통지서를 ~하다 serve (one) with a notice. こうふ

**교부(敎父)** ①《신부》 a [Catholic] father ②《대부》 godfather. しんぶ

**교분(交分)** friendship / ~이 두텁다 be good friends with; enjoy a close intimacy with. ゆうじょう

**교빙(交聘)** exchange of envoys / ~하다 exchange an envoy.

**교사(狡許)** clever fraud / ~하다 cheat by subtle trick / ~스럽다 (be) sly; tricky; crafty; foxy. こうさ

**교사(校舍)** a school-house; a school-building. こうしゃ

**교사(敎師)** a teacher; an instructor; a master; a schoolmaster / 여~ a schoolmistress; a lady teacher / ~자격증 a teacher's license[certificate] / ~직 instructorship. きょうし

**교사(敎唆)** instigation; incitement; abetment / ~하다 incite; instigate / ~ 방조죄 aiding and abetting. きょうさ

**교사(驕奢)** luxury; extravagance / ~하다 (be) luxurious; extravagant / ~를 다하다 live in grand style. きょうしゃ

**교살(絞殺)** strangulation / ~하다 murder by suffocation; strangle. こうしつ

**교상(咬傷)** an injury by biting / ~하다 injure by biting. こうしょう

**교생(敎生)** a student[pupil] teacher; school teacher in embryo. きょうせい

**교서(敎書)** a message / 대통령의 ~ the President's message (to Congress) / 연두 ~ 《미국 대통령의》 the annual State of the Union message. きょうしょ

**교섭(交涉)** ①《담론》 negotiation; bargaining; a parley; discussion / ~하다 negotiate (with) ②《관계》 relation; connection. こうしょう

**교성(嬌聲)** a lovely[charming] voice; seductive tone. きょうせい

**교수(絞首)** hanging; strangulation / ~하다 hang; strangle / ~용 밧줄 a halter / ~대 gallows; the gibbet / ~형(刑) death by hanging. こうしゅ

**교수(敎授)** teaching; instruction; tuition 《사람》 a professor 《전체》 the faculty / ~하다 teach; instruct; give instruction (in) / ~회 a faculty meeting / 개인 ~ private instruction. きょうじゅ

**교습(敎習)** training; instruction / ~하다 instruct; teach. きょうしゅう

**교시(敎示)** teaching; instruction / ~하다 instruct; teach. きょうし

**교식(矯飾)** ostentation; affectation; pomps / ~하다 display pomps; make outward show.

**교신(交信)** communication / ~하다 communicate (with); exchange telegraphic messages (with).

**교실(敎室)** a classroom; a schoolroom; a lecture room / 물리학 ~ a physics theater. きょうしつ

**교아절치(咬牙切齒)** teeth-grinding / ~하다 grind one's teeth with vexation.

**교안(敎案)** a teaching program[plan]; lesson plans / ~을 짜다 form a teaching plan. きょうあん

**교양(敎養)** culture; education; refinement / ~ 있는 cultured; refined; well-educated / ~학부 the general culture course; the liberal arts faculty [department]. きょうよう

**교언(巧言)** flattery; fair[fine] words /

~영색(令色) flattery; fine words and insinuating looks. こうげん
교역(交易) trade; commerce 《교환》barter/ ~하다 trade[barter] with; exchange. こうえき
교역(敎役) 【종】religious work/ ~자 a religious worker.
교열(校閱) revision; revisal; recension/ ~하다 revise/ ~자 a reviser/스미드 박사 ~ Revised by Dr. Smith. こうえつ
교열(咬裂) ~하다 bite off; tear off with teeth. かみさくこと
교오(驕傲) ~하다 (be) arrogant; proud; haughty. きょうごう
교외(校外) ~의 outside the school 《대학의》 extramural. こうがい
교외(郊外) the suburbs; the outskirts/ ~ 생활 a suburban life. こうがい
교우(敎友) 【종】a fellow believer; a fellow Buddhist[Christian].
교우(校友) 《동창》a schoolmate 《남자》an alumnus (pl. -ni) 《여자》an alumna(pl. -nae)〈미〉; an old boy; a graduate/ ~회 an alumni [graduates] association; an alumni meeting/ ~ 회지 an alumni bulletin. こうゆう
교우(僑寓) a temporary abode ⇨우거.
교우(交友) ①《사귐》companionship ②《벗》a friend; a companion; company; an acquaintance. こうゆう
교원(敎員) a teacher; an instructor 《총칭》the [teaching] staff/ ~ 자격증 a teacher's licence. きょういん
교유(敎諭) ①《가르침》instruction ②《선생》an instructor; a teacher; a middle-[high-] school master. きょうゆ
교유(交遊) companionship; friendship; acquaintance/ ~하다 associate (with); keep company (with).
교육(敎育) education 《교수》schooling 《훈련》instruction; training/ ~하다 educate; train/ ~가[자] an educationist; an educator/ ~행정 educational adminstration. きょういく
교의(交椅) 《의자》a chair/ ~에 기대다 lean on a chair. いす
교의(交誼) friendship; friendly relationship/ ~를 맺다 cultivate[promote] friendship with (a person)/ ~를 끊다 break friendship with. こうぎ
교의(校醫) a school doctor. こうい
교의(敎義) teachings; a dogma; a doctrine/ ~ 문답 catechism. きょうぎ
교인(敎人) a believer; an adherent; a follower. きょうと
교자(嬌姿) an attractive figure; a charming[bewitching] figure. きょうし
교자(交子) food set on a large table.
교자상(交子床) a large rectangular[dining] table.
교잡(交雜) confusion; disorder/ ~하다 be confused; be in disorder. こうざつ
교장(校長) ①《국민 학교》a schoolmaster; a schoolmistress(여자) ②《중학교》a principal ③《고등 학교》a director ④《주일학교》a superintendent/ ~ 회의 a headmaster's conference. こうちょう
교장(敎場) 《교련장》a drilling ground 《교실》a classroom; a schoolroom; a training field. きょうじょう
교장(校葬) a school funeral.
교재(敎材) teaching material; materials for teaching[instruction]. きょうざい
교전(交戰) ①《전쟁》war; hostilities ②《전투》a battle; an action/ ~하다 fight; engage in a battle/ ~국 belligerents; warring countries/ ~ 상태 a state of war/ ~군 embattled forces. こうせん
교전(敎典) a canon. きょうてん
교점(交點) an intesecting point 【천】a node. こうてん
교접(交接) 《성교》sexual intercourse; coition/ ~하다 have sexual intercourse (with). こうせつ
교정(交情) friendship; intimacy; friendly relations. こうじょう
교정(校正) proofreading; correction [of the press]/ ~하다 read proofs, correct the press/ ~원 a proofreader/ 쇄(刷) a proof-sheet; [printer's] proofs/ ~제 a proofreader. こうせい
교정(敎程) ①《교본》a text-book; a manual ②《과정》a course ③《방법》a method of teaching. きょうてい
교정(矯正) correction; remedy/ ~하다 correct; reform; remedy 《치료》cure/ ~법 a remedy; a cure. きょうせい
교정(校訂) revision/ ~하다 revise/ ~판(版) a revised edition. こうてい
교정(校庭) the [school] playground; the campus 〈미〉. こうてい
교제(交際) intercourse; association; friendship/ ~하다 associate with; hold intercourse with/ ~비 social expenses / ~가 넓다 have large social connections. こうさい
교조(敎祖) the founder of a religion; the head of a sect. きょうそ
교조주의(敎條主義) doctrinism/ ~자 a doctrinist.
교졸(巧拙) skill 《연기의》performance 《세공의》workmanship.
교종(敎宗) the various non-Zen sects of Buddhism; non-Zen Buddhism; the kyo sect. きょうしゅう
교죄(絞罪) a crime punished by hanging [strangling]. こうさつざい
교주(校主) the proprietor[founder] of a school. こうしゅ
교주(敎主) the founder of a religion; the head of a sect. きょうしゅ
교지(敎旨) tenets 《교리》doctrine.
교지(校誌) a school magazine. こうし
교지기(校─) a [school] janitor. がっこうをまもるひと
교직(交織) a mixed weave; mixtures; blended fabric/ 면모 ~ cotton and wool mixtures. まぜおり

교직(敎職) ①(교사직) the teaching profession ②(목사직) the ministry/ ~원 the teaching staff; faculty [members]. きょうしょく

교질(交迭) replacement; shift 《데이동》 shake-up(미)/~하다 replace; shift; change. こうたい

교질(膠質) stickiness; viscosity; adhesiveness. にかわしつ

교차(交叉) intersection; crossing/ ~하다 cross; intersect (each other)/ ~점 a crossing; a junction/~로 crossroads/입체 ~ grade separation; flyover 〈영〉. こうさ

교착(交錯) complication; intricacy; blending; mixing/ ~하다 be complicated [intricated]; be entangled. こうさく

교착(膠着) agglutination 《막다름》 stalemate/ ~하다 glue (to); adhere[stick] (to)/ ~상태 a deadlock; a standstill; a stalemate. こうちゃく

교체(交替) replacement; change/ ~하다 change; replace. こうたい

교치(咬齒) teeth-grinding/ ~하다 grind one's teeth.

교칙(校則) school regulations. こうそく

교칙(敎則) rules for teaching/ ~본 a manual. きょうそく

교탁(敎卓) a teacher's desk. きょうたく

교태(嬌態) coquetry/ ~를 부리다 play the coquette. きょうたい

교통(交通) 《왕래》 traffic; communication 《연락·교제》 intercourse; transport; transportation 《운수》 navigation (on a river)/~ 지옥 a traffic mess[jam]/~ 순경 a traffic policeman/~비 carfare; traffic expenses. こうつう

교파(敎派) a sect; a religious party; a denomination. きょうは

교편(敎鞭) a teacher's pointer/~잡다 teach [at a] school; stand on the platform; beengaged as a teacher. きょうべん

교폐(矯弊) reform of evil habits; remedy of abuses[evil]. きょうへい

교풍(校風) school morals[traditions]; school spirit. こうふう

교풍(矯風) moral reform/ ~하다 reform public morals. きょうふう

교합(交合) sexual union. こうごう

교향곡(交響曲) 【음】 a symphony ⇨교향악(交響樂). こうきょうきょく

교향시(交響詩) a symphonic poem. こうきょうし

교향악(交響樂) 【음】 symphony/ ~단 a symphony orchestra. こうきょうがく

교형(絞刑) strangling; [death by] hanging ⇨교수형. こうしゅけい

교혜(巧慧) ingenuity; cleverness; dexterity; cunning/ ~하다 (be) ingenious; clever; dexterous; cunning.

교호(交互) alternation; reciprocality/ ~하다 alternate with; be reciprocal/ ~ 계산 a current account. こうご

교화(敎化) education; culture; enlightenment/ ~하다 educate; enlighten; civilize/ ~ 운동 an educational campaign. きょうか

교환(交換) ①(교역) exchange; interchange; barter ②(대입) substitution; clearing/ ~하다 exchange; interchange 《어음을》 clear; barter/~수 a telephone operator[girl]; an operator. こうかん

교환(交歡, 交驩) an exchange of courtesies/ ~하다 exchange courtesies (greetings); fraternize with. こうかん

교활(狡猾) cunning; craftiness; artfulness/ ~하다 (be) cunning; sly; artful; crafty; tricky/ ~한 수단 a sharp practice; a trick. こうかつ

교황(敎皇) the Pope; the [Supreme] Pontiff/ ~의 papal/ ~청 the Vatican; the Holy See. きょうこう

교회(敎會) a church; a religious association/ ~당 a church 《사원》 a cathedral 《학교 등의》 a chapel/ ~에 가다 go to church. きょうかい

교회(敎誨) preaching; exhortation/ ~하다 preach; exhort/ ~사 a prison chaplain[missionary]. きょうかい

교훈(敎訓) ①(가르침) one's teachings; a precept ②(훈화) a lesson; an instruction/ ~적 instructive; edifying/ ~을 주다 give a lesson. きょうくん

구(九) nine/제~번 the nine; the ninth; No. 9. ここのつ

구(口) ①(입) a mouth ②(사람수) a mouth to feed; man. くち

구(灸) ①(구이) roast meat; grill ②(뜸) moxibustion; moxacautery. やく

구(區) ①(시의) a ward; a district/ ~청 a ward office ②(구역) a section; a division; a district/선거~ an electoral district; a constituency. く

구(球) a ball; a globe; a sphere. きゅう

구(句) ①(구절) a phrase 《절》 a clause 《문구》 an expression 《성구·숙어》 a [set] phrase 《문장》 a sentence 《구절》 paragraph; a passage 《일절》 a verse. く

구-(舊) old; former/ ~지사 an ex-governor. きゅう

-구(具) tool; implement/문방~ stationery/방한~ cold-weather gear.

구가(謳歌) glorification; praise; eulogy; applause/ ~하다 sing the praises of; eulogize; glorify/자유를 ~하다 sing the praises of liberty/인생을 ~하다 sing the joys of life. おうか

구각(舊殼) 알 ~을 벗다 break with tradition (of); shake off the fetters of customs and manners.

구간(軀幹) the trunk of the body; physique; build. くかん

구간(舊刊) 《잡지의》 a back number 《서적의》 an old edition. きゅうかん

구간(區間) the section (between A and B)/~ 버스 요금 the bus fare for a section/~ 열차 a local train. くかん

구갈(口渴) thirst. のどがかわくこと

구감(口疳) stomatitis.
구강(口腔) the mouth; the oral cavity／ ～위생 the hygiene of the mouth／ ～외과 dental surgery. こうこう
구개(口蓋) 【해】 the palate; the roof of the mouth／ ～의 palatal／ ～뼈 the palatine bones. こうがい
구거(溝渠) a ditch; a sewer; a drain. みぞ
구걸(求乞) begging／ ～하다 beg; ask alms[charity]. こじきをすること
구검(拘檢) 《제한》 a restriction; a restraint／ ～하다 restrict; restraint; put restraint on. こうりゅうしてしらべること
구격(具格) a formality; social rules／ ～하다 observe formalities.
かくしきをそなえること
구경 a visit 《관광》 sightseeing; pleasure-seeking／ ～하다 see; look at; visit／ ～감 a sight; a spectacle; an object of interest／ ～군 a spectator; an audience／ ～스럽다 be worth seeing／시내를 ～하다 do the sights of city. みもの
구경(九經) the Nine Chinese Classics.
구경(口徑) caliber; bore. こうけい
구경(究竟) ①《필경》 after all; in the long run; in the end ②《종국》 the final end; finality; extremity／～의 원인 the final[chief] cause. きゅうきょう
구경(球莖) a bulb. きゅうけい
구경가마리 an object of ridicule; a laughing stock. ちょうしょうのてき
구경거리 a sight; an attraction; an object of interest; a show 《흥행》 a circus.
みもの
구경군 ①《관광객》 a sightseer; a visitor ②《관객》 a spectator; the audience ③《방관자》 a looker-on; a bystander; a rubbernecks《미》. けんぶつじん
구경스럽다 (be) worth seeing; (be) spectacular. みものだ
구계(球界) the baseball world. きゅうかい
구고(究考) ①《조사》 investigation; inquiry ②《연구》 research; study ③《숙려》 consideration／～하다 inquire into; investigate; consider／고전을 ～하다 study classics／여러 가지 각도에서 ～하다 view (a problem) from all angles.
구고(舊稿) an old manuscript. きゅうこう
구곡(舊穀) grain produced in the year before. ふるいこくもつ
구공탄(九孔炭) a coal briquet with nine holes in it.
구관(舊官) the former governor.
むかしのかんり
구관(舊慣) old customs[practices]; established usages／～을 고수하다 keep [stick] to old customs. むかしのようす
구관조(九官鳥) 【조】 a mina; a myna[h].
구교(舊交) old friendship. きゅうこう
구교(舊敎) the [Roman] Catholic Church; the catholic church／～도 a [Roman] Catholic. てんしゅきょう
구구 《닭 부르는 소리》 chuck-chuck-chuck; ; cluck! cluck! と・と・と

구구(九九) a multiplication table／ ～하다 multiply／ ～표 a multiplication [t- able]. くく
구구(購求) purchase; procurement／ ～하다 purchase; procure.
구구하다(區區一) ①《변변찮다》 be poor; insignificant; silly; useless ②《각각이다》 be various; diverse／구구하게 uselessly; variously; lengthily. まちまちだ
구국(救國) national salvation／ ～운동 a save-the-nation movement. きゅうこく
구규(舊規) old regulations; conventional rules. きゅうこう
구균(球菌) a micrococcus. きゅうきん
구극(舊劇) an old play; a classical drama; a play of the old school.
きゅうきょく
구극(究極) finality; extremity／ ～의 final; ultimate. きゅうきょく
구근(球根) 《나리 따위의》 a bulb 《감자 따위의》 a tuber. きゅうこん
구금(拘禁) detention; confinement; custody／ ～하다 detain; confine; imprison; keep (one) in custody. こうきん
구급(救急) relief／ ～의 emergency; first aid／ ～차 an ambulance [car]／ ～약 a first aid medicine. きゅうきゅう
구기(枸杞) 【식】 a boxthorn／ ～자 the fruit of a boxthorn.
구기다, 꾸기다 crumple; wrinkle; rumple; crush. しわくちゃになる
구기적거리다, 꾸기적거리다 wrinkle; rumple; crumple (up); crush (clothes)／구기적구기적 crumpling. しわくちゃにする
구기지르다 crumple[wrinkle, crease, crush, ruffle] up.
구김살 creases; rumples; folds／ ～ 간 crumpled; rumpled／ ～을 펴다 smooth a wrinkle 《다리미로》 iron out. しわ
구깃구깃, 꾸깃꾸깃 ～하다 (be) creasy; crumpled; wrinkled. しわくちゃ
-구나 《감탄》 how; what; indeed／ 참 아름답~ How beautiful it is! ―だね
구나방 a nut; a crank; a screwball.
ひにくや
구내(構內) the premises; the compounds; the enclosure; the yard. こうない
구내(區內) ～에 within the section[district, area]. くない
구내염(口內炎) 【의】 stomatitis.
こうないえん
구년(舊年) the old[past] year／ ～ 친구 an old friend. きゅうねん
구눌(口訥) 《떠듬떠듬》 an impediment in speech; stammering ／ ～하다 have a speech impediment; stammer; stumble in getting one's words out. どもること
꾸다¹ 《꿈을》 dream／고향의 꿈을 ～ dream about one's home. ゆめをみる
꾸다² 《돈을》 borrow; have[get] the loan (of). かりる
구단(球團) a baseball team. きゅうたん
구대륙(舊大陸) the Old World; the Old Continent. きゅうたいりく

구더기 a maggot; a grub; a worm/ ~가 들끓다 be infested with maggots. うじ

구덩이 a hollow; a depression; a cavity; a pit. くぼみ

구도(構圖) composition; planning. こうず

구도(舊都) an old capital; an ancient seat of government. むかしのみやこ

구도(舊道) an old road; an old highway. むかしのみち

구도(求道) seeking after truth/ ~하 a seeker after truth. きゅうどう

구독(購讀) subscription/ ~하다 subscribe to/ ~료 subscription [rates]/ ~자 a subscriber; a reader. こうどく

구두 shoes; boots; high shoes〈미〉/ ~ 한 켤레 a pair of shoes/ ~솔 a shoes brush/ ~닦이 a shoeshine boy/ ~를 신다 put on shoes. くつ

구두(句讀) punctuation/ ~점 punctuation marks[points]/ ~점을 찍다 punctuate (a sentence). くとう

구두(口頭) word of mouth/ ~의 oral; verbal; spoken/ ~로 orally; verbally ; by word of mouth/~ 시험 an oral examination. こうとう

구두떨거리다 grumble. ぶつぶつついう

구두쇠 a grasping fellow; a miser; a close-fisted person. しゅせんど

구두질 cleaning out[repairing] a Korean hypocaust/ ~하다 clean[repair] a Korean hypocaust.

구두충류(鉤頭蟲類) 【동】 Acanthocephala (학명).

구둣발 feet with shoes on; [shoed] feet / ~로 차다 kick (a person) with boots on. くつばきのあし

구드러지다, 꾸드러지다 dry up; be parched; become hard and dry.

구들 flat pieces of stone used for flooring a Korean room. オンドル

꾸들꾸들 somewhat dry and hard/ ~ 하다 (be) hard-boiled; dry and hard.

구들방(-房) a room whose floor is paved with flat stones; a room with underfloor heating installed.
オンドルのへや

구들장 a piece of flat stone used for flooring a room over a Korean hypocaust. オンドルにつかういし

구들하다 be tasty; savory; appetizing. うまそうだ

구듭 painstaking service; undergoing troubles to help (a person)/ ~치다 undergo troubles to help (a person).
ひとのためのこくろう

구락부(俱樂部) a club; a clubhouse/ ~ 원 a member of a club; a clubman/ ~ 활동 social club activities. クラブ

구랍(舊臘) last December; the end of last year. さくねんのじゅうにがつ

구래(舊來) from old times; from times past/ ~의 old; ancient; traditional/ ~의 누습 old abuses.

구량(口糧) ration.

-꾸러기 an overindulger/심술~ a cross-grained[an ill-natured] fellow; a cynic /장난 ~ a mischievous boy; an urchin.

꾸러미 a bundle (in a wrapper)《작은》 a package; a parcel; a packet《큰》a bale. ほうそうもの

구럭 a straw network; anything[a small sack] made of straw netting (망태기) a mesh bag. なわあみのふくろ

구렁 ①[패인 곳] a depression; a hollow; a pit ②(구렁텅이) the bottom; the depths; abyss/절망의 ~텅이 the depths of despair. へこみ

구렁이 a big snake; a huge serpent; a boa [constrictor]《사람》an old fox; a tricky person. だいじゃ

구렁찰 【식】a kind of glutinous rice characterized by late-ripening.

구렁텅이 an abyss; a pit; the depth; a deep hollow; a gulf. ふかいほらあな

구레 the sides of one's waist; the flank. わきばら

구레나룻 whiskers. ほおひげ

구력(舊曆) the old calendar; the lunar calendar. きゅうれき

구련(拘攣) 【의】 convulsions of hands and feet.

구령(口令) a [word of] command; a verbal order/ ~하다 command; order/ ~대 a drill platform. こうれい

구령(救靈) salvation; the saving of a soul/ ~하다 save a soul.

구례(舊禮) ancient manners; old etiquettes. むかしからのれいぎほう

구례(舊例) a precedent; an old custom; a usage. きゅうれい

구루(傴僂, 佝僂) a hunchback/ ~병 rickets/ ~ 병에 걸린 rickety. せむし

구루마 a wag[g]on; a cart; a dray/ ~ 군 a carter; a drayman; a wagoner.
くるま

구류(拘留) detention; custody; remand; commitment/ ~하다 detain; keep (one) in custody. こうりゅう

구르다¹ roll (over); kick. ころがる

구르다² (발을) stamp one's feet noisily; pound. ふみとどろかす

꾸르륵 (배가) rumbling; with a rumble [of one's bowels]/ 뱃속이 ~거린다 the bowels rumble. ごろごろ

구름 a cloud; the clouds/ ~의 사이 a break[rift] in the clouds/ ~ 없는 cloudless/ ~낀 cloudy/ ~에 덮이다 be covered with clouds; be clouded over / ~ 위에 솟다 soar to the sky; rise above the clouds. くも

구름다리 a viaduct; a railway[land] bridge. りっきょう

구름 a nine-year-old.

구릉(丘陵) a hill; a hillock/ ~ 지대 hilly districts. きゅうりょう

구리 copper/ ~철 copper wire. あかがね

꾸리 a spindle[bobbin] of thread (뭉치) a spindle with its thread/실 ~ a

spindle[bobbin] of thread. いとまき
**구리**(究理) the study of truth[natural laws]. きゅうり
**구리귀신**(一鬼神) a tightfisted and stubborn[obstinate] person.
**구리다** ①《냄새가》 be stinking; bad-smelling／구린내 the smell of dung; stink ②《행동이》 be disgusting. だいべんくさい
**꾸리다** ①《짐을》 pack[wrap, do, tie] up; bundle; package《미》 ②《일을》 manage; make do (with)／살림을 ~ manage a household. ほうそうする
**구리때** 〖식〗 angelica.
**구리돈** copper[brass] coins.
**구리철** copper wire. あかがねのはりがね
**구린내** a bad[nasty, foul] smell; stench; stink; an offensive odor. くさみ
**구매**(購買) buying; purchase／~하다 buy; purchase. こうばい
**구멍** a hole; an opening 《틈》 《기다란》 a slit 《작은》 an orifice 《꿰뚫은》 a perforation 《관악기의》 a stop／~을 뚫다 make a hole. あな
**구멍가게** a small shop. こみせ
**구멍새** ①《구멍의》 the way a hole is shaped ②《얼굴의》 the way a face is shaped. あなのできばえ
**구메구메** on occasion; at odd moment; unnoticed. ひまごとに
**구메농사**(一農事) ①《소농》 small scale farming ②《농작》 an irregular crop.
**구메밥** food supplied to a prisoner through an opening in the wall.
ざいにんにやるごはん
**-구면** ①《사실의 발견·확인·추측·놀라움》¶아 그렇~ Oh is that it!, That's right!, So it is!, Well I'll be! ②《-는·-면·-더 다음에》¶비가 오는 ~ Well I see it's raining.
**구면**(舊面) an acquaintance; a familiar person. むかしからのしりあい
**구명**(救命) life saving／~정 a lifeboat／~부대 a life buoy. きゅうめい
**구명**(究明) study; investigation; inquiry／~하다 study; investigate; bring to light／문제를 ~하다 bring light on a subject. きゅうめい
**구명**(舊名) an old name. きゅうめい
**구몰**(俱沒) ~하다 lose both one's parents; be parted with both one's parents by death. ともにしぬこと
**구무럭거리다, 꾸무럭거리다** move slowly [sluggishly]; be slow; waste time; loiter; linger／꾸물거리지 말고 without [a moment's] delay. のろのろする
**구문**(歐文) European language. おうぶん
**구문**(舊聞) an old story; stale news.
**구문**(構文) sentence structure; construction of a sentence／~법 syntax／~의 불비 defective construction. こうぶん
**구문**(口文) commission; percentage; brokerage. こうせん
**구문**(究問) search; inquiry; exploration／~하다 inquire into; research; exp-

lore. きゅうもん
**구문서**(舊文書) an ex-proprietor's bill of sale. むかしのぶんしょ
**구물**(舊物) ①《옛 것》 antiquities; antiques ②《골동품》 curios ③《상속품》 a hereditary article; heirlooms. きゅうぶつ
**구물거리다, 꾸물거리다** 《벌레 따위가》 wriggle; squirm move slowly 《구무럭거리다》 dawdle. ゆっくりみをうごかす
**꾸미** beef shreds (for soup).
**구미**(口味) appetite; taste; flavour／~를 돋우다 stimulate one's appetite／~가 없다 have no appetite. しょくよく
**구미**(歐美) Europe and America／~의 European and American. おうべい
**구미**(舊米) old rice; rice produced in the year before. ふるいこめ
**꾸미개** ornamental strips along edges or borders. かざりもの
**구미납**(舊未納) unpaid taxes from last year; taxes that are a year overdue.
**꾸미다** ①《치장》 decorate; adorn; ornament; bedeck／방을 ~ decorate a room ②《조작》 make up; invent; concoct／꾸민 말 an invention. かざる
**구미수**(舊未收) uncollected taxes from last year.
**구미호**(九尾狐) an old fox; a sly dog; a tricky[cunning] person. こうかつなひと
**구민**(區民) the inhabitants of a ward [district]. くみん
**꾸민잠**(一簪) an ornamental hairpin.
ほうせきでつくったかんざし
**구밀 복검**(口蜜腹劍) A honeyed tongue, but a heart of gall., He has honey in his mouth, but gall in his heart.
**꾸밈** a decoration; an ornament／~없이 말하자면 in plain words／~새 the way one fixes up; the way one decorates／~씨 《문》 a modifier; a modifying word. そうしょくしたようす
**구박**(驅迫) cold treatment; maltreatment／~하다 maltreat; treat (one) badly; be hard upon (one). ぎゃくたい
**구배**(勾配) a slope; an incline 《철도의》 a gradient 《지붕의》 a pitch. こうばい
**꾸벅거리다, 꾸뻑거리다** ①《졸려서》 nod a doze; nid-nod; doze-off; drop (off) into a doze ②《머리를 숙이다》 bow and bow; repeatedly make respectful bows／웃사람에게 ~ cringe to one's superiors. こくりこくりする
**구법**(舊法) an old law; an ancient law. きゅうほう
**구벽**(口癖) a habit of speech; a way of talking. くちぐせ
**구변**(口辯) tongue; speech／~이 좋다 have a fluent tongue. べんぜつ
**구별**(區別) ①《차별》 distinction; difference; discrimination ②《분류》 classification; division／~하다 distingish; draw the line (between); discriminate (between, from); classify. くべつ
**구병**(救兵) a relief (person); reinforcem-

**구보(驅步)** ①《말의》a run; a canter; a gallop ②《군대의》double-time; double-quick. かけあし

**구복(口腹)** mouth and stomach/~지게 a means of living. くちとはら

**구부러뜨리다, 꾸부러뜨리다** bend; curve; crook. まげてしまう

**구부러지다, 꾸부러지다** bend; curve; be crooked. まがる

**구부리다, 꾸부리다** ①《몸을》stoop; bow ②《물건을》bend; curve; crook. まげる

**구부슴하다, 꾸부슴하다** be somewhat bent; be rather bent. いくぶんまがったようだ

**구부정하다, 꾸부정하다** be rather[slightly] bent[curved, arched]; somewhat crescent shaped. ややまがっている

**구분(區分)** ①《분할》division; demarcation ②《구획》a section; a partition. ③《분류》classification/~하다 divide; section; partition. くぶん

**구불구불, 꾸불꾸불** ~하다 (be) winding; meandering; curved. まがりくねっている

**구불텅구불텅, 꾸불텅꾸불텅** ~하다 (be) ever-bending; winding.

**구붓하다, 꾸붓하다** be slightly bent[curved]/구붓구붓[꾸붓꾸붓] all slightly bent[curved]. すこしまがっている

**구쁘다** feel an appetite. たべたい

**구비(口碑)** oral tradition; legend; folklore/~로 전하다 be handed down orally[by word of mouth]. こうひ

**구비(具備)** ~하다 have; possess; be endowed[furnished] with/모든 조건을 ~하다 fulfil all the conditions; satisfy all the requisites. ぐび

**구빈(救貧)** relief of the poor/~ 사업 settlement work/~ 제도 the poor-relief system. きゅうひん

**구사(求仕)** ~하다 seek a government post; seek an office; seek a government appointment. かんしょくをもとめること

**구사(驅使)** ①《자유 자재》free use ②《몰아 부림》driving/~하다 use freely; command the service of/영어를 자유 자재로 ~하다 have a good command of English. くし

**구사(舊師)** one's former teacher. きゅうし

**구사상(舊思想)** old ideas; out-of-date ideas. むかしのしそう

**구사 일생(九死一生)** a narrow escape from death/~하다 have a narrow escape. きゅうしにいっしょうをえること

**구산(口算)** oral calculation[arithmetic]/~하다 do [a sum in] oral arithmetic; calculate orally; calculate out loud. くちでけいさんすること

**구산(舊山)** one's ancestral graveyard.

**구상(具象)** concreteness; embodiment/~적 concrete/~적으로 in the concrete/~ 개념 a concrete concept/~ 예술 the plastic arts. ぐしょう

**구상(毆傷)** injury inflicted by assault and battery/~하다 injure (a person) by a blow; assault and injure. うってきずつけること

**구상(構想)** a plan; conception; plot; design/소설의 ~ the plot of a novel.

**구상(求償)** compensation; reparation; indemnification. こうそう

**구상(鉤狀)** ~의 hook-shaped/~골(骨) an unciform bone. つりばりのようなもの

**구상(球狀)** a spherical shape/~의 spherical; globular. きゅうじょう

**구상 유취(口尙乳臭)** being babyish[boyish, puerile] 《미숙》being green[unfledged, callow]. あおくさい

**구새먹다** become hollow; be eaten hollow/구새먹은 나무 a hollow tree. たちきのなかがくさってあながあく

**구새통** ①《통나무》a hollowed tree; the empty[hollow] trunk of a tree ②《굴뚝》a wooden chimney/~ 먹다 get hollow. くさってあながあいたきのかぶ

**구색(具色)** assortment; an assortment of goods/~이 갖추어져 있다 have an assortment of goods/~을 갖추다 assort. いろいろなものがぐびしていること

**구색(求索)** searching; looking for; seeking/~하다 search (for); look for; seek (after, for).

**구색(究索)** study; research; investigation/~하다 make an extensive study of.

**구생(舅甥)** ①《외삼촌과 조카》uncle and nephew ②《장인과 사위》father-in-law and son-in-law. きゅうそう

**구서(口書)** ①《입으로 쓴 글》writing done with the brush held in mouth ②《구공서》a written confession; a deposition; an affidavit. くちがき

**구서(具書)** ~하다 write [a Chinese character] in the square style.

**구석** a corner; a nook/~에 in a corner/~ 자리 a corner seat. すみ

**구석구석** every nook and corner; everywhere. すみごとに

**구석기(舊石器)** a paleolith; a paleolithic stone implement.

**구석지다** (be) secluded; out-of-the-way/구석진 곳 an out-of-the-way place; a nook; recess. ひととはなれている

**구설(口舌)** words of denunciation; strictures/~을 듣다 suffer from a slip of the tongue. こうぜつ

**구성(九成)** the second-best fineness of gold alloy.

**구성(構成)** constitution; composition; organization; formation/~하다 constitute; organize; make up; compose; form/~ 분자 a component; a constituent. こうせい

**구성없다** be ill-becoming; unsightly; awkward; clumsy. にあわない

**구성지다** be becoming; tasteful; elegant; artistic. おもしろい

**구세(救世)** salvation[redemption] of the world/~군 the Salvation Army/~

**구세주** the Savior; the Redeemer; the Messiah.
**구세(舊歲)** last year; the old year; the year passed. きょねん
**구세계(舊世界)** the Old Continent.
**구세대(舊世代)** the old generation.
**구세주(救世主)** the savio[u]r of the world; Christ; the Redeemer; the Messiah; the savio[u]r. きゅうせいしゅ
**구속(拘束)** restriction; restraint/ ~하다 restrict; restrain; bind/ ~력 a binding force/ ~을 받다 be placed under restraint. こうそく
**구속(救贖)** salvation; redemption.
**구송(口誦)** recitation/ ~하다 recite; read aloud. こうしょう
**구수(口授)** oral instruction (받아쓰기) dictation/ ~하다 instruct orally; dictate. こうじゅ
**구수(仇讐)** an enemy; a foe. かたき
**구수 응의(鳩首凝議)** a conference ⇒구수회의.
**구수하다** ①(맛·냄새가) be appetizing; savoury; rich in flavour ②(말이) be amusing うまそうだ
**구수 회의(鳩首會議)** conference; huddle /~하다 counsel together; lay (their) heads together. きゅうしゅかいぎ
**구술(口述)** an oral statement; an dictation / ~의 oral; verbal/ ~하다 state orally; dictate/ ~ 시험 an oral examination. こうじゅつ
**구슬** ①(보옥) a gem; a bijou; a jewel. ②(진주) a pearl. たま
**구슬구슬하다** (밥이) be cooked properly [well]; be cooked neither too hard nor too soft.
**구슬땀** beads of sweat; sweat in beads /이마에 ~이 났다 Beads of sweat stood on his brow. たまのあせ
**구슬덩** a sedan chair with bead-decorated screens.
**구슬려내다** wheedle (a person) out of (a thing); talk (a person) into doing (a thing). うまいことばではなしおとす
**구슬리다** coax; cajole; make sport of. よくおだてる
**구슬양피(一羊皮)** a curly sheepskin.
**구슬프다** (be) sad; sorrowful; mournful; plaintive/구슬픈 노래 a plaintive[doleful] song. ものかなしい
**구습(舊習)** old[time-honoured] customs /~을 묵수(墨守)하다 stick to old customs[practices]. きゅうしゅう
**구시(仇視)** hostility; enmity/ ~하다 look upon (one) as an enemy; be hostile to. きゅうし
**구시렁거리다** grumble; nag/구시렁구시렁 grumbling; nagging.
**구식(舊式)** old style [school, type, fashion]/ ~의 old-fashioned; antiquated; out-of-date/ ~ 사람 an old-fashioned person. きゅうしき
**구신(具申)** a representation/ ~하다 report [in detail]; make a representation to (a superior)/ ~서 a representation; a detailed report. ぐしん
**구실(직무)** a duty; a part; capacity (직능); a role/중요한 ~을 하다 play an important part. やく
**구실(口實)** an excuse; a pretext; a pretence/ ~을 만들다 find an excuse[a pretext]. こうじつ
**구실길** a trip on duty[official business].
**구실아치** a government exployee; a person in public office; yamen underling.
**구심(求心)** seeking the center/ ~력 centripetal force/ ~ 운동 centripetence/ ~적[으로] centripetal[ly]. きゅうしん
**구심(球心)** the center of a sphere/~적으로 centripetal[ly]. きゅうしん
**구심(球審)** an umpire on balls; a ball umpire. きゅうしん
**구십(九十)** ninety/제 ~번 the ninetieth. きゅうじゅう
**구악(舊惡)** a past crime[misdeed, offence]. きゅうあく
**구악(舊樂)** old music; ancient music. きゅうがく
**구안(苟安)** momentary ease (미봉) temporizing. いちじのやすらかさ
**구안(具眼)** a discerning eye; a critical talent/ ~자 a person with observant eyes. ぐがん
**구애(拘礙)** trouble; a hitch/ ~하다 be particular (about); stick[adhere] to; be wedded to. さしつかえ
**구애(求愛)** courtship/~하다 woo; court; make love to. きゅうあい
**구액(口液)** spittle; saliva. つば
**구약(口約)** a verbal promise. こうやく
**구약(舊約) (옛 약속)** an old[a former] promise. きゅうやく
**구약 성서(舊約聖書)** the Old Testament. きゅうやくせいしょ
**구어(口語)** the spoken[colloquial] language/ ~의 spoken; colloquial; conversational/ ~체 a colloquial style; colloquialism. こうご
**구어박다** ①(사람이) stick at home; stay inactive in one's place ②(쐐기 따위) drive in. どころにとじこもっている
**구역(區域)** ①(경계) the limits; the boundary ②(지대) an area; a district/ 위험 ~ a danger zone. くいき
**꾸역꾸역** in a steady stream; in [rapid] succession; one after another; one upon the heels af another. むれかかって
**구역질(嘔逆-)** nausea/ ~나다 feel nausea; feel sick/ ~나는 sickening; nauseating. はきけがすること
**구연(舊緣)** old ties; an old[a former] relationship. きゅうえん
**구연(枸櫞)** 【식】 lemon.
**구연(口演)** an oral narration/ ~하다 narrate orally; recite. こうえん
**구열(口熱)** fever[temperature] in the mouth. こうねつ

**구왕실(舊王室)** the Royal Household/~재산 Royal Household properties.

**구외(構外)** ~에서 outside the grounds (premises, compounds). こうがい

**구우(舊友)** an old friend[crony]; a friend of long standing. きゅうゆう

**구우 일모(九牛一毛)** a drop in the bucket. きゅうきゅうのいちもう

**구운석고(一石膏)** plaster of Paris.

**구워지다** (빵 따위가) be baked (불에 쬐어) be toasted (석쇠로) be grilled (고기가) be roasted.

**구원(久遠)** eternity; permanence; perpetuity/ ~한 eternal; perpetual; everlasting; permanent. くおん

**구원(救援)** relief; rescue; reinforcement (종교상의) salvation; redemption/ ~하다 rescue; relieve; succour; redeem/ ~대 a relief[rescue] party. きゅうえん

**구원(舊怨)** an old grudge. きゅうえん

**구월(九月)** September. くがつ

**구유** a manger; a trough. かいばおけ

**구은(舊恩)** old favours; kindness; shown in the past. きゅうおん

**구음(口音)** an oral sound.

**구읍(舊邑)** an old town; an old country. むかしのちいさいみやこ

**구의(舊誼)** old friendship/ ~를 존중하여 for old acquaintance's sake/ ~를 두텁게 하다 renew old friendship. きゅうぎ

**구이** (고기) roast meat (생선) broiled fish /돼지고기 ~ roast pork. やきにく

**꾸이다¹** dream; have a dream /…이 꿈에 ~ dream of. ゆめみられる

**꾸이다²** lend; loan; advance; accommodate (a person) with money. かしてやる

**구인(拘引)** arrest (구류) custody/ ~하다 arrest; apprehend/ ~장 a warrant of arrest. こういん

**구인(求人)** the offer of a situation/ ~광고 a help wanted advertisement; a want ad〈미〉; a situation vacant advertisement〈영〉. ひとをもとめること

**구일(九日)** ①(초아흐레) the ninth ②(9일 간) nine days. ここのか

**구입** a scanty livelihood; a bare living / ~하다 eke out; make[lead] a bare living. もとめいれること

**구입(購入)** purchase; buying; procurement/ ~하다 purchase; buy/ ~자 a purchaser[buyer]. こうにゅう

**구작(舊作)** one's old work. きゅうさく

**구잠함(驅潛艦)** a submarine chaser; a subchaser.

**구장(區長)** a village headman. くちょう

**구장(球場)** a baseball park[ground]; a stadium; a diamond. きゅうじょう

**구재** ashes and soot settled in the underfloor heating flues.

**구재(口才)** eloquence; the gift of gab/ ~있는 사람 an eloquent speaker; a gifted speaker[singer]. くちだっしゃ

**구재(鳩材)** accumulation of wealth/ ~하다 accumulate wealth.

**구저분하다** (be) shabby; filthy; untidy; rough and dirty. そまつできたないこと

**구적(口笛)** a whistle. くちぶえ

**구적(仇敵)** a bitter enemy; a foe; a sworn enemy. きゅうてき

**구적(求積)** 【수】 mensuration/ ~법 stereometry. きゅうせき

**구적(舊蹟)** remains; a historic spot; a place of historical interest. きゅうせき

**구적(寇賊)** an invading enemy; an aggressor; an invader; an invading enemy. こっきょうをおかすとうぞく

**구전(口傳)** information by word of mouth; tradition/ ~하다 inform by word of mouth. くでん

**구전(口錢)** commission; percentage (중개의) brokerage/ ~을 받다 take a commission. こうせん

**구전(舊典)** an ancient code of law (고전) a classic; a tradition. むかしのほうてん

**구전(俱全)** perfection; completeness; wholeness/ ~하다 be perfect; complete; whole. かんぜんにそなえている

**구절(句節)** a phrase and a clause; a paragraph. くとせつ

**구절 양장(九折羊腸)** a meandering path; a winding road.

**구절초(九節草)** 【식】 a kind of wild camomile.

**구점(口占)** ①(시작) improvisation of a poem ②(구전) handing down an information by word of mouth.

**구점(句點)** a punctuation [mark]. くてん

**구접스럽다** (be) dirty; shabby; messy; foul; nasty; mean; low. わいせつだ

**구정(舊情)** old friendship[acquaintance] / ~을 새로이 하다 renew one's old friendship (with). きゅうじょう

**구정(舊正)** the New Year Day according to the lunar[old] calendar. いんれきのしょうがつ

**꾸정꾸정하다** be straight and strong ⇒꼬장꼬장하다. まっすぐだ

**구정물** filthy water; slops; sewage.

**구제(舊制)** the old[former] system; the old order. きゅうせい

**구제(救濟)** relief; succor; help; aid; redress/ ~하다 relieve; succour/ ~책 a relief measure/~ 사업 relief work/빈민을 ~하다 relieve the poor/ ~할 수 없는 unrelievable. きゅうさい

**구제(驅除)** extermination/ ~하다 exterminate; get rid of. くじょ

**구조(久阻)** long neglect in writing/ ~하다 be long silent; be remiss in writing for a long time.

**구조(救助)** rescue; aid; help; relief; succour/ ~하다 save; rescue; relieve; help/ ~선 a rescue ship/인명을 ~하다 save a life. きゅうじょ

**구조(構造)** structure; construction; set-up (조직) organization; frame/인체의 ~ structure of the human body/~상 structually. こうぞう

구조개 《굴과 조개》 oysters and clams.
구족(九族) the nine generations of a family. きゅうぞく
구존(俱存) ~하다 have one's parents alive / 그의 양친은 ~하시다 His parents are both alive. りょうしんがいきていること
구좌(口座) an account / 진체 ~ a postal transfer account.
구주(歐洲) Europe.
구주(救主) 《그리스도》the Saviour; the Redeemer; the Messiah. きゅうせいしゅ
구주(舊主) one's former lord; one's former master. きゅうしゅ
구죽 piles of oyster shells on the seashore. かきがら
꾸준하다 be steady; unflagging; untiring; constant / 꾸준한 노력 steady[ceaseless] efforts. かんだんがない
구중(九重) ①《아홉 겹》ninefold ②《대궐》the Royal Palace. ここのえ
구중중하다 be frowzy; slovenly; filthy; dirty. しめっぽくてきたない
구지(舊趾) 《옛 터》ruins; historic remains. きゅうし
꾸지람 a scolding; a rebuke; a lecture / ~하다 scold; rebuke; give (a person) a lecture. きっせき
구지레하다 (be) dirty and untidy; be squalid and in disorder; (be) filthy. きたない
구직(求職) seeking work; job-hunting / ~하다 look out for a job; seek employment / ~자 a job hunter; an applicant. きゅうしょく
구진(具陳) a detailed[minute] statement / ~하다 state in detail; give a minute statement. ぐちん
구진하다(久陳一) ①《음식이》be stale ②《약이》ineffective.
しょくもつなどがしんせんでない
구질(九秩) ninety years of age. きゅじゅうさい
구질(丘垤) a hillock.
구질구질 indecently; in slovenly manners / ~하다 be indecent; slovenly.
きちんとしてないさま
꾸짖다 scold; rebuke; lecture; chide / 호되게 ~ give (a person) a good scolding. しかる
구차하다(苟且一) (be) poor; be in want; needy; destitute; miserable / 그들은 구차하게 살고 있다 They live poorly[in poverty]. ひじょうにびんぼうた
구창(口瘡) a sore in the mouth.
구책(舊債) an old debt. むかしのさいむ
구책(咎責) blame; rebuke; censure / ~하다 blame; rebuke; reprimand; reprove. とがめること
구척 장신(九尺長身) a giant; a person of extraordinary stature.
구천(九天) the sky; the highest heavens. きゅうてん
구천(九泉) the nether world; Hades; the grave. きゅうせん

구청(區廳) a ward office; a district office / ~장 the ward head[chief]; the mayor of a borough. くやくしょ
구체(具體) concreteness / ~적으로 concretely; definitely / ~화하다 make concrete 《실현》 materialize. ぐたい
구체(久滯) chronic dyspepsia; long-suffered indigestion. まんせいのいちょうびょう
구체(球體) a sphere; a globe. きゅうたい
구체제(舊體制) an old structure; an old order. むかしのたいせい
구축(驅逐) expulsion; ousting 《구대》 extermination / ~하다 drive away; expel.
くちく
구축(構築) construction / ~하다 build; construct.
구축함(驅逐艦) a [torpedo] destroyer.
くちくかん
구출(救出) rescue; help; save / ~하다 save (a life). きゅうしゅつ
구충(驅蟲) extermination of insects; getting rid of insects; getting rid of intestinal worms / ~하다 exterminate insects; get rid of worms. くちゅう
구충약(驅蟲藥) an insect-powder; an insecticide 《회충약》 a vermicide; vermifuge. くちゅうやく
구취(口臭) bad[foul] breath. こうしゅう
구치(臼齒) a molar [teeth]. きゅうし
구치(拘置) confinement; detention / ~하다 confine; detain; keep (one) in custody / ~소 a prison; a detension house. こうち
구치(驅馳) driving fast; gallop / ~하다 drive; gallop. ばしゃをはしらせること
구침(鉤針) a hook; a crochet needle.
구칭(舊稱) the old name. きゅうし
구타(毆打) assault and battery / ~하다 assault; beat / ~ 치사 an assault resulting in death. おうだ
구태(舊態) old condition; the old state of things / ~ 의연하다 remain unchanged[as it was]. きゅうたい
구태여 purposely; intentionally 《감히》 daringly 《알면서도》 knowingly 《적극적》 positively. わざわざ
구택(舊宅) one's old house; one's former residence. きゅうたく
구토(嘔吐) vomiting; emesis / ~하다 vomit; throw up; puke. おうと
구투(舊套) conventionalism. きゅうしき
구파(舊派) 《유파》an old school 《보수파》 the conservatives. きゅうは
구판(舊版) an old edition; an old book; the former edition. きゅうはん
구폐(舊弊) 《폐풍》old abuses[evils]; a standing evil. きゅうへい
구포(臼砲) a mortar.
꾸푸리다, 꾸푸리다 bend; bow / 몸을 ~ bend oneself; stoop. こしをかがめる
구풍(颶風) a hurricane; a whirlwind; a typhoon. たいふう
구피(狗皮) a dogskin. いぬのかわ
구필(口筆) writing with the brush held

구하다(灸―) ①(쑥으로) cauterize (*the skin*) with moxa ②(굽다) roast; toast; broil. やいとをすえること
구하다(求―) ①(언다) get; obtain; come by/구하기 힘든 hard to get; not easily obtained ②(고르다) choose ③(찾다) search for; look for. もらう
구하다(救―) ①(돕다) relieve; rescue; help; aid ②(구출) save[rescue, deliver] (*one*) from ③(병을) cure; heal. すくう
구학(丘壑) hills and hollows. おかとたに
구학(求學) pursuit of learning/~하다 pursue learning. まなぶみちをもとめること
구학문(舊學問) the old learning; Chinese literature; sinology. きゅしきのがくもん
구함(構陷) a false charge; slander; calumny/ ~하다 slander; make a false charge; calumniate.
구합(鳩合) gathering together; convocation/ ~하다 muster; convoke; call [gather] together.
구향(舊鄕) a family long settled in the country. むかしのこきょう
구허(丘墟) the ruins.
구험(口險) a foul mouth/ ~하다 (be) foul-mouthed.
구현(具現) embodiment/~하다 embody; materialize; realize. ぐげん
구혈(灸穴) the parts of the skin suited for moxa cauterization.
やいとをすえるあな
구혈(九穴) the nine openings of the human body [eyes, nostrils, mouth, ears, anus, urethra]. じんたいにあるななつのあな
구혐(舊嫌) an old suspicion.
むかしからのけんぎ
구형(求刑) prosecution/ ~하다 prosecute; demand a penalty (*for*). きゅうけい
구형(矩形) a rectangle/ ~의 rectangular. くけい
구형(球形) a globular form; globosity/ ~의 globular. きゅうけい
구형(舊型) ~의 outmoded (*cars*); old-fashioned.
구호(口號) a slogan; a rallying word; motto. となえること
구호(救護) relief; rescue; aid; help/ ~ 사업 relief work/ ~ 물자 relief supplies. きゅうご
구혼(求婚) a proposal[an offer] of marriage; courtship/ ~하다 court; propose to (*one*). きゅうこん
구화(構禍) ~하다 sew the seed of calamity; court disaster.
구화(歐化) Europeanization; Westernization/~하다 Europeanize; Westernize.
구화반자 a ceiling with a chrysanthemum design on it; a chrysanthemum *plafond*. きっかもようのてんじょう
구화장지 a sliding door with chrysanthemum design on it.
きっかもようのしょうじ

구할(久闕) long neglect[silence] in writing[correspondence]/ ~하다 remain silent. ながいあいだしょうそくのないこと
구휼(救荒) famine relief/ ~하다 relieve famine (sufferers). きゅうこう
구획(區劃) ①(구분) a division; a section ②(한계) a boundary; a limit/ ~하다 divide. くかく
구휼(救恤) relief; succour/ ~하다 relieve; succour. きゅうじゅつ
구희(球戲) a ball game; bowling; billiards; pinball. きゅうぎ
국 (먹는) soup; broth/ ~을 마시다 sip soup. しる
국 ①(누르는 모양) tightly; firmly; hard ②(참는 모양) patiently/모욕을 ~ 참다 bear an insult patiently. しっかり
국(國) a nation; a country; a state.
국(局) (관청의) an office; a bureau; a department; a board (전화국) the exchange; the central (우체국) a post office. きょく
국가(國家) a state; a country; a nation / ~적 national; state/ ~ 시험 a state examination. こっか
국가(國歌) the national anthem. こっか
국거리 soup makings; materials for soup. スープのさいりょう
국건더기 ingredients.
국경(國境) the border; the frontier; the boundaries [of a country]/사랑에는 ~이 없다 Love knows no frontier. / ~을 넘다 cross the border/~내[외] within[outside] the border. こっきょう
국경(國慶) national festival[feast]/~일 a national holiday.
국고(國庫) the [national] treasury/ ~ 수입 national revenues/ ~ 보조 a state subsidy. こっこ
국광(國光) national glory. くにのえいこう
국교(國交) diplomatic relations; national friendship/~를 맺다 enter into diplomatic relations (*with*). こっこう
국교(國敎) a state religion[church]/영국 ~회 Anglican Church. こっきょう
국구(國舅) the father-in-law of King; an emperor. こうごのちち
국국 closely; tightly; firmly; to the full.
국국물 the liquid part of soup; the broth.
국군(國君) the Sovereign; the King; the Emperor. おおさま
국군(國軍) the national army; the government army. こくぐん
국궁(鞠躬) prostration/ ~하다 prostrate [oneself] (*before*). きっきゅう
국권(國權) national power[prestige]/ ~을 신장하다 expand national power[prestige]. こっけん
국그릇 a bowl for containing soup[broth]; a soup bowl. しるのちゃわん
국금(國禁) the national prohibition/ ~ 하다 be prohibited [interdict] by the

government. こっきん

국기(國基) the foundation of a nation ⇒ 국초(國礎). くにのどだい

국기(國忌) an anniversary of the death of a king《queen》/ ～일 an anniversary of the death of a king.

국기(國技) a national sport[game]; national craftsmanship. こくぎ

국기(國紀) national discipline.

국기(國旗) the national flag[colours]/ 영국 ～ the Union Jack/미국 ～ the Stars and Stripes. こっき

국난(國難) a national crisis/ ～에 목숨을 바치다 die for one's country. こくなん

국내(國內) the interior/ ～의 internal; domestic; home/ ～ 문제 internal[domestic] affairs/ ～ 법 municipal[national] law/～ 사정 internal[domestic] affairs. こくない

국도(國都) the capital [of a country]; the metropolis. こくと

국도(國道) a national road; a highway; a state road《미》. こくどう

국란(國亂) a civil war; an internal disturbance. こくらん

국량(局量) calibre; ability; talent; capacity. きんど

국력(國力) national resources[power, strength]. こくりょく

국록(國祿) a stipend/ ～을 먹다 receive a stipend; be in government service. くにからくれるほうきゅう

국론(國論) public[national] opinion[sentiment]/ ～을 통일하다 unify the public opinion; unify the national view. こくろん

국리(國利) national welfare[interests, prosperity]. こくり

국립(國立) ～의 national; state; government/ ～ 극장 a national theater/～ 공원 a national park. こくりつ

국말이 cooked rice served in soup. しるにごはんをまぜること

국면(局面) the situation; the aspect/～을 타개하다 remove the bottleneck on the way/ ～이 일변하다 enter upon a new phase. きょくめん

국명(國名) the name of a country. こくめい

국명(國命) ①《사명》a national mission ②《명령》a government order. こくめい

국모(國母) the mother of the state; the Empress; the Queen. こくぼ

국무(國務) state affairs/ ～ 위원 a minister of state/ ～ 장관 the Secretary of State《미》/ ～ 총리 the Prime Minister; the Premier. こくむ

국무 회의(國務會議) a Cabinet council[conference, meeting]/임시 ～ an extraordinary Cabinet meeting. こくむかいぎ

국문(國文) ①《문학》national[Korean] literature ②《국어》the national[Korean] language ③《문자》the Korean alphabet. こくぶん

국문(鞠問) a trial for felony/ ～하다 try for a grave offense.

국물 soup; broth/김치 ～ kimchi juice. ·/ ～을 만들다 prepare soup. しるのみず

국민(國民) a nation; a people; a citizen; a national/ ～ 투표 a plebiscite; a referendum/ ～ 가요 a popular song/ ～ 장(葬) a people's funeral. こくみん

국민 학교(國民學校) an elementary school; a primary school/ ～ 학생 a [primary] schoolboy[schoolgirl]. こくみんがっこう

국밥 a dish of rice and soup preparation. しるにまぜたごはん

국방(國防) national defense/ ～부[장관] the Ministry[Minister] of National Defense/～비 national defense expenditure/ ～색 khaki [colour]. こくぼう

국법(國法) the national law; the laws of the country/～으로 금지하다 prohibit by national law. こくほう

국보(局報) ①《관청 전보》a service telegram ②《방송국 보도》an information [news] of a radio station. きょくほう

국보(國寶) a national treasure/ ～적 존재 a national asset. こくほう

국보 간난(國步艱難) national emergency.

국본(國本) the foundation of the country.

국부(局部) ①《일부》a locality; a part; a section ②《앓는 데》the affected part ③《음부》the private parts/ ～ 마취 local an[a]esthesia. きょくぶ

국부(國富) national wealth[resources].

국부(國府) the National Government of China; the Nationalist China. こくふ

국부(國父) a [founding] father of the country. くにのいだいなとうちしゃ

국비(國費) the national expenditure/～로 at the expense of the state. こくひ

국빈(國賓) a guest of the state; a national guest. こくひん

국사(國士) a distinguished citizen 《애국자》a patriot.

국사(國史) the national history/한국의 ～ the history of Korea Korean history. こくし

국사(國事) state affairs/～범 a political offence; high treason;《사람》a political offender. こくじ

국사(國師) ①《스승》the leader[light] of the nation ②《중》the Most Reverend Priest. こくし

국산(國産) home production/～의 home-made/ ～품 home products; a home-made articles. こくさん

국상(國喪) national mourning.

국새(國璽) the Seal of the State. こくじ

국색(國色) the most beautiful woman in the country; the reigning beauty 《모란꽃》the Peony. こくしょく

국서(國書) 《문서》credentials《신임장》《서적》national literature[works] 《친서》a sovereign's message. こくしょ

국선(國選) ～의 chosen[appointed] by the

government/ ~ 변호인 a defense counsel assigned by the court. こくせん
**국세**(國稅) a nation tax. こくせい
**국세**(局勢) 《판국》 the aspect of affairs; the situation/ ~가 일변하다 take a new turn; enter upon a new phase.
**국소**(局所) ①《국부》 a part; an affected part; local ②《관절》 joints [of the body] ⇒국부(局部). きょくしょ
**국속**(國俗) national manners and customs. くにのふうぞく
**국수** noodles; soup noodles; *spaghetti*(It); vermicelli/ ~를 말다 prepare a dish of noodles [with soup and pickles]/ ~를 a vermicelli-press. うどん
**국수**(國粹) national characteristics[virtues]/ ~주의 ultranationalism/ ~주의자 an ultranationalist. こくすい
**국수**(國手) a master[capital] hand; a national champion. こくしゅ
**국수맨드라미** 《식》 a kind of cockscomb.
**국숫물** a noodle broth. うどんのしる
**국시**(國是) a national[state] policy/ ~를 위반하다 act against a national policy. こくぜ
**국악**(國樂) Korean classical music; national classical music. こくがく
**국어**(國語) the national[Korean] language; *one's* mother tongue/ ~ 독본 a Korean reader. こくご
**국영**(國營) state operation/ ~의 nationalization; state-operated/ ~으로 하다 nationalize. こくえい
**국왕**(國王) a monarch; a king; a sovereign. こくおう
**국외**(局外) the outside/ ~의 outside; external/ ~에서 관찰하다 observe from the outside. きょくがい
**국외**(國外) ~에서[로] abroad; over seas; outside the country. こくがい
**국욕**(國辱) a national disgrace[humiliation, dishonour]; a disgrace to the nation. こくじょく
**국용**(國用) ①《비용》 nation expense[expenditure] ②《사용》 national use/ ~의 for national use. こくよう
**국운**(國運) the national fortunes; the destiny of a country/ ~의 발전 national development. こくうん
**국원**(局員) 《전원》 the staff of a bureau 《한 사람》 a member of a bureau.
**국위**(國威) national prestige[glory, honour]. こくい
**국유**(國有) state[government] ownership; nationalization/ ~의 state[government]-owned; state; nationalized/ ~림 a State forest. こくゆう
**국으로** within *one's* limitations; suitable to *one's* own ability/ ~ 가만히 있다 keep *one's* place. できたままに
**국은**(國恩) favo[u]rs benefited by *one's* country. こくおん
**국음**(國音) native pronunciation 《한국의》 Korean pronunciation. くになまり

**국자** a ladle; a dipper; a scoop. ひしゃく
**국자**(國字) 《한 나라의》 the national script 《한국의》 Korean characters. こくじ
**국장**(局長) the director of a bureau; a postmaster. きょくちょう
**국장**(國葬) a state[national] funeral/ ~으로 하다 inter at state expense. こくそう
**국장**(國章) the national emblem. こくしょう
**국재**(國財) national property; national funds; national wealth. くにのざいさん
**국재**(國災) a national disaster[calamity, misfortune]. くにのさいなん
**국적**(國賊) a traitor [to the country]; a rebel; an insurgent. こくぞく
**국적**(國籍) nationality/ ~ 불명의 비행기 a plane of unknown nationality/ ~을 취득하다 acquire citizenship. こくせき
**국전**(國典) ①《의식》 a State ceremony ②《전적》 national literature; Korean book ; a national code of law. こくてん
**국전**(國展) the National Art Exhibition. こくてん
**국정**(國政) administration; government/ ~에 참여하다 participate in the administration/ ~ 감사(監査) parliamentary inspection of the administration[government offices]. こくせい
**국정**(國定) goverement authorization/ ~의 state; national; statutory/ ~ 교과서 state textbooks. こくてい
**국정**(國情) the state of affairs in a country. こくじょう
**국제**(國際) ~적 international; world/ ~ 관계 international relations/ ~ 결혼 intermarriage; interbreeding/ ~법 international law. こくさい
**국제 연합**(國際聯合) the United Nations (略: U.N.)/ ~군 the United Nations Army/ ~ 총회 the United Nations General Assembly. こくさいれんごう
**국조**(國祚) the fortunes[destinies] of a state[country, nation]. こくうん
**국지**(一紙) paper scraps [produced by cutting the edges of paper]. かみのきれはし
**국지**(局地) a locality/ ~적 local/ ~화하다 localize. きょくち
**국채**(國債) a national debt[loan] 《증권》 a national bond/ ~를 모집[상환]하다 raise[sink] a national loan. こくさい
**국책**(國策) a national[state] policy/ ~ 회사 a national policy concern[company]. こくさく
**국척**(國戚) matrimonial relations of a king.
**국척**(跼蹐) ①《몸을 굽히다》 stoop ②《어물어물하다》 sneak about. きょくせき
**국철**(國鐵) the national[state] railways; the government railways. こくてつ
**국체**(國體) national constitution; nationality. こくたい
**국초**(國初) 《나라의》 the beginning of a state 《왕조의》 the beginning of a dynasty. こくしょ

**국초(國礎)** the foundation of a nation. ⇒국기(國基). こっかのきそ

**국치(國恥)** a national humiliation; a national disgrace/~일 National Humiliation Day. くにのはじ

**국태 민안(國泰民安)** national peace and prosperity.

**국토(國土)** a country; a territory/ ~방위 national defence/ ~계획 national land planning. こくど

**국판(菊版)** a small octavo; a medium octavo〈미〉. きくばん

**국폐(國弊)** national abuses. くにのへいがい

**국풍(國風)** national customs and manners. こくふう

**국학(國學)** Korean literature; the national literature. こくがく

**국한(局限)** localization/ ~하다 localize; set limits to. きょくげん

**국한문(國漢文)** Korean and Chinese literature. こくかんぶん

**국헌(國憲)** the national constitution; the laws of the country. こっけん

**국호(國號)** the name of a country. こくごう

**국혼(國婚)** a royal marriage.

**국화(國花)** a national flower. くにをしょうちょうするはな

**국화(菊花)** a chrysanthemum. きっか

**국화잠(菊花簪)** a hairpin shaped like a chrysanthemum.

**국회(國會)** the National Assembly(한국 프랑스); the Parliament(영국); the Congress(미국). こっかい

**군-** extra; superfluous; unnecessary/ ~음식 a snack/ ~식구 a boarder; a guest. よけいな

**-군** ①《짓군》a [skilled] gambler; an expert ②《성원》a member; a man; a hand. やく(役). もの(者)

**군(軍)** an army; a force; a team/ 제일 야전~ the First Field Army/백~ the white team. ぐん

**군(君)** you; Mister (略.Mr.)/김~ Mr. Kim. きみ

**군(郡)** a district; country. ぐん

**군가(軍歌)** a war song; a war chant/~를 부르다 sing a war song. ぐんか

**군거(群居)** gregarious life/ ~하다 live gregariously[together]. ぐんきょ

**군걸음** needless steps.

**군것질** enjoying to eat various things between meals/ ~하다 spend money on sweets. うんしょく

**군경(軍警)** the army[military] and the police/ ~ 유가족 the surviving[bereaved] families of the dead soldiers and policemen. ぐんけい

**군경(窘境)** a predicament; a fix; an awkward situation; a painful position.

**군계(群鷄)** a flock of fowls/~의 일학(一鶴) a jewel on a dung-hill; a triton among the minnows. にわとりのむれ

**군계집** a fornicatress; an adulteress.

**군고구마** a roast sweet potatoes. やきいも

**군고기** broiled beef; roast meat.

**군공(軍功)** meritorious services in war; distinguished military services ⇒전공(戰功). ぐんこう

**군관구(軍管區)** a military district/6~ 사령부 the 6th Military District Command.

**군국(軍國)** a militant nation/ ~주의 militarism/~주의자 a militarist/~주의적 militaristic. ぐんこく

**군글자** a superfluous [written] character; an expletive.

**군기(軍紀)** military discipline/ ~를 유지하다[문란케 하다] maintain[break] military discipline. ぐんき

**군기(軍氣)** morale; military spirit. ぐんき

**군기(軍旗)** the colours; a standard/~호위병 a colour party. ぐんき

**군기(軍器)** arms; weapons of war. ぐんき

**군기(軍機)** a military secret/ ~ 누설 leakage of military secrets. ぐんき

**군기(群起)** rising in a group/ ~하다 rise in a group. ぐんき

**군납(軍納)** supply of goods and services to the military/ ~업자 (물품의) a military goods supplier (용역의) service contractors for the military/ ~ 회사 military supply contract firm.

**군내** a bad smell; an unpleasant smell.; an extra smell. くさりかけたにおい

**군눈** eyes too curious[inquisitive] for their own good.

**군단(軍團)** a corps; an army corps/5~ the fifth army crops. ぐんだん

**군대(軍隊)** an army; troops; forces; the military/ ~ 생활 [an] army life/ ~수첩 a pocket-ledger. ぐんたい

**군대답(一對答)** a needless reply.

**군더더기** a superfluity. よけいなもの

**군던지럽다** be foul; mean; low; nasty; filthy. けがらわしい

**군데** ①《곳》a place; a spot; a point ② 《부분》a part. かしょ

**군데군데** here and there; sporadically; at places. ところどころ

**군도(軍刀)** a sabre; a service-sword; a sword. ぐんとう

**군도(群島)** an archipelago; a group of islands. ぐんとう

**군돈** money spent unnecessarily.

**군두목** writing in Chinese characters by phonetic equivalents. あてじ

**군두쇠** a large metal ring attached to one end of a log.

**군란(軍亂)** an insurrection of troops; an army rebellion. ぐんらん

**군략(軍略)** strategy; tactics/~가 a strategist; a tactician. ぐんりゃく

**군량(軍糧)** provisions; military supplies; food/~의 보급을 차단하다 cut off the supply of food. ぐんりょう

**군령(軍令)** a military command. ぐんれい

**군례(軍禮)** military honours.

**군림(君臨)** reigning/ ~하다 reign[rule]

군마(軍馬) ①(말) a military[war] horse; a charger ②(군사와 말) men and horses.
군막(軍幕) hangs[tents] for military use.
군말 an unnecessary remarks/ ~하다 say unnecessary things.
군매점(軍賣店) a canteen; a post exchange (略 P.X.).
군명(君命) a royal command/ ~을 받들어 in obedience to the royal command.
군모(軍帽) a military cap; an army[navy] cap.
군무(軍務) military affairs[service, duties].
군문(軍門) (군무)a military camp (문)a camp-gate/~에 들어가다 enlist in the army; enter the service; join the colors.
군물 ①(마시는 물) drinking water taken between meals ②(거듭치는 물) additional cold water added to a boiling liquid.
군민(軍民) the military and the people.
군민(郡民) the inhabitants of a country.
군밤 roast chestnuts.
군밥 food for uninvited guests; rice leftover; extra rice.
군번(軍番) the serial number.
군벌(軍閥) a military faction; a militarist party/~ 정치 militaristic government.
군법(軍法) martial[military] law/ ~회의 a court-martial.
군복(軍服) a military uniform; regimentals.
군부(君父) one's lord[king]; one's lord and father.
군부(軍部) the military [authorities]; army circles.
군불 ㉠~ 때다 heat the floor [of a Korean room].
군비(軍備) military[war] preparations; armaments/~ 축소[확장] reduction[expansion] of armaments.
군비(軍費) war expenditure.
군사(軍士) troops; forces; a soldier; a private.
군사(軍使) the bearer of a flag of truce; a military envoy.
군사(軍事) military affairs/~ 훈련 a military drill[training]/ ~ 우편 military post/ ~ 용어 a military term / ~ 고문 a military adviser/ ~상의 military; strategic.
군사람 a superfluous[an unnessary] person.
군사령관(軍司令官) an army commander.
군사령부(軍司令部) military headquarters.
군사설(一辭說) long and superfluous words; lengthy talk; a long and uncalled forlecture.
군살 superfluous flesh.
군상(群像) ①(조각) a group ②(족속) people.
군새 straw used to repair thatch roofs.
군색(窘塞) indigence; poverty/~한 indigent; poor; destitute/~하다 (be) destitute; poor.
군생(群生) 《생》 animate things;; living creatures/ ~하다 live[grow] in stocks.
군서(群書) a various books; many books.
군서(群棲) gregariousness/ ~하다 live in flocks; live gregariously.
군세(軍勢) ①(병대수)the number of soldiers ②(군) an army; a force; troops; military power.
군소 《동》 a seahare; Aplysia kuroda(학명).
군소(群小) minor; petty; lesser/ ~ 정당 minor political parties.
군소리 ①(군말) superfluous words; nonsense/ ~하다 talk nonsense ②(헛소리) delirious utterances/ ~하다 talk in delirium; utter ravings.
군속(軍屬) a civilian employee.
군손질 unnecessary handling[care].
군수(郡守) a country headman[governor]; the magistrate of a country; county leader.
군수(軍需) munitions of war/~품[물자] war supplies; munitions/~ 산업 a war[making] industry/~ 공장 a munitions factory.
군식구(一食口) an extra member of one's family; a dependant other than one's own family.
군신(君臣) soverign and subject; lord and vassal.
군신(軍神) the god of war.
군신(群臣) all officials; the whole body of officials.
군실거리다 itch/군실군실 all itchy; all crawly.
군아(郡衙) the country office.
군악(軍樂) military music/육군 ~대 a military band.
군액(軍額) ①(사람) the number of soldiers ②(곡식의 양) the amount of grains for military use.
군역(軍役) ①(신분) a serviceman; military personnel ②(군복무) military service.
군영(軍營) a military camp[base]; an encampment.
군왕(君王) a king.
군용(軍用) military use/~ 도로 a military road.
군용(軍容) ①(군장) military accouterments ②(진용) a formation of troops; military situat ion.

군웅(群雄) rival leaders／~ 할거 rivalry of local barons／ ~ 할거 시대 the age of rival war lords. ぐんゆう
군원 이관(軍援移管) transfer of the Military Assistance Program[me].
군위(軍威) military power; military dignity. ぐんたいのいりょく
군율(軍律) ①(군법(軍法)) martial law; the articles of war ②(군기) military discipline. ぐんりつ
군은(君恩) the Imperial benevolence; the favours of one's lord. くんおん
군음식(一飮食) extra food; food other than meals; snack. かんしょく
군의(軍醫) an army[a naval] surgeon／ ~관[장교] a medical officer. ぐんい
군인(軍人) a soldier; a serviceman／ ~정신 the military spirit／ ~ 생활 military life／ ~다운 soldierly. ぐんじん
군입정 eating extra eatables between meals／ ~하다 be given to get eatables [between meals].
군입질 eating[stuffing oneself] between meals; snacking. かんしょくするくせ
군자(君子) a man of virtue; a true gentleman; a wise man. くんし
군자금(軍資金) war funds; the sinews of war／ ~을 공급하다 supply the sinews of war. ぐんしきん
군장(軍葬) a military funeral.
군장(軍裝) ①(평시의) military uniform [equipment] ②(출정시의) war outfit [attire].
군적(軍籍) the army[naval, air force] list. ぐんせき
군정(軍政) military administration; ~부 a military government. ぐんせい
군정(軍情) military conditions. ぐんじょう
군제(軍制) a military system. ぐんせい
군졸(軍卒) soldiers; the rank and file. ⇨군사(軍士). ぐんそつ
군주(君主) a sovereign; a ruler; a monarch; a crowned head／ ~국 a monarchy／ ~ 정체 monarchism. くんしゅ
군중(群衆) a crowd [of people]; a multitude 《대중》 the masses／ ~ 심리 mob psychology. ぐんしゅう
군지럽다 be foul ⇨군던지럽다. けがらわしい
군진(軍陣) a military camp; an encampment. ぐんたいのじんえい
군집(群集) an assembly; a group; a crowd／~하다 gather; crowd together; congremate. ぐんしゅう
군청(郡廳) a county office.
군청(群靑) ultramarine [blue]; navy blue. こいあいいろ
군체(群體) a colony. ぐんたい
군축(軍縮) the reduction of armaments／ ~하다 reduce／~ 회의 a military reduction conference.
군침 excessive saliva／그 요리를 보자 그는 ~을 삼켰다 The sight of the dish made his mouth water. よだれ

군턱 a double chin.
군티 a slight flaw[defect].
군표(軍票) a military script; an army note; military payment certificate; military currency. ぐんぴょう
군핍(窘乏) ~하다 (be) straitened; pressed. ひじょうにまずしいこと
군학(軍學) military science; tactics; strategy. ぐんがく
군함(軍艦) a warship. ぐんかん
군항(軍港) a naval port; a naval station. ぐんこう
군현(郡縣) counties and prefectures／ ~ 제도 the prefectural system. ぐんとけん
군호(軍號) a military password; a watchword. ぐんのあんごう
군화(軍靴) military shoes; combat[army] boots. ぐんじんのくつ
군획 an extra stroke [in writing a character]. ふひつようなじかく
군후(君侯) a [feudal] lord. くんこう
굳건하다 (be) firm; steady. そうけんだ
굳다¹ become stiff[hard]; harden; stiffen; set; settle／풀이 굳었다 The paste has become hard. かたくなる
굳다² (형용사) (be) hard; solid／굳게 약속하다 give firm promise. かたい
굳세다 (be) firm; strong; stout; adamantine. つよい
굳어지다 become hard; harden.
굳은살 hardened skin 《손의》 a callus 《발의》 a corn.
굳이 positively; firmly; stubbornly／ ~ 사양하다 decline positively. かたく
굳히다 harden; stiffen. かためる
굴 【어】 an oyster／ ~ 양식장 an oyster bed[farm]. かき
꿀 honey 《꽃의》 nectar; molasses; honeydew／~같이 달다 be sweet like honey／ ~떡 honey cake／ ~범벅 honeyed pudding. みつ
굴(窟) ①(짐승의) a lair 《토끼의》 a burrow 《여우의》 an earth ②(동혈) a cave; a cavern ③(터널) a tunnel. いわや
굴갓 the hat of an office holding monks[priests].
꿀꺽 ①(삼키는 모양) at a gulp ②(참는 모양) patiently／ ~ 마시다 drink at a gulp; gulp down. ごくごく
굴검(掘檢) an inquest of a disentombed body／ ~하다 hold an inquest over a disentombed body.
굴곡(屈曲) winding; irregularity; crookedness; flexion. くっきよく
꿀꿀 ①(물 흐르는 소리) bubbling ②(돼지의) grunting／ ~하다 bubble; grunt／ ~거리다 grunt. ちよろちよろ
굴기(崛起) ①(산의) rising[towering, soaring] high ②(사람의) rising from obscurity.
굴다 behave; conduct oneself; act 《대하다》 treat. ふるまう
굴다리 a viaduct; a land bridge; an elevated bridge. りっきょう

굴대 an axle; an axis; a shaft. しんぼう
굴때장군(-將軍) a huge[burly] person with a dark[swarthy] complexion. せがたかくふといひと
굴도리 a cylindrical beam.
굴뚝 a chimney; a chimneystack; a [smoke] stack 《기선의》a funnel／～ 소제 chimney sweeping えんとつ
굴뚝새 《조》a wren.
굴렁쇠 a hoop／～를 굴리다 roll[drive] along a hoop.
꿀렁하다 ①《물이》splash; slush; slosh; make a splash inside ②《부풀어서》be baggy; be puffy. だぶだぶ
굴레 a bridle. くつわ
굴레미 a wooden wheel. もくせいのくるま
굴리다 ①《굴러가게》roll [over] ②《넘어지게》throw down ③《버려두다》neglect to take care ④《둥글게》round. ころがす
꿀리다 ①《쭈그러지다》be crumpled; be rumpled; be wrinkled ②《형편이》be impoverished; be hard up ③《켕기다》have something on one's conscience ④《기세・형세》be cornered; give in.
굴밤 an acorn. かしのみ
굴밥 rice boiled with oysters.
굴복(屈服) submission; surrender／～하다 yield; submit; surrender; give in (to). くっぷく
굴비 a dried yellow corvina. ほしぐち
굴속(窟-) the incide of cave[den, tunnel]; a dark place／～ 같다 be as dark as a cave. いわやのなか
굴슬(屈膝) submission; surrender／～하다 be brought to one's knees. ひざぐみ
굴신(屈伸) extension and contraction／～하다 bend and stretch; extend and contract／～ 자재의 flexible; elastic; pliable. くっしん
굴신(屈身) ①《겸손》self-depreciation; modesty／～하다 humble oneself ②《몸을 굽힘》bending oneself; bend oneself[forward]; bending the body.
굴왕신 같다 be old and shabby.
굴욕(屈辱) a humiliation; a disgrace; an insult／～을 주다 humiliate; insult／～을 느끼다 feel humiliated. くつじょく
굴우물(窟-) a bottomless well. ひじょうにふかいいど
굴이(掘移) reburial; reinterment／～하다 rebury; reinter.
꿀쩍 squashing; sniffling. ねちゃねちゃ
굴절(屈節) abandonment of one's integrity[principles]／～하다 abandon one's integrity[principles]. くっせつ
굴절(屈折) refraction／～하다 be refracted; bend／～각 the angle of refraction／～광선 a refracted ray. くっせつ
굴절어(屈折語) an inflected[inflectional] language. くっせつご
굴젓 pickled oysters. かきのしおから
굴젓눈이 a person suffering from cataract. めかち
굴조개 an oyster. かき

굴종(屈從) submission; servitude／～하다 submit (to); yield (to); succumb (to)／～시키다 keep (one) down. くつじゅう
굴지(屈指) counting on one's fingers／～의 leading; prominent／～의 실업가 a leading business man. くっし
굴총(掘塚) ～하다 open a grave; dig a grave open; violate a grave. たにんのはかをほること
굴타리먹다 be worm-eaten; become wormy. みがくさる
굴퉁이 a gimcrack; a trumpery; a gewgaw. びかびかしたやすもの
꿀풀 《식》the Asiatic selfheal; Brunella asiatica(학명).
굴피(-皮) ①an empty pocket[purse] ②《참나무 껍데기》oak bark. からさいふ
굴하다(屈-) 《복종》yield[submit] (to)／…에 굴하지 않고 in spite[defiance] of; undaunted. かがむ
굴혈(窟穴) a cave; a cavern; a den; a hollow. そうくつ
굴혈(掘穴) digging a hole／～하다 dig a hole. あなをほる
굴회(-膾) raw oysters; a dish of fresh oyesters.
굵기 thickness. ふとさ
굵다 (be) big; thick 《음성이》deep 《활자가》bold／굵은 팔 a big arm／굵다랗다 be very big[thick]. ふとい
굵다랗다 be very thick; very big. ひじょうにふとくておおきい
굵직굵직 severally thick[big, burly, deep, fat]／～하다 be all thick[big, burly, deep]. かなりふとい
굶기다 let (a person) go hungry; starve; make (a person) starve／굶겨 죽이다 starve (a person) to death. うえさせる
굶다 starve; go hungry; famish; go without food[eating]／나는 온종일 굶었다 I have not touched food all day.／I haven't eaten all day. うえる
굶주리다 starve; famish; hunger (for)／사랑에 ～ hunger for love. うえている
꿇다 bend one's knees; go down on one's knees／무릎을 꿇고 앉다 sit on one's knees. ひざまずく
꿇리다 make (a person) kneel down; force to yield. ひざまずかせる
꿇어앉다 kneel [down]; fall[drop] on one's knees／꿇어앉아 탄원하다 implore on one's knees. ひざまずく
꿈 a dream 《환상》a vision; an illusion／불길한 ～ an evil dream／청춘의 ～ the dream of youth／～나라 a dream land／～을 꾸다 have a dream. ゆめ
꿈결 a dreamy state／～같은 transient; ～같이 like a dream; in vain 《빠름》swiftly.
꿈꾸다 dream (of, about); have[dream] a dream 《바라다》dream of; fancy; hope; imagine. ゆめをみる
굼닐다 band and stretch [oneself]; keep bending and stretching. くっしんする

꿈땜 ~하다 console *oneself* that *one's* bad luck is simply the result of a bad dream that had foretold it. ゆめちがい

굼뜨다 be slow; dull; tardy. のろい

굼벵이 ①《벌레》a young cicada in its larval stage ②《사람》a laggard; a sluggard. ねきりむし

굼실거리다 writhe; wriggle; squirm/굼실굼실 wrigglingly. のたくる

꿈자리 a dream; the happenings in a dream. ゆめみ

굼적, 꿈적 ~거리다 budge; stir. ぐずぐず

꿈쩍없다 (be) unmoved; unperturbed; remain cool[calm]. びくともしない

꿈적이다 budge; stir; twist the body around in slow motion. のろくうごく

굼지럭, 꿈지럭 ~거리다 move slowly; stir sluggishly; be slow; be sluggish; be dilatory/굼지럭굼지럭〔꿈지럭꿈지럭〕 sluggishly. のろのろ

굼튼튼하다 (be) steady; solid; provident; tightfisted. せいじつがきょうけんだ

굼틀, 꿈틀 ~거리다 wriggle; squirm; writhe/굼틀굼틀〔꿈틀꿈틀〕 wrigglingly; convulsively. のたくるさま

굽 ①《마소의》a hoof/~이 있는 동물 a hoofed animal ②《구두의》a heel/나막신 ~ the base of a wooden shoes. ひづめ

굽갈리다 put new clog-supports on [a pair of wooden shoes]; put new supports into a clog. ぼくりのはをとりかえる

굽다 be bent; crooked; winding/굽은 나무 a crooked tree. まがっている

굽다 roast; broil 《감자 따위》bake 《빵 따위를》toast 《고기》do 《석쇠로》grill; parch/떡을 ~ toast ricecakes over a fire/빵을 ~ toast bread. やく

굽달이 a dish with a base [rim].

굽도리 the lower parts of walls of a room.

굽싸다 tie up the four feet [of an animal]; tie up by the hooves. けもののあしをしばること

굽슬굽슬하다 be curled; curly; crisp; wary; frizzled/머리가 ~ have curly hair. けがちぢみあがっている

굽실, 꿉실 ~거리다 cringe; wince; bow to/굽실굽실 obsequiously/상관에게 ~거리다 cringe to *one's* superiors/머리를 ~거리다 kowtow. ぺこぺこ

굽어보다 《내려다보다》look down; overlook. みくだす

굽이 a turn; a curve; a bend/~마다 at every turn[bend, corner]. まがり

굽이감다 wind; twist. まく

굽이굽이 ①《굽이마다》at every turn[bend] ②《흐르는 모양》windingly; meanderingly; in zigzag. まがりくねって

굽이돌다 wind around.

굽이지다 a bend[turn, curve] is made.

굽이치다 meander; roll. わんきょくになる

굽잡다 lay (*a person*) under restraint; make (*a person*) feel uneasy; have (*a person*) in *one's* grasp. おさえつける

굽잡히다 be made to feel small; be at (*a person*) mercy. おさえつけられる

굽적, 꿉적 with an awestricken bow/~하다 make an awestricken bow (with *one's body*).

あたまをさげてしんたいをかがめるさき

굽정이 a crooked article; something bent; a bent thing. まがったもの

굽질리다 run into a snag; (*a matter*) fail to go smoothly.

굽창 a leather reinforcing strip on the heel of a sandal. そこあてかわ

굽히다 bend [one's back]; bow [one's head]; stoop; curve; twist/허리를 ~ bend forward. かがめる

굿¹ 《구경거리》a spectacle; an object of interest 《연극 따위》a show. みせもの

굿² exorcism/~하다 exorcise.

굿거리 a tune[dance] performed during exorcism.

꿋꿋하다 ①《견고하다》(be) strong; firm; solid; tough ②《쪽바르다》straight; upright/꿋꿋한 의지 a firm will/꿋꿋이 버티다 take a firm stand. かたい

굿보다 ①《굿 구경하다》see a performance of exorcism ②《방관하다》remain unconcerned spectator; sit on the fence. ぼうかんする

굿중 a mendicant monk[priest]/~대 a band of mendicant priests. たくはつそう

굿하다 exorcise; perform an exorcism.

꿍 plump; with a thud[bump]. どすん

궁(宮) a palace/경복~ the *Kyungbok* palace. みや

궁(窮) ①《없어짐》exhaustion; being used up ②《궁박》poverty ③《막힘》being driven to the wall / ~하다 be in want; be reduced to poverty. こんきゅう

궁경(窮境) ①《가난》narrow circumstances; great straits ②《궁지》a fix; a sad plight; a dilemma/~에 빠지다 be in great difficulties[straits]. きゅうきょう

궁계(窮計) the last shift[resort]; the last[final] expedient; a desperate measure. きゅうけい

궁곡(窮谷) an abysmal ravine; a deep valley. やまのふかいたに

궁곤(窮困) poverty; destitution; straitened circumstances / ~하다 be needy; destitute; distressed. きゅうこん

꽝꽝 rattling and booming; popping and booming/대포가 ~거리다 the cannon is roaring. どん

궁구(窮究) thorough investigation[study, research] / ~하다 investigate thoroughly; master; make an exhaustive study of. ふかくげんきゅうすること

궁굴다 《그릇이》be larger than it looks; hold more than *one* might expect.

みかけよりおおきい

궁굴리다 be tolerant; forgive with kind words[remark]; be generous listen attentively. かんだいにとりはかる

꿍꿍 moaning; groaning/ ~하다 groan

궁궁이 with pain; utter a groan. うんうん
궁궁이 《식》*Angelica Polymorpha*(학명).
궁궁이셈 secret intention; a secret design[scheme] of *one's* own. しんさん
궁궁잇속 a secret design; an underlying motive/~이 있다 have a plot in mind; have a secret design. にえきらないいど
궁궐(宮闕) the royal palace. きゅうでん
궁극(窮極) finality; eventuality/ ~에 가서는 in the end; in the long run; in the final analysis. きゅうきょく
궁글다 ①(속이 비다)be hollow; empty; be left empty ②(소리가) be deep; hollow. みかけよりなかがひろい
궁글막대 the board that connects the front and back pieces of packsaddle.
궁금증(一症) anxiety. きがかり
궁금하다 be anxious; concerned (*about, for*); interested (*in*)/시험의 결과가 ~ be worried about the result of the examination. きになる
궁기(窮氣) wretchedness/ ~낀 사람 a poor-looking man. きゅうぼうなようす
궁끼다(窮一) be impoverished; be in narrow circumstances. きゅうちにおちる
궁내(宮內) the Court; the Imperial Household. きゅうでんのなか
궁녀(宮女) a court lady; a maid of honour. きゅうじょ
궁노(宮奴) a court servant; servants in the royal employ. きゅうでんのどぼく
궁노루 a muskdeer.
궁답(宮畓) rice-field owned by the royal family.
궁도(弓道) bowmanship; archery ⇨궁술(弓術). きゅうどう
궁도(窮途) straitened circumstances; a fix. こんきゅうしたきょうぐう
궁도련님(宮一) a green youth; a young buck; a greenhorn. ぼんぼん
궁도령(宮道令) a greenhorn ⇨궁도련님. わかだんな
궁뚱망뚱하다 (be) rustic; mean; miserable; be neglected and shabby [·looking].
궁둥방아 a pratfall(미)/~를 찧다 come down flop on *one's* bottom. しりもち
궁둥이 the hips; the buttocks/여자의 ~를 쫓아다니다 dangle after[about] a girl; philander. おしり
궁둥짝 either hip; both hips.
궁륭(穹窿) a dome; a vault. きゅうりゅう
궁리(窮理) consideration; thought a design 《고안》device/ ~하다 consider; think over.
궁마(弓馬) ①《활과 말》a bow and a horse ②《무술(武術)》archery and horsemanship. ゆみとうま
궁민(窮民) poor people; the needy; the destitute. きゅうみん
궁박(窮迫) straitened circumstances; distress needy; distressed destitute; hard pressed for. きゅうはく
궁벽(窮僻) ~하다 be secluded; remote; unfrequented; be out of the way.

궁상(弓狀) arch/ ~의 arched; bow-shaped.
궁상(窮狀) a distressed condition; a sad plight; straitened circumstances/농촌의 ~ the farmers distress. きゅうじょう
궁상(窮相) a meager face.
궁서(窮鼠) a cornered mouse; a rat at bay/ ~는 오히려 고양이를 문다 A stag at bay is a dangerous foe.
궁성(宮城) the Imperial Palace; the royal palace. きゅうじょう
궁수(弓手) an archer.
궁술(弓術) archery/ ~ 시합 an archery match. きゅうじゅつ
궁시(弓矢) bow and arrow. ゆみとや
궁실(宮室) a royal chamber; the royal palace. きゅうちゅうのへや
궁싯거리다 toss around sleeplessly.
궁여 일책(窮餘一策) the last resort; a desperate shift; a desperate measure. きゅうよのいっさく
궁인(宮人) a lady in waiting; a court lady ⇨나인. きゅうじょ
궁전(宮田) fields owned by the royal family.
궁전(宮殿) a [royal] palace/ ~ 같은 집 a palace of a house. きゅうでん
궁절(窮節) a time of straits for cereals.
궁정(宮廷) the Court; Court circles/ ~ 문학 Court literature/ ~ 시인 a Cavalier poet. きゅうてい
궁중(宮中) the Royal Court/ ~에서 봉사하다 serve at Court. きゅうちゅう
궁지(窮地) a difficult situation; a predicament; a fix; a dilemma; a sad plight/ ~에 몰아넣다 drive (*one*) into a corner. きゅうち
궁진(窮盡) exhaustion/~하다 exhaust. きわめつくすこと
궁창(穹蒼) the vault of heaven; the sky; the blue sky.
궁책(窮策) the last shift; a desperate measure. きゅうさく
궁체(宮體) the court style of writing the Korean script.
궁촌(宮村) a poor village. ひんそん
궁춘(窮春) the period of spring poverty.
궁태(窮態) extreme straits; distress ⇨궁상. きゅうじょう
궁터(宮一) the site of an old palace. ゆみば
궁핍(窮乏) want; destitution; poverty; penury; necessitous circumstances/ ~하다 poor; be destitute/ ~한 생활 a life of distress. きゅうぼう
꿍하다 (be) glum; sullen; moody and silent; he in a bad humor. ふきげんだ
궁하다(窮一) ①《살림이》be in distress[straitened circumstances]; be needy ②《입장이》be in an awkward position; be in a dilemma ③《처지에》be at a loss. びんぼうである
궁합(宮合) devination to decide if a proposed marriage is recommendable.

**궁행(躬行)** personal practice／～하다 act up to; carry out. きゅうこう

**궁향(窮鄕)** a remote[secluded] place.

**궁형(弓形)** a crescent form; 〖數〗 a segment of a circle／～의 arched; bow-shaped. きゅうけい

**궂기다** ①(일이) go wrong; fail; go amiss ②(상사나다) meet *one's* death; end *one's* life. しくじる

**궂다**[1] be bad; foul; ill; unlucky; nasty／궂은비 a long rain／궂은일 an unlucky affair; a disaster. てんきがわるい

**궂다**[2] 《눈이 멀다》 become blind; lose *one's* sight. めくらになる

**궂은고기** carrion; dead and putrefying flesh.

**궂은비** a long rain. ながあめ

**궂은살** superfluous flesh. ぜいにく

**궂은쌀** rice roughly hulled; rice of poor quality. よくつかれていないこめ

**궂은일** an unlucky affair; an untoward incident; a misfortune; a disaster.

**궂히다** be bereaved of (*a person*); lose (*a person*) in death; have (*a person*) die. しなす

**권(卷)** ①《책의》 a volume; a book ②《영화의》 a reel／3 ~으로 된 저서 a work in three volumes. かん

**권(勸)** ①《추천》 recommendation ②《권고》 advice; suggestion ③《장려》 encouragement／～하다 recommend; advise; suggest. かんこく

**-권(券)** document; ticket; card; bill; chit／100원 ~ a 100 *won* bill.

**-권(圈)** a circle; a range; a sphere 《반경》 a radius／태풍~내에 in the typhoon area. ―けん

**-권(權)** ①《권력》 authority; power ②《권리》 a right; a claim ③《이권》 a concession／재산~ the right of property／통치~ sovereignty. けん

**권계(勸戒)** ～하다 admonish; exhort; warn; remonstrate (*with*).

**권고(勸告)** advice; counsel; recommendation／～하다 advise; urge; recommend／～자 an adviser[advisor]／사직을 ～하다 advise to resign. かんこく

**권고(眷顧)** favo[u]r; patronage／～하다 look after; patronize; favo[u]r.

**권권 불망(眷眷不忘)** ～하다 bear (*a matter*) carefully in mind. けんけん

**권내(圈內)** ～에 within the circle[range, sphere]／당선~에 있다 be in the running; be within the bounds of possibility. けんない

**권농(勸農)** encouragement of agriculture／～하다 encourage[promote] agriculture[farming]. かんのう

**권능(權能)** power; authority; competency. けんのう

**권도(權道)** political expediency; the next best policy. けんりょくのみち

**권도(勸導)** ～하다 guide; lead; admonish.

**권두(卷頭)** the commencement[the opening, the beginning] of a book／~사[언] a foreword; a preface. かんとう

**권력(權力)** power; authority 《세력》 influence／~가 a man of power[influence]／~을 잡다 assume authority; come into power. けんりょく

**권련(眷戀)** a deep affection／～하다 have a deep affection (*for*); have a strong attachment (*to*). けんれん

**권리(權利)** a right 《요구권》 a claim 《소유권》 a title (*to*) 《특권》 a privilege／~금 a premium; key money／~가 있다 have a right; be entitled to. けんり

**권말(卷末)** the end of a volume; the end of a book. かんまつ

**권매(權賣)** conditional sale／～하다 sell (*a thing*) on the terms that reimbursement will be made in case the goods bought are returned. おしうり

**권면(券面)** the face of a bill; a denomination.

**권면(勸勉)** admonition; encouragement／～하다 admonish; encourage. けんめん

**권모(權謀)** a trick; an intrigue; an artifice. けんぼう

**권모 술수(權謀術數)** trickery; machination; diplomacy; finesse／~를 쓰다 resort to trickery[machination]; use diplomacy. けんぼうじゅっすう

**권문 세가(權門勢家)** a man of influence; an influential family; a powerful family. けんせいのあるうち

**권법(拳法)** boxing; *dangsu*. けんぼう

**권병(權柄)** power; authority; influence／~을 휘두르다 wield power; exercise authority[influence]. けんぺい

**권비(眷庇)** favo[u]r; protection; patronage／～하다 favo[u]r; patronize; take (*a person*) under *one's* wings.

**권선(勸善)** promotion of virtue; rewarding the good／～하다 encourage virtuous deeds; reward the good. かんぜん

**권선 징악(勸善懲惡)** promotion of virtue and reproval of vice; encouraging good and punishing evil. かんぜんちょうあく

**권세(權勢)** power; influence; authority／~부리다 wield power (*over*); exercise authority (*over*). けんせい

**권속(眷屬)** ①《식구》 a family; a household ②《아내》 *one's* wife. けんぞく

**권솔(眷率)** a family; the members of a household. かぞく

**권수(卷首)** ①《첫째 권》 the first volume ②《권두(卷頭)》 the beginning of a book. かんしゅ

**권수(卷鬚)** 〖植〗 a cirrus (*pl.* -ri). まきひげ

**권수(卷數)** the number of volumes. かんすう

**권신(權臣)** an influential vassal; a powerful courtier. けんしん

**권애(眷愛)** love; favo[u]r; loving and cherishing. あいすること

**권업(勸業)** encouragement of industry／～하다 encourage[promote] industry.

**권연(卷煙)** cigarettes ⇨권련. まきたばこ

**권외(圏外)** ~에 outside the circle[range, radius] (of)／당신~에 떨어지다 be outside the running. けんがい

**권우(眷遇)** warm treatment [by the king]／~하다 give warm treatment; favo[u]r.

**권운(卷雲)** a cirrus (pl·ri). まきぐも

**권위(權威)** ①(권세) authority; power; dignity ②(대가) an authority／~있는 authoritative. けんい

**권유(勸誘)** canvass[ing]; solicitation; invitation／~하다 canvass; invite; solicit／~원 a canvasser; an agent; a solicitor. かんゆう

**권유(勸諭)** admonition; counsel／~하다 admonish; councle. すすめさとすこと

**권익(權益)** rights and interests／우리들의 ~은 보호되어야 한다 Our rights and interests must be protected.／특수 ~ special interests. けんりとえき

**권장(勸獎)** recommendation／~하다 recommend. すすめてげきれいすること

**권적운(卷積雲)** a cirro-cumulus／~이 있는 하늘 a mackerel sky. けんせきうん

**권점(圈點)** a small circle for emphasis 《종지부》a period／~을 찍다 mark (words) with small circles. けんてん

**권주가(勸酒歌)** a Korean song at a drinking bout. さけをすすめるうた

**권지(勸止)** dissuasion／~하다 dissuade from (doing). すすめとめること

**권질(卷帙)** books; volumes.

**권척(卷尺)** a tape measure. まきじゃく

**권총(拳銃)** a pistol; a revolver／장난감 ~ a toy pistol／~ 강도 an armed robber; a gunman／6연발 ~ a six-chambered revolver. ピストル

**권축** a scroll. まきもののじく

**권층운(卷層雲)** a cirro-stratus／햇무리구름. けんそううん

**권태(倦怠)** fatigue; languor; ennui／~기《부부 생활의》 the turn of matrimonial life; a stage of lassitude. けんたい

**권토 중래(捲土重來)** ~하다 make another attempt with redoubled efforts; resume one's activities with redoubled energies. けんどじゅうらい

**권투(拳鬪)** boxing／~하다 box (with)／~시합 a boxing bout. けんとう

**권하다(勸一)** ①(권고하다) ask; exhort; advise; persuade ②(추천하다) recommend ③(먹을 것을) offer. すすめる

**권학(勸學)** the encourage of learning／~하다 encourage learning. かんがく

**권한(權限)** authority; power; competence／~ 다툼 conflict of attribution／~ 밖의 unauthorized. けんげん

**권화(勸化)** ①(감화시킴) inspiration／~하다 inspire; influence ②(보시를 청함) soliciting contributions for religious purpose.

**권화(權化)** incarnation／정의의 ~ an incarnate justice. ごんげ

**궐(闕)¹** 《궁궐》 the king's palace. きゅうじょう

**궐(闕)²** 《빠짐》 an omission; a vacancy; missing／~하다 be omitted; be missing. けつ

**궐궐** gurgling; gushing; with a gurgle; with a gush／~하다 gurgle[gush] out. とくとく

**궐기(蹶起)** ~하다 spring up; rise; rouse oneself to action. けっき

**궐나다(闕—)** cause a vacancy; vacate a post. たりない

**궐내(闕內)** the royal palace. きゅうてい

**궐련** a cigarette／~을 피우다 smoke a cigarette. たばこ

**궐문(闕門)** the main gate of a palace; a palace gate. きゅうじょうのもん

**궐문(闕文)** missing words; omitted letters. けつぶん

**궐방(闕榜)** failure in the examination／~하다 fail in the examination.

**궐석(闕席)** 【법】non-appearance／~재판 judg[e]ment by default. けっせき

**궐식(闕食)** ~하다 go without a meal; skip a meal. けっしょく

**궐직(闕直)** ~하다 fail to keep night watch.

**궐참(闕參)** non-attendance／~하다 fail to attend; absent oneself (from). ふさんか

**궐하다(闕—)** be omitted.

**꿩** 《동》a pheasant. きじ

**궤(几)** ①an armrest; an elbowrest ②《책상》a desk; a writing table; an altar table.

**궤(櫃)** a chest; a coffer; a box. ひつ

**궤계(詭計)** a trick; an artifice; a fetch; a ruse; wiles. きけい

**꿰다** ①(구멍에) pass[run] through; thread; string／구슬을 ~ thread bead ②(찔러 뚫다) pierce; thrust ③(입다) put on; wear. とおす

**궤도(軌道)** ①(천체의) an orbit 《유성의》 a circle 《철도의》 a [railway] line; a track 〈미〉／~에 오르다 be started along right lines. きどう

**꿰뚫다** ①(관통하다) pierce; pass[run] through (총알이) shoot through ②(정통하다) be well versed[informed] (in, on). つきとおす

**꿰뜨리다** puncture; break; burst; wear out[down]／창문을 ~ break a window.

**꿰들다** ①(꿰어 쳐들다) pierce[spear, skewer] and hold up ②(들추어 내다) expose; disclose; unmask; bring to light. つらぬきあげる

**궤란(潰爛)** ~하다 ulcerate; decompose.

**꿰매다** ①(집다) sew; stitch 《양말 따위》 darn; mend ②(탈없이 하다) patch up; make shift／터진 곳을 ~ sew up a rip／양말을 ~ darn stockings. ぬう

**궤멸(潰滅)** destruction; demolition 《전멸》annihilation／~하다 be destroyed; be ruined. かいめつ

꿰미 a string [for coins, fish, persimmons, mushrooms] 《꿴 것》 things of string/고기 ~ a string of fish. とおしひも
궤범(軌範) an example; a model; a pattern; a standard. きはん
궤변(詭辯) sophism; chicanery 《역설》 a paradox/ ~가 a sophist; a quibbler/ ~학파 the sophists. きべん
궤복(跪伏) kneeling down/ ~하다 kneel down; prostrate oneself.
궤산(潰散) a rout; a defeat/ ~하다 be defeated; be put to rout; collapse; be routed. かいさん
궤양(潰瘍) 《의》 an ulcer. かいよう
궤짝(櫃—) a box; a chest/감 한 ~ a box of persimmons. そまつなはこ
궤적(軌跡) ①《바퀴의》 the trace of wheels ②《선인의》 the deed of one's predecessors; 《수》 a locus(pl. -ci). きせき
궤조(軌條) a rail /합성〔편평〕 ~ a compound[flat] rail. きじょう
궤좌(跪坐) ~하다 kneel down; sit on one's feet きざ
궤주(潰走) a rout /~하다 be routed; be put to rout[flight]. かいそう
꿰지다 ①《미어지다》 rip [open]; be torn; tear ②《터지다》 rend; burst; be broken ③《해지다》 wear out ④《드러나다》 be exposed; lay bare. つぶれる
꿰찌르다 thrust through; run through; pierce/단도로 가슴을 ~ plunge a dagger into (a person's) breast. つきさす
궤휼(詭譎) a scheme; a trick; an evil design; wiles/~하다 be tricky[wily, treacherous]. きげつ
꿱 yelling; shrieking; shouting /~ 소리를 지르다 utter a cry; yell. おどろかすときまたはおこってさけぶこえ
귀 ①《사람의》 an ear 《청각》 hearing/~에 익다 be familiar ②《물건의》 an edge (끝); 《천의》 a list 《구석》 a corner; an edge; a margin. みみ
귀(句) a passage; a phrase 《절》 a clause 《한 줄》 a line 《시의》 a verse 《일련》 a stanza 《시》 a poem. く
귀가(歸家) returning home; home-coming / ~하다 come[go] home; return home/늦게 ~하다 be late in coming home. うちにかえること
귀감(龜鑑) a model; a pattern; a paragon; an exemplar; a good example/충신의 ~ a model of loyalty きかん
귀갑(龜甲) a tortoise shell. かめのこうら
귀객(貴客) a guest of honour. ききゃく
귀거칠다 be harsh to the ear; be unpleasant to bear. みみざわりだ
귀걸이 ①《방한용》 an earcap ②《장식용》 an earring. みみかざり
귀격(貴格) ①《상》 noble features; dignified appearance ②《체격》 a rare physique.
귀결(歸結) a conclusion; an end 《결과》 a result; a consequence/당연한 ~ a natural consequence. きけつ

귀경(歸京) return to Seoul/ ~하다 return to Seoul. ソウルにもどる
귀골(貴骨) ①《사람》 people of noble birth ②《골격》 noble features.
귀공자(貴公子) a young prince[nobleman]/ ~ 같은 princely. きこうし
귀교(歸校) ~하다 return to school. がっこうからかえること
귀국(貴國) your esteemed country. きこく
귀국(歸國) return to one's country; home-coming/ ~하다 return[come, go] home/ ~길에 오르다 leave for home; start on one's way home きこく
귀글(句—) a verse; a poetry.
귀금속(貴金屬) precious metals/ ~상 a dealer in precious metals; a jeweler 《미》/ ~ 상점 a jewelery store. ききんぞく
귀기울이다 listen (to); give ear (to); listen with attention.
귀나다 ①《모가》 warp; swerve; slant ②《의논이》 break down; come to a repture. つぶれる
귀남자(貴男子) a noble man; a precious young man; a young of noble birth. りょうかのわかむすこ
귀납(歸納) induction/ ~하다 induce (A from B); generalize/ ~법 the inductive method. きのう
귀넘어듣다 listen carelessly; give no heed to/아무의 말을 ~ pay no attention to what a person says. うわのそらできく
귀녀(貴女) ①《귀한 여자》 a noble woman ②《경칭》 you. りょうかのむすめ
귀농(歸農) ~하다 return to the farm; go back to the earth. きのう
귀느래 a horse with droopy ears; a fla-peared horse. みみがたれているうま
뀌다 release/ 방귀를 ~ break[make] wind; let a fare; fart.
귀다래기 cattle with small ears; a small-eared cattle. みみのちいさいうし
귀담아듣다 listen willingly; listen carefully; stuff one's ears with (a person's words).
귀때 a spout 《술통 따위의》 a tap. くち
귀댁(貴宅) your esteemed home; your esteemed house. あなたのうち
귀도(歸途) one's way home 《여행의》 one's return trip/ ~에 오르다 start on one's way home. きと
귀동(貴童) a beloved[precious] child; a dear child. とくにちょうあいされるこども
귀동냥 learning by the ear; ear-learning picked-up knowledge. みみがくもん
귀동이(貴童—) a precious[beloved] child.
귀동자(貴童子) one's dear[belove] son. とくべつにかわいがられるこども
귀두(龜頭) 《해》 the glans; the glans of the penis. きとう
귀뚜라미 《충》 a cricket; a grig. こおろぎ
귀뚤귀뚤 chirring; chirping. ころころ
귀둥귀둥 recklessly; thoughtlessly; blindly; indiscriminately.
귀뜨다 learn to hear things for the first

**귀뜨이다** time. きこえはじめる
**귀뜨이다** become interested (in); have one's attention drawn. ききみみをたてる
**귀띔** a hint; an intimation; a suggestion /먼저 가라고 ~했다 He suggested that I go first. あんじ
**귀로(歸路)** one's way home. きろ
**귀롱나무【식】** *Prunus padus*(학명).
**귀리【식】** an oat. からすむぎ
**귀머거리** a deaf person. つんぼ
**귀먹다** become deaf 《일시적으로》 be deafened. つんぼだ
**귀명(歸命)** conversion to Buddhism/ ~하다 convert oneself to Buddhism.
**귀명(貴命)** your orders[request, instructions]. あなたのめいれい
**귀목** Zelkova wood.
**귀문(貴門)** ①《명문》a noble family ②《남의 집안》your[his] family. みぶんのたかいうち
**귀물(貴物)** ①《진품》a rare articles; a curio ②《귀중품》an article of value; treasure 《총칭》valuables; a rare thing. めずらしいもの
**귀밑** the root of one's ear/ ~까지 빨개지다 blush to the roots of one's ears. みみしたのほっぺた
**귀밝다** (be) sharp-eared; (be) quick to hear; have good ears. みみがはやい
**귀방(貴邦)** your country. きこく
**귀부(龜趺)** the turtle base of a stone monument; a monument base in the shape of a turtle. きふ
**귀뿌리** the root of the ear.
**귀부인(貴婦人)** a lady; noblewoman; a society dame/ ~다운 ladylike. きふじん
**귀부인(貴夫人)** your esteemed wife.
**귀빈(貴賓)** an honored[a distinguished] guest; an important guest/ ~석 a distinguished visitor's gallery. きひん
**귀사(貴社)** your company[firm]. きしゃ
**귀살스럽다** '①《뒤숭숭하다》(be) all messed up; be tangled[scattered] ②《마음이 산란하다》complicated; worrisome; troublesome. こんらんしたかんがき
**귀상어【어】** a hammerhead shark.
**귀서(貴書)** your [esteemed] letter. きしょ
**귀선(龜船)** a turtle-shaped battleship ⇔ 거북선. かめかたのふね
**귀설다** be unfamiliar to one's ear; be unaccustomed; strange. みみがとおい
**귀성(歸省)** home-coming/ ~하다 return [go, come] home. きせい
**귀소 본능(歸巢本能)** homing instinct.
**귀속(歸屬)** ①《복귀》reversion; return ②《소속》possession/ ~하다 revert to~; be returned (to); belong to. きぞく
**귀순(歸順)** submission; allegiance/ ~하다 submit; do one's fealty. きじゅん
**귀신(鬼神)** ①《망령》a departed spirit 《유령》a ghost ②《마귀》an ogre; a fiend /~같다 be supernatual. きしん
**귀심(歸心)** 《집 생각》 longing for home 《사모》attachment. きしん

**귀아프다** be fed up with; have heard enough/귀아프도록 들어 왔네 I have heard enough of it. ききくるしい
**귀애하다(貴愛―)** love; favour; treat with love. かわいくおもってあいする
**귀약(―藥)** firelock powder/ ~을 넣다 apply eardrops. ひなわじゅうのかやく
**귀약통(―藥筒)** the container of firelock powder.
**귀얄** a paste brush; a paint brush. のりつけのぶらし
**귀얄잡이** a bewhiskered person.
**귀양** exile; banishment/ ~살이하는 사람 an exile/ ~가다 be exiled/ ~보내다 condemn (one) to exile; banish/ ~살다 live in exile. しまながし
**귀어(句語)** a phrase.
**귀에지** ear-wax; cerumen. みみあか
**귀엣고리** an earring; a pendant. みみわ
**귀엣말** a whisper; whispering. みみうち
**귀여겨듣다** listen attentively[with strained ears]. きをつけてきく
**귀여리다** (be) credulous. だまされやすい
**귀여워하다** love; pet; caress; hold (a person) dear; be attached to/개를 ~ treat a dog kindly; make a pet of a dog. かわいがる
**귀염** love; affection; attachment/ ~받다 be beloved (of); be favored (by); be liked (by). あいらしさ
**귀염성** loveliness; attractiveness; amiability; charm/ ~있는 얼굴 a lovely [sweet] face. あいきょう
**귀엽다** (be) lovely; pretty; sweet; cute; charming; attractive/귀여운 계집애 a cute little girl. かわいらしい
**귀영(歸營)** ~하다 return to barracks/ ~ 시간 the hour for returning to barracks. きえい
**귀의(貴意)** your will; your opinion.
**귀의(歸依)** conversion/ ~하다 be converted (to); become a believe. きえ
**귀이개** an ear-pick; an instrument for cleaning the ears; an ear swab.
**귀인(貴人)** a noble; a man of rank; a dignitary. きじん
**귀인성(貴人―)** nobility; nobleness/ ~스럽다 (be) likable; (be) attractive.
**귀일(歸一)** unity; unification/ ~하다 (be) united into one. きいつ
**귀임(歸任)** return to one's post/ ~하다 return to one's post. きにん
**귀잠** a sound sleep; a deep sleep/ ~들다 fall fast asleep. ふかいねむり
**귀적(歸寂)** death; demise/ ~하다 die; pass away. しぬ
**귀절(句節)** a phrase; a clause; a paragraph. くとせつ
**귀점(句點)** a punctuation mark; a punctuation point. くてん
**귀접스럽다** ①《더럽다》(be) dirty; filthy ②《천하다》mean; base. そざつできたない
**귀접이** rounding/ ~하다 round the edge off. もののかどをなくしておりこむこと

귀정(歸正) ~하다 come back to the right way.
귀젖 a skin adhesion near the ear.
귀조(歸朝) ~하다 return home (from *abroad*). きちょう
귀족(貴族) ①《총칭》the nobility; nobles; the peerage ②《개인》a noble [man]; a peer/~ 정치 aristocracy. きぞく
귀중(貴重) preciousness/ ~하다 (be) precious; valuable/ ~품 an article of value; a treasure. きちょう
귀중(貴中) Messrs/신한 출판사 ~ to the *Shinhan* publisher.
귀중중하다 (be) dirty; filthy; untidy; unclean/옷차림이 ~ be shabbily clad [clothed]. きたないかんじがある
귀지(貴地) your place[district]. きち
귀지(貴誌) your [valued] paper; your [esteemed] columns. きし
귀지(貴誌) your [valued] magazine. きし
귀질기다 (be) unresponsive; be slow to catch on[to understand]. かんかくがにぶい
귀착(歸着) ①~하다 《돌아옴》return; come back ~하다 ②《귀결》arrive at; come to; result in/의논의 ~점 the logical conclusion of an argument/서울에 ~했다 He arrived back in *Seoul*. きちゃく
귀찮다 (be) troublesome; annoying; bothering; irksome/ ···이 귀찮아지다 get tired of; feel weary of/귀찮게 굴다 bother; annoy. めんどうだ
귀척(貴戚) the royal relation on the queen's side. おおさまのいんせき
귀천(貴賤) high and low; the noble and the mean/ ~의 차별없이 irrespective of rank; high and low alike. きせん
귀청 the eardrum. こまく
귀체(貴體) you; your health. あいでのしんたい
귀추(歸趨) a trend; a tendency; a drift 《낙착점》issue; consequence.
귀축(鬼畜) a devil. きちく
귀축축하다 (be) foul; mean; low; nasty; indecent; obscene. きたない
귀태(貴態) a noble[an august] figure.
귀택(貴宅) your house; your [esteemed] home. きたく
귀퉁이 ①《모퉁이》a corner; an angle ② 《귀언저리》the root of the ear/책상 ~ the corner of a desk. つきでたところ
귀틀 a frame [work]/ ~집 a log hut; a blockhouse. ねだ
귀하(貴下) Mr.; Mrs.; Mdm[e].; Miss 《당신》you. きか
귀하다(貴一) ①《드물다》(be) rare; uncommon/귀한 물건 a rarity ②《지위가》 (be) noble; august; high/귀하신 분 an august person ③《귀중하다》(be) precious; valuable. めずらしい
귀한(貴翰) your [esteemed] letter[favor].
귀함(貴函) your [esteemed] letter[favor] / ~을 배수하였읍니다 I acknowledge receipt of your letter. きかん

귀함(歸艦) returning to one's warship/ ~하다 return to one's warship. きかん
귀항(歸航) a return passage; a homeward voyage[trip]/ ~하다 sail for home; make a homeward voyage; make a homeward trip. きこう
귀항(歸港) returning to port/ ~하다 return to port; put back to port. きこう
귀향(歸鄕) home-coming; going home/ ~하다 go[come] home; return to one's old home. ききょう
귀현(貴顯) ①《사람》a man of distinction ②《현달》eminence. きけん
귀형(鬼形) a ghastly figure; an ugly and haggard appearance. おにのかたち
귀화(鬼火) a corpse-candle; a jack-o'-lantern; a will-o'-the-wisp. きか
귀화(歸化) ①《국적 획득》naturalization/ ~하다 be naturalized/ ~인 a naturalized citizen. きか
귀환(歸還) return/ ~하다 return/ ~병 a returned soldier; a returnee. きかん
귀휴(歸休) release (of *a soldier*) before expiration of one's service/ ~병 a soldier on leave. ききゅう
귓가 the rim of the ear. みみのまわり
귓것 a demon ⇨신. きしん
귓결 ~에 [듣다] [hear of] by chance; casually. ねみみ
귓구멍 〖해〗the burr; an ear-hole/~을 쑤시다 pick one's ears. みみのあな
귓등 the back of an ear/ ~으로 듣다 do not listen carefully; take no notice of.
귓문(-門) an ear orifice. みみのあな
귓바퀴 a pinna; an auricle. みみわ
귓밥 ①《귓불의 두께》the thickness of an ear-lobe ②《귀에지》ear wax. みみたぶ
귓병(-病) an ear disease[ailment, trouble]. みみのびょうき
귓불 an ear-lobe; the lobe of an ear; a gunlock. みみたぶ
귓속 the inside of an ear; the inner ear / ~말로 in a whisper. みみのうちがわ
귓전 ~에 about one's ears. じかくのふち
귓집 earmuffs.
규각(圭角) ①《불일치》disagreement; disharmony ②《모》an angle; a corner.
규강(珪鋼) silicon steel.
규격(規格) a gauge; a standard/ ~품 a standardized article. きかく
규례(規例) rules and regulations; a standard. きそくとていれい
규명(糾明) a searching examination/ ~ 하다 examine closely. きゅうめい
규모(規模) ①《구조》a scale; scope; structure; plan ②《제도》a rule; a pattern ③《예산》a budget limit/ ~를 확장하다 enlarge the scope (of *the project*). きぼ
규문(糾問) a cross-examination; an interrogation; an inquiry/ ~하다 question (*a person*) closely. きゅうもん
규문(閨門) a boudoir. けいもん
규방(閨房) 《도장방》a boudoir 《침실》a bedchamber. けいぼう

규벌(閨閥) nepotism; matrimonial influence.

규범(規範) a standard; a criterion; a norm/ ~적 법칙 normative law. きはん

규보(跬步) 《가까운 거리》a very short distance; half a step[pace]. きほ

규사(硅砂) 【광】silica. けいしゃ

규산(硅酸) 【화】silicic acid/ ~염 a silicate. けいさん

규석(硅石) 【광】silex; silica. けいせき

규소(硅素, 珪素) silicon 【화】Si. けいそ

규수(閨秀) ①《처녀》a maiden; a spinster; a lady ②《글하는 여자》an accomplished lady[woman]/ ~ 작가 a lady [woman] writer. けいしゅう

규식(規式) rules and established forms. きしき

규암(硅岩) 【광】quartzite.

규약(規約) an agreement; a covenant; rules/ ~을 정하다 lay out rules/ ~을 맺다 enter into an agreement. きやく

규율(規律) ①《질서》order; discipline ②《조직》system/ ~ 바르게 in good order; in an orderly manner. きりつ

규정(規定) ①《조항》a provision, a stipulation ②《규칙》regulations; rules/ 하다 provide (for); stipulate (for)/ ~의 요금 a regulation charge. きてい

규제(規制) 《규칙》regulation 《제한》restriction 《통제》control/ ~하다 regulate; restrict; control. きせい

규조(硅藻) 【식】a diatom/ ~토(土) diatom earth.

규준(規準) a canon; a criterion. きじゅん

규중(閨中) a boudoir/ ~ 처녀 a maid; a spinster. けいちゅう

규칙(規則) a rule; regulations/ ~적인 regular; systematic; methodical/ 나는 조반을 ~적으로 7시에 먹는다 I make it a rule to take a breakfast at seven o'clock.

규탄(糾彈) censure; impeachment/ ~하다 censure; impeach/잘못을 ~하다 impeach with an error. きゅうだん

규합(糾合) rally; muster; convocation/ ~하다 rally; muster; convoke; call together/동지를 ~하다 muster[rally] kindred spirits. きゅうごう

규호(叫號) a shout; a cry; an exclamation/ ~하다 shout; cry; shriek; exclamate. きゅうごう

규화(硅華) 【광】siliceous sinter; geyserite.

규화(硅化) silicification/ ~하다 silicify / ~물 a silicide.

규환(叫喚) a shout; a cry; an outcry/ ~하다 shout; cry. きゅうかん

균(菌) a bacillus (pl. -li); a bacterium (pl. -ria); a germ/ ~ 배양 germ culture; cultivation of bacteria. きん

균등(均等) equality; uniformity/~하다 (be) equal; even; uniform. きんとう

균류(菌類) fungi (sg. -gus)/ ~학 fungology. きんるい

균배(均配) division into equal parts/~하다 divide equally; divide into equal parts. きんとうにぶんばいすること

균분(均分) dividing equally; equal division/ ~하다 divide equally; equalize. きんとうにぶんばいすること

균사(菌絲) a spawn; a hypha (pl. -phae).

균산(菌傘) 【식】a cap; a top; a pileus; a capitulum.

균열(龜裂) a crack; a cleft; a fissure 《교섭 등의》rupture; failure/ ~하다 crack; be cracked; break up; rupture; fail. きれつ

균일(均一) uniformity; equality/ ~한 uniform; equal/100원 ~ a uniform rate of 100 won. きんいつ

균점(均霑) ~하다 participate in; have a share in. ぎんてん

균제(均齊) symmetry. きんせい

균질(均質) homogeneity/ ~체 homogeneous substance. せいしつがひとしいこと

균평(均平) ①《균일》equality; uniformity ②《평평함》evenness; smoothness.

균형(均衡) balance; equilibrium/세력의 ~ the balance of power/ ~ 예산 a balanced budget/ ~이 잡힌 well-balanced. きんこう

귤(橘) an orange/~밭 an orange orchard[plantation]. みかん

그¹ 《사람》that[the] man; he; she; that [the] woman/ ~의 his; her/ ~가 왔다 He is here. そのひと

그² 《형용사적으로》that; the/ ~날 that [the] day/ ~때 then; that time/ ~ 곳 there; that place. その

그까지로 to that trifling extent. やっとそれまでに

그까짓 that kind of; so trifling[trivial, slight, little, worthless, poor]; such/ ~ 짓을 누가 하겠소 Who would do that sort of thing? やっとそれぐらいの

그같이 thus; so; like that; in that manner/ ~ 울어서는 안 된다 You must not cry like that. そのように

그것 it; that/ ~으로 충분하다 That much is enough for him. それ

그곳 there; that place/ ~에 there. そこ

그그러께 three years ago; two years before last. さきおととし

그그저께 three days ago; two days before yesterday. さきおととい

그글피 four days hence[from now]; three days after tomorrow. しあさって

그나마 even so; still; nevertheless; however; and that; at that/ ~ 없다 Even that one is gone. それまでも

그나불 ①《끈》a piece of string; a cord ②《앞잡이》a tool; an agent; a stool pigeon《미속》③《관계》connections; influence; medium; good offices. ひも

그날 that day; the same day/ ~의 일 the day's work/ ~로 서울에 돌아왔다 I returned to Seoul the same day./ ~중으로 before the day is over. そのひ

**그냥** as it is; as you find it; in that condition; intact 《줄곧》only; all the way／～두다 leave (a thing) as it is; leave (a thing) alone. そのまま

**그네**¹ a swing (곡예용) a trapeze／～를 매다 put up a swing／～를 뛰다 swing [get] on a swing. ぶらんこ

**그네**² those people; they; them.

**그녀** she. そのおんな

**그놈** that damn guy; he[him]; that damn thing; it. そいつ

**그느다** give an indication of having a call of nature; [a baby] show signs of having call of nature.

**그느르다** take care of; look after; take under one's wings; protect. せわする

**그느름하다** gloomy; overcast; (be) cloudy. くもってうすくらい

**그늘** ①(응달) shade／나무 ~ the shade of a tree／～진 shadowy ②(부모 슬하) parental care. かげ

**그늴거리다** ①(피부가) feel creepy ②(마음이) feel thrill. くすぐったい

**끄다** ①(불을) put out; extinguish 《불어서》blow out (전기를) turn[switch] off／촛불을 ~ blow out a candle／라디오를 ~ turn off[out] the radio ②(덩어리를) break; crush; crack／얼음을 ~ break[smash] ice ③(빚을) pay back; repay／빚을 꾸어 나가다 clear[pay] off one's debt. けす

**그따위** a thing or person of that kind [sort]; such a one; that kind[sort] of. そんなもの

**그다지** so much; particularly; to that extent[degree]; in that way; not so [much, very, too]／～ 예쁘지 않다 She is not so very attractive. そんなに

**그달** that month; the very same month. そのつき

**그대** you; thou／～들 you; ye. きみ

**그때** then; at that time／～의 교장 the principal at that time／～까지 by that time. そのとき

**그대로** like that; as it is; as it stands; thus; intact／~ 내버려두다 leave (a thing) as it is. そのまま

**끄덕거리다, 끄떡거리다** nod; make a slight movement／끄덕거리는 것은 동의의 표시다 A nod is a sign of agreement.／끄떡끄떡 with a nod. こっくり

**끄떡없다** ①(안전하다》(be) safe; secure; strong ②(병 따위에) immune (from) ③(물 따위에) proof (against) ④(태연하다) unmoved; calm. びくともしない

**끄덕이다, 끄떡이다** nod; nod approval／고개를 ~ nod the head. うなずく

**그덩이** 웅~잡다 take hold of a tuft of hair; catch (one) by the hair.

**그동안** the while; during that time; these[those] days／~ 안녕하셨읍니까? Have you been well all these days?

**그득하다** (be) full; filled. いっぱいだ

**그들** they／～의 their／～에 them.

**그들먹하다** (be) almost full; be nearly full. ほとんどいっぱいだ

**그래**¹ 《대답》Yes(긍정); No(부정); So it is; That's right. そう, ええ

**그래**² 《그래서》well／~ 어떻단 말인가 W-ell, so what? そして

**그래도** but; still; and yet. しかし

**그래서** upon this 《따라서》so 《그런데》then; and.

**그래야** only if one does[says] that; only if it is that way; only so; unless so. それで

**그래께** the year before last. おとどし

**그러나** but; hostill; wever. しかし. だが

**그러나저러나** at any rate; anyhow; anyway in any; case; setting aside; apart (from).

**그러내다** take out; rake out／난로에서 재를 ~ rake out the ashes from a stove. かきだす

**그러넣다** put into; rake in／바구니에 재를 ~ rake ashes into a dust basket.

**그러니까** so; for that[this] reason; therefore. かきあつめている

**그러니저러니** this or that; one thing or another／~할 것 없이 without saying this or that; without question; without useless objection. かれこれ

**그러담다** gather up and put in. かきあつめている

**그러당기다** gather up and pull[draw, drag]／판돈을 ~ rake in the money on a gambling table. かきあつめてひく

**그러들이다** collect; rake in／빚진 돈을 ~ collect debts. かきあつめている

**그러면** if so; in that case; if it is like that; then; if that happens／~ 내일 오겠읍니다 Well then, I shall come tomorrow. それでは

**그러면 그렇지** as [was, had been] expected; it should be so／~ 자네가 성공할 리가 있나 It is nothing strange that you have failed. おもったとおりだ

**그러모으다** gather up; scrape together; rake up／돈을 ~ scrape together a sum of money／낙엽을 ~ rake up fallen leaves. かきあつめる

**그러므로** so; hence; therefore／~ 그는 비관하고 있는 것이다 That explains his pessimism. それだから

**그러자** then; immediately.

**그러잖아도** even without this[that]; nevertheless; in spite of this; already; even so; moreover. そうでなくとも

**그러저러하다** (be) so and so; (be) such and such. かくかくである

**그러쥐다** seize; catch; grasp; grip; grab／손잡이를 ~ hold a handle; grip a strap／머리털을 ~ seize (a person's) hair.

**그러하다** (be) so; such; right／그러할 줄 알았다 I should not wonder. そのようだ

**그럭저럭** one way or another; in some

**그런고로** for that reason; therefore; hence.

**그런 대로** [such] as it is; anyway.

**그런데** but; however; yet; though; for all that; and. ところで

**그런듯 만듯** barely; slightly; hardly.

**그런 양으로** in that manner; in its own way; by itself.

**그런즉** therefore; so; then; accordingly such being the case.

**그럴 듯하다** (be) plausible; specious/그럴 듯한 거짓말을 하다 lie like the truth /그럴 듯한 말을 하다 tell a plausible story. もっともらしい

**그럴싸하다** (be) plausible ⇒그럴 듯하다. もっともらしい

**그럼** ①《물론》 certainly ②《그러면》 then; if that it so. それでは

**그럼그럼 ~하다**《눈물이》 be suffused with tears/눈물이 ~한 눈 eyes suffused[filled streaming] with tears; moist eyes. あふれそうに

**그렁성저렁성** this and that; something and other; somehow or other/~ 의견이 많다 There are many different opinions. どちらつかずに

**그렁저렁** one way or another 그저저럭. どうにかして

**그렇게** so; so much; that much; like that; that way; in that manner; particularly/~까지 안 해도 좋다 you need not go that[so] far. そんなに

**그렇고말고** indeed; of course; certainly; That's right. そうだよ

**그렇다** ①《그러하다》 (be) so; (be) like that/~고 하더라도 [and] yet; for all that; even so ②《대답》 yes; no. そうだ

**그렇지** So it is., That's right. そうだ

**그렇지** otherwise; unless; if…not so; [or] else. そうでなくては

**그루** ①《농사의》 a crop; a sowing ②《나무의》 a root; a stump; a stubble/나무한 ~ a stump of a tree/벼 ~ a stubble of rice plant.

**그루갈이**《모작》 two crops a year; semi-annual crop; an aftercrop/~하다 raise two crops a year. うらさく

**그루뒤** turn over the soil for a second crop.

**그루박다** ①《거꾸로》 drop[throw down] (a thing) headlong ②《연을》 turn a kite upside down ③《압박하다》 oppress; suppress. さかさまになげておく

**그루벼** rice plants raised after harvesting the barley.

**그루앉히다** consolidate the foundation for. あらかじめきそをつくっておく

**그루콩** an aftercrop of beans. うらさくのまめ

**그루터기**《나무의》 a stump (벼 따위의) a stubble. きのきりかぶ

**그루팥** an aftercrop of redbeans. うらさくのあずき

**그르다** ①《틀리다》 (be) wrong; mistaken; incorrect; blamable ②《품행이》 (be) bad; evil; ill; wrong/그른 짓 a wrong; a misdeed ③《가망없다》 (be) hopeless all over. まちがっている

**끄르다** undo; untie; unfasten; unpack; loosen 《잠근 것을》 unlock; take off/매듭을 ~ untie a knot/양복 단추를 ~ unbutton one's coat. ほどく

**그르렁거리다** wheeze; purr/고양이가 목을 ~ The cat is purring. ぜいぜいいう

**끄르륵** with a burp/~하다 keep burping[belching]. ごくごく

**그르치다** spoil; make a failure of; corrupt/판단을 ~ make an error of judgement/일생을 ~ make a failure of one's life. だいなしにする

**그릇¹** ①《용기》 a vessel; a receptacle/물한 ~ a cup of water ②《기량》 calibre; capacity; ability. きぐ

**그릇²** 《잘못》 wrong; erroneously; falsely mistake/ ~하다 mistake; do in the wrong way/ ~ 생각하다 misunderstand; mistake. あやまる

**그릇되다** go[become] wrong; be spoiled [ruined]; fail; end in failure/그릇된 생각 a wrong[an erroneous]; idea a mistaken notion. わるくなる

**그리** ①《그곳으로》 there; that way ②《그렇게》 so. そう

**그리고** and; and then; as well as; and also. そして

**그리다¹** 《그림을》 picture; draw (무채색) paint (채색화), sketch (약도를), portray (인물화); imagine(마음에); deserib; depict(묘사)/지도를 ~ draw a map/ 입술을 ~ rouge one's lips. えがく

**그리다²** 《사모하다》 yearn[long]_for; love (one) dearly. こいしたう

**그리마** 《동》 a milliped[e]; a galley worm. げじげじ

**그리움** yearning; attachment; longing; affection/~을 못 이기다 feel an irresistible yearning for.

**그리저리** at random; at[by] haphazard; in a hit-or-miss manner/ ~하다 try this way and that; do in a hit-or-miss manner. どうにかこうにか

**그림** a picture; a painting 《서화》 a drawing 《약도》 a sketch 《판화》 a print; 《삽화》 an illustration, a cut 《도표》 a diagram.

**그림쇠** a rule; a measure/ ~로 재다 measure with a rule.

**그림자** a shadow; a silhouette 《영상》 a reflection; an image 《환영》 a phantom 《모습》 figure. かげ

**그립다** 《동사적》 feel yearning for; long for; dear; dearest; be loved/고향이 ~ I am sick for my old home. こいしい

**그만** ①《그 정도로》 to that extent; there/ ~ 울어라 Don't cry any more. ②《곧》

as soon as; immediately/그는 나를 보더니 ~ 달아나 버렸다 He ran off the momen the saw me. そのていどで
**그만그만하다** (be) nearly[about] the same; much the same. まあまあだ
**그만두다** ①《중지》stop; cease; discontinue; give up; quit/장사를 ~ quit *one's* business ②《사직》resign; quit; leave /회사를 ~ leave (*the service* of) the company. やめる
**그만저만** ~하다 (be) about it; about the same. そのていだだ
**그만큼** that much; so much[many]; as much[many]; to that extent/ ~의 노력은 나도 했다 I too have done that much effort. それくらい
**그만하다** ①《정도》be in the same condition; be neither better nor worse; be about the same; be much the same ②《크기·양》be as much[many] as; be not less ③《중지》stop; cease; leave off. それぐらいだ
**그맘때** about that time 《나이》about the same age. ちょうどそのとき
**끄무러지다** cloud up; get[become] cloudy; get dim[smoky]. くもる
**끄무레하다** (be) cloudy; overcast; dull; (be) clouded over/ 끄무레한 날씨 cloudy weather; a cloudy day/ 끄무레한 하늘 a leaden[a sullen an overcast] sky. くもりかかっている
**그물** a net; a seine《끄는》a drag-net《그물 세공》a network 《던지는》a casting-net《총칭》netting/ ~을 짜다 net; make a net/ ~을 끌어 올리다 haul in a net/ ~에 걸리다 be caught in a net. あみ
**끄물거리다** become cloudy off and on; be unsettled. はれたりくもったりする
**끄물끄물** ~하다 (be) unsettled; fickle.
**그물코** meshes ﹝of net﹞/잔 고기는 큰 ~ 사이로 빠져나갔다 Small fish slipped away through large meshes of a net. / ~ 모양으로 reticulately. あみのあな
**그믐께** the last days of a month.
**그믐날** the last day of the month.
**그믐밤** the last night of a lunar month. みそかのよる
**그믐사리** yellow corvina caught around the end of the month.
**그믐초생** the end of the month and the beginning of the following month. みそかとしょじゅん
**그믐칠야(-漆夜)** the dark night of the last day of a month.
**그사이** the while; the meantime; the interval/ ~에 in the meantime; in the interval/ ~ 안녕하셨는지요 How have you been getting along. そのあいだ
**그새** the while ⇨그사이.
**그슬리다** burn; scorch; singe. やく
**그악스럽다** (be) fierce; mischievous; naughty 《부지런하다》hard-working. あまりひどい
**그악하다** (be) fierce ⇨ 그악스럽다.

**그야** it/ ~ 물론이지 It is a matter of course that… / ~ 그럴 수 있지 That is quite possible. それこそ
**그야말로** quite; really. それこそ
**그어주다** share; apportion.
**그 역시(-亦是)** too; also; as well; likewise/ ~ 사실이다 That also is true./ ~ 마음에 들지 않는다 I don't like it either. それもやはり
**그예** at last; finally; in the end; ultimately; after all.
**그외(-外)** outside[beyond] that; the others. そのほか
**그윽하다** ①《고요하다》(be) quite; still; secluded; hidden; solitary; lonely; peaceful ②《깊다》deep; profound/그윽한 생각 a deep thought/ 그윽한 마음씨 profound consideration. おくゆかしい
**그을다** ①《햇볕에》be sunburned; be browned ﹝with the sun﹞ ②《연기에》become sooty; be stained with soot; get covered[black] with soot/햇볕에 그을은 얼굴 be sunburned face. すすける
**그을음** soot/ ~이 끼다 become sooty; be soot-covered/ ~을 쓸어 내다 sweep away[wipe off] the soot. ゆえん
**그이** that person; he[him]. そのひと
**그저** ①《줄곧》constantly; continuously; all the time/ ~ 비가 온다 It keeps on raining ②《목적없이》casually; without particular purpose ③《그런 대로》just ④《제발》please. そのままずっと
**그저께** the day before yesterday/ ~ 밤 night before last. おととい
**그적** that time; last time/ ~에 at that time; in that occasion. そのとき
**그적거리다** scribble; scrawl; dash.
**그전** former times; the other days/ ~에는 formerly; before; in old days/ ~ 주소 former address /우리는 ~부터 아는 사이다 We have known each other for a long time. むかし
**그제야** then; for the first time; at length/그는 ~ 바다를 보았다 He saw the sea for the first time in his life. /며칠 지나서 ~ 그 사실을 알았다 It was not until a few days later that learned the truth. そのときはじめて
**그중** among them; among the rest《제일》the most[best]/너도 ~의 한 사람이다 You are one of the number.
**그즈음** about that time; around then. そのうち
**그쯤** ①《그 정도》that much ②《장소》around there.
**그지없다** (be) endless; boundless 《영원》eternal; in measurable/그지없는 사랑 deep love/그지없는 즐거움을 주다 give no end of pleasure. かぎりない
**끄집다** take[pick] up/여러 가운데서 하나를 ~ take one among many. ひく
**끄집어내다** ① take out; pull[draw] out; pick out/호주머니에서 편지를 ~ take a letter out of *one's* pocket ②《이야기를》

**끄집어내리다** take[bring, carry] down /사람을 의자에서 ~ drag (a person) out of a chair. ひきおろす

**끄집어당기다** pull; drag; draw /사람의 소매를 ~ pull by the sleeve. ひきよせる

**끄집어들이다** pull[take, carry, bring] in /자기 편으로) win[bring] over /짐을 ~ carry luggage in /사람을 자기 편으로 ~ win (a person) over to one's side.

**끄집어올리다** take up 《승진시키다》 promote /높은 지위에 promote (a person) to a high position ひきあげる

**그치다** stop; cease; end; be over /그칠 새 없이 without ceasing; unceasingly; continuously. とまる

**그토록** so [much]; such; to such an extent.

**고트러기** ①《나머지》 odds and ends ②《나무 조각》 chips; shasing. のこりもの

**고트머리** ①《맨끝》 an end; a tip; the tail end ②《실머리》 the beginning; a clue; the commencement. はし

**그후(一後)** 《이후》 after that; thereafter 《이래》 since; ever since. そのあと

**극(極)** 《절정》 the zenith; the height; the extreme 《지구 자석의》 a pole /북[남]~ the north[south] pole /영화의 ~ the height of glory / ~에 달하다 be at its height; reach its climax.

**극(劇)** a drama; a play /~적[으로] dramatic(ally) /~이 ~은 아주 호평이었다 The play made a tremendous hit.

**극광(極光)** the aurora; the polar lights 《남극의》 the aurora australis; the southern lights 《북극의》 the aurora borealis; the nothern lights. きょくこう

**극구 발명(極口發明)** ~하다 spare no pains to defend oneself; make every sort of excuses.

**극구 찬송(極口讚頌)** the highest praise /~하다 speak highly of; speak in high terms of; praise (one) to the skies. くちをきわめてほめること

**극권(極圈)** the polar circle /북~ the Arctic Circle. きょくけん

**극귀(極貴)** ~하다 《드물다》 (be) very rare 《귀중》 (be) very precious. ひじょうにとうといこと

**극기(克己)** self-control[-denial] /~하다 control oneself; be master of oneself /~심 most difficult; very hard. ひじょうにむつこと

**극기(極忌)** abhorrence; extreme dislike /~하다 abhor; detest.

**극난(極難)** ~하다 (be) most difficult; very hard. きわめてこんなんであること

**극단(極端)** an extreme; an extremity 《과도》 an excess /~하다 (be) extreme; excessive /~하게 extremely /~한 예 an extreme case /~론 an extreme view[opinion] /~론자 an extremist /~으로 흐르다 go too far; go to extremes. きょくたん

**극단(劇團)** a dramatic company. げきだん

**극단(劇壇)** the stage; the theatrical world.

**극대(極大)** the maximum /~치 the maximum value. きょくだい

**극도(極度)** the extreme 《최대한》 the maximum 《꼭대기의》 the zenith /~의 utmost; extreme; maximum /~로 extremely; in the extreme /~로 흥분하다 be extremely excited. きょくど

**극독약(劇毒藥)** a most drastic[powerful, terrible, deadly] poison. げきどくやく

**극동(極東)** the Far East /~의 the Far Eastern /~ 문제 the Far Eastern questions. きょくとう

**극락(極樂)** *Suhkavati*(Sans); the abode of the blessed; Paradise /~ 왕생하다 die a peaceful death. ごくらく

**극락 세계(極樂世界)** Paradise ⇨극락(極樂).

**극락 왕생(極樂往生)** a gentle and easy death /~하다 die a peaceful[a painless] death.

**극량(極量)** 《약의》 the maximum dose; a fatal dose.

**극력(極力)** 《부사적》 to the utmost; to the best of one's ability; strenuously /~ 부인하다 deny stoutly; try strenuously to deny the fact. きょくりょく

**극렬(劇烈)** violence; severity; intensity; vehemence; fierceness /~하다 (be) violent; severe; acute; keen. げきれつ

**극론(極論)** an extreme argument /~하다 make an extreme argument; go so far as to say…. きょくろん

**극무(劇務)** hard work げきむ

**극미(極微)** an atom; an iota /~하다 (be) microscopic; infinitesimal. きょくび

**극복(克服)** subjugation; conquest /~하다 conquer; overcome /악습을 ~하다 conquer bad habits /곤란을 ~하다 overcome the difficulty. こくふく

**극복(克復)** restoration; return /~하다 be restored; return.

**극본(劇本)** the script of a play; a drama; a scenario; the acting edition of a play /~을 쓰다 write a play. げきほん

**극북(極北)** the extreme north 《북극》 the north pole. きょくほく

**극비(極秘)** strict secrecy /~로 하다 keep in absolute secrecy. ごくひ

**극빈(極貧)** extreme poverty /~하다 (be) extremely poor; as poor as a church mouse. ごくひん

**극상(極上)** the first rate; the highest quality /~의 best; extra fine; excellent; superfine /~품 a choice article; an article of superfine quality; the best of *its kind*). ごくじょう

**극서(極暑, 劇暑)** intense heat. ごくしょ

**극성(極性)** polarity /~의 polar /~을 부여하다 polarize. きょくせい

극성(極星) 《북극성》 the north pole star 《남극성》 the south pole star. きょくせい

극성(極盛) ①《매우 성함》 the height of prosperity／～하다 (be) at the height of prosperity ②《성질의》 extremity／～하다 (be) extreme／～멸다 run to extreme. ひじょうにさかんでいる

극세포(極細胞) a polar cell.

극소(極小) minimum／～한 smallest; minimum; infinitesimal. ごくしょう

극시(劇詩) a verse drama; a drama in verse; dramatic poetry. げきし

극심(極甚) ～하다 (be) extreme; excessive; intense; severe; heavy; tremendous; terrible. きわめてはなはだしいこと

극악(極惡) atrocity; brutality／～하다 (be) heinous; atrocious; most wicked; (be) devilish. きょくあく

극약(劇藥) a powerful drug; a violent poison. げきやく

극양(極洋) the polar seas／～ 어업 the polar-sea fishery. きょくよう

극언(極言) unreserved criticism／～하다 go so far as to say; go [to] the length of saying. きょくげん

극영화(劇映畵) a dramatic movie. げきえいが

극우(極右) an ultra-rightist; the extreme right／～의 ultra-rightist／～파 the extreme right; an extreme right wing.

극작(劇作) play writing／～하다 write a play／～법 dramaturgy／～가 a dramatist; a playwright. げきさく

극장(劇場) a theatre[-er]; a playhouse／～가(街) a theatre[-er] district／～안내인 a theatre[-er] attendant; an usher／～주(主) the proprietor of a theatre[-er]／～ 경영자 a theatre[-er] manager. げきじょう

극적(劇的) theatrical; dramatic. けきてき

극점(極點) the extreme point; a climax; a height 《절정》 the summit; the zenith 《최하》 the bottom. きょくてん

극존(極尊) 《임금》 His Majesty《지위가 높음》 prominence.

극존대(極尊待) the most respectful treatment／～하다 treat most respectfully.

극좌(極左) an ultra-leftist／～의 leftmost; ultra-leftist／～파 the extreme left; the extreme left wing. きょくさよく

극중(極重) ～하다 《무게가》 (be) very heavy 《병세(病勢)가》 critical 《범죄(犯罪)가》 grave. ひじょうにおもいこと

극지(極地) the pole; the polar region／～ 탐험 a polar expedition. きょくち

극진(極盡) the height; the extremity; the utmost／～하다 (be) extreme; utmost／～히 extremely; to the utmost／～한 대우 the warmest treatment／～ 히 사랑하다 love deeply.

극치(極致) acme; ideal perfection; culmination／미의 ～ the ideal perfection of beauty. きょくち

극터듬다 climb up with much difficulty

극통(劇痛, 極痛) an acute pain; a severe pain; a pang. げきつう

극평(劇評) drama[theater] criticism／～가 a drama[theater] critic. げきひょう

극피 동물(棘皮動物) an echinoderm.
きょくひどうぶつ

극한(極寒, 劇寒) the intense cold; severe cold. ごっかん

극한(極限) ①《끝에》 [the last] extremity; bounds; limitation; limit／～에 달하다 reach the limit ②《수》 limit／～치 a limiting value. きょくげん

극형(極刑) capital punishment 《최대한의 형》 the maximum[extreme] penalty／～에 처하다 condemn (a person) to capital punishment. きょっけい

극호사(極豪奢) extravagance; luxury; sumptuousness／～하다 live like a prince; live in a grand style; live in extravagance. ひじょうにごうしゃなこと

극흉(極凶) ～하다 《성질이》 (be) extremely wicked; atrocious 《얼굴이》 (be) very ugly; very bad-looking
ひじょうにきょうあくなこと

극희(劇戲) a show; a drama.

극히(極-) 《심히》 very; highly 《가장》 most 《아주》 quite／～ 미묘한 most delicate／～ 아름다운 very beautiful. きわめて

끈 《줄》 a string; a cord 《끈[짠] 끈》 a braid; a lace 《가죽끈》 a strap; a thong／구두～ a bootlace: a shoestring. ひも

근(斤) a kuen; a pound〈영〉／설탕 한 ～ a pound of sugar. きん

근(根) ①《수》 a root; a radical／평방[입방]～ a square[a cubic] root ②《종기》 a core. こん

근(筋) 《근·육》 a muscle 《힘줄》 a sinew; a tendon／～ 운동 muscular movement[motion]. きん

근(近) about; near[ly]. きん

근가(近可) ～하다 (be) passable; fairly good; tolerably well. ややよい

근간(近刊) recent[forthcoming] publication[issue]／～서(書) a recent publication 《예정서》 a forthcoming book／～ 예고 announcement of books in preparation.

근간(近間) 《부사적으로》 shortly; before long; at an early date; in the near future; in a few days. ちかいうち

근간(根幹) ①《뿌리 및 줄기》 root and trunk ②《근본》 the basis; the root ③《기조(基調)》 the keynote; the fundamental.
こんかん

근거(根據) a basis; a base; a ground; a foundation 《전거》 authority／～지 a base／～ 있는 well-grounded[-founded]／～없는 groundless. こんきょ

근거리(近距離) a short distance／～ 경주 a short distance race. きんきょり

근검(勤儉) thrift [and diligence]; diligence and economy／～한 thrifty; frugal／～ 저축 thrift and savings／～한 가정 부인 a frugal housekeeper. きんけん

**근검하다** be blessed with many children. しそんがおおくてこうふくそうにみえる
**근경**(近頃) recently ⇒요즈음. ちかごろ
**근경**(根莖) a rootstock; a subterranean stem.
**근경**(近景) a near[close-up] view. きんけい
**근경**(近境) ①(곳) neighboring districts. ②(경우) the recent condition; the present state of affairs. きんきょう
**근고**(近古) the early modern age/ ～사 the history of the early modern age. きんこ
**근고**(勤苦) working hard[diligently]/ ～하다 work hard; apply oneself assiduously. きんべんとくろう
**근고하다**(謹告—) inform with respect; announce respectfully. つつしんでつげること
**근골**(筋骨) bones and sinews 《체격》 build; physique/ ～이 억센 muscular; sinewy. きんにくとほね
**근공**(勤工) hard study/ ～하다 study hard; work hard at one's studies. いっしょうけんめいにべんきょうすること
**근교**(近郊) a suburb; the suburbs; outskirts/ 서울 ～에 살고 있다 I live in the suburbs of Seoul. きんこう
**근국**(近國) a neighboring country.
**근근**(近近) shortly; before long; in a few days; in the near future.
**근근**(僅僅) narrowly; barely; with difficulty.
**근근 득생**(僅僅得生) ～하다 pick up a scanty living; eke out one's living; rub along. やっとくらしていくこと
**근근 부지**(僅僅扶持) ～하다 maintain with difficulty; manage with difficulty. やっとささえていくこと
**끈끈이** birdlime/ ～로 새를 잡나 catch a bird with birdlime. とりもち
**근근이**(僅僅—) barely; narrowly; with difficulty/ ～ 살아가다 make a scanty living; live barely. やっと
**근근 자자**(勤勤孜孜) industry and assiduity; diligence/ ～하다 industrious and assiduous; diligent. きんべいせいじつ
**근근하다** ①(물이) (be) full; brimful; stand full ②(가렵다) (be) itchy; feel itchy. みずがいっぱいみちている
**끈끈하다** ①(차지다) (be) sticky; adhesive; viscous/샤쓰가 땀으로 ～ one's shirt is sticky with sweat ②(검질기다) tenacious. ねばねばする
**끈기**(一氣) ①(끈끈한 기운) stickiness; viscosity; glutinousness ②(참을성) tenacity; pertinacity. ねばりけ
**근기**(根氣) perseverance; patience; endurance; energy/ ～있는 patient; persevering/ ～있게 patiently; with perseverance. こんき
**근년**(近年) recent years; late years/ ～에 보기 드문 큰 불 the biggest fire we have had for some years. きんねん
**근념**(勤念) a kind consideration/～하다

give a kind consideration (to). しんせつにしんぱいしてくれること
**근농**(勤農) diligent farming/ ～하다 farm diligently/ ～가 a most efficient farmer. のうじにつとめてどりょくすること
**근대** 《식》a [red] beet; a sugar beet; a [Swiss] chard. びーと
**근대**(近代) modern ages; recent times/ ～의 modern/ 、～인 modern people; a modern[er]/ ～사 modern history/ ～ 여성 modern women. きんだい
**근대다** bother; tease; annoy; aggravate. やっかいにふるまうこと
**근먹거리다, 끈먹거리다** be loose/이가 ～ A tooth is loose. ゆるんでいる
**끈먹지다** (be) sticky; tenacious; persevering; patient; tough; persistent/끈먹 지게 patiently. がまんつよい
**근동**(近東) the Near East. きんとう
**근들거리다** rock; sway. ゆらゆらする
**근래**(近來) recent time; these day/～의 recent; late/ ～에 recently; lately; in recent time. きんらい
**근량**(斤量) weight. きんりょう
**근력**(筋力) muscular strength; physical strength. きんりょく
**근로**(勤勞) labo[u]r; work; exertion; service/ ～하다 labo[u]r; work; serve/ ～ 소득 an earned income. きんろう
**근리**(近理) reasonableness/ ～하다 (be) reasonable.
**근린**(近隣) the neighbo[u]rhood. きんりん
**근면**(勤勉) diligence; industry/ ～하다 (be) industrious; diligent; labo[u]rious. きんべん
**근모**(根毛) the root hair. こんもう
**근무**(勤務) service; duty; work/ ～하다 serve work/ ～처 one's place of employment/ ～ 시간 office[working] hours. きんむ
**근묵자흑**(近墨者黑) He who touches pitch shall be defiled therewith. くろにちかづくものはくろくなる
**근방**(近方) the neighbo[u]rhood; vicinity; environs/이 ～에 near here; around here; in this neighbo[u]rhood/ ～ 의 neighbo[u]ring; near-by. きんぼう
**근배**(謹拜) 《편지의 끝말》Yours truly; Sincerely yours; Faithfully yours.
**근변**(近邊) the neighbo[u]rhood. きんぺん
**근본**(根本) ①(기초) the foundation; the basis ②(근원) the root; the source; the origin/ ～ 문제 a fundamental problem. こんぽん
**끈불다** a means of livelihood.
**근사**(近似) approximation/～하다 approximate 《좋다》 nice/ ～치 approximate quantity[value]. よくにていること
**근사모으다** make continued efforts for. ほねおってしあげる
**근상**(近狀) the recent state[condition, situation]; the recent state of affairs. ;one's daily life. きんきょう
**근성**(根性) nature; disposition; spirit/

~이 악한 ill-natured; crooked/상인 ~을 드러내다 betray a mercenary spirit /~이 썩은 depraved. こんじょう

**근세**(近世) modern age; recent times/~의 modern; recent day/~사 modern history. きんせい

**근소**(僅少) ~하다 《수효가》(be) a little 《수효가》a few; scanty; small; trifling/ ~한 차이 a shade of difference. きんしょう

**근속**(勤續) continuous service/ ~하다 be in continuous service; serve long/~자 a long-service man. きんぞく

**근수**(斤數) weight. きんすう

**근수**(根數) 〖수〗 a root; a radical/부진 ~ a surd root. こんすう

**근시**(近侍) an attendant; a page; a chamberlain/ ~하다 attend upon. きんじ

**근시**(近時) lately; recently. きんじ

**근시**(近視) near[short]-sightedness; near vision 《의》myopia/~안 near-sightedness; a myopia/ ~의 near[short]-sighted; myopic. きんし

**근신**(近臣) one's trusted vassal; a personal attendant. きんしん

**근신**(近信) the latest news; a newly arrived letter. きんしん

**근신**(謹愼) 《삼갈》 prudence; discretion/ ~하다 be on one's good behavio[u]r 《자제》self-control/~의 뜻을 표하다 show one's penitence. きんしん

**근실**(勤實) diligence; faithfulness/ ~하다 (be) diligent; faithful/ ~히 일하다 work diligently. きんべんせいじつ

**근실거리다** feel itchy/근실근실 itchy. むずむずする

**근심** anxiety; concern; worry; cares; trouble/ ~하다 be anxious about; be concerned about; feel uneasy. しんぱい

**근엄**(謹嚴) sobriety/ ~하다 (be) serious; grave; stern; rigorous. きんげん

**근역**(槿域) Korea.

**근엽**(根葉) root and leaf. ねとは

**근영**(近影) one's latest photograph.

**근왕**(勤王) loyalty/ ~하다 be loyal to one's sovereign. きんのう

**근원**(根源) ①《시초》the origin; the source; the beginning ②《근본》the cause; the root/모든 사회악의 ~ the root of all social evils. こんげん

**근위**(近衛) the Imperial[Royal] Guards/ ~대 the Imperial[Royal] Guard Corps.

**근육**(筋肉) muscles; sinews/ ~미 muscular beauty/ ~ 노동[자] manual labo[u]r[er]. きんにく

**근읍**(近邑) a near town; a neighbo[u]ring town. ちかいまち

**근인**(近因) the immediate cause [of a war]; the proximate cause; the immediate occasion. きんいん

**근일**(近日) soon; shortly; before long; in a few days; one of these days/그는 ~ 돌아올 것이다 He will be back in a few days. きんじつ

**근일점**(近日點) 〖천〗 the perihelion.

**근자**(近者) these days/~의 recent; late; laterday/ ~에 recently; lately; of late; these days. きんじつてん ちかごろ

**근작**(近作) one's latest work. きんさく

**근잠** a kind of rice-plant blight.

**근저**(近著) one's recent literary work; one's latest work. きんちょ

**근저**(根柢, 根底) the bottom; the basis; the root/ ~의 basic; radical.

**근저당**(根抵當) flexible mortgage. ねていとう

**끈적거리다** 《들러붙다》be sticky; be adhesive 《검질기다》persevere; stick (to); persist (in); be tenceious. べたべたする

**근절**(根絶) extermination; eradication/ ~하다 exterminate; eradicate; root out [up]; do away. こんぜつ

**근점**(近點) 《가까운》a near point 《근지점》 the perigee 《근일점》 the perihelion.

**근접**(近接) nearing; close contact; approximation; 〖천〗 appulse / ~하다 get near; near; approach; come into close contact. きんせつ

**근정**(謹呈) presentation 《책에》With the compliments of the author/ ~하다 give; present (a person with a thing, a thing to a person).

**근족**(近族) a near relative. きんしん

**근중**(斤重) weight. おもさ

**근지**(近地) near district; a neighbo[u]ring place. きんち

**근지럽다** (be) ticklish; scratchy/귀가 ~ My ears tickle. こそばゆい

**근직**(謹直) conscientiousness/ ~하다 (be) conscientious; scrupulous; faithful/ ~하게 근무하다 work conscientiously.

**근질거리다** feel ticklish. むずむずする

**끈질끈질하다** ①《오래 끌다》be longpending; prolonged; dragging ②《끈질기다》 (be) strong and sticky; strongly adhesive. べたつく

**근착**(近着) ~의 recently received; just [recently] arrived.

**근처**(近處) the neighbo[u]rhood; the vicinity/ ~에 in the neighbo[u]rhood [vicinity] (of); near. きんぺん

**근척**(近戚) a near maternal relation. きんしん

**근청**(謹聽) close attention; listening with attention/ ~하다 listen attentively [intently] (to); be all ears[attention]; give ear to きんちょう

**근촌**(近村) a near-by[neighbouring] village. ちかいむら

**근치**(根治) complete cure/ ~하다 cure completely[radically]. こんじ

**근칙**(謹飭) modesty; circumspection/~하다 be careful in one's behavior; (be) circumspect.

**근친**(近親) a near[close] relation[relative]; a kin/ ~ 결혼 intermarriage; consanguineous marriage/ ~ 상간[하다] [commit] incest. きんしん

근친(覲親) a bride's [first] call at her old home/ ~하다 make one's [first] call on one's parents after one's marriage. さとがえり

근태(勤怠) diligence and laziness; diligence and indolence. きんべんとたいまん

근포(跟捕) ~하다 pursue and catch.

근하(謹賀) cordial congratulation; congratulation with respect/ ~하다 congratulate cordially[respectfully], with respect] きんが

근하 신년(謹賀新年) [I wish you] a Happy New Year. きんがしんねん

근학(勤學) hard study; diligence; hard work/ ~하다 study hard[diligently]; grind. きんべんにまなぶこと

근해(近海) the neighbo[u]ring[home] waters; the near seas; the coast shore/ ~ 항로 a coastal service[line]/ ~ 어업 inshore fishery. きんかい

근행(覲行) a visit to parents/ ~하다 visit one's parents. さとがえりのりょこう

근화(槿花) the Rose of Sharon ⇒무궁화(無窮花). むくげ

근화(近火) a fire in the neighbo[u]rhood. きんか

근화향(槿花鄕) Korea. かんこくのむかしのな

근황(近況) the present condition; the recent state of affairs/무역의 ~ the present state of trade/우리 나라 외국 무역의 ~ the recent state of our foreign trade. きんきょう

끈히 tenaciously; persistently; pertinaciously. こんきつよく

끊기다 be cut; be broken; be snapped;

끊다 ①(자르다) cut off; sever; chop off ②(중단·차단) cut off; break; interrupt; stop; pause ③(전화를) ring off; hang up ④(전기를) shut off; switch off ⑤(인연을) sever; break off ⑥(그만두다) quit; give up ⑦(목숨을) kill [oneself]. きりとる

끊어지다 ①(절단되다) break 《실 따위가》 snap ②(중단·차단) break [off]; become broken; be cut off 《전화》be cut off ③(관계가) break [off]with; have done with; finish ④(기한이) expire; run out; terminate; be due ⑤(목숨이) expire; die. きられる

끊임없다 (be) ceaseless; incessant; continual; constant/끊임없이 ceaselessly; incessantly; continually. けいぞくする

글 ①(공부) learning; studies; letters ②(글자) writing; script; alphabet; characters ③(쓴 것) a piece of writing; a composition; an article. ぶん

끌 a chisel/ ~로 조각하다 chisel a statue out of [the marle]. のみ

끌꺽끌꺽하다 keep belching. さくりをする

글겅이 a currycomb. うまぐし

글겅이질 ①(털빗기기) currying ②(착취) exploitation; squeezing/ ~하다 curry exploit; squeeze. うまぐしでとくこと

글구멍 literary talent.

글귀(—句) ①(어구) a phrase; a clause ②(인용절) a passage ③(글) a sentence; a line 《시가》a poem; a verse/ ~를 외다 memorize a passage. もんく

끌끌 belching/트림을 ~하다 belch; burp /혀를 ~ 차다 click one's tongue.

끌끌하다 (마음이) (be) clean and pure; upright; honest; clean-handed (be) pure; innocent. しょうじきだ

끌다 ①(잡아당기다) pull; draw; give a pull; tug; tow 《갑자기》jerk/짐차를 ~ pull a cart ②《주의 따위를》 attract[draw] 《a person's attention》/사람들의 이목을 ~ attract public attention ③(인도하다) lead/노인의 손을 ~ lead an old man by the hand ④(늘어뜨리고 가다) drag; trail; draggle/치마를 끌고 걷다 walk with a trailing skirt ⑤(미루다) prolong; protract; delay; extend ⑥(시설하다) lay on [gas]; install.[a telephone]. ひきずる

글동무 a schoolmate.

글러지다 fail; worsen. わるくなっていく

끌러지다 come loose; get untied[undone]; become loosened. はずれる

끌리다 ①be drawn; be pulled; be dragged ②(지연되다) be prolonged; be protracted; be delayed ③(매력에) be attracted; be drawn; be caught ④(인도되다) be led. ひきずられる

글밋하다 (be) handsome; clearcut.

글발 ①(글씨) jottings; notes ②(글씨 모양) the appearance of one's letters ③(문맥) coherence. ぶんしょう

글방(—房) a private school; a village school. しょどう

끟발망이 a mallet; a chisel hammer. のみをうつふち

글벗 a literary friend.

글썽글썽 with tearful eyes/ ~하다 be about to cry/눈물이 ~하다 tears stand [gather] in one's eyes. なみだぐむ

글쎄 now 《불확실·의심·비난》well; let me see/ ~ 언제 도착할까 I wonder when he will arrive there. そうだね

글씨 a letter; a character 《글씨쓰기》 penmanship/ ~를 잘못 쓰다 write a poor hand. もじ

끌어내다 pull[take] out; bring[carry] out; drag out. ひきだす

끌어내리다 pull[drag, draw] down; haul down. ひきおろす

끌어넣다 take[pull, draw, drag] in; lead in; tempt in; entice; win[gain] over/소를 외양간에 ~ drag a cow into a barn. ひきいれる

끌어당기다 draw near; pull up; draw; attract; tug. ひきよせる

끌어대다 ①(돈을) finance ②(맞대다) refer to cite as an example; bring forward as a witness. ひきあわせる

끌어들이다 draw[drag] in[into]; pull in[into]; take[bring] into /수도를 ~ have water pipes laid; lay

**끌어인다**

on water; have water supplied ②《포섭하다》 win (a person) over to one's side; interest (a person) in; induce 《유혹》 tempt; entice/자기편으로 ~ win (a person) over to one's side. ひきいれる

**끌어안다** hug; embrace; hold in one's arm/어린아이를 ~ hug a child. いだきしめる

**끌어올리다** pull[draw, haul] up 《침물선을》 refloat; salvage. ひきあげる

**글** ①《글》 a writing 《저술》; a sentence 《문장》 ②《편지》 a letter; a note; a message. てがみ

**글자** a letter; a character 《표의 문자》 an ideography. もじ

**글재주** literary talent.

**글제(一題)** the title[subject, theme] of an article[a composition, a poem]/ ~를 내다 give a subject. もんのだいもく

**글줄** a line[some lines] of writing.

**글짓기** composition. さくぶん

**글체(一體)** [literary] style.

**끌탕** ~하다 be much worried[troubled] over. こころをこがすしんぱい

**끌팅** a stump ⇨그루터기.

**글피** two days after tomorrow; three days hence. しあさって

**글하다** engage in studies.

**긁다** ①《가려워서》 scratch ②《그러모으다》 rake[scrape] up; gather up ③《남을》 criticize; attack. かく

**긁어당기다** rake in; scrape in. かきこむ

**긁어먹다** ①《이로》 nibble ②《재물을》 extort; squeeze/돈을 ~ extort[squeeze] money from (one). かじってたべる

**긁적거리다** scratch successively/긁적긁적 scraping and scraping. ぼりぼりかく

**긁히다** be scratched. かきやぶれる

**긁히다** be scratched 《발톱에》 be clawed. すりきずがつく

**끓다** ①《물이》 boil [up]/끓어 넘치다 boil over ②《마음이》 burn; glow; be aflame ③《배가》 rumble ④《가래가》 wheeze; make a gurgling sound ⑤《우글우글하다》 swarm; be crowded with. わく

**끓이다** boil; make hot; heat/끓여 소독하다 sterilize by boiling. わかす

**금¹** 《값》 a price; a cost; value; worth/ ~을 올리다 raise[put up] the price / ~을 내리다 lower[put down, cheapen] the price. ねだん

**금²** 《선》 a line 《접은 자국》 a fold; a crease; a crack 《틈》 a crevice/ ~을 긋다 draw a line/ ~이 가다 be cracked/ ~간 찻잔 a cracked teacup. ひび

**금(金)** gold/ ~반지 a gold ring/ ~시계 a gold watch/ ~을 입히다 plate (a thing) with gold. きん

**금가다** crack; split; cleave; fissure; be cracked. ひびがはいる

**금가락지(金—)** a large gold ring. きんのゆびわ

**금강력(金剛力)** Herculean[a giant's] strength. こんごうりょく

**금강사(金剛砂)** emery [powder]; emery paper. こんごうしゃ

**금강석(金剛石)** a diamond/ ~처럼 굳은 물건은 없다 Nothing is harder than[so hard as] diamond. こんごうせき

**금계(禁界)** the limits of a restricted area; the forbidden ground.

**금계랍(金鷄蠟)** 【약】 quinine. キニイネ

**금고(今古)** ancient and modern ages. きんこ

**금고(金鼓)** ①《싸울 때 쓰는》 a war drum and a war gong ②《북 모양의 종》 a drum-shaped bell.

**금고(禁錮)** 【법】 imprisonment; confinement/10년의 ~형을 받다 be sentenced to 10 years' imprisonment.

**금고(金庫)** a safe; a strongbox 《은행 따위의》 a vault 《국고금 취급소》 a cash office/ ~ 방화 five-proof safe. きんこ

**금곡(金穀)** money and corn.

**금과 옥조(金科玉條)** a golden rule; most precious rules. きんかぎょくじょう

**금관(金冠)** a gold crown. きんかん

**금관 악기(金管樂器)** brass. きんかんがっき

**금광(金光)** golden colo[u]r; luster of gold. きんのひかり

**금광(金鑛)** a gold mine 《광석》 gold ore / ~을 발견하다 discover gold deposits. きんこう

**금괴(金塊)** gold bullion. きんかい

**금권(金權)** the power of money financial[monetary] influence/ ~ 정치 plutocracy. きんパん

**금궤(金櫃)** a cash box; a money chest; a money box 《금고식의》 a strong box; a coffer. きんでつくったひつ

**금귤(金橘)** 【식】 a kumquat; a cumquat; Citrus japonica《학명》.

**금긋다** draw a line. せんをひく

**금기(禁忌)** taboo 【의】 contraindication/ ~하다 avoid; abstain from. きんき

**금나다** ①《잔금이 가다》 be[become] creased[wrinkled] ②《값이 정해지다》 be priced; the price is fixed.

**금남(禁男)** forbidden to man/ ~의 집 a home without man/ ~의 섬 an isle of women. おとこをきんずること

**금낭화(錦囊花)** 【식】 a dicentra; a bleeding heart.

**금년(今年)** this year; the current[present] year. ことし

**금년생(今年生)** a baby born this year 【식】 a plant new this year. ことしうまれ

**금니(金—)** a gold tooth. きんば

**금니박이(金—)** a man who has gold teeth. きんばをいれたひと

**금단(禁斷)** prohibition/ ~하다 prohibit; forbid (one to do)/ ~의 열매 the forbidden fruit. きんだん

**금달맞이꽃** 【식】 the evening primrose.

**금닿다** reasonable (in price). ねごろだ

**금대(今代)** the present age; today. げんだい

**금대(金帶)** a golden band[belt, girdle]

⇨금떠.

**금덩이**(金―) a [gold] nugget. きんのかたまり

**금도**(襟度) generosity; magnanimity/ ～가 넓다 be broad-minded. きんど

**금도금**(金鍍金) gilding／～한 gilt; gold-plated／～하다 plate with gold／구리에 ～을 하다 plate copper with gold.

**금돈**(金―) a gold coin.

**금동**(今冬) this winter. ことしのふゆ

**금띠**(金―) a golden band[belt, girdle]. きんのおび

**금란지계**(金蘭之契) a Damon and Pythias friendship. きんらんのまじわり

**금란초**(金蘭草) 〖식〗a helleborine.

**금력**(金力) the power of money／～ 정치 plutocracy; timocracy／～ 만능 mammonism. きんりょく

**금렵**(禁獵) prohibition of shooting[hunting]／～기 the close season; the fence season[time]／～ 지구 a [game] preserve; a sanctuary. きんりょう

**금령**(禁令) an interdict; prohibition; a ban／～을 내리다 issue a ban (on).

**금리**(金利) interest; money rates. きんり

**금맞추다** adjust the price of (an article); set the price. ねだんをけっていする

**금맥**(金脈) a vein of gold. きんみゃく

**금메달**(金―) a gold medal.

**금명간**(今明間) today or tomorrow; in a day or two. こんみょうにちかん

**금모래**(金―) ①(사금) gold dust ②(금빛의) golden sand[s]. さきん

**금문자**(金文字) gold[gilt] letters／～의 gold-lettered. きんもじ

**금물**(禁物) [a] taboo; a prohibited[forbidden] thing. きんもつ

**금박**(金箔) gold-foil; gold-leaf. きんぱく

**금발**(金髮) golden hair (여자) blonde (남자) blond／～ 미인 a blonde. きんぱつ

**금방**(今方) just now; a moment ago; at once. ちょうどいま

**금방**(金房) a goldsmith's shop.

**금배**(金杯) a gold cup.

**꼼뻑, 꼼뻑** ～거리다 (불빛이) flicker; twinkle; waver (눈을) wink; blink／불이 ～거리다 a light flickers. ちらちら

**금번**(今番) this time (근자) recently; lately. こんど

**금법**(禁法) a prohibitive law; a law forbidding. きんしするほうれい

**금보다** bid a price on; put a value on; value (a thing). ねをつける

**금본위**(金本位) the gold standard／～국 a gold-using country／～제(制), the gold basis.

**금분**(金粉) gold dust. きんぷん

**금불**(金佛) a gold image of Buddha; a gilded statue of Buddha. きんのほとけ

**금붕어**(金―) a goldfish／～ 장수 a goldfish seller. きんぎょ

**금붙이**(金―) gold ware; an article made of gold. きんぞく

**금비**(金肥) chemical manure. きんぴ

**금비녀**(金―) a golden hairpin; an ornamental hairpin. きんのかんざし

**금빛**(金―) golden colo[u]r. きんいろ

**금사**(金絲) gold thread; spun gold. きんし

**금싸라기**(金―) a treasure; valuables. きんのつぶ

**금사작**(金絲雀) 〖조〗a canary [bird].

**금산**(禁山) a forest reserve; a reserved forest.

**금산**(金山) 《금광》a gold mine. きんざん

**금상**(金像) a gold statue; a gilt statue. きんのぶつぞう

**금상**(今上) the present King[Emperor]; His Majesty the Emperor. きんじょう

**금상 첨화**(錦上添花) ～하다 add luster to what is already brilliant; add something more to the beauty[honour, grace].

**금새** price／～가 비싸다[싸다] be dear[cheap]; be high[low] in price; be high [low]-priced. ねだん

**금색**(金色) golden colo[u]r／～의 구름 the golden cloud. きんいろ

**금서**(禁書) a banned book.

**금석**(今夕) this evening; tonight. こんせき

**금석**(今昔) the present and the past／～ 지감 a reminiscent mood. こんじゃく

**금석**(金石) minerals and rocks／～문 a monumental inscription／～학 (광물학) mineralogy 《금석 문자학》epigraphy／～ 지약(之約) a solemn promise; a deep pledge. きんせき

**금선**(金線) gold thread; gold stripes in a uniform 《복장의》gold braid. きんせん

**금설**(金屑) gold dust. きんぷん

**금성**(金星) ①〖천〗Venus; the daystar ② 《금빛 별표》a gold[en] star. きんせい

**금성 철벽**(金城鐵壁) a citadel; an impregnable fortress.

**금세** 《릿시에》in a moment; at once; immediately; without delay.

**금세**(今世) 〖종〗this[the mundane] world. げんせい

**금세공**(金細工) goldwork／～장이 a goldsmith. きんさいく

**금속**(金屬) a metal／～의 metal; metallic／～공 a metal worker／～판 a metal plate; a sheet metal／～ 공업 the metal working industry. きんぞく

**금수**(禽獸) birds and beast; [dumb] animals; a beast／～와 같은 beastial; beastly. きんじゅう

**금수**(錦繡) 《비단과 수》brocade and embroidery 《자연》a brocade of nature／～ 강산 the land of beautiful scenery; Korea (별칭). きんしゅう

**금수**(禁輸) embargo／～하다 place[put] an embargo on the export of; forbid [ban] the export of. きんゆ

**금슬**(琴瑟) a Korean harp and a Korean mandolin. きんしつ

**금시**(今時) the present time[moment]《부 사적》a moment ago; at once. いま

**금시계**(金時計) a gold watch. きんどけい

**금시 발복**(今時發福) ～하다 rise to wealth and hono[u]r in a day; spring at a bound into wealth and hono[u]r.

**금시 초견**(今時初見) seeing (*a thing*) for the first time. いまはじめてみること

**금시 초문**(今時初聞) hearing (*a matter*) for the first time.

**금식**(禁食) fasting／～하다 fast; go without food／～일 fast day. だんじき

**금실**(金-) gold thread; spun gold. きんし

**금실**(琴瑟) 《부부의 화목》conjugal harmony; connubial bliss／～이 좋다 live in conjugal harmony; lead a happily married life. きんしつ

**금압**(禁壓) suppression; prohibition; a ban／～하다 suppress; taboo; ban; prohibit. きんあつ

**금액**(金額) an amount of money; a sum of money. きんがく

**금야**(今夜) this evening; tonight. こんや

**금어**(禁漁) prohibition of fishing／～기 a closed season for fishing／～장 a marine preserve. きんぎよ

**금언**(金言) a golden[wise] saying; a proverb; a maxim. きんげん

**금연**(禁煙) prohibition of smoking 《게시》 "No Smoking"／～하다 give up smoking. きんえん

**금오**(金烏) the sun／～ 옥토(玉兎) the sun and the moon たいよう

**금옥**(金玉) gold and gems; jewels. きんぎよく

**금요일**(金曜日) Friday. きんようび

**금욕**(禁慾) asceticism; stoicism; self-denial《성욕의》continence／～하다 practise asceticism; repress the passions; be continent／～주의 stoicism; asceticism／～주의자 a stoic／～ 생활 an ascetic life. きんよく

**금원**(禁苑) a palace garden. きんえん

**금월**(今月) this month; instant(略:inst.); the present month. こんげつ

**금융**(金融) monetary circulation; the money market; finance／～계 financial circles／～ 기관 a banking[financial] organ／～업 financial operation; money lending[business]／～핍박 a tightness of the money market／～ 통제 monetary control. きんゆう

**금은**(金銀) gold and silver／～ 보배 money and valuables; treasures. きんぎん

**금의**(錦衣) clothes of silk brocade. きんい

**금의 옥식**(錦衣玉食) gorgeous dress and dainty food; an epicurean life; a good living. きんぎよくしよく

**금의 환향**(錦衣還鄕) ～하다 go[come] home in glory. せいこうしてこきようにかえる

**금인**(金刃) an edged tool; cutlery.

**금일**(今日) today; this day／～부터 from this day forward／～의 한국 the Korea of today; Korea today. こんにち

**금일봉**(金一封) an enclosure[a gift] of money.

**금자**(金字) gold letters; illuminated characters.

**금자동이**(金子童一) a precious child. きんのようにきちようなこども

**금자탑**(金字塔) a pyramid; a landmark／독서계의 ～ a monumental work. きんじとう

**금작화**(金雀花) 《식》a common broom.

**금잔**(金盞) a gold cup[goblet]／～ 한 벌 a set of gold cups. きんのさかずき

**금잔화**(金盞花) 《식》a common marigold; a yellow ox eye. きんせんか

**금잠초**(金簪草) 《식》a dandelion.

**금잡인**(禁雜人) ～하다 forbid the access of those who are without business.

**금장**(禁葬) prohibition of burying dead bodies.

**금장**(襟章) a collar badge[mark, ensign, bar]. えりしよう

**금장도**(金粧刀) a gold pocketknife 《도금한》a gilded pocketknife. きんでつくったかざりのかたな

**금장식**(金粧飾) gold[en] decoration／～하다 decorate with gold. きんのかざりもの

**금전**(金錢) money; cash／～ 출납부 a cash book／～상의 monetary; financial; pecuniary. きんせん

**금전 옥루**(金殿玉樓) a palatial residence; a stately mansion; a palace. きんでんぎよくろう

**금점**(金店) a gold mine 《금광업》the goldmining industry. きんこう

**금정**(金井) a four-sided frame for measuring proper size of a grave.

**금정틀**(金井一) a four-sided timber frame used in digging a grave.

**금제**(金製) [what is] made of gold; goldwork／～품 goldwork. きんせい

**금제**(禁制) prohibition; taboo; a ban ⇒ 금지(禁止)／～품 contraband[goods]; prohibited[banned] goods. きんせい

**금조**(今朝) this morning. けさ

**금조개**(金一) the shell of an abalone.

**금족**(禁足) confinement／～하다 confine keep (*one*) indoors／～령 an order of confinement. きんそく

**금종이**(金一) golden paper. きんし

**금주**(禁酒) abstinence [from drink] 《절대》teetotalism 《절주》temperance 《법령》prohibition／～하다 abstain [from drinking]; a give up drinking; go dry／～법 the prohibition law／～가 an abstainer; a total abstainer; a dry [man]／～ 운동 a temperance movement; a dry campaign. きんしゆ

**금주**(今週) this week. こんしゆう

**금준비**(金準備) 《경》gold reserves.

**금줄**(金一) a vein of gold ore. きんみやく

**금중**(禁中) the Court; the Imperial palace. きんちゆう

**금지**(金紙) gold-colo[u]red paper; gilt paper. きんし

**금지**(禁止) prohibition; taboo; a ban; an embargo 《금압》suppression／～하다 fo-

금지

rbid; prohibit; ban; taboo; place under a ban／수출입 ～ 품목 items on the contraband list／～ 구역 a restricted area／상영 ～ a stage ban／～세 a prohibitive tax. きんし

**금지**(禁地) a restricted area; an off-limit area. ひとのていりをきんしすること

**금지 옥엽**(金枝玉葉) 《귀여운 자손》 one's precious child／～으로 자라나다 be brought up like a prince. きんしぎょくよう

**금지환**(金指環) a gold ring. きんのゆびわ

**끔찍스럽다** (be) horrible ⇨끔찍하다.

**끔찍하다** ①《참혹하다》(be) horrible; terrible; frightful; extraordinary ②《극진하다》(be) whole-hearted; hearty; courteously kindly sincere.
ぞっとするほどだ

**금창**(金瘡) a cut; a wound inflicted by a blade. かたなでうたきず

**금추**(今秋) this autumn. こんしゅう

**금춘**(今春) this[coming] spring. こんしゅん

**금치다**(값을) name a price for; set a price on; appraise. ねだんをきめる

**금치산**(禁治産) 〘법〙 incompetency; interdiction／～자 an incompetent; an interdict／～ 선고 an interdiction／～ 선고를 받다 be interdicted from the management of one's property. きんちさん

**금침**(衾枕) bedclothes and a pillow; bedding. ふとんとまくら

**금테**(金—) 《안경의》gold rims 《사진틀의》a gold frame／～ 안경 gold[-rimmed] glasses.

**금파리**(金—) 〘충〙 a green bottle fly.

**금패**(金牌) a gold medal. きんぱい

**금품**(金品) money and other articles; cash and other possessions. きんぴん

**금풍**(金風) an autumnal breeze[wind].
しゅうふう

**금하**(今夏) this summer. ことしのなつ

**금하다** agree on a price of; fix the price of. ねだんをきめる

**금하다**(禁—) ①《금지》 forbid; prohibit; taboo 《규칙적으로》interdict; ban; embargo／소년들의 음주를 ～ prohibit minors from drinking ②《억제》suppress; repress; restrain／[웃음을] 금할 수가 없다 cannot help [laughing]. きんずる

**금혼식**(金婚式) a golden wedding anniversary. きんこんしき

**금화**(金貨) a gold coin[piece]. きんか

**금환식**(金環蝕) 〘천〙 an annular eclipse of the sun. きんかんしょく

**금회**(今回) this time ⇨이번. こんかい

**금후**(今後) after this; hereafter; in future／～의 future; coming／～ 계속하여 from this time forth／～ 5년 내지 10년 은 for five or ten years from now.
こんご

**급**(急) 《위급》[a] danger; an emergency; a crisis (pl. -ses). きゅう

**급**(級) a class; a grade; a form《영》／1년 ～ the first year class／6년 ～의 생도 boys of the sixth grade. きゅう

급비

**급각도**(急角度) an acute angle／～로 sharply; with a sudden turn／～의 전환을 보이다 take a sudden trun; make a face-about きゅうかくど

**급강하**(急降下) a sudden drop; a dive／～하다 《온도가》drop suddenly 《비행기가》dive／～ 폭격 dive bombing／～ 폭격기 a dive bomber. きゅうこうか

**급거**(急遽) in haste; in a hurry; hastily; hurriedly. きゅうきょ

**급격**(急擊) a sudden attack／～하다 take (the enemy) by surprise. きゅうげき

**급격**(急激) ～하다 (be) rapid; sudden; abrupt 《과격》radical／～하게 suddenly; rapidly／～한 변화 a sudden[radical] change. きゅうげき

**급경**(急境) an emergency; a crisis; a critical juncture. ききゅうなばあい

**급경사**(急傾斜) 《치받이》steep acclivity 《내리받이》steep declivity. きゅうけいしゃ

**급고**(急告) an urgent notice. きゅうこく

**급급하다**(汲汲—) (be) intent[bent] on; be engrossed[absorbed] in; busy oneself about. きゅうきゅうとしている

**급급하다**(急急—) (be) urgent; pressing; imminent. おおいそぎだ

**급기야**(及其也) at last; finally; in the end; as a last consequence. けっきょく

**급난**(急難) a sudden[impending] danger [calamity]. きゅうなん

**급등**(急騰) a sudden rise; a jump／～하다 rise suddenly; jump／물가의 ～ a speedy rising of prices. きゅうとう

**급락**(及落) success or failure; the result of an examination. きゅうらく

**급락**(急落) a sudden drop; a sharp decline／～하다 decline heavily; slump; fall suddenly.

**급료**(給料) pay; a salary; wages／～일 a payday／～가 적은[많은] poorly[well] paid. きゅうりょう

**급류**(急流) a rapid stream[current]; rapids. きゅうりゅう

**급무**(急務) an urgent necessity; a pressing need／초미(焦眉)의 ～ the pressing need of the hour. きゅうむ

**급박**(急迫) urgency; imminence／～하다 grow acute[critical, tense]／～한 pressing; imminent; urgent. きゅうはく

**급변**(急變) 《변고》a sudden change an accident／～하다 change suddenly; take a sudden turn for the worse. きゅうへん

**급병**(急病) sudden [attack of] illness; an urgent case. きゅうびょう

**급보**(急步) a quick pace; hurried steps／～하다 walk at a quick pace.

**급보**(急報) an urgent message[dispatch]／～하다 report promptly. きゅうほう

**급부**(給付) presentation; benefit; delivery／반대 ～ a counter-presentation／～ 연한(年限) a benefit year. きゅうふ

**급비**(給費) scholarship; supply [of expenses]／～하다 furnish (one) with expenses; allow (one) expenses／～생 a su-

**급사(急死)** sudden death／~하다 die suddenly. きゅうし

**급사(給仕)** 《사무실의》 an office boy[girl] 《여관의》 a page〈영〉; a bellboy〈미〉《식사의》 a waiter; a waitress(여자); 《선박의》 a cabin[ship] boy; a steward; a stewardess(여자). きゅうじ

**급사(急使)** an express messenger.

**급사면(急斜面)** a steep hill; a steep slope[decline]. きゅうしゃめん

**급살(急煞)** the most unlucky star; the worst fate. うんのわるいばつ

**급상승(急上昇)** a zoom／~하다 zoom; chandelle. きゅうじょうしょう

**급선무(急先務)** a matter of immediate necessity; a pressing need; the most urgent business. まっさきにすべきつとめ

**급선봉(急先鋒)** a leader; the vanguard.

**급설(急設)** rapid[hasty, hurried] installation／~하다 hastily install[provide, set up]. きゅうせつ

**급성(急性)** ~의 acute／~의 병 an acute case[disease]／~ 맹장염 an acute attack of appendicitis. きゅうせい

**급소(急所)** a vital point[part] 《약점》 a vulnerable spot／~를 찌르는 질문 a home question／~를 찌르다 《말이》 hit (*one*) in a vulnerable spot; touch (*one*) on the raw. きゅうしょ

**급속 냉동(急速冷凍)** quick freezing. きゅうそくれいとう

**급속하다(急速—)** (be) rapid; swift; prompt; fast. ひじょうにはやい

**급송(急送)** ~하다 send by express; dispatch [in haste]. きゅうそう

**급수(給水)** water supply[service]／~하다 supply (*a town*) with water／~관 a water pipe. きゅうすい

**급수(級數)** 《수》 progression; a series／산술[기하] ~ arithmetical[geometrical] progression. きゅうすう

**급습(急襲)** a sudden attack／~하다 raid; storm. きゅうしゅう

**급승(急昇)** ~하다 rise suddenly; swing upward rapidly.

**급식(給食)** supply of food; meal service／~하다 provide meals (*for*); furnish (*one*) with food. きゅうしょく

**급신(急信)** an urgent message; a dispatch; express mail. きゅうしん

**급여(給與)** allowance; grant; supply／~하다 grant; allow; supply[provide] (*one*) with. きゅうよ

**급용(急用)** urgent business. きゅうよう

**급우(級友)** a classmate. きゅうゆう

**급우(急雨)** a sudden rain; a shower.

**급유(給油)** oil supply; refueling／~하다 supply oil; refuel／~소 an oil[a gas] station. きゅうゆ

**급인(汲引)** ~하다 《물을》 draw up; pump up(펌프로); 《인재를》 appoint (*a person*) by merit; select (*a person*) for ability; promotion. みずをくみあげること

**급작스럽다** (be) sudden; abrupt; unexpected.

**급장(級長)** a monitor. きゅうちょう

**급전(急電)** an urgent telegram／~을 치다 dispatch a radio message. きゅうでん

**급전(急錢)** money for immediate use; urgently needed money.

**급전(急轉)** a sudden change[turn]／~하다 change suddenly; take a sudden turn／형세의 ~ an unexpected turn of event／~ 직하적으로 all of a sudden; all at once; precipitately. きゅうてん

**급전 직하(急轉直下)** precipitation; a headlong fall 《사건의》 a spectacular change[turn]／~하다 be precipitated; fall headlong. きゅうてんちょっか

**급전환(急轉換)** a sudden change [turn]. きゅうてんかん

**급정거(急停車)** a sudden stop／~하다 stop suddenly. きゅうていしゃ

**급제(及第)** ~하다 pass an examination; make it. きゅうだい

**급조(急造)** ~하다 build in haste; construct hurriedly.

**급조(急調)** 《음》 a quick movement; *allegro*(It).

**급증(急症)** 《급병》 a sudden illness 《급성병》 an acute disease. きゅうしょう

**급증(急增)** ~하다 increase[rise] suddenly[rapidly]. きゅうぞう

**급진(急進)** rapid progress 《과격》 radicalism／~하다 progress rapidly; push forward／~적 radical; extreme／~ 사상 radical ideas／~파 the radicals; the radicalists. きゅうしん

**급탄(給炭)** the supply of coal／~소 a coaling station／~선 a collier.

**급파(急派)** dispatch／~하다 dispatch; expedite; rush hurry／현장에 경관대를 ~하다 rush a police force to the scene.

**급하다(急—)** 《긴급하다》(be) urgent 《바쁘다》 hasty 《빠르다》 quick 《위중하다》 critical 《성급하다》 short-tempered／급한 볼일[로] (*on*) urgent business／급한 걸음[으로] (*with*) hurried steps／시간이 ~ be pressed fór time. きゅうだ

**급항(急航)** swift sailing／~하다 sail hurriedly (*to*).

**급행(急行)** 《열차》 an express [train]; a fast train／~하다 hurry[rush, hasten] to; go post-haste. きゅうこう

**급환(急患)** an emergency case; a sudden illness.

**급히(急—)** 《빨리》 quickly; fast; swiftly; rapidly; promptly 《바삐》 hastily; in a hurry.

**긋다** ① 《선을》 draw ② 《작정하다》 determine; decide ③ 《비가》 let up; stop; get out of the rain. (せんを)ひく

**긍경(肯綮)** the point; the most important part.

**긍고(亘古)** ~하다 go back to the distant past; range over old times.

끙끙 《신음 소리》groaning; moaning 《불평의 소리》grumbling/~하다 groan; moan; grumble; complain. むかしにおよぶこと うむうむ

긍긍하다(兢兢—) be in trepidation. せんせんきょうきょうとしている

긍낙(肯諾) consent; assent; acceptance/~하다 consent[agree, assent] to. しょうだくすること

긍민(矜憫) compassion; commiseration; pity / ~하다 feel compassion (for, toward); be touched with compassion (for); be moved with pity (for).

긍이 planting cotton[beans] as a side crop in a barley field. かんさくすること

긍정(肯定) affirmation; admission/~하다 affirm; confirm; acknowledge; bear out. こうてい

긍종(肯從) ~하다 obey[follow] willingly.

긍지(矜持) pride; dignity. じふしん

긍휼(矜恤) pity; sympathy; compassion/~하다 take pity on; feel pity for; have[take] compassion on/~이 with pity. あわれみめぐむこと

끝 ⇨별항 참조.

끝갈망 ~하다 settle; set (matters) right; wind up. とりきめる

끝끝내 to the last; to the [bitter] end; to the last extremity; persistently; stubbornly. さいごまで

끝나다 end; come to an end; close 《기한이》expire 《완성하다》finish 《완결하다》complete 《산회하다》break up; rise.

끝내다 end; finish; get[be] through with; complete; conclusion; settle/일을 ~ finish one's work. しまう

끝돈 the balance; the remainder. ざんきん

끝마감(一磨勘) closing; conclude/~하다 close; conclude; end. しめきり

끝막다 close; complete; finish. しめきる

끝장 《終結》a conclusion 《낙착》settlement/ ~나다 be over[settled]/ ~내다 bring to a conclusion[settlement]; put an end to. しまい

끝판 the last part [of a job, a game]; the end; the close. しゅうきょく

끼 a meal; a mealtime/하루에 세 ~를 먹는다 have three meals a day.

기(氣) ①《정기》spirit; essence; ether ②《원기》energy; vigo[u]r; vitality ③《힘》strength; energy; might 《노력》effort; exertions(기쓰다) ④《숨》a breath; breathing ⇨기막히다 ⑤《기세》spirit; ardour/ ~가 나서 in high spirits/ ~가 죽다 be in low spirits; lose heart; be dispirited ⑥《냄새》smell ⑦《공기》air/ 분위~ atmosphere.

기(忌) an anniversary of one's death; [a period of] mourning.

기(旗) a flag; a banner 《군기》the colo[u]rs/~를 올리다[내리다] hoist[lower] a flag; put up[take down] a flag/깃대 a flag-staff. はた

기(己) 《천간의》the 6th of the lo Heaven's Stems. き

기(期) 《기간》a period; a time 《기일》a date; a time 《시대》an age 《계절》a season 《병의》a stage/2~생 the second-term students/ 제1~의 폐병 tuberculosis in the first stage. き

기(記) an account; a narrative 《기록》a record; annals 《역사》a history. き

기(基) 【화】a radical 《수》radix(pl. ~es, -dices). き

기가(起家) ~하다 resuscitate a ruined family.

기가(妓家) a keesaeng house.

기각(棄却) abandonment; renunciation 《각하》rejection 【법】dismissal/~하다 《각하》turn down; reject; dismiss/공소를 ~하다 dismiss a suit. ききゃく

기간(期間) a period; a time; a term/일정한 ~내에 within a certain period of time. きかん

기간(基幹) a nucleus(pl. -clei); a mainstay/~ 산업 key industries. きかん

기간(起墾) ~하다 bring under cultivation; break up the soil. かいこん

기간(旗竿) a flag staff. はたざお

기간(既刊) ~의 already[previously] published[issued]. きかん

기갈(飢渴) hunger and thirst; starvation. きかつ

기갑 부대(機甲部隊) a panzer unit; an armo[u]red corps. きこうぶたい

기강(紀綱) 《관기》official discipline 《질서》public order; the laws. きこう

기개(氣概) spirit; mettle; pluck; pride; guts/~ 있는 [high-] spirited/ ~를 보이다 show one's mettle. きがい

기거(起居) 《일상 생활》one's daily life 《건강 상태》one's state of health/~ 동작 behavio[u]r; bearing/~를 같이하다 live together. ききょ

기꺼이 willingly; with pleasure; joyfully; delightfully; cheerfully. よろこんで

기걸(奇傑) a character; a remarkable man. きけつ

기껏 to the best of one's ability; to the utmost; as far[much] as possible; as far as one can. せいせい

기껏해야 at [the] best; at [the] most; at the utmost; at the [very] outside; at the ⋯est. よくても

기결(既決) ~의 decided; settled 《죄의》convicted/ ~ 사항 a matter settled [decided on]. きけつ

기경(起耕) farming; tillage; plowing; husbandry/ ~하다 farm; till (a field); plow (land).

기계(機械) a machine 《총칭》machinery / ~공 a mechanic/~ 공업 engineering industry / ~ 공장 an engineering works/ ~력 mechanical power/~ 수뢰 a mechanical mine/ ~유 machine [lubricating] oil/ ~학 mechanics/~화 mechanization. きかい

기계(器械) an instrument; an apparatus; an appliance; a divice; a gadget / 의료 ~ medical instruments[appliances] / ~ 체조(體操) heavy gymnastics / 물리 ~ a physical apparatus. きかい

기계(奇計) a trick; a clever scheme; a ruse. きけい

기계화(機械化) mechanization / ~하다 mechanize. きかいか

기고(起稿) ~하다 begin to write 《쓰기 시작》[frame a] draft(기초). きこう

기고(寄稿) a contribution 《기서(寄書)》a correspondence / ~하다 contribute to; write for [a magazine] きこう

기고(旗鼓) colo[u]rs and drums 《군대》an army. はたとたいこ

기고 만장(氣高萬丈) ~하다 be inflamed with rage 《성나서》be exasperated (기뻐서》be proud (of); be triumphant.

기골(氣骨) 《의기》 spirit; soul; backbone [of character]. きこつ

기골(肌骨) flesh and bones.

기공(技工) a craftsman / 치과 ~ a dental technician. ぎこう

기공(起工) ~하다 begin work 《철도 따위》lay down (토목업》break ground; set to work. きこう

기공(奇功) a signal success. きこう

기공(氣孔) 〖식〗a pore; a stoma 〖동〗a stigma. きこう

기관(機關) 《기계》an engine; a machine 《시설》facilities 《수단》an organ (기구》machinery / 증기 ~ a steam engine / 교육 ~ educational facilities / 운수 ~ means of transportation / ~고 an engine shed / ~수 an engineer / ~사 an engine driver〈영〉; a driver; a locomotive engineer〈미〉/ ~실 an engine

끝

①《첨단》a point 《펜촉 따위의》a nib; an end; a tip; a top; an extremity / 혀 ~ the tip of a tongue / 코 ~ the end [tip] of a nose / 연필 ~ the point of a pencil / 손가락 ~ the tip of a finger / 이 ~에서 저 ~까지 from this end to the other end / 책상 ~ an edge of the table / ~이 뾰족하다 be pointed [sharp] at the end / ~이 점점 가늘어지다 taper (to a point) / 머리 ~에서 발 ~까지 from head to toe / ~이 둥굿하다 be rounded at the end.

②《맨 마지막》the end; a close; conclusion; termination; tail end; finish / ~의 final; last; concluding; ultimate; terminal / 일 ~ the end of the job / ~에 가서 in the end; lastly; finally; at last; in the long run / ~까지 to the end[last]; to a finish; to the last extremity / ~ 순시 the last number of the program / ~까지 싸우다 fight to a finish; fight it out / 연설 ~에 at the conclusion of one's speech / 처음부터 ~까지 from beginning to end; from first to last / ~까지 남다 sit out / ~까지 저항하다 resist to the bitter end / ~까지 주장하다 persist in (one's opinion) / 누구의 이야기를 ~까지 듣다 hear a person out / ~까지 보다(듣다) sit through (a picture, a play) / 페이지의 ~까지 읽다 read down to the foot of the page / ~을 잘 맺다 come to a good[happy] end / 나는 ~까지 당신을 지원하겠다 I will stand by you to the last. / 할 말이 있으면 내 말을 ~까지 듣고 하여라 Say what ever you've got to say after you've heard me out. / 무엇이든지 ~이 있다 All things have an end. / 그 소설을 ~까지 읽었다 I read the novel through[to the end]. / 나의 이름은 명단 맨 ~에 있다 My name stands in the bottom of the list. / 즐거운 여행도 ~이 났다 Our pleasant tuur has come to a close. / 그는 여러 가지 죄를 지은 ~에 살인까지 하였다 He went to the extent of committing murder to top off the varieties of crime he had perpetrated.

③《차례·행렬 따위의》the last; the tail end / 행렬의 ~ the tail end of a procession / 맨 ~에 서서 가다 bring [close] up the rear.

④《일의 결과》result; consequence; an outcome; an effect 《결말》an end / 심사 숙고한 ~에 upon[on, after] mature consideration / ~이 좋다[나쁘다] be successful[unsuccessful] / 수술의 ~이 좋다 The surgical operation resulted in success. / ~이 재미 없구 the result does not come up to one's expectations[is not quite satisfactory] / 그는 방탕한 ~에 돈이 궁하여 절도를 했다 Want of money consequent upon his dissipation led him to commit theft. / 서로 양보한 ~에 사건은 곧 가라앉았다 We made mutual concessions with the result that the matter was settled at once.

⑤《한도》a limit; a bound; an end; limits; bounds / ~없이 without limit; without end; extremely; exceedingly / ~없다 be without end; be endless [unlimited, boundless, bottomless]; be infinite; be eternal.

⑥《단위》a roll (of silk) / ~으로 사다 buy a whole roll of(옷 따위).

⑦《어미》a suffix; an ending.

기관 room／ ~장 a chief engineer. きかん
기관(器官) an organ／ ~계통 the organ system. きかん
기관(氣管) the trachea; the windpipe／ ~염 《의》 trachitis. きかん
기관(奇觀) a singular spectacle; a novel sight. きかん
기관(汽管) a steam-pipe. きかん
기관(汽罐) a [steam] boiler／~실 a boiler-room; a stoke-hole／~압력 boiler pressure. きかん
기관 단총(機關短銃) a submachine gun. きかんたんじゅう
기관지(氣管支) the bronchus; a bronchial tube／~염 《의》 bronchitis. きかんし
기관차(機關車) an engine《영》; a locomotive《미》. きかんしゃ
기관총(機關銃) a machine gun; a maxim [gun]. きかんじゅう
기괴(奇怪) ~하다 (be) strange; mysterious 《못된》 outrageous. きかい
기괴 망측(奇怪罔測) ~하다 (be) very strange 《못되다》 really outrageous.
기괴 천만(奇怪千萬) extreme strangeness [mysteriousness]; extreme outrageousness. きかいせんばん
기교(技巧) technique; art; a trick; technical skill. ぎこう
기교(機巧) resources; tact.
たくらみとしゅだんがこうみょうなこと
기구(機構) structure; mechanism; setup; machinery; a system／ ~를 개혁하다 reorganize the system. きこう
기구(器具) a utensil; an implement; an apparatus 《붙어 있는》 fixtures. きぐ
기구(氣球) a balloon／계류[관측]~ a captive[an observation] balloon. ききゅう
기구(崎嶇) ①《운명이》adverse fortune; varied[checkered] fortunes／~하다 (be) checkered; varied 《기이》 strange ②《산길의》steepness. ~하다 (be) steep; rugged. よわたりのこんなんなこと
기국(器局) ability; talent; calibre; competency. さいのうとどりょう
기궁(奇窮) dire poverty; destitution; circumstances／ ~하다 (be) very poor; destitute.
기권(氣圈) 《기상》the atmosphere. きけん
기권(棄權) 《투표의》 abstention (from voting) 《권리의》the renunciation of one's right／ ~하다 abstain from voting; renounce one's right／ ~율 the abstention rate／ ~자 an abstentionist; an absentee. きけん
기근(飢饉) a famine; failure of crops 《결핍》scarcity／물~ water famine／큰 ~ a great[severe] famine. ききん
기근(氣根) 《식》an aerial root. きこん
기금(基金) a fund; a foundation; an endowment／구제 ~ a relief fund／ ~을 설정하다 establish a fund. ききん
기급(氣急) ~하다 《놀라다》be aghast; cry out in surprise[astonishment, amazement]. びっくりしてさけぶ

끼다 144 끼다
끼끗하다 (be) neat; clean; smart; spruce; fresh. せいけつでいきいきしている
기기(器機) machinery and tools. きき
기기 피괴(奇奇怪怪) ~하다 (be) abominable; extremely strange; monstrous; wildest. ききかいかい
기기 묘묘(奇奇妙妙) ~하다 (be) extremely strange; very curious[queer, odd]; wonderful. ききみょうみょう
기나무(幾那樹) 《식》a bark-tree; a cinchona.
기나염(幾那鹽) 《염산 키닌》salt of quinine.
기나피(幾那皮) cinchona[Peruvian quinine] bark.
기남자(奇男子) a man of no common ability. きだんし
기낭(氣囊) ①《물고기의》an air bladder ②《가스 주머니》a gas bag; an envelope ③ ⇨공기 주머니. きのう
기내(畿內) the districts around the capital city. きない
기녀(妓女) ①《관비》an official dancing girl ② ⇨기생. ぎじょ
기년(期年) one year [of the era]. きねん
기년(朞年) ①《복》mourning for one year ②《1주년》one year. きねん
기년(耆年) age over sixty years.
기념(記念) commemoration; memory／ ~물 a keepsake; token; a memorial; a memory／ ~비 a monument／ ~일 a memorial day; a commemoration day ／ ~제 a commemoration; an anniversary／ ~식 exercises marking the occasion; commemoration exercises／ ~우표 a commemorative stamp[postmark] ／ ~의 commemorative; memorial／ ~으로 as a memory[souvenir]; in memory[commemoration] of／ ~하다 commemorate; memorize. きねん
기능(技能) ability; skill; capability. ぎのう
기능(機能) function; faculty／소화 ~ digestive functions／ ~ 장애 a functional disorder／ ~적 functional／ ~을 하다 function. きのう
끼니 a meal; a repast／ ~를 굶다 fix into to keep the pot boiling 《결식》go without a meal. きまったしょくじ
끼니때 meal time; dinnertime／~를 굶다 skips a meal. きまったしょくじのじかん
기다 crawl; creep 《사지를 집고》go on all fours／기어오르다 climb up; climber [over] 《벼랑 따위를》scale／기어나오다 [나오다] crawl about[out]. はらばう
끼다¹ ①《들어박다》set (in); inlay ②《끗다》get[put, let] in; fix into 《소켓 따위를》seal 《구멍에》stick ③《장갑·반지 따위를》put on; pull on／장갑을 ~ draw [pull] on one's gloves ④《팔장을》fold (one's arms)／팔을 서로 끼고 arm in arm ⑤《옆구리에》hold[carry] under one's arm／책을 몇 권 끼고 with some books under one's arm ⑥《참가》join; participate in; be a party to／일행에 ~ join the party ⑦《따라서》 …을 끼고 al-

**끼다** ong; by／산을 끼고 along the mountains. さしこむ

**끼다²** ①《안개 따위가》settle; hang over; envelop／안개가 낀다 The mist is settling.／방에 연기가 끼었다 The room is smoky. ②《때 따위가》collect; gather／때가 낀 dirty. こもる

**기다랗다** (be) rather long; lengthy／～기다란 장대 a long pole. ひじょうにながい

**기다리다** wait (for); await 《기대》expect; anticipate／기다리게 하다 keep (one) waiting; let (one) wait／기회를 ～ watch an opportunity. まつ

**기담(奇談)** a strange story. きだん

**기답(起畓)** ～하다 reclaim (a plot) into paddy fields. すいでんをつくること

**기대(期待)** expectation; anticipation; hope／～하다 expect; anticipate; look forward to; hope for／…을 ～하고 in anticipation〔expectation, hopes〕 of／～에 어긋나지 않다 meet〔come up to〕〔one's〕 expectation. きたい

**기대다** ①《물건에》lean on〔against〕; rest against ②《의지》rely〔depend〕 on; lean on. よりかかる

**기도(祈禱)** a prayer《식사 전후의》grace／～하다 pray; offer〔utter〕 a prayer; say grace. きとう

**기도(企圖)** 《계획》a plan; a design; a project; a plot《시도》an attempt／～하다 plan; plot; design; try; attempt; intend; contemplate. きと

**기독교(基督教)** Christianity; the Christian religion〔faith〕.

**기동(起動)** ①《기계의》setup; starting／～의 motive／～기 a starter ②《몸을 움직임》moving; stirring／～하다 move; stir, starts up. きどう

**기동(機動)** maneuver／～하다 maneuver／～ 연습 a maneuver／～ 부대 a task force《해군》; a mobile unit《육군》／～성 mobility. きどう

**기동(奇童)** a remarkable child; a wonder boy; a child prodigy. きどう

**기동차(汽動車)** a diesel train. きどうしゃ

**기두(起頭)** ①《일의》the beginning; the start ②《글의》a foreword; a preface.

**기둥** ①《건축의》a pillar; a post; a pole 《둥근》a column／～을 세우다 put up a post ②《버팀목》a post; a pole ③《사람》a pillar; a support; a prop; a stay／나라의 ～ the pillar of the state. はしら

**기둥서방(一書房)** a pimp; a pander. きふ

**끼뜨리다** throw (water) away. ばらまく

**기득(既得)** ～의 already acquired; vested／～권 vested rights. きとく

**기라(綺羅)** a fine〔gorgeous, gaudy〕 dress; fine clothes／～성(星) glittering 〔bright〕 stars. きら

**기략(機略)** resources. きりゃく

**기량(技倆)** talent ⇒기능(技能). ぎりょう

**기량(器量)** capacity; caliber. きりょう

**기러기** 【조】 a wild goose (pl. geese)／～ 우는 소리 the cry of a wild goose／～가 울다 honk. がん

**기러기발** 《현악기의 줄받침》a bridge.

**기력(氣力)** ①《기운》energy; spirit; vigour／～이 왕성한 energetic; vigorous; full of vitality ②《압축 공기》pressed air. きりょく

**기력(汽力)** steam-power／～으로 움직이는 기계 a steamworked machine／～계 an airpressure gauge〔indicator〕.

**기로(岐路)** 《갈림길》a forked road; a crossroad／인생의 ～에 서다 stand at the crossroads of life. きろ

**기로(耆老)** a man aged above sixty.

**기록(記錄)** a record 《문서》a document 《관청의》archives 《학계의》transactions 《연대기》annals; a chronicle／～하다 record; register; write down; put on record／～계(員) a recorder; a scorer; an archivist／～ 영화 a documentary 〔film〕／～ 보지자 a record holder; a titleholder／～을 깨뜨리다 break〔smash〕 the record／～을 세우다 make 〔establish〕 a [new] record (in). きろく

**기롱(譏弄)** derision; ridicule; scoff／～ 하다 befool; ridicule; jeer (at). あざけり

**기뢰(機雷)** 【군】 a mine／～를 부설하다 lay〔place〕 mines [in the sea]. きらい

**기루(妓樓)** a house of ill fame; a brothel. ぎろう

**끼룩** ～거리다 stretch one's neck to see [something]; peep.

**기류(氣流)** an air〔aerial〕 current; a current〔stream〕 of air／악(惡)～대(帶) an air pocket. きりゅう

**기류(寄留)** temporary residence／～하다 reside temporarily (at)／～계 a report of temporary residence／～지 a place of temporary residence〔domicile〕／～인 temporary resident. きりゅう

**기르다** ①《사람 등을》bring up; rear; breed; raise／우유로 ～ feed (a child) on cow's milk ②《함양하다》cultivate; foster／도의심을 ～ cultivate moral sense ③《버릇을》from (a habit) ④《수염 따위를》grow (a mustache). そだてる

**기름** oil 《지방》fat 《비계》lard 《소·양의》suet 《바르는》grease 《짐승의》tallow 《머리》pomade. あぶら

**기름기** ①《고기의》the fat (of meat) ② 《기름 기운》oiliness; greasiness. あぶらげ

**기름먹이다** oil／종이를〔헝겊을〕 ～ oil paper〔cloth〕. あぶらをつける

**기름지다** ①《기름이 많다》(be) greasy; fatry; oily; fat《살찐》／기름진 음식 greasy〔fatty, rich〕 food ②《땅이》(be) fertile; rich; productive／기름진 땅 fertile 〔rich〕 field.

**기름콩** sprouting beans.

**기름틀** an oil press.

**-끼리** 예 같은 학생 ～ among fellow students／저희~ 싸우다 quarrel among themselves. なかま

**끼리끼리** each in a group 《명사적》people of like character. どうしごとに

기리다 praise; admire; extol. ほめる
기린(麒麟) 〚동〛 a giraffe; a camelopard / ～아(兒) a prodigy. きりん
기립(起立) rising; standing up 《호령》 Rise!, Everybody up!/ ～하다 stand up; rise; get to *one's* feet. きりつ
기마(騎馬) 《타는 말》 riding horse／ ～ 순경 a mounted policeman 《총칭》 the mounted police. きば
기막히다(氣—) ①《어이없다》 be dumbfounded; be struck dumb with amazement /기막힌 《형편 없는》 terrible 《고약한》 disgusting 《좋은》 wonderful／기막히게 terribly; wonderfully ②《숨막히다》 be choked; be suffocated; feel stifled[suffocated]. おどろきあきれる
기만(欺瞞) deception; imposition; trickery／ ～하다 deceive; impose on; cheat; play (*one*) a tricky. ぎまん
기말(期末) the end of a term.
기망(企望) hope; expectation; anticipation／ ～하다 hope; anticipate.
기망(旣望) the sixteenth night of a lunar month. きぼう
기망(欺罔) deception／～하다 deceive; commit fraud. きぼう
기맥(氣脈) 《연락》 connection／ ～을 통하다 conspire (*with*); be in collusion (*with*). きみゃく
기명(記名) register 《서명》 signature／ ～하다 register; sign／무～ 투표 an unsigned vote. きめい
기명(器皿) tableware; dishes.
기모(奇謀) an ingenious stratagem; a clever trick.
기묘(奇妙) strangeness; curiosity; a mystery; a wonder／ ～하다 (be) strange; curious; mysterious; wonderful／ ～한 이야기 a mystery story. きみょう
기묘(己卯) 〚민〛 the 16th binary term of the sexagenary cycle. きぼう
기문(氣門) 〚동〛 a stoma; stigma 《곤충 등의》 spiracle.
기문(奇聞) news; a curious story. きぶん
기물(器物) 《그릇》 a vessel 《기구》 an implement 《가구》 furniture. きぶつ
기미 《얼굴의》 a discoloration on the face; a liver spot; freckles. しみ
기미(己未) the 56th binary term of the sexagenary cycle. きみ
기미(氣味) ①《냄새와 맛》 smell and taste ②《심기》 feeling; sensation ③《취미》 taste; relish. きみ
기미(機微) secrets; inner workings; penetralia／ ～를 알아차리다 get a hint [an inkling] of (a *matter*). きび
기민(機敏) promptness; readiness; smartness; shrewdness／～하다 (be) prompt; smart; sharp; shrewd／～하게 promptly; smartly／～한 동작 quick action [movement]. きびん
기민(饑民) starved people; the famished. きみん
기밀(機密) secrecy 《일》 a secret／ ～의 secret; confidential／ ～비 secret. [service] funds／～ 누설 leakage of secrets / ～ 서류 secret[confidential] documents. きみつ
기밀실(氣密室) 〚항〛 an air-tight chamber. きみつしつ
기박(奇薄) sad fate; unhappiness; misfortune／ ～하다 (be) unfortunate; hapless; unlucky; ill-fated／팔자가 ～한 것을 한탄하다 grieve over *one's* ill[tough] luck. うんがわるくふこうなこと
기반(基盤) a base; a basis; a foundation／ ～을 이루다 form the basis. きばん
기반(羈絆) restraint; a yoke; fetters; bonds; shackles; ties／～을 벗어나다 set *one*self free (*from*); shake off the fetters. きはん
기발하다(奇拔—) (be) orignal; novel; smart; fanciful／～한 착상 an original idea; a novel conception.
기백(氣魄) spirit; soul; character. きはく
기백(幾百) hundreds.
기뻐하다 be pleased[delighted] with[at]; be happy with; be glad for; rejoice over[at]. うれしがる
기범선(機帆船) a steam-and-sail-driven boat. きはんせん
기법(技法) techniques. ぎほう
기법(記法) [a] notation.
기벽(氣癖) unwillingness to own[admit, acknowledge] *one's* defeat.
기벽(奇癖) an eccentric habit; an eccentricity; a peculiarity. きへき
기별(奇別, 寄別) information; notice／～하다 let (*one*) know; inform; send word; give (one) notice. しょうそく
기병(騎兵) 《총칭》 cavalry; horse 《한 사람》 a cavalryman; a horseman. きへい
기병(奇病) a strange disease.
기병(起兵) raising an army／～하다 raise an army; rise in arms.
기보(旣報) a previous report／ ～한 previously[already] reported. きほう
기보(棋譜) the record of a *badook* game.
기보법(記譜法) 〚음〛 music notation.
기복(起伏) ups and downs; undulation ／～하다 rise and fall; undulate. きふく
기본(基本) 《기초》 a foundation; a basis 《기준》 a standard／~ 법칙 fundamental law／~ 단위 a standard unit／ ~ 형(型) a basic pattern; the fundamentals (*of*)／~ 화폐 〚경〛 an archetype／ ～금 a fund; an endowment／～적 fundamental; basic; standard. きほん
기봉(起峰) a towering peak.
기부(寄附) subscription; contribution; donation／ ～하다 contribute; make a donation (*to, for, towards*); subscribe; donate／ ～자 a contributor; a subscriber; a donor／ ～금 a contribution; a donation money／ ～를 모집하다 raise subscriptions (*from*); collect contributions. きふ
기부(肌膚) flesh; skin. はだえ

기분(氣分) feeling; humour; mood; frame of mind/~ 전환 diversion/~이 좋다 feel well[fine]; be pleased/ ~이 나쁘다 feel unwell; be out of sorts; be displeased/ ~ 상하다 feel unpleasant; feel hurt; be offended/ ~이 안 나다 be in no mood (to *do*, *for*); do not feel like (*doing*). きぶん

기쁘다 (be) glad; delightful; happy 《유쾌》 pleasant; (be) joyous; joyful/기쁜 날 a happy[glad] day/기쁜 소식 glad [happy] news/기쁘게 하다 gladden; delight; please/기뻐하다 be glad; be pleased (*with*); be delighted (*with*, *at*); rejoice (*at*, *by*). うれしい

기쁨 《희열》 joy; gladness; delight; rejoice pleasure/~을 참을 수 없다 be unable to contain *one*'s delight. よろこび

기사(記事) ①《신문의》 news; a news item; an account; an article 《보도》 a report/특종 ~ a scoop; a beat/〈미〉삼면 ~ police-court news/~ 금지 a press ban ②《서술》 description; an account; a statement/~문(文) descriptive writing; a description. きじ

기사(記寫) a record/ ~하다 record; put on record. きろくすること

기사(己巳) 〖민〗 the 6th binary term of the sexagenary cycle. きし

기사(技師) an engineer; a technician/토목[광산] ~ a civil[a mining] engineer /건축 ~ an architect. ぎし

기사(騎士) a knight; horseman/ ~도 knighthood; chivalry. きし

기사(棋士) a *badug* player 《장기의》 a Korean chess player. きし

기사(饑死) death by starvation/ ~하다 die of hunger; starve to death. うえじに

기사(騎射) [horse-]riding and archery.

기사 회생(起死回生) resuscitation; revival/ ~하다 revive; resuscitate (*from death*). きしかいせい

기산(起算) ~하다 reckon from (*some date*); measure from (*some point*). きさん

기상(氣象) weather; atmospheric phenomena/ ~대 a meteorological observatory/ ~도 a weather map[chart]/ ~학 meteorology/ ~ 통보 weather reports/~학자 a meteorologist. きしょう

기상(氣像) nature; disposition; temper; spirit. せいしんとなりふり

기상(機上) 긔 ~에 오르다 get on [board] a plane. きじょう

기상(起床) rising [in the morning]/ ~하다 get up; rise/ ~ 시간 the hour of rising; the turn out/~ 나팔 the reveille; the morning bugle. きしょう

기상(奇想) a fantastic idea; a fanciful notion/~ 천외의 fantastic. きそう

기색(氣色) a look; looks; a countenance 《표정》 an expression. きしょく

기색(基色) the three primary colours.

기생(妓生) a *kisaeng*[-girl]; a singing girl. ぎせい

기생(寄生) parasitism/ ~하다 be parasitic on; live upon[in]/ ~ 생물[충, 식물] a parasite. きせい

기서(奇書) a rare book; a strange book. きしょ

기서(寄書) ①《편지》 despatch of a letter; sending a letter/ ~하다 send[despatch] a letter ②《기고》a contribution; a communicated article/ ~하다 contribute to; write for. きしょ

기선(汽船) a steamship; a steamer/~으로 가다 go by steamer. きせん

기선(基線) 《측량》 the basic line. きせん

기선(機先) forestalling/~을 제하다 forestall; have the start of (*one*); be beforehand. きせん

기설(既設) ~의 established; existing/~ 선 lines in operation. きせつ

기성(既成) ~의 《물품》 manufactured ready-made(다 되어 있는); 《일》 completed; accomplished/~하다 be in existence/ ~복 ready-made clothes; a slop/~ 정당 existing political parties/~ 작가 an established writer. きせい

기성(期成) resolution to carry out (*a design*)/ ~회 an association for the realization (of *a plan*). きせい

기성(奇聲) a queer[peculiar] voice. きせい

기성(氣盛) high spirits[morale]; vigour /~하다 be in high spirits; be full of life[energy]. げんきがさかんであること

기세(氣勢) spirit; vigor; ardour/ ~를 꺾다 dispirit; discourage. きせい

기세(棄世) death; decease; passing [away]/ ~하다 die; decease. よをさること

기세 양난(其勢兩難) a dilemma; a predicament/ ~하다 be in a dilemma.

기소(起訴) 《형사》 prosecution 《민사》 litigation/ ~하다 prosecute[indict] (*one for*) 《민사》 bring an accusation[a sue] against /~장 an indictment/불~ 처분 a disposition not to institute a public action. きそ

기송(記誦) recitation/ ~하다 recite from memory; say by rote. きしょう

기송(寄送) sending; forwarding 《금전의》 remittance/ ~하다 send; forward; remit. きぞう

기수(技手) an assistant engineer. ぎしゅ

기수(奇數) an odd number/~일(日) days in odd numbers; odd days. きすう

기수(氣數) fate; destiny; luck; fortune.

기수(基數) a cardinal number. きすう

기수(旗手) a standard-bearer 《군대의》 an ensign. きしゅ

기수(機首) the nose of a plane/ ~를 남으로 돌리다 head for south. きしゅ

기수(騎手) a horseman; a rider 《경마의》 a jockey. きしゅ

기수(既遂) ~의 completion; consummation/consummated; perpetrated/ ~범 (犯) a consummated crime. きすい

기수법(記數法) [the scale of] notation.

기숙(寄宿) 《식사 제공》 boarding 《셋방》 lo

dging 《기식 및 숙사》 board and lodging /~하다 lodge[board] with one [at one's house]. きしゅく

기술(技術) art; technique; skill/ ~적 technical/ ~상 technically/ ~자 a technical expert; a technician. ぎじゅつ

기술(奇術) magic; jugglery; a sleight of hand. きじゅつ

기술(記述) description; an account/ ~하다 describe; give an account of/ ~적 descriptive; narrative. きじゅつ

기쓰다(氣—) do one's utmost; make every possible effort; spare no labo[u]r /기쓰고 with all one's might. もがく

기스락 the edge [of the eaves]/~물 eavesdrop. こうばいのほとり

기슭 the edge; the foot; the base; the border: the corner. こうばい

기습(奇習) a strange[rare] custom[habit]. きしゅう

기습(奇襲) a surprise [attack]; a sudden attack/ ~하다 make a surprise attack (on); storm. きしゅう

기습(氣習) manners; customs; practices. きふうとしゅうせい

기승(氣勝) ~한[스러운] unyielding; unbending; spirited; strong-minded/ ~한 여자 a woman of spirit; a strong-minded woman.

기승(奇勝) a place of scenic beauty; a beauty spot.

기승 전결(起承轉結) 〖文〗 the four steps in composition the introduction, the development of the theme, conversion and summing up. きしょうてんけつ

기식(氣息) breath; breathing/~ 엄엄(奄奄)하다 gasp for breath 《비유적》 be on one's last legs. きそく

기식(寄食) dependence; parasitism/ ~하다 live with (one at one's expense); hang[feed, live] on. きしょく

기신(起身) ①《일어섬》 rising to one's feet; standing/ ~하다 stand[get] up ②《관계를 끊음》 secession; withdrawal/~하다 secede[withdraw] from; break [away] from. たちあがること

기신거리다 move limply; stir languidly; be sluggish. えっちらおっちらする

기신없다(氣神—) be unenergetic in body and unsound in mind. きりょくがない

기신호(旗信號) flag signaling[semaphore] 《군속》 flag-wagging.

기실(其實) the fack; the truth; the real [the true] state of affairs/ ~은 in reality[fact]; really. そのじつ

기심(欺心) ~하다 deceive oneself; do violence to one's conscience.

기아(饑餓) starvation; hunger/~선 the verge of starvation. きが

기아(棄兒) 《버리기》 abandoning a child 《아이》 an abandoned child; a foundling. すてご

기악(器樂) 〖音〗 instrumental music/ ~ 편성법 instrumentation. きがく

기안(起案) drafting/ ~하다 draft; draw up in written form. きあん

기암(奇岩) a curious rock; rocks of strange formation /~ 괴석 fantastic rocks and stones. きがん

기압(氣壓) atmospheric[air] pressure / 고~ high atmospheric[air] pressure/ ~계 a barometer. きあつ

기약(期約) promise; pledge/ ~하다 promise; pledge. やくそく

기약(氣弱) delicate; health; a weak constitution/ ~하다 (be) of delicate health; constitutionally weak; faint hearted.

기약 분수(旣約分數) 〖數〗 a simple fraction. きやくぶんすう

기어(綺語) 《좋은 말》 flourishes; flowery language; bon mot(F); 《교묘한 말》 fair words; flattery. きご

기어이(期於—) by all meahs; under any circumstances. きっと

기억(記憶) memory; remembrance; recollection/ ~하다 《외고 있다》 remember 《기억에 남다》 remain in one's memory 《상기》 recall; recollect 《잊지 않도록》 bear (a thing) in mind 《암기》 memorize /~력 memory/~술 the art of memorizing/~ 상실증 loss of memory/ ~할 만한 memorable (day)/~ 착오 paramnesia/나의 ~으로는 as far as l can remember/~력이 좋다[나쁘다] have a good[poor] memory. きおく

기언(奇言) a paradox; a play of words; a sophism. どくぜつ

끼얹다 pour; shower (on, over); splash (on, over, about). さんぷする

기엄기엄 carwling (along); creeping (up, down, about); on hands and knees; on all fours. よつばいになって

기업(企業) an enterprise; an undertaking/ ~가(家) a man of enterprise /~심 a spirit of enterprise/ ~ 형태 a form[type] of enterprise/ ~ 조합 a syndicate/ ~ 합동 a trust/ ~ 연합 a cartel/ ~의 합리화 rationalization of enterprises. きぎょう

기업(起業) promotion (of an enterprise); organization/ ~하다 start an enterprise; promote[organize] an undertaking. きぎょう

기업(機業) the textile[weaving] industry. きぎょう

기여(寄與) contribution; service/ ~하다 contribute to; add to; do much to. きよ

기여(其餘) the rest. そのあまり

기역시(其亦是) [that is] also; too; as well; likewise; again. やはり

기연(奇緣) strange relation[affinity]; a strange fate[chance]; an irony of fate; a curious coincidence. きえん

기연(機緣) ①《기회》 chance; opportunity; occasion ②《인연》 relation. きえん

기연미연하다 (be) confusing 《모호하다》 ambiguous; be uncertain [whether…or

not]. そうかそうでないかはっきりしない
**기연히(期然—)** in any case; at all events; by any means; whatever may happen. きっと
**기염(氣焰)** tall[big] talk; bombast／~을 토하다 talk big; speak with great vehemence. きえん
**기예(技藝)** arts 《수예》crafts; accomplishments. ぎげい
**기예(氣銳)** spiritedness; impetuousness／~의 spirited; energetic; pushing.
**기온(氣溫)** [atmospheric] temperature／~의 변화 a change of[in] temperature／~ 조절 air conditioning. きおん
**기와** a tile／~집 a tile-roofed house／~ 공장 a tilery／~ 가마 a tile-kiln／~ 지붕 a tiled roof. かわら
**기와(起臥)** one's daily life／~하다 get up and lie down. きが
**기왕(旣往)** the past／~의 past; by-gone／~증(症) the medical history of a patient; anamnesia. きおう
**기외(其外)** the rest; the others. そのそと
**기요(起擾)** ~하다 raise a disturbance; start a riot.
**기용(起用)** appointment; reappointment／~하다 appoint; employ the service (of); promote; reappoint. きよう
**기우(杞憂)** imaginary fears; groundless apprehensions. きゆう
**기우(奇遇)** a chance[strange] meeting; a strange encounter／~하다 meet by chance; meet unexpectedly. きぐう
**기우(祈雨)** praying for rain／~하다 pray[offer prayers] for rain. きう
**기우(寄寓)** ~하다 live[stay, lodge] (with). きぐう
**기우(氣宇)** large-mindedness; magnanimity. きう
**끼우다** ①《사이에 넣다》put[hold] (a thing) between ②《삽입》get[put, let] in; fix into; insert (in) 《소켓 따위를》seal ③《박아 넣다》set in; inlay／창에 유리를 ~ fix glass in a window. さしこむ
**기우뚱거리다, 끼우뚱거리다** rock; totter; shake; roll; sway from side to side／기우뚱기우뚱[끼우뚱끼우뚱] rockingly; totteringly; shakingly. ぐらぐら
**기우듬하다, 끼우듬하다** (be) somewhat slanting[aslant, oblique]; slant; be inclined a little. ややかたむいている
**기운** ①《힘》[physical] strength; energy; force; might／~이 세다 be strong; be mighty／~이 빠지다 lose strength ②《원기》vigour; energy; spirits／~찬 vigorous; energetic／~을 내다 brace oneself up ③《기미》a touch; a dash; a shade; a tinge／감기 ~ a touch of cold／술~이 있다 be under the influence of liquor; be tipsy／붉은 ~이 돌다 be tinged with red. げんき
**기운(氣運)** 《경향・형편》a tendency; a trend／개혁의 ~을 조성하다 pave the way for a revolution. きうん

**기운(機運)** ①《기회》an opportunity; the time ②《운수》fortune; luck ③《경향》a tendency. きうん
**기운(氣韻)** 《멋》atmosphere (in art, literature); elegance; tone.
**기울** 《밀 따위의》bran; the inner chaff of grain. ふすま
**기울다** ①《경사》incline (to); lean (to); tilt 《비행기가》bank; tilt 《배가》heel over; list 《갑자기》lurch ②《쇠하다》decline; fall／운(運)이 ~ one's star is on the wane; be down on one's luck《사람이 주어》③《해・달이》decline (toward); sink ④《경향》tend to; be incliend to. かたむいている
**기울어뜨리다** incline; list; lean; tip 《기구를》tilt 《배 따위를》heel (over).
**기울어지다** ①《경사》incline, lean; tilt 《배가》list; heel over ②《해・달이》decline (toward); be going down ③《경향》tend (to); be inclined (to). かたむく
**기울이다** ①《일반적》incline; bend; lean 《기구 따위》tip; tilt; slant／고개를 ~ incline one's head／귀를 ~ listen (to); give ear (to) ②《주주》devote (oneself) to; direct (one's attention) to; concentrate (one's energy) on／그는 공부에 정력을 ~ He devote his energy[himself] to his studies. かたむける
**기웃거리다** repeatedly incline[lean]; busily crane[stretch one's neck]; frequently get a peep (at). しきりにのぞく
**기웃하다** (be) somewhat inclined.
**기원(紀元)** an era; an epoch／서력 ~ 1973년에 in the year 1973 [of the Christian era] (略: 1973 A.D.)／서력 ~ 전 B.C. (=Before Christ). きげん
**기원(祈願)** a prayer; a supplication; a petition／~하다 pray; supplicate; petition／~문 an optative sentence. きがん
**기원(技員)** an assistant engineer[technician].
**기원(起源, 起原)** origin; beginning; genesis／~하다 originate in; have its origin in. きげん
**기월(期月)** one full month.
**기위(旣爲)** already ᄃ이미. すでに
**기유(己酉)** 【민】the 46th binary term of the sexagenary cycle. きゆう
**기율(紀律)** discipline; order／~있는 disciplined; orderly. きりつ
**기음(氣音)** 《음성》an aspirate.
**기음기(記音器)** an oscillograph; a kymograph.
**기음 문자(記音文字)** phonetic letters[symbol]. ひょうおんもんじ
**기이(奇異)** ~하다 (be) strange; curious; queer; odd. きい
**기이다** conceal; keep secret. かくす
**끼이다** get between／잇새에 ~ get in between the teeth. はさまれる
**기인(奇人)** an eccentric [person]; an odd fish[duck]. きじん
**기인(起因)** the cause; the root／~하다

기인 150 기차다

originate in; have origin in. きいん
**기인(基因)** a fundamental cause/ ～하다 be principally caused by; be fundamentally attributable to. きいん
**기인(棄人)** an abandoned person 《폐인》a disabled person. はいじん
**기일(忌日)** an anniversary of *one's* death; a death-day. きじつ
**기일(期日)** a [due, fixed] date; the appointed day; a time limit. きじつ
**기입(記入)** entry 《용지에》filling up/～하다 enter 《공란에》fill up. きにゅう
**기자(記者)** a writer 《신문・잡지의》a journalist 《외국 기자》a reporter 《통신원》a correspondent 《편집자》an editor/～회견 a press conference[interview]/～클럽 a press club/～석 《의사당의》a press gallery 《경기의》a press stand 《연예의》a press box. きしゃ
**기자(譏刺)** cynicism; a satire/ ～하다 satirize; innuendo.
**기장¹** 《식》millet; Panicum miliaceum 《학명》. きび
**기장²** length ⇨길이. はば
**기장(記章)** a badge; an insignia; a medal. きしょう
**기장(機長)** an aircraft[a plane] commander, the captain of a plane; the crew chief.
**기장차다** (be) long and straight. まっすぐでながい
**기장하다(記帳—)** make an entry (in) 《대장에》post up accounts. きちょうする
**기재(奇才)** 《사람》a genius; a prodigy 《재주》peculiar[remarkable] talent; an extraordinary talent; a man of no common ability. きさい
**기재(記載)** statement; description/～하다 state; record; mention/～ 사항 mentioned items. きさい
**기재(機材, 器材)** machine supplies; machinery and parts. きさい
**기저(基底)** a base; a foundation. きてい
**기저귀** a diaper; a wet napkin; a swaddling cloth; clouts. おしめ
**기적(奇蹟)** a wonder; a miracle/ ～적[으로] miraculous[ly]. きせき
**기적(汽笛)** a steam whistle; a syren; a siren〈미〉. きてき
**끼적거리다** scribble; dash/종이에 몇 자 끼적거려 놓다 dash off a letter. かきちらす
**기전(其前)** beforehand ⇨그전. そのまえ
**기전기(起電機)** an electric motor. きでんき
**기전력(起電力)** electromotive force (略: EMF). きでんりょく
**기절(氣絕)** fainting; a swoon/ ～하다 faint [away]; go faint; swoon; fall unconscious; lose *one's* senses. きぜつ
**기절(氣節)** 《기개》spirit; pluck; selfrespect 《절조》constancy; fidelity; integrity; hono[u]r. しせつ
**기점(起點)** a starting-point. きてん
**기점(基點)** cardinal point. きてん
**기정(既定)** ～의 established; foregone; previously arranged/～ 방침 prearranged programme[plan]/～의 사실 an established[accomplished] fact; *fait accompli*(F). きてい
**기정(起程)** departure; start/～하다 depart [on a trip]; start; set out. たびだち
**기정(汽艇)** a steam launch.
**기제(忌祭)** a memorial service held on an anniversary of *one's* death. きさい
**기제(既濟)** ～의 paid-up; already settled [finished]. きさい
**기조(基調)** the key-note; the basis; the underlying tone. きちょう
**기존(既存)** ～의 existing/～ 시설 the existing facilities.
**기주(嗜酒)** love[fondness] for liquor; a taste for drink. さけをこのむこと
**기준(基準)** a standard; a basis/ ～ 임금 standard wages/～점[선, 면] a datum [base] point[line, plane]. きじゅん
**기중(其中)** among the rest 《가장》most ⇒그중. そのなか
**기중(忌中)** [in] mourning. きちゅう
**기중기(起重機)** a crane; a derrick; a hoist. きじゅうき
**기증(寄贈)** a presentation/～하다 present; contribute; donate/ ～자 a contributor; a donator; a doner/～품 a gift; a donation/ ～ 도서 a presentation [complimentary] copy. きぞう
**기지(既知)** ～의 [already] known; familiar; well-known/ ～의 사실 a well-known fact; an established fact/ ～수 a known number[quantity]. きち
**기지(機智)** wit; tact; resources/ ～가 풍부한 witty; tactful; resourceful. きち
**기지(奇智)** acumen; rare wisdom.
**기지(基地)** a base/작전 ～ a base of operations/ ～촌(村) a military campside town. きち
**기지개** a stretch/ ～켜다[하다] stretch *oneself*; straighten *one's* back; take a good stretch. からだをのばすこと
**기직** a coarse strawmat.
**기진(氣盡)** exhaustion; fatigue/ ～하다 be exhausted; be tired out; be worn out/～ 맥진 complete[utter] exhaustion. きりょくがつきること
**기질(氣質)** disposition; nature; temper; character; spirit/학생 ～ the student character. きしつ
**기차(汽車)** 《열차》a [railway] train 《객차》a railway carriage; a railroad car〈미〉/～로 by train; by rail[way]/올라[내려]가는 ～ an up[a down] train/～ 운임 railway fares/기찻길 a railway line/～표 a [railway] ticket/ ～를 타다 get into[on] a train; board a train 《미》; take[catch] a train/～에서 내리다 leave[get off] the train/ ～를 놓치다[시간에 대다] miss[catch] a train/～ 시간표 a railway time table. きしゃ
**기차다(氣—)** be struck dumb with amazement; be dumbfounded; be disgusted

**기찻길**(汽車—) a railway [line]〈영〉; a railroad track〈미〉. てつどう

**기채**(起債) flo[a]tation of a loan; issuance of bonds/~하다 float[raise] a loan; issue bonds. きさい

**기척** a sign; an indication/ 인~이 있다 show signs of people present. あいず

**기체**(氣體) a gaseous body; gas; vapour/ ~의 gaseous/~ 연료 gaseous fuel/ ~화하다 gasify; vapourize. きたい

**기체**(機體) 《동체》 a plane; a body; a fuselage. きたい

**기체후**(氣體候) [your] state[condition] of health. ごきげん

**기초**(基礎) the foundation; the basis; the base/~공사 groundmaking; foundation work/~ 과목[학과] the fundamental studies[courses]; primary subjects of study/문법의 ~ 지식 elementary knowledge of grammar. きそ

**기초**(起草) drafting/~하다 draft; draw up; make a draft. きそう

**기초 시계**(記秒時計) a stop watch.

**기총 소사**(機銃掃射) machine-gunning 《비행기에서》 strafing/~ 하다 strafe; machine-gun/~를 받다 be machine-gunned; be strafed. きじゅうそうしゃ

**기축**(氣縮) discouragement/ ~하다 be discouraged; be daunted.

**기축**(機軸) 《중추》 an axis; an axle 《방안》 a device; a plan. きじく

**기축**(己丑) 《민》 the 26th binary term of the sexagenary cycle. きちゅう

**기치**(旗幟) 《기》 a flag; a banner 《군기》 a standard/ ~를 선명히 하다 define one's attitude; one's show. きし

**끼치다**[1] 《소름이》 shudder; shiver; thrill (with horror); feel a thrill; feel a chill creep (over one); feel one's flesh creep (all over); be goose-flesh all over 《사람의》 make one's blood run cold; curdle one's blood/무서워서 소름이 ~ shudder in horror. とりはだがたつ

**끼치다**[2] ①《원인이 되다》 cause; make; render 《공헌하다》 contribute to; make a contribution to 《폐를》 trouble (a person) ②《후세에 전하다》 bequeath; transmit; leave. めいわくをかける

**기침** a cough; coughing/ ~하다 have a cough/ ~약 a cough medicine/마른 ~ a dry cough. せき

**기침**(起枕) rising [in the morning]/ ~하다 rise; get up; turn out; rise from one's bed. きしょう

**기타**(其他) the others; the rest; and others; miscellaneous. そのほか

**기탁**(寄託) deposit[ion] 《법》 bailment/~하다 deposit (a thing with a person); entrust (a person with a thing)/~자 a depositor; a truster. きたく

**기탄**(忌憚) reserve; hesitation/ ~없는 frank; outspoken; unreserved/ ~없이 without reserve; frankly; candidly/

~없이 말하면 to be frank [with you]; plainly speaking. きたん

**기통**(氣筒) a [steam] cylinder.

**기특하다**(奇特—) (be) praiseworthy; laudable; commendable/기특한 마음씨 a praiseworthy intention/기특하게도 자진해서 하겠다고 나섰다 He had the grace to offer to do it. きどくである

**기틀** the key point; the pivot. かぎ

**기펴다**(氣—) feel relieved; feel at ease; feel spirited; be animated. きがはれる

**기포**(氣泡) 《주물의》 a blow-hole 《유리의》 a bubble.

**기포**(氣胞) an air cell; an air bladder; 【식】 an air vesicle. きほう

**기폭**(起爆) detonation; detonator/ ~약 the initial explosive/ ~ 장치 a triggering device.

**기품**(氣禀) nature; temper; disposition; character. きひん

**기품**(氣品) dignity; nobility; grace/ ~있는 noble; dignified; graceful/ ~있는 사람 a refined gentleman(남자); a dignified lady(여자). きひん

**기풍**(氣風) character; disposition 《단체의》 morale 《정신》 spirits/국민의 ~ the traits of a nation. きふう

**기피**(忌避) ①《징병 따위의》 evasion; shirking/ ~하다 evade; shirk; shun; avoid/ ~자 an evader [of service]; a shirker/징병 ~ evasion of conscription ②《법률상의》 challenge; exception/ ~하다 challenge; except (against)/ ~ 신립 a motion for challenge/ 판사를 ~하다 refuse a judge; take exception to[against] a judge. きひ

**기필**(期必) assurance of fulfil[l]ment/ ~코 by any means; in any case; without fail/ ~하다 assure the fulfil[l]ment of; be determined to bring about. きっと

**기하**(幾何) ①《얼마》 how many[much] ②【수】 geometry/~학적[으로] geometrical [ly]/ 평면[해석] ~ plane[analytical] geometry/ ~학자 a geometrician/ ~급수 geometrical progression. きか

**기하다**(忌—) avoid; loathe. いむ

**기하다**(期—) ① 《예기하다》 ②《전망하다》 fix ③《자신》 be confident[certain, sure] (of, that) ④《결의》 determine (to do) ⑤《기약하다》 promise [to meet again].

**기한**(期限) a term; a period; a time limit; a deadline〈미〉/ ~부의 with a time limit/ ~이 지나다 pass a fixed term; expire. きげん

**기한**(飢寒) hunger and cold. きかん

**기함**(旗艦) a flag-ship. きかん

**기합**(氣合) ①《호흡이 맞음》 breathing in harmoney ②《기세·소리》 concentration of spirit; will power; a yell/ ~이 충만한 일격 a stroke full of vitality/ ~을 걸다 shout at (a person); mesmerize with a yell/ ~술 the art of mesmerizing[hypnotyzing] by one's will power

/단체 ~ disciplinary punishment upon a group. きあい
**기항**(寄航) a call at a port/ ~하다 call [touch, stop] (at); put in (at)/부산에 ~하다 touch at Busan. きこう
**기해**(己亥) 【민】 the 36th binary term of the sexagenary cycle. きがい
**기행**(紀行) an account of travels/ ~문 an account of one's journey; a travel decription. きこう
**기행**(奇行) a strange[an eccentric] conduct; an eccentricity/그는 ~으로 알려진 사람이다 He is notorious for his eccentricity. きこう
**기행렬**(旗行列) a flag procession.
はたぎょうれつ
**기형**(畸形, 奇型) deformity/ ~아 a deformed[malformed] child. きけい
**기호**(記號) a mark; a sign; a symbol 《음》 a clef. きごう
**기호**(嗜好) taste; liking; fancy; a preference (for)/ ~하다 have a taste[fancy] for; like. しこう
**기혼**(既婚) ~의 married/ ~자 a married man[woman]. きこん
**기화**(氣化) evaporation/ ~의 evaporative/~하다 evaporate; etheralize; gasify/~기(器) a carburettor; a vaporizer. きか
**기화**(奇貨) 《물건》 a curiosity; a rarity 《호기》 a rare[good] opportunity/ ~로 하여 taking advantage (of). きか
**기화**(奇禍) an accident; a disaster; a misfortune. きか
**기화 요초**(琪花瑤草) pretty[lovely] flowers. きかようそう
**기황**(饑荒) a famine ➾기근. ききん
**기회**(機會) an opportunity; a chance; an occasion/~을 출세할 ~ a chance in life /~ 주의 opportunism/~ 균등주의 the principle of equal opportunity/ ~주의자 a timeserver; a trimmer; an opportunist/ ~를 잡다〔놓치다〕 seize[miss] an opportunity. きかい
**기획**(企劃) planning; a plan/ ~하다 plan; make a plan. きかく
**기후**(氣候) climate; weather /온화한〔해양성, 대륙성〕 ~ a mild[maritime, continental] climate. きこう
**기후**(其後) 《이후》 after that; later; afterward; thenceforth 《이래》 since that; ever since. そのあと
**기휘**(忌諱) displeasure; offence/ ~하다 dislike; abho[u]r/~를 사다 incur the displeasure (of). きき
**끽** shrieking; shouting; yelling/ ~하다 give[let out] a yell; give a scream; shout.
**끽겁**(喫怯) being frightened/ ~하다 be frightened; be struck with horror.
ひじょうにこわがること
**끽경**(喫驚) astonishment; amazement; fright/~하다 (be) astonished; amazed; frightened. きっきょう
**끽고**(喫苦) suffering hardships; going through difficulties/ ~하다 go through difficulties; suffer hardships.
**끽끽** shouting one's head off; yelling away; shrieking; screaming/ ~거리다 shriek; scream; give a scream; screech; squeak.
**끽긴**(喫緊) ~하다 (be) very important 《중요》 vital 《긴급》 urgent; pressing; necessary. きっきん
**끽다**(喫茶) drinking tea/ ~하다 drink [take] tea/ ~점 a coffee shop; a tea house. きっさ
**끽반**(喫飯) eating[taking] a meal/ ~하다 eat; take[have] a meal.
**끽소리** a yell (of protest)/~ 못하다 be complete silenced can't say a thing.
**끽연**(喫煙) smoking/~하다 smoke [tobacco, a pipe]/~실 a smoking room; a smoking saloon. きつえん
**긴급**(緊急) emergency; urgency/ ~하다 (be) urgent; pressing; emergent; burning/~ 동의 an urgent motion/~ 대책 an urgent countermeasure/~ 문제 an urgent question. きんきゅう
**긴긴날** a long day. ながいながいひ
**긴긴밤** a very long night.
ながいながいよる
**긴담**(緊談) an important conference[talk; consultation]; a talk of vital importance. きんようなだんわ
**긴대답**(一對答) a long-drawn reply/ ~하다 make a long-drawn[drawled] reply. ながくのばしてするへんじ
**긴등** a long ridge. ながくつきだしたおか
**긴말** a long talk. ながいはなし
**긴맛** 〔어〕 a razor-shell[-clam].
**긴밀**(緊密) closeness; compactness/ ~하다 (be) close; compact. きんみつ
**긴박**(緊迫) tension; strain/ ~하다 (be) tense; straitened; acute/ ~한 국제 관계 a tense[straitened] international relationship. きんぱく
**긴병**(一病) a long illness; a lingering disease 《고질》 a chronic disease; a protracted disease. ながいあいだのびょうき
**긴사설**(一辭說) a lengthy[long-winded] talk; a tedious speech; a tirade; a long speech. くちかずのおおいはなし
**긴살** rump of beef. うしのしりにく
**긴소리** a long-drawn sound[voice].
**긴요**(要要) burning necessity; importance/~하다 important; essential; (be) necessary. きんよう
**긴용**(緊用) ~하다 make good use of (a thing). きんよう
**긴장**(緊張) strain; tension/~하다 be strained; be on the strain[the stretch] /~ 상태 tense situation. きんちょう
**긴절**(緊切) ~하다 (be) urgent; pressing; (be) of vital importance. きんせつ
**긴중**(緊重) ~하다 (be) important; main; momentous. ひじょうにかんようなこと
**긴짐승** reptiles; a snake.

**긴찮다**(緊—) (be) unimportant; of little necessity. きんようでない

**긴촉**(緊囑) an urgent request/ ~하다 request urgently.

**긴축**(緊縮) 《경제적》strict economy retrenchment; contraction/~하다 economize; retrench; practise austerity/~ 생활 an austerity life/~ 정책 a retrenchment policy. きんしゅく

**긴하다**(緊—) (be) of burning necessity; of vital importance. きんようだ

**긴헐**(緊歇) importance and unimportance. じゅうようとじゅうようでないこと

**깁다** 《펌프로》 draw; pump/우물 물을 ~ draw water from a well. すくいだす

**길**[1] 《높이》 the height of a man 《깊이》 a fathom. せのたかさ

**길**[2] ①《윤》 patina; polish ②《숙련》 skill; dexterity ③《짐승 등의》 tameness; domestication. つや

**길**[3] ⇨별항 참조(page 1349).

**길**[4] 《등급》 a grade; a class. とうきゅう

**길**[5] 《책의》 series(총시). ちつ

**길가** the roadside; the wayside. ろじょう

**길거리** a street; a road; an avenue(미); a thoroughfare. がいろ

**길경**(吉慶) a matter for congratulation; an auspicious event. おめでたいこと

**길경**(桔梗) Chinese balloon flower. ききょう

**길군** a skilled gambler. じゅくれんしたひと

**길길이** high/~ 뛰다 start up high with anger/~ 자라다 grow high. ぎっしり

**길나다** ①《도로가》 a road is open; a road runs ②《습관이 되다》 become accustomed [habitual] ③《윤나다》 become glossy; become skillful. くせになる

**길년**(吉年) a good[a banner; an auspicious] year. きつねん

**길눈**[1] 《방향 감각》 one's sense of direction. よくみちをみわけること

**길눈**[2] 《적설》 snow deep as a man's height.

**길다** ①《물건이》 (be) long/긴 다리 a long leg/긴 막대 a long pole/길게 하다 make longer; lengthen; draw long/길고 짧은 것은 대어 보아야 안다 A real test will prove who is stronger[better] at doing something. ②《시간이》 (be) long; lengthy/긴 세월 long year/긴 장마 a long rainy season/긴 눈으로 보면 in the long run/ 긴 눈으로 보다 be patient; wait and see; take a long[-range] view of/앞날이 길지 못하다 He will not last long./점점 밤이 길어진다 The nights grow longer little by little. /애기가 길어졌다 our talk took time/인생은 짧고 예술은 ~ Life is short, art is long./사람은 길게 두고 봐야 안다 It takes a long time to understand a person./해가 차차 길어졌다 The days are getting longer [gaining on the nights]. ながい

**길닦이** road repairing/ ~하다 improve [repair] a road. どうろのしゅうり

**길동무** a traveling companion; a fellow traveler/~하다 keep (a person) company; travel together. みちづれ

**길들다** ①《동물이》 grow tame; become domesticated[housebroken, trained]/길 든 tame; domesticated/길든 고양이 a tame[house broken] cat/길들지 않은 새 a wild bird ②《윤나다》 take a good polish; get a polish/노상 닦아서 마루가 길이 들었다 The floor has a shine from constant polishing ③《익숙해지다》 get accustomed to; grow familiar with.
じゅくれんする

**길들이다** ①《동물을》 tame; domesticate; subdue; charm (a snake); housebreak /길들인 원숭이 a trained monkey/야수를 길들이는 trainer of wild animals/말을 ~ break a horse to the rein; train[break in] a bronco ②《익숙하게 하다》 inure; habituate; accustom; make (a preson) used to/몸을 추위에 ~ inure oneself to cold/곤란한 일에 ~ inure (a person) to hardships; habituate (oneself) to difficulties; harden (a person) to trouble ③《윤나게 하다》 put a polish on; give a polish[shine, gloss] to; make (it) glossy/가구를 문질러 ~ give a polish to furniture by rubbing it.

**길라잡이** a guide [who show the way]. みちのあんないじん

**길래** forever; for good; long. ながく

**길례**(吉禮) a happy ceremony. きちれい

**길리다** be brought up; be bred; be fed; be reared/유모 손에 ~ be fed by a wet nurse. そだてられる

**길마** a pack-saddle/~짓다 put a packsaddle on; fix a packsaddle. にぐら

**길모퉁이** a street corner; a corner. かど

**길목** ①《골목의》 a corner; a turn; a turning; a street corner/~에 있는 가게 a corner store ②《중요한》 an important position[post]; the main[a strategic] point. みちのいりぐち

**길몽**(吉夢) a lucky dream. きちむ

**길미** interest on money. りそく

**길바닥** the roadbed; the road surface; the paving. みちばた

**길바로** on the right way[path]/~ 들다 go the right way.

**길벗** a fellow-traveler; a traveling companion. みちづれ

**길보**(吉報) good news; glad news tidings; a good word. きっぽう

**길사**(吉事) an auspicious event. きつじ

**길쌈** weaving / ~하다 weave [on a loom]/ ~군 a weaver. はりしごと

**길상**(吉祥) a good omen; a lucky sign; a favourable auspice. きっしょう

**길상**(吉相) lucky physiognomy. きっそう

**길섶** the edge of a road; the roadside; shoulder of a road. みちばた

**길속** the inner working[of a job, of a line of business, etc.].

**길손** a travel[l]er; a wayfarer. りょじん

**길안내**(—案內) showing the way; guida-

**길운** nce of the road 《사람》a guide／ ～하다 show (*a person*) the way; guide (*a person*) to the way.

**길운**(吉運) luck; good fortune. こううん

**길이**¹ length; extent／～ 10센티미터 with a length 10cm. ながさ

**길이**² (오래) long; forever; eternally; permanently／～길이 for a long long time／～ 세상을 등지다 turn *one's* back on the world forever. ながらく

**길인**(吉人) 《착한 사람》a good man 《다복한 사람》a lucky person. ぜんにん

**길일**(吉日) a lucky[a propitious; an auspicious] day; a day of good／～을 택하다 choose a lucky day. きつじつ

**길잡이** a guide; a trail blazer／학회의 ～ the guiding star of the scientific world. みちのあんない

**길제**(吉祭) a memorial service held the 27th month after *a person's* death.

**길조**(吉兆) a good[lucky] omen; a favourable sign. きつちょう

**길쭉길쭉** severally longish; so that there are several rather long (*one's*); with all [of them] rather long／～하다 (be) severally longish; be all rather long; [such that] each is on the long side／대를 ～ 자르다 cut a piece of bamboo in long sections.

**길쭉스름하다** (be) longish; somewhat long. ほどよくながい

**길쭉이** so that it is longish. ながく

## 길³

①(도로) a road (탄탄대로); a street (건물과 건물 사이의); 《가로수 길》avenue 《갈 길》a way 《가도·공로》a thoroughfare; a highroad; a high-way 《산의 샛길》a path; a pass; a lane; an aisle (통로) a passage (보도) a footway (경로) a route／～ 건너편 집 a house across the street[road, way]／지름～ a short cut／에움～ a roundabout way／～ 없는 들판 pathless fields／～ 가는 사람 a wayfarer／ ～을 내다 make[build] a road／ ～참하다 take a rest on *one's* way／ ～을 묻다 ask (*a person*) *one's* way／～을 잘못 들다 take a wrong road／ ～을 잃다 lose[miss] *one's* way; get lost／ ～을 가르쳐 주다 show[tell] the way (to *the station*)／～을 가로막다 stand in the way／ ～을 트다 clear the way (for *a person*); keep a passage／ ～을 비키다 make way for; get out of (*a person's*) way／ ～이 막히다 a road is blocked[comes to a dead end]／ ～이 나다 a road[way] is open; There is a road [runs].／다른 ～로 귀가하다 go home another way／먼 ～을 오다 come all the way (*from*)／정거장으로 가는 ～을 가르쳐 주십시오 Please show me the way to the station.／ ～을 고르다 level a road 《불도자로》 bulldoze／후진을 위하여 ～을 열어 주다 make way for *one's* juniors; give the younger people a chance／승진의 ～을 열다 keep the door open to promotion; give an opportunity for promotion／ ～을 치우다 clear the way (*for*); keep the passage open／이 ～을 곧장 가시오 Go straight along this street.／ ～을 비키시오 Get out of my way.／ 스스로의 ～을 가다 go *one's* way／승진을 향한 ～ an avenue for promotion／멸망의 ～ the way to ruin／안전한 ～ a safe course／그 ～밖에 달리 도리가 없다 There is no other way., We have no alternative.

②(방법) a means; a way 《취할 길》 a course; a step／생활의 ～ a means of livelihood／성공하는 ～ the road[way] to success／안전한 ～ a safe course／그것을 행하는 ～ the means[way] of doing it／살아나갈 ～이 막연하다 I don't know how to make a living., Can hardly find a means of livelihood.／알 ～이 없다 There is no way to find out., There is no telling.／…으로의 ～을 트다 pave the way for[to].

③(도중 …하는 김에) the midst of a way[course]; incidental to a course of action／…하는 ～에 on the (*one's*) way; en route (*to, for*); while; as; on the occasion; as a side event to; in addition to／학교 가는 ～에 on *one's* way to school／오는 ～에 만나다 meet (*a person*) on the way back.

④(가르침, 지켜야 할 도리) a way (of *behaving*, of *life*); a path (of *conduct*); a duty; a moral principle[doctrine]; truth; teachings; the true way／우리의 갈 ～ our path of duty／세속의 ～ the way of the world／사람의 ～ *one's* path of duty／길이 아닌 ～을 가다 err [stray] from the path of duty[righteousness]／공자의 ～ the doctrines of Confucius.

⑤(전문 분야의) a profession; a speciality; a line of business／그는 이 ～ [방면]의 전문가이다 He is an expert in this line[trade].

⑥(여정) distance; journey／20마일의 ～을 가다 go a distance of twenty miles.

**길쭉하다** (be) longish; somewhat long; rather long. ややながい

**길쯔막하다** be about longish enough; be quite longish. ながすぎる

**길쯤하다** considerably long.

**길짐** government goods transported in relay by peasants who live along a main road.

**길짐승** a beast. 地上をはいあるくけもの

**길차다** be densely grown 《높이》be grown to a great height.

**길처(一處)** the area bordering one's way. ろぼうのちかく

**길하다(吉一)** (be) auspicious; lucky; propitious; fortunate. めでたい

**길항(拮抗)** rivalry; contention; competition/ ~하다 rival; contend[compete] with; stand against. きっこう

**길흉(吉凶)** good or ill luck; fortune; rights and shadows. きっきょう

**김¹** 《먹는》lever; green seaweed/~을 재다《굽다》season[toast] seaweed.

**김²** ①《증기》steam; a fume; a reek/~이 무럭무럭 나다 be steaming hot/~을 쐬다 fume; fumigate ②《입·코의》breath/입~ breath/콧~ breath through the nose ③《냄새·맛》smell; taste; savo[u]r; flavo[u]r.

**김³** 《기회·바람》[on the] impetus (of); while; when; as; as long as/술~에 under the influence of alcohol/홧~에 빰을 갈겼다 I boxed his ears in a moment of anger[rage].

**김매다** weed [root out]. くさかりをする

**김빠지다** 《냄새 따위가》flatten; become flat; lose its flavour 《더운 김이》send forth vapour; evaporate; exhale/김빠진 술 stale wine. ゆげがなくなる

**낌새** secrets; delicate signs; hint; a delicate turn/~ 채다 sense; take hint (of); get scent (of). かんづき

**김의털** 《식》a sheep's fescue; Festuca ovina(학명).

**김장** pickled vegetables for meals/~하다 pickle vegetables in preparation for the winter. つけもの

**김지이지** Kim and Lee; certain persons; every Tom, Dick and Harry.

**김치** pickled vegetables pickles. つけもの

**깁** silk gauze. きぬ

**깁다** 《꿰매다》sew [together]; stitch; mend 《헝겊을 대고》patch up 《양말 따위를》darn. ぬう

**깁바탕** a piece of silk on which a painting[writing] is made.

**깁옷** a garment made of silk gauze. きぬでつくったいふく

**깁창(一窓)** a window screened with silk gauze.

**깃¹** 《양복의》a collar 《샤쓰 따위의》a neckband/선《접은》~ a stand-up[turned-down] collar/외투 ~을 세우다 turn up the collar of one's overcoat. えり

**깃²** ①《날개털》a feather, plumage/~솔 a feather brush/~이 난 feathered ② ⇒새집. はねとけ

**깃³** 《외양간의》litter; horse bedding/~주다 litter down; litter with straw.

**깃⁴** 《몫》a share; a portion.

**깃광목(一廣木)** unbleached muslin.

**깃다** be overrun with weeds. しげる

**깃다듬다** smooth down the feathers (of a bird).

**깃대(旗一)** a flagstaff. はたざお

**깃들이다** 《새가》nest; roost 《짐승이》lair 《비유적으로》lodge; dwell/건전한 정신은 건전한 신체에 깃들인다 A sound mind [dwells] in a sound body. ねぐらにつく

**깃발(旗一)** a flag; a banner.

**깃옷** a raw-cotton garment, worn for the first three months, of mourning one's parents. もふく

**깃이불** a feather quilt.

**깃저고리** clothes with no collar.

**깃주다** litter (a stall) down; litter with straw/외양간에 ~ litter a stable down. しきわらをしく

**깃촉(一鏃)** a quill

**깃털** feathers and hair; bird down.

**깃펜** a quill pen.

**깊다** ①《깊이가》(be) deep/깊이 deep[ly] /깊은 데 a depth; a deep place/깊이 파다 dig deep ②《짙다》(be) thick; dense /깊은 숲[안개] a dense forest[fog] ③《정도》(be) deep; intense; strong 《관계가》(be) close; fast/깊이 deeply; heartily; intensely/깊은 인상 a strong impression/깊이 사랑하다 love (one) deeply[dearly] ④《생각이》(be) deep; profound/ 깊은 학문 profound[deep] learning/깊은 생각 a deep thought; deliberation ⑤《잠이》(be) deep; sound; heavy/깊은 잠 a deep[sound; heavy] sleep/깊이 잠들다 fall fast into a deep sleep ⑥《밤이》(be) late/밤이 깊어서 late at night/밤이 깊어지다 grow late; advance; wear on. ふかい

**깊다랗다** (be) somewhat deep; rather deep. ひじょうにふかい

**깊드리** a low-lying paddy field.

**깊숙이** deep; far. おくふかく

**깊숙하다** (be) deep; retired. おくふかい

**깊이¹** 《명사》depth; deepness/~가 없는 shallow thoughtless《생각이 없는》/~ 6피이트이다 (be) six feet deep/애정[연못]의 ~ the depth of affection[a pond]/~가 있다 be deep; be profound. ふかさ

**깊이²** deeply; profoundly; thoroughly/ ~ 생각하다 think deeply/ ~ 파다 dig deep/~ 연구하다 study deep into [a subject]/~ 사귀다 establish a close friendship with; be intimate terms with /~ 사랑하다 love deeply[dearly, intensely]/~ 사랑하는 사이 be[fall] deeply in love with. ふかく

**나¹** I; myself/~의 my/~에게[를] me/~의 것 mine/~로서는 as for me; for my part.  わたくし

**나²** age ⇨나이.  とし

**-나** ①but; though ②whether… or.

**나가다** ①(밖으로) go out; get out; step out/산책~ go out for a walk ②(진출) go forth (*into*); enter upon (*a political carrer*); go upon (*the world's stage*) ③(퇴거) move out; get away; take one's leave/집을 ~ leave home; get out of the house ④(근무) work in; serve (*in*); be in the service of/관청에 ~ Be in the service of the government. ⑤(출근·출석) be present at; attend/회사에 ~ go to office ⑥(참가) take part (*in*); enter; go out (*for*)/올림픽에 ~ Take part in the Olympic games. ⑦(팔리다) sell; get sold/책이 잘 ~ A book sells[goes] well., A book is in great demand[has a large circulation]./잘 나가는 책 the top[best] seller ⑧(닳음·꺼짐) be out; be broken; be worn out/불이 ~ the [electric] light is out[cut off] ⑨(정신이) go out of one's mind; go mad ⑩(가치·무게가) be worth; weigh ⑪(비용) be spent; be paid out.  でていく

**나가떨어지다** be thrown[knocked] down; fall down on one's back/차에 매달렸다가 나가떨어졌다 He was shaken off the car.  ころげおちる

**나가둥그러지다, 나가둥그러지다** tumble; fall head over heels [and rolls].

**나가자빠지다** ①(자빠지다) fall flat on one's back; sink to the ground; tumble down; be thrown down ②(손을 끊다) retire; withdraw (*from*); back out of (*a scheme*).  てんとうする

**나깨** inner husk of buckwheat/~떡 a coarse cake made with buckwheat husks.  そばのないひ

**나귀** an ass; a donkey.  ろば

**나그네** a person away from home; a stranger 《여행자》a traveler; a wayfarer; a tourist 《방랑객》a vagabond; a wanderer 《손》a visitor; a guest; a passenger.  りょじん

**나긋나긋하다** ①(음식이) (be) tender ②(살결이) (be) soft ③(태도가) affable; mild; benign.  なめらかだ

**-나기** a person from…; a man just out of…/서울~ a person from[born in, arrived from] *Seoul*/풋~ an inexperienced person; a green hand.

**나나니벌** 《충》 a digger wasp; a mud dauber; *Ammophila infesta*(학명).

**나날이** day by day; day after day; every day; daily/날씨가 ~ 추워진다 It is getting colder day by day.  まいにち

**나녀(裸女)** a nude[naked] woman.  おんなのらしん

**나누다** ①(분할) divide; part; sever; split; whack (*up*) ②(분배) distribute; divide (*among*); share; allot ③(구별) distinguish; classify; sort out/세 항목으로 ~ classify into three items ④(함께 하다) share 《합석해서》 drink[eat] together./저녁을 ~ have dinner together.  わける

**나누이다** be[get] divided.  わけられる

**나눗셈** [a] division/~하다 divide.  わりざん

**나닐다** fly[hover] about.  とびまわる

**나다** ①(출생) come into being[existence]; be born; come into the world ⇒ 태어나다 ②(돋아남) grow; sprout; bud (*out*); come out/풀이 ~ the ground sprouts grass ③(명성·소문 따위) acquire; get abroad/이름이 ~ come to fame; win a fame ④(감정·생각 다위가) occur ⑤(생산) be produced; be raised[grown] ⑥(잘 생김) be handsome; be well-formed ⑦(구멍·길이) be made; be open[ed].  しゅっしょう

**나다니다** gad[wander] about; go[move] about.  てあるく

**나다분하다** (be) untidy.  ごたごたしている

**나달** four or five days; several days.

**나도(糯稻)** 《찰벼》 glutinous rice plants.

**나돌다** (밖에) wander about (*outdoors*) 《말·소문이》 get around.  さまよう

**나들다** come in and go out.  ていりする

**나들이** going out; an outing/~옷 a street dress; a visiting dress; one's best clothes.  がいしゅつ

**나라** ①(국가) a state; a nation; a country/~를 위하여 for the sake of one's country/~를 위하여 목숨을 던지다 lay down one's life for one's country ②(세계) a world; a realm.  くに

**나락(奈落)** Hell; the infernal region; t-

he bottomless pit. ならく
**나란히** in a row[line]; side by side/ ~ 서다 stand in a row/~ 앉아 sit side by side with/우로~ Right, dress!, E. yes right! ならび
**나랏님** the king; the sovereign; the ruler. おおさま
**나래**¹ (농기구) a soil leveler/ ~질 leveling soil with a soil leveler. まぐわ
**나래**² (노) an oar; a pair of oars. かい
**나력**(瘰癧) 【의】 scrofula; the king's evil.
**나련하다** (be) languid ⇨나른하다.
**나루** a ferry; a ferry point/~터 a ferry / 나룻전 ferriage/~를 건너다 ferry over; cross a river by ferryboat/~질 ferrying. わたし
**나룻** whiskers; a beard; a mustache/ ~이 석자라도 먹어야 샌님《속담》 Long beards alone cannot make a gentlemen. ほおひげ
**나룻배** a ferryboat/~ 사공 a ferryman; a ferrymaster/~로 건너다 cross a river by ferryboat; ferry across/~를 타다 take a ferryboat. わたしぶね
**나르다** (운반) carry; convey; transport; move; send/짐을 ~ carry luggage/날라 가다 carry away/석탄을 트럭으로 ~ transport coal by truck. はこぶ
**나른하다** ①(피곤)(be) languid; limp; weary; tired; be "all in"/더워서 몸이 ~ The heat makes me feel languid. / 길을 걸었더니 몸이 ~ I am all in after the walk. ②(연약)(be) feeble; delicate/몸에 나른한 여자 a woman of delicate build. けだるい
**나름** depending on/네 ~으로 as you please/그 ~대로 in its own way/값은 물건 ~이다 The price varies with the quality. から
**나릅** a four-year old [animal].
**나룻** the two main poles on a carriage; the shafts. ながえ
**나리**¹ (존칭) sir; gentleman; your honour. さま
**나리**² 【식】 a lily; Lilium(학명). ゆり
**-나마** if only; though; even/변변치 못하~ 이 선물을 받아 주기를 바라네 I would like to offer you this gift, though I know it will fail to meet your satisfaction. ―でも
**나마**(喇嘛) 【종】《나마승》 a lama/ ~교 Lamaism/ ~교도 a Lamaist; a Lamaite/~ 사원 a lamasery.
**나막신** [wooden] clogs. ぼくり
**나맥**(裸麥) rye ⇨쌀보리. はだかむぎ
**나머지** ①(남은 것) the rest; the remainder (잔금) the balance ②(넘침) excess /기쁜 ~ in the excess of one's joy; elated by joy. のこり
**나무** ①(수목) a tree; a plant ②(재목) wood; lumber(미) ③(뗄나무) firewood; fuel/~ 장수 a firewood dealer/나뭇군 a woodman; a woodcutter; one who gathers firewood/~하다 gather fire-

**나무라다** reprove; reproach; reprimand; scold; take to task/생바리 짚바리 나무란다《속담》There is nothing to choose [little difference] between them./그녀의 성격은 나무랄 데가 없다 Her character is without blemish. しかる
**나무람** a blame; a censure; a reproof.
**나무아미타불**(南無阿彌陀佛) 【종】Save us, merciful Buddha! (명복을 빔) May his soul rest in peace! ナムアミタブツ
**나무하다** gather firewood; cut firewood. たきぎをとる
**나물** ①(생것) herbs; wild greens; salad makings ②(무친 것) seasoned vegetables[greens]; a Korean salad/~국 soup with greens in it/ ~군 a herb-picker. おひたし
**나미**(糯米) (찹쌀) glutinous rice. もちこめ
**나박김치** pickled sliced radished seasoned with pepper, garlic, onion, ginger and celery.
**나발** a trumpet; a bugle ⇨나팔. らっぱ
**나발꽃** 《나팔꽃》a morning-glory. あさがお
**나방** 【충】 a moth/불에 날아드는 ~격이다 It is a case of a moth flying into a flame to death.
**나변**(那邊) where/그 이유가 ~에 있는가 Where is the reason? なへん
**나병**(癩病) 【의】 leprosy; Hansen's disease/~원 a leprosarium; a leper's home/~ 환자 a leper; a leprous patient/ ~ 환자 수용소 a leper colony. らいびょう
**나부끼다** fly; flutter; flap; wave/온 거리에 깃발이 나부끼고 있었다 Flags were flying all over the street. なびく
**나부랑이** ①(조각) pieces; bits; scraps; slips; strips; odd pieces/헝겊 ~ piece [scraps] of cloth ②(사람) a petty official. きれはし
**나부죽이** bending humbly; gently.
**나부죽하다** (be) rather flat; lowishflattish. ややひろいようだ
**나분이** [flying] low.
**나불거리다** flutter ⇨나붓거리다. ゆらぐ
**나불나불** ①(나부끼다) fluttering; flapping ②(혀를) wagging one's tongue; chattering. ひらひらする
**나붓거리다** flutter; flap; wave; sway; keep blowing. ゆらぐ
**나붓나붓** fluttering; flapping; blowing; wavering. ゆらぐ
**나붓이** gently; softly (앉다) coming down lightly.
**나쁘다** ①(못되다)(be) bad; evil; ill; wrong 《사악》 wicked 《해로운》 harmful; injurious (품질이) inferior 《건강이》 unwell (기억이) poor; weak (길이) rough (명이 나쁜) unsavory/나쁜 것 a wrong; an evil deed/나쁜 동무 bad companions /나쁜 소식 sad news/나쁜 징조 an bad omen ②(모자라다)(be) not enough; not satisfied; insufficient; inadequate; be too low. わるい
**나비**¹ a butterfly/ ~ 넥타이 a bow tie

**나비²** / ~류 the butterflies; *Rhopalocera* (학명) / ~ 매듭 a bowknot.

**나비²** 《폭》width [of cloth]; breadth [of cloth]. おりもののはばのたんい

**나삐** bad; ill; insufficiently; unsatisfactorily; not enough. わるく

**나비잠** the sleep of a baby with outstretched arms. あかんぼうがちょうかたをしてねむること

**나비잠(一簪)** 《비녀》a butterfly bodkin.

**나비춤** a butterfly dance; dancing in the manner of a flying butterfly. ちょうのおどり

**나사(螺絲)** ①《못》a screw ②《나선》a spiral / ~ 층층대 a spiral staircase; screw stairs / ~못 a screw / ~ 송곳 a single-twist drill; a screw auger. ねじ

**나사(羅紗)** wool[l]en cloth / ~점 woo[l]-len dealer; a woo[l]len draper. らしゃ

**나상(裸像)** a nude figure[statue].

**나상선(螺狀線)** a spiral; a helical curve.

**나서다** ①《나가 서다》get out of (나가다); go into(들어가다); enter upon(시작); run for (입후보) / 교문을 ~ get out of the campus; leave the school / 실업계에 ~ go into business / 정계에 ~ enter upon a political career ②《구하는 것이》 turn up; present *one*self / 희망자가 하나도 나서지 않았다 No one applied for it.

**나선(螺旋)** 《나사》a screw; a spiral / ~총 a rifle / ~ 운동 screw motion / ~ 추진기 a screw propeller / ~ 펌프 a screw pump. らせん

**나선상(螺旋狀)** screw-shape; spirality / ~ 계단 a spiral staircase / ~ 성운《천》 spiral nubula. らせんじょう

**나스르르하다** (be) soft; fluffy; tender; shaggy. けばだる

**나슨하다** (be) loose; not tight; slack ⇨ 느슨하다. ゆるんでいる

**나아가다** ①《진진》advance; proceed; march; go forward; move on / 한 걸음 ~ make[take] a step forward ②《진보》 advance; [make] progress; improve ③ 《좋아지다》change for the better; take a favo[u]rable turn. こうじょうする

**나아지다** become[get] better; change for the better; improve; be improved; take a favorable turn. よくなる

**나약(懦弱)** enervation; effeminacy / ~하다 (be) weak; soft and spiritless; feeble-minded emasculate. だじゃく

**나열(羅列)** an array; marshal[l]ing / ~하다 marshal; arrange in a row; set forth. られつ

**나오다** ⇨별한 참조(page 1353).

**나을거리다** wave; undulate. ひらひらする

**나위** ① 더할 ~ 없이 perfectly / …은 말할 ~도 없고 not to mention that… / 말할 ~도 없이 네가 잘못이다 Needless to say, you are wrong. ゆうい

**나이** age; years / ~가 지긋한 old; well advanced in age / ~ 탓으로 due to[because of] *one's* age / ~ 차례로 according to age / ~를 먹다 grow old; become older / ~보다 젊어[늙어] 보이다 look y-oung[old] for *one's* age. とし

**나이배기** one looking young for his age.

**나인** a court lady; a maid of honor; lady attendant in the palace.

**나자 식물(裸子植物)** a gymnosperm; *Gymnospermace*(학명).

**나전(一錢)** money offered to a god or to Buddha in proportion to the years of *one's* age.

**나전(螺鈿)** mother-of-pearl《미》; nacre / ~ 세공 mother-of-pearl work. らでん

**나전어(羅甸語)** Latin / ~ 학자 a Latinist; a Latin scholar. ラテンご

**나절** the period of about half the daylight hours / ~반 ~ a quarter day; a fourth of the day. ひるまのひととき

**나졸(邏卒)** a patrol; a patrolman.

**나종대** a kind of reed torch burned at the bride's house as a sort of ceremonial candle.

**나중** ①《명사》the last; the latter part; the end; the conclusion; the finish / ~ 기차 a later train ②《부사》lastly; in the end; in the long run; at last; finally; in the future / ~[에] 왔다 He came later. あとに

**나지리보다** (더기다) look down on; despise; scorn; hold (*a person*) in contempt; sneeze at《속》. さげすむ

**나지막하다** (be) somewhat low / 나지막한 소리 a low voice; an undertone; *sotto voce* (It) / 나지막한 집 a low-built house. かなりひくい

**나직(羅織)** a false charge[accusation] / ~하다 put (*one*) under a false charge; bring a false charge against (*one*); accuse (*a person*) of falsely.

**나직나직** in an undertone; in whispers; secretly; softly.

**나직이** somewhat low. ひくく

**나직하다** 《높이가》 be low 《키》 short 《소리가》low; soft; in an undertone; subdued 《신분이》humble; lowly; mean. ややひくい

**나체(裸體)** a naked[a nude] body; nakedness; nudity / ~의 naked; nude; 《발가벗은》stark naked / ~화 a nude picture. らたい

**나치(拿致)** custody; arrest / ~하다 take (*one*) into custody; arrest. らち

**나침(羅針)** a compass[magnetic] needle / ~ 방위 a compass bearing. らしん

**나침반(羅針盤)** a compass; a box-and needle. らしんばん

**나타나다** ①《출현》come out; turn up; appear; emarge / 현장에 ~ appear on the scene ②《표현》show itself; come out; be expressed / 얼굴에 ~ be shown in *one's* face ③《시야에》come in sight [into view] ④《발각되다》be found (*out*) come to light; be revealed; be proved

# 나 오 다

①(밖으로) come[go, get] out (of *the room*); step out; emerge (*from, out of, on*); appear; make *one's* appearance; turn up; come forward; present itself/집에서 ~ get out of the house; leave home/극장에서 ~ come out of the theater/물에서 ~ come[emerge] out of the water/장보러 ~ be out shopping/무대에 ~ appear on the stage/산책을 ~ come out for a walk/기차가 터널에서 나왔다 The train emerged from a tunnel. /밖으로 나오지 않다 Keep to *one's* house. /달이 나왔다 The moon has risen. /별이 ~ The stars appear in the sky. 사과가 시장에 ~ Apples appear on the market. Apples are out on the market. /집을 나온 지 3년이다 It is already three years since I left home. /그 시대에는 많은 영웅이 나왔다 The age was productive of many heroes.

②(석방) be released/그는 교도소에서 갓 나왔다 He has just been released from prison.

③(싹이) shoot; sprout; bud/나무의 싹이 나오기 시작했다 The trees have begun to bud.

④(문제가) be given/시험에 다섯 문제가 나왔다 Five questions were given in the examination.

⑤(통하다) lead to; come to/이 길을 따라 곧장 가면 시장이 나온다 This road leads you to the market.

⑥(말이) be said[spoken, uttered] (버릇이) be revealed; assert[reveal, betray, express] itself; peep out; come out /고약한 버릇이 ~ *one's* bad habit peeps [crops] out/사투리가 ~ *one's* provincial dialect comes out[shows itself] /불멘 소리가 ~ angry words are spoken[uttered]/예의 고집이 ~ *one's* usual stubbornness asserts itself.

⑦(음식이) be served; be brought out; be given as a treat/술과 밥이 나왔다 We were treated with wine and food. /회합이 끝나고 다과가 나왔다 Fruit and cakes were served after the meeting. /저녁에는 비프스테이키 나왔다 Beefsteak was served at dinner.

⑧(액체가) flow out; run out; issue [forth]/샘물이 ~ a spring[fountain] flows/눈물이 ~ tears flow[fall]; tears come to *one's* eyes/굴뚝에서 연기가 ~ Smoke issues[rises] from the chimney. /콧물이 나오다 *one's* nose runs/하품이 ~ It makes me yawn. /재채기가 ~ have a fit of sneezing/상처에서 피가 나오고 있다 Blood is running from his wound.

⑨(발행) be out; come out; be published[issued, brought out]; be given to the world/책이 갓 나왔다 The book has just been published. /사전이 매일같이 새로 나온다 New dictionarys come out almost every day. /다음호가 곧 나온다 The next number will be out soon.

⑩(책·신문 따위에) appear[come out, be reported]; be found / 그런 말은 어느 책에나 나와 있다 The word is found [given] in any books. /신문에 ~ be in the paper/사전에 나와 있다 Be given [found] in a dictionary. /어떤 신문에 나왔소 What paper did it come out in?/그 강은 지도에 안 나와 있다 The river is not on the map.

⑪(졸업하다) graduate (*from, at*⟨영⟩); be graduated; finish ⇨졸업/학교를 ~ finish[graduate from] school/김군은 어느 대학을 나왔나?—서울대학교라고 하더군요 What university did Mr. Kim graduate from?—I hear that he graduate from Seoul University.

⑫(출석) be present (*at*); attend; put in *one's* appearance/그는 교회에 나오지 않았다 He was not present at the church. /그는 매일 학교에 나온다 He attends school every day.

⑬(참가) join; take part in; participate (*in*); enter; be entered (*in, for*); launch into/정계에 ~ enter upon a political career/시합에 ~ take part [participate] in a game/선거에 ~ run for an election/북한도 올림픽에 나온다 North Korea is also taking part in the Olympic games.

⑭(없어졌던 물건이) turn up; be found [restored]; get (*a thing*) back/잃어버렸던 책이 나왔다 The book which was lost has been found. /잃어버렸던 돈이 서랍에서 나왔다 The money I thought I had lost turned up in the drawer.

⑮(재배·산출) be raised; grow; be produced; be found; be turnen out/이 지방에서는 복숭아가 많이 나온다 The country produced a lot of peachs. /산에서는 많은 텅스텐이 나온다 Tungsten is found in the mountains.

⑯(사직) resign (from *one's office*); quit/회사에서 ~ leave[resign from] a company.

⑰(근원) come of[from]; originate in; be derived from; stem from/그 말이 누구에게서 나왔는가 Who started[first told] the story?/이 소식은 믿을 만한 소식통으로부터 나왔다 The news was obtained from reliable sources. /비용은 어디서 나오느냐 Who is to pay the expenses?/이 말은 라틴에서 나왔다 This word is of Latin origin. /질투에서 나

은 싸움 a quarrel originating in jealousy/확신에서 나오는 용기 courages springing from conviction/우리는 한 조상으로부터 나왔다 We are descended from a common ancestor.
⑱《태도》 assume (*an attitude*); take (*a move*)/그가 어떻게 나올지 볼 만하다 Let's wait and see what move he will take. /그런 태도로 나올 줄은 정말 몰랐다 His attitude was quite contrary to my expectations.
⑲《돌출》 project; stick out; protrude; jut out/이마가 ~ have a prominent forehead/눈이 툭 불그려져 나왔다 His eyes protrnde./윗니가 쑥 나왔다 His upper teeth projected./못대가리가 나왔으니 쳐 박아라. Hit the nail on the head, as it is out.
⑳《결과》 의 답이 여간해서 안 나온다 It is impossible to solve the problem./8을 4로 나누면 2가 나온다 Eight divided by four gives two.
㉑《노출》 be exposed/그의 책상 밑에서 발이 ~ legs stretch out of his desk.
㉒《출몰》 be infested[haunted] (*by*)/유령이 ~ a ghost walks[haunts the place]/유령이 나오는 집 a haunted house.

/본성이 ~ reveal the nature ⑤《언급》 mention/미국 문헌에 나타난 한국 Korea mentioned in American literature ⑥《알려지다》 become known. あらわれる
**나타내다** ①《표시》 show; indicate; manifest 《증명》 prove; speak for/성격을 ~ show the character ②《노출》 disclose; reveal; betray/정체(正體)를 ~ betray *one*self ③《표현》 express; describe ④《대표》 represent; stand for ⑤《상징》 symbolize ⑥《뚜렷이하다》 distinguish/두각을 ~ distinguish *one*self; cut a conspicuous figure. あらわす
**나태**(懶怠) idleness; laziness; indolence /~하다 lazy; idle; indolent; slothful; sluggish. なまけおこたること
**나팔**(喇叭) a bugle; a trumpet; a horn /~수(手) a bugler; a trumpeter/~불다 blow[sound] a trumpet 《술 따위를》 drink [beer] from a bottle. らっぱ
**나팔꽃**(喇叭—) a morning glory. あさがお
**나팔관**(喇叭管) 《해》 the oviduct; the trumpet/~염 salpingitis. らっぱかん
**나포**(拿捕) arrest; capture; seizure/~하다 arrest; capture; seize; make prize of/~선 a prize. だほ
**나푼거리다** flutter lightly; wave; flap gently. かるくひらめく
**나풀거리다** flutter[flap] roughly/나풀나풀 fluttering roughly. はためく
**나한**(羅漢) 《종》 the Buddha's disciples [followers]; *Arhan*(Sans). らかん
**나화**(裸花) 《식》 an achlamydeous flower.
**나획**(拿獲) capture; seizure; arrest/~하다 capture.
**나흗날** the fourth day of the month.
**나흘** ①《4일》 four days ②《나흗날》 the fourth [day] of the month. よっか
**낙**(樂) pleasure; delight; joy 《행복》 happiness 《향락》 enjoyment 《오락》 amusement/~으로 삼다 take pleasure in/낚시질을 ~으로 삼다 delight in fishing. らく
**낙가**(落價) a fall in price; a reduction of price/~하다 fall [off]; drop; come down; depreciate. ねだんがさがる
**낙관**(落款) [a painter's] sign and seal; [a writer's] signature/~하다 sign [and seal]; affix *one*'s signature[seal] /작자의 ~이 있다 bear a writer's[painter's] signature. らっかん
**낙관**(樂觀) optimism; an optimistic[a rosy, a hopeful] view; the bright side of things/~하다 be optimistic; take an optimistic[a hopeful] view (*of*); look on the bright side; take things easy/~적 optimistic/~론 an optimistic[rosy] view. らっかん
**낙구**(落句) the concluding[last] line of a poem. らっく
**낙길**(落—) a missing[lacking] volume. ひとそろいにならないほん
**낙낙하다** (be) enough; big enough; sufficient; adequate ⇒넉넉하다. ゆたかだ
**낙농**(酪農) dairy [farming]/~장 a dairy farm; a milk ranch/~ 제품 dairy products[produce]. らくのう
**낚다** ①《고기를》 angle [for fish]; fish with rod and line; catch ②《꾀다》 decoy; allure; entice. つる
**낙담**(落膽) discouragement; disappointment; despondency/~하다 be[get] discouraged; be disheartened[dispirited]; lose heart; be disappointed (*in*) /~시키다 discourage. らくだん
**낚대** a fishing rod. つりざお
**낙도**(落島) a remote[distant] island; a deserted island.
**낙락 장송**(落落長松) a tall and exuberant pine tree; a pine tree with trailing branches.
**낙뢰**(落雷) the falling of a thunderbolt /~하다 be struck by a bolt of lightning《맞는 것이 주어》; a thunderbolt falls《벼락이 주어》. らくらい
**낙루**(落淚) the shedding[dropping] of tears; weeping/~하다 shed tears; be moved to tears; weep. らくるい
**낙마**(落馬) falling from a horse; a fall from a horse/~하다 fall from[be thrown off] *one*'s horse. らくば
**낙망**(落望) despair; discouragement/~하다 despair (*of*); lose *one*'s heart; be discouraged. しつぼう
**낙명**(落命) losing *one*'s life; death/~하다 die; lose *one*'s life 《재난으로》 be killed (in *a traffic accident*). しぬ
**낙명**(落名) losing *one*'s reputation/~하다 lose *one*'s reputation; disgrace *one*'s

**낙방**(落榜) failure in an examination/ ~하다 fail in an examination; get plucked 《영·속》. らくだい

**낙백**(落魄) ①《영락》 reduced circumstances/ ~하다 sink in *one's* fortunes; descend in the social scale ②《넋을 잃음》 abstraction; stupefaction/ ~하다 be distrait; be stupefied; be entranced. おちぶれること

**낙사**(樂事) an amusement; a pleasure; a joy; a hobby. たのしいこと

**낙산**(酪酸) 【화】 butyric acid/ ~염(鹽) butyrate.

**낙상**(落傷) a hurt[bruise] from a fall/ ~하다 get hurt from a fall; fall and hurt *oneself*. たおれてけがをすること

**낙서**(落書) ①scribbling; a scrawl/ ~하다 scribble; on the wall scrawl ②《빠뜨리고 씀》 omission; skipping/ ~하다 omit; skip. らくがき

**낙선**(落選) 《선거의》 defeat[failure] in an election 《출품의》 rejection/ ~하다 be defeated in an election; be rejected/ ~ 의원 an unsuccessful candidate [for the Assembly]/ ~자 a defeated/ ~작 a rejected work. らくせん

**낙성**(落成) completion/ ~하다 be completed; be finished/ ~식 an inauguration[a completion] ceremony. らくせい

**낙수**(落水) eavesdrops ⇒낙숫물.

**낙숫물** raindrops [falling from the eaves]; eavesdrops/ ~ 소리 pattering of raindrops. あまだれ

**낚시** a [fish] hook/ ~를 드리우다 drop a line/ ~에 미끼를 달다 bait a hook; put a bait on a fishhook. つり

**낚시찌** a float; a cork; a quill; a buoy; a bob. うき

**낚시질** fishing; angling/ ~하다 fish; angle for fish. つり

**낚시터** a place for angling; a fishing place.

**낙심**(落心) disappointment; discouragement; despondency; despair/ ~하다 be disheartened; be discouraged/ ~천만하다 be much disappointed; be thrown into despair. ちからをおとすこと

**낚싯거루** a fishing boat[skiff]. つりぶね

**낚싯군** an angler; a waltonian; a fisherman. ちょうじん

**낚싯대** a fishing-rod; an angling rod.

**낚싯밥** a bait/낚시 바늘에 ~을 달다 fix a bait on the hook. えさ

**낚싯줄** a fishing-line; a fishline. つりいと

**낙엽**(落葉) fallen[dead] leaves/~기(期) defoliation/ ~색(色) yellowishbrown /~송(松) a larch tree/ ~수 a deciduous tree/~을 긁어 모으다 rake up dead leaves. おちば

**낙오**(落伍) straggling 《인생의》 a failure /~하다 straggle; drop[fall] behind; fall away[off]/~자 a straggler 《인생의》 a failure/인생의 ~자가 되다 make a failure of *one's* life. らくご

**낙원**(樂園) a paradise; Eden; Elysium. らくえん

**낙인**(烙印) a brand[-mark]; a stigma/ ~을 찍다 brand; stigmatize. らくいん

**낙일**(落日) 《태양》 the setting sun 《일몰》 sunset; sundown 《미》. らくじつ

**낙자**(落字) a missing word; an omission. おとしじ

**낙장**(落張) missing pages; a missing leaf. ほんのまいすうがかけていること

**낙장거리** falling outstretched on *one's* back/~하다 fall down outstretched on *one's* back. だいのじにひっくりかえること

**낙제**(落第) elimination 《실패》 failure 《거부》 rejection/ ~하다 fail in an examination; get plucked《속》. 《원급 잔류》 stay back in the class 《검사에》 be rejected. らくだい

**낙조**(落照) the setting sun; sunset; rays of the setting sun. ゆうひ

**낙종**(落種) sowing; seeding/~하다 sow seeds; seed. たねをまくこと

**낙지** 《어》 a small octopus; *Octopus vulgaris*《학명》. いいだこ

**낙지발송장개구리** 【동】 a reddish frog; *Ranatemporaria Coreana* 《학명》.

**낙질**(落帙) a wanting volume.

**낙차**(落差) 《물》 a head; a fall; a water level/고[저]위 ~ a high[low] head/ 유효 ~ an effective head. らくさ

**낙착**(落着) a settlement; an end; a conclusion/ ~하다 be settled; come to a conclusion; come to an end/~짓다 settle; bring 《a matter》 to an end[a close]. らくちゃく

**낙찰**(落札) a successful bid; awarding of a contract/~하다 make a successful bid; be awarded a contract; have *one's* tender accepted; have 《*an article*》 knocked down to 《*a person*》/~인 a successful bidder/ ~가(價) a contract price; the highest bid price/ ~물 an object knocked down. らくさつ

**낙천**(樂天) optimism/ ~가 an optimist; an easygoing person/~주의 optimism /~지 a paradise 《오락지》 an amusement center. らくてん

**낙체**(落體) 【물】 a falling body.

**낙타**(駱駝) 【동】 a camel/ ~직(織) mohairs/ ~털 camel's hair/단봉[쌍봉] ~ an Arabian[a Bactrian] camel. らくだ

**낙태**(落胎) 《의》 an abortion; a miscarriage/ ~하다 have an abortion; commit foeticide/인공 ~ an induced abortion/ ~약 an abortive [medicine]/ ~ 수술 an illegal operation. りゅうざん

**낙토**(樂土) paradise; Heaven; Elysium /지상 ~ an earthly paradise. らくど

**낙하**(落下) falling; dropping; descent/ ~하다 drop; fall[come] down [to the ground]; descend; make a descent/ 나선 ~ a corkscrew descent. らっか

**낙하산**(落下傘) a parachute/ ~ 부대 a

parachute troop; a paratroop/ ~병 a parachutist/~으로 내리다 make a parachute descent. らっかさん

낙한(落汗) lowering of fever after perspiration/ ~하다 the fever goes down after perspiration; sweat out fever. あせがでてねつがさがること

낙향(落鄕) rustication/~하다 rusticate; leave the capital for the country.

낙형(烙刑) burning the skin with a hot iron to punish a criminal; branding as punishment. ひあぶりのけいばつ

낙화(落花) the falling of blossoms 《진 꽃》 fallen[scattered] blossoms 《지는 꽃》 falling blossoms[petals]/ ~하다 flowers[petals] fall[scatter]; blossoms scatter. らっか

낙화(烙畫) a poker work[picture]; a poker engraving. やきえ

낙화생(落花生) a peanut; a groundnut; a pignut; a monkeynut(영). らっかせい

낙후(落後) falling behind/ ~하다 fall behind (others); drop[fall] out of line [the ranks]; drop out. らくご

난(亂) a disturbance; a war. らん

난(難) ①《접미어》 trouble; difficulty/식량 ~ difficulty in securing foodstuffs /주택 ~ a shortage of houses ②《접두어》 difficult; troublesome/~문제 a hard question[problem].

난(欄) ①《신문 따위의》 a column ②《기입란》 a blank; a column; a space/광고 ~ the advertisement column./운동 ~ the sports section[column page]. らん

난가(亂家) a family in turmoil; a disturbed family. へいわでないうち

난각(卵殼) an egg-shell.

난간(欄干) a railing; a rail 《계단의》 a balustrade/다리의 ~ a bridge-railing /배의 ~에 기대다 lean over the rail of a ship. らんかん

난감(難堪) ~하다 《견디기 어려움》 (be) unbearable; intolerable 《다루기 힘든》 insufferable; hard to deal with; be quite at a loss. たえにくいこと

난거지든부자(一富者) a person who puts up a front of poverty but is really rich. みせかけのびんぼうじん

난공 불락(難攻不落) impregnability/ ~의 impregnable; inexpugnable/ ~의 요새 an impregnable fortress/ ~이다 be hard of approach; defy attack. なんこうふらく

난공사(難工事) difficult construction work. なんこうじ

난관(難關) a barrier; an obstacle; a difficulty 《교착》 a deadlock; the crux of the situation/ ~을 돌파하다 overcome a difficulty. なんかん

난국(難局) a difficult[grave] situation [position]; a crisis. なんきょく

난국(亂國) a disturbed[disrupted] nation. みだれているくに

난군(亂軍) 《혼란에 빠진 군대》 a routed army. きりつがないぐんたい

난낭(卵囊) 【해】 an ovisac; an egg sac.

난다긴다하다 (be) nimble; smart; be quick[alert talented smart sharp; nimble]/난다긴다하는 사람 a man of great ability.

난당(亂黨) rioters; a mob; insurgents; rebels. じたいをこんなんさせるととう

난대(暖帶) 【지】 the subtropical zone; the subtropics. だんたい

난데없다 (be) unexpected; sudden; abrupt 《무근거》 unfounded; be out of the blue/난데없이 unexpectedly; abruptly; to one's surprise; all of a sudden; without warning 《당치 않게》 unreasonably; absurdly/ ~ 나타나다 make an abrupt appearance. でどころがわからない

난도질(亂刀一) mangling; hacking 《고기를》 mincing/ ~하다 mangle; hack to pieces. めちゃくちゃにつきさすこと

난독(亂讀) desultory reading/ ~하다 read desultorily; devour/ ~가(家) an omnivorous reader; a glutton for books.

난동(亂動) a thoughtless undertaking; an ill-considered attempt; a disturbance. みだりにこうどうすること

난든집나다 get practised; acquire skill; master; be[come] an old hand (in); be at home (on). てなれたぎじゅつ

난로(煖爐) a [heating] stove; a fireplace /석유 ~ an oilstove/전기 ~ an electric heater. だんろ

난류(暖流) a warm current. だんりゅう

난리(亂離) 《전쟁》 a war 《반란》 a revolt; a rebellion 《소요》 disturbance; tumult; riot; an uproar 《혼란》 confusion; commotion. ふんそう

난립(亂立) 《난잡》 disorderliness; confusion 《입후보자의》 running[standing] for election in a disorderly array/ ~하다 be all running for election at once; be adding to the election confusion/ 후보자 ~을 막다 check random candidacy. らんりつ

난마(亂麻) 《어지러운 상태》 chaos; anarchy/쾌도로 ~를 끊다 cut the Gordian knot; solve a knotty problem once and for all. もつれたあさ

난만(爛漫) splendo[u]r; luxuriance; being in full bloom; glory (of flowers)/ ~하다 (be) full-bloom; be at their glory [best]; glorious; splendid. らんまん

난망(難忘) unforgettable[ness]/ ~이다 be unforgettable. わすれにくいこと

난맥(亂脈) disorder; confusion; chaos/ ~상을 나타내다 be thrown into disorder; fall into chaos. らんみゃく

난무(亂舞) a wild dance; a boisterous dance/ ~하다 dance boisterously[wildly]. らんぶ

난문제(難問題) a difficult[hard, tough]; a knotty problem[subject]; a crux; a poser. なんもんだい

**난민(難民)** the destitute 《이재민》 sufferers 《피난민》 refugees/~ 구제 refugee relief; the relief of the destitute; aid to the destitute/~ 정착 사업 a refugee resettlement project. なんみん

**난반사(亂反射)** 〖물〗 diffused reflection. らんはんしゃ

**난발(亂發)** ①《총포의》 random[reckless] firing/~하다 fire[shoot] at random ②《증서의》 an indiscriminate issue; an overissue/~하다 issue in discriminately[recklessly]/어음의 ~ an over issue of bills. らんぱつ

**난발(亂髮)** dishevelled[ruffled, unkempt, uncombed] hair. みだれかみ

**난방(暖房)** 《데움》 heating; heater/~ 장치 a heating apparatus[system, arrangement]/~계(係) a janitor〈미〉 a caretaker/~ 시설 heating equipment/~차 a heater car/지역 ~ district heating. だんぼう

**난백(卵白)** the white [of an. egg]; the albumen. らんぱく

**난벌** a street dress; street wear; clothes for the street; one's best clothes; one's Sunday best. がいしゅつふく

**난봉** dissipation; debauchery; loose habits/~장이 a libertine; a prodigal; a debauchee; a Lothario/~부리다 live fast; lead a dissipated life/~나다 take to fast living; fall into evil ways. ほうとう

**난부자든거지(一富者一)** a person who puts up a front of wealth but is really poor. みかけうえのかねもち

**난비(亂飛)** fluttering[flying] wildly around/~하다 flutter[fly] around wildly[boisterously]. みだれとぶこと

**난사(亂射)** random firing/~하다 fire blindly[at random]. らんしゃ

**난사(難事)** a difficult matter[thing]; a difficulty; a hard task [undertaking]; a tough job. なんじ

**난사람** an outsanding[a prominent distinguished person, a remarkable person; prodigy. えらいひと

**난산(難産)** hard labo〔u〕r; a difficult delivery[birth]/~하다 have a difficult delivery; have a hard labo〔u〕r.《사물》 bring forth with difficulty. なんざん

**난삽(難澁)** hardship; difficulty/~한 hard; difficult. なんじゅう

**난색(難色)** disapproval; reluctance; unwillingness/~을 보이다 show disapproval; be opposed [to a plan]; hesitate [to do]. なんしょく

**난생(卵生)** 〖생〗 oviparity; oviparousness/~하다 bear [offspring] by egg; be oviparous/~ 동물 an oviparous animal/물고기는 ~이다 Fish are produced from eggs. らんせい

**난생처음(一生一)** for the first time in one's life; in all one's born days/~ 보는 사람 an utter stranger/~ 당하다 experience for the first time in one's life. うまれはじめ

**난생후(一生後)** after one's birth; since one's birth; this side of one's birth. うまれたいご

**난세(亂世)** troublous[troubled] times; turbulent days/~의 영웅 a hero in a warlike ages. らんせい

**난세포(卵細胞)** 〖생〗 an egg cell; an ovum.

**난소(卵巢)** 〖해〗 an ovary; the ovarium/~선 a nidamental gland/~염 ovaritis/~ 호르몬 ovarian hormones.

**난숙(爛熟)** ①《과일》 overripeness; overmaturity/~하다 (be) overripe; overmature ②《성숙의 극》 full maturity; full development; mellow ripeness/~하다 attain full maturity; reach complete maturity; (be) mature/~한 highly-developed. らんじゅく

**난시(亂視)** 〖의〗 astigmatism/~의 astigmatic/~ 안경 astigmatic glasses/~ 안 astigmatic eyes. らんし

**난시(亂時)** troublous times; turbulent days. みだれたじだい

**난신(亂臣)** ①a traitorous[treacherous] subject; a rebellious[mutinous] subject; a traitor ②《난세의 충신》 a loyal subject in turbulent days/~ 적자(賊子) rebellious statesman and ungrateful sons; inhuman wretches; traitorous. らんしん

**난심(亂心)** mental derangement; distraction; insanity. らんしん

**난외(欄外)** the margin 《신문의》 a marginal column/~ 기사 stop press news /~ 제목 a running title. らんがい

**난용(亂用)** misuse; abuse/~하다 abuse; misuse; misappropriate; use improperly[unlawfully]; divert. らんよう

**난원형(卵圓形)** an eggshape; ovalness; an ovoid figure. らんえんけい

**난의(暖衣)** warm clothes. だんい

**난이(難易)** hardness and[or] easiness; [relative] difficulty; hardness/일의 ~에 따라 according to the relative difficulty/일의 ~에 달려 있다 depend on how difficult the work is. なんい

**난입(亂入)** intrusion; trespass; forced entry/~하다 break into; intrude; trespass; force one's way into/~자 an intruder; a trespasser. らんにゅう

**난자(卵子)** 〖생〗 an egg cell; an ovum (pl. ova);《식물의》 an ovule. らんし

**난자(亂刺)** stabbing violently; 〖의〗 scarification/~하다 stab violently; pierce recklessly; hack; mangle 《피부를》 scarify. みだりやたらにさすこと

**난작(亂斫)** hacking; mincing; chopping /~하다 hack; mince. ほそくわること

**난작거리다** be rotten; be worn-out; be squashy; be flimsy/난작난작 flimsily; squashily. くさってたれさがる

**난잡(亂雜)** ①《혼잡》 disorder; confusion

/~한 disorderly; confused/~하게 in disorder[confusion]; disorderly; confusedly ②(문란) irregularity; lawlessness (추잡) indecency; foulness; obscenity/ ~하다 (be) irregular; lawless; indecent. らんざつ

난장(亂杖) random beating; reckless [wild] beating (형벌)indiscriminate flogging. らんだのむち

난장(亂場) a scene of confusion and disorder.

난장(亂帳) 〖인〗 erratic pagination.

난장이 a dwarf; a pigmy; a manikin; a shrimp. こびと

난장초(爛腸草) 〖식〗 a begonia (추해당) an elephant's-ear.

난장판(亂場一) a scene of confusion and disorder; a turmoil; disorder; chaos; bustle and confusion; a mess/회의가 ~이 되다 a meeting falls[is thrown] into disorder. むちつじょなきょくめん

난적(亂賊) a rebel; an insurgent; a traitors; rioters. らんぞく

난전(亂戰) confused fighting; a scuffle /~을 벌이다 get into a scuffle; fight in confusion.

난점(難點) (어려운 점)difficult[knotty] point; a crux of a matter; a rub (결점)a bad point; a fault. なんてん

난제(難題) (난문)a difficult problem; a knotty subject《무리한 제안》 unreasonable terms. なんだい

난중(亂中) the midst of turmoil[commotion]; time of war; a tumultuous [strife ridden] period/ ~에 during a war; in the midst of turmoil; during a revolt. らんちゅう

난중지난(難中之難) the most difficult of all things; the hardest thing to do.

난증(難症) a malignant disease; an incurable case; an intractable case; a serious disease. なんしょう

난질 forming a connection with a man; having illicit sexual intercourse with a man/~장이 a wanton woman. ふてい

난질거리다 feel squashy[pulpy, soft and mushy]; (be) flimsy/난질난질 squashy ; pulpy. ぐにゃぐにゃする

난처(難處) ~하다 (be) difficult; hard to deal with; awkward; embarrassing; be at a loss; be in a dilemma/ ~한 입장에 있다 be in an awkward position. しょりにくいこと

난청(難聽) hardness of hearing/ ~의 hard of hearing/ ~자 a person who has difficulty in hearing.

난초(蘭草) 〖식〗 an orchid; an iris; a canna. らんそう

난추니 〖조〗 the male Asiatic sparrow hawk; Accipiter nisus(학명).

난측(難測) immeasurability/~하다 immeasurable 《불확실》 uncertain 《예측 불능》 hard to foretell. はかりにくいこと

난층운(亂層雲) 《기상》 a nimbo-stratus; a rain cloud.

난치(難治) incurableness; incurability /~의 incurable; fatal/ ~의 병 disease hard to cure/ ~하다 be hard to cure. びょうきがなおりにくいこと

난침모(一針母) a day[visiting, nonresident, living-out] seamstress.

난타(亂打) pommeling; repeated knocking[blows]; random blows/~하다 strike violently; pommel; batter; knock repeatedly. らんだ

난투(亂鬪) a confused fight; a free fight; a free-for-all [fight]; a scuffle; a melee (F)/~하다 have a confused[free] fight; scuffle/ ~극 a scene of violence and confusion. らんとう

난파(難破) 《파선》 a shipwreck; a wreck /~선 a wrecked ship/~ 신호 a signal of distress; an SOS/~ 화물 wreckage. なんぱ

난폭(亂暴) violence; outrage; roughness; rudeness; wildness/~하다 (be) violent; outrageous; rough; rude; rowdy 《무법》 lawless; unlawful/ ~자 a wild fellow; a roughneck《속》. らんぼう

난필(亂筆) a [careless] scrawl/ ~을 용서하십시오 Excuse my writing in haste. らんひつ

난하다(亂一) (be) loud; gaudy; flashy; showy/난한 색 loud colo[u]r/치마 무늬가 ~ The pattern of her skirt is a bit too flashy. いやにはでだ

난항(難航) a stormy passage[voyage] 《비행기의》 a hard flight 《비유적》 hard sledding/~하다 have a difficult sailing. なんこう

난해(難解) ~하다 be hard[difficult] to understand; (be) hard; knotty; (be) hard to make out[solve]《심오한》 abstruse; unintelligible. なんかい

난행(難行) 《불교의》 asceticism; [self-]mortification; religious austerities/ ~하다 do penance; practise asceticism or austerity. なんぎょう

난형(卵形) an egg-shape; ovalness/ ~물 an ovoid. たまごがた

난형 난제(難兄難弟) (being) almost equal; hart to tell who is better / ~다 There is little to choose between the two. よくにてゆうれつつかない

난형성(卵形成) 〖생〗 oogenesis.

난호어(蘭胡魚) 〖어〗 《망둥이》 a goby.

난황(卵黃) the yolk; the deutoplasm/ ~의 deutomic / ~막(膜) a vitelline membrane/ ~분(粉) yolk powder/ ~소(素) vitellin. らんおう

낟 cereal grain[s]. こくもつのつぶ

낟가리 a stack of grain stalks.

낟알 a grain; a corn. こくもつのつぶ

날 ①《달력상의》 a day 《날짜》 a date 《시일》 time/어느 ~ one day/ ~마다 every[each] day; daily/ ~로 난로 day by[after] day ②《날씨》 weather ③《경우·때》 on the morrow of; in the

**날²** 《칼 따위의》an edge; a blade/~을 세우다 put an edge on; sharpen/~서다 be edged[sharpened]; sharpen/칼~ the blade of a knife/면도~ a razor blade/대팻~ the blade of a plane/무딘 ~ dull edge.

**날³** 《직물의》 the warp; the lengthwise threads.

**날-** 《익히지 않은》 uncooked; raw; green; unseasoned; crude/~계란 a raw egg/~목(木) unseasoned timber.

**날개** the wings/~ 있는[달린] 새 ~ the wings of a bird/비행기 ~ the wings of an airplane/~개미 a winged ant.

**날개죽지** a wing; the shoulder-joint of a wing.

**날것** raw stuff; uncooked food 《고기》 raw fish[meat] 《과실》 unripe fruit/~으로 먹다 eat raw.

**날고기** raw[uncooked] meat.

**날공전(-工錢)** daily wages; a day's wage.

**날기와** an unbaked tile; a raw tile.

**날김치** raw[unaged] pickles[pickled vegetables].

**날나다** fail; rupture; collapse; give way/일이 ~ matters fall through; a plan fails.

**날날이** ①day by day ⇒나날이 ②a kind of clarinet ⇒날라리.

**날다¹** ①《하늘을》fly; be flown off/높이 ~ fly high in the air 《빨리 가다》fly; hurry/나는 듯이 달리다 run like the wind/그 소식을 듣고 나는 듯이 집으로 달려 왔다 At the news I flew home like the wind.

**날다²** ①《색이》fade [away]; lose colo[u]r; discolo[u]r ②《냄새가》lose odor; vanish; go away 《알콜·수증기 따위가》evaporate/향내가 날아 버리다 Perfume loses its fragrance.

**날다³** 《실을》spin [a thread] 《베틀에》thread the warp of [a loom].

**날다람쥐** 《동》a flying squirrel; *Sciuropterus aluce* 《학명》.

**날도(-度)** 《지》degree of longitude.

**날뛰다** 《덤비다》act with reckless violence; be rash; be hasty/좋아 ~ leap for joy/성이 나 ~ rush about wildly with anger; rage/함부로 날뛰지 말게 You should be more careful.

**날뜀판** leaping[jumping] up and down; moving excitedly[violently]; rage; running amuck/지금은 좋아 ~이 아니다 This is no hour for joy.

**날들다** it clears [up]; it becomes fine weather/날들기 시작한다 It is clearing up.

**날라리** 《음》a Chinese horn[clarinet].

**날래다** (be) quick; fast; swift; nimble; agile/걸음이 ~ be swift of foot; walk fast.

**날려보내다** ①fly; make fly; set free; release; have (*a thing*) blown[snatched] off[away] ②《재산을》blow; waste; squander; lose.

**날렵하다** (be) sharp; acute; agile; smart 《어린 애가》 (be) cute.

**날로** ①《날것으로》raw; uncooked/~ 먹다 eat (*fish*) raw ②《나날이》daily; everyday; day by day.

**날름** 《잽싸게》quickly; with a quick snatch 《혀를》 [a tongue] darting in and out/~ 먹어치우다 eat up in a twinkling.

**날름거리다** 《혀 따위를》roll out and in [the tongue] 《탐내다》watch for; crane *one's* neck to see.

**날름날름** darting[taking] in and out repeatedly.

**날름쇠** ①《무자위의》a valve ②《총의》the hammer ③《물건의》a metal spring ④《자물쇠의》a tumbler; a tongue.

**날리다¹** ①fly; let fly; make fly; blow off ②《일을》scamp[skimp] *one's* work; do slipshod; do a hasty job ③《재산을》lose (*all*); waste ④《명성을》make famous.

**날리다²** 《바람에》wave; flap/깃발이 바람에 날리고 있다 A flag is flapping in the wind.

**날림** 《공을 안 들임》slipshod work; careless manufacture/~ 집 a jerry-built house/~ 글씨 sloppy handwriting/~ 공사 a jerry built; a hasty[careless, slipshod] job.

**날림치** a thing[article] of coarse manufacture; a thing made[a job done] in a slipshod manner.

**날마다** every[each] day; from day to day; day after day; per day.

**날목(-木)** unseasoned wood; unseasoned timber.

**날물** ①《나가는 물》outflowing water ②《썰물》a low tide; an ebb tide.

**날바닥** the bare floor[ground].

**날바람잡다** act frivolously[flippantly, absurdly].

**날밤** 《생밤》raw chestnuts; unroasted cheastnuts.

**날밤새우다** pass a night without sleep; sit up all [through the] night; kill the night.

**날부랑당** a barefaced swindlers[crooks]; shameless scoundrels.

**날불이** a cutting-instrument; an edged tool; bladeware; cutlery.

**날빛** sunlight; daylight.

**날사이** (*for*) the past several days; for some days now.

**날삯** daily wages; a day's wage/~군 a day labor.

**날쌍하다** (be) loose-woven; be [an] ope-

**nweave**/날쌍날쌍 all loose. めがあらい
**날새** the past several days ⇒날사이.
**날샐녘** dawn; daybreak; the early hours of the morning/ ~에 at down; at the peep of day[dawn]; at day break. よあけ
**날서다** be edged; be sharpened; sharpened/날선 칼 a sharp[keen] knife.
**날세우다** put an edge on; give an edge; sharpen (a knife). はをつける
**날수(-數)** ①(수효) the number of days ②(운수) the luck[fortune] of a particular day/ ~를 보다 tell[read] one's fortune for the day/~가 좋다[나쁘다] have a lucky[an unlucky] day. にっすう
**날숨** exhalation; expiration/~ 쉬다 exhale; breathe out; expire. はくいき
**날씨** the weather; weather condition; the look of the sky/좋은 ~ fine[fair, good, favorable] weather/궂은 ~ foul[bad, nasty, wretched] weather/거친 ~ stormy[rough] weather/~가 좋은 날 a fine day/~를 예보하다 make a weather forecast/ ~가 좋건 나쁘건 in all weathers. てんき
**날씬하다** (be) slender; slim; supple; lithe/날씬한 여자 a slim woman.
**날아가다** ①(공중을) fly away (날개로) take wings ②(없어짐) be gone/돈이 어느새 다 날아갔다 My money is all gone already. ③(파면) 그 모가지가 ~ lose one's neck《속》. とんでいく
**날염(捺染)** [textile] printing/~하다 print/~한 천 printed cotton; print; calico〈미〉/~기(機) a printing machine. そめる
**날인(捺印)** affixing a seal/~하다 seal; affix one's seal (to a paper). なついん
**날짜¹** ①(작정된) a date ②(일수) [the number of] days. ひづけ
**날짜²** ①(날것) raw stuff; uncooked food; untreated[unprocessed; unseasoned] article ②(미숙한) an unexperienced person; a greenhorn; a novice. なまもの
**날짝지근하다** (be) very languid; much weary; very dull. けだるい
**날조(捏造)** concoction; invention; a fabrication/ ~하다 forge; invent; fabricate; cook up; manufacture; frame up〈미〉/~ 기사 a fabrication; a fabricated report; a make-up story/~자 a fabricator. ねつぞう
**날짐승** birds; the feathered tribe.
**날치** 《어》 a flying fish.
**날치기** snatching (사람) a snatcher/ ~ 공사(工事) sloppy works; slipshod construction work. ひったくること
**날첫군** a master shot; an excellent hunter [so skilled as to shoot a bird on the wing]. つり
**날카롭다** (be) sharp; keen; cutting; acute; pointed /날카로운 비평 sharp criticism/신경이 날카로와지다 become nervous[touchy]. えいりだ

**날큰거리다** (be) soft and droopy ⇒늘큰거리다. ぐにゃぐにゃする
**날큰하다** (be) supple; lithe; limber; flabby. ぐにゃぐにゃする
**날탕** a person with no means; a penniless[empty-handed] person; a good for nothing. なにももたないひと
**날파람** ①(서슬에 나는 바람) a gust of wind raised by a swiftly passing object ②(기세) roaring spirits; keenness; fierceness. するどいきせい
**날포** several days. いちにちいじょう
**날품** day labo[u]r[work]/~삯 daily wages/~팔이 day labo[u]r (사람) a dayman; a day lobo[u]rer/~팔이하다 work by the day. にっきゅうやとい
**날피¹** (보습) a plowshare.
**날피²** a pauper with no character[morals].
**낡다** become old[antiquated] 《구식이 되다》 become old-fashioned/낡아빠진 worn; antiquated; obsolete. ふるい
**남** 《타인》 anothers; other people; another [person] 《낯선 사람》 a stranger 《친척이 아닌》 an unrelated person/~몰래 in secret/~같이 대하다 treat (one) like a stranger. たにん
**남(男)** (남자) a man; a male (아들) a son. おとこ
**남(南)** the south/ ~의 south[ern]/ ~으로 to the south/ ~으로 가다 go south. みなみ
**남(藍)** (남빛) indigo; indigo[deep] blue; Indian blue. あいいろ
**남가 일몽(南柯一夢)** a vain dream; an empty dream; an idle dream; a daylight dream 《덧없는 부귀 영영》 fleeting[passing] glory. はかないゆめ
**남계(男系)** the male line; the spear side / ~의 on the male line/~ 상속 succession in the male line/~ 친척 an agnate.
**남국(南國)** a southern country[land]; the south countries. なんごく
**남극(南極)** the South Pole/ ~의 antarctic/ ~광(光) aurora australis; the southern lights/~성 the South Pole-star/~ 탐험 an antarctic expedition/ ~ 대륙 Antarctica. なんきょく
**남기다** ①(뒤에) leave; leave behind (유산을) bequeath (안 쓰고) reserve; save spare ②(이를 보다) make[realize, secure, obtain] a profit; gain. のこす
**남날개** an ammunition pouch; a cartridge box (띠) a cartridge belt.
**남남동(南南東)** the south-south east (略: SSE). なんなんとう
**남남 북녀(南男北女)** In the South it is the man who are handsome and in the North it is the women.
**남남서(南南西)** the south-south west (略: SSW)
**남녀(男女)** man and woman; male and female; persons of different sexes;

both sexes/~ 공학 coeducation/~ 동등[평등] equality of the sexes/~ 동권 sex equality[relations]. なんにょ

**남녀 노소**(男女老少) young and old of both sexes; man and woman of all ages.

**남녀 유별**(男女有別) distinction between the sexes.

**남녀추니**(男女―) a hermaphrodite; an androgyne. ちゅうせいのひと

**남녘**(南―) the south; the south side; the southern districts. なんぽう

**남다** 《또 있다》 be left over; survive 《처져 있다》 remain; stay/남은 일 the remainder of work/남아나다 be abundant; be in excess/너의 추억은 영원토록 내 가슴에 남을게나 Your memory will be alive within me as long as I live. のこる

**남단**(南端) the southern extremity[end]. なんたん

**남달리** in a different way than others; out of the common; uncommonly; unusually; extraordinarily; especially; exceptionally. かわって

**남대문**(南大門) the South Gate of Seoul.

**남독**(濫讀) randomreading ⇨남독(亂讀).

**남동**(南東) the southeast/~풍 the southeastly wind. なんとう

**남루**(襤褸) 《누더기》 rag; shred 《헌옷》 tattered clothes; rags; tatters/~하다 (be) shabby; ragged; tattered; wornout; threadbare. ぼろ

**남만**(南蠻) 《남방의 만인》 barbarians from [in] the south/~ 북적(北狄) Southern and northern barbarians. なんばん

**남매**(男妹) 《둘》 a brother and a sister 《여럿》 brothers and sisters. あにといもうと

**남바위** a covering for the head worn in winter by women; a woman's hood for winter use.

**남반구**(南半球) the Southern Hemisphere. みなみはんきゅう

**남발**(濫發) overissue; excessive issue/~하다 overissue; issue recklessly[excessively]. らんぱつ

**남방**(南方) the south 《방향》 the direction of the south. なんぽう

**남벌**(濫伐) denudation; reckless; deforestation; indiscriminate felling [of trees]/~하다 denude; deforest; cut[fell] trees recklessly; fell indiscriminately. らんばつ

**남복**(男服) men's clothes[wear]; male attire; clothes in which a woman disguises as a man/~하다 be dressed like a man; be in men's clothes; disguise oneself as a man. おとこのふく

**남부**(南部) the southern part 《미국의》 the south/한반도의 ~ the southern part of the Korean Peninsula. なんぶ

**남부고럽다** (be) ashamed; front of others disgraceful; shameful in. はずかしくてひとにかおをあわせられない

**남부럽다** be envious of others/남부럽지 않게 살고 있다 be well off. うらやましい

**남부 여대**(男負女戴) ~하다 set out on a wandering life.

**남북**(南北) north and south/~ 전쟁 the War Between the States/~ 통일 reunification of North and South [Korea]. なんぼく

**남비** 《얕은》 a pan 《깊은》 a pot/ ~를 불에 올려 놓다 put a pan over the fire/~ 국수 scalloped[pot-boiled] macaroni/~ 뚜껑 a potlid/~ 손잡이 the bail of a pan; a pot bail. なべ

**남비**(濫費) waste; extravagance; dissipation. らんぴ

**남빙양**(南氷洋) the Antarctic Ocean. なんひょうよう

**남빛**(藍―) indigo; deep blue. あいいろ

**남사당**(男寺黨) 《민》 a travelling entertainer; a travelling clown/ ~패(牌) a troupe of players.

**남산골깍발이**(南山―) a wretched scholar.

**남산골샌님**(南山―) a penniless scholar.

**남살**(濫殺) blind[indiscriminate] execution/~하다 execute indiscriminately.

**남상**(男相) a woman with manly features; an unwomanly face/~지르다 have an unwomanly face. だんそう

**남상**(濫觴) the origin; the beginning; the rise; the source/연극의 ~ the origin of the drama. らんしょう

**남상거리다** stretch[crane] one's neck avidly [to see something] ⇨넘성거리다. ほしがってのぞきこむ

**남색**(男色) sodomy; unnatural vices; pederasty; buggery/~가 a sodomite; a pederast. だんしょく

**남색**(藍色) indigo ⇨남빛. あいいろ

**남생이** 《동》 a tortoise.

**남서**(南西) the southwest. なんせい

**남성**(男性) the male sex; the sterner sex 《언》 the masculine gender/ ~적 manly; virile / ~같은 mannish / ~미 masculine beauty/ ~화 virilism/ ~ 호르몬 male hormone. だんせい

**남성**(男聲) a male voice/~ 4중창 a male quartet/~합창 a male chorus/ ~ 중음 baritone. だんせい

**남성지다**(男性―) 《여자가》 (be) mannish.

**남수**(男囚) a male prisoner; a male convict. だんしゅう

**남승**(男僧) a Buddhist monk; a bonze; a priest. おとこのぞうりょ

**남실거리다** rubberneck; overflow ⇨넘실거리다. ほしがってのぞきこむ

**남아**(男兒) 《남자》 a boy[son] 《장부》 a man/~답게 in a manly manner. だんじ

**남양**(南洋) the South seas / ~군도 the South sea islands; Oceania; Polynesia. なんよう

**남여**(籃輿) a sedan chair; an open palanquin. かご

**남용**(濫用) abuse; misuse; misappropri-

**남우세** suffering other's derision; a disgrace／～하다 bring shame to; disgrace (*oneself*).

**남위**(南緯) the south latitude[parallel]／～선 a line of south latitude. なんい

**남유다르다** (be) extraordinary; uncommon. かわっている

**-남은** 접여 ～ ten odd.

**남의달** the month following the estimated month of childbirth. しゅっさんよていがつのつぎのげつ

**남의세** being a laughingstock ⇒남우세

**남자**(男子) ①(남성) a man; a male; the male sex／～같은 여자 a manly[manlike; mannish] woman ②(대장부) a hero man; a manly person／～다운 manly. だんし

**남작**(男爵) 《사람》 a baron 《작위》 baronage／～부인 a baroness／～에 서작되다 be created baron. だんしゃく

**남작**(濫作) overproduction; excessive production／～하다 overproduce; produce[write] at random; write recklessly. らんさく

**남장**(男裝) male attire[disguise]／～하다 disguise *oneself* as a man; wear men's clothes; dress *oneself* in male attire; be dressed like a man. だんそう

**남정**(男丁) a man who has reached the age of fifteen; an adult. わかいおとこ

**남정네**(男丁―) 《남자들》 menfolk 《남의 남편들》 the husbands. よそのおとこ

**남조**(濫造) overproduction 《조제》 careless manufacture／～하다 produce in [to] excess; overproduce; manufacture carelessly. らんぞう

**남쪽**(南―) the south／～ 나라 a southern country. なんぼう

**남존 여비**(男尊女卑) predominance of man over woman. だんそんじょひ

**남종**(男―) a male slave; a manservant.

**남종화**(南宗畵) the southern school of Chinese painting.

**남중**(南中) 《천》 southing; culmination／～하다 south; cross the meridian.

**남중 일색**(南中一色) an uncommonly handsome man; an Adonis. びだんし

**남진**(南進) southward advance; southern penetration／～하다 advance southward／～정책 the southward expansion policy. なんぽうにすすむこと

**남짓하다** (be) slightly over[above]／나이가 서른 ～ be little over thirty; be slightly over thirty. いくぶんあまる

**남징**(濫徵) improper collection; improper requisition／～하다 collect unduly; requisition[commandeer] excessively. みだりにちょうしゅうすること

**남창**(男娼) a male[homosexual] prostitute. なんしょく

**남창**(男唱) a song by a woman in a male voice; a woman singing in the man's part.

**남창**(南窓) a window facing the south; south window. みなみのまど

**남천촉**(南天燭) 《식》 a nandin; *Nandina domestica*(학명).

**남치마**(藍―) a deep-blue skirt.

**남태평양**(南太平洋) the South Pacific. みなみたいへいよう

**남편**(男便) a husband; *one's* man; *one's* worse half《속》; 《법》 a baron／～ 있는 married. りょうじん

**남포**[1] (다이너마이트) dynamite／～질하다 blast with dynamite. ダイナマイト

**남포**[2] (등) a lamp 《석유등》 an oil[a petroleum a kerosene] lamp. ランプ

**남풍**(南風) the south wind; the wind from the south. みなみかぜ

**남하**(南下) southward advance[movement]／～하다 go[come] south; advance southwards. なんか

**남해**(南海) the southern sea. なんかい

**남행**(南行) going south; southing／～하다 go [down to the] south／～ 열차 a southbound train. みなみする

**남향**(南向) a southern exposure; facing the south／～하다 face the south; be exposed to the south／～집 a house facing the south. みなみむき

**남향판**(南向―) a site[a place] with a southern exposure. みなみむきのいち

**남형**(濫刑) improper punishment／～하다 punish unduly.

**남혼**(男婚) the marriage of *one's* son. むすこのけっこん

**남회귀선**(南回歸線) the Tropic of Capricorn. みなみかいきせん

**남획**(濫獲) overfishing; overcatching; reckless fishing[hunting]／～하다 overfish; fish[hunt] recklessly; overcatch.

**납**(鉛) 《화》 lead; plumbum (기호: Pb); 《땜납》 solder／백～ soft solder pewter／～ 접착제 [soldering] flux. はんだ

**납**(蠟) wax; beeswax; white[refined] wax／～세공 waxwork. みつろう

**납가새** 《식》 a caltrop; a water chestnut; *Tribulus terrestris*(학명).

**납거미** 《충》 a spider; *Uroctea compactilis*(학명).

**납골**(納骨) laying *one's* ashes to rest／～당 a charnel house. のうこつ

**납공**(納貢) paying[offering] a tribute [tax, land tax]／～하다 pay in tribute[tax, land tax].

**납관**(納款) ～하다 offer loyalty; offer allegiance. しんぷくすること

**납금**(納金) 《지불》 payment; the money 《지불할 돈》; due the money paid 《지불한 돈》／～하다 pay (*money*). のうきん

**납기**(納期) the payment term; the time limit[appointed date]. のうき

**납길**(納吉) notification of the date fixed for the wedding／～하다 notify the date fixed for the wedding to the bride's house.

**납대대하다** be pleasantly flattish.

**납땜**(蠟—) soldering／～하다 solder／～인두 a soldering-iron. はんだづけ

**납득**(納得) understanding／～하다 understand／～시키다 convince (one) of; persuade／～할 수 있게 설명하다 explain to one's satisfaction. なっとく

**납량**(納凉) enjoying the cool [of the evening]／～하다 enjoy the cool [of the evening]／～음악회 a summer-evening concert. のうりょう

**납본**(納本) presentation of a specimen copy to the authorities; a persentation copy／～하다 present a specimen copy for censorship. のうほん

**납부**(納付) 《세금 따위》 payment 《물품의》 delivery／～하다 pay; deliver; supply (goods)／～금 payable collections; money due. のうふ

**납상**(納上) offering; presentation／～하다 offer; present.

**납석**(蠟石) 《광》 agalmatolite; pencil stone.

**납세**(納稅) tax payment／～하다 pay one's tax[es]／[다액] ～자 a [high] taxpayer／～액 the amount of taxes／～ 고지서 tax papers. のうぜい

**납시다** [the king] deign to come out; appear.

**납신거리다** talk glib and flippant; patter; gibber; chatter／납신납신 glibly; flippantly. べちゃくちゃしゃべる

**납월**(臘月) December of the lunar calendar ➪섣달. ろうげつ

**납의**(衲衣) black garments of priests; a prist's black cassock. のうえ

**납입**(納入) payment (of a tax, fee); delivery (of goods)／～하다 pay (a tax); deliver・(goods) のうにゅう

**납작** 《재빨리》 with quick motion 《모양》 lat; low／～ 엎드리다 lay down with quick motion.

**납작보리** 《식》 rolled barley おしむぎ

**납작코** a flat nose; a snub nose 《사람》 a flatnosed person. ひくいはな

**납작하다** (be) flat; low; thin／납작한 집 a low house／납작하게 찌부러지다 be crushed flat. ひくい

**납지**(蠟紙) wax paper. ろうがみ

**납지**(鑞紙) silver paper 《포장용》 tinfoil; lead foil. きんがみ

**납질**(蠟質) waxy substance／～의 waxen; waxy／～ 변성 waxy degeneration.

**납채**(納采) wedding presents sent from the bridegroom's house to the bride's house／～하다 send wedding presents to the bride's house. のうさい

**납촉**(蠟燭) a beeswax candle ➪밀초.

**납치**(拉致) seizure by force; hijacking; kidnapping; abduction／～하다 seize by force; hijack; kidnap. らち

**납폐**(納幣) wedding presents of silk.

**납품**(納品) delivery of goods 《납품된 물건》 delivered goods／～하다 deliver (goods)／～서 a bill of parcel; an invoice. のうひん

**낫** a sickle; a grain sickle; a reaping hook 《큰 낫》 a scythe／～으로 풀을 베다 cut grass with a sickle／～ 놓고 기역 자도 모르다 be illiterate[ignorant]; do not know A from B.

**낫낫하다** (be) tender; soft. なめらかだ

**낫다**¹ 《좋다》 be better (than); be superior to[over]; surpass; excel; (be) preferable; get the better of; be excellent／늦더라도 안하니보다는 ～ Better late than never. よい

**낫다**² 《병이》 recover (from) illness; get well; be cured (of)／《상처가》 heal up／병이 ～ be restored to health; recover from illness. なおる

**낫살** age; years／～을 먹다 get old／～ 깨나 먹은 사람답지 않게 in spite of one's age. とし

**낭군**(郞君) [my] dear husband. ろうくん

**낭당**(郞當) ～하다 (be) hard to deal with.

**낭떠러지** a cliff; a precipice 《바닷가의》 a bluff. だんがい

**낭독**(朗讀) reading aloud; declamation 《시를》 recitation／～하다 read aloud; recite; give a reading (of); declaim [verses]／～법 elocution／～자 a reader. ろうどく

**낭독 연설**(朗讀演說) a set[reading] speech／～하다 read an address; speak from one's notes. ろうどくえんぜつ

**낭랑**(朗朗) ～하다 《목소리가》 (be) clear and ringing; sonorous; full; clarion; silvery [voice]／《달빛 따위》 clear and serene／～한 음성 a clear[ringing, resonant] voice. ろうろう

**낭만**(浪漫) [being] romantic／～적 romantic／～주의 romanticism／～주의자 a romanticist／～파 romantic school; romanticism 《한 사람》 a romanticist／～ 문학 Romanticism. ろうまん

**낭보**(朗報) good[bright, glad, cheering] news; good tidings. ろうほう

**낭비**(浪費) waste; wasteful expenditure／～하다 waste; squander; throw away; use to no purpose／～자 a waster／시간의 ～ waste of time／～적 wasteful; extravagant／시간을 ～하다 idle [fool] away one's time. ろうひ

**낭상**(囊狀) sac-shape; sacciform／～관 a cystic valve／～선 a sac-like gland.

**낭설**(浪說) a false[an unfounded] rumor[report]; a groundless rumor／근거 없는 ～ a groundless rumor／～을 믿다 take rumor as it is／～을 퍼뜨리다 set a false rumor afloat. りゅうげん

**낭성**(狼星) 《천》 the Dog-Star; Sirius.

**낭송**(朗誦) recitation; reading／～하다 read aloud; recite／자본 ～ 《배우의》 re-

**낭독(朗讀)** recitation; recital／ ~하다 recite; sing. ろうぎん

**낭인(浪人)** a man out of employment [office]; a jobless man／ ~이 되다 be out of office[work]; lose one's position. ろうにん

**낭자(머리)** a chignon; a coiffure.

**낭자(娘子)** a virgin ⇒처녀. ろうし

**낭자(狼藉)** disorder; confusion／ ~하다 (be) in wild disorder; be in great confusion／유혈이 ~하다 be all covered with blood. ろうぜき

**낭잣비녀(娘子-)** a long hairpin worn in a chignon.

**낭종(囊腫)** 【의】 an encysted tumor.

**낭중(囊中)** one's pocket; the purse／ ~에 in a bag／ ~에 무일푼이 되다 become penniless／ ~ 취물 being very easy; an easy task. のうちゅう

**낭중물(囊中物)** things one has with one [on one]; what is in one's pocket.

**낭패(狼狽)** failure; frustration; bafflement／ ~하다 fail; be frustrated; be baffled／이거 ~났군 What a most awkward case this is! ろうばい

**낭하(廊下)** ①(복도) a corridor; a lobby; a hallway 〈미〉 ②(행랑) the servant's quarters. ろうか

**낮** 《주간》 day; daytime／ ~에는 in the daytime; by day／밤~ day and night／ ~이나 밤이나 공부에 여념이 없다 By night, as well as by day, he is absorbed in his study. ひる

**낮거리** sexual intercourse performed in the daytime／ ~하다 have sexual intercourse in the day. ひるまのせいこう

**낮다** (높이가) (be) low (비치하다) poor humble／낮게 low／낮은 지위 a humble position／낮은 소리로 in a low voice／낮아지다 become low; lower 《목소리 따위》 sink. ひくい

**낮도깨비** ①(사람) a shameless fellow. ②(도깨비) a goblin who does mischief in broad daylight. ひるのばけもの

**낮도둑** a greedy[grasping] fellow; a shark; a rapacious person; a shameless hog. どんよくなひとのたとえ

**낮번(一番)** the day shift.

**낮은말** ①⇒낮춤말 ②(상말) a vulgar word; a vulgarism. ひご

**낮은음자리표(一音一標)** 【음】 bass (F) clef.

**낮잠** a [midday] nap; a siesta／ ~을 자다 take a nap; take a siesta. ひるね

**낮잡다** estimate low; underestimate; rate low; underrate; appraise[evaluate] low; think little of; hold cheap; disparage／집 값을 ~ rate the price of a house low. もとねよりやすくきめる

**낮차(一車)** a day car[coach, train].

**낮참(점심)** a midday meal; lunch 《쉬는 시간》 a recess after lunch; a noon recess; a midday break. ひるげ

**낮추다** ①(낮게 하다) lower; bring down; make low 《음성을》 subdue 《라디오를》 tune down／목소리를 ~ lower[subdue, sink] one's voice／정도를 ~ lower the standard ②(말의 하대) lower one's style of speech. さげる

**낮추보다** look down upon[on]; hold (a person) in contempt; have a low opinion (of). みさげる

**낯** ①(얼굴) a face; a visage 《생김새》 features; looks 《표정》 a look a phiz 《속》 ②(면목) face; countenance; hono[u]r／ ~을 세우다 save one's face; keep (one's) in countenance／ ~이 깎이다 lose (one's) face／ 무슨 ~으로 그런 것을 해달라고 부탁하겠니? I cannot with any grace ask to do so. かお

**낯가리다** be afraid[by shy] of strangers; discriminate between persons／어린애가 ~ A baby shows likes or dislikes toward a person.／이 애는 낯가리지 않습니다 This baby takes to strangers. おやをみわける

**낯가죽** sense of honor[shame]／ ~이 두껍다 be thick-skinned[brazen-faced, shameless]. つらのかわ

**낯간지럽다** feel ashamed[abashed]; be bashful; feel small; be only too aware of one's own flattery. はじをかんじる

**낯나다** get credit (for); reflect credit (of); have the credit (on); feel oneself honored. めんもくがたつ

**낯내다** reflect credit to oneself (for); do honor to oneself; act so as to gain the respect of others. じまんする

**낯두껍다** (be) brazen[-faced]; shameless; cheeky; impudent; audacious／낯두껍게도 …하다 have the impudence [heart, audacity] to (do). あつかましい

**낯바대기** a face; a phiz 《속》. かおのひご

**낯붉히다** get angry; be red with anger ／부끄러워 ~ blush for shame／여간해선 낯붉히지 않다 be slow to get angry. かおをあかくする

**낯설다** (be) strange; unfamiliar; new; be not known／낯선 사람 a stranger／낯선 곳[타향] a strange place; a place strange to one. みなれない

**낯알다** know one by sight; remember one's face／낯아는 사람 an acquaintance. かおをしっている

**낯없다** be ashamed of oneself; be put out of countenance. めんもくがない

**낯익다** be familiar (to); be well known ／낯익은 사람 an acquaintance／낯익은 얼굴 a familiar face. みなれている

**낱** a piece; a unit; each piece. こ

**낱개** a piece 《묶지 않은 것》 bulk／ ~로 팔다 sell in bulk[loose pieces]. ひとつ

**낱낱이** 1《하나 하나》 one by one; individually; separately 2《모두》 in every case; entirely 3《산세히》 in detail; in full. ひとつずつ

**낱돈** small 'loose' money; coppers／small coins.

**낱뜨기** articles sold loose; merchandise sold by the piece. ひとつずつうるもの

**낱말** a word; a vocabulary; each word / 그는 나보다 영어의 ~을 많이 알고 있다 He has an English vocabulary larger than mine. たんご

**낱알** each grain. つぶ

**낳다**¹ ①(출산하다) bear; give birth to; be delivered of [a child]; bring forth (동물이) breed 《소가》calve 《개》drop [pup] 《고양이가》kitten ②(생기다) produce; bring forth/이자를 ~ draw interest. うむ

**낳다**² (실을) spin; make yarn 《피륙을》weave. つむぐ

**내**¹ (개울) a stream; a brook / ~를 건느다 go across a river / ~를 끼고 가다 go along a stream. とぶ

**내**² (연기) smoke /담배 ~ cigarette smoke / ~가 자욱하다 be full of smoke; be smoky /굴뚝에서 ~가 나다 smoke rises from a chimney. けむり

**내**³ (냄새) smell; odor; scent /구운 ~ the smell of something roasted. におい

**내**⁴ (나의) my (내가) I; myself / ~ 책 my book / ~가 했다 I did it. / ~가 가겠다 I will go. わたくしの

**-내** (…중) through; throughout /하룻밤 ~ all night through / 1년~ all the year round. ずっと

**내-**(來) next; coming; forthcoming / ~주 next week; the coming week. らい

**내가다** take[bring, carry] out[away]; remove /책상을 방에서 ~ take a desk out of the room. もちだす

**내각**(內閣) a Cabinet; a Ministry; the government / ~ 각료 Cabinet members / ~ 총사직 a general resignation of the Cabinet. ないかく

**내각**(內角) 【수】 an interior angle 《야구》 in-corner. たいかく

**내간**(內艱) the death of *one's* mother or grandmother. ないかん

**내갈기다** hit 《글씨를》dash off; scribble; scrawl.

**내강**(內剛) strong-mindedness; a strong will; inner strength / ~하다 (be) stouthearted; strong-minded; strong-willed. みかけよりこころがつよいこと

**내객**(來客) a caller; a visitor; a guest 《집합적》company. らいきゃく

**내거** 《내 것》 my thing; mine. わたくしの(おれの)もの

**내걸다** ①(물건을) hoist; hang ②(목숨 따위를) risk; stake; bet /생명을 ~ risk [stake] *one's* life. かかげる

**내경**(內徑) the inside diameter 《원통의》the caliber 《구경》the bore; the gauge / ~ 측정기 a calibrator.

**내계**(內界) the inner world[sphere] / ~ 의 inner; inward. ないかい

**내공**(耐空) endurance in flying / ~하다 make an endurance flight / ~ 비행 [기록] an endurance flight[record].

**내공**(內攻) 【의】retrocession; retrocedence / ~하다 retrocede; strike inwards.

**내공**(來貢) coming to pay tribute / ~하다 come to pay tribute. らいこう

**내공목**(內供木) coarse cotton cloth for lining.

**내과**(內科) 【의】 internal medicine; internal treatment[department] / ~ 병동 a medical ward / ~의(醫) a physician; a medical practitioner / ~병원 a hospital [for internal diseases]. ないか

**내과피**(內果皮) 【식】the endocarp.

**내관**(內官) ①(내시) a eunuch; an official of the Royal Household ②(고자) a man whose genital organs are underdeveloped. ないかん

**내관**(內觀) introspection / ~하다 introspect / ~적 introspective / ~적 작가 an introspective writer. ないかん

**내관**(來觀) attendance; inspection; a visit / ~하다 attend; inspect; visit / ~자 a visitor. らいかん

**내관**(內棺) an inner coffin.

**내교섭**(內交涉) informal[preliminary] negotiations / ~하다 carry on informal negotiations (*with*).

**내구**(內舅) *one's* maternal uncle; *one's* mother's brother.
ははのじつかのきょうだい

**내구**(耐久) (지구) durability (지속) persistence (항구) permanence / ~하다 endure; be durable; keep[last] long / ~력 durability; staying power; persistence. たいきゅう

**내구**(來寇) an invasion; an incursion; an inroad; a raid / ~하다 invade; raid; make a raid[an inroad] into (*on*).

**내국**(內國) home; the home country / ~의 home; domestic; national; native / ~ 인 a native / ~ 우편 domestic mail / ~ 항로 a coastwise service / ~ 통신 home news. ないこく

**내규**(內規) private rules[regulations]; tradition; unpublished[customary] rules; bylaws 《군》standard operating procedure(略;SOP). ないき

**내근**(內勤) indoor duty[service] / ~하다 work inside; be on room duty /. ~ 사원 an indoor service employee; a clerk.
ないきん

**내금**(內金) payment on account; partial payment in advance; token payment; deposit / ~으로 on account; as partial payment. うちきん

**내기** (도박) betting; staking; gambling / ~하다 bet (*on*); lay a wager (*on*); gamble / ~에 지다[이기다] lose[win] a wager[a bet]. かけ

**-내기** merchandise /전(廛)~ goods in stock; ready-made articles; mass-produced articles.

**내남없이** anyone; everybody; indiscriminately; with no discrimination between oneself and others/그것은 ~ 다 아는 사실이다 It is a fact known to everybody. だれでも

**내내** all along[through]; all the time; from start to finish; from beginning to end; all the way/3년 동안 ~ 수석이었다 He has been at the top of his class for the whole three year period. / ~ 혼자 여행하다 make the whole trip a lone. あいかわらず

**내내년**(來來年) the year after next ⇒후년(後年). さらいねん

**내내월**(來來月) the month after next. さらいげつ

**내년**(來年) next year; the coming year / ~ 봄 next spring/~ 이맘 때 about this time[next] year/~ 3월 next March. らいねん

**내다** ①《밖으로》put out 《주머니 속에서》take out; bring out; pull[draw] out ②《노출》expose; show; bare ③《발간》publish[issue, bring out] (a book) ④《제출》present; send in [an application]; give[set] (a question) ⑤《음식을》serve (wine). だしておく

**내다**¹ (연기가) smoke; smolder. けむる

**내다**² ⇒별항 참조(page 136C).

**내다보다** ①《밖을》look[peep] out ②《앞을》look forward into. ながめる

**내닫다** dart off; start off; run away suddenly; run off 《말이》break into a gallop. げんきよくはしる

**내달**(來—) next month; proximo(略: prox.). らいげつ

**내담**(來談) an interview; [a visit for] a talk/~하다 interview; visit [for a talk]. らいだん

**내대다** give the cold shoulder to; refuse with coldness/웃사람에게 ~ set oneself against one's superiors. つめたくあたる

**내떤지다** ①《힘있게》throw[hurl] away; throw[hurl] out ②《버리다》abandon; give[throw] up; throw up one's hands; forsake. ちからつよくなげる

**내도**(來到) arrival; coming / ~하다 come (to); arrive (at). とうちゃく

**내돌리다** hand[pass] (a thing) around carelessly[indiscriminately]. てからてにわたす

**내두르다** ①《흔들다》brandish; flourish ②《사람을》turn (one) round one's finger. ふりまわす

**내둘리다** ①《어지럽다》feel dizzy[giddy]; (be) shaky ②《남에게》be under (a person's) thumb; be led by the nose; be pushed around. ふりまわされる

**내뚫다** pierce; penetrate; go[pass, run] through; shoot through 《구멍을》perforate. とおす

**내뜨리다** throw[cast, fling] away/휴지를 문 밖으로 ~ throw wastepaper out of the window. なげすてる

**내디디다** step forward; advance; set foot (on); enter upon (a career).

**내락**(內諾) informal[private] consent/ ~하다 give informal consent/~을 얻다 obtain[secure] (a person's) informal consent. ないだく

**내란**(內亂) a civil war; internal disturbances[troubles]; a rebellion; an insurrection; a domestic conflict /~죄 high treason/ ~ 음모 conspiracy of a rebellion. ないらん

**내려가다** ①《아래로》go down; descend; 《시골에》go down [to the country] ②《물가가》get lower; fall; drop ③《열·온도가》subside; abate; fall/기온이 영하로 ~ fall down below zero. ④《지위가》come down in rank; sink; be demoted (to)/석차가 ~ come down on the list. くだる

**내려갈기다** flog down.

**내려깔리다** void[urine, feces] downrank. (しょうべんなどを) する

**내려긋다** draw a vertical line; draw (a line) down; underscore. せんをしたにひく

**내려놓다** set[put] down; take down; bring down; lower; let (a person) off (a vehicle)/책을 책꽂이에서 ~ take down a book from the bookshelf. おろしておく

**내려다보다** ①《밑을》overlook; look down ②《얕보다》look down upon; despise; hold (a person) cheap. みおろす

**내려뜨리다** let fall; drop; throw down /찻종을 ~ drop a glass[let a glass fall] to the floor. おとす

**내려디디다** step down.

**내려앉다** ①《옮겨 앉다》come down to a lower seat; take a lower seat ②《무너지다》collapse; fall[come] down; give way; sink; fall[cave] in/땅이 ~ ground sinks. うつってすわる

**내려오다** ①《위에서》come down; descend /나무에서 ~ come down from a tree ②《전해》be handed down (to)/가보로 전해 내려오는 칼 a sword handed down as an heirloom ③《차에서》get off; get down from; alight from/차에서 ~ get off a car. おりてくる

**내려지다** come[go] down. さがる

**내려찍다** cut with a downward blow.

**내려치다** give a downright blow; strike from above/책상을 주먹으로 ~ hit the table with one's fist. たたきつける

**내력**(來歷) one's personal history; one's past life; one's career; antecedents; an origin. らいれき

**내륙**(內陸) inland; inland area. ないりく

**내리** ①《아래로》down; downward ②《잇달아》through; successively; on end; without a break. うえからしたにむかって

**내리깎다** knock down the price; drive a hard bargain.

**내리깔다** lower[cast down] one's eye's down. しせんをおとす

**내리긋다** draw (a line) down; draw vertical line. せんをひきおろす

**내리내리** successively; continuously; on end; without a break; incessantly; ceaselessly.

**내리다**[1] ①《높은 데서》come[go] down; step down; descend 《하강》fall; drop 《차에서》alight; get[step] off 《말에서》dismount ②《값·기온 따위가》go down; drop; fall ③《먹은 것이》digest; be digested ④《신이》possess; take possession of ⑤《뿌리가》take [root]; strike [root]; live. くだる

**내리다**[2] ①《내려뜨리다》take down; lower; bring[put, pull] down drop／선반에서 책을 ~ take down a book from a shelf／포장을 ~ drop the curtain／불에서 남비를 ~ take the pot off the fire ②《하사(下賜)하다》give; grant; bestow ③《명령을》give; issue 《판결을》pass (judgement on one); give; pronounce／판결을 ~ give a descision. おりる

**내리닫이** a sash window; a vertically sliding window. じょうげするまど

**내리치다** beat down; give a downright blow／머리를 ~ strike (a person) a blow on the head. ぶんなぐる

**내림**[1] 《내력》heredity; [hereditary] transmission; inheritance／서적을 좋아하는 것은 우리집의 ~일쎄 A love of books is in my blood. いでん

**내림**[2] 《간수》frontage; a width. まぐち

**내림(來臨)** presence; attendance; a visit; an honored visit／~하다 attend; be present at. らいりん

**내림대** a rod used by a shaman [to be possessed by a spirit].

**내립떠보다** glare at (a person) casting down one's eyes; look at (a person) lowering one's eyes. にらみつける

**내막(內幕)** inside facts; private; circumstances; the inside／~ 얘기 the inside story (of)／~을 알고 있다 be familiar with the situation; be in the know《구》／~을 말하다 give (a person) the low-down (on). ないまく

**내막(內膜)** 【해】 the lining membrane. ないまく

**내맡기다** leave[entrust] (a matter entirely to a person); commit (a matter) to (a person's) care; leave[place] [it] in (a person's) hand. まかせる

**내면(內面)** the inside; the interior／~생활 one's inner life／~적[으로] internal[ly]／~관찰 an inside view. ないめん

**내명(內命)** an informal[a private, a secret] order／~을 내리다 issue an unofficial order.

**내명년(來明年)** the year after next. さらいねん

**내몰다** turn[send, drive] out; force out ／사람을 방에서 ~ drive[force] (a person) out of the room. ついだす

**내몰리다** be driven out[away]; be forced out／집 밖으로 ~ driven[forced] out of the house. ついだされる

**내무(內務)** home[domestic, internal] affairs／~반 《군》 quarters; barracks ／~부[성] the Ministry[Department] of Home Affairs／~ 장관[대신] the Minister for Home Affairs; the Home Minister; the Home Secretary of the Interior《미》. ないむ

**내밀(內密)** privacy; secrecy／~의 secret; private (비공식의) informal; unofficial／~히 조사하다 make confidential inquiries. ないみつ

**내밀다** ①《끝이 나오다》protrude; jut out; project ②《밖으로》push[thrust] out; stick out (of) ③《남에게 미루다》shift (on); throw (on); switch (over to) ④《물리쳐 쫓아내다》drive[force] out; expel. おしだす

**내밀리다** be pushed; be forced; be pressed; be thrust out／들 밖으로 ~ be thrust out of the garden／회사에서 ~ get shoved[pushed] out of one's job with the company. つきだされる

**내밀힘** pushing[forward] force; strength; drive (배짱) self-confidence; boldness. おしだすちから

**내발뺌** self-vindication; an excuse／~하다 defend[explain] oneself; talk oneself out. いいわけをすること

**내방(來訪)** a visit; a call／~하다 visit; call on; (one) pay (one) a visit; call at. らいほう

**내배다** ooze (out of); soak through; exude; transude; saturate; percolate. にじみだす

**내빼다** fly; flee; run away. にげる

**내뱉다** spit out; spew; spue／내뱉듯이 말하다 say disdainfully. はきだす

**내버려두다** 《그냥두다》leave (a thing) alone; let alone／병을 그대로 ~ let one's disease go untreated／일을 하지 않고 ~ leave one's work undone. すてておく

**내버리다** throw away; cast[fling] away; dump (refuse). すてる

**내보내다** ①《나가게 하다》turn[put, send, get] out／척후를 ~ send out scouts ②《해고하다》dismiss; fire《미》. おくりだす

**내복(內服)** ①《옷》underwear; underclothes ②《약》internal use／~하다 take [use] internally／~약 an internal medicine. ないふく

**내부(乃父)** his[her] father. かれのちち

**내부(內部)** the inside; the interior／~의 inside; internal; inner; interior／~에 inside; within／집의 ~ the inside [interior] of a house／신체의 ~ the inner parts of the body. ないぶ

**내분(內紛)** an internal trouble; domestic discord; a family dispute／~으로 고민하고 있다 suffer from internal trouble [dissension]. ないふん

**내분비(內分泌)** 【생】 internal secretion; endocrine／~선(腺) endocrine glands ／~액(液) endocrine[internal] hecretions; hormones／~학 endocrinology.

내불다 《(바람이)》 blow out 《(숨을)》 breathe out/입김을 ~ let one's breath out; blow upon. ふきだす

# 내 다²

①《(꺼냄)》 take out; bring out; carry out; put[let] out; pull out; draw from[out of]/주머니에서 담배를 ~ take cigarettes out of one's pocket/책상을 밖으로 ~ take a desk out/주머니에서 편지를 끄집어 ~ take[produce] a letter out of one's pocket/새장에서 새를 내주다 let a bird out of its cage.

②《(산출·배출)》 produce; turn out/100명의 졸업생을 ~ turn out 100 graduates/많은 수재를 ~ produce[turn out] many brilliant men/사태로 인하여 많은 사상자를 ~ The landslide caused heavy casualties./이 시에서는 뛰어난 정치가를 많이 내었다 The city has produced many able politicians.

③《(이름·명성을)》 raise; elevate; distinguish/이름을 ~ distinguish oneself; make a name for oneself.

④《(발휘)》 put forth; get up; muster[pluck up]; display/용기를 ~ summon [muster, pluck] up one's courage/기운을 내라 cheer up!/성을 ~ get angry/실력을 ~ display one's ability/있는 힘을 모두 ~ put forth all one's strength.

⑤《(제출)》 present; send in(원서) submit (의견); tender(사표); 《(출품)》 put (an article) on show file/원서를 ~ file[send in] an application/사표를 ~ hand in [submit] one's resignation/명함을 ~ present one's card/의안을 ~ present a bill/문제를 ~ present a problem; set [give] a question/답안을 ~ hand[give] in one's paper/전시회에 작품을 ~ exhibit one's paintings in an exhibition/보고서는 내일까지 내시오 You must hand in your report by tomorrow.

⑥《(발송)》 mail; post; send in[out]; dispatch/편지를 ~ send a letter; mail [post] a letter/초대장을 ~ send out an invitation.

⑦《(돈을)》 pay; give; contribute[donate] 《(투자)》 invest/각자가 비용을 ~ Each paid his share in the expenses. /자금을 ~ furnish (a person) with funds; advance [the] capital; invest in (an enterprise)/자선 사업에 돈을 ~ give[contribute] to charity/학비를 ~ pay one's school expenses/새로운 사업에 돈을 ~ Invest in a new enterprise./집세를 잘 안 ~ neglect to pay one's rent.

⑧《(발행·게재)》 publish; issue; bring out; give/책을 ~ publish a book/신문에 광고를 ~ publish[put] an advertisement/나의 이름은 내지 마시오 Please let me remain anonymous.

⑨《(발설)》 set forth; put forward; start/말을 ~ start talk[rumor]; broach [get on] a subject/소문을 ~ start [spread] a rumor.

⑩《(가게·살림 따위를)》 emanate[emit] 《(빛·열)》 radiate 《(먼지)》 raise/먼지를 ~ raise a dust/빛을 ~ emit[give out] light.

⑪《(음식을)》 serve; offer/점심을 ~ treat (a person) to lunch/손님에게 홍차를 ~ serve guests with tea/이것은 내가 내겠다 This is my treat., This is on me.

⑫《(가게·살림 따위를)》 open; start; set up; begin; run; keep/살림을 ~ set up one's own home/새로 가게를 ~ set up [start, open] a shop.

⑬《(운행)》 run; put/배를 ~ put out a boat/임시 열차를 ~ run a special train.

⑭《(속력을)》 put on[get up] speed/100마일의 속도를 ~ make 100 miles/이 차는 150마일까지 속력을 낼 수 있다 This motorcar develops a maximum speed of 150 miles./《(기선이)》 전속력을 ~ put on full steam.

⑮《(허가·빚 따위를)》 take out; get; obtain/허가를 ~ take out[get] a licence/빚을 ~ get[take out] a loan.

⑯《(팔다)》 offer; for sale; put up for sale/곡식을 ~ sell grain; put grain on sale[on the market]/쌀을 시장에 ~ put[place] rice on the market.

⑰《(시간·길 따위를)》 make; arrange (for); open; set up/시간을 ~ make[find, arrange] time for (something)/자리를 ~ make[arrange] a seat; leave room for (a person) to sit/길을 ~ build [make, open, cut] a road/구멍을 ~ put in[make] an opening/창문을 ~ put in a window/방을 ~ put a room in; build a room/틈을 내어서 같이 가도록 하겠다 I will manage to accompany you.

⑱《(소리를)》 utter; make/큰 소리를 ~ cry out; give a loud cry/이상한 소리를 ~ make a strange noise.

⑲《(비우다)》 empty; clear/방을 ~ clear [vacate] a room/병을 ~ empty a bottle.

⑳《(모를)》 transplant/모를 ~ set out [transplant] rice plants.

㉑《(선출)》 put forward; select; appoint; offer/대표자를 ~ offer[put forward] a representative/후보자를 ~ select a candidate.

**내뿜다** spout; gush out; spurt 《연기를》 shoot up／분수가 물을 ~ a fountain spouts water. はげしくはく

**내빈(來賓)** a guest; an invited guest／~석 the guests' seats／~실 a reception room. らいひん

**내빈(內賓)** a lady visitor; a woman guest. じょしのおきゃく

**내사(內査)** secret examination[inspection, investigation]／~하다 investigate [examine, inspect] secretly. ないみつにしらべること

**내상(內相)** ①《내무 장관》the Home Minister; the Minister of Home Affairs. ②《남의 부인》[your, his] esteemed wife. ないしょう

**내색(一色)** betrayal of *one's* emotions／~하다 betray *one's* emotions; give expression to *one's* feelings／~ 않다 give no expression to *one's* feelings. こころがかおにあらわれること

**내생(內生)** 〖생〗 endogeny／~ 식물 an endogen.

**내생(來生)** 《불교에서》the life to come; the future life[existence]; life after death. らいせい

**내서(耐暑)** proof against heat／~하다 stand[bear up against] heat／~의 heatproof. あつさにたえること

**내서(來書)** a letter [received].

**내선(內線)** 《전기의》 interior wiring 《작전상의》an inner line 《전화의》an extension／~ 번호 an extension number／~ 전화 an interphone. ないせん

**내성(內省)** 〖심〗 introspection; self-examination; reflection／~하다 introspect; reflect on *oneself*. ないせい

**내세(來世)** the future life; the other [next] world 《저승》the better land 《기독교의》kingdom; kingdom come《속》／~를 믿다 believe in the world beyond the grave／~의 명복을 빌다 pray for *one's* welfare in the future life. らいせい

**내세우다** ①《세게 하다》make (*a person*) stand ②《대표로》nominate; designate make (*a person*) represent ③《자기에게 유리하게》stand on; insist advocate; set forth ④《남이 보도록》put[set up, hang out] (*a sign*). もうしたてる

**내소박(內疏薄)** jilting [mistreating] *one's* husband／~하다 jilt[reject] *one's* husband. つまがおっとをれいぐうすること

**내손(來孫)** a great-great-great-grandchild [grandson]. げんそんのこ

**내솟다** spring surge, spurt] up[out].

**내수(耐水)** ~의 waterproof／~성 water-resisting qualities／~포(布) waterproofcloth; tarpaulin.

**내수장(內修粧)** interior decoration; room decoration／~하다 ornament[adorn] the interior of a house; decorate a room; upholster a room.

**내숭** treacherousness; trickiness／~하다 (be) tricky; crafty; sly; insidious; wily; treacherous; underhand; snaky／~스러운 웃음 an insidious smile／~한 사람 a snake. いんけん

**내숭스럽다** (be) insidious; tricky; treacherous. いんけんだ

**내쉬다** exhale; breathe out／숨을 ~ breathe out *one's* breath.

**내습(來襲)** an attack; a raid／~하다 attack; raid; assault; invade／적군의 ~에 대비하다 provide[guard] against the enemy's assault. らいしゅう

**내시(內侍)** a eunuch. かんがん

**내시(內示)** unofficial[informal] announcement／~하다 announce unofficially. ないし

**내신(來信)** a letter [received]; a message; an in-letter／~이 있다 have[receive] a latter from (*a friend*). らいしん

**내신(內申)** an unofficial report／~하다 report unofficially／~서《학교의》a school report; a record of *one's* previous schooling. ないしん

**내실(內室)** the inner room 《안방》the women's quarters 《남의》[your, his] wife. ないしつ

**내심(內心)** *one's* inmost heart; real inward feeling; *one's* mind; *one's* real intention 〖수〗 the inner center／~으로 at heart; in *one's* heart; within *one*／~으로는 …하고 싶어하다 have a secert desire to *do*. ないしん

**내야(內野)** 《야구》the infield; the diamond／~수 an infielder／~석 infield stands. ないや

**내약(內約)** a private agreement 《묵계》a tacit understanding 《밀약》a secret treaty／~하다 make private agreement. ないやく

**내역(內譯)** particulars; details; items／~을 밝히다 state the items (of *an account*); set down (*a bill*) by items／~표 a statement[list] of items. うちわけ

**내연(內燃)** internal combustion／~ 기관 an internal combustion engine／~ 기관차 a Diesel locomotive. ないねん

**내연(內緣)** 《법》 an unregistered marriage／~의 처 a common-law wife; a wife without wedlock／~의 남편 an unmarried husband. ないえん

**내열(耐熱)** heatproof; heat-resistant／~의 heatproof; heat-resisting; refractory／~성의 thermostable／~ 시험 a heat test; a heat-resistance test／~ 유리 heat-resisting glass. たいねつ

**내오다** take[carry, bring] out; remove／의자를 뜰로 ~ bring a chair out into the garden. もちだす

**내왕(來往)** 《왕래》coming and going; traffic 《교제》intercourse; association／~하다 come and go; pass; intercommunicate (*with*). おおらい

**내외(內外)** ①《안팎》the interior and exterior; within and without; the inside and outside ②《부부》husband and wi-

**내외과(內外科)** internal medicine and surgery; medical and surgical practice. ないがいか

**내외술집(內外—)** a public house without service girls.

**내외종(內外從)** cousins 《내종》cousins by a paternal aunt 《외종》cousins by a maternal uncle.

**내외척(內外戚)** relatives on one's father's side and mother's side. ないかいせき

**내용(內容)** contents; substance; subject matter; import/편지 ~ the contents of a letter/사건의 ~ the details of a case/형식과 ~ form and matter/ ~ 증명 우편 contents-certified mail. ないよう

**내용(內用)** ①《내복》internal use[application]/~하다 use[take] internally ②《가용》home expenditure. ないよう

**내우(內憂)** internal troubles/ ~ 외환 internal and external troubles; troubles at home and abroad. ないゆう

**내원(來援)** assistance; help; support/~ 하다 come to help[aid, assist]/~을 요청하다 ask (a person) to come and help [to come to one's assistance]. らいえん

**내월(來月)** next month; proximo(略: prox.)/ ~ 초하룻날 the first of next month; the 1st prox. らいげつ

**내유(來遊)** a visit/ ~하다 visit/ ~객 a visitor 《관광객》a tourist. らいゆう

**내응(內應)** a secret communication; collusion betrayal; treachery/ ~하다 collude[conspire] with; communicate secretly with. ないおう

**내의(內衣)** an undergarment; underclothes; an undershirt (부인용) woman's underwears(총칭); lingerie; scanties《미·속》; underwear; underclothing. したぎ

**내의(內意)** 《의중》one's mind; one's intention 《견해》one's private[personal] opinion. ないい

**내이(內耳)** 『해』 the internal[inner] ear; the labyrinth; Auris interna(학명). ないじ

**내인(內人)** (아낙네)a wife 《나인》a court lady; a maid of honour. ふじん

**내일(來日)** tomorrow/한국의 ~에 관하여 of Korea's tomorrow. あした

**내입(內入)** ①(돈의) partial[part] payment; payment on account/ ~하다 pay on account[as part, in part settlement] ②(궁중에 물건을 들임) delivery of goods to the Royal Court/ ~하다 deliver goods to the Royal Court. うちきん

**내자(內子)** my wife. じぶんのつま

**내장(內粧)** interior decoration[design]. うちのないぶをかざりととのえること

**내장(內臟)** the internal organs; the inward parts of the boby/~ 외과 internal surgery/ ~ 질환 an internal disease. ないぞう

**내장(內障)** 『의』(흑내장) amaurosis《백내장》cataract (녹내장) glaucoma.

**내재(內在)** 『철』immanence/ ~적 immanent/ ~ 철학 immanentism; immanence-philosophy. ないざい

**내적(內的)** inner 《유전의》inherited 《고유의》intrinsic (마음의)/ ~ 가치 the intrinsic value (of a thing)/ ~ 경험 inner experiences/ ~ 생활 inner life. ないてき

**내전(內殿)** 《왕비》a queen; an empress 《왕비(王妃)》. ないでん

**내전(來電)** a telegram; a dispatch〈미〉; a message. らいでん

**내전 보살(內殿菩薩)** feigned ignorance; pretending innocence 《사람》a person who feigns ignorance (about).

**내접(內接)** ~하다 『수』 be inscribed; touch internally/ ~원(圓) an inscribed circle. ないせつ

**내젓다** wag (the hand).

**내정(內定)** unofficial[informal, tentative, private] decision/ ~하다 decide unofficially[informally, tentatively]/ ~되다 be informally arranged[decided]/은행장으로 ~되었다 He has been informally designated as president of the bank. ないてい

**내정(內政)** domestic[home] administration; internal affairs. ないせい

**내정(內庭)** ①(안뜰)a courtyard; an inner garden ②(회교국에서의) a harem; a seraglio. ないてい

**내정(內情)** (내부 사정) inside affairs 《실정》the real state of affairs/ 회사 ~에 밝다 be familiar with the inside affairs of acompang. ないじょう

**내조(乃祖)** one's grandfather. そのひとのそふ

**내조(內助)** one's wife's assistance/ ~하다 help one's husband. ないじょ

**내조(來朝)** ①(외국 사신의) the arrival [visit] of foreign envoy ②(왕후의) the visit of a local lord to the King/~하다 [a foreign envoy] arrive; visit. らいちょう

**내종(內從)** cousins by a paternal aunt. こぼのこども

**내쫓기다** 《밖으로》be turned out 《해고》be dismissed; be fired. ついほうされる

**내쫓다** drive[force, send, turn, kick] out (지위에서)oust; relieve (퇴거시키다)eject; evict (해고하다)discharge; dismiss; give (one) the sack《영·속》; fire《미·속》. ついほうする

**내주(來週)** next week; the coming week/ ~ 금요일 Friday next week; next Friday. らいしゅう

**내주다** ①(금품을) take[bring, put] (a thing) out; and give it; give out[away]

/월급을 ~ pay one's salary ②《자리를》 give; offer; yield; resign; surrender / 자리를 ~ make room (for a person); give[offer] a seat. だしてやる

**내주장(內主張)** petticoat government/~하다 henpeck one's husband/그 집은 ~이다 The wife is the ruler in that house. かかあでんか

**내지(乃至)** (…부터 …까지) from… to; between… and (또는) or. ないし

**내지(內地)** the interior; inland; home/~의 inland; interior; home/ ~인 people at home. ないち

**내직(內職)** ①(본직 외의) a side job[business]; side[outside, extra, home]/~을 하다 do outside, work, take in (sewing) ②(가정 부인의) a job[work] for housewives. ないしょく

**내진(耐震)** proof against earthquakes; earthquake-proof/ ~ 된 건물 an earthquake-proof building/ ~ 구조 aseismatic structure. たいしん

**내착(來着)** arrival/~하다 reach; arrive (at in); come; get to. らいちゃく

**내찰(內札)** letters between women.

**내채(內債)** an internal[a domestic] loan / ~를 발행하다 raise[float] a domestic loan.

**내처** throughout; to the very end; without pause[intermission]; at a breath; at a stretch; at a dash; straight /길을 ~ 가다 go on one's way without pause/여섯 시간 ~ 일하다 work for six hours at a stretch. ずっと

**내청(來聽)** attendance/ ~하다 come to hear; attend (a lecture).

**내추(來秋)** next autumn[fall]; the coming autumn. らいしゅう

**내춘(來春)** next spring; the coming spring. らいしゅん

**내출혈(內出血)** 〖의〗 internal hemorrhage[bleeding]. ないしゅっけつ

**내치(內治)** ①(내정) home administration [policy]; internal affairs/~하다 administrate[administer] internal affairs [policy] ②(내과 치료) internal treatment/ ~하다 cure by internal medicine.

**내치다** throw away; cast away; abandon; desert[discard](a lover); reject (각하) turn down; drive back/쓰레기를 ~ throw away garbage; dump refuse. はねつける

**내치락들이치락** ①(변덕스럽게) capricious; fitful; blowing hot and cold / ~하다 (be) capricious; hot and cold / ~하는 사람 a man of moods; a capricious [whimsical] person ②(병세가) ~하다 change constantly/그의 병세는 ~ 한다 His illness hangs in the balance. きまぐれに

**내친걸음** having set about doing (a thing); having crossed the Rubicon. ついでに

**내침(內寢)** sharing one's wife's bed/ ~하다 share the same bed with wife. おっとがつまのへやにいってねること

**내켜놓다** remove farther; set farther ahead. とおくうつす

**내키다** 《마음이》 be inclined[disposed] (to do); have an inclination; care[like] to; feel like doing. /마음이 내키지 않다 take no interest in; have no inclination for; be in no mood to (do). するきになる

**내키다²** ①《마음을》 bring oneself to; put one's mind to/마음을 내키어 일하다 put one's mind to work ②《자리를》 make[leave] room for. するきにさせる

**내탐(內探)** a private inquiry; a secret investigation/ ~하다 make private inquiries/회사의 사정을 ~ 하다 investigate the inside affairs of a company. ないたん

**내탕금(內帑金)** a privy[a private] purse; the Imperial Privy Purse. ないどきん

**내통(內通)** ①《남녀의》 illicit intercourse; misconduct; intimacy/ ~하다 have improper relations (with) ②(내응) secret communication[understanding].

**내팽개치다** throw (a thing) out [forcefully]; toss (a thing) away.

**내평(內—)** the real state[of affairs]; the internal conditions.

**내포(內包)** 〖논〗 connotation; intention; comprehension/ ~하다 connote; contain; involve. ないほう

**내풀로** of one's own accord; voluntarily; on one's own initiative. じはつてきに

**내피(內皮)** 〖해〗 endothelium. ないひ

**내핍(耐乏)** austerity; voluntary privation/~ 생활 a life of austerity; an austerity life. たいぼう

**내한(耐寒)** proof against the cold; coldproof/ ~하다 endure[bear, stand] cold/ ~의 cold-proof. ないかん

**내항(內港)** the inner harbo[u]r. ないこう

**내항(內項)** 〖수〗 internal terms. ないこう

**내항(來航)** a visit (to this country)/ ~하다 visit; visit these[Korean] shores.

**내해(內海)** an inland sea; an arm of the sea; a big lake. ないかい

**내행(內行)** 《여행》 a woman on a journey 《행실》 the conduct of a wife at home.

**내향성(內向性)** 〖심〗 introversion 《형용사적》 introvert/ ~인 사람 an introvert. ないこうせい

**내형(乃兄)** his[her] elder brother. そのひとのあにき

**내홍(內訌)** an internal dissension[trouble]; domestic discord. ないこう

**내화(耐火)** proof against fire; fireproof / ~하다 (be) impervious to fire; fireproof/ ~ 구조 fire-resisting construction/저 집은 ~ 건물이다 The building is proof against fire. たいか

**내환(內患)** 〖병〗 the sickness of one's wife

**〈내우〉** domestic[internal] troubles／외우 ~ troubles both at home and abroad; troubles from within and without. ないかん

**내회(來會)** attendance; presence／~하다 attend; be present at a meeting; come and meet; assemble. らいかい

**내후년(來後年)** the year after next; three years hence. さらいねん

**내흉(內凶)** ~한[스러운] insidious; tricky; treacherous; wicked. いんけん

**냄새** smell; odo[u]r; scent 《방향》 fragrance; perfume 《악취》 stink; reek (of *tobacco*)／좋은 ~ a sweet smell; an agreeable smell／~가 없어지다 lose the odor. におい

**냅다¹** 《세차게》 with force; hard; actively; with all *one's* strength; violently／~ 달아나다 run for *one's* life; make a quick escape. はげしく

**냅다²** 《연기가》 (be) smoky／방이 ~ The room is smoky／연기가 ~ smoke stings [smarts]. けむる

**냅뜨다** venture (*on*); get gallantly started; sally forth.

**냇가** a riverside; the bank[edge] of a river. かわべ

**냇내** the smell of smoke. けむりのにおい

**냇버들** 【식】 a purple willow[osier].

**냇송어** 【어】 a bull-trout; a brook trout.

**냉(冷)** ①《대하증》 *fluor albus*; leucorrh[o]ea; whites ②《뱃병》 cold abdomen; a chill stomach ③《몸의》 a chill; a body chill. こしけ

**냉-(冷)** cold; iced／~맥주 iced beer／~커피 iced coffee. ひやし

**냉각(冷却)** cooling; refrigeration／~하다 refrigerate; cool down／~기 a freezer; a refrigerator／~ 기간 a cooling-off period. れいきゃく

**냉과리** half-burnt charcoal. けむるすみ

**냉국(冷—)** unboiled soup; soup prepared cold. つめたいすいもの

**냉기(冷氣)** 《찬 기운》 cold; chill 《추위》 a cold wave 《찬 공기》 cool air; a chilly draft／~를 느끼다 feel chilly. れいき

**냉담(冷淡)** ①《무관심》 coolness; indifference; lukewarmness; lack of interest／~하다 (be) cool; halfhearted; indifferent ②《냉정》 cold-heartedness; heartlessness; callousness／~하다 (be) cold; coldhearted. れいたん

**냉대(冷待)** cold treatment／~하다 treat (*one*) coldly; receive (*one*) with indifference; give the cold shoulder to; deal ill with. つめたいしうち

**냉돌(冷突)** a cold room[floor]; an unheated floor of a Korean room. つめたいオンドル

**냉동(冷凍)** freezing; refrigeration／~하다 freeze; refrigerate／~어 frozen fish／~기 a refrigerator. れいとう

**냉랭하다(冷冷—)** ①《차다》 (be) cold; coolly; chilly 《얼음장같이》 icy 《얼 것같이》 freezing ②《냉담하다》 (be) cool; indifferent. ひややかでさびしい

**냉면(冷麵)** a cold noodle dish; iced vermicelli. れいめん

**냉방(冷房)** a cold room; an unheated room／~ 장치 air conditioner[air conditioning apparatus]; an air cooler; a cooling apparatus. れいぼう

**냉소(冷笑)** a cold smile 《조소》 a sneer; a jeer／~하다 smile derisively; sneer (*at*). れいしょう

**냉수(冷水)** cold water／~ 마찰 a rubdown with a wet towel; cold-water rubbing／~욕하다 take a cold bath／~ 마찰하다 take a cold rubdown with a wet towel. れいすい

**냉수스럽다(冷水—)** (be) insipid. みずくさい

**냉습(冷濕)** ①《차고 습함》 being cold and damp; moisture／~하다 (be) cold and damp[moist] ②《병》 rheumatism. れいきとおんき

**냉엄(冷嚴)** ~하다 (be) grim; stern; stark／~한 현실 stark realities of life.

**냉연(冷然)** ~하다 (be) cold; indifferent; icy／~히 coldly; coolly; icily; indifferently. れいぜん

**냉온(冷溫)** coldness and warmth. れいおん

**냉우(冷遇)** cold[icy] treatment; frigid reception; inhospitality.

**냉이** 【식】 a shepherd's purse; a mother's-heart. なずな

**냉장(冷藏)** cold storage; refrigeration／~하다 keep (*a thing*) in cold storage; refrigerate／~고 《전기의》 a refrigerator; a freezer 《얼음의》 an ice chest; an icebox. れいぞう

**냉전(冷戰)** a cold war／~을 완화하다 ease cold war tensions／~ 외교 cold war diplomacy. れいせん

**냉정(冷靜)** calmness; composure; coolness; serenity／~하다 (be) calm; cool; serene／~히 calmly; coolly; serenely／~한 사람 a cool-headed person／~을 잃다 lose *one's* presence of mind; be upset. れいせい

**냉차(冷茶)** iced tea. ひやしたおちゃ

**냉천(冷泉)** a cold mineral spring.

**냉철(冷徹)** ~하다 (be) cool-headed; hard-headed. れいてつ

**냉큼** quickly; briskly; hastily; promptly; without delay; right away; readily／~ 대답하다 answer promptly[readily]. ただちに

**냉평(冷評)** a sarcastic remark; a sneer／~하다 sneer at; make a sarcastic remark (*on*). つめたいひひょう

**냉풍(冷風)** a chilly[cold] wind. れいふう

**냉하다(冷—)** (be) cold; chilly; icy; freezing 《마음이》 cold-hearted. つめたい

**냉한(冷汗)** a cold sweat. れいかん

**냉해(冷害)** cold-weather damage／~를 입다 suffer damage due to[from] cold

**냉혈(冷血)** 《온혈에 대한》 cold-bloodedness

《무정》cold-heartedness; callousness; heartlessness/〜의 cold-blooded[-hearted]; heartless; callous/〜 동물 a cold-blooded animal. れいけつ

**냉혹**(冷酷) cruelty; heartlessness/〜한 cruel; unfeeling; heartless; cold-hearted. れいこく

**냉회**(冷灰) cold ashes. れいかい

**-냐** 《의문》who; what; when; how/몇 살이〜 How old are you?/그 책을 읽었느〜 Did you read that book? —か

**냠냠** Yum-yum! [How tasty!]/〜거리다 smack *one's* lips.

**냠냠이** dainty food; a delicacy/ 〜대다 eat with much gusto; dine with a good appetite. おやつ

**냠냠하다** 《먹고 싶어》want[desire] to eat 《갖고 싶어》wish for; long[itch] for; be anxious for; covet. ほしがる

**냥**(兩) 《화폐의》a *nyang*; a tael 《중량의》a *nyang*(=1.325ounce, 37.5g). りょう

**너**[1] you; thou《고》/〜의 your; thy《고》/〜에게 to[for] you[thee]/〜 자신을 알다 Know yourself[thyself]. おまえ

**너**[2] 《넷》four/〜 발 four spans. し

**너겁** leaves or straws floating on the surface of water. じんかい

**너구리** 《동》a raccoon dog. あなぐま

**너그러이** leniently; tolerantly; liberally /〜 용시하다 forgive generously/〜 대하다 show clemency. かんように

**너그럽다** (be) broad-minded; generous; liberal; magnanimous; tolerant; indulgent; lenient; charitable/너그러운 사람 a generous person/너그러운 생각 a liberal idea/너그러운 처분을 바라다 plead for leniency. かんようだ

**너글너글하다** (be) large-hearted; broad-minded; generous; liberal/마음이 〜 be generous[liberal] (*with*). おおらかだ

**너더댓** about four or five. よつかいつつ

**너더분하다** ①《장황하다》(be) long and boring[tedious]; long-winded; diffuse ②《지저분하다》(be) untidy; disorderly/너더분하게 in disorder. ごたごたしている

**너덕너덕** patchily/〜 기운 patchy; full of patches/옷을 〜 집다 patch up *one's* clothes all over. つぎはぎだらけに

**너덜거리다** ①《여러 가닥이》dangle in tatters[in pieces] ②《주제넘다》behave fresh[forward, uppish]. ぶらぶらする

**너덜너덜** in tatters; in shreds; in rags and tatters/〜하다 (be) tattered; ragged; torn; worn-out. ぶらぶら

**너덧** about four. よつくらい

**너도밤나무** 《식》a beech [tree].

**너럭바위** a broad flat rock. ばんじゃく

**너르다** (be) wide; open; extensive 《집이》roomy. ひろい

**너름새** a talent for doing things on a large scale; managerial ability; resourcefulness. しゃこうせい

**너리** 《한》pyorrh[o]ea alveolaris/〜 먹다 have diseased gums. しそうのうろう

**너머** the opposite[other] side/산 〜 on the other side of the mountain/어깨 〜로 over *one's* shoulder. こえて

**너무** too [much]; over 《각별히》particulary/〜 진하다 《차가》be too strong; be oversteeped. あまりに

**너벅선**(一船) a flat-bottomed boat; a broad ferryboat. ひらたいそこのふね

**너부데데하다** have an unpleasantly flat face. かおがまるくてひらたい

**너부렁이** dangling odds and ends.

**너부죽이** ①《너부죽하게》somewhat flatly [evenly] ②《엎드리다》[lie] prostrate (*before*); [fall] prostrate[flat] (*upon the ground*). おもむろに

**너부죽하다** (be) somewhat flat and broad. ひらたくでややひろい

**너불거리다** flutter; flap; wave. ゆらぐ

**너비** 《폭》width; breadth/〜가 넓다 be wide; be broad [in width]. はば

**너비아니** slices of roast seasoned beef.

**너삼** 《식》*Sophora angustifolia*(학명).

**너새** 《조》a great bustard; *Otis tarda* (학명).

**너설** a rock-ribbed place; a rocky[craggy] spot. うねのあるどころ

**느스레** ①《아구리에 걸친》a frame-support made by criss-crossing twigs or sticks [used to cover a hole or to support things at the bottom of a pot] ② a tr:ck; an artifice; a catch.

**너울** a headpiece of black silk for lady /〜 쓴 거지 a beggar can't afford to be a gentleman.

**너울가지** affability; sociability/〜가 좋다 be sociable[amicable]. しゃこうせい

**너울거리다** 《물결 따위가》roll; undulate; wave 《나뭇잎 따위가》swing; sway; waver/너울너울 waving; undulating; surging; swaying; swinging/바닷물결이 〜 the sea surges/나뭇가지가 바람에 너울거린다 The tree branches are swaying in the wind. ひらひらする

**너저분하다** (be) shabby and untidy; dirty; sordid; filthy; nasty; disorderly; be out of order. ちらばっている

**너절하다** 《가치없다》(be) worthless 《쓸모없다》useless 《야비하다》mean 《추접하다》vulgar 《좋지 않다》poor 《초라하다》shabby. そまつできたない

**너털거리다**[1] 《흔들리다》dangle[sway] in a disorderly manner/너털너털 in a disorderly manner.

**너털거리다**[2] 《웃다》laugh loudly.

**너털웃음** loud laughter/〜을 웃다 laugh aloud. けらけらわらい

**너테** an added coating of ice on top of ice. こおりのかさね

**너펄거리다** flutter; flicker; wave/너펄 너펄 flutteringly. ひらひらする

**너푼거리다** lightly flutter[wave]. かるやかにひらひらする

**너풀거리다** flutter; wave; float; flap/ 너풀너풀 fluttering flapping/깃발이 바

람에 너풀거린다 The flag is flapping in the wind. ひらひらする

**너희** you; ye; you all. きみたち

**너희들** you; you all; you people. きみたち

**넉** four 《순서》 fourth/~ 달 four months/그 구절은 첫 페이지의 ~ 줄째에 있다 You will find the phrase in the fourth line of the first page. よつ

**넉가래** a grain-shovel 《눈을 치는》 a snow-shovel/ ~질 shoveling with a wooden shovel/ ~질하다 shovel with a wooden shovel.

**넉걸이** raking out vines/ ~하다 rake vines off (a melon field, etc.).

**넉넉하다** ①《족하다》(be) enough; sufficient; good; full; satisfactory; plenty ②《마음이》(be) magnanimous; generous; liberal; broad-minded. ゆたかだ

**넉살** audacity; impudence; shamelessness; cheekiness/ ~부리다 behave impudently/ ~좋다 (be) impudent; brash; shameless; sassy. むこうみず

**넉장** slowness; slow motion; sluggish behaviour/ ~부리다 be slow-going; be tardy; dally; dawdle. なまけること

**넉장거리** lying[falling] outstreched on one's back/ ~하다 fall[lie] down outstretched on one's back.

**넋** soul 《정신》the spirit; a ghost; one's spirit/죽은 ~ a shade/ ~이 없다 be absent-minded. たましい

**넋두리** ①《무당의》utterances of a shaman given as those of a deceased spirit / ~하다 [a shaman] speak in behalf of the dead ②《투덜거림》a complaint; a grumble; a murmur/ ~하다 grumble (at); complain (of).くちよせのことば

**넌더리** an aversion; a dislike; a disgust /~나다 be sick of; be tired up with; abhor/~대다 make (one) sick of (something) weary. ひどいいやき

**넌덕** smooth and witty talk/ ~부리다 have a smooth and witty tongue/ ~스럽다 be witty[facile, amusing]; be humorous. かいぎゃく

**넌지시** furtively; tacitly; covertly; indirectly; in a casual way/ ~ 말하다 hint (at); allude/ ~ 알리다 suggest; hint/그는 그 문제에 대해서 ~ 언급했다 He made a distant allusion to the question. ひそかに

**넌출** 《식》 a bine; a vine 《호박 따위의》a tendril 《고구마의》a runner/포도 ~ a grape vine/호박 ~ a pumpkin tendril / ~지다 tendrils dangle down. つる

**널** ①《널빤지》 a board; a plank ②《관》 a coffin/ ~에 넣다 lay in a coffin ③ 《널뛰기의》a seesaw board; a teetertotter. いた

**널감** ①《널의 감》wood for a coffin ② 《죽어 가는 이》an old man; a person with one foot in the grave.

**널다**¹ 《쥐가 쏠다》gnaw (a thing) into small pieces. ねずみなどがちらす

**널다**² 《퍼놓다》spread (out); stretch 《빨다》hang out to; dry air/빨랫줄을 ~ hang out (clothes) on a clothesline. ひらげておく

**널따랗다** (be) rather wide; extensive; roomy; spacious/널따란 이마 a broad forehead/널따란 길 a wide road/널따란 뜰 an extensive garden. ひじょうにひろい

**널다리** a wooden footbridge. いたばし

**널뛰기** seesaw; seesawing; teeter-totter [-ing]/ ~하다 ~널뛰다.

**널뛰다** play Korean seesaw; seesaw; teeter-totter.

**널름거리다** roll out and in; watch.

**널리** widely; far and wide 《일반적으로》 generally/ ~ 세상에 알려지다 be known all the world over. ひろく

**널리다**¹ 《흩어져 퍼지다》be spread (over); be scattered (about)/낙엽이 뜰에 널려 있다 Fallen leaves are spread all over the garden. ひろがる

**널리다**² 《넓히다》broaden[widen, extend, enlarge]. かくちょうする

**널마루** a wooden floor; a board-floor. いたどこ

**널문**(—門) a wooden gate. いたのもん

**널빤지** a board; a plank/ ~ 담 a wooden wall; a board fence.

**널브러지다** spread (out); extend; stretch widen. らんざつにひろがる

**널빈지** board[wooden] shutters. あまど

**널어놓다** spread out; hang out [a thing to air or dry it]. ひらげておく

**널장** a plank; a board. いた

**널조각** a piece of board.

**널찍이** somewhat broadly[widely, spaciously]/구멍을 ~ 파다 dig a hole big enough.

**널찍하다** (be) open; extensive; spacious 《집이》 roomy/널찍한 집 a roomy[spacious] house. ややひろい

**널판대기, 널판자** a big[long, broad and thick] piece of board.

**널판장**(—板墻) a board fence; a wooden wall. いたばり

**널평상**(—平床) a plank bed; a wooden bed. いたのしんだい

**넓다** ①《폭·넓이가》(be) broad; large; extensive/넓은 의미로 in a broad sense ②《마음이》(be) large-hearted; broad-minded; generous. ひろい

**넓데데하다** (be) unpleasantly flaffish. ややひらたくてまるい

**넓이** 《폭》width; breadth 《면적》extent; area; dimensions/ ~뛰기 running broad jump/《미》. ひろさ

**넓적다리** the thigh; the femur(pl. -mora). だいたい

**넓적부리** 《조》 a shovelbill.

**넓적스름하다** (be) somewhat flat; be rather flat. ややへんぺいだ

**넓적이** ①《사람》a person with a flat and broad face ②《넓적하게》flat; so that it is flat/떡을 ~ 썰다 cut a rice cake

넓적하다 (be) flat.
넓죽 ①(입을) with *one's* mouth wide open ②(엎드리다) flat; low.
넓죽하다 (be) flat and long.
넓히다 《널리다》widen; enlarge 《확장하다》extend; broaden; stretch[spread] out / 경험을 ~ enlarge *one's* experience / 길을 ~ widen[broaden] a road / 판도를 ~ extend the territory.
넘겨다보다 《넘어보다》look over; covet 《탐내다》gloat over.
넘겨씌우다 put (*a blame*) on another; lay (*a fault*) at another's door; impute; shuffle off.
넘겨잡다 guess [out]; suppose; conjecture.
넘겨짚다 guess; make a guesswork; make a random guess.
넘고처지다 be either too long or too short[too big or too small, too high or too low, *etc.*]; be too much one way or too much the other.
넘기다 ①(인도하다) hand [over]; turn over; transfer (권리 따위를) deliver up ②(넘어가게 하다) take (*a thing*) over ③(넘어뜨리다) fall; throw down; overthrow ④(기한·때 따위를) pass; spend; tide over ⑤(책장을) turn.
넘나다 be not suitable[proportionate] to *one's* means.
넘나들다 make free access (*to*); frequent; go and come often / 권문의 문턱이 닳도록 ~ frequent the house of an influential person.
넘노닐다 stroll around[to and fro].
넘늘거리다 wave; droop / 넘늘넘 swingingly; wavingly.
넘늘다 indulge *one's* humour without losing *one's* dignity.
넘늘어지다 droop at random.
넘다 ①(건느다) cross; go across[over]; go[get] beyond; clear (장애물을) hurdle ②(초과하다) exceed; pass; be in excess of; be over[above] ③(고비를) conquer[overcome, surmount] (*difficulties*) ④(칼날이) be turned ⑤(넘치다) overflow; run[flow] over.
넘보다 hold (*one*) cheap; make light of; look down upon; think meanly of; belittle.
넘성거리다 stretch[crane] *one's* neck avidly to see; look with *one's* neck stretched.
넘실거리다 ①(탐내다) be greedy for ⇨넘성거리다 ②(물·물결이) surge; roll; swell; be brimful; undulate; wave / 넘실넘실 swelling; rolling; full to the brim.
넘어가다 ①(지나가다) cross; go across; go over 《장애물을》hurdle ②(해·달이) sink; set; go down ③(남의 소유로) pass[fall] (*to, into*) *one's* hands ④(속다)

be taken in; be imposed upon; be deceived.
넘어다보다 look[peep] over (*a high thing*).
넘어뜨리다 ①(넘어지게 하다) throw[tumble] down; knock over; overthrow; fell / 바람이 나무들을 넘어뜨렸다 The wind blew down several trees. ②(지우다) defeat; beat ③(전복시키다) overthrow; undermine.
넘어오다 ①(오다) come over; come along ②(제 차지로) come into *one's* hand[possession]; come to *one's* turn; be transferred.
넘어지다 ① fall; come down; collapse; tumble down ②(지다) be defeated; be ruined;; be overthrown 《파산되다》go [become] bankrupt.
넘치다 ①(범람하다) overflow; flow[run] over; flood; be full of / 기쁨에 ~ be full of joy ②(초과하다) exceed; be above[beyond] / 분에 넘치는 영광 an undeserved hono[u]r.
넙데데하다 have an unpleasantly flat face ⇨너부레데하다
넙치 [어] a flatfish; a sole / ~눈이 a cross-eyed person.
넛손자(-孫子) a grandson of *one's* sister; a grandnephew on *one's* sister's side.
넛할머니 *one's* father's maternal aunt.
넛할아버지 *one's* father's maternal uncle.
넝마 old-clothes; rags / ~ 장수 a ragman; a junkman / ~주이 a trash[rag] picker.
넣다 ①(속에) put (*a thing*) in[into]; take in; let in (자물쇠로 잠가서) put [lock] away ②(끼우다) set (*a thing*) in; put in[into]; insert (채우다) stuff ③(수용하다) send[put] to(학교·병원 등에) ④(포함하다) include; account.
네¹ (너) you (너의) your.
네² (넷) four / ~사람 four people.
네³ (대답) yes; certainly; all right; very well; surely; sure; O. K.《미·속》.
-네 (들)all of / 우리~ we all / 당신~ you all / 그~ they.
네까짓 the likes of you; (*a person*) like you.
네거리 a crossroads; an X-road; a cross; an intersection / ~에 가게를 내다 set up a store at the crossroads.
네눈박이 a dog with a white spot above each eye.
네댓 about four or five / ~새 about 4 or 5 days; the better part of a week; a few days.
네뚜리 ①(업신여김) looking down on (*a person*); holding (*a person*) in contempt / ~하다 look down on (*a person*) ②(새우젓의) one fourth of a crock of pickled sprimps.

**네모** the four corners of a square/ ~난 four cornered; square. しかく

**네모꼴** a tetragon; a quadrangle; trapezium; a quadrilateral. しかっけい

**네발짐승** a quadrupeds; four-legged animals.

**네쌍동이** quadruplets.

**네째** the fourth; No. 4; the fourth place / ~의 fourth. よばんめ

**넨장[맞을]** 《간투사》 Damn!; Damn it!; 《주저할 때》 Damn him; Damn you!; Hang it 《형용사격》 damned; damnable; wretched; cursed; accursed; deuced.
くそっ

**녯** four/ ~으로 자르다 quarter; cut in four. よつ

**녀석** ①《경멸적으로》 a fellow; a guy; a rascal ②《귀엽게》 a little rascal; a chap; a boy/귀여운 ~ a sweet little rascal of a boy. やつ

**년** 《경멸적으로》 a woman; a bitch/이~ You wretched woman!/미친 ~ a crazy woman. あま

**년(年)** year/5~ 6개월 five years and six months. ねん

**념념하다** (be) wise and careful; sagacious and prudent; intelligent and cautious.

**녘** 《방향·지역》 (in) the area of(장소); 《무렵》 around; about 《방향》 (in) the direction of; towards. ほうこう

**노** 《끈 줄》 a string; a cord[rope]. なわ

**노(櫓)** an oar; a paddle; a scull / ~를 젓다 pull an oar; row; work a scull; scull (a boat). ろ

**노가주** 〖식〗 juniper; *Juniperus rigida*(학명). ねず

**노각(老-)** yellowish overripe cucumbers.

**노객(老客)** ①《늙은 손》 an aged caller[person] ②《늙은이》 an old man; an old 《손님》 an aged visitor. おいぼれ

**노경(老境)** advanced age[life]; one's declining years/ ~에 들다 be in the decline of one's life; be advanced in life; be well on in years. ろうきょう

**노고(老姑)** an old woman; a granny ⇒할미. おばあさん

**노고(勞苦)** labor; pains; toil/ ~하다 take trouble/ ~를 아끼지 않다 spare no pains. ろうく

**노고지리** 〖조〗 a skylark. ひばり

**노곤(勞困)** ~하다 (be) tired; exhausted; weary; languid. ひろう

**노골(露骨)** nakedness; frankness; candour; outspokenness; plainness. ろこつ

**노골적(露骨的)** ①《솔직》 plain; undisguised; frank; naked; open; candid/ ~인 사람 an outspoken person ②《음란》 broad (joke); lewd; indecent/ ~인 말 a broad story/저 그림은 너무 ~이다 The picture is too suggestive. ろこつてき

**노구(老軀)** one's old bones[body]; old and weak limbs; an advanced age/ ~를 이끌고[무릅쓰고] in spite of one's advanced age. ろうく

**노구(老嫗)** an old woman/ ~장이 an old-woman pimp. おばあさん

**노굿** the flowers of leguminous plants / ~일다 [beans] flower; blossom.

**노그라지다** ①《피로하다》 be tired out; be worn out; be exhausted; be dog-tired ②《마음이 쏠리다》 be infatuated with; give oneself up to. ふける

**노글노글** ~하다 (be) soft; elastic; pliant. ぐにゃぐにゃだ

**노급(弩級)** the dreadnought class.

**노긋노긋** ~하다 ①《촉감이》 (be) supple; elastic; soft to the touch ②《성격이》 (be) supple; adaptable; docile; compliant ⇒누긋누긋하다. ゆるゆるする

**노기(老妓)** an old singing girl; an old *keesaeng*. ろうぎ

**노기(怒氣)** anger; indignation; wrath/ / ~ 등등한 enraged; exasperated/ ~ 충천하다 be in a blaze of passion; be inflamed with rage. どき

**노년(老年)** old age; declining years; the winter of life/ ~기 senescence; old age. ろうねん

**노농(老農)** an expert[a skilled] farmer; an old farmer.

**노농(勞農)** laborers and farmers/ ~ 정치 Soviet rule/ ~당 the Farmer-Labour party. ろうのう

**노놓치다** let [a criminal] escape.
こっそりのがしてやる

**노느다** ①⇒나누다 ②《분배하다》 share; divide up/이익을 두 사람이 ~ divide the gain between the two. わける

**노느매기** distribution; sharing; division / ~하다 divide; share; distribute; deal out; allot. ぶんばい

**노는계집** a prostitute. ゆうじょ

**노닐다** stroll[ramble] about; saunter [lounge, loiter] along. ぶらぶらあるく

**노다지** a rich vein 《행운》 a bonanza 《늘 상》 any time; all the time. おおあたり

**노닥거리다** make a long and funny talk; prate; wag one's tongue; talk volubly. べらべらしゃべる

**노닥노닥** in patches. つぎはぎだらけ

**노닥다리(老-)** an an[aged] person ⇒늙은이. ろうじん

**노닥이다** talk volubly; make words; chatter. べらべらしゃべる

**노대(露臺)** 〖건〗 a gallery; a balcony.
ろだい

**노대가(老大家)** a veteran authority (on); a past master/국문학의 ~ a veteran student of Korean classics. ろうたいか

**노대국(老大國)** a senile great nation; a declining[withering] empire.

**노도(怒濤)** raging billows; angry waves; rough waters/ ~를 헤치고 나아가다 advance in the face of high seas.
どとう

**노독(路毒)** the fatigue of a journey; si-

**노동(勞動)** labo[u]r; manual labo[u]r; toil; work; industry／～하다 labor; work; toil／싸고 풍부한 ～력 cheap and plentiful labor／하루 8시간 ～제 daily eight-hour working system／～으로 생활하다 live by labor／～ 가치설 the labor value theory／～ 계약 a work contract／～ 공급 the labor supply／～ 관리 labor management／～ 능률 labor efficiency／～ 대회 a labor rally／～력 labor power; manpower／～ 문제 labor problems／～ 시간 working hours／～ 시장 the labor market／～ 인구 labor force; working population／～ 조건 working conditions／근육 ～ muscular labor／두뇌 ～ brain work／육체[정신] ～ physical[mental] work. ろうどう

**노동자(勞動者)** a labo[u]rer; a workman; a worker 《총칭》 labor／～ 계급 the worker[working] class[es]／～ 보호 protection of laborers／～ 수용소 a labor camp. ろうどうしゃ

**노동 조합(勞動組合)** a labor union; a trade union〈영〉／～ 간부 a union leader／～을 조직하다 organize a union; unionize (*company employees*)／한국 ～ 총연맹 The Federation of Korea Trade Union(略: F.K.T.U.).

**노두(露頭)** 《광》 a crop; an outcrop; a basset. ろとう

**노둔(魯鈍)** stupidity; stupid; dullness／～하다 (be) stupid; dull; muddle-headed. ろどん

**노둣돌** a horse block [for mounting and dismounting].

**노드리듯** in torrents; cats and dogs／～ 하다 pour down; rain in torrents; rain cats and dogs. どしゃぶりのさま

**노랑** yellow／～ 머리 a yellow head; yellow hair. きいろ

**노랑매미꽃** 《식》 a Japanese [yellow] rose; a multiflora rose.

**노랑이** ①《노란 것》 a yellow object ②《인색한 이》 a miser; a stingy person ③《개》 a yellow dog. きいろいもの

**노랗다** ①《색이》 (be) quite yellow; be a golden yellow／노란 저고리 a yellow coat／얼굴이 ～ one's complexion is yellow; look poor ②《싹수가》 ①싹수가 ～ have not dog's chance. きいろっぽい

**노래** a song; a ballad 《창가》 singing／～ 하다 sing [a song]／～를 부르다 sing a song／피아노에 맞춰 ～하다 sing to a piano accompaniment. うた

**노래(老來)** the later years of *one's* life.

**노래기** 《동》 a millipede; a myriapod; *Nipponoiulus truncatus*(학명).  やすで

**노략(擄掠)** pillage／～질 plundering; pillaging／～[질]하다 pillage; despoil; plunder.

**노려보다** glare[stare] at; stare fixedly [angrily, sharply] at／서로 ～ glare at each other; look daggers at each other／꼼짝 못하게 ～ scowl down (*a person*). にらみつける

**노력(努力)** endeavo[u]r; effort; exertion／～하다 endeavo[u]r; strive; make efforts; exert *oneself*／～가 a hard working person; a grinder／끊임없이 ～ 하다 persevere in *one's* efforts／～ 부족 a shortage of labo[u]r (*in*). どりょく

**노력(勞力)** 《수고》 trouble; pains; effort 《노동》 labo[u]r／～하다 take pains[trouble]; make efforts; labo[u]r; strive; work／～이 드는 일 labo[u]rious work／～을 제공하다 offer personal labo[u]r[services]. ろうりょく

**노련(老練)** being experienced[skilled]; mature experience／～하다 (be) experienced; long-practiced; veteran／～ 가 an expert; a veteran; an old hand. ろうれん

**노령(老齡)** old age; advanced years／～ 에 이르다 attain an advanced age; get old. ろうれい

**노루** 《동》 a deer; a roe deer; *Capreolus bedfordi*(학명). のろ

**노루발장도리** a claw hammer.

**노루잠** a broken sleep; an unsound slumber; a cat nap《미》.

**노르다** be yellow ⇒누르다. きいろい

**노르스름하다** (be) yellowish; somewhat yellow. ややきいろい

**노른자**《위》 the yolk of [an egg]; the vitellus. らんおう

**노름** gambling; gaming; betting／～하 다 gamble; play for money. とばく

**노름군** a gambler; a gamester／사기 ～ a card sharper; a rook. とばくうち

**노름빛** a gambling debt.

**노름질** gambling; betting.

**노름판** a gambling house; a place where people can gamble. とばくじょう

**노름패** ①a [playing] card ②a gang of gamblers[gamesters].

**노릇** a part; a role; a character／간사 ～을 하다 act[function] as a manager／햄릿 ～을 하다 act[play] the part of Hamlet; do Hamlet. やく

**노릇노릇** yellowish; spotted with yellow／～하다 (be) yellowish; spotted yellow.

**노리개** 《장신구》 trinkets 《장난감》 a plaything; a toy. おもちゃ

**노리다¹** ①《냄새가》 smell of fur-scorching; (be) foul-smelling; rank; smell like burning; burning fat[a skunk] ② 《마음씨가》 (be) mean; sordid; stingy.

**노리다²** 《눈으로》 glare at; keep an eye on; set *one's* eyes upon 《엿보다》 watch (*for*) 《겨누다》 aim at／기회를 ～ watch for a chance／이익을 ～ aim at profit making. ねらう

**노리다³** slice crosswise(칼로).

**노린내** (털의) fur-scorching smell (노래기의) stink of millipede. けだもののにおい

**노릿하다** smell somewhat of fur-scorching; (be) somewhat stinking[fetid]. ちょっとけだものくさい

**노망**(老妄) dotage; be senile/ ~한 senile; doting/ ~부리다 behave like a dotard. もうろく

**노망태기** a bag made of braided string [cord]. あみぶくろ

**노면**(路面) road surface/ ~을 개수하다 resurface the road. ろめん

**노모**(老母) one's old[aged] mother. ろうぼ

**노목**(老木) an old[aged] tree. ろうぼく

**노무**(勞務) labo[u]r; work; service/ ~관리 personnel[labo(u)r] management / ~자 a worker; a laborer/ ~를 제공하다 offer[render] one's service/ ~에 종사하다 give one's service. ろうむ

**노물**(老物) an old useless person.

**노뭉치** a ball of string[cord, twine]; coil wound in to a mass. ひものくくり

**노박이로** always; steadily; firmly; unmovingly. じっと

**노박히다** stick to one's work; be steady; be stuck. ずっととじこもる

**노반**(路盤) roadbed. ろめん

**노발 대발**(怒發大發) a big blowup; flaring up; wild rage/ ~하다 [be inflamed with] rage; get wild like a madman; flare up. ひどくおこること

**노방**(路傍) the roadside; the wayside / ~초 grass at the roadside[by the wayside]. ろぼう

**노변**(路邊) the wayside; the roadside ⇒ 노방(路傍). みちばた

**노변**(爐邊) the fireside; around the fireplace/ ~에서 by the hearth[fireside] / ~ 잡담 a fireside chat. ろへん

**노병**(老兵) an old soldier; a war veteran/ ~은 죽지 않는다 Old soldiers never die. ろうへい

**노병**(老病) senile infirmity/ ~으로 죽다 die of old age. ろうびょう

**노복**(奴僕) a man servant. どぼく

**노복**(老僕) an old man servant.

**노부**(老父) one's old[aged] father. ろうふ

**노부**(老婦) an old[aged] wife; an old woman. ろうふ

**노불**(老佛) ①(늙은 부처) an ancient image of Buddha ②(노자학과 불교) Laoism and Buddhism.

**노비**(奴婢) male and female servants; domestics. どひ

**노비**(路費) traveling expenses; travel money. りょひ

**노사**(勞使) labo[u]r and management; capital and labo[u]r/ ~ 관계 the relations between labo[u]r and management/ ~ 휴전 labo[u]r-management truce.

**노사**(老死) ~하다 die of old age. ろうし

**노사**(老師) an old teacher; an old master. ろうし

**노산**(老産) delivery in one's old age/ ~하다 deliver a child in one's old age. としをとってこをうむこと

**노상** (늘) always; all the time (버릇으로) habitually/ ~ 책만 읽다 always read books/아침이면 ~ 산보한다 He always takes a walk in the morning. いつも

**노상**(路上) on the road[way]; the road / ~에서 by the roadside; on the street / ~ 강도 a highwayman; a footpad; highway robbery. ろじょう

**노새** 【동】 a mule. らば

**노색**(怒色) anger; an angry face[look]. おこったかおいろ

**노선**(路線) a route; a way; a line; a course/강경 ~ a tough[hard] line/정책 ~ a policy line/항공 ~ an airline. ろせん

**노성**(怒聲) an angry voice; an excited voice. どせい

**노소**(老少) young and old; aged and youth/ ~를 막론하고 without distinction of age. ろうしょう

**노송**(老松) an aged[old] pine-tree/ ~나무【식】 the Japanese cypress; Chamaecyparis obtusa(학명). ふるいまつ

**노쇠**(老衰) age and infirmity; decrepitude; senile decay; senescence/ ~하다 be old and infirm; grow senile/ ~기 senescence/ ~하여 죽다 die of old age. ろうすい

**노숙**(老熟) matured experience; maturity; mellowness/ ~하다 (be) mature; mellow; attain maturity. ろうじゅく

**노숙**(露宿) camping-out/ ~하다 sleep [pass the night] in the open [air]; sleep under the open sky[stars].

**노승**(老僧) an old[aged] priest[bonze]. ろうそう

**노신**(老臣) a senior vassal; an old retainer. ろうしん

**노심**(勞心) anxiety; care; trouble/ ~하다 trouble oneself (about); worry; exert oneself mentally/ ~ 초사 끝에 after taking great pains; with a great deal of trouble. しんぱい

**노아가다** ①(배가) sail fast; scud ②(말이) run fast; gallop. はやくはしる

**노안**(老眼)【의】 presbyopia/ ~의 presbyopic/ ~인 사람 a presbyope/ ~경 spectacles for the aged; long-distance glasses. ろうがん

**노약**(老弱) infirmity with age/ ~하다 be infirm with age. ろうじゃく

**노어**(露語) Russian; the Russian language.

**노여움** anger; indignation; rage; fury; wrath; displeasure/ ~을 사다 arouse [excite] one's anger; incur one's displeasure; offend (a person)/ ~을 참다 restrain[hold in, master] one's anger / ~을 나타내다 betray one's anger/ ~을 풀다 relent towards (a person). おこり

**노여워하다** be offended; be given offense; feel hurt (*at*); be displeased (*at*). おこる

**노역**(勞役) work; labo[u]r; toil/~하다 do hard work; labo[u]r. ろうえき

**노염** anger ⇨노여움.

**노엽다** (be) irritating; provoking; reproachful/노여운 빛을 나타내다 betray one's anger/그의 말이 ~ I am offended by his remark. なごりおしい

**노영**(露營) encampment; camping-out; bivouac/ ~하다 encamp; camp out; pitch camp; bivouac. ろえい

**노예**(奴隷) a slave(사람) slavery(신분)/ ~ 같은 slavish; servile/~ 해방 emancipation [of slaves]/ ~ 매매 slave trade/ ~ 근성 a servile spirit/금전의 ~가 되다 let oneself be a slave of mammonism/ ~처럼 부리다 put (*a person*) to practically slave labor/~ 노동 slave labour. どれい

**노오라기** a piece of string. ひものきれ

**노옹**(老翁) an elderly gentleman; an old [aged] man. ろうおう

**노유**(老幼) young and old/ ~를 불문하고 irrespective of age. ろうよう

**노인**(老人) an old[an aged] man (총칭) the aged; the old/ ~의 old; aged/ ~을 공경하다 respect the aged/ ~병 the disease of old age/ ~[병]학 gerontology/ ~성 정신병 senile psychosis / ~ 의학 geriatrics. ろうじん

**노인경**(老人鏡) long-distance glasses; glasses for old folks.

**노임**(勞賃) wages/ ~을 지급하다 pay (*a person*)/싼 ~을 받고 일하다 work at low wages/ ~을 인상하다 raise[level up] the wages standard. ろうちん

**노자**(勞資) capital and labo[u]r; labo[u]r and management. ろうし

**노자**(路資) travel[l]ing expenses; road [travel] money. りょひ

**노작**(勞作) (역작) a labo[u]rious work; a work involving much elaboration/ 다년간의 ~ a labo[u]rious work taking years to finish. ろうさく

**노장**(老將) a veteran general. ろうしょう

**노장**(老壯) young and old; the old and the young. ろうねんとそうねん

**노장**(老莊) (노자와 장자) Lao-tzu and Chuang-tzu.

**노적**(露積) a stack[a rick] of grain; stacked grain/ ~가리 stacks of grain.

**노점**(露店) a street-stall; a booth/ ~ 상인 a stall[booth] keeper/ ~가(街) an open-air stall quarter/ ~을 벌이다 open[keep] a street stall. ろてん

**노점**(露點) 〖물〗 the dew point/~계 a dew indicator. ろてん

**노정**(路程) (이수) the distance; mileage 《여정》 an itinerary; a course; a route; a path/ ~계(計) a measuring wheel; a pedometer. ろてい

**노정**(露呈) exposure; disclosure/ ~하다 be exposed[disclosed]. ろてい

**노정골**(顱頂骨) 〖해〗 the parietal bone/ ~ 결절(結節) parietal eminence.

**노조**(勞組) a trade union〈영〉; a labo[u]r union〈미〉.

**노중**(路中) on the way; the middle[midst] of a journey; in one's journey; while traveling. とちゅう

**노질**(櫓─) sculling/ ~하다 work a scull; scull (*a boat*); pull an oar; row (*a boat*); paddle. ろをこぐこと

**노처**(老妻) one's old[aged] wife. ろうさい

**노처녀**(老處女) an old maid; a spinster; an elderly spinster/~ 같은 spinsterish / ~더러 시집가라 한다 make a superfluous remark. ろうしょじょ

**노천**(露天) the open; the open air/ ~의 out door; open-air/~광(鑛) a strip mine/ ~ 극장 an open-air theater[-re] / ~ 수업 open air classes. ろてん

**노체**(老體) old bones; an old body/~이다 be well advanced. ろうたい

**노총각**(老總角) an old bachelor. けっこんしていないどくしんのおとこ

**노출**(露出) exposure/ ~하다 expose; lay bare; disclose 《광맥이》 crop out/ ~된 uncovered; exposed; bare / ~ 시간 《사진》 time of exposure/~증 exhibitionism. ろしゅつ

**노친**(老親) one's old[aged] parents. ろうしん

**노태**(老態) looking old for one's age.

**노퇴**(老退) old-age retirement/ ~하다 retire due to one's old age.

**노파**(老婆) an old woman 《악의적으로》 a beldam[e]/~심 grandmotherly[excessive] solicitude/ ~심에서 out of kindness; for good/ ~심에서 이렇게 말하는 것입니다 I say this only for your own good. ろうば

**노폐**(老廢) superannuation/ ~하다 (be) superannuated/~물 effete[waste] matter. ろうはい

**노필**(老筆) 《노인의》 an old man's handwriting 《달필》 a skillful hand; a ready pen.

**노하다**(怒─) get angry; be offended; lose one's temper; take offense; get mad(미); get into a rage/노해서 in anger; angrily. おこる

**노형**(老兄) 《당신》 you. ろうけい

**노호**(怒號) a roar [of anger]; a bellow / ~하다 roar in anger]. どごう

**노환**(老患) the infirmities of old age; senile infirmity. ろうかん

**노회**(老獪) craftiness; astuteness; old roguery/~하다 (be) crafty; cunning; foxy/ ~한 사람 an old[a cunning] fox; a sly old dog. ろうかい

**노획**(虜獲) capturing alive/ ~하다 capture alive; take (*a person*) captive. ほりょにすること

**노획**(鹵獲) capture; seizure; plunder/ ~하다 capture; seize; plunder/ ~물

**노후(老朽)** superannuation; antiquation /~한 superannuated; antiquated /~선박 a superannuated vessel / ~화(化) deterioration. ろうきゅう

**노후(老後)** one's old age / ~의 낙 consolation of one's old age / ~를 시골에서 보내다 spend one's declining years in the country. ろうご

**녹(祿)** 《녹봉》 a stipend; a fief; a salary; a ration of rice / ~을 먹다 receive a stipend. ろく

**녹(綠)¹** 《금속의》 green / ~지대(地帶) a green belt. みどりいろ

**녹(綠)²** 《금속의》 rust; tarnish. さび

**녹각(鹿角)** an antler; a deer's horn. しかのつの

**녹나무** 【식】 a camphor tree.

**녹녹하다** (be) damp. やわらかい

**녹다** ①《열에》 melt; be melted; thaw; fuse; be fused ②《용해되다》 dissolve; melt ③《지다》 be beaten [들리다] be spoilt; suffer a serious setback ④《반하다》 be gone on (a girl); be fascinated[captivated] (by). とける

**녹두(綠豆)** small green peas; *Phaseolus radiatus*《학명》 / ~묵 green-pea paste / ~죽 green-pea gruel.

**녹로(轆轤)** a potter's wheel 《선반》 a lathe; a pulley / ~세공 turnery / ~군 a turner. ろくろ

**녹록하다(碌碌—)** (be) useless; of little value; trivial; of no importance; good for nothing. へいぼんである

**녹림(綠林)** ①《숲》 a green forest ②《도적 소굴》 a den of bandits. りょくりん

**녹말(綠末)** 【화】 starch; farina / ~질(質) 의 starchy; farinaceous. でんぷん

**녹봉(祿俸)** a stipend; a ration of rice; a salary. きゅうよん

**녹비** deerskin / ~에 "가로왈"자다 be easily swayed by others. しかのかわ

**녹비(綠肥)** green manure. りょくひ

**녹색(綠色)** a green colour; green / ~의 green. みどりいろ

**녹수(綠樹)** a green tree; a green-leaved tree; greenery《총칭》. りょくじゅ

**녹신녹신하다** (be) soft; tender; plastic; pliant; supple. ぐにゃぐにゃだ

**녹신하다** (be) soft and flexible / 녹신한 가죽 soft leather. じゅうなんだ

**녹실녹실하다** (be) pliant ⇨녹신녹신하다.

**녹야(綠野)** a green field. みどりののはら

**녹양(綠楊)** a green-leaved willow.

**녹엽(綠葉)** green leaves 《집합적으로》 green foliage. みどりっぱ

**녹용(鹿茸)** the young antlers of the deer. しかのやわらかなつの

**녹음(綠陰)** the shade of a tree; a shady nook / ~ 방초 green shades and fragrant plants[sweet grasses]. りょくいん

**녹음(錄音)** [sound] recording / ~하다 record; make a recording; transcription / ~ 방송 transcription[broadcast]; electro-transcription broadcasting / ~실 a recording room / ~가두 ~ a street-corner transcription. ろくおん

**녹이다** ①《녹게 하다》 melt; dissolve; liquefy / ~한 액화하다》 melt 《용해하다》 fuse; smelt [ore] ②《뇌쇄하다》 fascinate; enchant; captivate; bewitch ③《지게 하다》 beat; have (one) down. とかす

**녹죽(綠竹)** a green bamboo.

**녹지(綠地)** a green tract of land / ~화(化)하다 afforest. りょくち

**녹진녹진하다** be all soft and sticky ⇨녹신녹신하다. やわらかくねばりがある

**녹진하다** (be) soft and sticky.

**녹채(鹿砦)** an abatis; an entanglement; a palisade.

**녹초** ①《결딴남》 all tattered[out of shape] / 옷이 ~가 되다 one's clothes are worn to tatters ②《기진함》 utterly exhausted; dog-tired; to a pulp / 피곤해 ~가 되다 be ready to drop in one's tracks. つかれきったじょうたい

**녹초(綠草)** green grass. りょくそう

**녹화(綠化)** tree planting; afforestation / ~하다 plant [with] trees / ~ 계획 a plan for afforestation / ~ 운동 a tree-planting campaign. りょっか

**논** 《답(畓)》 a rice[paddy] field / ~도랑 water route around a paddy field / ~두렁[둑] a ridge[dike] between rice fields; a levee. すいでん

**논(論)** 《논의》 an argument; a discussion; a debate《토론》 《논평》 a comment; a criticism; an essay 《논설》 a treatise 《이론》 a theory 《의문·문제》 question 《얘기》 a talk / ~하다 argue; discuss; comment on; deal with; debate on / 법은 사람을 ~하지 않는다 The law has no respect of persons., All men are equal in the eyes of the law. ろん

**논객(論客)** a controversialist; a disputant; a polemic. ろんかく

**논거(論據)** grounds; data / ~가 확실하다 one's argument be well grounded / 당신의 ~는 박약하다 Your ground is anything but convincing. ろんきょ

**논꼬** an irrigation gate[a sluice] for irrigating a paddy-field.

**논고(論告)** the state's address; prosecutor's argument / ~하다 make the arguments; prosecute; address / 준엄한 ~ a scathing address / ~를 개시하다 open the arguments (on a case). ろんこく

**논공(論功)** ~하다 reward (one's services); grant honours / ~ the grant of rewards[honours] 《정당의》 the distribution of patronage / ~ 행상은 오늘 발표되었다 The grant of honours was announced today. ろんこう

**논구(論究)** an exhaustive discussion / ~하다 discuss thoroughly; make a full discussion of (a matter). ろんきゅう

**논급(論及)** ~하다 refer to; enter into; touch on. ろんきゅう
**논길** a paddy path.
**논난(論難)** adverse criticism ⇒논란.
**논농사(―農事)** rice farming; rice cultivation[culture]/ ~하다 do rice farming; cultivate rice. すいでんののうじ
**논다** divide up 《노느다》 share; distibute ⇒나누다.
**논다니** a woman of easy virtue; a prostitute. ばいしょうふ
**논단(論壇)** 《토론의》 the platform 《명론계》 the world of criticism; publicists' circles; the publicists. ろんだん
**논단(論斷)** a conclusion; a verdict/ ~하다 conclude; pass a verdict upon.
**논담(論談)** discussion/ ~하다 talk (over); discuss.
**논도랑** a ditch around a paddy-field.
**논두렁** a ridge between rice fields; a levee/ ~길 a footpath between rice fields.
**논둑** dikes[causeways] around a rice-field.
**논란(論難)** adverse criticism; denunciation; charge; censure/ ~하다 criticize; pass strictures (on); attack; censure. ろんなん
**논리(論理)** logic/~적[으로] logical[ly]; dialectical[ly]/ ~학 logic/ ~ 학자 a logician/비~적 illogical; fallacious/귀납 ~학 inductive logic/순수 ~학 pure logic/형식 ~학 formal logic. ろんり
**논마지기** some acres of rice field/그는 ~나 가지고 있다네 He is something of a landowner.
**논매다** weed a rice field.
**논문(論文)** 《학술적》 a treatise; a dissertation 《연구상의》 a thesis(pl. theses) 《학회 따위의》 a paper 《신문 따위의》 an article 《문학·평론》 an essay/박사 ~ a thesis for a doctorate; a doctor's degree/~을 제출하다 presentathesis. ろんぶん
**논물** water in a rice field. すいでんのみず
**논박(論駁)** refutation; confutation; disproof; wordy attack/ ~하다 refute; confute; disprove; attack [by argument]. ろんばく
**논밭** paddy-fields and dry fields; farms; fields. すいでんとはたけ
**논밭 전지(―田地)** paddy-fields and dry fields.
**논배미** a strip of paddy field; a parcel of rice field.
**논법(論法)** logic; reasoning/삼단 ~ a syllogism/이단 ~ an enthymeme/~을 쓰다 use an argument. ろんぽう
**논변(論辯)** an argument; a debate; a discussion/ ~하다 argue; debate; discuss. ろんべん
**논봉(論鋒)** the force of an argument 《논법》 logic/예리한 ~ an incisive[a keen] argument. ろんぽう

**논설(論說)** 《논문》 a discourse; a dissertation 《사설》 a leading article; a leader; an editorial/ ~ 기자[위원] a leader writer; an editorial writer(미)/ ~란 the editorial column. ろんせつ
**논술(論述)** statement/ ~하다 state; set forth. ろんじゅつ
**논어(論語)** the Analects of Confucius. ろんご
**논외(論外)** irrelevancy to the subject/ ~의 《문제 안 되는》 out of the question 《본제를 떠난》 beside the question.
**논의(論議)** discussion; debate; argument/ ~하다 discuss; debate; argue/정치상의 ~ a political discussion/ ~중이다 be under discussion[debate]/치열하게 ~되다 be hotly debated. ろんぎ
**논자(論者)** 《논객》 a disputant 《필자》 the writer 《주창자》 an advocate/개혁 ~ an advocate of reform. ろんしゃ
**논쟁(論爭)** a dispute; a controversy; a contention; an argument/ ~하다 dispute; contend; controvert; argue/ ~점 a point of dispute/ ~중이다 be in a controversy (with). ろんそう
**논전(論戰)** wordy warfare; a battle of words; passage of arms; an argument/~하다 fight with words; have wordy warfare. ろんせん
**논점(論點)** a disputed point; the point at issue[in question]/~을 벗어나다 be beside the point/~을 분명히 하다 make one's point clear/~을 파악하다 get a person's point. ろんてん
**논제(論題)** a subject (of discussion); a theme; a topic. ろんだい
**논조(論調)** the tone[tenor, drift] of an argument/신문 ~ press comments. ろんちょう
**논죄(論罪)** finding; ruling/~하다 rule; find; judge; try. ろんざい
**논증(論證)** proof; demonstration/ ~하다 demonstrate; prove. ろんしょう
**논지(論旨)** the drift[point] of an argument/ ~를 명백히 하다 make one's point [of argument] clear. ろんし
**논파(論破)** refutation; confutation/ ~하다 refute; confute; overthrow (a person's argument). ろんぱ
**논평(論評)** criticism; a comment; a review/ ~하다 critize; review; comment (on); give criticism (on)/이 문제에 관한 신문의 ~ newspaper[press] comments on this subject. ろんぴょう
**논풀다** ①《논을》 bring under cultivation; clear (a land) into a rice-field; cultivate (a land) into a paddy-field ②《오줌싸다》 a baby drenches its diaper.
**놀¹** 《하늘의》 glow/저녁 ~ the evening glow/아침 ~ a morning glow; a red morning; a red sunrise. ゆうやけ
**놀²** 《파도》 a big wave; a billow. なみ
**놀다** ⇒별항 참조(page 1367).
**놀라다** 《경악》 be surprised[astonished,

**놀리움** amazed, shocked〕(공포) be frightened/놀랄 만한 surprising; astounding; amazing/놀라게 하다 startle; surprise 《경이》 wonder〔marvel〕at/놀랄 만한 wonderful; marvellous. びっくりする

**놀라움** 《경악》 surprise; astonishment 《공포》 fright; horror 《경탄》 wonder; amazement; admiration. おどろき

**놀랍다** (be) wonderful; marvellous; surprising. ふしぎだ

**놀래다** surprise; astonish; shock; amaze; startle; astound; alarm; spring a surprise on 《소동시키다》 create a sensation〔a horror〕. びっくりさせる

**놀리다** ①(조롱) banter; ridicule; chaff; jeer at; make fun〔sport〕of ②(쉬게 하다) rest; give a holiday(휴일을 주다); let (a thing) idle(안 부리다); suspend(작업 중단) ③(돌다) play (a piece)(기계를); move (one's legs)(움직이다). あそばせる

**놀림** banter; raillery; chaff; fun; joke; teasing; kidding; making fun of; playing jokes on. からかうこと

**놀림감** an object〔a butt〕of ridicule; a mockery. なぶりもの

**놀림거리** an object of ridicule. なぶりもの

**놀아나다** fall into vicious courses; take to fast living. うわきする

**놀아먹다** lead a dissipated〔a dissolute〕life; be dissipated. ぶらぶらあそぶ

**놀음** merrymaking. あそびごと

**놀음놀이** pleasure; merrymaking; amusements; diversion; spree. こうらく

**놀음차** a tip; a gratuity. こころづけ

# 놀 다

①(유희) play; amuse〔enjoy〕oneself; divert oneself; make an excursion; visit/뛰어다니며 ~ play jumping〔romping〕about; gambol; frolic/놀러 가는 기분으로 ~ partly for pleasure; just for fun/소꿉장난〔숨바꼭질〕하며 ~ play house〔hide and seek〕/카드 놀이를 하며 ~ play cards/장난감을 가지고 ~ play with toys/놀고 있다 be at play/장기를 두며 ~ amuse〔enjoy, divert〕oneself playing chess/재미있게 ~ have a good〔nice, merry〕time; have fun/놀면서 시간을 보내다 play away one's time/놀기에 정신이 팔리다 be given to play/놀러 나가다 (어린이가) go out to play/일하고 놀지 않으면 사람이 못 쓰게 된다 "All work and no play makes Jack a dull boy."/휴가 중에는 무엇을 하며 놀았니 How did you amuse yourself during the vacation?/바닷가에 놀러 가다 go on an excursion to beach.

②(실직) be out of work; be jobless〔unemployed〕; have nothing〔no job〕to do/놀고 있는 사람 an unemployed person; a jobless man/그는 요즘 놀고 있다 He is out of work these days.

③(유휴) be not in use; lie〔stand〕idle; be unused〔unemployed〕; be out of operation/노는 돈 idle money/노는 자본 unemployed capital; idle〔sleeping〕funds/노는 기계 an unused machine/노는 땅 land lying idle/책상이 놀고 있다 The desk is not used./그 공장은 놀고 있다 The factory is lying idle./너의 재주를 놀려 두지 말라 Don't let your talent lie idle.

④(방문·소풍) visit/놀러 가다 make〔go on〕an excursion; go on a picnic; make a pleasure trip; visit/부산에 놀러 가다 visit Busan/산에 놀러 가다 go off to the mountains/놀러 오너라 Come and see me., Come see me./오늘 저녁에 놀러 오지 않겠소? How would you like to come and spend the evening with me?

⑤(유흥) make merry; have a spree; go on a spree; revel (방탕) lead a dissolute life; dissipate; visit the red-light district/놀러 나가다 go out for pleasure/오늘 저녁 한 잔 먹고 놀자 Let's have a spree tonight./그는 놀기 좋아하는 사람이다 He is a pleasure-seeker./어제 저녁은 밤새껏 신나게 놀았다 Last night we caroused around till dawn./간밤에는 여기저기 돌아다니며 진탕 놀았다 We painted the town red last night/그는 한때 많이 놀아먹었다 He sowed his wild oats.

⑥(박힌 것 따위가) totter; shake; give; be unstable〔unsteady, rickety, shaky, wobbly, loose〕/나사 못이 ~ a screw is loose/이가 ~ A tooth is loose. /바위가 ~ a rock shakes〔gives〕.

⑦(휴식·무위) relax; loaf (one's time) away; idle; have one's ease; be doing nothing/노는 사람 an idle man; an idler; a loafer/노는 시간 playtime (학교의) a recess; a break/노는 날 a holiday; an off day/하루를 쉬며 ~ take a holiday; take a day off/놀고 월급을 받다 be paid for no work/놀고 먹다 lead a lazy life; eat the bread of idleness; live a life of ease/놀며 지내다 live in idleness; do nothing but loaf; idle one's time away.

⑧(멋대로) behave as one likes; behave offensively; act〔have, take〕one's own way〔pleasure, course〕/멋대로 놀게 하다 allow one to go one's way; give (one) a free hand.

**놀이** 《유희》 play 《경기》 a game; a sport 《야외의》; 《오락》 amusement; pastime 《쾌락》 pleasure/ ～터 a playground; a pleasure resort(유원지 등)/놀잇배 a pleasure boat/～ 딱지 cards. こうらく

**놀잇군** a merry-maker; a carouser; junketer; a picnicker; an excursionist; a holidayer. こうらくしゃ

**놀다** a big wave rises[billows up].

**놀치다** billow; surge; swell; rise in great waves.

**놈** ①《경멸적》 a fellow; a chap a guy ②《동물·물건》 thing; one; damn thing [one]. やろう

**놈팡이** 《남자》 a man; a fellow; a guy 《전달》 a chap a bum; an idler. だんしのひご

**놉** a casual labo[u]rer paid by the day. ひやといろうどうしゃ

**놋** brass/ ～세공 brass-work/ ～ 닦는 가루 brass-polish/ ～빛의 brass-coloured; brassy/ ～대야 a brass basin/ ～대접 a brass bowl/～숟가락 a brass spoon. しんちゅう

**놋갓장이** a brazier; a brass-smith.

**놋그릇** brassware; brass tableware; a brass receptacle. しんちゅうのきぐ

**놋점**(一店) a brassware shop; a braziery.

**놋좆**(櫓一) an oar pivot; a pivot for twisting a scull on.

**놋칼** a brass knife; a brass sword.

**농**(弄) a sport; a joke; a jest; fun; a pleasantry/반 ～으로 half in fun; by way of amusement. じょうだん

**농**(籠) a basket; a cage; a clothes-box; a suit-case. かご

**농**(膿) pus ⇨고름.　うみ

**농가**(農家) a farm-house 《농민》 farmers; a farm household. のうか

**농간**(弄奸) a trick; an artifice; a craft; a design/ ～부리다 play a trick; make crafty designs. たくらみ

**농게**(籠一) 《동》 a rock crab.

**농경**(農耕) farming; cultivation; tillage; farm labour. のうこう

**농공**(農工) agriculture and industry 《사람》farmers and manufacturers/ ～업 agriculture and industry. のうこう

**농과**(農科) the agricultural department; 《과정》an agricultural course/ ～ 대학 an agricultural college. のうか

**농구**(農具) agricultural[farm] implements; farming tools. のうぐ

**농구**(籠球) basketball/～ 선수 a basketball player; a cage star; a cager《미·구》/～ 시즌 cage season. ろうきゅう

**농군**(農軍) a farmer; a peasant; a farm hand. のうふ

**농권**(弄權) an abuse of power/ ～하다 abuse one's power [authority]; usurp power. けんりをほしいままにすること

**농기**(農期) the farming season. のうき

**농기구**(農器具) ⇨농구(農具). のうきぐ

**농노**(農奴) a serf 《신분》 serfdom/ ～ 해방 emancipation of serfs. のうど

**농단**(壟斷) monopolization/ ～하다 monopolize; have (a thing) to oneself; engross. ろうだん

**농담**(弄談) a joke; a jest; fun; [a] pleasantry/ ～하다 joke; jest for/ ～으로 for fun; for a joke. じょうだん

**농대석**(籠臺石) the foundation[support] stone of a tombstone[monument].

**농도**(濃度) thickness; density; consistency; depth of [color; shade]; 《화》 concentration. のうど

**농들다**(膿一) form[generate] pus; fester; suppurate; maturate; [pus] be gathered. うむ

**농락**(籠絡) inveiglement; enticement/ ～하다 inveigle; entice; have (one) well in hand. ろうらく

**농림**(農林) agriculture and forestry/ ～ 장관[부] the Minister[the Ministry] of Agriculture and Forestry. のうりん

**농막**(農幕) a farmer's hut. かりごや

**농무**(濃霧) a dense[thick] fog. のうむ

**농무**(農務) agricultural affairs/ ～국 the Bureau of Agriculture. のうむ

**농민**(農民) farmers; peasants. のうみん

**농번기**(農繁期) the farmer's busy season/ ～ 휴가 school holidays in the [busy] farming season. のうはんき

**농병**(農兵) agrarian soldiers. のうふのへい

**농병아리** 《동》 a little grebe; a dadchick; Podiceps ruflcollis poggei《학명》.

**농본주의**(農本主義) physiocracy; the 'agriculture-first' principle. のうほんしゅぎ

**농부**(農夫) a farmer 《세농가》 a peasant; a farm hand. のうふ

**농사**(農事) agriculture; agricultural affairs; farming/ ～하다[짓다] engage in agriculture; follow the plough; farm / ～ 시험장 an agricultural experimental station; an experimental farm/ ～철 a farming season. のうじ

**농산물**(農産物) agricultural products; farm produce. のうさんぶつ

**농상**(農商) agriculture and commerce; farmers and merchants. のうしょう

**농상**(農桑) agriculture and sericulture; farming and silk-farming. のうそう

**농상**(農相) the Minister of Agriculture. のうしょう

**농성**(籠城) siege 《칩거》 confinement/ ～하다 be besieged; stand a siege; hold a castle. ろうじょう

**농숙**(濃熟) overripeness; full maturity /～하다 be overripe; mature fully; attain full maturity. ただれうむこと

**농아**(聾啞) deaf and dumb 《사람》 a deaf and dumb person; a deaf-mute/ ～ 학교 a school for the deaf and dumb; a deaf and dumb school. ろうあ

**농악**(農樂) instrumental music of peasants. のうがく

**농액**(濃液) a thick liquid. のうえき

**농약**(農藥) agricultural medicines[chem-

**농어**(-魚) 〖동〗 a [sea] bass; a perch; *Lateolabrax japonicus*(학명). すずき

**농어촌**(農漁村) farming and fishing villages[communities].

**농업**(農業) agriculture; farming; agricultural industry/~의 agricultural/~ 학교 an agricultural school/~ 정책 the farm policy. のうぎょう

**농예**(農藝) agricultural technology; agriculture and horticulture. のうげい

**농우**(農牛) farming cattle; a plow ox; a draft ox. のうさくようのうし

**농원**(農園) a farm; a plantation. のうえん

**농익다** be overripe; be over-mature. らんじゅくする

**농작**(農作) farming; husbandry; cultivation of land. のうさく

**농작물**(農作物) the crops; a harvest; farm produce. のうさくぶつ

**농장**(農場) a farm; a plantation/ ~ 관리인 a farm-bailiff/집단 ~ a collective farm. のうじょう

**농정**(農政) agriculture; agricultural administration. のうせい

**농지**(農地) agricultural land/~ 개혁 farmland[agrarian] reform. のうち

**농지거리**(弄—) gross pleasantries/ ~ 하다 indulge in gross pleasantries; joke; jest. ひどいじょうたん

**농촌**(農村) a farm[a farming] village; a rural community; an agricultural district/~의 agricultural/~ 경제 the rural economy/~ 문제 a rural[an agrarian] problem. のうそん

**농탕**(弄蕩) dissipation; prodigality; debauchery; fast life/ ~치다 flirt[dally] with (a woman); bill and cuo. わいせつ

**농토**(農土) farmland; agricultural land. のうど

**농하다**(弄—) ①(농담하다) joke; jest ②(부리다) indulge in. じょうだん

**농하다**(濃—) (빛깔이) (be) dark; deep 《액체가》 thick; dense; heavy. こい

**농학**(農學) [the science of] agriculture /~ 박사 Doctor of Agriculture/ ~자 an agronomist. のうがく

**농한기**(農閑期) farmer's slack[leisure] season. のうかんき

**농협**(農協) an agricultural co-operative [association]; a farmer's co-operative.

**농형**(農形) agricultural conditions; farm conditions.

**농회**(農會) an agricultural association [society]. のうかい

**농후**(濃厚) thickness; density/ ~하다 (be) thick; dense; heavy; strong/ ~하게 thickly; richly. のうこう

**높낮이** (고저) unevenness; undulations; high and low. こうてい

**높다** ①(be) high; lofty; tall 《코 따위》 elevated prominent ②(지위·명성이) (be) high; lofty; noble; elevated ③(값이) (be) dear; high; expensive; costly ④(소리가) (be) loud; high-pitched ⑤《온도가》 (be) high. たかい

**높다랗다** (be) very high; very tall; lofty; towering. ひじょうにたかい

**높으락낮으락** unevenly; undulatingly; high and low; up and down. でこぼこと

**높이**¹ (명사) height; elevation altitude(고도) (소리의) loudness; tone/ ~뛰기 a high jump. たかさ

**높이**² (부사) high; aloft; soaringly/하늘 ~ high up in the air. たかく

**높이다** raise; heighten; elevate; lift; enhance 《증진하다》 promote; increase 《개선하다》 improve 《존대하다》 hold (a person) in reverence. あげる

**높이뛰기** the [running] high jump/장대~ a pole vault[jump].

**높직이** rather[somewhat] high 《목소리를》 rather loud. ややたかく

**높직하다** (be) rather high. たかそうだ

**놓다**¹ ①(물건을) put; place 《뉘어》 lay 《세워》 set; lay down (a pen)/짐을 마루 위에 ~ rest luggages on the floor ②(남기다) leave (behind)/명함을 놓고 가다 leave a card ③(방치) leave; let 《어떤 상태로》 keep/그대로 놓아 두시오 Leave it as it is ④(잡은 것을) let it go[up, off]; relax; release/[잡았던] 손을 ~ take one's hand off; let go one's hold ⑤(마음을) ease; set one's mind at ease; give (one's mind) relief/한시름 ~ feel easy; set one's mind at rest ⑥(방화) set fire to; make a fire/집에 불을 ~ set fire to a house ⑦(사격) fire; shoot; discharge/총을 [한 방] ~ fire a gun ⑧(중간에 사람을) put in [as an intermediary]; send (a person) ⑨(기르다) keep; raise; rear /닭을 ~ raise chickens ⑩(파종) sow; plant; grow; cultivate ⑪(덫을) set [a trap] ⑫(주사·침을) apply; acupuncture [a needle ; syringe/침을 ~ needle; apply acupuncture ⑬(무늬·수를) embroider / 수를 ~ embroider; do embroidery ⑭(셈을) calculate; reckon; figure; compute; estimate ⑮(값을) bid; name; offer a price} ⑯(돈을·빚을) lend, loan [at interest] (미) ⑰(속력을) apply; put on [speed] ⑱(설비·가설) install; put in (a hypocaust, a telephone, a railroad, etc.) (다리를) build [a bridge over a river]; throw [a bridge across a river] /전화를 ~ install a telephone ⑲(기타) ⑳ 세목을 ~ 《바둑에서》 accept a three-stone handicap/엄포를 ~ make a threat. はなつ

**놓다**² Ⅰ(...해 두다) ⓐ논을 갈아 놓고 비를 기다린다 We have finished plowing the paddy field and are waiting for rain. 2 (...한 상태) ⓐ잠 못 자게 해~ keep (a person) awake.

**놓아두다** leave (a thing) as it is; let (a person) alone. おいておく

**놓아먹이다** graze (cattle); put (cattle) to grass; put to pasture. はなしかいする

**놓아주다** let go; set free; let loose; release; liberate. はなしてやる

**놓이다** ①(없히다) be put[set, laid, placed] ②(마음이) be at ease; be set at ease; feel relieved. おいてある

**놓치다** 《기회 따위》 miss; let slip 《범인 따위》 let escape; lose; fail to catch; drop. のがす

**뇌**(腦) the brain 《지력》 brains／ ～의 cerebral／ ～ 작용 a cerebration; brain action／ ～ 병원 a mental hospital／ ～매독〖의〗 syphilis of the brain／ ～를 쓰는 일 brain[mental] work／ ～를 지나치게 쓰다 overtax one's brains. のう

**뇌까리다** repeat[reiterate] the same remark unpleasantly; harp on the same string《子》.

**뇌격기**(雷擊機) a torpedo[-carrying] bomber[plane]. らいげきき

**뇌고**(牢固) firmness; solidness; inflexibility; steadfastness／ ～한 firm; strong; solid. ろうこ

**뇌관**(雷管) a percussion cap; a detonation cap; a detonator／ ～ 장치 a percussion lock. らいかん

**뇌다** ①(체로) pass through a sieve of finer mesh ②(같은 말을) repeat; reiterate; say over again. ふるいにかける

**뇌동**(雷同) ～하다 follow blindly; echo; fall in (with); chime in (with). らいどう

**뇌락**(磊落) open-heartedness; frank disposition／ ～한 frank; jolly; free and easy. らいらく

**뇌력**(腦力) mental capacity; intellectual power; brains. のうりょく

**뇌루**(腦漏) 〖의〗 softening of the brain.

**뇌리**(腦裡) the brain; one's mind; one's memory. のうり

**뇌막**(腦膜) 〖의〗 meninges／～염 meningitis; brain fever. のうまく

**뇌명**(雷鳴) thunder; thunder-clap; a peal[clap] of thunder. らいめい

**뇌문**(雷文, 雷紋) a fret／～ 세공 a fretwork; fretting.

**뇌물**(賂物) a bribe; boodle〈미〉; palm oil[grease]《속》／ ～을 먹다 be bribed; receive[accept, take] a bribe／ ～을 쓰다 bribe (a person). わいろのぶっぴん

**뇌병**(腦病) brain trouble; a brain disease. のうびょう

**뇌 병원**(腦病院) a mental hospital ⇒정신 병원(精神病院). のうびょういん

**뇌빈혈**(腦貧血) 〖의〗 cerebral an[a]emia. のうひんけつ

**뇌성**(雷聲) a thunder; a peal[a clap] of thunder／～ 벽력 [하다] [have] thunder and lightning. らいせい

**뇌쇄**(惱殺) ～하다 fascinate; enchant; captivate; bewitch. のうさつ

**뇌수**(牢囚) 《감금》 imprisonment 《죄수》 a prisoner; the imprisoned. ろうしゅう

**뇌수**(腦髓) 〖해〗 the brain. のうずい

**뇌 수술**(腦手術) brain surgery; a surgical operation on brain.

**뇌신경**(腦神經) 〖해〗 a cranial nerve／～ 세포 a brain cell. のうしんけい

**뇌약**(牢約) a firm promise／～하다 firmly promise.

**뇌염**(腦炎) brain inflammation; encephalitis; cerebritis／ ～의 발생 an outbreak of encephalitis／～에 걸리다 be stricken by encephalitis. のうえん

**뇌옥**(牢獄) a prison; a gaol〈영〉; a jail〈미〉

**뇌우**(雷雨) a thunderstorm; a thunder shower. らいう

**뇌일혈**(腦溢血) 〖의〗 cerebral h[a]emorrhage ／ ～을 일으키다 be stricken with a cerebral h[a]emorrhage. のういっけつ

**뇌장**(腦臟) the brains. のうしょう

**뇌전**(雷電) thunder and lightning; thunderbolts. いなびかり

**뇌조**(雷鳥) a ptarmigan; a snow-grouse.

**뇌진탕**(腦震蕩) 〖의〗 concussion of the brain; cerebral concussion. のうしんとう

**뇌척수막염**(腦脊髓膜炎) 〖의〗 cerebrospinal meningitis; brain fever.

**뇌척수액**(腦脊髓液) 〖의〗 the cerebrofever fluid.

**뇌척수염**(腦脊髓炎) 〖의〗 encephalomyelitis.

**뇌출혈**(腦出血) cerebral h[a]emorrhage ⇨ 뇌일혈. のうしゅっけつ

**뇌충혈**(腦充血) 〖의〗 a congestion of the brain. のうじゅうけつ

**뇌하다** (be) low and dirty; mean and foul; filthy. いやしくきたない

**누** who ⇨누구. たれ

**누**(累) trouble; complication; evil; involvement／ ～를 끼치다 bring trouble; to[upon] others; involve others in trouble. るい

**누**(樓) ①a two-storied house; an upper story; a turret 《성의》a look out 《망루》 belvedere ②a palace ⇨누각. ろう

**누가**(累加) accumulation; progressive [cumulative]／～하다 accmulate; increase progressively; accelerate. るいか

**누가 복음**(一福音) the Gospel of Luke.

**누각**(樓閣) a palace; a castle; a tall building. ろうかく

**누계**(累計) the total[sum]; the aggregate. るいけい

**누관**(淚管) 〖해〗 the tear duct[s]; the lachrymal duct. るいかん

**누구** ①(의문) who(누가), whose(누구의), whom(누구에게·누구를) ②(긍정·부정(不定)) any one; anybody; any; some[one]; whoever(누구든지·누구나·누구라도). たれ

**누그러지다** 《격감》 soften; moderate; be tempered 《눅어지다》 calm down; abate 《완화》 be mitigated 《노여움 따위가》 be appeased. おだやかになる

**누글누글** ～하다 (be) tender; soft; pulpy; pasty. やわらかい

**누긋하다** (be) soft; tender; flexible; placid. おおらかだ

**누기**(漏氣) moisture／ ～찬 wet; moist／

~찬 방 a damp room. しっけ
**누기차다**(漏氣一) (be) damp; dampish; moist; humid; wet. しっけがおおい
**누나** an elder sister; an older sister〈미〉; a big sister. あね
**누년**(累年) many years; several[some] years; successive years; [for] a series of years. るいねん
**누누이**(屢屢—) repeatedly 《장황하게》 tediously; a number of times; time after time. るる
**누님** one's elder sister. ねえさま
**누다**¹ 《똥·오줌을》 make; pass.
**누다**² 《옷감을》 bleach.
**누대**(累代) successive generations; a number of generations. るいだい
**누대**(樓臺) lofty structures; towers; a look-out; a turret. ろうだい
**누더기** rags; tatters [and rags]/ ~를 입은 사람 a person in rags. ぼろ
**누덕누덕** patchily; in patches/ ~하다 (be) full of patches. つぎはぎだらけ
**누되다**(累—) (be) harassing; troublesome. うるさくわずらわしい
**누두**(漏斗) a funnel; 【해】 infundibulum /~상(狀)의 funnelshaped; 【해】 infundibulate; infundibular.
**누락**(漏落) an omission; a lacuna/ ~하다 be omitted; be missing. だつらく
**누란**(累卵) imminent danger; a delicate [dangerous] situation. るいらん
**누렁** yellow dyes; yellow/ ~물 yellow water; dirty water. きいろ
**누렁우물** a well with impure water; a contaminated well. どろみずのいど
**누렇다** (be) deep yellow. きいろい
**누룩** yeast; leaven; malt. こうじ
**누룽지** scorched rice. こげめし
**누르께하다** be tinged[stained] with yellow. きいろみがかっている
**누르다**¹ 《빛이》 (be) yellow. きいろい
**누르다**² 《기압》 press [down ·]; weigh on 《위압》 overpower; overwhelm; dominate. おさえる
**누르락붉으락** turning[becoming] red with anger; flaring up.
**누르락푸르락** turning[becoming] pale with anger; changing countenance with anger.
**누르스름하다** (be) yellowish; a bit yellow. ややきいろい
**누르퉁퉁하다** be an unpleasant[unhealthy] yellow.
**누름적**(—炙) a kind of egg-coated shish kebab. おこのみやき
**누릇누릇** ~하다 (be) yellowy; yellow-spotted. てんてんときいろい
**누리**¹ 《우박》 hail. ひょう
**누리**² 《충》 a kind of locust; Pachytylus danicus(학명). いなご
**누리**³ 《세상》 the world; this world/온~ 에 all over the world. せじょう
**누리다**¹ 《냄새가》 smell of meat. なまぐさい
**누리다**² 《복을》 enjoy; be blessed with.

**누린내** a stench; a fetid[stinking] smell; a rancid smell. なまぐさいにおい
**누마루**(樓—) the upper storey; a balcony; a loft. たかどののどこ
**누만**(累萬) tens of thousands. すうまん
**누명**(陋名) dishonor; disgrace; a slur; a bad name/ ~을 쓰다 incur a bad name; be stigmatized/~을 씻다 clear oneself from dishonor. おめい
**누문**(漏聞) overhearing/ ~하다 overhear; hear casually. そくぶん
**누범**(累犯) repeated offence/ ~자 an old offender. るいはん
**누보**(累報) frequent reports; repeated informations/ ~하다 report repeatedly [frequently]. るほう
**누비** quilting; quilted work/~옷 quilted clothes/~ 이불 a quilt/ ~질하다 do quilting. さしぬい
**누비다** quilt/이불을 ~ quilt; form into a quilt. さしぬいする
**누삭**(屢朔) many months. すうかげつ
**누산**(累算) aggregation/ ~하다 aggregate; total.
**누상**(樓上) on the loft[tower]/~에 오르다 go up a tower. ろうじょう
**누선**(淚腺) 【해】 the lachrymal gland. るいせん
**누설**(漏泄) leakage; disclosure/ ~하다 leak; let out; reveal. ろうせつ
**누세**(累世) many generations. るいせい
**누속**(陋俗) an evil[a corrupt, a bad] custom. いやしいふうぞく
**누수**(漏水) a water leakage; a leakage of water; leaking water/~하다 water leak. ろうすい
**누습**(陋習) an evil[a corrupt] custom; an evil practice; an abuse. ろうしゅう
**누승**(累乘) 【수】 involution.
**누실**(漏失) ~하다 lose; let (a thing) slip. ろうしつ
**누심**(壘審) 【체】 a base[field] umpire; an umpire on a bases. るいしん
**누안**(淚眼) eyes suffused with tears; eyes full of tears; dew-lit eyes; tearful eyes. なみだぐんだめ
**누에** a silkworm/ ~ 나방 a silkworm moth/ ~를 치다 rear[raise] silkworms. かいこ
**누옥**(陋屋) a humble house; a wretched [squalid] hut; a hovel 《자기 집》 my humble dwelling[house]. ろうおく
**누운목**(—木) cotton cloth bleached in lye. ひょうはくしないもめん
**누운변**(—邊) interest paid back at the same time as the principal.
**누워먹다** live an idle life; eat the bread of idleness. ぶらぶらあそんでくらす
**누월**(屢月) many months. るいげつ
**누이** a sister 《손위》 an elder[a big] sister 《손아래》 a younger sister. しまい
**누이다** ①《대소변을》 hold out (a little child) to encourage urination(소변을);

**누이동생** a younger[little, small] sister; one's little sister. いもうと

**누일**(累日) many days; day after day.

**누적**(漏籍) ~하다 be left out of the domicile register. せきにもれていること

**누적**(累積) accumulation/~하다 accumulate; cumulate/~된 서류 accumulated papers on the table. るいせき

**누전**(漏電) 【물】 an electric leakage/~하다 short-circuit. ろうでん

**누정**(漏精) 【의】 spermatorrhea; involuntary emission of semen without orgasm.

**누지**(陋地) here; this place; my [humble] place. ろうち

**누지다** (be) damp; wettish. しっている

**누진**(累進) successive promotion/~하다 be promoted from one position to another; rise step by step. るいしん

**누차**(屢次) repeatedly; successively; many time. しばしば

**누추**(陋醜) filthiness; dirtiness/~하다 (be) dirty; filthy; humble 《옷차림 등이》 shabby. ろうしゅう

**누출**(漏出) leakage; leak; escape/~하다 leak (out); start[make, spring] a leak. ろうしゅつ

**누치** 〖어〗 Liza haematocheila(학명).

**누타**(壘打) 【체】 a base-hit.

**누풍**(陋風) a bad custom; vicious manners; an evil. ろうふう

**누하**(樓下) downstairs; [on] the lower floor of a loft[tower, turret]. ろうか

**누항**(陋巷) ①《더러운 거리》 a dirty alley; a narrow alley; wretched quarters ②《자기가 사는 곳》 my[our] town. ろうこう

**눅눅하다** (be) flabby; limp; damp humid; moist. ぐにゃぐにゃする

**눅느러지다** go limp; become flabby. ぐにゃぐにゃする

**눅다** 《반죽이》 (be) thin; limp; flabby 《부드럽다》 soft 《날씨가》 mild 《마음이》 lenient 《값이》 moderate.

**눅신하다** (be) soft and flexible; elastic; pliant; pliable; supple. じゅうなんだ

**눅실눅실하다** (be) elastic; pliant; flaccid ⇨눅신하다. ひじょうにぐにゃぐにゃする

**눅이다** ①《부드럽게》 soften; make soft ②《마음을》 pacify; calm (one's mind); quiet (one's anger). やわらかくする

**눅지다** become genial[mild]. おんわになる

**눅진하다** (be) soft and sticky. やわらかでねばねばする

**눈**[1] 《별항 참조(page 1370).

**눈**[2] ①《자·저울의》 a graduation; a scale; ②《나무의 싹》 sprout(돋아나온); a germ; a bud/~트다 bud; shoot; sprout ③《그물의》 a mesh; a stitch(편물의 코). めもり

**눈**[3] 《내리는》 snow 《강설》 a snowfall 《쌓인 눈》 snows/~길 a snowcovered road / ~을 이고 있는 snow-capped/ ~같이 흰 snow-white/ ~이 온다 It snows., Snow falls. ゆき

**눈가리개** 《사람의》 an eye bandage; blinkers 《말의》 blinders.

**눈가림** hoodwinking; deception/ ~하다 hoodwink; deceive; camouflage; temporize; pull the wool over (a person's) eyes; cover up. ずるさ

**눈가죽** an eyelid. まぶた

**눈까풀** an eyelid ⇨눈꺼풀. まぶた

**눈깔** an eye《비》. めのひご

**눈감다** ①《눈을》 close[shut] one's eyes ②《죽다》 die; breathe one's last. めをとじる

**눈감아주다** overlook; wink at; connive at; shut one's eyes (to). もくにんする

**눈깜작이** a blinkard. まばたきするひと

**눈거칠다** (be) offensive to the eye; unsightly. めざわりだ

**눈꺼풀** 《눈까풀》 an eyelid. まぶた

**눈겨룸** a staring match/ ~하다 play a staring match. にらみあいのしあい

**눈결** a glance; a glimpse. とたん

**눈꼴사납다** ①《아니꼽다》 be offensive to the eye; be hateful to see; (be) disgusting/눈꼴사나운 사내 a man of hard features ②《모양이》 (be) evil-looking; unsightly. みくるしい

**눈꼴틀리다** (be) disgusting disagreeable; hate to see. むかむかする

**눈곱** ①a discharge from the eyes; eye discharges; eye-wax ②《소량》 a bit; a whit. めあか

**눈곱자기** ①⇨눈곱 ②《미물》 a bit; a whit / ~만한 동정 a bit[particle] of sympathy/~만한 양심 a whit[bit] of conscience. めやに

**눈꽁댕이** 《눈초리》 the corner of the eye. めじり

**눈구녕**[1] 《안공》 the eye socket; the orbit of th eye 《눈》 an eye. がんこう

**눈구멍**[2] 《눈구덩이》 a pit in a snowdrift.

**눈구석** the corner of the eye. めのすみ

**눈금** ①《자의》 graduation; scale; a notch mark on a scale ②《눈짐작으로 그은 금》 a line drawn by eyesight. めもり

**눈기이다** hoodwink (one); deceive.

**눈길**[1] 《시선》 line of vision[sight]/~을 모으다 attract public gaze. しせん

**눈길**[2] 《눈 덮인 길》 a snowy road; a snow-covered road. ゆきのみち

**눈높다** (be) appreciative; over-nice (in choice); particular; fastidious (about); be a good judge of. めがたかい

**눈딱부리** 《사람》 a goggle-eyed[bug-eyed, pop-eyed] person; a popeye 《눈》 bulging eyes. ぎょろぎょろめ

**눈딱지** a dreadful look. わるいめつき

**눈대중** eye measure/ ~하다 measure (a thing) with the eye; estimate by looking/~으로 by [the] eye. もくそく

**눈독** eyeing; having an eye to; running one's eyes over [a thieg with a view to buying or stealing it later].

# 눈

①(일반적) an eye/가느다란 ~ narrow eyes; slit eyes/~의 ocular; optic[al]/~ 은행 an eye bank/날카로운 ~ sharp[alert] eyes/눈물 어린 ~ tearful eyes/멍청한 ~ dull[fishy] eyes/번뜩이는 ~ sparkling eyes/빛나는 ~ bright eyes/졸린 ~ sleepy[heavy] eyes/치켜 올라간 ~ peaked[slant] eyes/툭 불거진 ~ goggle-eyes/움푹 들어간 ~ sunken eyes/휘부리란 ~ big bright eyes/황홀한[꿈꾸는 듯한] ~ dreamy eyes; faraway look/ ~ 깜짝할 사이에 in an instant; in the twinkling of an eye/파란 ~의 blue-eyed/ ~의 운동 ocular movements/ ~을 감다 close [shut] one's eyes; die/ ~을 뜨다 open one's eyes; wake up; awake/ ~을 크게 뜨다 strain one's eyes/~에 차다 be satisfactory/ ~짓을 하다 wink at; make eyes at/ ~이 맞다 fall in love (with each other)/돈에 ~이 멀다 be blind with love of money/허욕에 ~이 멀다 get blind with avarice/부러운 ~으로 쳐다보다 see (a thing) with an envious eye/소매치기가 바로 그의 ~앞에서 그것을 훔쳤다 The pick-pocket took it right from under his nose./그 광경은 차마 ~을 뜨고 볼 수가 없을 만큼 비참했다 The sight was too miserable to look it./ ~이 휘둥그레지다 be pop-eyed; be surprised/ ~에 불이 나다 see stars; be indignant/ ~에 익다 be familiar; get[become] used to seeing/ ~에 설다 be unfamiliar; be strange/ ~에 선하다 be vivid to one's eyes/ ~을 속이다 deceive; hoodwink; pull the wool over eyes/ ~을 돌리다 take one's eyes off (a thing); look away/ ~을 부비다 rub one's eyes/ ~을 흘기다 look askance at; look angrily[sharply] at/ ~이 아프다 have sore eyes/ ~을 가리다 blindfold; bandage (a person) eyes/ ~이 닮다 bear a resemblance in the cast of the eyes/ ~이 핑핑 돌다 be[fed] dizzy; get giddy/ ~에 티가 들다 have a mote[get something] in one's eyes/ ~으로 알리다 wink at (a person); make a sign with the eye/ ~인사하다 [greet with a] nod; thank with one's eyes/ ~으로 말하다 give a significant look; wink at.

②(표정) a look; a gaze; eye/무엇인가 말하려는 ~ talking [eloquent] eyes/성난 ~으로 an angry look in the eye/시기하는 ~으로 보다 see with a jealous eye; look on green-eyed with jealousy/의심하는 ~으로 보다 regard with suspicion/경멸에 찬 ~으로 보다 gaze in contempt (upon a person).

③(마음의) eyes/[…의] ~에 들다 be in favor; be in good (with); find favor with [one's superior]/~에 드는 사람 a man after one's fancy/ […의] 눈밖에 나다 be out of favor; be in bad (with)/~을 즐겁게 하다 feast one's eyes (upon); delight one's eyes/ ~에 거슬리다 become an eyesore; obstruct[spoil] the view; offend the eye[sight].

④(안식) an eye; insight; judg[e]ment/내 ~은 틀림이 없다 I have an unerring eye./사람을 보는 ~이 있다 be a good judge of[have an eye for] character/ ~이 높다 aim high; be desirous of things beyond one's means/전문가의 ~ a professional eye; an expert's eye/골동품을 보는 ~이 있다 have an eye for curios; be a connoisseur of curios/예술가의 ~으로 보다 see with an artist's eye.

⑤(자각) awakening/시대에 ~을 뜨다 be awakened to the times.

⑥(시력) sight; eyesight; vision; eyes/밤~이 밝다 have the eyes of a cat/밤~이 어둡다 suffer from night blindness/ ~이 닿는 데까지 as far as the eye can reach; as far as one can see/ ~이 밝다[좋다] have good eyes[eyesight]; have a good sight/ ~이 어둡다[나쁘다] have bad eyes[defective vision]; have a poor sight/ ~을 멀다 be[become] blind; lose one's [eye] sight/~에 안 보이다 be invisible; be imperceptible/한쪽 ~이 멀다 be blind in one eye/최근에 ~이 나빠졌다 My eyesight has become poor recently./어두운 곳에서 책을 읽는 것은 ~에 나쁘다 Reading in a poor light is bad for the eyes.

⑦(주의·눈길) notice; attention; watch; observation; one's eyes/~에 띄지 않는 장소 a secret corner; a back seat 《미·속》/~ 감으면 코 베어 먹을 세상 a dog-eat-dog world/ ~을 떼다 look aside [away]; take one's eyes off/사람의 ~을 끌다 attract one's attention [notice]; be striking; catch[strike] one's eye; be attractive/남의 ~을 피하다 avoid another's observation/모든 ~이 나에게로 집중했다 All eyes were focused on me./도둑은 순경이 잠깐 ~을 떼는 순간 도망을 쳤다 The thief ran away while the policeman looked aside for a moment.

⑧(입장) one's eyes; a point of view; a viewpoint/공평한 ~으로 보다 look up (a person, a matter) with an impartial eye/그의 ~은 옳았다 He was right in his judgment. / 내 ~으로 보아서는 in my eyes; so far as I see; from where I sit[stand]/서양 사람의 ~으로 보면 from a Western point of view/법률의 ~으로 보면 in the eye of the law/공평한 ~으로 보면 이 사건은 무죄다 If we look upon this case with an impartial eye, he is guiltless.

⑨(기타) ¶~에 새롭다 be novel[fresh, original]/~ 딱 감고 with (a determined) effort; without hesitation.

눈동자(-瞳子) the apple[the pupil] of the eye. ひとみ
눈두덩 the protuberant parts of the eyelids. まぶちのりゅうきぶ
눈뜨다 ①(눈을) open one's eyes ②(깨닫다) be disillusioned; come to one's sense. めざめる
눈뜬장님 《장님》 an amaurotic person 《문맹》 an illiterate; an unlettered person; a blind fool. あきめくら
눈 띄다 attract another's attention/눈에 띄는 noticeable; conspicuous. めにつく
눈망울 an eyeball. がんきゅう
눈맞다 fall in love with each other. あいしあう
눈맞추다 ①(마주보다) look at each other; exchange glances ②(사랑을 표시하다) fall in love with each other ③(남녀가) make eyes at each other. めでものをいう
눈매 the shape of one's eyes. めつき
눈맵시 the shape of one's eyes. めつき
눈멀다 become blind; lose one's sight/눈먼 사람 a blind man. めくらになる
눈물¹ a tear/~을 머금은 목소리 a tearful voice/~겨운 얘기 a pathetic[touching] story/~ 없는 사람 a tearless [an unfeeling] person/~을 잘 흘리는 easily moved to tears; soft-hearted; sentimental/~어린 눈으로 with tearful[swimming] eyes/~을 흘리다 shed [drop] tears. なみだ
눈물² 《눈이 녹은 물》 melted snow.
눈바람 snow and wind 《찬 바람》 an ice-cold wind. ゆきかぜ
눈방울 an eyeball; the globe of an eye. いきいきとしためたま
눈발 snow-covered ground.
눈병(-病) 《의》 an eye disease[trouble]; sore eyes. がんしつ
눈보라 a snowstorm; a blizzard; a snowdrift; drifting[driving] snow. ふぶき
눈부라리다 glare; look with; ylaring eyes.
눈부시다 ①(빛이 부시다) (be) dazzling; glaring; blinding; radiant ②(빛나다) (be) bright; brilliant; dramatic. まぶしい
눈부처 a person's image reflected in the pupil of one's eye.
눈비음 dressing up for others' eyes/~하다 dress up for others' eyes. みせかけ
눈빛¹ 《안색》 the expression in one's eyes; eye-colo[u]r.
눈빛² [snow] white. ゆきいろ
눈사람 a snowman/~을 만들다 make a snowman. ゆきだるま
눈싸움¹ 《설전(雪戰)》 a snow[-ball] fight; snowballing/~하다 have a snowfight; snowball. ゆきがっせん
눈싸움² 《눈겨룸》 a staring match [contest]. にらめっこ
눈사태(-沙汰) a snowslip; a snowslide 《규모가 큰》 an avalanche. なだれ
눈살 the furrow[wrinkles] between one's eyebrows. りょうびかん
눈석임 thaw; slush; snow broth; melting[melted] snow; the thawing of the snow/~하다 the snow thaws[melts].
눈설다 (be) unfamiliar; strange; different; new. みなれない
눈썰미 sharp[dexterous] eyes; keen observation/~가 있다 have dexterous eyes. めのかんしきりよく
눈썹 the eyebrow/~먹 an eyebrow pencil/~을 그리다 pencil the eyebrows/짙은[굵은] ~ thick[bush] eyebrows. まゆ
눈썹차양 a narrow awning along the eaves.
눈속임 hoodwink[-ing]; deception; trickery. ひとのめをだますこと
눈송이 a snowflake. せっぺん
눈씨 the force of one's stare; the power of one's eyes. にらみつけるめつき
눈시울 the edge of an eyelid/~이 뜨거워지다 be moved to tears. めがしら
눈알 an eyeball/~을 굴리다 roll[goggle] one's eyes. がんきゅう
눈앞 in one's presence[face]; under one's eyes 《당장의》 immediate/당장 ~의 이익 an immediate profit. めのまえ
눈어림 eye-measurement. もくそく
눈여겨보다 look hard at; observe closely; watch[look at] carefully; get a good look into; scrutinize. みつめる
눈엣가시 an eyesore; an obstruction[offense] to the eye. めのどく
눈요기(-療飢) feasting one's eyes/~하다 feast one's eyes on (something); delight one's eyes.
눈웃음 a smile about one's eyes; a smile in[with] one's eyes/~치다[하다] wear a smile about one's eyes. しゅうび
눈익다 《사물이 주어》 be familiar (to a person) 《사람이 주어》 get[become] used to seeing. みなれている
눈인사(-人事) greeting with one's eyes /~하다 nod; greet with a nod.
눈자라기 an infant [who cannot sit down by oneself].
눈자위 the fringe of an eye/~꺼지다 dead. がんきゅうのふち
눈정기(-精氣) the gloitter of one's eyes. めのせいき
눈주다 give (a person) the eye; wink

**눈짐작** a guess ⇨눈대중.
**눈짓** winking/ ~하다 wink at; make a sign with the eyes. めくばせ
**눈초리** the outer corner of the eye. めじり
**눈총** a glare; a sharp look; looking daggers (at)/ ~맞다 be glared at; be hated.
**눈총기** keenness of the eye; sharp eyes; quick learning by seeing.
**눈치** ①《감지》sense; tact; intuition; flair; perceptiveness/~가 빠르다 be quick-witted ②《기색》sign; an indication 《태도》a manner; a look. かん
**눈치레** [a mere] show; display. みせもの
**눈치보다** try to read one's mind[face]; probe one's motives; study one's face [pleasure]; grasp a situation; see how the wind blows.
ひとのきげんをうかがうこと
**눈치채다** become aware of (a person's intention, motive, design, etc.); get a hint (of); scent; sense; get wind (of)/ 눈치 채이다 excite suspicion; be smelled out. きずく
**눈칫밥** a dinner for a guest[dependent] who is not entirely welcome/ ~먹다 eat another's salt; feed on (another).
いそうろうのしょくじ
**눈흘기다** glare sidewise (at); glare out of the corner of one's eyes (at).
**눋다** burn; be scorched/밥이 눋었다 The rice has got burned. こげる
**눌눌하다** be a dull yellow. うすきいろい
**눌러** in succession; consecutively/ ~앉다 stay on 《유임하다》remain in the same position. かんだいに
**눌러보다** treat with generosity[kindly, with good grace]. もくにんする
**눌리다**¹ be pushed[pressed] 《위압하다》be overawed[overpowered]. おさえられる
**눌리다**² 《눋게 하다》burn; scorch; singe /밥을 ~ burn the rice. こがす
**눌면하다** (be) rather[somewhat] yellow.
ややきいろがかっている
**눌변(訥辯)** slowness of speech/ ~가 a poor speaker. とつべん
**눌어(訥魚)** 《어》《누치》a cornet fish; Hemibarbus labeo (학명).
**눌어붙다** ①《타서》scorch and stick to ②《한 군데에》stick to; remain. こげつく
**눌언(訥言)** a stammering[stuttering] speech. とつべん
**눌외(─椳)** lateral[horizontal; cross] laths. ずりのよこぎ
**눌은밥** scorched rice. ごはんのおこげ
**눌하다(訥─)** have an irapediment in one's speech; stammer. どもる
**눕다** ①《드러눕다》lie down; lay oneself down; stretch oneself 《자리에》be[lie] in bed ②《앓다》be ill[sick] in bed; take to one's bed/병으로 누워 있다 be laid up; keep one's bed with illness/풀밭에 ~ lie on the grass. ねる
**눕히다** lay down; lay on the side; make [have] (someone) lie down. ねかせる
**눙치다** soothe (one); appease. なだめる
**뉘**¹ 《쌀의》a grain of unhulled rice.
**뉘**² 《누이》a sister. ねえさま
**뉘**³ 《누구》who; whose; someone's. だれの
**뉘반지기** chaffy rice; rice containing many grains of unhulled rice.
**뉘엿거리다** ①《해가》be about to set[sink] ②《뱃속이》feel sick[queasy]; have a desire. ひがまさにくれようとする
**뉘우쁘다** (be) penitential; repantant; regretful. ひじょうにこうかいしている
**뉘우치다** regret; repent (of); feel remorseful; be penitent/뉘우침 regret; repentance; remorse/죄를 ~ repent one's sin. こうかいする
**느글거리다** feel sick; feel nausea; keck; retch. むかむかする
**느긋거리다** feel sick; feel queasy[nauseated]; keck; retch. むかむか
**느긋하다** (be) satisfactory; enough; gratifying. まんぞくだ
**느끼다** ①《지각》feel; be conscious of; experience/불편을 ~ experience inconvenience/고통을 ~ feel a pain ②《감동하다》be impressed[struck, moved]/사물에 느끼기 쉬운 sensitive/비애감을 ~ be seized with grief/느끼는 바 있어 술을 끊었다 For reasons of my own I have given up drinking. ③《호느끼다》sob/ 느껴울다 weep silently. かんじる
**느끼하다** (be) too fatty[greasy, rich].
あぶらじみている
**느낌** 《인상》an impression 《기분》sentiment[feeling] 《촉감》touch[feel]/ ~표 an exclamation mark/…의 ~을 주다 impress[strike] (one) as; give an impression of. かんじ
**-느냐** 및가겠~ Are you going? ─か
**느닷없다** (be) sudden; abrupt; unexpected. とつさ
**느닷없이** suddenly; all of a sudden; unexpectedly; without notice. とつさに
**느럭느럭** sluggishly; idly/~ 일하다 work slowly. のろのろ
**느런히** 《나란히》in a row.
**느렁이** 《동》a doe; a hind.
**느른하다** (be) languid; weary; limp/느른하여 일하기가 싫다 I feel too lazy to work. つかれきっている
**느릅나무** 《식》an elm [tree].
**느리광이** a sluggard; an idler; a lazy fellow. のろま
**느리다** ①《속도가》(be) slow; tardy《완만하다》(be) slow; sluggish 《둔하다》(be) dull; slow ②《짜임새가》(be) loose/짜임새가 느린 천 loose fabric. のろい
**느림** 《장식술》a tassel. ふさ
**느림보** a sluggard ⇨느리광이. のろま
**느릿느릿** 《속도가》slowly; sluggishly; id-

느물거리다 ly 《짜임새가》 loose; slack. おそく
느물거리다 act craftily. ずるくふるまう
느슨하다 (be) loose 《매기 따위가》 not tight. たるんでいる
느즈러지다 ①《느슨해지다》loosen; slacken; become loose ②《기한이》 be put off; be postponed. ゆるむ
느지감치 rather late. ひじょうにおそく
느지막이 very late. おそく
느지막하다 (be) rather late. かなりおそい
느직이 ①very[rather] late／~ 일어나다 get up rather late in the morning ② 《느슨히》 rather slack[loose]. おそく
느직하다 be somewhat[rather] late; be rather slow. ややおそい
느치 《충》 a cadelle; Tenebroides mauritanicus(학명).
느타리 《식》 an agaric; Agaricuss subfunereus(학명). しいたけ
느티나무 《식》 a zelkova [tree]; Zelkova acuminata(학명). けやき
늑간(肋間) 《해》 intercostal／~ 신경통 intercostal neuralgia; costalgia／~근(筋) the intercostal muscle[nerve].
ろっこつとろっこつとのま
늑골(肋骨) 《해》 a rib; a costa／~ 동맥 the intercostal astery. ろっこつ
늑대 《동》 a Korean wolf. おおかみ
늑막(肋膜) 《해》 the pleura／건성[습성] ~염 dry[moist] pleurisy. ろくまく
늑목(肋木) wall-bars; Swedish bars. ろくぼく
늑연골(肋軟骨) 《해》 costal cartilage. ろくなんこつ
늑장 ~부리다 take one's time; be slow [in doing]; be tardy; loiter. のらくら
늑줄주다 supervise less strictly; exercise a lax supervision. ゆるめる
늑탈(勒奪) plunder; pillage; spoliation; looting; despoilment[despoliation]／~하다 plunder; loot; seize; pillage.
ぼうりょくでうばうこと
늑하다 (be) satisfactory. じゅうぶんだ
는 《토씨》 ¶ 국화는 지금 한창이다 The chrysanthemums are at their best. —は
-는 《어미》 ¶ 나는 새 a flying bird.
는개 a fine drizzle. ぬかあめ
-는구나 ¶ 글쎄 그가 나에게 거짓말을 하~ To my astonishment, he told me a lie.
—なあ. —ね
-는데 ¶ 김군은 왔~ 이군은 웬 일일까 Mr. Kim is here now. But what happened to Mr. Lee? —のに. —するのだが
는실난실하다 dally; flirt; take liberties.
いちゃつく
는적거리다 fall apart at a touch; feel squashy[pulpy] 《피륙 따위가》 be flimsy 《상한 생선이》 be crumbly; crumby; decomposed／~적거리는적 flimsily; all crumbly; crumby; decomposed.
ぐにゃぐにゃする
늘 《언제나》 always; ever; all the time; usually 《습관적》 habitually 《부단히》 constantly. いつも

늘그막 old age; declining years; the winter of life.
늘다 ①《증가하다》 increase; grow; swell; rise／두 개가 ~ increase by two／신용이 ~ rise in public confidence／회원이 ~ have an increased membership／체중이 두 관 늘었다 gain two kwan in weight ②《전진하다》 progress (in); advance (in); be improved／영어가 ~ make progress in one's English. ぞうかする
늘름 ①《날쎄게》 with a quick snatch ②《혀를》 [a tongue] darting out and in.
ぺろりと
늘름거리다 let (one's arm, one's tongue) dart out and in; take one's hand out and in. しきりにほしがる
늘리다 《양을》 increase; add to 《증액하다》 raise 《배가(倍加)하다》 multiply. ふやす
늘비하다 (be) in a row[line]; drawn up; be arrayed. つづいている
늘썽늘썽 all loose[slack, open]／~하다 be all loose[slack, open]; (be) loose -woven; be [an] open-weave.
늘썽하다 (be) coarse; loose. めがあらい
늘씬하다 (be) slender; slim／늘씬한 허리 a slender[slim] waist. すんなりしている
늘어가다 go on increasing; be on the increase. ふえていく
늘어나다 lengthen; grow longer; extend; expand. ふえる
늘어놓다 ①《여기저기》 scatter about; put in disorder; leave (things) lying about ②《길게》 talk away; rattle on; way one's tongue ③《배치하다》 post; station; detail; dispatch. ④《사업을》 carry on [various enterprises]. ならべておく
늘어뜨리다 《아래로》 hang down 《머리를》 trail 《개가 귀 따위를》 lop; droop.
늘어서다 stand in a row; form in a line 《열으로》 stand abreast. ならぶ
늘어앉다 sit in a row; sit in line; sit around. ならんですわる
늘어지다 ①《길어지다》 extend; lengthen; grow longer ②《처지다》 hang [down]; dangle; droop ③《시간이》 be prolonged; be protracted ④《몸이》 become limp; be exhausted. のびる
늘이다 ①《아래로》 hang down; suspend; dangle; slouch 《축 늘이다》 ②《증가하다》 increase; add (to) 《길이를》 lengthen; prolong; protract. ぶらさげる
늘임새 drawl; dragging one's words out.
늘자리 a bulrush-mat.
늘쩍지근하다 (be) dog-tired; fagged out; very languid; quite weary.
늘쩡거리다 be slow-moving; be lazy[slow] in doing something. のろのろする
늘채다 be far more than the expected number. あんがいおおい
늘컹거리다 act[be] all soft and doughy
⇒늘컹하다.
늘컹하다 act[be] all soft and doughy [droopy, flabby]／늘컹늘컹 [all] soft and doughy[droopy, flabby]; squashi-

**늘큰거리다** ly. ぐんにゃりたれる
**늘큰거리다** act[be] soft and droopy; act [be] flabby[pasty, doughy]/늘른늘른 squashily. ぐんにゃりする
**늙다** grow old; age; advance in age/ 늙은 old; aged/나날이 늙어가다 be getting old day by day. としとる
**늙다리** 《사람》 an old buffer 《짐승》 an old animal.
**늙바탕** old age; one's declining years/ ~에 들다 be advanced in life. ろうきょう
**늙수그레하다** (be) rather advanced in age; fairly old. ひじょうにとしとっている
**늙으신네** an old person.
**늙은이** an old man 《총칭》 the old; the aged. ろうじん
**늙히다** make (a person) old; age (a person)/처녀로 ~ let a girl become an old maid. ふけさす
**늚다** hull; shell.
**늠렬(凜烈)** ~한 (된) severe 《위풍있는》 majestic; intense/~한 추위 intense cold.
**늠름(凜凜)** ~하다 (be) gallant and forbidding; imposing; manly; commanding; dignified / ~한 태도 an imposing [awe-inspiring] attitude.
**늠실거리다** leer ⇨넘실거리다.
**늠연(凜然)** ~하다 (be) awe-inspiring; commandingly; commanding. りんぜん
**늡늡하다** (be) large-mined; open-hearted; liberal; magnanimous. きまえがよい
**능(能)** 《재능》 ability; capability; talent; capacity. のう
**능(綾)** a kind of thin silk. あや
**능(陵)** a royal[imperial] mausoleum[tomb]. りょう
**능(稜)** 〖수〗 an angle; an edge. りょう
**능가(凌駕)** ~하다 surpass; exceed; override; outstrip; get ahead of/노인을 ~ 하다 surpass old man. りょうが
**능간(能幹)** capability; ability; talent.
**능갈치다** devise clever excuses[pretexts]. じょうずにやりくりする
**능구렁이** 〖동〗①《뱀》 a kind of snake; Dinodon rufozonatum(학명) ②《사람》 old fox; a sly dog: a deep one. へびのいっしゅ
**능글능글** ~하다 (be) deceitful; sneaky; cunning; sly; insidious; wily; impudent. ずるがしこい
**능글맞다** (be) sly; sneaky ⇨능글능글하다.
**능금** an apple. りんご
**능놀다** do (something) slowly; take one's time [at a piece of work]. のばす
**능동(能動)** 《자반적》 spontaneity; spontaneousness; voluntariness 《활동적》 activeness; activity/~적 voluntary; active; spontaneously; lively/~태 《문법 의》 the active voice. のうどう
**능란(能爛)** ~하다 (be) skil[l]ful; dexterous; adroit; expert; proficient; good; clever. じょうず
**능력(能力)** 《역량》 ability; capability 《지력》 mental faculties; brain power 《성능》 capacity/생산 ~ productive capacity/지불 ~ solvency; the ability to pay/ …할 ~이 있다 be able to (do); be capable of [doing]; be competent (for a work). のうりょく
**능률(能率)** efficiency/~ 시험 an efficiency test/~급(給) efficiency pay/~ 적 efficient/~을 올리다[내리다] increase[diminish] efficiency. のうりつ
**능면체(菱面體)** rhombohedron.
**능모(凌侮)** slight; contempt; disdain; scorn/~하다 despise; scorn; disdain; slight; contempt. りょうぶ
**능변(能辯)** ①《언어》 eloquence; fluency; oratory ②《사람》 an eloquent speaker; an orator / ~의 eloquent; fluent/ ~ 가 an eloquent speaker. のうべん
**능사(能事)** 《적당한 일》 proper and suitable work 《잘하는 일》 a job that one can handle competently and easily; one's work; one's line [of business]. のうじ
**능소(陵所)** a Royal mausoleum.
**능소 능대(能小能大)** ~하다 (be) able and adaptable/ ~한 작가 a versatile writer. ばんじをじょうずにすること
**능소니** a bear cub; a cub bear. くまのこ
**능수(能手)** 《수완》 ability; capability; capacity 《사람》 an able man; a veteran; a tactician. じょうずなひと
**능수버들** a weeping willow. やなぎ
**능숙(能熟)** skill[fulness]; proficiency; expertness; adeptness/~하다 (be) skilled; skil[l]ful; proficient/…에 ~하 다 be skilled in. じゅくれんしている
**능욕(凌辱)** ①《모욕》 insult; affront; indignity; contempt/~하다 insult (a person) ②《여자를》 violation; outrage; rape; assault / ~하다 violate; commit rape on. りょうじょく
**능지기(陵一)** the caretaker of a royal mausoleum.
**능지 처참(陵遲處斬)** hacking a criminal to pieces/~하다 a hack (criminal) to pieces.
**능청거리다** move springily; swing; sway/능청능청 swayingly; swingingly. まがりやすい
**능청스럽다** (be) deceitful; cunning; artful; sly; crafty; wily; insidious/능청 스러운 사람 a sly dog. ずうずうしい
**능통(能通)** proficiency; mastery; skill; a full knowledge/ ~하다 (be) skillful; proficient/ …에 ~하다 be proficient in; be a master of; be versed in/영어에 ~하다 be versed in English.
**능필(能筆)** good writing 《사람》 a good penman[calligrapher]. のうひつ
**능하다(能—)** excel (in English); (be) capable; able; (be) expert (in); skilled; proficient (in). よくする
**능형(菱形)** a rhomb; a lozenge; a diamond [shape]/~의 rhombic; diamond [lozenge]-shape. りょうけい
**능히(能—)** well; easily; ably/ ~ 할 수 있다 can easily do; be able to do; be

equal to. うまく
**늦-** late; belated/~가을 late autumn.
**늦다** ①《시각이》(be) late; behind time《속도가》(be) slow; tardy/늦게 late/늦어도 at [the] latest/밤늦게 late at night; at a late hour/돌아오는 것이 ~ be a long time gone; come back [home] until a late hour/늦게 가다《시계가》lose /5분 ~ be five minutes slow /아침 늦도록 잠자다 sleep late into the morning/때는 이미 늦었다 It is too late now. ②《느슨하다》(be) loose; not tight/고삐가 ~ The rein is slack. おそい
**늦더위** the lingering summer heat; the second summer. ざんしょ
**늦동이**(一童—) ①《늦게 난》a child had late in *one's* life ②《늦된》a retarded child.
**늦되다** mature late; be slow in growing/늦된 아이 a retarded child.
**늦바람** ①《저녁 바람》an evening breeze ②《빠르지 않은 바람》a gentle[light, soft] breeze ③《난봉》dissipation in *one's* later years. ゆうがたおそくふくかぜ
**늦배** 《짐승의》late breeding《조류의》late hatching.
**늦벼** a kind of late-ripening rice. おくて
**늦봄** late spring.
**늦부지런** ①《뒤늦게》belated hasty diligence ②《늙어서》becoming diligent in *one's* old age.
**늦서리** a late frost. じきおくれのしも
**늦여름** late summer.
**늦잠** late rising; morning sleep/ ~자다 rise[get up] 'late; sleep late/~꾸러기 a late riser. あさね
**늦장마** a late rainy season; the rainy spell in late summer. じきおくれのつゆ
**늦추** ①《늦게》late ②《느슨히》loosely; slack/허리띠를 ~ 매다 tie *one's* belt loosely. おそく
**늦추다** ①《떠나 고삐를》loosen; make loose ②《속력을 느리게 하다》slow down ③《미루다》postpone; put off. ゆるめる
**늦추위** the lingering cold; late cold.
**늪** a swamp; a marsh; a bog; a pond.
**님** 《경칭》Mister; Mr.; Esq(남자); Miss (미혼 여자); Mrs(부인). 一さま
**닢** ♀동전 다섯 ~ five piece of copper.

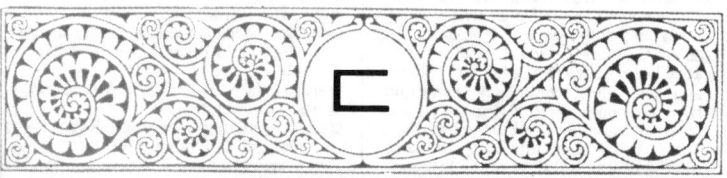

**다** 《모두》 all; each 《철저히》 completely; perfectly; indeed; thoroughly. すべて

**-다** ¶하늘을 찌를 듯이 높~ be sky-high/나의 형은 선생이~ My elder brother is a teacher./그 소녀는 아름답~ The girl is beautiful. －だ

**다가놓다** bring near; draw [up] near; put close. ちかよせておく

**다가서다** draw near (to); step[come] up (to). ちかよってたつ

**다가앉다** sit close; take one's seat closer. ちかよってすわる

**다가오다** 《공간적으로》 approach; near; come up to; get near 《시간적으로》 draw [come] near; draw close (to)/종말이 ~ draw to a close. ちかよってくる

**다각**(多角) many-sidedness/ ~의 many-sided; multiple; multilateral. たかく

**다각적**(多角的) diversified; many-sided; multilateral; versatile. たかくてき

**다각형**(多角形) 《수》 a polygon/ ~의 polygonal. たかくけい

**다갈색**(茶褐色) yellowish brown; liver-colour/~의 brown. ちゃかっしょく

**다감**(多感) sensibility; susceptibility; sentimentality; sentimentalism. たかん

**다겁**(多怯) cowardice; timidity; timidness; poor courage; faint-heartedness/~하다 (be) cowardly; timid; chicken-hearted.

**다과**(多寡) 《액》 amount 《양》 quantity 《수》 number. たか

**다과**(茶菓) tea and cake; light refreshments/~회 a tea-party. さか

**다구**(茶具) tea-things; tea utensils 《한 벌의》 a tea set. おちゃのどうぐ

**다그다** bring up near; draw close up [near]. ちかよせる

**다그치다** bring up nearer; draw close up. つめる

**따끔하다** feel prickly; prick; bite; tingle; have a tingling pain (in). ひりひりいたい

**다급하다** (be) imminent; impending; pressing; exigent; urgent/다급한 문제 a pressing question. きんきゅうである

**다기**(多岐) many divergences; many branches (of a road). たき

**다기지다**(多氣一) (be) courageous; brave; heroic; bold; daring; plucky; audacious; undaunted; gallant. だいたんだ

**다난**(多難) many difficulties; lots of trouble/~하다 be full of troubles[difficulties]; be eventful; be fraught with difficulties. たなん

**다녀가다** 《잠깐 들리다》 drop in for a short visit 《지나는 길에》 look (one) up; drop in (on a person). たちよってかえる

**다녀오다** return; drop in (on a person and then come back); come[get] back [home]; be back. いってくる

**다년**(多年) many[a number of] years/ ~간 many years 《부사적》 for [many] years; for a number of years; through the years; for a long time/~생 《식》 perennation. たねん

**다능**(多能) many-sidedness; many accomplishments; versatility/~하다 (be) many accomplished; many-sided; versatile.

**-다니** ¶그렇게 정직한 사람을 내쫓~ 기가 막히네 The idea of kicking out such an honest fellow!/여기서 자네를 만나~ 정말 의외일세 This is the last place, where I expected to meet you. －とは

**다니다** ①《왕래》 go back and forth; come and go; go to and from 《왕복》 go and return 《지나는 길에》 ply (between, from … to) 《기차 따위가》 run between ②《통근·통학》 attend; commute to; go to ③《들리다》 frequent; visit frequently; resort to; drop in; stop at. おうらいする

**다단**(多端) 《다항목》 many items; divergence; digression; ramification 《다망》 pressure of business/~하다 (be) busy; complicated. たたん

**다닫다** arrive at. とうたつする

**다달이** every month; per month; monthly/~ 부어 가다 pay by the month/~ 두 번씩 twice a month. まいつき

**다대** 《헝겊 조각》 a patch; a piece of cloth. つぎはぎ

**다대**(多大) (be) a great quantity/~하다 much; great; heavy; serious; considerable. ただい

**다독**(多讀) extensive reading/~하다 read much[widely, a great deal, extensively]. たどく

**다독거리다, 따독거리다** gather (things) up

**따님** your[his] daughter. れいじょう

**따다**¹ ①《잡아 떼다》 pick; pluck; clip; nip [off]; trim; deflower(꽃을); gather(모으다); cull ②《터뜨리다》 lance;

open; crush ③(발체) extract; pick out ④(얻다) get; obtain; take. つみとる
**따다²** (다르다) (be) different; separate; dissimilar; another; distinct. ちがう
**따다³** (면회 거절) refuse to a caller pretending to be away from home; pretend to be out; be not at home (to *some caller*) ②⇨따돌리다.
**다따가** suddenly; [all] of a sudden; abruptly. とちゅうできゅに
**다다르다** get to (*a place*); arrive at [in, on]; come up to; gain; reach／표준에 ~ come up to the standard. とうたつする
**다다 익선(多多益善)** The more, the better.
**다닥다닥** in clusters. ⇨더덕더덕.
**다닥뜨리다** hit against; run against; smash into; collide with. ぶつつかる
**다닥치다** collide with; draw near; approach; strike against; come near; run against; be imminent; crash [smash] into. しょうとつする
and press into order. とりまとめる
**따돌리다** exclude; neglect; boycott (*one*); leave (*one*) out in the cold; blackball; ostracize. じょがいする
**다듬다** (매만지다) arrange; smooth; face (석재 등을); finish; plume (깃 따위를); trim (나무 따위를) ②(푸성귀를) nip (*off*); trim ③(땅바닥을) [make] even; level; roll; smooth ④(옷을) full (*cloth*). そろえる
**다듬이** ①(옷감) cloth to be fulled [smoothed] ②⇨다듬이질. きぬた
**다듬이질** fulling cloth／~하다 full cloth. きぬたでうつこと
**다듬잇돌** a fulling block. きぬた
**다듬잇방망이** a fulling-club. きぬたのぼう
**다듬질** 〖미〗 finish; finishing touches／ ~하다 give the final touches to; do up; finish (*up*). しあげ
**따듯이** (열 따위) warmly ／~하고 있다 keep *oneself* warm ②(온정 따위) warm-heartedly; kindly; warmly. あたたかく
**따뜻하다** (온도가) (be) warm; mild (전이) (be) kindly; cordial; warm[-hearted]; genial. あたたかい
**따라가다** accompany; go with; follow (복종) obey; follow; yield to (뒤미쳐 오다) catch [come] up with／따라갈 사람이 없다 be peerless; stand unchallenged. ついていく
**따라서** ①(…대로) in accordance [conformity] with; according to ②(비례하여) in proportion to [as]; according to; as／능력에 ~ according to *one's* ability ／문명이 발달함에 ~ as civilization progresses ③(병행해서·끼고) along [with]; by; with (모방) after [the example of] ; in the manner of; in imitation of (함께)／강묵을 ~ along the river bank／어머니를 ~ with *one's* mother ④ (그러므로) consequently; accordingly; therefore／품질이 좋으니 ~ 값도 비싸다

The article is of fine quality, and consequently the price is high. したがって
**따라오다** ①(수행하다) come with; tag along with; accompany; follow (쫓아 오다) keep up with; follow at *a person's* heels ②(남이 하는 대로) follow suit; do likewise [the same]; catch up ③ (겨룸) compete; rival; equal; be a match for. ついてくる
**따라지** ①(난장이) a dwarf ②(노름판의 한 끗) one point.
**다라지다** (be) bold; daring; dauntless; spunky; plucky. びくともしない
**다락** a loft; a garret／~방 an upper [-story] room. たかどの
**다람쥐** 〖동〗 a squirrel; chipmunk. りす
**다랍다** ①(더럽다) (be) dirty; filthy; unclean ②(인색하다) (be) stingy; niggardly; mean. けちくさい
**다랑귀뛰다** cling to; hold on fast to; clutch. ぶらさがる
**다랑어(一魚)** 〖어〗 a tunny; a tuna 〈미〉.
**다랑이** a small strip of rice-paddy field. てのひらほどのはたけ
**다래** ①(다래나무의 열매) the fruit of the *Actinidia arguta* ②(목화의 열매) a cotton boll. さるなしのみ
**다래나무** *Actinidia arguta* (학명).
**다래다래** dangling in clusters. ふさふさ
**다량(多量)** a large quantity; a great deal; much／~의 much; great quantity of. たりょう
**따로** (별개로) separately; apart (추가로) besides; additionally; in addition (특별히) especially; in particular; particularly／~ 두다 keep [lay] aside／~ 말할 것이 없다 have nothing particular to say／~ 살다 live separately. べつに
**따로따로** separately; apart (개별로) severally; individually／~ 살다 live separately／형제들은 ~ 살고 있다 The brothers live each by himself. べつべつに
**다루다** ①(처리·대우) manage; handle; treat; deal with／다루기 힘든 unmanageable; hard to deal with ②(가죽을) tan; dress (*a skin*) (희게) taw／다루지 않은 untanned; raw (*hide*). とりつかう
**다르다** (be) different; dissimilar; unlike (동사적) vary; differ／다른 dissimilar; different; other (별개의) another／서로 ~ be different from each other [one another]. ちがう
**따르다¹** ①(수행) follow; go [along] with (*one*); accompany ②(수반) be followed by (병행) keep [in] step with／많은 곤란이 ~ be attended by various difficulties ③(복종) follow; obey (응하다) accede to; comply with／충고에 ~ follow *one's* advice ④(불좇다) become endeared [attached] (동물이) be tamed／아버지를 몹시 ~ be strongly attached to *one's* father ⑤(모방) follow; imitate; model (*after*)／전례에 ~ follow a precedent／본을 ~ follow from a model. したがう

**따르다²** (붓다) pour (*out, in*). そそぐ
**따르르** ¶ ~ 울리다 tinkle/~ 구르다 roll fast. ころころ
**따름** only; simply; merely/그는 일개 학생일 ~이다 He is nothing but a student., He is a mere student. ばかり
**다름아니라** be no more than; be nothing but/다름아닌 당신이니까 since it is you of all people. ほかでもない
**다름없다** (be) similar; be as good as; be not different; be the same/전과 ~ 이 just as it was before. ちがいない
**다름없이** in the same way; similarly; likewise; equally. ちがいなく
**다릅나무** 〖식〗 *Maackia amurensis*(학명).
**다리¹** (사람·동물의) a leg; a limb (물건의) a leg/~ 가 길다 be long-legged. あし
**다리²** (교량) a bridge/다릿목 the approach to a bridge/~ 난간 a bridge rail/~ 를 놓다 build[throw] a bridge (*across*) /~ 항구(桁構) a bridge girder. はし
**다리³** (머리의) a false lock of hair; artificial lock of hair. かもじ
**다리다** iron [out]; press; do the ironing /샤쓰를 ~ iron out a shirt/웃옷을 ~ iron clothes. ひのしをかける
**다리미** an iron; a flat-iron/~ 질하다 iron (*clothes*); do the ironing. ひのし
**다리쇠** a device which is put across a brazier to support things for heating; a trivet.
**다림** plumbing.
**다림보다** ①(겨냥대어) plumb ②(살피다) aim; watch. すいちょくをみる
**다림줄** a plumbing line.
**다림질** ironing/~하다 iron [out] (*clothes*); press; do the ironing. アイロンかけ
**다림추**(-錘) a plummet; a plumb [weight]. おもり
**다림판**(-板) a levelling plate.
**다릿돌** stepping stones. ふみいし
**다릿목** the approach[path] to a bridge. はしのあるようしょ
**다만** (오직)only; simply; merely; alone; but/~ 한 번 only[but] once (그러나) but; however; still/그건 ~ 소문에 불과하다 It is merely a rumor. ただし
**다망**(多忙) press[pressure] of work; business/~하다 (be) busy; busily engaged/~한 busy/~한 사람 a busy man. たぼう
**다망**(多望) a bright prospect; great promise/~하다 (be) promising; hopeful; rosy; of bright prospect/~한 전도 a bright[rosy] future. きぼうをおおいこき
**따먹다** ①(과실을) pick (*an apple*) and eat ②(장기 따위에) take a man[piece] in chess ③(여자를) defile[trifle with] a girl's chastity. つみとってくう
**다면**(多面) many sides/~체 a polyhedron/~ 성 many-sided; versatile. ためん
**다모류**(多毛類) 〖동〗 *Polychaeta*(학명).
**다모작**(多毛作) multiple cropping.
**다목** 〖식〗a Brazilwood; a sappanwood; *Caesalpinia sappan*(학명).
**다목다리** a dark-red leg. あかくろいあし
**다목적**(多目的) multipurpose/~ 댐 a multipurpose dam.
**다못** only ⇨다만. ただ
**다문**(多聞) much information /~ 박식 much information and wide knowledge. たぶん
**다문다문** once in a while ⇨드문드문.
**다물다** shut; close/입을 ~ be silent; be shut up. とじる
**다미씌우다** impute (*a crime* to); lay the blame on one. せきにんなどをおわせる
**다박나룻** a bushy beard; unkempt whiskers. もじゃもじゃひげ
**다박머리** dishevelled hair; unkempt hair. もじゃもじゃのかみ
**다발** a bundle; a bunch/꽃 한 ~ a bunch of flowers. たば
**다방**(茶房) a tea house[booth]; a tea room; a tea shop; a coffee house/~ 레지 a tea house waitress. きっさてん
**다방면**(多方面) (방향) many directions (문제) different subjects (취미) many -sidedness; versatility (측면) many sides/~의 varied; many-sided; all-round; versatile. たほうめん
**다변**(多辯) talkativeness/~가 a talkative person; chatterbox(여자)/ ~의 talkative. たべん
**다변형**(多邊形) 〖수〗a polygon/~의 polygonal. たへんけい
**다병**(多病) sickliness/~하다 (be) weak; sickly; frail; delicate; infirm/~한 사람 a sickly person. たびょう
**다보록하다** (be) bushy ⇨더부룩하다. けむくじゃらだ
**다복**(多福) being favo[u]red with good luck[fortune]/ ~하다 (be) happy; blessed; fortunate. たふく
**다복다복** in groves; thickly; in bunches.
**다복솔** a young pine tree with many twigs; bushy young pine tree.
**다부 일처**(多夫一妻) polyandry.
**다부지다** (be) dauntless; indomitable. けつだんりょくがある
**다북쑥** a mugwort ⇨쑥. にがよもぎ
**따분하다** ①(느른하다) (be) tired out; wearied; fatigued ②(난처하다) (be) awkward; helpless; embarrassing/따분한 세상 the dreary world. たいくつだ
**다분히**(多分-) much; mostly; for the most part. たぶんに
**다불과**(多不過) at [the] most. せいぜい
**다불다불** in tufts/~하다 (be) tufty; fringy. ふさふさ
**다붓다붓** at short intervals; close[ly].
**다붓하다** (be) dense; close; near/다붓이 close[ly]; densely. ちかい
**다붙다** come together; close in together. くっつく
**다붙이다** bring together. くっつける
**따비** 〖농기구〗 a small plough; a weeder. じょそうき

다비(茶毘) 《종》 cremation; *jhapita*(Sans)／～하다 cremate (*the remains*).  だび
따비밭 a field of small acreage.
다사(多事) ①《일이 많음》 pressure of work; busyness; bustling／～하다 (be) busy; eventful／～ 다난 eventfulness ②《간섭》 meddlesomeness; nosiness／～스럽다 (be) meddlesome; nosy; officious. たじ
다산(多産) productivity; fecundity／～의 productive; prolific／～부 a prolific woman.  たさん
다색(茶色) light brown／～의 brownish; light brown.  ちゃいろ
다섯 five／～배[의] fivefold; quintuple／～째 the fifth.  いつつ
다소(多少) 《수량의》 the amount[number, quantity] 《부사적》 somewhat; a little; more or less; in a way; to some extent.  たしょう
다소곳이 obediently; with *one's* head drooped.
다소곳하다 obedient; (be) silent with *one's* head drooped／다소곳한 태도 an obedient attitude. うつむいてだまっている
-다손치더라도 although; though; even if; no matter (*who, what, when, how*); admitting that／그렇у admitting that it is true／설령 무슨 일이 있у whatever[no matter what] may happen; come what may.  －としても
다수(多數) a majority; a large[great] number; many／～의 numerous; many; a large number of.  たすう
다수결(多數決) decision by majority／～하다 decide by majority／～에 좇다 abide by the decision of the majority.
다수굿하다 (be) obedient ⇨다소곳하다.
다스리다 ①《통치》 manage (*a household*); administer; govern (*a country*) ②《병을》 cure; treat ③《평정》 quiet; put down; suppress ④《죄를》 penalize; punish／죄를 ～ punish a crime.
다스하다, 따스하다 (be) somewhat warm; mild.  いくぶんあたたかい
다습다, 따습다 mild;(be) somewhat warm; gentle.  ほどよくあたたかい
다시 over again; again 《거듭》 once more; twice; a second time; again 《새로이》 anew／～ 한 번 once more; a second time／～ 시작하다 begin anew.  また
다시금 for the second time; again. また
다시마 《식》 a kelp; a sea tangle; a devil's apron; *Laminaria japonica*(학명). こんぶ
다시없다 (be) unique; unparalleled; matchless; unequalled／다시없는 일품 a unique article／이렇게 좋은 기회는 다시없을 것이다 Such an opportunity offers but once.  これいじょうない
-다시피 《같은 정도로》 nearly; almost; as good as 《마찬가지로》 like; as; similar to.  －ようсに
다식(多食) heavy feeding; gluttony／～하다 gluttonize; eat much[heavily]／～가 a glutton; a great eater.  たしょく
다식(茶食) a kind of coloured candy made of sesame seeds, honey, etc.
다신교(多神敎) polytheism／～도(徒) a polytheist; a heathen.  たしんきょう
다심(多心) excessive scrupulosity; over-cautiousness／～스럽다, ～하다 overanxious; overcautious; nervous; be given toworries.  おもいすぎること
다액(多額) a large sum[amount]／～의 considerable; a large sum of.  たがく
다언(多言) 《여러 말》 many words 《말 많음》 volubility; garrulity／～의 talkative; garrulous.  たげん

다염기산(多鹽基酸) 《화》 polybasic acid.
다오 ①《물건 따위를》 let me have; give me／우유 한 컵만 ～ Will you give me a glass of milk. ②《… 해 다오》이 편지를 부쳐 ～ Have this letter posted.  くれ
따오기 《조》 a sacred ibis; a crested ibis. とき
다용(多用) spending much; using much／～하다 spend lavishly; use much／～되다 be widely used.  たよう
다원(多元) 《철》 pluralism／～론 pluralism／～론자 a pluralist／～적 plural.
따위 《등등》 and others; and the rest; and so forth; like; et cetera(略：ect.)／예를 들면… ～ for example; such as／이 ～ 물건 an article of this kind／우리들 ～ 에게는 for such as we: for the like of us／너 ～ your likes.  など
다육(多肉) fleshiness／～의 pulpy; fleshy／～하다 (be) fleshy; pulpy; succulent.  たにく
다음 next; following; coming; ensuing 《인접한》 adjoining; adjacent 《둘째》 second 《계속》 the sequel (of *a story*); the rest／～의 following; next; second 《버금가는》／～에 in the next place; after／～ 일요일 next Sunday／～ 기사 the following article.  つぎ
다음가다 come after; be second[next] to／서울 다음가는 대도시 the greatest city next to Seoul.  にばんめである
다음 날 the next[following] day／도착한 ～ the day after[following] *one's* arrival.  つぎのひ
다음다음 next but one; the one after the next／～ 날 the next day after one; two days after.
다음 달 the following[the next] month.
다음자(多音字) a polyphone.
다음절어(多音節語) a polysyllabic word; a polysyllable.
다음 해 the following[the next] year; the year ensuing.  つぎのとし
다음 호(一號) the next number[issue]／～에 계속 To be continued.
다의(多義) diverse[various] meanings／～어(語) a multivocal word; a word with many meanings.
다짜고짜로 peremptorily; without [the slightest] warning; without preliminn-

aries; directly; abruptly./~ 사람을 치다 hit a person abruptly. めちゃくちゃに
다작(多作) prolificacy in writing/~의 prolific/~하다 write many works; be prolific in writing/~가 voluminous author; a prolific writer. たさく
따작거리다 scratch [and tear off]; claw.
다잡다 ①(마음을) turn over a new leaf; sober down ②(독려하다) control; supervise; urge. げんじゅうにしきかんとくする
다재(多才) great ability; versatile talents/~한 many-sided; versatile/~ 다능한 사람 a man of varied attainments; an all [a] round person. たさい
다정(多情) ①(인정・상냥) humaneness; kindness; cordiality; warm-[tender-]heartedness/~하다 (be) humane; kind; affectionate; cordial; warm-hearted; tender-hearted ②(교분) a close friend -ship. たじょう
다정 다감(多情多感) (감상) sentimentality (감정) passionateness/~하다 (be) sentimental; emotional; passionate; ardent/ ~한 사람 a man of sentiment[feeling]. たじょうたかん
다정 다한(多情多恨) sentimentality; sensibility; tears and regrets/~하다 (be) sentimental; emotional; ardent; be full of tears and regrets. たじょうたこん
다정 불심(多情佛心) tender-heartedness.
다정자(茶亭子) a tea table; a teacup holder.
다조지다 do in haste; urge[press] in haste. げんかくなとりしまりをする
다족류(多足類) 《동》 myriapods; millipedes; Myriapoda(학명). たそくるい
다지다 ①(다짐받다) make sure (of) ② 《단단하게》 ram; harden ③(고기를) mince. たしかめる
따지다 ①(시비를) distinguish [right from wrong]; inquire into [the rights and wrongs of a case]. ②(수를) count; compute [interest]; count; calculate. けいさんをはっきりする
다지르다 make sure of [that…]; insist on ascertaining. しっかりたしかめる
다질리다 be made sure of; get pressed for a definite answer; be assured; be pledged. しっかりたしかめられる
다짐 (보증) guaranty; reassurance (확약) a definite answer[promise]/~받다 get reassurance; make sure (of); secure a definite answer/~하다 pledge assure; guarantee. かくやく
다채롭다(多彩—) (be) colourful; variegated/다채로운 행사 variegated functions. たさいである
다처(多妻) a plurality of wives; many wives/일부 ~ polygamy.
다치다 be wounded[injured]; get[be] hurt; receive[sustain] a wound/다리를 ~ get hurt in the leg. けがする
다투다 ①(겨루다) contend; struggle; compete; vie with ②(논쟁) argue; dispute 《말다툼》 have words; quarrel/자리를 ~ scramble for good places. せりあう
다툼 《경쟁》 a contest; a competition (논쟁) an argument; a dispute; a quarrel /공명 ~ a contention for honors/자리 ~ the competition for a position.
다툼질 a quarrel; a conflict; a dispute; an argument; a contest/~하다 argue; dispute; quarrel; contest; struggle. せりあい
다팔다팔 flowing [in the wind]/ ~하다 flow in the wind. ひらひら
다팔머리 short hair flowing in the wind. すらりとたれたかみ
다하다¹ 《끝나다》 be over; end (없어지다) be all gone; be exhausted. つきる
다하다² ①(끝내다) get done; finish (완수하다) carry out; accomplish (이행하다) perform; fulfill/일을 ~ finish one's work/사명을 ~ accomplish[carry out] one's mission/본분을 ~ perform one's duty ②(다 들이다) use up; run through; exhaust/힘을 ~ put forth all one's strength/최선을 ~ do one's best. つくす
다항식(多項式) 《수》 a polynominal expression. たこうしき
다행(多幸) good fortune[luck]/~히 luckily; fortunately; be good luck /~한 happy; lucky; fortunate; blessed/ ~ 히도 …하다 be lucky enough to (do); have the luck to (do). たこう
다혈(多血) full-bloodedness; sanguineness /~한(漢) a hot-blooded fellow. たけつ
다혈질(多血質) a sanguine[hot] temperament/~의 full-blooded; sanguine; plethoric/~인 사람 a man of sanguine temperament; a full-blooded man/~증 plethoria; repletion. たけつしつ
다홍(—紅) crimson; deep red/~ 치마 a crimson skirt.
다화(茶話) a tea-talk[-gossip]; a talk over tea/~회 a tea party.
딱 ①(정확하게) exactly; accurately 《들어맞게》 to perfectly (꽉)closely; tight [ly]/~ 맞는 치마 a perfectly fitting skirt ②(벌린 모양) wide/가슴이 ~ 바라지다 have a strong chest/입을 ~ 벌리고 with an open mouth ③(버티는 모양) stiffly; firmly/~ 버티다 stand firmly against (one) ④(단호히) flatly; positively/~ 거절하다 decline positively; refuse flatly/~ 잘라 말하다 speak flatly ⑤(소리) with a snap. きっぱり
닥나무 《식》 the paper mulberry; Broussonetia kazinoki(학명). こうぞ
닦다 ①(윤내다) clean; polish; shine/구두를 ~ polish[shine] one's shoes/이를 ~ brush[clean] one's teeth ②(훔치다) mop; wipe/걸레로 ~ wipe (the floor) with a floorcloth ③(셈을) settle; balance; clear off(청산) ④(단련시키다) train; cultivate/기술을 ~ improve one's skill ⑤(길・터를 고르다) make even; level. ふく

딱다구리 〖조〗 a woodpecker.
닥다그르, 딱다그르르 thundering;《우회소리》 rumbling. ころころ
딱다기 《나무》 wooden clappers 《사람》 a night watchman.
닥닥 ①~ 긁다 scratch[noisily].
딱딱 with a snap; with a clap[rap].
딱 딱히다 《굳어서》(be) stiff; rigid 《엄격하다》(be) strict; rigid 《단단하다》(be) hard; solid 《문장의》(be) stiff; bookish 《학문이》(be) academic. かちかちだ
닦달질 ①《갈아서 다듬기》polishing; burnishing/~하다 burnish; give a polish ②《나무람》rebuke; scold. せきたてること
닥뜨리다 meet with; encounter; face; be confronted by. ぶつかる
딱바라지다 (be) pudgy and fat and short; squab; chunky; stocky/딱바라진 사람 a short and stout person; a stocky man; a chunky fellow.
딱부리 《사람》a lobster-eyed person; a bug-eyed person 《눈》protruding[projecting] eyes. ぎょろぎょろめ
딱새 〖조〗 flycatcher.
닦아세우다 brawl (one) out; blow up; take (one) roundly to task/잘못했다고 ~ take a person to task for his mistake. やっつける
닦음질 wiping; cleaning 《훔쳐내기》wipe; clean-up; sweeping/~하다 mop; wipe; clean. みがきあげること
닦이다 ①《닦음을 당하다》be wiped[polished, cleaned] ②《훌닦이다》have a good scolding; catch it; be strongly rebuked ③《경험이 많다》have a wide experience /세파에 닦인 사람 a man of ripe experience; a man of the world. みがかれる
닦이장이 a polisher; a shiner/구두 ~ a shoeshine [boy]. みがくひと
닦이질 polishing; burnishing/~하다 polish; burnish. みがくしごと
닥작닥작 thickly covered ㅡ덕적덕적.
딱장대 《사나운 사람》a rough[rude] person 《딱딱한 사람》a stern[a rigid, a stiff-laced] person.
딱장받다 torture; put [a thief] on the rack; use torture on [a burglar].
딱정벌레 ①〖충〗 a beetle ②〖동〗 a ground beetle. かぶとむし
딱지¹ 《부스럼의》a scab 《게·소라 등의》a carapace; a shell 《시계의》a watch case 《종이의 티》a speck. かさぶた
딱지² ①《엣벨》a label 《꼬리표》a tag 《우표》a [postage] stamp/~가 붙은(이름난) notorious; arrant; marked ②《놀이딱지》a card 《치는 딱지》a pasteboard dump. きって
딱지놀이 playing cards; a game of[at] cards/~하다 play [at] cards/이번 일요일에 ~를 하자 Let us play cards next sunday. カルタあそび
닥치다 draw near; approach; be imminent; be [close] at hand/닥치는 대로 without discrimination; at random/눈 앞에 닥친 imminent; pressing; pending. ちかよる

딱하다 ①《안되다》(be) sorry; regrettable 《가엾다》(be) pitiful; sad; pitiable/딱하게 여기다 take pity on; pity; regret; sympathize with/딱한 형편 a pitiable condition ②《곤란》(be) embarrassing awkward/딱한 처지 an awkward[a painful] position. かわいそうだ
단 《묶음》a bundle 《벼 따위》a sheaf; a bunch 《장작 따위》a faggot/~짓다 bundle; bunch; bind into a bundle; sheave. たば
딴 other; different; another/~ 곳 another[some other] place/~것 another; other things; the rest; the other/~ 방법 a different way; another method. ほかの
단(段) ①《인쇄물의 난》a column/2~ 표제 a two-column heading ②《지적의 단위》a dan(about 0.245 acres) ③《계급》a class; a grade; a rank; a level/7~의 사람 (바둑 따위에서)a seventh grader /단수가 틀리다 be not in a class with; stand on different levels belong to a higher class(낫다). だん
단(單) only/~ 한 번 only once. たん
단(壇) a platform; a raised floor; circles 《무대》a stage; a rostrum 《교회의 연단》a pulpit 《제단》an altar (…게) the world/~에 서다 occupy the platform[pulpit]. だん
단(但) but; provided that 《조건》however; only. ただ
단(團) 《악단》a band; a body; a corps; a group; a party 《경기단》a team 《악한 따위의》a gang/관광 ~ a tourist party /외교 ~ a diplomatic corps.
단(斷) decision; judg[e]ment; resolution /~을 내리다 make a final decision.
단가(短歌) a tan-ga [poem]; a Korean ode. たんか
단가(單價) a unit cost[price]/~ 100원으로 at 100won a piece. たんか
단가(檀家) 〖종〗 a supporter of Buddhist temple; a parishioner.
단가(團歌) the official song of an association.
단가살이(單家—) a small establishment; a small household family. ふうふくらし
단간(單間) a single room. ひとま
단갈(短碣) a small tombstone[gravestone].
단거리¹ 《재료》the only material.
단거리² 《나무》a faggot.
단거리(短距離) a short distance 《사정(射程)의》a shortrange/~ 선수 a sprint-runner; a sprinter/~ 경주 a short-distance race; a sprint[-race]; a dash. たんきょり
단건(單件) one's only suit.
단검(短劍) a short sword 《비수》a dagger. たんけん
단것 sweet things 《과자》sweets; candies

〈미〉/그는 ~을 즐긴다 He goes in for sweets. あまいもの

**딴것** another thing; a different thing; something else. ほかのもの

**단견(短見)** a narrow view; short-sightedness/~의 undiscering; short-sighted; shallow. たんけん

**단결(團結)** union; unity/~심 co-operative spirit; *esprit de corps*(F)/~력 power of combination/~하다 combine; unite; hold[band] together. だんけつ

**단결에** before it is too late; while it is hot (곧) immediately. いっぺんに

**단경(斷經)** stoppage of one's menses/~하다 (one's) menstruation ceases/~기(期) the turn of life. げっけいのていし

**단경(短徑)** 〖수〗 the minor axis. たんけい

**단계(段階)** a step; a stage; a phase/최종 ~ the final stage. だんかい

**단곡(短曲)** a short piece of music[poetry]; a *morceau*(F). たんきょく

**단골** a patron; a [regular] customer; a client; a regular visitor/~ 다방 one's favourite tea room. とくい

**단공류(單孔類)** 〖동〗 *Monotremata*(학명).

**단과 대학(單科大學)** a college.

**단광색(單光色)** 《사진》 the monochromatic ray.

**단교(斷交)** a rupture; a break of relations; a severance/~하다 break of relations (*with*). だんこう

**단교 경주(斷郊競走)** a cross-country race.

**단구(短軀)** short stature/~의 사람 a stockily built man. たんく

**단구(段丘)** a terrace; a bench.

**딴군(-軍)** a police underling; a police spy[agent].

**단꿈** a sweet dream/~을 꾸다 dream [have] a sweet[happy] dream.

**단권(單卷)** a work in one volume.

**단궤(單軌)** a monorail/~ 철도 a monorail[centripetal] railway.

**단귀(短句)** a phrase; a short sentence. たんく

**단근(單根)** ①〖식〗 a simple root ②〖화〗 a simple radical. またのないね

**단근질** burning skin with a hot iron stick to punish a criminal; branding.

**단금지교(斷金之交)** close friendship. しんみつなこうさい

**단급(單級)** a single class/~ 국민 학교 a single-class primary school. たんきゅう

**단기(單騎)** a single horseman; a lone horseman[rider]. たんき

**단기(短期)** a short term[time]/~ 대학 a junior college/~ 대부 a short[-term] loan. たんき

**단기(單機)** a single plane. たんき

**단기(團旗)** an association banner.

**단기(單記)** single entry/~ 투표 single vote. たんき

**단김에** at a breath ⇨단결에. いっきに

**단나무** a bundle of firewood; a faggot. たばねたたきぎ

**단내** burning smell. やけるにおい

**단념(斷念)** relinquishment; abandonment /~하다 abandon; relinquish; give up (*an idea*); forego; despaire. だんねん

**단단 상약(斷斷相約)** a solemn promise/~하다 make a solemn vow; plight one's faith.

**단단하다, 딴딴하다** (be) solid; hard 《세다》 strong 《굳건하다》 firm/단단한 땅에 물이 괸다《속담》 Only a frugal man can save money. かたい

**단단히, 딴딴히** 《꽉》 tightly 《세게》 strongly 《엄중히》 severely 《단연》 strictly firmly 《안 움직이게》 fast/~ 이르다 give strict orders/~ 결심하다 be firmly resolved. かたく

**단대목(單一)** the point; the most; important time 《섣달 그믐날》 the last day of December by the lunar calendar a pivot. きんようのしゅんかん

**딴데** some other place; other place; somewhere else. ほかのところ

**단도(短刀)** a short sword; a dirk; a poniard; a stiletto 《비수》 a dagger/~를 품고 with a dagger in one's bosom /~로 찌르다 give a thrust of cold steel. たんとう

**단도 직입(單刀直入)** straightforwardness/~적[으로] straightforward[ly]; point-blank; frank[ly]; without beating about the bush. たんとうちょくにゅう

**단독(丹毒)** erysipelas; the rose/~성의 erysipelatous. たんどく

**단독(單獨)** independence; singleness /~적[으로] independent[ly]; separate[ly]; individual[ly]; alone/~ 강화 a separate peace / ~ 행위 an independent [individual] action. たんどく

**단독 일신(單獨一身)** a solitary person.

**단돈** the small amount of [some money] /~ 백 원도 없다 haven't even got a hundred *won*. こくすくないおかね

**단두(斷頭)** decollation; beheading/ ~하다 decapitate; decollate; behead. だんとう

**단두대(斷頭臺)** a guillotine; a scaffold; the block/~의 이슬로 사라졌다 die on the scaffold; be guillotined.

**단락(段落)** 《문장의》 a section; the end of a paragraph 《일의 결말》 settlement; a conclusion; a full stop/~을 짓다 bring (*a matter*) to a conclusion. だんらく

**단락(短絡)** 〖전기〗 a short [circuit]/~하다 short-circuit; short; have a short circuit.

**단란(團欒)** 《원만》 harmony 《일가의》 a happy [family, home] circle; a fireside circle/~하다 (be) harmonious; sit in a happy circle/~한 가정 생활 a happy home life. だんらん

**단려(端麗)** gracefulness/~하다 (be) attractive; graceful/용자 ~ a graceful figure.

**단련(鍛鍊)** ①《금속의》 forging; temper ②《심신의》 drilling; training; discipline

/~하다 drill; train; discipline/심신을 ~하다 train *one's* body and mind.
**단로**(短路) 〖전기〗 a short circuit.
**단리**(單利) 〖수〗 simple interest/~법 the method of simple interest.
**단막**(單幕) one act/~극, ~물 a one-act drama[play].
**단말마**(斷末魔) the last moment[gasp, breath]/~의 고통 death agony; throes of death.
**단맛** a sweet taste; sweetness.
**단망**(斷望) hopelessness; despair.
**단면**(斷面) a section/~도 a cross section /사회 생활의 ~ a phase of social life.
**단명**(短命) a short life/~하다 (be) short-lived/재자(才子) ~ Whom gods love die young.
**단명수**(單名數) 〖수〗 a single unit number.
**단모음**(單母音) a single vowel.
**단문**(短文) ①《짧은 글》 a short sentence [composition, piece] ②《천학(淺學)》 superficiality; shallow learning.
**단문**(單文) 〖문〗 a simple sentence.
**단물** ①《맛이 단》 sweet water ②《담수》 freshwater/~의 limnetic.
**단물나다** become threadbare; be worn out.
**단박** immediately; instantly; at once; in a moment[an instant]; outright; on the spot/일을 ~ 해치우다 finish up *one's* work in a jiffy.
**단발**(短髮) short[cropped] hair; crop.
**단발**(斷髮) bobbed hair/~하다 have *one's* hair bobbed; bob *one's* hair/~ 머리 소녀 a bobbed girl.
**단발**(單發) ①《한 발》 a shot; a pop《구》 ~에 at a shot ②《발동기》 a single engine/~ 기 a single-loader.
**단방**(斷房) continence; sexual abstinence /~하다 abstain from sexual intercourse; practice continence.
**단방**(單放) ①《한 방》 a single; a single try ②⇒단번.
**단배** 《식욕》 a strong appetite 《소화력》 strong digestion.
**단백**(蛋白) albumen/~질 protein; albumen/~뇨증(尿症) albuminuria/~질이 많은 portein-rich.
**단백석**(蛋白石) 〖광〗 opal.
**단번**(單番) once for all; only once/~에 at a stroke[stretch]; by one effort.
**단벌**(單一) 《옷》 *one's* only suit/~사 one who has no spare suit/~ 나들이옷 *one's* sole Sunday best.
**단병전**(短兵戰) a hand-to-hand fighting.
**단본위제**(單本位制) 〖경〗 single standard system; monometalism.
**단봇짐** a handy bundle.

**단봉약대**(單峯―) 〖동〗 an Arabian camel; a dromedary.
**단분수**(單分數) 〖수〗 simple fraction.
**단비** a welcome[timely, seasonable] rain; a refreshing rain.
**단비**(單比) 〖수〗 simple ratio.
**단비례**(單比例) 〖수〗 simple proportion.
**단사**(丹砂) 〖광〗 cinnabar.
**단사리별**(單舍利別) simple syrup.
**딴사설**(―辭說) irrelevant remarks 《다른 얘기》 another story.
**단산**(斷産) ~하다 pass the age of bearing; terminate fetation; cease conceiving function.
**딴살림** 《부부간의 별거》 limited divorce; separation/~하다 live separately.
**단삼**(丹參) 〖식〗 a salvia.
**단상**(短喪) short-period mourning.
**단상**(壇上) (on) the platform/~에 on the platform[the rostrum, the stage]/~에 서다 stand in[take] the platform.
**단상 교류**(單相交流) 〖전〗 single-phase current.
**단색**(單色) a single[a simple] hue/~의 monochromatic; unicolored/~화 a monochrome.
**딴생각** another motive; a different intention 《속다른》 a secret purpose; an ulterior motive.
**단서**(但書) a provision; a proviso/ ~가 붙은 conditional.
**단서**(端緒) 《시작》 beginning 《기원》 birth; origin 《초보》 the first step 《실마리》 a clue; a trace/~를 잡다 have[get, gain] a clue.
**단선**(單線) ①《한 줄》 a single line ②《단체》 a single track/~ 철도 a single-track railway.
**단선**(斷線) ~ disconnection; breaking of a wire/~ 때문에 on account of a broken wires.
**단선**(團扇) a [round] fan.
**단성**(單性) 〖생〗 unisexuality; one sex/ ~ 생식 monogenesis/~화 a unisexual flower.
**단성**(丹誠) sincerity; *one's* true heart.
**단세**(單稅) the single tax.
**단세포**(單細胞) 〖생〗 a single cell/~ 동 〔식〕물 unicellular animals[vegetables] /~ 유기체 a monad.
**단소**(短小) littleness; smallness/~하다 (be) little; small.
**단소**(短簫) a short bamboo flute.
**딴소리** irrelevant remarks 《다른 소리》 another words.
**단속**(團束) 《감독》 supervision 《관리》 regulation; control; management 《기율》 discipline/~하다 regulate; manage; control; maintain control over; supervise.

**단속**(斷續) intermittence/~하다 intermit/~직[으로] intermittent[ly]. だんぞく

**단속곳**(單一) a kind of underwear worn by woman.

**단손** ①(혼자의 손) but one hand/~으로 single-handedly; without help ②(일격) one stroke[coup]/~에 at a stroke; with one coup.　いちどのほねおり

**단솥** a heated iron pot.

**단수**(斷水) suspension of water supply (물 기근) a water-famine/~하다 cut off water supply.　だんすい

**단수**(單數) 【문】the singular number/ 그 말은 ~로 쓰여 있다 The word is in the singular./~의 singular. たんすう

**단수**(短壽) a short life.　たんめい

**단수**(端數) a fraction; odds; a fractional amount; an odd sum.　はすう

**단순**(單純) simplicity; purity; singleness/~한 plain; simple 《사람이》 simple-minded;/~히 merely; simply/~한 사람 simple-minded person.　たんじゅん

**단순 호치**(丹脣皓齒) red lips and white teeth; a beautiful face. たんしんこうし

**단술** a sweet drink made from fermented rice.　あまざけ

**단숨에**(單一) at[in] a breath; at a stretch; at one effort 《한 모금에》 at a draught.　ひといきに

**단시**(短詩) a short poem[verse]; a sonnet/~ 작가 a sonneteer.

**단시간**(短時間) a short space of time/~에 in a short [space of] time.たんじかん

**단시일**(短時日) a short length[space] of time/~에 in a short time. たんじじつ

**단시합**(單試合) 【체】a single game at tennis.

**단식**(單式) 【수】a simple expression 《부기》 single entry.　たんしき

**단식**(斷食) fasting 《한번의》 a fast/~하다 fast; abstain from food/~ 파업 a hunger-strike/~일[요법] a fast day [cure].　だんじき

**단식구**(單食口) a single person; living alone.

**단신**(單身) 《부사적》 by oneself; alone; single-handed /~으로 single-handed/~ 여행하다 travel alone.　たんしん

**단신**(短信) a line; a brief letter[note, message].　かんたんなてがみ

**단심**(丹心) single-heartedness　⇨단성(丹誠).　まごころ

**단심제**(單審制) 【법】single-trial system.

**단아**(端雅) elegance; grace; refinement; delicacy/~하다 (be) elegant; graceful/~한 elegant; graceful.　たんが

**단안**(斷案) 《결론》 a conclusion 《결정》 a decision 《귀결》 consequence/최후의 ~을 내렸다 He made[gave, brought in] a final decision[verdict].　だんあん

**단안**(單眼) 《동》 an ocellus; a stemma.

**단애**(斷崖) a cliff; a precipice/~를 기어 오르다 clamber up[scale] a cliff/~ 절벽 an overhanging cliff/~ 위의 등대 a lighthouse on a bluff.　だんがい

**단야**(短夜) a short night 《여름밤》 the short summer nights.　みじかいよる

**단어**(單語) a word 《어휘》 a vocabulary /~집 a collection of words/기본 ~ a basic vocabulary; basic words. たんご

**단언**(斷言) an affirmation; a declaration; an assertion/~하다 assert; declare; affirm.　だんげん

**단역**(端役) a minor part[role]; a bit; a walk-on [part] 《사람》 an extra; a super《우》.

**단연**(斷然) resolutely; positively; firmly; decisively /~ 유리하다 have a decided advantage/~ 거절하다 refuse flatly/ ~ 1등이다 be by far the best of all/ ~ 반대다 be dead set against. だんぜん

**단연**(斷煙) abstinence from smoking/~하다 give up[quit] smoking.　きんえん

**단엽**(單葉) 【식】unifoliate/ ~ 비행기 a monoplane.　たんよう

**단예**(端倪) 《한(限)》 a limit.

**단오**(端午) the fifth day of May of the lunar month/~절 the *Dan-o* Festival.　たんご

**단옥**(斷獄) judgement of a grave crime /~하다 condemn; convict major crime.　ざいにんをしょちすること

**단원**(團員) a member (of *a party*).

**단원**(單元) ①【철】the monad/~론 monadology; monadism ②【교】a unit/~ 제도 the unit credit system.　たんげん

**단원제**(單院制) unicameral system/~의 unicameral.　いちいんせい

**단위**(單位) 《화폐의》 denomination; a unit /기본 ~ a standard unit/~가 같다 be commensurable.　たんい

**딴은** ①(…으로서는) as/내 ~ 하느라고 했읍니다 I put forth all my strength. ② 《과연》 indeed; really; I see/~ 그럴 듯한 말이오 Indeed you are right. /~ 그렇소 Well, so it is.　—としては

**단음**(短音) 【음】a short sound/~계 【음】 the minor scale.　たんおん

**단음**(單音) single sound; 《음》 a monotone /~절어 a monosyllabic word/~악 monophonic music.　たんおん

**단음**(斷飮) abstinence from wine 《절대 금주》 total abstinence/~하다 give up drinking; abstain from alcoholic beverages.　きんしゅ

**단일**(單一) singleness; uniqueness/~의 unique; single; simple/~화하다 simplify/~ 환율 a single exchange/~ 후보 sole candidacy.　たんいつ

**단자**(單字) 《글자》 characters representing a word.　たんご

**단자**(單子) ①【철】a monad ②《부의록》 a list of gifts.　ひめいのもくろく

**단자**(團子) a dumpling.

**단자론**(單子論) 【철】monadology; monadism.

**단자엽**(單子葉) 【식】a monocotyledon/ ~ 식물 a monocotyledonous plant; *Mo-*

*nocotyledonae*(학명).

**단짝** an intimate friend; a crony; a sidekick《미·속》. なかよし

**단작**(單作) a single crop/~ 지대 a single-crop region.

**단작스럽다** (be) dirty 넌적스럽다. けがた

**단잠** [a sound] sleep/~하다 wake up from a sound sleep/~이 들다 drop off into sound sleep. じゅくすい

**단장**(丹粧) 《화장》make-up; toilet/~하다 make *one's* toilet; beautify *one*self; make up. けしょう

**단장**(短杖) a walking stick《영》; a cane 〈미〉. みじかいつえ

**단장**(斷腸) heartbreak/~의 heartbreaking; heartrending/~의 비애를 느끼다 feel *one's* heart rent[torn to pieces]; *one's* heart bleeds. だんちょう

**단장**(團長) a head; a leader; a commandant/~ 소년 ~ a scoutmaster. だんちょう

**단적**(端的) ~으로 straightforwardly; directly; plainly; frankly/~으로 말하면 to be frank; frankly speaking. たんてき

**딴전** quite another business/~보다 do something else 《모르는 체》feign ignorance. ほかのかんがえ

**단전**(丹田) the abdomen. たんでん

**단절**(斷絕) 《소멸》 extinction 《중단》 interruption 《국교의》break; rupture/~하다 be broken off; be severed; become extinct/국교 ~ the rupture of diplomatic relations. だんぜつ

**단점**(短點) a defect; a weak point; a fault; a shortcoming/~을 고치다 remedy *one's* defects. じゃくてん

**단정**(端正) correctness; justness; decency; propriety; rightness/~하다 (be) right; correct; just; neat; decent; virtuous/~히 upright; neatly; tidily; properly/품행이 ~한 사람 a man of good moral character. たんせい

**단정**(斷定) judgement; conclusion/~하다 conclude; judge/~ draw a conclusion/~을 내리다 draw a conclusion; come to a conclusion. だんてい

**단정**(短艇) a boat/~ 경조(競漕) a regatta; a boat-race.

**단조**(單調) 《가곡의》 monotone 《변화 없는》 dullness; monotony/~로운[한] monotonous; dull; monotonic/~로운 생활 a monotonous[a dull] life/~로운 빛 a dull[flat] color. たんちょう

**단조**(短調) 《음》 a minor. たんちょう

**딴쪽** 《반대쪽》 the other side; another[different] direction. はんたいのほう

**단종**(斷種) 《의》 castration; sterilization/~ 수술을 하다 sterilize (one). だんしゅ

**단좌**(端座) ~하다 sit straight[upright, properly]. たんざ

**단죄**(斷罪) condemnation; conviction; judgement of a crime/~하다 condemn; convict. だんざい

**단주**(端舟) a boat; a small ship.

**단지** a crock; a pot; a jar/꿀 ~ a honey jar. つぼ

**단지**(斷指) cutting a finger/~하다 cut off a finger. ゆびをきること

**단지**(但只) only; merely; simply/~ 시간 문제 merely a question. ただ

**단찰**(短札) a short letter; a brief note. たんさつ

**단참**(單站一) at a stretch 단숨에.

**단처**(短處) a weak point; a drawback; a defect; a shortcoming/…의 ~ *one's* shortcomings. たんしょ

**단척**(短尺) a roll of cloth short of standard length. いっしゃくみまんのおりもの

**단철**(鍛鐵) wrought iron.

**단청**(丹靑) ①《색채》 colors; red and blue ②《그림》 a painting; a picture [of many colors and designs]. たんせい

**단체**(團體) a group; a body; a party; an organization/~ 행동 a collective[a mass] action/~ 실업 a business organization/~ 생활 a group life/~ 교섭 collective bargaining/~ 할인 a party-trip reduction/ ~ 정신 *esprit de corps*(F); a team spirit/~ 경기 collective sport. だんたい

**단총**(短銃) a pistol; a revolver/기관 ~ a submachine gun. たんじゅう

**단추** a button 《장식하는》 a stud 《누르는 장치》 a knob/~를 끼우다 button [up]; fasten a button/~를 빼다 undo a button; unbutton/커프스 ~ a sleeve link; cuff buttons/~를 달다 sew on a button/금 ~《제복의》a brass button. ボタン

**단축**(短縮) shortening; reduction; curtailment/~하다 shorten; reduce; cut [down]; curtail/시간을 ~하다 reduce the time (*of*)/조업 ~ the curtailment of operation/학년을 ~하다 shorten the school years. たんしゅく

**단출하다** be a family of small members [numbers]/단출한 식구 a small family /단출한 살림 a small establishment. すくないかぞく

**단충**(丹忠) true loyalty; utter devotion.

**단취**(團聚) a happy circle of relatives [bosom friends]/~하다 sit in a happy circle.

**단층**(斷層) 《지》 a dislocation; a fault/~ 지진 a dislocation earthquake/~면 a fault plane. だんそう

**단층**(單層) a single story; one-story/~집 a one-story house〈영〉; a one-storied house〈미〉. いっかい

**단침**(短針) 《시계의》 the short[hour] hand. たんしん

**단칭**(單稱) singular/ ~의 singular/ ~ 명제 《논》 a singular proposition/~ 명사 a singular term. たんしょう

**단타**(單打) 《야구》 a single [hit]/~하다 single.

**단파**(短波) a short wave-length/~ 방송 short-wave broadcasting/ ~ 수신기 a short-wave receiver. たんぱ

**딴판** a completely different state of

affairs/~이다 be quite[widely] different (*from*)/성격이 전혀 ~이다 Their characters are opposed to each other. ほかのきょくめん

**단판(單一)** a single round[game].

**단판에(單一)** easily; in a single round; at once.

**단패(單牌)** a single couple[pair].

**단편(短篇)** a short piece; a sketch/~ 소설 a short story; a novelette/~ 소설집 a collection of short stories/~집 a collection of short pieces[stories]. たんぺん

**단편(斷片)** a fragment; a piece/~적 fragmentary/ ~적 지식 fragmentary knowledge. だんぺん

**단평(短評)** short criticism[comment]. たんぴょう

**단풍(丹楓)** ① (나무) a maple[-tree] ② (잎) autumnal tints; red[yellow] leaves/~들다 put on autumnal tints; be tinged with red; turn red[yellow]/~ 구경 an excursion for viewing scarlet maple leaves. こうよう

**단풍나무(丹楓一)** a maple[-tree].

**단합(團合)** unity/~하다 be united ⇨단결(團結). だんけつ

**단항식(單項式)** 【수】 a uninominal expression. たんこうしき

**단행(斷行)** decisive action/~하다 take a resolute step; carry out[through, into effect]; dare. だんこう

**단행범(單行犯)** 【법】 single offence[-se]. たんこうはん

**단행법(單行法)** a special law. たんこうほう

**단행본(單行本)** a special volume; a book /~으로 in book form/~으로 발간하다 publish in book form. たんこうぼん

**단현 운동(單絃運動)** 【물】 simple harmonic motion.

**단호(斷乎)** ~하다 (결의) resolute 《결심》firm 《수단》decisive 《과단성》drastic/~히 resolutely; firmly; decisively/~히 말하다 use formal language; speak in set terms. だんこ

**단화(短靴)** shoes. たんぐつ

**닫다¹** (말이) canter; gallop (사람이) run/빠르게 닫는 말 a swift horse. かける

**닫다²** (문을 닫치다) close; shut/문을 ~ close the door[the gate]/쾅 ~ slam, [bang] (*the door*). とじる

**닫아 걸다** lock (*a door*).

**닫집** a canopy. てんがい

**닫치다** close; shut. もんをつよくとじる

**닫히다** be closed; shut/문이 닫혀 있다 The gate is shut./[문이] 저절로 ~ shut of itself/잘 안 ~ shut hard. とじられる

**달¹** ①(하늘의) the moon/초생~ a new moon/~ 세계 the moon/맑은 ~ a clear moon/~의 여신 Diana/~ 없는 moonless ②(달력의) a month/~마다 every month; monthly/전전 ~ the month before last (임신)의 ~수가 차지 않은 아이 a premature infant; a prematurely-born baby/~ 빛 moonlight; moonshine. つき ほかのきょくめん

**달²** 【식】 a kind of wild reed; *Phragmites japonica*(학명).

**달³** (연의) the frame of a kite.

**딸** a daughter/첫 ~ one's first daughter. むすめ

**달가닥거리다** rattle; clatter/바람에 문이 ~ a window rattles in the wind/수레가 달가닥거리며 지나간다 A wagon is clattering along the road/달가닥달가닥 rattling; clattering; with a rattle [clatter]. かたかたなる

**달가당거리다, 딸가당거리다** jingle; clink; tinkle/달가당달가당 jingling. がたがた

**달가락거리다** clatter; rattle/달가락달가락 rattling; tinkling. かたかたなる

**달가시다** an unlucky[evil] month passes. ふこうであったつきがすぎる

**달각거리다, 딸각거리다** make a rattling sound; clatter; rattle/달각거리며 지나가다 rattle along the road. かたかたなる

**딸깍발이** a penurious[poor] scholar, who has to wear wooden shoes all the time. まずしいがくしゃのべつめい

**달강어(達江魚)** 【어】 a sea robbin; *Lepidotrigla microptera*(학명).

**달걀** an egg/~의 흰자[노른자] the white [the yolk] of an egg/~ 모양의 egg-shaped/~ 껍질 an egg-shell/반숙의[갓난] ~ a soft-boiled[a new-laid] egg/~을 깨다 break[open] an egg/~ 빛 a light yellowish colo[u]r. たまご

**달게 굴다** tease; badger (*a person to do*); importune. ねだる

**달견(達見)** a far-sighted view; a fine idea; excellent views. たっけん

**달곰새곰하다** (be) somewhat sweet and sour. あまくていくぶんすっぱい

**달곰씁쓸하다** (be) somewhat sweet and bitter. いくぶんあまくてたいぶにがい

**달곰하다** (be) sweet[ish]; sugary; sweet-flavoured. ほどよくあまい

**달관(達觀)** far-sightedness; a long view/~하다 take a long[philosophic] view; take things philosophically. たっかん

**달구** a ground rammer. たこ

**달구다** heat; make hot. しゃくねつする

**달구지** a large cart; an oxcart. にぐるま

**달구질** ramming/~하다 compact earth with a rammer; ram; harden the ground.

**딸꾹질** a hiccough; a hiccup/딸꾹딸꾹 with repeated hiccoughs. しゃっくり

**달굿대** a rammer. たこのつきぼう

**달궁이** 【어】 a gurnard; *Lepidotrigla microptera*(학명).

**달그락거리다, 딸그락거리다** rumble; rattle/달그락달그락 rumbling. がらがらなる

**달그랑거리다, 딸그랑거리다** jingle; tinkle; clink/달그랑달그랑 tinkling.

**달금하다** (be) sweetish ⇨달곰하다.

**딸기** a strawberry (나무 딸기) a raspberry/~ 밭 a strawberry bed[patch]. いちご

**달기씨깨비** 【식】 a dayflower; a spiderwort; *Commelina communis*(학명).

**딸년** my daughter; a daughter. むすめ
**달다**¹ 《맛이》 (be) sugary; sweet 《맛있다》/단맛 쓴맛 다 본 사람이다 He has tasted the sweets and bitters of life./달게 먹다 eat with gusto 《입맛이》 have a good appetite. あまい
**달다**² ①《뜨거워지다》 get[become] hot; burn/불에 단 돌 a hot stone/빨갛게 ~ become red-hot ②《지나치게 익다》 be overdone ③《마음이 타다》 be anxious[impatient]/마음이 달아서 impatiently; irritatedly. ひじょうにあつくなる
**달다**³ ①《걸다》 put up[hang out] 《a sign》/간판을 ~ hang out[put up] a sign [-board] ②《붙이다》 affix; fix; attach /샤쓰에 단추를 ~ sew a button on a shirt/훈장을 ~ wear a decoration [medal]/문을 ~ fix in a door ③《올리다》 fly 《a flag》/기를 ~ fly[hoist] a flag ④《주(註)를》 annex[make] 《note》, annotate/토를 ~ supply the particle [s]. かける
**달다**⁴ 《무게를》 weigh/저울로 ~ weigh 《a thing》 in the balance. はかる
**딸따니** my dear little daughter.
**달달** trembling ⇨덜덜. ぶるぶる
**달달 볶다** torment ⇨들들 볶다.
**달떡** a round rice-cake. つきがたのもち
**달뜨다** become fickle[wanton]; grow restless. うわきしんがおこる
**달라다** request; ask for 《a thing》; demand/하룻밤 재워 ~ ask for a night's lodging/도와 ~ appeal 《to a person》 for aid. もとめる
**달라붙다** hold on; stick[cling, adhere] to ⇨들러붙다. くっつく
**달라지다** alter; be changed[altered]; vary; [undergo a] change/서울도 많이 달라졌다 Seoul has changed a great deal. /달라지지 않다 be[remain] unchanged. かわる
**달랑, 딸랑** ~하다 ①《가슴이》 be much surprised[startled, frightened, shocked] ②《방울이》 [a bell, ring] tingle; jingle.
**달랑거리다, 딸랑거리다** jingle; tinkle/달랑달랑, 딸랑딸랑 ringing; jingling; tinkling. りんりんとなる
**달래** 《식》 an allium; Allium monanthum (학명). のびる
**달래다** soothe; coax; appease; humo[u]r /화난 사람을 ~ calm down[placate] an angry man. なぐさめる
**달려가다** run; rush; dash; hasten 《to》/현장으로 ~ rush to the scene 《of murder》. はしっていく
**달려들다** jump[leap, spring] at[on]; run up; grapple with 《one》/고양이가 쥐에게 달려들었다 The cat pounced upon the mouse. とびかかる
**달려오다** run here; come running/ 말이 ~ a horse gallops over. はしってくる
**달력(-曆)** a calendar 《매일 들치는》 a block-calendar 《책력》 an almanac/매일 짓어내는 ~ a daily pad calendar. こよみ
**달리** dissimilarly; differently; in a different way 《따로》 separately/~하다 be different; differ 《from》/두 사람은 전연 성격을 ~하고 있다 They have nothing in common in character./견해를 ~ 하다 have a different opinion/색을 ~ 하다 be of different colors. ちがって
**달리다**¹ 《부족하다》 run short [of]; run [on]; lack; be shy of; be in need of; low. たらない
**달리다**² 《기운이》 be exhausted; be languid[tired, droopy]. ちからがおよばない
**달리다**³ 《질주하다》 run; rush; hurry 《차마를》 urge on 《a horse》; drive 《a car》/말이 ~ a horse runs[gallops]/달려가다 run[hurry, hasten] to/자동차를 달려 현장으로 가다 drive to the scene/달려오다 come in haste. はしる
**달리다**⁴ ①《걸리다》 be suspended 《from》; hang 《on, from》; be hung ②《의존하다》 depend on/달린 가족이 많다 have many dependents/그것은 사정 여하에 달렸다 It depends on the respective circumstances. ③《부속하다》 be attached/수도 달린 집 a house with city-water laid on. じゅうぞくする
**딸리다** ①《붙다》 be attached to; depend; belong to ②《부족하다》 be[fall, run] short 《of》/돈이 ~ run short of funds ③《수종하다》 attend/딸린 식구 dependents; a family depending upon me/가구 딸린 셋집 a furnished house to let.
**달마(達磨)** Dharma (Sans). だるま
**달마다** every month; monthly; per mensem (L)/~ 한 번 once a month.
**달막거리다, 딸막거리다** move up and down. あがりさがりする
**달맞이** enjoying[viewing] the moon/~ 하다 view the moon.
**달맞이꽃** 《식》 an evening-primrose; a sundrops.
**달무리** a halo; a ring[circle] around the moon. つきがさ
**달문(達文)** a clearly written composition; a lucid style. たつぶん
**달밤** a moonlight[moonlit] night/~의 moonshiny; moonlit. つきよ
**달변(-邊)** 《이자》 monthly interest.
**달변(達辯)** fluency; eloquence/~의 《대변의》 eloquent; fluent/~가 a good talker; a fluent speaker. たつべん
**달병(疸柄)** 《의》 jaundice.
**딸보** 《난장이》 a pigmy; a dwarf 《소견이 좁은 사람》 a narrow-minded person.
**달빛** moonlight 《한 줄기의》 a moonbeam; moonshine/~ 을 받은 호수 the lake in the moonlight/~ 을 받은 뜰 a moonlit garden. げっこう
**달싹거리다** shake ⇨들썩거리다. しょうかにうごかす
**달삯** monthly wage(s). げっきゅう
**달성(達成)** attainment; achievement; accomplishment/~하다 achieve 《a pur-

**달아나다** ①《도망가다》run away; take to flight; flee; [make one's] escape 《날라서》fly away/몰래 ~ sneak away/…을 가지고 ~ abscond with; run away with ②《빨리 가다》run fast; speed [away]; scuttle; scud.

**달아매다** 《매달다》hang (a thing) up 《묶다》tie (a thing) up.

**달아 보다** ①《무게를》weigh; check the weight (of) ②《사람을》gauge; fathom; sound; plumb.

**달아오르다** ①《쇠가》get very hot ②《얼굴이》feel hot; flush.

**달야(達夜)** a sleepless night; an all night sitting[vigil]/~하다 sit up all night; keep vigil.

**달음박질** running; a run/~하다 run; rush; dash; dart.

**달음질** running ⇨달음박질.

**달이다** decoct; boil [soy sauce]; infuse; make an infusion of/차를 ~ draw[brew] tea/약을 ~ make a medical decoction.

**달인(達人)** a great[master] mind; a far-sighted person.

**딸자식(-子息)** a daughter 《자기의》my daughter.

**달짝지근하다** (be) sweetish; somewhat sweet.

**달장근(-將近)** a month or so; about a month.

**달착지근하다** (be) somewhat sweet.

**달창나다** ①《해지다》be worn; wear 《옷 따위가》wear threadbare; become seedy ②《없어지다》be used up; become exhausted; run out/구두가 ~ one's shoes are worn out.

**달치다** 《끓이다》boil down[dry]; heat to excess.

**달카닥** clattering; clanging; rattling/~하다 clang; rattle.

**달카닥거리다** clatter; rattle; clang/달카닥달카닥 rattling; clattering.

**달카당** with a bang ⇨달카닥.

**달칵** with a click ⇨달카닥.

**달콤하다** (be) sweet; sugary/인생의 달콤한 맛 manna of life/달콤한 말 honeyed[sugared] words.

**달통(達通)** mastery; conversance/~하다 be phylosophical; be a master (of); familiar with.

**달팽이** 《동》a snail/~ 걸음 a snail's pace/~ 껍데기 a snail-shell/~ 뿔 the horns of a snail.

**달포** a month or so; more than a month; about a month/~ 동안 for more than a month.

**달품** monthly labo[u]r.

**달필(達筆)** 《솜씨》a good[skillful] hand 《글씨》skillful penmanship/~가 《문장의》a facile writer 《글씨의》a good penman.

**달하다(達-)** ①《목적을》accomplish; achieve; attain; carry out ②《수량이》amount to/천문학적 숫자에 ~ run into astronomical figures ③《도달하다》arrive in[at]; get to[at]; reach.

**닭** 《수탉》a cock 《암탉》a hen 《병아리》a chicken; domestic fowl/~쌈 a cockfight; cock-fighting/~을 치다 keep [raise] chickens; keep hens[fowls]/싸움 ~ a game[fighting]-cock/~어리 a hencoop/~고기 chicken.

**닭의장(-欌)** a hen-house[-cote, -coop].

**닭의홰** a [hen-]roost; a perch/~에 앉다 be on the perch.

**닭자치다** [a cock] crows at dawn; crow busily.

**닮다** be[look] like (a thing); resemble; look alike/꼭 ~ be quite alike/많이 ~ resemble (one) closely/그 소년은 아버지를 많이 닮았다 The boy takes after his father.

**닳다** ①《해지다》be worn[down]; wear/신 뒤축이 닳았다 My shoes are down at heel. ②《얼다》become red with cold ③《졸다》be boiled down ④《비유적》《세상에 닳고 닳은 사람》a sophisticated person.

**닳리다** 《해뜨리다》wear away[down]; rub off[down]/연필을 ~ wear down the lead of a pencil.

**담** 《집의》a wall 《울타리》a fence/~ 너머로 over a wall 《통해서》through a fence/~ 너머로 보이다 be able to see (a thing) over a hedge.

**땀¹** perspiration; sweat/~을 닦다 wipe the perspiration from (one's face)/구슬 ~ beads of sweat/손에 ~을 쥐고 breathlessly/~빼다 《혼나다》have a hard time of it 《수고하다》take pains/~ 흘려 번 돈 honestly earned money.

**땀²** 《바느질》a stitch.

**담(痰)** sputum; phlegm/~이 많이 나오다 expectorate much.

**담(膽)** the liver; the gallbladder 《담력》pluck; courage; nerve/~이 큰 bold; daring/~이 작은 faint-hearted; timid/~을 서늘하게 하다 frighten; curdle the blood.

**담가(擔架)** a stretcher.

**담그다** ①《물 따위에》soak; steep [in water]; dip ②《김치 따위를》pickle [vegetables] prepare 《양조하다》brew (sool); make (into).

**땀기(-氣)** a bit of sweat/~가 있다 be a little bit in sweat; have a bit of sweat (in one's palm).

**담기(膽氣)** pluck ⇨담력(膽力).

**담기다** be put in; be dished up; be served; contained; held.

**땀나다** sweat; perspire; the sweat comes out 《힘들다》be hard/땀나는 일 a hard job.

**담낭(膽囊)** 《해》the gall/~염 inflamma-

**땀내** smell[stink] of sweat/~나 smell sweaty; stink of sweat/~ 나는 옷 garments stinking with sweat.

**땀내다** sweat; perspire; induce perspiration. あせをながす

**담다** ①(그릇에) place; put in[to]; contain; hold 《음식을》 dish up; fill; serve/음식을 접시에 ~ serve food on a plate[in a dish]; dish up[out] the dinner ②(입에) use; employ/욕을 입에 ~ employ four letter words; use bad language ③⇒담그다. ものをいれる

**담담하다**(淡淡—) 《물이》 (be) clear; limpid; lucid 《마음이》 disinterested; (be) indifferent; serene 《빛·맛이》 (be) plain; light/담담한 심경 a serene state of mind. たんたんとしている

**담당**(擔當) charge/~하다 take charge of; be in charge of; be responsible for /~ 검사[아나운서] the prosecutor[announcer] in charge/~ 구역 a section under *one's* charge. たんとう

**담대**(膽大) boldness; fearlessness/~하다 (be) bold; daring; fearless. だいたん

**땀들이다** cool *oneself*; dry *one's* sweat.

**땀등거리** an undershirt for sweat.

**땀띠** prickly heat; heat rashes[spots] 《미》/~가 나다 have prickly heat/~약 prickly heat powder. あせも

**담략**(膽略) courage and resourcefulness; courage combined with resources/~이 있다 be courageous. たんりゃく

**담력**(膽力) pluck; courage; nerve; grit; spunk《속》/~있는 plucky; courageous; bold/~없는 timid; cowardly/~을 기르다 cultivate[foster, build up] courage. たんりょく

**담론**(談論) [a] talk;[a] discussion; [an] argument; [a] debate; [a] discourse/~하다 converse (*with*); talk; discourse; argue. だんろん

**담박**(淡泊) ~하다 《마음이》(be) candid; indifferent; frank 《맛·빛이》 plain; light/~한 사람 《욕심없는》 a man of few want 《솔직한》 an open hearted person; outspoken; candid. たんぱく

**땀받이** 《땀등거리》 an undershirt 《말의 안장 밑의》 sweat clothes 《모자의》 a sweatband.

**담방거리다** behave frivorously; flippant; make a fuss/담방담방 frivorously; thoughtlessly. うわつく

**담배** tobacco 《궐련》 a cigarette/코~ snuff/~를 피다 smoke a pipe. タバコ

**담배쌈지** tobacco-pouch.

**담배설대** a bamboo-stem of a pipe.

**담배칼** a tobacco-leaf cutter.

**담배갑**(一匣) a cigarette case; a tobacco box. タバコいれ

**담뱃값** money for tobacco 《사례금》 a small amount of money as reward; a tip.

**담뱃대** a tobacco-pipe; a pipe 《궐련의》 a cigarette pipe. キセル

**담뱃재** tobacco ashes. タバコのはい

**담뱃진** tobacco tar[s]; nicotine.

**담벼락** the surface of a wall 《사람》 a person of blockhead; understanding. かべのひょうめい

**담보**(擔保) ①《보증》 a guarantee; assurance/~하다 gurantee; assure; give[lay, put] to pledge 'in security' ②《법》《채무의》 a mortgage 《부동산의》 security /~ 없이 without security; unsecured/~ 물권 real rights granted by way of security/~로 넣다 give (*a thing*) as a security; mortgage. たんぽ

**담뿍** full; brimful/~ 웃음을 띠고 with smiles all over/~ 붓다 fill 'a glass' to the brim. たっぷり

**담북장**(一醬) a kind of bean paste.

**담불** a pile[heap] of corn[cereals]; a stack[rick] of grain.

**담불** a ten-year-old (*ox, horse*).

**담비** 《동》 a marten; a Korean sable.

**담쌓다** ①(담두르다) fence [up]; wall; enclose with a fence ②(관계를 끊다) break through with(미); break relations with.

**담색**(淡色) a light colour/~의 light-coloured. うすいろ

**담석**(膽石) 《의》 a gall-[bile-]stone/~병 chololithiasis. たんせき

**담소**(談笑) a friendly talk; a pleasant chat; chatting/~하다 'have a pleasant chat. だんしょう

**담소**(膽小) timidity 《비겁》 cowardice/~하다 (be) timid; poor-spirited; cowardly/~한 사람 a timid[a poorspirited] man. ひきょう

**담쏙담쏙** brimful; full to the brim; greedily. どっさり

**담수**(淡水) fresh-water/~호 a fresh-water lake/~어 a fresh-water fish.

**담예**(擔舁) ~하다 shoulder; carry[take, bear] a palankeen on the shoulder.

**담요**(毯—) a blanket もうふ

**담임**(擔任) charge; duty; business; responsibility/~하다 be in[take] charge of 《가르침》 teach/~ 사무 business under *one's* charge/~ 교사 a class teacher; a teacher in charge; an instructor in charge/~반 a class under *one's* charge.

**담장이** a mud-wall builder. たんにん

**담쟁이** 《식》 an ivy/~ 덩굴 ivy vines. つた

**담즙**(膽汁) bile; gall/~병 biliousness/~질 bilious temperament. たんじゅう

**담차다**(膽—) (be) daring; plucky; bold. だいたんだ

**담천**(曇天) cloudy weather[say]; an overcast sky. どんてん

**담청색**(淡青色) light blue.

**담총**(擔銃) ~하다 shoulder a gun. じゅうをかつぐこと

**담타**(痰唾) sputum; spittle. たんつば

**담틀** a frame used in building a mud wall.

담판(談判) a parley; negotiation; a talk; conversation/~하다 negotiate[converse, parley] with/외교 ~ diplomatic negotiations/강화 ~ peace negotiations.

담홍색(淡紅色) [rose-]pink; blush; blush tint/~의 pink.

담화(談話) [a] conversation; [a] talk 《성명》a statement; colloquy/~하다 talk; converse (with).

담황색(淡黃色) lemon-yellow; straw color; citrine.

답(答) an answer; a reply; a rejoinder; a response 《해답》a solution/~하다 answer; reply/~할 수 없는 질문 an unanswerable question/~을 내다 get[work out] an answer.

답곡(畓穀) grain from the paddy field; rice.

답농(畓農) rice culture; cultivation of a paddy field.

-답다 (be) like; becoming; -ly; -like/남자[여자]다운 manly[lady like]/숙녀다운[답지 못한] ~ feel heavy[unbecoming] a lady.

답답하다(畓畓—) ① 《가슴이》(be) heavy; stuffy; suffocating/가슴이 ~ feel heavy in the chest ② 《사물이》(be) irritating; boring/답답한 사람 a bore; a tedious person.

답례(答禮) 《인사에 대한》a return salute 《물건에 대한》a return present 《방문에 대한》a return call/~하다 return one's call; make a return present; salute in return/…의 ~로 in return for/ ~품 a return present.

답배(答—) an answer to a letter from one's inferior/~하다 reply to[answer] a letter from one's inferior; send a reply to one's inferior.

답배(答拜) a return salute; greet in return/~하다 salute in return; return a salute.

답변(答辯) 《답》a reply; an answer 《변명》[an] explanation 《피고의》a defense/~하다 answer; reply; explain; defend oneself.

답보(踏步) 《제자리 걸음》deadlock; stepping; a tread/~하다 mark time; step; be deadlocked.

답사(答辭) an address in reply; a response; a [formal] reply/~하다 make an address in reply.

답사(踏査) an investigation; a survey; exploration; prospecting/~하다 investigate; survey; explore/현지 ~ a field investigation; survey the place.

답서(答書) a reply; an answer/~하다 [send a] reply (to); reply to[answer] a letter.

답습(踏襲) following [a former policy] /~하다 follow in the steps; follow [suit].

답신(答申) a report/~하다 submit a report/~서 a report.

답안(答案) an examination; a paper/훌륭한[백지의] ~ a good[blank] paper /영어 ~ a paper in English/~지 examination paper.

답언(答言) a reply; an answer; a respondence.

답인(踏印) ~하다 set, fix, stamp [a seal].

답장(答狀) an answer; a reply/~하다 send a reply; reply to[answer] a letter/즉시 ~하마 I will answer you by return.

답전(答電) a reply telegram; a reply by wire[cable]/~하다 answer a telegram; wire back.

답주(畓主) the owner of a rice-field.

답지(遝至) rush; flood; influx; onrush; storming/~하다 rush to[in]; throng to (a place); storm/주문이 ~하다 have a rush of orders.

답치기 a rash[blind] act/~놓다 act on impulse; act recklessly; go it blind.

답토(畓土) a rice-[a paddy-]field; a paddy field.

답파(踏破) travel[l]ing on foot /~하다 travel on foot; traverse; tramp.

닷 five/~말 five mal.

닷곱 five hob; half a doi.

닷곱 장님 an extremely weak-sighted person.

닷새 ① 《닷샛날》the fifth day [of the month] ② 《다섯 날》five days.

닷샛날 ① 《다섯째 날》the fifth [day] ② 《초닷샛날》the fifth [day] of the month.

땅¹ ① 《대지》the earth 《지면》the ground /~을 파다 dig in the ground/~에 떨어지다 《퇴폐》be at a low ebb; fall to the ground ② 《영토》land; territory 《토양》soil; land 《토지》lands; an estate/~을 갈다 cultivate land/미국 ~을 밟다 set foot on American soil/~임자 a land owner/타국 ~에서 죽다 die in a strange land.

땅² 《총소리 따위》bang.

당(黨) ① 《단체》a faction 《당파》a party 《도당》a clique ② 《친족과 인척》relatives in blood and law/~에 가입하다 join the party.

당(當) ① 《이》this; the present 《그》that; the said 《문제의》in question; at issue /~역(驛) this station ② 《현재》ℚ~23세 aged twenty-three years at the time in question.

당(堂) ① shrine ⇒ 당집 ② a hall ⇒ 대청.

땅가래 【충】a blister beetle.

땅가물 a drought.

땅강아지 【충】a mole cricket.

당개나리 【식】a tiger lily; Lilium tigrinum(학명).

땅거미¹ 【충】a ground spider.

땅거미² 《어스레할 때》dusk; twilight; crepuscule/~가 질 때 at dusk; in the

**당고**(當故) ~하다 go into mourning for one's parent; lose one's parents.

**당고모**(堂姑母) one's grandfather's niece on his brother's side. ちちのじゅうしまい

**땅파리** 〖식〗 a ground cherry.

**땅광** (지하실) a cellar (동양식의) a go-down. ちかしつ

**당구**(撞球) billiards; pills／~장 a billiard-room／~를 치다 play billiards／~대 a billiard-table. たまつき

**당국**(當局) the authorities [concerned]; the government; official quarters[circles]／학교 ~ the school authorities／~의 명에 의하여 by order of the authorities; by police order. とうきょく

**땅꾼** (뱀 잡는) a snake catcher.

**당규**(黨規) the party regulations. とうき

**땅그네** a swing. ブランコ

**당근** a carrot. にんじん

**당금**(當今) these days; nowadays; today; at present／~ 청년 young men of today. とうこん

**당금**(唐錦) precious brocade produced in [ancient] China (귀한 것) something precious.

**당기**(黨紀) party discipline／~ 문란 a breach of party discipline.

**당기다**[1] pull; draw; tug (활을) bend (기일·시간을) advance; move[carry] up／연줄을 ~ handle[haul] in the string of a kite. ひく

**당기다**[2] (입맛이) stimulate[appeal to] one's appetite; [one's appetite] be stimulated. しょくよくをそそる

**땅기다** (가까이) pull in (팽팽히) be tense; be taut. ひっぱる

**당나귀** an ass; a donkey. ろば

**당내**(堂內) one's near relatives [for whose death he wears mourning]. しんぞく

**당년**(當年) (금년) this year (왕년) those years／~의(그 시대의) former; old; of those years; the then／~의 지사 patriots of those days. とうねん

**당년치기**(當年一) things[goods] with a year's life. とうねんかぎりのもの

**당뇨병**(糖尿病) 〖의〗 diabetes; glycosuria. とうにょうびょう

**땅딸막하다** (be) short and fat; dumpy; pudgy; stocky. ずんぐりしている

**땅딸보** a dumpy (person); a stocky man. ずんぐりしたひと

**당닭**(唐一) ①〖조〗 a bantam ②(난장이) a very small person; a midget; a pygmy.

**땅땅** (총소리) bang-bang (쇠붙이 소리) clang-clang.

**땅땅거리다** (호화롭게 살다) live in grand style (큰소리 치다) talk big[tall]; brag; boast. ごうしゃなせいかつをする

**당당하다**(堂堂一) (be) dignified; grand; (훌륭하다) brilliant (공정하다) fair; imposing (응·대하다) magnificent／당당한 태도 a stately appearance.

**당대**(當代) the present age; the day／~의 가인 the reigning beauty. とうだい

**당대 발복**(當代發福) ~하다 become prosperous in one's own generation.

**땅덩이** (지구) the earth; the globe (나라땅) a territory. ちきゅう

**당도**(當到) arrival; coming／~하다 arrive (at, in); reach; get to／~목전에 ~한 위험 a pressing danger. とうちゃく

**당돌**(唐突) ~하다 (be) abrupt; sudden／~히 abruptly; suddenly; of a sudden. とうとつだ

**땅뙈기** a plot [of field]. じゃっかんのとち

**당두**(當頭) ~하다 draw near; come close. ちかよること

**땅띔** lifting (something heavy) off the ground／~ 못하다 cannot lift[get] (something) off the ground. もちあげること

**당락**(當落) the result of an election; success [or defeat] at the polls.

**당랑**(螳螂) a [praying] mantis(pl. -tes, ~es). かまきり

**당략**(黨略) party politics; a party policy. とうりゃく

**당량**(當量) 〖화〗 an equivalent.

**당론**(黨論) the consensus of opinion in the party; a party opinion. とうろん

**당류**(糖類) saccharoid; sugars. とうるい

**당리**(黨利) party interests／~를 꾀하다 promote[advance] party interests／~당략(黨略) party politics. とうり

**당먹**(唐一) Chinese ink. ちゅうごくのすみ

**당면**(當面) facing; confrontation／~하다 face; confront／~한 present; urgent; pressing; immediate／~한 일 immediate work in hand／~한 문제 the matter[question] in hand; an urgent problem. とうめん

**당면**(唐麪) Chinese vermicelli.

**당목**(唐木) fine cotton cloth; calico; cotton[cloth]. もめん

**당무**(黨務) party affairs／~를 처리하다 manage[conduct] party affairs. とうむ

**당밀**(糖蜜) molasses; syrup; treacle〈영〉.

**땅바닥** the earth; the ground／~에 주저앉다 sit[squat] on the [bare] ground. じめん

**땅버들** 〖식〗 a sallow; a goat-willow.

**땅버섯** 〖식〗 a mushroom.

**당번**(當番) (당번중임) being on duty 《일반적인》 duty 《순번》 turn 《감시》 watch 《사람》 a person on duty／~하다 be[go] on duty／그날은 내가 ~이었다 On that day I was on duty. とうばん

**땅벌** 〖충〗 a digger wasp; a sphex; Sphex umbrous(학명).

**당벌**(黨閥) a faction; a clique／~ 싸움 dispute in factions.

**땅벌레** a grub; the larva of a ground beetle.

**당부**(當否) (적부) propriety; fitness; suitability (시비) right or wrong; justice. とうひ

**당부**(當付) ~하다 《요구》 ask; request 《명

**당분(糖分)** [amount of] sugar／쌀의 ~ the sugar content in the rice／~을 포함하다 contain sugar; be sugary／~ 측정기 a saccharometer.

**령)** tell; order; bid; instruct 《부탁》 entrust; trust／이 말씀을 전하라는 ~를 받았읍니다 I was told to see and tell you this. たのむ

**당분간(當分間)** 《현재》 for the present[time being] 《얼마 동안》 for some time [to come]; for a while 《한때》 temporarily／나는 ~ 바쁘다 I am rather busy for the present. とうぶんのあいだ

**당비(黨費)** party expenditure[expenses]／~를 기부하다 contribute toward party expenditure.

**당비름(唐—)** 〖식〗 a Joseph's coat; an amaranth; Amaranthus gangeticus(학명).

**땅비싸리** 〖식〗 kind of indigo plant.

**땅빈대** 〖식〗 a spurge; a euphorbia.

**당사(當事)** ~하다 attend to the business; be concerned in the affair／~국 the country concerned／~자 the person [party] concerned; a concerned party. とうじ

**당사기(唐沙器)** china [ware]; Chinese ceramics.

**당사자(當事者)** the person[party] concerned; a concerned party; a party to an affair／신문(訊問) examination of parties／결혼 ~ the contracting parties in a marriage. とうじしゃ

**당선(當選)** election; return〈영〉／~하다 win the election; be elected; be returned〈영〉／~ 무효 annulment of *one's* election／~자 a successful candidate; an elected person 《현상의》 a prizewinner／~ 소설 a prize winning novel／~ 권내에 있다 be in the running.

**당세(當世)** the present day[time]／~의 present-day; today's modern／~의 학생 the present-day[today's] students. とうせい

**당세(黨勢)** party influence[prestige]／~를 확장하다 extend party prestige; enhance party prestige. とうせい

**당수(黨首)** the leader of party; the party leader. とうしゅ

**당숙(堂叔)** a male cousin of *one's* father [by a grandfather's brother].

**당시(唐詩)** the poems of *Tang* age; Chinese Poetry(한시). とうし

**당시(當時)** 《그때》 [in] those days; [at] that time; then／~의 of those days; of the day; ~의 시장 the then Mayor／~의 청년들 the young people of those days. とうじ

**당시(黨是)** a party principle[platform].

**당신(當身)** 《2인칭》 you 《3인칭》 he; she／~의 your; his; her. あなた

**당아욱(唐—)** 〖식〗 a [common] mallow; Malva sylvestris(학명).

**당야(當夜)** that night. とうや

**당양하다(當陽—)** (be) sunny.

**당연(當然)** ~하다 (be) right; reasonable; proper; natural; due／~히 properly; justly; naturally; as a matter of course; deservedly／~한 일 a matter of course; that which is due／…하는 것은 ~하다 It is proper[but right] that one should …. とうぜん

**땅울림** a rumbling of the earth; earth tremor.

**당원(黨員)** a member of the party; a party man／~이 되다 join a party／~ 명부 the list of party members. とういん

**당월(當月)** this[that] month; the said month. とうげつ

**당의(糖衣)** a sugar coat.

**당의(黨議)** 《당회의》 a party council 《당의 결의》 a party decision 《당의 강령》 party policy[principle]／~에 의해서 결정되다 decided at a party council. とうぎ

**당인(黨人)** a member of party; a party man; a partisan／~ 근성 a partisan spirit.

**당일(當日)** the day; that day 《지정된 날》 the day appointed／~치기 여행 a day's trip. とうじつ

**당자(當者)** the person concerned[in question]. とうじしゃ

**당장(當場)** 《장소》 the spot 《그 자리에서》 on the spot; then and there／그 여자는 ~ 울 것 같았다 She was ready to cry. そのば

**땅재주** tumbling; acrobatic feat[performance]／~를 넘다 give acrobatic feat; tumble. じめんでするかるわざ

**당쟁(黨爭)** party strife[squabbles]; partisan wrangling／~에 초연하다 be above party strife[partisan wrangling]; keep clear of party strife. とうそう

**당적(黨籍)** the party register／~에서 떠나다 leave the party／~에서 제명하다 strike *one's* name off the party register. とうせき

**당조짐하다** teach (one) a lesson; give (one) beans; bear down on.

**당좌(當座)** 《예금》 a current deposit／~ 예금 a current account[deposit]／~ 계정 a current account／~를 개설하다 open a current account. とうざ

**당지(唐紙)** pith-[rice-]paper; Chinese paper. ちゅうごくのかみ

**당지(當地)** this place[district, city, locality]; here／~의 실업계 business circles here. とうち

**당지기(堂—)** 《당집의》 a shrine-keeper; the janitor [of a private school].

**당지다** harden; stiffen; become hardened. おさえられてかたくなる

**당직(當直)** duty; watch／~하다 be on duty[watch]／~ 수당 pay for night duty／~을 교대하다 relieve the watch／~ 장교 an orderly officer; an officer of the day[guard]. とうちょく

**당질(堂姪)** a second cousin; a cousin

once removed／～녀 one's second cousin; a daughter of one's cousin.

**당집**(堂―) a shrine; a temple.　しどう

**당차**(當次) ～하다 come to one's turn; one's turn comes round.

**당차다** (be) of small but sturdy build.　ずんぐりしてがんじょうた

**당착**(撞着) contradiction; conflict; inconsistency; clash／～하다 (be) contradictory (to); clash[conflict] (with); be inconsistent (with)／자가 ～ self-contradiction.　どうちゃく

**당찮다** (be) unreasonable; unjust; improper; absurd; unfair; out of question／당찮은 행동 an unreasonable[improper] act／당찮은 생각 an absurd idea.　まったくそうでない

**당책**(唐冊) a Chinese book.

**당철**(當―) the [proper] season.　とうせつ

**당첨**(當籤) prize winning／～하다 draw a lucky number; win a prize／～ 번호 a winning number; a lucky number／～자 a prize winner.　とうせん

**당초**(當初) the beginning; the outset; the first／～의 original; initial; first／～에 originally; at first; at beginning[outset]／～의 계획 one's original intention.　はじめに

**당칙**(黨則) the party rules[regulations].

**땅콩** a groundnut; a monkey nut〈영〉; a peanut〈미〉.　らっかせい

**당탄**(唐―) seed wool produced in China.

**당태**(唐―) cotton wool produced in China.　ちゅうごくのわた

**당파**(黨派) 《전파》 a party; a faction 《도당》 a clique; a league 《학파》 a school／～를 만들다 form a faction[clique]／～ 싸움 factional[partisan] wrangling／～에 속하다 belong to a party[faction]／～심 a partisan spirit.　とうは

**땅파기** a fool; an idiot; a dunce.

**땅파먹다** do farm work for a living; dig dirt for a living.　うふまたはこうふのせいかつをする

**당파창**(鐺把槍) a trident; a three pronged spear.

**당폐**(黨弊) party evils; party abuses／～를 제거하다 eliminate party evils.

**땅풍뎅이** 《충》 a kind of ground beetle; *Anomala rufocuprea*〈학명〉.

**당하다**(當―) ①《사리에》 (be) right; reasonable; proper; natural／당한 말을 하다 talk[speak] sense ②《이겨내다》 match; equal (one); be a match for; keep up with ③《감당하다》 face; confront／난국에 ～ cope with a difficult situation／당할 수 없다 be no match for.　あたる

**-당하다**(當―) 《입다》 receive; suffer; be subjected to; have; get; take／책망 ～ be charged with／거절 ～ be refused; get turned down.　―られる

**당한**(當限) ～하다 come to a close[fixed term]; become[fall] due.　きげんがせまること

**당해**(當該) proper 《소관의》 competent; concerned／～ 관청[관헌] the competent [proper] authorities; the authorities.　とうがい

**당혼**(當婚) ～하다 reach a marriageable age.　けっこんねんれいになったこと

**당화**(糖化) 《화》 saccharification／～하다 saccharify; make into sugar.　とうか

**당황**(唐慌, 唐慌) confusion; flurry; consternation／～하다 be confused; be consternated; lose one's head; be upset／～하게 하다 upset; confuse; perturb／그 소식에 나는 ～했다 The news took me aback.　あわてること

**닻** an anchor／～을 내리다[올리다] cast [weigh] anchor／～감다 weigh[pull up] anchor.　いかり

**닿다** 《도착하다》 reach; arrive at[in]; get to[at]; attain to／기차가 2시에 닿는다 The train is due at two. 《접촉하다》 be in contact with; touch; be close to／발이 바닥에 ～ touch the bottom.　いたる

**땋다** braid [one's hair]; plait／머리를 ～ wear one's hair in braids.

**닿소리** a consonant.　しおん

**대¹** 《식》 a bamboo／～로 만든 bamboo／～ 나무 세공 bamboo-work／～나무 숲 a clump of bamboo／～로 만든 비 a bamboo-broom／～바구니 a bamboo basket／～발 a bamboo flind[screen].　たけ

**대²** ①《줄기》 a stalk; a stem 《막대》 a staff 《～》 a holder; a pole／～저울 a beam balance; a steelyard／～가 약하다 《사람이》 be timid; be weak-kneed; be faint-hearted ②《담뱃대》 a [tobacco] pipe; a smoke(피는 도구); a fill (양)／담배를 한～ 피우다 have[take] a smoke; smoke a pipe ③《주먹 따위의》 a blow; a stroke; a hit.　みき

**때¹** ①《시각·시간》 time; hour; moment／～를 놓치지 않고 immediately; at once／점심 ～ lunch time／～늦은[늦게] late／이제 잘 ～다 It's time to go to bed. ②《경우》 case; occasion／어떤 ～는 sometimes; occasionally／실패했을 ～ in case I should fail; in the event of failure ③《기회》 chance; opportunity／마침 좋은 ～에 just at the right time; in good time 《시기》 season; time／～를 기다리다 a wait one's time／～를 못 만난 영웅 an unappreciated genius／～아닌 unseasonable ④《끼니》 a meal／세 ～의 식사 daily meals ⑤《시대·당시》 the day; the time[s]／불이 났을 ～ at the time oft he fire／내가 런던에 있을 ～ when[while] I was in London.　とき

**때²** ①《더러움》 dirt; grime; filth 《오점·얼룩》 a spot; a stain; a blot／～가 묻다 become dirty; become filthy[soiled]／～를 빼다 clean (a thing) of a blot (of ink); remove stain (from) ②《시골티 따위》 ㉠～를 벗지 못한 unpolished; rustic／～를 벗은 refined; elegant; smart ③《인색》 meanness.　あか

**대(大)** greatness 《크기》 size 《커다란》 great; large; big 《거대》 huge 《장대》 grand 《광대》 vast 《손해 따위의》 heavy 《대단히》 greatly; very much; strongly/~승리 a signal victory/~문제 a serious question. だい

**대(代)** 《시대》 an age 《치세》 a reign 《일대》 a lifetime/할아버지 ~에는 in grandfather's time/~를 끊다 let the family die out. だい

**대(隊)** 《군인의》 a company; a corps; a body; a squad 《악대의》 a band 《일행》 a party/비행 ~ a flying corps. たい

**대(臺)** ①《받침·걸이》 a rest; a stand 《시렁 따위의》 a rack 《탁자》 a table 《미석 따위의》 a pedestal 《기초》 foundation 《지주》 a support ②《단위》 a car/6~의 자동차에 분승하다 ride in six separate cars ③《액수》 a level/100원~에 달하다 the level of 100won rise to. だい

**대(對)** ①《짝》 a pair; a couple 《짝의 한 쪽》 a pendant/~가 되다 form a counterpart; make a pair ②《반대의 것》 the opposite 《대어》 an antonym/흑은 백의 ~다 Black is the opposite of white. ③《상대》 versus(略: v., vs.); against; between; 《미율》 to/민주주의 ~ 공산주의 democracy versus communism/서울 ~ 부산 Seoul vs. Busan game. つい

**대(帶)** 《지대》 a zone; a belt/한~ the frigid zone. おび

**대가(大家)** ①《대가옥》 a big house; a mansion; a large building ②《권위자》 an authority; a great master/그림의 ~ a master painter/음악의 ~ a great musician. たいか

**대가(大駕)** a state palankeen; an emperor's palanquin. たいが

**대가(代價)** a price; a cost; a charge; purchase money/어떤 ~를 치르더라도 at any price; at all costs. だいか

**대가(貸家)** a house to let; a house for rent 《광고의》 "To Let"; for rent/《미》 ~ 표찰 a "To Let" sign. かしや

**대가극(大歌劇)** a grand opera. おおかぞぐき

**대가다** get (somewhere) in time/기차 시간에 ~ catch a train/수업 시간에 ~ arrive at school on time. まにあうようにいく

**때가다** be taken up; be caught; be arrested; get[be] nabbed/경찰에 ~ be taken [walked off] to the police station; be taken up by the police. とらえられていく

**대가리** the head; the top[tip]/콩나물 ~ the tips of bean sprouts/생선 ~ the jowl. あたま

**대가족(大家族)** a large family/~ 제도 the large-family system. だいかぞく

**때까치** 〔조〕 a butcherbird; a shrike.

**대각(對角)** 〔수〕 the opposite angle/~선 a diagonal line/내~ the interior opposite angle. たいかく

**대각(大覺)** attainment of divine enlightenment; perception of absolute truth/~하다 see the truth; attain spiritual awakening. だいかく

**대각거리다** clatter; rattle/대각대각 clattering[ly]; rattling. がたがたする

**대갈** a horseshoe nail. ていてつのくぎ

**때갈** the shape and color of cloth; a pattern; design. しきさい

**대갈(大喝)** a loud cry; a great yell/~하다 yell at [in a thunderous voice]/~ 일성 in a thunderous shout. だいかつ

**대갈마치** ①《마치》 a farrier's hammer ②《사람》 a stout-hearted person who was schooled in adversity.

**대갈못** a nail with a big head. びょう

**대감(大監)** His[Your] Excellency.

**대감독(大監督)** a primate; an archbishop.

**대갓집(大家~)** a distinguished family.

**대강(大江)** a large river. おおきいかわ

**대강(大綱)** ①《대강령》 general principles [rules] ②《대략》 an outline; in general; generally 《얼추》 roughly; about 《빨리》 hurriedly 《거의》 almost; nearly/일을 ~하다 do a passing job. たいこう

**대강(代講)** teaching as a substitute/~하다 teach in one's place; teach for (another).

**대갚음(對─)** return; requital; repay; retaliation/~하다 repay; return; requite; pay back in kind. ほうふく

**대개(大概)** 《대략》 an outline; a summary 《대략》 generally; usually; mostly; mainly 《거의》 almost; nearly; practically/~의 most; general/~ 모두 nearly all; practically all/~의 경우 generally; in most cases. たいがい

**대개념(大概念)** 〔논〕 a major concept.

**대객(待客, 對客)** 《대접》 service; reception; entertainment 《향응》/~하다 entertain a guest[caller].
きゃくにたいすること

**대거(大擧)** 《총동원》 a united effort 《대기회》 great enterprise 《부사적》 in a body; in [great] force; in large numbers 《대규모로》 on a grand scale/~ 공격하다 attack [the enemy] in great force; take the offensive on a large scale. たいきょ

**대거리(對─)** retaliation; retort; measure for measure; tit for tat/~하다 retaliate; give tit for tat; pay back in kind. しかえし

**대검(帶劍)** wearing a sword 《검》 a sword at one's side/~하다 wear a sword; be armed with a sword. たいけん

**대검찰청(大檢察廳)** the Supreme Public Procurator's Office.

**대겁(大怯)** ~하다 (be) very timid; extremely coward. おおいにおびえること

**대견하다** ①《흡족하다》 (be) satisfactorily; sufficient ②《견디기가》 (be) unbearable; (be) hard to bear. じっぶんだ

**대결(對決)** confrontation; showdown 《미》/~하다 confront/~ 장면 a confrontation scene. たいけつ

**대경(大慶)** congratulations; great happiness; felicitation. おおきなよろこび

대경(大驚) great astonishment/～하다 be greatly surprised; be astounded [consternated]; be horrified. ひじょうにおどろくこと

대경 대법(大經大法) fair principles and fair laws.

대경 실색(大驚失色) turning pale from astonishment[fear]/～하다 lose colour with astonishment; turn pale with horror; be greatly startled. ひじょうにおどろいてかおいろかわること

대계(大計) a great policy/국가 백년의 ～ a far-reaching state policy. たいけい

대계(大系) an outline/세계사 ～ an outline of world history.

대고 (억지로) forcibly; intently 《열렬히》 strongly 《끊임없이》 incessantly; very hard/～ 책만 읽다 be intent on a book /～ 공부하다 keep at one's studies; keep studying without letup. やたらに

대고모(大姑母) a grandaunt[great-aunt] on the father's side. そふのしまい

때깝재기 bits of dirt[filth, grime].

대공 《건》 a king post. しんづか

대공(大功) ①《큰 공》 a great merit; a signal deed ②《복》 wearing mourn for nine months.

대공(對空) anti-air/～ 방어 anti-aircraft defence/～ 사격 flak; ack-ack[anti-aircraft] fire. たいくう

대공(大公) a grand duke/～국 a grand duchy/～비 a grand duchess.

대공 지정(大公至正) full justice; fairness /～하다 (be) just and proper; perfectly fair.

대과(大過) a serious error; a blunder; a grave[gross] mistake/～없다 be free from serious errors. たいか

대과거(大過去) 《언》 past perfect tense.

대관(大觀) a comprehensive view; a philosophical view/～하다 view in large relation; make a general survey (of). たいきょくをかんさつすること

대관(大官) a high official; a dignitary. こうかん

대관(戴冠) coronation/～식 the coronation [ceremony]. たいかん

대관절(大關節) on earth; in the world; the devil; the deuce/～ 무슨 일인가? What the deuce is the matter?/～ 너는 누구냐 What on earth are you?

대팔호(大括弧) 《수》 [square] brackets.

대교 경기(對校競技) an interschool[interscholastic] match[tournament] 《대학의》 an intercollegiate match[tournament]. たいこうきょうぎ

대꾸 a retort; a back-talk. くちごたえ

대구(大口) 《어》 a codfish; a cod/～ 알 the cod-roe. たら

대구루루, 때구루루 rolling/～ 굴리다 roll (a ball) over (the floor). ころころ

대국(大局) the general situation/～을 관찰하다 take a large view of things/ ～적 견지에서 보면 on a broad survey. たいきょく

대국(大國) 《총칭》 a great nation[power]; a large country. たいこく

대국(對局) a game/～하다 play [a game of] (chess, badook, etc.). たいきょく

대군(大軍) a big[great] army; a large force/～을 거느리다 lead[command] a strong army. たいぐん

대군(大君) a [Royal] prince.

대군(大群) a large crowd. たいぐん

대꾼하다, 때꾼하다 (눈이) be sunken[hollow] from exhaustion.

대굴대굴, 때굴때굴 rolling[rumbling] continuously. ころころ

대궁 the remains of a meal; left-over rice. くいのこりのはん

대권(大權) 《왕권》 the supreme power; sovereignty 《통치권》 the governing power/～을 장악하다 hold the supreme power. たいけん

대권(大圈) a great circle/～ 항로 the great circle route.

대궐(大闕) the Imperial Palace; the Court. おうきゅう

대규모(大規模) a large[a big, a grand] scale/～의 big[large]scale/～로 on a large[a big, an extensive, a grand] scale; in a big way. だいきぼ

대그럭거리다, 때그럭거리다 clatter; rattle /대그락대그락, 때그락때그락 clattering [rattling] repeatedly.

대그르르하다, 때그르르하다 be rather thick[big] among the thin[small] things. いっそうおおきい

대그릇 a bamboo-work[-bowl]; bamboo ware/～장이 a bamboo-ware maker. たけのようき

대극(大戟) 《식》 a spurge; Euphorbia pekinensis(학명).

대글대글하다 be rather thick[big] among all the thin[small] things.

대금(大金) a large sum [of money] 《고가》 a great cost/～을 내다 pay a handsome[big] sum.

대금(代金) a price; the money; cost; purchase money/～을 치르다 pay the price; pay for (a thing). だいきん

대금(貸金) a loan/～하다 make a loan [an advance] to/～업(고리대금) money lending business; usury. かしきん

대기(大忌) strong aversion; abhorrence /～하다 abominate; have a great aversion to; abho[u]r. おおいにいむこと

대기(大氣) the air; the atmosphere/～ 론 aerology/～의 압력 atmospheric pressure/～차(差) refraction. たいき

대기(大朞) the second anniversary of (a person's) death. まんにねんめのきねん

대기(大器) 《큰 그릇》 a large vessel 《큰 인물》 a great talent[genius]/～ 만성 A genius is slow to develop; Great talents mature late; Rome was not built in a day. たいき

대기(待機) waiting for a chance /～하

다 watch and wait; wait and see; stand ready for/~를 명하다 《관리에게》 order (one) to await orders.

**대길**(大吉) excellent luck; a great stroke of luck/~하다 be very lucky; have excellent luck.

**대낮**(白晝) the broad daylight; the daytime 《정오》 midday/~처럼 밝다 be as light as noonday.

**대내**(對內) 《형용사적》 home; domestic; interior/~의 domestic; internal; home; interior/~ 문제 domestic issues/~ 정책 a domestic policy.

**대노**(大怒) great anger ⇒대로(大怒).

**대뇌**(大腦) the cerebrum(pl. -bra); the brain proper/~막 the cerebral membrane/~ 피질(皮質) cerebral cortex/~ 엽(葉) a cerebral lobe.

**대다**¹ ⇒변항 참조.

**대다**² ①《물을》 draw [water] into; irrigate ②《공급·주선》 supply; provide; furnish.

**대다**³ ①《일러주다》 tell; indicate; show; inform of ②《사실을》 tell the truth]; speak up[out]; confess; spit it out《속》.

**대다**⁴ 《배·차 따위를》 pull[draw] up; bring to; berth[moor] (alongside); stop.

**때다**¹ 《잡히다》 be caught[arrested]; be rounded up.

**때다**² 《불을》 make[build] a fire; burn; heat with a fire/방에 불을 ~ heat a [hypocausted] room/석탄[장작]을 ~ burn coal[wood].

**때다**³ 《액운》 escape [evil].

**대다수**(大多數) a large majority; the great part (of)/~는 for the most part; mostly/~를 차지하다 hold a large majority.

**대단찮다** (be) trifling; slight; trivial/대단찮은 일 a trifling affair; a [mere] trifle.

**대단하다**(大端—) 《엄청나다》 (be) terrible; horrible 《중대》 (be) serious; grave awful 《많다·크다》 (be) great; many/대단히 very; greatly.

**대담**(對談) a talk; a conversation; an interview/~하다 talk[converse] with /~자 an interlocutor.

**대담**(大膽) boldness; daring/~하다 (be) bold; daring/~하게 boldly; daringly/~한 짓을 하다 do a daring thing.

**대담**(大談) tall talk; high-sounding words/~하다 talk big; speak boastfully.

**대답**(對答) [an] answer; [a] reply; [a] response/~하다 answer; reply/~할 수 없는 unanswerable; insoluble/모호한 ~ 《애매한》 a vague answer.

**대대**(大隊) a battalion/~장 a battalion commander.

# 대 다

① 《연결·대면》 bring into contact; connect; link/음극과 양극을 ~ bring the negative pole into contact with the positive/살 사람과 팔 사람을 ~ bring a buyer into contact with a seller; arrange a meeting between buyer and seller/김선생을 좀 대 주십시오《전화에서》 Will you get me Mr. Kim, please?, /그것은 누굴 대고 하는 말이오 And who is that remark aimed at?/회계과 좀 대 주십시오 Put me through to the accounts section. please.

②《갖다 댐》 put; place; apply; lay; hold; press/수화기를 귀에 ~ hold the receiver to one's ear/청진기를 가슴에 ~ put a stethoscope to a person's chest /눈을 망원경에 ~ apply one's eyes to a telescope.

③《손을》 touch; put [one's hand to]; 않다 do not eat at all; leave the food untouched.

④《도착》 arrive [on time]/ 서울까지 제 시간에 대려고 그들은 서둘렀다 They were in a hurry to get to Seoul on time.

⑤《핑계·성화를》 do; make/성화를 ~ behave badly/핑계를 ~ find[make] excuses/등쌀[을] ~ annoy.

⑥《착수·관계》 take to; put one's hand to [a task]; set to work; start [an enterprise]; set about (a thing); attempt/정치에 손을 ~ dabble[meddle] in politics/투기에 손을 ~ take to[dabble in] speculation/여자에게 손을 ~ have relations with a woman; possess a woman/일에 손을 ~ start[begin] one's work; set about one's business; start an enterprise/그는 자신 없는 일에는 손을 대지 않는다 He does not attempt a task he doesn't feel equal to.

⑦《비교》 compare (a thing) with/길이를 대보다 compare length/번역문을 원문과 대보다 compare a translation with original/이것은 그것과는 댈 수도 없다 This cannot bear[stand] comparison with that.

⑧《밀착·붙임》 fix; put; attach 《옷에 안감 따위를》 line/옷에 헝겊을 ~ put a patch on one's clothes/구두에 창을 ~ fix a sole on one's shoes/받침대를 ~ set up a prop; prop up a stick/벽에 판자를 ~ fix a board on the wall

**대대(代代)** successive generations; for generations/～의 hereditary. だいだい

**때때로** at times; occasionally; now and then; sometimes/～ 오다 come occasionally; come now and then. たびたび

**때때옷** a colourful dress for children. こどものはれぎ

**대대적(大大的)** grand; great; wholesale; immense; splendid/～으로 extensively.

**대도(大道)** a highway; a public street 《왕도》 a cardinal principle. だいどう

**대도(大盜)** an arrant robber; a notorious burglar. おおどろぼう

**대도구(大道具)** 《연극의》 stage-setting; a scene/～계(係) a scene-shifter.

**대도회(大都會)** a large[big] city; metropolis/～권(圈) the metropolitan area.

**대독(代讀)** reading by proxy/～하다 read for (another). だいどく

**대돈변(一邊)** the rate [of interest] of ten per cent per month.

**대동(大東)** Korea. だいとう

**대동(帶同)** accompaniment/～하다 be accompanied (by). たいどう

**대동(大同)** general similarity/～소이 하다 be practically[substantially] the same. だいどう

**대동 단결(大同團結)** a fusion; a union.

**대동맥(大動脈)** 【解】the main artery; the aorta/～염 aortitis. だいどうみゃく

**대동지론(大同之論)** the consensus of public opinion.

**대동지환(大同之患)** a generally-suffered trouble[disaster, affliction, calamity].

**대두(大斗)** a dry measure which contains ten dois. 一斗ます

**대두(大豆)** a soy bean. だいず

**대두(擡頭)** rise/～하다 raise (one) head; gathers trength/～하고 있다 come to the fore[the front]; gain force[power]. たいとう

**대두리** ①《싸움》a hot argument; a big quarrel/～하다 fight hard; have a great dispute ②《큰 판》a serious situation; aggravation/～하다 become serious; become aggravated. だいろんそう

**대득(大得)** a big[great] hit; a big success; a good luck/～하다 make a good haul; hit the jackpot〈미〉.

**대들다** stand against; stand up to fall upon; challenge; defy 《반항하다》resist 《말대꾸하다》retort/네가 나한테 대들 셈이냐 Do you mean to defy me? いどむ

**대들보(大一)** a girder; a large beam; the main beam of a roof. むなぎ

**대뜸** at once; outright; on the spot; then and there/～ 거절했다 I declined then and there. すぐさま

**대등(對等)** equality; equal terms/～한 equal/～하게 on equal terms; on an equal footing/～한 입장에서 on an equal footing. たいとう

**대란(大亂)** a great disturbance/～을 진 압하다 suppress[quell] a great rebellion. たいらん

**대략(大略)** 《개요》 an outline 《적요》 a gist; a summary; an epltome 《발췌》 an abstract 《거의》 nearly; mostly; almost 《약》 about; roughly; in round numbers/～의 rough; approximate/～을 말하다 give an outline of. たいりゃく

**대량(大量)** a large quantity; a mass/～ 수출하다 export (a thing) in large quantities/～ 생산하다 mass-produce/～ 검 거 a mass arrest. たいりょう

**대령(大領)** 《육군》a colonel 《略: Col.》; 《해군》a captain（略: Capt.）; 《공군》a group captain〈영〉; a flight colonel〈미〉. たいしゃ

**대령(待令)** awaiting orders/～하다 await orders. めいれいをまつこと

**대례(大禮)** an important ceremony 《결혼》a marriage-ceremony 《국가·황실》a state ceremony.

**-대로** ①《같이》according to; like; in accordance with; as/～규칙 ～ according to the rule/～본 ～ 얘기하다 tell as one saw /～예기한 ～ as I expected ②《곧》as soon as; immediately after; directly/형편 이 나아지는 ～ at your earliest convenience/～도착하는 ～ on arrival; as soon as one arrives. 一のまま

**대로(大怒)** wild rage; violent angry/～ 하다 rage; be enraged; be inflamed with rage; be exasperated; fly into a passion. ひじょうにおこること

**대로(大路)** a highway; a broad street; a main street. おおじ

**대롱** a slender bamboo-tube.

**대롱거리다** dangle; swing; sway [to and fro]; hang and swing loosely/대롱대롱 dangling[ly]; dingle-dangle/대롱대롱 매달린 물건 a dingle-dangle/바람에 흔들려 대롱거리다 dangle in the wind. ぶらぶらうごく

**대류(對流)** 【물】a convection [current]/ ～권(圈) the troposphere. たいりゅう

**대륙(大陸)** a continent/～의 continental /～적 continental/～적 기후 a continental climate/～ 정책 a continental policy/～적 사상 continentalism/～적인 인 간 a man of easy-going disposition/～ 횡단 철도 a transcontinental railway/ ～간의 intercontinental. たいりく

**대리(大利)** a big[an enormous] profit; a huge gain /～를 보다 make[reap] a big profit. たいり

**대리(代理)** procuration; representation; agency 《사람》a representative; a proxy/～의 acting; deputy/～하다 act for; act in place[in behalf] of/～점 an agency/～ 지배인 an acting-manager/ ～업 agency; factorage; commission agency〈미〉/～ 판매 sale by agent/～ 위임장 the letter of attorney. だいり

**때리다** ①《치다》strike (a person); hit; give a blow; thrash; beat; knock[rap] (at, on); slug; slap; flog; whip; smack;

smite; wallop; whack; pound[batter]《가볍게》tap (at, on) /때려 눕히다 knock (a person) down; beat (a person) to pulp; strike down/때려 부수다 knock (a thing) to pieces; smash (a thing) up/호되게 ~ give (a person) a sound thras hing; strike (a person)hard/지팡이로~ strike [hit] (a person) with a stick ②《비난하다·공격하다》attack; charge; denounce /신문에~ atack (a person) in the press /그는 어제 나를 때리는 말을 여러사람에게 하였다. He publicly denounced me yesterday. なぐる

**대리석**(大理石) marble/조상(彫像) ~ statuary marble/~[제]의 marble; of marble/~ 상 a marble statue/~ 무늬 있는 종이 marblepaper/~같이 단단하다 It is as hard as marble. たいりせき

**대리인**(代理人) a proxy; a substitute; a deputy; a representative/~을 내다 send a proxy/~을 쓰다 employ a substitute/…의 ~이 되다 stand[be] proxy for (another). だいりにん

**대립**(對立) 《대치》opposition; rivalry; standing face to face 《상호 관계》correlation/~하다 be pitted against; confront (each other); 《상대》stand face toface/ ~ 의견 conflicting views/~적 rival; opposing/민족의 ~ the antagonsim of one race to another. たいりつ

**대마**(大麻) 【식】a hemp/~계의 hempen /~유 hemp-seed oil/~인(仁) hemp-seed たいま

**대마루** the ridge [of a roof]. やねのむね

**대마루판** the crucial[decisive, critical] moment. しょうはいのわかれめ

**대만원**(大滿員) a full[a bumper] house. だいまんいん

**대망**(大望) a great ambition; a great desire; aspiration/~을 품은 ambitious; aspiring/~을 품은 사람 an ambitious [an aspiring] man/ ~을 품고 with a great ambition; with high aspirations /~을 품다 be full of ambition; have a high aim. たいもう

**대망**(待望) expectation; awaiting; anticipation/~하다 wait for; expect; anticipate/ ~의 hoped-for; long-awaited [-expected]. たいぼう

**대매** ①《매질》a single blow of whip[a rod] ②《결승》the decision (of a contest) /~하다 fight to the finish 《동점일 때》 break the ties.

**대매출**(大賣出) a great[big] sale. うりだし

**대맥**(大麥) barley 보리.

**대머리**《벗어진 머리》a bald head 《사람》 a bald-headed man/젊어서 벗어진 ~ a premature bald-head/일찍 ~가 된 prematurely bald. はげあたま

**대면**(對面) an interview/~하다 interview; meet; see; have an interview with /~자 an interviewer/초~ first meeting[interview]/~ 교통 walking on the rightside facing the traffic/오래간만에 ~하다 see (one) after a long interval [separation]. たいめん

**대명**(大命) an Imperial[King's] command; an Imperial[a King's] mandate/ ~을 받들어 in obedience to a word from the Throne. たいめい

**대명**(待命) awaiting order's; pending appointment/~하다 be on the waiting list/~이 되다 be placed on the waiting list. たいめい

**대명사**(代名詞) a pronoun/~의 pronominal/ 관계[지시, 인칭, 의문] ~ the relative[demonstrative, personal, the interrogative] pronoun/~로서 pronominally. だいめいし

**대명사**(大名辭) 【논】the major term.

**대명일**(代名日) a most widely celebrated holiday; a great fête day; a principal gala day.

**대모**(代母) a godmother. なづけはは

**대모**(玳瑁) ①《동》a hawksbill[turtle] ② 《귀갑(龜甲)》a tortoise-shell. たいまい

**대목** ①《시기》the most important time; vital moment/설달 ~ the last day of the year; New Year's Eve/~ 장 the year-end fair ②《자리》the vital; point /그는 제일 중요한 ~에 이르러 거절했다 When it came to the point, he declined. きんようなじき

**대목**(大木) a carpenter.

**대목**(臺木) 《총의》a stock; stock tree 《목수의》a block 《접목의》a parent stock /감나무 ~에 배를 접붙였다 A pear tree was grafted on the stock of a persimmon-tree. だいぎ

**대못** 《축전》a bamboo peg. たけくぎ

**대못**(人一) 《큰 못》a large nail[peg]. おおくぎ

**대못박이** a fool; a simpleton; a sluggard; a dunce; a blockhead; an ass. ぐどんなひとのたとえ

**때문** ground; reason; because (of) /~에 on account of; because of; owing to; due to; by reason of; through; in view of; thanks to; with/그 ~에 on this account/부주의 ~에 because of[through] carelessness/전쟁 ~에 owing to the war; as a result of the war/결과로/부지런하기 ~에 due to one's hard work ため

**대문**(大文) ①《원문》the text; the body ②《글의 부분》a passage. ほんぶん

**대문**(大門) the front[main] gate/~을 걸다 bolt the front gate. だいもん

**대문가**(對門家) the house opposite.

**대문띠**(大門一) a crosspiece on the door of a gate. だいもんのとびらのよこぎ

**대문자**(大文字) a capital [letter]/~로 쓰다 write in capitals. だいもんじ

**대문장**(大文章) 《글》a grand composition 《사람》a great master of「literary」style. だいぶんしょう

**때묻다** 《더러워지다》get dirty[soiled, stained] 《인색하다》(be) stingy; mean; di-

rty-minded. あかがつく
때물 unrefinedness; rusticity; boorishness; dirt./~을 벗다 be refined[urbane, smart, polished]; be free from boorishness.
대물(對物) objects; reality 《형용사적》objective; real/~의 real; objective/~경[렌즈] an object-glass[-lens]./~세(稅) a real tax. たいぶつ
대물리다(代一) hand down[leave, transmit, bequeath] to one's posterity/손자에게 재물을 ~ bequeath one's property to one's grandson.
대미(對美) ~의 with[towards] America/~ 관계 relations with America/~ 무역 trade with America/~ 정책 a policy towards America.
대바구니 a bamboo basket. たけかご
대반(大盤) a large dinner-table[-tray]. おおきなばん
대받다 《반항하다》 retort; contradict (a person). いいかえす
대받다(代一) ①《계승하다》succeed to; continue ②《상속하다》inherit.
대발 a bamboo blind[-screen].
대방(貸方) the credit side …대변(貸邊). かしかた
대방가(大方家) a master. だいがくしゃ
대밭 a clump of bamboo[s]; a bamboo thicket; a canebrake. たけやぶ
대번(代番) being on duty for[on behalf of] (another); a substitute/~하다 stand guard for; do duty for (another). だいりばん
대번에 《곧》at once; immediately; directly; promptly; instantly 《단숨에》at a breath;at a stroke《서슴지 않고》without hesitation 《쉽사리》easily; readily/~ 알다《이해하다》be easy to understand 《확인하다》be easy to recognize/그 책은 ~ 팔렸다 The book met with a ready[a rapid]sale. すぐに
대범(大凡) in general …무릇. およそ
대범(大凡, 大泛) broad-mindedness; large heartedness/~하다 be not overly fussy about trifles ; be not particula [fastidious] (about); be large-hearted [open-handed, broad-minded, liberalminded]/~한 태도 an air of magnanimity; lofty manners. おおざっぱ
대법(大法) 《원칙》fundamental principles 《국법》the law of the land 《불역(不易)의》immutable law. たいほう
대법원(大法院) the Supreme Court; the Court of Cassation/~장 the President of the Supreme Court; the Chief Justice/~에 상고하다 carry a case to the Court of Cassation. だいほういん
대법회(大法會) a [Buddhist] high mass; a great memorial[religious] service.
대변(大變) a serious trouble; a grave disturbance; a great accident; a calamity; a terrible accident. おおきなへんか
대변(大便) motions; excretions; faeces; dung; excrement; evacuation/~을 보다 evacuate; go to stool; ease oneself;/~보러 가다 go to the privy; go to the toilet room《이》. だいべん
대변(對辯) an answer; a reply/~하다 reply; answer [a question]. たいべん
대변(代辯) speaking by proxy/~하다 speak for; act as spokesman for (the family)/~자[인] a spokesman; a mouthpiece/신문은 세론의 ~자다 The newspaper is the mouthpiece of public opinions. だいべん
대변(貸邊) 《장부의》the credit side/~표 a credit note/~ 계정 credit account /~에 기입하다 enter on the credit side.
대변(對邊) 《수》 the opposite side; the subtense.
대별(大別) a general classification/~하다 classify roughly into; make a general classification/두 종류로 ~하다 divide into two main classes; classify into two groups. たいべつ
대병(大兵) a large military force …대군.
대병(大病) a serious[severe, critical] illness; a dangerous disease/~을 앓다 be in a serious[critical] condition; be seriously ill. じゅうびょう
대보(大寶) ①《보물》a treasure of great value; a priceless treasure ②《옥새》the Imperial[the Privy] Seal; the Seal of the Emperor たからもの
대보다 compare [one thing with another]; balance; measure 《대조하다》contrast/길이를 ~ compare length/…과 대보면 in comparison (with); as compared (with); if weighed against/번역을 원문과 ~ compare a translation with the original/그것에는 대볼 만한 것이 없다 It stands unchallenged[unparalleled, without a peer]. くらべてみる
대보름(大一) the 15th of January [lunar].
대복(大福) great happiness; great fortune; good luck. だいふく
대본(大本) 《원천》the foundation; the basis; the base; the source; the root; the fountainhead/국가[인륜]의 ~ the foundation of the state[human morality]. たいほん
대본(臺本) 《극의》a play-[text-]book 《영화의》a scenario 《가극의》a libretto. だいほん
대본(貸本) a book to be taken out; a book for[on] hire. かしほん
대본산(大本山) the headquarters; the cathedral of a sect . だいほんざん
대봉(代捧) payment in substitute/~하다 《주다》pay in substitutes 《받다》be paid in substitutes
대부(大富) 《대부호》a millionaire; a billionaire; a multimillionaire; a wealthy man. おおかねもち
대부(代父) 《종》a godfather. なづけちち
대부(貸付) 《돈의》loaning 《물건의》renting /~하다 lend; loan; advance; make

대부등 224 대서특필

an advance/~금 a loan; an advance/당좌 ~ a call-loan; a loan at call; a demand loan〈영〉;a day-to-day loan〈미〉/신용 ~ a loan on personal pledge; an open credit/은행 ~ a [commercial] bank loan/~계《은행의》a loan teller; a loan clerk. かしつけ

**대부등**(大不等) big round timber.

**대부분**(大部分) the majority; the major [best, greater] part (of)《부사적으로》mostly; for the most part/바다는 지구 표면의 ~을 이루고 있다 The ocean forms the bulk of the earth's surface. だいぶぶん

**대부인**(大夫人) Your[his] esteemed mother.

**대분수**(帶分數)《수》a mixed number. たいぶんすう

**대불**(大佛) a huge[big, colossal] statue of Buddha; a great image of Buddha. だいぶつ

**대불행**(大不幸) a great misfortune; a calamity; a disaster. だいふこう

**대비**(對比) ①《대조》contrast/~하다 contrast ②《비교》comparison/~하다 compare/~ 고찰하다 weigh (a thing) with[against] another. たいひ

**대비**(大妃) the Empress Dowager; the Queen Mother. せんのうのこうひ

**대비**(貸費)《학생에의》a loan; a loan scholarship/~하다 loan[advance] expenses; make a loan/~생 a loan student. たいひ

**대비**(對備) provision; preparation/~하다 be prepared for; provide against[for]/장래에 ~하다 provide for the future/만일에 ~하다 make provision[provide] against emergency/역습에 ~하다 provide[guard oneself] against an enemy attack/그는 위기에 ~하고 있다 He is ready for any risks. /우리들은 미래에 ~하지 않으면 안된다 We must provide for the future/최악의 경우에 ~하여야 하네 You must be prepared for the worst. じゅんび

**대빈**(大賓) a guest of honour; an important[a special] guest. きひん

**대빗** a bamboo comb. たけのくし

**대사**(大事)《소사에 대한》a great thing; a great undertaking; a great enterprise《중대사》a matter of grave concern; a serious[grave] affair《혼인》a marriage ceremony. だいじ

**대사**(大師) a saint; a great Buddhist priest. だいし

**대사**(大赦) amnesty; a general pardon/~령 a decree of amnesty/~를 행하다 grant[proclaim] an amnesty/~에 빠지다 be excluded from the amnesty. たいしゃ

**대사**(代謝) replacement ⇒신진 대사.

**대사**(臺詞) speech; dialogue; words; one's lines/독백 ~ a monologue/~를 말하다 speak one's part; read the lines/~를 잊다 forget one's lines/~가 서투르다 speak one's part badly. せりふ

**대사**(大寫)《영화의》a close-up/~를 하다 take[obtain] a close-up (of).

**대사**(大使) an ambassador; an envoy/~ 일행 the ambassadorial party/주미 한국 ~ the Korean Ambassador to America/~를 특파하다 dispatch a special envoy (to)/특명 전권 ~ an envoy extraordinary and ambassador plenipotentiary/~ 변리 ~ a resident ambassador/~ 부인 an ambassadress. たいし

**대사관**(大使館) an embassy/미국 ~ the American Embassy/~ 서기관 a secretary of an embassy/~ 참사관 a councillor [counsellor] of embassy/~원이다 be on the embassy staff. たいしかん

**대살**(代殺) executing a murderer/~하다 execute a murder; put a homicide to death.

**대살지다** (be) thin and tough; lean and hard; sinewy. やせておこりっぽい

**대상각** a bamboo-bat. たけかさ

**대상**(大祥) the second anniversary of a death.

**대상**(代償) ①《변상》compensation; reparation; indemnification/~하다 compensate; indemnify (for a loss)/~ 수입(輸入) compensation[in return] for ②《대신하는 변상》vicarious compensation/~하다 compensate on behalf of another ③《딴 것으로》compensation -in substitutes/~하다 compensate in substitutes. だいしょう

**대상**(隊商) a caravan.

**대상**(對象) an object/연구의 ~ an object of study/~성 objectivity. たいしょう

**대상자**(一箱子) a bamboo box[case]. たけのはこ

**대생**(對生)《식》opposition; symmetry/~엽 opposite leaves. たいせい

**대서**(大暑) the Korean midsummer day [occurring about July 23rd]《혹서》an intense heat. たいしょ

**대서**(代書) scrivenery/~하다 write for another/~인 a scribe; a scrivener/~소 a scrivener's office/~업 scrivenery. だいしょ

**대서다** ①《뒤따르다》follow; go in the wake of (one) ②《대들다》retort on《반항하다》fall on. うしろについてたつ

**대서양**(大西洋) the Atlantic [Ocean]/~의 Atlantic/~ 횡단 비행 a transatlantic flight/~ 함대 the Atlantic Fleet/~ 항로 an Atlantic line/~ 헌장 the Atlantic Charter/~ 저쪽[횡단]의 transatlantic. たいせいよう

**대서 특필**(大書特筆) special mention[writing]/~하다《좋게》write up; write in high terms of eulogy《나쁘게》write down; write against (one)/~할 만한 worthy of special mention; capital; remarkable; notable/~할 만한 사건 a big event; a capital event/신문은 모두

이 사전을 ~했다 The newspapers gave prominence to this incident.

**대석**(對席) sitting face to face/~하다 sit opposite (one) 《회견・회의》 sit face to face; attend together. たいせき

**대선**(大船) a big ship[boat]; a large vessel; a leviathan. おおきなふね

**대선거구**(大選擧區) a major constituency /~제(制) a major constituency system. だいせんきょく

**대설**(大雪) ①《절후》 [the season of] great snow [about February 8] ②《눈》 heavy snow. たいせつ

**대성**(大成) ①《완성》 completion; accomplishment; success/~하다 complete; accomplish; succeed in; be crowned with success; win distinction; attain greatness ②《집대성》 compilation/~하다 make a comprehensive compilation ③《인격의》 attainment of greatness/~하다 attain[come] to greatness/~할 인물 a man full of promise. たいせい

**대성**(大聖) a great sage; a mahatma. たいせい

**대성**(大姓) a prosperous clan. たいせい

**대성**(大聲) a loud voice[tone]/~으로 in a loud voice; loudly/~을 내다 bawl; speak[cry] in a loud voice/~ 질호(叱呼) violent denunciation; fulmination /~ 통곡 loud wail[weeping, lament]. おおごえ

**대성공**(大成功) a great[brilliant] success; a huge[great] success/저 친구도 서는 ~이었다 He has done very well. だいせいこう

**대성황**(大盛況) prosperity; prosperous condition/~을 이루다《극장 따위에서 속된 것이》 play to the gallery; be a gallery hit; strive for effect. だいせいきょう

**대세**(大勢) ①《형세》 the general situation 《추세》 the trend of affairs[the times]; the tide; the current; the general tendency/세계의 ~ the international situation; the trend of international affairs/~에 역행하다 go against the current ②《병의》 a serious[grave] condition; a critical state[stage]. たいせい

**대소**(大小) 《대와 소》 large and[or] small; big and[or] small 《큰 것 작은 것》 great and small ones 《크기》 size; measure/ ~에 불고하고 whether large or small; regardless of size/~에 따라 according to size. だいしょう

**대소**(大笑) a roar of laughter; a loud laughter; a cachinnation/~하다 roar with laughter; laugh [out] aloud; cachinnate; burst out laughing/가가 ~ 하다 burst into a roar of laughter; enjoy a hearty laugh. だいしょう

**대소**(代訴) litigation by proxy/~하다 sue[bring suit] on behalf of another.

**대소**(對訴) a counter-suit[-action].

**대소동**(大騷動) 《싸움》 a great uproar; a racket; a rumpus; a clamour 《혼잡》 a bustle; a hurly-burly; a turmoil 《소동》 a row; a tumult; great trouble[excitement] 《야단 법석》 a fuss/~하다 make a great uproar[to-do]; raise a hue and cry/회합에서 ~이 있었다 There was a great stir at the meeting. だいそうどう

**대소변**(大小便) urine and faces 《용변》 urination and defecation/~을 보다 go to the toilet-room; visit the lavatory; relieve oneself[nature]; ease nature. だいしょうべん

**대소사**(大小事) matters great and small; all sorts of matters. だいしょうじ

**대소상**(大小祥) the first and second anniversaries of one's death.

**대소수**(帶小數) 〖수〗 a mixed number.

**대소월**(大小月) odd and[or] even months.

**대소장**(大小腸) the large and the small intestines.

**대소쿠리** a bamboo basket. たけでつくったものいれ

**대속**(代贖) redemption[expiation, atonement] on behalf of another; 〖종〗 the Atonement.

**대솔**(大一) a great pine[-tree]/~잎 leaves of a big pine[-tree]. おおきなまつ

**대수**(大水) a flood ⇒홍수. おうみず

**대수**(大數) ①《큰 수》 a great[big, large] number ②《큰 운》 a good luck; good fortune. だいすう

**대수**(代數) algebra; literal arithmetic / ~ 기호 an algebraic symbol/~식〖함수, 방정식〗 an algebraical expression[function, equation]/ ~적(的) algebraic [al]/~로 풀다 solve (a problem) in algebra; work out a problem algebraically. だいすう

**대수**(對手) an antagonist; an opponent; a rival; a match. てきしゅ

**대수**(對數) 〖수〗 a logarithm/~표 a table of logarithm/~을 modulus of logarithm. たいすう

**대수롭다** 《중요하다》 (be) important; serious 《각별하다》 (be) particular; special /대수로운 용무는 없다 I have nothing particular to do. /병세에 대수로운 변화는 없다 There is no serious change in the patient. /그들은 남의 감정 따위는 대수롭지 않게 여긴다 They have no regard for other's feelings. /대수롭지 않은 일로 떠들지 마라 Don't make a fuss about trifles. たいしたことはない

**대수술**(大手術) a major [surgical] operation. だいしゅじゅつ

**대숲** a bamboo grove[thicket]. やぶ

**대승**(大乘) Mahayana(Sans); the greater vehicle/~적 견지에서 문제를 해결하다 settle a matter from a broad point of view. だいじょう

**대승**(大勝) ①《대승리》 a great victory/~ 하다 gain[win] a great victory ②《월등함》 ~하다 surpass; excel; be far better than. だいしょう

대승정(大僧正) 【종】 an archbishop; a chief abbot (카톨릭 교의) a cardinal.

대식(大食) ①(아침 저녁의 끼니) main meals [breakfast and supper] ②(많이 먹음) gluttony; voracity; heavy feeding /~하다 eat heavily; eat much; eat a heavy meal; eat gluttonously; gluttonize; gorge; gormandize; cram[stuff] oneself; eat like a horse. たいしょく

대식(對食) dining face to face (with); a tête-à-tête dinner / ~하다 take a tête-à-tête dinner; dine face to face (with). むかいあってたべること

대신(代身) ①(대리) vicariousness; substitution (사람) a substitute (교대자) a relief; a deputy /~의 vicarious; substitute /~하다 take the place of; take one's place; relieve (another) / ~에 in [the] place of; instead (of); for (one); on behalf of; vicariously / 사장을 ~하여 for[in palace of] one's director / ~으로 as a substitute /~하여 직무를 보다 act for; act on behalf of ②(대용) a substitute / ~의 substitute; alternative / ~에 instead of; for ③(대상(代償)) compensation; return (교환) exchange / ~에 by way of compensation; in return (for) (교환으로) in exchange /전번에 얻어 먹은 ~으로 오늘은 내가 한턱 내마 Let me pay the bill this time. ④(한편) but; though /값이 비싼 ~ 오래 간다 This wears long though a bit expensive. /가르치기 힘드는 ~에 즐거움도 있다 The pleasure of teaching makes up for toil.
たにんのみかわりになること

대신(大臣) a minister (of state); a cabinet minister; secretary / ~의 직 ministership /내[외]무~ the Home[the Foreign] Minister / ~ 비서실 the Minister's[the Ministerial] secretariate /~이 되다 become a minister; enter the cabinet. だいじん

대심(對審) 【법】(공판) a trial (대결) confrontation / ~하다 confront [the accused with the accuser]. たいしん

대아(大我) 【철】 absolute ego; the higher self; the inner man; one's larger self.
たいが

대악(大惡) atrocity; outrage; heinousness (대악인) a consummate[an arrant] knave; a thorough rascal. だいあく

대안(對岸) the other side of a river; the opposite bank /~의 집 a house on the opposite bank /~에 있다 be across the river /~의 적 the enemy on the opposite bank. たいがん

대안(代案) an alternative plan[proposal]; a substitute [measure, bill]. たいあん

대안(對眼) for the eye /~경 an ocular / ~ 렌즈 an eyelens; an eye glass; an eyepiece. たいがん

대액(大厄) (재화) a great misfortune [calamity, disaster].

대야 a washbasin; a washbowl. たらい

대양(大洋) the ocean; the main《사》/ ~의 oceanic; ocean / ~도(島) oceanic islands / ~ 한가운데에서 in the middle of the ocean /~을 항해하다 sail the ocean.
たいよう

대양주(大洋洲) Oceania / ~ 사람 an Oceanian.

대어(大語) big talk; a brag; a boast / ~하다 talk big[tall]; brag; boast.

대어(大漁) a large[good] catch; a good haul /~를 하다 have a large[big] catch of fish; make a good haul.

대언(大言) big talk; a boast; a brag; a bombast /~하다 talk big[tall]; brag (of); boast (that). たいげん

대언(代言) ~하다 speak for (another).
だいげん

대언 장담(大言壯談) big[tall] talk; loud-mouthed boasting; a loud boast; bragging /~하다 talk big[tall]; boast of [about]; talk in a grandiose style; use bombastic language; be full of hot air; rant.

대업(大業) an important task; a great achievement / ~을 맡다 be charged with an important task. たいぎょう

대여(貸與) lending; a loan /~하다 loan; lend; lease / ~금 a loan /~자 a lender /무료로 ~하다 lend free. たいよ

대여섯 about five or six; several. ごろく

대역(大逆) [high] treason; lese-majesty / ~ 사건 a lesemajesty affair; a high treason case. だいぎゃく

대역(大役) (역할) an important task[duty]; a heavy trust; an important part (사명) an important mission /~을 맡다 undertake[take up, accept] an important part /~을 완수하다 perform[discharge, accomplish] an important duty.
たいやく

대역(代役) a substitute; an alternate; a deputy; an understudy /~을 하다 act for another. だいやく

대역(對譯) a translation with the original /영한(英韓) ~으로 되어 있다 The English original has its Korean translation side by side[on the opposite page]. たいやく

대역 부도(大逆不道) heinous treason; regicide; hideous wickedness.
ひとのみちにひどくそむいたことをすること

대연(大宴) a big feast; a grand banquet.
せいだいなえんかい

대연습(大演習) grand maneuvers [manoeuvres《영》] / ~을 하다 hold grand mauvers. だいえんしゅう

대열(大熱) great heat 《체온의》 high fever. こうねつ

대열(大悅) exultation; rapture; ecstasy; unalloyed delight / ~하다 be overjoyed; be transported with joy; exult. たいえつ

대열(隊列) a line; ranks; formation / ~을 짓다 form ranks; get[form] in line;

fall in／~을 정돈하다 dress ranks; line up. たいれつ

**대엿새** about five or six days; several days. ごろくにち

**대영**(對英) ~의 with[towards] Great Britain／~ 무역 trade with Great Britain[the British Commonwealth].

**대오**(大悟) spiritual awakening[enlightenment]; 《종》 divine enlightenment／~하다 attain spiritual awakening; find one's philosophy of life; attain [divine] enlightenment／~ 철저 attainment of divine enlightenment; perception of absolute truth. だいご

**대오**(隊伍) 《대열》 the ranks; a line 《진열》 an array 《행렬》 a procession／~를 짜고 in line／~를 정돈하다 dress ranks／당당한 ~로 행진하다 march in grand order. たいご

**대오다** come[arrive] in time; get[be] [here] on time／약속한 시간에 ~ come by the appointed time. まにあわせてくる

**대오리** a narrow strip of bamboo.

**대왕**(大王) a Great King／세종 ~ Sejong the Great. だいおう

**대왕풀** 《식》 a kind of orchid.

**대외**(對外) foreign; abroad／~의 foreign; international; external; abroad 《외부》 outside／~ 관계 foreign[international] relations／~ 권익 foreign[overseas, international] rights and interest／~ 정책 a foreign policy／~ 투자 overseas investment. たいがい

**대요**(大要) 《개략》 an outline; an epitome; a summary 《내용》 the substance 《적요》 an abstract 《학문의》 general principles; elements; a [drief] résumé(F)／사건의 ~ the sum and substance of the matter／강연의 ~ an outline of the lecture／~를 설명하다 describe[give] the outline (of)／…의 ~를 말하다 epitomize; summarize; outline; give a summary [an outline] of; sum up. たいよう

**대욕**(大慾) avarice; greed; rapacity; great desire／~의 avaricious; covetous; greedy. だいよく

**대욕**(大辱) a major disgrace; a great insult; a deep disgrace. おおきなはじ

**대용**(代用) substitution／~하다 substitute; use one thing for another; substitute A for B; use A for[instead of] B／~의 substitute／~식 substitute food; a rice substitute／~품 a substitute article. だいよう

**대용**(貸用) borrowing; loan／~하다 borrow; have (thing, meney, etc.) on loan. かりてもちいること

**대우**(大雨) a heavy rain[rainfall]; a pouring rain; a downpour; a deluge of rain; torrents [of rain]; a cloudburst 〈미〉. たいう

**대우**(待遇) treatment 《접대》 reception 《여관 따위의》 service 《급료》 pay 《처지》 dealing／~하다 treat; receive; entertain／~ 개선 improvement of working conditions／~가 좋다 treat (one) well be hospitable to(손님에 대한)／pay (one) well(급료가)／정중한 ~를 받다 receive good[hospitable] treatment／~ 개선을 요구하다 demand for the increase of (wages)／그들은 혹독한 ~를 받았다 They were hardly treated. たいぐう

**대우**(對偶) ①《짝》 a pair／~법 《언》 antithesis ②《수》 contrapositive [proposition]／~ 정리 a contraposition ③《논》 opposition; antithesis. たいぐう

**대우깨** sesame grown as a catch-crop with wheat or barley.

**대우다** ①《깨어진 곳을》 solder (up); braze; tinker (up)／솥을 ~ solder[braze] a pot ②《집다》 patch (up) (the trousers); darn (stokings); put[add] a patch on (a coat); sew (in) a patch; mend ③《끼니를》 substitute／식빵 하나로 점심을 ~ substitute a loaf of bread for regular lunch. いかけする

**대우주**(大宇宙) 《철》 the great universe; a macrocosm.

**대우콩** bean grown as a catch-crop with wheat or barley. かんさくのだいず

**대우팥** redbeans planted as a catch crop with wheat or barley. かんさくのあづき

**대운**(大運) great fortune; [a] good luck. だいうん

**대울** a bamboo fence. たけがき

**대웅좌**(大熊座) 《천》 the Great Bear; the Big Dipper; the Plow; the Charles's Wain. おうくまざ

**대원**(大願) an earnest prayer; a great desire; one's cherished desire／~ 성취 the attainment of one's desire／나의 평생의 ~이 성취됐다 My lifelong desire has been gratified. だいがん

**대원수**(大元帥) the generalissimo; the commander-in-chief; of the Army and Navy. だいげんすい

**대월**(貸越) an outstanding account; an overdraft／~이 되어 있다 remain unpaid[due, outstanding]; overdraw one's accounts.

**대위**(大尉) 《육군·공군》 a captain 《해군》 a first lieutenant／~의 직 a captaincy; a lieutenancy.

**대위**(代位) 《법》 subrogation; substitution／~ 납부(納付) payment in subrogation／~ 납세 의무자 a subrogator／~ 변제 subrogated performance; subrogation. だいい

**대위**(對位) contraposition; coordination; counterpoint. たいい

**대위법**(對位法) 《음》 counterpoint／~의 contrapuntal／이중 ~ double counterpoint. たいいほう

**대유**(大儒) 《유학의》 a great Confucianist; a great scholar; a savant. たいじゆ

**대유성**(大遊星) 《천》 major planets.

**대음**(大飮) heavy[deep] drinking; a carouse／~하다 drink heavily; carouse;

대읍(大邑) a big town. おおきなまち

대응(對應) (필적) match (상응-) correspondence (조화) harmony (동형) homology (좌우의) symmetry／～하다 match; correspond to; cope with; be correspondent with／～책 a counter-measure／～변[각][수] homologous[corresponding] sides[angle]／시국에 ～하다 cope with the situation. たいおう

대의(大意) the gist; the substance 《개의 (概意)》 a general idea 《개략(概略)》 an outline. たいい

대의(大義) the law of justice; the great duty[moral obligation]; a great cause; loyalty and patriotism／～를 위하여 for the great cause (of a country)／～에 순(殉)하다 sacrifice oneself for justice; sacrifice one's life in the great cause／～ 명분 justice. たいぎ

대의(代議) popular representation／～원 a representative; a delegate; a mouthpiece／～ 정치 representative[parliamentary] government／～ 제도 a representative[parliamentary] system. だいぎ

대-를씨(代一) a pronoun ⇒대명사(代名詞). だいめいし

대인(大人) ①(남의 아버지) your father ②(어른) a man; a grown-up person ③ ⇒ 더인 군자(君子) ④(존칭) a gentleman ⑤(몸이 큰 사람) a giant. たいじん

대인(代印) signing for procuration／～하다 set a seal for (another)／～을 찍다 sign by proxy／～도 무방함 Signing per procuration would do. だいいん

대인(對人) ～의 personal; [concerning] personnel／～ 관계[신용, 담보] personal relations[credit, security]. だいじん

대인 군자(大人君子) a man of virtue; a great man. たいじんくんし

대인기(大人氣) a hit; a great popularity [vogue]; a great success; a big hit／～를 끌다 (극장에서 속된 것이)) play the gallery; be a gallery-hit／저 사람은 모든 사람에게 ～가 있다 He is highly spoken of by all people. だいにんき

대인물(大人物) a great man[character, figure]; a man of big caliber; a prominent[leading] figure; a big man [gun]／정계의 ～ a great figure in politics. だいじんぶつ

대일(對日) ～의 towards[with] Japan／～ 감정 the sentiment towards Japan／～ 관계[무역] relations[trade] with Japan／미국의 ～ 외교 방침 America's diplomatic policy towards Japan.

대임(大任) (임무) a great task; an important charge[duty] (책임) a heavy responsibility (사명) an important mission (요직) an important office[position]／～을 다하다 fulfill a great mission; carry through a great task／～을 맡다 undertake a great task／～을 맡기다 entrust (a person) with a great task. たいにん

대자 a bamboo measure; a bamboo foot-rule[r]. たけじゃく

대짜(大一) a big one (사냥감 따위의) big game／～가 걸렸다 (낚시터에서) I have got a bite from something big／～ 못 a big nail. おおきなもの

대자(大字) a large character／～로 in large characters／～로 쓰인 written in a large hand. おおきいもじ

대자 대비(大慈大悲) great mercy and compassion／～하신 관세음 보살 Avalokitêsvara of Great Love and Great Mercy. だいじだいび

대자리 a mat woven of bamboo strips; a split-bamboo mat. たけべつくったむしろ

대짜배기 a big[gigantic] one; an awfully big one／～로 in[with] a big one (일이) on a big scale; in a large[big] way／～로 한 잔 하다 have a drink in a large mug. おおきいもの

대자색(代赭色) red ochre.

대자연(大自然) nature; creation; Mother Nature; [Mighty] Nature. たいしぜん

대작(大斫) large splits of firewood; big chops of firewood. ふといわりぎ

대작(代作) ①(글의) writing for another; vicarious writing; ghost-writing／～하다 ghost-write; ghost (for one)／～을 vicarious work／～자 a ghost ② ⇒대파(代播). だいさく

대작(大作) a great work; a major work (결작) a masterpiece (미술) a work(picture, sculpture) of large size. たいさく

대작(對酌) ～하다 drink face to face; drink together; across the table each other; hobnob (with). たいしゃく

대장 (대장장이) a smith; a blacksmith (해학적으로) the knight of the hammer／～간 a blacksmith's shop; a smithy. かじや

대장(大將) (육군·공군) a [full] general (해군) an admiral. たいしょう

대장(大腸) 【해】 the colon; the large[great] intestine. だいちょう

대장(隊長) a commanding officer; a commander; a captain; a leader／소[중·대] 대장 a platoon[a company, a battalion] commander. たいちょう

대장(臺帳) (원장) a ledger 《등록 대장》 a register／토지 ～ a land register.

대장경(大藏經) the complete collection of Buddhist Sutras; Laws and Treatises; the complete Buddhist literature.

대장부(大丈夫) a hero; a brave[a great] man／～답게 굴어라 Be a man!, Play the man!／～라면 그런 짓은 못난다 You should be man enough not to do a thing like that. だじょうぶ

대장일 smithery. かじやのしごと

대장장이 a smith (직공) a black smith (해학적으로) the knight of the hammer. かじや

대재(大才) great abilities; a brilliant talent; a big talent. たいさい
대재(大災) a grave disaster; a serious calamity. おおきなさいがい
대저(大抵) generally [speaking]; on the whole; as a rule; in the main; on the average/~는 사람이라는 것은 하여야 할 본분이 있는 것이다 All men have their duties. たいてい
대적(大敵) a great foe[enemy]; heavy odds; a great[a formidable] rival[competitor]; a powerful enemy/그는 나의 ~이다 I have a formidable enemy in him/~이라도 두려워하지 말라 Don't hold even a formidable foe in awe. たいてき
대적(對敵) ①(적대) hostility; antagonism ②(적수) a [good] match; a worthy opponent; a rival; matching/~하다 fight against; oppose; be antagonistic to; contend against; match; equal; rival/~ 행위 hostile action; hostilities. たいてき
대전(大全) ①(완전) completeness; perfection ②(전집) a complete collection[works]. たいぜん
대전(大典) (의식) a great function; a state ceremony (법전) a code; a statute (종교의) a canon. たいてん
대전(大殿) His Majesty the King. おおさきのけいご
대전(大戰) a great war; a great battle/제 2차 세계~ World War Ⅱ/~ 전의 prewar; avant-guerre (F)/~ 후의 post-war. たいせん
대전(帶電) 【물】 electrification; electric charge/~하다 charge with electricity/~체 a charged body. たいでん
대전(對戰) (전쟁) a fight (경기) a match; a bout/~하다 fight; meet; be pitched against each other; oppose; be matched against/작년의 패자(覇者)와 ~하다 have[play] a game with the championship-holder of last year. たいせん
대전제(大前提) 【논】 the major premise; the sumption. だいぜんてい
대전차(對戰車) anti-tank/~포 an antitank gun/~호(壕) an anti-tank trench/~ 지뢰 an anti-tank mine. たいせんしゃ
대절(貸切) booking(영); reserving(미)/~하다 engage a whole (car, etc.)/~한 reserved/~차 a reserved carriage. かしきり
대절(大節) a great[lofty] principle[cause]. たいせつ
대접 ①(그릇) a large bowl; soup bowl ②(쇠고기의) beef shank. おおきなどんぶり
대접(待接) treatment; reception; entertainment; hospitality/~하다 treat; treat (a person) to (a drink); entertain; receive; give[show] (a person) hospitality/이렇게 친절한 ~을 받을 줄은 생각 못했다 I little thought of that I should meet with such a kind reception./은근한 ~을 받다 be given[accorded] hospitable treatment[a cordial reception]; receive hospitality/후하게 ~하다 give (a person) warm hospitality; lavish hospitality to; exercise great hospitality. もてなし
대정(大定) decision; conclusion/~하다 conclude; decide. だんてい
대정각(對頂角) 【수】 vertically opposite angles. たいちょうかく
대정맥(大靜脈) the vena cava (pl. venac cavae/상[하] ~ the ascending[the descending] vena cava. だいじょうみゃく
대정자(大正字) roman capitals.
대제(大帝) a great emperor. だいてい
대제(大祭) a great festival; a great fête. たいさい
대제사장(大祭司長) a high priest.
대조(對照) contrast; antithesis (비교) comparison/~하다 contrast; compare (A with B); set (A) against (B); check (A) up with (B)/좋은 ~ an excellent [a great] contrast/그 도시의 아름다운 모습은 딴 도시와 뚜렷한 ~를 이루고 있다 The beauty of the city presents a striking contrast to the aspects of other cities. たいしょう
대조(大潮) the flood[the spring]-tide; the major tide. おおしお
대족(大族) a powerful family; a prosperous clan. たいぞく
대종(大宗) the main stock[family line]; lineage of the head family/~가 the general head family/~손 the heir of the general head family.
대종(大鍾) a large bell. おおきなかね
대좌(對坐) sitting face to face/~하다 sit opposite[face to face, facing each other]. たいざ
대죄(大罪) a heinous crime; a grave offence; a felony; an enormity; an atrocity; a great sin (법률상의) a capital crime; a high[serious, foul] crime/~인 a felon; a great offender/~인은 교수형의 선고를 받았다 The felon was sentenced to death by hanging. たいざい
대죄(待罪) ~하다 await the official decision on one's punishment; wait for the judgment. たいざい
대주(大酒) heavy[deep, hard] drinking; carousal; a binge; a bender/~가(家) a heavy[hard] drinker; a toper; a sot; a soaker/~객 a heavy drinker; a soaker. おおのみや
대주(貸主) the lender (채권자) the creditor (토지·집 등의) the lessor. かしぬし
대주교(大主敎) an archbishop/캔터베리 ~ the Archbishop of Canterbury.
대주다 supply[provide, furnish, find] (a person with money); support/살림을 ~ give (one) financial aid; assist in getting a living/학비를 ~ supply (a student) with his school expenses/일감을 ~ provide (a person) with work; provide work to (a person). きょうきゅうする

대줄거리(大—) the essentials; a summary; a gist 《개요》 an outline.

대중 ①《겉어림》 estimation; calculation 《추측》 conjecture; guess/~하다 estimate; calculate; conject; guess ②《표준》 a standard; a level 《목표》 an aim 《한도》 measure/~을 잡다 set up a standard /무슨 말인지 ~을 잡을 수가 없다 I can't make head or tail of it. けんとう

대중(大衆) the masses; the mass of people; the multitude; the populace; the general public 《군중》 a crowd of people /~성 popularity/~ 문학 popular literature/~ 작가 a popular writer/~ 잡지 a low-brow magazine/~ 정책 a policy towards the masses/~ 심리 mass psychology/~적안 popular; for the masses; for everybody/~화하다 popularize; make (a thing) popular/~ 교육 mass education/~에게 인기가 있다 be popular (with, among); win popularity. たいしゅう

대중없다 ①《헤아리기 어렵다》(be) hard to foresee/사고란 언제 일어날지 대중없는 법이다 There is no knowing when accidents may happen. ②《표준이》(be) unsettled; uncertain 《애매하다》(be) vague/그의 말은 ~ His remarks are inconsistent. よそくしかねる

대증(對症) allopathy/ ~의 allopathic/ ~ 약제 allopathic medicine/~ 요법 allopathy; allopathic treatment/~ 요법을 하다 treat symptoms. たいしょう

대지(大旨) the substance; the gist 《대의》(大意). たいい

대지(大地) the earth; the ground; the solid earth; tread terra firma (L); mother earth《아》. だいち

대지(大志) a great ambition; an aspiration/~를 품고 with a great ambition /소년들아, ~를 품어라 Boys, be ambitious! たいし

대지(帶紙) a paper wrapping ribbon; a-[half-]wrapper.

대지(垈地) a [building] site; [a plot of] ground; a plot; a lot/건축 ~ a building site[lot]/~의 선정 the selection of a site (for).

대지(臺紙) pasteboard; board; ground paper 《사진의》 a mount 《그림의》 a mat /~ 없는 사진 an unmounted photograph/사진을 ~에 붙이다 mount a photograph. だいし

대지(臺地) 《고지》 heights; a terrace 《고원》 a table land; a plateau; an eminence/용암(熔岩) ~ a lava plateau.

대지(貸地) land to let[for rent]; a lot to let[for rent]. かしち

대지(人智) great wisdom 《사람》 a sage.

대지(人指) the thumb; the big finger. おやゆび

대지 공격(對地攻擊) a ground attack.

대지르다 thrust at (one with a knife) /대들다. つきさす

대지주(大地主) a great landowner; a lord of broad acres. だいじぬし

대지팡이 a bamboo cane; a walking stick of bamboo. たけのつえ

대진(代診) examination of a patient in behalf of another doctor/~하다 examine (a patient) in behalf of (another doctor)/~의(醫) a doctor's assistant; a locum tenens〈영〉; an intern〈미〉; a locum《속》. だいしん

대진(對陣) confrontation of armies/~하다 be encamped facing each other; confront each other/강을 끼고 ~하다 confront[face] each other across the river. たいじん

대진(大震) a violent earthquake. たいしん

대질(對質) confrontation/증인 상호간의 ~을 명하다 order witness to confront with each other/~ 신문 a cross-examination. たいしつ

때찔레 《식》 a sweet brier; Rosa eglanteria《학명》. かいどう

대집행(代執行) 《법》 execution by proxy.

대차(大車) 《큰 수레》 a large cart 《제조》 a giant swing. おおきなくるま

대차(大差) a great[material, wide] difference; a great discrepancy[disparity]; a great[striking] contrast/~가 있다 be much different from; differ much from. たいさ

대차(貸借) borrowing and lending; a loan 《장부상의》 debit and credit/~를 결산하다 strike a balance; sum up the debtor and creditor account/~ 관계 financial relations; accounts/~ 계약서 a charter/~ 기한 the term of a loan. たいしゃく

대찰(大刹) a grand temple; a cathedral 《이름난》 a noted temple. たいさつ

대창(大漲) a heavy flood/~하다 be heavily flooded[inundated].

대책(大責) a good scolding/~하다 give a good scolding. おおいにせめること

대책(對策) a counter-measure[-plan]/~을 강구하다 consider a counter-plan; devise a countermove; take a measure to meet the situation; study ways to cope with the situation. たいさく

대책(大册) a bulky volume; a big book; a tome/5천 페이지의 ~ a bulky volume of five thousand pages. おおきいほん

대처(對處) disposal/~하다 meet; deal with; cope with/정세에 ~하다 meet [cope with] the situation. たいしょ

대처승(帶妻僧) a married Buddhist priest. つまのあるぼうず

대척(對蹠) 《정반대의 위치》 diametrical opposition 《지구상의》 antipodism/~의 antipodal; antipodean; just the opposite/사회적 지위로 보아 ~적인 at the opposite social pole たいしょ

대천(大川) a big[large] river. おおかわ

대천지 원수(戴天之怨讐) an irreconcilable [a sworn, a life-long, a mortal, a deadly, the dearest] enemy[foe].

**대첩**(大捷) a signal[a great, a sweeping] victory/~하다 win a signal victory. たいしょう

**대청** the white membrane inside bamboo.

**대청**(大廳) the main floored room; a hall. おおびろま

**대청**(大靑) 【식】 a woad.

**대체**(大體) ①《요점》 the principal parts; the main points 《개략》 an outline 《개요》 substance; gist/~의 general; main; rough/~로 substantially; generally; in substance; on the whole/~로 말하여서 generally[broadly] speaking ② 《도대체》 on the earth; in the world/~너는 누구냐 What on earth are you?/~ 어떻게 된 셈이냐 What is the meaning of all this?. だいたい

**대체**(代替) alternation; change 《대용》 substitution/~하다 alternate; change; substitute/~ 식량 substitute food (for rice)/~ 원칙 the principle of substitution/~되다 be substituted (for)/~가능물 a fungible. だいたい

**대체**(對替) ①《상》 change; transfer/~하다 change (a bill); transfer/~ 전표 a transfer slip/~ 계정 a transfer account ②《주금의》 진체(振替). ふりかえ

**대초**(大一) a big candle; a large candle. おおきいろうそく

**대초**(大草) italic capitals.

**대촌**(大村) a large village. おおきなむら

**대총통**(大總統) 《중국의》 the Generalissimo; the Leader.

**대추** a jujube; a date/~나무 a jujube tree/~야자 《식》 a date-palm 《열매》 a date. なつめ

**대축**(對軸) a countershaft.

**대출**(貸出) a loan; lending; an advance credit/~하다 lend out; loan out; advance (money); let out on hire/비상 ~ emergency advances/~금 loaned money. かしだし

**대충** almost; nearly; about; roughly; loosely; grossly/~ 예산을 잡아 보다 make a rough estimate of expenses/일이 ~ 되다 one's work is almost done. ざっと

**대충**(代充) supplement in substitutes/~하다 supplement[replenish] in substitutes.

**대충 자금**(對充資金) the counterpart fund.

**대취**(大醉) dead drunkenness/~하다 be [get] dead drunk; be drunken; be drunk as a piper[a fiddler]. おうよい

**대치**(對峙) standing face to face (with); confronting each other 《적대》 keeping up rivalry; holding one's ground against (the enemy)/~하다 stand face to face with; confront each other; stand opposite to each other 《적대하다》 keep up rivalry; hold one's ground against (the enemy)/쌍방이 ~하여 굽히지 않는다 Neither would yield to the other in their rivalry. たいじ

**대침**(大針) a big needle. おおきなはり

**대칭**(對稱) 1.《수》 symmetry/~의 symmetrical/~적으로 symmetrical, ly,/~점 a point of symmetry 2.《어》 the second person/~ 대명사 a second personal pronoun. たいしょう

**대칼** a bamboo-knife.

**대컨** as a whole; generally. だいたい

**대탈**(大頃) a disastrous accident; a grave disaster/~이 났다 A disastrous accident happened to him., A serious thing befell him. おおきなじこ

**대테** a bamboo hoop/~를 메우다 bind with bamboo hoops; put a bamboo hoop on (a tub). たけのたが

**대토**(代土) 《바꿈》 exchange of land 《땅을》 substitute land.

**대통**(一筒) a bamboo-tube 《담뱃대의》 the bowl of a tobacco pipe. たけのつつ

**대통**(大通) prosperity/~하다 be in luck's way; fortune turns in one's favour/운수가 ~하다 have a spell of extremely good luck; fortune turns in one's favor. ひじょうにうんのよいこと

**대통**(大痛) severe[violent, intense] pain; great pangs 《심적 고통》 misery.

**대통**(大統) the Royal line; the Imperial line/~을 계승하다 succeed to the Royal[Imperial] line[the Throne]; continue the Royal line. たいとう

**대통령**(大統領) the President; the Chief Executive《미》/~의 presidential/~ 부인 the first lady [of the land]/~의 지위 presidency/~ 선거 presidential election/~ 임기 a presidential term/~에 취임하다 be sworn in as President/~ 관저 the Executive[Presidential] Mansion; the White House《미》/~ 교서 a Presidential message; the President's message. だいとうりょう

**대퇴**(大腿) 【해】 the thigh; the femur/~골 a thighbone; a femur/~부 the femoral region. もも

**대파**(大破) ①《깨짐》 ruin; decay; damage; dilapidation/~하다 be greatly damaged; be ruined; go to decay ②《격파》 a crushing defeat/~하다 defeat (an enemy) disastrously[overwhelmingly]; put (an enemy) to rout/~ 당하다 sustain[suffer] a crushing defeat; be routed. たいは

**대파**(代播) sowing in substitution/~하다 sow in substitution (for).

**대판**(大一) a large scale/~으로 on a large scale/~ 싸우다 fight hard[furiously]/~《논쟁》 argue hotly. おおじかけ

**대판**(大版) large size/~의 large-sized; of large size. おおきなかたち

**대판**(代辦) agency; comission management of another's affairs/~하다 represent; act for (another); act in[on] behalf of (another)/~인 an agent; a proxy; a factor.

**대패** a plane/~집 a plane stock; a stock of a plane/대팻날 a plane iron/대팻밥 [wood] shavings; planing refuse. かんな

**대패(大敗)** a crushing[heavy, serious, disastrous, terrible] defeat; an utter rout/~하다 sustain[suffer] a crushing defeat; be routed; be put to rout; be disastrously defeated./~를 당하다 meet a crushing defeat; be beaten hollow/~시키다 defeat utterly; put to rout. たいはい

**대패질** planing/~하다 plane (a board). かんなかけ

**대포(大砲)** ①《병기》a gun; a cannon; [a piece of] ordnance; artillery/~ 소리 the boom[roaring] of guns/~를 쏘다 fire a gun ②《거짓말》big[tall] talk; a high tale; tall talking/~를 놓다 talk big; brag; draw[shoot] a long bow; blow one's own trumpet. たいほう

**대폭(大幅)** ①《폭의》full breadth; full width ②《사이의》great jump/~적으로 sharply; steeply; by a large margin/~인상 a steep raise; a sharp increase; a heavy boost/~ 삭감 a drastic cut[curtailment] of expenses; a sharp cut. おおはば

**대표(代表)** representation; agency 《단체》a delegation 《개인》a delegate; a representative/ ~하다 represent; stand [act] for/~적 representative typical (전형적)/~하여 representing; on behalf of/~ 사원 a representative partner; an acting[a senior] partner/~작 a masterpiece. だいひょう

**대풍(大豊)** an abundant harvest; a bumper crop; a heavy[a record] crop/벼농사는 어느 모로 보든지 ~일 것이다 There is every prospect of a very large rice crop. だいほうねん

**대풍(大風)** a high[big, strong, violent] wind 《질풍》a gale. たいふう

**대풍자(大楓子, 大風子)** 《한》a chaulmoogra seeds/~유(油) chaulmoogra oil.

**대필(大筆)** a big writing brush; a big hair pencil. おおきなふで

**대필(代筆)** writing for (a person); ghost writing/~하다 write (a letter) for (a person); write (a letter) to (a person) dictation/어머니의 ~을 하다 write for one's mother.

**대하(大河)** a large river/~ 소설 a river [saga] novel; a roman-fleuve(F). たいが

**대하(大廈)** a large building; a large house; an edifice; a mansion. おおきくてひろいいえ

**대하(大蝦)** 《동》a lobster. おおきなえび

**대하다(對─)** ①《마주보다》face; confront; be opposite; be over against/서로 얼굴을 ~ face[confront] each other; be over against each other ②《…에 향하다·…에관하다》toward; to; in; by 《관하여》in regard to/물음에 대한 대답 an answer to a question/문학에 대한 흥미 interest in literature ③《대조하다》as opposed to; in opposition to; in contrast to/구어체에 대한 문어체 written[literary] style as opposed to spoken[colloquial] style ④《응대하다》address; receive; treat/교만한 태도로 손님을 ~ receive a visitor with a haughty style/부드러운 얼굴로 학생에게 ~ address oneself to one's students with a kindly look ⑤《대항하다》against/결정에 대한 항의 a protest against a decision ⑥《비교·비례하다》as compared with; as against; per; to; against/열 사람에 대하여 한 대의 라디오 one radio set to every ten persons/6에 대하여 3으로 by 6 to 3 ⑦《보수로서》for; in return for/그는 그 발명에 대하여 5만원의 보수를 받았다 He received a reward of fifty thousand won for the invention. あいみる

**대하증(帶下症)** 《의》leucorrhea; whites. こしけびょう

**대학(大學)** 《종합 대학》a university 《단과대학》college/~의 자유 academic freedom/~ 출신자 a university man[graduate]/~ 교수 a college[university] professor/~ 교수단 the faculty of university[college]/~ 교육 a university[college] education[training]/~생 a college[university] student; a college man[woman]/~원 a graduate school〈미〉; a postgraduate course/~ 학장 a dean; a president. だいがく

**대학자(大學者)** a great[prominent, profound] scholar; a man of great education. だいがくしゃ

**대한(大寒)** midwinter; the coldest season; the depth[the height] of winter; the midwinter occuring about January 21st/지독한 추위 intense cold. だいかん

**대한(大旱)** a severe drought. たいかん

**대한(大韓)** Korea/~ 해협 the Straits of Korea.

**대한 민국(大韓民國)** the Republic of Korea (略: R.O.K.).

**대합(大蛤)** 《어》a clam; Mertrix lamacki 《학명》. はまぐり

**대합실(待合室)** a waiting room/삼등 ~ the third class waiting room. まちあいしつ

**대항(對抗)** opposition; rivalry; confrontation; antagonism; emulation 《저항》counteraction/~하다 set up[against]; pit oneself against ; stand (against); oppose; cope with; rival/~자 an emulator; an antagonist; an opponent;/~력 opposing power/~ 운동 a counter movement/~책(策) a counterplot; a countermeasure/~책을 강구하다 counterplot against. たいこう

**대해(大害)** great damage[loss]; great harm[injury]/곡식에 ~를 주다 cause great damage to the grain. だいがい

**대해(大海)** an ocean; the open sea; the

**대행** high seas; the deep; the main 《시》/~의 일적(一滴) a drop in the bucket[the ocean]/우물 안의 개구리가 ~를 모른다 A frog in the well knows nothing of the great ocean. たいかい

**대행**(代行) vicarious execution/~하다 carry out[execute] as proxy/~ 회사 a [stock exchange] clearing corporation /~ 기관 an agency; a substitute machinery.

**대헌장**(大憲章) The Magna Charta; The Great Charter. だいけんしょう

**대현**(大賢) a man of great wisdom; a sage/~은 대우(大愚)와 같다 A great sage is often taken for a great fool.

**대형**(大兄) Mr.; you. たいけい

**대형**(大形, 大型) a large[a full] size/~의 large[full, over] sized; of a large size; big; large/~의 배 a large vessel.
おおきなかたち

**대형**(隊形) formation; order/전투 ~ a battle-formation/~을 짓다 form/~을 전연히 하고 in good formation.

**대화**(大火) a big[great] fire; a conflagration; a disastrous[destructive] fire /~를 만나다 be visited by a disastrous fire/~가 되다 spread; become serious. たいか

**대화**(大禍) a great disaster; a calamity; a woe/~를 입다 meet with a calamity. たいか

**대화**(對話) conversation; a chat; a dialogue/~하다 talk[converse] with; have a talk with (a person)/두 사람의 ~ a dialogue/~극 a dialogic play. たいわ

**대환**(大患) a great trial; a disaster/국가의 ~ great national trials[afflictions]. たいかん

**대황**(大黃) 【약】 rhubarb [root]/~환(丸) a rhubarb pill; Rheum undulatum(학명).

**대회**(大會) (모임) a great meeting; a mass meeting; a rally (총회) a general meeting; a conference; a convention (경기) a meet; a tournament; a tourney /~를 열다 hold a mass meeting; meet in [a] convention/국민 ~ a popular mass meeting/기념 ~ a commemoration meeting on a grand scale. たいかい

**대효**(大孝) (효성) great filial piety 《사람》 an affectionate and dutiful son/~로 부모를 섬기다 be very dutiful to one's parents. すぐれたこうこう

**대훈위**(大勳位) the Grand Order.

**대흉**(大凶) (흉년) a very bad crop; a very poor harvest; great failure of crops (불길) singular ill fortune; a black omen (극악) atrocity; brutality/ ~하다 ill-omened. だいきょう

**대희**(大喜) great delight; exultation; ecstasy/~하다 be overjoyed; be transported with joy; be ecstatic; be thoroughly delighted. おおいによろこぶこと

**댁**(宅) (집) one's house; one's residence

《당신》 you 《부인》 a lady; the wife (of one)/본~ one's home; one's principal house/~의 아이 your children/목요일에는 ~에 계십니까 Are you at home on Thursday? たく

**댁내**(宅內) your family/~가 다 무고하십니까 How are your people?, How is your family? おたく

**댁네** your wife (of).

**댁대구루루, 땍대구루루** rolling/~ 굴러 가다 roll over and over/~ 굴리다 roll (a pencil) over (the floor). ころころ

**멀나무** (잣작) firewood (섶) brushwood /~를 하다 gather firewood. たきぎ

**땜** soldering. いかけ

**땜질** soldering; brazing; patching (the trousers), 《수선》 tinkering; repairing; mending/~하다 tinker; solder; repair; mend. いかけ

**댓** about five/~ 번 about five times.
いつつくらいの

**댓가지** 1《가지》 a branch of bamboo ②
**댓개비** たけのえ

**댓개비** a slender piece of split bamboo.
'たけのこぎれ

**댓돌**(臺―) terrace stones 《섬돌》 step-stones.

**댓조각** a piece of bamboo.

**댓줄기** a bamboo stalk.

**댓진** nicotine[tar] accumulated in a pipe /~이 끼다 be chocked with nicotine.
キセルのやに

**땡감** an unripe and puckery[astringent] persimmon. なまかき

**댕그랑거리다, 땡그랑거리다** tinkle; jingle; clang; cling/댕그랑댕그랑[땡그랑땡그랑] tinkle-tinkle; ting-a-ling; ting-ting; jingling/풍경이 댕그랑거리기 시작했다 A hanging bell[wind bell] began to tinkle. ちりりんとなる

**댕기** a ribbon; a pigtail ribbon/~를 매다 wear[put on] a pigtail ribbon.
かざりひも

**댕기다** (불이) catch[take] fire (불을) light[make, kindle] a fire; ignite. ひがつく

**댕댕, 땡땡** clanging; jingling; ding-dong /종이 ~ 친다 The bell clangs., The bell is ringing. ちりんちりん

**땡땡이** a paper tambourine with beads inside; a kind of rattle.

**댕댕이덩굴** 【식】 Cocculus trilobus (학명).

**땡땡이중** a mendicant priest who goes around hitting a gong. たくはつそう

**댕댕하다, 땡땡하다** (be) tight; taut; compact; hard; solid/땡땡한 근육 a hard muscle/밧줄을 땡땡하게 매다 spread a rope tight[taut, tense]. はりきっている

**댕물갈다** (be) as hard as a brick; very solid. れんがのようにかたい

**더** 《수량·정도》 more; some more 《시간》 longer 《거리》 farther/~ 많이 more and more; still more/그만큼 ~ as many [much] more/~ 참을 수 없다 I can't stand it any more. もっと

**더가다** go past; go beyond; rise above;

**떠꺼머리 처녀(-處女)** an old maid with a pigtail. べんぱつをつけたとしよりのしょじょ

**떠꺼머리 총각(-總角)** an old bachelor with a pigtail. べんぱつをつけただんせいどくしんしゃ

**더껑이** scum; film; skin; cream 《녹인 쇠 등의》 dross. うきかす

**더께** layers of dirt; accumulated dirt. かさぶた

**더구나** moreover =더군다나. まして

**더군다나** besides; moreover; further [more]; in addition; what is more[is worse]; into the bargain 《설상 가상으로》 to make matters worse/~ 비까지 오고 있다 It is raining, into the bargain. なおまた

**더금더금, 더끔더끔** in heaps; on and on.

**더기** a plateau.

**떠나다** ①《출발》 leave; start (*from*); set out; depart (*from*)/서울을 ~ leave[start from] *Seoul*/부산을 ~ start for [set off to] *Busan*/세상을 ~ depart this life; die; pass away ②《손을 뗌》 leave; fall apart; part from/관계(官界)를 ~ leave one's official life/…에서 떠나서 apart from. しゅっぱつする

**떠내다** dip[scoop] up. くみだす

**더넘스럽다** (be) a little too big[large]; be a little too much. おおきすぎる

**더니** ¶마구 노름을 하~ 결국 가산을 탕진하고 말았다 He went on gambling until at last he lost all his fortune. —したが. —だったが

**떠다니다** drift[wander] about. ただよう

**떠다밀다** ①《밀다》 push ②《넘기다》 throw upon (*another*). おしのける

**더더귀더더귀** in clusters =더더덕.

**더더리** a stammerer; a stutterer. どもるひと

**더덕** 《식》 Codonopsis lanceolata(학명).

**더덕더덕** in clusters; in bunches/~하다 (be) clustered[thick]. ふさふさと

**더덜거리다** stammer; stutter; falter/더 덜더덜 stutteringly. どもる

**더덜못하다** (be) indecisive; irresolute; wishy-washy. けつだんりょくがない

**더덜이** addition and subtraction; increasing and decreasing. かげん

**떠돌다** 《표류》 drift about; be adrift; float 《방랑》 wander; roam 《소문이》 get about[abroad]. さすらいする

**더뜨리다** offend (*a person*).

**떠들다**¹ ①《큰소리로》 make a noise; clamour ②《술렁거리다》 be excited[agitated]. さわぐ

**떠들다**² 《쳐들다》 raise; lift [up]; jack up. もちあげる

**떠들썩하다** ①《시끄럽다》 (be) noisy; boisterous 《왁자하다》 uproarious; clamorous; turbulent; tumultuous ②《소문이》 (*a rumor*) (be) abroad; be noised about. やかましい

**떠들어대다** raise a clamour; make an uproar 《죽인다고》 set up a cry; make a terrible noise. さわぎたてる

**떠들치다** ①《비밀을》 reveal; disclose; divulge; expose ②《물건을》 lift up (one side of *a stone*). あげく

**더듬거리다, 떠듬거리다** ①《손으로》 grope; fumble (*in the darkness* for); feel about (*for*) ②《길을》 grope[feel] one's way ③《말을》 stammer; stutter. てさぐりする

**더듬다** ①《손으로》 grope; fumble (*in the darkness*) for (*a thing*); feel about for (*a thing*); feel after (*the handle*) 《길을》 grope[feel] one's way; pick one's way 《근원을》 trace ③《기억 따위를》 try to recall ④《말을》 stammer; stutter; falter. てさぐりする

**더듬더듬** 《말을》 stammeringly; stutteringly; faltering 《손으로》 by feel; gropingly. どもる

**더듬적거리다, 떠듬적거리다** be stammering[stuttering, faltering] (in one's speech)/더듬적더듬적[떠듬적떠듬적] stammering; stuttering; faltering.

**더디다** (be) slow (*in, of, at*); tardy (*at*); dilatory 《일손이》 ~ be slow in one's work. おそい

**-더라** I have found that; it is known that. —だったんだよ

**-더라도** if; even if; [even] though; although; admitting[granting, supposing] that. —であっても

**더러** ①《다소》 some; somewhat; a little ②《어쩌다》 occasionally; at times; once in a while; now and then; from time to time/~오다 come occasionally. いくらか

**-더러** 《에게》 to; toward/나는 그~ 나가 라고 명령했다 I ordered him out.

**더러워지다** 《불결해지다》 be stained; be soiled become[get] dirty[mean, sordid]; bepolluted; blemished 《지조가》 lose one's chastity. きたなくなる

**더럭** lots all at once/~ 겁이 나다 be seized with fear[struck with awe] all of a sudden; get into a funk.

**더럭더럭** pertinaciously; tenaciously; persistently 《귀찮게》 importunately.

**더럼타다** be easy to dirty[soil, stain]; be easily soiled. よくよごれる

**더럽다** (be) unclean; dirty; filthy 《비열》 mean 《추잡》 indecent 《인색》 stingy 《부 전》 impure/더러운 옷 dirty[soiled] clothes/더러운 계집 an impure[unchaste] woman/돈에 ~ 《인색하다》 be mean over money matters. きたない

**더럽히다** 《때묻히다》 make unclean[dirty]; soil; stain; taint; befoul; smear 《명예 따위를》 disgrace 《여자를》 violate; outrage; dishonour/몸을 ~ 《여자가》 lose one's chastity/말석을 ~ be given a seat among the rest. よごす

**떠름하다** ①《맛이》 (be) astringent; puckery ②《내키지 않다》 be indisposed to;

더리다 (be) reluctant; be unwilling to ③(꺼림하다) feel uncomfortable (about); feel uneasy. きがかりだ

더리다 ①(떠름하다)(be) awkward; poor; inadequate; be out of place ②(어리석다) (be) silly; soft-headed; asinine ③(야비하다) (be) mean; low; gross; dirty. ぶざまだ

떠맡기다 leave (a matter) to others; saddle (one) with/억지로 ~ force on; pass[impose] upon. まかせる

떠맡다 undertake; take upon oneself; be saddled with; take over/빚을 ~ hold oneself liable for a debt/책임을 ~ assume the responsibility. ひきうける

더미 a heap; a pile; a stack; an accumulation/돌 ~ a pile of rocks.

더미씌우다 shift the burden of responsibility (on to a person); throw the blame (on a person); pass the buck. つみかさね

떠받들다 ①(쳐들다) hold up; lift; raise; push up ②(공경) revere (추대) exalt (옹립) support; back ③(중시) make much of; hold (a person) dear. あげる

떠받치다 support; bolster; prop[shore] up. ささえる

더뱅기 lots of; heaps of/~가 되다 be covered with.

떠버리 a prattler (아녀자) a chatterbox; a braggart; gasbag; a rattler.ほらふき

더뻑 rashly; recklessly; blindly; thoughtlessly. けいそつに

더뻑거리다 act rashly.

더벅머리¹ dishevelled[unkempt] hair; bushy hair (소년) a lad with dishevelled hair. もつれかみ

더벅머리² (갈보) a prostitute [who is still very young]. しょうふ

떠벌리다 ①(과장) talk big; brag; exaggerate ②(크게 차리다) set up on a large scale. おおげさにいう

떠보다 ①(무게를) weigh; check the weight ②(사람됨을) measure; size up the caliber of a person ③(속뜻을) sound; fathom. はかってみる

더부룩하다 (풀이) (be) thick (머리·수염이) (be) bushy; shaggy; unkempt/수염이 ~ have a shaggy growth of whiskers.

떠뿌룩하다 feel stodgy; feel heavy on the stomach. はらいっぱいだ

더부살이 a living-in servant. いそうろう

더불다 ①(함께 하다) join in (something); do together; partake of ②(동행하다) take (a person) with (데리고 가다); bring (a person) with (데리고 오다); go with. ともにする

더불어 (함께) together; with/~ 즐기다 enjoy together. ともに

더새다 put up at; stay for the night. しゅくはくする

떠세 ~하다 make use of another's influence; shelter oneself under another's influence. けんせいによるいじつばり

떠오르다 ①(물위에) be afloat; rise to the surface (공중에) rise; go up; soar ②(생각나다) recall; come[flit, flash, shoot] across one's mind; occur to (one) ③(눈물·웃음 따위) be shown in one's face. うかびあがる

더우기 besides; moreover; in addition; what is more; particularly; especially; into the bargain; on to pof (that)/~ 좋은 것은 what is better. なお

더욱 more; more and more; still more/~ 중대한 것은 what is more important/~ 적어지다 grow less and less/~ 공부하다 work harder. かえって

더욱더욱 more and more; increasingly.

더운무대 (난류) a warm current.

더운점심 a hot lunch.

더위하다 be sensitive to the heat; complain of the heat. あつくかんじる

더위 the heat; hot weather/~를 먹다 be affected by the heat; suffer from hot weather/~타다 be sensitive to the heat; feel the heat あつさ

더위들다 affected by the heat.

더위먹다 be affected by the heat; suffer from hot weather. あつさにおかされる

더위잡다 clutch (a thing); catch; grasp at. すがる

떠죽거리다 ①(세체하고) boast; talk big ②(거짓 사양) make an outward show of declining. てしゃばる

떠지껄하다 be noisy; vociferous; boisterous; clamorous.

더지머리 a daring fellow; a busybody; a meddlesome person. せわやき

더펄개 a shaggy dog. むくげのいぬ

더펄거리다 ①(머리 따위가) bounce[fly] up and down ②(사람이) act[behave] helter-skelter; never sit down long enough to get anything done/더펄더펄 bouncing up and down.

더펄머리 hair flowing in the wind.

더하다¹ (늘이다) increase; add to (보태다) add up.; sum up/4에 5를 ~ add five to four/3에 2를 더하면 5이다 Three and two make[are] five/5에 6을 더해라 Add six to five. くわえる

더하다² (비교해서) (be) more/크기가 ~ be bigger. よりおおい

더할 나위 없다 (완전) (be) perfect (나은 것이 없다) unsurpassed (최상) the best, the finest.

떡 a shelf for drying grain.

떡¹ rice-cake. もち

떡² ①(버티는 꼴) firmly ②(벌리는 꼴) wide open. ぱっと

덕(德) (높은 덕) virtue; goodness; a merit (덕택) indebtedness; favour/~이 높은 사람 a man of virtue/…의 ~으로 by virtue[dint] of…; thanks to…. とく

떡가래 a piece of rice cake.

떡가루 rice-flour. もちのこな

**떡갈나무** 《식》 an overcup oak; *Quercus dentata* (학명).  かしわ
**떡고물** covering or coating for rice cake.  もちのつけこな
**덕교**(德敎) moral[ethical] teachings.
**덕기**(德器) virtue; moral character; goodness.  とっこうときりょう
**뙤다** become dirty; be soiled; be stained.  あかじみる
**덕담**(德談) well-wishing remarks.
**덕대**(德大) a miner who rents part of mine to work.
**덕량**(德量) broad-mindedness; greatness of mind.
**덕망**(德望) moral influence／～이 있다 have a moral influence (*over*).  とくぼう
**떡메** a mallet used to pound rice for rice cakes.  もちつきのきね
**떡무거리** rough rice flour sieved out as unsuitable for making rice cakes.
**떡방아** a mill [for flouring rice] 《일》milling of rice.
**떡벌어지다** ①(버지다) be wide open ②《소문이》the rumour get abroad; be in the everybody's mouth ③《잔치가》[a banquet] be given[held, thrown].
**떡볶이** a broiled dish of sliced rice cake, meat, eggs, seasoning etc.
**덕분**(德分) indebtedness.  おかげ
**떡쌀** rice for making rice cake.  もちごめ
**덕석** a straw-mat for covering the back of an ox [to protect it from cold].
**덕석밤** a big chestnut.  おおきなくり
**덕성**(德生) moral character; moral nature／～스러운 gentle; graceful／～을 함양하다 cultivate moral character.  とくせい
**떡심** ①(근육) strong and tough muscles ②《사람》an obstinate person.  きんにく
**덕업**(德業) virtuous deeds; a charitable undertaking; philanthropic work.
**덕육**(德育) moral training[education]; character-building.  とくいく
**덕의**(德義) morality; probity／～를 존중하다 have a high sense of honor.  とくぎ
**떡잎** a seed leaf; a bud; a sprout; a cotyledon; young leaves／될 성싶은 나무는 ～부터 알아 본다《속담》Genius will assert itself at an early age.
**덕적덕적** thickly covered.  こてこて
**덕정**(德政) benevolent[benign] government[rule].  とくせい
**덕조**(德操) virtue; chastity; morality.
**덕지덕지** thick (with *dirt*)／때가 ～ 끼다 be covered thick[encrusted] with dirt.  あかだらけのさま
**떡충이** a person who is crazy about rice cakes.  もちすきのひと
**덕택**(德澤)(=은혜) indebtedness; favour; grace; boon 《조력》help; aid; assistance 《후원》support; backing／노력한 ～으로 through hard work.  おかげ
**떡팥** boiled redbeans to be used in stuffing rice cake.
**덕행**(德行) virtuous[moral] conduct; virtue; well-doing; goodness.  とっこう
**덕화**(德化) moral influence[reform]; virtuous government.  とっか
**던적스럽다** 《비열》(be) mean; base; sordid; despicable 《추잡》(be) indecent; obscene; filthy.  けちだ
**던지다** ①(내던지다) throw; hurl; fling; cast／공을 ～ throw[pitch] a ball ②《투표하다》vote; ballot.／깨끗한 한 표를 ～ cast an honest[a clean] vote (*for*).  なげる
**던지럽다** (be) mean.  ひれつだ
**던테** ①a scab ②a layer of ice ③a door.
**덜** less; incompletely; little／～ 마른 half dried／～ 익은 underdone; half-cooked／～된 원고 an unfinished manuscript／～ 취한 half-drunk.  よりすくない
**멀거덕거리다, 떨꺼덕거리다** rattle; clatter.  かたかたなる
**멀거덩거리다** clatter; rattle.  がたがたなる
**떨거지** one's relatives.
**멀걱, 떨걱** rattling; clattering.  かたかた
**떨기** a cluster; a bunch; a plant／한 ～ 장미꽃 a rose.  ひとかたまり
**덜다** ①(절약하다) save; cut down; clip; slash 《감하다》lighten; mitigate; allay; diminish; reduce ②(빼다) subtract; deduct; take off; remove.  へらす
**떨다**[1] ①(빼다) clear away 《먼지를》dust 《흔들어》shake 《솔로》brush off ②《곡식을》thrash ③《최다》clear off; empty (*one's purse*) ④《부리다》show; display／애교를 ～ be all smiles; court favour.  とりのける
**떨다**[2] 《추위에》shake; tremble (for *fear*); shiver (with *cold*); quiver; quake; shudder (with *terror*).  ふるえる
**떨떠름하다** (be) somewhat puckery[astringent].  きがすすまない
**떨떨**[1] (떠는 모양) tremblingly; shiveringly.  ぶるぶる
**떨떨**[2], **떨떨** 《구르는 소리》rattling; rolling.  きいきい
**덜되다** ①(미완성) (be) incomplete; unfinished／덜된 원고 an unfinished manuscript ②(사람됨이)(be) silly; stupid; half witted／저 사람은 좀 덜됐다 He is wanting.  まぬけだ
**떨드리다** act haughty; give *one*self airs; hold *one's* head high; stand upon *one's* dignity.  もったいぶる
**떨렁거리다, 떨렁거리다** ①《소리가》tinkle; jingle; clink ②《행동이》be restless; conduct[behave] *one*self flippantly; act frivolously.  りんりんとなる
**떨렁이** a frivolous person; a flippant person.  けいはくしゃ
**떨렁이다** be restless.  けいそつにふるまう
**떨렁하다** 《소리가》jingle 《가슴이》feel a shock.  りんりんとなる
**떨름하다** (be) rather short.
**떨리다** ①(떨어지다) be subtracted; deducted; taken off[away, from] ②《경감·완화하다》be reduced; become less; les-

sen; decrease; become lower; be mitigated; be alleviated; be eased／걱정이 ~ one's anxiety is eased. へらされる

**떨리다¹** ①(떨어지다) be shaken off; be thrown off ②(쫓겨나다) be fired 《실직당하다》 be cashiered. おちる

**떨리다²** (몸이) shake; tremble; shiver; quiver; quake (이가) chatter 《무서워》 shudder 《진동》 vibrate／떨리는 목소리 a trembling[tremulous] voice. ふるえる

**떨미** the scruff[nape] of the neck ⇨뒷덜미.

**떨미잡이** ~하다 take[seize] (a person) by the scruff of the neck; catch (a person) around the neck. けいきんをつかむこと

**떨밉지 않다** be not so ugly[unsightly]; be rather fond of. そうみにくない

**떨어뜨리다** ①(낙하) drop; let fall; throw down ②(놓치다) miss ③(잃다) lose; drop ④(함락) take; capture; reduce; carry ⑤(지위를) debase; abase; degrade ⑥(실추) depreciate; detract (from one's merit); take from (the value) ⑦(낮추다); lessen; decrease ⑧(품질을) make worse; deteriorate ⑨(남기다) leave behind ⑩(시험에서) fail (a student) Ⅱ(경매에서) knock down (an article). おとしてしまう

**떨어먹다** squander; go[run] through (one's fortune); spend all (one's money); drain (the resources). なくす

**떨어지다** ⇨변항 참조(page 1394¹). おちる

**떨어치다** drop; let fall. なげおとす

**떨이** unsold goods; remnants. うれのこり

**떨치다** ①(이름·힘을) make well known in the world; make one's influence felt／이름을 ~ win fame ②(혼들어) shake off; throw [off]. ふりおとす

**떨커덕** ~거리다 rattle; clatter; make a rattling sound／떨커덕덜커덕 clicking; rattling; clatterling. がちゃり

**떨커덩** with a bang; with a crash; rattling; clattering／~거리다 keep banging[crashing, rattling, clattering]; with crashes. かたんかたん

**떨컥** ①(의외로 빨리) suddenly; unexpectedly／~ 죽어 버리다 die suddenly; pop; drop dead ②(소리) plump; thump with a thud[bump]／~ 떨어지다 fall plump [heavily]. どきん

**떨컹** with a bang ⇨덜커덕.

**떨떡이다** (be) plentiful; rich 《몸집이》 ample; plump; portly; corpulent 《여자의》 buxom. たっぷりた

**떨하다** ①(자동사) lessen; diminish; decrease ②(타동사) lessen; diminish; decrease ③(비교하여) (be) less.

**떫다** (be) puckery; astringent／떫은 감 a puckery persimmon. しぶい

**덤** an extra; anything thrown in; an addition 《추가·부가》 a throw-in 《상금·경품 따위》 a premium. わりまし

**덤덤하다** (be) speechless; remain silent silent; closemouthed; keep dumb[mum]; hold one's tongue. くちのきけない

**덤받이** a child of one's wife by a previous marriage. つれこ

**덤벙** 《물속에》 splashing; with a plop／~하다 make a splash[splatter]. どぶん

**덤벙거리다** ①(경솔하게) act frivolously／덤벙거리며 일을 함부로 하다 do one's work carelessly ②(물속에서) splash; splatter; bespatter／덤벙거리면서 걷다 go splashing (through the mud). うわつく

**덤부렁듬쑥** thick; dense／~하다 overgrown; luxuriant. もじゃもじゃ

**덤불** a thicket; a bush; a scrub; a jungle. やぶ

**덤비다** ①(달려들다) fall[turn] upon (one); fly at／맹호같이 ~ spring at (one) with tiger-like ferocity ②(서둘다) be hasty; make undue haste／덤비지 말라 Don't be in a hurry., Take your time about it.

**덤비어들다** ①(습격·저항하다) fall upon[turn upon, go at] (a person) ②(일을 시작하다) set to[about] work; get started (on a work). とびかかる

**덤터기** (짓) imputation 《허물》 a blame[a trouble] laid upon one.

**덥다** (be) hot; warm; heated／더운 날씨 hot weather／몸이 ~ have a fever[temperature]／물이 더웠다 The water is hot. あつい

**덥석** quickly; hastily; greedily; suddenly (단단히) tightly. ぐわっと

**덥적거리다** interfere[meddle] in. おせっかいする

**덥적이다** interfere in; meddle in; step in; put in a word. せかつく

**덧** a short time[while]; a spell／~없는 세월 flying[quick-passing] time. ま

**덧가지** a double branch.

**덧거름** fertilizer given to growing plants.

**덧거칠다** (be) going wrong; unfavourable. わるくなっていく

**덧나다** ①(병이) take a bad turn 《곪다》 form pus; fester ②(성나다) be offended. さらにわるくなる

**덧내다** ①(병을) make worse; cause to take a bad turn 《상처를》 fester; ulcerate ② ⇨덧드리다. あっかさせる

**덧니** a double tooth; a side tooth／~박이 a person with a double tooth. やえば

**떳떳하다** (be) just; fair; right; proper／떳떳이 justly; fairly／떳떳이 행동하다 act fair and square. せいとうだ

**덧두리** the cash supplement (in a barter deal); the difference in value between two articles being exchanged. よぶんのおかね

**덧들다** 《잠이》 be wakeful; be hard to get to sleep again. ねそこなう

**덧들이다** hurt one's feeling; offend; provoke (one) to anger; put (a person) out of temper. ひとのかんじょうをそこなう

**덧문**(-門) an outer[a double] door[window]. あまど

**덧물** (괸물) water which gathers above the ice. うわみず
**덧붙다** attach[stick] on in addition. つけくわえる
**덧붙이다** add (a thing) to; append/덧붙여 말하다 add; make an additional remark/담에 널판자를 ~ fix planks of wood on a wall. ついかする
**덧셈** addition/~하다 add [up figures].
**덧신** overshoes; rubber-shoes. うわぐつ
**덧신다** put on[wear] (a thing) over one's shoes. うわぐつをはく
**덧없다** (be) transient; vain; uncertain; momentary/덧없이 transiently; evanescently/덧없는 인생 a transient[an ephemeral] life. むじょうだ
**덧없이** fleetingly; transiently; ephemerally; evanescently/세월이 ~ 지나간다 Time flies fleetingly. はかない
**덧입다** put on[wear] (a coat) over a garment.
**덧저고리** an extra coat worn over one's regular coat. うわぎのうえにきるきもの
**덩굴** a vine 《권수(卷鬚)》 a tendril/~이 퍼지다 a vine creeps[climbs, trails]. /~이 뻗다 a vine creeps[climbs]. つる
**덩굴손** 〖식〗 a tendril; a cirrus.
**덩굴지다** grow creepers; creep; put on vines. つるばる
**덩그렇다** (be) solitary; lonely; stately /언덕 위에 집 한 채가 덩그렇게 서 있다 A lonely[solitary] house towers high over the hill.
**덩달다** follow suit; echo (another's view)/덩달아 웃다 laugh following suit. ひとのやりかたにならう
**덩떵거리다** live in great splendour; live like a prince/떵떵거리며 살다 be quite well off. ごうしゃにくらす
**덩두렷이** remarkably; conspicuously; strikingly; obviously. めだつ
**덩물하다** (be) foolish; stupid; nitwit. ぼかんとしている
**덩드럭거리다** give oneself airs; put on airs[frills]; be highbrowed; be high-hatted《미·속》. もったいぶる
**덩실거리다** dance merrily[cheerfully]/덩실덩실 merrily; gaily.
**덩신거리다** loll about lazily; wallow.
**덩어리** a lump; a mass (흙의) a clod/비누 ~ a cake of soap/흙 ~ a clod of earth. かたまり
**덩어리지다** lump; mass; form a mass; conglomerate/얼음이 ~ ice forms into a mass. かたまりになる
**덩이** a lump ⇨덩어리. かたまり
**덩저리** a piece of arger lump[mass, clod].
**덩지** bulk; size; volume/~가 크다 be bulky; be big. すんぼ
**덫** a snare; a trap; a hook/~으로 잡다 entrap; snare; ensnare; catch in a trap. わな
**덮개** ①(이불 따위) bedding; bedclothes; a quilt; a comfort[er]《미》 ②(뚜껑) a lid.
**덮다** (씌우다) cover; veil; overspread (은폐하다) hide; conceal; cover up; bury (닫다) shut; close/책을 ~ close[shut] a book. おおう
**덮어놓고** without any reason[cause]; causelessly/개인의 소원은 국가를 위하여 ~ 희생되어 왔었다 The wish of the individual has been sacrificed unquestioningly to the state. いやおうなしに
**덮어두다** ignore; disregard; pass (a matter) over unnoticed (비밀로) keep (a matter) scret[dark]/이건 그냥 덮어둘 수 없다 We should not let this pass without protest. つつみかくす
**덮어쓰다** take (another's guilt) on oneself.
**덮어씌우다** ①(가림) cover (a thing with…) put (a thing) over[on]; plate (a thing with gold) ②(죄를) charge (a person with a blame); pin (a fault on a person).
**덮이다** be covered; be veiled; be hidden; be concealed/안개에 ~ be enveloped in mist. おおわれる
**덮치기** a large fowling net; a bird net

## 떨 어 지 다

①(낙하·추락) fall; drop; have[get, take] a fall; come[go] down; be down /땅에 ~ fall to the ground/나무에서 ~ fall[drop] from a tree 《열매 따위가》 fall off a tree/배에서 ~ fall overboard/쿵하고 ~ fall with a thud/빗방울이 ~ raindrops start falling/비행기가 ~ an airplane is down; an airplane crashes/벼랑에서 ~ fall over a precipice/말에서 ~ fall from[off] a horse/계단에서 ~ fall down the stairs /접시가 상에서 떨어져 깨어졌다 The dish fell off the table and was broken.

②(시세 하락) become lower; fall; drop; go down; sag; decline; depreciate/물가가 ~ prices drop[go down]; prices are on the decline/시세가 멀어져 가고 있다 The market priceis on the decline[goes on declining]./견직물의 가격이 떨어졌다 Silk goods have sunken in price./100원이 ~ fall off by 100 won/시세가 1,000원대 이하로 ~ prices break[drop below] the level of 1,000 won.

③(흘러 빠지다) slip; drop/연필이 손에서 ~ a pencil fall out of[drop from] one's hand/쥐고 있던 책이 ~ a book falls out of one's hand/지갑이 주머니에서 ~ a pocketbook slips out of one's pocket.

④(가치 따위가) fall in value[merit]; depreciate; be debased; be impaired; be detracted/물건의 가치가 ~ the value of a thing is lowered[lessened]/사람의 품격이 ~ debase[degrade] oneself; lose one's dignity/신용이 ~ lose public confidence/인기가 ~ lose popularity [public favo'ujr]; decline in public favor; fall into disfavor; one's popularity wanes/위신이 ~ lose one's prestige/그의 명성은 떨어져 가고 있다 His reputation is on the wane.

⑤(거리가) be distant from[away from off] (a place); 《간격이》 keep off/좀 멀어져서 at a short distance (from)/멀리 떨어져서 at a long distance; a long way off; far away (from)/가족과 멀어져서 살다 live separated from one's family/경찰서는 여기서 5킬로나 떨어져 있다 The police station is five kilometers away[distant] from here. 그 집은 딴 집들과 떨어져 있다 The house stood apart from others. 그 마을은 큰 길에서 떨어져 있다 The village is off the highway. 2미터씩 떨어져 서라 Line up at intervals of two meters. 좀 떨어져서 보면 더 좋게 보인다 It looks better at a distance. /길에서 조금 떨어진 곳에는 큰 소나무가 있다 There stands a big pine tree a little way off the road.

⑥(뒤떨어지다) fall[drop] behind; be outstripped; be outrun; lag behind; be backward (in); be behindhand/다른 학생보다 영어가 ~ be behind the other students in English/경주에서 다른 선수보다 ~ fall behind another runner in a race; be outrun by another runner in a race/앓아서 공부가 ~ be behind in one's studies because of an illness /2년이나 먼저 배웠으나 지금은 그에게 떨어졌다 I began to learn it two years earlier, but have already been outstripped by him. /우리 나라는 여러 가지 면에서 서양보다 떨어졌다 Our country is lagging behind the West in many respects.

⑦(위에 남다) be left over[behind]/그 빚을 갚고도 돈이 좀 ~ There is a comfortable little sum left over after paying the debt. /저 어린아이는 집에 혼자 떨어져 있다 The child is left behind alone in the house.

⑧(해가) set; sink; go down/해가 서산에 ~ The sun goes down behind the western mountains./해가 지평선에 ~ The sun sinks[dips] below the horizon.

⑨(붙은 것이) come off; fall apart; be broken off; be removed/잎이 ~ leaves are shed/겨울이 되면 대부분의 나무는 잎이 떨어진다 In winter most trees are stripped of their leaves.

⑩(분리) separate; be detached; come off; fall apart; become disjoined/떨어질 수 없는 inseparable/떨어지기 쉬운 separable; severable/책상 다리가 ~ a leg of the table comes off[is disjoined]/붙어서 떨어지지 않다 stick[adhere, cling] to; stick like a bur/멀리 떨어져서 살다 live far apart/여러 해 동안 떨어져 살다 have been separated (from a person) for years/두 사람은 서로 떨어질 수 없는 사이다 They are inseparable from each other. /그 아이는 항상 어머니의 곁을 떨어지지 않는다 The child is always hanging on her mother's sleeve[is always at her mother's side]. /여자가 사내한테서 떨어지다 A woman is separated from her man.

⑪(온도·열 따위가) fall; drop; go down; descend/온도가 ~ the temperature [mercury] falls[drops, goes down] (to … degrees)/열이 ~ one's fever subsides [goes down, abates, falls].

⑫(감퇴) go down; decrease; diminish; fall (in one's estimation)/손님이 ~ The customers fall off./저 가게는 요즘 손님이 떨어졌다 The shop has lost its custom.

⑬(실패) fail; be defeated[unsuccessful]; lose/시험에 ~ fail[flunk] (in) an examination/선거에 ~ be defeated in [lose] an election/겨우 3표 차로 떨어졌다 He was shy of winning the election by only three votes./당 간부는 모두 선거에 떨어졌다 All the officers of the party failed to get elected.

⑭(해지다) be worn out; become threadbare/구두가 ~ one's shoes are worn out/옷이 ~ one's clothes are worn out.

⑮(목숨이) breathe one's last [breath]; die; expire/그는 막 숨이 떨어지려는 순간이었다 He lay at the point of death.

⑯(고립하다) isolate/혼자서 떨어져 살다 live[lead] an isolated life.

⑰(넘어가다) fall into; be carried away; be won/책략에 ~ play into a person's hand; fall into a person's trap [snare]/남의 수중에 ~ fall into another's hands/여자가 남자 유혹에 ~ a woman is seduced/그 그림은 경매에서 100만 원에 내 손에 떨어졌다 The picture was knocked down to me at an auction for 1,000,000 won.

⑱(없어지다) be exhausted; run out; be out; be out of stock/쌀이 ~ rice is exhausted; run out of rice/돈이 ~ run out of money; have no more money /기름이 ~ run out of oil; the oil is all gone[exhausted, used up]/식량이 ~ The provisions have run out., We have run out of provisions.

⑲(병·습관 따위가) be shaken off; be

got rid of/감기가 떨어지지 않는다 I can't shake off my cold./한 번 붙은 습관은 잘 떨어지지 않는다 A habit once made is not easily shaken off. ⑳(부합·나누어짐) tally with; (a number) divide evenly; be evenly divisible/10은 2로 나누어진다 Ten is evenly divided by two./책의 수가 생각했던 것과 맞아 떨어진다 The number of the books tallies with what I had expected. ㉑(유산) abort; miscarry/애가 ~ 하 ve an abortion[a miscarriage]. ㉒(일의 끝 따위) get finished; be completed/내일이면 일이 떨어진다 The work will be finished tomorrow.

with double handles.  カスミあみ
덮치다 ①(겹쳐 누르다.) lie one upon another; overlap one another; force down/폭풍우가 그 배를 덮쳤다 A storm overtook the ship. ②(한꺼번에) rush in/엎친 데 덮친다 Misfortune never comes singly.  おしつける
데 a place; a spot; a point 《경우》an occasion; a case/강한 ~ a strong; one's strength.  ばしょ
떼¹ 《무리》a group; a crowd 《사람》a throng 《마소》a herd 《양·새》a flock 《어류》a shoal 《벌레》a swarm/~지어 사는 동물 a gregarious animal.  むれ
떼² 《잔디》sod; turf/~를 입히다 sod/~를 뜨다 cut out sod.  しばふ
떼³ 《뗏목》a raft.  いかだ
떼⁴ 《고집》an impossible[unreasonable] 《핑계》quibbling 《궤변》sophistry; casuistry/~보 a quibbler/아버지를 ~를 써서 시계를 샀다 I teased father into buying me a watch.  いじっぱり
떼거리 impossible demand.  むれのこ
데걱거리다, 떼걱거리다 clatter; rattle/자물쇠를 데걱데걱[떼걱떼걱] 잠그다 lock the doors with rattling[clicking] sound/데걱데걱 떼걱떼걱 rattling.  かたかた
떼걸다 break off (relations with a person); cut connections.  わかれる
데구루루, 떼구루루 rolling; rumbling/~ 구르다 roll over and over.  ころごろ
데꾼하다, 떼꾼하다 (be) hollow (from exhaustion)/눈이 ~ one's eyes have sunken.  つかれきってめがくぼんでいる
데굴데굴, 떼굴떼굴 rolling[rumbling] continuously/~ 구르다 roll over and over.  ころごろ
데다 ①(화상을 입다) be[get] burnt; suffer a burn; scald oneself/손을 ~ get burnt in the hand; burn one's hand (on the stove) ②(진저리나다) have had enough of (a thing) 빚에는 아주 데었다 I know to my cost what it is to be in debt.  やけどする

떼다¹ ①(붙은 것을) take away; remove (a sign)/미닫이를 ~ take out off a paper sliding-door ②(갈라놓다) draw[pull, set] (a person, things) apart(잡아당겨서) ③(간격을) leave (space)/한 자씩 떼어서 at intervals of one foot ④《거절하다》refuse; reject; decline ⑤(절연) cut[sever] connections with (one); break off] with (one) ⑥(봉한 것을) break[open] (the seal); cut (a letter) open ⑦(수표 따위를) draw a bill (for a sum on one)/수표를 ~ issue a check ⑧(관직 따위를) deprive[strip] (a person) of (his official rank) ⑨(끊다) give up; stop/술을 ~ give up drinking ⑩(병을) get rid of; cure.  はなす
떼다² (안 갚다) do not pay back; fail to return《제것으로 하다》bilk.  かわさない
떼도둑 a gang of robbers; a pack of thieves.  ひとむらのどろぼう
떼도망(-逃亡) fleeing in a band; collective abscondence/~하다 flee in a band.  ひとむらとなってにげること
데되다 lack something; be short of perfection; leave something to be desired; be some what defective.  かけている
데려가다 take (along) with (one); take away; take (a person) home/아이를 학교에 데려갔다 He took a child to the school (with him).  つれていく
데려오다 bring (a person) along/왜 그를 데려오지 않았소 Why haven't you brought him along?  つれてくる
데리다 take[bring] with; be accompanied[be attended] by/그를 데리고 산 지가 10여 년이 되었다 We have been married more than ten years.  つれる
데릴사위 a husband who enters his wife's family/데릴사윗감 a model youth.  いりむこ
데림추 followers; an appendant; hangers on.  かげのようなもの
데면데면하다 (be) careless; thoughtless; heedless; negligent.  うかつぐ
데밀다 push[force] in.  おしこむ
떼밀다 push; thrust; shove; force out of the way/떼밀지 마라 Don't push me so much!  おしつける
떼버리다 ①(뜯다) take away ②(거절하다) refuse.  とってすてる
데삶기다 be half-done[-boiled]; be parboiled.  はんじゅくにされる
데삶다 parboil; boil (an egg) soft[lightly]/데삶은 underdone/달걀을 ~ boil eggs soft.  はんじゅくにする
떼새 ①《조》a plover ②(새의 무리) a flock of birds.  ひとむらのとり
데생기다 be immature; be raw.
데설궂다 (be) rough; rude; unrefined; loose.  きまきれ
데설데설하다 (be) rude[unrefined] in nature; loose.  きらくだ
데알다 know superficially.  なまはんかだ
떼어놓다 ①(경주에서) run ahead (of others); draw away (from a rival) ②(붙었던 것을) draw[pull, set] (person,

**떼어먹다** *things*) apart／두 애인 사이를 ～ separate the pair of lovers. おいこす

**떼어먹다** 《가로채다》 appropriate; embezzle 《안 갚다》 bilk; fail to pay[return]. ふみたおす

**데억지다** 《너무 크다》 be too big[large] 《너무 많다》 be in excess; be superabundant. おおきすぎる

**데우다** warm; heat [up]《술을》 mull／데 위먹다 eat hot／국을 데우다 heat up the cold soup. あたためる

**데익다** be half-cooked; half-done; rare. はんじゅくだ

**데치다** scald; parboil／야채를 ～ parboil vegetables [in hot water].

**떼치다** ①《달라붙는 것을》 shake *oneself* loose[free] from (*the grasp*); tear *oneself* away ②《거절하다》 refuse[brush aside] (*a request*).

**데퉁스럽다** (be) clumsy; awkward. まぬけだ

**떽데구루루** rolling ⇨데구루루. ごろごろ

**덴가슴** a bitter memory[experience]; a scalded cat fearing even cold water.

**덴겁하다** be flurried[disconcerted]; be confused. あわてる

**덴둥이** 《부푼》 a blister 《불에》 a burn 《물에》 a scald. やけどした所

**뗏목(一木)** a raft／～군 a raftsman／～ 을 지어서 목재를 운반하다 carry timbers on a float. いかだのき

**뗏장** a turf; a patch of grass; a piece of sod. しばふのひときれ

**뗑그렁거리다, 뗑그렁거리다** tinkle; jingle; clang／풍경이 바람에 뗑그렁[뗑그렁]거리 다 A hanging bell is tinkling in the wind. じゃんじゃんなる

**뗑뗑, 뗑뗑** clang-clang; ding-dong; jingle-jangle. がらんがらん

**도** ①《및》 and; as well as; both … and; too 《역시》 also／너도 그를 만났지만 나 ～ 만났다 You saw him, and so did I. ②《…이라 할지라도, 까지도》 even; although／하루～ even a single day／지금 ～ even now ③《어느 것도》 whether … or [not]; either … or／A～ B～ 아니다 not A either B; neither A nor B／언제라고 ～ 말할 수 없다 can not say when ④《어 림》 적어도 ～ at least／늦어도 ～ at the latest [the furthest] ⑤《강조》 부모를 부모로～ 여기지 않다 slight *one's* parents set parental authority at naught. —も

**또** ①《다시》 again; once more; another time; for the second time 《반복해서》 repeatedly 《계속해서》 in succession／승 리 ～ 승리 victory after victory／언제 든지 《나중에》 some other time; in another time／～ 일을 시작하다 begin *one's* work again ②《그 위에》 and; moreover; besides; further [more]; what is more ③《한편》 on the other hand; in turn; while／나는 ～ 누구라구 Well, it's you, I thought it was somebody else.

**도(道)¹** 《행정 구획》 a district; a province ／～ 행정 provincial administration／～ 지사 a provincial governor／～령(令) a provincial ordinance[order]. とう

**도(道)²** ①《도로》 a road ②《기예(技藝)》 an art; a cult／서～(書一) calligraphy; the art of handwriting ③《도리》 teachings 《교리》 doctrines 《진리》 truth／～를 구하 다 seek after truth. みち

**도(度)** ①《온도·각도》 a degree／오늘 아 침은 몇 ～입니까 What is the temperature of this morning? ②《정도》 moderation; degree; extent／～를 지나치사 go too far; carry to excess; be intemperate／무슨 일이고 ～를 넘으면 해가 된다 If you go beyond bounds in anything, it will do you harm. ③《척도》 measure; scale 《규준》 criterion. おんど

**도(都)** 《수도》 a metropolis; a capital 《도 시》 a city. みやこ

**도(途)** the way／도미(渡美)의 ～에 오르다 leave for America／도영(渡英)의 ～에 있 다 be on *one's* way to England. みち

**도(徒)** a party; a set; a clique. と

**도가(都家)** a club house of the same traders; a meeting house of allied traders.

**도가니** a meltingpot; a crucible／회장 (會場)은 흥분의 ～가 되었다 The assemblage went wild with excitement.／ 전쟁(政爭)의 ～ the whirlpool of political strife.

**도가자류(道家者流)** a Taoist; members of the Taoist school. どうかしゃりゅう

**도각(倒閣)** unseating[overthrowing] the Cabinet／～하다 overthrow[unseat] the Cabinet／～ 운동을 일으키다 start a movement to unseat[throw out] the Cabinet. とうかく

**도강(渡江)** crossing of a river／～하다 cross[go across] a river／～ 훈련 a river-crossing exercise.

**또깡또깡** clearly; distinctly; precisely ／～하다 (be) clear; distinct; precise. めいめい

**도개교(跳開橋)** a bascule bridge.

**도개그릇** earthenware; chinaware

**도깨비** a spectre; a devil; a ghost. おに

**도깨비바늘** 《식》 a Spanish needles; *Bidens bipinnata* (학명).

**도깨비부채** 《식》 a Rodger's bronzeleaf; *Rodgersia Podophylla*(학명).

**도깨비불** a will-o'-the-wisp; an elf-fire; a jack-o'-lantern. おにび

**도거리** the gross; bulk; mass／～로 togather; in a lump[the gross, bulk]／～값 the gross price／～로 사다 buy by bulk.

**도계(道界)** the boundary[the border] of a province; the province limits.

**도고(都庫)** selling (*goods*) in bulk on *one's* account／～하다 sell (*goods*) in bulk on *one's* account.

**도꼬마리** 《식》 a cocklebur; *Xanthium strumarium*(학명). みみなぐさ

**도공(刀工)** a swordsmith. とうこう

**도공(陶工)** a ceramist; a potter; a porcelain-maker.

**도관(導管)** ①《물 따위의》a conduit; a pipe ②《식물의》a vessel. どうかん

**도괴(倒壞)** collapse; destruction/~하다 fall down; crumble/가옥의 ~ 때문에 부상하다 be injured in the collapse of a house. とうかい

**도교(道敎)** Taoism/~의 신자 a Taoist. どうきょう

**도구(道具)** ①《공구》a tool; an implement/~ 상자 a tool box[chest] ②《부엌 도구》a utensil ③《용구 일체》an outfit ④《무대용》sets(대도구); property(소도구) ⑤《방편》a means; a stepping-stone ⑥《앞잡이》a tool; a cat's paw; a dummy. どうぐ

**도구(渡口)** a pass; a ford; a ferry[point]. わたしば

**도구(渡歐)** a visit to Europe/~하다 visit Europe/~의 도상에 있다 be on one's way to Europe. ヨーロッパにいくこと

**도국(島國)** an island country[kingdom, empire]/~적 insular/~근성 insularism. しまぐに

**도규(刀圭)** medicine/~가(家) a medical man; a physician/~술(術) the art of medicine[healing]/~계(界) the medical profession[world]. とうけい

**도금(鍍金)** gilding; plating 《물품》plated ware/~하다 plate; gild/전기 ~ electric gilding/~공 a plater; a depositor/~ 금시계 a goldplated watch. ときん

**도급(都給)** 《청부》undertaking; a contract (for *work*)/~맡다 contract for; undertake; take on/~주다 give[award] (*one*) a contract (*for*); contract (*a work*). うけおい

**도끼** an ax《미》;《손도끼》a hatchet/큰 ~ a broad-ax; a big hatchet/얼음 깨는 ~ an ice ax. おの

**도기(陶器)** 1.《오지그릇》pottery; porcelain; ceramic ware/~ 제조인 a potter/~ 제조소 a pottery ②《토기(土器)》china ware; crockery; earthenware/~상 a chinashop; a crockery-dealer/~제의 china; ceramic. とうき

**도끼눈** glaring eyes/~을 한 사람 an eagle-eyed person/~을 하고 보다 look daggers at; look menacingly at; glare fiercely at; scowl at.

**도난(盜難)** a burglary; robbery; theft/~품 stolen goods/~ 경보기 a burglar alarm/~ 당하다 be robbed; be burglarized《속》. とうなん

**도내(道內)** the inside of a province; throughout the province/~의 학교 the schools in the province.

**도닉(逃匿)** hiding; concealment/~하다 take[seek] refuge (*in*); conceal *oneself*; hide. にげてかくれること

**도닐다** go[walk] round (*a yard*); ramble about; walk up and down[to and from]/호숫가를 ~ ramble along the shores of a lake. しゅういをくるくるまわる

**또다시** 《한 번 더》again; once more; over [once] again 《재차》for the second time 《새로》afresh/~ 일어나다 recur; renew/~ 시작하다 resume; return to/~ 하다 repeat; do over again. また

**또닥거리다** tap; rap; beat; knock; pat/창문을 ~ tap against the window/귀여워서 가볍게 ~ give it an affectionate little pat/비가 지붕을 또닥거리며 운다 The rain is pattering on the roof. かちりかちりいう

**도달(到達)** arrival/~하다 arrive in[at, on]; reach; come to/~점 the place of destination/그 자경에 ~하다 arrive on the spot/같은 결론에 ~하다 come to [reach] the same conclusion. とうたつ

**도당(徒黨)** a faction; a band; a clique; a combination/~을 꾸미다 band together; form a clique[a faction]; conspire. ととう

**도대체(都大體)** on earth; in the world; under the sun/~ 무슨 의미냐 What on earth do you mean?/~ 어떻게 하란 말이냐 What on earth do you expect me to do? いったいぜんたい

**도덕(道德)** morality; virtue; morals/사회[산업] ~ social[commercial] morality/~상의 moral/~상 morally; from the moral point of view/~심 moral sense[sentiment]/~률 moral law/~의 문제 a moral question/~ 강화 a moral discourse/~관념 a moral sense/~가 a man of virtue/~적 moralistic; ethical/~적 교양 moral literacy/~적 감화 moral influence/~적 감정을 함양하다 moralize. どうとく

**도도록하다** (be) swollen; baggy; bulging; convex/도도록도도록 baggily; convexly; full of knobs/도도록한 지갑 a fat purse. もりあがる

**도도하다** 《거만하다》(be) triumphant; exultant/도도히 triumphantly; in triumph; exultantly; proudly; with elation/도도한 얼굴 a triumphant look/도도한 태도 a lofty air. ごうまんだ

**도도하다(陶陶─)** (be) peaceful; harmonious/도도히 harmoniously; in harmony [peace]; happily. ひじょうにわらくだ

**도도하다(滔滔─)** ①《물이》(be) rushing; rapid; swift/도도히 with a rush; rapidly; swiftly/도도히 흐르다 flow with a rush; run[flow] in a large stream [in a broad expanse] ②《말이》(be) eloquent; fluent; flowing/도도히 eloquently; fluently; effusively; flowingly/도도히 말하다 speak eloquently[fluently]; pour forth a flood of eloquence/그는 도도하게 연설했다 He rolled out his speech. とうとうとしている

**도독(荼毒)** 《심한 해독》heavy poison; enormous harm; a seriously evil[a contaminating, a baneful] influence/사회에 ~을 끼치다 poison[contaminate, corrupt] society tremendously; exert a seriously harmful influence on

**도두보다** overestimate; overrate; think too much of／그는 나를 도두보고 있는 모양이다 It seems he takes me for better than I am. かだいひょうかする

**도두보이다** look better [than actually is] 《낮게 보이다》 be overestimated[overvalued]; be seen distinctly[larger] 《두드러지게》 be seen distinctly; be vividly seen 《크게》 be seen larger; bulk largely in the eyes. じっさいよりよくみえる

**도둑** 《도둑놈》 a thief 《밤도둑》 a burglar; a robber 《강도》 a house-breaker 《좀도둑》 a pilferer 《도둑질》 theft; burglary; stealing／～맞다《사람이 주어》 have (a thing) stolen; be relieved of (one's purse) 《물건이 주어》 be stolen／～ 근성 a thievish[a sneaking] spirit／도둑이 제 발이 저리다《속담》 A guilty man apprehends danger in every sounds. ぬすみ

**도둑고양이** a stray cat. のらねこ

**도둑놈** a thief ⇨도둑.

**도둑질** theft; stealing; larceny 《좀스러운》 pilfering／～하다 commit theft; steal; rob; thieve; pilfer; filch／～ 행각 going round round against the sun／가난에서 나온 ～ theft through poverty／좀～ petty theft. せっとうすること

**도둑합례** (一合禮) a private wedding／～하다 be privately married.

**도둔** (逃遁) flight; bolt; scuttle／ ～하다 run away; fly; flee; lam.

**도뜨다** be above reproach in word and deed. めだっている

**도드라지다** stand conspicuous; be distinct[vivid, clear]; come in evidence distinctly. ろしゅつする

**도드미** a riddle.

**도라지** ①《식》 a Chinese balloon flower; a broad bell-flower; *Platycodon grandiflorum* 《학명》 ②《뿌리》 platycodon.

**도락** (道樂) 《방탕》 dissipation; debauchery 《기호》 taste; pleasure; hobby／～하다 dissipate; live fast; lead a dissipated life／～자 a libertine; a dissipated man. どうらく

**도란거리다** speak in undertones; whisper to each other; exchange whispers; murmur together 《연인이》 bill and coo; indulge in love talk／도란도란 in an undertone; in whispers. ささやく

**도랑** a ditch; a dike; a drain; a gutter／～을 치다 clear out a ditch／～을 메우다 fill in a ditch／～을 파다 dig a ditch; trench. みぞ

**도랑도랑하다, 또랑또랑하다** (be) very clear. はっきりしている

**도랑** mange. かいせんのひとつ

**도랑치마** a short skirt. みじかいスカート

**또래** (*of*) the age; (*of*) the size／모두 그 ～다 All of them are of the same age[size]. ほとんどどうねんぱい

**도래** (渡來) a visit; introduction; the influx (of *foreign goods*)／～하다 visit come over the sea; be introduced (*into*)／그리스도교의 ～ introduction of Christianity [into Korea]. とらい

**도래** (到來) arrival; advent／～하다 arrive; come; occur／호기가 ～하면 if a good opportunity presents itself; in [course of] time／나에게 기회가 ～했다 Here is my opportunity., My hour has struck. とうらい

**도래떡** round cakes. まるくてひらたいもち

**도래매듭** a double knot. にじゅうのむすびめ

**도래샘** a swirling fountain; a swirling spring. うずまくいずみ

**도래송곳** a round gimlet; a double-edged drill. らせんけいのきり

**도량** (跳梁) rampancy; domination／～하다 《이리저리 뛰어다니다》 gambol; romp 《발호》 be rampant; be dominant; prevail. ちょうりょう

**도량** (度量) ①《마음씨》 magnanimity; liberality; generosity／～이 큰 magnanimous; generous; liberal; broad-minded／큰 ～ a mind of great capacity／～이 좁은 사나이 a narrow-minded fellow ②《재능》 a talent of management; managerial ability; administrative ability. どりょう

**도량** (道場) 《종》 a seminary for the Buddhist priesthood. どうじょう

**도량형** (度量衡) weights and measures／～기 measuring instruments／～표 tables of weights and measures／～학 metrology. どりょうこう

**도려내다** cut off[out, away]; cleave／도려낸 조각《신문 등에서》 a cutting; a scrap; a clipping《미》／신문에서 도려낸 조각 news-paper／신문의 사진을 ～ clip pictures from a paper.

**도련** (刀鍊) trimming; cutting; the edge (of *paper*) even／～치다 trim; cut the edge (of *paper*) even／～칼 a paper-trimming knife. かみのきりとり

**도련님** Master; Darling 《주인 아들에게》 a young master 《시동생》 a young brother-in-law. ぼっちゃん

**또렷이** vividly ⇨뚜렷이. はっきり

**또렷하다** (be) clear ⇨뚜렷하다. めいはくだ

**도령** 《총각》 an unmarried man; a boy. みこんのだんし

**도령** (道令) 《행정 명령》 a provincial ordinance; the order of a province. どうれい

**도로** 《되짚어》 back 《먼저대로》 as ever[before, usual] 《또다시》 [over] again／～데려오다 bring back／～ 주다 give back. あらためて

**도로** (道路) a road; a street 《가로》 a way 《노정》 a route 《길거리》 a thoroughfare 《공도》 a highway／～를 보수하다 repair a road. どうろ

**도로** (徒勞) vain[sterile] effort; lost labour; an abortive scheme; waste of labour／～의 vain; futile; fruitless; lost. とろう

**도로 무익(徒勞無益)** vain effort. とろう

**도로아미타불(―阿彌陀佛)** a relapse/부주의 때문에 ~이다 From want of attention I am no better than before[than what I was]. もとのもくあみ

**도록** to; so as to; in order to[that]; so that one may …/…지 않— [so as] not to; that … may not; lest … ˙hould/나에게 …하~ 그가 말했다 It was suggested to me that I might…. するように

**도록(都錄)** (물품의) a list of articles; a roll (사람의) a list of names; a register. そうもくろく

**도롱고리** 〖식〗 a kind of millet.

**도롱뇽** ①〖동〗 a [giant] salamander ②〖동〗⇨영원(蠑蠑). ひとかげ

**도롱이** a rain cape [made of straw]; a straw raincoat. みの

**도롱태**¹ ①(수레) a simple wooden wheel ②(바퀴) a wheel. ろくろ

**도롱태**² 〖조〗①*Falco columbarius*(학명) ②(새매) an Asiatic sparrow-hawk.

**도료(塗料)** paints; pigments/~ 분무기 a paint sprayer; a spray gun/야광~ luminous paint. とりょう

**도루묵** 〖어〗 a kind of sandfish; *Arctoscopus japonicus*(학명). はたはた

**도륙(屠戮)** massacre; slaughter/~하다 massacre; slaughter; butcher. とりく

**도르다**¹ (게우다) vomit; cast up; spew; throw up; fetch up. はく

**도르다**² (분배하다) distribute; deal (*cards*); serve[hand] round; measure out (*food*) mete out (*reward*); dole out (*alms*) (배달) deliver (할당) assign; allot; apportion/신문을 ~ deliver newspapers/화투를 ~ deal cards. ぶんばいする

**도르다**³ (변통) tide over; [make] shift; shift and contrive; manage (with *what one has*); scratch along/돈을 ~ accommodate (*one*) with a loan[with …*won*]; advance (*money* to); spare (*wo-on*). へんつうする

**도르래** (장난감) pully a bamboo propeller; a whirligig made of bamboo.

**도르르, 또르르** round and round; with a twirl; coiling (구르는 모양) rolling/종이를 ~ 말다 roll paper up round and round/~ 감기다 coil[twine, wind itself] around (*tree, pole*)/실이 ~ 풀리다 thread is twirled off a reel. くるくる

**도리** 〖건〗 a beam; a crossbeam. けた

**도리(道理)** ①(조리) reason (정당) right; propriety (진리) truth (정의) justice (원리) principle/~에 맞는 reasonable; logical; consistent/~을 벗어난 unreasonable; inconsistent; illogical; absurd ②(방도) a way; a process; a procedure; a means; a plan; a measure/딴 ~가 있다 have two strings to *one's* bow; have an alternative plan ③(의리) duty; obligation/자식의 ~ filial duty/그런 짓을 하는 것은 학생의 ~가 아니다 It is not proper for a student to do such a thing. どうり

**도리깨** a flail/~아들 a swingle/~질 flailing/~질하다 thresh[thrash] with a flail; flail. からざお

**도리다** ①(베다) cut off[out]; scoop out (구멍을) hollow out; bore/강철판을 도려서 구멍을 내다 drill a steel plate ②(삭제하다) strike out; erase; cancel/도려내다. えぐる

**도리암직하다** (be) goodlooking; handsome; slim; neat and trim; smart; slick. こじんまりしている

**도리어** (반대로) instead; on the contrary (차라리) rather; more; all[only] the more/결점이 있기 때문에 ~ 당신이 좋다 I love you all the better for your faults./도리어 죄송합니다 That would place me all the more under your obligation. はんたいに

**도리질** ①(아기의) shaking the head following suit/~하다 shake the head following suit ②(거절) shaking head in denial/~하다 shake *one's* head in denial; say "No".

**도립(倒立)** standing on *one's* head [and hands] (체조) hand-standing/~하다 stand on *one's* head [and hands]/~해서 걷다 walk on *one's* hands. とうりつ

**도마** a chopping board; a kitchen block/~ 위에 오른 고기 a fish on the dressing board. まないた

**도마뱀** 〖동〗 a lizard (미국산) a blue-tail. とかげ

**도마뱀붙이** 〖동〗 a gecko (*pl.* ｰeｰs); a wall lizard.

**도막** a cut; a chop (나무의) a chip (어육의 두꺼운 도막) a fillet/생선 ~ a cut[a slice] of fish/고기 ~ a chop a meat. ひときれ

**도말(塗抹)** ①(칠하기) painting over; smearing/~하다 (채료를) paint over; smear (기름 따위를) smear; paint out(뭉개다) ②(미봉하다) temporizing; make shift/~하다 patch up; shuffle; varnish/~제 a liniment. ぬり

**도망(逃亡)** escape; flight; desertion/~치다[하다] run away; flee; fly; desert/~병 a runaway soldier; a deserter/~치게 하다 put (*one*) to flight/무사히 ~하다 make good *one's* escape (*to*); run away to (*a safe distance*). とうぼう

**도망군(逃亡―)** a runaway; a fugitive (탈주자) a deserter; an absconder; an escapee. とうぼうしゃ

**도망질(逃亡―)** flight/~치다[하다] flee to; take flight to; turn *one's* back (*upon*)/걸음아 날 살려라 하고 ~치다 take to flight. とうぼうすること

**도맡다** (책임을) answer for; be responsible for (부담·담당) undertake; take (*a matter*) in *one's* hands (맡다) take charge of; take over (*another's business*)/내가 그 아이를 도맡아 키우겠읍니다. I will take the child over and bring him・her〕it up./가게의 물건을 ~ take over all the goods in the store. そうせきにんをひきうける

**도매**(盜賣) selling (goods) by stealth/~하다 sell stolen good[things].

**도매**(都賣) wholesale/~하다 sell wholesale/~ 시세 (상점) a wholesale trade price/~상 (상점) a wholesale trade 《사람》a wholesale dealer; a wholesale store[business]/~ 값으로 at wholesale price. おろしうり

**도매**(都買) buying wholesale/~하다 by wholesale. ぜんたいをかいいれること

**도면**(圖面) a drawing; a sketch; a plan /건축 ~ 《청사진》 a blueprint/~을 그리다 draw a plan. ずめん

**도면**(圖免) ~하다 intend to escape; plan to evade (one's duty); devise to elude; try to get rid of (trouble).

**도모**(圖謀) device; contrivance; design; scheme/~하다 《꾀하다》plan; devise; contrive 《뜻하다》seek; intend (to do) 《노력》labour[work, strive] for; exert oneself for/사리를 ~하다 seek[look to] one's own interests/공익을 ~하다 labo[u]r for the good of the public; promote the public interest/일을 ~할온 인간이요 일의 성사는 하늘에 달렸다 Man proposes, God disposes. けいかく

**도무지** quite; at all; in the least; utterly; entirely; altogether; absolutely /~ 문제시하지 않는다 I don't care a fig/그를 ~ 만나 보질 못했다 I have seen nothing of him. ぜんぜん

**도미** 《어》a snapper 《어린것》 a red bream. たい

**도미**(掉尾) final efforts/~의 last; final; /~의 일약 the final leap. ちょうび

**도미**(渡美) going to America; a visit[an emigration] to America/~하다 visit America; go to America/~의 도에 오르다 leave for America. とべい

**도민**(稻米) rice. はくまい

**도민**(道民) a native of a province; the provincials. どうみん島

**도민**(島民) an islander; the inhabitants of an island. しまのひと

**또바기** 《꼭》without fail (한결같이) always; punctually 《완전히》completely/식전에 ~ 한 시간씩 산보를 한다 I make it a rule to take an hour's walk before breakfast. /~ 밤을 새웠다 I sat up all night. まちがいなく

**도박**(賭博) gambling; a gambling game; botting/~하다 gamble (돈을 걸다) play for money/~군 a gambler/~ 상습자 a confirmed[habitual] gambler/~장 a gambling house; a casino. とばく

**또박거리다** swagger; strut; mince (along) 뚜벅거리다. いばってあるく

**도발**(挑發) provocation; excitement; incitement; encouragement/~하다 provoke; excite; arouse/~적[으로] provokingly[ly]; suggestive[ly]; seductive[ly]/~적 연설[문장] inflammatory[seditious] speeches[writings]. ちょうはつ

**도배**(塗褙) facing; paper-hanging/~하다 face [a wall with paper]; paper [a wall]; coat (with); wallpaper/ ~지 wallpaper; paper hangings/~장이 a paper hanger.

**도배**(島配) exile; banishment/~하다 exile; banish (a criminal) to an island; maroon. しまながし

**도벌**(盜伐) the secret felling of trees/~하다 fell trees in secret/산림 ~ 사전 a forest tree theft scandal. とうばつ

**도법**(圖法) drawing; draftsmanship/평면 ~ projection. さくずほう

**도벽**(盜癖) a thieving habit; kleptomania/~이 있다 be larcenous; be kleptomaniac. とうへき

**도별**(道別) classification by province/~ 인구표 population by province. どうべつ

**도보**(徒步) going on foot; walking; pedestrianism/~하다 walk; go on a foot; foot it; pedestrianize/~로 on foot/~자 a pedestrian; a footpassenger/~ 경주 a foot race/~ 여행 a walking tour/~ 연락 train connections on foot. とほ

**도복**(道服) the garment of a Taoist. どうしゃのきもの

**도본**(圖本) a drawing ⇒도면(圖面). ずほん

**도부**(到付) 《행상》itinerant hawking/~치다 peddle; hawk/도붓장수 a peddler; a hawker. ぎょうしょう

**도불**(渡佛) a visit to France; going to France/~하다 go [over] to France; visit France.

**도비**(都鄙) the capital and the country. とひ

**도비**(徒費) waste; wastefulness/~하다 waste; cast away. とひ

**도사**(道士) 《도교의》a Taoist 《도승》an enlightened Buddhist. どうし

**도사**(導師) a spiritual father; a spiritual teacher in Buddhism. どうし

**도사공**(都沙工) a chief father[boatman]. せんどうのおやぶん

**도사리** ①《과일》an unripe fallen fruit ②《잡풀》weeds grown in the seedbed.

**도사리다** ①《앉다》sit cross-legged; sit with one's legs crossed ②《마음을》calm oneself; simmer down. うずくまる

**도산**(逃散) dispersion / ~하다 disperse; scatter; skedaddle; fly in all direction.

**도살**(屠殺) slaughter; butchery/~하다 slaughter; butcher/~장 a slaughterhouse/~자 a butcher. とさつ

**도상**(道床) roadbed. みちばた

**도색**(桃色) ①《빛》rose [colour] 《연한》pink/~의 rose-coloured; rosy ②《애정》love; amour; romantic attachment; love making/~ 잡지 a yellow journal /~ 유희 playing with love; an amorous[a love] affair. ももいろ

**도생**(倒生) 《식》~의 anatropous; obver-

**도생**(圖生) ~하다 earn *one's* livelihood; make a living; get *one's* living/근근히 ~하다 make a scanty living; eke out a living.

**도서**(島嶼) islands 《작은 섬》islets; isles 《군도》an archipelago. とうしょ

**도서**(圖書) books/~실 a library; book room/~ 열람실 a reading-room/~과 the library section/~ 해제(解題) a bibliography/~ 목록 a catalogue of books/~계 a librarian. としょ

**도서관**(圖書館) a library/국회 ~ the Library of National Assembly; the Library of Congress〈미〉/대학〔학교〕 ~ a university[a school] library/~장 the chief librarian/~원 a library clerk/~학 library science. としょかん

**도서다**[1] ①(바람이) change; shift; veer; ②(태아가) quicken. かえる

**도서다**[2] (농중이) (*smallpox*) be healing; become healed. いえる

**도석**(悼惜) lamentation/~하다 lament.

**도선**(導線) the leading[the conducting] wire. どうせん

**도선**(渡船) ferrying; ferry service 《배》a ferry-boat/~임(賃) ferriage/~장 a ferry. わたしぶね

**도설**(圖說) an explanatory diagram; an illustration. ずせつ

**도섭** caprice; wading; fording/ ~하다 wade; ford.

**도섭스럽다** (be) fickle; capricious; whimsical; uneven-tempered; mercurial. きまぐれ

**도성**(都城) a capital city. とじょう

**도성**(濤聲) the sound of waves. なみのおと

**도소주**(屠蘇酒) spiced *sool*; the New Year's ceremonial *sool*. とそ

**도수**(徒手) an empty hand/~ 체조 free gymnastics/~ 훈련 【군】 footdrill/~ 공권으로 with *one's* own bare hands; with *one's* naked fists(무기 없이). としゅ

**도수**(度數) the total [number]; the aggregate [number]. そうけい

**도수로**(導水路) a raceway.

**도수장**(屠獸場) a slaughter-house; shambles; a butchery/~에 끌려 가는 양같이 like a sheep going to be slaughtered. とじょう

**도술**(道術) Taoist magic; the magic of a Taoist. どうかのほうじゅつ

**도스르다** brace *one*self [up]; key *one*self up (*to do*); tighten[strain] *one's* nerves. げんきをだす

**도습**(蹈襲) ~하다 follow⇒답습. とうしゅう

**도승**(道僧) a Buddhist monk who has attained spiritual enlightenment. しゅうどうそう

**도시**(都市) a city; a town; urban communities/~의 municipal; city; urban /~ 계획 municipal planning〈영〉; city planning〈미〉/~ 국가 a city-state. とし

**도시**(都是) not at all ⇨도무지. ぜんぜん

**도시다** shave (*wood*); plane (*a plank*); whittle; trim (*one's nails*); finish (*a surface*). そる

**도시락** a small wooden box; a chip-box 《점심 그릇》a lunch-box/~밥 food packed in a chip-box; a lunch[eon] in a tiffin. べんとう

**도식**(圖式) a plan; a diagram; a schema (*pl.* schemata); 【논】 a figure/~으로 나타내다 graph; diagrammatize. ずしき

**도식**(徒食) idle life/~하다 lead an idle life; live in idleness; eat the bread of idleness/~하는 무리 the idlers; the drones of society. としょく

**도식**(倒植) 【인】 letters that are to be transposed. とうしょく

**도신**(刀身) a sword-blade.

**도신**(逃身) escape; flight; abscondence; decampment/~하다 flee; fly; run away; decamp. にげること

**도실**(桃實) a peach. もものみ

**도심**(都心) the heart[center] of the city /~지의 호텔 a midtown hotel. としん

**도심**(道心) ①(도의심) moral sense ②(신앙심) piety; faith in Buddhism/~자 a priest; a bonze. どうしん

**도심질** whittling; shaving/~하다 shave; whittle. すこしずつけずること

**도안**(圖案) a design; a plan; a device/ ~가 a designer/~과(科) the design course/~을 그리다 design/ ~화하다 make a design of. ずあん

**도액**(度厄) exorcism/~하다 exorcise.

**도야**(陶冶) education; cultivation; training/~하다 cultivate; train; build [up] /인격 ~ character building/품성을 ~하다 build[form, mould] *one's* character.

**도약**(跳躍) a jump 《경기》jumping; a spring/~하다 jump; leap 《말의》curvet/ ~ 운동 a jumping exercise/~자 a jumper; a leaper/~판 a spring-stand[-board]. ちょうやく

**도양 작전**(渡洋作戰) transoceanic operation.

**도어**(倒語) 【언】 inversion; transposition. とうご

**도연하다**(陶然—) (be) gloriously drunken /도연히 in a relaxed condition/도연히 취하다 be mellow and merry; be flushed with wine; be gloriously drunken. とうぜんとしている

**도연하다**(徒然—) (be) tedious; boring/ 도연한 세월 an insipid[a boring] daily life. ゆったりしている

**도열**(堵列) 《줄》a line (*of men*) 《늘어섬》 lining up/~하다 line[be drawn] up; form a line/~시키다 line (*people*) along (*a street*)/길 양편에 ~하다 line up on both sides of a road. とれつ

**도열병**(稻熱病) 【식】 rice-plant fever. いもちびょう

**도와**(陶瓦) an unglazed tile.

**도와주다** ①(조력) help; aid; give a helping hand; assist/일을 ~ hlep (*one*) in

**도외시(度外視)** disregarding; ignoring; neglecting／~하다 disregard; leave out of account／여론을 ~하다 disregard public opinion／우리는 이것을 ~할 수가 없다 We should never lose sight of this. どかいし

**도외 치지(度外置之)** ~하다 leave (a thing) out of consideration; take no account of; disregard; ignore／여론을 ~하고 in disregard of public opinion; apart from public opinion.

**도요새** 《조》 a snipe; a longbill.

**도용(盜用)** appropriation; peculation; using by stealth／~하다 steal; embezzle; peculate／전기를 ~하다 steal electric current／실인(實印)을 ~하다 make a fraudulent use of *one's* seal. とうよう

**도우(屠牛)** slaughtering cattle／~하다 slaughter cattle／~장 a butchery; a slaughterhouse／~한(漢) a butcher; a slaughterman. うしをころすこと

**도움** aid; help; assistance; support 《응원》 reinforcement 《구조》 rescue 《구제》 relief／~이 되다 be helpful; be a help／크게 ~이 되다 be of much help[assistance] to (one) たすけること

**도읍(都邑)** a capital [city]／~하다 (the dynasty) holds its court (at). とゆう

**도의(道義)** moral principles; morality; morals／~심 moral sense／~적 moral sentiment／~를 소중히 여기다 have high[strong] moral sense／~가 땅에 떨어졌다 Morality has lost its hold on the people. どうぎ

**도의회(道議會)** a provincial assembly／~의원 a member of a provincial assembly. どうぎかい

**도인(道人)** a Taoist ⇨도사(道士). どうじん

**도임(到任)** ~하다 arrive at[arrive to assume] *one's* new post. ふにん

**도자기(陶磁器)** pottery; chinaware.

**도작(稻作)** rice farming; rice-crop; the crop of rice. いなさく

**도작(盜作)** piracy; plagiarism; abstraction 《도작품》 a plagiarism／~하다 pirate; plagiarize. とうさく

**도장(道場)** ①《무예장》 an exercise-hall; a training place(훈련장); a fencinghall (검술의) ②《종》 도량(道場). とうじょう

**도장(圖章)** a seal; a stamp／~장이 a stamp[a seal]-engraver's [shop]／~칼 a seal-graver／~주머니 a seal-case／~을 파다 engrave a seal. はん

**도장(塗裝)** coating with paint／~하다 coat with paint／~재료 coating materials. とそう

**도저하다(到底一)** ①《매우 좋다》 (be) splendid; magnificent; excellent; superb ②《극진하다》 (be) cordial; warm-heart; careful; hospitable／그들의 나에 대한 대접은 ~ They gave me warm hospitality; すぐれている

**도저히(到底一)** not at all; possibly; [cannot] by any possibility; [none] at all; utterly 《결국》 after all／~ 비교가 안 된다 cannot for a moment compare with; it is beyond all comparison／…은 ~ 있을 수 없다 It is out of the bounds of possibility that…. とても

**도적(盜賊)** a robber; a burglar 《절도》 a thief 《강도》 a house breaker. とうぞく

**도전(挑戰)** challenge; defiance; provocation／~하다 challenge; bid defiance to; provoke a battle／~장 a written challenge／~적 challenging; aggressive／~에 응하다 accept a challenge; pick up the gauntlet. ちょうせん

**도전(盜電)** stealing of the electric current／~하다 make surreptitious use of electricity とうでん

**도정(道程)** distance 《여정(旅程)》 journey／버스로 두 시간 가량 걸리는 ~ about two hours ride by bus. どうてい

**도제(徒弟)** an apprentice／~ 교육 education of apprentice／~가 되다 be apprenticed to; be under articles to. とてい

**도조(賭租)** rice paid as land tax.

**도주(逃走)** escape; flight; desertion; fleeing／~하다 run away; flee; fly; have an escape; make off／~자 a runaway; a fugitive; a deserter／~를 꾀하다 attempt flight; make *one's* escape. とうそう

**도중(道中)** ontheway ⇨노중. どうちゅう

**도중(途中)** on the way／~에 on the road; by the way; *en route*(F); halfway／~의 역 stations on the way[the route]／이야기 ~에 in the course[the midst] of a conversation／~에서 하차하다 stop over [off]; break a journey／~에서 되돌아오다 turn back half-way. とちゅう

**도지(賭地)** sharecrop land; leased land; rented ground. しゃくち

**도지다¹** ①《심하다》 (be) extreme; severe; intense ②《단단하다》 (be) stout; (be) stiff; heavy. ひどい

**도지다²** 《사람이 주어》 relapse; have[suffer] a relapse; be seized with a relapse (병이 주어) relapse occurs／무리를 해서 병이 또 도졌다 He got a relapse through strain.; Strain brought on a relapse of his illness. さいはつする

**도지사(道知事)** the governor of a province. どうちじ

**도지소(賭地一)** rented cattle.

**도차지** monopoly; engrossment; exclusive possession[control]／~하다monopolize; engross; obtain the exclusive possession[control]. どくせん

**도착(到着)** arrival／~하다 arrive at[in]; reach; get to／~역[항] an arrival station[port]／서울에 ~하다 arrive in *Seoul*／현장에 ~하다 arrive on the scene[the spot]／비행기로 ~하다 arrive by air. とうちゃく

**도착**(倒錯) perversion/성욕 ~ sexual perversion/성욕 ~자 a sexual pervert.

**도찰**(塗擦) anointment; embrocation; inunction/~하다 anoint; embrocate/~제 an embrocation; an liniment. とさつ

**도처**(到處) everywhere; all over; throughout (the country); wherever one goes; far and wide; in every quarter; at every turn/국내 ~에서 all over Korea/throughout Korea/인간 ~에 유청산 A green hill fit for one's burial place is to be found anywhere. とうしょ

**도처 낭패**(到處狼狽) ~하다 fail in every attempt/그는 ~를 했다 Everything he put his hand to proved a failure.
とうしょろうばい

**도청**(道廳) the office of provincial government/~ 소재지 the seat of a provincial government. どうちょう

**도청**(盜聽) 《전화의》 wire tapping (《라디오의》 radio bootlegging[poaching]/~하다 《전화를》 wiretap; tap (a telephone wire) 《라디오를》 listen to the radio without a licence)/~자 a bootleg listener.
とうちょう

**도청 도설**(塗聽塗說) town talk; common gossip. まちのうわさ

**도체**(導體) 《물》《매개물》 a medium 《전기·열의》 a conductor/양[불량] ~ a good [a bad] conductor/반~ a semi-conductor/부~ a nonconductor.

**도충**(條蟲) 《동》 a tapeworm 촌백충.

**도취**(盜取) stealing/~하다 steal; pilfer; filch. ぬすみとること

**도취**(陶醉) intoxication 《깊은 감격》 fascination; rapture/~하다 be intoxicated; be fascinated; be enraptured/자기 ~ self-intoxication[-absorption]/자연미에 ~하다 be intoxicated with the beauty of nature. とうすい

**도치**(倒置) turning; upside-down; 《언》 inversion/~하다 invert; reverse/~법 《언》 inversion; hyperbation. とうち

**도침**(搗砧) fulling (cloth, paper, etc.)/~하다 be fulled. きぬ

**도탄**(塗炭) misery; distress/~에 빠지다 be in extreme distress/~에 빠진 민생고를 구하다 save the people from distress とたん

**도탑다** (be) warm; affectionate; kind; cordial/정의가 ~ be very friendly; be kind and warm-hearted. じょうふかい

**도태**(淘汰) selection/~하다 select; weed out; dismiss; comb out/자연[인위] ~ natural[artificial] selection/노후(老朽)~ the weeding out of superannuated persons/쓸데없는 인원을 ~하다 weed out superfluous members. とうた

**도토**(陶土) potter's clay; china-clay; kaolin 을. とうど

**도토리** an acorn/~ 나무 an oak; Quercus dentata(학명)/~ 깍정이 an acorn-cup; a cupule. どんぐり

**도톨도톨** unevenly; ruggedly; lumpy ⇒ 두툴두툴. でこぼこ

**도톰하다** be rather thick; (be) somewhat thick; thickish. いくぶんあつい

**도통**(道通) spiritual enlightenment/~하다 attain enlightenment; be spiritually awakened.

**도통**(都統) 《모두》 in all; all together; all told ⇒도합(都合). ごけい

**도투락댕기** a hair ribbon worn by a little girls. しょうじょのたれかみのリボン

**도투마리** a warp beam of a loom.

**도투리** all; entirely; altogether; in the total. まったく

**도포**(道袍) Korean full-dress attire [in olden days].

**도표**(道標) a sign-post; a guide-post[-stone]. どうひょう

**도표**(圖表) a chart; a diagram; a graph/《통계(統計)》~ a statistical chart/~로 나타내다 put (figures) into the form of a diagram; diagrammatize/점 ~ a point graph. いちらんひょう

**도품**(盜品) stolen articles[goods]; swag 《속》. とうひん

**도피**(逃避) a flight 《회피》 evasion; escape/~하다 flee; escape/~주의 escapism/~문학 escape literature/~행 a trip of recreation; an escape journey/자본의 ~를 방지하다 prevent the flight of capital. とうひ

**도하**(都下) the capital; the metropolis/~의 각 신문 the newspaper of the capital. とか

**도하**(渡河) crossing[fording] a river/~하다 cross a river 《강행하여》 force a passage of (a river)/~ 작전 river-crossing operations とか

**도학**(道學) ethics; moral philosophy/~자 a moralist/~ 군자 a virtuous gentleman. どうがく

**또한** ①too; also; as well; likewise; both … and; at once … and; and at the same time…; as well as ②《그 위에》 and; moreover; besides; further 「more ; what is more/그는 약속을 했으며 ~ 그 것을 실행했다 He made a promise and kept it., Besides making a promise, he kept it. また

**도한**(盜汗) night-sweat; sweating at night/~이 나다 have night-sweats; sweat at night. とうかん

**도합**(都合) 《총계》 the grand total 《전부 합해서》 in all; all told; altogether; the sum total. ごうけい

**도항**(渡航) a passage; a voyage/~하다 make a voyage; go abroad; go over to 《출발》 sail for 《이주》 emigrate to/~자 an emigrant/~ 면장(免狀) a passport. とこう

**도해**(圖解) ①《그림에 의한 설명》 a diagram; an illustration/~하다 illustrate by a diagram ; show in a graphic form ②《그림의 설명》 explanation ; interpr-

**도형**(圖形) a figure; a device; a diagram / 평면 ~ a plane figure.

**도형**(徒刑) penal servitude

**도호**(道號) a Buddhist name.

**도화**(桃花) a peach-blossom.

**도화**(圖畵) drawing; a picture / ~지 drawing paper.

**도화선**(導火線) a fuse; a primer 《탄약의》 a blasting fuse; a train of powder 《유인의(誘因)》 a cause; an agency; an incentive.

**도회**(都會) 《도시》 a city; a town / ~지[처] urban areas[district] / ~ 생활 city[town] life / ~인 city dwellers; urbanites / ~풍 urban manners / ~에서 자란 아이 a city-bred child.

**도흔**(刀痕) a sword cut[scar].

**독**[1] a jar; a jug; a pot / ~안에 든 쥐 같다 be like a rat in a trap; be quite in a helpless situation.

**독**[2] a dock / 부(浮)[건(乾)]~ a floating[dry] dock / ~에 넣다 dock a ship.

**똑**[1] 《두드리거나 떨어지는 소리》 with a tap [crack, rap, flop].

**똑**[2] 《틀림없이》 just; exactly; completely / 형제가 ~ 같다 The brothers are exactly alike.

**독**(毒) poison 《독사의》 venom 《병독》 virus 《해》 harm / ~이 있는 poisonous; venomous; harmful / ~을 마시다[먹이다] take [administer] poison.

**독가스**(毒―) poison gas; asphyxiating gas / ~ 마스크 a gas mask / ~ 탄 a poison-gas shell[bomb].

**독거**(獨居) solitude; solitary life / ~하다 live alone; lead a solitary life / ~성 동물 a solitary animal.

**독경**(讀經) sutra-chanting / ~하다 chant a sutra.

**독계**(毒計) a wicked design; an evil scheme; a trick / ~를 꾸미다 make a wicked[an evil] design

**독공**(篤工) hard work / ~하다 study hard; grind [away]; work hard at studies.

**독기**(毒氣) poisonous character; virulence 《악의》 malice; acrimony / ~ 있는 poisonous; malicious.

**독나방**(毒―) a brown-tail[-ed] moth.

**독납**(督納) tax dunning / ~하다 press (one for) tax payment; urge (one) to pay taxes

**독농**(篤農) a most efficient farming producer; a diligent[productive] farmer.

**똑딱거리다** click; clack 《시계가》 tick-tock / 똑딱똑딱 clicking; tick-tack / 《가슴이》 go pitapat; palpitate.

**똑딱선**(―船) a [steam] launch; motorboat.

**독단**(獨斷) arbitrary decision 《주장》 dogmatism / ~적 arbitrary; dogmatic / ~하다 decide arbitrarily; decide for oneself / ~ 으로 at one's own discretion [authority] / ~가 an arbitrary person; a dogmatist.

**독담**(獨擔) ~하다 take[be in] sole charge of; assume sole responsibility (for).

**똑똑** ①《두드리는 소리》 a tap; a rap; knocking / 문을 ~ 두드리다 knock[tap] at the door ②《부러지는 소리》 with a snaps ③《물이》 dripping; trickling; drop by drop.

**똑똑하다** ①《약다》 (be) clever; sharp; intelligent; bright; smart / 똑똑한 아이 a bright child ②《분명하다》 (be) clear; distinct; vivid; plain / 똑똑한 발음 clear[articulate] pronunciation.

**독두**(禿頭) 《머리》 a bald head 《사람》 a baldheaded person.

**독려**(督勵) encouragement / ~하다 encourage; stimulate; urge.

**독력**(獨力) one's own efforts; singlehanded efforts / ~으로 alone; singlehanded; for oneself.

**독립**(獨立) independence; self-reliance 《자활》 self-support / ~의 independent / ~하다 become independent (of); stand alone[on one's own legs] / ~으로 independently; for oneself / ~ 자존 self-respect and independence / ~국 an independent country[state] / ~심 the spirit of independence / ~ 전쟁 the war for independence; the Independence War / ~ 기념일 《미국의》 Independence Day.

**독목교**(獨木橋) a log bridge.

**독목주**(獨木舟) a dugout.

**독무대**(獨舞臺) the sole master of the stage / ~이다 have the stage all to oneself / 정계는 그의 ~다 He has the political stage all to himself.

**독물** a dark[deep] blue colour; blue-black.

**독물**(毒物) poisonous substance; poisonous stuff.

**독미나리**(毒―) 《식》 a water hemlock.

**똑바로** 《바르게》 in a straight line; straight 《꼿꼿이》 upright; erect 《순직히》 frankly 《정직하게》 honestly 《정확하게》 correctly; exactly.

**독방**(獨房) a room for one's exclusive use 《감옥의》 a solitary cell / ~ 감금 solitary confinement.

**독백**(獨白) a soliloquy; a monologue / ~하다 say to oneself; soliloquize; perform a monolog.

**독버섯**(毒―) a poisonous mushroom; a toadstool.

**독법**(讀法) the way of reading 《발음》 pronunciation.

**독보**(獨步) going on alone; having no rival / ~적인 unique; peerless; unrivaled; unequaled; unchallenged.

**독본**(讀本) a reader; a reading book / 영

**독부(獨夫)** a person left out in the cold 《사회의》 an outcast. どくしんのおとこ

**독불장군(獨不將軍)** 《독부(獨夫)》 a person who is left out in the cold 《자기 만족자》 a self-satisfied person 《고집장이》 a man of self-assertion; a man of self will. そっちのけにされたひと

**독살(毒殺)** poisoning/~하다 poison; kill [murder] by poison どくさつ

**독살부리다(毒殺一)** spit venom; speak bitterly. あくいのあるこうどうをする

**독살풀이(毒殺一)** giving vent to one's spite; going at (a person) in a wicked manner/~하다 give vent to one's spite.

**독살피우다(毒殺一)** spit venom; speak with acrimony; speak venomously.

**독생자(獨生子)** 《종》 Jesus Christ. キリストのいしょう

**독서(讀書)** reading/~하다 read books/~가 a reader; a great reader (다독가)/~력 reading ability; power of reading/~를 즐기다 be fond of reading; take kindly to books. どくしょ

**독선(獨船)** a boat hired for one's exclusive use かしきりしたふね

**독선(獨善)** self-righteousness/~적 self-righteous/관료 ~ bureaucratic self righteousness. どくぜん

**독설(毒舌)** a poisonous[malicious] tongue/~을 퍼붓다 speak with acrimony; use one's malicious tongue. どくぜつ

**독성(毒性)** poisonous character/~의 virulent; poisonous. どくせい

**독소(毒素)** poisonous matter; toxin/항(抗)~ an anti-toxin. どくそ

**독수(毒手)** a vicious means/…의 ~에 걸리다 fall a victim to (one). どくしゅ

**독수(獨修)** self-study; self-improvement/~하다 study[learn] by oneself; improve oneself. どくしゅう

**독수 공방(獨守空房)** living in solitude; a woman's leading solitary life in her husband's absence/~하다 live in solitude 《여자가》 be a lonely wife; live apart. ふうふがおなじへやできっきょしないこと

**독수리(禿一)** 《조》 a vulture; an eagle/~ 같은 vulturous. わし

**독습(獨習)** self-teaching/~하다 teach[educate] oneself; study by oneself/~서 a self-educator; a guide. どくしゅう

**독시(毒矢)** a poisoned arrow. どくや

**독시(毒弑)** ~하다 poison (one's superior); kill (one's superior) by poison. どくさつすること

**독식(獨食)** monopoly/~하다 monopolize/그는 이익금을 ~했다 He monopolized the gains. りえきをどくせんすること

**독신(獨身)** celibacy; a single life; bachelorhood(남자); spinsterhood(여자)/~자 a bachelor(남자); a spinster(여자)/~ 생활 a single life. どくしん

**독신(獨慎)** solitary confinement.

**독신(瀆神)** blasphemy; profanity; desecration; sacrilege. とくしん

**독신(篤信)** earnest belief; devotion/~하다 believe heartily in. とくしん

**독실(篤實)** sincerity; faithfulness/~하다 (be) sincere; faithful; true/~히 sincerely; faithfully. とくじつ

**독심(毒心)** malice; spite; venom/~있는 malicious; spiteful; venomous/~을 먹다 be filled with spite. どくしん

**독심술(讀心術)** mind[thought]-reading; telepathy. どくしんじゅつ

**독아(毒牙)** a [poison] fang/~에 걸리다 fall into one's clutches. どくが

**독액(毒液)** poisonous liquid 《과실즙》 poisonous juice 《나무 진》 poisonous sap.

**독약(毒藥)** poison; poisonous drug[medicine]/~을 마시다 take poison/~을 타다 put poison into (food). どくやく

**독어(獨語)** ①《독일어》 German; the German language ②《혼잣말》 soliloquy; monolog[ue]. どくご

**독염(毒焰)** a poisonous flame.

**독오르다(毒一)** become spiteful[venomous]. ゆうどくになる

**독와사(毒瓦斯)** poison gas ⇨독가스. どくガス

**독인(毒刃)** an assassin's dagger/~에 쓰러지다 be foully murdered. どくじん

**독자(讀者)** a reader 《구독자》a subscriber 《독서계》 the reading public/~난 the reader's column. どくしゃ

**독자(獨子)** 《외아들》 the only son 《자식》 the only child. ひとりご

**독자(獨自)** one's self/~의 original; characteristic; personal; individual of one's own unique/~성 individuality; originality. どくじ

**독장치다(獨場一)** stand without rivals; stand unchallenged; be the sole master of the stage. ひとりぶたいにする

**독재(獨裁)** dictatorship/~적 dictatorial; autocratic/~자 an autocrat; a dictator/~주의 dictatorship/~ 정치 dictatorial government. どくさい

**독전(督戰)** urging the soldiers to fight vigorously; leading in battle/~하다 urge the soldiers to fight still more vigorously; lead in battle/~대 a supervising army. とくせん

**독점(一店)** a pottery shop.

**독점(獨占)** monopoly; exclusive possession/~하다 monopolize; engross; have (something) to oneself/~주의 monopolism/~ 사업 a monopoly/~ 금지법 《법》 the Anti-Monopoly[-Trust] Law/~적 monopolistic; exclusive. どくせん

**독종(毒種)** 《사람》 a person of fierce character; a malicious person 《짐승》 a fierce animal. ちくしょう

**독좌(獨坐)** ~하다 sit alone. どくざ

**독주(獨奏)** 《악기의》 a recital 《성악의》 a solo/~하다 play a solo/~회 a recital/~자 a soloist/~곡 a solo. どくそう

**독지(篤志)** charity; benevolence/~가 a

독직(瀆職) corruption; bribery 《수회》 a graft/~ 사건 a corruption scandal; a bribery case;. とくしょく

독차지(獨一) monopoly; exclusive possession/~하다 monopolize; have to oneself/그녀의 사랑을 ~하다 get all of one's her love. どくせん

독창(獨唱) a [vocal] solo/~하다 sing[give] a solo/~자 a soloist. どくしょう

독창(獨創) originality/~적 original; creative/~력 creative power; originality とくそう

독채(獨一) an unshared house.

독처(獨處) 《독신 생활》 a single[an unmarried] life 《독거》 a solitary life/~하다 live alone; lead a single life.

독천(獨擅) surpassing others; lacking rivals/~장 (one's) field of monopoly; (one's) unrivaled sphere of activity; (one's) special province. どくせん

독초(毒草) 《독한 풀》 a poisonous plant [herb]; a noxious weed[plant] 《담배》 strong tobacco. どくそう

독촉(督促) pressing; urging/~하다 press (one) for; urge/~장 a collection [demand] note. とくそく

독충(毒蟲) a poisonous insect; a noxious insect. どくむし

독탕(獨湯) a private bath/~하다 take a private bath. せんようのふろば

독특(獨特) ~하다 be peculiar (to); (be) unique; original; be characteristic (of); (be) special/~한 방법으로 in one's own way. どくとく

독파(讀破) finishing reading; reading through/~하다 《끝까지》 read[go] through; finish reading 《다 읽다》 read all (the books)/단숨에 ~하다 read at a stretch. どくは

독판(獨一) monopoly/~치다 monopolize.

독필(禿筆) ①《붓》 a stump of a [writing] brush; a stubby brush ②《서투른 글씨》 clumsy writing ③《겸칭》 my humble writing. とくひつ

독필(毒筆) a spiteful pen; a pen dipped in gall. どくひつ

똑하다 《고지식하다》 (be) simple; frank 《정직하다》 very honest.
しょうじきでゆうずうせいがない

독하다(毒一) ①《독기가 있다》 (be) poisonous; virulent ②《술·담배가》 (be) strong /독한 담배[술] strong tobacco[wine] ③《잔인하다》 (be) cruel; cold-blooded; hard-hearted ④《굳세다》 (be) indefatigable; indomitable; stoical. ゆうどくだ

독학(獨學) self-study[-education]/ ~하다 teach[educate] oneself; study[learn] by oneself/~한 사람 a self-educated [-taught] person. どくがく

독학(篤學) a love of learning/~지사(之士) a devoted scholar. とくがく

독학(督學) supervision of study[school, work]/~하다 supervise school work [study]. とくがく

독해(毒害) poisoning/~하다 poison (one) kill by poison.

독행(篤行) good deeds; charitable work; upright conduct. とっこう

독행(獨行) going alone 《독립》 independence/~하다 go about alone 《자립하다》 stand on one's own legs. どっこう

독혈(毒血) 《한》 bad blood/~증(症) toxemia. ゆうどくなち

독회(讀會) a reading[meeting]/제일[이, 삼] ~ the [first the second, the third] reading. どっかい

독후(篤厚) sincerity; simplicity and honesty/~하다 (be) sincere; simple and honest; straightforward. せいじつ

독후감(讀後感) one's impressions of[after reading] a book.

돈¹ 《금전》 money; gold; cash 《재산》 wealth; riches/《적은》 ~ a large[small] sum of money/부정한 ~ ill-gotten money/~있는 rich; wealthy/~으로 살 수 없는 priceless/~지갑 a purse; a pocketbook\미/~이 많이 들다 be expensive; be costly/~을 벌다 make money/물건을 ~으로 만들다 change goods into money/~에 눈이 어둡다 be blinded by money/~을 물쓰듯 하다 squander [lavish, waste] money/~이면 안되는 일이 없다 Money governs[Gold rules] the world. おかね

돈² 《무게 단위》 a don(=0.1325 ounce, 3. 7565 grammes). いちもんめ

돈(噸) a ton/~수(數) tonnage/미터 ~ a metric ton. とん

돈견(豚犬) ①《돼지와 개》 a pig and a dog ②《미련한 사람》 a stupid person; a blockhead; a dullard. ぶたといぬ

돈구멍 ①《돈이 생길 길》 a source of revenue[profit] ②《돈에 뚫린》 the perforation on a coin. ざいげん

돈궤(一櫃) a money-chest[box]; a strong-box. かねいればこ

돈꿰미 《줄》 a string 《돈》 a string of coppers.

돈낭(一兩) some money; a number of coppers; a pretty[fine] penny./~께나 벌었다 He made a fortune/~께나 있는 집안에 태어났다 He was born to a fortune. じゃっかんのおかね

돈놀이 money-lending[business]/~하다 lend[out] money; practise usury/~하는 사람 a money-lender. かねかし

돈대(墩臺) high ground; an eminence.

돈독(敦篤) sincerity ›돈후(敦厚)

돈중(一重) a weight equivalent to several don. もんめ

돈등화(一燈花) the ball-shaped end of a burning candlewick.

돈만(一萬) tens of thousands of coppers; a sum of five figures. まんきん

돈목(敦睦) intimacy; friendly terms/~하다 be on good terms (with); be intimate (with); stand well with.

**돈바르다** (be) narrow-minded; hard to please; moody; particular; fastidious. にんじょうがない

**돈백**(一百) hundreds of coppers.

**돈벌이** moneymaking/~하다 make money/~가 되는 일 a lucrative[profitable] job/~를 잘 하다 be clever at making money. かねもうけ

**돈복**(一福) luck with money.

**돈복**(頓服) ~하다 take at once/~약 a draft of medicine; a dose/1회에 ~ 할 것 To be taken at once. とんぷく

**돈사** a small numbers of coppers; a little sum of money. はしたかね

**돈사**(頓死) a sudden[an abrupt] death/~하다 die suddenly; die a sudden death; drop[fall] dead.

**돈수**(頓首) ①(절) a bow; obeisance ②(편지의) Yours very respectfully; Yours truly[sincerely]. とんしゅ

**돈수**(噸數) tonnage; tons/실~ net tonnage[tons].

**돈아**(豚兒) my son. とんじ

**돈육**(豚肉) pork. ぶたにく

**돈절**(頓絶) a sudden cease[discontinuation]; an abrupt stop/~하다 cease suddenly; be cut off once and all; stop abruptly. にわかにへだてること

**돈점박이**(一點一) a brindled horse; a horse spotted with darker colour.

**돈주**(遁走) flight; abscondence/~하다 flee; run away; abscond; take [to] flight.

**돈주머니** a purse; a moneybag; a pocketbook(미)/~가 텅 비다 one's purse becomes empty.

**돈지**(頓智) wit; ready wit. とんち

**돈지갑**(一紙匣) a coin purse; a pocketbook

**돈지랄하다** spend money in a crazy way.

**돈책**(豚柵) a pigsty; a pigpen; a hogpen.

**돈천**(一千) thousands of coppers. せんきん

**돈치기** a kind of money-throwing game; coin-tossing. あないちあそび

**돈푼** some money/~이나 있다 have a fortune; be rich. じゃっかんのおかね

**돈피**(獤皮) marten; sable.

**돈후**(敦厚) simplicity and honesty; sincerity; naivety/~하다 simple and honest; naive. とんこう

**돌다**¹ ①(해가) rise; come up ②(싹이) bud [out]; sprout; put forth [buds]; grow ③(증기 따위가) form; break out (in nettle rash). あがる

**돌다**² raise ⇒돋우다. ひきあげる

**돋보기** ①(노인경) spectacles for the aged; glasses for far vision; long distance glasses ②(안경) spectacles ③(화경) a magnifying glass. ろうがんきょう

**돋보다** see in a favorable light ⇒돋우보다. あがめる

**돋보이다** look better [than actually is]; be shown to advantage. あがめられる

**돋우다** ①(심지를) turn up (the wick) ②(높이다) raise; elevate; make higher ③(화를) offend; provoke; aggravate(더욱)/남의 부아를 ~ offend one; aggravate one's anger(더욱) ④(일으키다) excite one's [curiosity]; stimulate ⑤(충동이다)instigate; incite; stir up. ひきあげる

**돋움** an underlayer; an underlay; a support. ささえもの

**돋을볕** the rays of the rising sun; morning sunshine. のぼるたいようのこうがた

**돋을새김** 《미》 relief; relievo; embossed carving. うきぼり

**돋치다** ①(내밀다) protrude/날개가 ~ grow wing ②(값이) rise (in price); go [run] up. ねだんがあがる

**돌**¹ 《광》 a stone 《잔돌》 a pebble 《라이터의》 a flint 「for the lighter]/~문 a stone gate/~을 깐 paved with stone/~ 많은 stony. いし

**돌**² ①(일주년) an anniversary/해방 열두 ~ 기념식 the 12th anniversary of the Liberation ②(첫돌) the first anniversary of one's birth. いっしゅうねん

**돌개바람** a whirlwind. つむじかぜ

**돌격**(突擊) a dash; a rush; a charge/~하다 dash at; charge; rush/~대 shock troops; a storming party. とつげき

**돌결** grain/~이 곱다 [거칠다] be fine[coarse]-grained.

**돌겻** a reel that has a form like an anemometer. かせ

**돌고드름** a stalactite. しょうにゅうせき

**돌고래** 《어》 a dolphin; a cowfish.

**돌곪기다** generate pus forming a hard lump.

**돌공이** a stone pestle(pounder); a pounder made of stone. いしのきね

**돌관**(突貫) a charge; a bayonet charge; a rush/~하다 charge (on the enemy); rush[dash]·at the enemy/일제히 ~ 하다 charge as one man. とっかん

**돌기** unripe fruits. みじゅくなくだもの

**돌기**(突起) ①(두드러짐) a projection; a protuberance/~하다 protrude; project ②(갑자기) rising suddenly; springing up/~하다 rise [suddenly]; spring up/충양 ~ an appendix. とっき

**돌기둥** a stone pillar. いしのはしら

**돌기와** a slate; slabs of stone for roofing/~집 a slate-roofed house. いしかわら

**돌김** 《식》 underwater stone moss. いわのり

**돌나물** 《식》 a sedum; a stonecrop.

**돌날** the first anniversary of one's birth. まんいちねんのたんじょうび

**돌능금** a wild apple. やせいのりんご

**돌다** ①(회전하다)[go] round; turn; revolve; rotate/오른쪽으로 ~ turn to the right/뺑뺑 ~ turn round and round/지구는 태양의 주위를 돈다 The earth moves[revolves] round the sun. ②(순회하다) make a round; go one's rounds (순유하다) tour; make a tour/동북 지방을 ~ make a tour of the Northeast. ③(우회하다) go[come] round/곳을 ~ (배가)

[go] round a cape ④《약·술 따위가》 take effect/독이 전신에 돌았다 The poison has passed into his system ⑤《소문이》 circulate; be abroad; get about; spread/내각 사직의 소문이 돌고 있다 Rumours are afloat that the Cabinet will step out. ⑥《융통》 circulate/불경기가 돼서 돈이 잘 안 돈다 Money is tight owing to the trade depression ⑦《눈이》 feel dizzy; get giddy ⑧《소생하다》 revive (from *a swoon*); come to life again. かいてんする

**돌다리**¹ 《석교》 a stone bridge.　いしばし

**돌다리**² 《조그만 다리》 a low flattish bridge built over a brook.

**돌담** a stone wall.　いしかき

**돌담불** piles of stones.　いしのつみかさね

**돌대가리** a stupid person; a stubborn person.　あほう

**돌떡** rice cake made for baby's first birthday.

**돌덩이** a piece of stone; a stone/~ 같다 be as hard as a rock.　いしころ

**돌도끼** a stone ax[e].

**돌돌, 똘똘** rolling up; curling up; with a twirl/종이를 ~ 말다 roll up a piece of paper/실이 ~ 풀리다 A thread is unwound with a twirl.　くるくる

**돌돌하다, 똘똘하다** (be) sharp; clever; smart; quick-witted.　りこうだ

**돌띠** a belt attached to the coat of a child.　こどものまわしおび

**돌라대다** ①《변통하다》swing a loan ②make a ready remark 둘러대다.へんかうする

**돌라막다** fence in; put a fence around …둘러막다.　かこむ

**돌라붙다** change sides; change fronts; turn around.　ひっつく

**돌라서다** stand in a circle.

**돌라앉다** sit in a circle; sit round.

**돌라주다** distribute; share; serve round; send out.　ゆうずうしてやる

**돌려내다** ①《물건을》 obtain by fraud; swindle; defraud ②《사람을》 leave (*one*) out in the cold.　だましててにいれる

**돌려놓다** ①《방향을》 turn (*around*); put the other way round/시계를 ~ turn the hands of a clock/책상을 ~ put a table the other way round ②《사람을》 leave out.　ほうこうをかえておく

**돌려보내다** 《반환》 return; give back 《원래의 자리로》 put back; restore 《반송》 send back.　かえす

**돌려쓰다** borrow (*money, things*).

**돌려주다** ①《반환하다》 give back; 《반송》 send back 《임자에게》 restore ②《변통하다》 lend; loan; accommodate (*one*) on loan.　かりたものをかえす

**돌리다**¹ ①《병을》 turn the corner ②《노염을》 cool down; calm down; relent (*toward one*) ③《융통하다》 borrow; have (*money*) on loan.

**돌리다**² ①《방향을》 turn; change; divert; convert/눈을 ~ avert[turn away] *one's* eyes from/화제를 ~ change the subject ②《회전하다》 turn [round]; roll; spin; revolve/핸들을 ~ turn a handle/팽이를 ~ spin a top ③《넘기다·보내다》 pass[send] round; hand round (*on*); 《전송하다》 forward 《회부》 transmit 《술잔을》 pass; offer/자동차를 사무실로 ~ send a car round to the office/행운의 편지를 ~ send on a "chain letter" ④《급한 것을》 take breath; pause for breath; take a rest/숨을 ~ get[recover] *one's* wind ⑤《원인 따위를》 attribute to; ascribe to; impute.　ほうこうをかえる

**돌림** ①《교대》 turn; rotation/~으로 alternately; by turns ②⊸돌림병. こうたい

**돌림감기**(一感氣) influenza; flu[e]《속》.

**돌림병**(一病) a contagious[an infectious] disease; an epidemic.　でんせんびょう

**돌림장이** a person left out in the cold; an outcast.　のけもの

**돌림턱** entertainment by rotation; a treat given by turns. こうたいしておごること

**돌림통** the period of prevalence of an epidemic.　りゅうこうのじき

**돌림편지**(一片紙) a circulating note; a circular [letter].　かいらんのてがみ

**돌멩이** a small stone; a piece of stone; a pebble.　こいし

**돌멩이질** stone-throwing; stone-slinging/~하다 throw a stone at (*a dog*); pelt (*one*) with stones; pelt at (*one*); sling a stone.　なげいし

**돌무더기** a pile[heap, mound] of stones.　いしのつみかさね

**돌무덤** a stone grave.

**돌미륵**(一彌勒) a stone Buddhist image.

**돌반지기** sandy rice; low-grade rice full of sand[grits].

**돌발**(突發) burst; outbreak/~하다 break [burst] out; occur suddenly/~ 사건 an unforeseen[unexpected] occurence [accident]; an accident/~적[으로] sudden[ly.; unexpected[ly].　とっぱつ

**돌방**(一房) a hollow in a rock. せきしつ

**돌배** 《식》 a wild pear.

**돌변**(突變) a sudden change[turn]/~하다 change (*one's* attitude) suddenly 《병이》 take a serious turn.　きゅうへん

**돌보다** 《보살피다》 take care of; care for; look[see] after (*one*) 《알선하다》 do (*one*) a service 《조력》 help; assist.　たすける

**돌부리** the projection of a rock.

**돌부처** a stone Buddhist image. せきぶつ

**돌비**(一碑) 《묘석》 a tombstone 《기념비》 a [stone] monument.　せきひ

**돌출**(突出) ~하다 fly out suddenly 《뛰어 나오다》 run[rush] out.

**돌비늘** 『광』 mica; isinglass.　うんも

**돌사닥다리** a stony mountain path.

**돌산**(一山) a stone mountain.　いしやま

**돌삼** 《식》 a wild hemp.　やせいのあさ

**돌샘** a spring gushing out of stony ground; a rock spring.

**돌소금** rock salt.

**돌솜** 『광』 asbestos.　せきめん

**돌아가다** ①(되돌아) go back; return; turn back／온 길을 ~ return one's steps; turn back／제자리로 ~ go back to one's seat ②(우회하다) take a roundabout way; make a detour／하와이로 해서 ~ go via *Hawaii* ③(원상으로) return (*to*); be restored to; resume／정상 상태로 ~ return to normal[cy] ④(귀착하다) come to; result in／수포로 ~ come to naught ⑤(뒤틀어지다) pout; sulk; turn sulky ⑥(죽다) die; be dead. かえる

**돌아내리다** pretend not to have a mind to accept; pretend to hesitate; hesitate in, its circling. しりごむふりをする

**돌아눕다** lie the other way round.

**돌아다니다** ①(싸다니다) walk[gad, wander] about ②(퍼지다) spread; prevail; be abroad. はいかいする

**돌아들다** return; come back. もどる

**돌아「다」보다** turn round; turn one's face; look back[round, behind] ②(회상하다) reflect; look back upon ③(고려) care; consider. ふりかえってみる

**돌아서다** ①(뒤로) turn one's back; turn on one's heels ②(등지다) break up with; fall out with; be alienated ③(병세가) take a favourable turn; take a turn for the better. うしろむいてたつ

**돌아앉다** sit the other way round. うしろむいてすわる

**돌아오다** ①(귀환하다) return; come back [home]; back ②(차례가) come round ③(책임이) be brought. もどってくる

**돌알** (안경 알) a crystal lens[of glasses].

**돌연**(突然) suddenly; on[all of] a sudden; unexpectedly; all at once／~한 sudden; unexpected; unlooked-for／~한 방문 a surprise visit. とつぜん

**돌옷** moss growing over a rock; a crustacious lichen. いわのり

**돌이키다** ①(고개를) turn one's face[head]; turn round ②(과거를) look back ②(회복) get back; regain; recover; restore; recuperate ③(재고하다) reconsider; reflect ④(달리 생각하다) think better of; change one's mind. ふりかえる

**돌입**(突入) inrush／~하다 dash in[into]; rush into (군사가) charge into／그는 적 중에 ~했다 He rushed at the enemy. ／자동차가 가게에 ~했다 The automobile dashed into the shop. とつにゅう

**돌자갈** a pebble; a gravel; a stone. じゃり

**돌잔치** the banquet given on a baby's first birthday.

**돌잡히다** celebrate the first anniversary of one's birth.

**돌쩌귀** a hinge／문은 ~로 여닫는다 The door opens and shuts on hinges.／~에 녹이 쓸지 않는다《속담》If I rest, I rust., Standing pools gather filth ちょうつがい

**돌절구** a stone mortar. いしのうす

**돌진**(突進) a rush; a dash; a charge／~하다 rush[dash] (*at*); charge／문을 향해서 ~하다 rush for the door／적을 향해서 ~하다 charge in upon the enemy. とっしん

**돌차**(咄嗟) ~하다 click one's tongue with regret; tut with regret. とっさ

**돌출**(突出) projection; protrusion; prominence／~하다 project; protrude; jut out; pop out／~한 projected; projecting; protruding／해중에 ~하다 project [jut out] into the sea. とっしゅつ

**돌층계**(一階層) a stone step; a flight of stone step. いしかいだん

**돌탑**(一塔) a stone tower; a stone pagoda. せきとう

**돌파**(突破) breaking through／~하다 break through; pass; overcome; exceed; cross／천원대를 ~하다 rise above the 1,000*won* level／난관을 ~하다 overcome the difficulties. とっぱ

**돌팔매** a throwing stone／~질하다 throw a stone. いしなげ

**돌팔이** a vagabond who is engaged in trade or sells what skill he has／~ 의사 a quack[-doctor]; a charlatan; a traveling healer. ぎょうしょうにん

**돌팥** a wild redbean. やせいのあずき

**돌풍**(突風) a gust of wind (강풍) a strong wind／배는 ~으로 말미암아 해안으로 밀려왔다 The ship was blown ashore by a sudden gust of wind. とっぷう

**돌피** wild millet; *Panicum crus*(학명).

**돌함**(一函) a stone case; a chest of stone; stone box. いしのはこ

**돌확** a stone mortar. いしのうす

**돐** ①(사전 따위의) a full year; the 1st anniversary (*of*)／창립 한 ~ 맞이 기념 행사를 하다 observe the first anniversary of the opening (of the[a] school) ②(출생의) a full year; the first anniversary of one's birth. しゅうねん

**돔발상어** 《어》a dog-fish; a mudfish; a lawyerfish; *Squalus Mitsukurii*(학명).

**돕다** help; assist; aid; stand by; support; give (one) a helping hand《구제하다》relieve《응원하다》reinforce／돕는 사람 a help[er]／그를 도우러 가다 go to his assistance／가난한 자를 ~ relieve the poor／그는 늘 약한 편을 도와주었다 He has always supported the weaker party. ／서로 ~ help each other. たすける

**돗바늘** a big needle; a matting needle; a darning needle. おおはり

**돗수**(度數) ①(얼마의 번수) the number of times; frequency／전화의 ~제(制) the message[the call]-rate system ②(각도・온도의) the degree. どすう

**돗자리** a rush-mat; a mat／~를 깔다 spread[make] a mat.

**동**¹ ①(마디) a joint; a juncture; a connection (식물의) a node ②(맥락) a chain [of reason]; a thread [of connection] (조리) reason; logic; consistency; coherent／~이 닿는 coherent; consistent; relevant; reasonable; justifiable; logical／~이 닿지 않는 말 incoherent talk／

네 말은 ~이 닿지 않는다 What you say does not sound to reason. ③(옷의) a sleeve of a baby's coat. あわせめ

**동²** (묶음) a bundle; a bunch. たば

**똥** dung; feces; stool; excrement/~ 푸는 사람 a night-soil man/~배짱 daredevil; foolhardiness/~ 마렵다 have a motion (급히) be taken short/~같이 여기다 make nothing of/얼굴에 ~칠하다 disgrace *one's* name. くそ

**동**(東) the east/~의 east; eastern/~에[으로] (동부) in the east (동방) to the east (동쪽) on the east/~남 south-east/~북 north-east/동남[북]-eastern/~풍 the east wind/~으로 가다 go east. ひがし

**동**(同) the same (상기의) the said (상당하는) corresponding/~번지 the same house number/~품(品) the said article/작년 ~일 the corresponding[the same] date of last year. おなじ

**동**(洞) (촌) a village; a hamlet (도회지의) a sub-ward; a *dong*/~사무소 a *dong* office. どう

**동**(垌) a dam; a great dike[bank]/~을 막다 build[construct] a dam/~이 터지다 a dam bursts. せき

**동**(銅) copper ((화)) Cu ⇒구리/~산(山) a copper mine/~을 입히다 copper; cover [coat] with copper. どう

**동**(胴) (몸의) the trunk [of the body] (격검의) the body armour. どう

**동가**(動駕) a royal journey.

**동가식 서가숙**(東家食西家宿) a man whf has no fixed abode; a floater; a wanderer; a vagabond.

**동갈**(恫喝) threat; intimidation; bluff/~하다 threaten; bluff; intimidate/~외교 bluff diplomacy. どうかつ

**동감**(同感) (같은 감정) the same sentiment (동정) sympathy; fellow-feeling (동의) agreement; concurrence/~하다 agree with (one); feel the same way; be of the same opinion/아주 ~입니다 I quite agree with you. どうかん

**동갑**(同甲) the same age; a person of the same age; contemporaries/ ~이다 be of an age/우리는 ~이다 We are oo the same age. とうねんれい

**똥값** a giveaway[ridiculous] price/~으로 팔다 sell for a mere song.

**동강**(식) a kind of mustard.

**동강** a piece; a bit; a cut; a scrap/촛~ a candle-end/칼이 두 ~ 나다 a sword is broken into two pieces. ひときれ

**동개** a quiver for arrows.

**동거**(同居) living with (*a family*)/~하다 live with; live in the same house/~인 an inmate [of the same house]/나는 아저씨댁에 ~하고 있읍니다 I live with my uncle. どうきょ

**똥거름** night soil; dung-manure (농장에서 얻는) manure/~을 치다 remove [the] night soil. ふんのひりょう

**동거리**(同距離) an equal distance; the same distance.

**동겨주다** hint; intimate; insinuate; let (*a person*) know. ほのみかす

**동격**(同格) (동지위) the same rank; (문) apposition (같은 대우) an equal footing/~의 co-ordinate; equal; equivalent to/그들은 ~의 사람이다 They are on a par with one another. どうかく

**동결**(凍結) freezing/~하다 freeze; be frozen/~ 자산 frozen assets/~을 해제하다 unfreeze; defreeze. とうけつ

**동경**(銅鏡) a copper mirror.

**동경**(憧憬) longing; yearning; aspiration/~하다 long[sigh] for; aspire[yearn, hanker] after (*for*)/···을 ~하는 마음 an aspiration after/자연미를 ~하다 long for natural beauty. どうけい

**동경**(東經) the east longitude/~ 20도 40분 20 degrees 40 minutes of east longitude; Long. 20°40′ E. とうけい

**동경이**(東京—) a short-tailed dog. おのみじかいいぬ

**동계**(冬季) the winter term/~ 휴가[방학] the winter holidays; the winter vacation/~ 올림픽 the winter Olympic games. とうき

**동계**(動悸) palpitation of the heart; pulsation/~하다 palpitate; pulsate; have a palpitation of the heart. どうき

**동계**(同系) ~의 agnate; akin; of the same stock /~ 회사 an allied company. どうけい

**동고 동락**(同苦同樂) suffering and rejoicing together/~하다 share *one's* joys and sorrows (*with*); participate in the joys and sorrows (*of*); share *one's* fortunes (*with*). どうくどうらく

**동고리** a round wicker suitcase; a small round willow basket. やなぎこうり

**동고비** (조) a nuthatch.

**동곳** a top-knot pin/~을 빼다 surrender; capitulate. ちょんまげさし

**동공**(瞳孔) (해) the pupil; the apple of the eye/~ 확대[수축] the dilatation [contraction] of the pupil/~ 막 the pupillary membrane. どうこう

**동공 이체**(同工異體) equal excellence in workmanship though different in style/~이다 be practically the same; there is little to choose between the two; it is six of one and half-a-dozen of the other.

**동관**(同官) a fellow official; a colleague. どうかん

**동광**(銅鑛) (광석) copper ore; crude copper (광산) a copper mine. どうこう

**동구**(東歐) Eastern Europe.

**동구**(洞口) the entrance to village; a village entrance. むらのいりぐち

**똥구멍** the anus; the anal passage[orifice]. こうもん

**동국**(東國) an eastern country (우리나라) Korea; the Nation of the East. とうごく

**동국**(同國) 《국토》the same[said] country/~인 a fellow countryman.

**동굴**(洞窟) a cavern; a cave; a grotto (pl. ~s, ~es). どうくつ

**동궁**(東宮) 《세자》the Crown Prince 《자궁》the Palace of the Crown Prince. とうぐう

**동권**(同權) equality; equal rights/남녀 ~ sex equality; equal rights for men and women. どうけん

**동그라미** ①《원형》a circle; a ring 《실·끈으로 만든》a loop/~를 그리다[만든다] describe[make, draw] a circle ②《권점(圈點)》a full stop; a period. まる

**동그랗다, 동글다** (be) round; circular 《구형》globular; spherical/동그랗게 round; in a circle/동그란 눈 round eyes. まんまるい

**동그스름하다** (be) roundish; globular; somewhat round. まるみがかっている

**동글납작하다** (be) round and flat/동글납작한 얼굴 a round and flat face.

**동글다** (be) round; circular 《구형》globular ⇒동글다. まるい

**동글동글** ①《구르는 모양》rolling; turning; ②《여러 모양이》all round/~하다 (be) all round; all globular/~한 조약돌 round pebbles. まるまると

**동글반반하다** (be) round and flat. まるくてなめらかだ

**동급**(同級) 《학급의》the same class[grade] 《동등》equality; same rank/나는 그와 ~이다 I am in the same class with him/~생 a classmate. どうきゅう

**동긋하다** (be) roundish; rather round. まるみがかっている

**똥꼴** the tip of excrement/~타다 feel anxious[worried]; worry oneself (about); be fidgeted (about). ひじょうになやむ

**동기**(同期) the same[corresponding] period/~생 a classmate/작년 ~에 비해 compared with the corresponding[the same] period of last year/우리들은 ~ 출신이다 We were contemporaries at the school. どうき

**동기**(同氣) 《남자》brothers 《여자》sisters/~간 sibling relationship. どうき

**동기**(銅器) a copper[bronze] vessel; copper ware/~ 시대 the bronze age. どうき

**동기**(動機) a motive; an inducement incentive/불순한 ~ an interested motive/행동의 ~는 좋았다 You have acted from worthy motives. どうき

**동기**(冬期) the winter [season]/~ 강습 a winter class[school]/~ 휴가 the winter holidays[vacation]. とうき

**동기**(童妓) a kisaeng in training; a young kisaeng girl. おさないぎせい

**똥기다** inform; tip off; hint; give a hint. あんじする

**동나다** run out of stock; be all gone; be exhausted 《상품이》be sold out/술이 동났다 The wine is all gone. しなきれる

**동나무** a small faggot. たきぎのたば

**동남**(東南) southeast/~의 southeast; southeasterly/~풍 the southeast wind. とうなん

**동남아**(東南亞) Southeast Asia.

**동냥** alms/~하다 beg[ask] for alms 《중이》go about as a begging priest/~을 주다 alms; give favour. ものもらい

**동냥아치** 《걸인》a beggar; a mendicant; a pauper. こじき

**동네**(洞一) a village/~ 사람 a villager; 《총칭》village folk. むら

**동년**(同年) the same year; the same age/~이다 be of the same age/너와 ~이다 I am [of] your own age. どうねん

**동녘**(東一) the east/~ east[ward]; eastern/~으로 toward[to] the east; eastward/~ 하늘이 밝아 온다 Day[Morning] dawns. とうほう

**똥누다** have a bowel movement; relieve oneself; move[evacuate] the bowel; shit《속》. だいべんをする

**동단**(東端) the eastern end/아시아의 ~에 위치하다 be situated at the eastern extremity of Asia.

**동답**(洞畓) village-owned rice-fields.

**동댕이치다** 《내던지다》throw[cast] away; fling away《포기하다》throw over[up]; give up/화가 나서 책을 ~ throw away the book in anger/하던 일을 중간에서 ~ give up one's work halfway through. なげつける

**동닿다** ①《조리가 맞다》be reasonable; be logical; be consistent ②《계속하다》continue; go in succession.

**동대다** ①《차례를》let go in succession ②《물건이》keep in stock ③《조리를》make reasonable. けいぞくさせる

**동떨어지다** 《떨어져 있다》be far apart; be separated from; far and away 《다르다》be different from/그들의 주장은 전혀 동떨어져 있다 Their contentions are poles asunder. とおくはなれる

**동떨어진 소리** ①《애매한》a cold manner of speaking ②《조리에 안 맞는》incoherent words; inconsistent talk; an absurd remark. あいまいないいかた

**동독**(董督) supervision; superintendence; control; management/~하다 supervise; superintend; manage; control; press. かんとくしとくそくすること

**동동**¹ 《북소리》tom-tom; boom-boom 동동/~치다 tom-tom. ぶかぶか

**동동**² ①《물 위에》¶~ 뜨다 float; drift; be adrift ②《발을》¶~ 구르다 stamp [one's feet] on (the floor). うかんでうごくさま

**동동거리다** jump up and down (with cold, impatience)/추워서 발을 ~ jump up and down with cold/어서 돈을 달라고 발을 ~ ask for money jumping up and down impatiently. かるくふみならす

**똥똥하다** (be) thick-set; fat [and short]; pudgy; plump. ぽってりしている

**동뜨다** ①《뛰어나다》(be) superior (to);

**far** better; be out[far] and away; (be) extraordinary; exceptional/동뜨게 out of the common[ordinary]; exceptionally; a long way/성적이 학급에서는 ~ be out and away[by far] the best student in class/키가 동뜨게 크다 He is exceptionally tall. ②《동안이 뜨다》 be far apart; have a space between./두 동네 사이가 ~ The two villages are far apart from each other. ぬきんでている

**동등**(同等) equality 《같은 수준》 a par 《동일》 oneness 《가격》 equivalence 《등급》 co-ordination/~하다 (be) equal; coordinate; on a par/~히 equally/~의 권리 equal rights/~으로 하다 equalize [all, one with others]; place (one) on an equal footing/~한 입장에서 an equal footing/돈의 가치는 전전(戰前)과 동등하지 않다 Money is not of the same value as it was before the war. どうとう

**동락**(同樂) enjoying together; sharing one's joy (with)/~하다 share one's joy (with); enjoy together. ともにたのしむこと

**동란**(動亂) agitation; disturbance; upheaval; cataclysm; a war/세계적 ~ a world cataclysm/한국 ~의 disturbance in Korea; the Korean War. どうらん

**동량**(棟樑) ①《기둥과 들보》 a beam and a pillar ②《큰 인재》 the pillar; the chief support [of the State]/~지재(之材) great ability/장래의 국가 ~ a future leader of the States. とうりょう

**동력**(動力) [motive] power/~계 a dynamometer/~학 dynamic. どうりょく

**동렬**(同列) the same rank[file]/~에 두다 put in the same category (with); plate on the same level with. どうれつ

**동록**(銅綠) verdigris; copper rust; green rust/~이 슬다 form green rust. あかがねのさび

**동뢰연**(同牢宴) a wedding reception; a wedding feast/미). さんさんくど

**동료**(同僚) one's colleague; an associate; a comrade; a co-worker. どうりょう

**동류**(同類) 《같은 종류》 the same class [kind, category] 《공모자》 an accomplice; a confederate/~ 의식 consciousness of kind. どうるい

**동리**(洞里) a village/~ 사람= the village folk; the villagers. むら. まち

**동마루** 《건》 the ridge of a tiled roof; a tile-roof ridge. やねのむね

**동막이**(垌—) embankment; banking/~하다 embank; dike. せきとめること

**동맥**(動脈) 《해》 an artery/~/대~ the main artery/~ 경화증 arteriosclerosis. どうみゃく

**동맹**(同盟) an alliance; a league 《연합》 a union/~하다 ally with; be allied [leagued] with; unite; combine/~국 an ally; an allied power/~군 allied forces[armies]/~ 파업 a strike/~ 휴학 a school strike/~ 파업중이다 be on strike; A strike is on. どうめい

**동맹국**(同盟國) an ally; an allied power; a confederate; a confederacy/프랑스는 영국의 ~이었다 France was once allied with England. どうめいこく

**동맹 파업**(同盟罷業) a strike; a turnout; a walk-out〈미〉/~하다 strike [work]; go on [a] strike; walk out/~자 a striker/노동자들은 요금 인상을 요구하여 ~을 했다 The labourers have gone on [a] strike for higher pay./~ 파괴자 blackleg. どうめいひぎょう

**동면**(冬眠) wintering; winter sleep; hibernation/~하다 winter; hibernate/~ 믈 hibernants. とうみん

**동명**(同名) the same name/~ 이인(異人) a namesake. どうめい

**동명**(洞名) the name of a *dong* [a village, a sub-ward]. そんめい

**동명사**(動名詞) 《언》 a gerund. どうめいし

**동명태**(凍明太) 《어》 a frozen pollack.

**동모**(同謀) 《공모》 collusion; conspiracy /~하다 conspire with; plot together [with]/~하여 in collusion[conspiracy] with/~하다 act in concert[collusion] with. きょうぼう

**동몽**(童蒙) a child; a boy. どうもう

**동무** a friend 《반려》 a companion 《짝패》 a comrade; a pal 《속》/길~ a fellow traveller; a travelling companion/여자 ~ a girl friend/나쁜 ~를 사귀다 fall into bad company. ともだち

**동문**(同文) the same[common] script. どうぶん

**동문 동종**(同文同種) the same script and the same race/한중(韓中) 양국은 ~이다 The Koreans and Chinese are of the same stock, using the same script.

**동문 서답**(東問西答) an irrelevant answer; an incoherent reply/~하다 answer incoherently; reply irrelevantly; say nothing to the purpose[point].

**동문 수학**(同門受學) ~하다 study under the same teacher (with one).

**동물** ①《똥이 풀린 물》 excremental water ②《구토(嘔吐)가 심할 때 나오는》 yellow water coming out in a heavy vomiting; bile. だいべんすい

**동물**(動物) an animal 《총칭》 animal life /~원 a zoo; a zoological garden/~성 animality/~ 시험 a biological test/~학자 a zoologist/~계 the animal life [kingdom]/~육식 ~ the carnivora/~을 애호하다 be kind to animals. どうぶつ

**동민**(洞民) a villager 《총칭》 the village folk. そんみん

**동바** a piece of string used to fasten the load on an A-frame. しばりひも

**동바리** 《건》 a support; a prop. しちゅう

**동박새** 《조》 a white[silver] eye.

**동반**(同伴) company/~하다 go with; be accompanied by; accompany; take (one) with; escort take with/~자 a companion/그는 가족 ~이다 He is accompanied by his family. どうはん

**동반구**(東半球) the Eastern hemisphere. ひがしはんきゅう

**동방**(東方) the east／~의 eastern; easterly／~에 towards the east; in an easterly direction. とうほう

**동방**(洞房) ①《신방》 the bridal bed-room ②《침방》 a bed-room[chamber]. ねや

**동방**(東邦) 《한국》 Korea 《동쪽 나라》 an Eastern[an Oriental] country 《동양》 the Orient; the East. とうほう

**똥배** a potbelly; a protuberant[protruding] belly; a big paunch. ふくれたはら

**동배**(同輩) one's equal 《동료》 a colleague／~ 중에 뛰어나다 rise above one's fellows／우리는 ~간이다 We are equals[friends]. どうはい

**동백**(冬柏) a seed of a camellia／~나무 a camellia; Camellia japonica(학명)／~ 기름 camellia oil. つばき

**동병**(同病) the same sickness[disease]／~ 상련하다 Grief is best pleased with grief's company. どうびょう

**동병**(動兵) military mobilization／~하다 mobilize (an army). どうへい

**동복**(同腹) brothers; sisters／~의 uterine／~ 동생(同生) uterine brothers[sisters]; brothers[sisters] of the same venter. どうふく

**동복**(冬服) winter-clothes[clothing]; winter wear. ふゆふく

**동복**(童僕, 僮僕) a page; a boy servant. どうぼく

**동봉**(同封) encloseing／~하다 enclose; inclose (a letter)／~ 서류 enclosures (略: encls.)／~한 편지 the enclosed[accompanying] letter. どうふう

**동봉**(動蜂) a working bee; a worker bee.

**동부** 《식》 a [ripe] cowpea. ささげのみ

**동부**(東部) the eastern part. とうぶ

**동부동**(動不動) 《꼭》 for sure; without fail; to a certainty／명령이니 ~ 거기에 갈 수밖에 없다 I have no alternative [choice] but to go there because it is the order. きっと

**동부인**(同夫人) going out with one's wife／~하다 go out with[accompany] one's wife; take one's wife along. どうふじん

**동북**(東北) the northeast／~동 east-northeast／~ 지방 the northeastern district／~풍 the northeast[erly] wind; a northeaster. とうほく

**동북향**(東北向) facing northeast; having a northeast exposure. とうほくむき

**동분모**(同分母) 《수》 the same denominator. どうぶんぼ

**동분 서주**(東奔西走) rushing east and west; being terribly busy／~하다 busy oneself about (a thing); be on the busy [rush, run]. とうほんせいそう

**동빙**(凍氷) freezing; frost／~하다 freeze over; be frozen over. けつぴよう

**동사**(同事) ~하다 go into business (with); run (a shop) in partnership. どうぎょう

**동사**(動詞) 《언》 a verb／~의 verbal. どうし

**동사**(凍死) death from cold／~하다 be frozen to death. とうし

**똥싸개** a child who is not able to control his bowel movements; a pants-soiler; a baby. だいべんをもらすこども

**똥싸다** ①《똥을》 have an uncontrollable bowel movement; pass evacuations uncontrollably ②《혼나다》 have a hard [bad] time of it (with a person); have a bitter[terrible] experience; have a hell of time. だいべんをもらす

**동산** a garden／~바치 a gardener.

**동산**(動產) movable estate; personal property; personalty; movables; things personal; chattels. どうさん

**동산**(銅山) a copper mine. どうざん

**동살** 《건》 the cross-strips of a lattice.

**동살**(東―) 《빛》 the faint rays of dawn; grow gray. あさのうすあかり

**동삼삭**(冬三朔) October, November and December of the lunar calendar; the winter season. ふゆのみっかげつ

**동상**(同上) the same as [the] above; ditto (略: do.) どうじょう

**동상**(銅像) a bronze statue; a copper image. どうぞう

**동상**(凍傷) [a] frostbite; [a] chilblains／~자 a frostbitten person; a case of frostbite／~에 걸리다 be frostbitten; have frostbite. とうしょう

**동상례**(東床禮) a wedding reception at the bride's house after the wedding ceremony.

**동색**(同色) ①《빛깔》 the same colo[u]r ②《당파》 fellow members of a party; the same faction. どうしょく

**동색**(銅色) copper colo'u.r. どうしょく

**동생**(同生) a younger brother; a younger sister. おとうと

**동생 공사**(同生共死) ~하다 share the fate with others.

**동서**(同壻) ①《자매의 남편》 the husband of one's wife's sister ②《형제의 아내》 the wife of one's husband's brother. あいむこ

**동서**(東西) 《동과 서》 the east and the west 《동서양》 the East and the West／~ 고금 all ages and countries／~ 남북 the [four] cardinal points／~ 남북도 가리지 못하다 do not know one's right hand from the left. とうざい

**동서**(同棲) cohabitation／~하다 live cohabit with; live together／~자(者) a cohabitant. とうせい

**동서**(同書) ①《같은 책》 the same book ②《그 책》 the said book／~에서 《출처 표시로》 ibidem(略: ib., ibid.).

**동서 남북**(東西南北) the [four] cardinal points; north, east, south, and west ―사방. とうざいなんぼく

**동석**(同席) sitting together／~하다 sit in company (with one)／~자 those present; the [present] company. どうせき

**동석**(凍石) 《광》 steatite; soapstone.

**동선**(同船) taking the same ship (같은 배) the same [sail] ship/~하다 take the same ship; sail on the same vessel /~자 a fellow passenger. どうせん

**동선**(銅線) copper wire; copper wiring. どうせん

**동설**(同說) the same opinion[view]; the same theory. どうせつ

**동성**(同性) ①(남녀의) the same sex; homosexuality/~의 homosexual/ ~ 연애 homosexual love; unnatural love 《여자간의》 Lesbianism ②(성질의) homogeneity; congeniality/~의 homogeneous; congenial. どうせい

**동성**(同姓) the same surname/~ 할머니 [할아버지] a paternal grandmother[grandfather]/~ 동본이다 be of the same surname belonging to the same family seat. どうせい

**동소**(同所) the same[said] place.

**동소체**(同素體) 【화】 an allotrope.

**동수**(同數) the same number/…과 ~의 as many [...as]; of the same number/가부 ~인 경우에는 in case of a tie.

**동숙**(同宿) lodging together/~하다 stay with; lodge together (with)/~자 a fellow lodger (호텔의) a fellow guest an inmate. どうしょく

**동승**(同乘) riding together/~하다 ride together (with)/~자 a fellow passenger. どうじょう

**동시**(同時) the same time/~의 simultaneous/~에 at the same time 《병발적》 concurrent; synchronous 《…과 동시에》 simultaneously (with) 《한꺼번에》 at a time; at once 《일방에서는》 while, on the other hand. どうじ

**동시**(同視) ~하다 treat alike; regard (A) in the same light with (B). どうし

**동시**(凍屍) the body of a person frozen to death. とうし

**동시**(童詩) children's verse; nursery rimes. どうし

**동식물**(動植物) animals and plants; fauna and flora. どうしょくぶつ

**둥실둥실** floating; buoyant[ly]/~ 뜨다 float; drift. ぶかぶか

**둥실둥실** ~하다 (be) plump; round.

**동심**(同心) ①(같은 마음) the same mind /~ 협력 harmonious co-operation ②(같은 중심) concentricity/~원 a concentric circle. どうしん

**동심**(童心) the child[juvenile] mind; the childish mind/~으로 돌아가다 become a child again. どうしん

**동심**(動心) inclination/~하다 be inclined (to do); have an inclination; take interest (in); waver. うごくこころ

**동아** 【식】 a white gourd-melon. とうが

**동아**(冬芽) 【식】 winter buds.

**동아**(東亞) East Asia 《동양》 the East 《극동》 the Far East. とうあ

**동아**(凍餓) hunger and cold. こごえること

**동아리** 《부분》 a part 《무리》 a group; confederates; companions. ぶぶん

**동아줄** a thick and durable rope. つな

**동안** ①(간격) an interval/일정한 ~을 두고 at regular intervals ②(기간) time; a space; a period 《부사적》 for; during; while/오랫 ~ for a long time/잠깐 ~ for a little while. あいだ

**동안**(童顏) a boyish face/~의 boyish-looking.

**동안뜨다** be an interval[a space] between; be few and far between; have a longer interval than usual. ひさしくなる

**동압**(動壓) dynamic pressure.

**동액**(同額) the same sum[amount] [of money]; a like sum. どうがく

**동야**(同夜) the same night; the night in question. どうや

**동야**(凍野) 【지】 the tundra.

**동양**(同樣) similarity/~의 similar; the same. どうよう

**동양**(東洋) the Orient; the East/~의 Oriental; Eastern/~화(化) Orientalization/~화(畵) painting in Oriental style; an Eastern painting/~ 사람 Orientals; Asiatics. とうよう

**동양**(動陽) man's sexual impulse.

**동어**(一魚) 【어】 《숭어 새끼》 a young mullet.

**동업**(同業) 《같은 직업》 the same trade [profession] 《신문의》 a contemporary 《공동의》 a joint enterprise/~하다 run business together (with)/~ 조합 a guild; a trade association/~자 man of the same profession[trade]. どうぎょう

**동옷** a man's coat. おとこのうわぎ

**동요**(動搖) tremble; quake; shake 《마음의》 agitation; perturbation; excitement 《소요》 disturbance; commotion 《불안》 restlessness; unrest/~하다 tremble; quake; shake; be agitated; be disturbed 《차가》 jolt 《배가》 rock; roll; pitch /사상의 ~ an agitation of thought /~하지 않고 composedly; calmly/정계의 ~ political disturbance. どうよう

**동요**(童謠) a children's song; a nursery rhyme. どうよう

**동우**(同友) friends of the same mind 《회따위의》 a fellow member. どうゆう

**동원**(凍原) 【지】 the tundra.

**동원**(動員) mobilization/~하다 mobilize (troops); set in motion/~령 a mobilization order. どういん

**동원**(同原) 【생】 isogeny.

**동월**(同月) the same[said] month; the said month. おなじつき

**동위**(同位) the same rank[position]; the same location; 【수】 the same digit/~의 coordinate/~각(角) corresponding angles/~ 원소 an isotope. どうい

**동유**(桐油) 【화】 tung oil. とうゆ

**동육**(凍肉) frozen meat. こおりつけたにく

**동음**(同音) the same sound 《음성》 homophony/~ 이의어(異義語) a homonym. どうおん

**동읍(同邑)** the same town; the said town. おなじまち

**동의(同意)** agreement; consent; assent／～하다 consent[assent, agree] (to); approve (of). どうい

**동의(同義)** synonymy; the same meaning／～의 synonymous (with)／～어 a synonym. どうぎ

**동의(胴衣)** 《조끼》 a vest; a waistcoat. おとこのうわぎ

**동의(動議)** a motion／～하다 move a motion／긴급 ～ an urgent motion. どうぎ

**동의 인자(同義因子)** 《생》 multiple factors.

**동이** a jar;／물～ a water jar. つぼ

**-동이** child; one／막내～ the youngest son／쫄개～ a frivolous urchin. こ(子)

**동이다** bind [up]; tie [up]; fasten. しばる

**동인(同人)** ①《뜻이 같은》 a mate; a member 《전체》 a coterie／～잡지 a coterie magazine [of an association] ②《같은 사람》 the same person. どうじん

**동일(同一)** identity; sameness 《동일성》 oneness／～한 the same; one and the same; identical with／～시하다 put in the same category; regard in the same light (with). どういつ

**동일(同日)** the same[said] day. どうじつ

**동일류(同一類)** 《논》 identical classes. どういつるい

**동일시(同一視)** ～하다 regard (A) in the same light with (B); class (A) with (B). どういつし

**동자** 《밥짓기》 cooking[preparing] of rice／～하다 cook the rice. めしたき

**동자(童子)** a child; a young boy; a youngster. どうじ

**동자(瞳子)** the pupil of the eye; 눈동자. どうし

**동자르다** ①《관계를》 sever[cut off] one's connection with; dissociate[break off, sever] oneself from; disconnect (교제를) be through with. ずたずたにする

**동자아치** a kitchen maid; a cook; a scullery maid. めしたきのおんな

**동자중(童子一)** a young[boy] priest; a priestling; an acolyte.

**동작(動作)** bearing; behaviour; action; movements 《태도》 manners／～하다 act; behave oneself. どうさ

**동장(洞長)** the headman of a subward; the chief of a dong office. そんちょう

**동장군(冬將軍)** a severe[hard] winter.

**동적(動的)** dynamic; kinetic. どうてき

**동전(銅錢)** a copper [coin]. どうせん

**동전(同前)** the same [as before, as above]; ditto. まえとおなじこと

**동절(冬節)** the winter [season]; winter time. ふゆのきせつ

**동점(同點)** a tie; a draw／～이 되다 tie with (one); draw with. どうてん

**동점(東漸)** ～하다 advance[proceed, penetrate] eastward.

**동접(同接)** a classmate; a fellow student／～하다 be a classmate (with). どうもん

**동정** 《웃깃의》 a collar [attached to the top border of a Korean coat]. えり

**동정(同情)** sympathy; compassion; fellow-feeling／～하다 sympathize with (one); feel for compassionate／～자 a sympathizer／～금 a gift of money; contribution; alms／～파업 a sympathetic strike. どうじょう

**동정(童貞)** chastity; virginity／～녀(女) a virgin. どうてい

**동정(動靜)** movements; a state of things; development／정계의 ～ development of political affairs. どうせい

**동정 서벌(東征西伐)** subjugation[conquest] of many countries／～하다 subjugate[conquer] many countries.

**동제(銅製)** made of copper／～의 copper[y]; made of copper／～품 copper manufactures[goods]. どうせい

**동조(同調)** 《보조 맞춤》 alignment／～하다 align oneself with; follow suit; act in concert with／～자 a fellow traveler; a sympathizer. どうちょう

**동쪽(東一)** the east／～의 east; eastern; easterly. とうほう

**동족(同族)** 《일족》 the same family[tribe]; one's kind／～ 회사 a family company／～ 결혼 endogamy／～애(愛) brotherly[fraternal] love. どうぞく

**동종(同宗)** the same blood; the same family. どうしゅう

**동종(同種)** the same kind. どうしゅう

**동좌(同坐)** ～하다 sit together (with); share company. どうせき

**동죄(同罪)** the same crime[sin]. どうざい

**동주(同舟)** ～하다 take the same boat／오월(吳越) ～ bitter enemies placed in the same boat [by fate]. どうしゅう

**똥줄빠지다** be startled and run away at top speed. ひどいめにあってにげる

**동지(冬至)** the winter solstice; the shortest day of the year. とうじ

**동지(同志)** 《사람》 men of the same view; comrades; friends 《마음》 the mind. どうし

**동지(同地)** the same place[district, locale] (그곳) the said place.

**동질(同質)** the same quality; homogeneity／～의 homogeneous. どうしつ

**똥집** ①《대장》 the large intestine ②《체중》 body-weight. いぶくろのひご

**동짓달(冬至一)** the 11th month of the lunar calendar. いんれきじゅういちがつ

**동차(同車)** ～하다 be in the same car[train] with; ride together. どうしゃ

**동차(童車)** a perambulator; a baby carriage(미). うばぐるま

**동차식(同次式)** 《수》 a homogeneous expression. どうじしき

**동차적(同次積)** 《수》 a homogeneous product.

**동창(東窓)** a window facing [to the] east; the east window. ひがしのまど

**동창(同窓)** a classmate; a school fellow; a fellow student 《졸업생》 a graduate／

**동처**(同處) ~하다 live together [in the same room]; share a room with.

**동천**(東天) the eastern sky; the sky in the east.

**동천**(洞天) a beauty[scenic] spot; a garden spot.

**동천**(冬天) 《날씨》winter weather 《하늘》 a winter sky.

**동철**(銅鐵) copper and iron.

**동철**(冬鐵) 《신의》 crampons 《편자의》 horseshoe spikes.

**동체**(動體) 〖물〗《움직이는》a body in motion 《유동체》 a fluid.

**동체**(胴體) 《비행기 따위의》the body; the fuselage; the hull 《몸체의》the trunk.

**동치**(同値) 〖수〗 the equivalent.

**동치다** bind up; tie up.

**동치미** turnips[chopped radishes] pickled in salt water.

**동침**(一鍼) an acupuncture needle.

**동침**(同寢) sleeping together; sharing the same bed (with)/~하다 sleep with [one's wife]; share the [same] bed with (a person).

**똥탈**(一頉) stomach trouble.

**동태**(凍太) a frozen pollack.

**동태**(動胎) quickening fetal movement.

**동태**(動態) movement/인구 ~ the movement of population.

**똥털** hair around the anus.

**동통**(疼痛) a pain; an ache.

**동트기** dawn; day break.

**동트다** (it) dawn; (the day) break/동틀 무렵에 at daybreak.

**동파**(同派) 《유파》the same[said] school [faction, clique].

**동판**(銅版) a copperplate print; a mezzotint/~ 인쇄 a copperplate [print]/~ 조각 mezzotint engraving.

**동패**(銅牌) a copper medal 《큰것》 a copper medallion.

**동편**(東便) the east[eastern] side/~에 on the east.

**동포**(同胞) 《형제》brothers 《같은 국민》 brethren; one's fellow countryman 《인간》 fellow creatures/~애 brotherly love; fraternity.

**동풍**(東風) the east wind; the wind from east; an easterly wind/마이(馬耳) ~ Bolt a door with boiled carrot; Turning a deaf ear to.

**동하다**(動—) ①《움직이다》move; stir ②《마음이》be perturbed[agitated, excited, shaken]/동하지 않다 be unperturbed; remain firm.

**동학**(同學) a fellow scholar [student, researcher].

**똥항아리** a chamber pot 《비유적》a useless person in superior position.

**동행**(同行) going together; travel[l]ing together/~하다 go [along] with; accompany (one); travel together/~자들 fellow travel[l]ers; [travel[l]ing] companions.

**동향**(同鄕) the same province[town, village]/그는 나와 ~입니다 He comes from the same province as I/~인 a person from the same province[town, village].

**동향**(東向) an eastern exposure[aspect] /~집 a house facing east; a house with an eastern aspect.

**동향**(動向) a trend; a tendency.

**동혈**(洞穴) a cave; a cavern 《인공적인》 a grotto.

**동형**(同型) the same[said] type[pattern]; a similar type/~이다 be of the same type[kind].

**동호**(同好) the same taste/~하다 share the same taste/~자 《이해 관계》interested persons 《취미》 men of similar taste /영화 ~자회 a movie-lover's society.

**동화**(同化) assimilation; 〖생〗 anabolism 《순응》 adaptation/~하다 assimilate (with) 《순응》 adapt oneself to./~하기 어렵다 be hard to assimilate; be unassimilable.

**동화**(銅貨) a copper [coin, piece]; a red cent〈미〉;《전체》copper coinage.

**동화**(童話) a fairy tale; a nursery story [tale]; a juvenile story/~극 a juvenile play/~ 작가 a fairy-tale writer; a nursery-tale writer.

**동화력**(同化力) assimilative power/~이 있는 assimilative.

**동화 작용**(同化作用) [the process of] assimilation 《세포의》metabolism 《음식물의》anabolism.

**동활차**(動滑車) a movable pulley.

**동회**(洞會) a village assembly; a block council/~ 사무소 a village office; a town-block office.

**돛** a sail; a canvas/~을 올리다 hoist [spread, put up] a sail/~을 내리다 lower[take down] a sail/순풍에 ~을 달고 달리다 sail before the[fair] wind; be under easy sail.

**돛단배** a sailing-ship[-boat, -vessel]; a sailer

**돛대** a mast; a stick/~를 잃은 배 a dismasted vessel.

**돠르르, 돠르르** gurgling; gushing; copiously/~ 흘러나오다 gush out (of); flow out [copiously].

**따리** 《도아리》 a head-pad.

**딸딸, 딸딸** 《배가》 rumble [because of indigestion].

**뙈기** a lot of field.

**돼지** ①《가축》a pig 《불깐》 a hog 《수컷》 a boar 《암컷》a sow 《단수·복수 동형》a swine/~고기 pork/~ 우리 a pigsty; a pigpen/~ 기름 lard/소금에 절인 돼지 고기 ham/~를 치다 keep a pig ②《사람》 a piggish person.

# 되 다³

①**(신분·지위 따위가)** become; (get to) be; turn into; grow to be/어른이 ~ become an adult; grow up; attain adulthood/장관이 ~ become a cabinet minister/부자가 ~ become a rich man; get rich.

②**(결과)** turn out; prove (to be); result in/거짓말이 ~ turn out false/한날 꿈이 ~ turn out (to be) just a dream/손해가 ~ result in[prove to be] a loss/치명상이 ~ prove (to be) fatal/그 결과는 어떻게 될까? What will be the result?, How will it turn out?, Where will it lead to?/밥이 잘 안 ~ the food does not turn out very well/선거가 어찌 될까? How will the election turn out?/될 대로 되어라! Go to the devil!, Devil take him!, I don't care a damn about it.

③**(시간·나이 따위가)** become; turn; reach; attain/열 다섯 살이 ~ turn[become] fifteen/성년이 ~ come of age/벌써 시간이 다 됐다 Time is up already.

④**(성립)** consist (of); be composed [formed, made, made up] of; form/집이 벽돌로 ~ a house is made of bricks/물은 산소와 수소로 되어 있다 Water is composed of oxygen and hydrogen./책은 5권으로 ~ The book consisits of [is published in] five volumes./국회는 양원으로 되어 있다 The National Assembly consists of two Houses./사회는 개인의 집합체로 되어 있다 A community is composed of individuals./그 회는 300명의 회원으로 되어 있다 The association is composed of 300 members.

⑤**(성취·완성)** be made[finished, completed, attained, accomplished]; succeed **(준비가)** be ready/일이 ~ one's work is done **(뜻대로)** succeed in one's attempt; a plan is effected; a project materializes/책이 ~ a book is completed/돈이 ~ succeed in getting money/사람이 ~ become a fine man; be a fine man/언제 다 되느냐 When will it be done[ready]?/계획이 제대로 됐다 A plan is effected, A plot is carried out./공사가 다 되었다 The work is finished[completed]./돈이면 안 될 일이 없다 Money is everything./만사가 제대로 되었다 All went well [with us]./되고 안 되고는 자네에게 달렸다 It's success or failure solely rests[depends] upon you./식사 준비가 됐습니다 Dinner is ready./일이 되고 안 되는 것은 운에 달리는 수도 있다 The success of failure of a plan sometimes depends upon luck.

⑥**(쓸모·적합)** serve the purpose; will do; work; be all right/이 의자면 되겠소ー그것이면 되오 Will this chair do you?—That will do me very well./되지 않은 말 nonsense; absurd remarks/그 돈이면 되겠다 That amount of money will do./이 짧은 끈으로 되겠읍니까ー예 됩니다 Will this short string do?—Yes, it will do./그것은 말도 되지 않는다 That is nonsense[absurd]./이것은 안 되겠군 This one's no good!/그렇게 해서야 되겠니? That won't do, You shouldn't do that./무어 좀 쓸 것이 필요한데ー이 연필이면 되겠읍니까? I want something to write with.—Does this pencil serve your purpose?

⑦**(계절·때가)** come; set in; become/봄이 ~ spring has come; spring is with us/초사흘이 ~ the 3rd of the month has come around.

⑧**(수가)** number; amount to; run up to; make; be **(무게가)** weigh **(용적·넓이·크기가)** measure **(면적이)** cover/그 수량이 약 300이나 된다 They number about three hundred., They are about three hundred in number./그는 키가 6피트나 된다 He is six feet tall., He stands six feet./몸 무게가 140파운드나 된다 I weigh one hundred and forty pounds./강폭이 100피트나 된다 The river measures[is] one hundred feet across./농장은 약 2천 평방미터 된다 The farm covers two about thousand square meters.

⑨**(흥성·생육)** grow; thrive; prosper/장사가 잘 ~ do good[prosperous] business; business is good/집안이 잘 ~ a family is prosperous; a family thrives./집안이 잘 안 되어 가다 a family is going downhill./채소가 잘 ~ vegetables grow well (in this soil).

⑩**(지나다)** pass; elapse; be [since]/저 나무를 심은 지 10년이나 된다 It is ten years since we planted that tree./얼마나 오래됩니까 How long has it been?/서울 간 지 10년이나 된다 It is ten years since he went to Seoul.

⑪**(관계)** ¶ 그는 나의 조카가 된다 He stands to me in the relation of nephew., He is my nephew.

⑫**(구실)** act as; serve as; play the role of/중매인이 ~ act as a gobetween/햄릿이 ~ play the role[take the part] of Hamlet 알코홀은 소독약이 된다 Alcohol acts as a disinfectant.

**되¹** 《계량기》 a measure 《곡식용》 a dry measure 《액체용》 a liquid measure 《한 되》 a doi [a unit of measure, 10 *hop*] / 다섯 ~들이 a five *doi* measure / ~를 속이다 give short measure. ます

**되²** 《만주인》 a Manchurian 《중국인》 a Chinese. まんしゅうじん

**되³** 《도로·다시》 back; again 《도리어》 on the contrary; instead / ~묻다 ask in return / ~사다 buy back / ~풀이하다 say again; repeat; reiterate. また

**되** ①though; although; even though; but / 아름답기는 하~ 지성미가 없다 Although she is beautiful, she lacks intellectual beauty ②and indeed[really]; and that; and… at that. —が

**되강오리** 《조》 a Chinese little grebe; a dabchick; a didapper; *Podiceps ruficollis poggei*(학명).

**되개고마리** 《조》 an indian red-tailed shrike; *Lanius cristatus*(학명).

**되걸리다** recur 《병이 주어》 return 《사람이 주어》 relapse. さいはつする

**되넘기** brokerage. なかがい

**되넘기다** resell; pass round.

**되놈** 《만주 사람》 a Manchurian 《중국 사람》 a Chinese. まんしゅうじん

**되뇌다** keep repeating 《*words*》/ 남의 말을 ~ echo *a person's* words. かさねていう

**되다¹** ①《짙지 않다》 (be) thick 《밥 따위》 hard ②《벅차다》 (be) hard; bitter ③《심하다》 (be) hard; heavy; severe; intense / 되게 hard; severely; heavily / 된 더위 intense heat ④《켕기다》 (be) tight; fast; tense / 되게 tightly; fast / 되게 동여매다 fasten; tight. かたい

**되다²** 《되질하다》 measure / 쌀을 ~ measure rice. ますではかる

**되다³** ⇒별단 참조. けつかになる

**되뚱하다** (be) rather heavy and thick.

**되때까치** 《조》 a red-tailed shrike[butcherbird]; *Lanius cristatus*(학명).

**되도록** ①《가능한 대로》 as…as possible; as much as you can / ~ 일찍 가라 Go as soon as you can ②《될 수 있게》 till [so that] it becomes / 일등이 ~ 힘써라 Try hard for first place. できるほど

**되돌아가다** turn[go] back; return 《온 길을》 retrace *one's* steps 《선박 따위가》 put back / 중간에서 ~ turn back halfway. もどっていく

**되돌아오다** return; come back / 길을 잃어서 되돌아오지 못했다 I could not find my way back. もどってくる

**되뜨다** (be) irrational; illogical; unreasonable; go against reason.

**되돌다** raise *one's* face defiantly.

**되룽거리다** dangle; sway; swing / 사과가 바람에 되룽거리다 Apples are dangling in the wind. ぶらりぶらりする

**되룽거리다** hold *one's* head high; be haughty; act stuck-up[high-hatted, high-browed]. たかぶる

**되리** a woman who has no pubes[pubic hair]. いんもうのないおんな

**되묻다** ①《다시 묻다》 ask again ②《반문하다》 counter a question by asking another; ask back. くりかえしてきく

**되바라지다** ①《성품이》 (be) sophisticated 《까진》; 《약다》 too smart[sharp] ②《장소가》 narrow-minded 《편협하다》 (be) conspicuous / 되바라진 데 a conspicuous place. ひんいのない

**되살다** ①《먹은 음식이》 remain undigested in the stomach; be heavy on *one's* stomach; feel uncomfortable because of indigestion ②《소생하다》 revive; return [come back] to life / 인공 호흡으로 되살아나다 be resuscitated by artificial respiration. いにもたれる

**되새기다** eat with apparent disrelish. はんすうする

**되술래잡다** turn the tables on 《*one*》; counter-attack. けいせいをぎゃくてんする

**되술래잡히다** go for wool and come home shorn; be counter-attacked.

**되씌우다** put a blame on another. かえってぬれぎぬをきせる

**되씹다** ①《말을》 harp on the same string; dwell 《*on*》 ②《되새기다》 eat with apparent disrelish; harp on the same thing. おなじことをくりかえしていう

**되알지다** ①《억지손 세다》 (be) aggresive; impudent; pushing; audacious ②《힘에 벅차다》 (be) beyond *one's* power; more than one can do. けちだ

**뙤약볕** the burning[scorching, dazzling] sun. やけこがすようなひ

**되어가다** turn out; go; come / 잘 ~ go well[all right]; succeed. なっていく

**되우** very; exceedingly; hard; awfully; extraordinarily; heavily; severely; bitterly / ~ 춥다 be very cold / ~ 무식하다 be quite ignorant / ~ 근심되다 be much worried. ひじょうに

**되우새** 《조》 a spectacled teal; *Anas formosa*(학명).

**되작거리다** ransack; rummage; forage for 《*something*》. ひっかきまわす

**되잡다** lay the blame on another ⇒되씌우다.

**되장이** a person who measures grain at a rice-dealer's.

**되직하다** (be) somewhat thick / 풀이 ~ The paste is a bit thick. しっこい

**되질** measuring / ~하다 measure.

**되짚어** soon; at once / ~ 가다 turn[go] back soon / ~ 보내다 send back at once; send right away. まもなく

**되창**(—窓) a door with a small window in it. ちいさいまど

**되치이다** be counter-attacked; go for wool and come home shorn; have the tables turned upon. はんげきされる

**되풀이¹** repetition; reiteration; doing over again / ~하다 do 《*a thing*》 over again; repeat / 역사는 ~한다 History repeats itself. くりかえし

**되풀이²** 《되로 계산》 figuring out the cost (of *something*); 《되로 팔기》 selling by the *doi*/~하다 figure[sell] by the *doi*. ますをたんいにしてけいさんすること

**된똥** hard stool[feces]. かたいだいべん

**된바람** 《강풍》 a rushing wind; a gale; a hurricane; a violent wind 《북풍》 a northerly wind. きょうふう

**된밥** rice cooked too hard. かたいめし

**된비알** a steep slope; a precipitous downhill. けわしいがけ

**된서리** a heavy frost; a severe frost/~ 맞다 suffer from a heavy frost. きびしいしも

**된장**(一醬) bean paste. みそう

**된풀** thick paste[starch].

**됨됨이** 《외관》 appearance 《본성》 one's nature 《성격》 character 《품질》 quality. ふうさい

**됫박** a gourd used as a measure. ます

**됫박질** measuring with a gourd bowl; buying by a gourd bowl /~하다 by grain by the *doi*; buy grain in small quantity.

**됫술** about one *doi* of rice wine.

**두** two; a couple/~ 배 double; two times/~ 번 twice; again; two times/같은 실패는 ~ 번 거듭하지 말라 Don't repeat the same failure [again]. ふたつの

**뚜** hooting; with a toot; honking; with a honk/기적이 ~ 울리다 a steam whistle hoots. ぶう

**두**(頭) a head/소 7 ~ seven heads of cattle. とう

**두각**(頭角) top of the head/~을 나타내다 rise above *one*'s fellows; distinguish *one*self; become distinguished/그는 뛰어난 재능으로 ~을 나타내고 있다 He stands out among men for his brilliant mental powers. とうかく

**두개**(頭蓋) 《해》 the cranium/~골 the skull; the cranium. ずがい

**두꺼비** 《동》 a toad. ひきがえる

**두꺼비집** 《전》 a [break and make] switch. かいへいき

**두건**(頭巾) a mourner's hempen cap; a hempen hood for a mourner. ずきん

**두겁** a cap/붓 ~ a sheath of a writing brush. さや

**두껍다** (be) thick/두껍게 하다 thicken; make thicker. あつい

**두껍다랗다** (be) rather thick; be rather heavy. ひじょうにあつい

**두껍조상**(一祖上) the most distinguished person among *one*'s ancestors. そせんのなかでさいもすぐれたひと

**뚜껑** 《시계 따위의》 a lid 《병·만년필의》 a cap 《붓 따위의》 a shield 《포켓 따위의》 a flap/~을 덮다 put on the lid; cover up. ふた

**뚜껑이불** padded quilts without sheets.

**두께** thickness/~가 5인치이다 be five inches thick[in thickness]. あつさ

**두견**(杜鵑) ① 《소쩍새》 a cuckoo ② 《진달래》 an azalea. ほととぎす

**두고두고** many times; from time to time; over and over again; over a long period 《영원히》 forever; for good and all 《잊지 않고》 hauntingly; unforgettably. なんしい

**두그르르, 뚜그르르** with a single roll of a large heavy thing. ごろっと

**두근거리다** go pitapat; palpitate; throb /두근두근 pitapat; palpitating; throbbing. どきつく

**두남두다** favo[u]r 《동정하다》 sympathize; have a bias for. みかたする

**두뇌**(頭腦) a head; brains/치밀[산만]한 ~ a close[loose] head/~가 던석한 사람 a clear-headed person. ずのう

**두다** ① 《놓다》 put; place 《세워서》 set 《뉘어서》 lay 《보존하다》 keep 《저장하다》 store ② 《사람을》 keep 《하숙인을》 lodge; engage 《고용하다》 employ/가정 교사를 ~ engage[have] a [private] tutor ③ 《배치하다》 put; station /보초를 ~ post a sentinel ④ 《사이를》 leave /5미터 간격을 두고 at five metre intervals/간격을 두지 않다 leave no space ⑤ 《마음을》 harbour; bear; cherish; entertain/존을 ~ regard 《*one*》 with affection ⑥ 《넣다》 stuff/이불에 솜을 ~ stuff a quilt with cotton ⑦ 《바둑·장기를》 play. おく

**두대박이** a two-masted ship; a two-master.

**두더지** 《동》 a mole/~ 가죽 moleskin/~ 혼인 같다 cherish an impossible hope.

**뚜덕거리다** knock; tap; rap/뚜덕뚜덕 rapping; tapping; rap-tap-tapping. こつんこつんたたく

**두덜거리다, 뚜덜거리다** grumble; complain; mutter/두덜두덜[뚜덜뚜덜] grumbling; complaining; griping; nagging; bitching 《속》. ぶつぶついう

**두덩** ① 《둑》 a bank; an embankment 《논의》 a levee/밭두렁 a bank around a field ② 《신체의》 a raised part of *one*'s body; a mount/눈 ~ *one*'s eyelids. うね

**두동지다** (be) self-contradictory; inconsistent; incoherent/너의 지금 이야기는 두동진다 There is no logic in your last remark. ちょうしはずれだ

**뚜뚜** toot-toot; hoot-hoot/나팔을 ~ 불다 blow a trumpet. ぶうぶう

**두두룩하다** (be) swollen; bulging out; puffy; full/두두룩한 돈지갑 a plump purse. ぷっくりふくらんだ

**두둑** a ridge between fields 《두덩》 a levee. あぜ

**두둑하다** 《두덥다》 (be) thick; heavy 《넉넉하다》 ample; plenty; satisfactory/두둑한 사례 an ample reward/호주머니에 두둑한 돈 a pocketful of money. ぶあつい

**두둔** favo[u]r; partiality; favo[u]ritism; protection/~하다 favo[u]r 《편들다》 side with/~하는 사람 a sympathizer. かばうこと

**두드러기** nettle rash; hives; urticaria /〜가 돋다 have urtication; break out in a rash.

**두드러지다** ①(내밀다) swell; bulge out ②(뛰어나다) (be) prominent; noted; conspicuous; remarkable. めだっている

**두드리다, 뚜드리다** strike; beat; hit; knock/문을 ~ knock at the door/가볍게 ~ tap/세게 ~ rap; bang. たたく

**두들기다** strike; hit; beat; knock/늘씬하게 ~ beat (one) to a jelly. たたく

**두럭** gamblers; the ranks of those who gamble.

**두런거리다** exchange murmurs/두런두런 murmuring. ひそひそはなす

**두렁** a ridge between rice-fields; a levee. あぜ

**두렁이** a baby's skirt. こどものスカート

**두렁허리** 〘어〙 a kind of eel; *Fluta alba* (학명). やつめうなぎ

**두레** (연장) a water scooper used in irrigation (모임) a farmer's co-operative group.

**두레박** a well-bucket/우물에서 ~으로 물을 긷다 draw water from a well with a bucket. つるべ

**두레박줄** a well-rope. つるべなわ

**두레박질** ~하다 draw water from a well with a bucket. へるべてみずをくむこと

**두레질** ~하다 water a rice-field with a pail.

**두려빠지다** come off from a center; an entire area sinks. えぐりとられる

**두려움** (공포) fear; dread; horror; awe; reverence; apprehension. きょうふ

**두려워하다** ①(무서워하다) fear; dread; be afraid of (근심하다) apprehend/그 일이 일어날까봐 나는 두려워하였다 I was afraid if it should happen ②(외경(畏敬)) fear; hold (one) in reverence; stand in awe of (one). こわがる

**두렵다** ①(무섭다) be afraid (of); be fearful (of); fear; (근심) be concerned about; terrified ②(외경(畏敬)하다) be awed. こわい

**두렷이, 뚜렷이** clearly; distinctly; plainly; vividly/그 광경은 지금도 내 마음 속에 ~ 남아 있다 The sight is vivid in my mind even now はっきり

**두렷하다, 뚜렷하다** (be) clear; distinct; vivid; plain/뚜렷한 기억 a vivid recollection/뚜렷한 대답 a definite answer/뚜렷한 목소리 a clear voice/뚜렷한 증거 a positive proof. めいはくだ

**두령**(頭領) a leader; a boss. おやぶん

**두루** (널리) universally; widely (전체적으로) all over; all around (골고루) equally; evenly (예외 없이) without exception. あまねく

**두루마기** a Korean overcoat; a *dooroomagi.*

**두루마리** a roll of paper 《편지지》 rolled letter paper; scroll.

**두루뭉수리** ①《사물》 a mess; a failure ②《사람》 a good-for-nothing; a ne'er-do-well. かたまり

**두루미** 〘조〙 a white crane with a red chest; the sacred crane. つる

**두루미냉이** 〘식〙 a Chinese artichoke; *Stachys sieboldii* (학명).

**두루주머니** a pouch; a money purse of cloth; a purse.

**두루치기**¹ 《음식》 a dish of boiled shellfishes. ゆでたもの

**두루치기**² 《둘러쓰기》 using a thing for various purpose. あまねくつかわれるもの

**두룽다리** a [high] fur cap; a tall fur hat. けがわのぼうかんぐ

**두류**(逗留, 逗留) a stay; a stop; a sojourn/〜하다 stop; stay/호텔에 〜하다 stay at a hotel/오래 〜하다 make a long stay. とうりゅう

**두르다** ①(원형으로) enclose (*with, in*); surround (*with, by*); encircle ②(가리다) envelop; cover ③(변통하다) obtain an accommodation (*of*) ④(사람을) manage (*a man*); have at *one's* beck and call. おおいかくす

**두르르, 뚜르르** 《말리는 모양》 round; with a twirl 《바퀴 소리》 rolling; rumbling. くるくる

**두름** a string of fish or vegetables; bunches of vegetable. ひとさし

**두름성** management (융통성) manipulation/〜이 있다 be versatility. やりくり

**두리기** dining together.

**두리기둥** a rounded column. えんちゅう

**두리반**(一般) a large[round] dining table. まるいおぼん

**두리번거리다** look around; stare around; look about (one) [wonderingly]/이상하게 생각하여 눈을 ~ look round in wonder. きょろきょろみる

**두리번두리번** with a startled look; restlessly; wonderingly (이상한 듯이) curiously/〜 휘둘러보다 stare round; look curiously at. きょろきょろ

**두말** 《이랬다저랬다 하는 말》 duplicity; a doubletongue; equivocation; double dealing/〜하다 be double-tongued[-faced]; break *one's* word; keep two tongues in one mouth; tell a lie/〜하지 않는 사람 a man of his word/〜 않고 frankly; honestly; without complaint; without objection; immediately/〜 말고 어서 돈을 내라 Pay me the money here and now. むだくち

**두멍** a cauldron[a large iron pot] used to store water. おおがま

**두메** a mountainous district; a remote village/두멧사람 mountain folk; inhabitants of a mountainous district; people in a remote village. さんきょう

**두메구석** a remote village; an out-of-the-way corner of a mountain district; a remote backwood. へきそん

**두목**(頭目) a chief; a head; a leader; a captain; a boss《의·속》. とうもく

**두문 불출**(杜門不出) ~하다 shut oneself up; lead a solitary life; remain[stay] indoors; confine oneself at home.

**두미**(頭尾) the head and the tail; beginning and end. あたまとお

**두미 없다**(頭尾—) (be) inconclusive; loose; desultory; incoherent／그의 이야기는 ~ He speaks incoherently.

**두발**(頭髮) the hair [of the head]／~ 탈락증〖의〗 alopecia. とうはつ

**뚜벅거리다** swagger; strut; walk gingerly. いばってあるく

**두벌갈이** a second sowing; a second crop／~하다 sow twice; raise a second crop.

**두부**(豆腐) bean-curd／~ 한 모 a cake of bean-curd／~ 장수 a bean-curd seller [dealer]. とうふ

**두부**(頭部) the head／~의 cephalic／~를 다쳤다 He was injured[wounded] in the head. とうぶ

**두상**(頭上) ~에 over[above, upon] one's head; over head. ずじょう

**두상화**(頭狀花) 〖식〗 a capitate flower; a flower head. とうじょうか

**두서**(頭書) a superscription／~의 superscribed; above-mentioned.

**두서**(頭緒) ①《단서》 a clue; the first step; the beginning; the commencement／일의 ~를 잡다 get a clue to a matter ② 《조리》 consistence; coherence; order; coherency／~ 없는 rambling; incoherent desultory; silly; absurd. たんしょ

**두서너** two or three-or-four; a few／~ 사람 a few people／~ 마디 a few words. ふたつかみっつくらいの

**두서넛** two or three; a few. ふたつかみっつくらい

**두세, 두셋** two or three; few／두세 번 two or three times. ふたつかみっつ

**두어, 두엇** about two; a few; a couple of. ふたつくらいの

**두억시니** 〖민〗 a [female] demon; a [she] devil. やしや

**두엄** 《거름》 a compost [heap]; barnyard manure. たいひ

**두옥**(斗屋) a hut; a shack; a shed. ちいさいいえ

**두우**(斗宇) the universe; the cosmos; heaven and earth; the macrocosm.

**두운**(頭韻) 〖언〗 alliteration／~법(法) alliteration／~을 밟다[맞추다] alliterate. とういん

**두유**(豆油) soy [bean] oil. まめあぶら

**뚜장이** a pimp; a pander／~ 짓을 하다 act as a pimp; pander. なこうど

**두전**(頭錢) a commission; brokerage／~을 받다 take a commission; charge for brokerage.

**두절**(杜絶) stoppage; cutting off; cessation; interruption／~하다 stop; cease; be interrupted; be paralysed; be at a deadlock[a standstill]／수출의 ~ the stoppage of export. とぜつ

**두족류**(頭足類) 〖동〗 *Cephalopoda*(학명)／~의 동물· a cephalopod. とうそくるい

**두주**(頭註) marginal notes; headnotes. とうちゅう

**두진**(痘疹) the smallpox and the measles; pustules. とうしん

**두찬**(杜撰) a careless work; a faulty book; a book without good authority. ずさん

**두텁다** (be) close; cordial; warm／두터운 우정〖친분〗 a close friendship[relations]. にんじょうぶかい

**두통**(頭痛) a headache／머리가 깨어지는 듯한 ~ a splitting[racking] headache／~이 나다 have a headache／~을 앓다 worry about (*a matter*). ずつう

**두통거리**(頭痛—) a headache; a source [cause] of constant anxiety[trouble]; a worry; a thorn in one's side／인구 문제는 아주 ~다 The population problem is a real headache. やっかいなもの

**두툴두툴** ~하다 (be) uneven; pimply rough; lumpy／길이 몹시 ~하다 The road is awfully rough. ぼこぼこ

**두툼하다** (be) somewhat thick／두툼한 입술 full lips. ややあつい

**두편**(—便) this side and that side; both sides.

**두호**(斗護) protection; patronage; looking after／~하다 protect; patronize; look after; favo[u]r／~ 아래 under the patronage (*of*)／약자를 ~하다 protect the weak／그가 나를 ~하여 주었다 He stood up for me. ほご

**두흔**(痘痕) a pockmark; a pit／~이 있다 be pitted[pockmarked]. とうこん

**둑** a bank; a dike; an embankment; a levee／~을 쌓다 build a dike; embank. ていぼう

**뚝** ①《갑자기》 suddenly／~ 그치다 come to a dead stop; stop suddenly ②《떨어지는 소리》 plump; flop ③《꺾는 소리》 with a snap. ぱっと

**뚝따거리다** ①《소리》 clatter; rattle ②《가슴이》 go pitapat; palpitate; throb. かちかちたたく

**뚝뚝** ①《물방울 소리》 dripping; trickling; drop by drop ②《부러지는 소리》 snappingly.

**뚝뚝하다** ①《애교가 없다》 (be) unsociable; unaffable; blunt; brusque／뚝뚝하게 bluntly; curtly; surlily ②《굳다》 (be) stiff; rigid. れいたんだ

**뚝발이** a cripple 、절뚝발이. びっこ

**뚝배기** an unglazed earthenware bowl.

**뚝별나다** (be) quick-tempered; touchy; peevish／그 더자는 나이 이야기만 나오면 매우 뚝별나게 군다 She is most touchy on the subject of age.／뚝별난 친구다 He is a testy fellow. おこりっぽい

**뚝별씨** hot temper; quick temper; touchiness; testiness; peevishness. だんき

**뚝심** physical strength; staying power 《당해 내는 힘》 endurance; sinews; tenacity／~이 센 사람 a man of mighty s-

둔각(鈍角) 《數》 a obtuse angle／~ 삼각형 an obtuse-angled triangle. どんかく

둔감(鈍感) dullness; insensibility; stolidity／~하다 (be) dull; insensible; thick headed[-skinned]. どんかん

둔갑술(遁甲術) occult arts; the art of invisibility. とんこうじゅつ

둔갑하다(遁甲—) disappear 《변신하다》 change[transform] oneself (into); take the form[shape] (of).

둔답(屯畓) ①《주둔군에 따른》 paddy fields cultivated by troops regularly stationed in the area ②《관청에 따른》 government owned rice fields.

둔덕 a hilly spot; a hill. おか

둔도(鈍刀) a dull[a blunt] sword[knife]. どんとう

둔병(屯兵) stationary troops 《수비병》 a garrison.

둔사(遁辭) an excuse; a plea; a pretext.

둔세(遁世) escape from life／~하다 renounce[retire] from the world. とんせい

둔열(鈍劣) stupidity; dullness／~하다 (be) stupid; dull ぐどん

둔영(屯營) a military camp[station]; barracks; a cantonment. とんえい

둔재(鈍才) dull wit; stupidity 《사람》 a dunce; a dullard／~의 dull-witted; dull. どんさい

둔적(遁迹) disappearing; vanishing; hiding oneself／~하다 cover one's trail; vanish; disappear (from); hide oneself (from).

둔전(屯田) a farm cultivated by stationary troops; a farm cultivated by the militia. とんでん

둔질(鈍質) stupidity; dullness; imbecility／~의 stupid; dull; imbecile.

둔치 the edge of the water; the waterside; a beach.

둔탁(鈍濁) dullness; slowness／~하다 (be) dull; slow; stupid; dull-witted; thick-witted. ぐどん

둔팍하다(鈍—) (be) thick-headed; slow-witted; stolid; stupid. おろかである

둔피(遁避) evasion; elusion／~하다 evade; elude. いんとん

둔필(鈍筆) 《글씨》 a poor handwriting 《사람》 a poor hand.

둔하다(鈍—) (be) dull; slow; stupid／둔 한 사람 a dull man. にぶい

둔한(鈍漢) a dolt; a stupid fellow; a stolid[dull] person. のろま

둘 two／~째 the second／~째로 secondly; in the second place／~씩 two at a time; by tows; in pairs／~로 접은 two-fold; twicefolded／~ 걸러 in[at] every third place／~ 중 하나 one of the two; one between the two／~도 없는 unique; peerless; matchless; the only; unrivaled; sole／~로 나누다 divide (a thing) in[into] two; divide by two／~ 중 어 느 이야기도 진실이 아니다 Neither story is true. ふたつ

둘- 《접두어》 sterile; barren／~게집 a sterile woman／~암소[암닭] a barren cow[hen]. ふにんの

둘되다 (be) stupid; dull; stolid; thick[-headed] 《상냥찮다》 curt; unpolished; blunt. むとんちゃくだ

둘둘, 똘똘 《말거나 감는 모양》 round and round; with a twirl／~ 감다 wind (a rope); round (a thing). くるくる

둘러대다 ①《변통하다》 manage to get a loan; swing a loan／집을 사려고 돈을 ~ swing a loan in order to buy a house ②《꾸며 대다》 put[cook] up (a good reason, excuse); make a ready remark [to get around a situation]／돈 못 갚는 이 유를 ~ put up good reasons why one hasn't been able to return the money. いいまわす

둘러막다 enclose; surround; environ; hem[shut] in. かこいをする

둘러보다 look round[about]. みまわす

둘러붙다 change front; turn around; change sides; go[flop] to the other party／유리한 쪽으로 ~ turn around to the favorable side. ひっつく

둘러싸다 《포위하다》 besiege; lay siege to 《에워싸다》 surround; enclose／바다에 둘 러싸인 나라 a sea-girt country／난로를 ~ gather about a stove. ほういする

둘러서다 stand in a circle. かこんでたつ

둘러앉다 sit in a circle. かこんですわる

둘러엎다 overturn; upset; overthrow 《하던 일을》 do away with／밥상을 ~ overturn a dining table. ひっくりかえす

둘러치다 ①《두르다》 surround; enclose／ 담을 ~ surround with walls ②《내던지다》 throw; fling; hurl. かこむ

둘레 circumference; girth／~에 round ／못의 ~ the circumference of a pond ／~ 5 피트 five feet round[in circumference]. まわり

둘레둘레 round; around; about 《빙둘러》 in a circle／~ 보다 look around; stare about／~ 앉다 sit round in a circle. きょろきょろ

둘리다 ①《둘러 막히다》 be surrounded; be enclosed; be environed; be embosomed; be fenced; be encompassed／사방이 산으로 둘러싸인 마을 a village surrounded[shut in, hemmed in] by mountains on all sides ②《싸여 가리어지다》 be put round; be wrapped in; be worn／ 머리에 수건이 ~ wear a towel around one's head ③《휘둘리다》 be controlled; be swayed; be wielded. かこまれる

둘소 a barren[sterile] cow.

둘이 two people; a couple; a pair／~ 서 로 사이가 멀어졌다 They became estranged from each other. ふたり

둘째 the second; number two／그는 ~ 번 으로 왔다 He was the second to come. にばんめ

둘하다 (be) stupid; dull; dull-witted; c-

뚫다 ①(구멍을) bore; punch; make [a hole]; drill 《관통하다》 pierce; cut[pass, run] through; shoot through; penetrate／구멍 뚫는 기구 a drill; a perforator; a punch ②(길을) bore; cut; excavate; build／터널을 ～ cut[bore, drive] a tunnel ③(이치에 통하다・통찰하다) pierce; penetrate; attain; get at; master／영원한 진리를 ～ attain to the eternal truth ④(틈을 비집다・무릅쓰다) go[elbow] through; penetrate 《곤란을》 weather 《무릅쓰다》 brave／인파 속을 뚫고 나아가다 penetrate a crowd ⑤(끓을 알아내다) find a way／돈 구멍을 ～ find a way to get money. あなをあける

뚫어내다 pierce out; bore out; manage to pierce／학문의 깊은 이치를 ～ manage to master the secrets of learning／험한 산길을 ～ open a path through a steep mountain. あなをあける

뚫어뜨리다 succeed[manage] to bore[pierce, perforate]; pierce[bore] out／나는 신발을 뚫어뜨렸다 I have worn out my shoes. あなをあけてとおす

뚫어지게 보다 stare (at); look hard (at); scrutinize／사람을 ～ stare at (a person). にらみつける

뚫어지다 (송곳 따위가) bore; drill; pierce; perforate (물건에 구멍이) be bored; be drilled; be pierced; be torn[broken]／이 송곳은 안 뚫어진다 This drill won't bore. あながあく

둥¹ rataplan; rub-a-dub; tomtom; boom／북을 ～ 치다 rataplan; tomtom; thump a drum. とん

둥² ◎그는 조반을 먹는 ～ 마는 ～ 외출하였다 He went out, taking his breakfast in a flurry. するようなしないような

둥개다 be at a loss; be upset; be disconcerted. てにおえない

둥그러지다 tumble (down); fall (down, over); have a tumble. ころぶ

둥그렇다, 둥그렇다 (be) round; circular 《공 모양》 globular. まんまるい

둥그스름하다 (be) roundish; somewhat round[circular, globular]／둥그렇게 round; in a circle. まるみがかっている

둥근톱 a circular saw. まるのこ

둥글다 (be) round; globular 《원만하다》 smooth; 《숭글숭글하다》 amicable. まるい

둥글둥글 ①(둥그렇게) round; in a circle ②(원만하게) harmoniously; smoothly; peacefully; amicably／～한 사람 an amicable person／그는 성격이 ～ 해졌다 The corners of his character are rounded off. まるまると

둥글리다 《깎아서》 round off; round; make round. まるくする

둥글뭉수레하다 (be) roundish; round and blunt-tip ped.

뚱기다 ①(튀기다) let spring back; let resile ②(깨닫게 하다) notice; inform.

뚱기치다 spring back. つよくはじきだす

뚱딴지 ①(사람) a log; a blockhead ②(전기의) an insulator. ばかもの

둥당, 둥땅 ～거리다 play musical 《박자를 치다》 beat time 《흥겹게 놀다》 make merry.

둥덩거리다 rataplan; tomtom; beat loudly. どんどんとうちならす

둥둥¹ (북소리) rub-a-dub; rat-a-tat; rat-a-plan; tom-tom; boom-boom; drumming; thumping／북을 ～ 울리다 beat a drum boom-boom. ぶかぶか

둥둥² floating ふうしむしむ

뚱뚱보 a corpulant fellow; a fatty; a plump person／그 여자는 ～다 She is a fat piece. でぶっちょ

뚱뚱하다 (be) fat; corpulent 《포동포동하다》 plump／그는 배가 ～ He is a pot-bellied man. ふとっている

뚱보 ①(뚱한 사람) a taciturn[glum, uncommunicative] person ②(뚱뚱보) a plump person; a fatso《속》; a cornfed person. むっつりしたひと

둥실 buoyantly; floating／배가 ～ 뜨다 a boat is floating buoyantly. ふわ

둥신거리다 move slowly[sluggishly, lazily]. からだをにぶくうごかすこと

둥우리 a basket. かご

둥치 the butt (밑둥) the base of a tree trunk. きのね

둥치다 tie up together; pack up; cut off the worthless part. いっしょにくくる

뚱하다 ①(말이 적다) (be) taciturn; silent; uncommunicative; quiet; reserved; reticent ②(못마땅하다) (be) moody; glum; sullen. むっとしている

뒈지다 kick the bucket; bite the dust; drop dead. しぬ

뒤 ◎별항 참조(page 1410).

뒤까불다 behave rashly; bear oneself frivolously. けいそつにふるまう

뒤꼍 the backyard; the back [side]; out in back／집 ～에서 놀다 play in the backyard; play out in back.

뒤꼭지치다 be dejected; get disheartened. らくたんする

뒤꽁무니 the tail; the for end こんむに

뒤꽂이 a hair-ornament.

뒤꿈치 the heel／구두 ～ the heel of a shoe. かかと

뒤끓다 ①(끓다) seethe; boil up ②(소란하다) be in uproar; infest ③(여럿이) swarm; quirm／장마당에 사람들이 뒤끓었다 A marketplace was crowded with people. わきたつ

뒤끝 (종말) an end; a close; a conclusion (낙착) settlement 《결과》 an outcome; an issue／～이 어떻게 될까 How will the metter end? まつり

뒤내다 shrink back (at, from); recoil; recede; hang[hold] back; back out of an agreement. てをひく

뒤넘기치다 (넘겨뜨리다) throw down; throw (a person) to the ground; get (a person) down／식탁을 ～ overturn a di-

ning table. なげおとす
**뒤넘다** (엎어지다) be overturned (넘어지다) fall on one's back/병풍이 뒤넘었다 The screen has turned over.
あおむきにたおれる
**뒤넘스럽다** (be) pert; impudent; forward/뒤넘스럽게도 …하다 have the impudence to…. なまいきだ
**뒤놀다** ①(흔들리다) be shaky ②(방랑하다) wander; roam; knock around《미·구》; jump about. ぐらつく
**뒤놀다** gambol; frisk; frolic; romp; play pranks. はねまわる
**뒤놓다** upset; overturn; overthrow; turn over. ひっくりかえす
**뒤늦다** be too late; be behind time/뒤늦게 too late. あまりおくれる
**뛰다**¹ ①(물·진흙 따위가) splash; spatter; sputter (불꽃이) spark ②(도망가다) run away; escape/국외로 ~ fly the country ③(두근두근하다) beat; palpitate; rush. はねあがる
**뛰다**² (도약하다) leap; spring; jump (뛰다) bound (가슴이) throb; palpitate (달리다) run. とびあがる
**뛰다**³ (그네를) swing (on a swing); have a swing (널을) seesaw; play seesaw.
ぶらんこにのる
**뒤따르다** follow; accompany; continue (행렬 따위를) bring[close] up the rear. おう
**뒤대다**¹ (공급하다) suppy (with); support; furnish with; provide (one with)/아들의 학비를 ~ supply one's son with school expenses. きょうきゅうする
**뒤대다**² (틀리게) misinform; make a false statement; tell a lie. やくにいう
**뒤떨다** tremble like an aspen; shiver; shudder. ひじょうにゆらゆらさせる
**뒤떨어지다** ①(처지다) fall behind; be outstripped (후진하다) be backward (in) (낙오하다) draggle/문화에 뒤떨어진 나라 a backward[a developing] country/유행에 뒤떨어지지 않도록 하다 keep pace with the styles ②(남다) remain; stay[drop] behind. うしろにひきはなされる
**뒤덮다** cover; overspread; hang over/그는 길을 걸으며 먼지를 뒤덮어 썼다 He was covered with dust while walking along the road. おおう
**뒤돌아보다** look back; look over one's shoulder; turn round/반생을 ~ look back one's past. ふりかえってみる
**뒤두다** reserve; leave undecided; leave for the future/내일 것으로 뒤두자 Let's save that for tomorrow. よゆうをおく
**뒤둥거리다** be shaky; be loose; totter/뒤둥뒤둥 걷다 walk with faltering steps. ふらふらする
**뒤둥그러지다** ①(뒤틀리다) be distorted; be bent ②(생각이) be come crooked; be perverse. まがる
**뒤뜨다** ①(들뜨다) warp and become loose ②(반항하다) oppose; resist; stand up.

ゆがんでゆるんでいる
**뒤뜰** a back garden; a backyard; a back lot. うらにわ
**뒤란** a backyard; an enclosure at the back of a house.
**뒤룩거리다** ①(눈알을) glare [one's eyes]; goggle ②(몸을) sway; waddle ③(화가 나서) make angry gestures; jerk with anger/뒤룩뒤룩 (눈알을) glaring (몸을) swaying; waddling (화가 나서) jerking with anger. おこつためつきをする
**뒤룽거리다** swing; hang swinging loose/뒤룽뒤룽 swingingly. ぶらりぶらりする
**뒤미처** (곧) soon after; before long (이어서) without intermission[a break]/점심 후에 ~ 그는 일을 시작했다 He set to work immediately after lunch. /~ 쫓아가다 follow a person right after he has left. すぐ
**뒤바꾸다** invert; reverse/순서을 ~ reverse the order; make a mistake in the sequence. さかさまにする
**뒤바뀌다** be inverted[reversed]; get out of order; get mixed over/순서가 ~ be out of order. さかさまにされる
**뒤받다** make a protest; retort; counterattack. いいかえす
**뒤버무리다** ①(섞다) mix up; mix together ②(말을) equivocate; prevaricate; quibble. よくまぜる
**뒤범벅** a hotchpotch; a jumble; a mixture; a muddle; a confusion/~되다 be mixed up. ごちゃごちゃなじょうたい
**뒤변덕스럽다** (be) very whimsical; fanciful; very capricious; fickle/뒤번덕스러운 여인 a fickle[capricious] woman.
ひじょうにきまぐれだ
**뒤보다**¹ (용변보다) go to stool; have a bowel movement; ease nature; evacuate the bowels. だいべんをする
**뒤보다**² (잘못 보다) make a mistake; misjudge/사람의 진의를 ~ misread (a person's) motives[intention]. みあやまる
**뒤보아주다** take care of; look after; help/그는 나를 친형제처럼 뒤보아준다 He takes quite a brotherly interest in me.
こうえんする
**뒤뿔치기** taking care of a person's menial task/뒤뿔치다 work for another; do hack work for. したづみのほねおりしごと
**뒤서다** fall behind; be outstripped; be backward. おくれる
**뒤섞다** mix up; mingle together; throw into confusion/흙과 모래를 ~ mix earth with sand; add sand to earth.
こんごうする
**뒤섞이다** be mixed [together up]; adulterated; be intermingled/우유에 물이 ~ milk is adulterated with some water.
こんごうされる
**뒤숭숭하다** (be) confused; disorder; restless; nervous; ill at ease/마음이 ~ feel restless[nervous]. そわそわしている
**뒤스럭거리다** ①(뒤지다) fumble[feel](for,

뒤스르다 arrange; put in order; move after, in, about); rummage; ransack ②《변덕부리다》(be) fickle; capricious; whimsical. てさぐりする

around to. てはいする
뛰어가다 go at a run; run; rush; dash /집까지 쭉 뛰어갔다 He ran all the way to house. はしっていく

# 뒤

①《후방》the back; the rear 「end」; behind/뒷방 a back room/~로 돌아 Right about turn[face]!. About turn!, About face!/고국을 ~로 하다 leave one's home country/~를 마주대고 앉다 sit back to back/~따라가다 walk behind (a person); follow (a person)/~돌아보다 look back; look behind/~돌아서다 turn back; turn on one's heels/~에서 부르다 call (a person) from behind/~로 넘어지다 fall backward/훨씬 ~에 앉다 sit far back /~에 남다 stay[remain] behind/~에 있는 사람 a person behind/동네 뒷산 a hill at the rear of the village/~를 쫓다 follow up; run after. /~에서 수레를 밀다 push a cart from behind/ ~에서 누가 부른다 Someone is calling from behind. /~를 돌아보지 말고 가라 Go ahead without looking back. /맨~에 가는 것이 기병대다 It is the cavalry that brings up the rear. /~에 혼자서 쳐져 있다 He is staying behind all alone.

②《미래·장래》the future; the time to come 뒷일/~를 떠맡다 answer for the consequences 《돌봄》look after a person's affairs/그는 ~에 사람이 되었다 He became a great man later on. /뒷날을 생각하다 think of the future /뒷날에 대비하다 provide for the future/내가 그 유가족의 ~를 돌보마 I will look after[take care of] the bereaved family.

③《나중·다음》later; later on; afterwards/닷새 ~에 after five days; five days after/아침 식사 ~에 after breakfast/텔레비전을 본 ~에 after watching television/~로 미루다 postpone; put off /~에 전화하겠다 I'll call you up later. /~로 미루어라 That can wait., Let it wait. /당신은 ~에 후회할 것이다 You'll be sorry afterwards. /성은 잘 내지만 ~는 없는 사람이다 He is quick to get angry and quick to get over it.

④《배후》background/ ~에서 남의 욕[험담]을 하지 말라 Don't speak ill of others behind their backs. /누군가가 ~에서 그를 조종하고 있는 것 같습니다 Somebody seems to be pulling the wires over bind him. /~에서 공작하다 maneber behind the scenes; pull the strings.

⑤《배경》backing; support; what is wanted; one's needs/그는 ~가 든든하다 He has strong backing. /~를 대다 keep in supply; supply one's needs; supply money/~를 밀어 주다 back up[support] (a person)/~를 밀어 주는 사람 a backer; a patron; a sponsor/공부하는 아들의 ~를 대주다 pay school expenses for one's son/장사하는 사람의 ~를 대다 supply a merchant with funds.

⑥《결과·뒤끝》the end; the conclusion; the latter part; consequences; aftermath/~는 내가 맡겠다 I will answer for the consequences. /그렇게 하면 ~가 재미 없을 것이다 You will have to pay dearly for doing so. /사건의 뒷처리를 하다 settle[wind up] an affair; get an affair straightened/뒷일이 어찌 되건 알게 뭐야 I do not care what may come of it. /~가 어떻게 되는지 나는 모른다 I shall not take responsibility for the results. /이 술은 ~가 좋지 않다 This liquor leaves[has] nasty aftereffects.

⑦《후손·자손》a descendant 《가독》inheritance; offspring; descent; posterity 《남은 가족》the bereaved [family]/ 그로써 그 집 ~는 끊어진다 The family will become extinct with his death.

⑧《계승》what is left behind by a predecessor; the footsteps (of)/~를 이을 사람 《남자》an heir 《여자》an heiress/~를 잇다 succeed to[take over] (a person's business); succeed [one's father as the head of the family] 《후임》succeed (a person) at the post; occupy a seat left[vacated] by (a person)/사장의 ~를 잇다 succeed to the presidency/전임자의 ~를 이어 사업을 운영하다 step into the shoes of one's predecessor and run the business.

⑨《행방》a trace; a track; a trail/~를 밟다[쫓다] shadow [follow] (a person); trail (a fox).

⑩《나머지》the rest; the remainder/ ~는 아시겠지요 You know the rest., You may guess the rest., The rest needs no telling.

⑪《대변》feces; excrement; stools; a bowel movement/~가 마렵다 have an urge to go to the bathroom; feel like having a bowel movement/~를 보다 go to stool; relieve[ease] oneself; relieve.

**뛰어나가다** run out; jump[leap] out/앞으로 ~ run forward. とびでる

**뛰어나다** 《남보다》 be superior (to); excel (in); surpass; stand[tower] high above (the others)/지능이 뛰어난 사람 a man of excellent intelligence/뛰어난 재주 a distinguished talent. よりすぐれている

**뛰어내리다** jump[leap, spring] down/말에서 ~ fling oneself from one's horse. とびおりる

**뛰어넘다** ①《몸을》 leap over; jump[skip, pass] over ②《거르다》 skip/한 계급 뛰어넘어 승진되다 be jumped one grade in rank. とびこえる

**뛰어들다** jump into; run into/창문으로 ~ leap in at the window. とびこむ

**뛰어보다** look for; hunt up[after]; search (for); ransack; rummage/나는 열쇠를 찾으려고 호주머니를 뛰어보았다 I searched[felt in] my pockets for the key. あさる

**뛰어오다** run; come running/학교에서 쭉 뛰어왔다 He ran all the way from school. かけてくる

**뛰어오르다** jump on; leap[spring] up/강단에 ~ spring up on a platform. とびあがる

**뛰어지다** die; kick the bucket《속》. しぬ

**뒤웅박** a gourd; a calabash. ひょうたん

**뒤재주치다** throw; turn over hurl; fling. たらにひっくりかえす

**뒤적거리다** make search; rummage; ransack/뒤적뒤적 rummaging. あさる

**뒤적이다** rummage (=뒤적거리다.

**뒤조지다** settle; set (matters) right; wind up (one's affairs). わんをおす

**뒤쫓아가다** follow (one); follow at another's heels; go in the wake of keep up with 《뒤를 밟다》 dog one's steps, track. うしろをおうていく

**뒤주** a rice-chest; a rice-bin; a grain-chest. こめびつ

**뒤죽박죽** topsyturvy; higgledy-piggledy; pellmell; all mixed up; all jumbled up; in mess; in confusion; in disorder/~으로 topsyturvy; in disorder; in confusion; pellmell. ごちゃごちゃ

**뒤쥐** 《동》 a shrew; a shrewmouse.

**뒤지**(一紙) toilet-paper; privy paper. おとしがみ

**뒤지다**¹ 《뒤떨어지다》 fall behind; lag behind; be backward (in)/남에게 뒤지지 않도록 하다 try to keep abreast of [keep up with] others/한국은 이 점에서 외국에 퍽 뒤졌다 Korea lags far behind other countries in this respect. おそれる

**뒤지다**² search (for); look for; hunt up; rummage; ransack. くまなくさがす

**뒤집개질** turning (a thing) over[upsidedown]/~하다 turn (it) over. うらかえし

**뒤집고 핥다** know thoroughly; understand thoroughly. しりつくす

**뒤집다** ①《겉을》 turn (a coat) out; turn over 《엎다》 upset; overturn ②《순서를》 reverse; invert/정상적 순서를 ~ reverse[change] the normal order ③《야단나게 하다》 throw into confusion/집안을 발칵 ~ put a house into utter confusion. うらかえす

**뒤집어쓰다** ①《온몸에》 pour (water) on (oneself); be covered with (dust) ②《이불 따위를》 draw[pull] over; pull over; pour on ③《죄를》 take (an other's fault) upon oneself/그는 내 죄를 뒤집어썼다 He took my fault[guilt] upon himself. うらかえしてかぶる

**뒤집히다** ①《뒤집어지다》 be upset[overturned]/형세가 뒤집혔다 The tables are turned./학설이 ~ a theory is upset ②《야단나다》 be turned topsyturvy; be in utter confusion. ひっくりかえる

**뒤차**(一車) 《다음 차》 the next[later] train; the following car 《끝차》 a car in the rear. つぎのくるま

**뒤채** a backhouse; a building in the rear.

**뒤채다** ①《많다》 be in excess; be superabundant; be superfluous ②《발에 채다》 obstruct the way. ありあまる

**뒤척거리다** rummage; search; fumble 뒤적거리다. ひっかきまわしてさがす

**뒤축** the heel/~이 높은[낮은] 구두 high [low]-heeled shoes/구두 뒤축이 한쪽만 닳다 wear down one's heels unevenly. くつのかかと

**뒤치다** turn over/책장을 ~ turn over the pages of a book; leaf through a book. おもむけにする

**뒤치닥거리** ①《돌봄》 care/병자의 ~를 하다 attend to the sick; tend the sick; after adjustment ②《정리》 clearing; clearance. しまつ

**뒤통수** 《해》 the occipital region; the back of the head. こうとう

**뒤틈스럽다** (be) imprudent; senseless; brusque; blunt/뒤틈스러운 짓 a blunder.

**뒤틀다** ①《비틀다》 twist; wrench; distort; wring ②《일을》 disturb; frustrate; baffle. ねじる

**뒤틀리다** ①《비뚤어지다》 be distorted; be twisted; go awry; warp 《마음이》 be crossgrained/무릎이 ~ get one's knee wrenched ②《일이》 go wrong; go amiss. ねじられる

**뒤틀어지다** be twisted; go awry; warp/일이 ~ a plan is thwarted[misses, goes wrong, falls]. ねじられる

**뒤틈바리** a blunt rude fellow; a rough. あばれもの

**뒤흔들다** shake violently; sway hard/과일을 따려고 나무를 ~ shake the tree for fruit. はげしくふる

**뜀** 《도약》 a jump; a leap 《구보》 a run/~뛰기 jumping/~박진 jumping 《구보》 running. とぶこと

**뜀들다** wrangle; quarrel; argue; brawl; dispute. いいあらそう

**뒷간(一間)** a toilet「room」(略); a water-closet(略: W. C.); a rest room; a privy.

**뒷갈망** settlement; winding up (an affair); putting in order／～이 큰일이다 It will be a terrific task to straighten things up.

**뒷걸음** stepping[walking, moving] backward／～하다 step[move] backward 《무서워서》shrink back.

**뒷골목** a back street; an alley; a by street.

**뒷공론(一公論)** 《소문》gossip in private 《험담》backbiting／～하다 backbite; gossip.

**뒷구멍** the back door; backstairs channels 《부정 수단》unjust means.

**뒷귀먹다** (be) dull-witted; slow of understanding; stupid; be slow to catch on.

**뒷길** 《샛길》a back-street; a by-road 《장래》one's future [prospects].

**뒷날** 《후일》days to come; another day 《장래》future.

**뒷다리** a hind leg／～ 잡히다 fall into (a person's) clutches; be caught in a snare.

**뒷담당(一擔當)** settling (matters) right; after adjustment; clearance work／～하다 answer for the aftergrowth; take care[charge] of the rest.

**뒷대문(一大門)** a back[rear] gate; the back entrance.

**뒷덜미** the neck; the back; the scruff [of the neck]／～를 잡다 take[grasp, seize] (a person) by the nape[scruff] of his neck.

**뒷돈** capital; ; funds; extra funds／～을 대다 supply (a person) with capital (for business).

**뒷동산** a hill at the back.

**뒷마당** a backyard; a backgarden; ground at the back of a house.

**뒷마루** a back floor; porch《미》; 《잇마루》a back veranda《h》.

**뒷말** backbiting : 뒷공론.

**뒷맛** after-taste／～이 나쁘다 leave a bad [unpleasant] taste behind.

**뒷맵시** the sight of one's back／그는 ～가 있다 He look smart when seen from the back.

**뒷모양(一貌樣)** back appearance; the sight of one's back／그는 ～이 그의 아버지와 비슷하다 He looks like his father from behind.

**뒷문(一門)** a back[rear] gate.

**뒷밀이** 《밀어주기》pushing (a cart) from behind《일》; 《사람》a pusher; a pushman／～하다 push (a cart) from behind.

**뒷바라지** backing; support／～하다 aid; support; back [up]／그 여자는 애들의 ～에 바쁘다 She is busy with the care of her children.

**뒷받침** backing; boosting《구》/그는 나의 사업에 ～이 되어 주었다 He backed me up in my business.

**뒷발** ①《동물의》a hind leg ②《발길》kicking with one's heel.

**뒷방(一房)** a back[rear] room.

**뒷보증(一保證)** endorsement／어음에 ～하다 endorse a note; back a bill／피～인 endorsee.

**뒷소리** 《응원》a shout of encouragement; a yell; a cheer 《경기의》root《구》／～치더 응원하다 yell[root] for a team.

**뒷소문(一所聞)** an after-talk.

**뒷손없다** (be) slovenly; loose; negligent.

**뒷수쇄(一收刷)** putting [things] in order／～하다 put to rights; wind up; settle／식사의 ～를 하다 clear the table after the dinner is over.

**뒷심** backing; help[aid, assistance] from behind／～이 든든하다 have a good backing.

**뒷일** ①《뒤의 일》the aftermath of an event; later happenings; the rest; the sequel ②《장래·사후의》future affairs; affairs after one's death.

**뒷자락** the rear train of one's clothes; the rear trail.

**뒷자리** a back seat.

**뒷전놀다** 《뒤치닥거리하다》wind up; deal with the aftermath; readjust; settle (matters) right.

**뒷조사(一調査)** a detailed investigation／～하다 thoroughly investigate.

**뒷짐 결박(一結縛)** ～하다 tie[bind] (a person's) hands behind his back.

**뒷짐** ～지다 fold one's hands behind one's back／～지우다 《결박짓다》tie one's arms behind one's back.

**뒷집** the house adjoining in the back.

**뒹굴다** ①《누워서》roll [about]; tumble about／잔디 위에 ～ roll about on a lawn ②《놀다》idle away; roll about; be on the loaf; loaf around《미》／일요일을 집에서 뒹굴며 지내다 pass Sundays idly at home.

**뜨개질** knitting; knitwork／～하다 knit; do knitting／～ 바늘 a knitting needle; a knitting pin.

**뜨겁다** (be) hot; too warm.

**뜨끈뜨끈** ～한 hot; warm／～한 감자 steaming[piping] hot potatoes; potatoes hot from the oven.

**뜨끔하다** (be) stinging; pricky／가슴이 ～ be shocked.

**드나들다** ①《출입하다》go in and out 《방문하다》visit[frequently]; frequent／그 집에는 식모가 자주 드나든다 Cooks are frequently changed in that house. ②《들쑥날쑥하다》be indented.

**드난** domestic service／～하다 be in domestic service／～군 a domestic.

**뜨내기** ①《사람》a tramp; a vagabond ②《일》an odd job.

**뜨내기 손님** a casual visitor; a transient guest. ふじのおきゃく

**뜨내기 장사** a casual[temporary] business. ぎょうしょう

**드넓다** (be) very wide; open; extensive; spacious／그는 드넓은 들판에서 말을 달렸다 He galloped his horse in an open field. ひろびろとしている

**드높다** (높이가) (be) very high; eminent／드높이 high; aloft／하늘에 드높이 high up in the air; way up in the sky〈미〉. ひじょうにたかい

**뜨다¹** ①(느리다) (be) slow／시계가 10분 ~ The watch is ten minutes slow. ②(둔하다) (be) dull; slow; slow-witted ③(입이 무겁다) be taciturn ④(무디다) (be) blunt; dull ⑤(사이가) be separated／부부 사이가 ~ the man and wife are estranged from each other ⑥(다리미 따위가) be slow to heat up. のろい

**뜨다²** ①(물·하늘에) float [on the water in the air] ②(해·달이) rise; come up [out] ③(사이가) be distant; be apart [from] ④(빌려준 물건·돈 따위가) be lost. うかぶ

**뜨다³** ①(썩다) become stale; grow moldy; go musty and fusty ②(발효하다) ferment; undergo fermentation. くさる

**뜨다⁴** (쑥으로) cauterize (the skin) with moxa. きゅうをすえる

**뜨다⁵** (자리를) leave[quit] (one's seat) (옮기다) move; clear out; remove／관직을 ~ throw up[quit, retire from] office. まがあく

**뜨다⁶** (물 따위에) scoop up (국자로) ladle 《바위 따위를》 cut[crack, hew]off[off]《벳장을》 shovel(삽으로); (고기를) slice (meat); 《갈드는》 cut in several parts; dismember 《종이를》 make; manufacture (paper); (옷감을) cut (a suit); (사다) buy. くみあげる

**뜨다⁷** ①(눈을) open one's eyes; be awake／눈을 ~ open one's eyes ②(귀를) hear; begin to understand／음악에 귀를 ~ begin to appreciate music. めざめる

**뜨다⁸** (털실로) knit (갈구리·바늘로) crochet (집다) darh (그물을) net; make. あむ

**뜨다⁹** (본을) copy; imitate／아버지 본을 ~ imitate one's father. かたどる

**뜨더귀** tearing apart to pieces／~하다 tear[pull] apart to pieces; dismantle. ずたずたにさくこと

**드던지다** throw at random; throw at wildly. てあたりしだいになげる

**뜨멈뜨멈** falteringly; with difficulty／글을 ~ 뜯어보다 construe a passage with difficulty. とぎれとぎれ

**뜨뜻이** [pleasantly] warm; hot／난로 앞에 앉아서 몸을 ~ 녹이시오 Sit down before the fire and have a warm. あたたかく

**뜨뜻하다** (be) warm／뜨뜻한 날씨 warm weather あたたかい

**드디어** at last[length]; finally／그는 ~ 시험에 합격했다 He passed the examination at length. ついに

**드러나다** ①(표면에) be revealed; show itself; come into evidence／표면에 ~ come to the front ②(노출하다) be exposed 《광맥이》crop out; be disclosed; be bared／거짓말이 드러났다 one's falsehood was found out. あらわれる

**드러내다** ①(나타내다) show; indicate; manifest ②(노출하다) reveal; bare; expose／비밀을 ~ divulge a secret／본성을 ~ betray oneself; reveal one's real character. めただせる

**드러눕다** lie down; lie on one's back; throw oneself down／병으로 ~ be laid up with illness. よこになる

**드러쌓이다** be piled up; accumulate; lie (on); collect; gather／눈이 10센티미터나 드러쌓였다 The snow lay ten centimeters deep on the ground. つみかさねる

**드렁드렁** roaring; thundering／코를 ~ 끌다 snore terribly. ぐうぐう

**드레드레** danglingly／~ 흔들리다 swing loose; dangle. ふさふさ

**드레지다** (be) imposing; dignified; commanding. いげんのある

**드레질** sizing up; weighing／~하다 size up (a person); try one's prudence; weigh (a thing). ひとのひんいをためすこと

**드렁거리다** snore loudly／드렁드렁 snoring heavily. ぐうぐうといびきをかく

**드르르¹, 뜨르르¹** ①(미끄럽게) without stopping; rolling; rumbling／~ 미끄러지다 go slipping; slip ②(떠는 모양) trembling'ly; shivering'ly ころころ

**드르르², 뜨르르²** (막힘없이) smoothly; without a hitch 《쉽게》easily 《유창하게》fluently. すらすら

**드리다¹** (주다) give; present; make (one) a present of (a thing); offer／기도를 ~ offer[put up] one's prayer. あげる

**드리다²** (꼬다) braid; twist (into a rope)／밧줄을 ~ braid[make] a rope. あむ

**드리다³** (방·마루 따위를) set (a room); construct.

**드리다⁴** (가게 문을) close the shop; put up the shutters (폐업하다) close up shop. とじる

**드리다⁵** (곡식을) winnow away[off] the chaff from the grain.

**드리우다** ①(늘어뜨리다) hang down; suspend ②(가르침을) teach; give lessons ③(전하다) hand down／자손들에게 ~ hand down to posterity. つりさげる

**드림** (기(旗)드림) a streamer (장막) a curtain; hangings. かけること

**드림셈** payment by installments; an installment plan. ぶんかつはらい

**드림흥정** transaction by installments／~하다 sell[buy] on installments.

**맑다** (be) very clear.ひじょうにあかるい

**드문드문** ①(공간적) at places(여기저기); sparsely／나무를 ~ 심다 plant trees at intervals ②(시간적) occasionally; once

뜨물 water in which rice has been washed. とぎしる

드물다 (be) rare; unusual; uncommon; few; scarce/그녀는 드문 미인이다 She is a rare beauty. まれだ

드새다 stay for the night; pass the night. よふかとをする

드세다 (be) powerful; influential; important. せいりょくがある

뜨악하다 reluctant; disinclined (to do); unwilling; unappealing. きがむかない

뜨이다 ①《눈이》wake up; awake; open 《비유적》come to one's senses; have one's eyes opened ②《발견하다》catch one's eye; come to one's notice/눈이 번쩍 ~ be wide awake. めをあける

드잡이 ①《싸움》a scuffle; a handgrip; a grapple; a scrimmage ②《차압》seizure; attachment; distraint/~하다 come to grips (with each other).

드티다 ①《공간적으로》move slightly away[aside] ②《시간적으로》postpone; extend/지불 기한을 ~ extend the term of payment/교섭이 ~ Negotiations are protracted. すこしずついどうする

드팀전(一廛) a draper《영》; a dry goods store《미》. ごふくや

득(得)《이익》profit; gain; interest《유리》advantage《유용》benefit/~보다 profit; gain. とく

득남(得男) begetting a son; 생녀(生女). おとこのこがうまれたこと

득녀(得女) begetting a daughter. じょしがうまれたこと

득도(得道)《불도》spiritual awakening [enlightenment]/~하다 be spiritually awakened; attain enlightenment[Nirvana]. とくどう

득돌같다 (be) satisfactory; gratifying; perfect. まんぞくだ

득득 ①《줄을 긋는 모양》[draw a line] firmly ②《얼어붙는 모양》[freeze] hard [solid] ③《긁는 모양》scratching hard.

득롱 망촉(得隴望蜀) Give him an inch, and he will take an ell.

득리(得利) ~하다 make[realize, obtain] a profit. いとく

득명(得名) ~하다 win[gain] fame; make a name/이 작품으로 그는 크게 ~했다 The work won[secured] him great fame. ゆうめい

득문(得聞) ~하다 hear of; be told[be informed] of; learn.

득배(得配) ~하다 take a wife; marry a woman. はいぐうしゃをえること

득병(得病) ~하다 get[fall, become, be taken] ill. びょうきにかかること

득보기 a blockhead; an ass; a fool; a dunce; an idiot; a moron. きたないひと

득세(得勢) ~하다 obtain influence; become influential; gain ground; rise to power. せいりょくをえること

득송(得訟) winning a lawsuit/~하다 win a lawsuit《사람이 주어》gain a case. しょうそ

득승(得勝) a win; a success/~하다 win [a victory]/시합에서 ~하다 win a game. しょうりをえること

득시(得時) ~하다 find an opportunity; get a chance. じきをえること

득시글득시글 in swarms; swarming/~하다 squirm; swarm. うようよ

득실(得失)《장단점》merits and demerits [defects]《손익》advantages and disadvantages; loss and gain; interest/~이 상반(相半)하다 The gains and losses are about on a par. とくしつ

득실득실 swarming⇨득시글득시글. うようよ

득의(得意) ①《성공》prosperity/~의 시대에 in one's best[one's bright, one's palmy] days ②《자랑》elation; self-complacency/성공을 ~하게 여기다 be elated over[with] one's success. とくい

득인(得人) ~하다 get[acquire] the right person; find one's win; find one's man. よいひとをえること

득인심(得人心) ~하다 win the hearts of the people. じんしんをえること

득점(得點) marks《경기의》a point《총괄적》a score/~하다 score [a point]/~표 a score book; scoreboard/~을 기록하다 score the runs. とくてん

득정(得情) ~하다 find out[get] the facts (of a crime).

득죄(得罪) ~하다 take the guilt upon oneself; hold oneself blamable; bear guilt. つみをうけること

득중(得中) moderation; temperance/~하다 he proper; be moderate.

득지(得志) realization of one's wish[aspiration]; attainment of one's desire[object]/~하다 realize one's wish; attain one's desire. もくてきをいたること

득책(得策) good policy; advisability; the best plan/~이다 be wise; be advisable; be politic. とくさく

득체(得體) maintenance of the appearance (of a gentleman); saving one's face/~하다 save the hono[u]r of; save appearances. たいめんをいじすること

득표(得票) the number of votes polled [got, obtained]/이(李)씨의 ~는 8만이었다 Mr. Lee polled[got] 80,000 votes. とくひょう

득하다《날씨가》grow cold suddenly.

득효(得效) ~하다 be effected a cure; get the effect. こうりょくをえること

-든 whether … or ⇨-든지. ーでも

뜬거지남부자(一富者) a person who looks rich but is really poor. みかけたおしのかねもち

뜬것《귀신》a wandering demon[devil, evil spirit, fiend]. きしん

뜬계집 a woman who happened to have connection with; a casual mistress. うわきおんな

**뜬구름** ①(구름) a drifting[floating] cloud; a cloud drift ②(덧없는 일) mutability; transience; evanescence/인생은 ~과 같은 것이다 Nothing is certain in this world. うきぐも

**뜬눈** unsleeping[wide-awake] eyes/~으로 밤을 새우다 sit up all night; have a sleepless night.

**뜬돈** money earned unexpectedly a windfall. ふいのしゅうにゅう

**든든하다** ①(굳세다) (be) firm; strong; steady/든든히 firmly; fast; solidly/마음을 든든히 먹다 take courage; keep out one's nerve ②(미덥다)(be) reliable, trustworthy/든든한 사람 a reliable man ③(배가) (be) stomachful/든든히 먹다 eat one's fill. しっかりしている

**든번(一番)** on duty; the on[-duty] shift /~이다 be on duty. とうばん

**든벌이** earning[making] money out of a casual job[an odd jobs].

**든부자난거지(一富者一)** a person who looks poor but is really rich. みかけはまずしいかねもち

**뜬소문(一所聞)** a wild[groundless]; a canard(F). うわき

**든손** at a breath; at once; instantly; in no time /서슴지 않고) without hesitation/~으로 일을 끝내다 finish one's work straight out. ちゃくしゅしたて

**뜬숯** used charcoal; cinders.

**뜬재물(一財物)** a windfall; an unexpected income. りんじしょとく

**-든지** either…or; whether … or/좋~ 나쁘~ good or bad/너~나~ either you or I. ようが

**든직하다** (침착하다)(be) sedate; composed 《위엄이 있다》 dignified/든직한 태도 a quiet attitude. おもみのある

**든침모(一針母)** a resident needlewoman [seamstress]. すみこみおはり

**뜯게** worn-out clothes.

**뜯그럽다** (be) noisy; clamorous; vociferous; boisterous. やかましい

**뜯기다** Ⅰ(빼앗기다) be extorted[squeezed, exploited] ②(물리다) get bitten (by a flea, a louse, etc.) ③(마소에게 풀을) graze; put on. むりにとられる

**듣다¹** ①(소리를) hear 《소문을》 bear of [that]/강의를 ~ attend a lecture ②(칭찬·꾸지람을) receive; suffer; be given /칭찬을 듣고 화낼 사람은 없다 Nobody feels offended at compliment ③(이르는 말·청 따위를) obey; take; follow; listen; mind ④(효력이 있다) take[have] effect (on); be efficacious; do (a person) ⑤(작용하다) work; act. きく

**듣다²** 《물·눈물 따위가》 drip; drop; trickle. ぽたぽたおちる

**뜯다** ①(메다) take away; take[pull, tear] down 《풀·털 따위를》 pluck; pick; tear/잡초를 ~ pluck out weed ②《악기를》 play[on] ③(얻다) get; extort; squeeze. ひきはなす

**듣보기 장사** speculative business; a venture. とうきしょう

**듣보다** search; seek; look for; keep on eye. そうさくする

**뜯어내다** ①(붙은 것을) take down[off]; remove; pick off ②(남을 졸라서) take; receive. つみとる

**뜯어말리다** pull apart/ 싸움을 ~ pull combatants apart. けんかをひきはなす

**뜯어먹다** ①(붙은 것을) pluck[tear] and eat 《작아서》 gnaw[bite] off/소가 풀을 ~ a cow grazes ②(졸라서) extort (money); sponge (upon). むしってくう

**뜯어버리다** tear (a thing) off and throw it away; take apart and throw it away; remove. つみとってすてる

**뜯어벌리다** ①(벌리다) take apart; pull to pieces; open up ②(얘기를) talk lengthily. かいたいする

**뜯어보다** ①(살펴보다) examine carefully; study closely/집을 이모저모로 ~ look a house over thoroughly ②(겨우 읽다) read with difficulty; make out ③(봉한 것을) open. せいみつにちょうさする

**뜯적거리다** scratch 「and tear off」; claw /뜯적뜯적 scratching. ひきちぎる

**들¹** a field (전답) the fields (평야) a plains/~에서 자라 wild/~가운데의 외딴 집 a lone[solitary] house in the middle of a plain. のはら

**들²** 《등등》 and other things; and others; and so forth; and the like/우리는 동물원에 가서 코끼리·범·곰 ~을 보았다 We went to the zoo and saw elephants, tigers, bears, and the like. など

**뜰** 《정원》 a garden 《울 안》 a yard; a ground/~에 심은 나무 a garden tree.にわ

**들까부르다** winnow briskly; fan briskly. はげしくしょうかさせる

**들개** a stray dog.

**들깨** 《식》 Perilla japonica(학명). えごま

**들것** a stretcher; a litter/~으로 나르다 carry on a stretcher. たんか

**들고나다** ①(간섭하다) interfere (in); meddle (in) ②(집안의 세간을) carry out for sale. かんしょうする

**들고뛰다** run away; flee; take to flight; make one's escape; take to one's heels /자동차를 타고 ~ make one's escape in a car. にげる

**들고주다** 《달아나다》 squander (낭비하다) run through; dissipate. ろうひする

**들고튀다** 《달아나다》 run away; take to flight (주다나다) break loose; get free.

**들국화(一菊花)** 《식》 a wild camomile[chrysanthemum]. のぎく

**들꿩** 《조》 a hazel grouse.

**들끓다** crowd; squirm/거지가 ~ be crowded with beggars. わいわいさわぐ

**들기름** perilla oil.

**들날리다** ①(이름·세력 따위를) be well known; become famous; be popular; flourish/시인으로서 이름이 온세상에 ~ be famous all over the world as a poet

**들내** ②《일을》 work in a slipshod(a perfunctory) manner. よくしられる

**들내** the smell(scent) of perilla.

**들녘** a plain; an open field flat country. のはらのほう

**들놀이** a picnic; an outing. やゆう

**들다**¹ ①《날씨가》 clear (up); become clear ②《많이》 stop; cease／장마가 들었다 The rainy season is over. はれる

**들다**² 《칼날이》 cut [well]; be keen; 잘 들지 않는 dull; blunt／잘~ cut well; be sharp／이 칼은 잘 든다 This knife cuts well. よくきれる

**들다**³ 《나이가》 grow older; take[put] on years／그는 아직 마흔인데 퍽 나이들어 보인다 He is forty, but he looks much older. としとる

**들다**⁴ ①《손에》 take[have carry] in one's hand; hold／펜을 ~ take a pen in hand; write ②《사실·예를》 give (an example); mention (a fact); cite／이와 꼭 같은 경우를 하나 더 들 수 있느냐 Can you cite another case at all like this one? ③《높이다》 raise; lift (up); hold up／얼굴을 ~ look up; lift one's face ④《음식을》 take; have; eat《마시다》drink／더 드시지요 will you take another helping? てにもつ

**들다**⁵ ⇨별항 참조(page 1414).

**들때밀** a wicked[a haughty] servant under the shelter of an influential family.

**들떠들다** make an uproar; make a fuss; be noisy. わいわいさわぐ

**들떠놓고** roundaboutly; indirectly; hintingly; insinuatingly; in a roundabout way. とおまわしに

**들떼리다** hurt one's feeling; hurt (one); offend (one).

**들돌** a lifting stone; a barbell stone.

**들두드리다** beat recklessly. やたらにうつ

**들뜨다** ①《들이》 become loose／구들장이 ~ a slab of floor stone gets loose ②《마음이》 be unsteady; be restless; be half-hearted／봄이 오면 마음이 들뜨기 쉽다 One's mind is apt to wander when spring comes. ③《살이》 sallow and swell. よくきかずにうきあがる

**들들** stirring; rummaging／~ 볶다 parch (beans)《괴롭히다》torment／깨를 ~ 볶다 parch sesame-seed torning upside down／~ 뒤지다 ransack; rummage／~ 타다 grind (wheat). しっこくせがむ

**들락날락** going in and out／~하다 go in and out frequently; come in and out incessantly. しきりにていりするさき

**들랑거리다** keep coming and going; frequent. しきりにていりするさま

**들러리** 《신랑의》 a best man《신부의》a bridesmaid. つけそい

**들러붙다** adhere[stick, cling, cleave] to ／집들이 들러붙어 있다 Houses stand close to each other. くっつく

**들레다** clamour; make a noise; be uproarious. わいわいさわぐ

**들려주다** 《말해 주다》 let one hear; tell《읽어 주다》read to《연주하여》play for《노래 불러》sing for／편지를 읽어서 ~ read a letter to (a person).

**들르다** 《도중에》 drop[look] in (at); stop off (at); call (at, on)／차 마시러 다방에 ~ stop[drop] in for tea at a coffeeshop. よる

**들리다**¹ ①《소리가》 be audible; be heard; hear《울리다》 sound; ring／내 말이 안 들리나 Don't you hear me? ②《소문이》 come to one's ears／너의 소식이 종종 들렸다 I've often heard of you. ③《듣게 하다》 let (one) hear; tell play for(연주해서); sing for(노래). きえる

**들리다**² ①《병이》 suffer from; be attacked; catch／감기가 ~ catch a cold ②《귀신이》 be possessed[obsessed] by／그는 귀신이 들렸다 He is possessed by the evil spirit. びょうきになる

**들리다**³ 《고갈되다》 run out; be exhausted; be out of stock／돈이 ~ be out of money. しなぎれる

**들리다**⁴ ①《올려지다》 be lifted[raised]／보따리를 ~ have (a person) carry a bundle ②《들게 하다》 let (one) raise[lift]; get to carry.

**들맞추다** humor; soothe; lick one's boots. きげんをとる

**들먹거리다, 뜰먹거리다** ①《움직이다》 move up and down; rise and fall; raise and lower／들먹들먹[뜰먹뜰먹] rising and falling ②《마음이》 one's heart leaps(뛰다); be restless; be fidgety／가슴이 ~ one's heart leaps. あげたりさげたりする

**들먹다** (be) dogged; perverse; bull-headed. がんこだ

**들메** ~하다 fasten one's shoes; tie straw sandals to one's feet. はきもののつけひも

**들메끈** shoe-string; bootlaces; shoe-ties. はきもののつけひも

**들메다** fasten one's shoes; tie to one's feet. はきものにひもをかける

**들보**¹ 《건》 a beam; a girder. はり

**들보**² 《샅에 차는》 a loin-cloth.

**들볶다** annoy; harass; torment; be hard on (one); be cruel to; treat (one) harshly／며느리를 ~ be cruel to one's daughter-in-law.

**들볶이다** be tormented; be annoyed; be handled roughly.

**들뽕나무** a wild mulberry tree.

**들부수다** break to pieces; smash; knock to pieces; crush. ぶちこわす

**들살** a prop; a stay; a support.

**들새** a wild fowl; wild birds.

**들썩거리다** ①《움직이다》 move up and down; raise and lower; rise and fall／들썩들썩 moving up and down ②《마음이》 be restless; be in a fidget《충동이다》stir up／들썩들썩 restlessly／그들은 들썩거리고 있었다 They were flurried and nervous. じょうげにうごく

**들썩하다**¹ 《그럴싸하다》(be) plausible; specious; verisimilar; sound plausible/들썩하게 거짓말을 하다 lie like the truth. もっともらしい

**들썩하다**² ①《떠들려 있다》be turned up [raised, lifted] slightly : 떠들썩하다 ②《물건을》lift[raise, move] (*something*) slightly. 《물건이》move slightly. くっついたものがうきあがる

**들썽거리다** itch; be nervous; be impatient; feel itch/그는 사실을 말하고 싶어 들썽거렸다 He was burning to tell the truth. おちつかない

**들소** a wild ox; a bison. やきゅう
**들손** a handle; a bail. とって
**들쇠** 《문을 거는》an iron hook for hanging a door 《손잡이》a handle 《서랍의》a drawerhandle. とって

**들쇠롱**(−籠) a bucket. バケツ
**들쑤시다** ①《쑤시다》smart; tingle/충치가 들쑤신다 A decayed tooth aches awfully. ②《충동이다》incite; abet; stir up/들쑤셔서 …하게 하다 entice[tempt] (*one*) to do (*something*); egg (*one*) on to (*an act*). ちくちくいたい

**들숨** Inspiration; inhalation. きゅうき
**들쓰다** ①《덮어 쓰다》draw[pull] over/이불을 머리까지 ~ pull the quilt over *one's* head ②《머리에》cover 《모자를》put on ③《물 따위를》pour (*water*) on *oneself*; be covered with ④《허물·책임을》take[blame] upon *oneself*; be charged (with *a crime*)/남의 죄를 ~ take upon *oneself* another's guilt.

**들씌우다** ①《이불 따위를》pull (*bed-clothes*) over (*a person's*) head ②《물 따위를》pour (*water*) all over (*a person*); 《먼지를》cover (*a person*) all over with dust ③《모자를》put (*a hat*) on (*a person's*) head casually ④《허물·죄 따위를》impute; shift (*responsibility*) to others. おおいかくす

**뜰아래채** an outer wing of a house; an outhouse.

**들아랫방**(−−房) a room separated by a garden from the main building.

**들어가다**¹ ①《안으로》enter; go[get, walk, step] in[into] 《침입하다》break into 《함부로》intrude in/몰래 ~ steal in ②《가입·참가하다》join; enter; go into 《회사 따위에》find service in/회사에 ~ enter the company/실업계에 ~ go into business ③《포함하다》hold; contain 《수용하다》accommodate; be included/이 과자에는 설탕과 우유가 들어갔다 This candy contains sugar and milk./그 회관은 1,000명이 들어간다 The hall accommodates[seats] 1,000 persons. はいる

**들어가다**² 《가져가다》take[carry] away; take along; make off with/누군가가 내 사전을 들어갔다 Somebody has taken away my dictionary. もっていく

**들어내다** ①《내놓다》take[bring] out; remove; carry out/의자를 뜰로 ~ bring a chair into the garden ②《쫓아 내다》drive[turn, send] out; expel 《지위에서》oust. もちだす

**들어맞다** 《적중하다》hit; strike 《끼운 것이》fit[fix] into 《예상이》come true; be [prove] correct/들어맞는 옷 well-fitting clothes/예언이 들어맞았다 The prediction came true. よくあう

**들어먹다** ①《탕진하다》squander; dissipate; run through/전재산을 ~ dissipate[play ducks and drakes with] *one's* fortune ②《남의 것을》pocket; peculate; appropriate [to oneself]/공금을 ~ embezzle[misappropriate] public funds[money]. つかいはたす

**들어박히다** ①《촘촘히》be packed; fall into; be stuffed/책이 가득 들어박힌 책꽂이 a shelf closely packed with books ②《칩거하다》be confined to *one's* home; stay indoors/집에 ~ keep indoors; take to *one's* home. be confined to *one's* home. いっぱいつまる

**들어붓다** ①《비가》pour on; fall heavily/들어붓듯 오는 비 a pouring rain; a streaming rain ②《그릇에》pour into; fill (*a jar* with *water*) ③《술을》guzzle; drink much. はげしくふる

**들어서다** ①《안쪽으로》step in[to] 《가까이》draw near; enter get in[to] go[come] into/구내에 ~ enter the premises ②《꽉 차다》be full (*of*); be filled (*with*); be crowded (*with*)/번화가에는 큰 건물들이 죽 들어섰다 Many great buildings stood in a row on the busy street. たちいる

**들어앉다** ①《안쪽으로》get nearer; sit nearer/화로 있는 쪽으로 들어앉아라 Take a seat nearer to the fireplace ②《집어치우다》retire from (*business*); go into retirement ③《자리에》enter; be installed; find service in/본처로 ~ become as a legal wife/아무의 자리에 ~ take *one's* place. ちかよってすわる

**들어오다** ①《안으로》enter; come[get] in; walk in[into]/일없는 사람은 들어오지 마시오. No admittance except on business., No unauthorized entry allowed. ②《수입이》have [an income of]; get; receive ③《직업·자리로》join[enter] a company/새로 사원 한 사람이 들어왔다 A new member joined our company. はいってくる

**들어차다** be packed; be crowded (*with*); be stuffed/집이 꽉 ~ be crowded with houses. いっぱいつまる

**들엉키다** coagulate; congeal; solidify; condense.

**들엎드리다** confine *oneself* to (*a room*); remain indoors; shut *oneself* up/온 종일 방안에 들엎드려 있다 Keep *one's* room all day long. うちにじっとしている

**들여가다** ①《안으로》take[bring, carry] in ②《사다》buy; purchase; get/좀 들여가시지요 Would you take some, ple-

# 들 다⁵

①(숙박·입주) settle; put up (*at*); stop (*at*) 《들어가다》 enter; go in[into]; get in[into]; step[walk] in live; dwell; reside/여관에~ put up[stop] at an inn/잠자리에 ~ go to bed; take to *one's* bed/병석에 ~ be confined to *one's* bed; be laid up/사람이 들지 않은 집 a vacant[an unoccupied, an empty] house/그 집에는 누가 들어 있는가 Who is the occupant of the house?/그 집에는 사람이 들지 않았다 The house is unoccupied.

②(가입) join (*a tennis club*); enter (*a company, a school*); go into; participate (*in*); associate *one*self (*with*)/모임에 ~ join a society[an association]/20세 미만의 사람은 이 모임에 들지 못한다 Nobody under twenty years is admissible to this club./그는 100만원짜리 생명 보험에 들었다 He insured himself [his life] for a million *won*.

③(마음에) be acceptable; be satisfactory; be satisfied[pleased] with; be to *one's* taste[satisfaction]; suit[catch, take, strike] *one's* fancy; find favor with (*a person*); be in *one's* favor; impress (*a person*) favorably; like/마음에 들도록 to *one's* satisfaction; so as to please (*a person*)/마음에 드는 자 a woman after *one's* heart[fancy]; a woman *one* likes[takes to]/마음에 드는 집 a house to *one's* taste; a house *one* likes/식모가 주인의 눈에 ~ a maid finds favor with her master/마음에 들지 않다 be not to *one's* taste[liking] be unacceptable; be unsatisfactory/저 그림이 마음에 든다 That picture appeals to my taste./모든 사람의 눈에 다 들기는 어렵다 It is hard to suit everybody./이것이 가장 마음에 든다 This suits my taste best./그가 하는 짓이 도저히 마음에 들지 않는다 I hate the way he behaves.

④(맛 따위가) set in; get a taste (to it); get tasty; become edible; get ripe; ripen; become mellow/술의 맛이 ~ wine mellows/사과의 맛이 ~ an apple gets some flavor in it; an apple is ripe/음식 맛이 들기 시작했다 The food is getting taste./한번 돈을 주면 맛을 들여서 또 온다 Once you give him money he is sure to come round again and again to ask for more/김치 맛이 들었다 The *kimchi* has ripened.

⑤(포함) hold; contain; be contained; be included; be among/그 속에는 내 몫도 들어 있었다 My part[share] was included in it./이 과자에는 설탕이 너무 많이 들었다 This cake has[contains] too much sugar in it./모래에 금이 ~ the sand has gold in it/모두 계산에 들어 있다 All expenses are included in the account./그 항목에는 무엇이 들어 있나 What items are included under the head?

⑥(침입) visit; attack; afflict; break [force one's way] into (*a house*)/아파트에 도둑이 들었다 A burglar broke into my apartment./잡념이 ~ be a victim of idle[worldly] thoughts/행운이 ~ be visited by good luck/감기가 ~ catch cold/도둑이 ~ a burglar breaks in/병이 ~ become ill; be afflicted with a disease/폐병에 걸려서 죽다 die consumption of by goodluck.

⑦(햇빛 따위가) shine (*upon*)/이 방은 햇빛이 잘 든다[안 든다] This room gets sunshine[no sunshine].

⑧(절기·상태 따위가) come round; set in; begin/철이 ~ get some sense/잠이 ~ go to sleep; fall asleep/정이 ~ fall in love/멍이 ~ get bruised; be hard hit/복(伏)이 ~ the dog days come round[begin]/장마철에 접어~ the wet weather sets in/풍년[흉년]이 ~ have a good[lean] year; have a bumper[bad] harvest/금년에는 풍년이 들 것 같다 We shall probably have a good harvest this year/이 달에는 춘분이 들어 있다 This month contains Spring[Vernal] Equinox Day.

⑨(소요) be needed; be required; be spent; take; cost/돈이 ~ take[cost] money/시간이 ~ take (*up*) time/힘이 ~ be hard[difficult, tough, trying]; require hard work; take effort/이래 저래 온통 돈드는 일뿐이다 There are a lot of drains on my purse./얼마나 들었소 How much did it cost you?

⑩(물들다) dye; be dyed; take colo[u]r 《죄악 따위에》 be stained; be tainted; be tinged/물이 검게 ~ be dyed black; be stained[tinged] with black/물이 잘 ~[들지 않다] dye well[badly]/나쁜 물이 ~ be tainted with vice; be steeped in vice/망바닥이 피로 물~ The ground are stained with blood.

⑪(버릇 따위가) take to a habit; get [fall] into a habit (*of*)/흡연이라는 나쁜 버릇이 ~ take to the bad habit of smoking; get [contract] the bad habit of smoking.

⑫(수용·용량) be included; hold; [can] accommodate; seat/드럼통에는 물 60갤론이 듭니다 a drum holds sixty gallon of water/강당에 3백 명이 ~ a lecture hall accommodates[holds] three hundred people/전부는 들지 못합니다 There is not room enough for all. ⑬(전역·시중 따위를) do/아무개의 시중을 ~ wait on[attend] a person/중매를 ~ serve as go-between/아무개의 역성[전역]을 ~ side with a person.

⑭(합격) enter (an institution); pass (an examination)/학교에 ~ enter a school/입학 시험에 ~ pass entrance examinations.

ase? もちこむ

들여 놓다 《발을》 set foot in; step into 《물건을》 bring[take] in/결상응 저 방에 들여 놓아라 Bring the chair in that room. とっておく

들여다보다 ①《밖에서 안을》 look (in); peep (into, through)/우물을 ~ look in [peep into] the well ②《빤히》 gaze; stare [intently] (at); watch intently/얼굴을 빤히 ~ gaze[stare] one in the face. ひとのぞきする

들여보내다 send in; let[allow] in; admit/아이를 학교에 ~ put[send] a child to school/이 증명만 있으면 그냥 들여보낸다 This certificate will gain you free admission. なかにはいらせる

들여오다 ①《안으로》 take[bring, carry] in ②《사들이다》 get; buy (something at a stop). もちこむ

들은 풍월(一風月) picked-up knowledge; learning by ear. きいたとおりのまねごと

-들이 containing/서 말- 뒤주 a rice-chest capable of containing three mal/2리터 ~ 병 a two-liter bottle/상자~ 물건 articles in a case. —いりの

들이굿다 《줄을》 draw inwards 《병이》 strike inwards. うちにむけてせんをひく

들이다 ①《안으로》 let (one) in[into]; admit ②《비용을》 spend (on); invest ③《힘을》 take pains; take trouble; make efforts/힘들여서 with great efforts; laboriously/큰돈을 들여서 at a great cost ④《맛을》 get[acquire] a taste for; take to/돈에 맛을 ~ get a taste for money ⑤《잠을》 induce sleep; make (one) sleep/어린애를 짐~ put a child to sleep ⑥《길을》 tame; train/사자를 길~ train a lion ⑦《물감을》 dye (black). はいらせる

들이닥치다 close in upon; gain upon; rush (to)/눈앞에 들이닥친 imminent; impending. おしよせてくる

들이대다 ①《뻣뻣한 말로》 defy; oppose; turn upon (one) ②《물건을》 thrust (a thing) before; point at; cover (one with a revolver)/증거를 ~ thrust proofs before (one); confront (one) with the proof. たいこうする

들이덤비다 ①《덤벼들다》 fall [turn] upon (one); defy; challenge; flare up/상관에게 ~ challenge one's superior/아무에게 ~ attack a person ②《서둘다》 bustle; busy oneself with/여럿이 들이덤벼 일을 잠깐 동안에 해치웠다 Several people went at the job and got it done in no time. いどむ

들이마시다 《기체를》 inhale; breathe in 《액체를》 drink in; suck in; sip 《술 따위를》 guzzle; swing; swill/국을 ~ sip soup. のみこむ

들이몰다 《안으로》 drive in 《마구》 drive violently[fast]/말을 ~ gallop a horse. ついこむ

들이받다 run[bump, ram] (a thing) into; knock (a thing) against/자동차가 나무를 ~ run one's motorcar into a tree. ばったりつきあたる

들이빨다 suck in; inhale; imbibe/담배를 ~ inhale the smoke of a cigarette. しきりにすいこむ

들이불다 ①《앞에서》 blow against; blow in[to] ②《세차게》 rage; blow violently [hard]/바람이 ~ a wind blows hard. うちのほうにむけてふく

들이붓다 ①《쏟아 붓다》 pour into/솥에 물을 ~ pour water into an oven ②《계속해서》 pour continuously[profusely]; keep pouring. そそぎこむ

들이지르다 ①《몹시》 push forcibly; thrust 《발길로》 give a hard kick/얼굴을 ~ strike (a person) in the face ②《소리를》 raise one's voice; shout louder; cry out/목청이 쉬도록 ~ shout oneself hoarse. ちからつよくつく

들이치다¹ 《비·눈이》 sweep[drive] into (a room); be blown in/비가 ~ rain into. ふきまくる

들이치다² ①《습격》 attack; assault; storm; raid/성 안의 적군을 ~ attack the enemy in the castle ②《안으로》 hit (a thing) this way; bat in/불을 물로 ~ bat a ball into the yard. しゅうげきする

들이키다 ①《다그다》 draw near; bring close ②《마시다》 gulp down; quaff out [off]/단숨에 ~ drink at a draught. ひきよせる

들일 farm work; field labour/~을 하다 do farm work; work on the farm[in the fields]. のはらのしごと

들입다 by force; violently; strongly 《열심히》 eagerly/~ 조르다 entreat (one to do). やたらに

들쩍지근하다 (be) sweetish; somewhat sweet. あまみがかった

들쭉나무 《식》 blueberry; Vaccinium uliginosum(학명).

들쭉날쭉 ~하다 (be) notched; notchy; indented; rugged; jagged. でこぼこ

들쥐 《동》 a field rat.

들짐승 a wild animals; a wild game. やじゅう

들차다 be sound in mind and body.

들창(一窓) a window which can be raised[propped] open; a small window

들척지근하다 (be) somewhat sweet; sweetish.

들추다 ①(뒤지다) ransack; rummage; forage for ②(일을) reveal; disclose /비밀을 ~ reveal a secret/남의 조상을 들추어 말하다 take a dig at another's ancestors. くまなくさがす

들추어내다 《폭로》 disclose; lay bare; bring to light 《뒤져서》 rummage out; find out; seek out; hunt out/서랍에서 돈을 ~ rummage money out of a drawer. くまなくさがしてあばく

들큼하다 (be) sweetish; somewhat sweet. たしょうあまい

들키다 be found out; be discovered; be caught (doing)/들키면 큰일난다 If you are found out, it will go hard with you. みつかる

들타작(-打作) thrashing in the fields.

들통(一筒) a pail; a bucket/~나다 be ruined[exposed]; get found out. ておけ

들판 a field; a plain; the green/허허 ~ a wilderness/~에 나가 일하다 work in the field. のはら

들피 emaciation from hunger/~지다 emaciate from hunger; get emaciated from hunger. うえてすいじゃくすること

듬¹ a rain[sun] screen[shelter] woven of straw[cattails].

듬² moxacautery; moxibustion/~ 뜨다 cauterize (the skin) with moxa; apply moxa (to)/머리에 ~을 뜨다 cauterize the head with moxa. きゅう

듬³ being well-steamed[-cooked]; an interval/~들이다 cook[steam] thoroughly. むし

듬⁴ a residential section (of a town); a block of houses.

듬깃 material to make a mat.

듬배질 horning; tossing; butt/~하다 toss; horn; butt. うしがつのでつくこと

듬부기 《조》 a Siberian ruddy crake; water rail. くいな

듬뿍 to the brim; brimfully; to the full; much; plenty/~하다 (be) full; brimful/술을 ~ 붓다 pour wine full to the brim/잔에 ~ 따르다 fill the glass to the brim. たっぷり

듬성듬성 sparsely; scatteredly; thinly; sporadically; here and there/털이 ~나다 hair grows thinly/나무를 ~ 심다 plant trees sparsely. まばらに

듬쑥 (굳게) tightly; firmly; fast; full; greedily/과자를 손에 ~ 그러쥐다 grasp a greedy handful of cake. どっさり

듬지근하다 (be) rather slow and dignified. どっしりしている

듬직하다 (be) dignified; measured; imposing. どっしりしている

듬질 cauterizing with moxa/~하다 cauterize with moxa. きゅうをすえること

듭하다 lull; abate; hold up; let up(비) /비가 듭해졌다 The rain is breaking; The rain is letting up a little.

~눈이 a person who is always lifting his eyelids/~코 an upturned[a turned-up] nose; a person with an upturned nose. ちいさいまど

듯 Q비가 울~ 말~ 했다 It was not sure if it would rain or not./너무 적어서 먹은 ~ 만~ 하다 I ate so little that I am hardly satisfied. ように

뜻 ①(의지) will; mind (의향) intention; motive 《야망》 ambition; aspiration 《희망》 desire[s]; wish[es] 《목적》 object; aim; purpose/~을 이루다 attain one's aim; realize one's aspirations/~을 거역하다 act against one's will ②《의미》 sense; meaning 《취지》 the effect; the intent/~있는 눈짓 a significant[a meaning] glance/~이 없다 be meaningless. いみ

뜻밖 being contrary to one's expectation; a surprise/~의 unexpected; unlooked for; surprising; unsuspected/~에 unexpectedly; accidentaly; suddenly 《우연히》 casually/~에 …하게 되다 happen [chance] to (do). いがい

뜻받다 receive (a command); obey (an order) 《잇다》 pursue (the will)/부모의 뜻을 받아 부모 하라는 대로 하다 yield to one's parents and do what they say; obey one's parents. したがう

듯이 like; as; as if[though]/그는 죽은 ~ 가만히 있었다 He remained motionless as if he were dead. ように

듯하다 look like; appear; seem/비가 울 ~ It looks like rain., It threatens to rain. ようだ

뜻하다 plan; intend; aspire to[after]; aim at; expect/뜻하지 않은 unexpected. もくろむ

등 the back 《발의》 the instep 《산의》 the ridge/~이 높은 high-backed; high in the instep. せ

등(等) ①《등급》 grade; class 《도》 degree 《질》 quality/~으로 나누다 classify ②《따위》 and so on; grade; and others; and what not; and so forth; etc.; and the like/사과나 배~ apples, pears, and what not. とう

등(燈) a light; a lamp/~불 lamplight /~을 켜다 light a lamp. とう

등(藤) 《식》 a rattan; a cane/~의자 a rattan[a cane] chair/~지팡이 a cane stick. ふじ

등가(等價) 【화】 equivalence 【경】 parity /~의 equivalent/~량 【화】 an equivalent. とうか

등각(等角) 【수】 equal angles/~의 equiangular/~삼각형 an equiangular triangle/~선 an isogonic line. とうかく

등갓(燈一) a shade; a lampshade. ランプのかさ

등거리 a sleeveless jacket; a lady's fur coat. そでのないジャケッ

등거리(等距離) equal distances; equidistance/~의 equidistant /~에 at equal

**등걸** a stump; a stub／나무 ~을 캐내다 dig up the stump of a tree／~불 stump fire／~숯 charcoal made from stumps.

**등걸음치다** ①《시체를》 remove[carry] a corpse ②《끌고 가다》 pull (one) by the neck. したいをうつる

**등걸잠** sleeping with *one's* clothes on and without any covering／~을 자다 sleep with clothes on. きたままのねむり

**등겨** 《쌀겨》 rice-bran 《왕겨》 chaff. ぬか

**등경걸이(燈檠—)** a lamp stand; a lamp pole. とうか

**등고선(等高線)** a contour／~ 지도 a contour[-line] map. とうこうせん

**등골** the spinal cord; the spine. せなか

**등골뼈** the backbone; the chine; the spinal column; the spine. せきついこつ

**등꽃(藤—)** wisteria blossoms／~빛 light purple; lilac.

**등과(登科)** passing the higher civil service examination／~하다 pass the higher civil service examination.

**등교(登校)** attending school／~하다 attend[go to] school. とうこう

**등귀(騰貴)** a price rise; an advance; appreciation／~하다 rise; go up; advance／미래 ~ a future rise in prices. とうき

**등극(登極)** accession to the throne; enthronement／~하다 accede to[ascend] the throne. とうきょく

**등글개첩(—妾)** a young concubine of an aged man わかいめかけ

**등긁이** a back-scratcher. まごのて

**등급(等級)** a class; a grade; a rank／~을 매기다[정하다] grade; classify; graduate. とうきゅう

**등기(登記)** registration; registry／~하다 register; have (a thing) registered／~우편으로 by registered post／~번호 the registered number. とうき

**등나무(藤—)** 《식》 a wisteria／~ 덩굴 wisteria-vine. かづらのき

**등널** the back board of a chair.

**등단(登壇)** ~하다 go on the platform; mount the rostrum. とうだん

**등달다** be flurried; be in hot haste; be impatient; be overanxious; be nervous／그렇게 등달지 않아도 좋다 Don't fret yourself like that. うろたえる

**등닿다** ①《마소의 동이》〔the skin of a horse〕 comes off ②《등대다》 shelter oneself under[rely upon] the man of influence.

**등대(等待)** waiting／~하다 wait for; await.

**등대(燈臺)** a lighthouse／~지기 a lighthouse-keeper／~불 a beacon lamp; lights／~선 a light ship. とうだい

**등대다** lean[depend] on; rely upon; look [turn] to (a person) for help. もたれる

**등덜미** the upper part of the back／~를 잡다 take[seize] (a person) by the scruff of the neck. せのじょうぶ

**등도(登途)** departure; setting out [on a journey]／~하다 start on a journey.

**등등(等等)** etc.; and so on; and others. とうとう

**등등거리(藤—)** a rattan shirt [worn in summer to keep sweat from coat].

**등등하다(騰騰—)** be triumphant; (be) wild／기세가 ~ be in high spirits／노기가 ~ be red-hot[-black] with rage; be in wild rage. きぐらいのたかいこと

**등락(騰落)** rise and fall; fluctuations; ups and downs. とうらく

**등렬(等列)** the same rank[file].

**등록(登錄)** registration; entry; record／~하다 [enter in the] register; enter; list／유권자의 ~ registration of voters／~금 a registration fee 《수업료》 tuition／~자 a registrant／~ 상표 a registered trademark. とうろく

**등롱(燈籠)** a hanging lantern; a garden lantern 《신전의》 a sacred lantern／~에 불을 켜다 light a hanging lantern. とうろう

**등루(登樓)** ~하다 go up tower; climb a tower 《창가(娼街)에》 visit a brothel [a sporting house]. とうろう

**등림(登臨)** ~하다 mount an eminence; climb a height.

**등마루** the spinal column; the spine／지붕 ~ the ridge of a roof. せきつい

**등메** a figured mat; a fancy mat. もようあみしたむしろ

**등명(燈明)** a sacred light／~을 올리다 offer a sacred light／~ 접시 a light-dish.

**등반(登攀)** ~하다 climb (up); scale; make a ascent of／~대 climbing party／~자 climber. とうはん

**등받이** the back of a chair.

**등본(謄本)** a copy; a transcript／호적 ~ a copy of the domiciliary register／~을 신청하다 apply for a copy. とうほん

**등분(等分)** equal parts; division into equal parts／~의 of equal parts; equal in measure／~하다 divide equally[in equal parts]; share equally／이익을 2~ 하다 divide[share] the profit among the two. とうぶん

**등불(燈—)** a light; a lamplight／~을 켜다 light[make] a light／~ 아래서 글을 읽다 read by lamplight. とうか

**등비(等比)** 《수》 equal ratio／~ 수열 geometric series／~ 급수 geometric[al] progression／~ 급수적으로 in a geometric ratio. とうひ

**등사(謄寫)** copy; transcription; mimeographing／~하다 copy; transcribe; mimeograph／~지 《복사용》 carbon-paper 《투사용》 tracing paper. とうしゃ

**등산(登山)** mountain-climbing; mountaineering／~하다 climb[scale] (up) a mountain; make an ascent of／~가 a mountaineer. とうざん

등살 the flesh[muscle] of *one's* back. せのきんにく

등쌀 torture; harass; annoyance; botheration/모기 ~에 잠을 못 자겠다 The mosquitoes are so annoying that I can't sleep. やっかい

등색(橙色) orange; orange colo[u]r/~의 orange-colo[u]red. だいだいいろ

등선(登船) going aboard; boarding a ship/~하다 go on board (*a ship*); board a ship; take ship. ふねにのること

등성마루 the ridge; the top of the back; the line of the backbone. せきつい

등성이 (잔등) the back (산의) a ridge.

등속(等屬) and the like; and so forth; et cetera(略:etc.)/과자 ~ cake and the like. など

등속(等速) equal speed 【물】uniform velocity./~ 운동 uniform motion. とうそく

등솔기 a seam down the back of a coat.

등수(等數) ①(차례)a grade; a rank/~를 정하다 grade; classify ②(같은 수) an equal number/찬반이 ~이다 The vote is equally divided. とうすう

등식(等式) 【수】an equality. とうしき

등신(等身) life-size/~상 a life-size statue. とうしん

등신(等神) a fool; a stupid person; a dunce; a noodle/~같은 stupid; foolish /~ 같은 짓을 하다 do a foolish[silly] thing; play the fool. おろかなひと

등심(一心) meat around the backbone of cattle.

등심(燈心) a wick. とうしん

등어리 the back ⇨등.

등에 【충】a horse-fly. うしあぶ

등온(等溫) ①~의 isothermal/~선【지】an isothermal [line]; an isotherm. とうおん

등외(等外) ~의 under the regular grades/~가 되다 fall under the regular grades.

등용(登用) 【임용】appointment/~하다 appoint; engage; employ/인재를 ~하다 engage men of ability; employ talent /위원으로 ~하다 appoint *one* to the committee. とうよう

등용문(登龍門) an opening to all honors; the only door to eminence/문단에의 ~ the only door to the literary world. とうりゅうもん

등위(等位) class; rank; grade/~ 접속사 【언】a co-ordinate conjunction. とうい

등유(燈油) lamp-[burning-, illumination-] oil; kerosene; [paraffin-oil(영). とうゆ

등자(橙子) 【식】a bitter orange/~나무 a bitter orange/~꽃 orange blossoms. だいだいのみ

등잔(燈盞) a lamp-oil container; a lamp /~ 밑이 어둡다《속담》One has to go abroad to get news of home. とうさん

등장(登場) appearance; entrance/~하다 set out on a journey; enter/~ 순서 the order of appearance/~ 인물 characters. とうじょう

등장(等狀) a petition under joint signature.

등재(登載) registration; record/~하다 record; register.

등정(登程) departure; setting out on a journey/~하다 depart; set out on a journey. りょていにつくこと

등줄기 the line of the backbone.

등지(等地) [and] like places/마산 ~ *Masan* and like places.

등지느러미 the dorsal fin.

등지다 ①(들어지다) turn against; break up with; fall out with/세상을 ~ turn *one's* back on the world ②(등뒤에 두다) lean *one's* back against. かんけいをたつ

등짐 a pack on *one's* back/~을 지다 carry a burden on *one's* back/~ 장수 a pack-man. せおうにもつ

등차(等差) 《균등한 차》 equal difference (등급) a grade/~를 정하다 graduate; discriminate/~ 급수 【수】arithmetical progression. とうさ

등창(一瘡) a swelling[a boil] on *one's* back. せなかのはれもの

등청(登廳) attendance at office/~하다 attend[go to] the office. とうちょう

등초(謄抄) copy; transcription; reproduction/~하다 copy; reproduce; transcribe.

등촉(燈燭) a light; a lamplight; a candlelight.

등치다 ①(치다) strike (*one*) on the back ; strike at the back ②(빼앗다) extort money by threats/등쳐 먹고 살다 live by racketeering.

등친(等親) the degree of kinship[consanguinity]/결혼 금지의 ~ forbidden degree.

등타다 go along the ridge [of a mountain].

등피(燈皮) (긴) a lamp chimney 《원형의》 a globe. ランプのかさ

등한(等閑) negligence; neglect; slight/ ~히 하다 neglect; slight; disregard; make light (*of*); leave to chance/일을 ~히 하다 slight[neglect] *one's* work. なおざり

등화(燈火) a light; a lamp-light/~ 관제 a black-out/~ 가친지절 the good season for spending evening hours in reading/ ~ 신호 signaling with a lantern. とうか

등화(燈花) the tip of a wick. とうか

등화(藤花) wisteria-flower.

등후(等候) waiting ⇨등대(等待).

띄다 (눈에) catch sight of; catch the eye (물건이) attract *one's* attention 《연 따위를》fly/사람의 눈에 ~ catch sight of a man. めにつく

띄어 쓰다 write leaving space; space/한 줄씩 ~ write on every other[second] line.

띄엄띄엄 brokenly ⇨띄엄띄엄. まばらに

띄우다 ①(물 위에)[set] float; sail (*a toy boat*) ②(공중에) float in the air/뗏목을

~ float a log raft down a river ③(훈김으로) ferment; mold ④(사이를) leave out; leave a space ⑤(편지 따위를) send out; mail.

**띠¹** (허리의) a belt (여자용의) a sash; a girdle (우편물의) a [half] wrapper/~를 매다 tie a girdle/허리 ~ a girdle.

**띠²** 〖식〗 a miscanthus. かや

**띠그르르** ~하다 (be) somewhat thick[big] among the rest. よりふとい

**띠다** ①(띠를) tie a girdle; do up a sash ②(지니다) wear; carry; be armed ③(용무 등을) be charged[entrusted] (with)/공무를 띠고 under government orders ④(빛·기색 등을) wear; assume; put on; carry; have/노기를 띠고 있다 look angry/붉은 빛을 띤 reddish (cheeks). むすぶ

**디디다** ①(땅을) step on; tread on/정계에 발을 내어 ~ enter upon a political career ②(누룩을) tread malted flour paste into cakes. ふむ

**디딜방아** a mortar [worked by treading].

**디딤돌** a stepstone (수단) a step; a stepping stone/~로 해서 over stepping-stones.

**디룽거리다** dangle; sway; swing/바람에 ~ dangle in the wind. ぶらりぶらりする

**띠앗머리** brotherly[sisterly] affection; fraternal love; love among brothers and sisters/~없다 lack in brotherly affection.

**띠엄띠엄** (단속적) brokenly; intermittently (여기저기) here and there; sporadically (사이를 두고) at intervals (느릿느릿) very slowly. まばらに

**띠톱** a band[belt] saw.

**띰목**(一木) a prop used in a pit.

**띳집** a miscanthus[imperata] thatched house. かやのいえ

**딩굴다** roll over[about]. ころがる

**딩딩하다, 띵띵하다** ①(힘이 세다) strong; robust; mighty; stout; sturdy ②(팽팽하다) (be) taut; tense; tight ③(기반이 튼튼하다) (be) stable; secure; firm; hard. ちからがつよい

**띵하다** ①(머리가 무겁다) feel heavy in the head ②(아프다) have a headache.

**라** 〖음〗 ① 《제6 계명》 la ② 《라 음》 re; D/~단조〔장조〕 D minor[major].

**-라** ① 《종결 어미》 ⓠ인명은 재천이~ Life and death are providential./그는 나를 해칠지라도 나는 그를 사랑하리~ Should he injure me, I would love him./효(孝)는 백행지본이~ Filial piety is the source of all vertues./생명으로 인도하는 문은 좁고 협착하여 찾는 이가 적음이니~ For the gate is narrow and the way is hard, that leads to life, and those who find it are few. ② 《연결 어미》 ⓠ그는 몸이 약한지~ 중노동은 못한다 He cannot do hard muscular labour because of his delicate health./그 일이 싫은 게 아니~ 틈이 없다 Not that I dislike the work, but that I have no time./우천인지~ 시합은 중지되었다 As it was rainy, the game was called off. ③《명령》서두르지 마~ Don't hurry./구하~ 그러면 너희에게 주실 것이오 Ask, it will be given you./가~ Go!, Get away!/정지하~ Stop!

**라고** ①《대용》[saying] that it is; calling it [by name]/이것은 진달래~ 하는 꽃이다 This is a flower called the azalea ②《비꼬는 투》ⓠ이것을 잡지~ 샀더니 볼 것이 하나도 없다 I bought this "magazine" and can't fine a thing in it to read. ―と

**-라고** to/들어오~ 해라 Tell him to come in./이것을 보~ 하시오 Tell him to take a look at this. ―せよと

**라는** called; named; styled; titled/메리~ 소녀 a girl called mary. ―という

**-라는** ⓠ그가 여기 오리~ 소문이 있다 It is rumoured that he will come here. ―せよという

**라니** ⓠ김씨가 첩자(諜者)~ 나는 깜짝 놀랐다 I am greatly surprised to hear that Mr. *Kim* is a spy. ―とは

**라도** (…까지도) even; the very (설사 … 일지라도) though; even if; however (어떤 …이라도) any (어느 것이라도) either … or/비가 오더~ even if it rains/결과가 어찌 되더~ whatever the consequence may be/내가 아니더~ besides me. ―でも

**라서** 《감히·능히》 indeed; possibly; by any audacity/뉘~ 나를 이기리오 Who indeed can best me!.

**라야, 라야만** only if it be; unless it be /너~ 능히 그 일을 하겠다 It is you that can do the job.

**라조(一調)** 〖음〗D ⓠ라장조〔단조〕 D major [minor].

**-락** ⓠ오~가~하다 go[walk] to and fro; wander; go back and forth/방안을 오~가~하다 walk up and down the room /비가 오~가~하다 rain off and on/정신이 오~가~하다 (one's mind) wander [stray]/저 전등은 붉으~파르~한다 Those lights become red and green by turns.

**-락말락** ⓠ담이 무너질~한다 The wall is on the brink[verge] of collapse.

**-래서** ⓠ그가 저녁을 먹으러 오~ 그의 집에 갔다 I went to his house, being invited to dinner./그를 오~ 같이 놀자 Let's ask him to come to play with us. ―せよというので

**-래서야** ⓠ이~ 됩니까 You shouldn't do this./두달도 못 되어 그만두~ 되겠소 It is unreasonable that you should ask me to quit within two months./이것이 100원어치~ 말이 됩니까 Are you kidding to say that this is worth 100 *won*?

**-래야** must; have to; should; ought to /사람을 보내어 그를 오~ 되겠다 I must send a person for him./그~ 마땅하지 You should do so., It should be so. ―といっては

**-랴** ①《반어》ⓠ 내가 설마 그러~ I would never do so./그가 차마 그런 말을 했으~ How could he dare to say so? ②《문의》ⓠ걸어가~ Shall I go on foot?/돈을 주~ Do you want some money?, Shall I give you some money? ―しようか

**-러** ⓠ너를 보~ 왔다 I have come to see you.

**-려고** ⓠ집을 사~ 은행에서 빚을 냈다 I took out a loan from the bank in order to buy a house. ―しに

**-려기에** on account of; owing to; as; because; since/비가 오~ 우산을 갖고 왔다 I took an umbrella with me, because it was going to rain.

**-려나** ⓠ대관절 내게 무엇을 시키~ What on earth do you expect me to do?/언제 돈을 주~ When shall I have the money? しょうとするのか

**-려네** I will; I intend[mean] to (*do*)/나

**려느냐** **ᄀ** 는 그것을 하~ I am going to (do) it/나는 내년에 미국에 가~ I intend[mean] to go America next year.  しようとするよ

**-려느냐** **ᄀ** 너는 무엇이 되~ What are you going to be?/언제 가~ When will you go? ―するつもりか

**-려는** **ᄀ** 직장을 구하~ 사람은 많다 There are many people who look out for a job./이것은 이제 우리가 만나~ 소녀의 사진이다 This is the picture of a girl whom we are going to see.

**-려는가** **ᄀ** 언제 떠나~ When are you going to leave?/너는 무엇을 하~ What are you going to do? ―しようとするのか

**-려는데** **ᄀ** 내가 막 외출을 하~ 그가 들어왔다 He came in just as I was going out.

**-려는지** **ᄀ** 그가 직접 오~ 모르겠다 I am uncertain whether he will come himself or not.

**-겨니** **ᄀ** 우리들은 그가 시험에 합격되~ 생각했다 We expected that he would pass the examination. ―だろう

**-려니와** ①(도한) not only … but …; as well as ②(한편) on the other hand/취직도 하~ 곧 결혼도 하겠다 Besides getting a job, I will get married soon. することはするが

**-려다가** **ᄀ** 소풍을 하~ 날씨가 흐려서 그만 두었다 As it was cloudy, I gave up the idea of going on a picnic.

**-려도** **ᄀ** 죽으~ 죽을 수 없다 I can't die in spite of myself./아무리 하~ 할 수 없다 However much I may try, I cannot do it. ―しようとしても

**-려면** **ᄀ** 싸우~ 끝까지 싸워라 If you do fight, fight it out. しようとすれば

**-려면야** **ᄀ** 이기~ 이길 수 있지만 I could win, if I would./하~ 할 수 있지만 I could, if I would.

**-려무나** may; had better/언제든지 들어오~ You may enter at will./좀더 누워 있으~ But you had better take a little more rest. ―せよ.  ―しないか

**-려야** **ᄀ** 나는 가~ 갈 수 없다 I do wish to go, but I am unable to go./잊으~ 잊을 수 없다 I shall never forget/…하지 않으~ …하지 않을 수 없다 cannot help …ing; cannot but (do). しようとしても

**-려오** I will[would]/다시는 그런 짓을 안 하~ I will never do such a thing again. しようとします

**-련만** **ᄀ** 좀더 열심히 공부를 했으면 좋으~ You ought to have[should have] studied harder. ―だろうに

**-렴** may ⇒려무나. ―せよ

**-렵니까** **ᄀ** 언제 떠나시~ When are you leaving?/신문을 좀 빌려 주시~ Will you please lend me the newspaper for a moment? しようとしますか

**-렷다** (틀림없음·추측·다짐) be sure[bound, agreed] to happen; will surely happen; probably be/비가 와도 그는 오~ He's bound to come even if it rains.
―だろうね

**로** ①(수단·기구) by; by means of; with; in; on ②(원인·이유) at; with; of; from; through; for; because of; on account of; owing to; due to ③(원료·재료) from; of/이 집은 나무~ 만들어져 있다 This house is made of wood. ④(척도·표준·단위·정도) by/파운드~ 팔다 sell by the pound ⑤(방향) to; for; forward ⑥(지위·신분·자격) as; in the capacity[position] of. ―へ

**로고** **ᄀ** 알 수 없는 일이~ What a mystery it is!/참으로 해괴한 일이~ What a strange thing it is! だね

**로구면** **ᄀ** 벌써 오정이~ It is already twelve o'clock!/참 아름다운 경치~ What a [beautiful] sight! だなだね

**로군** **ᄀ** 정말 아름다운 여자~ Truly, she is a fair woman!/이 진주는 모두 가짜~ These pearls are all shams./기상 천외 ~ What an idea! だな

**로다** **ᄀ** 그이야 말로 군자~ He is indeed a remarkable gentleman[a man of virtue]. だな.  てあるぞ

**로서** ①(기능·자격) as; for; in the capacity of/대표~ as a representative ②(인정된·알려진·생각된 상태·신분) to be; as; that; knowing it as; in view of/

교사~의 책임 one's duty as a teacher/나~는 ესო for me; on my [own] part; for my part/지도자~ 받들다 look up to (a person) for one's leader/그는 정치가~보다도 소설가~ 더 잘 알려져 있다 He is better known as a novelist than as a statesman. としてから

**로써** (수단) with; by; by means of; using (재료) with; of; [made] out of (원인) for; as; with; from; because of; due to (결과) as a consequence of; with; in accordance with/썰매~ 가다 go by sled/만년필~ 쓰다 write with a fountain pen. で もって

**-로 하여금** **ᄀ** …로 하여금 …을 시키다 (강제로) make (a person do); cause (a person to do); force (a person to do); compel (a person to do); (명령적으로) get (a person to do); (허락) allow (a person to do)/그~ 편지를 부치게 하다 get him to post a letter/나는 그~ 그 일을 하게 했다 I had him do the work., I got him to do the work.

**-론(論)** ①(논설) an essay; a treatise; a comment; a leading article ②(논의) argument; discussion; discourse; debate; controversy/예술~ an essay on art. ―ろん

**-롭다** be; be characterized by/향기~ be fragrant/ 호화~ be brilliant[gaudy]/해~ be harmful; be noxious/새 ~ be new. ―らしい. ―そうだ

**-류(類)** ①(강·綱) a class [of insects, ferns] ②(목·目) an order [of carnivores, hymenoptera] ③(유파) a type; a style; a mode. るい

-류(流) ①(형) a style; a type; a mode; a manner; a way; a system／자기~ one's own fashion ②(등급) order; rate; class; rank／일~의 출판사 a first-rate publishing company／2~ 시인 a poet of the second order.

럽 ①(동사의 목적어) 및 우표~ 수집하다 collect stamps／나에게 시계~ 주다 give me a watch／나에게 일자리~ 주다 find me a job ②(전치사의 목적어) 및 개~ 무서워하다 be afraid of dogs／머리~ 때리다 hit (a person) on the head.

리 (…할 리) [good] reason; possibility／못 올 ~가 없다 There is no reason why he can't come.／그 말이 거짓말일 ~가 없다 That couldn't be a lie.／아까까지 여기 있었던 것을 네가 모를 ~가 있나 You can't help knowing about a thing that was here a minute ago, can you?  はず

-리(裡) amid[st]; in ／갈채~에 단(壇)을 내리다 leave a platform amidst[in] the applause of the audience.

-리다 ①및 내가 하~ I'll be glad to do it.／필요하면 가~ I will go if necessary.／제가 맡아보~ I will take of that matter. ②(경계·경고) 및 빨리 서두르시오 늦으~ Make haste or you'll be late.
　　　　　　　　―するでしょう．―します

-리오 및 어찌 그 말을 할 수 있으~ How can I tell that?／어찌 말로 다할 수 있으~ No language can express it.／그 소식을 들으면 얼마나 기뻐 하~ How glad he will be to hear it!  しましょうか

마 【식】 a yam; *Dioscorea batas*(학명).
마(麻) 【식】 a hemp. あさ
마(碼) a yard/ ~로 팔다 sell by the yard/ ~자 a yard-measure 《줄자》 a yard-tape. ヤード
마(魔) a demon; a devil/ ~의 손 evil influence/ ~가 들다 be possessed by an evil spirit[a demon]. おに
마가목 【식】 a mountain ash; a rowan [tree]; *Sorbus commixta*(학명).
마가복음(-福音) 【성경】 [the Gospel of] Mark; The Gospel According to St. Mark.
마각(馬脚) a horse's legs/ ~을 드러내다 show the cloven hoof[foot]; reveal one's true character. ばきゃく
마감(磨勘) closing; finish; conclusion/ ~하다 close; bring to a close; finish; shut off/일을 ~하다 finish a job/모집 ~ the close of the subscription/편집 ~ editorial deadline; the final editing/기사 ~ 시간 the copy deadline [of a newspaper]. しめきり
마개 a stopper; a stopple; a cork; a plug/ ~를 막다 cork; plug; put a stopper (in)/ ~로 구멍을 막다 plug up a hole/ ~뽑이 a corkscrew; a cap opener/귀 ~ an earplug. せん
마고자 a Korean jumper.
마광(磨光) polish[ing]; burnish[ing]/ ~하다 polish; burnish.
마구 ①carelessly; at random; without discretion; without discrimination/글씨를 ~ 쓰다 write carelessly/말을 ~ 하다 be rough of speech ②(세차게) hard; much/비가 ~ 온다 It rains hard. てあたりしだいに
마구(馬具) harness 《장식》 trappings; horse equipment; saddlery/ ~를 달다 harness a horse/ ~ 상인[제조인] a saddler; a harness maker. ばく
마구간(馬廐間) a stable; a barn/ ~에 넣다 stable (*a horse*); put[lodge] a horse in a stable. うまや
마구리 the edge; the verge. はずれ
마구발방 rude speech and wild conduct; sloppy[outrageous] behavior/ ~하다 use wild words; behave outrageously; behave in a sloppy way; be sloppy.
ぼうげんぼうこう
마구잡이 random[careless] behavior; a reckless act. もうもくてきなこうどう

마군(馬軍) the cavalry ⇒기병.
마군(魔鬼) a person who puts a spoke in another's wheel.
마굴(魔窟) ①(마귀의) a lair of devils ②(악인의) a den (of *thieves, robbers*); an underworld hangout ③(창녀의) the brothel districts/ ~의 여자들 street girl ④(아편굴) an opium den. まくつ
마권(馬券) a pari-mutuel ticket; a pool ticket. ばけん
마귀(魔鬼) an evil spirit; a devil; a demon (기독교에서) the Devil; Satan/ ~ 같은 demoniac; diabolic/ ~ 할멈 a witch; a hag; an ogress; a harridan. おに

마기 ultimately; really; in reality.
마나님 《나이 많은 여자》 an elderly lady; an old woman 《호칭》 madam; your [good] lady. ろうふじんのけいご
마냥 as much as *one* wishes[wants]; till full; all the way; to *one's* heart's content/ ~ 즐기다 enjoy to *one's* heart's content/ ~ 먹었다 I have eaten all I wanted. もっぱら
마녀(魔女) a witch; a sorceress; a she-devil/ ~잡기 a witch-hunt. まじょ
마노(瑪瑙) 【광】 agate/얼룩 ~ onyx (*pl.* -es). めのう
마누라 《아내》 a wife/늙은 여자 an old woman/ ~를 얻다 take a woman to a wife/ ~로 삼다 have a woman for *one's* wife. つまのひご
마늘 garlic; a rocambole/ ~종 the stem [the stalk] of garlic. にんにく
마니교(摩尼敎) Manichaeanism/ ~ 교도 a Manichee; Manichaean.
마님 madam; a lady. りょうかのふじん
마다 every; each; at an interval of/5분 ~ every five minutes/날 ~ every day; daily/집집~ each and every house; at every door. まいに
마당 ①(뜰) a garden; a yard ②(경우) in a case; an occasion/ 이 ~에 무슨 소리냐 The case does not allow of saying such a thing. にわ
마당발 a wide foot. はばのひろいあし
마당질 threshing; flailing/ ~하다 thresh[flail] in the yard. だっこく
마땅하다 ①(적합하다) (be) suitable; becoming; befitting; worthy of ②(당연하다) (be) natural; just; deserved. てきとうだ
마땅히 ①(당연히) justly; properly; natu-

마도요 rally ②(적당히) suitably; adequately; appropriately. すべからく．
마도요 《조》 the Indian curlew; a sabre bill; *Numenius arquatus*(학명).
마도위(馬—) a horse broker. うまのちゅうかいにん
마똑하다 (be) satisfactory; agreeable. まんぞくだ
마들가리 ①(나무의) twigs; sticks; dead branches ②(솔기) seams of a worn-out garment. えのないみき
마디 ①(뼈마디) a joint; a knot; a knob ②(말·노래 따위의) a paragraph; a passage; a word. かんせつ
마디다 (be) durable; enduring; lasting; longwearing. もちがよい
마디마디 ①(관절) all the joints; every joint／～가 아프다 feel pain in every joint ②(말 따위) all the words[phrases]／～에 깊은 뜻이 있다 All the words are pregnant with meaning. ふしぶし
마디충 《동》 a rice borer; a pearl moth.
마디풀 《식》 a knotgrass; *Polygonum aviculare*(학명).
마래미 ①《어》 a young yellowtail [fish] ②(소작 관리인) the supervisor of a tenant farm.
마량(馬糧) fodder; forage; provender.
마력(馬力) 《물》 horse-power(h.p., HP)／800 ～의 기관 a 800 h.p. engine／～을 올리다 get up steam／그 발동기는 700 마력입니다 The motor develops 700 horse-power. ばりき
마력(魔力) magical power[virtues]; supernatural powers／그녀의 눈에는 일종의 ～이 있다 There is something in her eyes that captivates us. まりょく
마련 a plan; programme; arrangements／～하다 (준비하다) prepare; get ready; arrange 《조달하다》 supply; raise ／일을 ～하다 manage an affair／식사가 ～되었다 The meal is ready. したく
마렵다 have[feel] an urge; have a motion. べんいがおこる
마루 ①(집의) a floor; a veranda[h] ②《산·지붕의》 a ridge／산～ the ridge [of a mountain]. ゆか
마루터기 the top; the peak; the summit ／고개 ～ the summit of a pass／산 ～ the peak of a mountain.
마루폭 the waist [of a garment]. どうぶ
마룻귀틀 the joists of a floor.
마룻대 a ridge pole. むなぎ
마룻바닥 the floor／～에 앉다 sit on the floor. ゆかのめん
마룻줄 a halyard; a brace line for a sail.
마르다¹ (건조하다) dry; get dry; dry up; wither(꽃·잎이); (목재가) be seasoned (입술이) be parched (목이) be thirsty (야위다) becomes thin[lean]; lose flesh. かわく
마르다² (옷감·재목을) cut out／옷을 ～ cut out clothes. たつ

마른갈이 tillage of a dry rice-field. みずをいれずにたをたがやすこと
마른걸레 a dry floorcloth; a dry mop [cloth]; a dry house-cloth／～질하다 wipe with a dry cloth.
마른고기 dried meat[fish]. ほしこ
마른국수 ①(말린) dried noodles ②(삶지 않은) uncooked noodles／～로 먹다 eat noodles uncooked.
마른기침 a dry cough; a hacking cough ／～하다 hack; emit a short and dry cough; clear *one's* throat. からせき
마른나무 dried wood; dried fire-wood.
마른반찬 dried meat or fish eaten with rice as side dishes. ほしこ
마른빨래 drying muddy clothes and then scraping the dirt off.
마른밥 (주먹 밥) a rice-ball (국 없는 밥) boiled-rice eaten without soup.
마른버짐 《의》 a kind of ringworm.
마른번개 lightning in a clear blue sky.
마른신 ①(걸지 않은) unoiled leather shoes ②(마른 땅에 신는) dry-weather shoes.
마른안주 dried meat or fish tidbits to eat as a snack while drinking. つまみ
마른옴 《의》 the itch; scabies.
마른일 woman's room work; sewing; or weaving／～하다 do the dry part of the house work.
마른입 ①(국물 안 먹은) a mouth that has had no sup ②⇒잔입.
마른천둥 thunder in a clear blue sky.
마른하늘 a clear blue sky; a cloudless sky.
마른행주 a dish towel.
마름¹ 《식》 a water chestnut; a water caltrop／～죽 water chestnut porridge. ひし
마름² (소작 관리인) the supervisor of a tenant farm. こさくかんりにん
마름³ (이영의 단위) a bundle of woven straw for thatching.
마름모 a lozenge; diamond [shape]; 《수》 a rhombus. りょうけい
마름쇠 a caltrop; caltrap.
마름자 a yardstick used in cutting out clothes. さいだんようのしゃく
마름질 cutting out [clothes]／옷을 ～하다 cut out a dress. さいだん
마리 the number of animals. びき
마마 《의》 smallpox／～에 걸리다 suffer from smallpox; be taken ill of smallpox／～꽃 pox pustules. てんねんとう
마마(媽媽) Your[His, Her] Majesty[Highness]／대전～ H.M. the King／동궁 ～ the Prince; his Highness／중전～ H.M. the Queen.
마맛자국 a pockmark; a pit／얼굴에 ～이 있다 *one's* face is pitted with smallpox. てんねんとうのあと
마멸(磨滅) wear; defacement; attrition; abrasion／～하다 wear out; be worn out[away, down]; be defaced／도장이 ～되었다 The stamp has become defaced

/~ 시험 abrasion test. まめつ
마모(馬毛) horsehair.
마무르다 ①(일을) finish; complete; conclude ②(둘레·가장자리를) hem; fringe ③(끝손질) touch up. へりをつける
마무리 finish; finishing touches settlement; completion; conclusions/~가 잘 됐다 The finish is good. しあげ
마물(魔物) a thing of evil; a sprite; a spectre. ばけもの
마미(馬尾) a horsetail; horsehair.
마바리 a horse of burden; a packhorse.
마방(馬房) a horse stable.
마방집(馬房—) a livery stable.
마법(魔法) 《요술》 magic; black art; sorcery/~을 쓰다 practice the black art; use[work] magic/~을 걸다 cast spells (upon *a person*). まほう
마법사(魔法士) a magician; a wizard; a sorcerer; a sorceress(여자). まほうつかい
마병 junk(넝마); an old article; worn-out articles/~ 장수 a junk man. ぼろ
마병(馬兵) cavalry. きへい
마부(馬夫) a groom; a horsekeeper; stableman; a coachman; a driver. ばてい
마분(馬糞) horse-manure[-dung]; horse-droppings/~지(紙) strawboard; millboard. ばふん
마비(痲痹) paralysis; palsy; numbness/심장 ~ heart failure/소아 ~ infantile paralysis; polio/전신 ~ general paralysis/안면 ~ facial paralysis. まひ
마비풍(痲脾風) 『의』 diphtheria.
마사(馬事) horse affairs[matters].
마사회(馬事會) the horse affairs association/한국 ~ the Korean Horse Affairs Association.
마삯 the fee for hiring a horse. うまのちんぎん
마상(馬上) horseback/ ~에서 on horse-back/~에서 사람을 부르다 call out to another from on *one's* horse/ ~객 a rider; an equestrian. じょうばしていること
마상이 《작은 배》a [small] boat; a skiff; a canoe 《통나무 배》a dugout. こぶね
마성(魔性) devilishness; fiendishness.
마세(馬貰) horse hire 《마삯》 the fee for hiring a horse. うまのちんぎん
마소 horse and oxen[cattle]. うまとうし
마속 a measure; capacity of one-*mal*.
마손(磨損) friction loss; wear and tear 《화폐의》 abrasion.
마수(一數) quantity measured in *mal*.
마수(魔手) evil influence; an evil hand / ~를 뻗치다 exert *one's* evil influence. ましゅ
마수걸다 sell for the first time; make the first sale of the day.
はじめうんだめしのためにはんばいする
마수걸이 the first sale of the day/ ~ 하다 make the first sale of the day.
さいしょうんだめしのはんばい
마술(魔術) magic; the black art; sorcery; witchcraft/ ~을 걸다 throw a spell (over *a person*)/ ~을 쓰다 practice sorcery; use magic. まじゅつ
마술(馬術) horsemanship; equitation; the art of riding/~의 연습 riding practice /~ 연습소 A riding school. ばじゅつ
마시다 ①(액체를) drink; take; have; swallow ②(호흡하다) breath in; inhale; imbibe; inspire. のむ
마신(魔神) a devil; an evil spirit. まし
마신(馬身) a horse's length/그 말은 3 ~ 의 차로 이겼다 The horse won by three length. ばしん
마약(麻藥) a narcotic; an anesthetic; an opiate; a dope/~ 상용자 a drug[narcotic] addict/~ 중독 narcotic poisoning; narcotism. まやく
마왕(魔王) 《마귀의 왕》the Devil; Satan; the Prince of Darkness. まおう
마유(麻油) hempseed oil.
마육(馬肉) horseflesh; horse meat. ばにく

마을 ①(동리) a village; a rural community; a hamlet ②(옛 관청) a government office. むら
마을가다 visit *one's* neighboring village; visit *one's* neighborhood.
마을군 a habitual frequenter (to *one's* neighborhood); a woman who never stays home.
마음 ⇒변학 참조(page 1422). こころ
마음가짐 ①(마음 태도) *one's* mental attitude; *one's* state of mind ②(결심) determination; resolution; resolve.
마음껏 ①(실컷) to *one's* heart's content; to the full; to the utmost ②(충심으로) with *one's* whole heart; with devotion; with a single heart/~ 울다 cry *one's* heart out. こころのかぎり
마음결 disposition; temper; a turn of mind; grain; nature mind. きしつ
마음놓다 ①(안심하다) feel easy; feel at rest; set *one's* mind at ease ②(방심하다) relax *one's* attention; slacken *one's* effort. あんしんする
마음대로 as *one* pleases[likes, wishes]; at *one's* convenience. かってに
마음먹다 ①(의도하다) intend to; have a mind to; mean to; think of ②(결심하다) be determined; make up *one's* mind; make a resolution. しようとする
마음보 temper; nature; disposition; will; intention/~ 사나운 사람 an illnatured person. こころのつかいかた
마음성 ①(마음과 성질) heart and nature; mind and temper ②(성질) nature; disposition; character. しんせい
마음속 *one's* mind; *one's* heart; the bottom[the depths] of *one's* heart/ ~에 사무치다 sink deep into *one's* heart. かんがえ
마음쓰다 《생각·연구하다》use *one's* mind [head]; study; think; works *one's* brain 《유의하다》pay attention 《동정하다》

# 마 음

① **(생각·정)** mind; spirit; heart; idea; thought; mentality /~에 품다 have; harbor; cherish; entertain /~에 그리다 picture to oneself; imagine /~에 새기다 keep in memory; inscribe on one's mind; fix indelibly in one's mind /~ 든든하다 feel safe[secure, reassured] /~에 떠오르다 [good ideas] occur to (a person) /~에 걸리다 weigh[hang] upon one's mind; lie heavy on one's heart; trouble one's mind; feel uneasy about; be worried[concerned] about /~을 합하여 with one accord 《협력하여》 cooperatively /~을 합하다 act in concert with; be united /~을 사다 seek[court] a person's favor; curry favor (with a person); win a person's favor; ingratiate oneself (with a person); worm[insinuate] oneself into a person's favor /~을 주다 share one's confidence (with); trust; trust oneself (to); confide (in) /~을 고쳐먹다 reform oneself; turn over a new leaf /~을 모질게 먹다 steel[harden] one's heart /~을 진정하다 calm oneself; calm down; cool off; keep one's presence of mind /~을 잡아 개장사다 be a backslider; be still addicted to one's old vices /~을 잡다 take hold of oneself; get[keep] a firm grip on oneself; control[check] oneself; keep oneself from going astray; keep steady /~을 빼앗기다 be captivated[fascinated] by; be absorbed (in); lose one's heart (to) /~을 빼앗다 captivate [fascinate] (a person); charm[bewitch] (a person); magnetize; steal a person's heart /~속으로 in one's heart; inwardly; secretly; within; deep down inside /~속 one's heart of hearts; deep in one's heart /어린 ~ young ideas; a juvenile[puerile] mind /새 ~ a new heart /어리석은 ~ one's foolish heart /~을 쓰다 take care (of); give attention (to); beware (of) /~을 졸이다 be in a fidget; fret; stew; worry; trouble oneself; be anxious about /~이 변하다 change peace of mind /~을 가라앉히다 calm down one's feelings /좋은 생각이 ~에 떠오른다 A good idea occurs to me., I hit upon a good idea. /~이 흐뭇해지는 이야기 It is a heart-warming story. /그는 ~이 좋은 놈이다 He is a good fellow at bottom. /조금은 내 ~도 알아주시오 Kindly think about the matter from my point of view. /그는 ~속으로는 웃고 있다 He is laughing in his sleeve.

② **(의지)** will; intention; design; inclination; plan; mind; heart /~대로 at will; just as one likes[wishes, pleases]; as one will; at one's pleasure; at one's discretion /~은 굴뚝 같다 have a great mind to; be eager to /…할 ~이 없다 have no mind to do; be in no mood to do; have no inclination for; don't feel like doing /갈 ~이 있다 have a mind to go; want to go /~에 들지 않다 《사물이 주어》 be disagreeable one's mind; have a change of heart; be unfaithful; betray /~이 쓰이게 되다 be worried[concerned.anxious] about /~이 놓이다 be[feel] relieved; feel at ease; be assured /~이 크다 be large-minded[-hearted]; be broad-minded; be liberal; be generous; be big /~이 좁다 be narrow[-minded]; be illiberal; be ungenerous; be small /~을 쏟다 put[pour] one's heart [and soul] into; concentrate on; give[devote] one's whole mind (to) /여자 ~ a woman's heart[mind] /어머니 ~ maternal affection; a mother's love; a mother's feelings /~의 양식 mental nourishment /~이 기쁘다 be glad [at heart] /~이 상하다 one's heart breaks /~ 짚이다 know of; have [an idea] in mind /~이 약하다 be weak-hearted[-minded] /~이 아프다 be sorry; be grieved; be agonized /~의 평화

③ **(인정)** consideration; sympathy; tenderness; heart; kindness /~이 좋다 be gentle-hearted; be a good[nice] person at heart; be good-natured; have a tender heart; have a heart of gold /~을 쓰다 be sympathetic; be considerate /~이 나쁘다 be ill-natured; be cross-grained /매사는 ~먹기에 달렸다 Everything has its two sides to look at.

④ **(주의)** mind; attention; interest; care /~을 기울이다 direct one's attention to /~을 쓰다 give attention to; be attentive /그가 말한 것을 ~에 두지 마라 Don't mind what he says.

⑤ **(취미)** fancy; taste; liking; mind; heart /~에 드는 소녀 a girl after to (a person); 《사람이 주어》 go against the grain[stomach] /~에도 없는 소리를 하다 say what one does not mean /~이 내키거든 같이 갑시다 Let us go together if you want to. /그렇게 할 ~은 조금도 없다 I have not the slightest desire to do so. /오늘은 도무지 일할 ~이 없다 I don't feel like working today., I'm in no mood[humor] for working today. /그는 남에게 ~에도 없는 말을 한다 He speaks to others what is quite part from his real motive /이것은 그의 ~에서 나온 것은 아니다 It has not come of his own free will.

*one's heart*/ ~에 드는 옷 clothes to *one's taste*/~에 드는 집 a house to *one's fancy*[after *one's heart*]/ ~에 들다 be to *one's* liking; be after *one's* fancy; be satisfactory; be acceptable; suit[catch, take, strike] *one's* fancy; please; be in *one's* favor; find favor with (*a person*); impress favorably; take a shine to《미·구》/~이 내키지 않는다 be in no mood to; be unwilling (*to do*) /그 소녀는 나의 마음에 들었다 The young maiden captivated my heart/그 일 에는 ~이 내키지 않았다 I was not in the humor for the job.

**마음씨** a turn[cast] of mind; nature; motive; temper; disposition/~가 부드러운 사람 a man of a soft[sweet] temper/그녀는 ~는 좋은데 지혜가 부족하다 She has a sweet temper but poor sense. こころだて

**마음자리** heart; mind; nature/ ~가 좋은 사람 a good-natured person. しんじ

**마음졸이다, 마음졸이다** be worried; be anxious[concerned, nervous] about; fret; stew; fear/시험 결과가 어찌 될는지 몹시 마음조이고[졸이고] 있다 I am nervous about the examination results/~그의 모친은 그의 장래에 관해 몹시 마음 졸이고[조이고] 있다 His mother is very anxious about his future. きにかかる

**마의**(麻衣) hemp clothes. あさのきもの

**마이 동풍**(馬耳東風) pouring water on a duck's back; praying to deat ears[to the wind]. ばじとうふう

**마인**(魔人) a demon of a man.

**마작**(麻雀) mah-jong[g].

**마장** (거리)a *ri*/반 ~ half a *ri*.

**마장**(馬場) a grazing land for horse (목장) pasture land; a riding ground; a racecourse (경마장) a race track. ばば

**마장수** a peddler who carries his pack on horseback.

**마장스럽다** be a hindrance; be thwarting. せいこうのまぎわにじゃまがいる

**마저**[1] (토씨) even; also/하인들~ 주인을 업신여긴다 Even his servants despise him. までも、すら

**마저**[2] (부사)with all the rest; without living any.

**마적**(馬賊) mounted thieves; mounted bandits[brigands]. ばぞく

**마전**[1] bleaching/ ~하다 bleach/ ~장이 a bleacher; a laundryman/~터 a bleaching establishment; a laundry/~한 무명 bleached cotton. ひょうはく

**마전**[2] grain-measuring place.

**마제**(馬蹄) a horseshoe ⇨말굽. ばてい

**마조**(一調) tone E/마장조 E major.

**마주** opposite; face to face; *vis-a-vis*(F) /~보다 look each other in the face; look at each other.

**마주놓다** set (*things*) opposite each other.

**마주서다** confront [one]; come face to face with; stand opposite to; stand facing right ahead/서로 ~ stand face to face with (*a person*); stand opposite to (*a person*). むかいあってたつ

**마주앉다** sit face to face (with *a person*); sit across the table from (*a person*); sit opposite to (*a person*); sit opposite[facing] (*one*)/마주앉아 이야기하다 talk face to face (with *a person*). むかいあってする

**마주잡이** a bier carried by two bearers.

**마주치다** ①《부딪치다》 collide with; crash with; run against; knock[strike, bump] against ②《우연히 만나다》 meet with; be faced by[with]; fall in with; come upon. ぶつかりあう

**마주하다** put opposite.

**마죽**(馬粥) boiled horse food.

**마중** meeting (영접) reception; greet; receive/모든 정부 요인들이 그를 ~나왔다. All the high government officials came out to greet him. げいせつ

**마지**(摩旨) rice offered to Buddha.

**마지기** a *majigi*; a field wide enough to; be planted with one *mal* of seed/논 한 ~ a patch of rice paddy/밭 네 ~ four *majigi* of fields.

**마지막** the last; the end; a close/ ~으로 lastly; finally; at the conclusion/ ~에는 싸움이 되고 말았다 It ended in a quarrel. さいご

**마지못하다** be compelled; be obliged; be pressed/마지못하여 against *one's* will; unwillingly; reluctantly; with a bad grace; inevitably/마지못해 승낙을 하였다 He gave an unwilling consent/그는 마지못해 사과를 하였다 He apologized with a bad grace. やらざるをえない

**마지않다** can never (*thank*) enough.

**마진**(麻疹) 《한》 measles. はしか

**마질** ~하다 measure with a *mal* measure. こくもつをしょうでけいりょうすること

**마차**(馬車) a carriage; a coach; a cab; a cart; a wagon/쌍두 ~ a carriage and pair/ ~로 가다 go by carriage; drive (*to*). ばしゃ

**마찬가지** similarity; the [very] same; likeness; sameness/그 여자는 전과 ~로 대답했다 She gave the same answer as before./그것은 새것이나 ~다 It is as good as new. どうよう

**마찰**(摩擦) friction; rubbing/~하다 rub; chafe/나는 매일 아침 냉수 ~을 합니다 I take a rub-down with a cold wet towel every morning. まさつ

**마천루**(摩天樓) a sky-scraper. まてんろう

**마철**(馬鐵) a horseshoe. うまのひづめ

**마초**(馬草) fodder; hay; horse pasturage

/~를 주다 fodder[feed, give fodder to] a horse. まぐさ

**마추다** 《주문하다》 order; order from (*a person, a shop*); give an order for (*a thing*); place an order with/마추어 지은 양복 a suit made to order/나는 구두를 마췄다 I had a new pair of shoes made. ちゅうもんする

**마춤** the custom made; the article ordered/~의 tailor-made; ordered; custom [-made]〈미〉/~ 옷 custom clothes; tailor-made clothes/내가 입고 있는 샤쓰는 ~옷이다 My shirt is the custom made. ちゅうもん

**마취**(痲醉) anesthesia; narcotism/~시키다 anesthetize/~법 a method of anesthesia/~제 an anesthetic; a narcotic; an opiate/국부[전신] ~ local[general] anesthesia. ますい

**마취목**(馬醉木) 《식》 a mountain fetter bush; *Lyonia japonica*(학명).

**마치**[1] 《장도리》 a small hammer; a claw hammer 《망치》 a hammer/ ~로 못을 박다 drive a nail in with a hammer; hammer a nail in. かなづち

**마치**[2] 《흡사》 as if; as though; as if it were; just like; just as; as … as/그것은 ~ 눈처럼 희다 It is as white as snow./그는 그녀를 ~ 자기 딸처럼 사랑했다 He loved her as if she had been his own daughter. あたかも

**마치다**[1] 《끝내다》 finish; end; be through; complete; accomplish; fulfil/학업을 ~ complete[finish] a school course/대학을 ~ graduate from a university/일을 ~ finish *one's* work. おわる

**마치다**[2] ①《닿다》 be struck; hit; be obstructed/말뚝이 바위에 마치어 들어가지 않는다 The stake has hit a rock and won't drive in any deeper. ②《걸리다》 pinch; feel an acute pain/구두가 ~ *one's* shoes pinch. あたる

**마침** just; exactly; favorably; fortunately; opportunely; in the very nick of time/~ 그때 문을 두드리는 소리가 났다 Just then, there was a knocking at the door. ちょうど

**마침가락** the very thing wanted; the right thing/ ~으로 just in time; at the right moment; fortunately/그는 그 자리에 ~이다 He is the right man for the position. ぐうぜんのいっち

**마침내** at last; at length; in the long run; finally; ultimately/~ 그는 시험에 파스했다 At last, he passed the examination./~ 일이 끝났다 The work has come to an end at last. さいごに

**마침표**(一標) 《종지부》 a period; a full stop. しゅうしふ

**마탁**(磨琢) ①《연마》 polishing; shining ②《향상》 cultivation; training/~하다 polish; train; cultivate. たくま

**마태**(馬太) beans for horse feed; horse bean. ばりょうのだいず

**마태복음**(一福音) 《성경》 [the Gospel of] Matthew.

**마투리** odd measure; some odd *mal*/닷섬 ~ five *sem* and some odd *mal*.

**마파람** a south wind; a wind from the south; southerly wind. みなみかぜ

**마판**(馬板) ①《말 매는》 a horse paddock ②《마구간의》 floorboards of a stable.

**마포**(麻布) hemp 《삼베》 hemp cloth 《인도 마포》 jute/~대 a hemp sack; a gunny sack/~사(絲) hemp thread.

**마피**(馬皮) horsehide. うまのかわ

**마필**(馬匹) horses/~ 개량 horse improvement. ばひつ

**마흔** forty. よんじゅう

**막**[1] 《방금》 just; just now; (be) about to; (be) on the point of/그는 ~ 떠났다 He just left a moment ago. たったいま

**막**[2] 《함부로》 carelessly; at random; roughly; blindly; recklessly 《사납게》 severely; violently; wild; hard; terribly; awfully/그는 곤봉으로 개를 ~ 때렸다 With a stick he struck a dog blindly./그는 돈을 ~ 썼다 He spent money recklessly. てあたりしだいに

**막**[3] 《마지막》 the last/~차 the last train. さいご

**막**(膜) 《해》 a membrane/~질(質) membranous/~골(骨) a membrane bone/~상(狀) membranous. まく

**막**(幕) ①《집》 a booth; a hut; a cabin; a cottage; a shed; a shack; a lodge ②《휘장》 a curtain; a hanging screen; a tent ③《연극의》 an act ④《끝장》 an end; a close; a conclusion. まく

**막가내하**(莫可奈何) inevitability 무가내하. どうすることもできないこと

**막가다** 《행동이》 behave rambunctiously.

**막간**(幕間) an interval [between acts]; an enteracte; an intermission〈미〉/~에 가벼운 식사를 하다 eat a light meal between acts[during an intermission]/~극 an interlude; a middle piece; a skit between acts. まくあい

**막강지국**(莫强之國) the most powerful nation [country]. ひじょうにきょうだいなくに

**막걸리** a coarse fermented liquor; a raw [an unrefined] rice liquor. どぶろく

**막내** the lastborn; the youngest child./~ 아이 the youngest child. すえっこ

**막노동**(一勞動) physical labo[u]r; rough work; chore; toil.

**막다** ①《구멍 따위를》 stop up ②《방어·방지》 keep away[off, out] ③《칸을》 screen off; partition ④《차단·저지》 stop; check; hold in check. ふさぐ

**막다르다** come to the end of the road; reach an impasse; come to a deadlock/이 길은 막다른 골목이다 This is a blind alley. つきあたる

**막다른골** 《골목》 a blind[dead] alley; an impasse 《사태》 a standstill; a deadlock; a stalemate. いきづまり

**막다른집** a house at the end of a blind alley. つきあたりのいえ

**막대(莫大)** ~하다 (be) vast; huge; enormous; immense; prodigious/ ~한 돈 a huge[a very big] sum of money/ ~한 재산 immense wealth. ばくだい

**막대기** a stick 《곤봉》a rod; a bar; a club 《지휘봉》a baton/그는 ~로 개를 때렸다 He hit a dog with a stick. ちいさいぼうきれ

**막대잡이** ①(오른쪽) a blindman's right; the right ②《길잡이》a guide. あんないしゃの卑語

**막대패** a jack plane; a fore plane/ ~질 jack-planing/ ~질하다 use a fore plane. あらかんな

**막동이**《막내 the last[youngest] son 《사내종》a v servant; a page. すえっこ

**막되다** (be) ill-bred; ill-mannered; wild; rude; rough; unmannerly/막된 놈 a rude fellow/막된 소리 a barbarous speech/막되게 굴다 behave rudely[wildly, badly]. むてっぽう

**막론(莫論)** ~하다 go without question; stop discussion; be needless to say; there is no need to speak (of)/ …을 ~하고, not to speak of; to say nothing of/ 남녀를 ~하고 regardless of sex. ろんするよちがない

**막료(幕僚)** a staff officer 《총칭》the staff/해군의 ~ naval staff. ばくりょう

**막막(寞寞)** ~하다 lonesome; dreary 《쓸쓸함》desolate; deserted/~한 생활 a desolate life. ばくばく

**막막(漠漠)** ~하다 boundless; is vast; extensive; limitless/ ~한 벌판 a vast plain. ひろびろしている

**막말** random speech; rough[rude] talk/ ~하다 talk without thinking; speak roughly; talk at random; talk wild. けいそつなはなし

**막무가내(莫無可奈)** ~로 obstinately; stubbornly; resolutely; firmly/ ~로 듣지 않다 will not listen to; turn a deaf ear to; refuse flatly.

**막바지** the end; the very end; the dead end; the extremity/길 ~ the dead end of a road/골목 ~ the end of the alley/언덕 ~ the top of a hill. つきあたり

**막벌다** [make] earn by doing rough[hard] work; work as a day labourer; work as a day labourer. あらしごとをしてくらす

**막벌이** earning wages as a day labourer/ ~하다 earn wages as a day labourer. あらしごとかせぎ

**막벌잇군** a day labourer; an odd-jobber. あらしごとをするろうどうしゃ

**막부득이(莫不得已)** unavoidably; inevitably; necessarily. やむをえず

**막북겅이** rough shredded tobacco.

**막사(幕舍)** a camp; a barracke. ばくしゃ

**막사리** tidewater [before it is frozen].

**막살다** lead a rough[careless, haphazard, reckless] sort of life; lead a nondescript[drab, grubby] life/산골에 있을 때는 한동안 막살았다 I really roughed it for a while in the mountain village. そのひぐらしをする

**막살이** a rough[haphazard, reckless, planless, heedless] life/ ~하다 live a haphazard life. そのひぐらし

**막상** ultimately; really; actually; in reality/ 일이란 ~ 당해 보지 않으면 모르는 것이다 The proof of the pudding is in the eating. ほんとうに

**막상(莫上)** the best; the highest quality; the first-rate[grade].

**막상 막하(莫上莫下)** nothing better and nothing worse/ ~다 be equal; be even.

**막새** ①(수키와) convex tiles at the edge of eaves・②(암・수키와) [both concave and convex] tiles at the edge of eaves.

**막서다** (대들다) make a stand (against); show fight; turn upon; rise against (one's lord)/ 막서서 대들다 fight against (a person)/어른에게 버릇 없이 ~ defy one's elder rudely. はんこうする

**막심하다(莫甚一)** (be) at the furthest extreme; (be) immense; tremendous; enormous; heavy; hard; terrible/막심한 손해 a tremendous loss. すさまじい

**막아내다** ward off; keep away[out, off, back]; check; hold in check; hold off/ 추위를 ~ protect oneself from the cold. ぼうぎょする

**막엄(莫嚴)** ~하다 (be) supremely strict; very stern; extremely severe/학생에 대해서 ~하다 be extremely severe with one's pupils. あまりにもきびしい

**막역(莫逆)** intimacy; closeness; familiarity/ ~하다 (be) intimate; familiar; close/ ~한 친구 an intimate friend/ 한 사이 intimate relations. ばくぎゃく

**막연(漠然, 邈然)** ~하다 (be) vague; obscure; ambiguous; hazy/이 점에 대한 그의 답은 ~하다 His answer is rather hazy on this point. ばくぜんとしている

**막이** protection; defending; warding off; prevention; damming up; banking up 《부적》a charm 《간막이》a screen/서리 ~ a protection from frost/액~ a charm against evil influence/간로 방을 막다 partition the room with a screen. ぼうし

**막일** rough work; physical labor; toil; heavy work/ ~하다 labor; toil; do rough work/ ~군 a laborer. あらしごと

**막자** a medicine pestle. すりこぎ

**막잡이** a rough article used for any purpose; a coarse article. そせいひん

**막장** a blind end[front] in a mine gallery/ ~군 a miner; a digger; a pitman.

**막중(莫重)** ~하다 (be) very[extremely] precious; in valuable; priceless; costly; very important/ ~한 인명 precious

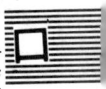

**막지르다** ①(앞을) stand in one's way; confront; block ②(함부로) thrust[jab, stab, kick] at random[with force] 《소리를》 shout loudly. やたらにけりとばす

**막질리다** ①(앞을) be interrupted; be blocked; be barred; be confronted ②(함부로) get thrust[jabbed, stabbed, pushed, kicked] at random[with force] やたらにけられる

**막차**(-車) the last train[car, bus]. さいしゅうのくるま

**막초**(-草) coarse[poor-quality, cheap] tobacco; cut tobacco; cut tobacco of inferior quality.

**막치** a coarse[low-grade] article; poor stuff; coarse manufactures. そせいひん

**막판** ①(마지막 판) the last round; the final scene 《중대한 때》 the last[critical] moment ②(뒤범벅판) a haphazard scene. さいしゅうのしょうぶ

**닥필**(-筆) a brush used for various purposes; a coarse writing-brush; a brush coarsely made. わるいふで

**막하**(幕下) a staff-officer 《전체》 the staff. ばくりょう

**막후**(幕後) behind the curtain; in the background/～의 인물 a man behind the scene/～에서 조정하다 pull the wires[strings]/～에 무엇인가 있다 There is something behind the scenes/～소극 an afterpiece.

**막히다** be closed; be shut; be clogged 《정지》 be stopped/말이 ～ be stuck for a word/길이 ～ 《차단되다》 the road is blocked. とざされる

**만**¹ 《때》 ❶ 이틀 ～에 on the second day/상경 후 5년 ～에 five years after *one* came up to *Seoul*. ―め

**만**² ①(다만·뿐) only; just/김군～ 왔다 Only Mr. *Kim* came. ②(만큼) just; to the extent of 《겨우 그 정도》 as much as; so trifling ③(비교) as⋯ as/내 키가 너～하다 I am as tall as you.―だけ.―のみ

**만**(萬) ten thousand; many; all; a myriad/그것은 ～인이 인정하는 바이다 It is universally recognized./그런 일은 만에 하나도 일어나지 않을 것이다 It is one in ten thousand that such a thing will happen. まん

**만**(灣) a gulf; a bay/인천～ *Inchun* Bay/～을 이루다 form a gulf[bay]. わん

**만**(滿) just; full; fully/～ 17세 full seventeen years old. まん

**만**(卍) the Buddhist cross; a Buddhist emblem; a fylfot; a swastika. まんじ

**만가**(挽歌) a dirge; an elegy; a lament.

**만가**(輓歌) ①(장례의) a funeral song ②(애가) an elegy; a dirge.

**만감**(萬感) a flood[crowd] of emotion/～이 북받쳤다 A thousand emotions [thoughts] crowded on my mind./～이 북받쳐서 말이 안 나왔다 My heart was too full for words. あらゆるかんじょう

**만강**(萬康) peace; tranquility; security; welfare; health. ぶじ

**만강**(滿腔) a full heart; full-heartedness; whole-heartedness/～ 하여 hearty; heartfelt; whole-hearted. まんこう

**만개**(滿開) full bloom/～의 at it's best; in full bloom[blossom, flower]/～가 되다 be in full bloom. まんかい

**만경**(晚境) old age; one's declining years/～에 접어들다 be advanced in life; become senescent. ばんきょう

**만경**(萬頃) vastness; extensiveness; boundlessness/～ 창파 the boundless expanse of water. ばんけい

**만경되다** one's eyes become dull[lifeless, lusterless]; one's eyes become lacking in vitality. めにせいきがなくなる

**만경 타령**(一打令) negligence; neglect; disregard; remissness. なげやり

**만고**(萬古) perpetuity; eternity/～에 유가 없는 unique for all generations.

**만고 불멸**(萬古不滅) being imperishable; lasting for ever. ばんふめつ

**만고 불변**(萬古不變) permanence; constancy; being unchangeable/～하다 be unchangeable; be immutable/～의 진리 immutable truths; eternal laws.

**만고 불후**(萬古不朽) being immortal; remaining intact[undecayed] for ever/～의 명작 a book of everlasting merit.

**만고 잡놈**(萬古雜―) a thorough-paced rascal; a thorough-going scoundrel.

**만고 절담**(萬古絶談) an unchangeable maxim; an eternal truth; an immortal saying.

**만고 절색**(萬古絶色) an unsurpassed beauty; the fairest of the fair.

**만고 절창**(萬古絶唱) 《노래》 a superb song unequalled in its beauty 《시》 a poem unexcelled in its beauty throughout the annals of literature.

**만고 풍상**(萬古風霜) long trials; all sorts of hardships and privations.

**만곡**(彎曲) a curve; a crook; a bend; a bow; curvature. わんきょく

**만구**(灣口) the entrance[mouth] of a bay. わんこう

**만구 전파**(萬口傳播) getting abroad among the public/～하다 spread about; be widely talked about; get abroad among the public. ばんこうでんぱ

**만국**(萬國) all[world] nations; all countries on earth/～사 a universal history/～ 박람회 an international exposition; a world fair/～ 신호 the international code signals/～ 우편 연합 the Universal Postal Union/～ 음성 기호 the international phonetic alphabet/～ 평화 회의 the International Peace Conference/～ 표준시 universal standard time. ばんこく

**만국기**(萬國旗) the flags of all nations 《총칭·장식용》bunting. ばんこくき

**만굴**(彎屈) a curve ⇨ 만곡. わんくつ

**만궁**(彎弓) drawing a bow/～하다 draw [bend] a bow.

**만권**(萬卷) ten thousand books; many books; a large library. まんがん

**만귀잠잠하다**(萬鬼潛潛一) be all quiet[silent, still, hushed]/만귀잠잠한 밤에 in the unearthly[ghostly] hour; at the still of the night; at dead of night. ひじょうにしずかなまよなかだ

**만근**(輓近) recent times; late years/～의 recent; late. ばんきん

**만금**(萬金) an immense sum of money /～을 던지다 invest an immense sum (in). まんきん

**만기**(滿期) expiration (of a term); expiry; maturity/～일 the day of maturity/～가 되다 expire; mature 《복역이》 fall due; serve out one's time. まんき

**만기**(萬機) ①《정사(政事)》 all state affairs ②《비밀》 all secrets. ばんき

**만끽**(滿喫) ～하다 《실컷 먹다》 have enough (of); have one's fill; eat[drink] to one's heart's content 《즐기다》 enjoy fully [to the full]. まんきつ

**만나다** ①《사람을》 see; meet 《면회하다》 interview/우연히 ～ come across[upon] (a person); fall in with (a person) ②《당하다》 meet with; suffer/화를 ～ suffer a calamity/소나기를 ～ be caught in a shower. あう

**만난**(萬難) all difficulties/～을 무릅쓰고 at any[all] cost; through thick and thin/～을 배제하다 surmount[overcome] all difficulties. ばんなん

**만날** always; all the time; usually; habitually/그는 ～ 같은 넥타이만 맨다 He always wears the same tie. いつも

**만냥판**(萬兩一) a large scale; a big way; luxurious circumstances.

**만년**(晩年) one's later[latter] years/～에 late in life/～에 접어들다 enter the twilight of one's life/～을 불우하게 보내다 live the rest of one's life in obscurity. ばんねん

**만년**(萬年) ten thousand years; eternity; perpetuity/～의 permanent; eternal; perpetual. まんねん

**만년필**(萬年筆) a fountain-pen; a selffeeding pen/파일용 ～ pilot fountain pen /～에 잉크를 넣다 fill a fountain pen /～에 잉크가 떨어졌다 The fountain pen has run out of ink[is dry]. まんねんひつ

**만능**(萬能) omnipotence; being almighty ;having an all-round capability/부(富)가 ～은 아니다 Wealth is not everything. /～ 선수 an all-round player[athlete] /～약 a cureall; a panacea. ばんのう

**만단**(萬端) all; everything/～의 준비가 되었다 All is ready/～ 설화 All sorts of stories; various stories/～ 수심 all kinds[lots] of worries/～ 개유(改諭) every possible admonition. ばんたん

**만달** 〖미〗 an arabesque design[painting].

**만담**(漫談) 《한담》 a gossip; a rambling talk; a general chat 《우스운 얘기》 a comic chat; a comic stage dialogue/～가 a comic-chat artiste. まんだん

**만당**(滿堂) the entire hall[house] 《청중》 all the audience/～은 쥐죽은 듯 잠잠하였다 A hust fell over the crowded hall. /～에 계신 신사 숙녀 여러분 Ladies and gentlemen! まんどう

**만대**(萬代) all generations; all ages; eternity/～ 불변의 eternal; everlasting /～의 영화 eternal prosperity and glory/～에 전해지다 be remembered for ages to come. ばんだい

**만도**(晩稻) late-ripening rice. おくて

**만도**(滿都) the whole[entire] city/～의 시민 all the citizens. ぜんと

**만동**(晩冬) late winter; the later part of winter. ばんとう

**만두**(饅頭) a bun/팥 ～ a bean-jam bun /고기 ～ a bun with meat stuffing/ ～소 bun stuffing/～ 송이 an individual bun. まんじゅう

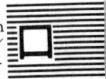

**만득**(晩得) ～하다 have[beget] a child in one's later days.

**만들다** ①《제조・요리하다》 make; manufacture; prepare ②《되게 하다》 make[turn] (a person, a thing) into ③《조직・창립하다》 set up; organize; form ④《창조하다》 make create; invent. つくる

**만듦새** ①《구조》 make; construction; formation ②《옷 따위의》 cut; style ③《세공》 workmanship. できばえ

**만래**(晚來) one's old age; one's declining years; the winter of life; the evening of life. ばんねん

**만력**(蠻力) brute force; violence; barbarous force/～을 부리다 resort to force [violence]; show reckless valor.

**만록**(漫錄) stray notes; random comments; light essays; jottings. まんぴつ

**만록**(萬綠) a myriad of green leaves/청중의 여사는 ～ 총중 홍일점 격이었다 She was the only lady in the whole audience, like a flower among vegetables.

**만뢰 구적**(萬籟俱寂) the hush of the midnight/～하다 (be) quiet; hushed.

**만료**(滿了) expiration; expiry; termination/～하다 come to an end/기한[임기]은 오늘 ～한다 The term expires today/～일 expiration date/계약 ～ the termination of an agreement/임기 ～ the termination of office. まんりょう

**만루**(滿壘) 《야구》 a full base/～가 되다 The bases are full. まんるい

**만류**(挽留) detention; keeping[holding] back; check/～하다 hold[keep] back; prevent; detain 《저지하다》 check/간곡히 ～하다 detain (a person) by the sleeve; hold (a person) by the button; buttonhole (one). ひきとめること

**만류**(灣流) the Gulf Stream.

**만리**(萬里) a long distance; thousands

of miles/~ 장성(長城) the Wall of China. ばんり

만리경(萬里鏡) a telescope; a field-glass ⇨망원경. ぼうえんきょう

만만(滿滿) ~하다 be abundant; be full of (*ambition*); be filled with (*courage*)/자신이 ~하다 be full of self-confidence/야심이 ~하다 be ambitious. みちみちている

만만(漫漫) vastitude; immensity ~하다 《멀고 지루하다》 be long and boring; tedious (넓은) vast; boundless/~한 바다 a vast sea; a boundless expanse of sea. はてしなくひろびろとしている

만만장이 a nobody; a man of straw; a mere cipher; a nonentity; a person easy to deal with. つまらないひと

만만하다 ①(보드랍다)(be) soft; tender; plastic; limp ②(용이하다)(be) easy [to deal with]; be ready to yield; not firm ③(우습게 보이다)(be) negligible; slight. やわらかい

만망(萬望) an ardent desire; an earnest wish/ ~하다 be anxious (*for*); wish [desire] earnestly. かつぼう

만면(滿面) the whole face/ ~에 희색을 띠고 smiling all over *one's* face/~수색 a face full of anxiety/~ 희색 a face beaming with joy. まんめん

만무(萬無) ~하다 cannot be; be hardly possible (*that*); be not likely at all (*that*); be out of the question; there is no reason why/그것은 진실일 리가 ~하다 That cannot be true./그럴 리가 ~하다 That cannot be the case. ぜんぜんない

만무방 rascals; scoundrels; knaves; outrageous people. ならずもののむれ

만문(漫文) (수필)an essay 《신문·잡지의》 causeries; jottings; stray[rambling] notes. まんぶん

만물 the final weeding of a rice paddy.

만물(萬物) all things [under the sun]; nature; creation/ ~의 영장 the lord of creation. ばんぶつ

만물상(萬物商) a general shop; a grocery [store]. ざっかしょう

만민(萬民) the whole nation; all the people. ばんみん

만반(萬般) all things; all kinds; all affairs; all sorts of matters/ ~의 준비를 갖추다 get everything in readiness (*for*). ばんばん

만반 진수(滿盤珍羞) a groaning board; a capital dinner; rich and dainty food. しょくたくいっぱいのごちそう

만발(滿發) full bloom/ ~하다 be at its best; come into full bloom/~한 장미 a full-blown rose; a rose in full bloom/벚꽃이 ~했다 The cherry trees are in full bloom. まっさかり

만방(萬方) all directions; every way; all possible means/ ~으로 in every way. ほうぼう

만방(萬邦) all nations; the nations of the world/ ~의 international; universal. ばんぽう

만병(萬病) all kinds of diseases/감기는 ~의 근원이다 Cold may lead to all kinds of illness. まんびょう

만보(漫步) a ramble; a stroll/ ~하다 [take a] stroll; ramble. まんぽ

만복(滿腹) a full stomach; satiety/ ~이 될 때까지 먹었다 He ate his fill./이제 ~입니다 I've had enough. まんぷく

만복(萬福) all sorts of good fortunes/댁내의 ~을 빕니다 pray for all blessings on your family. ばんぷく

만부당(萬不當) ~하다 be absurd; exorbitant; extremely improper; quite unreasonable/ ~한 말 an absolutely[utterly] unreasonable remark.
まったくふとうなこと

만분지일(萬分之一) a ten-thousandth; one in ten thousand. まんぶんのいち

만사(萬死) certain death; the jaws of death/ ~를 면하다 escape certain death.

만사(萬事) all things; everything/ ~가 잘 되었다 All went well./ ~가 돈이다 Money is everything./ ~가 허사이다 All is up[over, lost] [with me]. ばんじ

만사(輓詞) a funeral ode; an elegy ⇨만장(輓章). ちょうじ

만사 무심(萬事無心) ~하다 be utterly indifferent; be so worried that nothing can arouse interest.

만사 여의(萬事如意) ~하다 everything turns out as *one* wishes; all goes well. ばんじいのごとし

만사 태평(萬事泰平) all going well; nothing amiss/ ~하다 everything is all right. ばんじたいへい

만사 형통(萬事亨通) ~하다 all goes well; be prosperous in everything; everything turns out as *one* wished.

만삭(滿朔) parturiency; the month of parturience; the last month of pregnancy/ ~하다 be in the last month of pregnancy; be parturient/ ~한 부인 a parturient woman; a woman near her time. うみづき

만산(滿山) the whole hill[mountain]/벚꽃이 ~에 덮여 있다 The whole hill is covered with cherry blossoms. まんざん

만상(萬象) all things in the universe; the universe; [all] creation.

만생(晚生) begetting a child in *one's* later years/ ~하다 beget a child in *one's* later years.

만석군(萬石君) a rich man; a millionaire.

만성(晚成) being slow in maturing; maturing late/ ~하다 be slow in maturing/대기 ~ Great talents mature late [are slow to mature]. ばんせい

만성(慢性) 《의》 chronicity/~의 chronic; confirmed; inveterate/~ 위장병 inveterate[confirmed] dyspepsia/ ~병 a chronic disease/그의 병은 ~으로 변했

만성 ... 다 His disease passed into a chronic state. まんせい

**만성(蠻性)** barbarism; savagery; wild nature. ばんせい

**만세(萬世)** all ages〔generations〕; eternity／～에 전해지다 be transmitted into eternity. ばんせい

**만세(萬歲)** ①(만년) ten thousand years; a long time ②(외치는 소리) hurrah; cheers; long live／스미스군 ～ Hurrah for Smith!／～ 삼창하다 give three cheers (for *a person*). ばんざい

**만세력(萬歲曆)** a perpetual calendar; a thousand-year calendar〔almanac〕. ばんざいれき

**만세 불망(萬世不忘)** ～하다 keep in mind forever; remember long／귀하의 은혜는 ～이외다 I shall be eternally grateful to you. えいきゅうにわすれないこと

**만세 불역(萬世不易)** everlastingness; eternity; perpetuity／～의 everlasting; eternal; perpetual. ばんせいふえき

**만수(萬壽)** long life; longevity／～무강을 빕니다 Long life to you!／～ 무강 a long life. じゅみょうがないこと

**만수받이** ～하다 tolerate〔put up with〕 other's misbehavior. せわやきをする

**만시(晩時)** being too late／～지탄(之歎) repenting of *one's* missing a chance; mourning over what is too late. じきおくれ

**만신** a female shaman; a sorceress; a medium. みこ

**만신(滿身)** the whole body／～창이다 be covered all over with wounds. ぜんしん

**만심(慢心)** pride; self-conceit; a vanity swelled head／～하다 be consumed with pride; be proud; be self-conceited／그는 성공하여 ～하고 있다 He is puffed up with his success. ごうまんなこころ

**만안(萬安)** peace; tranquility; welfare; health／～하신을 비나이다 Peace be with you. ばんあん

**만약(萬若)** if; in case (*of*); provided〔supposing〕 that. もしも

**만억년(萬億年)** thousands of millions of years; eternity.

**만연(蔓延)** spread〔ing〕; diffusion／～하다 spread; sweep 「over」／～성의 progressive／～을 방지하다 prevent〔check〕 the spread (*of*). まんえん

**만연(漫然)** ～하다 be aimless; at random; rambling; discursive／～히 여행을 떠나다 go on a journey without any definite destination. ぼんやりする

**만열(滿悅)** great delight; satisfaction; ecstasy／～하다 be in raptures; be much delighted.

**만염(晚炎)** the late〔lingering〕 summer heat. じきおくれのあつさ

**만용(蠻勇)** brute〔venturous〕 courage; foolhardiness; recklessness; temerity／～을 부리다 resort to force; act with violence. ばんゆう

**만원(滿員)** a capacity audience〔crowd〕; no vacancy／～이다 be crowded to the limit; be filled to capacity／～을 이루다 be full〔up〕; be closely packed; be full to the doors.

**만월(滿月)** a full moon／～입니다 It is a full moon. まんげつ

**만유(萬有)** all things 〔under the sun〕; the creation; all things in the universe ／～ 인력(引力) universal gravitation／～ 의지론〔철〕 pantheism. ばんゆう

**만유(漫遊)** a tour; a 〔pleasure〕 trip／～하다 travel (for *pleasure*); tour; make a tour (*of*); make a pleasure trip／～객／세계～자 a round-the-world tourist／～하다 tour the world. まんゆう

**만이(蠻夷)** barbarians; savages. やばんじん

**만인(挽引)** traction; hauling. pull〔ing〕; towing／～하다 pull; drag; draw; haul; tow. ひっぱること

**만인(萬人)** all people; everyone／그것은 ～이 주지하는 바다 It is a matter of universal knowledge. まんにん

**만인(蠻人)** a savage 《토인》 a barbarian. やばんじん

**만인(萬仞)** ①(만 길) ten thousand fathoms ②(깊음) fathomless depth.

**만인계(萬人契)** mutual financing association of large scale. たのもし

**만일(萬 -)** If; in case; ten thousand to one; be any chance. まんいち

**만입(灣入)** 〔지〕 embayment／바다는 깊이 육지에 ～하고 있다 An arm of the sea penetrates far into the land. わんにゅう

**만자(卍字)** a fylfot; a gammadion; the Buddhist cross. まんじのじ

**만장(萬丈)** unfathomable height〔depth〕／～의 기염을 토하다 give full vent to *one's* feelings. ばんじょう

**만장(萬障)** all obstacles〔hazards, hindrances〕. ばんしょう

**만장(挽章, 輓章)** a funeral ode〔song〕; an elegy; a dirge; a lament.

**만장(滿場)** the entire audience; the whole assembly〔house〕／～ 일치 (一致) unanimity 〔of the whole assembly〕; unanimously. まんじょう

**만장봉(萬丈峰)** a lofty peak; a high mountain. ひじょうにたかいみね

**만재(滿載)** full load; a full〔capacity〕 cargo／～하다 carry a full load (*of*); load (*a ship*) to capacity (*with*)／석유를 ～한 선박 a ship carrying a full cargo of oil. まんさい

**만적거리다** finger; fumble with; fidget with／옷감을 ～ finger a piece of cloth. しきりにいじる

**만적만적** figering; handling; fumbling; toying; tampering; monkeying with; fooling with. しきりにいじる

**만전(萬全)** perfectness／～을 기하다 make assurance doubly secure. ばんぜん

**만점(滿點)** a full marks; a perfect score／그만하면 ～이다 that leaves nothing

만정(滿庭) the whole garden/~이 꽃 천지다 The whole garden is covered with flowers.

만져보다 feel; try touching; finger; test with *one's* hand.

만조(滿朝) the whole Court/~ 백관 all the civil and military officials of the court.

만조(滿潮) the high[full] tide; flood tide.

만조하다 be shabby 《초라하다》 poor-looking 《흉하다》 unsightly.

만족(滿足) satisfaction; contentment; gratification/~하다 be satisfied[gratified] (*with*); be content[pleased] (*with*)/행복은 ~에 있다 Happiness lies in contentment.

만족(蠻族) a savage tribe.
만종(蠻種) a barbarous race.
만종(晚鐘) the evening bell; a curfew [·bell].

만좌(滿座) the whole company; the entire assembled party/~ 중에서 창피를 당하다 be put to shame before the whole company.

만중(萬重) ①《만 겹》 ten-thousand fold; manifold ②《평안》 peace; quiet[·ness]/~하다 (be) quiet.

만지(蠻地) a savage land; a dark country; an uncivilized country.

만지다 finger; touch; feel; brush; handle; stroke; pass *one's* hand over/손가락으로 ~ feel[touch] with *one's* fingers.

만지작거리다 finger (*a button*); fumble with (*a key*); keep fingering; monkey with《속》.

만지작만지작 fingering; handling; touching; fumbling.

만질만질하다 be soft; tender/만질만질한 비단 soft silks.

만찬(晚餐) supper; dinner; the evening meal/ 그를 ~에 초대하다 ask[invite] him to dinner.

만천하(滿天下) the whole world; under the sun/~에 알려져 있는 사실이다 The whole world knows this fact.

만초(蔓草) a vine; a creeper; a climber.

만추(晚秋) late autumn[fall]/ ~의 어느 날 one day late in autumn/ in the autumn; in late fall.

만춘(晚春) late spring/~에 in late spring; towards the end of spring/~의 어느 날 one day late spring.

만취(滿醉) dead drunkenness/~하다 get dead drunk; steam up《속》; be boozy; be wet.

만큼 《긍정》as…as 《부정》 so…as/그녀 ~ 영어를 잘 했으면 좋겠다 I wish I could speak English as well as she.

만큼만 [just] as much as.
만태(萬態) a great diversity in form and figure; various phases/인생 ~ various phases of life.

만판 to the full; to *one's* heart's content; as much as one pleases/ ~ 놀다 enjoy *oneself* to the full; spend all *one's* time loafing/그는 ~ 놀기만 한다 He spends all his time loafing.

만평(漫評) rambling criticism; literary gossip/ ~하다 criticize desultorily/시사 ~ rambling comments on current events; current notes

만폭(滿輻) the full width.

만풍(蠻風) a savage[barbarous] custom; an uncivilized manners/ ~을 일소하다 do away with the whole barbarous customs[habits].

만필(漫筆) stray[random] notes; jottings/ ~가 a columnist.

만하(晚夏) late summer.

만하다 ①《상대·동작이》 be enough to…/ 나이가 일하기 좋을 ~ be old enough to work efficiently ②《가치·힘이》 be worthy of… ③《정도가》 be as … as. —くらいだ

만학(晚學) learning late in life; a late education/~하다 get a late education; study late in life.

만학 천봉(萬壑千峰) steep mountains and dark valleys; a remote mountains region.

만행(萬幸) good fortune; good luck/~하다 (be) very fortunate; terribly lucky.

만행(蠻行) an act of barbarity; a barbarism; an outrage; a brutality; an atrocity/그들의 ~을 규탄하다 impeach them for their brutalities.

만호(萬戶) ten thousand houses; numerous[many] houses/~ 장안 a capital city with many inhabitants.

만혼(晚婚) late[deferred] marriage/ ~하다 marry late (in *life*); get married late.

만홀(漫忽) carelessness; negligence/ ~하다 be careless; negligent/~히 negligently; carelessly.

만화 【해】 spleen and pancreas.

만화(漫畵) 《인물의》a caricature 《풍자적인》a cartoon; a comic picture/불량 ~ substandard comic books.

만화경(萬華鏡) a kaleidoscope.

만화 방창(萬化方暢) luxuriant growth of all things in spring.

만회(挽回) recovery 《명예의》 retrieval 《복구》 restoration/ ~하다 recover; restore; retrieve.

많다 ①《수가》 be many; numerous ②《양이》much ③《수·양이》plenty; abundant; plentiful; copious; exuberant ④《도수》(be) frequent; often; prevalent/이 지방에 바람이 ~ Winds are prevalent in this district

많이 ①《수량》 much; lots; plenty; in abundance; in profusion ②《대개》 often; lots; frequently.

맏 the eldest; the oldest／～며느리 the eldest daughter-in-law. ちょうしのいみ

맏물 the first product of the season 《과일》the first fruits.

맏배 the firstborn (of *animals*); the first batch. しょさんまたはそのこ

맏사위 the husband of *one's* firstborn [eldest] daughter. ちょうじょのむこ

맏상제(―喪制) the chief mourner; the eldest son of the deceased.

맏아들 the firstborn son; the eldest son; the heir. ちょうなん

맏이 the firstborn (*son*); the eldest [child].

말¹ a horse 《수말》a stallion 《암말》a mare 《망아지》a pony 《새끼 수말》a colt 《새끼 암말》a filly 《군용마》a steed 《경기용 말》a racer. うま

말² 〖식〗a duck-weed[-meat]. あおうきぐさ

말³ ①《언어》language; speech; words; a expression ②《잔소리》a scolding; a reprimand; a lecture ③《소문》a rumo[u]r; a report; gossip. ことば

말⁴ a unit of measure. ます

말(末)¹ 《가루》powder／분~ 잉크 powdered ink／분~ 우유 powdered milk. こな

말(末)² 《끝·끝장》the end; the close／4월~에 at the end of April. すえ

말갈기 a horse's mane. たてがみ

말감고(―監考) a person whose business is to measure grain in a market.

말갛다 be clear; clean; serene. きよい

말거리 ①《재료》a topic for conversation; material of conversation ②《말썽》a subject[target, an object] of criticism.  わだい

말거머리 〖동〗a horseleech; *Whitmania pigra*(학명).

말경(末境) ①《끝판》the end; the close ②《말년》the declining years of *one's* life. しゅうきょく

말결 chiming in with another's words; echoing another's remark.

말계(末計) the last resort; a desperate measure. きゅうさく

말고 not being／이것 ~도 또 다른것이 있지 않습니까 You have another besides this, surely? —でなくて

말고삐 reins; a bridle／~를 잡다 take [hold] a horse by the reins. たずな

말꼴 hay; fodder; feed; provender; forage／~을 주다 feed (*green grass*) to a horse. まぐさ

말공대(―恭待) polite language; courteous expressions. ていねいないいかた

말괄량이 a romp; a hussy; a minx; a vixen; a flapper. おてんばむすめ

말구유 a manger; a horse trough.  まぐさおけ

말구종(―驅從) a groom; a footman. ばてい

말군¹《말몰잇군》a packhorse driver; a horse driver. ばてい

말군² visitors [from the village]; a caller. きんじょからきたおきゃく

말굳다 stammer; falter; be stuttering; be stammering. どもる

말굴레 a bridle; a halter. ばろく

말굽 a horse's hoof 《편자》a horseshoe／~ 자석 a horseshoe magnet／~ 소리 the beat[clack, clatter] of a horse's hoof. うまのひずめ

말귀 《말의 뜻》the meaning of what one says／~를 못 알아듣다 can't make out what one says. はなしのいみ

말끄러미 fixedly; steadily; absent mindly／얼굴을 ― 들여다보다 stare (*a person*, in the face; look hard[steadily] at (*a person's*) face. じっと

말끔 all; entirely; wholly; totally／빚을 ~ 청산하다 pay all *one's* debt; clear off *one's* debt／집은 ~ 완성됐다 The house is now completely built. きれいに

말끔하다 (be) clean; neat; tidy; smart; nice 《매력적》good-looking; comely; attractive／말끔한 하늘 a clear sky／그의 방은 언제나 ~ His room is always clear and tidy. きれいだ

말끝 the end of words; the end of one's speech; the ending of a word／~마다 욕을 한다 He never opens his lips without curse and swear. ごび

말기 《치마의》the upper waistband of a Korean skirt[trousers].

말기(末期) the last years[period, days]; the end; the close; the last stage 조선~에 at the end[close] of the *Chosen* Dynasty. まっき

말나다 ①《논의하다》be broached; be proposed; be taken up 2《비밀이》get out; slip[leak] out. はなしかける

말내다 ①《얘기 삼아》bring into the conversation ②《비밀을》reveal; let out; disclose; betray. はなしはじめる

말녀(末女) the youngest daughter; the last daughter. すえのむすめ

말년(末年) ①《인생의》*one's* later years; *one's* declining years ②《말엽》the last years. ばんねん

말눈치 a suggestion; a hint; *one's* way of talking／그의 ~가 승낙할 것 같다 He gives us to understand that he will consent. ほのめかし

말다¹《둘둘》roll／기를 말아 주십시요 Roll up the flag, please. まく

말다²《음식을》put (*boiled rice*) into the soup[water]; mix (*foot*) with [water, soup].

말다³《중지하다》stop; cease; discontinue; leave off; drop; give up. とめる

말다⁴ ①《금지하다》don't; had better not／기다리게 하지 말라 You must not keep him waiting. ②《필경 …이 되다》끝그는 필경 가고 말았다 He went away at length. やめる

말다툼 a dispute; an altercation; an argument; a quarrel; a wrangle／~하다 dispute; altercate; have an argum-

**말단**(末端) the end; the tip;／기구 terminal organization／～관절 terminal joints／～의 terminal; 〖해〗distal／～까지 고루고루 퍼지다 diffuse every inch of *(the country)*. まったん

**말대**(末代) the last generation. まつだい

**말대꾸** a retort; answering back; a severe[an incisive] reply／～하다 talk [answer] back; reply in kind to／날카로운 ～ a sharp retort. くちごたえ

**말대답**(─對答) a retort; a back-talk／어른한테 ～하는 것은 실례가 된다 Talking back to older people is impertinent. くちごたえ

**말더듬다** stammer; stutter; falter／말더듬는 것은 고칠 수 있다 Stammering can be cured. どもる

**말더듬이** a stammerer; a stutterer／～ 교정기 an articulator. どもり

**말똥** horse dung; stable manure; horse droppings. うまのくそ

**말똥말똥** with wide fixed eyes; blankly; with a vacant stare; be wide awake／～하다 have *one's* eyes wide open [absent-mindedly, blankly]／눈을 ～ 뜨고서 천장만 바라보고 누워 있다 lie with a vacant stare at the ceiling. ぎょろぎょろ

**말동무** a companion 말벗. はなしあいて

**말되다** ①《이치에 맞다》make sense; be reasonable; be logical／말도 안 된다 It is quite out of the question. ②《말거리가 되다》become the focus[subject, target] of criticism. わだいになる

**말뚝** a pile; a stake; a post; a picket／～을 박다 drive in a stake[pile, picket]／～을 세우다 put[set] up a post. くい

**말라깽이** a living skeleton; a bag of bones; a lean[skinny] person. やせっぽち

**말라리아**(─의) malaria; malarial fever／～열(熱) malarial fever.

**말라빠지다** become thin[skinny, lean, emaciated]; grow gaunt; lose *one's* weight 《걱정으로》pine away／그는 볼면 날아갈 만큼 말라빠졌다 He is as thin as a lath[wafer]. やせこける

**말랑거리다** feel soft[tender]; be soft to the touch. ふにゃふにゃする

**말랑하다** be soft; ripe and tender 《성질이》soft[mild, meek]／말랑한 살 tender flesh. ふにゃふにゃする

**말려들다** be dragged (*into*); be[get] involved[entangled] (*in*); involve *oneself* in.

**말로**(末路) the last days; the final fate／그는 ～가 비참했다 He had a miserable end. まつろ

**말류**(末流) 《자손》descendants 《제자》disciples 《지류》a tributary. まつりゅう

**말리**(茉莉) 〖식〗a jasmine; *Jasmium grandiflorum*(학명).

**말리다**[1] be rolled [up]; be curled [up]／치마 끝이 ～ the end of the skirt is rolled [up]. まかれる

**말리다**[2] 《건조시키다》make dry 《재목을》dry season 《고갈시키다》drain; desiccate; dehydrate／말린 물고기 dried fish／볕에 ～ dry *(something)* in the sun／옷을 불에 ～ dry clothes over a fire. ほかす

**말리다**[3] 《못하게 하다》stop[dissuade] (*a person*) from; make (*a person*) stop／싸움을 ～ stop a quarrel; put an end[a stop] to a quarrel. やめさせる

**말림** conservancy (of *forest, pasture*); reservation／～하다 reserve (*a forest*); conserve／～구역 a restricted area; a reserved area／～풀 protected pasture. せいし

**말림갓** a reserved forest[pasture]; a forest reserve.

**말마디** a talk; a speech; a phrase; a clause; speech／그 사람 ～나 할 줄 안다 He knows how to put a talk over., He is quite a good speaker. はなしのくぎり

**말막음** ～하다 hush up; appease; allay; forestall another's words. いいわけする

**말말뚝** a horse post. うまをつなぐくい

**말매미** 〖충〗a kind of cicada; *Cryptotympana Coreana*(학명). くまぜみ

**말머리** the beginning of *one's* speech[talk]; introductory remarks; *one's* first few words. ことばのはじまり

**말먹이** horse feed; hay; forage; provender. ばりょう

**말목**(抹木) a pile ⇨말뚝. くい

**말몫** 《소작인의》a share of the tenant's grain according to the sharecropping system.

**말몰잇군** a packhorse driver. ばてい

**말못되다** be extremely poor[miserable, wicked]. いいあらわせないほどわるい

**말문**(─門) *one's* mouth when speaking／～이 막히다 be struck dumb (with surprise); lose *one's* speech. くちさき

**말미** leave [of absence]; furlough; day off／～를 얻다 get leave of absence／그는 ～를 얻어 고향에 돌아갔다 He went home on furlough[leave]. きゅうか

**말미**(末尾) the end; the close; the tip; finis. まつび

**말미암다** 《유래》be derived (*from*); 《원인》be due to; because by／말미암아 owing to; because of; in consequence. よる

**말미잘** 〖동〗a sea anemone.

**말밀**[1] 《되고 남은》grain left over after measuring with a *mal*.

**말밑**[2] ①《어원》the etymology[origin] of a word ②《말밑천》*one's* stock of words.

**말박** ①《큰 박》a large gourd ②《말 대용의》a gourd used in place of a *mal* measure. おおきなひょうたん

**말방울** a bell hung round a horse's neck. うまのくびにつけるすず

**말배**(末杯) the last glass at a banquet.

**말뱃대끈** a bellyband [of a horse]; a girth [of a horse].

**말버릇** the manner of speaking; a way

**말버짐** ringworm; psoriasis. かんせん
**말벌** 《충》 a [ground] wasp; a kind of hornet. くまんばち
**말벗** a companion; someone to talk with／좋은 ~ a boon companion; a pal／~이 되다 keep (a person) company／~이 있었으면 좋겠다 I want to have company to talk together with／~이 없다 have nobody to talk to. はなしあいて
**말뼈** 《뼈》 horse bone[s] 《거칠은 사람》 a rough person[fellow]. うまのほね
**말보** talkativeness from a usually taciturn person.
**말복**(末伏) the last of the dog days.
**말본** grammar ⇨문법. ぶんぽう
**말사**(末寺) 《불》 a branch temple. まつじ
**말살**(抹殺) erasure／~하다 erase; cross out; strike out 《부정》 deny. まっさつ
**말상**(一相) 《얼굴》 a long face; an extremely long face／~의 long-faced; horse-faced. うまずら
**말석**(末席) the lowest seat; the bottom／~을 차지하다 have the honor of being present at (a meeting). まっせき
**말선두리** 《충》 a water beetle.
**말썽** trouble; difficulties／~을 일으키다 lead to a dispute; cause trouble／~이 나고 있다 be in trouble／~꾸러기 a troublemaker. もんちゃく
**말썽거리** the cause[source] of trouble; a matter for complaint; a bone of contention／~가 되다 become a source of trouble. ふんそうのおこるりゆう
**말썽군** a trouble-maker; a grumbler. もんちゃくをおこすひと
**말세**(末世) a degenerate age; the end of the world／이렇게 되면 세상도 ~다 The world is going to the dogs. まっせ
**말소**(抹消) erasure; cancel; obliteration／~하다 erase; cancel; obliterate; strike[cross] out／등기의 ~ cancellation of registration／소송을 ~하다 withdraw a suit. まっしょう
**말소리** a voice 《소곤거리는》 a whisper; a murmur／~가 들리다 hear (a person) talk／~가 높다 have a loud voice; talk in a loud voice. こえ
**말속** the meaning[implication] of one's words; one's intention. ことばのおくぎ
**말속**(末俗) customs of a degenerate age; a bad custom; degenerate customs; a vicious manners. まつせのふうぞく
**말손**(末孫) a distant descendant; a scion; posterity. まっそん
**말솔** a horse brush. うまのはけ
**말솜씨** art of speaking／~가 없다 be poor at speaking[talking]／~가 좋다 be good at speaking[talking]／~ 없는 사람 a poor talker. ことばづかい
**말수** words; speech／그 여자는 ~가 많다 She speaks much., She is very talkative. ことば
**말쑥하다** smart; nice; tidy; neat／말쑥한 얼굴 nice features; a fair countenance／그녀는 항상 말쑥한 옷차림을 하고 있다 She is always neatly dressed. きれいですんなりしている
**말씀** speech; words; language; talk／친절한 ~ your kind words／당신의 ~이 옳소 What you say is true. おことば
**말승냥이** ①《이리》 a large wolf ②《키 큰 사람》 a tall person; a gangling fellow. おおかみ
**말씨** the use of words; one's way of speaking; the language; choice of words; diction／정중한 ~로 in courteous terms／그는 ~가 투박하다 He is crude in speech. くちぜ
**말씨말씨** ~하다 ①《연하다》 (be) soft; (be) tender ②《물씬하다》 flaccid; flabby. ひじょうにやわらかい
**말실수**(一失手) an impropriety in speech; a slip of tongue／~하다 make a tongueslip; one's tongue slips／~한 것을 따지다 blame (a person) for his improper language. いいそこない
**말 아니다** ①《언어 도단》 be unreasonable; nonsense; irrational; absurd ②《형편이》 be extremely poor[wretched, miserable]. はなしがりくつにあわない
**말 안되다** unreasonable; contrary to logic; be absurd. りくつにあわないはなし
**말약**(末藥) powdered medicine. こなくすり
**말없이** silently; in silence; mutely.
**말엽**(末葉) the end; the close／19세기 ~에 towards the end of the 19th century. まつよう
**말오줌나무** 《식》 a red-berried elder; Sambucus racemosa(학명).
**말일**(末日) the last day; the end／2월 ~에 at the end of February. まつじつ
**말자**(末子) the youngest[last] son.
**말짜**(一쭈) ①《물건》 the worst article; an article of inferior quality. ②《사람》 a man of low character; an unmannerly person.
**말잡이** one who measures grain.
**말장이**[1] 《마되질군》 a person who measures grain for pay.
**말장이**[2] 《수다장이》 a talkative person; a wordy person; a chatterbox; a prattler. くちじょうず
**말짱하다**[1] 《성질이》 be soft; be tender; be gentle. もろい
**말짱하다**[2] ①《깨끗하다》 be clean[ly]; pure; neat ②《흠 없다》 be flawless; faultless; free from blemish. かんぜんだ
**말째** the last; the bottom; the tail／그는 ~로 왔다 He was the last man to come. いちばんさいご
**말재간**(一才幹) a talent for words. わじゅつ
**말재기** a gossipmaker; a gossipmonger. むだくちをたたくひと
**말재주** a talent for words[language]; eloquence; the gift of gab／~가 없다

**말전주** tale-telling[-bearing]; a tale/ ~하다 tell tales; tell on/말전줏군 a tale-bearer[-teller]; a mischief-maker.
うわさはなしをいいふらすこと

**말절**(末節) 《문장의》 the last paragraph; trifles; the last part 《시의》 the last stanza. まっせつ

**말조심**(一操心) care in speaking/ ~하다 be careful of one's speech.

**말좌**(末座) the lowest seat; the bottom ⇨말석. まつざ

**말주변** talking ability; the gift of gab; oratorical skill[talent]/ ~이 좋다 have a ready tongue/~이 없다 be a poor talker[speaker]. ゆうべんのさいのう

**말죽**(一粥) boiled horse-feed/~통 a horse-feed tub. うまにくわせるぬかかゆ

**말즘** 《식》 a water-caltrop; a water chestnut; a curly pond-weed.

**말증**(末症) an incurable[a fatal] disease /~으로 고생하다 suffer from an incurable disease.

**말직**(末職) a small post; a terminal office; the lowest position. まっしょく

**말질** a dispute; an argument; a quarrel; a wrangle/그는 쓸데 없는 일로 ~했다 A mere trifle led to a quarrel between them. くちあらそい

**말질**(末疾) a terminal illness; an incurable disease.

**말집** a house with eaves on all sides.
こや

**말참견**(一参見) interfering; meddling/ ~하다 poke one's nose into; interfere in; make comment on. くちだし

**말채찍** a horsewhip/ ~질하다 whip[lash] a horse. むち

**말초**(末梢) a tree-top; a tip/ ~ 신경 the peripheral nervous system. まっしょう

**말총** horsehair. うまのたてがみまたはおのけ

**말치레** nice-talk; using fair[fine, pretty, honeyed] words; making a specious remark/ ~하다 nice-talk; use fair [fine, pretty, honeyed] words; say nice[pretty] things; make a specious remark. かざりことば

**말캉말캉** softly; flabbily/~하다 be soft; flabby; flaccid. ぐにゃぐにゃしている

**말코¹** a loom roller.

**말코²** the muzzle[nose] of a horse; a person's nose shaped like a horse's.
ししばな

**말코지** a branched hanger; a wooden hook. ものをかけるくぎ

**말투** one's way[manner] of talking/그는 무엇이든지 알고 있는 ~다 He talks as if he knew everything./ ~가 사납다 have a nasty way of talking/ 사람의 성격은 ~로 안다 You will be judged by your speech. ことづかい

**말판** a game board; a dice board.

**말편자** a horseshoe. ていてつ

**말하다** 별항 참조.

**말향**(抹香) incense [powder]/ ~고래 a spermwhale; a cachalot.

**말허두**(一虚頭) one's first few words ⇨ 말머리.

**말혁**(一革) reins attached to both sides of a saddle as decoration.

**맑다** ①《깨끗하다》 clear; pure; resonant ②《살림이》 poor; needy/맑은 마음 a lucid mind/맑은 하늘 a clear sky. きよい

**맑은소리** 【언】 a voiceless sound.
むせいおん

**맑은술** refined rice wine. せいしゅ

**맑은장국**(一醬—) clear[thin] meat soup.

**맑히다** make clear; purify; make neat /정신을 ~ refresh one's mind/물을 ~ clear the water. きよくする

**맘** mind ⇨마음. こころ

**맘마** food; rice/ ~하다 eat. かあさん

**맛¹** ①《음식의》 taste; flavor; savor/아무 ~도 없는 ill-tasting; unpalatable/ ~이 좋은 nice; tasty; palatable; savory; delicious; flavorous/ ~이 변하다 turn sour[stale] 《고기가》 get high ②《느낌》 relish; zest; taste/ ~을 알다 get[acquire] a taste for. あじ

**맛²** 【어】 a solen; a razor clam/~젓 pickled razor clams.

**맛깔** taste. みかく

**맛깔스럽다** ①《맛이》 be tasty; palatable; agreeable ②《마음에》 be pleasing; after one's fancy/맛깔스러운 집 a house too one's taste/저 그림은 ~ That picture appeals to my taste./이것이 나에게 제일 ~ This suits my taste best.
あじよい

**맛나다** (be) tasty; delicious; sweet; savory; palatable; taste good/아 ~ It tastes good/맛난 요리 a delicious[palatable] dish あじよい

**맛들다** become tasty; pick up flavor; turn sour; become good to eat[drink] /맛든 수박 watermelon ripe enough to eat. あじがつく

**맛들이다** ①《취미를 붙이다》 get[acquire] a taste for/돈에 ~ get a tast for money/여자에 ~ have a carnal knowledge of women ②《맛들게 하다》 make tasty /김치를 ~ get the *kimchi* well pickled.
あじをつける

**맛맛으로** according to one's taste[pleasure]; to one's liking. じぶんのきのままに

**맛바르다** have one's appetite still unsatisfied; want to eat more; have not eaten enough. じゅうぶんにたべたりない

**맛보다** ①《맛을》 taste; try the flavor of ②《경험하다》 experience; suffer; undergo; know; learn ③《즐기다》 enjoy/인생의 쓰라림을 ~ experience the bitterness of life. あじをみる

**맛부리다** behave in an insipid manner.
みずくさいこうとうをする

**맛살** the meat inside a razor clam.
かいのなかみ

**맛없다** ①《맛이 없다》 untasty; unpalatable; unsavory/맛없는 음식 unsavory food ②(흥미없다) be dry; flat; dull; insipid/맛없이 살다 lead a wretched life/맛없이 굴다 behave in an insipid manner. あじがない

**맛있다** ①(맛이) be delicious; sweet; nice; tasty; palatable ②(재미있다) be interesting; delightful/맛있는 농담 an amusing joke. あじがある

**맛장수** an insipid[a dull, a prosaic] person. みずくさいひと

**맛적다** 《맛이》have little taste to it; be flat 《재미·흥미가》unpleasant; bitter.

**맛젓** pickled razor clams. かいのしおつけ

**맛피우다** behave insipidly ~맛부리다.

**망(望)¹** ①(살림) watch; lookout; vigilance ②(명망) good reputation ③(천망) recommendation/~대 a watch tower; a lookout. みはり

**망(望)²** ①(만월) a full moon ②(음력 보름날) the fifteenth day of a lunar month. まんげつ

**망(網)** a net; a casting net 《조직》a network/방송~ a radio network. あみ

**망가(亡家)** 《망한 집》a ruined family 《결단냄》ruining a family/ ~하다 ruin [destroy] a family. ほろびたうち

**망각(忘却)** lapse of memory; forgetfulness; oblivion/~하다 forget; bury in oblivion; lose sight of/세상에서 ~되다 be buried in oblivion/ 사실을 ~하다 lose sight of the fact. ぼうきゃく

**망거(妄擧)** rash action; a leap in the dark; an ill-advised attempt. ぼうきょ

**망건(網巾)** a headband made of horsehair. あみのずきん

**망견(望見)** looking out over/~하다 look out over (a view). とおくながめること

**망계(妄計)** a reckless scheme; a rash plane; unjust[unfair, wrong, unrighteous] scheme. むてっぽうなけいかく

**망고** ①(연줄의) letting out[paying away]

---

## 말 하 다

①(이야기를) talk; speak; converse; utter; remark; chat (over); have a talk[chat] (with); tell; put (in); state; mention; relate 《설명하다》explain 《상세히》describe; say; bid; express/말할 수 없는 unspeakable; unutterable; indescribable/영어로 ~ speak in English/말하기 어려운 듯이 hesitatingly; falteringly/당신에게 말하고 싶은 것이 있다 I have something to tell you./이 사람이 당신에게 말한 이군이오 This is Mr. Lee I spoke of to you./나는 그 일에 대하여 아버지에게 말했다 I said the case before my father./아무한테도 말하면 안 된다 Not a soul must be told., This is strictly between you and me./모든 것은 나중에 말하겠읍니다 I will let you know all about it later on./말하면 이해가 간다 Talk[Discussion] will make the matter clear./이제는 내가 말할 차례다 It is now my say./말하고 싶은 것을 ~ speak one's mind; speak out; give rein to one's tongue/머리가 아프다고 ~ complain of a headache/사람을 좋게[나쁘게] ~ speak well[ill] of a person; say good[bad] things about a person; say a good[bad] word for a person/당시의 심정을 뭐라고 말할 수 없다 Words fail to express how I felt at the moment./그것은 세상 사람들이 흔히 말하는 일이다 It is a matter of common talk among people. /사람들은 그가 인격자라고 말한다 He is said to be a man of character./네가 말한 대로다 It is just as you say., What you say is true., You are quite right.
/이렇게 말하면 너는 저렇게 말한다 You contradict everything./말하기는 쉬우나 행하기는 어렵다 Easier said than done./그는 죄를 지었다고 말했다 He confessed himself to be guilty./남아답게 졌다고 말하라 Acknowledge your defeat with good grace./이것을 영어로는 뭐라고 말합니까 How do you say[put] this in English?/잠깐 말할 것이 있다 I'd like to have a word with you for a minute./그의 고심은 이루 다 말할 수가 없다 The troubles he took cannot be told in a few words./얼굴은 그 사람의 성격을 말한다 A man's face expresses his character.

②(부탁하다) ask; beg; wish; hope/그녀에게 결혼해 달라고 말했다 I asked her for her hand., I asked her to marry me./말하기 거북하더 hard to say/돈을 꾸어 달라고 말하기가 거북했다 I found it rather awkward to ask for money./그는 말하는 것을 다 들어준다 He is a very obliging[accommodating] man.

③(불평·만류·꾸짖음 따위) bring (a matter) to a person's attention; advise; complain; protest; scold/불평을 ~ complain; voice protest/아무리 말해도 듣지 않는다 Give him all the advice in the world, he won't listen./그 아이가 말을 듣지 않으니 한번 단단히 말해 주시오 I want you to give the boy a sound scolding, he is so disobedient.

④(어린애가) begin to speak[talk]/어린아이가 말하기 시작했다 The child started to babble.

all the kite string; come to the end of the kite string ②(파산) squandering; losing all *one's* fortune ③(끝판) an end; a conclusion.

**망구다** ruin; destroy; wreck. ほろばす

**망국**(亡國) the ruin of *one's* country; the national ruin[decay]/~지탄(之歎) lamentation[grief] over the national ruin. ぼうこく

**망군**(望軍) a watchman; a lookout; a guard; a keeper. みはり

**망그러뜨리다** break down; destroy; demolish; injure (망그지르다)/장난감을 ~ break a toy. ぶっこわす

**망그러지다** be damaged[destroyed]; get out of order; break down. ぶっこわす

**망극**(罔極) ~하다 (be) immeasurable; great; immense; extreme.

**망극지통**(罔極之痛) grief beyond expression; the greatest grief[lament].

**망나니** ①(사형 집행인) executioner ②(못된 사람) a scoundrel; a rogue.

**망녀**(亡女) ①(딸) *one's* late[deceased] daughter ②(망골 계집) an ill-mannered woman; a bad woman. しんだむすめ

**망년지우**(忘年之友) a young friend of an old man. ぼうねんのとも

**망년회**(忘年會) a year-end party/~를 열다 give a year-end party; celebrate the outgoing year. ぼうねんかい

**망념**(妄念) delusion ⇨망상. もうねん

**망녕** dotage; second childhood; senility; anility/~들다 be in *one's* dotage[second childhood]/~부리다 behave like a child; behave unreasonably[foolishly]. おいぼれ

**망녕그물** a net for catching rabbits[pheasants] 《새 잡는》 a fowling net; a rabbit net. しゅりょうようのあみ

**망녕되다** (be) childish; foolish; ridiculous; silly. ばかげたていろ

**망녕스럽다** (be) childish; foolish; ridiculous; silly. おいぼれがかる

**망단**(妄斷) a rash[hasty] conclusion/~하다 conclude rashly; jump to a hasty conclusion. あやまったはんだん

**망동**(妄動) ~하다 act blindly; behave rashly/경거 ~ a rash attempt and blind behavior. もうどう

**망둥이** 《어》 a goby; *Acanthogobius hasta* (학명). はぜ

**망라**(網羅) ~하다 ①(포함) include; comprise; contain ②(모으다) bring together; collect/모든 것을 ~한 comprehensive/모든 사실을 ~하다 cover[include] all the facts. もうらする

**망령**(亡靈) a departed soul[spirit] 《유령》 a ghost; an apparition. ぼうれい

**망령**(妄靈) dotage ⇨망녕. おいぼれ

**망론**(妄論) an absurd opinion; a silly talk/~을 하다 make absurd remarks. ばかげたりろん

**망루**(望樓) a watchtower; an observation tower; a belvedere. みはりだい

**망륙**(望六) fifty-one years of age/~에 이르다 reach[attain] *one's* 51st year of age. ごじゅういっさい

**망막**(網膜) 《의》 the retina/~염 retinitis. もうまく

**망막**(茫漠) ~하다 ①(넓다) (be) vast; boundless; extensive ②(막연하다) (be) vague; obscure/~한 전도 vague prospects.

**망망하다**(忙忙-) (be) very busy; in a whirl of business. ひじょうにいそがしい

**망망하다**(茫茫-) (be) vast; boundless; limitless/망망한 바다 a boundless ocean/망망한 평원 a vast stretch of lowland. ぼうぼうとしている

**망매**(茫昧) ~하다 (be) ignorant of the world; unenlightened.

**망명**(亡命) a flight from *one's* own country/~하다 flee from *one's* own country; exile *oneself*/~객 a [political] refugee; an exile/~ 전부 a government-in-exile. ぼうめい

**망모**(亡母) *one's* deceased mother. ぼうぼ

**망민**(罔民) imposing upon the public; deceiving the world/~하다 deceive the world[the people]; delude the public. こくみんをあざむくこと

**망발**(妄發) a reckless remark; absurd speech thoughtless words/~하다 use improper; language; make an ignominious speech. でまかせのことば

**망발풀이**(妄發—) a treat given to make up for *one's* absurd[reckless] remarks/~하다 give a treat[an entertainment] in apology for *one's* unreasonable remarks.

**망백**(望百) ninety-one years of age. きゅうじゅういっさい

**망보다**(望—) keep watch; look out for; stand watch; picket/엄중히 ~ keep strict watch/죄수를 방심 않고 ~ keep a careful watch on the prisoner. みはる

**망부**(亡父) *one's* deceased father. しんだちち

**망부**(亡夫) *one's* deceasee[late] husband. しんだおっと

**망사**(網紗) gauze.

**망상**(妄想) a wild fancy; a fantasy; a chimera/과대 ~증 megalomania/피해 ~ a delusion of persecution/~을 품다 nurse delusion. もうそう

**망상**(網狀) net shape; reticulation/~의 netlike; reticulate; reticular/~막 《의》 the reticulum. もうじょう

**망상**(望床) a large「dinner」table full of various eatables.

**망상스럽다** (be) crafty; saucy; tricky; impertinent; fickle. わるがしこい

**망새** a gargoyle; a ridge-end tile; a gargoyle.

**망석중이** a puppet; a marionette; puppetry 《남의 손에 노는 사람》 a puppet for another. あやつりにんぎょう

**망설**(妄說) a fallacious speech; an erroneous idea[opinion]; a groundless opi-

nion 《그릇된 풍설》 a false[baseless] report. でまかせのことば
**망설거리다** hesitate 망설이다.
**망설이다** hesitate; scruple; waver; think twice; be irresolute／망설이면서 hesitatingly; reluctantly／망설이지 않고 without hesitation／망설이지 않다 make[have] no scruple of. もじもじする
**망솔**(妄率) hastiness; rashness; recklessness／〜하다 be hasty; reckless; headlong.
**망쇄**(忙殺) busyness; pressure／〜하다 be very busy; be pressed with work. ぼうさつ
**망신**(亡身) a disgrace; a dishono[u]r; a shame／〜하다 be disgraced; be dishono[u]red／〜을 주다 put (a person) to shame／〜살 ill luck to bring disgrace. はじ
**망신**(妄信) blind faith; credulity／〜하다 believe blindly. もうしん
**망실**(亡失) loss／〜하다 lose／재산을 〜하다 lose one's fortune. ふんしつ
**망실**(忘失) ①(잃음) loss; missing ②(망각) forgetfulness; oblivion; lapse of memory／〜하다 lose memory; of miss; forget; be forgetful[oblivious] of.
わすれてなくすこと
**망아지** 《동》《수컷》a colt 《암컷》a filly 《총칭》a foal 《작은 말》a pony.
**망야**(罔夜) all night sitting; keeping awake all night／〜하다 stay up all night. よふかし
**망양 보뢰**(亡羊補牢) Locking the barn door after the horse is stolen. To cover the well after the child has been drowned in it.
**망양지탄**(望洋之歎) lamenting one's inability[incapacity]; a feeling of hopelessness／〜이 있다 feel one's object to be unattainable.
**망어**(妄語) a falsehood; a lie; an untruth; a prevarication. みだりなことば
**망언**(妄言) an absurd[improper] remark; a foolish talk; a reckless remark; thoughtless words／〜하다 make an absurd remark. ぼうげん
**망얽이** a net of ropes. ひもであんだあみ
**망연 자실**(茫然自失) 〜하다 be distrait; stupefied; entranced. ぼうぜんじしつ
**망연하다**(茫然—) ①(넓고 아득하다) be vast; boundless; extensive; limitless ②《명하다》(be) vacant; blank; abstracted; absent-minded／망연히 vacantly; blankly／어찌할 바를 몰라 〜 be quite at a loss what to do. ぼうぜんとしている
**망외**(望外) 〜의 unexpected; unlooked-for; unanticipated／〜의 기쁨 a pleasant surprise. ぼうがい
**망우**(亡友) one's dead[a deceased] friend. しんだとも
**망우초**(忘憂草) a day-lily ―원추리. わすれぐさ
**망운**(亡運) decline of fortune; declining fortune; adversity／〜이 들다 one's fortune sinks[declines]. ほろびるうんめい
**망울** ①(덩어리) lump; a ball; a kernel; a stone ②(꽃 따위) a flower bud; a bud ③(임파선종)《의》an inflammation of a lymphatic gland. かたまり
**망원경**(望遠鏡) a telescope; a field glass. ぼうえんきょう
**망원 렌즈**(望遠—) a telephoto-lens.
**망원 사진**(望遠寫眞) a telephoto／〜기 a telephotographic camera; a telecamera. ぼうえんしゃしん
**망월**(望月) ①(보름달) a full moon ②(달을 봄) watching the moon; gazing at the moon; viewing the moon／〜하다 gaze at[watch] the moon. もちづき
**망인**(亡人) a dead person; the deceased. しんだひと
**망일**(望日) a full moon day; the fifteenth day of the lunar month. じゅうごや
**망자**(亡子) one's dead[deceased] son. しんだこ
**망자**(亡者) a dead person; the deceased; the departed. しんだひと
**망자**(芒刺) a thorn; a prickle; a sticker.
**망자 존대**(妄自尊大) haughtiness; arrogance; self-importance; pomposity; superciliousness／〜하다 bear oneself haughtily; assume an air of importance; ride the high horse. うぬぼれじまん
**망제**(亡弟) one's deceased younger brother. しんだおとうと
**망조**(亡兆) omens of ruin／〜가 들다 show signs of ruin. ほろびるきざし
**망족**(望族) an illustrious[honorable, a reputable] family.
**망종**(亡種) a villain; a ruffian; a scoundrel; a bad boy; a rascal; a bad egg. あっかん
**망종**(亡終) the time[hour] of death; the last hour of one's life; one's last moment; one's deathbed; the dying hour. しにぎわ
**망종**(芒種) ①(곡식) grain with an awn. ②(절후) one of the 24 seasonal divisions [around 5 June].
**망주석**(望柱石) a pair of stone posts in front of a tomb. いっついのはかいし
**망중한**(忙中閑) moments snatched from a busy life.
**망지 소조**(罔知所措) 〜하다 be at a loss; do not know what to do.
おくどころをしらずとうわくすること
**망처**(亡妻) one's deceased wife. ぼうさい
**망초**(芒硝)【화】sulphate of soda.
**망측**(罔測) 〜하다 (be) inordinate; outrageous; atrocious／〜한 생각 an inordinate idea. はなはだしいこと
**망치** a hammer; a sledge[-hammer]／큰 〜 a maul; a sledge[-hammer]／〜 대가리 a hammerhead. ふち
**망치**(忘置) lapse[slip] of memory; forgetting; forgetfulness; oblivion／〜하다 forget; lose one's memory; be obli-

망치다 spoil; ruin; destroy; frustrate/신세를 ~ ruin oneself; make a failure of one's life. だいなしにする

망칠(望七) sixty-one years of age.

망태기(網—) a mesh[net] bag. あみぶくろ

망팔(望八) seventy-one years of age.

망패(妄悖) (be) absurd; unreasonable; improper; inordinate. はいり

망평(妄評) unjust criticism; abusive remarks/~하다 comment rashly[poorly]; criticize unjustly; make abusive remarks. しんらひょう

망하다(亡—) ①(멸망하다) go to ruin; be ruined[destroyed] (사업 따위가) fail ②(곤란하다) (be) hard; difficult/하기 싫은 hard[difficult] to do. ほろぶ

망형(亡兄) one's deceased elder brother. しんだあに

망혼(亡魂) a ghost; a soul; a spirit. ししゃのたましい

맞- facing; directly まっすぐ

맞갖다 be to one's taste[liking]; (be) agreeable; satisfactory; likable/맞갖은 여자 a girl after one's heart. きにいる

맞걸다 stake against; stake the same amount (of money) as the other party. あいかける

맞걸리다 ①(두 물건이) be linked together; be coupled ②(두 사람이) be pitted against each other.

맞고소(—告訴) a cross[counter] action; a countercharge/~하다 bring a counter[cross] action (for, against).

맞교군(—轎軍) a sedan chair [carried by two men].

맞교대(—交代) two shifts.

맞다¹ (정확하다) be right[correct] (명중하다) strike (적합하다) fit; suit; agree (with); (일치하다) correspond (to, with); (조화하다) be in harmony[accord] with. まちがいない

맞다² 《매 따위를》 be struck[beaten, knocked] 《총알을》 be shot (비·눈 따위를) be exposed to/비를 ~ be exposed to pelting rain/머리를 ~ be struck on the head. なぐられる

맞다³ (맞아들이다) receive; welcome; greet; hail (나가서 맞다) meet. むかえる

맞다⁴ (도둑을) have (a thing) stolen.

맞닥뜨리다 knock against; come face to face; come across. ばったりであう

맞닥치다 encounter; come face to face with; clash with/난관에 ~ be confronted with a difficult problem; hit[run into] a snag. おたがいにちかよる

맞담 a stone wall

맞담배 ~ 피우다[질하다] smoke to another person's face; sit smoking together.

맞당기다 draw[pull] each other; be pulled from both sides. たがいにひく

맞닿다 touch each other. たがいにとどく

맞대다 face; confront (접촉하다) bring in touch with/맞대 놓고 face to face; to one's face; in the presence. くっつけあう

맞대매 a play-off; a finish fight/~하다 play off a tie. けっしょうしあい

맞대면(—對面) a face-to-face interview [confrontation]/~하다 interview[confront] face to face. かおをみあわせること

맞대하다(—對—) face; confront. たいめん

맞돈 immediate[cash] payment/ ~으로 사다 buy for cash. げんきん

맞들다 hold up (a thing) together; lift together. むかいあっていっしょにあげる

맞금 a diagonal「line」. たいかくせん

맞물다 ①(이가) bite each other ②(톱니 바퀴 따위가) mesh together; [inter-]lock; engage (gears); put into gear.

맞물리다 gear with[into]; set the tooth /맞물림 《기계》 gearing.

맞바꾸다 exchange; barter; trade; truck (in). わりましなくこうかんすること

맞바느질하다 sew with two needles.

맞바둑 an unhandicapped match of checkers. あいご

맞바람 a head[an adverse, a contrary] wind. むかいかぜ

맞받다 (정면으로) receive[face] head-on 《호응하다》 respond at once (들이받다) crash head-on; crash into each other/태양 빛을 ~ receive the direct sunlight.

맞받이 an opposite side. むかいがわ

맞벌이 ~하다 work in double harness/~ 가정(生活) a double-income family[living].

맞벽(—壁) 《건》 the outer layer of a two-layer wall. ごうへき

맞보기 clear glasses; plane glasses. へいめんきょう

맞보다 watch each other; look at each other; look each other in the face/맞보고 웃다 smile at each other. さしむかってみる

맞부딪다 hit[scrape against] each other. ぶつかりあう

맞부딪치다 hit against; run into[against]; crash into. ぶつかりあう

맞붇다 stick together/맞붙어 싸우다 grapple with each other. たがいにくむ

맞붙들다 catch[hold] together[each other]; detain each other; help each other (권투에서) clinch. たがいにつかむ

맞붙이 (직접 교섭) a direct[face-to-face] negotiations. ちょくめん

맞붙이다 ①(사람을) bring them into contact 《경기 따위에서》 mach[pit] (A) against (B) ②(붙이다) stick[plaster, affix] together. ぐっつける

맞붙잡다 seize[grasp] each other.

맞상대(—相對) direct confrontation.

맞서다 ①(마주서다) stand face to face (with); confront ②(버티다) take a stand (against); hold out (against). たちむかう

맞선 a face-to-face sizing up of (a person); an interview to determine (a person's) suitability. みあい

**맞소송**(━訴訟) a counter-suit[-action,-complaint].

**맞수**(━手) a match; an equal; a peer/장기의 ~ one's equal in chess.

**맞아떨어지다** tally; be correct/계산이 ~ a calculation is correct; the figures tally.

**맞욕**(━辱) counter-abuse; answering back with abuse/~하다 call names back; answer back with abuse.

**맞은바람** a headwind 맞바람. むかいかぜ

**맞은바래기** the opposite side; the other side/~의 in front of. むかいかわ

**맞은편** the opposite side/~에 opposite; on the opposite side of. むかいかわ

**맞이** meeting/ ~하다 meet; receive; welcome; greet. むかえること

**맞잡다** ①《서로 잡다》hold each other ②《협동하다》cooperate with; get together. おたがいににぎりあう

**맞잡이** an equal; a match. ひってきしゅ

**맞장구치다** chime in with (one); echo [another's words]; fall in with (one's views). ふとであう

**맞장기**(━將棋) even-match chess; an unhandicapped chess-game.

**맞적수**(━敵手) a good match; a worthy opponent. ひってきしゅ

**맞절** ~하다 bow to each other.

**맞접다** fold together.

**맞추다** ①《조립·합치다》fix[fit] into; assemble; put together ②《시계·셈·수지 따위를》set (it) [right]; make (it) tally; correct (it) ③《조절·적응·적합하다》adjust; adapt; conform; set; fit; suit ④《대조하다》compare; check [up] (with). あわせる

**맞춤법**(━法) spelling/~ 통일안 a plan for standardizing[unifying] spelling/한글 ~ the rules of Korean spelling[orthography]. つずりじほう

**맞혼인**(━婚姻) a marriage arranged on equal terms.

**맞흥정** direct transaction/~하다 make a direct deal. ちょくせつのとりひき

**맞히다** ①《추측하다》hit; guess/바로 guess right (답을) give a right answer ②《명중하다》hit [the mark] ③《비·눈 따위를》expose/비 ~ expose to the rain; put out in the rain. いいあてる

**맡기다** ①《물건을》leave (a thing) in a person's charge; deposit[leave] (a thing) with (a person) ②《사람을》leave (a child) in the care of (a person); give (a person) charge of (a child) ③《위임하다》leave (a matter) to (a person); put (a matter) in[into] a person's hands; entrust (a person) with (a matter)/책임을 ~ place responsibility on (a person)/일체를 ~ leave everything to (a person). まかせる

**맡다** ①《보관하다》keep; receive (a thing) in trust[custody]; take charge of (a thing); take (a thing) in charge (담당·감독하다) take[have] charge of/5학년을 ~ have charge of the fifth-grade class ②《허가·인가를》get; obtain; receive; be permitted/~하가를 ~ obtain permission ③《냄새를》smell; scent; sniff/이 장미꽃 냄새 좀 맡아 봐요 Just have a smell of this rose ④《눈치채다》suspect; sense; scent out; get wind of. ひきうける

**매¹** ①《때리는》a whip; a rod; a cane; a lash/ ~를 때리다 whip; flog; lash; use a rod ②《매질》whipping; flogging; birching/사정없는 ~ merciless flogging. むち

**매²** ①《맷돌》a millstone; a grind mill ②《매통》a wooden grind mill.

**매³** 〖조〗 a hawk; a falcon; *Asturus gentilis*(학명)/~눈 같은 hawk-eyed/~부리코 a hooknose; a hawknose/~사냥 hawking; falconry. たか

**매⁴** 《맵시》figure; shape; form; cast/몸~ one's figure[shape];· one's physique; a pose/눈~ a look; the expression[cast] of one's eyes; one's eyes. すがた

**매⁵** quite; much [the same]/~한가지다 be much about the same; come to the same thing after all; be all the same.

**매**(每) each; every/~일요일 every Sunday. まい

**매가**(妹家) the family that one's sister is married into; the family of one's sister's husband. いもうとのうち

**매가**(買價) a purchase[buying] price. ばいか

**매가**(賣價) a sale[selling] price. ばいか

**매가**(賣家) a house for sale; selling a house/~하다 sell a house. うりや

**매가리** 〖어〗 a horse-mackerel; *Trachurus japonica*(학명).

**매각**(賣却) sale; disposal [by sale]; selling/ ~하다 dispose of; sell/~ 공고 a public notice of sale. ばいきゃく

**매갈이** hulling rice in a wooden mill/매갈잇군 a rice-huller. せいまい

**매개** the course of events/~보다 watch the situation. なりゆき

**매개**(每個) each one; every piece/이 수박은 ~ 당 30원입니다 These melons are thirty *won* apiece. ひとつ

**매개**(媒介) intermediation; mediation; agency; intervention/~하다 mediate; intermediate; act as an intermediary/전염병의 ~물 a vehicle of infection. ばいかい

**매개념**(媒概念) 〖논〗 the middle concept; the mean term. ばいがいねん

**매거**(枚擧) ~하다 enumerate; count; reckon; mention/일일이 ~할 수 없다 be too numerous to mention; it is virtually impossible to exhaust [the list of]. まいきょ

**매고**(賣高) the amount sold 매상고. うりだか

**매고르다** be all alike; be even; be of a sort. そろっている

**매골** [a bad] appearance; a figure.

**매관 매직**(賣官賣職) the sale of offices/ ~하다 sell government posts; sell appointments. ばいかんばいしょく

**매꾸러기** a naughty boy who is always given the rod. むちでうたれるいたずらっこ

**매국**(賣國) selling one's country; betrayal of[treachery to] one's country/ ~하다 sell[betray] one's country/ ~노 a traitor [to one's country]. ばいこく

**매끄럽다** (be) smooth; sleek; slick; slippery; velvety/매끄러운 종이 slick[sleek] paper. なめらかだ

**매끈거리다** feel slippery すべすべする

**매끈하다** (be) smooth; sleek; slick ⇒매끈하다. ひじょうにすべらかなかんじだ

**매기** ①《수퇘지와 암소의 트기》a cross between a boar and a cow ②《트기》 a hybrid; a mongrel; a cross; a half-breed.

**매기**(每期) every season[semester, time, period]; each term. まいき

**매기**(霉氣) mildew; mo[u]ld; must. かび

**매기다** ①《값을》put a price on; price; bid ②《점수를》give; grade/점수를 ~ score; give marks; rate/값을 비싸게 ~ put the price high (on an article). ねだんをつける

**매기단하다** wind up one's affairs; deal with the aftermath; put (things) in order; set matters right; bring to a conclusion. きちんとしあげる

**매나니** ①《빈손》an empty hand; a bare hand/ ~로 with empty[bare] hands; empty-handed ②《음식》a meal without side dishes; simple food. からて

**매년**(每年) every year; yearly; annually/ ~일 yearly; annual. まいねん

**매다**¹《동여매다》tie; bind; knot; fasten; link; join/개를 ~ chain a dog/ 구두끈을 ~ tie [up] one's shoes. むすぶ

**매다**²《김을》weed [out]; pick weeds out of; pull weeds/논의 김을 ~ weed a rice paddy. じょそうする

**매다**³ put [a price] on ⇒매기다. ねだんをつける

**매달**(每一) every month/ ~의 monthly/ ~의 지불 monthly payment/ ~한 번 once a month; monthly. まいげつ

**매달다** hang; suspend. ぶらさげる

**매달리다** ①be hung; be suspended; be tied down/시체가 나무에 매달려 있다 A dead body is hanging on a tree. ②《붙들다·늘어지다》hang on (another's neck); dangle; cling to (one's mother's skirt). ぶらさげられる

**매대기** smearing[daubing, besmearing] all over/벽에 진흙을 ~ 치다 smear a wall all over with mud.

**매도**(賣渡) sale and delivery/ ~하다 sell over/ ~ 계약 contract for selling/ ~인 a seller. うりわたし

**매도**(罵倒) condemnation; denunciation; scathing; abuse; severe criticism/ ~하다 denounce; decry; condemn; criticize severely; aduse; cry down. ばとう

**매독**(梅毒) 《의》 syphilis/ ~성의 syphilitic/ ~ 환자 a syphilitic person[patient]. ばいどく

**매득**(買得) ~하다 purchase 《싸게》 buy at a bargain. かいいれること

**매듭** a knot; a tie/ ~을 짓다[풀다] make [untie] a knot. むすびめ

**매듭짓다** ①make a knot; knot ②《끝맺다》conclude; complete; put an end (to); close; finish/일을 ~ conclude one's work. むすびめをつくる

**매듭풀** 《식》 a Japanese clover; a lespedeza; Kummerowia striata(학명).

**매력**(魅力) a charm; fascination/성적 ~ a sex appeal/ ~있는 charming; fascinating; attractive. みりょく

**매련장이** a stupid fool; an ass; a dullard; a thickhead; a coward. ばかもの

**매련퉁이** a dull[stupid] fellow; Mr. Thick Head. のろま

**매리**(罵詈) abuse; abusive language; reviling; vituperation/ ~하다 abuse; revile; rail (at); call (a person) names; use abusive language. ばり

**매립**(埋立) reclamation; filling-up/ ~하다 fill in (a moat); fill up (a pond with earth)/해면을 ~하다 reclaim foreshore (from the sea). うめたて

**매만지다** adjust; trim; tidy/옷 매무새를 ~ adjust[tidy] oneself/머리를 ~ tidy [arrange] one's disordered hair; give a smooth to the hair.

**매맛** a taste of the whip; whipping; flogging.

**매맞다** ①《매도》get flogged ②《얻어맞다》be whipped; be hit; be struck[beaten]; be thrashed; be knocked/또 매맞고 싶니 Do you want another thrashing?

**매매**(賣買) buying and selling; purchase and sale 《거래》dealing; trade; transaction; a bargain; traffic; a deal《속》/ 노예 ~ slave trade. ばいばい

**매명**(賣名) self-advertisement; self-publicity/ ~하다 seek publicity. ばいめい

**매명**(每名) each[every] person; per person. かくじん

**매목**(埋木) 《탄화목》lignite; bogwood; fossil-wood/ ~ 세공 fossil-wood work.

**매몰**(埋沒) burying/ ~하다 bury (in, under)/눈 속에 ~되다 be buried under snow. まいぼつ

**매몰스럽다** (be) cold; unkind; hard; harsh; cruel; heartless; callous/매몰스럽게 heartlessly; cruelly; coldly; harshly.

**매몰차다** (be) very unkind; very cold; callous; heartless. ざんこくだ

**매몰하다** (be) cold; icy; harsh; cold-hearted; unfeeling/매몰하게 굴다 treat (a person) coldly[in a cold way]; be unkind to. はくじょうだ

**매무새** dress; attire; personal appeara-

**매무시** primping; dressing up／～하다 primp; primp *oneself*; tidy [up]; dress; tidy up *oneself*／～단정하다 keep *oneself* neat and trim. きちんとしたふくそう

**매문**(賣文) literary hackwork／～하다 sling ink; peddle out *one's* knowledge／～업자 a hackwriter; a penny·a·liner. ばいぶん

**매물**(賣物) an article for sale／～로 내놓다 put (*a thing*) on the market; place (*a thing*) on sale. うりもの

**매미** a cicada; a'cicala／～ 소리 the shrill chirrup of a cicada. せみ

**매방**(賣方) a seller; the selling side 《증권》 a bear.

**매번**(每番) ①《때마다》each [every] time ②《자주》very often ③《늘》always.

**매복**(埋伏) ambush·ment／～하다 lie in; ambush／～했다가 습격하다 attack (*enemy*) from ambush. まいふく

**매복**(賣卜) fortunetelling; divination／～하다 tell fortunes; practice divination. かねをとってうらないをすること

**매부**(妹夫) the husband of *one's* sister; *one's* brother·in·law. しまいのおっと

**매부리**¹ 《매를 부리는 사람》a falconer; a hawker. たかつかい

**매부리**² 《매》a hawk's beak; hawk bill／～ 같은 hawk·billed／～ 징 《구두의》a kind of hobnail／～ 코 a hooked nose; a Roman nose; an aquiline nose.

**매사**(每事) everything／～에 in everything／～ 불성 failing in every undertaking. まいじ

**매사**(媒辭) 《논》the mean term.

**매사냥** hawking; falconry／～하다 go hawking; hawk. たかかり

**매사냥군** a falconer; a hawker; a falcon hunter. たかかりじん

**매싸리** a bush·clover whip [switch].

**매삭**(每朔) every [each] month; monthly. まいつき

**매상**(買上) purchase; buying 《전부의》procurement／～하다 purchase; buy／～가격 the Government's buying price. かいあげ

**매상**(賣上) sales; proceeds; receipts／～계정 sales account. うりあげ

**매상고**(賣上高) the sales; the amount sold; the proceeds of sale; the turnover; the returns; the takings／그날의 ～ the day's proceeds. うりあげだか

**매생이** a boat; a dugout 《마상이》a canoe.

**매석**(賣惜) an indisposition to sell; hoarding／～하다 be indisposed to sell; hold back.

**매설**(埋設) laying／～하다 lay [under the ground].

**매섭다** (be) fierce; sharp／매섭게 생기다 look sharp; look fierce. どうもうだ

**매세**(賣勢) ～하다 strut about in borrowed plumes; bluff under the shelter of *another's* influence.

**매소**(賣笑) prostitution; harlotry／～하다 practice prostitution; prostitute; walk the streets. ばいしょう

**매소부**(賣笑婦) a harlot; a prostitute; a streetwalker; a street girl. ばいしょうふ

**매수**(枚數) the number of sheets [leaves]. まいすう

**매수**(買收) purchase 《사람을》bribing; buying off／～하다 buy 《사람을》buy off; bribe; win over [by bribery]／부자에게 ～되다 sell *oneself* to the rich／～표를 ～하다 buy votes. ばいしゅう

**매수**(買受) buying over／～하다 buy over; take over; purchase／～인 a purchaser; a buyer; a vendee. かいうけ

**매스껍다** feel sick; feel nausea いメスきぱはきそうだ

**매시**(每時) every hour; per hour. まいじ

**매씨**(妹氏) ①《남의 누이》your [his] esteemed sister ②《자기의 누이》*one's* elder sister. たにんのあねのけいしょう

**매시근하다** dull; (be) languid. だるい

**매식**(買食) dining out; eating at a restaurant [an inn].

**매실**(梅實) a plum／～주(酒) plum wine. うめのみ

**매실매실하다** (be) sly; crafty; foxy. すれっからしだ

**매암돌다** spin *oneself* round; whirl till dizzy. くるくるまわる

**매암돌리다** 《제자리에서》spin [whirl] (*a person*) round. くるくるまわす

**매암운다** chirping／매미가 ～ 울다 A cicada is singing., A locust is chirping. ミーンミーン

**매암쇠** 《맷돌의》the rynd [of a millstone].

**매야**(每夜) every [each] night; nightly.

**매약**(賣約) a sales contract／～하다 conclude [strike] a bargain; contract to sell. ばいやく

**매약**(賣藥) a patent medicine／～하다 sell patent medicines. ばいやく

**매양**(毎樣) always; all the time; every time; constantly／그 여자는 ～ 아름답기만 하다 She is as beautiful as ever. ひじょうに

**매연**(煤煙) smoke; sooty smoke. ばいえん

**매염**(媒染) mordancy; colour·fixing by means of a mordant／～료 a mordant／～성의 mordant／～ 염료 mordant dyes.

**매움하다** (be) rather hot [pungent] somewhat hot. ちょっとからい

**매우** very; so; most; exceedingly; extraordinarily; greatly; remarkably much; much too／～ 아름다운 여자 a very [most] beautiful woman. ひじょうに

**매우**(梅雨) the long spell of rain in early summer／～기 the rainy [wet] season. つゆ

**매욱하다** (be) stupid; foolish. ぐどんだ

**매운바람** a sharp [biting] wind.

**매운탕**(一湯) a pepper·pot soup; a hot chowder.

**매움하다** (be) rather hot[spicy, sharp, pungent]. からいようだ

**매워하다** feel hot[pungent]; find (it) hot. からいようなかんじがする

**매원(埋怨)** ～하다 bear a grudge[hatred, resentment] against; bear (a person) hatred; have it in for (a person); bear (one) a grudge. うらみをいだいていること

**매월(每月)** every month; each month; monthly/～ 한 번 once a month; monthly. まいつき

**매음(賣淫)** prostitution; harlotry/ ～하다 practice prositution; prostitute oneself/～녀 a harlot, a prostitute; a street-walker[street girl]. ばいいん

**매이다** be bound up (with); be tied (to) /매인 데 없는 free; carefree/일에 ～ be occupied with one's work. むすばれる

**매인(每人)** each man; every one/ ～당 per head; for each person. かくじん

**매인목숨** not being one's own boss; being an underling[a slave]; an underling; a slave.

**매일(每日)** every day; each day; daily / ～의 daily; everyday/ ～의 일 daily works/ ～같이 almost every day. まいにち

**매일반(――般)** all the same; much the same/ ～이다 differ little; make little difference. けっきょくおなじ

**매입(買入)** buying; purchase/ ～하다 buy; purchase; lay in/대량 ～하다 lay in a large stock of (coal)/～ 가격 the purchase price. かいいれ

**매자(昧者)** a thickheaded[slow-witted] person; a dullard.

**매자(媒子)** a matchmaker; a go-between; a mediator. ちゅうばい

**매자기** 〖식〗 a kind of bulrush[club rush]; *Scirpus maritimus*(학명).

**매자나무** 〖식〗 the Korean barberry; *Berberis Koreana*(학명).

**매자목(賣子木)** 〖식〗 a snowbell; *Styrax japonica*(학명).

**매작(媒妁)** matchmaking ⇨중매(中媒). ばいしゃく

**매작지근하다** be tepid[cool, lukewarm]; be not warm enough ⇨미지근하다. なまぬるい

**매잡이¹** ①(매듭의) degree of tightness of a knot ②(일의) finishing up; winding up (a job).

**매잡이²** 《사냥》 hunting falcon 《사람》 a falcon hunter/ ～하다 hunt falcon.

**매장(埋葬)** 《시체의》 burial; interment; inhumation/～하다 bury; inter; entomb 《사회적으로》 ostracize; expel from society/～하다 ostracize; expel from society. まいそう

**매장(埋藏)** burying underground; deposits [of minerals]/～하다 hide underground; bury in the ground 《묻혀 있다》 lie underground; be deposited. まいぞう

**매장(買臟)** purchasing[receiving] stolen goods. ぬすんだものをかうこと

**매장(賣場)** a store; a counter; a shop; a place which sells.

**매점(賣店)** a booth; a stand; a stall/～을 내다 install a booth; set up a stand /신문 ～ a news stand/학교 ～ a school store(미).

**매점(買占)** cornering; a corner [on goods]; a bull corner/～하다 corner; buy up/쌀을 ～하다 corner rice; make a corner in rice. かいしめ

**매정스럽다** (be) cold; icy; heartless; unfeeling/매정하게 굴다 be hard on (one); treat coldly. はくじょうだ

**매제(妹弟)** a younger sister's husband; a brother-in-law.

**매조미쌀(一糙米―)** unpolished rice. まだついてないこめ

**매조지** "putting on" the finishing touches; the finish.

**매주(每週)** every week; each week/～의 weekly. まいしゅう

**매주(賣酒)** selling liquor; liquor for sale / ～하다 sell liquor; deal in liquor/ ～집 a wine shop; a liquor store.

**매주(買主)** a buyer; a purchaser; a vendee. かいぬし

**매주(賣主)** a seller; a vendor. うりぬし

**매죽(梅竹)** a plum tree and a bamboo. うめとたけ

**매지구름** a rain cloud. あまぐも

**매지근하다** (be) tepid; lukewarm ⇨미지근하다. なまぬるい

**매진(賣盡)** selling out/ ～하다 sell out; run out of (merchandise). うりつくすこと

**매진(邁進)** dash; pushing on/ ～하다 push on; dash[push] forward; strive for; struggle on/우리는 새로운 한국의 건설에 ～하자 Let all of us strive to build up [a] new Korea. まいしん

**매질** whipping; flogging; lashing; beating/ ～하다 whip; flog; beat; lash. むちうち

**매질(媒質)** 〖물〗 a medium. ばいしつ

**매질군** a man quick with the whip; a man of combative spirit; a fire-eater.

**매차(毎次)** each time; every time. まいじ

**매체(媒體)** a medium (pl. -dia)/공기는 소리의 ～이다 The air is a medium for sound.

**매초(賣草)** tobacco on sale. うるタバコ

**매초롭하다** (be) wholesome looking; possess a healthy beauty; (be) charmingly healthy. すらりとしている

**매축(埋築)** reclamation; filling up[in] / ～하다 reclaim; reclaim from the sea; fill up[in]/ ～ 공사 reclamation work/～지 filled-up land.

**매춘(賣春)** harlotry; prostitution; street walking/ ～하다 practice prostitution; *sell one's favors*/～ 방지법 an Antiprostitution Law/～부 a prostitute; a street girl. ばいしゅん

**매출(賣出)** a bargain sale 《특매》 a special sale／~ 가격 an offering price／특가 ~ special sales.

**매치광이** a madman; a maniac; a rash person.

**매치다** be crazy about; be eccentric; lose one's senses ⇨미치다.

**매캐하다** ①(연기내가) (be) smoky; stinging; burning ②(곰팡내가) (be) musty; mo[u]ldy; fusty.

**매콤하다** (be) hot pungent.

**매큼하다** (be) peppery-smelling／매큼한 냄새 a peppery smell.

**매토**(買土) purchase of land／~하다 buy [a piece of] land.

**매토**(賣土) selling land[a lot]／~하다 sell land[a lot].

**매통** a wooden mill for hulling rice.

**매파**(-派) a hawk.

**매파**(媒婆) an old woman go-between [match-maker].

**매판** an under mat for a handmill].

**매판 자본**(買辦資本) comprador capital.

**매팔자**(-八字) easy circumstances／~이다 be in easy circumstances.

**매표소**(賣票所) 《극장의》 a box office 《승차권의》 a booking office; a ticket office 〈미〉; 〈창구〉 a ticket[booking] window.

**매품**(賣品) an article for sale／비~ articles not for sale; Not to be sold／《게시》 Not for Sale.

**매한가지** the same; all the same; much the same／엇지나 잦지나~다 It is six of one and half a dozen of the other.

**매합**(媒合) matchmaking／~하다 bring about a match; go between.

**매향**(梅香) a fragrance of plum blossoms.

**매형**(妹兄) an elder sister's husband; a brother-in-law.

**매호**(每戶) every[each] house[door, family].

**매호**(每號) every number[issue].

**매혹**(魅惑) fascination; captivation; alluring charm／~하다 fascinate; charm; enchant／~적인 charming; captivating; fascinating.

**매화**(梅花) a plum blossoms 《나무》 a plum tree.

**매회**(每回) each[every] time 《권투 따위》 each[every] round.

**매흙** gray loam.

**매흙질** facing a wall with loam／~하다 face[plaster] a wall with loam.

**맥**(脈) ①(맥박) pulse; pulsation／~을 짚어보다 feel the pulse／~이 뛰다 pulsate; the pulse beats ②(혈맥) a blood vessel ③(광맥) a vein／~을 찾아내다 strike a vein of ore ④(맥락) a thread of connection.

**맥간**(麥稈) barley[wheat] straw.

**맥고**(麥藁) straw of barley[wheat].

**맥고 모자**(麥藁帽子) a straw hat.

**맥관**(脈管) 〖혈관〗 a blood-vessel.

**맥노**(麥奴) 〖식〗 the black ear [of barley].

**맥농**(麥農) cultivation of wheat[barley]; wheat[barley] farming.

**맥도**(脈度) pulse rate; pulse frequency.

**맥동**(脈動) pulsation.

**맥락**(脈絡) ①(혈맥) the blood vessel; an artery(동맥); a vein(정맥) ②(일의) a thread[line] of connection／적군과 ~을 통하다 have a dark connection of the enemy.

**맥랑**(麥浪) the waving[rippling] barley fields; a golden sea[waves] of wheat [barley].

**맥량**(麥凉) the cool weather at the barley harvest season.

**맥량**(麥糧) barley for summer use[provisions].

**맥령**(麥嶺) the barley hump 《보릿고개》 the period of food shortage just before the barley harvest in the early summer.

**맥류**(麥類) barley; wheat; oat.

**맥리**(脈理) ①(문맥의) a contextual connection; the thread of logic; the context ②(맥의 이치) the theory of the pulse.

**맥망**(麥芒) a wheat beard; an awn.

**맥맥하다** ①(코가) (be) stuffed up; congested; stuffy／코가 ~ My nose is stuffy ②(생각이) Be at a loss; be at one's wits' end／생각이 ~ be stuck for an idea.

**맥박**(脈搏) pulse; pulsation／~이 고르지 않다 The pulse is irregular.／~계 a pulsimeter; a sphygmometer／~ 묘사기 sphygmograph.

**맥반**(麥飯) boiled barley.

**맥보다**(脈-) ①(맥박을) feel[examine, take] the pulse ②(의향을) sound out (a person); feel out a situation; sound (one, one's view).

**맥분**(麥粉) wheat flour.

**맥비**(麥肥) fertilizer for barley farming.

**맥소**(脈所) a pulse point; that part of the wrist or ankle where the pulse can be felt.

**맥시류**(脈翅類) 〖충〗 Neuroptera(학명).

**맥아**(麥芽) malt／~당 maltose; malt sugar.

**맥암**(脈岩) 〖지〗 a dike lock.

**맥없다** (기운이 없다) feel tired; (be) enervated; dispirited; be in low spirits; be in the dumps; feel blue; dejected; feel tired[exhausted].

**맥없이** ①(힘없이) weakly; tiredly; spiritlessly; helplessly; disappointedly; in low spirits／~ 앉아 있다 sit exhausted ②(까닭없이) without much reason; at the slightest push／~ 울다 start crying at the least little thing.

**맥우**(麥雨) rain that falls in the season when barley is ripening.

**맥작**(麥作) cultivation of barley[wheat]; barley growing; barley crop. むぎさく

**맥적다** ①《심심하다》(be) tedious; dull; boring/맥적어하다 be bored; feel ennui ②《낮잡다》(be) put out of countenance/맥적게 되다 lose one's face[one's countenance].

**맥주**(麥酒) beer; ale 《흑맥주》 porter/생~ draught beer; beer on draught/김 빠진 ~ small beer/~를 한 모금 들이키다 take a pull at one's beer. ばくしゅ

**맥줄**(脈一) an artery. みゃくすじ

**맥진**(驀進) a dash; a rush/~하다 rush; dash forward[onward]; charge in[upon]/적을 향하여 ~하다 charge in upon the enemy. ばくしん

**맥추**(麥秋) barley[wheat] harvest season. ばくしゅう

**맥탁**(麥濁) cloudy *sool* of low qualty made from barley.

**맥풀리다**(脈一) ①《기운이 빠지다》lose one's energy[vigo[u]r, vim] ②《낙심하다》be disappointed; lose interest.

**맨**[1] 《오로지》 nothing but; just; full of/못에는 ~ 고기다 The pond is full of fish [swarms with fish].

**맨**[2] 《제일》 the very; the extreme/~ 처음에 at the very first; first of all; at the very beginning/복도 ~ 끝에 있읍니다 It's way down at the end of the hall./~ 왼편 집 a house at the very left. すっきり

**맨-** bare; naked; nothing but; just/~ 머리 a bare head; bareheaded.

**맨꽁무니** without resources; empty-handed/~로 장사를 하려 든다 He is going into business without a cent to back him up. からて

**맨 끝** the very end; the close; the last/~의 last; closing; final/소설을 ~까지 읽다 read a novel through[to the end]. いちばんおわり

**맨 나중** the very last[end]. さいごに

**맨둥맨둥하다** (be) bald; bare/맨둥맨둥한 산 a bald hill; a bare mountain.

**맨 뒤** the very last[end]; the tail [end]. いちばんうしろ

**맨드라미** 《식》 a cockscomb; *Celosia cristata*(학명). けいとう

**맨드리** ①《옷 맵시》 the style of dressing ②《모양새》 shape; form. できばえ

**맨망떨다** act frivolously[capriciously, flightly]. けいそつにこうようする

**맨망스럽다, 맨망하다** (be) imprudent; thoughtless; hasty; light; frivolous. かるがるしい

**맨 머리** a bare head; a hatless head/~ 바람으로 hatless; with a bare head. ぼうしなしのあたま

**맨 먼저** at the very first[beginning]; first of all. いちばんさきに

**맨 몸** ①《알몸》 a naked body; a nude/~으로 in the nude; with nothing on ②《무일푼》 being penniless/~으로 시집가다 be married with no dowry at all. はだか

**맨 몸뚱이** a naked body ⇨맨 몸.

**맨 밑** the very bottom. いちばんした

**맨바닥** the bare floor[ground].

**맨 발** a bare[naked] foot/~의 barefoot[ed]/~로 on barefoot[ed]; barefoot [ed]. すはだし

**맨 밥** boiled-rice served without any side dishes.

**맨 손** an empty[a bare] hand/~으로 with empty[bare] hands/~으로 적과 싸우다 fight the enemy with bare hands [naked fists]. からて

**맨송맨송하다** ①《털이 없다》 be hairless; bald ②《나무가 없다》 be bare; bald; treeless ③《술에 취하지 않다》 (be) unintoxcated; sober. はげている

**맨 아래** the bottom; the lowest/~의 the lowest; the nethermost/봉급은 ~가 10,000원이다 The monthly salary is 10,000 *won* at the lowest. いちばんした

**맨 앞** the head; the van; the foremost; the very front/~의 차 the foremost car/그의 이름이 ~에 나와 있다 His name lead the list.

**맨 위** the top; the summit; the peak 《최고》 the maximum 《최상》 the best/~의 topmost; uppermost; best; highest.

**맨 입** an empty mouth[stomach]/~으로 술을 먹다 drink on an empty stomach. しょくじをしていないくち

**맨 주먹** an empty hand; a bare hand/~으로 empty-handed 《빈 손으로》 with empty hands 《무기 없이》 with naked fists.

**맨 처음** the very first; the earliest; the original/~에 무엇을 할까요 What shall we do first?

**맵다** ①《맛이》 (be) hot; pungent; peppery; sharp; spicy/국이 ~ the soup is hot ②《독하다》 (be) severe; intense; harsh; strict. からい

**맵살스럽다** (be) hateful 밉살스럽다. にくらしい

**맵시** form; figure; appearance; shapeliness; smartness/~ 옷 ~ a style of dressing/그녀는 언제나 ~ 있게 옷을 입는다 She is always smartly dressed. したい

**맵자하다** have a tight[firm, solid] shape [form, figure, look].

**맷돌** a millstone; a hand mill; a grinding stone.

**맷돌 중쇠** the pivot and the gudgeon of a millstone.

**맷돌질** grinding/~하다 grind (*wheat*) into (*flour*).

**맷맷하다** slender; (be) slim 밋밋하다. しんたいがすらっとしている

**맷방석** a round straw-mat which is spread under the millstone.

**맷손** 1《맷돌의》 the handle of a millstone 2《매질의》 the degree of a beating[whipping].

**맷수쇠** the pivot of a millstone.

**맹격(猛擊)** a hard[severe] blow; a violent[fierce] attack; an onslaught/ ~을 가하다 deal (a person) a hard blow.

**맹견(猛犬)** a ferocious[fierce, savage] dog/~ 주의 Beware of the fierce dog!

**맹공격(猛攻擊)** a fierce attack; a violent [murderous] assault; an onslaught/ ~을 가하다 make a vigorous attack an onslaught] on (the enemy).

**맹꽁맹꽁** croaking [of a maenggongi frog]/~하다 croak.

**맹꽁이** ①(초류) a kind of small round frog; *Cacopides tornieri*(학명). ②(바보) an idiot; a moron.

**맹꽁이 자물쇠** a padlock.

**맹근하다** (be) somewhat warm ⇨밍근하다.

**맹금(猛禽)** 〖조〗 a bird of prey; a raptorial bird/~성의 hawk-like; accipitral /~류 rapacious birds; *Raptores*(학명).

**맹눈(盲一)** an illiterate eyes; an ignoramus.

**맹도견(盲導犬)** a seeing-eye dog.

**맹독(猛毒)** a deadly poison.

**맹동(孟冬)** ①(초겨울) early winter ②(음력 시월) October of the lunar calendar.

**맹동(萌動)** germination; budding; quickening; signs of forthcoming activity / ~하다 germinate; bud; start taking shape.

**맹랑하다(孟浪一)** ①(허망하다) (be) false; untrue 《근거없다》groundless; unfounded 《터무니없다》absurd; nonsensical; preposterous; fabulous 《믿을 수 없다》incredible; unbelievable/맹랑한 소문 wild rumors ②(허수롭지 않다) be not negligible; be quite contrary to *one's* expectation.

**맹렬하다(猛烈一)** (be) violent; furious; fierce/비가 맹렬히 퍼붓는다 It rains cats and dogs[in torrents, heavily, hard].

**맹목(盲目)** blindness/~의 blind; sightless/~적으로 blindly; recklessly/~적인 사랑 a blind love.

**맹문** the situation; circumstances; the state of things; details; the matter; the case/~ 모르고 without knowing the case/그는 ~이야 He has no sense.

**맹물** ①(물) water; tasteless water/이것은 술이 아니고 ~이다 This is not wine, it's dishwater. ②《사람》 an insipid person/ 그는 ~이다 He is a dull drink of water.

**맹반격(猛反擊)** ~하다 make a violent counterattack (on).

**맹방(盟邦)** an ally; a confederate; an allied nation.

**맹서(盟誓)** an oath ⇨맹세.

**맹성(猛省)** serious reflection[reconsideration]/ ~하다 reflect seriously on *one*self/~을 촉구하다 urge (a person) to reconsider seriously[to make serious reconsideration].

**맹세** 《신에 대한》 an oath; a vow 《서약》 a pledge 《약속》 a promise/~하다 swear; pledge; vow; make a vow/충성을 ~하다 swear allegiance/~를 지키다 keep *one's* vow.

**맹세지거리** swearing in vulgar language; a profane oath; a curse/~하다 swear profanely; utter curses.

**맹수(猛獸)** a ferocious beast; a fierce animal 《육식수》 a beast of prey/~ 사냥 big game hunting/~ 사냥을 하다 shoot big game.

**맹습(猛襲)** a vigorous[furious, heavy, hot] attack; a violent assault; an onslaught/ ~하다 attack hotly; make a fierce attack; make a vigorous attack on (the enemy).

**맹신(盲信)** credulity; a blind faith/ ~하다 be credulous.

**맹아(盲啞)** the blind and the dumb/ ~교육 education for the blind and the dumb/~학교 a blind and dumb school; an articulation school.

**맹아(萌芽)** ①(발아) germination ②《싹》 a bud; a germ; a sprout.

**맹악(猛惡)** savagery; barbarity; fierceness; ferocity / ~하다 (be) savage; barbarous; fierce; ferocious.

**맹약(盟約)** 《서약》 a pedge; a convanant; a pact 《동맹》 alliance; confederacy; a league/~국(國) a confederate[federal] state/ ~을 맺다 conclude a pact.

**맹연습(猛練習)** rigorous[intensive] practice/ ~하다 do hard training.

**맹위(猛威)** fury; fierceness; violence; ferocity/콜레라가 발생하여 ~를 떨치고 있다 Cholera has broken out and is raging with all its force.

**맹이** the body of a saddle.

**맹인(盲人)** a blind person ⇨소경.

**맹장(盲腸)** 〖해〗 the caecum (pl.-ca); the vermiform; appendix (pl.-dices); the blind gut/~ 수술을 받다 have[undergo] an operation[be operated on] for appendicitis/ ~염 appendicitis; caecitis/ ~염 수술 appendectomy.

**맹장(猛將)** a veteran fighter 《선수》 a champion.

**맹장지(盲障一)** an opaque paper sliding -door.

**맹장질(盲杖一)** a severe flogging[whipping]/~하다 flog severely; administer a hard whipping (to).

**맹점(盲點)** a blind point[spot]/법의 ~ a blind point of law/법의 ~을 이용하다 make an illicit use of law.

**맹종(盲從)** blind obedience[submission] /~하다 follow[obey, submit] (a pers-

**맹주**(盟主) the leader/ ～가 되다 become the leader (of); assume the leadership (of). めいしゅ

**맹진**(猛進) a dash; a drive; a thrust/ ～하다 dash forward; make a dash; make a drive (on). もうしん

**맹추** a stupid person; a fool; a thick-headed person; a blockhead; a dullard; a harebrain. おろかなもの

**맹추**(孟秋) ①《초가을》 early autumn[fall] ②《음력 7월》 July of the lunar calendar. はつあき

**맹춘**(孟春) ①《초봄》 early spring ②《음력 정월》 January of the lunar calendar. もうしゅん

**맹타**(猛打) a hard[severe] blow 《야구》 slugging; a heavy hit/ ～하다 strike [beat] violently; give a heavy hit/ ～자 a slugger; a heavy batter. もうだ

**맹탕** ①《국물》 insipid[tasteless] soup; flavorless soup; unseasoned soup ②《사람》 an empty person; an insipid person; a dull person.

**맹투**(猛鬪) a furious struggle[fight]/ ～하다 fight furiously; engage in hot fighting; make a bold fight. もうれつなたたかい

**맹폭**(盲爆) unscrupulous[blind] bombing/ ～하다 bomb[bombard] blindly. もうばく

**맹폭**(猛爆) heavy bombing[bombardment]; an intensive air-raid/ ～하다 bomb [bombard] heavily; strafe. もうばく

**맹풍**(猛風) a furious wind; a storm; a hurricane; a typhoon. もうふう

**맹하**(孟夏) ①《초여름》 early summer ②《음력 4월》 April of the lunar calendar

**맹한**(猛悍) ferocity and intrepidity/ ～하다 (be) fierce and intrepid. どうもう

**맹호**(猛虎) a ferocious[fierce, wild] tiger.

**맹화**(猛火) raging fire[flames]; conflagration/ ～ 속에 뛰어들다 rush[plunge] into the raging flames. もうか

**맹활동**(猛活動) full activity; active operations/ ～하다 be in full activity[swing]/사회 개혁가로서 ～하다 be actively engaged as a social reformer. もうれつなかつどう

**맹훈련**(猛訓練) intense[hard] training.

**맹휴**(盟休) a strike; a school strike/ ～하다 go on strike; down one's books /학생들이 ～했다 The students went on strike. どうめいきゅうぎょう

**맺다** ①《매듭을》 knot; tie/매듭을 ～ tie a knot; knot ②《결실》 bear; produce/ 열매를 ～ bear fruit; produce a result; be brought to fruition ③《관계를》 form; make; enter into a relation; contract /조약을 ～ conclude[enter into] a treaty/백년 가약을 ～ exchange the vows of marriage ④《완결하다》 finish; end; conclude; close; wind up/연설을 ～ conclude one's speech (with) ⑤《원한을》 harbor; bear; cherish; nurse/원한을 ～ bear a grudge. むすぶ

**맺음말** concluding remarks; conclusion. けつろん

**맺히다** ①《열매가》 come[develop] into fruit[bearing]; fruit; fructify; seed; go to seed/열매가 ～ fruit; be in fruit ②《매듭이》 be tied; be knotted/매듭이 ～ be knotted ③《원한이》 be pent up; be congested/가슴에 맺힌 원한 grudge smoldered in one's heart ④《눈물, 이슬이》 form/눈물이 ～ tears form; have tears.

**맺힌데** a bruised spot 《원한》 a point of rancor.

**머구리** a frog ⇨개구리.

**머귀나무** 〖식〗 a paulownia; Fagara ailanthoides(학명). きりのき

**머금다** ①《입에》 keep[hold] (something) in one's mouth; mouth(음식을)/물을 ～ 금고 with one's mouth full of water ②《마음에》 entertain; harbor; bear in mind; have/악의를 ～ entertain ill feeling ③《눈물을》 have tears in one's eyes ④《웃음을》 have a smile [on one's lips]; wear a smile. ふくむ

**머나멀다** ①《거리가》 (be) very far[long]; distant ②《시간이》 (be) very old; remote; ancient. はるかとおい

**머다랗다** (be) rather far; rather long [distant]/머다란 길 quite a long way.

**머드러기** a big[large] one; a large piece of fruit; a large fish. よりおおきいもの

**머루** 〖식〗 wild grapevines; wild grapes. やまぶどう

**머리** ①《두부》 the head; the pate《속》; the noddle《구》/ ～가 무겁다 one's head feels heavy; head feels heavy in the head ②《두뇌·사고력》 a head; a brain 《지력》intellect; mind/그 일은 ～가 필요하다 The job requires a lot of brains. ③《정신 상태》 mind/그는 ～가 돌았다 He is out of his mind. ④《머리털》 hair / ～를 깎다 have one's hair cut[trimmed] ⑤《꼭대기》 the top[head, point, tip] (of)/기둥 ～ the top of a pillar ⑥《맨 처음》 the beginning/말～ introductory remarks/일 ～ the beginning of a job ⑦《우두머리》 a chief; a leader; a boss/우두～가 되다 become a leader; take the lead. あたま

**머리감다** wash one's hair; have a shampoo. 洗髪する

**머리꾸미개** a hair-ornament.

**머리고덩이** a lock[clump] of one's hair / ～를 잡다 grab (a person) by the hair. かみのもつれ

**머리끝** the ends of one's hair; the crown of the head/ ～에서 발끝까지 from the crown of the head to the tip of the toes. かみのはし

**머리기름** hair oil; pomade.

**머리말** a foreword; an introduction; a preamble; a preface. かんとうのことば

**머리말** one's bedside／~에 at one's bedside; by one's pillow.
**머리쓰개** a headpiece; headgear; headdress; a hood; a kerchief. あたまの飾り物
**머리악쓰다** do one's best; make every possible effort ⇨기쓰다. もがく
**머리얹다** put up one's hair; do one's hair in a chignon 《비유적》 attain womanhood; get married; lose her virginity.
**머리채** a long tress of hair.
**머리 치장**(-治裝) hairdressing; hairdo／~하다 do up one's hair; dress[arrange, fix up] one's hair. かみのそうしょく
**머리카락** a hair [of one's head]／흰 ~ a white hair／~을 뽑다 pull out a hair.
**머리털** the hair on one's head／~이 빠지다 hair falls out[comes off]. とうはつ
**머리통** the bulk of one's head／~이 크다 have a big head. あたまのまわり
**머릿골** 《해》 the brain; brains; gray matter／~ 썩히다 《생각하느라고》 rack[tax] one's brains 《걱정으로》 bother one's brain 《about》; worry oneself 《about》; trouble 《oneself》. のう
**머릿니** head lice; vermin in the hair. かみのしらみ
**머릿방** a small back room.
**머릿살** nerves of the head／~을 앓다 be troubled. あたまのしんけい
**머릿살 아프다** have a headache; (be) troublesome; troubled; annoyed; worried.
**머릿장**(-欌) a single chest of drawers set at the bedside. 枕もとのたんす
**머릿줄** ①《연줄》 a string tied between the two ends of the top pole of a kite ②《부호》 a mark over a word to show a long vowel; a macron.
**머무르다** ①《묵다》 stay／오래 ~ stay long／친구 집에 ~ stay at a friend's house ②《서다》 stop; standstill ③《남아 있다》 remain; stay／현직에 ~ remain in one's present office. とどまる
**머무적거리다** hesitate; waver; wobble; be irresolute[hesitant]; linger; be slow; dawdle／머무적머무적 hesitatingly; waveringly／결단을 못 내리고 ~ be hesitant to make a decision. もじもじする
**머뭇거리다** hesitate ⇨머무적거리다. もじもじする
**머쓱하다** ①《키가 크다》 (be) lanky; spindly; rangy／그는 아주 키가 ~ He is quite a lamppost. ②《기가 죽다》 be in low spirits; dejected.
**머슴** a farm hand; a farmer's man／~애 a boy servant／~을 두다 keep a farm hand.
**머슴살이** serving as a farm hand; working as a farm hand; the life of a farmhand／~하다 work as a farm hand; take service as a farm laborer.
**머시** 《물건》 something 《사람》 somebody／송 ~ 라는 사람 Song somebody／이 ~ 라는 사람 a certain Lee. たれがし
**머위** 《식》 a bog rhubarb; a butterbur; a coltsfoot; *Petasites japonicus*(학명). ふき
**머줍다** (be) dull; slow; sluggish; tardy. にぶくてのろい
**머지다** break fooby itself in the wind.
**머춤하다** [it] stop for a while; break; lull up; let up; hold up／비가 ~ It stops raining for a while／열이 ~ The fever abates. いちじせいしする
**먹** an ink-stick; Chinese ink; Indian ink／~ 한 자루 a cake[stick] of Chinese ink／~을 갈다 rub an ink stick. すみ
**먹감** a persimmon blackend by the sun.
**먹구렁이** 《동》 a blacksnake. くろいおろち
**먹구름** dark clouds; a brewing／~이 하늘을 덮었다 The sky is overspread with dark clouds. こくうん
**먹그림** a colo[u]r picture with the basic groundwork done in black ink.
**먹다**¹ ⇨별항 참조(page 1435).
**먹다**² ①《귀가》 become deaf; lose one's hearing; go deaf; be deafened／시끄러워 귀가 먹겠다 The noise is deafening. ②《대패·톱 따위가》 bite; saw; plane; cut [well]／대패가 잘 먹는다 This tool planes well. ③《씨아·맷돌 따위가》 gin; grind／씨아가 잘 먹는다 gin well; a cotton gin gins well ④《물감이》 dye; be dyed; take colo[u]r 《풀이》 starch; be starched 《잉크 따위가》 spread／이 천은 물감이 잘 먹는다 This cloth dyes well. ⑤《소비하다》 consume; spend; be spent; be consumed／돈이 많이 ~ be costly; be expensive. みみがとおくなる
**먹도미** 《어》 a gilthead; a black porgy.
**먹똥** ①《먹물 찌끼》 dried sediment of Indian[Chinese] ink ②《먹물 자국》 a black ink-spot. くろあと
**먹두루마기** a garment smeared all over with ink. すみいろの周衣
**먹먹하다** have difficulty in hearing; be deafened; stunned. みみがよく聞えない
**먹물** India ink; Chinese ink; inky water／~이 들다 be stained with Chinese ink. ぼくじゅう
**먹병**(一甁) an inkpot; an ink-bottle.
**먹빛** an ink[y] black. すみいろ
**먹사과** 《식》 a kind of melon.
**먹성** appetite; capacity for eating／그는 ~이 좋다 He has a good[large] appetite. しょくよく
**먹실** (실) a string stained with ink 《문신》 tattooing. すみをつけたいと
**먹은금** ①《실비》 actual expense ②《원가》 cost price; prime cost. げんか
**먹을알** a superior gold vein; gold ore of superior quality.
**먹음새** ①《요리 범절》 the manner of cooking ②《식사 범절》 table manners. しょくじのしたど
**먹음직스럽다** (be) delicious looking; appetizing; tempting／이 참외는 ~ This melon looks very tempting.
**먹음직하다** (be) delicious looking ⇨먹음직스럽다. うまそうにみえる

**먹이** food; provisions／말 ~ provisions for horses／~가 떨어지다 run out of provisions／말에게 ~를 건초로 주다 feed a horse with hay.

**먹이다**[1] ①《음식을》 let someone eat[drink]; serve (*a person*) with; entertain (*a person*) with／친구에게 술을 ~ treat a friend to a drink ②《부양·사육하다》 feed; support; keep; provide for; maintain; raise／많은 가족을 먹여 살리다 support a large family ③《뇌물을》 bribe with; offer a bribe; corrupt／선거 민에게 돈을 ~ temper with the voters ④《겁을》 inflict on (*a person*); frighten; terrify; scare; threaten／욕을 ~ let (*a person*) get a scolding ⑤《때리다》 give; administer／한 대 ~ give[deal] a blow／뺨을 한 대 ~ slap (*a person*) on the cheek; give a box on the ear.

**먹이다**[2] ①《물감을》 dye; apply 《풀을》 starch 《초를》 wax 《기름을》 oil／머리에 물을 ~ dye one's hair ②《씨아에 솜을》 feed; gin; put in／씨아에 솜을 ~ feed a gin with cotton; feed cotton to a gin ③ 《돈을》 spend; put [money] in ④《연장에 재료를》 feed [a hay cutter] with [hay]. ⑤《돈을 들이다》 put [money] inispend [money on furniture].

**먹자** a carpenter's square for drawing ink lines.

**먹자판** a scene of riotous eating; a big feast; eating what there is. ほうとうせいかつ

**먹장** an ink-stick; a piece[stick] of Chinese ink／~구름 a very black cloud; an inky cloud.

**먹줄** an inking line; an inked string／~을 대다 stretch out an inking line.

**먹칠**(一漆) smearing with ink／~하다 smear with ink.

**먹칼** a carpenter's inking spatula. すみさし

**먹통**(一桶) 《목수의》 an ink-pad case 《먹 담는》 a kind of inkwell 《바보》 a fool.

**먹투성이** a person[thing] smeared all over with ink／~가 되다 be covered [be all stained] with ink. 墨だらけ

**먹히다** ①《먹음을 당하다》 be eaten [up]; get eaten; be swallowed(gulped); be devoured; be consumed／개구리가 뱀에 게 ~ A frog is eaten by a snake. ② 《빼앗기다》 be cheated of; be taken for; lose／…에게 돈을 ~ be cheated of money by (*a person*) ③《돈이》 be spent; be put in; cost. たべられる

**먼길** a long way[journey, distance]／ ~을 가다 make a long journey.

**먼나라** a faraway[distant] country; a far-off land.

**먼눈** ①《소경의》 a blind eye ②《먼 곳을 보는》 a far-off[faraway] look in one's eyes／~을 팔다 have a faraway look in one's eyes. めくら

**먼데** ①《먼 곳》 a far-off place; a distant place; a distance／~로 가다 go faraway ②《변소》 a toilet. はばかり

**먼동** the dawning eastern sky／~이 틀 무렵 출발했다 I started at the first gray of dawn. よあけのそら

**먼발치기** a distant place／그것은 ~서 보 아야 곱다 It looks to advantage at a distance.

**먼빛** a distant view; a spot far-off／~ 으로 보다 view from a distance.

**먼산**(一山) a distant mountain.

**먼일** the future; future[coming] events ／~을 예상하다 anticipate what is to come. とおいさきのこと

**먼저** ①《순위》 first; ahead; first of all; above all; before anything else／~ 가 겠읍니다 Please excuse my going first. ／~ 가십시오 Please go first. ②《이전에》 ago; previously; before; formerly; recently 《미리》 in advance; beforehand ／~ 말한 바와 같이 as previously stated ／돈을 ~ 치르다 pay in advance. さきに

**먼저께** the other day; sometime ago. せんじつ

**먼지** dust; a mote／~를 가라앉히다 lay dust／그 책상은 ~투성이다 The desk is covered with dust. ほこり

**먼지떨이** ①《살그머니 때림》 giving a slight rod; flogging (*a boy*) only for form's sake ②《오랜만의 나들이》 going out after keeping the house for a long while. ほこりはらい

**먼촌** ①《일가·친척》 a distant relative ② 《촌락》 distant village.

**멀거니** absent-minded[ly]; blank[ly]; vacant[ly]; with a blank[far-off] look ／그녀는 ~ 그를 보았다 She turned bemused eyes toward him.

**멀건이** an absent-minded person. あたまのわるいひと

**멀겋다** (be) light; thin; washy; dilute ／국을 멀겋게 만들다 dilute the broth／ 멀건 우유 washy milk. ややすんでいる

**멀게지다** clear a bit; go from dark to dull; become paler[clearer]. きはくだ

**멀구슬나무** 《식》 a bead-tree; a bastard cedar; *Melia japonica*《학명》.

**멀끄러미** [looking] vacantly ⇒물끄러미.

**멀끔하다** (be) clean ⇒말끔하다. きれいだ じっと

**멀다**[1] ①《눈이》 go blind; be blind 《총칭》 the blind／돈에 눈이 ~ be blinded by money ②《귀가》 be hard of hearing／ 귀가 ~ be hard[slow, dull] of hearing.

**멀다**[2] ①《거리가》 (be) far; distant／갈 길이 ~ have a long way to go ②《시간이》 (be) remote／먼 옛날 a long time ago; remote antiquity／머지않아 soon; before long; in the near future ③《관계가》 (be) distant／안 보면 멀어진다 Out of sight, out of mind. とおい

**멀떠구니** 《새의》 the craw; the crop; a maw. 食類のしょうかき

**멀뚱멀뚱** with a blank look; with bem-

멀리¹ far; far away[off]; a long way off; in the distance; afar/~ 여행하다 travel far. とおく
멀리² ~하다 keep (*a person*) away from; keep (*a person*) at a distance 《피하다》 avoid/사람을 ~하다 keep (*a person*) at arm's length.

멀미 ①《배·수레의》 sickness 《배》 seasickness 《비행기》 airsickness 《차》 carsickness/ ~하다 feel sick/나는 배 ~ 해 본 일이 없다 I have never been seasick in my life. ②《싫증》 an aversion;

---

# 먹 다¹

①《음식을》 eat; take; have/한입에 ~ eat at a mouthful; wolf it [down]/먹고 달아나다 run away without paying for *one's* food; bilk (*a restaurant*)./사흘 동안 아무 것도 먹지 않았다 He had taken no food for three days./아침을 일찍 먹었다 We took an early breakfast./그는 여섯 시경에 저녁을 먹는다 He takes dinner about six./조반을 ~ eat breakfast/밥을 ~ eat rice; eat; take [have] *one's* meal; manage to live; get along/배불리 ~ eat[have] *one's* fill; have a square meal; fill *one*self up; eat to *one's* heart's content/알맞게 ~ eat in moderation/먹을 수 있다 be edible; be eatable; be good to eat/아무거나 마음대로 집어 먹어라 Help yourself to anything you like on the table./이리 와, 잡아 먹지 않을 테니까 Come here, I won't bite you./참 잘 먹었읍니다 I've had enough, thank you./먹는 개도 아니 때린다《속담》 Refrain from beating or scolding a person while he is at his meal./먹지 않는 ون 투기 없는 아내《속담》 Don't expect too much [the impossible] of human nature./뱀은 개구리나 쥐를 먹는다 The snake lives on frogs, mice and rats.

②《먹고 살다》 live on; feed on; subsist on; live; subsist; live by; make a living; earn *one's* living; exist on/먹고 살기가 어렵다 find it hard to make *one's* living/먹기에 걱정 없다 have enough to live on; be well off/이럭저럭 먹고 살아가다 manage to live; keep body and soul together; make a scanty living; live by hook[crook]; manage to keep *one*self afloat/먹기 위해서 일한다 We work for bread./철학으로는 먹고 살 수 없다 Philosophy does not bake bread./무엇을 해서 먹고 지내나 What do you do for a living?/그는 빌어먹고 있다 He subsist entirely by begging./혼자서 먹고 살기가 빠듯하다 It's all I can do to feed myself.

③《담배·물 따위를》 smoke; drink/담배를 ~ smoke; smoke cigarettes/물을 ~ drink water/우물물을 ~ drink [water] from a well/술을 ~ drink [liquor]/약을 ~ take medicine/[유아가] 젖을 ~ suck [it's mother's] milk.

④《마음을》 fix; set; make/ 마음을 ~ make up *one's* mind; put *one's* heart (*into*); set[keep] *one's* mind (*on*); take special care; exercise great care; have a [broad, narrow] mind/그는 가려고 마음먹었다 He made up his mind to go./화가가 되려고 마음~ determine on becoming a painter.

⑤《남의 재물 따위를》 take; seize; appropriate; devour; swallow up; make (*it*) *one's* own unjustly[illegally]; cheat out of/뇌물을 ~ take[accept] a bribe; graft《미·구》/남의 재물을 ~ take another's property/공금을 ~ embezzle [misuse] public funds/그는 내 돈 천원을 먹었다 He cheated me out of one thousand *won*.

⑥《벌레 따위가》 eat into; be worm-eaten; be moth-eaten; be decayed/벌레가 있을 ~ Worms nibble green leaves./옷에 좀이 ~ a garment is moth-eaten./벌레먹은 이 a decayed tooth.

⑦《이문·구문 따위를》 get; receive; have/구문을 ~ get a commission[fee]/이익의 2할을 ~ get a 20% out of the profit.

⑧《나이를》 grow old[er]; get [years of age]; acquire [age]/나이를 ~ get older; acquire years/ …보다 세 살 더 ~ be three years older than…/나이먹은 사람 a man of years; an old man/보기보다는 나이를 먹지 않았다 be not so old as *one* looks.

⑨《욕·겁을》 get; undergo; suffer; catch/욕을 ~ get a scolding; catch it《구》; be abused[reviled; insulted]/겁을 ~ get scared; be intimidated/겁을 먹고 소리지르다 shriek in fear.

⑩《맞다》¶한 대 ~ be given a blow.

⑪《상금·판돈 따위를》 win[take] [the prize, wager].

⑫《더위를》 be affected by the heat; suffer from hot weather; be ill from the heat.

⑬《해치다》 put[cast] a slur; hurt; harm; injure/나를 잡아 먹으려고 온갖 중상을 다 한다 He resorts to all sorts of slander to hurt me.

**멀쑥하다** dislike; disgust; tiresomeness/그 일에는 아주 ~가 난다 I am about tired of that business., I am beginning to get fed up with the work.

**멀쑥하다** (be) lank; tall and slender.

**멀어지다** ①《관계가》be alienated (from); become estranged (from)/사이가 서로 ~ be[become] estranged each other ②《거리가》become more distant; go[get] away (from) ③《소리가》die away; grow faint/기적 소리가 멀어졌다 The whiles died away.

**멀쩡하다** ①《온전하다》(be) whole; complete; intact; sound; be free from damage/정신이 ~ have a clear mind ②《가식》(be) hypocritical; pretending; dissembling/멀쩡한 거짓말 a hypocritical lie.

**멀찌막하다** (be) pretty far; rather distant; be some distance away[apart]/정거장은 ~ The station is pretty far.

**멀찍멀찍** far apart; at distant intervals (between); at a good distance/~ 멀어져 앉다 take seats some distance apart.

**멀찍이** at a distant; far away; afar/그는 마을에서 ~ 멀어진 곳에 살고 있다 He lives in a secluded spot.

**멀찍하다** (be) pretty far; rather distant; be some distance away[apart].

**멈추다** stop; cease; put a stop to; bring to a stop[halt]; halt/차를 ~ stop a car; bring a car to a halt.

**멈칫** ~하다 stop suddenly; come to a sudden halt; flinch/하던 말을 ~하다 suddenly stop talking for a moment.

**멈칫거리다** hesitate; vacillate; dawdle/대답을 ~ be slow to answer/멈칫멈칫 hesitatingly.

**멋** ①《세련된 몸매》smartness; stylishness《맵시》foppery; dandyism; dudism/~ 있는 모자 a fanciful hat/~있는 be stylish; smart ②《풍취》taste; charm; elegance/그녀의 옷차림은 ~있다 Her dress is in good taste. ③《이유·원인》reason; cause; ground; the case/~도 모르고 달려들다 try to go at somebody [something] without knowing anything about him[it].

**멋거리** dandification; foppishness; foppery/~지다 be foppish; be dandified.

**멋내다** primp; prink; deck up; smarten oneself up; be in full feather.

**멋대로** in one's own way; willfully; waywardly; selfishly/~ 굴다 act at one's pleasure/~ 해라 do in your own way.

**멋들다** get interesting; take on flavo[u]r[charm]; be beautiful; be captivating.

**멋들어지다** (be) nice; glorious; grand; smart; stylish/멋들어지게 smartly; nicely 《능난히》 skillfully 《거뜬히》 successfully.

**멋부리다** spruce up; smarten[prettify, fancy, liven up].

**멋없다** (be) not smart; not stylish; unpolished; tasteless.

**멋장이** a dandy《남자》a fop《여자》a stylish woman.

**멋적다** ①《멋없다》lack flavor ⇨멋있다 ②《불쾌하다》(be) unpleasant; distasteful/멋적은 말 작작해라 Away with your distasteful remarks. ③《어색하다》feel embarrassed[awkward]; feel uncomfortable; feel small; be confused/또 부탁하기가 ~ I am embarrassed to ask a further favo[u]r.

**멋지다** be full of beauty《grace,fun》; (be) splendid; smart; fascinating/멋지게 춤추다 dance beautifully; dance with gusto.

**멋질리다** become dandified; get foppish; take to vanity.

**멍** ①《뻗친 피》a bruise; a contusion/눈에 ~이 들다 have[get] a black eye/~이 들게 때리다 beat (a person) black and blue ②《타격》a hit; a shock; damage; a real snag/사랑에 가슴이 ~들다 be lovesick; be lovelorn; languish for love.

**멍구럭** a large loose-knit straw net.

**멍들다** ①《피멍히다》have[suffer] a bruise; be bruised; have[suffer] an internal injury ②《일이》suffer a serious hitch [setback]; run into a real snag.

**멍멍**《개가》bowwow/~ 짖다 go[bark] bowwow; bark.

**멍석** a straw mat/~ 자리 a straw mat seat.

**멍석딸기**【식】the white-flowering raspberry; Rubus triphyllus《학명》.

**멍에** a yoke/소에게 ~를 메우다 put a yoke on an ox; yoke an ox/~를 벗다 cast[throw] off a yoke.

**멍엣줄**【인】the borderline of a printed page.

**멍울**《굳은 덩이》a lump《염증》an inflammation.

**멍울멍울** every lump; in a lump/~하다 (be) lumpy.

**멍청이** a stupid[thick-headed] person; a dullard; a dunce; a fool; a silly fellow; a simpleton; an ass.

**멍청하다** (be) stupid; dull; dumb; thick-headed; stolid slow-[dull-]witted/멍청한 사람 a stupid person/멍청한 짓을 하다 do a stupid thing; make an ass of oneself.

**멍추** a stupid person; a fool; a forgetful person; a weak-minded person.

**멍텅구리** ①【어】a sea fish; Aptocyclus ventricosus《학명》②《사람》a stupid pers-

**멍하니** absently; absent-mindedly; vacantly; blankly; with an air of abstraction/~ 경치를 바라보다 look absently at the landscape.

**멍하다** (be) abstracted; absent-minded; vacant; blank; dazed; woolgathering 《상심해서》 stunned; stupefied/멍한 얼굴을 하고 쳐다보다 gazé at (a thing) vacantly. ぼかんとしている

**메¹** 《제사밥》 rice offered to the gods[to departed spirits]. おそなえのめし

**메²** 《메꽃 뿌리》 the root of a bindweed [convolvulus]/ ~나물 seasoned roots of bindweed. ひるがおのね

**메³** 《방망이》 a hammer(철제); a mallet(목재); 《대장간의》 a sledge-hammer; a maul(큰 것)/~로 치다 strike[beat] with a hammer. つち

**메⁴** 《산》 a mountain; a hill. やま

**메-** 《차지지 않은》 nonglutinous; not sticky/~조 nonglutinous millet.
ねんちゃくせいのないものを表わすかたる

**메공이** a hammer-shaped pounder[pestle]. つきぎね

**메꽃** a convolvulus; a bindweed; the flower of convolvulus; Calystegia japonica(학명). ひるがおのはな

**메꽂다** ①《심술궂다》 cross-grained; cantankerous ②《고집세다》 (be) stubborn; headstrong. いじがわるい

**메귀리** 【식】 wild oats; Avena fatua(학명).

**메기** 【어】 a catfish; a wels; a sheatfish; a horned pout. なまづ

**메기다¹** fix [an arrow in one's bow]; put [an arrow on the string]. はめる

**메기다²** ①《소리를》 lead (a song, chant) ②《톱을》 take the lead on a two-man saw.

**메기입** a big long mouth; a catfish-like mouth. なまづくちのようなくち

**메기장** nonglutinous [India] millet.

**메다¹** 《어깨에》 shoulder; carry[bear] (a thing) on the shoulder/나는 무거운 짐을 멘 사람을 봤다 I saw a man carrying a burden on his shoulder. になう

**메다²** be stopped up; be[get] blocked; get clogged; be choked; be closed/목이 ~ one's throat is choked/굴뚝이 ~ a chimney is foul[choked up]. ふさがる

**메딱다구리** 【조】 a Korean black-naped green woodpecker; Picus canus jessoensis (학명).

**메떡** cakes made from nonglutinous grain. うるもち

**메떨어지다** (be) rustic; boorish; crude; unrefined; awkward (in one's actions); stiff[-mannered]. いなかくさい

**메뚜기** 【충】 a grasshopper 《벼메뚜기》 a locust. いなご

**메드다** (be) slow; tardy; sluggish; slow-moving/모든 일에 ~ He is slow-moving. のろい

**메마르다** (be) very dry; parched; arid; sterile; barren; waste 《마음이》 (be) severe; harsh/메마른 땅을 개간하다 open[develop] waste land. ふもうである

**메밀** buckwheat/~ 가루 buckwheat flour/ ~ 국수 buckwheat noodles/ ~밥 boiled buckwheat/ ~묵 buckwheat paste[jelly]. そば

**메벼** nonglutinous rice plants.

**메부수수하다** (be) boorish; rustic; countrified-looking/메부수수한 계집아이 a boorish girl. やぼだ

**메숲지다** (be) thick; luxuriant dense: bushy/메숲진 숲 a dense forest.
やまにきが茂っている

**메스껍다** ①《구역나다》 feel nausea; feel like vomiting; feel sick[queasy]/속이 ~ feel sick at the stomach ②《아주 불쾌하다》 (be) sickening; stomach-turning; nauseating; revolting; abominable; disgusting/메스껍게 굴다 act[behave] disgustingly/그의 잘난 체하는 꼴만 보면 ~ I am nauseated with his affectation. はきけがする

**메슥거리다** feel like throwing up[vomiting]; feel sick to one's stomach. むかつく

**메슥메슥** ~하다 feel sick [at the stomach]; feel like vomiting. むかむか

**메아리** an echo/~가 울리다 echo; resound; reverberate; be echoed. こだま

**메어붙이다** throw a person over his shoulder.

**메어치다** throw (a person) over one's shoulder; throw (a person) to the ground 《유도 따위에서》 buttock.

**메역취** 【식】 a goldenrod; Solidago virgaurea(학명).

**메우다¹** ①《빈 곳을》 fill up[in]; plug [up]; inlay (with)/여백을 ~ fill in a blank [space] ②《결손을》 fill up; make up for /결손을 ~ make up a deficit. みたす

**메우다²** 《통 따위의 테를》 put a hoop (on a tub) 《북통에 가죽을》 put a drumskin (on a drum) 《쳇바퀴에 쳇불을》 fix a sievenet (on its frame) 《짐 따위를 사람에게》 make (a person) carry [a burden on his shoulder]/세금을 ~ impose a tax; tax 《소에게 멍에를》 yoke [an ox]; put a yoke [on an ox]. たがのわをかける

**메이다** ①《테를》 make (a person) put a hoop on a tub ②《북을》 make (a person) put a drumskin on a drum ③《체를》 have (a person) fix a sieve net on its frame.

**메조** 【식】 nonglutinous[regular] millet.

**메주** a ball of bean paste/~콩 soybeans for making malt.

**메지¹** the conclusion of a job; the end of work; settling/일을 ~ 내다 bring a job to a conclusion; settle. だんらく

**메지²** 【전】 a seam of joint; a juncture.

**메지다** not be sticky; (be) nonglutinous /메진 쌀 nonglutinous rice.
ねんちゃくせいがない

**메지메지** [dividing something up] port-

**메질** hammering/~하다 hammer; strike with a mallet; pound [stones for road-making]. 槌打つこと
**메추라기** 《조》 a quail/ ~ 떼 a bevy of quails. うずら
**메키하다** ①(곰팡내 나다) (be) musty; moldy; fusty; frowzy/메키한 빵 moldy bread/방이 ~ A room is musty. ②(연기 냄새가) (be) smoky/부엌이 ~ A kitchen is smoky. かびくさい
**메탕(-湯)** 《국》 broth; soup (제사 때 쓰는) vegetable[kelp] soup offered in a memorial service to one's ancestors.
**멜대** a carrying pole/물건을 ~로 메다 carry (a thing) on a pole. しるもの
**멜빵** a rope[string] for shouldering; a sling (총의) a shoulder belt 《양복 바지의》 braces; suspenders.
**멥쌀** nonglutinous rice. うるち
**멥새** 《조》 a meadow bunting; Emberiza cioides castaneiceps(학명).
**멧갓** a reserved forest; a forest reserve.
**멧괴새끼** a wild fellow; a rough; a rowdy; a madcap《속》. やまねこ
**멧나물** edible mountain herbs; wild vegetables. さんさい
**멧누에** 《충》 a tussah; a wild silkworm; Antheraea pernyi(학명)/~ 고치 tussah cocoons/~나비 a tussah moth.
**멧닭** 《조》 a black grouse[cock]; Lyrurus tetrix(학명).
**멧돼지** a wild boar. いのしし
**멧두릅** 《식》 a spikenard; Aralia cordata(학명). かんしょう
**멧미나리** 《식》 Ostericum sieboldii(학명).
**멧부리** a peak; a summit; the top of a mountain. さんちょう
**멧부엉이** ①《조》 a mountain screech owl ②(사람) a rustic; countryman; a bumpkin; a boor. やまふくろう
**멧새** ①(산새) a mountain bird ②(멥새) a meadow bunting. ほおじろ
**멧종다리** 《조》 a Chinese mountain hedge sparrow; Prunella montanella pallas(학명).
**멧짐승** mountain animals.
**며** and/ 개~ 고양이~ 기타 여러 동물이 dogs, cats and many other animals. ―やら, ―や
**며** ①(어미) and; or/비가 오~ 말~ 하다 rain off and on ②(면서) while; as; over; during; with/술을 마시~ 얘기하다 talk over a bottle of wine. ―(し)て
**며느리** a daughter-in-law/ ~를 보다 get a wife for one's son. よめ
**며느리발톱** a spur; a calcar.
**며래** 《식》 a kind of nettle; Nanocnide japonica(학명).
**며루** 《충》 the larva of a crane fly[mosquito].
**며칠날** what day [of the month]/오늘이 ~인가 What day of the month is it today?. いくにち
**며칠** (시일) what day [of the month] (일수) how many days; how long/오늘은 ~입니까 What day of the month is this. いくにち
**멱¹** (목) a throat; a gullet/ ~을 그러잡다 grasp (a person) by his throat[neck]. のど
**멱²** (목욕) bathing; a cold bath/ ~감다 bathe; have[take] a cold bath/냇가로 ~감으러 가다 go to the river for a bath. わかめ
**멱³** (멱서리) a bag knitted of straw; a straw-bag. わら製のこくもついれ
**멱(冪)** 《수》 power/ ~수 an exponent /3승 멱 the third power. べき
**멱둥구미** a straw basket; a deep round grain basket woven of straw.
**멱미래** dewlap [beef]. うしのあごしたのにく
**멱부리** a chicken with feathery wattles.
**멱부지(一不知)** a chess player who does not know the rules of the game.
**멱살** throat (웃깃) a collar/그의 ~을 잡다 grab him by the throat. えりくび
**멱서리** a straw bag; a bag knitted of straw.
**멱씨름** handgrip; grips; a grapple/ ~하다 come to grips [with each other]. 頸のつかみあい
**멱신** woven shoes [of straw or hemp].
**멱통** the throat. 生きたどうぶつののど
**-면** if; in case (of); provided[supposing] that/시간이 있으시~ if you have time. ―たら. なら. れば
**면(面)¹** ①(얼굴) a face ②(체면) prestige; dignity; honor; reputation ③(표면) the surface; a side; a face/지구의 ~ the surface of the earth ④(방면) an aspect; a phase; a side; a field/어느 ~에서 보든지 in every respect/재정~에서 in finanical aspect ⑤(가면) a mask (검도의) a face guard/~을 벗다 take[throw] off one's mask ⑥(지면) a page/사회~ the society page/일~ the front page. かお
**면(面)²** (행정 구역) a township; a myon [a subdivision of a goon(county)]. めん
**면(綿)** cotton/ ~과 모의 교직 cotton-wool mixture; half wool. わた
**면경(面鏡)** a hand mirror; a small looking glass.
**면계(面界)** the border[boundary] of a township. めんのきょうかい
**면관(免官)** dismissal from office/의원 ~ dismissal at one's own request/징계 ~ disciplinary dismissal. めんかん
**면괴(面愧)** shamefacedness; abashment; shame/~하다 be shamefaced; be ashamed; be abashed.
**면구(面灸)** shamefacedness ⇒면괴/ ~스럽다 (be) shamefaced; abashed; feel awkward[embarrassed]. つらよごし
**면궁(免窮)** emergence/~하다 emerge from poverty; extricate oneself from p-

auperism. ひんきゅうをまぬかれること
**면급**(免急) escaping a danger[crisis, harm]/ ~하다 escape a danger[crisis]; get out of harm's way; stave off a crisis. きゅうをまぬかれること
**면급**(面給) spot delivery/ ~하다 deliver on the spot; hand [over] directly to (a person); deliver in the presence of a recipient. ちょくせつあたえること
**면나다**(面—) save *one's* face; get credit (for)/그렇게 하면 나도 면난다 That will save my face. かおがたつ
**면난**(面赧) a blush/ ~하다 blush (with *shame*); color up; be shamefaced; become red in *one's* face.
**면내다** ①(흙을 파다) dig out; gnaw; nibble/쥐가 벽에 ~ A rat makes a hole in a mud wall. ②(도둑질하다) steal bit by bit; filch[pilfer] bit by bit/쌀에 ~ steal rice little by little.
**면내다**(面—) save *one's* face; win honor; bring honor to/남을 면내 주다 keep (a person) in countenance. かおをたてる
**면담**(面談) an interview; a talk; personal conversation/ ~하다 have an interview (*with*); talk personally (*with*). めんだん
**면대**(面對) facing/ ~하다 face each other; meet[come] face to face/ ~하여 욕을 퍼붓다 abuse (a person) to his face. たいめん
**면도**(面刀) shaving/ ~하다 shave *oneself*; get a shave; get *oneself* shaved/나는 어제 ~했다 I shaved myself yesterday/ ~날 a razor blade.
**면도칼**(面刀—) a razor/ ~을 갈다 sharpen a razor; whet a razor; strap a razor.
**면려**(勉勵) ①(스스로) diligence; industry; assiduity/ ~하다 be industrious; be diligent; work hard ②(남을) encouragement; excitation/ ~하다 stimulate; urge; encourage. べんれい
**면류**(麵類) noodles.
**면류관**(冕旒冠) the imperial crown; a diadem. ていおうのせいふくのかん
**면리**(面吏) a township[*myon*] official.
**면마**(面痲) a pockmark; a pit. あばた
**면면**(面面) 《방면》 all[various] sides 《각기》 all faces; each one; every one. めんめん
**면면**(綿綿) ~하다 be continuous; endless; unbroken/면면히 끊이지 않다 be unceasing; be unending. れんめんと
**면모**(面毛) downy hair on the face; face fuzz.
**면모**(面貌) 《얼굴의》 countenance; looks; features 《일의》 aspect. めんぼう
**면목**(面目) ①《체면》 face; countenance; honor; dignity/신사의 ~ a gentleman's honor/ ~이 없다 be ashamed [of *oneself*]; be put out of countenance ②《양상》 appearance; an aspect/ ~을 일신하다 take on quite a new aspect; change the appearance[entire aspect];

undergo a renewal. めんもく
**면목 부지**(面目不知) ~하다 be unknown to one; be a total stranger; do not know the face.
**면밀**(綿密) minuteness; carefulness/ ~하다 (be) minute; careful; scrupulous/ ~한 조사의 결과 as a result of close investigation. めんみつ
**면바르다**(面—) (be) smooth; clean-cut; well-formed; nice and neat; shipshape /그는 면바르게 생긴 젊은이다 He is a nice-looking[clean-cut] young man. がいめんかなめらかだ
**면박**(面駁) personal reproof; refutation to (a person's) face/ ~하다 refute to face. かおとむかってののしること
**면벽**(面壁) 《종》 meditation facing the wall.
**면병**(麨餠) 《종》 the bread used in the Sacrament of the Lord's Supper.
**면보다**(面—) save appearances; put up a good front.
**면부**(面部) the face. かおのいちぶ
**면부득**(免不得) ~하다 (be) inescapable; unescapable; inevitable; unavoidable; ineluctable/그것은 ~이다 It cannot be helped. まぬかれることができないこと
**면분**(面分) a causal acquaintance; knowing by sight/ ~이 있다 know by sight; be on nodding terms. めんしき
**면사**(綿絲) cotton yarn[thread]. めんし
**면사**(面謝) ①《사과》 personal apology ②《치사》 personal thanks/ ~하다 thank personally. めんしゃ
**면사**(免死) escape from death/ ~하다 escape death. しをまぬかれること
**면사무소**(面事務所) the administrative office of a township[*myon*]. めんじむしょ
**면사포**(面紗布) a wedding veil; a bridal veil; a face veil. ベイール
**면상**(面上) (*in*) *one's* face/ ~에 미소를 띠고 with a smile on *one's* face. かお
**면상**(面相) looks; features; a countenance 《관상》 physiognomy/ ~이 좋지 않은 사람 an ill-looking person. めんそう
**면새**(面—) ①《표면》 the surface; appearance ②《체면》 honor; prestige.
**-면서** ①《불구하고》 though; yet; notwithstanding; in spite of; for[with] all /나쁜 줄 알~ 그는 거짓말을 했다 He told a lie though he knew it was wrong. ②《동시에》 as; while; at the same time that; with; between/걸으~ 책을 읽다 read a book as one walks. —ながら
**면서기**(面書記) a clerk of the administrative office of a *myon*. めんしょき
**면세**(免稅) exemption from taxation; tax exemption; immunity from taxes / ~되다 be exempted from taxation / ~ 수입품 duty-free imports; free goods. めんぜい
**면소**(免訴) dismissal (of a case); acquittal/ ~하다 dismiss (a case)/그는 증거 불충분으로 ~되었다 He was acquitted for

lack of evidence. めんそ

**면솔**(面―) a small brush for side burns [side-whiskers].

**면수**(免囚) a discharged convict[prisoner]; a released prisoner[criminal]／～보호 protection of discharged prisoners. めんしゅう

**면숙**(面熟) familiarity[acquaintance] with (a person)／～하다 be familiar[acquainted] with (a person); know.

**면시**(免試) exemption from an examination／～하다 be exempted from an examination. しけんをめんじょすること

**면식**(面識) acquaintance／～이 있는 사람 an acquaintance／그는 ～이 전혀 없다 He is quite a stranger to me. めんしき

**면식**(眠食) sleeping and eating; food and sleep. しんしょく

**면양**(緬羊) 〖동〗 a sheep (pl. sheep); a wool sheep. めんよう

**면업**(綿業) the cotton industry.

**면역**(免疫) 〖의〗 immunity／～하다 render immune; confer immunity／그들의 욕에 ～이 되었다 I am impervious to their abuse.／～자 an immune／～성 immunity. めんえき

**면역**(免役). 《노역의》 exemption from public labo[u]r 《병역의》 exemption from military service; immunity for conscription 《죄수의》 discharge[release] from penal servitude[prison]. めんえき

**면욕**(面辱) a personal humiliation; a personal insult[offence]／～하다 humiliate[insult, offend] (a person) to his face.

**면욕**(免辱) escaping a humiliation[shame]／～하다 escape a humiliation[shame]. ちじょくをまぬかれること

**면우**(面友) a mere acquaintance; a seeming friend. めんゆう

**면의회**(面議會) a *myon* council.

**면작**(棉作) cotton culture; cultivation of cotton 《수확》 cotton harvest[crop]. わたののうさく

**면장**(免狀) a license ⇨면허장. めんきょじょう

**면장**(面長) the chief magistrate of a *myon*.

**면적**(面積) area 《건물의》 floor space／그 도시의 ～은 10 평방 마일이다 The city covers ten square miles. めんせき

**면전**(面前) (a person's) presence／～에서 in the presence of. めんぜん

**면전**(面傳) direct delivery[report]／～하다 deliver directly; report directly.

**면접**(面接) an interview; a personal interview／～하다 see; receive; interview; have an interview／～ 시험치다 undergo an oral test; undergo a personal interview. めんせつ

**면정**(面情) friendship; amity.

**면제**(免除) exemption／～하다 exempt (*from*); remit／입학금 ～ exemption of the entrance fee. めんじょ

**면제품**(綿製品) cotton goods. めんじょひん

**면조**(免租) exemption from a land tax／～하다 exempt land from taxation／～지 land exempted from taxation; tax-[duty-]free land. めんそ

**면종**(面從) eyeservice／～하다 obey (a person) only in his presence; be obedient to (a person) only before his eyes. めんじゅう

**면종**(面腫) a furuncle[boil] on the face.

**면죄**(免罪) 〖법〗 acquittal; exoneration 《종교》 remission of sin／～하다 acquit／～부 an indulgence. めんざい

**면주**(麪酒) 〖종〗 the bread and wine used in the Sacrament of the Lord's Supper.

**면지**(面紙) 〖인〗 end paper; end leaf; the inside of a book cover.

**면직**(免職) removal[dismissal] from office; deprivation of office; discharge／～하다 dismiss (one) from office; relieve (one) of his post. めんしょく

**면직물**(綿織物) cotton fabrics[textiles, cloth]; cotton piece goods／～ 업자 cotton weavers. おりもの

**면진**(面陳) a direct statement; a direct [face-to-face] verbal report／～하다 make a direct[face-to-face] report; report directly.

**면질**(面叱) personal rebuke[scolding, reproof]／～하다 rebuke[reprove, reprimand] (a person) to his face. めんせき

**면질**(面質) confrontation; face-to-face questioning[controversy]／～하다 confront; question face-to-face. たいざしてろんずること

**면책**(面責) personal reproof／～하다 reprove (a person) to his face; cast a reproach in one's teeth. めんせき

**면책**(免責) exemption from responsibility[obligation]／～ 조항 an exemption [escape] clause. めんせき

**면청**(面請) a personal request; a direct demand; personal application／～하다 ask for (a thing) direct; request in person. たいめんしてねがうこと

**면추**(免醜) barely escaping ugliness／～하다 barely escape ugliness; be not quite ugly; be free from ugliness. かおがみにくいのをまぬかれること

**면치다**(面―) trim the surface (of a board).

**면치레**(面―) saving appearances; saving one's face／～하다 save one's face; save[keep up] appearances. そとうざり

**면탁**(面託) personal request; asking a favor in person／～하다 request (one to do) personally; ask a favor in person. たいめんしていらいすること

**면탈**(免脫) escape from punishment; acquittal of a charge; exoneration／～하다 escape punishment; be exonerated. めんざい

**면파**(面破) a personal cancellation; brea-

**면포(綿布)** cotton [cloth]; cotton stuff [tissue]／～류 cotton piece goods／～상 a dealer in cotton goods. めんぷ

**면포(麪麭)** bread.

**면품(面稟)** a personal report (to *a superior*)／～하다 report in person (to *a superior*).

**면피(面皮)** face skin; countenance／철~ brazen facedness; shamelessness; impudence; cheek《속》.

**면하다(免—)** ①(회피하다) escape; avoid／책임을 ~ shirk one's responsibility ②《면제하다》be exempted[exempt] (*from*)／병역 의무를 ~ be exempted from military duty. まぬかれる

**면하다(面—)** face (*towards, to*); front; look on; look out on[into]／그 집은 바다에 면하고 있다 The house fronts[faces] the sea. きんせつする

**면학(勉學)** study; pursuit of knowledge／～하다 study; pursue one's studies／～을 위해서 for study. べんがく

**면허(免許)** permission; license ／～하다 permit; license／～를 얻다 obtain[secure] a license／～증 a license card／~ 세 the license card. めんきょ

**면허장(免許狀)** ①(졸업·개업의) a diploma ②(일반의) a license; a certificate (증명서); a permit (허가증)／교원 ~ a teacher's certificate. めんきょじょう

**면화(免禍)** ～하다 escape disaster[calamity, mishap, misfortune]; keep out of harm's way. さいかをまぬかれること

**면화(棉花)** raw cotton／~씨 cottonseed／~씨 기름 cottonseed oil／~ 재배 cotton growing. めんか

**면화약(綿火藥)** guncotton. めんかやく

**면회(面灰)** lime mortar for the final coating; last coat／～하다 give the final coating of lime mortar [to the wall]. かべなどに上塗りするせっかい

**면회(面會)** an interview; a meeting／～하다 see; receive; meet; interview; have an interview with／환자는 ~ 사절이다 The patient is not allowed to see anyone. めんかい

**면흉(免凶)** escaping a famine[bad harvest]; escape a crop failure／～하다 be saved from a famine; escape a bad harvest. きょうねんをまぬかれること

**멸** 《식》 a kind of pepper plant; *Houttuynia cordata*(학명).

**멸각(滅却)** extinction; destruction; annihilation／~하다 extinguish; destroy; efface. めっきゃく

**멸공 정신(滅共精神)** the spirit to exterminate communism.

**멸구** 《충》 a small locust.

**멸균(滅菌)** sterilization 《살균》 pasteurization／～하다 sterilize; pasteurize／~제 a sterilizer; a germicide. めっきん

**멸도(滅度)** 〖종〗 *Nirvana* (Sans); the final emancipation; the complete annihilation of self. めつど

**멸망(滅亡)** downfall; fall; ruin; destruction; collapse／～하다 fall; be ruined; be destructed; collapse. めつぼう

**멸문(滅門)** ～하다 destroy one's whole family. めつもん

**멸시(蔑視)** contempt; disdain; disregard／～하다 regard (*a person*) with contempt; despise; disregard; disdain; look down upon／~받다 be held in contempt. けいべつ

**멸절(滅絶)** extermination; extirpation; eradication; extinction ㄷ절멸. ぜつめつ

**멸족(滅族)** extermination of a family [tribe]／～하다 exterminate a family [tribe].

**멸종(滅種)** extermination [of a stock]／~하다 exterminate [a stock]. たねをぜつめつさせること

**멸치** 〖어〗 an anchovy; *Engraulis japonicus* (학명)／~젓 salted anchovies. ひしこ

**멸치고래** 〖동〗 *Balaenoptera borealis*(학명).

**멸하다(滅—)** ruin; destroy; overthrow; exterminate; annihilate／나라를 ~ ruin [destroy] a nation／적을 ~ destroy[conquer] an enemy. ほろぼす

**명(名)** ①(사람) persons ②(이름) name; fame ③(유명한) noted (*wrestler*); celebrated (*place*); distinguished (*person*); great (*work*); star (*actor*). めい

**명(命)** ①(목숨) life／제 ~에 죽다 die a natural death ②(운명) a destiny; fate ③(명령) an order; a command; instructions; a dictation(지시)／~을 받다 receive orders. めい

**명(銘)** 《기념비의》 an inscription 《묘비의》 an epitaph. めい

**명가(名家)** 《집안》 a reputable family 《지명인》 an eminent person 《대가(大家)》 a great master. めいもん

**명가(名價)** fame; reputation; nominal value. めいよとせいか

**명가수(名歌手)** a famous[renowned] singer. ゆうめいなかしゅ

**명감(明鑑)** 《높은 식견》 a broad view and high intelligence 《올바른 식별》 bright discernment. こうめいなしきけん

**명개** loam along the riverside.

**명견(名犬)** a fine dog.

**명견 만리(明見萬里)** deep insight; far sightedness／～하다 have deep insight; be far-sighted.

**명경(明鏡)** ① a stainless mirror／마음이 ~ 지수(止水)와 같다 The mind is as bright and clean as a stainless mirror. ②(분명한 증거)definite[strong] evidence[proof]. めいきょう

**명계(冥界)** the nether world; the under world; Hades. めいかい

**명곡(名曲)** famous music／~ 감상 music appreciation. めいきょく

**명공(名工)** a master hand craftsman; an expert. めいこう

**명관(名官)** a celebrated governor; a good magistrate. ゆうしゅうなかんり

**명관(明官)** a wise governor[ruler].

**명관(鳴管)** 〖해〗 a syrinx [of a bird].

**명교(名教)** morals; morality. めいきょう

**명구(名句)** a fine expression; a famous phrase[line]; a wise saying; a well-known adage／~집 a collection of choice extracts. めいく

**명군(明君)** a wise ruler[king]; an enlightened monarch; a benevolent lord.

**명궁(名弓)** 《사람》an expert archer; a famous bowman 《활》 a noted bow. ゆみのめいしゅ

**명금(鳴禽)** a singing[song] bird; a songster. めいきん

**명기(名妓)** a celebrated[famous] gisaeng. めいぎ

**명기(明記)** ~하다 write[mention, state] expressly; write[put down] clearly; specify／그 암초는 해도에 ~되어 있다 The reef is clearly shown on the chart.

**명기(明氣)** ①《산천의》beauty [of a landscape] ②《얼굴빛의》a cheerful countenance. めいき

**명년(明年)** next year; the coming year. みょうねん

**명념(銘念)** ~하다 engrave[impress] on *one's* mind; lay (*a fact*) to heart; keep [bear] in mind roll. めいしん

**명단(明斷)** a judicious decision; a clear [wise, convincing] judgment／~을 내리다 pass a clear judgment (*on*).

**명단(名單)** a list of names[persons]; a roster. めいぼ

**명달(明達)** wisdom; sagacity; intelligence／~하다 (be) wise; sagacious; discerning.

**명담(名談)** a wise[gold] saying; a witty [sensible, felicitous] remark; a famous remark. めいげん

**명답(明答)** 《확답》a definite[decisive] answer／~하다 answer[reply] definitely; give (*a person*) a definite answer.

**명답(名答)** 《바른》a right[correct, excellent] answer 《교묘한》a clever[shrewd] answer／~이다 You are quite right., You have guessed right. めいとう

**명당(明堂)** ①《전전》the king's audience hall ②《무덤 앞 땅》the flat space in front of a grave ③《좋은 빛 자리》a propitious site for a grave. めいどう

**명도(名刀)** a fine[celebrated] sword; a noted sword.

**명도(冥途)** Hades; the nether world; the other world; the realm of shades. めいど

**명도(明渡)** surrender; evacuation; quitting／집을 ~하다 vacuate[quit] a house／~ 소송 an eviction suit／~ 통고 eviction notice. あけわたし

**명동(鳴動)** rumbling／~하다 rumble／대산 ~에 서일필(鼠一匹)《속담》Much cry and little wool., The mountain was in labour and brought forth a mouse.

**명란(明卵)** pollack roe／~젓 [salted] pollack caviar. めんたいのなまご

**명랑(明朗)** brightness; clearness; cheerfulness; gaiety／~하다 (be) bright; clear; cheerful; merry; sunshiny／가정을 ~하게 하다 fill *one's* home with happiness. めいろう

**명령(命令)** an order; a command 《지령》 instruction／~하다 order; command; instruct／그에게 무엇이라고 ~했느냐 What order did you give him?／~법 〖문〗 the imperative mood／~서 a warrant; a precept／~ 위반 violation of an order／~자 a commander; a dictator. めいれい

**명론(名論)** an excellent opinion; an excellent treatise／~ 탁설 sound arguments and eminent views. めいろん

**명료(明瞭)** clearness; plainness; lucidity; distinctness／~하다 (be) clear; plain; distinct／~하게 하라 make clear[plain]; clarify. めいりょう

**명류(名流)** a celebrated[prominent] person; a celebrity; a noted person／당대의 ~ prominent men of the time. めいりゅう

**명리(名利)** fame and wealth; name and fortune; riches and honor／~를 초월하다 be above riches and wealth／~ 심 a worldly spirit. めいり

**명마(名馬)** a fine horse 《군마》 an excellent steed; a renowned charger. めいば

**명막(冥漠)** ~하다 (be) vast; extensive; boundless.

**명망(名望)** reputation 《인망》renown; popularity／~을 잃다 lose *one's* popularity. めいぼう

**명망가(名望家)** a man of [high] repute [renown]; a popular man; a man high in public esteem／그는 상당한 ~이다 He now enjoys a fairly high reputation. めいぼうか

**명매기** 〖조〗 the large white-rumped swift; *Micropus pacificus*(학명).

**명맥(命脈)** life; the thread of life; existence／겨우 ~을 이어가다 barely keep *oneself* in existence. めいみゃく

**명멸(明滅)** ~하다 flicker; glimmer／~ 신호 a blinking signal. めいめつ

**명명(命名)** naming; christening／~하다 name; christen. めいめい

**명명백백(明明白白)** ~하다 (be) clear; plain; obvious; be as clear as day; be as plain as print. めいめいはくはく

**명모(明眸)** bright eyes. めいぼう

**명목(名目)** ①《명칭》a name; a title; an appellation ②《구실》a pretext／~상으로 nominally; titularly. めいもく

**명목(瞑目)** ~하다 《눈을 감다》close *one's* eyes 《죽다》die; pass away; breathe *one's* last; expire. めいもく

**명문**(名文) an excellent[a beautiful] composition; a literary gem; a beautiful passage／～가(家) a fine writer; a great master of style. めいぶん

**명문**(名門) a distinguished[an illustrious] family; noble lineage／～의 자제(子弟) children of noble birth[a good family]. めいもん

**명문**(明文) an express provision[statement]／법률에 ～이 없다 There is no provision in the law. めいぶん

**명문 천하**(名聞天下) world-wide fame[reputation]／～하다 be world-famous; gain world-wide fame.
名前がてんかにきこえること

**명물**(名物) 《산물》a special product; a speciality 《저명한 것》a feature; an attraction. めいぶつ

**명미**(明媚) beautifulness; picturesqueness／～하다 (be) beautiful; picturesque／풍광 ～한 땅 a picturesque site. めいび

**명민**(明敏) sagacity; intelligence／～하다 (be) sagacious; intelligent; sharp／두뇌가 ～하다 have a clear head. めいびん

**명반**(明礬) alum／～석 alum-stone; alunite. みょうばん

**명백**(明白) clearness; plainness／～하다 (be) clear; plain; obvious. めいはく

**명복**(名卜) a famous fortuneteller.
ゆうめいなぼくしゃ

**명복**(冥福) happiness in the other world; heavenly bliss／～을 빌다 pray for the repose of (a person's) soul. めいふく

**명부**(名簿) a list; a register; a roll／～를 작성하다 make a list (of)／선거인 ～ a poll book／회원 ～ a list of membership. めいぼ

**명부**(冥府) the other[nether] world; the underworld; Hades. めいふ

**명분**(名分) 《륜》one's duty; moral obligations 《명목》justification; pretext／～이 서다 be justified. めいぶん

**명사**(名士) a man of note; a distinguished[noted] person; a celebrity; a prominent figure. めいし

**명사**(名詞) 【언】a noun; a substantive／～ 변화 inflexion of nouns. めいし

**명사**(名辭) 【논】a term; a name／～주의 【철】terminism. めいじ

**명사**(銘謝) deep appreciation; heartfelt thanks／～하다 deeply appreciate; express one's heartfelt thanks.

**명산**(名産) a noted[special] product; a speciality. めいさん

**명산**(名山) a noted[celebrated] mountain／～ 대천(大川) noted mountains and large rivers; splendid mountains and rivers. めいさん

**명상**(瞑想, 冥想) meditation; contemplation／～하다 meditate[muse] (on); contemplate; muse (on)／～에 잠기다 fall into a brown study. めいそう

**명색**(名色) ①《명칭》a name; a title; a designation ②《구실》a pretext. な

**명석**(明晳) clearness; distinctness／～하다 (be) clear; distinct; lucid／그는 두뇌가 ～한 사람이다 He is a clearheaded person. めいせき

**명성**(名聲) fame; renown; reputation; celebrity／～을 유지하다 maintain one's reputation. めいせい

**명성**(明星) ①《천》Venus ②《새벽의》 the morning star; Lucifer ③《인기있는 사람》 a [singing] star. きんせい

**명세**(名世) a man of world-wide fame; a world-renowned person.

**명세**(明細) details; particulars／～하다 (be) detailed; full; minute／～히 기술하다 set forth in detail. めいさい

**명세서**(明細書) a detailed statement; a minute description; details; a list of particulars; a detailed account／선적 ～ shipping specifications. めいさいしょ

**명소**(名所) a place of interest[note]; a celebrated locality; a noted place; a beauty spot／～ 고적 places of note and historical interest. めいしょ

**명수**(名數) 《인원수》the number of persons 《명목수》a nominal number. めいすう

**명수**(命數) ①《수명》a person's natural span of life; a person's [length of] days. ②《운명》fate; destiny／～를 알다 know one's doom. めいすう

**명수**(名手) a master[capital] hand; a master; an expert／피아노의 ～ an accomplished pianist. めいしゅ

**명승**(名勝) a beauty[scenic] spot; a famous sight; a scenic beauty. めいしょう

**명승**(名僧) a distinguished[noted] priest; an eminent[a noted, a celebrated] Buddhist priest. めいそう

**명시**(明示) clear statement; elucidation／～하다 state clearly[plainly]; specify. めいじ

**명시**(明視) clear vision／～하다 see (a thing) clearly; see in a clear light／～거리[범위] the range of clear vision.

**명신**(名臣) an illustrious retainer.

**명실**(名實) name and reality[fact]／～ 상부하지 않다 The reality does not agree with the name. めいじつ

**명심**(銘心) bearing in mind／～하다 bear[keep] (anything) in mind; take (an advice) to heart／그 일을 항상 ～해야 한다 It must always be borne in mind. めいしん

**명아주** 【식】 a goosefoot; Chenopodium album(학명). あかざ

**명안**(名案) a good[capital, brilliant] idea; a splendid plan／～이 머리에 떠올랐다 A bright idea came to him.／그것은 ～이다 That's an idea. めいあん

**명암**(明暗) light and shade[darkness]／～도 brightness／～법 shading. めいあん

**명야**(明夜) tomorrow night[evening].
みょうばん

**명약 관화**(明若觀火) being as clear as daylight／～하다 be as clear[plain] as

**명언**(名言) a wise[golden] saying; a sage[witty] remark/ 만고의 ～ an immortal saying. めいげん

**명언**(明言) declaration; a definite statement; assertion/ ～하다 declare; say definitely[positively]. めいげん

**명역**(名譯) an apt[excellent] translation. すぐれたほんやく

**명연기**(名演技) an excellent[a beautiful] performance.

**명예**(名譽) hono[u]r 《영광》glory 《명예》distinction 《신망》credit 《명성》fame; reputation 《체면》dignity; prestige/～를 회복하다 restore one's hono[u]r. めいよ

**명왕성**(冥王星) 【천】 Pluto.

**명우**(名優) a great[celebrated] actor; a [famous] star/～가 되다 rise to stardom/～판 an all-star cast.

**명월**(明月) a bright moon 《보름달》 a full moon/중추의 ～ the harvest moon. めいげつ

**명유**(名儒) a famous Confucianist 《학자》 a prominent scholar. めいじゅ

**명의**(名義) ①《이름》name/～만의 사장 a president in name only/가옥을 처의 ～로 하다 transfer a house to the wife ②《명분》one's moral duty. めいぎ

**명의**(名醫) a noted doctor; a skilled physician. ゆうめいないし

**명인**(名人) a noted person; a [past] master; a master hand; an expert/그는 피리의 ～이다 He is a skillful performer on the flute. めいじん

**명일**(名日) a public holiday; a fete[-day]; a gala day; a festive day.

**명일**(明日) 《내일》tomorrow. みょうにち

**명일**(命日) 《기일(忌日)》the anniversary [date] (of one's) death.

**명자**(名字) 《이름자》the characters (of one's) name 《명판》fame.

**명작** (名作) a masterpiece; a fine piece (of literature); a fine work (of art)/근래의 ～ the greatest masterpiece in recent years. めいさく

**명장**(名匠) a master hand; a master craftsman; a skilled workman. めいしょう

**명장**(名將) a famous general; a great commander. めいしょう

**명재상**(名宰相) an able[a noted] premier. めいさいしょう

**명저**(名著) a notable[famous] book[work]; a masterpiece; a great[fine] work. めいちょ

**명절**(名節) festival[festive] days; big holidays; gala days; public holiday.

**명정**(酩酊) intoxication; drunkenness; inebriety/ ～하다 get[be] drunk; get tipsy; be intoxicated. めいてい

**명정**(銘旌) a funeral banner[streamer]; a streamer with an inscription of the name and the rank of the deceased.

**명제**(命題) 【논】 a proposition 《제목》a given subject for a composition/긍정 an affirmative proposition. めいだい

**명조**(明朝) ①《내일 아침》tomorrow morning ②《명나라》the Ming-dynasty. みょうちょう

**명조**(冥助) divine favo[u]r; providence.

**명조체**(明朝體) Ming-style printing type 《영자》roman type; the roman.

**명주**(銘酒) liquor of a famous brand; high quality liquor. めいしゅ

**명주**(明紬) silk 《견직물》silk fabric[cloth]/ ～실 silk thread/ ～안 silk lining/ ～옷 silk clothes. きぬおりもの

**명중**(命中) a hit/ ～하다 hit (the mark) strike 《예언이》come true/～탄 a [direct] hit/탄환이 눈에 ～하다 strike (a person) in the eye. めいちゅう

**명증**(明證) 《증거》clear evidence; evident proof 《증명》certification; verification / ～하다 prove clearly 《증명》certify [verify] as true. めいはくなしょうこ

**명징**(明澄) clearness; lucidity/ ～하다 (be) clear; lucid.

**명찰**(明察) insight; discernment; penetration/ ～하여 주십시오 I leave it to your good judg[e]ment. めいさつ

**명찰**(名札) a card; a business card; a name-plate 《문패》a door-plate 《간판》a sign on the door 《명함》a name-card/ ～을 내걸다 put up a name-plate. なふだ

**명창**(名唱) 《사람》a great[noted, celebrated] singer 《노래》an excellent singing. ゆうめいな歌又はかしゅ

**명철**(明哲) sagacity; intelligence 《사람》a wise man; a sage/ ～하다 (be) sagacious; wise; brilliant. めいてつ

**명추**(明秋) next autumn[fall]. らいしゅう

**명춘**(明春) next spring. らいしゅん

**명충**(螟蟲) 【충】a pearl-moth; a riceborer.

**명치** the pit of the stomach; the solar plexus/ ～뼈 the bone above the pit of the stomach. みぞおち

**명칭**(名稱) a name; a title; a term; a designation; a denomination/ ～을 바꾸다 change the name; rename; rechristen: retitle. めいしょう

**명쾌**(明快) clearness; lucidity; explicitness/그녀는 ～하게 대답했다 She answered clearly. めいかい

**명태**(明太) 【어】 a pollack. めんたい

**명토**(名一) indication/ ～박다 point out; indicate; lay a finger on; name.

**명투**(明透) conversance; mastery/ ～하다 (be) well-versed in; obtain the complete mastery of.

**명필**(名筆) ①《필적》an excellent handwriting[calligraphy]/ ～가 a good hand at writing[painting]/그는 ～이다 He is an excellent penman. ②《명화》an excellent drawing[painting] 《명화가》a master painter. めいひつ

**명하다**(命一) ①《명령하다》order; give orders; command; tell; bid/엄중히 ～ give strict orders ②《임명하다》appoint;

nominate assign. めいずる

**명함**(名銜, 名啣) ①a name card 〈사교용〉a visiting card; a calling card〈미〉;〈영업용〉a business card／ ~을 두고 가다 leave one's card ②〈성함〉(a person's) esteemed card.

**명현**(名賢) a noted wiseman[sage]; a man of great wisdom. ゆうめいなけんじん

**명호**(名號) ①〈이름과 호〉name and penname ②〈명목〉a title ⇒명목. めいごう

**명화**(名花) a famous[celebrated] flower 〈사람〉a beauty; celebrated courtesan.

**명화**(名畫) a famous[celebrated] picture; a notable painting; masterpiece; an old master ／루벤스의 ~ a masterpiece of Rubens. めいか

**명확**(明確) clearness; precision; definiteness／ ~하다 (be) clear and accurate; precise; distinct／이 점을 ~히 하다 clear up this point. めいかく

**몇** 〈약간〉some; a few; several 〈얼마〉how many／ ~이나 about how many; about so many; several／ ~ 사람이든 좋다 Any number of persons will do. ／~살입니까 How old are you? いくら

**몇몇** some; several; a few／ ~은 죽고 ~은 부상하였다 Some people were killed, others wounded. じゃっかん

**모**¹ 〈벼의〉a young rice plant 〈모종〉seedling 〈묘목〉a young plant[tree]／ ~판 a seedbed; a seedplot. なえ

**모**² ①〈각〉an angle 〈모서리〉an edge; a corner／ ~를 세우다 sharpen the edge ②〈성질이〉angularity; harshness; stiffness／ ~나게 굴다 act harshly. かど

**모**³ a cake; a block／두부 한 ~ a cake of bean curd.

**모**(毛) ①〈털〉hair; fur; wool ②〈단위〉a mo [one-tenth of a ri]／ ~사 woolen yarn／ ~사 worsted fabric. け

**모**(母) a mother. はは

**모**(某) 〈모인〉a certain person; someone 〈어떤〉a certain; som ; one; unnamed ／~처에서 at a certain place. ぼう

**모가비** a boss; a head; a chief; a gang leader. かしら

**모가지** a neck ⇒목. くび

**모가치** one's share ⇒몫. わりあて

**모감주나무** 〖식〗the soapberry plant; koelreuteria paniculata〈학명〉.

**모개로** all together; in the lump; wholesale; in bulk; in the gross／ ~ 사다 buy wholesale. まとめて

**모걸음질** walking[marching] off at an angle.

**모경**(暮景) an evening scene. ばんけい

**모경**(暮境) one's declining years; old age; the evening[winter] of life.

**모계**(母系) the maternal[mother's] line; the spindle[distaff] side; one's mother's side／ ~의 maternal. ぼけい

**모계**(謀計) a trick; a plot; an artifice; a machination; a stratagem／적의 ~에 빠지다 fall a prey to the enemy's stratagem. ぼうけい

**모꼬지** a meeting; a gathering; a party ／ ~하다 gather together.

**모골**(毛骨) hair and bone／ ~이 송연하다 shudder; shiver; thrill; feel a thrill; a shudder runs through one's frame. けとほね

**모공**(毛孔) pores [of the skin]. けあな

**모과**〖식〗a Chinese quince; a papaya. まるめろのみ

**모과나무**〖식〗a Chinese quince; a papaya tree; Chaenomeles sinensis〈학명〉.

**모관 현상**(毛管現象)〈모세관 현상〉capillary action[phenomenon]. もうかんげんしょう

**모교**(母校) one's old school; one's Alma Mater. ぼこう

**모국**(母國) one's mother country; the (one's) homeland; one's native country ／ ~을 방문하다 visit one's mother country. ぼこく

**모국**(某國) a certain country[nation]; an undisclosed country. あるくに

**모군**(募軍) ①〈인부〉a navvy; a coolie; a construction worker ②〈모병〉recruiting／ ~일 construction work; coolie work. にんぷ

**모권**(母權) mother's authority; maternal rights／ ~을 확장하다 raise the status of motherhood. ぼけん

**모근**(毛根)〖생〗the root of hair／ ~을 이식하다 implant a hair. もうこん

**모금** a draft; a gulp 〈조금〉a drop 〈차 따위〉a sip／물을 한 ~ 마시다 drink a draft of water. ひとのみ

**모금**(募金) money[fund] raising; a collection／ ~하다 collect contributions; raise subscriptions／ ~ 운동을 하다 canvass for subscriptions.

**모기**〖충〗a mosquito／ ~가 물다 mosquitoes bite[sting]／ ~가 앵앵거리다 mosquitoes buzz／ ~ 떼 a swarm of mosquitoes. か

**모기둥** a square pillar. かくちゅう

**모기장**(—帳) a mosquito net／ ~을 치고 자다 sleep under a mosquito net.

**모기향**(—香) a mosquito stick[coil].

**모깃불** a smudge; a mosquito-fumigator ／ ~을 피우다 smudge; fumigate to keep off[out] mosquitoes. かやりひ

**모나다** be pointed; be sharp; be rough; be angular ⇒모. かどたつ

**모내기** planting of young rice-plants; setting out rice-plants; rice-transplantation／ ~하다 transplant rice／ ~에 바쁘다 be busy planting the rice.

**모내다** ①〈벼의〉transplant young rice plants; set[bed] out rice plants ②〈각을〉make angular[square]; put corners on／기둥을 ~ make a pillar square. 角立たせる

**모녀**(母女) mother and daughter／ ~간 between mother and daughter.

**모년**(某年) a certain year. あるとし

**모년**(冒年) concealing one's age／ ~하다

모다기 | 328 | 모들뜨다

conceal *one's* age; give a false age. ねんれいをだますこと
**모다기** all at once; from all sides／모다깃매 blows from all-sides. いちねんの
**모닥불** be a campfire; a bonfire; fire in the open air／～을 피우다 make a fire [in the open air]. かがりひ
**모당(**一糖**)** cube sugar ⇨모사탕.かくざとう
**모당(**母堂**)** your[his, her] esteemed mother. たにんのははの敬稱
**모도(**母道**)** motherhood.
**모도록** thickly; luxuriantly; densely／～하다 (be) thick; luxuriant; dense. ほうがく
**모독(**冒瀆**)** defilement; debasement; pollution 《신성 모독》 blasphemy; profanity; desecration／～하다 profane; blaspheme; pollute. ぼうとく
**모동(**暮冬**)** late winter.
**모되** a square *doi* measure. せいしかっけいのます
**모두** all; everyone; everybody; everything 《합계》 in all; all told 《다 함께》 all together; al ogether; in a body 《몰아서》 in the gross／～ 너에게 주겠다 These are for you all. すべて
**모두(**冒頭**)** the beginning; the opening; the outset; the lead／그 장의 ～에 시가 실려 있다 The chapter opens with a poem. ぼうとう
**모두거리** a fall from having both feet tripped／～하다 fall plump
**모두뜀** leaping on both feet.
**모뜨다** ①《투사》 trace (*a drawing*) ②《흉내》 imitate; copy; ape／사람의 행동을 ～ imitate (*a person's*) conduct. まねる
**모드라기풀** 【식】 a sun-dew; a moor-grass; *Drosera rotundifolia* 〔학명〕.
**모든** all; whole; every／～ 경우에 on all occasions／～ 문제가 해결됐다 The problem is now completely solved. あらゆる
**모들뜨기** a cross-eyed person／～눈 a cross-eye. やぶにらみのひと
**모들뜨다** turn *one's* eyes inward[toward the nose]; have cross-eyes; squint convergently. やぶにらみでみる

# 모 르 다

①do not know; cannot tell; be unaware[ignorant] of; be not familiar (*with*); be not acquainted (*with*)／모르는 곳 a strange place／모르는 사람 a stranger／모르는 말 a word[language] *one* doesn't know／자기도 모르게 in spite of *one*self; unconsciously; unwittingly／모른다고 잡아떼다 stoutly maintain *one's* ignorance／전혀 ～ know nothing of; have not the slightest[remotest] idea of; be quite ignorant of／어찌 할 바를 ～ do not know what to do; be at a loss; be in a fog; be at *one's* wit's end／그 이유를 모르겠다 I cannot tell the reason. ／모르는 것이 약이다《속담》 Ignorance is bliss. ／하나만 알고 둘은 ～ You know only one side of the story.

②《깨치지 못하다》 do not understand; do not know; do not appreciate (*the value of money*); do not see[get]; cannot make out; do not follow／전혀 ～ do not understand at all; have not the slightest idea of／진의를 모르겠다 do not understand the meaning of it／왜 안 오는지 모르겠다 I don't see why he doesn't come. ／그의 마음을 모르겠다 I cannot make him out. ／뭐가 뭔지 모르겠다 It is all Greek to me., I cannot make head or tail of it／당신의 말을 모르겠다 I don't get you.

③《못 알아차리다》 fail to notice[see, perceive, realize, sense]; be not conscious of／자기 잘못을 ～ be blind to *one's* own faults[mistakes]; do not realize *one's* own mistakes／위험을 ～ do not realize[sense] the danger.

④《무감각하다》 do not feel; be unconscious of; be insensible of[to]; be impervious to／부끄러움을 ～ be dead[lost] to shame; be impervious to shame／은혜를 ～ be insensible of kindness／추운 줄을 ～ do not feel the cold／고마움을 ～ be insensible to kindness.

⑤《안면이 없다》 be not acquainted with; do not know／모르는 사람 a stranger.

⑥《몰라 보다》 do not recognize／그녀가 누군지를 모르겠다 I can scarcely recognize who she is. ／나를 모르겠나 Can't you recognize me?

⑦《기억을 못하다》 do not remember／그 당시 일을 전혀 모르겠다 I cannot remember anything of those days at all.

⑧《무관계하다》 be not concerned with; have nothing to do with／그 일은 나도 모른다 I have nothing to do with the matter., It's no concern of mine., That's none of my business., I can't help what you have done. ／죽거나 살거나 나는 모른다 He may be drowned for all I care.

⑨《경험이 없다》 have no experience; be ignorant of／가난을 ～ be ignorant of[free from] poverty／여자를 ～ have had no experience with women; be indifferent to women／세상을 ～ be unversed in the ways of the world; be ignorant of the world.

**모락모락** ①(힘차게) rapidly; well/ ~ 자라다 grow up quickly[rapidly] ②(김·연기가) thickly; densely; heavily/향수내가 ~ 나다 be heavily perfumed; reek of perfume. むくむく

**모란**(牡丹) a [tree] peony; *Paeonia suffrticosa*(학명).

**모란채**(牡丹菜) 〖식〗 a kind of cabbage; *Brassica oleracea*(학명).

**모래** sand; grit(거친) / ~ 장난을 하다 play with sand/쌀에 ~가 들어 있다 There are grits in the rice. / ~ 강변 a sandy shore[beach] / ~ 땅 sandy soil; sandy plain/밭 ~ 무더기 piles of sand; sand dunes/~ 밭 sandy spot[beach]; the sands/ ~ 사장 a sandy plain/~ 시계 a sandglass/ ~ 언덕 a sand dune; a sand hill/ ~ 주머니 a sandbag. すな

**모래무지** 〖어〗 a false[goby] minnow; *Pseudogobio esocinus*(학명). うぐい

**모래집** 〖해〗 the amnion (*pl*. -nia) / ~물 amniotic fluid; the water/ ~물이 터지다 the water breaks. ようすい

**모략**(謀略) strategy; a trick (음모) an intrigue; a plot; a ruse/ ~ 선전 strategic propaganda, ~을 꾸미다 devise a stratagem. ぼうりゃく

**모레** the day after tomorrow/ ~ 찾아가겠읍니다 I will visit you the day after tomorrow. あさって

**모려**(謀慮) practical ingenuity; resourcefulness and prudence. ちぼうしりょ

**모련**(慕戀) love; attachment; tender emotions/ ~하다 love; fall in love with become attached to; conceive love for. こいしたうこと

**모렴**(冒廉) going against *one's* sense of honor[decency].

**모로** (비껴서)aslant; obliquely (옆으로) crossways; sideways. よこに

**모록**(耄碌) dotage; senility/ ~하다 be senile; be in *one's* dotage. もうろく

**모롱이** (산의)a spur of a hill[mountain]. やまのまがりかど

**모루** an anvil. かなとこ

**모루채** a hammer; a sledge. つち

**모르다** ⇨변할 참조.

**모르면 모르되** if I guess right; most probably/ ~ 50은 넘었을 게다 If my guess is right, he must be over fifty.

**모르쇠** playing dumb; know-nothing-ism.

**모른 체** pretending not to know; pretended innocence; an unconcerned air; indifference/ ~하다 pretend not to know; pretend innocence.

**모름지기** by all means; necessarily (사람이 주어) should (do). すべからく

**모름하다** (be) stale; bad; be not fresh/생선이 ~ The fish is going. ちょっとくさりかけている

**모리**(謀利) profiteering/ ~하다 profiteer; make undue[unreasonable] profits / ~를 단속하다 control profiteering/ ~배 a profiteer/전쟁 ~배 a war profiteer. ふとういとくをあさること

**모만**(侮慢) insolence; arrogance; an insult; contumely/ ~하다 be insolent; arrogant; contumelious; insulting; treat with contempt. ぶまん

**모말** a square *mal* measure. せいろっかくけいのます

**모매**(侮罵) denunciation through scorn; condemnation through derision/ ~하다 deride to condemn; scorn to denounce. ぶば

**모맥**(牟麥) wheat and barley. おおむぎ

**모면**(謀免) evasion; escape/~하다 escape; get rid of; avoid; tide over/위기를 ~하다 escape[tide over] a crisis. けいをめぐらしてだっしゅつすること

**모멸**(侮蔑) contempt; scorn; disdain; slight/ ~하다 despise; scorn; disdain; slight; look down upon. ぶべつ

**모명**(冒名) an assumed[a fictitious] name; an alias; giving an alias[a false name]/ ~하다 assume a fictitious[false] name; give an alias. へんめい

**모모**(某某) some persons; such and such persons. ぼうぼう

**모모한**(某某—) prominent; distinguished; outstanding; influential/ ~ 사람 prominent people. ちょめいな

**모물**(毛物) furs; fur goods; a fell/ ~전 a fur store. けもの

**모밀잣밤나무** 〖식〗 the Japanese chinquapin; *Castanopsis cuspidata*(학명).

**모반**(一盤) a small hexagonal[octagonal] dining table.

**모반**(母斑) 〖해〗 a birthmark.

**모반**(謀叛) (반란) a rebellion; a revolt; an insurrection (반역) treason (음모) conspiracy/ ~하다 revolt; rebel; conspire; plot treason; plot against.

**모발**(毛髮) hair/ ~ 습도계 a hair hygrometer/ ~ 영양제 a hair tonic/ ~ 탈락 alopecia. かみ

**모방**(模倣) imitation; copying; mimicry / ~하다 imitate; copy (*from, after*); follow an example (*of*)/우리는 ~에 의해 많이 배운다 We learn many things by imitation. もほう

**모범**(冒犯) an intentional violation; a deliberate infringement/ ~하다 intentionally violate; deliberately infringe. 殊更にいはんすること

**모범**(模範) (본)a model (범례) an example (귀감)a pattern; a paragon/ ~으로 삼아야 할 사람 a model of what a man ought to be. もはん

**모병**(募兵) recruiting; conscription; draft/ ~하다 recruit[conscript, draft, enlist] (*soldiers*). ぼへい

**모본**(模本) (견본) a sample; a model; a pattern (표본) a specimen (작은 모형 模型)) a miniature/기계의 ~ the model of a machine. みほん

**모본단**(模本緞) a kind of Chinese silk. ひんしつのよいきぬおりもののいっしつ

**모붓다** sow rice-seeds [on a seedbed].

**모사**(毛絲) woolen yarn.

**모사**(茅舍) ①(자기집) my [humble] house ②(모옥) a thatched cottage.

**모사**(模寫) copying; a copy; a reproduction; a facsimile; a replica／～하다 copy; reproduce; trace; make a facsimile of.

**모사**(謀士) a strategist; a tactician.

**모사**(謀事) planning; making a plan (계획) a plan; a device; a scheme (군략) a stratagem (계략) a plot; a trick／～가 좌절 되었다 The plot has been frustrated.

**모사탕**(一砂糖) cube[lump] sugar; sugar cubes.

**모살**(謀殺) murder／～하다 murder; kill (a person) of malice prepense／～의 crime of murder／～ 사건 a murder case／～ 미수 attempted murder.

**모상**(母喪) one's mother's death／～을 당하다 lose one's mother; have one's mother die.

**모래** fine sand ⇒모래.

**모색**(暮色) shades of night; evening twilight[gloom, dusk].

**모색**(摸索) groping／～하다 grope／암중 ～하다 grope in the dark.

**모생약**(毛生藥) a hair restorer[grower].

**모서리** an angle; a corner; an edge／～를 죽이다 round off a corner[an edge].

**모선**(母船) a mother ship[vessel] (사령선) a command ship／포경 ～ a whaling mother ship.

**모성**(母性) motherhood; maternity／～ 예찬 adoration of motherhood.

**모세관**(毛細管) 【물】 capillary tube; a capillary／～ 현상 capillary; capillary action.

**모세 혈관**(毛細血管) 【해】 a capillary vessel; a capillary.

**모소**(某所) a certain place; somewhere.

**모손**(耗損) wearing out; friction loss; wear and tear; abrasion／～하다 wear out; undergo friction loss.

**모수자**(毛繻子) satin.

**모순**(矛盾) contradiction; conflict; inconsistency／～된 생각 an inconsistent idea／～이 많은 세상이다 This is a world of contradictions.／～ 개념 【논】 a contradictory concept[idea]／～ 대당 【논】 contradiction; contradictory opposition／～ 명사 contradictory terms／～성 contradictoriness.

**모숨** a handful (of grass); a lock (of straw).

**모습** (풍채) an appearance; one's features; one's image (용모) a face; a look (자취) trace; remnants／아버지의 ～을 닮다 have a look of one's father／옛 ～ one's former self／～을 나타내다 show one's face; show up.

**모시** ①ramie cloth; ramie fabric ② ⇒ 모시풀／～ 옷 clothes of ramie cloth.

**모시**(某時) a certain[undisclosed] time.

**모씨**(母氏) your mother; the mother of an inferior.

**모씨**(某氏) a certain person[gentleman]; an unnamed person; a man who shall be nameless.

**모시다** ①(웃어른을) attend[wait] upon; serve ②(신으로) deify (예배하다) worship (사당을) enshrine／부모를 ～ have one's parents with／조상을 ～ worship one's ancestors.

**모시풀** 【식】 a ramie; a China-grass; the ramie plant; Boehmeria nivea(학명).

**모심기** rice-planting ⇒모내기.

**모아들다** gather; come[get] together; flock; crowd; cluster; swarm; collect／곳곳에서 ～ flock from all[various] quarters.

**모야**(暮夜) a dark night; the dead of night; late at night.

**모양**(模様, 貌様) ①(형태) shape; form (자태) [personal] appearance; figure (맵시) looks (태도) an air／저고리의 ～ a cut of one's coat／초라한 ～ a miserable plight ②(동태) signs; indications; appearance／그는 돌아오지 않을 ～이다 There is no sign of his return. ③(상태) the state of affairs (방법) a way; a manner／이 ～으로 나가면 if things go at this rate／아버지가 하는 ～으로 하면 된다 You will make it if you do as your father does. ④(무늬) a pattern ⇒무늬.

**모양다리**(貌様一) form; shape; figure ⇒ 모양새.

**모양사납다**(貌様一) be unsightly; unbecoming; disgraceful／그의 옷차림이 ～ He is shabbily dressed.

**모양새**(貌様一) ①(생김새) shape; form; appearance; figure／～가 사납다 be bad-looking[ugly, shapeless] ②(체면) respectability; appearances; dignity／～가 없어지다 lose face; be put out of countenance.

**모어**(母語) the mother tongue; one's mother tongue.

**모여들다** gather; flock.

**모역**(謀逆) rebellion; an insurrection; a revolt; treason／～하다 rebel; revolt; conspire; plot against.

**모옥**(茅屋) a hovel; a straw-thatched cottage.

**모욕**(侮辱) insult; contempt; indignity; affront; dishonor／～하다 insult; treat with contempt／그것은 나에 대한 ～이다 It is a slap in the face to me.／～적인 언사 insulting remarks.

**모우**(牡牛) an ox(pl. oxen); (거세한 소) a steer (거세하지 않은 소) a bull.

**모우(暮雨)** evening rain; rain at nightfall. ゆうぐれのあめ

**모우(冒雨)** ~하다 brave[defy, face] the rain; go in spite of[in the teeth of] the rain; go in defiance the rain. あめをものともせずにこうどうすること

**모월(某月)** a certain month. ぼうげつ

**모유(母乳)** mother's milk; breast milk/ ~로 기르다 feed (a child) on mother's milk. ぼにゅう

**모으다** ①(여럿을) gather; get (things, people) together (수집하다) collect; make a collection of/우표를 ~ collect[make a collection of] stamps ②(집중하다) concentrate; focus/정신을 ~ concentrate[focus] one's attention on. あつめる

**모음(母音)** 【언】 a vowel [sound]/~ 변화 vowel gradation/중성 ~ a mixed[neutral] vowel/~ 조화 vowel harmony/~화하다 vocalize. ぼいん

**모의(謀議)** conference; consultation; deliberation (음모) conspiracy/ ~하다 hold a conference; consult; hold counsel. ぼうぎ

**모의(模擬, 模倣)** imitation; copy/ ~의 sham; mimic; mock/ ~ 법정 a moot court/ ~ 시험 a sham[trial] examination/ ~ 재판 a mock trial/ ~ 투표 a straw vote. もほう

**모의(毛衣)** furs; fur garments; fur pieces. けごろも

**모이** feed; food/새 ~ bird feed/~를 주다 feed; give food to. えさ

**모이다** ①(메지어) gather; come[get] together; flock; crowd; swarm/서로 ~ gather[flock] together ②(회의에) meet; assemble; congregate/회의하려고 ~ meet[assemble] for a meeting ③(돈·물건이) be collected; be gathered/눈이 모여 덩이가 되다 snow piles up into a heap. あつまる

**모인(某人)** a certain person. あるひと

**모일(某日)** a certain day. あるにち

**모임** a gathering; a meeting; an assembly; a party (종교적) a congregation; a social gathering/동민의 ~ a town meeting. しゅうかい

**모자(帽子)** (테 달린) a hat (차양이 있는) a cap (여자용) a bonnet 《사냥용》 a hunting[sporting] cap/~를 벗다 take off one's hat; remove one's hat. ぼうし

**모자(母姉)** mother and elder sisters. ははとあね

**모자(母子)** mother and son; mother and children/ ~ 모두 전재하다 Both mother and child are doing well. ははとこ

**모자라다** be not enough; be insufficient; be deficient; be short of/일손이 ~ be short of hands/식량이 ~ be short of provisions. たりない

**모자반** 【식】 gulfweed.

**모짝** at one sweep; all at once; in one big bite; in a sweep. ひっくるめて

**모잡이** a farm worker who transplants the young rice plants.

**모장(帽章)** a cap-badge; the badge on a cap.

**모전(毛氈)** a rug; a carpet/마루에는 두터운 ~이 깔려 있다 The floor is thickly carpeted. もうせん

**모정(慕情)** longing; love.

**모조(模造)** imitation/ ~하다 imitate; copy; pattern (after)/ ~ 진주 an imitation[artificial] pearl. もぞう

**모쪼록** as much as one can ⇒아무쪼록. なにとぞ

**모조리** all; one and all; wholly; entirely; all through; without an exception; completely/ ~ 털어 놓다 make a clean breast of. すべて

**모종** 【농】 a seedling; a young plant; nursery trees/ ~하다 transplant the seedlings of; bed out/배추를 ~하다 transplant cabbages/나무 ~ a sapling; a young tree/토마토 ~ a young tomato plant/벼 ~ a young rice plant. なえ

**모종(某種)** a certain kind[sort]/ ~의 certain; one; some; unnamed/ ~의 이유로 for a certain reason. あるしゅろい

**모종삽** a [garden] trowel.

**모주** ❶~꾼 a hard drinker; a confirmed drinker; a drunkard.

**모주(母酒)** raw spirit; crude liquor/ ~집 a crude liquor shop. はっこうを促すためにいれる元酒

**모주(母主)** mother. ははのけいご

**모지(某地)** a certain place. ぼうち

**모지다** ①(뾰족하다) be angular; pointed; square; sharp/모진 기둥 a square pillar ②(성질·일 따위) sharp; pointed; uncompromising; unsociable. かくばっている

**모지라지다** wear out; be worn down/붓끝이 모지라졌다 The writing brush is worn to a stump. すりへる

**모지락스럽다** be very harsh ⇒모질다. ややざんにんだ

**모지랑붓** a worn-out writing brush.

**모지랑비** a worn-out[stumpy] broom.

**모지랑이** something worn to a stump; a stump. すりへりきったもの

**모직(毛織)** 《방모》 woolen fabric[cloth] 《소모》 worsted/~물 woolen fabrics[textiles, goods]/~상 a woolen-draper. けおり

**모진(耗盡)** exhaustion; consumption; dissipation; using up; wearing out/ ~하다 consume; exhaust; dissipate; be worn out. もうじん

**모진목숨** a hard life; one's wretched[miserable] life/~이 아직 붙어 있다 I am still prolonging this damned life of mine. くなんのおおいじんせい

**모질다** ①(잔인하다) be angular; stiff; harsh; rough; uncompromising/모질게 말하다 speak harshly ②(능히 견디다) be persevering; indomitable. ざんにんだ

**모집(募集)** ①(지원자의) invitation; collection 《학생의》 registration 《군인의 징집》

**모집다** ①(지적하다) point out specifically; show ②(집다) grasp[hold] all/남의 허물을 ~ point out one's mistake specifically. あらわにしてきする

**모채(募債)** loan flotation; the flotation [raising] of a loan/ ~하다 float [raise, issue] a loan/ ~ 가격 the issue-price/ ~액 the amount of a loan. ぼさい

**모책(謀策)** a scheme; a plan; a stratagem; a tactic. さくりゃく

**모처(某處)** a certain place. あるところ

**모처럼** ①(오래간만에) at long last; finally; for the first time in many days [years]/ ~의 일요일을 비가 와서 망쳤다 Rain spoiled our long-awaited Sunday. ②(벼른 끝에) at great pains (특별히) especially (일부러) on purpose (친절히) kindly; expressly/ ~ 초대해 주셔서 감사합니다 Thank you for your kind[special] invitation. せっかく

**모체(母體)** the mother (중심) the mother's body; the kernel; the parent; the nucleus. ぼたい

**모추(暮秋)** late fall; late autumn. ばんしゅう

**모춘(暮春)** late spring. ぼしゅん

**모출** a bundle of rice seedlings.

**모출하다** be a little too much[many]; be a little too long. ちょっとあまる

**모친(母親)** one's mother⇒어머니. はは

**모탕** a block. まないた

**모태(母胎)** the mother's womb. ぼたい

**모퉁이** a corner; a turn; a turning/그 집은 ~에 있다 The house stands on the corner. まがりかど

**모판(一板)** a seedbed; a nursery; a plot of young rice plants. なえどこ

**모포(毛布)** a blanket; a rug.

**모표(帽標)** a cap-badge; the badge on a cap. ぼうしのきしょう

**모풀** grass used as a fertilizer for the rice seedbeds.

**모피(毛皮)** (부드러운) a fur (거친) a skin / ~ 외투 a fur[-lined] overcoat/ ~상 a furrier/ ~를 팔다 deal in furs/ ~목도리 a boa. けがわ

**모필(毛筆)** a writing brush; a hair pencil; a painting brush/ ~화(畫) a hair-pencil picture. もうひつ

**모하(暮夏)** late summer. ばんか

**모하다(模一)** copy; trace; reproduce; make a tracing of; duplicate; facsimile. もけいをとる

**모한(冒寒)** ~하다 brave[face, defy] the cold. さむさをものともしないこと

**모함(謀陷)** ~하다 trap; [en-]snare/ ~ 당하다 fall into a trap.

**모함(母艦)** a depot-ship; a tender/잠수 ~ a submarine tender. ぼかん

**모해(謀害)** a plot to do harm/ ~하다 do harm to; inflict injury upon. ぼうりゃくをつかって人をそこなうこと

**모험(冒險)** an adventure; a risk; a hazard/ ~하다 adventure; hazard; risk; venture to do (a thing)/ ~가 an adventurer/ ~담 an adventure story/ ~적 adventurous; risky; hazardous; perilous. ぼうけん

**모형(母型)** 【인】(활자의) a matrix (원형) a prototype. いんさつのぼけい

**모형(模型)** a model (기계 따위의) a pattern (주조의) a mold/ ~을 만들다 make a model (of). もけい

**모호(模糊)** ~하다 (be) vague; obscure; uncertain; ambiguous; equivocal. もこ

**목** ①(동물의) a neck/기다란 ~ a long [slender] neck/짧은 ~ a short neck/ ~을 자르다 cut off (a person's) head ②(인후) a throat; a gullet; a wind-pipe / ~이 마르다 be[feel] thirsty/ ~이 아프다 have a sore throat/ ~을 따다 cut one's throat ③(길의) the bottleneck in a way of escape; a strategic point/ ~을 지키다 fortify the points of strategic importance ④(물건의) a neck/버선 ~ the ankle of a sock/병 ~ the neck of a bottle. くび

**목(目)** ①(항목) an item (생물 분류상의) an order ②(바둑 돌) a piece; a stone (판의 눈) a cross/한 ~ 놓다 put a stone; give a piece. もく

**목가(牧歌)** a pastoral song[poem]; bucolics; bucolic verse/ ~적 pastoral; bucolic. ぼくか

**목각(木刻)** wood carving/ ~ 활자 a block letter/ ~ 화 a woodcut. もくはん

**목간(沐間)** (목욕탕) a bathhouse (목욕) a bath/ ~하다 bathe; have[take] a bath. もくよく

**목걸이** a necklace; a neckchain (보석의) a riviere(F)/진주 ~ a pearl necklace.

**목검(木劍)** a wooden sword; a singlestick. ぼくけん

**목격(目擊)** ~하다 witness; observe; see with one's own eyes/ ~자 an eye-witness/ ~자의 이야기 an eye-witness account; a first-hand account. もくげき

**목곧다** (be) stiff-necked. がんこだ

**목공(木工)** a woodworker (목수) a carpenter. だいく

**목관(木管)** a wooden pipe/ ~ 악기 a wood-wind instrument.

**목구멍** a throat; a gullet; a windpipe / ~이 아프다 have a sore throat/ ~이 포도청이다《속담》 The hungry belly has no ears. のど

**목근(木根)** a tree root. きのね

**목금(目今)** at present; now ⇒목하. もっか

**목금(木琴)** 【음】a xylophone. もっきん

**목기(木器)** a wooden container; wooden

vessels; wooden tableware／～전 a woodenware store. もくせいのきぐ
**목남청(睦郎廳)** a yes-man.
**목눌(木訥)** innocence and lack of eloquence; artlessness／～하다 (be) innocent[honest] and unstudied; artless; naive; unsophisticated. ぼくとつ
**목단(牧丹)** a peony ⇒모란. ぼたん
**목달이** worn-out socks／～양말 knee-length stockings. たびのじょうぶのおり返し
**목대야(木一)** a wooden washbasin. もくせいのせんめんき
**목대잡다** direct; control; supervise; command. おおくのひとをしきする
**목대잡이** a director; a supervisor; a commander. しきしゃ
**목덜미** the nape[back, scruff] of the neck／～를 잡다 take[seize] (one) by the scruff of his neck. うなじ
**목도** a pole [for shouldering]／～꾼 a shoulder-pole carrier.
**목도(木刀)** a wooden sword[stick] ⇒목검(木劍). ぼくとう
**목도(目睹)** witnessing ⇒목격. もくと
**목도리** a muffler; a neckerchief; a neck scarf; a comforter; a shawl(여자용); a [neck] wrap; a boa(여자용)／～를 하다 wear a muffler. えりまき
**목돈** a [good] round sum (of money); a sizable sum. まとまったかね
**목동(牧童)** a shepherd boy; a cow-boy; herdboy. ぼくどう
**목련(木蓮) 【식】** a magnolia; *Magnolia liliflora*(학명). もくれん
**목례(目禮)** nod／～하다 nod (to); recognize. もくれい
**목로(木壚)** a drinking stall／～주점 a grogshop; a public house. たちのみや
**목록(目錄)** ①《상품 따위의》a catalogue／재산 ~ an inventory ②《목차》[a table of] contents. もくろく
**목리(木理)** 《나뭇결》 the grain 《연륜》 an annual ring[layer]. もくめ
**목마(木馬)** a wooden horse; a rocking horse 《체조용》a vaulting horse／회전 ~ a merry-go-round. もくば
**목마(牧馬)** horse-raising[-pasturing]／～하다 raise horses; pasture horses. ぼくば
**목마르다** ①be[get] thirsty; thirst ②《갈망하다》 have a thirst for; crave[long, yearn, thirst, hunger] for; be anxious for; hanker after／지식에 ~ have a thirst for knowledge. のどがかわく
**목말** riding [on] another's shoulder／～을 타다 ride the shoulder of／～을 태우다 give (a person) a ride on one's shoulder. かたぐるま
**목매기 송아지** a tethered calf.
**목매다** ①《남을》strangle (a person to death) ②《스스로》strangle oneself with a cord).
**목매달다** ①《남을》hang (a person) by the neck; strangle (a person) to death ②《스스로》hang oneself (on a tree); strangle oneself (with a cord).
**목매아지** a tethered colt. こうし
**목맺히다** be choked (with); be stifled (by); be suffocated (with). むせぶ
**목메다** be choked (with); be stifled (by); be suffocated (with)／목멘 소리 a voice strangled with tears. のどにつまる
**목면(木綿)** ①【식】a cotton plant ②《목화》raw cotton ③《무명》cotton [cloth]／～직 cotton fabrics. もめん
**목목이** at key positions [on the road]; at every strategic point.
**목문(木紋)** the grain (of wood). もくめ
**목물** a bust bath／～하다 bathe the upper half of one's body; wash the bust. ひとのくびまでのみずのふかさ
**목물(木物)** wooden ware／～전 a woodenware shop. もくせいひんのそうしょう
**목민(牧民)** government [of people]／～하다 govern [people]. ぼくみん
**목본(木本)** a woody plant. じゅもく
**목부용(木芙蓉) 【식】** a cotton rosemallow; *Hibiscus mutabilis*(학명). もくふよう
**목불(木佛)** a wooden image of Buddha. もくせいのぶつぞう
**목불인견(目不忍見)** being unbearable to witness[see]／～이다 can not bear to witness[see].
**목사(木絲)** cotton thread[yarn].
**목사(牧師)** a pastor; a minister; a clergyman／교구 ~ 《보통 영국 국교의》a rector 《영국 국교 이외의》a parson／～직 order[s]; ministry. ぼくし
**목사리** an ox bridle くびづな
**목상(木商)** 《화목상》a wholesale merchant of firewood 《재목상》a timber dealer.
**목상(木像) 《조각품》** a wooden image; a wooden figure. もくそう
**목새¹** fine soft sand.
**목새²** 【농】rice-plant fever. いもちびょう
**목석(木石)** 《나무와 돌》trees and stones 《무감각물》inanimate objects; stocks and stones／~ 같은 unimpressionable; insensible. ぼくせき
**목선(木船)** a wooden vessel; a wooden ship. もくぞうのふね
**목성(木星) 【천】** Jupiter. もくせい
**목소(目笑)** a smile about one's eyes／～하다 have a smile playing about one's eyes; wear a smile about one's eyes.
**목소(木梳)** a wooden comb.
**목소리** a voice／큰 ~ a loud voice. こえ
**목송(目送)** ～하다 follow with the eye; gaze after. もくそう
**목수(木手)** a carpenter; a woodworker／～의 연장 a carpenter's tool[kit]／～가 많으면 집을 무너드린다 Too many cooks spoil the broth. だいく
**목수(木髓)** pith.
**목숨** life／～을 건지다[바치다] save[lay down] one's life／～을 내걸고 싸우다 fight to death (with). いのち
**목쉬다** become hoarse; grow husky／목쉰 소리 a hoarse voice. しわがれる

**목양(牧羊)** sheep-raising/ ~자 a sheep-raiser; a shepherd. ぼくよう

**목양(牧養)** stock-raising[-farming] ⇨목축. ぼくよう

**목양말(木洋襪)** cotton socks; cotton stockings もめんのくつした

**목어(木魚)** ①〖어〗 a sandfish ②〖목탁〗 a wooden clapper ③〖절에서 쓰는 제구〗 a wooden drum [in the shape of a carp in the Buddhist temple]. もくぎょ

**목엽(木葉)** a leaf; leaves [of a tree]. きのは

**목요일(木曜日)** Thursday(略: Thur.)/ 내주[지난 주] ~ next[last] Thursday; Thursday week. もくようび

**목욕(沐浴)** bathing; a bath/~하다 bathe oneself; take[have] a bath; bathe in/~실 a bath-room/~탕 a bath-house; a public bath/~물 the bath water/~값 bath charge/아이를 ~시키다 give a child a bath. もくよく

**목욕 재계(沐浴齋戒)** ablution/~하다 do [perform] ablution. もくよくさいかい

**목우(木偶)** a wooden figure[image]; a dummy. もくぐう

**목우(牧牛)** cattle-raising. ぼくぎゅう

**목운동(-運動)** a neck exercise. くびのうんどう

**목인(木印)** a wooden seal; a wooden stamp. もくせいのしるし

**목자(牧者)** ①〖목양자〗 a shepherd; a herdsman ②〖성직자〗 a shepherd; a pastor; a clergyman. ぼくしゃ

**목 자르다** ①〖목베다〗 cut off one's head; behead; decapitate ②〖졸라매다〗 strangle (one) to death ③〖해고하다〗 dismiss; discharge; fire〈미〉; cashier《속》/ 목 잘리다 be dismissed; be discharged; be fired〈미〉. くびをきる

**목작약(木芍藥)** 〖식〗 a peony ⇨모란.

**목잠(木簪)** an ornamental wooden hairpin. もくせいのかんざし

**목장(牧場)** a stock farm; a ranch〈미〉; a pasture; a meadow; a grazing ground [land]/ ~ 주인 the owner of a stock farm; a rancher; a ranchman〈미〉/ ~에서 일하다 work on a stock farm; ranch. ぼくじょう

**목재(木材)** wood 《건축용》 timber; lumber 〈미〉. ざいもく

**목적(目的)** a purpose; an aim; an object; an end/ ~하다 have an object; aim at/ …할 ~으로 with the object of (doing); with a view to (doing); for the purpose of (doing)/ ~을 정하다 set up a purpose/ ~격〖언〗 an objective [case]; an accusative/~론〖철〗 teleology/~물 the object[ive]; object matter/ ~어〖언〗 an object/ ~지 one's destination. もくてき

**목적(目賊)** 〖식〗 a scouring rush.

**목전(目前)** ~에 under one's eyes[nose] / ~의 immediate; impending/ …의 목전에서 in the presence (of)/ ~의 이익을 좇다 seek immediate gain/ 시험을 ~에 두고 with the examination coming soon. もくぜん

**목전(木栓)** a cork/ ~질 suberin/ ~층 phelloderm. コルクせん

**목정이** breaking one's neck/~하다 break one's neck bone.

**목정(木精)** wood spirit; methyl alcohol.

**목정강이** the neck bone. けいこつ

**목젖** 〖해〗 the uvula(pl. ~s, -lae)/ ~ 염증 uvulitis. のどびこ

**목제(木製)** ~의 wooden; make of wood / ~품 wooden articles[manufactures] / ~품 공업 the wooden article industry. もくせい

**목조(木造)** ~의 wooden; built[made] of wood/ ~ 건물[가옥] a wooden building [house]. もくぞう

**목조(木彫)** wood-carving/ ~의 carved in[out of] wood/ ~ 인형 a wooden doll/ ~기 a wood carving machine/ ~공 a woodcraftsman. もくちょう

**목조(木槽)** a wooden manger. もくせいのかいばおけ

**목조룡벌** 〖충〗 a kind of potter wasp; Eumenes japonica(학명).

**목줄기** the lines around the throat; throat lines.

**목 찌르다** pierce the neck (with a dagger); stab (one) in the throat. くびをさす

**목질(木質)** lignum/ ~의 woody; ligneous/ ~부(部) the wood parts (of a plant). もくしつ

**목차(目次)** [a table of] contents; the contents of a book. もくじ

**목찰(木札)** ①〖목패〗 a wooden ticket[tag] ②〖지저깨비〗 chips; scobs; sawdust; shavings.

**목책(木柵)** a wooden barricade[fence, picket]. きのさく

**목첩(目睫)** ①〖눈과 눈썹〗 eye and eyebrow ②〖가까움〗 nearness; closeness; imminence/~지간에 박두하다 be near[close] at hand; be imminent. もくしょう

**목청(-性)** the vocal chords 《목소리》 one's voice/~껏 at the top of one's voice/ ~을 울리다 vibrate the vocal chords. せいたい

**목초(牧草)** grass; pasturage/ ~를 뜯어 먹고 있다 be at grass; be grazing (in the fields). ぼくそう

**목촛대(木-)** a wooden candlestick. もくせいのしょくだい

**목축(牧畜)** cattle-breeding[raising]; stock-raising/ ~하다 raise[rear] cattle / ~장 a pasture/ ~업자 a stock-farmer/ ~업을 하다 engage in stock-raising. ぼくちく

**목측(目測)** eye-measurement/~하다 measure with the eye/ ~ 거리 distance measured with the eye. もくそく

**목침(木枕)** a wooden pillow. きまくら

**목탁(木鐸)** ①〖불교〗 a wooden gong; a bell with a wooden tongue/ ~을 두드

**목탄**(木炭) charcoal; fusain/ ~ 가스 charcoal gas/ ~지(紙) charcoal paper/ ~화(畫) a charcoal-drawing. もくたん

**목통** ① the throat; the gullet; the neck ②《욕심장이》a greedy person; a pig/ ~이 굵다 have a thick neck. いんこうぶ

**목통**(木桶) a wooden tub; a kit ⇨나무홈. もくせいのおけ

**목판**(木板) 《그릇》a wooden tray 《널판》board. もくせいのはん

**목판**(木版) a printing block; a woodcut / ~술 wood engraving; block printing/ ~화 a wood-block print; a wood-cut. もくはん

**목판장**(木板墻) a wooden wall; a board fence. いたばりのかき

**목편**(木片) a block of wood(큰 것); a chip[piece] of wood(작은 것). もくへん

**목포수**(一砲手) a hunter lying in wait for game animals.

**목표**(目標) 《표적》a mark; a sign; a target; an object; an aim (표준) standard / ~하다 aim at; have (a matter) as an object; set the goal at/ ~ 지짐 an objective point/공격 ~ the target for an attack/아무 ~ 없이 without any definite aim; aimlessly/ ~액을 돌파하다 pass the target/우리는 소나무를 ~로 해서 사격했다 We took aim at the pine-tree and fired. もくひょう

**목피**(木皮) bark; tan/초근 ~ roots and barks (약초) herbs. もくひ

**목하**(目下) now; at present/ ~의 present; existing / ~ 고려중인 사항 a matter now under consideration. もっか

**목합**(木盒) a wooden receptacle with high edges and a lid.

**목향**(木香) 《식》an elecampane 《뿌리》a root of an elecampane.

**목협**(木鋏) a trimmer; pruning-shears. せんていばさみ

**목형**(木型) a wooden pattern/구두의 ~ a shoetree; a boottree. きがた

**목화**(木花) 《식》a cotton-plant; a cottonwood tree 《솜》cotton/ ~를 따다 pick cotton/ ~를 틀다 gin cotton/ ~꽃 a cotton flower/ ~씨 cottonseed. わた

**목화**(木靴) deer-skin boots worn by old Korean officials. ぼくり

**목활자**(木活字) a printing type made of wood. もくせいのかつじ

**몫** a share; a portion; a part/한 사람 ~ a per head share/ ~을 나누다 divide; share; apportion/한 ~ 끼다 [have a] share in. わりあて

**몫몫이** in portions; into shares; separately/ ~ 나누다 share; apportion; allot (to)/ ~ 차지하다 take each one's own share. わけまえごとに

**몬다위** 《마소의》shoulders of a horse 《약대의》a camel's hump. ぎゅうのかた

**몬닥** falling apart from decomposition / ~ 떨어지다 fall apart flabbily[flaccidly, limply, squashily]. ぼたっと

**몬존하다** composed; (be) calm; collected. おちついている

**몰-**(沒) 《전부》all; exhaustively 《없음》without; lacking. まとめて

**몰각**(沒覺) ignorance and lack of understanding. むちでちこくのないこと

**몰각**(沒却) disregard; ignoring; effacement/ ~하다 《무시하다》disregard; ignor 《잊다》forget; efface/법의 정신이 ~되어 있다 The spirit of law is ignored. /자기 ~ self-effacement. ぼっきゃく

**몰강스럽다** (be) cruel; merciless; brutal; pitiless; harsh; outrageous/몰강스러운 짓을 하다 do a cruel thing. ざんこくだ

**몰골** unshapeliness; shapelessness/ ~스럽다 (be) unshapely; shapeless; ill-formed/ ~사나운 짓 unseemly behavior [conduct]. ぼっこつ

**몰교섭**(沒交涉) irrelevancy/ ~하다 have nothing to do (with); be unconcerned (in, with); be unrelated (to)/그는 세상과는 ~으로 지낸다 He stands aloof from the world. ぼっこうしょう

**몰년**(沒年) one's age at death. ぼつねん

**몰닉**(沒溺) 《익사》drowning 《침몰》sinking; submersion/ ~하다 drown; go down [to the bottom]; sink; submerge; be submerged.

**몰다** ①《자동차 따위를》drive (a car); urge on (a horse)/차를 몰고 …에 가다 drive to (a place) ②《쫓다》drive; chase; give chase to; run after; follow game/토끼를 ~ chase a rabbit ③《궁지에》corner; drive/궁지에 ~ drive (a person) to the corner[wall] ④《죄인·역적으로》impute (a guilt) to (a person); charge (a person) with (a guilt)/살인범으로 ~ charge (a person) with murder. かる

**몰두**(沒頭) absorption; preoccupation; devotion of oneself (to); engrossment of oneself (in); giving up oneself (to) / ~하다 be absorbed[engrossed, immersed, lost] in (one's studies). ぼっとう

**몰라보다** cannot[fail to] recognize 《무시하다》ignore; fail to appreciate/친구를 ~ fail to recognize a friend/남의 수고를 ~ fail to appreciate an other's efforts[kindness].

**몰락**(沒落) 《파멸》ruin; downfall 《파산》bankruptcy/ ~하다 go to ruin; fall; become bankrupt; be ruined/ ~시키다 ruin; bring to ruin. ぼつらく

**몰래** secretly; stealthily; in secret[private]/ ~ 눈짓하다 give a furtive wink / ~ 도망하다 steal away. こっそり

**몰려가다** ①《쫓겨가다》be driven; be pursued; be chased/모퉁이로 ~ be driven into a corner ②《떼지어》go in flocks /고기떼가 ~ a shoal of fish swim together. おしかける

**몰려나다** ①(쫓겨나다) be driven[turned, forced, kicked] out; be expelled; be ousted; be ejected 《해고되다》 be dismissed[fired]/ 회사에서 ~ be kicked out of a company ②(떼지어 나가다) go out in crowds[groups, flocks, swarms]. ついほうされる

**몰려다니다** ①(떼지어) go about in crowds[groups] ②(쫓겨) be driven round; be run after. むれがってあるきまわる

**몰려들다** ①(쫓아오다) be driven[chased, pressed, pushed] into/ 한편 구석으로 ~ be driven[pressed] into a corner ②(떼지어) come in crowds[flocks, shoals, droves]. むれがってはいる

**몰려오다** ①(떼지어) come in flocks[crowds]; flock[crowds] this way ②(쫓겨오다) come driven; be driven this way.

**몰리**(沒利) sinking one's personal interest/ ~하다 sink one's personal interest; take no account of one's interest. ぼつり

**몰리다** ①(쫓기다) be pursued after; be chased ②(일에) be pressed[driven] ③ (돈에) be pressed[hard up, pinched] for (money) ④(한군데로) throng; storm; surge. おわれる

**몰몰아** in all; all together; in toto (L); all told.

**몰박다** put[fix] all one place.

**몰방**(沒放) volley firing. れんぱつ

**몰분수**(沒分數) indiscretion; foolishness; stupidity/ ~하다 (be) indiscreet, foolish; stupid.

**몰사**(沒死) ~하다 (be) annihilated; be extinct; be totally dead. ぜんめつ

**몰살**(沒殺) massacre; annihilation; a wholesale murder/ ~하다 massacre; wipe out. ぜんめつさせること

**몰상식**(沒常識) ~한 wanting in common sense; nonsensical. ぼつじょうしき

**몰서**(沒書) a rejected contribution 《우편물》 a dead letter/ ~로 하다 reject; consign to a waste-paper basket; kill. ぼっしょ

**몰수**(沒收) confiscation; forfeiture; seizure/ ~하다 confiscate; forfeit; seize /~물 a confiscated article; a forfeit-[ure]/ 적산 ~ confiscation. ぼっしゅう

**몰수**(沒數) all; the whole [number] /~이 wholly; in all. ぜんぶ

**몰식자**(沒食子) a gall[-nut]/ ~산 gallic acid. ぼつしょくし

**몰씬** (물렁한 모양) soft; tender 《냄새가》 fragrant/ ~하다 (be) soft; tender 《냄새가》 nicely[strongly] scented/ 향수 냄새가 ~거리다 be strongly scented[reek] with perfume.

**몰아** in all; all; all together; in bulk; in the gross; in the aggregate; in a lump/ ~ 사다 buy up all. ひっくるめて

**몰아**(沒我) self-effacement; selflessness /~의 경지에 이르다 rise above self.

**몰아 가다** drive 《휩쓸어 가다》 sweep away 《몰아 사다》 make a blanket purchase; buy in the[a] lump. ひきつれていく

**몰아내다** expel; drive out; eject; oust.

**몰아넣다** (억지로) push[force, squeeze] in 《휩쓸어서》 herd[jam] into 《몰아서》 drive into 《a corner》. とじこめる

**몰아대다** drive; spur 《a horse》 on; urge on; press. せめたてる

**몰아들이다** drive[sweep] in.

**몰아 받다** ①(한꺼번에) receive[get] (it) all at one time[in a lump]/ 빚을 ~ collect the debt in one lump sum ②(한 사람이) receive all [as a representative of other people]; engross; monopolize. まとめてうける

**몰아붙이다** put[push] (the books) all to one side (of the room).

**몰아 사다** buy in a lump; buy in bulk; bulk purchase.

**몰아세우다** rebuke (one) strongly; take (one) roundly to task. ひどくひなんする

**몰아 오다** besiege; throng. 押しよせる

**몰아 주다** 《한꺼번에》 give [it][pay [it] up] all at once; give[pay up] the whole amount. まとめてあたえる

**몰아치다** ①(한군데로) drive in; corner ② (급히하다) make haste with 《one's work》; speed [up] 《one's business》; make short/ 일을 몰아쳐 하고 있다 The work is being pushed on as quickly as possible. せきたてる

**몰염치**(沒廉恥) ~하다 (be) shameless; impudent; have no shame/ ~하게도 shamelessly/ ~하게도 …하다 have the impudence to (do). はじしらず

**몰이** 《사냥의》 chasing; hunting; beating; running (after)/ ~하다 chase (from, out of, to); beat; hunt/ 도둑 ~ a thief-hunt/ 고기 ~ running fish; fishing. ついげき

**몰이포수**(一砲手) a chaser [in hunting].

**몰이해**(沒理解) lack of understanding[sympathy]/ ~한 unfeeling; heartless.

**몰인격**(沒人格) lack of character; impersonality/ ~하다 be lacking in character; have low moral character/ ~적 impersonal. じんかくがないこと

**몰인정**(沒人情) ~하다 (be) inhuman; cruel; hard-[cold-]hearted/ ~한 사람 a heartless person. にんじょうがないこと

**몰입**(沒入) (빠짐) immersion; devotion 《몰수》 confiscation/ ~하다 confiscate; forfeit; seize. ぼつにゅう

**몰잇군** a chaser [in hunting]; a beater; a hunter.

**몰자비**(沒字碑) an unlettered person; an illiterate. もじがないせきひ

**몰지각**(沒知覺) indiscretion; thoughtlessness/ ~하다 (be) indiscreet; thoughtless. ちこくがないこと

**몰취미**(沒趣味) lack of taste/ ~하다 be lacking of taste; (be) dry; vulgar; dull/ ~한 사람 a person wanting in taste. ぼつしゅみ

**몰풍**(沒風) tastelessness/ ~하다 (be) ta-

**몰풍정(沒風情)** inelegance; tastelessness; flavorlessness; vapidity／ ～하다 (be) inelegant; tasteless; vapid; prosaic. ふぜいがないこと

**몰풍치(沒風致)** lack of artistic effect／ ～하다 (be) tasteless. さっぷうけい

**몰하다(沒―)** die; pass away; be gone; expire; be dead. ぼっする

**몰후(沒後)** posthumously／～에 after one's death; posthumously. ぼつご

**몸¹** ⇨별항 참조.

**몸²** 《월경》 menses／～하다 be in the flowers; have one's periods; be unwell 〈미〉／～을 걷느다 skip a period／～이 없다 have a period suspended; one's period does not occur. げっけい

**몸가지다** 《임신하다》 conceive; become[be] pregnant. にんしんする

**몸가짐** 《거동》 one's behavior[conduct]; deportment; manner; bearing 《태도》 an attitude; a setup; an air／ ～이 점잖다 have gentlemanly behavior. きょどう

**몸가축** dress; make-up／ ～하다 dress oneself; make up.

**몸값** 《화대》 money paid for prostitution 《포로 따위의》 ransom／～을 치르다 buy out／～을 치르고 죄수를 구해 주다 redeem a prisoner. みのしろかね

**몸꼴** personal appearance 《몸차림》 attire. からだつき

**몸나다** grow fat; get stout; gain weight; put on flesh. からだがこえる

**몸닦달** training oneself; hardening one's body; self-discipline／ ～하다 train oneself; harden one's body. からだのくんれん

**몸단속(―團束)** watch; vigilance; guard ／～하다 be watchful (against); guard (against); be one's guard. からだのようおい

**몸단장(―丹粧)** decorating[embellishing] oneself／ ～하다 dress[equip] oneself.

**몸달다** be all hot and bothered; be eager[anxious]; fidget.

**몸때** the menstrual period. げっけいのじき

**몸뚱이** 《신체》 the body; the trunk 《체격》 physique; build; stature. からだつき

**몸말** the subject ⇨주어(主語). しゅご

**몸매** one's figure[form, shape]; one's carriage／ ～가 예쁘다 have a nice figure ／무용을 하면 ～가 예뻐진다 Dancing improves one's figure[carriage]. ふうさい

**몸받다** substitute oneself for; take anot-

---

# 몸¹

①《신체》 the body 《전신》 the system 《체격》 physique; build; construction; frame 《몸집》 size; stature 《모습》 figure ／ ～에 맞는 옷 well-fitting clothes／ ～이 큰 large[-sized]; big-bodied; big; of imposing[large] figure／ ～이 호리호리한 slim-figured; thin; slender 《girl》 ／ ～이 풍풍한 stout; corpulent; fat／ ～이 건장하다 have a strong constitution[frame, physique]; have a solid build; be sturdy[strong]／ ～이 약하다 have a weak consititutioñ; be delicately built; be weak[delicate, puny] ／온 ～에 all over the body／ ～을 단련하다 harden[strengthen] one's body; build up one's constitution／ ～을 녹이다 warm oneself (at the fire)／ ～을 가리다 cover oneself; clothe oneself ／～을 닦다 clean[polish] oneself.

②《건강》 health／～이 불편하다 be ill [sick]; be in poor[bad] health; be o← t of sorts; feel unwell／ ～에 좋다 be good for one's health; (be) healthful; wholesome; beneficial; do (a person) good／ ～에 나쁘다 be bad for one's health; be harmful[injurious, unwholesome]; do (a person) harm／ ～을 해치다 injure one's health; break down in health ／～이 튼튼하다 be strong; be in good health; be perfect.

③《지위·신분》 position; station; place; one's status[circumstances]／귀한 ～ a person of high[noble] birth; an important figure; an august[exalted] personage／천한 ～ a person of low[humble] birth.

④《몸통》 the body; the trunk; the torso ／비행기의 ～ the body of an airplane.

⑤《사람 자신》 one's own person; self; oneself／내 ～ my body; myself; I／첩의 ～에서 태어난 아들 a son begotten by a concubine／ ～에 익다 be accustomed to; be familiar with／ ～을 던지다 drown oneself; throw oneself into; engage in; enter into／～을 두다 stay in; live in／ ～을 의지하다 lean[rely] on; find shelter with (a person)／ ～을 감추다 conceal[hide] oneself／ ～을 아끼다 spare oneself[one's efforts]／ ～을 그르치다 ruin oneself; go astray／～을 더럽히다 《여자가》 be sullied; be dishonored; lose her chastity[purity]; stain her virtue／～을 팔다 《노예로》 sell oneself (into slavery); go into bondage 《악에》 sell oneself to vice 《마음을》 prostitute oneself; earn money on the streets／ ～을 맡기다 give oneself to (a man); place oneself at (a person's) disposal／ ～을 바치다 devote oneself[one's life]; offer one's life; give herself to (a man); lay down[sacrifice] one's life (for the country).

**몸보신**(補身) invigorating *one's* body／ ~하다 invigorate *one's* body.

**몸부림** struggle; wriggle; kicking and screaming／ ~하다 struggle; wriggle; flounder／고통으로 ~치다 writhe in the agony of pain. もがき

**몸살** illness from fatigue／~이 나다 suffer from fatigue. つかれびょうき

**몸서리** an aversion; disgust; a repugnance／ ~치다 have an aversion to; abhor; feel repugnance to／냄새만 맡아도 ~난다 Its smell disgusts me.

**몸소** for *oneself*; in person; personally／그는 ~ 부하에게 모범을 보였다 He personally set an example to his inferiors. みずから

**몸솔** a brush to scratch itchy spots.

**몸수색**(一搜索) a body search; a frisk[ing]／ ~하다 search *one's* person; frisk ／흉기를 숨기고 있지 않는가 ~을 하다 search (*a person*) for concealed weapons. からだをそうさくすること

**몸쓰다** perform a feat; [do] a stunt. 早わざをする

**몸시계**(一時計) a pocket watch. かいちゅうどけい

**몸약** a shot of dynamite; a mining blast. ばくはつしたダイナマイト

**몸엣것** (피) menstrual blood[discharge, flow, flux]《월경》 menses. げっけい

**몸있다** menstruate; have *one's* period 《월경중이다》be in the flowers.

**몸져눕다** lie on a bed of illness; be ill abed[in bed]; be laid up [with illness]; be sick in bed《미》. びょうきでねている

**몸조리**(一調理) taking care of *one's* health／ ~하다 take good care of *one's* health. けんこうかんり

**몸조심**(一操心)《건강에》care of health《근신》 behaving *oneself*／~하다 take care of *oneself*. けんこうにりゅういすること

**몸종** a lady's personal maidservant.

**몸주체** disposal of *oneself*. しんたいのしょち

**몸집** build; constitution／큰[작은] ~ a large[small] frame／나이에 비해 ~이 크다 be big for *one's* age. たいく

**몸짓** a gesture; conduct; action; movement; motion／ ~하다 make gestures; sign; motion／그는 ~으로 밖에 나가도록 알렸다 He motioned me to go out of the room.

**몸차림** dress; equipment; outfit.

**몸채** the main part of a house; the main building. せんかん

**몸치장**(一治粧) dress; equipment; outfit／ ~하다 dress *oneself*; equip *oneself*／그 여자는 ~을 잘 한다 She dresses well. みのよそおい

**몸통** the trunk; the body. たいく

**몸풀다** deliver a child; give birth; be brought to bed (*of a child*)／몸풀 때가 가까왔다 She is nearing her confinement. ぶんべんする

**몸피** physique; build; constitution; frame. からだのおおきさ

**몹쓸** wicked; vicious／ ~ 놈 a wicked man; a rascal／ ~ 짓 an evil deed; knavery; a vice. びどい

**몹시** very; very much; greatly; hard; extremely. ひどく

**못¹** 《연못》a pond 《작은》a pool《저수지》 a reservoir. いけ

**못²** 《박는》a nail 《나무·참나로 만든》a peg／~을 박다 drive [in] a nail; nail ／ ~을 빼다 unnail. くぎ

**못³** 《살가죽의》a corn; a callosity／발바닥에 ~이 생기다 have a corn on the sole／귀에 ~이 박히도록 들었다 I am sick[tired] of hearing it. たこ

**못⁴** 《불가능》[can] not／ ~보다 cannot [fail to] see.

**못걸이** a bar of wood with nails on it for hanging things. かけかぎ

**못나다** ①《용모가》(be) ugly; bad looking; plain ②《어리석다》(be) stupid; foolish; silly; dull／못난 생각 a foolish notion／못난 짓을 하다 play the fool; commit a folly. みにくい

**못난이** a stupid person; a no-good; a tomfool; a fool; a simpleton; a blockhead; a good-for-nothing; a ne'er-do-well. おろかなひと

**못내** forever; unforgettably; always／ ~ 잊지 못하다 never forget. なお

**못되다** ①《미달》(be) under; below; less than (*a year*) ②《악하다》(be) bad; wicked／못된 놈 a rascal なっていない

**못마땅하다** (be) unsatisfactory; displeased. こころにみたない

**못바늘** a pin. ピン

**못박다** drive a nail in 《남의 가슴에》wound *a person's* feelings.

**못박이다** ①《손발에》get[have] a corn[callus]／발바닥에 ~ have a corn on the soles of *one's* foot ②《가슴에》have a grudge (*against*); feel bitter (*against*). たこができる

**못 본 체하다** pretend not to see《관대하다》 connive(wink, blink) at; overlook.

**못뽑이** pincers; a nail-puller. くぎぬき

**못비** copious rain in the rice-planting.

**못 살게 굴다** tease; treat badly; torment; be hard upon (*a person*).

**못생기다** 《미운》(be) plain; ugly; ill-favoured; homely; plain-looking; uncomely／못생긴 남자 a plain-[a homely-]looking boy. できばえがわるい

**못 쓰다** 《행위·사람이》(be) bad; wrong; improper; no-good; worthless.

**못자리** ①《모판》a rice [-plant] nursery; a seed-bed ②《씨뿌리기》planting rice seeds／ ~하다 plant rice seeds. なえどこ

**못정** 《광산용》a pointed chisel. つち

**못주다** nail [down]; drive[put] a nail; knock in a nail; hammer a nail into (*wood*). くぎざけにする

**못줄** 〖농〗 a guide line for setting out

**못지 않다** be as good as; [do] as well as / 누구에게도 ~ be second [inferior] to none. おとらない

**못질** nailing / ~하다 nail; drive [in] a nail; hammer a nail into (wood) / 단단히 ~하다 nail tight. くぎをうつこと

**못하다**¹ (질·양이) (be) inferior to; worse than; not as good as. 一でない

**못하다**² (불능) be impossible; be unable to (do); cannot; fail / 까지 ~ fail to go / 우리들은 노력했지만 산꼭대기까지 오르지 못했다 In spite of our efforts, we failed to reach the top of the mountain. できない

**몽구리** a close-cropped head 《중의 별명》 a Buddhist monk. ぐりぐり坊主

**몽근벼** awnless rice. のぎのないいね

**몽글다** (be) beardless (낟알이) be awnless. こくもつにのぎやざつぶつがない

**몽글리다** ①(낟알을) take beard off; remove impurities; clear grains ②(단련하다) drill; train; discipline ③(맵시를) adjust oneself; tidy oneself; fix oneself 〈미〉. のぎなどを取ってきれいにする

**몽글몽글** ~하다 (be) clotty; lumpy ⇨몽글몽글. どろどろしている

**몽니** avarice / ~궂은 avaricious; grasping.

**몽따다** feign[pretend] ignorance; play the innocent. わざとしらんかおをする

**몽땅** altogether; [in] all. ばっさり

**몽당비** a stumpy broom; a worn-out broom. ちびれたほうき

**몽당이** ①(실뭉치) a ball of thread ②(몽동발이) a stump. きれのこり

**몽당치마** a skirt worn-out short; a short skirt. みじかいスカート

**몽똑** ~하다 (be) stumpy; blunt; dull; stubby / ~한 연필 a stubby pencil / ~ 몽똑 all stumpy. すれちびてまるいさま

**몽똥그리다** bundle it up crudely ⇨몽똥그리다. いいかげんにまるめてつつむ

**몽동발이** a worn-down stump.

**몽둥이** a stick; a club; a cudgel 《경관의 곤봉》 a truncheon; a baton〈미〉; a snag《속》. こんぼう

**몽롱(朦朧)** dimness; indistinctness; vagueness / ~하다 (be) dim; indistinct; vague / ~하게 dimly; indistinctly; vaguely. もうろう

**몽매(蒙昧)** ignorance / ~하다 (be) unenlightened; ignorant; uncivilized / 무지 ~한 benighted / ~한 백성 uncivilized people. もうまい

**몽매(夢寐)** sleeping and dreaming / ~ 간에도 even in sleep.

**몽몽(濛濛)** ~하다 (be) thick; dense; dim / ~한 먼지 clouds of dust. もうもう

**몽상(夢想)** a dream; a day dream; a vision; a fancy / ~하다 dream (of); fancy. むそう

**몽설(夢泄)** a wet dream; nocturnal pollution[emission] / ~하다 have a wet dream. むせい

**몽실몽실** ~하다 (be) plump ⇨몽실몽실 / ~한 몸 a fleshy body / ~ 살찌다 be fat and plump. ぽっちゃり

**몽외(夢外)** ~의 undreamed of; (a thing) never dreamed of. いがい

**몽유병(夢遊病)** 【의】somnambulism; sleep-walking. むゆうびょう

**몽은(蒙恩)** receiving a favor[benefit, grace, kindness] / ~하다 be indebted to. めぐみをうけること

**몽정(夢精)** a wet dream. むせい

**몽조(夢兆)** a dream; the omen of a dream; a prognostic from a dream / ~ 가 좋다[나쁘다] have a dream foretelling good[ill] luck. ゆめみ

**몽중(夢中)** (in) a dream / ~에 보다 see in a dream. むちゅう

**몽진(蒙塵)** royal flight from the palace / ~하다 the king flees from his palace. もうじん

**몽총하다** ①(냉정하다) (be) cold; indifferent; icy; frigid; blunt ②(몽똥하다) (be) short; stubby. ずんぐりだ

**몽치** club; a bar; a cudgel / ~질 clubbing; wielding; a cudgel / ~로 때리다 beat with a club / 쇠~ an iron club. みじかいこんぼう

**몽치다** lump together ⇨뭉치다.

**몽키다** gather together ⇨뭉키다.

**몽탕몽탕** [cut] in big lumps[in chunks].

**몽태치다** steal; take; purloin; swipe《속》. こっそりとる

**몽톡** ~하다 (be) stumpy; blunt; dull; thick. すれちびてまるいさま

**몽학(蒙學)** ①(아동의 공부) elementary studies ②(몽고어학) the science of Mongolian language. こどものべんきょう

**몽혼(夢魂)** one's soul [appearing] in a dream.

**몽혼(矇昏)** 【의】an[a]esthesia. ますい

**몽환(夢幻)** dreams and phantasms / ~극 a fantasy play. むげん

**뫼** a tomb; a grave; a mound / ~자리 the site for one's grave. はか

**묘(墓)** a grave; a tomb. はか

**묘(卯)** the Hare[Rabbit]. うさぎ

**묘(廟)** (문묘) a shrine 《종묘》 a mausoleum. たまや

**묘계(妙計)** an ingenious trick; a clever scheme; a wise[capital] plan. みょうけい

**묘곡(妙曲)** a lovely[sweet] tune[melody]; a fine piece of music. みょうきょく

**묘공(妙工)** exquisite workmanship; fine workmanship. みょうこう

**묘구 도적(墓丘盜賊)** a thief who digs open a grave and steal things there in.

**묘귀(妙句)** a clever expression; a beautiful phrase. みょうく

**묘기(妙技)** exquisite skill 《연예》 a wonderful performance 《곡예 등의》 a splendid feat; [a stunt]; (야구의) a fine play / ~를 보이다 exhibit one's feats. みょうぎ

**묘기(妙妓)** a beautiful keesaeng; a good

**묘년(妙年)** youth; blooming age ⇒묘령.

**묘당(廟堂)** (조정) the Court (내각) the Cabinet; the Government.

**묘령(妙齡)** youth; blooming age/ ～의 young; blooming [girl]/～에 달하다 arrive at a marriageable age.

**묘리(妙理)** an exquisite[abstruse] principle.

**묘막(墓幕)** a hut built near by a grave.

**묘망(渺茫)** ～하다 (be) vast and farreaching; broad; boundless; limitless/～한 대양 a vast expanse of water; a boundless ocean.

**묘맥(苗脈)** the clue; the beginning.

**묘목(苗木)** a sapling; a seedling; a young tree; a nursery tree; a set/ ～을 심다 plant a seedling.

**묘문(墓門)** the entrance to a grave yard (능의) the entrance to a mausoleum.

**묘미(妙味)** charms; beauty; exquisiteness; a nicety; a nice point; a fine point.

**묘방(妙方)** (처방) an excellent prescription (방법) an excellent means[method].

**묘법(妙法)** ①(처방) an excellent means [method] ②(불법) the marvelous[wonderful] law of Buddha.

**묘비(墓碑)** a tombstone; a gravestone/ ～를 세우다 set up a tombstone.

**묘사(描寫)** description; depiction; representation/～하다 (그림으로) draw; sketch; paint (글로) describe/인물 ～ character portrayal/～적 depictive; descriptive.

**묘산(妙算)** a wise plan ⇒묘책.

**묘상(苗床)** a nursery; a seedbed; a seed plot (못자리) a rice seedbed.

**묘수(妙手)** (솜씨) excellent skill (바둑 따위의) a capital move (사람) a master hand; an accomplished person; a proficient; an expert; an adept.

**묘안(妙案)** a happy[bright] idea; an excellent plan[scheme]/～을 생각해 내다 hit on[be struck with] a capital idea.

**묘안석(猫眼石)** 〖광〗 cat's-eye.

**묘약(妙藥)** a specific; a golden remedy /두통의 ～ an excellent remedy for headaches.

**묘연하다(杳然―)** (be) far; remote; dim; vague; unknown/ 그의 행방은 상금 ～ His whereabouts is still unknown.

**묘예(苗裔)** distant offspring; descendants.

**묘우(廟宇)** a shrine[mausoleum].

**묘의(廟議)** (회의) a Cabinet council (결정) a Cabinet resolution.

**묘전(墓前)** ～에 in front of a tomb; at a grave/～의 제사 a memorial service before the grave./ ～에서 곡하다 weep over one's grave.

**묘제(墓祭)** a religious service before the grave; a memorial service before the tomb.

**묘주(卯酒)** a morning drink; a morning draught/ ～를 하다 have a morning drink.

**묘지(墓誌)** an epitaph (묘지명(墓誌銘)) an inscription on a tomb.

**묘지(墓地)** a graveyard; a burial ground; a cemetery (교회의) a churchyard /공동 ～ a [public] cemetery/국립 ～ a national cemetery.

**묘지기(墓―)** the guardian of a grave; a grave keeper.

**묘책(妙策)** a clever[pet] scheme; a capital plan ⇒묘안.

**묘출(描出)** depiction; description; representation/ ～하다 depict; describe; represent; picture/이 소설에는 영국의 전원 생활이 ～되어 있다 In this novel is described the rural life of England.

**묘취(妙趣)** (묘미) an exquisite taste (기묘한) a curious taste[hobby, interest].

**묘판(苗板)** a seedbed ⇒못자리.

**묘포(苗圃)** a seedbed; a nursery.

**묘표(墓表)** a grave post; a grave marker.

**묘필(妙筆)** an excellent piece of brush -work[writing, painting].

**묘하(墓下)** a family burial ground; a family graveyard.

**묘하다(妙―)** (기이하다) (be) strange; curious (현묘하다) mysterious (절묘하다) exquisite; excellent (미묘하다) delicate.

**묘혈(墓穴)** a grave/스스로 ～을 파다 dig one's own grave; ask for trouble for oneself.

**무** a radish ⇒무우.

**무(戊)** 〖민〗 the 5th of the 10 Heaven's Stems.

**무(武)** military affairs (무예) military arts/ ～를 숭상하다 pursue the policy of militarism; glorify military power.

**무(無)** nothing; nonexistence; naught; nil; zero/～가 되다 go for nothing.

**무가(武家)** a military family[class] (무사) a warrior.

**무가내하(無可奈何)** ～하다 (응치 않다) would not listen (별무 대책) there is no help for it.

**무가치(無價値)** worthlessness/～하다 (be) worthless; of no value/그것은 ～하다 It is worthless.

**무간(無間)** ～하다 (be) intimate; close; friendly/ ～한 친구 a close[bosom] friend.

**무간섭(無干涉)** noninterference; nonintervention/ ～주의 a hands-off policy; a policy[principle] of noninterference.

**무감각(無感覚)** 《무지각》 insensibility; numbness 《무관심》 indifference; callousness; apathy; unconsciousnsess／수족이 ～하다 My hands and feet are numb[have no feeling]．

**무감사(無鑑査)** (being) not subject to the jury[a panel of judges]／～ 입선 "Not submitted to the jury[a panel of judges]."

**무감찰(無鑑札)** no license／～의 unlicensed; without a license.

**무강(無彊)** eternity; immortality; everlastingness／～하다 (be) endless; everlasting; eternal／만수～하옵소서 May you live long!

**무개(無蓋)** ～의 without a lid[cover]; unlidded; uncovered; open.

**무거리** screenings; bran; coarse flour／～체 a rough sieve.

**무겁** a mound in the rear of a target.

**무겁다** 《중량이》 (be) heavy; weighty 《중대하다》 (be) important; serious; grave 《신중하다》 (be) prudent; cautious 《기분이》 (be) oppressive; heavy／무거운 책임 a heavy responsibility／머리가 ～ feel heavy in the head.

**무게** 《중량》 weight; heaviness; burden 《중요》 importance 《위엄》 dignity／～가 있는 《물건이》 heavy 《위엄있는》 dignified／～가 없는 《사람이》 undignified; lacking in dignity／～를 달다 weigh (a thing).

**무결석(無欠席)** non-absence; whole attendance.

**무경고(無警告)** ～로 without warning[notice]／～ 정전 stoppage of electric current without warning.

**무경쟁(無競爭)** ～의 without competition [a rival]／～으로 당선되다 be elected unopposed／～ 선거구 an uncontested division.

**무경험(無經驗)** lack[want] of experience; inexperience／～의 inexperienced; green; unpracticed.

**무계출(無屆出)** ～의[로] without notice／～ 결근 absence without notice[leave]／～로 결근하다 absent oneself (from work) without notice.

**무계획(無計劃)** being planless／～하다 (be) planless; unplanned; haphazard; reckless／～한 짓 a rash act／～적인 지출 reckless expenditure.

**무고(武庫)** an armoury; an arsenal.

**무고(無故)** peace 《건강》 good health／～하다 (be) peaceful; well 《건강하다》 healthy／～하게 in peace; in good health; safe and sound.

**무고(無辜)** ～하다 (be) innocent; harmless; peaceable; lawabiding／～한 백성 innocent people.

**무고(誣告)** a false charge[accusation] 《문서의》 a libel; a slander 《구두의》 a calumny／～하다 accuse (one) falsely; make a false accusation; slander／～죄 a calumny／나는 억울하게 ～당했다 I was falsely accused.

**무곡(舞曲)** dancing and music; dance music.

**무골충(無骨蟲)** ①《벌레》 boneless warms ②《사람》 a spineless[wishy-washy] person.

**무공(武功)** military achievements[merits, feats, exploits]; distinguished military services／～을 세우다 render distinguished military service／～을 세워 훈장을 받다 be awarded a medal for outstanding[meritorious] military services.

**무공(無功)** lack of meritorious services／～하다 be without merit; be undeserving of merits.

**무과(武科)** the higher military service examination.

**무관(武官)** 《육군》 a military officer 《해군》 a naval officer.

**무관(無關)** having no concern with ⇒무관계(無關係).

**무관(無冠)** ～의 uncrowned／～의 제왕 a king without a crown; an uncrowned king.

**무관계(無關係)** ～의 unrelated; having no connection with／그것은 전혀 ～이다 It's absolutely out of the question.／그것은 문제와는 ～이다 That is neither here nor there.

**무관심(無關心)** indifference; unconcern; apathy; nonchalance／～하다 be indifferent (to); be unconcerned (about); have no interest (in)／명성에 ～한 사람은 거의 없다 Few men are indifferent to fame.

**무교육(無敎育)** without education／～의 uneducated; uncultured.

**무구(武具)** arms 《갑옷》 an armour; weapons of war／～ 장인 a maker of arms.

**무구(無垢)** purity; innocence／～하다 (be) pure; spotless; undefiled; immaculate; unspoiled／～한 처녀 an innocent virgin.

**무꾸리** a shaman's rites; a kind of shamanistic divination.

**무궁(無窮)** eternity; infinitude; immortality／～하다 (be) eternal; infinite; endless; immortal／～히 eternally; infinitely; forever.

**무궁 무진(無窮無盡)** ～하다 (be) infinite; endless; boundless; unlimited; inexhaustible.

**무궁화(無窮花)** 《식》 the rose of Sharon; *Hibiscus syriacus*《학명》《국화》 the national flower of Korea／～ 동산[삼처리] the beautiful land of Korea.

**무궤도(無軌道)** ～의 railless; trackless 《상궤를 벗어난》 aberrant／～성 one's eccentricities／～ 트랙터 a caterpillar tractor／～한 생활 a reckless[loose, dissip-

무균(無菌) 【의】 asepsis / ~의 without bacilli (살균된) sterilized / ~ 우유 sterilized milk / ~ 수술 aseptic surgery.

무극(無極) 【화】¶ ~ 분자[결합] nonpolar molecule(union). むきょく

무근(無根) ~의 groundless; unfounded / ~하다 (be) groundless / ~ 질의 a groundless[wild] rumour. むこん

무급(無給) ~의 honorary; unpaid; non-salaried; gratuitous / ~으로 without pay[salary]; for nothing. むきゅう

무기(武技) military arts ⇒무예. ぶぎ

무기(武器) arms; a weapon / ~고(庫) an armory (병기창) an arsenal / ~를 들다 take up arms; rise in arms (against) / ~를 버리다 give up[lay down] one's arms. ぶき

무기(無期) no limit / ~의 unlimited; indefinite (징역의) for life / ~로 indefinitely / ~ 정간 suspension of publication for an indefinite period / ~ 연기 indefinite postponement. むき

무기(無機) 【화】 ~의 inorganic / ~물 inorganic substance / ~ 화합물 an inorganic compound. むき

무기(舞妓) a dancing girl. ぶぎ

무기력(無氣力) enervation / ~하다 (be) spiritless; enervate; nerveless. むきりょく

무기명(無記名) ~의 unregistered; unsigned; uninscribed / ~ 투표 secret voting [ballot]. むきめい

무기 징역(無期懲役) penal servitude for life; perpetual penal servitude / ~자 a life-timer / ~의 선고를 받다 be sentenced to penal servitude for life.
むきちょうえき

무기한(無期限) no limit / ~ 공채[연금] a perpetual loan(annuity) / ~ 대부금 a dead loan / ~ 파업 a strike for an indefinite period. むきげん

무김치 pickled radishes.

무난(無難) ①(안전) safety; security / ~히 safely; successfully / 그렇이 ~하다 That's safer. ②(무결점) faultlessness / ~하다 (be) faultless; passable / 이만하면 그저 ~하다 This may pass, This is passable. ぶなん

무남 독녀(無男獨女) an only daughter.
むすこのないかていのひとりむすめ

무너뜨리다 break; pull down; bring down; destroy; demolish; level / 돌담을 ~ demolish a stone wall / 둑을 ~ break the bank. ぶちこわす

무너지다 crumble; go[fall] to pieces; collapse; break; give way; come down; be destroyed / 벽이 무너지기 시작했다 The wall has begun to crumble. / 흙이 ~ the earth breaks loose. くずれる

무녀(巫女) a [female] shaman 무당. みこ

무념(無念) freedom from distraction[all thoughts] / ~하다 be free from distraction / ~ 무상(無想) 【불교】 freedom from all ideas and thoughts; an impassive state of mind. むねん

무느다 demolish / 무너뜨리다. こわす

무능(無能) inability; inefficiency; incompetency; lack of talent[ability] / ~하다 (be) incapable; inefficient; incompetent / ~해서 해고당하다 be dismissed for incompetency. むのう

무능력(無能力) incompetence; disability; incapacity / ~자 an incompetent person; a person without legal capacity.
むのうりょく

무늬 a pattern; design; a figure / ~ 없는 plain; unadorned; unfigured. あや

무단(無斷) ~히 (예고없이) without warning[notice] (허가없이) without leave [permission]. むだん

무단(武斷) militarism (강행) enforcement; high-handedness / ~ 정치 military government[rule] / ~ 정치를 하다 govern by the bayonet / ~주의 militarism.
ぶだん

무담보(無擔保) ~의 unsecured; without collateral / ~ 대부금 an unsecured loan / ~로 돈을 꾸어 주다 grant (one) a loan without collateral. むたんぽ

무당(巫堂) a sorceress; a witch; a necromancer; a spirit medium. みこ

무당벌레 【충】 a lady-bird; a ladybug(미).

무당선두리 【충】 a water spider.

무대 (못난이) an ass; a fool; a goose; a dolt; a dimwit; a birdbrain. ばかもの

무대(舞臺) (연극의) the stage; the boards (활동의) a sphere[field] [of activity]; an arena / ~ 공포증에 사로잡히다 suffer from stage fright / ~를 떠나다 quit [retire from] the stage / ~를 장치하다 set the stage / ~에 서다 appear on the stage (배우가 되다) go on the stage; tread the boards[stage] / ~ 감독 stage management / ~ 장치 stage arrangement / ~ 효과 stage effects / 회전 ~ a revolving stage. ぶたい

무대상(無代償) ~으로 free; gratis; without payment; out for nothing / ~ 증정 "a free gift". だいしょうがないこと

무대소(無大小) elastic fabrics.

무더기 a heap; a pile; a mountain (of) / 설탕 ~ an overflowing heap[a mountain] of sugar / ~로 쌓다 heap up; pile up. たいせき

무더위 sultriness; [high] humidity; sultry[sweltering, humid] weather.

무덕(無德) virtuelessness; lack of virtue / ~하다 be of no virtue; lack virtue.
むとく

무덕지다 (be) plentiful; plenty; abundant. たっぷりだ

무던하다 ①(사람이) (be) generous; broad-minded; liberal; gentle / 무던한 사람 quite a nice man ②(정도가) (be) serviceable; passable; satisfactory (충분하다) enough (잘하다) nicely. かんだいだ

무던히 (어지간히) pretty; fairly; consid-

**무덤** a grave; a tomb; a sepulcher/ ~을 파다 dig a grave/자식의 ~ 앞에서 울다 weep over the grave of *one's* dead child. はか

**무덥다** (be) sultry; sweltering; hot and close; muggy.

**무도**(無道) inhumanity; brutality/~하다 (be) inhuman; brutal; cruel; heartless /~한 짓을 하다 treat (*one*) with cruelty; act brutally toward (*one*). むどう

**무도**(武道) military[martial] arts[science]; the spirit of chivalry; knighthood. ぶどう

**무도**(舞蹈) dance; dancing step 《두 사람의》 waltz 《네 사람의》 quadrille/ ~하다 dance/ ~회 a dancing party/~복 a balldress. ぶとう

**무독**(無毒) ①《무해》 being nonpoisonous [nontoxic]; innocuousness; innoxiousness; harmlessness ②《성질》 gentleness; mildness. むどく

**무두장이** a tanner. かわなめしたくみ

**무두질** ①《모피의》 tanning; tawing; dressing skin/~하다 tan; skin ②《고통》 a grinding pain; a piercing pain/~하다 gnaw; prick/가죽을 ~하다 tan leather; dress skin. かわをなめすこと

**무뚝뚝하다** curt; brusque; unaffable/무뚝뚝한 사람 a blunt person. やさしくない

**무둑지다** (be) plentiful; abundant; heaping. どっさり積んである

**무득 무실**(無得無失) no gain no loss/~하다 (be) neither advantageous nor disadvantageous; neither useful nor harmless. とくしつのないこと

**무득점**(無得點) ~의 scoreless. むとくてん

**무등**(無等) (being) peerless; matchless; supreme. むそう

**무디다** ①《성질・머리 따위가》 (be) dull; slow; thick-headed; slow-witted/술을 마시면 머리가 무뎌진다 Wine dulls the senses. ②《말씨가》 (be) blunt; curt; brusque ③《칼날이》 (be) blunt; dull/무딘 칼[칼날] a dull sword[blade]/ ~하게 하다 blunt. にぶい

**무람없다** (be) impolite; discourteous; rude; impudent. ぶれいだ

**무략**(武略) strategy; military design; tactics. せんりゃく

**무량**(無量) immeasurability; infinity; infinite quantity/ ~하다 (be) infinite; full; be beyond measure. むりょう

**무럭무럭** ①《자라다》 fast; [grow] rapidly 《힘차게》 vigorously; soundly ②《연기가》 densely; in a thick clouds 《냄새가》 strongly 《악취가》 rankly. すくすく

**무럼생선**(-生鮮) a jellyfish ⇒해파리.

**무럽다** (be) itchy [from bites]; itching. むずかゆい

**무려**(無慮) about; some; approximately; as many as; no less than; in round numbers; round about〈미〉/~ 2만 명이 회합에 참석했다 No less than twenty thousand people were present at the meeting. おおよそ

**무력**(無力) 《기력이 없음》 powerlessness; impotence 《능력이 없음》 incapacity incompetence 《재력이 없음》 lack of funds /~하다 (be) powerless; helpless; impotent; incapable/공격에 대하여 ~하다 be helpless[powerless] against an attack. むりょく

**무력**(武力) military power; force [of arms]; the sword/ ~전 an armed conflict/~ 공격 armed attack/~에 호소하다 appeal to arms/~으로 해결하다 settle by force. ぶりょく

**무렴**(無廉) ~하다 (be) ashamed (*of*); abashed; shy.

**무렵** 《때》 time 《즈음》 about; around; toward[s] 《…할 무렵》 about the time when…/ 벚꽃 필 ~ a cherry-blossom season/매년 이 ~에는 날씨가 거칠어진다 The weather is stormy in this season of the year. そのころ

**무례**(無禮) 《실례》 rudeness; discourtesy; disrespect; impoliteness 《모욕》 insult /~하다 (be) rude; discourteous/~한 놈 a rude fellow/~한 말을 하다 speak insolently; use insulting language; be free in talks/이 ~한 놈아 You insolent fellow!. ぶれい

**무론**(無論) naturally ⇒물론. むろん

**무뢰배**(無賴輩) bums; hoodlums; hooligans; roughnecks. ぶらいかんたち

**무뢰한**(無賴漢) a rogue; a rascal; a scoundrel; a hooligan.

**무료**(無聊) tedium; loneliness; dullness; *ennui*(F)/ ~하다 (be) tedious; dull/ ~를 풀다 beguile the tedium. りょう

**무릎맞춤** confrontation; a face-to-face controversy; a showdown〈미〉/ ~하다 confront. たいしつ

**무릎치기** ①《바지》 knee-pants ②《씨름에서》 a knee-whack.

**무리**¹ 《한꺼》 a group; conspirator; a party; a faction; a league 《군중》 a crowd /도둑의 ~ a band of robbers/ ~를 지어 in faction/노름군의 ~에 들다 associate with gamblers. しゅうだん

**무리**² 《사람의》 the rush hour 《생산물의》 the season/금년에는 딸기의 ~가 이르다 Strawberries have come in earlier this year.

**무리**³ 《해・달의》 a halo; a ring; a corona. かさ

**무리**(無理) ①《부조리》 unreasonable[ness]; irrationality/~하다 (be) unreasonable; unfair; unnatural/~한 요구 an unnatural demand.

**무료**(無料) no charge/~의 free [of charge]; gratuitous/~로 free; for nothing; gratis; without fee/ 책은 ~로 내주었다 The books were given away free. むりょう

**무릉태** a soft-headed person. とんま

**무루(無漏)** without omission[exception]; to everybody; one and all. もれないこと

**무르녹다** ①(무르익다) ripen; get fully ripe; mature; mellow 《꽃 따위가》 be at its best/복숭아가 ~ a peach is ripe ②(그늘이) be deep/신록이 ~ the fresh green [of spring] is at its best ③(시기가) be ripe (for); mature/기운이 무르녹기를 기다리다 wait for a ripe opportunity/때가 무르녹았다 The time is ripe for it. えんじゅくしている

**무르다¹** ①(연하다) (be) soft; tender; flabby; flaccid; limp/무른 감 a soft persimmon ②(마음·힘이) (be) weak; infirm; pliant; yielding; submissive/그는 사람은 ~ He has a soft head./무른 성질 yielding temper. やわらかい

**무르다²** ①(익어서) get soft; become tender/복숭아가 ~ The peach has got soft. ②(요리되어) get soft; become tender; be well cooked[done]/고기가 잘 물렀다 The meat has become tender enough.

**무르다³** ①(물러받다) get[obtain] a refund 《물러주다》 give a refund; make repayment (to); pay back; repay; refund; reimburse/대금을 ~ refund the price paid/샀던 시계를 ~ return a watch [and get one's money back] ②(상쇄하다) cancel each other's accounts; counterbalance/주고 받을 것을 ~ cancel the debts each owes the other ③(장기·바둑에서) turn around; retreat; go back; withdraw. もどす

**무르익다** ripen; become ripe; be mellowed; be matured/봄이 무르익었다[한창이다] spring has ripened[is now well on]. えんじゅくしている

**무르춤하다** stop short; come to sudden a halt; flinch; wince. しばらくとまる

**무르팍** a knee 〔무릎. ひざ

**무름하다** (be) rather soft[tender].

**무릅쓰다** ①(곤란을) risk; dare; brave; run; defy; face/···을 무릅쓰고 in spite [despite] of; in the face of/병을 무릅쓰고 in spite of one's illness/나는 그를 구하기 위해 생명의 위험을 무릅썼다 I ran the risk of losing my life to save him. ②(풍우를) weather; brave/폭풍우를 무릅쓰고 in the face[the teeth] of a storm/폭풍우를 ~ brave[weather] a storm. あえてする

**무릇¹** 〖식〗 a squill; a scilla; *Scilla sinensis*(학명). かいそう

**무릇²** generally speaking; as a general rule; on the whole/~ 사람은 자기 본분을 지켜야 한다 All men should be faithful to their duties. およそ

**무릇하다** (be) rather soft; somewhat tender[limp].

**무릎** a knee 《여자의》 a lap/~ 관절[마디] 〖해〗 the knee-joint/ ~덮개 a rug; a wrapper/~ 길이의 knee-deep/~을 꿇고 on one's bended knees/~을 세우다 draw up one's knee. ひざ reasonable[unfair] demand/그에게 그 것을 시키는 것은 ~다 It is not in reason to ask him to do that. ②(강제) compulsion/~하게 by force; against (a person's) will/ ~하게 결혼시키다 make (a person) marry against his[her] will; force (a person) into marriage/~하게 잡아당기다 pull by force ③(불가능) impossibility/ ~하다 (be) impossible; be beyond one's power/ ~한 일을 하려고 하다 attempt the impossible ④(과도·과로) excess; immoderation/~한 운동 immoderate exercise/~를 했더니 몸에 해로왔다 The overstrain affected my health/~ 방정식 an irrational equation. むり

**무릿매** stone-slinging/~질하다 sling stones; throw stones with a sling.

**무릿풀** rice starch[paste].

**무마(撫摩)** ①(손으로) stroking; patting ②(달램) soothing; pacification/~하다 《손으로》 stroke; pat 《달래다》 soothe; coax; pacify/~하기 어려운 inappeasable; implacable. なぐさめること

**무망(務望)** ~하다 earnestly desire; seriously hope.

**무망중(無妄中)** unexpectedly. むいしきで

**무면허(無免許)** ~의 unlicensed; without a license/~ 운전 unlicensed driving/~로 병원을 개업하다 practise medicine without a license. むめんきょ

**무명** 《옷감》 cotton; cotton cloth/ ~옷 [실] cotton clothes[thread]. もめん

**무명(武名)** military fame[glory, distinction]/~ 혁혁한 of distinguished military services. ぶめい

**무명(無名)** ~의 nameless; unnamed 《익명의》 anonymous; obscure 《알려지지 않은》 unknown. むめい

**무명(無明)** 〖종〗 ignorance; darkness in the mind; illusion. むみょう

**무명(無銘)** ~의 unsigned; nameless; bearing no (artist's) signature. むめい

**무명골(無名骨)** 〖해〗 an innominate bone; hipbone. むめいこつ

**무명조개** 〖어〗 a clam. びのすがこ

**무명지(無名指)** a ring finger. くすりゆび

**무모(無謀)** rashness; recklessness; imprudence/ ~하다 (be) rash; reckless; imprudent/ ~한 짓을 하지 마라 Don't do anything rash. むぼう

**무모(無毛)** ~의 hairless; 〖생〗 glabrous/ ~증 〖의〗 atrichosis.

**무문근(無紋筋)** 〖해〗 a smooth[an unstriated] muscle. むもんきん

**무미(無味)** ~하다 《맛없다》 (be) tasteless; flavorless 《무의미·몰취미》 dull; wearisome/~ 건조한 dry; insipid; dull; prosaic (life). むみ

**무미류(無尾類)** 〖동〗 an anuran; *Salientia* (학명).

**무방(無妨)** no hindrance[harm]/ ~하다 do no harm; be no hindrance; it does

**무방비**(無防備) ~의 defenceless; open (*city*). むぼうび

**무방침**(無方針) lack of fixed policy/ ~의 planless; unplanned.

**무배당**(無配當) ~이다 No dividend is paid (on *the stocks*).

**무법**(無法) 《불법》 injustice; unlawfulness; wrong 《이치에 어긋남》 unreasonableness 《난폭》 outrageousness; lawlessness/~하다 (be) lawless; unjust; unreasonable; outrageous/ ~한 짓을 하다 act unlawfully; do (*a person*) wrong/ ~자 an outrageous fellow; a desperado; an outlaw/~ 천지 a lawless world; an anarchy. むほう

**무변**(武弁) a military man; a warrior; a soldier/~ 기질 militarism. ぶかん

**무변**(無邊) ~의 boundless; limitless; infinite/~ 대해(大海) a boundless ocean. はてしのないこと

**무병**(無病) good health/~하다 (be) in good health; healthy. むびょう

**무보수**(無報酬) non pay; no compensation /~의 without pay; free of charge; for nothing/~로 일하다 give *one's* service free. むほうしゅう

**무복**(巫卜) shamans and fortunetellers. みことぼくしゃ

**무복친**(無服親) distant relatives [for whom one wears no mourning].

**무부**(武夫) a warrior; a man of courage; a brave man. ぶし

**무부모**(無父母) being parentless.

**무분별**(無分別) 《무사려》 indiscretion; thoughtless 《경솔》 rashness/ ~하다 (be) thoughtless; indiscreet; imprudent/ ~하게 thoughtlessly./~한 짓을 하다 do something rash. むふんべつ

**무불간섭**(無不干涉) indiscreet meddling in everything; indiscreet interference / ~하다 poke *one's* nose into everything; meddle constantly in all matters; interfere in everything.

**무불통지**(無不通知) ~하다 (be) omniscient; well-informed; learned much/~한 사람 a walking dictionary; a dictionary on legs; a living library

**무비**(武備) armaments; military preparations/적군의 ~ 해제는 끝났다 The disarmament of the enemy was completed.

**무비**(無比) ~하다 (be) peerless; unparalleled; unequalled; unique. むび

**무비판**(無批判) ¶~적[으로] uncritical[ly] 《무차별》 indiscriminate[ly]. むひはん

**무빙**(無氷) non-freezing/~하다 get unfrozen/~강(江) an ice-free river; a non-freezing river. よりどころがないこと

**무사**(武士) a warrior; a soldier; a knight/~도 knighthood; chivalry. ぶし

**무사**(無嗣) having no posterity. こうけいのないこと

**무사**(軍事) military affairs.

**무사**(無死) 《야구》 no down; none out/ ~ 만루(滿壘) full bases with no outs. むし

**무사**(無事) 《안전》 safety 《평온》 peace; quiet ness 《건강》 good health 《할일 없음》 *ennui*(F) ~하다 (be) safe; peaceful; quiet/~히 지내다 get along well. ぶじ

**무사**(無私) impartiality/~하다 (be) unselfish; disinterested/ 공평 ~한 fair and disinterested; just and fair. むし

**무사고 비행**(無事故飛行) accident-free flying without an accident. むじこひこう

**무사마귀** 《의》 a wart; a papula/~가 생기다 have a wart; a wart grows; a wart forms. いぼ

**무사 무려**(無思無慮) freedom from all cares and anxieties; an impassive state of mind/~하다 be free from care; feel no anxiety.

**무사 분주**(無事奔走) ~하다 be very busy about nothing. ぶじほんそう

**무사 불참**(無事不參) poking *one's* nose into everything; meddling in everything. やたらにたじにかんしょうすること

**무산**(無産) ~의 propertyless; without property; unpropertied; a proletarian. むさん

**무산**(霧散) dissipating[vanishing] like the mists/ ~하다 dissipate; vanish; disperse. むさん

**무상**(無上) the supreme/~의 the highest; the greatest; supreme/~의 영광 the supreme honour. むじょう

**무상**(無狀) ~하다 《무형》 (be) formless; shapeless 《무례》 have no manners; (be) graceless; rude. むじょう

**무상**(無償) no compensation/~으로 gratuitously; for nothing; free of charge; without compensation. むしょう

**무상**(無常) uncertainty; transiency; mutability/~하다 (be) uncertain; transient/인생의 ~을 느끼다 realize the uncertainty[vanity] of life. むじょう

**무쌍**(無雙) ~하다 (be) peerless; matchless; unequaled; unique; incomparable. むそう

**무상시**(無常時) any time at all; an irregular time; unstated times. おりおり

**무상 출입**(無常出入) going in and out constantly/~하다 go in and out constantly; frequent; have free access to; visit freely. じゆうにしゅつにゅうすること

**무색**(一色) dyed colo[u]r/ ~옷 a dyed dress.

**무색**(無色) ①《빛깔》《물》 achromatism/~의 colo[u]rless; achromatic [lens *etc.*] ②《부끄럼》 shame; disgrace/~해지다 feel shame; be put out of countenance/ ~케 하다 outshine; eclipse; put (*one*) to shame. むしょく

**무생물**(無生物) an inanimate object; a non-living thing/~학 abiology/~ 시

**무서리** the first frost of the year [the season]; an early frost/ ~가 내렸다 We have had the first frost the year.

**무서움** fearfulness; frightfulness; dreadfulness 《공구》 awe 《공포》 terror. きょうふ

**무서워하다** fear; be fearful (*of*); stand in awe (*of*); be frightened (*at*); be scared[terrified] at. こわがる

**무석인(武石人)** the statue of a warrior standing in front of a royal tomb.

**무선(舞扇)** a dancer's fan. まいおうぎ

**무선(無線)** wireless; radio. むせん

**무선 전보(無線電報)** a wireless [telegram]; a radio telegram[message]; a radiogram〈미〉/~를 치다 send[despatch] a wireless. むせんでんぽう

**무선 전신(無線電信)** wireless[telegraphy] radio/한미간의 ~ a wireless service between Korea and America/~국 a wireless[radio] station/~ 기사 a wireless operator. むせんでんしん

**무선 전화(無線電話)** 《기계》 a wireless[radio] telephone 《기술》 radio [tele]phony 《통신》 a wireless telephone message. むせんでんわ

**무선 조종(無線操縱)** wireless control/~ 전차[비행기] a radio-controlled tank [aeroplane]. むせんそうじゅう

**무섬** fear ⇨무서움. きょうふ

**무섬타다** be easily frightened; scare easily. おそろしい

**무섭다** ①《두렵다》(be) fearful; dreadful; terrible; horrible; frightful/무서운 죄 a horrible crime ②《사납다》(be) ferocious; fierce; formidable/무서운 사람 a fierce fellow. こわい

**무성(無性)** ~의 sexless; neuter/~ 생식 asexual generation. むせい

**무성(茂盛)** ~하다 (be) thick; dense; luxuriant.

**무성(無聲)** ~의 silent; voiceless/~ 영화 a silent picture/~음 a voiceless sound. むせい

**무성 무취(無聲無臭)** ①《천도가》 the inscrutability of providence; the mysterious ways in which God works ②《보람 없는 존재》 life in obscurity; unknown. むせいむしゅう

**무성음(無聲音)** 《음성》 a voiceless sound; a breath consonant. むせいおん

**무성의(無誠意)** insincerity/ ~하다 (be) insincere; unfaithful; be lacking in sincerity/너의 행위는 ~하다 Your conduct betrays want of sincerity. むせいい

**무세(無勢)** powerlessness ⇨무세력. ぶせい

**무세(無稅)** ~의 free; tax[duty] free/ ~로 free of duty; duty-free.

**무세객(無勢客)** a powerless[an uninfluential] man; a person living in obscurity. せいりょくのないひと

**무세력(無勢力)** ~하다 (be) powerless; uninfluential. むせいりょく

**무소** 《동》 rhinoceros; *Ceratotherium simum*(학명). すいぎゅう

**무소(誣訴)** a false accusation/~하다 accuse falsely. ぶそ

**무소 기탄(無所忌憚)** ~하다 be unreserved; make no scruple (to *do*); outspoken. いみはばかるところがないこと

**무소득(無所得)** ~하다 gain nothing (*from, by*).

**무소 부재(無所不在)** omnipresence; ubiquity/ ~하다 (be) omnipresent; ubiquitous.

**무소 부지(無所不知)** omniscience; infinite [universal] knowledge;. extensive learning/~하다 (be) omniscient; know everything; have infinite knowledge. しらないところがないこと

**무소 불능(無所不能)** omnipotence; almightiness /~하다 (be) omnipotent; almighty; all-powerful; be unlimited in power. できないところがないこと

**무소 불위(無所不爲)** ~하다 be capable of anything; would[dare to] do anything. しないところがないこと

**무소속(無所屬)** independence; being affiliated with no party/~의 neutral; independent/~ 의원 an independent member/~자 a free-lancer;a free lance. むしょぞく

**무소식(無消息)** no news/~하다 hear nothing[have no news] from/영 ~이다 Nothing has been heard from him since. しょうそくのないこと

**무소용(無所用)** uselessness/ ~하다 (be) useless; unserviceable; of no use[avail]; unwanted. むよう

**무손(無損)** ~하다 suffer no loss; be undamaged; be uninjured; be without loss. そんのないこと

**무솔다** 《푸성귀가》 decay from the dampness. くさる

**무쇠** pig[-iron]/단련한 ~ forged pig-iron /~ 솥 a pig-iron pot. せんてつ

**무수(無水)** 《화》 ~의 anhydrous/~산 (酸) anhydride/~ 화합물 an anhydrous compound. むすい

**무수(無數)** ~하다 (be) numberless; innumerable; countless/~히 innumerably; without number. むすう

**무수리** 《조》 an adjutant; an adjutant bird. はげこう

**무수입(無收入)** ~으로 without [any] income. しゅうにゅうのないこと

**무숙자(無宿者)** a homeless wanderer; a vagrant; a vagabond.

**무순(無順)** irregularity; disorder 《단서로》 "Not in order". じゅんじょのないこと

**무술** water used instead of wine in a sacrificial ceremony.

**무술(武術)** military arts/ ~ 교범 a manual of arms. ぶじゅつ

**무술(戊戌)** 《민》 the 35th binary term of the sexagenary cycle. ぼじゅつ

**무슨** what; what kind of; some; some kind of/~ 일에나 in anything and everything/ ~ 까닭인지 why; for what reason/~일이 생겼음에 틀림없다 Something must have happened./~ 일이 있어도 (긍정) by all means; at any cost (부정) by no means; on no account. なに

**무승부**(無勝負) a draw; a drawn game; a tie/~로 끝나다 end in a tie[draw]. しょうぶがないこと

**무시**(無視) ~하다 ignore; disregard; set at naught; defy (유린·거부하다) override; veto/…을 ~하고 in disregard of; in defiance of. むし

**무시근하다** (be) loose; slovenly; lazy and slipshod. しまりがない

**무시로**(無時─) on occasion; as occasion calls; irregularly; at any time (때때로) from time to time. おりおり

**무시무시하다** (be) terrible; dreadful; awful; frightful/무시무시한 광경 a terrible scene. ひじょうに恐しい

**무시 무종**(無始無終) 《천주교》 without beginning and without end 《불교》 the eternal nature of mahatman.

**무시험**(無試驗) no examination/~ 검정을 얻다 get a certificate without examination. むしけん

**무식**(無識) ignorance; illiteracy/~하다 (be) ignorant; uneducated/~의 소치로 due to ignorance. むがく

**무신**(戊申) 《민》 the 45th binary term of the sexagenary cycle. ぼしん

**무신경**(無神經) insensibility; callousness; apathy; stolidity/~하다 (be) insensible (of, to)/남이 하는 말 따위에는 ~이다 He is too thick-skinned to mind what others say. むしんけい

**무신론**(無神論) atheism/ ~적 atheistic/~자 an atheist. むしんろん

**무실**(無實) ~의 untrue; false; innocent [of the charge]/~의 죄 a false charge[accusation]. むじつ

**무심**(無心) ①(무의식) inadvertence (무감각) insentience (순진) innocence (무관심) indifference; being not interested (in) ②(불교에서) absence of the worldly desires; disinterested beatitude. むしん

**무아**(無我) self-effacement; absence of ego; selflessness/~경(境)에 들다 attain a spiritual state of perfect selflessness. むが

**무악**(舞樂) a court dance and music; an ancient pantomimic dance. ぶがく

**무안**(無顏) shame; disgrace; humiliation / ~하다 (be) ashamed; abashed; shy /~주다 put (one) to shame; humiliate. めんもくがないこと

**무안타**(無安打) 《야구》 no hit/~ 무득점 경기 a no hit, no run game.

**무애**(無涯) infinity; infinitude/~하다 (be) limitless; boundless; infinite. はてしないこと

**무애**(無碍) ~하다 be making smooth progress; have no obstacles; be going on without a hitch. むげ

**무애**(撫愛) caress; pet stroke/ ~하다 caress; pet. あいぶ

**무양**(無恙) free from sickness/ ~하다 be well; be in good health; be safe and sound. むびょう

**무어** ①(놀람·반대) why; well; what!/ ~ 동생이 죽어 What ! Brother dead?/ ~ 괜찮아 Never mind. ②(애들의 대답) yes; what ③(여러 말 할 것 없이) 9~ 남들도 다 그런 줄 아니 Does he think everybody else does so? ④(무엇) something.

**무언**(無言) silence; muteness; reticence / ~의 silent; reticent; dumb. むごん

**무언**(誣言) a slander; a calumny; a false accusation/ ~하다 slander; calumniate; make a false accusation; accuse (a person) falsely. ぶげん

**무언극**(無言劇) a pantomime; a dumb show. むごんげき

**무언 부답**(無言不答) ~하다 have too much to say in answer; keep silent without answering.

**무얼** ¶~ 달라고 What do you want?, What did you say[what was it] you wanted? なにを

**무엄**(無嚴) imprudence; indiscretion/~ 하다 (be) bold; imprudent; pert; cheeky; forward.

**무엇** what; which; something; anything/ ~이나 anything [at all]; whatever; everything/~보다도 above all things; before everything else; first of all/~ 때문에 what for/ ~이라 말할 수 없다 be beyond expression/~이 어쨌다고 What did you say?/목에 ~인지 생겼다 I seem to have some sort of growth on my neck. / ~보다도 먼저 그 버릇을 고쳐야 한다 You ought to correct that habit before everything else. なに

**무역**(貿易) trade; commerce; business/ ~하다 trade (with); carry on commerce/자유 ~ free trade/~품 trade goods/~풍 the trade wind/~에 종사하다 engage in foreign trade. ぼうえき

**무연**(無煙) ~의 smokeless/ ~탄 anthracite/~ 화약 smokeless powder. むえん

**무연**(無緣) (being) without relations; unrelated (불교) with no affinity to the Buddha in one's previous existence/ ~ 묘지 a potter's field/~ 분묘 an ownerless grave. むえん

**무연**(憮然) ~하다 (be) disappointed; disheartened; discontented/그는 잠시 ~히 있었다 He was thoughtfulf or a moment. ぶぜん

**무예**(武藝) military arts; feats of arms / ~를 갖춘 사람 a master of military arts/~를 닦다 practice military arts. ぶげい

**무오**(戊午) 《민》 the 55th binary term of the sexagenary cycle. ぼご

**무욕**(無慾) freedom from avarice; generosity/〜하다 generous; disinterested/지나치게 〜하다 be disinterested to a fault. むよく

**무용**(無用) 〜의 useless; of no use[avail] 《불필요한》 unnecessary; needless 《용무없는》 without business/〜자 출입 금지 "No admittance except on business" むよう

**무용**(武勇) bravery; courage; prowess; valour/〜담 a tale of heroism. ぶゆう

**무용**(舞踊) dancing; a dance/〜하다 dance; perform a dance/〜 선생 a dancing-master/〜 연구소 a dancing school. ぶよう

**무용 장물**(無用長物) a good-for-nothing; a nuisance. むようのちょうぶつ

**무용지물**(無用之物) a useless[superfluous] thing; a nuisance; a goodfor-nothing. むようのもの

**무우** a radish/〜 가는 채칼 a radish-grater/간 〜 grated radish. だいこん

**무우**(無憂) 〜하다 (be) carefree; free from care. うれいのないこと

**무우주론**(無宇宙論) 〖철〗 acosmism.

**무운**(武運) the fortune[s] of war; the fate of arms/〜이 기울어졌다 The fortunes of the day went against us./〜을 빌다 pray for (a person's) success in war. ぶうん

**무운**(無韻) 〖시〗 (being) unrhymed[unrimed]; blank/〜시 a blank verse; an unrimed poem. むいん

**무월사**(無月謝) free tuition/〜로 without tuition; tuition-free.

**무위**(無位) 〜의 without a rank/〜 무관의 사람 a plain citizen; a commoner. むい

**무위**(無爲) idleness; inactivity/〜의 생활 an idle life/〜로 세월을 보내다 idle [loaf] one's time away. むい

**무위**(無違) 〜하다 (be) secure; safe 《믿을 만하다》 reliable.

**무위**(撫慰) pacification; soothing; comforting/〜하다 pacify; soothe; humour. なぐさめたてること

**무위**(武威) military prestige[glory]/〜를 해외에 떨치다 exalt military prestige abroad. ぶい

**무육**(撫育) 〜하다 bring up; rear; foster; cherish 《백성을》 govern with clemency. ぶいく

**무의 무신**(無義無信) lack of integrity and trust/〜하다 (be) insincere; unfaithful; disloyal.

**무의 무탁**(無依無托) 〜하다 (be) helpless; wretched; homeless/〜한 고아 a helpless orphan. ひんこんでこどくなこと

**무의미**(無意味) nonsense; senselessness; meaninglessness/〜하다 empty; absurd; insignificant; nonsense/〜한 말 empty words; words devoid of sense/〜한 말을 하다 talk nonsense/〜한 생활을 하다 lead a meaningless life/그것을 따지는 것은 〜하다 There is little point in arguing about it. むいみ

**무의식**(無意識) unconsciousness; involuntariness/〜적 unconscious/〜적으로 unconsciously; involuntarily/〜 철학 philosophy of the unconscious/〜적 동작 an involuntary action/〜 상태 an unconscious condition. むいしき

**무의의**(無意義) meaninglessness; senselessness =▷무의미(無意味). むいみ

**무의촌**(無醫村) a doctorless village. むいそん

**무이다** 《머리털이》 fall out; become bald. はげる

**무이자**(無利子) no interest/〜의 without interest; interest-free/〜로 without [free of] interest/〜 공채 a flat bond. むりし

**무익**(無益) uselessness; futility/〜하다 (be) useless; futile; be no good; (be) vain; fruitless/유해 〜하다 do more harm than good/더 이상 수색을 계속하는 것은 〜하다 It is useless to continue the search any longer. むえき

**무인**(拇印) a thumbmark; a thumbprint/〜을 찍다 seal with a thumb (on a document). ぼいん

**무인**(武人) a soldier; a warrior.

**무인**(戊寅) 〖민〗 the 15th binary term of the sexagenary cycle.

**무인**(無人) 〜의 manless; unmanned; uninhabited; desert. むにん

**무인도**(無人島) a desert island; an uninhabited island. むじんとう

**무인 절도**(無人絶島) a desert islet; an uninhabited and isolated island. むじんぜつとう

**무인지경**(無人之境) an uninhabited region; no man's land; a pathless track/아군은 〜을 가듯이 진격했다 Our army marched on with an irresistible force. むじんのきょう

**무일푼**(無一分) (being) penniless/〜하다 be penniless; have not a penny in the world; be utterly broke〈미〉/〜이 되다 become[find oneself] penniless. むいちもん

**무임**(無賃) free of charge; free/〜 승차 free-passage/〜 승차권 have a free ride/〜 승차권 a free pass. むちん

**무임소**(無任所) 〜의 without portfolio; unassigned/〜 공사 a minister plenipotentiary at large/〜 장관 a Minister of State without portfolio. むにんしょ

**무자**(戊子) 〖민〗 the 25th binary term of the sexagenary cycle.

**무자격**(無資格) disqualification;〖법〗 incapacity/〜하다 (be) disqualified; unlicensed 《무면허》 uncertificated/〜 교원 an unlicensed teacher. むしかく

**무자력**(無資力) want[lack] of funds[means]/〜하다 (be) wanting in funds; insolvent; be without funds. むしりょく

**무자미**(無滋味) 〜하다 (be) dull; uninteresting; lack interest.

**무자본**(無資本) lack of capital[funds]／～으로 without capital[funds]; with nothing to start with. むしほん

**무자비**(無慈悲) mercilessness; cruelty; harshness; brutality; ruthlessness／～하다 (be) merciless; heartless; pitiless; cruel／그는 곤경에 빠진 친구를 ～하게 버렸다 He was cold-hearted enough to forsake a friend in need. むひ

**무자식**(無子息) (being) childless; heirless／～하다 (be) childless; heirless／～ 상팔자 Love of children is an eternal encumbrance. こどもがないこと

**무자위** a [water] pump. ようすいき

**무작정**(無酌定) recklessness; lack of fixed principle／～하다 (be) reckless; blind; devil／～하게 blindly; recklessly; without fixed principle. むけいかく

**무잡**(蕪雜) confusion／～하다 (be) confused; in disorder.

**무장** crude bean soy.

**무장**(武將) a military commander; a general; a warlord. ぶしょう

**무장**(武裝) arms 《나라의》 armament 《개인의》 equipment／～하다 arm; be under[in] arms; bear arms; equip oneself／～한 armed 《장갑한》 armored／～한 백만 대군 a million men under arms／～ 시위 행렬 armed demonstration／권총으로 ～ 하다 arm[equip] oneself with a pistol／～을 해제하다 disarm／～ 경관 an armed policeman／비～ 지대 a demilitarized zone. ぶそう

**무재**(無才) lack of ability; being untalented; incompetence／～하다 be lacking in ability; (be) untalented; ungifted; incompetent／～인 an untalented person. むさい

**무저항**(無抵抗) nonresistance; passive obedience／～으로 without offering any resistance／～주의 the principle of nonresistance. むていこう

**무적**(無敵) ～의 unrivalled; invincible; matchless／～ 함대 the Invincible Armada. むてき

**무적**(無籍) absence of a registered domicile; lack of a record／～자 a person without a registered domicile. むせき

**무적**(霧笛) 《고둥》 a fog siren; a foghorn. むてき

**무전**(無錢) being moneyless／～의 moneyless; penniless／～ 여행 a penniless journey; hitchhiking《미·속》／～ 여행하다 travel without money; go on a penniless journey. むでん

**무전**(無電) wireless; radio《미》 ～으로 by wireless[radio]／～ 장치 wireless [radio] apparatus. むでん

**무전 대변**(無前大變) an unprecedented catastrophe[calamity, disaster].

**무절조**(無節操) inconstancy; unchastity／～하다 (be) inconstant; inconsistent; unchaste; wanton／～한 정치인 an unprincipled politician／～한 여인 a wanton woman. むせっそう

**무정**(無情) hardness; heartlessness; inhumanity; cruelty／～하다 (be) hard; heartless; inhuman; merciless(무자비)；cruel(잔인)／～한 세상 an unfeeling world／～ 세월 pitiless time／～한 사나이 a heartless man; a man with a heart of stone. むじょう

**무정견**(無定見) lack of a fixed principle／～한 inconstant; unprincipled; fickle; wavering. むていけん

**무정란**(無精卵) an unfertilized egg; a wind egg. むせいらん

**무정부**(無政府) anarchy／～의 anarchical／～ 상태이다 be in a state of anarchy／～주의 anarchism／～주의자 an anarchist／당시 러시아는 ～ 상태였다 Anarchy prevailed in Russia at that time. むせいふ

**무정위**(無定位)《물》astaticism／～의 astatic／～ 전류계 an astatic galvanometer／～침(針) an astatic needle.

**무정차**(無停車) nonstop.

**무정형**(無定形) amorphousness; shapelessness／～하다 (be) formless; shapeless／～ 수정(水晶) massive quartz／～ 상태 amorphous state／～ 금속 amorphous metal. むていけい

**무제**(無際) infinity; infinitude／～하다 (be) boundless; unlimited; infinite. はてしがないこと

**무제한**(無制限) unlimitedness; unrestrictedness／～하다 (be) unlimited; without reserve／～으로 without any restriction; freely／이민의 ～ 입국 the unrestricted admission of immigrants／연령[인원]은 ～이다 There are no restrictions as to age[the number of persons]. むせいけん

**무조건**(無條件) ～의 unconditional; unqualified／～ 항복 unconditional surrender／～ 승낙하다 give an unqualified consent. むじょうけん

**무조지**(無租地) tax-free land; land exempted from taxation. むそち

**무족**(無足) ～의 《동》 apodous; apodal／～류 《동》 apodes. あしなしの

**무좀** athlete's foot; bath-itch;《의》water eczema／～먹다 have athlete's foot. みずむし

**무종교**(無宗敎) no religion; being without religion／～의 irreligious; atheistic.

**무죄**(無罪) innocence; guiltlessness; clean hands／～하다 (be) innocent; guiltless; not guilty／～가 되다 be found innocent[not guilty]／～로 하다[～를 언도하다] find[declare] (a person) not guilty; acquit (a person) of the charge [crime]／～ 석방 acquittal and discharge／～ 판결 a judgment of acquittal; a decision of "not guilty" むざい

**무주**(無主) being ownerless. むしゅ

**무주 고혼**(無主孤魂) a forlorn wandering spirit [who lacks posterity].

**무주 공당**(無主空堂) an ownerless house; a deserted house.

**무주 공산**(無主空山) an ownerless mountain[hill]; a deserted mountain. むしゅくうざん

**무주기**(無週期) ~의 《의》 acyclic. しゅうきのないこと

**무주의**(無主義) lack of fixed principle/ ~의 without any principle; unprincipled/ ~자 a person with no definite principle. むしゅぎ

**무증거**(無證據) lack of proof[evidence]; no proof. しょうこのないこと

**무지**(拇指) a thumb. おやゆび

**무지**(無知) ignorance; stupidity/ ~하다 (be) ignorant; uneducated; illiterate / ~한 백성 unenlightened people/ ~는 최악의 적이다 Ignorance is the most fierce enemy/자기의 ~를 모르는 것이 ~한 사람들의 폐단이다 To be ignorant of one's ignorance is the malady of the ignorant. むち

**무지각**(無知覺) indiscretion; imprudence; misguided feeling 《행위》 misconduct/ ~하다 (be) indiscreet; imprudent; unwise/ ~한 짓을 않도록 스스로 조심해야 한다 You must be on your guard against doing wrong/ ~한 짓을 하다 ommit an imprudence; act indiscreetly. ちこくのないこと

**무지개** a rainbow/ ~ 빛 rainbow colour [hue]; iridescence/ ~를 쫓는 사람 a rainbow chaser/ ~가 섰다 A rainbow appeared[hung, rose, formed] (the sky). にじ

**무지근하다** feel heavy[dull]/머리가 ~ have a slight[dull] headache/ 감기로 머리가 ~ A cold makes my head feel stuffy. おもぐるしい

**무지기** an underwear skirt; a slip. シミーズ

**무지러지다** get stumpy[blunt]; wear down to a stump; wear out; be worn out; be stumped/무지러진 비 a stumpy broom/붓이 무지러졌다 The writing brush is worn to a stump. ちびれる

**무지렁이** a fool; an ignoramus. あほ

**무지르다** cut off[away]; cut; sever/ 뭇가지를 ~ cut branches off a tree; lop off[down] branches. もののいちぶをきりすてる

**무찌르다** ①《살육하다》 kill off; mow[cut] down; kill recklessly; slaughter; butcher/닥치는 대로 ~ strike down everything that comes in one's way ②《공격하다》 attack; assault; launch an attack (on); set upon 《유린하다》 devastate; overrun/적의 성을 ~ assault[devastate] an enemy castle; devastate an enemy castle. むやみに攻め込む

**무지 막지** (無知莫知) ~하다 (be) ignorant and uncouth/ ~한 짓을 하다 commit an outrage. ぐどんでおうぼうなこと

**무지 몰각**(無知沒覺) ignorance; stupidity; illiteracy/ ~하다 (be) ignorant; unthinking and uninformed; stupid; uneducated. じょうしきのないこと

**무지스럽다**(無知-) (be) ignorant 《우악한》 cruel; rough; rude.

**무직**(無職) ~의 without[having no] occupation; jobless 《실업한》 unemployed; out of work[a job]/ ~자 a person out of work[without occupation]; a jobless man 《총칭》 the unemployed. むしょく

**무진**(戊辰) the 5th binary term of the sexagenary cycle. ぼしん

**무진**(無盡) ①《금융의》 the monthly lottery [of a savings-club]/~ 회사 a mutual loan company ②《무궁》 [with] no end; no limit/ ~하다 (be) unending; unlimited. むじん

**무진장**(無盡藏) an inexhaustible supply [treasury]; unlimited resources/ ~하다 (be) inexhaustible; unlimited; limitless /~의 보고 an inexhaustible mine of wealth/~의 공급원 unfailing sources of supply/돈을 ~으로 가지고 있다 He has a mint of money., He has no end of money. むじんぞう

**무질서**(無秩序) disorder; confusion 《혼돈》 chaos; anarchy/ ~하다 (be) disordered; confused; chaotic; anarchic; be at sixes and sevens. むちつじょ

**무차별**(無差別) indiscrimination; making no distinction/ ~하다 (be) indiscriminate; blind; without distinction/ ~로 indiscriminately; without distinction; equally. むさべつ

**무차일**(無車日) a no-vehicle day.

**무착륙**(無着陸) 《비행기의》 nonstop; without alighting/~으로 비행하다 make a nonstop flight; fly nonstop (to). むちゃくりく

**무참**(無慘) pitilessness; mercilessness; cruelty/~하다 (be) merciless; cruel 《비참하다》(be) tragic; pitiful/~하게 without pity[mercy]; mercilessly; cruelly/ ~한 광경 a horrible scene [to look at / ~한 죽음을 당하다 die a horrible death; meet with[come to] a tragic end. むざん

**무참**(無慚) shame; disgrace/~하다 be[feel] ashamed; feel mortified.

**무책**(無策) lack of policy; resourcelessness/ ~속수 ~이다 be resourceless; have no policy; lack policy; lack of means to deal with a situation. むさく

**무책임**(無責任) irresponsibility/ ~하다 (be) irresponsible; unscrupulous; negligent/~하게 irresponsibly; without a due sense of responsibility. むせきにん

**무척** very much; quite; exceedingly; extremely/ ~ 칭찬하다 praise highly / ~ 영리하다 be remarkably clever/ ~ 피곤하다 be dead tired/~ 춥다 It is very cold. ひじょうに

**무척추 동물**(無脊椎動物) an invertebrate

**무춤하다** halt; start back; hold back on c's steps; stop short; shrink back (at, from); recoil (from); flinch (form); hesitate. しりごみする

**무취**(無臭) ~의 odorless; scentless; inodorous. においかないこと

**무취미**(無趣味) lack of taste; vulgarity; prosaism; dullness／~하다 (be) uninteresting; prosaic; vulgar; dry／~한 사람 a man of no taste; a prosaic man. むしゅみ

**무턱대고** without rhyme or reason; for no good reason[cause]; unreasonably; with no prearrangement; with no preparation／~ 책망하다 scold (a person) for no good reason／~ 찾아가다 call on (a person) just like that／그가 왜 ~ 화를 내는지 모르겠다 I don't see any reason for his anger. むてつぽうに

**무테**(無-) ~의 brimless; unframed; frameless／~ 안경 [a pair of] rimless spectacles.

**무통**(無痛) ~의 painless; free from pain／~ 분만 painless delivery; twilight sleep. むつう

**무통제**(無統制) ①(무통일) lack of control [system] ②(통제를 받지 않음) ~이다 be placed underno control／~의 uncontrolled. とうせいのないこと

**무투표**(無投票) ~로 without voting／~당선(當選) return without voting.

**무표정**(無表情) dead-pan((미・속))／~하다 (be) expressionless; blank／~한 얼굴 an expressionless face; a poker face 《구》. むひょうじょう

**무풍**(無風) a dead[flat] calm／~의 windless; calm. むふう

**무학**(無學) 《무지》 ignorance 《문맹》 illiteracy／~하다 (be) illiterate; unlettered; unschooled／~에 몽매한 사람 an illiterate person; an ignoramus. むがく

**무한**(無限) infinity 《영구》 eternity／~하다 (be) limitless; endless; infinite; boundless 《영구하다》 eternal／~히 infinitely; boundlessly; eternally／~의 권력 unlimited power／~한 사랑[자애, 바다] boundless love[mercy, sea]／수요는 ~히 증가될 것이다 The demand will increase to an unlimited extent.／~ 궤도《공》 a caterpillar／~ 급수《수》 an infinite series／~소 infinitesimal／~ 책임《법》unlimited liability／~량 infinite quantity.

**무한정**(無限定) unlimitedness; infinity／~하다 (be) unlimited; infinite. げんていのないこと

**무함**(誣陷) a slander; a calumny; a false charge／~하다 slander; calumniate; make a false accusation; falsely implicate. におとすこと

**무해**(無害) harmlessness; innocuousness; innoxiousness／~하다 (be) harmless; innocuous; innoxious; inoffensive／~한 약품 a harmless drug／인축(人畜)~ no harm[harmless] to men and beasts. むがい

**무해 무득**(無害無得) ~하다 (be) neither harmful nor useful; neither advantageous nor disadvantageous. むがいのむとく

**무허가**(無許可) no permit; without a permit[license]／~의 unlicensed; non-licensed; without a licence／~ 판매[제조] non-licensed sale[production]. きょかのないこと

**무혈**(無血) ~의 bloodless; without bloodshed／~의 승리 a bloodless victory／~ 혁명 a bloodless revolution／~ 전쟁 a white war. むけつ

**무혐**(無嫌) ~하다 (be) free from suspicion; (be) unsuspected; clear; in the clear. けんぎのないこと

**무협**(武俠) chivalry; heroism／~적 chivalrous.

**무형**(無形) ~의 invisible 《추상적》 abstract; formless 《정신적》 moral／~ 물 an immaterial being／~의 세계 the immaterial world／유형 ~의 원조 material and moral support／지식은 ~의 재산이다 Knowledge is a moral asset. むけい

**무호 동중**(無虎洞中) a Triton among the minnows／~ 이작호(狸作虎) When the cat's away, the mice will play., Where there are no dogs, the fox is a king.

**무화과**(無花果) a fig／~나무 a fig tree. いちじく

**무환자**(無患子) 《식》a kind of soapberry; *Sapindus mukurossi*(학명).

**무효** invalidity; ineffectiveness; inefficiency; futility／~하다 《보라이 없다》(be) invalid; unavailable; of no effect 《효과가 없다》(be) ineffectual; fruitless; futile／~ 투표 a spoilt[an invalid] vote／~가 되다 become null[void, ineffective]; be fruitless 《무소용》; be of no use[avail]／그 법률은 ~가 됐다 The law has been annulled.／~도 간주되다 be regarded as not valid／~ 처분당하다 be dealt with as invalid. むこう

**무후**(無後) having no posterity／~하다 (be) sonless; be without offspring／~총(塚) the tomb of a sonless person. こうけいのないこと

**무훈**(武勳) a distinguished military service; military exploits[merits, feats, achievements]／~을 세우다 distinguish *one*self on the field of battle; win *one's* spurs. ぶくん

**무휴**(無休) no holiday; without holiday／~이다 have no holiday／연중 ~ open throughout the year. むきゅう

**무흠**(無欠) 《흠이 없음》flawlessness; faultlessness; perfection／~하다 (be) flawless; faultless; be free from blemish. むけつ

**무희**(舞姬) a dancer; a dancing-girl; a ballet-girl; a figurant; *a ballerina*(It);

*a danseuse*(F). まいひめ

**묵** a paste; jelly／도토리 ~ a paste made from the starch of the acorn.

**묵객**(墨客) 《서예가》a calligrapher 《화가》 a painter. ぼっかく

**묵계**(默契) a tacit[an implicit] understanding[agreement]／~하다 agree tacitly; make a tacit agreement／양국간에 ~가 성립된 모양이다 There seems to be a tacit agreement between the two countries. もっけい

**묵고**(默考) 《묵상》meditation; deep contemplation 《명상》reverie／~하다 meditate; muse (*on*); contemplate. もっこう

**묵념**(默念) meditation; contemplation／~하다 meditate; contemplate

**묵다**¹ 《오래되다》get old; get antiquated; get stale 《낡게하여》be off; lead a life away from／묵은 관습 old customs／묵은 사상 an old-fashioned[a moss-grown] idea／묵은 빚 an old debt; a debt of long standing／케케묵은 생각 a completely outmoded idea／케케~ the hackneyed; be threadbare; be stale.
ながくじかんがたつ

**묵다**² 《숙박하다》stay (*at, in, with*); put up (*at*); stop (*at, in*); lodge (*in, with*); put up[stop] (at *a hotel*); register (at *a hotel*)／아무리 밤이 늦어도 남의 집에서 묵는 일이 없다 I never stay out, but always come home, however late at night. とどまる

**묶다** ①《매다》bind; tie; fasten 《쇠사슬로》chain 《단을 지어》bind up; [tie up in a] bundle; fold／머리를 ~ bundle *one's* hair／원고를 ~ tie up Mss. ②《포박하다》bind; tie; arrest／손을 뒤로 ~ bind[tie] *one's* hands behind *one's* back. しぼる

**묵도**(默禱) a silent[tacit] prayer; a silent tribute／~하다 pray silently; offer a silent prayer／전몰 장병에 대하여 1분간 ~를 올리다 stand for a minute in silent tribute to the war dead; offer one-minute prayer for the repose of the souls of the war. もくとう

**묵독**(默讀) silent reading／~하다 read silently; look through. もくどく

**묵례**(默禮) a silent bow／~하다 bow to (*a person*); in silence make a silent bow／~를 교환하다 exchange bows with (*a person*). もくれい

**묵묵**(默默) ~하다 (be) silent; mute; tacit／~히 in silence; silently; mutely; tacitly／~ 부답하다 be silent and make no response. もくもく

**묵밭** a fallow field.

**묵비권**(默秘權) the right to keep silent／~을 행사하다 use the right of silence; stand mute [of malice]. もくひけん

**묵비지** the lees from filtering the greenpea liquid to make jelly.

**묵살**(默殺) ~하다 take no notice of; ignore [by keeping silence]／의안을 ~하다 shelve[pigeon-hole, kill] a bill／제안을 ~하다 smother up[burke] a proposal. もくさつ

**묵상**(默想) meditation; contemplation; musing; [a] reverie; a brown study／~하다 meditate (*on*); contemplate; muse (*on*); brood (*on*)／~적 contemplative; meditative／~에 잠기다 fall into [a] reverie; indulge in reveries [about the future]. もくそう

**묵새기다** make a long[an extended] stay.
ながくたいざいする

**묵수**(墨守) adherence／~하다 adhere to; cling to; stick to／구습을 ~하다 cling to an old custom. ぼくしゅ

**묵시**(默示) ①《신의》a revelation／~하다 reveal／~록 【종】the Book of Revelation; the Apocalypse ②《명시에 대한》implication／~하다 imply／명시 또는 ~의 계약 an agreement expressed or implied. もくし

**묵시**(默視) ~하다 overlook; pass over; tolerate 《방관》remain a mere spectator／그 사실을 ~할 수 없다 I cannot shut my eyes to the fact. もくし

**묶어치밀다** 《감정이》feel a lump rise in *one's* throat; be filled [with emotion]; have a fit (*of*)／가슴 속에 묶어치미는 증오 the hatred rising[heaving] within one／마음 속에 묶어치미는 슬픔 the sorrow welling up within one／노여움이 ~ have a fit of anger; feel a lump rise in *one's* throat.

**묵언**(默言) silence; muteness／~하다 keep silent; utter no words; be speechless. たまっていること

**묵연**(默然) silently; in silence／~하다 (be) silent; mute; tacit／~하게 silently; without saying anything; mutely; speechlessly／~중에 허락하다 give a tacit permission. もくぜんと

**묵은세배**(—歲拜) bowing *one's* greeting to elders on New Year's Eve.

**묵은해** the old year; the year that has been rung out; last year. きゅうねん

**묶음** a bundle; a bunch 《곡물·서류 따위의》a sheaf／나무 한 ~ a faggot of wood／짚 한 ~ a bundle of straw／서류 한 ~ a sheaf of papers／한 ~으로 하여[되어] in a bundle[bunch]／~으로 만들다 bundle; tie up in a bundle. たば

**묵이** an old thing. こぶつ

**묵인**(默認) tacit admission; connivance／~하다 permit tacitly; wink[connive] at／이런 부패가 ~되어 있는 것은 한탄할 노릇이다 It is a matter for sincere regret that such corruption should be overlooked. もくにん

**묵자**(默字) a mute [letter].

**묵정밭** a fallow field that has gone to waste; a deserted field.

**묵정이** an old article; second-hand goods; used articles[goods]《미》. 古くなったもの

**묵종**(默從) passive obedience; acquiesce-

**묵좌(默坐)** sitting in silence/~하다 sit in silence. もくざ

**묵주(默珠)** 【종】 a Roman Catholic rosary.

**묵죽(墨竹)** a Chinese-ink painting that depicts bamboo. すみにたけ

**묵중(默重)** taciturnity; reticence/~하다 (be) taciturn and dignified; reticent; reserved. とっしり

**묵즙(墨汁)** Indian ink/~으로 쓰다 write in Indian ink. ぼくじゅう

**묵지(墨紙)** copying paper; carbon paper/~를 받쳐 쓰다 take a carbon copy. ふくしゃし

**묵직이** heavily; massively; gravely; seriously/짐을 ~ 싣다 load a heavy cargo; pack a weighty load/입을 ~ 열다 talk in a grave[serious] manner.

**묵직하다** ①(be) rather heavy[weighty] ②(언행이)(be) rather grave[serious, solemn, dignified]/묵직한 음성으로 in a grave tone/입이 ~ be rather taciturn ③(뒤가) feel a bit heavy/뒤가 ~ feel as if the bowel movement is still incomplete. どっしりしている

**묵척(墨尺)** a carpenter's inking line.

**묵철(一鐵)** bullets for shooting birds.

**묵허(默許)** tacit consent 《법률》 connivance/~하다 consent tacitly; give tacit permission; connive (at); wink (at); pass over/그것을 ~하였다 He consented to it tacitly. もっきょ

**묵형(墨刑)** tattooing on the face.

**묵화(墨畵)** a paintings in black and white; an Indian-ink picture. すみえ

**묵흔(墨痕)** ink-marks (필적) handwriting/~이 선명하다 be written vividly; be written in bold strokes. ぼっこん

**묵히다** ①(버려두다) leave unused; leave wasted/묵혀 둔 땅 land lying idle/land in fallow/쌀을 ~ leave rice unused/돈[상품]을 ~ let funds[goods] lie idle/땅을 ~ lay land fallow; fallow [land, soil]. ②(나그네를) give[afford] shelter; accommodate (a person) with a night's shelter[lodging]/하룻밤 ~ give (a person) a night's lodging[shelter for the night]. 使わずにそのままおく

**문(文)** ①(문장) a sentence ②(학문·문화) literature; the pen (무(武)에 대하여)/~은 무보다 강하다 The pen is mightier than the sword. ③(글) [a piece of] writing; composition/의문~ an interrogative sentence/서술~ a declarative sentence/감탄~ an exclamatory sentence. ぶん

**문(門)** ①(입구) a gate; a door; a gateway; a portal/나가는 ~ the exit; the gate[door] out/~을 두드리다 knock at the door[gate]/~을 열어 주다 open a gate[door] (for a person); (기회) give an opportunity to; open the gate to ②(부류) a department; a special study ③(집안) a family/박씨 ~ Park's family ④(대포) cannons/대포 수 ~ several pieces of ordnance. もん

**문(紋)** 《전문(定紋)》 a crest 《문장(紋章)》 a coat-of-arms/~이 붙어 있다 bear a crest. もん

**문(問)** a problem 문제(問題). もんだい

**문간(門間)** a door; an entrance; a doorway/~에서 기다리다 wait at the door/~방 a room in the gate section/~에 들어서다 step just inside the gate.

**문갑(文匣)** a chest of drawers for papers and stationaries. ぶんぼうぐのいればこ

**문객(門客)** ①(식객) a hanger-on; a retainer ②(문안객) a frequent visitor. しょっかく

**문견(聞見)** one's experience[knowledge] 견문(見聞). けんぶん

**문경지교(刎頸之交)** 《친구》 lifelong[eternal] friendship; a friend in need; a sworn[devoted, bosom, boon] friend; devoted friendship/~를 맺다 pledge to eternal friendship. ふんけいのまじわり

**문고(文庫)** ①(서류 넣는) a hand-box (책장) a bookcase ②(서고(書庫)) a library (장서) a collection of books 《총서》 a library/통속 ~ Everyman's Library. ぶんこ

**문고리(門一)** a door handle; a door fastener an iron ring attached to a door/~를 걸다 fasten[latch] a door. もんのとり

**문공부(文公部)** the Ministry of Culture and Information/~ 장관 the Minister of Culture and Information.

**문과(文科)** ①(교육) a literary course; the department of literature ②(예 시험 제도) the higher civil service examination. ぶんか

**문관(文官)** 《무관에 대한》 a civil official; a civilian 《총칭》 the civil service 《군속》 a military civilian; a civilian in the military[the naval] service. ぶんかん

**문교(文敎)** education; culture/~를 관장하다 be in charge of education/~당국 the educational authorities/~부 the Ministry of Education/~ 정책 educational policy/~ 행정 educational administration. ぶんきょう

**문구(文具)** ①(문방구) stationery; writing materials ②(문식) rhetorical flourishes; literary embellishment. ぶんぐ

**문귀(文句)** words; phrases; an expression; a clause/화려한 ~ florid expression 《표현》 an expression/편지의 ~ the wording of a letter. もんく

**문구멍(門一)** a hole in a door[window]. もんのあな

**문기둥(門一)** a doorpost; a gatepost.

**문내(門內)** ①(대문 안) the inside of the gate; within the gate ②(문중) the whole family[clan]. もんない

**문단(文壇)** the literary world; the world of letters／～의 거성 a great man of letters／～의 경향 literary trends／～의 총아 a popular writer; a star writer／～에 이름이 나다 win literary fame／～ 시론 comments on current literary events／～인 a writer; a literary man.　ぶんだん

**문단속(門團束)** closing the doors and gates securely／～하다 fasten[lock, secure] the doors and gates／～을 잘 하다 fasten the door securely／세상이 어수선하니 ～을 잘 해야 한다 As we live in troublous times, we must see that all the doors are fastened.　とじまり

**문달(聞達)** reputation; fame; distinction.　ひょうばんがたかくなること

**문담(文談)** literary talk[causerie].　ぶんだん

**문답(問答)** questions and answers; a conversation 《대화》 a dialogue／～하다 《교리를》 catechize; hold a dialogue／～식 교수 《교리상의》 catechism／～식으로 in the form of questions and answers; in question and answer form／시국 ～ questions and answers on current problems.　もんどう

**문대다** rub; scrub／걸레로 ～ wipe[scrub] (the floor) with a floorcloth.　こする

**문덕[문떡]** falling apart (from); decomposition; crumbling to pieces／～ 떨어져 나가다 come off limply.　ぽたっと

**문도(門徒)** a disciple; a follower; a believer.　もんと

**문돋이(紋—)** patterned cloth; brocade; fabric with raised figures.　ぴかぴかする紗絹織

**문둥병(—病)** leprosy; Hansen's disease; lepra／～ 환자 a leper／～ 환자 수용소 a leper colony／～에 걸려 있다 be leprous.　らいびょう

**문둥이** a leper; a leprous patient 《거지》 a lazar／～ 요양소 a leper hospital[colony]; a lazaret.　らいびょうかんじゃ

**문드러지다** ulcerate; fester; be decomposed／시체는 무섭게 썩어 문드러져 있었다 The corpse was in a fearful state of decomposition.

**문득, 문뜩** suddenly; unexpectedly／그 사람과 만날 약속이 ～ 생각났다 It suddenly occured to me that I had an appointment.／～ 그가 사깃군이 아닐까 하는 의심이 일어났다 The suspicion flashed across his mind that they are impostors.　にわかに

**문띠(門—)** a crosspiece on a door or a gate.　とびらのよこぎ

**문란(紊亂)** disorder; confusion; chaos; breach／～하다 be in disorder; be disorganized[disordered]／～케 하다 disorder; disorganize; throw (a thing) into confusion; derange (social order)／～해지다 fall into disorder／관기 ～ a breach of official discipline／풍기 ～ an offense against public decency.　ぶんらん

**문례(文例)** an example; an illustration／～를 들다 give an example／～가 풍부하다 be full of examples.　ぶんれい

**문루(門樓)** the upper story of a castle [city] gate; a two-storied gate.　もんろう

**문리(文理)** ①《문맥》 the context; the line of thought／～상의 contextual; grammatical／～ 해석 grammatical interpretation ②《문맥이 전통함》 conversance; mastery; thorough knowledge ③《문과와 이과》 literature and science／～과 대학 the college of liberal arts and science.　ぶんり

**문망(文望)** literary fame[reputation, popularity].　がくもんのめいせい

**문맥(文脈)** context; the unity[the line] of thought／～상의 contextual／나는 이 글의 ～을 알 수가 없다 I cannot make out the construction of this sentence.　ぶんみゃく

**문맹(文盲)** illiteracy; ignorance 《사람》 an illiterate (person); an ignoramus／～의 illiterate; unlettered; ignorant／～ 타파 a crusade against illiteracy; the eradication of illiteracy.　もんもう

**문머리(門—)** the upper frame of a gate [door].

**문면(文面)** the contents[wording] of a letter／～에 의하면 according to[the wording of] a letter／편지의 ～은 다음과 같다 The letter reads as follows.　ぶんめん

**문명(文名)** literary fame[reputation]／～을 멸치다 win literary fame; make a name for oneself as an author.　ぶんめい

**문명(文明)** civilization; culture; enlightenment／～하다 (be) civilized; enlightened／～국 a civilized country[nation]／～ 사회 civilized society／～의 이기(利器) a factor of civilization／～에 뒤멀어진 국민 a backward nation; an uncivilized country.　ぶんめい

**문묘(文廟)** the Temple of Confucius; a Confucian shrine.　ぶんびょう

**문무(文武)** 《일》 civil and military affairs; the sword and the pen 《직권》 civil and military authority 《기예》 civil and military arts.　ぶんぶ

**문문하다** ①《부드럽다》 (be) soft; tender; supple／문문한 고기 tender meat／문문한 가죽 soft leather ②《우습게 보이다》 be easy to deal with; (be) soft; be not firm／문문한 사람 a pushover; a person easy to deal with; an easy mark 《주》.　つまらない

**문문히** ①《부드럽게》 softly; tenderly／가죽을 ～ 이기다 tan leather soft ②《우습게》 as a softy; not being firm／사람을 ～ 보다 make light of a person; look on a person as a softy; think little of a person.

**문물(文物)** 《문명》 civilization 《문화》 culture 《학예》 art and science 《학문》 lear-

**문미**(門楣) a lintel [of a door].

**문밖**(門—) ①(문의 바깥) outdoors/ ~의 outdoor; outside the house/~에서 out of doors; outside/ ~으로 내쫓다 give (*one*) the door ②(성(城)의) the outside of a castle (교외) the outskirts [of a city]; suburbs/ ~의 suburban/~에 살다 live in the suburbs. もんがい

**문발**(門—) a blind; a screen/ ~을 치다 hang a blind. もんのすだれ

**문방구**(文房具) stationery; writing materials/ ~점 a stationer's; a stationery [shop]. ぶんぼうぐ

**문뱃내** (술 냄새) a smell of drink[liquor].

**문벌**(門閥) (가문) lineage; pedigree (태생) birth (명문) good lineage; a good[distinguished] family/~이 좋은 집에서 태어나다 come of a good family; be of noble birth. もんばつ

**문범**(文範) model composition[s]; a model sentence. ぶんぱん

**문법**(文法) grammar/ ~상의 grammatical/ ~적으로 grammatically/~ 학자 a grammarian/~적으로 완전한 글이기는 하지만 관용적 어법은 아니다 Grammatically this sentence is all right; but it is hardly idiomatic.

**문병**(問病) an inquiry/ ~하다 a visit to a sick person; an inquiry after a sick person/입원중인 친구를 ~하다 visit a friend in hospital.

**문병**(門屛) a screen[wall] in the doorway.

**문복**(問卜) ~ 하다 have *one's* fortune told; consult a fortuneteller.

**문부**(文簿) documents; records; an account book. ちょうぼ

**문빗장**(門—) a door latch; a gate bar; a bolt/ ~을 지르다[빼다] latch[unlatch] the door. かんぬき

**문사**(文士) a literary man; a writer; a man of letters/ ~들 the literati/돌팔이 ~ a hack writer. ぶんし

**문사**(文詞, 文辭) words and sentences.

**문사극**(文士劇) amateur stage performances by literary men. ぶんしげき

**문살** the frame of a paper sliding door.

**문상**(問喪) condolence 조상. ちょうい

**문새**(門—) the look[style] of a door [gate].

**문서**(文書) (서류) a document; a paper (통신) correspondence; letters (기록) archives (공문서) a missive/ ~ 위조 forgery of documents/선전 ~ propaganda[publicity] literature/ ~로 적어

두다 commit to writing/보고서를 ~로 제출하다 submit all reports in writing/ ~철(綴) a file. ぶんしょ

**문석**(文石) (문석인) a stone statue of a civil official standing before a Royal mausoleum (마노) agate.

**문선**(文選) ①(인) type picking ②(선집) a selection of literary works; an anthology/ ~하다 select literary works; pick types. ぶんせん

**문설주**(門—) the side posts of a door [window, gate]. もんちゅう

**문세**(文勢) force of style/ ~ 절락(落) anticlimax. ぶんせい

**문소리**(門—) the noise made by opening or shutting a door[window, gate]; a sound at the door/~가 난다 I hear the door. もんのかい へいのおと

**문수**(文數) shoe size; the size of shoes. もんすう

**문식**(文飾) rhetorical embellishments[flourishes, ornaments]. ぶんしょく

**문신**(文身) a tattoo/ ~하다 tattoo/등에 용의 ~이 있다 have a dragon tattooed upon *one's* back. ぶんしん

**문신**(文臣) a civil official; a civil service subject. ぶんしん

**문아**(文雅) elegance; grace/ ~하다 (be) elegant; graceful; refined; artistic.

**문안**(門—) ①(문의 안) within the gate; inside the gate[door, window] ②(성(城)의 안) inside the city gate; the city proper. もんない

**문안**(文案) ①(초안) a draft / ~을 작성하다 make a draft (*of*); draft ②(문부) documents. ぶんあん

**문안**(問安) an inquiry after the health of (*a person*); sending kind regards/ ~하다 inquire after (*a person*); send kind regards; pay a visit of courtesy.
あんひをたずねること

**문야**(文野) civilization and barbarism; the civilized and the barbarous.

**문약**(文弱) effeminacy (나약) imbecility / ~으로 흐르다 become effeminate/~해지다 become effeminate; be given to polite pursuits at the expense of military arts. ぶんじゃく

**문어**(文魚) an octopus/ ~ 단지 an octopus trap/~ 데침 a boiled octopus.
おおかたのたこ

**문어**(文語) written language; literary language (표현) literary expression/ ~체 literary style. ぶんご

**문어귀**(門—) an entry. もんのいりぐち

**문얼굴**(門—) a door frame. もんのわく

**문예**(文藝) literary art (문학) literature; (문학 예술) art and literature/ ~의 소양 literary accomplishments/ ~에 조예가 깊다 be well versed in art and literature/ ~란 a literary column/ ~ 기자 a literary writer/~부 the literary section[critic]/ ~ 비평[비평가] a literary criticism[critic]/ ~ 잡보 a literary medley[miscellany]/ ~ 작품 a literary production/ ~에 종사하다 engage in literary pursuits/ ~ 활동 literary activity/~인 a literary man. ぶんげい

**문외**(門外) ~의 outdoor/ ~ 불출의 보물 a much-treasured heirloom. もんがい

**문외한**(門外漢) an outsider 《비전문가》a layman; a nonspecialist/~의 의견 an outsider's opinion; a lay opinion[idea] /그 문제에 대해서는 나는 전혀 ~ 입니다 I don't know the first thing about the subject. もんがいかん

**문우**(文友) a literary friend

**문운**(門運) the fortunes of a family. いちもんのうんめい

**문운**(文運) cultural progress; enlightenment; civilization. ぶんうん

**문원**(文苑) 《문단》a collection of literary masterpieces; the literary column[world] ぶんえん

**문의**(文義) the meaning of a passage; the purport of a letter]/이 편지는 ~가 통하지 않는다 This letter is quite unintelligible. ぶんぎ

**문의**(問議) an inquiry; enquiry; reference/ ~하다 make inquiry (about); ask / ~서 a letter of inquiry/ ~처 a reference/그에게 ~했지만 아무런 회답도 못 받았다 I have heard nothing from him in reply to my inquiry.

**문인**(門人) a pupil; a disciple; a follower. もんじん

**문인**(文人) a literary man; a man of letters 《총칭》literati/~ 사회 the literati/~화(畵) a picture of the calligraphic school. ぶんじん

**문일 지십**(聞一知十) ~하다 know all from hearing one.

**문자**(文字) ①《글자》a letter; a character 《자모》an alphabet/ ~의 literal/ ~판 a dial; the face (of *a clock*)/ ~ 그대로 to the letter; literally ②《숙어》a phrase; an idiomatic[a set] phrase; an idiom. もじ

**문자새**(門─) doors; gates; doors and windows. もん

**문짝**(門─) a leaf[flap] of a door/ ~을 열어 젖히다 push[pull] the door open. 一枚のとびら

**문장**(門帳) a hanging screen; a curtain. カーテン

**문장**(文章) a piece of writing 《작품》a composition 《구와 구별하여》a sentence 《논문》an essay; an article 《문체》a style 《사람》a good[fine] writer/~이 좋다 He is a good writer., He is clever with his pen. / ~가 an accomplished writer; a stylist; an essayist/~도 the art of writing/ ~론 syntax/ ~체 literary style. ぶんしょう

**문장부**(門─) a door pivot.

**문재**(文才) literary talent[ability]/ ~가 있다 have no little literary talent /~를 발휘하다 display[show] a talent for writing. ぶんさい

**문전**(文典) a grammar; a grammar book. ぶんてん

**문전**(門前) (*in*) front of a gate/ ~에 before[in front of] a gate/~ 성시 having a constant stream of callers/ ~ 걸식하다 go out begging. もんぜん

**문정**(門庭) a garden; a yard; an inner court[yard]. もんないのにわ

**문제**(門弟) a pupil; a disciple; a follower 《집합》a following. もんてい

**문제**(問題) a question; a problem 《연구 등의》a subject; an issue 《제목》a topic 《일》a matter/ 사회 ~ a social problem /금전 ~ a money matters/시험 ~ an examination question[paper]/ 사활 ~ a vital question/ ~의 다른 일면 the other side of the shield[medal]/~를 내다 set (*a person*) a question/~가 생기다 a question arises/ ~를 일으키다 raise a question[an issue]; raise discussion/~를 해결하다 solve a problem/ 정치 ~화하다 be made a political issue /그것은 취미의 ~이다 It is a matter of taste./계쟁 ~ the question at[in] issue. もんだい

**문제자**(門弟子) a disciple ⇒문제(門弟).

**문조**(文鳥) 〖조〗 a paddybird; a Java sparrow.

**문죄**(問罪) accusation; indictment; arraignment/~하다 accuse (*a person*) of a crime. もんざい

**문중**(門中) a family; the whole clan; near kin. どうせいどうほんの親類

**문지**(門地) 《문벌》lineage; pedigree; a family status. もんち

**문지**(知知) ~하다 be informed of; hear of; learn[know] of.

**문지기**(門─) a gatekeeper; a janitor(미); a gateman; a doorman; a guard; a *concierge*(F). もんばん

**문지도리**(門─) the hinges of a door.

**문지르다** rub; scrub/문질러 없애다 rub off[down]/문질러 바르다 rub (*the ointment*) into the skin/눈을 ~ rub *one's* eyes/마루를 걸레로 ~ scrub a floor with a floor cloth. こする

**문지방**(門地枋) a door[window] sill; the threshold. しきい

**문직**(紋織) figured texture. もんおり

**문진**(文鎭) a paperweight/ ~을 놓다 place a weight on. ぶんちん

**문질**(門疾) a hereditary disease/정신병이 ~이다 Insanity runs in the family.

**문집**(文集) a collection of works; an anthology; an analect/세익스피어 ~ a collection of Shakespeare's works. ぶんしゅう

**문창**(門窓) a door and a window.

**문채**(文采, 文彩) ①《문장의 광채》beautiful colo uring; a lovely sheen ②《무늬》a figure; a pattern; a design. ぶんさい

**문책**(問責) censure; reproof; reprehension/~하다 reprehend; censure; reprove; rebuke. もんせき

**문책**(文責) the sresponsibility for the wording of an article/~은 기자에게 있음 The reporter is responsible for the wording of this[the] article.

**문첩**(文牒) an official document.

**문체**(文體) a style; a diction／고~ an antiquated style／통속 ~ a colloquial style／구어적 ~ a colloquial style／평이한 ~로 in a plain[an easy] style／~론 stylistics. ぶんたい

**문초**(問招) questioning[interrogating] a criminal; an examination／~하다 question a criminal; cross-examine a criminal／경찰의 ~를 받다 be examined by the police／~중이다 be under investigation[examination]; inquiry is now in progress. とりしらべ

**문치**(門齒) an incisor; a fore-tooth. もんし

**문치**(文治) civil administration; administration by civilians／~파 a civilian party. ぶんち

**문치적거리다** dilly-dally; vacillate; act shilly-shally; dawdle; waver／문치적거리다가 기회를 잃다 dally away one's opportunity. ぐずぐずする

**문턱** the threshold; a doorsill／~에 걸터앉다 sit on a doorsill.

**문투**(文套) the manner of composition; style; a form. ぶんのくせ

**문틈**(門─) a chink between parts of a door[window, gate]／~으로 들여다보다 look through a chink in the door. もんのすきま

**문패**(門牌) a nameplate; a doorplate／~를 내걸다 put up a doorplate. もんぴょう

**문표**(門標) a gate pass; a pass. もんぴょう

**문표**(問票) a question mark; an interrogation mark.

**문풍**(文風) a tendency to set value on literary culture; literary spirit; holding letters in high esteem.

**문풍지**(門風紙) a paper flaps attached to the edges of window frames to cover the chinks.

**문필**(文筆) literary art; literary pursuits《신문·잡지업》journalism／~업 the literary profession／~가 a literary man; a writer／~에 종사하다 be engaged in literary pursuit; pursue literature／~에 재주가 있다 have a talent for writing／~로 생활하다 live by one's pen. ぶんぴつ

**문하**(門下) being under (a person's) instruction[guidance]／~생[인] a disciple; a student; a follower／그는 대학에서 나의 ~생이었다 He was a student under me at the university. もんか

**문학**(文學) literature; letters／~의 literary／기록 ~ documentary literature／대중 ~ popular literature／~계 the literary world[circles]／~회 a literary society／~부 the literature department／~개론 an introduction to literature／~과 a literary course／~론 comments on literature; the theory of literature／~ 작품 literary works／~사(史) history of literature／~ 청년 a literary youth／~을 논하다 talk on [discuss] literature／~에 뜻을 두다 aspire to literary honors. ぶんがく

**문한**(文翰) ①《문필》literary arts; writing ②《문필가》a writer; a literary man／~가(家) a family that has produced many men of letters. ぶんしょ

**문헌**(文獻)《문서》literature; a booklet《소책자》a leaflet《기록》records; documents《전거》authority／이 문제에 관한 ~ the literature on this subject／~학 philology／여러 가지 ~을 조사하다 refer to sundry records. ぶんけん

**문호**(文豪) a master writer; an eminent writer; a great man of letters; a literary celebrity. ぶんごう

**문호**(門戶) the door／~ 개방주의 the open-door policy[principle]／~를 개방하다 open the door (to)／~를 폐쇄하다 exclude (foreigners). もんこ

**문화**(文化) culture; civilization; cultivation／~적 cultural／~인 a man of culture; a cultured man／~재(財) cultural assets[properties]／~ 교류 a cultural exchange[interchange]／~ 단체 a cultural organization／~ 생활 cultural[cultured, civilized] life／~ 수준 a cultural level／~인 a cultured man; a man of culture／~ 주택 an up to-date[a modern] house／~ 활동 a cultural movement[activities]／~ 공로자 a person of cultural merits. ぶんか

**문화**(文華) ①《문명의》the glory of civilization ②《문장의》literary embellishments; (being) ornate; flowery ③《재능》literary talent. ぶんか

**문회**(文會) a family council.

**문후**(問候) ~하다 inquire after another's health; pay one's respect (to); send the compliments of the season. あんぴをとうこと

**묻다**¹ 《땅에》bury (in, under);《매장하다》inhume; inter; bury (in a grave, under the ground);《불을》cover; bank (up) (감추다) cover; conceal; keep (a matter) from (a person)／살인 사건을 비밀로 묻어두다 keep a murder case secret／계획을 묻어두고 일반에게 알리지 않다 keep a plan from the general public. うめる

**묻다**² 《들러붙다》stick (to); be stuck; adhere (to); be covered; be stained (with); be smeared (with)／피가 ~ be stained with blood／잉크가 ~ be smeared with ink. つく

**묻다**³ 《질문하다》ask; question; inquire of (a person) about (a thing); put[pose] a question to (a person)／값을 ~ ask the price／글 뜻을 ~ ask the meaning of a sentence／그의 계획을 ~ ask (a person) about his plan ②《책임 따위를》charge (a person) with (responsibility); call to account／책임을 ~ call (a person) to account; charge (a person) with responsibility ③《안부·소식 따위를》inquire[ask] after; inquire about／안부를 ~ ask after (a person, his health); inqu-

묻히다¹

ire after (a person's) safety/소식을 ~ ask how (a person) is getting along; ask for news about (a person).

**묻히다¹** 《칠 따위를》 smear; stain 《바르다》 apply/나물을 참기름에 ~ season vegetables with sesame-oil/구두에 흙을 ~ get[have] mud on one's shoes.

**묻히다²** 《덮이다》 be buried in[under]; be covered with 《숨겨지다》 be concealed/눈에 ~ be under snow; be snowed up/묻혀 살다 live in obscurity; be kept from the public eye.

**물¹** water; the water[s]/화초에 ~을 주다 water flowers[plants]/~을 타다 dilute; mix (wine) with water.

**물²** 《빛》 a colour; a hue/머리에 ~을 들이다 dye one's hair.

**물³** ①《빨래의》 a wash; the number of times clothes have been washed/이것은 두 ~ 빨았다 This has been washed twice. ②《과실·해산물 따위의 산출 시기》 a crop; a catch; a flush/나는 첫 ~ 딸기를 먹었다 I ate early strawberries.

**물가** water's edge; the beach/~에 집을 짓다 build a house close by the water.

**물가(物價)** prices [of commodities] 《시가》 the market price/ ~ 등귀(하락) a rise[fall] in prices/~ 통제 price control/~ 지수 the price index/~ 수준 price levels.

**물까마귀** 【조】 a water ouzel; Cinclus pallasii hondoensis(학명).

**물갈래** a branch; a tributary.

**물갈이** 【농】 plowing a paddy with water in it/~하다 plough watered ricefields.

**물갈퀴** a web; a webfoot.

**물감** a dye; dyestuffs.

**물개** 【동】 an otter

**물갬나무** 【식】 a Siberian alder; Alnus sibirica(학명).

**물거름** 《액체 거름》 liquid fertilizer[manure].

**물거리** 《땔나무》 dead branches; brushwood; faggot.

**물거리(一距離)** distance by water 《배의》 the navigable distance at high tide.

**물거미** 《충》 a water spider/ ~뒷다리《키가 큰 사람》 a beanpole.

**물거품** foam; froth; a bubble/~처럼 사라지다 burst like a bubble.

**물건(物件)** an article; goods; a thing; an object/이것은 내 ~이다 This belongs to me.

**물걸레** a wet floorcloth.

**물것** biting insects.

**물결** a wave; a billow 《잔 물결》 a ripple 《너울거리는》 a swell 《밀려오는》 a surf 《흰 물결》 a breaker/~을 헤치고 나가다 plow through the [heavy] seas; shear the sea/~치다 waves rise; rise and fall [like waves]; wave; roll.

**물결(勿驚)** to one's surprise/빚이 ~ 1천만 원이다 The debt adds up to a surprising amount of ten million won.

**물계(物一)** 《시세》 the current price; the selling price ruling.

**물계(物界)** the material world; the physical world.

**물꼬** a sluice gate; an irrigation gate.

**물고(物故)** death of an eminent[notorious] person/ ~나다 die; be dead/ ~ 내다 kill (a person); execute a criminal.

**물고기** a fish 《집합적》 fish/ ~ 장수 a fishmonger《영》; a fish dealer 《행상》 a fishpeddler/~를 낚다 angle for fish/~를 잡다 catch a fish/~ 뼈 a fish bone.

**물고 늘어지다** ①《입으로》 bite at something and hang on to it/개가 그의 목을 물고 늘어졌다 The dog sank his teeth in his throat and hung on. ②《집요하게》 stick to; hang[hold] on (to); get[have] a firm grip on (one's rival)/끝까지 ~ stick to one's last.

**물고동** a faucet《미》; a tap; a [water] plug/ ~을 틀다[잠그다] turn on[off] a faucet.

**물고랭이** 【식】 a bulrush; a club rush.

**물고의(一袴衣)** underwear worn by women while taking a bath or working in water.

**물곬** ①《도랑》 a drain; a ditch; a gutter ②《빠지는 길》 an outlet.

**물구나무서다** stand on one's head/물구나무서기 《체조》 hand-standing/물구나무서서 걷다 walk on one's hands.

**물구덩이** a pool; a [mud] puddle/ ~이에 빠지다 get[fall] into a puddle/ ~가 생기다 pools form.

**물굽이** a bend in a river; a turn of a stream/~ 지다 wind [in and out]; meander; bend; have a bend; curve; wind.

**물권(物權)** a real right; a right in rem/~법 the Law of Reality/ ~의 이전 [설정] the transfer[creation] of a real right.

**물귀신(一鬼神)** a water demon; the spirit of water/ ~이 되다 drown; be drowned [to death].

**물끄러미** fixedly; firmly; steadily/얼굴을 ~ 쳐다보다 gaze[look] abstractedly [blankly] at (a person's) face.

**물그릇** a water bowl.

**물그림자** shadows on the water.

**물금(一金)** 【광】 amalgam.

**물금매(一金梅)** 【식】 a primrose willow; Jussiaea repens(학명).

**물긋긋하다** (be) washy[weak]; very thin.

**물긋하다** 《묽다》 (be) somewhat washy[thin, watery].

**물기**(一氣) moisture/~ 있는 moist; damp; humid/~가 없나 be dry.
**물기둥** a column of water.
**물기름** hair oil.
**물길** a waterway; a watercourse/ ~을 따라 항해하다 sail along a waterway. すいろ
**물난리**(一亂離) a flood; flood damage; a flood disaster/ ~가 나다 have a flood disaster. こうずいのそうどう
**물납**(物納) payment in goods[kind]/ ~세(稅) a tax in kind.
**물내리다** 《기운이 빠지다》 become weak; lose one's strength[vitality, sap] 《먹여》 resift rice flour on a loose sieve while pouring water over it. けんきがない
**물너울** a swell; a roller/ 바다에 ~치는 waves roll[swell] on the sea. よは
**물놀이** ①《잔 물결》 rippling[wrinkling] of water ②《어린이들의》 dabbling in water/ ~하다 ripple; ruffle. さざなみ
**물다**¹ 《지불하다》 pay 《배상하다》 compensate (for); repay; return/ 책값을 ~ pay for a book/ 손해를 물어 주다 indemnify (a person) for damage/ 가난한 학생의 공납금을 물어 주다 pay a tuition fee for a poor student. しはらいつぐ
**물다**² 《상하다》 decay; molder; go bad/ 더위로 물고기가 곧 물었다 The fish soon went bad in hot weather. ふしくする
**물다**³ ①《깨물다》 bite/ 개가 사람을 ~ a dog bites [at] (a person) ②《입에》 put[hold] (a thing) in one's mouth/ 담뱃대를 물다 ~ put[hold] a pipe between one's teeth ③《벌레가》 bite 《모기가》 sting ④《톱니바퀴 등이》 gear with[into]; engage with /서로 물고 있는 톱니바퀴 engaged wheels. かむ
**물때**¹ 《물의》 fur; incrustation/ ~를 벗기다 clean fur (from a kettle)/ ~가 끼다 fur forms. みずあか
**물때**² 《조수의》 the tide hour 《만조시》 the high tide/ ~를 놓치다 miss the high tide/ ~가 이르다 It is too early for the high tide. さししおのじかん
**물멍덩술멍덩** recklessly; without settled views; flippantly/ ~하다 act blindly[naively]; go it blind. なるがままに
**물독** a water jar; a water jug. みずがめ
**물동** 《물방울》 a splash; a spatter/ ~을 튀기다 send up a spray. すいてき
**물동싸움** a water fight; kicking or splashing water on each other/ ~하다 have a water fight. みずかけしょうぶ
**물동이** a water pitcher[jar].
**물동튀기다** splash water; spatter water. 水泥などがはねとぶ
**물두부**(一豆腐) bean curds boiled in water. ゆどうふ
**물들다** ①《빛이》 dye; be dyed; take[put on] colo[u]r ②《감염(感染)하다》 be infected[stained] with (vices); be influenced by. いろがつく
**물들이다** dye (a thing)/ 장미색으로 ~ dye (a thing) rose colo[u]r. そめる
**물량**(物量) the amount[quantity] of materials[resources].
**물러가다** 《떠나다》 leave; take one's leave 《후퇴하다》 retrograde; recede; go back 《퇴각하다》 retreat. しりぞく
**물러나다** withdraw; fall[come] off; retire; resign/ 정계에서 ~ retire from the politics. ひっこむ
**물러서다** ① step[stand] back[aside]/ 뒤로 ~ move off to the rear ②《사임하다》 retire; resign; leave/ 그는 정년이 되어서 대학 교수의 직을 물러섰다 He reached the age-limit and retired from professorship. のちにしりぞく
**물러앉다** ①《뒤에 앉다》 move one's seat backward ②《지위에서》 retire; resign; leave. ひきさがってすわる
**물러오다** come back; withdraw; retreat /적이 ~ the enemy comes[falls] back in retreat/ 가던 길을 ~ retrace one's steps. もどってくる
**물러지다** soften; become tender/ 감이 ~ a persimmon softens up/ 마음이 ~ one's heart softens. ゆるくなる
**물렁팔죽** ①《사람》 a softy; a milksop; a pushover ②《물건》 soft stuff; a squash. ひじょうにじゅうじゃくなひとのたとえ
**물렁하다** ①《푹 익어서》 (be) overripe; mellow; soft ②《성질이》 (be) weak-hearted; weak-kneed/ 물렁한 성질 a yielding disposition[temper]/ 물렁한 사람 a flabby character; a person easy to deal with. ぶよぶよしている
**물레** a reeling instrument; a spinning wheel/ ~질 하다 spin on a spinning wheel. ぼうしゃ
**물레방아** a water mill[wheel]. すいしゃ
**물레새** 《조》 a forest wagtail; Dendronanthus indicus(학명).
**물려받다** take over; obtain by transfer /사업을 ~ take over the business/ 왕위를 ~ succeed to the throne.
**물려주다** hand[make] over; bequeath (property) to (a person)/ 재산을 자식에게 ~ hand over one's property to one's son.
**물려지내다** live under (another's) control; be kept under (a person's) thumb/ 아내에게 물려지낸다 He is under his wife's thumb. しがたなくすごす
**물력**(物力) ①《물건의 세력》 physical force; one's resources; wealth ②《재료와 노력》 materials and efforts. ぶつりょく
**물론**(勿論) [as a matter] of course; naturally/ 예외가 있는 것은 ~이다 It goes without saying that there are exceptions. もちろん
**물리**(物理) ①《이치》 the laws of nature ②《물리학》 physics/ ~적 현상 a physical phenomenon/ ~ 화학 physical chemistry. ぶつり
**물리다**¹ 《입으로》 be[get] bitten by (fleas) /나는 개한테 발을 물렸다 I was bitten

물리다² by a dog in the leg. かまれる

물리다² 《싫증나다》 get sick of; lose interest in; be fed up with 《음식을》 be cloyed／냉면에 ～ be fed up with cold noodle dishes. あきる

물리다³ 《돈을》 make (one) pay／깨뜨린 그 릇 값을 ～ make (a person) pay for a broken dish.

물리다⁴ 《익히다》 soften; mellow／감자를 ～ steam potatoes soft. えんじゅくさせる

물리다⁵ 《치우다》 clear away; put away; take away／밥상을 ～ take away the table; have finished eating. かたづける

물리다⁶ 《귀신을》 expel; drive out (evil spirits); exorcise・

물리다⁷ ①《연기하다》 postpone; put off; defer ②《옮기다》 let take away; remove ③《양도하다》 hand[make] over; transfer; convey 《주다》 give; offer 《지위를》 abdicate. えんきする

물리치다 《거절하다》 reject; refuse; turn down 《격퇴하다》 repulse; drive away／충고 를 ～ ignore(a person's) advice. しりぞける

물리학(物理學) physics; natural philosophy; physical science. ぶつりがく

물림 ①《연기함》 putting off; postponement ②《건》 an extra space of half a kan added to a regular room as a kind of porch ③《넘겨받음》 property handed down. えんき

물림쇠 a staple; a metal band; a clamp. とめかね

물마 an overflow; a flood; flood on the ground [caused by rain]. あふれてるみず

물마개 a drain plug.

물마루 the crest of waves; a swell. なみのみね

물만두(-饅頭) a stuffed bun boiled in water.

물말이 ①《밥》 cooked rice served in water ②《젖은 것》a thing drenched with water 《옷》 dripping-wet clothes.

물맛 the taste of water.

물망(物望) popular expectation; public confidence／～에 오르다 win public[popular] support. にんき

물망초(勿忘草) 【식】 a forget-me-not.

물맞이 taking[drinking, bathing in] mineral water.

물매¹ 《경사》 a slope[slant, pitch] of a roof／～가 싸다 The roof has a steep enough slant to it. けいしゃ

물매² 《매질》 sound thrashing; drubbing／～맞다 be flogged hard／～치다 punish (a person) with a good sound flogging. ひどいむち

물매암이 【충】 a whirligig beetle.

물매질 flogging[whipping] hard／～하 다 flog[whip] hard. ひどくむちうつこと

물매화(-花) 【식】 a grass-of-Parnassus; Parnassia palustris(학명).

물멀미 sickness caused by seeing a wave／～하다 feel sick by seeing a wave.

물면(一面) the surface of water. すいみん

물명(物名) names of articles. ぶつめい

물목 ①《물 어귀》 a point at which the water flows out; the fork of a river 《물 갈래》 a narrows／～을 지키다 stand watch at the fork of a river ②《사 광에서》 the spot where gold dust pans thickest. ながれのでぐち

물목(物目) a catalog of goods; a list of articles. ぶっぴんのひんもく

물몽둥이 a sledge.

물문(一門) a sluice; a floodgate; a lock [gate]; a penstock; a flash. すいもん

물물 교환(物物交換) barter; bartering; truck; dicker(미〉／소금과 식량을 ～하다 barter[trade] salt for eatables. -

물미 a spike／～ 작대기 a spiked prop on an A-frame.

물밀다 《만조가 되다》 rise; flow 《밀려오다》 advance; surge／물밀 때 the flow of the tide／물밀듯이 들이닥치다 be deluged (with tourist). しおがさす

물밑 《바다》 the bottom of the water[sea, river] 《해면 아래》 under the water／잠 수함은 ～을 다닌다 Submarines sail under the water. すいてい

물바가지 a gourd for dipping water.

물바람 a wind blowing over the water.

물방개 【충】 a Korean water beetle.

물방아 ①《물레방아》 a water mill／～에 곡 식을 찧다 grind grain in a water mill ②⇒방아 두레박. すいしゃ

물방아잠자리 【충】 a kind of dragonfly; Anotogaster sieboldii(학명).

물방앗간 a water mill. すいしゃこや

물방울 a drop of water; a water drop. すいてき

물뱀 【동】 a sea snake; a water snake; Oxystomus macrorhynchus(학명).

물벌레 a water insect; a water beetle.

물베개 a [rubber] water-pillow[-cushion]. みずまくら

물벼 undried rice.

물벼락 sudden down-fall[-pour] of water／～맞다 be suddenly poured over with water. みずのどしゃあび

물벼룩 a water flea.

물병(一瓶) a water-bottle; 【종】 a water bottle dedicated to the image of Buddha／유리 ～ a carafe. みずおけ

물보라 [cloud of] spray; a spray of water／～를 일으키다 send up a spray of water; spray. すいえん

물복숭아 a kind of peach. すいみっとう

물볼기 flogging[whipping] women with their underwear drenched; a wet flogging.

물봉숭아 【식】 a touch-me-not; a kind of snapweed.

물부리 ①《담뱃대》 a [tobacco] pipe; the mouthpiece of a pipe ②《권련의》 a cigarette holder; a mouthpiece. キセル

물분(一粉) a liquid face-paint; a liquid cosmetic[foundation].

물 불 water and fire／그녀는 그를 위해서

물비린내 a fishy smell.

물빛 ①(물감의) dyed colo[u]r ②(남색) light blue; water green. みずのいろ

물싸움 a dispute over irrigation water 《물똥 싸움》 a water fight; splashing water on each other. みずかけしょうぶ

물산(物産) 《농산물 따위》 a product; produces 《총칭》 production／~ 전람회 an exhibition of local products. ぶっさん

물살 the force of water[a current]; the flow of water／~이 빠르다 The current is swift. ながのそくど

물상(物像) the shape of an object; the image of a thing. ぶったいのけいしょう

물상(物象) ①《사물》 an object ②《현상》 material phenomena ③《교과》 the science of inanimate nature. ぶっしょう

물상 담보(物上擔保) a secured mortgage; real security／~부 사채 mortgage bonds. ぶつじょうたんぽ

물새 ①《수조(水鳥)》 a water bird; a waterfowl; an aquatic bird ②⇨물총새. すいちょう

물색(物色) ~하다 ①《찾다》 look for; search for; hunt for ②《고르다》 choose; select; pick[single] out／우리는 그의 후임자를 ~중이다 We are casting about for his successor. ぶっしょく

물색없다 (be) unreasonable; absurd; extraordinary. げんこうがどうりにあわない

물샐틈 없다 ①《틈이 없다》(be) watertight ／물샐틈 없는 변론 an watertight argument ②《경계가》(be) strict; watertight. すきがない

물써다 ebb; be on the ebb／물이 써고 있다 The tide is ebbing[on the ebb]., The tide is going out. しおがひく

물성(物性) 《물》 a property of matter. ぶっせい

물썽하다 《만만하다》(be) gullible; unstubborn; feeble; be easy to be fooled. こしがひくい

물세(物稅) a real tax; a tax on goods and possessions. ぶつぜい

물세례(一洗禮) 《종》 baptism [by immersion]. みずのせんれい

물소 《동》 a water buffalo. すいぎゅう

물소(物騷) ~하다 《불은하다》(be) troubled; disturbed 《불안하다》(be) dangerous 《불안전》 insecure. ぶっそう

물소리 the sound of water.

물속 in the water; deep in the water; at the bottom of the water. すいてい

물손 the quantity of water to be added in cooking (rice, etc.).

물수건(一手巾) a wet towel; a steamed [hot] towel. しぼりてふき

물수랄 a poached egg.

물수리 《조》 an osprey; Pandion haliaetus (학명).

물수세미 《식》 the Canada parrotfeather; Myriophyllum verticillatum (학명).

물수제비 ducks-and-drakes; skipping stones／~ 뜨다 play ducks and drakes; skip stones.

물쑥 《식》 a kind of wormwood; Artemisia Selengensis (학명).

물쓰듯하다 spend (money) like water; be a free spender; play (at) ducks and drakes with (one's money). しょうひする

물시계(一時計) a water clock 《수도 계량기》 a water gauge.

물신선(一神仙) an indifferent person.

물씬하다 ①(be) soft; tender／물씬한 고기 meat cooked tender ②《냄새가》 be nicely [strongly] scented／향수 냄새가 ~ be strongly perfumed. ぐなぐなする

물심(物心) matter and mind／~ 양면으로 both materially and morally; physically and spiritually. ぶっしん

물심부름 going to fetch water／~하다 go to fetch water.

물아(物我) 《철》 external objects and the ego; the ego and the non-ego. ぶつが

물안개 a wet fog; a rain-fog.

물안경(一眼鏡) swimming goggles.

물알 soft unripe grain／~들다 develop into soft unripe grain.

물앵두나무 《식》 a honeysuckle; Lonicera Ruprechtiana (학명).

물약(一藥) a liquid medicine.

물어내다 ①《퍼뜨리다》 reveal; disclose; let out (a domestic secret) ②《변상하다》 pay for; make good; indemnify.

물어넣다 reimburse; refund; repay; compensate for. べんしょうする

물어떼다 bite off; gnaw off[away]; cut off with the teeth. かみきる

물어뜯다 bite off; cut off with the teeth. かみちぎる

물어보다 《묻다》 ask; inquire; question／그것을 물어 보아야겠다 I will inquire about it. 《조회하다》 make inquiries. きく

물어주다 compensate[pay] (for); make reparation／아우의 빚을 ~ pay one's brother's debt. べんしょうする

물억새 《식》 a common[ditch] reed; Miscanthus sacchariflorus (학명).

물여우 《충》 a caddis worm／~나비 a caddis fly.

물역(物役) construction[building] materials／~ 장사 a dealer in construction materials. けんちくざい

물엿 millet jelly[honey].

물오르다 ①《초목에》 come to life ②《가난한 사람에》 get rich; make money; rise／봄이 되니 나무에 물오르기 시작한다 Spring has come and the sap of trees begin to rise. そせいする

물오리 《조》 a wild duck; a mallard 《수컷》 a drake.

물오리나무 《식》 a Siberian alder[tree]; Alnus sibirica (학명).

물외 a [water] cucumber. きゅうり

물욕(物慾) worldly desires; worldliness; a desire for material gain／~에 사로잡

히 worldly-minded. ぶつよく

물위 (표면) the surface of water (상류) the upper reaches of a river/배가 ~ 에 뜨다 a boat floats on the water.

물유리 (-琉璃) water glass.

물음 a question; an inquiry/~에 대답하다 answer a question/~표 a question mark.

물의(物議) (쟁론) public censure; dispute/~를 자아내다 arouse public discussion; raise a scandal. ぶつぎ

물이끼 a sphagnum (pl. -na).

물입(勿入) No admittance/Don't enter; Keep off/한인 ~ No admittance except on business.

물자 a [high] water mark; a water level gauge. すいいけい

물자(物資) (원료) goods; commodities; [raw] material (천연 자원) resources/~ 공급 a supply of goods. ぶっし

물자동차(一自動車) (살수차) a motor sprinkler. さんすいしゃ

물자체(物自體) 【철】 thing-in-itself; Ding an sich(D).

물잡다 draw water into (a paddy); supply (a paddy) with water. かんがいする

물장난 ①(어린애의) playing[dabbling] in water ②(홍수) a flood disaster/~하다 play[dabble] in water. みずあそび

물장사 (술집) a gay trade.

물장수 a water-carrier; one who carries water for sale. みずのしょうばいにん

물재(物財) goods and money; things and money. ぶっぴんとおかね

물적(物的) material; physical/~ 증거 material evidence/~ 자원 material resources ぶってき

물쩍지근하다 (be) stagnant; dull; tedious; standstill. まがぬけている

물정(物情) public feeling[opinion]; the state of affairs/세상 ~을 모르다 be ignorant of the world. ぶつじょう

물평하다 (be) faint-hearted; weak-willed; be a milksop. まぬけている

물종(物種) a kind; a sort; a description. ぶっぴんのしゅるい

물주(物主) (자본주) a capitalist; a financier (트럼프의) the dealer (도박의) the banker. しほんぬし

물주다 water (plants); give water (to)./나무에 ~ water a plant. みずをやる

물줄기 a watercourse; a current; a flow (구멍에서 뻗치는) a spout[jet, gush] of water. ぶんすい

물쥐 【동】 a water rat[vole, muskrat].

물지게 a frame for carrying water; a water-toting device. みずを運ぶ背負いこ

물찌똥 ①(똥) watery[loose] f[a]eces ②(물덩이) splashing waterdrops.

물질(物質) matter; substance/~적 material; physical/~ 명사[문명] material noun[civilization]/~계 material[physical] world/~주의자 a materialist/~주의 materialism. ぶっしつ

물집¹ (염색집) a dyer's; a dyeing house.

물집² (피부의) a [water-]blister/~이 잡히다 blister. みずぶくれ

물차(-車) (살수차) a motor sprinkler; a water-carrier. さんすいしゃ

물참 the high tide. まんちょう

물참나무 【식】 a Japanese oak; Quercus crispula (학명).

물체(物體) a body 【법】 a material; object; a physical solid; substance/~ 거리 (사진) the object distance/~학 somatology. ぶったい

물초 ~하다 be wet through[all over]; be dripping wet.

물총새 【조】 a common Indian kingfisher.

물치 【어】 a frigate mackerel.

물컥 strongly; stinkingly/곰팡 냄새가 ~ 난다 The stench of rot hits my nose. ぶんと

물컹이 (신체가 약한) a frail[delicate, tender, feeble] person (의지가 약한) a person of weak will[wanting in purpose]. ふにゃふにゃなもの

물컹하다 (be) soft; squashy; mushy/물컹물컹 softly; squashily/무엇인지 물컹한 것을 밟았다 I felt something squash under my feet. ひじょうにやわらかい

물크러지다 be reduced to pulp (시체 따위가) decompose (과일이) spoil; rot (종기가) fester; ulcerate. とろとろだたる

물타작(-打作) harvesting cut of rice while still wet.

물탄피 shallow resources[cunning]; superficial craftiness. あさはかなわるちえ

물탕 a hot spring; a hot-bath; a watering place. おんせんのふろば

물통(一桶) a water-pail; a [water-]bucket; a water tank. みずおけ

물편 a general name for all the kinds of rice cakes except steamed rice cake.

물표(物票) a ticket; a bill; a certificate. にふだ

물푸레나무 【식】 an ash tree; Fraxinus rhynchophylla (학명). せいようとねりこ

물품(物品) (물건) a thing; an article (상품) goods; commodities/~세(稅) the sale[commodity] tax/~세법 the commodity Tax Law/~ 임금제 a truck system.

물행주 a [wet] dishrag[dishcloth].

물형(物形) form; shape. もののかたち

물호랑이 【동】 a grampus; Grampus sakamata (학명).

물홈 a groove. みぞ

물화(物貨) goods (일용품) commodities (상품) merchandise. ぶっぴんとざいか

물활론(物活論) hylozoism.

물후미 an inlet.

묽다 ①(농도가) (be) thin; watery; washy/묽게 하다 thin; dilute ②(사람이) (be) weak; frail. みずっぽい

묽디묽다 ①(물이) be very[ever so] watery; be as thin as can be ②(사람이) very soft. ひじょうにみずっぽい

뭇¹ (묶음) a bundle; a faggot/장작 한 ~

a bundle of firewood. たば

**못²** 《여러》 many; numerous; a number of; all; all sorts of/~ 짐승이 떼를 지어 다닌다 All sorts of animals move around in groups. おおくの

**못갈림** a sharecrop system in which the rice sheaves are divided half-and-half between the landlord and the tenant.

**못나무** a faggot; a bundle of fire-wood.

**못매** sound thrashing; drubbing/ ~맞다 get[be under] a pelting rain of kicks and blows たいせいのおうだ

**못발길** 《발길》 kicking (a person) from all sides 《비난》 an attack from all quarters. たいせいのあしげ

**못방치기** intrusion; obtrusion 《사람》 an intruder; an obtruder/~하다 intrude; obtrude; intermeddle; in every thing. やたらにひとのことにかんしょうすること

**못소리** the voice of many people 《비난의》 hisses and boos 《여론》 public opinion/~가 일치하지 않는다 Opinions are divided. たいせいのひとのことば

**못시선** (—視線) everyone's eyes.

**못입** public rebuke; hisses and boos/~을 두려워하다 fear what people will say.

**못줄** a thick hemp rope; a Manila rope.

**뭉개다** ①《으깨다》 knead/《아이들이》 진흙을 ~ play[finger] with mud ②《일을》 shelve; smother up ③《자리에서》 dawdle. こねる

**뭉게구름** 《기상》 a cumulus (pl. -li); a towering mass of clouds.

**뭉게뭉게** densely; thickly; in thick clouds/연기가 ~ 나다 smoke rises up[rolls] in thick clouds. むくむく

**뭉그러뜨리다** destroy; demolish; throw down; let fall; level/쌓아 놓은 과일을 ~ throw[knock] down piledup fruit. こわしてしまう

**뭉그러지다** crumble; fall down; collapse. くずれる

**뭉그적거리다** dawdle; linger; move lackadaisically[listlessly] or aimlessly.

**뭉글뭉글** ~하다 (be) clotty; lumpy/ ~한 과자 a lumpy candy. どろどろしている

**뭉굿하다** ①《비스듬하다》 (be) sloping; inclined; gently sloped/고개가 ~ a hill slopes gently ②《휘우듬하다》 (be) warped; gently bent/뭉긋한 비탈 a gentle slope. ややけいしゃしている

**뭉기다** throw down; destroy; demolish; let fall. こわす

**뭉때리다** ①《시치미떼다》 pretend ignorance of; pretend innocence; pretend not to know ②《기피하다》 deliberately shirk (a job). おろそかにする

**뭉떵뭉떵** lump after lump; chunk after chunk; in big lumps. ばっさりばっさり

**뭉뚝** ~하다 (be) stumpy; stubby; blunt / ~한 사람 a stubby[stumpy] person. ばっさり

**뭉뚱그리다** wrap[bundle] at random; throw together hastily/짐을 ~ bundle up a package crudely. ざっにつつむ

**뭉실뭉실** ~하다 (be) plump; portly/ ~살이 찌다 be[grow] plump. ぼっちゃり

**뭉우리돌** a boulder; a smooth round stone.

**뭉치** a bundle; a ball; a lump; a mass /편지 한 ~ a bundle of letters. くくり

**뭉치다** ①《덩이지다》 lump; mass 《엉기다》 congeal 《피가》 clot/풀이 뭉친다 paste lumps ②《단결하다》 unite; stand together; combine/뭉쳐서 대항하다 stand together against. かためる

**뭉크러지다** crumble; collapse; break. さんざんにぶっこわれる

**뭉클뭉클하다** (be) round and smooth; be clotty. どろどろしている

**뭉클하다** ①《먹은 것이》 retch; keck; feel nausea ②《가슴이》 be filled[seized] with (sorrow)/노여움으로 가슴이 ~ 뭉클하여졌다 Indignation surged up with me. うっとおしい

**뭉키다** ①《덩이지다》 lump; mass; conglomerate/눈이 뭉키어 단단하게 되다 snow lumps into a hard mass ②《여럿이》 swarm; crowd 《송이송이》 cluster/뭉키어 in crowds. かたまる

**뭉텅** in lumps. ばっさり

**뭉텅이** a lump; a mass; a clod (of earth); a package/금 ~ a lump of gold /지폐 ~ a bundle[roll, wad] of bills [paper money]. かたまり

**뭉툭** ~하다 (be) stumpy. まるくなって

**뭍** land 《배에서 본》 the shore/~에서 멀리 멀어진 far off the coast (of). りくち

**뭐** what ⇒ 무엇. なに

**-므로** because; as; on account of; because of; on that account[ground]/비가 오~ 갈 수 없다 We cannot go, for it is raining. —ので

**미(美)** beauty; the beautiful/자연의 ~ natural beauty; beauties of nature/ ~육체~ physical beauty / ~적 감각 a sense of beauty. び

**미(未)** 〖민〗 ①The Sign of the Sheep[Goat] ②《미방》 the Direction of the Sheep (Southwest-by-south) ③《십이지의》 the zodiacal sign of the ram. ひつじ

**미-(未)** un-; in-;/~완성의 incomplete; unfinished. いまだー

**미가(米價)** the price of rice/~ 조절 control of the rice price. べいか

**미가공(未加工)** ~의 raw; crude; unprocessed. かこうがないこと

**미각(味覺)** the palate; the [sense of] taste; gustation/ ~ 신경 the gustatory nerve/~을 만족시키다 please one's palate. みかく

**미간(未刊)** ~의 unpublished; not yet published/~ 원고 an unfinished manuscript. みかん

**미간(眉間)** the middle of the forehead; the brow; 〖해〗 a glabella/ ~에 흠이 있다 have a scar between one's eyes.

**미간지**(未墾地) uncultivated land; virgin soil. りょうびかん／まだかいこんしてないとち

**미감**(美感) a sense of beauty; an esthetic sense[feeling]／~이 부족하다 be insensible to beauty. びかん

**미감**(米泔) 《쌀 뜨물》 rice water.

**미감**(味感) the taste ⇨미각(味覺). みかく

**미개**(未開) ①《문명의》~하다 (be) uncivilized; savage; barbarous／~인 a barbarian／~지 a backward region ②《꽃이》~하다 unblown; not open. みかい

**미개간**(未開墾) ~의 uncultivated／~지 uncultivated land; virgin soil ⇨미간지. みかいこん

**미개발**(未開發) 《형용사적》 undeveloped; unreclaimed 《저개발》 underdeveloped／~국(國) a backward country; an underdeveloped country.

**미개척**(未開拓) ~의 underdeveloped; unexploited; wild／과학계에도 아직 ~의 분야가 많다 Science has many fields still unexplored. みかいたく

**미거**(美擧) a commendable act; a praiseworthy[noble] undertaking. びきょ

**미거**(未擧) ~하다 (be) stupid; dumb; imbecile. もうまい

**미견**(迷見) a mistaken opinion; a wrong view; an erroneous idea.

**미결**(未決) ~의 undecided; unsettled; unconvicted; pending; open. みけつ

**미결산**(未決算) ~의 unsettled; outstanding.

**미결제**(未決濟) ~의 unsettled; outstanding 《미지불의》 unpaid／~ 계정 an outstanding account. けっさいがしないこと

**미경사**(未經事) ~하다 (be) inexperienced [unexperienced]; raw; green; be with no experience.

**미경지**(未耕地) uncultivated land; virgin soil. まだこうさくしてないとち

**미경험**(未經驗) ~의 inexperienced; unexperienced; new／~자 환영 Welcome, the inexperienced. けいけんがないこと

**미곡**(米穀) 《곡물》 rice; cereals; grain／~ 시장 the rice market. べいこく

**미골**(尾骨) 《해》 the coccyx. びこつ

**미관**(美觀) a fine[beautiful] sight[spectacle]; a fine[lovely] view／자연의 ~ the beauties of nature. びかん

**미관**(微官) 《관직》 an obscure[a low] position in government 《관리》 a petty official; a low official. したやく

**미관**(味官) the gustation organ; the taste organ. みかくきかん

**미광**(微光) a pale[faint] light; a shimmer／~등 a dim light.

**미구**(未久) ~에 before long; shortly; soon; in the near future／그는 ~에 돌아올 것이다 It will not be long before he returns. ひさしくないことのいみ

**미꾸라지** 《어》 a loach; a mudfish. どじょう

**미구 불원**(未久不遠) near future／~에 in the near future／~에 그날이 올 것이다 The day will not be far distant.

**미군**(美軍) the U.S. Armed Forces; American forces; the U.S. Army. べいぐん

**미궁**(迷宮) mystery; a maze; a labyrinth／그 문제는 여전히 ~에 빠져 있다 The question is as much in dark as ever. めいきゅう

**미균**(黴菌) a bacillus (pl. -li); a bacterium (pl. -ria)／~학 bacteriology／~설 the germ theory. さいきん

**미끄러지다** slide; glide; slip 《미끄럽다》 be slippery. すべる

**미끄럼** sliding／~타다 slide; ride a slippery slide.

**미끄럽다** (be) smooth; slimy; slippery／몸시 ~ be as slippery as an eel／미끄러운 길 a slippery road／미끄러운 종이 sleek paper. つるつるしている

**미끈거리다** (be) slippery[slimy]／길이 ~ A road is slippery[slick] (with mud). つるつるすべる

**미끈둥하다** (be) very smooth[sleek, slick]; quite slippery／미끈둥한 뱀장어 a very slippery eel. とてもすっべりしている

**미끈미끈** smoothly; sleekly; slickly; oily／~하다 be all slippery[oily]／한 머리 sleek hair／뱀장어가 ~하여 손에 잡히지 않는다 The eel is so slippery [that] I can't catch it. つるつるすべる

**미끈하다** (be) graceful; handsome; fine-looking; attractive／옷을 미끈하게 입다 be well dressed. しとやかだ

**미급**(未及) ~하다 fall short of; be not up to par 《열등하다》 be inferior (to); be no match (for)／생각이 거기까지는 ~했다 I was not far-sighted enough to think of it. いまだおよばないこと

**미끼** ①《낚시의》 a bait／낚시에 ~를 달다 bait a fish-hook／낚시 ~ a fish bait; a bait for fish ②《꾀는 물건》 a bait; an inducement; a lure; an allurement. えさ

**미기**(美妓) a beautiful[pretty] *keesaeng* [girl].

**미기**(美技) a brilliant[beautiful, neat] performance 《야구·정구》 a fine play.

**미나리** 《식》 parsley. せり

**미나리아재비** 《식》 a buttercup; a crowfoot; *Ranunculus acris*《학명》.

**미남자**(美男子) a handsome man; a good-[fine-]looking man／그는 진짜 ~이다 He is decidedly a handsome man. びだんし

**미납**(未納) nonpayment; default in payment／~의 unpaid; in arrears／~자 a person in arrears; a defaulter. みのう

**미녀**(美女) a beauty; a belle; a beautiful woman; a pretty girl; a knockout 《미·속》. びじょ

**미농지**(美濃紙) a kind of Japanese rice paper. みのがみ

**미늘** a barb／~창(槍) a halberd. あご

**미다**¹ 《머리가》 (one's hair) falls out; become bald／뒷머리가 ~ one's head gets bald in the back. はげる

미다² 《따돌리다》leave out in the cold; keep at a distance. れいぐうする

미다³ tear a hole in (*paper, leather*) / 잘못해서 종이를 ~ tear a hole in the paper by mistake. さく

미닫이 a sliding door / ~창 a sliding window. すべりもん

미담(美談) a beautiful[noble, an inspiring] story; a moving story. びだん

미대다 ①《전가하다》lay; throw; shift (*the blame*) ②《미루다》delay; put off; postpone; defer. おしつける

미덕(美德) a virtue; a moral excellency; a noble attribute; a good trait / ~을 지닌 사람 a man of virtue; a virtuous man. びとく

미덥다 (be) trustworthy; reliable; dependable / 미덥게 여기다 repose[place] trust in (*a person*) / 미더운 사람 a reliable[trustworthy] person. しんらいせいがある

미동(美童) a handsome[good-looking] boy 《면》a catamitte. びどう

미동(微動) a slight shock; a tremor / ~도 않다 be unshakable; stand adamant [as firm as a rock]. びどう

미두(米豆) speculation in rice; bucket-shop operation in rice / ~장(場) a rice exchange.

미뜨리다 push[shove] off; thrust; push [press] hard. ぶちやぶく

미등(尾燈) a tail-light.

미락(微落) 【경】 fractional decline.

미란(糜爛) 《염증》inflammation 《부란》decomposition / ~하다 be inflamed; fester; be decomposed / 시체가 몹시 ~되어 있었다 The corpse was in a fearful state of decomposition.

미래(未來) future; time to come 【언】 the future tense / ~의 future; coming; to come / ~에 in [the] future / ~사(事) future《coming》events / ~파 futurism(개인); the futurists(단체). みらい

미랭(微冷) slight coldness / ~하다 (be) slightly cold; coldish. すこし冷たいこと

미량(微凉) slight coolness / ~하다 (be) slightly cool. すこし涼しいこと

미량(微量) a very small quantity / ~분석 【화】 microanalysis / ~ 측정기 a microdetector.

미레자 a T-square. Tかたのしゃく

미려(美麗) beauty; elegance; loveliness / ~하다 (be) beautiful; elegant. びだい

미력(微力) one's small ability; the little one can 《자력》slender means / ~을 다하다 do *one's* bit; do what little one can. びりょく

미련 stupidity; dullness; clumsiness; awkwardness / ~하다 (be) stupid; dullwitted / ~장이 a stupid fool; an ass; a dullard. ぐどん

미련(未練) regret; attachment / ~이 있다 feel regret; be still attached to.

미령(靡寧) indisposition / ~하다 (be) indisposed; unwell; ill. みれん

미로(迷路) a maze; a labyrinth / ~에 빠지다 be[get] lost in a maze; be at a loss. めいろ

미료(未了) ~의 unfinished; unfulfilled; incomplete; unexecuted / ~안(案) a pending bill. みりょう

미루다 ①《연기하다》postpone; put off; defer; protract 《지체하다》delay ②《일·책임 따위를》impute; shift on; shuffle off; lay on ③《추측하다》infer; judge; gather; guess / 이것으로 미루어 보아 judging from this. えんきする

미륵보살(彌勒菩薩) Maitreya (Sans). みろくぼさつ

미리 beforehand; in advance; previously; in anticipation (*of*) / ~ 나에게 이야기를 했어야 했다 You ought to have told me before hand. あらかじめ

미립 a knack; the trick; tact / ~을 알으면 아주 쉽다 It's quite easy when you have the knack of it ようりょう

미립(微粒) a particle; a corpusc[u]le / ~체(體) 【생】 a microsome. びりゅう

미립자(微粒子) 【물】 a corpuscle / ~의 corpuscular / ~설(說) the corpuscular theory of light / ~ 현상 a corpuscular phenomenon. びりゅうし

미만(未滿) ~의 under; less than; not more than; below. みまん

미만(彌滿) spread; pervasion; diffusion / ~하다 pervade; extend all round; prevail; spread (*about*). びまん

미망(迷妄) [an] illusion; [a] delusion / ~설(說) illusionism / ~을 깨우치다 open (*a person's*) eyes; bring (*a person*) to his senses. めいもう

미망인(未亡人) a widow; a relict《고》/ 김씨의 ~ the widow of the late Mr. *Kim* / 전쟁 ~ a war-widow. みぼうじん

미맥(米麥) rice and barley. べいばく

미명(未明) early dawn / ~에 before dawn; in the early dawn; in the gray of the morning. みめい

미명(美名) a good[fair] name; fame; high reputation / 자선이란 ~하에 under the cloak of charity; in the name of charity. びめい

미모(美貌) a pretty[beautiful, handsome] face; good looks / ~의 여인 a beautiful lady; a Helen / ~가 그녀의 신세를 망치게 하였다 Her beauty was her ruin[downfall]. びぼう

미목(眉目) looks; features; a face / ~이 수려하다 have a handsome face; be handsome. びもく

미몽(迷夢) an illusion; a delusion / ~을 깨뜨리다 disillusion (*one*) / 그는 아직 ~에서 깨어나지 못하고 있다 He is not yet awakened from illusion. めいむ

미묘(美妙) elegance; exquisiteness; gracefulness / ~하다 (be) elegant; exquisite; graceful / ~한 음악에 매혹되다 be charmed with exquisite music.

미묘(微妙) delicacy; subtlety / ~하다

미문(美文) elegant prose; a literary essay／ ~학 polite literature; *belles-lettres*(F)／ ~체 a flowery[an ornate] style.

미물(微物) ①((작은 물건))a trifle; small articles ②((미생물))a microorganism; a microbe; an insect／ ~학 micrology.

미미(微微) insignificance／~하다(be) slight; little; small; trifling／~한 증가 an immaterial increase／그 회사는 처음에는 ~한 존재였다 At first the company was a petty affair.

미미(美味) ((맛))relish; a good flavor; daintiness; deliciousness ((음식))a dainty; a delicacy; a rich diet／~의 sweet; savory; tasty; palatable.

미반(米飯) boiled rice.

미발달(未發達) ~의 undeveloped ((저개발)) underdeveloped.

미복(美服) a pretty dress; fine clothes／ ~을 입다 be finely dressed.

미복(微服) disguise in dress／~ 잠행하다 travel incognito; go in disguise.

미봉(彌縫) temporizing; tinkering／~하다 temporize; patch up; make shift／ ~책 a makeshift ／잠시 ~하다 patch (*things*) up for the moment.

미부(尾部) a tail ((항공기의)) the empennage; tail unit.

미분(微分) differential; differentiation／~ 방정식 a differential equation／ ~학 differential calculus.

미분명(未分明) vagueness; uncertainty; obscurity／~하다 (be) vague; doubtful; uncertain obscure.

미분자(微分子) an atom; a corpuscle.

미불(未拂) arrears; arrearage／~의 unpaid; outstanding; unsettled／~의 봉급 back pay(salary)／~금 an account not yet paid.

미쁘다 (be) reliable; trusty; trustworthy.

미비(未備) ((부족))insufficiency ((불완전)) imperfection ((부적당))inadequacy／~하다 (be) insufficient; not enough／서류가 ~되어 있다 The documents are not in order.

미사(美辭) elegant language／ ~ 여구를 늘어놓다 marshal all sorts of flowery words; use euphuistic phrases.

미사(美事) a praiseworthy thing[conduct].

미사(彌撒) 〖종〗a [Christian] mass.

미삼(尾蔘) the root hair of ginseng.

미상(未詳) ~하다 (be) unknown; unidentified; be not exactly known／원인 ~이다 The cause still remains a mystery.

미상(米商) a rice dealer; a rice merchant.

미상(迷想) an erroneous idea; a mistaken notion; a fallacy.

미상(微傷) a slight wound[injury]／ ~을 입다 be slightly injured.

미상불(未嘗不) really; indeed; undoubtedly; truly; certainly／~ 이것은 편리한 기계다 This is a handy apparatus, to be sure.

미상환(未償還) ~의 outstanding; unredeemed／ ~액 outstanding issues.

미색(美色) ①((미인))a beautiful face [woman]; a beauty ②((빛깔))a beautiful colo[u]r.

미생물(微生物) a microbe／ ~ 학자 a microbiologist.

미설(未設) ~의 unestablished; uninstalled／~선(線) lines under project／~전화 projected telephones.

미성(美聲) a beautiful[sweet] voice.

미성(未成) incompletion／ ~의 unfinished; uncompleted／~숙(熟) immaturity; unripeness.

미성년(未成年) minority; nonage／ ~자 금주법 the law for prohibiting minors from drinking.

미성숙(未成熟) immaturity; unripeness／ ~하다 (be) immature; unripe; unfledged; callow.

미성안(未成案) an unfinished plan; an uncompleted scheme.

미성품(未成品) an unfinished article[product].

미세(微細) minuteness; details／~하다 (be) minute; delicate; nice.

미소(微小) minuteness／ ~하다 (be) minute; microscopic; infinitesimal／~ 식물 a microphyte.

미소(微少) a very small amount; extremely small quantities／ ~하다 (be) very little.

미소(微笑) a smile／ ~하다 smile; beam／ ~를 띠고 with a smile; smiling／그는 비웃는 ~를 머었다 He smiled an ironical smile.

미소년(美少年) a handsome youth; a good-looking boy; an Adonis(그리스 신화).

미송(美松) 〖식〗the Oregon pine; the Douglas fir[pine, spruce].

미수(未收) ~의 accrued; receivable; deferred; uncollected (*income*)／~ 수익 uncollected income.

미수(未遂) ~의 attempted／자살 ~ attempted suicide／ ~로 그치다 fail in the attempt.

미수(米壽) one's 88th birthday／~를 축하하다 celebrate one's 88th birthday.

미수범(未遂犯) an attempted crime; an unconsummated crime／암살 ~ ((범인)) a would-be assassin.

미숙(未熟) ①((덜 익음))unripeness; greenness; immaturity／ ~하다 (be) unripe;

**미숙련** green; immature; crude ②《숙달하지 못한》inexperienced; unskilled; callow; raw; poor／～한 자 an in experienced person; a green hand.

**미숙련**(未熟練) ～의 unskilled; unskilful／～공 an unskilled worker 《총칭》unskilled labo[u]r.

**미술**(美術) art; fine arts／～가 an artist／～상 a fine art dealer／～ 전람회 an art exhibition／～품 a work of art／조형 ～ formative arts. びじゅつ

**미시** sugared water containing glutinous rice flour. こがしこな

**미시**(未時) the Hour of the Ram; the hour from two o'clock to four in the afternoon.

**미식**(美食) dainty food; a luxurious diet; delicacies; dainties／～하다 have [live on] dainty food; be an epicure／～가 a gourmand; an epicure. びしょく

**미식**(米食) a rice diet／～하다 eat rice; live[feed] on rice／～ 국민 a rice-eating people. べいしょく

**미식 축구**(美式蹴球) American football.

**미신**(迷信) superstition; bigotry／～적인 superstitious; bigoted／～가 a superstitious person／～을 타파하다 do away with[break down] superstitions. めいしん

**미심**(未審) 《의심》doubt; suspicion; uncertainty／～하다 (be) doubtful／～쩍은 얼굴을 하다 look dubious[suspicious]／～한 데가 좀 있다 There is something that is not clear to me.
いまたつまびらかでないこと

**미싯가루** baked rice-granules; baked.
こがしのこな

**미아**(迷兒) ①《집 잃은 아이》a stray[lost] child／～를 찾아 search for a missing child ②《자기 아들》my son. まよいご

**미안**(未安) ～하다 ①《남에게》(be)sorry or regrettable; repentant／그 건에 대해서는 지금도 ～하게 생각하고 있다 That matter still troubles my conscience. ②《거북하다》(be) uneasy. すまないこと

**미안**(美顔) a beautiful face; handsome features／～술 beauty treatment／～수 a beauty wash[lotion]. びがん

**미안쩍다** (be) sorry; regretful; be ashamed; be out of countenance／바보 짓을 해서 ～ I am ashamed of my folly

**미약**(微弱) ～하다 (be) weak; feeble; insignificant; faint 《미미한》slight. びじゃく

**미약**(媚藥) an aphrodisiac [drug]; a [love-]philter; a love potion.

**미양**(微恙) an indisposition; a slight illness. びよう

**미어**(謎語) a riddle 《수수께끼》a puzzle. めいご

**미어**(美語) American English; an Americanism; American《어》. べいこくご

**미어뜨리다** tear a hole; let break; split.
ふちゃぶくあなをあける

**미어지다** 《종이·가죽이》be tattered; be torn; split; burst. やぶれる

**미역**¹ 《식》brown seaweed; *Undaria pinnatifida*(학명). わかめ

**미역**² 《목욕·수영 등》swimming; a swim; bathing; a bathe(목욕)／바닷가에 ～으러 가다 go to the beach for a swim.
からだをあらうこと

**미역국** 《국》 mee-yok soup／～먹다 ①eat me-e-yok soup ②《면직당하다》get dismissed [fired, sacked] 《시험에 실패하다》fail an examination.

**미연**(未然) ～에 before (*anything*) happens; previously／화를 ～에 방지하다 nip the evil in the bud. みぜん

**미열**(微熱) slight fever 《원인·불명의》febricula／～이 있다 be a bit feverish; have a slight fever.

**미온**(微溫) tepidity; lukewarmness／～적 indifferent; half-hearted／～적 정책[태도] a lukewarm policy[attitude]／～수 tepid water. びおん

**미완**(未完) ～하다 have not finished[completed]. みかんせい

**미완성**(未完成) incompletion／～ 교향악 the Unfinished Symphony (by *Schubert*). みかんせい

**미용**(美容) a beautiful face／～술 beauty art／～사 a beauty artist／～원 a beauty shop／～ 체조 calisthenics／～ 정형 cosmetic surgery. びよう

**미우**(微雨) a light rain; a drizzle; a mizzle. びう

**미우**(眉宇) the brow[s]. びう

**미욱하다** (be) stupid; silly; dull; asinine; thick-headed; dumb《미》／미욱한 사람 a foolhardy person. おろかだ

**미움** hatred; hate; enmity／～받다 be hated／그는 모든 사람들의 ～을 받고 있다 He is a common object of hatred.
にくしみ

**미워하다** hate; abhor; detest; have a hatred for; have a spite against／위선을 ～ hate hypocrisy. にくむ

**미음**(米飲) thin rice-gruel; water gruel rice water.

**미음**(美音) a sweet[beautiful] voice.
びおん

**미의**(微意) a humble desire／～를 표하여 as a small token of *one's* gratitude [appreciation]. びい

**미의식**(美意識) aesthetic consciousness.
びいしき

**미이다** be tattered ⇨미어지다. やぶれる

**미이라** a mummy.

**미익**(尾翼) 《비행기의》a tail; a tailplane.

**미인**(美人) ①《가인》a beautiful woman [girl]; a beauty／～ 대회 a beauty contest／놀라운 ～ a strikingly beautiful woman ②《미국인》an American; a Yankee《비》. びじん

**미인계**(美人計) *a mari complaisant*(F); using a beautiful woman to ensnare a person. びじんをつかったおとり

**미작**(米作) 《수확》rice crop[harvest, yield]

**미장**(재배) rice growing; culture; cultivation of rice. べいさく

**미장**(美粧) beauty culture[art]; beauty treatment; cosmetology/～원 a beauty parlor. びしょう

**미장**(美裝) fine dress; rich attire/～다 dress finely; be finely dressed; be richly dressed. びそう

**미장이** a plasterer. どこう

**미저골**(尾骶骨) 【해】 the coccyx (Pl. ~es, -cyges)/～ 신경 the coccygeal nerve.

**미적**(美的) aesthetic/～ 가치 an aesthetic value/～ 관념 an aesthetic sense/～ 생활 an aesthetic life. びてき

**미적거리다** ①(밀다) push forward little by little ②(연기) put off from day to day; procrastinate time again and again. すこしずつぜんしんする

**미적미적** ～하다 put off from day to day; delay for a long time.

**미적분**(微積分) 【수】 differential and integral calculus; infinitesimal calculus. びせきぶん

**미적지근하다** (be) tepid; lukewarm (미온적)(be) half-hearted/미적지근한 태도 a lukewarm attitude. なまぬるい

**미전**(美展) an art exhibition.

**미점**(美點) a [point of] beauty; a merit; a virtue. びてん

**미정**(未定) ～의 undecided; unsettled; unfixed (불확실한) uncertain/계획은 이다 my plan is unsettled/～고(稿) an unfinished manuscript. みてい

**미제**(未濟) ～의 《미불의》 unpaid 《미필의》 unfinished. みさい

**미제**(未製) ～의 unfinished; unmanufactured; raw/～품 unfinished goods; an unfinished product[article].

**미제**(美製) ～의 American[U.S.] made; of American make; made in U.S.A.

**미조**(美爪) beautiful[cared-for] nails/～사(師) a manicurist/～원(院) a manicure parlor. うつくしいつめ

**미족**(未足) insufficiency; shortage; inadequacy/～하다 (be) not yet sufficient. また足らないこと

**미죄**(微罪) a minor offence; a peccadillo.

**미주**(美酒) excellent wine; a good drink. びしゅ

**미주 신경**(迷走神經) 【해】 the vagus; the pneumogastric nerves.

**미주알** the anus. こうもん

**미주알고주알** inquisitively 《모두》 thoroughly; to the last details/～ 캐묻다 ask inquisitively. あれやこれやと

**미증유**(未曾有) ～의 unheard-of; unprecedented/～의 대전 the greatest battle in history[on record, ever fought]. みぞう

**미지**(一紙) wax paper. ろうがみ

**미지**(未知) ～의 unknown/～수 an unknown quantity/～의 친구 a friend whom one has not yet seen; an unknown friend. みち

**미지**(微志) one's humble intention ⇨미의 (徽意).

**미지근하다** (be) lukewarm; tepid 《미온적》(be) half-hearted/미지근한 대답 a half-hearted reply. あまぬるい

**미진**(微震) a faint[slight] earthtremor; a slight shock [of earthquake]/계(計) a trometer. びしん

**미진**(微塵) an atom; a particle; fragments. みじん

**미진**(未盡) ～하다 (be) unfinished; remaining. まだちゃくしないこと

**미질**(美質) good character; fine quality.

**미착**(未着) unarrival; non-arrival/～의 not yet arrived 《미배달의》 not yet delivered/～품 goods to arrive[in transit]. みちゃく

**미착수**(未着手) ～의 not yet started/～ 공사 works[constructions] not yet started. みちゃくしゅしないこと

**미채**(迷彩) camouflage; dazzle painting/～를 베풀다 camouflage [a ship].

**미처** [not] yet/～ 예상도 못하다 not to come up to one's expectation. まだ

**미천**(微賤) a low rank; a humble position; obscurity/～하다 humble; obscure; ignoble; of low origin/～한 몸 a person of humble station. びせん

**미첩**(美妾) a beautiful concubine. うつくしいめかけ

**미추**(美醜) beauty or ugliness 《용모》 personal appearance/용모의 ～를 불문하고 whether fair or otherwise. びしゅう

**미추룸하다** be healthy and fair; be of healthy beauty. すんなりしている

**미충**(微衷) one's inmost feelings; one's true heart 《성의》 sincerity. びちゅう

**미취**(微醉) slight intoxication; mellowness; elevation/～하다 be tipsy; be slightly intoxicated. びすい

**미치광이**(狂人) a madman; an insane[a crazy] person; a lunatic 《열광자》 a maniac. きょうじん

**미치다**¹ ①《정신이》 go[become, run] mad; get crazy; go[become] insane/～게 mad; insane; lunatic; crazy/그 사람은 미친 사람이다 He has a screw loose. ②《하고 싶어》 run mad after; be infatuated with (one); give oneself up to; be crazy about/그는 그 여인에 미쳤다 He is wild about her. くるう

**미치다**² ①《이르다》 reach; come up to come[amount] to 《걸치다》 extend; range/멀리 미치지 못하다 fall far below; be far behind one in (a thing) ②《영향을》 influence; tell; affect/영향을 have (good) influence (on). および

**미칭**(美稱) euphemism.

**미쾌**(未快) being unwell/～하다 (be) not yet recovered [from an illness]; be not quite well; be still unwell.

**미타**(彌陀) 【종】 Amita Buddha; beautiful. あみだぶつ

**미태**(美態) beautiful posture[appearance]. うつくしいたいど

**미태(媚態)** coquetry; coquettish behavior/ ~를 부리다 be coquettish; flirt with; cast sheep's eyes at (*a person*).

**미투리** hemp-cord sandals. あさのくつ

**미품(美品)** an article of fine quality; excellent goods. うつくしいひん

**미풍(美風)** a beautiful[fine] custom; a virtue. びふう

**미풍(微風)** a breeze; a breath of air; a gentle wind; a light wind. びふう

**미필(未畢)** incompletion/ ~하다 have not finished yet/~의 unfinished; incomplete. まだおわらないこと

**미학(美學)** 【철】 [a]esthetics/~자(者) an aesthetician. びがく

**미해결(未解決)** ~의 unsolved; unsettled; outstanding/ ~의 문제 an unsolved problem[issue]. みかいけつ

**미행(尾行)** following. びこう

**미행(微行)** incognito travelling; a private visit/ ~하다 travel incognito; pay a private visit/ ~의 공주 a princess incognito. びこう

**미행(美行)** a praiseworthy conduct; a commendable act. びこう

**미혹(迷惑)** 《미망》 a delusion; an illusion 《미신》 superstition 《망설임》 perplexity / ~하다 《사도에 빠지다》 be tempted (유혹) 《여자에》 be enamoured of; fall a victim to 《헤매다》 wander; be at a loss; be in two minds; be captivated (by). めいわく

**미혼(未婚)** ~의 unmarried; single/ ~자 an unmarried person; not-yet-weds; a bachelor(남자); a maiden [lady]; a spinster(여자). みこん

**미화(美化)** beautification/ ~하다 beautify; make beautiful; refine; embellish 《장식》 adorn/도시 ~ 운동 a city-beautiful movement. びか

**미화(美貨)** American money[currency]; the American dollar 《화물》 American goods/ ~로 in American money. べいこくのかへい

**미흡(未洽)** 《부족》 insufficiency 《불완전》 imperfection/~하다 (be) insufficient; unsatisfactory; imperfect; defective/ ~한 점이 있다 leave something to be desired. まだたらないこと

**미희(美姬)** a beautiful girl[maiden]; a beauty. びき

**민가(民家)** a private house; a commoner's house. みんか

**민간(民間)** ~의 《공에 대한》 private; non-official 《군에 대한》 civil; civilian/ ~ 사업 a private enterprise[business]/ ~ 방송 private broadcasting/ ~ 항공 civil aviation. みんかん

**민간인(民間人)** a [non-official] civilian. みんかんにん

**민감(敏感)** sensibility; sensitiveness/ ~하다 (be) sensitive; impressionable; susceptible (to). びんかん

**민국(民國)** 1《인민과 국가》 the people and the state ②《공화국》 a republic/대한 ~ The Republic of Korea. みんこく

**민군(民軍)** militia :민병(民兵). みんぺい

**민권(民權)** civil[the people's] rights/ ~ 운동 democratic movements/ ~ 유린 an outrage on the people's[civil] rights. みんけん

**민날** a sharp edge 《칼》 a naked sword. するどいやいば

**민낯** an unpainted face.

**민단(民團)** a settlement corporation; a foreign settlement group. みんだん

**민달(敏達)** adroitness; deftness/ ~하다 (be) adroit; deft.

**민대가리** a bald head ▫민머리. はげあたま

**민도(民度)** the conditions[cultural standard] of people; the level[stage]/ ~가 낮다 have a low level of culture[standard of living]. みんど

**민둥민둥하다** (be) treeless; bare; bald; hairless. はげている

**민둥산(一山)** a bald[bare] hill; a barren [treeless] mountain. はげやま

**민들레** 【식】 the dandelion. たんぽぽ

**민란(民亂)** a riot; a rising; an insurrection; a revolt 《농민의》 a peasants' uprising.

**민력(民力)** national power[resources]/ ~을 기르다 foster[build up] national power; store up national resources. みんりょく

**민망(民望)** 《신망》 public confidence 《기대》 popular expectation. みんぼう

**민망(憫惘)** ~하다 (be) sorry; regrettable; pitiful; sad/~한 생각이 들다 feel sorry (for); have compassion (on); feel [pity] (for).

**민머리** a bald head 《사람》 a bald-headed person. はげあたま

**민며느리** a girl who is brought up by the family of the husband-to-be.

**민멸(泯滅)** extinction/~하다 be extinct; go out of existence. びんめつ

**민물** fresh-water/ ~의 limnetic/ ~고기 fresh-water fish. たんすい

**민박(民泊)** ~하다 take lodgings at a private house.

**민방위(民防衛)** civile defense; civilian defense.

**민법(民法)** the civil law 《법전》 the civil code/ ~학의 권위 an authority on the civil law/ ~ 학자 a scholar of the civil law 《로마법의》 a civilian. みんぽう

**민병(民兵)** a militiaman; a colonial soldier; the militia. みんぺい

**민복(民福)** well-being of the people; national welfare/ ~을 도모하다 look to [promote] the welfare of the people. こくみんのこうふく

**민본주의(民本主義)** democracy. みんぽんしゅぎ

**민비녀** a plain silver ornamental bar for the[ladies'] hair. かざりのないかんざし

**민사(民事)** civil affairs 《소송》 a civil

**민사** case/ ~ 소송 a civil suit[action]/ ~ 재판 a civil trial. みんじ

**민사(悶死)** death in agony/ ~하다 die in agony [of vexation]; writhe oneself to death. くもんしてしぬこと

**민생(民生)** national life/ ~ 안정 stabilization of national life. みんせい

**민선(民選)** popular election/ ~의 elected by the people; popularly elected/ ~ 의원 a representative elected by the people[by popular vote]. みんせん

**민성(民聲)** the popular voice; public opinion. みんせい

**민속(民俗)** manners and customs of the people/ ~학 folk-lore/ ~학자 an expert on folk-lore. みんぞく

**민속(敏速)** quickness ⇒민활(敏活).

**민수(民需)** civilian[popular] needs/ ~ 산업 the civilian[popular] industry. みんじゅ

**민숭민숭하다** ①((산이))(be) bare; treeless; bald ②((머리가)) be bald/민숭민숭한 머리 a bald head. はげている

**민습(民習)** convention; usage; popular [national] customs. みんかんのしゅうかん

**민시(民時)** the farming season.

**민심(民心)** popular feelings; the minds of men/ ~을 선동하다 inflame the popular passion. みんしん

**민약설(民約說)** the Theory of Social Contract. みんやくせつ

**민어(民魚)** 【어】 a croaker; *Sciaena albiflora*(학명).

**민업(民業)** a private enterprise[business]. みんぎょう

**민연(憫然)** ~하다 (be) worried; concerned; miserable. かわいそうだ

**민영(民營)** a private enterprise[business] / ~의 privately operated; private; non-government[al]. みんえい

**민예(民藝)** folk arts; folk crafts/ ~품 a folk art article.

**민완(敏腕)** ability; capacity; skill/ ~ 의 able; capable; astute/ ~가 an able man/ ~을 휘두르다 show[give full play] to one's ability. びんわん

**민요(民謠)** a folk song; a ballad; a popular song. みんよう

**민요(民擾)** a revolt ⇒민란(民亂).

**민원(民怨)** public hatred[grievance]/ ~을 사다 become the object of public hatred. こくみんのうらみ

**민원(民願)** ¶ ~ 상담소 the Civil Service Consultation Center.

**민유(民有)** the people's possession; private ownership/ ~의 privately-owned; private/ ~ 철도 a privately-owned railway. みんゆう

**민의(民意)** the will of the people/ ~ 를 묻다 appeal to the judgment of the people; consult the will of the people. みんい

**민의원(民議院)** the Lower House; the House of Representatives[Commons] / ~ 의원 a member of the House of Representatives; a member of Parliament.

**민재(民財)** privately-owned property; an estate in private possession; the people's possessions. じんみんのざいさん

**민적(民籍)** ((등록)) census registration ((등본)) a census register; a family register. こせき

**민정(民情)** ①((정상)) the conditions of the people ②⇒민심(民心). みんじょう

**민정(民政)** ((군정에 대한)) civil administration[government]. みんせい

**민족(民族)** a race; a people; a nation/ ~ 성 racial characteristics[traits]/ ~ 정신 national spirit/ ~주의 racialism; nationalism/ ~ 의식 national[racial] consciousness/ ~ 주체성 national identity / ~ 자결주의 principle of the self-determination of nations. みんぞく

**민주(民主)** democracy/ ~적인 democratic/ 비~적인 undemocratic/ ~ 공화국 a democratic republic/ ~ 정치 democratic form of government/ ~ 제도 the democratic system. みんしゅ

**민주대다** detest; hate. いみきらう

**민주주의(民主主義)** democratic principles; democracy; democratism/ ~ 국가 a democratic state. みんしゅしゅぎ

**민줄** a plain[unpowdered] kite string. なにもつけないひも

**민중(民衆)** the people; the masses/ ~ 적 popular; democratic/ ~ 운동 a popular movement/ ~화하다 popularize/ ~ 오락 mass entertainment. みんしゅう

**민지(民智)** the people's intellect. じんみんのちえ

**민지(敏智)** ready wit; tact; resourcefulness. びんしょうなちえ

**민첩(敏捷)** agility; alacrity; quickness /~하다 (be) quick; nimble; ready; sharp; acute. びんしょう

**민촌(民村)** a village inhabited by the common people. へいみんのむら

**민치(民治)** civil administration; government. みんじ

**민툿하다** (be) smoothly aslant. なだらかにけいしゃしている

**민패** a plain thing; an artless article. かざりのないもの

**민폐(民弊)** an abuse suffered by the public; harm inflicted upon the people. じんみんのへいがい

**민풍(民風)** ethnic[folk] customs; folkways. みんぷう

**민하다** (be) senseless; thoughtless; stupid; silly; foolish. ちょっとおろかだ

**민화(民話)** folklore; folk tale[story]. みんわ

**민활(敏活)** promptitude; quickness; alacrity; activity/ ~하다 (be) prompt; active; brisk; quick; swift. びんかつ

**믿다** ⇒별항 참조(page 1463).

**믿음** faith; belief; creed/ ~이 없는 un-

**믿음성** (一性) 《신임(信任)》 confidence; trust; faith; credence 《신뢰(信賴)》 dependence; reliance/~ 있는 trustworthy; t-rusty; reliable/~ 없는 untrustworthy; unreliable; not to be depended upon; doubtful. しんらいせい

believing; impious/~이 두터운 pious devout; godly. しんらい

**믿음직하다** (be) reliable; trusty; encouraging; reassuring; hopeful 《유망하다》 promising. たのもしい

**밀**¹ 〖식〗 wheat/~의 wheaten/~짚 wheat straw.

**밀**² 《밀랍》 wax; beeswax/~로 만든 w-ax; waxen/~을 먹이다 wax (a thing)/~먹인 종이 wax-paper. みつろう

**밀가루** wheat flour; American flour. こむぎこ

**밀감** (蜜柑) 〖식〗 a mandarin orange; Citrus nobilis (학명). みかん

**밀깜부기** the black ear of wheat.

**밀계** (密計) a secret plan[design, plot, stratagem]/~를 꾸미다 plot secretly; frame a secret plot; devise a secret stratagem. みつけい

**밀계** (密啓) a secret memorial to the Throne/~하다 submit a secret report to the Throne.

**밀고** (密告) [secret] information/~하다 inform against (one); betrayal/~자 an informant. みっこく

**밀골무** a wax-thimble.

**밀교** (密敎) Esoteric Buddhism. みっきょう

**밀국수** wheat vermicelli.

**밀기** (密記) a secret record 《비밀 서류》 a confidential document. ひみつなきろく

**밀기름** a pomade made of beeswax and sesame oil.

**밀기울** the wheat bran. こむぎのぬか

**밀낫** a reaping-hook.

**밀다** ①《떠밀다》 push; shove; thrust/밀어 넘어뜨리다 push down/밀어 젖히다 push[brush] aside/밀고 들어가다 force oneself into/밀어 내다 push out ②《칼로》 shave (off); 《대패로》 plane (off, away)/수염을 ~ shave oneself; have a shave/대패로 판자를 ~ plane a board ③⇨미루다. おす

**밀담** (密談) a secret conversation; confidential talk/~하다 talk secretly; have a confidential talk with. みつだん

**밀대** ①《막대》 a push stick ②《총의》 the recoil mechanism (on a carbine). こむぎのくき

**밀떡** an ointment[a plaster] made of honeyed wheat flour. こむぎのもち

**밀도** (密度) 〖물〗 density/~계 a densimeter/~측량 densimetry. みつど

**밀도살** (密屠殺) illegal butchery.

**밀둘레** a [globular] lump of beeswax. みつろうのかたまり

**밀뜨리다** push hard; give a shove.

**밀랍** (蜜蠟) beeswax. みつろう

**밀려들다** advance[press] on (a castle); make[rush] for (the door); 《파도가》 beat upon (the shore); surge into.

**밀렵** (密獵) poaching/~하다 poach [on a preserve]; steal game. みつりょう

**밀리다** ①《일이》 be delayed; be belated; be behind with/일이 ~ leave over[lay by] one's work/주문이 ~ orders pile up ②《지불이》 fall[be] in arrears; be overdue/밀린 overdue; outstanding; back ③《떠밀리다》 be pushed[thrust, jostled]/밀려 나가다 be pushed out; be forced out/밀려들다 《파도가》 beat upon (the shore); surge into ④《내밀리다》 be pushed back; be beaten a retreat/전군이 밀려 나오는 중이다 be in full retreat. のばされる

**밀림** (密林) a thick[dense] forest; a jungle 《관목의》 a close thicket/~지대 a jungle area. みつりん

**밀막다** refuse under a pretense; decline on the pretext of. こうじつをつけてことわる

**밀매** (密賣) illicit sale/~하다 sell secretly; smuggle. みつばい

**밀매음** (密賣淫) an unlicensed prostitution/~하다 live on[walk] the streets without license/~녀 an unlicensed prostitute. みつばいいん

**밀모** (密謀) a plot; a machination; a conspiracy/~하다 plot secretly; conspire; machinate; lay a plot. みつぼう

**밀무역** (密貿易) smuggling/~하다 smuggle/~ 업자 a smuggler. みつぼうえき

**밀물** the flowing[high] tide 《만조》 flood tide/~이 들어오다 The tide is rising [coming in]. あげしお

**밀범벅** wheat-and-pumpkin pudding.

**밀보리** ①《쌀보리》 rye; naked barley ②《밀과 보리》 wheat and barley. おおむぎ

**밀봉** (蜜蜂) 〖충〗 a [honey-]bee. みつぷう

**밀봉** (密封) sealing up/~하다 seal hermetically; seal up. みつばち

**밀사** (密使) a secret messenger[envoy]; a secret-service agent. みっし

**밀사** (密事) a secret. みつじ

**밀상** (密商) a smuggler; a secret dealer.

**밀생** (密生) ~하다 grow thick[in clusters]; be tickly wooded. みっせい

**밀서** (密書) a secret letter. みっしょ

**밀선** (密船) a smuggling-vessel; a smuggler; a runner.

**밀썰물** high tide and low tide.

**밀송** (密送) ~하다 send[despatch] secretly[in secret]. みっそう

**밀수** (密輸) smuggling; contraband/~하다 smuggle; import[export] through illegal channels/~자 a smuggler/~단 a smuggling ring/~선 a smuggling vessel/~입 smuggling/~출 smuggling abroad. みつゆ

**밀수제비** a dish[piece] of wheat dough boiled in soup.

**밀실** (密室) a secret room[chamber]; a c-loset. みっしつ

**밀약** (密約) 《약속》 a secret promise[agree-

밀어(密語) a confidential[private] talk; lover's whispers. みつご
밀어(密漁) poaching/ ~하다 poach; fish illegally/ ~자 a poacher. みつりょう
밀운(密雲) dense[heavy] clouds. みつうん
밀월(蜜月) a honeymoon. みつげつ
밀유(密諭) private admonition round -about instruction.
밀의(密議) a chamber-council; a private[closed] consultation/ ~하다 hold a secret conference; have a private consultation (with). みつぎ
밀입국(密入國) smuggling/ ~하다 smuggle oneself into a country 《배로》 stowing away. みつにゅうこく
밀장지 a paper sliding door. しょうじ
밀접(密接) ~하다 (be) close; intimate; near/ ~한 관계가 있다 be closely related (with); be intimately associated.
밀정(密偵) a spy; a secret agent; an emissary; an agent provocateur. みってい
밀조(密造) illicit manufacture; illicit distilling/ ~하다 manufacture[brew] secretly. みつぞう
밀주(密酒) home-brew; bootleg; a moonshine《미·속》/ ~를 담그다 brew clandestinely[secretly, illicitly]; moonshine《미·속》.
밀지(密旨) secret orders. みっし
밀집(密集) massing/ ~하다 mass; crowd; concentrate; swarm. みっしゅう
밀짚 wheat[barley] straw/ ~ 모자 a straw hat. こむぎのわら
밀착(密着) 《동식물》adnation; close adherence/ ~하다 adhere closely to; stick fast to (a thing). みっちゃく
밀책(密策) a secret plan ⇒밀계. みっけい
밀초 a candle made of beeswax; a wax candle. ろうそく
밀초(蜜炒) honeyed medicinal herbs that are roasted.
밀치다 push away; thrust/ 옆으로 ~ push[thrust] aside. つよくおす
밀칙(密勅) a secret royal order. みっちょく
밀타승(蜜陀僧) 【약】 litharge.
밀탐(密探) secret detective work; secret investigation; espionage/ ~하다 spy (on one, into a secret);investigate secretly. ひみつにたんさくすること
밀통(密通) ①《내통(內通)》secret communication; betrayal/ ~하다 communicate secretly with (one); betray/~자 a betrayer ②《간통》intercourse; illicit; adultery/ ~하다 make an illicit love (to); commit adultery with. みっつう
밀폐(密閉) hermetic sealing/ ~하다 shut[close] up tight; make airtight.
밀풀 wheat flour paste.
밀항(密航) a secret passage; smuggling /~하다 stow away; steal a passage; make a secret passage/ ~선 a smuggler vessel. みっこう

## 믿다

①《신용하다》believe; put belief (in); credit; put credit (in); give credit[credence] (to); be convinced of /믿을 수 없는 애기 an unbelievable[incredible] story; a story that passes belief/ 믿을 수 있다 be credible; be believable/ 믿을 수 없다 be incredible; be unbelievable; be doubtful/내가 믿는 바로는 in my opinion; to the best of my belief; my belief is (that)/남의 말을 잘 ~ be credulous; be ready to believe anything one hears/굳게 ~ have a firm belief (that); firmly believe (that) /옳다고 믿는 바를 행하다 do anything one believes right/나는 그의 말이 사실 이라고 믿고 있다 I place credit in his statement as being true./그가 죽었다 는게 믿어지지 않는다 I cannot persuade myself that he is dead[of his death]. /그녀의 말은 믿을 수가 없다 I cannot believe her., I cannot give credit to her statement.

②《신뢰하다》trust (in); put trust (in); put[place] confidence (in); put[have] faith (in); pin[attach] one's faith (to) 《의지하다》rely (on); look[turn] to (a person) for help; depend[count, lean, reckon, calculate] (on); trust (to); 《기대하다》expect/믿을 만한 보도에 의하면 according to reliable[trustworthy] information/믿을 만하다 be trustworthy; reliable; authentic; authoritative/자기 힘을 ~ have confidence in[rely on] one's strength/권력을 ~ turn to[lean on] one's power/믿지 못할 것을 ~ lean on [turn to] a broken reed; hope against hope/아저씨를 믿고 상경하다 come up to Seoul, counting on one's uncle's help /자네를 믿고 이 일을 맡기네 I will trust to you for the performance of the task.

③《확신하다》be sure of; be confident of/성공하리라 be sure of success/그녀는 신의 존재를 믿고 있다 She is positive as to the existence of God. /지식은 힘이라고 믿는다 It is my firm belief that knowledge is power.

④《신앙》believe in; have belief in/불교를 ~ believe[profess] in Buddhism. /나는 귀신 따위를 믿지 않는다 I don't believe in ghosts.

**밀행**(密行) a prowl / ~하다 prowl (*about*); go[patrol] secretly. みっこう

**밀환**(蜜丸) a honey-coated pill. はちみつでまるめたじょうざい

**밀회**(密會) a clandestine[secret] meeting; a rendezvous / ~하다 meet in secret; meet (*one*) secretly / ~ 장소 a place of assignation; a secret rendezvous / ~를 즐기다 enjoy a stolen meeting with *one's* lover. みっかい

**밉광스럽다** (be) hateful; abominable; detestable; spiteful. ひじょうにくい

**밉다** (be) hateful; abominable; detestable; spiteful. にくい

**밉살머리스럽다** (be) [very] hateful ⇨밉살스럽다

**밉살스럽다** (be) [very] hateful; spiteful; provoking / 밉살스러운 웃음 a malicious smile. にくったらしい

**밉상**(-相) a disgusting face[appearance, act].

**밋밋하다** (be) straight and smooth; slim; slender. ながくてまっすぐだ

**밍밍하다** ①《맛이》(be) tasteless; insipid ②《술·담배 등이》light; mild; weak; thin; dilute. あまりみずくさい

**및** both… and; besides. また

**밑** ①《하부》the bottom; the base; the underpart; the foot / ~의 lower; under; subordinate / ~에 down; under; beneath; below / 테이블 ~에 under a table / 계단 ~에 at the foot of the stairs ②《근본》the root; the origin ③《음부》the private parts; the secrets ④《바닥》the bottom / 바다 ~에 at the bottom [depths] of the sea ⑤《뿌리》root a tuber ⑥《수》a base angle. そこ

**밑거름** 〘농〙 fertilizer used at sowing time.

**밑그림** 《그림의》a rough sketch 《도안》a draft; a design.

**밑넓이** 〘수〙 the bottom dimensions. そこはば

**밑동** the root; the base / 나무의 ~에 at the root of a tree.

**밑둥치** the root [of a tree, *etc*.]. ね

**밑들다** 《밑이 들다》form a root[bulb]; grow big. ねづく

**밑머리** original hair. もとのかみ

**밑면적**(-面積) the bottom dimensions.

**밑바닥** ①《바닥》the bottom; the base / 구두의 ~ th esole of a shoe / 독의 ~ the bottom of a jar / ~이 빠지다 the bottom comes[falls] out ②《마음 속》*one's* inmost thoughts[desire] / ~ 생활 life in the gutters[slumbs]. そこ

**밑바탕** 《물건의》the foundation; the ground; the element 《사람의》birth《혈통》; nature; disposition《성질》. ほんしつ

**밑받침** an underlay; an underlying object; a support; a rest. ささえもの

**밑밥** 《낚시질의》ground bait.

**밑변**(-邊) 〘수〙 the base the; base line of a geometrical figure]. ていへん

**밑불** starter fire; a light; live coals.

**밑살** ①《미주알》anal sphincters ②the vulva ⇨음부.

**밑술** crude liquor; raw spirits.

**밑씨** 〘식〙 a germinal vesicle.

**밑씻개** toilet paper. おとしかみ

**밑알** an egg kept in an egg-laying box.

**밑짝** the under piece [of a two part object]. じょうげ一對のしたのもの

**밑절미** the foundation; the basis; the base. うまれつきのもの

**밑조사**(-調査) 《예비 조사》a preliminary inveistgation; spadework.

**밑줄** an underline. アンダーライン

**밑줄기** the lower part of the trunk (of *a tree*). みきのかぶ

**밑지다** lose; suffer[sustain] a loss; be [come off] a loser / 밑지고 팔다 sell at a loss[sacrifice] / 밑지는 장사 a losing business[transaction].

**밑창** the bottom piece / 구두 ~ the sole of a shoe. くつぞこ

**밑천** 《상업 자본》capital; funds 《자산》resources / ~을 투자하다 put[invest] capital in (*a thing*). しほん

**밑층**(-層) 《아래층》the ground floor; the bottom layer. かいか

**밑판**(-板) the bottom board plate. とこ

**바**[1] what/그가 말하는 ~ what he says.
**바**[2] (밧줄) a rope/~를 치다 stretch a rope. みっつよりのなわ
**바**[3] 〖음〗 fa; F. /울림 ~조 F sharp(기호: F#)/내림 ~조 F flat(기호: F♭)/~장조 F major/~ 단조 F minor.
**바가지** a [dipper made of] gourd/~를 긁다 snarl at one's husband. ひさご
**바가지쓰다** pay through the nose; pay exorbitantly.
**바각, 빠각** gratingly; with a scrape/~거리다 rattle; clatter/~하다 scrape; grate; make a grating sound/쥐가 문을 ~거린다 A mouse is scratching at the door. ぎいぎい
**바깥** the outside/~의 outer; outside; exterior/~쪽 away/~ 양반 one's husband/~쪽 the outside. そと
**빠개다** ①split; cleave/장작을 ~ split firewood ②(어긋내다) spoil; ruin. わる
**바꼳**[1] (송곳) a drill with a metal sidehandle. てつのえのついたきり
**바꼳**[2] 〖식〗 an aconite; a wolfsbane; a monkshood. とりかぶと
**바구니** a wicker basket. かご
**바꾸다** ①(교환하다) [ex]change (물품 교환) barter; replace; renew; cash/물지을 돈으로 ~ convert[exchange] goods into money ②(변경하다) change; alter; modify; amend/바꾸어 말하면 in other words/방향을 ~ change the direction ③(피륙을) buy [cloth]. とりかえる
**바구미** 〖충〗 a rice weevil. こくぞうむし
**바꾸이다** be[get] changed ⇨바뀌다. とりかえられる
**바꿈질** exchange; change; interchange; switching. とりかえること
**바뀌다** be changed[altered, varied]; (변형되다) be transformed. とりかえられる
**빠그러지다** get broken. われてしまう
**바그러움** (수치) shame; disgrace (수줍음) shyness. はずかしさ
**바그럽다** be[feel] ashamed ⇨부끄럽다. はずかしい
**바그르르, 빠그르르** (물·거품이) simmering; foamly/~하다 simmer; bubble up; foam. ぐらぐら
**빠근하다** feel heavy ⇨뻐근하다. けだるい
**바글바글** seething; boiling; bubbling/~ 끓다 seethe. ぶくぶくあわだつ

**빠끔하다** (be) open ⇨뻐끔하다. ぽっかりひらいている
**빠기다** boast ⇨뻐기다. たかぶる
**바느질** sewing; needlework/~하다 sew; do needlework (~품을 팔다 earn one's living by needlework. はりしごと
**바늘** a needle (핀) a pin (낚시 따위의) a hook (시계의) a hand/~겨레 a needle pad; a pincushion/~꽃 a kind of willow-weed/~ 구멍 a hole made by a needle/~귀 a needle's eye/~밥 thread remnants/~ 방석 ①(바늘 겨레) a pincushion ②(자리) a mat of needles/~쌈 a packet of needles. はり
**바다** the sea (대양) the ocean/불~ a sea of flames/바닷 바람 a sea breeze/~로 나가다 go out to sea. うみ
**바따라지다** (be) rich[thick] and tasty [savory].
**바다매** Peale's peregrine falcon.
**바다뱀** a sea snake[serpent].
**바다비오리** a red-breasted merganser.
**바다오리** a guillemot.
**바다제비** a fork-tailed petrel.
**바다표범** a seal; *Phoca vitulina*(학명). あざらし
**바닥** ①(평면) the floor; the ground ②(밑부분) the bottom (강 따위의) the bed (신의) the sole ③(끝) end; close ④(짜임새) texture/~이 고운 fine in weave ⑤(번잡한 곳) a congested area/서울~ the *Seoul* area. そこ
**바닥나다** run[give] out; be all gone; be drained[exhausted]. そこをつく
**빠닥빠닥** ~하다 be dried out stiff ⇨뻐덕뻐덕. ざらざらしている
**바닥보다** (밑천이) run out of capital (실패하다) fail; fall through. しきんがきれる
**바닥짐** (배의) ballast.
**바닥첫째** the first from the bottom; the last; at the bottom. まっせき
**바닷가** the shore (대양의) the coast; the beach; the seashore. かいへん
**바닷개** 〖동〗 a fur seal. おっとせい
**바닷게** a [saltwater] crab. うみがに
**바닷고기** a sea fish. うみのさかな
**바닷귀신** (一鬼神) a sea goblin[monster].
**바닷물** sea water; salt water/~고기 sea-fish. うみのみず
**바닷장어** (一長魚) a sea-snake[-serpent].
**바동거리다** struggle; writhe; flounce;

**wriggle**／바동거리지 마 Don't make a scene!《미》. もがく

**바둑** [the game of] *badook*／～돌 *badook* pieces; a *badook* stone／～판 a *badook* board／～을 두다 have a game of *badook*.

**바둑말** a piebald(dapple); a dappled horse. しまうま

**바둑무늬** a pattern[figure, design] with black and white spots; a speckled design.

**바둑이** a white and black dog; a spotted dog; Spot[ty].

**바둑점(一點)** a spot; a speck／～이 있는 a spotted; a speckled. まるいてん

**바드득, 빠드득** with a grating sound; ～하다 grind; creak; squeak; grate／이를 ～갈다 grit one's teeth. ぎいぎい

**바드득거리다, 빠드득거리다** creak; grate; grind; squeak. ぎいぎい

**바드름하다** protrude ⇨버드름하다.

**빠뜨리다** ①《물 따위에》throw into; drop 《함정에》entrap 《유혹에》lead into ②《누락하다》omit; miss [out]; pass over; leave out ③《잃다》lose; drop; let it fall. おとしいれる

**바득바득** doggedly; perversely; obstinately; importunately／～ 우기다 stand firm on one's opinion. しっこく

**빠득빠득하다** ①(be) headstrong; disobedient; perverse ②《떫다》(be) astringent; puckery ③《눈이》(be) dry and tired; burn. おとなしくない

**바들거리다** quiver ⇨부들거리다.

**바듬하다** (be) somewhat prominent.

**바듯하다, 빠듯하다** ①《겨우 차다》be on the margin; be barely enough ②《꼭 맞다》fit perfectly; (be) tight[close](꼭 끼다). ぎりぎりだ

**바라(哱囉)** 《자바라》a small cymbal 《소라》a shell trumpet. どら

**바라기** a porcelain dish of small size; a kind of small food dish. ちいさいさら

**바라다** 《예기·기대하다》expect; hope for; count on; look forward to ②《소원하다》wish; desire; hope ③《간원·부탁하다》beg; request; entreat. ねがう

**바라보다** 《건너다보다》see; look (*at*); watch 《응시하다》gaze (*at, on*); 《관망하다》view 《방관하다》look (*on*). ながめる

**바라보이다** be looked over; command; overlook. ながめられる

**바라지** care; service; provision／～하다 provide[supply] (*one*) with.

**바라지다**¹ ①《몸이》(be) stumpy; stuggy; pudgy ②《그릇이》(be) shallow ③《속이》(be) shallow[-brained]; superficial ④《야무지다》(be) cheeky. しりすぼみだ

**바라지다**² 《갈라지다》split off 《열어지다》be wide open. さける

**바락바락** desperately; doggedly／～ 기를 쓰다 make desperate efforts; become frantic. かっと

**바람**¹ ①《대기의 유동》a wind 《미풍》a breeze 《강풍》a gale; a draught(틈으로 들어오는); a blast; a gust(한바탕 부는)／찬～ a cold wind／～이 센 windy／～이 없는 windless／～이 잘 통하다 be well ventilated; be airy／저녁 ～을 쐬다 enjoy the cool of the evening／～이 인다[잔다] The wind rises[drops]. ②《들뜬 마음》fickleness; inconstancy 《바람난 행동》amours／～나다 take to amours; have a secret love affair／～난 fickle; inconstant; wanton／～장이 a flirt; a fickle man[woman] ③～풍병(風病). かぜ

**바람**² ①《기세》heat; act／일어나는 ～에 in rising ②《차림》without *one's* (*clothing*) on／샤쓰 ～으로 in shirt sleeves. —のせい

**바람개비**¹ a weather vane; a weather-cock. かざぐるま

**바람개비**² 《조》a Korean jungle nightjar; *Caprimulgus indicus*(학명).

**바람결** a rumour／～에 들으니… It has come to my ear that…. うわさ

**바람꽃**¹ a hazy atmosphere around the top of a distant mountain presaging a high wind. ふううん

**바람꽃**² 《식》a windflower; *Anemone narcissiflora*(학명).

**바람 구멍** a wind hole; an air hole; a vent; an air shaft.

**바람기(一氣)** the force[feel] of wind.

**바람끼다** take to fast living; become "quite the gay blade".

**바람나가다** become insipid; grow dull; get lifeless. すいびする

**바람나다** ①lead a loose life; keep fast company ②《신바람나다》warm up; get warmed up; get under way. うわきする

**바람둥이** ①《허풍선이》a braggart; a boaster; a windbag ②《바람장이》a flirt; an inconstant lover; a playboy; a fickle woman(여자). ほらふき

**바람들다** ①《탈나다》(*something*) goes wrong (*with*) ②《바람나다》take to amours; play with love ③《무우가》form vacuoles. うわきする

**바람막이** a windscreen; a shelter from the wind. かぜよけ

**바람맞다** ①《속다》be deceived[cheated]; be swindled ②《풍병에 걸리다》be stricken with paralysis. かぜをひく

**바람맞히다** reject (*a suitor*); give the cold shoulder (*to*); give the gate (*to*);《기다리는 사람을》keep (*a person*) waiting in vain.

**바람받이** a place exposed to the wind; a wind-swept place. かぜあたり

**바람벽(一壁)** a wall; a partition. かべ

**바람비** wind and rain. ふうう

**바람세(一勢)** 《풍세》wind force. ふうせい

**바람자다** ①《바람이》the wind dies down; the breeze stops blowing ②《들뜬 마음이》calm down; quiet down. かぜがやむ

**바람잡이** be fickle; take to amours; commit absurdity. うわきをする

**바람잡이** a frivolous characters; a fast

liver; a playboy; a fast[loose] woman.
**바람직하다** (be) desirable; advisable.
**바람켜다** be fickle[inconstant]; dissipate. うわきなこうどうをする
**바랑** a Buddhist's sack. はいのう
**바래다**¹ ①(변색하다) fade; discolour/바래지 않는 fade-proof; fast; standing ②(표백하다) bleach (*cloth*) [in the sun]. あせる
**바래다**² (배웅하다) see (*one*) off; send off /바래 주다 see (*one*) to (*one's house*).
**바로** ①(옳게) rightly (정직히) honestly (정확히) correctly; certainly; surly (진실히) truly (곧장) directly; straight (불과) only (꼭) just; very /~ 말하나 tell the truth/~ 집으로 가다 go straight home/~ 알아 맞추다 guess right /~ 이웃에 살다 live close by/~ 이 근처에서 그를 보았다 I saw him just about here. ②(구령) Eyes front!. すぐに
**바로잡다** ①(굽은 것을) straighten; make straight ②(교정하다) correct; redress; remedy; reform. ただす
**바르다**¹ ①(곧다) (be) straight; straight forward ②(정당하다) (be) right; righteous; just (정직하다) (be) honest; upright (적당하다) (be) proper (합법하다) (be) lawful (정확하다) (be) correct. まっすぐだ
**바르다**² ①(종이 따위를) stick; paste; plaster (장지 따위를) paper; cover ②(칠하다) paint(채색을); plaster(벽도 따위를); coat(칠 따위를); apply(고약·페인트 따위를); rub(문질러서); (분 따위를) powder; put on; rouge(연지를)/버터를 바른 빵 bread spread with butter. ぬる
**바르다**³ (껍질을) split; cleave; break; crack (단단한 껍질을) crush. はぐ
**빠르다** ①(속도가) (be) quick; fast; swift; speedy; rapid; fresh(배가); (민속하다) (be) brisk ②(시간이) (be) early; premature(시기 상조). はやい
**바르르** ①(끓는 소리) seething; bubbling; fizzing ②(성냄) in a huff/~ 화를 내다 simmer ③(떨다) shiveringly; trembling /추위로 ~ 떨다 shiver with the cold. かっと
**바르작거리다** struggle; writhe; wriggle; strain at. しきりにもがく
**바른길** (곧은 길) a straight way (옳은 길) the right path. せいどう
**바른말** (옳은 말) a reasonable[right, proper] word (직언) plain speaking; a straight talk/~하다 speak reasonably.
**바른쪽** the right side[hand]. うそく

**바리**¹ (밥그릇) a brass bowl. しょっき
**바리**² (짐) a pack[load]; a horse load.
**바리나무** firewood carried on a horseback.
**바리때** a wooden rice bowl used by temple priests. しょっき
**바리전**(-廛) a brassware shop; a brazier's shop.
**바리집다** ①(폭로하다) exposed; disclose ② (과장하다) exaggerate; make too much of; overdraw. きりひらく
**바보** a fool (백치) an idiot (미련퉁이) a dunce; a blockhead/~같은 silly; foolish/~같은 소리를 하다 talk silly; sound like an idiot. あほう
**바쁘다** (be) busy/바쁘게 busily; hurriedly/여행 준비에 ~ be busy preparing for a journey. いそがしい
**바삐** (바쁘게) busily (급히) hurriedly; in haste (이제 at once; immediately/~ 일하다 work busily. いそがしく
**바사기** (덜 된 사람) a simpleton; a half-wit. あほう
**바삭** with a rustle[crinkle]; with a crunch/~하다 give a rustle[crinkle]; crunch. ばさばさ
**바싹** ①(소리) rustlingly; with a rustle ②(마른 모양) [dried up] entirely ③(죄는 모양) fast; tightly (가깝게) closely. ぐいと
**바삭거리다** [make a] rustle; crunch [again and again]; crinkle. かさかさ
**바삭바삭** rustlingly; with a rustle[crunch]. かさかさ
**바서지다** break; be crushed; crumble; go smash. こわれる
**바소** (침) a needle used for cutting a boil. やまいを治すはり
**바소쿠리** a basket made of bush clover used for carrying earth; a wicker basket used as a dirt-carrier.
**바수다** break; smash (*into*); crush (찧다) grind (빻다) pound. おしつぶす
**바스대다** fidget; move about restlessly; be never still. そわそわする
**바스라기** crumbs; scraps; odds and ends; shreds; bits. くず
**바스락** faint[ly]; indistinct[ly]; stealthy /~하다 make a muffled[indistinct] sound. ばさばさ
**바스러뜨리다** crush; smash; break into crumbs. ふんさいする
**바스러지다** (조각이 나다) be broken to pieces; fall to pieces. こなごなに砕ける
**바스스** with long unkempt hair; gently; softly; lightly. ばさばさ
**바슬바슬** crumbly/~하다 be crumbly.
**바심**¹ (풋바심) threshing and milling unripe grain. だっこく
**바심**² (재목의) trimming timber/~하다 smooth the surface of timber; plane. ざいもくのひょうめんをなめらかにすること
**바야흐로** (한창) at the height of; in full swing (이제 막) about to/~ 기차는 떠나려고 간다 The train is about[just going] to start. まさに
**-바에야** (이왕 …이면) at all (차라리) rather; sooner…than; as soon.
**-바와 같이** as; like.
**바위** a rock/~가 많은 rocky/~ 너설 rugged rocks. いわ
**바위솔** [식] a houseleek.
**바위옷** [식] rock moss; lichen/~이 끼다 be mossy. がんせきのこけ
**바위옹두라지** the spur of a rock; a jag of a rock. がんせきの突端

**바위채송화**(-菜松花) 【식】 a sedum; a stone crop; *Sedum polystichoides*(학명).

**바이** at all; in the least／~ 없는 일이로 다 I cannot help it. ぜんぜん

**바자** network of wooden strips／~을 a fence made of reed or bamboo. まがき

**바자위다** (be) niggardly; stingy; tight. どりょうがせまい

**바짝** completely; closely ⇒바삭. ぐいと

**바작바작** crackling; nervously／~거리다 crack; crackle. ばちんばちん

**바장이다** stroll aimlessly. はいかいする

**바조**(-調) 【음】 the note F.

**바지** the outer garment covering the lower half of the body (양복의) trousers; pants(미). ズボン

**바지게** ①(지게) an A-frame with a mat-like rack attached ②(발채) a rigid matlike rack; any mat-like rack.

**빠지다** ⇒별항 참조(page 1467).

**바지락조개** 【어】 short-necked clam.

**바지랑대** a clothes pole; a laundry pole.

**바지런하다** (be) diligent; industrious／~ 부지런하다. きんべんだ

**바지저고리** ①trousers and coat ②(비유적으로) a goof-for-nothing (등신) a stupid person. ズボンとじょうい

**바지지** with a hissing[ripping] sound／~하다 hiss; give[let out] a hiss rip. じゅうじゅう

**바짓가랑이** a trouser leg. ズボンのまた

**-바치** an artisan; a worker.

**바치다**¹ (드리다) offer; present; consecrate(신에게); devote; give up(신심을); dedicate(건물・서적 등을); (납부하다) pay in／수업료를 ~ pay in *one*'s tuition fee／일생을 ~ devote[dedicate] *one*'s life. ささげる

**바치다**² (즐기다) have an excessive liking for (*sexual intercourse*); be mad about. できあいする

**바퀴**¹ a wheel／~통 the hub／큰수레 ~ a large wheel／~ 자국 ruts; wheelmarks; a furrow; the print of a wheel. わ

**바퀴**² (충) a cockroach.

**바퀴살** a spoke.

**바탕**¹ (기질) the foundation; the basis (소질) making; qualities (바탕 빛) the ground (품질) quality／~이 좋다 be of good quality. きそ

**바탕**² for some [a] time.

**바투** close; closely. ちかづいて

**바특하다** (국물이) (be) thick; stodgy; dry／바특이 a little bit; closely (국물이) thick. つまっている

**박** a bottle gourd; a calabash. ひさご

**박**(箔) (두꺼운) foil (얇은) leaf. はく

**박**(拍) a [musical] clapper.

**밖** ①(바깥) the outside (외면・외부) the exterior (옥외) out-of-doors; the open [air]／~에 나가다 go out [of doors, of the house]／~에서 놀다 play outdoors; be out playing ②(그외) the rest; the others; another／그 ~에 besides; else; in addition／그 ~의 사람들 the rest; the others. そと

**박격**(迫擊) a close assault[attack]／~하다 make a close attack on; storm／~포 (一砲) a [trench] mortar. はくげき

**박공**(牌栱) 【건】 a gable／~ 지붕 a gable roof.

**박구기** a [small] gourd dipper[ladle]. ひょうたんのひしゃく

**박근**(迫近) pressure; urgency／~하다 draw near; press; be imminent.

**박다**¹ (못 따위를) strike in; drive in; hammer in(큰못을); (보석 따위를) set in; inlay. うちこむ

**박다**² (인쇄 따위를) print; get (*a thing*) printed; impress. いんさつする

**박다**³ (바느질) sew with sewing machine stitches.

**박달나무** 【식】 a kind of birch; *Betula Schmidtii*(학명).

**박답**(薄畓) a barren[an unproductive] rice field. ひよくでないはたけ

**박대**(薄待) a cold treatment／~하다 treat (*one*) coldly; give (*one*) a cold reception. れいぐう

**박덕**(薄德) want[lack] of virtue; possessing little virtue. とくのすくないこと

**박도**(博徒) a gambler; a gamester／~의 두목 a boss gambler. ばくと

**박두**(迫頭) pressure／~하다 approach; draw near; be imminent. さしせまること

**박락**(剝落) peeling off／~하다 fall[come, peel] off; exfoliate. はくらく

**박람**(博覽) wide reading; extensive knowledge／~회 an exhibition; a fair; an exposition(미)／만국 ~회 an international exhibition. はくらん

**박람회장**(博覽會場) the exhibition[fair] grounds. はくらんかい

**박래**(舶來) ~의 foreign-make; imported／~품 imports; imported goods; foreign-made articles. はくらい

**박력**(迫力) force; intensity／~있다 strong; powerful; convincing. はくりょく

**박론**(駁論) refutation／~하는 refute; confute. ばくろん

**박리**(薄利) small profits／~ 다매(多賣) small profits with quick returns／~ 다매주의 a quick returns policy. はくり

**박멸**(撲滅) extermination; eradication; extirpation／~하다 eradicate; exterminate; stamp[wipe] out／결핵 ~ 운동 a crusade against tuberculosis. ぼくめつ

**박명**(薄命) misfortune illuck／~하다 (be) unfortunate; unlucky. はくめい

**박모**(薄暮) dusk; twilight. はくぼ

**박문**(博聞) erudition／~하다 (be) well-informed; erudite. はくぶん

**박문**(駁文) a written refutation[confutation]. ばくぶん

**박물**(博物) ①(넓은 견문) wide knowledge ②(박물학) natural history／~ 군자 a man of erudition. はくぶつ

**박물관**(博物館) a museum／국립 ~ the

National Museum. はくぶつかん
**박물학**(博物學) natural history; the study of nature／～자 a naturalist. はくぶつがく
**박박**¹, **빡빡**¹ 《긁는 소리》 hard; roughly 《찢는 소리》 shredding. がりがり
**박박**², **빡빡**² ①《얽은 모양》 be pitted ②《머리 깎은 모양》 having one's hair cut close. ぶつぶつ
**빡빡하다** ①《꽉 차다》 (be) close; closely; packed; chock-full ②《고지식하다》 (be) unadaptable; strait-laced ③《음식 따위가》(be) heavy. かさかさだ
**박복**(薄福) misfortune; sad fate／～하다 (be) unlucky; unfortunate.
ふくのすくないこと
**박봉**(薄俸) a small[low] salary; small pay／～자 a poorly-paid person; a low-salaried person.
**박빙**(薄氷) thin [coat of] ice. はくひょう
**박사**(博士) a doctor(略;Dr.)／～호 a doctor's degree／～ 논문 a thesis for a doctorate. はくし
**박사**(薄謝) a small consideration; a slight token of one's gratitude. はくしゃ
**박살**(撲殺) clubbing[beating] to death／～하다 beat to death. ぼくさつ
**박새** 《조》 a great-tit; a titmouse.
**박색**(薄色) an ugly face 《사람》 a plain woman. みにくいかお
**박세**(迫歲) ～하다 come close to the end of the year.
**박소**(朴素) simplicity／～하다 (be) simple.
**박소**(薄少) ～하다 (be) scarce; uncommon.
**박속** the flesh[edible part] of a gourd.
**박수** a male diviner[shaman].
**박수**(拍手) hand clapping／～하다 clap [one's hands]／우뢰 같은 ～ a thunderous hand clapping／～ 갈채 cheers; applause; plaudits. はくしゅ
**박식**(博識) wide[extensive] knowledge／～하다 (be) erudite; well-informed.
**박신거리다** squirm; swarm. ごたごたする
**박신박신** in swarms; in crowds／～ 모여 들다 gather in swarms. ごたごたする
**박애**(博愛) philanthropy／～의 philanthropic／～가 a philanthropist／～주의 philanthropism. はくあい
**박약**(薄弱) feebleness／～하다 (be) feeble; weak; infirm. はくじゃく
**박언학**(博言學) philology; linguistics ⇒ 언어학.
**박옥**(璞玉) an uncut gem. はくぎょく
**박음질** sewing; sewing-machine stitches.
**-박이** an inlaip one a backstitch. さしぬい
**박이다** ①《인쇄하다》 print ②《사진을》 take; have one's picture taken ③《마음에》 sink deeply into one's mind. ひょうたんをのこぎりでひいてわる
**박이부정**(博而不精) wide but shallow knowledge. おおくしっている
**박이옷** clothes sewn with sewing-machine stitches. さしぬい着物
**박자**(拍子) time; rhythm; beat／3 ～ triple time／～를 맞추어 in time with; keeping time with. ひょうし
**박작거리다** be crowded; be swarming; bustle. こみあう
**박작박작** in a bustle; full of stir.
**빡작지근하다** feel heavy. びりびりいたむ
**박장**(拍掌) hand-clapping; clapping.
**박장 대소**(拍掌大笑) applause mingled with laughter／～하다 engage in applause mingled with laughter; laugh aloud clapping one's hands.
**박재**(薄才) lack of ability; incapacity; incompetence. さいのうのないこと
**박재**(雹災) a hail disaster.
**박절**(迫切) ～하다 (be) cold-hearted; unfeeling; heartless; inhuman. れいこく
**박절기**(拍節機) 【음】 a metronome.
**박정**(薄情) ～하다 (be) cold-hearted; heartless; unfeeling. はくじょう
**박제**(剝製) stuffing／～한 새 a stuffed bird／～자 a taxidermist／～술 taxidermy. はくせい
**박주**(薄酒) untasty[poor] liquor; unpalatable sool. あじのうすいさけ
**박주가리** 【식】 milkweed; Metaplexis japonica(학명) ⇨새박덩굴.
**박쥐** 【동】 a bat. こうもり
**박쥐구실** opportunism; wait-and-see policy. しそうのないひとのたとえ
**박쥐오입장이** one who goes out pleasure seeking at night.
**박쥐우산**(一雨傘) an umbrella 《양산》 a parasol. こうもりがさ
**박지**(薄志) 《약한 의지》 infirmity of purpose／～ 약행(弱行) weakness of mind and lack of decision. はくし
**박직**(樸直) simplicity; honesty／～하다 (be) naive[simple] and honest.
**박진**(迫眞) truthfulness to life; verisimilitude. まことにせまること
**박차**(拍車) a spur; a rowel spur／～를 가하다 spur (one's horse); give impetus to; accelerate. はくしゃ
**박차다** kick away[off]; 《거절하다》 reject.
**박찬**(薄饌) poor[unsavory] side dishes. そまつなおかず
**박처**(薄妻) cold treatment to one's wife; mistreatment of one's life／～하다 treat one's wife coldly. つまをれいぐうすること
**박치기하다** bumb(knock) one's head against (a person); give a butt [of a head] (to a person). あたまでつくこと
**박타**(縛打) binding and beating／～하다 bind[tie up] and beat.
**박타다** ①《박을》 split a gourd in two ②《낭패하다》 be disappointed in one's expectations; have one's hopes frustrated. ひょうたんをのこぎりでひいてわる
**박탈**(剝奪) 《재산·권리 따위》 deprivation; divestiture; deplumation 《죄·과실에 의한》 forfeit; forfeiture／～하다 deprive [strip] (one) of [his office]; divest (one) of. はくだつ
**박통**(博通) erudition; extensive learning／～하다 (be) erudite. はくつう

**박피**(薄皮) a thin skin 《액체의》 a film 《박막》 a membrane.

**박하**(薄荷) 〔식〕 peppermint／~유 mint oil; peppermint oil.

**박하다**(薄一) 《인색하다》(be) niggardly／인심이 ~ be inhospitable; be unkind／점수가 ~ be strict[severe] in marking.

**박학**(博學) erudition; great learning／~하다 erudite; learned.

**박해**(迫害) persecution／~하다 persecute; oppress; torment／~자 a persecutor.

**박흡**(博洽) wide knowledge.

**박히다** 《못이》 be driven into; be nailed 《인쇄물이》 be printed 《사진이》 be taken.

**반** a flattened sheet[layer]／솜~ a flattened layer of cotton.

**반**(半) ①《절반》[a] half／컵 half a cup／한 다스 ~ a dozen and a half／세 시 ~ half past three／전~ the first half／후~ the latter half ②《반쯤》 half in part; partly《일부》／~은 무의식 중에 half unconsciously.

**반**(班) 《학급》 a class 《동네의》 a neighbo[u]rhood association 《군대》 a corps; a squad 《조(組)》 a party; a company; a circle; a set.

**반-**(反) anti-／~제국주의 anti-imperialism.

**반가**(半價) half the price; half-price ⇒ 반값.

**반가**(班家) a noble family; a house of nobility.

**반가공품**(半加工品) semi-manufactured[processed] goods.

**반가부좌**(半跏趺坐) sitting with one's legs [half-]crossed, as in Buddhist statues.

**반가와하다** be glad[pleased, delighted] about.

**반가움** delight; joy; gladness.

**반가이** gladly; delightedly; with joy; with pleasure.

**반각**(返却) return／~하다 return; give

# 빠 지 다

①《떨어지다》 fall[get] into; be drowned[sunk into]《물에》; fall[be led, sink down]《어떤 상태에》／개골창에 ~ be mired in a ditch／곤경에 ~ get into trouble[difficulties]; run up against a snag／물에 빠진 사람은 지푸라기라도 붙잡는다 A drowning man will catch at a straw.／물에 빠진 사람을 건지다 save (a person) from drowning／혼수 상태에 ~ lapse[fall] into a [state of] coma [delirium, stupor]／진흙에 ~ stick[be caught] in the mud／물에 ~ fall into a river; sink under the water.

②《탐닉하다》 indulge[wallow] (in); be given up (to); give oneself up (to); be addicted (to)／주색에 ~ give oneself up to women and wine; wallow in sensual pleasur／유혹에 ~ yield[give in] to temptation.

③《누락되다》 get left out; be omitted; be missing[wanting]; be not included; be dropped／일곱 페이지가 ~ There are seven pages missing.／전문이 온통 ~ The whole passage is left out.

④《박혔던 것이》 come off[out]; fall out; be taken off; get removed／못이 빠져 있다 A nail is missing.／이가 빠졌다 A tooth came off.／병마개가 ~ a cork come out.

⑤《흘러나가다》 drain; flow off／고였던 물이 빠지기 시작한다 A pool of water begins to flow off.／하수구의 물이 잘 안 빠진다 It does not drain well.

⑥《제외되다》 be left out; be excluded [exempted] (from); be not included／초대에 ~ be left out of the invitation／입선에서 빠진 것 중에도 가작이 있다 Some of those that have not been accepted are good.

⑦《야위다》 become[grow] thin; lose weight[flesh]; get lean; become skinny [peaked]／빠져 보이다 look peaked／살이 빠진 것 같다 You appear to have lost weight[flesh].

⑧《탈출하다》 escape; slip out; get off; avoid; shun; avert／빠져 나갈 수 없는 골목 a blind alley／위험한 고비를 빠져 나가다 escape danger; find one's way out of danger／오늘밤 송별회에는 빠질 수 없다 I can't excuse myself from the farewell party this evening.

⑨《없어지다》 come off; be gone; be got rid of／빨아도 빛깔이 빠지지 않는다 The colo[u]r stands the wash.／힘이 빠졌다 All my strength is gone.／빠지기 쉬운 물감 a fugitive dye; a dye that washes out [easily]; a dye that will fade.

⑩《뒤떨어지다》 fall[lag] behind; be inferior／그는 학식에 있어서 누구에게도 빠지지 않는다 In scholarship he falls behind none.／그녀의 옷차림이 그 중 빠졌다 Her dress was the least attractive one there.

⑪《속다》 be cheated; be taken in; be imposed upon／계략에 ~ fall into a trap／그런 속임수에 빠질 내가 아니다 That trick won't do with me., I don't fall for such a trick.

⑫《제비뽑히다》 draw[cast] (a winning number); win (in a lottery).

back; hand back. へんきゃく
**반간**(反間) alienation; estrangement ⇨ 이간(離間). はんかん
**반간**(半間) a half *kan*《반간 방》a half-size room ⇨ 간. はんげん
**반감**(反感) antipathy; ill-feeling／～을 품다 harbo[u]r ill-feeling／～을 사다 incur (*one's*) ill-feeling. はんかん
**반감**(半減) ～하다 reduce by half; cut in half; halve. はんげん
**반감기**(半減期) 【물】a half life; a half [-life] period.
**반갑다** (be) joyful; glad; happy; delightful; pleasant／반가운 소식 glad[happy, joyful] news／반갑잖은 손님 an unwelcome guest. なつかしい
**반값**(半—) half the sum; half-price／～으로 at half-price. はんか
**반개**(半個) half a piece.
**반개**(半開) ～하다 (be) half-open[ed]；《꽃이》half in bloom《문화가》half-civilized. はんかい
**반거**(蟠踞) ～하다 hold a vast sphere of influence. ばんきょ
**반거들충이**(半—) a half-trained person.
**반걸음**(半—) half a step. はんぽ
**반격**(反擊) a counter-attack／～하다 make a counter-attack. はんげき
**반결**(盤結) entanglement; complication intricacy; involvement.
**반경**(半徑) 【수】a radius; a semidiameter／～을 그리다 describe a radius. はんけい
**반고지**(反古紙) waste paper; old scraps of paper. かみくず
**반공**(反共) anti-communism／～의 anticommunist／～ 운동 an anticommunism movement. はんきょう
**반공**(半空) midair; the air. はんくう
**반공식**(半公式) (being) semi-official.
**반공일**(半空日) a half holiday; Saturday. はんきゅうじつ
**반과거**(半過去) 【언】the imperfect tense.
**반관 반민**(半官半民) ～의 semi-governmental [company]; semiofficial／～ 신문 a semiofficial organ. はんかんはんみん
**반구**(半球) a hemisphere. はんきゅう
**반군**(叛軍) a rebel army. はんらんぐん
**반군**(反軍) ～의 anti-militaristic／～주의 anti-militarism.
**반궁**(半弓) a short bow.
**반근**(盤根) entangled roots. ばんこん
**반금**(返金) repayment／～하다 pay back; repay. へんきん
**반기** a tray of eatables to be distributed among guests after a party.
**반기**(反旗) the standard of rebellion／～를 들다 raise the standard of revolt; be up in arms (*against*). はんき
**반기**(半旗) a flag at half-mast. はんき
**반기**(半期) ～의 half-yearly; semi-annual／전[후]～ the former[latter] half of the year／～ 결산 a half-yearly [closing] account. はんき
**반기다** rejoice; be glad (*of*); be delighted[pleased] (*at*). うれしがる
**반기생**(半寄生) 【생】semiparasitism／～의 hemiparasitic; semiparasitic／～ 생물 a hemiparasite. はんせい
**반깃반**(一盤) a tray; a refreshment tray.
**반나마**(半—) more than half. はんぶんいじょう
**반나절**(半—) a quarter of a day; half the morning. はんにちのはん
**반나체**(半裸體) ～의 half-naked; semi-nude／～화 a semi-nud [picture].
**반날**(半—) half a day. はんにち
**반납**(返納) return; restoration／～하다 return; give back; restore. へんのう
**반년**(半年) half a year; a half-year(미)／～마다 half-yearly. はんねん
**반단**(半—) a half-bundle; a cabinet; a half-bunch; a half-sheaf.
**반달이**(半—) a cabinet. じょうぶだけにとびらのあるたんす
**반달**(半—) ①《반개월》half a month ②《달의》a half moon. はんつき
**반당**(反黨)《반역자》traitors《반당 행위》anti-party activities／～ 분자 anti-party elements. とうのきていにはんすること
**반대**(反對) ①《반항》opposition [or] objection; dissension／～의 opposite; hostile／～하다 dissent from; object to; be against; be opposed to／～어 an antonym／～자 an opponent; an opposer／～당《정부의》the Opposition [party]／～를 받다 meet with opposition; be opposed ②《역》opposite; reverse／～의 opposite; reverse; contrary／～로 the other way; conversely; on the contrary. はんたい
**반도**(半途) halfway; midway. はんと
**반도**(半島) a peninsula／～의 peninsular. はんとう
**반도**(叛徒) rebels; insurgents.
**반도미**(半搗米) half-cleaned[-polished] rice. はんつきまい
**반도이폐**(半途而廢) ～하다 do (*things*) by halves; stop[*working*] halfway. ちゅうとでやめること
**반독립**(半獨立) halfway; independence; part independence. はんどくりつ
**반독립국**(半獨立國) a semi-independent state[country]. はんどくりつこく
**반동**(反動) reaction; rebound《총 따위의》kick; recoil／～하다 react; rebound; kick; recoil／～적 reactionary／～파 the reactionaries／～ 혁명 a counter-revolution. はんどう
**반두** a scoop-net; a dip-net. すくいあみ
**반둥거리다, 빤둥거리다** idle *one's* time away; live an idle life. ふらふらなまける
**반둥건둥** by halves; halfway／～하다 do by halves; take half measures.
**반드럽다** ①《매끈매끈하다》(be) smooth; glazed ②《약빠르다》(be) smart; slick; sharp; glossy. なめらかだ
**반드르르, 빤드르르** glossily／～하다 (be) smooth; glassy; lustrous; bright. つるつる

**반드시** 《확실히》 certainly; surely; without fail(틀림없이); 《꼭》 by all means; at any cost 《늘》 always; ever; habitually (필연) necessarily; inevitably/그는 ~ 이긴다 He is bound to win./그는 ~ 출석한다 He never fails to attend the meeting. きっと

**반득, 빤득** shining; flashing; flickering/~하다 shine; flash; glisten. ちらつく

**반들거리다, 빤들거리다** be smooth[slippery]. つるつるする

**반들반들** smoothly. つるつるする

**반뜻** in a flash ⇒번듯. ちらり

**반듯하다, 반뜻하다** (be) straight; upright; erect; even/반듯이 straight; upright; even. まっすぐだ

**반등**(反騰) 《경》 reactionary rise/~하다 rice in reaction; rally.

**반디** a firefly. ほたる

**반딧불** the glow of a firefly[lightningbug(미)]. ほたるのひかり

**반락**(反落) 《증권》 a reaction/~하다 react.

**반란**(反亂, 叛亂) revolt; rebellion; insurrection/~군 a rebel[an insurgent] army; mutinous troops/~을 일으키다 rise in revolt; rebel. はんらん

**반려**(伴侶) a companion. はんりょ

**반려**(返戾) return; restoration/ ~하다 give back; return. へんかん

**반례**(返禮) 《예물》 a return present 《방문》 a return call/~하다 make a return (for); 《선물을》 give (a person) a present in return. へんれい

**반로**(返路) the way back; a return trip.

**반론**(反論) a turn; a conversion/~하다 turn to; get converted to. はんろん

**반만**(半萬) half a myriad; five thousand.

**반말**(半—) words lacking in respect.

**반맥**(班脈) a noble family line.

**반면**(半面) 《사물의》 one side; a half 《얼굴의》 a profile/~상(像) a profile; a silhouette. はんめん

**반면**(反面) the other side; the reverse/ ~에 on the other hand. はんめん

**반명**(班名) a title of nobility. はんめい

**반모음**(半母音) a semi-vowel.

**반목**(反目) antagonism; hostility; enmity/~하다 be in antagonism with 《each other》. はんもく

**반몫**(半—) half a share; a half-share.

**반문**(反問) ~하다 ask in return. はんもん

**반문**(斑紋) a spot; a speckle.

**반물** blue black; indigo/~집 a dyeing establishment. くろばんだあいいろ

**반미**(飯米) rice for meal; cooking rice. ごはんようのこめ

**반미**(反美) ~의 anti-American.

**반미개**(半未開) semi-barbarism. はんみかい

**반미치광이**(半—) a slightly mad person; a half-crazed person. はんきちがい

**반바닥** the base of the thumb.

**반박**(反駁) confutation; refutation/~하다 confute; refute; retort. はんばく

**반반**(半半) ①《절반》 half and half; fifty fifty ②《반의 반》 one fourth; half of half. はんはん

**반반하다** ①《바닥이》 (be) smooth; even ②《생김새가》 (be) handsome; fine/얼굴이 ~ have a handsome[beautiful] face ③《지체가》 (be) decent; respectable; noble. なだらかだ

**빤빤하다** (be) impudent; shameless; unabashed. ずうずうしい

**반발**(反撥) repulsion/~하다 repel; repulse/~력 repulsive power; repulsive force. はんぱつ

**반백**(半白) 《머리털이》 (being) gray-haired; half-white; grizzled. はんぱく

**반백**(半百) fifty years of age; half a hundred. ごじゅうさい

**반벌**(班閥) noble lineage. はんばつ

**반벙어리**(半—) a man of inarticulate pronunciation. ひじょうなどもり

**반베**(班—) towel cloth woven of indigo threads mixed with white.

**반벽**(返璧) return; giving back; restoration.

**반병신**(半病身) ①《불구자》 a slightly disabled person; a half paralytic (반신 불수) ②a half-wit(반편이). はんびょうしん

**반보**(步步) half a step. はんぽ

**반복**(反覆) 《언행의》 fickleness; flightiness 《생각의》 switching (one's opinion, decision, etc.)/~하다 switch. はんぷく

**반복**(反覆) repeat; repetition/~하다 repeat/~하여 repeatedly; over again/ ~설(說) 《철》 the recapitulation theory/~ 기호 《음》 a sign of repetition; a repeat/ ~ 발생 《생》 palingenesis. はんぷく

**반봇짐**(半—) a small parcel which one can carry in the hand.

**반봉건**(半封建) semi-feudalism/~ 사회 a semi-feudalistic society. はんほうけん

**반분**(半分) half/~하다 halve 《나누다》 divide into halves 《자르다》 cut in half. はんぶん

**반불겅이**(半—) 《고추》 a half-red pepper 《담배》 reddish tobacco [leaves].

**반비**(飯婢) a female[woman] cook.

**반비**(反比) 《수》 inverse ratio. はんぴ

**반비례**(反比例) 《수》 inverse proportion; a reciprocal proportion/~하다 be in inverse proportion to. はんぴれい

**반빗**(飯—) a woman[female] cook in charge of making side dishes.

**반빗간**(飯—間) a kitchen. だいどころ

**반빙**(半氷) half-frozen ice.

**반사**(反射) reflexion; reflection〈미〉/~하다 reflect; reverberate/~ 작용 reflection; reflex action/~열 reflected heat/~ 운동 reflex action[movement]/ ~경 a reflecting mirror; a reflector. はんしゃ

**반사회적**(反社會的) (being) anti-social. はんしゃかいてき

**반삭**(半朔) half a month; a half month;

a fortnight. はんつき
**반산**(牛產) 《낙태》abortion; miscarriage. りゅうざん
**반상**(返償) repayment; redemption／〜하다 refund; pay back; repay.
**반상**(班常) the high and the low; the nobles and the means. きぞくとへいみん
**반상기**(飯床器) a table service; a dinner-set; a set of tableware.
**반색하다** be pleased (*at*); rejoice at; be delight at; delight in; be glad. ひじょうにうれしがる
**반생**(半生) half *one's* life; half a lifetime. はんせい
**반생 반사**(半生半死) (being) half-alive and half-dead.
**반생 반숙**(半生半熟) (being) half-done 《빵》 half-baked 《고기》 half-roasted.
**반서**(反噬) 〜하다 return evil for good; repay kindness with evil. はんぜい
**반석**(盤石) a rock; a crag／〜같은〔같이〕 as firm as a rock. ばんじゃく
**반성**(反省) reflection; self-examination／〜하다 reflect (*on*)／〜을 촉구하다 ask (*one*) to reconsider. はんせい
**반성양**(半成樣) 〜하다 be half finished; be halfway through; semimanufactured. はんしあげ
**반성 유전**(伴性遺傳) sex-linkage.
**반세**(半世) half *one's* life; half a lifetime. はんせい
**반소**(半燒) partial destruction by fire／〜하다 be half-burned.
**반소**(反蘇) anti-Soviet.
**반소**(反訴) a cross action. はんそ
**반소경**(半－) (being) half-blind; purblind.
**반소매**(半－) a half-sleeve; a half-length sleeve. はんそで
**반송**(返送) returning／〜하다 send back; return. へんそう
**반송**(伴送) 〜하다 deliver[send] (*a thing*) along with.
**반송장**(半－) a dotard. おいぼれ
**반수**(半數) half the number; the half. はんすう
**반수**(伴隨) 〜하다 accompany; follow; attend upon. どうはん
**반수 반성**(半睡半醒) broken sleep; doze／〜하다 have a broken sleep; doze. ゆめうつつ
**반숙**(半熟) 〜의 half-done[-boiled] 《과일》 half-ripe; unripe 《달걀 따위》 halfcooked; soft-boiled. はんじゅく
**반시**(半時) half an hour. はんじ
**반시**(盤柿) a flat persimmon.
**반시간**(半時間) half an hour; thirty minutes. はんじかん
**반시류**(半翅類) 《동》 *Hemiptera*《학명》
**반신**(半身) half the body／〜상 a half-length statue／〜 불수 hemiplegia／〜 불수의 paralyzed on one side; hemiplegia. はんしん
**반신**(返信) a reply; an answer／〜하다 send a reply to／〜료 return postage.

**반신**(半信) 〜하다 be suspicious of; mistrust; be half in doubt. はんしん
**반신**(叛臣) a traitorous minister; a rebel retainer. はんしん
**반신**(半神) a demigod.
**반신 반의**(半信半疑) doubt／〜의 dubious; half in doubt; incredulous／〜하다 be [half] in doubt. はんしんはんぎ
**반실**(半失) 〜하다 lose about half. はんぶんをうしなうこと
**반심**(叛心) a rebellious[treacherous] intent[heart]. はんしん
**반암**(斑岩) 《광》 porphyry. はんがん
**반액**(半額) half the amount[sum, price, fare]; half-price[-fare]／〜으로 at half-price. はんがく
**반야**(半夜) 《한밤중》 midnight; the middle of night.
**반야경**(般若經) 《종》 *Prajna-paramitasutra* (Sans). はんにゃきょう
**반어**(反語) irony／〜적 ironical. はんご
**반역**(叛逆) treason; rebellion／〜하다 rebel[revolt] (*against*); rise in revolt／〜자 a traitor; a rebel. はんぎゃく
**반영**(反英) 〜의 anti-British.
**반영**(反映) reflection／〜하다 reflect; be reflected (*in*). はんえい
**반영**(反影) a reflection;.a reflected shadow. はんえい
**반영**(半影) penumbra; partial[imperfect] shadow. はんえい
**반영구적**(半永久的) (being) semi-permanent. はんえいきゅうてき
**반영식**(半影触) 《천》 a penumbral eclipse of the sun[moon].
**반올림**(半一) rounding off to the nearest integer. ししゃごにゅう
**반원**(半圓) a semicircle／〜 〔형〕의 semicircular. はんえん
**반월**(半月) a half moon／〜형의 semicircular; crescent[-shaped]. はんげつ
**반유동체**(半流動體) [a] semifluid; [a] s-emiliquid.
**반음**(半音) 《음》 [chromatic] semitone／〜부 a minim. はんおん
**반응**(反應) reaction 《반향》 response 《효과》 effect／〜을 보이다 react; effect; respond to; act upon. はんのう
**반의반**(半－半) one fourth; a quarter. はんぶんのはんぶん
**반의식**(半意識) 《심》 sebconsciousness／〜적 subconscious; half-conscious.
**반의어**(反意語) 《언》 an antonym.
**반이**(搬移) moving; removal／〜하다 remove; move. やうつり
**반일**(半一) half the work; half-day's work. はんにち
**반일**(半日) half a day; a half day. はんにち
**반일**(反日) 〜의 anti-Japanese.
**반입**(搬入) carrying in／〜하다 carry[bring, take] in. はんにゅう
**반자** a ceiling／〜지(紙) ceiling paper.
**반자**(半字) a simplified character; a si-

반작, 빤짝 glittering; sparkling; in flashes. きらっと

반짝 ①(쉽게) lightly; easily; without effort ②(높이) high. さっと

반작(半作) 〖농〗 sharecropping; tenancy／～하다 sharecrop; tenant (a farm). こさく

반작용(反作用) 〖물〗 reaction. はんさよう

반장(班長) 《학급의》 a monitor 《직공의》 a foreman 《동네의》 the head of a neighbourhood association. はんちょう

반장(叛將) a rebel leader.

반장(返葬) bringing a body for burial.

반장화(半長靴) half boots.

반적(叛賊) a rebel; a traitor. はんぞく

반전(反戰) ～의 anti-war／～파[운동] an anti-war party[campaign]. はんせん

반전(反轉) a reverse turn. はんてん

반전(返電) a reply telegram／～하다 wire [telegram] back. へんでん

반절(半—) a half bow.

반절(半折) half size. せっぱん

반절(反切) 《한글의》 a paradigm of the Korean alphabet arranged as a syllabary. はんせつ

반점(半點) 《점》 a half point; half a point 《시간》 a half hour; half an hour. はんてん

반점(斑點) a spot; a speckle／～이 있는 spotted; speckled.

반정(反正) restoration; renovation／～하다 take over the throne. はんせい

반정립(反定立) 〖철〗 antithesis.

반정부(反政府) (being) antigovernment; anti-ministerial. はんせいふ

반정신(半艇身) a half-length／～의 차로 이기다 win a race by a half-length

반제(返濟) repayment; refundment／～하다 pay back; repay; refund／～기간 the term of repayment. へんさい

반제국주의(反帝國主義) anti-imperialism／～적 anti-imperialistic. はんていこくしゅぎ

반제 운동(反帝運動) anti-imperialistic movement.

반제품(半製品) half-finished goods[products]; partly manufactured articles; semimanufactures. はんせいひん

반조(返照) reflection; evening glow; reflexion／～하다 reflect. せきよう

반족(班族) a noble family.

반쪽(半—) [a] half. はんきれ

반주(伴奏) 〖음〗 accompaniment／～하다 accompany／～하는 an accompanist／～부 the accompaniment. ばんそう

반주(飯酒) liquor taken at meal time. しょくじのときのさけ

반주(半周) a semicircle.

반주권국(半主權國) a semi-dependent country. はんしゅけんこく

반주그레하다 (be) rather nice-looking; attractive ふうさいがややよい

반죽 kneading; dough／～하다 knead [flour]; work[mortar]. ねり

반죽음(半—) half death.

반중간(半中間) half-way; the middle.

반증(反證) evidence to the contrary; contrary evidence; disproof. はんしょう

반지(斑指, 半指) a [finger] ring／약혼 ～ an engagement ring／결혼 ～ a wedding ring／～를 끼다 put[slip] a ring on one's finger. ゆびわ

반지(半紙) ordinary writing paper. はんし

반지기 adulterated with. こんごうぶつ

반지랍다 (be) smooth; glossy; sleek; glabrous. なめらかだ

반지르르 smoothly. なめらかなさま

반지름(半—) 〖수〗 a semidiameter; a radius ＝반경(半徑). はんけい

반지빠르다 ①(약밉도록) pert; presumptuous; impudent ②(어중되다) (be) awkward to handle; inconvenient; troublesome. でしゃばりだ

반지반(半之半) a quarter; one fourth. はんぶんのはんぶん

반지화(斑枝花) 〖식〗 a kapok tree.

반직업적(半職業的) semi-professional. はんしょくぎょうてき

반짇고리 a work-box; a needle case; a housewife.

반질거리다, 빤질거리다 ①(매끄럽다) be glossy[smooth, slippery] ②(교활하다) be crafty[cunning]. つるつるする

반질반질, 빤질빤질 sleekly／～하다 (be) glossy; smooth; sleek. つるつるする

반찬(飯饌) a side-dish; subsidiary articles of diet／～ 가게 a grocer's shop; a grocery. かず

반창고(絆瘡膏) a plaster; an adhesive plaster[tape]. ばんそうこう

반청(半晴) (being) partly clear. はんはれ

반추(反芻) rumination; cud-chewing／～하다 ruminate; chew the cud／～ 동물 a ruminant. はんすう

반출(搬出) ～하다 carry[take] out (화재 때) save. はんしゅつ

반춤 gentle swaying of the body.

반취(半醉) ～하다 (be) half-drunk. はんすい

반측(反側) ～하다 《뒤척거리다》 turn over; toss about. はんそく

반칙(反則) a foul; an irregularity／～하다 play foul. はんそく

반침(伴寢) putting up at the same hotel ＝동숙(同宿). どうしゅく

반침(伴寢) a closet; a small room attached to a large room.

반타작(半打作) ～하다 share the crop equally.

반토(礬土) 〖화〗 alumina ばんど

반투명(半透明) ～의 semitransparent[body]; translucent. はんとうめい

반편(半偏) a simpleton; a fool. はんぶん

반포(頒布) distribution／～하다 promulgate; circulate. はんぷ

반포(反哺) repaying one's indebtedness to parents. はんぽ

반푼 《엽전》 a half phun.

**반품**(半—) a half-day['s] work.
**반품**(返品) returning goods 《물건》 returned good/〜하다 return goods. へんぴん
**반하다**[1] 《매혹당하다》 fall in love with; be enamoured of; lose *one's* heart to; be charmed with. あいにおぼれる
**반하다**[2], **빤하다** ①《환하다》 (be) light; bright ②《틈나다》 be at leisure; be free ③《병세가》 be in a state of lull ④《분명하다》 (be) obvious. みえすいている
**반하다**(反—) 《반대되다》 be contrary to; be against; contradict/이에 반하여 on the contrary; on the other hand/의사에 반하여 against *one's* will.
**반하다**(叛—) go against ⇨반항하다. そむく
**반할인**(半割引) 50% reduction[discount]; half rate. はんわりびき
**반합**(飯盒) a canteen. はんごう
**반항**(反抗) resistance; opposition; defiance/〜하다 resist; oppose; defy/〜심 a rebellious spirit. はんこう
**반향**(反響) an echo; reverberation 《반응》 a response; comment 《신문 따위의》《더 평판》 sensation/〜하다 echo; resound; reverberate/〜을 일으키다 create a sensation. はんきょう
**반혁명**(反革命) a counterrevolution/〜적 counterrevolutionary. はんかくめい
**반현**(半舷) the broadside.
**반환**(返還) return/〜하다 return; give back; restore.
**반휴일**(半休日) a half holiday. はんきゅうじつ
**반흘림**(半—) semi-cursive writing. はんそうしょ
**받다** ①《수령·수납하다》 receive; accept; be given; have; take; get/교육을 ~ receive an education; be educated (*at*)/환영을 ~ receive[meet with] a warm welcome ②《입다》 receive; suffer; sustain/손해를 ~ suffer[sustain] a loss/혐의를 ~ fall[come] unde suspicion ③《겪다》 undergo; go through/치료를 ~ undergo medical treatment/취조를 ~ undergo an examination ④《공·물 따위를》 stop; catch; receive/공을 ~ catch a ball ⑤《우산을》 put up an umbrella ; hold ⑥《뿔 따위로》 gore; toss; knock down/황소에 받치다 be gored by a bull ⑦《빛을》 be bathed (*in*) ⑧《애를》 deliver/아이를 ~ deliver a child ⑨《음식이》 agree with (*a person*); suit *one's* palate. うける
**받들다** ①《옹립하다》 set up; have (*a person*) as *one's* leader 《승복하다》 obey ②《들어올리다》 lift[hold] up ささえる
**받들어총**(—銃) 《호령》 Present arms!/〜하다 present arms.
**받아들이다** accept; receive; assent to; comply with. うけいれる
**받아쓰기** dictation/〜하다 have dictation.
**받아쓰다** write[take, put] down/받아쓰게 하다 dictate (*to one*).
**받을 어음** bills receivable(略: B/R, b. r. ).

**받치다** ①《괴다》 prop[bolster] up; support; hold ②《먹은 것이》 lie heavy on the stomach ③《당소리를》 attach a consonant. ささえる
**받침** 《괴는》 a support; a mat. ささえ
**받히다**[1] be butted; be gored; be struck; be hit. ささえられる
**받히다**[2] sell wholesale; supply. きょうきゅうする
**발**[1] 《사람·동물의》 a foot 《개·고양이 따위 발톱이 있는》 a paw 《문어의》 tentacles/〜등 the instep/〜바닥 the sole of a foot/〜을 멈추다 stop; halt/〜을 맞추다 keep pace[step] with (*one*). あし
**발**[2] 《가리는》 a bamboo[rattan] blind; a reed screen. すだれ
**발**[3] 《길이·깊이의 단위》 the span of both arms; a fathom.
**발**(發) ①《출발》 departure; leaving/오후 5시~ 급행 the 5 P.M. express ②《탄수(彈數)》 a round; a shot 《소총의》 a shell 《대포의》/탄약 5천~ 5,000 rounds of ammunition. はつ
**발**(跋) an epilogue; a postscript (*to a book*) 《시가의》 an envoy. ばつ
**발가락** a toe. あしゆび
**발가벗기다** strip (*a person*) to the skin; denude. よだかにさせる
**발가벗다** strip *oneself* bare[stark-naked]; bare *oneself*. らたいになる
**발가숭이** a naked body; a nude.
**발깍** in a sudden outburst. むくっと
**발각**(發覺) 〜되다 be detected; be brought to light; be found out. はっかく
**발깍거리다** 《술·빨래 따위》 bubble up 《진흙 따위》 make mud squash underfoot.
**발간, 빨간** utter; downright; barefaced; sheer. かんせんた
**발간**(發刊) publication; issue/〜하다 publish; issue. はっかん
**발간**(發柬) 〜하다 send an invitation.
**발감개** leggings; footcloth; spats; foot-wrapping in place of socks.; gaiters. あしにまくもんん

**발강이, 빨강이** 《물건》 a red-colored article 《공산주의자》 a Red; a Communist/〜가 되다 go[turn] Red あかいろのもの
**발갛다** (be) bright-red; scarlet 뺨이 ~ have red cheeks. うすあかい
**빨갛다** (be) deep-red; crimson 《빨갛게 되다》 redden; turn r d/성이 나서 ~ be red with anger. あかい
**발개지다, 빨개지다** turı red; redden/얼굴이 ~ blush; flush. あかくなる
**발거리** 《남을 속임》 artif ·e 《알 :줌》 forewarning. たくらみ
**발걸음** gait; step; pace.
**발걸이** 《의자 따위의》 a rung 《자전거의》 a pedal 《발 놓는 데》 a f otrest; a foot rail [as at a bar.
**발검**(拔劍) drawing sword/〜하다 draw *one's* sword. ばつけん
**발견**(發見) discovery; revelation/〜하다 find (*out*); discover/〜자 a finder; a

발광(發狂) madness/~하다 go mad; become insane.
발광(發光) radiation; emitting light/~하다 emit light.
발구 (썰매) a sleigh; a sledge (걸채) a saddle rack.
발구르다 stamp one's feet noisily.
발군(拔群) ~의 distinguished; pre-eminent; conspicuous; unparalleled.
발군(發軍) the dispatch of troops; an expedition/~하다 dispatch troops; send an expedition.
발굴(發掘) excavation/~하다 dig [out]; unearth; excavate; exhume.
발꿈치 a heel.
발굽 a hoof.
발권(發券) note issuing/~ 은행 a bank of issue.
발그대대하다 be a dirty red.
발그뎅뎅하다 be a messy[smeared; dirty].
발그레하다 (be) somewhat red; ruddy.
발그림자 a footmark; a trail; a trace; a shadow/~도 안하다 never come; do not appear.
발그스름하다 be tinged with red; (be) reddish.
발그족족하다 (be) meanly reddish[unevenly]; ruddy.
발긋집다 disclose; divulge; expose (another's crime); reveal (a secret).
발끈 in a fit of rage.
발근(拔根) eradication/~하다 eradicate; root[stamp] out.
발끈거리다 be hot-tempered.
발금(發禁) sale prohibited.
발급(發給) ~하다 issue/여권을 ~하다 issue a passport.
발긋발긋, 빨긋빨긋 ~하다 dotted with red spots.
발끝 the tip of the toes.
발기(一記) a catalogue.
발기(勃起) (근육의) erection/~하다 stand erect; become rigid[stiff].
발기(發起) (안(案)) projection; suggestion; proposal (사업) promotion (순서) initiation (주최) auspices/~하다 project; suggest; promote/~인 a projector (회사 따위의) a promoter/…의 ~로 at the proposition of (주최) under the auspices of.
발기계(一機械) a foot-operated machine; a machine with a treadle.
발기다 tear to pieces; split open; shell.
발기름 fat of the abdominal region.
발기발기 to pieces; to shreds/~ 찢다 tear to pieces.
발길 (걸어차기) a kick (왕래) coming and going (교제) association.
발길질 kicking; a kick (at something).

발노(發怒) ~하다 get angry; take offence; lose one's temper.
빨다¹ (입으로) suck; sip; smoke; puff at (흡수하다) absorb; suck in.
빨다² (세탁하다) wash; cleanse.
빨다³ (뾰족하다) (be) pointed; sharp; tapering.
발딱 (갑자기) suddenly; jerk (반듯이) flat /~ 자빠지다 fall on one's back.
발딱거리다, 빨딱거리다 ①(맥이) beat rapidly ②(가슴이) go pit·a·pat; throb.
발단(發端) (근원) the origin (개시) the opening (최초) the beginning; the inception; the commencement/사건의 ~ the origin of an affair.
발달(發達) development; growth(생장) (진보) progress; advance[·ment]/~하다 develop; grow; progress; advance /심신의 ~ physical and mental development.
발대 a straw; a hollow paper tube [used in drinking some beverages].
빨대대다 ①(빨대를) put in a straw ②(빨아 먹다) sponge.
발덧 sore feet from much walking/~이 나다 have a sore foot.
발돋움 standing on tiptoe (발판) something to stand on/~하다 stand on tiptoe; stretch oneself.
발동(發動) ~하다 move; take action.
발동기(發動機) a motor; an engine/~선 a motorboat; a motor ship.
발뒤꿈치, 발뒤축 a heel.
발등 the instep of a foot.
라내다 tear[peel] off; pare; shell; clean.
발라맞추다 flatter; oil one's tongue; adulate; wheedle.
발란(撥亂) suppression of a disturbance.
발랄(潑剌) ~하다 (be) fresh; lively; vivid; vigorous; be full of life.
발랑거리다 act nimbly[smartly]; move agilely.
빨랑빨랑 hurriedly; in a hurry; in haste; quickly.
빨래 wash; washing; laundry/~터 a wash·place/~판 a washboard.
빨래질 washing; laundry/~하다 do washing; launder.
발령(發令) gazetting; official announcement/~하다 announce officially/~되다 be gazetted.
발로(發露) expression; manifestation/ ~하다 express; manifest.
발론(發論) proposition; motion/~하다 propose; move; suggest/~자 a proposer; a mover.
빨룩거리다 inflate and deflate alternately; quiver; wiggle; palpitate.
발룸거리다 quiver ⇒빨룩거리다.
빨리 fast; rapidly; quickly/~하다 hasten; quicken; expedite.
발리다¹ (사이를) widen; broaden (속을)

**발리다²** open; crack 《펴다》unfold; stretch 《늘어놓다》lay out.

**발리다²** be opened; be cracked open.

**빨리다** 《흡수당하다》be sucked 《착취당하다》be fleeced of 《빨아 먹이다》suckle; give the breast (to). すわれる

**발맘발맘** slowly; step by step／~하다 walk slowly. いっぽいっぽ

**발맞다** fall into step／발이 맞지 않다 get out of step. ほちょうがあう

**발맞추다** keep pace (with); fall[get] into step (with);《행동면으로》act in concert (with). ほちょうをあわせる

**발매(伐賣)** felling; deforestation／~하다 cut down; fell [trees]. さんりんのばっさい

**발매(發賣)** sale; issue／~하다 sell; put on sale／~중 on sale. はつばい

**발명(發明)** ①《고안》invention／~하다 invent; devise／~가 an inventor／~품 an invention ②《변명》explanation／~하다 explain. はつめい

**발목** an ankle／~을 삐다 sprain one's ankle. あしくび

**발목잡히다** be chained to one's business; give a handle to the enemy; be busy [with work]. あしかせをかけられる

**발묘(拔錨)** weighing anchor／~하다 weigh[raise] anchor; set sail (from); get under way. ばつびょう

**발문(跋文)** an epilogue; a postscript; an envoy. ばつぶん

**발문(發文)** sending out a notice.

**발밑** ~에 under[at] one's feet.

**발바닥** the sole of the foot. あしのうら

**발바리** a lap dog; a Pekingese [dog]; a spaniel. スパニエルのいぬ

**발바심** ~하다 thresh by treading[stepping] (on). あしでふんで穀をおとすこと

**발발¹** shivering; shaking. ぶるぶる

**발발²** easily; asunder／~하다 tear easily. ぼろぼろに

**빨빨** profusely; dripping; freely. あわただしく

**발발(勃發)** outbreak; outburst; sudden occurrence／~하다 break[burst] out; occure suddenly. ぼっぱつ

**발밤발밤** ~하다 walk on aimlessly; walk on as fancy leads one. ぶらぶらと

**발빼다** quit; wash one's hands. みをひく

**발뺌** an excuse; a pretext. みをひくこと

**발버둥이치다** stamp [one's feet]; wriggle; struggle. あしをふみならす

**발버둥질** stamping; wriggling.

**발벗다** be barefoot[ed]; have bare feet／발벗고 나서다 throw oneself into a matter with enthusiasm.

**발병** a canteen; a water bottle.

**발병(一病)** a sore foot. あしのいたみ

**발병(發病)** ~하다 be taken ill[sick]; fall ill[sick]. はつびょう

**발병(發兵)** ~하다 dispatch[send] of troops. ぐんたいをしゅつどうさせること

**발보이다** ①《재주를》display proudly one's ability ②《일의 끝말을》give a hint; reveal a part (something) of. みせびらかす

**발복(發福)** a favorable change in fortune. こううんがとうらいすること

**발본(拔本)** eradication／~하다 root out; eradicate; up root. ばっぽん

**발본 색원(拔本塞源)** ~하다 eradicate sources of evil. ばっぽんそくげん

**발부(髮膚)** hair and skin. かみとはだ

**발부리** the tip of the toes. つまさき

**발분(發憤)** ~하다 be roused to action; bestir oneself. はっぷん

**발분 망식(發憤忘食)** ~하다 give oneself up entirely to; devate oneself to.

**발빈(拔貧)** ~하다 emerge from poverty.

**발사(發射)** firing; discharge／~하다 fire; shoot; discharge; blast-off. はっしゃ

**발사(跋辭)** an epilogue ⇒발(跋). ばっぷん

**발싸개** foot wrapping cloth[paper]; footwrappers. あしをまくもめん

**발싸심** fidgeting. おちつかないたいど

**발산(發散)** 《증기의》evaporation 《빛의》radiation／~하다 give out; radiate; evaporate; diffuse. はつさん

**발상(發喪)** ~하다 announce one's death.

**발상(發想)** 〖음〗 expression 《사상》 conception.

**발상지(發祥地)** the cradle [of]; the birth place. はっしょうち

**발샅** the space between the toes. あしゆびのまた

**발생(發生)** 《돌발》occurrence 《기원》origination 《생육(生育)》growth; generation 《출현》appearance／~하다 occur; break out; originate; grow／~학 genetics; embryology. はっせい

**발선(發船)** sailing; departure of a ship／~하다 sail; set sail: leave [port]. しゅっぱん

**발설(發說)** ~하다 announce; make public; make known; give out. はつびょう

**발섭(跋涉)** ~하다 travel about; rove; roam; traverse. しょう

**발성(發聲)** articulation; utterance／~하다 utter; speak／~기(器) a vocal organ; a talking apparatus／~ 영화 a talkie; a talking[sound] picture／~법 vocalization. はっせい

**발소리** the sound of footsteps／~를 죽이고 with stealthy steps. あしおと

**발송(發送)** dispatch; sending／~하다 《물품을》send out; dispatch 《우편물을》post; mail〈미〉／~인(人) a sender 《출하주》a consignor／~선(先) address; a destination (of goods). はっそう

**발송전(發送電)** generation and transmission of electricity.

**발솥** a three-legged[tripod] pot. あしがついているかま

**발쇠** informing on others. みってい

**발쇠군** a spy; an informer. かんちょう

**발수(發穗)** ~하다 come into ears; be in [the] ear. ほがでること

**발씨** skill with one's feet. あるきぶり

**발씨름** ankle[shin] wrestling.

**발신(發身)** ~하다 rise in the world. ひせんなみぶんからしゅっせすること
**발신(發信)** ~하다 send; dispatch a letter [message]/~인 an addresser/~지 the place of dispatch/~기 a transmitter /~국 the sending office. はっしん
**발심(發心)** spiritual awakening/ ~하다 have spiritual awakening. ほっしん
**발아(發芽)** germination; sprouting/~하 다 bud; germinate; sprout. はつが
**빨아내다** suck[draw] out. すいだす
**빨아들이다** 《기체를》 breathe[draw] in 《액체를》 suck in; inhale.
**빨아먹다** ①《음식을》 suck; imbibe; sip ② 《우려내다》 suck; squeeze out; sponge. ちびちびのむ
**발악(發惡)** ~하다 rail against[at]; rave; revile; inveigh against; abuse. いさいかまはずどなりちらすこと
**발안(發案)** suggestion 《발의》 proposal 《동의》 motion/~하다 suggest; propose; move 《계획하다》 originate/~자 a proposer an originator. はつあん
**발양(發揚)** ~하다 raise; exalt. はつよう
**발언(發言)** speaking; speech; utterance /~하다 speak; utter 《의원이》 take the floor/~자 a speaker/~권 the right to speak. はつげん
**발연(發煙)** emitting smoke/~통 a smoke-candle/~[폭]탄 a smoke shell/~제 a fumigant. はつえん
**발연(勃然)** ①《갑자기》 suddenly; all at once ②《분연》 in a fit of passion; in a flare. ぼつぜん
**발열(發熱)** ①《열의 발생》 generation of heat/~하다 generate heat/~량[력] calorific value ②《병열》 pyrexia /~하 다 be attacked with fever. はつねつ
**발원(發源)** ~하다 originate (in); rise (in); spring 「up」 (from). はつげん
**발원(發願)** a prayer/~하다 make[offer] a prayer. きがんすること
**발육(發育)** growth; development/~하다 grow; develop/~기 the period of development. はついく
**발음(發音)** pronunciation 《음절》 articulation/~하다 pronounce; articulate/~ 학 phonetics/~ 부호 phonetic symbols /~ 기관 a vocal organ. はつおん
**발의(發意)** an initiative; a suggestion/ ~하다 suggest; originate. はつい
**발의(發議)** an instance 《제안》 a proposal 《동의》a motion/~하다 propose; move; make a proposal; suggest. はつぎ
**발인(發靷)** ~하다 carry a coffin out of the house; carry out of bier fo burial.
**발자국** a footprint; a footmark; a footstep; a trail; a track. あしあと
**발자귀** an animal's footprint.
**발자취** ①《발자국》a footprint; a footmark; a footstep; a trail ②《발소리》 the sound of footsteps; a footstep; tread; a trace; a wake. あしあと
**발작(發作)** a fit; a paroxysm; a spasm /~적[으로] spasmodic[ally]; paroxysmal[ly]; fitful[ly]. ほっさ
**발짧다** 《먹는 자리에》 (be) late for; unlucky; unfortunate.
**발장구치다** 《헤엄치다》 kick; do one's kick 《태평하게》 pass one's days in indolence. あしでばたばたする
**발장단(一長短)** beating time with the foot.
**발전(發展)** 《발달》 development; growth 《융성》 prosperity/~하다 develop; grow; prosper/~성 possibilities/~적 해소 dissolution for the better/~성 있는 산업 industries with futures. はってん
**발전(發電)** ①《전기의》 generation of electric power/~하다 generate electricity /~소 a power plant[station]/~기 a generator ②《전보의》 telegraphing / ~ 하다 send a telegram; wire; cable; dispatch of a telegram. はつでん
**발정(發情)** sexual excitement/~하다 be [get] excited with the desire/ ~기 [the age of] puberty 《동물의》 the mating season; heat. はつじょう
**발정(發程)** ~하다 set off; start on a journey; take the road. しゅつぱつ
**발족(發足)** ~하다 starting; beginning/~ 하다 start functioning. はっそく
**발주(發注)** ~하다 place an order.
**발진(發疹)** 《의》 eruption; rash/ ~하다 break out [in a rash]; effloresce/~티 푸스 eruptive typhus. はっしん
**발진기(發振器)** 《통신》 an oscillator. はっしんき
**발차(發車)** departure/~하다 start; leave /~ 시간 the time for departure/~ 신호 a starting signal/~계 a starter. はっしゃ
**발착(發着)** departure and arrival/~하 다 arrive and depart/~ 시간표 a time-table; a railroad schedule. はっちゃく
**발췌(拔萃)** 《빼기》 extraction; selection 《빼낸 것》 an extract; an excerpt; a selection/~하다 extract; select/~곡(曲) a selection. ばっすい
**발치** direction of one's foot when one lies down. ねているときのあしのほうこう
**발치(拔齒)** pulling out a tooth. ばっし
**발칙하다** ①《버릇없다》 (be) ill-mannered; rude ②《괘씸하다》 (be) insolent; outrageous; abominable. けしからない
**발탁(拔擢)** selection; choice/~하다 select; single out; choose. ばってき
**발톱** 《사람의》 a toenail 《짐승의》 a claw 《맹수의》 a talon 《마소의》 a hoof 《고양이의》 a bill. あしゆびのつめ
**발틀** 《재봉틀》 a treadle sewing machine.
**발파(發破)** blasting/~하다 blast. はっぱ
**발판(一板)** a [foot]stool; a step; a foot-rest; a stage; a foothold. あしがかり
**발포(發布)** promulagation/~하다 promulgate; proclaim; issue. はっぷ
**발포(發砲)** ~하다 fire (on); discharge (a gun); open fire (on). はっぽう

**발표(發表)** 《공표》 announcement; publication; presentation 《표현》 expression／～하다 announce; make public; make known; release; express. はっぴょう

**발하다(發─)** ①《방사하다》emit(불·빛·연기 따위를); emanate(빛을); radiate(빛·열을); give forth[out]; shed(향기 따위를) ②《명령 따위를》issue; give; publish; send out 《소리를》utter; give utterance to 《발표하다》announce; make public ③《출발하다》leave; start; set out ④《피어나다》bloom; blossom; open; blow ⑤《기원하다》originate (in); spring (up). あばく

**발한(發汗)** perspiration／～하다 sweat; perspire／～제 a diaphoretic.

**발항(發航)** departure of a ship／～하다 depart; set sail／～지 a home port of; a port of departure. しゅっぱん

**발행(發行)** ①《도서의》publication; issue／～하다 publish; issue／～인 a publisher／～금지[정지] suppression[suspension] of publication ②《어음 따위의》drawing; issue／～하다 draw up on (a bank) for (an amount); issue／～지[일] the place[date] of issue／～인 a drawer ③《지폐·채권 따위의》floatation／～하다 float; issue／～고 issued amount／～가격 the issue-price. はっこう

**발향(發向)** leaving for; starting for／～하다 leave for; go to; proceed to; start for.
しゅっぱつしてもくてきちにむかうこと

**발헤엄** treading water／～하다 tread water; swimming by legs.

**발현(發現)** ～하다 be revealed[manifested]; manifest itself. はつげん

**발호(跋扈)** domination; prevalence／～하다 be rampant; be dominant. ばっこ

**발화(發火)** ～하다 catch fire; originate／～점 the firing point／～장치 an ignition device／자연 ～ spontaneous combustion／～기 an exploder. はっか

**발회(發會)** ～하다 open a meeting／～식(式) an opening ceremony; an inaugural meeting. はっかい

**발효(發效)** effectuation／～하다 become effective; come into effect. はっこう

**발효(醱酵)** fermentation／～하다 ferment／～소(素) yeast. はっこう

**발휘(發揮)** exhibition／～하다 show; display; exhibit. はっき

**발흥(勃興)** ～하다 rise suddenly [into power]; come to the front. ぼっこう

**밝다¹** ①《환하다》(be) light; bright／밝은 데 a light place／밝게 하다 lighten; light up ②《능통하다》(be) familiar with; versed in／미국 사정에 ～ be conversant with American affairs ③《귀·눈이》(be) sharp; keen／귀가 ～ have a sharp ear; be quick of hearing. あかるい

**밝다²** 《날이》dawn; break; grow light／밝아 오는 하늘 the dawning sky／날이 밝기 전에 before dawn. よるがあける

**밝을녘** daybreak; dawn; the early hours of the morning.

**밝히다** ①《밤을》sit[stay] up all night ②《불을》brighten; lighten; light up; make brighter ③《분명하게》make (a matter) clear; disclose; bring to light; make it public. あかるくする

**밟다** ①《디디다·쫓다》tread (on); step (on); stamp one's feet (on) ②《순서·절차 따위를》go through; complete[finish] (a course); undergo. ふみつける

**밤¹** 《야간》night; evening(저녁)／～에 at night; in the evening／～ 경치 a night scene／～ 거리의 여인 a street girl; a woman of the street／～마다 every night; nightly; night after night／～을 얘기로 새우다 talk the night away／～이 깊었다 The night is far advanced.／～이고 낮이고 night and day. よる

**밤²** 《식》a chestnut／～나무 a chestnut-tree／～색[의] chestnut; bay. ぐり

**밤³** 《놋그릇 틀》a die; a mlod. いがた

**밤거리** night street; the town at night. よるのがいろ

**밤꾀꼬리** 《동》a nightingale.

**밤글** reading at night; studying at night. よるのどくしょ

**밤길** a walk at night; a night trip; a journey by night.

**밤낮** night and day; at all hours; day in and day out. ちゅうや

**밤놀이** night pleasure[amusement]／밤놀잇군 a nightbird. よあそび

**밤눈¹** night vision; seeing at night. よるのめ

**밤눈²** 《내리는 눈》snow in the night.

**밤대거리** night shift; night crew; night relief. よるのこうたいきんむ

**밤도와** all night; all throughout the night.

**밤들다** [the night] be advanced; grow late; wear on. よるがふかまる

**밤마다** nightly; every night; night after night.

**밤바람** a night-wind; a night-breeze.

**밤볼** a plump[chubby] cheek; a full cheek. こえたかお

**밤비** rain in the night. よるのあめ

**밤사이, 밤새** the night time. やかん

**밤새도록** all night [long]; overnight; all the night through.

**밤새우다** sit[stay] up all night; keep awake all night through. よふかしする

**밤새움** staying up late／～하다 sit up all night; hold a wake. よふかし

**밤색(─色)** a chestnut color; maroon.

**밤샘** staying up all night 밤새움. よふかし

**밤소경** night blindness.

**밤소일(─消日)** night amusement／～하다 go out in the evening for pleasure; a night outing. よるのたのしみ

**밤손님** a night thief[bird]; a burglar; a night prowler. よるのどろぼう

**밤송이** a chestnut bur. くりのいが

**밤안개** a night fog[mist].

**밤알** a single chestnut. くりのみ

밤얽이 a kind of knot. にじゅうのむすび
밤엿 a taffy; a toffee.
밤윷 *yuch* sticks small as chestnuts. こがたのさじ
밤이슬 the night dew.
밤일 night work 《야근》 a night shift/ ～하다 work at night. やぎょう
밤자갈 pebbles (for *paving*). じゃり
밤잔물 a bowl of drinking water left overnight at the bedside.
밤잠 sleeping at night; night sleep. よるのねむり
밤장(一場) a night market. よみせ
밤재우다 keep overnight.
밤저녁 late evening; night. よふけ
밤중(一中) the middle of the night.
밤차(一車) a night train; an owl train.
밤참 a midnight meal[snack]. やしょく
밤톨 a chestnut. くりのみ
밤하늘 a night sky.
밥¹ 《쌀밥》 boiled[cooked] rice 《식사》 a meal; food 《생계》 living; liveliness/ ～을 먹다 《생계를 세우다》 take a meal; earn one's bread. めし
밥² waste material produced in cutting /가윗～ scraps of cloth[paper] /대팻～ shavings/실～ bits of thread/톱～ sawdust. かんなやのこぎりのくず
밥값 food costs; board. しょくひ
밥그릇 a rice bowl. しょくつ
밥내다 torture a confession out of (a *criminal*). ごうもんにかける
밥맛 《식욕》 appetite. しょくよく
밥물 《밥짓는》 water for boiling rice 《넘는 물》 rice-water. めしたきようのみず
밥밀 beans[*harley, etc.*] boiled with rice.
밥벌레 a useless mouth; a good-for nothing; an idler.
밥벌이 earning *one's* daily bread/～하다 make a living; earn *one's* daily bread. くうためのかせぎ
밥보자(一褓子) a covering for boiled-rice container; a table-colth.
밥쌀 rice for boiling; eating rice.
밥상(一床) a dinner table. しょくたく
밥소라 a large brass food bowl. おすきなしんちゅう製のしょっくき
밥솥 a rice pot. すいじようのかま
밥쇠 a dinner bell [in a Buddhist temple].
밥술 a spoonful of boiled rice. さじ
밥알 a grain of boiled-rice. めしつぶ
밥자배기 a earthen bowl.
밥잔치 a small simple dinner party.
밥장사 restaurant business/～하다 sell meals; run an eating house. めしや
밥장수 one who sells meals; a restaurant.
밥주걱 a spatula. しゃもじ
밥주머니 《사람》 a good-for-nothing.
밥줄 *one's* means of livelihood/～이 끊어지다 lose *one's* means of livelihood. せいかつのみち
밥집 an eating house; a chophouse. めしや
밥짓다 boil rice; cook food. めしをたく
밥통(一桶) ①《그릇》 a wooden container for boiled rice ②《위》 the stomach ③《밥벌레》 a good-for-nothing. めしおけ
밥투정 ～하다 grumble[complain] about meals[food]. しょくじにたいするへい
밥풀 ①《풀》 rice paste ②《밥알》 a boiled rice-grain. めしつぶ
빳빳하다 ①《꼿꼿하다》 (be) stiff; straight ②《성질이》 (be) headstrong; firm; unyielding; willful. こっている
빵¹ bread.
빵² 《소리》 pop; bang. ばちん
방(放) 《총알 따위의》 a shot; a round 《대포》 a shell. ばつ
방(房) a room; a chamber; an apartment. へや
방(榜) ①《방목》 the list of successful candidates ②《방문》 a placard; a public notice. かきょのごうかくしゃのめいぶ
방(磅) a pound.
방(方) 《방위》 direction. ほう
방(房) 《댁》 care of (略 ; c/o)/이선달～ 홍길동씨 Mr. *Hong Kill Dong* care of Mr. *Lee*.
방가(邦家) a state; a nation ⇨나라. くに
방가(放歌) singing loudly/～하다 sing noisily. おおごえにうたう
방가위지(方可謂之) indeed; really; true.
방갓(方一) a wide-brimmed bamboo hat [worn by a mourner].
방게 《동》 a kind of small crab.
방계(傍系) ～의 collateral; subsidiary/ ～회사 a subsidiary company. ぼうけい
방고래(房一) a flue of a hypocaust. オンドルの炕道
방공(防共) defense against communism; anti-Comintern. ぼうきょう
방공(防空) air defense/～호 an air-raid shelter; a dugout. ぼうくう
방과(放課) dismissal of a class/～후 after school [hours]. ほうか
방관(傍觀) ～하다 remain a spectator; stand by idly; look on [unconcerned] /～자 a spectator; a looker-on/～적 indifferent attitude. ぼうかん
방광(放光) ～하다 give out[emit] light; radiate. ひかりを放こと
방광(膀胱) 【해】 the bladder/～염(炎) inflammation of the bladder; cystitis. ぼうこう
빵꾸 a blowout; a puncture; a hole/～ 나다 blow out; puncture. パンク
방구들(房一) a hypocaust. オンドル
방구멍 the center hole of a Korean kite.
방구석(房一) the interior of a room.
방귀 wind; a fart/～를 뀌다 break wind; fart. おなら
방그레 smilingly; beamingly/～웃다 smile; beam. にっこりと
방글거리다 smile; beam. にこにこわらう
방글방글 with a bland smile; beamingly; smilingly. にこにこ
방금(方今) just now; a moment ago.
방금(防禁) prohibition; a ban; a restriction; a taboo.

**방긋거리다** smile; beam. にこにこわらう
**방긋방긋** with a bland smile; beamingly. にこにこ
**방긋이** ①(웃는 모습) smilingly; with a smile ⇒방그레 ②(열린 모양) ajar/문을 ~ 열다 open the door a little. にこやかに
**방긋하다** be ajar; be partly opened. じゃっかん廣がっている
**방기**(放棄) abandonment 《권리를》 surrender; relinquishment/~하다 give up; abandon; renounce. ほうき
**방나다** run bankrupt; be brought to ruin; be ruined. はさんする
**방나다**(榜一) [the list of successful candidates] be released[made public].
**방년**(芳年) blooming age; the sweet age of a young girl. ほうねん
**방놓다**(房一) build a room; remodel a room. オンドルをつくる
**방뇨**(放尿) ~하다 urinate; make[pass] water; relieve nature [oneself]. ほうにょう
**방담**(放談) a random[free] speech; an irresponsible[unreserved] talk/~되а gabfest《미·구》; a bull session《속》.
**방대**(尨大) ~하다 (be) bulky; massive; huge; enormous; vast; colossal. ぼうだい
**방도**(方途) a means; an art; a way; a method; a measure. ほうと
**방독**(防毒) anti-gas/~실 an anti-gas room[shelter]. ぼうどく
**방둥이** the rump. こしのまがったもの
**방랑**(放浪) ~하다 wander[roam] about; rove/~객 a wanderer; a vagabond/~ 생활 a vagabond life. ほうろう
**방략**(方略) 《정책》a policy 《계획》a plan 《책략》a stratagem; tactics 《수단》 means. ほうりゃく
**방령**(芳齡) blooming age ⇒방년(芳年). ほうれい
**방론**(放論) a harangue; a rant/~하다 speak irresponsibly.
**방류**(放流) ~하다 《물을》 discharge 《고기를》 stock [the streams] with/강에 잉어를~하다 stock a stream with carp.
**방리**(方里) a square ri.
**방만**(放漫) ~하다 (be) lax; loose; careless.
**방망이** a mallet; a stick; a cudgel/요술 ~ the magic mallet. ぼう
**방망이들다** disturb; prevent; interfere. かんしょうする
**방매**(放賣) selling; sale/~하다 sell off/특가 ~ a special sale/~가 house to sale. ぶっぴんをだしてうること
**방면**(方面) 《방향》a direction 《지방》a quarter; a district 《일의 분야》a line; a field 《국면》an aspect. ほうめん
**방면**(放免) ~하다 set (one) free; acquit; release; discharge; liberate. ほうめん
**방명**(方命) disobedience of orders/~하다 disobey (a person's) order; run counter to orders. めいれいにさからうこと
**방명**(芳名) your [respected] name/~록 a list of names; a visitors-list. ほうめい

**방목**(放牧) grazing; pasturage/ ~하다 pasture; graze (cattle)/~지(地) a grazing land. ほうぼく
**방목**(榜目) the [field] list of successful candidates [in the higher civil service examination].
かきょのごうかくしゃのめいぶ
**방문**(訪問) a call; a visit 《기자 등의》an interview/~하다 call on (a person); call at (a person's house); visit; make a call (on)/~을 갔다 He went out for a visit./~객 a caller; a visitor/~ 기자 a reporter. ほうもん
**방문**(榜文) a public notice/~하다 post [put up] a notice. こうじぶん
**방문**(方文) prescription ⇒약방문.
**방문**(房門) a door (of a room). へやのしゅつにゅうもん
**방물 장사** hawking women's items.
**방물 장수** a peddler[hawker] selling women's items.
**방밑**(坊一) the lower part of a wall.
**방바닥**(房一) the floor of a room. オンドルのとこ
**빵빵** ①(소리) sound after explosion ②(모양) with hole after hole; gaping and gaping. ぼこぼこ
**방방 곡곡**(坊坊曲曲) the whole length and breadth of the land/~에서 throughout the length and breadth of the land.
**방범**(防犯) prevention of crime/~ 주간 Crime Prevention Week. ぼうはん
**방법**(方法) 《하는 법》a way; a method 《과정》a process 《수단》a means 《계획》 a plan; a system 《조치》a step; a measure 《젯법》 a formula 《방안》 a scheme 《수속》 a procedure /…하는 ~ how to make…/~론 methodology. ほうほう
**방벽**(防壁) a barrier; a protective wall; a bulwark/민주주의의 ~ a bulwark of democracy.
**방부**(防腐) prevention against putrefaction; antisepsis; preservation 《시체의》 embalmment/~하다 preserve [from decay]; mbalm/~의 antiseptic/~제 an antiseptic/~처리를 하다 apply antiseptic treatment 《시체에》embalm. ぼうふ
**방불**(彷彿, 仿佛, 髣髴) close resemblance /~하다 resemble closely/~케 하다 remind (a person) of (a thing); adumbrate. ほうふつ
**방비**(房一) an indoor broom.
**방비**(防備) defence; defensive works; fortifications; safeguard/~하다 defend; fortify; guard/~가 없는 defenseless; undefended/~가 없는 도시 an open city. ぼうび
**방비**(芳菲) fragrance; beauty/ ~하다 (be) fragrant; beautiful; smell sweet; aromatic. ほうひ
**방사**(放射) 《군·열의》 radiation 《빛·열·냄새 따위의》emission; emanation 《발사》firing; discharge/~하다 radiate; emit; discharge; fire/~선 radiant

**방사** rays/~상의 radiated; radial/~능 radioactivity/~능이 있는 radioactive/~성 원소 a radioactive isotope. ほうしゃ

**방사(房事)** sexual intercourse/~를 삼가다 be contained. ぼうじ

**방사(放肆)** willfulness; waywardness/~하다 (be) self-indulgent; licentious; libertine; unrestrained. ほうし

**방사(放飼)** pasturage; grazing/~하다 pasture (cattle); leave (a dog) at large; keep loose. はなしがい

**방사(倣似)** a close resemblance/~하다 resemble closely. まったくよくにていること

**방사림(防沙林)** an erosion control forest; trees to arrest sand-shifting. ぼうしゃりん

**방산(放散)** ①(헤침) diffusion; radiation 《열·빛의》 evaporation(수증기); emanation(방사등)/~하다 radiate; diffuse ②《흩어짐》 dispersion; scattering/ ~하다 disperse; scatter.

**방석(方席)** a cushion/~에 앉다 sit[seat oneself] on a cushion. じゃぶとん

**방석(放釋)** release; discharge; liberation /~하다 set (a person) free[at liberty]; release.

**방선(傍線)** a side line. ふちのせん

**방설(防雪)** protection against[from] snow/~림 a snowbreak; a snow forest.

**방성 대곡(放聲大哭)** weeping loudly and bitterly/~하다 cry loudly; weep bitterly; lament. おおごえでなくこと

**방세(房貰)** a room rent; the charge for [the rent of] a room.

**방세간(房—)** [room] furniture; furnishing. しつないのかぐ

**방송(放送)** 《라디오》 broadcasting; a broadcast(1회의); 《석방》 release; liberation/~하다 broadcast; send [out] (a drama) on the air/~을 듣다 listen in on the radio service/~국 a radio[TV] [broadcasting] station/~극 a [radio] drama/~망 a radio[TV] network[circuit]/~ 실 a radio[TV] studio/~ 주파수 radio frequency/~중이다 be on the air. ほうそう

**방수(防水)** ①(being) watertight; waterproof ②《군함의》 torpedo defense/~하다 make (cloth) watertight/~관(管) a watertight pipe/~화(靴) rain-shoes; rubbers/~ 외투 a mackintosh. ぼうすい

**방수(放水)** drainage/~하다 drain water off.

**방수(防守)** defense; defensive; guard/ ~하다 defend; act on the defensive/ ~ 동맹 a defensive alliance. ふせぎまもること

**방수(傍受)** ~하다 pick up; intercept/무전을 ~하다 intercept a radio message.

**방술(方術)** method and technique. ほうじゅつ

**방습(防濕)** ~의 damp-proof. ぼうしつ

**방시(榜示)** ~하다 post[put up] a notice.

**방식(方式)** 《형식》 a form 《방법》 a method; a process 《정식》 a formula (pl. ~s, ·lae); 《수속》 formalities 《관례》 usage/생활 ~ the mode of living/사고 ~ one's way of thinking/~에 따라서 in due [proper] form. ほうしき

**방식제(防蝕劑)** an anti-corrosive.

**방실거리다** smile (at a person); beam (upon a person). にこにこわらう

**방심(放心)** ①absent-mindedness; abstraction [of mind]/~하다 be absent-minded/~하지 않다 be on one's guard ②(안심) relief; peace of mind/그 점에 대하여는 ~해도 무방합니다 Set your mind at rest about it. ほうしん

**방아** a mill/물~ a water mill.

**방아깨비** 《충》 a grasshopper; a locust.

**방아굴대** the water wheel shaft. すいしゃのじく

**방아쇠** a trigger; a gunlock/~를 당기다 pull the trigger. ひきがね

**방아확** a mortar.

**방안(方案)** a plan; a device; a scheme; a program/~을 세우다 draw up[formulate] a plan. ほうあん

**방안지(方眼紙)** section[graph, squared] paper. ほうがんし

**방알** ~하다 prevent; check.

**방앗간(—間)** a rice[-cleaning] mill; a flour[corn] mill; a mill. せいまいしょ

**방앗공이** a pestle; a pounder. きね

**방앗군** a miller.

**방약 무인(傍若無人)** arrogance; audacity; outrage/~한 arrogant; audacious; outrageous/~하다 (be) audacious; arrogant/~한 짓을 하다 behave outrageously[audaciously]. ぼうじゃくぶじん

**방어(防禦)** defense; protection; safeguard/~하다 defend; protect oneself (against)/~선(線) a line of defense/~율 《야구》 earned run average(略: ERA.) /~전 a defensive war/~ 진지 a defensive position. ぼうぎょ

**방어(魴魚)** 《어》 the yellowtail. おしきうお

**방언(方言)** a dialect; a provincialism/~ 연구 dialectology. ほうげん

**방언(放言)** a bombastic[random, big] talk; an unreserved talk; free speech /~하다 talk big [at random]. ほうげん

**방역(防疫)** prevention of epidemics[infectious disease]/~하다 prevent an epidemic of/~관 a health official; an epidemic control commissioner. ぼうえき

**방연광(方鉛鑛)** 《광》 galena.

**방열(放熱)** radiation/~하다 radiate/~기 a radiator. ほうねつ

**방영(放映)** ~하다 《텔레비전》 telecast.

**방외인(方外人)** an outsider; an unconcerned person. きょがいしゃ

**방우구(防雨具)** waterproofs.

**방울** ①(쇠방울) a bell/~ 소리 the tinkling of a bell ②(물의) a drop/물~ a water drops/빗~ rain drops/~ 방울 떨어지다 fall in drops/그후 술이라고는 한 ~도 안 마셨다 I have not tasted

a drop of wine since.
**방울벌레** 〖충〗 a bell-ring insect.
**방울새** 〖조〗 a goldfinch; a greenfinch; a green linnet.
**방울 집게** pincers; a nail-puller; nippers.
**방위**(方位) a direction; azimuth/~각 bearing; target[track] angle; magnetic declination; azimuth/~권 an azimuth circle.
**방위**(防衛) defense; protection; safeguard/~하다 defend; protect/~군 a defense corps/~ 협정 a defense agreement /~대 a defense force.
**방음**(防音) sound arresting; sound absorption/~하다 arrest sounds/~의 soundproof/~ 장치 soundproofing; a silencer; a sound arrester.
**방일**(放逸) ~하다 (be) dissolute; loose; unrestrained; riotous.
**방임**(放任) non-interference; non-intervention/~하다 《사람을》 let[leave] (one) alone/~주의 a let-alone policy; liberalism.
**방자** invoking evil[curses] upon (a person); imprecation.
**방자**(芳姿) a beautiful[graceful] figure.
**방자**(房子) a servant; a footman; a valet.
**방자**(放恣) license; self-indulgence; impudence; rampancy/~하다 (be) impertinent; self-indulgent; licentious; uppish.
**방자고기** roasted meat seasoned with salt only.
**방잠망**(防潛網) an antisubmarine net.
**방장**(房帳) a mosquito net[curtain]; room curtains; hangings.
**방장**(方丈) 《주지》 a chief priest; an abbot 《주승의 처소》 an abbot's chamber; the priest's quarters.
**방재** a [wooden] boom.
**방적**(紡績) [cotton] spinning/~ 공장 a spinning mill/~ 기계 a spinning machine/~ 회사 a spinning company/~업 cotton-spinning industry.
**방전**(防戰) a defensive war/~하다 defend; fight in defense.
**방전**(放電) 〖물〗 electric discharge/~하다 discharge electricity/~관 a discharge tube.
**방점**(傍點) a side dot[point]/~을 찍다 mark with a side dot.
**방접원**(傍接圓) 〖수〗 an escribed circle.
**방정** a rash act/~맞다 be outrageously rash/~떨다 behave rashly.
**방정**(芳情) good wishes; kindness.
**방정**(方正) ~하다 《언행이》(be) irreproachable; good; upright/품행이 ~한 사람 a man of good conduct 《물건의》 neat and square.
**방정꾸러기** a light-headed[rash] person 《특히 여자》 a madcap; a daredevil.

**방정떨다** act imprudently[rashly]; act on impulse.
**방정맞다** (be) light-headed; frivolous; rash; flippant.
**방정식**(方程式) 〖수〗 an equation/1차[2차 3차] ~ a simple[quadratic, cubic] equation/고차 ~ an equation of higher degree.
**방조**(幇助) assistance; 〖법〗 aiding and abetting; help; backing/~하다 assist; aid; help; aid and abet.
**방조**(傍助) assistance; help; support/~하다 assist; get behind (a person).
**방종**(放縱) dissoluteness; license; looseness/~하다 be loose; be dissolute/~한 self-indulgent; dissolute.
**방주**(方舟) an ark/노아의 ~ Noah's ark.
**방주**(旁註) marginal notes 《각주(脚註)》 foot notes.
**방죽** an embankment; a dike; a bank/ ~을 쌓다 build a dike.
**방증**(傍證) circumstantial evidence; corroboration.
**방지**(防止) prevention; check; preclusion /~하다 prevent; stop; check; hold/ ~책(策) a preventive measure.
**방직**(紡織) spinning and weaving; textile manufacturing/~업자 a textile manufacturer.
**방진**(方陣) a square; a phalanx.
**방책**(方策) 《계획》 a plan; a scheme 《방침》 a policy 《수단》 a means.
**방책**(防柵) a palisade; a paling; a stockade.
**방척**(放擲) abandonment/~하다 abandon; give up; lay aside.
**방천**(防川) a dike; an embankment; a levee/~하다 shore up the river[s].
**방첩**(防諜) prevention of espionage; counter-intelligence; anti-espionage; protection from[against] spying/~대 (隊) Counter Intelligence Corps《略: C.I.C.》.
**방청**(傍聽) hearing; attendance 《입장》 admission/~하다 hear; attend; listen to; sit in on; visit/~권 an admission ticket/~인 a hearer/~석 《회의 따위의》 seats for the public.
**방초**(芳草) fragrant[green] grass.
**방촌**(方寸) 《사방 한 치》 a square chi 《마음》 the mind.
**방추**(紡錘) a spindle.
**방추**(方錐) a square drill/~의 pyramidal/~형 a pyramid shape; square pyramid.
**방축**(防築) a dike; a bank; an embankment/~이 무너지다 a dike breaks.
**방축**(放逐) ~하다 expel (a person); drive (a person) out of 《국외로》 deport; banish.

**방축 가공**(防縮加工) ~한 pre-shrunk 《상표 이름》 Sanforized.

**방춘**(芳春) ①《봄》 the flowering spring ②《방년》 blooming age.

**방출**(放出) ~하다 《방산하다》 emit; radiate 《배출하다》 discharge; release/~물자 released goods.

**방충**(防蟲) ~ 가공의 moth-proof/~제 insecticide 《좀약》 a moth ball.

**방취**(防臭) deodorization/~하다 deodorize/~제 a deodorizer.

**방치**(放置) leaving alone; negligence/~하다 leave[let] (*a thing*); leave (*a matter*) as it is.

**방침**(方針) a course (of *action*); a policy 《주의》 a principle 《계획》 a plan 《목적》 a purpose; an aim; an object/일정한 ~ a definite policy.

**방탄**(防彈) ~의 bulletproof; bombproof/~하다 shield from bullets/~ 유리 bulletproof glass/~ 조끼 a bulletproof vest[jacket].

**방탄**(放誕) big talk; bragging; loudmouthed boasting/~하다 speak wildly.

**방탕**(放蕩) dissipation; debauchery/~하다 be dissipated; lead a dissipated[dissolute] life/~ 생활 a dissipated[fast] life/~자 a libertine; a rake; a dissolute person.

**방토**(邦土) a country; a land; a realm.

**방파제**(防波堤) a breakwater; a bulwark; a mole.

**방판**(方板) a square board.

**방패**(防牌) a shield; a buckler/~막이 a pretext/~삼아 on the strength[plea] of.

**방편**(方便) 《융통》 expediency; an expedient 《수단》 means 《도구》 an instrument 《방법》 a scheme/일시적 ~ a temporary expedient.

**방포**(放砲) a blank shot/~하다 fire a blank shot.

**방풍**(防風) protection against wind/~림(林) a shelter belt; a windbreak [forest]; a tree belt.

**방하다**(放—) discharge; release 《방매하다》 put on sale; sell off.

**방학**(放學) a vacation; school holidays/~하다 go on vacation; close the school.

**방한**(防寒) protection against the cold/~하다 keep the cold away/~구 cold weather gear/~모 a winter cap/~화 [복] winter boots[clothes].

**방한**(訪韓) a visit to Korea/~하다 visit to Korea.

**방해**(妨害) 《장해》 an obstacle; a hindrance 《폐해》 obstruction; disturbance/~하다 obstruct; disturb; hinder; interfere with/~물 an obstacle/의사(議事) ~ a filibuster; obstructive tactics/~ 방송 jamming/치안 ~ the disturbance of public peace.

**방해석**(方解石) 〖광〗 calcite; calcareous spar.

**방향**(方向) ①《방위》 direction; bearings/서울 ~으로 in the direction of *Seoul* ②《침로》 a course; a line/~ 탐지기 direction finder ③《방침》 one's course ④《목적》 an aim[object].

**방향**(芳香) a sweet smell; perfume; fragrance/~ 있는 sweet-smelling/~제 an aromatic.

**방형**(方形) a square.

**방호**(防護) protection; defense/~하다 protect; defend/~자 a protector; a defender; a custodian.

**방혼**(芳魂) the spirit of a lovely young woman.

**방화**(放火) 〖법〗 arson 《화재》 an incendiary fire; incendiarism/~하다 set fire (*to*)/~죄 arson/~범 an incendiary; a arsonist.

**방화**(防火) prevention of fire;/~ 건축 a fireproof building/~ 설비 fire protection.

**방화**(邦貨) 《화폐》Korean money[currency]; 《화물》Korean goods.

**방화**(邦畵) a Korean film[motion picture, movie].

**방황**(彷徨) wandering/~하다 wander[roam] about; rove.

**밭** a field; a farm; a garden/감자 ~ a potato patch/대 ~ a bamboo thicket/사과 ~ an apple orchard.

**밭갈이** plowing; tillage; cultivating/~하다 plow; till; farm; cultivate.

**밭고랑** a furrow.

**밭곡식**(—穀) dry field grain; corps of field.

**밭귀** a corner of a field.

**밭농사**(—農事) dry field farming.

**밭다**¹ ①《인색하다》 (be) stingy; miserly; illiberal ②《절박하다》 (be) near; close by; imminent.

**밭다**² 《거르다》 filter; strain 《물을》 leach; percolate.

**밭도랑** a ditch between fields.

**밭두둑** a ridge between fields.

**밭둑** an embankment around the end of a field.

**밭뒤다** 〖농〗 repeatedly plow a field.

**밭매기** weeding a dry field/~하다 weed `in` a dry field.

**밭문서**(—文書) a ˈtitleˈ deed.

**밭벼** a dry-field rice plant.

**밭보리** barley `planted in a dry field`.

**밭사돈**(—査頓) father of one's son-in-law [daughter-in-law].

**밭은기침** a short-breathed cough; a hack.

**밭이다** be[get] filtered[strained, drained]; filter (*out*); strain (*through*, *out*).

**밭이랑** a ridge in a field.
**밭일** field farming／～하다 work in the field.
**발장다리** a bow-legged person／～의 X-legged; bow-legged.
**발장이** a kitchen gardener.
**밭치다** filter; strain; leach ⇨밭다.

**배**¹ ①《복부》 the abdomen; the belly 《창자》 the bowels 《위》 the stomach／큰～ a big paunch; a potbelly／～가 아프다 have a stomachache ②《마음 속》 heart; mind ③《태(胎)》a womb／～가 다르다 be born of a different mother／～가 부르다 be big with child; be in the family way.
**배**² 《선박》 a ship; a vessel; a boat 《기선》 a steamer 《총칭》 a craft／～로 by ship／～를 타다 get[go] on board [a ship]／～에서 내리다 leave[get off] a ship.
**배**³ 〖식〗 a pear／～나무 a pear tree.
**배**(胚) 〖식〗 an embryo; 〖동〗 an embryo; a fetus.
**배**(倍) ①《갑절》 double; twice; two times; twofold ②《곱절》 times; fold／3～ three times／4～ quadruple／5～ quintuple／7～ septuple／8～ octuple／10～ decuple／백～ centuple.
**배가**(倍加) doubling／～하다 [make] double; increase double／수입을～ double the income.
**빼각거리다** squeak; creak; grate.
**배갈** Chinese liquor.
**배겨나다** bear up (under); put up (with) suffer patiently (through).
**배격**(排擊) rejection; denouncement／～하다 reject; denounce; drive out; oust.
**배견**(拜見) inspection; looking at／～하다 inspect; see; look at; have a look at.
**배경**(背景) ①《후면》 a background ②《무대의》 scenery; setting; a scene／～을 그리다 paint scenes ③《배후 세력》 backing; support; protection; pull《미·속》;《후원자》 a backer; a supporter／유력한～ strong backing.
**배계**(拜啓) Dear Sir; Dear Mr. [Mrs.]; Dear Madam.
**배꼬다** twist ⇨비꼬다.
**배고프다** (be) hungry; feel hungry／배고파 죽을 지경이다 be dying with hunger.
**배곯다** have an empty stomach.
**배꼽** the navel; the umbilicus.
**배꼽노리** the neighborhood of the navel.
**배관**(拜觀) inspection; visit／～하다 inspect; look at; view.
**배관**(配管) pipe laying／～하다 lay a pipe／～공사 piping work.
**배관**(陪觀) viewing (something) in the company of a superior／～하다 see in attendance upon a superior.
**배교**(背敎) apostasy; perversion; renegation／～자 a pervert; a renegade.
**배구**(排球) 〖체〗 volleyball／～시합 volleyball game.
**배구**(倍舊) redoubling (one's efforts)／～의 redoubled; increased.
**배금**(拜金) money worship／～주의 mammonism／～주의자 a mammonist; a money worshipper.
**배급**(配給) distribution 《통제 배급》 rationing; supply／～하다 distribute (to, among); supply (with); ration／～제도 [조직] distributing system[structure]／～소 distributing station[centre].
**빼기** 〖수〗 subtraction.
**배기**(排氣) ventilation; exhaust 《폐기》 used steam／～관 an exhaust pipe／～스 exhaust gas.
**배기다**¹ endure; stand; put up with; with-stand; hold out／배길 수 있는 bearable endurable／배길 수 없는 insufferable; unendurable.
**배기다**² (마치다) be hard; pinch; squeeze ·／의자가 등에～ a seat is hard on one's back.
**빼나다** excel (a person) in (sport); surpass (a person)／빼 난 eminent; distinguished.
**배나무** a pear tree.
**배낭**(背囊) a knapsack; a pack; a rucksack(D).
**배낭**(胚囊) 〖식〗 an embryo sac; a megaspore.
**배내**¹ from birth; in born; a baby's; of a newborn baby／배냇내새 the smell of a newborn baby／배냇니 a milk tooth／배냇병신 a congenital deformity.
**배내**² breeding animals from another person's stock and sharing the offspring with him／배냇닭 chickens raised on a share-basis.
**빼내다** ①《뽑다》 pull[draw] out; extract／못을～ pull out a nail ②《골라내다》 select; pick[single] out／지원자 100명 중 2명만～ select two only out of 100 applicants ③《돌라내다》 pilfer; steal／돈을～ pilfer from money ④《붙들린 몸을》 ransom (a person); secure (a person's) liberty ⑤《꾀어내다》 lure[entice] (a person) out 《고용인을》 hire (a person) away.
**배내밀다** turn one's nose up (at); sneer (at).
**빼놓다** ①《제쳐 놓다》 exclude; leave (a person) out; set aside; omit;· boycott (a person)／일요일을 빼놓고는 매일 사무실에 있다 I am always at office except Sunday. ②《뽑아 놓다》 draw[pull] out extract 《뿌리를》 uproot ③《골라놓다》 select; pick[single] out.
**배뇨**(排尿) urination／～하다 urinate; pass one's urine; pass water; make water.

배다¹ 《잉태하다》 conceive; get[become] pregnant /애를 ~ be with child; be pregnant; be in the family way; be knocked up《미·속》. はらむ

배다² ①《침윤하다》 soak[pierce] through; transude; permeate /피가 밴 붕대 a bandage saturated with blood ②《익숙하다》 get used; become accustomed /손에 밴 일 accustomed work /일이 손에 ~ get skilled (in). ひたる

배다³ 《조밀하다》 (be) close; dense; thick /나무를 배게 심다 plant trees close together. かんかくがせまい

빼다 ①《빼내다》 draw out[up]; take out 《칼 따위를》 draw; unsheathe; bare 《이 따위를》 extract; pull out ②《감산하다》 subtract[deduct, takeaway] (from) / 20에서 5를 ~ subtract[take] 5 from 20 ③《삭제하다》 remove; cancel; strike out /잉크의 얼룩을 ~ remove an ink-spot ④《꾸미다》 affect; assume; put on airs; pose (as) /점잔을 ~ be prudish[genteel]; do the genteel ⑤《회피하다》 evade; shirk; avoid /공무니를 ~ shirk one's responsibility ⑥《차려 입다》 dress[doll] up ⑦《함락하다》 capture; seize; carry ⑧《관계를 끊다》 /이 발을 빼겠다 I will wash my hands /이 사업에서 발을 빼겠다 I will wash my hands of this business. ぬく

배다르다 be born of a different mother; be half-blood /배다른 형제 half-brothers[sisters]; a steptorother[stepsister]. どうふくでない

배다리 a pontoon bridge. うきばし

빼닫이 a drawer ⇨서랍. ひきだし

배달(倍達) [the earliest name for] Korea /~ 민족[겨레] the Korean[Baidal] race.

배달(配達) delivery /~하다 deliver; distribute /~군 a carrier /~료 the delivery charge /우편 ~부 a postman; a mailman; a letter carrier /우유 ~원 a milkman /신문 ~부 newsboy; a newscarrier /~ 증명서 a delivery receipt. はいたつ

배당(配當) allotment 《주식의》 a dividend /~하다 allot; pay a dividend /이익 ~이 없다 pass a dividend /이익 ~을 받다 share in the profits. はいとう

배당금(配當金) a share; a dividend /특별 ~ an extra dividend. はいとうきん

배때벗다 (be) arrogant; haughty; insolent.

배덕(背德) immorality; demoralization; curruption /~의 immoral; currupt /~ 행위 immoral conduct.

배돌다 keep to oneself; avoid mixing with people; keep aloof from others. なかまにはいらない

배두렁이 a belly band for a baby 한두렁이. はらおび

배뚜로 aslant; obliquely; slope-wise. なめに

배뚜름하다, 빼뚜름하다 (be) inclined; slant; crooked. かたむいている

빼뚝거리다 wobble; limp ⇨비뚝거리다. よたよたあるく

빼뚤어지다 be tilted; be perverse ⇨비뚤어지다. かたむく

배란(排卵) 《생》 ovulation / ~하다 ovulate. はいらん

배랑뱅이 a beggar; a tramp; a hobo. こじき

배래 the offing; the open sea /~에 in the offing; offshore. さかなのふくぶ

배래기 《물고기의》 the abdominal region [belly] of a fish 《웃소매위》 strip of cloth along the sleeve-seam.

배려(配慮) care; concern; consideration 《진력》- trouble 《알선》 good offices /세 심한 ~ careful concern. はいりょ

배례(拜禮) a salutation; a salute; worship ~하다 salute; bow down; worship. はいれい

배롱나무 《식》 a crapemyrtle.

배리(背理) irrationality; unreasonableness /~의 irrational; absurd.

배리다 fishy; bloody ⇨비리다. なまくさい

배릿배릿 disgusting; sickening ⇨비릿비릿. けちけち

배릿하다 (be) somewhat fishy ⇨비릿하다. なまくさい

배맞다 make an illicit intercourse.

빼먹다 《빠뜨리다》 omit; leave out; skip 《돌려내다》 pilfer; filch; walk off with /몇 마디 빼먹은 게 있다 leave out few words. おとす

배면(背面) the back; the rear / ~ 공격 a rear attack /적의 ~을 치다 attack the enemy in the rear. はいめん

배명(拜命) ~하다 《명령을》 receive an order; have the word 《임명을》 accept an appointment. はいめい

배문(拜聞) ~하다 hear; be informed of. はいぶん

빼물다 《거만하게》 pout one's lips in a lordly manner.

배미 a strip[piece, patch] of rice paddy; an individual rice paddy.

배밀이¹ 《어린아이의》 crawl; creeping /~ 하다 crawl; creep.

배밀이² 《대패》 a three-groove plane.

배반(背反) betrayal /~하다 betray; turn against; rebel against /~자 a betrayer; a traitor /친구에게 ~당하다 be betrayed by one's friend. はいはん

배반(胚盤) 《식》 the germinal disk; 《동》 the blastodisk. はいばん

배백(拜白) "Yours very truly"; "From".

배번(背番) a uniform number.

배변(排便) a movement /~하다 evacuate [open] the bowels.

배별(拜別) leave-taking; saying good-by /~하다 part with; bid farewell to; leave; say good-by. おわかれ

배복(拜伏) prostrating oneself /~하다 humbly prostrate oneself. はいふく

배복(拜復) in reply to your letter[favor]; Dear Sirs. はいふく

**배본**(配本) distribution of books／～하다 distribute (*books*). はいほん

**배부**(配付) distribution／～하다 distribute (*among, to*); divide (*among*); deliver (*to*).

**배부 개가**(背夫改嫁) ～하다 betray *one's* husband and marry another person.

**배부 도주**(背夫逃走) ～하다 betray *one's* husband and run away.

**배부르다** full; have a full stomach 《임신하여》 be large with a child／배부르게 지내다 be well off／배부른 소리 하다 talk high and mighting. じゅうぶんにたべる

**배부른흥정** a take-it-or-leave-it sale[deal, proposition]; an indifference to the outcome (of *a transaction*).

**배불뚝이** a person with a potbelly. たいこばら

**배불리** eating one's fill heartily／～먹었다 I have had more than enough. まんぷくに

**배불리다** fill *one's* stomach. はらをふくらます

**배비**(配備) disposition; arrangement／～하다 dispose; arrange. はいび

**배빈**(陪賓) a person invited with the guest of honor. ばいひん

**배사**(拜辭) refusal／～하다 decline; refuse [to accept]. はいじ

**배사**(拜謝) thanking; acknowledgement; appreciation／～하다 thank (*one*) cordially; express *one's* gratitude. はいしゃ

**배사**(背斜) 《지》 anticline／～의 anticline／～ 습곡 anticline. はいしゃ

**배삭**(排朔) monthly allocation／～하다 allocate by the month.

**배상**(賠償) reparation; indemnity; compensation／～하다 compensate; pay (*one*) for; make reparation[amends]／～금 an indemnity; reparation／～책임 a liability of reparation／～자 an indemnitor／～을 청구하다 demand reparation. ばいしょう

**배상군** a person who is insolent and sly.

**배색**(配色) a colour scheme; colouring／～하다 arrange the colours. はいしょく

**배서**(背書) [an] endorsement／～하다 endorse (*a check*); back (*a bill*)／～인 an endorser／피～인 an endorsee.

**배석**(陪席) sitting with a superior／～하다 sit with [one's superior]; (재판 따위에) be present as an assistant／～판사 an assoaiate judge. ばいせき

**배선**(配線) 《전선》 wiring／～하다 wire a power line (*a house*). はいせん

**배선**(配船) allocation[arrangement, assignment] of vessels[ships].

**배설**(排泄) excretion; evacuation／～하다 excrete; evacuate; discharge／～물 excrements／～기관 the excretive organs. はいせつ

**배설**(排卨) clearing[removing] of snow／～하다 clear[remove] snow／～차 a snow-plough.

**배설**(排設) arrangement; preparation; provision／～하다 arrange [vessel for offering on the altar on a fête day or fesitival in the religious celebration].

**배속**(配屬) attachment; assignment／～하다 attach; assign／～장교 a military officer attached to a school. はいぞく

**배수**(排水) drainage; sewerage／～하다 drain; pump out／～량 displacement [tonnage]. はいすい

**배수**(拜受) receiving with thanks／～하다 receive; accept. はいじゅ

**배수**(倍數) a multiple; a double number／공～ a common multiple／～비례 multiple proportion. ばいすう

**배수**(配水) supply[distribution] of water／～하다 supply[distribute] water／～관 a conduit pipe／～지(池) a distributing reservoir. はいすい

**배수성**(背水性) 《식》 negative hydrotropism.

**배수진**(背水陣) a position taken up with a river behind the troops; burning the bridges／～을 치다 fight with *one's* back to the wall. はいすいのじん

**배숙**(一熟) boiled pear preserved in honey.

**배스듬하다** be slightly inclined; be a bit askew／모자를 배스듬히 쓰다 have *one's* hat on askew. ややななめになっている

**배승**(陪乘) riding in the same car[carriage]／～하다 ride in the same car[carriage].

**배시**(陪侍) attending[waiting] upon *one's* superior／～하다 wait upon *one's* superior. ばいじ

**배식**(陪食) dining with [one's superior]／～하다 dine with [one's superior]; partake of a dinner with. ばいしょく

**배신**(背信) a breach of faith; betrayal／～하다 betray *one's* ccnfidence; break faith／～행위 a breach of faith. はいしん

**배심**(背心) a traitorous mind; a treacherous mind. はいしん

**배심**(陪審) jury／～하다 hold jury／～제도 jury system／～원 《총칭》 a jury 《개인》 a juror. ばいしん

**배아**(胚芽) a germ; an embryo bud／～미(米) wholesome rice. はいが

**배안**(拜顏) ～하다 have the honor of seeing (*a person*). はいがん

**배알** entrails; guts ○창자. はらわた

**배알**(拜謁) an audience (with *the king*)／～하다 be granted an audience; have an audience of. はいえつ

**배앓이** 《의》 colic; gripes; stomach trouble's. ふくつう

**빼앗기다** ① 《탈취》 be taken (*a thing*) away 《도난》 be robbed of (*a thing*); 《약탈》 be plundered 《박탈》 be deprived of (*a thing*)／돈을 ～ be robbed of *one's* money ② 《매혹》 be fascinated; be captivated; be absorbed／음악에 넋을 ~ be e-

빼앗다 ①《탈취하다》snatch (a thing) from (a person); take (a thing) away from (a person); 《훔치다》rob (a person) of (a thing); 《약탈하다》plunder/왕위를 ~ usurp the throne ②《매혹하다》fascinate; charm/넋을 ~ captivate (a person) ③《짓밟다》seduce[violate, dishonor]《정조를》; 《인권을》infringe /정조를 ~ violate[seduce, dishonor] a woman. うばう

배액(倍額) double the amount (of); twice the cost. ばいがく

배양(培養) culture; cultivation/~하다 cultivate; grow; breed/~소《세균의》a nursery; a farm. ばいよう

빼어나다 excel (in) ⇨빼나다. めだつ

배역(配役) the cast (of a play)/~을 정하다 cast[assign] a part to (players). はいやく

배역(背逆) betrayal; turning against[upon]; rebels/~하다 betray; turn against; rebel against; turn upon.
おんにさからうこと

배열(排列) arrangement; disposition/~하다 arrange; dispose; put in order; array. はいれつ

배엽(胚葉)《식》a germinal layer.

배영(背泳) the backstroke [swim]/~ 선수 a backstroke swimmer. はいえい

배외(排外) anti-foreign/~하다 exclude as foreign/~ 사상 anti-foreign ideas/주의 exclusionism/~주의자 an exclusionist. はいがい

배우(俳優) a player《남자》an actor《여자》an actress/인기 ~ a star/무대 ~ a stage actor[actress]/ 영화~ a film actor[actress]. はいゆう

배우다 《학습》learn; be taught; take lessons in[on]; 《연구하다》study; take a course in《연습하다》practice; be trained in/수영을 ~ learn how to swim. まなぶ

배우자(配偶者) a match; a life partner; a spouse/적당한 ~를 고르다 get a suitable match for one. はいぐうしゃ

배우자(配偶子) 《생》a gamete.

배움 study; learning/~의 길 the pursuit of studies; learning. まなび

배움배움 scholarly attainments; learning. がくしき

배움터 a school; a place where learning is taking place. がっこう

배웅 seeing (a person) off; a send-off/~하다 show (one) out; see (one) off.

배유(胚乳) 《식》an albumen; an endosperm. はいにゅう

배율(倍率) magnification; magnifying power. ばいりつ

배은 망덕(背恩忘德) ingratitude/~하다 be ungrateful; lose one's gratitude/~한 사람 an ungrateful person[man]; an ingrate. おんをわすれてそむくこと

배음(倍音) 《물》harmonics; 《음》an overtone; a harmonic [tone]. ばいおん

배일(排日) anti-Japanese. はいにち

배일성(背日性) 《식》negative heliotropism; apheliotropism. ごこうせい

배임(背任) breach of trust; misappropriation/~ 행위 an act in violation of one's duty. はいにん

배자(排字) arrangement of letters/~하다 arrange letters.

배자(胚子) an embryo. はいし

배자(褙子) a kind of vest[waistcoat].
からぎぬ

배재기 a pregnant woman. にんぷ

배짱 1《버티는 힘》self-confidence; boldness; pluck; nerve · ~센 daring; bold; plucky; spunky ~없는 white-livered; faint-hearted 2《속마음》mind; heart; intention. たんりょく

배적(配謫) banishment; deportation; exile; condemnation to exile/~하다 banish; deport.

배전(配電) supply of electric power/~하다 supply electricity; distribute power/~선 a service wire/~ 회사[소] a power distribution company[station].
はいでん

배점(配點) distribution[allotting] of marks.

배정(拜呈) presentation; offering/~하다 present; compliment. はいてい

배정(配定) allocation; assignment; apportionment/~하다 allot[assign] (work) to (each student); assign. はいぶん

배정과(一正果) sliced pears preserved in honey.

배제(排除) exclusion; elimination; removal/~하다 exclude; eliminate; remove /~법《논》the method of exclusion/물을 ~하다 pump out water. はいじょ

배제(配劑) dispensation; prescription.
はいざい

배종(陪從) attendance/~하다 wait upon [attend on] one's superior. ばいじゅう

배종(胚種) 《식》a germ; a germinal vesicle/~ 세포 a germinal cell.

배주(胚珠) 《식》an ovule; germinal vesicles. はいしゅ

배죽거리다, 삐죽거리다 twist one's mouth; pout one's lips 《경멸하다》curl[screw up] one's lips. ふくれつらをする

배중률(排中律) 《논》the principle of the excluded middle.

배증(倍增) doubling; growing double/~하다 be doubled; increase double; redouble ばいぞう

배지기《씨름》a belly grab; a belly throw. こしなげ

배지성(背地性) 《식》apogeotropism; negative geotropism. はいちせい

배진(背進) backing 《철수》withdrawl/~하다 fall back; retire; withdraw.

배질 rowing; sailing. ふねをこぐこと

배차(排次) arrangement of the order;

배차(配車) allocation of cars; marshalling of cars／〜하다 allocate[marshall] cars はいしゃ
배참 venting one's anger [for being scolded] on (someone else)／〜하다 vent one's anger on. おこりをぶちまけること
배척 a kind of hammer-claw for pulling out large nails. くぎぬき
배척(排斥) rejection; exclusion; a boycott／〜하다 reject; exclude 《상품을》 boycott 《부정한 수단으로》 oust (a person from a place). はいせき
배청(拜聽) hearing／〜하다 hear; listen (to); give one's ear (to). はいちょう
배추 Chinese cabbage; celery cabbage／ 〜 김치 pickled cabbage. はくさい
배출(排出) 〜하다 discharge; exhaust; issue／〜관 an exhaust[a discharge] pipe. はいしゅつ
배출(輩出) coming forward in succession; appearing one after another／〜하다 《내다》 produce a large[great] number of 《나오다》 appear in numbers; appear one after. はいしゅつ
배치(背馳) contrariety; contradiction／ 〜하다 be contrary to; run counter to; contradict (each other)／이것은 사실과 완전히 〜한다 This is utterly opposed to the fact. はいち
배치(排置) arrangement／〜하다 arrange; place in a row; lay out. はいち
배치(配置) arrangement; disposition／〜하다 arrange; distribute 《부서에》 post; station; detail. はいち
빼치다 《빠져나오게》 let get away; let go of 《끝을 빨게》 sharpen; taper; put a point on. ぬけるようにする
배타(排他) exclusion／〜적 exclusive; cliquish／〜주의 exclusivism; exclusionism. はいた
배탈(一頉) a stomach upset[disorder, trouble]／〜나다 have a stomach ache; suffer from indigestion. ふくつう
배태(胚胎) ①《임신》 pregnancy; germination ②《원인》 origin; germ／〜하다 be pregnant; originate (in). はいたい
배토기(排土機) earth-moving equipment.
배통기다 turn up one's nose (at)／〜배내밀다. おごりたかぶって強情がる
배통이 belly; stomach. はら
배트작거리다 stagger 비트적거리다. よちよちあるく
배틀거리다 stagger; reel; falter; shamble／배틀거리며 with faltering[tottering] steps. よろめく
배틀다 twist; wrench; screw; wring. ねじる
배틀리다 get twisted; be distorted; be wrenched. ねじられる
배편(一便) shipping[steamer] service／〜으로 by ship[boat]／〜으로 물건을 보내다 send a thing by boat. ふなびん
배포 scale[breadth] of thinking; one's capicity／〜가 크다 be magnaninmous.
배포(排布, 排鋪) planning; scheme 《배치》 arrangement. けいかくすること
배풍(背風) a fair[tail] wind. うしろかぜ
배필(配匹) a spouse; a partner for life; a mate; a consort／〜하다 vent choose a suitable match (for one)／천생 〜이다 be a well-matched couple (pair). はいぐうしゃ
배하(拜賀) congratulations; greetings／ 〜하다 congratulate／신년 〜식 the New Year's ceremony. はいが
배하다(拜一) receive [a government appointment]. かんしょくをはいじゅする
배합(配合) 《결합》 combination 《조화》 harmony; match 《혼합》 mixture／〜하다 match; combine; harmonize; mix／그 〜은 잘 어울린다 The combination is a becoming one. はいごう
배행(陪行) attendance 《배웅》 going along partway with a departing person.
배혁(背革) a leather-back／〜 제본 quarter -binding.
배화(排貨) a boycott [movement] (against); boycotting／〜하다 boycott. はいか
배화교(拜火敎) 《종》 fire-worship; Zoroastrianism; Parsiism.
배회(徘徊)／〜하다 loiter[knock] about; stroll／여기저기 〜하다 wander from place to place. はいかい
배후(背後) the rear; the back／〜에 at the rear[back] (of); behind／〜 조종자 a wirepuller; a man behind the scene. はいご

빽 ①《소리》 whistling; piping ②《빽빽하게》 closely; densely; thickly. きゃあっ
백(白) white. はく
백(百) a[one] hundred／〜 번째 the hundredth. ひゃく
백(伯) 《백작》 a count; an earl〈미〉;《맏형》 the eldest brother. はくしゃく
백가서(百家書) the books of all scholars. おおのがくしゃのちょしょ
백계 노인(白系露人) White Russians.
백곡(白穀) all kinds of grain[crops].
백골(白骨) 《뼈》 a white bone; a skeleton 《목기・목골》 wooden vessels(아무 칠도 하지 않은)／〜 난망이다 be unforgettable. はっこつ
백곰(白一) 《동》 a white bear.
백공(百工) 《장색》 all sorts of artisans 《백관》 all officials. ひゃっこう
백과(白瓜) 《식》 a white cucumber[muskmelon].
백과(百科) all kinds[branches] of learning／〜 사전 an encyclopedia. ひゃっか
백관(百官) all the government officials ／문무(文武) 〜 civil and military officers. ひゃっかん
백구(白鷗) 《조》 a white [sea] gull. かもめ
백군(白軍) 《역》 the white Russian Army

**《경기에서》** the white team. はくぐん
**백금**(白金) platinum; white gold;《화》Pt. はっきん
**백기**(白旗) a white flag《항복》a flag of truce. しろいはた
**백날**(百一) ①《아이의 백일》a hundredth day of a child's birth ②《많은 날》a hundred days; a very long time. こどもがうまれてひゃくにちになるひ
**백납**(白一)《의》vitiligo; leucoma／〜먹다 have a leucoma. はくろう
**백내장**(白內障)《의》cataract.
**백년 가약**(百年佳約) a plight of eternal love; a marriage bond／〜을 맺다 become man and wife for weal or woe; cast in one's lot with a partner for life. ふうふのぶかいちぎり
**백년초**(百年草)《식》a cactus (pl. 〜es, -ti). サボテン
**백년 해로**(百年偕老) growing old togeter in wedded life／〜하다 grow old together in wedded life.
**백대**(百代) one hundred generations; a very long time. ひゃくだい
**백대하**(白帶下)《의》leucorrh[o]ea; whites《속》.
**백도**(白桃) a white peach.
**백동**(白銅)《합금》nickel《백동화》a nickel [coin]. はくどう
**백두**(白頭) a white head. はくとう
**백랍**(白蠟)《초의 원료》white[refined] wax《벌레집》insect wax. はくろう
**백랍**(白鑞) solder; pewter. はくろう
**백련**(白蓮)《식》《연꽃》a white lotus《목련》a white magnolia. びゃくれん
**백로**(白鷺)《조》an egret; a snowy[white] heron. しらさぎ
**백로**(白露)《이슬》white dew《계절》the 16th of the 24th seasonal divisons of a year. はくろ
**백마**(白馬) a white horse. はくば
**백막**(白膜)《해》the sclerotic; the sclera／〜염 scleritis.
**백만**(百萬) a[one] million／〜 원 one million won. ひゃくまん
**백만 장자**(百萬長者) a millionaire; a multimillionaire. ひゃくまんちょうじゃ
**백면**(白麵)《가루》buckwheat flour《국수》buckwheat vermicelli.
**백면 서생**(白面書生) a stripling; a green horn; a novice. はくめんしょせい
**백모**(伯母) an aunt; an auntie《아줌마》an aunty. はくぼ
**백목**(白木) cotton cloth. もめん
**백목련**(白木蓮)《식》a yulan; a white magnolia. しろもくれん
**백묵**(白墨) a chalk : 분필. はくぼく
**백문**(白文) ①《관인이 없는 문서》a written statement without government seal ②《주석이 없는 한문》an unpunctuated Chinese composition[text].
**백문 불여 일견**(百聞不如一見) Seeing is believing., An eye finds more truth than two ears. ひゃくぶんいっけんにしかず

**백물**(百物) all sorts of goods[things]. もろもろのもの
**백미**(白米) polished rice; cleaned rice／〜병《각기》beriberi. はくまい
**백미**(白眉) the best (of); the finest example [of the kind]. はくび
**백반**(白礬) alum. みょうばん
**백반**(白飯) boiled rice; cooked rice [not mixed with any other cereals]. はくはん
**백발**(白髮) white[gray] hair; snowy hair／〜의 white[gray]-haired. はくはん
**백발 백중**(百發百中) all hits; a hundred hits to a hundred shots／〜하다 never miss the mark. ひゃっぱつひゃくちゅう
**백방**(白放) acquittal; exculpation／〜하다 exculpate. むざいほうめん
**백방**(百方) ①《여러 가지 방법》various ways; every way／〜으로 손을 쓰다 try all means available／〜으로 노력하다 make every effort ②《여러 방향》every direction; all sides／〜으로 사람을 구하다 all over for a person. あらゆるほうほう
**백배**(百倍) a[one] hundred times／〜의 centuple／〜하다 centuple. ひゃくばい
**백배**(百拜) bowing many times／〜 사죄하다 make[offer] an apology by bowing many times. ひゃっぱい
**빽빽하다** ①《촘촘하다》(be) close《조밀하다》(be) dense; thick《가득차다》(be) packed [to the full]／빽빽하게 closely; thickly; densely; tightly ②《구멍이 막혀》be choked《갑갑하다》stuffy／코가 〜 My nose is clogged[stuffy]. ③《소견이 좁다》(be) fussy[narrow-minded]／그는 빽빽한 사람이다 He is a narrow-minded person. こんもり茂っている
**백범**(白帆) a white sail／〜선 a boat with a white sail. しらほ
**백변**(白邊) sap [wood]; alburnum.
**백병**(百病) all kinds of diseases[illnesses]. ひゃくびょう
**백병**(白兵) a naked sword／〜전 hand-to-hand fight; a close combat; fighting at close quarters. はくへい
**백부**(伯父) an uncle; one's father's elder brother. はくふ
**백분**(白粉) face powder; toilet powder／〜을 바르다 powder one's face. はくふん
**백분**(百分) one-hundred part／〜하다 divide into a[one] hundred parts／〜의 20 twenty-hundredths; twenty percent／〜율 percentage.
**백비탕**(白沸湯) boiling water. わかしたゆ
**백사**(白沙) white sand／〜장 sandy beach.
**백사**(百事) all kinds of matters.
**백사과**(白一)《식》a white melon.
**백삼**(白蔘) white ginseng. しろにんじん
**백색**(白色) white [color]／〜 인종 the white race; white people. はくしょく
**백서**(白書) a White Paper; a White Book／경제[외교] 〜 the Economic[Diplomatic] White Paper. はくしょ
**백서**(白鼠)《동》a white rat.
**백석**(白石) a white stone. はくせき

**백석**(白晳) white [incomplexion]/ ～하다 (be) white[-skinned]; be of white complexion. はくせき

**백선**(白癬) 『의』favous. はくせん

**백설**(白雪) white snow; snow/～같이 흰 snow-white; white as snow/～이 덮인 산 a snowcapped mountain. はくせつ

**백설기**(白一) steamed rice-cake.

**백설탕**(白雪糖) white sugar; castor-sugar.

**백성**(百姓) 《국민》the people; a nation 《서민》the common people. ひゃくしょう

**백세**(百世) one hundred generation; forever. ひゃくせい

**백수**(白首) a head of white hair; a white-haired person. はくしゅ

**백수**(百獸) all kinds of animals/～의 왕 the king of beasts. ひゃくじゅう

**백수건달**(白手乾達) an idler. のらくらもの

**백수 풍신**(白首風神) a white-haired gentleman of fine[distinguished] appearance. ろうじんのりっぱなふうさい

**백숙**(白熟) a dish of fish or meat boiled in plain water.

**백씨**(伯氏) your[his] elder brother.

**백십자**(白十字) the white cross.

**백악**(白堊) 《백회》chalk 《흰 벽》a white wall/～관 the White House/～기 『지』 the cretaceous period/～질 cement/～층 『지』 chalk pit. はくあ

**백안시**(白眼視) ～하다 《흘겨보다》 frown upon; look with indifference 《냉정하게》 look coldly upon 《의심하여》 look askance at. はくがんし

**백야**(白夜) a white night.

**백약**(百藥) all kinds of medicines/～지장 the best of all medicines/～이 무효하다 All medicines prove useless.

**백양**(白楊) 『식』a white poplar. はくよう

**백양**(白羊) 『동』a white sheep.

**백양궁**(白羊宮) 『천』the Aries; the Ram.

**백어**(白魚) 『어』a whitebait. しらうお

**백연**(白鉛) white lead 《분 만드는》 ceruse.

**백열**(白熱) 《온도》white heat; incandescence 《열정》a climax; enthusiasm/～전 hot fighting/～등(燈) a glow lamp /～화하다 glow white. はくねつ

**백옥**(白玉) a white gem[bead]; a white precious stone. はくぎょく

**백옥**(白屋) a hovel; a humble cottage. まずしいひといえ

**백운**(白雲) white clouds. はくうん

**백운모**(白雲母) 『광』white[common] mica.

**백운석**(白雲石) 『광』dolomite.

**백의**(白衣) a white robe[dress]/～ 민족 the Korean people; the white-clad folk /～ 용사 a hero in white. はくい

**백인**(白人) a white man; a Caucasian; a white《속》/～종 the white race; the whites. はくじん

**백인**(白刃) a drawn[naked] sword[saber] a naked blade. はくじん

**백일**(白日) 《백주》broad daylight; the daytime 《맑은 하늘》bright day/～몽 a day-dream; a revery/～하에 드러나다 be brought to light. はくじつ

**백일**(百日) 《어린이의》one hundredth day 《백 일 간》a[one] hundred days/～ 잔치 the feast[celebration] of a hundred-days-old baby. ひゃくにち

**백일 기도**(百日祈禱) praying for a hundred days. ひゃくにちきとう

**백일재**(百日齋) 『종』a Buddhist memorial service on the hundredth day after (*a person's*) death.

**백일초**(百日草) 『식』a zinnia; a youth-and-old-age. ひゃくにちそう

**백일해**(百日咳) 『의』whooping cough; pertussis. ひゃくにちぜき

**백일홍**(百日紅) 『식』a crape-myrtle; a garden zinnia. さるすべり

**백작**(伯爵) a count; an earl《영》/～ 부인 a countess. はくしゃく

**백장** a butcher 《욕》son-of-a-bitch; a bastard. はくちょう

**백저**(白苧) grass-cloth bleached white.

**백전**(白戰) 《무기 없는 싸움》fist fighting [fighe]; 《글 시합》a verse-writing contest. はくせん

**백전 노장**(百戰老將) a veteran; an old timer; an old campaigner; a person of experience. ひゃくせんろうしょう

**백전 백승**(百戰百勝) ～하다 win every battle [that is fought]; be ever-victorious; be invincible. ひゃくせんひゃくしょう

**백절 불굴**(百折不屈) ～의 indefatigable; indomitable. ひゃくせつふっくつ

**백점**(百點) a[one] hundred points 《만점》 full marks; a perfect score. ひゃってん

**백정**(白丁) a butcher ⇒백장. はくちょう

**백조**(白鳥) 『조』《고니》a swan 《해오라기》 a white heron. はくちょう

**백종**(百種) various kinds; all kinds. ひゃくしゅう

**백주**(白晝) broad daylight; the daytime /～에 blindly. はくちゅう

**백주**(白酒) white liquor[wine].

**백중**(伯仲)¹ *one's* eldest brother and second brother.

**백중**(伯仲)² 《맞섬》being equal (*to*)/～하다 be equally matched 《경기에서》 be well contested. はくちゅう

**백중**(百中) ㉠ ～날 July 15th of lunar month.

**백지**(白紙) ①《흰종이》white paper ②《상태》 a clean slate ③《공지》 a clean[blank] sheet of paper/～ 동맹 sending in blank examination. はくし

**백지도**(白地圖) a blank[an outline] map.

**빽지르다** shout; shriek. きゃっとさけぶ

**백척 간두**(百尺竿頭) extremities; the last extremity. ひじょうにきけんなじょうたい

**백천 만사**(百千萬事) everything; all sorts of things. あらゆること

**백철광**(白鐵鑛) 『광』marcasite; white iron pyrites.

**백청**(白清) honey of fine quality; refined honey. しろくひんしつのよいはちみつ

**백출**(百出) ～하다 arise[appear, pop up]

in great numbers／그 문제로 의논이 ~하다 The matter become the subject of heated discussion. ひゃくしゅつ

**백치**(白痴, 白癡) idiocy; imbecility 《사람》 an idiot; an imbecile. はくち

**백탄**(白炭) fine charcoal; charcoal of superior quality. はくたん

**백태**(白苔) ①《혓바닥의》 a coating on the tongue ②《눈의》 a morbid coating on the eyeball that interferes with vision.

**백토**(白土) white clay; terra alba(L.). はくど

**백통** nickel; white brass. はくどう

**백판**(白板) ①《흰 널빤지》 a white board ②《형편》 having nothing. しろいた

**백팔**(百八) one hundred and eight／~ 번뇌《종》 the hundred-and-eight torments of mankind／~ 염주 a Buddhist rosary of 108 beads.

**백팔십도**(百八十度) ¶ ~ 전환하다 make a complete face about (in one's stand).

**백편**(白―) steamed rice-cake.

**백포도주**(白葡萄酒) white wine 《프랑스산》 sherry. 《독일산》 hock.

**백학**(白鶴) a crane. はくつる

**백합**(白蛤) 《어》 a kind of clam.

**백합**(百合) a lily. ゆり

**백해 무익**(百害無益) ~하다 do more harm than good. ひゃくがいむえき

**백혈구**(白血球) 《해》 a white blood corpuscle. はっけっきゅう

**백혈병**(白血病) 《의》 leukemia. はっけつびょう

**백형**(伯兄) one's eldest brother. ちょうけい

**백호**(白狐) a white[silver] fox; a blue [an arctic] fox. しろぎつね

**백호**(白濠) White Australia／~주의 the White Australia principle[policy].

**백화**(百花) all varieties of flowers.

**백화**(白話) Chinese as spoken. はくわ

**백화점**(百貨店) a department store; the stores《영》. ひゃっかてん

**밴대질** sexual practice between women; Lesbianism／~하다[치다] a woman has sexual relations with another woman. どうせいあい

**밴댕이** 《어》 a big-eyed herring.

**밴둥거리다** loaf away; idle away one's time. ぶらぶらなまける

**밴들거리다** loaf[idle] away one's time. なまけてあそんでいる

**뺄셈** subtraction. げんぽう

**뱀** a snake 《구렁이》 a serpent／~ 같은 snaky. へび

**뱀딸기** 《식》 Indian[mock] strawberry; Duchesnea indica《학명》. へびいちご

**뱀벌이** upbringing; breeding; training／ ~가 있다 be well brought up.

**뱀장어**(―長魚) 《어》 an eel.

**뱁새** 《조》 a Korean crow-tit; Suthora webbiana fulvicauda《학명》. しじゅうから

**뱁새눈이** a person with slitted[narrow] eyes. ひじょうにちいさくほそいめ

**뱃가죽** flesh[skin] of the belly.

**뱃고동** a boat whistle.

**뱃구레** the abdomen. せんたい

**뺏기다** get grabbed; be robbed of ⇨빼앗기다. うばわれる

**뱃길** a [ship's] course; a waterway／~ 안내자 a pilot. かいろ

**뱃노래** a boatman's song; a chant[e]y; a sailor's song.

**뱃놀이** boating [excursion]; a boat ride 〈미〉／~ 가다 go for a sail; go rowing [boating]. ふねあそび

**뱃놈** a sailor; a seaman.

**뺏다** grab ⇨빼앗다. うばう

**뱃대끈** 《여자용》 a woman's bloomer sash 《마소용》 a cinch. おび

**뱃덧** a stomach disorder; disagreement of food.

**뱃머리** the bow; the prow; the head／~ 를 돌리다 wind a ship. せんしゅ

**뱃멀미** seasickness; nausea／~하다 get seasick／~하는[하지 않는] 사람 a bad [good] sailor. ふねによう

**뱃바람** a wind that one is sailing directly into. ふねのかぜ

**뱃밥** oakum; ca[u]lking.

**뱃병**(―病) stomach trouble; intestinal upsets／~이 나다 have stomach trouble; have a stomach upset.

**뱃사공**(―沙工) a boatman(pl.-men); a sailor; a seaman(pl.-men).

**뱃사람** ①《선주》 a shipowner ②《뱃사공》 a sailor; a seaman; a mariner／~이 되다 go to sea. せんしゅ

**뱃삯** 《승객의》 passage; a fare 《나룻배의》 ferryboat charge 《용선료》 charterage 《화물의》 freight [rates].

**뱃살** abdominal muscle／~을 잡다 shake with laughter; split one's sides.

**뱃소리** a boatman's song ⇨뱃노래.

**뱃속** ①《복부》 the stomach／~이 아프다 have a stomach-ache ②《속마음》 mind; heart; intention／~이 검다 be black-hearted; be evil minden. はらのなか

**뱃심** greediness; impudence／~ 좋다 be shameless and greedy; be impudent.

**뱃일** work aboard ship.

**뱃자반**(―佐飯) fish salted at the fishing ground. ぎょじょうで干したさかな

**뱃장사** peddling with a boat／~꾼 a bumboat man.

**뱃장작**(―長斫) firewood brought in by boat[ship].

**뱃전** the sides of a boat／~이 기울어지다 A boat lists to one side. ふなばた

**뱃줄** a boat line[rope]; a hawser.

**뱃지게** an A-frame carrier used by stevedores.

**뱃짐** a [ship's] cargo; a freight／~을 싣다 take in cargo.

**뱅**, round; around〈미〉／~ 둘러싸다 surround completely. ふらふら

**뱅그레, 벵그레** smiling ⇨빙그레. にっこり

**뱅그르르, 뺑그르르** ¶ ~돌다 turn round and round. くるくる

**뱅글거리다** smile; beam. にっこりする
**뱅뱅, 뺑뺑** round and round. ふらふら
**뺑소니** flight; fleeing; running/~치다 run away. とうそう
**뱅어(一魚)** 【어】 an icefish; a whitebait /~젓 salted whitebait. しらうお
**-뱅이** one; person /가난~ a poorman; a pauper/비렁~ a beggar.
**뱅충맞다** (be) stupid; thickheaded; bashful; clumsy ⇨뱅충맞다/뱅충맞게 clumsily. おろかではにかみやだ
**뱅충맞이** a stupid and bashful person; a dolt; a coward. おろかなはにかみや
**뱉다** ①(입밖으로) spit out; spew (숨을) breathe out/가래를 ~ cough up phlegm/뱉듯이 say disdainfully/그는 먹을 것을 다 뱉어 버렸다 He threw all he had eaten ②(물건을) disgorge; give up; vomit. はく
**빠드득** grinding; creaking ⇨바드득. きいきい
**뱌비작거리다** rub and rub ⇨비비다. しきりにこする
**뱌슬거리다** avoid coming to grips with (a job, a problem); keep aloof. のがれる
**뱐둥거리다** idle away one's time ⇨뱐둥거리다. ぶらぶらなまける
**뱐미주룩하다** (be) slightly bulging out. ちょっとつきでいる
**뱐뱐하다** (be) handsome ⇨반반하다. ちょっとよさそうだ
**뱐주그레하다** (be) rather nice-looking ⇨반주그레하다. だいたいよさそうだ
**뱐죽거리다** pert; act flippantly; act flip. しきりにみせびらかす
**뺨** a cheek/복스럽게 생긴 ~ plump cheeks/불그레한 ~ a ruddy[rosy] cheek/~을 때리다 slap (a person) on the cheek /~을 불룩하게 하다 puff out one's cheeks (불만이 있어) be sulky. ほほ
**뱜뛰어가다** caper; jump about. びょんびょんとんでいく
**버걱, 뻐걱** creaking; squeaking; grating. きいきい
**버겁다** (be) hard to handle; beyond one's control; unmanageable/이 일은 나에게 ~ This work is beyond my capacity. おさえられない
**뻐꾸기** 【조】 a cuckoo. かっこうとり
**뻐꾹** the call of the cuckoo. かっこう
**버그러뜨리다** crack; split; loosen. そらす
**버그러지다** loosen; separate.
**뻐그러지다** get broken. そらされる
**버그르르, 뻐그르르** simmering ⇨바그르르.
**버근하다** (be) ajar[open]. すきがある
**뻐근하다** ①(몸이) feel heavy[stiff]; grow stiff/어깨가 ~ feel stiff in the shoulders ②(일이) (be) hard; tiring; exhausting. けだるいかんじがする
**버글거리다** ①(끓다) boil; seethe; simmer ②(거품이) bubble up ③(많이 모여) swarm[be crowded] (with); teem; wriggle. ぶくぶくあわだつ
**버글버글** (물이) seethingly (거품이) foamily; bubbling. ぶくぶくあわだつ
**버금** the next; the second in order/~가다 be in the second place; rank next up. ついでのばん
**빠끔하다** be open. ぽっかりひらいている
**버긋하다** (be) gappy; open; be loosened a bit; be ajar. すきまがあいている
**빼기다** 《잘난 체하다》 put on airs; give oneself airs. たかぶる
**뻐덕뻐덕** ~하다 be dried out stiff[hard]. ざらざらしている
**버덩** a barren plateau; a waste land overrun with weeds. こうげん
**버둥거리다** wriggle; squirm [kick and]; struggle. しきりにもがく
**버드나무** a willow. やなぎ
**버드러지다, 뻐드러지다** ①(밖으로) warp; be prominent/버드러진이 a prominent tooth ②(뻣뻣해지다) stiffen; get stiff; become rigid ③(죽다) [stiffen and] die; drop death. でっぱっている
**뻐드렁니** a projecting[prominent] tooth.
**뻐드렁이** a person with protruding tooth. でっぱのひと
**버드름하다** (be) slightly protruding; somewhat prominent. てっぱっている
**뻐득뻐득하다** (언행이) (be) rude (눈이) grim; fierce (입안이) astringent; puckery. すなおでない
**버들** a willow. やなぎ
**버들개지** a pussy willow. やなぎのはな
**버들고리** a willow[wicker] trunk; a hamper. やなぎこうり
**버들눈** a willow bud.
**버들치** 【어】 Moroco oxycephalus (학명). あぶらはや
**버듬하다** protrude; somewhat prominent ⇨버드름하다. てっぱっている
**버러지** an insect ⇨벌레. むし
**버럭** suddenly; [all] of a sudden/~ 화를 내다 explode with rage. かっと
**버렁** ①(범위) a scope; an extent; a sphere ②(장갑) thick gloves used in hawking. はんい
**버력**¹ (광) rock with no mineral content; low-grade ore.
**버력**² (천벌) a curse; an evil spell/~입다 be cursed. のろい
**버르장머리** a habit; manners ⇨버릇. くせ
**버르장이** a habit; manners ⇨버릇. くせ
**버르적거리다, 뻐르적거리다** writhe; squirm; struggle. しきりにもがく
**버르집다** ①(숨은 일을) reveal; disclose; expose; lay bare ②(벌려 펴다) cut open; cut and enlarge; stretch ③(과장하다) exaggerate. あばく
**버름 하다** (be) slightly open; ajar; have a crack between. すきまがあいている
**버릇** ①(습관) a habit; a way; a customary/고치기 힘든 ~ an inveterate/술 마시는 ~ an intemperate[a liquor] habit /담배 피우는 것이 ~이 되었다 Smoking has grown into a habit with me. ②(성벽) a peculiarity; a characteristic

**버릇다** 《경향》a propensity／말~ one's peculiar way of speaking ③《에의》manners; etiquette 《품행》breeding 《행실》behaviour／~없다 be badly brought up; be ill-mannered／~ 들이다 discipline. くせ

**버릇다** dig open; scatter. 掘りさらえる

**버리다**¹ ①《내던지다》throw away; cast [fling] away; cast aside／쓰레기를 ~ dump refuse ②《포기·방기》abandon; forsake; desert; give up／버림받다 be abandoned[forsaken, deserted]／남편에게 버림받다 be deserted[left] by one's husband／아이를 ~ ruin; spoil／매를 아끼면 아이를 버린다 Spare the rod and spoil the child. すてる

**버리다²** 《끝마치다》finish; [get] through; get done; up／다 읽어 ~ read through (a book)／다 써 ~ use up.

**버림치** an useless thing; a waster. くず

**버마재비** 〖충〗a [praying-]mantis; a rearhorse.

**버무리다** mix up; compound／나물을 ~ fix[mix] a salad. こんごうする

**버물다** be involved (in a crime); be mixed up. かんけいする

**버물리다** ①《피동》get mixed ②《사역》get (a person) to mix. まじる

**버새** 〖동〗a hinny.

**버석** rustlingly; with a rustle; with a rustling sound ⇒바삭. ばさっと

**버썩** [dried up] completely ⇒바삭. しっかりと

**버석거리다** rustle; make a rustle／낙엽이 바람에 ~ The fallen leaves are rustling in the wind. ばさっとおんする

**버선** Korean socks; sweatsocks.

**버섯** 〖식〗a mushroom; a fungus (pl. gi)／~을 따러 가다 go mushroom hunting. きのこ

**버성기다** ①《틈이》(be) rough; coarse; have a crevice[crack] ②《사이가》be estranged[alienated]. すきまができている

**■세다** (be) tough; stiff and tough; be unyielding. ごういんだ

**버스러지다** ①《분쇄되다》be crushed[smashed]; crumble; break give way; go to pieces／컵이 마루에 떨어져 버스러졌다 The glass fell on the floor and went to pieces. ②《벗겨지다》come[fall] off; be worn off ③《빗나가다》miss; go wrong[astray] ④《상반되다》be against [contrary to]. ぼろぼろになる

**버스럭거리다** rustle; make a rustle／~스럭거리다. ばさりと

**버스름하다** 《틈이》be slightly 《관계가》be estranged[alienated].

**버슷하다** 《관계가》be a bit estranged; do not get on together. したしくない

**버쩍** ①《마른 모양》entirely; [dried up] completely／우물 물이 ~ 말랐다 The well has all dried up. ②《조이는 모양》tightly; firmly／~ 조이다 tight fast ③《우기는 모양》stubbornly; doggedly ④《느는 모양》a great deal; considerably／~ 늘다 increase markedly. からからに

**버적버적** with a crunching sound; with crunches ⇒바작바작. ばりばり

**버젓하다** ①《당당하다》(be) fair and square 《상당하다》(be) respectable; decent／버젓이 fairly 《떳떳이》openly; decently. こうめいせいだいだ

**버정이다** walk idly back and forth. さまよう

**버찌** a cherry 《꼭지에 달린》a cherry-bob／~씨 a cherry-stone. さくらのみ

**버지다** ①《베어지다》be cut／잘 버지는 칼 a knife that cuts well ②《긁히다》be scratched ③《젖어지다》wear; be worn out; fray／소매가 버졌다 The cuff was frayed. きれる

**버짐** scabs; a scabby 《진 버짐》pityriasis 《마른 버짐》psoriasis. かんせん

**버캐** scum; crystallized substance. うきかす

**버커리** a withered old woman; a hag. おいてやせたおんな

**버티다** ①《쓰러지지 않게》support; prop [up]; bolster up／막대기로 나무를 ~ prop up a plant with a stick ②《맞서다》contend(compete) with; resist; hold one's ground／순경한테 ~ resist a policeman ③《부지하다》maintain; sustain; endure; hold [out]／버티어 나가다 endure through／모든 어려움을 ~ stand all hardships. ささえる

**버팀목(-木)** a wooden support; a prop; a stay. つっかいぼう

**벅벅**¹ hard; roughly ⇒박박¹. ぼりぼり

**벅벅²** all over ⇒박박². びりびり

**뻑뻑** 《담배를 ~ 피우다 puff away at a cigarette. すぱすぱ

**벅신거리다** squirm; swarm. うようよする

**벅적거리다** be crowded[thronged]; swarm; bustle／거리는 몹시 벅적거렸다 The street was full of bustle. うようよする

**뻑적지근하다** feel heavy and painful. しくしくいたい

**벅차다** ①《힘에 겹다》(be) beyond one's power[ability]; (be) unbearable／이 일은 나에게 ~ I am not equal to this task. ②《가슴》(be) too full; be in great force／가슴이 벅차서 말이 나오지 않는다 My heart is too full for words. あふれそうだ

**번(番)** ①《당번》duty 《숙직》night duty ②《차례》turn ③《회수》a time／여러 ~ many times／몇 ~이고 again and again ④《번호》a number. ばん

**번가(煩苛)** ~하다 (be) troublesome. はんか

**번가루** extra flour in kneading dough properly.

**번각(翻刻)** a reprint; reprinting／~하다 reprint／~자 reprinter. はんこく

**번갈아** by turns; alternately; one after another; in turn／그들은 ~ 나를 찾아 왔다 They came to see me by turns. こうたいに

**번개** [a flash of] lightning; lightning flashes/번갯불 a bolt of lightning/~처럼 빨리 as swiftly as lightning; with lightning speed. いなびかり

**번거롭다** ①(복잡하다) (be) troublesome; complicated ②《시끄럽다》be noisy.

**번거를히다** (귀찮게 함) trouble; bother; keep (*a person*) busy; cause (*a person*) trouble; put (*a person*) into trouble.

**번극**(煩劇) pressure of business[work]; busyness/~하다 (be) busy. はんげき

**번나다**(番—) be off duty; be relieved of *one's* watch. ひばんになる

**번뇌**(煩惱) worldly passions[concerns] /~하다 be harassed by consuming[worldly] passions. ぼんのう

**번다**(煩多) ~하다 (be) multitudinous; troublesome. はんた

**번답**(反畓) converting a field into a paddy-field. はたけをすいでんにかえること

**번데기** a chrysalis(*pl.* ~es, -lides); a pupa(*pl.* ~s, -pae). さなぎ

**번둥거리다** idle away; lead an idle life; loiter/하는 일 없이 ~ be at a loose end.
なにもせずぶらぶらする

**번드럽다** (미끄럽다) (be) glossy; smooth 《약다》(be) smartish; clever; shrewd; sharp. つやつやしている

**번드르르, 뻔드르르** glossily; smoothly/ ~하다 (be) glossy; smooth. つやつやと

**번득, 번뜩** with a flash/~~거리다 flash.
ちらつく

**번들거리다** be glossy; be smooth; be slippery; be slimy/번들번들 smoothly; glossily. つやつやする

**번들다**(番—) be on duty; go on guard.
とうばんになる

**번듯하다, 번뜻하다** (be) even; well-balanced; be in harmony. むらがない

**번로**(煩勞) trouble; worry. はんろう

**번론**(煩論) complicated[troublesome] arguments. はんろん

**번롱**(翻弄) ~하다 trifle with; make a fool of/여자를 ~하다 trifle with a woman. はんろう

**번루**(煩累) troubles; cares/인생의 ~ the curse[worries] of life. はんるい

**번망**(煩忙, 繁忙) busyness/~하다 (be) busy. はんぼう

**번무**(煩務) troublesome affairs. はんむ

**번문 욕례**(繁文縟禮) red-tape; red-tapism; officialism. はんぶんじょくれい

**번민**(煩悶) agony; worry; anguish; pang /~하다 be in agony; agonize; suffer /~을 잊으려고 술을 마시다 take drinking to drown *one's* agony[mental anguish]. はんもん

**번바라지**(番—) food to be delivered to the man on duty.

**번방**(番房) a guard room; a night duty room.

**번번이** whenever; every[each] time; always/서울에 올 때마다 ~ every time I come to Seoul. ときどき

**번번하다** ①《물건이》even; (be) smooth ②《생김새가》(be) fair. きれいだ

**뻔뻔하다** (be) shameless[brazen-faced, impudent, cheeky]/뻔뻔하기 짝이 없군 Well, all cheek! ずうずうしい

**번복**(翻覆) ~하다 change; turn; reverse; upset/생각을 ~하다 change *one's* mind.
くり返しへんぎょうすること

**번본**(翻本) a reprint; a reprinted book.
さいはんぼん

**번서다**(番—) go on guard; stand guard; be on duty. とうちょくする

**번설**(煩屑) troudlea; **vexations**/사전을 찾는 ~을 피하다 spare *oneself* the trouble of consulting a dictionary.

**번설**(煩說) boring[tedious] talk 《소문》 gossiping.

**번성**(蕃盛) prosperity 《수목 따위가》luxuriance of growth/~하다 prosper; flourish. はんじょう

**번성**(繁盛) prosperity/~하다 prosper; flourish; thrive/사업이 ~하다 *one's* business prospers. はんじょう

**번쇄**(煩瑣) subtlety; messiness/ ~하다 (be) messy/~한 subtle; troublesome; complicated/~ 철학자 a schoolman/~ 철학 scholasticism. はんさ

**번식**(繁殖) breeding; propagation; increase/~하다 increase; propagate/~력 propagating power/~기 a breeding season. はんしょく

**번안**(翻案) ①《안건의》~하다 change; switch; reversal ②《작품의》an adaptation /~하다 adapt; rehash/~ 소설 an adapted story. ほんあん

**번역**(翻譯) translation/~하다 translate (*English*) into (*Korean*); render; put (*into*); decipher 《암호를》decode/~관 an official translator/~권 translation right/~자 a translator/~물 a translation. ほんやく

**번연**(翻然, 幡然) ~히 suddenly; with a sudden turn; clearly. ほんぜん

**번열증**(煩熱症) a fever; a febrile disease.
はんねつしょう

**번영**(繁榮) prosperity; flourish/~하다 prosper; flourish; thrive/국가의 ~ the prosperity. はんえい

**번요**(煩擾) annoyance; complexity; disturbance/~하다 be complicated; disturbing. はんじょう

**번육**(燔肉) roast meat; grill. やきにく

**번의**(翻意) changing *one's* mind; reversing *one's* decision/~하다 change *one's* mind; reverse *one's* decision; go back on *one's* resolution. ほんい

**번인**(藩人) 《토착민》an aboriginal(*pl.* -nes); 《야만인》a savage; a barbarian.

**번잡**(煩雜) 《복잡》complexity 《빈번》frequency/~하다 be complicated/~한[스러운] complicated; troublesome/~한 거리 crowded streets. はんざつ

**번쩍** at a breath; easily; lightly; without any effort. ぱっと

번적거리다, 번쩍거리다 glitter; glisten 《별 따위》 twinkle 《섬광》 glare; flash 《보석 따위》 sparkle. ひらめく
번쩍하면 easily; on the slightest movement. ややもすれば
번전(反田) converting a rice-field into a [dry] field.
번족(蕃族) a savage tribe. ばんぞく
번주그레하다 (be) rather nice looking; attractive. こぎれいだ
번죽거리다 vex; provoke; annoy／그는 항상 나한테 번죽거리다 He always annoys me. なぶる
번지(番地) a house number; an address ／댁은 몇 ~입니까 What is the number of your house?. ばんち
번지다 ①《물 따위가》 blot; spread; run／이 잉크는 종이에 번진다 This ink spreads on the paper. ②《확대하다》 spread; extend ③spread affect《영이》.
번지럽다 (be) smooth; sleek; glossy; bright; lustrous. つやつやしている
번지르르, 뻔지르르 sleekly; brightly; glossily (be) sleek; bright／~한 머리가락 sleek hair. つるつると
번질거리다, 뻔질거리다 《윤이 나다》 be lustrous[slimy]; 《약가 굴다》 be shrewd; be wide-awake. つやつやする
뻔질나게 continuously coming and going; frequenting. たびたび
번차례(番次例) a turn; an order／~를 기다리다 await[wait for] one's turn. とうちょくのじゅんばん
번창(繁昌) prosperity; flourish／~하다 prosperous; thriving. はんじょう
번철(燔鐵) a frying pan. せんてつ
번초(蕃椒) red pepper.
번폐(煩弊) a troublesome abuse; implication. はんざつなへいがい
번하다¹, 뻔하다¹ ①《훤하다》 (be) light; bright ②《분명하다》 (be) clear; evident; obvious; plain／뻔한 사실 an obvious fact 《확실》 (be) certain ③《여가가 있다》 (be) free; unoccupied; have a short leisure ④《병이》 be in a state of lull／병세가 좀 ~ A patient gets a bit better. ぼんやりしている
번하다², 뻔하다² be[come, go] near (doing); almost; nearly／죽을 뻔했다 I was nearly death.
번호(番號) a number 《부호》a mark 《호령》 Number!／~ 순으로 in numberical order／~를 매기다[달다] number／~표 a number ticket[plate]／수령 ~ an examinee's seat number. ばんごう
번화(繁華) ~한 flourishing; thriving; bustling; busy／~가(街) a busy street; amusement quarters. はんか
벋가다, 뻗가다 stray; deviate; swerve (from); go astray. はずれる
벋나다 protrude; stick out. そとへむく
벋놓다 turn loose; give a free rein to.
벋니 a projecting[protruding] tooth; a bucktooth. でっぱ

벋다¹ be protruding／번은이 a protruding tooth. つき出ている
벋다², 뻗다¹ 《가지 따위가》 spread; stretch; extend 《힘이》 spread out／나뭇가지들이 햇빛 쪽으로 벋고 있다 The branches are spreading toward the sun.／세력이 벋다 one's influence is extended. のびる
뻗다² stretch out／팔을[다리를] ~ stretch one's arm[leg]. のびる
벋대다, 뻗대다 《버티다》 hold[stand] out; stand firm; hold fast to 《맞서다》 oppose; stand against; resist. ささえる
벋디디다, 뻗디디다 ①《힘을 주어》 step[stand] firmly ②《금 밖으로》 step out of (bounds). しっかりふむ
벋버듬하다 have a gap between the two ends. そってすきができている
벋버슬하다 be on bad terms with; be at odds with.
벋서다, 뻗서다 resist; oppose; rise against ⇒버티다. たいこうする
뻗치다 《내밀다》 stretch; extend; reach; hold out／구조의 손을 ~ give (a person) a helping hand. のばす
벌¹ 《들》 field; a plain; a prairie／황량한 ~ a wilderness. はら
벌² 《충》 a bee 《황봉》a wasp／~떼 a swarm of bees／~집 a [bee]hive／꿀~ honey bee／~집을 건드리다 have a hell of time interfering carelessly in a matter／~에 쏘이다 be stung by a bee. はち
벌³ 《그릇 따위》 a set 《옷 따위》a suit 《즈봉이》 a pair 《서류 따위》a copy／옷 한 ~ a suit of clothes. ちゃく
뻘 《혈족 관계》 standing; status; the role of／그는 내 아저씨 ~이다 He is an uncle to me.
벌(罰) punishment; penalty 《천벌》 judgment／~하다 punish; bring (one) to punishment; penalize／~을 주다 inflict penalty on (a culprit)／~을 받다 be punished; suffer punishment. ばつ
벌(閥) a clique; a faction 《동인》 a coterie 《종교·학문상의》 sectarianism／학~ an academical clique／재~ a great industrial family. ばつ
벌개지다, 뻘개지다 turn red; redden; color／얼굴이 벌개지게 하다 put (a person) to the blush. あかくなる
벌거벗다, 뻘거벗다 become naked; strip oneself naked; strip to the skin／벌거벗은 여자 a naked woman／벌거벗기다 unclothe; strip (one) naked; strip of his clothes. はだかになる
벌거숭이, 뻘거숭이 a nude; a naked body／~의 naked; nude; bare. はだか
벌꺽 outburst; suddenly; a rage／~ 화를 내다 flare up. むくっと
벌꺽거리다 《술·빨래 따위가》 bubble up 《진흙 따위를》 make mud squash underfoot. ぶくぶくとおんをたてる
벌건 《아주·온통》 utter; downright／~ 거짓말 a downright[plump] lie; pure fabrication. すっかり

**벌겅, 뻘겅** red 《진홍》 scarlet; crimson. あか

**벌겋다, 뻘겋다** (be) red; crimson 《얼굴이》 ruddy／벌겋게 red; ruddily／벌건 얼굴 a ruddy face. ひじょうにあかい

**벌그데데하다** be a coarse and unpleasant red. いくらかあかいがげひんである

**벌그뎅뎅하다** be a messy red. いくらかあかいがかくにあわない

**벌그레하다** be tinged with red; be aglow. あかみがかっている

**벌그스름하다** (be) reddish; be a dirty red. あるていどまですこしあかい

**벌끈** ①《성내는 모양》 in a fit of passion; in a rage; all of a sudden／～하다 fly into a rage ②《시끄러운 모양》 in an uproar; in commotion／～ 뒤집히다 be in a great disturbance. かっと

**벌금(罰金)** a fine; a penalty／～을 과하다 [punish with a] fine／～을 물다 be fined; pay a penalty／～형 punishment with a fine. ばっきん

**벌기다** open; crack[cut] open. ひらく

**벌노랑이** 〖식〗 a bird's-boot trefoil.

**벌다**¹ 《사이가》 open; be opened; get wider／사이가 ～ the crack gets wider; a chink forms. あく

**벌다**² 《돈을》 earn; make; make a profit／돈을 [잘] ～ make [good] money／고생해서 번 돈 hard-earned money／생활비를 ～ gain one's livelihood. もうける

**벌떡** suddenly; quickly／～ 일어서다 spring to one's feet; rise with a spring; get up with a jump. さっと

**벌떡거리다** ①《가슴이》 go pitapat; palpitate; throb／가슴이 벌떡거렸다 My heart throbbed violently. ②《마시는 모양》 gulp down; drink at a gulp／벌떡벌떡 pitapat. どきどきする

**벌럼거리다** act nimbly; behave lightly. かるくうごいている

**벌렁벌렁** 《민첩하게》 nimbly; agilely; quickly 《들떠서》 gadding about.

**벌렁코** a flaring nose.

**벌레** 《곤충》 an insect; a bug 《속》; 《유충》 a worm 《부나비·좀 따위》 a moth 《해충》 vermin／～먹은 이 a decayed tooth ／～먹은 worm-[moth-]eaten. こんちゅう

**벌룩거리다** 《열렸다 닫혔다 하다》 open and shut. ぶらぶらする

**벌름거리다** swell and subside alternately. ばくばくする

**벌름하다** (be) wide open.

**벌리다** ①《사이를》 widen; open; leave space 《펴다》 stretch out; outstretch／입을 딱 ～ open one's mouth wide ②《늘어놓다》 lay out; place 《things》 in order; arrange; spread 《진열하다》 display 《goods》 ③《일의 시작》 open 《a shop》; start; begin. ひらく

**벌리춤** ㅁ～이다 It is too late to change your mind.

**벌림새** 《상품 따위의》 the mode of display. はいれつ

**벌매듭** a bee-shaped knot.

**벌모** 〖농〗 rice plants growing outside the seedbed.

**벌목(伐木)** felling; cutting／～하다 cut down; fell; lumber／～기(期) a felling season. きをきること

**벌물** 《논·그릇의》 spilt water; slop.

**벌물(罰-)** water forced on 《a person》 to drink as punishment.

**벌바람** wind on an open field. はらのかぜ

**벌벌** shiveringly; tremblingly／～ 떨다 tremble; shake; shiver／추워서 ～ 떨다 shiver with the cold. ぶるぶる

**벌봉(罰俸)** a monetary penalty.

**벌부(筏夫)** a raftsman; a rafter.

**벌불** a side prong of a flame.

**벌써** ①《이미》 already 《의문에》 yet 《지금은》 by now[this time]／～ 7시다 It's already 7 o'clock. ②《오래 전》 long ago; a long time ago／～ 오랜 옛날 ages ago; long long ago.

**벌쐬다** get stung by a bee／벌쐰 사람 같다 be like a man stung by a bee.

**벌쓰다(罰―)** be punished. ばちをうける

**벌씌우다(罰―)** punish; penalize. ばちする

**벌어먹다** earn one's bread[living, livelihood]; work for one's living／벌어먹기 힘들다 find it hard to make a living.

**벌어지다** ①《사이가》 split; crack; open; be separate ②《몸이》 grow stout[firm] ③《사건이》 occur; come about; take place／원유회가 벌어졌다 The garden party took place. すきまができる

**벌열(閥閱)** a distinguished family[clan].

**벌이** 《돈벌이》 money-making; earning money 《일》 work 《번돈》 earnings 《수입》 income／～ 잘 되다 make good money ／～하러 가다 go to[for] work. かせぎ

**벌이다** ①《일을》 set about; embark on ／새로운 사업을 ～ embark on an enterprise ②《가게를》 open; establish／가게를 ～ open a shop ③《물건을》 stretch; spread. しごとをはじめる

**벌이줄** a cord; a tie string. ながいと

**벌전(罰錢)** a cash penalty; a fine.

**벌점(罰點)** a demerit; black marks／～을 주다 give black mark 《for》.

**벌족(閥族)** a distinguished family[clan].

**벌주(罰酒)** the wine forced to 《a person》 as punishment ばつし

**벌주다(罰―)** punish; inflict penalty on 《a culprit》. ばちをあたえる

**벌집** a beehive; a honeycomb a nest of hornets／～을 건드리지 마라 Let sleeping dogs lie. はちのす

**벌창** ～하다 《물이》 overflow; run over; flood 《물건이》 be flooded. はんらん

**벌채(伐採)** felling; lumbering／～하다 cut down; fell; hew. ばっさい

**벌책(罰責)** reproof; rebuke; reprimand; censure／～하다 reprimand; rebuke; reprove; censure／～ 처분 reprimand.

**벌초**(伐草) mowing/~하다 mow; cut to-he grass (around a grave).

**벌충** recovery; supplement; compensation/~하다 recover; make up (for); make good; supply/손해를 ~하다 make up for the loss. ほじゅう

**벌치** a wild cantaloupe.

**벌칙**(罰則) penal code[regulation]; punitive rules/~에 의거하여 according to the penal regulation. ばっそく

**벌컥** all of a sudden ⇒벌컥. むくっと

**벌타령**(一打令) doing at random; doing without any thought; doing as one pleases. でたらめ

**벌통**(一桶) a beehive.

**벌판** 《명야》 field; a plain 《황야》 a wilderness; a moor. のはら

**범** a tiger 《암컷》 a tigress /새끼 ~ a tiger cub; a tiger kitten/~의 굴에 들어가야 ~을 잡는다 Nothing venture, nothing have[gain]. /자는 ~에게 코치주다 wake a sleeping dog. とら

**범**(犯) an offence; a violation/~하다 commit; perpetrate; violate; infringe /강력~ a violent offence[criminal] /상습~ a habitual offence[criminal] /절도~ a larceny/지능~ an intellectual criminal.

**범-**(汎) Pen-/~아시아 Pan-Asiatic/~아메리카주의 Pan-Americanism.

**범계**(犯界) a border violation; border transgression/~하다 violate a border. きょうかいせんをおかすこと

**범고래** 〖동〗 a grampus; a killer whale.

**범골**(凡骨) an ordinary person. ぼんこつ

**범과**(犯過) a fault; a wrong; wrongdoing/~하다 commit a fault; do a wrong. つみをおかすこと

**범국민**(汎國民) pan-national/~ 운동 a pan-national campaign[movement, drive].

**범금**(犯禁) violation of restrictions infringement; transgression; contravention/~하다 violate restrictions break a prohibition. きんせいをおかすこと

**범나비** 〖충〗 a swallowtail [butterfly]. あげはちょう

**범독**(泛讀) ~하다 reading at random.

**범람**(氾濫) overflowing; flood; inundation 《분수에 넘침》 presumption/~하다 overflow; flow over/강이 ~하고 있다 The river is in flood. はんらん

**범령**(犯令) violation of the law/~하다 violate the law. ほうれいをおかすこと

**범례**(凡例) introductory remarks; explanatory notes. はんれい

**범론**(汎論, 氾論) a summary; general remarks.

**범론**(汎論) a vague remark.

**범류**(凡類) ordinary person[minds]; a mediocrity. へいぼんなにんげんのたぐい

**범리론**(汎理論) 〖철〗 Hegelism; pan-logicism. はんりろん

**범민**(凡民) a commoner; the common people.

**범방**(犯房) having sexual intercourse/~하다 have sexual[marital] intercourse. せいこうすること

**범백**(凡百) ①《온갖 것》 all sorts of things; all matters ②《범례》 manners; etiquette; breeding 《행위》 behaviour/~을 가르치다 tell the etiquette. ぼんぴゃく

**범벅** ①《음식》 pudding prepared with rice; flour and pumpkin ②《일》 a medley; a mess; a pell-mell; a hotchpotch /~이 되다 go to pie; be in muddle; be mixed up.

**범범하다**(泛泛一) (be) careless; heedless; inattentive/범범한 사람 a careless person. おうざっぱだ

**범법**(犯法) breaking the law; violation of the law/~하다 violate the law; break the law. ほうをおかすこと

**범부**(凡夫) 《범인》 an ordinary person; a mediocrity 《속인》 a layman. ぼんぷ

**범분**(犯分) ~하다 forget one's own place. ぶんべつをぼうきゃくすること

**범사**(凡事) ①《모든 일》 all matters; everything; all things ②《평범한 일》 an ordinary matter; a common affair [event]. すべてのこと

**범상**(凡常) ~한 common[place]; ordinary; usual; average; normal/~치 않은 《병적인》 abnormal. ぼんじょう

**범색**(犯色) immoderate sexual intercourse. いろごとのふせっせい

**범서**(凡書) a mediocre book. ぼんしょ

**범서**(梵書) 《범문》 Sanskrit literature 《불경》 the Buddhist scriptures. ぼんしょ

**범선**(帆船) a sailing-vessel a sailing boat; a sailer. はんせん

**범속**(凡俗) mediocrity; banality; vulgarity/~한 (be) mediocre; vulgar/~하다 ordinary; common. ぼんぞく

**범수**(犯手) 《손찌검》 hitting; beating; striking/~하다 hit; beat; strike.

**범신교**(汎神敎) 〖종〗 pantheism/~도 a pantheist. はんしんきょう

**범심론**(汎心論) pan-psychism. はんしんろん

**범아귀** the distance between the thumb and the forefinger

**범안**(凡眼) ordinary intelligence; a layman's eye. ぼんがん

**범애**(汎愛) philanthropy; universal love /~주의 philanthropism. はんあい

**범야당 전선**(汎野黨戰線) pan-opposition front.

**범어**(梵語) Sanscrit; Sanskrit; pali /~학자 a Sanskritist. ぼんご

**범연**(汎然, 泛然) ~하다 (be) indifferent; careless; heedless; inattentive /~히 carelessly. ぞんざいに

**범용**(凡庸) mediocrity; commonplace/~한 mediocre. ぼんよう

**범용**(犯用) ~하다 misappropriate; peculate; embezzle; use illegally.

**범월**(犯越) border transgression.

**범위(範圍)** a scope; an extent; a sphere; a range; a province 《제한》 limits; bounds/활동 ~ the sphere of activity/넓은 ~에 걸쳐 cover a wide scope[range]. はんい

**범의(犯意)** 【법】 a criminal intent. はんい

**범의귀** 【식】 a creeping saxifrage.

**범인(凡人)** an ordinary person; a common mortal; a mediocrity; a man of mediocre talent. ぼんじん

**범인(犯人)** a criminal; an offender; a culprit; a convict/~ 은닉 concealment of an offender. はんにん

**범일(汎溢, 氾溢)** inundation; overflowing; flooding/~하다 inundate; overflow; flood. はんらん

**범입(犯入)** illegal entry/~하다 illegally enter.

**범자(梵字)** Sanskrit. ぼんじ

**범재(凡才)** common[ordinary] ability; mediocrity of capacity. ぼんさい

**범절(凡節)** manners; etiquette; decorum.

**범죄(犯罪)** a crime; an offense 《행위》 a criminal act/~하다 commit a crime; violate the law/~ 심리학 criminal psychology/~ 사회학 criminal sociology /~ 소설 criminal story/~학 criminology. はんざい

**범주(範疇)** a category; a class/~에 들다 come[fall] under the category of/미적 ~ an esthetic category. はんちゅう

**범주(泛舟)** floating a boat/~하다 set a boat afloat. ふねをうかべること

**범천(梵天)** 【종】 Brahma.

**범청(泛聽)** inattentive listening/~하다 listen inattentively.

**범칙(犯則)** violation/~하다 infringe; violate; break. はんそく

**범칭(泛稱, 汎稱)** a general title[term]; a popular name. はんしょう

**범타(凡打)** 《야구》 poor batting

**범태평양(汎太平洋)** Pan-Pacific.

**범퇴(凡退)** ~하다 《야구》 be easily put out.

**범포(帆布)** canvas; sailcloth. ほのぬの

**범하다(犯―)** 《죄를》 commit 《법률 등을》 violate; infringe; break/죄를 ~ commit a crime[sin]/학칙을 ~ break the school regulations. おかす

**범행(犯行)** a crime; an offence /~을 자백[부인]하다 confess[deny] one's crime /~ 현장 the scene of an offence/대담한 ~ a bold crime. はんこう

**범홀(泛忽)** careless; negligence; inattention.

**법(法)** ① 《법률》 a law 《총칭》 the law 《법칙》 a rule 《법전》 a code 《조례·규정》 a regulation/~을 지키다 observe[keep, obey] the law/~의 정신 the spirit of the law ② 《방법》 a method; a way/교수~ a teaching method/글 쓰는 ~ how to write ③ 《도리》 reason; justification /~에 어긋나다 be wrong ④ 《본보기》 an example. ほう

**법계(法系)** the legal system; a code of law /로마 ~ Roman law /중국 ~ Chinese law. ほうりつたいけいのりゃくご

**법계(法界)**¹ 《법조계》 legal circles; the judicial [world]. ほうそうかい

**법계(法界)**² 《종》 the realm of Buddhism. ほうかい

**법과(法科)** the law faculty[department] 《과정》 a law course/~ 대학 a law college; a school of law/〈미〉/~ 학생 a law student. ほうか

**법관(法官)** a judicial officer; a judge《총칭》 the judiciary 《집합적》 the bench. ほうかん

**법권(法權)** a legal right. ほうけん

**법규(法規)** the law; the regulations/~상의 수속을 마치다 go through all legal formalities. ほうき

**법금(法禁)** a prohibition; a restriction; a ban. ほうきん

**법당(法堂)** the sanctuary. ほうどう

**법도(法度)** a law; regulations. はっと

**법등(法燈)** 《종》 the light of Buddhism.

**법랑(琺瑯)** enamel. ほうろう

**법령(法令)** a law; a statute; laws and ordinances. ほうれい

**법례(法例)** the law governing the application of laws. ほうれい

**법률(法律)** a law; a statue 《총칭》 [the] law/도박을 금하는 ~ a law against gambling/~의 legal; juridical/~학 jurisprudence/~가 a jurist/~ 고문 a legal adviser/~ 사무소 a law office/~ 행위 a legal act[action]. ほうりつ

**법리(法理)** a principle of law; legal principle/~학 jurisprudence; the science of law. ほうり

**법망(法網)** the net of the law; justice/~에 걸리다 fall into the meshes of the law. ほうもう

**법명(法名)** a sacred name; one's Buddhist name. ほうみょう

**법무(法務)** judicial affairs/~관 《군》 a judge advocate a judiciary. ほうむ

**법무부(法務部)** the Ministry of Justice; the Justice Department/~ 장관[차관] the Minister of Justice. ほうむぶ

**법문(法文)** ① 《법》 the law; written laws 《법률과 문학》 law and literature ② 《종》 Buddhist writings. ほうぶん

**법문(法門)** Buddhism; the Buddhist priesthood. ほうもん

**법복(法服)** 《재판관의》 a judge's robe; a gown 《변호사의》 a lawyer's robe; a barrister's gown 《승려의》 a sacerdotal [clerical] robe. ほうふく

**법사(法師)** a Buddhist priest[monk]; a bonze. ほうし

**법석** a fuss; a ado; a tumult; an uproar; a noise; a row /~ 떨다 make a lot of noise. わいわいさわぎ

**법수(法手)** a means; a method.

**법식(法式)** 《형식》 a form 《방법》 a method; a process 《정식》 a formula (pl. ~s,

·lae); 《수속》 formalities 《관례》 usage／일정한 ~ a regular form. ほうしき

**법안**(法案) a bill; a measure／~을 제출하다 introduce a bill／~을 가결하다 pass a bill. ほうあん

**법언**(法言) canonical remarks.

**법열**(法悅) ①《즐거움》 ecstasy; rapture; transport ②《종》 religious exaltation. ほうえつ

**법왕**(法王) ①《불교》 Tathagata(Sans); Buddha ②《천주교에서》 the pope; the pontiff／~ 제도 the papal system. ほうおう

**법외**(法外) (being) unreasonable; exorbitant. ほうがい

**법원**(法院) a court; a court of justice／~장 the president of a court／지방 ~ a district court／고등 ~ an appellate court／대 ~ the Supreme Court. ほういん

**법의**(法衣) 『종』 a sacerdotal robe; canonical dress ほうい

**법의**(法意) the spirit[intent] of the law. ほうい

**법의학**(法醫學) medical jurisprudence／~의 medicolegal. ほういがく

**법인**(法人) 『법』 a juridical[legal] person; a corporate body／~세 the juridical person tax／~단체 the body corporate／사단 ~ a corporation aggregate／재단 ~ a juridical foundation. ほうじん

**법적**(法的) (being) legal; legalistic／~근거 a legal basis. ほうてき

**법전**(法典) a code of laws; a statute《종교》a canon. ほうてん

**법정**(法庭) a [law] court; a court of justice; the bar／~에 나가다 appear in court. ほうてい

**법정**(法定) ~의 legal; statutory／~ 대리인 a legal representative／~ 상속인 an heir-at-law／~ 화폐 legal tender／~ 가격 the legal price. ほうてい

**법제**(法制) legislation; laws; legislative system／~(처處) the Legislative Office. ほうせい

**법조**(法曹) judical officers; judges and lawyers／~계 legal circles; the legal word. ほうそう

**법주**(法主) a Buddhist high priest.

**법치**(法治) constitutional government／~ 국가 a constitutional state; a law-governed country／~주의 constitutionalism; legalism. ほうち

**법칙**(法則) a law; a rule／자연의 ~ a law of nature; a natural law／~론 nomology. ほうそく

**법폐**(法幣) 『경』 a Chinese legal tender.

**법하다** may／그가 올 ~ He might come. ―らしい

**법학**(法學) law 《법리학》 jurisprudence／~박사 a doctor of laws(略: LL. D.)／~사 bachelor of laws(略: LL. B.)／~ 통론 a compendium of law. ほうがく

**법호**(法號) 『종』 a posthumeus Buddhist name. ほうごう

**법화**(法幣) 『경』 legal tender; lawful money. ほうか

**법화**(法話) a sermon; a homily.

**법화경**(法華經) 『종』 the Saddharma Pundarika Sutra.

**법회**(法會) a Buddhist mass; memorial service. ほうえ

**벗** a friend 《반려》 a companion 《동아리》 comrade 《일반》 company; a pal《속》／친한 ~ an intimate friend／책을 ~삼다 have books for companions. とも

**벗가다** have one's own way; go beyond the limit ⇒벗나가다.

**벗개다** clear up. はれわたる

**벗겨지다** come[go, wear, fall] off; slip [fall] off 《머리가》 grow[get] bald 《금박이》 fret 《구름이》 clear up 《색칠이》 fade[discolor]／구두가 잘 벗겨지지 않는다 My shoes will not come off／이 빛깐은 썻어도 벗겨지지 않는다 This colo[u]r will standthe wash. ぬげる

**벗기다** ①《옷을》 unclothe; undress; strip [take] off／아이의 옷을 ~ undress a child ②《껍질을》 peel; skin; pare; flay; strip off／바나나 껍질을 ~ strip a banana ③《제거하다》 remove; take off／뚜껑을 ~ take off the lid／그의 가면을 벗기고 말겠다 I will show up his false face. ぬかす

**벗나가다** deviate; swerve (from); go astray; go beyond the limit／벗나간 짓 an improper behavior. それる

**벗놓다** let go astray; leave alone／let stray from the right path.

**벗다** ①《옷 따위를》 take[put] off; divest [strip] oneself of; slip off／외투를 ~ take off[get out of] one's overcoat ②《누명・빛・짐 따위를》 clear oneself of; remove; rid oneself of／누명을 ~ clear oneself of a false charge／짐을 ~ put one's load down／책임을 ~ rid oneself of responsibility ③《티를》 get rid of／시골티를 ~ get polished ④《허물을》 leave the cocoon／허물을 ~ 《뱀 따위가》 slip out of its skin. ぬく

**벗바리** a backer; a supporter／~좋다 have strong backing.

**뻣뻣하다** (be) straight; stiff ⇒빳빳하다. しこっている

**벗어나다** get out of; escape from; free oneself of; shake oneself from; get rid of; be contrary to／악습에서 ~ get rid of a bad habit／곤경에서 ~ get out of difficulties. まぬがれる

**벗어 버리다** take off; throw[cast] off 《신을》 kick off／그는 저고리를 벗어 버리고 일을 시작했다 He threw off his coat and started work.

**벗어지다** ①《가죽 따위가》 peel [off]; come [go] off; be taken off／햇볕에 탄 살갗은 벗어진다 Sunburnt skin will peel. ②《머리가》 become bald／그는 젊은데도 머리가 벗어졌다 He became baldheaded before his time. ぬげる

**벗트다** become intimate; get so one can

벗하다 dispense with formalities in talking (with). ともだちにする

벗하다 make friends with; associate with; become a good friend/책과 ~ have books for companions/자연을 ~ make friends with nature. ともだちにする

뻥 ①《소리》bang; pop ②《거짓》a lie; an invention; a falsehood. ばん

벙거지 a felt hat; a hat; headgear. むかしのへいそつのぼうし

벙글거리다 smile; beam/기쁜 듯이 ~ smile happily. にこにこする

벙긋거리다, 뻥긋거리다 smile; beam ⇒벙글거리다. にこにこする

벙긋하다 (be) ajar; open; be slightly opened/문이 벙긋하게 열려 있다 The door left is ajar. すこしあいている

뻥나다 be disclosed[exposed]/그 일이 뻥 났다 The thing was ruined. ばれる

뻥놓다 reveal; divulge; let out; disclose; spoil; lay bare. ほらをふく

뻥뻥 《소리》popping and popping 《구멍》with hole after hole. ぽかりぽかりと

벙벙하다 be dumbfounded/벙벙해서 in mute amazement/나는 어안이 벙벙해서 어쩔 줄을 몰랐다 I was quite at a loss what to do. あきれてものいえない

벙실거리다 smile ⇒벙글거리다 / 벙실벙실 beamming. にこにこわらっている

벙어리 ①《사람》a dumb person; a deaf-mute ②《저금통》a saving-box; a piggybank. おし

벙태기 headgear. むかしのへいそつのぼうし

벚꽃 cherry blossoms/~놀이 a cherry-blossom viewing party. さくら

벚나무 a cherry tree. さくらのき

베 《삼베》hemp cloth. あさのぬの

베개 a pillow/공기 ~ an air cushion/~를 베다 rest one's head/팔~를 베다 make a pillow of one's arm.

베갯머리 the end of a pillow/~에서 by[at] one's beside.

베갯모 embroidered pads attached to both sides of a pillow for decoration.

베갯밀공사(一公事) love talk; soft nothings; a private request given by a wife to her husband; a curtain lecture.

베갯속 the stuffing of a pillow; fillings for a pillow. まくらのつめもの

베갯잇 a pillow-slip. まくらカバー

베거리 sounding; probing (a person's) mind. さぐりしんだん

베끼다 copy; make a copy of/책에서 문제를 ~ copy out a problem from a book. うつす

베내다 cut off ⇒베어내다. きりだす

베다¹ 《베개를》rest[lay] one's head on [a pillow]. まくらをする

베다² 《자르다》cut; chop 《잘게》hash 《톱으로》saw 《가위로》shear; clip 《얇게》slash 《난도질》hack [to pieces]; slice 《저미다》shave 《나무를》fell 《곡물을》reap 《풀을》mow /목을~ cut off one's head. きる

베풀다 remain apart from; keep aloof from; keep to oneself; do not mix with. なかまからこりつする

베풀이 a bad mixer; an unsociable person. なかまはずれのひと

베먹다 cut off and eat ⇒베어먹다.

베물다 bite off; cut off[sever] with one's teeth. はでかみきる

베버리다 cut ⇒베어버리다.

베불이 hemp cloth. ぬのるい

베슬거리다 try to get away; try to back out of; shrink; recoil. ずるくのがれる

베실 twine; hemp yarn; linen thread. あさいと

베어내다 cut off[away]; cut out 《나무를》cut down/고기 한 점을 ~ cut off a slice of meat. きりだす

베어먹다 ①《칼로》cut[chop, hash] and eat ②《침식》erode; wear out; eat away; bite. きってたべる

베어버리다 cut; cut down[off]/한 칼에 ~ cut down with one sword stroke.

베옷 hemp clothes. ふい

베이다 get it cut; get cut on. きられる

베짱베짱 《베짱이의》chirping; chirring/ ~ 울다 chirrup; chirre. ちいちい

베짱이 《충》a grass-hopper.

베틀 a loom. はた

베풀다 ①《주다》give; bestow 《은혜를》grant 《조력을》render /자선을 ~ render aid to the poor /잔치 따위를 ~ give; hold /잔치를 ~ hold a feast.

벼 a rice plant/~를 심다 plant rice/~를 베다 harvest[reap] the rice/~농사 rice farming. いね

뼈 ①《골》a bone 《동물의》;《갈비》a rib 《유골》ashes/~가 많은 고기 a bony fish ②《핵심》the gist; main points ③《저의》a hidden meaning; the connotation/~ 있는 말 words full of hidden meaning ④《기골》guts; backbone; spirit/~ 없이 좋은 사람 a simple-minded person. ほね

뼈다귀 a bone.

뼈대 frame; build; physique/~가 작다 one has a small frame. こっかく

벼락 thunder; a thunderbolt/~이 친다 It thunders., The thunder rolls. かみなり

벼락감투 a mushroom office[post] obtained through the moneyed power.

벼락공부(一工夫) cramming/~하다 cram up; get up (for an examination).

벼락대신(一大臣) a tough nut [to crack]; a tough guy. にんたいのできるひと

벼락맞다 be struck by lightning. らいげきをうける

벼락바람 a sudden and impetuous charge; a sudden attack[brunt].

벼락부자(一富者) an upstart; a mushroom millionaire.

벼락불 ①《번갯불》a flash of lightning; lightning flashes ②《사나운 위협》tyranny; abuse of power. でんこう

벼락치다 a thunderbolt falls/그 건물에

벼락이 쳤다 A thunderbolt struck hte house. かみなりがおちる
**벼랑** a cliff; a bluff; a precipice. がけ
**벼루** an inkstone. すずり
**벼룩** 〖虫〗 a flea. のみ
**벼룻길** a narrow road leading to a precipice. でっぽう
**벼룻돌** stone used as an inkstone. すずり
**벼룻집** an inkstone case. すずりのはこ
**벼르다** ①《분배하다》divide; distribute; share ②《꾀하다》be firmly determined to (do); plan; intend. ぶんぱいする
**벼름, 벼름질** equal division; apportionment; distribution; sharing; allotment; apportionment/〜하다 share (with); portion out; divide equally; apportion; distibute (among). ぶんばい
**벼리** 《그물의》the border ropes of a fishing-net 《책의》index. あみのふち
**벼리다** sharpen; temper; forge.
**벼물다** 《웃치하다》dress up 《성내다》be touchy 《벼르다》plan; lay one's plan; be determined to. どなる
**벼슬** a official rank; a government post/〜하다 take office/〜이 높다[낮다] be of high[low] government position.
**벼슬길** the way [to get] into the government service. かんしょく
**벼슬살이** an official life; a government service. かんりせいかつ
**벼슬아치** a government official. かんり
**뼈저리다** pierce deeply into one's mind; cut to the heart. つうせつにかんずる
**뼈지다** 《말이 여무지다》(be) sharp; pithy 《속어》solid. なるほどとおもわせる
**벼훑이** a rice hackling. だっこくき
**벽** sodomy ⇨비역 だんしょく
**벽(壁)** a wall; a partition/〜을 칠하다 plaster a wall. かべ
**벽(癖)** a habit; a characteristic/도〜 a thieving habit. くせ
**벽개(劈開)** cleavage; crevice.
**벽걸이(壁—)** a wall tapestry.
**벽견(僻見)** a prejudiced opinion. へきけん
**벽계(碧溪)** a blue stream. へきけい
**벽공(碧空)** the blue [azure] sky; the blue heaven. へきくう
**벽난로(壁煖爐)** a hearth.
**벽도(碧桃)** ①《과일》a peach that is supposed to exist in fairyland ②《꽃》a blossom of the double-flowering peach. へきとう
**벽돌(壁—)** [a] brick. れんが
**벽두(劈頭)** the outset; the first/〜에 at the very beginning. へきとう
**벽력(霹靂)** a [thunder] bolt. へきれき
**벽로(壁爐)** a fireplace.
**벽론(僻論)** a biased[one-sided] argument; a prejudiced. へきろん
**벽루(僻陋)** 《장소》a remote place 《성격》eccentricity. へきろう
**벽보(壁報)** a bill; a poster; a wall newspaper; a placard.
**벽색(碧色)** dark[deep] blue. あおいろ

**벽서(壁書)** 《광고》a placard; a bill; a poster. へきしょ
**벽서(僻書)** a rare and curious book.
**벽성(僻姓)** an unusual surname; a rare surname. まれなせい
**벽시계(壁時計)** a wall clock.
**벽신문(壁新聞)** a wall newspaper.
**벽안(壁眼)** blue eyes. へきがん
**벽오동(碧梧桐)** 〖식〗a sultan's-parasol; Firmiana platanifolia 《학명》. あおぎり
**벽옥(碧玉)** green jade; jasper. へきぎょく
**벽원(僻遠)** 〜하다 (be) remote; secluded. へきえん
**벽자(僻字)** an odd and rare character; an unusual letter. あまりつかわないじ
**벽장(壁欌)** a wall closet.
**벽장코** a snub nose. ひらたいはな
**벽지(僻地)** a remote place; an out-of-the-way place. へきち
**벽지다(僻—)** (be) secluded; isolated; lonely.
**벽창호** a pig-headed person; a bigoted[stubborn] person. いっこくもの
**벽채** a mine hoe[pick].
**벽촌(僻村)** a remote village; an out-of-the-way hamlet. へきそん
**벽토(壁土)** plaster; wall mud; stucco. かべつち
**벽하다(僻—)** 《장소가》(be) remote; out of the way; isolated 《성질이》eratic; rare; odd. とおくかけはなれている
**벽항(僻巷)** a remote village; an isolated village. へきそん
**벽해(碧海)** the blue sea. へきかい
**벽향(僻鄉)** a remote village. へききょう
**벽화(壁畵)** a mural painting; a painting in fresco. へきが
**변** 《결말》a jargon; a password; a countersign; a watchword. いんご
**변(邊)¹** 《수》《측(側)》a side/삼각형의 세 〜 the three sides of a traingle. くにざかい
**변(邊)²** 《변리》[rate of] interest/높은[낮은] 〜으로 at a high[low] rate of interest. りし
**변(邊)³** 《한자의》a left-hand radical (of a Chinese character). へん
**변(變)** 《변화》change 《재앙》a calamity; a mishap; an accident; a disaster 《동란》a disturbance 《사변》an emergency. へんか
**변(便)** 《대변》motions; feces; excrements/〜보다 ease oneself. だいべん
**변개(變改)** change; alteration; modification. へんこう
**변격(變格)** ①《변칙》irregularity ②《변칙활용》irregular conjugation. へんかく
**변경(邊境)** a frontier [district]; a remote region; a border district. へんきょう
**변경(變更)** change; alteration; modification 《명의의》transfer/계획의 〜 a change of one's plan. へんこう
**변계(邊界)** the border [land]; the frontier /〜를 침범하다 violate a frontier.

변고(變故) an accident; a misfortune; a disaster/~없이 살다 get along all right. へんじ

변광성(變光星) 【천】 a variable star.

변피(變―) an extraordinary calamity. いじょうなさいへん

변기(便器) a chamber pot; a night chair [stool]; a urinal; a bedpan. べんき

변놀이(邊―) usury; moneylending.

변덕(變德) fickleness; whim; caprice/~장이 a fickle person. むらっき

변돈(邊―) a loan; money lent at interest. りがつくおかわ

변동(變動) change; alteration/~하다 change 《시세가》 fluctuate/격심한 ~ violent fluctuations. へんどう

변두리(邊―) 《가·끝》 the end; the outskirts 《가장자리》 a brim; an edge; a border/도시 ~에 on the outskirts of a city. くにざかい

변두통(邊頭痛) 【의】 megrim ⇒편두통.

변란(變亂) a disturbance; a disorder; a civil war 《반란》 an uprising. へんらん

변론(辯論) discussion; argument 《토론》 debate 《법정의》 pleading/~하다 discuss; argue; debate; plead in court/~가 a debater. べんろん

변류기(變流器) 【공】 a converter; a current transformer.

변리(邊利) interest [on money]. りし

변리(辨理) management/~하다 manage; conduct/~ 공사 a minister resident/~사 an attorney[agent]. べんり

변명(變名) 《가명》 an assumed[a fictitious] name; an alias/~하다 《개명》 change one's name. へんめい

변명(辨明) an explanation 《사과》 an apology 《구실》 a pretext 《변호》 a defence/~하다 apologize; offer an apology; explain oneself; defend oneself/졸렬한 ~ a poor excuse. べんめい

변모(變貌) transfiguration. へんぼう

변모없다 ①《무뚝뚝하다》(be) blunt; brusque; unaffable ②《변통없다》(be) unadaptable; hide-bound; strait-lined. がんこだ

변민(邊民) border folk; people in the border district. くにざかいのひと

변박(辯駁, 辨駁) refutation; confutation/~하다 refute; confute/~의 여지가 없다 be irrefutable. べんばく

변발(辯髮) a pigtail; the Chinese queue.

변방(邊方) edges; a remote region; the border areas; sides. くにざかい

변변치 않다 (be) worthless; insignificant; small; poor; trashy; badly-made/변변치 않은 선물 a small present.

변변하다 《좋다》(be) good 《만족하다》(be) satisfactory 《상당하다》(be) proper; decent 《충분하다》(be) sufficient; enough/물건이 ~ The thing is tolerably good. なみいくじょうだ

변별(辨別) discrimination; distinction/~하다 discriminate (A from B); distinguish (A from B, between A and B)/~력 [power of] discrimination; judg[e]ment. べんべつ

변보(變報) news about a calamity[an uprising]. へんぼう

변복(變服) disguise/~하다 disguise; change the dress/여자로 ~하다 disguise oneself as a woman. へんそう

변비증(便秘症) 【의】 constipation; constiveness/~에 걸렸다 My bowels have stopped. べんぴしょう

변사(辯士) 《연설하는》 a speaker; an orator 《무성 영화의》 a film interpreter; a movie talker. べんし

변사(變死) an accidental death/~하다 meet one's death accidentally/~자 a person accidentally killed; a person whose death is unexplained. へんし

변사(變事) an accident; a mishap; a calamity; a disaster. へんし

변사(變辭) changing one's previous words/~하다 change one's previous words.

변상(辨償) payment; compensation; reparation/~하다 pay for; reimburse; indemnify; make good/~금 an indemnity; reparations. べんしょう

변색(變色) discoloration/~하다 fade; discolo[u]r. へんしょく

변설(辯舌) speech; eloquence/~이 유창한 eloquent; fluent. べんぜつ

변성(變成) rebirth; regeneration/~ 작용 【지】 metamorphism. へんせい

변성(變性) denaturalization; degeneration/~하다 《바뀌다》 degenerate 《바꾸다》 denaturalize; denature. へんせい

변성(變姓) 《이름》 changing one's surname/~하다 change one's surname[family name]. へんせい

변성(變聲) the change of voice/~하다 (voices) change/~기 puberty. おんせいのかわること

변성명(變姓名) changing one's name/~하다 change one's name; assume another name. せいめいをかえること

변소(便所) a water-closet (略:W.C.); a lavatory; a toilet-room《미》; a privy; a rest room/~에 가다 go to pay a call of nature/공중 ~ a public lavatory/수세식 ~ a flushtoilet. べんじょ

변속(變速) change of speed/~ 장치 the transmission [of un automobile, etc.]. へんそく

변수(變數) 【수】 a variable; a fluent. へんすう

변스럽다(變―) (be) odd; queer; funny; peculiar. へんだ

변신(變身) disguise; transformation/~하다 disguise oneself (as). へんしん

변심(變心) change of mind[heart]; infidelity/~하다 change one's mind; undergo a change of heart. へんしん

변압(變壓) 【전기】 transformation/~하다 transform/~기 a transformer. へんあつ

변역(變易) change; transition/~하다 c-

**변위(變位)** 【물】 displacement. へんい

**변음(變音)** 〖음〗 a flat. へんおん

**변이(變異)** change; 〖생〗 variation 〖돌연변이〗 mutation. へんい

**변자(邊子)** decoration around the edge [end] of (a thing). ふち

**변작(變作)** alteration 《위조》 forgery／~하다 alter; forge; remodel. へんぞう

**변장(變裝)** disguise／~하다 disguise oneself (as); make up (as a woman)／그는 ~을 하고 적진에 잠입했다 He went among the enemy in disguise.／~술 the art of disguise. へんそう

**변재(辯才)** oratorical talent[skill]; the gift of the gab《속》; eloquence／~가 있다 be gifted with eloquence. べんさい

**변전(變轉)** mutation; change; vicissitude／~하다 change; transmute／국제 정세의 ~ inconstant[ever-changing] international situation. へんてん

**변전소(變電所)** a [transformer] substation.

**변절(變節)** apostasy; treachery; betrayal／~하다 apostatize; backslide; change sides／~자 a turncoat; an apostate; a renegade. へんせつ

**변제(辨濟)** repayment; payment; reimbursement／~하다 repay; pay back; reimburse. べんさい

**변조(變造)** alteration; forgery／~하다 alter; forge; counterfeit. へんぞう

**변조(變調)** 〖음〗 a change of tone 《불규칙》 irregularity (이상) abnormality; anomaly／《라디오의》 modulation／~기 a modulator. へんちょう

**변종(變種)** a variety; a variant; a sport; a mutation; a freak. へんしゅ

**변주곡(變奏曲)** 〖음〗 a variation [on a theme]. へんそうきょく

**변죽울리다(邊―)** allude to; hint; intimate; suggest; glance at. ほのめかす

**변증(辨證)** demonstration／~법 〖철〗 dialectic. べんしょう

**변지(邊地)** a remote place; the edge of land; the borderland. へんち

**변지변(邊之邊)** compound interest; interest on the interest. へんちのへん

**변질(變質)** change in quality; deterioration／~자 a degenerate; a pervert. へんしつ

**변천(變遷)** change; transition 《성쇠》 vicissitude; ups and downs／~하다 change; undergo a change／시대의 ~ the changes of the times. へんせん

**변체(變體)** an anomalous state; anomaly; abnormality／~의 anomalous; abnormal. へんたい

**변칙(變則)** irregularity; anomaly／~의 irregular; anomalous／~ 동사 〖문〗 an irregular verb. へんそく

**변칭(變稱)** changing the name／~하다 change the name. へんしょう

hange; undergo a change; shift; mutate; modify. へんえき

**변태(變態)** 《생물의》 transformation; metamorphosis (이상) abnormality; anomaly／~ 심리[성욕] abnormal psychology［sexual desire］. へんたい

**변통(變通)** 《융통》 makeshift; shifting; contrivance 《처치》 management arrangement／~하다 manage; contrive; devise means; make shift; arrange matters／임시 ~ a rough makeshift／~성 adaptability. へんつう

**변통(便通)** a passage; bowels; the action of the bowels. べんつう

**변통수(變通數)** a resource; a contrivance; a makeshift. へんつうするほうほう

**변폭(邊幅)** hemming; a hem; a selvage; a list.

**변하다(變―)** change; become different; vary／영원히 변하지 않는 eternal／서울이 많이 변했다 Seoul has changed a great deal. かわる

**변함없이** unchangeably; invariably; forever.

**변해(辯解)** an explanation; a defense; an excuse; a vindication. べんかい

**변혁(變革)** a change; a reform 《혁명》 a revolution／~하다 revolutionize; reform. へんかく

**변형(變形)** metamorphosis; a variety; transformation／~하다 《바꾸다》 change; transform; metamorphose; turn. へんけい

**변호(辯護)** defense; pleading; justification 《자기 변호》 self-defense／~하다 defend; plead (for)／사건을 ~하다 defend [plead] (a person's) case. べんご

**변호사(辯護士)** a lawyer; a barrister [at law]; a solicitor／~ 사무소 a law office／~회 a bar association. べんごし

**변화(變化)** change 《변경》 alteration 《다종 다양》 variety 《변형》 transformation 《동사의 활용》 conjugation／~하다 change; alter; transform; conjugate／정세의 ~ a change in situation. へんか

**변환(變換)** change; conversion; transformation／~하다 change; convert; divert. へんかん

**변환(變幻)** transformation. へんげん

**별** 【천】 a star／~이 밝은 밤 a starlit night. ほし

**별가(別家)** ①《작은집》 a concubine ②《딴집》 a separate house.

**별가락(別―)** a different[separate] tone [key, beat, rhythm]. べつのちょうし

**별갑(鼈甲)** tortoiseshell／~ 세공 tortoise[-shell] work.

**별개(別個)** a different[distinct] one; a separate one／그것은 ~의 문제이다 That is another question. べっこ

**별거(別居)** living separately; separation／~하다 live separately. べっきょ

**별건(別件)** ①《물건》 an unusual thing; something unusual ②《사건》 an unusual event[case]. べつのもの

**별것(別―)** a rarity; a curiosity; an od-

**별격(別格)** a special status.

**별견(瞥見)** a glance; a glimpse; a cursory view. べっけん

**별고(別故)** ①《뜻밖의 사고》an untoward event; a hitch; a trouble ②《까닭》a specific reason. ふいのじこ

**별곡(別曲)** 《문》a new tune; a special tune. べっきょく

**별꼴(別─)** an extraordinary spectacle; an obnoxious thing. おかしなたいど

**별꽃** 〔식〕a chickweed.

**별과(別科)** a special course. べっか

**별관(別館)** an annex; an outhouse; an outbuilding. べっかん

**별궁(別宮)** a detached palace; a secondary palace; a royal villa. べつぐう

**별기(別記)** a separate paragraph[note]/~하다 write in separate paragraph; make a separate note. べっき

**별나다(別─)** (be) peculiar; queer; strange; eccentric/별난 사람 an eccentric; an odd duck. おかしい

**별나라** starland.

**별납(別納)** paying separately/~하다 pay separately. べつのう

**별놈(別─)** an eccentric person.

**별다르다(別─)** be of peculiar kind; uncommon. いじょうだ

**별달리(別─)** differently/~ 굴다 behave differently. べつに

**별당(別堂)** a separate house. はなれや

**별도(別途)** a separate way 《용도》separate use. べつと

**별도리(別道理)** an alternative; a choice; a better way/~ 없다 have no choice but to (do). べつのどうり

**별똥** a shooting star; a meteor. いんせき

**별동(別棟)** an annex.

**별동대(別動隊)** a detached force; partisans; flying column. べつどうたい

**별로(別─)** especially; particularly/~ 할 일도 없다 I am not particularly engaged. べつに

**별록(別錄)** a special record. ほかのきろく

**별리(別離)** separation; parting/~하다 part (from)/~의 슬픔 the sorrow of parting. べつり

**별명(別名)** a nickname; a by-name; an alias; another name. べつめい

**별 무늬** a star[red] design.

**별문제(別問題)** another question; another thing. べつもんだい

**별물(別物)** 《물건》a peculiar thing 《사람》a queer one; an odd duck. べつのもの

**별미(別味)** a delicacy; a tidbit/~적다 (be) queer; odd; peculiar; unusual; abnormal; weird. とくべつなあじ

**별반(別般)** particular[ly]; especial[ly]. べつだん

**별배(別杯)** a parting cup. べっぱい

**별배달(別配達)** special-delivery mail. とくべつはいたつ

**별법(別法)** another way; a different method. べっぽう

**별별(別別)** of various and unusual sorts/~ 일 unusual things of all sorts. べつべつ

**별보(別報)** special news. べっぽう

**별봉(別封)** a letter under separate cover. べっぷう

**별빛** starlight; the stars. せいこう

**별사(別使)** a special envoy; a special messenger. とくべつなししん

**별사건(別事件)** a strange affair; a strange event. べつのじけん

**별사람(別─)** an eccentric; a queer bird; a mess; an odd duck. べつのひと

**별석(別席)** another room[seat]; a special seat; a seat apart. べっせき

**별설(別設)** special establishment. とくべつなせつび

**별세(別世)** ~하다 die; pass away; depart this life; decease. しぬこと

**별세계(別世界)** another world; a world of it's own. べつせかい

**별소리(別─)** unreasonable remarks. べつのことば

**별송(別送)** ~하다 send by separate post [under separate cover].

**별수(別數)** ①《운수》special luck; extraordinary good fortune ②《수단·방법》the magic formula; the magic touch; the (be) secret (to); a secret key.

**별스럽다(別─)** (be) queer ⇒별나다. おかしい

**별식(別食)** a dainty; specially-prepared food; a rare dish. とくべつないしょく

**별실(別室)** a separate room; another room; a special room. べっしつ

**별안간(瞥眼間)** suddenly; all of a sudden; all at once; abruptly/~의 sudden; unexpected; abrupt/~ 죽다 die suddenly/~ 환해지다 become bright suddenly. にわか

**별일(別─)** a strange event; an oddity 《사고》an accident 《특별한 일》something particular/~없이 safely; in safety; without any accident. おかしいこと

**별자(別者)** ①《사물》a peculiar thing; a strange thing ②《사람》a crank; an odd fellow; a queer fish[duck]. おかしいもの

**별자리** 〔천〕a constellation; an asterism. せいざ

**별장(別莊)** a villa; a summer house/해변의 ~ a seaside villa. べっそう

**별재(別才)** special[extraordinary] talent. べっさい

**별제(別製)** ~의 specially made; deluxe; of special manufacture. べっせい

**별종(別種)** ①《종류》a special[different] kind ②《선물》a gift of special kind. べっしゅ

**별주(別酒)** ①《별제의》a specially-prepared liquor ② a parting drink ⇒이별주(離別酒). とくべつなさけ

**별쭝나다** strange ⇒별나다. おかしい

**별증(別症)** a complication; a deuteropa-

**별지**(別紙) an annexed[accompanying] paper/~와 같이 as stated in the accompanying letter[document]. べっし

**별찬**(別饌) a rare dish; a dainty. とくべつなおかず

**별책**(別冊) a separate volume 《잡지의》 an extra number[issue]. べっさつ

**별천지**(別天地) another world. べってんち

**별체**(別體) an odd style; a peculiar style. とくべつなたいせい

**별칭**(別稱) another name. べつめい

**별파**(別派) 《종파》 a separate sect; another[a different] party[school].

**별판**(別—) an unexpected improvement of the situation. べつのきょくめん

**별표**(一票) 《별꼴》 a star; an asterisk/~가 있는 asterisked.

**별표**(別表) an attached table; an annexed list/~ 양식 an attached form. べっぴょう

**별항**(別項) separate paragraph; another section[clauses]. べっこう

**별행**(別行) another line. べつぎょう

**별호**(別號) 《호》 pen name; *nom de plume* (F); 《별명》 a nickname. べつごう

**볌** a piece of cloth[paper] inserted to make something fit tighter; a filler.

**뼘** a span; the span of a hand/길이를 ~으로 재다 span length.

**뼘다** span (*length*); measure by the span. ゆびではかる

**뼘들이로** in quick succession; one after another; consecutively.

**볍씨** rice seed. いねのたわ

**볏** a cockscomb; a crest; a crown. とさか

**볏가락** awns on a rice plant.

**볏가리** a stack of rice straw. いねむら

**볏가을** rice-harvest/~하다 harvest rice. いねのしゅうかく

**볏단** a rice-sheaf.

**볏모** a young rice plant. いねのなえ

**볏섬** a sack of rice.

**볏성내다** flare[blow] up [in anger]. かんしゃくをおこす

**볏짚** rice-straw/~을 깔다 spread rice-straw. いねわら

**병**(瓶) a bottle 《약병》 a phial 《플라스크》 a flask/~에 담은 bottled; in bottles. びん

**병**(病) a disease; indisposition; illness 〈영〉; sickness〈미〉; 《국부적》 a trouble; an ailment; a disorder; a complaint/~난 sick; ill; unwell; indisposed; diseased/~ 때문에 on account of illness; owing to ill-health/가벼운 ~ a slight illness/~ 문안 a visit to a sick person/~이 낫다 get well; recover from illness. やまい

**병**(丙) 《성적 등의》 a third [class]; C. ひのえ

**병가**(兵家) a tactician; a strategist; a man of arms; a soldier. へいか

**병가**(病家) a patient's house; a sick family/~에 문병가다 pay a sick call.

**병가**(病暇) sick leave.

**병갑**(兵甲) armour; arms.

**병객**(病客) a sick person. びょうにん

**병거**(兵車) a [war] chariot.

**병결**(病缺) absence on account of[due to] illness.

**병고**(病故) sickness; a disease; illness. びょうきになったじこ

**병고**(病苦) suffering[pain] from sickness/~에 시달리다 labour under *one's* disease. びょうく

**병골**(病骨) a man of delicate constitution; a weak person. びょうじゃくしゃ

**병과**(兵戈) ①《창》 a spear ②《싸움》 a war; a conflict. へいか

**병과**(兵科) a branch of the service; an arm (of *the army*)/~ 장교 a combatant officer.

**병구**(病軀) a sick body; *one's* sickly constitution/~를 무릅쓰고 in spite of *one's* illness.

**병구완**(病—) nursing; care/~하다 nurse; care for; tend. びょうにんのかんご

**병권**(兵權) military power/~을 잡아 possess military power. へいけん

**병권**(秉權) taking the power/~하다 take the power; come into power; seize power. けんりょくをにぎること

**병균**(病菌) disease germs 《전염병의》 an epidemic bacillus. びょうきん

**병근**(病根) the cause of a disease ⇨병원(病源). びょうこん

**병기**(兵器) arms; weapons of war; ordnance/~고 an armoury; an arsenal/~ 제조 manufacture of arms. へいき

**병나다**(病—) ①《병이》 become sick; fall ill ②《탈이》 get out of order; go wrong/차가 병났다 The car has gone wrong; The car is out of order. びょうきになる

**병내다**(病—) ①《몸에》 make ill; let fall ill ②《탈을》 break down; cause a breakdown; bring out of order. びょうきにさせる

**병단**(兵端) war ⇨전단(戰端). せんたん

**병단**(兵團) an army corps.

**병대**(兵隊) an army/~ 군대. へいたい

**병독**(病毒) disease germs; a virus/~ 보유자 a germ-carrier. びょうどく

**병동**(病棟) a ward. びょうとう

**병들다**(病—) be taken[fall] ill/병든 ill; sick; laid up; in poor health/그 여자는 병들었다 She was affected by a disease. びょうきにかかる

**병란**(兵亂) a war; a disturbance; trouble/~의 터로 변하다 become a scene of war. へいらん

**병략**(兵略) strategy; tactics. へいりゃく

**병력**(兵力) military force; force of arms/소수 ~ a small force. へいりょく

**병력**(病歷) anamnesis; a case history.

**병렬**(竝列) a row/~하다 stand in a line; be in a row/~ 회로 《물》 a paralle

**병리**(病理) pathology／~학상의 pathological／~학 교실 a pathology [class] room.

**병립**(並立) ~하다 stand abreast[side by side]; coexist.

**병마**(兵馬) 《군사》 military affairs 《전쟁》 war 《군대》 troops／~의 대권을 잡다 assume supreme military power.

**병마**(病魔) a malady; a cursed disease／~에 사로잡히다 be attacked by a disease.

**병마개**(瓶—) a stopper 《콜크제의》 a cork 《쇠로 된》 a capsule.

**병막**(病幕) an isolation hospital; a detention hospital.

**병명**(病名) the name of a disease／~을 알 수 없는 병 an unidentified disease.

**병목**(瓶—) the neck of a bottle.

**병몰**(病沒) death from sickness.

**병무**(兵務) military affairs／~국 the Military Service Bureau.

**병발**(竝發, 倂發) concurrence 《병의》 a complication／~하다 concur; develop [accompany] (another disease).

**병방**(丙方) 【민】 south by southeast.

**병배**(瓶—) a bottle-shaped pear.

**병법**(兵法) tactics; strategy／~가 a tactician; a strategist.

**병변**(兵變) a war ⇨병란(兵亂).

**병부**(病夫) one's sick husband; a sick man.

**병비**(兵備) armaments.

**병사**(兵士) a soldier; a service-man; a private.

**병사**(兵舍) barracks.

**병사**(兵事) military affairs／~과 a military affairs section.

**병사**(病死) death from sickness; a natural death／~하다 die of sickness; die from a disease.

**병사**(病舍) an infirmary; a hospital.

**병살**(倂殺) 《야구》 double play[killing].

**병상**(病床) a sickbed／~ 일지 a clinical diary.

**병상**(病狀) the condition [of a disease, a patient]; one's condition.

**병상병**(病傷兵) the sick and the wounded [soldiers]; disabled soldiers.

**병색**(病色) a sick complexion／~이 보이다 look sickly.

**병서**(兵書) a book on tactics.

**병서**(竝書) writing same characters in a lateral line.

**병석**(病席) a sickbed／~에 있다 be ill in bed.

**병선**(兵船) a warship.

**병세**(兵勢) military force; the number of soldiers; an army; a force.

**병세**(病勢) the condition of a disease patient]／~가 나아지다 get better; improve／~가 악화되다 take turn for the worse.

**병소**(病巢) a focus(pl. ~es, -ci).

**병술**(瓶—) bottled sool.

**병술**(丙戌) 【민】 the 23rd binary term of the sexagenary cycle.

**병신**(病身) ①《기형물》 a malformed article; odds ②《병든 몸》 a sick body 《병자》 a sickly person ③《바보》 a fool; a dunce 《천치》 an idiot ④《불구》 deformity; malformation 《불구자》 a cripple; a deformed person.

**병신**(丙申) 【민】 the 33rd binary term of the sexagenary cycle.

**병신 구실**(病身—) unworthiness; uselessness.

**병신성스럽다**(病身—) (be) foolish; stupid; silly; dump《미·속》.

**병실**(病室) a sick-room 《병원의》 a [sick] ward 《군함의》 a sick-bay 《학교·공장의》 an infirmary〈영〉.

**병아리** a chick; a chicken／~ 감별사 a chicken sexer.

**병아리 오좀** a chickenhearted[fainthearted] person; a weakling. つまらないもの

**병약**(病弱) [constitutional] infirmity; delicate constitution／~하다 (be) sickly; delicate.

**병역**(兵役) military service; conscription; service in the army.

**병영**(兵營) barracks.

**병오**(丙午) 【민】 the 43rd binary term of the sexagenary cycle.

**병와**(病臥) ~하다 be ill in bed; be ill abed.

**병용**(竝用) ~하다 use together[at the same time].

**병원**(兵員) strength; military personnel.

**병원**(病院) a hospital 《학교·공장 등의》 an infirmary／~장 the director of a hospital／~차 an ambulance.

**병원**(病原, 病源) the cause[origin] of a disease／~균 germs; a bacillus(pl. -cilli, -lai).

**병유**(倂有, 竝有) ~하다 possess together; combine (one thing) with (another).

**병인**(兵刃) a weapon; a sword.

**병인**(病人) a sick person.

**병인**(病因) the cause[origin] of a disease; the cause of one's illness[malady]; an etiological factor.

**병인**(丙寅) 【민】 the 3rd binary term of the sexagenary cycle.

**병자**(病者) a sick person; an invalid 《의사가 보아》 a patient; a case.

**병자**(丙子) 【민】 the 13th binary term of the sexagenary cycle.

**병작**(竝作) share tenancy[sharecropping] by half／~하다 tennant share and share alike.

**병장**(兵長) a lance corporal.

**병장기**(兵仗器) a weapon; arms; ordnance.

**병적**(病的) morbid; diseased; abnormal; unsound; pathological. びょうてき
**병적**(兵籍) the army roll. へいせき
**병점**(病占) divination for sickness/~하다 diagnose a case of sickness by divination. びょうきのうらない
**병정**(兵丁) a soldier (해군) a sailor (공군) an air-man (군대) troops. へいてい
**병제**(兵制) a military system. へいせい
**병조**(兵曹) a warrant officer/~장 a chief warrant officer. へいそう
**병졸**(兵卒) a soldier; a private 《총칭》 the ranks. へいそつ
**병종**(兵種) a branch of the army ⇒병과(兵科).
**병종**(丙種) the third class. へいしゅ
**병중**(病中) during one's illness; while one is ill/~이다 be ill in bed; be laid up (with illness). びょうきちゅう
**병증**(病症) the nature of a disease; a case. びょうしょう
**병진**(竝進, 倂進) ~하다 keep abreast; keep pace with. へいしん
**병진**(兵塵) the tumult of war; the dust of the battlefield. せんじょうのほこり
**병진**(丙辰) 【민】 the 53rd binary term of the sexagenary cycle. へいしん
**병집**(病-) a fault; a flaw; a defect; a weakness. けっかん
**병참**(兵站) communications/~ 장교 a commissary/~부 the commissariat; a supply department. へいたん
**병추기**(病--) a sickly[weak] person; an invalid; a person in delicate health. びょうじゃくしゃ
**병충해**(病蟲害) damages by blight and harmful insects. びょうちゅうがい
**병칭**(竝稱) ~하다 rank[class] (one) with; rank them together. へいしょう
**병탄**(竝呑, 倂呑) annexation/~하다 annex (to); swallow up. へいどん
**병태**(病態) the condition [of a patient]. びょうたい
**병통**(病-) trouble (with a thing); malfunction; something wrong (with); a hitch; a snag. けっかん
**병폐**(病廢) disablement[deformity] by disease/~하다 be disabled [by a disease].
**병폐**(病弊) an evil ⇒폐해(弊害).
**병풍**(屛風) a [folding] screen. びょうぶ
**병학**(兵學) strategy; military science; tactics. へいがく
**병합**(倂合) annexation; amalgamation 《병탄》absorption/~하다 annex (to); amalgamate (into). へいごう
**병합죄**(倂合罪) 【법】 the concurrence of offenses. きょうごうはん
**병행**(竝行) ~하다 go side by side; keep pace with; go abreast of. へいこう
**병혁**(兵革) 《무기》 arms; weapons 《전쟁》 warfare. へいかく
**병화**(兵火) the fires of war/~의 와중 a battlefield/~에 짓밟히다 be destroyed [devastated] by fire in a battle. へいか

**병환**(病患) illness: sickness. ごびょうき
**병후**(病後) ~의 convalescent/~의 조섭 aftercare. びょうご
**볕** sunshine; sunlight; sunbeams/~에 쪼이다 expose to the sun. にっこう
**볕기**(-氣) heat of the sun; the force of the sunlight. ようき
**볕들다** shine (into, in, upon)/방에 ~ The sun shines[streams] into the room.
**보** (들보) a crossbeam; a beam. はり
**보**(步) (걸음) a step; a pace/제 1~ the first[initial] step/1~ 전진[후퇴]하다 make a step forward[backward].
**보**(保) (보증) guarantee; security 《보증인》 a guarantor/~서다 stand surety [security] for. ほしょう
**보**(洑) (저수지) a reservoir for irrigation; an irrigation pond. いせき
**보**(褓) a [small] wrapping[covering] cloth. むつき
**보**(補) assistant; probationary/서기 ~ an assistant clerk[secretary]/외교관 ~ a probationary[student] diplomat/차관 ~ an assistant vice-minister.
**보가지**(-어) a swellfish; a blowfish.
**보글**(술 따위가) with a bubble[pop]/~ 보글 bubbling; popping/~거리다 bubble; pop. ぶくぶく
**보각**(補角) 【수】 a supplementary angle; a supplement. ほかく
**보감**(寶鑑) a thesaurus; a handbook; a manual. ほうかん
**보강**(補强) reinforcement; invigoration /~하다 reinforce; invigorate/내각의 ~ 공작을 하다 take measures to strengthen the Cabinet/~ 공사 reinforcement work/~ 증거 【법】 corroboration. ほきょう
**보강**(補講) a supplementary lecture/~하다 make up for missing lecture.
**보깨다** have a stomach trouble; suffer from indigestion. いがおもい
**보건**(保健) health; preservation of health 《위생》hygiene; sanitation/~소 a health center/이것은 국민 ~에 중대한 문제이다 This is vital question for health of the nation[s]. ほけん
**보검**(寶劍) a treasured sword 《의장용》 a formalless sword. ほうけん
**보결**(補缺) supply of deficiency; supplement; filling a vacancy/~하다 fill a vacancy; cover a deficiency/~생 supplementary students/~ 선거 a by-election. ほけつ
**보고**(報告) a report; an account 《정보》information 《계산의》 returns 《학회의》 a paper 《연구·조사의》 a memoir/~하다 report; inform (one) of/~자 a reporter/~서 a report; returns /회의에 대한 ~를 하다 give a report of the conference. ほうこく
**보고**(寶庫) a treasure-house; a treasury. ほうこ
**보관**(保管) custody; [safe-]keeping; cha-

rge/~하다 keep; take custody[charge] of/~인 a custodian; a keeper/~료 storage; custody fee.

**보관**(寶冠) 《왕의》 a crown 《귀족·왕족의》 a coronet; a diadem.

**보교**(步轎) a sedan[-chair]; a palankeen/~를 타다 ride[have a ride] in a sedan chair/~로 가다 go by palankeen.

**보국**(報國) patriotic service; patriotism/~심 patriotism; patriotic spirit/납세 ~ patriotic service by taxation.

**보국 안민**(輔國安民) ~하다 promote national interests and welfare of the people.

**보군**(步軍) a foot-soldier; a footman.

**보굿** a piece of bark; a net float.

**보균**(保菌) carrying germs; being infected/~하다 carry germs; be infected/~자 a germ carrier; an infected person.

**보글보글** boiling; simmering/~ 끓다 simmer; be at a simmer.

**보금자리** a nest; a roost/사랑의 ~ a love nest/~를 짓다 build a nest/~에 들다 [go to] roost; fly home to roost.

**보급**(普及) diffusion; spread; propagation; pervasion 《민중화》 popularization/~하다 diffuse; spread; propagate/교육의 ~을 도모하다 prompt the spread of education.

**보급**(補給) supply; replenishment/~하다 supply; replenish/연료를 ~하다 refuel; replenish fuel.

**보기** ①《예》 an example; an instance 《본보기》 a case/~를 들면 for example [instance] ②《보는 각도》 a way of looking at 《things》.

**보기**(寶器) a treasured article; a treasure.

**보기**(補氣) invigoration of one's energy [vitality] by taking medicine/~하다 invigorate[animate] one's energy by taking medicine.

**보내기**(洑―) making an irrigation ditch.

**보내다** ①《물품을》 send; forward; transmit; consign 《배로》 ship 《돈을》 remit 《편지를》 write 《증정》 present (one with a thing); make (one) a present; give; send/책을 ~ send a book to (one); present (one) with a book ②《사람을》 send; dispatch; despatch/심부름을 ~ send (one) on errand/부르러 ~ send for (one)/짐 가지러 하녀를 ~ send maid-servant for one's luggage/아이를 학교에 ~ send (a boy) to school/나는 아이들을 해변가에 보냈다 I send the children off to the seaside. ③《이별》 see off; give a send -off/성대하게 ~ give a good send-off ④《세월을》 pass (one's life); spend (one's time); live (a life, an existence)/시간을 ~ take up one's time/말년을 편안히 ~ live the rest of one's life happily/그녀는 깨끗한 생애를 보냈다 she led a clean life.

**보늬** the inner skin of a chestnut.

**보다**¹ ⇨별항 참조(page 1488).

**보다**² ①《시험삼아》 try; have a try (at)/새옷을 입어 ~ try on a new suit/구두를 신어 ~ try shoes on ②《경험》 Q영국에 가 보았느냐 Have you been to England?

**보다**³ 《추측·의향》 seem; it seems [to me] (that); look like; appear/눈이 올려나 ~ It looks like[is likely to] snow.

**보다**⁴ 《비교의》 than; rather than/~ 더 나쁘다[좋다] be worse[better] than; be inferior[superior] to/홍차ー 커피를 즐기다 like coffee better than tea/그는 내가 생각했던 것ー 키가 컸다 He was taller than I thought he would be. ―より

**보따리**(褓―) a bundle; a package; a parcel/~ 장수 a packman; a peddler; a hawker.

**보다 못해** being unable to refrain from interfering; being unable to pass unnoticed/~ 그가 사이에 끼어들었다 Being unable to remain a mere spectator, he intervened.

**보답**(報答) 《보상》 recompense; a reward/~하다 return; requite; reward; recompense/노력에 ~하다 recompense (one) for his labo[u]r.

**보덕**(報德) requital; reward for service [kindness]/~의 뜻 a sense of gratitude.

**보도**(步度) pace; step; cadence.

**보도**(步道) a footpath; a sidewalk; a footway; a pavement/횡단 ~ a pedestrians' crossing.

**보도**(輔導) guidance; direction; lead; protection and guidance/~하다 lead; guide; direct/직업 ~ vocational guidance/~과 a guidance section.

**보도**(寶刀) a treasured sword/전가의 ~를 빼다 have recourse to one's best [and rarely-used] weapon; play one's trump card.

**보도**(報道) a report; news; information; intelligence/~하다 report; inform/~부[반] a press section[corps]/~ 관제 news black-out.

**보도독거리다** creak; graze; grind; grate.

**보독**(報毒) revenge; vengeance; retaliation/~하다 vent one's spite; satisfy one's grudge; revenge oneself on (one).

**보동보동** plump/~하다 (be) plump; chubby; full/~ 살이 찐 아기 a chubby baby.

**보두다**(保―) endorse; stand[go] security.

**보드기** a dwarf tree.

**보드득, 뽀드득** grinding ⇨바드득, 빠드득.

**보드랍다** (be) soft ⇨부드럽다.

**보득솔** a dwarf pine tree.

**보들보들하다** (be) very soft; tender; su-

보듬다. embrace; hug; clasp (*a person*) in *one's* arms[to *one's* bosom].

pple; flexible/보들보들한 살결 very soft skin.

보라매 a young hawk [tamed for hawking].

보라빛 [royal] purple; violet/~의 purple; violet/~이 도는 purplish/~ 수정 amethyst/연~ lilac/진~ fluorite violet; dark lilac.

보라장기(一將棋) a slowmoving chess game.

보람¹ worth; effect; result/~있는 fruitful; effective/~ 없는 useless; fruitless; vain; worthless; futile/~도 없이 in vain; to no purpose; without result; uselessly/~있는 수고 fruitful labo[u]rs/~없는 인생 a fruitless life/노력한 ~이 있어 시험에 합격했다 Thanks to his efforts[hard work], he passed the examination./수고한 ~이 없었다 I have labo[u]red to no purpose.

보람² a note; a mark; a sign/~하다 mark; sign.

보령(寶齡) the age of the king.

보로통하다, 뽀로통하다 ①(종기가) (be) swollen up; tumid ②(성나서) (be) sullen; sulky; in the sulks/보로통해서[뽀

보모(保姆) a nurse; a nursery governess; a kindergarten[nursery-school] teacher.

보무(步武) precise[measured, marching] steps/~ 당당히 전진하다 march[advance] in fine array; go on proudly; strut.

보무라지 rubbish; scraps; dust; bits; lint 《실의》 ravellings/실~ waste pieces of thread.

보물(寶物) a treasure; a treasured article (가보) an heirloom.

보배 a treasure; precious[valuable] things; valuables; a jewel/숨은 ~ a buried[hidden] treasure/나라의 ~ a national treasure/그는 우리나라의 ~다 He is the pride of our nation.

보배스럽다 (be) precious; valuable.

보법 dignity and the law[rule].

보법(步法) one's walk; step; gait; pace.

보병(步兵) an infantryman; a foot soldier/~대 an infantry corps[action]/~총 a [an infantry] rifle/~포 an infantry gun.

뽀뽀 kiss-kiss 《애기에게》 Give us a kiss.

보보(步步) step by step; each step.

보복(報復) retaliation; revenge; reprisal/~하다 retaliate (*upon*)/~적 retaliatory; reprisal.

보본(補本) ~하다 make up for (*one's* loss); recover (*one's* loss); compensate for (*one's* loss); recoup *one's* losses [oneself for *one's* losses].

보부상(褓負商) a peddler; a packman.

보비리 a miser; a stingy[close-fisted] fellow; a scrape-penny; a cheap skate.

보비위(補脾胃) pleasing another's humour; propitiation/~하다 humour; please another's humour; propitiate.

보싸기 wrapping cherry bark around the grip of an archer's bow.

보산(寶算) the king's age.

보살(菩薩) ①[종] *Bodhi-sattva*(Sans); a Buddhist saint; a Buddha elect ②(늙은 신령) an old She-Buddhist ③《점장이》 a fortuneteller.

로통해서] 입술을 쀼쭉 내밀다 pout; thrust out the lips in displeasure.

보료 a fancy mattress used as cushion.

보루(堡壘) a battery; a bulwark; a fort; a rampart/~를 구축하다 fortify; rampart; entrench.

보류(保留) reservation/~하다 reserve; hold back 《연기》 defer/~ 조건 a reserve; a reservation.

보름 ①(15일) fifteen days; half a month ②(보름날) the fifteenth day of a lunar month/~달 a full moon on the fifteenth night.

보름보기 a one-eyed person.

보름사리 ①(조수) the high tide on the fifteenth of the lunar month ②(조기) a yellow corvina fish caught at the time of the high tide.

보리 (대맥) barley/~차 barley water [tea]/~밭 a barley-field/~밥 boiled barley [and rice]/보릿짚 barley straw/보릿고개 the period of spring poverty/~ 타작하다 thresh barley.

보리(菩提) 《불》 *Bodhi*(Sans); 《정각(正覺)》 the Supreme Enlightenment; the way of salvation/~심 a devout disposition; aspiration for Buddhahood.

보리새우 《동》 a kind of small shrimp; *Acetes japonicus*(학명).

보리수(菩提樹) 《식》 a bo-tree; a linden-tree; a lime[-tree]; *Bodhendrum*(Sans).

보린(保隣) neighbourhood/~회 a neighbourhood association/~관 a settlement house/~ 사업 settlement[social] work; social service.

보릿가을 the time of barley harvest.

보릿고개 the period of pring poverty.

보릿재 ashes used to fertilize barley.

보릿짚 barley straw.

보막이(洑一) building a dammed pool [of water]/~하다 make[build] a dammed pool.

보매 apparently; seemingly; judging from appearance/얼핏 ~ at the first glance[sight]/~ 슬픈 것 같다 appear to be sad.

**보명(保命)** conservation[preservation] of life/~하다 conserve[preserve, maintain] one's life.　せいめいをたもつこと

**보살피다** look[see] after; take care of; care for; attend to.

**보살할미** a Buddhist nun with her hair unshaven.　あまさん

**보상(報償)** requital; remuneration; consideration; compensation/~하다 recompense; requite; remunerate; reward; repay.　ほうしょう

**보상(補償)** compensation; indemnity; reparation/~하다 indemnify; make reparation (for); compensate for/~금 an indemnity; compensation [money]/~안 a compensation bill.　ほしょう

**보새(寶璽)** the Royal[Privy] Seal; the king's seal.　ぎょじ

**보색(補色)** a complementary[complement] color.　美ほしょく

**보서다(保—)** go security for; stand surety for.　ほしょうにんになる

**보석(步石)** ①《디딤돌》a stepping-stone ②《돌층계》stone-steps; a flight of stairs of stone.

**보석(保釋)** bail/~하다 bail (a person) out/~인 a bailer; a bail/~금 bail. ほしゃく

**보석(寶石)** a jewel; a gem; a precious stone/~류 jewellery/~상 a jeweller; a jeweller's shop.　ほうせき

**보선(保線)** maintenance of railway tracks/~하다 keep the tracks in good condition/~공 a lineman(pl. -men)〈영〉; a track-walker〈미〉;《구간의》a section m-

## 보 다¹

①《눈으로》perceive; see; set eyes on; look (at)/보시는 바와 같이 as you see/어느 모로 보나 to all appearances/한 번 보아서 at first glance; at a glance; at first sight/ …을 보자 at the sight of/슬그머니 steal a glance at/얼핏 ~ catch a glimpse (of)/자세히 ~ have a good look (at)/죽 훑어 ~ glance over (a thing); look through (a book)/못 본 체하다 pretend not to see [not to have seen]; wink[blink, connive] (at)/차마 볼 수 없다 cannot bear to see; be unable to bear the sight of/보기 좋다 be nice to look at/보기 싫다 hate (a person); hate the sight (of a person)/어디 보자 let me see[think]…; let me take[have] a look/그것 보라구 I told you [so]! There you are!/어디 두고 보자 You will see!, We'll see about that./이것 보게 Look here!/볼지어다 Behold!/도둑은 순경을 보자마자 도망갔다 At the sight of the police man, the thief took to his heels./상자 안에 무엇이 들었는지 보고 싶어 죽겠다 I'm dying to see what's inside of this chest./좌우지간 가서 보고 나오게 At any rate, go and have a look at it./이 그림은 보면 볼수록 좋다 This picture improves on acquaintance.

②《구경하다》see (the sights); visit/영화를[연극을] ~ see a movie[play]/볼 만하다 be worth seeing[visiting]/공장을 보러 가다 visit a factory.

③《일을》manage; transact; attend to/사무를 ~ attend to business/일을 ~ take care of a business; conduct affairs; handle a job; work/나의 아들은 우체국에서 일을 본다 My son works at the post office.

④《고찰·간주》consider; judge; view; look (at); regard (as)/내가 보기에는 from my point of view; in my opinion; to my mind; as I take it/어느 모로 보나 in every respect; from every point of view/보는 바가 다르다 look at (a matter) differently; view differently/그의 침묵은 동의하는 것으로 보아도 무방하다 His silence can be read as consent./나를 몇 살로 보는가 How old do you take me for?/대체로 보아 on the whole; considered as a whole.

⑤《읽다》read; see 《대충 훑어봄》look through[over]/신문을 ~ read[see] the newpaper/너 그것을 잡지에서 보았니 Did you read that in the magazine?

⑥《치르다》take/시험을 ~ take[sit for] an examination; undergo an examination.

⑦《돌보다·차리다》look after; take charge of; watch/아이를 ~ look after [nurse] a baby; baby-sit〈미〉; keep an eye on the baby (주의하여)/집을 ~ look after a house (while a person is away).

⑧《당하다》experience; go through; undergo; encounter; enjoy; suffer/경사[상사]를 ~ have a happy[an unhappy] occasion ~ suffer loss[damage]/이익을 ~ make a profit/욕을 ~ be insulted; be disgraced; have [rough] time of it; be put to shame; be humiliated; be abused.

⑨《누다》relieve nature/대변을 ~ have a bowel movement/소변을 ~ urinate 《장을》buy[sell] (in a market)/장 보러 가다 go to market; go shopping 《값을》offer (a price); bid《자손·사위·며느리를》get (a new relative)/며느리를 ~ get a daughter-in-law《점치다》tell (fortune); read [one's fortune in]; have one's fortune told/손금을 ~ read one's palm.

보선 · 보이다²

**보선**(普選) popular[universal] suffrage. ふつうせんきょの略語

**보세**(保稅) 【법】 bond/~ 창고 a bonded warehouse/~ 창고에 넣다 store in bond [a bonded warehouse]/~ 창고에서 내다 take out of bond/~ 화물 bonded goods. ほぜい

**보소**(譜所) an office for compilation of genealogical tables[family records].

**보송보송하다** (be) dry; parched; dried up. ぼっとりしている

**보수**(保守) conservatism/~적 conservative/~당 the Conservative Party/~ 세력 conservative force/~주의 conservatism. ほしゅ

**보수**(報酬) remuneration; a reward 《의사 등의》 a fee 《급료》 pay/…의 ~로서 in recompense for; as a reward for/무 ~로 without pay[fee]/~를 주다 remunerate[reward] (a person); pay (a person) a fee. ほうしゅう

**보수**(補修) mending; repair/~하다 mend; repair/~ 공사(工事) repair works. ほしゅう

**보수계**(步數計) a pedometer.

**보슬보슬** gently; softly. ぼろぼろ

**보슬비** a drizzle; a drizzling rain/~가 내리고 있다 It is drizzling. きりさめ

**보습** a plowshare[ploughshare]; a share.

**보습**(補習) supplementary work; supplement/~ 교육 supplementary education /~ 학교[과] a supplementary school [course]. ほしゅう

**보시**(布施) an offering (at a temple); alms; charity. ふせ

**보시기** a small bowl. つぼ

**보신**(補身) self-preservation; self-protection/~지책 the means of self-protection. ほしん

**보신**(補身) ~하다 build oneself up by taking tonics/~탕 soup of dog's meat. げんきをつけること

**보신**(補腎) invigoration by taking tonics /~제 a tonic; a cordial; an invigorant. せいりょくをほきょうすること

**보아** for one's sake; out of consideration for/나를 ~서라도 그를 용서해 주게 Forgive him for my sake.

**보아라듯이** showily; for show[display]; to attract attention. これみよがしに

**보아주다** take care of; take trouble; look after. きをつけてみまもってやる

**보아한들** upon reflection; if one considers the matter carefully. かんさつしたとて

**보안**(保安) the preservation of public peace/~과 the public peace section/~ 관 a sheriff〈미〉. ほあん

**보약**(補藥) a restorative; a tonic; a bracer; an adjuvant. きょうそうざい

**보양**(保養) a rest; recreation; relaxation 《병후의》 recuperation/~하다 recreate oneself; have relaxation 《병후에》 recuperate oneself/눈의 ~ a feast to the eye; a sight for sore eyes/~하는 사람 a health seeker/형은 시골에서 병후의 ~을 하고 있다 My brother is now recuperating in the country. ほよう

**보양**(補陽) ~하다 aid[strengthen] virility/~제 medicine to aid[strengthen] virility. せいりょくをやしなうこと

**보얗다, 뽀얗다** (be) whitish; milky; creamy; hazy. かすんでいる

**보어**(補語) 【언】 a complement/주격[목적격] ~ a subject[an objective] complement. ほご

**보여주다** let (one) see; show.

**보옥**(寶玉) a jewel ⇒보석(寶石). ほうぎょく

**보온**(保溫) keeping (a thing) warm; retaining warmth/~하다 keep warm/~ 을 위해서 for keeping warmth; to keep (a thing) warm. ほおん

**보우**(保佑) protection; help; assistance; aid/~하다 protect; help; assist; aid. ほゆう

**보위**(寶位) the throne; the crown/~ 계 승 succession to the throne/~를 잇다 succeed to the throne.

**보유**(補遺) a supplement; an addendum (pl. -da); an appendix (pl. -dices)/~의 supplementary/~하다 supplement; complement. ほい

**보유**(保有) possession; [a] holding/~하 다 hold; possess; keep; retain/~물 【법】 tenement/~미 rice holdings/금~고 g- old holdings/정부 ~미 governmentstocked rice. ほゆう

**보유스름하다, 뽀유스름하다** (be) whitish; milky; frosty.

**보육**(保育) nurture; upbringing/~하다 bring up; nurse/~원 a nursery school /~아동 ~ the bringing up[care] of children. ほいく

**보은**(報恩) requital of a favor; repayment of a kindness/~하다 requite [repay] another's kindness. ほうおん

**보음**(補陰) lessening the virile powers /~하다 strengthen the negative principal in one's nature; lessen the virile powers. いんきをほきょうすること

**보응**(報應) retribution; nemesis; a reward in accordance with a deed.

**보이다**¹ ①《눈에》 see; catch sight of 《사물이 주어》 be seen; be visible; show; be in sight; be open to the view/눈에 보이는 visible [to the naked eye]/보이 지 않다 be not seen; be out of sight/ 우리집에서 지리산이 잘 보인다 Our house commands a good view of Mt. Chiri./ 바다가 보이기 시작했다 The sea came into view. ②《…인 것 같다》 look; seem; appear/건강해 ~ look well/장삿군같이 ~ look like a merchant/이 계획은 잘 될 것같이 보인다 This plan is likely to work well. みえる

**보이다**² 《보게 하다》 show; let (a person) see[look at]; display; exhibit; evince

/앨범을 ~ show (a person) one's photo album/실력을 ~ show[display] one's ability.

**보익**(補翼) aid; help; assistance; support/~하다 aid; help; assist; support.

**보익하다** (be) somewhat milky; misty.

**보자기**¹ a wrapping cloth; a cloth-wrapper.

**보자기**² a diver [as for pearl or seaweed].

**보잘것 없다** (be) worthless; insignificant; trifling; good-for-nothing; small; useless/보잘것 없는 남자 a good-for-nothing fellow/그것은 보잘것 없는 일이다 That is a matter of no consequence./그의 세력은 ~ His influence is about as much use as a rope of sand.

**보짱** ①(담력) courage; pluck; heart; nerve; mettle; grit《미》; guts《속》 ②(마음 속) heart; mind; intention/~이 검다 be black-hearted.

**보장**(寶藏) 《보고》 a treasury; treasure house 《비장》 treasuring/~하다 treasure; store in secrecy.

**보장**(保障) guarantee; security/사회 ~ [제도] social security.

**보재**(寶財) a treasure; valuables; precious[valuable] things; a highly-prized article.

**보전**(保全) integrity; preservation; conservation; maintenance/~하다 preserve; keep intact/국토 ~ conservation of national land/영토 ~ territorial integrity.

**보전**(寶典) 《귀중한 법전》 a precious code 《사전》 a thesaurus (pl. ~es, ·ri) 《편람》 a hand-book.

**보정**(補正) revision; correction/~하다 revise; correct.

**보제**(補劑) a restorative; a tonic.

**보조**(補助) assistance; aid; support/~하다 support; aid; assist; subsidize/정부의 ~ a government grant/남의 ~로 생활하다 live on the bounty of another.

**보조**(步調) step; pace/경쾌한 ~ a light step/빠른 ~로 at a fast[good, great] pace/~가 맞지 않다 be[walk] out of step; break step/~를 맞추어 행진하다 walk in step.

**보조개** a dimple/그 여자는 웃으면 ~가 생긴다 Her face dimples with a smile.

**보조금**(補助金) a subsidy; a bounty; a grant-in-aid; a grant of money/~을 내다 subsidize; make grants for (a research).

**보족**(補足) a complement; a supplement/~하다 complement; supplement; make good/~적 complementary; supplementary.

**보존**(保存) preservation 《저장》 storage/~하다 preserve; keep intact; save/잘 ~되어 있다 be well preserved/영수증을 ~하다 keep a receipt.

**보좌**(補佐) aid; assistance/~하다 aid; assist; advise/~인[관] an assistant 《고문》 a counsellor.

**보좌**(寶座) the Imperial throne.

**보주**(補註) a supplementary note.

**보중**(保重) conservation[preservation] of one's health; taking care of oneself/~하다 conserve[preserve] one's health; take care of oneself.

**보증**(保證) guarantee; security; assurance/~하다 guarantee; warrant; assure; vouch[answer] for/~부(附) guaranteed; warranted/~금 security[caution] money; a deposit/~인 guarantor; a surety/~ 수표 a certified check/신원을 ~하다 vouch for (one)/품질을 ~하다 guarantee the excellence of the quality (of goods).

**보지** the vulva(pl. ~s, ·vae).

**보지**(保持) maintenance; preservation/~하다 maintain; preserve; hold; keep/기록 ~자 a record holder/선수권을 ~하다 hold the championship.

**보지**(報知) information; news; a report/~하다 inform (a person) of (a matter); communicate (a matter) to (a person); let (a person) know; report.

**보직**(補職) assignment to a position; appointment/~되다 be assigned[appointed] [to the post of..

**보채**(堡砦) a fort[ress]; a fortification; a stronghold; a citadel; a rampart.

**보채다** tease (for); clamour (for); fret/과자를 달라고 ~ clamour for candy.

**보철**(補綴) supplement; complement; replenishment/~하다 supplement; complement; replenish.

**보첨**(補添) an addition; a supplement/~하다 add (to); supplement.

**보첩**(譜牒) a genealogical table; a family tree; a genealogy book.

**보청기**(補聽器) a hearing aid.

**보초**(步哨) a sentry; a sentinel; a picket/~선 a sentry-line/~ 근무 sentry duty/~를 세우다 post a sentry.

**보충**(補充) supplement; replacement/~하다 supplement; replenish; fill up; replace/~ 계획 a replacement program/~병 a recruit/~의 supplementary; complementary.

**보칙**(補則) supplementary rules.

**보태다** ①《보충하다》 make up; supplement/보탬이 되다 go toward; be an aid (to) ②《가산하다》 add [up]; sum up.

**보통**(普通) ~의《통상의》 usual; general; ordinary; common 《전상적인》 normal; ordinal 《평범한》 commonplace 《평균의》 average/~으로 usually; commonly; generally／~ 교육 common[ordinary] education／~ 명사 《언》 a common noun／~ 선거 universal suffrage／~ 열차 an accommodation train／~ 사람 an ordinary[average] man; a common being／~ 우편 ordinary post／~ 수단으로는 with chaff／~ 아닌 uncommon; unusual／~대로 as usual／~ 이상[이하]의 above[below] the average; above[below] mediocrity／~으로 지내다 make a decent living／~ 사람과 다름없이 말하다 talk like an ordinary man／그는 ~의 인간이다 He is the man in the street.／어선은 ~ 저녁에 나가 아침에 돌아온다 As a rule fishing smacks go out in the evening and return in the morning. ふつう

**보퉁이**(褓─) a bundle; a package; a packet; a parcel.

**보편**(普遍) 《보편성》 universality; pervasion; the universal 《보급》 diffusion／~적으로 universal[ly]; general[ly]／~ 타당성 universal validity／~주의 universalism. ふへん

**보폭**(步幅) a stride; a pace.

**보표**(譜表) 《음》 a staff(*pl.* -ves); a score; a stave. ふひょう

**보푸라기** nap ⇨보풀. けば

**보풀** fine nap (of *cloth*); fuzz (of *paper*)／~ 명주 nubby[rough] silk. けば

**보풀다** nap; have a nap (on *cloth*); have fuzz (on *paper*). けばたつ

**보풀리다** raise a nap (on); nap. けばたたせる

**보풀보풀** with a nap; with fuzz／~하다 have a nap; (be) nappy; downy; fuzzy. もしゃもしゃ

**보필**(輔弼) assistance to the throne／~ 하다 assist; counsel. ほひつ

**보하다**(報─) report 《알리다》 inform; notify; acquaint; communicate to; let (*one*) know; tell.

**보하다**(補─) ①《보직》 appoint; choose; select ②《몸을》 nourish; nurse; invigorate. ほにんする

**보학**(譜學) genealogy／~자 a genealogist.

**보합**(步合) rate; percentage／~산 the calculation of percentage／~고 the amount of percentage／~ 청부 a percentage contract／~을 내다 give (*one*) a percentage. ぶあい

**보행**(步行) walking／~하다 walk; go on foot／~자 a walker／~객 a walker; a pedestrian; a foot-passenger／~의 자유를 잃다 be crippled. ほこう

**보험**(保險) ①《보증》 guarantee; warrant ②《생명・화재 등의》 insurance; assurance／생명 ~ life insurance[assurance]／화재[상해] ~ fire[accident] insurance／~금 insurance money／~료 insurance due; a premium／~ 계약자 a policy holder／~금 수취인 a beneficiary／~ 증서 an insurance policy／~에 들다 be insured. ほけん

**보혈**(補血) ~하다 nourish the blood／~제 a hematic. ほけつ

**보혈**(寶血) 《기독교》 the precious blood [of Jesus].

**보호**(保護) protection; shelter; safeguard／~하다 protect; shelter 《옹호하다》 safeguard 《돌봐 주다》 take care 《애호하다》 patronize 《보존하다》 preserve／~ 무역 protective trade／~ 관세 a protective tariff／~국(國) a protectorate／~색(色) a protective colo[u]r; protective colo[u]ring／~자 a protector; a guardian; a patron／~조(鳥) a protected bird. ほご

**보화**(寶貨) a treasure; a highly prized article; valuables. ほうか

**복** 《어》 a swellfish; a globefish; a puffer／~ 중독 swellfish poisoning. ふぐ

**복**(伏) the dog days; midsummer; the hottest period. ふくじつ

**복**(福) happiness; felicity; bliss; blessedness; a blessing／~된 happy; felicitous; blessed／그런 어머니가 계시니 너는 ~도 많구나 You are fortunate to have such a mother. ふく

**복**(蹼) a web[-foot]. みずかき

**복-**(複) double; complex; compound; compositive.

**복각**(伏角) 《물》 a dip (of *the compass*)／~계(計) an inclinometer; a dip needle／무-선 an aclinic line. ふかく

**복간**(復刊) reissue; revived publication.

**복강**(腹腔) the abdominal[peritoneal] cavity.

**복거**(卜居) ~하다 take up[choose, fix] [one's abode]. ぼっきょ

**복걸**(伏乞) ~하다 prostrate *one*self and beg. ふしてこうこと

**복고**(復古) 《정치상의》 restoration; revival／~하다 return to the old regime／~ 주의 reactionism. ふっこ

**복고**(腹稿) a literary plot [in one's mind] idea／~하다 map out[draw up, formulate] a plan. ふっこ

**복교**(復校) reinstatement [at school]; return to school／~하다 be reinstated [at school]; return to school; be at school again／~를 허락하다 allow (*a boy*) to return to school; readmit (*a boy*) into school. ふっこう

**복구**(復舊) restoration／~하다 be restored to normal [conditions]／~ 공사 repair[s] [restoration] works. ふっきゅう

**복권**(福券) a lottery ticket[card]／~이 맞았다 The lot fell on me.

**복권**(復權) rehabilitation; reinstatement; restoration of rights／~시키다 rehabilitate; reinstate. ふっけん

**복귀**(復歸) return; reversion／~하다 return (*to*); revert (*to*); make a comeback／구제도로 ~하다 return[revert] to the old system／직장에 ~하다 return to work. ふっき

**복날**(伏─) the dog day[s]; the hottest period in [the] midsummer. ふくじつ

**복놀이**(伏―) merrymaking on the dog day; a midsummer outing/~하다 hold [keep] merrymaking on the dog day; ~ 가다 go on a midsummer outing.

**볶다** ①(불에) parch; roast (기름에) fry /차를 ~ fire tea ②(들볶다) bully; tease; annoy; torment; torture.

**복달임**(伏―) the hottest period of summer; dog days.

**복당**(復黨) rejoining the party/~하다 rejoin the party; be reinstated in the party.

**복대기** 〖광〗 the dross of gold; slag; residue left after gold is panned/~ 삭히다 extract gold from slag.

**복대기다** fuss about; be uproarious.

**복대기치다** be boisterous.

**복더위**(伏―) a heat wave during the dog days; a midsummer hot spell.

**복덕**(福德) good fortune; happiness and prosperity.

**복덕방**(福德房) a real estate agent.

**복도**(複道) a corridor; a passage; a lobby; a hallway 〈미〉.

**복리**(複利) 〖경〗 compound interest/~법 the compound interest method.

**복리**(福利) welfare; well-being/ ~ 시설[사업] a public welfare facilities[work].

**복마**(卜馬) a packhorse.

**복마전**(伏魔殿) an enchanted hall; an abode of demons; a pandemonium; a hotbed/정계의 ~ a hotbed of political iniquity.

**복막**(腹膜) 〖해〗 the peritoneum (pl. -nea) /~염 peritonitis.

**복망**(伏望) ~하다 desire earnestly; sincerely hope; humbly beg.

**복면**(覆面) a mask/~하다 wear a mask /~의 masked.

**복명**(復命) a report/~하다 report [back]; submit a report to (a person)/~서 a report.

**복명**(腹鳴) intestinal[stomach] rumbling /~하다 (the bowels) rumble.

**복모**(伏慕) adoration/~하다 hold (a person) in the high esteem.

**복모음**(複母音) 〖언〗 a diphthong.

**복무**(服務) [public] service/~하다 serve; be in the service/~ 규정 the Public Service Regulations; 〖군〗 the standing orders/~ 시간 office hours.

**복문**(複文) 〖언〗 a compound sentence.

**복물**(伏―) heavy rains during the dog days[midsummer]/~지다 It rains heavily during the dog days[midsummer].

**복받치다** well up 〈북받치다〉.

**복발**(復發) recurrence; fresh return (of sadness, worries); 〖병의〗 relapse/~하다 return; recur; break out again; relapse.

**복백**(伏白) 〈편지〉 Yours [very] truly.

**복벗다**(服―) get over wearing[put aside] one's mourning garb.

**복벽**(腹壁) 〖해〗 the abdominal walls/~ 절개 수술 laparotomy/~의 abdominal.

**복벽**(復辟) reinstatement to the throne; restoration of the royal regime/~하다 restore the royal regime; reinstate an abdicated king to the throne/~ 운동 a monarchist movement.

**복병**(伏兵) an ambush; an ambuscade; men in ambush.

**복본위**(複本位) 〖경〗 bimetallism; the double metallic standard/~ 주의자 a bimetallist.

**복부**(腹部) 〖해〗 the abdomen; the abdominal region; the belly/~의 abdominal/~ 수술 an abdominal operation; abdominal surgery; ventrotomy/~ 임신 abdominal pregnancy.

**복비**(複比) 〖수〗 compound ratio.

**복사**(複寫) reproduction; reprint; a copy; 〈복사물〉 a reproduction/~하다 reproduce; take a copy/~용 잉크[지] copying ink[paper].

**복사**(輻射) radiation/~하다 radiate/~ 열 radiant heat.

**복사**(卜師) a fortuneteller; a diviner; a soothsayer; an augur.

**복사**(伏射) ~하다 fire prone/~호(壕) a sheltered trench.

**복사**(服事) obedient attendance; submission/~하다 serve[attend] obediently; obey; submit oneself to.

**복사**(蝮蛇) a viper; an adder.

**복사뼈** the ankle[-bone].

**복사화채**(―花菜) a peach punch.

**복상**(服喪) wearing mourning/~하다 wear mourning; go into the mourning.

**복상**(福相) a happy look; a radiant face.

**복색**(服色) dress; attire; personal appearance/~이 좋다 be well dressed/~ 에 무심하다 be indifferent about one's personal appearance.

**복서**(卜筮) ~하다 divine; foretell; presage /길흉을 ~하다 tell fortunes.

**복서**(卜書) 〈연극〉 stage directions.

**복선**(複線) a double track[line]/ ~으로 하다 double-track.

**복선**(伏線) an underplot (of a novel); preparation; ground work.

**복선**(覆船) capsizal/~하다 capsize; be capsized.

**복성**(複姓) a family name composed of two Chinese characters.

**복성**(複星) 〖천〗 multiple stars.

**복성**(福星) 〖목성〗 Jupiter.

**복성스럽다** (be) happy-looking; full faced; plump.

**복소수**(複素數) 〖수〗 a complex number.

복속(服屬) obedience; submission／~하다 obey; submit. ふくぞく

복수(復讐) revenge; avenge; vengeance 《보복》 retaliation; reprisal; a vendetta／~하다 revenge (oneself) on／나는 그에게 ~하겠다 I will get even with him. ふくしゅう

복수(複數) the plural number; plural; compound numbers. ふくすう

복수(復水) condensed water.

복수(腹水) 〘의〙 abdominal dropsy; dropsy of the belly; ascites. ふくすい

복수초(福壽草) 〘식〙 an Adonis; a pheasant's-eye; a garden pink; *Adonis amurensis*(학명).

복술(卜術) the art of divination; fortunetelling. ぼくじゅつ

복숭아 〘식〙 a peach [tree]; *Pranus persica* (학명). もも

복스럽다(福─) (be) happy-looking; fat and well-looking; prosperous-looking. ふくぶくしい

복습(復習) review／~하다 review; go over[through]; repeat *one's* lesson／프랑스 말을 ~해야겠다 I will have to brush up[on] my French. ふくしゅう

복시(複視) 〘의〙 diplopia; double vision.

복시합(複試合) 〘정구〙 doubles／남녀 혼합 ~ a mixed doubles. ふくしあい

복식(服飾) dress and its ornament／부인용 ~ ladies trimmings. ふくしょく

복식(複式) ~의 《부기》 double-entry 《투표의》 plural 《기계의》 compound; engine. ふくしき

복식 호흡(腹式呼吸) abdominal breathing [respiration]; the abdominal type of respiration. ふくしきこきゅう

복신(福神) the God of Wealth; the mother of good luck. ふくじん

복심(腹心) ~의 confidential; bosom; trusty. ふくしん

복심(覆審) 〘법〙 retrial; re-examination; a renewal of procedure; a review／~하다 hear again; retry. ふくしん

볶아대다 pester[bother, annoy] (*a person*) to death[persistently].

볶아치다 hurry (*through, over*); rush about. せきたてる

복안(腹案) a plan[scheme] in *one's* mind; a program[me]. ふくあん

복약(服藥) ~하다 take medicine. ふくやく

복어 a globefish; a swellfish; a puffer／~에 중독되다 be poisoned by swellfish.

복역(服役) [penal] servitude／~하다 serve *one's* term[sentence]／~ 기간 a term of sentence／만기 ~하다 serve *one's* full time. ふくえき

복염(伏炎) the heat of midsummer.

복엽(複葉) 〘식〙 a compound leaf／~의 symphyllous. ふくよう

복용(服用) 《약의》 internal use; dosage／~하다 take; use internally／~량(量) dosage; a dose. ふくよう

복욱(馥郁) ~하다 (be) fragrant; mellow; sweet-smelling; odorous. ふくいく

복원(伏願) ~하다 humbly request[beg]; sincerely hope (*for*); desire earnestly. ふしてねがうこと

복원(復元) restoration／~력 〘공〙 dynamic stability. ふくげん

복원(復員) demob; demobilization／~하다 be demobilized. ふくいん

복위(復位) restoration; rehabilitation; reinstatement; 〘의〙 reduction／~하다 be restored. ふくい

볶음 a roast; a broil; roasted[panbroiled] food／떡 ~ broiled rice-cake.

복음(複音) 《음성》 a compound sound. ふくおん

복음(福音) 《반가운 소식》 glad tidings; good[welcome] news; a godsend 《복음서》 the Gospels／그것은 월급장이에게는 ~이다 It is good news for salary men. ふくいん

복이나인 a servant to a lady-in-waiting at court.

볶이다 ①《불에》 be parched; be fired ②《들볶이다》 be teased; be annoyed; be tormented; be worried／아이들에게 ~ be pestered by *one's* kids. せきたてられる

복입다(服─) wear mourning. もふくをきる

복자 brass cup used for measuring oil. あぶらのけいりょうき

복자(踏子, 伏字) 〘인〙 a piece of printing type that is set wrong end to. ふせもじ

복자(福者) a person who is beatified; the Blessed. ふくしゃ

복작거리다 jostle; swarm.

복잡(複雜) complication; complexity／~한 complicated; intricate; complex／그의 논증은 아주 ~하다 His Proof[demonstration] is very involved. ふくざつ

복장(腹臟) the center of the thorax[chest].

복장(服裝, 服章) dress; costume; attire; clothes／훌륭한[단정한] ~을 하고 있다 She is well[neatly] dressed. ふくそう

복재(伏在) concealment; latency／~하다 lie concealed[dormant, latent]; lurk in[under] (*a thing*). ふくざい

복재기(服─) a person wearing mourning.

복쟁이 〘어〙 a globefish; a swellfish; a puffer. ふぐ

복적(復籍) return to *one's* original domicile／~하다 transfer *one's* name back to *one's* original family. ふくせき

복제(服制) dress regulation[system]; 《상복의》 the traditional system of mourning attire 《복식》 costume. ふくせい

복제(複製) reproduction／~하다 reproduce 《책의》 reprint／~를 불허함 All rights Reserved. ふくせい

복종(服從) obedience; submission／~하다 obey; submit[yield, bow] (*to*) ／~적 obedient. ふくじゅう

복죄(服罪) a plea of guilty／~하다 plead guilty (*to*); enter a plea of guilty／~자(者) a tonvict. ふくざい

**복주감투** a kind of winter cap worn by monks or old people.

**복중**(伏中) [the period of] the dog days; the hottest period of summer.

**복중**(服中) the period in mourning. もちゅう

**복지**(福地) blessed[promised] land; a land of bliss. うんのよいとち

**복지**(福祉) welfare ⇒복리(福利). ふくし

**복직**(復職) rehabilitation; reinstatement; reappointment/~하다 be reinstated/~ 발령이 났다 I was restored to my former position[reinstated in the service]. ふくしょく

**복처리**(福—) a person out of luck. ふくのないひと

**복철**(覆轍) the rut left by a capsized carriage/~을 밟다 follow in the wake of another. ふくてつ

**복태**(卜駄) a pack-load on horseback.

**복통**(腹痛) a stomach-ache 《복통의》a colic; a bellyache; an abdominal pain. ふくつう

**복판** the middle[center, heart]/~의 middle; central part.

**복표**(福票) a lottery ticket[card].

**복합**(複合) ~의・compound; composite; complex/~ 개념 a complex concept/ ~어 a compound [word]. ふくごう

**복화술**(腹話術) ventriloquy; ventriloquism; the ventriloquial art/~을 사용하다 ventriloquize.

**본**(本) ①《본보기》an example; a model ②《옷 등의》a pattern/종이로 ~을 뜨다 make a pattern out of paper (for a dress) ③《고향》(貫鄉). もと

**본**-(本) (이・현재의)this; the same; the present 《주요한》the head; the main; principal 《진짜의》real; regular.

**본가**(本家) ①《본집》the main[head] family; the head house; a main stock ② 《친정》the maiden home of a married woman. ほんけ

**본값**(本—) the cost price; the prime cost /~에 팔다 sell at cost. げんか

**본거**(本據) the headquarters; a base; a stronghold. ほんきょ

**본건**(本件) this affair[case, matter]; the case in question.

**본격**(本格) a genuine[regular] style/~적 regular; real/~적으로 in earnest/ 이제 ~적인 장마철이다 The rainy season has come in earnest. ほんかく

**본견**(本絹) silk fabric; silks. ほんけん

**본고**(本稿) this manuscript[article, piece, of writing].

**본고장**(本—) 《원산지》the original home one's native place. げんち

**본고향**(本故鄉) one's native place; one's old home. もとのこきょう

**본과**(本科) the regular course/~를 수료하다 finish the regular course. ほんか

**본관**(本官) ①《임시직에 대한》a regular office 《겸직에 대한》the principal post ② 《지칭》the present official. ほんかん

**본관**(本館, 本舘) the main building; this building. ほんかん

**본관**(本管) a main [pipe]; a water main.

**본관**(本貫) one's ancestral home; family origin. ほんかん

**본교**(本校) this[our] school 《분교에 대한》 the principal school. ほんこう

**본국**(本國) one's native[home] country; home. ほんごく

**본국**(本局) 《지국에 대한》the main[head] office. ほんきょく

**본금**(本金) principal [sum]. がんきん

**본금새**(本—) the proper price. げんか

**본기**(本期) this[the current] term; this [the current] quarter.

**본남편**(本—) one's legal husband; one's first husband. せいしきのおっと

**본년**(本年) this year; the current[present] year. ほんねん

**본능**(本能) instinct/~적으로 instinctively/~주의 instinctivism. ほんのう

**본당**(本堂) the main[inner] temple; the main hall (of a temple).

**본때** 《본보기》a pattern; a model; an example/~ 없다 be unattractive; be poor-looking; be unshowy. みほん

**본대**(本隊) 《군대의》the main body[force]. ほんたい

**본댁**(本宅) 《본집》one's home 《전실》 legal wife. ほんけ

**본댁네** one's legal wife; one's first wife. ほんさい

**본데** good manners; discipline; experience/~있다 be experienced. きょうよう

**본뜨다** model after a pattern; make (a thing) after a pattern; copy from a model. かたをとる

**본뜻**(本—) 《본 생각》one's real intention 《본 의미》the real meaning. ほんい

**본디**(本—) originally; from the first; by nature/~의 original; primary. もと

**본래**(本來) originally; primarily; essentially; naturally/~의 original; essential; natural. ほんらい

**본령**(本領) 《본분》one's province; one's element 《특성》one's speciality; a characteristic/~을 발휘하다 be in one's element. ほんりょう

**본론**(本論) the main subject. ほんろん

**본루**(本壘) 《본거》the base; the main fort 《야구》the home base[plate]/~타 a home run[hit]; a homer. ほんるい

**본류**(本流) the main stream. ほんりゅう

**본리**(本利) principal and interest. がんり

**본말**(本末) means and ends; cause and effect; the substance and the shadow /~을 전도하다 put the cart before the horse; reverse the right order of things. ほんまつ

**본맛** the original taste[flavor].

**본망**(本望) 《열원》one's [long-cherished] desire[dream]; hope; aim; ambition. ほんもう

**본명**(本名) one's real name. ほんみょう
**본무**(本務) 《본분》 one's duty 《본직》 one's regular[proper] work. ほんむ
**본무대**(本舞臺) the main stage.
**본문**(本文) the body (of *a letter*); the text (of *a treaty*). ほんぶん
**본문제**(本問題) 《본래의》 the original problem[question]; 《기본의》 the fundamental[main] problem 《이 문제》 this problem. ほんもんだい
**본밑천**(本―) capital; stock; funds. がんきん
**본바닥**(本―) the home; the place of origin; a native place. しゅっしょうち
**본바탕**(本―) essence; [real] substance; essential quality. ほんしつ
**본받다**(本―) model after a pattern.
**본방**(本邦) this[our] country. ほんぽう
**본보기**(本―) 《모범》 an example 《본뜨는 자료》 a model; a pattern. みほん
**본봉**(本俸) the basic[regular] salary; pay proper. ほんぽう
**본부**(本夫) one's legal husband; one's first husband. ほんぷ
**본부**(本部) the headquarters; the head [main] office 《대학의》 an administrative building. ほんぶ
**본분**(本分) duty; part; function / ~을 다하다 do[perform, fulfil] one's duty; do one's part. ほんぶん
**본사**(本社) 《본점》 the head office 《우리 회사》 our company[firm]; we / ~의 통신원 our correspondent. ほんしゃ
**본사**(本寺) 《불교에서》 the temple where *one* first became a Buddhist priest 《자기가 있는》 this[our] temple.
**본사내**(本―) 《본 남편》 one's ex-husband; one's real husband. せいとうなおっと
**본산**(本山) the head temple. ほんざん
**본새**(本―) 《생김새》 the original looks [features]; 《본바탕》 the nature; basic quality / ~가 곱다 be nice-looking; look nice; have good features. うまれつき
**본색**(本色) one's real character; one's true colo[u]rs. ほんらいのいろ
**본생가**(本生家) an adopted person's original home; family into which *one* was born. うまれたうち
**본서**(本書) this book; this volume.
**본서**(本署) the chief police station; the principal office. ほんしょ
**본선**(本線) the main line. ほんせん
**본선**(本船) this[our] ship; a depot ship / ~ 인도(引渡) free on board(略: f. o. b.).
**본성**(本性) the original nature (*of*); real [true] character; true colors. ほんせい
**본성**(本姓) one's original surname; one's original family name. ほんせい
**본소**(本訴) the original suit.
**본숭만숭하다** glance (*over*); take a cursory view (*of*); skim (*over*).
**본시**(本是) 《부사적》 originally; primarily; from the first. ほんらい

**본식**(本式) orthodox style; the regular way / ~의 regular; formal. ほんしき
**본실**(本室) one's legal wife; one's first wife.
**본심**(本心) 《진의》 one's real intention; one's heart / ~은 at heart / ~으로 돌아가다 come to one's senses. ほんさい
**본안**(本案) 《이 안건》 this proposal[bill]; 《본 안건》 the original proposal; the original bill. ほんあん
**본얼굴**(本―) one's original[unchanged, unpainted] face.
**본업**(本業) one's main business; one's regular work[trade] / ~ 외의 일 a side work[business, job]; a side-line. ほんぎょう
**본연**(本然) ~의 natural inherent / ~의 성질 one's true character. ほんぜん
**본영**(本營) the headquarters. ほんえい
**본원**(本源) the origin; the source 《근원》 the root. ほんげん
**본원**(本願) one's heart's desire. ほんがん
**본월**(本月) this month; the current month; instant. ほんげつ
**본위**(本位) 《기준》 standard 《주의》 principle 《기초》 a basis / 금~ the gold standard / ~ 화폐 legal tender. ほんい
**본유**(本有) ~의 innate; inborn; natural / ~ 개념(概念) an innate idea. ほんゆう
**본의**(本意) 《참 의도》 one's will; one's real intention 《진심》 one's heart / ~ 아닌 against one's will; unwilling. ほんい
**본이름**(本―) one's real[original] name 《본명》(本名). ほんみょう
**본인**(本人) the person himself 《대리인에 대한》 the principal 《당자》 the person in question. ほんにん
**본일**(本日) today; this day. ほんじつ
**본임자**(本―) the original owner[master]. もとのしゅじん
**본적**(本籍) 《원적》 one's [permanent] domicile; one's home address; 《본적지》 one's place of register. ほんせき
**본전**(本錢) 《원금》 principal 《밑천》 capital. がんきん
**본점**(本店) 《지점에 대한》 the head office; the main shop. ほんてん
**본정**(本情) one's true colo[u]rs 《참된 심정》 one's real intention. ほんしん
**본제**(本第) one's house back home; one's home.
**본제**(本題) the main subject[topic, issue]; the original subject / ~로 돌아가다 return to the subject.
**본존**(本尊) 《종》 the object of worship; the idol; the principal image. ほんぞん
**본종**(本宗) relatives on one's father's side.
**본주**(本主) 《원주인》 the original proprietor[owner]; 《소유자》 the owner[proprietor, possessor]. もとのしゅじん
**본줄기**(本―) the main line.
**본지**(本旨) the main[principal] object [purport]; the object in view. ほんし

**본지**(本紙) this[our] newspaper. ほんし
**본지**(本誌) this journal; our magazine. ほんし
**본직**(本職) ①(본업) regular occupation [profession]; principal business ②(자신) I; me; myself. ほんしょく
**본진**(本陣) military headquarters. ほんじん
**본질**(本質) (진수) essence (실질) true nature; substance/~적[으로] essential[ly]; substantial[ly]. ほんしつ
**본집**(本—) one's [own] home; one's parents' home. ほんけ
**본처**(本妻) a lawful[legal] wife. ほんさい
**본체**(本體) (본래의 자태) the true form (실체) substance (실재) reality/~론 ontology. ほんたい
**본체만체** pretending not to have seen/ ~하다 neglect; slight; do not care for; show indifference to.
**본초**(本草) (한약재) medical plants (한약학) Chinese medical botany/~가(家) a herbalist.
**본초 자오선**(本初子午線) the prime[first] meridian.
**본촌**(本村) (본 마을) the main village (이 마을) this[our] village. ほんそん
**본치** appearance; figure. がいかん
**본토**(本土) the mainland; the country proper/중국 ~ China proper/~박이 natives; aborigines. ほんど
**본형**(本刑) (법) a regular penalty.
**본형**(本形) the original form. ほんけい
**본회담**(本會談) the full-dress talks; the main conference. ほんかいだん
**본회의**(本會議) a plenary session; a general[regular] meeting. ほんかいぎ
**볼** ①(뺨) a cheek ②(물건의 넓이) width; breadth. ほお
**볼가심** a morsel of food; a bite/~하다 have[take, eat] a bite.
**볼가지다** protrude; project; jut[stick] out; bulge out. はれあがる
**볼강거리다** take a lot of chewing; be chewy; be leathery; be lumpy.
**볼강볼강** hard to chew; leathery; lumpy.
**볼꼴** [outward] appearance; show; look. がいかん
**볼꼴사납다** (be) ugly; unseemly; unsightly. めざわりだ
**볼그레하다** (be) reddish; rubicund; be tinged with red.
**볼그무레하다** (be) reddish; red-hued うすくあかみがかっている
**볼끈** (갑자기) all of a sudden (쑥) tightly/~ 성내다 flare up. ばっと
**볼근거리다** chew on. もぐもぐかむ
**볼끈거리다** fly into a rage easily; get mad easily.
**볼긋하다, 뽈긋하다** be splashed with red. ややあかいようだ
**볼기** the buttocks[hips, rump]/~치다 spank; beat on the buttocks; be spanked しり

**볼기짝** the buttocks; the hips; the back side. しりべた
**볼되다** ①(벅차다) be a strain on one's; (be hard ②(억세다) (be) very tight.
**볼록거리다** palpitate; swell and subside. ふくらんだりへっこんだりする
**볼록거울** 《물》 a convex mirror. とつめんきょう
**볼록렌즈** 《물》 a convex lens.
**볼록면**(—面) a convex surface. とつめん
**볼만하다**¹ (보암직하다) be worth seeing; be worthy of notice. みるかちがある
**볼만하다**² (방관하다) look on silently; remain a spectator; hold one's tongue. ぼうかんしている
**볼맞다** ①(손발이 맞다) go cahoots; make good partners; be hand in glove (with) ②(걸맞다) fit like a glove; go together nicely; be well matched. ちょうしがあう
**볼멘소리** sullen[sulky] words; an angry voice/~로 in angry tone.
**볼모** ①(물건) a security; a pledge ②(사람) a hostage; a prisoner/~로 잡아두다 take (one) as hostage/~로 잡히다 be held as a hostage. たんぽ
**볼받다** patch [up]; put a patch on [Korean socks]. つぎをあてる
**볼썽** outward appearance; show; look/ ~사납다 be ungainly[unseemly, awkward, indecent]. がいかん
**볼쑥거리다** keep sticking out abruptly.
**볼일** business; engagement (심부름) an errand/~로 on business (남의 부탁으로) on an errand/~이 있다 be engaged; have something to do/~이 없다 be free; be disengaged. ようむ
**볼장 다보다** be all up[over, lost] with.
**볼통거리다** speak bluntly; surly. でっぱっている
**볼통스럽다** (be) blunt; brusque; rough/ 볼통스러운 말씨 a brusque way of speaking. ぶっきらぼうだ
**볼통하다** (be) bulgy; protruding.
**볼품** appearance; show; look's/~이 있다 make[have] a good appearance[show, figure]; be[look] seemly[decent, nice]/~이 없다 make[have] an ill appearance[show, figure]/책이 ~이 있다 This book is of elegant format. みかけ
**볼호령**(—號令) angry roars/~하다 roar; bellow; howl. どごう
**봄** (계절) spring time / ~의 spring; vernal/인생의 ~ the spring of life; the flower[prime, heyday] of youth/이른 [늦은] ~에 in the early[late] spring / ~날[밤] a spring day[night] /~기운 a feel[an air] of spring; spring in the air/~아지랑이 ~ in angry tone. a spring haze/~바람 a spring breeze/~옷 spring wear/~비 spring rain/~빛 spring scene ry ; a spring view/~새 spring time/~추위 cold weather in the early spring/~ 풀 spring grass[es]. はる
**봄갈이** spring plowing[ploughing]/~하

다 do the spring plowing[ploughing].
**봄내** all through[throughout] the spring. はるのあいだ
**봄내다** 《체하다》 affect; assume[put on] airs; give *one*self airs; pose (*as*);《자랑하다》boast; be proud (*of, that*); take pride (*in*)／봄내며 걷다 walk affectedly swagger／봄낼 일이 못 된다 That is nothing to boast of. いばる
**봄눈** spring snow／~ 녹듯하다 melt like spring snow (사라지다) vanish[disappear] into thin air (소화가 잘 되다) melt in *one*'s mouth; go down[digest] easily. はるのゆき
**봄맞이꽃** 《식》a rock jasmine; *Androsace saxifragaefolia*(학명).
**봄볕** spring sun shine.
**봄철** the springtime; the spring season. はるのきせつ
**봄타다** be susceptible to spring weather; suffer from spring weather. はるまけする
**뽑다** ①《빼내다》 pull out[up]; take out 《칼·권총을》 draw 《이를》 extract[pull out]／잡초를 ~ pull up weeds; weed [a garden] ②《가려내다》 select; pick out; single out 《선거하다》 elect ③《모집하다》 receive applicants for; book 《병사를》 recruit[enlist] [troops]. ぬく
**봇논**(洑─) a paddyfield watered by a reservoir[dammed pool]. いせきのみずようするすいでん
**봇도랑**(洑─) an irrigation ditch. いせきのみぞ
**봇돌** ①a support stone on either side of the fireplace ②a stone used to press down the wooden pieces over a roof.
**봇둑**(洑─) a dam; a bank.
**봇물**(洑─) a dam water ; water confined by dam; water in a reservoir. いせきのみず
**봇일**(洑─) irrigation dam[reservoir] work.
**봇줄** draw-cords on a draft animal.
**봇짐**(褓─) a package[parcel] carried on the back of a person. にもの
**봉**[1] dissipation ☞난봉. どうらくしゃ
**봉**[2] 《낚시의》 a sinker ☞봉돌. おもり
**봉**[3] 《땜질에서》 a solder patch／~박다 solder on a patch; solder up a hole／솥에 ~을 박다 solder up a hole in a kettle. あてがね
**봉** 《식》 a mulberry [leaf]／~잎을 따다 pick mulberry leaves／~나무 a mulberry tree. くわのは
**봉**(峰) a peak; a top; a summit. みね
**봉**(封) a paper bag／약 한 ~ a packet of medicinal herbs; a dose of medicine.
**봉**(鳳) a male phoenix. ほうおう
**봉건**(封建)《제도》 feudalism; the feudal system／~적 feudal feudalistic／~시대 the feudal age[days, times]; the era of feudalism (시대에 뒤떨어진) old-fashioned; too conservative (전체적) despotic／~ 사상 a feudalistic idea／~적 사상 feudalistic idea／그것은 ~ 시대의 사상이다 That idea is a relic of feudal days／~주의 feudalism; feudality.
ほうけん
**봉견**(奉見) ~하다 see[look at] with reverence. はいけん
**봉고도**(棒高跳) a pole jump; a polevault 《미》. ほうたかとび
**봉공**(奉公) public duty[service];《봉직》government service／~하다 work for the country[government]; serve the public. ほうこう
**봉급**(俸給) a salary; pay; wages／낮은 ~의 under-paid; low-salaried／비싼 ~의 high-salaried／무~으로 without pay／~을 인상하다[인하하다] raise[lower] (*a person's*) salary／~ 봉투 a pay-envelope／~ 생활자 a salaried man; a salary earner (총칭) the salaried class／~일 pay day／월 4만 원의 ~ a salary of 40,000 *won* a month. ほうきゅう
**봉기**(蜂起) uprising; insurrection; revolt／~하다 rise in revolt[arms, rebellion]; rise (*up*) against／농민 ~ an uprising of the peasants; an agrarian revolt.
ほうき
**봉나다** be disclosed[divulged]; be brought to light. ひみつがばれる
**봉납**(捧納) dedication; offering; presentation [to a deity]／~하다 dedicate; offer; present; consecrate／~물 an offering; a votive offering[object]／~액 a votive[dedicated] tablet／~자 an offerer; a dedicator.
**봉놓다** disclose; reveal; expose; divulge.
**봉답**(奉答) a deferential reply [to a superior]／~하다 reply with due respect.
ほうとう
**봉당**(封堂) the unfloored[dirt-floored] area between two rooms／~ 마루 a dirt floor／~을 빌려 주니 안방까지 달란다《속담》 Give him an inch and he'll take an ell. どま
**봉대**(烽臺) a signal fire post; a beacon post. ほうかだい
**봉대**(奉戴) ~하다 have (*a personage*) over; be presided over by (*a personage*); live under (*a ruler, a master*)／총재로 ~하다 install (*a person*) as the president; be under the presidency of (*a person*).
**봉독**(奉讀) reading reverentially[deferentially]／~하다 read with reverence; read reverentially. ほうどく
**봉돌** a sinker; a sink; a bullet／줄에 ~을 달다 weight a line. おもり
**봉두**(峰頭) the top; the summit; the peak. やまのみね
**봉두 난발**(蓬頭亂髮) unkempt hair[locks]; a shaggy head of hair; a rat's nest.
ほうとうらんはつ
**봉랍**(封蠟) sealing wax／~으로 봉하다 seal (*a letter*) with wax.
**봉리**(鳳梨) a pineapple.

**봉명**(奉命) receiving orders[commands] from the king/~하다 receive orders [commands] from the king. ほうめい

**봉물**(封物) a present; a gift.

**봉밀**(蜂蜜) honey ⇨꿀. はちみつ

**봉바리** a kind of brass rice bowl for women.

**뽕빠지다** sustain[suffer] a heavy loss; go into bankruptcy; fail; be broke; have a hard time 《지치다》 be exhausted /시험 치르기에 나는 뽕빠졌다 I'm done in from exams. はさんする

**봉박다** solder on a patch; solder up a hole; patch up a hole/이에 ~ plug [up] a decayed tooth. あてがねをつける

**봉박다**(封一) add something extra to a package. ふうにゅうする

**봉방**(蜂房) a honeycomb; a [honey] cell.

**봉변**(逢變) ①《욕을 당함》 receiving insult; having bitter experience; an insult ②《화를 당함》 encountering a mishap; a misfortune; a calamity/~하다 be insulted[humiliated]; have bitter experiences; have a bad[rough] time (of it); 《화를 당함》 meet with[encounter] an unlucky accident[a mishap]; suffer an unexpected calamity. ぶじょくされること

**봉사**(奉仕) service; attendance/~하다 serve; render service; attend[wait] on (a person)/~사업 public welfare work /근로 ~ labor service/사회 ~ social service/사회 ~로서 as a service to the public. ほうし

**봉사**(奉祀) religious service for one's ancestors/~하다 perform a religious service for one's ancestors. ほうし

**봉사**(奉事) ①《장님》 a blind man ②《섬김》 service; attendance/~하다 serve; attend; wait on. もうじん

**봉상**(封上) presentation [submission] [of a thing to the king]/~하다 present[submit] [to the king].

**봉서**(封書) a sealed letter. ふうしょ

**봉선화**(鳳仙花) a [garden] balsam; a touch-me-not. ほうせんか

**봉송**(奉送) seeing [a superior] off; sending off/~하다 see [a superior] off; send off. おくりものをとどけること

**봉송**(蓬鬆) ~하다 (be) bushy; shaggy; dishevelled; ragged/~한 머리 shaggy [dishevelled] hair.

**봉쇄**(封鎖) a blockade; blocking up; freezing/~하다 blockade; block up; seal [bottle] up/경제 ~ an economic blockade/대륙 ~령 the Continental System /~를 풀다 lift the blockade/해상 ~ a naval[sea] blockade. ふうさ

**봉수**(逢授) trust; charge/~하다 entrust (one with a thing); place (a thing) in a persons charge.

**봉수**(逢授) custody; trust; deposit; charge/~하다 be entrusted[charged] with (a thing); have the custody of (a thing). たしかにじゅりょうすること

**봉수**(捧受) receiving; collecting/~하다 receive; collect.

**봉수**(烽燧) a rocket ⇨봉화(烽火). ほうか

**봉수표**(逢受票) a receipt; a voucher; an acknowledgement.

**봉숭아** 【식】 a balsam; Impatiens Balsamina(학명). ほうせんか

**봉승**(奉承) ~하다 comply with the will (of a superior); obey/성지(聖旨)를 ~하여 in obedience to the Imperial command. ほうしょう

**봉아술**(蓬莪茂) 【식】 a zedoary; Curcuma zedoaria(학명).

**봉안**(奉安) enshrinement/~하다 enshrine; lay in state. ほうあん

**봉양**(奉養) support; maintenance/~하다 support (one's parents); serve one's parents faithfully/그의 노모를 ~할 사람은 그뿐이다 He is the sole support of his aged mother.

**봉영**(奉迎) welcome/~하다 welcome[hail] His Majesty. ほうげい

**봉오리** a bud/꽃~ a [flower] bud/피어 나는 꽃~ bursting buds/~를 맺다 bud; put forth[shoot out] [the] buds; have buds. つぼみ

**봉요**(蜂腰) a slender waist.

**봉욕**(逢辱) ~하다 suffer an insult; be put to shame; be humiliated; meet with humiliation. ぶじょくをうけること

**봉우리** a peak; a summit; a top/산 ~ mountain top[peak]. みね

**봉인**(鋒刃) 《창·칼 따위의》 a blade; a spearhead. やいば

**봉인**(封印) a seal; sealing/~하다 seal; put the seal upon a letter; put a letter under seal/~을 뜯다 break[take off] the seal. ふういん

**뽕잎** mulberry leaves/~을 따다 pick mulberry leaves. くわのは

**봉자채**(逢子菜) 【식】 a bedstraw; Galium verum(학명).

**봉작**(封爵) investiture[investment] with the titles of nobility/~하다 dedicate; present; offer.

**봉적**(逢賊) meeting with a burglar; suffering robbery/~하다 meet with[encounter] a burglar; suffer[meet with] robbery. とうぞくにあうこと

**봉접**(蜂蝶) bees and butterflies. はちとちょう

**봉접**(鳳蝶) 【충】 a swallow tail.

**봉정**(奉呈) presentation; dedication/~하다 present; dedicate; offer. ほうてい

**봉조**(奉助) help; aid; assistance/~하다 help; aid; assist; give (one) assistance. じょりょく

**봉지**(封紙) a paper-bag/약 한 ~ a packet of medicinal herbs. ふうじがみ

**봉직**(奉職) government[public] service/ ~하다 serve (at, in); be in government service/학교에 ~하다 be on the staff of a school/~처(處) one's place of employment/~처를 찾다 look for a posi-

**봉착**(逢着) ~하다 face; confront; encounter; be faced[confronted] with/난관에 ~하다 be confronted with a difficulty.

**봉창**(封窓) 《창을 봉함》 sealing up the window 《봉한 창》 a sealed-up window 《구멍 창》 a small blind window/~하다 seal up a window.

**봉창질** hoarding things/~하다 《물건을》 hoard things 《손해를》 make up for (a loss); recover; cover.

**봉축**(奉祝) celebration/~하다 celebrate (an occasion).

**봉치** gifts from the bridegroom's family to the bride presented prior to the wedding.

**봉친**(奉親) the support of one's parents/~하다 support one's parents.

**봉토**(封土) a fief; a feud; feudal territory.

**봉투**(封套) an envelope; an envelope.

**봉피**(封皮) an envelope; a cover/~를 뜯다 open[unseal] an envelope.

**봉하다**(封一) ①《붙이다》 seal 《a letter》; close up; fasten 《봉해 넣다》 enclose; confine/봉한《봉하지 않은》 편지 a sealed [an unsealed] letter/봉하여 보내다 send (a thing) under seal ②《다물다》 shut; close one's mouth/입을 ~ be silent; hold one's tongue.

**봉함**(封緘) a seal; sealing/~ 엽서 a letter-card[-sheet]/~을 뜯다 break[open] the seal[envelope].

**봉합**(封合) suture/~하다 suture; stitch together.

**봉행**(奉行) observance/~하다 observe; obey; carry out/명령을 ~하다 obey [follow] (a person's) order.

**봉헌**(奉獻) dedication; presentation; consecration/~하다 dedicate[consecrate, offer] to (a superior, shrine).

**봉화**(烽火) a signal-fire; a rocket; a warning-light; a beacon/~를 올리다 light a signal-fire.

**봉환**(封還) ~하다 turn down one's resignation.

**봉황**(鳳凰) a phoenix; a Chinese phoenix; a fabulous bird.

**봐하니** so far as my observation goes; so far as the appearances go; to all appearance.

**뵙다** 《웃어른을》 see (one); meet (one); have an audience[interview] with/찾아 ~ call on (one).

**뽀로통하다** pout; (be) sulky/그 아이는 조금만 야단쳐도 뽀로통해진다 The boy gets sulky at the slightest scolding.

**뽀롱뽀롱** ~하다 (be) ill-tempered; cross-grained.

**뽀루지** an abscess; a skin eruption; a pimple; a boil; a tumor/얼굴에 ~가 나다 pimples break out on one's cheeks.

**뾰족하다** (be) pointed; sharp/뾰족한 머리 a peaked head/뾰족한 코 a sharp nose/~같이 ~ be pointed at the end/손가락이 ~ have tapered fingers.

**부**(父) a father.

**부**(否) no (pl. -es(명사형에서)); nay/가~ aye and no; pro and con; for and against/~가 많았다 The noes had it.

**부**(部) ①《부분》 a part; a portion; a section/3~로 된 소설 a novel in three parts ②《분과》 a department; a bureau; a division 《내부의》 a section; a department/편집~ an editorial department/~장 the head[chief] of a section[division, department] ③《서적의》 a copy (책); a volume(권).

**부**(富) wealth; riches; a fortune/~를 이루다 grow rich[wealthy]; make[amass] a fortune/~의 분배 distribution of wealth.

**부**(賦) poetical prose; an ode; verses of six feet.

**부-**(副) assistant; deputy; vice-; sub-/~독본 a supplementary reader/~의장 a vicechairman/~지배인 an assistant manager/~총재 a vice-president/~통령 a vice-president.

**-부**(附) ①《날짜》 dated; under date of ②《부속》 attached to; in attendance upon; belonging to; bearing/대사관~ 육[해]군 무관 a military[naval] attaché to an embassy.

**부가**(附加) addition; supplement/~의 additional; annexed/~하다 add; supplement; affix/~를 an addition/~세 (稅) a supplementary[an additional] tax.

**부가**(富家) a wealthy family.

**부각** fried kelp.

**부각**(負角) 《수》 a negative angle.

**부각**(俯角) 《수》 a dip; an angle of depression[declination].

**부감**(俯瞰) ~하다 overlook; command a bird's-eye[an aerial] view (of the city); look out upon.

**부강**(富強) wealth and power/나라의 ~을 증진하다 promote the prosperity and power of the country.

**부걱거리다** bubble up; foam/부걱부걱 bubbling; foamily.

**부검지** waste[refuse] straws.

**부결**(否決) rejection; voting down; negation/~하다 reject; vote[decide] against; vote down/~권(權) a negative voice.

**부계**(父系) the father's side; the male [paternal] line/~의 on the father's side/~의 친족 an agnate; a relative on the father's side.

**부고**(訃告) a report of one's death; the news of one's death; an obituary/~를 받다 receive the news of one's death.

부골(富骨) the physique of a man of wealth; wealthy feature.

부과(賦課) levy; imposition; incidence; ~하다 levy[impose] (a tax) on/소득세를 ~하다 levy an income tax (on)/~액 the amount imposed/~금 《세관 따위의》 dues; taxes. ふか

부관(副官) an adjutant; an aide; an aide-de-camp (F)/고급 ~ a senior adjutant/연대 ~ a regimental adjutant. ふくかん

부광대(富鑛帶) a bonanza.

부교(父敎) the precepts[teachings] of one's father. ちちのきょうくん

부교(浮橋) a pontoon[floating] bridge; a floating-log bridge. うきばし

부국(富國) a rich[wealthy] country/~강병 a wealthy country and a powerful army/~론 the Wealth of Nations/~책 a plan[measure] for enriching one's country. ふこく

부군(夫君) one's husband. ふくん

부권(父權) paternal authority[rights]. ふけん

부권(夫權) the husband's rights; marital authority. ふけん

부권(婦權) women's rights.

부귀(富貴) riches and honors; wealth and fame[rank]; prosperity/~를 타고나다 be born rich; be born with a silver spoon in one's mouth/~ 공명 wealth, rank and fame; luxury; sumptuousness/~ 공명 속에 살다 live in honor and wealth. ふき

부끄러움 shyness ⇨부끄럼. はにかみ

부끄러워하다 ①《수줍어하다》 be bashful[shy] around ②《창피해 하다》be ashamed of; consider something shameful[a shame]. はにかむ

부끄럼 《수줍음》 shyness; bashfulness; coyness 《수치》 shame; disgrace; dishonor/~타다 be shy; feel bashful/~을 알다 dread shame; respect honor; have a sense of shame. はにかみ

부끄럽다 ①《양심에》 (be) shameful; disgraceful/신사로서 부끄러운 일 an act unworthy of a gentleman 《창피하다》 be ashamed (of) ②《수줍다》 (be) shy; bashful; coy/그녀는 사람을 부끄러워한다 She is bashful in company./나는 사진 찍히는 것이 ~ I am camera shy. はずかしい

부그르르 ①《끓어서》 on the simmer; with a sizzling sound ②《거품이》 bubbling; foamingly. ぶくぶく

부근(附近) neighbourhood; vicinity/~의 neighbouring; near-by/~에 near; in the neighbourhood of/서울 ~ the vicinity of Seoul; Seoul and [its, the] vicinity/이 ~에 near here. ふきん

부글거리다 ①《끓어서》 simmer /부글부글 on the simmer; with a sizzling sound ②《거품이》 bubble /부글부글 bubbling; foamily/부글부글 거품이 일다 bubble up. ぶくぶくあわだつ

부기 a stupid fool; a simpleton; a dolt; an idiot; a ninny; a dunce.

부기(簿記) 【경】 book-keeping/~를 달다 keep books[accounts]/~계 a book-keeper; a ledger clerk/~학 [the art of] book-keeping/~가계 domestic book-keeping/단식[복식] ~ book-keeping by single[double] entry. ぼき

부기(附記) an addition; an appendix/~하다 add; write in addition. ふき

부기(浮氣) swelling 《수종증》 dropsy/~가 가라앉다 The swelling subsides[goes down]. はれけ

부나비 【충】 a tiger moth. ひとりが

부내(部內) circles; the department/정부 ~ government circles. ぶない

부녀(父女) father and daughter. ちちとむすめ

부녀자(婦女子) 《부인》 a woman 《총칭》 womenfolk; the fair sex/~를 학대하다 bully the fair sex. ふじょし

부농(富農) a rich[wealthy] farmer.

부닐다 act amiably[friendly, affably]/착착 ~ stick close (to a person); eager to be helpful. あいそうよくふるまう

부닥뜨리다 be confronted with. ぶつかる

부닥치다 face; confront; encounter; come face to face with/곤란《적》에 ~ encounter[be faced with] difficulties [the enemy]/그는 어려운 문제에 부닥쳤다 He is confronted with a hard problem. てくわす

부단(不斷) continuity; constancy; steadiness/~하다 (be) constant; continual; ceaseless/~한 노력 constant exertions; a sustained effort/~한 주의 constant attention. ふだん

부담(負擔) a burden 《지불》 a charge 《책임》 a responsibility 《경비의》 defrayment/~하다 bear; assume; shoulder; pay/자기의 ~액 one's share [in the expenses]; an allotment/비용을 ~하다 bear[defray] expenses/무거운 ~을 주다 impose a heavy burden on (a person). ふたん

부당(不當) injustice; wrongfulness; unreasonableness/~하다 (be) unjust; unfair; unreasonable 《과하다》 undue; excessive/~한 요구 an excessive demand /~한 조치 an unfair dealing/~ 이득 excessive profits; profiteering. ふとう

부대(負袋) a [burlap] bag; a bale; a sack /밀가루 한 ~ a sack of flour. ふくろ

부대(部隊) a unit; a corps; a force 《파견대》 a detachment 《분대》 a squad/~기 a guidon; a squad flag/~장 commander; a leader/기동 ~ a task force/외인 ~ a foreign legion/전투 ~ a fighting unit/후방 ~ rear-guard units. ぶたい

부대(富大) ~하다 (be) fat; plump; corpulent; stout. ひまん

부대(浮帶, 浮袋) a lifebuoy; a lifebelt; a swimming tube; a life preserver 《수

**부대끼다** be troubled (*with*); be pestered (*by*); be afflicted (*with*); suffer (*from*)/가난에 ~ be tormented by poverty; feel the pinch of poverty/세상에 나가서 좀 부대껴 봐라 You had better go out into the world and school yourself. くるしむ

**부덕**(不德) lack[want] of virtue; unworthiness; vice 《패덕》 immorality/~하다 (be) unworthy; lack virtue; immoral/~한 짓 an immoral act; an evil deed/그것은 모두 저의 ~한 소치입니다 I am solely to blame for it., It is all my fault. ふとく

**부덕**(婦德) womanly[female] virtues; womanhood. ふとく

**부도**(婦道) woman's duties; womanly virtues/~를 다하다 perform the duties of womanhood. ふどう

**부도**(不渡) 〖경〗 dishonor; nonpayment/~나다 be dishonored/~ 수표 a dishonored[bad] check; a check that bounces [is dishonored]/~ 어음 a dishonored [bad] bill/~ 수표를 남발하다 pass a bad check. ふわたり

**부도**(附圖) an appended[attached] chart [map, diagram]. ふず

**부도덕**(不道德) immorality; bad morals; lack of morality/~하다 (be)immoral; unprincipled/~한 행동 immoral conduct. ふどうとく

**부도옹**(不倒翁) a toy tumbler; a Dharma doll; a tumbling doll. おきあがりこぼし

**부도체**(不導體) 〖물〗 a non-conductor of heat[electricity]; a nonconducting substance/유리는 전기의 ~이다 Glass is a nonconductor of electricity. ふどうたい

**부독본**(副讀本) a supplementary reader. ふくどくほん

**부동**(不凍) nonfreezing/~제(劑) [an] antifreeze [agent]/~항(港) an ice-free port; a nonfreezing port. ふとう

**부동**(不同) 〖차이〗 difference; dissimilarity 《고르지 않음》 inequality; irregularity 《불평균》 unevenness/~하다 (be) unequal; uneven; irregular/~이다 vary in size; be uneven in quality/순서 ~ not in order. ふどう

**부동**(符同) ~하다 collude (*with*); conspire (*with*); group[gang] together; go (*in*) cahoots. ふわ

**부동**(浮動) floating; wafting/~하다 float; be float 《변동》 fluctuate/ ~하는 floating; fluctuating; unsettled; unsteady/~성 instability; fluctuation/~주 floating stocks/~표(票) a floating vote. ふどう

**부동**(不動) immobility; immovability; firmness/~의 immovable; firm; fixed /~ 자세 an immobile posture;《군》 attention/~의 신념 immovable belief; a firm belief. ふどう

**부동산**(不動産) immovable property; immovables; realty; things real; real[fixed] estate/~을 매매하다 deal in real estate/~ 대부 a loan on real property /~ 매매업자 a realty dealer; a realtor 〈미〉~ 소득 an income from immovables/~ 취득세 property transaction[acquisition] tax. ふどうさん

**부동의**(不同意) disagreement; disapproval. ふどうい

**부동항**(不凍港) an ice-free port; a nonfreezing port. ふとうこう

**부두**(埠頭) a quay; a pier; a wharf/~ 인부 a stevedore; a longshoreman /~ 사용료 wharfage; pierage. ふとう

**부뚜막** a cooking fireplace; a kitchenrange; a cooking-range/~의 소금도 집 어넣어야 짜다《속담》 Everything demands some work. かまど

**부둑부둑** pretty well dry; damp-dry; dry enough for ironing. からから

**부둑하다** (be) dryish. かわききっている

**부둣가**(埠頭—) a quay; a pier; the wharfside.

**부둥키다** 《안다》 embrace (*one*) closely; hug (*one*) tightly; clasp (*one*) in a tight embrace 《붙잡다》 hold on fast to (*one*)/두 사람은 부둥켜 안고 울었다 The two threw themselves into each other's arms and wept.

**부드득, 뿌드득** with a grinding[grating, creaking] sound/~하다 grind; grate; grit; creak/이를 ~ 갈다 grind[grate, grit, gnash] one's teeth. かりかり

**부드럽다** 《유연하다》 (be) soft 《온화하다》 tender; (be) gentle; mild 《음·색 따위가》 (be) soft; delicate; compliant/부드럽게 softly; gently; tenderly/부드러운 음성 a soft voice/부드럽게 말하다 speak gently. やわらかい

**부득부득** persistently; obstinately; stubbornly; doggedly/~ 고집을 부리다 stick doggedly to *one's* idea/~ 조르다 importune; ask importunately. しっこく

**부득불**(不得不) out of sheer necessity; unavoidably; necessarily 《본의 아니면서》 against *one's* will/~ 그렇게 했다 I had no option but to do so./~ 그렇게 하지 않으면 안 되었다 Necessity obliged him to that action. どうしても

**부득 요령**(不得要領) (being) vague; ambiguous; evasive/~의 대답 an evasive answer/그의 이야기는 ~이다 He does not speak to the point., He is ambiguous.

**부득이**(不得已) unavoidably; inevitably; out of necessity/~하다 (be) unavoidable; inevitable/~한 용무로 owing to [on account of] an unavoidable engagement/~한 일이다 It can't be helped. やむえず

**부득책**(不得策) no policy; no plan/~하다 (be) unwise; inexpedient; disadvantageous; have no policy[plan].

**부들** 〖식〗 a cattail; a read mace; a bulrush; *Typha orientalis*(학명). がま

**부들부들** tremblingly; shiveringly/~ 떨리다 quiver (with *emotion*); tremble; shiver/추워서 ~ 떨다 shiver with[from] cold/손이 ~ 떨려서 쓸 수 없었다 I could not write as my hand shook. ぶるぶる

**부들부들하다** (be) soft; tender; supple; flexible/부들부들한 가죽 a supple leather. はだざわりがやわらかい

**부들자리** a cattail[bulrush] mat.

**부듯하다, 뿌듯하다** ①《꼭 맞다》(be) tight; close/부듯하게 tight[ly]; closely;/부듯이 맞다 fit tightly; suit to a T/부듯한 신 perfectly-fitting shoes ②《꼭 차다》(be) full; close. ぴっしりつまっている

**부등(不等)** inequality/~의 unequal/~하다 (be) unequal; incongruent/~식 an inequality/~ 부호 a sign of inequality/~속(速) 운동『물』 ununiform[accelerated] motion. ふとう

**부등가리** a substitute for a fire-shovel. とうきのはへん

**부등깃** the soft feathers of a young bird; fluff; pinfeathers. とりのうぶけ

**부등변(不等邊)** ~의 scalene/~ 삼각형 a scalene triangle.

**부등부등하다** (be) plump; full; fat/부등부등 살쪄다 be plump[like a dumpling]; be a sheer hump of fat.

**부디** [if you] please; kindly; pray/~ 안부 전해 주십시오 Please give him my best regards./~ 몸조심하십시오 Take good care of yourself. どうぞ

**부딪다** knock; strike; beat; dash (*against*)/벽에 머리를 ~ knock *one's* head against the wall/노도는 바위에 와서 부딪쳤다 The angry waves dashed against the rocks. ぶっつかる

**부딪뜨리다** knock against; dash against /몸을 문에 ~ dash[throw] *oneself* against the door/그는 머리를 기둥에 부딪트렸다 He knocked[bumped] his head against the post. つよくぶっつける

**부딪치다** 《충돌하다》run(knock, clash, dash) against; collide with 《곤난 따위에》clash; tackle; bear the brunt/곤난에 ~[마주치다] meet with[come across] a difficulty/암초에 ~ strike[run on] a sunken rock. ぶっつかる

**부딪히다** be bumped[crashed] into; be bumped[run] against/배가 바위에 부딪히었다 A boat was dashed against a rock./나는 어린아이한테 부딪히었다 I was run into by a boy. ぶっつかる

**부라리다** glare; look with glaring eyes /화가 나서 눈을 부라리며 with an angry glare/그들은 서로 눈을 부라리며 서 있었다 They stood glaring at each other. めにつのをたてる

**부라퀴** a screw; a grasping fellow; a tough guy. しつこいひと

**부락(部落)** a village; a village community/~민 people of the [village] community; village folk/~회 a village meeting. ぶらく

**부란(腐爛)** 《시체의》 putrefaction; rottenness/~하다 putrefy; be rotten; rot; decompose/~ 시체 a decomposed[putrefied] body.

**부란(孵卵)** incubation; hatching/~하다 hatch; incubate. ふらん

**부랑(浮浪)** wandering; vagrancy; vagabondage/~의 wandering; roaming/~하다 wander; roam; lead a vagrant life/~아 a vagrant; a juvenile vagrant/~인 a wanderer; a vagabond/~아는 전부가 전쟁 고아는 아니다 Every juvenile vagrant is not a war orphan. ふろう

**부랴부랴** hurriedly; in a great hurry; in deadly haste; pell-mell/~ 달려갔으나 이미 늦었다 I rushed to the scene but it was too late. せかせか

**부러** on purpose; purposely; intentionally 《알면서》 knowingly/그는 ~ 못 알아듣는 척했다 He would not understand me./~ 그렇게 했다고는 생각할 수 없다 It is not likely that he did it on purpose. わざと

**부러뜨리다** break 《딱 소리를 내며》 snap 《뼈를》 fracture/나뭇가지를 ~ break off a branch of a tree/왼팔을 ~ break *one's* left arm; suffer a broken left arm. おる

**부러워하다** envy; be envious of; regard (*one, a thing*)/부러워하며 enviously; with envious eyes/남을 부러워하게 하다 make others envious; excite others to envy. うらやむ

**부러지다** break; be broken; snap; give away 《뼈가》 fracture/잘 부러지지 않는 막대기 a tough stick/둘로 ~ break in two/의자 다리가 하나 부러졌다 One of the legs of the chair is broken. おれる

**부럽다** be enviable/부럽지 않다 be unenviable; be not to be envied/부럽게 하다 make (*others*) envy[envious]; excite *one's* envy/그의 행운이 ~ I envy him his good luck. うらやましい

**부레** an air-bladder/~풀 fish glue; isinglass. さかなのうきぶくろ

**부레끓다** get mad; be enraged; boil (w-ith *rage*). げきどする

**부레질** gluing [by fishglue]/~하다 glue (*one thing*) to (*another*); fasten (*it*) with fishglue. にかわつけにすること

**부력(浮力)** 『물』 buoyancy; the floating 《비행선의》 lifting power; lift/~의 중심 the center of buoyancy/~계 a buoyancy gauge. ふりょく

**부력(富力)** wealth; resources. ふりょく

**부령(部令)** a departmental ordinance[order]/문교~ an Education Ministry ordinance. ぶれい

**부로(父老)** elders; aged persons. ふろう

**부로(俘虜)** a prisoner (of *war*); a war prisoner; a captive. ほりょ

**부록(附錄)** an appendix; a supplement/타임지(誌)의 ~ a supplement to the

"Time"/~을 붙이다 add an appendix (to a book). ふろく

부루나가다 last[keep] longer than expected.

부루말 ①(길들지 않은 말) an unbroken horse ②(흰 말) a white horse.

부루퉁이 a thing which bulges out; a swollen[bloated, bulging, baggy, plump] thing. つきでたもの

부루퉁하다, 뿌루퉁하다 (be) swollen; bloated (불만스러워서) sullen; sulky; morose/부루퉁한 손 a swollen hand/뿌루퉁한 얼굴 a sullen[sulky] look/뿌루퉁하니 말이 없었다 He kept a sullen silence. はれあがっている

부룩 catch-cropping/~ 박다 grow (some vegetable) between rows of another crop. かんさく

부룩소 a small ox. ちいさい雄牛
부룩송아지 an unbroken calf.
くんれんされていないこうし

부룻 the bulk of a heap; the amount in a heap. かさ

부류(部類) 《종류》 a class; a kind 《항목》 a head 《범주》 a category/~로 나누다 classify (into, as, with); catalogue/같은(다른) ~에 속하다 belong in the same [a different] classification. ぶるい

부류(浮流) ~하다 float; drift/~ 기뢰 a floating mine/~물 floating matters; flotsam (나무) drift wood.

부르걷다 roll[turn, pull] up (one's sleeves)/팔을 부르걷고서 with bare arms; with one's sleeves turned over his elbows. まくりあげる

부르다¹ ①(배가) (be) satiated; sated (with)/배부르게 먹다 eat heartily; eat one's fill; eat to one's heart's content ②(통통하다) (be) swollen; bloated; bulging; plump. はらいっぱいだ

부르다² ①(소리를 내어) call; call [out] to; hail 《소환하다》 summon/부르면 닿을 곳에 그는 서 있었다 He was standing within call. ②(외치다) cry; shout/만세를 ~ cry "Hurrah!" ③(노래를) sing; chant /피아노에 맞추어 노래를 ~ sing to a piano accompaniment ④(청하다) send for; send after; summon; procure (a doctor); 《불러오다》 call in ⑤(일컫다) call; name; style (학술상으로) term; designate (악명을 붙여서) brand/…이라고 ~ call; give (it) the name of ⑥(값을) ask; charge/부르는 값 the price asked [named]. よぶ

부르르 ①(떠는 모양) trembling; shivering /~ 멸리는 손으로 with trembling hand /~ 멸다 tremble (with fear); shiver (with cold); temble like an aspen leaf ②(끓는 모양) seething; boiling/물이 ~ 끓기 시작하다 The water comes to a bubbling boil. ③(타오르는 모양) in a sudden burst of flame. ぶるぶる

부르릉 with a cough/~하다[거리다] sp-lutter.

부르쥐다 clench (one's fist); double up (one's fist)/주먹을 ~ clench one's fist /주먹을 부르쥐고 치다 strike a person with a clenched fist. こぶしをにぎる

부르짖다 ①(외치다) shout; cry; utter [give] a cry (비명을 울리다) exclaim; scream/벽력같이 ~ cry out; roar; howl /목이 쉬도록 ~ shout oneself hoarse ②《창도(唱導)》 cry (for); clamour (for); advocate; advance/여성 교육의 필요를 ~ espouse the cause of education for women; urge the necessity of education for women. おおごえでさけぶ

부르짖음 《외침》 a shout; a cry; an outcry; an exclamation 《비명》 a shriek; a scream 《노호》 a roar; a howl/개혁의 ~ a cry[clamor] for reform/임금 인상의 ~ a cry[clamor] for a raise in pay /민족의 ~ the voice of the race.

부르트다 (물집이) get a blister; have a corn (물린 자리가) swell up/발이 부르텄다 I have got a corn on the sole of my foot./장작을 팼더니 손이 온통 부르텄다 My hands are all blistered from chopping wood. はれあがる

부릅뜨다 strain one's eyes; open one's eyes wide (성을 내어) make one's eyes glare/눈을 부릅뜨고 with angry[glaring] eyes/그는 눈을 부릅뜨고 나를 노려보았다 He glared at me with angry eyes. にらむ

부리 ①(새의) a bill (매의 부리 따위) a beak ②(물건의) a pointed end[head].
くちばし

뿌리 ①(식물의) a root (부스러기의) a nucleus (밑동) the root[base]/이 ~ the root of a tooth/~를 박고 싹이 터서 잎을 냈다 They took root, sprouted and sent forth leaves./그 개나리 가지는 벌써 ~가 붙었다 The forsythia branch has already struck root. ②(근본) the root; the cause[origin, source]; the bottom/질병의 ~ the cause of a disease /사건의 ~를 캐다 a probe a case to the bottom; dig into the bottom of a case.

부리나케 precipitately; hurriedly/~ 물러가다 beat a hasty retreat/~ 달아나다 run away with the tail between the legs/ ~ 계단을 올라가다[내려가다] rush up[down] the stairs/ ~일하다 rush one's work. かきゅうに

부리다¹ ①(사람·말을) manage; handle; use; keep; employ/하인을 ~ keep a servant; work a servant/사람을 잘 ~ be clever in handling[using] one's men ②(기계·기구를) work (a machine); operate/기계를 ~ operate a machine /자동차를 ~ drive a car ③(재주·피를) play [a trick]; start [trouble]/말썽을 ~ start [trouble]; start a quarrel (with) /수단을 ~ play a trick; think up a ruse /재주를 ~ exercise one's talent; perform a trick. させる

**부리다²** 《짐을》 drop; discharge; unload; get (*a bundle*) off／짐을 ~ cargo[goods]／트럭에서 짐을 ~ unload a truck unload. にもつをおろす

**뿌리다** 《비 따위가》 drive; be driven[blown] into 《끼얹다》 sprinkle 《씨를》 sow 《낭비하다》 spend freely／빗방울이 방 안으로 뿌리었다 The rain swept into the room. ふりまく

**부리망**(一網) a cow muzzle made of straw.

**부리부리하다** (be) big and bright／부리부리한 눈 big bright eyes.

**부리잡히다** come to a head.
できものにさねができる

**뿌리치다** shake off; disengage *oneself* from (*a person's grasp*); 《만류·권고를》 turn a deaf ear (*to*); refuse; reject／뿌리치고 도망가다 tear *oneself* away (from *a person's grasp*)／손목을 ~ shake off (*a person's*) hand／유혹을 ~ thrust temptation away. ふりはなす

**부마**(駙馬) a son-in-law of the king; a princess's husband. ふば

**부명**(父命) one's father's instruction[order]. ちちのめいれい

**부모**(父母) father and mother; parents／~의 parental／~의 사랑 parental love／~의 마음 the heart of a parent／~ 슬하에 있다 live under *one's* parental roof. ふぼ

**부모 처자**(父母妻子) one's parents, wife and children. ふぼとさいし

**부목**(副木)【의】a splint／~을 대다 splint; apply splints (*to*). そえぎ

**부문**(訃聞) the report[news] of *one's* death. しんだしらせ

**부문**(部門) a class; a group; a department; a section／~으로 나누다 divide (*things*) into classes／…의 ~에 넣다 classify (*things*) under／…의 ~에 들어가다 fall[come] under the head of. ぶもん

**부민**(富民) wealthy[rich] people; the rich.

**부민**(浮民) vagabonds; tramps; nomadic race; gypsies.

**부박**(浮薄) fickleness; frivolity; levity; insincerity／~하다 (be) frivolous; fickle; insincere／~한 문학 frothy literature／사람이란 자칫하면 ~으로 흐르기 쉽다 The people are apt to become frivolous. ふはく

**부반장**(副班長) a vice-president (of *a class*). ふくはんちょう

**부벽**(付壁) pictures and writings pasted on the wall; wall pastings／~서 writings pasted on the wall.

**부복**(俯伏) prostration／~하다 lie prostrate; prostrate *oneself*. ふふく

**부본**(副本) 《복사》 a copy; a duplicate 《여벌》 a reserve／~을 만들다 make[take] a copy of. ふくほん

**부부**(夫婦) man[husband] and wife; a married couple; a pair／~의 conjugal; connubial／젊은 ~ a young couple／~ 싸움 a quarrel between husband and wife／~ 이별 divorce; separation／신혼 ~ a newly married couple; the newlyweds〈미〉／~의 애정 conjugal affection; married love／~ 사이가 좋다 He is happy with her. ふうふ

**부분**(部分) a part; a portion; a section／~적으로 partially; in part／대~ a large part; the greater part (*of*); the majority／~식 a partial eclipse (of *the sun*, *of the moon*)／~품(品) parts; accessories／네 생각은 ~적으로 옳다 You are partly right. ぶぶん

**부분 색맹**(部分色盲)【의】partial colo[u]r blindness／~의 partial colo[u]r blind.
ぶぶんしきもう

**부비**(浮費) expense; expenditure; cost; outlay. ひよう

**부빙**(浮氷) floating ice. ふひょう

**부사**(副使) a vice-envoy; a deputy delegate. ふくし

**부사**(副詞)【언】an adverb／~적[으로] adverbial[ly]／~구 an adverbial phrase／~절 an adverbial clause. ふくし

**부사리** a goring bull.

**부사장**(副社長) a vice-president (of *a firm*). ふくしゃちょう

**부산물**(副産物) a by-product; a residual [an accessory] product. ふくさんぶつ

**부산하다** 《떠들썩하다》 (be) noisy; uproarious 《붐비다》 (be) thronged; bustling／부산한 장소 a bustling quarter; a crowded place／거리는 ~ The streets are alive with people. そうぞうしい

**부삽**(一鋪) a iron fire shovel. じゅうのう

**부삽하다**(浮澁—) (be) crumbly.

**부상**(父喪) the death of *one's* father; mourning for *one's* father.

**부상**(負傷) a hurt; an injury 《전상》 a wound 《벤 상처》 a cut 《타박상》 a bruise／~하다 get[be] injured; get hurt; be wounded／~병[자] a wounded soldier [person]／팔을 ~하다 be injured in the arm. ふしょう

**부상**(副賞) an extra prize. ふくしょう

**부상**(富商) a rich merchant.

**부생**(浮生) transient life; ephemeral existence; mutable life.

**부서**(部署) one's post [of duty]; one's place／~로 가다 go to *one's* post; take *one's* position[place]／~를 지키다 keep [remain at] *one's* post. ぶしょ

**부서**(副署) countersignature／~하다 countersign; endorse; back／각 장관이 ~한 countersigned by the ministers.
ふくしょ

**부서지다** break; be[get] smashed[broken, wrecked] 《파손되다》 be damaged 《기계가》 get out of order／부서진 broken; damaged／부서지기 쉬운 fragile; easy to break; frail; delicate／산산이 ~ be smashed[be broken] into fragments.
こわれる

**부썩** 《갑자기》 rapidly 《우기는 모양》 stub-

부석부석 slightly swollen/~하다 (be) slightly swollen/~한 얼굴 a slightly swollen face. むくむく
부선(艀船) a sampan; a lighter; a barge /~료 the sampan fare; lighterage.
부선거(浮船渠) a floating dock. うきドック
부설(附設) ~하다 attach; annex. ふせつ
부설(浮說) a wild rumo[u]r; an unfounded report/그것은 ~에 불과하다 That is nothing but a wild rumo[u]r. ふせつ
부설(敷設) laying; building; construction /~하다 lay; build/~권(權) a right of construction/철도를 ~하다 build[construct] a railway. ふせつ
부성분(副成分) an accessory ingredient. ふくせいぶん
부성애(父性愛) father's[paternal] love.
부세(賦稅) taxation; imposition of taxes /~하다 tax; impose a tax; levy duties (on). ふぜい
부세(浮世) the world; fleeting life. うきよ
부속(附屬) affiliation; attachment; addendum/~하다 belong to; be attached to/~를 adjuncts; appendages/~품 accessories/~ 병원 a hospital in affiliation. ふぞく
부속(部屬) being attached[annexed] to a body[department]; a section; a division.
부손 a small fire shovel. じゆうのう
부송(付送) sending; forwarding/ ~하다 send; forward.
부수(附隨) accompanying; following/~하다 accompany; be annexed (to); be incidental (to)/~적 accompanying; incidental; attendant/~적 비용 incidental expenses. ふずい
부수(負數) 【수】 a negative number; a minus [quantity]. ふすう
부수(部數) the number of copies; the circulation; the edition/~에 제한이 있다 The number of copies is limited.
부수다 break; smash; destroy; demolish /산산이 ~ break to bits; smash up/접시를 ~ break a dish. とりこわす
부수수 in disorder; disheveled; untidy /~하다 (be) disheveled; disorderly; untidy. ごたごた
부수입(副收入) an additional[a side] income; the income from a side job. ふくしゅうにゅう
부숭부숭하다 《마르다》 (be) dry; parched; be dried up[out] 《곱다》 fair; refined; clean. からからにかわいている
부스대다 fidget; be never still/부스대는 아이 a restless child/그는 항시 부스댄다 He is always in a fidget. そわそわする
부스러기 a bit; a fragment; scraps 《빵의》 crumbs 《나무의》 chips/고기 ~ scraps of meat. かけら

부스러뜨리다 break; break down; destroy; crush; demolish/산산이 ~ break (a thing) to pieces; smash (a thing) to bits. おしつぶす
부스러지다 break; crumble; fall[come] to pieces; collapse/빵이 ~ bread crumbles/부스러지기 쉽다 be easy to break; be fragile. こなごなになる
부스럭거리다 rustle; make a rustle[rustling sound]/낙엽이 바람에 부스럭거린다 The fallen leaves are rustling in the wind. ばさばさ
부스럼 a boil; an ulcer; a tumor; a blotch; an eruption/발에 ~이 생기다 get a boil on one's foot; a boil forms on one's foot. はれ
부스스 lightly; gently/~ 일어나다 (a person) gently rise/머리가 ~하다 have unkempt hair. そっと
부슬부슬 《눈·비가》 lightly; gently 《눈이》 in flakes/~ 내리는 비 drizzling[softly falling] rain/비가 ~ 내린다 It rains gently., A light powdery rain falls. ざらざら
부시 a metal striking piece used with flint to make fire/~를 치다 make sparks with metal on flint; get a light from a flint/~ 쌈지 a pouch for a flint fire-making set.
부시다¹ 《눈이》 (be) dazzling; glaring; blinding/눈이 부시도록 아름다운 여자 a lady of dazzling beauty; a radiant beauty/눈이 부셔서 들 수가 없다 My eyes are so dazzled that I cannot open them. まぶしい
부시다² 《그릇을》 wash (out); rinse; cleanse; clean out. きれいにあらう
부시치다 strike fire; strike a flint[spark]. ひうちする
부식(扶植) implantation; spread; extension 《확립》 establishment/~하다 spread; extend; establish; increase/자기의 세력을 ~하다 establish one's influence. ふしょく
부식(腐蝕) corrosion; erosion/~하다 corrode; rot 《산에 의한》 erode 《녹슬다》 rust/~ 작용 erosion/~제 a corrosive /~토 mold; humus [soil]. ふしょく
부식물(副食物) a side dish; a subsidiary article of diet; food to eat with rice. ふくしょくぶつ
부신(副腎) 【해】 a suprarenal [body]/~의 adrenal; suprarenal. ふくじん
부실(副室) a concubine; mistress ⇒소실 (小室). めかけ
부실(不實) ~하다 ①《불성실》 (be) unreliable; insincere; faithless/~한 친구 a false friend/~한 아내 an undeserving wife/~한 짓을 하다 act falsely; break faith with (a person)/그는 일을 ~하게 한다 He is not a conscientious worker. ②《내용이》 (be) incomplete; unsatisfactory; poor; short/결과가 ~한 회의 a conference poor in results; an

unfruitful conference/연구가 ～하다 There is something yet to learn. ③《(몸이)》(be) weak; feeble; delicate/몸이 ～하다 be weak; be in delicate health/그는 원래 몸이 ～ He is naturally delicate.

**부심**(副審) a subveferee.

**부심**(腐心) care; worry; pains; labor/～하다 take pains (*to*); rack *one's* brains; be vexed. ふしん

**부싯깃** tinder/～통 a tinderbox. ほくち

**부싯돌** a flint [stone]. ひうちいし

**부아** 《예》lungs 《분개》exasperation; anger; rage/～가 나다 be exasperated; feel offended; feel sore (*at*). はいぞう

**부앙**(俯仰) ～하다 look up and down/～하여 천지에 부끄러움이 없다 My conscience is quite clear. ふぎょう

**부액**(扶腋) support; help/～하다 support; help; assist; second. ふえき

**부양**(扶養) support; maintenance/～하다 support; maintain; sustain/양친을 ～할 의무가 있다 We are under obligations to support our parents./～ 가족 a dependent family/～자 a supporter; a sustainer. ふよう

**부양**(浮揚) floating (*up*); floatage; floatation; refloating/～하다 float; be floated 《침몰선이》be refloated/기구를 ～하다 float a balloon/～력 buoyancy; floatage/～성 floatability/～작업 salvage operation. ふよう

**부언**(附言) additional remark; a postscript/～하다 add (*a remark*). ふげん

**부언 유설**(浮言流説) a wild rumor; a groundless report. ふげんりゅうせつ

**부얼부얼** ～하다 (be) plump; chubby 《털이》 plump and hairy. ふくぶく

**부업**(副業) a side line[job, business]; an avocation/유리한 ～ a profitable[remunerative] sideline/～으로 하다 do (*a thing*) on the side. ふくぎょう

**부엉이** 〖조〗an owl; a hoot owl; *Otus scops stictonotus*(학명)/～가 운다 The owl hoots. ふくろう

**부엌** a kitchen 《호텔 따위의》a cuisine 《아파트의》a kitchenette/～일 kitchen work/～칼 a kitchen knife/～일을 하다 do scullery work. すいじば

**부여**(附與) giving; grant; bestowal; investment/～하다 give; grant; vest; invest (*a person*) with/칭호를 ～하다 invest (*a person*) with a title. ふよ

**부여**(賦與) endowment/～하다 endow (*a person*) with; bless (*a person*) with/우리들에게는 양심이 ～되어 있다 We are all endowed[gifted] with a conscience/～능이 ～되다 be endowed with talent. ふよ

**부여잡다** grab hard [with a twist]. つかむ

**부역**(賦役, 夫役) statute labour; compulsory labo[u]r[service]; *a corvée*(F.)/～을 과하다 put (*a person*) to slave labo[u]r; exact statute labor[*corvée*] from (*people*). ふえき

**부역**(負役) statute labor; drafted labo[u]r; *corvée*(F). ふえき

**부연**(敷衍) expatiation; enlargement; dilation/～하다 expatiate; extend; develop/그는 그 문제를 ～하여 설명했다 He dilated upon that subject. ふえん

**부연**(附椽) 〖건〗tilted eaves attached to the edge of rafters.

**부영**(浮榮) worldly[transitory] prosperity[glory]. はかないえいが

**부영사**(副領事) a vice-consul. ふくりょうじ

**부옇다, 뿌옇다** (be) whitish; grayish hazy; misty/안개가 ～ the fog is heavy/먼지로 하늘이 ～ The sky is hazy with dust.

**부예지다** get misty[hazy]; thicken; blur. しろみがかる

**부외 채무**(簿外債務) off-the-book loans.

**부요**(富饒) wealth/～하다 (be) rich; wealthy. ふゆうなこと

**부용**(芙蓉) ①〖식〗〖연꽃〗a lotus ②《목부용》a kind of rosemallow. ふよう

**부용**(附庸) dependency (on *a stronger power* or *person*)/～국 a dependency; a tributary [state]; a subject[vassal] state. ふぞく

**부운**(浮雲) a floating[drifting] cloud; a cloud drift/～처럼 덧없는 인생 the transience of human life. うきぐも

**부원**(部員) a member of the staff; a staff [member]; a staff man/편집 ～(의 한 사람) [a man on] the editorial staff. ぶいん

**부원**(富源) natural resources; sources of wealth/무진장의 ～ an inexhaustible mine of wealth/～을 개발하다 develop [exploit] the natural resources (of *a country*). ふげん

**부월**(斧鉞) 《도끼》an ax[e]; 《큰 도끼》a broad ax[e]; a battle-ax[e]; 《정벌》conquest; subjugation 《중형》severe punishment 《의장의》a kind of ceremonial grayish/～을 가하다 impose a punishment (*on*); punish [severely]. おのとまさかり

**부유**(富裕) wealth; plenty; affluence; opulence; prosperity/～하다 (be) wealthy; be well provided for/～한 사람 a well-off person; a person of easy means/～하게 살다 live[be] in easy means. ふゆう

**부유**(浮遊) wafting; floating/～하다 waft; float; drift/～물 a floating matters/～ 생물 a plankton /공중에 ～하다 float in the air. ふゆう

**부유**(腐儒) a [dull] pedant; a doctrinaire; a book-worm; a dry-as-dust. ふじゅ

**부유스름하다, 뿌유스름하다** (be) somewhat pearly[milky, frosty, misty]; grayish. せんめいでなくしろみがかっている

**부육**(腐肉) tainted meat; putrid flesh; carrion. くさったにく

**부음**(訃音) a report of *one's* death; an obituary notice/～에 접하다 hear[be informed] of (*a person's*) death. ふいん

**부응**(副應) ~하다 meet; conform to; satisfy; suit. つきしたがうこと

**부의**(賻儀) a condolatory present; 「obituary」 offerings/~하다 give (*money a gift*) to ward funeral expenses/~금 donation for funeral expenses.

**부의**(附議) submission for consideration; presentation for discussion/~하다 present[submit] for consideration[discussion]; refer [a bill] to [a committee]. ふぎ

**부의장**(副議長) a vice-president; a vice-chairman. ふくぎちょう

**부익**(副翼) a [wing] flap.

**부익부 빈익빈**(富益富貧益貧) the rich-get-richer and the poor-get-poorer.

**부인**(夫人) a wife; Mrs. (경칭) Madam /~께서도 안녕하십니까 How is your wife? ふじん

**부인**(婦人) a woman; a lady (총칭) the fair[weaker, tender] sex; womankind; women/~다운 womanly; lady like/~과 gynecology/~병 women's diseases /~복 women's dress[clothes]/~회 a women's society. ふじん

**부인**(否認) (부정) denial; repudiation; disapproval (거부) veto/~하다 deny; repudiate; disclaim; ·say no (*to*) / ~할 수 없다 be undeniable/법안을 ~하다 veto a bill/~권 the veto power/~자 a denier. ひにん

**부임**(赴任) ~하다 leave[start] for one's [new] post; proceed to one's post/~지 the place of appointment; one's [new] post/~의 도중에 on the way to one's post. ふにん

**부자**(夫子) a sage; a master; a learned man. ふし

**부자**(父子) father and son. ふし

**부자**(富者) a rich[wealthy] man/~ 계급 the moneyed class/~가 되다 become rich; make a fortune. ふうしゃ

**부자집**(富者—) a wealthy family; a rich man's house/~에 장가들다 marry a rich heiress. /~에 태어나다 be born rich.

**부자 상전**(父子相傳) transmission; from father to son. ふしそうでん

**부자연**(不自然) unnaturalness/~하다 (be) unnatural; against nature 《인위적》 artificial 《무리》 forced/~스러운 태도 an affected manners. ふしぜん

**부자유**(不自由) 《불편》 inconvenience 《불쾌》 discomfort 《궁핍》 want of comforts; poverty/~하다 (be) inconvenient; poor; needy; disabled 《몸이》 crippled/~한 생활 a life of want/~를 참다 put up with inconveniences/~한 것 없이 지내다 live in comfort; be comfortably [be well] off. ふじゆう

**부자지** testicles and penis; male genitals. こうがんといんきょう

**부작용**(副作用) [evil] reaction; subsidiary ill effect; by effect; secondary effect /~ 없는 harmless/~을 일으키다 give rise to[produce] ill effects; cause harmful effects. ふくさよう

**부잔교**(浮桟橋) a floating stage[pier]. うきさんばし

**부잡**(浮雜) wantonness; fickleness; unreliableness/~하다 (be) naughty; wanton; unreliable; flighty/~한 아이들 naugnty[wanton] boys. ふまじめ

**부장**(部長) the head[chief, director] of a department; a department manager /인사 ~ the chief of the personnel department ぶちょう

**부장품**(副葬品) an article buried in a tomb. ふくそうひん

**부재**(不在) absence/~하다 (be) absent; be out; be not at home/~중 during *one's* absence/~자 an absentee/~ 투표 voting by mail/~ 투표자 an absentee. ふざい

**부쩍** 《우기는 모양》 obstinately; stubbornly; persistently 《갑자기》 rapidly; quickly/~ 우기다 persist stubbornly/그는 영어 실력이 ~ 늘었다 He has made a remarkable improvement in english. ぐいと

**부적**(符籍) a divine tablet; an amulet: a talisman; a charm.

**부적격**(不適格) ~의 disqualified/~이 되다 be disqualified. ふてきかく

**부적당**(不適當) unfitness; unsuitableness; inappropriateness/~하다 (be) unfit (*for*); unsuited (*to*); inappropriate (*to*) 《성질상》 inapt/그 일은 저 사람에게는 ~ 하다 He is not the right man to undertake the task. ふてきとう

**부적임**(不適任) inadequacy; unsuitableness; unfitness/~의 inadequate; unsuitable; unfit; unqualified. ふてきにん

**부전**(附箋) a slip; a tag; a label/~을 붙이다 tag; label/그 편지는 ~이 붙어서 돌아왔다 The letter was mailed back with a tag explaining its nondelivery. ふせん

**부전**(不戰) antiwar; renunciation of war/~ 조약 an antiwar pact[treaty]/양국간에 ~ 조약이 체결되었다 An antiwar treaty was concluded between the two countries. ふせん

**부전승**(不戰勝) an unearned win/~이 되다 get a win without playing[fighting] 《추첨으로》 draw a bye. ふせんしょう

**부전 자승**(父傳子承) transmission from father to son; transmission through the eldest male branch/~하다 hand down from father to son/~의 handed down from father to son.

**부전 자전**(父傳子傳) transmission from father to son ⇨부전 자승(父傳子承).

**부절**(不絕) ~하다 (be) incessant; ceaseless; continuous/~히 all the time; without interruption; incessantly; continuously. たえないこと

**부절제**(不節制) excess; intemperance; immoderation/~하다 be intemperate; commit excesses/~한 intemperate/~한 생활을 하다 lead an intemperate life.

**부점**(附點) 〖음〗 having a dot; dotted/~음부 a dotted note/~ 2분[4분, 8분] 음부 a dotted half[quarter, eighths] note /복~ a double-dotted note.

**부접못하다** ①be kept from approaching; be denied access to (*a person*)/어떤 방문객도 그에게는 부접못한다 He is always inaccessible to any visitor. ②cannot stand[endure]/시어머니 구박에 며느리가 부접못했다 Harsh treatment by her mother-in-law was more than she could bear.

**부젓가락** fire tongs.

**부정**(不淨) uncleanliness; pollution; impurity/~하다 (be) unclean; dirty; impure; filthy/~한 재물 ill-gotten wealth.

**부정**(不貞) frailty; unfaithfulness/~하다 (be) frail; unchaste; disloyal/그 여자는 ~한 아내다 She is a faithless wife to her husband.

**부정**(不定) uncertainty; indefiniteness/~하다 (be) uncertain; unfixed; unsettled/~ 관사 〖언〗 the indefinite article/~ 기간 an indefinite period of time/~ 대명사 〖언〗 the indefinite pronoun/~법 〖언〗 the infinitive mood/~ 수입 anirregular[incidental] income/~형 an indeterminate form/주소 ~의 사람 a man of no fixed abode; a vagabond; a tramp.

**부정**(不正) (불공정) injustice; unfairness; unjustness (비행) wrong (부정직) dishonesty (위법) illegality (악덕) vice; ~하다 (be) dishonest; unfair; wrong; corrupt; practices/~ 경기 a cross; a fixed fight; a got-up affair/~취득한 돈 ill-gotten money/~ 수단 unlawful means/~ 소득 illicit gains/~ 사건 a scandal.

**부정**(否定) negation; denial; contradiction/~하다 deny; contradict; gainsay; say no/~적 negative/~할 수 없는 undeniable; indisputable/~적 판단 negative judgment/~문 a negative sentence/~하기 어려운 사실 an undeniable[a stubborn] fact.

**부정기**(不定期) irregularity; [having] no schedule/~의 irregular; unfixed; nonscheduled/~선 a tramp steamer; a tramper/~ 열차 an extra train/~형 an indeterminate sentence.

**부정당**(不正當) injustice; iniquity/~하다 (be) unjust; unrighteous; iniquitous.

**부정 명색**(不正名色) ill-gotten wealth; wealth obtained by unjust methods.

**부정직**(不正直) dishonesty; untruthfulness/~하다 (be) dishonest; intruthful.

**부정확**(不正確) inaccuracy; uncertainty; incorrectness/~하다 (be) uncertain; incorrect/~하게 uncertainly; incorrectly; inexactly/그 일에 관해서는 나의 지식은 ~하다 I have no certain knowledge of it.

**부제**(不齊) irregularity; unevenness; lack of uniformity[symmetry]/ ~하다 (be) unsymmetrical; irregular; uneven.

**부제**(不悌) lack of courtesy/~하다 (be) impolite; uncourteous.

**부제**(副題) a subtitle; a sub heading.

**부조**(父祖) ancestors; forefathers/~의 영(靈) the memory of *one's* ancestors/~ 전래의 hereditary.

**부조**(不調) bad condition; disorder; slump; irregularity/~하다 be in a bad condition; be in disorder (운동 선수가) be out of form; be not *one's* usual self /일기 ~ unfavorable weather condition.

**부조**(浮彫) relief; relievo/~ 세공 raised [relief] work.

**부조**(扶助) ①(도움) help; aid; assistance ; support/~하다 support; aid; assist/~료(料) an allowance in aid/상호 ~ mutual aid ②(돈) a congratulatory gift; a money offering.

**부조리**(不條理) irrationality; absurdity; unreasonableness/~한 irrational; unreasonable.

**부조화**(不調和) disharmony; inharmoiousness; incongruity; discordance/~하다 do not harmonize[match] (*with*); be out of keeping (*with*)/~한 색 (色) inharmonious colours.

**부족**(部族) a tribe.

**부족**(不足) (결핍) shortage; lack; want; scarcity; deficiency (금액) a deficit (불만족) dissatisfaction; discontent/~하다 (be) insufficient; lacking; short (*of*); in want of/~액 shortage; a difference/~량 ullage/~을 보충하다 make good[up] a deficiency/~한 점이 없다 leave nothing to be desired/식량이 점점 ~해지고 있다 The food supplies are running short.

**부종**(浮腫) 〖의〗 edema.

**부주** a hereditary trait; a famity strain.

**부주의**(不注意) carelessness; inattention; heedlessness; neglect/~하다 (be) careless; inattentive/운전수의 ~로 차가 전복됐다 The car was upset through the carelessness of the driver.

**부주제**(副主題) 〖음〗 the subsidiary theme.

**부중**(浮症) 〖의〗 a [pathological] swelling.

**부지**(不知) ignorance/~하다 do not know; be ignorant of/~의 진술(陳述) a plea of ignorance of fact.

**부지(敷地)** a [building] site; a plot; a lot; ground／~의 선정 the selection of a site (for)／건축 ~ a building site [lot].

**부지(扶支)** ~하다 bear; endure; stick to; hold out／~ 못하다 cannot stand; be unable to remain.

**부지깽이** a poker.

**부지거처(不知去處)** whereabouts unknown; missing.

**부지기수(不知其數)** (being) innumerable; countless; numberless.

**부지런하다** (be) diligent; assiduous; industrious; hard-working／부지런히 일하다 work hard; be industrious in one's work／부지런히 공부하다 work hard; study with diligence; be diligent in one's lessons.

**부지배인(副支配人)** an assistant manager.

**부지불식간(不知不識間)** ~에 unconsciously; unwittingly; in spite of oneself; without intention／~에 나쁜 짓을 하게 되다 drift[slip] into an evil course.

**부지사(副知事)** a deputy[lieutenant] governor.

**부지중(不知中)** unconsciously; unintentionally; unawares.

**부지하세월(不知何歲月)** not knowing when something is going to be completed／그것은 언제 될지 ~이다 Nobody can tell when it will be completed.

**부직(副職)** an additional post.

**부진(不振)** dullness; inactivity; depression; stagnation／~하다 (be) dull; inactive; slack／사업의 ~ business depression; stagnation of trade; a slump in business.

**부진(不進)** ~하다 make no progress／지 ~하다 make slow progress; progress at a snail's pace.

**부진(不盡)** inexhaustibleness; endlessness／~하다 (be) inexhaustible; endless; unfailing／~근 《수》 a surd root／~근 수 《수》 an irrational number; a surd.

**부질없다** (be) vain; futile; useless／부질없이 idly; to no purpose; in vain／부질없이 시간을 보내다 idle away one's time／부질없는 짓을 하다 do a foolish thing.

**부집게** [flame] snuffers; fire nippers; a candle snuffer.

**부집 존장(父執尊長)** one's father's friend; a man about the same age with one's father.

**부차적(副次的)** secondary／~ 원인 a secondary cause.

**부착(附着)** sticking; adherence; adhesion; cohesion／~하다 adhere[stick, cling] to; attach[fasten] itself to／~력 adhesive power; adhesion／~어 《언》 an agglutinative language.

**부채** a fan; a folding fan／~를 부치다 fan oneself; use a fan／~ 꼭지 the rivet[pivot] of a fan.

**부채(負債)** (빚) a debt 《채무》 liabilities／~자 a debtor／~를 지다 run[get, fall] into debt／~를 지불하다 pay off debts／겨우 ~를 다 벗어버렸다 With much difficulty, I have got out of debt.

**부채살** the ribs of a fan.

**부처(석가모니)** Buddha 《성인》 a Buddhist saint／~님 가운데 토막같은 사람 tin man too saintly to be true; a little a Jesus／그는 ~ 같은 사람이다 He is a saintly man.

**부처(夫妻)** husband and wife; a couple／윌슨씨 ~ Mr. and Mrs. Wilson.

**부처꽃** 《식》 a purple loosestrife.

**부처손** 《식》 a selaginella.

**부첨(副尺)** a vernier [scale].

**부첨(富籤)** a lottery; a lottery ticket.

**부촌(富村)** a wealthy village; a rich village.

**부총리(富總理)** the Deputy Prime Minister.

**부총재(副總裁)** a vice-president.

**부추** 《식》 a leek; a scallion; a shallot; Allium odorum 《학명》.

**부추기다** incite; urge; stir up; instigate; agitate 《개 따위를》 set (a dog) on／부추기어서 싸움하게 하다 incite (a person) to a quarrel.

**부축** helping by holding a person's arms／~하다 help (a person); give one's arm to.

**부치다¹** (힘에) be beyond one's strength／힘에 ~ be beyond one's power; be beyond one／힘에 부치는 일을 하려고 하지 마라 Attempt nothing beyond your strength.

**부치다²** (부채를) fan／부채를 ~ fan oneself; use a fan／손수건으로 ~ fan oneself with a handkerchief.

**부치다³** (편지·물건을) send; mail (돈을) remit 《짐을》 forward／기차로 상품을 ~ ship goods by rail／이 편지를 항공편으로 부쳐 주시오 Please mail this letter by air-mail.

**부치다⁴** (논·밭을) till; plow; cultivate; work a farm／논을 ~ cultivate rice／밭을 ~ cultivate a field.

**부치다⁵** (음식을) fry; griddle; cook on a griddle／달걀을 ~ fry eggs.

**부친(父親)** a father; a paternal parent.

**부침(浮沈)** ups and downs; rise and fall; vicissitudes／인생의 ~·ups and downs of life; life's vicissitudes／일생의 ~에 관계되다 affect the whole course of one's life.

**부침하다** sow[seed] the field; prepare fields for farming; make a farm.

**부탁(付託)** a request; a favor; solicitation/~하다 ask; request; make a request; ask a favor of/…의 ~으로 at (*a person's*) request/~을 거절하다 refuse (*a person's*) request; refuse (*a person*) a request[favor]/~이 있읍니다 I have a favor to ask of you., I should like to make a request.

**부터** ①(…에게서) from; of; through/멀리 있는 친구로~ 온 편지 a letter from a friend far away/…으로~ 독립하다 become independent of… ②(장소) from; out of; off; through; at; in; by; with; on; down/서울~ 인천까지 from *Seoul* to *Inchon*/창으로~ 내다보다 look out of the window/지붕[계단]으로~ 떨어지다 fall off the roof[staircase] ③(시간) from at; in (이래) since (이후) after (며칠 이후) on and after /세 시~ 다섯 시까지 from three to five/이 법률은 1973년 1월 1일~ 시행한다 This law shall come into force on January 1,1973. ④(견지·표준) from; by/이러한 사실로~ 판단하면 judging from these facts/사회적 견지로~ 본다면 from a social point of view ⑤(범위) [ranging] from…to ⑥(순서) beginning with; first; starting from/당신~ 하시오 You do first. /무엇~ 시작할까 What shall I begin with?

**부통령(副統領)** a vice-president(略: V.P.).

**부패(腐敗)** ①(물질적) rotting; spoiling; decomposition; putrefaction /~하다 (음식물 따위가) go bad; rot; be spoiled; decomposed (달걀이) addle (우유가) turn/~한 rotten; addled (*eggs*)/~하기 쉬운 perishable; corruptible ②(정신적) corruption; decay; depravity; degeneration/~하다 become corrupt; decay /사회[정치]의 ~ the corruption of society[politics]/~한 spoiled; corrupt/~한 정치인 a corrupt politician/~균 a saprogenous bacillus; a saprophyte /~물 decomposing matter/ ~ 중독 septic poisoning.

**부평초(浮萍草)** duckweed.

**부표(浮標)** (표지) a buoy (낚시찌) a float; a cork; a quill/~를 달다 a buoy light /~ 설치 buoyage/정박 ~ a mooring buoy.

**부표(否票)** a negative vote; a vote"no"; a "nay" vote.

**부표(浮表)** floating; floatage/~물 a floater/~ 식물 duckweed; duckmeat.

**부표(付票)** an attached tag/~하다 attach a tag (*to*).

**부풀** fine nap [on the surface of cloth]; fuz [on the surface of paper].

**부풀다** (물건이) swell [out] (팽창하다) expand (빵이) rise.

**부풀리다** swell; bulge; expand; inflate (마음을) puff out/풍선을 ~ inflate a toy balloon/나는 그것을 터지도록 부풀리었다 I expanded it to the breaking-point.

**부품(部品)** parts (부속품) accessories/~을 조립하다 assemble parts into a complete whole.

**부풋하다** ①(be) thick and bulky; unwieldy ②(말이) (be) exaggerated; magnified.

**부프다** ①(부피가) (be) bulky/그것은 부프나 가볍다 It is bulky but light. ②(성급하다) (be) impatient; hasty; rash/그는 성미가 부픈 사람이다 He is a rash person.

**부피** bulk; volume; size/~가 큰[있는] bulky; copious; voluminous; unwieldy; of great bulk[size]/~ 큰 물건 articles of a bulky nature/~가 크다 be bulky; be voluminous.

**부하(負荷)** ①(짐) carrying a burden; a burden; a load/~하다 carry a load[burden]; be loaded ②(전기) [carrying] an electrical load/~ 전동기 a loaded motor.

**부하(部下)** a subordinate; *one's* men; a follower; an adherent; a henchman/~ 장병 soldiers[men] under *one's* command/~를 삼다 place (*a person*) under *one's* orders.

**부하다(富─)** ①(부자) (be) rich; wealthy ②(살지다) (be) fat; plump; corpulent.

**부하다(附─)** attach; affix.

**부합(符合)** coincidence; agreement; correspondence/~하다 agree; coincide; correspond (*with*)/~하지 않는 discrepant; contradictory/현실과 ~하다 correspond to the reality.

**부항 항아리(附缸─)** a cupping glass.

**부허(浮虛)** frivolity; levity; fickleness/~하다 (be) showy; foppish; frivolous; fickle.

**부형(父兄)** parents and brothers/~회 a parent's association.

**부호(符號)** a mark; a sign; a symbol; a cipher (전신의) a code.

**부호(富豪)** a rich man; a man of wealth; a millionaire/~가 되다 become rich; amass a fortune.

**부화(孵化)** hatching; incubation/~하다 hatch; incubate; sit (on *eggs*)/병아리를 ~하다 hatch out chickens/인공 ~ artificial incubation/인공 ~기 an[artificial] incubator.

**부화(浮薄)** frivolity (허영) vanity; idle show (허식) ostentation/경조 ~ frivolity/~로 흐르다 become frivolous.

**부화(附和)** blind following/~하다 follow (*another*) blindly; echo (*another's views*); chime in with/~ 뇌동 blind following/그는 ~ 뇌동을 일삼는다 He is ready to follow another's example.

**부활(復活)** (갱생) resurrection; rebirth

**부회(回復)** revival 《부흥》 restoration/～하다 revive; resurrect; come to life again/～시키다 revive; restore; bring to life/예수의 ～ the Resurrection/～전야 Easter eve/～제[절] Easter/～주일 Easter Sunday. ふっかつ

**부회(附會, 傅會)** a forced analogy; a farfetched interpretation; distortion; sophistry/～하다 make a forced analogy to; give a farfetched interpretation to[of]; distort; twist. ふかい

**부회장(副會長)** a vice-president; a vice-chairman. ふくかいちょう

**부흥(復興)** 《재건》 reconstruction 《부활》 revival; restoration 《정신상의》 renaissance; renascence/～하다 reconstruct; be reconstructed; rebuild; be revived; restore/인도의 ～ the renaissance of India/한국의 ～은 현저하다 Remarkable is the rehabilitation of Korea/～회 a revival [service]/경제 ～ economic rehabilitation; an economic comeback/문예 ～ 〖역〗 the Renaissance; the Revival. ふっこう

**북**[1] 〖음〗 a drum/～ 소리 the sound of a drum/～을 치다 beat a drum/～치는 사람 a drummer. たいこ

**북**[2] 《베틀의》 a spindle 《방직기의》 a shuttle. ひ

**북**[3] 《뿌리의 흙》 the earth covering roots/～을 주다 earth up.

**북(北)** the north/～의 north; northern; northerly/～으로 north; northward[s]. きた

**북광(北光)** the aurora borealis; the Northern Lights.

**북구(北歐)** Northern Europe; Scandinavia/～의 Scandinavian/～ 신화 the Norse mythology. ほくおう

**북국(北國)** a northern country; the north/～ 사람 a northerner. きたぐに

**북벌(北伐)** subjugation of the northern countries/～하다 subjugate the northern countries. ほくばつ

**북부(北部)** the north; the northern part. ほくぶ

**북북** noisily/～ 긁다 scratch.

**북북동(北北東)** north-northeast(略: N.N.E.). ほくほくとう

**북북서(北北西)** north-northwest(略: N.N.W.). ほくほくせい

**북빙양(北氷洋)** the Arctic Ocean.

**북상(北上)** northing/～하다 go[come] north; proceed northward. ほくじょう

**북새** disturbance; bustle; tumult/～놓다 cause disturbance; bustle about. さわぎまわること

**북서(北西)** northwest(略: N.W.)/～풍 a northwesterly wind. ほくせい

**북슬개** a shaggy[ragged] dog; a poodle. もじゃもじゃしたけなみのいぬ

**북슬북슬** ～하다 (be) bushy; shaggy; plump and hairy もじゃもじゃ

**북안(北岸)** the northern coast; the north shore. ほくがん

**북양(北洋)** the northern sea/～ 어업 northern-seas fisheries.

**북어(北魚)** a dried pollack.

**북위(北緯)** north latitude(略: N.L.)/～30도 30 degrees[30°] North latitude. ほくい

**북잡이** the drummer in a band of mendicant priests. たいこをうつひと

**북장지** a paper sliding door.

**북적거리다** jostle; throng; bustle (about); be clamorous/북적북적 in a bustle; full of stir; tumultuously. うようよする

**북조(北朝)** the North Dynasty.

**북쪽(北-)** the north/～의 north; northern; northerly/～으로 north; northward[s]. きたのかた

**북지(北地)** the north; northern region.

**북진(北進)** ～하다 go north; march[sail] northward. ほくしん

**북채** a drum-stick. たいこのばち

**북천(北天)** the northern sky; 〖천〗 the sky north of the zodiac. ほくてん

**북춤** a court dance by *geesaeng* around a drum. たいこおどり

**북치** a small cucumber. ちいさいうり

**북통(-筒)** a drum frame; a drum; a wooden body of a drum. たいこのどう

**북틀** a drum stand. たいこのたい

**북편(北便)** the northern part[side]; the north/～에 on the north side (of). きたのほう

**북풍(北風)** the north wind; the northerly wind. きたかぜ

**북한(北韓)** North Korea.

**북향(北向)** a northern aspect[exposure]/～집 a house with a northern aspect; a house facing [the] north. きたむき

**북행(北行)** going north; northing/～하다 go [up] north. きたゆき

**북회귀선(北回歸線)** the Tropic of Cancer. きたかいきせん

**분** 9이～ this gentleman[lady]/한두 ～ a couple of people. かた

**분** merely; alone; only; but/～만 아니라 moreover; besides; in addition; what is more/나는 내 의무를 다했을 ～이다 I have done nothing but my duty/믿을 사람은 너 ～이다 I have no one but you to rely upon. だけ

**분(分)**[1] 《시간 등의》 a minute/15～ a quarter of an hour. ぶん

**분(分)**[2] 《부분》 a part; a portion/5～의 3 three-fifth 《몫》 a share; a part; a portion 《일정량》 amount; quantity/식사 5인～ dinner for five/3일～의 양식 food for three days 《본분》 duty 《신분》 social position[standing]; lot; means/～에 맞게 살다 live within *one's* means; live up to *one's* income. わりあて

**분(粉)** 《화장용》 [toilet] powder; face powder[-paint]/물～ liquid powder/～을 바르다 powder[paint] *one's* face; put powder on. ふん

**북극**(北極) the North Pole／~의 Arctic; polar; pole／~ 지대 the Arctic Circle／~ 탐험 an Arctic[a polar] expedition／~성 the pole star; the North Star／~양 the Arctic Ocean. ほっきょく

**북녘**(北―) the North; the northern part. きたのかた

**북단**(北端) the northern end[extremity]. ほくたん

**북대서양**(北大西洋) the North Atlantic [Ocean]／~ 조약 기구 the North Atlantic Treaty Organization(略: NATO).

**북더기** waste-straw; dust-heap. くず

**북덕지**(―紙) crumpled paper.

**북돋우다** ①**(식물을)** earth up ②**(고무시키다)** arouse; stir up; prompt; excite／용기를 ~ summon[muster, pluck up, screw up] *one's* courage. ばいようする

**북동**(北東) northeast(略: N. E.)／~풍 a northeasterly wind. ほくとう

**북두칠성**(北斗七星) the Great Bear; the Plough; the Dipper⟨미⟩. ほくとしちせい

**북등**(―燈) a kind of drum-shaped lamp.

**북류**(北流) ~하다 flow north (into *the sea*).

**북면**(北面) ①**(북향)** facing north ②**(면)** the north side[face]. ほくめん

**북미주**(北美洲) North America.

**북반구**(北半球) the Northern Hemisphere. きたはんきゅう

**북받치다** 《감정이》 be filled with (*emotion*); have a fit of; well up; fill *one's* heart 《일이 주어》

**북방**(北方) the north[ward]／~의 northern; notherly／~에 in [the direction of] the north／~으로 northwards; toward the north. ほっぽう

**분**(盆) a pot／~받침 a flow stand. ぼん

**분**(憤, 忿) indignation; resentment; anger; rage／~을 참지 못하다 lose *one's* temper; get angry; get out of patience. ふんど

**분**(糞) excrement[s]; feces; dung《속》《새・짐승의》 droppings. ふん

**분가**(分家) a branch family; a cadet house／~하다 create a new family; set up a branch[separate] family. ぶんけ

**분간**(分揀) ①**(분별)** distinctoin; discrimination; discernment／~하다 distinguish (between *two things*, *one* from *others*); know[tell] (*from*); discern; discriminate／~하기 어려운 indistinguishable ②**(죄를 용서함)** forgiveness; pardon／~하다 forgive; pardon; excuse. ぶんべつ

**분감**(分監) a branch prison.

**분갑**(粉匣) a puff box 《휴대용》a compact. コンパクト

**분개**(分介) 《부기》 journalizing／~하다 journalize／~장(帳) a journal.

**분개**(憤慨) indignation; resentment／~하다 be indignant at; resent／~하여 in a rage; in resentment; indignantly. ふんがい

**분격**(憤激) excitement; inspiration／~하다 be inspired[roused, stirred]／~시키다 stir; inspire; animate. ふんげき

**분격**(奮擊) a fierce attack[onset]／~하다 make a fierce attack. ふんげき

**분견**(分遣) detachment／~하다 detach; detail／~대 a detachment; a contingent; a draft. ぶんけん

**분결같다**(粉―) (be) tender and spotless; fair-skinned／그 여자의 얼굴은 ~ She has a fair-skinned face.

**분계**(分界) a boundary; demarcation／~하다 demarcate; delimit／~선을 긋다 draw a demarcation between the two. ぶんかい

**분골 쇄신**(粉骨碎身) ~하다 make *one's* best exertions. ふんこつさいしん

**분공장**(分工場) a branch factory; a branch plant[mill].

**분꽃**(粉―) 《식》 a four-o'clock; a marvel-of-Peru. はくふんのはな

**분과**(分課) a subdivision (of *a section*); a section; a branch／~하다 divide (*an office*); divide (*a bureau*) into sections. ぶんか

**분과**(分科) a department; a branch／~회 a sectional meeting／과학은 학문의 한 ~이다 Science is a branch of learning. ぶんか

**분관**(分館) an annex; a detached building. ぶんかん

**분광**(分光) dispersion of light; spectrum／~기 a spectroscope／~학 spectroscopy／~ 분석 spectroscopic analysis／~ 사진 a spectrogram. ぶんこう

**분괴**(憤愧) remorse; regret／~하다 regret; suffer remorse. ひどくくいはじること

**분교**(分校) a branch school. ぶんこう

**분교장**(分敎場) a detached classroom.

**분국**(分局) a branch office; a branch bureau. ぶんきょく

**분권**(分權) decentralization [of authority power]. ぶんけん

**분규**(紛糾) complication; tangle; confusion; a trouble 《분쟁》 a dispute／~에 싸인 문제 a vexed question. ふんぎゅう

**분극**(分極) 《물》 polarization.

**분근**(分根) division of plants／~하다 part the roots (of *a plant*).

**분급**(分給) division; distribution; apportionment／~하다 distribute; allocate; apportion. ぶんきゅう

**분기**(分岐) divergence; ramification; forking／~하다 divide; distribute; apportion／~점 crossroads; a fork. ぶんき

**분기**(憤氣) anger; resentment; indignation. ふんき

**분기**(奮起) rising; rousing; awakening／~하다 rouse *oneself*; be stirred up; rise. ふんき

**분기**(噴氣) spouting; ejection; jet／~하다 eject; emit／~공 《공》 a steam valve; 《지》 a fumarole. はいき

**분김**(忿―) a fit of anger[rage]／~에 in

**분납(分納)** installments/~하다 《돈을》 pay by installments 《상품을》 deliver in parts.

**분내(分內)** ⁋~에서 살아가다 live within one's means. みのほど

**분내(粉—)** the smell[ing] of powder.

**분네** ①《분들》 esteemed persons ②《분》 an esteemed person. かたたち

**분노(忿怒, 憤怒)** anger; wrath; rage/~하다 get angry; be enraged/~를 가라앉히다 soothe another's anger. ふんど

**분뇨(糞尿)** excrements; stool; night-soil. ふんにょう

**분단(分團)** a branch; a section; a [local] chapter〈미〉. ぶんだん

**분담(分擔)** partial charge; assignment 《분업》 division of works 《분장》 allotment/~하다 《금전을》 take partial charge (of)/~금 a share; an allotment/~시키다 allot a part of (the work). ぶんたん

**분당(分黨)** 《나눔》 splitting[dividing] a political party 《당》 a party split; a splinter party/~하다 split[divide] a political party/~파 the seceders; the separatists.

**분대(分隊)** 《육군》 a squad 《분견대》 a detachment 《해군》 a division/~장《육군》 a squad-lea der[-commander] 《해군》 a divisional officer. ぶんたい

**분대(粉黛)** ①《분과 먹》 powder and paint ②《미인》 a beauty; a belle(F). ふんたい

**분대질** meddling; complication/~치다 make trouble. もんちゃくをおこすこと

**분대군** a troublemaker; a roughneck; a meddler; an intruder; an interloper. もんちゃくをおこすひと

**-뿐더러** as well as;not only but…[also].

**분도기(分度器)** a graduator; a protractor. ぶんどき

**분돋음(忿—)** offence/~하다 stir one's bile. かんじょうをそこなうこと

**분동(分銅)** a [metal] weight. ふんどう

**분등(分等)** grading; classification/~하다 grade; classify. とうぶん

**분등(奔騰)** a jump; a sudden rise/~하다 soar [up]; jump; boom; advance[rise] suddenly. ほんとう

**분등(噴騰)** spouting; a spout/~하다 blow up; spout. ふんとう

**분디나무** 《식》 *Fagara schinfolia*〈학명〉. さんしょうのき

**분란(紛亂)** 《혼잡》 confusion; excitement 《문제》 trouble 《소란》 bustle/~하다 (be) in a tangle; in confusion/~을 일으키다 complicate matter; muddle things; throw into disorder. ぶんらん

**분량(分量)** quantity; a measure 《약의》 a dose. ぶんりょう

**분려(奮勵)** exertion; energetic endeavors; great assiduity/~하다 make strenuous efforts[exertions]. ふんれい

**분력(分力)** 《물》 a component [of a force]; a component force. ぶんりょく

**분력(奮力)** putting forth one's strength/~하다 put forth one's strength; rouse [call forth] one's energy. ふるってちからをだすこと

**분로(分路)** 《전》 a shunt. わかれみち

**분류(分流)** a tributary; a branch/~하다 branch from (a large river). ぶんりゅう

**분류(分類)** classification; division 《품별로》 assortment/~하다 classify (as, into); assort; divide (things) into classes. ぶんるい

**분류(奔流)** a torrent; a rapid stream 《폭류》 rapids/~하다 rush; flush; run with rapidity; dash along. ほんりゅう

**분류(分溜)** fractional distillation; fractionation/~시키다 fractionate; crack.

**분리(分利)** division of profits; profit sharing/~하다 share the profit; divide profits. りえきをぶんばいすること

**분리(分離)** separation; solution; secession/~하다 separate (from); divide; part; detach; split; be divided. ぶんり

**분립(分立)** separation; independence/~하다 separate[segregate, secede] from; set up independently. ぶんりつ

**분마(奔馬)** a galloping horse. ほんば

**뿐만** nothing but; only ⇒뿐.

**분만(分娩)** childbirth; parturition; delivery/~하다 give birth to; be delivered of/여아를 ~하다 give birth to[be delivered of] a daughter. ぶんべん

**분만(憤懣)** anger; resentment. ふんまん

**분말(粉末)** powder/~의 powdered/~로 만들다 reduce (a thing) to powder; powder; pulverize. ふんまつ

**분망(奔忙)** pressure of work; busyness/~하다 (be) busy; busily engaged[occupied]. たぼう

**분매(分賣)** selling separately/~하다 sell separately[singly]. ぶんばい

**분면(粉面)** 《얼굴》 a powdered face. おしろいをつけたかお

**분멸(焚滅)** incineration; destruction by fire/~하다 be incinerated; be destroyed by fire. やけてなくなること

**분명(分明)** clearness/~하다 (be) clear; plain; distinct 《자명》 evident; apparent; obvious 《확실》 certain; sure/…임이 ~하다 It is apparent that …/~히 기억하다 remember clearly. ぶんめい

**분몌(分袂)** parting/~하다 part from (one); part with; bid (one) farewell. ぶんけつ

**분모(分母)** 《수》 a denominator/공~ a common denominator. ぶんぼ

**분묘(墳墓)** a tomb; a grave. ふんぼ

**분무기(噴霧器)** a spray[er]; a vaporizer 《향수 따위의》 an atomizer 《치료용》 a nebulizer. ふんむき

**분문(噴門)** 《생》 the esophageal orifice [of the stomach]; the cardia. ふんもん

**분바르다(粉—)** powder [one's face]; put

powder on [one's face]; plaster [one's face] with powder.

**분반(噴飯)** ~하다 burst into laughter; burst out laughing. ふんぱん

**분받침(盆—)** a pottery flowerpot holder. ぼんだい

**분발(奮發)** effort; exertion; endeavo[u]r/~하다 make an effort; endeavo[u]r; be eager (*for, to do*)/~심 a spurt; the spirit of exertion. ふんぱつ

**분방(奔放)** being wild [free, unfettered]. ほんぽう

**분배(分配)** distribution; division; allotment/~하다 distribute (*among*); divide (*between, among*); allot; share (*with*)/이익 ~ distribution of profits. ぶんばい

**분벽(粉壁)** a white washed wall. しらかべ

**분변(分辨)** discrimination; distinction/~하다 discriminate (*A from B*); distinguish (*A from B, between A and B*).

**분별(分別)** (분류) classification; assortment; division (분변) distinction; discrimination/~하다 classify; assort; distinguish; discriminate (*A from B, between A and B*)/~있는 사람 a man of sense. ふんべつ

**분복(分福)** one's lot; one's destined luck.

**분봉(分封)** ①(제후의) enfeoffment/~하다 enfeoff; invest (*one*) with a fief ②⇒분봉(分蜂). ぶんぽう

**분봉(分蜂)** hiving off; splitting the hive/~하다 hive off; split the hive.

**분부(分賦)** assignment; allotment; allocation/~하다 assign; allot.

**분부(分付, 吩咐)** (명령) an order; command (지시) directions; instructions/~하다 tell· order; command; appoint; bid; request; give instructions[directions]/~를 내리다 give[issue] orders/그들은 선생님의 ~를 소홀히 했다 They did not mind what their teacher told them. めいれい

**분분하다(紛紛—)** (be) in confusion; in disorder; in a tangle; pellmell/분분하게 confusedly; in disorder/의견이 ~ 하다 Their opinion is divided. ふんぶんとしている

**분비(分泌)** 【생】 secretion (배설) excretion/~하다 secrete; excrete/~액 secreting fluid/~ 기관 a secretory organ/~약 a secretive drug. ぶんぴつ

**분사(分社)** a branch office. ししゃ

**분사(憤死)** ~하다 destroy *oneself* in a fury; die of indignation. ふんし

**분사(噴射)** jet/~식 비행기[전투기] a jet-plane[fighter]. ふんしゃ

**분사(分詞)** 【언】 a participle/현재[과거]~ a present[past] participle/~ 구문 a participial construction. ぶんし

**분산(分散)** ①(흩어짐) break-up; dispersion; decentralization/~하다 scatter; disperse; break-up/위험의 【경】 diversification of risks ②(물) dispersion/~하다 disperse (*rays into colours*)/빛의 ~ dispersion of light. ぶんさん

**분산(墳山)** a mountain used as a burying place. はかのあるやま

**분상(粉狀)** ~의 powdered; pulverized; powdery; powder-like.

**분서(焚書)** book burning; burning books/~하다 burn books. ふんしょ

**분석(分析)** analysis (광석의) assay (검사) examination/~하다 analyze; assay/~학 analytics/~표 an analysis table/~적 analytical. ぶんせき

**분선(分線)** a branch line. ぶんせん

**분설(分設)** establishment of a branch/~하다 establish (*a branch*).

**분성(分性)** 【물】 divisibility.

**분손(分損)** 【경】 partial loss. ぶぶんてきなそんがい

**분쇄(粉碎, 分碎)** pulverization; tearing (*a thing*) into pieces/~하다 pulverize (가루로) reduce to powder (부수다) crush; break into fragments; shatter[smash] to pieces; annihilate/~당하다 be smashed[blown] to pieces. ふんさい

**분쇠(粉—)** lead used in making powder.

**분수** ①(한도) a limit; an extent 《자기 분수》 one's social position; one's station in life/~를 지키다 keep to *one's* sphere in life; cut *one's* coat according to *one's* cloth/제 ~를 모르다 forget *one's* station in life ②(분별) judg[e]ment; discretion; wisdom; good sense/~ 없는 짓 a rash act/~없다 have no sense of propriety; be impertinent; be impudent/그는 ~없이 말을 한다 He doesn't know when to shut up.

**분수(分數)** 【수】 a fraction/~의 fractional/~로 나누다 fractionize/진[가]~ a proper[an improper] fraction. ぶんすう

**분수(噴水)** (샘) a fountain 《솟아나는 물》 a jet (of *water*)/~기(器) a waterspout/~가 솟고 있다 The fountain is playing. ふんすい

**분수(分手)** parting/~하다 part from; part with; separate from.

**분수령(分水嶺)** a divide〈미〉; a watershed〈영〉. ぶんすいれい

**분승(分乘)** riding separately/~하다 ride separately/2대의 자동차에 ~하여 in two separate cars. ぶんじょう

**분식(分蝕)** 【천】 a partial eclipse (of *the sun, etc.*). ぶんしょく

**분식(扮飾)** dressing/~하다 dress *oneself*.

**분식(粉食)** powdered[pulverized] food; flour; flour-based meals/~하다 eat flour/~을 장려하다 encourage the use of flour for food.

**분식(粉飾)** embellishment[s]; make-up/~하다 adorn; decorate; paint (화장하다) make up. ふんしょく

**분신(分身)** the other self; an incarnation of the Buddha. ぶんしん

**분신**(焚身) burning oneself to death; suicide by burning oneself.

**분실**(紛失) loss; losing/~하다 lose; miss; be lost; be missing/~계 a report of the loss of an article/~된 lost; missing. ふんしつ

**분실**(分室) 《관청 등의》 a branch[detached] office 《병원의》 an isolated room. ぶんしつ

**분야**(分野) a sphere; a field; a branch; a division/과학의 ~ the sphere[field] of science. ぶんや

**분양**(分讓) lotting out; sale in lots; allotment/~하다 sell (land) in lots; share (a thing) with (one); 《분배하다》 distribute (among)/ ~지 land for sale in lots. ぶんじょう

**분업**(分業) the division of labour; specialization/~하다 divide (work); specialize. ぶんぎょう

**분연**(忿然) in a rage; indignantly/그녀는 ~히 돌아섰다 She went away in indignation[a huff]. ふんぜん

**분연**(奮然) resolutely; courageously; boldly/~히 vigorously. ふんぜん

**분열**(分列) filing off/~하다 file off/~식 a march past/~식을 하다 [have a] march past. ぶんれつ

**분열**(分裂) division; disruption; disunion; split 《해체》 disorganization; break up /~하다 break up; be disrupted; be split; be disunited/~ 생식 fissiparism. ぶんれつ

**분외**(分外) ~의 《분수에 넘치는》 undeserved; unworthy 《과도의》 undue/~의 지위 an undeserved position. ぶんがい

**분요**(紛擾) 《분란》 trouble; complication 《요란》 agitation; uproar; disturbance 《소요》 disorder/국제적 ~ international complication[trouble]. ふんじょう

**분운**(紛紜) a dispute; a trouble; complications; dissension/ ~을 조정하다 mediate in a dispute. もつれ

**분울**(憤鬱) indignation; resentment; grudge/~하다 burn with indignation; be in deep resentment.

**분원**(分院) a detached building; a branch hospital[institute]. ぶんいん

**분위기**(雰圍氣) 《대기》 an atmosphere 《환경》 surroundings/종교적인 ~ a religious atmosphere/자유스러운 ~에서 in an atmosphere of freedom. ふんいき

**분유**(粉乳) powdered milk/탈지 ~ nonfat dry milk. ふんにゅう

**분자**(分子) 《요소》 an element; a factor 《원자》 a molecule 《분수의》 a numerator /~량 molecular weight/~식 a molecular formula/~설(說) a molecular theory. ぶんし

**분잡**(紛雜) confusion; a mess; disorder/ ~하다 (be) crowded; confused; disordered. こんざつ

**분장**(分掌) ~하다 allot office duties; dispose dignities; take charge of part (of). ぶんしょう

**분장**(扮裝) a make-up; disguise; impersonation/~하다 dress[make] up (as); impersonate 《변장》 be disguised as/여자로 ~하다 dress as a lady. ふんそう

**분재**(分財) distribution of property; settlement/~하다 distribute one's property among. ざいさんをぶんぱいすること

**분재**(盆栽) culture of plants in pots 《나무》 a potted plant/~하다 culture plants in pots. ぼんさい

**분쟁**(紛爭) a trouble; a dispute; difficulties; a strife; complications. ふんそう

**분전**(奮戰) a desperate fight; hard fighting/~하다 fight desperately[furiously]/끝까지 ~하다가 죽다 fight to death. ふんせん

**분점**(分店) a branch shop[store].

**분점**(分點) 【천】 equinoctial points; equinoxes/~월 a tropical month/평균 ~ mean equinox. ぶんてん

**분종**(盆種) a potted plant ⇨분재(盆栽).

**분주**(奔走) ~하다 (be) busy; busily engaged/~하게 busily/항상~하다 be always kept busy. ほんそう

**분지**(盆地) a basin; a hollow. ぼんち

**-분지**(分之) a part; a fraction/3~ 1 a third part; one third/3~ 2 two thirds.

**분지르다** break 《딱하고》 snap 《뼈를》 fracture. おる

**분책**(分冊) a separate volume. ぶんさつ

**분첩**(粉貼) 【화장용】 a [powder] puff 《글쓰는》 a kind of cardboard slate for children's writing practice.

**분초**(分秒) a moment; an instant; a minute and a second. ふんびょう

**분출**(噴出) spouting; jet; sudden outburst /~하다 gush; spout; jet; emit/~물 ejecta 《화산의》 eruptions. ふんしゅつ

**분침**(分針) the minute hand; the long hand. ぶんしん

**분칭**(分秤) a small balance beam.

**분탄**(粉炭) slack; dust coal 《석탄가루》 powdered coal. ふんたん

**분탕**(焚蕩) squandering; dissipation/~하다 squander; run through; dissipate. ざいさんをつかいはたすこと

**분토**(糞土) decayed soil; rotten earth; black earth. ふんど

**분통**(憤痛) great indignation/~이 터지다 get enraged[infuriated]; fly into a passion. げきふん

**분투**(奮鬪) a fight; a struggle/~하다 fight desperately; make strenuous efforts; exert oneself [hard]/자유를 위하여 ~하다 fight for liberty. ふんとう

**분파**(分派) a sect; an off-shoot; a branch 《당파의》 a faction. ぶんぱ

**분파**(分破) ~하다 break; split; rupture. わること

**분패**(憤敗) ~하다 be defeated by a narrow margin; lose by a whisker; nose out. せきはい

**분포**(分布) distribution/~하다 be distr-

**분풀이(憤—)** retaliation／~하다 blow off steam; satisfy *one's* resentment[grudge]; vent *one's* anger[rancour] on(*one*). うさばらし

**분필(分筆)** division of a lot.

**분필(粉筆)** chalk／~로 쓰다 write with chalk／~로 쓰여 있다 be written in chalk. はくぼく

**분하다(憤—)** ①(원통하다) (be) vexing; vexatious; mortifying／분하게 생각하다 be vexed[chagrined] (*at*) ②(아깝다) (be) regrettable／분하게도 to my regret. くやしい

**분한(分限)** ①(한계) a limit; an extent ②(분수) *one's* status; *one's* social position[standing]; *one's* station in life (자력) means／자기의 ~을 지켜라 Remember who you are and what you are. ぶんげん

**분할(分割)** division; partition; dismemberment／~하다 divide [up]; cut up; split; partition; dismember／~ 지불 easy payment／~할 수 없는 indivisible ／~ 상속 divided succession／~ 지배 divide and rule. ぶんかつ

**분할(分轄)** ~하다 divide for an administrative purpose. ぶんかつ

**분할불(分割拂)** an easy payment plan; payment in[by] installments; hireurchase system／~로 사다 buy on the installment[hire-purchase, easy-payment] plan.

**분해(分解)** 《분석》 analysis 《환원》 resolution; decomposition 《용해》 solution／~하다 analyse; decompose; dissolve; disjoint; dismantle; disassemble 《기계 따위를》 take [up] to pices; break up／~ 작용 disintegration 《생물 따위의》 catabolism／~할 수 있는 resoluble; decomposable. ぶんかい

**분향(焚香)** ~하다 burn incense. ふんこう

**분홍(粉紅)** [rose-]pink. ももいろ

**분화(分化)** differentiation; specialization ／~하다 specialize; differentiate; be specialized. ぶんか

**분화(噴火)** an eruption; volcanic activity ／~하다 become active; erupt; burst into eruption／~구 a crater／~산 a volcano. ふんか

**분회(分會)** a branch [of an organization, of a society]; a [local] chapter. ぶんかい

**붇다** ①(물에 젖어서) get soaked; become sodden ②(늘어가다) gain; increase; grow; swell／식구가 ~ the family grows larger.

**불¹** ①(타는 현상) fire 《화염》 flame; blaze ／~붙기 쉬운 inflammable／~이 붙다 catch fire／~을 때다 light a fire／~을 붙이다 fan the fire ②(등화) a light; an electric light; a lamp／~을 켜다 [make a] light; light a lamp; switch [turn] on the light[s]／~을 끄다 put out the light[a lamp] ③(화재) a fire; a conflagration (큰불)／~을 내다 start [cause] a fire; have a fire started (in *a house*)／~조심하다 look out for fire ④(비유적) 정열의 ~ fire of passion. ひ

**불²** 《음낭》 the scrotum 《불알》 the testicles; the balls《속》. いんのう

**불(佛)** ①Buddha 《불교》 Buddhism ②(프랑스) France. ほとけ

**불(弗)** a dollar. ドル

**불가(不可)** ~하다 (be) wrong; bad; improper; unadvisable／가~ right or wrong; good or bad.

**불가(佛家)** 《신도》 a Buddhist; a Buddhist family 《절》 Buddhist temple 《승려》 a Buddhist priest. ぶっけ

**불가결(不可缺)** indispensability; absolute necessity／~하다 (be) indispensable (*to*) essential (*to*). ふかけつ

**불가능(不可能)** impossibility; unattainableness／~하다 (be) impossible; unattainable; impracticable／~한 일 an impossible thing. ふかのう

**불까다** castrate; emasculate; geld／불깐소 a bullock. きょせいする

**불가래** a wooden fire shovel.

**불가무(不可無)** indispensability; absolute necessity／~하다 (be) absolutely necessary; indispensable; essential.

**불가물** a severe drought. ひどいかんばつ

**불가분(不可分)** indivisibility／~의 indivisible／양자는 ~의 관계에 있다 Both are inseparably related (to *each other*). ふかぶん

**불가불(不可不)** whether one will or not; whether willing or not／~ 해야 한다 have no choice but to do. どうしても

**불가사리** 《동》 a starfish; an asteroid.

**불가사의(不可思議)** a mystery; a wonder; a riddle; a miracle／~하다 (be) mysterious[miraculous, inscrutable, strange] ／~론 《철》 agnosticism. ふかしぎ

**불가서(佛家書)** the Buddhist scriptures; Buddhist literature. ぶっしょ

**불가시 광선(不可視光線)** 《물》 an invisible ray.

**불가역 현상(不可逆現象)** an irreversible phenomenon.

**불가지(不可知)** unknowableness; inscrutability／~론 《철》 agnosticism／~론자 《철》 an agnostic.

**불가침(不可侵)** nonaggression; inviolability／~의 inviolable／양국간에는 ~ 조약이 체결됐다 A non-aggression pact was concluded between these two countries.

**불가피(不可避)** inevitability; unavoidability／~하다 (be) unescapable／죽음은 ~하다 Death is inevitable. ふかひ

**불가항력(不可抗力)** irresistable force; an act of God／~의 uncontrollable; beyond control. ふかこうりょく

**불가해(不可解)** an inscrutability; a mystery; a riddle／인생은 ~하다 Life is a

**불각(佛閣)** a Buddhist temple[shrine] ⇨ 불당(佛堂). ぶっかく

**불깍정이** a real stinker.

**불간섭(不干涉)** nonintervention; noninterference/~주의 a nonintervention[hands-off] policy. ふかんしょう

**불감증(不感症)** 〖의〗 frigidity/~의 여자 a frigid woman. ふかんしょう

**불강아지** a lean puppy.

**불개** a mythical dog thought to cause eclipses of the sun and the moon.

**불개미** 〖충〗 a mound-building wood ant; Formica rufa(학명).

**불개입(不介入)** non-intervention/~ 정책 a non-intervention policy. ふかいにゅう

**불거웃** pubic hair; pubes. いんもう

**불거지다** project; protrude; jut out; bulge out; swell out. ふくらむ

**불걱거리다** 〖섭다〗 chew away 《빨래를》 scrub; rub briskly. かりかりがみくだく

**불건강(不健康)** unhealthiness; bad[ill] health/~하다 (be) unhealthy; unwholesome. ふけんこう

**불건전(不健全)** unwholesomeness; unsoundness; morbidness/~하다 (be) unwholesome; unhealthy; unsound; morbid/~한 사상 unsound ideas. ふけんぜん

**불검속(不檢束)** nonrestraint. ふけんそく

**불결(不潔)** dirtiness/~하다 (be) dirty; unclean; filthy; foul; unsanitary/~을 dirt; filth. ふけつ

**불결과(不結果)** a poor[an unfavourable] result; a failure. ふけっか

**불경(不敬)** disrespect; irreverence 《신에 대한》 blasphemy[profanity]/~죄 〖법〗 lese-majesty. ふけい

**불경(佛經)** 〖종〗 the Buddhist scriptures; the sutras. ぶっきょう

**불경기(不景氣)** 《일반의》 hard[bad] times; dullness 《상업의》 depression; slump. ふけいき

**불경제(不經濟)** poor[bad] economy; extravagance; waste/~하다 (be) uneconomical[unthrifty]/그런 짓을 하는 것은 시간의 ~이다 It is a sheer waste of time to do such a thing. ふけいざい

**불고(不顧)** ~하다 disregard; take no notice of; pay no heed[attention] to; ignore; neglect/가사를 ~하다 neglect the home. かえりみないこと

**불고기** roast meat. やきにく

**불공(不恭)** disrespect; impoliteness/~하다 (be) insolent; impolite. ふそん

**불공(佛供)** a Buddhist mass/~드리다 hold[offer] a Buddhist mass. ぶっく

**불공대천지수(不共戴天之讐)** a mortal[deadly] enemy; a sworn foe. ふぐたいてんのあだ

**불공정(不公正)** (be) unfair; inequity ⇨ 불공평. ふこうせい

**불공평(不公平)** unfairness; partiality; injustice/~하다 (be) unfair; partial; unjust; discriminate/~한 조처를 취하다 take partial measures. ふこうへい

**불꽃** a flame; a blaze; a spark/~이 굴뚝으로 날아오른다 Sparks fly up the chimney. ほのお

**불과(不過)** only; merely; no more than/~하다 be nothing but[no more than, only]/구실에 ~하다 That is only an excuse. すぎないこと

**불과(佛果)** Buddhahood; Nirvana(Sans)/~를 얻다 attain Buddhahood; enter Nirvana; achieve supreme enlightenment. ぶっか

**불관(不關)** not minding/~하다 do not concern oneself in; have no connection with. かんけいしないこと

**불교(佛敎)** 〖종〗 Buddhism/~의 Buddhist[ic]/~도 a Buddhist; a follower of Buddhism. ぶっきょう

**불구(不具)** 《기형》 deformity; malformation 《얼굴의 손상》 disfigurement 《절름발이》 a cripple/~자 a deformed person; a cripple/일생의 ~자가 되다 be crippled [disabled] for life. ふぐ

**불구(不久)** ~하다 (be) not long (before)/~에 before long; in a short time; shortly. ひさしくないこと

**불구(佛具)** [Buddhist] altar fittings. ぶつぐ

**불구(不拘)** ~하다 disregard; be not deterred[bothered, hindered] (by)/~하고 regardless of; in spite of; despite/비가 오는데도 ~하고 in spite of the rain. かかわらないこと

**불구속(不拘束)** nonrestraint/~으로 without physical restraint. ふこうそく

**불굴(不屈)** fortitude; indomitability/~하다 (be) indomitable; inflexible/~의 정신 an indomitable spirit. ふくつ

**불귀객(不歸客)** a dead[deceased] person/~이 되다 die; pass away; join the majority. ふきのきゃく

**불규율(不規律)** disorderliness; lack of discipline; irregularity. ふきりつ

**불규칙(不規則)** irregularity; lack of system/~하다 (be) irregular; fitful/~하게 irregularly; unsystematically/그는 ~한 공부를 하고 있다 He studies by fits and starts. ふきそく

**불균형(不均衡)** want of balance; inequality; disproportion/~하다 (be) illbalanced; unequal; disproportioned. ふきんこう

**불그데데하다** (be) gaudily red.

**불그레하다** (be) reddish; be tinged with red.

**불끈** 《갑자기》 suddenly; casually 《단단히》 tightly; fast; hard; forcibly/주먹을 ~쥐다 clench one's fists. ばっと

**불근(不勤)** idleness; laziness; indolence/~하다 (be) idle; lazy; indolent. きんべんでないこと

**불근거리다** be touchy; be oversensitive.

**불근신(不謹愼)** indiscretion/~한 imprudent; indiscreet. ふきんしん

**불금(不禁)** ~하다 do not prohibit; permit; cannot bear[help] doing 눈물을 ~하다 cannot help shedding[hold back] tears. きんじないこと

**불급(不及)** ~하다 be inferior to; be no match for; be behind. およばないこと

**불급(不急)** ~한 nonurgent/~하다 be not urgent[pressing]; be in no hurry. ふきゅう

**불굿불굿** ~하다 be splashed[dotted] with red.

**불긍(不肯)** ~하다 be unwilling to [do]; be disinclined; be reluctant; have no inclination; cannot give one's mind to; disapprove of. こうていしないこと

**불기(一氣)** fire/~없는 unheated; fireless.

**불기(佛紀)** the Buddhist Era(略: B.E.). ぶっけのねんき

**불기(不羈)** freedom from restraint; independence/~하다 be unrestrained; unshackled. ふき

**불기둥** a pillar of fire[flames]. ひばしら

**불기소(不起訴)** nonprosecution/~로 하다 drop not to prosecute (a person). ふき

**불기운** the heat of a fire (화력) the force[spread] of the fire.

**불긴(不緊)** ~하다 (be) of little importance; of no consequence. きんようでないこと

**불길** the fire[flames, blaze]. かえん

**불길(不吉)** bad[ill] luck/~하다 (be) unlucky; ominous; sinister; inauspicious /금요일은 ~한 날이라고 한다 Friday is believed to be an unlucky day. ふきつ

**불김** the heat[warmth] from fire/젖은 옷이 ~에 말랐다 The wet clothes dried out by the fire. ひのき

**불깃** burning a swath of trees ahead of a forest fire to prevent its spread.

**불나다** a fire breaks out[occurs]/그의 집에 불났다 His house is on fire. ひがでる

**불난리(一亂離)** a fire.

**불납(不納)** default; nonpayment/~자 a defaulter/~결손 losses due to nonpayment.

**불내다** accidentally set fire (to).

**불녕(不佞)** your humble servant; I; myself. じこのけんしょう

**불놀이 (불장난)** playing with fire (총사냥) shooting/~하다 play with fire (총사냥) go shooting.

**불놓다 (방화하다)** set fire to (a house); (도화선에) light a fuse. ほうかする

**불놓이** shooting; hunting/~하다 shoot [game]; hunt.

**불능(不能) (불가능)** impossibility (무능력) inability; incapacity; lack of ability /~하다 (be) impossible; incapable; unable.

**불다** ①(바람이) blow/바람이 어느 쪽에서 불어 오느냐 Where does the wind sit? ② (입으로) blow; breathe upon (a thing) /촛불을 불어 끄다 blow out a candle ③ (악기를) blow; play (on)/나팔을 ~ blow a trumpet/피리를 ~ play a flute ④(고백하다) confess; own up; come clean; make a clean breast (of)/죄상을 ~ confess to a crime. ふく

**불단(佛壇)** a Buddhist altar; a family Buddhist alter[shrine]. ぶつだん

**불당(佛堂)** a Buddhist temple[sanctum, shrine]. ぶつどう

**불당그래** a fire rake.

**불땀** heat/~이 세다 have strong caloric force; bo loaded with heat. ねんしょうのきょうじゃく

**불때다** make[build] a fire (지피다) put fuel on a fire (때다) burn/교실에 ~ heat a classroom/불땔 나무가 없다 have no wood to make a fire (with).

**불덩어리** a fireball/~가 되어 in a mass of flames.

**불도(佛道)** Buddhism; Buddhist doctrines; the teachings of Buddha. ぶつどう

**불도(佛徒)** a Buddhist. ぶつと

**불도두개** a metal device for raising the wick of a lamp.

**불돌** a stone used for covering the fire in a brazier. とねにつかういし

**불동** ①(탄 심지) the snuff (of a candle); the charred portion (of a candlewick) ②(작은 불덩이) a spark/~이 튀기다 spark; give off sparks. ひばな

**불되다** be extremely oppressive; intolerably harsh[cruel].

**불두덩** the groin. いんぶ

**불뚱거리다** get sulky; scowl; grouch(미·구). むっとする

**불뚱이** hot[peevish] temper; irritability; quick-temper; irritable disposition; a choleric person. たんきなひと

**불등걸** pieces of glowing charcoal.

**불량(不良) (행실이)** wickedness; delinquency (질이) badness; inferiority/~하다 (be) bad; evil; wicked; delinquent; poor; inferior/그는 학교 성적이 ~하다 He stands low in his school work./사람이 ~해지다 go to the bad; become deliquent/~품 inferior goods/~배 the depraved. ふりょう

**불러내다** call out; call (a person) to (before)/문간으로 ~ call (a person) to the door.

**불러먹기** blackmail; extortion/~하다 blackmail (a person); extort (a thing) by intimidation. ゆすり

**불력(佛力)** the power[influence] of Buddha. ぶつりょく

**불령(不逞)** outlawry; insubordination/ ~의 무리 lawless people; rebels; outlaws. ふてい

**불로(不老)** eternal youth/~하다 (be) ever-young[ageless]/~ 불사(不死) the land of perennial youth and immortality/~초 an elixir of life. ふろう

**불로 소득(不勞所得)** unearned income; a windfall income; investment income. ふろうしょとく

**불로 장생(不老長生)** eternal youth; pere-

**불룩거리다** quiver; vibrate/좋아서 코를 ~ be puffed up with pride.
ふくらんだりへこんだりする

**불룩하다** be swollen; baggy; bulging/과자로 불룩한 주머니 a bulging pocket with candies/임신하여 배가 ~ be big with child.
とっきしている

**불륜**(不倫) immorality; impropriety/~의 immoral; illicit.

**불리**(不利) disadvantage; a drawback; a handicap/~하다 unfavorable; be disadvantageous/형세가 우리에게 ~하다 The odds are against us.
ふり

**불리다**¹ (배를) fill (one's) stomach; satisfy (one's appetite);(비유적) enrich; oneself; feather one's own net/공금으로 자기 배를 불렸다 He enriched himself with public fund.
みたす

**불리다**² (쇠를) temper; anneal (곡식을) winnow; fan (away).
きたえる

**불리다**³ (부름을 받다) be called; be summoned; be invited/법정에 ~ be summoned to the court/잔치에 ~ be invited to a feast/선생님에게 불리어 가다 be called before a techer.
よばれる

**불리다**⁴ (바람에) be blown/먼지가 바람에 ~ dust flies in the wind.

**불리다**⁵ (액체에) soak; steep/쌀을 물에 ~ soak rice in the water (재물을) increase; add to/재산을 ~ increase[add to] one's fortune.
ふやす

**불리다**⁶ (악기를) make (a person) blow (자백시키다) make (a person) admit oneself guilty/그에게 나팔을 ~ have him blow a trumpet.
すいそうされる

**불림**¹ (쇠의) tempering metal.
きたえること

**불림**² (죄인의) confession of one's partners in the crime.

**불만**(不滿) discontent; dissatisfaction/~하다 (be) dissatisfied[displeased]; unsatisfactory[malcontent]/나는 지위에 ~을 가지고 있다 I am discontented with my position.
ふまん

**불만족**(不滿足) dissatisfaction ⇨**불만**.
ふまんぞく

**불망**(不忘) ~하다 de not forget; always remember; keep in mind all the time.
わすれないこと

**불매 동맹**(不買同盟) a boycott[against purchasing]; a buyers' strike; a boycott movement.
ふばいどうめい

**불매증**(不寐症) insomnia. ふみんしょう

**불면 불휴**(不眠不休) ~하다 deny oneself sleep and rest; forget food and sleep; work day and night. ふみんふきゅう

**불면증**(不眠症) (의) insomnia; sleeplessness/~에 걸리다 suffer from insomnia /~ 환자 an insomniac. ふみんしょう

**불멸**(不滅) (정신적) immortality (물질의) indestructibility/~의 immortal; inde- structive/영혼의 ~ immortality of the soul. ふめつ

**불멸**(佛滅) 〖종〗 Buddha's death.

**불명**(不明) ~한 indistinct; obscure; vague (행명치 않음) unwise/신원 ~의 시체 an undetified body. ふめい

**불명**(佛名) (부처의) the name of Buddha (불호) the name of a Buddhist saint (신자의) one's Buddhist name. ぶつめい

**불명료**(不明瞭) indistinctness; obscurity; ambiguity/~하다 (be) indistinct; obscure; be not clear. ふめいりょう

**불명예**(不名譽) dishono[u]r; disgrace; shame/~하다 be disgraceful; dishono[u]rable; inglorious/~ 제대 dishono[u]rable discharge. ふめいよ

**불모**(不毛) barrenness; sterility/~의 barren; sterile; waste/그들은 ~의 땅을 개간했다 They reclaimed the waste land /~지(地) barren land; a desert. ふもう

**불목** the part of the floor of a Korean room nearest to the fuel hole.

**불목**(不睦) disharmony; [family] discord; trouble; dissension/~하다 be in discord (with).
むつまじくないこと

**불목하니** a cook in a temple.

**불무하다**(不無―) be not lacking[wanting]; definitely exist. ないものがない

**불문**(佛門) a Buddhist family. ぶつもん

**불문**(不文) ①(무식) illiteracy ②(불성문) unwritten (rule). ふぶん

**불문**(不問) taking no notice; giving no heed/~하다 take no notice of; ignore /남녀 노소를 ~하고 regardless sex and age. ふもん

**불문 가지**(不問可知) being easily understandable without asking/~의 일이다 It goes without saying.
きかなくてもよくわかること

**불문 곡직**(不問曲直) ~하다 do not inquire into the right or wrong/~하고 regardless of merits; without inquiring into the right or wrong.

**불문율**(不文律) an unwritten law[rule]; common law/~ 헌법 an unwritten constitution. ふぶんりつ

**불미**(不美) ~하다 (be) ugly; unsavory; scandalous; nasty; disgraceful; shame /~스러운 일 a shameful thing; a shame.
みにくいこと

**불민**(不敏) stupidity; dullness; incompetency/~하다 (be) dull-witted; incompetent; stupid; dull. ふびん

**불바다** a sea of flames/~를 이루었다 The flames have steadily spread.
ひのうみ

**불발**(不發) ①(탄환의) misfire/~하다 misfire; fail to be fired[exploded] ②(떠나지 않음)~하다 do not depart[leave]/~탄 a blind shell; a dud. ふはつ

**불발**(不拔) firmness; steadfastness/~하다 (be) firm; indomitable invincible/~의 정신 an indomitable spirit. ふばつ

**불범**(不犯) ①(침범하지 않음) not trespass-

**불법** 452 **불순하다**

**불법**ing[encroaching, intruding] ②《불교》abstinence from sexual intercourse.

**불법**(不法) 《위법》 unlawfulness; illegality 《부정》 injustice; outrageousness／～하다 unjust; illegal; (be) unlawful／～한 짓을 하다 do wrong. ふほう

**불법**(佛法) 《종》 Buddhism 《부처의 교법》 the law of Buddha. ぶっぽう

**불벼락** ①《번갯불》 a bolt of lightning ② 《비유적》 a tyrannical decree.

**불변**(不變) constancy; unchangeability; permanence／～하다 (be) constant[unchangeable, invariable, immutable]／～의 법칙 an immutable law. ふへん

**불병풍**(一屛風) a small folding screen to protect a brazier fire from the wind.

**불볕** a broiling sun／～이 나다 the sun comes out blazing.

**불복**(不服) disobedience／～하다 disobey; protest against; object to; be dissatisfied (with); disagree. ふふく

**불부채** a fan used in fanning the fire.
ひをおこすおうぎ

**불분명**(不分明) indistinctness; obscurity ／～하다 (be) indistinct; obscure; be not clear; be ambiguous. ふめい

**불뿔이** scattered; in all directions／～흩어지다 be scattered; disperse; break up／가족이 ～ 헤어졌다 The family broke up. ばらばらに

**불붙다** catch fire／불붙기 쉽다 be easy to catch fire; be combustible. ひがつく

**불비**(不備) defect; deficiency; unpreparedness／～하다 (be) unprepared; defective; incomplete; imperfect／위생 설비의 ～ lack of proper sanitation／교통 기관의 ～ defective means of communication／～한 점 a defect; imperfections.

**불빛** a light; a flicker. ひのひかり
**불사**(佛寺) a Buddhist temple. ぶつじ
**불사**(佛事) a Buddhist service[mass]／～를 행하다 hold a Buddhist service.

**불사**(不死) immortality; eternal life／～하다 (be) immortal; undying; deathless ／～조(鳥) a phenixo. しなないこと

**불사**(不辭) ～하다 do not decline; act in an unreserved way／…하기를 ～하다 be ready[willing] to (do). やめないこと

**불사르다** burn; fire 《태워 버리다》 commit to the flames; lay in ashes 《방화하다》 set (a house) on fire／불살러 재로 만들다 reduce to[lay in] ashes.

**불사신**(不死身) invulnerable life; invulnerability／～의 invulnerable; insensible to pain／그는 ～이다 He is invulnerable life.

**불상**(不祥) ～하다 《불길하다》 (be) ill-omened; ominous; inauspicious; sinister; 《언짢다》 disgraceful; scandalous／～사(事) a scandal; a disgraceful affair; an untoward incident. ふしょう

**불상**(不詳) ～하다 (be) unknown; unidentified ⇨ 미상(未詳). しょうさいでないこと

**불상**(佛像) an image of Buddha; a Buddhist image[statue]. ぶつぞう

**불상놈** a very vulgar person; a very lowborn[humble] person.

**불상당**(不相當) ～하다 (be) unsuitable; inappropriate; improper; undue／신분에 ～한 생활을 하다 live beyond one's means.

**불쌍하다** (be) poor; pitiable; pitiful; sad; pathetic; touching／불쌍한 고아 a poor orphan／불쌍한 처지 a wretched plight[lot]. かわいそうだ

**불서**(佛書) the Buddhist scriptures; Buddhist literature. ぶっしょ

**불선**(不善) evil; vice; mischief 《잘하지 못함》 lack of skill; clumsiness. ふぜん

**불선명**(不鮮明) indistinctness; obscurity; unclearness 《사진》 blurring／～하다 (be) indistinct; obscure; (be) not clear; dim; blurred. ふせんめい

**불설**(佛說) Buddha's teachings; Buddhistic doctrines. ぶっせつ

**불성공**(不成功) failure; ill success／～하다 be unsuccessful[abortive]; fail at; meet with a failure; prove abortive[fruitless]; end in failure. ふせいこう

**불성립**(不成立) failure; miscarriage; fiasco／～하다 fail; fall through; miscarry. ふせいりつ

**불성실**(不誠實) insincerity; dishonesty／～하다 insincere; dishonest; false; untruthful. ふせいじつ

**불성 인사**(不省人事) unconsciousness; a coma／인사 불성／～하다 lose consciousness; become unconscious. じんじふせい

**불세지재**(不世之才) an extraordinary talent[gift]; 《사람》 a man of rare talent; a prodigy [with few parallels].

**불소**(不少) ～하다 be not a little[few]; be quite much[many]; be considerably. すくなからず

**불소**(弗素) 《화》 fluorine(기호 : Fl)／～의 fluoric／～산(酸) fluoric acid.

**불쏘시개** kindling-wood; kindlings; a fire starter; material for starting a fire／～로 쓰기에 알맞다 be good to start a fire with. たきつけ

**불손**(不遜) insolence; arrogance／～하다 (be) insolent; haughty; arrogant／그는 ～때문에 지위를 잃었다 His insolence lost him his situation. ふそん

**불수**(不隨) paralysis／반신 ～ paralysis of one side／～가 되다 be paralysed (in an arm).

**불수의**(不隨意) ～의 involuntary／～근(筋) involuntary muscles. ふずいい

**불쑥** abruptly; all of a sudden／～ 나오다 protrude all of a sudden／～ 질문을 하다 ask one point-blank. ぴょこんと

**불쑥거리다** 《내밀다》 protrude repeatedly 《말을》 speak out abruptly.

**불순**(不純) impurity; adulteration／～물 impurities／～ 분자(分子) an impure element. ふじゅん

**불순하다**(不順一) 《성질이》 (be) disobedie-

**불승인**(不承認) disapproval; refusal to consent; veto 《정권의》 non-recognition /~의 not recognized.

**불씨** a live coal.

**불시**(不時) 《제 때가 아닌》 unseasonableness; untimeliness 《의외》 unexpectedness 《응급》 emergency/~의 《때아닌》 untimely 《뜻밖의》 unexpected 《우연의》 unforeseen; accidental; incidental 《응급의》 emergent/~에 unexpectedly; without notice[warning]/그는 ~에 나에게 달려들었다 He sprang upon me unawares.

**불시착**(不時着) an emergency landing; a forced landing/~하다 make an emergency landing/~ 비행장 an emergency landing field.

**불식**(佛式) Buddhist rites.

**불식**(拂拭) wiping out; sweeping off; cleaning/~하다 wipe out; sweep off; clean.

**불식**(不息) ~하다 do not take a rest[break]; do not relax.

**불식**(不食) a fast; fasting/~하다 do not eat; fast; abstain from food.

**불신**(不信) 《신의 없음》 insincerity 《신용 없음》 discredit 《불신임》 discrust 《신앙 없음》 unbelief/~하다 distredit; distrust; don't believe; refuse to believe/~하게 되다 lose faith in/~ 행위 a breach of good faith.

**불신용**(不信用) distrust ⇨불신. 신용

**불신임**(不信任) lack[want] of confidence; non-confidence/~하다 have no confidence (in); distrust/~ 결의 a non-confidence resolution.

**불심**(佛心) 《부처의 마음》 the mercy 《해탈》 deliverance.

**불심**(不審) 《의심》 doubt; suspicion 《기이》 strangeness 《알 수 없음》 unaccountability/~하다 (be) doubtful; suspicious; strange/~ 검문 questioning.

**불심 상관**(不甚相關) ~하다 affect slightly; have little effect upon; make little difference/누가 당선되든 나에게는 ~다 It matters little to me who is elected.

**불심 상원**(不甚相遠) ~하다 be about right; be not far from the truth; make little difference.

**불안**(不安) uneasiness; anxiety; unrest/~한 uneasy; insecure/~하게 여기다 feel uneasy/~감 a feeling of uneasiness.

**불안정**(不安定) instability; unrest/~하다 (be) unstable[unsettled, insecure]/~한 지위 a precarious position/~ 참 unrest; insecurity.

**불알** testicles; a testis (pl. -tes); the balls《속》/~을 까다 castrate; emasculate/~을 긁어 주다 curry favo[u]r (with a person).

**불야성**(不夜城) a nightless city; an all-night city; a nightless quarter/밤엔 전 도시가 ~을 이룬다 At night the whole city is brilliantly illuminated.

**불양**(祓禳) exorcism; a purification ceremony/~하다 exorcise[drive out] evil spirits; purify.

**불어**(佛語) ①French; the French language ②《종》 Buddhist terms.

**불어나다** increase; multiply.

**불어 세우다** exclude; leave (a person) out [in the cold]; boycott shun.

**불언 가지**(不言可知) ~하다 be obvious; be easily to be inferred; it goes without saying (that).

**불언 실행**(不言實行) action before words; work before talk/~은 나의 생활 신조 (信條)다 Deeds but not words is my principle in life.

**불여귀**(不如歸) 《조》 a cuckoo ⇨소쩍새.

**불여우** 《동》 a red fox; Vulpes kiyomasai 《학명》/~ 같은 계집 a shrew; a vixen; a spitfire.

**불여의**(不如意) ~하다 go wrong[amiss]; go contrary to one's wishes/매사가 ~하다 Things never turn out as I wish.

**불역**(不易) immutability; unchangeableness; constancy/~의 immutable; unchangeable; invariable/~성 immutability.

**불연**(不然) ~하다 (be) not so; (be) far from it/~이면 other wise; else/공부하라 ~이면 낙제한다 Work hard or you will fail in the examination.

**불연**(佛緣) providence of Buddha.

**불연**(怫然) ~하다 (be) indignant; angry; wrathful; furious/~히 indignantly; in a rage; angrily.

**불연성**(不燃性) incombustibility/~의 incombustible; non-inflammable/~ 물질 incombustibles.

**불연속선**(不連續線) 《기상》 a line of discontinuity.

**불염포**(不鹽脯) dried slices of meat unsalted.

**불온**(不穩) unrest; disquiet/~하다 (be) disquieting; threatening; subversive/~한 언사를 쓰다 use improper words/~ 분자 a disturbing element.

**불온당**(不穩當) inappropriateness; impropriety/~하다 (be) unfair; unjust; improper; unreasonable.

**불완전**(不完全) imperfection; incompleteness; defectiveness/~하다 (be) imperfect; incomplete; defective; faulty/구조가 ~하다 be defective in construction/다소 ~한 데가 있다 leave somet-

**hing** to be desired／～ 고용 underemployment. ふかんぜん

**불요**(不撓) tenacity; inflexibility; indomitableness／～하다 (be) indomitable／～ 불굴의 정신 an indomitable spirit.

**불용**(不用) disuse; inutility; uselessness／～하다 do not use; make no use／～이 되다 become useless／그것은 ～입니다 It can be done without. ふよう

**불우**(不遇) misfortune; adversity; obscurity／～하다 (be) unfortunate; adverse／～함을 한탄하다 complain of *one's* ill fate. ふぐう

**불우**(不虞) unexpectedness; suddenness／～의 unforeseen; unexpected／～의 변(變)에 대비하다 provide against emergencies. ふぐ

**불우리** a flame guard to protect a lamp [brazier] from the wind.

**불운**(不運) misfortune; ill luck; adverse fortune; a hapless fate／～하다 (be) unlucky; ill-fated／그녀는 일평생 ～했다 She led an ill-fated life. ふうん

**불원**(不遠) ～하다 (be) not distant; not far off; not remote／그는 ～간 완쾌할 것이다 It will not be long before he gets well. ちかいこと

**불유쾌**(不愉快) unpleasantness; discomfort; disagreeableness／～하다 disagreeable; gloomy; uncomfortable／그는 아주 ～한 태도를 한다 He has a very offensive manner. ふゆかい

**불은**(佛恩) the grace[mercy] of Buddha; Buddha's blessings.

**불의**(不意) unexpectedness; suddenness; unlooked-for／～에 unexpectedly; suddenly; without warning／나는 ～의 습격을 당했다 I was caught napping. ふい

**불의**(不義) immorality; impropriety; infidelity; perfidy; injustice; iniquity／～하다 (be) immoral; improper／～의 씨 a child out of wedlock. ふぎ

**불이익**(不利益) a disadvantage; inadvisability／～의 disadvantageous; unprofitable／자기에게 ～이 되는 짓을 하다 act against *one's* own interests. ふりえき

**불이행**(不履行) nonfulfilment; breach; nonobservance／의무의 ～ failure in duty／조약 ～ a treaty violation. ふりこう

**불인**(不仁) heartlessness; hardness／～하다 (be) unkind; inhuman. ふじん

**불인가**(不認可) rejection; refusal; disapproval／～ 되다 be rejected; be refused.

**불인견**(不忍見) cannot bear witnessing [to see]／～이다 cannot bear to see; be unable to bear the sight of.
みるにしのびないこと

**불인정**(不人情) inhumanity; heartlessness; unkindness／～한 남자 a hard-hearted man. にんにんじょう

**불일**(不一) ①(불일치) disharmony; discord; disagreement ②(고르지 않음) irregularity; unevenness; lack of uniformity／～하다 lack uniformity.
ひとしくないこと

**불일내**(不日內) shortly; soon; before long; in a few days. ちがいうち

**불일치**(不一致) discord; discordance; disagreement; dissonance／～하다 (be) discordant; be in discord (*with*)／～를 초래하다 lead to a discord. ふいっち

**불임**(不姙) sterility; ～의 sterile; barren／～증 sterility／～증이 되다 become sterile; lose *one's* reproductive power.
ふにん

**불입**(拂入) payment; subscription／～하다 pay in; pay up／주금 전액을 ～하다 pay up shares. はらいこみ

**불자**(佛者) 《불제자》 a Buddhist. ぶっし

**불자동차**(一自動車) a fire engine; a fire truck. しょうぼうじどうしゃ

**불잡다** ①《진화하다》 put out a fire; bring a fire under control ②《켜다》 hold up a light. ひをけす

**불장**(佛葬) a Buddhist funeral／～으로 하다 bury (*a person*) according to the Buddhist rites. ぶっそう

**불장난** playing with fire 《남녀간의》 playing with love; an idle love affair／～하다 play with fire; play with love.
ひいたずら

**불쩍거리다** rub and rub; scrub; away [at laundry]. じゃぶじゃぶあらう

**불전**(佛殿) a Buddhist sanctum. ぶつでん

**불전**(佛前) before the Buddhist altar.
ぶつぜん

**불전**(佛典) Buddhist classics 《경전》 the Sutras. ぶってん

**불제**(祓除) purification; exorcism／～하다 exorcise; purify. ばつじし

**불제자**(佛弟子) a Buddhist; a believer in Buddhism.

**불조심**(一操心) caution[guarding] against fires／～하다 be careful not to start [have] a fire; guard against fire.
ひのようじん

**불종**(一鐘) a fire bell; a fire alarm.
はんしょう

**불종**(佛鐘) a Buddhist temple bell.

**불좌**(佛座) the seat of a Buddhist idol.
ぶつざ

**불쬐다** warm *oneself* by the fire; enjoy the fire; warm (*a thing*) over a fire／불쬐세요 Please warm yourself by the fire. ひにあたる

**불줄** 《송전선》 a power-transmission line [wire]. そうでんせん

**불지르다** set fire to (*a house*); burn; set on fire. ほうかする

**불지피다** make[build] a fire／아궁이에 ～ make a fire in the fireplace.

**불질** ①making a fire (in *the fireplace*) ②《총질》 shooting; firing (*a gun*)／～하다 make a fire 《발사하다》 fire; shoot.
はっぽう

**불집** a fire hazard／～을 건드리다 bring a hornet's nest about *one's* ears; arou-

**불집게** ①(심지 자르는) snuffers ②(《불집는》 fire nippers[pincers]. ひばさみ

**불충분**(不充分) insufficiency; imperfection; shortage; inadequacy／자금이 ~하다 be short of capital. ふじゅうぶん

**불충실**(不忠實) ~하다 (be) disloyal; unfaithful／직무에 ~하다 be unfaithful to *one's* duty; be neglectful of *one's* duties. ふじゅうじつ

**불측하다**(不測—) ①(be) bad; wicked ② (be) unforeseeable; unfathomable; inscrutable; incomprehensible. ふそくだ

**불치**(不治) incurability／~의 incurable; fatal／결핵은 오랫 동안 ~의 병이라고 생각되었다 Tuberculosis was for a long time considered as an incurable disease.

**불친소** a bullock; a steer. きょせいしたうし

**불친절**(不親切) unkindness; unfriendliness／~하다 (be) unkind; unfriendly; inhospitable. ふしんせつ

**불착**(不着) nonarrival; nondelivery 《연착》 overdue／~ 우편 a lost letter.

**불찬성**(不贊成) disapproval; disapprobation; dissension; dissenting／~하다 disapprove (*of*); do not agree (*with, to*)／나는 그 혼담에는 절대 ~이다 I am dead set against that match. ふさんせい

**불찰**(不察) a mistake; a blunder. かご

**불찰**(佛刹) a Buddhist temple. ぶっさつ

**불참**(不參) absence; non-attendance／~하다 be absent (*from*); fail to attend／~자 an absentee. ふさん

**불철저** (不徹底) ~하다 (be) not thoroughgoing; inconsistent; unconvincing; insufficient; half／그 설명은 아주 ~하다 That explanation is extremely unconvincing. ふてってい

**불철 주야**(不撤畫夜) day and night; by day and by night／~일하다 work day and night; work double tides[shifts]. ちゅうやのべつをつけないこと

**불청**(不聽) ~하다 do not listen to; do not pay attention to; do not consent to. きかないこと

**불청객**(不請客) an uninvited guest; a surprise party.

**불초**(不肖) an unworthy son; your unworthy son; I; me; myself／~ 자식 one unworthy of *one's* father. ふしょう

**불출**(不出) ①(못난이) a failure; a good-for-nothing; a stupid fellow ②(나가지 않음) confining *one*self at home／두문~하다 keep[stay] indoors; confine *one*self at home. ふしゅつ

**불출**(拂出) payment; defrayal; defrayment／~하다 pay; defray; disburse. しはらい

**불충**(不忠) disloyalty; unfaithfulness; infidelity; perfidy／~하다 (be) disloyal; unfaithful／나라에 ~하다 be disloyal to *one's* country. ふちゅう

**불침략**(不侵略) nonaggression／~ 조약 nonaggression pact[treaty, agreement]. ふしんりゃく

**불침번**(不寢番) night watch; vigil 《사람》 a night watchman／~ 서다 keep a night watch; keep vigil.

**불켜다** kindle; light (*a lamp*); turn[switch] on (*an electric lamp*). ひをつける

**불쾌**(不快) ①unpleasantness; displeasure; discomfort／~하다 (be) unpleasant; uncomfortable／~한 날씨 nasty weather／~지수 the Discomfort Index ②(편찮음) indisposition／~하다 be unwell; be indisposed／다소 ~하다 feel rather poorly; feel a bit out of sorts. ふかい

**불타**(佛陀) 《종》 Buddha. ぶつだ

**불타다** burn; blaze; flame; be in flames／불타는 사랑 flaming love／불타기 쉽다 be easy to burn.

**불탑**(佛塔) a pagoda. ぶっとう

**불통**(不通) ①(《교통, 통신의》) interruption; suspension ②(언어 사정에) no understanding; no association／언어 ~이다 have language difficulty. ふつう

**불퇴전**(不退轉) determination; a firm resolve; an indomitable spirit／~의 노력을 하다 make unremitting exertions [efforts]. ふたいてん

**불투명**(不透明) opacity; obscurity／~하다 (be) opaque; obscure; be not clear [lucid]／~색 an opaque color／~체 an opaque body[substance]. ふとうめい

**불룩그러지다** bulge (*out*); protrude; become protuberant. ふくらんでくる

**불룩불룩** ①(내민 꼴) protuberantly／~하다 (be) protuberant; bulging out ②(퉁명스럽게) bluntly; curtly／~하다 (be) curt; blunt. ふくれている

**불룩스럽다** (be) curt; gruff; blunt. ぶあいそうだ

**불룩하다** (be) bulging out. ふくれている

**불티** sparks; embers; fire-flakes／~를 둘러쓰다 be covered with sparks／~가 튀어오르다 sparks shoot up in the air. ちいさいひばな

**불편**(不便) inconvenience; inexpediency; unhandiness 《몸이》 discomfort; sickness／~하다 (be) inconvenient; incommodious; unhandy 《몸이》 be feeling unwell／나는 몸이 좀 ~하다 I feel a bit out of sorts., I am not quite well. ふべん

**불편 부당**(不偏不黨) impartiality; nonpartisanship; neutrality; independence／~하다 (be) impartial; fair; nonpartisan／~의 신문 an independent newspaper. ふへんふとう

**불평**(不平) discontent; dissatisfaction; a complaint; displeasure; a grievance 《정치상의》 disaffection／~의 소리 a voice of discontent／쌓인 ~이 드디어 폭발했다 The pent-up discontent at last found its vent.／~가 a grumbler; a malcontent／~ 분자 a discontented disaffected element.

불평등(不平等) inequality／～하다 (be) unequal; unfair／～ 조약 an unequal treaty. ふびょうどう

불포화(不飽和) being unsaturated／～ 화합물 an unsaturated compound.

불품행(不品行) misconduct; immoral conduct; loose morals 《방탕》 profligacy. ふひんこう

불풍나게 busily／～ 돌아다니다 bustle around busily. しきりに

불피우다 make a fire. ひをおこす

불필요(不必要) ～하다 (be) unnecessary; needless; unessential／～하게 unnecessarily; needlessly／이런 것은 ～ We can dispense with this. ふひつよう

불하(拂下) disposal／～하다 dispose of; sell; transfer. はらいさげ

불학(佛學) Buddhist learning[lore]; Buddhology／～자 a Buddhism scholar; a Buddhologist. ぶつがく

불학 무식(不學無識) illiteracy; utter ignorance／～하다 (be) utterly ignorant; illiterate; uneducated. ふがくむしき

불한당(不汗黨) a group of robbers; bandits; brigands. やくざもの

불한 불열(不寒不熱) ～하다 (be) neither cold nor hot; mild.

불합(不合) disagreement; discord; disharmony／～하다 be in disagreement (with). ふごう

불합격(不合格) disqualification; failure; rejection; elimination／～하다 be disqualified／～품 a rejected article／～자 rejected person. ふごうかく

불합리(不合理) ～하다 (be) irrational; illogical; unreasonable; absurd. ふごうり

불행(不幸) unhappiness; misfortune; ill [bad] luck; misery／～하다 (be) unhappy; unfortunate; unlucky; miserable／～을 면하다 escape misfortune. ふこう

불허(不許) nonpermission; disapproval／～하다 do not permit; do not allow. ゆるさないこと

불허가(不許可) disapproval; disapprobation; disallowance; rejection／～하다 disapprove; disallow; turn down; do not permit. ふきょか

불현듯이 suddenly; all of a sudden; abruptly; unexpectedly／～ 약속이 생각났다 It suddenly dawned upon me that I had an appointment. いきなり

불협화음(不協和音) 〖음〗 dissonance; discord. ふきょうわおん

불호(佛號) 《부처의》a Buddha's name 《불교도의》a Buddhist name.

불호령(一號令) an impetuous order／～하다 issue an impetuous[a fiery] order; give a strict command. きびしいおこり

불호박(一琥珀) red-amber. あかいろのこはく

불혹(不惑) the age free from vacillation; the age of forty／～을 지나다 be over forty years old. ふわく

불화(不和) disagreement; discord; dissension; differences; trouble; disunion／～하다 be in discord (with); be at odds (with); be on bad terms (with)／가정 ～ family troubles[discord]. ふわ

불화(弗貨) dollars; American money; an American dollar.

불화(佛畫) a Buddhist[Buddhistic] painting[picture]. ぶつが

불화(弗化) 〖화〗 fluoride／～ 수소 hydrogen fluoride.

불확대(不擴大) localization／～ 방침 a policy of localization.

불확실(不確實) ～하다 (be) uncertain; unreliable; insecure. ふかくじつ

불확정(不確定) ～하다 (be) indefinite; uncertain; unsettled; undecided. ふかくてい

불환 지폐(不換紙幣) an inconvertible note; a fiat money《미》; an irredeemable banknote. ふかんしへい

불활발(不活潑) inactivity; dullness; indolence 《시장의》 stagnation; depression; slackness／～하다 (be) dull; inactive／시장 거래가 아주 ～하다 The market is extremely dull[stagnant].

불황(不況) depression; slump; bad[slack] business／세계적인 ～ world-wide depression[slum] (in business).

불효(不孝) undutifulness[impiety] to one's parents; disobedience (to parents). ふこう

불효(拂曉) dawn; daybreak; early morning. ふつきょう

불후(不朽) immortality; imperishability／～하다 (be) immortal; undying; undecaying. ふきゅう

붉다 《색》(be) red 《심홍》 crimson 《진홍》 scarlet／붉어지다 redden; turn red／붉은 빰 red cheek. あかい

붉덩물 a muddy [turbid] stream.

붉디붉다 (be) deep red; crimson. ひじょうにあかい

붉은가시딸기 〖식〗 a raspberry; a wineberry.

붉은거북 〖동〗 a toggerhead [turtle].

붉히다 blush (with shame); colo[u]r up; turn red; be shame-faced／그녀는 얼굴을 붉혔다 A pink glow mounted to her cheeks. あからめる

뿜다 《액체를》 spout; spurt; gush out; burst 《연기・불을》 belch (smoke); shoot up 《방출하다》 emit／분수가 물을 뿜고 있다 The fountain is playing／고래가 물을 ～ The whale spouts water. ふきだす

붐비다 (be) congested; crowded; packed; thronged; jammed; jampacked／거리가 ～ The street is busy with traffic. ごたごたしている

붐하다 be dawn gray. ぼうっとしむ

붓 a writing brush; a brush; a pen／～을 놓다 lay down one's pen／～장난 wielding one's brush／～집 a pen-case／～통 a pen-stand. ふで

붓꽃 〖식〗 an iris; a blue flag. いちはつ

붓끝 the tip of a [writing] brush; the

**붓날다** point of a pen 《필봉》 a stroke of the pen[brush]/~이 닳았다 The tip of this brush has worn out. ひったん

**붓날다** be frivolous; be light; be flippant/언행이 ~ be flighty; be giddy.

**붓날리다** make one's words[deeds] superficial; do in a shallow way/언행을 ~ be flighty. うきかされる

**붓다**[1] ①《살·가죽이》swell; become swollen; tumefy; bloat/다친 팔목이 몹시 부었다 The injured wrist swelled up badly. ②《성나서》get sulky; get angry; sulk; grow sullen/부어 있다 be sulky; be in the sulks/부은 얼굴 a sulky face [look]; a sullen looks. はれる

**붓다**[2] ①《쏟다》pour (into, out); fill (a cup) with (tea)/술을 ~ fill a glass with wine/목욕탕에 물을 ~ pour water into a bath-tub ②《씨앗을》cast; sow; seed down/모판에 씨앗을 ~ sow seed in a seedbed ③《곗돈·월부금》pay by[in] installment. そそぐ

**붓대** the stem of a writing brush; a brush handle. ふでのじく

**붓두껍** the sheath of a writing brush.

**붓방아** halting strokes in writing; hesitation with the pen.

**붓순** 《식》 a Japanese star anise.

**붕괴**(崩壞) collapse; breaking/~하다 collapse; crumble; break down. ほうかい

**붕긋붕긋** 《솟다》in little hills 《들뜬 모양》loose here and there/~하다 rise in little hills; be loose here and there.

**붕긋하다** ①《언덕이》(be) slightly elevated ②《물건이》(be) heaved.

**붕당**(朋黨) a faction; a clique. ほうとう

**붕대**(繃帶) a bandage; dressing/~를 감다 bandage (the arm); dress. ほうたい

**붕락**(崩落) a slump/~하다 slump; fall sharply. ほうらく

**붕배**(朋輩) a companion; a mate; a comrade; a friend; a fellow. ほうばい

**뽕뽕** with a poop-poop!/~ 소리를 내다 honk; hoot/~ 경적을 울리며 달리다 run honking. ぶんぶん

**붕붕거리다** hum; buzz. ぶんぶん

**붕사**(硼砂) borax 《천연적》tincal/~뺨 plastering up with borax. ほうしゃ

**붕산**(硼酸) 《화》boracic acid. ほうさん

**붕소**(硼素) 《화》boron (기호: B).

**붕어** 《어》a crucian [carp]; a gibel; a Prussian carp. ふな

**붕어**(崩御) death; demise; passing away/~하다 (the king) die. ほうぎょ

**붕우**(朋友) a companion; a friend/~신 confidence among friend. ほうゆう

**붕장어**(一長魚) 《어》a conger; a sea-eel.

**붕정**(鵬程) a long way/~ 만리의 항해 a long voyage. ほうてい

**불다** ①《맞닿다》cling (to); stick (to); adhere (to)/젖은 옷은 몸에 붙는다 Wet clothes cling to the body. ②《불이》burn; catch fire ③《생기다》bear; form /살이 ~ take on flesh/3부 이자가 ~ bear three percent interest ④《싸움이》begin; arise; develop (into). くっつく

**불당기다** grab and pull; yank (on); jerk (along).

**불들다** ①《손으로》catch; seize; grasp; 《쥐다》take hold of ②《만류하다》detain; keep ③《체포하다》catch; capture; arrest ④《도와주다》help; assist; aid. つかむ

**불들리다** be caught; be detained; be arrested[apprehended]/붙들리지 않고 있다 remain at liberty [large]./그 친구한테 붙들리면 도망갈 수가 없다 You can not get out of his clutches. つかまれる

**불매이다** be caught; be detained; be subordinated; be tied (to); be bound up (with). れいぞくされる

**불박이** a fixture; a fixed article/~가 되어서 움직일 수 없다 It is stationary and not removable. すえつけ

**불박이다** be held in position; be fastened immovably. こていして\'る

**불어다니다** follow (a person) about; dangle about[after, round] (a person); shadow.

**-불이** things of (a class, a group); things of (the same kind); things made (of) things belonging (to).

**불이다** ⇒ 별항 참조 (page 1508).

**불임불임** in a friendly way; affably.

**불임성** amiability; affability/~있는 태도[친구] an affable manner[fellow].

**불임판** a metal vice for holding pieces of wood which are being joined.

**불잡다** 《쥐다》clasp; clench; grasp; hold; catch 《체포하다》arrest; capture; seize /꼭 붙잡고 있어라 Don't release[let go] your hold[grasp] on it. つかむ

**불잡히다** be caught ⇒ 붙들리다. つかまる

**불장**(一欌) a kitchen closet; a cupboard.

**불좇다** respect; follow [as a disciple or retainer]. ふくじゅうする

**비**[1] 《강우》rain; a rain 《일회의 강우》a rainfall 《소나기》a shower/~가 억수같이 쏟아졌다 It rained cats and dogs. /비에 젖다 get wet. あめ

**비**[2] 《쓰는》a broom 《마당비》a besom /~로 쓸다 sweep with a broom; besom.

**비**(碑) 《묘비》a tomb[grave] stone 《기념비》a monument/ ~를 세우다 erect a monument. ひ

**비**(妣) the deceased mother; one's late mother.

**비**(妃) 《왕비》a queen; an empress/태자~ acrown princess. ひ

**비**(比) 《비율》ratio; proportion 《비교》comparison 《대조》contrast 《필적》an equal; a match/~하다 compare (a thing) with (another)/나이에 ~해 젊다 be[look] young for one's age. ひ

**비-**(非) 《반》un-; anti-; non-/ ~애국적 unpatriotic. ひ-

**비가**(悲歌) an elegy; a dirge. ひか

**비각**(碑閣) a monument[tablet] house; a building erected over a monument.

**비감**(悲感) [the feeling of] sorrow; grief/~하다 grieve (at, over); [feel] sorrow; a sad feeling. ひかん

**비강**(鼻腔) 【해】 the nasal cavity[fossa, passages]. びこう

**비거**(飛去) ~하다 fly away.

**비걱거리다, 삐걱거리다** creak; squeak/의자가 ~ The chair creaks/비걱거리는[삐걱거리는] 소리 a creaking sound. きいи

**비겁**(卑怯) cowardice/~하다 (be) cowardly 《남자답지 못하다》 unmanly/~한 행동을 하다 play foul; act cowardly. ひきょう

**비게질** rudding; chafing/~하다 rub; chafe (against). こすること

**비격**(飛檄) an urgent written appeal; a manifesto admitting of no delay/~하다 give a manifesto priority. ひげき

**비견**(鄙見) one's humble opinion[view]/~을 말하다 tell[offer] one's humble opinion. ひけん

**비견**(比肩) ~하다 rank with; stand beside (a person); be comparable with[to]/투수로서 그와 ~ 할 수 있는 선수는 별로 없다 Few players can compare with him as a pitcher. ひけん

**비결**(秘訣) a secret; a key/장수의 ~은 절제다 The secret of longevity is to be moderate in everything. ひけつ

**비결정론**(非決定論) 【심】 indeterminism.

**비경**(悲境) a sad condition; distress; adversity; adverse circumstances/~에 빠지다 fall into adverse circumstances; be reduced to distress. ひきょう

**비계**[1] 《돼지의》 [hog] fat. あぶらみ

**비계**[2] a footing; a foothold; a staging 〈미〉; a scaffolding plank.

**비계**(飛陛) a footing; a foothold; a scaffold.

**비계**(秘計) a trump card; one's last resort/~를 쓰다 play one's best card. ひけい

**비고**(備考) a note; a remark; a reference /~난에 기입하다 write in[fill up] a remarks column. びこう

**비꼬다** ①《꼬다》 twist; twine ②《말을》 give a sarcastic twist (to one's words). ねじる

**비꼬이다** ①《끈이》 get twisted ②《마음이》 be perverse[contrary, obstinate]/그는 마음이 비꼬여 있다 His heart is not in the right place. ねじられる

**비곡**(悲曲) a plaintive[doleful] melody. ひきょく

**비곡**(秘曲) a most treasured piece of music; a secret music. ひきょく

**비곤**(憊困) exhaustion; fatigue/~하다 (be) exhausted; be fagged out; fatigued; be tired out. こんぱい

**비공**(鼻孔) nostrils ⇨콧구멍. びこう

**비공개**(非公開) (being) not open to the public/~ 회의 a closed meeting. ひこうかい

**비공식**(非公式) informality/~적으로 unofficially; informally. ひこうしき

**비과세**(非課稅) tax exemption/~품 a tax-free article. ひかぜい

**비과학적**(非科學的) (being) unscientific. ひかがくてき

**비관**(悲觀) pessimism/~하다 be pessimistic (about, of); take a pessimistic view (of)/그녀는 나쁜 소식에 몹시 ~했다 She was terribly cut at the bad news. ひかん

**비교**(比較) comparison; parallel/~하다 compare (a thing) with (another)/A와 ~하면 B가 낫다 Compared with A, B is better. ひかく

**비구**(飛球) 【체】 a fly [ball]. ひきゅう

**비구니**(比丘尼) a Buddhist nun; a bhiksuni. びくに

**비구름** a rain cloud 《천》 a nimbus (pl. ~es, -bi). あまぐも

**비구승**(比丘僧) a Buddhist monk; a bhiksu. びく

**비국가적**(非國家的) (being) unpatriotic. ひこっかてき

**비국민**(非國民) an unpatriotic person; a traitor. ひこくみん

**비군사적**(非軍事的) (being) nonmilitary; civilian. ひぐんじてき

**비군사화**(非軍事化) demilitarization. ひぐんしか

**비굴**(卑屈) meanness; servility/~하다 (be) mean; servile; sneaking 《사내답지 못하다》 unmanly/~한 자 an unmanly fellow; a sneak. ひくつ

**비극**(悲劇) a tragedy/~ 배우 a tragedian /~적 tragic. ひげき

**비근**(卑近) ~하다 (be) familiar; common; plain; simple/~한 예를 들다 give a familiar example. ひきん

**비근거리다** be shaky[rickety]; wobble; shake. ぐらぐらする

**비금**(飛禽) flying creatures. ひきん

**비금비금하다** be much the same. ほとんどかわらない

**비금속**(卑金屬) a base metal. ひきんぞく

**비금속**(非金屬) nonmetal/~의 nonmetallic. ひきんぞく

**비끗거리다, 삐끗거리다** ①《잘 안 되다》 come [fall] short of one's expectation; go wrong[amiss] ②《어긋나다》 do not fit in properly. できそうでできない

**비기**(秘記) a writing of divination. ひき

**비기다**[1] 《승부를》 end in a tie[draw]; come out even; tie (with)/시합에 ~ The game ended in a tie[draw]. /비기기 a tie. そうさつする

**비기다**[2] 《견주다》 compare to; liken to/인생을 여행에 ~ liken[compare] life to a journey. ひかくする

**비기다**[3] 《때우다》 patch up; put a patch (on). そうさいする

**비끼다** ①《놓이다》 lie aslant; hang at an angle ②《비치다》 shine at on angle; light obliquely. ななめにおかれる

**비김수**(一手) 《장기 따위의》 a tying move

비나리치다 flatter (a person); fawn upon (a person); curry favo[u]r with (a person). へつらう

비난(非難) criticism; reproach; blame; condemnation 《공공연한》 denunciation /~하다 criticize; reproach; blame; condemn; denounce; attack; disapprove (of)/~의 대상이 되다 be the target of criticism. ひなん

비녀 an ornamental hairpin/~를 꽂다 wear an ornamental hairpin. かんざし

비녀(婢女) a woman slave. げじょ

비녀장 a linchpin

비논리적(非論理的) (being) illogical; irrational. ひろんりてき

비뇨(泌尿) 〖의〗 urination/~기 the urinary organs/~기과 urology; urinology. ひにょう

비누 soap/비눗물 soap-suds; lather/~로 손을 씻다 wash one's hands with soap and water. せっけん

비늘 scales/~을 벗기다 scale (a fish). うろこ

비능률(非能率) inefficency/~적 inefficient. ひのうりつ

비다 be empty[vacant]; 《손이》 be free 《속이》 be hollow/빈 방[집] an empty room[house]/좌석이 ~ become less crowded. あいている

삐다¹ 《물이》 subside; drain (away, off); go down. こうずいがひく

삐다² 《뼈를》 break; sprain; dislocate/발목을 ~ sprain one's ankle. ひねる

비다듬다 preen oneself; arrange; smooth (down, out). なめらかにする

비딱, 삐딱 ~하다 (be) rickety[shaky]. けいしゃしている

비딱거리다, 삐딱거리다 be shaky[rickety]; wobble. よろめく

비단(但) not only; not merely; as well as/~ 그뿐 아니라 not only that. ただ―でなく

비단(緋緞) silk fabrics; silks/~이불 silk bedding. きぬおりもの

비단결(緋緞―) the texture of silk; a velvety texture/~ 같다 be soft as velvet.

비단벌레 〖충〗 a buprestid [beetle].

비당파적(非黨派的) (being) nonpartisan; nonparty. ひとうはてき

비대(肥大) portliness; corpulence 〖의〗 hypertrophy/~하다 (be) fat; portly; corpulent. ひだい

비대다 assume another's name /남의 이름을 ~ assume a false name; give a wrong name. なすりつける

삐대다 put (a person) to trouble; bother; annoy; embarrass. くっついてなやむ

비대발괄 entreaty; solicitation/~하다 beg; entreat; appeal (to); beseech. あいがんすること

비도(匪徒) bandits; outlaws; insurgents; rebels. ひと

비도(悲悼) sorrowful mourning condolence; grief; lamentation/~하다 grieve (at); regret. ひとう

---

## 붙 이 다

①《부탁·첨부하다》attach; fix; put on; put up; paste; apply /우표를 ~ put a stamp; on (a letter) /광고를 ~ post a bill/꼬리표를 ~ attach a tag (to a parcel)/포스터를 ~ put up a poster /고약을 ~ apply a plaster.

②《이름을》name; give a name; christen/별명을 ~ give a nickname (to a person)/그 책에 신한 사전이라는 이름을 붙였다 The book was christened the Sinhan Dictionary.

③《불을》 light; kindle; ignite; apply /담배에 불을 ~ light a cigarette.

④《중개하다》arrange; bring two parties together for (an enterprise, a negotiation) /흥정을 ~ arrange a bargain; get two parties to strike a bargain/싸움을 ~ make (persons) quarrel; set (dogs) to fighting/노름을 ~ arrange gambling.

⑤《사람을》have (a person) in attendance/환자에게 간호원을 ~ have a nurse in attendance upon a patient; have a patient attended by a nurse/피고에게 변호사를 붙여 주다 provide the defendant with a lawyer.

⑥《의견을》give one's opinion; make an additional comment/조건을 ~ attach a condition.

⑦《기식하다》 live on; sponge on; hang on; rely on (someone) for (one's care); put oneself under a person's care/몸 붙일 곳이 없다 have nobody to turn to [for help]; have no place to go.

⑧《때리다》 slap/뺨을 ~ slap (a person); box a person's ears.

⑨《교미시키다》 mate; copulate; pair/개를 ~ mate a dog.

⑩《노름 돈을》 bet; stake; wager/100 원을 ~ bet hundred won.

⑪《가입하다》 let (a person) in[into]; take (a person) in; admit (a person) into/붙여 주지 않다 keep (a person) out of (a group)/저 사람을 붙이지 말자 Let's not let him in.

**비도(非道)** 《무도》 injustice 《횡포》 tyranny 《잔인》 cruelty 《비인도》 inhumanity／~한 cruel; inhuman; unjust. ひどう

**비도덕적(非道德的)** (being) unmoral; immoral. ひどうとくてき

**비동맹(非同盟)** nonalignment／~ 회의 Conference of Non-allied Countries／~주의 nonalignment. ひどうめい

**비뚜로, 삐뚜로** diagonally; obliquely; aslant. かたむいて

**비뚜름하다, 삐뚜름하다** (be) inclined 《주부정하다》 slant; crooked. かたむいて

**비뚝거리다, 삐뚝거리다** ①《흔들거리다》 totter; be shaky; reel; shake ②《걸음을》 waddle; shamble; reel along 《다리가 짧아》 walk lame. びっこをひく

**비뚝비뚝, 삐뚝삐뚝** in a tottering manner; unsteadily; with faltering[tottering] steps. びっこをひく

**비둔(肥鈍)** ~하다 (be) corpulent; fleshy fat 《동작이》 clumsy; slow-moving 《껴입어서》 heavily clothed. こえてにぶいこと

**비툴거리다, 삐툴거리다** ①《흔들거리다》 stagger; totter; reel 《마차가》 jolt／비틀거리는 마차 a ramshackle[rickety] carriage／무거운 짐으로 ~ stagger with a heavy load ②《구부러지다》 wind; curve; meander. よろめく

**비둘기** a dove 《기르는》 a pigeon／전서(傳書) ~ a carrier pigeon. はと

**비둘다, 삐둘다** (be) crooked; wrong; slanting; be at the wrong angle／코가 ~ have a crooked nose／그림이 비둘어졌다 The picture is crooked. かたむいている

**비둘비둘, 삐둘삐둘** 《흔들흔들》 staggeringly; totteringly 《꼬불꼬불》 meanderingly; crookedly／~한 길 a winding road／걷다 reel along; walk zigzag. よろよろ

**비둘어지다, 삐둘어지다** ①《기울다》 incline; lean (to); tilt／비둘어진 나무 a crooked tree ②《쏠리다》 be bent; bend; curve; swerve; be crooked ③《마음이》 become perverse; get cranky. かたむく

**비둘이, 삐둘이** a person with a twisted body[limb]；《비탈진 땅》 the skirt of slope. ひねくれたもの

**비드득, 삐드득** grinding; creaking. きいきい

**비듬** dandruff; scurf／~약 a hair lotion [tonic]／~이 끼다 Dandruff accumulates. ふけ

**비등(比等)** ~하다 be a match (for); be equal (to); be about the same／이것과 그 것은 크기에 있어 ~하다 That is equal to this in size. ひとしき

**비등(沸騰)** boiling; seething 《거품이 남》 effervescence 《흥분》 agitation; excitement／~점 the boiling point／~하다 boil; seethe 《의논이》 be agitated; [excited]／여론이 ~하다 Public opinion is agitated[aroused]. ふっとう

**삐라** a [hand] bill; a leaflet; a placard [poster]／~를 뿌리다 distribute leaflets／~를 붙이다 put up[stick] a bill; post a placard.

**비래(飛來)** ~하다 come flying; come by air. ひらい

**비량(鼻梁)** the ridge[bridge] of the nose.

**비럭질** begging; pauperism; mendicancy／~하다 go begging; beg one's bread.

**비렁뱅이** a beggar ☞거지. こじき

**비련(悲戀)** tragic love; disappointed love. ひれん

**비례(比例)** proportion 《비율》 ratio 《비교》 comparison／~하다 be in proportion (to); 《비하다》 be in proportionate (to)／~ 대표제 proportional representation／~수 a proportional number／~식 a proportion／반~ inverse proportion／~정 direct proportion. ひれい

**비례(非禮)** discourtesy; impoliteness; rudeness; incivility. ひれい

**비로소** for the first time; first／죽은 후에야 ~ 그의 존재 가치를 깨달았다 It was not until his death that I realized how much he meant to me.／밤이 늦어서야 ~ 그가 왔다 He did not come until late in the evening. はじめて

**비록** if; even if; though／~ 나이는 어리지만 though he is young. たとえ

**비록(秘錄)** a secret memoir; a confidential document.

**비롯하다** begin; commence; open; start; make a start; originate; initiate／…을 비롯하여 including; headed by; as well as. はじまる

**비료(肥料)** manure; fertilizer／인조 ~ artificial fertilizer／~를 주다 manure; fertilize. ひりょう

**비루** 《의》 mange／~먹다 suffer form mange; be infected with mange. かいせん

**비루(鄙陋)** meanness; baseness／~하다 (be) vulgar; mean; base／~한 근성 a base[mean] spirit. ひろう

**비류(比類)** a parallel; a peer; an equal; a match／~가 없다 be unparalleled[peerless, matchless, unique]／역사상 그 ~가 없다 It is without parallel in history., It is unique in history. ひるい

**비륜(比倫)** a peer; a match; an equal／~하다 (be) equal (to); parallel (with).

**비름** 《식》 *Amantus Blitum*《학명》. ひゆ

**비리(非理)** irrationality; unreasonableness; absurdity. ひり

**비리다** 《생선이》 be fishy; smell of raw fish 《피가》 be bloody／비린내 a fish-like[fishy] smell.

**비리비리** thin[skinny] and dry／~하다 (be) thin[skinny] and dry. がりより

**비린(鄙吝)** stinginess; parsimony; miserliness／~하다 (be) stingyniggardly; miserly; near／~한 사람 a miser; an old screw; a skinflint. ひりん

**비린(比隣)** a neighbor; neighborhood; vicinity／~ 제국 neighboring countries. ちかいとなり

**비린내** a fishy[bloody] smell／~나다 smell fishy.

**비릿비릿** disgustingly; sickeningly/~하다 (be) sickening; disgusting. けちけち

**비릿하다** be slightly fishy; smell somewhat fishy.

**비마자**(萆麻子) a castor bean/~유 castor oil. ひまし

**비만**(肥滿) fatness; portliness; corpulence/~하다 (be) fat; plump; fleshy; corpulent/~해지다 become fat[portly, plump, fleshy]. ひまん

**비말**(飛沫) a splash; a spray/~을 일으키다 splash (in the river). ひまつ

**비망록**(備忘錄) a memorandum (pl. -da); a note; a memo; a reminder; a commonplace-book; a scribbling diary; a pocket-book〈영〉. びぼうろく

**비매 동맹**(非買同盟) a boycott; boycotting/~을 맺다 stage a boycott; boycott [taboo] goods. ひばいどうめい

**비매품**(非賣品) an article not for sale 《게시》 "Not for Sale." ひばいひん

**비명**(悲鳴) a scream; a shriek/~을 올리다 cry; scream; shriek (for help). ひめい

**비명**(非命) an accidental[unnatural, untimely] death/~에 죽다 meet (with) a violent death; die an unnatural death; die with boots on. ひめい

**비명**(碑銘) an epitaph; an inscription on a monument. ひめい

**비명**(秘命) a secret order.

**비모**(鼻毛) the hairs of the nostril; vibrissa.

**비목**(費目) an item of expenditure.

**비목어**(比目魚) a flatfish ⇒넙치. ひもくぎょ

**비몽사몽**(非夢似夢) a dreamy state; trance/~간에 between asleep and awake; between sleeping and waking; dreamily. ゆめうつつ

**비무장**(非武裝) demilitarization/~ 지대 a demilitarized zone/~ 도시 an open city. ひぶそう

**비문**(碑文) an epitaph; an inscription [on a monument]. ひぶん

**비문명**(非文明) ~의 uncivilized; barbarous/~국 an uncivilized nation. ひぶんめい

**비문화적**(非文化的) (being) uncivilized[uncultured, unenlightened, preliterate). ひぶんかてき

**비밀**(秘密) 《내밀》secrecy; privacy 《신비》mystery 《밀사》a secret; a mystery/~하다 (be) secret; confidential/공공연한 ~ an open secret/~히 secretly; in secret; privately/~을 밝히다 reveal [divulge, disclose] a secret/~을 지키다 observe secrecy; keep a secret/~ 결사 a secret society/~ 결혼 a clandestine marriage/~ 서류 a confidential document/~ 회의 a secret[closed] meeting. ひみつ

**비바람** rain and wind; a rainstorm/~을 무릅쓰다 brave a rainstorm; go in the teeth of a rainstorm. あめかぜ

**비방**(誹謗) slander; abuse; calumny; defamation/~하다 abuse; slander; libel; cast aspersion on (a person)/~하는 자 a slanderer; a vilifier. ひぼう

**비방**(秘方) a secret method[recipe]; 《약의》 a secret formula. ひほう

**비번**(非番) off duty/오늘은 ~이다 This is an off day for me. ひばん

**비범**(非凡) ~하다 (be) remarkable; uncommon; unique/~한 사람 a remarkable man; a man of unusual ability/~한 재주 an unusual gift[talent]. ひぼん

**비법**(非法) illegality; unlawfuness ⇒불법(不法). ひほう

**비법**(秘法) a secret recipe; a secret method[process]; the secret. ひほう

**비보**(悲報) a sed[heavy] news. ひほう

**비보**(秘寶) treasure[s]; a treasured article. ひほう

**비보**(飛報) an express message; a dispatch; a despatch. ひほう

**비복**(婢僕) female and male servants. ひぼく

**비분**(非分) (being) unbecoming to one's status; beyond one's means.

**비분**(悲憤) resentment; indignation/~의 눈물 tears of indignation/~ 강개하다 be full of righteous[moral] indignation[wrath]; deplore [evils]. ひふん

**삐삐**¹ gaunt; haggard/~ 마른 사람 a living skeleton; a mere shadow/~ 마르다 be gauntlooking; be haggard; be worn to a shadow. がりがり

**삐삐**² screeching; bawling/~ 울다 squall. びいびい

**비비**(狒狒) 《동》 a baboon.

**비비**(霏霏) ~하다 be falling thick and fast. しとしと

**비비꼬다** twist over and over again; knot together tight. なう

**비비꼬이다** be twisted many times. よる

**비비다** ①《문지르다》 rub (against)/손을 ~ chafe one's hands ②《둥글게》 round; make round; make into a ball ③《뒤섞다》 mix (up) ④《송곳을》 drive a gimlet (into). こする

**비비대기치다** jostle; shove and push; throng.

**비비대다** rub repeatedly. しきりにこする

**비비송곳** a drill. きり

**비비적거리다** rub on. しきりにこする

**비비적비비적** rubbing and rubbing. しきりにこする

**비비틀다** twist[wrench, turn] again and again. よる

**비비틀리다** get[be] twisted tight[hard]. よくねじられる

**비빈**(妃嬪) the queen and the royal concubine. ひひん

**비빔 국수** a noodle hash.

**비빔밥** a rice hash; rice food mixed with seasonings. ごもくめし

**비사**(秘事) a secret; private affairs. ひじ
**비사**(秘史) a secret history. ひし
**비사교적**(非社交的) (being) unsociable; uncompanionable. ひしゃこうてき
**비싸다** (be) dear; expensive; costly; high/터무니없이 비싼 가격 a ridiculously high price; an exorbitant price/기껏 비싸야 at most/비싸게 받다 charge too much. こうかだ
**비사리** the bark of a bush-clover. はぎのかわ
**비사치다** inform gently (in *an indirect way*). ほのめかす
**비사회적**(非社會的) (being) anti-social. ひしゃかいてき
**비산**(飛散) ～하다 fly away; scatter; disperse/사방으로 ～하다 fly in all directions. ひさん
**비산**(砒酸) 〖화〗 arsenic acid. ひさん
**비상**(非常) ①(사변) emergency; contingency/～하다 (be) emergent; urgent/～ 소집 an emergency call ②(극단) extraordinariness; extremity/～하다 (be) extraordinary; extreme/～한 관심을 집중하고 있다 be a matter of great concern. ひじょう
**비상**(砒霜) arsenic. ひそ
**비상**(悲傷) bitter grief; deep sorrow; pathos. ひしょう
**비상**(飛翔) flight; flying/～하다 fly; take a flight; soar. ひしょう
**비상 간고**(備嘗艱苦) going through every hardship/～하다 endure every hardship; taste every bitters of life.
もろもろのかんくをたいけんすること
**비상구**(非常口) an emergency exit. ひじょうぐち
**비상 사태**(非常事態) a state of emergency/～를 선언하다 declare[proclaim] a [state] of emergency/～에 있다 be under a state of emergency/～에 대비하다 provide against emergencies; be ready for emergencies. ひじょうじたい
**비상선**(非常線) a [police] cordon; a patrol line/화재의 a fire line/～을 치다 post a cordon ひじょうせん
**비상시**(非常時) an emergency; a crisis/국가의 ～ a national emergency/～에는 in case of emergency; in an emergency. ひじょうじ
**비상식**(非常識) senselessness; lack of [common] sense/～적 senseless; eccentric; thoughtless. ひじょうしき
**비쌔다** 《안 그런 체하다》 decline reluctantly[begrudgingly]; pretend to decline [an offer]; 《어울리기를 싫어하다》 avoid company; keep[hold] aloof.
ことわるふりをする
**비색증**(鼻塞症) 〖의〗 occlusion of the naris (*pl.* -es). はながつまるびょうき
**비생산**(非生産) unproductivity; nonproductiveness/～적 unproductive; nonproductive/～적인 사업 a nonproductive enterprise. ひせいさん

**비서**(秘書) ①(비장한 책) a treasured book ②(비서역) a private secretary/～실 a secretariat [office]/장관 ～ a secretary to the Minister (*of*). ひしょ
**비석**(砒石) →[광] arsenic. ひせき
**비석**(碑石) a stone monument; a monumental stone. ひせき
**비성**(鼻聲) (음성) a nasal [sound].
はなごえ
**비소**(砒素) 〖화〗 arsenic (기호: As.).
**비소**(鼻笑) sneering ⇒코웃음. ちょうしょう
**비소**(誹笑) a derisive[sardonic] smile; a scornful laugh/～하다 laugh scornfully; smile derisively. そしりわらい
**비속**(卑俗) vulgarity; vulgarism/～하다 (be) vulgar; coarse; low. ひぞく
**비송 사건**(非訟事件) a noncontentious case; a nonlitigation case.
**비수**(匕首) a dirk; a dagger; a dart; a knife/～로 찌르다 stab (*a person*) with a dagger. ひしゅ
**비수**(悲愁) a pathos; a grief. ひしゅう
**비술**(秘術) a secret art; stratagem/～을 전수하다 initiate (*one*) into the mysteries ひじゅつ
**비스듬하다** (be) slightly tilted; be a bit askew/모자를 비스듬히 쓰다 wear a hat tilted to one side. ななめだ
**비스러지다** get out of shape; be illshaped [unshapely]. ねじける
**비스름하다** (be) somewhat like[alike].
**비쓱거리다** stagger; reel; totter; walk with faltering steps/비쓱비쓱 staggeringly; totteringly. ひょろひょろする
**비슬하다** ①(일을) neglect; slight; be neglectful of ②(베돌다) keep away from…; do not mix with. おろそかにする
**비슬비슬** reeling; tottering. ひょろひょろ
**비슷비슷하다** (be) all alike; all similar; of a sort/모두 ～ They are of a sort/생김새가 ～ the two look like. にている
**비슷이** 《같게》 alike; similar; likely 《비스듬히》 leaning a bit to one side.
**비슷하다**¹ be alike; (be) similar; like; resemble/비슷한 사건 a similar case; a case similar to (*a thing*)/비슷이 닮다 bear some resemblance to (*a person*)/성격이 ～ They are much alike in character. にている
**비슷하다**² (기욺) have a slight tilt to one side; be a bit askew[slanted]/비슷이 기울어진 벽 a wall with a slight lean. ななめだ
**비신** rain shoes.
**비신사적**(非紳士的) (being) ungentlemanly; ungentlemanlike. ひしんしてき
**비실제적**(非實際的) (being) unpractical; unrealistic. ひじっさいてき
**비아냥거리다** make cynical remarks; be sarcastic (*about*). いやらしくひにくをいう
**비악, 삐악** ❶～ 울다 peep; cheep; pule.
びよびよ
**비애**(悲哀) sorrow; grief; sadness; pathos; misery/인생의 ～ the sorrows of

life; the pathos of life/~를 느끼다 feel sad. ひあい

**비애국적**(非愛國的) (being) unpatriotic. ひあいこくてき

**비약**(飛躍) a flying jump; a leap《발전》rapid progress《활동》activity/~하다 leap; jump《발전하다》make rapid progress《활동하다》be active; play an active part/논리의 ~ a leap in argument; a jump of logic. ひやく

**비약**(秘藥) a secret remedy[medicine]; a nostrum. ひやく

**비약**(秘鑰) the secret; the key; the cardinal principle; the links. ひやく

**비양**(飛揚) flying; a flight《뽐냄》swaggering/~하다 swagger; throw *one's* weight around; fly [in the air]. ひよう

**비어**(飛語, 蜚語) a slanderous report; a wild rumour/~를 퍼뜨리다 spread a false report[rumour]. ひご

**비어**(鄙語, 卑語) a slang; a vulgarism. ひご

**비어지다**《밖으로 내밀다》jut out; protrude; project; stick out《드러나다》come to light; be exposed[disclosed, revealed]. つきでる

**비언**(鄙諺) a vulgar proverb[saying].

**비역** sodomy; unnatural vice; pederasty; buggery/~하다 practise sodomy; go after strange flesh. けいかん

**비열**(卑劣) meanness; baseness/~하다 (be) mean; base; cowardly/~한 수단 a mean[dirty] trick/~한 정신 a low spirit/~한(漢) a sneak; a hound; a cad. ひれつ

**비열**(比熱)『물』specific heat.

**비영리**(非營利) monprofit-making/~ 사업 a nonprofit[-making] undertaking. ひえいり

**비영비영하다** (be) weak; feeble; emaciated. ひょろひょろしている

**비예**(睥睨) a glare; a sharp look/~하다 glare at; look contemptuously at/천하를 ~하다 have the world at *one's* feet; reign over the world as a conqueror. へいげい

**비예술적**(非藝術的) (being) inartistic.

**비오리**『조』a goosander. がちょう

**비옥**(肥沃) fertility; richness (of *the soil*)/~하다 (be) fertile; rich; productive/~안 땅 fertile[rich] soil ひよく

**비옥**(翡玉) green jade with red spots.

**비옷** a raincoat/~을 입다 wear a raincoat. あまぎ

**비용**(費用) expense[s]; expenditure; cost; outlay/~을 절약하다 cut down[retrench, save] expense/여행 ~ traveling expenses. ひよう

**비우다** empty (*a box*); clear (*a room*);《명도》vacate; quit (*a house*); absent *one*self from《비워 두다》stay away from (*home*)/가게를 비우지 말라 Don't stay away from the shop. あける

**비우호적**(非友好的) unfriendly (*act*).

**비운**(非運) misfortune; ill luck/~에 빠지다 bad days fall on me. ひうん

**비웃**〘어〙a herring/~ 백숙 boiled herring soysauce. にしん

**비웃다** laugh with scorn (*at*); laugh derisively (*at*); deride; scoff (*at*); jeer (*at*); mock/비웃음을 사다 a jeer; a laugh/비웃음을 사다 be mocked[derided]; excite ridicule. あざけりわらう

**비웃적거리다** ridicule again and again; make cynical remarks 、빈정거리다. しきりにあざけりわらう

**비위**(脾胃) ①《비장과 위》spleen and stomach ②《기분》humour ③《기호·미각》taste; palate; choice/~에 맞는 음식 a favorate food/~에 맞다 be to *one's* taste; suit to *one's* taste[palate] ④《뻔뻔스러움》impudence; audacity; cheekiness/~가 좋다 have a nerve to (*do*); be brazen-faced. ひぞうとい

**비위생**(非衛生) carelessness about *one's* health; insanitation/~적 unhealthy; unwholesome; unsanitary. ひえいせい

**비유**(比喩, 譬喩)《은유》a metaphor《직유》a simile《우화》a fable[parable];《이언》a proverb《예》an example[illustration]/~하다 liken (*to*); compare (*to*); speak figuratively/~적 figurative. ひゆ

**비육지탄**(髀肉之嘆) 日~이 있다 be eager for the fray; be all eagerness to do something; get sick of staying behind the scenes. ひにくのたん

**비율**(比率) proportion; rate; ratio/남녀의 ~ the proportion of males to females. ひりつ

**비음** gala dress 、빔.

**비음**(鼻音) a nasal sound. びおん

**비익**(裨益) benefit; profit; good/~하다 benefit; profit (*one*); do (*a person*) good/…에 의하여 ~ derive benefit from; profit by/인류에 ~하다 benefit mankind. ひえき

**비익**(比翼) wing's abreast/~조(鳥) an imaginary pair of male and female birds each with one eye and one wing and always flying together. ひよく

**비인**(非人) an inhuman wretch; a beast; a brute. ひとらしくないこと

**비인도**(非人道) inhumanity/~적 inhumane. ひじんどう

**비인정**(非人情) heartlessness《인정 초월》detachment. ひにんじょう

**비일 비재**(非一非再) frequent occurrence; taking place time and again[many times]/그런 일은 ~하다 It is just one of those common things.

**비자**(榧子)〘식〙a torreya nut/~나무 Torreya nucifera(학명). かや

**비장**(脾臟)〘해〙the spleen/~병(病) splenetic [disease]. ひぞう

**비장**(秘藏) treasuring; storing in secrecy/~하다 treasure; prize; cherish; store

**비장** in secrecy/~물 a treasure; a treasured article. ひぞう

**비장(悲壯)** ~하다 (be) tragic; pathetic; grim 《슬프다》plaintive/~한 결의 a grim[heroic] resolution/~한 죽음을 하다 die a tragic death. ひそう

**비재(非才)** lack of ability; want of talent; incapacity; incompetence. ひさい

**비적(匪賊)** a bandit; a rebel; an insurgent. ひぞく

**비적비적** protruding[coming out] here and there. ずるずる

**비전(秘傳)** a secret; a recipe; the mysteries (pl. ·na). ひでん

**비전(費錢)** waste of money/~하다 waste money. おかねをろうひすること

**비전(非戰)** renunciation of war; outlawry of war; anti-war/~론 pacifism/~론자 a pacifist; a peace advocate/~론을 부르짖다 advocate peace.

**비전(飛電)** 《전보》a telegram 《번개》a flash of lightning. はやいいなびかり

**비전략 물자(非戰略物資)** non-strategic goods.

**비전투원(非戰鬪員)** a noncombatant; a civilian. ひせんとういん

**비전하(妃殿下)** 《3인칭》Her Imperial Highness《略：H.I.H.,H.R.H.》; 《2인칭》Your Imperial Highness.

**비접** a change of air; a change of scene/~나가다 take a change of air and scene. てんちりょうよう

**비정(秕政)** maladministration; misgovernment; misrule. ひせい

**비정(非情)** ~의 cold-[hard-, stone-]hearted; heartless; cruel; hard; false. ひじょう

**비정당적(非政黨的)** (being) non-party[-partisan]. ひせいとうてき

**비제(鄙第)** my humble house.

**비조(飛鳥)** a flying bird; a bird on the wing. とぶとり

**비조(鼻祖)** the founder; the father 元祖(始祖). びそ

**비조(悲調)** a plaintive tone; a mournful [pathetic] tone/~를 띤 plaintive; sad; pathetic. ひちょう

**비족(鄙族)** my [humble] relatives.

**비좁다** (be) narrow small 《사람이 주어》be cramped[confined] for room/비좁은 마을 a small hole of a town. ひじょうにせまい

**비종교적(非宗敎的)** (being) nonreligious. ひしゅうきょうてき

**비쭈기나무** 《식》Sakakia ochnacea 《학명》.

**비주룩하다** (be) jutting out; protruding. ちょっとつきでている

**비쭉** poutingly/입술을 ~ 내밀다 pout [one's lip]; stick out one's lip/창문 밖으로 머리를 ~ 내밀다 pop one's head out of the window.

**비죽거리다, 비쭉거리다** pout [one's lips]; make up a lip. くちをとがらす

**비준(批准)** ratification/~하다 ratify (a treaty)/~ 교환 exchange of ratifications. ひじゅん

**비준(比準)** 《비율》proportion 《표준》a standard/《대조》comparison 《대조》contrast/~하다 compare; contrast. ひじゅん

**비중(比重)** 『물』specific gravity/~계(計) a hydrostatic balance. ひじゅう

**비지** bean-curd dregs. おから

**비지(鄙地)** my humble place of residence.

**비지땀** profuse perspiration; copious sweating/~을 흘리다 perspire profusely; have heavy sweating. あせしずく

**비질** sweeping with a broom/~하다 sweep with a broom.

**비집다** ①《틈을》force apart ②《눈을》rub and open one's eyes. むりにあける

**비참(悲慘)** misery; distress; wretchedness/~하다 (be) miserable wretched; sad; tragic; pitiable/~한 광경 a pitiable scene; a pathetic sight/~한 생활 a wretched[miserable] life/~한 죽음을 하다 die a miserable death. ひさん

**비창(悲愴)** a pathos; a grief; sadness; a sorrow/~하다 (be) pathetic; sorrowful. ひそう

**비척거리다** totter; stagger; reel. よろめく

**비척걸음** tottering; waddling; a staggering walk. よろよろあるき

**비척비척** totteringly; unsteadily/~ 걷다 totter; waddle; walk with an unsteady gait. よろよろ

**비척지근하다** (be) slightly fishy; smell somewhat of raw fish.

**비천(卑賤)** humbleness; lowliness; humble circumstances; obscurity/~하다 (be) lowly humble; obscure/~한 태생 a man of low birth/~한 신분에서 출세하다 rise from obscurity. ひせん

**비철(非—)** off season; out of season.

**비철금속(非鐵金屬)** nonferrous metals.

**비첩(婢妾)** a concubine of low birth. ひしょう

**비추(悲秋)** lonely autumn; grieving over the autumn/~하다 feel sorrow at autumn.

**비추다** ①《빛을》shine on; shed light on; light [up]; illuminate/달빛이 교교하게 사번을 비치고 있었다 The moon was shedding her silvery rays all around. ②《그림자를》reflect/호수는 산 그림자를 비추고 있었다 The lake reflected the mountain. ③《비교·참조하다》compare (with); refer (to); check up on (a matter)/법에 비추어 according to the law/사실에 비추어 in view[the light] of facts ④《속이 드러나게》hold (a thing) up to [against] the light/편지를 불빛에 비추어 보다 hold a letter closely to the light. てらす

**비축(備蓄)** saving for emergency/~하다 save for emergency.

**비취(翡翠)** 《동》a kingfisher 《보석》green jadeite; jade/~색 jade green/~옥 green jadeite; jade/~잠 an ornamental

**jade hairpin.**

**비치(備置)** placement; equipment; provision/~하다 place; equip[furnish] with; provide with/이 방에는 무전이 ~ 되어 있다 This room is equipped with a wireless apparatus. そなえておくこと

**비치다** ①《빛이》shine/햇빛이 찬란하게 ~ The sun shines brightly. ②《그림자가》 be reflected[mirrored]; fall upon/창문에 비친 사람의 그림자 the shadows of men falling on the window ③《드러내다》 show [through]; be seen [through] /인쇄가 뒷면에 비치다 The printing shows through on the other side. ④《암시》 hint (at); drive (at); feel[sound] (a person) out on (a thing)/사의를 ~ hint at resignation. うつる

**삐치다** be languid; be dull; be weary. はねる

**비칭(卑稱)** a humble title. ひしょう

**비켜나다** fall back; draw back; move aside; step aside; get out of the way. /비켜나서 마차를 보내다 step back to let the cart pass. わきへよる

**비켜서다** step[tand] back; move aside; get out of the way /한두 발 ~ fall[draw] back a step or two. わきによる

**비키다** leave; get away; get out of the way; move aside; remove; clear/길을 ~ clear the road; get out of the way/자동차를 ~ dodge a car; get out of the way of a car. わきによる

**비탄(悲嘆)** grief; sorrow; anguish; lamentation/~하다 grieve; mourn; sorrow (over, on); lament/~에 잠기다 abandon oneself to grief; be heart-broken (at). ひたん

**비탄(飛彈)** flying bullets. ひだん

**비탈** a slop; an incline; a hill/~지다 slop; be sloped/~진 a slope; an uphill [ascending] road. さか

**비통(悲痛)** grief; bitterness; sorrow/ ~하다 (be) grievous; bitter; sorrowful; sad/~한 생각에 잠기다 be filled with deep sadness. ひつう

**비통제(非統制)** ~의 uncontrolled; unregulated. ひとうせい

**삐트적거리다** stagger; totter reel. よろめく

**비틀거리다** stagger; totter; falter; reel/ 비틀거리며 걷다 walk with faltering steps; totter along. ひょろひょうする

**비틀걸음** faltering steps; reeling[unsteady] steps/~으로 걷다 reel along; walk zigzag. ひょろひょろあるき

**비틀다** twist; twirl; wrench; turn 《나사를》 screw /팔을 ~ wrench[twist] one's arm/목을 비틀어 죽이다 wring the neck (of a chicken). よる

**비틀리다** be wrenched; be twisted. よれる

**비틀비틀** with faltering steps; totteringly; staggeringly/~ 일어서다 stagger to one's feet/술에 취해 ~하다 reel under the influence of liquor. ひょろひょろする

**비틀어지다** get twisted; get bent; be distorted/열쇠가 ~ the key gets bent. よられる

**비틈히** [say] in a round about way; vaguely; by hinting; indirectly.

**비파(琵琶)** a lute; a Korean mandoline /~장이 a lute-player; a lutist/~를 타다 play [on] the lute. びわ

**비파(枇杷)** 《식》a Japanese medlar; a loquat. びわ

**비판(批判)** critique; criticism; comment /~하다 criticize; comment (on); pass judg[e]ment upon/~ 철한 critical philosophy. ひはん

**비평(批評)** criticism; comment 《문예 작품의》 critique 《신간 서적의》 review/~ 하다 criticize; comment (on); review (a book)/~가 a reviewer; a critic/~할 가치가 없다 It is beneath criticism/문예 ~ a literary criticism. ひひょう

**비품(備品)** fixtures 《집·방안의》 furnishings 《집합적》 equipment. びひん

**비하(卑下)** 《자신을 낮춤》 abasement; self-humbling 《땅이 낮은》 low level of ground 《지위가 낮은》 low standing[position]; humbleness. ひか

**비하다(比一)** compare; contrast. くらべる

**비학술적(非學術的)** unscientific; unacademic. ひがくじゅつてき

**비합리(非合理)** 《철》 irrational[ity]; illogical/~ 주의 irrationalism. ひごうり

**비합법적(非合法的)** illegal; unlawful. ひごうほうてき

**비행(非行)** a misdeed; a misdemeanour; a misconduct; an evil deed/타인의 ~을 폭로하다 expose[reveal] other's misdeeds. ひこう

**비행(飛行)** flying; a flight 《비행술》 aviation/~하다 fly; make a flight/~가 [사] an aviator; an airman; an airplane pilot/~ 시간 flying hours/단독 ~ a solo flight/무착륙 ~ a nonstop flight /세계 일주 ~ a round-the-world flight /시험 ~ a test flight. ひこう

**비행기(飛行機)** an aeroplane〈영〉; an airplane〈미〉; 《총칭》 a plane; aircraft/~ 에 타다 get aboard[board] a plane/무인 ~ a pilotless plane/수상 ~ a seaplane[hydroplane]/여객 ~ a passenger plane/연습~ a training plane/정기 ~ an air liner; a clipper / ~를 조종하다 pilot a plane. ひこうき

**비행선(飛行船)** an airship; a dirigible/ 경식[연식, 반경식] ~ a rigid[nonrigid, semi-rigid] dirigible. ひこうせん

**비행장(飛行場)** an airfield[airport, airstrip]; an airdrome〈미〉. ひこうじょう

**비현실적(非現實的)** not real; unreal/~ 인 계획 an unfeasible[impracticable] plan/~인 생각 a rather fantastic idea /가장 ~이다 be far from the reality [actuality]. ひげんじつてき

**비호(飛虎)** an agile tiger/~ 같이 as quick as lightning/ ~ 같다 be as fast as a

**비호**(庇護) protection; patronage/~하다 protect; shelter; take (a person) under one's wing 《범인을》 harbor /~하에 under the patronage (of); under the protection (of)/~자 a protector; a patron. ひご

**비화**(飛火) a leap of the fire; leaping flames/~하다 flame; leap to (another house)/강 건너로 ~한다 The fire leaps across a river. とぶひばな

**비화**(悲話) a sad[pathetic] story. ひわ

**비화**(秘話) a secret story; a secret history; a behind-the-scences story (of). ひわ

**비화수소**(砒化水素) 〖화〗 arseniuretted hydrogen.

**비훼**(誹毀) slander; defamation of character 《신문지상의》 libel/~하다 slander; defame/~죄 slander; libel.

**비희**(悲喜) joy and sorrow/~의 감이 교착하다 have a mingled feeling of joy and sorrow; joy and grief alternate in one's heart. ひき

**비희극**(悲喜劇) a tragicomedy. ひきげき

**빽** 《배게 들어선 모양》 thickly; densely 《소리》 with a whistle; whistling.

**빽빽하다** (be) close ⇨빽빽하다. こんもりしげっている

**빅수**(一手) a move to end (a game) in a draw/~를 보다 make a move to end in a tie[draw]. ひきわけのて

**빈가**(貧家) a poor family/~에 태어나다 be born poor. ひんか

**빈개념**(賓概念) 〖논〗 an objective concept.

**빈객**(賓客) a visitor; a guest. ひんきゃく

**빈고**(貧苦) hardship of poverty[destitution]; pressure of poverty. ひんく

**빈곤**(貧困) poverty; indigence 《궁핍》 need[want]/~하다 (be) poor; needy; destitute/~한 사람의 the poor; the needy/~에 빠지다 be reduced to extreme poverty/이 나라 청년 남녀의 사상은 한심하도록 ~하다 The young men and women of this country are sadly barren of ideas. ひんこん

**빈광**(貧鑛) lean[poor, low-grade] ore.

**빈국**(貧國) a poor[destitute, needy] country. ひんこく

**빈궁**(貧窮) destitution; extreme poverty/~하다 (be) destitute; poverty-stricken. ひんきゅう

**빈궁**(嬪宮) the wife of heir apparent.

**빈농**(貧農) a poor farmer; a needy peasant. ひんのう

**빈대** 〖충〗 a bed-[house-] bug. なんきんむし

**빈대떡** a green-bean cake.

**빈대코** a flat nose.

**빈도**(頻度) frequency/높은〔낮은〕 ~수 high[low] frequency/사용하는 ~수에 따라서 in the order of frequency in use. ひんど

**빈둥거리다, 삔둥거리다** loaf around; loiter about; lead an idle life; away one's time/빈둥빈둥 idly; aimlessly; leisurely/빈둥빈둥 세월을 보내다 loaf away one's days/집안에서 ~ loaf at home. のらくらする

**빈들거리다, 삔들거리다** be[live] idle; loaf; loiter/빈들빈들 leisurely; idly; aimlessly/빈들빈들 놀기만 하다 do nothing but idle about; idle one's time away. のらりくらりする

**빈랑나무**(檳榔一) a betel-nut palm.

**빈마**(牝馬) a mare. めうま

**빈말** [an] idle[empty] talk; an empty promise; empty words/~하다 have an idle talk; talk idly/~이 지나치다 carry the joke too far. むだぐち

**빈모**(鬢毛) whiskers; sideburns. びんづら

**빈민**(貧民) the poor; the needy/~굴 a slum; poor quarters/~을 구제하다 relieve the poor. ひんみん

**빈발**(頻發) frequent occurrence/~하다 occur frequently; be frequent/교통 사고가 ~하다 Traffic accidents occur very often; a motor accadent in a common occurrence. ひんぱつ

**빈방**(一房) 《가구가 없는》 an empty room 《사람이 쓰지 않는》 a vacant room.

**빈번**(頻繁,頻煩) frequency/~하다¨(be) frequent; incessant/~히 frequently; repeatedly/~히 일어나는 일 a matter of frequent occurence/왕래가 ~한 거리 a busy[bustling] street. ひんぱん

**빈부**(貧富) wealth and poverty 《사람》 rich and poor/~의 현격 the gulf between rich and poor/~의 차별 없이 rich and poor alike. ひんぷ

**빈빈하다**(頻頻一) (be) frequent/빈빈히 frequently. ひんびんとしている

**빈사**(賓辭) 〖논〗 the predicate; 〖언〗 an object [word]. ひんじ

**빈사**(瀕死) a dying condition/~의 dying /~의 환자 a dying patient/~상태에 있다 be in dying condition; lie at death's door. ひんし

**빈삭**(頻數) frequency; oftenness/~(be) frequent; often. ひんぱん

**빈상**(貧相) a countenance that bespeaks poverty; a meager[haggard] look. ひんそう

**빈소**(殯所) the place where a coffin is kept until the funeral day. ひんしょ

**빈소리** useless[pointless] words.

**빈속** an empty stomach/~에 술을 마시다 have a drink on an empty stomach. すきばら

**빈손** an empty hand/~으로 with empty hands; without taking any present with one からて

**빈약**(貧弱) poorness; scantiness/~하다 (be) poor; scanty; limited/내용이 ~한 책 a book poor in substance/~한 지식 scanty[smattering] knowledge. ひんじゃく

**빈우**(牝牛) a cow. ひんぎゅう

**빈자**(貧者) a poor man; the poor; needy [indigent] people／～의 일등(一登) the widow's mite. ひんじゃ

**빈자떡**(貧者—) a kind of pancake made from lentil flour／～을 지지다 make lentil pancakes.

**빈자리** a vacancy; an opening (공석) a vacant seat／～를 메우다 fill a vacancy.

**빈정거리다** 《공위》 make cynical[sarcastic, ironical, cutting] remarks; satirize／자꾸 ～ make (one) sarcasm after another／빈정빈정 jokingly; teasingly; caustically. ひにくをいう

**빈주먹** an empty hand／～으로 empty-handed. からこぶし

**빈집** a vacant[an unoccupied, an empty] house／그 집은 ～이다 The house is left vacant.

**빈차**(—車) an empty car.

**빈척**(擯斥) 《배척》 rejection; exclusion 《경멸》 disdain／사회의 ～을 받다 be socially[publicly] ostracized. ひんせき

**빈천**(貧賤) poverty [and lowliness]／～하다 (be) poor and lowly／～한 가문에 태어나다 be born poor. ひんせん

**빈천지교**(貧賤之交) a friend in need. ひんせんのまじわり

**빈촌**(貧村) a poor village. ひんそん
**빈총**(—銃) an unloaded gun. くうほう
**빈축**(嚬蹙) a frown; a grimace／～하다 frown[scowl] (at, on); look on (something) with scorn[disdain]; be scandalized at／～할 만한 scandalous; despicable; objectionable. ひんしゅく

**빈탕** emptiness; vacancy; blank[-ness]; 《알이 없는》 an empty nut; a blank (in a lottery). あきがら

**빈털터리** a penniless fellow; a penniless person; a person destitute of money／～가 되다 go[be] broke; become penniless. いちもんなしのもの

**빈틈** ①《간격》 an opening; an aperture; a gap; a crevice／～없는[없이] close[ly]; compact[ly]／중이와 형겊 조각으로 ～을 들어막다 stuff the crevice with paper and rage ②《불비》 unpreparedness; a blind side; an opening (for attack)／～없이 경계하다 be on the alert; be on (one's) guard／일이 ～없이 잘 되어 있다 The work leaves nothing to be desired. すきま

**빈핍**(貧乏) poverty; indigence／～하다 (be) poor; needy; indigent. びんぼう

**빈한**(貧寒) poverty; want; destitution; indigence／～하다 (be) poor; needy; indigent. ひんかん

**빈혈**(貧血) anemia; anaemia／～증 anemia／～증의 anemic／～증에 걸리다 become anemic; be impoverished of blood. ひんけつ

**빌다**¹ ①《차용하다》 borrow; have (money) on loan 《세내다》 hire; rent (a house, land); take (a house) ②《힘을》 have[get] (a person's) help ③《방을》 rent; take／집을 ～ rent[take] a house. かりる

**빌다**² ①《구걸하다》 beg; solicit／빌어먹다 go [about] begging; beg food[one's bread] ②《간청하다》 ask; request; beg; entreat ③《사죄하다》 ask (a person's) pardon; beg[make] an apology (for). こう

**빌리다** ①《대여하다》 lend; advance; loan 〈미〉/이름[됨]을 ～ lend one's name[aid] (to a project) ②《임대하다》 let[hire] out (부동산을) hire rent; let; lease／말을 ～ hire horses out. かす

**빌미** a curse; an evil spell／～가 내린 cursed; ill-fated. のろい

**빌붙다** curry favour with a person; win one's favour by flattery; flatter; grovel. へつらう

**빌어먹다** beg one's bread; go begging; live as a beggar. こじきする

**빌어먹을** Damm…!, Damm it! ちくしょう

**빔** one's best clothes; gala dress／～하다 dress up; be faily dressed／～을 차리다 dress up for the New Year.

**빕더서다** ①step back ②《약속을》 shirk to fulfil one's promise. わきによる

**빗** a comb／～살 the teeth of a comb／～으로 머리를 빗다 comb one's hair／～을 꽂다 wear[put on] a comb. くし

**빗-** mis-; mistaken; crooked; sidewise; wrong; astray.

**빗가다** miss; go astray. わきへそれる
**빗금** a deviant crease[fold, line].
**빗기다** comb[dress] (one's) hair. くしげしてやる

**빗나가다** turn away[aside]; deviate; wander (from); 《빗맞다》 glance off; miss; go astray／과녁에 맞지 않고 ～ miss the mark; go wild. わきへそれる

**빗다** comb／머리를 ～ comb the hair; brush one's hair. くしげする

**빗대다** ①《비꼬다》 make an insinuating remark; insinuate (that…); hint at／그는 분명히 내게 빗대고 있다 He is really referring to[speaking of] me. ②《고백을》 make a false statement 《위증하다》 give false evidence. ねじる

**빕더서다** ①《방향을》 face askance at ② step back ⇨비켜서다. わきへよる

**빗돌**(碑—) a stone monument; a monumental stone. ひせき

**빗뜨다** look out of the corner of (one's eye); look sidewise／눈을 ～ look out of the corner of one's eyes.

**빗듣다** hear wrong; mishear; be misinformed. ききまちがう

**빗디디다** miss one's foot[step]; lose one's footing; make a false step／계단을 ～ miss one's footing on the stairs. ふみあやまる

**빗맞다** ①《빗나가다》 miss (the mark); go wide (of the mark) ②《뜻못》 fail; go wrong／계획이 ～ be baffled in one's design. あてそこなう

**빗먹다** saw obliquely. ななめにひける

**빗물** rain-water. あまみず
**빗반자** an inclined ceiling.
**빗발** falling of rain/～치듯 하다 rain [down]; fall like rain. あまあし
**빗방울** a raindrop/～ 소리 pattering of raindrops. しずく
**빗변** 《수》 a hypotenuse; an oblique side /직각 삼각형의 ～ the hypotenuse of a right-angled triangle.
**빗살** the teeth of a comb. くしのは
**빗소리** the sound of rain. あめのおと
**빗솔** a comb-brush. くしのはけ
**빗장** a bolt; a [cross]bar/～은 a gate with a cross-bar/문에 ～을 걸다 bar [bolt] the gate. かんぬき
**빗장고름** a bow-tied ribbon. かんぬきのようなむすびめ
**빗장뼈** the collarbone; the clavicle.
**빗접** a comb-case. くしばこ
**빗줄기** great streaks[sheets] of rain/～가 세차다 It rains cats and dogs., It pours down. あまずじ
**빗질** combing/～하다 comb; dress *one's* hair/～하지 않은 머리 unkempt hair. くしげすること
**빗치개** an instrument for parting hair and cleaning combs.
**빙, 삥** round; in a circle/～ 돌다 a circle [turn] round. ぐるりと
**빙거**(憑據) authority; ground; foundation/～하다 be based on; be founded on; prove; evidence. ひょうきょ
**빙결**(氷結) freezing/～하다 freeze; be frozen [over]; be ice-bound. ひょうけつ
**빙고**(氷庫) an ice-house; a refrigerator. ひむろ
**빙고**(憑考) examination; scrutiny; investigation/～하다 refer to; consult (*a book*). さんしょう
**빙과**(氷菓) ices; ice-candy; ice-cakes. ひょうか
**빙괴**(氷塊) a lump[piece, block] of ice 《떠도는》 an ice floe. ひょうかい
**빙그레, 뻥그레** with a beaming face; smilingly/～ 웃다 beam; chuckle. にやっと
**빙그르르, 뻥그르르** round and round; around smoothly/～ 돌다 turn round and round. くるくる
**빙글거리다, 뻥글거리다** smile (at *a person*); beam (upon *a person*).
**빙글빙글, 뻥글뻥글** around and around smoothly/～ 웃는 얼굴 a beaming face. くるくる
**빙굿거리다, 뻥굿거리다, 뻥끗거리다** ⇒빙글거리다. にこにこわらう
**빙낭**(氷囊) an ice-bag; an ice-pack/～ 줄 ice bag suspender. ひょうのう
**빙당**(氷糖) sugar candy ⇒빙사탕(氷砂糖).
**뻥등거리다** shake (*one's* head) to show a negative reaction.
**빙모**(聘母) the wife's mother. つまのはは
**빙벽**(氷壁) an ice ridge.
**빙부**(聘父) the wife's father ⇒장인(丈人).
**빙빙, 뻥뻥** round and round/～ 돌다 turn round and round; circle.
**뻥뻥매다** go about busily; bustle about; be at a loss (*what* to do). せかせかする
**빙사탕**(氷砂糖) sugar candy.
**빙산**(氷山) an iceberg. ひょうざん
**빙상**(氷上) ～에서 on the ice/～ 경기 ice-skating. ひょうじょう
**빙석**(氷釋) ～하다 thaw 《의문 따위가》 be cleared; be dispelled; be resolved. ひょうしゃく
**빙설**(氷雪) ice and snow/～에 둘러싸이다 be icebound/～에 갇힌 icebound. ひょうせつ
**빙수**(氷水) shaved ice; iced water 《음료》 ice flakes with syrup. こおりみず
**빙신**(憑信) reliance; trust/～하다 rely on; place reliance upon; trust/～할 만한 reliable; trustworthy. ひょうしん
**빙실**(氷室) an icehouse; a refrigeratory. ひむろ
**빙실거리다, 뻥실거리다** smile; beam; chuckle. にこにこわらう
**빙어**(一魚) 《어》 a pond smelt; a smelt.
**빙원**(氷原) an ice field. ひょうげん
**빙자**(憑藉) ①《평계》 an excusel /～하다 make a pretext[plea] of; make an excuse of; use (*a thing*) as an excuse for /…을 ～하여 under the pretence of; on the pretext of ②《의지》 reliancel /～하다 be under the shelter of another's influence. かこつけること
**빙점**(氷點) the freezing-point. ひょうてん
**빙충맞다** (be) foolish; stupid; dull-witted. おくびょうだ
**빙충[맞]이** a fool; a stupid person.
**빙침**(氷枕) an ice-pillow/～을 베다 rest *one's* head on a pillow of ice. こおりまくら
**빙탄**(氷炭) ①《얼음과 숯》 ice and charoal ②《비유적》 contradiction/～ 불상용이다 be as incompatible as oil and water. ひょうたん
**빙퉁그러지다** go wrong; take an unfavourable turn; do not turn out as one wishes. ゆがんでいる
**빙판**(氷板) a frozen road; a passage covered with ice; an icy road.
**빙하**(氷河) 《지》 a glacier/～ 시대 the glacial age. ひょうが
**빙하다** (be) fuddled with drink; in a drunken stupor. ぐらぐらする
**빙해**(氷解) clearance ⇒빙석. ひょうかい
**빙해**(氷海) a frozen sea. ひょうかい
**빙활**(氷滑) ice-skating. こおりすべり
**빚** a debt; liability/～을 갚다[물다] pay off debts. ふさい
**빚거간**(一居間) 《영업》 a loan agent[broker]; a loan agency[brokerage].
**빚내다** borrow money; get[float] a loan /부동산을 저당으로 은행에서 ～ get a loan from a bank on *one's* real estate.
**빚놀이** lending money; making a loan.
**빚놓다** lend money; loan (*out*)/고리(高利)로 ～ lend money at a high rate of

빚다 ①(가루·반죽을) shape dough for (*rice cakes*); roll into balls (as *dumplings*) ②(술을) brew (*rice wine*); ferment ③(사태를) cause; breed; bring about [on]. ちょうごうする

빚돈 a loan; a debt／~을 내다 make a loan／~이 있다 be in debt. しゃっきん

빚장이 《채권자》a creditor 《수금원》a [bill] collector 《고리 대금업자》a loan shark 《미·속》. しゃっきんとり

빚주다 lend money; loan.

빚지다 get into debt; contract[incur] a debt／빚지고 도망가다 run away leaving *one's* debt unpaid. しゃっきんする

빚지시 an intermediary party to a loan／~하다 serve as intermediary party to a loan.

빛 ①《광명》light 《광선》a beam; a ray 《섬광》a flash; a gleam (어둠 속의); 《광휘》a luster; glow; radiance; twinkle(별의); a sparkle(보석 따위의); a glitter 《희미한》a glimmer／~이 잘 드는 방 a sunny room／태양 ~ sunlight; the sun's rasy／~을 발하다 emit[give out] light／가로등 불~을 빌어 책을 읽다 read by the light of a street lamp／어슴프레한 불~ 밑에서 일하다 work in the faint light ②《빛깔》a colo[u]r; a hue; a tint; a shade／겨울 ~ winteral tints／밝은[어두운] ~ a bright[dark] colo[u]r／푸른 기운이 도는 붉은 ~ red of [with] a blue tint ③《얼굴빛 따위》an expression; a look／피로한 ~이 보이다 tired; show signs of fatigue／그는 그 소식을 접하다 얼굴~이 달라졌다 He changed colo[u]r at the news. あかるさ

빛깔 a shade of colo[u]r; a colo[u]r; a hue. いろ

빛나다 ①《비치다·번쩍이다》shine; sparkle; glitter; be bright; be radiant ②《영광스럽다》be glorious; become distinguished ③《두드러짐》shine; be prominent; be outstanding. ひかる

빛내다 《비치게 하다》make (*a thing*) shine; brighten; polish 《영광스럽게 하다》bring glory[fame, distinction] to; glorify. ひからす

빛살 rays of light. こうせん

빛없다 feel humiliated[deflated].

빛접다 be something to be proud of; (be) shining／그가 한 일이 ~ He did himself proud. もったいづけている

**사 (단추 구멍의)** a buttonhole stitch／ ~뜨다 buttonhole; hemstitch; cross-stitch.

**사(士)** ①(선비) a man (인사) a figure／독학지~ a scholarly man ②(장기의) a chessman in Korean chess.

**사(巳)** 〖민〗①the zodiacal sign of the Snake ②⇨사방(巳方) ③⇨사시(巳時).

**사(四)** four (제4) the fourth／제~계급 the fourth estate／~배하다 increase fourfold; quadruple／~차원 the fourth dimension.

**사(死)** death ⇨죽음／자연~ a natural death.

**사(寺)** a temple／불국(佛國)~ the Boolkook Temple.

**사(私)** (공에 대한) privateness (자기) privacy (사리) self-interest／~의 private; personal; confidential／ ~가 있는 selfish; self-interested／ ~가 없는 unselfish; disinterested.

**사(邪)** (부정) wrong; injustice; unrighteousness (사악) evil; vice.

**사(社)** (회사) a company; a corporation 〈미〉a firm (사무소) an office.

**사(赦)** pardon; clemency; leniency; indulgence／~하다 pardon; forgive; absolve; discharge; grant clemency[leniency] to (a person).

**사(詞)** a written word (용어) a term (문구) a phrase.

**사(紗)** [silk] gauze; gossamer.

**사(辭)** (인사) an address; a message (공식적인) a formal message／송별~ a parting[farewell] message／환영~ an address of welcome.

**-사(史)** history (연대사) annals; chronicles／현대~ a contemporary.

**사가(史家)** a historian.

**사가(私家)** (집) a private residence (가정) one's [private] home.

**사가(賜暇)** leave of absence (장기의) furlough／~하다 give[grant] (one) a leave of absence.

**사가(死街)** a deadly quiet street.

**사각(四角)** ~의 four-cornered; square／~이다 It is square[fourcornered].／ ~주(柱) a square pillar／ ~형 〖수〗 a quadrilateral; a tetragon; a quadrangle; a square.

**사각(死角)** 〖군〗the dead angle[ground] (of a gun).

**사각(射角)** an angle of fire.

**사각(斜角)** 〖수〗an oblique angle; a bevel.

**사각거리다** crunch; be crisp[crunchy] to the teeth／배를 사각사각 먹다 crunch a pear／무우를 사각사각 먹다 crunch a radish／감자가 덜 익어서 사각거린다 This potato is half-done and is still hard to eat.

**사각모자(四角帽子)** a square-shaped cap; a mortarboard.

**사갈(蛇蝎)** (뱀과 전갈) snakes and scorpions (사람) a malignant person.

**사감(私憾)** (원한) personal grudge; a bitter feeling; spite.

**사감(舍監)** a dormitory inspector; a dormitory superintendent.

**사개** 〖건〗a dovetail [joint].

**싸개¹** a wrapper; cover material; a slip cover; wrapping paper／ ~질 upholstering.

**싸개²** one who urinate or defecate／오줌~ a bed wetter／ 똥~ pantswetter.

**사거(死去)** death; decease／ ~하다 die; pass away; expire.

**사건(事件)** (큰) an event (사소한) an incident (음모) a plot (일) an affair; a matter (봉기) an outrage (사고) an accident (소송) a case (알력) a trouble (추문) a scandal.

**사격(射擊)** firing; shooting／ ~술 marksmanship／~하다 shoot; fire at／~ 대회 a rifle meeting.

**사견(私見)** one's personal opinion[view]; one's point of view.

**사견(邪見)** a heretical views; an evil[a wrong] idea.

**사경(四更)** the small hours.

**사경(死境)** (생사지경) the gates of death (궁경) a deadly pass.

**사경제(私經濟)** 〖경〗 private[individual] economy.

**사계(四季)** (사철) the four seasons.

**사계(射界)** a field of [gun]fire.

**사계(斯界)** the line [of business]; the subject; the profession／~의 권위자 an authority on the subject.

**사고(四顧)** ~하다 look around／ ~ 무친 하다 have no one to turn to for help; be without kith or kin.

사고(社告) an announcement; a notice.
사고(事故) 《사건》 an incident(예측하지 못한); an accident 《고장》 a hitch; a trouble/ 철도 ~ a railway accident/ ~를 일으키다 cause an accident.
사고(思考) thought/ ~하다 think; consider; regard (*a thing*) as/ ~력 thinking power.
사고 팔고(四苦八苦) 《분투》 hard struggle 《고경》 dire distress 《고통》 agony.
사곡(邪曲) crookedness; evil-mindedness / ~하다 (be) crooked; wicked; evil-minded; crafty.
사곡(私穀) privately-owned cereals[grain].
사공(沙工) a boatman; a sailor; a sea-man.
사과(沙果) an apple/ ~나무 an apple tree/ ~산(酸) malic acid/~술 cider/ ~를 깎다 pare an apple.
사과(絲瓜) 【식】 a snake[towel] gourd.
사과(謝過) apology; pardon/ ~하다 apologize; make[offer] an apology; beg *one's* pardon/~장(狀) a written apology.
사관(士官) an officer/육군[해군] ~ 학교 a military[naval] academy/ ~ 후보생 an officer on probation.
사관(史觀) a historical view.
사광(砂鑛) an alluvial gold mine; a placer mine.
사교(司敎) 【종】 a bishop.
사교(社交) society; social intercourse [life]/ ~ society; social circles/상류 ~계 fashionable society/ ~적 social/ ~실[층] a social hall[dance]/ ~계의 부인 a society woman/ ~가 사교적인 사람 a good mixer; a 술의 art of social intercourse/ ~성 있는 social; sociable.
사교(邪敎) a heretical religion; heresy / ~도 a heretic.
사구(砂丘) a sand hill; a dune.
사구(四球) 【체】 four balls; walking
사구(死球) 【체】 a dead ball.
사군자(四君子) plum-blossoms, orchids, chrysanthemums and bamboos 《그림》 oriental paintings of plum-blossoms, orchids, chrysanthemums and bamboos.
사군자(士君子) a gentleman; a man of honor; a scholar; a learned person; a man of letters; the *literati*(L).
사권(私權) 【법】 a private right.
사귀(邪鬼) an evil spirit; a devil.
사귀다 associate with (*one*); keep company with; mix with; hold intercourse with.
사귐성 affinity; sociability/ ~ 있는 sociable; congenial.
사그라지다 《썩어서》 decompose 《녹아서》 melt away 《종기 등이》 be resolved.
사극(史劇) a historical play[drama].
사근사근하다 ①《성질이》(be) amiable; aggreeable; pleasant; affable ②《먹기에》(be) fresh.
사금(砂金) gold dust; alluvial gold/ ~채집 alluvial mining.
사금(賜金) a government grant of money; a money grant.
사금(謝金) a reward; a fee; a remuneration; an honorarium; a tip.
사금융(私金融) private loan.
사금파리 broken pieces of chinaware; chips.
사기(士氣) morale; fighting spirit/ ~가 떨어지다 be demoralized/~를 고무하다 raise the morale.
사기(史記) a historical book[work].
사기(死期) the hour of death.
사기(沙器) china; crockery 《자기》 porcelain/~ 접시 porcelain dishes.
사기(邪氣) ①《사심》 malice; an evil intention ②《독기》 noxious vapor.
사기(社旗) a flag with an emblem denoting a commercial firm.
사기(詐欺) fraud; fraudulence; swindling / ~하다 swindle; commit a fraud/ ~군 a swindler; an impostor.
사기업(私企業) 【경】 an individual[a private] enterprise.
사나이 ①《남자》 a man; a male ②《남성》 man[hood]; the male sex ③《사내다움》 manliness/ ~다운 manly; manlike; manful/ ~답게 like a man; in a manly manner.
사날¹ three or four days; several days.
사날² *one's* own way; willfulness; ُfishness; having *one's* own way; behaving as *one* pleases.
사납다 (be) fierce; wild; violent; rude; rough; ferocious/사납게 fiercely; roughly; violently; wildly/사나운 짐승 a fierce beast; a wild animal/사납게 생긴 rough-[fierce-]looking/사나운 사람 a rough; a savage.
사낭(砂囊) 《모래의》 a sandbag 《닭짐승의》 a gizzard.
사내 ①a man ⇒사나이/ ~아이 a boy/ ~종 a man servant ②《남편》 *one's* husband.
사내(社內) within the firm/ ~에 in the company[firm, office].
사내(舍內) within the dormitory.
사냥 《수렵》 hunting 《총렵》 shooting/ ~하다 hunt; shoot/~갓 《짐승》 game; a game animal/~가다 go hunting; go on a shooting expedition.
사냥개 a hound; a hunting dog/ ~를 풀어 놓다 slip a hound.
사냥군 a hunter; a huntsman; a sportsman.
사냥질 hunting; shooting/ ~하다 hunting; shoot.

**사냥터** 《개인의》 a [game] preserve; a hunting ground[field].

**사녀**(士女) man and woman; male and female; gentleman and gentlewoman. しんしとふじょ

**사념**(邪念) evil[depraved] thoughts; an evil mind[intention]; a vicious mind 《간계》 a sinister design[scheme] / ~없는 마음 a heart pure of evil / ~을 버리다 free oneself of evil thoughts. じゃねん

**사농공상**(士農工商) the scholar, the farmer, the artisan and the merchant. しのうこうしょう

**사느랗다** (be) cool; (be) chilly ⇒사늘하다. ひやっとする

**사늘하다, 싸늘하다** 《날씨가》 (be) cool; chilly; icy 《무섭다》 be chilled; feel a chill 《태도가》 (be) cool; chilly; distant. ひやっこい

**사다** ①《물품을》 buy; purchase / 싸게 [비싸게] ~ buy cheap[dear]; make a good [bad] bargain / 외상으로 ~ buy (a thing) on credit / 그녀는 급료를 타면 다 책을 사 버린다 She spends all her salary on books. ②《가져오다》 incur; invite; bring (upon) / 환심을 ~ win[gain] another's favor / 아첨으로 환심을 ~ buy (a person's) patronage with flattery. かう

**싸다**¹ ①《덮다》 cover; wrap; envelop ②《꾸리다》 wrap up [paper] 《종이로》. つつむ

**싸다**² 《대·소변을》 excrete.

**싸다**³ ①《입이》 (be) talkative; voluble ②《걸음이》 (be) quick; fast ③《불이》 intense. ぐちまめだ

**싸다**⁴ ①《값이》 (be) cheap; low; lowpriced; inexpensive / 싸게 cheap; cheaply; at a low price / 싸게 사다 buy cheap; get[buy] at a low price ②《처벌이》 deserve; merit; be due. やすい

**싸다니다** run[bustle] about / 사방으로 ~ bustle in and out. はしりまわる

**사다리** a ladder ⇒사닥다리. はしご

**사다리꼴** 《수》 a trapezoid. はしごがた

**사다새** 《조》 a pelican. がらんちょう

**사닥다리** a ladder / ~ 층계 a staircase; a flight of stairs. はしご

**사단**(社團) a corporation / ~ 법인 an incorporated body; a corporate juridical person. しゃだん

**사단**(事端) 《발단》 the origin[cause] of an affair; beginning / ~을 일으키다 stir up troubles. じけんのいときぐち

**사단**(師團) a[an army] division / 수도 ~ the Capital Division / ~장 a divisional commander / ~ 사령부 divisional headquarters. しだん

**사담**(史談) a historical tale[story].

**사담**(私談) a private talk / ~하다 have a private talk with (one); talk privately with. こじんてきなはなし

**사답**(私畓) a privately-owned rice field. こじんのはたけ

**사당**(寺黨) a gang of low girls that sell singing and dancing.

**사당**(邪黨) scoundrels; rascals; villains. よこしまなやから

**사당**(私黨) a faction; a private party.

**사당**(祠堂) a shrine; a sanctuary. しどう

**사대**(事大) submission to the stronger; worship of the powerful / ~ 사상[주의] flunkeyism; toadyism / ~주의자 a truckler; a time-server. じだい

**사대**(私大) a private university[college].

**사대문**(四大門) the four main gates of old Seoul. よんだいもん

**사대부**(士大夫) a man of noble birth. もんばつのたかいひと

**사대삭신**(四大一) flesh and bones [of a human being]; the whole[high] body. しんたいぜんたいのこつにく

**사대 육신**(四大六身) the whole body.

**사또** 《주장·원님에게》 My lord!

**사도**(私道) a private road. しどう

**사도**(使徒) an apostle / ~행전 《종》 The Acts of the Apostles. しと

**사도**(邪道) evil ways[courses]; vice; heresy. じゃどう

**사도**(師道) the duty of a teacher.

**사도**(斯道) 《문제》 the subject 《방면》 the line 《기술》 the art / ~의 대가 an authority[expert] in the line; a master of the art. しどう

**사돈**(査頓) a member of the family of one's daughter-[son-]in-law / ~집 a house[family] of in-laws. あいやけ

**사동**(使童) an office[errand] boy; a page; a messenger. きゅうじ

**사두**(四頭) four horses[oxen] / ~ 마차 a coach-and-four; a four-horse coach.

**사들이다** buy in (goods); stock [a shop with goods]; purchase.

**사뜻하다** (be) clean ⇒산뜻하다. さっぱりしている

**싸라기** 《쌀》 half-crushed rice; broken bits of rice 《눈》 tiny pellets of hail.

**사라사** printed cotton; chintz; print; calico〈미〉.

**사라쌍수**(沙羅雙樹) a couple of sal trees. さらそうじゅ

**사라지** a tobacco pouch made of oiled paper.

**사라지다** 《소실하다》 vanish; disappear; fade away; go out of sight 《소멸하다》 die[melt] away. きえてなくなる

**사람** ①《인류》 man; mankind; 《개인》 a man; a person; a human being / ~ 서리가 crowd; a throng / ~의 일생 a human life / ~을 보내다 send a messenger / ~은 만물의 영장이다 Man is the soul of the universe. ②《인재》 a man of talent; a capable man 《성격·인물》 character; nature; personality / ~이 좋은[나쁜] good-[ill-]natured / ~을 잘[잘못] 보다 be a good[bad] judge of character ③《성인》 a man; an adult / ~이 되다 become a man. ひと

**사람구실** behaving as a person should; living up to one's role / ~하다 behave

사람답다 (be) humane; decent; modest. ひとらしい
사람멀미 ~하다 feel sick from the jostling of a crowd. ひといきにようこと
사랑 love 《애정》 affection 《애착》 attachment; tender passion／~하다 love; be fond of; be attached to／순결한 ~ Platonic love／불의(不義)의 ~ illicit love／거짓~ false love／~하는 이 one's sweet heart; a lover(남자); a love(여자)／~의 보금자리 a love nest. あい
사랑(舍廊) a detached room used as man's quarters／~채 a detachedhouse／~문 the door of the party room.
사랑니 a wisdom tooth. おくば
사랑 양반(舍廊兩班) one's husband.
사랑스럽다 (be) lovable 《매력 있는》(be) lovely; charming. かわいらしい
사래 ⑨ ~논[밭] wet(dry) fields allowed [a grave keeper or tenant supervisor] for his services.
사래질 winnowing; fanning／~하다 winnow; fan. ふるいにかけること
사략(史略) an outlined history. しりゃく
사량(思量) consideration／~하다 consider; think; take into consideration. しりょう
사레 being choked by the entrance of food or drink into trachea／~들리다 be choked. むせぶこと
사려(思慮) 《생각》 thought; consideration 《분별》 sense; prudence／~하다 ponder; meditate; think over carefully／~가 깊은 사람 a man of discretion／~ 있는 thoughtful; considerate. しりょ
사려중(思慮症) worrying[nervous, solicitous] temperament; anxiety; psychosis.
사력(死力) a desperate effort. しりょく
사력(私力) private power. こじんのちから
사력(思力) thinking power. しこうりょく
사련(邪戀) unlawful love; guilty love; wicked love. じゃれん
사령(司令) command／~관 a commander; a commandant／~부 the headquarters／~탑 a conning tower／총 ~관 the commander-in-chief／연합군 최고 ~관 The Supreme Commander for the Allied Powers(略: SCAP). しれい
사령(死靈) a departed soul; a ghost.
사령(赦令) a decree of amnesty; an act of grace[oblivion]. しゃれい
사령(辭令) 《사령서》 a written appointment; a writ of appointment; a government order 《인사》 diction; address; manner of speaking. じれい
사례(事例) an example; an instance; a case 《선례》 a precedent. じれい
사례(謝禮) 《감사》 thanks 《보수》 a remuneration／~하다 reward; remunerate; recompense (one for); fee (one for)／~금 a reward; a recompense; a remuneration. しゃれい
사로자다 have a restless sleep; sleep uneasily; can not fall asleep soundly／잠을 ~ sleep a troubled sleep. まどろむ
사로잠그다 lock halfway; bolt (the door) insecurely. はんぶんかける
사로잡다 catch (an animal) alive; capture (one);《생포하다》 take (one) prisoner 《매혹하다》 captivate; charm. いけどりする
사로잡히다 be captured [alive]; be taken prisoner 《매혹하다》 be captivated 《구애하다》 be seized with; be a slave of [honour and gain].
사록(史錄) historical records. しろく
사론(史論) a historical essay. しろん
사론(私論) one's personal opinion. しろん
사뢰다 tell; in inform ⇨아뢰다.
사료(史料) historical materials／~ 편찬원(員) an official historian. しりょう
사료(思料) consideration／~하다 consider; deem; regard; think. しりょう
사료(飼料) fodder; feed; forage. しりょう
사륙 배판(四六倍判) 【인】 a large[royal] octavo. しろくばいばん
사륙판(四六判) 【인】 duodecimo; 12mo; crown octavo. しろくばん
사르다¹ 《불을》 set fire (to); 《피우다》 make a fire; kindle 《태우다》 burn; set (a thing) on fire. ひをおこす
사르다² 《곡식을》 winnow (from, out, away). ふるう
사르르 gently; softly. じわじわ
사름 a three-year-old horse[ox].
사리¹ 《감은》 a coil ⇨사리다.
사리² 《만조 때》 time of high tide／~ 고기 fish caught at high tide.
싸리 《식》 a bush clover. えぞやまはぎ
사리(私利) one's own interest; self-interest; personal gain[profit]. しり
사리(舍利) 《유골》 Buddha's bones; a relic of the Buddha; sarira 《경전》 Buddhist scriptures; the Sutras. しゃり
사리(事理) reason 《사실》 facts 《당부》propriety／~에 닿다 stand to reason; be reasonable; be logical／~ 분별하다 be sensible; have good sense. じり
사리(射利) love of gain; seeking profit／~심 mercenary spirit.
사리다 ①《말다》 coil [up]; wind (rope, etc.) round ②《몸을 아끼다》 spare oneself [pains]. ぐるぐるまく
싸리버섯 an edible mushroom; Clavaria botrytis(학명). ははきたけ
사리별(舍利別) syrup; sirup〈미〉.
사리염(瀉利鹽) 【화】 sulphate of magnesium.
사린(四隣) the surrounding countries; the whole neighbourhood. しりん
사린교 a four-man palanquin; a palankeen carried by four men.
사립(私立) private establishment／~의 private; privately-controlled／~ 학교 a private school／~ 학교법 the Private School Law.
사립문(一門) a brushwood gate; a twig gate. しばのとびら

**사립짝** a brushwood door-flap.
**사마귀**¹ a mole (《무사마귀》) a wart. いぼ
**사마귀**² 《충》 a praying mantis. かまきり
**사막**(沙漠) a desert. さばく
**사망**(死亡) death; decease; mortality/ ～하다 die; pass away/ ～자 the dead [person]; the deceased (단수); ～률 mortality; the death-rate/ ～신고 a notice of death. しぼう
**사매**(私—) illegal flogging; lynch[ing]/ ～질 lynching. しけいのむち
**사맥**(事脈) the cause; the origin; the circumstances 《사실》 facts. じゆう
**사면**(四面) the four sides; all directions / ～팔방에 on all sides; in every direction. しめん
**사면**(死面) a death mask/ ～을 뜨다 take a death-mask of (one). デスマスク
**사면**(斜面) a slope; an inclined plane/ 급～ a steep incline[slope]. しゃめん
**사면**(赦免) pardon 《대사》 amnesty/ ～하다 pardon; remit; grant (one)/ ～장 (狀) a letter of pardon. しゃめん
**사면**(辭免) resignation; retirement from office/ ～하다 resign; retire from office. にんするこ と
**사면발이** ①《충》a crab-louse(pl. -lice) ② 《사람》a flatterer. けじらみ

**사면 초가**(四面楚歌) enemies on every side / ～이다 have the world against (one); be surrounded by foes on all sides; be forsaken by everybody. しめんそか
**사멸**(死滅) extinction; annihilation; destruction; death/ ～하다 die out; be annihilated; become extinct; perish. しめつ
**사명**(死命) 《죽을 운명》a doomed life; fate 《생사의 고비》life or death/ 적의 ～을 제압하다 seal the fate of the enemy. しめい
**사명**(使命) a mission; an appointed task; a commission; an errand/ ～을 떠다 be charged with a mission. しめい
**사명**(社名) the name of a company [firm, corporation].
**사명**(社命) an order [a directive] of the company. しゃめい
**사모**(思慕) longing; yearning; deep attachment/ ～하다 be attached to; long for; yearn after. しぼ
**사모**(師母) 《스승의 아내》the wife of one's teacher 《호칭》 Madam; your [good] lady.
**사무**(社務) the company's business [affairs]
**사무**(事務) business; affairs; office [clerical] work/ ～적인 practical; business-like/ ～가 a man of business[affairs] / ～원 a clerk; an office worker 《총칭》 the office force/ ～관 a secretary; an administrative official/ ～장 a head official 《배의》 a purser/ ～ 총장 secretary general/ ～실 an office [room] / ～소 an office; a place of business / ～국 a secretariat/ ～ 당국 authorities directly in charge/ ～복 a working suit/ ～ 인제를 하다 hand over the charge of an office. じむ
**사무치다** strike one home; sink deeply into one's mind. いたる
**사문**(沙門) a Buddhist monk [priest]; a friar. さもん
**사문**(査問) inquiry; inquisition/ ～하다 interrogate; examine; inquire (into a matter)/ ～회 a court [commission] of inquiry. さもん
**사문**(死文) a dead letter.
**사문서**(私文書) a private document; private papers. しぶんしょ
**사문석**(蛇紋石) 《광》《사문 대리석》 serpentine; ophite. じゃもんせき
**사물**(事物) things; a matter; an affair 《만사》 everything; all things. じぶつ
**사물**(私物) private thing. しぶつ
**사물**(死物) a dead [lifeless] thing; an inanimate object/ ～ 기생 《식》 saprophytism. しぶつ
**사뭇** quite 《몹시》 very much 《거리낌 없이》 without reserve; boldly. しぶつ
**사미**(沙彌) a Buddhist acolyte; a sramanera (Sans).
**사민**(四民) the four classes; all estates of the nation. しみん
**사바**(娑婆) Saha; Sabha (Sans); this world/ ～의 earthly; worldly; mundane/ ～ 속심 worldly desires. しゃば
**사바사바** saba-saba/ ～하다 dispose of (a matter) by using backstair means; make interest with (one).
**사바 세계**(娑婆世界) 《불교》the world of suffering; this world/ ～가 싫어졌다 I am sick of this world. しゃばせかい
**사박거리다** crunch softly. さくさくかむ
**사박사박** with a soft crunch/ 모래밭을 ～ 걷다 walk across the sand with a soft crunch. さくさく
**사박스럽다** (be) rude; boorish; rough. ぶれいだ
**사반**(四半) a quarter/ ～기 a quarter/ ～기의 quarterly.
**사발**(沙鉢) a [porcelain] bowl/ 밥 ～ a rice bowl.
**사발**(四發) 《발동기의》 four-engine; four-motored/ ～ 폭격기 a four-motored bomber.
**사발 농사**(沙鉢農事) begging [one's bread]; mendicancy.
**사방**(四方) the four sides; all directions [quarters]/ ～에 [으로] on all sides; on every side; in all directions; all round / 4피트 ～ four feet square/ 산지 ～으로 in all directions; far and wide. しほう
**사방**(砂防) erosion control; sand-bank fixing/ ～ 공사 sand arrestation work; sand guard. さぼう
**사방등**(四方燈) a square hand-lantern.
**사방형**(斜方形) a rhombus; a rhomb/ ～의 rhombic しゃほうけい
**사배**(四倍) four times; quadruple.

**사백**(舍伯) one's eldest brother. じぶんのあに

**사백**(詞伯) a great[master] poet; a major poet. しはく

**사백**(四百) four hundred. よんひゃく

**사번**(事煩) complexity; intricacy; pressure of business/~하다[스럽다] (be) complicated; intricate. はんざつなこと

**사범**(師範) 《교사》 a teacher; a master; an instructor; a tutor/~ 학교 a normal school. しはん

**사범**(非犯) an offence; a crime/선거 ~ election illegalities. じはん

**사법**(司法) administration of justice; the judicature/ ~의 judicial; judiciary/ ~권 judicial power/ ~관 a judicial officer 《전체》 the judiciary/ ~관 시보(試補) a probationary judicial officer/ ~ 서사 a judicial scrivener/ ~ 제도 the judicial system/~ 행정 judicial administration. しほう

**사법**(死法) a dead law. しほう

**사법**(私法) 《법》 private law. しほう

**사법**(邪法) black arts; sorcery; witchcraft.

**사변**(四邊) 《사변형의》 the four sides/ ~형 《수》 a quadrilateral. しへん

**사변**(事變) 《사고》 an accident; a disaster; a mishap 《변란》 a trouble; a disturbance 《급변》 an emergency; exigency. じへん

**사변**(思辨) speculation; discrimination/ ~적 speculative/ ~ 철학 speculative philosophy. しべん

**사변**(斜邊) 《수》 the hypotenuse/삼각형의 ~ the leg of a triangle. しゃへん

**사별**(死別) separation by death; bereavement/ ~하다 be bereaved. しべつ

**사병**(士兵) a private; a [common] soldier; [enlisted] men(복수); the ranks 《총칭》 the rank and file. しへい

**사병**(死病) a fatal[mortal] disease. しびょう

**사보**(私報) 《보고》 a private report 《사전》 a private telegram[message]. しほう

**사복**(私服) plain[civilian] clothes/ ~ 경관 a plain-clothes policeman. しふく

**사복**(私腹) 9 ~을 채우다 fill one's own pocket; enrich oneself. しふく

**사본**(寫本) a manuscript [copy]; 《부본》 a duplicate 《등사물》 a transcript/ ~을 만들다 copy. しゃほん

**사부**(四部) four parts/~작 a tetralogy /~ 합주《음》 a quartet/~ 합창 a vocal quartet.

**사부**(師父) 《스승》 one's teacher 《스승과 부친》 one's father and master. しふ

**사부**(師傅) 《스승》 a teacher 《왕자의》 a prince's fosterer and tutor. しふ

**사부랑거리다** chatter; prattle; gabble; tattle. ぺちゃくちゃいう

**사부랑삽작** lightly and nimbly; with agility; with a light jump. はしこく

**사부랑하다** (be) loosely-piled; loosely-bound. しまりがない

**사부자기** with ease; effortlessly; stealthily. こそっと

**사북** 《부채의》 the rivet; the pivot 《요점》 the point; a pivot. かなめ

**사뿐** with a soft[muffled] step; softly; lightly. そっと

**사분**(私憤) personal spite[grudge, resentment].

**사분**(四分) ~하다 divide in four; quarter/ ~의 일 one fourth; a quarter/ ~의(儀) a quadrant/ ~ 음부《음》 a crotchet〈영〉; a quarter note〈미〉.

**사분거리다** ①《사근거리다》 tease (one) using funny remarks ②《가만가만》 whisper; talk in a low voice. ささやく

**사분사분하다** 《친걸하다》 (be) kindly; good 《유화하다》 (be) gentle; tender 《붙임성 있다》 (be) amiable; sweet. やさしい

**사분 오열**(四分五裂) disruption / ~하다 go to pieces; be torn up[asunder]; be disrupted. しぶんごれつ

**사분하다** (be) slightly loose; look a bit precarious; be not quite tight[properly stacked].

**사뿟사뿟, 사뿟사뿟** gently;quietly; lightly; softly. しずしず

**사비**(私費) private expense/ ~로 at one's own expense[cost]; at private expense. しひ

**사비**(社費) the company's expenses/~로 at the expense of the company. しゃひ

**사비**(舍費) 《식비 포함》 boarding expenses [charges].

**사사**(私事) personal affairs. しじ

**사사**(事事) in everything/ ~건건 in everything; all cases. じじ

**사사**(師事) ~하다 become a pupil; study under (one); sit at one's feet. しじ

**사사**(謝辭) declination; a humble refusal. しゃじ

**사사로이**(私私一) on personal business [affairs]; for private purposes[use]; informally.

**사사롭다**(私私一) (be) personal; private. こじんてきなことだ

**사사 오입**(四捨五入) ~하다 count fractions of 5 and over as a unit and disregard the rest. ししゃごにゅう

**사사일**(私事一) a private matter; private affairs. してきなこと

**사산**(四散) dispersion / ~하다 disperse [scatter] in all directions. しさん

**사산**(死產) a still birth/~하다 give birth to a stillborn child. しさん

**사살** 《잔소리》 a scolding; a rebuke; a lecture; a nagging.

**사살**(射殺) shooting to death/ ~하다 shoot (one) dead. しゃさつ

**사삼**(沙參) 《식》 a wild plant ⇒더덕.

**사삿집**(私私一) a private home[house]. こじんのうち

**사상**(死相) the seal of death. しそう

**사상**(死傷) casualties/ ~자 the killed

**사상(事狀)** the situation; the state of things; the aspect of affairs; how things stand. ことのじょうたい

**사상(事象)** a phenomenon(*pl.* -na); an aspect; an event. じしょう

**사상(思想)** thought; an idea／신(구) ~ new[old] ideas／ ~가 a thinker／위험 ~ "dangerous" ideas; nefarious ideas／ ~ 단속 thought control／~범 thought[political] offence 《사람》a political offender. しそう

**사상(絲狀)** ~의 filiform; thready／~균 《식》a filamentous fungus. しじょう

**사상(寫象)** an image／~파 imagists.

**사상(史上)** in history／~에 이름을 남기다 abide in history. しじょう

**사색(思索)** thinking; contemplation; meditation／ ~하다 think; contemplate; speculate on／~가 a thinker／~에 잠기다 be given to speculation; be lost in meditation. しさく

**사색(四色)** the Four Factions [of the *Lee* Dynasty].

**사색(辭色)** words and looks. じしょく

**사생(私生)** illegal birth. しせい

**사생(死生)** life and[or] death／ ~ 결단하고 at the risk of *one's* life. ししょう

**사생(寫生)** sketching from nature／~하다 sketch from nature[life]／~화 a sketch. しゃせい

**사생아(私生兒)** an illegitimate child; a natural[love] child; a bastard. しせいじ

**사생활(私生活)** *one's* private life; personal life. しせいかつ

**사서(司書)** a librarian. ししょ

**사서(四書)** the Four Books [of Confucianism]／~ 삼경 the Three Classics and the Four Books; the Seven Chinese Classics. ししょ

**사서(史書)** a history book. ししょ

**사서(私書)** a private document 《사신》a private letter／[우편] ~함 a post-office box(略：P.O.B.).

**사서(辭書)** a dictionary ⇨사전(辭典). じしょ

**사석(私席)** an unofficial occasion／ ~에서 at a private occasion. してきなせき

**사석(沙石)** sand and stones. しゃせき

**사석(捨石)** a riprap; a rubble mound.

**사선(死線)** the deadline. しせん

**사선(私線)** a private[privately-owned] line. しせん

**사선(私船)** a private boat. しせん

**사선(射線)** a trajectory. しゃせん

**사선(斜線)** 《수》an oblique line. しゃせん

**사설(社說)** a leading article; a leader; an editorial／ ~난 the editorial column／ ~ 기자 an editorial[a leader] writer. しゃせつ

**사설(邪說)** a heretical doctrine. じゃせつ

**사설(私設)** a private establishment／ ~의 private. しせつ

**사설(辭說)** a scolding; a rebuke; a lecture／ ~하다 scold; rebuke; lecture; give a lecture.

**사성(四聖)** the four greatest sages of the world. しせい

**사성(四聲)** the four Chinese accents; the "Four Tones" of classical Chinese. しせい

**사성(賜姓)** ~하다 confer[bestow] a surname on *(one)*.

**사세(事勢)** the situation; the state of things[affairs]／~ 부득이 unavoidably; out of sheer necessity. じせい

**사세(辭世)** ~하다 die; depart this life; leave the world. じせい

**사세국(司稅局)** the Revenue[Taxation] Bureau.

**사세청(司稅廳)** the Office of Tax.

**사소** where to die; a place where *one* should die. ししょ

**사소(些少)** ~하다 (be) trifling; trivial; small; petty; slight; inconsiderable. さしょう

**사소설(私小說)** a novel dealing with the author's own life; an "I" story; a private life novel. ししょうせつ

**사수(死守)** a desperate[stubborn] defence／ ~하다 defend to the last [ditch]. ししゅ

**사수(査收)** receipt／ ~하다 receive.

**사수(射手)** a shooter; a marksman 《포수》a gunner／명~ a crack shot. しゃしゅ

**사숙(私塾)** a private school. しじゅく

**사숙(私淑)** ~하다 admire; take as *one's* model; pattern after *(one)*. ししゅく

**사숙(舍叔)** my uncle. しゅくふ

**사순재(四旬齋)** 《그리스도교의》Lent.

**사순절(四旬節)** 《기독교》[Christian] Lent.

**사술(邪術)** witchcraft; black arts; an evil trick. じゃじゅつ

**사슬** a chain 《개를 매는》a tether／~ 고리 a link／ ~에 묶다 chain. てつのくさり

**사슴** a deer(*pl.* deer); 《수컷》a stag 《암컷》a hind／ ~ 가죽 deer skin／ ~ 고기 venison／ ~뿔 an antler. しか

**사습(私習)** self-study; self-culture.

**사승(史乘)** a history book. しじょう

**사승(四乘)** 《수》the fourth power.

**사시(四時)** the four seasons 《부사적》all the year round; throughout the year; at all seasons [of the year]. しき

**사시(斜視)** a side glance; squint eyes／ ~하다 look askance[sidewise] at (*a person*)／왼쪽 눈이 ~다 have a cast in the left eye. しゃし

**사시(史詩)** a historical poem. しし

**사시나무** 《식》a poplar／~ 떨듯 하다 tremble like an aspen leaf. やまならし

**사시 장청(四時長青)** ~하다 (be) evergreen; verdant at all seasons.

**사시 장춘(四時長春)** 《늘 봄이다》everlasting spring／~하다 《늘 봄》be spring all the year round 《잘 지내다》be well-off.

**사식(私食)** meals sent in to a prisoner at private[his own] expenses. さしいれのしょくじ

**사신**(私信) a private letter[message]; a private communication. ししん

**사신**(使臣) an envoy; an ambassador. ししん

**사신**(邪神) a false god; an evil deity; a demon; a devil. じゃしん

**사실**(史實) a historical fact. しじつ

**사실**(事實) a fact; an actual fact **(진실)** truth/확고한 ~ an established fact/기정의 ~ an accomplished fact/ ~상 in fact; actually; really; as a matter of fact. じじつ

**사실**(査實) a survey of the fact; an actual inspection.

**사실**(寫實) realism/ ~적[으로] realistic-[ally]; graphic[ally]/ ~주의 realism/ ~주의자 realist. しゃじつ

**사실**(私室) a private room. ししつ

**사심**(私心) selfishness; self-interest; a selfish motive/ ~이 없는 unselfish; disinterested. ししん

**사심**(邪心) evil mind; malicious intention/ ~에 찬 full of malice. じゃしん

**사십**(四十) forty/ ~대(代)다 be in one's forties. しじゅう

**사악**(邪惡) wrong; evil; vice/ ~하다 (be) wicked; vicious; evil; wrong. じゃあく

**사안**(私案) one's private plan. しあん

**사안**(史眼) a historical view.

**사암**(砂岩) 【지】 sandstone. さがん

**사약**(死藥) a deadly drug; poison.

**사약**(賜藥) bestowal of poison as a death penalty/ ~하다 give[bestow] poison (to one) as a death penalty.

**사양**(斜陽) the setting sun; the evening sun shine[lights]. しゃよう

**사양**(飼養) raising; breeding; keeping / ~하다 raise; keep; breed/ ~자 a keeper; a breeder / ~장 a farm **(목축용)** a ranch. しよう

**사양**(辭讓) **(사퇴)** declination; declining **(겸양)** reserve; deference; modesty/ ~하다 decline; excuse oneself (from); refrain[keep] from; stand on ceremony/ ~하지 않고[말고] freely; unreservedly; without ceremony[reserve]. えんりょ

**사양채** 【식】 Anthriscus Sylvestris(학명).

**사어**(私語) **(은근한 얘기)** secret talk; a private talk **(속삭임)** whisper[ing]/ ~하다 talk secretly; whisper. しご

**사어**(死語) a dead language **(폐어)** an obsolete word. しご

**사업**(事業) **(일)** work; a task **(기업)** an enterprise; undertaking; a project **(상업)** business **(실업)** [a line of] business **(산업)** an industry **(사적)** an achievement; a deed/교육[사회] ~ educational[social] work/ ~가 an enterprising man **(기업가)** an industrialist/~ 연도 a business year/ ~비 working expenses/ ~에 성공[실패]하다 succeed[fail] in business. じぎょう

**사역**(使役) employment; work; service/ ~하다 employ; use; set (one) to work /~ 동사 **(문)** a causative verb. しえき

**사연**(事緣) circumstances; the matter; the case. じゆう

**사연**(辭緣) content[s] **(의미)** import **(대강)** the gist.

**사열**(四列) four lines[rows]/ ~로 행진하다 go[march] by fours.

**사열**(査閱) inspection/ ~하다 inspect; examine / ~관 an examiner **(교련의)** an inspecting officer. さえつ

**사염화**(四鹽化) 【화】 tetrachloride.

**사영**(私營) private operation[management]/ ~의 private. しえい

**사영**(射影) 【수】 projection/ ~ 기하학 projective geometry. しゃえい

**사영**(斜影) a slanting shadow. しゃえい

**사오**(四五) four or five/ ~ 일 four or five days; several days.

**사옥**(社屋) the building [of a company]. しゃおく

**사욕**(私慾) self-interest; selfishness/ ~ 있는 selfish; interested/ ~없는 unselfish; disinterested. しよく

**사욕**(邪慾) **(못된 욕심)** an evil desire; a selfish ambition **(육욕)** an evil passion; a sinful lust. じゃよく

**사용**(私用) private[personal] use **(용무)** private[personal] business/ ~하다 turn to private use; appropriate to oneself/ ~으로 가다 go on private business. しよう

**사용**(使用) use; employment/ ~하다 use; employ; apply/ ~법 use; how to use; directions/ ~료 rent; hire/ ~인 an employee; a hired person〈미〉/ ~량 the amount used. しよう

**사용**(社用) company business/ ~으로 on business. しゃよう

**사우**(祠宇) a shrine. しう

**사우**(社友) **(동료)** a colleague **(사의 관계자)** a "friend" of the firm. しゃゆう

**싸우다** ①**(투쟁하다)** fight (with, for, against); struggle (with, against); combat (with); engage in battle **(다투다)** contend with/적과 ~ engage with one's enemy/곤란과 ~ fight against difficulties/유혹과 ~ struggle with temptation ②**(쟁론하다)** [have a] quarrel; wrangle **(손찌검하다)** come to blows **(불화하다)** be at variance[discord] (with); be at issue/…의 원인으로 ~ quarrel with (one) over. あらそう

**싸움** ①**(투쟁)** a fight **(전투)** a battle **(교전)** an engagement **(격투)** a combat **(맞붙어 싸우기)** a scuffle **(전쟁)** a war; warfare **(시합)** a contest/ ~하다 fight a battle; engage in a battle; wage[make] war on/인생의 ~ the battle of life /노자간의 ~ a struggle between capital and labour/ ~을 좋아하는 warlike / ~에 이기다 win[gain] a battle[the day] ②**(말다툼)** a quarrel; a wrangle; a row **(논쟁)** a dispute; an argument

**싸움터** 《논전》 a controversy 《분쟁》 a trouble/ ~하다 have a quarrel[dispute]/집안 ~ a family fight; an internal trouble / ~거리 the apple of discord/~을 걸다 seek a quarrel.

**싸움터** a battlefield; a scene of carnage.

**싸움판** the scene of a quarrel[fight].

**싸움패**(-牌) hoodlums; roughs.

**사원**(私怨) a personal[private] grudge[spite, enemity]/~을 품다 have a grudge against (one); bear (one) malice.

**사원**(社員) a member; an employee; a clerk 《총칭》 the staff.

**사원**(寺院) a [Buddhist] temple; a monastery; a church.

**사월**(四月) April; the fourth month of the year.

**사위**[1] 《서랑》 a son-in-law; a bridegroom.

**사위**[2] 《꺼림》 abominating[avoiding] anything new as an ill omen[a portent].

**사위**(四圍) surrounding; environment; environs; neighbourhood.

**사위**(詐僞) betraying one's conscience; falsehood; deception.

**사위다** burn up; burn to nothing; go die[out].

**사위스럽다** weigh on one's mind; be ominous; be abominable.

**사유**(私有) private ownership[possession] / ~의 privately-owned/ ~물[재산] private possessions[property].

**사유**(思惟) thinking/ ~하다 think[speculate] about consider.

**사유**(事由) a reason; a cause; a ground; conditions.

**사유**(赦宥) forgiveness; pardon/ ~하다 forgive; pardon.

**사육**(飼育) breeding (of cattle); raising /~하다 raise; rear; breed; keep; bring up/~자 a fancier; a breeder/ ~장 a farm.

**사육제**(謝肉祭) the carnival.

**사은**(私恩) personal obligations.

**사은**(謝恩) expression of gratitude; repaying a kindness/ ~회 a testimonial dinner.

**사은**(師恩) the favo[u]r of one's master; one's obligation to one's master.

**사음**(舍音) a land owner's agent.

**사음**(邪淫) lasciviousness; immorality; lewdness 《간통》 adultery.

**사의**(私意) self-will; a selfish motive; one's own will.

**사의**(私議) private discussion (of a thing) / ~하다 discuss (a matter) in private.

**사의**(謝意) ①《감사》 thanks; gratitude; appreciation ②《사죄의 뜻》 apology/ ~를 표하다 offer one's apology.

**사의**(辭意) 《사퇴할 마음》 one's intention to resign/ ~를 표시하다 hint at resignation to resign.

**사이**[1] ①《공간》 interval(간격); space 《거리》 distance/ ~에 《둘의》 between 《셋 이상의》 among 《통하여》 through 《한가운데》 amidst/ 10미터 ~를 두고 at intervals of 10 metres/ ~를 두다 leave a space (for) ②《시간》 interval; time/ ~에 《공간》 between 《하는 동안》 while/외출한 ~에 while one is out/어느 ~에 before one knows ③《관계》 relations/ ~에 among; between/ ~가 틀리다 estranged; alienated/ ~에 들다 mediate between (two parties); act as go-between / ~를 가르다 separate; estrange/ ~가 좋다[나쁘다] be on good[bad] terms (with).

**사이**[2] 《목재량의 단위》 a sai (207.36 cubic inches).

**싸이다** be[get] wrapped; be covered; be enveloped.

**사이비**(似而非) false; sham; make-believe; pretended/ ~ 학자 a pretended scholar; a charlatan.

**사이사이** 《공간》 spaces (between); intervals; gaps; distances.

**사이참**(-站) 《휴식》 a rest 《휴게 시간》 recess; an intermission; a break.

**사익**(私益) self-interest ⇒사리(私利).

**사인**(私人) a private person.

**사인**(死因) the cause of death/ ~ 통계 statics of death causes.

**사인**(私印) a private seal; a signet/ ~ 위조 forgery of a private seal.

**사인교**(四人轎) a four-man palanquin.

**사인조**(四人組) a quarter; a foursome.

**사임**(辭任) resignation ⇒사직/~하다 resign (one's post).

**사자**(四者) ~[간]의 quadripartite.

**사자**(死者) a dead person; the deceased 《총칭》 the dead 《사고에 의한》 the fatalities; loss of life.

**사자**(私資) private funds.

**사자**(使者) a messenger.

**사자**(寫字) copying; transcription.

**사자**(獅子) a lion 《암컷》 a lioness.

**사자**(嗣子) an heir 《여자》 an heiress; a successor.

**사자후**(獅子吼) 《열변》 harangue; fiery eloquence.

**사장**(沙場) a sandbank; a bar; a shoal; a sandy beach; the sands.

**사장**(社長) the president of a company the director.

**사장**(死藏) ~하다 hoard; keep (a thing); idle; keep idle on stock.

**사장**(師匠, 師丈) a teacher; a master.

**사장**(査丈) senior relatives by marriage.

**사장**(師長) teachers and elders.

**사장**(射場) a shooting[firing] range; a target practice range.

**사장**(寫場) a photo[graphic] studio[atelier]. しゃじょう
**사장**(謝狀) a letter of appreciation[thanks].
**사장**(社葬) a company funeral.
**사재**(私財) private means[funds]. しざい
**사재**(社債) a company's property; a firm's assets. しゃさい
**사재발쑥** 〖식〗 mugwort.
**사저**(私邸) one's private residence. してい
**사적**(史的) historic[al]／~ 고찰 historical researches. してき
**사적**(史蹟) a historic[al] spot[place]; a place of historical interest. しせき
**사적**(史積) historical works. しせき
**사적**(私的) (being) personal; private／~ 생활 private[home] life. してき
**사적**(事績) 《업적》an achievement; an accomplishment; a deed 《공적》services; merits. じせき
**사적**(事蹟) an evidence; a trace; a vestige. じせき
**사적**(射的) a target; a mark. しゃてき
**사전**(私田) privately-owned fields. してん
**사전**(私錢) counterfeit money[coin]／~ 군·a counterfeiter; a coiner.
**사전**(私電) a private telegram. してん
**사전**(死戰) a death struggle; a desperate fight[struggle]／~하다 fight desperately. しせん
**사전**(謝電) a telegram of thanks.
**사전**(事前) ~에 before the fact 《미리》beforehand; in advance／~ 검열 pre-censorship. じぜん
**사전**(辭典) a dictionary; a lexicon; a wordbook／~을 찾다 look up (a word) in a dictionary; consult[refer] a dictionary. じてん
**사절**(四節) the four seasons ⇨사철. しき
**사절**(四折) a quarto; being folded in four／~하다 fourfold; folded in four.
**사절**(死絕) ~하다 be extinct 《사멸》die out. しぜつ
**사절**(使節) 《일행》a mission 《일인》an envoy; an ambassador／미국으로부터의 방한 경제~ an American economic mission to Korea. しせつ
**사절**(謝絕) denial; refusal／~하다 excuse oneself (from); refuse; decline; deny; turn down／외상 ~ "No Credit allowed". しゃぜつ
**사정**(使丁) a servant; a school[an office] servant; a janitor(미). こつかい
**사정**(私情) personal[private] feelings／~을 두다 be influenced by personal sentiment; be partial. しじょう
**사정**(事情) ①《처지·곡절》circumstances; conditions; reasons 《형세》the state of things[matters, affairs]／식량 ~ food situation／자세한 ~ the details; the whole circumstances／~이 허락하는 한 as far as circumstances permit／부득이한 ~이 있어서 for some unavoidable reasons; under unavoidable circumstances ②《하소연》~하다 beg for one's favour[pardon]; supplicate／~없다 be merciless[relentless]. じじょう
**사정**(邪正) right and wrong; justice and evil. じゃしょう
**사정**(査定) assessment; revision／~하다 assess; revise／~액 an assessment; a revision. さてい
**사정**(射程) a [shooting] range／유효 ~ the effective range.
**사정**(射精) ejaculation／~하다 emit semen; ejaculate／~관(管) an ejaculatory duct. しゃせい
**사정사정** pleadingly; pleading one's case; imploringly／~하다 implore; plead (for); beseech; appeal (to, for).
**사정없다**(事情—) (be) merciless; unsparing; relentless; severe; ruthless. たのみにたのんで
**사제**(司祭) 《카톨릭》a priest; an officiant; a pastor. しさい
**사제**(私製) private[illicit] manufacture／~의 privately made／~ 담배 privately made cigarettes／~품 privately made goods; an article of private manufacture. しせい
**사제**(舍弟) ①《자기 아우》my younger brother ②《형에게》me; I who am your younger brother. しゃてい
**사제**(師弟) teacher and pupil; master and disciple／~간 the relationship between teacher and pupil. してい
**사제**(瀉劑) 〖의〗 a laxative.
**사조**(—調) 〖음〗[the key of] G／사장[단]조 [a sonata in] G major[minor].
**사조**(査照) an investigation; a survey; a check／~하다 investigate; survey; check.
**사조**(思潮) the trend[current] of thought; the drift of public opinion／근대 ~ modernism／시대 ~ the spirit of the time[s]. しちょう
**사조**(詞藻) 《문체》rhetorical flourishes 《시문》prose and poetry.
**사족**(四足) ①《네 발》four legs ②《사지》the limbs／~을 못 쓰다 be spellbound; be crazy (about)／~발이, ~백이 a horse with all four hooves white. しそく
**사족**(蛇足) a superfluity; a redundancy／~을 가하다 make an unnecessary addition; add a fifth wheel. だそく
**사족**(士族) a descendant of a noble family／~ 출신이다 come of a noble family. しぞく
**사졸**(士卒) a private ⇨군사(軍士).
**사종**(四從) a fourth cousin.
**사죄**(死罪) a capital crime[offense]; a crime punishable with death 《사형》crime punishment. しざい
**사죄**(赦罪) 《용서·사면》pardon; remission 《천주교》absolution／~하다 pardon; remit (a punishment); absolve (a person from[of]). しゃざい
**사죄**(謝罪) [an] apology／~하다 apolog-

**사주**(使嗾) instigation/ ~하다 instigate; incite; egg (one) on/ …의 ―로 instigated by (one)/ ~하여 반란을 일으키다 incite to rebellion. しゃざい

**사주**(砂洲) a sand-bar[-bank];(하구 등의) a delta. さす

**사주**(四柱) fate/~ 팔자 one's lot; destiny; fate/~ 장이 a fortuneteller; a diviner. しかくちゅう

**사주**(私鑄) counterfeit coinage/ ~하다 counterfeit; forge [coins]. しちゅう

**사주**(社主) the head[proprietor] of a firm[company].

**사주체**(斜柱體) an oblique cylinder. しゃちゅうたい

**사주 팔자**(四柱八字) **《운수》** destiny; one's lot **《행운》** fortune; kismet/ ~가 좋다[세다] be born under a lucky[an unlucky] star; be born with good[bad] destiny.

**사중**(四重) ~주[창] a quartet[te] / 현악 ~주 a string quartet. しじゅう

**사증**(査證) visé(F); visa/~하다 visé; endorse/ ~료 the visé fee/ ~한 visé'd; visa'd. さしょう

**사지**(四肢) the limbs; the legs and arms; the members. したい

**사지**(死地) the jaws of death; a fatal position/ ~로 들어가다[를 벗어나다] go into[escape from] the jaws of death/ ~ 속에 활로를 찾아 seek salvation by taking a desperate step. しち

**사지**(邪智) perverted talent; craft; wiles. じゃち

**사지춤** a dance with a lion's mask.

**사지코** a pug[snub] nose / ~의 pug[snub] nosed.

**사직**(司直) the judicial authorities **《법관》** a judge **《총칭》** the bench. しちょく

**사직**(社稷) the guardian deities of the State **《국가》** the State/ ~지신 a pillar of the State. しゃしょく

**사직**(辭職) resignation/ ~하다 resign; resign [from] office; give up one's office; quit[leave] office / ~자 a resigner/ ~을 강요하다 urge[call upon] (one) to resign. じしょく

**사진**(仕進) attendance at office; going to office ⇒출근(出勤)/ ~하다 attend one's office; present oneself; go on duty. ししん

**사진**(沙塵) dust/ ~을 일으키다 raise a cloud of dust/지독한 ~이군 How dusty it is! さじん

**사진**(寫眞) a photograph; a photo; a picture 《스냅》 a snapshot/ ~첩 a photograph album / ~틀 a picture frame/ ~판 a photogravure(요판(凹版)); a phototype(철판(凸版))/ ~기 a camera; a kodak/ ~관 a photographic studio/ ~사 a photographer/ ~반 newspaper cameramen/ ~ 도락 a photofad[hobby]/천연색 ~ a [natural] colour photograph/ ~ 결혼 a picture-bride marriage/~을 찍다 take a photograph of; photograph (남이 찍게 하다) have one's picture taken. しゃしん

**사질**(舍姪) my nephew. じぶんのおい

**사차**(四次) ~의 biquadratic [equation]/ ~원 the fourth dimension / ~ 방정식 a biquadratic equation / ~식 a quartic.

**사찬**(賜饌) a state banquet at the court.

**사찰**(寺刹) a temple ⇒절. じさつ

**사찰**(私札) a private letter. こじんのたより

**사찰**(査察) inspection; investigation/ ~하다 inspect; investigate / ~과 a thought control section; an inspection section. ささつ

**사창**(私娼) **《업》** unlicensed prostitution **《사람》** an unlicensed prostitute; a streetwalker/ ~굴 a house of ill-fame; a brothel/ ~ 검색을 하다 hunt up unlicensed prostitutes. ししょう

**사창**(紗窓) a gauze window.

**사채**(私債) a personal debt; private liabilities/ ~ 동결 loan freeze. しさい

**사채**(社債) a bond; a debenture/ ~권 a bond; a debenture bond/ ~를 발행하다 issue bonds[debentures]. しゃさい

**사책**(史冊) a history book. しさく

**사처**(死處) where to die; a place where one should die/ ~를 얻다 die[lay down one's life] to some purpose.

**사천** (몰래 모은) pin money (개인 돈) private funds. おんなのへそくり

**사천왕**(四天王) the Four Devas; the Big Paladins. してんのう

**사철**(四―) the four seasons; seasons of the year (부사적으로) throughout the year; all the year round. しき

**사철**(私鐵) a private line; a privately owned railway. してつ

**사철**(砂鐵) 《광》 iron sand. さてつ

**사철나무** 《식》 a spindle-tree. もちのき

**사철쑥** 《식》 *Artemisia capillaris*(학명). かわらよもぎ

**사체**(四體) the limbs; members. したい

**사체**(死體) a [dead] body; a corpse (동물의) a carcass ⇒시체(屍體). したい

**사초**(莎草) ①《식》 a nut grass ②(잔디) lawn; turf ③(잔디입히기) turfing a tomb/~하다 turf a tomb.

**사촌**(四寸) a [first] cousin. いとこ

**사춘기**(思春期) adolescence; [the age of] puberty/ ~의 pubescent/ ~의 소녀 an adolescent girl; a girl at puberty/ ~에 달하다 reach puberty. ししゅんき

**사출**(射出) emission; shooting out/ ~하다 shoot out; project; emit; radiate 《항공》 catapult/ ~기(機) 《비행기의》 catapult. しゃしゅつ

**사춤** ①(틈) a crack; a cleft; a chasm; a split ②(흙메우기) stuffing[stopping

사취(砂嘴) 〖지〗a sand bank[bar].

사취(詐取) fraud; swindle/~하다 obtain by fraud; swindle money from one); defraud (one of a thing)/돈을 ~하다 obtain money by false pretences; swindle money.

사치(奢侈) luxury; extravagance/ ~하다 be extravagant (in food, etc.); indulge in luxury/ ~품 a luxury; a luxurious article/ ~스러운 l uxurious; extravagant/ ~하는 사람 an extravagant person; a high liver. しゃし

사칙(四則) 〖수〗the four operations[rules] in arithmetic. しそく

사칙(社則) the [company's] regulations

사친회(師親會) a Parent-Teacher Association(略: P. T. A.)

사칭(詐稱) false assumption/ ~하다 assume another's name/~하에 on false prete. さしょう

사타구니 the groin.

사탑(斜塔) ¶ 피사의 ~ the Leaning Tower of Pisa.

사탕(砂糖) ①〖설탕〗sugar/모~ lump[cube] sugar/얼음 ~ sugar[rock] candy / ~ 수수 the sugar cane/ ~ 무우 the white beet; the sugar beet/ ~을 친 sugared ②〖과자〗sweets; candy/눈깔 ~ toffees. さとう

사탕 발림(砂糖—) sugar-coated words; cajolery; flattery 《감언》honeyed words / ~하다 flatter; cajole; coax with honeyed words. かんげんでつること

사태(死胎) a dead f[o]etus/ ~ 분만 a still birth. したい

사태(沙汰) ①〖산 따위의〗a landslip; a landslide ②〖많음〗a flood 《풍부》superabundance/사람 ~ a flood of overflowing people; crowds/편지~ an influx of letters. さた

사태(事態) a matter; a situation; the state[position] of affairs[things]/극동의 새로운 ~ the new situation in the Far East/ ~를 알다 realize the situation. じたい

사택(私宅) one's home; one's private house[residence]. したく

사택(社宅) a company's house (for its employees). しゃたく

사토(沙土) sandy soil.

사통(私通) ①〖밀통〗illicit intercourse; [illicit] liaisons/~하다 misconduct oneself with ②〖편지〗unofficial correspondence between officials. しつう

사통 오달(四通五達) ~하다 run[radiate, stretch] in all directions.

사퇴(仕退) leaving office/ ~하다 leave [withdraw from] office. たいきん

사퇴(辭退) ①〖사양〗declination; refusal / ~하다 decline (an offer); refuse to accept ②〖퇴거〗withdrawal; leave-taking/ ~하다 take one's leave; leave; retire[withdraw] (from). じたい

사투(私鬪) a personal[private] strife/ ~하다 strive[fight] privately.

사투(死鬪) a [life or] death struggle/ ~하다 fight desperately; struggle for life. しとう

사투리 a dialect; a brogue 《와전》a corruption/지방[고향] ~ one's provincialism. ほうげん

사특(邪慝) viciousness/~한 wicked; vicious/ ~하다 (be) wicked; vicious; sinister. よこしまでわるいこと

사팔눈 a squint[-eye]; cross eyes 《심하지 않은》a cast in the eye/ ~의 squint[cross]-eyed. やぶにらみ

사팔뜨기 《안쪽으로 보는》a cross-eyed man 《바깥쪽으로 보는》a wall-eyed man. やぶにらみのひと

사포(砂布) sandpaper; emery-[glass-]paper. かみやすり

사표(師表) a model; a pattern; a paragon/세상의 ~ a model character. しひょう

사표(辭表) a written resignation; a letter of resignation/~를 제출하다 tender [give in] one's resignation/ ~를 철회하다[각하하다] withdraw[turn down] one's resignation. じひょう

사푼 softly; with a soft[muffled] step; lightly/ ~사푼 걸어가다 walk lightly; go with soft steps; tread softly. そっと

사품 《겨를》time; leisure 《기회》a chance; an opportunity. ひま

사풋 with a light-footed step. そっと

사풍(邪風) rash conduct and speech; imprudent words; indecent behaviour; indecent manners/ ~맞다[스럽다] (be) out-rageous.

사풍(砂風) a sandstorm.

사필 귀정(事必歸正) Right will prevail in the end.

사하다(赦—) forgive; pardon; excuse; remit; absolve. つみをゆるす

사학(史學) history [as science]; historical science/ ~자 a historian. しがく

사학(私學) ①〖사설 학교〗a private school ②〖자기 학설〗one's own theory [doctrine]. しがく

사학(斯學) this study; this field; the subject/ ~의 권위 an authority on the subject. しがく

사항(事項) 《일》matters; subjects 《항목》items; articles; particulars/ 조사 ~ matters for investigation/회의 ~ an agendum (pl. -da); a program《미》/주요 ~ a main point. じこう

사해(四海) the four seas; the seven seas 《천하》the whole world/ ~ 동포 the brotherhood of mankind; universal fraternity. しかい

사해(死海) 《중동의 염호》the Dead Sea.

사해(死骸) a dead body; a corpse; remains. しがい

사행(私行) ①〖행위〗one's private conduct [doing] ②〖여행〗a private[personal] tr-

사행(射倖) speculation; adventure／～심 a speculative[gambling] spirit. しゃこう

사행(蛇行) meandering／～하다 snake along; go zigzag; meander; crawl meanderingly. じゃこう

사향(思鄕) yearning for *one's* home; homesickness; nostalgia／～하다 yearn for *one's* home; think of *one's* native home／～병 nostalgia; homesickness. しきょう

사향(麝香) musk／～수 musk water／～초〖식〗a wild thyme. じゃこう

사혈(死血) virulent blood; impure blood. どすくろいち

사혈(瀉血) depletion／～하다 deplete [blood]／～제(劑) depletive.

사혐(私嫌) private malice; a personal grudge; personal spite. してきなけんぎ

사형(私刑) lynch; lynching／～을 가하다 lynch (one). しけい

사형(舎兄) 〖형〗my elder brother (아우에게) I. しゃけい

사형(死刑) death penalty[sentence]; capital punishment／～ 선고 sentence of death; a capital sentence／～ 집행인 an executioner; a hangman／～수 a criminal under sentence of death; a condemned man／～죄 a capital offence／ ～에 처하다 put to death; execute; condemn to death. しけい

사형(詞兄) Mr …; you sir. しけい

사화(士禍) the massacre of scholars; the calamity of literati／갑자 ～ the *kabcha* calamity of savants.

사화(史話) a historical tale[story]. れきしものがたり

사화(死貨) dead money; a dead coin. しか

사화(私和) ①(화해) reconciliation／～하다 be reconciled (*with*); make peace ② (송사의) settlement out of court; a private settlement／～하다 settle (*a matter*) out of court. わかい

사화산(死火山) an extinct[a dead] volcano. しかさん

사환(使喚) a servant; a [shop] boy; an errand boy. きゅうじ

사활(死活) life and[or] death／～ 문제 a matter of life and[or] death. しかつ

사회(司會) chairmanship (사회자) a chairman／～하다 preside at[over]; take the chair／～자 the chairman; a master of ceremonies. しかい

사회(死灰) cinders; ashes. しかい

사회(社會) society; the community (세계) the world (공중) the public／～의 social; public／～적인 social／～적 계급 social rank[scale]／상류[하류] ～ high [low] society／～ 경제 social economy ／～ 교육 social education／～ 구조 social structure[organization]／～ 문제 a social problem／～ 사업 social work; public-welfare service／～ 운동 a social movement.／～인 a social being; a member of society／ ～ 인류학 social anthropology／～장(葬) a public funeral ／～ 정세 social conditions／～ 제도 the social system／～ 조직 social structure[organization]／～주의 socialism ／～ 길드 ~주의 Guild socialism／수정 ~주의 revised socialism／～ 질서 public[social] order／～학 sociology／ ～학자 a sociologist／～ 혁명 a social revolution／～화 a social phenomenon／～화 socialization／인간 ～ human society／일반 ～ the general public; the public in general[at large]／문명 ～ a civilized community／봉건[시민] ～ feudal[civic] society. しゃかい

사후(死後) ～의 after death; future; posthumous／～에 after *one's* death; posthumously／～ 강직(强直) stiffening after death. しご

사후(事後) ～의 after the fact; *ex post facto*(L)／～에 after the fact; *post factum*(L)／～ 승낙 *ex post facto* approval[consent]. じご

사후(伺候) ～하다 wait upon (*one*); pay *one's* respects to; go to／궁중에 ～하다 go[proceed] to the Palace. しこう

사흗날 the third [day of the month]／ 4월 ～ the third of April. みっか

사흘 ①(3일) three days／～째 the third day／～걸러 every fourth day ②⇒사흗날. みっか

삭¹ (베는 모양) at a stroke／～ 베다 cut at a stroke (모두) completely; all; thoroughly／～ 변하다 change completly ／～ 쓸다 sweep out. さっと

싹² ①(씨앗의) a sprout; a shoot／～트다 sprout; put forth shoots; bud ② ⇒싹트. め

삭(朔) 〖달〗a month／사오～ several months. さく

삭갈다 〖농〗plow[plough〈영〉] just once [before transplanting rice plants].

삭감(削減) reduction; curtailment; retrenchment／～하다 curtail; retrench; reduce; cut[down]; slash. さくげん

삭거(削去) elimination; cancellation; striking out／～하다. eliminate; cancel; strike out; erase. けずってしまうこと

삭과(蒴果) 〖식〗a capsule.

삭다 ①(소화하다) be digested; digest ② (썩다) decompose; crumble; moulder; decay ③(종기가) get resolved ④(마음이) melt away; calm down; be appeased ⑤(익다) get ripe; ripen; mellow (술 따위) ferment ⑥(품어지다) become sloppy. くちる

싹둑거리다 snip; mince; chop／싹둑 snip-snip. ほそかくきる

삭막(索莫, 索漠) ～하다 (be) vague; dim; obscure; indistinct／～한 기억 vague remembrance; a faint recollection[memory]. さくばく

삭망(朔望) 〖천〗syzygy; the first and

fifteenth days of the lunar month.   さくぼう
**삭모**(槊毛) decorative tassels.
**삭발**(削髮) hair cutting 《체발》 tonsure/ ~하다 have *one's* hair cut; have *one's* hair tonsured.   さくはつ
**싹** Q~ 빌다 supplicate[beg *one's* pardon] with joined hands.   もみもみ
**싹싹하다** (be) affable; amiable.
**싹수** Q ~가 노랗다 be hopeless; have no prospect of.   ぜんと
**삭월**(朔月) the new moon.   しんげつ
**삭월세**(朔月貰) a house rent by the month; monthly rent.
**삭이다** digest/잘 먹고 잘 ~ eat well and digest well.   しょうかさせる
**삭일**(朔日) the first day of a lunar month.   さくじつ
**삭정이** dead branches on a tree; a withered twig[sprays].
**삭제**(削除) elimination; erasure; cancellation; expurgation / ~하다 eliminate; erase; cancel.   さくじょ
**삭치다**(削一) 《없애다》 cancel; erase; cross [mark] out; void; nullify 《맞비기다》 s-ettle (*accounts*); balance (*books*).
**삭탈 관직**(削奪官職) deposition of *one's* office.
**싹트다** bud; sprout; put forth shoot; germinate; (*a matter*) begin to develop.   めがでる
**삭풍**(朔風) the north wind; of winter a wind from the north.   さくふう
**삭히다** 《소화하다》 digest; make (*a thing*) ripe; mellow 《발효하다》 cause to ferment 《풀기 따위를》 resolve.
**삯** 《요금》 charge 《삯삯》 fare 《운송료》 carriage; freight 《품삯》 wages; pay; hire 《보수》 remuneration; a reward/~전 wages; pay / ~짐 a load / ~품 wage labo[u]r / ~군 a wage earner; a hired man / ~바느질 needle work for pay.   ろうちん
**산**(山) ① a mountain; Mt. (관두에 붙이는 약자); 《동산》 a hill 《고지》 a height 《봉우리》 a peak / 백두 ~ Mt. *Backdoo* / ~꼭대기 the top[summit] of a mountain / ~줄기 a chain of mountains ② a grave : 산소(山所).   やま
**산**(算) 《계산》 computation; reckoning; calculation 《수》 number / ~놓다 compute; reckon; calculate; count; number.   けいさん
**산**(酸) an acid / ~의 acid / ~류 acids.   さん
**-산**(産) 《산출》 production 《산물》 a product / 외국~ foreign-made.   ―さん
**산가**(山家) a cottage in a mountain; a mountain house.   さんか
**산가**(産家) a house delivered of a child.
**산가지**(算一) a counting stick[block]; 《점치는》 a divining stick.
**산각**(山脚) the foot of a mountain.   やまのふもと

**산간**(山間) ~의[에] among[in] the mountains; place among the mountains / ~ 벽촌 a mountain village.   さんかん
**산감독**(山監督) 《산림의》 a forest ranger 《광산의》 a mine superintendent. ばっさい
**싼값** cheap price / ~으로 물건을 사다 buy a thing cheap; make a good bargain.   れんか
**산개**(散開) extension; development 《군대의》 deployment / ~하다 extend; form in open[extended] order.   さんかい
**산거**(山居) dwelling in the mountains / ~하다 live[dwell] in the mountains.   さんきょ
**산경**(山景) mountain scenery.   さんけい
**산계**(山系) a mountain system; a mountain chain[range] / 알프스 ~ the system of the Alps.   さんけい
**산고**(産故) childbirth; delivery.
**산고**(産苦) birth pangs; labo[u]r pains.
**산고양이**(山一) 《동》 a wild cat.
**산곡**(山谷) a mountain valley : 산골짜기.   さんこく
**산꼭대기**(山一) the mountain top; the top [summit] of a mountain.   さんちょう
**산골**(山一) a remote[secluded] place in [among] the mountains.   さんかん
**산골짜기**(山一) a ravine; a gorge; a glen.   たに
**산과**(産科) obstetrics / ~ 병원 a maternity hospital / ~ 의사 《여자》 an accoucheuse 《남자》 an accoucheur / ~학 obstetrics; midwifery.   さんか
**산광**(散光) 《물》 scattered[diffused] light.   さんこう
**산국화**(山菊花) a wild chrysanthemum.   やまぎく
**산굴**(山窟) a mountain cave.
**산굽이**(山一) a mountain bend.
**산금**(山禽) a mountain bird.   やまどり
**산금**(産金) production of gold / ~하다 produce[mine] gold / ~ 지대 a gold field.   さんきん
**산기**(産期) the time of parturition / ~ 가 닥쳐온다 Her time is near.
**산기**(産氣) travail; labo[u]r 《진통》 pangs of childbirth / ~가 있다 begin to labor; begin to feel the pains of childbirth.   さんけ
**산기슭**(山一) the foot[base, bottom] of ,a mountain / ~에 at the foot[bottom] of a mountain; go along mountain road.   やますそ
**산길**(山一) a mountain road / ~을 가다 go along a mountain road.   やまみち
**산나물**(山一) edible mountain herbs / ~ 을 캐다 pick wild greens.   さんさい
**산놀이**(山一) a mountain excursion[picnic, hike].
**산놓다**(算一) calculate with sticks[on an abacus].   そろばんをはじく
**산다**(山茶) 《식》 a camellia tree.   さんちゃ
**산달**(山一) the higher[hilly] sections.   やまのあるところ

산달(産—) the month of giving birth.
산더미(山—) a heap; a pile; a great mass / ～ 같이 쌓인 a mountain[heap] of. やまなりにつまれたもの
산도(酸度) 【화】 acidity. さんど
산돼지(山—) 【동】 a wild hog; a wild boar. いのしし
산드러지다 (be) sprightly; vivacious; lighthearted; cheerful.
산득, 산뜩 with a sudden chill ⇒선득.
산들거리다 [the wind] blow cool and gentle. そよぐ
산들다 fail; go wrong[amiss]. ぜつぼうだ
산들바람 a gentle[light] breeze. そよかぜ
산들산들 gently; softly. そよそよ
산뜻하다 《선명하다》 (be) clear; fresh; vivid; bright 《보기 좋다》 (be) neat; tidy; trim; clear; smart; nice. あざやかだ
산등성이(山—) a [mountain] ridge / ～를 따라서 along the ridges. やまのせ
산디 【민】 a makeshift stage for a medi[a]eval masked drama.
산란(産卵) ～하다 lay egg[s]; 《물고기가》 spawn / ～기 a breeding season; spawning-time. さんらん
산란(散亂) ～하다 be scattered about; lie about in disorder. さんらん
산로(山路) a mountain road[path]. やまじ
산로(産勞) 《진통》 labour-pains; birth pangs; travail. しゅっさんのくるしみ
산록(山麓) the foot[base, bottom] of a mountain. さんろく
산류(酸類) 【화】 [the] acids. さんるい
산림(山林) a forest; woodlands / ～ 간수 a [forest] ranger / ～학 forestry; dendrology / ～ 보호 forest conservancy. さんりん
산마루(山—) a mountain ridge.
산막(山幕) a mountain lodge; a hut. やまごや
산만(散漫) ～하다 (be) diffuse; vague; desultory. さんまん
산말 a living language.
산망스럽다 (be) thoughtless; imprudent; flighty; flippant. けいそつだ
산매(散賣) retail sale; retailing / ～하다 [sell] retail. こうり
산맥(山脈) a chain of mountains; a mountain range / 알프스 ～ the Alps; the Alpine range. さんみゃく
산멱통 the live throat; the gullet. いんこう
산명(山鳴) a mountain rumbling. やまなり
산명 수려(山明水麗) beautiful scenery; scenic beauty. しぜんの美景
산모(産母) a woman in childbed; a woman in her confinement; a woman who delivered a child. さんぷ
산모롱이(山—) the spur of a mountain.
산모퉁이(山—) the spur of a mountain; the corner of a mountain foot.
산목숨 a life; a living creature. せいめい
산무애뱀 【동】 *Elaphe quadrivirgata* (학명). しろすじしまへび

산문(山門) 1.《산의 어귀》 the entrance of a mountain 2.《절의 문》 the gate of a Buddhist temple. さんもん
산문(産門) the vulva; the vagina. ほうもん
산문(散文) prose; prose writings / ～ 작가 a prose writer / ～체 prose style; prosaism / ～시 a prose-poem / ～적이 prosaic. さんぶん
산물(産物) d product; production 《총칭》 produce 《성과》 a product; a result / 주요 ～ staple products. さんぶつ
산미(産米) the rice produced. さんまい
산미(酸味) acidity; sourness. さんみ
산밑(山—) the foot[bottom, base] of a mountain. やまのした
산바람(山—) a mountain wind[blast]; a wind from the mountain 《산의 공기》 mountain air. やまかぜ
산발(散發) sporadic occurrence; scattered hits(야구의) / ～하다 occur sporadically. さんぱつ
산발(散髮) dishevelled hair / ～하다. become dishevelled. さんぱつ
산법(算法) arithmetic. さんぽう
산벼락 a horrible experience / ～맞다 undergo a horrible experience. ひどくびっくりすること
산벼랑(山—) a mountain cliff[precipice].
산병(散兵) a skirmisher 《일》 loose[extended] order / ～호 a shelter[fire] trench / ～선 a skirmish[ing] line. さんぺい
산보(散步) a walk; a stroll / ～하다 go [out] for a walk; take a walk[stroll]; take the air. さんぽ
산복(山腹) a mountainside; a hillside; the side of a mountain. さんぷく
산봉(山峰) a summit ▷산봉우리. さんぽう
산뽕나무(山—) a wild mulberry tree. やまくれ
산봉우리(山—) a peak; the summit[top] of a mountain. やまのね
산부(産婦) a woman in childbed. さんぷ
산부리(山—) a mountain crag[jutting out]; a spur.
산부인과(産婦人科) obstetrics and gynecology / ～ 의사 《산과》 an obstetrician 《부인과》 a gynecologist. さんふじんか
산부처 a living Buddha; a virtuous person. いきぼとけ
산불(山—) a forest[hill] fire.
산붕(山崩) a landslide; a landslip / ～하다 have a landslide. やまくずれ
산비(酸鼻) ～하다 (be) pitiable; sad / ～를 극한 very pitiable; disastrous. さんび
산비둘기(山—) 【조】 a wood pigeon; a ringdove. やまばと
산비탈(山—) the slope of a mountainside[hillside]; a steep mountain slope. やまのきゅうけいしゃめん
산사(山寺) a mountain temple. さんじ
산사(山査) 【식】 a hawthorn. さんざし
산사람(山—) a wild man [of the mountains]; a woodsman. やまびと

**산사태**(山沙汰) a landslide; a landfall.

**산삭**(產朔) the month of parturition [giving birth]; the last month of pregnancy. おうみのつき

**산삭**(刪削) elimination; erasure／ ～하다 eliminate; erase; cancel. さんさん

**산산이**(散散-) 《조각남》 to[in] pieces 《흩어짐》 scatteredly. さんさん

**산산조각**(散散―) q ～나다 be broken to pieces; be smashed to fragments.

**산산하다** (be) cool; refreshing ⇨선선하다. すずしい

**산삼**(山蔘) a wild ginseng.

**산상**(山上) ～의[에] on the top of a mountain[hill]／ ～ 수훈(垂訓) 《성경》 the Sermon on the Mount. さんじょう

**산새**(山-) a mountain bird. やまどり

**산색**(山色) mountain scenery; a hillscape. さんしょく

**산성**(山城) a mountain fortress; a castle on a mountain top. さんじょう

**산성**(酸性) acidity／ ～의 acid／ ～ 산화물 an acid oxide／ ～화하다 acidify; acidulate. さんせい

**산세**(山勢) geographical features of a mountain; the physical aspect of a mountain. さんせい

**산소**(山所) a grave; a tomb 《표소》 an ancestral graveyard. はかば

**산소**(酸素) 《화》 oxygen(略：O)／ ～ 화합물 an oxide／ ～ 요법 oxypathy／ ～ 흡입 oxygen inhalation／ ～ 용접 oxyacetylene welding. さんそ

**산소리** ～하다 do not yield (to); do not give in; talk big. ごうご

**산속**(山-) the recesses[heart] of a mountain.

**산송장** a living corpse; a decrepit person.

**산수**(山水) 《경치》 landscape; scenery 《산과 물》 mountains and waters／～화 a landscape painting. やまとみず

**산수**(算數) mathematics; calculation. さんすう

**산수소**(酸水素) oxyhydrogen／ ～ 용접 oxyhydrogen welding.

**산수화**(山水畵) 《화법》 landscape painting 《그림》 a landscape. さんすいが

**산술**(算術) arithmetic／ ～의 arithmetical. さんじゅつ

**산승**(山僧) a Buddhist priest living in the mountain. さんじのそう

**산식**(算式) 《수》 an arithmetic expression; a formula. さんしき

**산신**(山神) the god of a mountain. さんじん

**산신령**(山神靈) the god of mountain; the guardian spirit of a mountain. やまのかみ

**산실**(散失) get[be] scattered and lost; scatter and lose. さんしつ

**산실**(產室) a lying-in room; a maternity ward. さんしつ

**산아**(產兒) a newborn baby／ ～ 제한[조절] birth control. さんじ

**산악**(山岳) mountains／ ～회 in alpine society／ ～부 a mountaineering club／ ～병[전] mountain sickness[warfare]. さんがく

**산액**(產額) the yield (of rice); the output (of gold); the [amount of] production. さんがく

**산야**(山野) fields and mountains. さんや

**산약**(散藥) powder medicine; a medicinal powder. さんやく

**산양**(山羊) ①《염소》a goat ②《영양》an antelope. やぎ

**산언덕**(山-) a hillock; a hill; a mound. ひくいやま

**산언저리**(山-) the ridge of a mountain; the edge[brim] of a hill.

**산업**(産業) industry／ ～의 industrial／ ～계 the industrial world／ ～ 조합 an industrial guild／ ～ 혁명 the Industrial Revolution／ ～별 노동 조합 an industrial union／～ 자금 industrial funds／～ 도시 an industrial city. さんぎょう

**산역**(山役) tomb work; construction[repair] of a tomb／ ～하다 dig a grave／ ～꾼 a grave digger; a sexton. はかをつくるこうじ

**산욕**(産褥) childbed; confinement／ ～열 (熱) puerperal fever／ ～에 눕다 be in childbed; be lying-in. さんじょく

**산용**(山容) the figure[looks] of a mountain. さんよう

**산용 숫자**(算用數字) Arabic figures[numerals]. さんようすうじ

**산울림**(山-) an echo ⇨메아리. やまびこ

**산울타리** a living[growing] hedge.

**산원**(產院) a maternity[lyingin] hospital. さんいん

**산월**(產月) month of parturition ⇨산삭.

**산육**(產育) bearing and raising／ ～하다 bear and bring up. うみそだてること

**산음**(山陰) the shady side of a mountain: the northern side of a mountain. さんいん

**산읍**(山邑) a mountain town. やまなかのむら

**산인**(山人) mountain folks ⇨산사람.

**산인**(散人) a man in retirement[seclusion]; a man of leisure. さんじん

**산일**(散佚) getting[being] scattered and lost／ ～하나 get[be] scattered and lost. さんいつ

**산입**(算入) inclusion／～하다 include in: count[reckon] in. さんにゅう

**산자 수명**(山紫水明) beautiful scenery; scenic beauty. さんすいめい

**산장**(山莊) a mountain villa[retreat]; a hillside cottage. さんそう

**산재**(散在) being scattered; lying here and there／ ～하다 be[lie] scattered; be strewn; lie sporadically. さんざい

**산재**(散財) waste of money; a wasteful use of money; dissipation; extravagance／ ～하다 squander; run through one's fortune. さんざい

**산적**(山積) ~하다 form a mountain; accumulate; lie in a heap. さんせき

**산적**(散炙) skewered slices of seasoned meat/~꼬챙이에 꿰다 spit (meat).

**산적**(山賊) a bandit (pl. ~s, -ti); a brigand. さんぞく

**산적도둑**(散炙—) 《미식가》 an epicure; a gourmet 《딸》 one's married daughter.
よりこのみしてたべるひと

**산전**(山田) a field among hills.

**산전**(産前) before childbirth; before delivery. さんぜん

**산전 수전**(山戰水戰) 이~다 겪다 experience every sort of difficulties; go through the ups and downs of life.

**산정**(山亭) a mountain arbour. さんてい

**산정**(山頂) the summit[top] of a mountain. さんちょう

**산정**(算定) computation; calculation 《평가》 estimate/ ~하다 calculate 《평가하다》 estimate; appraise. さんてい

**산주**(山主) the owner of a mountain.
さんしゅ

**산줄기**(山—) a mountain range; a chain of mountains. さんみゃく

**산중**(山中) a mountain recess; the bosom of the hills/ ~에 among[in] the mountains. さんちゅう

**산지**(山地) a mountainous district; a hilly country. さんち

**산지**(産地) the place of production[origin]; 《동식물의》 the home 《말 따위의》 a breeding center 《식물의》 a growing district. さんち

**산지기**(山—) a [forest] ranger. やまもり

**산질**(散秩) odd volumes/~하다 get scattered; be incomplete.

**산짐승**(山—) mountain beasts; a wild beast. やまのけもの

**산채**(山菜) wild edible greens; edible mountain herbs. さんさい

**산채**(山寨) a mountain fastness[stronghold]; 《산적의》 a den of mountain bandits.

**산책**(散策) a walk; a stroll/~하다 take a walk; stroll; ramble. さんさく

**산천**(山川) mountains and rivers/ ~ 초목 nature; landscape. さんせん

**산초**(山椒) 《식》 Chinese pepper /~나무 a prickly ash. さんしょう

**산촌**(山村) a mountain village. さんそん

**산출**(産出) production; yield; output/ ~하다 produce; yield; bring forth; turn out. さんしゅつ

**산출**(算出) computation; calculation/~하다 compute; calculate; reckon/ ~된 세액 a calculated tax amount. さんしゅつ

**산칠**(山漆) 《식》 a wild lacquer tree.
やまうるし

**산코골다** pretend to snore.
ねむったふりをする

**산탄**(霰彈) case shot; slugs 《알이 굵은》 buckshot 《유산탄》 a shrapnel/ ~총 a shotgun. あめあられのようなだんがん

**산턱**(山—) the crest of a mountain.

**산토끼**(山—) 《동》 a hare; a wild rabbit; a jack-rabbit. やまうさぎ

**산통**(算筒) a divining-stick case/ ~ 깨뜨리다 spoil; ruin (a scheme, a plot, etc); put a spoke in one's wheel.

**산파**(産婆) a midwife; a maternity nurse/ ~술 midwifery. さんば

**산판**(山坂) a forest preserve. やまさか

**산패**(酸敗) acidification/~하다 acidify; turn sour. さんはい

**산포**(山砲) a mountain gun; a [mountain] howitzer. さんほう

**산포**(散布) ~하다 scatter; distribute; diffuse/ ~약 dusting powder. さんぷ

**산포도**(山葡萄) 《식》 wild grapes ~むらう.

**산표**(散票) scattered votes. さんぴょう

**산하**(山下) the foot[bottom] of a mountain. やまのした

**산하**(山河) mountains and rivers. さんか

**산하**(傘下) ~의[에] under the influence [command] of. さんか

**산학**(算學) arithmetic. さんがく

**산학**(山學) orography; orology.

**산해**(山海) mountains and seas/ ~진미 (珍味) dainties of all lands and seas; a sumptuous repast. さんかい

**산허리**(山—) a mountainside; a hillside.
やまのちゅうふく

**산협**(山峽) 《계곡》 a gorge; a ravine.
さんきょう

**산호**(珊瑚) coral/ ~충(蟲) a coral insect/ ~초(礁) a coral reef 《환초》 an atoll/ ~도(島) a coral island/ ~해 (海) the Coral Sea. さんご

**산화**(山火) a forest[hill] fire.

**산화**(酸化) 《화》 oxidation; oxygenation 《유기체의》 combustion/~하다 oxidize; oxidate; oxygenate/~철 oxidized steel /~물 an oxide. さんか

**산회**(散會) adjournment/ ~하다 break up; adjourn; disperse; close. さんかい

**산후**(産後) after childbirth/~의[에] after childbirth/ ~가 좋다[나쁘다] be doing well[poorly] after the birth of one's child. さんご

**살¹** 《동물의》 flesh 《근육》 muscles 《과실의》 flesh/ ~이 많은 fleshy/ ~이 오르다 put on[gain] flesh. にく

**살²** 《벌의》 a bee's sting.

**살³** 《뼈대》 a frame 《장지 따위의》; 《우산·부채 따위의》 a rib 《빗의》 a tooth 《바퀴의》 a spoke.

**살⁴** 《어살》 a weir 《화살》 an arrow. や

**살⁵** 《나이》 age; years/스무 ~ twenty years of age. とし

**쌀** rice/ ~가루 rice flour/ ~겨 rice bran/ ~알 a grain of rice/~밥 boiled rice/ 찧은 ~ hulled rice. こめ

**살**(煞) evil influence; an evil spirit.

**살가죽** the skin. 피부 ひふ

**살갈퀴** 《식》 a tare; a vetch; Vicia sativa (학명).

**살갑다** 1 《넓다》 (be) rather spacious; ra-

ther roomy ②《다전하다》(be) affable; kind; amiable; genial.
**살강** a plate-rack; a tableware shelf.
**살갗** the skin; complexion／～이 희다 be white-complexioned; be fair-skinned／～이 거칠다 have a rough skin. ひふ
**살거름** manure mixed with seeds.
**살거리** state of flesh. にくづき
**살걸음** the speed of an arrow. やのそくど
**살결** the [texture of] skin／～이 고운 close[delicate] texture. はだ
**쌀골집** a kind of sausage.
**살구** 《식》 an apricot. あんずのき
**살균**(殺菌) sterilization／～하다 sterilize; pasteurize／～제 a sterilizer／～우유(乳) sterilized milk. さっきん
**살그머니** secretly; stealthily; quietly; by stealth. そっと
**살근거리다** rustle; rub together. こする
**살금살금** softly; with stealthy steps; stealthily; noiselessly. こっそり
**살긋하다** (be) tilted; slanting; be leaning to one side. ややかたむいている
**살기**(一氣) state of flesh; fattiness. にくづきのぶんりょう
**살기**(殺氣) death; excitement; bloodthirstiness／～를 띤 threatening; ferocious／～를 띠다 grow excited; be bloodshot. さっき
**살기 충천**(殺氣衝天) widespread bloodthirstiness[excitement, ferocity]／～하다 death is in the air; there is a widespread thirst for blood.
さっきがてんをつくこと
**살길** a means to live; a livelihood.
**살깃** the feathers [of an arrow]; an arrow feather. やばね
**살날** the rest of one's life; [the remainder of] one's days.
**살내리다** lose flesh; get thin. やせる
**살다** live 《살아 있다》 be alive 《생활하다》 make a living 《거주하다》 dwell[reside] 《생동하다》 be enlivened／잘 ～ be well-off／어렵게 ～ make a poor living／부산에 ～ live in *Busan*; make one's home in *Busan*. いきる
**살담배** cut[pipe] tobacco. きざみたばこ
**살닿다** cut into one's capital.
がんきんがへる
**살대¹** 《화살대》 an arrow-shaft.
**살대²** 《버팀나무》 a prop; a stay; a support／～로 버티다 prop[shore] up.
**살덩어리, 살덩이** a lump[piece] of flesh.
**살돈** principal; funds. とばくのしきん
**살똥스럽다** (be) snappish; virulent; bitter 《당돌하다》
**살뜰하다** 《애정이 깊다》(be) affectionate [toward]; attached (to); fond (of)／《알뜰하다》(be) frugal, thrifty／살뜰한 주부 a frugal housewife. まめまめしい
**살랑거리다** rustle; murmur／살랑살랑 ustling; murmuring; with a rustle.
さらさらとそよぐ

**살랑하다** (be) cool; chilly. ひやっとする
**살래살래** wagging; waving／～하다 wag; wave／머리를 ～ 흔들다 shake one's head gently. ふらふら
**살략**(殺掠) killing and plundering; massacre and despoilment／～하다 kill and plunder; slay and loot[pillage].
さつりゃく
**살려내다** rescue; deliver (a person) out of／죽음에서 ～ save (a person) from death. すくいだす
**살려주다** save; rescue; spare. すくう
**살륙**(殺戮) massacre; slaughter／～하다 massacre; slaughter; butcher. さつりく
**살리다** ①《구명하다》save; rescue; spare 《소생하다》restore (one) to life; revive 《살려두다》keep (an animal) alive; let (one) live ②《활용하다》make the most [best use] of 《교전에서》stet. たすける
**살림** 《생계》 living; livelihood; life 《살림살이》 housekeeping 《형편》 circumstances; one's affairs／～하다 keep house 《처음으로》 start housekeeping／～이 넉넉하다[넉넉하지 못하다] be well[badly] off; be in easy[bad] circumstances.
せいかつ
**살림군** 《맡은 이》 the mistress of the house 《잘하는 이》 a good house-wife.
**살림맡다** take charge[care] of the household; keep house.
**살림살이** a household; house-keeping 살림. せいかつ
**살림집** a residential house; a house for dwelling; a home. せいたいするいえ
**살맛** the touch of skin.
はだのふれあうかんじ
**살망하다** (be) long-legged; lank; be slender from the waist down.
**살맞다**(煞—) be struck with the influence of evil spirits; get sick suddenly.
**살며시** 《슬그머니》secretly; stealthily; quietly 《소리 나지 않게》quietly; softly; lightly. そっと
**살몃살몃** stealthily; quietly; lightly／～걷다 walk lightly. こっそりこっそり
**살목**(一木) a stay; a support; a prop.
**살몽혼**(一朦昏) an[a]esthesia／～하다 an[a]esthetize locally. ますい
**살무사** a viper; an adder. まむし
**살문**(一門) a lattice door.
**살밑** the arrow-head[point]. やじり
**살바람** a chilly wind. はるのつめたいかぜ
**살박다** press a pattern into a cake; decorate a cake.
**살받이** a target board; a mark; the ground around a target. ゆみのまと
**살방석**(一方席) a device for polishing arrows. やをみがくどうぐ
**살벌**(殺伐) ～하다 (be) bloody; bloodthirsty; brutal; savage; violent. さつばつ
**살별** 『천』 a comet. けいせい
**쌀보리** a kind of barley; *Hordeum sativum*(학명). ▸はだかむぎ
**살보시**(一布施) sexual relations with a

**실붙이** Buddhist priest/~하다 have illicit sexual relations with a priest.
**살붙이** a relative; a relation 《총칭》 kinsfolk. おなじけっとうのひと
**살빛** flesh colo[u]r[tint]; carnation.
**살사리** a sneak; a sneaker; a schemer. げんこうのかんきょうなひと
**살살**[1] gently; softly; slowly; quietly; lightly; stealthily. そろそろ
**살살**[2] 《다리로》 with a brisk crawl; at a lively pace 《머리로》 with a gentle shake; gently. ぐらぐら
**살살**[3] with a slight pain [in the stomach]/ ~하다 (one's stomach) aches. しくしく
**살살하다** ①《간사하다》 (be) cunning; sly; crafty; sneaky ②《곱다》 (be) delicate; slim; slender. はらはらする
**쌀쌀하다** (be) chilly; [rather] cold; distant/쌀쌀한 바람 a chilly wind/쌀쌀한 태도 a distant air[manner]/쌀쌀한 대답 a cold reply. ひえびえしている
**살상**(殺傷) killing and wounding; casualties; bloodshed/ ~하다 kill and wound; shed blood. さっしょう
**살생**(殺生) taking[destroying, destruction] of [animal] life/ ~하다 take [destroy] life; kill animals/~을 즐기는 cruel; merciless. せっしょう
**살성** grain; texture. はだのせいしつ
**살수**(撒水) watering/ ~하다 water (the street); sprinkle with street water/~차 (車) a water cart; a sprinkler.
**살수건**(—手巾) a piece of cloth used to polish arrows. やをみがくぬのきれ
**살신성인**(殺身成仁) ~하다 make a martyr of oneself; sacrifice oneself for the good of others.
**살아나다** ①《소생하다》 revive; be resuscitated; be restored to life ②《구명하다》 be saved[rescued]; 《조난의 경우》 survive ③《곤경에서 벗어나다》 escape [death, danger]. よみがえる
**살아생전**(一生前) one's lifetime/~에 during one's lifetime.
**살얼음** thin ice; a thin sheet of ice/~판 atsicky situation.
**살오르다** get[become] fat; gain flesh. にくがつく
**살오르다**(煞—) an evil influence[spirit] ascends [within one]; 《며앗》 a household is torn with disharmony.
**살육**(殺戮) killing; slaughter ➪살륙.
**살의**(殺意) [conceive] a murderous desire; intent to kill. さつい
**-살이** ①《생활》 living; life ②《옷》 garb; clothes.
**살인**(殺人) homicide 《모살》 murder 《고의적》 manslaughter/ ~범 a homicide; a murderer/~광(狂) homicidal insanity [maniac]/ ~광선 death ray/~ 사건 a murder case. さつじん
**살짝** ①《재빠르게》 quickly; nimbly ②《힘들이지 않고》 easily; readily ③《가볍게》 lightly; slightly; softly. そっと
**살잡다** rebuild; reerect.
**살잡히다** ①《구김살지다》 wrinkle; crumple ②《살얼음이 덮다》 [a thin coat of ice] forms. しわがよる
**살쩍** the hair before the ears. びん
**살점**(—點) a piece of meat; a chop; a cut. にっかのきれ
**살조개** 《어》 an ark shell; Anadara granosa(학명). はいがい
**살지다** 《몸이》 (be) fat; fleshy; corpulent 《땅이》 rich; fertile. こえる
**살찌다** grow[get] fat; put on[gain] flesh 《비옥하다》 grow fertile[rich]/살찐 fat 《기름지다》 fertile. こえる
**살찌우다** make fat; fatten. こえさせる
**살집** fleshiness/~이 좋다 be fleshy[plump, stout].
**살차다** ①《혜성이》 have a long tail ②《성질이》 (be) cold and unapproachable; be a cold fish.
**살창**(—窓) a lattice window. こうしまど
**살촉**(—鏃) an arrowhead; a barb of an arrow. やじり
**살충**(殺蟲) killing[destroying] insects; fungicide/ ~제 an insecticide 《가루》 an insect powder. さっちゅう
**살코기** lean; flesh part. にっかい
**살통** a jack; a prop supporter.
**살팍지다** (be) muscular; brawny; sinewy; stout. きんにくがこえてかたい
**살판나다** strike it rich; come into a fortune; one's ship comes in.
**살펴보다** look about; watch; see; study. みる
**살평상**(一平床) a slat bed.
**살포** a spade for irrigation work.
**살포**(撒布) scattering; sprinkling/ ~하다 scatter; sprinkle; spread. さんぷ
**살풀이**(煞—) exorcism; casting out evils / ~하다 exorcise; drive out evils.
**살품** the bosom; the breast. むねとふくとのあいだ
**살풍경**(殺風景) tastelessness; inelegance; lack of refinement; prosaism/ ~하다 (be) tasteless; graceless. さっふうけい
**살피** a land mark; a dividing mark.
**살피다**[1] ①《잘 보다》 look about[out]; watch; see ②《판단하다》 judge; gather ③《동정하다》 sympathize with; feel for. よくみる
**살피다**[2] 《천 따위가》 (be) thin and coarse; loose; gauzelike.
**살해**(殺害) murder; killing/ ~하다 murder; kill; put (one) to death; slay; slaughter 《암살하다》 assassinate/~ 사건 a murder case. さつがい
**삵괭이** 《동》 a wildcat; a lynx; a tiger cat. やまねこ
**삵피**(一皮) the skin of a wildcat.
**삶** life; living/ ~에 지치다 get tired of living. いきていくこと
**삶다** ①《물에》 boil; cook/계란을 ~ boil eggs ②《사람을 구슬리다》 appease; coa-

**삶이지다** x; win over ③(흙을) till. にる
**삶아지다** boil; be boiled; be cooked/ 너무 ~ be overdone.
**삼**¹ hemp; a hemp/~씨 hemp-seeds/ ~으로 만든 hempen. あさ
**삼**² (태아의) the fetus membrane[amnion] and the placenta. たい
**삼**³ (눈동자의) a pupil[l]ary speck[dot]. がんきゅうにできるほし
**쌈**¹ seasoned rice rolled in vegetable [laver, etc.].
**쌈**² a struggle ⇨싸움. あらそい
**삼**(三) three/~게 ~ the third. さん
**삼**(蔘) geenseng ⇨인삼. にんじん
**삼가** respectfully; humbly. つつしで
**삼가다** ①(조심하다) be discreet[prudent, careful]/언행을 ~ be discreet in word and deed ②(억제하다) abstain[keep, refrain] from 《절제하다》be moderate (in)/술을 ~ abstain[keep] from drinking. うやうやしくする
**삼가르다** cut off the navel cord.
**삼각**(三角) a triangle/ ~의 triangular; three-cornered/ ~ 관계 the eternal triangle; triangular love/~법 trigonometry/~ 함수(數) trigonometrical function. さんかく
**삼각**(三脚) a tripod/ ~의 three-legged; tripodal/ ~가(架) a tripod/ ~이인 경기 a three-legged race. さんきゃく
**삼각형**(三角形) a triangle/ ~의 triangular; triangle-shaped. さんかくけい
**삼간 초가**(三間草家) a thatched cottage (hut). きぼのちいさいくさや
**삼강**(三綱) the three bonds/ ~ 오륜 the three bonds and the five moral rules in human relations. さんこう
**삼거리**(三一) a crossing with three corners; three-forked road.
**삼겹실**(三一) three-ply thread.
**삼경**(三更) midnight; the small hours; the dead of night. さんこう
**삼경**(三景) the three famous views[beauty spots]/한국 ~'의 하나 [one of the scenic trio[three noted views] of Korea.
**삼광조**(三光鳥) a Korean paradise flycatcher. さんこうちょう
**삼교**(三校) the third proof.
**삼국**(三國) three countries[states]/ ~ 동맹 a triple alliance/~ 협상 a triple entente/~제 a third power[state]. さんごく
**삼군**(三軍) a great army; the armed forces/ ~을 지휘하다 command a great army/ ~ 총참모장 the chief of staff of the armed forces. さんぐん
**삼권 분립**(三權分立) separation of three powers. さんけんぶんりつ
**삼남**(三南) the six southern provinces of Korea.
**삼년**(三年) three years/~생 《학생》a third-year student/ ~마다 every three years/~생 식물을 a triennial.

**삼노** a hempen twine; a hemp cord[rope].
**삼노끈** twine. あさなわ
**삼눈** a pupillary white[red] speck. ほしふ
**삼다** ①(인연을 맺다) make (something) of a person/벗으로 ~ make a friend of (one); associate with ②(사용·생각하다) use one as (something); regard… as; have as… ③(짚신 따위를) make [strawshoes]; (감을) spin. する
**삼단** a bunch of hemp. あさのたば
**삼단계**(三段階) three stages; the third stage. さんだんかい
**삼단 논법**(三段論法) 『논』a syllogism/ ~으로 논하다 syllogize.
**삼단뛰기**(三段一) 『체』hop, step, and jump; a triple jump.
**삼대** a hemp stalk. あさのみき
**삼대**(三代) three generations.
**삼도내**(三途一) the River Styx/ ~를 건너다 cross the Styx. さんずのかわ
**삼독**(蔘毒) ginseng poisoning.
**삼독회**(三讀會) the third reading (of a bill).
**삼동**(三冬) the three winter months 《겨울》winter. さんとう
**삼동**(三同) having three parts joined together; (being) in three sections.
**삼동네**(三洞一) neighbours. ちかいまち
**삼두근**(三頭筋) 『해』the triceps.
**삼두 정치**(三頭政治) triumvirate.
**삼등**(三等) the third class[rate]/ ~ 여객 a third-class passenger 《배의》a steerage passenger/ ~ 차표[석] a third-class ticket[seat].
**삼등분**(三等分) trisection/ ~하다 cut[divide] into three equal parts; trisect.
**삼라 만상**(森羅萬象) 'all' creation[nature]; everything under the sun; the universe. しんらばんしょう
**삼루**(三壘) 『체』the 3rd base/ ~수(手) the third-baseman/ ~타(打) a three-base hit; a triple. さんるい
**삼류**(三流) the third rate[class]/ ~의 third-rate[-class]; of the third order/ ~ 극장 the lower-class theater.
**삼륜차**(三輪車) a tricycle. さんりんしゃ
**삼릉**(三稜) a triangle. みっつのかど
**삼림**(森林) a wood; a forest/ ~대(帶) a forest belt[zone]/ ~ 보호 forest conservation/ ~학 forestry. しんりん
**삼립**(森立) ~하다 stand close together; bristle. りんりつ
**삼막물**(三幕物) a three-act play.
**삼매**(三昧) 『불』ecstasy; absorption/ ~ 경에 들어가다 sink into a blissful state of self-forgetfulness. さんまい
**삼면**(三面) three sides[faces]/ 《신문의》the third page/ ~ 기사 police news; stories of human interest. さんめん
**삼모작**(三毛作) 『농』three crops a year. さんもうさく
**삼문**(三文) a farthing/ ~ 문사(文士) a scribbler; a hack writer/ ~ 소설 a cheap shocker; a dime novel〈미〉.

**삼민주의**(三民主義) 《손 문의》 [Dr. *Sun Moon*] Three Principle of the People; Sunwenism. さんみんしゅぎ

**삼박거리다** [one's eyes] blink lightly. まばたきする

**삼박자**(三拍子) 《음》 triple time.

**삼반규관**(三半規管) 《해》 semicircular canals. さんはんきかん

**삼발이**(三一) a tripod; a trivet. ごとく

**삼배**(三倍) three times; thrice/ ~의 three times [as many as, as much as, as large as]; treble/ ~하다 treble; multiply by three.

**삼배**(三拜) bowing thrice.

**삼백년제**(三百年祭) the three hundredth anniversary; a tercentenary.

**삼베** hemp cloth. あさのぬの

**삼복**(三伏) the period of summer heat; the hottest period of summer; midsummer; three dog days/~의 더위 the midsummer heat. さんぷく

**삼봉낚시**(三鋒一) a three forked fishing hook.

**삼부**(三部) three parts; three copies 《서적의》 three volumes 《부처》 three departments/~작 a trilogy/~ 합주 a trio; a terzetto. さんぶ

**삼분**(三分) trisection 《시간》 three minutes/~하다 divide (*a thing*) into three [parts]; trisect; 《수》 divide by three/ ~의 2 two-thirds. さんぶん

**삼분 오열**(三分五裂) disruption/~하다 be disrupted; be torn asunder. ちりぢりばらばらになること

**삼사**(三思) ~하다 reflect on; think over and over again. さんし

**삼삭**(三朔) the three months of a season.

**삼삼오오**(三三五五) (*by*) twos and threes /~로 by two and three; in groups [of two or three]. さんさんごご

**삼삼하다** be not salty but tasty. みずくさい

**삼삼하다**(森森一) (be) thick; luxuriant.

**삼색**(三色) three [primary] colo[u]rs/~의 three-colo[u]r; tricolo[u]r/~기 the tricolo[u]r [flag]. さんしょく

**삼선**(三選) election for the third term/ ~되다 be elected for the third term.

**삼성**(三聖) ①《한국의》 the three founders [of Korea] ②《성인》 the three sages ③《세계의》 the Buddha, Confucius and Christ. さんせい

**삼성들리다** eat to *one's* heart's content. むさぼりくう

**삼세**(三世) the three states of existence; the Triple Universe. さんせい

**삼세번**(三一番) just three times. ちょうどさんかい

**삼승**(三乘) 《수》 cube/~하다 cube; multiply (*a number*) by its square[twice by itself]. さんじょう

**삼씨** hemp seeds. たいまのたね

**삼시**(三時) three daily meals [of breakfast, lunch and supper];《때》 morning, noon and evening. さんじ

**삼신**(三神) ①《우리나라의》 the three founders of ancient Korea ②《아이를 점지하는 신》 the three gods governing childbirth. さんじん

**삼십**(三十) thirty; XXX 《로마 숫자》/제~ the thirtieth. さんじゅう

**삼십육계**(三十六計) escape; flight/ ~ 놓다 beat a retreat; show a clean part of heels. さんじゅうろっけい

**삼십팔도선**(三十八度線) the 38th Parallel; 38 degrees north Latitude/여기가 ~입니다 This is on the 38th Parallel.

**삼엄**(森嚴) ~하다 (be) solemn; sublime; awe-inspiring; grave/~한 분위기 awe-inspiring atmosphere. しんげん

**삼오야**(三五夜) a full moon night; the fifteenth night of a lunar month.

**삼옷** baby garment ⇒배내웃.

**삼용**(參茸) ginseng and antler.

**삼원색**(三原色) the three primary colo[u]rs. さんげんしょく

**삼월**(三月) March (略: Mar.). さんがつ

**삼위일체**(三位一體) trinity; consubstantiality. さんみいったい

**삼이웃** the neighbourhood; the vicinity.

**삼인**(三人) three men/ ~조(組) a triumvirate; a trio. さんにん

**삼인칭**(三人稱) the third person/~ 단수 [복수] the third person singular[plural]. さんにんしょう

**삼일**(三日) ①⇒사흘 ②《해산·결혼·일요일 후의》 the third day after childbirth [marriage, Sunday]. みっか

**삼일 예배**(三日禮拜) 《종》 Wednesday evening church service.

**삼일 운동**(三一運動) the 1919 Independence Movement [of Korea].

**삼일장**(三日葬) burial three days after death.

**삼일절**(三一節) March 1st.

**삼일 천하**(三日天下) a three day[short-lived] rule; a three-day[very brief] reign. みっかてんか

**삼자**(三者) ①⇒제삼자(第三者) ②《삼인》 three persons/~간의 tripartite/ ~ 회담 a tripartite meeting. さんしゃ

**삼재**(三災) three calamities [of fire, flood and storm]. さんさい

**삼족**(三族) the three sets of relatives. さんぞく

**삼종**(三從) a third cousin. ふたいとこ

**삼줄** umbilical cord ⇒탯줄. へそのお

**삼중**(三重) ~의 threefold; treble; triple /~주〔창〕 a trio; a terzetto. さんじゅう

**쌈지** a [tobacco] pouch. たばこいれ

**삼지창**(三枝槍) a three-pronged spear; a trident. さきがさんさになったやり

**삼진**(三振) 《체》 a strike-out; a fan.

**삼질**(三一) March 3rd of the lunar month[calendar].

**삼차**(三次) the third time/ ~식 a cubic expression/ ~원 three dimensions/~ 방정식 a cubic equation. さんじ

**삼차**(三叉) ①~로(路) a three-forked road /~ 신경《해》 the trigeminal [nerve]; the trigeminus. さんさ

**삼창**(三唱) 《만세의》 three cheers/ ~하다 give three cheers/ 만세 ~하다 give three cheers (for). さんしょう

**삼척 동자**(三尺童子) a mere child. さんじゃくのどうじ

**삼척 장검**(三尺長劍) a long[big] sword; a three-feet sabre. さんじゃくけん

**삼천 세계**(三千世界) the universe; the whole world. さんぜんせかい

**삼촌**(三寸) ①《세치》 three inches ②《아버지의 형제》 an uncle; a father's brother. さんずん

**삼촌설**(三寸舌) the tongue. さんずんのした

**삼총사**(三銃士) a triumvirate; a trio/ 회사의 ~ the triumvirate of the firm.

**삼추**(三秋) ①《가을의 석달》 the three autumn months ②《3년》 three years. さんしゅう

**삼춘**(三春) ①《봄의 석달》 the three spring months ②《3년》 three years. さんしゅん

**삼출**(滲出) transudation/ ~하다 ooze out; exude; transude through. にじみでること

**삼층**(三層) the second floor〈영〉; the third floor[story]〈미〉/~집 a three-storied[-story] house. さんかい

**삼치**《어》 Scomberomorus niphonius(학명).

**삼칠일**(三七日) the 21st day of a child's birth.

**삼키다** swallow; gulp down.

**삼태**(三胎) triplets/ ~세쌍둥이. みつつこ

**삼태기** a carrier's basket.

**삼투**(滲透) saturation; infiltration; permeation/ ~하다 saturate; permeate; infiltrate/ ~압 osmotic pressure/ ~작용 osmotic action. しんとう

**삼파전**(三巴戰) a triangular contest; a three-cornered contest[fight].

**삼판선**(三板船) a sampan(Chin); 《거룻배》 a lighter.

**삼판 양승**(三一兩勝) best two out of three [games].

**삼팔선**(三八線) the 38th parallel [dividing Korea]⇨삼십팔도선(三十八度線).

**삼포**(參圃) a ginseng field. にんじんのさいばいはたけ

**삼하**(三夏) ①《여름의 석 달》 the three summer months ②《3년》 three years.

**삼하다** (be) fretful; short-tempered.

**삼한 사온**(三寒四溫) alternation of three cold days and four warm days. さんかんしおん

**삼할미** an old midwife; a maternity nurse. ろうばのじょさんぷ

**삼합사**(三合絲) three-ply thread.

**삼항식**(三項式) 《수》 a trinomial [expression]. たこうしきのひとつ

**삼현**(三絃) three strings/ ~의 trichord; three-stringed. さんげん

**삽**(鋪) a shovel; a scoop/ ~질하다 shovel. シャベル

**삽괭이** a narrow-bladed hoe with a long shaft.

**쌈사래하다** (be) a bit bitter. ややしぶい

**삽살개** 《동》 a shaggy dogs. むくいぬ

**쌈살하다** (be) slightly bitter; bitterish. ちょっとにがい

**삽상하다**(颯爽一) (be) refreshing; cool.

**삽시간**(霎時間) a twinkle; a moment; an instant/ ~에 in a twinkling; in an instant; in less than no time; quicker than thought. しゅんかん

**삽앙**(挿秧) planting of young rice-plants /~하다 transplant rice.

**삽연**(颯然) ~하다 (be) refreshing.

**삽입**(挿入) insertion; interposition; incorporation/ ~하다 insert; put (a thing) in[to]; interpose; incorporate/ ~구 a parenthesis (pl. -ses). そうにゅう

**삽주**《식》 Tractylis ovata(학명). おけら

**삽지**(挿紙) 《인》 paper feeding/ ~하다 feed paper.

**삽체**(澁滯) delay; retard; congestion/ ~하다 be delayed; be retarded; be congested. じゅうたい

**삽화**(挿話) an episode/ ~적 episodic/ ~의 episodic; episodical. そうわ

**삽화**(挿畵) an illustration; a cut/ ~를 넣다 illustrate; insert[put in] an illustration. さしえ

**삽화**(挿花) flower arrangement/ ~하다 put flowers in (a vase). そうか

**삿갓** a bamboo-hat 《사초로 만든》 a sedge-hat; a braided hat. かさ

**삿대** a [row] pole ⇨상앗대. ふねのさお

**삿반**(一盤) a rush-tray; a reed-tray. あしでつくったざるのようなもの

**삿자리** a rush-mat; a reed-mat. あしでつくったこざ

**상**(喪) mourning/ ~을 입다 be in[go into] mourning (for one). そう

**상**(上) 《상등의》 superior; first-class; best 《상부의》 upper 《제일권》 the first volume 《견지》 from the viewpoint of. じょう

**상**(床) a [small-]table/ ~보다 lay[spread] the table (for dinner); set a dinner table. おぜん

**상**(賞) a prize 《보수》 a reward/ 1등~ the first prize; first honors/ ~타다 win[get] a prize. しょう

**상**(相) 《모습》 an aspect; a phase 《인상》 physiognomy 《얼굴》 a face; a look/ ~을 찌푸리고 with a frown. そう

**상**(商) 《상업》 trade; business; a dealer; 《수》 the quotient. しょう

**상**(想) an idea; a conception. そう

**상**(像) a figure; a statue; an image 《화상》 a picture; a portrait. ぞう

**상가**(喪家) a house of mourning. そうか

**상가**(商街) downtown; the business section[quarters]. しょうてんがい

**상가**(商家) a shop; a store 《상인》 a shopkeeper; a merchant. しょうか

**상각**(償却) repayment; refunding; rede-

**상감**(上監) (임금) the king; the Lord; His Majesty.

**상감**(象嵌) inlaying; damaskeening (세공물) inlaid work; an inlay.

**상강**(霜降) the 18th of the 24 seasonal divisions. そうこう

**상객**(上客) (상빈) a guest of honour; a chief guest. じょうきゃく

**상객**(常客) a regular customer[patron]; a frequenter.

**상거**(相距) distance; interval; the space between. おたがいのきょり

**상거래**(商去來) a commercial transaction; a business deal.

**상거지**(上―) the most wretched of beggars.

**상건**(上件) an article of superior quality; fine goods. じょうとうのぶっぴん

**상건**(床巾) (식탁용) a table cloth (장식용) a table cover; a table linen.

**상격**(相格) physiognomy. かおかたち

**상격**(相隔) ~하다 be distant from each other; be separated each other; be apart. おたがいのかんかく

**상견**(相見) ~하다 look at each other; exchange looks. そうけんのれい

**상경**(上京) ~하다 go[come] up to capital [Seoul]. じょうきょう

**상계**(上計) the best policy; a capital plan; the wisest thing. じょうけい

**상계**(相計) a setoff/ ~하다 offset; set off; cancel each other/ ~ 계정 an offset account.

**상계**(商界) the business world; the world of commerce. しょうかい

**상고**(上古) ancient times[days]; remote ages; remote antiquity/~의 ancient; of remote antiquity/~사(史) an ancient history. じょうこ

**상고**(上告) ①(재판) an appeal to the Supreme Court/ ~하다 appeal to/ [신립]인 an applicant for revision/대법부에 ~하다 appeal to the Supreme Court ②(보고) a report/~하다 report. じょうこく

**상고**(詳考) close reference; consultation in detail/~하다 consult (a book) in detail; refer closely to.

**상고**(尙古) worship of ancient civilization/~주의 classicism. しょうこ

**상고대** frost on the tree/~하다 be frost-covered. そうもくにおりたしも

**상고머리** a square-cut hair.

**상공**(上空) the upper air; the sky; high in the air[sky]. じょうくう

**상공**(商工) (상공업) commerce and industry/~의 commercial and industrial/~부 The Ministry of Commerce and Industry/서울 ~ 회의소 the Seoul Chamber of Commerce and Industry. しょうこう

**상공**(翔空) soaring; flying in the air/~하다 soar; fly high in the air. そらをとびまわること

**상공업**(商工業) commerce and industry/~의 commercial and industrial/중소 ~ 자 small and medium merchants and industrialists. しょうこうぎょう

**상과**(商科) a commercial course/~ 대학 a commercial university[college]. しょうか

**상관**(上官) a higher[superior] officer; a commanding officer; a chief. じょうかん

**상관**(相關) ①(관계) mutual relation/ ~ 하다 interrelate; correlate; be related to each other/ ~격 correlative; interrelative; mutually related ②(개의) concern (간섭) interference/ ~하다 take part in; concern oneself in; be involved in; interfere/ ~없다 (무관계) have nothing to do with (괜찮다) do not matter/네가 ~할 게 아니다 It's none of your business. そうかん

**상관례**(商慣例) a business[commercial] practice. しょうかんしゅう

**상권**(上卷) the first volume; Vol.1; volume one. じょうかん

**상권**(商權) commercial power (권리) commercial rights. しょうけん

**상궤**(常軌) the normal course/ ~를 벗어나다 break bounds; go off the track; be abnormal. じょうき

**상규**(常規) established rules. じょうき

**상그레** with beaming eyes; blandly/ ~ 웃다 beam; smile blandly. にやっと

**상극**(相剋) (충돌) conflict; rivalry; discord; disagreement/ ~하다 fight against each other; disagree with each other. そうこく

**상근**(常勤) ~의 full time/~자 a full timer/ ~ 촉탁 full time engagement.

**상글거리다** beam; smile blandly[gently]. にやにやする

**상글방글, 상글상글** beaming; smiling. にこにこ

**상금**(尙今) up to now; still (부정) yet; until now. いまなお

**상금**(賞金) a [money] prize; a purse (현상금) a reward. しょうきん

**상금**(償金) an indemnity. しょうきん

**상급**(上級) a high rank; an upper class /~의 upper; higher; superior; senior/ ~생 an upperclass student/ ~ 학교 a school of higher grade; an advanced school. じょうきゅう

**상급**(賞給) a reward; a prize. しょうきんをあたえる

**상긋** with a [sudden] smile/ ~거리다 smile blandly. にやっと

**상긋방긋, 상긋상긋** smiling; beaming.

**상기**(上氣) a rush of blood to the head; dizziness; swimming of the head/ ~하다 have a rush of blood to the head; be dizzy. じょうき

**상기(上記)** the above statements ⇨상술.
**상기(詳記)** a minute description; a full account/ ~하다 describe minutely; state in detail; give a full account (of). しょうき
**상기(商機)** a business opportunity.
**상기(想起)** ~하다 remember; recollect; call to mind/ …을 ~시키다 remind (one) of; put (one) in mind of. そうき
**상기(喪期)** the period[term] of mourning. そうき
**상길(上一)** the highest[finest] quality; prime quality. じょうとう
**상납(上納)** payment [to the authorities] /~하다 pay to the authorities[government]; offer/ ~미(米) rice paid as a tax. じょうのう
**상냥하다** (be) gentle; tender 《온순하다》 (be) meek; kind; sweet; affectionate; amiable; affable. せいしつがにゅうわだ
**상년(常一)** a mean[vulgar] woman; a bitch. みぶんのひくいおんな
**상년(上年)** last year ⇨지난해. さくねん
**상념(想念)** a notion; conception. そうねん
**상노(床奴)** a page; a [chore-]boy; a boy-servant. きゅうじ
**상놈(常一)** a mean[vulgar] fellow; a beast. みぶんのひくいおとこ
**상늙은이(上一)** the eldest[dean] of a group of old men. ちょうじょうのろうじん
**상다리(床一)** table legs.
**상단(上段)** 《인쇄면의》 the upper portion [division] 《상렬》 the upper row 《상좌》 a place of honor 《높은 자리》 a dais. じょうだん
**상단(上端)** the top; the upper end; the head. じょうたん
**상달(上一)** October; Harvest month.
**상달(上達)** a report (to a superior)/ ~하다 report (to a superior).
**상닭(常一)** a scraggly[misbred, misformed, ugly] chicken.
**상담(相談)** consultation; counsel; conference/ ~하다 consult (one); take counsel (with); talk (over a matter with one)/ ~소 an information bureau/결혼 ~소 a matrimonial advice office. そうだん
**상담(商談)** negotiations; business; bargaining/~을 결정하다 close a deal.
**상답(上畓)** a rich rice field.
**상답(上答)** an answer to one's superior / ~하다 answer[reply to] one's superior. めうえのひとにこたえること
**상당(相當)** ~하다 《알맞다》 (be) fit; proper; suitable; corresponding《대응하다》; 《적응하다》 befitting; appropriate 《지당하다》 fair; reasonable 《필적》 equivalent 《어지간하다》 fair; considerable; decent/ ~히 pretty; fairly; considerably/ ~한 보수 a due reward/ ~한 교육[수입] a good education[income]/ ~한 인물 a respectable person/ ~한 값 a reasonable price. そうとう

**상대(上代)** ancient times; remote ages.
**상대(相對)** ①《서로 대함》 facing each other/ ~하다 face each other ②《짝패》 a companion; a mate; a fellow; a partner/ ~하다 keep company with/이야기 ~ a companion to talk to; one's crony ③《적수》 an opponent; a rival《필적자》a match 《상대방》the other party /~하다 deal with (one); contend with 《경기에서》play (against) ④《대상》the object /연애 ~ the object of one's love ⑤《절대에 대한》 relativity/ ~적[으로] relative[ly]/~성 원리[이론] the principle[theory] of relativity. そうたい
**상대(商大)** a college of commerce.
**상대자(相對者)** a companion; a mate; one's partner ⇨상대(相對).
**상대편(相對便)** the other party.
**상도(常道)** a regular[normal, proper] course. じょうどう
**상도(想到)** ~하다 think of; consider; hit upon (a plan). そうとう
**상도덕(商道德)** business[trade] morality / ~ 앙양 enhancement of business morality.
**상동(相同)** the same[similar] relation; 《생》homology. そうどう
**상되다(常一)** (be) vulgar; low; mean; base; indecent. いやしい
**상두** a [funeral] bier ⇨상두. まげ
**상득(相得)** agreement/ ~하다 agree with each other; be in accord with each other.
**상등(上等)** the first class/ ~의 first-class[-rate]; superior; fine/ ~품[석] a first-class article[seat]. じょうとう
**상동(相等)** equality/ ~하다 (be) equal. じょうとうしいこと
**상등병(上等兵)** 《육군·해병》 a corporal 《해군》 seaman 《공군》 an airman second class.
**상란(上欄)** 《위의 난》 the top column 《앞의 난》 the preceding column.
**상람(上覽)** imperial inspection. じょうらん
**상략(上略)** omitted so far; the preceding part omitted/ ~하다 omit [the preceding part]. じょうりゃく
**상량(商量)** consideration; deliberation; discussion/ ~하다 consider; deliberate (on); discuss; weigh. しょうりょう
**상량(爽凉)** ~하다 《날씨가》 (be) cool; refreshing さわやかですずしいこと
**상량(上樑)** putting up the ridge-beam; setting up the framework / ~하다 set up[raise] the framework [of a house]; put up the ridge-beam. むね
**상량대(上樑一)** a ridgepole; a ridge-beam.
**상련(相連)** connection; linking/ ~하다 be connected[linked] with (each other, one another); connect; join. たがいにつらなること
**상련(相憐)** mutual sympathy.
**상례(常例)** a[an established] usage; a custom; a usual practice. じょうれい

상례(喪禮) the ceremonies of mourning; funeral rites. そうれい
상로(商路) commercial pursuits; trade.
상록(詳錄) a full record; record in detail / ~하다 record (a speech) in detail. しょうろく
상록(常綠) ~의 evergreen; indeciduous / ~송 an evergreen pine/ ~수 an evergreen [tree]; (총칭) evergreens. じょうりょく
상론(詳論) full discussion[treatment] / ~하다 discuss at length[large]; treat (a matter) in detail; deal with (a matter) in detail. しょうろん
상류(上流) (강의) the upper stream[reaches]; (사회의) the upper classes/ ~의 upstream; upper. じょうりゅう
상륙(上陸) landing; disembarkation/ ~하다 land (in a country, at a port); get to land 《선원이》 go[come] on shore 《군대 등의》 disembark 《태풍 등이》 strike. じょうりく
상리(常理) a matter of course; a proper way; the natural course to take; a sound principle. じょうり
상마(一馬) a stallion. せいちょうしたうま
상막하다 (be) dim; obscure; not clear; faint; vague. おぼろげだ
상말(常一) vulgar words; a vulgarism; a four-letter word. いやしいことば
상망(想望) (우러러봄) admiration/~하다 admire. たがいにみること
상머리(床一) the head of the table.
상머슴(上一) a heavy-duty farmhand.
상면(上面) the surface 《테이블의》 the top side/ …의 ~에 over; on. うわべ
상면(相面) meeting for the first time / ~하다 meet (one) for the first time; interview おたがいにあうこと
상명(詳明) minuteness and clearness/~하다 (be) minute and clear. しょうめい
상모(狀貌, 相貌) features; physiognomy; looks; a face.
상목(桑木) a mulberry tree ⇨뽕나무.
상몽(祥夢) an auspicious dream ⇨길몽.
상무(尙武) militarism; warlike spirit/ ~하다 pursue the policy of militarism / ~의 기상 a martial[military] spirit. しょうぶ
상무(常務) regular business; routine work/ ~취체역 a managing director/ ~위원 the standing committee. しょうむ
상무(商務) commercial affairs/ ~관(官) a commercial attache. しょうむ
상문(上文) the foregoing paragraphs; the above [statement]/ ~과 같이 as mentioned above. じょうぶん
상문(上聞) imperial hearing. じょうぶん
상문(尙文) encouragement of learning.
상문(喪門) (민) a baleful direction.
상미(上米) first-class rice; rice of fine quality. じょうまい
상미(上味) fine taste; good flavour. じょうとうのあじ

상미(賞味) relish; appreciation/ ~하다 prize; eat with relish; relish; appreciate. あじみ
상미(賞美) admiration; praise; applause / ~하다 praise; admire; prize; value.
상민(常民) the common people; the lower classes. へいみん
상박(上膊) 〖해〗 the upper arm; the brachium/ ~골 the humerus/ ~부 the humeral region/ ~ 동맥 the brachial artery. じょうはく
상반(相反) being contrary to each other; conflicting with each other; contradiction; reciprocity/~하다 be contrary to each other; conflict with each other. そうたいすること
상반기(上半期) the first half of the year. かみはんき
상반신(上半身) the upper half of the body; the bust/ ~ 사진을 찍다 have one's bust photoed. じょうはんしん
상밥(床一) a sold meal set on a table/ ~집 a chop house.
상방(上枋) the upper lintel.
상방(上方) the upper part/ ~의 upper / ~에 above; upward[s].
쌍방(雙方) both parties; both sides; either party. そうほう
상배(喪配) the death of one's wife/ ~하다 lose one's wife. つまにしべつすること
상배(賞盃) a prize cup; a trophy cup; challenge cup. しょうはい
상벌(賞罰) reward and punishment; justice/ ~ 없음 No reward and no punishment.
상법(商法) the commercial law[code]; business law. しょうほう
쌍벽(雙璧) (옥) a pair of jewels 《사람》 the two great masters[authorities]; the matchless twin stars. そうへき
상병(上兵) a corporal ⇨상등병(上等兵).
상병(傷兵) a wounded soldier 《제대 후의》 a war-disabled ex-service man.
상병병(傷病兵) the sick and wounded soldier's/ ~ 포로 sick and wounded prisoners of war. しょうびょうへい
상보(床褓) a table-cloth; a table-cover. おぜんかけ
상보(詳報) a detailed[full] report; details; particulars[a full account] of; report at length. しょうほう
상보(商報) a business[shop, store] bulletin.
상보다(床一) set the table.
상보다(相一) tell a person's fortune by reading his physiognomy; read the countenance of (a person).
상복(喪服) mourning dress; sables. もふく
상복(常服) everyday wear; home wear; workaday clothing; weekday clothes. ふだんぎ
상봉(相逢) meeting each other/ ~하다 meet each other. たがいにあうこと
상부(上部) the upper[top] part; the top

**(위쪽)** the upside **(표면)** the surface **(상관)** one's superiors／ ~ 구조 a superstructure.　じょうぶ

**상부**(上府) high-ranking officials. じょうし

**상부**(喪夫) the death of one's husband／ ~하다 lose one's husband; be widowed; meet the death of one's husband.　おっとにしべつすること

**상부**(孀婦) a young widow.

**상부 상조**(相扶相助) mutual aid; interdependence.

**상비**(常備) ~의 standing; permanent; regular／ ~하다 reserve (for); have (something) always ready／ ~군(軍) a standing army; ready troops／ ~약(藥) a household medicine.　じょうび

**상사**(上士) **(육군·해병·공군)** master sergeant **(해군)** a chief petty officer.

**상사**(上司) the authorities **(상관)** one's superiors.　じょうし

**상사**(相似) resemblance; similarity; similitude; 〖생〗 analogy; pseudo／ ~하다 be similar; be alike; resemble／ ~의 similar／ ~형 similar figures.

**상사**(相思) mutual love／ ~하다 think of each other.　ぞうし

**상사**(商社) a [commercial] firm; a commercial house.　しょうしゃ

**상사**(商事) business affairs[matters]／ ~계약 a commercial contract.　しょうじ

**상사**(常事) a common occurrence; the way of the world.　じょうじ

**상사**(喪事) death; mourning／ ~가 나다 have mourning.

**상사**(殤死) dying at (one's) teen age／ ~하다 die at teen age.　しょうし

**상사람**(常—) a commoner **(전체)** the common people.　へいみん

**상사발**(常沙鉢) a coarsely-made[crude] bowl.　ひんしつのわるいはし

**상사병**(相思病) lovesickness. そうしびょう

**상사치다** groove; put a groove in.

**상상**(想像) imagination **(공상)** fancy **(가정)** supposition; conjecture **(추측)** speculation／ ~하다 imagine; fancy; suppose; conjecture; guess; speculate／ ~적 imaginative power; imaginay／ ~력 imagination.　そうぞう

**상상봉**(上上峰) the highest peak.

**쌍쌍이**(雙雙—) by twos; in pairs; in couples; two by two.　組ごとに

**상상치**(上上—) choice goods; exclusive merchandise; a top-quality article.

**상서**(上書) **(웃어른께)** a letter to one's senior／ ~하다 send a letter to one's senior.　じょうしょ

**상서**(相書) a guide book to phrenological interpretation; a book of physiognomy.

**상서**(祥瑞) a good omen; a lucky omen; a happy augury; a propitious sign／ ~롭다 (be) of good omen; (be) auspicious; (be) propitious.　しょうずい

**상석**(上席) **(고위)** seniority **(상좌)** an upper seat; the top seat **(주빈석)** the seat [place] of honour.　じょうせき

**상석**(床石) a stone-stand in front of a tomb.

**상선**(商船) merchant ship[vessel]; a merchantman **(총칭)** the merchant marine／ ~대(隊) a merchant fleet. しょうせん

**상설**(常設) permanent esatblishment／ ~하다 regular／ ~ 위원 a standing committee／ ~의 permanent　じょうせつ

**상설**(詳說) expatiation; enlargement; detailed[full] explanation／ ~하다 explain in detail; state in full[at length].　しょうせつ

**상설**(霜雪) frost and snow.　そうせつ

**상세**(上世) ①antiquity ⇨상고(上古) ②(윗대) the older generation.　じょうせい

**상세**(詳細) details; particulars／ ~하다 (be) full; detailed; minute／ ~한 보고 a detailed[full] report.　しょうさい

**상소**(上疏) a memorial to the Throne／ ~하다 present a memorial to the Throne.　じょうそ

**상소**(上訴) an appeal／ ~하다 appeal to [a higher court].　じょうそ

**상소리** four-letter words; vulgar language; indecent talk **(욕설)** abuse／ ~하다 use abusive language.　いやしいことば

**상속**(相續) succession **(재산의)** inheritance／ ~하다 succeed (to); inherit／ ~인 a successor **(남자)** an heir **(여자)** an heiress／ ~세 an inheritance tax; death duties／ ~권 the right of succession [inheritance]／ ~ 재산 an inheritance; inherited property.　そうぞく

**상쇄**(相殺) an offset; a setoff; a counter-balance; cancelling each other／ ~하다 offset[cancel] each other; set off (a merit against a fault)／ ~ 계정 an offset account.　そうさつ

**상수**(上手) a better hand; an adept; a superior.　じょうず

**상수**(上壽) a longevity.　じょうじゅ

**상수**(常數) 〖수〗 a constant; an invariable [number].　いっていふへんのすう

**쌍수**(雙手) both hands／ ~를 들어 찬성하다 give one's hearty support.　そうしゅ

**상수도**(上水道) water-works／ ~ 시설 water supply facilities.　じょうすいどう

**상수리나무** 〖식〗 a kind of oak; *Quercus serrata*(학명).　くぬぎのき

**상순**(上旬) the first part[the ten days, the decade] of the month／ 5월 ~에 at the beginning of May; early in May.　じょうじゅん

**상술**(床—) wine sold at tables with tidbit on them.

**상술**(上述) the above statements ⇨상기(上記).　じょうじゅつ

**상술**(詳述) expatiation; enlargement; a detailed explanation／ ~하다 fully explain; make a detailed explanation; dwell on.

**상스럽다**(常—) (be) vulgar; low; mean;

상습(常習) 《사회의》 a common custom; a regular practice; a usage; a convention 《개인의》 a habit/ ~적 customary/ ~범(犯) 《범죄》 a habitual crime 《범인》 a habitual criminal. じょうしゅう

상승(上昇) rise; rising; ascension; upturn/ ~하다 rise; ascend; climb; go up; soar [up]/~ 기류 an ascending currente. じょうしょう

상승(常勝) ~의 invincible; undefeated; ever-victorious/ ~군 an ever-victorious army.

상승(相乘) multiplication/~ 하다 multiply/ ~비(比) geometrical ratio.

상시(常時) ①normal times ⇒평상시. ②always ⇒항시. じょうじ

상식(上食) offering of meals to a departed soul.

상식(常食) staple food; daily food; a normal diet. じょうしょく

상식(常識) common sense; good sense/ ~ 있는 사람 a man of common[good] sense/ ~적 common-sense; sensible; practical/ ~적으로 생각하여 in the name of common sense. じょうしき

상신(上申) a report (the superior department etc.)/ ~하다 report (to the authorities)/ ~서(書) a written report/ ~자 a reporter. じょうしん

상실(喪失) loss; forfeiture/ ~하다 lose; be deprived of; forfeit. そうしつ

상심(喪心) trance; abstraction; stupefaction/~하다 fall into trance; be abstracted; be depressed; be dejected; be cast down. そうしん

상심(詳審) full investigation; minute inspection/~하다 investigate fully; inspect in detail. しょうしん

상심(傷心) grief; sorrow; heart-break/ ~하다 be grieved; grieve. しょうしん

상아(象牙) ivory/ ~세공 ivory work/ ~질(質) 《이의》 a dentin[e]/ ~탑 an ivory tower; the tower of ivory. ぞうげ

상악(上顎) 【해】 the upper jaw. じょうがく

쌍안경(雙眼鏡) [a pair of] binoculars; opera glasses. そうがんきょう

상앗대 a [row] pole; a punting pole; a boatman's pole. ふなのさお

상애(相愛) mutual love/ ~하다 be in love with each other. そうあい

상약(相約) a promise; an engagement; an agreement/ ~하다 promise with each other; make an engagement[appointment]. たがいにやくそくすること

상약(常藥) a private medicine[remedy].

상어 a shark/ ~ 가죽 sharkskin; shagreen; fishskin; sea leather. さめ

상업(商業) commerce; trade; business/ ~의 commercial; merchantile/ ~ 영어 business[commercial] English/ ~ 학교 a commercial school/ ~화하다 commercialize. しょうぎょう

상없다(常—) (be) unreasonable; absurd. じょうりにもとっている

상여(喪輿) a bier/ ~군 a bier bearer.

상여금(賞與金) a reward 《회사 등의》 a prize; a bonus/연말 ~ the year-end bonus. しょうよきん

상연(上演) presentation; performance/ ~ 하다 play; present; stage; put (a play) on the stage[the boards]/ ~권 performing rights. じょうえん

상영(上映) screening/ ~하다 screen; show; put on the screen. じょうえい

상오(上午) the forenoon; a.m.; A.M./ ~ 네 시에 at four in the morning; at 4 a.m. こぜん

상오리(常—) 【조】 a greenwing; a greenwinged teal.

상온(常溫) the normal temperature. じょうおん

상옷(喪—) mourning clothes ⇒상복. もふく

상완(賞玩) appreciation; admiration/ ~하다 appreciate; enjoy 《귀히 여기다》 prize; admire. たのしんでみること

상왕(上王) the abdicated king.

상용(常用) common[habitual, daily, everyday] use/~의 in common[ordinary, everyday]/ ~ 한자 Chinese characters in common use. じょうよう

상용(商用) business; a business-engagement/ ~으로 on business/ ~어 a commercial[business] term. しょうよう

상우다(傷—) wound; injure; hurt; harm; damage; impair. きずつける

상운(祥雲) auspicious clouds. しょううん

상운(祥運) good luck; auspicious fortune. めでたいうん

상원(上元) January fifteenth of the lunar month.

상원(上院) the Upper House; the House of Lords 《영》; the Senate 《미》/ ~ 의원 a member of the Upper House; a senator 《미》. じょういん

상원(桑園) a mulberry plantation[field]. そうえん

상위(相違) difference; dissimilarity; disagreement; discrepancy; a gap/ ~하다 differ; be different (from); disagree; be at variance (with). そうい

상위(上位) a high[superior] rank; precedence. じょうい

상응(相應) ①《호응》 acting in concert/~하다 act in concert (with); respond to (a request) ②《상당》 suitability; fitness/ ~하다 (be) suitable; fit; suited (to); proper. そうおう

상의(上衣) a coat 《군복의》 a tunic; a blouse 《부인복의》 a jacket. じょうい

상의(上意) a command of the Emperor; the Emperor's wish. じょうい

상의(相議, 商議) consultation; conference 《담판》 negotiation; a parley/ ~하다 consult (with one); take consel (with); confor with; talk (over a matter with one); negotiate. そうだんすること

**상이(傷痍)** wound; injury/ ~의 disabled; wounded/ ~ 군인 a disabled[maimed, crippled] ex-service man; a wounded soldier. しょうい

**상인(商人)** a merchant; a tradesman; a shopkeeper〈영〉; a storekeeper〈미〉/ ~ 근성 a mercenary spirit. しょうにん

**상인(上人)** a saint.

**상인(常人)** the common people. へいみん

**상인(喪人)** a mourner. もちゅうのひと

**상인(霜刃)** a burnished blade.
えいりなあおいやいば

**상인방(上引枋)** 【건】 a lintel. かもい

**상일(常一)** a chore; manual work; miscellaneous services; odd jobs/ ~군 a manual labourer.

**상임(常任)** a permanent post/ ~의 standing; permanent/ ~ 위원회 a standing committee/ ~ 서기 a permanent clerk/ ~ 위원 a trustee; a permanent member [of a council]; a standing committee/ ~ 이사 an executive director 〈미〉. じょうにん

**상자(箱子)** a box; a case (작은) a casket. はこ

**상자성(常磁性)** 【물】 paramagnetism.

**쌍자엽(雙子葉)** a double seed leaf[cotyledon]; dicotyledonous/ ~ 식물 【식】 a dicotyledonous plant/ ~ 종자 a dicotyledonous seed. そうしよう

**상잔(相殘)** struggling with each other/ ~하다 struggle with each other/ 동족 ~ dog eating dog; internal strife; internecine feud; domestic dissension.
たがいにけんかあらそいをすること

**상장(喪杖)** a mourner's walking stick.
もしゆがつくつえ

**상장(喪章)** a mourning badge; a crape.
もしょう

**상장(賞狀)** a certificate of merit; an honorary certificate; honourable mention. しょうじょう

**상장(上場)** ~하다 《증권율》 list [stocks]/ ~주(株) listed stocks.

**상재** 〖불교〗 a monk who is first in line to succeed his master[teacher].

**상재(上梓)** publication; printing/ ~하다 publish; print. しゅっぱんすること

**상재(商才)** business ability[capacity, acumen]; a knack for business.

**상재(霜災)** frost damage/ ~를 입다 suffer from frost. しものひがい

**상쟁(相爭)** dissension; conflict; dispute / ~하다 be at feud with each other; compete with one another; contest; struggle against each other; fight one another. たがいにあらそうこと

**상적(相敵)** antagonism (필적자) an opponent /~하다 rival; match; equal: compare with. たがいにひってきすること

**상적(商敵)** a trade rival (상점) the other shop.

**상전(上典)** the master; the employer.

**상전(相戰)** fighting against each other; quarrel/ ~하다 fight against each other. たがいにたたかうこと

**상전(相傳)** inheritance/~의 hereditary; inherited/~하다 hand down; inherit; transmit. そうでん

**상전(桑田)** a mulberry field/ ~ 벽해 Things are subject to change. そうえん

**상전(詳傳)** a full[detailed] biography.

**상점(商店)** a shop; a store〈미〉/ 대명 ~ the Daemyung firm/ ~가 a shopping street (주요한) a shopping centre.
しょうてん

**상접(相接)** 〖수〗 contact/ ~하다 come in contact[touch] with each other; meet (만나다) get together. くっつくこと

**상정(上程)** ~하다 (일정에) introduce[present, put] (a bill) on the order of the day (의회에) lay before the House (토의에) bring up (a bill) for discussion.
じょうてい

**상정(常情)** [ordinary] human nature[feeling]. ふつうのにんじょう

**상정(想定)** hypothesis(pl. -ses); a supposition; assumption/ ~하다 suppose; imagine; assume (어림하다) estimate.
そうてい

**상정(傷情)** ~하다 injure one's feeling; hurt another's feeling; hurt (a person).
じょうぎをそこなうこと

**상제(上帝)** God; the Creator; Providence; the Lord. じょうてい

**상제(喪制)** ①(사람) a man who is in mourning for his parents or grand-parents; a mourner ②(제도) mourning practice [custom]; the ritual of mourning.
もちゅうのひと

**상조(尙早)** ~의 too early[soon]; premature. しょうそう

**상조(相助)** mutual aid[help, assistance] /~하다 help each other[one another]; be interdependent; cooperate.

**상종(相從)** association; intercourse; friendly relations/~하다 associate[keep company] with each other; mix with each other.

**상좌(上座)** the top seat; an upper seat (주빈의) the seat[place] of honour (식탁의) the head (of a table). じょうざ

**상주(上奏)** a report[an address] to the Throne/ ~하다 report to the Throne / ~문 a memorial to the Throne.
じょうそう

**상주(常住)** constancy; eternity/ ~ 인구 a settled population. じょうじゅう

**상주(喪主)** the chief mourner. もしゅ

**상주(詳註)** copious notes.

**상중(喪中)** mourning. もちゅう

**상중하(上中下)** the first, the second and the third class; good, better, best; the three grades of good; fair, and poor.
じょうちゅうげ

**상지(上肢)** the upper limbs; the arms.
じょうし

**상지(相地)** geomancy.

**상지(相持)** mutual stubbornness; praise; applaud; extol[1]; speak highly 각 maintains his own opinion [idea, view]; refuse to give in each other. とちのきっきょうをうらなうこと

**상지(相知)** an acquaintance. そうち

**상지(常紙)** coarse paper; paper of poor quality. ふつうのかみ

**상지상(上之上)** the very best.

**쌍지팡이** [a pair of] crutches. まつばづえ

**상징(象徵)** a symbol; an emblem;/~하다 symbolize; be symbolic of/ ~주의(主義) symbolism/~적 symbolical. しょうちょう

**상찬(賞讚)** admiration; praise; commendation; applause/ ~하다 praise; admire; speak highly of; commend; extol[1]. しょうさん

**상찰(詳察)** careful observation; full consideration/ ~하다 observe carefully; consider in full. しょうさつ

**상창(傷創)** a wound; an injury; a cut.

**쌍창(雙窓)** a window consisting of two panes.

**상채(償債)** repaying one's debt/ ~하다 repay one's debt. しゃっきんをかえすこと

**상책(上策)** a capital plan; the best policy. じょうさく

**상책(商策)** a business policy.

**상처(喪妻)** the death[loss] of one's wife; bereavement of one's wife/ ~하다 be bereaved of[lose] one's wife; (one's wife) die[pass away]. つまにしべつすること

**상처(傷處)** a wound; an injury; a hurt; a cut (타박상) a bruise (깊은) a gash.

**상천(上天)** ①(하늘) the sky; the heavens ②(하느님) God ③(겨울 하늘) the winter sky. そら

**상체(上體)** the upper part of the body. じょうたい

**상초(上草)** cut tobacco of finest quality. じょうとうのたばこ

**상춘(賞春)** enjoying spring;  admiring the spring scenery/ ~객 admirers for the spring scenery.

**상층(上層)** 《지층 따위》the upper layer [stratum]; 《하늘의》the upper air[region]; 《건》the upper stories 《사회》the upper classes. じょうそう

**상치** lettuce/~쌈 lettuce-wrapped rice. ちしゃ

**상치(上一)** 《물건》an article of superior quality choice articles. じょうとのもの

**상치(相値)** coincidence. さしつかえ

**상침(上針)** a needle of superior quality. じょうとうのはり

**상쾌(爽快)** refreshingness; exhilaration /~한 refreshing; fresh; crisp/~하다 exhilarating. そうかい

**상큼상큼** with light steps. ぴょんぴょんと

**상큼하다** have slender legs; be lanky. すらっとしている

**상타다(賞一)** win[get] a prize; be awarded a prize. しょうをうける

**상탄(賞嘆)** admiration/ ~하다 admire; praise; applaud; extol[1]; speak highly of/~할 만한 admirable; praiseworthy. しょうたん

**상태(狀態)** a condition; the state (of thing, affairs); a situation/생활 ~ living conditions/정신 ~ a mental state. じょうたい

**상태(常態)** a normal condition[state]; normality/ ~로 돌아가다 be restored to a normal condition. じょうたい

**쌍태(雙胎)** a double[twin] fetus. そうたい

**상통(相一)** face; countenance; phiz《속》; ugly mug《속》/ ~을 찌푸리고 with a grimace. かおかたち

**상통(相通)** ①(연락) communication (교환) exchange; interchange/ ~하다 communicate (with); exchange ②(의사의 소통) mutual understanding/~하다 be mutually understood.

**상통(傷痛)** grief; distress; sharp sorrow; heartache; heartbreak/ ~하다 be greatly grieved at heart; suffer distress. こころがきずついていたこと

**상투** a topknot [of hair]. ちょんまげ

**상투(相鬪)** fighting with each other; exchanging blows/ ~하다 fight with each other. たがいにうちあいあらそうこと

**상투(常套)** ~의 commonplace; conventional; hackneyed/ ~ 수단 an old[a common] trick. じょうとう

**상파(翔破)** flying [a distance]; covering a flight distance/ ~하다 fly; cover [a distance]. しょうは

**상판대기** ugly mug. かおかたち

**상팔자(上一)** good fortune; a happy[the best] lot; high living. よいみぶん

**상패(賞牌)** a medal. しょうはい

**상편(上篇)** the first volume[piece]; Book I. じょうべん

**상포(喪布)** cloth for funeral use/ ~계 a mutual-aid society to cover funeral costs.

**상표(商標)** a trademark; a brand; a label/등록 ~ a registered trademark. しょうひょう

**상품(上品)** first-grade articles; superior article. じょうひん

**상품(商品)** goods; merchandise; commodities (매입품) stock/~권 a gift[merchandise] certificate; an exchange ticket; a credit voucher/ ~학 the study of commercial products/ ~ 견본 a commercial sample/ ~ 목록 a catalogue. しょうひん

**상품(賞品)** a prize. しょうひん

**상풍증(傷風症)** 《의》a stuffed-up nose; a nose cold. はなかぜ

**상피(上皮)** 《생》the epithelium.

**상피(象皮)** elephant skin/ ~병 elephantiasis. ぞうひ

**상피(相避)** incest/~붙다 commit incest.

**상피리** 《어》*Scombrops boops*(학명). むつ

**상하(上下)** ①(위와 아래) up and down;

상하 upper and lower sides; top and bottom ②(귀천) the upper and lower classes; high and low; superiors and inferiors ③(전후) the first and second ④(관민) the government and the people. じょうげ
상하(常夏) everlasting summer.
상하다(傷—) ①(손상하다) be hurt[injured, damaged]; (썩다) rot; go bad/감정을 상하게 하다 hurt one's feeling ②(속이) be worried (about); trouble one's mind; be distressed[troubled] with. きずつく
상학(上學) beginning of lessons[school] / ~하다 begin[start] school[lessons].
상학(相學) physiognomy; phrenology. そうがく
상학(商學) commercial science.
상한(上限) maximum; the upper limit.
상한(象限) 【수】 a quadrant/ ~의(儀) 【천】 a quadrant. しょうげん
상합(相合) coincidence; agreement; conformity/~하다 coincide with one another; agree with each other. そうごう
상항(上項) the above; the above-mentioned part; the said item.
상항(商港) a commercial harbour[port]. しょうこう
상해(傷害) injury; harm; casualty/~하다 injury; do (one) an injury/ ~치사(致死) bodily injury resulting in death/ ~ 보험 accident[casualty] insurance. しょうがい
상해(詳解) a detailed explanation; minute explanation; a full commentary/~하다 explain minutely; give a detailed explanation (of). しょうかい
상해(霜害) damage by[from] frost; frost-damage.
상행(上行) ~의 up/ ~선[열차] an up-line[-train].
상행위(商行爲) a business[commercial] transaction. しょうこうい
상현(上弦) 【천】 the first quarter [of the moon]/~달 a waxing moon; a young moon. じょうげん
상혈(上血) hemoptysis. ちをはくこと
상형(常衡) avoirdupois [weight].
상형 문자(象形文字) a hieroglyphic character; a hieroglyphics; a pictograph. しょうけいもんじ
상호(相互) (부사적) mutually; reciprocally/ ~의 mutual; reciprocal/ ~ 작용 reciprocal action/ ~ 원조 조약 mutual assistance pact/ ~ 부조 mutual aid. そうご
상호(商號) (상점명) a firm[shop] name (품명) a trade name. しょうごう
상혼(商魂) a commercial spirit. しょうこん
상황(相換) exchange; interchange/ ~하다 exchange; interchange/대금 ~ cash on delivery. たがいにかえること
상환(償還) repayment; redemption/ ~하다 repay; redeem; refund. しょうかん
상황(狀況) the state of things[affairs]; conditions; circumstances. じょうきょう
상황(上皇) the abdicated emperor. じょうこう
상황(商況) business[trade] conditions (시황) the market [condition]; 【경】 the tone of a market. しょうきょう
상회(商會) a firm; a company; a concern. しょうかい
상훈(賞勳) citation of merit/~과 the Section of Decoration. しょうくん
상흔(傷痕) a scar. しょうこん
샅 the crotch; the groin.
샅바 ①(씨름할 때에) a cloth band worn about legs in Korean wrestling ②(죄인의) a leg-band for a prisoner.
샅샅이 all over; in every nook and corner; everywhere. くまなく
쌓다 ①(겹겹이 포개다) pile up; heap (up); stack; lay ②(구축하다) build; erect; raise; construct ③(축적하다) accumulate; gain; acquire; store up; amass. つむ
쌓이다 be piled up; be heaped; get accumulated (눈 따위가) lie (on). つまれる
새¹ (동물) a bird; a fowl (가금) poultry / ~ 소리 a bird call; the song[note] of a bird; wood notes/~장수 a poultry man; a bird-fancier. とり
새² interval ⇒사이. あいだ
새³ (새로운) new (신기한) novel (신선한) fresh (최근의) recent. あたらしい
새⁴ (띠) sod; turf (억새) purple eulalia (이엉) straw thatch. いわとだしば
새– (짙은) deep; dark/~파랑 deep blue; navy blue(미). まー
새(璽) the Great Seal ⇒국새. こくじ
새가슴 a chicken[pigeon] breast/ ~의 chicken-breasted. とりのようなむね
새겨듣다 listen carefully to ⇒새기어듣다.
새경 the annual salary given to a farm servant.
새고막 【어】 a bloody clam. あかがい
새골(鰓骨) 【어】 branchial skeleton[bones] of a fish. えらのほね
새곰하다 (be) sour acid. すっぱい
새공(鰓孔) 【어】 a branchial pore; a gill slit. えらのあな
새근거리다 ①(뼈마디가) ache ②(숨을) pant; gasp. ずきずきいたむ
새근하다 have a slight pain; ache. ふしぶしがずきずきうずく
새금새금하다 all sourish. ちょっとすっぱい
새금하다 (be) sourish/이 사과는 ~ This apple tastes a bit sour. ちょっとすっぱい
새끼¹ (끈) a [coarse] straw rope/ ~를 꼬다 make[twist] a rope/~발 a straw-rope blind. なわ
새끼² ①(동물의) [the] young; a cub (한배의) a litter (소의) a calf (말·사슴의) a colt (개의) a puppy (고양이의) a kitty (양의) a lamb (물고기의) fry (새의) a young bird; a chicken / ~를 낳다 bring forth (its) young; litter; cub (양이) lamb (개가) pup (고양이가) kitten (소가) calf ②(자식) a child; a son (아들);

새기다 a daughter(딸) ③(육) a fellow; a guy /저 ~ that fellow. どうぶつのこ

새기다¹ ①(파다) carve (an image); engrave (a seal); chisel; incise /도장을 ~ engrave a seal ②(기억하다) bear[keep] (a thing) in mind; take (a thing) to heart; engrave (an image) on one's mind. きざむ

새기다² interpret; explain; construe; accept; take / 바르게 ~ interpret variously. かいしゃくする

새기다³ 《반추하다》 ruminate; chew the cud. はんすうする

새끼발가락 a little toe. あしのこゆび

새끼발톱 the little toenail. あしのこゆびのつめ

새끼 벌레 larva(pl. ·vae). ようちゅう

새끼손가락 the little finger. こゆび

새끼손톱 a little[small] fingernail. こゆびのつめ

새기어듣다 listen carefully to; pay attention to.

새김 ①(뜻의) interpretation; paraphrase; explanation ②(번역) translation ③(조각) carving; engraving; sculpture. かいしゃく

새김질 ①(조각) carving; engraving; sculpture/ ~하다 carve; engrave; chisel ②(반추) ruminating/ ~하다 ruminate; chew the cud. ちょうこくすること

새김칼 a carving knife; a graver; a burin.

새나다 (비밀이) get[slip] out; be disclosed; leak out. ばれる

새노랗다 (be) [golden] yellow; be a vivid yellow. まっきいろ

새다 ①(날이) dawn; break ②(기체·액체 따위가) leak [out]; (흘러나오다) trickle out; escape (빛 따위가) come through (말소리가) be heard outside ③(비밀이) get[slip] out; be disclosed; leak out. あける

새달 next month; the coming month. らいげつ

새때 between meals.

새떡 a bride ⇒새색시. しんこんのおんな

새되다 (be) sharp; shrill; soprano. かんだかい

새둥주리 a bird['s] nest. とりのす

새뜨다 (be) separated; be at a distance; be spaced [at intervals]; (be) slow. かんかくあいている

새득새득 slightly dry; withered/ ~하다 (be) somewhat dry; withered; wizened. しなしな

새들새들 slightly wilted/ ~한 somewhat withered. しなしな

새뜻하다 (be) fresh and neat; new and bright. あたらしくすがすがしい

새로 new[ly]; freshly; anew; afresh; [over] again. あたらしく

새로에 (도리어) anything but; far from (…은 물론 …도) not to mention; not to speak of. —はさておいて

새록새록 in succession. つぎつぎと

새롭다 (be) new (전기하다) novel (신선하다) fresh (최근) recent /새롭게 newly; freshly /아직도 기억에 ~ be still fresh in one's memory. あたらしい

새롱거리다 babble; gabble; jabber; patter; prattle; rattle; chatter; dally; flirt. べちゃくちゃしゃべる

새마을운동(—運動) the new community movement.

새막(—幕) a hut built in a field to scare sparrows.

새맛 freshness; novelty/ ~을 내다 display originality (in).

새매 《조》 an Asiatic sparrow hawk.

새머루 《식》 a kind of grapevine. ぎょうじゃのみず

새머리 beef from between the ribs; spare ribs.

새무룩하다 ①(기색이) (be) sulky; glum; sullen ②(날씨가) (be) leaden; murky; gloomy; sullen. ことばがない

새물 ①(과일·생선 따위) the first product of the season ②(옷) fresh washed clothes. あたらしいもの

새물내 the laundry scent of clothes.

새물청어(—青魚) ①《어》 the first herring on the market ②(무경험자) a new [green, raw] hand; a froshman; a greenhorn. はつでのにしん

새박 milkweed seeds. かがいも

새빨갛다 ①(빛깔이) (be) deep red; crimson ②(거짓말이) barefaced. まっかだ

새밭 a field [full] of eulalia.

새벽¹ (아침) dawn; the break of the day; daybreak/ ~에 at break[peep] of day/ ~부터 저녁까지 from dawn till dusk/ ~녘 the time of dawning. よあけ

새벽² (전) the second layer of plaster; the third coating of wall.

새벽같이 early in the morning; at an early hour. あさはやく

새벽 동자 cooking at dawn/ ~하다 cook food at dawn; boil rice at daybreak. あかつきにつくるごめし

새보다 chase birds away from crops; watch for[against] birds. とりを近づけない

새봄 early spring. しんしゅん

새부랑거리다 gabble; wag one's tongue; talk garrulously.

새사냥 fowling; bird shooting.

새사람 ①(신인) a new figure ②(신부) a new bride ③(갱생한) a new man; another man. あたらしいひと

새싹 a sprout; a shoot; a bud/ ~이 나다 bud; sprout.

새살 new skin.

새살거리다 carry on[behave] flippantly; chatter merrily; be not serious. にやにやしながらおしゃべりする

새살스럽다 (be) flippant; frivolous; shallow. ふざけている

새삼 《식》 a dodder. ねなしかずら

**새삼스럽다** (be) new; fresh/새삼스럽게 anew; afresh 《다시》 again 《특히》 specially 《형식적으로》 formally 《이제서야》 now/새삼스럽게 anew/새삼스럽게 굴 열려고 있나 You needn't make yourself so uneasy now? ことあたらしい

**새새틈틈** ①《공간》 every nook and cranny [corner] ②《시간》 at intervals; at one's odd moments.

**새색시** a bride. しんこんのおんな
**새서방**(一書房) a bridegroom. しんこんのおとこ
**새실새실** grinningly/～웃다 laugh mischievously. べちゃくちゃ
**새아가씨** 《새아기》 a bride; a young wife; one's new daughter-in-law. あたらしいよめ
**새알** a sparrow egg. すずめのたまご
**새알심** rice dumplings [in red-bean soup]. ぜんざいにいれるだんご
**새암** jealousy; envy/～하다 be jealous [covetous, envious]. ねたみ
**새앙** 《식》 ginger. しょうが
**새앙머리** one's hair done up to two locks.
**새앙쥐** 《동》 a mouse(pl. mice).
**새옹** a small brass kettle.
**새옹지마**(塞翁之馬) 옛 인간만사 ～ Inscrutable are the ways of Heaven.
**새완두**(一豌豆) 《식》 a hairy vetch.
**새우**[1] 《동》 a lobster 《대하》 a crawfish; 《작은》 a shrimp/～로 잉어를 낚다 throw a sprat to catch a whale. えび
**새우**[2] 《기와 밑의》 the clay laid under a tile.
**새우나무** 《식》 a hop hornbeam; *Ostrya japonica*(학명).
**새우다**[1] 《밤을》 sit[stay] up all night; keep vigil/밤을 새워서 공부하다 burn the midnight oil; study till late at night. よるをあかす
**새우다**[2] 《시기를》 be jealous (of); be envious of. しっとする
**새우등** a stoop; a bent back; round shoulders. ねこせ
**새우잠** sleeping all curled up/～ 자다 lie huddled up in bed.
**새우젓** pickled shrimps. えびのしおから
**새장**(一欌) a bird cage/～ 속의 새 a caged bird; a cageling. とりかご
**새전**(賽錢) an offertory. さいせん
**새조개** 《어》 a cockle. しおふき
**새쪽** the east; the direction of the east wind. とうほう
**새중간**(一中間) the very middle.
**새집**[1] 《신축한》 a new house; a newly-built house. しんちくのいえ
**새집**[2] 《새의》 a nest [of sparrow]. とりのす
**새창** the lower intestine of an ox. うしのないぞう
**새척지근하다** (be) sourish.
**새초** 《미역》 a kind of dried seaweed.
**새총**(一銃) 《공기총》 an air gun; an air rifle 《고무총》 a slingshot. ちょうじょう
**새출발**(一出發) a fresh start/～하다 make a fresh start.

**새치** white hair in youth.
**새치기** ①《일》 an odd job; a side job/～하다 do other work at odd moments ②《차례를》 cutting; snatching/ ～하다 cut in; snatch; intercept.
**새치름하다** paly the innocent; wear an innocent look/그녀의 새치름한 태도 her cold attitude. そしらんかおをする
**새치부리다** behave *oneself* with reserve; pretend diffidence.
**새침데기** an ostensibly modest person. おとなしいふりをするひと
**새침하다** play the innocent ⇨새치름하다.
**새카맣다** (be) pitch-dark; jet-black. まっくろだ
**새콤하다** (be)sour; acid. さっぱい
**새큰거리다** ache. ふしぶしがずきする
**새큰하다** aching. ふしぶしがずきずきする
**새털** a feather; plume 《솜털》 down.
**새털구름** 《천》 a cirrus(pl. cirri). けんうん
**새파랗다** (be) deep blue 《안색이》 (be) deadly pale; as white as a sheet/새파란 하늘 the deep blue sky. まっあおだ
**새하얗다** (be) pure[snow] white; (be) dazzling[immaculately] white. まっしろだ
**새해** new year; the New Year/～ 복 많이 받으십시오 [I wish you] a Happy New Year!/～를 맞이하다 greet the New Year. しんねん
**새해 문안**(一問安) the New Year's greetings.

**색**[1] 《소리》 with a hiss. しゅう
**색**[2] 《자루》 a sack 《통·짐 따위》 a case (for *glasses*); 《피임구》 a condom; a rubber.
**색**(色) a colour 《농담》 a shade 《농색》 a tint 《피부의》 complexion 《여색》 love/진한[연한] ～ a deep[light] colour. いろ
**색각**(色覺) 《심》 the colour sense. しきかく
**색깔**(色一) colo[u]r ⇨빛깔. いろ
**색갈다** change; make a change; diversify.
**색감**(色感) the color sense; color sensation.
**색골**(色骨) a sensualist; an admirer of the fair sex; a Don Juan. こうしょくか
**색광**(色狂) an erotomaniac 《남자》 a satyr 《여자》 nymphomaniac/～증 sexual insanity; erotomania. いろきちがい
**색구**(索具) rigging.
**색다르다**(色一) (be) novel; new; fresh 《기이》 (be) unusual; uncommon/색다른 모자 a fancy hat. めあたらしい
**색대** a sharp-pointed bamboo or metal instrument for testing rice in a bag.
**색떡**(色一) coloured rice-cake. いろだんご
**색덕**(色德) [a lady's] beauty and virtue. おんなのびぼうとびとく
**색도**(索道) a cableway; a ropeway.
**색동**(色一) colo[u]red patches/～ 저고리 a child's coat with multi-coloured sleeves.
**색등**(色燈) a colored lantern[light].
**색마**(色魔) a libertine; a sexual pervert; an erotomaniac; a slave of lust. しきま

**색맹**(色盲) colour-blindness.

**색미투리**(色—) brightly decorated hemp sandals for children.

**색사**(色事) sexual relation[intercourse].

**색사진**(色寫眞) a color picture.

**색상**(色傷) a disease caused by sexual excess.

**색상자**(色箱子) a colo[u]r-papered box.

**색색** [breathe] in light little gasps/～ 잠을 자다 sleep sweetly[calmly, peacefully].

**색색거리다** pant; gasp [for breath]; breathe hard.

**색색이**(色色—) with various colo[u]rs.

**색소**(色素) colouring matter; pigment/～체 chromatophore; chromatogen/～액 a staining solution.

**색쓰다**(色—) have[practice] sexual intercourse.

**색시** (신부)a bride 《아내》 a wife 《처녀》 a maiden; a lass.

**색신 검사**(色神檢査) examination of colo[u]r sense.

**색실**(色—) dyed[colo[u]red] thread; dyed cord.

**색심**(色心) 《성욕의》 lustful mind; sensual desire; sexual desire.

**색안경**(色眼鏡) tinted glasses; colored spectacles; sunglasses.

**색약**(色弱) colo[u]r blindness.

**색연필**(色鉛筆) a coloured pencil.

**색옷**(色—) dyed 무색옷.

**색욕**(色慾) lust; sexual[carnal] desire; sexual appetite.

**색유리**(色琉璃) stained glass; coloured glass; flashed glass.

**색의**(色衣) dyed clothes; coloured garments.

**색인**(索引) an index/자구(字句) ～ index verborum.

**색정**(色情) sexual desire[passion]; carnal desire; lust/～광 sexual mania; erotomania 《사람》 a sexual maniac.

**색종이**(色—) colored paper.

**색주가**(色酒家) a barrel house; a night club; a brothel; a bawdy house.

**색채**(色彩) colouration; colouring; colour; tint.

**색책**(塞責) ～하다 talk out of rebuke; dodge reprimand; shuffle out of responsibilities.

**색체**(色褅) a colourless face.

**색출**(索出) ～하다 search[seek, ferret] out; hunt[round] up; track down.

**색칠**(色漆) colouring; painting; staining/～하다 colour; paint; stain; apply colored lacquer.

**색탐**(色貪) lewd desire; lust/～하다 dangle after woman; have lecherous desires.

**색태**(色態) good manners; charming conduct; lovely behaviour.

**색판**(色版) ¶ ～ 인쇄 colour printing/～화 colour-prints.

**색향**(色香) beauty; charm; attractions.

**색황**(色荒) libertinism; dissipation.

**샌님** a weak-kneed and bigoted person.

**샐녘** 《여명》 dawn; daybreak.

**샐룩거리다** twitch; be cramped; have the cramp.

**샐쭉** ～하다 (be) distorted 실쭉.

**샘¹** 《물의》 a spring 《우물》 a fountain; a well 우물.

**샘²** 《시기》 jealousy; envy / ～ 하다 be jealous; be jaundiced; envy 《선망하다》 be envious of.

**샘구멍** a fountainhead; a headspring; a source.

**샘물** spring water; fountain water.

**샘솟다** [water] rise in a fountain; gush [spring] out[forth].

**샘터** a washing place watered by a spring.

**샘터지다** ①《새로》water starts to gush from a fountain ②《다시》a spring revives.

**샛강**(—江) a large river which divides to pass around an island.

**샛거리** work-break snacks.

**샛검불** fire-weeds.

**샛길** a lane; a narrow path; a by-pass; a by-road; a byway.

**샛문**(—門) a side gate.

**샛바람** an east wind.

**샛밥** ①《곁두리》snack for farmhands ②《끼니 외의》 a snack; a meal taken at an irregular time.

**샛별** 《계명성》 the morning star; Lucifer.

**샛서방**(—書房) an adulterer ⇨ 샛이서방.

**생**(生)¹ 《생명》 life 《삶》 living; existence /～의 철학 philosophy of life; life philosophy.

**생**(生)² 《자기》 I; me/ ～이 전에 말씀 드린 바와 같이 as I have informed you before.

**생**-(生) 《조리하지 않은》raw; uncooked 《자연 그대로의》 crude 《신선한》 fresh 《익지 않은》 green; unripe 《살아 있는》 live; living; green 《공연한》 unreasonable/～우유 raw milk.

-**생**(生) ①《청년》 young man's title/김 ～ young Mr. Kim ②《학생》a student of ③《생년의》 born in (a year); born on (a date).

**생가**(生家) the house of one's birth; one's parent's home; one's paternal home;

생가슴 　　　　　　　　　　503　　　　　　　　　　생리

the house of *one's* birth. 　せいか
**생가슴** an aching heart. 　つらいこころ
**생가죽**(生一) a raw hide; a pelt; untanned skin.
**생가지**(生一) a live [tree] branch. 　なまきのえだ
**생각** ⇨별항 참조.
**생각나다** 《기억나다》 recollect; remember; recall; call to mind; have a glimmering [an inkling] of; have a reminiscence of 《착상》 occur (to *one's* mind); hit upon; flash on; have an idea. おもいだす
**생각되다** 《보이다》 appear; look; seem (*to*) 《타인에게》 be thought of: be regarded as/좋게[나쁘게] ~ be well[ill] thought of.
**생각해 내다** 《안출》 think out (*a plan*); invent; contrive; devise 《상기하다》 recall; remember; call to mind; recollect; be reminded of.
**생강**(生薑) ginger ⇨새앙. しょうが
**생거름**(生一) raw manure; unmixed fertilizer. りょくひ
**생것**(生一) raw food; unripe fruit. なまのもの
**생계망게하다** (be) incomprehensible; unaccountable; inexplicable.
**생견**(生絹) raw silks.
**생경**(生硬) crudeness; immaturity/ ~하다 (be) crude; raw; stiff; unrefined.
**생경**(生梗) discord between two persons.
**생계**(生計) livelihood; living; subsistence/ ~비 living expenses/ ~가 넉넉[곤란]하다 make a good[poor] living/ 문필로 ~를 세우다 make a living by literary work; live by *one's* pen. せいけい
**생고무**(生一) crude rubber.
**생과**(生果) raw green fruits.
**생과부**(生寡婦) a neglected wife; a grass widow.
**생과실**(生果實) unripe fruit; raw fruit. なまのくだもの
**생과자**(生菓子) [a] cake; [a] pastry.
**생굴**(生一) raw[uncooked] oyster; a fresh oyster. なまのかき
**생글거리다** smile/생글거리며 with a smile; smilingly. にこにこする
**생금**(生金) rude gold; unrefined ore; gold ore. せいれんしないきん
**생금**(生擒) capture/ ~하다 catch[take, capture] (*a tiger*) alive. いけどり
**생급스럽다** (be) abrupt; brusque.
**생긋거리다** smile; chuckle. にこっと
**생기**(生氣) animation; life; vitality/ ~있는 animated; vital; lively; spirited. せいき
**생기다** 《발생하다》 happen; occur; take place; come about; come into existence /직업이 ~ get a job 《유래하다》 originate (*from, in*); result (*from*). おこる
**생김새** personal appearance; looks features. うまれつき
**생김생김** features; looks; a face; [personal] appearance. ようぼう

**생나무**(生一) green wood; wet faggot [wood]. なまき
**생남**(生男) the birth of a son; delivery of a boy/~하다 be delivered of a boy; give birth to a boy 《아버지가》 beget a son. おとこのこがうまれること
**생남례**(生男禮) celebration of the birth of *one's* son/ ~하다 stand treat for friends to celebrate the birth of *one's* own son.
**생녀**(生女) delivery of a girl/ ~하다 be delivered of a girl; give birth to a girl. おんなのこがうまれること
**생년**(生年) the year of birth/ ~월일 the date of *one's* birth. うまれたとし
**생니**(生一) a healthy tooth. かんぜんなは
**생담배**(生一) a cigarette butt still burning.
**생땅**(生一) uncultivated land; wild land; untouched soil. せいち
**생당목**(生唐木) unbleached cotton cloth. ひょうはくしないカナキン
**생때같다** (be) healthy; sound; robust; fine and dandy. じょうぶだ
**생떼거리** obstinacy; stubbornness; obduracy; pertinacity. しっこう
**생도**(生徒) a scholar 《국민학교·중학교의》 a school-boy[-girl]; a pupil 《국민학교의》 school children. せいと
**생도**(生道) a living; a livelihood; a means of living. せいけい
**생돈**(生一) money spent to no purpose.
**생동** 《鑛》 an unexploited mineral vein. はっけんしただのこうみゃく
**생동**(生動) lifelikeness/ ~하다 be lifelike. せいどう
**생동**(生銅) unrefined copper. せいどう
**생동생동하다** (be) vigorous[lively, light-hearted] as ever. いきいきしている
**생되다**(生一) (be) immature; inexperienced; unskilled; green; clumsy/생지 말 crude speech. しろうとくさい
**생득**(生得) nature/ ~의 natural; inborn; innate/ ~ 관념 innate ideas/ ~권 *one's* birth-right. せいとく
**생래**(生來) by nature; naturally; by birth/ ~의 natural; innate; born; inborn. せいらい
**생략**(省略) abbreviation; abridg[e]ment /~하다 abbreviate; abridge; omit (*from*). しょうりゃく
**생량**(生凉) early autumn; the beginning of the cool season/ ~하다 the cool autumn weather sets in/~머리 the early autumn. すずしくなること
**생력군**(生力軍) a vigorous person; a strong fellow. じょうぶなひと
**생령**(生靈) souls; lives; people. せいめい
**생로**(生路) living ⇨생계(生計). せいけい
**생리**(生利) ~하다 yield a profit. りえきがでるようにすること
**생리**(生理) physiology/~의 physiological/ ~적 physiological/ ~학 a physiology/~학자 a physiologist. せいり

생마(生馬) an unbroken horse. やせいば
생매(生埋) burying alive/ ~하다 bury alive. いきうめ
생맥주(生麥酒) draught[draft] beer; beer on draught[draft].
생먹다 ①(말을 안 듣다) do not take[follow] (a person's advice); do not obey ②(모른 척하다) take no notice of; feign [pretend, affect] ignorance.
생면(生面) (처음 대면) a first meeting [interview] (with one)/~하다 see[meet, interview] (one) for the first time. しょたいめん
생면 부지(生面不知) an utter stranger.
생면주(生綿紬) raw silk cloth. きいとのきぬおりもの

생명(生命) life 《중대한 사물》the soul (of thing)/ ~을 걸고 at the risk of one's life/ ~ 보험 life insurance/ ~선 a life line/ ~수 a life giving water/ ~을 내던지다 lay down one's life (for). せいめい
생모(生母) one's real mother. せいぼ
생모시(生一) unbleached ramie cloth.
생목(生一) regurgitated food.
생목(生木)¹ 《직물》unbleached cotton cloth. きもめん
생목(生木)² green wood ⇒생나무. なまき
생목숨(生一) ①《목숨》 life ②《죄없는 사람의 목숨》an innocent [person's] life. いのち
생무지 a raw novice; a green hand; a

# 생 각

①(사고) thinking 《사상》a thought; an idea 《관념》a notion; a concept; a conception/ ~하다 think (of, about); give thought (to); conceive; reflect; meditate/좋은 ~ a happy[good] idea; a capital[splendid] idea/표한 ~ a queer notion/~에 잠기다 be lost in thought/~은 좋으나 실행할 수가 없다 That is a good idea but it won't work. /~을 전하다 convey thoughts/~이 다르다 have a different way of thinking (from)/혼자 ~하다 think to oneself/ ~하지 않을 수 없다 I cannot get off my mind./좋은 생각이 떠올랐다 A good idea occurred to me. /~하기도 싫다 I dislike the very thought of it.
②(추억·숙고) recollection; remembrance/ ~하다 ponder; reflect; think over/ ~이 나다 remember; recall; have the recollection/장래를 ~하다 reflect upon the future/~에 on reflection/내일까지 ~할 여유를 달라 Let me think it over till tomorrow. /그런 말을 한 ~이 나지 않는다 I have no recollection of having said that.
③(의도) an intention; a plan; an idea; a view/ ~하다 intend (to do); have in mind; think of (doing); plan to; be going (to)/이번 여름에는 소설이나 쓸까 ~한다 I am thinking of writing a novel this summer./학자가 될 ~으로 공부하다 study with the intention of becoming a scholar/나는 선생이 될 ~이었다 I intended to become a teacher.
④(그리움·욕망) desire; longing; wish / ~하다 desire; long; pine/사과 ~이 나다 feels like [having] an apple/임이 ~이 나다 long for one's sweetheart/만사가 ~과 같이 되지 않는다 Things don't go as we wish., Everything goes wrong with me. /집 ~이 난다 I began to think of home.
⑤(상상) imagination; supposition/~하다 think; believe; imagine; suppose / ~ 좀 해 봐 Just imagine !/~할 수 없는 unimaginable; unthinkable.
⑥(기대) expectation; supposition; hope/ ~하다 expect; hope/ ~이 어긋나다 be disappointed in one's expectations /결과가 ~대로 되다 the results turn out just as one expects/만사가 ~대로 안 된다 Everything goes wrong[amiss] with me., Things don't go as we wish. / ~했던 것보다는 일이 쉬웠다 I found the work easier than I had expected.
⑦(분별·배려) discretion; prudence; [good] judgment/ ~하다 consider; take into consideration; care for; think of; pay attention to/ ~ 없이 thoughtlessly; imprudently; rashly/내 ~으로는 in my judgment; to my thinking/내일을 ~하다 take thought for the tomorrow/ 건강을 ~하다 take one's health into consideration/그 여자는 남편을 조금도 ~지 않는다 She never give her husband a thought[second thought]. /그것은 ~할 문제다 It is a matter for consideration.
⑧(각오) a resolution/네가 정 그렇다면 이쪽도 ~이 있다 Two can play at that game.
⑨(의견) opinion; views 《제안》a suggestion/ ~하다 ponder; reflect; think over/정해진 ~ a settled[definite] opinion/흔들리는 ~ an irresolute mind/ 내 ~으로는 to my mind; in my opinion /내 말을 잘 ~해 봐라 Think over what I told you. /나는 네 ~과 다르다 I have a different opinion from yours. /내 ~으로는 당신이 옳은것 같습니다 In my opinion[To my mind] you are right.

tenderfoot. ずぶのしろうと

**생물**(生物) a living[an animate] thing; a creature **(총칭)** life/ ~계 animals and plants; the animate creation/ ~학 biology/ ~학자 a biologist / ~학적 biological/ ~ 화학 biochemistry/ ~ 발생설 biogenesis. せいぶつ

**생민**(生民) the people. こくみん

**생밤**(生—) raw chestnuts. なまぐり

**생방송**(生放送) **(라디오의)** a live broadcast **(텔레비전의)** live[television] coverage (of *an event*)/ ~하다 cover (*a musical play*) live (by *television*).

**생배**(生—) ¶ ~를 앓다 be sick with envy.

**생번**(生蕃) aborigines [of Formosa]; unsubmitted tribesmen. せいばん

**생베**(生—) unbleached hemp-cloth.

**생벼락**(生—) an accidental disaster; a sudden calamity. とつぜんさいなん

**생병**(生病) a sickness caused by over-work.

**생복**(生鰒) a raw abalone.

**생부**(生父) one's real father. せいふ

**생부모**(生父母) one's own[real] parents.

**생불**(生佛) a living Buddha; an incarnation of Buddha. しょうぶつ

**생사**(生死) life or[and] death **(안부)** safety **(운명)** fate/ ~에 관한 문제 a matter of life or death; a vital question / ~를 같이하다 share *one's* fate (*with*) / ~ 지경을 헤매다 hover between life and death. せいし

**생사**(生絲) raw silk. きいと

**생사람**(生—) an innocent person/ ~잡다 **(살해하다)** kill an innocent person **(모해하다)** inflict injury upon an innocent person.

**생산**(生產) production/ ~하다 produce; turn out/ ~자 a producer/ ~물 produce/ ~고 [an] output **(농업의)** [a] yield/ ~ 능력 producing capacity/ 과잉 overproduction/ ~재 producers' goods/ ~ 관리 production control. せいさん

**생살 여탈**(生殺與奪) sparing life and killing/ ~권을 쥐다 hold the power of life and death. せいさつよだつ

**생색**(生色) a credit/ ~나다 reflect credit on (*one*); do (*one*) credit/ ~내다 pose as a benefactor. めんもく

**생생가**(生生家) one's paternal home; the house of *one's* real father. じっぷのせいか

**생생하다**(生生—) (be) vivid; lively; fresh; full of life/생생히 vividly; true to the life. なまなましい

**생석회**(生石灰) limestone; quicklime. さんかカルシューム

**생선**(生鮮) [a] fish; fresh [raw] fish/ ~ 장수 a fishmonger; a fish dealer/ ~ 회(膾) sliced raw fish. せいせん

**생성**(生成) creating; formation **(철학의)** becoming; generation/ ~하다 create; form; generate. せいせい

**생소**(生疎) unfamiliarity **(미지)** ignorance **(무경험)** inexperience/ ~하다 (be) unfamiliar; not acquainted with; strange. なれてないこと

**생소리**(生—) an unreasonable talk; an absurdity; a nonsense.

**생수**(生水) spring water/ ~받이 a rice field irrigated with spring water. なまみず

**생시**(生時) ①**(태어난 시간)** (*one's*) birth hour; the time of *one's* birth ②**(깨어 있을 때)** waking hours/ ~에 in waking hours ③**(생전)** *one's* lifetime. うまれたじかん

**생식**(生食) eating (*something*) raw[uncooked]/ ~하다 eat (*something*) raw. せいしょく

**생식**(生殖) generation; reproduction; procreation/ ~하다 reproduce; procreate; generate/~ 작용[기능] the generative reproductive[function]/ ~력 generative power; fecundity/ ~기(器) the generative[sexual] organs; genitals/ ~ 세포 a germ cell. せいしょく

**생신**(生辰) a birthday. たんじょうび

**생아버지**(生—) *one's* real father ⇒생부(生父). せいふ

**생안발** a sore toe; a boil on the tip of a toe.

**생안손** a swelling on the tip of a finger; a sore finger.

**생애**(生涯) a career **(생활)** life; living; **(생계)** livelihood. しょうがい

**생양목**(生洋木) unbleached calico.

**생어**(生魚) ①**(산 물고기)** a live fish ②**(생선)** fresh fish(절인 것의 대); **(말린 것의 대)** raw fish. せいぎょ

**생어머니**(生—) one's real mother ⇒생모(生母). せいぶつ

**생억지**(生—) irrational insistence on having *one's* own way; stubbornness; perversity. いいつけ

**생업**(生業) an occupation; a calling/ ~자금 a rehabilitation fund; a fund for operating business. せいぎょう

**생옥양목**(生玉洋木) unbleached cotton.

**생울타리** a hedge.

**생원**(生員) **(옛 제도)** a person who had passed the minor state examination **(성 밑에)** Mister…; Mr…; …Esquire(略: Esq.).

**생유**(生乳) raw milk. なまちち

**생육**(生肉) raw meat; uncooked meat. なまにく

**생육**(生育) bringing up; rearing; raising /~하다 bring up; rear; raise; foster; nurse. せいいく

**생으로**(生—) ①**(날것으로)** uncooked; raw /~ 먹다 eat raw ②**(억지로)** forcibly; unreasonably ③**(까닭없이)** without any reason; causelessly. なまで

**생의**(生意) intention; inclination/ ~하다 intend; have a mind to do; be inclined to do. きとしん

**생이별**(生離別) a lifelong separation[parting]; separation by circumstances/ ~하다 part (from *a person*) forever [for life]. いきわかれ

**생이지지**(生而知之) ~하다 know without being taught.

**생일**(生日) a birthday; *one's* natal day / ~을 축하하다 celebrate *one's* birthday. たんじょうび

**생짜**(生一) (음식) uncooked food (고기) raw fish[meat] (과실) unripe[green] fruits. なまのもの

**생자**(生子) delivery of a boy ⇨생남(生男)/ ~하다 give birth to a boy. おとこのこがうまれること

**생자**(生者) (산사람) a living person (생명이 있는 것) living beings / ~ 필멸(必滅) Man is mortal., Life is subject to decay. せいしゃ

**생장**(生長) growth; increment/ ~하다 grow; thrive. せいちょう

**생장작**(生長斫) wet firewood.

**생재**(生財) accumulation of property; increase of *one's* fortune[goods] / ~하다 accumulate[increase] *one's* property; add to *one's* fortune; increase *one's* goods. ざいぶつをふやすこと

**생전**(生前) lifetime / ~에 during[in] *one's* life[time]; while alive. せいぜん

**생존**(生存) existence; being; life/~하다 exist (살아 남다) survive/ ~권 the right to live/ ~자 a surviver/ ~ 경쟁 the struggle for existence (생태) competition. せいぞん

**생죽음**(生一) a violent[an unnatural] death (참사) a tragic death (변사) an accidental death/~하다 die[meet] a violent[tragic, unnatural, accidental] death; die by violence. おうし

**생쥐** musk rat ⇨새앙쥐.

**생지**(生地) untouched soil ⇨생땅. せいち

**생지옥**(生地獄) a hell on earth. いきじごく

**생질**(甥姪) *one's* sister's son; a nephew.

**생채**(生菜) salad; lettuce.

**생채**(生彩) brilliance; vividness; life; vitality. せいさい

**생채기** a [nail] scratch. ひっかいたあと

**생철**(一鐵) tin plate/~통 a tin[-can].

**생청**(生清) unrefined honey.

**생청스럽다** (be) inconsistent; contradictory. ふごうりだ

**생체**(生體) a living body/ ~ 해부 vivisection.

**생초**(生綃) silk gauze.

**생치**(生雉) an uncooked pheasant. りょうりしてないきじ

**생칠**(生漆) (안 달인) unboiled lacquer (정제하지 않은) unrefined sap of lacquer tree. なまうるし

**생탈**(生頉) deliberately caused trouble; intentional disturbance. こいのいんえん

**생태**(生態) an organism/ ~학 ecology; bionomics/ ~ 변화 ecological adaptation. せいたい

**생트집**(生一) an unreasonable dispute; purposeful fault-finding/ ~하다 lead to an unreasonable dispute; find fault (with *one*) purposefully/~잡지 마라 Stop riding me! むりないいがかり

**생파리** a cool and distant person; "a cold fish". ぶあいそうなひと

**생판**(生板) ①(백지) blank; groundless; unfounded; false; empty; complete ignorance[unfamiliarity]; (사람) an ignoramus; a greenhorn ②(부사) groundlessly; unjustly; unreasonably; outrageously. なにもないこと

**생포**(生捕) capture; catching alive/ ~하다 (사람을) take (*one*) prisoner (동물을) catch (*an animal*) alive. いけどり

**생풀**(生一) (풀) raw starch (풀질) starching a whole bale of cloth/ ~하다 starch a whole bale of cloth.

**생피**(生一) fresh[-drawn] blood; warm blood.

**생핀잔**(生一) undeserved reproaches. ふそうおうなしっせき

**생혈**(生血) vital blood; life-blood (of)/ ~을 빨아 먹다 suck the lifeblood. なまち

**생호령**(生號令) unreasonable scolding/ ~하다 scold (*a person*) unreasonably.

**생화** (장사) business (벌이) earnings (직업) profession. もうけ

**생화**(生花) a live[fresh] flower. せいか

**생환**(生還) returning alive; 〖체〗 reaching the home plate/ ~하다 return alive; 〖체〗 reach the home plate; score. せいかん

**생활**(生活) life; living (생계) a livelihood/ ~하다 live; exist (생계를 세우다) live; make a living; support *oneself*/ ~ 양식 a mode of life/ ~고 the grim realities of life/ ~난 hard living/ ~수준 the standard of living/ ~ 상태 living condition/ ~ 필수품 necessaries of life/ ~ 설계 a plan for living/ ~력 vital powers/ ~비 living expenses; the cost of living/ ~ 환경 life environment/ ~ 개선 the betterment of living. せいかつ

**생황**(笙簧) (악기) a panpipe; a reed instrument. しょう

**생회**(生灰) quicklime. せいせっかい

**생획**(省劃) omission of strokes of a Chinese character/ ~하다 omit [strokes of a character].

**생후**(生後) after[since] *one's* birth. せいご

**생흙** uncultivated soil.

**서** (셋) three/ ~ 되 three [Korean] quarts.

**서**(序) (서문) a preface; a foreword; an introduction. じょ

**서**(西) west/ ~풍 the west wind. にし

**서**(書) (서적) a book (서간) a letter (서도) calligraphy (필적) handwriting.

**서**(署) ①an office; a station ②(경찰서) a police station. しょ

**서-**(庶) half-blood [relationship]/ ~동

**서가(書架)** a book-stand; book-ends; a book-case[-shelf]. しょか

**서가(書家)** a calligrapher; a calligraphist; a penman. しょか

**서까래** a [house] rafter. たるき

**서각(犀角)** a rhinoceros' horn; *Cornu rhinocerotis*(학명). さいかく

**서간(書簡)** a letter; a note (총칭) correspondence/ ~문 letter writing/ ~체 epistolary style of writing. しょかん

**서거(逝去)** death; demise/ ~하다 die; pass away; demise. せいきょ

**서걱거리다** crunch ⇨사각거리다. ぼりぼりいう

**서경(西經)** the west longitude/ ~ 30도 longitude 30 degrees west.

**서경(書經)** the Book of History; the Canon of History.

**서경(敍景)** description of scenery.

**서고(書庫)** a library. しょこ

**서곡(序曲)** 『음』 an overture; a prelude; a prologue. じょきょく

**서관(書館)** (책사) a bookshop; a book-store (출판사) a publisher; a publishing company. しょかん

**서광(曙光)** the [first streaks of] dawn; dawning/ 희망의 ~ a flash of hope. しょこう

**서구(西歐)** Western Europe (서양) the West.

**서국(西國)** a Western country (서양 제국) the Western countries[nations].

**서그러지다** (be) magnanimous; gentle ⇨ 서글서글하다. どりょうがひろくなる

**서글서글하다** (be) magnanimous; gentle broad-minded (사귐성 있는) sociable. おおまかである

**서글프다** (be) sad; plaintive; melancholy. やるせない

**서기(西紀)** the Christian Era; *Anno Domini*(略: A.D.). せいき

**서기(書記)** a clerk; a secretary/ ~장 a chief secretary. しょき

**서기(暑氣)** the summer heat; hot weather. しょき

**서기(瑞氣)** auspicious signs; a good omen. ずいき

**서남(西南)** southwest/ ~의 southwestern; southwesterly/ ~풍 a southwester; a southwesterly wind/ ~향 a southwestern exposure[aspect]; facing [the] southwest. せいなん

**서낭** a local deity; the guardian god of a village; a tutelary deity.

**서낭당** a village[tutelary] shrine.

**서너** three or four; a few; some/ ~ 달 three or four month; three months or so. さんし

**서너너덧** three or four.

**서넛** three or four; about three. さんし

**써넣다** write in; fill in; insert [by writing]. きにゅうする

**서녀(庶女)** an illegitimate daughter; a daughter born of a concubine. しょじょ

**서녘(西一)** the west; the westward. せいほう

**서느렇다** ①(온도가) be chilled; chill feel ②(마음 속이) have a thrill of horror. ひやっとする

**서늘하다** (be) cool; refreshing. すずしい

**서다** ①(기립하다) stand up; rise [to one's feet]; get up ②(정지하다) stop; [make a] halt (말 따위가) draw up (시계가) run down ③(건립하다) be built[erected]; be established; be set up ④(장이) be opened[held] ⑤(칼날이) be sharpend[edged] ⑥(명령이) be obeyed; be followed; be carried out ⑦(이론이) hold good; be made good (이유가) pass; be admissible ⑧(계획이) be formed [established]; be worked out ⑨(면목이) save *one's* face; relieve (*one*) from disgrace. たつ

**써다** (조수가) ebb; fall; go out. ひく

**서당(書堂)** a private school. しょどう

**서덜** (강변) a pebbly[stony] river-side.

**서도(書道)** calligraphy; penmanship. しょどう

**서두(書頭)** the opening sentence[paragraph]; the beginning. もじのはじめ

**서두르다** (급히 하다) hurry; hasten; make haste (재촉하다) press; urge (조급해 하다) be impatient/서둘러서 in haste [a hurry]. あわてる

**서랍** a drawer.

**서랑(壻郞)** your[his] son-in-law.

**서러워하다** sorrow[grieve] (*at, over*); feel sad[sorrowful] (*at*); be distressed (*over*). かなしむ

**서럽다** (be) sad; sorrowful; mournful; grievous. かなしい

**서력(西曆)** the Christian Era; *Anno Domini*(略: A.D.). せいれき

**서로** each other (셋 이상) one another (함께) mutually; together. たがいに

**서로치기** doing the same thing for each other/ ~하다 each does for the other. たがいにこうたいしてやること

**서론(序論, 緒論)** introduction; an introductory remarks; foreword; preface/ ~을 말하다 make introductory remarks; preface [*one's speech, etc*]. じょろん

**서류(書類)** papers; documents (관청 비치의) archives/ ~함[상자] a filling cabinet. しょるい

**서른** thirty/ ~ 살 thirty years of age/ ~째 thirtieth. さんじゅう

**서름서름하다** ①(서툴다) (be) unpracticed; inexperienced; unfamiliar; unacquainted ②(태도가) (be) reserved; distant; lacking in intimacy/서름서름한 태도 distant air. みじゅくだ

**서릊다** ①(쓸다) sweep; clear ②⇒설겆다. はく

**서리¹** (가루 얼음) frost; hoar[white] frost/ ~맞다 be killed[nipped] by the frost. しも

**서리²** 《훔치기》 stealing (*fruits, chickens, etc.*) in a band [out of a mischievous motive].

**서리³** 《무리》 a mass; a group.

**서리(署理)** administering as an acting director(일); (사람) an acting director/ ~하다 administer (*affairs*) as an acting director/국무 총리 ~ an acting premier. しょくむのだいり

**서리다¹** ①(김이) condense ②(기가 꺾이다) be discouraged[disheartened].

**서리다²** (새끼 따위를) coil; wind; twine 《뱀이》 coil itself. まるくまく

**서리맞다** ①(서리가 내리다) be nipped by the frost ②(기운이) be discouraged [dispirited] 《타격받다》 be hit; receive a set-back. しもにあたる

**서리서리** in a coil; round and round. くるくる

**서림(書林)** a bookshop; a bookstore〈미〉. しょりん

**서릿바람** a wintry blast; a chilly wind; a frosty wind. あさのつめたいかぜ

**서막(序幕)** ①(극의) the opening[first] scene ②(시초) a prelude (to *an entertainment*); beginning. じょまく

**서머하다** (면목없다) be ashamed (of oneself). はずかしい

**서먹서먹** ~하다 feel awkward[nervous] (before *an audience*); feel small[embarassed] (in *company*); be self-conscious; feel ill at ease. びくびくする

**서먹하다** feel awkward ⇒서먹서먹. おどおどする

**서면(書面)** a letter (총칭) correspondence (문서) writing; a document/~으로 by letter; in writing. しょめん

**서명(署名)** a signature; an autograph / ~하다 sign *one's* name (*to*); affix *one's* signature/~ 운동 signature-seeking campaign/~장 an autograph album/~날인하다 sign and seal. しょめい

**서명(書名)** the name of a book. しょめい

**서모(庶母)** *one's* father's concubine. しょぼ

**서목(書目)** a catalogue of books 《참고 서목》 a bibliography. しょもく

**서몽(瑞夢)** an auspicious dream.

**서무(庶務)** general affairs/ ~과 the section of general affairs. しょむ

**서문(序文)** a foreword; a preface; an introduction. じょぶん

**서민(庶民)** (평민) common people; commoners 《대중》 the masses/ ~ 금융 petty loans for the working classes. しょみん

**서반구(西半球)** the Western Hemisphere. にしはんきゅう

**서발(序跋)** a preface and a postscript (to *a book*); prolog[ue] and epilogue. じょぶんとばつぶん

**서방(西方)** the west/ ~의 western; westward/ ~ 세계 the Western world/ ~ 정토 paradise; the blissful Buddha land in West. せいほう

**서방(書房)** ①(남편) a husband; *one's* man / ~맞다 get married to a man ②(호칭) Mr. (*Lee*). おっと

**서방질(書房—)** adultery; cuckolding/ ~하다 commit adultery; cuckold.
おんながほかのおとことしつうすること

**서벅거리다** yield easily to the teeth. さくさくする

**서벅돌** a frail stone.

**서법(書法)** a style of handwriting; calligraphy. しょほう

**서변(西邊)** the westward ⇒서쪽. せいへん

**서부(西部)** the western part; the west /~의 western/~극 a wild West drama (영화) a western [film]〈미〉. せいぶ

**서부렁하다** (be) loose. しまりがない

**서북(西北)** ①(서쪽과 북쪽) north and west ②(서북간) the northwest/ ~의 northwesterly/~풍 a northwestern[northwesterly] wind. せいほく

**서북향(西北向)** (서북으로 면한) a northwestern exposure[aspect]; looking towards [the] northwest; facing the northwest. せいほくむき

**서분서분하다** (be) docile ⇒사분사분하다. こころがやさしい

**서분하다** ①(서부렁 하다) (be) somewhat loose; loose a little ②⇒서운하다.
ややしまりがない

**서뿟서뿟** with springy[nimble] steps. そっと

**서사(叙事)** narration; description/ ~문 a description; a narrative/~시 descriptive poetry; an epic/ ~적 descriptive; narrative. じょじ

**서사(書肆)** a bookshop; a bookstore. ほんや

**서사(書寫)** transcription; copying/ ~하다 copy; transcribe. しょしゃ

**서사(誓詞)** an oath; a pledge. せいし

**서산(西山)** a western mountain.

**서상(瑞相)** a good omen; an auspicious [happy] sign. ずいそう

**서색(鼠色)** dark gray; slate. ねずみいろ

**서색(曙色)** the color of the dawn; down; aurora. しょしょく

**서생(書生)** (학생) a student (남의 집 일을 돕는) a house boy. しょせい

**서서히(徐徐—)** slowly; gradually ⇒천천히. じょじょに

**서설(序說)** an introduction; introductory remarks. じょせつ

**서성거리다** walk up and down restlessly; go back and forth uneasily. うろうろする

**서속(黍粟)** millet. きびとあわ

**서수(序數)** 《수》 an ordinal [number].

**서술(叙述)** description; narration; depiction/ ~하다 describe; narrate; depict / ~어〖언〗 the predicative/ ~적 descriptive; narrative/ ~체 a descriptive style. じょじゅつ

**서슬** ①(칼날) a burnished blade; a sharp edge ②(기세) the brunt (of *an attack, argument*); an impetuous charge. するどいこと

**서슴거리다** hesitate; waver; have scruples about／서슴서슴 hesitatingly; waveringly; irresolutely. ためらう

**서슴다** hesitate; waver; vacillate／서슴지 않고 without hesitation. ためらう

**서슴없다** have no scruples about; make no scruple of; do not stick at／서슴없이 unhesitatingly. ためらわない

**서식(書式)** a [fixed, prescribed] form. しょしき

**서식(棲息)** habitation; inhabitation／〜하다 inhabit (the *earth*); live (in *water*)／〜지 a habitat. せいそく

**서신(書信) (왕래 편지)** correspondence **(편지)** a letter. しょしん

**서악(序樂)** a prelude; an overture. じょきょくのおんがく

**서안(西岸)** the west coast.

**서안(書案)** a desk; a [writing] table. しょあん

**서약(誓約)** an oath; a pledge; a vow／〜하다 swear; vow; take an oath; pledge *one*self／〜서 a written oath[promise]. せいやく

**서양(西洋)** the West; the Occident／〜의 Western; European; Occidental／〜 사람 a Westerner; a European; a foreigner／〜 문명[사상] Western civilization[ideas]／〜식 Western style; Occidentalism／〜화(畵) a painting in oils／〜사 European history／〜화하다 Westernize; Europeanize. せいよう

**서어(齟齬)** 〜하다 ①**(의견이)** (be) inconsistent[contradictory, discrepant]; be contrary (*to*); disagree; be at variance ②**(탐탁잖음)** (be) frustrated; be not happy (*about*). そご

**서언(西諺)** a Western proverb. せいげん

**서언(序言, 緒言)** a foreword; a preface ㆍ머리말. じょげん

**서열(暑熱)** the heat (of *the summer*).

**서열(序列)** order; grade; rank.

**서염(暑炎)** intense heat; extreme heat. こくしょ

**서운(瑞雲)** auspicious clouds. ずいうん

**서운하다** (be) regrettable; sad; disappointing／서운해 하다 be sorry (*for*); regret; be disappointed. ものたりない

**서운해하다 (주로 2·3인칭 주어)** be sorry; be saddened by; miss.

**서울** Seoul **(수도)** the capital; the metropolis／〜나기 a Seoulite／〜 시민 a citizen of Seoul; a Seoulite《子》／〜 장안 (*in*) all Seoul. みやこ

**서원(書院) (글방)** a lecture-hall; an auditorium. しょいん

**서원(署員)** a member of the police force. しょいん

**서원(誓願)** a vow; a pledge; an oath／〜하다 vow[mak a vow] to; swear[oath]; pledge *one*self to. せいがん

**서이 (세 사람)** three persons **(셋)** three. さんにん

**서임(敍任)** appointment; in stallation;

investiture／〜하다 appoint. じょにん

**서자(庶子) (첩자식)** a child born of a concubine **(사생아)** an illegitimate child. しょし

**서작(敍爵)** ennoblement／〜하다 raise to the nobility; ennoble. じしゃく

**서장(書狀)** a letter; a note. しょぢょう

**서장(署長)** the head of a government office／경찰 〜 a police superintendent; the chief constable. しょちょう

**서재(書齋)** a study; a library. しょさい

**서적(書籍)** books **(출판물)** publications／〜상 **(사람)** a bookseller **(가게)** a book-shop; a bookstore. しょせき

**서절(暑節)** the hottest season. あついきせつ

**서점(書店)** a bookstore; a bookshop／그것은 어느 〜에서나 구할 수 있다 You can get it through any bookseller. しょてん

**서점(西漸)** a westward drive.

**서정(庶政)** all administrative business.

**서정(敍情, 抒情)** description[expression] of feelings[passion]; **(총칭)** lyricism／〜하다 delineate／〜 시 lyric poetry **(개별적)** a lyric poem; a lyric／〜 시인 a lyricist／〜적 lyric[al]／〜적으로 lyrically. じょじょう

**서조(瑞兆)** a good[an auspicious] omen. ずいちょう

**서쪽(西一)** the west／〜의 west; western／〜으로 to the west. せいほう

**서족(庶族)** descendants from a person bron of a concubine. しょぞく

**서중(暑中)** summer; the hot season; midsummer. しょちゅう

**서지(書誌)** bibliography／〜학자 a bibliographer／〜학 the bibliography. しょし

**서진(書鎭)** a [paper] weight. ぶんちん

**서차(序次)** order; turn; precedence; arrangement. じじ

**서창(西窓)** a window open to the west. せいほうのまど

**서책(書冊)** a book **(저서)** a work. しょさつ

**서천(西天)** the western sky. せいてん

**서철(西哲) (사람)** a Western philosopher **(철학)** Western philosophy. せいてつ

**서첩(書帖)** an album of excellent hand-writings. めいしょをつづったほん

**서체(書體)** a style of penmanship; handwriting. しょたい

**서체(暑滯)** indigestion due to hot weather. あつさざわり

**서출(庶出)** 〜의 illegitimate; bastard; born out of wedlock. しょしゅつ

**서취(書取)** dictation ㆍ받아쓰기. かきとり

**서캐** nits. しらみのたまご

**서퇴(暑退)** falling of the heat; abatement of hot weather／〜하다 become cool. あつさがさること

**서투르다 (미숙하다)** (be) unskilful; clumsy; poor; awkward; inapt／계산이 〜 He is bad at figures. へただ

**서파(庶派)** descendant from a person born out of wedlock. しょしのしそん

**서편(西便)** the west／〜의 west; weste-

**서평**(書評) a book review.
**서표**(書標) a bookmark. ほんのしおり
**서푼**(―分) a farthing／ ～의 가치도 없다 be not worth a penny.
**서푼서푼** with light[soft] steps; lighty. そっと
**서풍**(西風) the west wind; westerly [wind]; zephyr. にしかぜ
**서풍**(書風) a style of penmanship.
**서한**(書翰) a letter ⇨서간(書簡). しょかん
**서해**(西海) the western[yellow] sea.
**서행**(徐行) going slow[ly]／～하다 go slow[ly]; crawl; slow down. じょこう
**서향**(西向) a western exposure. にしむき
**서향나무**(瑞香―) 【식】 a sweet-smelling daphne; *Daphne odora*(학명).
**서혜**(鼠蹊) 【해】 the groin／ ～의 inguinal.
**서화**(書畫) paintings and writings. しょが
**서회**(敍懷) an effusion of *one's* thoughts [and feelings]／～하다 relate *one's* thoughts; express[pour out] *one's* reminiscences. じょかい
**서훈**(敍勳) [conferment of a] decoration ／～하다 confer a decoration (on *one*); decorate. じょくん
**석** 《셋》 three／ ～ 달 three months.
**썩** ①《아주》 very much; greatly; exceedingly; awfully ②《곧》 right away; immediately. すばらしく
**석**(錫) tin. しゃく
**―석**(席) a seat; a place. せき
**석가산**(石假山) an artificial[a miniature] hill; a rockery. にわのいしやみ
**석각**(石刻) stone carving／ ～하다 carv in a stone. いしにもじなどをきざむこと
**석간**(夕刊) an evening paper[edition]. ゆうかん
**쉬갈리다** 《이야기 따위가》 get confused[mixed, tangled]. もつれる
**석경**(夕景) evening scenery.
**석경**(石鏡) a [looking] glass. いしかがみ
**석계**(石階) stone steps. いしだん
**석고**(石膏) gyps[um]; plaster of Paris／ ～세공 plaster work. せっこさ
**석공**(石工) a stonemason. せっこう
**석관**(石棺) a stone coffin. せきかん
**석광**(錫鑛) a stannary. すずのこうさん
**석교**(石橋) a stone bridge ⇨돌다리. いしばし
**석구**(石臼) a stone mortar. せっきゅう
**석굴**(石窟) a cavern; a grotto. せっくつ
**석권**(席卷) ～하다 overwhelm; carry everything before (*one*); sweep (over *a place*); make a conquest of.
ひろいちいきにせいりょをひらめること
**석기**(石器) a stone implement. せっき
**석남**(石南) 【식】 a rhododendron; *Andromeda Polifolia*(학명). しゃくなげ
**석녀**(石女) a sterile[barren] woman; a childless woman. うまずめ
**석년**(昔年) ①ancient times ⇨옛날 ②last year ⇨작년.

**석다** 《눈이》melt; thaw 《양조물이》 mellow／～술이 ～ rice wine mellows.
なかからとける
**썩다** ①《부패하다》go bad 《물건이》rot 《음식이》spoil 《우유 따위가》turn sour; decompose; corrode; stale; decay ／썩은 생선 rotten fish ②《속이》(*one's heart*) become heavy; break 《재주가》(*one's knowledge*) gather dust[rust]; get[become] rusty. くさる
**쉬다** mix; commix; mingle; blend 《불순물을》adulterate (*with*). まぜる
**석돌** a soft[crumbly] stone. もろいし
**석랍**(石蠟) 【화】 paraffin; coal-oil. せきろう
**석류**(石榴) 【식】 a pomegranate[·tree]. ざくろ
**석류석**(石榴石) 【광】 garnet. ざくろいし
**석면**(石綿) 【광】 asbestos. せきめん
**석명**(釋明) explanation／ ～하다 explain; give an explanation of; make clear; clear up. しゃくめい
**석묵**(石墨) 【광】 graphite; black-lead; plumbago. せきぼく
**석문**(石門) a stone gate. せきもん
**석물**(石物) stone figures [of men and animals] placed before a tomb.
はかのまえにたてるせきぞうのもの
**쉬바꾸다** mix up; mistake (*one*) for (*the other*); take the wrong one. まぜかえす
**쉬바뀌다** be mixed up; be mistaken 《위쉬이다》run into each other.
**석박**(錫箔) tinfoil. すずのはく
**석반**(夕飯) supper; the evening meal.
ゆうはん
**석방**(釋放) release; discharge; acquittal; liberation／～하다 set (*one*) free[at liberty]; release; liberate; let (*one*) go [off]. しゃくほう
**석벽**(石壁) ①《낭떠러지》a cliff; a stone wall ②《벽》a stone wall. せきへき
**석별**(惜別) reluctance to leave; unwillingness to part／ ～하다 be unwilling [sorry, loath] to part (from *one's friend*); be reluctant to leave; express regret at parting. せきべつ
**석부**(石斧) a stone-axe. せきふ
**석불**(石佛) a stone image[idol] of Buddha. せきぶつ
**석비**(石碑) a stone monument. せきひ
**석사**(碩士) ①《학위》Master／문학 ～ Master of Arts ②《선비》a confucian scholar without any rank.
たいがくいんそつぎょうのひと
**쉬사귀다** mix with a person of different social standing.
**석산**(石山) a stony[rocky] mountain.
いしやま
**석삼년**(―三年) nine years. くねん
**석상**(石像) a stone image; a stone statue. せきぞう
**석상**(席上) during the meeting; in company. せきじょう
**썩썩**[1] imploringly ⇨싹싹. もみもみ
**썩썩**[2] 《피륙 따위를 베다》with *one* clean

stroke after another. すっすっと
썩썩하다 (be) frank; open-hearted ⇒싹싹하다. やさしい
석쇠 a grill; a gridiron.
석수(石手) a stone-mason; a stone-cutter /~질 masonry. せっこう
석수 (汐水) the evening tide.
석수어(石首魚) a yellow corvina fish ⇒조기. いしもち
석순(石筍) 【광】 stalagmite. せきじゅん
석양(夕陽) the setting sun. せきよう
석얼음 ①(뜬 얼음) floating ice; drift ice; a floe ②(유리창 위의) frostwork [on a windowpane]. みずのうえにうかむこおり
석연하다(釋然—) (사람이 주어)(be) satisfied (with *the explanation*); 《사물이 주어》 satisfactory. しゃくぜんとしている
석염(石鹽) 【광】 rock salt. がんえん
석영(石英) 【광】 quartz/ ~암 quartzite. せきえい
석유(石油) 【광】 petroleum (등불용) kerosene; earth oil/ ~등 an oil[a kerosene] lamp. せきゆ
석음(惜陰) husbanding[making the best use of] *one's* time. せきいん
석의(釋義) a commentary; an exposition. しゃくぎ
석이(石耳, 石栮) 【식】 a manna lichen; *Gyrophora esculenta*(학명). いわたけ
쉬이다 be mixed[mingled]; mix; mingle; blend. まざる
썩이다 ①(부패하다) let (*a thing*) rot[decay]; corrupt; spoil ②(방치하다) leave unemployed; let go to waste ③(속을) eat *one's* heart out (*with*); make *one* sick at heart; make *one's* heart break. ふはいさせる
석인(石人) a stone image; a stone statue. せきじん
석일(昔日) old days ⇒옛날. むかし
석임 fermentation; undergoing fermentation. はっこうすること
석자 a big scoop with meshes like those of a net.
석장(錫杖) 《불교》 a monk's staff. しゃくじょう
석재(石材) [building] stone. せきざい
석전(石戰) a fight stones. いしなげ
석전(石田) a stony field. せきでん
석전(石典) 《불경》 Buddhist scriptures.
석전(釋奠) a festival held twice a year to honour Confucius. しゃくてん
석조(夕照) the evening glow. せきしょう
석조(石造) (being) stone-built; [of] stone; things made of stone/ ~의 stone [·built]/~ 건물 a stone building. せきぞう
석존(釋尊) Buddha; Sakyamuni.
석종유(石鍾乳) 【광】 stalactite. せきじゅん
석주(石柱) a stone pillar. せきちゅう
석죽(石竹) a pink; a China pink; *Dianthus sinensis*(학명). せきちく
석차(席次) (자리의) the order of seats; precedence 《학교의》 standing; *one's* rank in class. せきじ
석찬(夕餐) dinner; supper; the evening meal. ゆうはん
석창포(石菖蒲) 【식】 a sweet rush.
석천(石泉) a spring coming out of the stones. せきせん
석청(石清) 《야생꿀》 wild honey; honey found in the crevices of rocks. はちみつのいっしゅ
석축(石築) a stone wall for reinforcement. いしがき
석탄(石炭) coal/ ~광 a coal mine; a coal-pit; a colliery/ ~ 가스 coal gas / ~차 a coal truck/~고(庫) 《배의》 a coal bunker; a coal hole/~ 상인 a coal dealer. せきたん
석탄산(石炭酸) 【화】 carbonic acid; phenol. せきたんさん
석탑(石塔) a stone pagoda; a stone tower. せきとう
석판(石板) a slate. せっかいせきのへいばん
석판(石版) 【인】 《석판화》 lithography 《석판화》 a lithograph/~ 인쇄 lithography; lithographic print[ing]/~사진 ~술 photolithography. せきはん
석패(惜敗) a regrettable defeat; a defeat after hard fighting/~하다 be defeated by a narrow margin. せきはい
석필(石筆) a slate pencil. せきひつ
석학(碩學) a man of erudition; a great scholar. せきがく
석함(石函) a stone box[case]. いしのはこ
석화(石火) 《몹시 빠름》 flash 《불꽃》 a flint fire[spark]/ ~ 광음 fleeting time. せっか
석화채(石花菜) 【식】 agar-agar ⇒우뭇가사리.
석회(石灰) lime; calcium carbonate/ ~석 limestone/~수 limewater. せっかい
썩히다 let (*a thing*) rot ⇒썩이다.
섣 (노염) passion; a fit of anger 《의심》 a doubt; suspicion/ ~삭다 《노염이》 relent 《의심이》 be solved. げきじょう
선 (혼사의) an interview with a view to marriage/ ~보다 have an interview with a prospective bride[·groom]. じんぶつのよしあしをみること
선(先) ①《장기·바둑에서》 the first move ②《죽은》 deceased ③《먼저》 first [of all]. せん
선(善) good; goodness; virtue/ ~과 악 good and evil/ ~을 행하다 do [what is] good. ぜん
선(線) a line/호남~ the *Honam* line / ~을 긋다 draw a line. せん
선(腺) a gland. 【해】 a gland.
선(縇) an edge; edging; a frill; a border; trim[ming]/ ~이 좁다 have a narrow edge[edging].
선(禪) religious meditation; *Dhyana* (Sans); 《불》《종파》 the *Seon* sect 《선학》 the *Seon* doctrine. ぜん
선가(船價) shipping charges ⇒뱃삯.
선가(禪家) a *Seon* temple[·priest]. ぜんか
선각(先覺) foresight; seeing[perceiving]

in advance／～자 a man of foresight; a pioneer; a forerunner. せんかく

**선감**(善感) 【의】an effectual vaccination. ぜんかん

**선객**(先客) a preceding visitor. せんきょく

**선객**(船客) a passenger／일등 ～ a first-class passenger. せんきゃく

**선거**(船渠) a dock／건～ a dry dock. せんきょ

**선거**(選擧) election／～하다 elect; vote for; return〈영〉／총～ a general election／～장 a polling station[place]; the polls〈미〉／～ 운동 election campaign; electioneering／～위반 election irregularities／～일 the election day／～참관인 a referee of an election／～위원 an election committee／～사무소 an election[a campaign] office／～전 an election contest[compaign]／～연설 a campaign speech／～위원회 an Election Management Committee／～구 an electoral district; a constituency／～권 the suffrage; the right to vote／～법 election laws. せんきょ

**선겁다** (be) surprising; startling; astonishing. おどろく

**선견**(先見) foresight; outlook; anticipation; foreknowledge; divination／～지명(之明) far-sightedness. せんけん

**선견 부대**(先遣部隊) advance troops; vanguards.

**선결**(先決) a previous decision／～하다 decide[settle] beforehand／～ 문제 a prior question; a precondition; a prerequisite; a previous question. せんけつ

**선경**(仙境) a fairy-land; an enchanted land; an elfland. せんきょう

**선고**(先考) my deceased[late] father. しんだちち

**선고**(宣告) sentence; verdict 〈판결〉 judg[e]ment 《공포》pronouncement／～하다 pronounce; proclaim; sentence; pass a sentence on (one)／사형의 ～ a sentence of death. せんこく

**선공**(先攻) 《야구》batting first／～하다 [go to] bat first. せんこう

**선과**(善果) good fruit[results]／～를 맺다 bring forth good fruit. ぜんか

**선과**(選科) an elective course. せんか

**선광**(選鑛) concentration[dressing, separation] of ores. せんこう

**선교**(宣敎) missionary work; preaching; proclamation／～하다 preach; propagate／～사 a missionary. せんきょう

**선교**(船橋) 《배다리》a pontoon [bridge]; 《배의 갑판의》a bridge.

**선구**(船具) ship's fittings 《색구》rigging; gearing 《조종 도구》tackle／～상 a ship chandler; a tackle store. せんぐ

**선구**(先驅) a pioneer ⇒선구자. せんく

**선구안**(選球眼) 《야구》[a] batting eye／～이 좋다 have a sharp[good] batting eye.

**선구자**(先驅者) ①《지도자》a pioneer; a herald; a precursor; men of light and leading ②《차마의 선도자》an outrider 《차》a pilot-car ③《먼저 알리는 자》a forerunner; a precursor; a herald. せんくしゃ

**선근**(善根) good [deeds]; a deed of charity. ぜんこん

**선금**(先金) advances; payment in advance; prepayment. さきがね

**선급**(先給) payment in advance; prepayment／～하다 pay in advance; make on advances. まえばらい

**선남 선녀**(善男善女) pious people[folk]; votaries; the faithful. ぜんなんぜんにょ

**선납**(先納) payment in advance; prepayment／～하다 pay in advance. よのう

**선내**(船內) [in] the ship.

**선녀**(仙女) a fairy; a nymph. せんにょ

**선다형**(選多型) a multiple choice system.

**선단**(船團) a fleet of vessels.

**선대**(先代) the predecessor [in the family line]; the former[last] generation. せんだい

**선대**(善待) a warm reception; kind treatment; hospitality／～하다 give a warm reception to; treat (a guest) kindly [well]; receive (one) warmly; a kind reception. よくもてなすこと

**선대**(船隊) a fleet of ships.

**선떡** half-done rice cake.

**선도**(先導) guidance; leadership／～하다 guide; lead; take the lead／～자 a leader; a guide. せんどう

**선도**(鮮度) freshness／～가 높은 very fresh.

**선도**(善導) proper guidance／～하다 lead[guide] properly; guide aright／～받다 be influenced for good. ぜんどう

**선돌** 【역】a menhir. せんしじだいのけんぞうぶつのいっしゅ

**선동**(煽動) instigation; incitement; agitation; stirring up／～하다 instigate; abet; incite; stir up; set on; agitate／～자 an agitator; an instigator; a setter-on／～연설 an inflammatory[a seditious] harangue[speech]／소동을 ～자 a mischeif-maker; a firebrand／～정치가 a [seditious] demagogue. せんどう

**선동이**(先童—) the firstborn of twins.

**선두**(先頭) the lead; the head; the van／～에 서서 at the head[in the van] of／～에 서다 lead; be in the van; take the lead. せんとう

**선두**(船頭) the bow; the prow; the stem; the head. せんとう

**선두르다** fringe; border; margin; frame; hem. いんえんをつける

**선드러지다** (be) light-hearted; cheerful; buoyant. さらっとしている

**선득, 선뜩** ～하다 《추워서》(be) chilled; fell chilly; feel a chill〈cold〉《놀라서》shudder (at); have a thrill of horror／나는 가슴이 ～했다 A cold shiver ran through me., My blood ran cold.／선득

선득[선뜩선뜩]; 《추워서》chilly 《놀라는 느낌》shudderingly; with a thrill of horror. ひやっと

선득거리다 ①《추워서》feel chilly ②《놀라서》shudder (at to see).

선들거리다 [coll breezes] blow gently／바람이 선들거린다 A refreshing breeze blows gently. そよそよふく

선들바람 a cool[gentle] breeze. そよかぜ

선뜻 《가볍게》lightly 《쾌히》readily; willingly 《빨리》at short notice; at one's bidding 《즉석에서》offhand／ ~ 응낙하다 comply readily with; give a ready consent. さらっと

선뜻하다 《선명하다》(be) clear; fresh; bright 《보기 좋다》(be) neat; tidy; trim; smart／선뜻하게 차리다 be neatly dressed. さらっと

선등(先等) the lead; the initiative; the vanguard／~하다 take the lead[initiative]; go ahead; precede.
たにんよりさきにすること

선량(善良) goodness／~하다 (be) good; excellent; virtuous; right／ ~한 사람 a good man／ ~한 사람들 good people; law-abiding people. ぜんりょう

선량(選良) a representative of the people; the nation's choice. せんりょう

선려(鮮麗) resplendent beauty／ ~하다 (be) bright; vivid; gay.

선령(船齡) a ship's age.

선례(先例) a precedent; a previous instance／ ~ 없는 일 an unprecedented matter／ ~를 깨뜨리다 violate precedents／~로 삼다 take (a thing) as a precedent. せんれい

선로(船路) a ship's route[course]; a sea route; a seaway ⇨뱃길. せんろ

선로(線路) a [railway] line[track]／ ~ 인부 a lineman; a trackman〈미〉／ ~를 깔다 lay a [railway] tracks. せんろ

선린(善隣) (being) good neighbors; neighborly friendship; a good-neighbor relationship／~ 정책 a good neighbor policy. せんりん

선망(羨望) envy／ ~하다 [feel] envy; be envious of／ ~의 대상이 되다 become an object of envy (among). せんぼう

선망 후실(先忘後失) forgetfulness; a short memory／ ~하다 be forgetful; be apt to forget.

선매(先賣) an advance sale; selling ahead／~하다 sell in advance; sell beforehand／~권 pre-emption; right of prior purchase.

선머슴 a naughty boy. わんぱくこども

선명(宣明) proclamation; announcement; declaration enunciation; promulgation／~하다 proclaim; declare; announce.
せいめい

선명(鮮明) clearness; distinctness; lucidity; vividness／~하다 (be) clear; distinct; vivid; clear-[sharp-]cut／ ~ 하지 못하다 lack clearness. せんめい

선모(旋毛) the vortex[whirl] of hair on the crown of one's head. せいもう

선모(腺毛) a tentacle; glandular hairs.
せんもう

선무(宣撫) placation; pacification／~반 a placation squad; authorized placators. せんぶ

선무당 a new[novice] shaman／~이 장구 나무란다 He is not a mason who refuses a stone. みじゅくなみこ

선문(禪門) Zen[Dhyana] Buddhism; a Buddhist[Zen] monk／ ~에 들어가다 become a Zen monk. ぜんもん

선물(先物) ①：만물 ②〈경〉futures／ ~을 사다 deal in futures; buy futures.
じぜんのうわさ

선물(膳物) a gift; a present 《기념품》a souvenir／축하 ~ a congratulatory present／하느님의 ~ a gift of Heaven／연말[크리스마스] ~ a year-end[Christmas] present／이별의 ~ a parting present [gift]. おくりもの

선미(善美) the good[fine] and the beautiful／ ~하다 be good[fine] and beautiful. ぜんび

선미(船尾) the stern／ ~에 astern; aft／ ~포 a stern-chaser. せんび

선미(鮮美) brightness; clearness／ ~하다 (be) bright; clear; fair. ぜんび

선민(選民) the chosen people; the elect.
せんみん

선박(船舶) a vessel; ship 《총칭》shipping; craft／항내 ~ vessels in port; shipping in port[the harbour]／ ~ 국적 증서 the certificate of a ship's nationality／ ~ 관리료 husbandage／~법 the marine act; the shipping law／ ~ 보증 ship's warrant／ ~ 서류 the ship's papers／ ~ 임대료 《사용료》charterage／ ~ 입항[출항] 신고 a ship's clearance inward[outward]／ ~ 회사 a shipping company. せんぱく

선반(一盤) a shelf; a rack／~에 얹다 put (a thing) on a shelf; shelve. やらい

선반(旋盤) a lathe／~공 a lathe operator; a turner; lathemen／ ~ 공장 a lathe shop. せんばん

선발(選拔) selection; choice／~하다 select; choose; pick[single] out／ ~ 경쟁 an elimination match／~ 시험 a selective examination／~ 야구 시합 elimination baseball games／ ~ 위원회 a selection committee／ ~에서 빠지다 be left out in the select list. せんばつ

선발(先發) starting[going] in advance; getting[taking] a head start／ ~하다 start[go] in advance; go ahead (of); get[take] ahead start／~대 an advance party[unit]; forerunners. せんばつ

선배(先輩) a superior; an elder／대(大) ~ a big senior／~연하다 assume a patronizing attitude; pose［give oneself airs] as a senior／4년 ~다 be one's senior by four years. ぜんぱい

**선변(先邊)** interest paid in advance (on loan). さきばらいりそく

**선병(腺病)** 《醫》 scrofula / ~질 scrofulosis; scrofulous tendency. せんびょう

**선보다** pay a preliminary visit to [the prospective bride[bridegroom].

**선보름(先—)** the early half of a month. せんぼう

**선복(船腹)** 《배의 내부》 bottoms; [freight] space 《수송 능력》 [shipping] tonnage. せんぷく

**선복(船卜)** a [ship's] cargo; a freight.

**선봉(先鋒)** the van [guard]; the advance guard; the scouting line / ~이 되다 lead the van. せんぼう

**선부(先父)** one's deceased father; one's late father. せんぷ

**선부(先夫)** one's deceased[late] husband. せんぷ

**선불** a stray bullet / ~ 맞은 호랑이 뛰듯 hopping mad; furious / ~걸다 get hoist with his own petard.

**선불(先拂)** payment in advance / ~하다 pay in advance; prepay. さきばらい

**선불선(善不善)** good and[or] evil.

**선비** a scholar; a classical scholar; a gentleman; a student of Chinese classics. かんしょくにつかないがくしゃ

**선비(先妣)** one's dead mother; one's late mother. せんぴ

**선사** 《선물》 presentation / ~하다 give[make] (one) a present; send (one) a gift / ~받다 get (a thing) as a gift. おくりもの

**선사(先史)** ~의 prehistoric[al] / ~ 시대 the prehistorical age. せんし

**선사(善事)** 《공양》an offering / ~하다 offer / 절에 ~하다 make a monetary offering to a temple. ぜんじ

**선사(先師)** one's deceased[late] teacher. せんし

**선사(禪師)** a Seon priest; an esteemed priest / 달마 ~ Saint Dalma. ぜんし

**선산(先山)** a mountain where one's ancestors are buried; an ancestral graveyard.

**선상지(扇狀地)** a fan; an alluvial fan or cone; a fan delta. せんじょうち

**선생(先生)** a teacher; a master; an instructor 《의사》 a doctor 《호칭》 Sir; Madam / 영어 ~ a teacher of English; an English teacher. せんせい

**선서(宣誓)** an oath; swearing-in; parole / ~하다 swear; take an oath / ~문 a deposition; an affidavit / ~식 a swearing-in[an oathtaking] ceremony / ~ 증언 deposition; sworn testimony / ~ 증인 a deponent / ~를 위반하다 break one's parole / 취임 ~를 하다 administer the oath of office. せんせい

**선선하다** ①《시원하다》 (be) cool; refreshing / 조석으로 선선해졌다 It is now cool in the mornings and evenings. ②《성질이》 (be) light-hearted; cheerful; cheery; vivacious; sprightly; open-minded

/ 선선히 cheerfully; vivaciously 《쾌뜻》 with a good grace; without reluctance. すずしい

**선세(先貰)** prepaid [house] rent; rent in advance. かりちんのさきばらいすること

**선셈(先—)** payment in advance; advance payment. さきばらいうけい

**선소리** foolish[silly] talk; an absurd remark; nonsense / ~를 하다 talk nonsense; make an absurd remark.

**선손(先—)** ①《먼저 착수함》 forestalling; forestallment / ~쓰다 take[seize] the initiative; forestall (another); get the start (of) ②《선손질》 first blow / ~ 걸다 give the first blow; get the start of a fist fight. せんて

**선손질(先—)** starting a fight ⇒선손.

**선수(先手)** 《선손》 forestalling; the initiative 《바둑·장기에서》 the first move; an opener [in a chess game] / ~를 놓다 make the first move. せんて

**선수(船首)** the prow [of a ship] ⇒이물. せんしゅ

**선수(選手)** a player; a champion 《전체》 a team 《단정(短艇)》 the eight 《야구》 the nine 《축구》 the eleven 《농구》 the five / ~권 보지자 a champion[title] holder / ~단 a team / ~가 되다 become a player / 올림픽 ~로 뽑히다 be chosen an Olympic player. せんしゅ

**선수권(選手權)** a championship; a title; a crown / ~을 다투다 scramble for a championship; play for the title / ~을 방어하다 defend the title / ~ 시합 a title match.

**선술(仙術)** Taoist [occult] magic; magic arts; wizardry; the secret of immortality. せんじゅつ

**선술집** a [stand] bar; a [drinking] tavern. たちのみや

**선승(禪僧)** 《종》 a Zen priest. ぜんそう

**선승하다(先勝—)** win the first game; score the first point.

**선시 선종(善始善終)** ~하다 start well and finish well; do a consistently good job; do well consistently.

**선실(船室)** a cabin 《1등의》 a state room; the passenger's quarters / 2등 ~ a second-class cabin / ~ 배당표 a berth list; ~을 예약하다 reserve a passage; book a berth. せんしつ

**선심(善心)** ①《착한 마음》 virtuous mind; kind heart ②《남을 돕는 마음》 generosity; kindness / ~을 쓰다 do something nice (for a person). ぜんしん

**선심(線審)** 《체》 a line umpire; a linesman. せんしん

**선악(善惡)** good and evil 《정사(正邪)》 right and wrong / ~의 구분을 알다 know right from wrong; distinguish right from wrong. ぜんあく

**선약(仙藥)** the elixir of life; a wonderful remedy 《만병의》 a panacea. せんやく

**선약(先約)** a previous engagement[appoi-

선양 515 선전

ntment]; a prior contract[promise]/ ~순으로 in the sequence of the orders received/ ~이 있다 have a previous engagement.

**선양**(宣揚) enhancement; exaltation; promotion/ ~하다 raise; enhance; promote/국위를 ~하다 enhance the prestige of *one's* country. せんよう

**선어**(鮮魚) fresh fish.

**선언**(宣言) declaration; proclamation/ ~하다 pronounce; declare; profess; announce/ ~서 a manifesto; a declaration/ 독립 ~ the Declaration of Independence/폐회를 ~하다 declare the meeting closed. せんげん

**선언 명제**(選言命題) 〖논〗 a disjunctive proposition; disjunction.

**선업**(善業) good work; a good deed. せんぎょう

**선열**(先烈) the patriot of old/순국 ~ the martyred patriots. せんれつ

**선왕**(先王) the late king. せんのう

**선외**(選外) being left out of selection[choice]/ ~ 가작(佳作) good work left out of selection/ ~가 되다 be left out of selection; be rejected.

**선용**(善用) a good use/ ~하다 make a good use of; make the most of/여가의 ~ making a good use of spare time[hours]/지식을 ~하다 make a good use of *one's* knowledge. せんよう

**선웃음** a forced[an affected] smile; a simper/~을 웃다 force[affect] a laugh; pretend to smile; simper. つくりわらい

**선원**(船員)**(총칭)** the crew; a ship's company**(한.사람)** one of the crew[the ship's company] / ~ 수첩 a seaman's pocket ledger /~실 the crew's quarters/하급 ~ the forecastle. せんいん

**선위**(禪位) abdication [of the throne]/ ~하다 abdicate. ぜんい

**선유**(船遊) boating; rowing /~하러 가다 go for a row[sail]; go rowing[boating] ふなあそび

**선율**(旋律) melody/~적인 melodious; of a harmonized melody /~학 〖음〗 melodics. せんりつ

**선의**(善意) good intention; good faith; good will/~의 well-intended; *bona fide*(L)/~로 해석하다 interpret (*a thing*) for the best. ぜんい

**선의**(船醫) the ship's doctor[surgeon].

**선의권**(先議權) the right to prior consideration (of *the budget*).

**선인**(善人) a virtuous person; a good man ぜんにん

**선인**(仙人)**(은자)** a hermit **(선녀)** a fairy 〖초속(超俗)적인 존재〗 a superhuman being/~ 같은 생활을 하다 live a hermit life. せんにん

**선인**(先人)**(선친)** my deceased father **(이전 사람)** *one's* predecessors; forerunners; precursors. せんじん

**선인**(船人) a sailor ⇨뱃사람. ふなびと

**선인 선과**(善因善果) the results[fruits] of good deeds; the rewards of virtue. ぜんいんぜんか

**선인장**(仙人掌) 〖식〗 a cactus; a prickly pear. さぼてん

**선임**(先任) seniority **(선임자)** a predecessor/~ 장교(將校) a senior officer. せんにん

**선임**(選任)**(선거)** election **(임명)** appointment **(지명)** nomination / ~하다 select and appoint; elect; nominate/변호인의 ~ designation of counsels [by the government]. せんにん

**선입**(先入) prior entry /~하다 enter first; preoccupy; prepossess/~관 preconception; a prejudice / ~관을 가지다 have a preconceived idea. せんにゅう

**선입감**(先入感) preconception; prejudice; bias. せんにゅうかん

**선입견**(先入見) preconception; prepossession; preoccupation. せんにゅうかん

**선자**(選者) a selector; a judge. せんじゃ

**선잠** a light[dog] sleep **(불안한 잠)** an uneasy sleep **(자주 깨는 잠)** a broken sleep/~을 자다 have a poor[bad] sleep; sleep poorly[badly]; be a light sleeper. うたたね

**선장**(船長) a [ship's, sea] captain; a commander; a master mariner **(소상선의)** a skipper/~ 면허장 a master's certificate of competence/~실 a captain's cabin/~직 captaincy; mastership/~ 해난 증명서 captain's protest. せんちょう

**선장**(船匠) a shipwright; a ship-carpenter **(배 타고 다니는)** a ship's carpenter. せんしょう

**선재**(船材) [ship-building] timber[lumber] ふねのしざい

**선저**(船底) a [ship's] bottom/~ 도료 bottom paint. せんてい

**선적**(船籍) ①**(국적)** the nationality of a ship ②**(등기부)** the registry of a ship /~항 a port of registry. せんせき

**선적**(船積)**(발송)** shipping; shipment **(적재(積載))** loading; lading/~ 송장 a shipping invoice/~항(港) a port of shipment.

**선전**(宣戰) declaration[proclamation] of war/~하다 declare[proclam] war (*upon, against*)/~ 포고(布告) a declaration [proclamation] of war. せんかん

**선전**(旋轉) rotation; circulation; revolving/~하다 rotate; circulate; revolve. せんてん

**선전**(善戰) fighting a good fight; fighting admirably[well]/ ~하다 fight a good fight; fight admirably[well].

**선전**(宣傳) **(사상적)** propagandism; propaganda **(광고적)** publicity **(종교적)** propagation **(광고)** advertisement/ ~하다 propagate; propagandize; give publicity to; make propaganda **(광고하다)** advertise/~ 삐라 a propaganda-bill; a leaflet; a handbill/~부 a publicity department／∼비 advertising expenses／ ∼ 효과 propaganda effect. せんでん

**선점**(先占) 〖법〗 prior occupation／∼하다 preoccupy; acquire by occupancy／∼권자 an occupant／∼ 취득 acquisition by occupancy. せんせん

**선정**(選定) selection; choice／∼하다 select; choose. せんてい

**선정**(善政) good government[administration]; just rule／∼을 베풀다 govern well; rule wisely. ぜんせい

**선정적**(煽情的) (being) sensational; suggestive; lascivious; sex-appealing／∼적 소설 a lascivious novel; a suggestive story.

**선제**(先帝) 《죽은》 the late Emperor; an ex-Emperor. せんてい

**선제 공격**(先制攻擊) ∼하다 attack [the enemy] first.

**선조**(先祖) an ancestor; a forefather; ancestry／∼의 ancestral; family (tomb, etc.). せんぞ

**선조총**(旋條銃) a rifle.

**선종**(禪宗) the Seon sect; Zen Buddhism. せんしゅう

**선주**(船主) a ship's owner. せんしゅ

**선줄** a longitudinal vein of ore; a lengthwise mineral vein.

**선중**(船中) the interior of a ship／∼에서 in a ship; on board [a ship]／∼ 생활 ship life. せんちゅう

**선지** the blood taken from a slaughtered animal. いきち

**선지자**(先知者) a prophet [who knows the future]; a seer; a predictor. せんちしゃ

**선진**(先進) seniority; advance／∼의 advanced; senior／세계의 ∼국 the advanced nations of the world. せんしん

**선진**(先陣) 〖군〗 the van [of an army]; the advanced guards 《전초선》 a scouting line／∼이 되다 lead the van. せんじん

**선집**(選集) a selection; a choice selection. せんしゅう

**선착**(先着) first[early] arrival／∼순으로 by order of arrival; in the order of receipt. せんちゃく

**선창**(先唱) chorus leading／∼하다 lead the chorus 《주창하다》 take the lead (in)／∼자 《노래의》 a chorus leader. さきに

**선창**(船窓) a porthole. せんそう

**선창**(船艙) 《잔교》 a wharf 《배의》 a hatch／∼가 a bund. さんばし

**선채**(先綵) betrothal presents; engagement gifts.

**선책**(善策) a good scheme; a capital plan; a good policy. ぜんさく

**선처**(善處) adequate management; proper dealing[step]／∼하다 make the best (of); tide over (difficulties)／시국에 ∼하다 meet[cope with] the situation properly. ぜんしょ

**선천**(先天) apriority; innateness; inbornness; inherence／∼적 native; inborn;

innate; inherent／∼적으로 by nature; naturally／∼적 불구 a congenital deformity／∼병 a congenital[hereditary] disease. せんてん

**선철**(先哲) ancient sages. せんてつ

**선철**(銑鐵) pig iron ⇨ 무쇠. せんてつ

**선체**(船體) a hull 《배의》 a ship. せんたい

**선출**(選出) election／∼하다 elect; return 《영》／서울에서 ∼되다 be elected[returned] for Seoul. せんしゅつ

**선충**(線蟲) 〖동〗 an eelworm; a nematode／∼류 Nematoda 《학명》.

**선취**(先取) taking first／∼하다 take first; preoccupy／한 점을 ∼하다 score a point in advance. せんしゅ

**선취 특권**(先取特權) the right of priority; a prior right; a priority; a preferential right／∼이 있다 hold prior rights. せんしゅとっけん

**선측**(船側) the ship's side; the side of a ship／∼ 인도 free alongside [ship] 《略: F. A. S.》.

**선치**(善治) good government／∼하다 rule benevolently; govern well. ぜんち

**선친**(先親) my deceased[late] father.

**선키** one's height when standing.

**선탁**(宣託) an oracle; a revelation; an inspiration／신의 ∼이 있다 have a divine revelation. しんのおつげ

**선태**(蘚苔) a moss; a bryophyte／∼류 Bryophyta 《학명》. こけ

**선택**(選擇) selection; choice／∼하다 select; choose／∼ 과목 an optional subject; an elective [subject]／∼의 자유 freedom of choice; option／∼법 a method of selection／직업을 ∼하다 choose a vocation[profession]／∼의 여지가 없다 I have no alter native. せんたく

**선통**(先通) advance[prior] notice; informing beforehand／∼하다 communicate [notify] in advance; give prior notice. まえにしらせること

**선팽창**(線膨脹) 〖물〗 linear expansion／∼계수 coefficient of linear expansion. せんぼうちょう

**선편**(先鞭) the initiative; leading／∼하다 take the initiative; lead. せんべん

**선편**(船便) steamer service／∼으로 by ship[steamer, water]／다음 ∼을 기다리다 wait for the next boat. ふなびん

**선포**(宣布) proclamation／∼하다 proclaim 《포고하다》 propagate a religion. せんぷ

**선표**(船票) a steamboat[ship, vessel] ticket. じょうせんけん

**선풍**(旋風) a whirl wind; a cyclone; a tornado 《pl. -es, -s》／∼을 일으키다 《비유적》 create a great sensation／∼에 휩쓸리다 be caught up in a cyclone. せんぷう

**선풍기**(扇風機) an electric[a mechanical] fan; a motor-fan／회전 ∼ an oscillating fan／∼를 돌리다 set an electric fan going[in motion]／∼를 끄다 turn[switch] off an electric fan. せんぷうき

**선하**(船荷) a cargo; freight／∼ 증권 a

**선하다** 《눈에》 be vivid before *one's* eye; live vividly in *one's* memory/그 광경이 눈에 ~ I have a vivid recollection of it.

**선학**(禪學) the doctrine of the Zensect.

**선함**(船艦) 《군함과 배》vessels of war and other ships; warships and other vessels 《배》vessels.

**선행**(先行) going first; walking ahead; preceding/ ~하다 go first; walk ahead of/ ~ 조건 a precedent condition.

**선행**(善行) a good deed; good conduct/ ~을 표창하다 officially recognize (*a person's*) good deed/ ~을 쌓다 keep on doing good deeds.

**선향**(先鄕) *one's* ancestral home ⇒관향(貫鄕)

**선향**(仙鄕) a land of eternity; a fairyland; an elf land.

**선향**(線香) a joss stick; an incense-stick / ~을 피우다 burn incense-sticks/모기 ~ a mosquito incense-stick.

**선험**(先驗) *a priori*(L); transcendental/ ~적 인식 transcendental cognition/~적 확률 a priori probability.

**선헤엄** treading water; standing stroke /~을 치다 tread water.

**선현**(先賢) ancient sages.

**선혈**(鮮血) [fresh] blood; life blood.

**선형**(扇形) a fan shape; 《수》a sector/ ~의 fan-shaped.

**선형**(船型) type[class] of ship.

**선호**(船號) a ship's name; the name of a vessel.

**선혹**(煽惑) agitation; stirring up; instigation/ ~하다 agitate; stir up; instigate.

**선화**(仙化) natural death/ ~하다 die a natural death.

**선화**(線畵) line[lineal] drawing[engraving].

**선화**(禪話) a talk on Seon philosophy.

**선화지**(仙花紙) reclaimed paper.

**선황**(先皇) the late Emperor.

**선회**(旋回) turning; circling; revolution; rotation/ ~하다 circle; turn[revolve] round; rotate/ ~ 운동 a turning movement/ ~ 비행 circuitous flying; circling/~축 a pivot.

**선후**(先後) 《앞뒤》front and rear; beginning and end 《순서》order; sequence/ ~의[에] before and after; fore and aft /말의 ~가 뒤바뀌다 get confused in *one's* talk.

**선후책**(善後策) a remedial[relief] measure; remedies/ ~을 강구하다 consider the remedies.

**선훈**(船暈) seasickness ⇒뱃멀미.

**섣달** the last month of the year; December; the year-end/~ 그믐 New year's Eve.

**섣부르다** (be) clumsy; awkward; tactless.

**섣불리** awkwardly.

**설** 《새해》the New Year [season]; 《설날》the New Year's Day/ ~ 음식 festive dishes for New Year/ ~을 쇠다 celebrate the New Year.

**설**(說) ①《의견》an opinion; a view; ~을 바꾸다 change *one's* views ②《학설》a theory; a doctrine/다윈의 ~ Darwin's theory ③《풍설》a rumour; a talk /그런 ~이 세상에 떠돌고 있다 Rumours to that effect are in the air.

**설겅거리다** 《밥·콩 따위가》taste lumpy; chew hard/콩이 설어서 설겅거리다 These beans are not well done so they are hard to eat.

**설겆다** wash; do [the dishes]/그릇을 ~ do the dishes.

talk (*one*) over/ ~력 persuasive power / ~하여 승낙시키다 persuade[reason]

**설겆이** ①《식후의》dish-washing; washing-up/ ~하다 wash[do] dishes; wash up ②《비 올 때의》taking away (*things*) to shelter from the rain/ ~하다 take away (*things*) to keep out rain.

**설경**(雪景) a snow-covered scene[landscape]; a landscape of snow; a snowscope.

**설계**(設計) a plan; a design/ ~하다 plan; design; project/ ~도 a plan 《청사진》a blueprint/ ~서 specifications / ~ 약도 an outline plan/ ~자 a designer; a projector/생활의 ~ life planning/정원을 ~하다 lay out a garden design/신생활을 ~하다 make *one's* plan for a new life.

**설계**(雪溪) a snow valley[gorge, ravine].

**설골**(舌骨) 《해》hyoid bone.

**설교**(說教) ①《설법》a sermon; a preaching; a discourse/ ~하다 preach; preach a sermon (*on*)/ ~자 a preacher ②《잔소리》a lecture/ ~하다 lecture (*one*); read (*one*)/ ~를 듣다 be scolded; be lectured.

**설날** the New Year's Day/ ~에 on the New Year's Day; on the first day of the year.

**설다** ①《서투르다》(be) not familiar; not accustomed (*to*); poor/ 선 솜씨 poor ability ②《덜 익다》be half-done[-boiled] ③ sad ⇒서럽다.

**썰다** chop; mince; dice; slice 《키다》spin off 《쎠리다》harrow /잘게 ~ cut into small pieces.

**설다루다** mismanage; handle wrongly; do a halfway job.

**설대** 《식》an arrow bamboo; *Arundaria japonica*(학명).

**설득**(說得) persuasion/ ~하다 persuade;

**설듣다** half-hear; hear but doesn't quite understand. じゅうぶんにきかない

**설라마**(雪羅馬) a white horse with black spots ⇒서라말.

**설렁** a [call] bell; a doorbell/ ~줄 a bell rope; a bellpull.

**설렁거리다** ①《바람이》 blow gently/바람이 설렁설렁 분다 There is a gentle breeze. そよそよふく ②《걷다》 walk briskly.

**설렁탕**(一湯) a kind of meat and rice soup.

**설렁하다** be somewhat chilly[cold]; (be) chilly; cool/비가 오더니 설렁해졌다 The rain has cooled the air. ひやっとする

**쎌레놓다** manage to accomplish a hard job. できるようにじゅんびする

**설레다** ①《가슴이》 flutter; feel uneasy; fidget; pitapat; palpitate/마음이 ~ feel uneasy ②《서성거리다》 move about uneasily; be restless/설레지 말고 한자리에 앉아 있어라 Don't be so restless. —Keep your seat. むねがたかなる

**설레설레** swingingly; waveringly; in a wavering manner/아니라고 머리를 ~ 혼들다 shake one's head in denial. ふりふり

**설령**(設令) if; even if; though; even though; whatever⋯ may⋯; although/~ 돈깨나 있다손 치더라도 however rich one may be. たとえ

**설립**(設立) foundation; establishment; organization; institution/ ~하다 establish; institute; create; set up/ ~자 a founder; an organizer/ ~ 등기 registration of incorporation/ 도서관을 ~ 하다 institute a library. せつりつ

**설마** impossible; that cannot be; by no means/ ~ 그럴라구 It is not at all likely./ ~ 그가 그런 짓이야 안 하겠지 He is the last man to do such a thing. まさか

**설맞다** go wide of the mark; miss the mark; go wide/총알에 설맞었다 I received a flesh wound. てきがはずれる

**설맞이** welcoming the New Year.

**썰매** a sled; a sleigh; a sledge/자동 ~ a motor sledge/ ~를 타다 sled; drive in a sledge. そり

**설맹**(雪盲) snow-blindness.

**설면하다** ①《소원하다》 (be) estranged; alienated ②《정답지 않다》 (be) on cold[bad] terms with; want in familiarity. かおなじみおなじみがうすくなる

**설명**(說明) explanation; description 《도해》 illustration; elucidation/~하다 explain; make plain; illustrate; describe/ ~도(圖) a diagram/ ~서 an explanation/ ~자 an explainer; an interpreter/별로 ~할 필요가 없다 It tells its own tale. せつめい

**설문**(設問) a question/ ~하다 question; put a question to/다음 문장을 읽고 아래의 ~에 답하라 Read the following and answer the questions given below.

**썰물** an ebb; ebb tide/ ~ 때에 at low tide. かんちょう

**설밤** snow falling on New Year's day.

**설백**(雪白) snow-[milk-]white; pure white. ゆきのようにしろいこと

**설법**(說法) a Buddhist sermon; preaching/ ~하다 preach [a sermon]; preach to (one). せっぽう

**설보다** mistake [in seeing]; see unclearly or wrongly /그를 김군으로 설보았다 I glanced at him and thought he was Mr. Kim. ふじゅうぶんにみる

**설복**(說服) persuasion/ ~하다 persuade; prevail on; convince (a person) of (his error); argue down/나는 함께 오도록 그를 ~했다 I prevailed upon[with] him to come with me. せっぷく

**설봉**(舌鋒) the tongue/ ~이 날카롭다 have an incisive[a trenchant] tongue. ぜっぽう

**설분**(雪憤) venting one's rage.

**설비**(設備) equipment; provision 《수용의》 accommodations/ ~하다 equip[fit, provide, furnish] with; accommodate/ 그 공장은 ~가 완전하다 This workshop is perfectly equipped. せつび

**설빔** the New Year's garb/~하다 dress up for the New Year's/ ~ 옷 a New Year's garment.

**설사**(泄瀉) loose bowels; diarrhea[diarrhoea]/ ~하다 have loose bowels/ ~약 a binding medicine/ ~를 막다 bind the bowels. げり

**설사**(設使) even if ⇒설령(設令). まさか

**설상**(舌狀) ~의 ligulate; linguiform/ ~ 기관 [동] a lingua(pl. -guae)/ ~화 [식] a ligulate flower.

**설상**(雪上) (on) top of the snow/ ~ 가상(加霜) misfortune on top of misfortune; misfortunes never come single/ ~ 가상으로 to make things[matters] worse. せつじょう

**설선**(雪線) [지] the snow line. せっせん

**설설**[1] gently heating/방이 ~ 끓다 a room is comfortably warm. ごとごと

**설설**[2] ①《기는 모양》 crawl; cringe; cower/ ~ 기다 cringe (before) ②《고개를》 with a gentle shake of the head; be awestruck.

**쎌쎌하다** feel hungry/배가 ~ I feel hungry. ひもじい

**설소차**(雪搔車) snow-plough; a rotaryplough. ゆきかきぐるま

**설쇠다** greet the New Year.

**설술** wine to celebrate the New Year.

**설암**(舌癌) [의] tongue cancer; cancer of the tongue. せつがん

**설연**(設宴) spreading a banquet/ ~하다 give[hold] a dinner; hold a banquet.

**설영**(設營) ~하다 《세우다》 construct 《준비하다》 prepare; arrange.

**설왕 설래**(說往說來) arguing back and forth/ ~하다 bandy words (with); wran-

**설욕(雪辱)** vindication of *one's* honour/ ~하다 clear *one*self of a disgrace; exonerate *one*self (of) / ~전(戰) a return match.

**설움** sorrow; grief; lamentation; sadness; distress/ ~을 못 이기다 be overcome with sorrow. かなしみ

**설원(雪冤)** exoneration; clearing *one*self of a false charge/ ~하다 clear *one*self [of a false charge]. せつえん

**설원(雪原)** a snowfield; the frozen waste.

**설유(說諭)** admonition 《견책》 reproof/ ~하다 admonish; exhort; reprove; give (*one*) a talking-to 《속》. せつゆ

**설음(舌音)** 【언】 a lingual sound. ぜつおん

**설음질** dishwashing ⇨설것이.

**설익다** 《과실이》 (be) half-ripe 《음식이》 (be) half-done; half-boiled/ 설익은 밥 half-cooked rice. みじゅくだ

**설인(雪人)** 《히말라야의》 a[an abominable] snowman; a yeti.

**설자다** sleep fitfully[poorly].

**설잡다** drop (*a thing*) from *one's* grasp. ふじゅうぶんにつかむ

**설전(雪戰)** snowballing ⇨눈싸움.

**설전(舌戰)** a verbal[wordy] battle; a war of words; an argument/ ~하다 engage in a wordy[verbal] battle (with *one*). ぜっせん

**설정(雪程)** a snow-covered road. ゆきのつったみち

**설정(設定)** establishment; creation; institution; fixing/ ~하다 establish; create; institute/ ~ 행위 an action of creation[establishment]/권리를 ~하다 create a right. せってい

**설주(―柱)** a side post; a support [pillar].

**설죽다** be half-alive. かんせんにしなないこと

**설중(雪中)** ~에 in the snow/ ~ 행군 a snow march/ ~에 행군하다 march through the snow. せっちゅう

**설차림** preparing the New Year's festive dishes.

**설천(雪天)** a snow sky; a snowy day. せってん

**설철(屑鐵)** scrap iron. くずてつ

**설측음(舌側音)** 【언】 a lateral [sound]. ぜっそくおん

**설치(雪恥)** vindication of *one's* honour / ~하다 clear *one*self of a disgrace; vindicate *one's* honor. はじをそそぐこと

**설치(設置)** establishment; foundation; institution 《설비》 installation 《조직》 organization/ ~하다 establish; institute; set up; found; create/학교를 ~하다 establish[found] a school. せっち

**설치다¹** leave (*something*) half-done; do (*a thing*) by halves/간밤에는 잠을 설쳤다 I slept badly last night.

**설치다²** run wild; riot; ·be unruly. あばれめぐる

**설치레** New Year's garb ⇨설빔. がんたんようのいふく

**설컹** hard chewing; lumpy-tasting. ごりごり

**설탕(雪糖)** sugar/각~ lump[cube] sugar /모래 ~ granulated[crystallized] sugar/ 흑~ muscovado/ ~물 sugared water/~을 넣다 sugar; sweeten [food] with sugar. さとう

**설태(舌苔)** the coat on *one's* tongue; a coated tongue; tongue fur[fuzz].

**설통발** a fish trap; a fishweir; a fish garth.

**설파(說破)** ①《밝힘》 exposure ②《깨뜨림》 confutation; refutation/ ~하다 expose; confute; refute/진리를 ~하다 give an expression to the truth. せっぱ

**설편(雪片)** a snowflake. せっぺん

**설피다** (be) rough; coarse 《직물이》 loose in weave/이 직물은 설피게 짰다 This fabric is loose in weave. うとらである

**설피창이** loose-woven stuff; gauze.

**설핏설핏** ~하다 (be) all rather loose woven; gauze-like.

**설핏하다** (be) somewhat coarse. うとらだ

**설하선(舌下腺)** 【해】 a sublingual gland. ぜっかせん

**설한(雪寒)** cold weather following snow fall/엄동 ~ the cold of winter. ゆきがおってさむいこと

**설해(雪害)** snow damage. せつがい

**설형(楔形)** ~의 cuneiform; wedgeshaped / ~ 문자 a cuneiform character; cuneiform letters. きっけい

**설혹(設或)** even if ⇨설령(設令). たとえ

**설화(舌禍)** an unfortunate slip of the tongue/ ~ 사전 *one's* incriminating public utterance. ぜっか

**설화(雪花)** ①《눈송이》 snowflakes ②《나무 위의 눈》 silver thaw; rime deposit/~석고 alabaster. せっか

**설화(說話)** ①《이야기》 a tale; a story; a narration ②《훈계》 a sermon; preaching; a dissertation/그는 툭하면 일장 ~를 한다 He is ready to preach. せつわ

**섬¹** ①《용기(用器)》 a straw sack/쌀 ~ a rice bag ②《단위》 a unit of volume; a *sem*. かます

**섬²** 《층계의》 a flight of stonestairs; a flight of steps. いしだん

**섬³** an island; an isle 《작은 섬》 an islet /~에 살다 live in an island/ ~나라 an island country. しま

**섬(纖)** small; fine; delicate. せん

**섬거적** straw matting; a straw mat/~에 싸다 wrap in a straw mat.

**섬게** 【동】 a sea urchin. うに

**섬광(閃光)** a flash/ ~ 사진 flash-light photography/ ~ 전구 a flashing lamp [bulb]/ ~을 발사하다 flash. せんこう

**섬교(纖巧)** delicacy; exquisiteness/ ~하다 (be) delicate; exquisite/ ~한 세공 exquisite workmanship. せんこう

**섬기다** serve 《고용되다》 be in the serv-

**섬니리** ice of; work under another; work for [a firm]; 《모시다》 minister to; wait on / 스승을 ~ obey *one's* teacher / 신을 ~ serve God. つかえる

**섬나라** an island[insular] country / ~ 근성 insular spirit. しまぐに

**섬놈** an islander; a native of an island. しまのもの

**섬누룩** malt of inferior quality; coarse malt.

**섬돌** 《단층》 a stone step; [a flight of] stone steps. いしだん

**섬뜩하다** have a fright; be taken by surprise; (be) frightened; startled; shocked; feel a shock / 섬득하여 with a start; startingly; in amazement. びっくりする

**섬멸**(殲滅) annihilation; total[complete] destruction; a crushing defeat / ~하다 annihilate; destroy totally / ~전 annihilation operation. せんめつ

**섬벅, 섬뻑, 썸벅, 썸뻑** cutting with light stroke [with knife]. すぱっ

**섬벅거리다, 썸벅거리다** wink; blink. まばたきする

**섬서하다** (be) unkindly; cool; curt.

**섬섬**(纖纖) being delicate / ~하다 (be) slender; slim; supple; delicate / ~ 약골 a man of delicate constitution / ~ 옥수 supple hands. せんせん

**섬섬**(閃閃) ~하다 (be) flashing; sparking; gleaming; glittering. ぴかぴか

**섬세**(纖細) delicacy / ~하다 (be) light; slender; delicate; exquisite / ~하게 만들어진 lightly-constructed. せんさい

**섬약**(纖弱) frailty; delicacy / ~하다 (be) frail; fragile; delicate.

**섬어**(譫語) ①《헛소리》 delirium ②《잠꼬대》 talking in *one's* sleep. たわごと

**섬유**(纖維) a fiber; textile / ~ 공업 the fiber[textile] industry / ~ 조직 a fibrous tissue / ~질 fibroid material / ~증(症) fibrosis / ~층 a fibrous layer / ~품 textile goods / ~ 상(狀)의 fibriform. せんい

**섬흘하다**(閃忽—) flash; twinkle. ひらめく

**섬화**(閃火) a flash; a spark / ~ 방전(放電) spark discharge. せんか

**섭금류**(涉禽類) 〖조〗 wading birds; *Grallatores* (학명).

**섭력**(涉歷) versatile experience; wide experience / ~하다 gain[have] versatile experience; become[be] widely experienced / 그는 젊지마는 ~한 것이 많다 He is young in years, but old in experience.

**섭렵**(涉獵) extensive reading / ~하다 read extensively; range over / 널리 문헌을 ~하다 range over an extensive literature. しょうりょう

**섭리**(攝理) [Divine] Providence / 신의 ~ Divine Providence / 자연의 ~ the dispensation of nature. せつり

**섭새기다** emboss; carve in relief / 섭새김 embossed carving; relief. うきぼりする

**섭생**(攝生) care of health; preservation of *one's* health; 《의》 regimen / ~하다 take care of *one's* health; observe the rules of health / ~가 a person careful of his health / ~법 the rules of health; hygiene. せっせい

**섭섭하게** to *one's* regret; regretfully; unfortunately / ~도 그는 오지 않았다 To my disappointment, he did not come.

**섭섭하다** 《떠나는 것이》(be) unwilling; reluctant; loath; regretful; sorry 《아깝다》(be) regrettable; pitiful; disappointing; sorry (사람이 주어) / 그가 못 와서 ~ I regret[It is regrettable, It is too bad] that he can't come.

**섭씨**(攝氏) Celsius(略: C) / ~ 온도계 a centigrade thermometer; a Celsius.

**섭양**(攝養) care of health ⇒섭생(攝生). せっせい

**섭외**(涉外) negotiation; liaison / ~계원 a public relations man; a liaison clerk / ~과 the public relations section / ~ 사무 public-relations work; liaison business. しょうがい

**섭정**(攝政) 《사람》 a regent 《직위》 regency / ~하다 rule as regent / ~을 두다 set up a regency; appoint a regent / ~ 황태자 the Prince Regent. せっしょう

**섭취**(攝取) intake; adoption / ~하다 take; partake of 《문화 따위를》 assimilate / ~물 ingesta / 칼로리 ~량 caloric intake. せっしゅ

**섭호선**(攝護腺) the prostate [gland] / ~염 prostatitis.

**섰다** a kind of Korean card game.

**성** anger; indignation; rage; wrath / ~나다 be off ended; be angered; become [get] angry; be enraged. いかり

**성**(姓) a family name; a surname.

**성**(性) ①《남녀의》a sex 《문법의》a gender / ~적 sexual / ~적 생활 sexual life / ~병(病) a venereal[sexual] disease / ~도덕 sexual morality / ~행위 sexual intercourse / ~ 호르몬 a sex hormone / ~교육[문제] a sex education[problem] / ~에 눈뜨다 wake up[be awakened] sexually ②《본성》 nature 《품성》 character. せい

**성**(城) a castle; a fortress; a citadel; a city wall / ~터 the ruins of a castle / ~을 함락시키다 take a castle; carry a fortress. じょう

**성**(省) 《행정부의》a ministry; a department [of the government]; 《중국의 행정 구역》a province / 국무 ~ the Department of State.

**성**(聖) sanctity; holiness 《성인》a holy man; a sage; a saint / ~스럽다 (be) holy; sacred; saint / ~ 바울 St. Paul. せい

**성가**(成家) ①《학문·기술을》 establishing

**성가** *one*self as a master[an authority]; developing a style of *one's* own/ ～하다 develop a style of *one's* own; make a name for *one*self ②(집을) establishment of *one's* own household; success in life /～하다 establish *one's* own household; succeed in life/자수 ～하다 make *one's* own efforts.

**성가(聲價)** reputation; repute; fame; popularity/ ～를 높이다 enhance *one's* reputation. せいよ

**성가(聖歌)** a sacred song; a hymn/ ～대 a choir/ ～집 a hymnal; a hymn-book. せいか

**성가시다** (be) annoying; troublesome; bothering; harassing; pesky(미); persistent/성가신 사람 an importunate/성가시게 굴다 give (*one*) trouble; bother; annoy/성가시게 굴지 마라 Don't trouble me. わずらわしい

**성깔** a sharp temper; an irritable disposition. するどいせいしつ

**성게** 【어】(식용 성게) a sea-urchin; paste of seasoned sea-urchins.

**성격(性格)** character; personality 《개성》 individuality/ ～ 묘사 character drawing[delineation]/ ～ 배우 a character actor[actress]/ ～의 차이 dissimilarity[disparity] in character/ 좋은 ～을 갖추다 bear[possess, have] a good character. せいかく

**성결** nature; disposition; temperament; temper/ ～이 곱다[사납다] have a lovely[nasty] disposition.

**성결(聖潔)** sanctity and purity/ ～하다 (be) holy and pure/ ～ 교회 the Holiness Church. しんせいできれいなこと

**성경(聖經)** the Bible; the Book; the Scriptures; sacred books; a holy book/ ～의 Biblical; scriptural/ ～ 이야기 a Bible story/ ～학자 Biblicist. せいけい

**성경 현전(聖經賢傳)** the works of the sages. せいけいけんでん

**성공(成功)** success; achievement 《성취》 accomplishment 《연극·영화 등의》 a hit / ～하다 succeed (*in*); be[prove] successful/ ～자 a successful man; a success/ ～을 빕니다 I wish you success. せいこう

**성과(成果)** a result; a product; fruit; an outcome/노력의 ～ the fruit[product, result] of *one's* labour[efforts]. せいか

**성곽(城廓)** 《성》 a castle; a citadel 《곽》 a castle-wall 《성채》 a fortress; a stronghold/ ～을 수호하다 keep a castle. じょうかく

**성교(性交)** sexual intercourse; *coitus* (L) / ～하다 have sexual intercourse/ ～ 불능 impotence; impotency/ ～ 연령 a copulation age. せいこう

**성교(聖敎)** ①《성훈(聖訓)》 the sacred teachings ②《기독교》 the Christian religion ③《교파》 the Holy Church. せいきょう

**성교육(性敎育)** sex education; sex information. せいきょういく

**성군(星群)** asterism; a cluster of stars; a group of stars. せいぐん

**성군(聖君)** a wise and virtuous king. せいくん

**성군 작당(成群作黨)** forming a gang[cabal, faction]; conspiracy/ ～하다 form a gang; gang[band] together; cabal.

**성궁(聖躬)** the Imperial[Royal] person; His Majesty's person. せいきゅう

**성귀(成句)** a set phrase; an idiomatic/ ～어 an idiom. せいく

**성규(成規)** regulations; prescriptions/ ～의 regular; formal; established. せいき

**성극(聖劇)** a biblical drama. せいげき

**성글벙글** smilingly; beamingly; with a bland smile. にやにや

**성금** (효과) effect; fruit; result 《보람》 worth 《효용》 avail; use. こうか

**성금(誠金)** a donation; a contribution; a gift of money; a subscription/ ～을 내다 subscribe; contribute; donate. まことからたすきん

**성급(性急)** ～하다 (be) hasty; quick-[short-]tempered; impatient /성급하게 impatiently; hastily/성급한 사람 a hot headed man; a hotspur. せいきゅう

**성기(成器)** ①《완성한 그릇》 a finished vessel[instrument, tool]/ ～하다 bring a vessel[tool, instrument] to perfection ②《재기(材器)를 완성함》 a perfected ability/ ～하다 refine *one's* abilities; perfect *one's* talents. せいき

**성기(星期)** a wedding date. けっこんのひ

**성기(性器)** genitalia; the reproductive [sexual, genital] organs. せいき

**성기다** ①《거리·간격이》 be sparsely[thinly, scatteredly] spaced; be far apart/성기게 난 수염 a thin moustache ②《관계가》 (be) estranged; alienated: be not on good terms. うとらだ

**성깃성깃** thinly; scatteringly; sparsely; here and there/벌판에는 나무가 ～ 서 있었다 The field was sparsely dotted with trees.

**성깃하다** (be) rather thin; somewhat sparse; loose a little. うとらのようだ

**성나다** get[grow] angry[offended] with (*a person*) [*at a thing*]; lose *one's* temper; take offense; get mad(미)/성이 나서 얼굴이 파래지다 become pale with anger. いかる

**성내(城內)** inside a fortress[city wall, castle]; within the city; the city. じょうない

**성내다** get angry ⇒성나다. いかる

**성냥** a match/ ～갑 a matchbox/ ～개비 a match stick/ ～불 the light of a match/ ～을 켜다 light[strike] a match. マッチ

**성냥일** blacksmithing; smith work.

**성냥하다** temper; forge; anneal.

**성녀(聖女)** 《천주교》 a woman saint; a

**성년(成年)** majority; full[coming of] age／ ～자 an adult; a major; person of legal age／ ～이 되다 come of age; attain *one's* majority. せいねん

**성년(盛年)** the prime of life[manhood].

**성능(性能)** ability; capability／ ～ 검사 an ability test 《지능》 a mental test. せいのう

**성단(星團)** 【천】 a group[cluster] of stars. せいだん

**성단(聖壇)** an altar; a pulpit.

**성당(聖堂)** a church; a Catholic Church; a sanctuary.. せいどう

**성대(盛大)** 《번영》 prosperity; flourish 《훌륭함》 splendour; grandeur; magnificence／ ～하다 (be) prosperous; flourishing 《당당하다》 be grand／ ～해지다 become prosperous; grow in prosperity; prospes.

**성대(聲帶)** the vocal cords／ ～ 모방 vocal mimicry. せいたい

**성덕(聖德)** 《성인의》 saint's virtues; saintly virtues 《임금의》 royal virtues[favor]. せいとく

**성도(成道)** mastering the secrets (of *a religion*); mastering (of *the art*)／ ～하다 go to[see into] the heart of …; become expert as (*a writer*). どうをなすこと

**성도(聖都)** the Holy City.

**성도(聖徒)** a [Christian] saint; an apostle; a disciple of Christ／ ～전 hagiology; lives of the saints／ ～ 베드로 Saint Peter. せいと

**성도(星圖)** 【천】 a celestial map. せいず

**성랑(城廊)** a castle tower.

**성량(聲量)** volume of *one's* voice／ ～이 풍부하다 have a powerful[rich] voice. せいりょう

**성려(聖慮)** the King's wish[thought, pleasure]. せいりょ

**성력(誠力)** sincerity and energy; whole-hearted devotion／ ～을 다하다 devote *oneself* whole-heartedly. まこととちから

**성령(聖靈)** the Holy Ghost; the Holy spirit／ ～ 강림절 the Pentecost／ ～을 받다 receive divine inspiration. せいれい

**성례(成禮)** completion of ceremonies of marriage／ ～하다 complete the ceremonies of marriage.

**성례(聖禮)** 《예식》 a sacred ceremony 《기독교》 Christian ceremonies.
しんせいなぎしき

**성루(城壘)** a fort; a fortress; ramparts／ ～에 육박하다 press upon a fortress／ ～를 함락시키다[빼앗다] take[carry] a fortress. じょうるい

**성루(聲淚)** a tearful voice／ ～로써 말하다 speak with tears in *one's* eyes.

**성리(性理)** human nature and the rule of Heaven／ ～학 philosophy; metaphysics. せいり

**성립(成林)** ～하다 [a group of small trees] grow into a forest.

**성립(成立)** ①《이루어짐》 coming into existence[being]; 《실현》 materialization; realization／ ～하다 come into existence [being]; be materialized／ ～시키다 bring[call] into existence[being]; materialize; effect ②《조직》 formation; organization／ ～하다 be formed; be organized／내각이 ～했다 The cabinet was formed. ③《결성》 conclusion; completion／ ～하다 be completed; be concluded／혼담은 ～되지 않았다 The proposed match was broken off. せいりつ

**성마르다** be narrow-minded and hottempered.

**성만찬(聖晩餐)** the Holy Communion; the Sacrament of the Lord's Supper; Eucharist. せいばんさん

**성망(聲望)** reputation; fame; popularity／ ～이 있는 popular (*with*); of high reputation／ ～이 높다 be highly reputed; be very popular. せいぼう

**성명(姓名)** *one's* family name and given name／ ～ 판단 onomancy; onomatomancy／ ～을 대다 give *one's* name (*as*). せいめい

**성명(盛名)** renown; fame; reputation／ ～이 높은 far-famed／ ～을 떨치다 command admiration[renown]. せいめい

**성명(聲名)** reputation; fame; popularity／ ～을 올리다 rise[raise *oneself*] in public estimation. せいめい

**성명(聲明)** [a] declaration; [a] statement; [an] announcement／ ～하다 declare; make a statement; announce／ ～서 a [public] statement／ ～서를 발표하다 issue a statement (*on*). せいめい

**성모(聖母)** the Holy Mother; our Lady／ ～ 마리아 the Holy Mother Mary／ ～ 숭경(崇敬) hyperdulia／ ～ 잉태 Immaculate Conception. せいぼ

**성묘(省墓)** visiting *one's* ancestral tombs／ ～하다 visit[pay *one's* homage to] a grave／ ～객 a visitor to his ancestral tomb.

**성문(成文)** reducing to writing／ ～의 written／ ～ 법[률] a statute; a law; a written[positive] law; *lex scripta* (L); *jusscriptum*(L). せいぶん

**성문(城門)** a castle-gate. じょうもん

**성문(聲門)** 《해》 the glottis. せいもん

**성미(性味)** nature; disposition; temperament; character／ ～가 급한 hot-[quick-, short-]tempered／ ～에 맞는 친구 a congenial friend／그들은 ～가 안 맞는다 They are not suited to each other. せいしつ

**성벽(性癖)** *one's* natural disposition; a mental habit／그는 이상한 ～이 있다 He has a curious habit. せいへき

**성벽(城壁)** a castle-wall; a rampart／ ～을 쌓다 build a rampart／ ～이 둘러싼 시가 a walled town. じょうへき

**성별(性別)** sex distinction. せいべつ

**성병(性病)** a venereal disease(略: V. D.); D); a social disease〈미〉／ ～ 감염 (感染)

**venereal** infection／~ 예방 prevention of venereal diseases／~ 치료소 a V.D. clinic／~ 환자 a person venereally infected. せいびょう

**성보**(城堡) a fortress; a citadel; a fort; a rampart. じょうほう

**성복**(成服) wearing mourning clothes／~하다 go into mourning (for *one*); be in mourning [black].

**성부**(聖父) 《종교》 Holy Father. せいふ

**성분**(成分) 《혼합물의》 an ingredient 《조직상의》 a component[part]／주요 ~ the chief[principal] ingredient／조미료의 ~은 무엇입니까 What are the ingredients of seasoning? せいぶん

**성불**(成佛) attaining Buddhahood; entering Nirvana／~하다 attain Buddhahood; enter Nirvana; become a Buddha／고이 ~하소서 May thy soul rest in peace. じょうぶつ

**성불성**(成不成) success and[or] failure; the outcome. ことのせいひ

**성사**(成事) success; attainment of an end[a result]／~하다 succeed in; accomplish; effect; attain *one's* end; achieve success. せいじ

**성사**(盛事) a splendid enterprise; a great event／이 ~를 함께 기뻐하자 Let us rejoice together on this great occasion.
せいじ

**성산**(成算) confidence of success; prospects of sure success; chances of success／~이 있다 be confident[have little hope] of success. せいさん

**성상**(星霜) years; time／십년의 ~ ten year's time. せいそう

**성상**(聖上) His Majesty; the Emperor; the king. せいじょう

**성상**(聖像) an icon／~ 연구 iconography／~ 예배 iconolatry／~ 숭배 iconolatry. せいぞう

**성상학**(性相學) physiognomy／~의 physiognomical／~자 physiognomist.

**성색**(聲色) demeanor; voice and countenance. せいしょく

**성서**(聖書) the [Holy] Bible; the Scriptures; the Book [of books]／~ 협회 a Bible society／~에 있는 구절 a biblical expression. せいしょ

**성석**(成石) hardening into stone／~하다 harden into stone; turn to stone.

**성선설**(性善說) the ethical doctrine that man's inborn nature is good; the view of human nature as fundamentally good. せいぜんせつ

**성성하다**(星星-) (be) gray; grizzled／백발이 성성한 머리 grizzled hair; hair shot with gray. とうはつがしろい

**성세**(聖世) an age of sage rulers; an era of wise rule. せいせい

**성쇠**(盛衰) ups and downs; rise and fall; vicissitudes／로마의 ~ the rise and fall of Rome. せいすい

**성수**(聖壽) the King's age／~ 만세 Long live the King! せいじゅ

**성수**(星宿) 【천】 constellations; the stars. せいしゅく

**성수**(星數) a star; fortune／~를 보다 consult a fortune-teller. うん

**성수**(聖水) holy water.

**성수기**(盛需期) high-demand season／~를 맞이한 상품 things most in demand.

**성숙**(成熟) ①《과실의》 ripening／~하다 ripen; be ripe／~할 대로 ~한 overmature ②《발육》 full[complete] growth; maturation／~하다 attain full growth; mature／~한 처녀 a mature[marriageable] girl ③《숙성》 maturity; ripeness／~하다 mature; ripen／기운이 ~하다 An opportunity ripens[matures]. せいじゅく

**성숙기**(成熟期) puberty; adolescence; the age of puberty[maturity]／~에 달하다 arrive at puberty; become adolescent. せいじゅくき

**성스럽다**(聖-) (be) holy; sacred; august; divine. いだいでこうけつだ

**성습**(成習) forming[contracting] a habit／~하다 acquire[contract, form] a habit; fall into the habit (*of*).
しゅうかんになること

**성시**(成市) opening a fair[market]／~하다 open a fair.

**성시**(城市) a castle-town; a walled town; a walled city. じょうし

**성시**(盛時) the prime of life; a prosperous age. せいじ

**성신**(星辰) the stars; heavenly bodies／~ 숭배 astrolatry. せいしん

**성신**(聖神) the Holy Heaven[God]／~ 강림 the advent[descent] of the Holy Spirit.

**성실**(誠實) sincerity; fidelity; honesty; integrity／~하다 (be) sincere; faithful; truthful; honest／~하게 일하다 work faithfully／그는 ~한 사람이다 He is a man of integrity. せいじつ

**성심**(誠心) sincerity; wholehearted; devotion／~ 성의로 sincerely; heartily／~ 성의를 다하다 deal with (*a matter*) in all sincerity. せいしん

**성악**(聲樂) vocal music／~가 a vocalist／~과 a vocal music course／~ 연습 voice culture／~을 배우다 study vocal music; study voice. せいがく

**성악설**(性惡說) the ethical view that human nature is evil; the doctrine of original sin. せいあくせつ

**성안**(成案) a definite plan[draft]; a concrete program／~하다 form a definite plan; draft. せいあん

**성안**(聖顏) His Majesty's countenance; the Royal countenance. せいがん

**성애** ①《대접함》 treating friends[bystanders] after striking a good bargain ② 《덤받음》 receiving something extra goods at shopping.

**성애**(性愛) sexual love.

성야(星夜) a starlit night. せいや
성어(成語) ①(어귀) a [set] phrase ②(말을 이룸) forming aword[set phrase]. せいご
성업(成業) the completion of one's work / ~하다 complete one's work[studies] / ~의 희망이 없다 be unpromising; be not hopeful. せいぎょう
성에¹ frostwork.
성에² (쟁기의) the handle of a Korean plow.
성엣장 an ice-drift; a floe; a drifting-ice. りゅうひょう
성역(聖域) sacred precincts; holy grounds. せいいき
성연(盛宴) a magnificent banquet; a grand feast / ~을 베풀다 hold[give] a grand banquet. せいえん
성염(盛炎) intense heat; the hottest weather. こくしょ
성왕(聖王) a wise and virtuous king ⇨ 성군(聖君). せいおう
성외(城外) beyond the wall /~에 outside [the walls of] a castle. じょうがい
성욕(性慾) sexual desire[appetite] / ~ 도착(倒錯) sexual perversion /~ 만족 gratification of sexual desire /변태 ~ abnormal sexuality /~을 만족시키다 gratify one's carnal appetite. せいよく
성우(聲優) a radio actor[actress, performer]. せいゆう
성운(星雲) a nebula (pl. -e) /~의 nebular /~설 the nebular hypothesis[theory]. せいうん
성운(盛運) prosperity; good fortune.
성원(成員) [one of] a quorum; a constituent [member]/ ~ 미달 lack of a quorum. せいいん
성원(聲援) encouragement; [moral] support (유희의) cheering / ~하다 shout encouragement; encourage; cheer; root (for a team)〈미〉/ ~자 a supporter /~대 a band of supporters. せいえん
성월(星月) the moon and star.
성위(星位) 〘천〙 the position or a fixed star; the configuration.
성유(聖油) 《천주교》 chrism; consecrated oil. せいゆ
성은(聖恩) 《왕의》 royal favo[u]r /신의) divine favo[u]r. せいおん
성음(聲音) a sound; a vocal sound/ ~학 phonetics / ~ 문자 phonetic letters [script]. せいおん
성읍(城邑) a town.
성의(誠意) sincerity; good faith; 《법》《선의》 bona fides (Sans) / ~를 피력하다 show one's good faith; lay bare one's heart. せいい
성인(成人) an adult; a grown-up man; a grown-up/ ~ 교육 adult education / ~부(部) an adult division. せいじん
성인(聖人) a sage; a saint; a holy man / ~ 같은 생활을 하다 live a holy life. せいじん
성자(姓字) a family name; a surname.

성자(聖者) 《성현》a sage 《성인》a saint; a holy man. しょうじゃ
성자(聖子) the Son of God; the [Holy] Son. せいし
성자(盛者) a prosperous person. じょうしゃ
성작(聖爵) 《천주교》a communion cup.
성장(成長) growth / ~하다 grow (up); be brought up/ ~점 the growing point / ~이 빠르다 grow quickly /너 굉장히 ~했구나 How you have grown up! せいちょう
성장(盛裝) a gala dress; beautiful attire / ~하다 dress up; be in full dress; be dressed in one's best / ~시키다 dress up (one's daughter). せいそう
성적(成績) result; record; a grade; merit; academic standing /시험 ~ the result of an examination /학교 ~ one's school record[work]/ ~표 a list of students' records /~이 좋다[나쁘다] do well[poorly] (in English) /좋은 ~을 얻도록 열심히 공부하라 Work hard to show good results. せいせき
성적(性的) sexual / ~ 욕망 sexual appetite[desire] / ~ 충동 a sex impulse /~ 매력 a sex appeal / ~ 흥분 sexual excitement[arousal] /~으로 조숙하다 know the sex early. せいてき
성전(聖典) the Scriptures; the Sacred books 《성서》the Bible. せいてん
성전(盛典) a grand[an imposing] ceremony. せいてん
성전(聖殿) a sacred hall; a sanctuary; a temple. せいでん
성전환(性轉換) sex reversal[change] /~ 수술 a sex exchange operation.
성정(性情) nature; temper. せいじょう
성조(性燥) ~하다 be quick[hot]-tempered; be irritable; be hasty. せっかち
성조기(星條旗) the Stars and Stripes. せいじょうき
성좌(星座) a constellation; an asterism /오리온 ~ the constellation of Orion. せいざ
성주(聖主) a wise and virtuous king; a good and wise king. せいしゅ
성주(城主) the castle owner; the lord of a castle. じょうしゅ
성중(城中) the inside of a castle / ~에 inside a castle.
성지(城址) the ruins[remains] of a castle[fortress]. じょうし
성지(聖旨) the Imperial[Royal] will[wish] せいし
성지(聖地) a sacred ground; the Holy Land; Palestine / ~ 순례 《순례자》a pilgrimage to sacred places a pilgrim to the Holy Land. せいち
성직(聖職) holy orders; the ministry; the clergy / ~자 a churchman; a minister. せいしょく
성질(性質) 《기질》nature; disposition; temper 《특성》property; qualities 《종류》

nature; character; kind; sort／일의 ~ the character of the business／이 두 문제는 ~이 다르다 The two questions are of different character. せいしつ

**성찬**(盛饌) a sumptuous[capital] dinner; a feast; good table／~을 베풀다 give a feast; set a good table; entertain. せいせん

**성찬**(聖餐) 《기독교》the Lord's Supper. せいさん

**성찬식**(聖餐式) the Holy Communion; the Lord's Supper. せいさんしき

**성찰**(省察) reflection; self-examination; introspection. せいさつ

**성채**(城砦) a fortress and a stockade; a fortified and garrisoned city. じょうさい

**성책**(城柵) a castle and a stockade; a fortress and a palisade. じょうさく

**성철**(聖哲) a sage; the wise. せいてつ

**성체**(成體) 〖생〗 an adult [animal]. せいたい

**성체**(聖體) 〖왕의〗 the person of the king 〖천주교〗Eucharist; the body／~ 강복 Benediction of the Blessed Sacrament／~ 봉헌(奉獻) oblation／~ 성사 the Sacrament; the Holy Communion. せいたい

**성총**(聖寵) 〖왕의〗royal grace[favo[u]r]／〖천주교〗 divine grace[favo[u]r]. ていおうのちょうあい

**성충**(成蟲) 〖동〗 an imago(pl. ~s, -gines); an adult insect. せいちゅう

**성충**(誠忠) true[unswerving] loyalty. せいちゅう

**성취**(成娶) taking a wife; marrying a woman／~하다 marry a woman; take to wife[a woman in marriage]. つまをめとること

**성취**(成就) completion; accomplishment; attainment; achievement; fulfil; ment realization／~하다 accomplish; attain; achieve; fulfil／소원을 ~하다 obtain a wish／사업을 ~하다 accomplish[achieve] an undertaking. じょうじゅ

**성층권**(成層圈) the stratosphere／~의 stratospheric／~ 연구자 a stratospherist／~을 비행하다 fly through the stratosphere. せいそうけん

**성층암**(成層岩) sedimentary rock; aqueous rock. せいそうがん

**성층 화산**(成層火山) a cone; a conical volcano. せいそうかざん

**성큼성큼** with big strides／~ 걷다 stride; walk with long strides; stalk. ぬきあしさしあし

**성탄**(聖誕) the sacred birth (of a saint or king); birth of a sage. せいたん

**성탄목**(聖誕木) a Christmas tree. クリスマスツリー

**성탄절**(聖誕節) Christmas(略 : X'mas). せいたんせつ

**성터**(城−) the ruins[remains] of a castle; a ruined castle; the site of an ancient castle.

**성토**(聲討) censure; debate／ ~ 대회[를 열다 stage a rally.

**성패**(成敗) success and[or] failure; hit and[or] miss; victory or defeat／~하 에 해 보자 run the risk; try one's chance. せいはい

**성풀이** satisfying one's resentment／~하다 vent one's anger[rage].

**성품**(性品) 《천품》 one's nature; one's disposition 《기품》 one's character. てんぴん

**성하**(城下) a castle-town／~지맹 surrender; capitulation. じょうかのした

**성하**(盛夏) midsummer; high summer／~ 염열 the extreme heat of midsummer. せいか

**성하다** ①《온전하다》(be) intact; unimpaired／성한 생선 fresh fish ②《탈없다》(be) healthy; in sound[good] health／몸성히 잘 있다 be as sound as a horse [roach]; be as fit as a fiddle; be doing quite well. いきいきしている

**성하다**(盛−) ①《초목이》(be) dense; thick; luxuriant; rampant／정원에 풀이 성하게 자라고 있다 The garden is overgrown with grass. ②《기운·세력이》(be) prosperous; flourishing; thriving／성해지다 grow in prosperity.

**성학**(星學) astronomy 천문학. せいがく

**성함**(姓銜) (your, his) esteemed name／~이 무엇입니까 May I ask your name? せいめいの敬語

**성행**(性行) character and conduct. せいこう

**성행**(盛行) prevalence; vogue／ ~하다 prevail; be prevalent[rampant, fashionable]. さかんにおこなうこう

**성행위**(性行爲) sexual intercourse.

**성향**(性向) disposition; propensity; inclination／소비[저축] ~ propensity to consume[save]. せいこう

**성현**(聖賢) saints; sages／ ~의 가르침 the teaching of the sages; the words of the wise. せいけん

**성혈**(聖血) sacred blood [of Jesus]. せいけつ

**성형**(成形) 《형용사적》 plastic; orthopedic／ ~ 수술[을 받다] [have, undergo] a plastic operation／ ~ 외과 plastic[cosmetic] surgery. せいけい

**성혼**(成婚) a marriage; a wedding. せいこん

**성홍열**(猩紅熱) 《의》 scarlet fever; scarlatina. しょうこうねつ

**성화**(成火) annoyance; irritation; vexation; a bother; a trouble／ ~ 거리 a source of irritation; a bother; a nuisance. ひどくはんもんすること

**성화**(星火) ①《운성》meteor ②《불빛》a shooting light ③《급한 일》an urgent matter; an emergency／ ~같이 재촉하다 make an urgent request (for); press [hard] (for). りゅうせい

**성화**(聖火) sacred fire. さかんにもえるひ

**성화**(聖化) sanctification／ ~하다 be sa-

**성화**(聖畵) a holy[sacred, religious] picture. しゅうきょうが
**성화**(聲華) great renown[reputation]; world-wide fame. よのひょうばん
**성황**(盛況) prosperity; prosperous condition; success/ ~을 이루다 be in a prosperous condition; enjoy prosperity. せいきょう
**성황당**(城隍堂) a village shrine. 서낭당.
**성회**(盛會) a successful meeting/어젯밤 ~은 ~었다 Last night's meeting was splendid. せいかい
**성훈**(聖訓) 《가르침》 the teachings[instructions] of a wise man[saint]; the instructions of a king. せいくん
**성히** healthily; in good health /몸~ 잘 있다 be well.
**섶**¹ 《나무》 brushwood; kindling. は
**섶**² 《지탱》 a support; a prop; a stay.
**섶**³ 《웃의》 outer collar of a coat /안~ an inturned jeogori collar.
**섶나무** brushwood.
**세** three/ ~ 사람 three men. さん おくみ
**세**(稅) a tax 《물품에 대한》 a duty 《지방세 따위》 rates 《과세》 taxation /납~하다 pay a tax /징~하다 collect taxes. ぜい
**세**(貰) rent 《사용세》 hire; loan /집〔방〕 ~ house[room] rent. ぜい
**세**(勢) power 세력(勢力). せい
**-세**(世) a generation; an age/헨리 5~ Henry V[the Fifth]. 一せい
**세가**(世家) a noble family. せいか
**세가**(勢家) a powerful family; an influential person. せいか
**세간** household effects[goods, belongings]; furniture and effects. かぐ
**세간**(世間) the world; society; life; 《불》 the mundane world. せけん
**세간나다** set up housekeeping on *one's* own; start a branch family.
べっきょする
**세간 치장**(一治粧) fastidious taste in household goods/ ~하다 have fastidious taste in *one's* household effects.
**세거**(世居) residing (in *a place*) for generations/~하다 reside (in *a place*) for generations.
**세거리** a three-forked road; a three-way intersection ⇨삼거리. みっつじ
**세경**(細徑) a lane; a path ⇨소로(小路).
**세계**(世界) ①《지구》 the world; the earth / ~적 international; worldwide; all over the world/ ~에서 가장 큰 the world/ ~ 일주 여행을 하다 make a round the world trip ②《우주》 the universe; the cosmos ③《세상》 the world ④《특수한 사회》 a society; circles; a realm; sphere/ ~ 경제 world[international] economy/ ~관 an outlook on the world/ ~ 정책 a world[global] policy / ~주의 cosmopolitanism/ ~어 a universal language/ ~ 연방 the World Federation/전 ~에 퍼지다 spread all over the world/ 이상의 ~ an ideal world. せかい
**세계**(歲計) an annual budget. さいけい
**세곡**(稅穀) grains offered for tax payment.
**세공**(細工) craftsmanship; ware; handiwork; workmanship/ ~하다 work; craft/ ~품 [a piece of] work; handiwork; ware/ ~인 a worker; an artisan/ 보석에 ~하다 cut precious gems. さいく
**세공**(細孔) a small cavity; a pore.
**세관**(稅關) a custom-house; the customs / 인천 ~ the *Inchun* Custom-House/ ~장 the superintendent of the customs/ ~ 수속 customs formalities/ ~ 보고 a custom's bill of entry/ ~ 화물 취급인 a custom-[house-] broker. ぜいかん
**세광**(洗鑛) 《광》 ore washing/ ~하다 wash ore. せんこう
**세교**(世交) old family friendship.
**세궁민**(細窮民) the indigent; the poor [needy]; paupers. さいみん
**세궁 역진**(勢窮力盡) ~하다 be pushed to the wall; be driven to the last logiex-tremity.
**세균**(細菌) a bacillus(*pl*. bacilli); a bacterium(*pl*. bacteria); a microbe; a germ/ ~학 bacteriology; microbiology / ~성 질환 a bacterially caused disease. さいきん
**세금**(稅金) a tax; a duty; a charge; dues ⇨세(稅)/ ~을 체납하다 fail to pay a tax on the date due. ぜいきん
**세기**(世紀) a century/21~ the 21th century. せいき
**세기**(貰器) vessels for hire.
**세기말**(世紀末) the end of the century; the *fin-de-siècle*(F)/ ~적 불안 a fin-de-siècle unrest. せいきまつ
**세나다**¹ get worse ⇨덧나다. あっかする
**세나다**² 《잘 팔리다》 sell well; sell like fun[wildfire, hot cakes]; enjoy a good demand. ひっぱりだこだ
**세납**(稅納) payment of tax; tax payment. のうぜい
**세내다**(貰一) hire (*a boat*, *etc.*)/차를 ~ take hire a car. ちんしゃくする
**세농**(細農) small farming; a poor farmer; a needy peasant.
**세놓다**(貰一) let out on hire; hire out (*a car*); rent (*to*); lease. ちんしゃくする
**세뇌**(洗腦) brain-washing; indoctrination/ ~하다 indoctrinate/ ~ 공작 brain-washing. せんのう
**세다**¹ ①《강력하다》 (be) strong; powerful; might 《근력이》 muscular ②《강렬하다》 (be) violent; strong; hard; severe /세게 hard; severely; strongly; powerfully /기운이 센 사람 a strong man / 콧대가 센 사람 a braggart; a blusterer/ 세어지다 grow strong[powerful] /세게 때리다 beat (*one*) a sound thrashing/

바람이 세어졌다 The wind stiffened. つよい

**세다²** 《머리털이》 become white; one's hair turns gray; be gray-haired / 그는 머리가 세기 시작한다 He is growing gray. とうはつがしろくなる

**세다³** 《계산하다》 count; number; calculate; take a count of / 이루 다 셀 수 없는 numberless; countless; innumerable; incalculable; too many to be enumerated / 잘못 ~ miscalculate; count wrong 《투표 수를》 miscount / 빠짐없이 ~ keep count of. けいさんする

**세대**(世代) a generation / 젊은 ~ the rising[younger] generation / ~ 교체 alteration of generations. せだい

**세대**(世帶) a household; house-keeping / ~주 a householder / ~수 the number of households. せたい

**세도**(世道) public morals / ~ 인심 public morals and popular sentiments. せどう

**세도**(勢道) 'seizure[of] political power; [holding] the reins of government / ~하다 have one's own way about state affairs; seize political power; assume the reins of the government.

**세력**(勢力) influence; power; might; strength 《물리학의》 energy / ~있는 influential; powerless / ~ 범위 the sphere of influence / ~ 투쟁 a struggle [scramble] for power / ~ 보존 conservation of energy / ~권 a sphere of influence. せいりょく

**세련**(洗練, 洗鍊) polish; refinement / ~하다 polish up; refine / ~된 polished; refined; elegant / ~된 문장 a polished style. せんれん

**세례**(洗禮) baptism; christening / ~식 [the rite of] baptism; the baptismal ceremony / ~명 a baptismal name; a name of baptism. せんれい

**세로** 《길이》 length《명사》; lengthwise; lengthways《부사》 vertically / ~의 vetical; longitudinal. たて

**세로지**(一紙) 《종이 결》 paper grain that runs lengthwise 《긴 조각》 slip of paper [cloth].

**세론**(細論) a detailed discussion / ~하다 discuss in detail. さいろん

**세루** serge / ~ 옷 a serge suit.

**세루**(世累) troubles of the world; worldly cares.

**세류**(細流) a streamlet; a small stream; a brooklet. さいりゅう

**세류**(細柳) a weeping willow. さいりゅう

**세리**(稅吏) a tax collector; a revenue officer. ぜいり

**세마**(貰馬) a hackney.

**세마치** a large [three-man] blacksmith's hammer.

**세말**(細末) powder / ~하다 pulverize; comminute; powder. さいまつ

**세말**(歲末) the close of the year; the year-end. さいまつ

**세면**(洗面) washing one's face / ~하다 wash one's face / ~대 a wash-basin stand / ~소 a lavatory; a wash-room; a toilet room〈미〉 / ~기 a wash-basin; a washbowl. せんめん

**세모** [a] triangular (thing) / ~꼴 a triangle / ~뿔 a trigonal pyramid / ~나다 have three corners; be triangular. さんかく

**세모**(歲暮) 《연말》 the end[close] of the year; the year-end / ~ 판매 year end sale. せいぼ

**세모래**(細一) fine sand.

**세모시**(細一) ramie cloth of close texture. さいもくのいちび

**세목**(細目) details; particulars / 교수 ~ the particulars of instruction; a teaching syllabus. さいもく

**세목**(稅目) items of a tariff; items of texation; tax items. ぜいもく

**세무**(細務) sundry duties[tasks]; trifling affairs; matters of unimportance. さいむ

**세무**(世務) public affairs; worldly affairs / ~에 통하다 be well versed in worldly matters. せいむ

**세무**(稅務) taxation business / ~관 a revenue officer / ~서 a tax[revenue] office / ~ 서장 the superintendent of a revenue office. ぜいむ

**세물**(貰物) rented objects; objects for rent / ~전 a renter's store / ~전 영감이다 be well-informed. ちんたいぶつ

**세미**(細美) slenderness and beauty / ~하다 (be) slender and beautiful; fine and lovely. ほそくうつくしいこと

**세미**(細微) minuteness; dimunitiveness; delicacy; fineness. さいび

**세민**(細民) the poor; paupers / 박봉 ~ low[small] salaried clerks. さいみん

**세밀**(細密) minuteness / ~하다 (be) minute; detailed; fine; close; elaborate / ~히 minutely; in detail; closely / ~히 조사하다 inquire minutely into (a matter). さいみつ

**세밀**(歲一) the year-end; the end of the year. さいまつ

**세발뛰기** hop-step-and-jump; hop-skip-a-nd-jump.

**세배**(歲拜) a New Year's greetings[call] / ~하다 make a New Year's call.

**세버들**(細一) a weeping willow. さいりゅう

**세법**(稅法) the taxation law. ぜいほう

**세별**(細別) subdivision; breaking down / ~하다 subdivide; itemize; break down[into parts]. さいべつ

**세보**(世譜) a genealogy. せいふ

**세부**(細部) details; the fine parts; the minutiae. さいぶ

**세부득이**(勢不得已) by force of circumstances; owing to unavoidable circumstances / ~하다 (be) unavoidable / ~한 경우에는 when unavoidable.

**세분**(細分) subdivision / ~하다 subdiv-

**세비**(歲費) 《수당》 an annual allowance 《비용》 yearly expenditure. さいひ
**세사**(細沙) fine sand ⇨세모래.
**세사**(世事) worldly affairs; mundane matters; the ways of life／ ~에 어둡다 know little of the world[ways of the world]. せじ
**세사**(細事) a trifles; a trivial[small] matter／ ~에 구애하다 trouble oneself about trifles. さいじ
**세 살** three years of age／ ~ 버릇이 여든까지 간다 The child is [the] father of[to] the man.
**세살부채**(細—) a narrow-ribbed fan; a fan with fine ribs.
**세상**(世上) ①《세계·사회》the world; society; the times 《시대》an age／ ~은 넓은 것 같아도 좁다 The world is not so wide as it appears. ②《사람들》people; the world; the public／ ~에 알려지다 be made public; come to light; get abroad ③《인생》life; one's lifetime／ ~을 떠나다 depart this life; pass away; leave this world ④《독무대》without rivals. せじょう
**세상**(世相) social conditions; the world ⇨세태. せそう
**세상살이**(世上—) a living; getting on in the world／ ~하다 go[walk] through the world; get on in the world 《살림》 make a living／ ~하는 법 the art of living. よのなかのくらし
**세상없어도**(世上—) under[in] any circumstances; whatever may happen; by all means／~ 이 일만큼은 해야 한다 Nothing shall hinder me from accomplishing my purpose.
**세상에**(世上—) in the world; on earth／ ~에 이게 무슨 일이람 What on earth is it?
**세석**(細石) a pebble; a gravel. さいせき
**세설**(細說) ①《설명》a detailed[full] account; a minute explanation; expatiation／ ~하다 explain fully; expatiate ②《잔소리》faultfinding. さいせつ
**세세**(世世) generation after generation 대대(代代). よよ
**세세하다**(細細—) (be) detailed; minute; circumstantial; particular 《계산 따위》close／세세히 말하다 give full details; tell all the details. とてもくわしい
**세소**(細小) minuteness. さいび
**세속**(世俗) the world 《세상의 풍습》popular customs／ ~의 worldly; popular; mundane／ ~적 명성 worldly fame. せぞく
**세수**(洗手) washing one's face and hands／ ~하다 wash oneself[one's face and hands]／세숫대야 a [wash]basin／세숫대 wash-hand stand.
**세수**(稅收) tax revenues; tax yields.
**세습**(世襲) transmission by heredity; descent／ ~하다 transmit from generation to generation／ ~ 재산 freehold; patrimony; heritage. せしゅう
**세시**(歲時) the beginning of the year; the New Year. さいじ
**세신**(世臣) a vassal by heredity.
**세실**(細—) fine thread. ほそいと
**세심**(細心) prudence; circumspection; caution; carefulness／ ~한 주의를 하다 pay close[scrupulous] attention (to). さいしん
**세안**(歲—) before the current year is out; within the present year. ねんないのふゆのあいだ
**세액**(稅額) the amount of a tax; an assessment／ ~을 정하다 assess. ぜいがく
**세약**(洗藥) a lotion; a wash. せんやく
**세업**(世業) hereditary occupation. だいだいついでくたせいぎょう
**세요**(細腰) a slender[delicate] waist 《미인》a beauty with a slender figure.
**세우**(細雨) a drizzle; a fine[misty] rain. さいう
**세우다** ①《일으키다》stand; raise; set up; erect; put up (긴 것을) stand on end 《기둥 따위를》plant／일으켜 ~ make (one) stand／귀를 쫑긋 세우고 듣다 prick one's ears and listen ②《정지하다》stop; put a stop to; hold up／말을 ~ rein up a horse; stop the horse; bring the horse to a stop ③《건축하다》build; erect; construct; set up／집을 ~ build a house ④《설립하다》establish; found; create; set up／도서관을 ~ establish a library ⑤《정하다》establish; lay down (regulations); enact (a law)／보증인을 ~ appoint a surety ⑥《조직하다》organize; institute; constitute ⑦《학설을》advance; set up; bring forward; put forward (an argument); advocate; lay down (a proposition)／새로운 학설을 ~ advance a new theory ⑧《계획을》mark out; map out; prepare; lay down ⑨《공훈을》render (distinguished services); perform (meritorious deeds)／큰 공을 ~ achieve a great thing ⑩《생계를》support[maintain] oneself; earn one's living ⑪《뜻을》have (an object) in view; set (an object before one) ⑫《날을》sharpen; set ⑬《계산하다》make; calculate ⑭《지위에 앉히다》put up ⑮《체면을》save one's face[honor]. たてる
**세운**(世運) the luck of the times[age]. せいうん
**세원**(稅源) a source of revenue; tax sources. ぜいげん
**세월**(歲月) ①《시간》time and tide／ ~이 유수 같다 Time flies like an arrow. ②《시세》[the] times; things; business; conditions／ ~이 좋다[나쁘다] Times are good[bad]. さいげつ
**세위**(勢威) power; authority influence. せいい

**세율(稅率)** tax rates; a tariff/ ~표 taxrate scales; a table of tax rates.

**세의(世誼)** generations of family friendship ≡세교. せんぞだいだいからのじょうぎ

**세의(歲儀)** a year-end gift.

**세이레** the 21st day of a baby's life [celebrated with a party].

**세인(世人)** people; the world; the public / ~의 이목을 피하다 avoid public notice; slip from the sight of the world. せじん

**세입(歲入)** 《국가의》an annual revenue 《개인의》an annual income/ ~ 예산액 estimated revenues/ ~ 세출 revenue and expenditure. さいにゅう

**세입(稅入)** revenue; tax income[yield, intake]; income from tax.

**세자(世子)** the Crown Prince. せいし

**세자(洗者)** a baptist; one who baptizes.

**세자(細字)** small type; small[fine] characters[letters]. さいじ

**세전(世傳)** handing down from generation to generation/ ~지물(之物) things handed down from generation to generation. せいでん

**세전(歲前)** before the New Year. せいぼ

**세정(世情)** the affairs of the world ~ 세상〈世上〉. せじょう

**세정(洗淨)** washing; cleaning/ ~하다 wash; rinse (*a bottle*); clean. せんじょう

**세정(稅政)** tax administration. ぜいせい

**세제(稅制)** a system of a taxation; a tax system/ ~ 개혁 tax reform[s]/ ~ 정리 readjustment[overhaul] of the tax system. ぜいせい

**세제(歲除)** New Year's Eve; the last day of the year. さいじょ

**세제(洗劑)** cleaning material; a detergent; a detersive; a cleanser.

**세제곱** 《수》cubing; cube/ ~하다 cube; multiply (*a number*) by its square/ ~근(根) a cube root. さんじょう

**세족(勢族)** a powerful clan[tribe, family].

**세주(細註)** detailed notes.

**세주다(貰—)** lease; let[for rent]; rent /집을 ~ rent a house to (*a person*). ちんたいする

**세차(歲差)** precession (of *the equinoxes*).

**세차다** (be) violent; intense; furious; powerful; mighty; vigorous; energetic; lively/비가 세차게 부리고 있다 It is raining heavily[hard]. つよい

**세찬(歲饌)** 《음식》food for treating New Year's guests (선물)New Year's gifts.

**세책(貰册)** a book for lending; a book from a rental library. かしほん

**세척(洗滌)** washing; lavation; lavage; rinsing; 《분만·수술 후의》toilet/ ~하다 wash; rinse; swill; rinse out (*impurities*)/ ~기 a washer; a syringe/ ~약 a cleansing lotion; a wash/위를 ~하다 carry out a lavage of the stomach.

**세초(歲初)** the beginning of the year. せんじょう

**세출(歲出)** annual expenditure[s]/ ~예 산액 estimated expenditures. さいしゅつ

**세칙(細則)** detailed rules; bylaws; minor regulations/~시행 ~ rules for operation; regulations relative to the application of the law. さいそく

**세칭(世稱)** what is known as; what people call; the so-called. せしょう

**세탁(洗濯)** laundry/ ~기 a washing machine/ ~ 비누 laundry soap/ ~소 a laundry [establishment]. せんたく

**세태(世態)** the prevailing state of society; social conditions; the way[order] of the world/ ~ 인정 the way[s] of the world; life and men. せたい

**세톱(細—)** a fine-tooth saw.

**세파(世波)** ups and downs[vicissitudes] of life/ ~에 시달리다 be tossed about in the storms of life; go through the whirlpools of life. どうぞくのぶんば

**세파(細波)** ripples; wavelets; tiny waves. さざなみ

**세평(世評)** 《평판》public opinion; popular judgment[verdict];《인기》popularity 《소문》hearsay; rumor/ ~에 의하면 people[they] say (*that*)/ ~을 두려워하다 be afraid of what people say. せひょう

**세평(細評)**. detailed comments; minute criticism. さいひょう

**세폐(歲幣)** an annual tribute.

**세포(細布)** fine-textured hemp cloth.

**세포(細胞)** 《생》a cell/ ~의 cellular/ ~ 분열 cell division; segmentation/~ 조직 cellular tissue/ ~학 cytology/ 생식 ~ a generative cell. さいぼう

**세하(細蝦)** a shrimp.

**세후(歲後)** after the New Year. ねんしがすぎたのち

**센개** a white dog.

**센둥이** a white puppy. いろのしろいこいぬ

**센머리** a gray head; gray hair/ ~의 gray-haired; gray-headed. はくはつ

**센물** 《경수(硬水)》hard water.

**센털** gray hair; white hair. はくはつ

**셈¹** ①《계산》count[ing]/ ~하다 count; reckon; calculate ②《회계》account / ~하다 keep accounts/ ~을 치르다 settle accounts ③《분별》sense; discretion / ~이 없다 have no sense. けいさん

**셈²** ①《추측·결과》the calculation; supposition; conjecture ②《예정》intention; idea; expectation/ …할 ~이다[으로 있다] intend to *do*; will have a mind to *do*; mean to *do*. すいそく

**셈나다** attain *one's* years of discretion; cut *one's* wisdom-teeth. ぶっしんがつく

**셈들다** become sensible; grow in intelligence; come to have discretion/그도 셈 들 나이가 되었는데 He ought to know better at his·age. ぶんべつがつく

**셈본** arithmetic/ ~의 arithmetical/ ~문제 an arithmetical problem. けいさんのほうそく

**셈속** the real state of affairs; the internal conditions; the private circumstances. ことのないよう

**셈치다** think of …ing; mean; expect; have the intention of …ing/죽을 셈치고 해 보자 Let us do or die. ことにする

**셈판** ①(사정) circumstances; conditions; the situation 《원인》 reason/어떻게 된 ~인지 for some unknown reason; somehow ② ⇨주판(籌板). ないよう

**셈평** the money outlook; good prospects [especially of money]; favourable circumstance/~이 된다 It figures to pay off.

**셈평펴이다** live in ease[comfort, plenty]; be in easy circumstances; be well to do. ややゆたかになる

**셋** three/~째로 thirdly.

**셋돈**(貰―) hire 《가옥·토지의》 rent/이 사무실은 ~이 싸다 This office has a low rent.

**셋방**(貰房) a rented room/ ~살이 living in a rented room/ ~있음 Rooms for rent.

**셋붙이** a three-piece suit[jacket, vest, trousers].

**셋집**(貰―) a house for rent《미》; a house to let〈영〉; a rental house 《게시》 To let; For rent/ ~을 구하다 seek[look] for a house to let. かしや

**소¹** 《암소》a cow 《황소·종우》a bull 《거세된》an ox(pl. -en); 《총칭》cattle/ ~가죽 cowhide/ ~떼 a herd of cattle /~ 잃고 외양간 고친다《속담》 To lock the stable door after the horse is stolen., After death, the doctor. うし

**소²** a seasoned mixture used as a stuffing for bun; stuffing/빵에 ~를 넣다 stuff a bun[dumpling]. あんこ

**소**(小) smallness; littleness; small; little; minor; lesser/ ~규모 small scale /~도시 a small town/~아시아 Asia Minor/ ~전제 《논》 the minor premise. しょう, こ

**소**(少) 《적은》 little; few; scarce 《젊은》 young/ ~량 a little; some/ ~수 a few; some. しょう

**소**(沼) a swamp; a marsh; a bog; a pond/ ~택지 a marshy place. ぬま

**소가**(小暇) a bit of leisure; a short break[respite]; a brief moment of spare time/ ~를 틈타서 독서하다 read in the short intervals of business; read at odd moments. しょうか

**소가**(小家) one's concubine. しょうか

**쏘가리** a mandarin fish. こうらいけつぎょ

**소가족**(小家族) the small-family system / ~ 제도 the small-family system. しょうかぞく

**소가지** nature; disposition/~가 좁은 사람 a narrow-minded person; an illiberal person. しんせい

**소각**(消却) 《지움》erasure; effacement 《소비》expenditure/ ~하다 erase; efface; expend. しょうきゃく

**소각**(燒却) destruction by fire; incineration; burn up/~하다 destroy by fire; burn up; reduce to ashes/ ~기 an incinerator /쓰레기를 ~하다 burn up the rubbish. しょうきゃく

**소간**(所幹) business ·소간사. ようむ

**소간사**(所幹事) business; a thing to do /일상 ~ the daily round[routine]; everyday business. ようむ

**소갈머리** disposition; temper; nature 《심성》 mind; spirit 《생각》 thought/ ~가 좁은 illiberal; ungenerous; narrow-minded. しんし

**소감**(所感) impressions; one's opinions; one's thoughts/ ~을 말하다 give one's impressions (of something). しょかん

**소강**(小康) a lull; a respite/그의 병이 ~상태에 있다 There is a slight improvement in his condition. しょうこう

**소개**(紹介) introduction; presentation 《추천》recommendation/ ~하다 introduce (to, into); present (to); recommend/자기 ~ self-introduction / ~자 an introducer. しょうかい

**소개**(疎開) dispersion; dispersal; evacuation/ ~하다 disperse; evacuate; move to (the country) for safety; thin out 《전물을》 remove. そかい

**소거**(繰車) a spinning wheel.

**소거**(消去) elimination/ ~하다 eliminate/ ~법 《수》 climination. しょうきょ

**소건**(訴件) 《법》 a case.

**소격**(疎隔) estrangement; alienation/~하다 estrange[alienate] (one) from; drift apart. そかく

**소견**(所見) 《견해》one's views[opinions]; 《인상》impressions/~을 말하다 express one's views; express oneself. しょけん

**소견**(消遣) killing time; wasting time; beguiling idle hours/ ~하다 kill[waste] time. しょうけん

**소경** a blind man; a sightless person 《총칭》 the blind/ ~ 놀이 blindman's buff/ ~ 막대 a blindman's stick/ ~이 되다 become[go] blind; lose one's sight. めくら

**소경사**(所經事) one's [accumulated] experience.

**소계**(小計) a total/~ 4천 원이다 It totals four thousand won. しょうけい

**소계**(小憩) a short rest; a brief recess / ~하다 take a short rest.

**소고**(溯考) tracing back; looking back on the old time/ ~하다 trace[look] back (anything) to the old time.

**소고**(小鼓) a tabor. しょうこ

**소곡**(小曲) a short piece. しょうきょく

**소곤거리다** whisper; talk in whispers; speak under one's breath/소곤소곤 in whispers; in an undertone/ 소곤소곤

**애기하다** talk in whispers. ささやく
**소곳하다** be drooping[hanging] low; be bowed[lowered]. うつむきかげんだ
**소공업**(小工業) a small industry/ ~자 small-scale industrialists.
**소관**(所管) jurisdiction 【권능】 competency/ ~ 다툼 jurisdictional rivalry/ ~청 the competent authorities/외무부 ~ 사항 matters under the jurisdiction of Ministry of Foreign Affairs/ ~ 밖이다 be beyond the jurisdiction (of).
**소관**(所關) relation; relationship; matters concerned/ ~사 one's business/ ~ 서류 all the documents related to (the matter). かんけいするところ
**소구**(小球) a small ball[globe]; 【혈구 따위】 a globule.
**소구**(小丘) a hillock; a small hill.
**소구잡이** a tabor[small-drum] player. しょうこもち
**소국**(素—) soup prepared without meat.
**소국**(小國) a small country; a minor power/ ~민 a small nation 【소년】 the young children. しょうこく
**소국**(小局) 【도량의】 narrow-mindedness; a shortsighted[circumscribed] view 【판국의】 a small situation. せまいどりょう
**소굴**(巢窟) a den; a nest 【짐승의】 a lair 【범죄의】 a breeding-place/도적의 ~ a den of robbers. そうくつ
**소꿉질** playing with a doll house; playing house/ ~하다 play house; play at housekeeping; play with a doll house. ままごとあそび
**소권**(訴權) 【법】 the right of action.
**소규모**(小規模) a small scale/ ~의 on a small scale; in a small way/ ~ 가족 a peanuts size family. こきぼ
**소극**(消極) the negative pole; negativity/ ~적[으로] negative[ly]; passive [ly]/ ~주의 negativism. しょうきょく
**소극**(笑劇) a farce. しょうげき
**소극장**(小劇場) a little theater. しょうげきじょう
**소금** salt/ ~에 절이다 salt (fish); preserve in salt/생선에 ~을 뿌리다 sprinkle salt on fish; sprinkle fish with salt/ ~으로 간을 맞추다 season with salt. しお
**소금기** saltiness; salty taste / ~있는 salty. しおけ
**소금물** salt water; brine/ ~에 담그다 steep in brine water.
**소금버케** coagulation of salt; salt that has hardened. しおのかたまり
**소금엣밥** plain food; a plain[simple] diet; a poor meal.
**소금쟁이** 【충】 a water-spider. あめんぼ
**소급**(遡及) going back to the past; retroaction; 【법】 relation (to) / ~하다 go back to the past; be retroactive/ ~력 retroactive power; retroactivity/ ~법 a retroactive law. さっきゅう
**소기**(小朞) the first anniversary of a death. しょうしょう
**소기**(笑氣) 【화】 laughing gas; nitrous oxide.
**소기**(沼氣) marsh gas; 【화】 methane. しょうき
**소기**(所期) expectation; anticipation/ ~의 목적을 달성하다 achieve the desired end/ ~의 성과를 올리다 achieve the expected results. しょき
**소나기** a shower; a passing rain/ ~가 오다 it showers/ ~가 올 것 같다 It looks like shower., It is going to shower. にわかあめ
**소나무** a pine[tree]/ ~ 잎 pine needles / ~ 숲 a pine-grove. まつ
**소나무겨우살이** 【식】 a species of Spanish moss; Usnea longissima(학명). さるおがせ
**소납** requisites; necessaries. ようけん
**소녀**(少女) a young girl; a lass; a maid/ ~ 소설 a story for girls/ ~ 시절 [young] girlhood/ ~다운 girlish; maidenlike. しょうじょ
**소년**(少年) a boy; a lad; a youth/ ~ 단 the Boy Scouts/ ~ 단원 a boy scout/ ~원 a [juvenile] reformatory [school]/ ~ 시대 one's boyhood; one's early days. しょうねん
**소농**(小農) a small farmer/ ~ 제도 the intensive agricultural[small-farming] system. しょうのう
**소뇌**(小腦) 【해】 the cerebellum(pl. ~s, -bella). しょうのう
**쏘다** ① shoot; fire; discharge/권총으로 ~ shoot (a person) ②【벌레가】 sting; bite/벌에 쏘이다 get strung by a bee ③【말로】 blow (a person) up; storm at (a person). いる
**쏘다니다** run around; roam; wander; gad (about, out)/일자리를 구하러 ~ pound the pavement[sidewalks] looking for a job. あるきまわる
**소달구지** an oxcart.
**소담**(小膽) timidity 【비겁】 cowardice/ ~ 하다 (be) timid; faint-hearted; cowardly/ ~자 a timid person. しょうたん
**소담**(笑談) a funny story. しょうだん
**소담스럽다** (be) delicious; dainty; palatable; tasty; good; nice. ふうがにみえる
**소담하다** (be) good; nice; delicious; dainty; palatable; tasty. ふうがだ
**소당**(小黨) a small[minor] [political] party.
**소대**(小隊) a platoon; a section/ ~장 a platoon leader[commander]. しょうたい
**소대상**(小大祥) the first and second anniversaries of a death.
**소댕** the lid of a kettle. かまのふた
**소도**(小刀) a knife. こがたな
**소도**(小島) an islet; a small island; a cay. こじま
**소도구**(小道具) stage property; props. こどうぐ
**소도둑놈** ①【도둑】 a cattle thief; a cattle rustler ②【욕심많은】 a greedy and ba-

소도리 a small hammer. ちいさいつち
소도시(小都市) a small[er] town; a tank town (미).
소독(消毒) disinfection (살균) sterilization (우유 등의) pasteurization (증기로) fumigation /～하다 disinfect; sterilize; pasteurize /일광～ disinfection by sunlight. しょうどく
소동(小童) a kid; a little boy (종) a boy servant. しょうどう
소동(騷動) (소란) disturbance; agitation (다툼) a strife; a dispute (혼란) confusion; disorder; a row; a tumult (폭동) a riot; a rising /～이 일어나다 a riot arises /～을 진압시키다 put down a riot. そうどう
소두(小斗) a half-*mal* measure.
소두(小豆) redbean. あずき
소드락질 pillage; plunder /～하다 plunder; pillage. うばいとること
소득(所得) income; incomings (수익) gain; earning /～세 an income tax /～층 an income group /국민～ the national income /근로～ earned income /불로～ unearned income /순[총][gross] income /실질～ real income /현물～ an income in kind. しょとく
소득밤 an unshelled dried chestnut.
かわのままかわしたくり
소득소득 ～하다 (be) withered; dry.
かさかさ, しなしな
소들소들 ～하다 (be) withered; dry.
しなしな, くなくな
소들하다 be not enough; be not sufficient. きにいらない
소등(消燈) putting out lights; blackout /～하다 put out the lights /～기 an extinguisher /～시간 the hour for putting out lights; lights out. しょうとう
소라 ①(조개) a top-shell; a wreath-shell; *Turbo cornutus* (학명) ②(악기) a conch; a trumpet-shell /～를 불다 blow a trumpet-shell. さざえ
소라게 〖어〗 a hermit-crab; a soldier crab. やどかり
소라고둥 〖어〗 a trumpet-shell; a conch; a triton. ほらがい
소락(小落) 〖경〗 a slight decline; a petty recess.
소락소락 thoughtlessly; rashly /～하다 (be) thoughtless; rash. ちょろっか
소란(小欄) a railing; a reinforcing or protecting strip /～을 치다 attach the broider pieces. ちいさいらんかん
소란(騷亂) (소동) disturbance; confusion; (훤조) noise; clamour /～하다 (시끄럽다) (be) noisy; clamourous (수선수선하다) (be) turbulent; agitated /세상을 ～케 하다 disturb society.
そうらん
소란반자(小欄—) a coffered[compartment] ceiling; a coffering.
소략(疎略) carelessness; roughness; rudeness /～하다 (be) careless; rude; rough /～한 취급 (물건의) rough handling; uncourteous treatment. そりゃく
소량(少量) a small quantity; a little (약) a little dose /～의 a little (*water*); a small quantity[dose] of. しょうりょう
소렴(小殮) shrouding; covering of a corpse with a winding sheet.
소렴포(小殮布) a shroud; a winding sheet.
소령(少領) (육군) a major (해군) a lieutenantcommander (공군) a wing commander /보병～ an infant major.
소로(小路) a narrow path; a lane (골목길) an alley. しょうろ
소론(所論) one's opinion; one's view.
ろんずるところ
소롱하다(消—) squander; waste.
ろうひする
소루(疎漏) (부주의) carelessness; oversight; inadvertence (태만) negligence /～하다 (be) careless; thoughtless; negligent /～한 점이 없도록 해라 See that all is right. そろう
소르르 ①(풀어지는 모양) easily ②(졸리는 모양) drowsily; gently; quietly ③(바람이 부는 모양) quietly; gently; softly. すらすら
소름 gooseflesh; goose skin /～이 끼친다 get goose-skinned.
소리 ①(음향) a sound (잡음) a noise (우렁찬) a din (문 따위를 여는) a bang (파쇄음) a crash (파도의) a roar (총성 따위의) a report (음조의) tone; note ②(음성) a voice (외침) a cry; an outcry; a shout (새·벌레의) chirp; notes; call ③(말) talk; a chat; what one says; a remark ④(소문) a rumour; a report; news; an account ⑤(노래) a song; a ballad; singing /～하다 sing [a song]. おと
소리(小利) a small profit; a little gain /눈앞의 ～에 눈이 흐려지다 be blinded by a small immediate profit. しょうり
소리값 phonetic value. おんか
소리개 〖조〗 a [black] kite. とび
소리결 a sound wave.
소리굽쇠 a tuning fork. おんさ
소리마디 a syllable. おんせつ
소리맵시 tone quality[color].
소리소리 yelling; roaring /～지르다 yell; roar. こえ
소리장이 a singer (여자) a songstress.
かしゅ
소리지르다 shout; cry[call] out; raise [strain, lift up] the voice (요란하게) clamour; bawl /가라고 ～ shout (to *one*) to go.
소리치다 shout; bawl; utter[give] a cry; yell; rise one's voice /소리쳐 도움을 청하다 yell for help. さけぶ
소리판(一板) a [phonograph] record.
ろくおんばん
소림(疎林) a thine[sparse] wood[grove].
そりん

**소립자**(素粒子) 〖물〗 an elementary particle. そりゅうし

**소마** urine／～보다 urinate.

**소마소마** timidly; in fear and trembling; nervously／～하다 (be) timid; nervous; be in fear and tremble. びくびく

**소망**(所望) wish; desire; request／당신 ～대로 하지요 I am entirely in your hands. しょもう

**소망**(素望) one's long cherished desire. そぼう

**소매** a sleeve 《양복의》an arm／～ 없는 코트 a sleeveless coat／～가 긴 long-sleeved／～를 잡아당기다 pull (one) by the sleeve; entice 《매춘부가》solicit. そで

**소매**(小賣) retail sale; retailing／～하다 retail; sell by retail／～상인 a retailer／～점 a retail shop[store]／～가격 a retail price. こうり

**소매치기** pocket-picking 《사람》a pickpocket／～하다 pick (one's) pocket／～주의 "Beware of pickpockets". すり

**소매뽕** the breadth of a sleeve／～이 좁은[넓은] tight[wide]-sleeved.

**소맥**(小麥) wheat 밀. こむぎ

**소면**(素麵) vermicelli; noodles. すうどん

**소멸**(消滅)《절멸》extinction《소실》disappearance／～하다 become extinct; cease to exist; go out of existence; disappear《무효가 되다》become null and void／권리의 ～ the lapse of one's rights. しょうめつ

**소멸**(燒滅) destruction by fire／～하다 destroy (a thing) by fire; reduce to ashes. しょうめつ

**소멸**(掃滅) a [clean] sweep; extermination／～하다 sweep away[off]; drive off; clear away[off];《상처 따위를》deterge《근절하다》make an end of; stamp [root] out／해적을 ～하다 sweep[scour, clear] (the sea) of pirates. そうめつ

**소명**(召命) summons [from His Majesty]／～을 받들어 in response to a royal summons. おうがしんかをよぶめいれい

**소명**(昭明) cleverness; brightness／～하다 (be) clever. しょうめい

**소모**(消耗)《소비》consumption《마손》wear and tear《감쇠》waste／～하다 consume; use up; dissipate; waste／～품 articles for consumption; expendables〈미〉／정력을 ～하다 dissipate one's energy. しょうもう

**소모**(梳毛) carded wool／～기 a carding machine.

**소목장이**(小木—) a cabinetmaker; a joiner.

**소몰이** a cowherd; a cowboy; a cowman; a cattleman〈미〉. うしかた

**소묘**(素描) rough drawing; a rough sketch[ing];《단채화(單彩畵)》a monochrome picture. そびょう

**소문**(小門) ① a small gate ②《보지》vulva《속》. いんもん

**소문**(所聞) a rumor; a report; hearsay; gossip; common talk／～이 나다 a rumor get started[stirred up]／～을 퍼뜨리다 spread[air] a rumor; shout it about. うわさ

**소밀**(疎密) density; thickness. そみつ

**소바리** loading an ox; an ox load.

**소박**(素朴) simplicity; artlessness／～하다 (be) simple; artless; rustic; crude; unsophisticated; naive. そぼく

**소박**(疎薄) ill-treatment[maltreatment] to one's wife／～하다 ill-treat one's wife; reject one's wife《내쫓다》abandon [cast forth] one's wife／～맞다 be neglected[rejected] by one's husband. そはく

**소박데기**(疎薄—) a neglected[rejected] wife; a grass widow. おっとにうとんじられたつま

**소박이** stuffed cucumber pickles.

**소반**(小盤) a small dining table; a tray. ちいさいぜん

**소반**(素飯) a plain meal. そしょく

**소밥**(素—) meatless food; a no-meat meal. そしょく

**소방**(消防) fire-fighting; a fire-brigade [arrangement]／～관 a fire fighter／～기구 fire fighting equipment／～대 a fire brigade; a fire company〈미〉／～서 a fire department／～연습 a fire-drill／～차 a fire engine／～용 사닥다리 fire-ladder／～에 진력하다 fight the fire; arrest the spread of a fire; get fire under control. しょうぼう

**소변**(小便) urine; water; piss／～소 a lavatory; a toilet／～보다 pass water [urine]; void urine; urinate／～이 마렵다 Nature calls me. ／～ 금지 "Decency forbids", "No nuisance here". しょうべん

**소복**(素服) a white [mourning] dress. しろいふく

**소복소복** brimfully; to the full; to the brim; overflowingly.

**소복하다** (be) brimful; heaping full; full to overflowing. みちている

**소분**(小分) a subdivision／～하다 subdivide (into);《세분하다》itemize.

**소비**(所費) expenses; expenditure; outlay. しょようのひよう

**소비**(消費) consumption; spending／～하다 consume; spend; expend／～ 경제 consumer economy／～ 단위 a consumption unit／～ 도시 consuming[consumer] cities／～ 물자 consumer goods／～세 the consumption tax／～자 a consumer《소비 대중》the consuming public／～재 consumer goods／～제 공업 consumer industry／～ 제한 restriction on consumption／～ 조합 a consumers' cooperative society／시간을 ～하다 spend time. しょうひ

**소사**(小史) a short history. しょうし

**소사**(小辭) 〖논〗 a minor term.

**소사**(小使) an errand boy; a servant; a

janitor; a messenger; an office boy. こづかい

**소사**(掃射) 《기관총의》 machine-gunning. そうしゃ

**소사**(燒死) death by fire／〜하다 be burned to death; meet death in the flames; perish[lose *one's* life] in the flames[by fire]／〜자(者) a person burnt to death. しょうし

**소사스럽다** (be) sly; cunning; crafty; foxy; loopy／소사스러운 녀석 a tricky guy; a crafty fellow; a sly dog. こすそうだ

**쏘삭거리다** incite; instigate; induce; stirup／군중을 쏘삭거려 반대케 하다 stir up people against (*the government*). おだてる

**소산**(所産) ①《소산물》a product; a production 《집합적으로》produce／주요 〜 staple products[produce] ②《성과》a product; a result; an outcome／시대의 〜 a creature of a day. しょさん

**소산**(消散) dissipation; dispersion; disappearance／〜하다 disappear; vanish 《증발하여》evaporate 《안개 따위가》lift. しょうさん

**소살**(燒殺) burning to death／〜하다 burn to death; burn alive. やきころすこと

**소삼**(蕭森) ①《쓸쓸함》loneliness; desolation; desolateness; bleakness／〜하다 (be) lonely; desolate; bleak ②《울창》 thickness; denseness; luxuriance／〜 하다 (be) thick; dense; luxuriance.

**소삽하다**(蕭颯一) (be) sobbing／소삽한 바람 소리 sobs of wind. かぜがものさびしい

**소상**(小祥) the first anniversary of *one's* death. しょうしょう

**소상**(塑像) a plastic[plaster] image; a clay figure／〜 예술 plastic arts. ねんどちょうこくのぞう

**소상**(小像) a statuette.

**소생**(蘇生) revival; resuscitation; reanimation／〜하다 revive; resuscitate (from *death*); be restored[brought] to life; come back to life; return to life／그를 〜시킬 수는 없었다 We could not resuscitate him. そせい

**소생**(所生) a child; issue《자손》offspring.

**소생**(小生) I; me／〜의 my. しょうせい

**소석고**(燒石膏) 【화】 plaster of Paris. しょうせっこう

**소석회**(消石灰) 【화】slaked lime; calcium hydroxide. しょうせっかい

**소선거구**(小選擧區) a smal electoral district. しょうせんきょく

**소설**(小說) a story; a novel《총칭》fiction《전기적》a romance／〜가 a story [fiction] writer; a novelist／〜적 the world of fiction／단편 〜 a short story; a novelette. しょうせつ

**소설**(所說) *one's* view; *one's* opinion／〜을 말하다 give *one's* opinion (on).

**소성**(小成) a small success; a humble lot in life／〜에 만족하다 be contented with a small success. しょうせい

**소성**(笑聲) laughter; a laugh. しょうせい

**소성**(素性) nature; character; disposition; temperament／〜이 정직하다 be honest by nature. すじょう

**소세**(梳洗) washing *one's* face and combing *one's* hair; dressing／〜하다 wash *one's* face and comb *one's* hair; dress *oneself*.

**소소리바람** a chilly spring wind[breeze]. はるのひややかでさびしたかぜ

**소소리패** frivolous youngsters.

**소소하다**(小小一) (be) minor; trifling; insignificant. わずかだ

**소소하다**(昭昭一) (be) clear; plain; distinct; evident; obvious／소소하게 clearly; plainly; distinctly; evidently. あきらかだ

**소소하다**(蕭蕭一) (be) dreary; bleak; sobbing; whining. しょうしょうとしている

**소속**(所屬) *one's* position[post place]／〜 하다 belong to be attached to／〜 관리 officials attached to (*the office*)／〜 부대 *one's* regiment[unit]; *one's* home post／〜시키다 attach; assign. しょぞく

**소솔**(所率) *one's* whole family; *one's* people. じぶんのかぞく

**소송**(訴訟) a lawsuit; a suit; an action; a legal action; an litigation／〜하다 sue (*one for*); go to law (*with*); institute[take] legal preceedings; bring an action[a suit] (*against one*)／〜법 the law[code] of legal procedure／〜인 a plaintiff／〜 사건 a [legal] case; a law suit／〜을 걸다 go to law against (*one*) ／〜을 취하하다 drop[discontinue] a suit. そしょう

**소쇄**(瀟灑) 〜하다 (be) elegant; smart; neat; chic／〜한 모습 *one's* smart appearance.

**소쇄**(掃灑) 〜하다 sweep clean and sprinkle with water.

**소수**(小數) 【수】 a decimal fraction／〜점 a decimal point. しょうすう

**소수**(少數) a small number; a few; a minority／〜당[파] a minority[party] ／〜의 사람 a few[handful of] persons. しょうすう

**소수**(素數) 【수】 a prime number. そすう

**소수**(疎水) drainage／〜 공사 drainage work.

**소스라치다** be frightened; be taken aback; start (with *fright*)／그 광경을 보고 〜 be frightened at the sight; start up at the sight. びっくりぎょうてんする

**소슬하다**(蕭瑟一) (be) sobbing; soughing; wailing; whining／소슬한 가을 바람 a sobbing autumnal wind[blast]. さびしい

**소승**(小乘) 【종】 *Hinayana* (Sans); the Lesser Vhricle／〜 불교 *Hinayana*[Southern] Buddhism／〜적 견지 a narrow point of view. しょうじょう

**소승**(少僧) a young priest.

**소시**(少時) *one's* early days; *one's* youth

/ ～적에 in *one's* earliest day[childhood]．
쏘시개 tinder／불～ tinder; kindling wood．
소시민(小市民) a petit bourgeois．
소식(小食, 少食) light eating; a spare diet／ ～하다 eat sparingly／ ～가 a light[spare, small] eater．
소식(素食) a meatless meal; meatless food; a no-meat meal．
소식(蔬食) vegetable food; a vegetable diet．
소식(消息) news; tidings; information; intelligence; a letter／슬픈 ～ sad tidings／～통 a well-informed person; well-informed quarters／～이 없다 hear nothing[none] from (*a person*)．
소신(所信) conviction; belief (의견)opinion／～을 피력하다 speak *one's* mind; express[give] *one's* opinion．
소실(小室) a concubine (첩·정부) a mistress／～ 자식 a child by a concubine．
소실(消失) disappearance; vanishing／ ～하다 vanish; disappear．
소실(燒失) destruction by fire／ ～하다 be burnt down; be destroyed by fire; be reduced to ashes／ ～ 가옥 destroyed houses by fire; houses burnt down．
소심(小心) ～하다 (담이 작다)(be) timid; cowardly; fainthearted (주의 깊다) prudent; cautious; scrupulous／～자 a coward; a timid person．
소아(小兒) a child; a baby; an infant; ／～마비 infantile paralysis; poliomyelitis／～병 a child's disease; infantilism．
소아(小我) 【철】 relative[empirical] ego．
소아과(小兒科) pediatrics; pediatry／ ～ 병원 a children's hospital／ ～ 의사 a children's doctor; a child specialist; a pediatrist[pediatrician]／ 그 의사는 ～ 전문의다 The doctor specializes in pediatrics.
소안(笑顔) a smiling face．
소액(少額) a small amount[sum] [of money]／ ～ 지폐 a small note／ ～ 대부금 a small loan／～ 국채 a small government bond; a baby bond．
소야곡(小夜曲) a serenade．
소양(小恙) a minor illness; a complaint．
소양(素養) (지식) knowledge (교양) culture; cultivation; accomplishments (수양) training／국어에 ～이 있다 be well grounded in Korean．
소양증(搔癢症) 【한】 pruritus; itching．
소양지판(霄壤之判) a great[wide] difference (*between*)．
소연(小宴) a small feast; an informal dinner[party]; a dinnerette; a collation ／～을 베풀다 hold a small [dinner] party．
소연하다(蕭然─) (be) bleak; dreary; desolate (쓸쓸하다)(be) lonely; lonesome ／소연해지다 become desolate／소연한 장소 a lonely spot．
소연하다(昭然─) (be) clear; distinct; plain; evident; obvious／소연하게 plainly; clearly; doubtless．
소연하다(騷然─) be in commotion[an uproar]; be agitated; be disturbed．
소엽(小葉) 【식】 a small leaf; leaflet．
소영사(所營事) *one's* undertakings; *one's* business．
소옥(所屋) a shed; a shack; a hut; a cabin; a cottage; a small house．
소외(疎外) alienation／ ～하다 avoid *one's* company; keep (*a person*) at a distance; be cool (*toward*)．
소요(所要) need; requirement; what is needed[required]／～ 금액 the necessary[required] sum／ ～ 시간 the time required; the necessary time／ ～ 조건 required conditions; requisites．
소요(逍遙) a ramble; a stroll; a turn／ ～하다 stroll[ramble] about／뜰을 ～하다 take a turn[stroll] (in the garden); stroll about the garden．
소요(騷擾) a disturbance; an agitation (폭동) a riot[ing]; an uprising／ ～죄 [the crime of] sedition．
소욕(所欲) *one's* wish; *one's* desire．
소용(所用) need; want; demand; necessity; use／ ～되는 absolutely; necessary; essential; eddy．
소용(笑容) a smiling face．
소용돌이 a whirlpool; a swirl (작은) an eddy／ ～치다 whirl．
소용없다(所用─)(불필요하다)(be) needless; unnecessary; useless; of no use ／소용없는 이야기 an idle talk．
소우(小雨) a drizzle; a drizzling[light] rain／～가 온다 It drizzles．
소우주(小宇宙) 【철】 a microcosm．
소웅좌(小熊座) 【천】 the Little Bear [Ursa Minor]; the Little Dipper．
소원(所願) desire; wish (기원) a prayer ／ ～을 들어 주다 comply with *one's* wishes／ ～ 성취하다 realize *one's* cherished wishes／이루지 못한 ～ an unfulfilled desire．
소원(素願) *one's* long-cherished desire／ *one's* heart's desire．
소원(溯源) investigation of the origin (of *a matter*)／ ～하다 trace (*it*) back; trace (*a thing*) to its origin．
소원(訴究) ～하다 call out[appeal] to (*the court*)．
소원(疏遠, 疎遠) 《무소식》 long silence[ne-

**소원**(訴願) a petition; an appeal／～하다 petition; appeal／～인(人) a petitioner／～을 제기하다 persent a petition. そがん

**소위**(所謂) the so-called; as it is called; what they call／그는 ～ 귀공자다 He is what is called a young prince.／～ 운명이란 것은 사람이 스스로 친 거미줄이다 What a man calls fate is web of his own weaving. いわゆる

**소위**(少尉) 《해군》an ensign 《육군》a second lieutenant. しょうい

**소위**(所爲) an act; action; a deed; *one's* doing[work]／그 사람의 ～가 틀림없다 It must be his doing. しょい

**소위원회**(小委員會) a subcommittee. しょういいんかい

**소유**(所有) ownership; possession 《소유물》property／～하다 posses; own; be in possession of／～권 ownership; proprietorship; dominium／～권 보호 protection of property／～권 침해 infringement of ownership／～격《언》the possessive[genitive] case／～ 본능 acquisitive instinct／～욕 a desire to possess (*a thing*); possessiveness／～자 an owner; a proprietor; a possessor／～지 land owned by (*a person*)／～가 되다 come[pass] into (*a person's*) possession／이씨의 ～지(地) Mr *Lee's* land. しょゆう

**소유성**(小遊星) minor[lesser] planets; an asteroid. しょうゆうせい

**소음**(騷音) a noise; cacophony／～ 받지 arrest of noise／요란한 ～ car-splitting noise; the din (of *a factory*). そうおん

**소음기**(消音器) a silencer; a muffler; a damper.

**소읍**(小邑) a small town. こむら

**소이**(小異) slight difference; small[minor] differences／대동 ～이다 be in substantial agreement with each other; be much alike. しょうい

**소이**(所以) the reason;[the reason] why／내가 사직한 ～는 바로 여기 있다 This is the reason why I have resigned my office. ゆえん

**쏘이다** ①(벌레에) be stung／벌에 ～ get stung by a bee ②(볕에) expose to sun ─쐬다. むしにさされる

**소이연**(所以然) a reason; [the reason] why. ゆえん

**소이탄**(燒夷彈) an incendiary[a fire] bomb. しょういだん

**소인**(小人) a little man 《난장이》a dwarf; a pigmy 《어린이》a child 《소인물》a small man; a little man[mind]; 《나》I／～국 《난장이 나라》a land of pigmies; a Lilliput. しょうにん

**소인**(消印) a postmark; a cancellation stamp／～하다 postmark; cancel with a stamp／서울의 ～이 찍혀 있는 편지 a letter bearing the *Seoul* postmark. けしいん

**소인**(素人) an amateur; a non-professional／～극 amateur theatricals; an amateur dramatic performance. しろうと

**소인**(素因) a factor; a principle; a primary cause; a fundamental; 《병》 predisposition／폐병의 ～ a predisposition to consumption. そいん

**소인**(訴因) 《법》a charge.

**소인수**(素因數) 《수》a prime factor. そいんすう

**소일**(消日) diversion／～하다 divert; beguile *one's* idle hour／나는 독서로 ～하고 있다 I beguile my idle hour by reading.／～거리 the object of diversion[recreation]; a beguiler. しょうじつ

**소임**(所任) *one's* duty[office, task]; 《사명》 *one's* mission／～을 다하다 accomplish *one's* mission. にんむ

**소입**(所入) expenses; requirements; expenditure. ようしたおおかねやもの

**소자**(小字) a small letter. しょうじ

**소자**(小子) 《부모에게》I; me.

**소작**(小斫) slender firewood.

**소작**(小作) tenancy／～ 농 tenant a farm／～농 tenant-farming／～권 tenant-rights. こさく

**소작**(小作) a work; a production／김 동인의 ～ a work by *Kim Dongin*.

**소장**(少將) 《육군》a major-general 《해군》a rear admiral 《공군》an air commodore. しょうしょう

**소장**(所長) the head [of an office, a factory, *etc.*]; a superintendent／연구 ～ the director[head] of a laboratory. しょちょう

**소장**(小壯) vigorous youth; the young／～파 younger members[set]／～학파 the young school. しょうそう

**소장**(小腸) 《해》the small intestines 《돼지 따위》chitterlings／～ 간막(間膜) mesentery／～선(腺) glands of the small intestines／～염 enteritis. しょうちょう

**소장**(所掌) matters under *one's* management. しょかつのしごと

**소장**(消長) rise and fall; ups and downs; ebb and flow; welfare／일국의 ～ the welfare[the prosperity and decline] of a nation. しょうちょう

**소장**(訴狀) a [written] complaint 《청원장》a petition. そじょう

**소장**(所藏) collection; possession／～ 골동 *one's* collection of curios; curios in *one's* possession／～ 서화 *one's* collection of writings and paintings／백씨 ～의 owned by [in the possession of] Mr. *Back*. しょぞう

**소재**(素材) material 《작품의》a subject matter. そざい

**소재**(所載) ～의 printed; published; reported／전호(前號)에 ～된 바와 같이 as reported [stated] in the previous number[issue].

**소재**(所在) 《위치》whereabouts; position 《건물 따위의》location/《도청》~지 the seat [of provincial governnment]/그의 ~는 모르고 있다 His whereabouts is unknown. しょざい

**소저**(小姐) a young lady; a young mistress. おんな

**소쩍새** 《조》a cuckoo. ほととぎす

**소전**(小傳) a biographical sketch; a brief life. しょうでん

**소전제**(小前提) 《논》a minor premise. しょうぜんてい

**소절**(小節) 《예절》minor matter of etiquette or protocol 《절조》minor points of honor; trifles;《음》a bar. しょうせつ

**소정**(所定) ~의 fixed; prescribed; designated; established/~의 위치에 자리잡다 take one's place./~의 위치에 자리잡다 take one's place. しょてい

**소제**(掃除) cleaning; clean-up 《쓸기》sweeping 《먼지를 털기》dusting/ ~하다 clean; sweep; dust; wash/ ~부(夫) a cleaner; a sweeper; a scavenger/ ~부(婦) a scrub woman/실내를 ~하다 clean (up) a room; sweep a room clean. そうじ

**소조**(小潮) the neap; the neap-tide.

**소조**(小鳥) a little[small] bird. ちいさいとり

**소조**(蕭條) ~하다 (be) dreary; desolate; bleak. うらさびしい

**소주**(小註) brief notes/ ~를 달다 add detailed notes[comments, remarks] to.

**소주**(燒酒) [distilled] spirits; ardent spirits; alcohol. しょうちゅう

**소죽**(一粥) boiled fodder.

**소중**(所重) importance; significance; valuableness/ ~하다 (be) important; weighty; significant; valuable; dear / ~히 seriously; carefully/ ~한 물품 a valuable[treasured] article; a treasure; valuables/ ~한 일 the main [important] thing/~한 자식 a precious [beloved, dear] child/나는 돈보다 시간을 ~하 여긴다 I consider time more important than money. きちょう

**소지**(所持) possession/ ~하다 have [in one's possession]; possess; carry/~품 one's personal effects/ ~자 a holder; an owner; a possessor. しょじ

**소지**(小指) 《손의》the little finger; the ear-finger; the pinkie 《발의》the little toe. こゆび

**소지**(素地) a foundation; a basis.

**소지**(素志) one's original intention; one's cherished intention[desire, object]. そい

**소지**(燒紙) sacrificial paper [burned to departed spirit].

**소진**(消盡) disappearance; vanishing/~하다 vanish; disappear. しょうじん

**소진**(燒盡) entire destruction by fire/ ~하다 be burnt down [to the ground]; be totally destroyed by fire; be reduced to ashes. しょうじん

**소질**(素質) makings; nature; qualities; character 《체질》constitution 《병의》predisposition/그는 의사가 될 ~이 없다 He has no makings of a doctor. そしつ

**소집**(召集) a call; a summons 《징집》a levy 《의회 따위의》convocation 《동원》mobilization. しょうしゅう

**소차**(小差) a small[slight] difference/ ~로 이기다 win by a narrow margin; nose out〈미〉. しょうさ

**소찬**(素饌) plain side dishes without meat or fish. やさいだけのおかず

**소창**(消暢) 《오락》amusement; recreation; diversion; pastime/ ~하다 divert[recreate] oneself (with baseball). こころをくつろげること

**소창옷**(小氅一) a small outercoat without reinforcing strips.

**소채**(蔬菜) vegetables; greens; garden products; garden truck〈미〉/ ~원 a kitchen garden. そさい

**소책자**(小冊子) a pamphlet; a booklet; a brochure. しょうさっし

**소천지**(小天地) a small world.

**소철**(蘇鐵) 《식》a sago palm; a cycad. そてつ

**소첩**(小妾) I; me (said by women).

**소청**(所請) an entreaty; one's request/ ~에 의하여 at request. たのむこと

**소촌**(小村) a small village; a hamlet. こむら

**소총**(小銃) a rifle 《총칭》small-arms/~탄 a rifleshot; a bullet. しょうじゅう

**소추**(訴追) legal action; prosecution; proceedings; charges/ ~하다 file charges (against); prosecute. そつい

**소춘**(小春) October of the lunar calendar. こはる

**소출**(所出) crops; yield[s]; products. しょしゅつ

**소치**(所致) 《결과》result 《이유》reason/ 그것은 그녀가 근면한 ~이다 That is due to her diligence. りゆとけっか

**소침**(消沈) depression; gloom; melancholy/ ~하다 get depressed; sink into gloom; feel blue/~하여 with a dejected air; pulling a long face. しょうちん

**소쿠라지다** 《물결이》leap up.

**소쿠리** a bamboo basket 《큰 것》a crate. かご

**소탈**(疏脫) unworldliness; unconventionality/ ~하다 (be) unworldly; uncoventional; free and easy.

**소탐 대실**(小貪大失) suffering a heavy loss by pursuing a small profit/ ~하다 suffer a heavy loss by pursuing a small profit.

**소탕**(掃蕩) sweeping; clearing/ ~하다 sweep (the enemy) from; mop up; clear (the land) of; clear up/ ~전 a mopping[clean]-up campaign. そうとう

**소태** 《식》《나무》a kind of sumac; Picrasma ailanthoides(학명); 《껍질》sumac bark. にがき

소택(沼澤) bogs; marshes; swamps. しょうたく

소톱(小—) a small saw. ちいさいのこぎり

소통(疏通) ①《물 따위의》drainage/ ~하다 cut a channel through; draw[drain] off ②《의사의》understanding; explanation/ ~하다 understand each other; come to an explanation[understanding] with/의사가 ~하다 come to a mutual good understanding. そつう

소파(小波) ripples; rippling waves; wavelets. しょうは

소편(小片) a small piece; a bit; a fragment. しょうへん

소포(小包) a pracel; a package; a packet/~ 우편[으로] (by) parcel post/~ 우편료 parcel-post charge. こづつみ

소품(小品) 《물건》a trifle article 《문예의》a short piece; a sketch. しょうひん

소풍(逍風) ①《산보》a walk; a stroll; an outing; an airing/ ~하다 go for a walk/ ~나가다 go out for a walk. ②《원족》an excursion; a long walk; a walking tour; a hike; a picnic/ ~하다 go on excursion[a hike]; take a long walk. さんぽ

소피(所避) going to the toilet; relieving oneself/ ~보다 go to the toilet; relieve.

소하(消夏) summering; spending[passing] the summer/~하다 avoid the heat of summer; summer/~법 a way of spending the summer. しょうか

소하다(素—) abstain from fish and meat; stick to a vegetarian diet.
にくしょくをしない

소하물(小荷物) a package; a parcel/ ~ 취급소 the parcels office. こにもつ

소학교(小學校) an elementary school; a primary school. しょうがっこう

소한(小閑) a bit of leisure; a little[spare] time; a short break. すこしのひま

소한(小寒) the period of lesser cold.
しょうかん

소할(所轄) jurisdiction; competency/ ~ 관청 the competent[proper] authorities. しょかつ

소해(掃海) sweeping of the sea; dragging (for *mines*); mine sweeping[dragging]/. ~하다 sweep the sea (for *mines*)/~대 a sea-clearing party/ ~ 작업 clearing[dragging] operation; mine sweeping. そうかい

소행(所行) one's doing; a work; an act; a deed/ ~이 사납다 be ill-behaved/이 것은 그 사람의 ~임에 틀림없다 It must be his doing. しょうぎょう

소행(素行) conduct; behaviour; one's natural character/ ~이 좋아지다 improve in one's conduct/ ~을 삼가다 be prudent in one's conduct. そこう

소향(所向) one's destination; the objective. むかうところ

소향(燒香) burning incense/ ~하다 burn incense. しょうこう

소허(少許) a small quantity. すこしばかり

소형(小形, 小型) a small size/ ~의 small sized; of small size; under-sized; small; little; diminutive; miniature/ ~ 비행기 a moth[tiny, midget] plane/ ~ 판 a mind ature[pocket] edition. こがた

소형(素馨) a jasmine/ ~말리(茉莉). まつり

소호(小毫) the least thing; an atom; a bit; a jot; a fragment. ちいさいこと

소호(沼湖) marshes and lakes/~의 lacustrine.

소혼(消魂) vacancy; absent-mindedness /~하다 be absent-minded; be abstracted. しょこん

소홀(疏忽) 《부주의》carelessness 《태만》negligence; neglect 《실례》inattention / ~하다 (be) careless; heedless; hasty; thoughtless; negligent; remiss; neglectful; inattentive/ ~히 하다 neglect; slight; be neglectful of; disregard. そそっかしいこと

소화(小話) a short story[tale]; an anecdote; a vignette. しょうわ

소화(笑話) a funny[humorous] story; joke. しょうわ

소화(消化) digestion; absorption; consumption/ ~하다 digest; absorb/ ~기 the digestive organs 《계통-》the digestive system/ ~기 질환 digestive trouble/ ~력 digestive power/ ~ 불량 indigestion; dyspepsia/ ~액 digestive fluid[juice]/ ~ 작용 the digestive process/ ~제 a digestive; a peptic; an aid to digestion/ ~가 빠르다[느리다] be quick(slow) of digestion/ ~를 돕다 promote[help, aid] digestion/ ~하기 쉬운 digestible. しょうか

소화(消火) fire extinguishing; fire fighting/ ~하다 extinguish[put out] a fire/ ~기 a fire extinguisher/ ~전 a hydrant; a fireplug/~에 힘쓰다 fight a fire. しょうか

소환(召喚) recall/~하다 recall; call back; summon to return/ ~장 a summons; a subpoena/본국에 ~되다 be recalled; be summoned home. しょうかん

소환(召還) a call; a summons; 《법》subpoena/ ~하다 summon; call; subpoena/ ~장 a summons; a subpoena.
しょうかん

소활(疏闊) slovenliness; looseness; negligence 《부주의》carelessness/ ~하다 (be) slovenly; loose; negligent; careless.

소회(所懷) a view; an opinion/ ~를 말하다 express one's thoughts[views, opinions]. しょかい

소회(小會) a small meeting[gathering].

소회하다(溯洄—) go[sail, steam] up.

소휴지(小休止) 《음》a short halt[rest]; a pause.

속 ①《마음의》the depth; the bottom/마음 ~ the bottom of one's heart/ ~이

검은 black-hearted; scheming／～을 썩이다 worry oneself about (*a matter*); be worried; feel anxious about ②《안의 깊은 곳》 the interior; the back; the inner part; the depth; the heart 《핵심》 a core／산 ～ the heart of a mountain／말 ～의 숨은 뜻 the hidden meaning of words ③《속에 든 것》 contents (내용); 《실질》 [the] substance 《충전물》 the filling／연필의 ～ lead. なか

쏙 《동》 a kind of crab; *Upogebia major* (학명). ぽこんと

속(屬) a family; a tribe; a series; 《생》 a genus. ぞく

속(續) continuation; a sequel; an installment; a continuation (*of*); a sequel (*to*); 《부분의》 a series／～편 a supplement volume; a follow-up; a sequel to a preceding volume. ぞく

속(贖) 《속죄》 atonement; expiation 《속전》 ransom 《배상》 indemnity／～하다 atone[expiate] for; indemnify. ぞく

속(束) bind ⇨ 뭇, 단. ぞく

속가(俗家) a layman's house. ぞっか

속가(俗歌) a popular song; a folksong; a ditty; a ballad. ぞっか

속가량(一假量) a rough estimate [based on one's feelings]. こころづもり

속가죽 inner part of hide[leather]. ないひ

속간(俗間) the world; the public at large; people [in general]. ぞっかん

속간(續刊) continuation of publication／～하다 continue to publish; publish consecutively. ぞっかん

속개(續開) continuation; resumption／～하다 continue; resume (*a meeting*)／국회는 내일 ～한다 The Assembly will resume its session tomorrow. ぞっかい

속객(俗客) ①《속물》 a worldling ②《불가 (佛家)에 대한》 a layman 《총칭》 the laity. ぞっかく

속껍질 the inner layer of skin or cover; the derma. ないひ

속겨 inner chaff[bran]. ふすま

속결(速決) a prompt[immediate, quick] decision／～하다 decide promptly[immediately].

속계(俗界) the world; the earthly world; earthly life／～를 초월하다 keep aloof from the world. ぞっかい

속고(續稿) remaining manuscripts; the sequence. ぞっこう

속고갱이 the heart／캬베스 ～ the heart of a cabbage. しん

속곳 a slip; a petticoat; underwears worn by women／～ 바람에 with nothing on but a slip. おんなのはだぎ

속공(屬公) reversion to the public (of *an ownerless article*).

속공하다(速攻—) lose no time in attacking (*the enemy*).

속관(屬官) a subordinate government official; a government clerk. ぞっかん

속구(速球) 《야구》 a fast[speed] ball; a speeder; a sweeper／～ 투수 a fast-ball pitcher; a sharp-shooter; a speed-baller《미·속》.

속국(屬國) a vassal state; a dependency; a subject[tributary] state. ぞっこく

속궁리(一窮理) reflecting to oneself; considering／～하다 mull over.

속굿 a copy; ～넣다 set (*one*) a copy; write a copy (*for*)／～을 받쳐 쓰다 write after a copy.

속기(俗氣) vulgarity; worldliness; worldly ambition／～가 없다 be above the world. ぞっけ

속기(速記) ①《빨리 씀》 quick[rapid] writing[copying]／～하다 write[copy] rapidly[quickly] ②《속기법》 shorthand; stenography 《기록》 stenographic records[notes]／～하다 take down in shorthand; write shorthand／～사 a stenographer; a shorthand writer／～록 stenographic records. そっき

속나깨 fine bran of buckwheat. ふすま

속내 mind; intention／～를 모르겠다 be unable to read (*a person's*) inner thought. ないじょう

속내다 sharpen [the blade of a plane[drill]]; put an edge[point] on. かたなをたてる

속내평 the internal conditions; the inside (of *a matter*); the real state (of *affairs*)／～을 떠보다 inquire into the real state. ないじょう

속념(俗念) worldly thoughts[ambitions]; earthly desires; worldliness. ぞくねん

속눈썹 the eyelashes／긴 ～ long lashes／인조 ～ a false eyelashes. まつげ

속눈치 [an inkling of] one's real attitude.

속다 be cheated; be deceived; be imposed upon; be taken in; be duped; be fooled／그에게 속아 넘어갔다 He has made a dupe of me.／아, 속았구나 Alas! I've been duped! だまされる

솎다 thin [out]／무[배추]를 ～ thin out the rows of radish[cabbage].

속닥거리다 talk secretly; have a talk in an undertone (*with*)／속닥속닥 《비밀히》 in secret 《작은 소리로》 in an under-tone; in whispers. ささやく

속단(速斷) ①《지레 짐작》 a hasty[rash] conclusion／～하다 decide[conclude] hastily; jump to a conclusion; come to a rash conclusion ②《빠른 판단》 an immediate judgement; a prompt decision／～하다 give an immediate judgement. そくだん

속달(速達) express[special] delivery／～하다 send (*a letter*) by express; express (*a parcel*)／～로 by dispatch[express]／～ 우편 express-delivery post; special delivery mail(미). そくたつ

속달거리다 lay heads together in secret consultation; talk in whispers／속달속

**속달다** 달 secretly 《작은 목소리로》 in whispers.

**속달다** be worried; be annoyed; be irritated; be impatient. やきもきする

**속달뱅이** a small scale.

**속담(俗談)** a proverb; a [common] saying/ ~에도 있듯이 as the proverb says. ぞくだん

**속대** the heart of vegetable.

**쑥대기** 〖식〗 a kind of laver.

**속대중** one's personal estimate; a rough guess based on one's feelings.

**속도(速度)** rate 《속력》 speed 《풍속》 velocity/제한 ~ the regulation speed/ ~를 놀이다[줄이다] increase[decrease] the speed. そくど

**속독(速讀)** rapid reading/ ~하다 read (a book) fast[rapidly].

**쑥독새** 〖조〗 the Korean goatsucker; Caprimulgus indicus jotaka(학명).

**속돌** 〖광〗 a pumice [stone].

**속되다(俗—)** 《비속》(be) vulgar 《통속》(be) common; popular 《세속적》(be) worldly; earthly; mundane 《현세의》(be) lay; secular/속된 말로 하면 to use a common word[phrase]; in common parlance; as is commonly said[called]/ 속된 것을 좇다 follow the crowd. つうぞくだ

**속등(續騰)** a further advance/ ~하다 continue to rise; continue its advance.

**속락(續落)** 〖경〗 a continued[persistent] fall/~하다 continue falling[to fall]; fall steadily. ぞくらく

**속량(贖良)** emancipation [of slaves]/ ~하다 emancipate (one); free.

**속력(速力)** speed; rate 《바람의》 velocity/ ~ 범위 a speed range/ ~ 시험 a speed trial/ ~ 제한 speed limit/경제 ~ an economical speed/대 ~ a great [headlong] speed /최대 ~ the greatest[maximum] speed/ ~이 빠른 fast; speedy/ ~이 느린 slow; slow-going/전 ~으로 at full speed; with all speed; with the throttle wide open/~을 가하다 accelerate [the] speed; speed up. そくりょく

**속령(屬領)** a possession; a dependency/ ~지 a dominion. ぞくりょう

**속례(俗例)** a popular custom; a common usage; a common way; convention.

**속례(俗禮)** conventional etiquette; ceremonial customs. ふうぞくからきたれいぎ

**속론(俗論)** vulgar[popular] opinion; conventional views. ぞくろん

**속료(屬僚)** subordinates 《속칭》 the staff. ぞくりょう

**속류(俗流)** the vulgar[common] crowd; the herd; people. ぞくりゅう

**속리(俗吏)** a bumble; a Jack-in-office/ ~ 근성 bumbledom.

**속마음** one's inmost heart; real inward feeling; one's mind. ないしん

**속말** a confidential talk; a frank talk; a confession/ ~하다 talk frankly[without reserve] (to); give (one) the lowdown (on)《미·속》.

**속명(俗名)** ①《속된 이름》 a common[popular] name/나의 ~은 영호이다 My common name is Young-Ho ②《법명에 대한》 a secular name ③《본명 이외의》 a popularname. ぞくめい

**속명(屬名)** 〖생〗 a generic name.

**속무(俗務)** worldly affairs[matters]; daily affairs. ぞくむ

**속문학(俗文學)** vulgar literature.

**속물(俗物)** a worlding; a worldly[-minded] man; a philistine; a man of low taste/ ~ 근성 Philistinism; snobbery. ぞくぶつ

**속바치다(贖—)** pay [as] ransom.

**속박(束縛)** restraint; restriction; fetters; a yoke/ ~하다 restrict; restrain; shackle; bind; fetter/ ~력 constraining force/자유를 ~하다 restrict (a person's) freedom/ ~을 받다 be restricted/ ~을 벗어나다 free oneself from restraint; get rid of restraints; throw off the yoke. そくばく

**속발(束髮)** ①《조발》 hair-dressing/ ~하다 do up one's hair; dress one's hair; bind one's hair ②《상투의》 tying of a top-knot/ ~하다 tie a top-knot. そくはつ

**속발(續發)** successive[frequent] occurrence/~하다 occur frequently; follow/ 요즘 화재가 ~한다 Fires are frequent these days. ぞくはつ

**속방(屬邦)** a subject state ⇨속국.

**속배(俗輩)** the common crowd.

**속배포(一排布)** one's inmost bosom; one's heart; one's design.

**속병(一病)** an internal disease[complaint]; 《탈》 an internal disorder.

**속보(速報)** a prompt report; a quick announcement/ ~하다 report promptly; announce quickly/~판 a flash board. そくほう

**속보(續報)** further news; additional[further] particulars. ぞくほう

**속보이다** reveal one's heart; give oneself away; disclose one's intention; wear one's heart on one's sleeve. ないしんをみせる

**속뽑다** sound (a person) out; read (a person's) mind. ないしんをさぐる

**속뽑히다** be made to, reveal one's heart /속뽑히는 말 remarks which betray oneself.

**속사(速寫)** 《사진외》 a snapshot/~하다 snapshot; take a snapshot/ ~기 a snapshot camera. そくしゃ

**속사(俗事)** worldly affairs[matters]; daily routine; business/ ~에 쫓기다 be engrossed in daily affairs. ぞくじ

**속사(速射)** quick[fast] firing; quick fire/ ~하다 fire quickly/ ~포 a quick-firing gun; a rapid-fire gun. そくしゃ

**속사정(一事情)** the inside[unrevealed] c-

**속삭이다** whisper; murmur; speak under one's breath; talk in whispers 《시냇물이》ripple/사랑의 달콤한 속삭임 soft nothings; billing and cooing. ささやく

**속산**(速算) rapid calculation.

**속살** ①《옷 속의》parts of the body ordinarily covered by clothing/〜이 희다 have fair skin ②the inner meat of (a lobster).

**속살거리다** whisper; murmur; talk in whispers/속살속살 in an undertone; in whispers. ささやく

**속살다** (be) unbending; unyielding; obstinate; repulsive; revolting.

**속살찌다** ①《살찌다》(be) fat ②《실속있다》(be) substantial; solid; rich.

**속상하다**(—傷—) ①be distressing[worrisome, annoying, exasperating]; get on one's nerves ②be distressed[worried, annoyed, exasperated, vexed]/무엇이 그렇게 속상합니까 What are you sore[mad] at?

**속새** ①《식》the scouring rush; a horsetail [plant] ②《사포》sandpaper. とくさ

**속새질** rubbing with sandpaper; sandpapering down/ 〜하다 rub with sandpaper; sandpaper. とこさでみがくこと

**속생각** inward thoughts; thinking to oneself/ 〜하다 think to oneself.

**속샤쓰** an undershirt; underwears.

**속설**(俗說) common talk; a common[popular] saying; a popular version (of an incident); 《전설》folklore; tradition. ぞくせつ

**속성**(俗姓) one's secular surname. ぞくせい

**속성**(速成) rapid completion; quick mastery/ 〜하다 complete rapidly; train quickly; give a quick training/ 〜법 a quick-mastery method; a royal road; a short cut./〜과 a short[brief] course. そくせい

**속성**(屬性) 《논》an attribute. ぞくせい

**속세**(俗世) the [workaday] world; earthly life/〜를 버리고 renounce the world/〜에서 초연하다 stand aloof from the world; stand isolated from every day life. ぞくせい

**속세간**(俗世間) the [mundane] world; earthly existence; the public; the people. ぞくせけん

**속셈** an intention; a design; a purpose; an estimate; a calculation.

**속소위**(俗所謂) to use a common word; as is commonly said; what in commonly called. そくせいでいうところ

**속속**(續續) successively; one after another; in rapid succession/주문이 〜 밀려든다 Orders pour in./보도가 〜 들어온다 Reports pour in. ぞくぞく

**속속곳** underpants worn by women. おんなのはだぎ

**속속들이** all; wholly; thoroughly/〜 알다 know everything about; know the ins and outs of (a matter). すみずみ

**속속이풀** 《식》a marsh cress.

**속속히**(速速—) rapidly; fast; apace/ 〜 나아가다 advance rapidly 《진행》make rapid progress 《걸어서》 go ahead at a rapid pace. はやばやと

**속손톱** 《해》lunula of a fingernail. てのちいさいつめ

**속수 무책**(束手無策) helplessness; resourcelessness/어떻게 처리하면 할지 〜이다 I am at a loss how to do it.

**속습**(俗習) a [popular] custom; convention; usage. ぞくしゅう

**속심**(俗心) a worldly mind; worldliness.

**속아넘어가다** be deceived ⇒속다.

**속악**(俗樂) popular music. ぞくがく

**속안**(俗眼) a common eye; a popular view; a layman's opinion. ぞくがん

**속어**(俗語) a slang word[expression]; 《집합적》slang 《일상 회화 용법》a colloquialism; a colloquial expression/〜를 쓰다 use vulgar speech. ぞくご

**속어림** an estimate; a calculation.

**속언**(俗言) a vulgar saying; common talk; slangy speech. ぞくげん

**속언**(俗諺) a common[popular] saying; a household word; a proverb. ぞくげん

**속없다** (be) unsubstantial; empty; lack depth[content]. はいりょがない

**속연**(續演) continuous show[performance]; the continuation of a show/ 〜하다 show continuous; continue to present (a play). ぞくえん

**속옷** underwear; underclothes; undergarments. はだぎ

**속요**(俗謠) a popular song; a folk song; a ballad; a ditty. ぞくよう

**속음** thinning [out]/ 〜하다 thin[cull] [out] (plants).

**속음**(俗音) the popular phone of a Chinese character. ぞくおん

**속이다** deceive; cheat; swindle; fool; gull; dupe; trick; impose on; hambug; put upon (one); take (one) in; play (one) false; play a trick on; make a fool of 《거짓으로 말하다》[tell a] lie; cook [up] 《장부 따위에서》/사람의 눈을 〜 hoodwink; delude (one)/자기 자신을 〜 deceive oneself. だます

**속인**(俗人) ①《속물》a worldling; a vulgar person ②《불문에 대한》a layman; the laity. ぞくじん

**속인주의**(屬人主義) 《법》the personal principle. ぞくじんしゅぎ

**속임수** a trick; trickery; deception; cheat[ing]; fraud; swindle/ 〜를 쓰다 play a trick on (a person); serve (a person) a trick/ 〜에 넘어가다 fall a victim to fraud; be cheated. だましほう

**속잎** an inside leaf.

**속자**(俗字) the popular[simplified] form of a Chinese character. ぞくじ

**속장**(一章) 《인》an inside leaf [of a ne-

**속장**(束裝) 《여장》 preparations for a journey/ ~하다 make preparations[prepare, equip *oneself*] for a journey.

**속적삼** an undershirt; underwear.

**속전**(贖錢) a ransom.

**속절없다** (be) hopeless; futile; vain; unavailing/ 속절없이 futilely; in vain; as there is no help/ 속절없는 세상 a futile world.

**속정**(俗情) worldly passion[concerns, mind].

**속종** *one's* view[opinion]; *one's* inmost thoughts.

**속죄**(贖罪) atonement; expiation (of *sins*); redemption 《고생을 쌓고서》 purgation (from *sins*)/ ~하다 atone for; expiate (*sins*); redeem /죽음으로써 ~하다 pay with death for a crime; atone for *one's* fault with *one's* life.

**속주다** take (*one*) into *one's* confidence; disburden *one's* mind (*to*); open *one's* heart (*to*); unbosom *oneself*.

**속지**(屬地) a possession; a dependency; a territory; a dominion/ ~주의 《재판상의》 the territorial principle; the principle of territorial privilege for jurisdiction.

**속진**(俗塵) the world; earthly[mundane] affairs/ ~을 멀리하다 keep aloof from the madding crowd; live secluded from the world.

**속짐작** *one's* personal[mental] estimation.

**속창** an insole; a sock.

**속체**(俗體) ①《속인》 the laity ②《속된 체재》 vulgarity; philistinism; vulgar style.

**속출**(續出) successive occurrence/ ~하다 appear[occur] in succession; follow one after another.

**속취**(俗趣) vulgar[bourgeois] taste; philistinism.

**속취**(俗臭) vulgarity 《속기》 worldliness/ ~가 나는 of low taste; vulgar; worldly-minded.

**속치레** interior decoration/ ~를 하다 decorate the interior.

**속치마** a chemise; an underskirt; a petticoat.

**속치장**(一治裝) interior decoration[design].

**속칭**(俗稱) a popular[common] name/ ~하다 call[name] popularly; be popularly known as/ ~을 …라고 한다 be popularly known (*as*).

**속타다** be worried (*about*); be concerned (*about*); be anxious (*for*); be troubled; be annoyed.

**속타점**(一打點) decision in *one's* heart/ ~하다 decide in *one's* heart.

**속탈**(一頉) a stomach upset[disorder].

**속태**(俗態) vulgar[low] appearance.

**속태우다** ①《남을》 vex; fret; worry; irritate; annoy; trouble ②《스스로》 worry [*oneself*] (*about*); fret (*about*); be concerned (*about*).

**속편**(續篇) a sequel; an afterpiece/ ~ 소설 a serial novel.

**속필**(速筆) quick[rapid] writing; a hasty scribble; a fast hand (with *pen*)/ 그는 ~이다 He writes fast.

**속하다**(速—) (be) fast; quick; rapid; swift/대답을 속히 해라 Answer promptly.

**속하다**(屬—) 《소속하다》 belong (*to*); appertain (*to*); 《가입하다》 be affiliated with; join/그것은 나의 직무에 속한다 That belongs to my duties./ 고래는 동물에 속한다 A whale belongs to the animal life.

**속학**(俗學) popular learning; secular learning[studies].

**속한**(俗漢) a philistine; a person of low taste; a snob; a worldly[-minded] person; a snooty fellow《미·구》.

**속행**(速行) 《걸음》 walking fast 《행동》 prompt action/~하다 go[walk] quickly; carry out speedily; take prompt action.

**속행**(續行) continuance; continuation/ ~하다 continue; go on (*with*); proceed (*with*); carry on/경기를 ~하다 proceed with the game.

**속현**(續絃) remarriage (by *a man*)/ ~ 하다 (*a man*) remarry; marry again.

**속화**(俗化) vulgarization; popularization; secularization/ ~하다 vulgarize; popularize; secularze 《속화되다》 be vulgarized[popularized]; be secularized.

**속화**(俗畵) a commonplace painting; an uninspired picture.

**속회**(續會) resumption of a meeting/ ~ 하다 [a meeting] resume.

**속효**(速效) immediate effect/ ~가 있다 have[produce] immediate effect; 【의】 be active.

**속히**(速—) rapidly; swiftly; speedily; quickly; promptly.

**손**[1] ⇒별항 참조.

**손**[2] 【민】《꺼리는 방향》 an unlucky direction.

**손**[3] a guest[customer].

**손**(孫) descendants; posterity; offspring; sons and grandsons ⇒후손.

**손**(損) 《손실》 loss 《불리》 disadvantage 《손해》 damage/ ~을 보다 lose [heavily]; suffer a loss.

**손가락** a finger/엄지 ~ the thumb/ 가운데 ~ the middle[medium] finger / 둘째 ~ the fore[index, marginal] finger/ 약 ~ the third finger; the earfinger/ 새끼 ~ the little finger; the earfinger/ ~ 끝 the tip of a finger.

**손가락질** ①《지시》 pointing with the finger/ ~하다 point at (*a thing*); point

**손가방** 〔loc: 543〕 **손님**

(one's) finger at ②《비평》 pointing with the finger [of scorn]／~하다 point a finger [of scorn] at; talk about (one) with scorn. ゆびさし
**손가방** a briefcase; a portfolio; a valise; a handbag.
**손거스러미** a hangnail. さかむけ
**손거울** a hand mirror.
**손거칠다** (be) light-fingered; have thievish habits; be a kleptomaniac; have light fingers／저 친구는 손이 거칠다 His fingers are light[lime-twigs].
**손겪다** entertain a guest.
**손결** the texture of the skin of the hand.
**손곱다** (be) stiff; numb; benumbed (with *cold*)／추워서 ~ My hands are stiff [benumbed] with cold. てがこごる
**손꼽다** count on *one's* fingers／손꼽는 사업가 a leading businessman／손꼽아 기다리다 look forward to; anticipate／아버지의 귀가를 손꼽아 기다렸다 We waited for father's return.
**손공**(―功) manual work[labour].
**손구루마** a handcart. ておしくるま
**손그릇** domestic utensils.
**손금** the lines in the palm of *one's* hand／~을 보다 read *one's* palm.

**손금**(損金) pecuniary loss. そんきん
**손끝** the finger-tip; the tip of a finger.
**손끝 맵다** have an evil hand; have a contaminating touch／그는 모든 일에 손끝이 맵다 He fouls up everything he touches.
**손끝 맺다** remain idle; look on with folded arms; stand by with *one's* arms folded／손끝 맺고 있을 때가 아니다 This is no time for us to remain idle. なまける
**손기계**(―機械) a hand[-operated] machine.
**손길** an outstretched hand／~잡다 join [clasp] hands.
**손넘기다** ①《잘못 세다》 skip numbers in counting; miscount; short-count; short ②《시기를 잃다》 miss an opportunity; lose *one's* chance.
**손녀**(孫女) a granddaughter. まごむすめ
**손놓다** 《손떼다》 wash *one's* hands of; get (*a thing*) off *one's* hands; retire; withdraw (*from*). なしおわる
**손누비** quilting by hand／~ 버선 hand-quilted bootees[socks].
**손님** ①《내방객》 a caller; a visitor; a guest／~을 접대하다 entertain company ②《고객》 a customer; a patron; custom;

# 손

①《사지의》 a hand／오른[왼] ~ the right[left] hand／~을 들다 raise *one's* hand 《찬성의 뜻으로》 show *one's* hand 《때리고자》 lift *one's* hand against (*a person*)／ ~을 내밀다 hold out *one's* hants／ ~이 닿는 곳에 있다 be within *one's* reach; be within *one's* grasp／~을 쥐다 《주먹》 clench *one's* fists; close *one's* hands 《남의 손》 grasp another's hand 《악수》 shake hands; clasp hands (*with*); shake (*a person*) by the hand.／~을 흔들다 wave *one's* hand／손들어 《강도가》 Hold up! 《항복의 뜻》 Throw up your hand!／~대지 마시오 《게시》 Hands off《미》.

②《관계》 connection; meddling／ ~을 끊다 wash *one's* hands of (*one's* business)／ ~을 대다 have relations (*with*); start; set *one's* hand to／정부(情婦)와 ~을 끊다 break with *one's* mistress／당신이 만약 그것을 주장한다면 나는 당신과 ~을 끊겠다 If you insist upon it, I wash my hands of you.／그 업체는 전국에 ~이 뻗쳐 있다 The firm is branching out[has branches] all over the country／투기에 ~을 대다 dabble in speculation.

③《구타》 strike; a blow／ ~을 대다 strike; hit; give a blow to／누가 먼저 ~을 댔느냐 Who started the fight?, Who struck the first blow?

④《소유》 the hands (*of*); possession; power／남의 ~에 넘어가다 fall into another's hands／미인을 ~에 넣다 win [the heart of] a belle／물건이 ~에 들어오다 a thing comes into *one's* hands; *one* gets; come by; put *one's* hands on (*a thing*); obtain／서울이 적군의 ~에 들어갔다 Seoul fell into the enemy's hands.／새로운 정보를 ~에 넣었다 I am in possession of new information.

⑤《일손・도움》 a hand; a helping hand／ ~을 빌려주다 give (*a person*) a hand／~이 모자라다 be short of hands／이 일은 여러 사람의 ~이 필요하다 This work calls for many hands.／빈민에게 구호의 ~을 뻗치다 extend help [a helping hand] to the poor／여러 사람의 ~ 으로 된 번역 a translatoin by various hand／~이 비다 be free; be at leisure.

⑥《수고》 care; trouble／~이 가다 take [need] a lot of care; require attention; be troublesome／이 집은 이모저모로 ~ 볼 데가 많다 There is a lot of slapdash [work] about this house.／이 일은 ~이 많이 간다 This is painstaking work.

⑦《관대》 liberality; generosity／ ~이 큰 사람 a generous giver／~이 크다 be generous; be liberal.

trade 《배·차 따위의》 a passenger; a fare / ~이 적다 attract few customers. とまりきゃく

**손때** dirt from the hands; finger marks / ~가 묻다 become hand-stained; be well thumbed / ~를 묻히다 soil (anything) with the hand.

**손대다** ①《만지다》 touch; lay one's hands on / 손대지 말라 Do not touch it. ②《착수하다》 begin; start; set about; set one's hand to / 일에 ~ set about one's work / 이것부터 손댑시다 Let's begin with this one. ③《때리다》 strike; hit; give (a person) a blow; take a fist (to); give a blow (to) / 얼굴에 ~ strike (a person) in the face ④《관계하다》 take a hand (in the matter); try one's hand (at a thing). てをつける

**손대야** a hand basin. ちいさいせんめんき

**손대중** hand-measurement / ~하다 measure with one's hand; estimate [judge] by the hand [rule of thumb].

**손떼다** 《끝내다》 finish; complete; get (a thing) off one's hand 《관계를 끊다》 finish; break (one's connection) with; wash one's hands of; be through with / 그들은 서로 손뗄 수 없는 사이다 They are closely [inseparably] connected. / 정치에서 손을 떼다 withdraw oneself from politics. なしおわる

**손도끼** a hatchet. ておの

**손도장**(一圖章) a thumb-mark / ~을 찍다 seal with the thumb (on a document). ぼいん

**손독**(一毒) hand poisoning. てのどくけ

**손동작**(一動作) hand movement[s]; manual activity.

**손들다** ①《거수하다》 raise [hold up] one's hand ②《공격하다》 lift one's hand (against).

**손등** the back of a hand.

**손료**(損料) hire; rent [fee] / ~를 받고 빌리다 hire out (a thing); let out (a thing) on hire. そんりょう

**손맑다** ①《생기는 게 없다》 (be) inept in moneymaking poor ②《다랍다》 (be) stingy; close; miserly. けちできたない

**손맵다** have an evil hand; have a contaminating touch. てをつけたけっかがよくない

**손맺다** remain idle; look on with folded arms; fold one's arms. なまける

**손모**(損耗) waste; wastage; wear and tear. そんもう

**손목** the wrist / ~을 잡다 catch one's wrist; take (one) by the wrist.

**손바느질** sewing by hand. てぬい

**손바닥** the palm [of the hand] / 《우묵한 데》 the hollow of the hand / 맨 ~ an open palm. てのひら

**손바람** the swish [swing] of a hand / 일에 ~이 나다 get into the swing of one's work. しごとのやりほう

**손발** hand and foot; the limbs / ~을 묶다 bind (one) hand and foot / ~이 큰 big-limced. しゅそく

**손버릇** 《도벽》 a habit of stealing / ~이 사납다 be lightfingered.

**손뼉** the flat of one's hand / ~치다 clap one's hands; applaud. てのひら

**손보기** harlotry; prostitution. ていれ

**손봐주다** give a hand; lend a [helping] hand; help; assist.

**손부**(孫婦) the wife of one's grandson; a granddaughter-in-law. そんのつま

**손붙이다** begin; start; set about. ちゃくしゅする

**손비비다** rub [chafe] one's hands.

**손빌다** ask (one) a [helping] hand; be given a hand. てをかりる

**손싸다** (be) deft; dexterous; nimble-fingered; quick-handed.

**손사래** waving one's hand / ~하다 wave one's hand. てのゆびのあいだ

**손상**(損傷) injury; damage / ~하다 damage; injure; impair; damnify; ruin; spoil / 명예 ~ libel; defamation 《구두의》 slander / ~되다 get damaged; be injured; suffer a loss. そんしょう

**손살** the fork of the hand.

**손색**(遜色) inferiority / ~이 있다 be inferior to (another); suffer by comparison with; yield the palm to. そんしょく

**손서**(孫壻) a grandson-in-law; the husband of one's granddaughter.

**손서투르다** be a poor hand at; be weak in. ぶきようだ

**손속** a hand / ~이 나쁘다 have a wretched hand / ~이 좋다 play a good hand.

**손수** with one's own hands 《몸소》 in person; personally / ~ 만든 homemade; of one's own making. おのずから

**손수건**(一手巾) a handkerchief. てふき

**손숫물** water for washing hands. てあらいみず

**손쉽다** (be) easy; simple; light / 손쉽게 해치우다 toss off. たやすい

**손쓰다** do one's best; exert oneself; make every effort.

**손시늉** hand gestures [mimicry] / ~하다 gesture; make gestures / ~으로 말하다 talk by signs [in sign language].

**손실**(損失) a loss / ~액(額) the loss; the amount of loss / ~을 입다 suffer [sustain] a loss. そんしつ

**손심부름** a petty errand.

**손씻이** a gift sent in remuneration [reward] of one's help.

**손아귀** the space between the thumb and the index finger; hand / ~에 들다 fall into one's hands. しゅちゅう

**손아래** ①《나이》 being junior [younger] / ~의 younger; junior / 손아랫 사람 a junior ②《항렬》 being low in the degree of kinship ③《지위 따위》 inferiority / ~의 inferior; subordinate / 손아랫 사람 one's inferior; a subordinate; an unde-

**손양**(遜讓) modesty; humility/ ~하다 be modest; be humble. めした, そんじょう

**손어림** rough estimation; hand measurement/~하다 estimate by the hand; make a rough estimation.

**손위** ①(나이) being older[elder]; seniority/ ~의 older; elder/손윗사람 an elder; a senior ②(항렬) being senior in the degree of kinship ③(지위 따위) superiority; seniority/ ~의 superior; senior/손윗사람 a superior; a senior; one's betters. めうえ

**손익**(損益) profit and loss; loss and gain /~ 계산 a profit and loss account. そんえき

**손익다** become experienced (in); be skilled; get used to; be versed (in)/손익은 사람 an old hand (at). てなれる

**손일** manual work; handiwork; handicraft.

**손자**(孫子) a grandchild; a grandson. まご

**손자귀** a flat adze; a hand adze/~로 깎다 adze. ちいさいておの

**손잡다** have one's hands full; have one's time fully engaged; be busy; be engaged/일에 손잡겨서 나갈 수 없다 I have my hands too full to go out. てがぬけない

**손잡이** a handle (둥근) a knob (문의) a catch/~ 끈 (전차 따위의) a strap/~를 돌리다 turn a knob. とって

**손장난** toying with one's hands; trifling; fumbling/ ~하다 trifle; fumble; fidget. つまらないいたずら

**손장단** beating time with the hand. てびょうし

**손재수**(損財數) the doom to loss one's possessions. ざいさんをなくすうん

**손재주** cleverness; skillfulness; dexterity; ingenuity/~가 있다 be skillful with one's fingers; be deft-fingered; be smart with one's hand. てかみ

**손전등**(-電燈) a flashlight; an electric torch. かいちゅうでんとう

**손찌검** striking; hitting; beating/ ~하다 strike (a person); beat; hit.

**손질** ①(수선) repair; mending/ ~하다 repair (a house); mend (shoes) ②(가꿈) trimming(나무 따위); 《전돈》 keeping/ ~하다 trim. ていれ

**손짓** a signal with the hand; a gesture; a gesticulation; signs/ ~하다 beckon to (one); [use] sign; [make a] gesture; motion.

**손치르다** entertain guests; give a party; play host (to). おきゃくをもてなす

**손치다**[1] (여관에서) take in lodgers. おきゃくをもてなす

**손치다**[2] ①(매만져 바로잡다) smoothe; put in order ②(흐트러지다) get out of order; get messed up; get scattered.

**손크다** ①(후하다) (be) liberal; generous; open-minded; free-handed; magnanimous ②(수단이 많다) (be) able; capable. てあつい

**손톱** finger-nails/~ 자국 a nail-mark/ ~을 깎다 cut one's nail/~깎이 nail scissors; nail clippers. つめ

**손톱눈** [해] the corners of a nail.

**손틀** a hand-operated sewing machine.

**손티** (주근깨) freckles; flecks 《마마 자국》 a pockmark; a pit. あばた

**손풀무** a hand[-operated] bellows. ふきだけ

**손풍금**(-風琴) a hand-organ; a concertina; an accordion. てふうきん

**손해**(損害) 《손상》 damage; injury; harm 《손실》 loss 《사상》 casualties; loss/막대한 ~ heavy damage/~ 배상 damages; reparation; recompense 《돈》 indemnity / ~하다 pay for damage; indemnify (one) for damage. そんがい

**손회목** [the most slender part of] a wrist.

**쏟다** pour out; spill; drop; empty 《마음을》 be bent on; devote oneself; be devoted to/땅 위에 물을 ~ dash water over the ground/통의 물을 ~ empty out the water from a pail. こぼす

**쏟뜨리다** pour out; spill ⇨쏟다. こぼす

**쏟아지다** pour (out, in, down); get[be] spilt/비가 쏟아진다 The rain is pouring down. おちる

**솔**[1] (터는) a brush/~질을 하다 brush (a hat).

**솔**[2] 《식》 a pine; a pine tree. まつ

**솔**[3] 《표적》 a mark; a target.

**솔가지** pine twigs[branches].

**솔권**(率眷) taking away one's family/ ~하다 take[lead] one's family away.

**솔기** a seam [in clothing]/~ 없는[있는] seamless[seamy].

**솔깃하다** (be) inclined (to); interested (in); attracted. かたむく

**솔다**[1] ①(가렵다) (be) itchy and sore; irritating ②(좁다) (be) narrow; small; cramped/이 웃이 품이 ~ This coat is tight under the arm. むずむずする

**솔다**[2] ①(귀가) (one's ears) ache; have sore ears/시끄러워 귀가 ~ the noise is nerve-racking/잔 소리에 귀가 ~ I am tired of her complaining. ②(말라 쬐어들다) dry up; tighten up with dryness ③(무솔다) (a vegetable) decay from the damp. みみにたこができる

**쏠다** (쥐 따위가) gnaw; chew; bite/벽을 쏠아 구멍을 내다 gnaw a hole through a wall. かじる

**솔대** a [thin] slat; a lath.

**솔래솔래** gradually vanishing. こそこそ

**쏠리다** 《기울다》 incline (to); lean (to, toward)/탑이 한쪽으로 쏠려 있다 The tower leans from the perpendicular. かたむく

**솔바탕** a scope; a [shooting] range.

**솔발**(鐸鈸) a small brass handbell; a handbell/~놓다 《소문내다》 set (a rumo-

**솔방울** a pine cone.
**솔밭** a pine grove[wood]/애～ a grove of young pines.
**솔보굿** a pine bark.
**솔봉이** a young rustic; a boorish young man.
**솔비** a whisk; a whisk broom.
**솔새** 《조》 an arctic willow-warbler; *Phylloscopus borealis*(학명).
**솔선**(率先) taking the lead[initiative]/～하다 lead; take the lead[initiative] (*in*); be a pioneer[leader]/그는 ～하여 그 운동을 일으켰다 He took the initiative[lead] in the movement.
**솔솔** gently; softly/～ 부는 바람 a gentle[light] breeze.
**쏠쏠하다** (be) so-so.
**솔숲** a pine wood[forest]; a pinery.
**솔잎** pine needles.
**솔직**(率直) plainness; frankness; openheartedness; straight/～하다 (be) plain; frank; open; candid; openhearted; straight/～히 말하자면 frankly speaking.
**솔질** brushing/～하다 brush.
**솜** cotton; cottonwool/ ～덩이 a ball of cotton/ ～뭉치 a wad of cotton/ ～바지 padded trousers/귀를 ～으로 막다 stop one's ears with cotton; cottonwool one's ears.
**솜돗** a willowing mat [for cotton].
**솜반** a thin layer of cotton; a thin slice of cotton.
**솜사탕** cotton candy; spun sugar.
**솜솜** ～하다 (be) pockmarked.
**솜씨** 《기술》 skill 《교묘》 cleverness; dexterity 《세공의》 make; workmanship; hand 《수완》 ability; capacity 《교제상의》 tact/ ～있다 (be) skilful; clever; dexterous; adroit; ingenulous.
**솜옷** wadded[padded, quilted] clothes.
**솜저고리** a padded jacket.
**솜털** down; fluff 《새의》 pinfeathers/～방석 a downy cushion.
**솜틀** a willow; a willowing machine.
**솜화약**(一火藥) cotton powder; guncotton.
**솟고라지다** ①《끓어오르다》 boil up ②《용솟다》 leap [up].
**솟구다** draw[perk] up (the *shoulders*); raise; shrug/어깨를 ～ raise[shrug] *one's* shoulders.
**솟구치다** raise quickly; make a quick rise.
**솟다** ①《높이》 rise[soar, tower] high/ 종달새가 하늘 높이 솟는다 A skylark soars to the sky. ②《샘 따위가》 gush[spring] out[forth]; flow out; well out; /샘물이 ～ A well flows.
**솟보다** have a bad bargain; buy dear; pay too much (*for*); overestimate the value of a thing.

**솟아나다** gush[spring] out [forth]; flow [stream] out [forth]; well up [out, forth]/눈물이 ～ tears well (*up*) in *one's* eyes.
**솟을대문**(一大門) a tall gate; a lofty gate.
**솟치다** raise; set higher; elevate; lift up/몸을 ～ stand on tiptoes.
**송**(頌) a eulogy; a panegyric; laudation.
**송가**(頌歌) a hymn; a song of praise/ a doxology.
**송골매**(松鶻―) 《조》 a Siberian peregrine falcon; a duck hawk.
**송곳** 《나사로 된》 a gim[b]let 《작은 구멍 파는》 an awl 《금이나 돌을 파는》 a drill.
**송곳니** an eye-tooth; a canine [tooth].
**송곳칼** a knife with a drill; a combination knife-drill.
**송구**(悚懼) ～하다 be filled with awe; be overwhelmed (with *shame* or *gratitude*) /친히 돌봐 주시니 ～스럽습니다 To be helped by you, sir, is too great an honor[u]r for me.
**송구**(送球) handball.
**송구 영신**(送舊迎新) ～하다 see the old year out and the new year in; ring out the old ring in the new.
**송금**(送金) remittance/～하다 remit money to; send (*one*) money/ ～인 the remitter/ ～ 수취인 the remittee/ ～ 액 the amount of remittance.
**송기**(送氣) air supply/ ～하다 supply/ ～관(管) an air-pipe.
**송기떡**(松肌―) pine endodermis cake.
**송년**(送年) bidding the old year out [and the new year in].
**송달**(送達) delivery; conveyance; forwarding/ ～하다 send; deliver; forward; convey 《교부》 serve/～처(處) the destination.
**송당송당** with hasty[random] whacks/ 무를 ～ 썰다 whack away at a radish.
**송덕**(頌德) eulogy/ ～하다 extol[l] *one's* virtue/ ～비(碑) a monument in *one's* hono[u]r.
**송독**(誦讀) recitation; recitation from memory/ ～하다 recite; recite from memory.
**송두리째** root and branch; all; completely; thoroughly/ ～ 없애다 eliminate root and branch.
**송로**(松露) ①《이슬》 dew on pine needles ②《버섯》 a truffle; a mushroom.
**송료**(送料) postage; haulage; carriage 《바다의》 shipping charge/인삼의 ～ the postage of a ginseng.
**송림**(松林) a pine wood[forest]; a pinery.
**송목**(松木) a pine tree ⇒소나무.
**송백**(松柏) the pine and the nut pine/

~과 coniferae／ ~과 식물 a conifer; a coniferous plant. まつとこのてがしも

**송별**(送別) a farewell; a send-off／ ~사(辭) a farewell speech[address]／ ~연 a farewell dinner／~회(會) a farewell party[meeting]; a sand-off dinner; a good-bye party. そうべつ

**송부**(送付) sending; forwarding; remittance／ ~하다 send; forward 《돈을》 remit.

**송사**(訟事) a lawsuit; a suit; litigation／ ~하다 sue; file suit; go to law (with); take legal proceedings (against); litigate. しょうじ

**송사**(頌辭) a laudatory address; a eulogy; a memorial; a panegyric. しょうじ

**송사리** 〖어〗 a minnow; a killifish. めだか

**송송** ①(잘게) into small pieces; finely; mincing ②(구멍 따위가) full of small holes; perforated／파를 ~ 썰다 chop scallion into small pieces／솥에 구멍이 ~ 뚫려 있다 The oven has holes all over the bottom. こまごま

**송수**(送水) water supply／ ~하다 supply water／ ~관 a water-pipe 《본관》 a water-main.

**송신**(送信) transmission (of a message)／ ~하다 transmit[dispatch] a message／ 무전 ~기 a wireless[radio] transmitter. そうしん

**송아지** a calf／ ~를 낳다 calve. こうし

**송알송알** ①(땀이) in profuse drops ②(거품이 피어서) fermenting; bubbling／땀이 ~ 나다 perspire profusely. だらだら

**송액**(松液) rosin; pine resin. まつやに

**송어**(松魚) a trout; a salmon trout. かつお

**송연**(悚然) ~하다 be horror-struck; be terrified[horrified] (at); shudder with fright. しょうぜん

**송영**(送迎) welcome and send-off; greeting and farewell／ ~하다 welcome and send off; receive (a person) and (another) off／ ~ 위원회 a reception committee. そうげい

**송영**(誦詠) welcome and send-off; greeting and farewell／ ~하다 welcome and send off; greet and bid farewell; receive (one) and see (another) off／ ~ 연설(演說) a speech of greeting and farewell. しょうえい

**송유**(松油) turpentine. まつのえだからとったあぶら

**송유**(送油) oil supply／ ~하다 supply oil／ ~관(管) an oil pipe [line].

**송이** 《꽃·과실의》 a bunch; a cluster 《귤의》 a segment 《눈의》 a flake／포도 한 ~ a bunch of grapes. ふさ

**송이**(松栮) a pine mushroom／ ~를 캐러 가다 go mushroom gathering[hunting]. まつたけ

**송이송이** in clusters; in bunches. ふさふさ

**송이술** undiluted liquor.

**송이재강** lees; grains.

**송장** a dead body; a corpse; a cadaver 《유해》 one's remains／그는 산 ~이다 He is a living corpse.

**송장**(送狀) an invoice; a dispatch note／ 획정 ~ definite bills. おくりじょう

**송장메뚜기** 〖동〗 Patanga succincta(학명). せすぢつちいなご

**송전**(送電) power[electric] transmission; transmission of electricity; electric supply／ ~하다 transmit power; supply the [electric] current／ ~선 a power-transmission line[wire]／ ~ 전차선 a live trolley wire／ ~을 끊다 cut[shut] off the current. そうでん

**송죽**(松竹) pine and bamboo.

**송지**(松脂) pine resin; rosin. しょうし

**송진**(松津) pine resin; rosin. まつやに

**송채**(送綵) sending skirt materials [of red and blue] from the bridegroom to the bride.

**송청**(送廳) committal for trial／ ~하다 send to the procurator's office; commit (a person) for trial.

**송축**(頌祝) admiration and blessing; commendation and benediction／ ~하다 praise and bless. ほめたたえいわうこと

**송충이**(松蟲―) a hairy[pine-eating] caterpillar. まつむし

**송치** a calf in the uterus.

**송치**(送致) sending; dispatch; commitment／ ~하다 send; forward; dispatch; make a commitment／불량 소년의 ~를 받다《소년원이》 receive juvenile delinquents.

**송판**(松板) a pine board. まつのいた

**송편** a rice cake stuffed with bean-jam.

**송풍**(松風) the sighing[whispering] of the wind among the pines; the wind passing through the pine-trees. しょうふう

**송풍**(送風) air-blast; ventilation／ ~기 a blower; a ventilator. そうふう

**송하**(送荷) forwarding; sending; shipment／ ~ 통지 an advice of shipment [sending].

**송화**(松花) pine pollen. まつのはな

**송화**(送話) transmission (of speech)／ ~ 하다 transmit／ ~구 a mouthpiece／ ~기 a [voice] transmitter; a sender／ ~료 telephone charges／ ~선 a transmitting line. そうわ

**송환**(送還) sending back [home]; 《본국에》 deportation 《포로의》 repatriation／ ~하 다 send back; deport; repatriate 《부상병을 본국에》 invalid (one) home. そうかん

**솥** an iron pot; a kettle 《가마솥》 a cauldron／ ~뚜껑 the lid of a kettle; a pot lid. かま

**솥귀** an ear of a kettle. かまのみみ

**솥떔장이** a tinker.

**솥전** the rim of a kettle[pot].

**쇠, 쌔** with a cool gust; briskly; whistling／바람이 ~ 분다 The wind whistles

[hisses, pipes].　びゅっ
**쏼쏼** without stopping; profusely; flowingly/ ~ 흐르다 flow without stopping.　こぢゃこぢゃ
**쇄골(鎖骨)** 《해》 the collarbone; the clavicle.　さこつ
**쇄광기(碎鑛機)** a crushing machine; a crusher.　さいこうき
**쇄국(鎖國)** national isolation; seclusion; exclusion of foreigners/ ~하다 close the country; close the door (to *foreigners*); seclude (*a country*) from the world/ ~ 정책 a national isolation policy; a policy of seclusion/~주의자 a seclusionist.　さこく
**쇄도(殺到)** ruch; a flood/ ~하다 rush in; sweep in; storm; pour in; throng to (습래하다) descend upon.　さっとう
**쇄빙선(碎氷船)** an ice-breaker; an iceboat.　さいひょうせん
**쇄소(灑掃)** watering and sweeping/ ~하다 water down and sweep.
**쇄신(刷新)** reform; renovation; a clean-up/ ~하다 reform; introduce[make] a reform; renovate; innovate; clean up/정계(政界)의 ~ political reform.　さっしん
**쇄신(碎身)** ~하다 exert *one*self to the utmost; do *one's* best; make *one's* best exertions; do everything possible [in one's power].　さいしん
**쇄편(碎片)** a fragment; a splinter; a broken piece.　さいへん
**쇄항(鎖港)** closing the ports/ ~하다 close the ports; exclude foreigners form the ports.　さこう
**쇄환(刷還)** repatriation/ ~하다 repatriate.
**쇠** ①(철) iron; 《화》 Fe. /~의 iron/~빛 reddish-black ②(열쇠) a key/ ~를 채우다 turn a key on; lock ③(지남철) a compass.　てつ
**쇠가죽** oxhide; cowhide.　ぎゅうひ
**쇠고기** beef/ ~ 장수 a butcher.　うしのにく
**쇠고랑** handcuffs; manacles/ ~을 채우다 manacle (*one*); handcuff.
**쇠고래** 《동》 a gray whale.
**쇠고리** (둥근) an iron ring; clasp/ ~를 걸다 fasten the clasp.
**쇠곤(衰困)** exhaustion; fatigue/ ~하다 be exhausted; be fatigued; be tired out.　すいじゃくしてつかれること
**쇠골(一骨)** the brain of cattle.
**쇠공이** an iron pestle; a pounder.
**쇠귀** the ears of a cow/ ~에 경 읽기 《속담》 praying to deaf ears.　うしのみみ
**쇠귀나물** 《식》 an arrow-head; *Sagittaria sagittifolia*(학명).
**쇠기름** beef tallow.
**쇠기침** a chronic cough.　ぜんそく
**쇠나다** ①(솔녹이 슬다) soak into ②(덧나다) develop worse symptoms; get worse; become inflamed.　さびる

**쇠뇌** a bow capable of discharging several arrows at one time.
**쇠다**¹ ①(채소가) (*vegetables*) become tough [and stingy] ②(병이 덧나다) get worse; take a bad turn; take a turn for the worse/윗병이 ~ *one's* stomach trouble becomes worse.　かたくなる
**쇠다**² (명절을) celebrate; observe; keep (*one's birthday*)/성탄절을 ~ keep[commemorate] Christmas/한국에선 설을 쉽니다 New Year's Day is kept as a festival in Korea.
**쐬다** expose [to the sun]; air; bare/이불을 햇볕에 ~ air bedding; let the bedding get some sun.　あたる
**쇠다리** an ox's legs.　うしのあし
**쇠달구** an iron ground-leveler.
**쇠똥**¹ (쇠부스러기) iron slag; dross; scoria.　てっぷん
**쇠똥**² ①cattle dung ②(쇠딱지) dirt an children's heads.　うしのくそ
**쇠로(衰老)** senility; senile decay[weakness]; decrepitude; anility; infirmity of old age/ ~하다 become[grow] senile; become decrepit; become infirm with age; grow old and infirm.　すいろう
**쇠망(衰亡)** ruin; decay; collapse; downfall/ ~하다 fall; decay; go to ruin; be ruined.　すいぼう
**쇠망치** an iron hammer.
**쇠머리** the head of an ox.　うしのあたま
**쇠먹이** fodder; forage; provender.
**쇠멸(衰滅)** decline and fall; go the way to destruction; become extinct.
**쇠못** an iron nail; a nail.　てつくぎ
**쇠몽둥이** an iron rod; a metal rod[bar]; a crow.　てっつい
**쇠몽치** an iron bar; a short metal truncheon.
**쇠뭉치** a clump of iron.
**쇠미(衰微)** decline; wane; ebb tide; decadence/ ~하다 be on the decline[the wane]/ ~하여지다 decline; go to[fall into] decay; wane.　すいび
**쇠백장** a slaughterer; a slaughterman; a butcher.　うしのとさつしゃ
**쇠버짐** a kind of ringworm.　はたけ
**쇠북** a bell (징 따위) a gong/ ~을 치다 strike a bell.
**쇠뿔** an ox horn/ ~은 단김에 빼라 《속담》 Strike the iron while it is hot., Make hay while the sun shines.　うしのつの
**쇠붙이** metal/ ~의 metallic.　きんぞく
**쇠비름** 《식》 a pursla[i]ne.　すべりひゆ
**쇠사슬** a chain (개의)a tether/ ~을 풀다 unchain.　つっさ
**쇠새** 《조》 a kingfisher; a halcyon.
**쇠스랑** a rake; a forked rake.　すき
**쇠약(衰弱)** weakness; debility; sinking; breakdown; emaciation; 《의》 asthenia; collapse/ ~하다 (be) feeble; weak; weakened; debilitated/ ~증 a wasting[consumptive] disease.　すいじゃく

**쇠양배양하다** (be) indiscreet; imprudent; thoughtless. ぶんべつがない

**쇠운**(衰運) declining fortune; the decline of one's fortune; one's waning star. すいうん

**쇠자루** a metal handle.

**쇠잔**(衰殘) ~하다 (쇠약) become emaciated; lose vigour; become enfeebled (쇠퇴) fall off (기운 따위가) sink; wane/ ~한 emaciated; worn-out. すいざん

**쇠족**(一足) ox-hoot.

**쇠죽** boiled food for cattle. うしのしりょう

**쇠줄** iron[steel] wire.

**쇠지레** a crow-bar.

**쇠진**(衰盡) decline; exhaustion; decay; wane; decadence/ ~하다 decline; exhaust; decay; wane; go to[fall into] decay. おとろえつすっかりなくなること

**쇠코뚜레** a nose-block. はながい

**쇠테** an iron[a metal] frame[rim].

**쇠톱** a hack saw.

**쇠통**(一桶) (철통) an iron tub; a tank. てっせいのおけ

**쇠퇴**(衰退) decline; decadence; wane; decay/ ~하다 decline; decay; wane. すいたい

**쇠파리** a warble fly. にくばえ

**쇠패**(衰敗) infirmity of old age; senile decay[weakness]/ ~하다 become[grow] senile; become infirm with age. すいはい

**쇠폐**(衰弊) ruin; downfall; collapse; fall / ~하다 go to[fall into] ruin; fall; be ruined; collapse. すいへい

**쇠푼** a small[petty] sum of money; a little money. わずかなきんせん

**쇠하다**(衰—) (쇠약하다) become weak; lose vigour; be emaciated; be enervated; be broken[run] down; be enfeebled; be weakened; waste away; languish; flay (위축하다) wither (쇠망되다) decline; wane (감퇴하다) fall off. おとろえる

**쇳내** a metallic taste/ ~를 빼다 remove a metallic taste. てっぷんのにおい

**쇳돌** an ore (광물) a mineral. てっぷんをがんゆうしたこうせき

**쇳물** rusty water. てつさびのみず

**쇳소리** a metallic sound/ ~가 나다 sound something metallic. きんぞくのおん

**쇳조각** a piece[a scrap] of iron. てっぺん

**쇳줄** a vein of ore.

**수¹** (수컷) a male (새의) a cock (코끼리·고래·붙소 따위의) a bull/ ~말 a stallion (거세한 말) a horse. おす

**수²** ①(수단) a means[way]; a hand (가능성·능력) possibility; ability; capacity. しゅだん

**수**(手) (장기 따위의) a move. て

**수**(數) ①(운수) luck; fortune/ ~가 좋다 [나쁘다] have good[bad] fortune ②(수효) a number; a figure/ ~ 많은 many; numerous; a great many; a large number of ③(몇) a few; several/ ~년 뒤에 after several[a few] years. すう

**수**(壽) ①(장수) long life; longevity ②(연령) one's age/ ~가 짧다 be short lived. ことぶき

**수**(繡) embroidery/ ~놓다 embroider/ ~를 an embroidery frame. ししゅう

**수**(首) a poem; a piece/ 한 ~을다 compose an ode[a poem]. しゅ

**수간**(樹幹) a trunk; a shaft. じゅかん

**수간**(數間) several[a few] can; a small space/ ~ 두옥 a small house. すうけん

**수감**(隨感) occasional thought[impressions]; random thoughts/ ~록 stray notes; essays. ずいかん

**수감**(收監) confinement; commitment; imprisonment/ ~하다 put in jail; confine; imprison/ ~중이다 be in confinement. しゅうかん

**수갑**(手匣) handcuffs; manacles; darbies《속》/ ~을 채우다 put[slip] handcuffs on (one).

**수갑**(水閘) a lock.

**수강**(受講) attendance [at a lecture]/ ~하다 attend at a lecture; listen to (a lecture). じゅこう

**수개**(數個) several (items); a few (pieces). すうこ

**수개**(修改) repair; mending/ ~하다 repair; mend; improve.

**수건**(手巾) a towel/ ~걸이 a towel-hanger. てふき

**수검**(搜檢) inspection; examination/ ~하다 inspect; examine.

**수결**(手決) a signature; a monogram; a written seal/ ~두다 sign; affix one's signature. しょめい

**수경**(水耕) hydroponics; tank farming/ ~ 농장 a hydroponic farm.

**수계**(授戒) 【불】 Buddhist confirmation; the consecration ceremony; giving commandments [of Buddhism]. じゅかい

**수계**(水系) water system; river system; the waters.

**수계**(受戒) 【불】 receiving Buddhist confirmation. じゅかい

**수고** trouble; labour; pains; efforts; service; toil/ ~하다 take pains[trouble]; (진력) do (one) a service/ ~를 아끼지 않다 spare no efforts (to do); do not mind work. しんく

**수고롭다** (be) troublesome; toilsome; laborious; tiresome; painstaking/수고롭지만 이 편지를 좀 부쳐 주시겠습니까 May I trouble you to post this letter for me?

**수고스럽다** (be) troublesome; toilsome; hard; labo[u]rious; painful/수고스럽지만… I am sorry to trouble you, but….

**수공**(手工) manual work[training]; handiwork; handicraft/ ~ 교육 manual training/ ~업 manual trade[labor] / ~업자 a handicraftsman/ ~업품 handiworks/ ~품 a piece of handiwork/ ~이 들다 take much trouble; involve much labo[u]r. しゅこう

**수공**(水攻) flooding／ ～하다 flood／성을 ～하다 flood a castle. みずぜめ

**수관**(水管) a water-pipe[-main]; a spout; a conduit. すいかん

**수괴**(首魁) a ringleader; a chief. しゅかい

**수괴**(羞愧) shame; humiliation; disgrace. はずべきこと

**수교**(手交) handing／ ～하다 hand over (*a thing*) directly; deliver into one's hands; hand over (*to*). しゅこう

**수교**(修交) amity; friendship; friendly relations. しゅうこう

**수구**(守舊) conservatism; adherence to traditional customs／ ～하다 be conservative／ ～ 세력 conservative force／ ～파 the conservatives.

**수구**(水球) (경기) water polo. すいきゅう

**수구**(壽具) graveclothes; cerements. かりもがり

**수국**(水國) a flooded[flood-stricken] district; a watery area. すいこく

**수국**(水菊) 〖식〗 a hydrangea. あじさい

**수군**(水軍) the naval forces. すいぐん

**수군거리다** talk in whispers; talk in an undertone; have secret counsel／수군수군 in an undertone; secretly. ささやく

**수궁**(守宮) 〖동〗 a gecko(*pl*. -oes, -os); a wall-lizard. やもり

**수권**(水圏) the hydrosphere. すいけん

**수그러지다** ①(머리가) become low; lower; drop; sink ②(바람의 강세가) go(die, calm) down; subside; abate ③(병세가) be suppressed; be put down; be subdued ④(분노 따위가) be appeased ⑤(더위가) abate. うつむく

**수그리다** lower; drop; hang [one's head] ／그는 머리를 수그리고서 걷고 있었다 He walked keeping her head down. たれる

**수금**(水禽) a water-bird[-fowl]. すいきん

**수금**(囚禁) confinement; commitment; imprisonment／ ～하다 put in jail; confine; imprison. しゅうきん

**수금**(收金) collection [of money]; bill-collection／ ～하다 collect money[bills] ／ ～인 a bill-collector／ ～이 잘 되다 The collection of bills is good. しゅうきん

**수급**(需給) demand and supply／ ～ 계획 a supply and demand program. じゅきゅう

**수급**(首級) a decapitated head. しゅきゅう

**수급자**(受給者) a recipient (of *a pension*).

**수긍**(首肯) assent; consent; a nod [in approval]／～하다 nod assent; assent to; give consent; be convinced of ([해)) understand. しゅこう

**수기**(水氣) dampness ⇒물기. すいき

**수기**(手技) skill; art. しゅぎ

**수기**(手記) a note; a memorandum (*pl.* -da, -dums)／ ～를 적다 note[put] down; take notes of; make a memorandum of. しゅき

**수기**(手旗) a flag／ ～ 신호 flag signaling [semaphore]; flag-wagging《속》. しゅき

**수기목** 〖식〗 a Japanese cedar; a cryptomeria ⇒으루나무. すぎのき

**수나다** hit a jackpot; have unexpected luck.

**수나사** a male screw.

**수난**(受諾) acceptance ⇒수락(受諾).

**수난**(水難) a disaster by water／ ～ 구조 rescue at sea／ ～을 당하다 (배가 조난하다) be drowned (배가 조난하다) be shipwrecked. すいなん

**수난**(受難) sufferings; crucifixion; ordeals; severe trial; misfortune／ ～일 Good Friday. じゅなん

**수납**(受納) acceptance; receipt／ ～하다 accept; receive／ ～자 a recipient.

**수낭**(水囊) a water-bag. すいのう

**수냉식**(水冷式) ～의 water-cooled／ ～ 엔진 water-cooled engine.

**수녀**(修女) a sister of charity／ ～가 되다 take the veil.

**수년**(數年) some[a number of, several, a few] years／ ～간 for some years／ ～ 전 some years ago. すうねん

**수놈** a male. おす

**수뇌**(首腦) (수뇌자) the head; the brains ／한국 정부의 ～ the heads of the Korean Government. しゅのう

**수뇨관**(輸尿管) 〖해〗 the urethra.／～염(炎) 〖의〗 urethritis. ゆにょうかん

**쑤다** cook (*hot cereal, porridge*); boil; prepare; make／풀을 ～ prepare paste.

**수다**(數多) ①(다수) a great many; plenty; a heap; a mass (다량) plenty; an abundance／ ～하다 (다수) (be) [a great] many; a large number of; numerous 《다량》 (be) much; a great[good] deal of (여러 가지) (be) various; varieties of ②(말이 많음) garrulity; loguacity; loquaciousness; talkativeness; volubility／ ～하다 (be) garrulous; chatty; loquacious; talkative／ ～장이 a talkative person; a tattler; a prattler; a babbler (여자 등의) a chatter-box. すうた

**수다스럽다**(數多―) (be) talkative; garrulous; wordy; prattling; chattering／그 여자는 여간 수다스럽지 않다 she is a confirmed gossip.

**수단**(手段) a means; a measure; a way; a step (궁리) device (방편) an expedient; a shift／정당한 ～ a justifiable means[step]／～과 방법 ways and means／부정한 ～ a foul means ／외교적 ～ diplomatic means[steps, moves] ／비열한 ～ a dirty trick／최후의 ～ the last measure[shift, resort] ／갖은 ～을 다 쓰다 exhaust every means; leave no means untried／그 외에는 ～이 없다 No other means[No alternative] is left. ／할 수 있는 ～을 다하다 take all possible steps; adopt all the means in one's power. しゅだん

**수단추** a male snap[fastener]; a stud; a button.

**수달**(水獺) 〖동〗 an otter／~피 an otter skin[fur]. あざらし

**수답**(水畓) a paddy field; a wet field. みずのあるすいでん

**수당**(手當) an allowance 《상여》 a bonus／가족 ~ a family allowance／근무지 ~ a duty place allowance／연말 ~ a year-end bonus／초과 근무 ~ overtime allowance／퇴직 ~ a retiring[severance] allowance／~이 많다 have a good allowance／~을 주다 give an allowance／시간외 근무에는 초과 ~을 받는다 You are paid extra for overtime. てあて

**수더분하다** (be) simple and honest; artless; unsophisticated; naive／수더분한 시골 노인 an old countryman; simple and honest by nature. そぼくだ

**수도**(水道) ①《설비》 water works; water service[supply]; 《수로》 an aqueduct; a water duct; a water course 《용수》 city water; service water; service pipes／~ 공사 water[·supply] works／~료 water rates[charges]／~료 city[service] water／~ 수원지(水源地) a catchment area／~ 철관 a water pipe; a water main; a water lines／~를 놓다 have water pipes laid; have water supplied／~를 틀다[잠그다] turn on[off] water. すいどう

**수도**(水稻) a waterfield[moist·land] rice plant; aquatic rice. すいとう

**수도**(受渡) receipt and delivery／~하다 [receive payment and] deliver (goods); transfer (property); hand over. うけわたし

**수도**(囚徒) a prisoner; a convict; an inmate; a jailbird. しゅうと

**수도**(首都) a capital [city]; a metropolis／한국의 ~ 서울 Seoul, capital of Korea. しゅと

**수도**(修道) cultivation of oneself; asceticism; spiritual discipline／~사 a monk; a friar／~ 생활 monasticism; monastery life／~승 a monk／~원 a monastery; a cloister 《수녀원》 a convent; a nunnery／~원장 an archimandrite／~회 order [of religious regulations]; congregation. しゅうどう

**수도**(隧道) a tunnel. トンネル

**수동**(受動) passivity; passiveness／~의 passive／~적으로 passively／~성 범죄 〖법〗 a passive crime／~태(態) 〖언〗 the passive voice／그는 ~적인 기질의 소유자다 He is man of passive disposition. じゅどう

**수동**(手動) ~의 hand·operated[·worked]／~ 펌프 a hand·pump. じゅどう

**수두**(水痘) 〖의〗 chicken pox; varicella. みずぼうそう

**수두룩하다** (많다) (be) abundant; plentiful 《흔하다》 be [very, quite] common; met with everywhere. きわめておおい

**수득수득** dried up hard[severely]／~하다 be all dried up. かさかさ

**수들수들** dried up partially／~하다 be partially dried up; be [a bit] withered. かさかさ

**수라**(水刺) a royal repast.

**수라장**(修羅場) a scene of bloodshed[strife]／~이 되다 be turned into shambles. しゅらじょう

**수락**(受諾) acceptance／~하다 accept; agree (to)／취임을 ~하다 accept the post (of). じゅだく

**수란**(水卵) a soft·boiled egg; a poached egg. はんじゅくのたまご

**수란관**(輸卵管) 〖해〗 the Fallopian tube; the oviduct. ゆらんかん

**수람**(收攬) grasping／~하다 take hold of; grasp; win. しゅうらん

**수량**(水量) water volume／~계 a water·gauge. すいりょう

**수량**(數量) quantity; volume; measure／~이 불다[줄다] increase[decrease] in quantity.

**수럭수럭** lively; vivacious／~하다 (be) lively; vivacious. はきはき

**수럭스럽다** (be) vivacious; lively; cheerful; gay; sprightly. いきいきしている

**수렁** a swamp; a marsh; a bog; a marshy place.

**수레** a waggon; a dray; a cart. くるま

**수려**(秀麗) grace; beauty／~하다 (be) graceful; beautiful; handsome; fine; comely／~한 산 모습이 보인다 We see the graceful figure of the mountain. しゅうれい

**수력**(水力) water[hydraulic] power／~ 발전소 a hydroelectric[water] power station／~ 전기 hydroelectricity／~ 기계 hydraulic machinery. すいりょく

**수련**(修練) training; practice; drill; discipline culture／~하다 practice; train; cultivate. しゅれん

**수련**(睡蓮) 〖식〗 a water·lily. すいれん

**수련하다** (be) gentle; tender; meek; kind; sweet／마음이 수련한 소녀 a kindhearted girl. おとなしい

**수렴**(收斂) ①《추렴》 joint contribution; sharing the expense／~하다 collect together; pool; contribute jointly ②《가세(苛稅)》 levying and collecting of heavy taxes; exaction／~하다 exact; collect strictly ③《오그라듦》 astriction; contraction; 〖물·생·수〗 convergence／~하다 be astringent ④《행동의》 sobriety; continence／~하다 sober down; be continent. あつめること

**수렵**(狩獵) hunting 《총렵》 shooting／~하다 hunt; follow game; have a hunt 《새를》 shoot／~가 a sportsman; a hunter／~ 금지기 the close season／~지(地) a hunting·ground. しゅりょう

**수령**(守令) a magistrate; a local governor.

**수령**(首領) the head; a leader; the chief; a boss 《속》／정당의 ~이 되다 assume the leadership of.

**수령(受領)** acceptance; receipt; acknowledg[e]ment/ ~하다 accept; receive; be in receipt (of); be placed in one's hands/ ~증 a receipt. じゅりょう

**수령(樹齢)** the age of a tree. じゅれい

**수로(水路)** a waterway; a water-course [-route]; a channel 《항해로》 a lane/ ~ 표시 a beacon. すいろ

**수록(收錄)** gethering; collection 《기재》 recording; mention/ ~하다 gather; collect 《기재》 record; write down; mention. しゅうろく

**수뢰(水雷)** a torpedo 《부설》 [naval] a mine/ ~정 a torpedo boat; a mosquito boat. すいらい

**수뢰(受賂)** accepting a bribe/ ~하다 accept a bribe. じゅぞう

**수료(修了)** completion/ ~하다 complete; finish/제 2학년을 ~하다 finish the second-year course. しゅうりょう

**수류(獸類)** beasts; animals; brutes/ ~의 bestial. じゅうるい

**수류(水流)** a current; a watercourse; a flow.

**수류탄(手榴彈)** a hand-bomb[-grenade]; a pineapple 《속》/ ~병 a grenade-thrower/ ~을 던지다 throw a hand grenade at (a person). しゅりゅうだん

**수륙(水陸)** land and water/ ~ 공동 작전 amphibious operation/ ~ 양서 동물 an amphibian; an amphibious animal. すいりく

**수르르** smoothly; easily/~ 풀어지다 《허리띠가》 slip off. すらすら

**수리 《조》** an eagle/ ~부엉이 an eagle-owl. いぬわし

**수리(修理)** repair; mending/ ~하다 repair; make repairs; mend; fix 《미·구》/ ~ 공장 a repair shop/ ~중이다 be under repair; be undergoing repair/시계를 ~하다 have a watch mended. しゅうり

**수리(水利)** utilization of water; water supply 《관개》 irrigation 《운송》 water transport; water-carriage/ ~ 조합 an irrigation association. すいり

**수리(受理)** acceptance/ ~하다 accept; receive; take up/사건을 ~하다 take cognizance of a case. じゅり

**수리(數理)** a mathematical principle/~학 mathematics. すうり

**수리수리** ~하다 have one's sight dimmed with fever; (be) feverish. ぼんやり

**수리치** 《식》 a kind of marsh plant; Synurus deltoides 《학명》. やまぼち

**수림(樹林)** a wood; a grove; a forest/ ~ 속을 헤매다 wander about in the woods. しんりん

**수립(樹立)** establishment; founding; setting-up/ ~하다 establish; found; set up; plant. じゅりつ

**수마(睡魔)** somnolence; Morpheus; the sandman 《의인적으로》 the dustman 《졸음》 sleepiness; drowsiness. すいま

**수마(水魔)** a flood; an inundation.

**수만(數萬)** tens[scores] of thousands/ ~의 청중 scores of thousands of spectators. すうまん

**수맥(水脈)** a water-vein; a [subterranean] channel. すいみゃく

**수면(水面)** the surface of the water; the sea-level/ ~에 뜨다 come up[rise] to the surface of the water. すいめん

**수면(睡眠)** sleep; slumber/~하다 sleep; slumber; have a sleep/ ~ 시간 hours of sleep/ ~ 부족 lack of sleep/ ~제 a sleeping drug[draught]. すいみん

**수명(壽命)** life; the length of life [one's days]; the span of life/사람의 평균 ~ the average span of a man's life. じゅみょう

**수모(受侮)** scorn; disdain; slight/ ~하다 be insulted; be humiliated; suffer insult[humiliation]. ぶじょくをうけること

**수모(誰某)** certain ones; so and so. たれがし

**수모(手母)** a bridesmaid.

**수모자(首謀者)** a ringleader; a prime mover; the chief plotter. しゅぼうしゃ

**수목(樹木)** trees [and shrubs]; arbors/ ~이 우거진 woody; wooded (hill); arboreous. じゅもく

**수묵(水墨)** ①《먹》pale Indian ink ②《묵화》a painting in Indian ink. すいぼく

**수문(水紋)** a [water-]ring. すいもん

**수문(水門)** a sluice; a flood-gate; a lock. すいもん

**수문(手紋)** 《손금》 the lines in the palm of the hand. しゅもん

**수문(守門)** gate-keeping/ ~하다 keep the gate.

**수문 수답(隨問隨答)** a ready[prompt] answer to a question/ ~하다 make a prompt reply to a question.

**수미(首尾)** beginning and end; alpha and omega. しゅび

**수미(愁眉)** the knitted eyebrow; a worried look. しゅうび

**수밀(水密)** ~의 watertight/ ~ 시험 a watertight test. すいみつ

**수밀도(水蜜桃)** a peach. すいみっとう

**수박** a water-melon/ ~ 겉 핥기 a superficial knowledge; a smattering. すいか

**수반(水盤)** a flower tray. すいばん

**수반(隨伴)** accompaniment; concomitance/~하다 accompany; go[come] with; be concomitant with/ ~자 an attendant; a follower 《총칭》 a suit. ずいはん

**수반(首班)** the head [position]/ ~이 되다 stand at the head; head the list/ 내각 ~ the chief executive. しゅはん

**수발(鬚髪)** beard and hair. あごひげととうはつ

**수방석(繡方席)** an embroidered cushion.

**수배(手配)** disposition of men 《경찰의》 search instruction/~하다 make dispositions for. てはい

**수배(數倍)** several times/~가 되다 increase several times.

**수백**(數百) hundreds／ ～명 several hundred people. すうひゃく

**수범**(首犯) a principal [offender]／그가 ～이다 He committed the offence as the principal. はんにんのかしら

**수범**(垂範) setting an example／ ～하다 set an example／솔선 ～하다 take the initiative and set an example (to *others*). すいはん

**수법**(手法) technique; technical skill; mechanism; style; mannerism. しゅほう

**수변**(水邊) the water's edge; the edge of the water; the waterside. すいへん

**수병**(繡屛) an embroidered folding screen.

**수병**(水兵) a sailor; a seaman; a blue jacket; a [Jack] tar《속》; a devil dog 《미·속》／ ～모 a sailor['s] hat／ ～복 a sailor suit〔uniform〕／1등〔2등〕～ a first 〔second〕class seaman. すいへい

**수보**(修補) repairing; mending／ ～하다 repair; mend; patch. しゅうほ

**수보다**(數—) tell〔read〕 *one's* fortune; have *one's* fortune told. こううんにあう

**수복**(收復) reclamation; recovery／ ～하다 reclaim; recover; repatriate／ ～민 repatriated people／ ～ 지구 a reclaimed area.

**수복**(修復) ～하다 repair; mend 《답장하다》 reply.

**수복**(壽福) good fortune blessed with longevity 《수와 복》 longevity and happiness／～ 강녕 longevity; happiness and healthiness. ちょうじゅのこうふく

**수부**(水夫) a sailor; a seaman／ ～장 a boatswain. すいふ

**수부**(首府) the capital 《상업상의》 the metropolis. しゅふ

**수부종** planting seed directly in a paddy [without transplanting]／ ～하다 plant seed directly in a paddy.

**수북수북** so that all are heaped up／ ～ 하다 all are heaped up／밥을 ～ 담다 fill a bowl heaping full of rice.

**수북하다** (be) filled to the brim; brimful; in a heap／수북히 to overflowing; to the brim.

**수분**(水分) moisture; water; juice／ ～을 흡수하다 suck up water. すいぶん

**수분**(守分) ～하다 be content with *one's* lot; keep to *one's* status in life. しょくぶんをまもること

**수분**(授粉, 受粉) 【식】 pollination／ ～하 다 pollinate／인공 ～ artificial pollination. じゅふん

**수불**(受拂) receipts and disbursements [payments]／ ～하다 receive and pay. うけばらい

**수비**(守備) defence; defensive preparations; 【체】 fielding／～하다 defend; guard; garrison／～병 a garrison; guards. しゅび

**수빙**(樹氷) silver thaw.

**수사**(修士) a monk; a regular; a friar. しゅうどうし

**수사**(修辭) rhetoric; a figure of speech; a rhetorical flourish／ ～학 rhetoric／ ～학자 a rhetorician／～적 기교 a rhetorical device／ ～학상의 rhetorical. しゅうじ

**수사**(數詞) 【언】 numerals. すうし

**수사**(手寫) copying／～하다 copy／～본 a written copy. しゅしゃ

**수사**(搜査) search; detection; investigation／ ～하다 investigate; search[look] for／～과 a criminal investigation section／범죄 ～ criminal investigation. そうさ

**수사납다** (be) unlucky; unfortunate. あくうんだ

**수사돈**(—査頓) the father of *one's* son-in-law. むこのちち

**수산**(授産) providing work; industrial training／～하다 provide work. じゅさん

**수산**(水産) aquatic products; marine products／ ～업 the marine products industry／ ～ 조합 an aquatic products guild. すいさん

**수산**(蓚酸) 【화】 oxalic acid／～철 oxalate ／～염 oxalate. しゅうさん

**수산화**(水酸化) 【화】 hydration／ ～물 a hydroxide／ ～아연 zinc hydroxide／ ～철 hydrated iron／～칼슘 calcium hydroxide. すいさんか

**수삼**(水蔘) raw ginseng.

**수삼차**(數三次) several times.

**수상**(水上) 《물 위》water surface 《상류》 the upper reaches of a river／ ～ 경기 aquatic[water] sports／ ～ 경찰 the water police ／ ～목 timber carried downriver on floats／～ [비행]기 a waterplane; a seaplane; a hydro·air·plane; a hydro《구》／ ～ 생활 aquatic life／ ～ 선수권 the swimming[aquatic] championship／～ 운송 transportation by water／ ～에 뜨다 float on the water. すいじょう

**수상**(首相) the Premier; the Prime Minister／ ～ 관저 the official residence of the Prime Minister. しゅしょう

**수상**(受像) a tele[television]·image／ ～ 기(機) a television receiver. じゅぞう

**수상**(手相) the lines of the palm／ ～술 palmistry; chiromancy. しゅもん

**수상**(受賞) receiving a prize[reward]／ ～하다 win[receive] a prize; be awarded a prize／～자 a prizeman; a prize·winner 《박람회 따위의》a medal·winner. じゅしょう

**수상**(授賞) awarding a prize; prize giving; recognition／ ～하다 award[give] a prize; recognize. じゅしょう

**수상**(隨想) occasional[random, stray] thoughts／ ～록 essays; stray notes. ずいそう

**수상**(殊常) suspiciousness; strangeness／ ～하다 (be) suspicious[·looking]; dubi-

수상스럽다 ous; doubtful; questionable; strange; peciliar (이상) queer／〜한 자 a suspicious[-looking] fellow／〜히 여기다 have a doubt; be doubtful of[about]; suspect; feel suspicious about (one). あやしいこと

**수상스럽다**(殊常—) (be) suspicious; doubtful; dubious; odd; peculiar.

**수색**(羞色) a blush; an ashamed look. はじらいをおびたかお

**수색**(愁色) a worried look; melancholy [gloomy] air／〜을 띠다 wear a worried look; look concerned[anxious, gloomy, worried]. しゅうしょく

**수색**(搜索) a search; searching; a hunt 《임검》 a raid／〜하다 search; look; hunt; make a search for; raid／〜영장 a search-warrant／가택 〜 a domiciliary visit. そうさく

**수생**(水生) aquatic; living[growing] in water.

**수서**(水棲) aquatic; living in water／〜 동물 an aquatic animal. すいせい

**수서**(手書) *one's* own handwriting; an autographic [letter]. しゅしょ

**수석**(首席) 《사람》the head; the chief 《석》the top[head] seat／〜의 head; chief; senior／〜 판사 the chief judge. しゅせき

**수선** fuss; ado; bustle／〜부리다 make a fuss; fuss; make much ado; bustle about／〜하다 (be) fussy; noisy／〜떨다 make a fuss; fuss; bustle; make much ado 《까불다》frolic／〜장이 a fussy person.

**수선**(垂線) 《수》a perpendicular [line]. すいせん

**수선**(修繕) repair; mending／〜하다 repair; mend 《수선시키다》get mended[repaired]／〜비 repair expenses／〜 공장 a repairshop／〜중이다 be under repair; be being repaired. しゅうぜん

**수선화**(水仙花) 《식》a daffodil; a jonquil; a narcissus. すいせんか

**수성**(水性) the property of water／〜 도료 water paint. すいせい

**수성**(水星) Mercury. すいせい

**수성**(水成) ¶ 바위가 〜인 hydrogenous／ 〜 광상 a sedimentary deposit／〜암 aqueous rock; sedimentary rock.

**수성**(獸性) beastliness; bestiality; brutality／〜적인 bestial; brutal／〜화하 다 animalize; bestialize; brutalize. じゅうせい

**수세**(受洗) 《기독교》receiving[taking] baptism／〜하다 be baptized. じゅせん

**수세**(水勢) the force of water[a current]. すいせい

**수세**(水洗) washing; flushing／〜하다 wash／〜식 변소 a flush toilet; a water closet (略：W.C.).

**수세**(收稅) collection of taxes; tax collection; taxation／〜하다 collect[gather] taxes／〜과 the section of revenue.

**수세**(守勢) the defensive position／〜를 취하다 take[assume] the defensive; remain on the defensive. しゅせい

**수세미** a scrubbing-brush／〜외 a snake [towel] gourd. たわし

**수소** a bull; an ox. おうし

**수소**(水素) 《화》hydrogen／〜 가스 hydrogen gas／〜산 hydracid／〜 폭탄 a hydrogen bomb; an H-bomb; a fusion bomb／〜 화물 a hydride／중~ heavy hydrogen. すいそ

**수소문**(搜所聞) inquiring into rumors／ 〜하다 inquire into rumors／〜하여 잃은 아이를 찾다 search for a lost child by tracing rumors.

**수속**(手續) process; procedure; formalities; steps 《소송의》proceedings／〜하다 go through formalities; take steps; take proceedings／입항[출항] 〜 clearance inwards[outwards]／입학 〜 entrance formalities. てつづき

**수송**(輸送) transport[ation]; conveyance ／〜하다 convey; transport; deport; carry／〜기 a transport plane／〜난 transport difficulties／〜량 the volume of traffic; carloadings／〜력 transport capacity／〜로 a transport route ／〜 보험 transport insurance／〜선 (船) a line of transportation／〜선(船) a transport ship／〜 시설 transportation facilities／〜 열차 a transport train／ 항공 〜 air transport; airlift／군대를 〜 하다 transport[convey] troops. ゆそう

**수쇠** the pivot of a quern.

**수수** 《식》Indian millet. もろこし

**수수**(授受) giving and receiving; delivery or receipt; transfer／〜하다 deliver or receive; deliver; transfer. じゅじゅ

**수수께끼** a riddle; an enigma; a puzzle; a quiz／〜의 인물 a mysterious man／ 〜 같은 enigmatic; puzzling; mysterious／〜를 풀다 solve[work] a riddle; puzzle out. なぞなぞ

**수수료**(手數料) a fee; a commission; brokerage. てすうりょう

**수수 방관**(袖手傍觀) indifferent observation／〜하다 look on with folded arms; stand idle／〜하고 있을 때가 아니 다 This is no time for us to remain idle. しゅうしゅぼうかん

**수수하다**¹ 《맵시 따위가》(be) plain; quiet; sober; simple; modest; moderate 《보수 적》conservative 《검소하다》frugal／수수 한 옷 a quite dress. ふつうだ

**수수하다**² 《시끄럽다》(be) noisy; clamourous; tumultuous. さわしい

**수술** 《식》a stamen. おしべ

**수술**(手術) an[a surgical] operation／〜 하다 operate on (one) for; perform surgical operation／〜실 an operating room／〜비 charges for an operation ／대 〜 a major operation. しゅじゅつ

**수습**(收拾) control; coping (*with*)／〜하

다 deal[cope] (*with*); control; have in hand／시국을 ~하다 save[cope with] the situation; have the situation in hand／인심을 ~하다 win the hearts of the people.　　　　　しゅうじゅう

**수습(修習)** apprenticeship; probation／~하다 receive training; practise *oneself* (*at*)／~ 제도 service training system〈미〉.

**수시(隨時)** 《부사적》at any time 《필요에 응해서》on demand; as occasion calls／~ 응변으로 as occasion arises[demands, calls]／~ 변통하여 accommodating *oneself* to circumstances.　　ずいじ

**쑤시다** ①(아프다) twinge; tingle; smart; prickle; feel prickly; feel sharp pains／다리가 ~ have a twinge in *one's* leg／이가 ~ I have a toothache., My teeth ache. ②(찌르다) pick; poke／이를 ~ pick *one's* teeth.　　さす

**수식(水蝕)** erosion／~ 방지 preparations against erosion.　　すいしょく

**수식(修飾)** ornamentation; embellishment; 《언》 modification／~하다 embellish; ornament; modify／ ~어 《언》 a modifier.　　しゅうしょく

**수신(水神)** 《여신》a naiad; the god of water; a water-nymph.　　すいじん

**수신(受信)** the receipt of a message; reception／~하다 receive a message[letter]／ ~인 an addressee／~기 a receiver; a receiving set.

**수신(修身)** morals 《수양》 moral training／~책 a text-book on morals／~ 강화 a lecture on morals.　　しゅうしん

**수신 제가(修身齊家)** moral training and home management／~하다 order *one's* life and manage *one's* household.
　　　　　　　　　　　　　しゅうしんせいか

**수심(水深)** the depth of water／ ~계 a hydrobarometer／~이 20미터다 The water is 20 meters deep.　　すいしん

**수심(獸心)** a bestial mind; a brutal heart／인면(人面) ~ man in face; brute in mind; a beast with a human face.
　　　　　　　　　　　　　じゅうしん

**수심(垂心)** 《수》 an orthocenter. すいしん

**수심(愁心)** worry; anxiety; gloom; melancholy; sorrow; heaviness of mind／~에 잠기다 be in a state of deep anxiety; be lost in apprehension.　　しゅうい

**수십(數十)** scores／ ~년 scores of years.
　　　　　　　　　　　　　すうじゅう

**수알치새** 《조》 a horned owl; a long-eared owl.　　　　　　　　わしみみづく

**수압(水壓)** water[hydraulic] pressure／~계 a water-pressure gauge; a piezometer／ ~관 a hydraulic pipe／ ~ 기관 a hydromotor／~이 약하다 The water pressure is low.　　すいあつ

**수액(水厄)** a disaster by water; a deluge.　　　　　　　　みずによるさいやく

**수액(樹液)** sap [of a tree]; milk／ ~이 많은 sapful; sappy.　　じゅえき

**수약(水藥)** a liquid medicine.

**수양(收養)** adoption; fostering／~하다 adopt; fostering／ ~ 아들[딸] a foster-son [-daughter]; an adopted-son[-daughter]／ ~ 아버지[어머니] a foster father [mother].　　しゅうよう

**수양(修養)** culture; cultivation／ ~하다 improve *oneself*[*one's* mind]; cultivate; train／ ~서 a book on self-culture／ 정신 ~ mental culture／정신을 ~하다 improve[cultivate] *one's* mind(character)／ ~을 쌓다 do a great deal in self-culture.　　しゅうよう

**수양버들(垂楊─)** the weeping willow.
　　　　　　　　　　　　　しだれやなぎ

**수어(數語)** several words; a few words.

**수업(受業)** taking lessons; receiving instruction／ ~하다 receive instruction; take lessons; be taught.　　じゅぎょう

**수업(授業)** teaching; instruction; school [work]; lessons／ ~하다 teach; instruct give lessons／ ~료 school-fee; tuition-fee／ ~ 시간 school-hours／ ~중에 during school hours／~을 받다 be taught; take lessons.　　じゅぎょう

**수업(修業)** study; pursuit 《수료》 completion of a course／ ~하다 study; prosecute *one's* studies 《수료하다》 complete a course／ ~ 연한 a term of school years; a course of study. しゅうぎょう

**수없다** ①(도리없다) be unable to do; (be) impossible; helpless ②(재수없다) (be) unlucky; unfortunate／나는 그 문제를 풀 수 없었다 The problem was utterly beyond me.／그건 도저히 참을 ~ It is more than I can bear.／인간의 힘으로 할 수 없는 것은 없다 Human power is equal to anything.　　ほうほうがない

**수없다(數─)** (무수하다) (be) innumerable; countless; numberless／수없이 innumerably; countlessly; without number (with *a thing*).　　かぞえられない

**수여(授與)** awarding; conferment; distribution／~하다 confer (*a degree* on *a person*); award(*a medal*); give; grant; present (*a thing* to *a person*)／학위를 ~하다 confer a degree on (*a person*)／졸업 증서를 ~하다 present a diploma. じゅよ

**수여리** 《충》 a queen bee.　　めばち

**수역(水域)** waters／중립 ~ neutral waters.　　　　　　　　　　　すいいき

**수역(殊域)** a foreign country[land]; alien parts.

**수역(獸疫)** a cattle-disease[-plague]; an epizootic.　　　　　　　　じゅうえき

**수연(水鉛)** 《화》 wulfenite; molybdenum (기호: Mo).　　　　　　　　すいえん

**수연(水煙)** water spray[mist].　すいえん

**수연(垂涎)** watering at the mouth／ ~하다 covet; hanker after; long for; (*one's*) mouth) water for (*a thing*).　　すいえん

**수연(晬宴)** a banquet given in celebration of *one's* birth; the celebration of a birth.

**수예**(手藝) manual arts; handicrafts／~품(品) fancy works. しゅげい

**수온**(水溫) [water] temperature. すいおん

**수완**(手腕) ability; skill; capability; talent／~가 a man of capacity; an able man／~있는 able; capable; talented. しゅわん

**수요**(需要) demand; request; want; requirement／~와 공급 supply and demand. じゅよう

**수요일**(水曜日) Wednesday. すいようび

**수욕**(水浴) bathing／~하다 take a bathe (in a river); bathe. すいよく

**수욕**(獸慾) animal[carnal] desires; sexual appetite; lust／~을 채우다 satisfy one's carnal desires. じゅうよく

**수욕**(受辱) ~하다 be[get] humiliated; be insulted; be disgraced.

**수욕**(羞辱) humiliation; shame; disgrace. はずかしいこと

**수용**(水溶) (being) water soluble／~성 solubility in water.

**수용**(收用) expropriation／~하다 expropriate／토지 ~법 the law of expropriation of land. しゅうよう

**수용**(收容) accommodation; admission; reception 《불량 소년 등의》 consignment; custody／~하다 take in; accommodate; admit; hold; seat 《형무소에》
a concentration camp 《귀환자의》 a repatriate reception center／~인원 the number of persons to be admitted／~자《양로원 따위의》 inmates 《병원의》 patients 《형무소의》 a prisoner.
commit 《a person》 to jail／~ 능력 capacity; accommodation／~ 좌석 a seating capacity／~소 a home; an asylum 《포로의》

**수용**(受容) acceptance; recipiency／~하다 accept; receive／~성 receptivity; receptiveness. しゅうよう

**수용**(需用) consumption／~자 a consumer. じゅよう

**수우**(水牛) a buffalo. 물소.

**수우**(殊遇) special treatment; cordial treatment; a warm reception 《애고》 [high] favour／~를 받다 receive a cordial treatment; be in great favour with 《one》. とくべつなたいぐう

**수운**(水運) water transportation／~의 편리가 좋다 have[enjoy] good water transportation facilities. すいうん

**수원**(水源) the sourse[head] of a river 《수도의》 a sourse of water supply／~지(地) a watershed; the head-waters. すいげん

**수원**(隨員) [a member of] one's suite; an attendant 《집합적》 a suite; a retinue／~을 데리고 accompanied by one's suite. ずいいん

**수월**(數月) several months.

**수월내기** a formidable person; a man of no mean strength. あつかいやすいひと

**수월스럽다** (be) easy; not hard; not tough.

**수월찮다** (be) not easy; not simple; hard; be some trouble. ないがしろにできない

**수월하다** (be) easy; simple; light／수월한 일이 아니다 be no easy thing to 《do》. たやすい

**수위**(首位) the premier[leading] position; the first place／~를 차지하다 occupy [the] first place; hold [the] first position. しゅい

**수위**(水位) water-level／~표 a water gauge.

**수위**(守衛) a guard 《문지기》 a door-keeper／~장 the chief guard／~실 a guard office; a [porter's] lodge. しゅえい

**수유**(須臾) a little while. 잠시. しばらく

**수유**(授乳) nursing／~하다 nurse; suckle 《a baby》; give the breast to 《a baby》／~기(期) the lactation. じゅにゅう

**수유관**(輸乳管) 〖해〗 a lactiferous duct.

**수유자**(受遺者) 〖법〗《동산의》 a legatee 《부동산의》 a devisee.

**수육** cooked beef. むしにく

**수육**(獸肉) meat; flesh of animals. じゅうにく

**수은**(受恩) reception of favo[u]rs／~하다 receive favor; receive kindness. おんけいをうけること

**수은**(水銀) 〖화〗 mercury; quicksilver (기호: Hg)／~ 온도계 a mercury thermometer／~주(柱) a column of mercury 《온도계의》 the mercury. すいぎん

**수음**(手淫) self-abuse; masturbation; onanism／~하다 practise masturbation; masturbate; commit self-abuse. しゅいん

**수음**(樹陰) the shade of a tree. こかげ

**수응**(酬應) ~하다 meet the demand of others; give as requested.

**수의**(壽衣, 襚衣) grave-clothes; a shroud.

**수의**(遂意) accomplishment of one's purpose／~하다 fulfil one's wish; realize a hope; have 《a thing》 as one wishes.

**수의**(隨意) voluntariness; option; pleasure／~의 voluntary; optional; free／~로 freely; at will; as one pleases; at one's pleasure. ずいい

**수의**(獸醫) a veterinary surgeon; a vet-

수이(殊異) ~하다 (be) markedly different (*from*); remarkably distinguished (*from*).

수익(收益, 受益) earnings; profits《수익액》proceeds《투자의》returns/ ~세(稅) profit tax/ ~을 올리다 make profits; realize.

수익다 become skil[l]ful; become expert; get accustomed.

수인(囚人) a convict; a prisoner/ ~을 호송하다 send the prisoners under guard to (*a place*).

수인(數人) several[a few, some] persons.

수일(數日) several[a few] days/ ~전 a few days ago/ ~간 for several days.

수일(隨一) ~의 the best; number one(略: No. 1).

수임(受任) ~하다 accept an appointment; be nominated/ ~자 an appointee; a nominee.

수입(收入) 《개인의》an income; earnings 《법인·국가의》a revenue 《영수금》receipts 《매상금》proceeds; takings/고정 ~ fixed income/월~ a monthly income [takings]/실제 ~《세금을 뺀》one's net receipts; an actual income.

수입(輸入) importation; import《물건》imports《도입》introduction/~하다 import; introduce/ ~ 초과 an excess of imports over exports/ ~세 an import duty/ ~품 imported ariticles[goods]/ ~을 금하다 prohibit the importation.

수있다 《가능하다》can; be able; be capable of; be equal to; be possible《능숙하다》be proficient《무방하다》may; be entitled to/될 수 있는 대로 as [much] as one can; as [much] as possible/할[될] 수 있으면 if you can; if possible/될 수 있는 대로 그녀에게 말하지 마시오 Don't tell her as long as you can help.

수자리 《국경 수비》frontier guards《경비원》frontier guards/~하다 guard the frontier.

수자원(水資源) water resources/ ~ 개발 development of water resources.

수작(酬酌) ①《말의》an exchange of words/ ~하다 exchange words ②《술같의》an exchange of *sool* cups/~하다 exchange cups of *sool*.

수작(授爵) ennoblement; elevation to the peerage/ ~하다 confer a peerage (*on*); ennoble; elevate to the peerage; make (*a person*) a peer/ ~식을 행하다 hold an investiture.

수잠 a light sleep; an easy sleep.

수장(水葬) a burial at sea/ ~하다 bury (*one's body*) at sea/ ~ 당하다 be buried at sea.

수장(修粧) remodeling; embellishment/ ~하다 remodel; repair; embellish/ ~기둥 a temporary pillar for remodeling purposes.

수장(收藏) 《농작물의》garnering《일반적으로》collection/~하다 garner up; collect.

수재(水災) a flood; a flood disaster/ ~민 flood sufferers.

수재(手才) handicraft ⇨손재주.

수재(秀才) a brilliant[talented] man/ ~ 교육 a genius[talent] education/그는 천하의 ~다 He is a genius of nationwide fame.

수저 ①《순가락》a spoon《수프용》a tablespoon ②《순가락과 젓가락》spoon and chopsticks.

수저(水底) the bottom of the water/ ~에 가라앉다 sink[go down] to the bottom of (*the sea*).

수적(手迹) handwriting; a holograph; an autograph.

수적(讎敵) an enemy; a foe.

수적(水賊) a pirate; pirates/~질 piracy.

수전(水田) a paddy field; a rice field; a wet field ⇨논.

수전(水戰) a naval battle; a sea fight/ ~하다 fight on sea; have a naval battle.

수전(水電) hydroelectric[ity].

수전노(守錢奴) a miser; a niggard; a skinflint; a screw; a tightwad《미·속》a pennypincher.

수전증(手戰症)《한의학》palsy in the hand.

수절(守節) maintaining *one's* integrity; faithfulness/~하다 maintain *one's* integrity; reamin faithful[chaste, true] to *one's* husband.

수정(修正)《의안·조문 따위의》amendment; revision; modification《사진의》retouching/~하다 amend; modify; revise; retouch; correct/ ~안 an amended bill; an amendment/ ~ 예산 revised budget/ ~자 an amender《사진의》a retoucher/ ~ 자본주의 revised capitalism/ ~주의자 a revisionist/헌법의 ~ an amendment of the Constitution/의안을 ~하다 amend a bill/사진을 ~하다 retouch a negative.

수정(水晶) [rock-]crystal/자색 ~ amethyst/ ~체 crystalline; crystal/ ~체《해》the crystalline lens《수정액》the crystalline humour.

수정(受精, 授精)《생》fecundation; fertilization,《식》pollination/~하다 be fertilized; be pollinated; fertilize/동화[이화] ~ close[cross]-fertilization.

수정(修整) adjustment/ ~하다 adjust.

수정과(水正果) sugared[honeyed] water flavoured with dried persimmons, gingers and other fruits.

수정관(輸精管)《해》the spermaduct; the

deferent canal[duct]. ゆせいかん

**수제**(手製) (being) hand-made 《자가제의》 homemade; of domestic make 《수제품》 handiwork／～하다 make by hand.てせい

**수제비** pieces of dough boiled in meat soup.

**수제자**(首弟子) one's best pupil; the most able student. いちばんのでし

**수조**(水藻) duckweed; water plant; a hydrophyte. すいそう

**수조**(水漕) a water-tank; a cistern. すいそう

**수족**(手足) hands and feet; hand and foot; the limbs; the extremities／～을 못 쓰게 되다 lose the use of one's limbs. しゅそく

**수족**(水族) aquatic animals; the finny race[tribe]; sea creatures; water life／～관 an aquarium. すいぞく

**수졸**(守拙) ～하다 cling to one's stupidity; stick to one's folly; remain foolish.

**수종**(隨從) 《시중》 attendance (on); service 《사람》 an attendant; a servant／～하다 attend; serve; wait upon. ずいじょう

**수종**(水腫) 〖의〗 dropsy／～ 다리 dropsical legs. すいしゅ

**수죄**(首罪) a cardinal crime しゅざい

**수죄**(數罪) ①《여러 죄》 several crimes ②《들춤》 disclosure／～하다 disclose (one's crime). すうざい

**수주**(受注) ～하다 receive an order／～고(高) order awarded.

**수주머니**(繡一) an embroidered pouch.

**수준**(水準) water-level 《정도》 a level; a standard／생활 ～ the standard of living／～에 못 미치다 fall short of the standard. すいじゅん

**수줍다** (be) shy; bashful; timid／그 여자는 수줍어 말도 못한다 She is too shy to speak／그 여자는 사람들 앞에 나서면 수줍어한다 She is bashful in company. はじる

**수줍음** shyness; bashfulness; timidity; self-consciousness. はじらい

**수중**(水中) underwater; submarine／～ 발사관 a submerged tube／～ 속력 submerged speed／～ 안경 《관측용》 a hydroscope; water glasses 《수영용》 swimming goggles／～ 전파 탐지기 a sonar; an asdic〈영〉／～ 청음기 a hydrophone; a subaqueous sound locator／～ 폭발 an underwater explosion[detonation]／ ～으로 사라지다 disappear[sink] in the water; go under／～에 살다 live in water. すいちゅう

**수중**(手中) in the hands 《세력 안에》 within one's power／～에 넣다 secure; capture; possess oneself of; come by／～에 들어오다 fall into one's hand. しゅちゅう

**수중다리** 〖의〗 dropsical legs.→수종.

**수중익**(水中翼) a hydrofoil／～선(船) a hydrofoil craft.

**수증**(受贈) acception of a gift／～하다 accept a gift. じゅぞう

**수증기**(水蒸氣) vapour; steam. すいじょうき

**수지**(一紙) 《휴지》 scraps of paper; wastepaper; facial tissue paper; toilet paper ／～통 a wastpaper basket. ちりがみ

**수지**(手指) fingers. しゅし

**수지**(樹脂) 〖점성〗 resin 〖고체〗 rosin／～ 광택 resinous luster／～를 바르다 resin (a thing). じゅし

**수지**(收支) income and expenditure; receipts and expenditures／～ 일람표 a balance sheet; a statement of income and expenditure／～를 맞추다 make both ends meet; make (it) pay／～ 결산을 하다 strike a balance. しゅうし

**수지**(獸脂) grease; animal fat; tallow／ ～를 칠하다 grease. じゅうし

**수지맞다**(收支—) 《어떤 일이》 pay; be profitable; be paying 《사람이》 find one's account in; find it profitable／수지맞는 장사 a paying business; a good bargain／수지맞는 remunerative 《직업 따위》 paying 《거래 따위》 profitable 《위치 따위》 advantageous. しゅうしがあう

**수직**(守直) keeping; guard; watch／～하다 keep; guard; watch; take care of. ひきうけてまもること

**수직**(垂直) perpendicularity／～ 강하 a vertical descent; a nose-dive／～선 a perpendicular line／～ 안전판 a vertical stabilizer [of an airplane]／～ 이착륙기 a vertical take-off and landing craft／～으로 교차하는 두 직선 two lines crossing at right angles／～이 아니다 be out of plumb. すいちょく

**수직**(手織) handweaving／～의 home-woven; hand-loomed; homespun／～ 무명 homespun cotton cloth. ており

**수진**(袖珍) pocket size[book]; a manual ／～ 사전 a pocket[vest] dictionary. ぶんこほん

**수질**(水疾) sea-sickness. ふねよい

**수질**(水質) the quality of water／～이 좋은 우물 a well whose water is good for drinking. すいしつ

**수집**(收集) collection; gathering／～하다 collect; gather. しゅうしゅう

**수집**(蒐集) collection; gathering／～하다 collect; compile／～가 a collector／～ 표 the collection of postagestamps; philately. しゅうしゅう

**수차**(水車) a water-mill[-wheel].すいしゃ

**수차**(收差) 〖물〗 aberration／구면(球面) ～ spherical aberration. しゅうさ

**수차**(數次) several times; time and again／～의 방문 several visits.

**수찬**(修撰) editing (a book); redaction; compilation／～하다 edit; redact; compile. しゅうせん

**수찰**(手札) a letter; a note; an epistle. しゅさつ

**수창**(首唱) advocacy; pioneering; origin-

ating/ ~하다 advocate; promote; be first to [do]; pioneer (in); advance/ ~자 an advocate; a promoter; a pioneer; a prime mover. しゅしょう
**수채** a drain; a ditch. げすいどう
**수채움**(數—) filling up/ ~하다 fill up.
**수채화**(水彩畵) a water-colour [painting]/ ~ 물감 water-colour paints; water-colours/~를 그리다 paint with water-colours. すいさいが
**수처**(數處) several places.
**수척**(瘦瘠) emaciation/~하다 (be) thin; haggard; gaunt; emaciated/슬픈 나머지 얼굴이 ~해졌다 Sorrow has left its traces on her face. やせること
**수천**(數千) thousands; several thousands / ~의 사람 thousands of people.
**수첩**(手帖) a note book; a memo-book; a pocket-book/ ~에 써 넣다 note; jot [write] down in one's note-book. てちょう
**수청들다**(守廳—) (a geesaeng) give her body from time to time to the local magistrate; serve one's magistrate.
**수초**(水草) a water[an aquatic] plant. すいそう
**수축**(收縮) contraction; shrinking/ ~하다 contract; shrink/ ~성 contractibility/통화의 ~ the contraction of currency exports. しゅうしゅく
**수축**(修築) repair (of a building); improvement; mending; restoration/ ~하다 repair; renovate; make improvements (in); mend; restore/ ~중이다 It is under repair., It is being repaired. しゅうちく
**수출**(輸出) export; exportation; improvement/ ~하다 export; ship abroad/ ~업[무역] the export business[trade]/ ~ 장려 the encouragement of export trade / ~품 export articles/ ~ 허가 [서] an export permit. ゆしゅつ
**수출입**(輸出入) exportation and importation; imports and exports/ ~ 금지품 contraband goods.
**수취**(收取) 〖법〗 collection; acquirement / ~하다 collect; acquire. しゅうしゅ
**수취**(受取) receipt; receiving/ ~하다 receive; accept; take. うけとり
**수치**(羞恥) shame; disgrace; dishonour; humiliation/ ~스럽다 be shameful; be disgraceful/ ~를 드러내다 wash one's dirty linen in public. しゅうち
**수치질**(—痔疾) external[protruding] hemorrhoids.
**수침**(水沈) sinking/ ~하다 sink under water.
**수캉아지** a he-puppy. おすのこいぬ
**수캐** a he-dog. おすのいぬ
**수컷** a male 《날짐승의》a cock/ ~의 male; cock; he.
**수코양이** a tom-cat. おすねこ
**수키와** a convex roofing tile. おすかわら
**수탁**(受託) trust 《상품 판매의》 consign-ment/ ~하다 be given in trust; be entrusted with (a thing); take charge of (a thing). じゅたく
**수탄**(愁嘆) grief; sorrow. しゅうたん
**수탄**(獸炭) animal charcoal.
**수탈**(收奪) 《착취》 exploitation/ ~하다 exploit (one's workers).
**수탉** a rooster〈미〉; a cock. おんどり
**수탐**(搜探) investigation; search/ ~하다 investigate; search. さぐる
**수태**(受胎) conception; impregnation 〖생〗 fecundation; fertilization/ ~하다 conceive; be impregnated; become pregnant; be fecundated/성모 마리아의 ~ the Immaculate Conception/ ~ 능력 〖생〗 fertility/ ~ 현상 〖생〗 fertilization; fecundation; impregnation. じゅたい
**수토**(水土) water and soil 《풍토》 climate. すいど
**수통**(水桶) a water; a water pail bucket 〖물통〗. みずおけ
**수통**(水筒) a [water] flask; a canteen.
**수퇘지** a boar. おすぶた
**수틀**(繡—) an embroidery-frame 《둥근 것》 a tambour.
**수펄** a drone. おばち
**수펌** a tiger. おすとら
**수평이** a hedge; a forest; a thicket; a bush 《관목숲》 a shrubbery.
**수평**(水平) the water-level; the horizon / ~의 level; even; horizontal/ ~으로 horizontally; at a level with (a thing)/ ~각 a horizontal angle/ ~ 거리 horizontal distance/~선 the sea line; the horizon. すいへい
**수포**(水泡) 《거품》 foam; bubble 《헛수고》 naught; nothing/ ~로 돌아가다 come to naught[nothing]; prove[result in] a failure; be brought to naught; end in smoke. すいほう
**수포**(水疱) 〖의〗 a blister. すいほう
**수폭**(水爆) a hydrogen bomb; an H-bomb/~ 실험 an H-bomb test; a thermonuclear test.
**수표**(手票) a cheque; a check〈미〉/ ~장 a cheque book/ ~를 발행하다 issue [make out] a cheque.
**수풀** a forest; a wood 《입목지》a grove 《덤불숲》 a copse; a thicket. しんりん
**수피**(樹皮) the bark of a tree. じゅひ
**수피**(獸皮) the skin of an animal; a fur; a pelt. じゅうひ
**수피둘기** a male pigeon; a cock-dove[pigeon]. おすはと
**수필**(隨筆) stray notes; [fugitive] essays; miscellaneous writings/ ~가 an essayist; a columnist/ ~집 a collection of one's essays; literary jottings; essays. ずいひつ
**수하**(手下) a subordinate; a retainer; a henchman; an underling; a follower 《총칭》 a following; men under one's order; staff/ ~가 되다 be placed under one's command. てした

**수하**(水下) the lower stream; the lower reaches[courses] of a river; an estuary. かりゅう

**수하**(誰何) ①《검문》 challenge／～하다 challenge (one) ②《누구》 anyone; who; what／～를 막론하고 regardless of who it may be. だれかれ

**수하물**(手荷物) luggage〈영〉; baggage〈미〉; 《휴대할 수 있는》 hand luggage[baggage]; personal effects／～ 취급소 a luggage office〈영〉; a baggage room[office]〈미〉. てにもつ

**수학**(受學) being taught; receiving instruction／～하다 receive instruction; study; learn. がくもんをうけること

**수학**(修學) pursuit of knowledge; study; learning／～하다 study; learn; pursue knowledge／～ 여행 a school excursion; a study tour; a trip for educational purposes. しゅうがく

**수학**(數學) mathematics; math[s]〈구〉／～ 문제 a mathematical problem／～자 a mathematician. すうがく

**수할치** a falconer.

**수해**(水害) 《손해》 flood damage; a flood disaster 《홍수》 a flood; an inundation／～를 입다 suffer from a flood; be damaged by a flood／～ 대책 anti-flood measures／～ 지구 a flooded[flood stricken] district. すいがい

**수해**(樹海) a wavy sea of emerald leaves; a sea of leafage[foliage, trees].

**수행**(修行) 《수련》 training; practice 《수학》 study 《종교상의》 ascetic practices／～하다 receive training; train oneself; practice asceticism; study／～을 쌓다 get experienced; be well-trained. しゅぎょう

**수행**(獸行) bestiality; a bestial act 《폭행》 an assault (on a woman). けもののようなおこない

**수행**(遂行) accomplishment; execution; achievement; discharge／～하다 accomplish; carry out[through]; execute; perform／직무의 ～ the performance[discharge] of one's duties. すいこう

**수행**(隨行) attendance／～하다 attend (one on a journey); accompany (one); be in one's suite／～원 a member to the suite; attendants; a suite 《총칭》 a retinue. ずいこう

**수향**(水郷) a waterside[riverside, lakeside] village. すいきょう

**수험**(受驗) sitting for an examination; taking[undergoing] an examination／～하다 take[undergo, sit for, go through] an examination／～ 과목 subjects of examination／～료 an examination fee／～ 번호 an examinee's seat number／～생 a candidate for an examination; an examinee／～표 an admission ticket for examination. じゅけん

**수혈**(輸血) blood transfusion／～하다 transfuse [blood]; give a blood transfusion (to). ゆけつ

**수형**(受刑) being under sentence／～하다 serve time [in prison]／～자 a convict; a convicted person; a prisoner under sentence. じゅけい

**수호**(守護) protection; guard; safeguard／～하다 protect; guard; safeguard; watch over (a person)／～신 a guardian [protecting] deity; a patron saint. しゅご

**수호**(修好) friendship; comity; amity／～ 조약(條約) a treaty of amity[friendship]. しゅうこう

**수화**(水火) fire and water／～ 불통(不通)하다 be at enmity; be like cats and dogs. すいか

**수화**(繡畫) an embroidered picture. ししゅうしたえ

**수화**(水化) 《화》 hydration／～물 a hydrate. すいか

**수화기**(受話器) a [telephone] receiver 《무전의》 radio earphones／～를 메다[걸다] unhook[hang up] the receiver. じゅわき

**수화법**(手話法) chirology.

**수확**(收穫) a harvest; a crop; a yield／～하다 harvest; reap; gather in／～고 the crop; the yield／～ 체감《경》 diminishing return. しゅうかく

**수황증**(手荒症) kleptomania.

**수회**(收賄) acceptance of a bribe; corruption; corrupt practices; graft〈미〉／～하다 take[receive, accept] a bribe; graft／～ 사건 a bribery affair[case]／～자 a bribee. しゅうわい

**수회**(數回) several times; on several occasions／～ 시도하다 make several attempts.

**수효**(數爻) a number; an amount／사람 ～ the number of people.

**수훈**(垂訓) a precept; a lesson; teachings／산상(山上) ～ the Sermon on the Mountain.

**수훈**(殊勲) distinguished[meritorious] services／～자 a person who has rendered distinguished services／～을 세우다 distinguish oneself; render distinguished service 《전쟁에서》 win one's spurs. しゅくん

**쑥**[1] wormwood; mugwort; artemisia; sagebrush.

**쑥**[2] shame; impropriety; indecency／너도 ～이다 Shame on you! ぐしゃ

**쑥**[3] ①《내민 모양》 way out 《들어간 모양》 way in／～ 들어간 눈 deep-set eyes ②《힘차게》 with a jerk／칼을 ～ 뽑다 draw one's sword in a flash; whip out one's sword. ぼこっと

**숙가**(宿痾) a chronic[an inveterate] disease.

**쑥갓** a crowndaisy; Chrysanthemum coronarium 《학명》. しゅんぎく

**숙고**(熟考) [mature] consideration; deli-

**숙군**(肅軍) a purge in the army; restoration of military discipline.

**숙근**(宿根) an old root／～초(草) a perennial plant. しゅっこん

**숙녀**(淑女) a lady. しゅくじょ

**숙다** ①(앞으로) droop; bow; be bent ② 《기운이》 go[die] down; subside. うつむく

**숙달**(熟達) proficiency; skill; mastery／～하다 (be) skilled; proficient; expert; adept／～한 기수(騎手) a complete horseman. じゅくたつ

**숙당**(肅黨) a purge in the party.

**쑥대강이** disheveled[unkempt] hair. ほうとうらんばつ

**숙덕**(淑德) womanly graces; a feminine virtue. すゅくとく

**숙덕거리다** whisper; talk in whisper; exchange whispers. こそこそとはなす

**쑥덕공론**(—公論) exchanges of subdued remarks; secret counsel. みつぎ

**숙덕숙덕** in whispers; in a subdued tone 《비밀히》 secretly. こそこそ

**쑥덕이다** talk in a subdued tone; exchange subdued remarks.

**숙독**(熟讀) careful reading; perusal／～하다 read [a book] carefully[thoroughly]; peruse. じゅくどく

**숙려**(熟慮) mature deliberation／～단행 Deliberate slowly, execute promptly. じゅくりょ

**숙련**(熟練) skill; expertness; dexterity／～된 skilled; skillful; expert; experienced／～공(工) a skilled worker 《총칭》 skilled labour. じゅくれん

**숙망**(宿望) a long cherished desire; ambition; one's heart's desire／～을 이루다 attain one's long cherished desire. しゅくぼう

**숙맥**(菽麥) beans and barley. まめとむぎ

**숙면**(熟眠) a sound[heavy, deep] sleep／～하다 sleep well[soundly, heavily]; have a good sleep. じゅくみん

**숙명**(宿命) fate; destiny; fatality; predestination; one's fated lot／～론 fatalism／～적인 fatalistic. しゅくめい

**숙모**(叔母) an aunt. しゅくぼ

**숙박**(宿泊) lodging; staying; putting up; stopping; accommodation／～하다 lodge (at, in); stay[stop] at; put up; for the night; take up one's lodgings／～소 a lodging-house; one's lodgings; one's quarters／～료 hotel[lodging, inn] charges; hotel bill[expenses]; the fare. しゅくはく

**숙부**(叔父) an uncle. しゅくふ

**숙부드럽다** ①(《얌전하다》) (be) gentle; mild; meek; quiet ②(마음이) (be) tender; mild; sweet; gentle. ぜんりょうだ

**숙사**(宿舍) a hotel; lodgings; quarters; 《군대의》 a billet／～ 할당 allocation of quarters. しゅくしゃ

**숙사**(熟絲) boiled silk thread.

**숙상**(肅霜) a heavy frost. きびしいしも

**숙설거리다** talk in whispers ⇨속살거리다. ささやく

**숙성**(夙成) precocity; early maturity／～하다 (be) precocious; be wise above one's age 《몸집이》 be big for one's age／～한 사람 a precocious man. ねんよりせいじゅくしている

**숙세**(宿世) one's previous life; one's former [state of] existence[life]. せいぜんのせかい

**숙소**(宿所) one's address; one's place of abode; one's quarters／～를 옮기다 change one's lodgings[quarters, hotel]; remove. しゅくしょ

**숙수**(熟手) a fancy cook; a caterer. りょうりにん

**숙수**(熟睡) a sound sleep. じゅくすい

**쑥스럽다** (be) unbecoming; unseemly; indecent; improper／쑥스럽게 굴다 cut an awkward[a ridiculous] figure; expose oneself to ridicule.

**숙시**(熟視) steady gaze; stare; scrutiny／～하다 gaze (at, on); stare (at); look hard[steadily, intently]; scrutinize; examine; inspect. じゅくし

**숙씨**(叔氏) [your, his] esteemed third brother.

**숙식**(宿食) board and lodging; bed and board／～하다 board and lodge／～비를 지불하다 pay for one's board and lodging. しんしょく

**숙야**(夙夜) morning and evening; day and night; always. しゅくや

**숙어**(熟語) an idiom; an idiomatic phrase; a [set] phrase／～집 a phrase book; a dictionary of phrase. じゅくご

**숙어지다** hang down; droop; be bowed ⇨수그러지다. うつかたむく

**숙연**(宿緣) destiny; fate; 【불】 a karma (Sans). しゅくえん

**숙연**(肅然) ～하다 (be) solemn; reverential; silent／～히 silently; quietly; solemnly. おごそかでととのっている

**숙영**(宿營) billeting; quartering 《숙사》 military quarters; billets／～하다 be billeted[quartered] (on a town); bivouac; camp. しゅくえい

**숙우**(宿雨) a long rain; a long spell of rainy weather. しゅくう

**숙원**(宿怨) an old grudge[score, rancor]; deep-rooted enmity; an old feud／～을 갚다 satisfy one's old grudge; work off an old grudge; pay off old scores. しゅくえん

**숙의**(熟議) [careful] deliberation; exhaustive discussion; careful consultation [consideration]／～하다 deliberate [fully] on (a matter); consider[consult] carefully; talk (a matter) over／～한 후에 after careful consideration. じゅくぎ

숙이다 hang down; droop/고개를 ~ hang down one's head; hang[bend, drop, lower] one's head. まえにうつむく

숙장(宿將) a veteran general. しゅくしょう

숙적(宿敵) an old enemy; an ancient foe. しゅくてき

숙정(肅正) regulation/ ~하다 enforce; regulate/관기를 ~하다 enforce official discipline. しゅくせい

숙제(宿題) a home work[task]; (현안) a pending question/ ~를 내다 set (one) a home work. しゅくだい

숙죄(宿罪) 《기독교의》 the original sin 《불교의》 sins committed in one's previous existence. しゅくざい

숙주(宿主) 〖생〗 a host. しゅくしゅ

숙주나물 a kind of bean sprouts. ぶんどうのもやし

숙지(宿志) a long cherished desire.

숙지(熟知) familiarity; full knowledge /~하다 know well; be well[fully, thoroughly] aware of 《정통하다》 be familiar with. じゅくち

숙직(宿直) night-duty/ ~하다 be on night-duty; keep vigil[night-watch]/ ~원 a person on night-duty/ ~실 the night-duty room. しゅくちょく

숙질(叔姪) uncle and nephew. しゅくふとめい

숙채(宿債) old debts. しゅくさい

숙철(熟鐵) pig iron. じゅくてつ

숙청(肅淸) a purge; a clean-up; liquidation/ ~하다 clean up; stage a purge; liquidate/ ~ 운동 a "purge" campaign (against). しゅくせい

숙체(宿滯) chronic indigestion[dyspepsia].

숙취(宿醉) a hangover; a sickhead; the morning-after/~하다 have a hangover; suffer from the aftereflects of the previous night's`drink. しゅくすい

숙친(熟親) close friendship; intimacy/ ~하다 (be) intimate (with); close.

숙폐(宿弊) old[deep-rooted] evils; an inveterate vice/ ~를 일소하다 do away with old evils. しゅくへい

숙학(塾學) a purge in the university [school].

숙혐(宿嫌) an old grudge; deep-rooted rancour; long-harboured resentment. いぜんからのけんぎ

숙환(宿患) a chronic disease; an old complaint; an old spell〈미〉/~으로 병상에 눕다 be confined to bad by an attack of a chronic disease.

숙흥 야매(夙興夜寐) early rising and late lying down; assiduity/ ~하다 rise up early and lie down late.

순(旬) (10일) a period of ten days (10년) ten years; a decade/상~ the first ten days of a month. じゅん

순(筍) 《싹》 a sprout; a bud/죽~ a bamboo shoot[sprout]. たけのこ

순(巡) ①《활쏘기의》 a round [of a shooting 5 arrows) ②《차례》 order of rounds. じゅん

순-(純) 《사물의》 pure; genuine; chaste; innocent; fine; sterling 《진정한》 unalloyed; unmixed; absolute; true; unadulterated 《이익 따위》 net; clear 《사람 등》 a trunborn; born and bred; out-and-out/ ~이익 net profit/ ~서울나기 a Seoul man[woman] to the core; a true[bred, born] Seoul man[woman]. じゅん

순간(瞬間) a moment; a second; an instant; a twinkle/ ~의 momentary; instantaneous/ ~에 instantaneously; in a moment[an instant]. しゅんかん

순간(旬刊) ~의 published every ten days. じゅんかん

순강(巡講) a lecturing tour/~하다 make one's rounds for lectures; make a lecturing tour.

순검(巡檢) ①《순찰》 a tour of inspection; a round/ ~하다 make a tour of inspection; make one's rounds/ ~자 an inspector ②a policeman.

순견(純絹) pure silk/~의 all-silk; sheer silk/ ~ 양말 sheer silk hose[stockings]. じゅんけん

순결(純潔) purity; cleanliness; integrity / ~하다 (be) pure; clean; unspotted; chaste/ ~한 사랑 pure[platonic] love /~한 처녀 a virgin. じゅんけつ

순경(巡更) night watch; night patrol/ ~하다 go the rounds at night. やけい

순경(巡警) a policeman; a [police] constable〈영〉; a patrolman〈미〉; a cop〈미·속〉 /교통 ~ a traffic policeman. じゅんけい

순경(順境) a favourable condition; prosperity; good fortune; favourable circumstances/ ~에서 자라나다 be bred in favourable circumstances. じゅんきょう

순교(殉敎) martyrdom; baptism of blood / ~하다 die a martyr for one's faith; be martyred/ ~사(史) martyrology. じゅんきょう

순국(殉國) dying[sacrifice of one's life] for one's country/~하다 die for one's faith; martyr in[to] the cause of one's country/ ~ 열사 a martyr; the brave men who laid down their lives for their country. じゅんこく

순국산(純國産) ~의 of entirely Korean make; all-Korean (productions)/ ~품 an all-Korean product.

순금(純金) pure gold; solid gold/ ~ 반지 a solid gold ring. じゅんきん

순난(殉難) martyrdom being involved in a disaster/~하다 die for one's country; sacrifice[lay down] one's life for one's country. じゅんなん

순대 a sausage.

순도(殉道) religious martyrdom ⇨순교. じゅんきょう

순도(純度) purity. じゅんど

**순두부** uncurdled bean curd.

**순라(巡邏)** a patrol; a round／ ～하다 patrol; go *one's* rounds[beat]／～선 a patrol-ship; a ground-boat 《밀수 감시의》 a revenue-cutter. じゅんら

**순람(巡覽)** a tour of sightseeing; a tour of inspection／ ～하다 go sightseeing; go on a tour of inspection[round of visit]; tour. じゅんらん

**순량(純良)** being pure[genuine, good]／ ～하다 (be) pure; pure and good; genuine; wholesome. じゅんりょう

**순량(馴良)** being well tamed／～하다 (be) tame; gentle; meek. じゅんりょう

**순량(順良)** being good and obedient／ ～하다 (be) good and obedient; meek; law-abiding.

**순량(純量)** net weight.

**순력(巡歷)** a tour; an itinera[n]cy／ ～하다 [make a] tour (round); travel about[through]. じゅんれき

**순례(巡禮)** a pilgrimage 《사람》 a pilgrim; a palmer／ ～하다 make[go on] a pilgrimage／여러 나라를 ～하다 make a pilgrimage through various provinces. じゅんれい

**순로(順路)** the usual[regular] route. じゅんろ

**순록(馴鹿)** 〖동〗 a reindeer. じゅんろく

**순류(順流)** drifting with the tide／ ～하다 go with the current. じゅんりゅう

**순리(順理)** submission to reason; reasonableness／ ～하다 be reasonble; accord with reason.

**순리(純利)** a net profit／～ 100원을 얻다 net a profit of 100 *won*. じゅんり

**순리(純理)** pure reason; logic／～론 rationalism／～적 rational; logical／～론적 결론 rational conclusion. じゅんり

**순만(順娩)** easy childbirth. あんざん

**순망간(旬望間)** the period from tenth to fifteenth of a lunar month.

**순면(純綿)** pure cotton／ ～의 all-cotton. じゅんめん

**순모(純毛)** whole wool／ ～의 all-wool. じゅんもう

**순무** 〖식〗 a turnip; Brassica rapa(학명).

**순문학(純文學)** polite literature; belles literature; *belles-lettres*(F)／ ～파 a belletrist. じゅんぶんがく

**순물** water strained out from bean-curds.

**순미(純味)** unalloyed taste; pure flavo[u]r. まじりきのないあじ

**순미(純美, 醇美)** unalloyed[absolute] beauty／ ～하다 (be) absolutely beautiful. じゅんび

**순박(純朴, 淳朴)** Arcadianism; simplicity; naive; homeliness／～하다 《성질이》 (be)simple; naive; simple-hearted; ingenuous; innocent; unsophisticated 《풍속》 (be) homely simple-mannered (*one*); Arcadian (*life*). じゅんぼく

**순배(巡杯)** passing cups round／ ～하다 pass cups round.

**순백(純白)** a pure[snowy] white; sheer [virginal] white／ ～하다 (be) snowwhite; immaculate. じゅんぱく

**순번(順番)** order 《순서》 sequence 《교대》 turn／ ～으로 서다 stand in a queue. じゅんばん

**순보(旬報)** a ten-day report. じゅんぽう

**순복(順服)** obedience; submission; subordination 《복종》 acquiescence／ ～하다 obey; be obedient to; submit (*oneself*) to 《복종하다》 acquiesce in.

**순분도(純分度)** 《금·은의》 fineness 《금의》 carat. じゅんぶんど

**순사(殉死)** suicide upon the death of *one's* lord; self-immolation on the death of *one's* master 《과부의》 suttee ／ ～하다 immolate[kill] *oneself* on the death of *one's* lord; follow *one's* lord[*one's* master] to the grave. じゅんし

**순산(順產)** an easy delivery[birth]／ ～하다 have an easy delivery. あんざん

**순색(純色)** a pure[an unmixed] colour. じゅんすいのいろ

**순서(順序)** 《차례》 order; sequence 《방법》 system; method 《수속》 procedure; course／ ～있게 in good[proper] order; in regular sequence; systematically／ ～를 바로잡다 correct the order／ ～를 밟다 go through due formalities／ ～가 틀리다 be in wrong order／ ～표 a list; a programme. じゅんじょ

**순석(巡錫)** a preaching tour／ ～하다 make a preaching tour. じゅんしゃく

**순성(馴性)** ①《사람의》 submissiveness; docility; gentleness; meekness ②《짐승의》 tameness; domestication.
なれるせいしつ

**순성(順成)** easy achievement／ ～하다 accomplish smoothly; achieve without a hitch. じゅんちょうになること

**순소득(純所得)** net income. じゅんしょとく

**순수(巡狩)** an Imperial tour; a Royal progress／ ～하다 make a tour[progress].

**순수(純粹)** purity; pureness; genuineness／ ～하다 (be) pure; real; genuine; unmixed; unalloyed; straight; absolute 《순혈의》 full-blooded; true-born／ ～ 소설 pure fiction. じゅんすい

**순수입(純收入)** net income.

**순순하다(諄諄—)** (be) earnest; patient／순순히 타이르다 inculcate; exhort; talk earnestly. ねんごろでしんせつだ

**순순하다(順順—)** 《성질이》 (be) gentle; docile; obedient; submissive／순순히 tamely; quietly; smoothly; without trouble; obediently. せいしつがおとなしい

**순시(巡視)** an inspection; a patrol; a round of visits[inspection]; 《사람》 a guard／ ～하다 go[make] *one's* rounds; make a tour of inspection; inspect; patrol／ ～인 a patrol[man]; a floor-walker; a watchman. じゅんし

순시(瞬時) a moment; an instant／～라도 [even for] a moment. しゅんじ

순식간(瞬息間) a brief instant／～에 in the twinkling of an eye. またたくあいだ

순실(純實) naivety; purity; naiveté(F)／～하다 (be) naive; pure; genuine; sincere／그녀의 마음은 ～하다 She is pure in heart.  すなおでまじめであること

순실(淳實) simplicity; naiveté(F)／～하다 (be) simple and honest; unsophisticated naive; simple-hearted.
しつぼくでまじめであること

순양(馴養) domestication／～하다 tame; domesticate.

순양(巡洋) a cruise; cruising／～하다 cruise; sail about／～함 a cruiser.

순업(巡業) a provincial tour〈영〉; a tour of country〈미〉／～하다 tour [the country]; take a show on the road 《지방을》 hit the road〈미〉.  じゅんぎょう

순여(旬餘) more than a decade. じゅんよ

순역(順逆) right and wrong 《군주 등에 대한》 obedience and disobedience; loyalty and treason.  じゅんぎゃく

순연(順延) postponement; deferment／～하다 postpone; defer; put off.

순연(純然) ～하다 (be) pure; absolute; perfect; outright; out-and-out; veritable.  じゅんぜん

순열(順列) 【수】 permutation; [linear] arrangement.  じゅんれつ

순열(巡閱) a tour[round] of inspection／～하다 make a tour of inspection; go a round of inspection. じゅんえつ

순외(順外) an extra／～의 extra; special／～ 연주 an extra number[performance]; an addition to the scheduled programme.

순위(順位) order; rank; ranking; precedence／～를 결정하다 decide ranking.
じゅんい

순유(巡遊) a tour; an itinera[n]cy／～의 itinerary／～하다 make a tour of [Korea]; go on a tour of 《Busan》; travel through[about].  じゅんゆう

순은(純銀) pure[solid] silver. しゅんぎん

순음(脣音) 【언】 a labial [sound]. しんおん

순응(順應) adaptation; accommodation; adjustment; sympathy／～하다 adapt [accommodate] oneself (to 《circumstances》); adjust oneself (to)／～성 adaptability／사회 환경에 ～하다 adapt oneself to social surrounding.  じゅんのう

순이익(純利益) net[clear] profit／～ 천만원을 올리다 net[clear, gross, realize] a profit of ten million won. じゅんりえき

순익(純益) net profit.  じゅんえき

순일(旬日) ①《열흘》 a period of ten days; a decade  ②《초열흘》 the tenth [day of the month].  じゅんじつ

순일(純一) purity; genuineness／～하다 (be) pure; genuine／～ 무구의 성격 pure and unstained character.  じゅんいつ

순잎(筍一) young[new] leaves; young foliage; leaflets.

순장(旬葬) burial on the tenth day after death.

순전(純全) purity; spotlessness／～하다 (be) pure [and simple]; absolute; downright; perfect; sheer; utter; entire／～한 악당 an absolute knave／～히 absolutely.  まじりきのないこと

순절(殉節) dying in defense of one's chastity[integrity].

순정(純正) simplicity; purity; honesty／～하다 (be) honest; upright; pure; genuine／～ 과학 pure science／～ 철학 metaphysics.  じゅんせい

순정(純情) a pure heart[mind]; naivety; self sacrificing devotion／～ 소설 a boy-meets-girl story.  じゅんじょう

순조(順調) 《일의》 a favourable[normal] condition; favourableness; smoothness 《천기의》 seasonableness／～로운 favourable; well; satisfactory; smooth; 《정상적》 normal 《날씨》 seasonable／～롭게 favourably; satisfactorily; normally; well; smoothly／～롭게 나가다 progress satisfactorily; proceed favourably; go well; go on nicely[smoothly]／만사가 ～롭다 All goes well.
じゅんちょう

순종(純種) a full[pure] blood; a thoroughbred.  まじりきのないしゅるい

순종(順從) docility; obedience; submissiveness; acquiescence／～하다 obey; submit; acquiesce; yield (to).
おとなしくしたがうこと

순주(醇酒) choice wine.

순직(純直) simplicity and uprightness／～하다 (be) simple[·minded] and upright; honest; straight.
じゅんしんでしょうじきなこと

순직(殉職) dying at one's post of duty; death in harness／～하다 die[be killed] in the pursuit of one's duties; die at one's post of duty／～자 a victim to one's post of duty.  じゅんしょく

순진(純眞) innocence; simplicity; purity; artlessness／～하다 (be) pure; innocent; artless; simple; genuine; naive／～한 소녀 a maiden pure in heart; an innocent girl; a virgin／～한 마음 a pure [and simple] heart; a heart pure of any taint.  じゅんしん

순차(順次) order 《순번》 turn／～적으로 in [regular] order; in regular succession; successively.  じゅんじ

순찰(巡察) a patrol; a round of inspection／～하다 patrol; make[go] a round of inspection.  じゅんさつ

순채(蓴菜) 【식】 a water-shield; Brasenia Purpurea 《학명》.  じゅんさい

순초(巡哨) scouting; patrolling／～하다 scout; patrol／～군 a scout.

순치(馴致) ①《길들임》 domestication; taming  ②《초래》 bringing about; giving

순치다 / 565 / 술서

rise to/ ~하다 tame; domesticate; naturalize; habituate; lead to; bring about[forth, on]; give rise to. ちゅんち

**순치다**(筍―) cut off sprouts[buds, shoots]; trim (*a plant*); cut (*a plant*) back.

**순탄**(順坦, 純坦) ①(성질이) even-mindedness/ ~하다 (be) equable; even-minded ②(길이) evenness; flatness/ ~하다 (be) even; flat; level; smooth.
せいしつがむずかしくないこと

**순풍**(淳風) a good custom. じゅんぷう

**순풍**(順風) a favourable[seasonable] wind; a fair wind 《뒤에서 부는 바람》 a tailwind/ ~에 돛을 달다 sail before a fair wind; hoist the sails in a fair wind; be under easy sail. じゅんぷう

**순하다**(順―) ①(성질이)(be) gentle; docile; obedient; amiable; meek; tender ②(맛이)(be) mild; smooth ③(일이)(be) smooth; go well. おとなしい

**순하다**(殉―) sacrifice oneself[one's life] (*to*); die a martyr (to *one's principle*).

**순항**(巡航) a cruise; cruising/ ~하다 sail; cruise/ ~선 a cruiser. じゅんこう

**순행**(巡行) a patrol; a tour; a round/ ~하다 make a tour [round]; go on a patrol. じゅんこう

**순행**(巡幸) an Imperial tour/ ~하다 make a tour[progress]. じゅんこう

**순혈**(純血) pure blood/ ~의 pure blooded; pure-bred 《말 따위》 thorough-bred.
じゅんけつ

**순화**(醇化) refinement; sublimation/ ~하다 refine; polish; chasten; sublimate; idealize; purify. じゅんか

**순화**(純化) purification/ ~하다 purify.
じゅんか

**순환**(循環) 《동》 circulation; rotation; cycle/ ~하다 circulate (*through*); rotate; cycle; recur; revolve/ ~ 곡선 recurring curve/ ~ 급수 recurring series / ~기 a cycle/ ~론 circular reasoning; a vicious circle/ ~ 소수 circulating decimals/ 혈액 ~ circulation of blood/계절은 ~한다 The seasons rotate. じゅんかん

**순회**(巡廻) a trip; a patrol; a tour; a round/ ~하다 patrol; go round; go [make] *one's* rounds[tour]; make a tour of/ ~ 강연 a lecturing[lecture] tour/읍내를 ~하다 go round the town.
じゅんこう

**순후**(醇厚, 淳厚) pure-mindedness; warm-heartedness/ ~하다 (be) pure-minded; warmhearted. じゅんこう

**술가락** a spoon/한 ~의 설탕 a spoonful of sugar/ ~으로 뜨다 spoon out[up].
しゃもじ

**술**¹ rice wine; wine; liquor; spirits; intoxicant/ ~꾸러기 a tippler/ ~독 a liquor jug/ ~독(毒) alcohol poisoning/ ~을 마시다 drink/ ~을 빚다 brew [make] rice wine/ ~에 취하다 get drunk; become intoxicated/ ~을 삼가다 refrain[abstain] from liquor/ ~을 끊다 cut out wine/ ~을 맡다 pour[fill] out wine. さけ

**술**² (장식용) a tassel; a tuft; a fringe/ ~ 달린 기 a tasselled flag. かさ

**술**³ 『식』 the pistils and stamens of a flower/ 수~ a stamen/ 암~ a pistil.
かさ

**술**⁴ (부피) the thickness of a book or paper.

**술**(戌) the zodiacal sign of the dog/ ~년 the year of the Dog. いぬ

**술가**(術家) a diviner; an augurer.
せんじゅつ

**술값** drink-money; a tip/ ~을 주다 tip; give one drink-money.

**술객**(術客) a conjurer. せんじゅつ

**술계**(術計) a stratagem; an artifice; a trick/적의 ~에 빠지다 play into the enemy's hand. じゅっけい

**술구더기** a grain of rice floating on *sool*.

**술국** soup taken with *sool*[wine].

**술군** a drinker; a tippler; a sot; a thirsty soul; a bacchant〈미〉. しゅかく

**술길** the influence of liquor/ ~에 under the influence of liquor; in a drunken fit. よいまえに

**술래** a tagger 《눈 가리고 하는》 a hood-man/ 내가 ~다 You are it. おに

**술래잡기** tag 《눈 가리고 하는》 prisoner's base; blindman's baff; hoodman-blind 《고》/ ~하다 play catch who catch can; play blindman's baff; play tag.
かくれんぼう

**술렁거리다** be perturbed; be disturbed; be unsettled; be agitated/그 소식을 듣고 학생들은 술렁거렸다 The students were agitated by[with] the news./술렁술렁 tumultously. がやがやする

**술망나니** a vicious[quarrelsome] drinker. のむんだくれ

**술명하다** (be) fair; decent; moderate.
おとなしくにあっている

**술밑** boiled-rice mixed with yeast for brewing.

**술바닥** a sole of a plow.

**술밥** boiled-rice for brewing.
さけをつくるめし

**술법**(術法) magical tricks; conjury; magic; mysteries/ ~을 쓰다 practice magic; lay a spell (*upon*). うらないかた

**술병**(一瓶) a wine-holder[-bottle].
さけのびん

**술병**(一病) a disease caused by drinking.

**술부대**(一負袋) a heavy drinker; a drunkard; a sponge; a soaker; an insatiable drinker. のむんだくれ

**술사**(術士) an augurer ⇨ 술가(術家).
じゅっし

**술상**(一床) the table laden with *sool* and some eatables/ ~을 보다 lay *sool* and some eatables on the table.

**술서**(術書) a book on magic[witchcraft]. うらない書

술수(術數) conjury; an artifice ⇨술법. うらないかた

술술 ①《순조롭게》smoothly; without a hitch 《유창하게》fluently; facilely; with facility 《쉽게》easily; with ease; readily/ ~ 대답하다 give a ready answer ②《바람이》gently; softly/ 바람이 ~ 분다 The wind blows gently., There is a gentle breeze. さらさら

술안주(-按酒) a relish [taken with wine]; an accompaniment of[for, to] *sool*; a side dish/술과 ~ *sool* and some eatables. さけのさかな

술어(述語) 〖언〗 the predicate/~ 동사 a predicate verb. じゅつご

술어(術語) a technical term; professional language; [scientific] terminology 《총칭》technics. じゅつご

술업(術業) magic; witchcraft; conjury; divination.

술자리 a drinking party; a banquet; a feast/ ~에 모시다 wait at a banquet. しゅせき

술잔 a wine cup; a wine bowl; a wine glass (다리가 있는) a goblet/ ~을 받다 accept a cup/ ~을 돌리다 pass the wine cup round; circulate the wine cup. さかずき

술잔치 a drinking party; a feast. しゅえん

술장사 the liquor-selling business.

술주자 a tub for straining *sool*[wine]; a liquor cask[strainingtub].

술집 a bar; a bar-room; a drinking establishment; a saloon《미》/ ~ 주인 a barkeeper. さかや

술책(術策) an artifice; a stratagem; a trick; wiles; tactics; a policy/ ~을 부리다 resort to tricks. じゅっさく

술청 the counter of a stand-up bar 《술집》 the bar. たちのみのだい

술추렴 collecting money for a drinking bout/ ~하다 have everyone chip in for a drinking party.

술타령(-打令) drinking/ ~하다 keep [go] on drinking; do not leave off drinking/ ~꾼 a drunkard; a sot; a heavy drinker.

술탈(-頉) an upset due to drinking.

술통(-桶) a wine barrel; a wine keg.

술판 a drinking party.

술회(述懷) 《회상》recollections; reminiscence 《토로》an effusion of *one's* thoughts/ ~하다 speak[say] reminiscently; recall; relate[express] *one's* thoughts/ ~담 *one's* reminiscences; *one's* memories. じゅっかい

숨¹ a breath; breathing; respiration/ 단~ 에 all in a breath/ ~가쁘게 out of breath; panting; breathlessly/ ~차게 달리다 run *oneself* without breath / ~을 쉬다 breathe; respire; draw a breath/ ~을 들이쉬다 breathe in; inhale. こきゅう

숨² 《채소 따위의》the crispness of fresh vegetables; harshness/배추가 ~이 죽었다 The cabbage has lost its crispness. やさいなどのしんせんさ

숨쁘다 (be) gasping; panting; be short [out] of breath/숨쁘게 gaspingly; panting; breathlessly.

숨결 breathing; respiration/ ~이 가쁘다 breathe hard. こきゅうのはやさ

숨고다 be suffocated; be asphyxiated; be choked[stifled, smothered]; pant. ちっそくする

숨구멍 〖해〗 the trachea; the windpipe. きゅうするあな

숨기(-氣) signs of breathing/ ~가 없다 show no sign of life/아직 ~가 있을 동안에 while one is alive. こきゅうするいき

숨기다 hide; conceal 《은닉》harbour; shelter; screen 《비밀로 하다》keep secret [dark]; keep (*a matter*) from (*one*); keep (*a matter*) to *oneself*; hide (*a matter*) from (*one*); 《덮어 두다》cover; veil; cloak 《속이다》disguise 《안 보이게 하다》keep[put] out of sight/사실을 ~ conceal the fact. かくす

숨김없다 (be) frank; openhearted; unreserved; straight-forward/숨김없이 without reserve; frankly.

숨넘어가다 breathe *one's* last; expire; die. こきゅうしなくなる

숨다 ①《안 보이게》hide [*oneself*]; take over ②《피난하다》take shelter; seek refuge/숨어 있다 be in hiding; be concealed; be behind. かくれる

숨막히다 be suffocated; be chocked/숨막히는 choking; oppressive (*silence*); breath-taking; suffocating.

숨바꼭질 hide and seek/ ~하다 play hide and seek. かくれんぼう

숨소리 a breath/ ~를 죽이고 hardly daring to breathe. こきゅうするおん

숨숨하다 (be) pockmarked; (be) pitted/ 숨숨한 얼굴 a pitted face.

숨쉬다 breathe; respire; draw *one's* breath; take breath/숨쉴 사이도 안 주다 give (*a person*) not a moment's respite. こきゅうする

숨어들다 lie concealed; hide *oneself* (*behind, in, from, under*).

숨지다 breathe *one's* last; expire; gasp *one's* life away; die; give up *one's* breath. いきをひきとる

숨차다 pant; be out[short] of breath; breathe with difficulty/숨찬 gasping; panting; broken-winded. いきせく

숨통(-筒) the windpipe ⇨숨구멍. きかん

숫- pure; unspoiled; spotless; undefiled; innocent/ ~처녀 a virgin; an innocent[unsophisticated] girl. はじめの一. きれいな-

숫간(-間) a lean-to; a penthouse.

숫것 untouched food.

숫구멍 〖해〗 the fontanel[le].

숫기(-氣) innocent; openness/ ~ 좋다

be unashamed[unabashed, bold, outgoing].

**숫돌** a whetstone; a grindstone 《면도칼용》 a hone/ ~에 갈다 sharpen [a knife] on a whetstone; whet; grind.

**숫되다** (be) innocent; a simple-minded; naive. そぼくだ

**숫보기** a simple man. きいなひと

**숫사람** a simple[an unsophisticated] person. きいとなひと

**숫색시** an innocent young girl; a virgin. きいとなおんな

**숫실(繰—)** embroidery thread.

**숫자(數字)** a figure; a numeral/로마 ~ Roman numerals/ ~로 표시하다 state [express] in figures.

**숫접다** (be) pure; innocent; chaste; sincere/숫저운 색시 an innocent girl. じゅんぼくでまじめだ

**숫제** ①《차라리》 rather; preferably/수모를 당할 바엔 ~ 죽는 편이 낫겠다 Death is preferable to dishonor. ②《진심으로》 sincerely; wholeheartedly/~ 마음을 바치다 completely devote oneself to (one's husband) ③《전적으로》 [not] at all; from the first[beginning]/ ~ 안가는 게 좋다 You better not go at all. まことに

**숫지다** (be) simple and honest; naive.

**숫처녀(—處女)** an immaculate[undefiled] virgin. おぼこむすめ

**숫총각(—總角)** an innocent bachelor. どうていのおとこ

**숫하다** (be) many; naive; numerous; plenty (of).

**숭고(崇高)** loftiness; grandeur/ ~하다 (be) lofty; noble; sublime/ ~한 정신의 high-minded. すうこう

**숭굴숭굴** plump 《태도가》amiable/ ~하다 (be) chubby; plump; happylooking 《태도가》 affable; amiable; easygoing/그 사람은 누구에게나 ~하다 He makes himself agreeable to everybody.

**숭늉** scorched-rice tea.

**숭덩숭덩** thickly; largely; in big parts / ~ 자르다 chop thickly[in large parts]. あらあら

**숭배(崇拜)** worship; admire; adoration/ ~하다 worship; admire; adore 《열광적으로》 mark an idol of; idolize/ ~자 an admirer; a worshipper; an adorer; a votary/영웅[조상] ~ hero[ancestor] worship/우상 ~ the worship of idols /나는 이 순신을 진심으로 ~하고 있다 I have a sincere admiration for Lee Su-nsin. すうはい

**숭상(崇尙)** respect; esteem; [high] regard; deference/ ~하다 respect; esteem; value; have a regard for[to]; deem highly of. うやまいあがめること

**숭숭** ①thickly ②《바느질》 with large stitches; coarsely/ ~ 호다 sew with large stitches. あらあら

**숭어(—魚)** 【魚】 a grey mullet. まぼら

**숭엄(崇嚴)** dignity; majesty; augustness / ~하다 (be) solemn; sublime; majestic. すうげん

**숯** charcoal/ ~덩이 a lump of charcoal/ ~불 a charcoal fire/ ~을 굽다 make charcoal (in a kiln). すみ

**숯가마** a charcoal pit; a charcoal kiln [oven]. すみやくかま

**숯검정** charcoal soot. すみのすす

**숯내** poisoning smell of carbonic gas/ ~가 나다 smell burning. すみのにおい

**숯덩걸** a half-burned piece of charcoal.

**숯머리** a headache caused by inhaling carbonic gas. すみのにおいによるずつう

**숯먹** an ink stick made of pine soot.

**숯장수** ①《숯 파는》 a charcoal dealer ②《얼굴이 검은》 a dark-faced[-skinned] person. すみしょうにん

**숯장이** a charcoal maker.

**숱** thickness; density; richness 《수량》 quantity/ ~하다 (be) plentiful; thick; rich/ ~이 많은 머리 tufty[flowing] hair; thick hair.

**숲** a bush; a thicket; a cluster[clump] of trees; a grove; a wood 《큰》 a forest 《밀림》 a jungle/대나무 ~ a bamboo-bush[-grove]. やぶ

**숲길** a forest path[road]. やぶみち

**쉬** 《새 쫓는 소리》 Shoo! しー

**쉬¹** the eggs of the fly; flyblow. はえのたまご

**쉬²** 《조용히》 Hush!, Sh!, Hist!, Whist! / ~ 조용히 해라 Hush! Be quiet!

**쉬³** 《어린이 오줌눌 때》 Pass!, Tinkle-tinkle! しいしい

**쉬⁴** ①《곧》 soon; presently; before long; shortly/ ~ 돌아오겠습니다 I will be back soon. ②《쉽게》 easily; readily ⇒ 쉽다. たやすく

**쉬다¹** ①《일을》 rest from one's work; lay off 《휴가로》 take a vacation[holiday, day]; 《결석·결근하다》 be absent; miss (school); stay away from (school, work) / 회사를 ~ be absent from one's office ②《휴식하다》 rest; take[have] a rest; stop (from work); 《한숨 돌리다》 breathe; take a breath/쉬지 않고 continually; without rest ③《중지하다》 lie idle; be at a standstill/쉴새 없이 지껄이다 talk without a pause; rattle on ④《취침하다》 sleep; go to sleep 《자리에 들다》 go to bed; retire; turn in/편안하게 ~ sleep soundly; have a good night. やすむ

**쉬다²** 《상하다》 spoil 《음식이》 go bad 《우유 따위가》 turn sour. かされる

**쉬다³** 《숨을》 breathe; take breath/그는 안도의 숨을 내쉬었다 The man heaved a sigh of relief. こきゅうする

**쉬다⁴** 《목이》 get[grow] hoarse; become husky; hoarsen/쉰 목소리 a hoarse [husky] voice.

**쉬다⁵** 《피륙을》 soak [cloth] in water in which rice has been washed; gloss.

**쉬쉬하다** hush up (*a matter*); suppress; keep (*a matter*) secret/그 일에 대하여 쉬쉬하고 있다 They are gaged about it. かくしておく

**쉬슬다** flyblow/쉬슨 고기 flyblown meat.

**쉬엄쉬엄** with frequent rests; intermittently; in easy stages; off and on/~ 일하다 work taking frequent breaks; do a job in easy stages. やすみやすみ

**쉬지근하다** (be) rather stale-smelling; musty; sourish. くさってすっぱい

**쉬척지근하다** (be) sour; acid.
ひどくくさってすっぱい

**쉬파리** a blue-bottle [fly]; a blow-fly.
しまはえ

**쉬하다** (*a child*) "tinkle"; urinate.

**쉰** fifty 《쉰째》 the fiftieth/~ 살 fifty years of age. ごじゅう

**쉰둥이** a child born to a person 50 years of age.

**쉽다** 《용이하다》 (be) easy; simple; light; plain 《경향》 (be) apt[liable, susceptible] to./쉽게 easily; simply; in a simple way; without trouble[difficulty, effort]. やすい

**쉽사리** easily; without difficulty/~ 알 수 있다 《인식》 be easy to recognize 《이해》 be easy to understand.

**스님** 《중》 a priest 《스승 중》 master[teacher] of a Baddhist priest. ぼうず

**쓰개** a headpiece. こうむりもの

**쓰다**¹ 《글씨를》 write 《글을》 compose (*a poem*); write; pen (*a story*); 《적다》 put[write, note] down/잉크로 ~ write in ink/연필로 ~ write in[with a] pencil/글씨를 잘 ~ write a letter/잡지에 글을 ~ write for a magazine. かく

**쓰다**² ⇒별항 참조.

**쓰다**³ put on; wear; cover/모자를 ~ put on[wear] a hat; have a hat on; be bareheaded/안경을 ~ put on glasses/먼지를 ~ be covered with dust/남의 죄를 ~ take upon *oneself* another's fault. こうむる

**쓰다**⁴ 《묘를》 choose the site of a grave [by geomancy]/묘를 ~ set up a grave.

**쓰다**⁵ 《맛이》 taste[be] bitter/쓴 맛 a bitter taste/쓴 약 bitter medicine/쓴 맛을 보다 taste a bitted[hard] experience. にがい

**쓰다듬다** stroke (*one's beard*); pat (*a child* on *the head*); pass *one's* hand over (*one's face*); rub (*a person's chin*)/턱을 ~ touch[rub] *one's* chin. なだめる

**쓰디쓰다** (be) extremely bitter.
とてもくるしい

**쓰라리다** (be) sore; smart /쓰라린 경험 bitter experience /가슴이 ~ (*it*) wring *one's* heart/연기 때문에 눈이 ~ The smoke makes my eyes smart. くるしい

**스라소니** ①《동》 a lynx ②《무능자》 a good-for-nothing.

**스란치마** a trailing skirt[*chima*].

**쓰러뜨리다** throw down; knock[bring] down 《발을 걸어서》 trip up; fell 《바람이》 blow down/사람을 때려서 ~ knock (*a person*) down/나무를 ~ fell a tree 《바람이》 blow down a tree.

**쓰러지다** ①《서 있던 것이》 fall[come] down 《도괴하다》 collapse; go[roll] over /마루 위에 ~ fall down on the floor /지진으로 많은 집이 쓰러졌다 Many houses were destroyed by the earthquake ②《병고·피로 따위로》 break down(fr-om *exhaustion*); go[be] down (with *an illness*); 《기절하여》 fall in a faint; be laid up (with *cold*)/기진하여 ~ sink down on[to] the ground ③《몰락하다》 be ruined; be overthrown 《파산하다》 fail; go[be] bankrupt/이 회사는 쓰러져 가고 있다 This company is on the verge of bankruptcy. ④《죽다》 die; fall down dead; fall a victim to/… 의 손에 ~ fall[meet *one's* end] at the hand of. たおれる

**-스럽다** be; be like; seem; suggest/변덕 ~ be capricious/사랑~ be lovely/신비~ be mysterious. —らしい

**쓰레기** dirt; rubbish; refuse; garbage; dust; trash/~ 통 a dust-bin.

**쓰레받기** a dustpan. ごみとり

**쓰레질** sweeping and cleaning; housework/ ~하다 sweep. はくこと

**쓰르라미** 《충》 a kind of cicada; *Meimuna opalifera*(학명). ひぐらし

**쓰르르** smoothly; easily; gently / ~ 눈을 감다 close[shut] *one's* eyes gently.
さらさら

**스리** a bite in the interior of *one's* mouth.

**쓰리다** ache; smart; tingle; burn/가슴이 ~ have heartburn/눈이 ~ My eyes are smarting. ペこぺこだ

**스멀거리다** itch; be itchy; feel crawly [creepy]/스멀스멀 crawling; itching.
こちょこちょとこそばい

**스무** twenty/ ~ 날 the twentieth day of the month 《20일 동안》 [for] twenty days/ ~ 번째 the twentieth/ ~ 고개 《라디오에서》 "Twenty Questions".
にじゅう

**스물** twenty; a score. にじゅう

**스미다** infiltrate into; percolate[permeate] through; soak[sink] into; penetrate into/[빗물이] 지붕으로 스며들다 soak through a roof/[교훈이] 마음에 ~ sink into *one's* mind/물이 땅 속으로 스며들다 The water sinks into the ground./그의 충고가 가슴에 스며들었다 H-is advice was well imprinted on our minds. そまる

**스스럽다** ①《정분이 두텁지 못해》 be ill at ease; feel constrained; feel awkward ②《부끄럽다》 be overwhelmed with shyness; be abashed; be shy. よそよそしい

**스스로**¹ 《자가 자신》 oneself; by *oneself*; in person/자기 일은 자기 ~로 해라 Look after yourself/너 ~로 가 봐라 Go

스스로² ①(저절로) of itself; of its own accord (자동적으로) automatically／그것은 ~ 명백해질 것이다 It will become clear of itself. ②(자진해서) of one's own accord; of one's free will; of one's own initiative／그는 ~ 사임했다 He resigned voluntarily. てずから

스승 a teacher; a master／~의 은혜 favours of one's teacher. せんせい

쓰이다¹ (글씨가) write; be written (쓰게 하다) let (a person) write／이 펜은 글씨가 잘 쓰인다 This pen writes well.／그는 아들에게 편지를 쓰게 하였다 He had his son write a letter. かかれる

쓰이다² ①(들다·소용되다) be spent; be consumed; take; lost／그 일에는 사람 손이 많이 쓰인다 The work takes[requires] quite a number of hands. ②(사용되다) be used; be made use of; be employed; serve／흔히 ~ be in common use／널리 쓰이게 되다 get[go] out of use／이 방은 서재로 쓰인다 This room now serves as my study. つかわれる

쓰적거리다 ①(비비어지다) rub[chafe] against each other ②(대강대강 쓸다) a sweep slovenly. される

스쳐보다 cast a side glance at; glance sidewise at (사람을) give (one) a sidelong glance.

스치다 graze (past, by, along); shave; touch slightly／문득 공상이 나의 심중을 스쳤다 suddenly a fancy flitted through my mind.

쓱 (슬쩍) (slip away) quickly and quietly (척) (bolt) abruptly (빨리) (pass by) rapidly (슬쓸) (rub) deftly. 삿さっ

쓱싹 ~하다 ①(돈 따위를) pocket; peculate; embezzle; sneak《미·속》/남의 돈을 ~하다 embezzle money from (a person) ②(상쇄하다) offset[cancel] each other; wipe off (a debt); square up《속》. ③(얼버무리다) cover up. ごしごし

쓴웃음 a bitter[grim] smile／~을 짓다 smile a bitter smile. にがわらい

쓸개 【해】 the gall-bladder; the gall／~ 머리 beef from the top of the gallbladder／ ~ 빠진 녀석 a spiritless person. きも

슬겁다 (be) spacious at the rear; wider at the rear than at the entrance.

슬그머니 stealthily; secretly; by stealth; on the sly／~ 나가다 steal out of／~ 훔치다 pick and steal. そっと

슬근슬근 rub[chafe] gently together／ 슬근슬근 rubbing gently.

슬금슬금 stealthily; sneakingly; on the sly／~ 달아나다 run away stealthily; slip away. こっそり

슬금하다 (be) wise and generous; sagacious and broad-minded. かしこい

슬기 wisdom; wits; brains; intelligence; sagacity; resources／~있는 wise; clever; intelligent; intellectual. ちえ

슬기롭다 (be) wise; sagacious; bright; intelligent; clever[-headed]／슬기롭게

---

## 쓰 다²

①(사용하다) use; make use of; employ; put to use (something) to a bad use／머리를 ~ use one's brain; do brain work／연장 쓰는 법을 배우다 learn the use of a tool／이것은 무엇에 쓰는가 What is this used for?／내 차를 써라 My car is at your service.／외출중에는 내 방을 마음대로 쓰시오 I will give[allow] you the run of my room while I am out.／구두 만드는데 가죽을 ~ use leather for making shoes.／배운 것을 실지로 ~ put what one has learned to practical use.

②(고용하다) employ; hire; use; take (a person) into one's service; keep (a servant)／그 일에 나를 써 주시오 Use me for the work.／시험삼아 써 보다 take (a person) on trial／아무개를 국어 선생으로 ~ employs a person as a language teacher／그 공장에서는 직공을 200명 쓰고 있다 The factory employs two hundred hands.

③(소비하다) use; spend／돈을 물처럼 ~ spend money like water／다 써 버리다 use up; run[go] through (money); consume; exhaust／버는 대로 죄다 써 버리다 He spends all he earns.／책[옷]에 많은 돈을 ~ spends a lot of money on books[for clothes].

④(구사하다) use; speak／전방진 말을 ~ use haughty language／이탈리아에서는 무슨 말을 쓰느냐 What language is spoken in Italic?／

⑤(색을) have sex; copulate／색을 ~ have sex; copulate.

⑥(술법을) practice; do; deal in／마술을 ~ do conjuring tricks; deal with the devil; practice magic／수단을 ~ take a measure.

⑦(힘을) exert oneself(노력하다); apply [use] one's force(폭력을); use one's strength[energy](정력을).

⑧(약을) administer (medicine); dose; use; apply／약을 ~ administer a medicine (to a patient); (바르다) apply a medicament (to a diseased part)／이 약을 쓰면 병이 나을 것이다 This medicine will cure you of your disease.

wisely; intelligently; cleverly/슬기로운 사람 a man of wisdom. ちえがある
슬다¹ 《알을》 oviposit (곤충이); 《파리가》 blow; spawn 《물고기 따위가》 shoot[deposit] spawn. たまごをうみつける
슬다² ①《푸성귀가》 wither ②《없어지다》 vanish; disappear; fade away; die [melt] away. かれていく
쓸다¹ sweep/마루를 ~ sweep the floor /쓸어 모으다 sweep up together; sweep into a heap/유행병이 한 고을을 쓸었다 The epidemic swept[prevailed throughout] the town. はく
쓸다² 《줄로》 rasp; file/줄로 쓸어서 매끈하게 하다 file (a thing) smooth; file away roughness. (やすりで)かける
쓸데 없다 be of no use[value]; (be) useless; worthless/쓸데 없이 unnecessarily; to no purpose; in vain/쓸데 없는 책 a book of no value; a stupid book/쓸데 없이 돈을 쓰다 waste money; spend money wastefully.
쓸리다¹ ①《쓸게 하다》 let[make] sweep/하인에게 방을 ~ have a servant sweep the room ②《피동》 be swept; get swept/홍수에 다리가 쓸려 나갔다 The bridge was washed away by the swollen river. はかれる
쓸리다² 《줄·톱으로》 get rasped[filed]. さすりむける
슬며시 secretly; furtively; privately; stealthily; in secret[private]; by stealth/~ 집을 나가다 slip out of the house; sneak off. そっと
쓸모 use; usefulness; utility/~가 있다 be of use; be useful[serviceable]/~가 없다 be useless[of no use]; be good-for-nothing; be no good/~가 많다 be of wide[extensive] use. じつり
슬미지근하다 (be) lukewarmish; tepid/그녀를 다루는 방법이 너무 ~ That's too mild a way of dealing with her. なまぬるい
슬슬 ①《가볍게》 softly; quietly; gently; tenderly; lightly/바람이 ~ 분다 The wind blows gently. ②《은근히》 cajolingly; skilfully/우는 아이를 ~ 달래다 soothe a crying baby gently. こっそり
쓸쓸하다 《적적하다》 (be) lonely; lonesome 《날씨가》 dreary; gloomy; dismal/쓸쓸한 웃음 a wan[melancholy, sad] smile /쓸쓸하게 지내다 lead a lonely life/네가 없어 매우 쓸쓸했다 We missed you badly. さびしい
슬쩍 ①《몰래》 secretly; in secret; furtively; stealthily; by stealth/그는 모임에서 ~ 빠져 나왔다 He slipped away from the meeting. ②《쉽게》 easily; cleverly/주먹을 ~ 피하다 lightly parry a blow. さっと
슬퍼하다 sorrow[grieve] (at, over); feel sad[sorrowful] (at); be distressed (over); 《애석히 여기다》 mourn (for, over); regret/슬프게 하다 make (a person) sad;

grieve (a person)/아버지의 죽음을 ~ grieve[mourn] over one's father's death.
슬프다 (be) sad; sorrowful; pathetic; doleful 《유감스럽다》 regrettable; touching/기쁠 때나 슬플 때나 in joy and in sorrow/슬퍼하다 sorrow; grieve (at, over); be sad; feel sorrow; mourn (for, over); regret/그는 아직도 아내의 죽음을 슬퍼하고 있다 He still nurses his wife's death./너무 슬퍼서 눈물도 안 나온다 My grief is too deep for tears. かなしい
슬픔 sorrow; sadness; grief 《비탄》 lamentation/남모르는 ~ a hidden sorrow/ ~에 잠기다 be in deep grief[sorrow]; be buried in grief; yield to sorrow. かなしみ
슬피 sorrowfully; sadly; mournfully/ ~ 울다 cry sorrowfully.
슬하(膝下) the care of one's parents/부모 ~를 떠나다 leave [one's parental] home. しっか
슭다 polish [grain].
씀바귀 a sowthistle; Lactuca dendata (학명). にがな
슴베 a tang (of a sword etc.).
습격(襲擊) an attack; an assault; a raid; a storm; a charge/~하다 attack; raid; charge; assault; swoop down upon/불의에 ~하다 make a surprise attack/적진을 ~하다 attack[storm] an enemy position. しゅうげき
습관(習慣) 《습성》 habit 《상습》 practice 《관용》 usage 《풍속》 custom/~적 habitual; customary/~을 기르다 form a habit; accustom oneself to (a task, do) /~이 붙다 get into[acquire] a habit; take to (idling, drinking)/~을 고치다 break (a person, oneself) of a habit / ~은 제 2의 천성이다 Habit a second nature./그것은 그의 ~이 되어 있다 It is a habit with him. しゅうかん
습기(濕氣) damp[ness]; moisture; humidity/ ~없는 dry/ ~있는 damp; moist; humid/ ~없는 장소에 두다 keep (a thing) in a dry place. しっけ
습답(襲踏) ~하다 follow in (a person's) footsteps; follow; follow suit.
습도(濕度) humidity/높은 ~ a high percentage of humidity/ ~계 a [wet and dry bulb] hygrometer/ ~를 재다 determine the humidity. しつど
습득(拾得) picking up/ ~하다 pick up; find (lost property)/ ~물 a find; a found article/ ~자 a finder. しゅうとく
습득(習得) learning; acquirement/ ~하다 practise; be trained in; learn; master/ ~시키다 get (one) trained[drilled] in/5개 국어를 ~하다 master five languages. しゅうとく
습래(襲來) an attack; an invasion; an incursion; a raid/ ~하다 invade; attack; raid; make an inroad[incursion] into 《폭풍 따위》 visit; strike. しゅうらい

**습성(習性)** a habit; a habitude; a second nature / ~이 되다 become a habit; grow into a habit. しゅうせい

**습성(濕性)** wetness.

**습속(習俗)** convention; usage 《전통》a tradition / ~에 따르다 be true to the tradition. しゅうぞく

**씁쓸하다** (be) somewhat bitter; bitterish. ややくるしい

**습습하다** (be) manly; manful; manlike; valiant. おとこらしい

**습신** shoes for a dead person.

**습용(襲用)** using[employing] hereditarily / ~하다 follow; adopt. しゅうよう

**습유(拾遺)** an addendum; a supplement 《낙수》gleanings / ~하다 add a supplement to [a main work]. しゅうい

**습윤(濕潤)** dampness; moisture; humidity / ~하다 (be) damp; wet; moist. しつじゅん

**습의(襲衣)** a shroud; the dress for a dead body for burial.

**습자(習字)** penmanship; handwriting 《모필》calligraphy / ~하다 learn handwriting; practise penmanship / 영어 ~ English penmanship. しゅうじ

**습작(習作)** an essay; a study; étude(F). しゅうさく

**습작(襲爵)** succesion to the title[peerage] / ~하다 succeed to the title[peerage]. しゅうしゃく

**습전기(濕電氣)** galvanic electricity.

**습전지(濕電池)** 【물】a galvanic battery.

**습종(濕腫)** abscesses and ulcers (on the leg).

**습증(濕症)** a disease caused by damp.

**습지(濕地)** swampy land; boggy[damp] ground; marsh; wet land. しっち

**습진(濕疹)** 【의】eczema.

**습하다(濕—)** (be) damp; dampish; humid; moist; soppy; wet / 습한 공기[기후] damp[muggy] air[weather]. じめじめする

**습하다(襲—)** wash a dead body; prepare [a corpse] for burial. したいをきよめる

**승(升)** a measure of capacity [=1.588 quarts, 0.48 gallons]. しょう

**승(乘)** 【수】multiplication / ~하다 multiply / 5에다 4를 ~하다 multiply five by four. じょう

**승(僧)** a priest; a bonze; a monk / 순례~ an itinerant priest; a wandering monk. そう

**승(勝)** a victory; a win.

**승가(僧家)** 《중》a monk. そうか

**승강(昇降)** ①《오르내리기》going up and down; ascent and descent 《높이가 변함》rise and fall / ~하다 go up and down; ascend and desend; rise and fall / ~기 a lift〈영〉; an elevator〈미〉/ ~구 an entrance 《배의》a companion-way ②《옥신각신》a petty quarrel; bickering; wrangle / ~하다 have a petty quarrel; wrangle (with). しょうこう

**승강이** a petty quarrel; wrangling; altercating / ~하다 have a petty quarrel; wrangle (with). いざこざ

**승객(乘客)** 《택시 따위의》a passenger; a fare / ~수 the number of passengers carried / ~ 안내소 an inquiry office; for passengers / 이등 ~ second-class passengers. じょうきゃく

**승검초(—草)** 【식】 Angelica Uchiyamai(학명). とうき

**승격(昇格)** elevation of the status; the raising of status; promotion in status / ~하다 raise in status; be promoted [elevated] in status raise / 공사관을 대사관으로 ~시키다 raise a legation to the rank[status] of an embassy. しょうかく

**승경(勝景)** a fine view; a beauty[scenic] spot. しょうけい

**승계(承繼)** succession; continuation ➾계승. しょうけい

**승교(乘轎)** a palanquin; a sedan-chair.

**승급(昇給)** an increase[a rise] in pay [salary] / ~하다 obtain[get, win, receive, attain] promotion; be promoted [advanced]. しょうきゅう

**승급(昇級)** promotion; advancement; rise / ~하다 be promoted; be advanced; rise; rise in rank / ~시키다 promote; advance (one) / 과장에서 국장으로 ~하다 be promoted from sectional chief to bureau director. しょうきゅう

**승기(勝機)** a chance of victory.

**승낙(承諾)** consent; assent; acceptance; agreement; compliance / ~하다 consent[agree, assent] to;· give one's consent to; comply with; acquiesce in / ~없이 without (a person's) consent; without leave / ~서 a written consent / ~을 구하다 ask (a person's) consent / ~해 주시겠읍니까 Have your consent ? しょうだく

**승냥이** 【동】a jackal. やまいぬ

**승당(僧堂)** the priest's quarters of a Buddhist temple. ぼうずのいえ

**승도(僧徒)** [Buddhist] priests[monks]. そうと

**승려(僧侶)** a monk 《목사》a clergyman 《총칭》the clergy / ~가 되다 become a priest; enter the priesthood 《목사》take holy orders. そうりょ

**승률(勝率)** the percentage of victories [to the total number of matches]. しょうりつ

**승리(勝利)** victory; triumph; conquest 《경기의》a win / ~자 a victor 《경기의》a winner / 사랑의 ~자 a successful lover / ~를 얻다 win[gain, achieve] a victory; score[achieve] a triumph; win [carry] the day / 최후의 ~을 얻다 gain the final victory; win in the long run / ~는 우리의 것이다 The day is ours., The victory is an our side. しょうり

**승마(乘馬)** 《말타기》 horse-riding; riding 《말》 a riding horse/ ~하다 ride a horse; mount[get on] a horse; take [a] horse; be across a horse's back/ ~복(服) a riding-suit 《부인용》 a riding-habit. じょうば

**승명(乘冪)** 〖수〗 a power. じょうべき

**승명(承命)** receiving an order[a command] (from *one's king, father*)/ ~하다 receive an order[a command].

**승무(僧舞)** a Buddhist dance.

**승무원(乘務員)** 《기차의》 a train-man 《전차의》 a car-man 《기선·비행기 따위의》 a crew 《배의》 a complement 《총칭》 man on car service. じょうむいん

**승문(僧門)** Buddhism ⇨불가. ぶっけ

**승방(僧房)** a nunnery; a cloister. そうぼう

**승법(乘法)** 〖수〗 multiplication/ ~의 multiplicative. じょうほう

**승벽(勝癖)** an unyielding spirit; a competitive spirit/ ~이 있는 사람 a man of spirit.

**승병(僧兵)** a monk soldier; a warrior-monk. そうへい

**승복(僧服)** ①《자백》 confession of a crime ②《따름》 submission/ ~하다 confess a crime; submit; yield to (*another's view*). そうふく

**승복(承服)** ①《굴복》 submission/ ~하다 submit to (*anything*); yield[bend, bow] to (*another's views*) ②《자백》 confession /~하다 confess (*one's guilt*); own (to *a fault*).

**승부(勝負)** the issue [of a battle]; victory or[and] defeat; the utcome/ ~를 결하다 fight it out; fight to the finish. しょうぶ

**승산(勝算)** a chance[prospect] of victory; chances of success; odds/전혀 ~이 없다 The chances are dead against us. /우리 편에 ~이 있다 The odds[chances] are in our favor. しょうさん

**승상(承相)** a prime minister. しょうじょう

**승서(陞敍)** promotion; advancement/ ~하다 promote; advance.

**승선(乘船)** embarkation; boarding/ ~하다 embark; go aboard; get on board [a ship]; join a ship/ ~권 a passage-ticket/급히 ~하다 board [a ship];take ship. じょうせん

**승세(乘勢)** taking advantage of the circumstances; seizing the right moment / ~하다 take advantage of the circumstances; seize the right moment. しょうせい

**승소(勝訴)** winning a lawsuit/ ~하다 《사람을 주어로》 win a .suit[case]/ 《재판을 주어로》 result[be decided] in favour of. しょうそ

**승수(乘數)** 〖수〗 a multiplier/피 ~ a multiplicant. じょうすう

**승순(承順)** submission/ ~하다 submit to; yield to. しょうじゅん

**승 장구(乘勝長驅)** pressing hard on the heels of enemy; making a long drive taking advantage of victory/ ~하다 make a long drive taking advantage of victory; press hard on the heels of enemy; seize[avail *one*self of] an opportunity.

**승아** 〖식〗 a sorrel; a dock. すいば

**승안(承顏)** a meeting with a superior/ ~하다 pay a visit to [a superior]. しょたいめんすること

**승야 도주(乘夜逃走)** ~하다 escape in the night; run away taking advantage of darkness of night.

**승용(乘用)** ~차 a motorcar[an automobile] for riding; a passenger car. じょうよう

**승원(僧院)** a Buddhist monastery; a cloister. そういん

**승인(勝因)** the cause of the victory.

**승인(承認)** recognition; acknowledg[e]ment 《인가》 admission / ~하다 approve; recognize; admit / ~을 얻어 with (*a person's*) approval/ ~을 바라다 seek [ask for] the approval of (*a person*) /독립을 ~하다 recognize the independence of [a country]. しょうにん

**승임(陞任)** promotion/ ~하다 promote; advance. しょうにん

**승자(勝者)** a winner; a victor.

**승적(僧籍)** the priesthood; the holy orders/ ~에 들다 enter the priesthood; become a priest. そうせき

**승전(勝戰)** victory; triumph; conquest / ~하다 win a war[battle]/ ~고(鼓) the drum of victory. かちいくさ

**승전(承前)** "continued (*from*)". しょうぜん

**승정(僧正)** a bishop.

**승제(乘除)** 〖수〗 multiplication and division/가감 ~ the four[elementary] rules of arithmetic; addition; subtraction, multiplication and division; the four operations. じょうじょ

**승지(勝地)** a scenic[beauty] spot; a place of natural beauty. しょうち

**승직(勝職)** the priesthood; holy orders 《목사직》 the ministry/ ~에 취임하다 enter the priesthood; take holy orders.

**승직(陞職)** [receiving] promotion; advancement in office.

**승진(昇進)** promotion; advancement;rise / ~하다 be promoted[advanced](*to*); rise (*to*); get[obtain] promotion/ ~시키다 raise[promote, advance] (*a person*)/ ~이 빨랐다 His promotion has been rapid. しょうしん

**승차(乘車)** taking[mounting]·a train [car]/ ~하다 take a train[car]; get on[into, in] a train; board a car; get aboard (*a train*)〈미〉/~구 an entrance to a platform/ ~권 a free pass. じょうしゃ

**승차(陞差)** advancement to a higher post / ~하다 advance to a higher post.

승척(繩尺) a measurement cord.
승천(昇天, 陞天) ascension/ ~하다 go [ascend] to heaven/ ~일(日) Ascension Day. しょうてん
승통(承統) succession to a lineage/~하다 succeed to[carry on] the lineage. そうけのだいをつぐこと
승패(勝敗) victory or[and] defeat/ ~를 결정하다 try conclusions with (one); decide the issue (of the battle, etc.). しょうはい
승평(昇平, 承平) peace; tranquillity; quiet/ ~하다 (be) peaceful; tranquil; quiet. くにがたいへいであること
승하(昇遐) the death[demise] of a king / ~하다 [a king] die[demise]. おうがしぼうすること
승하다(乘一) multiply/ 7에다 4를 ~ multiply seven by four. かける
승하다(勝一) ①《뛰어나다》be excellent; stand out (*from*); be outstanding ②《낫다》surpass; be superior to; lead; outdo (*others*). すぐれる
승합(乘合) riding together; sharing a vehicle. のりあい
승홍(昇汞) 《화》corrosive sublimate; bichloride of mercury/ ~수 a solution of corrosive sublimate. しょうこう
승화(昇華) 《화》sublimation/ ~하다 sublimate; sublime/ ~물 a sublimate. しょうか

씌우다 《모자 따위를》put [a hat] on (*a person's head*); cover (*a thing*) with 《죄 따위를》impute (*a fault*) to (*a person*); lay[put, fix] (*a fault*) on (*a person*). ぬりつける
씨¹ ①《종자》a seed; a stone 《사과 따위의》a pip 《핵 속의》a kernel/ ~를 뿌리다 sow seed; sow/ ~를 받다 gather the seeds ②《동물의》a breed 《혈통》a stock; a lineage 《아이》a child/ ~가 좋다 be of[bred from] a good[fine] stock ③《원인·재료》cause; source; a subject. しゅ
씨² (피륙의) woof; weft; the widthwise treads/ ~와 날 woof and warf.
씨³ 《품사》a part of speech; a grammatical category of words. ひんし
시(是) right; righteousness; justness. ぜ
시(時) 《시간》hour 《시각》o'clock; time /다섯 ~ five o'clock; the hour of five/ 4 ~ 15분 a quarter past four/ 3 ~ 5분 전 five to three [o'clock]. じ
시(詩) 《총칭》poetry 《운문》verse 《한 수》a poem/ ~의 poetic/ ~를 짓다 compose[write] a poem; turn to writing poetry. し
시(市) a city; a town; a municipality 《시장》a market; a fair/ ~당국 the municipal[city] authority/ ~청 a city hall.
씨(氏) 《경칭》Mister(略: Mr.); Missis (略: Mrs.); Miss 《가계·혈통》a lineage; birth; a clan; a family 《성》a family name; a surname/백~ Mr. *Back*/이~ Mr. *Lee*. さん
시가(市價) the market price[value]/ ~의 변동 the market fluctuations. しか
시가(市街) [city] streets 《시》a city; a town/ ~전 street fighting/ ~지 a town; a city; an urban district. しがい
시가(時價) the current price; the market price/ ~로 in current prices. じか
시가(媤家) the family of *one's* husband; a wife's in-laws. おっとのうち
시가(詩歌) [Chinese and Korean] poetry; songs and poems. しか
시각(視角) 《물》the visual angle; an angle of vision; the optic angle. しかく
시각(時刻) time; hour; a short time/ 약속한 ~ the appointed time/이런 ~ 에 어디를 쏘다니고있었느냐 Where have you been fooling around at this time of night? しこく
시각(視覺) [the sense of] sight; eyesight/ ~ 교육 visual education. しかく
시간(時間) ①time 《한 시간》an hour ②《학교의》a class hour; a lesson; a class/ 한 ~ an hour /정확한 ~ correct[right] time/국어 ~ a Korean language lesson/한두 ~마다 every hour or two / ~에 맞추어 punctually; on time; at the appointed[fixed] time; as regular as a clock/ ~가는 줄도 모르다 be unaware[unconscious] of the passage of time/기차 ~에 대다 be in time for a train/야간 통행 금지 ~ curfew hours/생각할 ~을 주길 바란다 ask for time to consider/아침 식사 ~은 7시이다 Our breakfast hour is at seven o'clock./노는 ~ recess/이제 잘 ~이다 It is about time to go bed./그곳은 서울에서 2~ 걸린다 The town is two hours distant from *Seoul*/사고가 일어난 ~은 오후 5시 37분이었다 The time of the accident was 5 : 37 P. M. / ~ 문제 a question of time/ ~표 a timetable; a schedule 〈미〉/수업[영업] ~ school[business] hours/ ~ 제한 a time limit/ ~ 엄수 punctuality. じかん
시객(詩客) a poet; apoetess. しかく
시꺼멓다 (be) deep black; jet-black; coal-black/시꺼멓게 타다 be scorched black. まっくるだ
시거에 first [of all]; in the first place; at once; instantly; on the spot. すぐ
시건방지다 (be) saucy and pert. です
시게 cereals[corn, grain] for sale [at market].
시겟바리 a market-bound cart laden with cereals [for sale].
시경(詩經) the *Shi-Kyung*; the Book of Songs.
시경찰국(市警察局) 《서울의》the Metropolitan Police Board[Bureau, Headquarters]/~장 Metropolitan Police Director.
시계(時計) 《괘종·책상 시계》a clock 《회중》

시계 a watch 《괄목》 a [wrist] watch 《종류불문》 a timepiece／탁상 ~ a table-clock／전기 ~ an electric clock／야광 ~ a luminous watch; a watch[clock] with a luminous[an illuminating] dial／~탑 a clock tower／~방 a watch-repair shop／~를 맞추다 set the watch／~를 보다 look at[consult] one's watch. とけい

시계(視界) sight; the field of vision 《볼 수 있는 정도》 visibility. しかい

시고(詩稿) a draft poem. しこう

시고모(媤姑母) one's husband's aunt; one's aunt by marriage; a sister of one's father-in-law. おっとのしゅくぼ

시골 the country; a rural district; the provinces 《고향》 one's home[country]; one's home town〈미〉～의 country; 《전원적》 rural 《촌스러운》 rustic／~에 가다 go into the country／~에서 살다 live in the country. いなか

시골고라리 a stupid countryman; a bumpkin; an awkward clumsy yokel.

시골구석 a remote place[corner]; a remote village; an out-of-the-way place [corner]; the black woods〈미〉／~에서 살다 live in a remote country place いなか

시골나기 a country person; a farmer; a rustic; rural folk. いなかっぺい

시골뜨기 a country bumpkin; a hick; a yokel: a hillbilly. いなかっぺい

시골말 a country dialect; backwoods talk; a local expression; a localism. ほうげん

시공(施工) carrying out; execution; operation／～하다 carry out; execute; operate. しこう

시구(市區) streets; urban districts; a municipal district.

시구(詩句) a verse; a stanza; a stave. しく

시구식(始球式) opening ceremony of a ball game／～을 하다 throw[pitch out, kick] the first[commencement] ball. しきゅうしき

시국(時局) the situation; the state of things[affairs]／～에 관한 의견 one's view of[considering] the [current] situation／～을 수습하다 save[improve] the situation／～을 타개하다 tide over a critical situation. じきょく

시굴(試掘) prospecting; a prospect／~하다 prospect (for gold); bore for (oil)／~권 prospecting rights／~자 a [mining] prospector. しくつ

시굼하다 (be) sourish; acidulous. すっぱい

시궁창 a ditch; a gutter; a drain; a sewer／~에 빠지다 fall into a ditch. ぬかるんだところ

시끄럽다 《소란하다》 (be) noisy; boisterous; clamorous; uproarious／시끄러운 소리 a tumult of noise／시끄러운 세상 a troubled world／시끄럽게 떠들다 make much noise[clamor]; make clamor／시끄러워 Be quiet! さわがしい

시극(詩劇) a verse drama. しげき

시근거리다, 씨근거리다 ①《숨결을》 pant; gasp [for breath]; puff [and blow] hard／시근시근[씨근씨근] gasping[ly]; panting ②《신경이》 twinge; tingle; smart; ache; have a tingling pain／시근시근[씨근씨근] with a twinge; tinglingly; smartly. さしこむ

시근하다 have a twinging ache[tingling pain]. うずく

시글시글 swarming. うじゃうじゃ

시금(試金) assaying／~하다 assay; make an assay of／~석 a touchstone 《시련》 an acid test; a crucial test.

시금떨떨하다 (be) sourish and astringent; acidulous and rough.

시금치 【식】 spinach; spinage. ほうれんそう

시금하다 (be) sourish; acidulous; (be) a bit sour. すっぱい

시급(時急) urgency; imminence／～하다 (be) urgent; imminent／이것은 ~히 해결을 요하는 문제다 The matter must be settled without delay. せっぱくしていること

시기(時期) season; time; the times; period 《경우》 an occasion／매년 이 ~에는 at this time every year／~가 절박하다 Time presses. じき

시기(時機) a chance; an opportunity; an occasion／~를 포착하다 take[seize] an opportunity／~를 놓치다 lose[let slip] one's chance. じき

시기(猜忌) 《염오》 hatred; disgust 《샘》 jealousy; envy; a green eye／~하다 abhor; abominate 《미워하다》 adverse to; be jealous[envious] of; envy; view with a jealousy. さいき

시나브로 in one's leisure hours; at one's leisure. ときどき

시난고난 gradually getting worse／병이 ~ His sickness grows worse.

시내 《냇물》 a [mountain] stream; a rivulet; a brook／시냇가 the edge of a stream／시냇물 the water of a stream／~가 벌판을 조용히 흐르고 있다 A little quiet creek is running through the fields. おがわ

시내(市內) the city [proper]／~ 거주자 city residents／~ 전차 a [city] streetcar／~판 the city edition／~에 살다 live in the city. しない

시녀(侍女) a waiting-maid[-woman]; a lady in waiting; a lady-attendant 《귀부인의 시중을 드는》 a lady's maid. じひ

시누렇다 (be) bright yellow. まっきろいだ

시누이 one's husband's sister; a sister-in-law. おっとのしまい

시뉘올케 one's husband's sister and wife of one's brother; sisters[-in-law] by marriage.

시늉 feigning; pretence／ ～하다 feign; pretend／우는 ~ pretending to cry; fa-

시다 lse tears. しぐさ

시다¹ 《맛이》 (be) sour; acid; tart/신맛이 나다 taste sour. すっぱい

시다² 《뻐가》 (b3) stinging; painful (in the joints)/발목이 ~ feel a dull pain in one's ankle. ずきずきする

시다³ 《눈이》 (be) dazzling; glaring; blinding/눈이 시어서 뜰 수가 없다 My eyes are so dazzled that I cannot keep them open. めのどくだ

시단(詩壇) the poetry world; poetical circles; the world of poetry. しだん

시달(示達) instructions; directions/~하다 instruct; give directions. じたつ

시달리다 be troubled (with); be annoyed (by); be bothered (by); be afflicted (with)/병에 ~ suffer from[be afflicted with] disease/생활에 ~ be harassed by the problem of living/빚에 ~ be harassed with debts. いじめられる

씨닭 a hen raised for breeding.
たねをとるにわとり

시담(示談) 《법》 settlement out of court; a mutual concession 《채무자·채권자간의》 composition. じだん

시당숙(媤堂叔) a cousin of one's father-in-law.

시대(時代) ①《시기》 a period; an age; a time; an era; an epoch/원자 ~ the atom[atomic] age ②《시세(時世)》 the times/~의 요구 the demands[needs] of the times ③《고풍》 q ~극 a historical play[drama]. じだい

시댁(媤宅) one's husband's home; the family of one's husband. おっとのいえ

시도(示度) a reading; registered[recorded] degree/온도계의 ~는 영하 20도 다 The thermometer shows a reading of 20 degrees below zero.

시도(試圖) an attempt; a venture; an experiment/~하다 attempt; make an attempt; try out; test/그 방법을 ~하다 give the method a trial. しと

시도식(始渡式) the opening ceremony of a newly built bridge.

시동생(媤同生) one's husband's younger brother. おっとのおとうと

시드럭부드럭 slightly wilted/~하다 (be) slightly wilted. しなしな

시들다 《초목이》 wither; die; fade [away]; be shriveled; wilt; droop 《기세가》 be dejected; be dispirited/서리에 꽃이 시들어 버렸다 The frost killed the flowers. しおれる

시들방귀 dull[disagreeable] stuff.
けいしすること

시들하다 (be) not contented with; not satisfactory/시들하게 여겨지다 be not satisfied; feel something wanting.

시뜻하다 (be) unsatisfactory; undesirable; distasteful 《싫증나다》 be tired of; be fed up with. いやできにいらない

시디시다 (be) very sour[acid, tart]; be sour as sour can be. ひどくすっぱい

시랑(豺狼) a wolf and a jackal.
やまいぬとおおかみ

시래기 dried radish leaves.

시량(柴糧) food and fuel/~을 대다 provision and fuel. たきぎとしょくりょう

시렁 a shelf 《그물 모양의》 a rack; a bracket 《포도 시렁》 a trellis 《벽의 툭 불거진》 a ledge 《난로 양쪽의》 a hob 《난로 위의》 a mantelpiece.

시력(視力) sight; eyesight; vision; visual power/~이 약하다 have bad sight; be weak-sighted/~을 잃다 lose one's sight[eyesight]/~ 검사 a test of vision[visual power]. しりょく

시련(試鍊) a test; a trial; an ordeal/~하다 try; make a trial; give an ordeal/~을 당하다 be tried; undergo a trial/~을 견디다 stand the test[trial].
しれん

시론(詩論) poetics; a criticism of poems; an essay on poetry. しろん

시론(時論) 《시사평》 comments upon current events 《일반적 견해》 a current[contemporary] view 《세론》 public sentiments [of the day]. じろん

시료(施療) free medical treatment/~하다 treat (one) free [of charge]; give (one) free medical treatment/~원 a free dispensary[clinic]. せりょう

시료(試料) 《광석의》 a sample ore.

시루 an implement used to steam rice cakes. こしき

시룽거리다 be chatty; be talkative; talk garrulously[loquaciously]; prate; jabber; joke; romp/시룽시룽 romping about; joking. ! しゃべくる

시류(時流) 《풍조》 the current of the times; the trend of the world 《시대》 the times 《유행》 the fashion/~를 따르다 follow the fashion. じりゅう

시르죽다 be in poor spirits; be out of sorts; be depressed. きがぬける

시름 trouble; anxiety; worry; cares/한 ~ 놓다 be relieved of worry.

씨름 wrestling 《승부》 a wrestling match/~하다 wrestle/~군 a wrestler/영어와 ~하다 wrestle with English/~을 한 판 하다 try a fall (with). すもう

시름없이 (be) worried; anxious; absent minded/시름없이 창 밖을 내다보다 look out the window absent mindedly.
ぼうぜんとしている

시리다 《손발이》 (be) cold. つめたい

시립(市立) 《형용사적》 municipal; city-established/~의 municipal; city/~ 도서관 a city library/~ 병원 a municipal hospital/그 병원은 ~이다 The hospital is maintained at municipal expense.

시말서(始末書) a written explanation[apology]. しまつしょ

시매기다(時一) place a limitation on time; set limits to time.
じかんをせいげんする

씨명(氏名) family name and personal

시모(媤母) a mother-in-law [by marriage]; one's husband's mother. おっとのはは
시묘(侍墓) mourning at the graves of one's parents/ ～하다 mourn at the graves of one's parents during the mourning period.
시무(時務) the requirements of the time; current affairs.
시무(始務) the opening of government offices for the year; reopening of office business after the New Year holidays/～식(式) the opening ceremony.
시무(視務) performance of one's duties; execution of one's business/～하다 attend to one's business[duty]; work/～시간 business hours.
시무룩하다 (be) sullen; sulky; ill-humoured; displeased/시무룩해지다 become [look] ill-humoured. むっとする
시문(詩文) prose and poetry. しぶん
시문(時文) contemporary writing; current writing/～체 current style of writing. じぶん
시문(試問) a question; an examination; an interview/～하다 question; put a question to (one)/구두～ an oral examination. しもん
시민(市民) a citizen; the townspeople; people [of a city]; (총칭) citizenry/～계급 bourgeoisie(F)/～권 citizenship/～사회 civil society/서울～ the citizens of Seoul. しみん
시발(始發) the first train[car]; the start/～역 the starting station[suburbs] of a train; a terminal. しはつ
시방(時方) now ⇨지금. ただいま
시방서(示方書) specification.
시뻘겋다 (be) crimson; deep red/성이 나서 얼굴이 시뻘겋게 되다 be black[crimson, purple] with anger.
시범(示範) a model for others; showing an example of/ ～하다 set an example (to); show[give] a good example (of).
시변(市邊) ①(변두리) the outskirts of a city ②(시장 변리) market interest. しのしゅうへん
시보(試補) a probationer/사법관～ a probational judge; a judicial officer on probation.
시보(時報) current news (공보) a bulletin (평론) a review (시간 알리는) correct-time broadcasting (라디오 방송의) anntouncement of time (고동의) time siren [signal]. じほう
시복(諡福) beatification/ ～하다 beatify (a person)/ ～식 beatification.
시봉(侍奉) serving[waiting on] one's parents/ ～하다 serve one's parents filially.
시부(媤父) a father-in-law [by marriage]; one's husband's father; a woman's father-in-law. おっとのちち

시부(詩賦) poem and improvisational poetic writing; Chinese poetry. しふ
시부렁거리다, 씨부렁거리다 chatter; jabber; talk nonsense; gabble out words of no account; have redundant[worthless] words. しゃべくる
시부룩하다 ①be unsatisfied ②(be) unsatisfactory to one. むっとする
시부모(媤父母) one's husband's parents; one's father-and-mother-in-law by marriage. おっとのふぼ
시분(一分) a line drawn with powder.
시쁘다 (be) unsatisfying; be not contented with ⇨시들하다. まんぞくでない
시비(侍婢) a waiting woman[maid]; a lady attendant; a lady in waiting; a maidservant. じひ
시비(市費) municipal expenses (경비) city expenditure.
시비(施肥) dressing; fertilization; manuring; soiling/～하다 dress; fertilize; manure; soil (a field); apply dung[compost] to. せひ
시비(是非) right and[or] wrong; the propriety (of)/～하다 quarrel[dispute] with (one)/ ～를 가리다 discriminate [distinguish] between right and wrong; tell right from wrong/ ～ 곡직 the right and wrong/하찮은 일로 ～하다 quarrel[argue] about trifles. ぜひ
시사(時事) the events of the day; current events(affairs, questions); (시세) the times (형세) the situation things /～ 문제 a current question[issue]/～해설 news comment/～ 해설자 a news commentator/ ～를 해설하다 comment on issues of the day. じじ
시사(試射) test[trial] firing/～하다 fire out; test [a rifle,a gun]/～탄 a trial shot/～장 a firing range. ししゃ
시사(侍史) (편지 겉봉에) Esquire(略：Esq.). じし
시사(試寫) a preview; a private show [ing]/ ～하다 preview/～실 a projection room/ ～회를 하다 give a preview (of a film). ししゃ
시사(示唆) suggestion; a hint; an inkling/ ～하다 hint; suggest/그의 강연은 매우 ～적이었다 His lecture was full of suggestions. しさ
시산(試算) a trial (calculation)/ ～하다 calculate; try/ ～표 a trial balance. しさん
시살(弑殺) a regicide; murdering one's master[one's parents]/ ～하다 murder[kill] one's master[parents]; assassinate the king of a country; commit regicide. しぎゃく
시삼촌(媤三寸) one's uncle by marriage; one's husband's uncle/～댁 one's aunt by marriage; one's husband's aunt. おっとのしゅくふ
시상(施賞) awarding prize; prize giving / ～하다 award a prize.

**시상(詩想)** a poetical sentiment[idea]; the idea of a poem. しそう

**시새** fine sand.

**시새우다** hate[abhor, detest, abominate] each other. やきもちをやく

**시생(侍生)** I; your junior.

**시서늘하다 (음식이)** (be) quite cold. ひえてつめたい

**시석(矢石)** arrows and stones; weapons in olden times.

**시선(視線)** one's eye; the line of vision [sight, collimation]; the level of vision /~을 피하다 avoid (a person's) eye/~이 맞았다 Their eyes met. しせん

**시선(詩選)** a selection of poems; an anthology of poems; a selected[chosen] ode. しせん

**시설(施設)** establishment; institution; equipment **(시설물)** facilities; establishments/~하다 establish; equip; institute/교육 ~ educational facilities/군사 ~ military establishments/산업 ~ industrial facilities/환자의 치료 ~이 있다 have facilities for the treatment of patients. しせつ

**시설(柿雪)** bloom/곶감에 ~이 앉았다 The cried persimmons have bloom on them.

**시설스럽다** (be) unsociable; uncompromising; harsh; rough.

**시성(詩聖)** a great poet. しせい

**시성식(示性式)** 【화】a rational formula. しせいしき

**시세(市稅)** a municipal tax[duty, rate].

**시세(市勢)** ①**(도시의)** the condition of a municipal life ②**(시장의)** market conditions municiipal census-taking. しせい

**시세(時勢)** ①**(그때의 형세)** the current [the situation] of the times **(시대 풍조)** the tendency[the drift, the trend] of the times; the signs of the times; the spirit of life ②**(세상(世相))** the condition of life ②**(시가)** the current price; the market price; business conditions /거래소의 ~ exchange quotation/~가 내리다 fall[decline] in price ③⇒시세(時世). じせい

**시세(時世)** the times; the days; the era; the age/ ~에 뒤지다 fall behind the times/그는 ~에 앞서 가고 있다 He is far ahead of his times. じせい

**시세닿다(時勢―)** rise[advance] moderately in price; rise up to a satisfactory price.

**시속(時速)** speed per hour **(바람의)** velocity per hour/ ~ 50마일 50miles per hour(50 m. p. h.). じそく

**시속(時俗)** the manners and ways of the age; the mores of the times. じぞく

**시솔(侍率)** attention to the old and to the young.

**시숙(媤叔)** brothers of one's husband. おっとのきょうだい

**시술(施術)** a surgical operation/ ~하다 operate. しゅじゅつをおこなうこと

**시습(時習)** frequent review/~하다 review (one's lesson) at times; go over[through](one's lesson) occasionally.

**시승(試乘)** a trial ride[trip]/~하다 have a trial ride (in). しじょう

**시시 각각(時時刻刻)** hourly; every hour [moment, minute]; moment by moment; constantly/날씨가 ~으로 변한다 The weather varies from hour to hour. じじこっこく

**시시덕거리다** laugh and talk over nothing; laugh sillily; talk nonsense.

**시시부지** ~하다 be buried in oblivion; drift into abscurity; vanish/돈이 ~하게 없어졌다 My money seemed to have evaporated. /무슨 일이든지 ~하게 하기는 싫다 I hate leaving things half done. うやむや

**시시 비비(是是非非)** ~하다 argue about what is wrong and what is right/ ~ 주의 a free and unbiased policy; a fair attitude. ぜぜひひ

**시시하다 (사소하다)** (be) trifling; trivial; petty **(미미하다)** (be) insignificant **(하찮다)** (be) of little importance; of no account **(가치 없다)** (be) worthless; unworthy; good-for-nothing **(쓸데 없다)** (be) of no use; useless; vain **(흥미없다)** (be) dull **(빈약하다)** (be) poor; humble **(어리석다)**, (be) foolish; stupid; senseless; silly **(상스럽다)** (be) low/시시한 말을 하다 talk nonsense/시시한 것**(물건)** a matter of no importance; a trifle/시시한 일 a thing of no value. つまらない

**시식(試食)** tasting; sampling; demonstration/~하다 sample [the cake]; taste; try; obtain a foretaste (of)/~회 a sampling party. ししょく

**시식(時食)** seasonable foods; food in season.

**시식(試植)** trial planting/ ~하다 plant for trial.

**시신(侍臣)** an attendant; a courtier; an immediate vassal; an immediate follower; an offical in attendance.

**시신(屍身)** a dead body; a corpse. しかばね

**시신경(視神經)** the optic[visual] nerve.

**시심(詩心)** poetic sentiment[instinct].

**씨아** a cotton gin/ ~로 목화의 씨를 빼다 gin cotton.

**시아버지(媤—)** a father-in-law [by marriage]; one's husband's brother. おっとのちち

**시아주버니(媤—)** a brother-in-law [by marriage]; one's husband's brother; a woman's brother-in-law. おっとのきょうだい

**시안(試案)** a tentative plan[proposal, draft]; a draft policy. しあん

**씨암탉** a brood hen. たねめんどり

**시앗** one's husband's concubine. おっとのめかけ

**씨앗** a seed/~을 뿌리다 sow seed; sow /배추의 ~ cabbage seeds. しゅし

**시야**(視野) a visual field; a field[range] of vision; view/~에 들어오다 come in sight of/~를 넓히다 widen[broaden] one's mental vision/~에서 사라지다 go out of sight. しや

**시야비야**(是也非也) right and[or] wrong; true or false/~하다 argue right and wrong. よしあしをいうこと

**시약**(試藥) a trial; 【화】 a reagent/~병 a trial bottle. しやく

**시약 불견**(視若不見) pretending not to have seen/~하다 pretend not to have seen[noticed].

**씨양이질** ~하다 bother a busy person. うるさくすること

**시어**(詩語) poetic diction. しご

**시어머니**(媤―) a mother-in-law [by marriage]; one's husband's mother. おっとのはは

**시업**(始業) opening; commencement of work; inauguration/~하다 commence [begin, start] work; open/~식 the opening ceremony[exercises]. しぎょう

**시여**(施與) a contribution; an offering; a donation/~하다 give; dispense; donate; contribute; give free; give (money, things) in charity. しよ

**시역**(市域) the city limit[s]; the municipal area.

**시역**(始役) starting[beginning] construction work/~하다 begin[start] a construction work[job].

**시역**(弑逆) regicide; the murder of one's lord ⇒시살(弑殺). しぎゃく

**시연**(試演) a demonstration; a trial performance [of a play]; a rehearsal; a preview/~하다 give a trial performance; rehearsal [a play]/공개 ~ a public rehearsal[demonstration]. しえん

**시영**(市營) municipalization; municipal management[operation, ownership]/~버스 a city[municipal] bus/~ 주택 a municipal dwelling house/~의 가스와 수도 사업 municipal trading[enterprise] in gas and water.

**시외**(市外) the outskirts of a city; the suburbs/~ 전차 a suburban streetcar /~ 전화 an out-of-town call; a trunk line/~에서 살다 live in a suburb[in the suburbs] (of Seoul).

**시외가**(媤外家) one's husband's mother's house[family]. おっとのははのいえ

**시용**(試用) a test; trial/~하다 try; use for trial. しよう

**시우**(時雨) a seasonable rain. じう

**시우쇠** pig iron. きたいがね

**시운**(時運) the tide/~이 불행하다 The condition is unfavourable to us. じうん

**시운전**(試運轉) 《기차 따위》 a trial trip[run, voyage]; 《기계 따위》 a test [working] /~하다 make a trial run/전차의 ~을 하다 conduct[have] a trial run of the electric train. しうんてん

**시원섭섭하다** feel relieved but sorry; make oneself easy about (a thing) but feel as if something were missing. さっぱりするがさびしい

**시원스럽다** 《태도가》 (be) brisk; quick; active 《성질이》 frank; forthright/시원 스럽게 처리하다 dispose of (a matter) lightly; dismiss (a matter) summarily. さっぱりする

**시원시원하다** (be) open-hearted; unreserved; cheerful; agreeable; exciting; sprightly/시원시원히 일하다 work willingly. かっぱつだ

**시원찮다** (be) unsatisfactory; dull; lack liveliness[briskness]/시원찮은 사람이다 He does not know his own mind. うっとうしい

**시원하다** ①《상쾌하다》 feel refreshed; be refreshing 《안심하다》 feel relieved/목욕을 하고 나니 시원하다 My bath refreshed me ②《언행이》 (be) bright ⇒시원스럽다.

**시월**(十月) October(略 : Oct.). じゅうがつ

**시위**[1] a bowstring. ゆみのけん

**시위**[2] 《홍수》 a flood; an inundation/~나다 be flooded; be inundated; be overflowed. こうずい

**시위**(示威) demonstration; display; showing/ ~하다 demonstrate; display; show off/ ~ 운동 a demonstration/~운동자 a demonstration/학생 ~ a student demonstration. しい

**시위**(侍衛) the imperial guard[s]; royal body guard[s]; the lifeguard[s] of a king; escort/ ~하다 escort; guard; convoy. じえい

**시위적거리다** do in an easy-going manner. のろのろする

**시유**(市有) city[municipal] ownership/ ~의 municipal; city/~를 municipal property/~로 하다 municipalize. しゆう

**시육**(屍肉) dead flesh; carrion.

**시율**(詩律) rules of meter[er] [for poems]; metrics. しりつ

**시은**(施恩) doing (a person) a favor/~하다 do (a person) a favor; bestow favors on (a person); confer favor.

**시음**(試飮) sampling [a drink]/ ~하다 《상품 따위를》 sample [a beverage]; 《약 따위를》 try out [a drink]. しいん

**시읍면**(市邑面) cities towns and village; municipalities.

**시의**(侍醫) a court physician; a physician to the king. じい

**시의**(時宜) circumstances; the occasion /~에 맞づ be opportune;/ be seasonable; be timely. じぎ

**시의**(猜疑) 《의혹》 suspicion 《불신》 distrust 《시기》 jealousy/~하다 suspect; doubt; distrust; be jealous/~의 눈으로 보다 look upon (one) with suspicious eyes; suspect. ねだみうたかうこと

**시의회**(市議會) a city[municipal] assembly/~ 의원 a member of a municipal assembly/~ 의원 선거 a municipal election. しぎかい

시인(是認) approval; approbation; endorsement 《허용》 admission／~하다 approve of; endorse; admit／나는 내가 잘못했다는 것을 ~한다 I admit that I was wrong.　ぜにん

시인(時人) people of the times; one's contemporaries.　そのときのひと

시인(詩人) a poet 《여류》 a poetess／엉터리 ~ a poetaster.　しじん

시일(時日) 《때》 time; days; hours 《날짜》 the date; the day／~이 경과함에 따라 as time passes; as the days go by／~과 장소 time and place.　じじつ

시자(侍者) an attendant; [a member of] retinue.

시작(試作) 《기계·상품》 trial manufacture 《재배》 trial growing 《예술품》 a study 《문장·그림 따위》 an essay／~하다 manufacture for trial; cultivate[grow, raise] for trial; compose as an experiment／~ 전시회 a study exhibition／~품 trial product.　しさく

시작(詩作) verse-making; writing[composing] [of] poems.　しさく

시작(始作) the beginning; the commencement; the start; the outset 《기원》 the origin／~하다 begin; commence; start; go into; launch／새로 ~하다 begin afresh／회를 ~하다 open the meeting／일을 ~하다 set about one's work; go to work／그는 사업을 ~했다 He set up in a business／~이 반이다 A good beginning is half the battle., Well began is half done.　はじめること

시장 hunger; an empty stomach／~하다 be hungry; feel empty／~기를 달래다 appease[alleviate] one's hunger／몹시 ~하다 be savagely hungry.　くうふく

시장(市場) a market[-place]; a fair; a m. art／~에 내다 put (a thing) on the market; market／~을 개척하다 open the market.　しじょう

시장(市長) a mayor 《직위》 mayoralty／~ 관사 a mayor's mansion／ ~ 선거 a mayoral election／서울 ~ the Mayor of Seoul.　しちょう

시재(時在) supplies or cash on hand 《현대》 the present time; at present.

시재(試才) selecting talented persons through examination／~하다 examine and select as talented persons.

시재(詩才) a poetic gift[genius]; a gift for verse／~를 나타내다 display one's poetic genius.　しさい

시재(詩材) a subject for a poem; verse material; material for poetry.

시저(匙箸) spoon and chopsticks.　さじとはし

시적(詩的) poetic; poetical／~미(美) poetic beauty／~ 정서 poetic feeling／그 여자는 ~ 성벽(性癖)을 가지고 있다 She has a taste for poetry.　してき

시적거리다 do reluctantly[un willingly]／시적시적 without enthusiasm; with little spirit; listlessly.　しぶしぶする

시전지(詩箋紙) paper to write poems or letters on; note-paper; letter-paper.　しせんし

시절(時節) 《계절》 the season; the time of [the] year 《시세(時世)》 the times 《시기》 [due] time; a period; occasion; chance; opportunity／매년 이 ~에는 일기가 거칠다 the weather is stormy in this season of [the] year.　じせつ

시점(視點) a visual point 《관점》 A point of view.　してん

시정(市井) 《거리》 the town; streets 《사람》 a trademan; a marchant; townsmen.　しせい

시정(是正) correction; readjustment; revision／~하다 correct; [set] right; rectify; readjust／잘못을 ~하다 correct a mistake; correct errors.　ぜせい

시정(施政) administration; government; statemanship／ ~ 방침 an administrative policy; a ministerial program／~연설 a speech on administrative policies／ ~ 방침을 정하다 decide upon the administrative policy.　しせい

시정(市政) municipal government; city administration; civic affairs／ ~을 개혁하다 reform municipal government.

시정(詩情) poetic feeling[sentiment].　しじょう

시제(時制) 【언】 the tense／현재[과거, 미래] ~ the present[past, future] tense.　じせい

시제(詩題) a poetic theme; a subject for a poem.　しだい

시제(市制) municipality／ ~를 실시하다 municipalize; organize as a municipality.

시제(時祭) ancestor-memorial services performed in each season of the year.

시조(始祖) the founder; the originator; the father; the progenitor／노동 운동의 ~ the father of labor movement.　しそ

시조(時調) a Korean verse[ode]; shijo／~를 읊다 recite a poem.

씨족(氏族) a family; a clan／ ~ 사회 a clan society／ ~ 제도 the family system.　しぞく

씨종 an inherited servant; a family slave.

시종(始終) the beginning and the end／ ~ 일관하다 be consistent.　しじゅう

시종(侍從) a lord in waiting; a chamberlain／ ~ 무관 a military aide-de-camp to His Majesty／~장 the grand chamberlain.　じじゅう

시주(施主) 《일》 offering; oblation; alms-giving 《물건》 an offering 《사람》 an offerer; a dedicator／~하다 offer; make an offering (to a temple).　せしゅ

시주(詩酒) verses and wine.

씨주머니 a seed bag; an ascus.　しのう

시준(視準) collimation／ ~하다 collimate [a telescope]／~기 a mercury colli-

시중 service 《모심》 attendance 《간호》 nursing／ ～하다 serve; attend (one); nurse/환자를 ～하다 attend[care for] a patient. せわ

시중(市中) ①《거리》 the city; the town; streets ②《시장》 the open market／～은행 a city[commercial] bank. しちゅう

시즙(屍汁) water from a corpse.

시지르다 doze; drowse ⇒졸다. いねむりする

시집(媤—) one's husband's home[family]／～ 보내다 marry off [one's daughter]／～가다 marry; get married. おっとのいえ

시집(詩集) an anthology of poems; poetical works／바이론 ～ [a collection of] Byron's poetical works. ししゅう

시집살이(媤—) married life[housekeeping] in the home of the husband's parents／～에 고생하다 lead a hard married life.

시차(時差) a time difference; difference in time; 〖천〗 the equation of time／～계(計) an equation timepiece. じさ

시차(視差) 〖천〗 parallax. しさ

시찰(視察) inspection; observation／～하다 inspect; observe; make an inspection (of); visit／～관 an inspector／～단 an inspection／현장을 ～하다 take a view of the scene. しさつ

시창 the poop deck [of a ship].

시찾다(時—) be at death's door; be on the verge of death. しにかかっている

시채(市債) municipal bond[loan, obligation]／～를 발행하다 issue a municipal loan. しさい

시책(施策) a measure; a policy. しさく

시척지근하다 (be) sourish. ややすっぱい

시청(視聽) sight and hearing 《주목》 attention 《감흥》 sensation 《시청각》 audiovisual／～을 집중시키다 attract [public] attention[interest]. しちょう

시청(市廳) 《건물》 the city hall; the municipal building; a city office.

시청(試聽) an audition／～하다 audition／～실 an audition room. しちょう

시체(屍體) a dead body; a corpse; one's remains／～를 인수하다 claim the body. したい

시체(時體) the customs of the times; the fashion of the day.

시체(詩體) a style [of verse]. したい

시초(始初) the beginning; the start; the origin; the outset／일은 언제나 ～가 어려운 것이다 Beginnings are always hard. はじめ

시초(詩抄) a selection of poems; selected poems／～하다 select poems. ししょう

시초(柴草) dry grass used for fuel. たきぎにするくさ

시축(詩軸) a verse scroll; scroll of poems.

시취(屍臭) the smell of a dead body; a putrid smell／～가 코를 찔렀다 the smell of the dead was horrible. したいからはっさんするにおい

시취(詩趣) poetical interest[sentiment, feeling]／～가 풍부하다 be full of poetical interest. ししゅ

시치다 baste; tack／시침질 basting／시침실 basting thread.

시치미 feigned innocence[ignorance]; feigned indifference; dissimulation／～떼다 pretend not to know; play the innocent; feign indifference. しら

시침(時針) the hour-hand [of a watch].

시커멓다 (be) jet-black; deep-black; be as black as coal. まっくろだ

시큰거리다 tingle; twinge; feel a dull pain (in one's joints). あえぐ

시큰둥하다 (be) impudent; fresh; impertinent; pert; cheeky.

시큼하다 (be) sourish. すっぱい

시키다 《하게 하다》 make (one) do; let (one) do; get (one) do 《주문하다》 order／억지로 일을 ～ force to work. させる

시탄(柴炭) firewood and charcoal; fuel／～비(費) fuel[firing] expenses／～상 a fuel[wood-and-coal] dealer. しんたん

시태(時態) the current situation; the times; a sign of the times. じたい

시통스럽다 (be) impertinent; impudent; pert.

시틋하다 《싫증나다》 be fed up with; be sick of; be tired of 《시들하다》 (be) unsatisfactory; reluctant. きにいらない

시판(市販) marketing／～하다 [put on the] market／～되고 있다 be on the marketing.

시퍼렇다 (be) deep blue 《창백하다》 deadly pale 《권세가》 powerful; influential; (be) purplish. まっさおだ

시편(詩篇) 〖종〗 the Book of Psalms. しへん

시평(時評) comments on current events [topics]／～가 a commentator／문예 ～ comments on current literature／～난 editorial columns. じひょう

시폐(時弊) the existing evils[abuses]; the evils of the time[s]／～에 개탄하다 deplore the abuses of the times. じへい

시필(試筆) writing for trial／～하다 write for trial. しひつ

시하(侍下) a person with both parents living; being under one's parental roof.

시하(時下) now; at present; at this time of [the] year／～ 엄동지절에 in this season of cold winter. じか

시학(詩學) poetics; poetry; poesy 《운율학》 prosody. しがく

시한(時限) a time limit; limit of time 《문 닫는 시간》 lock-up 《통금 시간》 curfew／～ 폭탄 a time bomb. じげん

시할머니(媤—) one's husband's grandmother. おっとのそば

시할아버지(媤—) one's husband's grandfather. おっとのそふ

**시합**(試合) a match; a game; a contest; a round; a bout 《여러 사람들의》a tournament/~하다 have a game[match, bout, contest] (*with*); play against; meet/~장 (경구) a court (야구) a [ball] park (권투) a ring (축구) a field/ ~에 나가다 take part in a game/농구 ~을 하다 have a basketball game (*with*)/현상 ~ a prize fight. しあい

**시해**(弑害) a regicide ⇒시살(弑殺).

**시행**(施行) operation; enforcement; carrying out/~하다 put (*law etc.*) in operation[force, effect]; carry into effect; enforce/ ~ 규칙 regulations relative to the application of a law/ ~되어 있다 be in force[operation]. しこう

**시행 착오**(試行錯誤) 【심】 trial and error. しこうさくご

**시허열다** (be) pure white; snow white. まっしろだ

**시험**(試驗) ① an examination; a test; an exam《속》/~하다 examine (*a person*); test/ ~을 치르다 take[sit for] an examination/~ 준비를 하다 prepare[read, study] for an examination/ ~공부를 하다 cram for an examination ② (실험) an experiment; a test; a trial / ~하다 test; try; put to the test/ ~관(官) an examiner/~관(管) a test tube/ ~기 a tester; a testing machine/~ 답안지 an examination paper / ~ 문제 an examination question/~ 비행사 a test pilot/ ~실 a laboratory / 구두 ~ an oral examination/입학 ~ an entrance examination/자격 ~ a qualifying examination/필기 ~ a written examination/학기말 ~ a term examination/~을 해 보다 put (*a thing*) to the test. しけん

**시험관**(試驗管) a test tube/~ 배양 (세균의) a [test tube] culture. しけんかん

**시험지**(試驗紙) ① examination[test] paper ②【화】 litmus paper. しけんし

**시현**(示現) revelation; showing/ ~하다 reveal; show. じげん

**시형**(詩形) a poetic form; a meter/ ~학 prosody. しけい

**시호**(詩號) a poet's pen name. しじんのがごう

**시호**(諡號) a posthumous name[title] / ~를 추증하다 grant (*a person*) a posthumous epithet. しごう

**시호**(時好) the current fashion; the vogue[mode]/ ~에 따르다 catch the public fancy

**시화**(視話) (벙어리의) lip language[reading]/ ~법 visible speech.

**시황**(市況) the market; market conditions/~ 보고 a market report/주식 ~ the stock market/ ~이 한산하다 The market is quiet. しきょう

**시회**(詩會) a poetry club[party]. しかい

**시효**(時效, 時效)【법】 prescription/~ 기간 the period of prescription/ ~ 정지 suspension of prescription/~에 걸리다 be barred by prescription; prescribe.

**시후**(時候) (계절) season (기후) climate; weather/불순한 ~ unseasonable weather. じこう

**시흥**(詩興) poetical inspiration/~이 나다 be inspired to verse; have poetical inspiration. しきょう

**-씩** each; apiece; respectively / 조금~ little by little; little at a time/하나~ at a time; one by one/매일 10시간~ 일하다 work the hours every day. ーずつ

**식**(式) ①(식전) a ceremony; rites; rituals /졸업~ a graduation ceremony; the commencement〈미〉 ②(양식) form (형) type; style; model; fashion; plan (방법) a method; a system/서양~으로 경영하다 operate on European[Western] lines ③(수학·화학의) an [algebraic] expression; a [chemical] formula.

**식**(蝕) 【천】 an eclipse; occultation.

**식간**(食間) ~에 between meals/ ~에 약을 먹다 take medicine between meals.

**식객**(食客) a dependent; a hanger-on; a sponge. しょっかく

**식견**(識見) (판단력) knowledge; insight; discernment; vision (의견) views/~있는 사람 a man of broad view and understanding. しきけん

**식곤증**(食困症) languor after a meal; drowsiness; the stupor induced by a full.

**식구**(食口) a family; a household; members of a family/우리집은 ~가 많다 My family is a large one. かぞく

**식권**(食券) a meal[food]-ticket[card]. しょっけん

**식기**(食器) tableware; a dinner set (주발) a bowl/ ~장 a pantry. しょっき

**식다** ①(냉각) cool; get[grow] cold/ 커피가 식습니다 Your coffee will get cold. ②(감퇴) abate; subside (열의 따위가) flag; be dampened; cool down (흥이) be chilled/열이 ~ lose interest; grow less enthusiastic. ひえる

**식단**(食單) a menu; a bill of fare.

**식당**(食堂) a dining room[hall]; a restaurant (간이 식당) a cafeteria (군대의) a mess hall/ ~차 a dining car; a buffet car. しょくどう

**식도**(食刀) a kitchen knife.

**식도**(食道) 【해】 the gullet; the esophagus/ ~염 esophagitis. しょくどう

**식도락**(食道樂) epicurism/ ~가 (미식가) an epicure/저 사람은 ~가이다 He is an epicure., He is addicted to the pleasures of the table. しょくどうらく

**식되** a measure of capacity for domestic use.

**씩둑거리다** chatter[prattle] over useless things; talk idly; take glibly. ごちゃごちゃいう

**식량(食糧)** food; foodstuffs; provisions/ ~ 문제 the food problem/ ~ 사정 the food situation/ ~을 공급하다 provision (a district)/우리들은 배에 ~을 실었다 We victualled the ship. しょくりょう

**식량(食量)** capacity for eating. しょくりょう

**식량(識量)** knowledge and talent; discernment and ability/그는 지도자가 될 ~이 있다 He is smart enough to lead others. けんしきとどりょう

**식료(食料)** 《식물》 food; articles of foods; provisions; rations/ ~품 articles for food; provisions; groceries/ ~품점 grocery; a provisions shop/ 좋은 ~가 되다 be edible; be good to eat; be fit for food. しょくりょう

**식리(殖利)** bringing in interest[profit] / ~하다 bring[bear] interest; bring in return; contribute profit. しょくり

**식림(植林)** afforestation; tree planting / ~하다 plant trees; afforest; reforest (land) with trees/ ~계획 a reforestation plan. しょくりん

**식모(食母)** a kitchenmaid; a cook.

**식목(植木)** planting trees; forestation; tree planting/ ~하다 plant trees; transplant trees/ ~일 Arbor Day〈미〉 うえき

**식물(食物)** [an article of] food; eatables; a fare; a diet; victuals/ ~을 섭취하다 take food. しょくもつ

**식물(植物)** a plant 《총칭》 vegetation; plant[vegetable] life 《한 지방의》 a flora /~원 a botanical garden/~ 채집 plant collecting/ ~학 botany/ ~학자 a botanist/고산 ~ an alpine plant/열대 ~ a tropical plant/ ~의 분포 the geographical distribution of plants. しょくぶつ

**식민(植民)** colonization; settlement 《사람》 a colonist; a settler/ ~하다 settle / ~ 사업 colonization/ ~ 정책 a colonial policy/ ~주의 colonialism/ ~지 a colony/ 브라질에 ~를 colonize Brazil; plant settlers in Brazil. しょくみん

**식반(食盤)** a small food table. しょくたく

**식빵(食一)** bread/~ 한 덩어리 a loaf of bread.

**식별(識別)** discrimination; discernment /~하다 distinguish (between, from); discriminate; tell (things) apart/ ~력 power of discernment; discrimination /선과 악을 ~하다 discern good from evil. しきべつ

**식보(食補)** taking nourishments/ ~하다 take nourishing food; diet on nourishments.

**식복(食福)** luck in eating; luck to be treated with food/~이 있다 be blessed with things to eat. しょくもつのとく

**식비(食費)** food expenses[cost]; 《하숙의》 the charge for board/ ~를 포함하다 include board/~를 얼마나 내고 있나 What do you pay for your board? しょくひ

**식사(式辭)** 《축사》 a formal address a congratulatory address. しきじ

**식사(食事)** a meal; fare; diet; board/ ~하다 take a meal; dine/~ 준비를 하다 prepare a meal 《식탁의》 set the table/~ 시간입니다 It is time for dinner. しょくじ

**식산(殖産)** increase of production; industry; production/ ~하다 increase production; foster [national] industry/ ~ 공업 productive industry. しょくさん

**식상(食傷)** 《물림》 surfeit 《중독》 food poisoning 《불소화》 indigestion/ ~하다 be surfeited[sated] (with); be poisoned by food. しょくしょう

**식색(食色)** appetite for food and sex; appetite and sexual desire. しょくよくとしきよく

**식생활(食生活)** dietary[food] life; eating habits/ ~조차 어렵다 find it hard to earn one's daily bread.

**식성(食性)** taste; palate/ ~에 맞는 음식 agreeable food / ~이 까다롭다 be fastidious about food.

**식수(植樹)** tree planting; planting trees / ~하다 plant a tree/ ~일 Arbor Day〈미〉/ ~ 운동 afforestation movement. しょくじゅ

**식수(食水)** drinking water; potable water. いんりょうすい

**식순(式順)** the contents[order] of a ceremony. しきじゅん

**식식, 씩씩** ~거리다 breathe heavily; gasp; pant/ 그는 ~거리며 뛰어왔다 He came running out of breath. はあはあ

**씩씩하다** (be) manly; valiant; brave; courageous; gallant; vigorous/ 씩씩한 남자 a fine strapping fellow/ 씩씩하게 싸움터로 나가다 go out to war most gullantly.

**식언(食言)** eating one's word; breaking a promise/ ~하다 eat[break, go back upon] one's word. しょくげん

**식염(食鹽)** table salt; common[culinary] salt/ ~수 a solution of salt/ ~ 주사 salt injection. しょくえん

**식욕(食慾)** appetite; desire to eat/~ 증진 promotion of appetite/ ~을 채우다 satisfy one's appetite. しょくよく

**식용(食用)** edibility; table use/ ~ 개구리 an edible frog/~ 색소 food coloring/ ~ 식물 esculent plants; plants for food/ ~품 articles of food; eatables; food/~에 적합하다 be edible; be good (suitable) to eat. しょくよう

**식육(食肉)** meat; meat-eating/ ~하다 eat meat; be carnivorous/ ~류 the carnivorous[meat-eating] animal; Carnivora(학명). しょくにく

**식은땀** a cold sweat/ ~을 흘리다 be in a cold sweat. ひやあせ

**식음(食飮)** eating and drinking/~을 전

**식이(食餌)** 폐하다 give up eating and drinking; fast. のみくい

**식이(食餌)** food; a diet/~ 요법 a dietary treatment. しょくじ

**식인(食人)** cannibalism/~의 man-eating; cannibal; cannibalistic/~종 a cannibal race; cannibals. しょくじん

**식일(式日)** ① a ceremonial day ② (날마다) every day.

**식자(植字)** 〖인〗 typesetting; typography/~하다 set [up] type/~공 a compositor; a typesetter/사진 ~ photo-letter composition; photographic lettering. しょくじ

**식자(識者)** a learned man; intelligent [informed] people; men of intelligence; a person with good sense/~ 우환 ignorance is bliss. しきしゃ

**식장(式場)** the hall of ceremony; a ceremonial hall. しきじょう

**식적(食積)** indigestion; dyspepsia.

**식전(食前)** ~에 before a meal (아침 식사 전) before breakfast/~에 기도를 하다 say grace. しょくぜん

**식전(式典)** a ceremony; rituals; rites. しきてん

**식주인(食主人)** a proprietor of an inn[eating house].

**식중독(食中毒)** food poisoning/~에 걸리다 be[get] poisoned (by fish); (음식이 주어) disagree with (one).

**식지(食指)** the fore[index, marginal] finger. しょくし

**식지(食紙)** oiled paper for covering food.

**식체(食滯)** indigestion; dyspepsia.

**식초(食醋)** vinegar/~산 〖화〗 acetic acid/~를 치다 vinegar (food).

**식충(食蟲)** 〖동〗〖식〗 insect-eating (대식가) a glutton; a gourmand/~류 the insectivora/~ 식물 an insectivorous plant; a carnivore (pl.-ra).

**식칼(食-)** a kitchen knife; a carving knife (고기 베는 큰칼) a cleaver/~질하다 carve with a kitchen knife; chop with a cleaver. しょくたくナイフ

**식탁(食卓)** a [dinner] table; the board/~용의 for table use/~에 앉다 sit [down] at [the] table/~을 보자 lay the cloth; set the table. しょくたく

**식탈(食頉)** (식상(食傷)) disagreement of food; food-poisoning (불소화) indigestion/~이 나다 be poisoned by food.

**식품(食品)** food; articles of food; groceries ⇒식료품. しょくひん

**식피(植皮)** 〖의〗 skin grafting/~하다 graft/~법 skin grafting; transplanting of skin. しょくひ

**식혜(食醯)** a sweet drink made from fermented rice/~ 가루 dried malt used for fermenting rice.

**식후(食後)** ~에 after dinner[a meal]. しょくご

**식히다** cool; let (a thing) cool/더운 물을 ~ cool hot water; let hot water cool (불어서) blow hot water to cool it/열을 ~ reduce[bring down] a fever. さます

**신¹** (발에 신는) footgear; footwear (구두) shoes (나막신 따위) clogs/~을 신다(벗다) put on[take off] one's shoes/~을 신은 채 올라가다 enter with one's shoes on. くつ

**신²** (기분) joy; delight; amusement; enthusiasm; excitement/~이 나다 get excited; be keyed up; become enthusiastic/~이 나서 설교하다 preach with great fervor.

**신(申)** (십이지(十二支)) the ninth of the twelve horary signs; the Ape/~년 the year of the Ape. さる

**신(臣)** (신민) a subject (가신) a retainer; a vassal (자기) Your Majesty's servant; I; me. しん

**신(信)** (신용) credit; trust; credence (신회) confidence; faith (신의) fidelity (신념) belief. しん

**신(神)** (일신교의) God; the Almighty; Providence; the Lord; the Creator (다신교의) a god; a deity (인신) a deified hero/~의 divine; heavenly/~의 심판 divine judgment/~에게 기도드리다 pray to God/~을 믿다 believe in God. しん

**신(腎)** ①(자지) the penis ②(신장) the kidney. じん

**신-(新)** new; modern; latest; novel; up-to-date/~무기 a new weapon/~여성 the modern woman. しん

**신가정(新家庭)** a new home[housekeeping]/~을 꾸미다 make a new home; set up house

**신간(新刊)** a new publication; a newly-published book; a recent release/~하다 publish (a new book)/~ 목록 a list of new publications/~서적 a new book[publication]. しんかん

**신간(新墾)** (형용사적) newly reclaimed[tilled]/~하다 reclaim (new land).

**신거어** an insipid person; a bore; a humourless fellow; a dull person.

**신격(神格)** godhead; divinity.

**신경(神經)** nerves/~ 계통 the nervous system/~ 과민 hypersensitivity; nervousness/~ 쇠약 nervous breakdown [prostation, debility]; neurasthenia/~염 neuritis/~전 psychological warfare/중추 ~ a nerve center/~질 nervousness; nervous temperament/~통 neuralgia/~이 날카롭다 be sensitive; be nervous/그는 ~ 과민이다 He is thin-skinned/~통을 앓다 suffer from neuralgia. しんけい

**신경지(新境地)** new ground/~를 개척하다 break new ground.

**신경향(新傾向)** a new tendency[trend].

**신고(申告)** (신립) statement (보고) report (소득세의) a return (가격 등의) decla-

신고 584 신도

ration/ ~하다 state; report; declare; make[file] a return/ ~서 a report; a return/ ~자 an applicant; a reporter/세관에서 허위 ~를 하다 make a false customs declaration. しんこく

**신고**(辛苦) hardships; trials; tribulations; adversity (고심) labor; pains; trouble; toil/ ~하다 go through hardships; take pains/ ~를 겪다 suffer hardships. しんく

**신곡**(神曲) 《단테의》 The Divine Comedy.

**신곡**(新穀) the new crop 《햅쌀》 new rice. しんこく

**신곡**(新曲) a new musical composition; a new tune. しんきょく

**신골** the [shoe] last; shoetrees; shoe [boot] stretchers/ ~에 맞추다 put [set] (one's shoes) on the last.

**신공**(神功) divine help; god's grace. しんこう

**신관**(信管) a fuse [of an explosive charge]/시한 ~ a time fuse/~을 끊다 cut a fuse. しんかん

**신관**(新官) a newly appointed official; a new appointee.

**신관**(新館) a new building 《증축한·별관》 an annex; an extension 《미》.

**신교**(信敎) religious belief; faith; belief / ~의 자유 religious freedom[liberty]; freedom of worship. しんきょう

**신교**(新敎) Protestantism; the Reformed /~도 a Protestant. しんきょう

**신구**(新舊) the new and the old/ ~의 old and new/~ 장관 the incoming and outgoing Ministers/ ~ 관리 incoming and outgoing officials. しんきゅう

**신국면**(新局面) a new phase [aspect, situation]/ ~을 전개하다 develop[enter upon] a new phase. しんきょくめん

**신권**(神權) divine right/~ 정치 theocracy/ 제왕~설 the doctrine of the divine right of kings. しんけん

**신규**(新規) a new regulation; new project/ ~의 new; fresh/ ~ 사업 a new undertaking/ ~로 채용하다 hire[employ] a new hand. しんき

**신극**(新劇) a new play [drama]; 《과(派)》 a new school of acting/ ~단 a new-drama association. しんげき

**신금**(宸襟) the king's mind[heart]/ ~을 괴롭히다 give great anxiety to His Majesty. しんきん

**신기**(神技) superhuman skill; unsurpassed abilities/ ~에 가깝다 That is beyond human power. かみわざ

**신기**(神奇) marvellousness; strangeness 《신기한 일》 a mystery; a wonder; a miracle/ ~하다 (be) marvellous; strange 《신비》 mysterious 《기적적》 miraculous/ ~하게 생각하다 wonder; marvel (at). しんき

**신기**(神氣) vigor; vitality; spirit; the mind/ ~가 쇠하다 become less energetic; fall into low spirits. しんき

**신기**(神祇) the gods of heaven and earth. じんぎ

**신기**(神器) a sacrificial[ritual, sacred] vessel; a sacred treasure. しんき

**신기**(神機) ①《계기》 a marvelous moment; a golden opportunity ②《기략》 divine expedients[providence, intervention].

**신기**(腎氣) virile power; virility.

**신기**(新奇) novelty; originality/ ~하다 (be) new; novel/ ~한 방법으로 in a novel way/ ~를 좋아하다 be fond of novelty. しんき

**신기다** let (one) wear; help (one) to put on (his shoes).

**신기록**(新記錄) a new record[mark]/ 세계 ~ a new world record/~을 세우다 make[create, establish] a new record. しんきろく

**신기루**(蜃氣樓) a mirage/ ~가 나타나다 a mirage appears. しんきろう

**신기원**(新紀元) a new era[epoch]; a turning-point/ ~을 열다 make[mark, open] an epoch[era]/ ~을 이루는 사건 an epochal event. しんきげん

**신기축**(新機軸) a new device[contrivance, departure]; an originality/~을 보이다 show[display] an originality. しんきじく

**신나다** get in high spirits; be[get] elated; feel triumphant (over)/ 그 영화 참 신나더라 The picture thrilled[excited] me a great deal.

**신나무** 《식》 Acer aizuense《학명》. からこぎかえで

**신남**(信男) 《불》 a Buddhist; a man who believes in Buddhism.

**신낭**(腎囊) the scrotum.

**신내리다**(神―) (a shaman) go into a trance; be possessed by a spirit.

**신녀**(信女) a female believer in Buddhism. しんにょ

**신년**(新年) 《설날》 a new year; New Year's Day/ ~을 맞이하다[축하하다] greet [celebrate] the New Year/ 근하(謹賀) ~ I wish you a Happy New Year! しんねん

**신념**(信念) belief; faith 《확신》 conviction /강한 ~을 가지고 있다 have a strong [firm] conviction (that). しんねん

**신다** wear; have on; slip on; put on/ 그는 단화를 신었다 He put on a pair of shoes.

**신당**(神堂) a shrine; a joss house. かみをまつってあるしどう

**신당**(新黨) a new political party/ ~을 결당하다 form[organize] a new political party.

**신대륙**(新大陸) a new continent; the New World. しんたいりく

**신덕**(神德) the grace[goodness, benevolence] of a god; divine help. しんとく

**신도**(信徒) a believer; a devotee; a follower; an adherent 《총칭》 the faithful

**신동**(神童) an infant prodigy[genius]; an extraordinary child.  
/불교 ~ a Buddhist.

**신뒤축** a shoe heel/ ~이 닳았다 The heels are worn [down].

**신랄**(辛辣) ~하다 (be) sharp; severe; bitter; cutting; poignant; pungent/ ~한 비평을 하다 make a severe[vitriolic] criticism/ ~한 언사를 쓰다 make caustic[cutting] remarks; have a biting tongue.

**신랑**(新郎) a bridegroom/ ~감 a suitable [likely] bridegroom/ ~ 신부 the bride and the bridegroom; the bridal pair; newlyweds《미·속》.

**신력**(神力) divine power; superhuman strength.

**신력**(新曆) the new[solar] calendar/ ~으로 according to the new calendar.

**신령**(神靈) a divine spirit; the soul/ 산~ the god of a mountain; the guardian spirit of a mountain/ ~의 가호 divine protection.

**신록**(新綠) tender green; fresh verdure; new foliage/ ~의 계절 the season of fresh green/ ~으로 덮이다 be covered with verdant vegetation.

**신뢰**(信賴) 《신임》 confidence; trust; credit 《의뢰》 reliance/ ~하다 trust; put trust[faith] in; believe[confide] in/ 세인(世人)의 ~를 받다 win public confidence.

**신뢰**(迅雷) a sudden peal of thunder; a thunderclap.

**신망**(信望) 《신용》 confidence 《인망》 popularity/ ~이 두텁다 enjoy[possess] the confidence (of)

**신면목**(新面目) a new aspect[phase, side]/ ~을 나타내다 present a new aspect.

**신명**(身命) one's life/ ~을 걸고 at the risk of one's life/ ~을 바치다 lay down one's life.

**신명**(神明) a deity; a divinity; God/ 천지 ~께 맹세하다 swear before Heaven.

**신묘**(神妙) being my sterious and marvelous/ ~하다 (be) my sterious; marvelous.

**신문**(訊問) questioning; an examination (of a witness); a query; an inquest/ ~하다 question; examine; interrogate/ ~자 an examiner/ ~ 조서 an interrogatory.

**신문**(新聞) a newspaper; a paper 《총칭》 the press/ ~의 newspaper; press/ ~ 광고 newspaper advertising/ ~ 구독료 subscription for[to] a paper/ ~ 구독자 a newspaper reader[subscriber]/ ~기자 a pressman; a reporter; a newsman《미》/ ~ 배달[인] a newsman; a newsboy/ ~사 a newspaper office/ ~ 용지 newsprint [paper]/ ~팔이 a newsboy; a news vendor/석간 ~ an evening paper/영자 ~ an English language paper/일간[주간] ~ a daily[weekly] newspaper/ ~을 배달하다 deliver newspapers/ ~을 발행하다 publish [issue] a newspaper/ ~에 나다 appear [be reported] in the paper[s].

**신물** acid water that comes out of stomach when vomiting.

**신미**(辛味) a sharp[pungent] taste.

**신미**(新米) new rice ▷햅쌀.

**신미**(新味) a hot[spicy] taste.

**신민**(臣民) subject[s].

**신바닥** the soles of shoes; a sole.

**신바람** excitement ▷신².

**신발** footwear ⇨신¹.

**신발명**(新發明) a new invention; a recent invention/ ~의 newly-invented; of recent invention.

**신발족**(新發足) a new[fresh] start/ ~하다 make a new[fresh] start; start a fresh.

**신방**(新房) bridal room; a bridal bed/ ~에 들다 go[get] into bridal bed.

**신벌**(神罰) divine punishment; divine retribution/ ~을 받다 be punished by God.

**신법**(新法) ①《법률》 new regulations; a new law ②《방법》 a new method.

**신변**(身邊) [by] the side of (a person); on the person/ ~이 위태롭다 be in personal danger/ ~을 걱정하다 be anxious about one's personal safety.

**신병**(身病) illness; sickness〈미〉; a diseas 《만성의》 a malady/ ~으로 쓰러지다 succumb to disease.

**신병**(新兵) a new conscript; a [raw] recruit/ ~ 훈련 boot training.

**신보**(新報) news; a new report.

**신복**(臣僕) subjects and servants.

**신복**(信服) submission/ ~하다 be convinced; submit to/ ~시키다 convince (a person).

**신볼** the width of a shoe.

**신봉**(信奉) belief; faith/ ~하다 believe in; profess; embrace/ ~자 an adherent; a devotee; a believer/그리스도교를 ~하다 embrace[believe in] Christianity.

**신부**(神父) a father/ ~가 되다 be ordained to a priest.

**신부**(新婦) a bride; a newlywed wife 《결혼식 전의》 a bride-to-be.

**신분**(身分) 《지위》 a social position[standing, status]; a station[situation] in life 《신원》 identity; origin; birth/ ~을 증명하다 identify oneself.

**신불**(神佛) gods and Buddha/ ~의 가호 divine protection.

**신비**(神秘) mystery/ ~경 a land of mystery/ ~극 a mystery drama/ ~주의 mysticism/ ~ 철학 esoterics; mystic

**신빙(信憑)** credence; credit; trust/ ~하다 credit; place confidence (in); give credence (to); put trust (in)/ ~성 authenticity; credibility. しんぴょう

**신사(神祠)** a shrine. しんし

**신사(紳士)** a gentleman; a man of honor 《단정한 사람》 a fine-looking man/ ~도 the code[ideals] of a gentleman/ ~ 협정 a gentleman's agreement/ ~인 척하다 play a gentleman. しんし

**신사복(紳士服)** a lounge-suit 《영》; a sack coat; a business-suit 《미》. しんしふく

**신사업(新事業)** a fresh[new] enterprise; a new undertaking[project]; a new promotion. しんじぎょう

**신산(辛酸)** hardships; trials; privations / ~을 맛보다 go through hardships; have reverses of fortune. しんさん

**신상(身上)** 《운》 one's fortune; one's lot 《경력》 one's history; one's career 《처우》 one's personal affairs; one's circumstances; one's condition 《안부》 welfare/ ~ 얘기를 하다 tell one's life story. しんじょう

**신상(紳商)** a great[wealthy, rich] merchant; a merchant prince. しんしょう

**신상 필벌(信賞必罰)** dispensation of justice both to services and crimes; never fail to reward a merit or let a fault go unpunished.

**신색(神色)** looks; countenance/ ~ 자약하다 be calm and self-possessed. しんしょく

**신생(新生)** new birth; rebirth; newborn; renascence/ ~대(代) 《지》 the Cenozoic[Cainozoic] era[period]. しんせい

**신생명(新生命)** a new life/ ~을 부여하다 reanimate; revivify; resuscitate. しんせいめい

**신생애(新生涯)** a new [stage of] life; a new career/ ~로 들어가다 begin life anew. しんしょうがい

**신생활(新生活)** a new life/ ~에 들어가다 start a new life; start one's life anew[afresh]; start one's life all over. しんせいかつ

**신서(新書)** a newly published book ☞신간(新刊). しんしょ

**신서(信書)** a letter 《총칭》 [personal] correspondence/ ~의 비밀을 침범하다 violate the privacy of [personal] correspondence. しんしょ

**신석기(新石器)** a neolith/ ~ 시대 the neolithic era.

**신선(神仙)** a Taoist hermit with supernatural powers; a wizard/ ~경 a fairly land. しんせん

**신선(新鮮)** freshness/ ~하다 (be) new; fresh/ ~한 공기 〖야채〗 fresh air[vegetables]/ 공기는 아주 ~하였다 The air was cool and crisp. しんせん

**신선(新選)** 《책》 new selection; a new anthology/ ~하다 newly select 《선출하다》 newly elect/ ~ 의원 a newly elected member of the National Assembly. しんせん

**신선로(神仙爐)** a cook-pot with a tube for burning charcoal in the center.

**신설(伸雪)** wiping away a disgrace.

**신설(新雪)** freshly fallen snow.

**신설(新設)** new establishment[organization]; creation/ ~하다 establish[organize] newly; create; found/ ~ 공장 a new factory/ ~ 회사 a newly-formed company/ 학교를 ~하다 establish[found] a school. しんせつ

**신설(新說)** a new theory[doctrine]/ ~을 내세우다 advance a new theory. しんせつ

**신성(神聖)** sacredness; sanctity; holiness; inviolability/ ~하다 (be) sacred; holy; sanctified; hallowed; consecrated; divine/ ~ 동맹 the Holy Alliance / ~ 불가침이다 be sacred and inviolable. しんせい

**신성(神性)** divinity; divine nature. しんせい

**신세** indebtedness; a debt of gratitude; an obligation/ ~를 지다 be under indebtedness.

**신세(身世)** ①《처지》 one's personal affairs; one's lot; one's circumstances; one's condition ②《남의 은혜》 kindness; favour; indebtedness/ ~진 것을 갚다 repay one's kindness; return another's kindness. みのきょうぐう

**신세계(新世界)** a new world 《미대륙》 the New World. しんせかい

**신세대(新世代)** the new era/ ~의 젊은이 the coming[young] generation.

**신소리**[1] a caustic remark/ ~하다 talk saucy; have a saucy tongue; give cheek.

**신소리**[2] 《신발의》 the echo of footsteps; sound of walking shoes. くつのおん

**신속(迅速)** rapidity; swiftness; promptitude/ ~하다 (be) rapid; swift; quick; prompt; speedy/ 이 명령을 ~히 수행하라 Be prompt to carry out this order. じんそく

**신수(身手)** one's appearance; look/ ~가 환하다 have a fine appearance; have a good bearing.

**신수(身數)** one's star; fortune; luck/ ~를 보아 주다 tell[read] one's fortune.

**신술(神術)** a divine art.

**신승(辛勝)** ~하다 win (a game, a race) after a hard fight[struggle]; win by a narrow[close] margin; nose out (the opposing team) 《미·속》.

**신시(新詩)** modern poem. しんし

**신시대(新時代)** a news age[epoch, era]. しんじだい

**신식(新式)** a new style[type]; 《방법》 a new method/ ~ 무기 a new-type weapon / ~의 new-style 《현대적》 up-to

**신신 부탁**(申申付託) earnest request; solicitation/ ~하다 request earnestly; solicit. くれぐれのむこと
**신신하다**(新新―) (be) fresh. しんせんだ
**신실**(信實) sincerity; honesty; truth; faithfulness; good faith.
**신심**(信心) faith; devotion; piety/ ~이 없는 impious; unbelieving; godless. しんじん
**신안**(新案) a new idea[design, plan]/ ~ 특허 a new design patent/ ~ 특허를 얻다 take out a new design patent (on). しんあん
**신앙**(信仰) faith; belief/ ~하다 believe [have faith] in/ ~의 자유 religious liberty; freedom of worship/ ~ 생활 a life of faith/~인 a believer; a devotee/ ~ 생활을 하다 lead a religious life. しんこう
**신약**(信約) a covenant; an agreement; a compact.
**신약**(神藥) wonderful[a miraculous, sovereign] remedy. しんやく
**신약**(新藥) a new medicine. しんやく
**신약**(新約) 《성경》the New Testament/ ~ 시대 New Testament times. しんやく
**신어**(新語) a new word; a newly coined [newfangled] word; a new coinage/ ~ 사용 neologism/ ~ 사용자 a neologist/ ~를 만들다 coin new words; neologize. しんご
**신여성**(新女性) the modern girl; the new woman. しんじょせい
**신역**(新譯) a new translation[version]. しんやく
**신열**(身熱) fever [body] temperature/~ 이 나다 have a fever. ねつ
**신예**(新銳) new and superior/~의 new; fresh/ ~ 병기 a new weapon of war. しんえい
**신용**(信用) 《신뢰》 confidence; trust; faith 《명망》 reputation 《경제상의》 credit 《진위에 대한》 credence/~하다 trust; place[put] confidence in/ ~ 거래 dealing [sales] on credit/ ~ 보험 《대부의》 credit insurance 《고용인의》 fidelity insurance/ ~장 a letter of credit(略: L/C) / ~ 조합 a credit association/~을 얻다 win[gain] a confidance of. しんよう
**신용 대부**(信用貸付) [open] credit; credit loan; loan on credit/ ~하다 give[allow, grant] credit to; extend credit to / 장기 ~ long credit. しんようかしつけ
**신원**(身元) one's birth and parentage; one's identity/ ~ 보증서 a reference; a character/ ~ 증명서 an identification card/ ~을 조회하다 refer to (a company) for (a person's) character. みもと
**신원**(新元) the New Year; the New Year's Day. がんたん
**신월**(新月) a new[young] moon; a crescent/ ~ 형의 crescent[-shaped]. しんげつ

**신위**(神位) an ancestral tablet. しんい
**신음**(呻吟) moaning; groaning; a groan 《고민》 pining/ ~하다 moan; groan; be harassed (by poverty); pine/ 병상에서 ~하다 be confined to bed suffering severely. しんぎん
**신의**(信疑) belief or disbelief; credit or discredit/ ~가 반반이다 I can't tell whether it is credible or not. しんぎ
**신의**(神醫) a wonderful physician. かみわざのいし
**신의**(神意) God's will; divine will; Providence. しんい
**신의**(信義) faith; fidelity; truthfulness / 국제 ~ international faith/ ~를 지키다[깨뜨리다] keep[break] faith (with a friend). しんぎ
**신인**(神人) ① a man of god; a godlike person; a prophet ② god and man/그의 죄는 ~ 공히 용서치 않으리라 He has sinned against God and man. しんじん
**신인**(新人) a new figure[man]; 《한창인 사람》 a rising man 《연예계 등의》 a new face. しんじん
**신임**(信任) confidence; trust; credence/ ~하다 confide in; trust; put confidence in/~ 투표 a vote of confidence /~장 credentials/ ~을 얻다 win[obtain, gain] the confidence of. しんにん
**신임**(新任) new appointment /~의 newly appointed/~하다 newly appoint to office/ ~ 대사 a newly accredited Ambassador/~식 an installation ceremony/ ~ 인사를 하다 make an inaugural address. しんにん
**신입**(申込) application → 신청. もうしこみ
**신입**(新入) [newly] entering; incoming; new/ ~의 new; incoming; entering/ ~생 an entering[a new] student/ 어제 ~생의 환영회가 있었다 We had a welcome meeting yesterday for the freshmen. しんにゅう
**신자**(信者) a believer; a devotee; an adherent 《총칭》 the faithful/불교 ~ a believer in Buddhism; an adherent of Buddhism/그는 그리스도의 ~다 He is a believer in Christianity. しんじゃ
**신자**(新字) a newly made letter[character]. しんじ
**신작**(新作) a new work; a new production 《작곡》 a new composition/~을 발표하다 publish a new [piece of] work. しんさく
**신작로**(新作路) a newly constructed road; a highway.
**신장**(―欌) the shoe chest; a boot cupboard. くつをいれるはこ
**신장**(伸張) elongation; expansion; extension/ ~하다 extend; expand; exalt/ ~률 the coefficient of expansion/외국 무역을 ~하다 expand[increase] foreign trade. しんちょう
**신장**(身長) height; stature/ ~이 자라다 grow[advance, increase] in stature/

**신장** ~을 재다 take[measure] *one's* height. しんちょう

**신장**(神將) a great commander. かみのようなしょうぐん

**신장**(腎臟) 【해】 the kidneys / ~결석 a kidney stone; a nephrolith / ~병 kidney trouble / ~염 nephritis; Bright's disease. じんぞう

**신장**(新裝) a new dress; new attire 《장정》new binding / ~된 newly finished / ~하다 give a new look to 《개축하다》; furnish up. しんそう

**신저**(新著) a new work 《신간서》a new publication /~ 한 권을 증정합니다 Kindly accept a copy of my work just out. しんちょ

**신전**(伸展) expansion; extension / ~하다 expand; extend.

**신전**(神前) before God[gods] / ~에 before the shrine / ~에 바치다 offer (a thing) to the god[deity]. しんぜん

**신전**(神殿) a shrine; a sanctuary. しんでん

**신절**(臣節) loyalty [to one's lord] / ~을 다하다 remain loyal to *one's* lord to the end.

**신접**(새살림) setting up a new home 《이사하여 삶》 taking up *one's* abode [in a new place].

**신접살이**(新接─) a new home[house-keeping] / ~하다 make a new home; set up house.

**신정**(神政) theocracy.

**신정**(新政) 《정부》a new government; a reformed administration. しんせい

**신정**(新正) the New Year 《정월》the first month of the new year. しんねんのしょうがつ

**신정**(新訂) a new revision /~판 a newly reised edition. しんてい

**신정**(新情) a newly developed affection; a new love; young love. あたらしいじょう

**신제**(新制) a new system. しんせい

**신제**(新製) new manufacture /~하다 newly make / ~의 new; newly-made. しんせい

**신조**(神助) divine grace[aid]; providence. しんじょ

**신조**(信條) a creed; an article of faith 《신념》a principle; a belief / ~을 지키다 keep[follow, be true to] *one's* creed. しんじょう

**신조**(新造) 《건설》new construction / ~하다 build; construct; lay down 《말을》 coin / ~ 군함 a newly-built warship / 배를 ~하다 build a ship. しんぞう

**신종**(信從) believing and following; reliance / ~하다 believe and follow; obey; trust; rely on.

**신주**(神主) an ancestral tablet / ~를 모시다 enshrine *one's* ancestral tablet. しんしゅ

**신중**(愼重) prudence; discretion; circumspection; caution; care / ~하다 (be) prudent; cautious; careful; circumspect; discreet; judicious; deliberate / ~한 태도를 취하다 use prudence and caution; take a cautious attitude / ~히 심의하다 give careful consideration to (*a matter*). しんちょう

**신지식**(新知識) up-to-date knowledge[information]; advanced ideas. しんちしき

**신진**(新進) rising; coming forth / ~의 rising; promising; new /~ 작가 a rising writer. しんしん

**신진 대사**(新陳代謝) renewal; replacement; regeneration 《육체의》 anagenesis; metabolism / ~하다 be renewed; be regenerated. しんちんたいしゃ

**신착**(新着) a new[fresh] arrival / ~하다 newly arrive; be a new arrival /~품 new arrivals; newly arrived[imported, received] goods / ~ 양서 newly -imported foreign books.

**신찬**(新撰) new compilation / ~하다 newly compile[select, edit] / ~ 국어 독본 The New Language Readers. しんせん

**신참**(新參) 《고참에 대한》a newcomer; a new hand; an incomer 《미숙자》a green hand; a novice /~의 new 《신임의》 newappointed 《미숙한》 green. しんざん

**신창** a shoe sole /~을 갈다 resole shoes. くつのそこ

**신천옹**(信天翁) 【조】 an albatross. あほうどり

**신천지**(新天地) a new world / ~를 개척 하다 open up a new field of activity. しんてんち

**신청**(申請) application; a petition; request; filing; 【법】 motion / ~하다 apply (*for*); make an application; petition (*for*); file (for *a licence*); 【법】 move / ~인 an applicant 《배상의》a claimant / ~ 서 a written application /정부에 허가를 ~하다 apply to the Government for permission / ~서를 제출하다 send in a written application. しんせい

**신청부갈다** 《걱정이 많다》be beset with worries; (be) harassed 《불만족》 dissatisfied; disappointed.

**신체**(身體) the body 《체격》the physique 《체질》the constitution / ~의 bodily; physical; personal / ~ 검사 a physical examination; a physical check-up〈미〉 / ~ 장해자 a physically handicapped person / ~를 단련하다 build up a healthy body. しんたい

**신체시**(新體詩) the new style poetry; a new style poem. しんたいし

**신체제**(新體制) a new structure[system]. しんたいせい

**신축**(新築) building; construction 《집》 a new building / ~하다 newly build [construct] / ~중의 집 a house under construction. しんちく

**신축**(伸縮) expansion and contraction

**(탄성)** elasticity; flexibility/~하다 expand and contract; be elastic/~을 주다 give elasticity to. しんしゅく

**신축 자재**(伸縮自在) elasticity/elastic; flexible; telescopic/ 이것은 ~입니다 This may be expanded or contracted as one pleases.

**신춘**(新春) **(신년)** the New Year **(초봄)** early spring/ ~을 맞이하다 welcome the New Year. しんしゅん

**신출 귀몰**(神出鬼沒) elusiveness; preternatural swiftness; sudden appearance and disappearance/~하다 suddenly appear and suddenly disappear/~의 행동 elusive movements. しんしゅつきぼつ

**신출나기**(新出—) a novice; a green hand a tenderfoot; a beginner [in the trade]. みじゅくなひと

**신코** a toe-cap. くつのせんたん

**신탁**(信託) trust/~하다 trust (a person) with (a thing); leave (a thing) in trust with (a person)/~ 계약 a trust agreement/~ 기금 trust funds/ ~ 예금 a trust deposit/~ 증서 a trust deed/~ 통치 trusteeship/ ~ 통치 이사회 the Trusteeship Council/ ~ 회사 a trust company/ ~ 기금을 설정하다 provide [create] the trust fund. しんたく

**신탁**(神託) an oracle; a revelation; a divine message; an inspiration/ ~을 받다 receive an oracle. しんたく

**신탄**(薪炭) firewood and charcoal; fuel / ~비 fuel(firing) expenses. しんたん

**신통**(神通) **(신기)** mystery; strangeness **(통달)** skill/~하다 (be) mysterious; strange; efficacious; miraculous; skillful; versed (in)/이 책은 그리 ~치 않다 This book does not appeal to me. じんとう

**신트림** belching up a bit of sour vomit.

**신파**(新派) a new school/~ 배우 an cator of the new school/ ~ 연극 a new-school play; the new drama/ ~를 이루다 form[organize] a new school. しんぱ

**신판**(新版) a new publication; a new edition/최~ the newest edition. しんばん

**신편**(新編) a new edition. しんぺん

**신품**(新品) a new article/ ~과 똑같다 look brand-new; look as good as new; be only slightly used/ ~ 샤쓰를 입다 put on a new shirt. しんぴん

**신풍스럽다** (be) harassed [마음에 안 차다] dissatisfied ⇒신청부같다.

**신필**(宸筆) the Emperor's autograph. しんぴつ

**신하**(臣下) a subject; a retainer; a vassal; a minister. しんか

**신학**(神學) theology/ ~교 a theological school[seminary]; a divinity school/ ~자 a theologian/ ~ 박사 a Doctor of Divinity(略:D.D.). しんがく

**신학기**(新學期) a new [school] term; the new semester. しんがっき

**신학문**(新學問) new learning; modern education. しんがたがくもん

**신한**(宸翰) an Imperial[a Royal] letter. しんかん

**신형**(新型) a new[the latest] style[fashion, model]/ ~ 자동차 a new style car. しんがた

**신호**(信號) a signal; signaling/ ~하다 signal; make a signal **(신호기로)** put up a signal/ ~기(旗) a signal flag/ ~기(機) a signal apparatus; a railroad signal/~등 a signal lamp/~수 a signalman; a flagman〈미〉;**(군대)** a buzzer / ~탑 a signal tower/ 교통 ~ a traffic signal/위험 ~ a signal of danger /자동 ~ an automatic signal/조난 ~ a distress signal/~를 무시하고 횡단하다 jaywalk《미·구》/파란 ~가 켜졌다 The signal showed "Proceed"./배에서 조난 ~를 보냈다 The ship signaled its distress[sent an SOS]. しんごう

**신혼**(新婚) a new marriage/ ~하다 be newly married; become a newlywed/ ~ 부부 newly-married[wedded] couple; newlyweds/~ 생활 newly-married life / ~ 여행 a honeymoon/ ~ 여행을 떠나다 go[off] on a honeymoon. しんこん

**신화**(神化) deification/ ~하다 deify; get deified. しんか

**신화**(神話) a myth **(총칭)** mythology/~ 시대 the legendary[mythological] age /~학자 a mythologist/그리스 ~ Greek mythology. しんわ

**신환자**(新患者) a new patient. しんかんじゃ

**신효**(神效) wonderful efficacy/ ~하다 (be) wonderfully efficacious. しんこう

**신흥**(新興) newly rising; up-and-coming / ~하다 newly rise/ ~국 a rising nation/ ~ 계급 a newly risen[rising] class/ ~ 산업 a rising industry/ ~ 회사 a newly established company. しんこう

**신희**(新禧) New Year congratulations [greetings, good wishes]. しんき

**싣다** ①**(적재하다)**load; take on **(배에)** take on board ship/수레에 수하물을 ~ load a cart with luggage/말에 장작을 ~ pack firewood on a horse ②**(기록하다)** record; publish; insert/광고를 ~ put[insert] an advertisement (in) ③**(논에 물을)** water (a rice-field). つむ

**실** **(바느질용)** thread **(방적사)** yarn; a string; a line; twine/ ~밥 waste thread; silk waste/ ~패 a spool; a reel/바늘에 ~을 꿰다 thread a needle. いと

**실**(室) a room; a chamber **(한 개 이상으로 된)** an apartment/1등~ **(기차의)** a first class compartment/ ~내[외] inside[outside] a room. しつ

**실**(失) **(과실)** an error **(불리)** disadvantage **(손실)** loss.

실(實) 《진실》 the truth[reality]; 《현실》 actuality 《성실》 sincerity 《실질》 substance. じつ
실가(實家) the family one was born into; one's parents' home; one's original house. じっか
실가(實價) 《진가》 intrinsic[true] value; sterling worth 《원가》 cost [price]; 《가격》 actual[real] price 《정가(正價)》 netprice. じったいのかち
실각(失脚) a downfall; fall; loss of one's position/ ~하다 lose one's position; fall; be overthrown/~한 정치가 a knock-out politician. しっきゃく
실감(實感) actual feeling[sensation]; solid sense/~하다 feel actually; realize; experience/ ~나게 말하다 say feelingly. じっかん
실감개 a spool; a reel.
실개천 a brook [let]; a rivulet; a streamlet; a rill; a creek〈미〉.
실격(失格) disqualification; elimination; 《법》 incapacity/ ~하다 be disqualified (for a post, from doing something); 《의원이》 be unseated from (the Diet); 《경기에서》 be eliminated (from, out of)/ ~자 a disqualified person. しっかく
실경(實景) the actual view; the [actual] scene; nature/이 그림은 ~을 그린 것이다 That picture is drawn from nature. じっけい
실고추 shred[ded] red pepper.
실골목 a narrow back-street; an alley.
실과(實科) a practical course. じっか
실과(實果) fruit/ ~점 a fruit shop[store] : 과실(果實). かじつ
실꾸리 a ball of thread[yarn].
실국수 thin[thread-like] noodles. そうめん
실국화(-菊花) 《식》 a daisy.
실군(實軍) a good hand; a competent worker.
실굽 the base [stand] of vessels[receptacles, dishes].
실권(失權) 《권리》 loss of one's rights; disfranchisement 《권력》 loss of power[authority]/~하다 lose one's rights; be disfranchised; lose one's power. しっけん
실권(實權) actual[real] power /정치의 ~을 쥐다 assume the helm of state; hold the reins of government. じっけん
실그러지다, 씰그러지다 get out of shape [balance]; get distorted; be pushed out of shape; wobble.
실금 a crack; a fissure. ほそいひび
실기(失期) missing an opportunity/ ~하다 miss an opportunity; let slip[let go] a chance. きかいをうしなうこと
실기(失期) missing an appointed time; failing in one's promise/ ~하다 fail to keep an appointed time; fail in one's agreement[promise].
실기(實記) a true record; an authentic record[account]; a history/한국 동란 ~ a history of Korean War. じっき

실기(實技) practical[real] talent/ ~시험 practical [talent] examination/미술 ~ 시험 fine arts talent test. じつぎ
실낱 a strand; a ply; a single thread/ ~ 같은 목소리 a feeble voice. いとのより
실내(室內) the [interior of a] room/ ~악 chambermusic/ ~ 장식 interior decoration/ ~를 장식하다 upholster a room. しつない
실념(失念) a lapse of memory/ ~하다 forget 《인의 주의》 escape one's mind[memory]; 《사람이 주어》 forget. しつねん
실농(失農) missing the season for farming/ ~하다 miss the season for farming.
실농군(實農軍) a solid[steady] farmer. のうぎょうにじゅうじつなひゃくしょう
실눈 narrow eyes/ ~을 뜨고 보다 narrow one's eyes; look through half closed eyes.
실담(實談) a true story. じつわ
실답다(實-) (be) true; reliable. しんじつらしい
실답지 않다(實-) (be) untrustworthy; unreliable; untrue; insincere; not to be depended upon. しんじられない
실당(失當) ~하다 fail to be reasonable. どうりにはずれること
실덕(失德) loss of virtue/ ~하다 meet dishonor; lose one's virtue. しっとく
실떡거리다 talk nonsense; say useless things. ざつだんばかりする
실뚱머룩하다 (be) disinclined; unwilling uninterested; reluctant; reluctant. いやいやながらである
실뜨기 cat's cradle. あやとり
실락원(失樂園) 《밀턴의 서서명》 Paradise Lost. しつらくえん
실랑이[질] bothering/~하다 pester; bother; trouble. わずらわすこと
실량(實量) real quantity.
실력(實力) 《능력》 one's real ability[talent]; 《진가》 worth; merit 《무력》 force; arms/~이 있다 be able/~자 an influential person's; a power; a potentate/ ~ 테스트 an achievement test/ ~ 행사 use of force/학력보다는 ~을 중시하다 I esteem real ability more than academic titles. じつりょく
실력(實歷) actual experiences; one's life; one's career/ ~담(譚) the story of one's life. じつれき
실련(失戀) a broken heart; a disappointed/ ~하다 be disappointed in one's love. しつれん
실례(失禮) rudeness; impoliteness; discourtesy; impudence; disrespect; bad manners; a breach of etiquette/~를 저지르다 act rudely; commit a breach of etiquette/잠깐 ~합니다 Excuse me a moment. /이만 ~합니다 I must be going now. しつれい
실례(實例) an example; an instance 《예증》 an illustration 《선례》 a precedent/

실로 ~로 증명하다 explain it with examples.

실로(實-) really; indeed; in fact; in truth; truly/ ~ 아름답다 How fine it is!

실록(實錄) an authentic record[history] /이조 ~ a true record of the Yi Dynasty.

실룩거리다, 씰룩거리다 with repeated twitching[jerking, quivering]; in a jerky way/실룩실룩, 씰룩씰룩 with repeated twitching[jerking, quivering]; in a jerky way.

실리(失利) [financial] loss/ ~하다 suffer [financial] loss.

실리(實利) utility; profit; material interests[gain]/ ~의 utilitarian/ ~주의 utilitarianism/~적 utilitarian; practical.

실리다 ①(기재되다) be printed[reported]; be recorded; be given in a dictionary]; be mentioned; be put (on the list) /광고를 ~ put[insert] an advertisement in (a paper) ②(실어서 보냄) get (something) loaded; load (배에) make ship /쌀을 짐차에 ~ load a wagon with rice.

실마리 ①(실끝) the end of a thread ②(단서) a beginning; the first step (사건 해결의) a clue/~를 얻다 find a clue.

실망(失望) disappointment; discouragement; despair/ ~하다 be[feel] discouraged; (be) disappointed (at)/그것은 나를 대단히 ~시켰다 It was a great disappointment to me.

실명(失名) name unknown/~의 anonymous/ ~자 an anonymous person.

실명(失明) loss of eyesight[sight]/ ~하다 lose one's sight; become sightless; become[go] blind/~다 a blind; a sightless person/두 눈 다 ~하다 lose the sight of both eyes.

실명(失命) loss of life/ ~하다 lose one's life.

실모(實母) one's real mother.

실무(實務) [practical] business[affairs]; actual affairs/ ~에 익숙하다 be versed in business.

실물(失物) loss of goods[things]/ ~하다 lose goods[things].

실물(實物) the real thing; an actual object; a substance 《진짜》 a genuine article[thing]/ 《사진의》 the original (사생의) life/ ~ 묘사 model drawing/이 사진은 ~보다 훌륭하다 This picture is better than the original.

실뭉치 a bundle of thread.

실미적지근하다 (be) lukewarm; tepid.

실바람 a wisp of breeze.
실반대 a bundle[bunch] of thread.
실밥 ①(실보무라지) waste [pieces of] thread[yarn] ②(솔기) a seam/ ~을 뜯다 rip up the seams.

실백(實柏) a pine-nut kernel.

실버들 a weeping willow.

실보무라지 waste [pieces of] thread[yarn].

실부(實父) the real father; one's own.

실비(實費) (비용)actual expense; [real] cost/ ~ 제공 service at actual expense/~ 진료소 a clinic operated at cost / ~로 판매하다 sell (a thing) at cost.

실사(實事) an actual event[fact]; a fact; a really.

실사(實査) an actual inspection[survey]; a working survey; a survey on the spot/ ~하다 inspect actually; survey / ~를 거쳐 through an actual inspection (of)

실사(實寫) a real picture; a picture[photograph] taken from life; 《영》 an actuality film/~하다 take a picture[photograph] on the spot.

실사회(實社會) the real[actual] world/ ~에 나가다 go into the world; get a start in life[the world].

실상(實相) real facts (of a case); actual circumstances; the actual condition; the real state of affairs; reality/사회의 ~ the true picture of life.

실상(實狀) the actual[real] state of affairs; the real situation; the true state /한국의 ~ the real state of affairs in Korea.

실상(實像) 《물》 a real image.

실색(失色) changing countenance; loseing color/~하다 lose color; turn pale [white]; change countenance.

실선(實線) a solid line.

실성(失性) madness; insanity; mental derangement; distraction/ ~하다 become insane; go mad; lose one's mind [reason, wit]/~한 사람 a mad man; an insane person.

실세(失勢) loss of power/ ~하다 lose power[influence]; forfeit one's influence.

실소(失笑) laughter/ ~하다 burst out laughing; laugh outright/ ~를 금치 못하다 cannot help laughing (at something); cannot repress laughter; be laughable.

실속(實-) content; substance; material gain[interest]/이 책은 ~이 없다 This book is poor in contents.

실솔(蟋蟀) 《충》 a cricket.

실수(失手) ①(실책)a blunder; a slip; a mistake; bungle; a miscarriage; a stumble; an error ②discourtesy ⇒실례 (失禮)/ ~하다 make a blunder; commit a fault; bungle; blunder/젊었을 적에는 ~가 없을 수 없다 Slips in youth

**실수(失手)** are unavoidable. しくじり

**실수(實收)** 《수입》an actual income[return]; 《수확》an actual yield／10만원의 ~를 올리다 realize 100,000 *won* (*from*). しっしゅう

**실수(實數)** ①《실제의 수》an actual number ②《수》a real number[quantity]; 《피승수》a multiplicand. じっすう

**실수요(實需要)** consumption requirement; actual consumption.

**실습(實習)** practice; actual training 《연습》drill; training; 「practical」 exercise／ ~하다 practise; have[practical] training; be apprenticed to／ ~ 기간 practice hour／ ~생 a student apprentice; an apprentice. じっしゅう

**실시(實施)** execution; operation; enforcement／ ~하다 put in operation[force, practice]; put in effect; enforce (*a law*); give effect to／그 법률이 ~되었다 The law was put in force. じっし

**실신(失神)** a swoon; a faint; fainting／ ~하다 swoon; faint 《의식을 잃다》lose consciousness／ ~ 상태에 빠지다 fall into unconsciousness; fall faint.

**실실** with a silly snicker[snigger]／ ~ 웃다 laugh like an idiot; snicker; snigger; giggle. にやにや

**실심(失心)** 《망연자실》distraction; stupefaction; abstraction 《낙담》dejection; dispiritedness／ ~하다 (be) absentminded; distracted; dejected; dispirited／슬픔으로 ~하다 be distracted with grief. しっしん

**실안개** a thin mist. うすいきり
**실액(實額)** actual amount. じつがく
**실어증(失語症)** 〖의〗aphasia. しつごしょう

**실언(失言)** a slip of the tongue; an improper remark; misstatement／ ~하다 misstate; make a slip of the tongue／ ~을 사과하다 apologize for *one's* slip of the tongue. しつげん

**실업(失業)** unemployment／ ~하다 lose *one's* job[work, place]; be thrown out of work; be unemployed／ ~ 대책 a relief measure for the unemployed; unemployment policy／ ~ 문제 an unemployment surance／ ~자 an unemployed person; a person out of work[employment]／ ~자를 구제하다 relieve unemployed people. しつぎょう

**실업(實業)** 《산업·실무》business 《생산업》industry／ ~의 business 《산업》industrial 《상업》commercial／ ~가 a businessman／ ~ 학교 a vocational school／ ~ 교육 vocational education／ ~에 종사하다 engaged in business. じつぎょう

**실없다** (be) untrustworthy; unreliable; insincere; idle; vain; silly／ 실없는 남자 a false man. したらない

**실없이(實—)** frivolously; nonsensically; rubbishly; uselessly／ ~ 말하다 make idle[flippant] remarks.

**실연(失戀)** a disappointed[an unreturned] love; a disappointment in love; a broken heart 《짝사랑》an unrequited [a one-side] love／ ~하다 be crossed[disappointed] in *one's* love; have *one's* heart broken／그 여자한테 ~당했다 He was disappointed in love for the girl. しつれん

**실연(實演)** stage performance; acting; execution 《공연》a [public] demonstration; an exhibition／ ~하다 give a stage performance; give an exhibition[a demonstration]. じつえん

**실외(室外)** outdoor[s]／ ~에서 outside [of] a room; outside; out of doors. しつがい

**실용(實用)** utility; practical use／ ~의 practical; utilitarian; serviceable／ ~품 《필수품》necessaries／ ~ 영어 practical English／ ~주의 pragmatism; practicality／ ~ 본위 a commercial unit. じつよう

**실은(實—)** really; in truth; in fact; as a matter of fact; in reality; to tell the truth…; to be frank with you.

**실의(失意)** disappointment; despair; dejection／ ~하다 be disappointed; be disheartened; despair／그는 지금 ~의 구덩이 속에 있다 He is at the lowest ebb now. しつい

**실익(實益)** 《실수》a net profit; an actual profit 《실리》practical use; utility; benefit／취미와 ~을 겸하고 있다 It is useful as well as beautiful. じつえき

**실인(實印)** the legal seal; a registered [name-]seal. じついん

**실인심(失人心)** ~하다 become unpopular; lose the hearts of the people.

**실자(實子)** *one's* real[*one's* own] child. じっし

**실재(實在)** actual[real] existence; reality／ ~하다 exist／ ~론 〖철〗realism／ ~론자 〖철〗a realist／ ~하지 않다 be unreal; be non-existing. じつざい

**실적(實績)** [actual] results[accomplishments]; 《영업의》business showings／아직 ~이 오르지 않고 있다 The work has not yet borne fruit. じっせき

**실전(實戰)** actual fighting[fight, warfare]; an actual battle; actual service／ ~하다 serve in campaign／ ~에 참가하다 engage in actual fighting; be in the field. じっせん

**실점(失點)** a mark obtained by the opponent 《감점》a bad mark.

**실정(失政)** misgovernment; maladministration; misrule／ ~하다 misgovern; misrule. しっせい

**실정(實情)** actual circumstances 《실상》the actual[real] state of affairs; the real situation; the true state／ ~을 알다 know the actual circumstances. じつじょう

**실제(實弟)** a younger blood brother. じってい

**실제**(實際) 《사실》the truth; a fact 《이론이 아닌》practice 《현실》reality; actuality 《실정》an actual condition／ ~ 교육 practical instruction／ ~ 생활 practical life／ ~로 응용하다 put a theory in practice. じっさい

**실족**(失足) stumbling 《실패》a failure／ ~하다 stumble (*over, against*); take a false step 《실패》fail／계단에서 ~하다 miss *one's* footing on the stairs.

**실존**(實存) existence／ ~주의 existentialism／ ~주의자 an existentialist. じつぞん

**실종**(失踪) disappearance; missing／ ~하다 disappear (from *one's house*); run away; be missing／ ~자 a missing person／돈을 가지고 ~하다 abscond with the money. しっそう

**실주**(實株) a real stock; a spot share.

**실쭉** ~하다 ①《물건의 모양이》(be) distorted; misshapen ②《얼굴이》look sullen; (be) sulky; be in the sulks[pouts]／ ~해서 말도 않다 keep a sulky silence.

**실쭉실쭉** 《물건의 모양이》distorting; distorted 《얼굴이》sullen; sulky／실쭉하다.

**실증**(實證) an actual proof／ ~하다 prove; corroborate (*a proof*); establish (*a fact*); establish by evidence; substantiate／ ~주의 positivism／ ~주의자 a positivist／ ~ 철학 positive philosophy／그는 나의 진술을 ~했다 He confirmed my statement. じっしょう

**실지**(失地) lost territory／ ~를 회복하다 recover lost territory. しっち

**실지**(實地) practice; actuality; reality／ ~의 practical; actual; real／ ~ 경험 practical experience／ ~ 검사 personal inspection／ ~ 시험 a trial practic／ ~ 답사 an actual survey／ ~로 응용하다 apply to practice. じっち

**실직**(失職) unemployment／ ~하다 lose *one's* employment[job, place]; be out of work／ ~자 a zobless person; the unemployed. しっしょく

**실질**(實質) 《본질》substance; essence 《소질》quality 《재료》material; matter 《내용》contents 《진가》worth／ ~적 substantial; essential／ ~ 임금 real[substantial] wages／ ~에 있어서는 큰 차이가 없다 They are little different in essence. じっしつ

**실착**(失錯) a fault; a mistake; an error; a blunder. しっさく

**실책**(失策) a faulty policy; an error; a mistake; a slip; a blunder／큰 ~을 저지르다 make a great[gross] mistake. しっさく

**실천**(實踐) practice／ ~하다 practice; put (*a theory*) in practice; live up to action; reduce (*a doctrine*) to practice／ ~ 이성[도덕, 철학] practical reason [morality, philosophy]／ 그 교훈을 ~하라 Carry those precepts into practice. じっせん

**실체**(實體) 〖철〗substance; matter; the true nature (*of*)／ ~법 substantive law／ ~론 〖철〗substantialism; ontology／ ~경(鏡) a stereoscope／ ~적 substantial; masterial／ ~화하다 substantialize. じったい

**실총**(失寵) the loss of [royal] favor／ ~하다 lose [royal] favor.
ちょうあいをうしなうこと

**실추**(失墜) loss／ ~하다 lose; fall／권위를 ~하다 lose *one's* prestige. しっつい

**실측**(實測) survey; actual measurement／ ~하다 survey; make a survey of (*a forest*); measure／ ~도 an ordnance map／산림을 ~하다 survey a forest. じっそく

**실컷** to *one's* heart's content; as much as one wishes; heartily; to the full／ ~ 웃다 laugh heartily; laugh *one's* head off／ ~ 먹었읍니다 I have done ample justice to the meal. じゅうぶんに

**실켜다** reel [silk off cocoons].

**실탄**(實彈) 《소총의》a ball[live, loaded] cartridge 《대포의》shell; a loaded shell; a solid[round] shot／ ~ 사격 《소총의》ball firing 《대포의》target practice with live shells. じつだん

**실태**(失態) 《실패》a blunder; a fault; indiscretion 《불면목》disgrace／ ~를 부리다 commit a blunder. しったい

**실태**(實態) the actual condition[state]; the realities／ ~ 조사 research on the actual condition／ ~ 조사 위원회 a fact-finding committee. じったい

**실토**(實吐) the true confession; telling the whole truth／ ~하다 tell the whole truth; speak with sincerity; tell the fact／ ~하게 하다 get the truth out of (*a person*).

**실톱** a kind of jigsaw; a fret saw.

**실투**(失投) 및 그의 홈런은 피처가 ~한 탓이다 It was because the pitcher delivered a careless ball that he swatted a homer.

**실파** a thready stone-leek.

**실팍지다** (be) solid; strong; stout／실팍진 사람 a man of solid build; a man strongly built. かたい

**실패** a spool; a bobbin／ ~에 실을 감다 wind thread on a spool.

**실패**(失敗) failure; miscarriage; a fiasco 《실수》a blunder／ ~하다 fail; be unsuccessful; go wrong; end in a failure miscarry／ ~자 a failure／나는 시험에 ~했다 I failed in the examination.／그는 결혼에 ~했다 His marriage was a failure.／ ~는 성공의 어머니 Failure is but the threshold of[a stepping stone to] success. しっぱい

**실하다**(實一) ①《건강하다》(be) very strong; robust; stalwart; vigorous ②《재산이》(be) wealthy; rich ③《내용이》(be) full; substantial; replete／이 책은 내용이 ~ This book is very substantial. ④

**실학**《믿을 만하다》(be) trustworthy; reliable; solid; substantial／실한 친구 a stanch[solid] friend. けんじつだ

**실학(實學)** practical science; realism／～파 a positive school. じつがく

**실행(失行)** 〖법〗 abatement. しっこう

**실행(實行)** 《실천》practice; deed; action 《수행》execution; performance 《미행》fulfilment 《실시》execution; operation 《실현》realization／～하다 practise; carry out (a plan); fulfil; put into effect[operation]／～에 옮기다 carry out a scheme; execute a plan／약속을 ～하다 perform a promise. じっこう

**실험(實驗)** 《개개의》an experiment; a test 《실험을 하는 일》experimentation／～하다 experiment (on); make[conduct] an experiment (on, with)／～ 과학 an empirical science／～ 농장 an experimental farm／～ 대 a testing bench／～ 물리학 experimental physics／～실 a laboratory／～ 심리학 experimental psychology／동물 ～을 하다 experimental stage. じっけん

**실현(實現)** realization; actualization; materialization／～하다 realize; make [become] a reality 《희망 따위가》come true／이상을 ～하다 realize one's ideals; act up to one's ideals. じつげん

**실혈(失血)** loss of blood／～하다 lose blood. しっけつ

**실형(實兄)** one's own elder brother. じっけい

**실형(實刑)** imprisonment 《기간》the real term of imprisonment. じっけい

**실화(失火)** an accidental fire／～하다 have an accidental fire. しっか

**실화(實話)** a true story; an authentic account／범죄 ～ a factual account of crime. じつわ

**실황(實況)** 《실정》the real condition; the actual state of things 《광경》the [actual] scene／～을 시찰하다 inspect the real condition. じっきょう

**실효(失效)** a lapse; losing effect; abatement; invalidation／～하다 lapse; lose effect; become null and void／조약의 ～ the lapsing of a treaty. しっこう

**실효(實效)** effectiveness 《약의》efficacy 《능률》efficiency／～가 있다 do good work; give satisfactory results.

**싫다** ①《사물이 주어》(be) disagreeable; unpleasant; hateful; disgusting; loathsome; detestable; offensive ②《사람이 주어》do not like; dislike; hate／싫은 기색을 하다 look displeased／세상이 싫어진다 I grow sick of the world[life]／거저 주어도 ～ I would not have it even as a gift. きらいだ

**싫어하다** dislike; have a dislike to[for]; hate; abhor; detest; be unwilling／공연히 ～ be disgusted with the world／나는 싫어하는 음식이 없다 I am not particular about food. きらう

**싫증(-症)** dislike; disgust; repulsion; aversion; repugnance／～이 나다 be tired of; get sick of; be fed up with; be bored with／나는 그 일에 ～이 나기 시작했다 I was about tired of that business. いやけ

**심** 《소 심줄》beef's tendon. うしのきん

**심(心)** ①《마음》mind; heart; feeling; emotion／애국～ patriotism ②《핵심》the core ③《심지》a wick ④《연필의》lead. こころ

**심(審)** a trial; a hearing／제 1～ 에서 at the first trial.

**심각(深刻)** seriousness; gravity; acuteness; poignancy／～하다 (be) serious; grave; keen; acute; poignant／～한 인생 문제 a serious problem of life／～한 얼굴을 하다 look serious. しんこく

**심간(心肝)** the heart. しんかん

**심경(心境)** a state[frame] of mind; a mind; a mental state／～의 변화 a change of mind; a change in one's mental attitude. しんきょう

**심경(深更)** the dead of night; midnight. しんこう

**심경(深耕)** deep plowing[ploughing〈영〉]／～하다 plow deep. しんこう

**심계원(審計院)** the Board of Audit.

**심계 항진(心悸亢進)** 〖의〗 palpitation [of the heart].

**심고** a sinew used to tie the bowstring to the end of the bow.

**심곡(深谷)** a deep valley. しんこく

**심규(深閨)** the woman's apartments[quarters]; the back end of the house. しんけい

**심근(心筋)** 〖해〗 the heart muscle; a myocardium (pl. -dia). しんきん

**심금(心琴)** heartstrings; the deepest emotions／～을 울리다 touch a string in (a person's) heart.

**심기(心氣)** feeling; sensation. しんき

**심기(心機)** the mind; a mental attitude／～ 전환 the diversion of one's mind. しんき

**심난(甚難)** extreme difficulty／～하다 (be) very difficult.

**심낭(心囊)** 〖해〗 the pericardium. しんのう

**심뇌(心惱)** anguish [of heart]; mental affliction; sufferings. しんのぼんのう

**심다** ①《식물을》plant 《씨뿌리다》 《재배하다》grow／묘목을 ～ grow young shoots; set out seedlings ②《활자를》set up (type). うえる

**심대(甚大)** ～하다 (be) very great; enormous; immense; tremendous; heavy; serious／그들은 ～한 피해를 입었다 They suffered heavy damage. じんだい

**심덕(心德)** virtue; moral character／～ 이 있는 사람 a man of virtue; a man of high moral character. しんのとく

**심도(深度)** depth／～계 a sea gauge; a deep sea indicator／～를 재다 measure the depth; sound [the sea]; fathom.

**심돋우개** a wick-raiser; a wick control.

**심동**(深冬) 《엄동》 a severe winter 《중동》 midwinter. げんとう

**시드렁하다** linger (on); drag (on); hang (on)/시드렁한 신병 a protracted[lingering] disease; a long illness.
きんきゅうでない

**심란**(心亂) disturbance[confusion] of mind/ ~하다 (be) uneasy[confused] in mind; nervous; fidgety/ ~한 하룻밤을 지내다 pass the night in anxiety.
こころがみだれること

**심려**(心慮) prudence; thoughtfulness; deliberation 《선견》 fore sight/~를 끼치다 give (a person) to feel anxiety. しんりょ

**심력**(心力) mental power[faculty].
しんりょく

**심령**(心靈) the spirit; the soul/ ~계 the spiritual world/ ~술 spiritualism/ ~학 psychics; spiritism/ ~ 현상 a spiritual phenomenon. しんれい

**심로**(深勞) worry; distress; cares; trouble; anxiety; mental fatigue/ ~가 되다 be mentally fatigued. しんろう

**심록**(深綠) dark[deep] green.

**심리**(心理) a mental state; mentality; the mind; psychology/ ~극 psychodrama/~ 묘사 psychological description / ~ 상태 a mental state; mentality/ ~ 소설 a psychological novel/ ~ 작용 psychosis; mental process/ ~ 현상 a psychological phenomenon/ ~적으로 나쁜 영향을 주다 be bad in its psychological effect (on a child). しんり

**심리**(審理) trial; examination; inquiry 《형사 사건의》 hearing/ ~하다 try (a case); examine; inquire into (a case); handle/ ~서 a document of trial/ ~에 붙이다 try. しんり

**심리학**(心理學) psychology; mental psychology[science]/ ~자 a psychologist /교육 ~ educational[pedagogical] psychology/범죄 ~ criminal psychology /아동 ~ child psychology/행동 ~ behavioristic psychology. しんりがく

**심마니** diggers of wild ginseng.

**심문**(審問) a trial; a hearing; an inquiry; an inquest; an examination/ ~하다 hear (a case); examine; try/증인을 ~하다 interrogate[examine] a witness. しんもん

**심미**(審美) appreciation of the beautiful / ~가 an aesthete/ ~주의 aestheticism/ ~파 an aesthetic school/ ~학 aesthetics/ ~적 견지 aesthetic point of view. しんび

**심방**(心房) 〖해〗 an atrium (pl. -ia).
しんぼう

**심방**(尋訪) a call; a visit/ ~하다 call on (one); call at (a house); visit; make a call. ほうもん

**심병**(心病) ①《근심》 anxiety; sickness at heart; worry ②《졸도》 syncope; a fainting fit. こころのびょうき

**심보**(心—) character; nature; disposition/ ~가 비뚤어지다 have a crooked [wicked] mind. こころ

**심복**(心服) admiration and devotion/ ~하다 be devoted to; serve faithfully; have a high regard for/ ~받고 있다 enjoy the esteem of. しんぷく

**심복**(心腹) ①《가슴과 배》 the heart and the stomach ②《긴 요한 것》 the indispensable ③《믿는 사람》 one's confidant/ ~부하 a devoted retainer; a confidential follower. しんぷく

**심부름** a mission; an errand; a message / ~하다 go on an errand; do[run] errand/ ~군 an errand boy; a messenger 《지참자》 the bearer/ ~보내다 send (a person) on an errand[a message].
つかい

**심사**(心事) ①《생각》 thinking; thought; an idea ②《마음씨》 disposition; temper; spirit; a turn of mind/ ~가 복잡하다 be disturbed[confused] in mind. しんじ

**심사**(心思) ill nature; cross temper; malice; perverseness; crabbedness/ ~가 사납다 be malicious; illnatured; crooked; spiteful. しんし

**심사**(審査) 《검사》 inspection; examination 《감사》 judging/ ~하다 inspect; examine; judge; inquire; investigate/~관[원] an examiner; a judge/ ~ 위원 a jury 《그림의》 a judging[hanging] committee/ ~의 결과를 보고하다 report on one's finding. しんさ

**심사**(深思) meditation; contemplation; deep thought/ ~하다 meditate (on); contemplate; ponder (on, over)/ ~ 숙고하다 consider (a matter) carefully.
しんし

**심사**(深謝) hearty[sincere, cordial] thanks; deep gratitude/ ~하다 express one's sincere gratitude; thank heartily. しんしゃ

**심산**(心算) intention; purpose; calculation; a design/어떻게 할 ~이냐 What do you intend to do?/ ~이 들어지다 be frustrated in one's design. しんざん

**심산**(深山) the heart[depth] of a mountain; a deep[remote] mountain; a mountain recess/ ~ 유곡 high mountains and secluded valleys. しんざん

**심살내리다** have something to worry about all the time.

**심상**(心像) 〖심〗 an image. しんぞう

**심상**(尋常) ~하다 (be) common; ordinary; usual 《보통의》 average 《전형적》 normal 《평범》 commonplace/사태가 ~치 않다 The affair has taken on a bad [an ugly] look. じんじょう

**심성**(心性) nature; disposition; mind; mentality. しんせい

**심수**(深邃) profundity; abstruseness/ ~하다 (be) profound; abstruse.

**심술**(心術) cross-temper; perverseness;

**crabbedness／ ~꾸러기** an ill-natured person; a cross-grained person／ **~부리다** be cross with (*a person*).

**심신(心身)** mind and body; body and spirit／ **~의** mental and physical／ **~의 건강** both physical and mental health／**청년의 ~을 단련하다** train both bodies and spirits of the young. しんしん

**심신(心神)** mind; mentality／ **~이 산란하다** be deranged; be unhinged in mind. しんしん

**심실(心室)** 〖해〗 the ventricles of the heart. しんしつ

**심심 소일(─消日)** waste of time; a killing time／ **~하다** kill[waste] time; while away *one's* time／ **~로 바둑을 두다** play *badook* to kill time.

**심심풀이 (소일)** killing time; whiling away the hours; beguiling *one's* hours; pastime／ **~하다** kill[waste] time; beguile *one's* hours／ **~로 정구를 치다** play tennis to kill time.

**심심하다¹** feel ennui; be bored; find time hanging heavily[heavy] on *one's* hands／ **말동무가 없어 심심했다** I felt ennui having no one to talk to.

**심심하다² (싱겁다)** (be) not salted. みずくさい

**심악하다(甚惡─)** (be) harsh; cruel; merciless; devilish; inhuman. ひどくわるい

**심안(心眼)** the mind's eye／ **~을 뜨다** open *one's* spiritual eyes. しんがん

**심야(深夜)** the dead of night; midnight／ **~ 방송** midnight broadcasting／ **~ 작업** midnight labor; a night shift／ **~까지 공부하다** burn the midnight oil. しんや

**심약(心弱)** feeble-mindedness; weakmindedness／ **~하다** (be) feebleminded; weak-minded; irresolute. しんがよわいこと

**심연(深淵)** an abyss; a gulf; a profound depth／**절망의 ~** an abyss of despair. しんえん

**심오(深奧)** profundity; abstruseness／ **~하다** (be) profound; abstruse／ **~한 연구** recondite studies. しんおう

**심원(心願)** *one's* heart's desire; *one's* earnest wish[prayer]. しんがん

**심원(深怨)** deep resentment[grudge]／ **~하다** deeply resent. しんえん

**심원(深遠)** profundity; depth／ **~하다** (be) profound (*theory*); deep (*meaning*); abstruse (*idea*)／ **~한 학리** a profound theory. しんえん

**심의(審議)** deliberation; consideration; discussion; review／ **~하다** deliberate on (*a matter, subject*); consider; discuss／ **~회** a [deliberate] council／**문제를 ~하다** deliberate on the question. しんぎ

**심이(心耳)** 〖해〗 the auricles of the heart. しんじ

**심장(心臟)** the heart／ **~병** a heart-disease[-trouble]／ **~ 마비** heartfailure／ **~파멸** the rupture of the heart／ **~이 약하다** suffer from a weak heart. しんぞう

**심장(深長)** **~하다** (be) profound; deep／ **의미 ~하다** It is full of significance. しんちょう

**심재(心材)** heartwood; duramen. しんざい

**심적(心的)** mental; psychological／ **~상태** a mental state; a state of mind／ **~ 작용** a mental[psychical] action／ **~현상** a mental phenomenon. しんてき

**심정(心情)** *one's* heart; *one's* feelings／**남의 ~을 살피다** feel for (*one*); enter into another's feelings. しんじょう

**심줄** a sinew; a tendon. きん

**심중(心中)** at heart; in *one's* heart; inwardly／**~을 털어 놓다** unburden[unbosom] *oneself*／**남의 ~을 알아채다** read another's thought. しんちょう

**심중(深重)** prudence; discretion; caution／ **~하다** (be) prudent; discreet; circumspect. しんちょう

**심증(心證)** an impression; 〖법〗 conviction. しんしょう

**심지(心─)** a wick／ **~를 끊다** (초의) snuff the candle (남포의) crick[trim] a wick／**남포의 ~를 낮추다** lower[turn down] a wick. とうしん

**심지(心志)** will; intention; mind. しんし

**심지(心地)** disposition; nature; temperament; the way of mind; *one's* heart／ **~가 사납다** be perverse; be crooked. しんじ

**심지어(甚之於)** what is worse; worst of all; to crown all; the extreme case is (그 위에 또) besides; in addition／**그는 ~ 결혼 반지까지 팔았다** He went so far as to sell his wedding ring.

**심책(深責)** a severe reprimand／ **~하다** reprimand severely. ふかくせめること

**심천(深淺)** the depth／ **~을 재다** sound the depth (of *the sea*). しんせん

**심청(深靑)** dark[deep, navy] blue. こんいろ

**심축(心祝)** earnest congratulations[good wishes, blessings]／ **~하다** offer hearty congratulations (*to*); celebrate.

**심취(心醉)** fascination; absorption; a mania (for *a thing*)／ **~하다** be fascinated with; come under the spell of (*a person*); be infatuated (*with*)／**서양 문명에 ~하다** be fascinated with occidental civilization. しんすい

**심토(心土)** subsoil.

**심통(心統)** [bad] disposition／ **~이 사납다** be crooked; be perverse ⇨**심지(心地)**. こころのほんしつ

**심통(心痛)** mental suffering; agony of mind; heartache; concern; worry／ **~하다** be troubled (in *mind*); be worried about.

**심판(審判)** (경기의) umpireship; refereeing (신의) judg[e]ment; trial／ **~하다** [act as] umpire／ **~관** a judge／ **~부**

**심하다**

(특허 따위의) the Judg[e]ment Division／최후의 ~ the Last Judge. しんぱん

**심하다**(甚―) (격렬하다)(be) extreme; great; gross; intense; hard; terrible; excessive／심한 통증 an acute[a severe, a violent] pain／기침이 ~ I have a bad cough. はなはだしい

**심해**(深海) a deep sea; deep waters／~어 a deep-sea fish／~ 어업 deep-sea fishing; ocean fishery; hard; terrible; deep-sea salvage [work]. しんかい

**심혈**(心血) heart's blood／~을 기울이다 put one's blood into (one's work); put one's heart [and soul] into. しんけつ

**심호흡**(深呼吸) deep respiration[breathing]; a deep breath／~하다 draw a deep breath; practise[take] deep breathing. しんこきゅう

**심혼**(心魂) one's heart[soul]／~을 기울이다 put one's heart and soul into (one's work). しんこん

**심홍**(深紅) crimson; scarlet／~의 crimson; cardinal.

**심화**(心火) anger; passion／~가 솟다 burn with wrath[jealousy]. こころからのつっしり

**심황** 〘식〙 turmeric[-plant]; *Curcuma Longa*(학명). うこん

**심황**(深黃) saffron [colour].

**심회**(心懷) thoughts of the heart; the mind; the heart. しんかい

**심후**(深厚) ~하다 (be) deep; profound／~롭다 (감사·우정이) (be) profound; deep. しんこう

**심히**(甚―) very; very much; most; greatly; exceedingly; highly; badly; excessively; awfully; terribly／그는 ~ 피를 흘리고 있었다 He was bleeding to death.

**씹** ①(음부) the vulva; the vagina ②(성교) sexual intercourse; *coitus*(L)／~하다 have sexual intercourse (*with*); copulate. いんもく

**십**(十) ten; the tenth／~ 배 tenfold; ten times／~의 1 one tenth／~중 팔구 in nine cases out of ten; ten to one. じゅう

**십각형**(十角形) a decagon／~의 decagonal.

**십간**(十干) the ten calendar signs; the ten celestical stems. じっかん

**씹웃** a woman's pubic hair; pubes. いんもう

**십계**(十戒) the Ten Commandments; the decalogue／~를 지키다[어기다] keep [break] the commandments. じっかい

**십년**(十年) ten years; a decade／~제 the tenth anniversary／~ 감수하다 be scared to death; have a hard time of it／~이면 강산도 변한다《속담》Ten years is an epoch. じゅうねん

**씹다** chew; masticate／음식을 잘 ~ chew one's food well. かむ

**십대**(十代) the teens／~의 사람들 teenagers.

**씹두덩** the pubic part of the female.

**십만**(十萬) a hundred thousand／~ 기(騎)를 거느리고 달려가다 run to meet at the head of 100,000 horses.

**십맹일장**(十盲一杖) a friend in need. おおくのひとにきんようなこと

**십면체**(十面體) 〘수〙 a decahedron／~의 decahedral.

**십분**(十分) ①(시간) ten minutes ②(충분히) enough; well; fully ③(수) division in ten／~의 tenth; decimal／자기 실력을 ~ 발휘하다 make the most of what one has. じっぷん

**십상** (어울림) just right; just the [right] thing; the thing wanted; perfect／재떨이로 쓰기 ~이다 It make an admirable ashtray.／그 사람이라면 ~ 해낼 것이다 He would be fully equal to the task.

**십상 팔구**(十常八九) ten to one; in nine cases out of ten; probably; in all probability／내일은 ~ 비가 올 것이다 It is probable that it will rain tomorrow.

**십생 구사**(十生九死) ~하다 escape from the zaws of death; escape by a hair's breadth; have a narrow escape; have a close shave〈미〉.

**십시 일반**(十匙一飯) making a united effort to help a person.

**십억**(十億) a thousand million; a billion〈미〉. じゅうおく

**십이궁도**(十二宮圖) the horoscope.

**십이월**(十二月) December(略: Dec.). じゅうにがつ

**십이지**(十二支) the twelve zodiacal signs. じゅうにし

**십이지장**(十二指腸) 〘해〙 the duodenum／~ 궤양 duodenal ulcer／~ 충 a hookworm; *Dochmius duodenalis*(학명); a dochmius／~ 염 duodenitis. じゅうにしちょう

**십인 십색**(十人十色) so many men, so many minds; no man is alike ⇒각인각색 (各人各色). じゅうにんといろ

**십일월**(十一月) November. じゅういちがつ

**십자**(十字) a cross／~의 crossed; crucial; cruciate; cruciform／~군 a crusades／~가(街) a crossroads／~를 긋다《기도》cross oneself; make the sign of cross on one's breat[forehead]／~로(路) a crossroads／~로에 서다 be[stand] at the crossroad／~형 a cross [shape]／~ 포화 a cross fire／~ 포화를 퍼붓다 cross-fire. じゅうじ

**십자가**(十字架) ①(형구) a cross／~에 못박다 crucify ②(종) the Holy Rood／~ 상(像) a crucifix. じゅうじか

**십자매**(十姉妹) 〘조〙 a lovebird.

**십자형**(十字形) a cross-shape.

**십장**(什長) ① a foreman [of navvies]; the chief workman ②(옛날 병제에서) the corporal of a file of ten.

**십전 구도**(十顛九倒) ~하다 go through the ups and downs of life; see many hardships; taste the bitters of life.

**십종 경기**(十種競技) 〖체〗 the decathlon／～ 참가자 a decathlon contestant. じっしゅきょう

**십중 팔구**(十中八九) 《부사적》in nine cases out of ten; ten to one; most likely; in all probability. じゅうちゅうはっく

**십진**(十進) progressing by tens／～의 decimal; denary／～법 the decimal system／～ 분류법 《도서의》 decimal classification.

**씹히다** be chewed[masticated];《씹게 하다》let (a person) chew／밥에 돌이 ～ bite on a grit in the rice. かます

**씻가시다** wash and rinse. あらいきよめる

**씻기다** wash; be washed《풍랑에》be carried away《씻게 하다》have (a person) wash／큰비에 길이 ～ A road is washed[carried away] with heavy rains. あらわせる

**싯누렇다** (be) vivid yellow. まっきいろだ

**씻다** ① wash; cleanse; rinse／얼굴을 ～ wash one's face ②《누명을》clear oneself of／누명을 ～ wipe off a dishonor; clear oneself of a 「false」 charge ③《닦아내다》wipe off; mop／눈물을 ～ dry one's eyes; wipe one's tears away. あらう

**싯뻘겋다** (be) vivid red. まっあかだ

**씻부시다** wash (dishes) clean; cleanse; clean. あらいきよめる

**씻은 듯이** clean; bright; completely; thoroughly／하늘이 ～ 맑다 The sky is as clear as can be. あらったように

**싯퍼렇다** (be) deep blue 《안색이》deadly pale ⇨시퍼렇다. まっあおだ

**싯허옇다** (be) snow white ⇨시허옇다. まっしろだ

**쌩** whistling; hissing; whizzing／바람이 온 종일 ～쌩 불었다 The wind whistled all day long. びゅっ

**싱겁다** ①《맛이》(be) not salted enough; insufficiently flavoured／이 음식은 ～ This dish is not salty enough. ②《언행이》(be) absurd; silly; nonsensical; unbecoming; vacant／싱거운 소리를 하다 talk nonsense ③《술맛이》(be) washy; insipid.

**싱겅싱겅하다** (be) cool; (a room) be chill[y]. ひえびえする

**싱그레, 쌩그레** gently smiling／～ 웃다 grin; smile sweetly. にこっと

**싱글거리다** grin／싱글거리는 얼굴 a smiling[beaming] face; a radiant look. にこにこわらう

**싱글싱글** grinningly／～ 웃다 grin; give a broad grin; smile sweetly. にこにこ

**싱동싱동하다** (be) still lively; hale and hearty; be full of life[energy]; be in high spirits／그 늙은이는 아직도 ～ The old man still remains hale and hearted.

**싱숭생숭** uneasiness／～하다 feel restless[nervous, fidgety]; be in a fidget; have a birdlike restlessness／그가 떠난 후로 어쩐지 마음이 ～하다 I have been ill at ease since he left home. うきうき

**싱싱하다** (be) fresh [and vivid]／싱싱한 야채[과일] fresh vegetables[fruit]／풀잎이 ～ The leaves of the grass are all fresh. しんせであるん

**싶다** ①《욕구》want (to); wish (to); be desirous of (doing); feel like (doing); should[would] like to; inclined to (do); hope／꼭 …하고 ～ be anxious[eager, dying] to do／울고 ～ I feel like crying.／가고 싶지 않다 I don't want do go., I don't feel like going.／집에 돌아가고 ～ I wish I could see him.／집에 돌아가고 ～., I want[wish] to go home., I should[would] like to go home.／차 한 잔 마시고 싶니 Would you like a cup of tea?／내일은 날씨가 좋았으면 ～ I hope it will be fine tomorrow.／이렇게도 하고 싶고 저렇게도 하고 싶지만 무엇 하나 한 것이 없다 I want to do this and that, but so far have done nothing.／콧노래라도 부르고 싶은 기분이다 I feel like humming／새 자동차를 가지고 ～ I want a new car. ②《추측》look; appear; seem; be likely to／그가 올 성～ He is likely to come.／그녀의 목소리를 들은 성～ I seem to hear her voices.／내일도 날이 좋을 성～ It promises to be another fine day tomorrow. したい

**싶어하다** 《2·3 인칭이 주어》want to; feel like (doing); be desirous of (doing)／그 여자는 그를 만나고 싶어한다 She longed to see him. したいしたがる

아 《감동》 Ah!, Oh! 《놀람》 O dear!, Oh, Dear me!, Good gracious!, Good Heavens!, Why!, Good bless me! 《하품》 ho; hum/~ 이제 생각나는군 Oh! I remember it now! あっ

아-(亞) sub-; near-; secondary/~열대 the subtropics/~황산 sulphurous acid. あー

아-(阿) Africa; African. あー

아가 a baby; a babe 《호칭》 My darling!, Baby!, Daughter!, Daughter-in-law! あかんぼう

아까 some time[a little while] ago/~부터 for some time. さっき

아가딸 a daughter 《소녀》 a girl. むすめ

아가리 a mouth; a muzzle; a snout/~를 벌리다 open one's trap/~질 talking; shouting angrily. くち

아가미 a gill; the gills of a fish; the branchia. えら

아가씨 a young girl[lady]; an unmarried lady; a maid[en]; 《호칭》 Miss; you; Young lady!/~ 어디서 오셨읍니까 Where are you from, Miss? むすめさん

아가위 the fruit of the hawthorn; a haw/~나무 the Chinese hawthorn. さんざしのみ

아감 gills/~구멍 gill slit/~뼈 branchial arch/~뚜껑 gill cover.

아깝다 《애석하다》 (be) pitiful; disappointing; regrettable 《귀중하다》 (be) dear; precious; valuable; too good; ill-spared 《과분하다》 (be) wasteful; too good (for) /아까운 일이군 What a pity it is! おしい

아교(阿膠) glue/~로 붙이다 glue; fasten (a thing) with glue. にかわ

아교(阿嬌) a charming girl[woman].

아구맞추다 round of the number; make it come out even[as it should]. しゅうしをあわせること

아국(我國) our country[land, nation]; this country [of ours]. わがくに

아군(我軍) our forces[troops, army]; friendly forces. わがぐん

아궁이 a fuel hole; a fireplace. たきぐち

아귀 ①《갈라진 곳》 a fork; a crotch ②《씨의》 a budding[sprouting] spot. ぶんきてん

아귀(餓鬼) 《주린 귀신》 a hungry ghost [devil, demon]; Preta(Sans); 《대식가》 a glutton; a gourmand. がき

아귀 다툼 argument; a spat ⇨말다툼. いいあらそい

아귀세다 (be) tough; firm; strong-minded; have a strong grip/아귀센 아이 a tough boy. いしがけんごだ

아귀차다 (be) tough ⇨아귀세다.

아기 ①a baby; an infant; a child; a babe《시》 ②《딸・며느리》 dear; darling; pet. あかんぼう

아끼다 ①《인색하다》 grudge; spare; be sparing of; be stingy; be a miser; be stint /용돈을 ~ spare expense ②《소중히 여기다》 value; prize; hold (a thing) dear/시간을 ~ value time. おしむ

아기살 a short arrow. ちいさいや

아기서다 be[become] pregnant; be with child. こをはらむ

아기자기 ~하다 ①《예쁘다》 (be) pretty; fine; lovely ②《재미있다》 (be) thrilling; tingling with pleasure; very happy/~한 이야기 a juicy story. ほれぼれと

아기집 《자궁》 the womb; the uterus(pl. -ri). しきゅう

아낌없이 ungrudgingly; unsparingly; generously; freely; without stint/~ 주다 give freely. おしまない

아나 ①《아이에게》 Hey!, Hey there! ②《아나 나비야》 Here puss!, Kitty-kitty! おい

아낙 a boudoir; woman's quarters.

아낙네 a woman; a wife. ふじょし

아내 a wife; one's better-half 《배우자》 a spouse/그 여자는 훌륭한 ~가 될 것이다 She will make a good wife. つま

아녀자(兒女子) children and women; minor and women; a skirt《속》.

아늑하다 (be) cozy; snug; comfortable /아늑한 사무실 a snug[cozy] office/아늑한 방 a snug room. ふかぶかとし

아는체하다 feign knowledge/아는체하는 놈 a knowing fellow.

아니¹ ①《부정의 대답》 no; nay; not at all; yes(긍정)/~라고 대답하다 say no /~, 그렇지 않다 No, you are wrong. ②《감탄사》 O!, Oh!, Bless me!, Oh my!, My eye!, What!/~ 또 늦었나 What Are you late again? いや

아니² 《부정》 [do] not/~ 가다 do not go.

아니꼽다 ①《불쾌하다》(be) disgusting; loathsome/아니꼬운 자식 a disgutful fellow ②《구역이 날 듯하다》 feel vomiting

**아니꾸다** [nauseous]. しゃくにさわる
**아니나다를까** as was expected; sure enough; just as was expected／~ 그는 나타나지 않았다 As was expected, he failed to turn up. やはりそうだ
**아니다** (be) not; no／이것은 상상이 아니고 실제다 This is not imagination but reality. そでない
**아니라고** saying that it is not／그것은 내 것이. ~ 주지 않았다 He said it was not mine and wouldn't give it to me.
**아니하다** be not; do not ⇒않다. —しない
**아닌게아니라** 《과연》 indeed; really／~ 네 말이 옳다 To be sure, what you say is right. いうまでもなく
**아닌밤중** (一中) q~에 홍두깨 a great surprise; a thunderclap. いがいなよあい
**아따** [oh] boy; well／~ 말도 많다 Oh boy, you really talk, don't you! まあ
**아담** (雅淡) ~하다 (be) refined; elegant; neat; tidy; dainty／~한 집 a refined [nice] house. がだん
**아동** (兒童) a child (pl. ·ren); a juvenile 《생도》 pupil 《총칭》 boys and girls／~문학 juvenile literature／~ 심리학 child psychology／~ 복지법 the Juvenile Welfare Law. じどう
**아둔하다** (be) dull; slow of apprehension; dull[slow-]witted; stupid／아둔하기도 하다 How stupid can you get! うとい
**아드님** your[his, her] son.
**아드득** with a crunching sound／~거리다 crunch; be crunchy／이를 ~ 갈다 grind one's teeth. がりがり
**아드등거리다** bicker with each other; spat; fuss／아드등거리며 살다 lead a cat and dog life. いがみあう
**아득하다** (be) far; distant; remote; far off; far-away／아득한 옛날에 in the far off days. ほのかだ
**아뜩하다** (be) suddenly dizzy; giddy／그 소식에 정신이 ~ be stunned by the news. ふらふらする
**아들** a son; a boy 《자기의》 my son／~딸 son[s] and daughter[s]. むすこ
**아등** (我等) we; us／~의 our.
**아등그리다** get warped; get twisted out of shape.
**아람** 《밤·상수리 따위의》 (being) fully ripened on the tree／밤~ tree-ripened chestnuts.
**아랑** the sediment[dregs] left from brewing liquor. さけかす
**아랑곳** concern; interest／~하다 concern oneself 《with》／그 일에 네가 ~할 필요가 뭐냐 What concern is it of yours?
**아랑곳 없다** have nothing to do 《with》; have no interest 《in》／그것은 내게 아랑곳 없는 일이다 That's none of my business. かんしょうのひつようない
**아랑주** (一紬) cloth woven of silk and cotton.
**아래** ①《하방(下方)》 the low part; the foot; the bottom; the base／~의 lower; under 《다음의》 following／~에[서] below; down; under; beneath／책상 ~에 under a desk ②《하위(下位)》 ~의 lower; inferior subordinate; below 《이하의》 under. した
**아래위** up and down; above and below 《신분의》 the upper and lower classes; high and low. しょうか
**아래쪽** down; lower position[direction]; the south.
**아래채** the outer wing building.
**아래층** (一層) the downstairs. かいか
**아래턱** the lower[under] jaw[chin]. したあご
**아래통** the lower part [of the body]／~이 가늘다 have a slender waist. もののかぶ
**아랫녘** 《아래쪽》 lower part[side]; the south 《전라·경상도》 the south. したのかだ
**아랫니** the lower teeth. したば
**아랫도리** 《하체》 the lower part [of the body]; 《옷의》 lower garment[s]; bottom[s]. かはんしん
**아랫동** the lower part (of a thing)／나무의 ~ the base of a tree. もののほう
**아랫목** a top seat of a room; the part of a Korean room nearest to the fuel hole.
**아랫방** (一房) an outer wing room.
**아랫배** the belly; the abdomen／~가 아프다 have a bellyache. したばら
**아랫벌** the lower garment. したぎ
**아랫사람** 《나이가》 one's junior 《지위가》 one's inferior; a subordinate.
**아랫사랑** (一舍廊) a guest room in the outer wing of a house.
**아랫수염** (一鬚髥) a beard; chin-whiskers／~을 기르다 grow a beard. したあごひげ
**아랫입술** the lower lip／~을 깨물다 bite one's lower lip. したくちびる
**아량** (雅量) generosity; liberality; magnanimity; greatness of soul／~있는 사람 a man of magnanimity. がりょう
**아련하다** (be) dim; vague; faint; indistinct／기억이 ~ remember dimly. げんきがない
**아렴풋이** faintly; dimly; vaguely.
**아렴풋하다** (be) faint; dim.
**아령** (啞鈴) iron dumb-bells／~ 체조 exercise with dumb-bells.
**아로새기다** engrave／돌에 이름을 ~ engrave a name on a stone. しさくする
**아롱다롱** ~하다 (be) spotted; dotted; speckled／무늬가 ~한 천 cloth speckled with designs. まだらだ
**아뢰다** tell; inform; let (one) know; say: mention. つたえる
**아류** (亞流) an adherent; a follower; a second (to). ありゅう
**아류산** (亞硫酸) 【화】 sulphurous acid.
**아른거리다** 《물건이》 flicker; flit 《눈이》 be dazzled 《마음이》 haunt (one)／그의 모습이 눈 앞에 ~ His image flit before my eyes. ちらちらする

이름 601 아비신

아름 an armful／한 ~의 장작 an armful of firewood.

아름답다, (be) beautiful; pretty; lovely; fine; picturesque 《용모가》 charming／아름다운 여자 a beautiful woman; a beauty. うつくしい

아름드리 an armful／~ 나무 a tree measuring more than an arm's span around.

아름아름 ①《말을》 mumblingly ②《일을》 at random; half-way.

아름차다 (be) unmanageable; be too much for (one)／나 혼자서는 ~ I can not manage it alone. ちからにあまる

아리다 ①《맛이》 (be) pungent; -acrid; sharp ②《상처가》 (be) tingling; smarting ③《얼어서》 (be) numbed; benumbed; asleep. ひりひりする

아리땁다 (be) lovely; charming; coquettish／아리따운 처녀 a charming young lady. うつくしい

아리송하다 (be) ambiguous ⇨아리숭하다.

아릿아릿하다 (be) absent-minded; be; be in a baze. よろめく

아릿하다 taste sharp; have a biting[burning] taste. ぴりっとする

아마 《대개》 probably; perhaps; maybe; likely; possibly; presumably; in all probability 《십중 팔구》 in nine cases out of ten; ten to one. たぶん

아마(亞麻) 【식】 flax hemp. あま

아명(兒名) one's childhood name. おさな

아무 ①《긍정·부정(不定)》 anyone; anybody any; whoever; [every] one; all; everybody／~라도 할 수 있다 Anyone can do it. ②《부정(否定)》 no one; nobody; none; anyone; anybody／~도 그것을 할 수 없다 No man can do that. だれ

아무개 Mr. [Miss, Mrs.] so and so; such and such a person; a certain person; some person or other. だれそれ

아무때 any time; any day; whenever; always; all the time／~나 좋다 Any time will do. いついつ

아무데 《부정 의문》 any place; anywhere／~도 안 간다 I am not going anywhere. 《아무 곳》 somewhere; a certain place. どこそこ

아무래도 ①《어떻든》 anyhow; anyway; in any case 《결국》 after all; in the long run 《아무리 봐도》 in all respects; in every respect／~ 저이가 수상하다 I have every reason to suspect that man. ②《무관심》 ①그까짓 일은 ~ 좋다 That does not matter. ③《결코 …이 아닌》 by no means; on any account; never／~ 그의 이름이 생각나지 않았다 I cannot, for the life of me, remember his name. どうしても

아무러면 ①《결코·설마》 [not] in any way; [not] in any case ②《아무런들》 [no matter, it make no difference] whatever it is; however it is. なにはともあれ

아무런 《부정》 any sort of; no／~ 사고 없이 without any accident. どのような

아무렇거나 anyhow; anyway; in any case; at any rate／~ 출발하자 Let's start anyway. どうであっても

아무렇게나 in any manner one pleases; carelessly／~ 대답하다 give a random answer. どのように

아무렇게도 ①~ 생각지 않다 make little [nothing] of; do not care about.

아무렇든지 anyhow; no matter what／~ 방법을 강구해 보겠읍니다 I will find some means to do so. どのようでも

아무렴 Of course!, Certainly!, To be sure／가겠 느냐고 ? ~ 가야지 ! Will I go you say? Sure, I will. そうですとも

아무리 however; how [much]／~ 일해도 however hard you may work. どれほど

아무말 [not] any word／~도 할 것이 없다 I have nothing to say.

아무일 something; anything 《부정》 nothing／종일 ~도 없었다 Nothing happened all day.

아무짝 any use／~에도 쓸모가 없다 It is of no use whatever.

아무쪼록 《꼭》 by all means; in any way 《아뭏든》 anyway; at'any rate 《가능한 한》 [if you] please; pray. なるだけ

아물거리다 ①《물체가》 (be) dim[hazy]; 《마음의》 haunt (a person) ②《불투명하게》 talk[act] ambiguously.

아물다 heal (up); be healed／상처가 ~ a wound heals up; be healed of one's wound. いえる

아물리다 ①《낫게 하다》 make (a wound) heal／고약으로 상처를 ~ help heal a wound with an ointment ②《일을》 finish up; conclude; wind up／일을 ~ finish up one's work. いやす

아물아물하다 flicker ⇨아물거리다.

아미(娥眉) lovely[beautiful] eyebrows; crescent; eyebrows. がび

아빠 papa; daddy; dad; pop《미·속》.

아버님 《경칭》 one's father ⇨아버지. おとうさま

아버지 a father 《어린이 말》 papa; daddy; dad／~ 없는 fatherless／근대 음악의 ~ the father of modern music／~의 사랑 paternal affection. おとうさん

아범 《비칭》 father 《하인》 an elderly manservant. ちち

아부(阿附) flattery／~하다 flatter (a person); fawn (upon)／상사에게 ~하다 ingratiate oneself with one's superiors. へつらうこと

아뿔싸 Dear me!, Darn it!, Gosh!, Damn!／~ 이 일을 어쩐담 O my! What shall I do! あちゃー

아비 father／~ 없는 자식 a fatherless child; an illegitimate child. ちち

아비 규환(阿鼻叫喚) agonizing cries; appalling confusion. あびきょうかん

아비산(亞砒酸) 【화】 arsenious acid／~염 arsenite. あひさん

**아사(餓死)** death from hunger; death by starvation/~하다 starve[be starved] to death; die of starvation. がし

**아삭** ~하다 be crispy; crunchy.

**아삭거리다** be crispy; munch at (a cake). ぼりぼり

**아삭아삭** crunching/~하다 be crisp[crunchy, crispy]. ぼりぼり

**아서라** Oh no!, Quit!, Stop!, Don't!, Come now!, Nonsense!/~ 남을 욕하지 마라 Now now! Don't run other people down!

**아성(牙城)** inner citadel; the stronghold (본부) the headquarters. がじょう

**아성(亞聖)** sage[saint] of second rank.

**아성층권(亞成層圈)** the substratosphere/~비행 a substratospheric flight.

**아속(雅俗)** culture and vulgarism; the stylish and the common (사람의) the refined and the vulgar (언어의) the classical and the colloquial. がぞく

**아수라(阿修羅)** Asura(Sans)/ ~왕 the King of the Asura. あしゅら

**아수룩하다** (be) cheap; low; low-priced; inexpensive. うしろぐらい

**아쉬워하다** miss; feel the lack of; be incovenienced by not having/이별을 ~ be unwilling[reluctant] to part with (a person).

**아쉰대로** lacking anything better; by way of a makeshift/~ 이것을 쓰시오 Use this as a makeshift. せめても

**아쉽다** (be) inconvenient; lacking/응접실이 없어서 ~ It is inconvenient not to have a reception room. ふべんだ

**아스라하다** be far off[up].

**아스러지다** ①(덩어리가) crumble ②(살이) be abraded; get rubbed raw.

**아슬렁거리다** shuffle along ⇒어슬렁거리다. のろのろわきまわる

**아슬아슬** ~하다 ①(위태하다)(be) dangerous; risky; critical; thrilling; exciting (위기일발)(be) close ②(춥다) feel a chilly; shiver. ひやひや

**아씨** (하인의) young mistress (호칭) a married lady; your lady; Mrs. (명칭) madam. むすめさん

**아식 축구(一式蹴球)** Association football; soccer; socker.

**아아** (일이 잘못된 때)Oh-oh! (감동)Ah!

**아아(阿亞)** Africa and Asia; Afro-Asian; Afro-Asiatic/~어족 the Afro-Asiatic [Hamito-Semitic] language family.

**아악(雅樂)** court[ceremonial] music/~을 연주하다 play ceremonial music. ががく

**아야** Ouch!/~ 아파라! Ouch, it hurts. あいた

**아얌** a fur cap worn by women in winter.

**아양** coquetry; winsomeness; flattery/~스럽다 be coquettish; coy/~을 부리다 play the coquette. あいきょう

**아어(雅語)** refined diction[speech]; an elegant word.

**아역(兒役)** (역)a child's part (in a play); a juvenile part (사람) a child actor.

**아연(亞鉛)** 【화】zinc(略：Zn)/ ~광 zinc ore/~판(板) a zinc sheet/~판(版) a-nastatic printing. あえん

**아연(俄然)** suddenly; all of a sudden; abruptly/~ 긴장하다 become suddenly tense[strained]. がぜん

**아연(啞然)** (부사격)agape (with wonder); aghast; speechless; in amazement/~하다 be aghast; be stunned. あぜん

**아열대(亞熱帶)** the subtropics; the subtropical zone/~ 식물 a subtropical plant. あねったい

**아예** from the very first; never; altogether/~ 그런 생각은 없었다 I never intended to do so. はじめから

**아용** a miaow; with a miaow; mew/~하다 miaow; mew. にゃあお

**아옹거리다** gripe; bicker; squabble. ぶつぶついう

**아옹다옹하다** be disgruntled; be griped; be complaining[griping] to oneself.

**아우** ①(동생) a younger brother ②(나이 적은 이) a junior (in age); a junior colleague. おとうと

**아우러지다** (조화하다) match (with); harmonize (합치다) join together. あわせられる

**아우르다** (보태다) add (to); (병합하다) amalgamate; merge/아울러 also; in addition/힘을 ~ work together. あう

**아우성** a war[battle-]cry; shouting/~치다 raise[shout] a war-cry; shout. かんせい

**아우타다** (젖먹이가) [a child] get thin from premature weaning as a result of the mother's new pregnancy. ようじがやせる

**아욱** 【식】a mallow. つゆあおい

**아울러** [joining] together/~ 가지다 possess together (with); possess (a thing) in addition (to).

**아울리다** join; (be) becoming ⇒어울리다.

**아유(阿諛)** flattery; adulation/~하다 flatter (one); adulate. あゆ

**아음(牙音)** 【연】velar sounds; a velar.

**아이** (자식) a child (사내아이) a boy (계집애) a girl (아들) a son (딸) a daughter/~를 가지다[배다] get[conceive] a child. こども

**아이고** Oh!, Ah!, Oh dear!, Dear me!/~ 좋아라 Oh! how glad I am!/~ 죽겠다 Oh, I am dying. ああ

**아이종** a young servant. おさないとび

**아장거리다** toddle; totter/아장거리는 아기 a toddler. ちょこちょこあるく

**아장걸음** toddling step[gait].

**아재** (아저씨)an uncle (아주버니) one's husband's brother; a brother-in-law. おじ

**아저씨** 《삼촌》an uncle 《부모 연배의》a man of one's parents age. おじさん

**아전(衙前)** a petty official of provincial

**아전 인수**(我田引水) drawing water to one's own mill/~의 self-seeking/~의 설(說) a selfish view.

**아제** 《아씨》 an uncle 《자매의 남편》 the husband of a girl's sister.

**아주** ①(전혀) very; quite; really; perfect[ly]; altogether; exceedingly; utterly; entirely; [not] at all/~ 기분이 좋다 feel quite well/~ 피곤하다 be dead tired ②(감탄사) Oh really?, /Damn it!, Hang it!

**아주까리** 〖식〗 a castor-bean [plant]; *Ricinus communis*(학명).

**아주머니** 《숙모》 an aunt 《아줌마》 an auntie; an aunty 《일반 부인》 a lady.

**아주먹이** ①(정미) polished rice; refined rice ②(솜옷) clothes with permanently stitched cotton padding.

**아주버니** one's husband's elder brother.

**아지랑이** heat haze[wave]; shimmering [air]/~가 끼었다 The air is shimmering.

**아지작거리다** crunch; crush noisily/사과를 ~ munch an apple.

**아직** yet; as yet; still/~ 미해결이다 It is yet to be solved. /그는 ~ 오지 않았다 He has not come yet.

**아직까지** so[thus] far; up to now; till now; up to the present/~는 일이/수월했다 So far the work has been easy.

**아질하다, 아찔하다** be[feel] dizzy[giddy]; feel faint/머리가 ~ I feel have vertigo dizzy;.

**아집**(我執) egoistic attachment; egotism; tenacity; obstinacy.

**아차** Heavens!, By Jove!, My goodness!, Dear me!

**아첨**(阿諂) flattery; adulation/~하다 flatter (*a person*); fawn upon (*a person*) /~잔이 a flatterer; a sycophant.

**아청**(鴉靑) a dark blue.

**아취**(雅趣) elegance; tastefulness; charm; artistry; refinement/ ~있는 생활을 하다 lead a tasteful life.

**아치**(雅致) good taste; elegance; grace; artistry; gusto/~있는 별장 a tasteful cottage.

**아침** ①《때》 morning; morn《아》/~에 in the morning/~ 다섯 시에 일어났다 I turned out at five o'clock in the morning. ②(밥) breakfast; the morning meal/~잠 a morning nap.

**아침 저녁** morning and evening/~으로 제법 쌀쌀하다 We have cooler mornings and evenings now.

**아탄**(亞炭) lignite; brown coal.

**아파하다** feel pain; hurt; complain of pain.

**아편**(阿片, 鴉片) opium; an opiate/~ 전쟁 the Opium War/~ 중독 opiumism; opium poisoning/~ 중독자 an opium addict/~을 피우다 smoke opium.

**아프다** pain; ache; have[feel] a pain; be painful; be sore/머리가 몹시 ~ I have a splitting headache.

**아하** Dear me!, My goodness!, Well!, What-do-you-know!/~ 그것을 깜박 잊었구나 Oh my goodness!—it slipped right out of my mind!

**아한대**(亞寒帶) the subarctic zone; the subfrigid zone.

**아형**(雅兄) Sir; You sir.

**아호**(雅號) a pen name; a *nom de plume* (F)/단원이란 ~로 쓰다 write under the pen name of *Danwon*.

**아홉** nine/~째 the ninth; No. 9.

**아황산**(亞黃酸) 〖화〗 sulfurous acid/~가스 sulfurous acid gas/~염 sulfite.

**아흐레** the ninth day of the month 《아홉 날》 nine days.

**아흔** ninety/~째 the ninetieth.

**아희**(兒戱) a child's play; a playgame /~ 같은 childish; puerile.

**악**¹ (몹시 놀랄 때) Oh!, Dear me!/~ 호랑이다! Oh! there's a tiger!

**악**² (모짐) excitement; desperation; franticness/~이 받친 desperate/~이 받쳐 술을 먹다 take to drink out of desperation.

**악**(萼) 〖식〗 a calyx(*pl.* ~es, -lyces); of a flower; a cup; a vase.

**악**(惡) badness; evil (잘못) wrong(악덕) vice 《사악》 wickedness/~하다 (be) bad; evil; ill; wrong; immoral; sinful; wicked; vicious/~을 선으로 갚다 return good for evil/사회~ social vice.

**악감정**(惡感情) ill feeling[will]; ill blood; animosity/~을 품다 bear (*a person*) an ill will.

**악곡**(樂曲) a musical piece[composition]; a piece of music; a tune.

**악골**(顎骨) 〖해〗 a jawbone; a maxillary bone.

**악공**(樂工) a court musician.

**악귀**(惡鬼) an evil spirit; a devil; a demon; the Evil One/~가 들리다 be possessed by[with] a devil.

**악극**(樂劇) an opera; a music[al] drama /~단 a musical troupe.

**악기**(惡氣) noxious air[gas]; miasma.

**악기**(樂器) a musical instrument/관(현, 건타, 타, 취주)~ a wind[string, key, percussion, brass] instrument.

**악기류**(惡氣流) a treacherous[dangerous] aircurrent; air turbulence.

**악녀**(惡女) a wicked woman; a virago; a witch 《용모의》 an ugly woman.

**악념**(惡念) a bad[an evil] intention[thought]; malice; spite.

**악다구니** a name-calling quarrel; bicke-

**악단(樂壇)** the musical world; musical circles.

**악단(樂團)** an orchestra/교향~ a symphony orchestra/~원 a member of an orchestra.

**악담(惡談)** abuse; slander; abusive language/~하다 abuse; speak ill of; call (a person) names.

**악대(樂隊)** a [musical] band 《취주악단》 a brass band 《관현악단》 an orchestra/~원 a bandsman/~장 a bandmaster.

**악대소** a bullock; a castrated bull.

**악덕(惡德)** vice; immorality; corruption; evil conduct/~ 기업주 vicious entrepreneurs/~ 상인 wicked dealers.

**악도리** a tough guy; a ruffian; a roughneck.

**악동(惡童)** a bad[naughty] boy 《도회지의》 a street Arab.

**악독(惡毒)** viciousness; perversity; harshness/~하다 (be) vicious; naughty; venomous; harsh/~한 짓 vicious practices.

**악랄(惡辣)** craftiness; knavishness/~하다 (be) mean; nasty; knavish/~한 수단 knavish tricks.

**악력(握力)** grip; grasping power/~이 세다 have a strong grip/~계 a hand-dynamometer.

**악례(惡例)** a bad example 《선례》 a bad precedent/~를 남기다 establish a bad precedent.

**악리(樂理)** theory of music; music theory.

**악마(惡魔)** an evil spirit; a devil; a demon; a fiend 《마왕》 Satan/~ 같은 devilish; fiendish.

**악머구리** a croaker; a frog/~ 끓듯 하다 make a lot of noise.

**악명(惡名)** an evil reputation; a bad name; notoriety/~이 높아지다 become notorious.

**악모(岳母)** one's mother-in-law; the mother of one's wife.

**악몽(惡夢)** a bad[an evil] dream; a nightmare/~에서 깨어나다 start from a nightmare.

**악물다** (이를) gnash; set; clench [one's teeth]; shut [one's teeth] hard; compress (one's tips)/이를 악물고 with one's teeth set.

**악미(惡米)** rice of an inferior quality; poor rice.

**악바리** a bad[wicked] man; a rogue; a villain; a scoundrel.

**악벽(惡癖)** a bad[vicious, ill] habit; a vice/~을 바로잡다 overcome a bad habit; cure of bad habit.

**악병(惡病)** a malignant[foul, virulent] disease.

**악보(樂譜)** a musical note; music; a score/~를 읽다 read music.

**악보(惡報)** bad[sad] news; ill[evil] tidings 《결과》 an evil effect.

**악부(岳父)** the father of one's wife; a father-in-law.

**악사(樂士)** a band[s]man; a musician/~장 the chief music master.

**악사(惡事)** evil; evil-doing; an evil thing [deed]; a wrong; villainy 《죄악》 a crime/가난 때문에 ~를 저질렀다 Poverty drove him to evil-doing.

**악설(惡說)** abusive language; slander; backbiting; curse/~하다 speak ill; abuse; curse.

**악성(惡聲)** a bad voice 《욕》 scandal; evil-speaking; abuse 《악평판》 evil reputation; ugly rumo[u]rs.

**악성(樂聖)** a celebrated musician/~ 베토벤 Beethoven, the master.

**악성(惡性)** malignancy; viciousness/~의 malignant; vicious/~ 감기 a malignant influenza.

**악세다** (be) strong; tough.

**악소년(惡少年)** a bad[naughty] boy; an urchin.

**악속(惡俗)** a bad practice; vicious[evil] manners; evil ways[habits, customs]. /~을 일소하다 extirpate evil practices.

**악수(握手)** a handshake 《화해》 reconciliation 《제휴》 a union/~하다 shake hands (with); 《제휴하다》 join hands (with); 《화해하다》 make peace (with).

**악순환(惡循環)** 《경》《의》 a vicious circle.

**악쓰다(惡一)** be[become] desperate; be driven to desperation.

**악습(惡習)** (나쁜 버릇) a bad habit 《나쁜 풍습》 an evil[acorrupt] practice 《악폐》 abuses/~을 일소하다 extirpate evil practices.

**악식(惡食)** 《음식》 coarse[gross] food; plain food 《먹기》 gross feeding/~하다 live[feed] low; live on plain diet.

**악심(惡心)** an evil intention/~을 품다 become evilly inclined.

**악어(鰐魚)** 《동》 a crocodile 《북미산》 an alligator 《중남미산》 a cayman/~ 가죽 alligator[crocodile] leather.

**악업(惡業)** karma(Sans)/전세의 ~은 피할 수 없다 There is no escape from the karma.

**악역(惡役)** a villain's part/저 배우는 ~을 잘한다 That actor plays a villain's part very well.

**악역(惡疫)** a plague; a pestilence; an epidemic/~이 만연중이다 A pestilence rages[is prevalent].

**악연(惡緣)** 《운명》 an evil destiny 《나쁜 인연》 an evil connection; a fatal relation 《남녀간의》 an unhappy marriage.

**악연(愕然)** aghast; appalled; shocked; in surprise; amazedly/~하다 be amazed[astonished, shocked].

**악영향(惡影響)** bad effect[influence]; harm/~을 끼치다 have[exert] a bad influence (upon).

**악용(惡用)** abuse; misuse/~하다 abuse; misuse; use for a wrong purpose; make a bad use (of)/권력을 ~하다 abuse one's authority.

**악우(惡友)** a bad[an evil] companion [friend]/~와 사귀지 않도록 주의해라 Don't keep company with bad friends.

**악운(惡運)** ill luck; bad[adverse] fortune; an evil fate/그에게는 ~이 따른다 An evil fate pursues him.

**악음(樂音)** a musical tone[sound].

**악의(惡意)** an evil intention; ill will; malice; grudge; spite; ill feeling/그는 나에게 아무런 ~도 품지 않고 있다 He bears no malice to me.

**악의 악식(惡衣惡食)** coarse clothing and gross food; a plain dress and a poor meal/~하다 be ill-clad and poorly fed.

**악인(惡人)** a bad[wicked] man; a rogue; a villain; a scoundrel.

**악장(樂長)** a bandmaster; a conductor; a music director.

**악장(樂章)** 〖음〗 a movement/제1[2]~ the first[second] movement.

**악장치다** quarrel[dispute] with each other noisily.

**악전 고투(惡戰苦鬪)** hard fighting; a hard[-fought] battle; a hard[desperate] fight (경기의) a close game; a tight match (경쟁의) a close contest/~하다 fight desperately; fight with one's back to the wall/선거전에서 ~하다 have a close contest in the election.

**악정(惡政)** misgovernment; misrule; bad government.

**악조건(惡條件)** adverse[unfavo[u]rable] conditions[factors].

**악조증(惡阻症)** 〖의〗 morning sickness; nausea accompanying pregnancy.

**악종(惡種)** a rogue; a bad seed[character]; a villain; a rascal.

**악증(惡症)** 〖병〗 a malignant disease; a violent disorder (못된 짓) a bad habit.

**악질(惡疾)** a malignant[virulent] disease/~에 걸리다 be seized with a malignant disease.

**악질(惡質)** (악성) evil nature (열등) inferior quality; malignancy; wickedness /~의 bad; evil; vicious; ill-natured/~ 분자 bad elements.

**악착(齷齪)** ①(잔인) villainy; wickedness /~하다 (be) nasty; atrocious; diabolical ②(도량이 좁음) narrowmindedness /~하다 (be) narrowminded; ungenerous.

**악착스럽다** worry [oneself]/악착스럽게 fussily; busily; hard; sedulously.

**악처(惡妻)** a bad wife[wicked]/~는 일생을 두고 말썽을 부린다 A bad wife is a lifelong dearth[the shipwreck of her husband].

**악취(惡臭)** an offensive[evil] smell[odour]; a bad[nasty] smell; a stink; stench/묵은 생선은 ~를 풍긴다 An old fish stinks.

**악취미(惡趣味)** bad[vulgar] taste.

**악치듯** harshly ⇒악패듯.

**악패듯** harshly; relentlessly; ruthlessly; violently.

**악평(惡評)** (평판) a bad reputation; ill repute (비난) an adverse criticism/~ 하다 speak ill of; make malicious remarks/그는 세상의 ~을 받고 있다 He is ill spoken of.

**악폐(惡弊)** an evil; an abuses; evil practices/~를 타파하다 do away with abuses.

**악풍(惡風)** a bad custom[habit]; evil manners; a vicious practice.

**악필(惡筆)** bad handwriting; a bad[poor] hand/그는 지독한 ~이다 He writes an awful scrawl.

**악하다(惡—)** (be) bad; evil; ill; wrong; immoral/성질이 ~ be ill-natured/악한 일을 하다 do wrong.

**악한(惡漢)** a rascal; a villain; a rogue; a scoundrel.

**악행(惡行)** (부정) malpractice (비행) misconduct; wrong[evil] doing/~에 빠지다 be given to evil ways.

**악혈(惡血)** bad[impure, black] blood.

**악형(惡刑)** a severe punishment[penalty] /~을 과하다 inflict a severe punishment (on).

**악화(惡化)** (형세·상태) a change for the worse; aggravation (품질) deterioration (심성·풍속) degeneration; debasement /~하다 make[become, grow] worse; degenerate; take a turn for the worse /사태는 점점 ~하고 있다 The situation is growing from bad to worse.

**악화(惡貨)** bad coins[money]/~는 양화 (良貨)를 구축한다 Bad money drives out the good.

**악희(惡戱)** a prank; a practical joke; a mischievous act[trick]/~하다 play pranks.

**안¹** ①(내부) the inside; the interior/~ 에 within; inside; in (집 안에) indoors /~에서 from the inside ②(한도 내) within; inside of; in; less than; not more than/일주일 ~에 within a week ③(이면·내편) the back; the wrong side; the reverse side; the other side /천의 ~쪽 the wrong side of the cloth ④(옷의) the lining; doubling/~을 대 다 line (clothes) ⑤(내실) the woman's quarters; the inner room ⑥(아내) one's wife ⑦(여자) 및 ~부모 a mother/~주 인 a mistress.

안² not ⇒아니.

안(案) 《의안》 a bill; a measure 《제안》 a proposal; a suggestion; a proposition 〈미〉;《고안》 an idea; a conception 《계획》 a plan; a scheme; an idea 《초안》 a draft／～을 세우다 make a plan. あん

안간힘 ill-contained resentment／～쓰다 give vent to one's ill-contained resentment.

안감 lining; cloth for lining.

안강(安康) peace and good health／～하다 (be) well; healthy; safe and sound. あんこう

안갚음 repaying one's indebtedness to one's parents／～하다 show one's appreciation of one's parents.

안개 [a] fog; a mist; haze／～에 싸인 산 hills veiled in mist／～ 구름 stratus clouds／사건이 ～ 속에 싸이다 a case is shrouded in mystery. きり

안거(安居) a quiet[tranquil, peaceful] life／～하다 live quietly. あんきょ

안건(案件) a matter; a case; an item; 중요한 ～ an important matter. あんけん

안경(眼鏡) glasses 《귀에 거는》 spectacles 《코안경》 eyeglasses 《비행사용》 goggles／～테 a spectacles frame／～ 너머로 보다 look over [the edge of] one's glasses. めがね

안계(眼界) prospect; sight／～가 in prospective／～에 들어오다 come into view; appear[come] in sight. がんかい

안고나다 be responsible for; answer for／내각에 대한 비난을 그가 전부 안고났다 He took upon himself the criticism levelled at the cabinet. せきにんをおう

안고 수비(眼高手卑) an appreciative eye with an incompetent hand.

안고지고 fall into the pit one dug for anothers.

안공(眼孔) an eyehole; an eye socket. がんこう

안과(眼科) 《의》 ophthalmology／～ 병원 an ophthalmic hospital／～학 [the study of] ophthalmology. がんか

안광(眼光) the brightness of the eye 《통찰》 penetration. がんこう

안구(眼球) an eye-ball; the globe of an eye／～ 은행 an eye bank. がんきゅう

안구(鞍具) saddlery; saddle gear; horse gear; harness.

안기다¹ 《팔에》 be embraced; be in one's arms[bosom]; be carried in the arms／어머니 품에 안겨 있는 아기 an infant nestling in mother's bosom ②《닭한테 알을》 set eggs [under a hen]. いだかれる

안기다² ①《물건을》 force on; thrust on 《가짜를》 pass[foist, impose] upon; palm [fob] off upon／《강제로》 물건을 ～ force a sale on (one) ②《책임을》 fix responsibility upon; charge; impose／빚을 ～ hold (one) liable for the debt.

안날 the previous[preceding] day; the day before／출발하기 ～ the day before one's departure.

안내(案內) ①《향도》 guiding; conducting 《현관에서의》 answering the door 《안내자》 a guide／～하다 guide; conduct; show 《좌석으로》 usher 《앞장서서》 lead the way／～소 an inquiry office; an information bureau／～서 a guide[-book]／그는 나를 자기 집으로 ～했다 He guided me to his house. ②《통지》 advices; information; notice／～하다 advise; notify. あんない

안녕(安寧) ①《평온・질서》 public peace; tranquillity; welfare 《복지》 well-being ②《건강》 good health／～하다 (be) well; sound; uneventful／～하시다 be in good health; live in peace; get along well ③《인사》 good-bye; bye-bye; adieu 《멀리 갈 때》 farewell 《낮에》 good day 《오전에》 good morning 《오후에》 good afternoon 《저녁에》 good evening 《밤에》 good night. あんねい

안노인(一老人) an old woman (of the household).

안다 ①《팔에》 hold[carry] in one's arm[s]; embrace; hug／잠깐만 애기를 안아 주세요 Hold the baby in your arms a minute, please. ②《새가 알을》 sit on (eggs); brood／암탉이 알을 안고 있다 The hen is sitting on eggs. ③《책임 따위를》 be responsible for; answer for／빚을 ～ shoulder another's debt. いだく

안달 fretting; impatience／～하다 fret (over); fret oneself／～하지 마라 Don't be so impatient. いらだち

안대(眼帶) an eye bandage／～를 하다 have one's eyes in bandage.

안댁(一宅) [your, his] esteemed wife; Madam.

안도(安堵) relief／～하다 be[feel] relieved; feel at ease; breathe again／～의 숨을 내쉬다 heave a sigh of relief. あんど

안되다 ⇒별항 참조 (page 1584).

안락(安樂) ease; comfort／～하다 (be) easy; comfortable; cozy／～한 생활 an easy life／～ 의자 an armchair. あんらく

안락사(安樂死) euthanasia; an easy and painless death. あんらくし

안력(眼力) sight; eyesight; vision; visual power／～이 쇠퇴하다 one's eyesight is falling／날카로운 ～ an acute insight; acute observation. がんりょく

안료(顔料) 《화장용》 cosmetics; face-paints 《채료》 a colo[u]r; a paint; a pigment. がんりょう

안마(按摩) massage; shampooing／～하다 shampoo (one); massage (one's back)／～장이 a shampooer／～ 치료 a massage treatment; osteopathy. あんま

안마당 an inner court. にわ

안마루 the floor of the main building.

안면(安眠) peaceful[quiet] sleep／～하다 sleep well[peacefully]／～을 방해하다 distrub one's sleep. あんみん

안면(顔面) ①《얼굴》 the face／～의 facial

**안모**(顏貌) the face; appearance; a countenance. がんめん

**안목** inside measurement; interior width.

**안목**(眼目) an eye; a discerning[critical] eye; discernment/예술가로서의 ~을 기르다 train artistic judgement. がんもく

**안무**(按撫) plaction; pacification/ ~하다 placate; pacificate.

**안무**(按舞) arrangement of a dance; dance composition 《발레의》 choreography/ ~하다 design (dancing); compose (a ballet).

**안받침** inner[inside] support.

**안방**(-房) the inner room; the woman's quarters.

**안배**(按排, 按配) arrangement; disposition 《배분》 distribution; assignment/ ~하다 set in order; arrange; distribute; assign. あんばい

**안벽**(-壁) the inner wall.

**안보**(安保) security/국가의 ~ 문제 national security problems/~외교 diplomacy for national security. あんぽ

**안부**(安否) one's state of health; safety; welfare; health/~하다 inquire after one's health/~를 묻다 ask[inquire] after (one's health). あんぴ

**안부모**(一父母) one's female parent; one's mother. はは

**안부인**(一夫人) [your, his] esteemed wife; madam.

**안분**(安分) content; satisfaction with one's lot/~하다 be content [with one's lot].

**안빈 낙도**(安貧樂道) ~하다 be contented with honest poverty.

**안사돈**(一査頓) a daughter's mother-in-law; a daughter-in-law's [real] mother.

**안사람** [my] wife. つま

**안사랑** the party room in the main wing of a Korean house.

**안산**(案山) a hill on the opposite side; a mountain on the opposite side of a house or a grave. あんざん

**안산**(安産) easy labour[delivery]/~하다 have easy delivery/그녀는 사내아이를 ~했다 She gave an easy birth to a boy. あんざん

**안살림** home life.

**안색**(顏色) ①《얼굴빛》 complexion/ ~이 좋다[나쁘다] look well[pale, unwell] ②《얼굴 표정》 a look; a countenance; an expression. がんしょく

**안석**(案席) a cushion for the back; a chair back

**안성마춤**(安城一) the most suitable; the very thing desired[wanted]/~의 right; just; ideal; suit for/그것은 나에게 ~이다 It is just the thing to me.

**안섶** an in-turned jeogori collar.

**안손님** a lady visitor; a woman caller; a guest of one's wife.

**안식**(安息) rest; repose; relaxation; sabbatical/~하다 rest; take a rest; relax/ ~일 the Sabbath.

**안식**(眼識) insight; discernment; discrimination; penetration; a critical eye/ 전문가의 ~ an expert's eye. がんしき

**안식구**(一食口) female members of a family. おんなのかぞく

**안식처**(安息處) a place for peaceful living.

**안식향**(安息香) 【화】 benzoin. あんそくこう

**안신**(雁信) a letter; news; tidings. かりのつかい

**안심** lean meat of short ribs. うしのあばらにく

**안심**(安心) 《안도》 relief 《평안》 peace of mind 《근심없음》 ease of mind; freedom from care 《안정》 safety; security/~하다 feel at rest; feel easy (about); rest assured/나는 두려워할 것 없다고 그 여자를 ~시켰다 I satisfied her that there was no cause for fears. あんしん

**안심찮다**(安心一) (be) uneasy; ill at ease; anxious; uncertain; insecure; precarious/안심찮게 여기다 feel uneasy. あんしんできない

**안아말다** bear[assume, accept, shoulder, undertake] the responsibility; hold oneself responsible for/빚을 ~ shoulder (a person's) debt. せきにんをおう

**안아일으키다** raise[lift up] (a person) in one's arms; help (a person) to sit up. いだきあげる

**안약**(眼藥) eye-water[-lotion]/~을 넣다 apply eye-lotion. がんやく

**안양반**(一兩班) the lady of the house; the mistress; the wife.

**안어버이** one's own mother; the female parent. はは

**안여**(晏如) tranquility ⇒안연. あんぜん

**안연**(晏然) ~하다 (be) easy; comfortable; calm; quiet/~히 지낼 때가 아니다 This is no time for idling. あんぜん

**안염**(眼炎) 【의】 ophthalmia; inflammation of the eyes. めのえんしょう

**안온**(安穩) peace; quiet; tranquility; calmness/~하다 (be) peaceful; quiet; tranquil; calm/~한 세상 peaceful[tranquil] times. あんのん

**안올리다** paint the inner surface (of a thing).

**안옷고름** inside coat-strings.

**안위**(安危) fate; safety; welfare/국가의 ~에 관한 중대사 a matter of vital importance to the welfare of the State. あんき

**안이**(安易) easiness; ease/~하다 (be) easy; easygoing/~한 생활 an easy life. あんい

**안일** housework; woman's work.

**안일**(安逸) ease; idleness; indolence/~ 하다 (be) easy; at ease; idle; indolent /~한 생활을 하다 live in ease. あんいつ

**안짝** ①(이내) within; inside a limit; less than; not more than/5만원 ~의 수입 an income short of 50,000 won ②(글귀의) the first half (of *a poem etc.*).

**안잠자기** a resident woman servant. うばまん

**안장**(安葬) burial; interment/~하다 bury; inter; entomb/~지 a burial ground.

**안장**(鞍裝) a saddle/~을 얹다 saddle (*a horse*). くら

**안장코** a flat nose. はなぺちゃ

**안짱다리** a bow-legged person; a knock-kneed person/~의 knock-kneed/~로 걷다 walk intoed.

**안저지** a nurse[ry] maid.

**안전** the inside rim (of *a jar*).

**안전**(一殿) the inner palace; the king's residence.

**안전**(安全) safety; freedom from danger; security/~하다 (be) safe; secure; free from danger; sure; all right/~히 safely/그의 말은 믿어도 절대로 ~합니다 You are perfectly safe in believing what he tells you. あんぜん

**안전**(眼前) ~의 광경 a view before *one*/~바로 ~에서 under *one's* very nose.

**안절부절 못하다** be restless[nervous, anxious]; be on pins and needles/그녀는 안절부절 못하며 시간이 지나가기만 기다리고 있었다 She was greatly impatient with the slow passage of time.

**안정**(安靜) rest; repose; quiet; peace/~시키다 ease; put at rest[ease]; relieve/~ 요법 a rest cure. あわてふためく あんせい

**안정**(安定) stability 《평형》 equilibrium 《안정화》 stabilization 《침착》 settlement; composure/~하다 be[become] stabilized; be settled; settle/생활의 ~ security/~감 a sense of stability. あんてい

**안정**(眼睛) the pupil[apple] of the eye. がんせい

**안조**(贋造) counterfeiting; forgery; fabrication; fake/~하다 counterfeit; forge; fabricate. がんぞう

**안쪽** the inside; the inner part/~의 inside; inner/~에 inside; within/~에서 from the inside/문의 ~에 열쇠가 잠겨 있다 The door hooks on the inside. うちがわ

**안존**(安存) ~하다 (be) gentle; genial; graceful; amiable; quiet; be at peace. おとなしくおんこうなこと

**안주**(安住) peaceful living; a comfortable life/~하다 lead a peaceful living/~할 땅을 찾다 seek a place for peaceful living. あんじゅう

**안주**(按酒) relish [taken with wine]; an accompaniment of wine; a side-dish/이것은 술~에 좋습니다 This goes very well with wine. さけのさかな

**안주머니** an inside[inner] pocket; the bosom/~에 넣다 keep (*it*) in *one's* in-

## 안 되 다

①(금지) must not; should not (*do*) (해서는 안 되다) ought not to (*do*); (안시키다) shall not (하지 말라) don't (금지되어 있다) be forbidden[prohibited]; (허가되지 아니하다) be not allowed (안되게 되어 있다) be not supposed/버스 안에서 담배를 피워서는 안 된다 You are forbidden[not allowed] to smoke in bus., You are prohibited from smoking in bus., Smoking is prohibited[forbidden] in bus./들어가면 안 될까요 May I not come in?/네 안 됩니다 No, you must[may] not./그것에 손을 대서는 안 된다 Don't touch it., You are not allowed[forbidden] to touch it; You must not touch it./거짓말을 해서는 안 된다 You should not[ought not to] tell a lie/다섯 시 이후에는 학교에 남아 있어서는 안되게 되어 있읍니다 We are not supposed to stay in school after five.

②(필요·의무) must (않으면 안 된다) have [got] to (필요가 있다) need; (요구되고 있다) be required/오늘은 학교에 안 가면 안 된다 I have [got] to go to the school today./대학에 추천되려면 85점 이상을 따지 않으면 안 된다 You are required to take more than 85 marks [if you want] to be recommended to the college./뜰의 잡초를 뽑지 않으면 안 된다 The garden needs weeding./싫든 좋든간에 그의 지시를 따르지 않으면 안 된다 It is imperative that we should obey his instruction./미안하지만 초대를 거절하지 않으면 안 되겠군요 I am sorry to decline your invitation./늦어도 8시까지 학교에 도착하지 않으면 안 된다 I must[have to, have got to] be in school at the latest at eight o'clock.

③(예방) ¶ …하면 안 되니까 lest … should; [so] that … may not; so as not to; for fear that/젖으면 안 되니까 in case you should get wet/지각하면 안 되니까 서둘러라 Let us hurry up, so that we may not be too late[behind time]./선생님께 꾸지람을 들으면 안 되니까 가만히 있자 Let's not tell our teacher, [so] that he may not scold us[so as not to be s-colded by him]/비가 오면 안 되니까 우산을 가지고 가거라 Take your unbrella with you lest[for fear] it [should] rain.

**안주인**(-主人) the landlady; the mistress; the hostess. しゅふ

**안중**(眼中) ~에 in the eye/그 따위는 ~에도 없다 I take no notice of such a fellow.

**안중문**(-中門) the inner gate.

**안질**(眼疾) an eye disease[trouble]; sore eye/그는 ~을 앓고 있다 He is suffering from an affection of the eyes. がんしつ

**안집** the inner building; the main building.

**안집** 《안감》 lining material 《내장》 the viscera of an animal; the guts 《관》 a coffin.

**안차다** (be) bold; plucky/안찬 사람 a bold man.

**안착**(安着) 《사람의》 safe arrival 《물품의》 safe receipt/~하다 《사람이》 arrive safe 《무사히 돌아오다》 be safe home again 《물품이》 reach in good condition/그가 목적지에 무사히 ~했다는 소식을 들었다 I heard that he had got to his destination safe and sound. あんちゃく

**안창** 《구두의》 an inner sole/구두에 ~을 깔다 Put liners in shoes.

**안채** the main building (of a house).

**안출**(案出) contrivance 《발명》 invention/~하다 contrive; devise; originate; invent; study out; project/~자 a contriver; an inventor; an originator. あんしゅつ

**안치**(安置) installation/~하다 install; enshrine 《관 따위를》 lay in state/유해를 ~하다 lay (a person's) body in state. あんち

**안치다**¹ ①《중책을 맡다》 take a heavy trust on oneself ②《앞에 와서 닿다》 reach; arrive. たちふさがる

**안치다**² 《밥을》 prepare rice for cooking 〔boiling〕. しかける

**안타**(安打) 《야구》 a hit; a safe〔base〕 hit; a safety/~를 치다 hit a safety/조군은 오늘 시합에서 4개의 ~를 쳤다 Mr. Cho made four hits in today's game. あんだ

**안타까와하다** ①《애태우다》 be anxious about; be frustrated by ②《애처로와하다》 be heartbroken at; be distressed by. あわれがる

**안타깝다** feel pitiful〔painful〕; be tantalized〔vexed, irritated〕/그 광경은 정말 안타까왔다 The sight touched my heart. せつない

**안타깝이** an eager-beaver; an impatient person. あわれがるひと

**안태**(安泰) peace; welfare; security/국가의 ~를 빌다 pray for the country's peace and security.

**안태우다** 《스스로》 be worried; worry oneself 《남을》 worry; tear one's heart; give (one) trouble; bother; keep in suspense. こころをいためる

**안택**(安宅) calming the household got for the peace of the household.

**안팎** ①《안과 밖》 the interior and exterior; the inside and outside/~으로[에] within and out ②《표리》 two sides/~이 있는 사람 a double-dealer/사람이 ~이 있어서는 안 된다 You must not be one thing in a person's presence and another behind his back. ないがい

**안팎곱사둥이** a person with a hump-back and a protruding chest.

**안팎노자**(一路資) the round trip fare/부산까지 ~가 얼마 들까요 How much is it round-trip to Busan? おうふくのりょひ

**안팎심부름** inside and outside chores.

**안편지**(-便紙) 《내간》 a letter from a woman to a woman.

**안표**(眼標) a sign; a mark; a earmark 《비행장의》 a pylon/~하다 mark; put a mark. めじるし

**안하**(眼下) ~에 right beneath the eyes; under one's eyes/시가 전체를 ~에 내려다보다 overlook the whole city.

**안하무인**(眼下無人) 《자만》 over-bearance; arrogance 《뻔뻔스러움》 audacity; effrontery 《무법》 outrage 《거만·오만》 insolence; defiance/~의 overbearing; arrogant; domineering; audacious/~으로 audaciously; impudently/그는 하는 짓이 ~격이다 He behaves audaciously. ないがしろにすること

**안한**(安閑) ~하다 (be) peaceful; tranquil; leisured/~히 지내다 pass one's time in idleness. やすらかでひまなこと

**안형제**(一兄弟) a girl's sisters.

**앉다** ①《자리에》 take; assume (a seat); take a seat; be seated; set oneself; sit〔squat〕 down/식탁에 ~ sit at a table/단정히 앉아라 Be seated here properly. ②《지위에》 take up; engage in; be installed/좋은 자리에 ~ occupy a good position ③《새 따위가》 perch〔alight, sit-settle〕 on 《보금자리에》 roost/새가 창가에 앉았다 The bird alighted on our window sill. すわる

**앉은검정** soot collected under a pot.

**앉은뱅이** a cripple; a wheel-chair case/그는 ~다 He is crippled/ ~ 저울 a platform scale. いざり

**앉은일** sedentary work; seated work; bench work/~을 하다 have a sedentary job.

**앉은자리** one's seat/~의 immediate; ready; instant; prompt 《즉흥의》 extempore/~에서 글을 짓다 compose a sentence extempore. そくせき

**앉은장사** a sedentary trade〔business〕.

**앉은저울** a platform scale.

**앉은키** one's height when seated. ざこう

**앉을깨** the seat of the weaver at a loom.

**앉을자리** a place to sit/~를 가리키다 motion to a seat.

**앉음새** the way one sits; one's seated posture. すわりかた

**앉히다** ①(앉게 하다) make (one) sit down; seat (one)/상좌에 ~ seat (one) at the head (of a table) ②(주대하다) place (one in a position); install (one in a place)/교장 자리에 ~ appoint (one) principal (of) ③(버릇을) train; discipline ④(장부에) set down as an item. すわらせる

**않다** be not; do not/그녀는 사흘 동안이나 아무것도 먹지 않고 지냈다 He went without food for three days./그는 정직하지 ~ He is not honest. よくない

**알¹** an egg 《물고기·조개 따위의》 spawn/~을 낳다 lay eggs 《물고기가》 spawn. たまご

**알²** ①(낟알) a grain/한 ~의 쌀 a grain of rice ②(작고 둥근 것) a ball; a bead 《연필의》 lead. つぶ

**알-** bare; naked; uncovered/~몸 a naked body/~부피 net bulk.

**알깍정이** ①(지독하게 인색한 사람) a real tightwad; a real "stinker" ②(망근) a true-to-life snake-catcher 《부랑자》 a sure-enough boy tramp. いたずらっこ

**알갱이** a kernel; a grain; a berry 《작은》 a granule. つぶ

**알거지** a man with no property but his own body; a person as poor as a crow [church mouse].

**알게 하다** let (a person) understand[comprehend]; teach; let (a person) know; tell; inform (a person of, that…); make (a matter) known.

**알껍질** an egg shell.

**알겨먹다** trick a weaker person out of some small thing/가련한 소녀의 돈을 ~ defraud[cheat] a poor girl of her money. だましとる

**알결다** cackle [to call a cock to mate]. おんどりをよぶ

**알곡** (一穀) (곡식) corn; cereals; grain 《콩》 [thrashed] bean 《팥》 [thrashed] red bean. はくまい

**알궁둥이** the bare buttocks.

**알다** ⇒변향 참조(page 1586)

**알땅** naked land. さらしとち

**알독배기** a small earthen bowl.

**알뜰살뜰** ~하다(be) extremely frugal ⇒ 알뜰하다. まめまめしく

**알뜰하다** (be) prudent; thrifty; frugal; assiduous/알뜰하게 돈을 모으다 save money frugally. つつましい

**알랑거리다** seek to gain favor by flattery; curry favor with (a person); (여자가) coquet; play the coquette/그에게 알랑거려도 소용없다 He is above flattery. こびる

**알랑쇠** flatterer; an apple polisher《미》, a door mat《속》. こびるひと

**알랑알랑** cunningly; with flattery.

**알랑하다** (비꼬는 투) (be) just fine[dandy, ducky, grand]/알랑한 소리를 하다 make grand talk indeed/알랑한 녀석 Oh, a fine fellow! みるべきものがない

**알려지다** be[become] Known (to); come to (a person's) knowledge 《유명해지다》 become famous; become well-known/그것은 널리 알려져 있다 It is common knowledge. しられる

**알력** (軋轢) friction; discord; quarrel; jar; strife/이것이 ~의 원인이다 This is the apple of discord. あつれき

**알로하다** (몸시 약다) (be) cocky; shrewd; astute; sharp/알로 깐 녀석 a sharp customer. そうめいだ

**알록달록** mottled ⇒얼룩덜룩.

**알른거리다** glisten; glitter; sparkle; flicker (빛이) shine; blink→어른거리다. ほのかにみえる

**알리다** let (one) know; tell; inform (one) of; break the news to (one)/전화로 ~ let (one) know by telephone/편지로 ~ write to (one)/출발 날짜를 ~ let (one) know when one leaves. しらせる

**알맞다** 《적도하다》(be) modest; moderate 《적당하다》(be) fit; right; proper; befitting; adequate; suitable; appropriate 《상당하다》 reasonable; fair 《어울리다》 (be) becoming; suitable; wellmatched/알맞는 때에 at a right moment/술도 알맞게 마시면 약이 된다 When it is taken in moderation, wine has medicinal qualities. ぴったりする

**알맹이** 《과실의》 a stone; a kernel 《실질》 substance; matter; contents/이 책은 전혀 ~가 없다 This book is poor in content. つぶ

**알몸뚱이** ①(나체) a naked body stark-nakedness/~의 naked; nude/더워서 ~가 되다 strip because of the heat ②(빈털터리) pennilessness/~가 되다 go broke; lose the shirt off one's back. らたい

**알바늘** a needle without its thread. はりそのもの

**알밤** 《밤톨》 a[shelled] chestnut.

**알배기** 《알든 생선》 a fish full of roe. たまごをはらんださかな

**알부랑자** (一浮浪者) a notorious rascal.

**알싸하다** (be) acrid; pungent; hot; peppery; sharp/알싸한 맛 pungent flavour/맛이 ~ taste peppery. ぴりぴりする

**알쌈** a meat omelet[te].

**알선** (斡旋) intercession; recommendation; good offices; mediation/~하다 intercede; recommend; put in a good word (for one); say a good thing (for)/그의 ~으로 쟁의는 해결되었다 Through his mediation the strike came to an end. あっせん

**알쏭달쏭하다** ①(무늬가) motley; jumbled; intricated/알쏭달쏭한 무늬 a bewildering patten ②(뜻이) (be) vague, (idea); obscure; ambiguous (meaning); hazy (nation)/알쏭달쏭한 말을 하다 speak (of a matter) in general terms. まだらに

**알슬다** lay[deposit] eggs; spawn 《어류》 shoot spawn 《곤충》 oviposit 《파리 따위》 blow. たまごをうみつける

**알씬거리다** hang around in *a person's* presence [to curry his favor]; flatter. ちらつく

**알심** 《동정》 hidden sympathy 《힘》 hidden strength 《고갱이》 core; kernel. どうじょうしん

**알아내다** notice; perceive; find out; ferret out; take notice/그의 거처를 알아냈다 I found out[located] his whereabouts. さとる

**알아듣다** understand; catch/알아듣도록 설명하다 explain to *one's* satisfaction/알아듣게 말하다 convince (*a person*); persuade (*a person*). ききわける

**알아맞히다** guess right/누가 알아맞히는지 보자 Let us see who guesses right. おもいあてる

**알아보다** 《조사하다》 look up; inquire into; investigate; study; inspect 《탐지하다》 search for 《인식하다》 recognize/원인을 ~ inquire into the cause/취직 자리를 ~ look out for a job. たんちする

**알아주다** ①《인정하다》 acknowledge; recognize; admit; appreciate/이 사정을 알아주는 사람은 거의 없다 Very few understand this situation. ②《도와 주다》 help; aid; assist; stand by. みとめる

**알아차리다** 《주의하다》 be precautions[heedful, careful]; 《준비하다》 provide (*for*); prepare (*for*); make preparations. さとる

**알아채다** catch; understand; notice 《있고 없음을》 observe 《그 자리의 분위기 등을》 take in (*the situation*)/나는 위험이 닥쳐옴을 알아챘다 I sensed the danger that was coming upon me. さとる

**알아하다** do at *one's* discretion; do as *one* thinks fit; act for *oneself*; do with care /알아서 해라 Do as you please. ぜんしょする

**알알이** grain after grain; berry after berry; egg after egg.

**알알하다** (be) acrid; pungent; hot; peppery; sharp. ひりひりする

**알암** a mature chestnut.

**알약** a tablet; a tabloid.

**알은체** ①《간섭》 interference; intervention; meddling/~하다 interfere (in *a matter*); meddle in[with]; step in/내 일이 아니면 ~하고 싶지 않다 I don't want to interfere in what is not my business. ②《인사하는 표정》 notice; recognition; greething/~하다 recognize (*one*); greet; salute/~하지 않다 refuse to recognize; cut (*one*).

**알음** ①《안면》 an acquaintance; intimacy; familiarity ②《이해》 understanding; comprehension; apprehension.

**알음알음** 《아는 관계》 mutual acquaintance 《친분》 shared intimacy.

**알음알이** 1《친지》 an acquaintance/그녀는 거기에 많은 ~가 있다 She has many acquaintance in the place. ②《재능》 cleverness; knowledge. ちき

**알음장** winking/~하다 wink[cock *one's* eyes] at; make a sign with the eyes. めくばせ

**알짜** the cream; the essence; quintessence; the best thing[part]; the choice. もっともじゅうようなもの

**알짝지근하다** (be) rather hot[spicy, peppery]; taste a bit sharp. ひりひりいたむ

**알짱거리다** 《알랑거리다》 curry favor with; fawn upon 《할일 없이》 loaf around idly; hang about (*a person*). ぺこぺこしながらだます

**알젓** salted roe; salted caviar[e].

**알주머니** the spawn sac of fish 《가오리・상어 등의》 a sea-purse.

**알탄**(―炭) an oval briquet[te]; an egg-shaped briquet[te].

**알통** muscles/~을 내다 flex *one's* biceps.

**알현**(謁見) an imperial audience/~하다 have an audience with; be presented to. えっけん

**앎** knowledge; wisdom; information/~이 많다 be well-informed; know a lot of (*a thing*); have seen much of life.

**앓는소리** complaints/~하다 make complaints; betray weakness/그는 항상 ~를 한다 He always draws in his horns.

**앓다** ①《병을》 be ill; be sick; be afflicted with; suffer from[with]/감기를 ~ suffer from cold ②《비유적》 have a headache; feel annoyed (*at*)/골치를 ~ suffer from head trouble. いたむ

**-앓이** ache; sickness /가슴~ a pain in the chest/이~ a toothache. やまい

**암** ①《암컷》 a female; a she 《새의》 a hen·bird ②《기와 따위의》 concave; internal. めす

**암²** 《감탄사》 Of course!, Naturally!, To be sure!, Surely!, Certainly!/~ 그렇지 Why of course!, But definitely! そうだとも

**암**(癌) 【의】 cancer/위~ cancer of the stomach/자유의 속박은 민주 정치의 ~이다 Restriction on freedom is an impediment to democracy. がん

**암**(庵) a monk's cell; a small Buddhist temple. あん

**암가격**(闇價格) black-market prices; private quotations.

**암갈색**(暗褐色) dark brown; dun/ ~의 dark brown.

**암거**(暗渠) a culvert; an underdrain/~ 배수 drainage by culvert. あんきょ

**암거래**(闇去來) black marketeering; black-market dealings; underhand transactions; an off-the-book deal/~하다 sell [buy] on the black market; black-market.

**암꽃** a pistillate flower; a female flower. しか

**암군**(暗君) an incompetent king; an imbecile ruler. あんくん

**암굴**(岩窟) a cave; a [rocky]cavern; a grot[to]. がんくつ

**암글다** heal up; be cured ⇨아물다.

**암기** jealousy; envy. やきもち
**암나사**(一螺絲) a female[an internal] screw.
**암기**(暗記) memorizing; learning by heart; memory work/~하다 learn[get] by heart; commit to memory; memorize 〈미〉/그는 무엇이든지 ~하고 있다 He commits everything to memory. あんき
**암내** ①《곁땀내》 the [offensive] smell of the armpits; axillary odour; body odour(略: B.O.)〈미〉 ②《암컷의》 the odour of a female animal in heat/~나다 rut; go on heat/~내다 be in rut; be in heat. わきがのにおい

**암단추** a female button[snap].
**암담**(暗澹) ~하다 (be) dark; gloomy; dismal/장래가 ~하다 The future looks grey. あんたん
**암따다** ①《비밀 기질》 be a person who loves secrets ②《숫접다》 be easily embarrassed.
**암록색**(暗綠色) dark green.
**암루**(暗淚) silent tears. あんるい
**암류**(暗流) an undercurrent; a hidden drift[tendency]. あんりゅう
**암만** 《값・수량》 a certain amount. どのくらい
**암만해도** from every point of view; by

## 알 다

①《일반적으로》 know; have[get] a knowledge (of); be well aware (of); learn; be familiar (with); be acquainted (with)/자기를 ~ knows oneself/널리 알려진 widely known/미국에 대해 잘 ~ have first-hand knowledge of America /알지 못한 사이에 before one knows/내가 알고 있는 바로는 so far as I know; to [the best of] my knowledge/거의 알지 못하다 know very little; have little knowledge of/그를 알지 못하는 사람이 없다 He is known to everybody. /정확히는 알지 못한다 I don't know for certain. /자기의 결점을 알고 있다 be aware of one's shortcomings. /나는 작년에 그 일을 알았다 I knew about the matter last year. /아는 것이 병이다《속담》 Ignorance is bliss. /그는 범어도 약간 알고 있다 He has some knowledge of Sanskrit, too. /그가 겁장이라는 것을 알았다 He proved to be a coward /어떠한 사태가 일어날지 알지 못한다 There is no telling [knowing] what may happen.
②《이해하다》 understand; see; get; comprehend 《의미 따위를》 grasp 《어려운 것을》 make out 《설명・강의 따위를》 follow 《음악 따위를》 appreciate/알았읍니다 I see., Sure, I get you〈미〉. /너의 기분은 잘 안다 I am sensible of your feeling. /아, 이제 알았다! Ah, that accounts for[explain] it!/건강의 진가를 ~ appreciates the value of health./네 말은 도무지 알 수 없다 I haven't a remote [the remotest] idea of what you mean. /네 말뜻이 무언지 알겠다 I know what you mean. /그는 자연의 아름다움에 대하여 잘 알지 못한다 He hasn't much feeling for natural beauty. /그녀는 그림을 볼 줄 안다 She has an eye for picture. /나를 진정으로 알아 주는 사람은 그녀뿐이다 She is the only on that really understands me. /그 계획이 현명하지 못함을 알았다 We saw that the plan unwise. /어떻게 했으면 좋을지 알 수 없다 I am [feel] doubtful [about] what I ought to do.
③《아는 사이》 be acquainted with; know 《아는 사이가 되다》 become[get] acquainted with; make (a person's) acquaintance/알지 못하는 얼굴 strange [unfamiliar] faces; strangers/대개는 내가 알지 못하는 사람들이였다 Most of them were strangers to me. /그녀를 어떻게 알게 되었느냐 How did you come to know her? 내가 알고 있는 사람 중에는 그런 사람이 없다 There is no such person that know of.
④《발견하다》 find; notice; perceive; sense; realize/가난의 고통을 ~ go through[know] poverty/그의 사무실을 이내 알았다 I soon found his office., I had no difficulty [in] finding his office. /세상 물정을 아는 사람 a sensible man; a man of sense; a person of understanding.
⑤《관지(關知)하다》 have to do with; be concerned with/내가 알 바 아니다 It is none of my business., That is my lookout. /하나를 들으면 열을 안다 A word to the wise is sufficient.
⑥《인정하다・깨 닫다》 recognize; realize; see; find; notice; be convinced of/자기의 잘못을 ~ be convinced of one's error/그의 결점을 잘 알고 있다 I am wide awake to his weak points. /못 알아볼 만큼 자라다 grow out of recognition.
⑦《느끼다》 feel; be alive to; be conscious of; be sensible of[to]/부끄러움을 ~ be alive to a sense of hono[u]r; be sensible to shame/고마움을 ~ be sensible of kindness.
⑧《간주하다》 regard [as]; look upon [as]; consider; think of [as]; take (for) /우리들은 그가 바보인 줄 알았다 We considered him [to be] a fool. /그들은 계약이 파기된 것으로 알았다 They considered that the contract was canceled. /그것을 명예로 안다 We regard it as an honor.

all means; at all costs/~ 그는 실패하겠다 From every point of view he is likely to fail. どうしても

**암말** any word/~ 않고[없이] without a single word.

**암말** a mare; a female horse.

**암매**(暗昧) stupidity; foolishness/~하다 (be) stupid; foolish; dull. おろかなこと

**암매매**(暗賣買) black-market dealings/~하다 black-market.

**암매상**(暗賣商) a black-market dealer; a black-markete[e]r a secret[an illegal] dealer.

**암묵**(暗默) silence; tacit[ness]; withholding of comment/~리에 tacitly/~ 계약 an implied contract. あんもく

**암반**(岩盤) a base rock. がんばん

**암산**(暗算) mental arithmetic/~하다 do (a sum) in mental arithmetic. あんざん

**암살**(暗殺) assassination/~하다 assassinate; murder/~을 기도하다 make an attempt on (a person's) life /~자 an assassin. あんさつ

**암상** jealousy; envy/~꾸러기 a jealous person/~부리다 nurse jealousy; have [feel] envy. ねたみ

**암상인**(暗商人) a black-market dealer; a black markete[e]r.

**암새** a female bird.

**암석**(岩石) a rock; a crag; a boulder/~이 많은 rocky; craggy/~학 the study of rocks. がんせき

**암소** a cow. うし

**암송**(暗誦) recitation; memorization/~하다 recite; recite from memory; say by rote/시를 ~하다 recite a poem. あんしょう

**암쇠** ①(열쇠·자물쇠) a keyhole plate ②《맷돌의》 the bottom[pounding] plate of a mill.

**암수** female and male.

**암수**(暗數) a foul play; a trick; a means of deception/~를 쓰다 play (a person) a trick/~에 걸리다 fall into a trick. きぼう

**암술** 《식》 a pistil. めしべ

**암시**(暗示) a hint; a suggestion; an allusion; an intimation/~하다 hint (at); suggest; allude (to); intimate; imply/~를 주다 give (one) a hint/자기 ~ autosuggestion. あんじ

**암시세**(暗市勢) a black-market price; off-the-books quotations.

**암시장**(闇市場) 《경》 a black market. やみいちば

**암실**(暗室) a dark room. あんしつ

**암실**(庵室) a hermit's cell; a hermitage; a hermit's cottage.

**암암리**(暗暗裡) ~에 tacitly; obscurely; secretly; stealthily/~에 tacitly; secretly/~에 처리하다 dispose of (something) in secrecy. あんあんり

**암야**(暗夜) a dark night/~를 틈타서 under cover of night[darkness]. あや

**암약**(暗躍) behind-the-scene manoeuvring /~하다 manoeuvre; engage in secret manoeuvres. あんやく

**암연**(黯然) ~하다 (be) sad[tearful] (at parting). あんぜん

**암염**(岩鹽) 《광》 rock-salt; halite. いわしお

**암영**(暗影) 《그림자》 a [dark] shadow 《장애》 a gloom; an obstruction/~의 전도에 ~을 던지다 cast a gloom[shadow] over the future of …. あんえい

**암우**(暗愚) imbecility; weak-mindedness /~하다 (be) stupid; idiotic; slow-witted.

**암운**(暗雲) dark clouds; murky clouds/~이 감돌다 Dark clouds are hanging (on the horizon, over the political world). あんうん

**암유**(暗喩) a metaphor/~적 metaphorical.

**암자**(庵子) a monk's cell; a small Buddhist temple.

**암자색**(暗紫色) a dark purple color; a dark mauve.

**암장**(暗葬) secret burial/~하다 bury secretly [in another's lot]. あんそう

**암전**(暗轉) 《연》 a dark change (of scenery); changing sets during a stage black-out. あんてん

**암쪽** a counter-foil; a duplicate of a counter-stock.

**암종**(癌腫) 《의》 a cancer; a cancerous growth. がんしゅ

**암죽**(─粥) thin rice soup [as baby food]; pap; hot cereal. おもゆ

**암중**(暗中) [in] the dark; [in] darkness /~ 모색하다 grope in the dark.

**암초**(暗礁) a reef; a submerged[sunken] rock/배가 ~에 걸려 부서졌다 The ship was wrecked on a reef. あんしょう

**암치** a dried [and salted] croaker.

**암치질**(─痔疾) 《의》 anal fistula; internal hemorrhoids.

**암캉아지** a female puppy.

**암캐** a she-dog; a bitch a female dog. めすいぬ

**암컷** a female [animal]; a she 《새의》 a hen-bird/~인지 수컷인지 모르겠다 I can't tell its sex. めす

**암케** a female crab. めすかに

**암코양이** a female cat. めすねこ

**암꿩** a hen pheasant. めすきじ

**암키와** a female roof-tile. めんかわら

**암탉** a hen 《병아리의》 a pullet. めんどり

**암톨쩌귀** a gudgeon; a female joint of a hinge. つがね

**암퇘지** a sow. めんぶた

**암투**(暗鬪) a secret strife[feud]; an undercover struggle; veiled enmity; discord/그들 사이에는 끊임없는 ~가 벌어지고 있다 There is constantly veiled enmity among them.

**암팔스럽다** (be) bold; daring; plucky.

**암팡지다** (be) plucky; daring 《담에》 bold.

**암펌** a tigress. めすとら

**암평아리** a pullet; a female chick. めすひよこ

**암표**(暗標) winking; a secret mark[sign]. やみじるし

**암하다** (be) jealous. しっとふかい

**암행**(暗行) incognito travelling; a private visit/~하다 travel incognito; pay a private visit (to)/~ 어사 a regius secret inspector. みっこう

**암호**(暗號) 《암호문》 a cryptograph; a cryptogram (전신용) a cipher(비밀 암호); (상업용) a code (군호) a pass-word; a sign/~를 대다[말하다] give a pass-word. あんごう

**암흑**(暗黑) darkness; blackness/~가 the dark quarters/~ 시대 the dark age. あんこく

**압각**(壓覺) 【심】 pressure sensation. あっかく

**압권**(壓卷) the best; the masterpiece; the best part. あっかん

**압근**(狎近) ~하다 get[become] overfamiliar (with).

**압도**(壓度) [degree of] pressure. あつど

**압도**(壓倒) ~하다 overwhelm; overcome; overpower; weigh down; surpass; crush; excel/~적 승리 an overwhelming [a sweeping]/~적 다수로 당선되다 be elected by a sweeping[an overwhelming] majority of votes. あっとう

**압력**(壓力) pressure; stress/~을 가하다 press (one) for/~계 a manometer. あつりょく

**압박**(壓迫) push; pressure; heft; oppression; tyranny; coercion/~하다 exert pressure upon (one); oppress; suppress; coerce/언론의 자유를 ~하다 suppress the freedom of speech. あっぱく

**압사**(壓死) death from pressure/~하다 be crushed to death/기계에 깔려 ~하다 be crushed to death under a machine. あっし

**압살**(壓殺) killing by pressing/~하다 cruch (one) to death. あっさつ

**압송**(押送) ~하다 escort (a criminal); send (a person) in custody (to). ごそう

**압수**(押收) seizure; confiscation; attachment/~하다 seize; take over; attach; confiscate; impound; take legal possession of. おうしゅう

**압승**(壓勝) an over whelming victory; a landslide [victory]/~하다 win an overwhelming victory (over); swamp.

**압연**(壓延) rolling/~하다 roll.

**압운**(押韻) rhyming/~하다 rhyme; rime 〈미〉. おういん

**압인**(押印) seal[ing]/~하다 seal; affix one's seal to.

**압정**(押釘) a [thumb] tack; a fastener; a push-pin/~으로 고정시키다 tack down (a carpet).

**압정**(壓政) 《학정》 tyranny 《전제》 despotism/~에 신음하다 groan under tyra-nny. あっせい

**압제**(壓制) 《압박》 oppression 《강제》 coercion 《학정》 tyranny 《전제》 despotism/~하다 oppress; keep down 《학정》 tyrannize 《위압》 overpower/~에 신음하다 groan under tyranny/~ 정치 despotism. あっせい

**압지**(壓紙) blotting paper; a [paper] blotter. すいとりがみ

**압착**(壓搾) compression/~하다 compress; press/~ 가스 compressed gas/~ 공기 compressed air. あっさく

**압축**(壓縮) compression; constriction; condensation/~하다[com]press; condense/~ 공기 compressed air. あっしょく

**앗** Oh!, O dear!, O my!, Heaven!/~ 모자를 잃고 왔다 Dear me! I've left my hat behind. あっ

**앗기다** have something taken[stolen] ⇒ 빼앗기다. とられる

**앗다** ①《빼앗다》 take (a thing) away from (a person); (마음을) fascinate; charm; captivate ②《씨를 빼다》 gin (cotton) ③pay for labor in kind/품을 ~ exchange labor. うばう

**앗아가다** snatch (a thing) away (from a person).

**앗아넣다** twist in; force in.

**앗아라** (금지) Oh no!, Stop!/~ 싸우지 마라 Oh no! Stop fighting. よせ

**앙가발이** bandy legs; bow legs. がにまたのひと

**앙가슴** the part of the chest between the two breasts; the middle of the bosom. むね

**앙감질** hopping [on one leg]/~하다 hop. ぴょんぴょんとぶこと

**앙갚음** revenge; retaliation; repayment; blow for blow; measure for mesure; reprisal/~하다 revenge oneself on (a person)/그에게 ~을 하겠다 I will pay him out. ほうふく

**앙뺑이그리다** blacken one's face; daub black on one's face. かおにくるいものをぬる

**앙구다** 《식지 않게》 keep (food) warm (여러 가지 음식을) put (several kinds of food) on the same plate (사람을) accompany or see (a person) on his way. あたためておく

**앙금** (커피 따위의) deposit; grounds 《술찌꺼기》 dregs; lees (밑바닥의) settlings; sediment/~을 가라앉히다 settle the lees. ちんでんぶつ

**앙금앙금** crawlingly; sprawlingly/~ 기다 crawl; go on all fours/우리 애기가 ~ 기는 것을 배웠다 Our baby has learned to go on all fours. ちょこちょこ

**앙달머리** a person swollen with inordinate[audacious] ambition/~스럽다 be inordinate; be ambitious; be pert; be forward.

**앙당그러지다** be curved; be contorted; be distorted; shrink up; shrivel; be hud-

**잉당그리다**

dled up/몸이 앙당그러질 정도로 춥다 It is cold enough to shrivel one up. かがむ

**앙당그리다** huddle[curl] [oneself] up/추워서 ~ be huddled up with the cold/아파서 ~ be doubled up with pain. かがめる

**앙등(昂騰)** a sudden rise; an advance; a jump/~하다 rise suddenly; jump; soar /쌀값이 ~하다 Rice soars in price. こうとう

**앙망(仰望)** ~하다 hope; desire; solicit (for)/곧 답장해 주십을 ~하나이다 Kindly favour me with an early answer. ぎょうぼう

**앙모(仰慕)** ~하다 look up to with respect; regard (a person) with love and respect; admire; adore/그는 그들의 은인으로 ~를 받고 있다 He is looked up to as their benefactor. あおぎしたうこと

**앙바틈하다** (be) short and broad; fat and short; stocky; squabby; stumpy/앙바틈한 남자 a stocky man; a chunky fellow. ずんぐりしている

**앙버티다** stick; cling; hold on to; resist to the bitter end; bear down/끝까지 ~ hold out to the last; keep at it.

**앙살** a noisy protest; loud opposition/~하다 make a noisy protest; retort; oppose/그녀는 늘 ~부린다 She is always fussing about something or other.

**앙상궂다** (be) terribly gaunt. ひどくやつれている

**앙상하다** (be) haggard; gaunt; thin; spare/뼈만 ~ be nothing but skin and bones; be a mere bag of bones. やつれている

**앙숙(怏宿)** ~이다 be on bad terms (with); 《특히 부부가》 lead a cat-and-dog life. なかがわるいこと

**앙심(怏心)** spite; malice; grudge/~먹다 feel one's vengeance; bear (one) a grudge/~깊은 여자 a vindictive woman. うらみ

**앙앙(怏怏)** ~하다 be discontented[dissatisfied]; be despondent; be unhappy; be disconsolate; be heartsick/마음이 ~하다 be low-spirited; be disconsolate.

**앙양(昂揚)** elevation; exaltation; enhancement/~하다 exalt; enhance; promote; raise; uplift/사회 도의의 ~ uplifting of the standard of public morals. こうよう

**앙얼입다(殃孽—)** be brought evil upon; be cast an evil spell on (one)/저 집은 앙얼입었다 There is a curse on that house. たたりをうける

**앙짜** an irritatingly; jealous man 《점잔뺌》 putting on airs; giving oneself airs; assuming an air of importance/~ 지 마라 Stop acting so prim. ひがんだひと

**앙증스럽다, 앙증하다** (be) disproportionately small; tiny; little/앙증한 계집애 a chit of a girl.

**앙진(昂進)** rise;〖의〗acceleration; exasperation/~하다 rise; grow; accelerate; exasperate/병세가 ~하다 one's condition grows worse.

**앙천 대소(仰天大笑)** a great[hearty] laugh; a roar[burst] of laughter/~하다 laugh loudly; burst out laughing; have a hearty laugh.

**앙칼스럽다, 앙칼지다** (be) fierce; vehement; stubborn; unyielding; dauntless/그녀는 앙칼스럽게 말대답했다 She gave a sharp retort. ごうじょうだ

**앙큼앙큼** with short steps; toddling; stealthily/~ 걷다 walk with short steps. ちょこちょこ

**앙큼스럽다, 앙큼하다** audacious; (be) overambitious; presumptuous. ずるい

**앙탈** ~하다 scheme to evade; try to be delivered from; fuss/그는 그 일을 안 하려고 ~했다 He tried frantically to get out of the work. いいのがれ

**앙토(仰土)** plaster between rafters/~장이 a rafter plasterer/~질 rafter plastering.

**앙판(秧板)** a seed bed; a seedplot; a nursery bed[ground].

**앙혼(仰婚)** a morganatic marriage; marriage with a person of higher standing/~하다 marry above one.

**앙화(殃禍)** disaster; woe; misfortune; calamities/~를 피하다 keep out of harm's way. おうか

**앞** ⇨별항 참조( page 1589).

**앞가림** having just enough education to get by/~하다 have just enough education to get by. ややがくしきがあること

**앞가슴** the breast; the chest. むね

**앞길** future; prospects; an outlook/~의 행복을 빕니다 I hope you have a happy future before you./~을 걱정하다 be anxious about one's future. しょうらい

**앞날** the future; the days ahead[to come]; the remainder of one's life [days]; the rest of one's life/그의 ~은 멀지 않다 His days are numbered/~의 즐거움 expection. しょうらい

**앞니** a front tooth; a fore-tooth/~가 나다 cut one's front teeth. まえば

**앞다리** ①《짐승의》 the forelegs; fore limbs/~를 들고 서다 sit erect on the haunches with the forepaws raised; beg ②《이사할 집》 one's new residence[house] ③《앞잡이》 an intermediary; an agent. ぜんさく

**앞마지** a protruding plank[board].

**앞당기다** move (a date) up; advance (a date); make (anything) earlier/이틀 ~ shift two days ahead/기일을 ~ advanced the date. よていよりさきにする

**앞대** the southern region[section] (of a country, a province).

**앞대문(—大門)** the front gate. まえのほうのだいもん

**앞두다** have (*a distance*) ahead／일주일 ~ have a week to go／40마일 ~ have forty miles ahead to cover.

**앞뒤** 《전후》 before and behind; the front and the rear 《순서》 order; sequence 《결과》 consequences／~ 생각 없이 without thought; regardless of the consequences. ぜんご

**앞뒷집** the neighboring house; the neighbors; houses in front and in the rear.

**앞뜰, 앞마당** a front yard[garden]. まえにわ

**앞머리** ①《전두》 the forehead; the sinciput ②《물건의》 the front end ③《선두》 the vanguard; the van; the front. ぜんとうふ

**앞못보다** ①《소경》 be blind; can't see what is going on ②《무식》 be ignorant; be not farsighted. めくらになる

**앞문**(一門) a front gate; the front door; the street door. まえもん

**앞바닥** the fore part of a sole.

**앞바람** ①《마파람》 a south[southerly] wind ②《역풍》 a head wind. ぎゃくふう

**앞바퀴** a fore[front] wheel.

**앞발** 《개·고양이의》 a paw 《네발짐승의》 a forefoot [of a quadruped]／~질 kicking (*with*) the forefeet. ぜんそく

**앞산**(一山) the mountain in front (of *a house*). まえのやま

**앞서** ①《이전에》 before; already; previously／~ 말한 바와 같이 as previously stated／어머니는 누구보다 ~ 일어나신다 Mother gets up earliest of all. ②《미리》 beforehand; in advance; previously; in anticipation; formerly; the other day; some time[a few days] ago／출발에 ~ 알리겠다 I will let you know before I leave. まえもって

**앞서다** 《선행하다》 go before[ahead of]; precede; go in advance of; take the lead; leave (*a person*) behind 《탁월하다》 excel; outdo; surpass (*a person*)／부모보다 앞서서 죽다 die before one's parents／무엇보다 앞서는 것은 돈이다 Money is the first consideration. まえにたつ

**앞서서** before; previous to／이에 ~ prior [previous] to this. さきだって

**앞세우다** make (*a person*) go ahead; let (*a person*) lead[precede]／행렬에 악대를 ~ place a band at the head of a procession. まえにたたす

**앞앞** for each one; in front of each person; apiece; respectively／~ 그 책을 한 권씩 가지고 있다 We have each a copy of the book. それぞれ

**앞이마** the front forehead. まえひたい

**앞일** 《미래》 the future／~에 어둡다 have no foresight; be short-sighted／~에 대비하다 prepare for the future. みらい

**앞자락** the front part (of *a skirt, coat*).

**앞잡이** ①《안내》 a guide 《관광객의》 a cicerone; a leader／~가 되다 lead (*a party*); act as a guide ②《주구》 an agent; a tool; a cat's paw／경찰의 ~ a stool pigeon. せんどうしゃ

**앞장** 《일》 the lead; the head 《사람》 the leader; a pioneer; the vanguard／~서서 at the head of／행렬에 ~서 가다 walk at the head of a parade. せんとう

**앞지르다** forestall; anticipate; steal a march upon; get beforehand with; get [have] the start of／남이 말하려는 것을 앞질러 말하다 take the words out of another's mouth.

**앞집** the house in front.

**앞차** an earlier departing car[train]; the car[train] ahead.

**앞차다** (be) reassuring／앞차게 여기다 feel emboldened. たのしい

**앞참**(一站) the next stage[post-town]. まえのうち

**앞창**(一窓) the front window. まえまど

**앞채** the front building[wing].

**앞치마** an apron; a slip; a lap 《어린애의》 a pinafore／~를 두른 소녀 a girl wearing an apron／~를 두르다 put on an apron. まえかけ

**애**¹ 《수고》 troubles; efforts 《걱정》 worry; solicitude; annoyance; impatience; anxiety／~태우다 be anxious／생활 문제로 ~타다 be harassed by the question of life. うれい

**애**² å child ⇒아이／~를 업다 carry[have] a child on one's back／~를 밴 여인 a woman with child; a pregnant woman ／~를 기르다 rear a child. こども

**애-** 《처음》 the very first 《어린》 little; tiny 《미숙한》 the very young; green ／~숭이 a novice／그는 전혀 ~숭이다 He is as green as grass.

**애가**(哀歌) a dirge; an elegy; plaintive song. あいか

**애개** What a small amount!, How poor [little, paltry]! これぼっち

**애걸**(哀乞) pleading; supplication; entreaty／~하다 implore; plead[beg] for; appeal／그는 그녀에게 가지 말라고 ~했다 He implored her not to go. あいがん

**애걸 복걸**(哀乞伏乞) ~하다 beg earnestly; implore; supplicate. あたまをさげてあいがんすること

**애견**(愛犬) one's pet[favorite] dog／~가 a dog lover; a lover of dogs; a dog-fancier. あいけん

**애경**(哀慶) sorrow and joy; sad events and happy events.

**애경**(愛敬) love and esteem; loving respect; affection and respect／~하다 venerate; love with respect; hold (*a person*) in high esteem. あいけい

**애고** Oh!, Dear me! ⇒아이고. ああ

**애고**(愛顧) favor; patronage; love; custom; care／~하다 patronize; favor／~를 받고 under the patronage of. あいこ

**애고머니** 《감탄사》 Heavens!, Dear me!, Good God!, O my. あら

**애곡(哀哭)** wailing; mourning; lamentation; grief; plaint／～하다 mourn (over); lament (for); wail. あいこく

**애교(愛嬌)** attractiveness;[personal] charms; winsomeness 《장사아치들의》courtesy／～있는 charming; winning; winsome／그녀는 ～가 넘쳐 흐른다 She is overflowing with smiles. あいきょう

**애교심(愛校心)** love of one's school; attachment to one's Alma Mater.

**애꾸눈이** a one-eyed person; blind of one eye／～가 되다 lose [the sight of] one eye. かためのひと

**애국(愛國)** love of[for] one's country; nationalism; patriotism／불타는 ～심 patriotism glowing in one's heart／～자 a patriot／～정신 patriotism／～심을 고취하다 infuse[instil] patriotism into the heart of (people)／～단체 a patriotic society[organization]／～운동 a patriotic movement. あいこく

**애국가(愛國歌)** a patriotic song 《국가》 the national anthem. あいこくか

**애꿎다** be innocent; be to be pitied; guiltless／애꿎은 사람 a blameless[innocent] person.

**애끊다** feel one's heart rent[torn to pieces]／그 말을 듣고 나는 애끊는 듯했다 My heart bled to hear that.
はらわたがちぎれそうだ

**애끓다** worry [oneself] about; fret about; be overanxious; be all roiled up; go into a stew (about) ／애끓어 병이 나다 worry oneself ill. やきもきする

**애금가(愛禽家)** a bird-lover; a bird-fancier; a lover of birds.

**애긍(哀矜)** pity; compassion; sympathy ／～하다 be pitiable[piteous, pathetic].

**애기(愛機)** one's favorite[own] plane. あいき

**애기미나리아재비** 〖식〗 a buttercup; a crowfoot; Ranunculus acris(학명). こきんぽうげ

**애기잠** the first dormant period of the silkworm.

**애늙은이** a young person who behaves like an old person.

**애달다** overanxious; be anxious (to); be impatient (at)／그녀는 너를 다시 만나려고 애달고 있다 She is impatient to see you again. やきもきする

**애달프다** aching; (be) heartbreaking; sorrowful; pathetic; painful; distressing／애달픈 마음을 털어 놓다 confess a heartrending sorrow. ふびんだ

**애당초** the start; the outset; the beginning; the commencement; [from] the very first time／～에는 회원이 겨우 3명이었다 We had only three members to start with. はじめ

**애도(哀悼)** sorrow; grief; condolence; regret; mourning／～하다 mourn (for, over); regret; lament／～의 뜻을 표하다 express one's regret[sorrow] at (a person's) death. あいとう

**애독(愛讀)** love of reading; reading [for pleasure]; bibliophilia／～하다 read (a book) with pleasure; read and enjoy／나는 셰익스피어를 ～하고 있다 I am a lover of Shakespeare., Shakespeare is my favorite author.，～자 a devoted [an appreciative] reader. あいどく

**애돝** yearling pig. いっさいのぶた

**애락(哀樂)** grief and joy; grief and pleasure. あいらく

**애련(哀憐)** pity; mercy; compassion／～하다 pity; take pity (on); feel compassion (for); have mercy (on)／～의 정을 금치 못하다 be overwhelmed with pity (for); be greatly moved with compassion (for); have[take] great compassion (on). あいれん

**애로(隘路)** a narrow path 《산중의》 a defile 《일의》 a bottle-neck／이 계획에는 많은 ～가 있다 There are series of bottlenecks in the way of the program. あいろ

**애림(愛林)** forest conservation[protection]; loving[cherishing] the forests／～녹화 Keep the Trees Green., Save the Trees／～주간 Arbor Week. あいりん

**애마(愛馬)** one's favorite[pet] horse; one's trusty steed. あいば

**애매(曖昧)** vagueness 《말뜻의》 ambiguity 《용어의》 equivocation／～하다 (be) vague; ambiguous; doubtful 《회피적》 evasive／그는 ～한 대답을 했다 He gave me an equivocal answer. あいまい

**애매하다** be falsely charged; be wrongly accused (of stealing); be unjustly convicted (of a forgery charge)／애매한 사람을 죽이다 kill an innocent person.
あいまいだ

**애먹다** have bitter experience; have a hard time of it; be troubled; be worried (about); be in distress; be harassed／돈이 없어 애먹고 있다 He is hard up for money.

**애먹이다** annoy; harass; bewilder; embarrass; give (a person) trouble／어려운 질문으로 선생님을 ～ annoy one's teacher with hard questions.

**애모(愛慕)** affection; attachment; love; yearning／～하다 love; be attached to; yearn after[for]／～를 받고 있는 선생 a beloved teacher. あいぼ

**애무(愛撫)** love; endearment／～하다 love; pet; fondle; caress. あいぶ

**애물** ①《애매움》 a [cause of] worry ②《죽은 자식》 a son who died young.

**애바르다** be alive to one's interests; be money-mad; be keen on[about] money-making.

**애바리** a shrewd man of business; a greedy person; a miser.

**애벌** a rough job of it; the first time [round]／일을 ～하다 make short work of it; dispose of it lightly; make a rough job of it. したごしらえ

**애벌레** 〖虫〗 a larva; a newborn insect. ようちゅう

**애사**(哀史) a tragedy; a sad[pathetic] story[history]. あいし

**애상**(哀傷) grief; sorrow/~하다 grieve; lament; mourn/~의 곡 a song of sorrow; elegy. あいしょう

**애서**(愛婿) one's [beloved] son-in-law. あいせい

**애서**(愛書) fondness for books; love of books; one's favorite books/~가 a book-lover; a bibliophile/~광 bibliomania; craze for books.

**애서다** get with child; become pregnant.

**애석**(哀惜) lamentation; grief; sorrow /~하다 grieve; lament; mourn/정말 ~하구나 What a pity it is! あいせき

**애석**(愛惜) ~하다 be loath to (part); hold precious; be reluctant to part with/ 떠나게 되어 매우 ~합니다 I am very loath to part from you. あいせき

**애소**(哀訴) an appeal; a petition; supplication; entreaty; pleading/~하다 plead; implore; make an appeal (to)/ 구원을 ~하다 appeal (to a person) for help. あいそ

**애솔** a young pine tree/~밭 a grove of young pines.

**애송**(愛誦) recitation of one's favourite poem/~하다 love to recite; sing often /~시 one's favourite poems/~집 one's favorite anthology. あいしょう

**애송아지** a young calf; a newborn calf.

**애송이** a very young person; a greenhorn; a novice. こどもぽいひと

**애수**(哀愁) sorrow; sadness; grief; pathos/~를 자아내다 make (a person) feel sad/~를 느끼다 feel sad. あいしゅう

**애순** a young buds; fresh sprouts; sprouts; shoots. あたらしいめ

**애숭이** a very young person; a greenhorn. こどもぽいひと

**애쓰다** exert[strain] oneself; work hard; endeavor; do one's best; take pain [trouble]; make an effort/애쓰지 않으면 얻는 것도 없다 Nothing can be obtained without effort. どりょくする

**애아**(愛兒) one's beloved child; one's dear [favorite, pet] child; one's darling [child]. あいじ

**애아버지** my husband. おっと

**애애**(藹藹) ~하다 (초목이)(be) lush; thick; exuberant 《많은 모양》swarm; form [a large group]. あいあい

**애애**(靄靄) ~하다 (be) hazy; misty; cloudy; dark 《화기》 peaceful/화기가 ~하다 be peaceful and harmonious. あいあい

**애연가**(愛煙家) a habitual smoker; a person who indulges in[enjoys] tobacco /대단한 ~ a heavy smoker. あいえんか

**애오라지** 〖좀〗 somehow; somewhat; but; only; but … somewhat. とにかく

**애옥살림** indigent life; narrow circums-

# 앞

①**(미래)** the future; the time to come; a prospect/~을 내다보다 look into the future; look ahead/너희들은 ~날이 요원하다 You have a long way to go. /~으로 그런 일은 다시 않겠다 I won't ever do it again./~으로 5년 후 five years from now/출판 사업은 ~이 퍽 유망하다 The publishing business has great[excellent] prospects/이 장사는 ~으로 장래성이 없다 This business has no future.

②**(전면)** the front; the fore [part]/ ~으로[에] in front of; before; forward; ahead; away; off; farther; beyond 《맞은편》opposite/~ 줄 the front row /5마일 ~에 five miles ahead[away]/ 앞으로 가 《구령》 Forward march!/~에 앉다 sits in front; takes a front seat /1등 차는 ~에서 네 번째 차량이다 The first-class coach is the forth one from the head of the train.

③**(면전)** presence/~에서 in (a person's) presence; in the face of (a person) /그녀는 사람들 ~에 나서는 것을 싫어한다 She doesn't like to be seen in company./사람들 ~에서 그런 말을 하는 게 아니야 You should not say such things in company. /신 ~에서 모든 인간은 평등하다 In the sight of God all men are equal.

④**(편지에서)** addressed[directed] to (a person);**(어음에서)** drawn in one's favo-[u]r/이씨의 자택 ~으로 편지를 쓰다 write Mr. Lee at his home/여기 네 ~으로 온 편지가 있다 Here is a letter for you./김씨[B은행] ~으로 어음을 발행하다 draw a check in front of Mr. Kim [upon B Bank].

⑤**(순위)** the former (이전) previous /~서 before; ahead of; in advance of; first; earlier; formerly; previously /~을 달리다 get ahead of (a person); get[have] the lead/~을 다투어 ···하다 struggle to (do)/악대를 ~세우고 headed by a brassband/~서 말한 바와 같이 as previously stated/~서 걷다 lead the way.

⑥**(몫)** a share; a portion/그는 한 사람에 100원씩 주었다 He gave 100 won to each [one] of us./그의 재산은 거의 장남 ~으로 갔다 Most of his estate went to the eldest son.

**애옥하다** tances/~하다 be in narrow circumstances; live in poverty; lead an indigent life. ひんこんせいかつ

**애옥하다** (be) poor; in want; needy; indigent; destitute. ひんこんだ

**애완**(愛玩) ~하다 be fond of; fondle; make a pet of; prize; treasure/~가 an adorer; an admirer; a fancier/ ~물 one's pet. あいがん

**애욕**(愛慾) love and lust; passion/~의 노예가 되다 fall a prey to passion. あいよく

**애용**(愛用) habitual use/~하다 use regularly; patronize/국산품을 ~하다 patronize home production. あいよう

**애원**(哀怨) tearful[bitter] resentment; sad reproach/~의 소리 sounds of grief and resentment. かなしみうらむこと

**애원**(哀願) an appeal; supplication; pleading; an entreaty/~하다 entreat; implore/~자 an implorer; a supplicant. あいがん

**애육**(愛育) tender nurture/~하다 bring up (a child) with tender care; coddle up. あいいく

**애음**(愛飮) fondness of drinking/~하다 be fond of drinking; love to drink/~가 a regular[habitual] drinker. あいいん

**애인**(愛人) (남자) a[her] lover (여자) a [his] love; a dear heart (공통) a sweetheart/그녀는 나의 ~이다 She is a my love. あいじん

**애자**(愛子) a beloved child; one's darling; one's dear child/~지정(之情) parental love. あいし

**애잔하다** (be) slender; weak; delicate; frail; naive. かよわい

**애장**(愛藏) ~하다 treasure; cherish; store up carefully for future use/~의 골동품 one's treasured antiques.

**애저**(—猪) a suckling pig/~찜 《음식》 steamed suckling pig.

**애절하다**(哀切—) (be) sad; touching; pathetic/애절한 이야기 a sad[pathetic] story.

**애젊다** look younger than one's age; be still a bit boyish[girlish]/애젊은 이 a youngster; a lad. こどもぽくわかい

**애정**(哀情) sadness; [a feeling of] sorrow; grief/~을 느끼다 feel sad/~을 자아내다 make one feel sad; excite one's grief. あいじょう

**애정**(愛情) love; affection; a tender feeling/~이 없는 결혼 a loveless marriage[match]/~을 표시하다 show one's love (for). あいじょう

**애제자**(愛弟子) one's favorite disciple[pupil].

**애조**(哀調) a plaintive tone; a mournful melody;《음》 a minor key/~를 띤 말씨; mournful; plaintive. あいちょう

**애족**(愛族) loving one's people/~하다 love one's people/애국 ~ devotion to one's country and to one's people.

みんぞくをあいすること

**애주**(愛酒) love of wine/~하다 be fond of liquor; love wine; drink habitually /~가 a habitual drinker; a lover of wine. さけをこのむこと

**애중**(愛重) ~하다 love and prize; make [think] much of. あいちょう

**애증**(愛憎) love and hatred; likes and dislikes/~은 근본을 따져 보면 다른 것이 아니고 같은 것이다 Love and hatred are one in the final analysis. あいぞう

**애지중지**(愛之重之) ~하다 dote on; treasure/자식을 ~하다 dote upon one's children. おぼれたあい

**애착**(愛着) attachment; affection; love /나는 이 직업에 아무런 ~을 느끼지 않는다 I am not attached to this job at all.

**애처**(愛妻) one's beloved wife/~가 a devoted husband/그는 ~가다 He is devoted to his wife. あいさい

**애처롭다** 《슬프다》 (be) lamentable; sad; wretched; mournful 《가엾다》 (be) pitiful; (be) miserable/굶주린 아이들은 보기에도 애처로왔다 The starving children were a piteous sight. かわいそうだ

**애첩**(愛妾) one's favorite concubine; one's mistress. あいしょう

**애초** the begiňning; the first; the commencement/~의 계획은 그가 가기로 되어 있었다 According to original plan, he was to go. はじめ

**애칭**(愛稱) a pet name; a term of endearment/미스 김의 애칭은 고양이다 "Cat" is the nickname for Miss Kim.
あいしょう

**애타**(愛他) loving others; altruism/~적 altruistic/~주의 altruism/~주의자 an altruist. あいた

**애타다** be much worried; worry oneself sick; be overanxious; be quite uneasy (about)/그녀는 지각하지 않나 하고 애가 탔다 She was anxious lest she should be late for school. きがきでない

**애태우다** ①《스스로》 worry oneself (about); feel anxiety; concern oneself (about)/ 그녀는 하찮은 일에 애태우고 있다 She worries about little thing. ②《남을》 worry; annoy; vex/부모를 ~ worry[grieve] one's parents.

**애통**(哀痛) deep lamentation/~하다 lament; grieve; deplore/사람의 불행을 ~하다 feel sorry for (a person's) misfortune. あいつう

**애틋하다** painful; (be) heart-rending; distressing; deplorable/애틋한 사랑을 고백하다 confess one's ardent love.

**애티** childishness; puerility/~나다 be childish/~를 벗다 grow up; leave childhood behind. こどもらしさ

**애해** Eh! Well!, Oh yeah! へえ

**애햄** ahem; hem. えへん

**애향**(愛鄕) love of one's home/~심 local patriotism; love of one's home[native place]/그는 ~심이 있다 He loves his

애호 home town. あいきょう
애호(愛好) love (for, of); a liking (for)/～하다 be fond of; like; love; have a liking for; take much delight in/술을 ～하다 be addicted to drink. あいこう
애호(愛護) (보호) protection; kindly treatment; loving care (애용) patronage. あいご
애호박 a green[young] pumpkin. みじゅくなかぼちゃ
애화(哀話) a sad[pathetic] story; a tragic tale. あいわ
애환(哀歡) joy and sorrows (of life).
애휼(愛恤) compassion; charity/～ 운동 a charity campaign. あいじゅつ
액(厄) misfortune; mishap; disaster; ill-luck/무서운 ～이 그들에게 닥쳤다 A frightful calamity befell them. やく
액(額) (금액) an amount; a quantity; a sum 《채권의 액면》 a denomination/거～에 달하다 amount to big figures; reach a vast amount/생산～ the volume of manufacture. がく
액(液) (액체) liquid; fluid (용액) solution (즙) juice (과일); sap (나무의)/～을 짜내다 squeeze out juice. えき
액기(腋氣) (암내) underarm[armpit] odor; the [offensive] smell of the armpit. わきが
액난(厄難) a misfortune; a calamity; an ill luck; a misadventure/～을 당하다 have a misfortune[mishap]; suffer a calamity.
액날(厄一) an evil[unlucky] day; a black[bad] day; (농가에서)a critical day.
액년(厄年) an unlucky[an evil, a bad] year; a critical age/농가의 ～ a bad year for farmers. やくどし
액달(厄一) an unlucky[an evil, a bad] month/이달은 ～이다 This month is an unlucky [month]. やくづき
액때우다(厄一) escape[get rid of] a misfortune by undergoing beforehand one of lesser degree.
액뗌(厄一) an escape from evil; exorcism.
액량(液量) liquid measure. えきたいのぶんりょう
액막이(厄一) 【민】 exorcism; warding off evil/～ 부적 a talisman against evils/～굿 a yearly exorcism by a shaman.
액면(額面) a denomination; par value; face·value/그 소문은 ～대로 받아들일 수 없다 We cannot take the rumor at its face value. がくめん
액모(腋毛) underarm[armpit, axillary] hair; hair of the armpit. わきげ
액사(縊死) death by hanging/～하다 die by hanging; hang[strangle] oneself. いし
액살(縊殺) murder by strangling/～하다 strangle (a person) to death. いさつ
액수(額數) a sum; an amount; a volume /엄청난 ～에 달하다 reach a colossal amount.
액운(厄運) disaster; misfortune; calamity; adverse fortune; ill luck/～을 면하다 escape a disaster[calamity]/～을 당하다 come to grief. やくうん
액자(額字) letters written on a signboard.
액체(液體) a liquid; a fluid/～ 공기 liquid air/～ 동력학 hydrodynamics/～ 온도계 a liquid thermometer. えきたい
액취(腋臭) underarm[armpit] odor; the [offensive] smell of armpit. えきしゅう
액화(厄禍) calamity; misfortune; disaster. やくのわざわい
액화(液化) liquefaction/～하다 become liquid/석탄 ～ liquefaction of coal/～ 가스 liquefied gas. えきか
앵생이 a weak person[thing]; a weakling; a fragile thing. かよわいひと
앳되다 look young[new]. こどもぽい
앵 a buzz; a hum; a zoom; a whiz/벌이 ～하고 달아났다 A bee droned away. ぶん
앵돌아지다 make an abrupt turn; turn one's back; turn sulky; get cross; be angry with (a person)/그녀는 조금만 야단쳐도 앵돌아진다 She gets sulky at the slightest scolding. ねじれる
앵두 【식】a cherry/～나무 a cherry tree; Punus tomentosa(학명). さくらんぼみ
앵무새(鸚鵡—) a parrot; a parakeet/～처럼 남의 말을 외다 repeat[echo] (a person's) words. おうむ
앵미 rice of an inferior quality; poor rice. くずまい
앵앵 humming; buzzing; droning/모기가 ～거리는 소리를 들었다 I heard the faint hum of a mosquito.
앵하다 (be) regrettable; feel bitter (about); vexing; mortifying/손해를 보고 ～ feel bitter about one's loss. おしい
야 ①《놀라서》Oh!, Oh dear!, Good heavens!, Dear me!, O my! ②《부를 때》Hey!, Hey there/～ 너는 누구냐 Hey there, who are you? やあ
야(野) ①(들) a field; a plain; a farm ②(야당) an opposition party/～에 있다 remain out of office/그는 ～에 있은 지 벌써 10년이다 He has been ten years out of government service. のはら
야간(夜間) night; the night time/～ 근무 night duty/～ 시합 a night game/～ 통행 금지 a curfew. やかん
야거리 a one·mast boat/야거릿대 the single mast of a one·mast boat.
야견(野犬) a stray dog; a homeless[ownerless] dog. やけん
야경(夜景) a night view[scene]/베니스의 ～ a night view of Venice/～화(畵) a night piece[scene]; a nocturne. やけい
야경(夜警) night watch; a night watch man/～단 a guard; a vigilance corps. やけい
야경스럽다(夜警—) (be) noisy[clamorous] in the night. さわがしい

**야곡(夜曲)** 〖음〗《야상곡》 a nocturne; a serenade. やきょく

**야광(夜光)** noctilucence／〜의 noctilucent／〜 도료 a luminous paint／〜 시계 a luminous watch／〜충(蟲) the noctiluca (*pl*. -cae). やこう

**야구(野球)** baseball; ball [game]／〜를 하다 play baseball／고려대학과 연세대학의 야구 시합 a baseball game between *Korea* University and *Yon-sei* University／〜계 baseball circles; the baseball world／〜선수 a baseball player／직업 〜 선수단 a professional baseball team. やきゅう

**야근(夜勤)** night duty; night work; nightshift／〜하다 take night duty／〜 수당 a night-work allowance 《시간외 수당》 an overtime pay. やきん

**야금(冶金)** metallurgy／〜학 metallurgy／〜학자 a metallurgist／〜술 [technique, art of] metallurgy. やきん

**야금(野禽)** a wild fowl; a wild bird. やきん

**야금거리다** take repeated little bites. ぐずぐずいう

**야금야금** little by little; bit by bit; bite by bite／〜 먹어 들어가다 eat into little by little 《침입》 invade gradually; encroach.

**야굿야굿하다** jagged; (be) notched; have teeth; rugged. ぎざぎざしている

**야기(夜氣)** 《밤공기》 night air 《냉기》 the cool of the night. やき

**야기(惹起)** 〜하다 cause; bring about; arouse; provoke; lead to／문제를 〜하다 raise a problem／그의 연설은 교육계에 문제를 〜했다 His speech occasioned a stir in educational circles. じゃっき

**야기부리다** grumble (*at*); complain (*of*); make a complain; whimper; murmur (*at*)／그는 화가 나면 누구에게나 야기부린다 He works off his anger[bad temper] on everybody around him. さわがしく

**야뇨증(夜尿症)** 〖의〗 bed-wetting; enuresis. やにょうしょう

**야단하면** if there is no help for it; if compelled[forced]／〜 그만두어라 If you are in a fix, don't trouble yourself further. どうしょうもなければ

**야단(惹端)** ①《소란》 a clamor; an uproar; a row; a commotion 《곤란》 a trouble; a plight; a fix／〜하다 be uproarious [in commotion]／급료를 올리라고 〜이다 clamor for a high wage ②《호명·호통》 scolding; rebuke; chiding; giving (*a person*) a scolding／장난하는 아이를 〜치다 scold a boy for his mischief. くちゃかましくしかること

**야단법석(野壇法席)** a boisterous merry-making; a spree; a racket／〜하다 have high jinks; go[be] on the spree.

**야담(野談)** a historical romance; an unofficial historical story[tale]／〜가 a [professional] historical story-teller／〜 책 a story book.

**야당(野黨)** a nongovernment party; an opposition party; a party out of[not in] power 《2대 정당의 경우》 the opposition; the outs／〜의 영수(領首) the Opposition leader／〜 연합 a combination of parties out of power. やとう

**야독(夜讀)** reading at night; night study／〜하다 read in the night; study till late at night. よるおそくまでよむ

**야들야들하다** (be) soft and delicate; soft; shiny／감촉이 〜 feel soft; be soft to the touch. ぴかぴかしている

**야료(惹鬧)** interruption; heckling; catcalling; jeering; hooting; denouncing／〜하다 disturb; heckle; jeer／그는 청중들로부터 〜를 당했다 He was jeered by his audience.

**야릇하다** strange; odd; peculiar; (be) queer／야릇한 사람 a queer person／야릇한 기분이다 feel strange／운명이란 〜 Fate plays strange tricks. おかしい

**야리다** ①《안 질기다》(be) frail; weak; tender ②《모자라다》(be) a little short of; wanting; be short (*of*)／옷감이 〜 The material is a little short to make a suit of clothes. もろい

**야만(野蠻)** savagery; savageness; barbarity; barbarism／〜하다 (be) savage; barbarous; barbaric／이 습관은 〜 시대의 유물이다 This custom is a relic of the barbaric times. やばん

**야말로** indeed; just; only; exactly／너〜 잘못이다 It is you that are in the wrong. —こそは

**야망(野望)** personal ambition; aspiration／〜을 실현하다 have *one's* ambition realized／〜을 품다 ambitious. やぼう

**야맹(夜盲)** 〖의〗 nyctalopia; nightblindness.

**야멸스럽다** unfeeling; heartless; callous; inconsiderate; insensible／저 사람들은 야멸스러운 데가 있다 They are people without feelings. むじょうだ

**야멸치다** (be) cold-hearted ⇨야멸스럽다／너는 정말 야멸치구나 How inconsiderate you are! むじょうだ

**야무지다** (be) firm; solid; steady; reliable; staunch／야무진 사람 a man of firm character／그는 야무진 데가 없다 He lacks firmness of character. しっかりしている

**야물다** ①《익다》 get ripe; ripen; mature ②(be) stout. しめている

**야바위** trickery; swindle; fraud; imposture; deception／4만 원을 〜당했다 be swindled out off 40,000 *won*.

**야박(野薄)** heartlessness; stinginess／〜하다 (be) hard-hearted; unkind; unfeeling; stingy／그들은 〜한 인간들이다 They are people without feelings.

**야반(夜半)** midnight; the middle of the night／〜까지 공부하다 work till late in the night. やはん

**야밤중**(夜—) the middle of the night/~까지 till late at night. まよなか

**야번**(夜番) night watch; duty at night/~군 a night-watchman; a night guard/~을 하다 keep night-watch; be on duty at night. やばん

**야비**(野卑) meanness; boorishness; bad taste; vulgarity/~하다 (be) vulgar/그의 얘기는 듣기에 너무 ~하다 His talk is too low to listen to.

**야비다리치다** pretend modesty; affect humility. ねこをかぶる

**야사**(野史) an unofficial[unauthorized] history[chronicle]. やし

**야산**(野山) a hill; a hillock. のやま

**야살** crabbedness; perverseness; peevishness/~스럽다 be perverse; be peevish; be impertinent; be saucy; be crabbed/~ 떨다 be cross. ひがみ

**야상곡**(夜想曲) 〖음〗 a nocturne. やそうきょく

**야색**(夜色) a night view[scene].

**야생**(野生) ~의 wild; uncultivated/~하다 grow wild; grow without cultivation/벼는 ~하지 않는다 Rice does not grow wild./~ 과일 wild fruit. やせい

**야성**(野性) wild[savage, unpolished] nature; brutal nature; rusticity; boorishness; uncouthness/~녀 a wild girl. やせい

**야속**(野俗) unfriendly; unkind; cruel; inconsiderate; heartless; unfeeling/나는 그런 ~한 짓은 못 하겠다 It is not in my nature to do such a thing. はくじょうなこと

**야수**(野獸) a wild beast[animal]/~ 같은 beastly; beastlike; brutal/~성 brutality/~성을 나타내다 show *one's* brutality/~파 〖미〗 Fauvists; Fauves. やじゅう

**야수**(野手) (야구) a fielder/내~ an infielder/외~ an outfielder.

**야수다** watch for a chance; wait for an opportunity; watch and wait/뱀이 개구리를 야수고 있다 The snake is watching a frog. きかいをねらう

**야순**(夜巡) night watch; night patrol/~하다 beat the round at night; be on night patrol. やけい

**야습**(夜襲) a night attack[raid, assault]; a surprise by night/~하다 make a night attack on (*the enemy*). やしゅう

**야시**(夜市) a night fair/~점 a night stall/~점을 내다 open[set up] a night stall.

**야식**(夜食) 《저녁밥》 supper 《밤참》a late snack; a midnight meal/~을 먹다 have a midnight snack. やしょく

**야심**(夜深) being late at night/~하다 be late at night/~토록 일하다 work far into the night. よいち

**야심**(野心) 《야망》 ambition 《포부》 aspiration 《음모》 a sinister design; an intrigue/~을 품다 have an ambition.

**야업**(夜業) night work; evening work 《야근》a night shift/~하다 work at night; do a night shift; do night work/~ 수당 an allowance for night work. やぎょう

**야연**(夜宴) an evening party[banquet]/~을 베풀다 give[hold] an evening party. やえん

**야영**(野營) a camp; camping 《행동》 encampment/~하다 camp; make camp/~지 a camping ground. やえい

**야옹** mewing/~을다 mew.

**야외**(野外) 《들》 the field 《옥외》the open air/~극 an outdoor play/~ 사생 outdoor sketching/~로 산보 나가다 take a stroll out of town. やがい

**야우**(夜雨) rainfall at night. よるのあめ

**야위다** become[grow] thin 《병으로》 lose flesh 《근심으로》pine away/그녀는 야위려고 애쓴다 She is trying to reduce her weight. やせている

**야유**(揶揄) banter; raillery/~하다 make fun[sport] of; poke fun at; rally; ridicule. やゆ

**야유**(野遊) a picnic/~회 a picnic party/~하러 가다 go on a picnic. やゆう

**야유**(夜遊) night pleasure[amusement]/~하다 go out in the evening for pleasure/~객 a night-bird. やゆう

**야음**(夜陰) the darkness; the dark of night/~을 타고 under cover of darkness [the night]. やいん

**야인**(野人) 《촌사람》 a rustic; a boor; a bumpkin; a countryman; a farmer 《재야인》 a person out of official position. やじん

**야자**(椰子) 〖식〗 a coconut palm; a coconut tree/~ 열매 a coconut/~유 palm oil; coconut milk. やし

**야전**(野戰) field operation; field warfare; a plain[an open] battle/~군 the field army/~ 병원 a field hospital/~포 a field gun; a fieldpiece. やせん

**야전**(夜戰) night operation/~하다 engage in night warfare. やせん

**야조**(夜鳥) a night-bird; a nocturnal bird.

**야조**(野鳥) a wild fowl; wild birds.

**야죽거리다** ①《말하다》 wag *one's* tongue in a flattering manner ②《씹다》 chew lightly. たわむれをいう

**야지**(野地) a field; a plain. やち

**야지러지다** wane; chip; have a piece break off ⇨이지러지다. かける

**야차**(夜叉) 〖민〗 a female demon; a *yaksa* (Sans)/보살 같은 외면에 ~ 같은 속심《속담》 An angel without, a devil within.

**야찬**(夜餐) a midnight snack.

**야채**(野菜) vegetables; greens; greenstuff 《시판용의》 garden truck/~를 가꾸다 raise[grow] vegetables; grow garden truck/~ 요리 greens; dish of cooked green vegetables. やさい

**야청**(—靑) a dark blue colo[u]r.

**야초(野草)** wild grass[plants]/~를 캐먹다 gather wild plants for eating.

**야취(野趣)** rural scenery; rusticity/~가 풍부하다 be rich in rustic beauty.

**야포(野砲)** a field-gun; a fieldpiece 《총칭》 field artillery/~대 a field-artillery corps.

**야하다(冶—)** ①《난하다》 (be) gorgeous; showy; gaudy; tawdry/야한 옷 gaudy clothes ②《속되다》 (be) vulgar; mean; low; coarse.

**야학(夜學)** an evening school/~생 an evening school student/~에 다니다 attend[go to] an evening school; attend an evening class.

**야합(野合)** an illicit union[connection]; 《공모》 collusion; conspiracy/~하다 form an illicit connection 《공모하다》 plot together.

**야행(夜行)** night-traveling; a night trip; nocturnal travel; travel by night/~하다 go[travel] by night.

**야화(野花)** wild flowers.

**야화(野火)** a field[bush] fire; a prairie fire.

**야화(夜話)** a tale by the fireside; an anecdote.

**야회(夜會)** an evening party 《무도회》 a ball/~복 an evening dress/~를 열다 hold[give] an evening party.

**약(略)** 《축소》 abbreviation; curtailment 《생략》 omission 《약자》 an abbreviation/~하다 abridge; omit 《단축하다》 cut short 《생략하다》 dispense with/의례를 ~하다 dispense with formalities/이하는 ~합니다 The rest is omitted.

**약(葯)** 〖식〗 the another [of a flower].

**약(約)** 《대략》 about; some; round; nearly around; approximately/수출 총액은 ~ 18억 불이다 The total export value is in round figures 1,800 million dollars.

**약(藥)** ①medicine, a drug 《알약》 a pill 《특효약》 a specific 《강장제》 a tonic 《치료제》 a remedy/~을 먹다 take medicine/이 ~은 잘 낫는다 This medicine does me good./이것은 감기에 잘 듣는 ~이다 This is a good medicine for a cold./~병 a medicine bottle; a bottle of medicine/가루~ powdered medicine /두통~ a headache remedy ②《화학 약품》 chemicals; chemical preparations [pastes, powder, pills] ③《이익》 good; benefit/그것은 ~이 된다 It is good for the health./모르는 게 ~이다 Ignorance is bliss.

**-약(弱)** 《모자라다》 a little less than; a little short of; a little under/1할 ~ a little less than 10 percent.

**약가심(藥—)** chasing the after-taste [of a medicine]/~하다 cut the after-taste [of a medicine]/~으로 사과를 먹었다 eat an apple to chase the bitter taste of the medicine.

**약간(若干)** some; a little; a bit; a few; somewhat/오늘은 기분은 ~ 좋은 편이다 I feel a little better today.

**약값(藥—)** the price of medicine; the charge for a medicine; a medical fee; a doctor's bill/~을 치르다 pay for medicine; pay a doctor's bill.

**약골(弱骨)** delicate health; a weak[delicate] constitution 《사람》 a weakling/그는 ~이다 He is a weak[delicate] constitution., He is delicately built.

**약과(藥果)** ①《과즐》 a cake made from wheatflour; oil and honey ②《쉬운 일》 an easy thing; a sure thing; a cinch/그를 이기는 것은 ~다 It's a child's play to beat him.

**약관(弱冠)** twenty years of age; a youth of twenty; a young man; youthfulness/그는 ~으로 등과했다 He passed the higher civil service at an early age of twenty.

**약관(約款)** a stipulation; an agreement; a provision; a contract; an article; a clause.

**약국(藥局)** a pharmacy; a chemist's shop; an apothecary; a drugstore 《병원의》 a dispensary; a pharmacist office.

**약꿀(藥—)** honey prepared as a medicine.

**약기(略記)** a brief[short, rough] sketch; an outline; a quick write-up/~하다 outline; jot down/이름은 ~하지 말 것 Your name should be written in full.

**약년(藥碾)** a muller ⇒약연(藥碾).

**약다** (be) clever; wise; sharp; shrewd; smart/약은 녀석 a shrewd man; an old fox; a smart guy/약게 놀다 behave shrewdly; be tactful.

**약단지(藥—)** a medicine pot; a clay pot for making a medical decoction.

**약대** 〖동〗 a camel ⇒낙타.

**약대(藥大)** a college of pharmacy.

**약대접(藥—)** a dish to drink medicine.

**약도(略圖)** a rough sketch 《지도》 an outline map; a sketch map 《계획》 a rough plan/너희 집까지의 ~를 그려 달라 Please make a sketch map showing the way to your house.

**약동(躍動)** a lively motion; a stir; a throb; a movement; a palpitation/~하다 move lively; be quick with life/가슴이 ~하는 것을 느끼다 feel a stir in one's heart.

**약동이(—童—)** a smart boy; a clever [shrewd] child.

**약되다(藥—)** be effective as medicine; be good medicine.

**약두구리(藥—)** a brass pot in which medical decoction is prepared.

**약력(略歷)** a brief personal history; a

**brief personal record; a sketch of** *one's* **life; a brief survey of** *one's* **career (고인의) a memoir.** りゃくれき

**약령(藥令) a medicine-market/~보다 s-hop for drugs at the drug market/~서다 hold a drug market.**

**약막대기 a stick on each side of the medicine-straining cloth.**

**약문(略文) an abridged sentence.**

**약물(藥—) ①(약수) medicinal waters; mineral waters ②(탕약 달인 물) water heated for a medicinal decoction/~터 a mineral spring; a spa.**

**약물(藥物) drugstuffs; drugs; medicines /~ 소독 disinfection by disinfectant/~ 요법 medication; medical therapy/~학자 a pharmacologist.** やくぶつ

**약물터(藥—) a mineral spring; a spa ⇨ 약수터.**

**약빠르다 cunning; clever; smart; sharp; (be) shrewd/약빠른 사람 a shrewd fellow/약빠르게 굴다 act tactfully; move smartly/거래에 있어서 ~ be smart in** *one's* **dealings.** すばしこい

**약밥(藥—) flavored glutinous rice mixed with honey, dates, chestnuts.**
やくごはん

**약방(藥房) a drug store〈미〉; a pharmacy 〈영〉/~에 감초 Jack-of-all-trades.**

**약방문(藥方文) a prescription [slip]; a recipe/~을 받다 have a prescription filled[made up].**

**약복(略服) an ordinary dress; an abbreviated clothes; informal attire; undress/그는 ~을 입고 있다 He is in undress.**

**약봉지(藥封紙) a paper-bundle of medicine; a medicine packet.** やくのつつみ

**약분(約分) 【수】 reduction of a fraction [to its lowest terms]/~하다 reduce a fraction; abbreviate; cancel/~할 수 있는 reducible.** やくぶん

**약사(略史) a short[brief; an abridged] history; a historical sketch; an outline history/한국 ~ an outline history of Korea.** りゃくし

**약사발(藥沙鉢) a poison bowl/~을 내리다 offer (***a person***) a cup of death; put (***a person***) to death.**

**약삭빠르다 (be) clever; sharp; smart; shrewd/약삭 빠르게 굴다 behave alertly [cunningly].** すばしこい

**약석(藥石) medicine/~의 효과 없이 in s-pite of careful medical treatment.**
やくせき

**약설(略說) a summary; a brief explanation/~하다 give an outline of; resume; sum up; summarize.** りゃくせつ

**약설(略設) informal establishment; simple[limited] fittings/~하다 set up [establish] simply.**

**약소(略少) (being) little; scanty; few/~하다 (be) scanty; few; little; insignificant.** わずか

**약소(弱小) the weak and small; the weak; the minor/~하다 (be) small and weak/~ 국가 a lesser Power; a minor Power; a small nation/~ 민족 a lesser race.** じゃくしょう

**약속(約束) an engagement; an agreement; an appointment; a promise (관습) a convention; a date〈미〉/그는 ~을 지킨다 He keeps his promise.** やくそく

**약속 어음(約束—) a promissory note; an advance note; a note of hand/~을 발행하다 issue a promissory note.**
やくそくてがた

**약속 우편(約束郵便) contract mail matter; second-class postal matter〈미〉; promissory post.** やくそくゆうびん

**약손(藥—) a soothing touch of the hand; a comforting hand.** くすりのて

**약손가락(藥—) the third finger; the ring finger.** くすりゆび

**약솜(藥—) surgical cotton; absorbent [sanitary] cotton.** だっしめん

**약수(藥水) medicinal water; mineral water ⇨약물(藥—).** くすりみず

**약수(約數) 【수】 a divisor [of a number] /공~ a common measure.** やくすう

**약수건(藥手巾) a hemp cloth for straining herb medicine.**

**약수터(藥水—) a mineral spring resort; a spa.**

**약쑥(藥—) medicinal wormwood[moxa].**
やくようよもぎ

**약술(略述) a brief account; an outline; a summary; a brief[short, rough]. sketch/~하다 summarize; give a rough sketch (***of***); sketch; outline.**
りゃくじゅつ

**약스럽다 wicked; (be) ugly.** おかしい

**약시(弱視) 【의】 weak sight; weakness of sight; amblyopia/~의 amblyopic; weak-eyed[-sighted].** じゃくし

**약시시(藥—), 약시중(藥—) the administering of medicine/~하다 administer medicine to (***one***).**

**약식(略式) informality/~의 informal; unceremonious; summary/~으로 informally; without formality; in an informal way/혼례는 ~으로 거행되었다 The marriage ceremony was gone through without due formality/~ 복장 an ordinary dress[clothes]; abbreviated clothes/~ 처분 summary disposition.**
りゃくしき

**약식(藥食) flavored glutinous rice ⇨약밥.** やくごはん

**약실(藥室) (약국) a pharmacist's office; a pharmacy; a drugstore; a doctor's medicine room (총의) a powder[cartridge] chamber.** やくしつ

**약약하다 unwilling; (be) reluctant.**

**약어(略語) an abbreviation; a contraction; an abbreviated[a shortened] word /~ 풀이 a key to an abbreviation.**
りゃくご

**약언(略言) a brief statement; an outline;**

a summary／~하다 state briefly; summarize; sum up／~한다면 in short; in a word; to make a long story short. りゃくげん

**약연(藥碾)** a druggist's mortar; a muller／~으로 갈다 bray in a mortar.

**약오르다** 《사람이 주어》 get angry[mad]; be offended; get irritated; be stung to the quick／저 녀석의 말투에 약오른다 I get sore about that remark of his.／그의 싸늘한 태도에 나는 바짝 약이 올랐다 His coldness cut me to the quick. はらがたつ

**약올리다** make (a person) angry; vex; provoke (a person) to anger／그의 말은 그녀를 약올렸다 His remarks stung her to the quick. はらをたたさせる

**약용(藥用)** medicinal use／~의 medical; medicinal／~ 식물 medical plant[herb]. やくよう

**약육 강식(弱肉强食)** the law of the jungle; The weak are the prey of the strong. じゃくにくきょうしょく

**약은피** shrewd wiles.

**약자(略字)** an abbreviation; an abbreviated word／~로 쓰다 write a character in simplified form. りゃくじ

**약자(弱者)** the weak; the underdog／~의 소리 the voice of the weak／~의 보호 protection of the weak／~의 편을 들다 stand by the weak. じゃくしゃ

**약장(略章)** a miniature medal[decoration]; a miniature.

**약장(藥欌)** a medicine-chest[cabinet].

**약재(藥材)** medicines; drugs; drugstuffs; medica; pharmaceuticals. やくのざいりょう

**약저울(藥—)** pharmacy scales. やくのはかり

**약전(藥典)** the pharmacopoeia.

**약전(略傳)** a brief life; a biographical sketch 《고인의》 a memoir; a sketch of a person's life. りゃくでん

**약전기(弱電機)** light electric appliances.

**약점(弱點)** a weakness; a flaw; a defect; a vulnerable point[spot, side]; 《불리한 점》 a disadvantage; one's blind side／적에게 ~을 잡히다 give a handle to the enemy. じゃくてん

**약정(約定)** an agreement; a contract; a promise; an engagement／~하다 agree; contract; promise／~ 기한 stipulated time／~서 an agreement. やくじょう

**약제(藥劑)** drugs; chemicals; medicine／~사 a chemist; a pharmacist. やくざい

**약조(約條)** 《언약》 a promise; a pledge 《규정》 rule; an agreement; a condition／~하다 promise; pledge／~를 지키다 keep one's pledge. やくじょう

**약졸(弱卒)** a cowardly[weak] soldier／강장(强將) 밑에 ~ 없다 Brave soldiers under a brave general. じゃくそつ

**약종(藥種)** pharmaceutical supplies; pharmacopoeia; materia medica(L)／~상 a seller of; materia medica a drug merchant; a chemist. やくしゅ

**약주(藥酒)** 《약술》 a medicinal wine 《술》 rice wine.

**약주름(藥—)** a pharmaceutical broker.

**약진(躍進)** rush; dash 《군대의》 onslaught 《말의》 prance／~하다 dash for[on]; advance on; rush on[against]／~에 약진을 거듭하다 advance leaps and bounds. やくしん

**약진(弱震)** a minor shock of earthquake／~이 있었다 A slight earthquake was felt. じゃくしん

**약질(弱質)** a weak[delicate] constitution; a person of feeble strength; a weakling. じゃくしつ

**약차약차(若此若此)** ~하다 (be) so and so [such and such, this and that]／~한 사람 such and such a person／그가 하지 않은 이유는 ~하다 The reason he didn't was so and so. このように

**약체(弱體)** a weak body／~의 weak; effete; weakbodied／지난 정부는 다소 ~ 다 The last Government is making rather a poor show. じゃくたい

**약초(藥草)** medicinal herbs; a medical plant／~상 a herbalist／~학자 a herbalist; a medical botanist. やくそう

**약칭(略稱)** an abbreviation; an abbreviated name; a short designation／FBI 는 연방 수사국의 ~이다 FBI is short for the Federal Bureau of Investigation.

**약탈(掠奪)** plunder; pillage; despoilment／~하다 pillage; despoil; plunder／~자 a despoiler; a plunderer; a marauder. りゃくだつ

**약탕관(藥湯罐)** a clay pot preparing medicines.

**약뿌리** the body of a round carrot; ginseng root, etc.

**약포(藥圃)** a herbal garden. やくほ

**약포(藥脯)** beef slices dried and flavored with spices.

**약품(藥品)** medical supplies; medicines 《매약》 drugs 《화학 약품》 chemicals／~부 a drug section[department]／~ 회사 a pharmaceutical company. やくひん

**약하(若何)** How then!, What if!, How about. いかが

**약하다(弱—)** 《연약하다》 (be) weak 《섬약하다》 (be) frail; delicate 《미약하다》 (be) faint feeble 《술 따위에》 (be) light; mild; weak／약한 사람 a weak person／약한 담배 mild tobacco／그 여자는 의지가 ~ S- he is infirm of purpose. よわい

**약하다(略—)** abbreviate; abridge; shorten 《생략하다》 cut out; omit; leave out／의식을 ~ dispense with formalities.

**약학(藥學)** pharmacy; pharmacology／~자 a pharmacologist／~과 a pharmaceutical department. やくがく

**약해(略解)** a rough explanation; a brief explanation[interpretation]／~하다 give a brief explanation of outlines.

**약호**(略號) a code address; an abbreviation; a short designation／전신 ~ a telegraphic code address. りゃくごう

**약혼**(約婚) a promise of marriage; engagement; betrothal／~ 반지 an engagement ring／그는 딸을 부자의 ~시켰다 He betrothed his daughter to a rich man.

**약화**(略畵) a rough sketch／~를 그리다 make a rough sketch (of); sketch. りゃくが

**약화**(弱化) weakening／~하다 weaken; become weakened／~시키다 weaken; enfeeble; unnerve. じゃっか

**약효**(藥效) remedial result; the effect [virtue, power] of a medicine／이 약은 곧 ~를 나타냅니다 This drug will soon work upon[on] you. やっこう

**얄궂다** perverse; nasty; (be) treacherous; queer; quaint; curious／얄궂은 얼굴을 하다 make a queer face. へんだ

**얄궂거리다** be shaky; be crazy; be rickety; quiver／얄궂거리는 의자 a rickety [shaky, rocky] chair. ぶらつく

**얄궂하다** (be) distorted; contorted; twisted; sagged. くいちがっている

**얄기죽거리다** sway one's hips to and fro. ふらつく

**얄따랗다** (be) very thin. うすっぺらだ

**얄라차** (감탄사)Heavens!, Why!, O my! (젠장) Gee!, Gosh! おかしいな

**얄망궂다** (be) imprudent; frivolous; uncompliant; crossgrained／얄망궂게 imprudently; frivolously; crossgrainedly／얄망궂게 굴다 act imprudently; behave erratically. きむずかしい

**얄망스럽다** (be) ill-tempered; ill-natured; cross-grained; cantankerous; malicious. きむずかしい

**얄밉다** (be) offensive; mean and nasty; (뻔뻔스럽다)(be) saucy; cheeky; pert; hateful; detestable／얄미운 태도 an impudent manner／그녀는 얄미울 정도로 노래를 잘한다 She is an enviously good singer. にくらしい

**얄밉상스럽다** (be) rather hateful. にくらしい

**얄팍하다** (be) rather thin／얄팍한 책 a thin book. うすっぺらだ

**얇다** (be) thin; lack thickness／얇게 thinly／얇은 옷 thin clothes／입술이 ~ 하다 have thin lips／고기를 얇게 썰다 slice meat thin／창이 얇은 구두 thin-soled shoes／얇게 썬 빵 a thin slice of bread. うすい

**얌냠하다, 얌냠거리다** smack one's lips; go "yum-yum!"

**얌심** jealousy; spite; green envy; malice／~스럽다 be mean and jealous; be spiteful／~꾸러기 a mean and jealous person. さいきしん

**얌전하다** ①(행동이)(be) gentle; well-behaved; graceful; modest; decent; nice／얌전한 처녀 a modest[well-behaved] girl／얌전하게 걷다 walk gracefully ②(일·작품이)(be) good; fine; excellent; nice; neat／글을 얌전하게 쓰다 write neatly／옷을 얌전하게 입다 dress neatly[nicely]. おとないち

**얌치** a sense of honor ⇒염치. れんち

**양**(胖) tripe; the cud pouch; the wall of ox stomach. うしのいのにく

**양**(羊) a sheep (수컷) a ram (암컷) a ewe (거세한) a wether (새끼 양) a lamb／~치는 사람 a shepherd／~같이 순하다 be as gentle as a lamb／~고기 mutton／~떼 a flock of sheep. ひつじ

**양**(陽) the positive／~과 음 the positive and the negative; the male and female／음으로 ~으로 openly and coverly; explicitly and implicitly. よう

**양**(量) ①(분량) quantity; amount; volume／~의 증가 an increase in quantity／술의 ~을 줄이다 reduce one's drinking ②(식량) one's capacity for food[wine]／~보다 질을 택하다 I prefer quality to quantity／~껏 마시다 drink one's fill [as much as one likes]. りょう

**양**(良) fine; good／~답(畓) a fertile ricefield／~서(書) a good book. りょう

**양**-(兩) both; two; a pair; a couple／~면(面) two faces; both sides／~인(人) both persons.

-**양**(洋) an ocean; the sea／대서~ the Atlantic [Ocean]. よう

-**양**(孃) 《처녀》 Miss／김~ Miss Kim. じょう

**양가**(良家) a respectable family; a good family／~의 처녀 a daughter of a good family[parentage]／~집 태생이다 come of a respectable family; be wellborn. りょうか

**양가**(兩家) both[two] houses[families].

**양가**(養家) an adoptive family; the adopting household／~의 어버이 one's adoptive parents. ようか

**양가구**(洋家具) Western-style furniture.

**양각**(陽刻) engraving in relief; embossed carving; raised carving／~으로 하다 emboss; carve in relief／~ 세공 relief work; embossed work ようこく

**양각기**(兩脚器) a pair of compasses.

**양간**(陽乾) drying in the sun／~하다 dry in the sun／~ 벽돌 a sun-dried brick; an adobe. ひぼし

**양갈보**(洋—) a foreigners' whore; a prostitute who are patronized by foreigners.

**양감**(量感) massiveness; volume／~이 있다 be massive; be voluminous.

**양견**(洋犬) a foreign dog; a dog of foreign[Western] breed; an European dog.

**양견**(兩肩) one's [both] shoulders. りょうけん

**양계**(養鷄) poultry farming; chicken raising/~하다 raise poultry[chickens]/~장 a poultry farm; a chicken farm/~업자 a poultry farmer[raiser].　ようけい

**양곡**(糧穀) provisions; cereals; corn; grain/~상 a grain[corn] merchant/~시장 the grain[corn] market/~창고 a granary/~증산 increased grain production[output].　りょうこく

**양공**(良工) a skilled artisan[workman].　りょうこう

**양과자**(洋菓子) Western-style cakes[confections].　ようがし

**양관**(洋館) 《서양식 집》 an European[Western] style building 《공관》 legations of the foreign countries.　ようかん

**양광**(陽光) sunshine; sunbeams; [spring] sunlight.　ようこう

**양광**(佯狂) feigned insanity; pretending to be mad.

**양국**(兩國) both countries/~간의 유대 [friendly] ties between the two countries.

**양군**(兩軍) both armies 《야구·축구 따위의》 both teams/치열한 싸움이 ~간에 벌어졌다 A fierce fight broke out between the two troops.

**양귀비**(楊貴妃) 〖식〗 a [opium] poppy/~씨 a poppy-seed.　ようきひざくら

**양극**(陽極) 〖전기〗 the positive pole; the anode/~광[선] an anode glow[ray]/~판(板) the positive [plate].　ようきょく

**양극**(兩極) both extremities; the two poles; the north and south poles; the positive and negative poles/~성 polarity/~지방 the polar circles[areas].　りょうきょく

**양극단**(兩極端) the two[both] extremes/~은 일치한다 Extremes meet.

**양근**(陽根) 〖화〗 a positive radical 《음경》 the penis.

**양금**(洋琴) a kind of zither/~채 a zither stick; a stick with which *one* strikes the strings of a Korean zither/~채 같은 몸이다 be of delicate health.

**양끝**(兩―) both ends/~을 끊다 cut (*a stick*) at both ends.

**양기**(凉氣) cool[refreshing] air.　りょうき

**양기**(養氣) nursing[preserving] one's energy; cultivating one's mental strength/~하다 cultivate[develop] courage; build oneself up.　よき

**양기**(陽氣) ①《볕》 sunlight; sunshine ② 《남자의》 the male[positive] element in nature; vigor; vitality; energy/~가 왕성하다 be full of energy; have great vigor.　ようき

**양난**(兩難) a dilemma/진퇴 ~이다 be in dilemma; be in a fix.　しんたいきわまること

**양날**(兩―) ~의 double-bladed; two-edged/~의 칼 a double-edged sword.

**양녀**(洋女) an Western[European, American] woman.

**양녀**(養女) a foster daughter; an adopted daughter/~로 기르다 foster a girl as *one's* daughter.　ようじょ

**양념** spices and condiments; dressing materials/~이 든 spicy; seasoned/이 수프는 ~이 적다 There is not enough seasoning in this soup.　やくみ

**양놈**(洋―) a foreigner; a white; a Westerner.

**양단**(兩端) both ends; both extremes; either end.　りょうたん

**양단**(兩斷) ~하다 break[cut] in two; bisect/~되다 get split in two/그 배는 ~되어 버렸다 The ship has broken in half[twain].　りょうだん

**양단간**(兩端間) anyway; anyhow; at any rate; somehow or other/~에 손해는 없다 Whatever may be the issue, he has nothing to lose/~에 그것은 사실이다 Belive it or not, it's a fact.　どうあろうと

**양달**(陽―) a sunny place[spot]/~쪽 the sunny side/~에서 볕을 쬐다 sit in the sun/~에서 말리다 dry (*a thing*) in a sunny spot.

**양딸**(養―) an adopted daughter.　ようじょ

**양딸기**(洋―) the Alpine strawberry.

**양달력**(洋―歷) a hanging[wall] calendar.

**양담배**(洋―) imported tobacco; American cigarettes[tobacco].

**양떼** a herd of sheep/~구름 《기상》 a cumulocirrus [cloud].

**양당**(兩黨) the two political parties/~제도 the two-party system〈미〉.

**양도**(糧道) supply of provisions/적의 ~를 끊있다 We cut off the enemy's supply of provisions.　りょうどう

**양도**(兩刀) two swords; a sword in either hand/~논법 a [logical] dilemma.

**양도**(讓渡) transfer; conveyance 《권리의》 assignment 《영토의》 cession 《어음의》 negotiation/~하다 transfer (*to*); hand (*a thing*) over (*to*); dispose of/소유권을 ~하다 yield possession/그는 사업을 아들에게 ~했다 He handed over his business to his son./~가격 a transfer [sale] price/~인 a transferer; an assigner.　じょうと

**양도체**(良導體) a good conductor/구리는 전기의 ~이다 Copper is a good conductor of heat.　りょうどうたい

**양돈**(養豚) pig keeping; hog farming; swine keeping; hog[pig] raising[breeding]/~가 a hog[pig] raiser/~업 a hog raising industry.　ようとん

**양동이**(洋―) a metal tub; a metal bucket/~에 물을 붓다 pour water into a [metal] bucket.

**양동 작전**(陽動作戰) demonstration; a faint operation; diversionary activities/~으로 나오다 create[make] a diversion.

**양돼지**(洋―) a pig of a foreign breed.

**양두**(兩頭) ~의 double-headed; bicephalous/~사(蛇) 《뱀》 an amphisbaena/~

**양두 구육(羊頭狗肉)** crying up wine and selling vinegar; using a better name to sell inferior goods; all outside show. ようとうくにく

**양득(兩得)** double gain ⇒일거 양득. りょうとく

**양력(揚力)** 〖물〗upward force; lift [on the wing of an airplane]. ようりょく

**양력(陽曆)** the solar calendar; Julian calendar. ようれき

**양로(養老)** taking care of the aged; provision for old age; living at ease in *one's* old age/~ 연금 an old-age pension/~원 an old people's home; a public assistance institution. ようろう

**양론(兩論)** both arguments; both sides of the argument. りょうろん

**양류(楊柳)** 〖식〗a willow. ようりゅう

**양륙(揚陸)** landing; unloading; disembarkation/~하다 land; unload; disembark/~료 landing charge/~장 landing place[stage]. ようりく

**양립(兩立)** compatibility; coexistence/ ~하다 be compatible (*with*); coexist (*with*); stand together/자본주의와 사회주의는 ~ 못한다 Capitalism is incompatible with socialism. りょうりつ

**양막(羊膜)** the amnion(*pl.* ~s, ·nia). ようまく

**양말(糧秣)** provisions and fodder/~차 a forage-cart. りょうまつ

**양말(洋襪)** 《짧은》socks 《긴》stockings; hoses〈미〉/~을 신지 않은 stockingless; no-stocking/~ ~대님 sock-suspenders; garters. くつした

**양면(兩面)** both[two] faces[sides]/~의 double-faced; both-sided/인생의 ~ both bright and seamy sides of life/~ 인쇄 printing on both sides of the paper. りょうめん

**양명(揚名)** gaining fame; making *one's* name/~하다 gain fame; make *one's* name/그는 천하에 ~하려고 뜻하고 있다 He has an aspiration after distinction. ようめい

**양명학(陽明學)** the doctrines[philosophy, teaching] of *Wang Yangming*/~자 a scholar of the *Wang Yangming* school. ようめいがく

**양모(養母)** a foster mother; an adoptive mother. ようぼ

**양모(羊毛)** a wool; pile/~의 woolen/~를 깎다 fleece[shear] sheep/~ 공업 the woolen and worsted industry/~ 제품 woolen goods. ようもう

**양모제(養毛劑)** a hair tonic.

**양목(洋木)** cotton cloth. もめんおり

**양미(糧米)** provisions; food; rice.

**양미간(兩眉間)** the middle of the forehead; the brow/~을 찌푸리다 knit *one's* brows; frown (*at*, *on*). りょうびかん

**양민(良民)** good citizens[people]; peaceable people; law-abiding[peaceable] citizens/~ 학살 massacre[slaughter] of the innocent people. りょうみん

**양반(兩班)** a nobleman; a gentleman; an aristocrat; the two upper classes of old Korea/주인 ~ the master (of *a house*).

**양방(兩方)** both; either; the two; each of the two 《부정》neither/그렇게 하면 ~이 다 만족할 것이다 That will satisfy both parties. りょうほう

**양배추(洋一)** [an imported variety of] cabbage/~ 밭 a cabbage patch. かんらん

**양버들(洋一)** 〖식〗a poplar.

**양변(兩邊)** both sides; either side/~에 on both sides/길의 ~에 구경군들이 인산 인해를 이루고 있다 The street was lined with spectators on either side. りょうへん

**양병(養兵)** building up[raising] military forces/~하다 build up[train] military forces; maintain an army.

**양병(養病)** recuperation; curing a disease 《악화》aggravating a disease/~하다 cure a disease; improve *one's* health 《악화하다》aggravate a disease/그녀는 해변으로 ~하러 갔다 She has gone to the seaside to recuperate.

**양보(讓步)** concession; conciliation; compromise/~하다 concede; make a concession/조금도 ~하지 않다 make no concession; do not yield a single point. じょうほ

**양복(洋服)** foreign clothes; European [Western] clothes; a European dress [suit]/~을 입다 put on Western clothes/~감 cloth; stuff. ようふく

**양봉(養蜂)** bee-keeping; bee-culture; apiculture/~하다 keep bees; engage in apiculture/~가 a bee-keeper/~ 상자 a wooden beehive; a movable comb hive. ようほう

**양부(良否)** good or bad; quality/승진은 성적의 ~에 따른다 Promotion depends upon *one's* service. /~를 알아내다 ascertain the quality (of *a thing*). りょうふ

**양부(養父)** a foster father; an adoptive father. ようふ

**양부모(養父母)** foster parents. ようふぼ

**양부인(洋婦人)** 《서양 부인》a foreign lady 《창녀》a foreigners' whore.

**양분(兩分)** bisection; dividing[cutting] into two/~하다 bisect; halve; cut [divide] (*a thing*) into two. りょうぶん

**양분(養分)** nourishment; nutriment; nutritious substance[matter]; nutritional elements/~을 흡수하다 take nourishment (*from*). ようぶん

**양산(陽傘, 洋傘)** a parasol; a sunshade; an umbrella/~을 쓰다 put up an umbrella[a parasol]. ひがさ

**양산(量産)** mass production/~하다 mass-produce.

**양살구** 〖식〗a medlar; a loquat.

**양상**(樣相) an aspect; a phase; a condition; 〖논〗 a modality/~을 일변시키다 change the whole appearance. ようそう

**양상 군자**(梁上君子) **(도독)** a thief[robber] **(쥐)** a rat.

**양생**(養生) **(보건)** care of health; preservation of *one's* health **(보양)** recuperation/~하다 take care of *one's* health **(병후에)** recuperate *oneself*. ようじょう

**양서**(洋書) a foreign book; European and American books, ようしょ

**양서**(良書) a good book; a valuable work /~는 적다 There are few good books among many. りょうしょ

**양서**(兩棲) ~의 〖동〗 amphibious/~ 동물 an amphibian; an amphibious animal /~류 the Amphibia. りょうせい

**양성**(良性) 〖의〗 ~의 benign (*tumor*). ようせい

**양성**(兩性) both sexes; the [two] sexes/ ~의 bisexual/~ 관계 sex relations/~ 생식 amphigony; gamogenesis; digenesis/~화(花)〖식〗a bisexual flower. りょうせい

**양성**(陽性) positivity/~의 positive; active/~ 반응 positive reaction/투베르크 린 반응은 ~이었다 The tuberculin test proved positive. ようせい

**양성**(養成) training; education **(함양)** cultivation; nurture/~하다 train; educate; cultivate; bring up; nurse/교원 을 ~하다 train teachers.

**양속**(良俗) a fine custom; a good custom/미풍 ~ a good and beautiful custom. りょうぞく

**양손**(養孫) an adopted grandchild; the adopted child of *one's* son.

**양수**(讓受) acquisition by transfer; inheritance; taking over/~하다 obtain by transfer; take over; receive/~인 a grantee. ゆずりうけること

**양수**(兩手) both hands/~를 쓰는 사람 ambidextrous persons. りょうしゅ

**양수**(羊水) amniotic fluid; the water/ ~가 나오다 the water breaks. ようすい

**양수기**(量水器) a water meter. りょうすいき

**양수기**(揚水機) a water pump. ようすいき

**양순**(良順) ~하다 meek; (be) good and obedient; docile; peaceable/~하게 말 을 듣다 do as told without objection/서 커스의 동물은 대개 ~하다 Most circus animals are tame/~한 성격 a gentle nature. おとなしいこと

**양식**(洋式) European[Western] style/~ 가옥 Western-style houses. ようしき

**양식**(洋食) Western food; foreign cookery[dishes]/~ 먹는 법 Western table manners/~ 요리법 Western cooking. ようしょく

**양식**(良識) good sense/~ 있는 사람 a sensible[intellectual] person; a person of sense; a person of sound judgment/ 그의 ~을 의심하다 doubt if he is really sound in judgment. りょうしき

**양식**(養殖) culture; farming; raising; rearing; breeding/~하다 rear; raise; cultivate/~장 a nursery; a farm/~ 진주 a culture pearl. ようしょく

**양식**(樣式) a mode; form; modality/~ 화 하다 conventionalize/생활 ~을 변화 시키다 change *one's* mode[style] of living. ようしき

**양식**(糧食) provisions; food; bread; supplies; rations; victuals/~이 충분하다 have an ample supply of food/그날 그 날의 ~을 벌다 earn *one's* daily bread. りょうしょく

**양실**(洋室) a Western-style room; a room furnished in foreign style. ようしつ

**양심**(良心) conscience; the inner voice; the still small voice/~적 conscientious/~의 가책 the stings of conscience. りょうしん

**양아들**(養―) an adopted[a foster] child [son]. ようし

**양아버지**(養―) an adoptive father; a foster father. ようふ

**양아욱**(洋―) 〖식〗 a geranium. あるてあ

**양아치** a ragpicker.

**양악**(洋樂) Western music/~가(家) a musician of Western music. ようがく

**양안**(兩眼) both eyes/~이 다 멀다 be blind in both eyes. りょうがん

**양안**(兩岸) either bank.

**양약**(良藥) a good medicine/~은 입에 쓰 다 A good medicine tastes bitter. りょうやく

**양약**(洋藥) a Western remedy[medicine, drug].

**양양**(洋洋) ~하다 (be) vast; broad; boundless **(유망하다)** bright/당신의 전도는 ~한 메가 있다 A rosy future is smiling on you. ようよう

**양양하다**(揚揚―) ~하다 (be) triumphant; exultant. ようようする

**양어**(養魚) fish-breeding[-farming]/~장 a fish-farm/~지 a fishpond; a breeding pond. ようぎょ

**양어머니**(養―) a foster-mother. ようぼ

**양어버이**(養―) a foster parent. ようふぼ

**양언**(揚言) speaking publicly; announcement; declaration/~하다 say publicly; announce; declare; assert. ようげん

**양여**(讓與) transfer **(영토의)** cession **(이 권의)** concession **(포기)** surrender; alienation/~하다 transfer; assign/권리 를 ~하다 transfer *one's* rights to (*a person*). じょうよ

**양옥**(洋屋) a Western[European] style house.

**양요리**(洋料理) foreign food[dishes]; Western cooking[cookery]/~점 a foreign-style restaurant.

**양용**(兩用) (*for*) double use/수륙 ~ 비행 기[전차] an amphibian plane[tank].

**양우**(良友) a good friend[companion]; **(집 합적)** good company/~를 사귀다 keep

**양우리**(羊―) a sheep pen.
**양원**(兩院) both Houses[Chambers]; the two Houses/~ 의원 members of both Houses/~ 협의회 a joint conference of the two Houses/~을 통과하다 pass both Houses. りょういん
**양위**(讓位) abdication; demise of the Crown/~하다 vacate the Throne. じょうい
**양유**(羊乳) sheep's milk. ひつじのちち
**양육**(養育) nurture; bringing up/~하다 rear; bring up/그녀는 두 아이를 ~했다 She took over two children and brought them up. よういく
**양육**(羊肉) mutton 《새끼의》 lamb.
**양으로**(陽―) 《드러나게》 openly; publicly. あらわに
**양은**(洋銀) nickel[German] silver. ようぎん
**양의**(洋醫) a Western medical doctor; a physician of the new school. ようい
**양의**(良醫) a good[clever, skillful] physician; a Hippocrates. りょうい
**양의**(兩義) two meanings; a double meaning; ambiguity/이 말은 ~로 해석된다 This word bears a double interpretation.
**양이온**(陽―) 『물리』 a positive ion.
**양익**(兩翼) both wings 《대열의》 both flanks. りょうよく
**양인**(兩人) two persons; a pair; a couple /~이 모두 both [of them]; either [of the two]. ふたり
**양인**(洋人) a Westerner; a foreigner; an Occidental. ようじん
**양일간**(兩日間) for[in] two days; with [in] two days.
**양입 계출**(量入計出) measuring *one's* spending by *one's* means.
**양자**(兩者) both (*persons, parties, events, things*) together/~ 합의하에 under joint[bilateral] agreement. りょうしゃ
**양자**(量子) 『물』 quantum/~론 the quantum theory/~ 역학 quantum mechanics. りょうし
**양자**(陽子) 『물・화』 a proton. ようし
**양자**(養子) a foster child(son, daughter); an adopted son[daughter]; *one's* son by adoption; a son-in-law/그는 지체 있는 집에 ~로 들어갔다 He was adopted into a respectable family. ようし
**양짝**(兩―) both counterparts; two pairs [couples].
**양잠**(養蠶) raising silkworms; silk raising; silk culture; sericulture/~하다 raise[rear] silkworms/~업 the silk-raising[sericultural] industry/~ 농가 a silk-raising farmer. ようさん
**양장**(洋裝) ①《양복》 foreign[Western] style of dress/그 여자는 ~이 어울린다 She looks better in Western dress./~ 부인 a lady in foreign dress ②《제본》 binding a book in Western style. ようそう

**양장**(羊腸) ①the entrails of a goat ②a winding[twisting, tortuous] path; a narrow meandering road/~의 winding; zigzag/~ 같은 산길 a winding mountain path. ようちょう
**양재**(洋裁) foreign style dressmaking/~사 a dressmaker; a seamstress/~ 학원 a dressmaking school. ようさい
**양재**(良材) 《재목》 a good timber; good material 《인제》 a man of ability; a competent person. りょうざい
**양재기**(洋―) enamelware. せとひきのきぐ
**양잿물** caustic soda; lye.
**양적**(量的) quantitative/~으로 quantitatively. りょうてき
**양전**(兩全) ~의 advantageous to both sides/나는 피차 ~지책을 강구했다 I found a plan advantageous to both sides. りょうぜん
**양전기**(陽電氣) plus electricity; positive [vitreous] electricity/~선 positive rays. ようでんき
**양전자**(陽電子) 『물』 a positron. ようでんし
**양젖**(羊―) goat['s] milk. ひつじのちち
**양조**(釀造) brewing; distillation; brewage/~하다 brew; distill/~장 a brewery; a distillery/맥주를 ~하다 brew beer. じょうぞう
**양조모**(養祖母) a foster[an adoptive] grandmother.
**양조부**(養祖父) a foster[an adoptive] grandfather.
**양쪽**(兩―) both sides; either side 《사람》 both; the two; either; each of the two; neither/~ 다 결석이다 Both are absent. りょうほう
**양종**(洋種) a foreign breed; Western kind[seeds]/~닭 a chicken of foreign stock. ようしゅ
**양주**(洋酒) foreign wine[liquors]/~상 a wine merchant; a dealer in foreign liquors/~류 liquors and drinks. ようしゅ
**양주**(兩主) husband and wife; man and wife; a couple; a pair. ふうふの俗称
**양지**(陽地) a sunny place/~의 sunny; in the sun/~에서 말리다 dry in the sun.
**양지**(諒知) understanding/~하다 know; understand; grasp. うかがいしること
**양지머리** beef ribs; the bricket of beef /~뼈 the ribs of an ox[a beef].
**양지바르다**(陽地―) be sunny; be full of sunshine/이 방은 ~ This room is exposed to the sun. ひあたりがいい
**양지쪽**(陽地―) the sunny side; a sunny spot/~에 나가 놀아라 Go out and play in the sunny side. ひのあたるそく
**양질**(良質) good quality/~의 of good quality; superior. りょうしつ
**양차**(兩次) two times; twice.
**양차렵** light cotton padding worn in spring and autumn. あいふく
**양찰**(諒察) consideration; sympathy/~

하다 consider; take into consideration; sympathize with／이런 사정이니 ~하십시오 Such being the case, I beg you will kindly excuse me. りょうさつ

**양책**(良策) a good plan[scheme]; a capital plan; a good policy. りょうさく

**양처**(兩處) two[both] places.

**양처**(良妻) a good wife／현모 ~ a good wife and wise mother／현모 ~주의 교육 an education for making good wives and wise mothers. りょうさい

**양철**(兩凸) double convex／~렌즈 a biconvex lens.

**양철**(洋鐵) galvanized iron; tinned iron; tin-plate／~통 a tin pail; a metal bucket／~판 a tin-plate sheet. ブリキ

**양청**(洋靑) deep[Prussian] blue; ultramarine.

**양초**(洋—) a candle 《가는 것》 a taper／~를 켜다 burn[light] a candle／~ 심지 the wick [of a candle]／양촛대 a candlestick／~ 동강 a candle ends. せいようろうそく

**양초**(糧草) provisions and fodder. しょくりょうとばりょう

**양추**(凉秋) the cool autumn; September of the lunar calendar. りょうしゅう

**양춘**(陽春) spring; the springtime／~ 가절 the pleasant days of springtime. ようしゅん

**양측**(兩側) both sides; either side／길의 ~에 on either side of the street; on both sides of the street／길의 ~에 늘어서다 be lined on either side of the street.

**양치**(養齒) brushing one's teeth; rinsing the mouth／~하다 brush one's teeth; rinse [out] one's mouth／소금물로 ~하다 rinse out one's mouth with salt and water. うがい

**양치기**(羊—) sheep-raising.

**양치류**(羊齒類) 《식》 the ferns. しだるい

**양치질** brushing one's teeth; rinsing the mouth. うがいすること

**양친**(兩親) parents; one's father and mother／~의 parental／그녀는 ~이 없는 아들 셋을 인수했다 She took in three orphaned children. りょうしん

**양코**(洋—) a foreigner's nose; a large protruding nose; a foreigner. たかいはな

**양탄자**(洋—) a carpet; a rug 《갈》 rugcloth; carpeting／마루에는 두꺼운 ~가 깔려 있었다 The floor was thickly carpeted. カペット

**양태** ①《갓의》 the brim of a Korean hat ②《어》 a flathead; a dragonet.

**양털**(羊—) wool; sheep's hair. ようもう

**양토**(養兎) rabbit raising[farming]; rabbit rearing／~하다 raise[breed] rabbit ／~장 a rabbit farm; a rabbitry. うさぎをかうこと

**양파**(洋—) an onion. たまねぎ

**양팔**(兩—) two[both] arms.

**양편**(兩便) either side; both sides／~에 은행나무가 줄지어 있다 On either side of the road grows a long line of gingko trees. りょうほう

**양편−**(兩便−) both sides[parties]; 《부정》 neither／~ 다 모른다 I know neither of them.

**양푼** a large brass basin[bowl].

**양품**(洋品) foreign articles[goods]／~점 a foreign[an imported] goods shop [store]. ようひん

**양풍**(良風) a good custom／~ 미속 a good and beautiful custom／~을 함양하다 cultivate good customs. りょうふう

**양풍**(洋風) a foreign[an European, a Western] style[fashion]／~의 European; Western／~의 건물 a building in foreign style. ようふう

**양풍**(凉風) a cool[refreshing] breeze. りょうふう

**양피**(羊皮) sheep skin; goat skin 《무두질하지 않은》 a roan／~ 구두 goatskin shoes; sheepskin shoes／~지 parchment. ようひ

**양하**(蘘荷) 《식》 Zingiber mioga《학명》.

**양학**(洋學) Western[European] learning ／~을 배우다 study Western science／ ~자 a scholar of European learning.

**양항**(良港) a good harbor. りょうこう

**양해**(諒解) 《승낙》 consent 《동의》 agreement 《이해》 understanding 《찬동》 approval; approbation／~하다 consent to; agree with; appreciate. りょうかい

**양행**(洋行) ①《외국행》 foreign travel; going[travelling] abroad／~하다 go abroad; a travel abroad／그는 회사 일로 ~하였다 He has been sent abroad by his firm. ②《점포》 a foreign business firm 《중국의》 a hong. ようこう

**양형**(量刑) weighing of offense／~상의 정상 참작 extenuating circumstances in the examination of an offense.

**양호**(養護) protection; nursing; protective care／~하다 protect; take (one) under one's protection／~ 시설 a protective institution. ようご

**양호**(良好) good／~하다 (be) good; excellent; favourable; satisfactory／경과가 ~하다 make satisfactory progress. りょうこう

**양호 유환**(養虎遺患) Keeping a tiger will only bring trouble upon oneself.

**양화**(洋畵) ①《그림》 a Western painting; an oil painting／~가 an oil painter ② 《영화》 a foreign movie[film]. ようが

**양화**(洋貨) foreign[imported] goods. ようか

**양화**(洋靴) leather shoes 《단화》 shoes 《반장화》 boots／~점 a shoe store／~점 직공 a shoemaker. くつ

**양화**(陽畵) 《사진》 a positive [picture]. ようが

**양화**(良貨) good money／악화는 ~를 구축한다 Bad money drives out good money.

**양회**(洋灰) cement. セメント

**얕다** ①《깊이가》(be) shallow/물이 얕은 곳에서 헤엄쳐라 You should swim in shallow water. ②《천박하다》(be) shallow; superficial/그녀의 영문학 실력은 ~ She has a smattering knowledge of English literature. ③《빛깔이》(be) light; pale/얕은 초록빛 light green ④《관계가》be not close; (be) slight/나와 그이는 교제가 ~ I am only slightly acquainted with him. ⑤《높이가》(be) low 《키가》short ⑥《지위가》(be) low; humble; lowly/지위가 ~ be low in position. あさい

**얕보다** look down upon; make light of; despise; belittle; hold (*a person*) in contempt/그는 우리를 가난한 친척이라고 얕보고 있다 He looks down upon us as poor relations. みくびる

**얕은꾀** shallow brains; shallow wit; transparent subterfuge[guile]/체면을 살리려고 ~를 부리다 resort to malingering and some other subterfuge to save face. あさはかなちえ

**얕잡다** despise; neglect; make light of; treat with contempt/사람을 얕잡아 보면 안 된다 You ought not to hold people cheap. さげすむ

**얘** 《호칭》sonny; you; there; hey 《이 애》this child《boy, girl》/~야 Hey, you! /~야 이리 오너라 Hey you, come here. このこ

**어** 《감탄》Oh!, well; why 《대답》yes; yea. あ·お

**-어**(語) a word 《전문어》a term 《언어·국어》a language/법률 ~ legal terms/비속 ~ a slang; a vulgarism/외국 ~ a foreign language. ご

**어가**(御駕) a royal carriage. おうのみこし

**어가**(漁歌) a fishermen's song. ぎょか

**어간** a gap; a space; an interval [of a time, space].

**어간**(御間) a large space in a house/~ 대청 a large floored hall between two rooms/~ 마루 the floor between two rooms.

**어간**(語幹) the stem of a word; a stem. ごかん

**어간유**(魚肝油) 【약】 cod-liver oil.

**어감**(語感) a linguistic sense; sensitivity to language; a feeling for words,/~이 예민하다 have a keen sense of language. ごかん

**어깨** the shoulder/벌어진 ~ square shoulder/~을 에 메고 with a gun on *one's* shoulder/~가 뻐근하다 have stiff shoulders. かた

**어개**(魚介) 《어류와 조개》fish and shellfishes 《해산물》marine products. ぎょかい

**어깨걸이** a shawl.

**어깨넘엇글** odd pieces of information acquired by overhearing other persons learning their lessons; picked-up knowledge.

**어깨동무** 《동무》an old playmate; a bosom friend from childhood; a childhood friend 《동작》putting arms around each other's shoulders/~하고 걷다 walk arm in arm. かたをくむこと

**어깨뼈** the shoulder blade; the *scapula* (pl. ~s, ·lae)(L)/~가 부러지다 get *one's* blade bone broken. かたのほね

**어깨차례**(一次例) the order of turns 《키》order of height. うえからのじゅんばん

**어깨총** ①shouldering *one's* rifle ②《구령》Shoulder [arms]! になえつつ

**어깨춤** a shoulder dance; moving *one's* shoulders up and down/~을 추다 dance with *one's* shoulders moving up and down. かたでおどるおどり

**어깨바람** wiggling *one's* shoulders with delight; swaggering. きょうしゅ

**어깻숨** a shoulder-heaving breath.

**어깻죽지** the shoulder joint. かたさき

**어깻짓** moving *one's* shoulders.

**어리풍년**(一豊年) a bumper[·crop] year. たいほうねん

**어거하다**(馭車—) 《마소를》drive (*ox* or *horse*); urge (*a horse*); 《게어하다》manage;control; bring under control; lead/부하를 잘 ~ manage *one's* men well/어거하기 쉬운 easy to manage. ぎょする

**어구**(漁具) fishing gear; fishing implements 《총칭》fishing tackle. ぎぐ

**어구**(漁區) a fishing place[area]; a fishing-ground[district]; a fishing-bank. ぎょく

**어구수하다** (be) tasty; juicy; palatable; dainty; good 《말씨가》pleasing; delightful/그의 말투는 ~ He speaks in a tactful[pleasing] manner/어구수한 음식 a tasty dish. みばえがよくてうまい

**어굴**(語屈) being argued down to silence; being silenced in an argument/~하다 be at a loss for an answer; be put to silence. ことばがつまること

**어귀** an entrance; a way in; an ingress; the mouth; an approach (to *a tunnel*); an entry 〈미〉.

**어귀**(語句) phrases; words and phrases/~의 용법 the use of words and phrases; phraseology. ごく

**어귀어귀** ravenously; voraciously; greedily/~ 먹다 eat ravenously; eat away with a savage appetite. ばくばく

**어귀차다** (be) strong; firm; strong-minded. いしがけんだ

**어그러지다** 《빗나가다》be put out of joint; be twisted; deviate[swerve] from 《붙일치하다》be contrary to; conflict with 《사이가》become estranged from; go badly /법에 ~ be against law/기대에 어그러지지 않게 노력하겠읍니다 I will do my best to act up to your expectation. くいちがう

**어근**(語根) the root[radical] of a word; an etymon(*pl*. ~s, ·ma). ごこん

**어근버근** not fitting into each other pr-

**어금니** a grinder; a back tooth; a molar [tooth]. きゅうし

**어금지금하다** be rather even; be much alike; be of little difference; be much the same／모두 ～ They are much the same., There is little difference between them. たいさがない

**어긋나다** ①(엇갈리다) cross each other; wedge into each other ②(길이) cross [pass] each other; miss each other on the road／길에 어긋나서 그를 못 만났다 We took different paths, so I missed him. ③(빗나가다) go wrong with; go amiss／예상이 ～ guess wrong ④(삐 위가) be dislocated. くいちがう

**어긋매끼다** stack[insert] crisscross. こうさせる

**어긋물리다** fit securely; put in gear; dovetail／어긋물린 톱니바퀴 a skew gear. くみあわせる

**어긋버긋하다** (교차하다) cross each other (어긋나다) go crisscross with; be in discord with; be contrary to; (be) bose; uneven. たがいちがいだ

**어긋하다** be a bit out of joint; be [a bit] off. たがいちがいだ

**어기**(漁期) a fishing season. ぎょき

**어기다** go against; act[offend] against; run counter (to); (위반하다) break; violate; transgress／신임을 어기지 않겠다 I will try to be worthy of your trust. まもらない

**어기대다** disobey; oppose; go against; be insubordinate to／어기대지 말고 하라는 대로 해라 Don't talk back, just do what you are told.

**어기뚱하다** (be) haughty and insolent; audacious; inordinate; impertinent; pert; saucy (허슨하다) be a bit loose. ずうずうしい

**어기어지다** (틀려지다) be violated; be contrary to; depart from (길·가르침 따위에) deviate(swerve) from. くいちがう

**어기적거리다** totter; waddle; walk listlessly; trudge along; shuffle along. よたよたあるく

**어기중하다**(於其中—) (be) [near the] middle; medium; average; mediocre.

**어기차다** be sturdy[courageous]／어기찬 아이 a headstrong child. がんきょうだ

**어김** a miss; failure／월말까지는 ～없이 그 돈을 주겠다 You shall have the money without fail by the end of the month.

**어눌**(語訥) ～하다 be slow of speech; stammer; stutter. ことばをどもること

**어느** ①(한) a; one; a certain; some／～ 한 가지 일에 전념해라 Devote yourself to some one subject. ②(어떤) which; what (모든) every (어느 것이나) any (부정) none. どの

**어느것** which; any／～이든지 whichever; any／～이나 (둘 중에서) either; any; every (부정) neither／～이나 하나 either… or／～도 …하지 않다 neither…nor….

**어느 겨를에** in what spare moments; when with so little time to spare. いつのまに

**어느때** when; [at] what time; what hour; how soon (어느 때나) any time.

**어느덧** before one is aware; unawares; unnoticed. いつのまに

**어느새** before one is aware; unnoticed; without *one's* knowledge／겨울 방학도 ～ 지나가 버렸다 The winter vacation has passed all too soon. いつのまに

**어느 정도**(一程度) to some degree; to a certain extent; somewhat; more or less／사나운 폭풍우도 ～ 가라앉았다 The violence of the storm lulled to some extent. どのくらい

**어느 쪽** (의문) which (무엇이든) whichever (선택) either… or; neither…nor (두쪽 다) both; either; neither(부정); (방향) which direction[side]／～이든 간에 in either case; either way／～도 소용없다 Neither will answer my purpose／～이나 다 결석이다 Both are absent.

**어느 틈** in so little t.me; in no time [at all]; so soon; quickly; already. いつのま

**어따** Here!, Hey! まあ

**어떠하다** (be) how ⇒어떻다. どうだ

**어떠한** what ⇒어떤.

**어떤** ⇒별항 참조(page 1598). どんな

**어떻게** how／～보아도 to all appearance; in every respect／～ 해서라도 by all[any] means; at any cost／[이 편지를] ～할까요 What shall I do [with this letter]? ／나는 ～하면 좋을지 모른다 I am at a loss what to do. どのように

**어떻게 되다** turn out somehow or other; be managed.

**어떻게 하다** take some measure; do somehow; manage somehow; manage to do／어떻게 해서든지 도와 주어야 한다 Something must be done to help him.

**어떻다** ①how; what／어떠하십니까 How are you? ②(권하면서) 잉 어떻습니까 산책이나 할까요 What do you say to a walk? ③somehow／요즘 날씨는 어떻다고 말할 수 없다 There is no telling about the weather nowadays. どうだ

**어떻든지** (좌우간) at any rate; anyhow; at all events; be that as it may (젖혀 놓고) to say nothing of.

**어떻씨** adjective ⇒형용사. けいようし

**어두움** darkness ⇒어둠. くらさ

**어두 육미**(魚頭肉尾) The most delicious part of fish is [found] in the head and the best part of flesh in the tail.

**어두커니** in the morning twilight.

**어두컴컴하다** (be) dim; darkling; dusk; gloomy／이 방은 ～ This room is poorly

**어둑어둑** ~하다 (be) dim; gloomy; dusk.

**어둑하다** be a bit dark; get dark 《어수룩하다》 (be) simple; simple-hearted.

**어둔하다(語鈍―)** (be) slow of speech (be) tongue-tied. ことばがのろい

**어둠** darkness; [the] dark; dimness 《저녁 어둠》 dusk; twilight; the shades of evening; night／~의 dark／~ 속을 더듬어 가다 grope one's way in the dark. くらさ

**어둠침침하다** (be) obscure; somber; dark; gloomy; dim／전등이 ~ The electric light is dim. くらくてうっとうしい

**어둡다** ①(암흑이다)(be) dark 《희미하다》 dim 《음침하다》 gloomy／그에게는 어두운 일면이 있다 He has a gloomy turn of mind. ②(무지하다) know but little of; be badly-[ill-]informed of／저 사람은 법률에 ~ His knowledge of law is very limited. くらい

**어득삐득** ①(불손) improperly; imprudently／~하다 (be) improper; imprudent ②(줄이) sinuously zigzagging／~하다 (be) sinuous zigzag. だらしなく

**어디**¹ ⇒별항 참조 (page 1599). どこ

**어디**² well; now; well now; let me see／~ 영어 한번 해 보아라 Well now, let me hear you speak some English.／~ 산보나 할까 Let's see now, shall we take a walk?

**어딘가, 어딘지** somehow; in some way; without knowing why／~ 이상하다 Somehow, it seems strange.

**어란(魚卵)** fish eggs; spawn. ぎょらん

**어람(御覽)** his majesty's inspection; royal inspection. ごらん

**어런더런** at a dizzy rate; with bewildering rapidity. ごみごみ

**어렵쇼** Oh!, Heavens!, My goodness!, I say!, Gee!《미·속》／~ 벌써 1시네 Why! It is one. いけない

**어레미** a coarse sieve; a riddle; a bolter／~질을 하다 sieve. ふるい

**어려워하다** feel constrained; be[fee] ill at ease; have scruples about (doing); be afraid[shy] (of)／어려워하지 말고 편히 앉으시오 Make yourself at home and sit comfortably.

**어려무던하다** (be) quite satisfactory; nice; be free of faults. おとなしい

**어련하다** (be) certain; sure／그가 하니 어련하랴 We may trust him.

**어련히** naturally; certainly; undoubtedly; in the natural course of events.／내버려 둬, ~ 잘 알아서 할라구 Let him alone, he will take care of himself.

**어렴성** reserve; deference; modesty／그의 태도와 말은 ~이 너무 없다 His manners and speech are too free／~없는 친구 a candid friend; a friend on frank terms. きたん

**어렴풋이** dimly; faintly; vaguely; indistinctly／피리 소리가 ~ 들렸다 There came to my ears the distant music of a flute.

**어렴풋하다** (be) dim; hazy; indistinct; faint; misty 《애매하다》 vague／어렴풋한 기억 a dim memory. ぼうっとしている

**어렵(漁獵)** fishing; fishery／~하다 fish. ぎょりょう

**어렵게** in a hard[a difficult, an awkward] way.

**어렵다** ①(곤란·난해하다) (be) hard; difficult; hardly possible (…할 수 없다) cannot; be unable to (…을 주저하다) hesitate (to do)／어려운 입장에 있다 be in a difficult[delicate] situation／설명하기 ~ It is hard to explain[of explanation]. ②(가난하다)(be) poor; needy; indigent; destitute／어려운 집안에 태어나다 be born poor; be born of[in] a poor family／살림이 ~ be badly off. むずかしい

**어령칙하다** (be) faint; dim; vague／어령칙히 faintly; dimly／기억이 ~ have a vague memory. ぼうっとしている

**어로(漁撈)** fishing; fishery／~하다 fish ／~법 the art of fishing; halieutics／~장 a piscary; a fishing place. ぎょろう

**어로 불변(魚魯不辨)** ignorance; illiteracy.

**어록(語錄)** analects; sayings. ごろく

**어뢰(魚雷)** a torpedo／~정(艇)a torpedo boat (flotilla)／~를 발사하다 discharge [fire] a torpedo. ぎょらい

**어룡(魚龍)** (고생물) an ichthyosaur.

**어루꾀다** wheedle; coax; lure[seduce] with flattery.

**어루더듬다** grope; fumble (in the darkness) for; feel about for.

**어루러기** 【의】leucoderma; a white macula; albinism. なまず

**어루만지다** ①(문지르다) stroke; pass one's hand over ②(위무하다) pacify; soothe; appease. なでる

**어루쇠** an iron mirror. てっせいのかがみ

**어룰** stammering; stuttering. どもること

**어룽** spots; dapples; mottles／~지다 be mottled. はんてんのもの

**어룽더룽하다** (be) spotted; dappled; variegated. まだらだ

**어류(魚類)** fishes; the finny tribe／~학 ichthyology／~학자 an ichthyologist／~지(誌) ichthyography. ぎょるい

**어르다** amuse; humour; coax／우는 어린 애를 ~ humor a crying baby. あやす

**어르신네** (남의 아버지) your esteemed father; your[his] father 《존칭》 an esteemed elder; sir; you.

**어른** ①(성인) a man; an adult; a grown-up [person]; grown-ups; a full-grown man／~답지 않다 be childish[puerile] ②(웃사람) one's senior 《연장자》 one's elders; the head／집안의 ~ the head of a family. おとな

**어른거리다** 《불빛이》 flicker; flit 《눈이》 be dazzled 《마음에》 haunt (one)／눈앞에 ~ flit before one's eye. ちらつく

**어른스럽다** 《온순하다》 (be) gentle; mild; m-

어른어른 (의젓하다)(be) well-behaved[-mannered]; 《깜찍하다》(be) precocious/어른스럽게 굴다 behave like[assume an air of] a grown-up (*person*).

어른어른 coming in and out of sight; flickering; glimmering; wavering. ちらちら

어름 ①《가운데》the middle; halfway ②《끝 닿은 데》a point of contact. なかば

어름거리다 ①《언행을》equivocate; prevaricate; quibble/어름어름 equivocally; quibblingly ②《일을》scamp[fudge] (*one's work*)/어름어름 cursorily; at random; inattentively.

어리¹ 《전》a door-frame[-case]; a frame.

어리² 《병아리의》a hencoop; a wicker cage for chicks/~ 장사 poultry peddling/~전 a poultry store. おり

어리광 playing the baby/~부리다 behave like a spoilt child; play the baby. あまったれること

어리굴젓 oysters pickled with red pepper. かきのしおから

어리눅다 pretend to be foolish[stupid]. おろかなふりをする

어리다¹ 《유소하다》(be) young; juvenile; youthful《유치하다》(be) childish; infant 《미숙하다》(be) green; inexperienced/나이는 어리지만 생각하는 것은 어른이다 have an old head on young shoulders. おさない

어리다² ①《눈물이》be streaming[suffused] with tears/슬픈 소식을 읽고 그 여자의 눈에 눈물이 어렸다 Her eyes moistened as she read the sad news. ②《엉기다》coagulate; curdle; congeal.

어리다³ 《눈이》be dazzled; be glared; be blinded/강한 빛 때문에 눈이 어리었다 The strong light dazzles my eyes. うるむ

어리대다 loiter under *one's* nose. ぶらつく

어리둥절하다 be disconcerted; become confused; be at a loss 《당황하다》lose *one's* presence of mind/처음으로 연단에 서면 어리둥절해진다 The inexperienced feel nervous on the platform. ぼうっとなる

어리벙벙하다 be confounded; be disconcerted; bewildered. ぼうっとなる

어리보기 a stupid person; a blockhead; a coward; a dimwit. おろかなひと

어리석다 (be) foolish; silly; dull; stupid/어리석은 사람 a foolish person; a fool/어리석은 짓 a foolish act; a folly. おろかだ

어리숭하다 ①《사람이》look stupid[foolish]; be dull-witted; be dull ②《사물이》(be) indistinguishable; vague; obscure. はっきりしない

어리어리하다 (be) all dim[hazy, indistinct, vague]; be all a little foolish [-looking]. はっきりしない

어리전(一廛) a poultry shop.

어리치다 swoon; faint.

어리칙칙하다 (be) so impudent as to pretend to be a fool; saucy and wily. ずうずうしい

어린것 a little one; a young one; a youngster; a kid/집에 ~이 많다 have a lot of kids [in one's family]. おさないもの

어린녀석 a little chap; a brat; an urchin.

어린년 a little girl; a little wench.

어린애 a child(*pl.*·ren); a little one; youngster; an infant; a baby; a kid 《속》~ 같은 소리를 하다 talk like a child; say childish things/~가 생기다 be pregnant [with child]/그는 아직도 ~다 He is a mere child. おさないこ

어린이 children; infants 《미성년자》minors/~ 날 Children's Day/~ 시절에 익힌 것은 평생 잊혀지지 않는다 What is learned in the cradle is carried to the grave. ようじ

어림 a rough guess; an estimate/이렇게 되면 당초의 ~과는 크게 틀린다 This is very much different from the original estimate. しんざん

어림없다 《능력이》(be) beyond (*one*); 《상상도 못하다》beyond the stretch of imagination 《불가능》impossible/그것은 내 힘으로는 어림도 없다 It is quite beyond me. とんでもない

어림장이 a blockhead; a simpleton; a dunce. ていけんのないひと

어림짐작 a rough-and-ready guess; guesswork; an estimate/~으로 잘 맞추다 make[give] a random guess; talk at random. がいりゃくのみつもり

어릿거리다 be in a daze; be dull[absentminded]; be dazed. ぐずぐずする

어릿광대 a comic actor; a clown.

어마 《놀람》My!; oh!; Good Heaven[s]!/~ 참 많이 컸구나 Oh my! What a big boy you've grown to be! まあ

어마나 《놀람》Oh!, Why!, Dear me!/~ 가엾어라 what a pity! あ, あっ

어마어마하다 《당당하다》(be) dignified; grand; magnificent 《과장적》(be) ostentatious; pompous. ものものしい

어망(魚網) a fish[ing] net 《끄는 것》a drag net 《투망》a casting-net. ぎょもう

어머니 ①《모친》a mother; *one's* real mother《생모》/~의 mother's; maternal/~의 사랑 mother's love[affection]/~날 Mother's Day/~다운[같은] motherly; maternal ②《사물의 근본》cause; motive/필요는 발명의 ~ Necessity is the mother of invention. はは

어멈 《하인》a housemaid; an amah; a maidservant 《어머니》a mother.

어명(御名) the Emperor's name. ぎょめい

어명(御命) a royal command[mandate]; an order from the king/~을 내리다 issue a royal command. おうのめいれい

어물(魚物) dried fish; stockfish/~전 a dried-fish shop. ひもの

어물거리다 equivocate; prevaricate.

**어물다** (be) immature; undeveloped/어물어 빠졌다 be utterly immature.

**어물어물** equivocally; evasively; carelessly; slowly; lazily/~하다가는 음악회에 늦겠다 Hurry up or, you'll be late for the concert.

**어물쩨거리다** equivocate; skimp; do slapdash/태도를 ~ maintain an uncertain attitude (*toward*).

**어미** ①(동물의) a mother animal/~ 고양이 a mother cat/~새 a parent[mother] bird ②(어머니) a mother.

**어미**(語尾) the ending of a word (접미어) a suffix/~ 변화 inflection; declension; conjugation.

**어민**(漁民) fishermen; fisherfolk.

**어빡자빡** irregularly; unmethodically; disorderly.

**어버이** parents; father and mother/~ 슬하에 있다 be under *one*'s parental roof/~를 공경하다 be respectful towards *one*'s parents.

**어벌쩡하다** (be) evasive; mystify; hoodwink; distract attention.

**어법**(語法) diction; phraseology; wording (문법) grammar/~에 어긋나다 make a grammar slip/~ 위반 a breach of syntax.

**어부**(漁夫) a fisher[man]/~지리(之利)를 얻다 fish in troubled water.

**어뿔싸** Alas!, woe!

**어불성설**(語不成說) lack of logic; illogants/~이다 (*one's argument*) do not hold water; lack logic.

**어비**(魚肥) fish manure[fertilizer].

**어사**(語辭) a word; a term; a phrase; language.

**어사**(御史) a Royal secret inspector travelling incognito.

**어사리** net-fishing/~하다 net (*fish*).

**어살** a weir; a wooden fence in the water to trap fish.

**어상**(一商) (소장수) a cattle dealer.

**어상반**(於相半) likeness; similarity; resemblance/~하다 be much like; be almost simiar; be nearly alike.

**어새**(御璽) the Imperial Seal; the Seal of the Emperor.

**어색**(語塞) ~하다 ①(말이 막히다) be stuck for a word; stumble over a word; (be) silenced ②(열쩍다) feel awkward; feel [be] ill at ease/여자와 같이 있기가 ~하다 feel ill at ease in the presence of ladies ③(서투르다) clumsy; crude/어색한 웃음을 하는 a forced smile.

**어서** ①(빨리) quick[ly]; fast; promptly; rapidly; without delay/~ 등불을 가져오너라 Bring a light quickly. ②(환영)[if you] please/~ 들어오십시오 Come in, please.

**어석거리다** crunch; champ; munch/사과를 ~ munch (*at*) an apple.

**어선**(漁船) a fishing-[fisher-]boat/~대(隊) a fishing fleet.

**어설프다** ①(페이지 않다)(be) coarse; rough; loose ②(탐탁찮다)(be) no good; clumsy (부주의하다) (be) careless; negligent/어설프게 하는 일이 잘될 리 없다 A half measure is always a failure.

**어섯** a bit part (모자라는) less than completely.

**어성**(語聲) [the sound of] the voice/~을 크게 하지 말라 Don't talk so loudly.

**어세**(語勢) emphasis; stress/~를 높이다 lay stress (on *a word*).

**어수룩하다** (be) naive; unsophisticated; simple/그 여자는 어수룩하지 않았다고 본다 I suppose she is sophisticated.

**어수선산란하다**(一散亂—) (be) much confused; in a muddle; in utter confus-

---

# 어 떤

①(더하한·어떠한) what kind[sort] of; what …like/~ 이유로 why; for what reason; what for/~ 까닭인지 somehow; for some reason or other/~ 투로 how; in what way/~ 사람인가 What is he like?, What sort of a man is he?/~ 사람이라도 그것을 알고 있다 Anybody knows that./최근에 ~ 영화를 보았읍니까 What movie have you seen lately?/~ 일이 있더라도 whatever may happen; under any circumstances/소설이란 ~ 것인가 What is a novel like?

②(어떤 …라도) every; any; no…/~ 사람이라도 anybody; everybody; any [every] person; nobody(부정); (어떤 사접 아래서도) under[in] any circumstances (결코(…않다))(*not*) for all the world; on no account; under no condition/나는 ~ 일이라도 개의치 않는다 I don't mind any work./~ 짓을 해서라도 at all costs; at any cost; at all hazards; by any means/~ 도 담배도 일체 피우지 않는다 He never uses tobacco in any form/~ 사정이 있더라도 약속은 지켜야 한다 You must keep your promise under any circumstances./너 때문이라면 ~ 일이라도 한다 I will do anything I can for you[your sake].

③a certain; some/~ 날 one day/~ 사람 a certain person; someone; a Mr. So-and-so(모씨)/ ~의 미로는 in a sense; in a way; in a manner/외출하셨을 때 ~ 분이 찾아오셨읍니다 Some one came to see you while you were out.

**어수선하다** ion. まったくみだれている
**어수선하다** (be) disorderly; confused/어수선하게 in disorder[confusion]/어수선해지다 fall into disorder[confusion]; get confused. みだれている
**어순(語順)** 〖언〗 word order.
**어숭그러하다** 《일이》turn out pretty good [favorable, satisfactory smooth, well] 《사람이 주어》be easy to get along with. まあよろしい
**어스러기** a distorted part of a seam.
**어스러지다** ①《말·풍채가》become[get] abnormal ②《어슷하게 되다》be distorted/그 사람은 좀 어스러진 성품이다 He is a queer sort of fellow. せいじょうでない
**어스럭송아지** a big[hefty] calf. おおきくなったこうし
**어스레하다** (be) dusky; dim; gloomy; murky/어스레한 저녁 a dusky evening. ほのぐらい
**어스름** dusk/~ 속에서 독서하다 read in the twilight[dim light].
**어슬렁거리다** walk at a leisurely pace 《만보》 stroll[ramble] about/어슬렁어슬렁 slowly; lazily.
**어슬하다** (be) dusky.
**어슴새벽** dawn; daybreak/~부터 일하다 work from early dawn. みめい
**어슴푸레하다** (be) dim; vague; indistinct; misty; hazy. ぼうっとしている
**어슷거리다** drag one's feet listlessly. よぼよぼとあるく
**어슷비슷하다** (be) much the same; somewhat alike; be of a sort/그 점에 있어서는 양자가 ~ There is little to choose between the two in that respect.
**어슷하다** (be) slanting; oblique/어슷하게 on the slant/어슷하게 자르다 cut diagonally. かたむいている
**어시장(魚市場)** a fish market.
**어아리나무** a golden-bell; Forsythia kareana(학명).
**어안이 벙벙하다** be dumbfounded; be struck dumb; be amazed; be dazed/그 대답에 어안이 벙벙했다 I was dumbfounded by the answer. あぜんとする
**어어** Oh-oh! ⇨아아. おー
**어언간(於焉間)** before one knows[is aware]; unawares; unnoticed; in no time at all/~ 겨울이 왔다 Winter has stolen upon us. いつのまに
**어업(漁業)** fishery; fishing industry/원양[근해] ~ deep-sea[coast] fishery/~조합 a fishing guild. ぎょぎょう
**어여머리** a [peri]wig worn by women as a part of ceremonial costume.
**어여차** Heave-ho!, Yo-heave-ho! よいしょ
**어연간하다** (be) moderate; temperate; tolerable. てきとうだ
**어연번듯하다** be honest and respectable to all appearances. どうどうとしている
**어엿하다** (be) dignified; grand; imposing; magnificent/어엿하게 in a dignified manner. どうどうとしている

**어용(御用)** government service/~학자 a government patronized scholar/~ 신문 a subsidized organ of the Cabinet; a government organ. ごよう
**어우르다** put together; unite; combine; connect; join together. あわせる
**어울리다** ①《조화하다》match; suit; become; harmonize with; be fit; look well[nice]/어울리지 않는 결혼 an ill-assorted marriage ②《참가하다》join; go over to; associate/어울리는 친구를 보면 어떤 사람인가를 안다 A man is known by company he keeps. ちょうわする
**어웅하다** (be) hollow; empty; vacant/어웅한 눈 hollow eyes. うつろだ
**어원(語源)** the derivation of a word; etymology/~학 etymology/~을 조사하다 trace a word to its origin. ごげん
**어유(魚油)** fish oil. ぎょゆ
**어육(魚肉)** 《생선》fish 《생선과 수육》 fish and flesh/~을 많이 먹다 eat much fish and meat. ぎょにく
**어음** 〖경〗 a draft; a bill; a note/~ 발행[수취]인 the drawer[payee] of bill/약속 ~ a promissory note/~이 만기가 되다 The bill falls due. てがた
**어음(語音)** pronunciation; the sound of a word. ごおん
**어의(語義)** the meaning of a word/일반적인 ~로는 in the common acceptation of the word. ごぎ
**어이¹** 《짐승의 어미》a mother animal/~새끼 a mother and her cubs[puppies].
**어이²** 《어찌》why; how/당신이 모르는데 내가 ~ 알겠소 How should I know if you do not. どうして
**어이³** 《부를 때》Hey!/~ 기다려 Hey, wait!
**어이구** 《놀람》Oh!, Wow! うん. いたい
**어이딸** mother and daughter.
**어이새끼** mother and litter.
**어이아들** mother and son.
**어이어이** Alas!, Woe!
**어이없다** (be) amazing; surprising; absurd; egregious/어이없어하다 be taken aback; be dumbfounded; be amazed at 《전멸어지다》be disgusted at[with]. どうしようもない
**어일싸** 《경별》Hum!, Hah! へえーっ
**어장(漁場)** fishing grounds; fishing place. ぎょじょう
**어째[서]** why; for what reason; how it is that/~ 그가 자살했을까 Why did he kill himself/~ 그러냐 How so? どうして
**어쨌든** anyhow; anyway; at any rate; in any case[event]. どうあろうとも
**어저께** yesterday 어제. きのう
**어저귀** 〖식〗 an Indian mallow. いちび
**어쩌다가** accidentally; casually; by chance/~ 그를 길에서 만났다 I met him by accident on the street. いがいに
**어쩌면** ①《추측》possibly; perhaps; likely/~ 그가 옳을지도 모른다 He is perhaps[probably] right. ②《감탄》how; what/~ 사람이 저럴까 How can he be

**어적거리다** munch; crunch; champ/어적어적 with a munching. ぼりぼりする

**어전**(御前) the presence (of *a king*).

**어쩐지** ①(웬일인지) somehow; without knowing why/~ 무섭게 느껴지다 have an unaccountable fear ②(그래서) so; [it is] no wonder [that]/~ 기쁜 얼굴을 하고 있더라 That explains his happy look. どうしたのか

**어정거리다** walk at a leisurely pace (만보) stroll[ramble] about; take a stroll; saunter. あるきめぐる

**어정뱅이** ①(갑자기 잘 된 사람) a person suddenly elevated [to wealth or position] ②(어정거리는 사람) a negligent[sloppy] person. なまけもの

**어정버정** sauntering; rambling/~ 걷다 take a stroll; ramble about. のらくら

**어정쩡하다** (be) doubtful; dubious; suspicious; disputable (애매하다) evasive; vague (확실잖음) not sure. いかがわしい

**어제** yesterday/그를 만난 것은 바로 ~다 It was only yesterday that I met him. /어젯밤 last night. きのう

**어제**(御製) a king's ode[poem]. ぎょせい

**어조**(語調) a tone; a key; euphony; accent (표현) a turn of expression/그는 아주 진지한 ~로 말했다 His tone was very earnest. ごちょう

**어조사**(語助辭) 〖언〗 a particle in classical Chinese. かんぶんのじょし

**어족**(語族) 〖언〗 a family of language; related language /우랄 알타이~ the Ural Altaic language family. ごぞく

**어족**(魚族) fishes; the finny tribe; Pisces. ぎょぞく

**어좌**(御座) the Royal throne[seat]; the King's chair. ござ

**어줍다** (언동이) (be) dull; inanimate (저리다) become numb; be asleep. にぶい

**어쭙지않다** (be) ridiculous; contemptible; pert; frisky; conceited. おかしい

**어중간**(於中間) halfway; the middle/영동은 서울과 부산의 ~에 있다 *Yungdong* lies halfway between *Seoul* and *Busan*. どっちつかず

**어중되다** (be) excessive; immoderate; undue; be not perfectly fit.

**어중이떠중이** [anybody and] everybody; all the world and his wife; all sorts and conditions of men. やじうま

**어찌** ①(방법) how; in what way; by what means/~ 해서 why/~ 해서든지 by all means; in any way/~ 할 수 없이 unavoidably; inevitably/이 일을 ~하나 What shall I do? ②⇒어찌나. どうして

**어지간하다** (상당·우연만하다) (be) fair; passable; considerable (넉넉하다) enough; sufficient/어지간히 fairly; passably; considerably. かなりよい

# 어디

①(의문) where; what place/~가 아프냐 Where do you feel the pain?/여기가 어딥니까 Where are we now?/~ 사십니까 Where do you live?

②¶ ~에도 anywhere (부정) [not] anywhere; nowhere/ ~에 가도 wherever [no matter where] you [may] go/나는 ~에도 안 갑니다 I am not going anywhere. /~든지 마찬가지다 Everywhere you go, you will find the same thing. /~나 휴일을 즐기는 사람들로 붐볐다 There were lots of holiday-makers everywhere/~든지 가도 좋다 you may go anywhere.

③¶ ~에서 from where/ ~에서인지 모르게 나타나다 appear from nowhere/~ 에서 왔읍니까 Where have you come from?, Where do you come[are you] from?(출신지).

④¶ ~까지 how far; to what extent (어느 정도)/요전번에는 ~까지 했읍니까 (수업에서) How far did we go last time?, Where were we last time?/~까지 고집을 부리련 속이 후련하겠느냐 How persistent must you be?

⑤¶ ~까지나 endlessly(끝없이); to the end[last](최후까지); completely; thoroughly(완전히); persistently(고집 세게); stubbornly/논쟁은 ~까지나 계속되었다 The dispute lasted endlessly., There was no end to the dispute. /그 여자는 ~까지나 숙녀다 She is every inch a lady. /그는 ~까지나 자기 의견을 고집했다 He persisted in his opinion to the bitter end. /나는 ~까지나 당신을 돕겠소 I will stand by you to the last[through thick and thin].

⑥¶ ~나[든지] anywhere at all/서울이라면 ~든지 알고 있다 I know every inch of *Seoul*.

⑦¶ ~엔가 somewhere; anywhere(의문문에)/주말에 ~엔가 가셨나요 Did you go anywhere over the weekend?/그는 이 근처 ~엔가 살고 있다 He lives somewhere near[about] here. / ~엔가 수상한 점이 있어 There's something shady about him. /~엔가에서 본 사람이다 I remember seeing him somewere.

⑧¶ 어딘가[의] some; any (의문문에서)/그는 어딘가 미국의 대학에서 공부한 사람이다 He went to school at some university in America

**어찌나** too; so／~ 기쁜지 in the excess of one's joy. どんなにか

**어지럼** dizziness; giddiness; loss of equilibrium; vertigo(pl. ~s, -tiginess). めまい

**어지럽다** ①(눈·머리가) be dizzy; feel giddy; swim／어지럽게 변천하는 세상 the giddy whirl of modern life; the dizzy[dazing] bustle of life ②(무질서하다) be troubled[turbulent, disturbed]; be in disorder／어지러운 세상 troubled [troublous] times／방이 ~ The room is in wild disorder. みだれている

**어지르다** litter (with); disarrange; put out of order[in disorder]／이 방은 몹시 어질러져 있다 This room is in wild disorder. みだす

**어지빠르다** be too big or little to be right; be not what is wanted; (be) unsuitable. どっちつかずだ

**어찌씨** an adverb ⇨부사. ふくし

**-어지이다** (기원) wish[desire] (it) to happen／뜻이 하늘에서 이룬 것같이 땅에서도 이루~ Thy will be done on Earth as it is in Heaven. 一ならんことを

**어지자지** a hermaphrodite; an epicene person／~의 hermaphroditic. ちゅうせいのにんげん

**어진(御眞)** the portrait of a king.

**어질다** (be) merciful; generous; kindhearted; benevolent; humane／어진 마음 benevolence. ぜんりょうだ

**어질어질, 어쩔어쩔** dizzily; dazedly; giddily／~하다 be dizzy; dazing; giddy ／수면 부족 때문인지 ~하다 My head swims, perhaps from lack of sleep.

**어찔하다** be dizzy; feel giddy; have vertig. あたまがくらっとする

**어차피(於此彼)** anyhow; anyway; in any [either] case; at any rate／자네는 ~ 실망할 걸세 Whatever you may choose, you will be disappointed. どっちにしても

**어처구니** a very big person[thing]; a real[regular] monster; a giant[whale]. きょだいなひと

**어처구니없다** (be) amazing; surprising; absurd; egregious／어처구니없어하다 be amazed at; be disgusted at[with](정말 어처다). とんでもない

**어촌(漁村)** a fishing village[hamlet, settlement]; a sea village. ぎょそん

**어치** 【조】 a jay; *Garrulus glandarius*(학명).

**-어치** worth／과자를 100원~ 사다 buy one hundred won worth of cakes.

**어치렁거리다** trudge[trod, jog] along／어치렁어치렁 trudgingly; totteringly. のそのそあるく

**어칠거리다** toddle; stagger; saunter.

**어투(語套)** a way[habit] of saying; one's way of talking. ことばのくせ

**어폐(語弊)** a faulty[misleading] expression／~가 있다 be misleading; be liable to be misunderstood／이 말은 ~가 있다 The word is misleading. ごへい

**어포(魚脯)** dried slices of fish seasoned with spices.

**어필(御筆)** a king's handwriting; the writing of a king. おうのひっせき

**어학(語學)** language study; linguistics／~의 linguistic／~자 a linguist／~에 소질이 있다 have a talent for learning languages. ごがく

**어항(魚缸)** a fish basin; a globe (유리제의); a glass fish bowl. きんぎょばち

**어항(漁港)** a fishing port. ぎょこう

**어허** oh; well; indeed; I see／~ 참 잘못했군 Bless my soul! お一. あ一

**어험** hem!, ahem! えへん

**어형(語形)** 【언】 the form[shape] of a word; a [language] form／~ 변화 conjugation. ごけい

**어화(漁火)** a fishing fire; a fisherman's fire [to lure fishes]. ぎょか

**어회(魚膾)** slices of raw fish; sliced[minced] raw fish／~를 만들다 slice raw fish. ぎょかい

**어획(漁獲)** a catch／이 근해에서는 고등어의 ~이 많다 Large quantities of mackerel are caught off this coast.／~기 fishing season. ぎょかく

**어휘(御諱)** the king's name. おうのな

**어휘(語彙)** a vocabulary; a glossary; one's stock of words／~집 a word-book; a vocabulary／이 사전은 ~가 많다 This dictionary includes an extensive vocabulary. ごい

**억(億)** a[one] hundred million／10~ a milliard(영); a billion(미). おく

**억강 부약(抑強扶弱)** coercing the strong and helping the week／~하다 coerce the strong and help the weak.

**억겁(億劫)** countless ages [of this world and the future]. おっこう

**억견(臆見)** a conjecture; a guess; speculation; a supposition. おっけん

**억누르다** 《진압하다》 suppress 《제지하다》 repress; restrain; prevent; control 《억제하다》 master; hold; stay; check; keep under; curb 《압박하다》 oppress／눈물을 ~ repress[keep back, force back] one's tears. あっぱくする

**억단(臆斷)** a conjecture; a supposition; a surmise; a guess [work]; an inference; a hasty conclusion／~하다 conjecture; suppose; infer／실정을 살펴보지도 않고 ~하다 pass judgment without careful inquiry into the circumstances. おくだん

**억류(抑留)** detention; internment／~하다 detain[keep] by force; seize; hold; apprehend／~자 a detainer; an internee. よくりゅう

**억만(億萬)** 【억】 a hundred million 《무수한》 myriads; countless numbers／~의 countless; numberless／~년 countless years／~ 장자 a billionaire. おく

**억매(抑賣)** forcing a sale／~하다 force

**억매(抑買)** forced purchase/~하다 buy [up] by force. おさえつけてかうこと

**억매흥정(抑賣一)** a forced trade; forced transaction/물건을 ~으로 사다 be forced to buy a thing.

**억병** hard[excessive, heavy] drinking/~같이 마시다 drink heavily/그는 ~으로 취해 돌아왔다 He came home dead drunk.

**억설(臆說)** ①(억측) a conjecture; a surmise; speculation/~하다 [make a] conjecture; speculate (about) ②(억지) distortion; a self-styled explanation/~하다 strain (the interpretation); force the meaning. おくせつ

**억세다** ①(세차다) (be) stubborn; dogged; strong; stiff; unbending; tenacious/억센 경상도 사투리 broad Kyongsangdo dialect ②(뻣뻣하다) (be) tough; hard; stiff/이 배추는 ~ This is a tough cabbage. かたい

**억수** a pouring[heavy, torrential, drenching, downpour of] rain[shower]; downpour(미)/비가 ~같이 내린다 It rains cats and dogs. ごうう

**억수 장마** a long spell of heavy rain.

**억압(抑壓)** check; restraint; suppression; pressure/ ~하다 check; restrain; suppress; hold (one) down/언론의 자유를 ~하다 repress freedom of speech. よくあつ

**억양(抑揚)** (음조의) intonation; modulation; áccent/~있는 modulated; intoned/~을 붙이다 modulate; intone/~ 부호 a circumflex. よくよう

**억울(抑鬱)** ①(원통함) regret; depression; mortification; chagrin ②(죄의 누명) distress/~하다 (be) distressing (사물이 주어) unjust (사람이 주어) distressed /~하게 죄를 입다 be falsely charged (with); be falsely accused (of) /~한 조처 unfair treatment. よくうつ

**억제(抑制)** control; restraint; suppression control/~하다 repress; suppress; 감정을 ~하다 suppress[smother] one's feelings. よくせい

**억조(億兆)** 의~ 창생 the [common] people; the multitude[masses]. おくちょう

**억지** (고집) obstinacy (궤변) sophistry /~센[스러운] obstinate; stubborn; self-willed; sophistic[al]/~부리다(쓰다) chop logic; insist obstinately (on); sophisticate.

**억지로** by force[compulsion]; forcibly; compulsorily; against one's will. むりに

**억지손** a strong measure; high-handedness/~으로 wilfully/~쓰다 take a strong measure; be high-handed with (a person). むりなやりかた

**억지춘향이** doing against one's will; compelling; compulsion; coercion; forcing. むりにすること

**억척** being unyielding; toughness; stiffness; stubbornness/~배기 a tough [stubborn] child/저렇게 ~스러운 사람은 처음이다 His obstinacy really beats me. かどに

**억측(臆測)** an inference; speculation; a supposition; a guess; a conjecture/~하다 suppose; guess; conjecture; surmise; speculate (upon). おくそく

**억탈(抑奪)** extortion; exaction/~하다 extort; exact; get by force. よくだつ

**억판** extremely strained circumstances; dire poverty; a bare living; indigence /사는 것이 ~이다 live in dire poverty. すっからかん

**억패듯** without mercy; relentlessly; threateningly (억지로) compulsorily.

**언감 생심(焉敢生心)** How dare you…?/ ~ 내 앞에서 그런 말을 하느냐 How dare you say such a thing in spite of my presence?

**언감히(焉敢一)** how; why. どうしてあえて

**언거번거하다** (be) talkative; garrulous.

**언걸** 9~먹다 suffer heavily being involved in another's affairs. とばっちり

**언구럭** honeyed words/~부리다 take(cajole, wheedle] (one) into. かんげん

**언급(言及)** ~하다 refer[allude] to (a matter); touch on/이 이상 ~하지 말라 Don't touch it any more. げんきゅう

**언니** an elder brother[sister]. あねさん

**언덕** a hill; a hillock; a height; a rising ground/가파른 언덕 a steep slope/~질 a sloping[an 、ascending, an uphill] road. おか

**언도(言渡)** a sentence; a judgement; a pronouncement/~하다 sentence; pronounce/사형 ~ a sentence of death/어제 그에게 판결 ~가 있었다 Judgement was passed[was pronounced] on him yesterday. いいわたし

**언동(言動)** speech and conduct/~을 삼가다 be careful[discreet] in one's speech and conduct[action]. げんどう

**언뜻** (별견) at a glance (별안간) suddenly; [all] of a sudden (우연히) by chance; by accident/울타리 사이로 그의 뒷모습이 ~ 보였다 The opening in the fence gave a glimpse of his back view. さっと

**언론(言論)** speech; discussion/~의 자유 freedom of speech/~계 the press/~기관 an organ of expression. げんろん

**언막이** an irrigation dam[barrage].

**언명(言明)** declaration; assertion/~하다 declare; affirm/사직을 ~하다 make definite statement of one's intended resignation. げんめい

**언문(諺文)** the Korean script; the Korean letters. げんぶん

**언문(言文)** the written and spoken language/~ 일치 the identity of the written and spoken language. げんぶん

**언변(言辯)** (연설) eloquence; fluency; speaking/~이 있는 사람 an eloquent speaker. はなしかた

**언사**(言辭) 《표현》 words; speech; language; expression/불손한 ~를 쓰다 use improper language. げんじ

**언설**(言說) a statement; a remark; views; utterances. げんせつ

**언성**(言聲) a tone [of voice]/~을 높이다 raise (one's voice)/그는 감정이 치밀어 ~이 높아졌다 His voice was getting thick with emotion. はなすこえ

**언약**(言約) one's word; a [verbal] promise; an oral agreement; a pledge; a vow/~하다 [make a verbal] promise; give one's wold; pledge [oneself]/그와 만날 ~을 하다 make an appointment to see him. ことばのやくそく

**언어**(言語) language; speech; words/그 풍경의 아름다움은 ~로 표현하기 어렵다 The beauty of the scenery beggars description. げんご

**언어 도단**(言語道斷) ~의 inexcusable; outrageous; abominable; absurd (터무니없는) preposterous/그의 행동은 ~이다 His conduct cannot be too severely criticized. ごんごどうだん

**언어학**(言語學) the science of language; linguistics/~적, ~상의 philological/ ~과 the department of linguistics/민족 ~ ethnolinguistics. げんごがく

**언어 행동**(言語行動) words and actions; speech and behavio[u]r/~을 삼가다 be careful in one's speech and behavior /감정을 ~에 나타내다 betray [one's emotions] in speech and action. げんこう

**언언 사사**(言言事事) words and works; speeches and actions.

**언짢다** (be) bad; feel bad/내 말을 언짢게 여기지 말라 Don't feel bad about what I said. きにいらない

**언재**(言才) oratorical talent; eloquence /~가 있다 have the gift of the gab; be eloquent. ことばのさいのう

**언쟁**(言爭) a dispute; a quarrel; an altercation/~하다 dispute; quarrel; altercate; have words (with)/~이 싸움으로 번졌다 They proceeded from words to blows.

**언저리** circumference; vicinity/강~ [the side of] a river.

**언제** when; [at] what time; what hour; how soon; any time/~부터 from what time; since when; how long/~ 출발합니까 When are you going to start?/ ~ 한번 만납시다 I should like to see more of you some time. いつ

**언제까지** how long; till when; by what time; how soon/~나 as long as one likes (영구히) for ever/이 행복이 ~나 계속되기를 빕니다 I wish this blessing would last forever[for ever].

**언제나** always; all the time (평소에) usually (습관적으로) habitually (…할 때마다) whenever; every time/그는 ~ 아침 산책을 한다 He is in the habit of going for a walk in the morning. いつも

**언제든지** 《어느 때라도》 [at] any time (항상) always; all the time; whenever/그는 일요일에는 ~ 집에 있다 He is always at home on Sunday. いつでも

**언제부터** from what time; since when; how long/~ 그가 행방 불명이 되었읍니까 Since when has he been missing?

**언젠가** (미래의) some time; some day; one day; one of these days (과거의) once; at one time; before/~ 후회할 때가 올 것이다 The time will come when you will repent it.

**언죽번죽** shamelessly; brazen-facedly; impudently. ふてぶてしく

**언중 유골**(言中有骨) ~이다 speak it up with implicit bitterness.

**언중 유언**(言中有言) a significant word.

**언질**(言質) a pledge; a commitment/~을 잡히지 않게 말하다 make a noncommittal statement/~을 주다 give a pledge[one's word] (to do); 《무의식중에》 commit oneself to …. げんしつ

**언책**(言責) 《책임》 responsibility for one's words/~을 어기다 break one's promise [word]. げんせき

**언청이** [a person with] a harelip; [a person with] a cleft palate; a hare-lip. いぐちのひと

**언치**[1] 《조》 a jay.

**언치**[2] (마소의) a pad; a saddle cloth.

**언턱** an edge; 《건》 an arris. かいきゅう

**언턱거리** the cause (of a dispute, of a quarrel)/싸움의 ~를 만들다 sow the seeds of strife. ろんそうのげんいん

**언들먼들** ~하다 (be) uneven; rough.

**언필칭**(言必稱) always; habitually; every time one opens one's mouth. いつも

**언해**(諺解) Korean annotation[translation] of Chinese classics/~하다 translate Chinese classics into Korean. げんかい

**언행**(言行) speech and conduct; words and actions[deeds]/~록 a chronicle of one's sayings and actions; a memoir /~ 일치 conformity of one's action to one's word/~이 일치하다 act up to what one says. げんこう

**얹다** 《놓다》 put on; place[lay, set] (a thing) on 《짐을》 load/어깨에 손을 ~ put one's hand on (a person's) shoulder. のせる

**얹히다** ①《놓이다》 be placed; be put; be set; be laid ②《좌초하다》 be stranded; run aground/배가 목포 해안에서 얹혔다 The ship ran aground on the coast of Mogpo. ③《음식이》 heavy/생선을 먹고 얹힌 것 같다 I'm afraid the fish disagreed with me. ④《붙어 살다》 be a dependant on; live with; hang[live] on (one's relations). のせられる

**얻다** ①《획득하다》 get; gain; obtain; earn; achieve; win; command 《이득이다》 profit[gain] (by, from); 《배우다》 learn

**(from)**/나는 자네에게 휴가를 얻도록 권한다 I recommend you to take a holiday. ②(결혼하다) marry (*a woman*)/아내를 ~ take a wife.

**얻어듣다** hear from others; learn by hearsay/얻어들은 지식이 많다 have a smattering knowledge of many things.

**얻어맞다** receive a blow; be struck/얼굴을 호되게 얻어맞았다 He was beaten badly in the face.

**얻어먹다** ①(음식을) be treated[entertained]; (걸식하다) beg *one's* bread ②(욕 따위를) be reprimanded; be scolded/그는 친구로부터 잔뜩 욕을 얻어먹었다 He was basely slandered by his friends.

**얼¹** (홈) a scratch (과일의) a bruise; a flaw; a fault/이 사과는 거의가 ~이 있다 These apples are much bruised.

**얼²** (넋) the soul (정신) the spirit/~빠진 초상이다 This portrait has no soul [life].

**얼간** ~한 slightly salted/~ 고등어 lightly salted mackerel.

**얼간망둥이** a simpleton; a blockhead.

**얼간이** a fool; a dunce/지갑을 소매치기 당하다니 ~로군 Got your pocket picked!—What an ass you are!

**얼갈이** ①(논밭의) winter tillage ②(채소) winter-sown greens.

**얼거리** the general[overall, schematic] structure; an outline; the layout.

**얼결** the confusion of the moment.

**얼굴** ①(낯) a face (용모) features/~이 잘 나다 have a handsome face/~을 내놓다 show *one's* face; put in an appearance/~이 팔리다 become popular/~을 똥칠하다 disgrace (*a person*) ②(안색이) a look; a countenance (표정이) an expression/실망한 ~ a disappointed look/그 여자의 ~은 기쁨으로 아름답게 빛났다 Her face fairly shone with joy.

**얼굴빛** ①(안색) complexion; color (창백한) turn pale [as white as a sheet] ②(표정) a face; a look/~을 살피다 read (*a person's*) face[countenance].

**얼근하다** ①(술이) (be) half tipsy; mellow; slightly intoxicated ②(매워서)(be) hot; spicy; pungent.

**얼금뱅이** a pockmarked person; a person with a pitted face.

**얼금숨숨** ~하다 (be) pitted; pockmarked.

**얼기설기** in complete disorder; entangled/~ 얽힌 complicated; complex; intricate; entangled/~ 얽힌 사정 a perplexed state of things.

**얼김** an impulse/~에 on the spur[impulse] of the moment/~에 기차를 잘못 탔다 In my hurry I took a wrong train.

**얼김덜김에** in the confusion of the moment; taking advantage of the confusion.

**얼다** freeze; be frozen (몸이) be benumbed with cold/언 frozen/언 손 numbed hands.

**얼떨결** ~에 in the confusion of the moment/~에 그렇게 말해 버렸다 He said so in his bewilderment.

**얼떨떨하다** (be) confused; flurried/얼떨떨하여 in confusion[consternation, a flurry]/얼떨떨해지다 get confused; be upset; lose *one's* head; be puzzled[bewildered]; get flurried.

**얼떨하다** ①(바빠서) (be) flurried; confused; disconcerted ②(머리가) (be) dizzy; giddy/잠을 못 자서 정신이 ~ I feel groggy[stupefied] from lack of sleep.

**얼뜨기** a stupid; a blockhead; half-witted fellow.

**얼뜨다** (be) stupid; cowardly/얼뜬 짓을 하다 do a stupid thing.

**얼락녹을락** now freezing and then melting.

**얼락뺄락하다** now rise and then fall; prosper and decline by turns.

**얼러맞추다** humour; please another's humour; lick another's boots; flatter (아첨) curry favour with/얼러맞추기 힘들다 be hard to please.

**얼러먹다** eat together; share (*in*).

**얼러방망이질** threatening with *one's* fists.

**얼러붙다** grapple with; close with/얼러붙어 싸우다 fight hand to hand; come to grapples (*with*).

**얼러치다** ①(때리다) strike[hit, score] two or more at one time ②(셈을) make a combined price (for *the pair*, for *the lot*).

**얼럭** (오점) a stain; a blot (반점) a mottle; spots; dapple.

**얼럭덜럭** in spots[patches]/~하다 (be) spotted; mottled (작은 점이) speckled; dappled.

**얼럭지다** become stained[blotted].

**얼럭질** (양식이) a house of mixed styles (재료가) a house with part tile-roofing.

**얼렁거리다** humour; soothe; please another's humour (아첨하다) flatter; curry favour with.

**얼렁뚱땅** (꾀듯) wheedlingly (교묘히) trickily (교활하게) cunningly/~하지 말고 정신차려 일해라 Don't be so sloppy, pay more attention to your work.

**얼렁장사** joint business; partnership/~하다 go into business in partnership with (*one*).

**일레** a reel/~에서 실을 풀다 unwind from a reel.

**일레빗** a coarse-tooth comb.

**얼레살** a reel spoke.

**얼룩** 《오점》 a stain; a spot; a blot; a smut 《반점》 a speckle; a blotch; dapples; mottles/~ 있는 spotted; stained; smeared; dappled/~고양이 《동》 a tabby cat/~말 《동》 a zebra/~을 빼다 remove a stain[blurs].

**얼룩덜룩** in parti-colour; with marks [patches] of different colours/~하다 (be) parti-coloured; variegated; motley. だんだら

**얼룩얼룩** ~하다 (be) spotted; dappled; mottled; motley; speckled; variegated /볕과 그늘로 ~한 잔디밭 a lawn checkered with sunlight and shade. だんだら

**얼룩지다** become stained[blotted]/얼룩지게 하다 stain. まだら

**얼퉁덜퉁하다** (be) variegated; mottled; dotted. まだら

**얼른** quickly; rapidly; promptly; with despatch; at once/~ 해라 Make haste!, Hurry up!/~ 대답해라 Answer promptly. すぐ

**얼리다**¹ 《얼게 하다》 freeze; let (a thing) freeze; expose (a thing) to cold weather/생선을 ~ freeze[refrigerate] fish. こおる

**얼리다**² ①《어울리다》 cooperate with; club [band] together; form partnership ②《얽히다》 be entangled 《분규하다》 be complicated; be in a tangle ③《속이다》 deceive; play a trick on. ちょうわする

**얼마** ①《의문》 how many 《수》; how much 《양》; how much 《금액》; what/~입니까 How much is it?/여기서 서울까지는 거리가 ~나 되느냐 How far is it from here to Seoul? ②《비율》 by/하루 ~로 by the day ③《다소》 some 《조금》 a little; a bit/~든지 원하는 대로 as many [much] as one wants/~ 있다가[후에] after a while[time]. いくら

**얼마나** 《수》 how many 《양》 how much 《정도》 how; how far 《시간》 how long 《거리》 how far 《크기》 how large 《높이》 how high 《무게》 how heavy 《금액》 how much; what/돈이 ~ 필요합니까 How much money do you need? いくらぐらい

**얼마든지** any; any amount 《한없이》 without limit; as much[many] as one wants[likes]/~ 가져도 좋다 You may take as much[many] as you like. いくらでも

**얼마르다**¹ be frozen into drying. こおったりかわいたりする

**얼마르다**² be not quite dry; be only half dry. かんぜんにかわかない

**얼마큼** ①⇨얼마나 ②《정도》 some; something; somewhat; a little; partly/그는 ~ 음악가 기질이 있다 He has something of the musician in him. いくらぐらい

**얼멍멍** ~하다 (be) lumpy; be full of lumps/~ 말하다 stammer. つぶつぶ

**얼밋얼밋** hesitantly/~하다 hesitate; be hesitant. ぐずぐず

**얼바람둥이** a crazy person; a crackpot; an absurd person. たわいないひと

**얼빠지다** be disconcerted; be absent in one's mind; be consternated/얼빠져 vacantly; stupefiedly/얼 빠진 사람같이 보인다 have a vacant[stupid] look. しっしんする

**얼 빼다** ①《착란하다》 disconcert; consternate ②《매혹하다》 enchant; fascinate; charm. しっしんさせる

**얼뺨붙이다** slap (a person) in the heat of the moment.

**얼버무리다** 《말을》 equivocate; cover up by talking; quibble.

**얼보다** can not see straight[clearly]; see blurred[incorrectly]. はっきりみない

**얼보이다** ①《흐릿하게》 be dimly seen; loom ②《바로 안 보이다》 be not seen properly/집이 안개 속에 ~ The house looms through the mist. はっきりみえない

**얼부풀다** expand by freezing. こおってたいせきがふえる

**얼싸** Bravo!, Hurray!. あらえっさっさ

**얼싸안다** hug; embrace/소년은 기뻐서 어머니를 얼싸안았다 The boy hugged his mother for joy. いだきしめる

**얼쑹덜쑹** ~하다 (be) checkered; cross-stripped. だんだら

**얼씨구** What a delight!, What a pleasure. よいやよいや

**얼씬거리다** flicker; flit. ちらちらする

**얼씬못하다** dare not come around[show up]; do not appear before (a person's) eyes at all. めにとまらない

**얼씬아니하다** never turn up; do not come in sight at all/적들은 얼씬도 아니 하였다 Not a shadow of the enemy was to be seen. あらわれない

**얼안** within the limits (of); within the enclosure; within the scope[range, sphere].

**얼어붙다** be frozen hard[fast to]/이 길은 아침 나절은 얼어붙어 있다 This road is frozen hard all morning. こおりつく

**얼얼하다** 《아프다》 smart 《맛이》 taste hot; bite/상처가 ~ The cut smarts. ひりひりする

**얼없다** be just the same; (be) quite correct[certain].

**얼요기** a mere morsel (of food); a small meal/~하다 eat just a bite (of food). はらふさぎ

**얼음** ice/인조 ~ artificial ice/~집 an ice-shop/~ 배달군 an iceman/~ 사탕 sugar candy/~ 과자 ices; ice-candy/~ 냉수 iced water/~ 벌차 an ice-field /~장[덩이] a cake[lump] of ice/~베개 an ice-pillow/~ 같은 icy/~이 언 frozen/~에 채다 cool (a thing) with ice /~을 지치다 skate[slide] on the ice. こおり

**얼음박이다** 《국부가 주어》 become frostbitten; be affected with chilblains 《사람

**얼음판** an icy ground; an iced ground; an ice/~에서 얼음지치다 skate on an ice rink. こおったところ

**일입다** suffer a loss from *another's* fault; suffer undeservedly due to *another's* failure. ひがいをこうむる

**일찍지근하다** (be) tingling 《상처가》 smarting/까진 데가 아직도 ~ The scratch still smarts. ずきずきいたい

**일쭝거리다** upon by flattery; coax; wheedle; get around/일쭝거리며 사람을 속이다 impose upon by flattery.

**일추** 《거의》 nearly; almost; roughly; about. ほとんど

**일추잡다** roughly estimate[put] at/계획을 ~ outline a plan. さんていする

**일치기** something half-and-half; a thing of double aspect; a half-and-half person 《사람》 a fool 《일》 things half-done/~로 일을 하다 do (*something*) by halves; leave half done.

**얼크러지다** get entangled[involved, complicated, messed up]. もつれる

**얼큰하다** 《술이》 (be) intoxicated; be feeling *one's* liquor 《맛이》 be a bit spicy; have a hot taste/그는 얼큰하게 취했다 He is slightly intoxicated. ほろよいだ

**얼키설키** entangling/~ 얽히다 be entangled; knot. ごちゃごちゃ

**얼토당토 아니하다** (be) irrelevant; extravagant; absurd; bear no relation/얼토당토 않은 말을 하지 말라 Don't talk nonsense. とんでもない

**얽다**¹ ①《엮다》bind; tie up/새끼로 ~ bind (*a thing*) with a rope ②《꾸며 대다》cook[frame] up; forge/이야기를 ~ make up a story. あむ

**얽다**² ①《마마자국》become marked with pits/그의 얼굴은 얽었다 His face is pitted[scarred] with smallpox. ②《흠이 생기다》flaw; have many flaws/이 사과는 얽었다 This apple is bruised. あばただ

**얽동이다** 《짐짝을》tie up; bind [up]; 《사슬로》chain/상자를 끈으로 ~ bind [up] a box with a cord. あみむすぶ

**얽둑배기** a person with a pocky face. あばたかおのひと

**얽둑얽둑** ~하다 (be) pitted; pocky; pockmarked. あばた

**얽매다** ①《결속하다》bind; tie; fasten ②《구속하다》bind; fetter; tie; restrict (by *rule*). しばる

**얽매이다** 《속박당하다》be tied[fettered] by (*affection, etc.*); be bound; be put in bonds 《분주하다》be taken up with (*business*); be busy/규칙에 ~ be rule-bound. しばられる

**얽배기** a pockmarked person. あばたかお

**얽어매다** bind up; tie up/사슬로 개를 ~ chain up a dog. あむようにしばりつける

**얽이** 《얽는 일》tying[trussing, binding] up securely 《일의 순서·배치》[getting] an overall picture[an outline] of a things. あみようにむすぶこと

**얽적얽적** ~하다 (be) slightly pitted[pockmarked]. ぽつぼつ

**얽히다** twine round; coil itself round 《엉키다》get entangled 《감기다》be involved 《복잡해지다》get complicated/얽힌 complicated; tangled. もつれる

**엄** a check 느어음. てがた

**엄격(嚴格)** strictness; sternness; severity; rigour; austerity/~하다 (be) strict; stern; rigorous; severe; austere/그 소녀는 ~한 가정에서 자랐다 The girl was brought up in a stern family. げんかく

**엄금(嚴禁)** strict prohibition; a ban/~하다 prohibit[forbid] strictly; interdict; taboo. げんきん

**엄나무** 〖식〗the thorny ash [tree]; *Kalopanax pictum*《학명》. はりぎり

**엄동(嚴冬)** a severe[hard] winter/~全 한에 in the depth of winter. げんとう

**엄두** the very thought (of *doing*); daring/~를 못 내다 can hardly think of doing; cannot hope to do/그들은 올 느도 못 냈다 They did not dare to come.

**엄마** 《어린이 말》ma; mama; mammy; mummy. おかあちゃん

**엄명(嚴命)** a strict command; a stringent mandate/~하다 give strict orders. げんめい

**엄밀(嚴密)** strictness; exactness; rigidity /~하다 (be) exact; close; strict/~한 의미에서 in the strict sense. げんみつ

**엄벌(嚴罰)** a severe punishment/~하다 punish severely/~주의 rigorous measures; strict discipline. げんばつ

**엄벙덤벙** rashly; frivolously/~하다 be rash[frivolous].

**엄벙하다** (be) rash; not serious; frivolous. ごたごたしている

**엄부(嚴父)** 《엄한 아버지》a stern[strict] father 《아버지》*one's* father. げんぷ

**엄부렁하다** (be) slovenly; loose; sloppy /그 사람은 ~ He wants screwing up [needs winding up].

**엄비(嚴秘)** strict secrecy/~에 부치다 keep (*a matter*) a strict secret; classify (*a matter*) top-secret. げんぴ

**엄살** pretending pain/~하다 pretend pain[hardship]; exaggerate. ふり

**엄선(嚴選)** careful selection/~하다 select carefully; choose with care/~된 물건 a choice article. げんせん

**엄수(嚴守)** strict observation/~하다 observe strictly/너는 약속을 ~해야 한다 You should always keep your promises/비밀을 ~하다 keep a secret strictly. げんしゅ

**엄숙(嚴肅)** seriousness; solemnity; gravity/~한[히] solemn[ly]; serious[ly]; grave[ly]/인생을 ~하게 보다 take a solemn view of life. げんしゅく

**엄습(掩襲)** a surprise attack/~하다 make a sudden[surprise] attack; take

엄시하(嚴侍下) having only one's father alive to serve.

엄연(儼然) ~하다 (be) solemn; grave; stern; majestic; authoritative/그는 ~히 말했다 He spoke with a magisterial air. げんぜん

엄전(嚴全) ~하다 (be) decent; modest; well[mild]-mannered; well-conducted.

엄정(嚴正) ~하다(be) exact; strict; fair; impartial; unprejudiced/~히 strictly; fairly; without partiality/~ 과학 an exact science. げんせい

엄쪽 one half of a bill[transaction paper] torn off and given to each party].

엄중(嚴重) strictness; severity/ ~하다 (be) strict; severe/~히 처벌하다 punish (a person) severely. げんじゅう

엄지 《손의》 the thumb; the big finger 《발의》 the big toe. おやゆび

엄지(一紙) a draft; a bill; a note; used for a check. てがたようし

엄지발가락 the big toe. あしのおやゆび

엄지발톱 the nail of the big toe. あしのおやゆびのつめ

엄지손톱 the nail of the thumb; the thumb nail. てのおやゆびのつめ

엄징(嚴懲) a severe[heavy] punishment[chastisement]/~하다 punish[chastise] (one) severely. きびしくちょばつすること

엄책(嚴責) a severe reproof/~하다 give (one) a sharp rebuke. げんせき

엄처 시하(嚴妻侍下) a henpecked husband; petticoat government/~에 살다 be tied to one's wife's apron strings.

엄청나다 《놀랍다》 (be) surprising 《가량없다》 (be) extraordinary; awful; exorbitant/그렇게 엄청난 이야기가 있단 말인가 How can that be? よそうにすぎる

엄친(嚴親) 《아버지》 father 《자기의》 my father. げんしん

엄탐(嚴探) ~하다 search strictly for; be on a sharp lookout for/범인을 ~중이다 The police are hot on the trail of the culprit. げんたん

엄평소니 a trick; a swindle; a sharper's trade/~를 쓰다 trick[swindle] (a person); take (a person) in.

엄폐(掩蔽) ~하다 cover up; mask 《사실을》 suppress 《죄를》 conceal/~호(壕) a covered trench; an entrenchment; a bunker. えんぺい

엄포 a bluff; bluffing/~ 놓아 쫓아내다 scare (a person) away.

엄하다(嚴一) 《엄격一》 (be) strict; severe; stern; rigorous 《심하다》 (be) intense; severe; extreme 《가혹하다》 (be) harsh; bitter 《용서치 않다》 unsparing 《신문이》 searching; close/선생님은 학생에게 ~ That teacher is severe with his pupils. おごそかしい

엄한(嚴寒) intense[severe] cold. げんかん

엄형(嚴刑) severe[heavy, harsh] punishment.

엄호(掩護) covering; protection/~하다 cover; protect; shelter/해병대의 상륙을 ~하다 cover the marines' landing. えんご

업 《민》 a household mascot/~두꺼비 a mascot toad.

업(業)¹ 《직업》 an occupation; a calling 《전문의》 a profession 《상공업》 business; trade; industry/그는 변호사를 ~으로 하고 있다 He is a lawyer by profession. ごう

업(業)² 《종》 Karma(Sans). ごう

업다 ①《등에》 bear; carry on one's back ②《꼬들여가다》 implicate/아무를 업고 들어가다 drag a person in ③《교미하다》 copulate. おんぶする

업무(業務) business; business matters; service; duty; operations; affairs/~를 방해하다 impede[interfere with] one's business. ぎょうむ

업보(業報) 《종》 retribution for the deeds of a former world. ごうほう

업신여기다 despise; hold in contempt; slight; make light[little] of/업신여김을 받다 of be held in contempt of/사람을 업신 여기지 말라 Don't hold me cheap.

업왕(業王) the God of wealth.

업원(業寃) 《종》 a retribution in this world for the sins of a previous life; Karma effects.

업자(業者) the trade; traders[dealers, businessmen] concerned; makers[manufacturers] concerned/~ 단체 a trade association. ぎょうしゃ

업적(業績) 《개인의》 work; achievements; results; contributions 《회사 따위의》 business result/~ 보고 a business report/~을 올리다 produce achievements. ぎょうせき

업종(業種) a types of industry; a category of business/~별로 분류하다 classify by industry. ぎょうしゅ

업태(業態) business condition[status]/ ~ 조사 a business conditions survey.

업히다 ride[get] on one's back; be carried on one's back/아이가 등에 ~ a child gets on (a person's) back. おんぶされる

없다 《존재하지 않다》 there is no … 《안가지고 있다》 have not 《결여하다》 want; lack; be wanting; be lacking (in); 《없어지다·탕진하다》 run short; be out of 《보이지 않다》 be not found; be gone; be missing 《결점 따위가》 be free from/전송하는 사람이 없었다 No one came to see me off./그녀는 없는 집에서 태어났다 She was born poor. ない

없애다 《제거하다》 remove; get rid of 《낭비하다》 waste; squander; run through 《분실하다》 lose/재산을 ~ lose one's fortune/장애물을 ~ remove obstacles.

없어지다 《분실하다》 be missing; be[get] l-

**없이** without/할 수 ~ unavoidably/틀림[의심]~ without fail[doubt].

**없이살다** live in poverty; be badly off. まずしくくらす

**엇** obliquely; aslant; diagonally. くいちがって

**엇가다** ①《비뚜로 나가다》go astray ②《언동이》become perverse; be cross. ふらっちになる

**엇갈리다** cross [each other]; miss each other on the road. いきちがう

**엇걸다** cross; intersect; join. すじちがいにかける

**엇걸리다** 《교차하다》intersect; cross; join /두 선이 엇걸리는 점 the junction of two lines. こうさくする

**엇결다** cross (each other); weave at an angle. たがいちがいにする

**엇결** the cross grain [of wood].

**엇구수하다** ①《맛이》(be) nice; tasty; rich in flavour ②《말이》(be) pleasing; interesting. しょくよくをそそる

**엇그루** the stump of a tree that has been cut off diagonally.

**엇대다** apply[lay, hold] obliquely. ななめにあてる

**엇되다** 《건방지다》(be) snobbish; self-important; uppity/엇된 녀석 a snob.

**엇뜨기** a cross[squint]-eyed person.

**엇뜨다** squint (one's eyes). しゃしする

**엇먹다** be cross; say spiteful things. そとれさす

**엇메다** strap under one arm and over the other shoulder. たすきがけにする

**엇바꾸다** exchange [with each other]; interchange. たがいにこうかんする

**엇베다** cut diagonally. ななめにきる

**엇보(一保)** mutual guarantee/두 사람이 ~를 서다 Two persons stand surety for each other.

**엇비슷하다** (be) much the same; much alike; of a sort. ややにている

**엇셈** an offset; a setoff/~하다 offset [cancel] each other; set off. そうさつ

**엇스다** (be) perverse; selfcentered; cross-grained.

**엉거능축하다** (be) crafty; wily; full of sly ways. かんにたけている

**엉거주춤하다** ①《몸자세가》(be) in a half-rising posture; half-sitting ②《주저하다》(be) wavering; hesitant; half-hearted. うずくまっている

**엉겁결에** unexpectedly; before one knows it. ふいに

**엉겅퀴** 【식】a thistle. やまあざみ

**엉구다** firm (a plan) up; arrange; manage; fix; conclude.

**엉글벙글** with a smile/~ 웃다 be all smiles. にこにこ

**엉금엉금** on all fours/~ 기어가다 go on all fours. のそっのそっ

**엉기다** 《응축하다》curdle; solidify; freeze; congeal 《뒤얽히다》be all tangled up /우유가 ~ milk curdles. こりかたまる

**엉기정기** pell-mell; confusedly; in disorder; in a jumble. ばらばら

**엉너리치다** [please another's] humour; curry favour (with); flatter. かんしんをかおうとしてへつらう

**엉너릿손** the skill of ingratiating oneself. へつらいて

**엉덩방아** the rump hitting the ground; pratfall/~ 찧다 fall on one's buttocks [seat].

**엉덩이** the hips; the buttocks/~를 때리다 《벌로서》spank a child. しり

**엉덩이짓** swaying[swinging] one's hips; hip movements.

**엉덩춤** a hip dance; a dance characterized by the swinging of the buttocks. しりふりおどり

**엉덩판** the hips; the buttocks; the backside/~이 크다 have big hips. しり

**엉두덜거리다** express discontent; complain (of); grumble (at); mutter (at, about). ぶつぶついう

**엉뚱하다** (be) extraordinary; exorbitant; unreasonable; inordinate; immoderate. かどである

**엉망, 엉망진창** confusion; disorder; mess; muddle/~이다 be confused; be in a muddle; be at sixes and sevens; be upset. いりみだれ

**엉성하다** ①《마르다》(be) lean; haggard; emaciated ②《눈에 설다》(be) unfamiliar ③《안 째이다》(be) thin; sparse; loose; coarse. あらい

**엉세판** poverty; indigence; destitution.

**엉엉거리다** ①《울다》cry loudly; wail; weep bitterly ②《하소연하다》deplore one's poverty; lament one's ill luck. わんわんとなく

**엉클다** tangle; entangle; knot. もつらす

**엉클어지다** be tangled; get entangled; be complicated/실이 엉클어졌다 The thread is tangled. もつれる

**엉큼성큼** with long[big, great] steps/~ 걷다 stalk; stride; walk with long steps. のしのし

**엉큼스럽다** (be) exorbitant; foxy; wily; inordinate; crafty. ほうがいである

**엉큼엉큼** with long steps; with big steps. のそっのそっ

**엉큼하다** (be) exorbitant; inordinate; foxy; crafty/엉큼한 짓을 하다 do inordinate things. ほうがいである

**엉키다** get tangled. もつれる

**엉터리** ①《터무니없는 사람》an unreliable person; a gasbag; a humbug 《터무니없음》humbug; sham; fraud/~ 작가 a back writer/~ 회사 a bogus company ②《윤곽》an outline ③《근거》a foundation; ground/~ 없는 소문 an unfounded rumour. はったり

**엊그저께, 엊그제** 《수일 전》 a few days ago 《그저께》 the day before yesterday.

**엊저녁** last night[evening]. さくばん

**엎다** 《전복하다》 overturn; upset 《쓰러뜨리다》 tumble [down]; 《뒤집다》 turn upside down; *turn down[over]. かえす

**엎드러지다** fall[tumble] down. うつむけにたおれる

**엎드려팔굽히기** 《체조》 push-up.

**엎드리다** lay *one*self down flat; lie flat. ふせる

**엎어놓다** put (*a thing*) face[top] down. かえしておく

**엎어지다** 《전복되다》 upset; overturn; fall [down]; 《넘어지다》 tumble down; bite the dust 《속》/엎어지면 코 닿을 데에 《속담》 within stone's throw. ひっくりかえる

**엎지르다** slop; drop; spill/엎지른 물은 다시 담지 못한다 《속담》 It is no use crying over spilt milk. ひっくりかえす

**엎치락뒤치락** ~하다 turn over 《자리 속에서》 toss about [in bed]. ころげまわる

**엎친 데 덮치다** Misfortunes seldom come singly[never come single]./엎친 데 덮치느라고 to make matters worse. なんじかがさなる

**엎친물** spilt water/~은 다시 담을 수 없다 It is no use crying over spilt water.

**에**[1] ①《때》 at(시작); in(연·월·주); on (날)/5시 20분~ at 20 minutes past 5 o'clock/일주일~ in a week/일요일~ on Sunday ②《장소》 at(지점); in(나라·도·도시·가로); on(현장·구내); 《위치》 in(속); on(표면)/오른편~ on the right hand/100페이지~ on page a hundred/한국~ in Korea ③《목적》 in; to; for; on(속에); into(향해서); at/상자~ 넣다 put (*a thing*) in a box/학교에 가다 go to school ④《가격》 at [the price of]; for; in/100원~ at[for] a hundred *won* ⑤《나이》 in; at/여덟 살~ 학교에 가다 go to school at the age of eight/30세~ at [the age of] thirty ⑥《비율·마다》 per; for/100원~ 팔다 sell for a hundred *won* ⑦《기타의 관계》 to; on; in; with; of/어떤 일~ 관계하다 relate to a certain matter. に

**에**[2] well; let me see. え

**에게** for; to; with 《피동》 by (*a person*)/아버님~ 편지를 쓰다 write to *one*'s father/아무~ 말을 걸다 speak to a person/미국 사람~ 배우다 be taught by an American. に. へ

**에게로** to; for/그녀의 사랑이 그~ 옮겨 갔다 Her love drifted to him. に. へ

**에게서** from; through; of/누구~ 샀니 F- rom whom did you buy this?/그 말을 친구~ 들었다 I heard that from a friend of mine. から. より

**에끼** Damn…!, Damn it!, Curse!, Go to hell! えい

**에널느레하다** (be) scattered about. ちらかっている

**에누리** 《지나친 값》 an overcharge; two prices/~하다 overcharge; have two prices 《깎음》 a discount/~하다 reduce; lower (*the price*); take off.

**에는** for; in; to /일기가 좋은 날~ on a fine day/내 생각~ in my opinion [view].

**에다** into; onto; for; to/책상 위~ 책을 놓다 put a book on the desk/5~ 6을 보태다 add six to five. に

**에도** 《까지도》 even 《…도 또한 …에 대해서도》 also; too; as well. にも

**에돌다** [make a] detour; go clear of.

**에두르다** 《둘러싸다》 enclose; surround 《둘러 말하다》 hint; talk in a roundabout way; suggest/말을 에둘러 하다 talk in a roundabout way. はりめぐらす

**에라** ①《실망》 No help for it!, Let me forget it! ②《비켜라》 Get out of my way!, Get away! えい

**에멀무지로** ①《시험삼아》 on trial; as a test; tentatively/~ 해 보다 have a trial [try] ②《느슨히》 loosely/ ~ 묶다 tie loosely. こころみに

**에서** ①《장소》 in (*Seoul*); at (*Mapo*); on (*the table*)/집~ 공부하다 study at home ②《시작되는 장소》 from; out of; off; in; over/학교~ 돌아오다 come back from school ③《동기》 out of; from [motives of]/호기심~ out of curiosity ④《견지·표준》 in; from; by; according to/교육적 견지~ 보면 from an educational point of view ⑤《범위》 from/한 시~ 네 시 사이에 between one and four o'clock. で

**에우다** ①《둘러싸다》 enclose; surround; fence [around]; 《지우다》 cross out; strike off; eliminate/계약서에서 한 조약을 ~ cross an item off a written contract. ほういする

**에움길** a detour; a circuitous route. うかいどう

**에워가다** ①《우회하다》 take a roundabout way; make a detour; go a long way around ②《장부를 지우다》 cross out[liquidate] an account. うかいしていく

**에워싸다** surround; enclose; encircle 《사람이》 gather about 《포위하다》 besiege; lay siege to. ほういする

**에이다** scoop [out]; hollow out/에이는 듯한 아픔 shooting pain/살을 에이는 듯한 찬 바람 a searching[cutting, piercing] wind. えぐる

**에잇** 《불쾌》 Pshaw!, O!/~ 빌어먹을 Damn it!, Hang it! ちえっ

**에크** 《놀람》 Oh!, Dear me!, Heavens!, Wow! あっ

**에헴** Hem!, Ahem! えへん

**엔간하다** 《적당하다》 suitable; (be) proper 《상당하다》 reasonable; (be) fair; tolerable/엔간히 pretty; fairly/엔간한 수입 a handsome income. てきとうだ

**엔굽이치다** wind its way (through *the plain*); meander/엔굽이치는 winding; serpentine; meandering; crawling.

엔들 also; even／명공~ 실수가 없으랴 Even Homer sometimes nods. うずまいてながれるにても

여 《물 속의 바위》a sunken rock in the sea; a reef. あんしょう

여(女) a girl; a woman ⇨여자. おんな

-여(餘) 《이상》above; over; more than／20~ 년 more than twenty years. —よ. —あまり

여가(餘暇) spare time; leisure [hours]; odd moments／~를 이용하다 make use of one's spare time／~가 없다 have no leisure[time to spare]. よか

여각(餘角) 〖수〗 the complementary angle. よかく

여간(如干) some; a little／~ 아니다 be uncommon; be extraordinary; be great／~해서는 살아날 것 같지 않다 His recovery is beyond hope. ちょっとやそっと

여간내기(如干—) a man of mediocre abilities; a mediocrity. ちょっとやそっとのやっこ

여감(女監) a prison ward[cell] for females. じょかん

여객(旅客) a traveler; a tourist 《차의》a passenger／~ 열차[기] a passenger train[aeroplane]. りょかく

여걸(女傑) a great woman; a heroine. じょけつ

여겨듣다 listen to [attentively]; be all attention[ears]／어머니의 말씀을 ~ listen attentively to what the mother has to say.

여겨보다 keep an eye on; fix the eye on.

여경(餘慶) recompense; the merits (of one's virtues)／적선지가에 필유 ~이라 Virtue brings its own reward. よけい

여공(女工) a factory girl; a woman worker; a female operative. じょこう

여과(濾過) 〖물〗filtering／~하다 filter; filtrate; pass filters／~액 filtrate／~지(池) a filter bed／불순물을 ~해 내다 filter out the impurities. ろか

여관(女官) 《나인》a court lady; a lady-in-waiting 《내전의》a maid of hono[u]r. じょかん

여관(旅館) an inn; a hotel; a lodging-house; a public-house／~에 들다 put up[stop] at a hotel. りょかん

여광(餘光) 《빛》afterglow; lingering [remaining] light. よこう

여교사(女敎師) a school mistress; a woman [school-]teacher. じょきょうし

여구(旅具) trip equipment; travel gear; luggage.

여구하다(如舊—) be as of old; remain unchanged. むかしとかわらない

여국(與國) an allied power[nation]; an ally. よこく

여군(女軍) a woman soldier 《군단》Women's Army Corps.

여권(旅券) a passport／~을 신청[발부]하다 apply for[issue] a passport／~ 사증 a visa. りょけん

여권(女權) woman's rights 《참정권》woman's suffrage／~의 확장 the extension of women's rights／~ 확장 운동 a feminist movement. じょけん

여뀌 a kind of water-pepper. たで

여급(女給) 《급사》a maid 《접대부》a waitress 《바의》a barmaid. じょきゅう

여기 this place; here／~에서 here; in this place／~가 어디냐 What place is this?. ここ. ここに

여기(餘技) a hobby. よぎ

여기다 regard[consider] (a thing) as; take (a thing) for 《믿다》believe／진실로 ~ take (it) seriously／귀찮게 ~ regard (it) as a bother. みなす

여기자(女記者) a lady[woman] reporter 《잡지의》a female[woman] magazinist. じょせいのきしゃ

여기저기 here and there; hither and thither; from place to place 《군데군데》in places 《산재하여》sporadically. あちこち

여낙낙하다 (be) gentle; tender; meek; good tempered; kind. おとなしい

여난(女難) danger from women; troubles[misfortunes] through women.

여남은 some ten odd; somewhat over [more than] ten. あまり

여년(餘年) the remaining years; the unexpired years. よねん

여년묵다 age; be time-honored／여년묵은 고목 a venerable old tree.

여념(餘念) distraction／…에 ~이 없다 be absorbed in (one's studies, one's work, etc.); be devoted to. よねん

여느 《보통의》ordinary; commonplace 《그밖의》other; different. つうじょうの

여느때 ordinary times／~의 《평상의》usual 《매일의》everyday 《보통의》common／~와 같이 as usual; in the usual way.

여단(旅團) 〖군〗a brigade／~장 a brigade commander／~혼성 ~ a mixed brigade／~으로 편성하다 form into a brigade. りょだん

여닫다 《문을》open and shut; open and [or] close (the door). かいへいする

여닫이 ①《열고 닫음》opening and shutting[closing] ②《미닫이》sliding doors and windows. かいへいすること

여담(餘談) 《나중 이야기》the follow-up story 《이야기의 계속》the sequel (of a story); 《지엽》a by-talk; a digression／~은 그만하고 to return to the main subject. よだん

여당(餘黨) the remnants of a party; the rest of the bandits. よとう

여당(與黨) the government[ministerial] party; a party in office／~[측]의 ministerial／~ 의원 the ministerialists. よとう

여대(女大) a women's college／~생 a student at a women's college 《남녀 공학》a coed.

여덕(餘德) the influence of great virtue／선조의 ~ the influence of one's ance-

**여덟** eight／～째 the eighth／～번 eight times. はち

**여덟팔자**(一八字) the chinese numeral of eight／～ 걸음 a splay-footed walk／～ 모양[의] (in) the shape of the Chinese numeral of eight. がにまたあるき

**여독**(餘毒) lingering poison. よどく

**여동** 〖종〗 putting aside a small spoonful of rice before eating／～밥 the rice put aside.

**여동생**(女同生) a younger sister; one's little sister. いもうと

**여드렛날** the eighth day [of the month].

**여드름** a pimple／～이 있는 pimpled; pimply-faced／～ 난 얼굴 a pimpled[pimply] face. にきび

**여든** eighty; a fourscore／～째 eightieth／～이 넘다 be over eighty. はちじゅう

**여든대다** over assert oneself; be willful [obstinate]. しゅちょうする

**여들없다** (be) clumsy; ungainly.

**여듭** an eight-year old horse[ox].

**여래**(如來) 〖종〗 Buddha. にょらい

**여러** many; a large number of／～ 식구 a big family／～ 사람 several people／～ 학교 many schools; various schools. おおくの

**여러 가지** various kinds; varieties／～의 many kinds of; various; a variety of; diverse (잡다한) miscellaneous／～로 in many[various] ways; variously. おおくのしゅるい

**여러 날** many days; several days／～ 비가 오다 it rains several days running. おおくのひ

**여러 달** many months; several months／～째 행방 불명이다 be missing for many months. おおくのつき

**여러 대**(一代) many generations／～에서 살다 have lived in Seoul for generations. おおくのだい

**여러 번**(一番) many times; on several occasions／～ 시험해 보다 make several attempts／그 사람은 ～해서 실패했다 He repeatedly tried in vain., Every time he tried, he failed. おおくのばん

**여러분** all gentlemen[ladies]; all of you; all people; everybody／신사 숙녀 ～ Ladies and Gentlemen!. みなさん

**여러 차례**(一次例) time after time; many a time; over and over again.

**여러 해** many years; a number of years／～ 동안의 연구 many years' study／～에 걸치다 extend over many years [over a long period of years]

**여러해살이**[풀] 〖식〗a perennial plant. たねんせい

**여럿** ①(많은 사람) a crowd [of people]; a great number of people／～이 크로즈 wds; in great numbers ②(많은 수) a large[great] number; a multitude; numbers／～의 many; a [large] number of／～ 있다 be abundant; abound in; be full of. おおくのすう

**여력**(餘力) reserve power[strength, energy]; (금전의) money to spare／～이 충분히 있다 have a great[plenty of] reserve energy. よりょく

**여로**(旅路) a journey／～에 오르다 start on a journey／먼～ a long journey. たびじ

**여록**(餘錄) a record of the rest; a follow-up story. よろく

**여론**(輿論) [public] opinion; general sentiment／～을 일으키다 arouse[stir up] public opinion／～에 호소하다 appeal to public opinion よろん

**여론**(餘論) complementary discussion.

**여류**(女流) a lady; a woman／～의 female; lady; woman・미／～ 작가 a lady [woman]-writer[-novelist]; an authoress／～ 시인 a poetess／～ 비행사 a woman aviator(pl. women aviators). じょりゅう

**여름** summer／～날 a summer day／～철 summertime; the summer season／～ 옷 summer clothes／～ 방학 the summer vacation／초～에 early in summer／한～에 in the height of summer; at midsummer. なつ

**여름타다** lose weight in summer; suffer from the summer heat. なつまけする

**여리다** ①(단단하지 않다) (be) soft; tender; weak; delicate ②(부족하다) (be) not enough; short of／옷 짓는 데 감이 약간 ～ The material is a little short to make a suit of clothes. よわい

**여립켜다** lure customers with a shill.

**여릿군** a shill (for a shop); a customer-baiter; a decoy.

**여마릿군** a spy; a person spying. スパイ

**여망**(輿望) (인망) popularity (신임) confidence; esteem／국민의 ～을 몸에 지니다 enjoy the confidence[trust] of the whole nation. しゅうじんのきたい

**여망**(餘望) the remaining hope. まだのこっているのぞみ

**여맥**(餘脈) what [little] pulse[strength] is left. のこっているみゃく

**여명**(黎明) dawn; daybreak／～에 at dawn; at break of day／～기 the dawning／～ 문학 literature at the dawn of a new era[age]. れいめい

**여명**(餘命) one's remaining days; the remainder of one's life. よめい

**여모**(女帽) women's headgear. おんなようのぼうし

**여무**(女巫) a female shaman.

**여무지다** (be) stout; sturdy; firm; solid／더무지게 stoutly; firm[ly]; solidly／여무진 나무 hard wood／여무지게 다문 입 a firm mouth. がっちりした

**여물**[1] (마소의) feed; provender; forage／～통 a crib／～을 주다 feed (a horse)／～ 구유 a manger. まぐさ

**여물**[2] (첫열매) the first product of the season.

여물(餘物) surplus goods. あまりもの

여물다 ①(열매가) ripen; grow[become] ripe ②(일이) go well[right]; go on smoothly/계획이 잘 여물어 간다 The plan is working beautifully[smoothly]. みのる

여물죽 boiled fodder. にるまぐさ

여미다 adjust; arrange/옷깃을 ~ adjust the neckband of *one's* clothes. ただす

여반장(如反掌) (being) very easy; like falling off a log/~으로 without effort[the least trouble]/그런 일은 ~이다 It is as easy as falling off a log.

여배우(女排優) an actress/~ 지원자 a prospective actress. じょはいゆう

여백(餘白) space; blank (종이 끝) a margin/~을 메우다 fill in[up] the blank [space]/~을 남기다 leave space; leave a margin. よはく

여벌(餘一) remainings; spare articles/ ~의 reserved; spare/~ 옷 a spare suit /~ 침대 a spare bed/~이 하나 있다 There is an extra.

여병(餘病) complications; an after effect [of an illness]; a secondary disease/~을 병반하다 have a complication arise[set in]. よびょう

여보 hello; [I] say; [look] here; hey (미); there (부부간) [my] dear (남편에게); [my] darling (아내에게). もしもし

여보시오 [I] say; excuse me (전화에서) Hullo!, Hello!, Hallo!, Are yout here?. もしもし

여복(女卜) a woman fortune-teller.

여복(女服) a female dress; female attire [costume]. おんなふく

여봐라 hello ⇒여보. おい

여부(與否) ①(부정(不定)) if; or/성공 ~ success or failure ②(가부) right or wrong; good or bad; propriety/~를 논하다 argue the right or wrong (of *one's* position). かひ

여부없다 (be) sure; infallible; unfailing; certain. たしかだ

여북 how [much]; very; greatly/~ 원통하랴 He must be awfully grievous. どれほど

여분(餘分) extra; surplus; excess/~이 없다 have no surplus/~이 생기다 remain in excess. よぶん

여비(旅費) travelling expenses; travel costs/~를 지급하다 grant a travel allowance (to *a person*). りょひ

여사(如斯) ~하다 (be) like this; of the kind[sort]; such/~히 thus; like this; so/~한 바에는 since it has come to this; now that …. かくのごときこと

여사(餘事) other things; the rest/~는 차치하고 setting aside other things; to return to the subject. よじ

여사(女史) (기혼자) Madame; Mrs. (미혼자) Miss. じょし

여사무원(女事務員) an office girl; a female clerk. じょじむいん

여상(女相) womanish features. にょそう

여상하다(如上一) be as above.

여색(女色) (미색) feminine beauty; a woman's charm (색욕) carnal pleasures[desire]/~에 빠지다 indulge in lewdness/~광 debauchery; philandering. じょしょく

여색(餘色) a complementary colo[u]r. よしょく

여생(餘生) the rest[remainder] of *one's* life; *one's* remaining years/~을 조용하게 보내다 live a quiet life for the rest of *one's* days. よせい

여서(女壻) a son-in-law; *one's* daughter's husband. にょせい

여섯 six/~째 the sixth. ろく

여성(女性) womanhood; feminity (부인) a woman (총칭) the feminine; the fair [weaker, gentle] sex; 〖언〗 the feminine gender/~관 a view of womanhood /~적 태도 a feminine attitude. じょせい

여성(女聲) a female voice/~ 합창 a female chorus. じょせい

여송연(呂宋煙) a cigar/~을 피우다 smoke a cigar.

여수(女囚) a female prisoner. じょしゅう

여수(旅愁) ennui[tedium] of a journey /~를 술로 달래다 relieve *one's* loneliness on a journey in drink. りょしゅう

여수(與受) delivery or receipt; giving and receiving/~하다 deliver or receive; transfer. あたえることとうけること

여수(餘數) remainder; surplus; excess.

여습(餘習) surviving customs/봉건 시대의 ~ customs handed down from the feudal days. よしゅう

여승(女僧) a [Buddhist] nun; a priestess /~이 되다 become a Buddhist nun; take the veil. にょそう

여식(女息) a daughter. むすめ

여신(女神) a goddess/자유의 ~ the Goddess of Liberty. じょしん

여신(餘燼) embers (불난 자리의) smouldering ruin. よじん

여실(如實) reality/~하다 (be) true; lively/~히 truly; true to life; realistically/인생을 ~히 그리다 delineate life just as it is. にょじつ

여심(女心) woman's heart (처녀의) maidenly feelings.

여아(女兒) (딸) a daughter; a [baby, young] girl. じょじ

여앙(餘殃) nemesis; retribution. むくい

여액(餘額) (차액) balance (잉여) surplus [money]; money left. ざんがく

여액(餘厄) remains of ill luck; lingering misfortune. のちにまたうけるさいやく

여염(閭閻) a street; residential quarters /~집 a dwelling [house]; a house.

여왕(女王) a queen/~ 같은 queenly; queenlike/~벌 〖충〗 a queen bee/~개미 a queen ant. じょおう

여우 ①〖동〗a fox (암컷) a vixen/~ 가죽

a fox-fur[-skin]/~에 홀리다 be possessed by a fox ②(비유적) a sly fellow; a fox/~ 사냥 fox-hunting. きつね
**여우**(女優) an actress/~를 양성하다 train actress/~가 되다 go on the stage; become an actress. じょゆう
**여우별** a short sunshine while the rain falling.
**여우비** a short spell of sunshine with the rain falling.
**여우오줌풀** 〖식〗 *Carpesium macrocepalum* (학명).
**여운**(餘韻) the swell (of *the hymn*); (시사적) suggestiveness/~이 있는 trailing; suggestive/~이 많은 full of suggestions. よいん
**여울** a swift current; a rapid; a shoot (분류) torrents/~목 the neck of the rapids/~을 건너다 ford a rapid. せ
**여위다** grow thin; become emaciated; lose flesh/여윈 thin; wornout; emaciated/여윈 얼굴 a haggard face. やせる
**여윈잠** a light sleep; a bad[poor] sleep/~을 자다 sleep badly; pass a poor night. うたたね
**여유**(餘裕) (잉여) a surplus; a margin (여지) room; scope (시일의) time [to spare]; (침착) placidity; composure/~가 있다 have (*a thing*) in reserve; have (*time, money*) to spare; have enough and to spare/마음의 ~ latitude of mind; inner resources/그는 ~만만하다 He has much in reserve. よゆう
**여의**(女醫) a lady[female, woman] doctor; a doctress. じょい
**여의**(如意) ~하다 turn out as *one* wishes/~하게 되다 go[work] well; come up to *one's* expectations/매사가 ~치 않았다 Everything has gone wrong with me. にょい
**여의다** ①(사별하다) lose; be bereaved of/양친을 ~ lose[survive] *one's* parents ②(출가하다) marry off (*a daughter*). しべつする
**여의주**(如意珠) a magic stone that bestows omnipotence on him who acquires it. にょいほうじゅ
**여인**(女人) a woman/~ 금제(禁制) no admittance to women/~ 천하 petticoat government/그 절은 ~ 금제다 The temple is closed to women. にょいん
**여인**(麗人) a beauty; a belle. れいじん
**여인숙**(旅人宿) an inn; a hotel; a lodge/싸구려 ~ a flophouse〈미〉; a doss house《영·속》.
**여일**(餘日) days remaining; time left. よじつ
**여일**(如一) constancy/~하다 (be) consistent; changeless; immutable/ ~하게 constantly; invariably/시종 ~하게 consistantly; from first to last.
**여잉**(餘剩) surplus ⇨잉여. じょうよ
**여자**(女子) a woman; a lady; a girl (총칭) the fair sex (산아) a baby girl/~

의 female; woman; lady['s]; girl['s]; feminine/~ 친구 a girl-friend/~다운 womanlike; ladylike; womanly/~를 좋아하는 amorous; susceptible to female charms; fond of women; lustful/~용의 lady's; for ladies' use/~ 교육 women's education; education of girls. じょし
**여장**(旅裝) traveling outfit; traveler's equipment/~을 차리다 make preparations for a journey/~을 풀다 take a rest after a travel. りょそう
**여장**(女裝) a female dress; female attire [costume]/~하다 put on a female [woman's] dress/~하고 있다 be dressed up like a woman. じょそう
**여장부**(女丈夫) a heroine; a virago; an Amazon; a brave[spirited] woman. おとこまさりのおんな
**여재**(餘財) remaining fortune (여유 있는 자금) money to spare. よさい
**여전**(如前) ~하다 (be) unchanged; as before; constant; the same/~히 as usual; as … as ever; still; as before/~히 아름답다 be as beautiful as ever. まえとおなじこと
**여점원**(女店員) a saleswoman; a shopgirl. おんなのてんいん
**여정**(旅程) distance; journey. りょてい
**여정**(旅情) the weary thoughts of a traveler; the heart of a traveller/~을 위로하다 beguile to monotony of *one's* journey. りょじょう
**여정하다** (be) much[about, pretty, nearly] the same; practically equal. ほとんどおなじだ
**여제**(女弟) a [younger, little] sister. いもうと
**여제**(女帝) an empress; a queen. じょてい
**여존**(女尊) respect for woman/~ 남비(男卑) respect for woman at the expense of man/~주의 petticoatism. じょそん
**여종**(女-) a female slave[servant].
**여좌**(如左) ~하다 it is[runs] as follows; it is to the following effect; be as on the left. さのごときこと
**여죄**(餘罪) an additional charge; other crimes/~를 추구하다 make further inquiries about some other crimes suspected. よざい
**여주** 〖식〗 the balsam-pear; *Momordicach-arantia*(학명). つるれいし
**여주인공**(女主人公) a heroine. おんなのしゅじんこう
**여줄가리** left-overs; leavings; remains. じゅうようでないざんぶつ
**여쭙다** tell; say/잠깐 여쭤 보겠읍니다 Excuse me, but. いう
**여중**(旅中) during *one's* journey; while [one is] travelling. りょこうちゅう
**여중 군자**(女中君子) a lady of eminent [high] virtue.
**여중 호걸**(女中豪傑) a heroine; a brave [spirited] woman; an Amazon; a lady

of firm character.

**여지**(荔枝) 〖식〗 a litchi; a lichi 《열매》a litchi nut. つるれいし

**여지**(餘地) room; a margin; a scope 《여백》a blank/변명의 ~가 없다 There is not the slightest excuse./개량의 ~ room[margin] for improvement.

**여진**(餘震) a secondary shock. よしん

**여질**(女姪) a niece.

**여짓거리다** keep hesitating (to speak)/여짓거리며 hesitatingly; hesitantly; nervously. ためらう

**여차** a trifle; a trifling matter[thing]. つまらないこと

**여차**(如此) being such; being like this/~하다 (be) like this; such/~하면 at the last moment; when the moment arrives 《할 수 없으면》 if compelled; in case of need. かくのごときこと

**여창**(女唱) singing with a woman's voice.

**여창**(旅窓) a traveller's room; the room in which one stay as a traveller.

**여천**(餘喘) the lingering life/~을 이어가다 keep a lingering life. よせん

**여천지 무궁**(與天地無窮) being eternal as heaven and earth/~하다 be eternal as heaven and earth.

**여청**(女一) a woman's[female] voice/~으로 말하다 talk in a womanish voice. おんなのこえ

**여축**(餘蓄) 《저금》savings 《저장》a store; a stock 《잔익》hoarding 《예비》reserve; supplies/~하다 save up; hoard; put aside; lay[set] by 《저장》store/한 푼의 ~도 없다 have not a penny saved[laid by]. ちょちく

**여치** 〖충〗 a noisy cricket; *Mecopoda elongata*(학명). くつわむし

**여탈**(與奪) giving and depriving/생살 ~지권 the power of life and death; the power over life and property. よだつ

**여탕굿** a ritual held to offer thanks for an happy occasion to the souls of one's ancestors through sorceress practices.

**여탕**(女湯) the women's[ladies'] section of a bathhouse.

**여태까지** till now; until[up to] now; up to date; by this time[now]/~ 없었던 사전 an unprecedented event/~ 사람들에게 알려지지 않은 비밀 a secret hitherto unknown to people. いままで

**여택**(餘澤) blessings which remain behind/문명의 ~ the blessings of civilization. よたく

**여투다** 《저장하다》keep; store; preserve/쌀을 ~ lay in rice. ちょぞうする

**여파**(餘波) an aftermath; an after-effect/~를 받다 be under the influence (of). よは

**여편네** ①《아내》 a wife/~를 얻다 take (to oneself) a wife; be married to a woman ②《어른된 여자》 a woman; a female. ふじょ

**여폐**(餘弊) a surviving evil; a relic; a hold-over (from *the Dark Ages*). よへい

**여품**(餘風) a relic; a hold-over/시대의 ~ a relic of barbarism; a holdover from barbaric times. よふう

**여필**(女筆) woman's hand [writing]/이것은 ~이다 This is a feminine handwriting. にょひつ

**여필종부**(女必從夫) Wives should follow their husbands.

**여하**(如何) what: how/~한 what; what kind[sort] of; what like/~히 how; in what way/~한 경우에도 at all times; in any case/~한 일이 있더라도 whatever may happen/~한 희생을 내더라도 at any cost/~한 이유로 why; for what reason. いか

**여하간**(如何間) anyway; in any case; at any rate; at all events/~ 해 보는 것이 좋을 것이다 At all events you had better try. どうであろうとも

**여하튼**(如何一) anyway; in any case; at all events; at any rate/~ 지금 불경기이니깐 considering the hard times.

**여학교**(女學校) a girls' [high] school. じょがっこう

**여학생**(女學生) a girl student; a schoolgirl 《남녀 공학의》 a co-ed《미·구》. じょがくせい

**여한**(餘恨) a smouldering[surviving] grudge. のこったえんこん

**여한**(餘寒) the lingering cold[winter]; the after-winter cold/~이 아직 가시지 않다 the cold still lingers. よかん

**여행**(旅行) a travel; a journey; a travelling 《만유》a tour 《유람》an excursion 《단거리》a trip 《항해》a voyage/~하다 travel; journey; make[go on] a journey[trip, tour]/~의 계절 a tourist season/~가 a 〖great〗 traveller; a tourist/~ 안내서 a guide-book; a Baedeker/~ 가방 a traveling bag; a portmanteau; a glad-stone bag/~지 one's destination in travel. りょこう

**여행**(勵行) enforcement/~하다 carry out; enforce; observe. れいこう

**여권권**(旅行券) a passport · 여권(旅券).

**여향**(餘香) a faint scent; a smack (of). よこう

**여향**(餘響) an after-effect; an aftermath; a repercussion. よきょう

**여혼**(女婚) marriage of one's daughter. むすめのけっこん

**여흥**(餘興) amusement; an entertainment; a side-show/~으로 by way of entertainment. よきょう

**여희**(如一) as like/~하기와 ~ as follows; as in the following/신기와 ~ as above as in the preceding.

**역**(譯) translation; rendering. やく

**역**(亦) 《역시》too; also; likewise; as well. また

**역**(役) 《연극의》 a part; a character; a

role/어린이 ~ a juvenile part/일인 이 ~을 하다 play a double rôle.

**역**(逆) the wrong way 《거꾸로 된 것》 inverse 《반대》 reverse; 《수》 converse/~의 contrary; inverse; reverse; opposite/~으로 by converse; the other way; by contraries/~은 반드시 진(眞)이 아니다 converses are not always true. ぎゃく

**역격**(逆擊) a counterattack; a counter-offensive/~하다 counterattack; make a counterattack (on, against).

**역결**(逆—) an interlocked grain. もくめがさからなこと

**역경**(逆境) adversity; a reverse of fortune/~에 있다(빠지다) be in[fall into] adversity/~과 싸우다 struggle with adversity. ぎゃくきょう

**역경**(易經) the Book of Changes; the Yi-king. えききょう

**역광선**(逆光線) 《물》 counter-light/~ 사진 a shadowgraph(미)/~으로 사진을 찍다 take a picture against the light.

**역군**(役軍) a coolie; a navvy; an earth worker; a construction labourer.

**역기**(力技) weight-lifting. じゅうりょうあげ

**역년**(歷年) one year after another; lapse[passage, flight] of year/~하다 elapse; pass; go by. れきねん

**역년**(曆年) a calendar[civil] year. れきねん

**엮다** ①《엮어 만들다》 plait; knit; together/울타리를 ~ make a fence ②《편찬하다》 edit; compile/이야기를 ~ weave a story. あむ

**역단층**(逆斷層) 《지》 a diagonal fault.

**역대**(歷代) successive generations[reigns]/~의 왕 successive kings 《표로 만든》 a chronological list of sovereigns. れきだい

**역도**(逆徒) [a group of] rebels; traitors; insurgents. ぎゃくと

**역도**(力道) weight lifting/~ 선수 a weight lifter. じゅうりょうあげ

**역독**(譯讀) translation/~하다 translate (English) into (Korean). やくどく

**역두**(驛頭) the station; the front of the station. えきとう

**역들다** support ~옹성들다

**역량**(力量) 《체력》 strength; power 《기능》 capacity; ability; talent/~있는 able; capable; competent/~을 시험하다 try one's talent. きりきりょう

**역력**(歷歷) ~하다 (be) clear; plain; obvious; fresh/~히 plainly; clearly; vividly. ありあり

**역류**(逆流) 《조류의》 a countercurrent; an adverse tide 《역류함》 flowing backward 《혈액의》 regurgitation/~하다 flow backward. ぎゃくりゅう

**역리**(逆理) ①《도리의》 absurdity; irrationality; unnaturalness; paralogism/~의 unreasonableness; irrational; absurd ②《역결》 an interlocked grain. ぎゃくり

**역리**(疫痢) 《의》 children's dysentery. えきり

**역마**(驛馬) a post-horse. えきば

**역마차**(驛馬車) a stage-coach. えきばしゃ

**역모**(逆謀) a design to revolt; a conspiracy to rise in revolt/~하다 conspire to rise in revolt; plot treason (against). ぎゃくぼう

**역문**(譯文) a translation; a rendering; a version.

**역반응**(逆反應) 《물》 inverse reaction.

**역방**(歷訪) a round of visits[calls]/~하다 visit (places, persons) one after another. れきほう

**역병**(疫病) an epidemic; a plague; a pestilence/~이 발생하다 an epidemic breaks out. えきびょう

**역부**(驛夫) a station porter; a redcap. えきふ

**역불급**(力不及) ~하다 be beyond one's power[ability]; find oneself unequal (to the task). ちからがおよばないこと

**역비례**(逆比例) an inverse proportion [ratio]. ぎゃくひれい

**역사**(力士) a man of great physical strength; a strong man. りきし

**역사**(役事) building; construction; erection 《수선》 repairs.

**역사**(轢死) death from a vehicular[car, train] accident/~하다 be run over and killed. れきし

**역사**(歷史) ①《학문·기록》 history 《사서》 a history/~가 a historian; a historiographer/~상의 historic; historical/~에 남다 be recorded in history/~적 historic; history-making/~ 이전의 prehistoric/한국의 ~ Korean history; the history of Korea ②《내력》 history 《전통》 tradition/~ 있는 학교 a historic school. れきし

**역산**(逆産) ①《도산》 cross birth; footpresentation ②《역적의 재산》 a property of a traitor. ぎゃくさん

**역서**(曆書) an almanac. れきしょ

**역서**(譯書) translated books; translations. やくしょ

**역선전**(逆宣傳) counterpropaganda/~하다 carry out counterpropaganda.

**역설**(力說) emphasis; stress/~하다 emphasize; lay stress on; accentuate/그 점은 ~할 필요가 있다 It deserves special emphasis. りきせつ

**역설**(逆說) a paradox/~적 paradoxical/~적으로 말하면 paradoxically speaking. ぎゃくせつ

**역성** partiality; favo[u]ritism/~들다[하다] favo[u]r; side with; show (one) favo[u]ritism; take one's part.

**역수**(逆水) a counter current. ぎゃくすい

**역수**(逆數) 《수》 a reciprocal number. ぎゃくすう

**역수**(易數) the art of divination.

**역수입**(逆輸入) reimportation; reimport/~하다 reimport. ぎゃくゆにゅう

**역수출**(逆輸出) reexportation; reexport/~하다 reexport. ぎゃくゆしゅつ

**역술**(譯述) translation/~하다 translate; render/~자 a translator. やくじゅつ

**역습**(逆襲) a counterattack/~하다 [make a] counterattack; retort; turn the tables upon/~을 받다 have the tables turned upon (*one*). ぎゃくしゅう

**역시**(亦是) [또한·같이] too; also; as well 《의연히》 still; all[just] the same 《결국》 after all 《…에도 불구하고》 but; in spite of; not with-standing/나 ~ 그렇습니다 So am I. やはり

**역신**(疫神) [민] the spirit of smallpox; the god of plague; a jinx《미·속》/~에 붙들리다 be seized by a plague. えきじん

**역어**(譯語) words[terms] used in a translation; a Korean[an English, *etc.*] equivalent. やくご

**역연**(亦然) ~하다 be[also] the same.

**역연**(歷然) ~하다 (be) clear; manifest; evident; plain; unmistakable/~히 clearly; manifestly; evidently; plainly/~한 사실 a glaring[an obvious, an undeniable] fact. ぶんめいである

**역용**(逆用) a reverse use/~하다 make a reverse use (of). ぎゃくよう

**역원**(役員) an officer; an official 《전체》 the board/~ 선거 the election of officers. やくいん

**역원**(驛員) a station employee 《총칭》 the station staff.

**역임**(歷任) successive service in various posts/~하다 successively fill[hold] various posts. れきにん

**역자**(譯者) a translator. やくしゃ

**역작**(力作) a fine literary effort; an elaborate work/~하다 take great pains in writing. りきさく

**역작용**(逆作用) [a] reaction; [a] reverse action.

**역장**(驛長) a stationmaster; a station agent《미》/~실 a stationmaster's office. えきちょう

**역저**(力著) a labo[u]red work. りきちょ

**역적**(逆賊) a rebel; a traitor; an insurgent/~의 누명을 쓰다 be branded as a traitor[rebel]/~ 모의하다 conspire to rise in revolt. ぎゃくぞく

**역전**(力戰) a good[hard, desperate] fight/~하다 fight desperately[well]. りきせん

**역전**(歷戰) long record of active service/~의 용사 a veteran; a hero of many battles. れきせん

**역전**(逆轉) reversal; inversion 《비행기의》 loop/~하다 reverse (*itself*)/형세가 ~ 됐다 The tables are turned. ぎゃくてん

**역전**(驛前) the station front; a station plaza/~의 거리 a station road; a depot street《미》/~ 광장 a station square. えきまえ

**역전 경주**(驛傳競走) a long-distance relay race. えきでんきょうそう

**역점**(力點) ①《강조》 [the point of] emphasis[stress] ②《물》 [better] dynamic point. りきてん

**역정**(逆情) anger; wrath; rage; resentment; indignation/~나다 be angry; be out of temper/~내다 get[become] angry (with *one*, at *a thing*); be fired up. いかり

**역조**(歷朝) successive dynasties[reigns]. れきちょう

**역조**(逆潮) head-tide; weather tide; adverse current. ぎゃくちょう

**역조**(逆調) an adverse[unfavorable] condition/무역의 ~ an adverse balance of trade.

**역주**(譯注) translation and annotation; translation with notes.

**역진**(力盡) exhaustion/~하다 be spent up 《힘이 주어》 one's strength is gone. ちからがつきること

**역참**(驛站) a post town; a post-stage; a relay station.

**역천**(逆天) flying in the face of providence/~하다 fly in the face of providence give offence to the will of god. てんめいにそむくこと

**역청**(瀝青) [광] bitumen; asphalt/~질 (質)의 bituminous/~암 pitch-stone/~탄 bituminous coal. れきせい

**역투**(力鬪) a mighty struggle; a hard fight/~하다 fight hard[with might and main]. りきとう

**역풍**(逆風) an unfavo[u]rable wind; a head-wind. ぎゃくふう

**역하다**(逆─) (be) nauseous; disgusting; offensive. はきそうである

**역학**(力學) [물] dynamics/~적 dynamic[al]/~자 a dynamist/양자 ~ quantumdynamics. りきがく

**역학**(易學) the art[science] of divination. えきがく

**역할**(役割) 《구실》 a part; a role; personnel 《극의》 a role 《전체의》 a cast (of *characters*)/~을 정하다 assign a part allot duties. やくわり

**역해**(譯解) translation [with explanatory notes]; paraphrase 《암호의》 decoding. やくかい

**역행**(力行) strenuous efforts; endeavour; exertion/~하다 make an energetic[a strenuous] effort. りっこう

**역행**(逆行) retrogression; retrogressive motion; reverse movement/~하다 《반대로 나가다》 go back; move backward; retrogress; retrograde 《상반하다》 run counter to. ぎゃっこう

**역혼**(逆婚) marriage in reverse order.

**역효과**(逆效果) a counter result; an adverse reaction/~를 내다[가져오다] have[produce] a reverse effect. ぎゃっこうか

**연**(鉛) [광] lead; [화] plumbum. えん

**연**(鳶) a kite/~을 날리다 fly a kite.

**연(緣)** 《관계》 relation; connection; relationship 《혈연》 blood relation; affinity 《결연》 a bond; a tie 《결혼》 marriage/부부의 ~을 끊다 divorce one's wife; break off conjugal relations.　えん

**연(蓮)** 〖식〗 a lotus; a Chinese water-lily /~꽃 a lotus flower.　たこ　れん

**연(年)** a year,/~에 a year; yearly; per annual/~ 1회 once a year / ~ 1회의 yearly; annual.　とし

**연(輦)** the Royal carriage.

**연(延)** 《~인원 《여객의》 the total number of passengers carried 《일의》 man-day/~일수 the total[running] number of days.

**연(連)** 《양지의》 a ream\ 양지 2~ two reams of paper.

**연가(戀歌)** a love song; an amatory poem.　れんか

**연간(年間)** for a year; during the course of a year/~ 계획 the program for the year/~ 생산고 yearly output.　ねんかん

**연감(軟—)** 《연시》 a ripe[mellowed] persimmon.

**연감(年鑑)** a yearbook; an annual/경제 ~ the economy yearbook/통계 ~ the statistics yearbook.　ねんかん

**연강(軟鋼)** soft steel.

**연거푸(連—)** continuously; consecutively; in succession; successively/그는 ~ 담배를 피운다 He is a chain smoker.

**연결(連結)** connection; coupling/~하다 connect; attach; couple; interlink; join.　れんけつ

**연계(軟鷄)** a grown chicken; a chicken.　ひなにわとり

**연고(年高)** being old[aged].　としかさ

**연고(軟膏)** an ointment; an unguent; a salve/붕산 ~ boracic ointment/수은 ~ mercurial boracic.　なんこう

**연고(緣故)** ①《까닭》 a reason; a ground; conditions ②《관계》 relation; connection /~자 a relative/~가 없다 have no connection (with); have no thing to do (with).　えんこ

**연고로(然故—)** therefore; consequently; because of that; so that.　そんなりゆうで

**연골(軟骨)** 〖해〗 《쇠고기 따위의》 a cartilage/~ 조직 a cartilage tissue/~막 the perichondrium.　なんこつ

**연공(年貢)** an annual tribute.　ねんぐ

**연공(年功)** 《근속》 long[continued] service 《공로》 long and meritorious service 《경험》 long experience/~에 의하여 through long continuous service/~을 쌓다 have long experience.

**연관(聯關)** connection/~이 있다 be connected with.　れんかん

**연관(鉛管)** a lead pipe/~ 장치 plumbing fixture.　えんかん

**연광(年光)** 《경치》 the seasonal changes in the scenery 《나이》 young age.

**연구(研究)** study; research [work];《조사》 investigation; inquiry/~하다 study; make a study (of); conduct researches (in science);《조사》investigate; inquire into/~실 a laboratory/~심 the spirit of inquiry/~ 문제 a subject of study /~적 태도 a studentlike attitude.　ねんこう

**연구(軟球)** a soft ball.　けんきゅう

**연구개(軟口蓋)** 〖해〗 the soft palate; palatum molle; the velum.　なんきゅう

**연귀(聯句)** a couplet.　なんこうがい

**연극(演劇)** ①《극》 a play; a drama; a theatrical performance 《소인극》 a farce《소극(笑劇)》/~ 운동 a dramatic movement/~ 애호가 a play-goer; a theatre-goer/~에 미친 stage-struck[-mad] /~을 보러 가다 attend[go to] theatre/ ~ 대본 a play-book/~ 학교 a dramatic school/~계 the theatrical world ②《허위》 a trick; a sham; a made-up affair /~을 부리다[꾸미다] play[act] a part; act.　えんげき

**연근(蓮根)** a lotus rhizome; a lotus root.　れんこん

**연금(年金)** an annuity; a pension/퇴직하여 ~으로 생활하다 retire to live on a pension.　ねんきん

**연금(軟禁)** 《집안에》 domiciliary confinement/~하다 confine informally.　なんきん

**연금술(鍊金術)** alchemy/~사 an alchemist.　れんきんじゅつ

**연급(年級)** a year; a form〈영〉; a grade.

**연급(年給)** an annual[a yearly] salary.　ねんきゅう

**연기(年紀)** 《나이》 one's age 《연보》 a life-story in chronological order.　ねんき

**연기(延期)** postponement; deferment; putting off 《회의의》 adjournment/~하다 postpone; defer; put off; adjourn /~되다 be postponed; be put off[over]/무기 ~되다 be postponed indefinitely.　えんき

**연기(煙氣)** smoke/검은 ~ black[murky] smoke/~를 뿜다 send[puff] up smoke /아니 땐 굴뚝에 ~ 날까《속담》 There is no smoke without fire., Out of nothing, nothing comes.　けむり

**연기(演技)** performance; action; acting; playing; a tournament/~자 a performer/~가 자연스럽다 acting is natural [stiff].　えんぎ

**연기(緣起)** ①《징조》 an omen; a luck 《흉사의》 a portent/~가 좋은 lucky; of a good omen; auspicious ②《유래》 the history; the origin.　えんぎ

**연기(連記)** ~하다 list; write down together; catalogue/~제 《투표의》 the plural ballot system.　れんき

**연기(年期)** a term; a fixed period [of years].　ねんき

**연내(年內)** within[before the end of] the

**연년(年年)** every year; year by year; yearly; annually. ねんねん

**연년(連年)** years after[by] year; for a series of years; one year after another. れんねん

**연년생(連年生)** a child born within a year of another's birth/그들은 ~이다 They are brothers born within a year of each other.

**연놈(~)** man and woman; Jack and Jill. やろうとじょろう

**연단(演壇)** a platform; a rostrum (敎壇) a dais (說敎壇) a pulpit/~에 오르다[에서 내리다] ascend[leave] the platfrom. えんだん

**연달(鳶-)** (연의) a bamboo-frame of a kite.

**연달(練達)** skill; dexterity/~하다 (be) expert; experienced; veteran/~한 사람 an expert; a veteran; an old hand. れんたつ

**연달다** continue; be continuous; keep on (…에 이어) follow/ 연달은 continued; continuous; successive; frequent/연달아 one after another; successively; continuously; in rapid succession. のちにつづく

**연당(蓮堂)** a shrine on the bank of a lotus pond.

**연당(蓮塘)** a lotus pond. はすいけ

**연대(年代)** an age (시대) an epoch; a period (기원) an era/~표 a chronological table/~기 chronology/~순으로 in chronological order. ねんだい

**연대(連帶)** solidarity/~의 joint/~하다 be jointly and severally liable to; be collectively responsible (to one for a thing)/~로 jointly/~ 책임 joint liability[responsibility]/~ 보증 joint liability on guarantee/사회 ~ social solidarity. れんたい

**연대(聯隊)** 【군】 a regiment/~의 regimental/~ 본부 the regimental headquarters/~장 the regimental commander. れんたい

**연도(年度)** a year; a term (달력의) a calendar year (회계의) a fiscal year (학교의) a school year/~ 초[말]에 at the beginning[end] of the fiscal year. ねんど

**연도(連禱)** 【종】litany; rogations.

**연도(沿道)** ~에 along the route[road]; by the roadside. えんどう

**연독(煙毒)** smoke pollution. えんどく

**연독(鉛毒)** lead-poisoning; plumbism/~에 걸리다 suffer from lead poisoning. えんどく

**연돌(煙突)** a chimney ⇨굴뚝. えんとつ

**연동(聯動)** gear[ing]/~하다 be connected[linked, coupled] (with)/~기(機) a clutch/~ 장치 a gear (of a machine).

**연동(蠕動)** peristalsis; vermiculation/~하다 creep; worm. せんどう

**연두(~)** 【빛】 light green.

**연두(年頭)** the beginning of the year (설날) New Year's Day. ねんとう

**연락(宴樂)** merrymaking; festivities; revery; gaieties; jollity.

**연락(連絡)** ①(접속) connection; junction; communication/ ~ 하다 join; connect with/~이 끊어지다 lose contact with ②(통신) communication; correspondence/~하다 communicate (a matter) to; inform (one)/~을 끊다 cut off[sever] communications ③(접촉) contact; touch (연결) liaison (관계) connection/~병 a connecting file/~을 맺다 establish a connection with. れんらく

**연래(年來)** for years;[for] some years; these years/~의 희망 a long-cherished desire/10 ~의 벗 a friend of ten years' standing. ねんらい

**연령(年齡)** age; years/~에 불구하고 regardless of age/결혼 ~ the age of marriage/~ 제한 the age limit. ねんれい

**연례(年例)** ~의 yearly; annual/~ 대회 an annual general meeting. ねんれい

**연로(年老)** old[advanced] age/~하다 (be) old; aged. ねんろう

**연로(沿路)** the route ⇨연도. えんろ

**연료(燃料)** fuel/~비 cost of fuel; fuel expense/~를 절약하다 save fuel/~가 부족하다 Fuel is badly needed (for the winter). ねんりょう

**연루(連累)** (연좌) implication; complicity; involvement (관계) connection; relation/~하다 be implicated[involved] (in); be connected with/~자 a confederate; a person concerned. れんるい

**연륜(年輪)** an annual ring[layer] (of a true); age. ねんりん

**연리(年利)** an annual interest[rate]/~6푼으로 at an annual interest of six percent. ねんり

**연립(聯立)** union; alliance; coalition/~ 내각 a coalition cabinet/~ 정부 a coalition government. れんりつ

**연마(硏磨)** ①(갈기) ~하다 give a polish; grind; brush up ②(연구) study; research/~하다 study hard; make a study (of); research. けんま

**연마(練磨)** training; improvement; exercise; practice/~하다 train; drill; improve.

**연막(煙幕)** a smoke screen/~을 치다 lay down a smoke screen/~으로 가리다 cover (a ship) with a smoke-screen. えんまく

**연만(年滿)** old age/~하다 (be) old enough; aged. としがおけていること

**연말(年末)** the end of the year; the year-end/~의 year-end/~ 대매출 a year-end sale. ねんまつ

**연맥(燕麥)** 【식】 an oat. えんばく

**연맹(聯盟)** a league; a union; a federation; a confederation/국제 ~ the League of Nations. れんめい

**연면**(連綿) ~하다 (be) continuous; uninterrupted; unbroken/~히 continuously. れんめん

**연명**(延命) ~하다 《살아남다》 survive (another); 《오래 살다》 live long 《목숨을 건지다》 escape death/간신히 ~하다 make a bare living; eke out a precarious living. えんめい

**연명**(連名) joint signature/~하다 sign jointly. れんめい

**연몌**(連袂) cooperation; joint action/~하다 act together/~로 in a body; in concert. どうはんすること

**연모** 《도구》 an implement; a tool; an instrument 《재료》 material; stuff. どうぐ

**연모**(戀慕) love; attachment; tender emotions/~하다 [fall in] love; become attached (to); be charmed (with)/~를 받다 be loved. れんぼ

**연목**(椽木) 《건》 a [common] rafter ⇨서까래. たるき

**연목 구어**(緣木求魚) ~하다 seek a fish on a tree; fish in the air; go to a tree for fish. ふとうなやしん

**연못**(蓮─) a lotus pond; a pond. はすいけ

**연무**(延袤) extent; expanse; area.

**연무**(煙霧) mist; haze; vapour. えんむ

**연무**(鍊武) military drill/~하다 train oneself in warlike arts; practice military exercise. れんぶ

**연무**(演武) military exercise/~하다 train oneself in warlike arts/~장 a military exercise hall; a drill hall. えんぶ

**연문**(戀文) a love letter. こいぶみ

**연문**(衍文) pleonasm; a redundant sentence[phrase].

**연문학**(軟文學) sentimental literature; erotic[amatory] literature. なんぶんがく

**연미복**(燕尾服) an evening dress; a swallow-tail; a swallow-tailed coat. えんびふく

**연민**(憐憫) compassion; commiseration; mercy; pity/~하다 show mercy to (one); take compassion[pity] on/~의 정을 느끼다 be touched[moved] with pity[compassion]; feel pity. れんびん

**연발**(連發) a volley; firing in succession; running fire/~하다 fire in volleys; fire in rapid succession/~로 쏘다 fire a volley/~총 a magazine rifle[gun, pistol]. れんぱつ

**연밥**(蓮─) a lotus pip. はすのみ

**연방** continuously. つけてすぐ

**연방**(聯邦) a [federal] union; a federation; a confederation; a federal state/~의 federal; confederal/~ 정부 the Federal Government/~ 재판소 a federal court. れんぽう

**연배**(年輩) age; years/자비 ~의 청년 young men of your age/상당한 ~의 사람 an elderly person; one well on in years. ねんぱい

**연방**(連放) running fire. れんぱつ

**연백**(鉛白) white lead; lead foil.

**연번호**(連番號) a serial number.

**연변**(年邊) an annual[a yearly] interest. ねんり

**연변**(沿邊) the area along a river[railroad, border]/철도 ~의 집들 houses on[along] a railway line. えんどう

**연병**(練兵) military drill; military exercise/~하다 drill; parade/~장 a parade[drill] ground. れんぺい

**연보**(年報) an annual report/무역 ~ the annual report[returns] of foreign trade. ねんぽう

**연보**(年譜) a chronological personal history. ねんぷ

**연보**(捐補) alms-giving; charity 《보시물》 alms/~하다 give alms (to).

**연봉**(蓮─) a lotus flower-bud.

**연봉**(年俸) a yearly stipend; an annual salary. ねんぽう

**연봉**(連峰) a chain of mountains; a mountain-range[-chain]. れんぽう

**연봉잠**(蓮─簪) a floral hairpin. はすのはなかたのかんざし

**연부**(年賦) an annual[a yearly] installment/~로 by yearly installments/~ 산환 redemption by yearly installments. ねんぷ

**연분**(年分) ①《전세율(田稅率)》 an yearly field tax rates ②《일년의 몫》 a yearly amount ③《일년의 어느 때》 a season of the year. ねんぶん

**연분**(緣分) connection; affinity; relation 《친분》 acquaintance/~이 없다 be unfortunate in matrimonial chances/~을 끊다 break off (with a person); have done with (a person, a matter). いんえん

**연분수**(連分數) 《수》 a continued fraction.

**연분홍**(軟粉紅) light[pale] red. うすいももいろ

**연비**(聯臂) indirect introduction/~하다 introduce indirectly.

**연비**(連比) 《수》 a continued ratio. れんひ

**연비례**(連比例) 《수》 continued proportion. れんぴれい

**연사**(演士) a speaker; a lecturer; an orator. えんし

**연사 장치**(連射裝置) a draft gear.

**연산**(連山) a range[chain, group] of mountains; a mountain range. れんざん

**연산**(年産) annual[yearly] production[output]/~ 능력 annual capacity of production. ねんさん

**연산**(演算) 《수》 operation. えんざん

**연상**(年上) 《사람》 elders; seniors/~의 elder; older; senior. としうえ

**연상**(聯想) association [of ideas]/~하다 associate (one) with (another); be reminded of/~시키다 remind (a person) of; suggest. れんそう

**연서**(連署) joint signature countersigna-

**연석**(宴席) a banquet; hall a dinner-party/~에 참석하다 attend a banquet. れんせき

**연석**(硯石) an inkstone. すずりいし

**연선**(沿線) ~의[에] on a railway [line]; along a railway [line]/철도 -에 있다 be on a railroad line. えんせん

**연설**(演說) a speech 《의식에서의》 an oration 《강연》 a lecture; an address/~하다 address (an audience); speak (on a subject); lecture/~회 a lecture meeting/~법 elocution/~자 a speaker 《웅변가》 an orator. えんぜつ

**연성 하감**(軟性下疳) 【의】 a chancroid; a soft chancre/~의 chancroidal. なんせいげかん

**연세**(年歲) age; years; time of life/~가 많다 be advanced[well up] in years [age]; be an old man. おとし

**연소**(年少) tender age[years]; childhood; youth/~하다 (be) young [in years]/~자 a youth 《미선년자》 a minor. ねんしょう

**연소**(延燒) the spread of the fire/~하다 《불이》 spread 《건물이》 burn down by the spreading fire; catch fire/~를 방지하다 check the spread of the flames. えんしょう

**연소**(燃燒) combustion/~하다 burn; ignite/~성의 combustible; inflammable/~물 combustibles; inflammable articles. ねんしょう

**연소**(燃素) phlogiston. ねんそ

**연소배**(年少輩) 《청년》 a youth; young fellows[men]; a youngster 《미숙한 사람》 a raw youth; a greenborn. ねんしょうのひとたち

**연속**(連續) continuity; continuation; succession; a series 《연쇄》 a chain/~하다 continue; last; continuous/~적으로 continuous[ly]; successive[ly]/~물 a sequel; a serial/~ 비행 a nonstop flight/~ 소설 a serial story/~ 방송극 broadcast of dramatic series. れんぞく

**연송**(連誦) recitation from the beginning to the end/~하다 recite (a book) from first to last. つけてあんしょうすること

**연쇄**(連鎖) a chain; a series; a link; a connection/~법 《논》 sorites/~ 반응〈물〉 chain reaction/~극 a play combined with moving picture; a screen -and-stage play. れんさ

**연수**(年數) a number of years/~가 늘어감에 따라 as years go by; with lapse of time. ねんすう

**연수**(延髓) 【해】 the medulla oblongata; the afterbrain. えんずい

**연수**(研修) study and training/ ~하다 study (science); master [English]; pursue the study (of history)/~생 a trainee/~ 제도 the service training system (미). けんしゅう

**연수**(年收) an annual income.

**연수**(軟水) soft water. なんすい

**연숙**(鍊熟) dexterity; mastery; expertness/~하다 become skillful; get skilled (in); become expert (in, at); acquire skill. れんじゅく

**연습**(練習) practice; training; exercise/~하다 practice; train; [have] exercise; drill 《연극에서》 rehearse/~이 부족하다 lack training[practice]/~곡 《음》 a study/~ 문제 exercises/~생 a student/~ 비행 a practice[training] flight/무대 ~ a stage rehearsal/~소 a training school[institute]. れんしゅう

**연습**(演習) 《익힘》 practice; an exercise 《기동 훈련》 maneuvers 《모의전》 a sham battle/~하다 practice; hold[carry out] manoeuvres/~림 an experimental plantation. えんしゅう

**연승**(連勝) straight[consecutive, successive] victories/~하다 win[gain] consecutive[successive] victories; win victory after victory/연전 ~하다 win every battle. れんしょう

**연승**(連乘) 【수】 continual multiplication/~하다 multiply continually.

**연시**(年始) the beginning of the year. ねんし

**연시**(軟柿) 【식】 a ripe persimmon.

**연식**(軟式) nonrigid[soft] type/~ 야구 kittenball; softball; kitty ball/~ 정구 softball tennis. なんしき

**연실**(鳶―) a kite-string/~을 감다 haul in the string of a kite.

**연실**(蓮實) a lotus pip ⇨연밥(蓮―). はすのみ

**연안**(沿岸) the coast; the shore/~에 along the coast/~ 무역 coastal[coastwise] trade/~ 어업 coastal[inshore] fishery/~ 항로 a coasting route[service line]. えんがん

**연애**(戀愛) love; affection; amour; love making/~의 erotic/~하다 fall in love (with one); get off (with one)/정신적 ~ platonic love/~ 문제 the love problem[affair]/~ 결혼 a love marriage/~ 소설 a romance; a love-story. れんあい

**연액**(年額) a yearly amount; an annual sum/~ 보장 노임제[도] guaranteed annual wage system. ねんがく

**연야**(連夜) night after night; every night. れんや

**연약**(軟弱) weakness; effeminacy/~하다 (be) tender; weak; effeminate/~해지다 weaken; [grow] effeminate. なんじゃく

**연어**(鰱魚) 【어】 《단복수 동형》 a salmon; Onchorhynchus peta(학명). さけ

**연역**(演繹) deduction/~하다 deduce (from); evolve/~적[으로] deductive[ly]; a priori/~적 추리 deductive inference

**연연(娟娟)** a light colo[u]r/~하다 (be) light-colo[u]red. えんえき

**연연(涓涓)** trickling; murmuring. けんけん

**연연(戀戀)** ~하다 (be) ardently attached to; clinging to; unwilling to let go. れんれん

**연염** beef rump; shin.

**연예(演藝)** a performance; entertainments/~인 a performer; an artiste; an entertainer/~계 an entertainment world[business]. えんげい

**연옥(煉獄)** 《종》 purgatory; hell/~의 고통을 겪다 go through purgatory[hell]. れんごく

**연옥색(軟玉色)** light[pale] blue. うすいたまいろ

**연와(煉瓦)** a [piece of] brick ⇒벽돌. れんが

**연운(年運)** the fortune[luck] of the year. そのとしのうん

**연원(淵源)** an origin; a beginning; a source/~하다 come from; originate; issue out of. えんげん

**연월일(年月日)** a date/~을 기입하다 date (a letter); give the date. ねんがっぴ

**연유(緣由)** 《사유》 a reason; a ground; a cause 《유래》 origin; derivation/~하다 originate (in); be derived (from); be caused (by); be due to. えんゆ

**연유(煉乳)** condensed milk. れんにゅう

**연유(燃油)** fuel oil/~선 an oil-burning ship.

**연의(演義)** 《주해》 a commentary; an exposition 《통속적 개작》 an adaptation for popular reading/~하다 explain; elucidate; comment (on the text). えんぎ

**연이나(然一)** however; but; still; and yet; nevertheless. だが

**연이율(年利率)** annual rate of interest ⇒연리. ねんりりつ

**연익(年益)** the profit per annum; an annual profit.

**연인(延引)** prolongation; extension; elongation/~하다 draw out; prolong; extend 《금속을》 beat out. えんいん

**연인(戀人)** 《남자》 a lover 《여자》 a [lady-]love 《남녀》 a sweetheart/한 쌍의 ~ a pair of lovers. こいびと

**연일(連日)** every day; day in and day out; day after day; from day to day/~ 비가 내린다 It rains day in and day out./~의 시험 the continuous examination of several days. れんじつ

**연일수(延日數)** the total number of days; a man-day〈미〉. のべにっすう

**연잇다(連一)** continue; be continuous/연이어 continuously; successively/연이은 불행 a train[series, chapter, succession] of misfortunes.

**연잎(蓮一)** a lotus leaf. れんよう

**연자매(硏子一)** a millstone worked by horse or ox.

**연장** a tool; an instrument; a utensil; an appliance; a gadget/~ 주머니 a tool-bag. どうぐ

**연장(年長)** seniority/~의 older; elder; senior/~자 《원로》 an elder 《연산》 a senior. ねんちょう

**연장(延長)** extension; extent; prolongation; length/~하다 extend; prolong; lengthen/~전 extra innings/철도를 ~하다 extend a railway. えんちょう

**연재(連載)** serial publication/~하다 publish serially; give in serial form/~ 소설 a serial story. れんさい

**연적(硯滴)** an ink-water container; a water-holder. けんてき

**연적(戀敵)** a rival suitor; a rival in love. こいがたき

**연전(年前)** some[a few] years ago; formerly.

**연전(連戰)** series of[successive] battles; every battle/~하다 fight a series of battles/~ 연승[연패] a succession of victories[defeats]. れんせん

**연접(連接)** connection; junction/~하다 connect; combine 《열차를》 interlock 《전화를》 switch. れんせつ

**연정(戀情)** [a feeling of] love; attachment; tender passion/~을 고백하다 confess one's love/~을 느끼다 feel attached (to). れんじょう

**연제(演題)** the subject (of a lecture); 《설교의》 a text. えんだい

**연제(年祭)** an anniversary/10년제 the tenth anniversary/50년제 the semi-centennial.

**연좌(連坐)** implication/~하다 be implicated[involved] in (an affair). れんざ

**연주(演奏)** a musical performance 《독주》 a recital/~하다 play; perform; render/~회 a concert 《독주회》 a recital/~법 execution; technique. えんそう

**연주창(連珠瘡)** 《의》 scrofula; struma; the king's evil. るいれき

**연죽(煙竹)** a tobacco pipe.

**연줄(緣一)** connections; pull 《중개》 medium/~을 구하다 make interest; hunt up connections/…의 ~로 through the influence[medium, good offices] (of). つながり

**연줄(鳶一)** 《연실》 the string of a kite.

**연줄연줄(緣一緣一)** through one connection after another; on the strength of some connection.

**연중(年中)** the whole year round; winter and summer; throughout the year/~ 행사 the year's celebrations; annual functions. ねんじゅう

**연즉(然則)** in that case; if [it be] so; then. それでは

**연지(蓮池)** a lotus pond. はすいけ

**연지(臙脂)** [cheek] rouge; cochineal/~를 찍다[바르다] apply[put on] rouge; rouge (one's cheeks, one's lips)/~분

**연차(連次)** many times; repeatedly.

**연차(年次)** ①《나이 차례》priority of age; order by age/~로 according to age 〔years〕 ②《해》a year/~의 annual; yearly/~ 계획 a long term yearly plan /~ 보고 an annual report. れんじ

**연차(聯借)** a joint debt〔loan〕/~하다 borrow money on joint liability〔responsibility〕.

**연착(延着)** 〔a〕 delay/~하다 arrive late; be delayed〔overdue〕/~한 우편물 belated mail. えんちゃく

**연찬(研鑽)** study; prosecution of one's studies/~하다 study; accomplish oneself. けんさん

**연창(一窓)** a storm window.

**연천(年淺)** being short/~하다 (be) short; not long. としのわかいこと

**연철(鍊鐵)** wrought iron/~로 a puddling furnace. れんてつ

**연체(延滯)** delay; procrastination; retardation/~하다 be delayed; be put off; stop on the way/~금 arrears; arrearages. えんたい

**연체 동물(軟體動物)** a mollusc; the mollusca. なんたいどうぶつ

**연초(煙草)** tobacco ⇨담배. たばこ

**연출(演出)** production; representation/ ~하다 produce; stage; perform/~가 a producer/~ 효과 stage effect/~ 각본 an acting copy. えんしゅつ

**연출대(筵―)** a board used for setting up a mud wall.

**연충(蠕蟲)** a worm; a vermin. みみず

**연치(年齒)** 〔years of〕 age. とし

**연타하다(連打―)** 《종 따위를》 clang (a bell) repeatedly 《구타하다》 deliver a shower of blows (on a person).

**연탄(煉炭)** a briquet/~ 난로 a briquet stove/~ 가스 coal gas. れんたん

**연통(煙筒)** a stove pipe; a chimney; a smokestack/~ 소제 chimney sweeping. えんとう

**연파(軟派)** the moderate party; the moderates. なんぱ

**연파(煙波)** ①《연기》 volumes〔billows〕 of smoke ②《물결》 the hazy sea; the hazy horizon. えんば

**연판(鉛版)** a stereotype; a plate/~공 a stereotyper/~ 인쇄 stereotypography. えんばん

**연판(連判)** joint signature〔seal〕/~하다 sign〔seal〕 jointly/~장 a list of signers to the compact.

**연패(連敗)** a series of reverses; defeats in succession/연전 ~하다 lose every battle; be a constant loser. れんぱい

**연포(練布)** glossed〔boiled-off〕 cloth.

**연폭(連幅)** joining (paper); piecing together/~하다 join〔piece〕 together. つなぎはば

**연표(年表)** a chronological table 《연대기》 chronology. ねんぴょう

**연풍(軟風)** a gentle breeze; a light 〔soft〕 wind. なんぷう

**연필(鉛筆)** a 〔lead〕 pencil/~심 a pencil lead/~을 깎다 sharpen a pencil. えんぴつ

**연하(嚥下)** swallowing/~하다 take〔get〕 down; swallow; drink-in.

**연하(煙霞)** a haze; a mist. えんか

**연하(年賀)** New Year's greetings/~장 a New Year's card/~객 a New Year's caller〔visitor〕. ねんが

**연하다(軟―)** ①《무르다》(be) tender; soft /연하게 하다 soften; make soft ②《빛이》(be) light/연한 빛깔 a light color. やわらかい

**연하다(連―)** connect; link; join. つける

**연하다(然―)** pretend to be; act as if (one were); have〔put on〕 the airs of. そうである

**연한(年限)** a period; a term/복무 ~ a term of office/~이 찼다 The term has expired. ねんげん

**연합(聯合)** 《연결》 combination 《동맹》 alliance 《조합》 union 《일치》 concert 《합동》 amalgamation 《정당의》 coalition/ ~하다 combine; join; unite; ally/~국 the Allies; the Entente Powers/~ 단체 a federation. れんごう

**연해(連―)** continuously; unceasingly/ ~ 비가 온다 It continues rainning. つづいて

**연해(沿海)** the coast; the sea; the inshore/~의 coastal; long-shore/~ 항로 a coastwise line〔service〕/~ 지대 the littoral zone. えんかい

**연해(煙害)** smoke pollution. えんがい

**연해안(沿海岸)** the coast; the shore/~ 지대 coastland.

**연해연방** successively; continuously; one after another.

**연행(連行)** ~하다 take〔walk〕 (one) to (the police station). れんこう

**연혁(沿革)** 《발달》 the 〔origin and〕 development 《역사》 the history. えんかく

**연호(年號)** the name of a chronological era. ねんごう

**연화(煙火)** smoke rising from kitchens. えんか

**연화(蓮花)** 【식】 a lotus flower. はすのはな

**연화(軟化)** softening weakening/~하다 become soft; soften. なんか

**연화(軟貨)** soft money.

**연회(宴會)** a dinner〔·party〕; a banquet; a feast. えんかい

**연회(年會)** an annual convention〔meeting〕. ねんかい

**연후(然後)** after that; afterwards/~에 after that; thereafter; thenceforth.

**연휴(連休)** consecutive holidays/~를 즐기다 enjoy straight holidays.

**연희(演戲)** a play; theatricals/~하다 give a play; perform a play on the stage. えんぎ

열 ten 《열째》 the tenth/~ 남짓한 ten odd (people).

열- young; new/~무 new turnips.

열(列) a line; a row; a file 《종렬》 a column 《횡렬》 a rank/~을 짓다 form a line[row, file]/~ 밖에 out of the ranks.

열(熱) ①《열기》 heat/~의 caloric; thermal; thermic/~ 단위 a heat[thermal] unit/~을 가한 heated/태양의 ~ the solar heat ②《체온》 temperature 《병열》 fever 《염증》 inflammation/높은[얕은] ~ a high[low] fever/~을 재다 take one's temperature/~을 식히다 reduce fever ③《열심·유행》 mania; craze; fever; enthusiasm/~이 있는 earnest; enthusiastic/~이 식다 cool down/~이 없는 indifferent.

열각(劣角) 〖수〗 a minor angle.
열강(列强) the [great] powers.
열거(列擧) enumeration/~하다 enumerate; list; array.
열고나다 hurry; hasten; press; urge.
열광(熱狂) [wild] enthusiasm; excitement; passion/~하다 be wildly excited; go wild with enthusiasm/~적 wild; frantic 《광신적》 fanatic.
열구름 a cloud drift; a drift of cloud.
열구자탕(悅口子湯) a stew served in a cook-pot of brass.
열국(列國) the powers; all countries; the nations of the world.
열기(熱氣) ①《더운 공기》 heat; hot air/방에 ~가 차 있다 The room is filled with heat. ②《신열》 temperature; fever.
열기(列記) enumeration; listing/~하다 enumerate; list.
열김(熱一) the heat of passion/~에 in a fit of anger; in the heat of passion.
열나다(熱一) ①《몸에》 develop fever; come to have fever ②《열중하다》 become enthusiastic (over) ③《화나다》 be offended; take offence; feel irritated/열나는 《말 따위》 provoking; vexatious; aggravating.
열나절 a very long time.
열녀(烈女) a heroine; a heroic woman.
열다¹ ①《열어 젖히다》 open; throw open 《펴다》 unfold 《꾸러미를》 undo 《열쇠로》 unlock/비틀어 ~ wrench open/문을 열어 놓다 keep[leave] the door ②《개시하다》 open; start; begin/가게를 ~ open a shop[store]/학교를 ~ start a school ③《개최하다》 hold; give; open/회를 ~ hold a meeting ④《길을》 open; clear/후진을 위하여 길을 ~ give the young fellows a chance.
열다² 《열매가》 bear [fruit]; fruit 《나무가 주어》 be in fruit 《열매가 주어》 grow (on a tree).
열대(熱帶) the tropics/~의 tropical/~ 식물 tropical plants[flora].
열댓 about fifteen/~ 살 about fifteen years of age.
열도(列島) a chain of islands; an archipelago.
열도(熱度) 《열》 [degree of] heat 《온도》 temperature.
열독(閱讀) perusal; reading/~하다 peruse; read; go over.
열등(劣等) inferiority/~의 inferior; low-grade/~감 inferiority complex; a feeling of inferiority/~생 a poor student/~품성이 ~하다 be of low character.
열락(悅樂) joy; pleasure; delight/~하다 enjoy.
열람(閱覽) reading; inspection; perusal/~하다 peruse; read; inspect; give (a book) a perusal/~실 a reading room/~인 a reader.
열량(熱量) calorie; calory/~이 많다[적다] be high[low] in calories/~계 a calorimeter.
열력(閱歷) a career; a personal history.
열렬(熱烈) ~하다 (be) ardent; fervent; fiery 《열성이다》 (be) hearty; enthusiastic/~히 ardently; fervently; passionately/~한 사람 passionate love.
열루(熱淚) hot[burning] tears.
열리다 ①《열어지다》 open; be opened 《자물쇠 따위가》 be unlocked/창이 모두 열려 있다 All the windows are open. ②《개최하다》 be held; take place; be given ③《개발하다》 be modernized; become civilized ④《열매가》 bear [fruit]; 《나무가 주어》 (be) in fruit 《열매가 주어》 grow (on a tree) ⑤《귀가》 hear; catch.
열망(熱望) an ardent wish; a longing (for)/~하다 thirst (for); desire earnestly.
열매 fruit 《견과(堅果)》 a nut 《장과(漿果)》 a berry 《양귀비씨 따위》 a seed/~를 맺다 bear fruit 《비유적》 produce a result.
열명(列名) listing of names; enrollment/~하다 list; enroll; enter names in a list.
열반(涅槃) Nirvana(Sans)/~에 들어가다 pass into Nirvana.
열변(熱辯) an impassioned[eloquent] speech/~을 토하다 make an impassioned [a fiery] speech; deliver a fervent speech.
열병(熱病) ①《열이 나는 병》 a fever/~에 걸리다 suffer from a fever ②《장질부사(腸窒扶斯)》.
열병(閱兵) a review; an inspection of troops/~하다 review; inspect/~식 a formal military inspection[review].
열복(悅服) willing submission/~하다 s-

**열부**(烈婦) a heroine ⇨열녀(烈女). れっぷ
**열분해**(熱分解) 〖화〗 pyrolysis／～하다 pyrolyze.
**열비**(劣比) 〖수〗 a minor ratio; ratio of lesser inequality.
**열사**(烈士) a patriot; a man of fervid loyalty; a hero／순국 ～ a martyr. れっし
**열사병**(熱射病) heat-stroke; heat prostration／～에 걸리다 suffer from[be affected by] heatstroke. ねっしゃびょう
**열상**(裂傷) a laceration; a lacerated wound／～을 입다 have (one's face) lacerated. れっしょう
**열쌔다** (be) quick; prompt; nimble; active／열쌔게 quickly; promptly; nimbly. すばやい
**열석**(列席) attendance; presence／～하다 attend; be present at; sit at／명사의 ～ a galaxy of notables. れっせき
**열선**(熱線) 〖물〗 thermic[heat] rays. ねっせん
**열성**(熱誠) earnestness; ardour; zeal; enthusiasm／～적인 warm; earnest; enthusiastic／～스럽다 be ardent; be earnest; be zealous. ねっせい
**열성**(列聖) successive kings. れっせい
**열성**(劣性) 〖생〗 inferiority; recessiveness／～감 inferiority complex／～형질(形質) a recessive character. れっせい
**열세**(劣勢) inferiority in numbers; numerical inferiority. れっせい
**열쇠** a key／한 다발의 ～ a bunch of keys／～ 구멍 a keyhole／～를 채우다 turn a key on; lock. かぎ
**열씨**(列氏) Réaumur／～ 온도계 a Réaumur thermometer.
**열심**(熱心) enthusiasm; zeal; ardor; eagerness／～하다 (be) enthusiastic; eager; earnest／～히 zealously; ardently／～히 노력하는 사람 a strenuous worker. ねっしん
**열십자**(一十字) a cross／～의 cross-shaped／～로 crosswise.
**열악**(劣惡) ～하다 (be) inferior; poor; coarse; deteriorated.
**열애**(熱愛) ardent[passionate] love／～하다 love (one) passionately; be devoted (to). ねつあい
**열어젖뜨리다** push[throw, fling] open. あけひろげる
**열없다** ①(부끄럽다) (be) awkward; a bashed; shy／열없이 bashfully; awkwardly ②(겁이 많다) (be) weak; feeble; effeminate; weak-kneed. ちょっとはずかしい
**열없장이** a coward; a weak-kneed person; a poltroon. しまりきのないひと
**열역학**(熱力學) 〖물〗 thermodynamics. ねつりきがく
**열연**(熱演) a superb play; ardent performance／～하다 perform (a part, a play etc.) enthusiastically. ねつえん
**열용량**(熱容量) 〖물〗 heat[thermal] capacity. ねつようりょう

**열원**(熱源) heat-source; heating sources. ねつげん
**열위**(列位) gentlemen.
**열의**(熱意) zeal; enthusiasm／～있는 zealous; ardent. ねつい
**열이온**(熱—) 〖물〗 thermion／～ 전류 a thermionic current.
**열자**(劣者) an inferior; the weak.
**열자기**(熱磁氣) 〖물〗 thermomagnetism.
**열적다** shy; weak ⇨열없다.
**열전**(熱戰) a fastfight 《경기》 a hot contest; a close game 《권투》 fast going. ねっせん
**열전**(列傳) a series of biographies; lives. れってん
**열전기**(熱電氣) 〖물〗 thermal electricity／～ 온도계 a thermoelectric thermometer. ねつでんき
**열전도**(熱傳導) thermal conduction／～율 thermal conductivity ねつでんどう
**열정**(熱情) passion; fervour; ardour; fire／～적 passionate; ardent; fervent／청년의 ～ youthful zest. ねつじょう
**열정**(劣情) the low passions; carnal desire. れつじょう
**열좌**(列座) the whole company[assemblage]; those present／～하다 be present (at a party). れんざ
**열중**(熱中) enthusiasm; zeal; mania／～하다 devote oneself; give oneself up (to); be bent 《여자에》 be infatuated with／～하는 성질의 enthusiastic; ardent; earnest. ねっちゅう
**열증**(熱症) 〖의〗 inflammation.
**열차**(列車) a train／～편으로 by train／급행[직행] ～ an express[a through] train. れっしゃ
**열채** a whip with a lash.
**열탕**(熱湯) 〖물〗 boiling water／～ 소독을 하다 scald. ねっとう
**열퉁적다** (be) clumsy; gawky／열퉁적은 사람 an awkward fellow; a gawk. のろまだ
**열파**(熱波) 〖물〗 a heat wave.
**열패**(劣敗) defeat／～하다 be defeated; be worsted; be beaten. れっぱい
**열팽창**(熱膨脹) thermal expansion／～율 the coefficient of thermal expansion. ねつぼうちょう
**열품**(劣品) a low[er] class[an inferior] article; an article of the lower grade.
**열풍**(熱風) a hot wind; a simoom. ねっぷう
**열하다**(熱—) heat; make hot 《고온으로》 ignite; heat intensely.
**열흘** 《열흘날》 eleven days 《열하루째》 the eleventh [day]
**열학**(熱瘧) malarial fever.
**열학**(熱學) 〖물〗 thermotics; calorifics. ねつがく
**열혈**(熱血) hot blood; fervent zeal; ardor; fieriness／～ 남아 a hot-blooded young man; a passionate[sanguine]

**열호(劣弧)** 【수】 a minor arc.

**열화(烈火)** a blazing[raging] fire; furious[devastating] flames/～같이 노하다 flush with anger[fury]; burn[boil] with anger.

**열화(熱火)** furious flames; a blazing fire/～ 같은 더위 fiery heat/～ 같은 연설 a fiery speech.

**열화학(熱化學)** thermochemistry.

**열흘** (10일) ten days 《열흘째》 the tenth day of the month/～도 못되어 in less than ten days/초～ the tenth day [of the month].

**열흡수(熱吸收)** absorption of heat.

**엷다** ①《두께가》(be) thin/엷게 thinly/입술이 ～ have thin lips ②《빛이》(be) light; pale; faint; thin/엷은 빛 a light color 《흐리하게》 dimly/엷게 화장한 얼굴 a slightly powdered face ③《천박하다》 (be) shallow; shallowminded; superficial [learning]/속이 엷은 사람 a shallow person; a shortsighted person/정이 ～ be not close[intimate]; be rather cool.

**엷붉다** (be) pale[light] red.

**염(炎)** an inflammation/늑막～ pleurisy; pleuritis/폐～ pneumonia; inflammations of the lungs.

**염(殮)** shrouding.

**염(鹽)** salt/～류 salts/정～ normal salt/중성～ neutral salt.

**염가(廉價)** a moderate[cheap, low] price/～의 cheap; moderate-[low-]priced; inexpensive/～로 사다 buy cheap[at a bargain price]/～로 팔다 sell cheap[at a reduced price, at a bargain price]/《재고품 정리로》 clear off/～판 a cheap [popular] edition/～ 대매출 a bargain sale/～품 low[popular] priced goods.

**염갱(鹽坑)** a brine[salt] pit.

**염결(廉潔)** integrity; uprightness; probity; honesty/～하다 (be) pure; upright; honest; high-minded; cleanhanded; disinterested/～한 사람 a man of probity[integrity]; a man of upright character.

**염고(厭苦)** dislike; abhorrence/～하다 dislike; abhor; detest.

**염광(鹽鑛)** a salt mine.

**염교** 【식】 a scallion; a shallot; *Allium Bakeri*(학명).

**염글리다** bring to success[pass]; bring (a plan) off; accomplish; carry out.

**염기(厭忌)** dislike; detesting/～하다 dislike; detest; abhor.

**염기(鹽基)** 【화】 a base/～성의 basic; positive; electropositive/～도 basicity/～류 the bases; the basic group/～성 반응 basic reaction/～성 산화물 a basic oxide.

**염낭(―囊)** a purse; a money pouch; a small moneybag.

**염담(恬淡)** unselfishness; simplicity/～하다 (be) simple; unselfish; undemanding/～도 무욕하다 be indifferent to worldly gain.

**염두(念頭)** mind; thought; the head/～에 두다 bear (*a thing*) in mind; keep in mind/～에 두지 않다 give no thought[heed] to; take no thought of/～에서 사라지다 dismiss (*a matter*) from *one's* mind.

**염라국(閻羅國)** 【종】 Hades; the nether world; the land[kingdom] of the dead; the infernal regions.

**염라대왕(閻羅大王)** Yama(Sans); Pluto(L); the King[Judge] of Hades; the King [Ruler, Judge] of Hell.

**염량(炎凉)** ①《한서》 heat and cold ②《분별》 discernment; discretion; good sense ③《성쇠》 rise and fall; ups and downs; vicissitudes.

**염려(念慮)** anxiety; worry; apprehension; misgivings; a weight on *one's* mind/～하다 worry; be[feel] anxious; be concerned (*about*)/～되다 feel anxious[uneasy] about 《사람이》 worry about 《일이》 weigh on *one's* mind; lie at *one's* heart.

**염려(艶麗)** [voluptuous] beauty; charm/～하다 (be) charming; enchanting; beautiful; coquettish/～한 여자 a voluptuous beauty[woman]; a glamor girl.

**염력(念力)** will[-power]; energy/～은 바위를 뚫는다 Will is all-powerful.

**염료(染料)** dyes; dyestuffs/～가 좋다[나쁘다] The dye is fast[weak]./～ 공업 the dye industry/무기 ～ mineral dyes/인조[합성] ～ artificial[synthetic] dyes/천연 ～ natural dyes.

**염류(鹽類)** 【화】 salts/～천(泉) a saline spring; a mineral salt spring.

**염마(閻魔)** 《염라대왕》 Yama(Sans); Pluto(L).

**염마장(閻魔帳)** a black list 《염라대왕의》 book used by Yama for marking[listing] person's sins.

**염매(廉賣)** a bargain[cheap] sale; selling at small profits/～하다 sell cheap; sell at low prices/～일 a bargain day/～ 시장 a bargain[cheap] market.

**염모제(染毛劑)** a hair-dye.

**염문(艶文)** a love letter; a *billet-doux*(*pl.* billets-doux)(F).

**염문(艶聞)** a love-affair; a rumour of love; a romance 《추문》 a scandal/～이 퍼지다 give rise to scandal; become the talk of the town for *one's* love affairs.

**염전(鹽―)** a salt farm[field, garden]; a saltern; a salina.

**염백(廉白)** uprightness; integrity; hon-

**염병(染病)** ①(장질부사) enteric fever; typhoid [fever]; abdominal typhus/~을 치르다 get over[recover from, be cured of] typhoid fever ②(전염병) a contagious disease; an epidemic.

**염복(艶福)** good fortune in love/~가 beau; a ladies' pet.

**염분(鹽分)** salt; salt content; salinity /~있는 saltish; saline/바닷물에는 다량의 ~이 있다 Sea-water contains much salt.

**염불(念佛)** a Buddhist invocation/~하다 offer prayer to Amida Buddha; chant a prayer; tell one's beads/~을 외우다 repeat[chant] prayers.

**염산(鹽酸)** 【화】 hydrochloric acid/~가리 potassium[kalium] chlorate; chlorate of potash/~아연 butter of zinc; ~염 hydrochloride.

**염색(染色)** dyeing/~하다 dye/~기 a dyeing range/~공 a dyer / ~공장 dye works/~법 a process of dyeing/~체 【생】chromosome/성~체 a sex chromosome/머리 ~약 hairdye.

**염서(炎暑)** intense heat; a heat wave; ~지절(之節) the hot weather; (at) this time of hot summer days.

**염서(艶書)** a love-letter; a billet-doux (pl. billets-doux)(F).

**염세(厭世)** pessimism; weariness of life [the world]/~적인 pessimistic; world-weary/~ 자살하다 commit suicide from an unconquerable disgust for existence/ ~가 a pessimist; a misanthrope /~주의 pessimism/~ 철학 pessimistic philosophy.

**염소** a goat/~가죽 goatskin/~ 새끼 a kid; a goatling/~ 수염 a goatee.

**염소(鹽素)** chlorine/~와 화합하다 chlorinate; chloridize/~산 chloric acid/~산염 a chlorate.

**염수(鹽水)** salt water; brine/~선 brine assortment/~호 a saline lake.

**염습(殮襲)** shrouding/~하다 wrap[clothe] dead body in a shroud; dress the deceased; shroud.

**염연(恬然)** ~하다 (be) tranquil; carefree; (be) calm[peaceful] with no desires in mind.

**염열(炎熱)** intense[extreme] heat; sultriness/~이 찌는 듯한 날 a scorching[sweltering, burning hot] day.

**염오(厭惡)** dislike; hatred; aversion; disgust/~하다 dislike; hate; be averse (to)/~할 사건 an abominable incident; a scandal/몹시 ~하다 regard (a person) with great aversion.

**염원(念願)** one's heart's desire; one's dearest wish; a cherished desire; one's prayer/~하다 desire; wish (for)/오랜 ~ one's long-cherished desire/나의 ~이 이루어졌다 My prayer has been answered.

**염의없다** (be) shameless.

**염장(鹽醬)** (조미료) seasonings; condiments; spices 《소금과 장》 salt and soy sauce.

**염장이(殮-)** a professional engaged in preparing the dead for burial; an undertaker in washing and dressing the dead.

**염전(鹽田)** a salt farm[field, garden]; a salina; a saltern.

**염접** tucking in the edge/~하다 tuck in the edge.

**염좌(捻挫)** a sprain/~하다 sprain [one's ankle].

**염주(念珠)** a rosary;[a string of] beads; a chaplet/~ 알 a bead 《첸 구슬》 the beads of a rosary / ~를 세다 finger[tell] one's beads.

**염증(厭症)** an aversion; dislike; disgust; a repugnance (to)/…에 ~이 나다 feel a repugnance to; be tired of …/일에 ~이 났다 He grew sick [and tired] of his work., He was fed up with the work.

**염증(炎症)** an inflammation/~을 일으키다 be[become] inflamed; start inflammation/~열 an inflammatory fever.

**염직(染織)** dyeing and weaving/~하다 dye and weave.

**염직(廉直)** integrity; honesty; probity; uprightness/~하다 (be) honest; just; clean-fingered[-handed]/~한 사람 a man of integrity; an upright man.

**염천(炎天)** the hot[blazing,' broiling] sun; the heat of the day; hot weather/~하에 under a burning sun / ~하에서 일하다 work in a burning[blazing] sun.

**염출(捻出)** ~하다 ①(의안을) contrive; devise/재무 변상의 방법을 ~하다 work out a plan for financing one's obligations ②(비용 따위를) contrive to raise / 재원(財源)을 ~하다 contrive to raise funds.

**염치(廉恥)** a sense of honor; a sense of shame/~가 있다 have a sense of honor/~가 없다 have no sense of honor; be shameless.

**염탐(廉探)** spy; secret observation; espionage/~하다 spy (upon); pry (upon); make secret observations/적정을 ~하다 spy on the enemy/~군 a spy; a scout; a secret agent.

**염통** the heart.

**염포(殮布)** winding sheet; a shroud.

**염하다(廉-)** ①(값이) (be) cheap; low[moderate-]priced; inexpensive ②(청렴하다) (be) upright; clean-handed; disinterested; incorruptible.

**염화(鹽化)** chloridation/~하다 chloridize

**엽견(獵犬)** a hunting dog; a hound; a gun dog〈미〉.

**엽관 운동(獵官運動)** office-hunting[-seeking]; place-hunting/~을 하다 run[hunt] for office.

**엽권련(葉卷煙)** a cigar/~을 물고 with a cigar in *one's* mouth[between *one's* teeth]/~을 피우다 smoke a cigar; puff at *one's* cigar.

**엽기(獵奇)** bizarrerie hunting; hunting after grotesqueries/~하다 seek[hunt] the bizarre/~적 curiosity-seeking/~심에서 out of curiosity/~소설 a bizzare story/~심 [wicked] curiosity.

**엽기(獵期)** the hunting[shooting, open] season/~가 되었다 The shooting season has opened., The close season is over.

**엽록소(葉綠素)** 《식》 chlorophyll.

**엽맥(葉脈)** 《식》《지맥》 a vein 《맥리》 a nerve 《주맥》 a nervure.

**엽부(獵夫)** a hunter; a huntsman.

**엽서(葉書)** a postcard; a postal card〈미〉/~를 내다 send a postcard (*to*)/관제[사제] ~ an official[a private] postcard/그림 ~ a picture postcard; a postcard〈미〉.

**엽전(葉錢)** a Korean brass coin.

**엽초(葉草)** leaf tobacco.

**엽초(葉鞘)** 《식》 a vagina; a sheath.

**엽총(獵銃)** a hunting[sporting] gun 《조총》 a fowling piece; a shot-gun 《맹수용》 a hunting rifle.

**엽치다** hull [barley] roughly.

**엿** wheat-gluten; glutinous rice jelly/~ 세공(細工) wheat-gluten figures/~장수 a wheat-gluten vendor/~을 빨아먹다 suck wheat-gluten.

**엿-** six/~말 six *mal*.

**엿가락** a stick of taffy; a piece of taffy.

**엿기름** malt; germ[germinated] barley; a dry barley sprout/~을 만들다 malt ~ 가루 powdered malt.

**엿듣다** overhear; listen secretly to; eavesdrop/엿듣는 사람 an eavesdropper/전화를 ~ tap the wires; listen in on a (*person's*) telephone conversation.

**엿밥** dregs of glutinous rice jelly.

**엿보다** watch[wait] for; look [out] for 《상태를》 see; spy out[on]; search out/기회를 ~ watch[look] for a chance/형세를 ~ see how the wind blows/틈새를 통해서 ~ peep through a crack.

**엿새** 《엿샛날》 the sixty day [of a month] 《6일》 six days.

**엿치기** a taffy-breaking game.

**영(令)** 《명령》 an order; a command 《법규》 an ordinance; a law; an act/~을 내리다 order; command; dictate; issue [a decree]/~을 거역하다 disobey[protest against] (*a person's*) order.

**영(永)** forever; eternally; perpetually; for good [and all]/고향을 ~ 떠나다 leave *one's* native place for good[permanently].

**영(零)** zero(*pl*, -s, -es); nought; nothing; a cipher/~하 10도 ten degrees below zero/시험에 ~점 맞다 get zero in an examination; get no marks/~도(度) freezing point/~봉 《체》《정구》 a love game 《야구》 a shoutout.

**영(嶺)** a ridge; a [mountain] pass; a high hill.

**영(靈)** the spirit; the soul 《유령》 a ghost/~과 육(肉) the spirit and the flesh/~의 세계 a world of spirits/~적 spiritual/선조의 ~을 모시다 worship the spirits of *one's* ancestors.

**영감(令監)** 《존칭》 Your Excellency 《노인》 an old man; an elderly man; a patriarch 《남편》 *one's* husband/시골 ~ a gaffer.

**영감(靈感)** inspiration; intellectual intuition; afflatus 《신리》 extrasensory perception/~을 받다 be inspired.

**영걸(英傑)** ①《인물》 a great man; a hero; a master mind ②《기상》 heroic qualities[character].

**영검(靈—)** miraculous virtue; a wonderful responsive to prayers/~이 신효한 wonderfully responsive to prayers.

**영겁(永劫)** eternity; perpetuity.

**영격(迎擊)** a responsive-[counter-]attack; interception/~하다 intercept; counter [an enemy attack].

**영결(永訣)** an eternal separation by death; the last[final] parting[farewell]/~하다 be separated by death eternally; part forever/~을 고하다 bid *one's* last farewell (*to*)/~식 a ceremony of the last farewell.

**영계(—鷄)** a spring chicken/~ 백숙 boiled chicken with rice.

**영계(靈界)** 《영적인 세계》 the spirit[ual] world 《종교계》 the religious world/~의 현상 spiritual[psychic] phenomena.

**영고(榮枯)** prosperity and decline; ups and downs; rise and fall/개인과 마찬가지로 일국에는 ~ 성쇠가 있다 Like an individual a nation goes through many ups and downs.

**영관(領官)** 《군》《육군》 a field-officer; a captain 《해군》 a commander/~급 장교 field grade officers.

**영관(榮冠)** the crown [cf glory]; the laurels; the palm/승리의 ~을 쓰다 win laurels; be crowned with victory; bear [carry away] the palm.

**영광(榮光)** honour; distinction; glory/

**~스럽다** (be) glorious; honourable; h-onoured/**~스러운 역사** a glorious history/**~으로 여기다[생각하다]** esteem it an honour; feel honoured/**분에 넘치는 ~이올시다** The honor is more than I deserve.

**영구**(永久) permanence; eternity; perpetuity/**~하다** (be) lasting; a permanent; eternal/**~히** eternally; permanently/**반 ~적인** semi-permanent/**~성** permanency/**~ 운동** perpetual motion/**~치(齒)** the permanent[second] teeth. えいきゅう

**영구**(靈柩) a coffin; a hearse; a casket/**~ 열차** a funeral train/**~차** a [motor] hearse; a funeral carriage; an obituary[a mortuary] car. れいきゅう

**영귀**(榮貴) high rank and distinction/**~하다** (be) high and noble. えいたつ

**영금** a bitter[dreadful] experience[humiliation]/**~을 보다** undergo a bitter humiliation; have a bitter experience. からいけいけん

**영내**(營內) inside barracks/**~의** within [in] barracks; barrack/**~ 근무** service in barracks/**~ 생활** a barrack life/**거주** living in barracks.

**영년**(永年) a long time; many[long] years; for many years; for ages; for a long time. えいねん

**영농**(營農) engaging in agriculture; farming/**~하다** engage in farming[agriculture]/**~ 자금** farming fund. えいのう

**영단**(英斷) a decisive[drastic] measure; a resolute step; prompt decision/**~을 내리다** take a decisive measure; act decisively/**이 일은 일대 ~이 필요하다** The case calls for a drastic[decisive] measure. えいだん

**영단**(營團) a corporation; a management foundation/**주택 ~** a housing corporation.

**영달**(榮達) distinction; wordly fame; advancement/**~을 바라다** hanker after [aim at] distinction; aspire to[after] high honors. えいたつ

**영대**(永代) eternity/**~의** perpetual; eternal/**~ 차지권** a perpetual lease; a lease in perpetuity/**~ 소유권** a perpetual ownership; perpetuity. えいだい

**영도**(零度) zero degree; the freezing[zero] point/**~ 이하의** the degrees of frost⟨영⟩/**~ 이상으로 오르다[이하로 내리다]** rise above[fall down below] zero. れいど

**영도**(領導) leading; leadership; direction; guidance/**~하다** take the lead/**~자** a leader/**정당을 ~하다** lead[steer] a political party. りょうどう

**영독**(獰毒) fierceness; ferocity/**~하다** (be) fierce; ferocious; savage; truculent/**~한 얼굴을 하고 있다** look fierce.

**영락**(零落) ruin; downfall; comedown/**~하다** go to ruin; be in reduced[needy] circumstances; be in distress/**~한 사람들** ruined people/**그는 ~했다** He is in reduced circumstances. れいらく

**영락없다** (be) sure; unfailing; certain; evident/**영락없이** infallibly; without fail/**영락없는 일** a certain fact. たしかである

**영랑**(令郞) your[his] son. れいろう

**영령**(英靈) the spirit[soul] of the dead. えいれい

**영롱**(玲瓏) **~하다** (be) brilliant; translucent; clear and bright; lucid; serene/**~한 구슬** bright gems/**~한 문체** a crystal-clear style. れいろう

**영리**(營利) profit[-making]; moneymaking; gain/**~적인** commercial; money-making; mercenary/**~에 급급하다** be bent solely upon profit/**이것은 ~적인 계획이 아니다** This is not a money-making scheme./**~ 사업** an undertaking for profit; a commercial enterprise/**~주의** commercialism/**~회사** a company established for profit. えいり

**영리**(怜悧) cleverness; wisdom; intelligence; brightness/**~하다** (be) wise; clever; sagacious; intelligent 《눈치빠름》saucy 《빈틈없음》 shrewd/**~하게 보이는** intelligent-looking/**~한 여자** a clever woman/**~한 수법** a wise policy. れいり

**영림**(營林) forest management[administration]; afforestation; forestry/**~국** a forestry bureau[office]. えいりん

**영마루**(嶺—) the top of a mountain pass; a summit.

**영망**(令望) good reputation; high repute; renown. よいめいぼう

**영매**(令妹) your[his] younger sister. れいまい

**영매**(靈媒) a spirit medium. れいばい

**영매**(英邁) **~하다** (be) wise and masterful; brave and sagacious/**~한 사람** a master mind; a man of parts. えいまい

**영면**(永眠) eternal sleep[rest]; death; passing away; quietus/**~하다** pass away; sleep the long sleep. えいみん

**영명**(英明) clear-sightedness; perspicacity/**~하다** (be) clever; clear-sighted; intelligent; perspicacious. えいめい

**영명**(令名) a fair name; reputation; good repute; renown/**~있는** noted; distinguished; famous; celebrated; of high reputation/**~이 높다** be highly renowned; enjoy an excellent reputation; be famed; be reputed (cs). れいめい

**영몽**(靈夢) a vision; a dream which tells the truth; an inspired[a true] dream; a prophetic vision[dream]/**~을 꾸다** have[dream] an inspired dream [vision].

**영묘**(靈妙) **~하다** (be) ethereal; inexplicable; unutterable; subtle; inscrutable/**~한 미(美)** ethereal beauty/**영묘[불가사의]한 일** an inscrutable fact. れいみょう

**영문** ①(까닭) a reason; a cause; a ground; why／무슨 ~인지 모르지만 for some unknown reason; for some reason or other／~모를 소리 words that do not make sense／왜 화를 내고 있는지 ~을 모르겠다 I don't see any reason for his anger. ②(형편) circumstances; the matter; the case／~을 캐묻다 inquire into the circumstances／그는 처음부터 ~을 알고 있었다 He was in the secret from the beginning. わけ

**영문(英文)** English; English composition [writing]; an English sentence／~으로 쓰다 write (a matter) in English／~과 the English department／~ 편지 a letter in English; an English letter／ ~학 English literature／~학을 전공하다 major in English literature(미)／~학사 a history of English literature／~학자 a scholar of English literature／~법 English grammar. えいぶん

**영문(營門)** the barrack gate. えいもん

**영물(靈物)** a spiritual[sacred] being. れいぶつ

**영민(英敏)** cleverness; sharpness; [mental] acuteness／~하다 (be) quick-witted; sharp; sagacious／~한 두뇌 a clear head; a keen intellect／머리가 ~한 사람 a nimble-witted person. えいびん

**영바람** high spirits; exhilaration; elation／~이 나서 exultantly; triumphantly; in fine[good] feather／~이 나다 be in high spirits; be elated[exhilarated]. げんき

**영법(英法)** 《법》 English law.

**영법(泳法)** a swimming style[form].

**영별(永別)** parting forever; eternal farewell; the last[final] parting[farewell]／~하다 part forever; be separated by death／~을 고하다 bid one's last farewell (to). えいべつ

**영봉(靈峰)** a sacred mountain. れいほう

**영부인(令夫人)** your[his] wife; Madame (F). れいふじん

**영사(映寫)** projection (on a screen)／~하다 project; throw (a picture) on a screen／~막 a screen／~기 a projector／~실 an operating room. えいしゃ

**영사(領事)** a consul; a consular representative／~관 a consulate／~관원 a consular attaché[official]; the staff of a consulate／~ 재판[권] consular jurisdiction／~ 재판소 a consular court／명예 ~ an honorary consul／부~ a vice-consul／총~ a consul general. りょうじ

**영사(營舍)** barracks; cantonments. えいしゃ

**영상(領相)** the Premier; the Prime Minister; the Minister-President.

**영상(映像)** an image; a reflection (그림자) a silhouette. えいぞう

**영상(零上)** above zero／~ 5도 five degrees above zero.

**영색(令色)** servile looks／교언 ~을 농하는 무리 flatterers; sycophants. れいしょく

**영생(永生)** eternal life; immortality／~하다 live eternally; enjoy immortality. えいせい

**영생이** 《식》 peppermint. はっか

**영서(令壻)** your[his] [esteemed] son-in-law. れいせい

**영서(永逝)** death ⇒영면(永眠).

**영서(英書)** an English book (영문) English literature. えいしょ

**영선(營繕)** building and repairs; repairs／~하다 build and repair／~과(課) a building and repairs section. えいぜん

**영성(靈性)** spirituality; divinity. かみのみたまのようなせいしつ

**영세(永世)** eternity; permanence; everlasting generations／~의 eternal; perpetual／~토록 forever; eternally; perpetually／~ 중립 permanent neutrality／~ 중립국 a permanent neutral country. えいせい

**영세 불망(永世不忘)** ~하다 keep the matter in view forever; hold in remembrance for all days. えいえんにわすれないこと

**영속(永續)** everlastingness; permanency; perpetuity; continuation／~하다 last long; be permanent; be long-lived／~적 lasting; permanent; perpetual／~하지 않다 be of short duration; be short-lived／이 장사는 ~성이 없다 This business will not last long. えいぞく

**영손(令孫)** your[his] grandchild[grandson, granddaughter]. れいそん

**영솔(領率)** command; supervision; direction; leadership／~하다 command; lead; take the lead of／군대를 ~하여 진군하다 march at the head of an army.

**영송(迎送)** welcome and send-off; greeting and farewell／~하다 welcome and send off; meet and see off. そうげい

**영쇄(零瑣)** ~하다 (be) trivial; trifling.

**영수(領收, 領受)** receipt／~하다 receive; acknowledge; receipt (of); be in receipt of (a letter)／~증을 쓰다 make (out) a receipt[voucher]／~자 a receiver; a recipient／~증 a receipt; an acknowledgment／가~증 an interim receipt. りょうしゅう

**영수(領袖)** a leader; a chief; a boss(미); a protagonist／정당의 ~ a leader of a political party; a political leader.

**영시(零時)** twelve o'clock; the zero hour (정오) noon (밤) midnight／~ 30분[에] (at) half past twelve [o'clock.]; twelve thirty. れいじ

**영시(英詩)** (전체) English poetry[verse]; (시편) an English poem; a poem in English. えいし

**영식(令息)** your[his] son. れいそく

**영아(嬰兒)** an infant; a baby; a new-born child; a suckling／~ 살해 infanticide; child-murderer／~ 위탁소 a baby-f-

**영악(獰惡)** savage; fierceness; ferocity; cruelty/~하다 (be) fierce; ferocious; savage/~한 사람 a fierce fellow; a Tartar. arm; a nursery/~ 사망률 infant mortality/~ 살인죄 infanticide. えいじ

**영악하다** (be) clever; bright; assiduous.

**영애(令愛)** your[his] daughter. れいあい

**영약(靈藥)** a miraculous medicine; a wonderful remedy; a royal れいやく

**영양(羚羊)**【동】 an antelope. れいよう

**영양(營養, 榮養)** nourishment; nutrition; alimentation/~이 좋은 well-nourished [-feú]/~ 부족의 ill-fed[-nourished]; underfed/~가(價) nutritive[food] value; nutritive qualities/~ 과다 supernutrition/~ 부족 undernourishment; insufficient nutrition/~ 섭취량 caloric intake/~ 실조 malnutrition/~학 dietetics. えいよう

**영양(令孃)** a daughter; a young lady; a miss; *a mademoiselle*(F). れいじょう

**영어(英語)** English; the English language[tongue]/~의 English/~로 쓴 편지 a letter [written] in English/정확한[바른] ~ correct[proper] English/세련된 [저속한] ~ polished[vulgar] English/산 ~ living English/순수한 ~ the King's[Queen's] English/~를 쓰다 speak English(말을); write English(글씨를)/ ~가 늘다 improve[make progress] in *one's* English/~ 강습회 an English class/~교사 a teacher of English; an English teacher/~ 시험 an examination in English/상업 ~ commercial[business] English/시사 ~ current English/실용 ~ practical[living] English /표준 ~ standard English. えいご

**영어(囹圄)** a prison; a jail/~의 몸이 되다 be put in prison[jail]. れいご

**영업(營業)** business; trade/~하다 do business; engage in[carry on] business; operate; trade in/~ 이익 trading profits/~ 과목 lines of business/~부 a business department/~주 a proprietor /~ 시간 business hours/~비 business [working] expenses/~ 방법 *one's* business method/~정지 prohibition[suspension] of business. えいぎょう

**영역(英譯)** an English translation[version]/~하다 translate[render, put, turn] into English/다음 문장을 ~하시오 Put the following sentences into English. えいやく

**영역(靈域)** a sacred ground; holy precincts. れいいき

**영역(領域)** ①《영토》 a territory; a domain; a possession/타국 ~을 침범하다 encroach on another country's territory ②《지배 범위》 jurisdiction; a province; a field/…의 ~이다 be in *one's* line [province]/자기 ~을 벗어나다 move in another's sphere/여기까지 나의 ~이다 This is the extent of my sphere/정신병학의 ~ the field of psychiatry. りょういき

**영영(永永)** forever; eternally; perpetually; for good [and all]/~ 조국을 떠나다 leave *one's* homeland permanently[for good]. えいえい

**영영(營營)** ~하다 (be) assiduous; strenuous; busy; diligent; strive hard [after fame[gain]]. えいえい

**영영 무궁(永永無窮)** eternity; perpetuity; infinitude; immortality/~하다 (be) eternal; everlasting; infinite; immortal /~토록 forever; eternally; perpetually; immortally.

**영예(榮譽)** honour; distinction; glory; splendour/~로운 honourable; glorious; renowned/~로운 날 a glorious[splendid] day/국가의 ~ the glory of a nation/~를 지니다 have the honour of. えいよ

**영외(領外)** ~에 outside[beyond] the territory (*of*).

**영외(營外)** outside barracks/~ 거주 living out of barracks.

**영요(榮耀)** 《영예》 honour 《영광》 glory 《명예》 fame 《면목》 credit.

**영욕(榮辱)** glory and shame; honor and contempt; reputation and disgrace. えいじょく

**영웅(英雄)** a hero; a great man/~심 ambition; aspiration/~ 숭배 hero-worship/~적 행위 a heroic deed/국민적 ~ 이 되다 become a national hero/그는 ~다운 기질이 있다 He is cast in heroic mold. えいゆう

**영원(永遠)** eternity; permanence; perpetuity; immortality/~하다 (be) eternal; everlasting; permanent; imperishable /~히 eternally; forever; permanently; perpetually/~한 잠 eternal sleep/~한 진리[생명] an eternal truth[life]/~한 평화 a lasting[permanent, everlasting] /~성 eternal nature; eternity. えいえん

**영원(蠑蚖)**【동】 a salamander; a newt; a water lizard; an eft. いもり

**영위(營爲)**《관리》 management; administration; operation〈미〉/~하다 carry on; operate[run] (*a hotel*); manage; conduct. えいい

**영위(榮位)** an exalted[eminent] position; a high rank/~에 오르다 attain to a high[an honorable] position; gain distinction. えいい

**영위(零位)** zero/~법 the zero method.

**영유(領有)** possession/~하다 possess; set possession of; take[be in] possession of/…의 ~로 되다 be annexed to; come under *one's* way. りょうゆう

**영육(靈肉)** soul and body; body and spirit/~ 일치 the union[coincidence] of body and soul. れいにく

**영윤(令胤)** your[his] son.

**영이(靈異)** a wonder; a miracle/~하다 (be) wonderful; miraculous.  れいい

**영인(英人)** an Englishman 《여자》 an English woman 《총칭》 the English 《별명》 John Bull.

**영일(寧日)** a peaceful[quiet] day/ ~이 없다 be kept busy all the time; Not a single day passes quietly.  ねいじつ

**영자(英字)** an English letter[character] /~ 신문 an English paper; an English-language news paper.  えいじ

**영자(英姿)** an impressive[a gallant] figure; a majestic[dignified] appearance; a noble mien/그가 늠름한 ~를 나타냈다 He made his majestic appearance.  えいし

**영자(影子)** a shadow; a silhouette; an image.  かげぼうし

**영작(榮爵)** peerage; a title.  えいしゃく

**영장(令狀)** a warrant; a writ; a written order/~을 발부하다 issue a warrant/~을 집행하다 execute a warrant; serve a writ on (one)/가택 수색 ~ a search warrant/소환 ~ a [writ of] summons/체포 ~ a warrant of arrest/차압 ~ a writ of affachment.  れいじょう

**영장(永葬)** burial; interment.

**영장(靈長)** a supreme creature/사람은 만물의 ~이다 Man is the lord of [all] creation./~류《동》 Primates(학명).  れいちょう

**영재(英才)** brilliant qualities; talent; high intelligence 《사람》 a brilliant[gifted] man; a genius/저 학교는 많은 ~를 배출했다 The school has turned out a lot of talented men./~ 교육 special education for the gifted children[the precocious].  えいさい

**영전(榮轉)** transfer on promotion/~하다 be promoted [and transferred] to (a higher post); be transferred on promotion/그는 본사로 ~됐다 He was transferred to the head-office on promotion.  えいてん

**영전(靈前)** ~에 before the spirit of the departed[deceased]/고인의 ~에 바치다 offer (a thing) to the spirit of the departed.  れいぜん

**영절스럽다** (be) plausible; specious; likely; appear to be true/영절스러운 아기 an admirable child; a likely lad.  そうらしい

**영점(零點)** ①《무득점》 zero; the zero point; no marks 《경기 득점》 a duck; a duck's egg〈미〉/~을 맞By get no marks 《경기에서》 get a duck ②《빙점》 the freezing point.  れいてん

**영접(迎接)** reception; welcome 《출영》 meeting/~하다 welcome; receive; meet 《출영하다》 go out to meet/~ 위원[회] a reception committee.  げいせつ

**영정(影幀)** a portrait scroll.  えいぞう

**영제(令弟)** your[his] younger brother.  れいてい

**영조(營造)** building; construction; erection/~하다 build; construct; erect.  えいぞう

**영조(靈鳥)** a sacred bird.

**영존(永存)** durability; permanence; perpetuity/~하다 remain[exist] forever /~성 perpetuity.  えいきゅうにあること

**영주(英主)** a wise ruler; an illustrious sovereign; an enlightened monarch; a heroic king.  えいしゅ

**영주(永住)** a permanent residence/~하다 reside permanently (in); settle down (in a place); make one's home (at, in) /~권 denizen-ship/~민 permanent residents; settlers/~지 a permanent domicile; one's permanent home/~권을 얻다 be denizened/이 곳에 ~하고 싶다 I should like to settle here permanently.  えいじゅう

**영주(領主)** a feudal lord; the lord of the manor.

**영준(英俊)** 《재주》 talent; genius; sagacity 《사람》 a man of talent; a talented man/~하다 (be) sagacious; gifted; talented; perspicacious.  えいしゅん

**영지(領地)** ①《영토》 a territory; a possession; a dominion; a domain ②《봉토》 a fief; feudal tenure; a vassalage.  りょうち

**영지(靈芝)** 【식】 a Japanese touchwood; Formes japonicus(학명).  れいし

**영지(靈地)** a holy ground; a sacred place.

**영진(榮進)** promotion; advancement; preferment; rise/~하다 be promoted [advanced] (to a higher position); get promotion.  えいしん

**영질(令姪)** your[his] nephew.

**영차** Yo-ho!, Yo-heave-ho!.  よいしょ

**영창(映窓)** a window for admitting light.

**영창(營倉)** a guard house; detention barracks; a military jail[lock up]/~에 갇히다 be confined in the guardhouse/중~ detention in the guardroom for a serious offense.  えいそう

**영창(咏唱)** 【음】 an aria.  えいしょう

**영채(映彩)** brilliant[radiant] color; brilliancy; splendor.

**영천(靈泉)** a magical fountain 《온천》 a hot spring with miraculous virtues.  れいせん

**영철(英哲)** great discernment; wisdom; perspicacity 《사람》 a man of great discernment/ ~하다 (be) sagacious; perspicacious; be of great discernment.  えいてつ

**영체(零替)** ruin ⇒영락.  おちぶれること

**영총(榮寵)** royal favor[grace, benevolence]/~을 입다 get into favor with a king; become a king's favorite subject.

**영탄(詠嘆)** 《읊음》 recital of a poem 《감탄》 exclamation 《찬탄》 admiration/ ~하다 recite a poem; exclaim; admire.  えいたん

**영토(領土)** a territory; a possession; a domain/~권 territorial rights/~ 확장열 land-hunger/~적 야심을 품다 harbour territorial ambitions. りょうど

**영특하다(英特—)** (be) wise; sagacious; perspicacious; intelligent.

**영판** ①(꼭) just like 《아주》very ②(길흉을 맞힘) true fortune telling.

**영패(零敗)** a shutout; a whitewash; a skunk《미》/~하다 be nosed out; fail to score; be skunked 《정구》be defeated in a love game/~시키다 whitewash; skunk; shut[nose] out.

**영피다** put out[forth] one's strength [energy]; show spark. げんきをだす

**영하(零下)** below zero; sub-zero/~ 10도 ten degrees below zero/~의 기온 sub-zero temperature. れいか

**영하다(靈—)** 《영험이》be marvelously responsive to prayers (효험이) (be) wonder-working; wonderfully efficacious; be magical in its effect/영한 의사 a wonderful doctor; an excellent physician. かみがかりである

**영학(英學)** [the study of] English; English studies/~자 an English scholar /~생 a student of English.

**영한(英韓)** English-Korean/~ 사전 an English-Korean dictionary/~ 양문으로 in English and Korean.

**영합(迎合)** flattery/~하다 flatter/~주의 opportunism; time-serving/~적 태도를 취하다 assume an ingratiatory attitude/여론에 ~하다 go with the current of the time. げいごう

**영해(領海)** territorial waters; the closed sea/~ 내[외]에서 within[outside of] territorial waters/외국 ~ foreign waters. りょうかい

**영향(影響)** influence; consequence[s]; 《결과》effect 《일시적》affection/~하다 influence; have an effect on; exert influence on; affect; tell on/전쟁의 ~ the effect of a war/~을 미치다 have[exert, exercise] a bad effect[an evil influence] (upon)/~을 받다 be influenced[affected] by /환경이 주는 ~은 크다 Environment is a potent influence./그 사건은 그의 전생애에 ~을 주었다 The incident colored his entire life. えいきょう

**영험(靈驗)** miracle ⇒영검. れいげん
**영현(英顯)** the spirit of the departed.
**영형(令兄)** your[his] elder brother. れいけい

**영혼(靈魂)** a soul; a spirit/~ 불멸[설] [the doctrine of] the immortality of the soul. れいこん

**영화(榮華)** 《번영》glory; prosperity; splendor; pomp 《호화》luxury; extravagance/~로운 glorious; prosperous; luxurious/속세의 ~ the pomps and glories of the world; vain glories/~롭게 살다 live in luxury; live sumptuously.

**영화(映畵)** a motion picture; a film; a moving picture; a cinema〈영〉; movies 〈미〉; (발성) talkies/~계 filmdom; the film[screen, cinema] world/~인 a movieman/~극 a photoplay; a screen drama/단편 ~ a short motion picture; a shorty《미》; a short《속》/~관 a cinema; a cinema[movie] house [theater]/~감독 a film director; a producer〈영〉/~ 제작자 a film producer /~ 회사 a film company/~를 만들다 produce a film/~화하다 picturize (a novel); scenarize/~를 찍다 film; take a moving picture of. えいが

**영화(英貨)** British currency[money]; sterling; the pound/~의 하락[등귀] a fall[rise] of the pound/~로 환산하다 convert into English currency.

**옆** the side; the flank/~의 side; next; adjoining/~에[서] aside; by; beside/ ~으로 on[to] one side; sidewards; sideways/~얼굴 the side face/~방 an adjoining room/~에 앉은 사람 a person sitting next to one/문 ~에서 by the gate/~을 지나가다 pass by/~을 보고 앉다 sit sideways/~으로 밀다 push (a thing) aside/ ~에서 말참견을 하다 poke one's nose into (a matter); meddle in (another's affair). そば

**옆구리** the flank; the side [of the chest] /~에 under one's arm/왼편 ~ the left side/~가 아프다 have a pain in the side/~가 드끔드끔하다 I have stitches in my side. わき

**옆길** a side road. わきみち
**옆널** a sidepiece of a woodenware; a side board. わきいた
**옆뎅이** the side/~에 at one side; at the side. そば
**옆들다** give assistance; extend help to; lend a helping hand.
**옆면(—面)** a side; sides.
**옆모습** a profile; a side face; a face in profile/~를 그린 초상화 a portrait drawn in profile/~을 그리다 draw a profile of (a person)/~이 아름답다 have a good[fine] profile.
**옆바람** a side wind.
**옆발치** the side of either of one's feet when he lies down.
**옆방(—房)** a side room; the next room.
**옆쪽** the side; the flank/~의 side; flank/~에 앉다 sit by (a person); sit by (a person's) side.
**옆줄** a side line.
**옆찌르다** give a nudge in (someone's) side (with one's elbow).
**옆집** the next door[house]; a neighboring house; an adjacent house/~의 next; next-door; neighboring/그 여자는 우리 ~에 산다 She lives in the house-next to ours./~ 사람 a neighbor.
**옆폭** a side board; a sidepiece.

**엎홀이** a corner chisel; a side grooving [fluting] plane[chisel].

**예¹** ①(옛적) antiquity; ancient[old] times; days gone by; former years/～로 부터 from old[ancient] times/～나 지금이나 같다 It is the same now as in old times. ②(과거) old days; former years. むかし

**예²** ①(대답) yes; certainly; all right; very well 《출석의 대답》 here; present; /～ 알았읍니다 Yes, certainly., All right sir. ②(반문) Eh?; what?/～ 그러세요 Is it?, Is that so?, Really. はい

**예³** here; this point ⇒여기. ここ

**예(例)** ①(실례) an instance; an example; an illustration/～를 들면 for instance [example]/～를 들다 cite[draw, give] an instance/이 이상 ～를 들 필요가 없다 I need not multiply instance. ②(경우) a case /이러한 ～ such a case/유사한 ～ a similar case ③(관례) a custom; a habit; a record 《전례》a precedent; 《유례》parallel/～의 usual; habitual; customary/～와 같이 according to the usual manner. れい

**예(禮)** ①(절) a salutation; a salute; an obeisance/～하다 bow; salute; make a bow[an obeisance] to drop[make] a courtesy ②(예의) etiquette; courtesy; civility; decorum/～를 잃다 be impolite[uncivil]; be rude[ill-mannered]; be wanting in courtesy/～를 다하다 extend (a person) every courtesy; show (a person) every civility. れい

**예각(銳角)** 〖數〗 an acute angle/～ 삼각형 an acute-angled triangle. えいかく

**예감(豫感)** a presentiment; a premonition; a presage; foreboding/～하다 have[experience] a presentiment[foreboding] (of)/불길한 ～ a gloomy foreboding/죽음을 ～하다 have a premonition of death/그의 ～이 들어맞았다 His presentiment came true. よかん

**예견하다(豫見─)** foresee; forestall/…을 예견하고 in anticipation of…. よけんする

**예고(豫告)** an advance[a previous] notice; a preliminary announcement; a notice; heralding in advance 《경고》a warning/～하다 give an advance notice [a notice in advance]; warn (one) of /～ 없이 without [previous] warning[notice]; 《즉석에》 at a moment's notice/ ～한 대로 as previously[already] announced/～한 것보다 못하다 It does not come up to what we expected from the preliminary announcement. /～편 a preview; a trailer/신간 ～ the announcement[notice] of new[forthcoming] books. よこく

**예과(豫科)** 《과정》preparatory course; a preparatory department/～생 a preparatory course student; a prep student 《미·구》/～를 수료하다 complete the preparatory course. よか

**예광탄(曳光彈)** a tracer shell[bullet]; a light[flame] tracer.

**예규(例規)** an established rule[regulation]/～에 따라 처리하다 dispose of (a matter) in accordance with the established regulations. れいき

**예금(預金)** a deposit; a bank account; money on deposit/～하다 deposit in the bank; place money on deposit/～ 계정 deposit account/～ 이자 interest on[of] deposits/～자 a depositor/～ 통장 a [deposit] pass-book/통지 ～ a deposit at notice[call]/～을 찾다 draw[withdraw] one's money[deposit] from the bank /아직 ～이 남아 있다 I have still a balance at my bank. よきん

**예기 (욕)** Damn it[you]!/～ 나쁜 놈 You rascal!/～ 더러운 놈 You filthy dog! やい

**예기(銳氣)** 《기세》spirit; dash; ardor 《원기》vigor; energy/～있는 젊은이 young [fresh] blood/～를 기르다 conserve one's energy; foster high spirits/～를 꺾다 break (a person's) spirits. えいき

**예기(豫期)** 《기대》expectation; anticipation 《희망》hope 《선견》foresight/～하다 expect; anticipate; hope for; look forward to/～치 않은 unexpected; unlooked for/…을 ～하고 in expectation [anticipation] of/～에 어긋나서 contrary to expectations/～한 대로 as was expected; as one expected. よき

**예기(藝妓)** a Korean keesaeng; a singing girl; a professional entertainer. げいぎ

**예기지르다(銳氣─)** break (a person's) spirits.

**예납(豫納)** payment in advance; advance payment; prepayment/～하다 pay in advance; prepay/반신료 ～ 전보 a reply-paid telegram. よのう

**예년(例年)** a normal[an ordinary] year 《평년》the average year 《매년》every year/～의 annual; usual/～의 행사 an annual function[event]/～대로 as usual; as in other years/～에 비해 compared with other years. れいねん

**예능(藝能)** accomplishments; acquirements; attainments/～인 an artiste; a player/～과(科) art course. げいのう

**예니레** six or seven days. ろくしちにち

**예닐곱** six or seven. ろくしち

**예단(豫斷)** prediction; presupposition/ ～하다 predict; presuppose. よだん

**예답다(禮─)** (be) courteous; decorous; polite; civil/그는 언행이 ～ He has good manners., He is well-mannered. れいがあつい

**예대(禮待)** an honourable treatment; a cordial reception/～하다 receive (one) courteously[cordially]; treat (one) with respect. れいぐう

**예도(藝道)** an art/～에 전념하다 devote oneself to the pursuit of an art.

**예둔(銳鈍)** sharpness and dullness; kee-

**예라** Quit!, Don't!, Get away!/~ 그런 짓 하지 말라 Look here!, None of that./~ 울지 마라 There, my boy, don't cry.

**예령**(豫鈴) the first bell.

**예로부터** from old[ancient] times; from very early[remote] ages; from the remotest days; since the days of antiquity/~의 풍습 time-honoured[long-established] customs.

**예리**(銳利) sharpness; keenness/~ 하다 (연장이) (be) sharp; cutting; sharp-edged 《두뇌・판단이》 keen; acute/~한 연장 a sharp instrument; a sharp-edged tool/~한 비평 biting[scathing, sharp] criticism/~한 논법 a keen argument/머리가 아주 ~하다 be (as) keen as a razor.

**예망**(曳網) a seine; a towing net; a drag-net.

**예매**(豫買) advance purchasing; purchasing in advance/~하다 buy in advance.

**예매**(豫賣) advance sale[subscription]; sale in advance/~하다 sell [tickets] in advance/~권 a ticket sold in advance.

**예명**(藝名) a professional name; a stage [screen] name.

**예모**(禮帽) a silk[ceremonial] hat; a top hat.

**예모**(禮貌) decorum; [good] manners; etiquette/~ 바른 사람 a well-bred person/~ 없는 ill-mannered; discourteous/~가 없다 have no manners; be ill-mannered.

**예물**(禮物) a gift; a present/신랑 신부가 ~을 교환했다 The bride and bridegroom exchanged wedding presents.

**예민**(銳敏) acuteness; sharpness 《감성》 sensitiveness; mental acuteness 《지성》 acumen/~한 관찰 a keen observation/~한 통찰 a penetrating insight/~한 머리 a clever head/~한 감각 a keen [quick] sense.

**예바르다**(禮—) (be) courteous; decorous; polite; civil/예바르지 않다 be wanting in politeness;. be discourteous.

**예방**(豫防) 《방지》 prevention; protection (against);《경계》 precaution/~의 preventive; precautionary/~하다 prevent; protect oneself[take precautions] against/~법 a method of prevention; a protection (against)/~ 의학 preventive medicine/~할 수 있는 preventable/~책 a precautionary measure/~책을 강구하다 take precautionary measures [steps].

**예방**(禮訪) a courtesy call/~하다 pay a courtesy call on (a person).

**예배**(禮拜) worship 《교회의》 church[divine, devotional] service 《십자가・성체에의》 adoration/~하다 worship; adore; pay homage to/~당 a chapel; a place of worship/~자 a worshipper/~에 출석하다 attend divine service/교회에서 ~가 있었다 The services were held in the church.

**예법**(禮法) courtesy; decorum; etiqette; propriety; manners/식탁 ~ table manners/~에 맞다[어긋나다] conform to[be against] etiquette/~을 배우다 learn good manners; take lessons in manners.

**예보**(豫報) forecast[ing]; prediction/~하다 predict; forecast/~한 바와 같이 [was] previously reported[announced]/일기를 ~하다 forecast the weather/일기 ~에 의하면 이따금 소나기가 내릴 것이라 한다 The weather forecast predicts occasional showers.

**예복**(禮服) full dress; a dress-suit; a ceremonial dress 《야회의》 evening dress/평상 ~ a frock coat; a morning coat/~을 입다 be in full dress/《부인용의》 a robe *décolletee*(F).

**예봉**(銳鋒) the brunt of an attack[argument]; a trenchant attack/~을 꺾다 blunt the point of an attack/~을 꺾을 수 없다 They carry everything before them.

**예쁘다** (be) pretty; lovely; beautiful 《매력적》 charming; handsome 《귀여운》 sweet 《모양이》 shapely/예쁜 인형 a pretty doll/예쁜 꽃 a beautiful flower.

**예쁘장스럽다** pretty.

**예쁘장하다** (be) lovely; pretty; be on the pretty side/예쁘장한 얼굴 lovely face; sweet-faced/예쁘장한 계집아이 a sweet girl.

**예비**(豫備) ①《준비》 preparation ②《마련》 reserve; spare/~하다 prepare[provide] for; reserve/~의 preparatory; introductory/~로 가지고 있다 have (a thing) in reserve/~ 조사를 하다 make a preliminary inquiry/~ 검사 a preliminary inspection/~ 교섭 preliminary negotiations/~금 reserve funds/~ 수단 preliminary step/~ 시험[회의] a preliminary examination[conference]/~실 a spare room/~ 지식 preliminary[previous] knowledge.

**예사**(例事) a commonplace event; an affair of common[everyday] occurrence; an ordinary affair/~하다 (be) usual; ordinary; commonplace/~가 아닌 unusual; extraordinary; uncommon/분위기로 보아 ~가 아닌걸 The atmosphere is charged.

**예산**(豫算) ①《수입・지출의》 an estimate; a budget/~의 budgetary; estimated/

**예상** 총~ the total[general] budget[estimates]/지불 ~ the payment estimates/~안 a budget bill; a bill of budget/~ 초과 an excess over the estimates/~을 세우다[편성하다] make[draw up] an estimate/~의 수지를 맞추다 balance the budget ②(예상) forecast; expectation; anticipation (계획) a plan; an intention (의도) a design (목적) an object/~하다 (예상하다) estimate; expect (계획하다) forecast; project; form[lay] a plan/~이 있다 have (some object) in view/~ 없이 행해지다 be done without calculation.　よさん

**예상(豫想)** (예기) expectation; anticipation (예측) forecast; presumption; an estimate/~하다 expect; anticipate; forecast; estimate/~ 외의 unexpected; unlooked-for/~ 외로 unexpectedly; beyond *one's* expectations/~ 외로 좋다 be better than [was] expected/장래를 ~하다 forecast[anticipate] the future/정치적인 반응이 일어날 것으로 ~하다 anticipate a political reaction/~액 estimates/~ 이익 an imaginary[estimated, anticipated] profit; paper profit/~ 생산고 estimated production.　よそう

**예상사**(例常事) a common place event ⇒ 예사(例事).　いつもあること

**예상외**(豫想外) being outside anticipation [expectation]; being unlooked-for/성적이 ~로 좋다[나쁘다] The result is better [worse] than I expected.　よそうがい

**예서(隷書)** a seal character.　れいしょ

**예선(豫先)** beforehand; in advance; previously; in anticipation.　まえもって

**예선(豫選)** a preliminary match[contest]; a provisional selection[election]/~하다 hold a preliminary contest; preelect/~에서 통과[탈락]되다 be qualified[dropped off, disqualified] at a preliminary contest.　よせん

**예속(隷屬)** subordination/~하다 be under the control[authority] of; be subordinate[subjected] to; belong to/ ~국 a subject nation; a dependency/~시키다 subjugate.　れいぞく

**예순** sixty.　ろくじゅう

**예술(藝術)** art 《학술》 the arts 《미술》 fine arts/~가 an artist/~ 작품 a work of art/~ 지상주의[예술을 위한 예술] art for art's sake/~ 비평 criticism of art/~가 기질의 사람 a man of artistic temperament/~적 가치가 있다 be of artistic value.　げいじゅつ

**예스럽다** (be) antiquated; archaic/예스런 말투 an archaic expression/예스런 습관 old customs.　ふるめかしい

**예습(豫習)** preparations of lesson 《극・음악 따위》 rehearsal/~하다 prepare lessons; rehearse/~ 시간 study hours/~ 하지 않고 학교에 가다 go to school without doing *one's* preparation.　よしゅう

**예시**(例示) illustration; exemplification /~하다 illustrate; exemplify.　れいじ

**예시**(豫示) indication; foreshadowing /~하다 indicate; show a sign of; foreshadow.　よし

**예식**(例式) an established form; a form/~에 따라서 in due form.　れいしき

**예식(禮式)** 《예의》 etiquette; manners 《의식》 a ceremony; formalities; a rite.　れいしき

**예심(豫審)** a preliminary hearing[trial, examination] *sub*; *judice*(L)/~ 중이다 be *sub*; *judice*/~ 재판소 the preliminary court of inquiry/~ 판사 an examining judge; a preliminary court judge.

**예악(禮樂)** social code of etiquette and music 《교육의 방편》 a means of culture.　れいほうとおんがく

**예약(豫約)** 《좌석・배 따위》 booking; reservation 《출판물》 subscription 《기부금 등》 a pledge/~하다 book in advance; subscribe for; sell in advance 《기부금》 promise; pledge/~금 the subscription price; a deposit/~ 모집 invitation for subscription/~ 출판 publication by subscription/~자 a subscriber/좌석을 ~하다 book a seat [in advance]; reserve a seat/좌석을 ~해 두는 것이 좋다 You had better book your seat.　よやく

**예언(例言)** a preface; a foreword; introductory remarks; an introduction.　れいげん

**예언(豫言)** a prophecy; a prediction; a forecast/~하다 prophesy; foretell; predict; make a prediction/~할 수 있는 predictable; foreseeable/~이 적중했다 The prediction was fulfilled[came true, proved correct]/~자 a prophet [prophetess(여자)]; a predictor.　よげん

**예외(例外)** an exception/~의 exceptional/~적인 용법 an exceptional use/~ 없이 without exception/~없는 규칙은 없다 Every rule has its exceptions., There is no rule without exceptions.　れいがい

**예우(禮遇)** honorable treatment; cordial reception/~하다 receive (*a person*) courteously[warmly, cordially]; treat (*a person*) with respect.　れいぐう

**예의(銳意)** zealously; energetically; assiduously; with zeal/~ 전심하다 devote *oneself* to; apply *oneself* heart and soul to/~ 검토하다 inquire into (*a matter*) assiduously; examine (*a matter*) in earnest.　えいい

**예의(禮儀)** courtesy; politeness; civility 《예절》 manners; etiquette; good form/외교상의 ~ diplomatic etiquette/~ 바른 courteous; polite; civil/~를 모르는 discourteous; rude; ill-mannered[-bred]/~상 as a matter of courtesy/~를 무시하고 in disregard of etiquette/~를 지키다 observe the proprieties/~ 범절 the rules of etiquette/형식적 ~ sham courtesy; outward decorum.　れいぎ

**예장(禮狀)** a letter of thanks; a letter of acknowledgement[appreciation]《상품 따위의 효과를 인정하는》a testimonial/~을 내다 send a letter of thanks; write to (one) in acknowledgement of one's kindness. れいじょう

**예장(禮裝)** a ceremonial dress; a full dress/~하다 wear a ceremonial dress; be in full dress/~을 하고 in full dress/그는 ~으로 점잖게 차렸다 He stood imposing in full dress. れいそう

**예전(-前)** old days[times]; former days; the past/~ 사람들 men of old times/~부터 from old times/~에 in old [ancient] times; in the old days/~대로 as of old; as usual; unchanged; as it was before. このまえ

**예절(禮節)** propriety; politeness; decorum; etiquette; manners/~을 중히 여기다 attach great importance to propriety/~을 닦다 cultivate manners; promote courtesy. れいせつ

**예정(豫定)** previous arrangement; programme; schedule《예상》expectation; anticipation《예산》estimate/~의 prearranged; appointed; expected/~하다 arrange; plan; prearranged; map out《시일을》set; schedule/~액 the estimated amount/~의 행동 a prearranged course of action/~한 시간에 on scheduled time; at the appointed time/~이 들어지다 have a hitch in the programme. よてい

**예제**《여기저기》here and there; everywhere; far and wide. あちこち

**예제(例題)**《보기》an example《연습 문제》an exercise. れいだい

**예증(例證)** an illustration; an exemplification; an example; an instance/~하다 illustrate; exemplify/~으로서 by way of illustration; as an example [instance]/이론을 ~하는 여러 가지 사실을 들다 enumerate facts in illustration of one's theory. れいしょう

**예지(叡智)**, supreme intelligence; wisdom; intellect. えいち

**예지(豫知)** foreknowledge; foresight/~하다 foresee; know beforehand; forebode/지진을 ~하다 foretell an earthquake. よち

**예진(豫診)**《의》a preliminary medical examination[check-up]/~하다 make a diagnosis in advance.

**예진(豫震)** a preliminary tremor.

**예찬(禮讚)** praise; glorification; worship; admiration/~하다 admire; glorify; worship; praise; idolize/모성 ~ the glorification of motherhood/미의 ~ a beauty cult; glorification of beauty/~자 a worshiper; an admirer/자연의 ~ the cult of nature. らいさん

**예측(豫測)** prediction; forecast; expectation《어림》estimation/~하다 predict; forecast; estimate/~이 어긋나다 The prediction didn't come true./내년의 일을 ~할 수 없다 I can't make a prediction about next year. よそく

**예탐(豫探)** detection; spying; espial/~하다 spy upon; search; throw out[put up] a feeler/~군 a spy; a secret agent/적정을 ~하다 spy upon the enemy's movements. まえもってさぐること

**예편(豫編)** ~하다 transfer to the (first) reserve; place on the reserve list.

**예포(禮砲)** a salute [gun]/12발의 ~를 쏘다 fire a salute of 12 guns. れいほう

**예풍(藝風)** one's artistic taste《연극의》acting《음악의》one's personal technique.

**예항(曳航)** tow; towing/~하다 tow; take (a ship) in tow/우리는 요함을 ~했다 We had our consort in tow.

**예해(例解)** an example; an illustration; an exemplification/~하다 exemplify; illustrate; give example.
(Sans). ごかい

**오계(誤計)** a mistaken step[plan]; blunder; misjudg[e]ment; false scheme. まちがったけいかく

**오가다** come and go; go back and forth/오가는 사람들 streams of people going and coming; the busy coming and going of people. いったりきたりする

**오곡(五穀)** the five grains [rice, millet, beans, wheat and barnyard millet]/~밥 boiled-rice mixed with four other cereals/풍요한 ~ bumper crops. ごこく

**오관(五官)** the five sensory organs [of hearing, seeing, tasting, smelling and feeling]. ごかん

**오그라뜨리다** dent ⇒오그리다.

**오그라지다** be crushed; be battered; get curled[rolled] up; be broken/오그라진 남비 a dented pan/오그라진 차 a dented car/나뭇잎이 오그라진다 The leaves curl up. ちぢむ

**오그랑이** ①《물건》a shrunk object ②《사람》a cranky person; a perverse character; a crooked stick.

**오그랑장사** a failing business; an unprofitable[a losing] business.

**오그랑하다** (be) battered; bent in; shrunk. くぼんでいる

**오그르르** in swarms《끓이》boiling; simmering/~하다 simmer; boil; swarm. うじゃうじゃ

**오그리다** shrink; contract; draw/오그리고 자다 sleep curled up/개는 잔뜩 몸을 오그리고 떨었다 Curling himself up, the dog was shivering with cold. ちぢめる

**오글거리다** ①《끓음》simmer; boil with a sizzling sound/오글오글 simmering; with a sizzling sound ②《벌레 따위가》wriggle; squirm/오글오글 in swarms. うじゃうじゃとうごめく

**오글쪼글** ~하다 (be) crumpled; rumpled; wrinkled; withered/오글쪼글한 할멈 an old withered woman; a crone/노인의 오글쪼글한 손발 the shrunken limbs of

old age. くしゃくしゃ
**오금** the crook[hollow, inside curve] of the knee[elbow]; the popliteal region; ham/~을 못 쓰다 be unable to move around 《비유적》 be intimidated /그는 마누라 앞에서 ~을 못 쓴다 He is under his wife's thumb. ひざのうら
**오금뜨다** gad about hunting for love affairs. しりがかるい
**오금박다** attack (one) for his discordance between his previous words and actual actions; cavil at one's previous words.
**오금탱이** the inner angle of a bend[curve].
**오굿하다** be pressed in; be dented; be crushed a little out of shape; be sunk /찻 주전자 밑이 오굿하게 들어갔다 The teakettle has a dent on its bottom. ややくぼんでいる
**오기**(傲氣) an unyielding[a competitive, an indomitable] spirit; an obstinate mind/~부리다 stick to one's own opinion; ごうまんなきせい
**오기**(誤記) a mistake in writing; a clerical error; a slip of the pen/~하다 miswrite; write wrong; make a mistake in writing.
**오나가나** always; all the time; wherever one goes; everywhere you turn; making no difference/그는 ~ 사람을 골탕 먹인다 He always takes peoples in. いってもきても
**오냐** 《대답》 yea; yes; all right/~ 그렇지 면 좋다 Okay, if that is the way you want it. /~ 알았다 Yes, I see. /~ 두고 보자 You shall soon smart for this. よろしい
**오뇌**(懊惱) mental anguish/~하다 have a mental struggle. おうのう
**오누이** brother and sister; siblings. あにといもうと
**오뉘죽** rice gruel mixed with mashed red bean.
**오뉴월**(五六月) May and June/~ 긴긴 해 the livelong summer day/~ 염천 the hot weather of midsummer. ごろくがつ
**오는** coming; next/~ 토요일 next Saturday.
**오늘** today; this day/~ 저녁 this evening/~ 밤 tonight/~부터 from this day forth/~은 며칠[무슨 요일]이냐 What day of the month[the week] is this? きょう
**오늘날** these days; the present time; nowadays; today/~의 of these day; of the present time; contemporary/~의 한국 the Korea of today/생존 경쟁이 심 한 ~ in these days of severe struggle for existence /~에는 at the present time. きょう
**오늬** the notch of an arrow; the nock/ ~를 시위에 걸다 fit an arrow on the string; nock an arrow/~ 무늬 a herringbone [pattern].

**오다** ①《일반적으로》 come; come up[down]; come over[along]; turn up/오는 사람마다 each and every person that comes in /오자마자 잘 차리나 Are you going? You have been here only a little while. ②《도착하다》 reach; arrive (at); 《기 차가》 be in 《편지가》 come to hand ③《방 문하다》 call (on, at a house); make call; come to see; visit/그는 약속해 놓고 끝 내 안 왔다 He never turned up in spite of his promise. ④《비·눈이》 come on/ 비가 온다 Rain comes on., It begins to rain. /눈이 차차 덜 온다 The snow has becomeless severe. ⑤《계절·기한이》 come [round]; set in; be due/봄이 왔 다 Spring is here. ⑥《가까이 오다》 approach; be at hand; draw near ⑦《되다》 become; grow/따뜻해 온다 It is getting warmer. ⑧《전래하다》 come from; be brought[introduced] from/그는 미국에서 왔다 It has been introduced into Korea from America. ⑨《유래하다》 derive from; come of; be due to; originate in. くる
**오다가다** occasionally; at times; now and then; once in a while; sometimes; by chance/~ 만나다 meet by chance/ 그에게서 ~ 소식이 있다 I hear from him once in a while. /~ 있는 일 a rare occurrence; a thing of infrequent occurrence. ときどき
**오달지다** (be) full; replete; rich; solid; substantial.
**오도**(悟道) 【종】 apprehension of the truth; spiritual awakening; enlightenment/~하다 attain enlightenment; be awakened; attain supreme wisdom. ごどう
**오도깝스럽다** (be) abrupt and frivolous; flippant; imprudent/오도깝스런 수작 flippant remarks/오도깝스럽게 굴다 act rashly. けいそつだ
**오도방정** a rash act; a harebrained deed; a flighty[reckless] act; giddiness. けいそつなこと
**오도카니** blankly; vacantly; idly; absentmindedly. つまらなく
**오똑** high; aloft. ぽつんと
**오독**(誤讀) misreading/~하다 misread; read wrong/신호를 ~하다 misread a signal. ごどく
**오똑이** a tumbling doll; a tumbler. だるま
**오돌오돌** hard and lumpy; gristly; fibrous; tough/~하다 (be) hard and lumpy; gristly; tough. こわいさま
**오동**(烏銅) oxidized[blackened] copper.
**오동**(梧桐) 【식】 a paulownia; Paulownia imperialis(학명)/~나무로만 된 장 an all -paulownia chest of drawers. あおぎり
**오동지**(五冬至) May and November of the lunar month.
**오동통하다** (be) short and fat; dumpy; corpulent/오동통한 계집애 a plump girl

/오동통한 얼굴 a bonny face; a buxom face.

**오두막**(一幕) a [temporary] hut; a shed; a shack/~집 a hut; a hovel; a dug-out/~을 짓다 put up a shed.

**오드득** with a crunching sound/~거리다 crunch.

**오드득뼈** cartilage; gristle.

**오들오들** tremblingly; shiveringly/~ 떨다 tremble; be all of a tremble; quiver; quake; shake/무서워서 ~ 떨다 tremble for fear; shudder (at) with fright/추워서 ~ 떨다 shiver with cold. ぶるぶる

**오등**(吾等) we; us.

**오디** a mulberry.

**오라**[1] (오라줄) a red rope formerly used for binding a criminal; a rope to bind a criminal with/~로 묶다 bind[tie up] a criminal; seize[arrest, take up] a culprit.

**오라**[2] right; true; correct; yes/~ 네가 옳다 Yes, you are right. よろしい

**오라기** a piece; a scrap; a bits of thread [cloth, paper]/실 ~ a scrap of thread /헝겊 ~ a piece[scrap] of cloth.

**오라버니** one's elder brother. あにさん

**오락**(娛樂) amusement; recreation; entertainment; pleasure/~으로 by pleasure; for one's pastime; as a pastime/독서는 좋은 ~이다 Reading is a good pastime./~가 an amusement center[quarter, district]/~관 an entertainment hall/~ 시설 recreation facilities/~실 an amusement hall; a recreation room /~ 잡지 a magazine for amusements. ごらく

**오락가락** ~하다 come and go; go back and forth; wander; mill around/비가 ~하다 rain off and on; rain by fits and starts/정신이 ~하다 one's mind wanders[strays]. いったりきたり

**오랑캐** a savage; a vandal.

**오랑캐꽃** 《식》a violet. すみれ

**오래** long; for a long time; for an age; old-fashioned (음식이) 《기한 넘어》 over-due/~전 long time ago/~된 old; ancient; antique 《고풍의》 old-fashioned/~ 계속되는 longcontinued/~ 사귄 친구 a friend of long standing/~ 걸리다 take a long time/~ 머무르다 stay long; make a long stay. ながらく

**오래가다** (견디다) last long; be durable; keep[wear] well; live long/오래가는 durable; enduring; lasting/오래 못가다 be short lived; never keep[last] long; wear ill/이 신은 오래잘 것입니다 These shoes will last for a long time.

**오래간만** after a long time[interval, silence, absence, separation]; a long time since/~입니다 We haven't met for ages., It is an age[ages, a long time] since I saw you last[I last sow you]./~에 날이 개었다 It is a long while since we had such a fine day. ひさしぶり

**오래다** be a long time since[ago]; be of long standing; be long continued; (be) long; extended/오랜 습관 a custom of long standing; an old custom/오랜 교제 an intercourse of long standing/오랜 옛날 many years/오랜 옛날 great antiquity; time immemorial. ひさしい

**오래도록** for long; a long while; for a long time; long (영구히) forever; eternally; for ever and ever/그녀는 ~ 남편으로부터 소식을 듣지 못했다 She hasn't heard from her husband for a long time. えいきゅうに

**오래뜰** an outdoor court; a ground outside the house[in front of the gate].

**오래오래** for a long; long time (영원히) forever; eternally/이름을 ~ 전하다 immortalize one's fame/~ 살다 live long; live on. えいきゅうに

**오랫 동안** for a long time; very long/~ 편지 못 드려 죄송합니다 I must apologize [Excuse me] for my long silence./~ 소식이 없다 hear nothing (from a person) for long. ながいあいだ

**오량**(五樑) five-beam construction/~집 a house with five main beams; a large house.

**오려내다** clip [out]; cut out[away, off]; carve out[away, off]/기사를 ~ clip an article (from the newspaper).

**오련하다** (be) light; faint; pale/빛이 ~ be light in colour; be of a light colour [shade]. かすかだ

**오로지** 《주로》chiefly 《전혀》entirely; exclusively; wholly; solely 《전심하여》earnestly; intently; whole-heartedly /문학 연구에 전념하다 devote oneself to the study of literature/어학의 습득은 ~ 연습에 있다 Practice is the only way of mastering a language. ただ

**오롱이조롱이** variously; diversely.

**오류**(誤謬) a mistake; an error; a fallacy/~를 범하다 commit a fault; make an error/~를 시정하다 mend one's ways; correct an error/~를 적발하다 expose an error. ごひゅう

**오륜**(五倫) moral rules to govern the Five Human Relations [of master and servant, of father and son, of husband and wife, of brothers, of friends]. ごりん

**오륜 대회**(五輪大會) the Olympic Games; the Olympiad. ごりんたいかい

**오르내리다** ①《고저》rise and fall 《시세 따위가》fluctuate 《열이》be intermittent 《등락하다》fluctuations/계단을 ~ go up and down the staircase ②《남의 입에》be talked[gossiped] about; become the talk (of); be in everybody's mouth/그녀는 행실이 좋지 않아서 남의 입에 오르내렸다 Her conduct gave rise to scandals., Her conduct was on everybody's lips. あがったりさがったりする

**오르다** ①(산 따위에) go up; climb; ascend; rise (타다) mount/기차에 ~ board a train/왕위에 ~ come to the throne/월급이 ~ get a salary raise/기세가 ~ be in high spirits/열이 ~ The fever rises. ②(게재하다) be registered; be included; be entered/그의 공적이 역사에 올랐다 His achievement is recorded in history. ③(전염하다) be infected; be contracted (때가) be soiled; get dirty/옴이 ~ be infected with the itch[scabbies] ④(입에) be talked about; become the talk of; be gossiped about ⑤(기타) ¶ 약이 ~ get angry/얼굴에 술이 ~ one's face is flushed with liquor/살이 ~ put on flesh. あがる

**오르락내리락** rising and falling; going up and down. あがったりさがったり

**오르르** all in a rush; rumbling; simmering; shivering/~ 떨다 tremble; shiver. ちょこちょこ

**오르막** an uprise; an upward slope; uphill/~길 an uphill road.

**오른** the right. みぎ

**오른손** the right hand; the whip-hand. みぎて

**오른쪽** the right side/~에 on the right side (of)/~으로 가다 keep to the right/첫째 모퉁이에서 ~으로 돌아가라 Take the first turning to the right. うそく

**오른편** the right [side]/~의 right/~에 on the right side/…의 ~에 on the right of. うそく

**오름세** an upward tendency (of the market); a rising market.

**오리**¹ 〖동〗 a duck; a drake/새끼 ~ a teal; a duckling. あひる

**오리**² a strip/대 ~ a strip of bamboo/나무 ~ a strip of wood.

**오리**(五厘) half a jun.

**오리**(五里) five ri [Korean miles].

**오리**(汚吏) a corrupt official. おり

**오리나무** 〖식〗 a [black] alder.

**오리너구리** 〖동〗 a duck-bill.

**오리다** cut off[away]; cut out; carve out; cut into strips/신문에서 광고[기사]를 오려내다 cut[clip] an advertisement [article] from a newspaper/잡지에서 그림을 오려내다 cut out pictures from magazines.

**오리목** (건축용) a lath.

**오리무중**(五里霧中) ¶ ~이다 be in a fog [cloud]; be at sea; be mystified/우리는 아직 이 문제에 대해서는 ~에 놓여 있다 We are still all at sea on this subject. ごりむちゅう

**오리발** ①(물갈퀴) a web; a webfoot (사람) a web-fingered hand ②(단작) a chum; a sidekick. みずかきのあるしゅそく

**오막살이** [living in] a grass hut[humble cottage]; a hovel life/~하다 lead a hut life; be a hut-dweller.

**오만**(傲慢) haughtiness; arrogance; pompousness/~하다 (be) haughty; arrogant; consequential; overbearing; proud/~하게 haughtily; proudly/~부리다 give oneself airs; act haughtily [arrogantly]/그녀는 ~한 태도로 말한다 She always speaks with an air of importance. ごうまん

**오만**(五萬) ever so much; innumerable; thousands/~ 가지 일 ever so many things to do/~ 가지 수단을 다 쓰다 leave no stone unturned; try every possible means.

**오망**(迂妄) ~하다 (be) cranky; cantankerous; flighty.

**오망떨다**(迂妄—) do cranky[whimsical, flighty] things; be hare-brained; be flighty.

**오망부리** a disproportionate[deformed] figure; an unbalanced style.

**오매**(寤寐) waking and sleeping; awake or asleep. ごび

**오매 불망**(寤寐不忘) ~하다 remember when awake or asleep; bear in mind all the time.

**오명**(汚名) disgrace ➾누명(陋名). おめい

**오목**(五目) a game of Badook with five checkers placed in a row. ごもく

**오목렌즈** a concave lens.

**오목오목** ~하다 (be) hollow; sunken; concave. ぽこっとくぼんでいる

**오목하다** (be) pressed[pushed] in; (be) depressed; dented; sunk/눈이 ~ be hollow-eyed; have deepset[recessed] eyes. ぽこっとくぼんでいる

**오묘**(奧妙) 〖심오〗 profundity; depth (현묘) abstruseness; mystery/~하다 (be) profound; deep; abstruse (현묘(玄妙)하다) recondite/ ~하게 profoundly; deeply; abstrusely; reconditely/~한 인간 행동의 동기 the recondite motives of human action.

**오무래미** a toothless old person; a shrivel-gummed old person.

**오문**(誤聞) mishearing/~하다 hear amiss; mishear. ごぶん

**오물**(汚物) filth; dirt; dust; muck; impurities (부엌의) garbage; ash (하수의) sewage/~ 처분 disposal of garbage/~ 운반인 a dust-man; a garbage-man; an ash-man(미). おぶつ

**오물거리다** ①(벌레 따위가) swarm; teem with; be alive with; wriggle in great numbers/벌집에 벌들이 오물거린다 The hive is alive with bees. ②(음식을) mumble; chew on /잇몸으로 ~ chew on one's gum ③(말을) mumble/말을 ~ mumble one's word. うようよする

**오므라드리다** make narrower; shut; close. へっこましてしまう

**오므라들다** become narrower; narrow close; wither/오므라든 입 a puckered [pursed] mouth/상처가 오므라들었다 The wound has closed. へっこむ

**오므라지다** 〖닫히다〗 be closed; be shut; 〖좁아지다〗 become narrower; closed;

**오므리다** close; pucker up; shut/입을 ~ pucker up one's mouth[lips]; purse up one's lips /우산을 ~ shut[close, fold] an umbrella /몸을 ~ make oneself small; huddle up. へっこます

**오미**(五味) the Five tastes [of sour, bitter, pungent, sweet and salty]. ごみ

**오미자나무** 《식》 *Maximowiczia chinensis* (학명). ごみしのき

**오빠** a girl's elder brother. あにさん

**오발**(誤發) 《총기의》 accidental firing; firing by accident/~하다 go off of it's own accord. まちがっていうこと

**오변형**(五邊形) a pentagon. ごへんけい

**오보**(誤報) an incorrect[erroneous] report; a false report; misinformation /~하다 misinform; give a false report /그것은 ~였다 The report turned out [to be] incorrect., The information was wrong. ごほう

**오보록하다** (be) massed; thick; crowded. うっそうとしている

**오복**(五福) the Five Blessings [of longevity, wealth, health, love of virtue, peaceful death]. ごふく

**오붓하다** ①(be) enough; ample; substantial; sufficient/오붓하게 살다 lead a comfortable living; be well[comfortably] off ②(be) comfortable; cozy; snug/오붓한 자리 a cozy corner.

**오비다** scoop out; gouge; pick; bore /오비어 넣다 cram; stuff; squeeze (into). ほじくる

**오사바사하다** be likable but capricious; (be) affable but fickle.

**오싹오싹** chilling; shivering. ますます

**오산**(誤算) a miscalculation/~하다 miscalculate; miscount; make an erro in calculation/전략상의 ~ a strategic miscalculation/~하지 않도록 주의하다 be careful not to miscalculate. ごさん

**오살**(誤殺) manslaughter by mistake/~하다 kill (*a person*) by mistake.

**오살**(鏖殺) wholesale massacre; slaughter; extermination; annihilation/~하다 massacre; exterminate. おうさつ

**오색**(五色) the five cardinal colors [of blue yellow, red, white and black]; variegated colors/~이 영롱하다 shine brilliantly in various colors; be very colorful; be resplendent. ごしき

**오서**(誤書) a clerical error; a slip of the pen; incorrect writing/~하다 make an error in writing; write incorrectly. あやまってかくこと

**오선지**(五線紙) 《음》 music paper. ごせんし

**오소리** 《동》 a badger. あなぐま

**오손**(汚損) stain; soil; damage/~하다 stain; damage; be spoiled[stained]. おそん

**오수**(午睡) a nap; a siesta.

**오수**(汚水) sewage; foul[filthy] water 《개숫물》 slops/~관 a soil pipe/~ 처리 sewage disposal. おすい

**오순도순** harmoniously; on good terms; in amity/~ 잘 지내다 live happily together/~ 잘 놀다 chum up with; play together well.

**오슬오슬** shivering/~하다 feel[be] chilly; (be) shivery/~한 날씨 chilly weather/~ 떨다 shiver with cold/~ 춥다 feel chills/열이 나서 ~하다 have chills [shakes] with the fever. ぞくぞく

**오시**(午時) the Hour of the Horse; noon. ごじ

**오식**(誤植) a printer's error; a misprint; an erratum/ ~투성이다 be full of misprints/~ 정정표 errata/~을 교정하다 correct errors in proof. ごしょく

**오신**(誤信) a fallacy; a misbelief/~하다 misbelieve; hold an erroneous belief/~자 a misbeliever. ごしん

**오심**(誤審) [a] misjudg[e]ment 《경기의》 wrong refereeing; 《법》 [a] mistrial/~하다 misjudge; referee wrongly. ごしん

**오십**(五十) fifty 《제 오십》the fiftieth/~대에 in one's fifties/인생 ~이다 Man's allotted span of life is fifty., Our life is two score and ten./~보 백보다 be six of one and half a dozen of the other. ごじゅう

**오얏** a plum/~나무 a plum [tree]. すもも

**오언 절귀**(五言絕句) 《문》a quatrain with five Chinese characters in each line.

**오역**(誤譯) mistranslation/~하다 mistranslate; make a mistake in translation/~한 곳 a mistake in translation/~을 지적하다 point out mistakes in a translation/~이 없다 be free from errors of translation. ごやく

**오연**(傲然) arrogance; haughtiness/~하다 (be) proud; arrogant; haughty; show the attitude of haughtiness /~히 arrogantly; haughtily; proudly/~히 굴다 show the attitude of haughtiness[arrogance]; behave arrogantly[haughtily, overbearingly]. ごうぜん

**오열**(嗚咽) a sob; sobbing; choking with sobs; weeping/~하다 sob; weep. おえつ

**오열**(五列) the Fifth Column; the Fifth Columnists; secret agents. かんちょう

**오염**(汚染) pollution; contamination/~하다 be contaminated[polluted]; be soiled[stained]; be imbued /공기 ~ air pollution. おせん

**오엽송**(五葉松) 《식》 *Pinus pentaphylla*(학명). ちょうせんまつ

**오예물**(汚穢物) filth; dirt; muck 《인분》 night-soil /《부엌 쓰레기》 garbage/~ 청소인 a night-soil man; a night-farmer. きたないもの

**오욕**(汚辱) dishonour; ignominy; disgrace 《모욕》 insult; contumely/~하다 disgrace; dishonour; bring disgrace upon /~을 입다 be disgraced/~을 참다 endure obloquy; eat dirt. おじょく

**오용**(誤用) misuse; wrong use; misapplication/~하다 misuse; misapply; use (*a thing*) for a wrong purpose. ごよう

**오월**(五月) May/~의 여왕 a May queen/~ 단오(端午) the May Festival. ごがつ

**오유**(烏有) reverting to nothing; vanishing away/~로 돌아가다 be reduced to ashes; be burnt down; be laid level with the dust. うゆう

**오의**(奧義) the secrets; the mysteries; profound meaning; recondite principles/~를 터득하다 master the art of; dive into the secrets of. おうぎ

**오이** a cucumber/~채 hashed cucumber seasoned with vinegar and other seasonings. きゅうり

**오인**(吾人) ①《나》 I; me ②《우리》 we; us ③《인류》 mankind; human being.

**오인**(誤認) misconception; misunderstanding; an erroneous assumption; a mistake/~하다 misconceive; mistake [take] (*one thing*) for (*another*). ごにん

**오일**(五日) five days; the fifth day of the month.

**오입**(誤入) whoring/~하다 visit a brothel; consort with a whore; whore/~장이 a man who frequents a brothel/~판 the demimonde.

**오자**(誤字) a wrong word 《잘못 씀》a clerical error 《인쇄의》 a misprint/이 판은 ~투성이다 This edition is full of wrong words. ごじ

**오작**(烏鵲) crow and magpie 《까막까치》. うじゃく

**오장**(五臟) the five viscera [of heart, liver, spleen, lungs and kidneys]. ごぞう

**오장 육부**(五臟六腑) the five viscera and the six entrails. ごぞうろっぷ

**오쟁이** a small straw-bag/~지다 be cuckolded; have *one's* wife cheat on (*a person*); wear the horns.

**오전**(午前) the forenoon; the morning/~에 in the morning 《略: a.m.》/~ 9시에 at nine in the morning; at 9 a.m./그는 ~에는 집에 있다 He is at home in the morning. ごぜん

**오전**(誤傳) a false report; misinformation/~하다 give a false report. ごでん

**오점**(汚點) a stain; a blur; a blemish 《결점》a flaw 《얼룩》a fleck; a speckle; a tarnish; a blot/~없는 stainless; spotless/~을 찍다 stain/이 일은 그의 인격의 ~이었다 This was a blot on his character. おてん

**오정**(午正) noon; midday; the meridian huor/~에 at noon. しょうご

**오조** early-ripening variety of millet. わせのくり

**오졸거리다** move rhythmically; keep dancing (swaying). ゆらゆらさせる

**오종종하다** 《빽빽하다》 (be) dense; thick; compact 《얼굴이》 (be) small and boring. ずんぐりしている

**오죽** how; how much; to what extent/그것을 보면 네 어머니가 ~ 좋아하시겠니 How glad your mother will be to see it?/~이나 낙담했을까 I can well imagine your disappointment./~ 못 났으면 그런 짓을 하랴 How stupid you are to do so! どれくらい

**오줌** urine; piss/~의 urinary; uric/자다가 ~싸는 버릇 bed-wetting; wetting the bed at night/~을 누다 pass urine; piss/~마렵다 have a desire to urinate [pass water]. ゆばり

**오줌똥** feces and urine; human waste; excreta.

**오줌싸개** a child who urinates involuntarily. おむつ

**오줌통** ①《그릇》 a tub for urination ②《몸의》 the [urinary] bladder; the vesica.

**오지**(奧旨) recondite principles; inner intention; deep thought. おうし

**오지그릇** china; earthenware; crockery; pottery.

**오지끈** with a snap; smash; crackling/~하다 crackle; smash/~ 부러지다 break with a snap. がちゃ

**오지랖** the front; the breast.

**오지직** ~거리다 ①《타는 소리》crack; crackle 《물이》 seethe ②《먹는 소리》munch; crunch. ばちばち

**오직** 《단지》 merely; only 《오로지》 wholly; solely/어학의 습득엔 ~ 연습이 있을 뿐이다 Practice is the only way of mastering a language/~ 한 가지 이유 the only [sole] reason. ただ

**오진**(誤診) an erroneous [a wrong, mistaken] diagnosis/~하다 make a wrong diagnosis; diagnose erroneously. ごしん

**오징어** 《어》 a cuttle-fish/말린 ~ a dried cuttle-fish. いか

**오차**(誤差) an error/~의 법칙 the theory of error/관측 ~ an observational error. ごさ

**오착**(誤錯) a mistake; an error/~하다 err; make an error [mistake]. あやまり

**오찬**(午餐) a lunch; a luncheon/~회 a luncheon party/~을 들다 take a lunch/~에 초대하다 invite (*a person*) to a luncheon/~을 같이하다 lunch with (*a person*). ごさん

**오채**(五彩) five colours. ごさい

**오체**(五體) the [whole] body; the whole frame; the limbs/~가 멀쩡하다 He is without any physical defect. ごたい

**오촌**(五寸) *one's* cousin's son [daughter]; *one's* father's cousin/~ 조카 a cousin once removed.

**오탁**(汚濁) impurity/~하다 (be) dirty; impure; turbid; filthy.

**오톨도톨** ~하다 (be) uneven; rough. ぼこぼこ

**오한**(惡寒) a chill; a cold fit; 《의》 rigor algor; ague/~이 나다 feel [have] a chill; catch a chill. おかん

**오합지졸**(烏合之卒) a conglomeration of

**오해**(誤解) misunderstanding; misconception; misapprehension/~하다 misunderstand; misconceive 《어귀를》 misconstrue/~를 받다 be misunderstood/~를 사다 cause[invite] misunderstanding/~를 초래하기 쉽다 be liable to lead misunderstanding/너는 ~하고 있다 You labor under a mistake./그 ~는 너 자신이 풀어야 할 일이다 It is you that are to remove that misunderstanding.

**오호**(嗚呼) Alas!/~ 슬프다 그녀는 가고 이젠 없도다 Alas! She is dead and gone!

**오호호** 《웃음》 ha! ha!

**오활**(迂濶) thoughtlessness; stupidity; ignorance; unfamiliarity/~하다 (be) careless; thoughtless; inattentive; stupid; ignorant; unfamiliar.

**오후**(午後) afternoon/~의 afternoon/오늘[어제, 내일] ~ this[yesterday, tomorrow] afternoon/토요일 ~에 on Saturday afternoon.

**오히려** rather [than]; better [than]; sooner [than]; preferably; for preference/치욕을 받느니보다 ~ 죽는 게 낫다 I would rather[sooner] die than suffer disgrace./그는 학자라기보다 ~ 작가다 He is not so much a scholar as a writer. むしろ

**옥**(玉) a precious stone; a gem; a jewel/~에 티 a flaw in a precious stone; a fly in the ointment.

**옥**(獄) a prison; a jail; a goal《영》; a lockup/~에 가두다 imprison (one); throw (one) into prison; put (one) in prison/~에 갇히다 be imprisoned; be thrown into prison/~에서 나오다 be released from prison; come out of prison.

**옥고**(玉稿) your manuscript.

**옥내**(屋內) the inside [of] a house/~의 indoor/~에서 indoors; within doors/~ 전화 an interphone.

**옥니** front teeth that turn in/~배기 a person with front teeth that turn in.

**옥다** bend inwards.

**옥답**(沃畓) rich[fertile, fat] paddy-fields.

**옥당목**(玉唐木) calico of inferior quality; inferior calico.

**옥도**(沃度) iodine/~전기 tincture of iodine; iodine tincture/~게 an iodine preparation. ヨード

**옥돌**(玉—) a precious stone; a gem.

**옥동자**(玉童子) an angel[a gem] of a boy; a precious son.

**옥란**(玉蘭) 《식》 Chinese[white] magnolia; a yulan; *Magnolia denudata*《학명》.

**옥문**(獄門) a prison gate; the gate of a jail.

**옥바라지**(獄—) sending in clothes and food to a prisoner/~하다 send in clothes and food to a prisoner.

**옥사**(獄舍) a prison house.

**옥사**(獄死) death in prison/~하다 die in prison.

**옥사장이**(獄舍—) a jailer; a gaoler《영》; a turnkey; a hellhound.

**옥살이**(獄—) prison life; life behind bars.

**옥상**(屋上) a roof; the house top/~에서 on the roof/~ 정원 the roof garden.

**옥새**(玉璽) the Imperial[Privy] Seal; the Seal of the Emperor/~관 the Lord Keeper of the Privy Seal.

**옥색**(玉色) light blue.

**옥생각** misunderstanding; misapprehension; perversion; a distorted view/~하다 distort; pervert/남의 말을 ~하다 pervert another's words.

**옥석**(玉石) ①《옥돌》 precious stones; jade ②《옥과 돌》 precious stones and pebble stones; jades[gems] and stones ③《좋은 것과 나쁜 것》 wheat and tares.

**옥석 구분**(玉石俱焚) Gems and stones are destroyed together. The good and the bad are ruined together.

**옥석 혼효**(玉石混淆) a mixture of wheat and chaff; a jumble of wheat and tares; thread and thrum.

**옥셈** miscalculation/~하다 miscalculate; make a miscalculation.

**옥소**(沃素) 《화》 iodine → 옥도.

**옥쇄**(玉碎) a death for honor/~하다 die honorably; die but never surrender; suffer an honorable death/대장부는 ~할지언정 와전(瓦全)은 원치 않는다 A man of honor would rather die with his name unstained than survive with disgrace.

**옥수**(玉水) crystal water; clear water.

**옥수**(玉手) 《왕의》 the king's hand 《미인의》 a beautiful [woman's] hand.

**옥수수** 《식》 maize; Indian corn[millet]《영》; corn《미》/~ 기름 corn oil.

**옥신각신** ~하다 wrangle; altercate; squabble; argue/서로 ~ 말다툼하다 wrangle with each other.

**옥신거리다** ①《북작거리다》 swarm; crowd; throng/벌이 수없이 ~ bees swarm by the thousands/사람들이 ~ be thronged; with people ②《환부가》 tingle; ache; rankle; throb with pain/어제 베인 상처가 자꾸 옥신거린다 The wound keeps smarting from a cut I got yesterday.

**옥안**(玉顔) 《왕의》 the king's face; the royal visage 《미인의》 a beautiful [wo-

**옥야**(沃野) a fertile[rich] field[plain]/ ~ 천리 a vast stretch of fertile plain.

**옥양목**(玉洋木) calico.

**옥외**(屋外) the open air; the exterior of a house; outside the house; the outdoors/~의 out-of-door; outside/~ 연설 an outdoor[open-air, a stump] speech/~ 운동 outdoor[open-air, field] exercise[sports].

**옥우**(屋宇) a house; houses.

**옥인**(玉人) ①(옥장이) a lapidary ②an angel of a person ③(인형) a jade doll.

**옥잠화**(玉簪花) a plantain lily; *Hosta undulata*(학명).

**옥장이**(玉匠—) a lapidary; a jewel cutter.

**옥졸**(獄卒) a jailer.

**옥좌**(玉座) the Imperial throne; the Emperor's chair/~에 앉다 sit on the throne; take The Imperial seat.

**옥죄이다** be tight; be fitting too closely /옥죄이는 옷 a tight clothes/옷의 겨드랑이가 너무 옥죄인다 the coat cuts me under the arm.

**옥중**(獄中) the inside of a jail 《옥중에서》 in jail[prison]/~기 a diary written in prison.

**옥체**(玉體) ①(임금의) the person of the king; His Majesty's person[health] ②(미인의) the body of a beautiful woman ③(존체) the noble body; your body; you.

**옥토**(沃土) fertile[rich, fat] land[soil]/ 메마른 땅을 ~로 만들다 make barren soil fertile.

**옥토끼** ①(흰 토끼) a white rabbit ②(달 속의) the man rabbit in the moon.

**옥편**(玉篇) a Chinese-Korean dictionary; a dictionary of Chinese characters.

**옥호**(屋號) a shop[store] name.

**옥황상제**(玉皇上帝) the highest of the heavenly gods of Taoism; the Lord; the king of kings.

**온** 《전부》 all; whole/~ 하늘 the whole sky[heavens]/~ 누리 the whole universe/~몸 the whole body/~ 세계에 all over the world/~ 힘을 다하여 with all one's might[strength].

**온각**(溫覺) sensation of warmth; temperature sensation.

**온갖** all kinds[sorts] of; every kind of; all manner of; every [possible]; whatever … all/~ 것 all; everything/~ 기회 every and any occasion/~ 사람 all sorts of peple/~ 고생을 다하다 go through all kinds of hardship imaginable/~ 준비를 갖추다 make every preparation (*for*)/그는 목적을 달성하기 위하여 ~ 수단을 쓴다 He uses every available means[He leaves no stone unturned] to attain his object.

**온건**(穩健) moderateness; moderation; soundness/~하다 (be) moderate; slow and steady/~한 생각 moderate views /~한 의론 a sound argument/ ~주의 moderatism/~파 the moderateparty/ 나의 사상은 ~ I have a sound mind.

**온고 지신**(溫故知新) ~하다 review the old and learn the new; carry the knowledge gained into new field; take a leaf out of a wise man's book.

**온골** the overall width.

**온공**(溫恭) politeness; civility; courtesy /~하다 (be) polite; respectful; reverent; courteous.

**온기**(溫氣) warmth; warm air/~가 있다 be warm/~가 없다 be not warm; have no warmth.

**온난**(溫暖) warmth; being warm[mild]/ ~하다 (be) warm; mild.

**온당**(穩當) ~하다 (be) proper; just; right; reasonable / ~히 properly/~한 말 proper language; a statement proper for the occasion/~한 요구 a reasonable claim/그 해석은 ~하다 That is a sensible interpretation of the passage.

**온대**(溫帶) the temperate[variable] zone; the warm latitudes[belt]/~ 식물 the flora of the temperate zone/~ 지방 the temperate regions.

**온도**(溫度) temperature/높은[낮은] ~ a high[low] temperature/일년의 평균 ~ the annual mean temperature/실내 ~ shade temperature/ ~ 조절 thermostatic control/절대 ~ the absolute temperature.

**온도계**(溫度計) a thermometer; the mercury/~가 영도로 내려가면 물이 언다 When thermometer is below zero, water will freeze. /섭씨[화씨] ~ a centigrade [Fahrenheit] thermometer/최고[최저] ~ a maximum[minimum] thermometer.

**온돌**(溫突) the Korean under-floor heating system; a hypocaust.

**온량**(溫良) gentleness/~하다 (be) gentle; amiable; benign.

**온면**(溫麵) hot noodle soup; warm noodle.

**온몸** the whole body 《부사적》 all over the body; from head to foot/그녀는 ~에 화상을 입었다 She got scalded all over his body.

**온반**(溫飯) hot beef soup with rice.

**온밤** the whole night/간밤엔 ~을 꼬박 뜬눈으로 새웠다 I couldn't sleep a wink throughout last night.

**온상**(溫床) a hot-bed; a warm nursery /악의 ~ a hot-bed of vice /자유의 ~ the cradle of liberty.

**온색**(溫色) a warm colour.

**온수**(溫水) warm water; hot water.

**온순**(溫順) gentleness; obedience; docility/~하다 (be) gentle; meek; obedient; submissive; compliant.

**온습**(溫習) review; exercise/~하다 review; keep in practics.

**온실**(溫室) a greenhouse; a hothouse; a glasshouse〈영〉; a greenery/~장 hothouse growth/~ 식물 a hothouse[greenhouse] plant[flower]/~ 재배 glass culture.

**온아**(溫雅) ~하다 (be) refined; graceful; elegant; affable/~한 말 graceful[refined] language/~한 사람 a person of quiet grace.

**온안**(溫顏) an amiable[kindly] face; a gentle countenance[look].

**온양**(醞釀) ~하다 ①《양조》 brew ②《모함》 entrap; ensnare; cherish a secret.

**온오**(蘊奧) profundity 《깊은 이치》 mysteries/~를 체득하다 make a profound study of; master the secrets of; delve deeply into the mysteries of.

**온욕**(溫浴) a hot[warm] bath/~하다 take a hot[warm] bath/~ 요법 the hot-water cure; treatment by warm water.

**온유**(溫柔) gentleness; tenderness; mildness/~하다 (be) gentle; mild; tender; amiable; sweet.

**온장**(一帳) 《전 지면》 the whole surface of a sheet of paper; the whole[entire] space 《of a newspaper》; 《자르지 않은 종이》 uncut paper.

**온전**(穩全) soundness; intactness/~하다 (be) sound; whole; intact; perfect/집안에 ~한 접시라고는 하나도 없다 There isn't a whole plate in the house.

**온정**(溫井) a hot spring.

**온정**(溫情) warm-heartedness; a warm feeling; warmth; heartiness; geniality/~주의 the kind-feeling policy/~있는 warm[-hearted]; cordial; kind-hearted.

**온종일**(一終日) all day [long]; the whole day; all through the day; from morning to[till] night/어제는 ~ 비가 왔었다 It rained yesterday from morning till night./~ 기다리고 있었다 I was kept waiting all the day.

**온집안** the whole family; all the family; all over the house/~을 찾다 search all over the house.

**온채** the whole[entire] house/~를 새로 짓다 build a whole new house; rebuild the entire house.

**온천**(溫泉) a hot spring; a thermal[medicinal] spring 《광천》 a spa/~장 hot springs; a hot-bath resort/~ 여관 a hotel at hot spring; a hot spring hotel/~에 가다 visit[go to] a spa; take the baths[waters].

**온축**(蘊蓄) 《지식의》 a stock of knowledge; profound knowledge; erudition.

**온탕**(溫湯) 《온천》 a hot spring; thermal waters 《욕탕》 hot[warm] water[bath]; 《국》 hot soup.

**온통** all; wholly; entirely; altogether; completely.

**온폭**(一幅) overall[whole] width of cloth [paper].

**온혈 동물**(溫血動物) a warm-blooded animal.

**온화**(溫和) ~하다 (be) gentle; mild; quiet; pacific 《기후》 (be) mild; temperate; clement/~한 기후 a mild climate/~한 사람 a gentle person/성질이 ~하다 be of a gentle character.

**온후**(溫厚) gentleness; mildness; suavity/~하다 (be) gentle; mild; affable/~한 신사 a courteous gentleman/그는 ~ 성실한 사람이다 His personality is gentle and sincere.

**올**¹ 《가닥》 ply 《짜임새》 texture/~이 고운 직물(織物) close texture/~이 성긴 coarse/~이 고운[거친, 촘촘한] 천 cloth of fine[coarse, loose] texture.

**올**² this year/~ 안에 in the course of this year; before the year-end/~ 여름 휴가 the coming summer vacation 《지나간》 the last summer vacation/~에는 비가 많이 왔다 We have had a lot of rain this year.

**올-** early ripening/ ~벼 early ripening rice/ ~감자 early potato/~복숭아 early peach.

**올가미** ①《틀》 a snare; a trap/~를 놓다 lay a snare; set[lay] a trap/~로 잡다 entrap; gin, ensnare; catch in a trap/~에 걸리다 be caught in a trap; fall into a snare; be entrapped ②《꾀》 a trick; a plot; an intrigue; a conspiracy.

**올강올강** chewing; mumbling; mouthing/~ 씹다 chew on 《a thing》.

**올고둥** 《동》 a marine snail; *Cancellaria spenglerriana*《학명》.

**올곧다** 《사람이》 (be) upright; straight; honest; right-minded 《줄이》 straight; direct/올곧은 사람 an upright person/올곧은 줄 a straight[direct] line.

**올내년**(一來年) this and next year; this year and the next.

**올되다** ①《피륙이》 (be) fine; close ②《사람이》 (be) precocious; wise above *one's* age; forward for *one's* years/올된 아이 an over-developed[a precocious] child ③《곡식이》 (be) rareripe; ripening early.

**올라가다** ①《상승하다》 rise; go up; ascend; mount 《타고》 climb 《분출하다》 belch; soar /산에 ~ climb[go up] a mountain; ascend[make an ascend of] a mountain/지붕에 ~ get[go up] on th-

**올라오다**

e roof ②《상륙하다》land; go ashore ③《상경하다》go up to (Seoul) ④《승진·선양하다》be[get] promoted; be advanced; be raised; gain/그는 대위로 올라갔다 He was promoted to captain. ⑤《동귀하다》advance (in *prise*); go up; rise《대단히》jump/값이 ~ rise in price ⑥《거슬러》go[sail, steam] up (*a river*). のぼっていく

**올라오다** go up; rist. のぼってくる

**올랑출랑** lapping; splashing; spattering/~ 물가를 씻고 있는 물결 the water lapping the shore. ちゃぶちゃぶ

**올리다** ①《위로》elevate; lift [up]; put up; put (*a thing*) on; hoist《손을》hold up; put (*a thing*) on; hoist《손을》hold up《불꽃을》set off/손을 ~ hold[lift] up *one's* hand; raise *one's* hand/돛을 ~ unfurl a sail ②《선양하다》exalt; raise (획득하다) win; achieve/명성을 ~ become famous; win fame[*one's* spurs]/국가의 위신을 ~ raise national prestige ③《승진하다》promote; raise; elevate/계급을 ~ raise *one's* rank/한 급 ~ promote (*one*) to a higher class ④《거행하다》hold; observe; solemnize/결혼식을 ~ celebrate a marriage[wedding] ⑤《양륙하다》land; up shore; discharge; unload/육지에 ~ land (*goods*) ⑥《소리를》set up; raise (*one's voice*)/환성을 ~ set up a shout of joy ⑦《증정하다》give; present; offer ⑧《기재하다》record; put on record; enter; make an entry/사건을 역사에 ~ record an event in history/이름을 ~ register[enter] *one's* name/장부에 ~ enter[make an entry] in a book. あげる

**올막졸막** all kinds of small things in cluster/~하다 (be) of various small sizes. ごちゃごちゃ

**올망** a net for deep-sea fishing.

**올망졸망** variously; diversely; with various sizes/~한 어린이들 little children of about the same size/사과가 ~ 여러 개 있다 There are a lot of small apples of about the same size. すずなり

**올목졸목** all kinds of small things in cluster. ごちゃごちゃ

**올무** a snare; a trap; a noose. となみ

**올바로** ①《바르게》rightly; right; aright; justly; lawfully《정직하게》honestly《정확하게》correctly; exactly/~ 말하면 properly[strictly] speaking/~ 발음하다 pronounce correctly/~ 세상을 살아가다 lead an honest life; pursue an honest career; live straight ②《곧게》straight; direct; upright/~ 서다 stand upright. ただしく

**올밤** an early chestnut. そうじゅくのくり

**올빼미** an owl/~ 새끼 an owlet/~ 우는 소리 a hoot. ふくろう

**올벼** the early-ripening rice plant.

**올봄** this spring. こんしゅん

**올새** texture; weave《뜨갯 따위의》a stitch/~가 촘촘한 직물 a fabric with close[fine] texture/~가 거친 rough; open in weave.

**옮기다**

**올연(兀然)** [standing] bolt upright; aloft. こつぜん

**올차다** ①《사람이》(be) substantial; sturdy; stout; small but solid; be of compact build/올찬 사람 a man of compact[substantial] build ②《곡식이》grow [become, get] ripe and hard early; ripen early. だいたんだ

**올챙이** a tadpole. おたまじゃくし

**올케** a sister-in-law; *one's* brother's wife.

**올콩** an early-ripening variety of bean. そうじゅくのまめ

**올통볼통** ~하다 (be) lumpy; rough; uneven; rugged. でこぼこ

**올팥** early red beans. そうじゅくのあずき

**올해** this year; the current[present] year/~ 겨울 this winter/~도 며칠 남지 않았다 We have only a few days left before the end of the year., The year is drawing to a close./~는 풍년이다 This is plenteous year. ことし

**옭걸다** tie up and hang; bind. かさねてかける

**옭다** ①《잡아 매다》tie up; fasten; bind/사람을 ~ bind a person; tie a person up/새끼줄로 짐을 ~ tie a bundle with a rope ②《올가미로》noose [a rope around the neck of]; put the noose on ③《피를 써서 사람을》[en]trap; [en]snare. くくる

**옭매다** tie a secure[fast] knot; fasten. しばりつける

**옭아내다** ①《올가미로》put a rope around the neck and drag out; noose (*an animal, a thing*) out ②《남을 속여서》cheat [wheedle, swindle, squeeze, do] (*a person*) out of (*a person's money*). しばりつける

**옭아매다** bind to; tie to; fasten to. むすびつける

**옭히다** ①《올가미에》get roped[noosed]; be tangled/여우가 올가미에 ~ A fox is caught in a snare. ②《얽히다》be[get] tangled[entangled, knotted]/실이 옭히어 풀어지지 않는다 Thread is so tangled up that it is impossible to straighten it out. ③《걸리다》be dragged [sucked] in; be involved; be entangled in/그는 살인 사건에 옭히어 큰 욕을 봤다 He is mixed up in a murder case and gets a rough going over.

**옮기다** ①《이전하다》remove; move (*to, into*); transfer/주거를 시외로 ~ move[change *one's* abode] to the suburbs/학교를 ~ change shools; transfer to another school ②《돌리다》transfer; carry (*to*)/본점에서 지점으로 ~ be transferred from the head office to a branch ③《그릇 따위에》transfuse (붓다) pour; empty (*into*)/물을 통에서 병으로 ~ pour water from the case into a bottle; empty the cask into bottle ④《전염하다》give; communicate (*a disease to another*) ⑤《번역하다》translate (*into*); render[turn,

옮다 ①(이선되나) remove to〈영〉; move into〈미〉/신축한 집으로 ~ move into a new house ②(사람이 병에) be infected (with a disease); take; catch; contract 《병이 사람에게》 be communicated to; infect /옮기 쉬운 병 an infectious disease / 병이 옮은 사람 an infected person /옮기 쉽다 be catching[infectious, contagious] ③(물이) be stained[smeared] (with dye) ④(말·소문이) spread; pass on /말이 ~ words spread[pass on]. うつる

옮아가다 ①(이사하다) remove; move; change quarters/종로로 ~ remove to the *Chongro* District ②(퍼져가다) spread; overspread; expand; widen; stretch/ 불은 사방으로 옮아 갔다 The fire spread in all directions. ③(이동하다) pass (*to, into*); turn (*to*)/남의 수중으로 ~ pass into another's hands/애기는 정치 문제로 옮아 갔다 The conversation turned on political problems. ④(병·유행 등이) prevail. うつっていく

옮아오다 move into ⇨옮다. うつってくる

옰 compensation; recompense; indemnity; reparations. むくい

옳다¹ ①(정당하다) (be) right; rightful / 옳은 일 right conduct /옳은 은 일 what is right; a right thing/하는 일이 ~[그르다] go about (*anything*) in the right [wrong] way ②(정의) (be) righteous; just/옳은 사람 a righteous man/그는 자기가 ~고 생각하면 아무것도 두려워하지 않았다 When he knew he was in the right, he feared nothing. ③(정직하다) (be) honest; upright 《진실하다》 truthful/옳고 꿋꿋하라 Be just and fear not. ④(적절하다) (be) proper /옳은 방법 the proper way; the correct method ⑤(틀림없다) (be) correct 《정확하다》 (be) accurate 《순정》 (be) genuine; pure ⑥(합법적이다) (be) lawful; legal; legitimate /옳지 않은 unlawful; illegal ⑦(건전하다) (be) sound; healthy. ただしい

옳다² 《감탄사》 Right!, O.K.!, All right!, Right you are!/~ 됐다 Now I've got it., That's fine., I am sure of my game. そうそう

옳은 길 (바른 길) the path of righteousness[virtue, duty]; the straight path; the right track 《도리》 righteousness /~에서 벗어난 짓 an unrighteous act /~ 로 인도하다 guide (*people*) into the right path. せいどう

옳은 말 right words; righteous remarks; an honest speech /~을 하다 tell the truth; say right things; tell what is right/~을 하는 사람 a person who speaks truly[true].

옳지 Good!, Right!, Yes!/~ 그만하면 됐다 Good! That will do. そうそう

옴¹ 《의》 the itch; scabies 《개·고양이·소 따위의》 mange; scotch fiddle《속》.

옴² the tiny process around the nipple of a new mother. かいせん

옴나위 room to budge; elbowroom/ ~ 없다 be jammed[packed] in tight; have no elbowroom /버스는 하도 사람이 많아서 ~ 없었다 The bus was so closely packed that I could not move. わずかなよゆう

옴두꺼비 a warty old toad. ひきがえる

옴살 bosom friendship; intimacy; one flesh; two hearts beating as one.

옴쏙 ~하다(be) hollow; sunken/눈이 ~ 하다 His eyes are sunken. むしゃむしゃ

옴실거리다 swarm; wriggle; teem with. うごめく

옴장이 an itch sufferer. かいせんかんじゃ

옴종(-腫) a sore caused by itch.

옴죽거리다 squirm; wriggle. うごめく

옴쭉달싹 with a very slight[the slightest] move; budging slightly/ ~ 않다 don't turn a hair do not budge[stir, move] an inch/ ~ 못할 지경이다 be in a fix[pinch]. びくびく

옴질거리다 squirm; wriggle. うごめく

옴질거리다 ①(오물거리다) mumble; chew on ②(벌레 따위가) swarm; squirm ③ 《망설이다》 waver; vacillate/ ~가 기회를 놓치다 dally away *one's* opportunity. ぐずぐずする

옴츠러뜨리다 shrink; draw; contract.

옴츠러들다 shrink up; cower; flinch; quail; recoil. うずくまる

옴츠리다 cringe; cower/몸을 ~ make *oneself* small. うずくまらせる

옴켜잡다 grasp; seize ⇨옴켜잡다.

옴켜쥐다 grasp; seize ⇨옴켜쥐다.

옴큼 a handful.

옴파다 dig; delve; core (*out*); cave (*a rock*); sink (*a well*). ほじくりにぎる

옴파리 a bellied[belly-swollen] chinaware bowl.

옴팍눈 sunken[deep-set] eyes 《사람》 a person with sunken[deep-set] eyes; a hollow-eyed person.

옴패다 be digged [down]; be delved; be cored [out]; be sunken/옴패인 곳 a sunken place; a depression /폭우로 땅이 옴팼다 The ground was pitted by heavy rains. うちがわにふかくほじくる

옴폭 ~하다 (be) hollow; deep; sunken; dented/눈이 ~하다 have deep-set[sunken] eyes. ぼこっと

옷 《의복》 clothes; a garment 《총칭》 clothing; apparel; costume 《복장》 a dress 《직장복》 a garb 《제복》 a uniform/얇은 ~ a light dress; thin clothing/갈아 입을 ~ spare clothing[clothes]/ ~ 갈아 입는 곳 《공장 등의》 a dressing-room; an outfit room/~을 입다[벗다] put on [off] clothes; dress[undress] *oneself*/ ~이 날개 Clothes make the man., Fine feathers make fine birds. いふく

옷가슴 the breast [of a coat]; 《샤츠의》 th-

**옷가지** [several kinds of] garments.
**옷감** cloth; stuff/얇은 ~ light stuff; thin cloth/~을 마르다 cut cloth/~에 물을 들이다 dye cloth
**옷거리** outward appearance; one's form; the appearance of one's clothes. ふくのきこなし
**옷걸이** 《매다는 것》a coat hanger 《거는 것》a clothes rack. いか
**옷고름** a breast-tie; a coat string. ふくのむすびひも
**옷기장** the length of a garment. ふくのながさ
**옷깃** the collar[neck] of a coat/~을 세우다 turn up one's collar. えり
**옷단** a hem; a fly/~을 감치다 hem.
**옷밥** 《옷과 밥》clothing and food 《생계》living; livelihood/~있고 예컨이라 W-ell-fed; well-bred; It is hard for an empty sack to stand straight.
**옷보**(一褓) ①《보》a cloth for wrapping clothes; a cloth wrapper/~에 옷을 싸다 wrap up a dress in a kerchief ②《사람》a clothes-conscious person. いふくつつみ
**옷자락** the lower ends of clothes; the skirt; the train/~을 끌다 trail[drag] the skirt/~을 걷어 올리다 tuck up the skirt. すそ
**옷차림** one's attire; personal appearance. いふくのきこなし
**옷치레** dressing up; rich attire/~하다 dress up; wear fine clothes.
**-옹**(翁) an aged[old] man/김~ the old Mr. Kim. おう
**옹고집**(壅固執) obstinacy; stubbornness; bigotry 《사람》a stubborn person.
**옹골지다** (be) well-filled; substantial; solid. けんじつである
**옹골차다** (be) solid; firm; stout; sturdy /옹골찬 사람 a person of sturdy build. けんじつでじゅうまんしている
**옹구** a [kind of] pack-saddle.
**옹그리다** crouch; squat down/다리를 ~ draw in one's legs. うずくめる
**옹기**(甕器) pottery with a dark brown glaze. とうき
**옹기장수**(甕器一) a pottery dealer; an earthenware dealer.
**옹기장이**(甕器匠一) a potter. とうこう
**옹기전**(甕器廛) an earthenware shop.
**옹기중기** thickly ⇒웅기중기.
**옹달** a hollow; a depression/~샘[우물] a small spring[well]/~솥 a small kettle. ちいさくくぼむ
**옹동그라지다** be shortened[contracted]. まりにまがる
**옹동이**(甕一) a small earthen jar; a crock.
**옹두리** a knot; a gnarl; a node.
**옹립**(擁立) enthroning/~하다 enthrone; give backing to; help (a person) to a position; support. ようりつ
**옹배기** a small earthen vessel; a tiny earthenware bowl.
**옹색**(壅塞) ~하다 ①《궁핍하다》be hard up; be in straitened circumstances; be in a fix/~하게 살다 be badly off; live in poverty/돈에 ~하다 be hard up for money; be pinched for money ②《좁은》(be) narrow; cramped/~한 방 a marrow room/집이 ~하다 The House is too small. こんきゅうすること
**옹생원**(壅生員) an illiberal person; a bigoted; a narrow-minded person.
**옹서**(翁壻) father-in-law and son-in-law. へんきょうなひと
**옹송그리다** curl up (one's body); double up; cower/추워서 몸을 ~ huddle oneself up with cold. みをかがめる
**옹송옹송하다** (be) hazy; confused; stupefied. ぼんやりする
**옹알거리다** mutter; murmur; grumble; grunt/혼자서 ~ grumble[mutter] to oneself. つぶやく
**옹위**(擁衛) safeguard; escort/~하다 guard; escort. ひだりとみぎからささえまもること
**옹이** a knot; a gnarl; a knob/~ 있는 gnarled.
**옹잘거리다** murmur[grumble] [to oneself]. ぶつぶついう
**옹졸하다**(壅拙—) (be) narrow-minded; illiberal; intolerant/그는 옹졸한 위인이다 He is a narrow-minded man. へんきょうなこと
**옹주**(翁主) a princess; a king's daughter by a concubine.
**옹추** one's bitter enemy/그들은 서로 ~다 They are bitter enemies to each other. にくみきらうひと
**옹크리다** shrink; curl[huddle] oneself up; double up; draw[pull] in/옹크리고 자다 sleep curled up/무서워서 몸을 ~ be huddled up with fear. みをかがむ
**옹호**(擁護) 《보호》protection; safeguard 《엄호》cover 《원조》support; assistance /~하다 protect; defend; safeguard; support/~하에 under the protection (of)/정책을 ~하다 support a policy /자기의 권리를 ~하다 safeguard one's own rights/자유를 ~하기 위하여 싸우다 fight in the cause of freedom/ ~ 자 a defender; a supporter; a protector. ようご
**옻** lacquer/~칠한 lacquered; japanned /~칠한 제품 a lacquerware/~오르다 be poisoned with lacquer/~을 타다 be allergic to poison ivy/~나무 a lacquer [varnish-]tree. うるし
**와**[1] 《및》and/너~ 나 you and I.
**와**[2] with a rush 《시끄럽게》loudly; with a great roar/~ 울다 burst out crying /~ 달아나다 run away in a panic/~ 웃음이 터지다 burst into laughter. わあー
**와가**(瓦家) a house roofed with tiles; a tile-roofed house. かわらぶきのいえ

**와각거리다** clatter; rattle. がじゃつく

**와글거리다** ①swarm; crowd; throng／시장에 사람들이 와글거린다 The market is jammed inside. ②be clamorous[boisterous, tumultuous, noisy]／와글거리는 사람들 a clamorous crowd of people. うようよする

**와다닥** suddenly; with a rush; abruptly. ばたばたと

**와당탕** thumping; boisterously; noisily／~하다 make a thumping sound; make a noise／아이들이 마루 위에서 ~거린다 Children romp around boisterously on the floor. ばたん

**와당탕퉁탕** thump; plump; bang; clamourously. ばたんどしん

**와드등와드등** with thud[thump]; rumbling and clattering／~하다 thump; clatter. がちゃがちゃ

**와들와들** shivering; trembling／추위서 ~ 떨다 shiver from cold／무서워서[성이 나서] ~ 떨다 tremble with fear[anger]／손이 ~ 떨려서 쓸 수가 없었다 My hand trembled so much that I could not write. ぶるぶる

**와락** all at once; suddenly; with a rush [start]／문을 ~ 열다 jerk a door open／청중이 ~ 몰려 나왔다 The audience poured out／개가 어린애에게 ~ 달려들었다 The dog sprang upon the child. とつぜん

**와르르** ①《사람이》 with a rush ／우리들은 ~ 역으로 몰려갔다 We rushed to the station.／군중이 ~ 몰려 들어갔다 The crowd poured[surged] in. ②《물건이》 clattering; crumbling; all in a heap／~ 떨어지다 clatter down. がらがら

**와륵**(瓦礫) pieces of broken tile; broken tiles. がれき

**와병**(臥病) lying on a bed of illness／~하다 be ill in bed; lie on a bed of illness. がびょう

**와사**(瓦斯) gas. ガス

**와삭거리다** rustle／와삭와삭 rustlingly／낙엽이 바람에 와삭거린다 The dead leaves rustle in the wind. かさっとする

**와상**(臥狀) a bed; a bedstead; a berth. がしょう

**와석**(瓦石) tile and stone. がせき

**와식**(臥食) ~하다 live in idleness; eat the bread of idleness; vegetate／~자 an idler; a drone. あそんでくうこと

**와신상담**(臥薪嘗膽) struggling against difficulties for the sake of vengeance; sustained determination and perseverance／~하다 go through unspeakable hardships and privations／~도 굳이 사양치 않는 바이다 I am ready to go through thick and thin., I vow to wade through all changes of fortune. がしんしょうたん

**와언**(訛言) ①a false story; a groundless rumor ②《사투리》 dialect. かげん

**와우**(蝸牛) the snail 달팽이. かぎゅう

**와음**(訛音) a corruption; a corrupted pronunciation. かおん

**와짝** ①forcefully; vigorously／줄을 ~ 잡아당기다 give a rope a vigorous pull ②all at once; all of a sudden; abruptly／날씨가 ~ 추워진다 The weather gets cold suddenly. ばっと

**와전**(瓦全) completing one's span of life; content with mediocrity／~을 부끄럽게 여기다 be ashamed of having led a safe but mediocre life.

**와전**(訛傳) a misrepresentation; a false [distorted] report／~하다 misrepresent; give a false[distorted] report. かでん

**와중**(渦中) a whirlpool; a vortex／전쟁의 ~에 휩쓸려 들다 be embroiled in war／정쟁(政爭)의 ~에 말려들다 be involved in political strife. かちゅう

**와지끈** with a crash; snappingly; with a snap. がちゃん

**와해**(瓦解) collapse; fall; breakup; downfall; crumbling; disintegration／~하다 collapse; fall to pieces; disintegrate／정당의 ~ the collapse of a political party／내각은 불원간에 ~할 것이다 The Cabinet will soon be dissolved. がかい

**왁자지껄하다** (be) noisy; clamorous; boisterous; uproarious. さわがしい

**완강**(頑強) obstinacy; stubbornness; doggedness／~하다 (be) stubborn; obstinate; strong／~하게 obstinately; stiffly; stoutly／그들은 ~히 저항했다 They offered a stubborn[stout, strong] resistance. がんきょう

**완결**(完結) conclusion; completion; termination; finish; end／~하다 conclude completely; terminate; finish／~되다 be completed[concluded]; be brought to an end／사전의 편찬은 일단 ~되었다 The compilation of the dictionary has practically been finished. かんけつ

**완결**(完決) definite decision／~하다 decide conclusively; determine definitely. かんけつ

**완고**(頑固) 《고집》 obstinacy; stubbornness 《완미》 bigotry／~하다 (be) obstinate; stubborn 《외고집》 headstrong／~하게 obstinately; persistently／~한 늙은이 an obstinate old man／저러 ~한 사람은 드물다 Such a pig-headed person is rarely met with. がんこ

**완곡**(婉曲) a roundabout way [of speaking]; circumlocution; euphemism／~하다 (be) euphemistic; roundabout; periphrastic／~히 circuitously／~히 말하다 insinuate; say in a roundabout way; beat about[around] the bush／그는 ~하게 말하는 법이 없다 He does not mince matters. えんきょく

**완구**(玩具) a toy; a plaything／~점 a toyshop. がんぐ

**완급**(緩急) 《늦고 빠름》 fast and slow motion; high and low speed 《위급》 emergency. かんきゅう

**완납**(完納) payment in full; full paym-

**완두**(豌豆) 【식】 a pea. えんどう

**완력**(腕力) physical[muscular] strength; brute force; brawn/~으로 이기다 win by force/~을 사용하다 use[appeal to] force; resort to force[violence]/~으로는 도저히 그를 이길 수 없다 I am no match for him in mere physical strength. わんりょく

**완롱**(玩弄) ~하다 toy; play with; make sport[a plaything] of. がんろう

**완료**(完了) completion; conclusion; finish; end; termination/~하다 complete; finish; conclude/~되다 be concluded; be finished; be completed. かんりょう

**완만**(緩慢) slowness 《불활발》 dullness laxity; slackness/~하다 (be) slow[-moving, -going]; slack; inactive/~한 시장 《상》 a dull market 《금융》 slackness of the money market/그는 동작이 ~하다 He is slow-moving., He is slow in action. かんまん

**완명**(頑冥) stupidity; asininity/~하다 (be) stupid; foolish; imbecile. がんめい

**완미**(頑迷) asininity; bigotry; obstinacy; stubbornness/~하다 (be) asinine; bigoted; stupidly/저런 ~한 사람은 드물다 Such a bigoted person is rarely met with./그는 ~하여 여론의 동향을 깨닫지 못한다 He is so bigoted in his views that he is blind to the tide of public opinion. がんめい

**완벽**(完璧) perfection; completeness/~하다 (be) perfect; complete; faultless; free from blemish/~을 기하다 aim at perfection. かんぺき

**완보**(完補) supplementation/~하다 supplement; complement. かんぜんにおぎなうこと

**완보**(緩步) a slow walk/~하다 walk slowly. かんぽ

**완본**(完本) a complete book[volume]; complete works. かんぽん

**완비**(完備) perfection; completion; complete provision[arrangement, preparation]/~하다 perfect; complete; make (a thing) perfect; equip[furnish] completely/국방의 ~ the completion of national defense/그 호텔은 시설이 ~되어 있다 The hotel is completely furnished., You will find perfection of accommodation, service and cuisine at the hotel. かんび

**완상**(玩賞) 《감상》 appreciation; admiration 《즐김》 enjoyment/~하다 appreciate; enjoy 《중히 여기다》 prize; admire 《즐기다》 relish. たのしんでみること

**완성**(完成) completion; perfection; accomplishment; consummation/~하다 complete; perfect; finish; accomplish; bring (a thing) to perfection/~에 가깝다 (be) near completion /죽기 전에 이 사업을 ~하고 싶다 I hope to see the work accomplished before I die. かんせい

**완소**(完燒) total destruction by fire/~하다 be completely burnt; be totally destroyed by fire/집이 ~되었다 The house was totally destroyed by fire.

**완수**(完遂) successful execution; completion; accomplishment/~하다 bring to a successful completion; perfect; complete/직책을 ~하다 perform[do] one's duties. かんすい

**완습**(頑習) an inveterate habit. がんこなしゅうかん

**완승**(完勝) a complete victory/ ~하다 win a complete victory.

**완악**(頑惡) wickedness; stubbornness; obstinacy; bigotry/~하다 (be) wicked; stubborn; obstinate; bigoted. かたくなでわるいこと

**완연**(宛然) ~하다 (be) clear; obvious; evident; patent; distinct; vivid/~히 clearly; vividly. はっきり

**완연**(蜿蜒) ~하다 (be) wiggly; snakelike; serpentine; winding; meandering; sinuous/~히 기복하는 산악 rolling mountains. えんえん

**완완**(緩緩) slowness/~하다 (be) slow; tardy. かんかん

**완우**(頑愚) stupidity; obstinacy/~하다 (be) stupid and obstinate; pig-headed. がんぐ

**완월**(玩月) viewing the moon/~하다 enjoy the moonlight; view the moon. つきをみてたのしむこと

**완인**(完人) 《흠없는》 a perfect person 《병이 나은》 a person perfectly recovered.

**완자**[1] a meatball fried in egg batter; a kind of wonton/~탕(湯) a kind of wonton soup.

**완자**[2] 《만자》 a swastika; a gammadion; a fylfot; the Buddhist cross/~창 a window with a swastikashaped frame.

**완장**(腕章) an armband; a brassard 《계급장》 a chevron. わんしょう

**완전**(完全) perfection; completeness; consummation/~하다 (be) perfect; complete; whole; consummate/~히 perfectly; to perfection; completely; thoroughly; wholly/~하게 하다 perfect; make perfect; bring to perfection; be near perfection. かんぜん

**완전 무결**(完全無缺) absolute perfection/~하다 (be) perfect and faultless; absolutely perfect; flawless.

**완초**(莞草) 【식】 a rush. わんぐる

**완충**(緩衝) shock-absorbing; concussion-deadening; buffing/~하다 buff; absorb shock; deaden concussion/~국 a buffer country[state]/~ 지대 a buffer [neutral] zone. かんしょう

**완치**(完治) a perfect cure; a complete recovery/~하다 be completely cured [recovered]/6개월 만에 상처는 ~되었다

At the end of six months the last bandages were removed. かんぜんになおすこと

**완쾌(完快)** complete recovery (from *illness, of health*)/~하다 recover completely (*from*); be restored to health; get well. かんぜんになおすこと

**완패(完敗)** a complete defeat/~하다 suffer a complete defeat.

**완하다(緩-)** (be) slow; tardy. ゆるい

**완하제(緩下劑)** a laxative; an aperient.

**완행(緩行)** going[running] slow/~하다 go[run] slow/~ 열차 a slow train; a local train. ゆっくりいくこと

**완화(緩和)** relief mitigation; alleviation/~하다 ease; relieve; lighten; soften; allay; temper. かんわ

**왈가닥거리다** clatter; rattle/창문이 ~ The window rattles. からころとなる

**왈가닥달가닥** rattling and clattering/~하다 rattle and clatter. からころ

**왈가왈부(曰可曰否)** an argument pro and con/~하다 argue pro and con; argue for and against. かひをろんずること

**왈왈** copiously; in a copious flow; streaming[ly]; plentiful[ly]. とくとく

**왈왈하다** (be) impetuous; hasty; quick; tempered.

**왈칵** 《별안간》 suddenly 《세게》 with a jerk/~ 잡아당기다 pull (*a thing*) with a jerk. げっ. はっと

**왈패(日牌)** ①《망나니》 a wild fellow; an unruly person; a rough ②《말괄량이》 a hussy; a flapper.

**왔다갔다** ~하다 come and go; walk about; loiter; stroll 《배회》 wander/거리를 ~하다 stroll aimlessly through the streets/해변을 ~하다 take a stroll on the beach. いったりきたり

**왕(王)** a king 《군주》 a monarch 《통치자》 a ruler; a prince/~의 royal/짐승의 ~ the king of beasts/꽃 중의 ~ the queen of flowers. おう

**왕가(枉駕)** attendance; presence; visit ⇒ 왕림. おうが

**왕가(王家)** a royal family. おうか

**왕개미(王-)** 《충》 a Hercules ant; an army ant; *Camponotus ligniperdus*(학던). くろおうあり

**왕거미(王-)** 《충》 a large spider. おにぐも

**왕겨(王-)** chaff; rice bran.

**왕고(往古)** remote antiquity; time immemorial; ancient times. おうこ

**왕고모(王姑母)** a sister of *one's* father's father. いちばんめのしゅくぼ

**왕골** a rush; a bulrush/~ 자리 a rush mat. わんぐる

**왕관(王冠)** a crown; a diadem. おうかん

**왕국(王國)** a kingdom; a monarchy. おうこく

**왕궁(王宮)** the King's Palace; the Royal Palace. おうきゅう

**왕권(王權)** sovereign powers[rights]; royal authority; regality; royal prerogatives 《왕위》 the throne; royalty; sovereignty; the sceptre/~ 신수설 the divine right of kings. おうけん

**왕기(王族)** a royal standard; a king's colour.

**왕녀(王女)** a Royal princess; a princess; a princely daughter.

**왕년(往年)** former years; the years gone by; the past; former times/~의 대 선수 a star player in gone days by. おうねん

**왕눈이(王-)** a person with large eyes; a large-eyed person. めのおおきいひと

**왕당(王黨)** the Royalists 《영국의》 the Tories.

**왕대(王-)** 《식》 a kind of large bamboo.

**왕대비(王大妃)** the Empress Dowager; the Queen Mother. おうたいひ

**왕도(王道)** the rule of right; righteous government; the principles of royalty/~와 패도 the rule of right and the rule of might/~로써 다스리다 rule *one's* people with justice/학문에는 ~가 없다 There is no royal road to learning. おうどう

**왕돈(王-)** a large coin.

**왕래(往來)** ①《통행》 come-and-go; comings and goings 《인마의》 [street] traffic; passing of people [on the road]/~가 많은 거리 a bustling street; a busy thoroughfare; a much-frequented road/~가 많지 않은 거리 a lonely street/사람의 ~ the traffic of men ②《교우》 intercourse 《서신의》 communication/~하다 have intercourse[keep company] with 《서신 왕래》 exchange letters with. おうらい

**왕로(往路)** an outward trip[journey].

**왕림(枉臨)** attendance; presence; visit/~하다 attend; visit/당신의 ~을 고대합니다 We look forward to your attendance. おうが

**왕마디(王-)** a biggest knot[joint]. いちばんおおきいふし

**왕명(王命)** the king's order; a royal order[command]/~으로 by royal order/~에 따라 in obedience to a royal command. おうめい

**왕모래(王-)** coarse sand; grit. あらいすな

**왕밤(王-)** 《식》 a large[giant] chestnut. おおきいくり

**왕방(往訪)** paying a visit; a call/~하다 pay a visit to; go and see; call on (*a person*) at (*a place*); visit/~한 기자 a pressman who called (on *a person*). おうほう

**왕방울(王-)** a big bell.

**왕벌(王-)** 《충》 a hornet. くまばち

**왕법(王法)** the king's law. おうほう

**왕복(往復)** going to and from; coming and going; going and returning; correspondence; communication/~하다 go

**왕봉**(王蜂) 〖충〗 a queen bee.
**왕부**(王父) *one's* grandfather.　おうふ
**왕비**(王妃) a queen [consort]; an empress.　おうひ
**왕사**(王事) the king's business; the affairs of the Emperor; the cause of royalty.　おうじ
**왕사**(往事) past events; bygones; things past[of old]; the past／〜는 불귀라 The past is beyond recall.　おうじ
**왕생**(往生) death; (*one's*) end; extinction of life; passing to the next world／〜하다 die; depart this life; pass away [to the next world]／〜 극락을 빌다 pray for rebirth in paradise.　おうじょう
**왕생 극락**(往生極樂) euthanasia; an easy passage into enternity／〜하다 go to paradise; die an easy and peaceful death; pass away peacefully.　おうじょうごくらく
**왕석**(往昔) olden times; old days.　おうせき
**왕성**(王城) the capital of a kingdom.　おうじょう
**왕성**(旺盛) a prosperous[flourishing, thriving] condition; a fine[an excellent] condition／〜하다 (be) excellent; prosperous; flourishing; thriving; vigorous; energetic／사기가 〜하다 be in excellent spirits.　おうせい
**왕세손**(王世孫) the eldest son of the Crown Prince; the eldest grandson of the king (in *a direct line*).　おうのうえのまご
**왕세자**(王世子) the Heir Apparent to the Throne; The Crown Prince.　おういをつぐこ
**왕손**(王孫) a grandson of a king.　おうそん
**왕수**(王水) 〖화〗 *aqua regia*(L).　おうすい
**왕시**(往時) old[former] times; old days.　おうじ
**왕신** a cantankerous person; a crossgrained person.　ねじれたひと
**왕실**(王室) the royal household; the royal family[house].　おうしつ
**왕업**(王業) kingcraft; the principles[science] of royalty; the Imperial cause 《지배·통제》 rule 《통치자의 지위 또는 직》 rulership.　おうぎょう
**왕왕**(往往) occasionally; now and then; from time to time; once in a while; more often than not; at times／학생들에게 〜 있는 일이지만 as is often the case with students／이런 일이 〜 있다 Such things are apt to happen.　おうおう

**왕위**(王位) the throne; the crown／〜 계승 succession to the throne.　おうい
**왕일**(往日) bygone days; old days; former days[times]; the past.　おうじつ
**왕자**(王子) a prince; a royal prince.　おうじ
**왕자**(王者) a king; a monarch; a sovereign; a ruler／정구계의 〜 the champion of the tennis world.　おうしゃ
**왕자**(往者) a former time.　おうしゃ
**왕정**(王政) the royal regime; the kingly rule; monarchy／〜 복고 the restoration of the royal regime; Restoration／〜 복고 주의자 a monarchist.　おうせい
**왕조**(王朝) a dynasty／〜의 dynastic.　おうちょう
**왕족**(王族) the royal family 《한 사람》 a member of royalty.　おうぞく
**왕좌**(王座) the throne 《패권》 supremacy 《수위》 the premier position／〜를 차지 하다 occupy the premier position.　おうざ
**왕지**(王旨) an Imperial order[command].
**왕지네**(王一) 〖동〗 a large centipede.
**왕진**(往診) a visit to a patient／〜하다 visit; make a call on (*a patient*); make a professional visit; go and see a patient at his house／〜료 a fee for a doctor's visit.　おうしん
**왕참**(往參) 〜하다 go and attend; go to take part in.
**왕청되다** be poles apart; be as different as light and darkness.　さいがおおきい
**왕콩**(王一) 〖식〗 a soy bean.
**왕토**(王土) the royal domain.　おうど
**왕항**(往航) outward voyage[passage].
**왕화**(王化) civilizing influence of (*a king*); the benevolent rule of the sovereign.
**왕후**(王侯) princes; crowned heads 《총칭》 royalty.　おうこう
**왕후**(王后) an empress; a queen.　おうごう
**왜** why; how; for what reason／〜냐 하면 because; for; The reason is …／〜 그런지 without knowing why; somehow／〜 너는 캔디를 좋아하지 않느냐 How is it you don't like candy?　なぜ
**왜**(倭) Japan; Japanese.　わ
**왜가리** 〖조〗 a common heron.　あおさぎ
**왜간장**(倭一醬) Japanese soysauce[soy].
**왜골** a boor; a large fierce person; a rude fellow.
**왜구**(倭寇) Japanese invaders[pirates]; Japanese pirate raiders.
**왜귤**(倭橘) a mandarin orange.　みかん
**왜기**(倭器) a Japanese vessel.
**왜기름** kerosene ⇒석유.
**왜녀**(倭女) a Japanese woman.　にほんおんなの卑語
**왜놈**(倭一) a Japanese 《총칭》 the Japanese.　にほんじんの卑語
**왜림**(矮林) a brushwood.　ひくいきのもり
**왜말**(倭一) Japanese; the Japanese language.　にほんご

**왜바람** a fickle wind. ぼうふう
**왜반물** dark blue dyestuffs.
**왜색(倭色)** Japanese manners [and customs]; Japanese ways; things Japanesque. にほんしき
**왜선(倭船)** a Japanese ship. にほんのふね
**왜소(矮小)** small stature; dwarfishness／~한 (be) small; diminutive; dwarfish; of small build; small-statured. たんしょうなこと
**왜수건(倭手巾)** a towel.
**왜식(倭式)** Japanese style. にほんしき
**왜식(倭食)** Japanese food[cuisine]／~집 a Japanese restaurant. にほんのたべもの
**왜옥(矮屋)** a small flat house. ちいさいいえ
**왜인(倭人)** 《총칭》a Japanese; a Jap 《한 사람》a Japanese. にほんじん
**왜인(矮人)** a dwarf; a pigmy; a pygmy 《미》. こびと
**왜자하다** (be) in everybody's mouth; abroad 《풍문이》(be) widespread.
**왜장(倭將)** a Japanese general[commander].
**왜장녀(一女)** a virago; a termagant; an amazon.
**왜적(倭敵)** the enemy Japan; the Japanese foe.
**왜적(倭賊)** Japanese invaders[pirates].
**왜정(倭政)** Japanese rule. にほんせいふ
**왜축(矮縮)** contraction; shrivelling／~하다 contract; shrivel. いしゅく
**왜태(一太)** a big pollack.
**왜틀비틀** totteringly; reelingly. ひょろひょろ
**왜풍(一風)** a violent wind.
**왜풍(倭風)** Japanese style; Japanese manners [and customs]. にほんしき
**왱그랑댕그랑** clink; clank; with a clang. ちゃりんちゃりん
**왱뎅** noisily; uproariously; clamorously. わいわい
**왱왱** whistling／~하는 바람 소리 a whistling sound. がんがん
**외** a cucumber ⇨오이. きゅうり
**외-** 《홑》one; single／~눈깔이 a one-eyed person.
**외(椳)** a lath; a lattice-strip.
**외(外)** ①《이외》except; but; save／그 ~ the rest／바보 ~에는 그런 말을 하지 않는다 Nobody but a fool would say such a thing. ②《바깥》outside; out (of)／~권한 ~의 행위를 하다 do an act in excess of one's authority. そと
**외가(外家)** one's mother's family; one's mother's old home.
**외가닥** a single strand.
**외가서(外家書)** books on subjects other than ethics and history.
**외각(外殼)** a shell; a crust; integumentary covering. がいかく
**외각(外角)** 【수】an exterior angle 《야구》 the outcorner. がいかく
**외간(外艱)** mourning for a father／~을

당하다 go into mourning for one's father. がいかん
**외감(外感)** ①《감기》a cold ②《감각》sense; sensation; feeling.
**외객(外客)** a guest; a visitor. がいかく
**외견(外見)** external aspect; [external] appearance. がいけん
**외계(外界)** the external [outer] world; the outside; 【철】external phenomena the physical world／~론【철】externalism. がいかい
**외고집(一固執)** [single-minded] stubbornness; obduracy; obstinacy; mulishness／~의 obstinate; obdurate; stubborn; mulish; pigheaded; unyielding／그는 ~장이다 He is a stiff-necked person.
**외골** an unforked road; a road without a fork all along. いっぽうにのみ通じたみち
**외과(外科)** surgery／~ 수술 a surgical operation／~ 의원 a surgery. げか
**외과피(外果皮)** 【식】an exocarp; an epicarp. がいかひ
**외곽(外廓)** ①《성》the outer wall [of a walled city] ②《바깥 테두리》an outer ring; the outline. がいかく
**외관(外觀)** external appearance; an outward show; an exterior view／~으로 사람을 판단하다 judge of a person by appearance. がいかん
**외교(外交)** diplomacy 《관계》diplomatic relations 《정책》foreign policy 《권유》soliciting; canvassing／~ 관계를 수립하다 establish diplomatic relations (with)／~가 a diplomatist; a diplomatic person／~ 정책 a foreign policy. がいこう
**외교원(外交員)** an agent; a representative; a sales agent; a canvasser; a solicitor 《미》. がいこういん
**외구(畏懼)** awe; reverential fear／~하다 be awe-stricken; be struck with awe. いく
**외구(外寇)** a foreign enemy; a foreign invader. がいこう
**외국(外國)** a foreign country[land]; a foreign nation[power]／~에서 abroad; overseas／~ 무역 foreign trade／~ 사절 a foreign envoy／~환[시세] foreign exchange [rate].
**외국어(外國語)** a foreign language[tongue]／~로 자기 생각을 말한다는 것은 매우 어렵다 It is very hard to express oneself in a language that is not one's own. がいこくご
**외국인(外國人)** a foreigner; a foreign national; an alien／~ 관광객 a foreign tourist／~ 촌 the foreign quarter of a city. がいこくじん
**외근(外勤)** outside duty[service]; 《외교원의》canvassing／~하다 be on outside duty; work outside／그는 ~입니다 He works outside.／~ 기자 a legman; a reporter. がいきん
**외기(外氣)** the [open] air. がいき

**외기 노조**(外機勞組) the Foreign Organizations Employees Union(略: FOEU).
**외길** the only road; a single path／～목 a narrow entrance to a blind alley.
**외김치** cucumber pickles.
**외나무다리** a log bridge; a single bridge／원수는 ～에서 만난다《속담》 Evildoing always catches up with you.
**외날** a single edge／～ 면도칼 a single-edged razor.
**외다** 《암기하다》 recite from memory; learn by heart; memorize／시를 ～ recite a poem ⇨외우다. あんきする
**외따로** separated; isolated; lonely; all alone; solitarily／벌판에 조그만 집이 ～서 있다 In the middle of the field [there] stands a solitary cottage.
**외딴집** an isolated house; a solitary [lonely] house.
**외딸다** [be] alone; solitary; isolated; sequestered; remote; secluded; lonely. となりがない
**외대**(外待) unkind[cold] treatment; cold reception; inhospitality／～하다 treat (*a person*) unkindly. れいぐう
**외대다** ①《푸대접》 treat unkindly; give (*one*) a cold reception ②《배척》 reject. れいぐうする
**외도**(外道) ①《오입》 whoring ②《나쁜 길》 an evil course; a wrong course. せいどうをあやまること
**외동이** *one's* beloved only son. ひとりご
**외등**(外燈) an outdoor lamp. がいとう
**외람**(猥濫) impudence; presumptuousness; audacity／～하다 (be) impudent; presumptuous; audacious／～스럽지만 Allow me to tell you that …
**외래**(外來) ～의 foreign; imported／～ 사상 a foreign[an imported] ideas／～어 a word of foreign origin; a bor rowed word; a loan word. がいらい
**외력**(外力) 【물】 external force／～이 가해 지다 be pressed by external force. がいりょく
**외로이** lonelily; solitarily／～ 살다 live a lonely[lonesome] life.
**외롭다** (be) lonely; lonesome; solitary; isolated／외로운 생활을 하다 lead a solitary life. こどくだ
**외마디 소리** a single cry; an outcry of pain; a scream／～를 지르다 scream; shriek; utter a piercing cry. たんちょうなこえ
**외면**(外面)¹ outward appearance; the outside; the exterior／～치레 showing off. がいめん
**외면**(外面)² ～하다 turn away (*one's face*); look away (*from*); cut [dead]／그는 나를 ～하고 지나갔다 He passed by with his face averted. そっぽむくこと
**외모**(外貌) [outward] appearance; external features[aspect]; externals／그녀는 ～가 단정한 사람이다 She is a woman of decent appearance. がいぼう

**외무**(外務) foreign affairs／～부 the Ministry[Department] of Foreign Affairs; the Foreign Office／～부 장관 the Foreign Minister. がいむ
**외문**(外聞) reputation; publicity 《체면》 decency. がいぶん
**외물**(外物) an outward thing; a foreign matter; an extraneous substance. がいぶつ
**외미**(外米) foreign[imported] rice; rice from abroad. がいまい
**외박**(外泊) stopping[staying] out／～하다 sleep out; stay out; stop out 《군인의》 stop out of the barracks. がいはく
**외벌** a single set／～ 매듭 a single[simple] knot.
**외벽**(外壁) 【건】 an outer wall. がいへき
**외부**(外部) the outside; the exterior／～와 교통이 두절되다 be cut off from the outside world. がいぶ
**외분**(外分) 【수】 external division／～하다 divide externally. がいぶん
**외비**(外備) defense against foreign invasion. がいてきにそなえること
**외빈**(外賓) 《외국 손님》 a foreign visitor [guest]; 《외부 손님》 a guest.
**외사**(外事) external[foreign] affairs／～과 the section of foreign affairs. がいじ
**외사**(外史) ①《외국 역사》 history of a foreign country ②《야사》 an unofficial [unsanctioned] history. がいし
**외사촌**(外四寸) a maternal cousin.
**외삼촌**(外三寸) a maternal uncle; an uncle on *one's* mother's side. ははほうのしゅくふ
**외상** credit; trust／～값 a credit account; accounts／～으로 해 주시오 Charge it to my account.／～ 거래 credit transaction.
**외상**(一床) a table for one; an individual table.
**외상**(外傷) an external wound; a traumatic injury. がいしょう
**외상**(外相) the Foreign Minister ⇨외무부 장관. がいしょう
**외서**(外書) a foreign book. げしょ
**외설**(猥褻) obscenity; lewdness; indecency; immorality／～하다 (be) obscene; nasty; filthy; indecent／～죄 public indecency／～ 소설 an obscene[a hot] novel. わいせつ
**외세**(外勢) ①《바깥 형세》 outward conditions; external circumstances; exterior situation ②《외국 세력》 the power[influence] of a foreign country／～에 의존하다 depend on the power of a foreign country. がいせい
**외손** one hand／～의 one handed; single-handed.
**외손**(外孫) a child of *one's* daughter; a grandchild by *one's* daughter. がいそん
**외손지다** get deprived of the use of one hand.
**외숙**(外叔) an uncle on *one's* mother's side; a maternal uncle／～모 the wife

**외숙(外叔)** of a maternal uncle. がいしゅく
**외숙(外宿)**《외박》 staying out [away from home]; sleeping out／～하다 stay away from home; sleep out. がいしゅく
**외식(外食)** eating[dining] out／～하다 dine[eat] out; board out(미).
**외식(外飾)** external ornament; a show off／～하다 put on outside appearance; show off. がいめんだけかざること
**외신(外信)** foreign news; a foreign telegram; an overseas dispatch／～부[장] [editor of] the foreign news department. がいしん
**외실(外室)** an outer room; man's quarters. しゅじんのいま
**외심(外心)**〖수〗 a circumcenter; an outer center (of *a similitude*)／～각 an eccentric angle／～점 the metacenter. がいしん
**외씨버선** small shapely socks.
**외아들** an only son. ひとりご
**외야(外野)**〖야구〗 the outfield／～석 outfield bleachers／～수 an outfielder. がいや
**외양(外洋)** the open sea[ocean]. がいよう
**외양(外樣)**〖의견〗 look; show; aspect; [outward] appearance《용모》 looks; features《풍채》 personal appearance／그는 ～이 반반하다 In person he is handsome／～이 그럴 듯하다 have a good appearance. がいぶのようぼう
**외양간(喂養間)**《말의》 a stable《소의》 a cow-house[-shed].
**외양치레(外樣～)** putting on a fair show. がいぶをかざること
**외어서다** step aside; ger out of the way. ほうこうをかえてたつ
**외연(外延)**〖논〗 extension; denotation. がいえん
**외올** a single strand／～베 cloth woven of single strands／～실 singlestrand thread.
**외외(巍巍)**《산이》(be) lofty; towering; soaring《인격이》 be of noble character; lofty. ぎぎ
**외외가(外外家)** *one's* maternal grandmother's maiden home[family]. ははほうのははのうち
**외용(外用)** external[topical] use[application]／～약 a medicine for external use [application] only. がいよう
**외우(外憂)** ①《부친상》 *one's* father's death ②《외적 근심》 foreign troubles; external alarms. ちちやそふのそう
**외우(畏友)** an esteemed friend; a respected[venerated] friend. そんけいするとも
**외우다**《암기하다》 learn by heart[rote]; commit to memory《암송하다》 recite [speak] from memory; say by heart／그것을 잘 외우시오 You must bear it well in your mind. あんきする
**외유(外遊)** a foreign travel[tour]／～하다 travel abroad／～에서 돌아오다 return from *one's* foreign tour. がいゆう

**외의(外衣)** an outer garment. がいい
**외이(外耳)**〖해〗 external ear; auricle; concha／～염 otitis externa; conchitis.
**외인(外人)** ①《외국인》 a foreigner; an alien／～부대 the Foreign Legion ②《남》 outsiders《가족이》 an unrelated person／이 일은 ~이 알아서는 안 된다 This is between ourselves. がいじん
**외자(外字)** foreign lotters[characters]／～ 신문 a foreign-language newspaper. がいじ
**외자(外資)** foreign capital[currency, money, funds]／～ 도입 introduction[importation] of foreign capital／～ 유입 the inflow[influx] of foreign capital. がいし
**외짝** an odd[unmatched] member of a pair;a single member[side, part].
**외장골(外腸骨)**〖해〗 iliaca external; the external flank bone／～ 동맥[정맥] arteria[vena] iliaca externa. がいちょうこつ
**외적(外敵)** a foreign enemy[invader]／～의 침입을 받다 suffer from foreign invasion[attack, raid]. がいてき
**외적(外的)** external; outward／～ 증거 an external evidence. がいてき
**외전(外電)** a foreign dispatch; a foreign telegram; a cable[gram]. がいでん
**외접(外接)**〖수〗 circumscription／～하다 circumscribe; be circumscribed／～원 a circumscribed circle. がいせつ
**외정(外征)** a foreign expedition[campaign]／～하다 go on a foreign expedition; invade a foreign country. がいせい
**외조모(外祖母)** a grandmother on *one's* mother's side; a maternal grandmother. ははほうのそぼ
**외조부(外祖父)** a grandfather on *one's* mother's side;a maternal grandfather. ははほうのそふ
**외족(外族)** the maternal line of relatives; a relative on the mother's side. がいぞく
**외종(外從)** a cousin on *one's* mother's side; a maternal cousin. ははほうのいとこ
**외주(外周)** circumference. そとのまわり
**외줄** a single line[stripe].
**외줄기** a single stalk[stem].
**외지(外地)** a foreign[an alien] land; an overseas land／～ 근무 overseas service. がいち
**외지(外紙)** a foreign newspaper《총칭》 the foreign press. がいし
**외지다** get isolated[secluded, sequestered]. こどくである
**외직(外職)** a government post away from the capital; a local[provincial] government post.
**외진(外診)** consultation at a patient's home.
**외채(外債)**〖경〗《차관》 a foreign loan《증권》 a foreign bonds《채무》 an external debt／～를 모집하다 raise[float] a fore-

**외척**(外戚) a maternal relation; relatives on one's mother's side. がいせき
**외청도**(外聽道) 【해】 an external auditory canal. がいちょうどう
**외촌**(外村) a village outside a town; outlying[outside] villages. むらのそとにあるむら
**외축**(畏縮) ~하다 quail; cower; shrink up; flinch; recoil; wince/그는 그만한 일에 ~할 사람이 아니다 He is not a man to flinch from such a thing. いしゅく
**외출**(外出) going out; an outing/~하다 go out/김군 집에 책을 빌리러 갔더니 ~ 중이었다 I called at Mr. *Kim's* to borrow a book and found him out./~ 시간 《군인의》 leave-time/~ 금지령 a curfew order. がいしゅつ
**외치**(外治) ①《외과적 치료》external treatment/~하다 treat externally ②《외교》 a foreign policy. がいぶからちりょうすること
**외치다** shout out; shout; utter[give] a cry; exclaim (큰 소리로) cry[call] out 《비명을 지르다》shriek; scream 《소리를 지르다》yell/살려 달라고 ~ cry for help. さけぶ
**외탁**(外—) ~하다 take after one's mother's side in appearance[character].
**외톨** a single ripened chestnut/~밤이 《마늘》single-bulb garlic 《밤》a single-bur chestnut.
**외투**(外套) an overcoat; a great-coat; a topcoat. がいとう
**외풍**(外風) ①《바람》a draught; a draft /이 방에는 ~이 있다 There is a draft in this room ②《외국풍》 foreignism; exotic fashion; foreign ways[manners, style]. そとからのかぜ
**외피**(外皮) 《딱지》a crust; a shell 《과실의》a husk 《곡식의》a hull. がいひ
**외할머니** a [maternal] grandmother. ははほうのそぼ
**외할아버지** a [maternal] grandfather. ははほうのそふ
**외항**(外港) an outer port; an outport. がいこう
**외항선**(外航船) an ocean-going ship; a ship for overseas service.
**외해**(外海) the open sea; the high seas /~로 나가다 go out into the open sea. がいかい
**외향성**(外向性) 【심】 extroversion/~의 extroversive/~인 사람 an extrovert. がいこうせい
**외형**(外形) an external form; shape/~이 둥글다 be round in shape. がいけい
**외화**(外貨) 【경】foreign money[currency] /~ 획득 the obtaining of foreign money/~는 받지 않음 《게시》Foreign money is refused. がいか
**외화**(外畵) a foreign film[movie].
**외환**(外換) foreign exchange/~ 은행 a foreign exchange bank.
**외환**(外患) external[foreign] troubles; the pressure[invasion] of foreign enemy/내우 ~ internal and external troubles. がいかん
**왼** left/~쪽 the left [side]. ひだり
**왼발** the left foot. ひだりあし
**왼소리** a report of one's death.
**왼손** the left hand/~으로 글을 쓰다 write with the left hand. ひだりて
**왼손잡이** 《사람》a left-handed person; a left hander/~ 투수 a left-handed pitcher; a southpaw《미·속》. ひだりてきき
**왼쪽** the left side/~으로 돌다 turn to the left. さそく
**왼팔** the left arm.
**왼편** the left side. さそく
**욋가지** a lath; lath strips.
**요**¹ ①《얕잡을 때》this little [one]; these/ ~까짓 … such a[little] …/~같이 like this/~놈 you small thing ②《시간·거리》right near at hand/~ 근처에 in this neighborhood. この
**요**² 《의문》 이 저이는 누구~ Who is he?
**요**(褥) beddings; a mattress/~를 깔다 [개다] spread[put away] the mattresses. じょく
**요**(要) 《요점》the main[chief] point; the aim [목적] the purpose/~는 연습에 있다 The essential thing is practice.
**요강**(要綱) 《중요 사항》the outline; a summary; the general idea 《계획》the general plan 《취지서》a prospectus. ようこう
**요강**(尿綱) a chamberpot; a commode; a [night-]stool. おまる
**요건**(要件) 《필요 조건》a requisite; an essential condition 《요긴한 일》an important business[matter]/건강은 행복의 첫째 ~다 Health is the first requisite for happy. ようけん
**요격**(邀擊) an ambush; interception; a surprise attack/~하다 ambush; intercept; attack by surprise/~용 미사일 an interceptor missile. ようげき
**요결**(要訣) 《비결》a key; a secret 《뜻》an essential meaning; a vital point (of)/건강의 ~은 일찍 일어나는 것이다 Early rising in the morning is a key to good health. ようけつ
**요관**(尿管) 【해】the ureter. ゆにょうかん
**요괴**(妖怪) a ghost; an apparition; a specter 《괴물》a goblin; a hobgoblin. ようかい
**요괴스럽다**(妖怪—) (be) wicked and mysterious; eerie; weird; uncanny.
**요구**(要求) 《요청》a demand 《권리에 의한》a claim 《청구》a request 《필요》a requirement/~하다 demand; request; claim; call for; call upon (*a person* to *do*); require/손해 배상을 ~하다 present a claim for damages. ようきゅう
**요귀**(妖鬼) an apparition; a ghost; an evil spirit. あやしいきしん
**요금**(料金) a charge; a fee; a fare; a

**요기** rate／～을 징수하다 collect fees／수도〔전기〕～ water〔power〕rate. りょうきん

**요기** right this place; right here. ここ

**요기(療飢)** appeasing〔relieving〕／～하다 appease〔relieve〕 one's hunger.

**요기(妖氣)** a weird〔ghostly〕 air／～가 서려 있다 There is something ghostly in the atmosphere. ようき

**요긴(要緊)** essential importance／～하다 be essentially important; be of vital importance. じゅうようできんきゅうなこと

**요녀(妖女)** a temptress; a siren; an enchantress; a vamp《속》. ようじょ

**요다음** next／～ 일요일에 방문하겠읍니다 I shall come and see you next Sunday. このつぎ

**요담(要談)** an important 〔business〕 talk／～하다 have a talk with (a person)／～중이다 be in the middle of an important talk. ようだん

**요때기(褥一)** shabby〔dirty〕 bedding.

**요도(尿道)** 【해】 the urethra／～염 urethritis. にょうどう

**요도(腰刀)** a sword; a sabre. こしがたな

**요독증(尿毒症)** 【의】 uremia; urine〔uremic〕 poisoning. にょうどくしょう

**요동(搖動)** shaking; shake; rocking／～하다 shake; quake; rock; pitch and roll／천지를 ～하다 shake heaven and earth. ようどう

**요란(擾亂)** a commotion; a disturbance; a fuss; a bustle／～하다 (be) noisy; clamorous; boisterous; uproarious／밖이 ～하다 There is a commotion outside. じょうらん

**요람(要覽)** a survey; a summary; an outline 《안내서》 a handbook; a directory. ようらん

**요람(搖籃)** a cradle／문명의 ～지 the cradle of civilization／～에서 무덤까지 from the cradle to the grave. ようらん

**요략(要略)** an outline; a summary; an epitome. ようりゃく

**요량(料量)** 《짐작》 guess; calculation; estimate 《생각》 a plan; an intention; an idea 《판단》 judgment; discretion／～하다 guess; calculate; plan out／내 ～으로는 그 계획이 성공할 것 같지 않다 I don't think the plan will prove successful. のちのことをしゅっこうすること

**요런** such; this; like this／～ 식으로 in this manner〔way〕／～ 식으로 하라 Do like this. こんな

**요령(要領)** 《요점》 the〔essential, main〕 points; the 《개략》 a summary; an outline／～있는 연설 a pointed speech／간단하면서도 ～이 있다 be brief and to the point. ようりょう

**요령(搖鈴)** a handbell. すず

**요령 부득(要領不得)** pointlessness; irrelevancy; impertinence／～하다 (be) pointless; be not to the point.

**요로(要路)** 《고위》 an important position; a high office 《당국》 the authorities 《길》 a principal road; a main artery／～에 아는 사람이 많다 have many friends in the authorities. ようろ

**요론(要論)** an important discourse; a discussion of importance〔consequence〕 a vital argument. ようろん

**요리** 《요렇게》 in this way; like this; so 《요리로》 this way; this direction; here. こちらへ

**요리(料理)** ①《만들기》 cooking; cookery; cuisine 《음식》 a dish; food; fare／～하다 cook (food); dress (fish); prepare (a dish)／그녀는 ～ 솜씨가 좋다 She has the right touch about cooking. ②《처리》 management; handling／～하다 manage; handle; dispose of／국정을 ～하다 manage〔conduct〕 state affairs. りょうり

**요리조리** here and there; this way and that way. ここかしこに

**요마(妖魔)** a goblin; a demon; a bogey; a hobgoblin. ようま

**요마적** lately ⇨이마적. ついさっき

**요만치** this small〔little〕 bit／～도 모르느냐? Don't you even know this. これくらいのもの

**요만큼** this 〔little〕 bit; to this small extent〔degree〕 ⇨이만큼. これくらい

**요망(妖妄)** ～스럽다 (be) flighty; fickle; frivolous; capricious; erratic; treacherous. じゃあく

**요망(要望)** a demand (for); a desire; a longing; a cry (for)／～하다 demand; desire; request earnestly／혁신을 ～하는 소리가 높다 There is a cry for reform. ようぼう

**요망(遙望)** ～하다 gaze into the distance after; see (something) far away; look afar off. とおくながめること

**요망(瞭望)** ～하다 watch (the enemy movement) from the heights.

**요망떨다(妖妄―)** act frivolously〔flightily, capriciously〕. けいそつなことをする

**요면(凹面)** a concave surface; concave; concavity／～경 a concave mirror. おうめん

**요목(要目)** principal items; a syllabus; a conspectus; the [main] points; the essence; the kernel; the gist (of a speech). ようもく

**요무(要務)** important business／～를 띠고 on an important business. ようむ

**요물(妖物)** 《괴물》 a goblin; a monster; a hobgoblin 《사람》 a wicked person; a crafty fellow. あやしいもの

**요민(饒民)** the people of ample means; the well-off subjects〔citizens〕. ゆたかなこくみん

**요민(擾民)** disturbing people／～하다 disturb people.

**요밀요밀하다** (be) meticulous scrupulous／요밀조밀한 사람 a meticulous person.

**요밀조밀하다** 《면밀하다》 (be) meticulous; scrupulous／요밀조밀한 필치 a meticulous bit of writing. 細かである

**요배(遙拜)** worshiping from afar／～하다 bow to the direction of (*one's home*).

**요번(一番)** this time. こんど

**요법(療法)** a remedy; a method of treatment; a medical treatment／전기 ～ electropathy. りょうほう

**요변(妖變)** 《사건》 a mysterious happening; a phantom case 《행동》 suspicious behavior／～스럽다 (be) strange suspicious; fishy; erratic. ようへん

**요부(妖婦)** an enchantress; a temptress; a vamp[ire]; a witch／～형의 여자 a woman of the vampire type. ようふ

**요부(要部)** the principal part; the essential part. ようぶ

**요부(饒富)** affluence; opulence; prosperity; easy means／～하다 (be) rich; wealthy; affluent; opulent; well-to-do. ふゆうなこと

**요부(腰部)** the waist; the loins. ようぶ

**요사(夭死)** an early death; premature death／～하다 die young; die at an early age／그녀는 ～했다 She died young [an early age]. ようし

**요사(妖邪)** capriciousness; fickleness; treacherousness; wickedness; craftiness／～스럽다[하다] (be) wicked; vicious; wily; capricious. こしまであること

**요산(尿酸)** 〖화〗 uric acid.

**요새** 《근래》 recently; of late; lately; now 《저번》 the other day; a few days ago 《요전부터》 for some time past; these few days 《현재》 nowadays; in these days; at this time of day／～ 혼히 볼 수 없는 책이다 Such a book is rarely to be met with nowadays. このごろ

**요새(要塞)** 〖군〗 a fortress; a stronghold; fortification／～를 구축하다 construct a fortress. ようさい

**요서(夭逝)** a premature death ⇒요사(夭死). ようさい

**요소(要素)** an element; a factor; an essential part 《필요 조건》 a requisite 《소질》 makings／행복의 ～ a factor of happiness. ようそ

**요소(要所)** an important position[post]; a strategic point[position]／～ 요소를 설명하다 explain the important points (*of*).

**요소(尿素)** 〖화〗 urea.

**요술(妖術)** magic; a magical practice; black art; witchcraft; tricks; jugglery／～쟁이 a juggler; a conjurer 《마술사》 a magician 《남자》 a wizard 《여자》 a witch. ようじゅつ

**요승(妖僧)** a vicious priest; an evil-working Buddhist priest. せいとうをみだすぼうず

**요시찰인 명부(要視察人名簿)** a black list; a surveillance list／～에 오르다 be "put" on the black list.

**요식(要式)** formal formalities／～ 계약 a formal contract／～ 행위 a formal act.

**요신(妖神)** Satan; an evil-spirit; a devil; a demon. あくま

**요악(妖惡)** wickedness; viciousness; vice; evil／～하다 (be) wicked; vicious; malicious; sinister. あやしくわるいこと

**요약(要約)** summary; condensation; summing up／～하다 summarize; give an outline of; epitomize／～해서 말하자면 in a word; in brief. ようやく

**요양(療養)** medical treatment[care]; [rest and] recuperation／～하다 recuperate; receive medical treatment／～소 a sanitarium〈미〉; a sanatorium〈영〉／자택 ～ home treatment. りょうよう

**요언(妖言)** crafty remark; wicked talk 《주문》 magic spells. ようげん

**요언(要言)** summarizing the essential points. ようげん

**요업(窯業)** 〖공〗 the ceramic industry; ceramics[keramics]. ようぎょう

**요연(瞭然)** ～하다 (be) clear; evident; plain; obvious; manifest／그것은 일목 ～하다 It is clear at a glance. りょうぜん

**요염(妖艶)** voluptuous beauty; amorousness; sensual charm; the witchery／～하다 (be) fascinating; bewitching. ようえん

**요요(擾擾)** noise and disturbance／～하다 (be) noisy; uproarious; tumultuous. じょうじょう

**요요하다(遙遙—)** (be) far away; distant. はるかかなただ

**요용(要用)** useful employment／～하다 make good use of; put (*a thing*) to a good use. ようよう

**요우(僚友)** a colleague; a comrade; a fellow official; a fellow worker; a coworker. りょうゆう

**요원(要員)** workers required; needed[necessary] personnel.

**요원(遙遠)** (being) very far away; far distant／～하다 (be) far distant; far off[away]; remote. ようえん

**요인(要人)** a key figure; an important person; a prominent man; a notable (*person*). ようじん

**요인(要因)** a factor; an element／중대한 ～ an important element. よういん

**요일(曜日)** a day of the week 《일요일을 제외한》 a week-day／오늘은 무슨 ～입니까 What day of the week is this? ようび

**요임(要任)** 《책임》 a heavy responsibility; an important duty[mission]; 《지위》 a responsible post; an important post of duty. じゅうようなにんむ

**요전(—前)** ①《며칠 전》 a few days ago; not long ago; a short time ago／～의 late; recent／바로 ～까지 until quite recently ②《전》 last; before; last time／～ 일요일 last Sunday. いぜん

**요절(夭折)** early[premature] death／～하다 die young[early]; die in the prime

요절(腰絕) ~하다 be convulsed with laughter; shake with laughter.

요절나다 ①(못 쓰게 되다) become unfit for use; do not stand use; become unserviceable 《부서지다》 break; get broken; be damaged ②(일이) be spoiled; fall through/내 구두가 요절났다 My shoes are worn out.

요점(要點) the main[essential] point; the gist; the substance; the pith; the essence; nub《미》/~을 찌르다 come to the point.

요정(了定) 《결정》 decision 《결말》 conclusion; settlement/~나다 be decided; be settled/~짓다 decide (upon); conclude.

요정(妖精) a fairy; a spirit/숲의 ~ a dryad/바다의 ~ a mermaid/샘의 ~ a naiad/물의 ~ a nymph.

요정(料亭) a [Korean-style] restaurant; a gisaeng house.

요조(窈窕) modesty; chastity; decency/~하다 (be) graceful; refined; modest; chaste; decent/~ 숙녀 a chaste and modest woman; a lady of refined manners.

요족(饒足) affluence 〓요부(饒富).

요즈막 recently; lately; these days; nowadays; last few days.

요즈음 recent days; these [last few] days; nowadays; just recently; lately/~ 그런 생각은 통하지 않는다 Your way of thinking won't do nowadays.

요지(要地) an important place; a strategic point[place].

요지(要旨) 《요점》 the point; the gist 《요령》 substance; amount 《취지》 purport 《서적·의론의》 an argument/~를 말하다 set forth the essential points.

요지경(瑤池鏡) a magic glass; a toy peep-show.

요지부동(搖之不動) steadfastness/~하다 be steadfast; be adamantine.

요직(要職) an important post[position, office]; a key position/정부의 ~에 있다 hold an important post in the government.

요진(要津) 《나루》 an important ferry 《요로》 an important[a principal] road.

요처(要處) a strategic[an important] point.

요처(凹處) a concave; concavity.

요철(凹凸) prominence and depression; unevenness; irregularity/~하다 (be) bulgy and hollow; uneven.

요청(要請) demand; request; claim/~하다 demand; request; claim; ask for ; ask (one) to/나는 그에게 보고를 제출하라고 다섯 차례나 ~했다 I have asked him five times to send in his report.

요추(腰椎) 《해》 the lumbar vertebra/~ 마취 lumbar anesthesia.

요충(要衝) an important spot 〓요충지.

요충(蟯蟲) a seat worm; a pinworm.

요충지(要衝地) an important spot 《군사상의》 a point of strategic importance.

요컨대(要─) in short[a word, sum, fine]; after all; all things considered; to sum up; to make a long story short/~ 그 문제는 이렇게 된다 After all, the question boils down to this.

요탁(料度) conjecture; surmise 〓촌탁.

요통(腰痛) lumbago; crick in the back; lumbar affection/~이 일어나다 have an attack of lumbago.

요판(凹版) 《인》 intaglio/~ 인쇄 intaglio printing.

요포대기(褓─) a baby quilt.

요하다(要─) require; be required to; need; want; take; have [the] need of; demand; call for/휴식을 ~ need a rest.

요함(僚艦) a comrade vessel; a consort ship.

요항(要項) essential points; essentials; an important item; the staple 《요의》 the gist.

요항(要港) an important port; a strategic naval port.

요해(要害) ①《요새》 a stronghold 《요지》 a strategic point ②《신체의》 the vital parts of the body.

요행(僥倖) [good] luck; chance; good fortune; a godsend; a windfall/참 ~ 이로군 What a stroke of good luck!

요행수(僥倖數) a lucky[happy] chance; a piece[stroke] of good luck; a fortunate move.

요혈(尿血) hematuria/~증 《의》 hematuria.

요형(凹型) concavity/~의 concave.

요희(妖姬) a temptress; an enchantress; a vamp; a witch.

욕(辱) ①(욕설) abuse; abusive; language; an insult 《독설》 a biting tongue 《중상》 slander; scandal/~하다 abuse; call (one) names; speak ill of (one); 《조소》 jeer at 《중상》 scold; slander/그는 나를 ~했다 He called me names. ②(치욕) shame; disgrace/오래 사는 것은 ~ 이다 To live long is to outlive much. ③(고난) hardships; trials; distress; misery; sorrows/~을 보다 have a bitter experience.

-욕(慾) a desire/금전~ desire for wealth/명예~ desire for fame/소유~ possessiveness/지식~ a thirst/그는 지식~에 불타고 있다 He is thirsty for knowledge.

욕가마리(辱─) the butt of abuse.

**욕감태기**(帑—) a person who is called bad names by many people. おおくのひとからぶじょくされるひと

**욕객**(浴客) a bather; a bathing guest; a visitor at a hot spring. よっきゃく

**욕계**(慾界) the world to avarice; the world of desire. よくかい

**욕구**(慾求) desire; craving; urge; want; aspiration/~하다 desire; want; crave (for); aspire (after)/~ 불만 [심] frustration. よっきゅう

**욕기부리다**(慾氣—) covet; envy; be greedy; be avaricious; be rapacious/너무 욕기부리지 마라 You must not be so grasping. よくけをだす

**욕념**(慾念) desire; wish; appetite 《정욕》 passions/육체적 ~을 억제하다 crucify the lusts of the flesh. よくねん

**욕되다**(辱—) bring disgrace upon oneself/내가 그 말을 하면 오히려 내게 욕이 됩니다 I would be ashamed to say that. めんもくがなくなる

**욕망**(慾望) a desire 《야망》 an ambition 《욕구》 wants/~을 일으키다 arouse a desire/~을 채우다 gratify [satisfy] one's ambition [desire]. よくぼう

**욕먹다**(辱—) ①《욕설을 당하다》 suffer an insult; be insulted; be slighted; be abused; be slandered ②《악평을 듣다》 have one's name scandalized; be stigmatized 《신문 따위에서》 be criticized unfavourably; be attacked/그는 정직하지 못하다고 욕먹는다 He has a bad reputation of being dishonest. ののしられる

**욕보다**(辱—) ①《곤란을 겪다》 try hard; make great efforts; strive; struggle; labour; take pains/그 범인의 수사에 무척 욕보았읍니다 I had work hard to hunt up the culprit. ②《치욕을 당하다》 be disgraced; be dishonoured; be subjected to humiliation; be abused. くろうする

**욕보이다**(辱—) disgrace; dishonour; insult; bring shame on (one); make (one) ashamed; put (one) to shame; humiliate. はずかしめる

**욕설**(辱說) evil-speaking; slander; abusive [foul] language/~하다 call (one) names; abuse; speak ill of; revile; talk scandal about/~을 퍼붓다 curse and swear. ののしり

**욕실**(浴室) a bathroom; a bath; a toilet room 〈미〉. よくしつ

**욕심**(慾心) 《탐욕》 greediness; covetousness; avarice; cupidity 《욕망》 a desire; a passion; an appetite; a hunger 《이기심》 selfishness; self-interest/그는 매우 ~이 많다 He is very avaricious. よくしん

**욕의**(浴衣) a bathrobe; a dressing gown; a bathdress. よくい

**욕장이**(辱—) a foul-mouthed [-tongued] person; a knocker; a slanderer 《험담군》 a scandal-monger.

**욕정**(欲情) [a] desire; craving 《색욕》 passions; [a] lust; sexual desire/~을 채우다 gratify one's lust. よくじょう

**욕조**(浴槽) a bathtub.

**욕지거리** abuse 《독설》 a biting tongue 《야유·비난》 jeers; hisses/~하다 say bitterly; call (one) names. ののしり

**욕지기** nausea; qualm; queasiness; a sickly feeling; sickness at the stomach/그것을 보니 ~가 난다 At the sight of it nausea rises in me. むかつき

**욕창**(蓐瘡) a bedsore; [의] decubitus.

**욕탕**(浴湯) a bath house; a public bath. よくとう

**욕하다**(辱—) abuse; call (a person) names; speak ill of (a person); revil (at, against); scold; slander /그는 화가 나서 욕하기 시작했다 He was so angry that began calling them names.

**욕화**(浴化) the influence of virtue/~하다 be influenced by virtuous examples. とくのきょうかをうけること

**욕화**(慾火) burning [ardent] desire.

**옷속**(帑—) quilting; filling; cotton-wool stuffing; wadding; batting.

**옷잇**(帑—) a bed sheet; sheeting.

**용**(用) ①《용돈》 pocket money ②《비용》 expenses ③《쓰임이》 for [the use of]/남자~ for men/어린이~ 책 books for children. ひよう

**용**(茸) 《녹용》 an antler. しかのつの

**용**(龍) 《상상의 동물》 a dragon 《큰 것》 a large thing/~이 되다 rise to greatness. りゅう

**용가마** a big rice pot; a caldron. おおきなかま

**용감**(勇敢) bravery; courageousness; boldness gallantry; heroism/~하다 (be) brave; courageous; heroic; gallant; valiant/그는 ~하게 죽었다 He died a brave death. ゆうかん

**용강**(勇剛) intrepidity; stout-heartedness; stalwartness; sturdiness/~하다 (be) intrepid; stout-hearted; stalwart; sturdy; brawny. ゆうもう

**용건**(用件) ~ business; a matter of business/빨리 ~을 말하시오 Come to the point at once.

**용고뚜리** a heavy [chain] smoker.

**용골**(龍骨) 《선박의》 the keel 《동물의》 mastodon bones.

**용공**(容共) pro-Communist/~ 정책 a pro-Communist policy.

**용관**(冗官) a supernumerary.

**용광로**(鎔鑛爐) a melting [smelting] furnace; a blast furnace. ようこうろ

**용구**(用具) 《기구》 a tool; implements 《장치》 an appliance; an apparatus/가정 ~ household appliances/운동 ~ sporting goods. ようぐ

**용꿈**(龍—) a lucky dream; a dream about a dragon/~꾸다 dream [have] a lucky dream.

**용궁**(龍宮) the Dragon Palace; the palace of the dragon king. りゅうぐう

**용귀**(踊貴) a rise in price. とうき

**용기**(用器) a tool; an instrument. ようき

**용기**(勇氣) courage; bravery; pluck; valour; grit《미·속》/그들은 그 광경을 보고 새로운 ~를 냈다 They drew fresh courage from the scene. ゆうき

**용기**(容器) a container; a vessel; a receptacle. ようき

**용기병**(龍騎兵) a dragoon.

**용납**(容納) 《허용》 permission; allowance; admission 《용서》 pardon; forgiveness/~하다 permit; admit; allow; pardon; forgive/변명을 ~하지 않다 allow no excuse. きょよう

**용녀**(龍女) the Dragon Princess; the princess of the Dragon.

**용녀**(傭女) a maid; a maidservant; a hired girl. やといおんな

**용뇌**(龍腦) 〖약〗 refined Borneo[Sumatra] camphor; borneol; camphol.
りゅうのう

**용단**(勇斷) a decisive measure; a resolute[drastic] step/~을 내리다 make a resolute decision (on *a matter*).
ゆうだん

**용달**(用達) errand; messenger[delivery] service/~사 a delivery agency.
ようたし

**용담**(用談) talk on a matter of business; business talk/~하다 have a talk with (*one*) on business/~중이다 be engaged with (*one*). ようだん

**용도**(用度) expenditure; expense. ようど

**용도**(用途) use; service/~가 넓다 have many uses. ようと

**용돈**(用-) pocket-money; money for current use; money for incidental use 《남편이 아내에게 주는》 pin-money/ ~이 떨어지다 run out of *one's* pocket-money.

**용두**(龍頭) the stem of a watch/~ 시계 a keyless watch.

**용두레**(농업) a large water dipper; a scoop bucket.

**용두사미**(龍頭蛇尾) good beginning and dull finish; a weak conclusion/~로 끝나다 end in a fiasco. りゅうとうだび

**용두질** masturbation; self-abuse; self-pollution; onanism/~하다 practise masturbation; masturbate; commit self-abuse. しゅいん

**용략**(勇略) courage and strategy; valour and stratagem; bravery and artifice.
ゆうりゃく

**용량**(容量) capacity; content; volume; measure of capacity/~ 분석 〖화〗 volumetric analysis. ようりょう

**용량**(用量) 《약의》 a dose; dosage.
ようりょう

**용력**(用力) [mental] exertion;[physical] labor/~하다 exert *one*self; labor; set *one's* heart on. みこころをつかうこと

**용력**(勇力) manly strength; undaunted power. ゆうりょく

**용렬**(庸劣) 《우둔》 stupidity; foolishness; tomfoolery 《용졸》 mediocrity; the commonplace/~하다 (be) silly; stupid; awkward; clumsy; bungling; mediocre; commonplace/~한 짓을 해서 미안하오 I am sorry for the blunder I have committed. ようれつ

**용례**(用例) an example; an illustration; an instance/~를 들다 take an example.
ようれい

**용로**(鎔爐) a cupola [furnace]. ようろ

**용립**(聳立) rising; soaring; towering/ ~하다 rise[tower, soar] high (*over*)/ 산봉우리가 구름 위에 ~하고 있다 The mountain rears its crest into the clouds. しょうりつ

**용마**(龍馬) a swift horse; a fleet steed. りゅうま

**용마루** a ridge of a [tiled] roof.

**용마름** the cover[ing] of a roofridge or a mud wall.

**용매**(溶媒) 〖화〗 a solvent [agent]; a menstruum(*pl.* -strua). ようばい

**용맹**(勇猛) courage; dauntlessness; intrepidity; valour; bravery; daring/~하다 (be) intrepid; undaunted; daring /~심 an intrepid spirit. ゆうもう

**용명**(勇名) a fame for bravery/~을 떨치다 win a fame for bravery. ゆうめい

**용모**(容貌) a face; looks; a countenance; features/매력적인 ~ a charming face.
ようぼう

**용무**(用務) business; a thing to do; a matter of business; a concern/급한 ~로 on urgent business/~가 무엇입니까 What is your business? ようむ

**용무**(冗務) a trifle[trivial] business.

**용법**(用法) the way to use 《사용 지시서》 direction/~을 잘 읽고 이 약품을 사용하시오 Apply the medicine after carefully reading the direction. ようほう

**용변**(用便) easing nature; going to the lavatory/~를 보다 relieve *one*self; ease nature; go to the closet.

**용병**(用兵) tactics; manipulation of troops/~하다 manipulate the troops/~ 술 tactics; strategy; the science of war. ようへい

**용병**(冗兵) superfluous soldiers; an uncalled-for army.

**용병**(勇兵) a brave soldier; a soldier of fearless courage. ゆうへい

**용병**(傭兵) a mercenary [soldier]; hired troops. ようへい

**용봉탕**(龍鳳湯) soup of carp and chicken boiled together.

**용부**(勇夫) a brave[courageous] man; a man of prowess.

**용부**(庸夫) a mediocrity; an inferior man; a mediocre man. ようふ

**용부**(勇婦) a brave woman; a heroine.

**용불용**(用不用) use and disuse/~설 〖생〗 Lamarckism; the theory of use and disuse. ようふよう

**용비**(用費) expense; expenditure; cost; outlay. ひよう

**용비**(冗費) unnecessary[avoidable] expenditure. じょうひ

**용빙**(傭聘) engagement/~하다 engage; employ/전문가를 ~하다 secure the services of an expert (on). ようへい

**용사**(勇士) a brave man; the brave; a hero. ゆうし

**용상**(龍床) the king's seat; the [royal] throne. おうざ

**용색**(用色) sexual union/~하다 have a sexual intercourse.

**용서**(容恕) pardon; forgiveness/~하다 pardon; condone; forgive; excuse; overlook; pass over/저의 무례를 ~하십시오 I beg you to forgive my rudeness.
ゆるしてやること

**용석**(熔石) 〖지〗 lava; volcanic rock.

**용선**(傭船) chartering 《선박》 a chartered vessel/~하다 charter[hire] a ship.

**용설란**(龍舌蘭) 〖식〗 an agave; a pita.
りゅうぜつらん

**용소**(龍沼) a linn; the basin of a waterfall.

**용속**(庸俗) ~하다 (be) mediocre; banal; ordinary; common; vulgar; commonplace.

**용솟음** 《끓음》 boiling up 《뒤끓음》 leaping up; bubbling up; gush/~하다 《끓다》 boil up; seethe; bubble up 《솟다》 well [up, forth, out]; gush[spring] out/샘물이 ~치듯 한다 A fountain gushes out.
たぎること

**용수**(用水) water 《빗물》 rainwater 《수도》 city water 《우물물》 well water 《관개용》 irrigation water 《사용》 using water/~권 water rights/~지(池) a reservoir.
ようすい

**용수뒤** the dregs[lees] of the wine in the bottom of the barrel.

**용수철**(龍鬚鐵) a spring/~ 장치의 worked by a spring. スプリング

**용신**(容身) ①《몸을 놀림》 moving [around]; getting about to move/~하다 move one's body; stir/좁아서 ~을 못 하다 have no room to move ②《살아감》 living; getting along/~하다 get along; lead a life. やっとせいかつすること

**용신**(龍神) the Dragon God[King]/~제 the Dragon God festival. りゅうじん

**용심**(用心) ①《주의》 care; heed; caution /~하다 attend; take care (of); be cautious (of) ②《심술》 malice; spite.
ようじん

**용심부리다** wreak one's jealousy (upon); take one's grudge out.
ひとをきらいわるだくみしてがいする

**용심지** a large wick.

**용안**(龍眼) 〖식〗 a longan; Nephelium longana(학명). ようがん

**용안**(龍顔) the royal countenance.
りゅうがん

**용암**(熔岩) 〖지〗 lava; molten rock/~이 분출하다 Torrents of lava pour forth.
ようがん

**용액**(溶液) a solution; a solvent. ようえき

**용약**(勇躍) elation; exultation; high spirits/~하다 exult; take heart; become high-spirited. ゆうやく

**용어**(用語) 《말씨》 wording; phraseology 《술어》 a term; technics 《총칭》 terminology 《어휘》 vocabulary/전문 ~ technical terms[terminology]/~에 주의하다 be careful about wording. ようご

**용언**(用言) 〖연〗 a declinable word.
ようげん

**용언**(冗言) unnecessary words; a jest; a joke; fun.

**용왕**(龍王) The Dragon King. りゅうおう

**용왕 매진**(勇往邁進) advance in a dashing spirit; dashing forward/~하다 advance bravely; dash forward/그는 ~의 기상이 있다 He is full of push and go.

**용용**(溶溶) full and gentle flow of water /~하다 [the flow of water] be gentle and full.

**용원**(傭員) a temporary employee; an extra hand. かんちょうのりんじこようにん

**용의**(用意) 《준비》 readiness 《조심》 precaution; prudence/~ 주도하 very cautious/~가 되어 있다 be ready (to, for); have (a thing) in one's sleeve. ようい

**용의**(容儀) manner; mien; bearing; deportment; demeanor. ようぎ

**용의**(庸醫) a mediocre doctor.

**용의자**(容疑者) 〖법〗 a suspect; a suspected person; an alleged culprit[criminal]/살인 ~ a suspected murderer.
ようぎしゃ

**용이**(容易) easiness; ease; facility; simplicity/~하다 (be) easy; simple/그건 ~한 일이 아니다 It is no easy matter/하기가 ~하다 be easy to do; be easily done. ようい

**용인**(容認) admission; approval; toleration/~하다 admit; approve of; tolerate. ようにん

**용인**(用人) employment of a person; employ; hire/~하다 employ (a person); hire (a person).

**용인**(傭人) an employee ⇨고용인.
ようにん

**용인**(庸人) a mediocrity; a mediocre person. ようにん

**용자**(容姿) the face and feature; look; personal appearance/꽃다운 ~ a blooming face. ようし

**용자창**(用字窓) a lattice window.
ようのじけいのこうしのまど

**용잠**(龍簪) an ornamental hairpin in the shape of a dragon's head.
りゅうのあたまのかたちにつくったかんざし

**용잡**(冗雜) uselessness; triviality/~하다 be of no use; (be) trifling; trivial; petty. じょうざつ

**용장**(勇將) a brave general; a great soldier/~밑에 약졸이 없다 As is the master, so are his men.

**용장**(勇壯) bravery/~하다 (be) brave;

**용재**(用材) materials to make use of; raw materials 《재목》 timber; lumber 〈미〉. ようざい

**용재**(庸才) mediocre ability; mediocrity; a person of common ability; commonplace capacity.

**용적**(容積) 《용량》 capacity 《체적》 volume 《부피》 bulk;《수》 content; cubical[solid] measure[content]. ようせき

**용전**(勇戰) brave fighting/~하다 fight heroically; fight a brave fight. ゆうもうにたたかうこと

**용전**(用箋) writing paper; stationery; a writing pad; a form. ようせん

**용전여수**(用錢如水) spending money like water/~하다 spend money like water.

**용점**(熔點) 《물》 the melting point. ようてん

**용접**(鎔接) welding/~하다 weld (to)/~공 a welder/~관 a welded pipe/가스 ~ gas welding. ようせつ

**용접**(庸接) reception; interview/~하다 receive (a guest); go[come] out to welcome.

**용졸**(庸拙) clumsiness; shabbiness/~하다 clumsy; shabby; be below; mediocrity; (be) stupid. せつれつなこと

**용지** a flambeau; a torch.

**용지**(用紙) paper [to use]; a [blank] form; a printed form/시험 ~ [a sheet of] examination paper/전보 ~ a telegraph form/신문 ~ paper [used] for newspaper. ようし

**용지**(用地) land required; a lot; a site /군~ a military reservation/주택 ~ a housing lot[site].

**용지판**(一板) 《건》 a wainscot; a wainscotting.

**용진**(勇進) dashing forward; a brave advance/~하다 dash forward bravely.

**용질**(溶質) 《화》 solute. ようしつ

**용출**(湧出) gush; eruption/~하다 gush out[forth]; erupt; well (up).ゆうしゅつ

**용출**(聳出) rising[towering] above/~하다 rise; tower[rise] above; soar. たかくそびえること

**용출추다** be annoyed; be harassed; be pestered; be bothered; give in to flattery. ひとになやまされる

**용충줄** a soil rope; rigging.

**용퇴**(勇退) voluntary retirement[resignation]/~하다 retire voluntarily[with good grace]/정계에서 ~하다 retire from political life. ゆうたい

**용툼하다** (be) insensible; stupid; stolid; very stupid.

**용트림** belching in an affected manner/ ~하다 let out a big burp.

**용틀임**(龍—) a dragon picture[engraving] in a building; dragon embellishments [decorations]. りゅうのちょうこく

**용품**(用品) supplies; an article (for the use of)/가정 ~ household goods. /사무 ~ office supplies. ようひん

**용품**(庸品) 《물건》 an article of poor quality 《계급》 inferior [lower] official rank.

**용필**(用筆) the use of a [writing] brush /~하다 use a brush/도화 ~ a painting brush. ようひつ

**용하다** ①《잘하다》 (be) deft; skilful; dexterous; good; clever/용하게 처리하다 dispose of (a case) skilfully ②《훌하다》 (be) admirable; praiseworthy; wonderful/혼자서 그 일을 다 했다니 참 용한 일이다 It is admirable that he did such a great work by himself. りっぱだ

**용해**(溶解) melting; solution/~하다 melt; dissolve/물에 ~하다 be soluble in water. ようかい

**용해**(鎔解) 《금속의》 melting; fusion/~ 하다 melt; fuse/~성 fusibility/~점 the melting point.

**용호**(龍虎) ①《용과 범》 the dragon and the tiger ②《뛰어난 글》 a powerful style of writing ③《두 영웅》 the two rival heroes/~ 상박 a well-matched contest. りゅうこ

**용화**(熔化) melting; liquefaction; fusion /~하다 melt; liquefy; fuse; dissolve /금속의 ~ the fusion of metals. ゆうか

**용훼**(容喙) making comments (on); meddling; interference/~하다 put in a word (in); but in/남의 일에 ~하다 meddle in another's affairs.

**우** all at once; with a rush/사람들이 현장으로 ~하고 몰려갔다 A crowd of people rushed to the scene. どやどや

**우**(優) 《채점 등급》 excellent; an "A"; superior. ゆう

**우**(右) the right/~로 나란히 《구령》 Right, dress!, Eyes right!/~향 ~《구령》 Right turn! みぎ

**우각**(牛角) cow's horns; oxhorn. うしのつの

**우거**(寓居) a temporary abode[residence] /~하다 reside[live] temporarily (at). ぐうきょ

**우거지** ①《채소의》 outer leaves of cabbage or other vegetables ②《절인 것의》 the dry and tasteless top layer of a crock of salted shrimps of pickles.

**우거지다** be[grow] thick; overgrow; be overgrown with; grow luxuriant[ly] [thickly]/나무가 우거진 산 a thickly -wooded hill. しげる

**우거지상**(一相) a sour[wry] face; a scowl; distorted features; a frown; a grimace/~의 sulky; morose. ふくれつら

**우걱뿔** an inflexed horn; arched horns (of cattle). うちがわにまがったつの

**우걱우걱** swinging side to side with creaks.

**우겨대다** hold fast to; persist/그는 자기의 말이 옳다고 우겨대고 있다 He asserts his statement to be true.

**우겨싸다** surround; wrap ⇒욱여싸다. そとからうちにむけてかこむ

**우격다짐** high-handedness; forcible compulsion; coercion/~하다 force (*a person*) to do; browbeat/모든 일을 ~으로 하다 resort to high-handed measures in everything.

**우격으로** (거역해서) high-handedly; against (*a person's*) will 《무리로》 by force [compulsion]; forcibly/~ 그의 승낙을 받으려는 것은 어리석은 일이다 It is quite silly of you to try to force him to consent. むりに

**우견(愚見)** ①(자기 의견) my humble opinion[view] ②(어리석은 의견) foolish [stupid] opinion. おっかなかんがえ

**우경(右傾)** veering[turning, tending] to the right side; rightist/ ~하다 swing [turn] to the right/~화하다 turn rightist. うけい

**우곡(紆曲)** winding/~하다 wind; zigzag; take a meandering course/~한 winding; roundabout; zigzag. うきょく

**우골(牛骨)** cow bones; oxbone. うしのほね

**우구(雨具)** (우비) rain-gear 《비옷》 a raincoat 《우산》 an umbrella. あまぐ

**우구(憂懼)** worry; anxiety; fear; dread; apprehension/~하다 worry about; be anxious over; fear; dread; be apprehensive of[for].

**우국(憂國)** patriotism/~지사(之士) a patriot/~지정(之情) patriotism; a patriotic spirit/~ 충정 one's intense patriotism. ゆうこく

**우군(友軍)** friendly forces; an allied army. ゆうぐん

**우군(右軍)** the right wing of an army; the right-hand troops.

**우그러뜨리다** crush[beat] [out of shape]; make dent in; push in; dent/의자를 ~ break a chair/밀집 모자를 ~ crush a straw hat out of shape. へこます

**우그러지다** be crushed [out of shape]; be[get] dented/자동차 옆이 우그러졌다 The car is dented on the side. /우그러진 모자 a battered hat. へこむ

**우그르** in swarms 《물이》 simmering 《벌레가》 swarming; in swarms. ぐらぐら

**우그리다** crush; dent ⇒오그리다. くぼます

**우글거리다** swarm; be crowded; be alive (*with*); teem (*with*)/거리에 거지가 우글거린다 The streets swarm with beggars. うごめく

**우글다** get[be] dented[crushed out of shape].

**우글우글** (모인 모양) in swarms/~하다 squirm; wriggle (*about*); (떼를 짓다) swarm/물통에 장구벌레가 ~하다 The water-trough teemed with mosquito larvae. うごめく

**우글쭈글** crumpled; rumpled; wrinkled /~하다 (be) crumpled; rumpled; wrinkled; withered/옷에 주름이 ~ 잡혔다 The clothes are all wrinkled. しわくちゃ

**우금(于今)** till now; until now; up to the present; by this time. いままで

**우기(雨期)** the rainy[moist, wet] season /~에 접어들었다 The wet season has set in. うき

**우기(雨氣)** signs of rain; a slight promise of rain/~를 머금은 하늘 a watery sky. うき

**우기(右記)** ~의 the above noted; the above mentioned; the aforesaid. うき

**우기다** demand one's own way; force (*one's ideas* on); persist in; insist; impose; assert oneself/그는 모른다고 우겼다 He persisted in denying his knowledge. of it. しゅちょうする

**우김성(一性)** egoistic attachment; obstinacy; adherence; persistence; stubbornness/~이 많다 be pig-headed.

**우내(宇內)** the whole world; (*in*) the universe.

**우는소리** a complaint; a whimper/~하다 whimper; whine; complain.

**우단(羽緞)** velvet. ベルベット

**우담(牛膽)** ox-gall. うしのきも

**우당(友黨)** a friendly[an allied] party. うよくのせいとう

**우당탕** a thump; bump; plump/그는 ~ 소리를 내며 계단을 내려왔다 He clattered down the stairway. どしんと

**우당탕퉁탕** a thump; plump; heavily; with a thud[bump]/무엇인지 마루에 ~ 떨어졌다 Something fell heavily on the floor. どしんがたん

**우대(優待)** courteous[considerate, good, kind, generous, warm] treatment; a warm reception 《관대》 hospitality 《환영》 welcome/~하다 treat (*one*) courteously; receive (*one*) considerately/손님을 ~하다 be hospitable to one's guest /~권 a complimentary ticket. ゆうたい

**우도(友道)** the rules of friendship.

**우두(牛痘)** cowpox; inoculation/~를 맞다 take vaccination; be vaccinated/~를 놓다 vaccinate; inoculate (*a person*) for[against] smallpox. しゅとう

**우두둑** (깨물다) crunchingly; with a crunching sound 《부러지다》 snappingly; with a snapping sound. かりかり

**우두망찰하다** fluster; be[come] confused; be perplexed; be disconcerted; be at a loss/그는 그 소식을 듣고 우두망찰하였다 The news struck him speechless[dumb] for a while. うろたえる

**우두머리** 《꼭대기》 the top; the head 《장(長)》 a chief; a leader; a boss; the head/회사의 ~ the boss of a company. かしら

**우두커니** idly; listlessly/그는 창가에 ~ 서 있다 He is standing idly by the window. ぼさっと

**우뚝** high; aloft/~하다 (be) high; lofty; tall; towering 《뛰어나다》 eminent; pr-

**ominent; outstanding**／산이 ～ 솟아 있다 a mountain rises high. たかく

**우둔(愚鈍)** stupidity; dullness; silliness／～하다 (be) stupid; dull-witted; thick-headed; silly. ぐどん

**우둔우둔하다** go pit-a-pat; pound; throb; palpitate. どきどきする

**우둘우둘** ～하다 (be) hard and lumpy; fibrous; gristly. ぼろぼろ

**우둥퉁하다** (be) stout and fat; fleshy; portly; dumpy. ふとくみじかい

**우드득** crunchingly.

**우들우들** trembling; shivering／무서워서 ～ 떨다 tremble with fear. ぶるぶる

**우듬지** a treetop, the top branches of a tree. こずえ

**우등(優等)** the top[superior] grade; excellency; superiority／～상 an honor prize／～상을 타다 win an honor prize／～생 an honor student. ゆうとう

**우락부락** (난폭) rudely; roughly; wildly; harshly／～하다 (be) rude; rough; wild; harsh／～한 사람 a rough fellow／～ 말하다 talk rudely. ぞんざいに

**우람하다** (be) imposing; grand; majestic; magnificent／우람한 경치 a grand sight. ゆうそうである

**우량(雨量)** rainfall; rain／～이 적어서 저수지의 물이 줄었다 Lack of rain sank the reservoirs.／～계 a rain gauge; a hyetometer. うりょう

**우량(優良)** excellence; superiority／～하다 (be) superior; excellent; high grade／～아(兒) an ideal child／～품 superior goods; articles of superior quality[grade]. ゆうりょう

**우러나다** come out[off]／이 옷에서는 검은 물감이 우러났다 When this cloth was steeped black dyes came off. にじみでる

**우러나오다** spring up; well up／바위 틈에서 물이 우러나온다 Water springs from the rock. にじみでる

**우러러보다** 《쳐다보다》 look up (at); look upward; lift the eyes 《앙모하다》 look up to; admire; respect／우리들은 그분을 스승님으로 모시고 우러러보았다 We looked up to him as our teacher.

**우러르다** lift one's head up; look up (to). あおぎしたう

**우럭우럭** flaring up; actively; furiously／술이 얼굴에 ～ 오르다 one's face flushes up with wine. ぼうぼう

**우렁우렁** thunderingly; rumblingly／천둥이 멀리서 ～ 울렸다 The thunder rolled[rumbled] in the distance. ごろごろ

**우렁이** 〖어〗 a pond[mud] snail; a freshwater snail. たにし

**우렁이속** a complicated state of affairs.

**우렁차다** ①《소리가》 (be) ringing; resonant; resounding; loud／우리는 우렁차게 애국가를 불렀다 We sang our national anthem loudly. ②《으리으리하다》 (be) magnificent; imposing. こえがたかい

**우려(憂慮)** anxiety; concern; fear; apprehensions; cares; solicitude／～하다 be [feel] anxious; fear; worry; be apprehensive of; have apprehension／시국에 관하여 ～하다 worry over the situation. ゆうりょ

**우려내다** extort; wring; squeeze; exploit／돈을 ～ squeeze[wring, extort] money out of (a person). おどしてださせる

**우렴하다** (be) dim; obscure; vague; faint; hazy; misty／배 한 척이 안개 속에 우렴하게 나타났다 A ship loomed through the mist. あきらかでない

**우로(雨露)** rain and dew／～를 막다 shelter oneself from the weather. うろ

**우로(迂路)** a roundabout way.

**우롱(愚弄)** mockery; derision; scoff; jeer／～하다 mock (at); deride; fool; ridicule; make fun[a fool] of／사람을 ～ 하다 hold up (a person) to ridicule. ぐろう

**우뢰** thunder; thundershower; thunderstorm／～같은 thunderous／～ 소리가 난다 It thunders. かみなり

**우료(郵料)** postage. ゆうびんりょうきん

**우르르** ①《사람이》 rushingly《떼를 지어》 in a crowd／그들은 ～ 그 방으로 몰려갔다 They poured noisily into the room. ②《우뢰 소리》 thundering; rolling; rumbling ③《무너지는 소리》 clattering; all in a heap ④《물이 끓는 소리》 boiling up noisily. どっと

**우리**¹ ①《맹수의》 a cage《가축의》 a pen[corral]; 《양 따위의》 a fold. おり

**우리**² we 《우리의》 our 《우리에게》 us／～ 한국인 we Koreans. われ

**우리나라** our country.

**우리다** ①《물에 담가서》 soak [out]／옷에 묻은 잉크를 ～ soak an ink stain out of clothes ②《우려내다》 extort; squeeze; wring／돈을 ～ wring money out of (a person) ③《때리다》 slap hard; strike／뺨을 ～ slap (a person) in the face.

**우리우리하다** 《눈이》 (be) fierce; menacing／그의 눈매가 ～ He has fierce eyes.

**우마(牛馬)** oxen and horses; [horses and] cattle／～차 carts. ぎゅうば

**우매(愚昧)** stupidity and ignorance／～하다 (be) stupid and ignorant; silly; thick-headed／～한 사람들을 계몽하다 enlighten the ignorant. ぐまい

**우멍거지** 〖의〗 phimosis; a foreskin-covered adult penis. かわかぶり

**우멍하다** be sunken in. へこんでいる

**우모(羽毛)** feathers; plumes; plumage. はね

**우무** vegetable gelatine; agar-agar; gelidium jelly.

**우무리다** depress; make hollow; dent; indent.

**우묵우묵** ～하다 (be) hollowed here and there; dented all over.

**우묵하다** (be) hollow, dented; depressed; sunken. へこんでいる

**우물** a well／~안의 개구리는 대해(大海)를 모른다《속담》 The frog in the well does not know the ocean. いど

**우물거리다**¹ (여럿이) squirm in swarm; be alive with (fish). うごめく

**우물거리다**² (입속에서) mumble 《말을》 m-ump／우물우물 씹다 mumble[chew] something. もぐもぐする

**우물귀신**(-鬼神) the spirit[soul] of a person drowned in a well.

**우물마루** 〖건〗 a checkered floor.

**우물반자** 〖건〗 a checkered ceiling.

**우물쭈물** hesitantly; hesitatingly; indecisively; with hesitation／~하다 hesitate; vacillate; waver; boggle／~ 대답하다 make a vague answer. ぐずぐず

**우물지다** ①(보조개가) dimple; dimples appear on the cheeks／그녀는 미소지으면 우물진다 Her face dimples with a smile. ②(우묵 패다) become hollow; form a hollow; sink. えくぼができる

**우뭇가사리** 〖식〗 agar-agar; Ceylon moss; *Gelidium Amansii* (학명). テングサ

**우므러들다** become narrower; narrow; pucker. せまくなる

**우므리다** pucker up; purse up; shut／입을 ~ pucker up one's lips[mouth]. せまくする

**우미**(優美) grace; elegance; comeliness; refinement／~하다 (be) graceful; elegant; refined; gainly; delicate. ゆうび

**우민**(愚民) ignorant people; the stupid masses／~ 정치 mobocracy／~ ぐみん

**우민**(憂悶) worry;[mental] agony／~하다 worry oneself (about); be worried [troubled]; be in agony. ゆうもん

**우박**(雨雹) hail (한알) hailstone／~이 오다 It hails. あめあられ

**우발**(偶發) accidental[incidental] occurrence／~하다 happen accidentally／~사건 an accident／~ 전쟁 an accidental war. ぐうはつ

**우방**(友邦) a friendly nation[country]; an ally. ゆうほう

**우방**(右方) the right side. うほう

**우변**(右邊) [the edge on] the right side. うそくのほう

**우보 전술**(牛步戰術) stalling tactics.

**우부**(愚夫) a stupid fellow; a foolish man; a dolt. ぐふ

**우부**(愚婦) a stupid[foolish] woman. ぐふ

**우비**(雨備) (준비) preparation for rain (제구) rain-gear (비옷) a raincoat (우산) an umbrella／~를 입다 put on a raincoat. あまぐ

**우비다** poke; scrape[scoop] out; bore; pick／귀[코]를 ~ pick one's ear[nose]／구멍을 우비다 scrape out[bore] a hole. えぐる

**우비어넣다** twist (a thing) into (a hole); force in. こじいれる

**우비어파다** scoop out; hollow out; scrape out; gouge; carve／벽에 구멍을 ~ bore a hole in the wall. ほじくりだす

**우비적거리다** keep poking／우비적우비적 poking; scraping; boring; picking. ほじくる

**우비칼** a scooping[an engraving] knife; a gouge; a router. まるのみ

**우사**(牛舍) a cowshed; a cowhouse.

**우산**(雨傘) an umbrella／~을 쓰다 put up an umbrella／그녀는 나에게 ~을 받쳐 주었다 She held her umbrella over my head. あまがさ

**우상**(偶像) an image; an idol; an icon／~화하다 idolize; make an idol of／~ 숭배 idolatry; idol worship／~ 숭배자 an idolater. ぐうぞう

**우색**(憂色) a worried[an anxious] look; a melancholy[gloomy] air; the traces of sorrow (in one's face)／~을 띠다 wear a worried look. ゆうしょく

**우생학**(優生學) eugenics／~적인 eugenic[al]／~자 a eugenist. ゆうせいがく

**우서**(郵書) a letter; a mail; a communication (짧은 편지) a note. ゆうびんでおくるてがみ

**우선**(郵船) a mail steamer[boat]; a packet ship／외국행 ~ an outgoing mail. ゆうせん

**우선**(于先) first; first of all; before everything; in the first place／~ 건강이다 Health first.／~ 비용이 문제다 The question of expense takes precedence of all others.／~ 일을 끝내고 놀기로 합시다 Business first and pleasure afterwards. まず

**우선**(優先) preference; priority; precedence／~의 preferential; prior／~권 a preference; a prior[preferential] right; a priority (채권자의) the first claim／~하다 have priority (to, over); have perference (to); be prior to／~적으로 perferentially; on the preferential basis／공익은 사익에 ~한다 Public interest takes precedence of private interest.／이 의무는 다른 모든 의무에 ~한다 This duty is prior to all others.／~권 a priority; a prior[preferential] right／~권을 얻다 acquire a priority; acquire the first claim／~ 동의 a privileged motion／~ 배당 preference[preferred] dividends／~주 preference[preferred] stocks[shares]／ ~ 채무 a preferential debt／공익 ~ precedence of public interest. ゆうせん

**우설**(雨雪) rain and snow. うせつ

**우성**(偶性) 〖논·철〗 accident; accidental quality[nature].

**우성**(優性) 〖생〗 a dominant [character]; dominance／~의 dominant／~ 유전 prepotency／~ 형질 a dominant [character]. ゆうせい

**우세** shame; humiliation／~하다 be put to shame; be humiliated; be subjected to humiliation／~스럽다 be humiliating. はずかしいこと

**우세**(郵稅) postage; postal charges; rate

of postage. ゆうぜい

**우세(優勢)** superior power; superiority; predominance; ascendancy; an advantage 《다수》 superiority in number; super numbers; heavy odds／~하다 (be) superior; predominant; gain in power [strength]; outnumber／~를 보이다 show a preponderance／~를 차지하다 prevail over[against]; get[gain] the better of 《경기에서》 lead／그들은 수에 있어서 우리들보다 ~하다 They are superior in number to us., They outnumber us. ゆうせい

**우송(郵送)** posting; mailing／~하다 post; mail; send by post[mail]. ゆうそう

**우수** ①《덤》 an addition; an extra; anything thrown in ②change · 우수리.

**우수(偶數)** an even number／~의 even; even-numbered／~의 날이 휴근이다 We are off duty on days bearing even numbers. ぐうすう

**우수(雨水)** ①《빗물》 rain water ②《절기》 second of the 24 seasonal divisions.
うすい

**우수(右手)** the right hand. みぎて

**우수(優秀)** excellence; superiority; superbness／~하다 (be) good; excellent; superior／~한 성적으로 with excellent results; with honors[high marks]／단연 남보다 ~하다 He is definitely superior to the others. ゆうしゅう

**우수(憂愁)** melancholy; gloom／~의 melancholy; gloomy／~의 빛 a melancholy air. ゆうしゅう

**우수리** ①《거스름 돈》 change／~를 내주다 give [back] the change／~를 받다 get the change／~는 받아 두시오 You may keep the change., Keep the rest for yourself. ②《단수》 an odd sum; a fraction／~를 메다 ignore fractions.

**우수 사려(憂愁思慮)** melancholy and anxiety; gloom and solicitude／~하다 be deeply apprehensive; be anxious about.

**우수수** falling; rustling; [fall] in a multitude／~하다 rustle／바람에 나뭇잎이 ~ 떨어졌다 A gust of wind shook a multitude of leaves off the trees.／나뭇잎이 바람에 ~ 떤다 The leaves are rustling in the wind. さらさらと

**우순 풍조(雨順風調)** ~하다 have rain and wind seasonably; have seasonable weather.

**우스개** jocularity／~ 소리 a joke; a jest／~ 소리를 하다 make joke (on)／~ 짓 clowning; drollery; comicality; waggery.

**우스꽝스럽다** (be) funny; ludicrous; comic[al]; ridiculous; laughable／우스꽝스럽게 여기다 think ridiculous／우스꽝스러운 짓 하지 말라 Do not make yourself ridiculous.／그 양복을 입으니까 우스꽝스럽게 보인다 You look funny[ridiculous] in that suit. ひじょうにおかしい

**우습게 보다** despise; look down on; hold in contempt; think little of; slight／사람을 ~ look down upon (a person)／돈을 ~ make light of money／부자는 가난한 사람을 우습게 보기 쉽다 The rich are apt to despise the poor. けいしする

**우습게 여기다** despise. みくびる

**우습다** ①《재미있다》(be) funny; amusing 《가소롭다》(be) laughing; laughable; ridiculous; absurd; droll; funny《익살 맞다》(be) comic／우스운 죽겠다 be tickled to death／우습게 들리다 sound funny／우스운 소리를 하다 say a funny thing／무엇이 그렇게 우스우냐 What is so funny? ②《하찮다》(be) trifling; trivial; small 《쉽다》(be) easy／우습게 여길 일이 아니다 It is not a small matter., It is not an easy job. ③《기이하다》(be) strange; unusual; singular; queer; funny; grotesque. おかしい

**우승(優勝)** 《승리》 victory 《우월》 predominance; superiority 《선수권》 championship／~하다 win a victory[the championship]; win (a game); cop first 《속》／~기 the championship flag[banner]; a pennant／~자 a [championship] winner／~팀 a winning[championship] team／~배 a championship cup; a trophy [cup]／그는 정구에 ~했다 He won[captured, gained] the tennis championship／우리 팀이 ~했다［~기를 탔다］ Our team won[the championship flag]. ゆうしょう

**우승 열패(優勝劣敗)** the survival of the fittest／~하다 The superior gains and the inferior loses., The weakest goes to the wall. ゆうしょうれっぱい

**우시장(牛市場)** a cattle fair[market].

**우심하다(尤甚—)** (be) extreme; excessive 《추위가》 severe 《손해가》 heavy.
さらにひどい

**우아(優雅)** elegance; grace; refinement; tastefulness／~하다 (be) elegant; graceful; refined; urbane／~한 문체 a polite[elegant] style／동작이 ~하다 be graceful in manner; move with grace.

**우악(優渥)** graciousness; benevolence／~하다 (be) gracious. ゆうあく

**우악(愚惡)** ~스럽다 (be) ferocious; cruel; violent; wild; rough／우악스럽게 rudely; wildly; roughly／~스러운 사람 a rough fellow／우악스럽게 생기다 have a ferocious look about one／그는 말버릇이 ~스럽다 He is roughspoken[crude].
おろかなこと

**우안(愚案)** 《자기 안》 my [humble] opinion 《어리석은 안》 a foolish plan. ぐあん

**우안(右岸)** the right bank (of a river).

**우애(友愛)** friendship; friendly feeling; brotherliness; fellowship／~롭다 be friendly; be brotherly ゆうあい

**우애 결혼(友愛結婚)** a companionate marriage. ゆうあいけっこん

**우양(牛羊)** cattle and sheep.

**우언**(寓言) an allegory; a fable. ぐうげん
**우없다** (be) unsurpassed; unexcelled.
**우엉** 〖식〗 a burdock; *Arctium Lappa*(학명). ごぼう
**우여 곡절**(迂餘曲折) 《굴곡》 windings, zigzags 《파란》 vicissitudes (of *fortune*); complications; ups and downs/인생의 ~ the vicissitudes of life/~을 겪은 뒤에 after much meandering. うよきょくせつ
**우역**(牛疫) cattle-plague; rinderpest. ぎゅうえき
**우연**(偶然) [a singular] chance; accident; fortuity/~하다 (be) casual; fortuitous; accidental; incidental/~히 by chance [accident]; incidentally/~의 일치 a coincidence/~한 일 an accident/~것 발견 a chance discovery/우리가 만난 것은 순전히 ~한 일이 아니었다 Our meeting was not quite accidental./~히 만나다 meet by chance; happen to meet/~론 accidentalism/~성 contingency/~ 변화[변이] mutation. ぐうぜん
**우연만하다** 《쓸 만하다》 (be) passable; usable; serviceable; tolerable; helpful 《가깝다》 (be) nearly the same; practically equal; not much different. まずよい
**우열**(優劣) superiority and[or] inferiority; merits and[or] demerits/~이 없는 level; even; equal; evenly matched /~을 겨루다 struggle for mastery/~을 논하다 discuss merits and demerits (*of*). ゆうれつ
**우완**(愚頑) stupid obstinacy; asininity /~하다 (be) asinine; stupidly obstinate; pig-headed. おろかでがんこなこと
**우왕 좌왕**(右往左往) ~하다 go this way and that; move about busily; run [move] about in [utter] confusion; run pell-mell; rush about to no purpose. うおうさおう
**우울**(憂鬱) melancholy; dejection; gloominess/~하다 (be) melancholy; doleful; dejected; gloomy/~해지다 be seized with melancholy/~증 melancholia; hypochondria. ゆううつ
**우월**(優越) superiority; predominance; supremacy/~하다 (be) superior; supreme/~감 superiority complex. ゆうえつ
**우위**(優位) predominance; ascendancy; a predominant position; superiority/~를 차지하다 gain the upper hand (*of*). ゆうい
**우유**(牛乳) [cow's] milk/~를 짜다 milk a cow/~를 배달하다 deliver milk/~배달부 a milkman. ぎゅうにゅう
**우유 부단**(優柔不斷) irresolution; indecision/~하다 (be) indecisive; irresolute; dilatory. ゆうじゅうふだん
**우육**(牛肉) beef. ぎゅうにく
**우음 마식**(牛飮馬食) heavy eating and drinking; immoderation in food and drink.

**우의**(友誼) friendship; fellowship; friendly relations/~를 맺다 form a friendship with/국제 ~ international comity[friendship]. ゆうぎ
**우의**(羽衣) a robe of feathers. うい
**우의**(雨衣) a raincoat. うい
**우이**(牛耳) ①《쇠귀》 the ears of an ox ②《우두머리》 the leader/~ 잡다 lead; head. うしのみみ
**우이 독경**(牛耳讀經) pouring water on a duck's back; to preach to the wind. うまのみみにかぜ
**우익**(右翼) ①《열》 the right wing[flank, column] ②《야구》 the right field/~수 a right fielder ③《정당》 the Rightists; the Right Wing/극단적인 ~ an ultraconservative/~ 단체 a right wing organization. うよく
**우자**(愚者) a fool; a dunce; a simpleton; a goose. ぐしゃ
**우장**(雨裝) rain-gear; rainwear; a rain outfit; a raincoat. あまぐ
**우적우적** ①《씹다》 munching; crunching ②《무너지다》 creaking; squeaking ③steadily. どんどん
**우정**(友情) friendship; friendliness; fellowship; friendly feelings[spirit]/~있는 amiable; friendly/~이 두텁다 be kind to *one's* friend. ゆうじょう
**우정**(郵政) postal service/~국(局) the Bureau of Postal Administration. ゆうせい
**우제**(雩祭) a shamanist service to pray for rain. あまごいのまつり
**우제**(虞祭) a sacrificial rite at the conclusion of a burial.
**우족**(右族) ①《적자 계통》 the descendants of the legitimate son ②《귀족》 the nobles. せいりょくのあるうちがら
**우졸**(愚拙) stupidity; folly; foolishness; absurdity/~하다 (be) stupid; silly; foolish; absurd. ぐせつ
**우주**(宇宙) the universe; the cosmos; heaven and earth/~의 universal; cosmic/~ 과학 space science/~복 a space suit/~ 시대 the cosmic[space] age/~선 the cosmic ray;《수》 the world line/~ 인력 universal gravitation/~론 cosmology/~ 개발 계획 a space development project. うちゅう
**우죽** twigs; sprigs; upper branches; the top boughs. こずえ
**우쭉우쭉** 《몸을》 dancing *one's* body up and down 《커지는 모양》 rapidly and steadily; quickly/~ 자라다 become taller with rapidity. どんどん
**우쭐거리다** move (*one's* body) rhythmically. ぶらぶらする
**우줄우줄** 《몸체를》 dancing; swaying 《걸음을》 swaggering/~하다 swing in the wind; sway to the wind.
**우줅거리다** walk slowly; trudge.
**우줅이다** go ahead and do; persist in doing *one's* own way. むりにおこなう

**우중(雨中)** ~에 in the rain／~에 나가다 go out in the rain.

**우중충하다** (be) gloomy; somber; dusky; dim／우중충한 방 a gloomy old room.

**우지끈** with a crash[crack]; ~하다 crackle; smash; snap／~거리다 crackle; crack; keep popping

**우지직** (타는 소리) with a crackle; cracking 《부러지는 소리》 with a snap[crack]／나뭇가지를 ~ 꺾다 break twigs with a snap／~거리다 (타다) crackle; crack; pop 《나무가》 creak; crack／~우지직 (타는 소리》 with crackling[cracking] sounds 《부러지는 소리》 with snaps.

**우직(愚直)** simplicity and honesty; stupidity and tactlessness.

**우집다** look down upon (a person); despise; scorn.

**우짖다** scream 《새가》 chirp.

**우차(牛車)** an ox cart.

**우천(雨天)** (날씨) rainy[wet] weather. 《날》 a rainy[wet] day／~ 순연(順延) "To be postponed till the first fine day in case of rain".

**우청(雨晴)** rain or shine; rainy or fair weather; weather conditions.

**우체(郵遞)** post; mail《미》; postal[mail] service／~국 a post-office／~부 a mailman《미》; a postman〈영〉／~통 a post; a pillar box〈영〉; a mailbox〈미〉.

**우측(右側)** the right side／~에 on the right／~ 통행 Keep to the right.

**우치(愚癡)** stupidity; silliness; imbecility／~하다 (be) imbecile; stupid; silly.

**우툴두툴** ~하다 (be) rugged; knotty; rough; uneven／~한 길 a bumpy road.

**우파(右派)** the right wing[wingers]; the Rightist.

**우편(右便)** the right side／~에 on the right side of; on one's right.

**우편(郵便)** post; mail《미》; the mail service／~ 배달부 a mailman〈미〉; a postman〈영〉／~으로 보내다 send by post[mail]／군사 ~ military post／항공 ~ air mail／~ 번호 zip code〈미〉; a code number〈영〉／~ 저금 postal[post office] savings.

**우표(郵票)** a stamp; a postage stamp／~를 수집하다 collect stamps.

**우피(牛皮)** oxhide; cowhide.

**우합(偶合)** accidental agreement; coincidence／~하다 coincide[agree by accident] with.

**우향(右向)** 우~ 앞으로 기 (구령) Right wheel!

**우현(右舷)** (배) starboard 《호령》 Starboard!／키를 ~으로 잡다 starboard the helm.

**우호(友好)** comity; friendship／~ 관계를 유지하다 maintain friendly relations (with)／~ 조약 a treaty of friendship [amity].

**우화(羽化)** ①《벌레의》 emergence／~하다 grow wings ②《사람의》 flight up into the sky／~하다 fly into the sky.

**우화(寓話)** an apologue; an allegory; a fable.

**우환(憂患)** (병) illness; sickness 《근심 따위》 trouble; worry; anxiety／~이 있다 have anxieties; be agonized.

**우회(迂廻)** ~하다 take a roundabout way; make a detour; go round／~선 a loop line; a loop／산을 ~해서 가다 go round a mountain.

**우회전(右回轉)** ~하다 turn to the right.

**우후(雨後)** after the rain; after a rain. fall／~ 죽순처럼 나오다 spring up like [so many] mushrooms after a rainfall.

**욱기(一氣)** impetuosity; hot-headedness; hot temper; rashness; wildness／~가 있다 be hot-tempered[hotheaded].

**욱다** ①《굽다》 (be) dented; battered; crushed ②《힘이》 (be) weak; weakened／기운이 ~ lose one's pep.

**욱대기다** ①《위협하다》 scare; intimidate; oppress ②《딱딱거리다》 snarl[bark] at.

**욱박지르다** intimidate; scare; threaten; oppress.

**욱시글거리다** swarm together／많은 개미가 ~ ants swarm by the thousands.

**욱시글득시글** ~하다 swarm; throng; teem with.

**욱신거리다** ①《쑤시다》 tingle; throb with pain; smart／벌에 쏘인 손가락이 ~ My finger smarts from a sting. ②《떼가》 swarm; throng; teem (with).

**욱신덕신** in swarms.

**욱신욱신** (북적임) in swarms; pricking 《쑤심》 throbbing[smarting] with pain.

**욱실욱실** swarming together.

**욱여싸다** surround; beset; wrap; cover／김치독을 얼지 않도록 짚으로 ~ wrap a picklecrock up in straw to prevent freezing.

**욱이다** dent; crush; batter／양철을 욱여 넣다 bend a tin plate in.

**욱일(旭日)** the rising sun／~ 승천지세다 be in the ascendant.

**욱적거리다** jostle all at one place.

**욱죄이다** feel cramped; be too tight for one.

**욱지르다** intimidate; browbeat／욱질러 말을 못하게 하다 shut (a person) down.

**욱질리다** be intimidated; get browbeaten.

**욱하다** flare up impulsively; get impetuous; lose one's head; be distracted (with, by)／그는 걸핏하면 욱한다 He gets like a madman on the slightest provo-

**운(運)** fortune; luck 《운명》 fate; destiny 《기회》 chance/~좋은 lucky; fortunate/~나쁜 unlucky; unfortunate/~ 좋게 fortunately; luckily; by good fortune [luck]/~ 나쁘게 unluckily; unfortunately; by ill luck/~이 좋으면 if fortune smiles upon one/~이 좋아 …하다 be lucky enough to; have the good fortune to (do)/~이 트이다 be in luck's way/~에 맡기다 leave (a matter) to chance. うん

**운(韻)** a rhyme; a rime〈미〉/~이 맞다 rhyme with. いん

**운각(雲刻)** cloud-shaped designs carved on the edges of a utensil.

**운기(運氣)** ①《열병》an epidemic fever ②《운수》good luck and bad luck. うんき

**운김** ①《남은 기운》a trace of warm air [vapo[u]r]/방에 ~이 아직 있다 There is still a little warmth lingering in the room ②《…하는 바람》a sequel; a consequence [of joint effort].

**운니(雲泥)** 《운니지차》a great[wide] difference (between).

**운동(運動)** ①《물체의》motion; movement /~하다 move; be in motion/~의 법칙 laws of motion/~량 momentum ②《몸의》[physical] exercise 《경기》sports; athletics; games 《체조》gymnastics/~하다 [take] exercise/실내 ~ indoor games/호외[야외] ~ outdoor[field] sports/~ 경기 athletic sports/~《경기》회 an athletic meet/~ 선수 an athlete; a sportsman/~ 신경 a motor nerve/~ 정신 sportsmanship/~장 a playground 《경기장》an athletic field/~구 sporting [sport, athletic] goods/~복 a sporting uniform[suit]/~을 하면 식욕이 생긴다 Exercise gives (a person) a good appetite. ③《노력·알선》an effort 《집단적》a movement; a campaign; an agitation; a drive 《의회에서의》lobbying/~하다 make an effort; conduct a campaign; lobby (for a bill)/선거 ~ electioneering〈영〉; campaign[ing]〈미〉/노동 ~ a labour movement/모금 ~을 일으키다 start a campaign for subscriptions. うんどう

**운동화(運動靴)** sports shoes; sneakers〈미〉; tennis shoes.

**운두** height/~가 높은[낮은] 신 a high [low]-cut shoes.

**운명(殞命)** death/~하다 die; expire; breathe one's last. しぬこと

**운명(運命)** fate; destiny; fortune; one's lot; kismit/~의 장난 a whim[an irony] of life/~의 총아 a child of fortune; a fortune's favourite/~론 fatalism/…과 ~을 같이하다 share one's fortune; throw in one's lot with another/~의 날 the fatal day. うんめい

**운모(雲母)** 【광】 mica/~판 a mica plate /백~ muscovite. うんも

**운무(雲霧)** cloud and mist[fog]/~에 싸이다 be enveloped in a fog. うんむ

**운문(雲紋)** a cloudlike[wavelike] pattern; moiré(F). うんもん

**운문(韻文)** verse 《시》poetry; a poem/~극 verse drama. いんぶん

**운반(運搬)** conveyance; transportation; carriage/~하다 carry; convey; transport/~비 carriage; portage/~인 a carrier 《인부》a porter. うんぱん

**운봉(雲峰)** a gigantic column of clouds; a bank of clouds; cloud banks.

**운산(雲山)** a mountain covered by[shrouded with] cloud; a cloud-shrouded mountain. うんざん

**운산(運算)** operation; calculation/~하다 operate; work; calculate; figure out. うんざん

**운석(隕石)** 【광】 a meteoric stone; a meteorite. いんせき

**운성(隕星)** 【천】 a meteor; a shooting star. りゅうせい

**운세(運勢)** one's fortune[stars]/~가 좋다[나쁘다] be born under a lucky[an unlucky] star; be lucky[unlucky].

**운송(運送)** conveyance; transport; transportation; fowarding/~하다 carry; transport; convey; forward/해상[육상] ~ transportation by sea[land]/~업 the carrying trade; transportation business/~점(店) a forwarding agency/ ~ 업자 a carrier; a forwarding agent/~료(料) carriage; freight [rates]; forwarding charges/~비 cost of transport 《선편의》shipping expenses. うんそう

**운수(運輸)** conveyance/~ 기관 means of conveyance[transportation]/~ 사업 the transportation business/~ 회사 a transportation company. うんゆ

**운수(運數)** one's star; luck; fortune; chance/이제 그는 ~가 났다 His star is in the ascendant. うん

**운신(運身)** moving one's body/~하다 move one's body; move around. しんたいをうごかすこと

**운영(雲影)** the shade of a cloud. うんえい

**운영(運營)** management; operation; administration/~하다 manage; run; operate; administer/사업을 ~하다 conduct a business. うんえい

**운용(運用)** application; working; employment/~하다 apply; employ; use; make use of. うんよう

**운운(云云)** 《이러이러함》so and so; thus and thus; such and such (…따위) and so on; and so forth; etc./~하다 speak about 《비평하다》criticize. うんぬん

**운유(雲遊)** wandering/~하다 wander about like a floating cloud. しゅうゆう

**운율(韻律)** a rhythm; a metre/~의 rhythmical; metrical. いんりつ

**운임(運賃)** 《화물의》goods rates〈영〉; freight [rates]〈미〉; 《사람의》fare 《총료》carriage [charges]; 《해운비》shipping exp-

운전(運轉) working; operation; motion 《회전》 revolution 《차량》 running 《수송업무》 traffic [service]; 《운용》 employment/~하다 work; operate; put[set] in motion; run; manage 《운용하다》 employ/~ 자본 a working capital/~ 계통 《차의》 a route; the operation system/시계의 움직임을 멈추다 supend the operation of a machine/자동차를 ~하다 drive a motorcar.　うんてん

운전사(運轉士) 《자동차》 a driver 《기차》 an engineer/~ 면허 시험 driver's licence test.　うんてんし

운조(運漕) marine transportation; shipping; freighting.　うんそう

운집(雲集) gathering in swarms/~하다 swarm; gather in swarms[crowd]; crowd; throng (a place); flock.
　うんしゅう

운철(隕鐵) 【광】 meteoric iron.　いんてつ

운치(韻致) taste; elegance/~있는 tasteful; elegant/그것에는 ~라고는 조금도 없다 It is of sheer boorishness.　がち

운필(運筆) strokes of the brush; 【필】 the use of the brush.　うんぴつ

운하(運河) a canal; a waterway/파나마 [수에즈] ~ the Panama[Suez] Canal/~ 통과료 canal tolls/~를 파다 dig[build] a canal.　うんが

운하(雲霞) clouds and haze 《봄》 the spring [season].　うんか

운항(運航) service; operation/~하다 operate; run; ply/인천 목포간을 ~하는 기선 a steamer that plies between *Inchon* and *Mokpo*.

운해(雲海) the sea covered by clouds.
　うんかい

운행(運行) movement; revolution; motion; a march; race; operation; service/~하다 revolve; go[move] round; run/유성은 그 궤도를 ~한다 The planets roll on in their courses.　うんこう

운휴(運休) suspension of the (*bus*) service.　うんきゅう

울¹ 《떨거지》 relations; relatives; kinfolk/~을 믿고 행패하다 play the bully; relying on his cousins to back him up.

울² ①《울타리》 an enclosure; a fence/~을 뛰어넘다 jump over a fence; clear a fence ②《신의》 the outer rim of shoes.

울가망하다 (be) in low spirits; cheerless; depressed; melancholy; blue.
　こころがやすまることがない

울걱거리다 gargle/양치질하느라고 ~ gargle (*one's* mouth).　うがいする

울결(鬱結) ~하다 feel heavy in the chest; feel oppressed; have a feeling of *one's* breath smothered.
　こころがふさがること

울근거리다 chew; mumble.

울근불근 ~하다 be at war (*with*); be in discord (*with*); be on bad terms (*with*).
　ちぐはぐ

울긋불긋 ~하다 (be) colorful; multicolored; picturesque/들에 꽃이 ~ 피어 있다 The blooming field is ablaze with glaring color.　いろとりどり

울기(鬱氣) pent-up resentment; pent-up anger.　うっき

울다 ①《사람이》 weep; cry《소리지르며》; sob《흐느껴 가며》; wail《통곡》; blubber《엉엉하고》; shed tears《눈물 흘리며》/기뻐서 ~ weep[cry] for[with] joy ②《동물이》 cry; howl《짖다》; bark《개》; mew; purr《고양이》; bellow; low《소》; neigh; whinny《말》; bleat《양·염소》; howl《늑대》; roar《범·사자》; trumpet《코끼리》; croak《개구리》; chirp; sing; twitter《벌레·새》; caw《까마귀》; crow《수탉》; cluck《암탉》; quack《오리》; hoot《부엉이》; cuckoo《뻐꾹새》; coo《비둘기》; chirr; chirrup《귀뚜라미》/말이 하늘을 향해서 운다 The horse neighs to the sky. ③《종 따위》 sound; ring/고동이 ~ The sirens blow [whistle].　なく

울도(鬱陶) ~하다 (be) heavy-hearted; depressed; gloomy.　うっとう

울렁거리다 feel *one's* heart leaping; get nervous; be excited/기뻐서 가슴이 ~ *one's* heart flutters[throbs] with joy.

울렁울렁 ①《가슴이》 pitapat; palpitating; throbbing; thumping ②《물결이》 tossing; rolling.　どきどきする

울력 combined strength; cooperation; collaboration; joint effort/~하다 join forces; get together; make a united effort.

울룩불룩 rough; bumpy; coarse; uneven/~하다 (be) rough; bumpy; coarse; uneven.　でこぼこ

울름대다 threaten; menace; intimidate; frighten; scare.　おどす

리다 ①《울게 하다》 make (*one*) cry; move [touch] (*one*) to tears《감루》; 《슬프게 하다》 grieve; bring sorrow upon (*one*)/[사람을] 울리는 이야기 a touching[pathetic, moving] story ②《소리를 내다》 ring; sound 《땡그랑땡그랑》 clang 《기적을》 blow 《북을》 beat/경적을 ~ sound the horn ③《소리가 들리다》 sound; ring (*out, forth*); 《반향》 resound; echo; reverberate; be echoed 《산·지면이》 rumble ④《떨치다》 ring; resound (through *the world*)/명성이 전국에 ~ win nation-wide fame.　なかせる

울림 《음향》 a sound; a noise 《진동》 a vibration 《반향》 an echo 《굉음》 a roar 《포성의》 a boom 《우뢰의》 a peal.

울민(鬱悶) dolefulness; melancholy; anguish; gloom[iness]; low spirit/~하다 (be) doleful; melancholic; gloomy; lowspirited.

울밀(鬱密) denseness; thickness/~하다 (be) dense; thick; compact.

울바자 a marsh-reed screen used for fence.

울보 a crybaby; a blubberer.

**울부짖다** howl; wail; scream/울부짖는 부녀자와 아이들 screaming women and children.

**울분(鬱憤)** resentment; rancour; grudge; wrath; [pent-up] anger/~을 풀다 control one's resentment[grudge]; let off the steam; vent one's anger[rancor] (on a person).

**울상(一相)** a face about to cry/~을 하다 be about to cry; look sad.

**울섶** branches[twigs] used in making a fence

**울세다** have many relatives; have a large number of relatives.

**울쑥불쑥** toweringly here and there; soaringly at different quarters/산이 ~하다 The mountains are jagged.

**울안** a fenced-in place; an enclosure.

**울연하다(蔚然—)** (be) dense; thick; luxuriant; rank.

**울울(鬱鬱)** ~하다《우울하다》(be)melancholy; gloomy; heavy-hearted/~하게 세월을 보내다 mope one's time away.

**울울창창하다(鬱鬱蒼蒼—)** (be) luxuriant.

**울음** weeping; crying; lamenting/~ 소리 a tearful voice; a cry/~이 터지다 burst into tears/~을 참다 repress one's tears/~을 그치다 stop weeping.

**울적(鬱寂)** ~하다 (be) melancholy; desolate; depressed; lonesome; cheerless /기분이 ~하다 be in low spirits; be in the blues; be cast down.

**울창(鬱蒼)** luxuriant growth; luxuriance; exuberance/~하다 (be) luxuriant; exuberant; thick; dense/수목이 ~하게 자랐다 The trees have grown thick[luxuriant].

**울타리** a fence; a hedge; an enclosure; a hurdle/~를 뛰어넘다 jump over a fence; clear a fence.

**울퉁불퉁** uneven; rugged; rough; bumpy /~하다 (be) uneven; bumpy (road); rugged (features); jagged (rocks).

**울혈(鬱血)** 〖의〗 blood congestion; engorgement/~이 생기다 be congested with blood.

**울화(鬱火)** wrath; pent-up resentment/ ~병 a sickness caused by pent-up resentment.

**욹하다** fly into a rage; flare up impulsively; get impetuous/그는 걸핏하면 욹한다 He gets like a madman on the slightest provocation.

**움¹** 《싹》a tiller; a sprout; a shoot; a bud; an offshoot; a second growth/~이 트다 sprout; shoot; bud; tiller.

**움²** 《움막》 a dugout mud hut; a cellar; a dugout mud hole/~을 파다 dig out a mud hole[hut]/~에서 살다 live in a dugout mud hut.

**움딸** the second wife of one's disowned son-in-law.

**움돋다** bud; sprout; put forth shoots.

**움돋이** a tiller; a bud; a sprout; a shoot.

**움막(一幕)** a mud hut; a dugout/~살이 life in a mud hut[dugout].

**움매** moo/~하고 울다 (소가) moo; low.

**움묻다** dig out a mud-hut[cellar]; make a cellar.

**움버들** a sprouting willow tree.

**움벼** shoots from rice roots.

**움뽕** second growth of mulberry leaves.

**움쑥** ~하다 (be) dented; depressed; hollow.

**움실거리다** swarm; squirm; wriggle in a great numbers.

**움찔하다** flinch; draw back (with fear); shrink; wince/주사침을 보고 ~ flinch before a doctor's needle.

**움쭉달싹** with a very slight move; budging/ ~ 않다 do not budge; be unshakable; be unmoved; remain calm.

**움직거리다** budge; stir; move slowly[slightly]/지렁이가 움직거린다 An earthworm wriggles along./움직거리면 너는 죽는다 If you dare budge, you are a dead man.

**움직씨** a verb ⇨동사.

**움직이다** ① move; stir; shift; change the position (of); budge; shake; act; be moved; be shaken/이가 움직인다 A tooth is loose. ②《기계 따위를》 put[set] (a machine) in motion; operate[run] (a machine)/이 기관은 증기로 움직인다 The engine is driven by steam. ③《마음을》 move; touch; affect; inspire; influence 《마음이》be moved[touched, affected]; be influenced[swayed]/그 광경은 그 여자의 마음을 움직였다 The scene touched[moved] her [heart]. ④《변경하다》change; alter/움직일 수 없는 의지 an immovable purpose.

**움직임 (이동)** movement; motion 《활동》 activity 《동향》trend; drift; movement; development/세계의 ~ the trend of the world/여론의 ~ the drift of public opinion.

**움질거리다** move timidly; dawdle; mumble.

**움집** a dugout hut; an underground shack; a cellar used as a residing place /~살이하다 live in a dugout hut

**움츠리다** shrink back; flinch; crouch; draw in/어깨를 ~ shrug one's shoulders.

**움찔** with a start[flinch, jump]/~하다 start; flinch; be jumpy; be startled.

**움켜잡다** grab; grasp; seize; clutch/멱살을 ~ grasp (a person) by the throat.

**움켜쥐다** ①《쥐다》 seize; grab; grasp;

**움큼** clutch ②(일움) have in *one's* power; have at *one's* own disposal/주먹을 ~ tighten *one's* fist. ぎゆっともつ

**움큼** a handful/쌀 한 ~ a handful of rice. ひとにぎり

**움키다** clench; grasp; clasp; clutch; seize; catch hold of/독수리가 병아리를 움키었다 An eagle grabbed a chick. ぎゆっとつかむ

**움트다** sprout; bud; shoot; put forth shoots/그 둘 사이엔 사랑이 움텄다 Love budded between the two. めがではじめる

**움파** scallions grown in an underground cellar.

**움파리** ①(움집) a cellar·hovel; an underground shack ②(웅덩이) a puddle.

**움패다** become hollow[depressed]; form a hollow. ほじくりおこされる

**움펑눈** a person with sunken eyes; a hollow-eyed person. くぼみめ

**움푹** pitted; sunken; dented/~하다 (be) sunken; pitted; dented; hollow/~움쪽 in hollows[pits, depressions]. ぼこん

**움쌀** genuine rice put on top of minor cereals to boil rice.

**웃기다** make (*a person*) laugh; set (*a person*) to laughing; raise[provoke] a smile; cause a laughter; excite (*a person's*) laughter; 청중을 ~ move the audience to laughter. わらわす

**웃날들다** (날씨가) clear up; become clear /웃날들었다 The sky [It] cleared up.

**웃녘** the upper part; the upper side/~ 아가씨 a girl living in the upper village. うえのほう

**웃다** ① laugh (미소) smile (깔깔) giggle (껄껄) chuckle/소리내어 ~ laugh loudly/웃는 얼굴로 맞이하다 welcome with a smile/웃지 않을 수 없다 cannot help laughing ②(조소) laugh at; sneer[jeer] at; ridicule; deride/그의 협박에 웃어 버렸다 I laughed at his threats. ③(꽃이) bloom beautifully; be in full bloom/들에는 꽃들이 활짝 웃고 있다 The field is a bloom with flowers. わらう

**웃더껑이** 《덮개》 a cover 《뚜껑》 a lid 《호주머니의》 a flap. ふた

**웃도리** ①(상체) the upper part of the body (웃옷) a coat; an upper garment /~를 벗다 strip to the waist; remove *one's* coat ②(십장) a foreman; a gaffer. じょうたい

**웃돈** the difference/~을 치르다 pay the difference in cash. たしきん

**웃목** the upper part of a room; an ordinary[lesser] seat.

**웃물** 《상류》 the upper stream; the upper waters of a river (질물) water[liquid] floating on another without mixing with it/~이 맑아야 아랫물이 맑다《속담》 A servant is only as honest as his master. じょうりゅうのみず

**웃비 걷다** cease[stop] raining; hold up 〈미〉; the rain lifts[ceases, stops]; it clears.

**웃변** (一邊) 〖수〗 the topside of a polygon.

**웃사람** *one's* seniors; *one's* elders; *one's* superiors; *one's* betters/~에게 순응하라 Obey your betters. めうえのひと

**웃아귀** the crotch between the thumb and the index finger.

**웃어른** *one's* elders. めうえのひと

**웃옷** 《거죽옷》 an outer garment; overclothes; a coat 《상의》 an upper garment. うわぎ

**웃음** a laugh; laughter (미소) a smile (조소) a derision/~을 터뜨리다 break out[into] a laugh; laugh out. わらい

**웃음거리** a laughing·stock; an object[a butt] of ridicule; a byword/그는 친구들 사이에서 ~가 되고 있다 He is the laughingstock[scorn] of his companions. わらいもの

**웃음판** a scene of boisterous laughter/그의 이야기로 좌중에 ~이 벌어졌다 At his story the whole party burst into laughter.

**웃자리** the upper[higher] seat; the top seat 《주빈석》 the seat[place] of honor. じょうせき

**웃통** the upper half of *one's* body; the upper part of (*a thing*)/그는 ~을 벗고 나한테 덤벼들었다 He took his coat off and hit into me. うわぎ

**웅거** (雄據) ~하다 hold and defend *one's* own territory; stand *one's* ground.

**웅건** (雄健) majesty and vigor/~하다 (be) virile; stout; sturdy; vigorous/~한 기상 a virile spirit. ゆうけん

**웅걸** (雄傑) a hero; a great man; an extraordinary man/당대의 ~ the greatest hero of the age. ゆうけつ

**웅그리다** crouch; squat/웅그리고 앉다 squat down; squat down on *one's* hams. すくませる

**웅긋쫑긋** sprouting up[standing out] here and there; bristling/굴뚝이 ~ 솟아 있다 The sky bristles with smokestacks. でこぼこ

**웅담** (熊膽) bear's gall. くまのきも

**웅대** (雄大) grandeur; magnificence; sublimity; majesty/~하다 (be) grand; magnificent; sublime; majestic/~한 구상 a grand conception. ゆうだい

**웅덩이** a mud puddle; a pool; a bog; a plash/~지다 form a puddle. ちいさいぬま

**웅도** (雄圖) a grand plan[scheme]; an ambitious project/~가 수포로 돌아갔다 One has been frustrated in *one's* great enterprise. ゆうと

**웅변** (雄辯) eloquence; fluency (of *speech*) /~은 은이요 침묵은 금이다 Speech is silver, silence is gold. /~ 대회 an oratorical contest/~가 an eloquent speaker; an orator. ゆうべん

**웅보** (雄—) broad·mindedness; magnani-

웅봉 711 원동력

mity; large-heartedness. ゆうそうなどりょう
**웅봉**(雄蜂) 〖충〗 male bees; drones. おすばち
**웅비**(雄飛) a great leap[flight]; a flying jump; a great achievement／～하다 take a flying jump; soar up.
**웅성거리다** be noisy; be in a commotion. ざわめく
**웅그리다** crouch ⇨웅그리다. すくめる
**웅숭깊다** (be) deep; profound; inscrutable; subtle; broad[-minded]; magnanimous／웅숭깊은 사람 an unfathomable character. どりょうがおおきくてひろい
**웅시**(雄視) looking down on predominantly／～하다 predominate over; hold sway over; gain an ascendency. ゆうし
**웅신하다** ①(덥다) (be) warm; well-heated ②(불기운이) be burning dully. おもいやりふかい
**웅어** 〖어〗 *Coilia ectenes*(학명). えつ
**웅얼거리다** mutter; murmur; grumble／혼자 ~ mutter to *oneself*. ぶつぶついう
**웅예**(雄蕊) 〖식〗 a stamen. ゆうずい
**웅자**(雄姿) a gallant figure; a splendid style／～를 나타내다 make a brave[gallant] appearance. ゆうし
**웅장**(雄壯) grandeur; magnificence; sublimity; splendor／～하다 (be) grand; magnificent; sublime; splendid／～한 건물 a splendid[magnificent] building. ゆうそう
**웅천** an unreliable person. うかつなひと
**웅크리다** crouch; pull in a limb. すくませる
**웅편**(雄篇) a masterpiece; a great literary. ゆうへん
**웅필**(雄筆) an outstanding piece of writing; a magnificent handwriting. ゆうひつ
**웅혼**(雄渾) grandeur; sublimity／～하다 (be) grand; sublime; magnificent／～한 문체 a grand[sublime] style. ゆうこん
**웅화**(雄花) male(sterile) flowers. ゆうか
**워낙** (본디) by nature[origin]; constitutionally; primarily; originally／그는 ~ 몸이 약하다 He was born weak. なにせ
**워석** rustling. かさおと
**원**(員) ①(벼슬) a country magistrate ② a member; an employee. いん
**원**(院) an institution／대학~ a graduate school／과학~ an academy of science. いん
**원**(圓) a circle／～을 그리다 draw a circle.／~ 운동 circle[circular] movement [motion]. えん
**원**(願) (소망) a desire; a wish (부탁) a request 《간청》 an entreaty 《기원》 a prayer／～하다 desire; wish; have a desire (to); (부탁하다) ask; request (간청하다) beg; entreat (기원하다) pray／부모는 그가 의사가 되기를 ~했다 His parents wanted him to be a doctor. がん
**원**(元) (본디) former; original／~ 주소 original residence. もともと
**원가**(原價) 〖경〗 the cost; the prime cost／~ 계산 cost accounting／생산 ~ cost of production. げんか
**원거리**(遠距離) a great[long] distance 《사정 거리》a long range／ ~에서 사격하다 shoot at a long range.
**원거인**(原居人) a native; the native[indigenous] population.
**원격**(遠隔) ~하다 be far apart (*from*); be widely separated (*from*); be distant from／~ 조작 remote control／~ 투시 〖심〗 telesthesia. えんかく
**원경**(遠景) a distant view; perspective. えんけい
**원고**(原告) a plaintiff; an accuser; a complainant. げんこく
**원고**(原稿) a manuscript(略: MS., *pl.* MSS.); a copy; a draft／～료 money for a manuscript; contribution fee／~ [용]지 copypaper 《한 묶음의》a writing pad. げんこう
**원공**(元功) the most distinguished merit [service].
**원광**(圓光) a halo; a nimbus. えんこう
**원광**(遠光) a distant view seen from afar.
**원교**(遠郊) a place remote from a city. えんこう
**원군**(援軍) relief; a reinforcement／~을 요청하다 ask for reinforcements／~을 보내다 reinforce. えんぐん
**원근**(遠近) far and near; distance／~을 불구하고 regardless of distance／~에서 모여들다 come flocking from far and near. えんきん
**원금**(元金) 〖밑천〗 the capital 《이자의》 the principal. がんきん
**원급**(原級) 〖문법의〗 the positive degree; the original class[rank]／~에 머물다 stay down in the same class.
**원기**(元氣) vigor; energy; vitality; spirits／~를 회복하다 restore *one's* energy／~가 넘쳐 흐르다 brim over with good spirits. げんき
**원내**(院內) in[within] the institution[Diet, House, Parliament, hospital]／~ 총무 a Parliamentary manager; the leader of the House. いんない
**원년**(元年) the first year (of *an era, a king's reign, etc.*). がんねん
**원단**(元旦) New Year's Day／~의 이른 아침 early on the morning of New Year's Day. がんたん
**원대**(遠大) ~하다 grand; great; (be) far-reaching[-sighted]／~한 목적 far-reaching aims. えんだい
**원대**(原隊) *one's* [home] unit／~에 복귀하다 return to *one's* unit.
**원동**(原動) a motive for action; a prime mover／~기 a motor; a prime mover; a motive power. げんどう
**원동력**(原動力) motive power[force]; the prime[first] mover; generative power;

driving force/생산의 ~ the basic production factors.

**원두막**(園頭幕) a look-out [shed] for a melon field.

**원둘레**(圓-) circumference/~가 1미터다 be a meter in circumference.

**원래**(元來, 原來) originally; primarily; naturally; by nature; from the first/그는 ~ 정직한 사람이다 He is honest by nature.

**원래**(遠來) coming from afar/~하다 come from afar/~의 손님 a visitor [come] from afar.

**원려**(遠慮) long-sightedness; forethought; foresight; prudence/~가 없다 be lacking in forethought; be imprudent.

**원령**(怨靈) a vindictive[revengeful] spirit 《유령》 a specter.

**원로**(遠路) a long way[distance]; a long journey/~를 무릅쓰고 오다 come a long way.

**원로**(元老) an elder[a senior, a veteran] statesman 《고참》 an elder; a senior [member]; an old-timer; a veteran 《고대 로마의》 the conscript fathers/문단의 ~ a literary magnate.

**원론**(原論) a theory; the principles (of)/경제학 ~ the principles of economics/의학 ~ the principles of medicine.

**원뢰**(遠雷) distant thunder; a distant roll[clap] of thunder.

**원료**(原料) raw material; materials/~를 확보하다 secure[procure] raw materials/공업 ~ raw material industry.

**원리**(元利) principal and interest/~ 합계액 an amount with interest added [included].

**원리**(原理) a principle; a theory; the fundamental truth; fundamentals/궁극적 ~ the ultimate principle.

**원만**(圓滿) 《조화》 harmony; peace 《원활》 smoothness 《완전》 perfection/~하다 (be) amicable; satisfactory; peaceful; harmonious/~히 해결되다 settle (a dispute) amicably.

**원망**(怨望) 《원한》 grudge; resentment; reproach; spite 《증오》 hatred 《불평》 a grievance/~하다 bear a grudge against (a person); reprach; resent.

**원망**(遠望) a distant view[prospect]; a perspective/~하다 view from a distance; look afar at/성곽을 ~하다 get a distant view of a castle.

**원망**(願望) a desire; a wish 《큰 뜻》 an aspiration/~하다 desire; wish.

**원면**(原綿) raw cotton.

**원명**(原名) original name; real name.

**원모**(原毛) raw wool.

**원모**(遠謀) foresight; forethought; a farsighted scheme; a long-range plan.

**원무**(圓舞) a waltz; a circle dance; a round/~곡 a waltz.

**원문**(原文) 《본문》 the text 《원서》 the original/~에 충실하게 번역하다 make a translation faithful to the original; translate literally.

**원반**(圓盤) a disk 《투원반용》 a discus/~던지기 discus throw[ing].

**원방**(遠方) a distant place; a remote area; a distance; a great distance/~에서 오다 come from a distance/~으로 여행가다 make[go on] a long journey.

**원방**(遠邦) distant countries; a far-off [remote] land.

**원배**(遠配) exile to a remote place/~하다 exile (a person) to a remote place.

**원범**(正犯) 《정범》 the principal offender/그 사람이 ~이다 He committed the offense as the principal.

**원병**(援兵) a relief; reinforcement[s]; a relieving force/~을 보내다 send reinforcements (to).

**원본**(原本) the original (work); the original copy[document]; the text; 《법》《사본에 대하여》 the script.

**원뿔**(圓-) a cone; a circular cone.

**원사**(寃死) being put to death on a turmped-up charge.

**원산**(原産) the origin of a product/커피의 ~지 the home of the coffee plant/감자는 미국이 ~지다 The potato is native to America./~물(物) a primary products.

**원상**(原狀) the original state; the former condition; the status quo/~으로 복구하다 restore to the original state[former condition, status quo].

**원색**(原色) a primary color; original color[s]/~ 사진 a heliochrome; a color picture/삼~ three primary colors.

**원생**(原生) ~의 primeval; primary; proto/~림 a virgin[primeval] forest/~식물 a protophyte.

**원서**(原書) the original (work, text)/셰익스피어를 ~로 읽다 read Shakespeare in the original.

**원서**(願書) an application; a written request/~를 제출하다 send in[submit] an application/입학 ~ an application for admission [into a school].

**원성**(怨聲) a complaint; a grievance.

**원소**(元素) 《화》 an element; a chemical element/~ 분석 ultimate[elementary] analysis/~ 주기율 the periodic law of the elements.

**원수**(元首) the chief of the state; a ruler; a sovereign.

**원수(元帥)** 《육군》 a general of the army; a [field-]marshal 《해군》 a fleet-admiral 《공군》 an air-marshal. げんすい

**원수(員數)** the number of persons. いんすう

**원수(怨讐)** an enemy; a foe; the object of *one's* grudge[grievance]/~를 만나다 come across the object of *one's* vengeance/~를 갚다 take revenge[vengeance] (for *one's father's* death). あだ

**원숙(圓熟)** maturity; mellowness; ripening; perfection/~하다 (be) mature; mellow; ripe; become perfect; fully developed/~해지다 come to maturity. えんじゅく

**원숭이** a monkey 《꼬리 없는》 an ape/~도 나무에서 떨어지는 수가 있다《속담》 A monkey may fall from the tree. さる

**원시(元是, 原是)** originally; primarily; from the beginning. もとより

**원시(原始, 元始)** the beginning; origin; genesis; the original[primitive] state of nature/~ 동물 a protozoan/~인 인간 the primitive man. げんし

**원시(遠視)** looking far-off at 《원시안》 far-sightedness; a long-sighted eye; 《의》 hypermetropia/~인 사람 a long-sighted person. えんし

**원심(怨心)** a bitter feeling; a heartburning; a grudge; a spite/~을 품다 have a grudge against (*a person*). えんぼうのこころ

**원심(圓心)** 【수】 the center (of *a circle*).

**원심(原審)** the original decision.

**원심력(遠心力)** 【물】 the centrifugal force. えんしんりょく

**원아(園兒)** kindergarten children. えんじ

**원안(原案)** 《초안》 the [original] draft 《의안》 the original bill 《계획》 the original plan/~대로 가결하다 pass a bill in its original form. げんあん

**원안(遠眼)** 【의】 a far-sighted eye; hypermetropia. えんがん

**원앙(鴛鴦)** a mandarin duck; a pair of love-birds/~의 인연을 맺다 plight *one's* troth; vow eternal[unchanging] love. おしどり

**원액(元額, 原額)** the original sum[amount]. もとのがく

**원야(原野)** waste land; a wilderness; a moor; a prairie; a wild plain. げんや

**원양(遠洋)** an ocean/~의 pelagic; pelagian/~ 동물 a pelagian/~ 항해 ocean navigation; a long cruise/~ 어업 deep sea[pelagic] fishery[fishing]. えんよう

**원어(原語)** the original language[word].

**원영(遠泳)** a long-distance swim/~하다 swim a long distance. えんえい

**원예(園藝)** gardening; horticulture 《꽃 재배》 floriculture/~가 a gardener; a horticulturist/가정 ~ home gardening. えんげい

**원외(員外)** non-membership; supernumerary [status]/~의 supernumerary/~ 교수 a professor extraordinary/~자 a non-member. いんがい

**원외(院外)** ~의 outside the institution [House, academy, temple, monastery, board, chamber, hospital]; non-parliamentary. いんがい

**원원이(元元一)** originally; primarily. ほんらいから

**원유(原油)** crude petroleum[oil]. げんゆ

**원유회(園遊會)** a garden party; a pienic/~를 개최하다 give[hold] a garden party. えんゆうかい

**원음(原音)** the original pronunciation [sound]; 【음】 the fundamental tones. げんおん

**원의(原意, 原義)** original intention; original[primary] meaning. げんぎ

**원의(院議)** the decision of the House/~를 존중하여 in deference to the decision of the House. いんぎ

**원인(願人)** 《지원자》 an applicant 《바라는 사람》 one who wants. がんにん

**원인(原因)** the origin; the cause/~하다 originate; result from; be caused by /간접 ~ mediate cause/직접 ~ immediate cause/~ 결과 cause and effect; causality/~ 불명의 죽음 death of unknown cause/실패의 ~ the cause of *one's* failure/~을 밝히다 trace (*a thing*) to its origin/주된 ~ a major cause (*for*)/~이 없이 결과가 생기지 않는다 An effect presupposes a cause./이것이 이 사건의 ~이다 This is at the bottom of the trouble., This stands in a causal relation to the event./이 소동의 ~은 전적으로 교장의 무능에 있었다 The incompetency of the principal is solely responsible for the disturbances./~론 etiology; the philosophy of causation/간접 ~ indirect[mediate] cause/궁극 ~ the ultimate cause/직접 ~ direct[immediate] cause. げんいん

**원인(遠因)** a remote cause; an underlying cause/그것이 전쟁의 ~을 이루고 있다 It is[forms] a remote cause of the war. えんいん

**원일(元日)** New Year's Day. がんじつ

**원일점(遠日點)** 【천】 the aphelion; the higher apsis. えんじつてん

**원입(願入)** application/~하다 apply for admission.

**원자(原子)** 【물】 an atom/~의 atomic /~가 atomic value/~량 atomic weight/~력 관리 atomic control/~력 평화 이용 peaceful use of atomic energy/~론 atomic theory; atomism/~병 an atomic disease/~ 시대 the atomic age /~ 폭탄 an atom[ic] bomb/~핵 분열 nuclear fission. げんし

**원작(原作)** the original [work] (of *art*)/~자 the author; the artist. げんさく

**원장(園長)** the chief; the head; the superintendent (of *a zoo, a kindergarten, etc.*). えんちょう

**원장(院長)** 《병원의》 the director 《학원의》 the president. いんちょう

**원장(元帳)** the ledger; the blotter《속》. もとちょう

**원저(原著)** the original work/~자 the author; the writer. げんさく

**원적(怨敵)** a spiteful[sworn, bitter] enemy; a mortal[deadly] foe. うらみのあるあだ

**원적(原籍)** the domicil[e]; an [original] domicile; the place of origin/~지 the place of one's domicile; the domicile of origin. げんせき

**원전(原典)** a source book; the original text. げんてん

**원전(圓轉)** revolution; rotation; gyration /~하다 revolve; rotate. えんてん

**원정(園丁)** a gardener. えんてい

**원정(遠程)** a long way[distance] ⇒원로

**(遠路).** えんろ

**원정(遠征)** an expedition; an invasion; ~하다 go on an expedition; invade; make a foray/~대 an expeditionary force[team]/~대를 조직[파견]하다 organize[dispatch] an expeditionary force /~ 시합 an out-match. えんせい

**원조(元祖)** the founder; the father; the originator. がんそ

**원조(援助)** help; support; assistance; aid/~하다 assist; help; support; encourage; aid; give assistance[support] to/~를 청하다 ask (a person) for assistance[help]/~를 얻다 receive[secure, derive] assistance/나는 그를 ~하고 싶다 I am disposed to help him./~국 an aid country/~금 an aid fund/~ 물자 aid goods/재정 ~ financial aid. えんじょ

**원족(遠族)** distant relatives of the same family origin.

**원족(遠足)** an excursion; a trip; an outing; a picnic; a hike〈미〉/~하다 take a long walk; go on an excursion; make a trip to. えんそく

**원죄(原罪)** the original sin. げんざい

**원죄(冤罪)** a false charge[accusation]/~를 입다 be falsely accused of; be falsely charged with. えんざい

**원주(圓柱)** a column/~상(狀)의 columnar; cylindrical. えんちゅう

**원주(圓周)** circumference/~율 the ratio of the circumference of a circle to its diameter; pi(기호：π). えんしゅう

**원지(原紙)** 《등사용》 a stencil paper 《잠란지》 an egg-sheet. げんし

**원지(遠地)** a remote area ⇒원방(遠方). えんぼう

**원지(遠志)** a great ambition; a lofty aspiration; vast ambition[s]. えんだいないし

**원질(原質)** a protyle/〈유전〉 ~ a gene/불가분(不可分)~ a protyle. げんしつ

**원차(怨嗟)** grievance; grudge; resentment. えんさ

**원채** by nature ⇒워낙. なにせ

**원챗집** a house hired exclusively by a family ⇒몸채.

**원천(源泉)** the fountain head; the headspring; the wellspring; a source; an origin/지식의 ~ the source of knowledge[information]/~ 과세 taxation on the source (of income); withholding tax〈미〉/~ 징수 제도 the withholding system. げんせん

**원체(元體)** the original form. もともと

**원촌(遠村)** a distant village.

**원촌(遠寸)** a distant relation/~의 distantly[remotely] related/~이 되는 사람 a distant relative/그는 나의 ~이 된다 He is a remote relative of mine., He is a distant kinsman of mine.

**원추(圓錐)** 《원추체》 a cone; conical shape/~형의 conical/모래 주머니가 ~형으로 쌓여 있다 Sand bags are piled up in conical shape./~ 곡선 a conic; a conic section /~대 a truncated cone/~면 a conical surface.

**원추리** 《식》 a day lily; Hemerocallis`aurantiaca(학명). わすれぐさ

**원칙(原則)** a principle; a rule/~적으로 as a [general] rule; in principle/~을 세우다 establish a principle/~적으로 동의하다 agree in principle/본교 입학자는 ~적으로 기숙사에 넣기로 되어 있다 Our school expects new students to enter the dormitory/~ 협정 a formula /근본 ~ a cardinal[basic] principle. げんそく

**원컨대(願—)** I hope; I pray; It is to be hoped that…/신이여 이 불쌍한 소녀에게 복을 내리소서 Have mercy on this poor girl, O God! ねがわくば

**원탁(圓卓)** a round-table/~ 회의 a round-table conference. えんたく

**원통(冤痛)** resentment; mortification; chagrin; regret/~하다 (be) resentful; mortifying; chagrined/~해 하다 regret; be mortifiled[vexed] (at); be galled.

**원판(原版)** 《사진의》 a negative 《영화의》 a film 《환등의》 a magic lantern slide. げんばん

**원하다(願—)** desire; wish; hope; be desirous; want; intend; please; care for 《간원》 beg; entreat; implore/원하는 대로 as one please. ねがう

**원한(怨恨)** 《원망》 grudge; resentment; a bitter feeling; spite; grievance (증오) enmity; ill will; animosity 《유감》 regret/~을 갚다 vent one's spite; revenge oneself on (the offender); work off a grudge/~을 사다 incur enmity; earn (a person's) grudge/~을 잊다 forget one's grudge (against)/나는 그에게 ~을 품고 있다 I owe him a grudge./나는 그에게 아무런 ~도 없다 I bear him no grudge. えんこん

**원항(遠航)** ocean navigation; a long

원해어 cruise/~하다 set out on ocean navigation/~ 중이다 be on a long[-distance] cruise.

원해어(遠海魚) a pelagic fish.

원행(遠行) a long trip/~하다 make[go on] a long trip. えんこう

원형(原形) the original form/~을 유지하다 retain its original form; remain intact/~을 잃다 lose its original form/~을 찾아볼 수 없을 정도로 부서지다 be broken[destroyed] beyond recognition. げんけい

원형(原型) the archetype; the prototype; the type; the model. げいけい

원형(圓形) a round shape[form]; a circle; circularity/~의 circular 《식물의》discoid/~으로 circularly; in a circle/~으로 만들다 make a circular; circularize/~ 극장 an amphitheater. えんけい

원형질(原形質) 〖생〗 protoplasm. げんけいしつ

원호(援護) backing; protection; relief; support/~하다 back; support; protect; lend support to/~회 a relief association/~ 기금 a relief funds. えんご

원호(圓弧) a circular arc/~를 그리다 describe[trace] circular arcs. えんこ

원혼(冤魂) malignant spirits; the spirit of *one* put to death on a trumped-up charge.

원화(原畵) the original picture/이 초상화는 ~와 비슷하지 않다 The portrait does not resemble[come near] the original.

원활(圓滑) harmony; smoothness/~하다 (be) smooth; harmonious; peaceful/~하게 smoothly; peacefully; amicably 《지장없이》 without a hitch/만사가 ~히 진행된다 Things go on smoothly./예의는 사회 생활을 ~하게 한다 Good manners serve to oil the wheels of social life. えんかつ

원훈(元勳) a veteran statesman 《원로》 an older statesman. げんくん

원흉(元兇) a ringleader; the chief instigator; the prime mover; the head; the leader (of *a gang*); an archvillain; an archtraitor. あくにんのとうもく

월 《문장》 a sentence. ぶんしょう

월(月) 〖천체〗 the moon; a month/~평균 a monthly average/5~ May. つき

월간(月刊) monthly issue[publication]/~의 monthly/~ 잡지 a monthly magazine. げっかん

월갈 〖언〗 syntax. ぶんしょうろん

월경(越境) border transgression; violation of the border; border jumping/~하다 cross the frontier into another country/~ 사건 a border incident. えっきょう

월경(月經) 〖의〗 catamenia; menstruation; menses; the flowers; the monthlies; the courses/~의 menstrual/~시에 at the period of menstruation; during *one's* period/~이 있다 have the menses [monthlies]/~중이다 be in the flowers; be off the sports list 《미》/~ 과다 profuse menstruation; menorrhagia/~ 불순 menstrual irregularity. げっけい

월계(月計) a monthly account. げっけい

월계관(月桂冠) laurels; a laurel crown [wreath]/~을 차지하다 win laurels; bear the palm/ ~을 쓰다 be crowned with the laurel fo victory/~은 그에게 돌아갔다 The laurel of the day fell on his head. げっけいかん

월계수(月桂樹) a bay tree; a laurel tree; *Laurus nobilis* 《학명》. げっけいじゅ

월계화(月季花) 〖식〗 the Chinese rose; *Rosa chinensis* 《학명》.

월광(月光) moonlight/ ~곡 《베토벤의》 "The Moonlight Sonata". げっこう

월권(越權) presumption; abuse of confidence; going beyond *one's* powers; arrogation/~하다 arrogate power; exceed[overstep] *one's* authority; override *one's* commission/그런 짓은 ~이다 You have no warrant for doing that./~ 행위 an [act of] arrogation. えっけん

월급(月給) a monthly salary[pay]; a [monthly] salary[wage]; 《지불 급료의 총액》the payroll/많은 ~ a large[high] salary/ ~을 받다 draw[get] a salary/~이 오르다 have *one's* salary raised; get a rise in *one's* salary /~으로 살다 live on *one's* salary/~ 날 a pay day; a salary day/~ 봉투 a pay-envelope/~장이 a salaried man; a white-collar worker. げっきゅう

월남(越南) coming-south [from North Korea]/~하다 come down [the 38th Parallel] into South Korea.

월내(月內) ~에 within a month; in less than a month そのつきのうち

월단(月旦) ①《초하루》 the first [day of a month] ②《인물평》 a character sketch; comments on personalities.

월당(月當) monthly share[allowance].

월동(越冬) passing the winter/~하다 tide over the winter; winter/~ 자금 a winter relief fund; a winter allowance /~ 준비 preparations for passing the winter. えっとう

월등(越等) a vast difference in degree; excellence; superiority/~하다 (be) out of the common; extraordinary; outstanding/~히 out of the common[ordinary]; exceptionally; by far/ ~히 낫다 be far better[superior]/ ~히 크다 be gigantic; be huge.

월력(月曆) a calendar. つきのこよみ

월령(月齡) 〖천〗 the age of the moon; the month's age. げつれい

월례(月例) ~의 monthly/~ 회의 a monthly meeting. げつれい

월말(月末) the end of the month /~에 at the end of the month/~ 지불 month-end payment[settlement]. げつまつ

**월맹증**(月盲症) 《수의학》 periodic ophthalmia.

**월면**(月面) the surface of the moon/~도(圖) a selenographic chart; a selenograph. つきのひょうめん

**월명**(月明) moonlight. げつめい

**월번**(月番) monthly duty[turn]. つきばん

**월변**(月邊) a monthly interest. まいつきのりし

**월보**(月報) a monthly report[bulletin]. げっぽう

**월봉**(月俸) a monthly pay. げっぽう

**월부**(月賦) a monthly installment[payment]/~로 천원씩 물다 pay by monthly instalments of 1,000 won/~로 구두를 한 켤레 마추다 have a pair of shoes made on the monthly instalment system/~ 판매법 the hire purchase plan〈영〉; instalment selling[sale]〈미〉; the piano system〈미〉; the easy payment plan〈미〉. げっぷ

**월불**(月拂) monthly installments[payment]/~로 하다 pay by monthly installments.

**월비**(月費) monthly expenses. まいつきのひよう

**월사**(月事) 〖생〗 menstruation ⇒월경.

**월사금**(月謝金) a monthly fee 《학교 등록금》 a monthly school[tuition] fee/비싼 ~ a heavy charge for tuition/~을 면제하다 remit [a student] the fee. げっしゃきん

**월삭**(月朔) the first [day of a month]. つきのはじめ

**월산**(月產) a monthly output; a monthly production. げっさん

**월색**(月色) moonlight; moonbeam[s]. げっしょく

**월석**(月夕) a moonlight night; the night of the 15th day of the 8th lunar month. げっせき

**월세**(月貰) monthly rent/이 집은 ~ 만원입니다 This house rents at ten thousand won a month.

**월세계**(月世界) the lunar world; the moon/~ 여행 a moon trip/~로 로케트를 발사하다 Shoot a rocket at the moon.

**월수**(月收) 《수입》 a monthly income 《빚》 a loan at monthly interest/~ 8만 원이 되다 have[draw] a monthly income of 80,000 won. げっしゅう

**월수당**(月手當) a monthly allowance. つきのてあて

**월식**(月蝕) 〖천〗 a lunar eclipse /개기(皆既)[부분] ~ a total[partial] eclipse of the moon. げっしょく

**월액**(月額) the monthly amount. げつがく

**월야**(月夜) a moonlight night. つきよ

**월여**(月餘) more than a month/~간이나 more than a month; over a month. げつよ

**월영**(月影) the shade of the moon; the moon. げつえい

**월요일**(月曜日) Monday(略: Mon.). げつようび

**월일**(月日) the moon and the sun; the manth and thd day; the date/생년 ~ the date of *one's* birth. つきひ

**월전**(月前) ~에 a month ago.

**월정**(月定) contracting[arranging] by the month/~고용 month-to-month engagement; hiring by the month. つきぎめ

**월정 독자**(月定讀者) a regular subscriber; a subscriber by the month.

**월초**(月初) the beginning of a month/~에 at the beginning of the month.

**월파**(月波) moonlight; moonbeams. なみのようにみえるげっこう

**월편**(越便) the other[opposite] side/~에 on the opposite[other] side. むかいがわ

**월평**(月評) a monthly review/문단 ~ a monthly survey of the literary world. げっぴょう

**월표**(月表) a monthly list[table]; monthly returns. げっぴょう

**월하**(月下) ~의 moonlit/~에서 in the moonlight/~ 빙인(氷人) a matchmaker; a go-between. げっか

**월화**(月華) moonlight.

**월훈**(月暈) a halo[ring] around the moon.

**웬** what; what sort of; what kind of/~일인지 with out knowing why; somehow/~ 일이냐 What is the matter [with you]? どんな—

**웬만큼** 《알맞게》 properly; moderately; within measure 《어느 정도》 to some extent 《어지간히》 fairly; pretty /독일어를 ~하다 speak German fairly well/~마셔라[먹어라] Take it easy on the liquor[food]. /~농담도 ~해라 Do not go too far with your jokes. /우리의 계획은 ~ 성공했다 Our plan was successful to some extent. いいかげん

**웬만하다** (be) passable; serviceable; tolerable; fairly good/~ 김새가 ~ be quite good-looking. ふつうである

**웬셈** what is intended; what is going to be done/~인지 나도 모르겠다 I don't know what all this is about. どうしたこと

**웬일** what; what business; what cause /~인지 for some reason [or other]/~이야 What is all this about?

**웽그렁뎅그렁** clang; clank. からんからん

**웽웽** noisily; boisterously; with the hum. ぶんぶん

**위** ①《상부》 upside; upper part/~의 upper; upside; upward/~에 above; over; upwards; up; on; upon/~로 오르다 rise up; go up ②《꼭대기·상부》 the top; the summit; the head 《포장의 표기》 the top; top/맨 ~의 top-most; uppermost/~에서 아래까지 form top to bottom/언덕 ~에 교회가 있다 There is a church at the head of the slope. ③《비교》 superiority/~의 《높은》 higher 《…이

위(상의) more than; above; over; beyond 《나은》 superior 《연상의》 older／훨씬 ~다 be far better／기는 놈 ~에 나는 놈《속담》 There is no limit to those above us.／~를 바라다보면 한이 없다 Don't compare yourself with those above you. ②《신분·지위》그는 나보다 지위가 ~다 He is above me in rank. ⑤《표면》the surface／호수 ~에 달이 비치고 있다 The moon is shining over the the lake. ⑥《문장 등의》 the above. うえ

위(位) ①《위치》 situation ②《지위》 rank; grade／1~를 차지하다 hold the first rank. い

위(胃) the stomach／~의 gastric／~가 튼튼하다[약하다] have a strong[weak] stomach[digestion]／~가 아프다 have a stomach-ache／~를 상하다 put the stomach out of order. い

위거(偉擧) a great deed 《계획》 a splendid plan. すばらしいけいりゃくまたはじぎょう

위격(違格) disagreement with established formalities.

위경(危境) a critical situation; danger; a crisis／~을 당하다 face a crisis／~을 벗어나다 tide over[pass through] a crisis. きけんなたちば

위경련(胃痙攣) 【의】 convulsion of the stomach／~을 일으키다 have a cramp of the stomach. いけいれん

위계(位階) court rank／~가 높은 사람 a person high in rank. いかい

위계(危計) a dangerous[risky] plan. あぶないはからい

위계(僞計) a deceptive plan; a fraudulent stratagem／~를 쓰다 use a deceptive scheme. ぎけい

위곡(委曲) details; [full] particulars／~하다 (be) minute; detailed; particular; full. いきょく

위공(偉功) a meritorious service; a great deed／~을 세우다 render great services; achieve a great success. いこう

위관(偉觀) a grand[magnificent] sight; grandeur. いかん

위관(尉官) 《육군》 a company officer; officers below the rank of major; a subaltern《중·소위》;《해군》officers below the lieutenant commander. いかん

위광(威光) authority; power; influence. いこう

위구(危懼) fear; apprehensions; misgivings／~하다 fear; be afraid (of); apprehend; have misgivings. きぐ

위국(危局) a crisis; a critical situation. ききょく

위국(爲國) ~하다 serve one's country; render service to one's country. くにのため

위권(威權) authority; influence.
위궤양(胃潰瘍)【의】 gastric[stomach] ulcer; an ulcer of the stomach. いかいよう

위급(危急) an emergency; a crisis; an exigency／~하다 (be) critical; crucial; imminent／~시에 in case of emergency; in time of need／~하게 되다 be in peril; be at stake. ききゅう

위기(危機) a crisis; a turning point; a critical moment／~의 critical; acute／~를 벗어나다 tide over a crisis. きき

위기 일발(危機一髮) the critical moment [juncture]; the psychological moment.

위기(委寄) trust; charge ⇨위임(委任). いたくすること

위기(委棄) abandonment／~하다 abandon.

위기(違期) ~하다 fail to keep the time limit. きをちがうえる

위기(圍碁) playing badook／~하다 play badook. いご

위난(危難) danger; distress; peril／~을 피하다 keep out of danger's way; escape danger／~에 당면하다 encounter a danger. きなん

위대(偉大) greatness; grandeur; mightiness／~하다 (be) great 《강대하다》 mighty 《숭고하다》 grand／~한 국민 a great nation／~한 인물 a great man; a master mind. いだい

위덕(威德) virtue and dignity; virtuous dignity. いとく

위도(緯度) latitude／~의 측정 determination of latitude／고[저]~ high[low] latitudes. いど

위독(危篤) ~하다 (be) dangerously[hopelessly] ill; in danger; in a critical condition／부친이 곧 귀가하라 《전문》 Father seriously ill, return immediately. きとく

위락(萎落) withering and falling／~하다 wither and fall. なれておちること

위략(偉略) an outstanding stratagem; a grand tactics. すばらしいさくりゃく

위력(威力) power; authority; might; force／~있는 powerful; mighty／~을 행사하다 exercise one's power. いりょく

위력(偉力) great power[influence]; efficiency／국가의 ~ the national authority／돈의 ~ the power of wealth[money]. いりょく

위령(威令) authority. いれい
위령(違令) violation of laws and ordinances.

위령제(慰靈祭) a memorial service／전몰 장병 ~ a memorial service for the war dead. いれいさい

위로(慰勞) ①《치사》 recognition of another's services; thanks for another's services／~하다 recognize another's services／~금 a bonus ②《위안》 ~하다 console; solace 《위자》 sympathize. いろう

위막(胃膜) the coats of the stomach.
위망(威望) influence and popularity. いりょくとめいぼう

위망(位望) position and fame[popularity].
위명(威名) a glorious name; prestige; fame. いめい

위명(僞名) a false name. ぎめい

**위무**(威武) authority and force. いぶ

**위무**(慰撫) pacification; soothing/~하다 pacify; soothe; appease/그들은 흥분한 부하의 ~에 전력을 다했다 They did all they could to appease their excited subordinates. いぶ

**위문**(慰問) (위자) consolation 《문병》 an inquiry after *another's* health 《조위(弔慰)》 condolence/~하다 console; condole (*with*); inquire after *another's* health/~금 a consolatory present of money. いもん

**위미**(萎靡) decline; decay/~하다 decline; droop; decay.

**위반**(違反) 《법규의》 violation; infringement 《약속 등의》 breach 《명령 등의》 disobedience/~하다 violate; break; be against; disobey/~ 행위 an offense/법을 ~ an offense against the law/~자 an offender. いはん

**위배**(違背) violation ⇨위반(違反). いはい

**위법**(違法) unlawfulness; illegality/~의 unlawful; illegal/~ 행위 an illegal act/~ 조치 an illegal disposition/~ 처분 illegal disposition[measures]. いほう

**위병**(胃病) a stomach trouble; stomachic disorder. いびょう

**위병**(衛兵) a sentry; a guard; a sentinel/~을 세우다 post a guard/~소 a guardhouse/~ 근무 guard duty. えいへい

**위복**(威服) ~하다 awe (*one*) into obedience; frighten (*one*) into submission. いふく

**위본**(僞本) a fabricated book; a spurious copy 《해적판》 a pirate edition.

**위부**(胃部) the stomach. い

**위부**(委付) 《법》 abandonment/~하다 abandon. いふ

**위불위없다**(爲不爲—) (be) unquestionable; certain; indubitable. うたがうよちがない

**위산**(胃酸) acid in the stomach/~ 과다 excess acid in the stomach. いさん

**위산**(胃散) medicinal powder for the stomach.

**위상**(位相) 《전기》 phase/~ 속도 《물》 phase velocity. いそう

**위생**(衛生) health; sanitation/정신 ~ mental hygiene/~적 sanitary; healthful; hygienic/공중 ~ public health/~ 설비 health facilities/학교 ~ school hygiene. えいせい

**위서다**(후행하다) accompany the bride [bridegroom].

**위선**(胃腺) 《해》 peptic glands. いせん

**위선**(緯線) a parallel [of latitude]. いせん

**위선**(僞善) hypocrisy/~적 hypocritical/~자 a hypocrite; a cant/~을 행하다 play the hypocrite. ぎぜん

**위선**(爲先) to begin with. まず

**위성**(衛星) a satellite/~국 a satellite state/인공 ~ an artificial satellite. えいせい

**위세**(威勢) influence; power; prestige; authority/~있는 powerful; influential; mighty/~를 부리다 exercise *one's* authority over (*others*); domineer over. いせい

**위수**(衛戍) a garrison/~ 근무 garrison duty/~ 사령관 the commadant of a garrison/~지 a garrison town[place]. えいじゅ

**위시**(爲始) ~하다 ①(비롯하다) originate (*in*) ②(시작하다) begin; commence/대통령을 ~하여 including President himself. はじめ

**위신**(威信) dignity; authority; prestige 《명예》 honour/~있는 of high repute/~이 떨어지다 lose authority; fall in public estimation. いしん

**위아래** up and down; the upper and lower; top and bottom 《신분》 high and low/~ 구별 없이 both high and low. うえとした

**위아랫물지다** do not mix up well (*with*); liquids seek separate level. えきたいがよくゆうごうしない

**위안**(慰安) (위자) comfort; consolation 《소창》 recreation/~하다 comfort; console; solace/~을 구하다 seek comfort [consolation] in (*music*)/생활의 ~ comforts of life/~을 주다 give comfort to; afford solace. いあん

**위암**(胃癌) 《의》 cancer of the stomach; gastroscirrhus. いがん

**위압**(威壓) coercion; overpowering/~하다 coerce; overpower; overawe/~적[으로] coercive[ly]. いあつ

**위액**(胃液) 《해》 gastric juice/~선(腺) peptic glands. いえき

**위약**(胃弱) dyspepsia; indigestion/~하다 (be) dyspeptic. いじゃく

**위약**(違約) breach of promise/~하다 infringe a contract; break a promise/~금 a penalty; damages for breach of contract. いやく

**위엄**(威嚴) dignity; stateliness; majesty/~있는 dignified; majestic; stately/~을 지키다 keep[maintain] *one's* dignity [*one's* gravity]/~을 더하다 increase [add to] *one's* dignity. いげん

**위업**(偉業) a great work; a great achievement/~을 성취하다 achieve a great work[thing]. いぎょう

**위없다** (be) unsurpassed; unexcelled; unparalleled. それいじょうない

**위여 일발**(危如一髮) a critical moment; the eleventh hour ⇨위기 일발.

**위염**(胃炎) 《의》 gastritis; inflammation of the stomach. いえん

**위요**(圍繞) ~하다 surround/…을 ~하여 in connection with…. いじょう

**위용**(偉容, 威容) a dignified[stately, commanding, grand] appearance[air]; a majestic air. いよう

**위원**(委員) a member of a committee; a commissioner; a committeeman/~장 a chairman/집행 ~ an executive committee/국무 ~ a Cabinet Member; a Minister/상임 ~ a standing committ-

**ee.** いいん

**위원회**(委員會) a committee; a commission; a board; a meeting of a committee/~를 소집하다 call a committee meeting. いいんかい

**위의**(威儀) dignity; solemnity/~있는 dignified; solemn; stately/~를 갖추고 in a dignified manner; with a solemnity of manner. いぎ

**위인**(偉人) a great man[mind]; a hero/역사상의 ~들 the great names of history. いじん

**위인**(爲人) character; nature; disposition; personality; one's character[personality, make-up]. ひととなり

**위임**(委任) trust; commission; charge (전권의) delegation; 【법】 mandate/~하다 (권한을) entrust (one) with (대표자로서) delegate/~장 a procuration/~자 the mandator. いにん

**위임장**(委任狀) a power of attorney; a procuration. いにんじょう

**위임 통치**(委任統治) mandate; mandatory rule/~권 a mandate/~국 a mandatory power[territory]; a mandatory. いにんとうち

**위자**(慰藉) comfort; consolation/~하다 comfort; console/~료 consolation money/~료를 청구하다 demand compensation (for). いしゃ

**위작**(位爵) title and court rank; peerage. いとしゃく

**위장**(胃腸) the stomach and bowels/~의 gastroenteric/~이 튼튼하다[약하다] have a strong[poor] digestion/~병 a gastroenteric disorder[trouble]. いちょう

**위장**(僞裝) camouflage/~하다 camouflage; disguise/~의 camouflaged; sham/~ 수출 fraud export. ぎそう

**위재**(偉才) a great man; a great talent. いさい

**위적**(偉績) an exploit; distinguished services. いせき

**위정자**(爲政者) a statesman; an administrator. いせいしゃ

**위조**(僞造) forgery; fabrication; falsification/~하다 counterfeit; forge; falsify; fabricate/~ 지폐 a false note; a forged bank-note/서류를 ~하다 forge a document/~품 a counterfeit; a sham; a forgery/~ 문서 a spurious document/~ 증서 a forged bond. ぎぞう

**위쪽** the upper direction. うえにむかたほう

**위족**(僞足) 【생】 pseudopodium (pl. -dia). ぎそく

**위주**(爲主) putting first [in importance]/~하다 make (a thing) the prime object; give the first consideration to 《목적》 aim at

**위중**(危重) ~하다 (be) in critical condition; critically ill. びょうがきもいこと

**위증**(僞證) 【법】 perjury/~하다 forswear; perjure (oneself); give false evidence/~자 a perjurer/~죄로 기소되다 be accused of perjury. ぎしょう

**위증**(危症) a dangerous symptom; a critical condition of an illness. きけんなびょうじょう

**위지**(危地) a dangerous position; a critical situation/~에 빠뜨리다 endanger; jeopardize. きち

**위집**(蝟集) gathering in a swarm/~하다 throng; crowd together. いしゅう

**위차**(位次) order of seats[ranks, positions]. せきじゅん

**위채** the "upper" wing of a Korean house.

**위촉**(委囑) entrusting; commission (의뢰) request (담당) charge/~하다 commit (a matter) to (one); request; ask/~에 의해 at one's request. いしょく

**위축**(萎縮) withering; contraction; 【의】 atrophy/~하다 (사람이) be daunted (by); shrink (물건이) wither. いしゅく

**위층**(一層) the upper floor[story, storey〈영〉]; upstairs. うえのかさなり.

**위치**(位置) 《장소》 position; place; location (대지) site (입장) stand (지위) position; standing; place/~ 에너지 【물】 potential energy/~ 감각 【심】 consciousness of bodily position. いち

**위탁**(委託) a trust; trusteeship/~하다 entrust (one with a thing); charge (one with a task); (상품을) consign (일을) commit (a matter) to/~ 판매 consignment sale/~을 받다 be entrusted/~품 consignment/~금 trust money. いたく

**위태**(危殆) danger; peril; risk/~하다 (be) dangerous; risky; perilous.

**위턱** the upper jaw; the maxilla.

**위통**(胃痛) 【의】 gastralgia; a stomach-ache. いつう

**위패**(位牌) a memorial tablet 《조상의》 an ancestral tablet. いはい

**위품**(位品) grade of official ranks. かんしょくのいかい

**위풍**(威風) dignity; a commanding presence; a majestic air/~ 당당한 majestic; imposing/~에 압도되다 bow[bend] to (a person's) dignity. いふう

**위필**(僞筆) forged handwriting 《그림》 a forged picture/~하다 forge; counterfeit. ぎひつ

**위하다**(爲一) 《사랑하다》 love 《존중하다》 value 《존경하다》 respect 《잘되기 바라다》 wish (one) well/자식을 ~ love[be affectionate to] one's children; wish one's children well/부모를 ~ be dutiful to one's parents. ためになる

**위하수**(胃下垂) 【의】 gastroptosis; falling of the stomach. いかすい

**위하여**(爲一) ①《이익·편의를》for; for the sake[benefit] of; in the interests[favour, honour] of (…을 대신하여) in[on] behalf of/조국을 ~ for the sake of the fatherland/사회를 ~ in the interests

**위해(危害)** injury; harm (위험) danger /～를 가하다 hurt (one); inflict an injury on; do (one) an injury. きがい

**위헌(違憲)** a violation of the constitution; unconstitutionality/～의 unconstitutional; against the constitution. いけん

**위험(危險)** danger; risk; hazard/～하다 (be) dangerous; hazardous; perilous/～ 신호[지대] a danger signal[zone]/～에 빠뜨리다 endanger; jeopardize/～을 당하여 in case[time] of danger/～ 인물 a dangerous character/～에 빠지다[을 벗어나다] get into[out of] danger. きけん

**위협(威脅)** threat; menace; intimidation /～하다 threaten; be a menace to (peace); frighten/평화의 ～ a menace [threat] to peace/생활을 ～하다 threaten one's livelihood/～적 menacing; threatening.

**위확장(胃擴張)** 【의】 dilation of the stomach; gastric dilation. いかくちょう

**위훈(偉勳)** a great service; a brilliant achievement; conspicuous merit. いくん

**윗길** superior quality; better grade; top grade. じょうとう

**윗니** the upper [set of] teeth.

**윗배** the upper part of the abdomen; the stomach.

**유(類)** (종류) a kind; a sort; a description (부류) a class (유속(類屬)) an order; a family; a form; a species. るい

**유(有)** (존재) existence; being/무에서 ～는 생기지 않는다 Out of nothing, nothing comes. ゆう

**유가(有價)** valuableness; having a fixed /～ 증권 securities. ゆうか

**유가(儒家)** a Confucian [scholar]; a Confucianist.

**유가족(遺家族)** a bereaved family/군경 ～ the bereaved families of the war dead. いかぞく

**유감(遺憾)** regret; a pity/～된 regrettable; sad; deplorable (불만족) unsatisfactory/～없이 perfectly; most satisfactorily/～으로 생각하다 be sorry (for); regret/～ 천만이다 It is deeply to be regretted. いかん

**유개(有蓋)** ～의 covered; closed (car).

**유객(幽客)** a hermit; a recluse; an anchorite.

**유객(遊客)** ①(유람객) a tourist; a traveller ②(놀고 사는 사람) a man of leisure; an idle fellow. ゆうかく

**유거(幽居)** (장소) a hermitage (생활) seclusion/～하다 live in seclusion; lead a retired life. ゆうきょ

**유건 악기(有鍵樂器)** a keyed musical instrument; a clavier.

**유격(遊擊)** 【군】 a raid; a diversion/～대 (육군)a flying column (해군)a flying squadron/～수 《야구》 a shortstop/～전 guerrilla[a partisan] warfare[war]. ゆうげき

**유견(謬見)** erroneous[wrong] view. びゅうけん

**유경(有莖)** 【식】 being caulescent/～의 caulescent/～ 식물 a cormophyte.

**유경(幽境)** a solitude; a solitary place [spot].

**유계(幽界)** Hades; Hell. ゆうかい

**유계(遺戒)** one's dying instructions; injunctions left by one dead. いかい

**유고(有故)** ～하다 an accident happens; have a reason (for it); be owing to some trouble. じこがあること

**유고(遺稿)** writings left by a deceased person; posthumous works/변영로의 ～를 출판하다 publish in book form the manuscripts left by the late Mr. Yung Ro Byun. いこう

**유고(諭告)** ①(타이름) advice; warning; counsel; instructions; admonition/～하다 give instructions ②(관청의) an official notice[instruction, announcement]. ゆこく

**유고(油庫)** an oil bunker.

**유곡(幽谷)** a deep valley; a deep[dark] glen/심산 ～ deep mountains and dark valleys. ゆうこく

**유골(遺骨)** ashes; remains/～을 모으다 gather (a person's) remains. いこつ

**유공(有功)** merit/～하다 (be) meritorious/～증 a certificate of merit/～장(章) a medal. ゆうこう

**유공충(有孔蟲)** 【동】 Foraminifera(학명). ゆうこうちゅう

**유과(乳菓)** an emulsion.

**유곽(遊廓)** licensed[gay, prostitute] quarters; a red-light district〈미〉/～에 드나들다 frequent houses of ill fame. ゆうかく

**유괴(誘拐)** kidnapping; abduction/～하다 abduct; lure away; carry off (어린이를)kidnap/～ 사건 an abduction case; a snatch case〈미〉/～자 an abductor; a kidnap[p]er/～죄 abduction. ゆうかい

**유교(遺敎)** one's will; one's dying injunctions. いきょう

**유교(儒敎)** Confucianism/～도(徒) a Confucianist/～ 사상 Confucian ideas. じゅきょう

**유구(悠久)** eternity/～하다 (be) eternal; everlasting/～한 옛날부터 from time immemorial. ゆうきゅう

**유구(類句)** a synonymous phrase/～집 (集) a collection of similar phrases.

**유구 무언(有口無言)** ～이다 have no word to say in excuse. へんめいすることばがない

**유군(幼君)** a young lord[master]; a princeling.

**유권자(有權者)** a voter; an elector〈영〉. ゆうけんしゃ

**유권 해석(有權解釋)** an authoritative interpretation.

**유금(遊金)** idle money[capital]. ゆうきん

**유금류(游禽類)** 【조】 the swimmers; *Natatores*(학명).

**유급(有給)** ~의 paid; salaried/~ 휴가 a paid holiday; a holiday with pay. ゆうきゅう

**유기(有期)** ~의 terminable; limited/ ~형(刑) penal servitude for a term/~ 공채 a terminable loan. ゆうき

**유기(有機)** ~의 organic/~물 organic matter[substance]/~ 화학 organic chemistry. ゆうき

**유기(遺棄)** abandonment; desertion/~하다 abandon; leave behind/~ 시체 an abandoned corpse/~자 a deserter. いき

**유기음(有氣音)** 《음》 an aspirate; an aspirated sound. ゆうきおん

**유기적(有機的)** organic; systematic/~으로 organically/~ 세계관 the organic view of the world. ゆうきてき

**유나(柔懦)** effeminacy; effeminateness/~하다 (be) effeminate.

**유난 (보통이 아님)** unusualness; uncommonness (괴팍) fastidiousness/ ~하다 (be) unusual; uncommon; exceptional.

**유년(幼年)** infancy; childhood; boyhood/~의 juvenile/~공 a child worker/~ 시대에 in *one's* childhood. ようねん

**유념(留念)** attention; heed; regard/~하다 mind; care about; attend to; pay regard to; give heed to.
こころにとどめること

**유뇨증(遺尿症)** 【의】 enuresis.

**유능(有能)** ability; capability; competence/~하다 (be) able; capable; talented/~한 선생 a competent teacher. ゆうのう

**유다르다** (be) uncommon; extraordinary; unusual/유달리 unusually (특히) especially; uncommonly.

**유단자(有段者)** a grade-holder (in *wrestling, fencing, chess, etc.*). ゆうだんしゃ

**유당(乳糖)** milk sugar; lactose. にゅうとう

**유대류(有袋類)** 【동】 the marsupial [animal]; *Marsupialia*(학명).

**유덕(有德)** ~하다 (be) virtuous; good. いとく

**유덕(遺德)** posthumous influence. ゆうとく

**유도(柔道)** *jujutsu*(J); a Japanese art of self-defence/~복 a suit for *jujutsu* practice. じゅうどう

**유도(誘導)** inducement; leading; 【물】 induction/~하다 induce; lead/ ~ 전기 induced electricity/~체 【물】 a conductor/ ~ 장치 a guidance system. ゆうどう

**유도(儒道)** Confucianism. じゅどう

**유도 신문(誘導訊問)** a leading question/~하다 lead (*a criminal suspect*) to the point in question. ゆうどうじんもん

**유독(有毒)** poisonousness; noxiousness/~하다 (be) poisonous; noxious/~ 식물 a poisonous[noxious] plant. ゆうどく

**유독(惟獨)** only; uniquely; singly/~ 돈벌이만이 인생의 목적은 아니다 Money-making is not the sole end and aim of existence. だだひとり

**유동(流動)** a flow; flowing/~하다 flow/~성 liquidity; fluidity; 【사】 mobility/~ 자본 circulating capital. りゅうどう

**유동(遊動)** ~하다 move freely/~대 a mobile corps/~ 활차 a loose pulley/~ 원목 a swinging pole. ゆうどう

**유두(流頭)** June 15th of the lunar month.

**유들유들** ~하다 (be) audacious; impudent; cheeky. ふてぶてしいさま

**유락(遊樂)** pleasure; amusement/~하다 enjoy[amuse] *one*self; make merry/~에 빠지다 give *one*self up to pleasure; be given to pleasure. ゆうらく

**유람(遊覽)** sightseeing; excursion 《유람여행》 a pleasure-trip; a sightseeing tour/~하다 go sightseeing; do[see] the sights (*of*)/~ 여행을 하다 go on a sightseeing tour[pleasure trip]/ ~객 sightseers; tourists; excursionists/~ 단체 a tourist party; a sightseeing[an excursion] party/~ 버스 a sightseeing bus/~선 an excursion ship; a pleasure boat/~ 안내소 a tourist guide; an itinerary/~지 a pleasure ground; a tourist resort. ゆうらん

**유랑(流浪)** vagrancy; wandering/~의 wandering; vagrant; roaming; roving/~하다 wander[roam, rove] about/세계를 ~하다 roam[wander, knock] about the world/~ 생활을 하다 lead a roving [wandering] life/ ~민 a nomadic people; nomads/~ 민족 nomadic tribes/~벽 vagrant habits/~ 생활 a wandering[nomadic, Bohemian] life; nomadism/~자 a wanderer; a nomad; a vagabond; a vagrant. ろろう

**유래(由來)** 《기원》 origin; genesis 《내력》 history 《출처》 derivation; source 《원인》 cause/~하다 originate (*in*); result (*from*); be derived (*from*); derive itself[its sorigin](*from*)/~를 더듬다 trace (*a thing*) to its origin; trace (*a custom*) to its source; inquire into the origin (*of*)/그 이름은 여기서 ~했다 Hence the name. ゆらい

**유량(流量)** 【물】 flux/~계 a flow meter.

**유려하다(流麗—)** (be) flowing; fluent; smooth/유려한 문장 a flowing and elegant style; a fluent and flowery style. りゅうれいだ

**유력(有力)** ~하다 (be) powerful; influential; strong; effective/~한 증거 a valid[strong] evidence[proof]/~한 소식통 some influential quarters; a reliable source/~한 신문[실업가] an influential newspaper[businessman]/~한 용의자 a highly probable offender; a

**유력(有力)** strongly supported suspect/~자 an influential person; a power; a potentate.

**유력(遊歷)** a tour/~하다 tour; make a tour of; travel about/~자 a tourist; a traveller/세계를 ~하다 make an extensive tour of the world.

**유렵(遊獵)** sport; shooting〈영〉; hunting〈미〉/~하다 hunt; shoot; kill game/~가 a sportsman/~기 the shooting [open] season/~하러 가다 go hunting [shooting].

**유령(幽靈)** a ghost; an apparition; a spectre; a supernatural visitor/~같은 ghostlike/~의 집 a haunted house/~이 나오다 be haunted [by a ghost]; a ghost walks on the earth/그 집에는 ~이 나온다는 소문이 있다 It is rumored that the house is haunted/~ 인구 bogus population; fraudulently registered population/~ 회사 a bogus company; a long firm〈영〉.

**유례(類例)** a similar example[instance]; a parallel case; an analogy/사상(史上) ~가 없다 be without parallel in history.

**유록(柳綠)** light green.

**유료(有料)** ~의 charged; feed; toll; paid/~ 도로 a toll highway; a turnpike/~ 변소 a pay toilet/~ 시사회 a charged preview/~입니다 be charged for.

**유루(遺漏)** omission; neglect/~하다 omit; leave out; miss out; look over/만사 ~ 없도록 하시오 See that everything is done well.

**유류(遺留)** ~하다 leave behind/~품 lost articles.

**유리(有理)** rationality; reasonableness/~하다 (be) reasonable; rational/~수 [식]《수》 a rational number[expression]/~ 함수 《수》 a rational function.

**유리(有利)** ~하다 (이익되다) (be) profitable; lucrative; paying; gainful 《좋은》 (be) advantageous; favourable/~한 조건 remunerative terms/~한 장사 a paying business/그 여자는 그에게 ~한 증언을 했다 She testified for him.

**유리(瑠璃)** 《광》 emerald/~빛 emerald; bright blue.

**유리(遊離)** isolation; separation; 《화》 extrication/~하다 isolate; separate; set free; be isolated[separated]/현실에서 ~되다 be isolated[removed] from reality.

**유리(流離)** vagrancy; wandering/~하다 vagabond; wander[roam] around; rove/~ 개걸(丐乞) roving around begging.

**유리(琉璃)** glass 《창유리》 a pane/~ 자르는 칼 a glass cutter/색 ~ colored glass/~ 가게 a glass-shop/~병 a glass bottle/~창[문] a glass-window[door]/~를 끼우다 《창 따위에》 glaze (a window).

**유리론(唯理論)** 《철》 rationalism/~자 a rationalist.

**유린(蹂躙)** trampling down; overrunning 《겁탈》 violation; outrage/ ~하다 trample on[down]; tread down[under foot] 《황폐하게》 overrun; deyastate 《겁탈하다》 violate; outrage 《침해하다》 infringe upon/인권을 ~하다 infringe[trample] upon human rights/정조를 ~하다 violate[dishonor] a woman/적국을 ~하다 overrun[override, trample down] an enemy country/~자 a devastator; a harrier/인권 ~ infringement of personal[people's] rights.

**유림(儒林)** Confucianists.

**유만부동(類萬不同)** ~하다 be different one from another; be of all different kinds.

**유망(流網)** a drift-net/~ 어업 driftnet fishing.

**유망(有望)** a bright prospect; great promise; rosy prospects; hopefulness/~하다 (be) promising; hopeful; favorable; have a bright future; be full of promise/전도 ~한 청년 a promising youth; a young man of [great] promise.

**유명(幽明)** this and the other world/~을 달리하다 pass away[beyond]; join the majority.

**유명(幽冥)** darkness; gloom; dimness/~계(界) the other world/~객이 되다 depart from this life; go down to the shades.

**유명(遺命)** dying command; one's will/아버지의 ~에 의하여 by one's dead father's will; according to one's father's will.

**유명(有名)** fame; renown 《나쁜 뜻으로》 notoriety/~하다 (be) famous; noted; renowned; celebrated/~한 사람들 celebrities; men of distinction/~한 소설가 a noted novelist/일약 ~하게 되다 leap to fame/그여자는 ~한 작가이다 She is a celebrated author./그는 박학으로서 ~하다 He is famous[noted, celebrated, famed] for erudition./ ~세 a penalty of greatness/그는 어째서 그렇게 ~해졌는가 What gained him such a reputation?

**유명론(唯名論)** 《철》 nominalism.

**유명 무실(有名無實)** ~하다 (be) nominal; titular; little more than a mere name/~한 회장 a nominal[titular] chairman; a chairman in name only/~한 지도자 a titular leader without any power.

**유모(乳母)** a nurse; a wet nurse/~를 대다 place (a baby) under the care of a nurse.

**유목(遊牧)** nomadism/~하다 nomadize/~민 nomadic people; a nomad/~ 생

활 a nomadic life. ゆうぼく
유무(有無) existence; presence/~ 상통하다 supply each *other's* needs/유령의 ~ the existence of a ghost/출석할 의사의 ~를 묻다 ask (*a person*) whether he will be present or not. うむ
유문(幽門) 【해】 the pylorus. ゆうもん
유문(遺文) one's posthumous writings; literary remains. いぶん
유물(唯物) ¶ ~론 『철』 materialism/~론자 a materialist/~사관 historical materialism; the materialistic conception of history. ゆいぶつ
유물(遺物) (유품) a relic; remains (유증물) a legacy; a bequest/과거의 ~ a relic of the past/구시대의 ~ antiquities; a survival of olden days/석기 시대의 ~ remains[vestiges] of the Stone Age. いぶつ

유미(乳糜) chyle/~관(管) a lacteal. にゅうび
유미(柳眉) fair eyebrows; woman's crescent eyebrows/~를 곤두세우다 raise *one's* eyebrows with anger; get into a rage. りゅうび
유미(唯美) ¶ ~적 aesthetic/~주의 aestheticism/~주의자 an aestheticist.
유민(流民) drifting[wandering] people; the migrants.
유민(遊民) idle people; idlers; nonworkers (무직자) the unemployed 《총칭》 unemployment; drones/고등 ~ educated idlers. ゆうみん
유밀과(油蜜菓) honey-and-oil candy.
유방(乳房) the breast; the nipple. にゅうぼう
유방(遺芳) posthumous honours[fame, reputation]; honours after death.
유배(流配) banishment; exile/~하다 banish[exile] (*a criminal*) to an island maroon. ざいにんをりゅうけいにすること
유별(有別) ~하다 differ (*from*); have distinction (*between*). くべつのあること
유별(類別) classification; assortment/~하다 classify; assort; grade. るいべつ
유별나다(有別-) (be) distinctive; different/유별난 사람 a peculiar person; a queer man/유별난 대조 a striking[sharp] contrast. とくべつである
유보(留保) reservation/~하다 reserve; hold over; keep back for a later occasion.
유복(有福) ~하다 (be) blessed; fortunate; lucky. ゆうふく
유복(有服) near relatives for whose death *one* goes into mourning.
유복(裕福) affluence; opulence; prosperity/~하다 (be) rich; wealthy; affluent; opulent; well-off; well-to-do; prosperous/~한 가정에서 자라나다 be bred up in luxury. ゆうふく
유복자(遺腹子) a posthumous child[son]. にんしんちゅうにちちのなくなったこ
유부(油腐) [a piece of] fried bean curd.

유부녀(有夫女) a married woman.
유비(油肥) fertilizer made of animal fat. しぼうでつくったひりょう
유사(遺事) reminiscences; memories; overlooked historic remains. いじ
유사(有事) emergency/~시에 in time [case] of emergency[need]; in an emergency/~시에 대비하다 provide for all emergencies; prepare for the worst. ゆうじ
유사(類似) resemblance; similarity; likeness; analogy; affinity/~의 similar; like; kindred; akin to; analogous (비슷한) pseudo/~하다 be similar (*to*); be analogous; resemble; be alike; be akin (*to*)/~한 similar; like; analogous /이 문제는 그것과 ~하다 This question is similar to that./그들은 성격이 ~하다 They are alike in character./~ 사건 a similar[like] case/~품 an imitation/~품에 주의하시오 Beware of imitations. るいじ
유사(有史) history/~ 이래 in history; since the dawn of history/~ 이전의 prehistoric; of prehistoric times/~ 이래 오늘날까지 from prehistoric times to the present. ゆうし
유사시(有事時) emergency/~에는 in an emergency; if need be (곤란할 때)/in a pitch/~에 대비하다 prepare for the worst. ゆうじのこと
유산(有産) ~의 propertied/~ 계급 the propertied classes; de bourgeoisie(F)/~자 a man of property; a propertied man. ゆうさん
유산(硫酸) 【화】 sulphuric acid ⇒황산(黃酸). りゅうさん
유산(乳酸) 【화】 lactic acid/~균 lactic ferments/~염 a lactate. にゅうさん
유산(流産) an abortion; an abortive birth; a miscarriage/~하다 have a miscarriage[an abortion]; miscarry; abort 《실패》 fail/그의 계획은 모두 ~되었다 All his plans failed[miscarried]./그 녀자는 ~했다 She had an abortion[a miscarriage]. りゅうざん
유산(遺産) an inheritance; an estate[property] left behind; a legacy/~을 남기다[상속하다] leave[inherit, come into, take over] property[a fortune, an estate]/~을 분배하다 divide (*a person's*) property/~ 다툼 a quarrel over an inheritance/~ 상속 succession to property/~ 상속세 succession duty. いさん
유산(遊山) a picnic; an excursion; an outing; a jaunt/~하다 go on[have] a picnic[an excursion]; jaunt/~객 a picnicker; a holiday-maker; a vacationist. ゆさん
유산탄(榴散彈) a shrapnel [shell]. りゅうさんだん
유상(油狀) being oily/~의 oily; like oil. ゆじょう
유상(有償) compensation; consideration

유상무상 724 유습

/~ 계약 a contract made for a consideration/~ 몰수(沒收) onerous confiscation.

**유상 무상(有象無象)** ①(어중이떠중이) all sorts and conditions of people; the rabble ②(삼라만상) all things in nature; the universe; creation.

**유색(有色)** ~의 colo[u]red/~인종 the colo[u]red races/~체 a chromatophore.

**유생(儒生)** a Confucian scholar; a Confucianist.

**유생(有生)** ~의 living/~기원설 biogenesis/~물 the animate; life; living beings.

**유서(由緒)** a history; a story/~있는 historic; storied/~ 깊은 가문 a historic family; ancient lineage/~ 깊은 땅 a place with its old associations; a place with a historic background.

**유서(類書)** books of the same kind; similar[allied] books.

**유서(遺書)** a note left behind by a dead person; a testament; a [written] will/~를 쓰다 make[draw up] one's will [testament]/~를 남기고 죽다 die testate/자살의 이유를 쓴 ~가 있었다 He left a note giving the cause of his suicide.

**유선(乳腺)** 【해】 the mammary gland/~염(炎) mastitis.

**유선(有線)** wire/~방송 wire[d] radio/~전신[전파] wire telegraph[telephone]/~식 the wire system.

**유선형(流線型)** stream-lining; streamline form/~의 streamlined/~ 자동차 a streamlined car[automobile]; a streamliner.

**유설(謬說)** a false view[opinion]; a fallacy 《오보·오전(誤傳)》 a false report; a wild rumour.

**유성(流星)** a meteor; a shooting-star/야아 ~이다 There goes a shooting star!/~우(雨) a meteoric shower.

**유성(遊星)** 【천】 a planet/~의 planetary/대~ the major planets/소~ a planetoid.

**유성(有性)** ~의 sexual/~ 생식 sexual reproduction; gamogenesis.

**유성(有聲)** ~의 sound; voiced/~ 영화 a sound picture/~음 a voiced sound.

**유성기(留聲器)** a phonograph〈미〉; a gramophone〈영〉; a talking machine〈미〉/~를 틀다 play a record[phonograph]; turn the phonograph on/~를 끄다 turn[put] off a phonograph/~ 바늘 a phonograph needle; a recording stylus/~ 판 a [phonograph] record; a disk.

**유세(有勢)** ~하다 powerful; strong.

**유세(遊說)** 《선거의》 electioneering〈영〉; stumping; stump-speaking〈미〉;《선전》 a propaganda 《유세 여행》 a speaking tour; a stumping tour[trip]/~하다 stump; take the stump; go electioneering[canvassing, campaigning]/전국을 ~하다 stump the whole country; go about the country electioneering/~원 a campaign[stump] speaker; an electioneerer; a stump orator; a vanvasser.

**유세(有稅)** ~의 taxable 《관세》 dutiable/~품 dutiable[taxable] goods[articles]; goods subject to duty.

**유소(類燒)** ~하다 be destroyed by a spreading fire; catch fire/~를 당하다 have one's house burnt (down) by catching fire [from another burning house]/~를 면하다 escape the fire [flames]/~ 가옥 houses burnt by a [spreading] fire.

**유소(幼少)** childhood; infancy/~하다 (be) young; juvenile early life; in one's infancy/~시에 in one's infancy; in one's childhood; in one's early days/~시부터 from the infant years; from infancy[childhood, a child]; from the cradle.

**유속(流俗)** convention; prevalent customs/~을 따르다 follow the beaten track; swim with the stream.

**유속(流速)** the speed of a current/~계(計) a current meter/~ 측정 tachometry.

**유속(遺俗)** customs[manners] handed down from ancient times[preceding generations]; hereditary customs.

**유수(流水)** running water/세월은 ~와 같다 Time flies.

**유수(幼樹)** a young tree[plant]; a sapling.

**유수(有數)** ~의 prominent; leading; foremost; distinguished/~하다 (be) prominent; leading; distinguished; foremost/그는 우리나라 ~의 과학자다 He is one of the foremost scientists in this country.

**유수(幽邃)** ~하다 (be) sequestered; secluded; quiet and retired/~한 마을 a quiet and sequestered village/~의 경(境) a retired spot.

**유수류(遊水類)** 【동】 Natatores《학명》.

**유숙(留宿)** lodging; stopping; boarding/~하다 lodge (in, at); stay (at); stop (in); put up (at)/~시키다 put up (a person) at (an inn); give (a person) accommodation (for the night)/~자 a lodger.

**유순(柔順)** submission; obedience; docility/~하다 (be) submissive; obedient; docile; meek; gentle/~한 아이들 obedient children/매우 ~하다 be as gentle [meek] as a lamb.

**유술(柔術)** jujitsu(J).

**유습(遺習)** a custom handed down from preceding generations; hereditary customs.

**유시**(流矢) a stray arrow. ながれや
**유시**(幼時) childhood; infancy; early life. ようじ
**유시**(諭示) instruction; admonition; injunction; a message／～하다 admonish; give an instruction. ゆし
**유시류**(有翅類) 【蟲】 *pterygogenea*(학명).
**유식**(有識) ～하다 (be) intelligent; well-informed; (be) learned; educated／～하게 말하다 speak in a refined way／～계급 the learned[intellectual] class; the intellectuals; intelligentsia／～자 an intelligent[a well-informed] person; men of learning; the wise[learned]. ゆうしき
**유식**(遊食) ～하다 live in idleness; live an idle life; eat the bread of idleness／～생활 an idle life; a life of ease／～자 an idler; a lounger; a drone. ゆうしょく
**유신**(有信) being trustworthy[reliable]／～하다 (be) faithful; reliable; true. しんようのあること
**유신**(維新) restoration 〔혁신〕 renovation／～하다 renovate; restore. いしん
**유신**(遺臣) a surviving retainer. いしん
**유신론**(有神論) theism／～[자]의 theistic／～자 a theist. ゆうしんろん
**유실**(遺失) loss／～하다 lose; leave behind／～물 a lost article; lost property／～자 a loser; the owner of lost property[article]／～물 보관소 a lost article; lost property. いしつ
**유실**(流失) ～하다 be swept[carried, washed] away; lose to the waves[to the flood]／다리가[집이] 홍수에 ～되었다 A bridge[house] was washed away by the flood. りゅうしつ
**유심**(有心) attention／～하다 be attentive; pay attention to／～히 attentively; carefully. ゆうしん
**유심론**(唯心論) 【철】 spiritualism; idealism／～자 a spiritualist; an idealist. ゆいしんろん
**유아**(幼兒) a baby; an infant; a little child／～사망률 the infant mortality rate. ようじ
**유아**(乳兒) a suckling; a nurs[e]ling／～각기〔脚氣〕 infantile beriberi／～식〔食〕 baby food. にゅうじ
**유아**(幼芽) a young sprout; the germ.
**유아**(遺兒) 《유복자》 a posthumous child 《고아》 an orphan 《내버린》 an abandoned child. いじ
**유아 독존**(唯我獨尊) ◎ 천상 천하 ～ I am my own Lord throughout heaven and earth., Holy am I alone, throughout heaven and earth., I am not any man's man but my own. ゆいがどくそん
**유아등**(誘蛾燈) a light trap; a luring lamp. ゆうがとう
**유아차**(乳兒車) a perambulator; a pram〈영〉; a baby-carriage[-car]〈미〉／～를 밀다 wheel[trundle] a perambulator[baby carriage]. うばぐるま

**유안**(硫安) 【화】 ammonium sulphate. りゅうあん
**유안**(留案) a pending question[problem]; pendency; suspension／～하다 leave (a *matter*) in abeyance; leave (a *question*) undecided [for future settlement].
**유암**(乳癌) 【의】 cancer of the breast; mammary cancer. にゅうがん
**유액**(乳液) ①【식】 latex; milky liquid (*in plants*) ②《화장품》 milky lotion.
**유야무야하다**(有耶無耶—) (be) noncommittal; vague; ambiguous; sloppy; indecisive／유야무야하게 되다 be dropped; be buried in oblivion; become hazy／유야무야로 덮어두다 hush up (a *matter*); suppress[smother] (a *matter*)／소문은 유야무야하게 사라졌다 The rumor blew over.／뜻하지 않은 사건으로 교섭이 유야무야하게 되어 버렸다 Owing to the unforeseen incident, the negotiations were allowed to drop. うやむやだ
**유약**(幼弱) ～하다 (be) juvenile and weak; young and fragile. ようじゃく
**유약**(柔弱) weakness; unmanliness／～하다 (be) weak; unmanly. じゅうじゃく
**유약**(釉藥) glaze; enamel／～을 칠하다 enamel; glaze.
**유어**(類語) a synonym／A와 B는 ～다 A is synonymous with B. るいご
**유어**(游魚) fish swimming in the water. ゆうぎょう
**유언**(遺言) a will; one's dying wish; one's last injunctions 《구두의》 one's last words; death-bed injunctions 《서면의》 a testament／～하다 make[leave] a will; will; express one's dying wish／～에 의해서 by (a person's) will／～을 집행하다 administer (a person's) will／～자 a testator 《여자》 a testatrix／～장 a will; a testament／～을 남기지 않고 죽다 die intestate. ゆいごん
**유언**(流言) a groundless rumour; a false report; a *canard*(F)／～비어〔蜚語〕 a groundless[wild] rumour／～비어를 퍼뜨리다 spread [a sensational] rumor／여러 가지 ～비어가 퍼지고 있다 All sorts of rumors are in the air[noised abroad]. りゅうげん
**유업**(遺業) work left by someone; an unfinished work／부친의 ～을 계승하다 carry on the work left unfinished by one's father. いぎょう
**유역**(流域) a drainage-basin; a catchment-basin; a valley 《큰강의》 a river valley／양자강 ～ the Yangtze valley／미시시피강 ～ the Mississippi valley. りゅういき
**유연**(悠然) repose; composure. ゆうぜん
**유연**(柔軟) softness／～하다 (be) soft; pliant; supple; elastic; flexible／～체조 callisthenics／～성 softness; suppleness; pliability. じゅうなん
**유연**(油煙) lamp soot; lampblack; carbon black. ゆえん

유연(油然) 등~히 freely; abundantly/~히 솟아오르다 well up. ゆうぜん
유연탄(有煙炭) bituminous coal; soft coal. ゆうえんたん
유영(游泳) swimming/~하다 swim/~기관(器官) 《동》 the flipper/~술 the art of swimming/~장 a swimming pool.
유예(猶豫) 《지연》 delay 《연기》 an extension of time 《지불 따위의》 grace 《주저》 hesitation 《형의》 a respite; a reprieve/~하다 put off; postpone; allow[grant] delay[grace]; give (a day's) grace; hesitate/~없이 without (a moment's) delay; without hesitation/지불 ~ indulgence; a grace of payment. ゆうよ
유요(有要) ~하다 (be) necessary; needed. ゆうよう
유용(流用) diversion/~하다 divert; appropriate/그들은 가끔 공금을 ~했다 They often made use of[misappropriated] government funds. りゅうよう
유용(有用) ~하다 (be) useful; valuable; serviceable; good (for a thing); be of use/~한 사람[물건] a useful man[thing]/국가에 ~한 인물 a man useful to the state; a man of service to the country/돈을 ~하게 쓰다 make the best use of one's money. ゆうよう
유우(乳牛) a milk[milking] cow 《총칭》 dairy cattle. にゅうぎゅう
유원(悠遠) remoteness 《영집》 eternity/~하다 (be) remote; eternal. ゆうえん
유원지(遊園地) a public pleasure[recreation]-ground; an amusement park〈미〉. ゆうえんち
유월(六月) June(略: Jun.). ろくがつ
유월절(踰越節) the Passover.
ユダヤじんのしゅくじつのひとつ
유위(有爲) ~하다 (be) able; capable; efficient 《유망하다》 promising/~지사 a man of ability[great promise]. 
유유낙낙하다(唯唯諾諾—) do quite willingly[readily, submissively, meekly]; work at (a person's) beck and call.
ただいはいする
유유 상종(類類相從) "Birds of a feather flock together"/~하다 Birds of a feather flock together.
유유아(乳幼兒) babies and infants.
유유 자적(悠悠自適) living in easy[comfortable] retirement; living free from worldy cares.
유유하다(悠悠—) ①《한가하다》 (be) leisurely; slow; deliberate 《침착하다》 quiet; calm; self-composed/유유히 quietly; calmly; in a leisurely way; deliberately/담배를 유유히 피우다 smoke serenely[at ease]/우리는 적을 앞에 두고 유유히 식사를 했다 We sat down composedly to a hearty meal in the face of the enemy. ②《아득하다》 (be) boundless; vast; eternal/유유한 천지 the immense universe. ゆっくりする

유음(溜飮) water pyrosis; sour stomach.
유의(留意) attention; heed; regard/~하다 heed; regard; mind; take heed[account] of/~해야 할 noteworthy; notable/~해서 듣다 hear attentively[with attention, with care]/~하지 않다 give no heed to; pay no attention[regard] to/타인의 이익에 ~하지 않다 take no notice of other's interests/~ 사항 matters to be attended to. りゅうい
유의(有意) ~하다 《의식하다》 conscious 《자원하다》 be voluntary 《의사》 be intentional/~ 행위 a voluntary action. ゆうい
유의범(有意犯) 《범죄》 a deliberate offence 《사람》 a deliberate[an itentional] offender. ゆういはん
유의의(有意義) significance; meaningfulness/~하다 (be) significant/~한 생활을 하다 lead a useful life; live to some purpose. ゆういぎ
유익(有益) ~하다 (be) profitable; lucrative 《교훈이 되다》 (be) instructive; edifying; salutary 《유용하다》 (be) useful; serviceable/~하게 usefully; to good advantage; serviceably/~한 교훈 an instructive[edifying] discourse[lesson]/~한 경험 a useful experience/~한 충고 wholesome advice. ゆうえき
유익(遊弋) ①《군함이》 cruise; range ②《사냥》 game hunting/~하다 cruise; range; sail; go hunting/황해를 ~하다 cruise in the Yellow sea.
유인(幽人) a hermit; a recluse. ゆうじん
유인(誘引) temptation; allurement; enticement; seduction/~하다 allure; tempt; entice; seduce/나쁜 짓을 하도록 ~하다 tempt (a person) into evil doing; lead (a person) astray/~해 내다 lure (a person) out. ゆういん
유인(誘因) an occasion; a cause; a motive; an inducement; a proximate[contributing] cause/전쟁의 ~ the cause of war/~이 되다 be the cause of; occasion; cause; lead (up) to; induce.
ゆういん
유인물(油印物) printed matter. すりもの
유인성(柔靭性) flexibility; elasticity/~이 있다 be flexible; be elastic.
じゅうじんせい
유인원(類人猿) 《동》 an anthropoid.
るいじんえん
유일(唯一) ~의 the only; the sole; the one; solitary; unique/~하다 (be) unique; single/~ 무이한 the one and only; unique; peerless/~한 벗 one's only [sole] friend; the one and only friend one has/~의 방책 the only measure left; one's only resource/~신교 monotheism. ゆいいち
유임(留任) remaining in office/~하다 remain in office/~을 권고하다 advise (a person) to stay in office/~하시기를 바랍니다 I hope you will stay. りゅうにん
유입(流入) inflow; influx; incoming/~

하다 flow in; stream in／외자(外資)의 ～ an inflow[influx] of foreign capital. りゅうにゅう

유자(柚子) 【식】 a citron. ゆず
유자(遊資) 【경】 idle capital[funds]; floating money[funds]. ゆうし
유자(儒者) a Confucian scholar; a Confucianist. じゅせい
유자(孺者) 《소아》 a child 《소년》 a lad; a youngster 《풋나기》 a stripling; a greenhorn. としのおさないおとこ
유자격자(有資格者) a properly-qualified person; an eligible 《총칭》 the qualified／교원 ～ a licensed teacher.
유자생녀(有子生女) ～하다 bring forth many sons and daughters.
유작(遺作) one's posthumous works.
유작자(有爵者) a peer 《집합적》 the peerage.
유장(乳漿) whey; plasma.
유장(悠長) ～하다 (be) long; lengthy.
유저(遺著) a posthumous work; books that one has left behind. いちょ
유적(遺跡) ruins; remains; relics／고대 문명의 ～ the remains[relics] of ancient civilization／역사상의 ～ a place of historic interest; a historic site[relic]／～을 방문하다 visit a place of historic interest. いせき
유적(幽寂) solitude; quiet／～하다 (be) sequestered.
유전(遺傳) heredity; inheritance; hereditary transmission／～하다 be inherited; be hereditary; run in the blood[family]; be transmitted (from parents)／～성의 hereditary; of hereditary nature; transmissible／～에 의한 범죄자 a criminal from heredity／병을 자손에게 ～하다 transmit a disease to one's children／저 집안은 정신병이 ～한다 There is hereditary insanity in the family.／어떤 버릇은 ～한다 Some habits are inherited.／～론 hereditism／～법 the law of heredity／～병 a hereditary disease; a constitutional disease／～학 the study of heredity; genetics. いでん
유전(誘電) induced electricity／～체 a dielectric.
유전(油田) an oil-field; oil land. ゆでん
유전(流傳) 《퍼짐》 spread; propagation; circulation／～하다 spread; propagate; circulate. りゅうでん
유전(流轉) 《유랑》 vagrancy; wandering 《변전》 vicissitude; impermanency 《윤회》 transmigration／～하다 wander about; rove; roam 《영혼이》 transmigrate／만물은 ～한다 All things are set in motion and flow., Impermanency is the nature of things. るてん
유전기(流電氣) 【전】 galvanic[voltaic] electricity.
유전물(油煎物) fried food.
유전지(流電池) a voltaic[galvanic] battery.

유절(有節) Q～음 an articulate sound／～어(語) an articulate speech.
유정(遺精) 【의】 involuntary emission of semen; nocturnal pollution; wet dreams《속》. いせい
유정(有情) sentience; warm-[tender-]heartedness; sympathetic[compassionate] feelings humaneness／～하다 be sentient; warmhearted; humane／천지 ～ There is feeling in everything in the universe. ゆうじょう
유정(油井) an oil-well.
유제(制) hereditary system[institution]. いせい
유제(類題) similar questions. るいだい
유제(乳劑) 【약】 an emulsion. にゅうざい
유제(幼帝) a young emperor; a boy king.
유제류(有蹄類) 【동】 Ungulata(학명).
유제품(乳製品) dairy products; a milk product.
유조(有助) ～하다 (be) helpful; useful; beneficial. たすけがあること
유조(油槽) an oil tank／～선 a tanker／～차 a tank-car. ゆそう
유조(遺詔) the king's dying wish; the king's last injunction. いしょう
유족(遺族) a surviving[bereaved] family; the survivors／전사자의 ～ the war bereaved／～ 부조 a survivor's pension ／～부조 aid to a surviving family／～ 부조금 an allowance to a bereaved family; survivor's benefits. いぞく
유족하다(裕足—) (be) sufficient; abundant／유족하게 살다 be well off; live in affluence[opulence]; live[be] in easy circumstances.
유종(乳腫) 【의】 mastitis; a breast tumo[u]r[abscess].
유종(有終) having an end; perfection／～의 미 crowning glory; consummation (of wisdom and virtue); perfection／～의 미를 거두다 bring (a thing) to a successful conclusion; crown (a thing) with perfection. ゆうしゅう
유죄(有罪) guiltiness; culpability 《유죄의 선고》 conviction／～의 guilty; culpable／～하다 be found guilty; (be) culpable／～을 선고하다 convict (a person) of crime; give (a person) the verdict of guilty／～라고 인정할 만한 증거가 있다 There is an evidence to convict him.／～인 a guilty person／～ 판결 conviction ／～ 판결을 받다 be convicted; be found guilty／～ 혐의자 a suspected criminal. ゆうざい
유죄(流罪) exile; transportation. るざい
유주(幼主) ①《임금》 a young emperor [king] ②《주인》 a young master[lord]. ようしゅ
유즙(乳汁) milk. にゅうじゅう
유증(類症) similar diseases[cases].
유증(遺贈) 《동산의》 bequest 《부동산의》 devise／～하다 leave (a thing) by will 《동산》 bequeath 《부동산》 devise／～물 a be-

quest; a legacy/~자 a legator; a devisor/그는 조카에게 재산을 ~했다 He left his nephew a fortune by will. いぞう

**유지**(油紙) oil[oiled] paper. ゆし

**유지**(油脂) oils and fats/~ 공업 the oil and fat [manufacturing] industry. ゆし

**유지**(遺志) one's dying wishes[will]; the intention of a deceased person/아버지의 ~를 받들어 in pursuance of[in obedience to] one's father's will/~에 의하여 according to the deceased's will/~를 따르다 follow up the intention of the deceased. いし

**유지**(遺址) an old site; remains; ruins; relics. いし

**유지**(維持) maintenance; preservation; upkeep 《지지》 support/~하다 maintain; hold; keep [up];《지지하다》 support/~비 maintenance expenses/~책 a measure for maintenance/~금 a maintenance fund/건강을 ~하다 maintain one's health/지위를 ~하다 maintain one's position/사회 질서를 ~하다 preserve the order of society/평화를 ~하다 maintain[keep] peace. いじ

**유지**(有志) interest 《사람》 an interested person[party]; a volunteer; a supporter; a sympathizer/~의 voluntary; interested/~하다 (be) voluntary; interested; sympathetic; intend; aim at/~들에 의해서 기금이 마련되었다 Funds have been collected by people interested./~일동 all the persons concerned/지방 ~ those who work for the good of the local community. ゆうし

**유직**(有職) having a job; being employed/~자 the employed.

**유질**(流質) 〖법〗 a forfeited[an unredeemed] pledge/~하다 forfeit a pawn/~ 공개 처분 a foreclosure sale. りゅうしち

**유착**(癒着) 〖의〗 adhesion; union; conglutination; healing-up/~하다 heal up; adhere; knit/상처가 완전히 ~되었다 The wound has completely healed[closed] up./늑막 ~ 〖의〗 pleural adhesion./~ 불능 《골절의》 nonunion. ゆちゃく

**유착하다** (크다) (be) very big; huge; colossal.

**유찬**(類纂) a classified collection in book form/법규 ~ a classified compilation of laws. りゅうけいにすること

**유창하다**(流暢—) (be) fluent; flowing; facile; smooth/유창하게 fluently; with fluency; smoothly/유창한 문장 a flowing[an easy] style/그는 말이 ~ He is a fluent[ready] speaker./그의 영어가 유창한 데 놀랐다 I was surprised at the fluency with which he spoke English. りゅうちょうだ

**유체**(流體) 〖물〗 fluid/~ 역학 hydrodynamics. りゅうたい

**유체**(有體) ~의 material; corporeal; tangible/~물 〖법〗 materiality; corporeal things/~ 자산 tangible assets.

**유체스럽다** (be) uncommon; unusual; out of the common; be affected. げんこうがつねでない

**유촉**(遺囑) entrusting (a person) with everything after one's death; leaving last instructions[requests]/~하다 entrust with everything after one's death; leave a last request. いしょく

**유추**(類推) analogy; analogism; analogical influence/~하다 analogize; reason by analogy; infer/~적 analogic[al]/일부로써 전체를 ~하다 analogize the whole out of a part/~법 analogy/~해석 analogical construction. るいすい

**유출**(流出) effluence; outflow/~하다 flow[run] out; issue; discharge/금의 ~ an outflow[a drain] of gold/정화의 ~ the outflow of specie/~구 an outlet/~물 effluence/금이 ~되다 Gold flows out of the country. りゅうしゅつ

**유충**(幼蟲) a larva (pl. -vae)/~의 larval/~기(期) the larval stage. ようちゅう

**유취**(類聚) assortment 《배열의》 arrangement 《배합》 combination/~하다 group in classes; assort; classify. るいじゅう

**유층**(油層) a pool of oil; an oil stratum.

**유치**(誘致) inducement 《꾀어내기》 luring/~하다 induce; bring about; lure/외자를 ~하다 attract foreign capital/외국인 관광객의 ~책을 강구하다 try to attract foreign tourists. ゆうち

**유치**(幼稚) ~하다 (be) childish; puerile 《미숙하다》 crude; raw; immature; primitive/~한 생각 a childish[crude, an infantile] idea/지능이 ~하다 be young in wisdom. ようち

**유치**(乳齒) a milk tooth; the first set of teeth; one's baby teeth. にゅうし

**유치**(留置) 《억류》 detention; custody; lockup/~하다 detain; keep (a person) in custody; hold; lock up; remand/~ 당하다 be detained; be locked up/~장 a house of detention; a detention cell/경찰서에 ~하다 take (a person) into custody of the police; detain (a person) at a police station. りゅうち

**유치원**(幼稚園) a kindergarten/~ 선생 〖보모〗 a kindergarten teacher; a kindergartener. ようちえん

**유쾌**(愉快) pleasure; delight; enjoyment; merriment; mirth/~하다 (be) pleasant; merry; delightful; joyful; jovial; gay/~하게 pleasantly; delightfully; happily/~한 여행 a pleasant trip/~한 기질 a pleasant[cheerful] disposition/~한 이야기 an exhilarating story/~히 지내다 live happily/~하게 하루를 보내다 pass the day pleasantly; have a very enjoy·able day. ゆかい

**유탄**(榴彈) a shell/~포 〖군〗 a howitzer. りゅうだん

**유탄**(流彈) a stray bullet[shot]; a random shot/~에 맞다 be struck by a stray bullet. りゅうだん

**유탈**(遺脫) omission [of type]. いだつ

**유탕**(遊蕩) dissipation; profligacy; riotous living/~하다 (be) dissipated; dissolute; profligate; riotous/~으로 재산을 탕진하다 run through one's fortune in riotous living/~문학 pornographic literature/~아 a rake; a dissipated person. ゆうとう

**유통**(流通) 《금전의》 circulation 《어음의》 negotiation/~하다 circulate; pass current/~화폐의 the circulation of money/공기의 ~ the ventilation of air/신화폐를 ~시키다 put new coins in[into] circulation/공기의 ~이 좋다 be well ventilated/이 방은 공기의 ~이 나쁘다 This room is poorly ventilated./~고《화폐의》 the amount of current money/~성《어음의》 negotiability/~어음 a negotiable bill/~자본 a circulating [floating] capital/~증권 a negotiable security[instrument]. りゅうつう

**유파**(流派) a school; a sect. りゅうは

**유폐**(幽閉) confinement; imprisonment/~하다 confine; shut up; imprison/~되어 있다 be in confinement. ゆうへい

**유폐**(流弊) a deep-rooted evil[abuse].

**유포**(油布) wax[oil] cloth. あぶらをひいたぬの

**유포**(流布) circulation; spread/~하다 circulate; run current; be [put] in circulation; spread; get about/~되고 있다 be in circulation; be current; be prevalent/풍설을 ~하다 set a rumor afloat/소문이 ~되고 있다 There is a rumor abroad. るふ

**유포**(遊匍) 《체》 a short grounder.

**유표**(有表) ~하다 (be) marked; striking; remarkable; conspicuous. とくにあらわれること

**유품**(遺品) an article left by the departed. いひん

**유풍**(遺風) a tradition; an old custom; a relic; a survival/조상의 ~ a custom handed down by one's forefathers/봉건시대의 ~ a relic of feudalism/그의 ~을 따르는 사람이 많다 Quite a few people follow in his footsteps./거기에는 봉건 시대의 ~이 아직도 남아 있다 Some customs of the feudal age still survive there. いふう

**유피**(鞣皮, 柔皮) dressed skin; tanned leather; buff/~법 [the art of] tanning; tawing. なめしかわ

**유하다**(柔一) ①《물건이》 (be) soft; flexible ②《성격이》 (be) mild; gentle; not hot-tempered. やわらかい

**유하다**(留一) stop; stay (at, in). とどまる

**유학**(留學) studying abroad/~하다 study abroad; go abroad to study/국비로 ~하다 study abroad at government expense/~을 마치고 귀국하다 return home from studying abroad/~생 a student studying abroad/~가다 go abroad for study りゅうがく

**유학**(遊學) study; prosecution of one's study/~하다 prosecute one's studies [study] away from home/해외에 ~하다 go abroad for study. ゆうがく

**유학**(儒學) Confucianism/~자 a Confucianist. じゅがく

**유한**(有限) limitedness; finiteness/~하다 (be) limited; finite/~급수 a finite series/~법화 limited legal tender/~소수 a finite decimal/~직선 a finite straight line/~책임 limited liability/~회사 a limited company. ゆうげん

**유한**(有閑) leisure; spare time/~하다 (be) leisurely; leisured/나는 ~마담 노릇 할 만한 여유가 없다 I cannot afford to be a woman of leisure./~계급 the leisure[d] class/~부인 a leisured[an idle rich] woman; a woman of leisure. ゆうかん

**유한**(流汗) sweat; perspiration. りゅうかん

**유한**(遺恨) grudge; rancour; enmity/~을 품다 owe (a person) a grudge; have a spite[grudge] against (a person)/~을 갚다 pay off one's old scores; get even with (a person)/그에게 아무런 ~도 없다 I bear him no grudge. いこん

**유해**(遺骸) remains; a corpse; a [dead] body 《유골》 ashes. いこつ

**유해**(有害) noxiousness; harmfulness; hurtfulness/~하다 (be) injurious; harmful; noxious; bad; malignant; baleful/건강에 ~하다 be injurious to one's health; be bad for health/풍기상 ~하다 be prejudicial[destructive] to public morals/사회에 ~하다 be detrimental to society/~ 무익하다 be more injurious than beneficial; do more harm than good/~물 a hazardous article; a harmful object. ゆうがい

**유행**(流行) fashion; vogue 《병의》 prevalence/~의 fashionable; prevailing; popular; epidemic/~하다 be in fashion [vogue]; be fashion[able]; be widely liked/최신 ~ the latest fashion; the latest fad[rage]/일시적인 ~ a [mere] passing vogue/ ~을 따르다 follow the fashion/~에 뒤지지 않도록 하다 keep up with the fashion; keep pace with the current style/~의 첨단을 걷다 lead [set] the fashion/~은 반복한다 Fashion repeats itself./독감이 전국에 ~하고 있다 Influenza is prevailing throughout the country/~어 a word in fashion; a popular saying/재건이라는 말이 ~어가 되어 있다 Reconstruction is the word on everybody's lips./~작가 a popular writer. りゅうこう

**유행**(遊行) ①《사람의》 a tour; wandering/~하다 make a tour; wander ②《천체의》 movement; revolution/~하다 move; revolve; travel. かくちをあそびまわること

**유행가**(流行歌) a popular song/~ 가수 a popular song singer; a vocalist; a cro-

**유행병**(流行病) an epidemic; a pestilence /~이 발생하다 an epidemic rages[breaks out]. りゅうこうびょう

**유행성 감기**(流行性感氣) influenza; flu《속》/~에 걸리다 be seized with influenza; have an attack of influenza/~가 퍼지고 있다 There is an epidemic of influenza.

**유행지**(流行地) an infected district[locality]/호열자의 ~ a cholera infected district.

**유향**(乳香) frankincense.

**유현**(幽玄) mystery; profundity/~하다 (be) profound; occult; abstruse; recondite. ゆうげん

**유현**(儒賢) the sages of Confucianism.

**유혈**(流血) bloodshed; shedding of blood /~의 참사 [an affair of] bloodshed; a sanguinary accident/~로 끝나다 result in bloodshed. りゅうけつ

**유협**(遊俠) a chivalrous man. ゆうきょう

**유형**(有形) materiality/~의 material; corporeal; tangible/~하다 (be) concrete; material; corporeal; tangible/~무역 visible trade/~ 문화재 tangible cultural properties/~물 a material[concrete] object/~ 자본 a corporeal capital/~ 재산 corporeal property/~체 a material body. ゆうけい

**유형**(流刑) transportation; banishment; exile/~에 처하다 condemn (*a person*) to exile; banish; transport/~수 a transported criminal/~지 a penal colony [settlement]; a place of exile. りゅうけい

**유형**(類型) a [similar] type/~적 typical /~학 《신》typology. るいけい

**유형 무형**(有形無形) material[ity] and immaterial[ity_]; visibility and invisibility/~으로 그 사람의 도움을 받았다 I received material and moral support from him., I was supported by him both materially and spiritually.
ゆうけいむけい

**유혹**(誘惑) temptation; allurement; enticement; seduction/~하다 tempt; entice; lure; seduce/도시의 ~ the allurements[temptations] of a big city/~을 견디다 resist[withstand] temptation /바다의 ~ the lure[call] of the sea/~을 이겨내다 overcome[get the better of] a temptation/~과 싸우다 wrestle with a temptation; fight[struggle] against a temptation/~에 빠지기 쉽다 be easily led astray; be easily overcome by temptation/~물 a decoy/~자 a tempter; an enticer. ゆうわく

**유화**(油畫) an oil painting; a painting in oil/~가 an oil painter. あぶらえ

**유화**(柔和) gentleness; tenderness; mildness; meekness/~하다 (be) gentle; mild; meek; tender; bland/눈매가 ~한 사람 a meek-eyed person/사람들은 그녀의 ~한 태도가 마음에 들었다 Her suavity of manner pleased all around her. にゅうわ

**유화**(宥和) appeasement/~하다 appease; pacify/~ 정책 a policy of appeasement /~론자 an appeaser/~ 정책은 패배를 뜻한다 Appeasement signifies subjection. ゆうわ

**유화**(類化) assimilation; 《생》 anabolism /~하다 assimilate. るいか

**유화**(乳化) emulsification/~하다 emulsify.

**유화**(硫化) 《화》sulphuration/~하다 sulphurate; sulphurize/~물 a sulfide/~ 암모늄[은, 수소, 철] ammonium[silver, hydrogen, iron] sulfide/~ 작용 sulphurization.

**유화 식물**(有花植物) flowering plants; *Phanerogamia*(학명). はながあるしょくぶつ

**유환류**(有環類) 《동》*Annulata*(학명).

**유황**(硫黃) sulphur; sulfur;《화》S. /~의 sulphur[e]ous. いおう

**유황화**(硫黃華) sublimed sulphur; flowers of sulphur; hot-spring incrustations.

**유회**(流會) adjournment of meeting/~가 되다 be adjourned; prove abortive/참석자가 적어서 ~되었다 The meeting was adjourned owing to scanty attendance.
りゅうかい

**유효**(有效) 《법규 따위》validity; effectiveness 《표 따위》availability 《약(藥)》efficiency/~하다 (be) valid; effective; available; efficacious; good/시간을 ~하게 쓰다 use *one's* time effectively; make good use of *one's* time; put *one's* time to good use/이 기차표는 한 달 동안 ~하다 This train ticket is good [available] a months. /~ 기간 the term of validity; the available period/~ 수요 an effective demand/~ 증명 a certificate of validity; a testimonial/~ 투표 a valid ballot. ゆうこう

**유훈**(遺訓) *one's* last injunctions; teachings of the departed; dying injunctions /조상의 ~을 받들다 follow the testament left by *one's* ancestors. いくん

**유훈자**(有勳者) holders of decorations.

**유휴**(遊休) ~의 idle; unused; unemployed; out of operation/~ 물자를 활용하다 desterilize/~ 생산력 idle production capacity/~ 자본 idle capital[funds] /~ 자재 idle materials; materials lying unused[idle]. ゆうきゅう

**유흥**(遊興) pleasure; merrymaking; a spree; junketing 《오락》amusements; /~하다 make merry; disport *one*self; be on the spree/~에 빠지다 indulge in pleasures/~비 entertainment costs; the expense of pleasure/~세 the entertainment tax/~ 음식세 the tax on amusement, food and drink/~장 an amusement quarter. ゆうきょう

**유희**(遊戲) 《어린이의》play 《오락》a pastime 《시합》a game 《경기》a sport /~

하다 play a game; [be at] play／～ 본능 a sportive instinct; the play instinct／～장 a playground. ゆうぎ

**육**(六) six《제 6》the sixth／～분의 1 one -sixths; a sixth part／～분의 3 three -sixths. ろく

**육**(肉) the flesh／～과 영(靈) flesh and spirit. にく

**육각**(六角) a hexagon; a sexangle／～의 hexagonal; sexangular／～형 hexagon; sexangle.

**육감**(六感) the six sense／제 ～을 쓰다 exercise one's sixth sense; give free play to one's sixth sense. ろっかん

**육감**(肉感) carnal desire; sexual feeling; sensuality; lust／～적인 sensual[sex-appealing, voluptuous]／～적인 미인 a voluptuous beauty／이 그림은 ～적이다 The picture appeals to sensuality.／～주의 sensualism. にっかん

**육개장**(肉—) broth seasoned with various relishes.

**육계**(肉桂) 【식】 cinnamon《계피(桂皮)》cassia bark. にっけい

**육괴**(肉塊) a lump of flesh[meat];《살찐 사람》a plump fellow; a corpulent person. にっかい

**육교**(肉交) carnal relations; sexual intercourse／～하다 have carnal relations [sexual intercourse]. だんじょかんのせいこう

**육교**(陸橋) a viaduct; a railway[land] bridge. りっきょう

**육군**(陸軍) the army; the military service／～의 military; army／～에 입대하다 join[enter, go into] the army; be drafted into the army／～에서 제대하다 leave[be discharged from] the army／～ 대학 a Military Staff College／～ 병력 land power／～ 병원 a military[an army] hospital／～ 비행대 the Army Flying[Aviation] Corps. りくぐん

**육담**(肉談) vulgarism; vulgar language; vulgar talk. ひぞくなことば

**육대주**(六大洲) the Six Continents. ろくだいしゅう

**육도**(陸稻) 《밭벼》 upland rice; the upland rice plant.

**육력**(戮力) cooperation 협력. りくりょく

**육로**(陸路) a land[an overland] route／～로 by land; overland; by an overland route／～ 여행 a land[an overland] journey. りくろ

**육류**(肉類) flesh; meat. にくるい

**육륜**(肉輪) the two [upper and lower] eyelids. まぶた

**육면체**(六面體) a hexahedron／～ 의 hexahedral／정 ～ a regular hexahedron; a cube. ろくめんたい

**육모**(六—) a hexagon; a sexangle／～의 hexagonal／～정(亭) a hexagonal arbour／～ 방망이 a hexagonal club.

**육미**(六味) the six flavours. りくみ

**육미**(肉味) animal food; flesh food; meat meals／～를 먹지 않다 abstain from flesh meals[foods]. にくみ

**육박**(肉迫) ～하다 《전쟁에서》 press (the enemy) hard; close with (the enemy); come to close quarters 《경기에서》 tread close one's heels／적진에 ～하다 carry the fighting to the enemy's camp／우리 보병이 적군에 ～ 해 갔다 Our infantry closed in upon the enemy.／～전 a hand-to -hand fight; a close contest[game]; a close battle. にくはく

**육발이**(六—) a person of six toes; a six -toed person 《추럭의》 a six wheeler. あしのゆびがろっぽんあるひと

**육배**(六倍) six times; sextuple／～의 sextuple; sixfold; six times as large[big, many, much] as／～하다 sextuple; multiply by six.

**육백육호**(六百六號) 《약》 the "606" remedy; salvarsan.

**육법**(六法) the six codes of laws／～ 전서 a Compendium of Laws; the Statute Books; a complete book of the six major laws. ろっぽう

**육보**(肉補) nourishing one's body by eating meat／～하다 eat meat one's health.

**육봉**(肉峰) a hump.

**육부**(六腑) the six viscera[bowls]. ろっぷ

**육붕**(陸棚) 【지】 a continental shelf. りくだな

**육산**(陸産) land products; products of the soil. りくさん

**육삼삼제**(六三三制) 【교】 the six-three-three system of education; the American type school system.

**육상**(陸上) land; ground; shore／～ 경기 athletic sports; field and track events／～ 수송 land carriage[transportation]; ground[overland] transport／～ 운동회 an athletic meet[ing]; a field-and-track meet; a track meet. りくじょう

**육상**(陸相) the War[Army] Minister; the Minister of War.

**육색**(肉色) flesh colour[tint]; carnation. にくいろ

**육서**(陸棲) 【동】 living on land／～의 terrestrial; living on land; land-inhabiting／～ 동물 terrestrial animals; a land animal.

**육성**(育成) upbringing; rearing／～하다 rear; nurture; bring up; train up; nurse 《조성》 foster／～ 재배 rearing and cultivating. いくせい

**육성**(肉聲) a natural voice; a [human] voice／～과 같은 음색을 내다 produce the correct sounds of the human voice. にくせい

**육속**(陸續) continuity; continuation; succession／～하다 continue; be continuous／～하여 successively; continually; one after another; in succession; consecutively／～하여 탈당하다 leave[resign from] the party one after another. りくぞく

**육손이**(六—) a person of six fingers; a six-fingered person.

**육수**(肉水) meat stock; gravy.

**육시**(戮屍) posthumous decapitation/~하다 behead (*the dead*) posthumously.

**육식**(肉食) 《사람의》 meat-diet 《동물의》 flesh-eating/~의 《동물》 carnivorous/~하다 eat flesh[meat]; be carnivorous/~을 끊다 abstain from meat and flesh/나는 ~보다 채식을 좋아한다 I prefer a vegitable diet to animal food./~가 meat-eater/~ 동물 a carnivorous[predatory] animal; predator/~조 a predatory bird; a bird of prey.

**육신**(肉身) the body; the flesh.

**육십**(六十) sixty; threescore/~대의 사람 a sexagenarian/~ 갑자 the sexagenary cycle.

**육아**(育兒) child care; nursing; upbringing of a child/~하다 bring up; rear; raise; nurse/~법 the art of rearing infants/~실 a nursery [room]/~원 an orphanage; an orphan asylum; a foundling hospital; a baby farm.

**육아**(肉芽) 【식】 a granula/~가 생기다 granulate.

**육안**(肉眼) the naked[unaided] eye/~으로 쉽게 볼 수 있는 곳에 within easy range of one's eye/~으로 보다 see with the naked eye; examine with the unaided eye/~으로는 보이지 않다 be invisible to the naked eye.

**육양**(陸揚) 《배에서》 unloading 《뭍에》 landing/~하다 unload (*a ship*); land; discharge (*a cargo*); take ashore/그 배는 ~중이다 She is discharging her cargo./~ 수속 landing formalities/~장 a landing place/~항 a port of discharge.

**육영**(育英) education/~하다 educate; instruct/~ 사업 educational work/그는 ~ 사업에 일생을 바쳤다 He devoted his life to education./~ 자금 scholarship.

**육예**(六藝) the six accomplishments [of etiquette, music, archery, riding, writing and mathematics].

**육욕**(戮辱) ignominy; shame.

**육욕**(肉慾) carnal desire; sensual pleasure; pleasures of the flesh[senses]; the animal passions/~을 채우다 satisfy one's sensual appetites; gratify one's lusts/~에 빠지다 indulge in[be given to] sensual pleasures/~을 억제하다 restrain one's passions; be continent/~주의 sensualism; carnalism.

**육우**(肉牛) beef cattle.

**육운**(陸運) overland transportation; transportation by land; land carriage [transportation]/~국 the Land Transportation Bureau.

**육장**(肉醬) meat preserved in soy.

**육적**(肉炙) roast meat; a roast; a steak.

**육전**(陸戰) land-fighting; warfare by land/~하다 fight on land/~대 landing forces; the marines/~ 법규 the Articles of War.

**육정**(肉情) carnal desire ⇒육욕(肉慾).

**육정**(六情) the six feelings[emotions] [of joy, anger, sorrow, pleasure, love and hatred].

**육종**(肉腫) 【의】 a sarcoma(*pl*. -mata).

**육종**(育種) breeding (of *animals*); rearing/~하다 breed; rear.

**육중**(肉重) heaviness/~하다 heavilybuilt; heavy; weighty; ponderous 《말이》 (be) exaggerated; excessive/~하게 걷다 walk heavily.

**육즙**(肉汁) meat juice; gravy; broth.

**육지**(陸地) land 《배에서 본》 the shore/~의 동물 a land animal/~가 보이다 come in sight of land/~에 오르다 go ashore/~로 둘러싸이다 be landlocked.

**육찬**(肉饌) a meat dish/~으로 밥을 먹다 eat boiled rice with meat as an accompanying dish.

**육척**(六尺) six feet/~ 남자 a six footer.

**육체**(肉滯) indigestion caused by eating meat.

**육체**(肉體) the flesh; the body/~의 bodily; fleshly; physical; sensual; carnal; corporeal/~적 고통 physical suffering/~ 노동 physical labor/~ 문학 sensual literature.

**육초** a candle [made] of suet.

**육촌**(六寸) ①《치수》 six inches ②《친척》 a second cousin.

**육축**(六畜) the six domestic animals.

**육친**(六親) the six blood relations.

**육친**(肉親) a blood relation; one's flesh and blood; one's immediate relative/~의 of one blood; real.

**육탄**(肉彈) a human bullet; a human bomb/~전 a hand-to-hand struggle [fight].

**육탕**(肉湯) meat soup.

**육태**(陸駄) a cargo/~ 인부 a stevedore.

**육태질**(陸駄—) landing/~하다 land ⇒육양(陸揚).

**육통터지다**(六通—) fail on the brink of success; collapse on the point of completion.

**육포**(肉脯) dried slices of beef; jerked beef; jerk/~를 뜨다 jerk.

**육표**(陸標) a landmark.

**육풍**(陸風) a land breeze; a land wind.

**육필**(肉筆) an autograph; a handwriting

/~의 handwritten/~의 편지 a handwritten letter; a letter in *one's* own handwriting. にくひつ

**육합**(六合) 《우주》the universe; the cosmos. りくごう

**육해공군**(陸海空軍) a land, air and sea forces; army, navy, and air force; armed forces/~ 합동 작전 a joint operation of the army, navy and air forces. りくかいくうぐん

**육행**(陸行) travelling by land/~하다 travel by land[overland]. りくろでいくこと

**육혈포**(六穴砲) a pistol; a six-chambered revolver; a six-shooter. ピストル

**육혹**(肉—) a sarcoma; a flesh lump. にくのかたまりのこぶ

**육화**(六花) snow; flakes of snow. ろっか

**육회**(肉膾) slices of raw meat; sliced[minced] raw meat; a dish of raw beef. にくのなます

**육후하다**(肉厚—) (be) fat; fleshy; corpulent; plump. にくがあつい

**윤**(潤) 《광택》gloss; lustre; brightness; brilliance; polish. じゅん

**윤**(閏) embolism; intercalation/~의 leap; intercalary/~년[달] a leap year [month].

**윤가**(允可) permission; sanction; authorization/~하다 permit; approve/~를 얻다 obtain permission. おうのきょか

**윤간**(輪姦) a gang[group] rape/~하다 attack[violate, rape] a woman in turn[by turns]. りんかん

**윤감**(輪感) influenza; flu[e]; *grippe*(F).

**윤강**(輪講) reading and explaining (*a book*) in turn; construing the contents (of *a book*) by turns /~하다 read (*a book*) in turn.

**윤곽**(輪廓) 《개관》an outline 《외형선》a contour; a skeleton 《그림 따위의》a rough sketch/~ 지도 an outline map/얼굴의 ~ the contour of *one's* face/~을 잡다 《비유적》get (*a matter*) into shape/ ~이 잡히다 take shape[form]; be in shape. りんかく

**윤기**(倫紀) morals and discipline; ethics and public order. りんりのきこう

**윤기**(潤氣) shine; luster. じゅん

**윤나다**(潤—) become glossy; become lustrous; grow bright; be shiny; be polished; be sleek. こうたくがでる

**윤납**(輪納) payment by rotation/~하다 pay by turns; take turns paying. りんばんにおさめること

**윤내다**(潤—) gloss; glaze; bring out the lustre; brighten; put a polish on; make (*it*) glossy; give a shine (*to*). つやをだす

**윤년**(閏年) a leap[an intercalary] year. うるうどし

**윤달**(閏—) a leap[an intercalary] month. うるうづき

**윤독**(輪讀) reading in turn; reading by rotation/~하다 read by turns; take turns reading. りんどく

**윤똑똑이** a smart guy; a shrewd fellow.

**윤락**(淪落) ruin; fall/~하다 be ruined; go to ruin/ ~ 여선 a ruined[fallen, lost] woman; a woman of the underworld. りんらく

**윤리**(倫理) ethics; morals; a code of conduct[ethical practice]/~적 ethical; moral/~적 행위 a moral act/~적 종교 an ethical religion.

**윤리학**(倫理學) ethics; moral philosophy [science]/~자 an ethicist; a moralist /동양 ~ Oriental ethics/실천 ~ practical ethics. りんりがく

**윤몰**(淪沒) sinking; submersion; foundering/~하다 sink; submerge 《죄에 빠짐》 sink into vice りんぼつ

**윤무**(輪舞) a round dance; a circling dance/~곡 a rondo. りんぶ

**윤번**(輪番) turn; rotation/~하다 take turns; alternate/~으로 by turns; in turn; by rotation; alternately /~으로 의장이 되다 rotate the chairmanship of the conference/~제 a rotation system. りんばん

**윤삭**(閏朔) an intercalary month 《윤달 (閏—)》. うるうづき

**윤상**(輪狀) ~의 annular; ring-shaped.

**윤색**(潤色) flourish (꾸밈) embellishment; colouring/~하다 embellish (*one's story*); colour; adorn; give colour (*to*) /~한 문장 an ornate style of writing. こうたく

**윤생**(輪生) 《식》verticillation/~의 verticillate; verticillated/~엽 verticillate leaves. りんせい

**윤월**(閏月) a leap month 《윤달》. うるうづき

**윤음**(綸音) the Emperor's word; an Imperial message[mandate]. おうのことば

**윤일**(閏日) a leap[an intercalary] day.

**윤작**(輪作) crop rotation; shift of crops /~하다 rotate crops/밭을 ~하다 rotate crops in *one's* fields. りんさく

**윤전**(輪轉) rotation/~하다 rotate; revolve; turn round/~기 a cylinder press; a rotary press/초고속도 ~기 a superhigh speed rotary press.

**윤지**(綸旨) the king's words; a royal message. りんし

**윤차**(輪次) *one's* turn in rotation. まわるじゅんじょ

**윤창**(輪唱) a troll; a round/~하다 troll; sing a round.

**윤척없다**(倫脊—) (be) confused; incoherent; disjoined/윤척없는 말을 하다 talk incoherently; utter an incoherent remark; contradict *oneself*.

**윤택**(潤澤) ①《광택》gloss; luster; shine ②《풍부》abundance; plenty; richness/ ~하다 be glossy; shiny; abundant; ample; plentiful/~한 자금 abundant funds/~한 지식 a great store of knowledge/생활이 ~하다 live in comfortable circumstances; be well-off. じゅんたく

윤필(潤筆) painting and writing; wielding the brush/~료 a fee for one's writing[painting]. じゅんぴつ

윤허(允許) leave; permission; sanction/~하다 (be) permitted[sanctioned] (by *the king*). おうのきょか

윤형(輪形) a circle; ring [shape]/~의 ring-shaped; cyclical/~으로 서다 stand in a ring. りんけい

윤형(輪刑) leading a prisoner about; public exposure.

윤화(輪禍) an automobile accident; a traffic accident/~를 당하다 have a traffic accident; be injured in a traffic accident.

윤환(輪奐) magnificence; grandeur (of *a building*); splendor.

윤활(潤滑) lubrication/~하다 (be) lubricious; smooth; lubricative/~유 a lubricating oil/~제 a lubricant[antifriction]/~유의 역할을 하다 serve to remore the friction (*between*). じゅんかつ

윤회(輪廻) *Samsara*(Sans); the transmigration of souls; the cycles of life/~하다 transmigrate; make a motion constantly; rotate. じゅんばんにめぐること

율(率) ①(비율) a rate; a ratio (비율) a proportion; 《물》 an index; 《수》 a constant/~을 나타내다 show the percentage[rate] of/~율 높이다[낮추다] raise [lower] the rate/~을 정하다 fix the rate; designate the percentage ②(능률) efficiency. りつ

율(律) 《법률》 a law; a regulation; a statute 《계율》 a commandments 《기율》 a discipline (운율) a rhythm; a meter/자연~ the natural law. りつ

율격(律格) ①(규칙) a rule; a statute ② 《시 형식》 rules of versification. りっかく

율동(律動) rhythm; rhythmic movement /생의 ~ the rhythm of life/~적인 미 rhythmical beauty/빠른 ~으로 연주하다 play in quick rhythm/~ 체조 rhythmical gymnastics. りつどう

율려(律呂) the Chinese system of musical sounds; melody; rhythm; music. りつりょ

율령(律令) a law; a statute; an ordinance; a mandate. りつりょう

율례(律例) an established usage[precedent] of a criminal code; the penal code; a statute; a law. はんれい

율로기 a species of snake with red and blue spots on its head.

율문(律文) 《본문》 the text (of *regulation*); 《조문》 provision; 《문》 literature written in *yul* verse. りつぶん

율시(律詩) verse/~를 짓다 versify; compose verse. りっし

율어(律語) verse.

율연(慄然) ~히 with horror/~케 하다 terrify; horrify; strike (*one*) with terror; make (*one*) shudder.

율학(律學) criminal jurisprudence.

융(絨) cotton flannel. じゅう

융기(隆起) a projection; a protuberance 《지표의》 elevation; upheaval/~하다 protrude; upheave; bulge; rise/~ 해안 an uplifted coast. りゅうき

융단(絨緞) a carpet/~을 깔다 spread a carpet; carpet (*a floor*).

융동(隆冬) a severe[cold] winter. げんとう

융로(隆老) an old person [above 70].

융모(絨毛) wool; 《해》 a villus(*pl.* -li).

융병(癃病) 《의》 senile atrophy.

융비술(隆鼻術) nasal plastic surgery 《수술》 [make] a rhinoplastic operation. りゅうびじゅつ

융성(隆盛) prosperity/~하다 (be) prosperous; flourishing; thriving/극히 ~하다 be in full flourish; be at the zenith of prosperity/그 당시 국운이 크게 ~했다 The nation was in full flourish at that time. りゅうせい

융숭(隆崇) high respect[regard, esteem, deference]; hospitality/~하다 highly respect[regard]; think highly of; pay high[deep] esteem to; entertain warmly[cordially]/~히 heartily; cordially; kindly/~히 대접하다 entertain (*a person*) cordially; give (*a person*) warm hospitality; receive (*one's visitors*) kindly. ひじょうにあがめること

융자(融資) 《자금》 funds; money 《대부》 a loan; financing/~하다 finance; furnish funds (to *a company*); accommodate (*a person*) with funds/~금 a loan/~ 알선 loan facilitation/~ 회사 a finance company/단기 ~ a short-term loan; a call loan(미). ゆうし

융점(融點) the melting point; the fusing [fusion] point; the point of fusion. ゆうてん

융통(融通) ①(유통) circulation (of *capital*); accommodation (어음의) negotiation/~하다 accommodate (*a person*) with (*money*); provide[advance] money; circulate; lend/돈을 ~해 주다 accommodate (*a person*) with a loan; advance money (to *a person*) ②《재주·성질》 adaptability; elasticity; versatility/ ~ 어음 an accommodation bill/~ 자금 a circulating[floating] capital/~ 증권 a negotiable instrument. ゆうずう

융통성(融通性) adaptability; flexibility; resourcefulness (어음 따위의) negotiability/~이 있다 be adaptable; be versatile; be resourceful/~없다 be unadaptable; be straitlaced; be rigid; be narrow-minded/~을 발휘하다 adapt oneself to circumstances/고창 관리들은 ~이 없다 Superannuated officials cannot prove of use in other walks of life. ゆうずうせい

융합(融合) 《결합》 fusion 《융화》 harmony 《일치》 unity/~하다 fuse; harmonize; be in harmony with; unite/~ 유전 bl-

**융해(融解)** fusion; melting; dissolution /~하다 fuse; melt; dissolve; liquefy /~열 the heat of fusion/~점 the melting point. ゆうかい

**융화(融化)** deliquescence/~하다 deliquesce; soften/~성의 deliquescent. ゆうか

**융화(融和)** melting; softening; soothing; propitiation; harmony; reconciliation /~하다 harmonize; reconcile; placate; soothe; soften/~를 꾀하다 try to be reconciled (*with*); take a measure to bring about reconciliation/저 사람하고는 ~하기 힘들다 Somehow I cannot hit it off with him. ゆうわ

**융흥(隆興)** revival; restoration; reestablishment; rehabilitation/~하다 revive; restore; rehabilitate. りゅうこう

**윷** four chips of wood used in *yoot*-game; the *yoot*/~놀이 playing *yoot*; a game of *yoot*/~밭 a quarter of the *yoot* board/~짝 the sticks used in playing *yoot*/~짝 가르듯 흑백을 가르다 discriminate clearly between good and bad [right and wrong]/~판 a *yoot* board; a scene of *yoot* playing.

**윷놀다** play *yoot*.

**으깨다** ①(눌러서) crush; smash; junk; squash 《감자 따위를》 mash ②(깨다) mash; soften up; beat 《뭉개다》 knead. おしつぶす

**으그러뜨리다** crush; smash; squash. おしつぶす

**으그러지다** be crushed; be squashed; be battered/으그러진 양철통 a battered tin-can. おしつぶれる

**으그르르** rumbling. ごろごろ

**-으나** ①(…하지만) do[be] but; though it is[does]/애는 많이 썼으나 보람이 없었다 I tried very hard, but all in vain. ②《모두 …간에·어쨌든》[whether …] or; or the like/좋~싫~ 해야 한다 You must do it whether you like it or not. ③《쾌 …한》 that is very[quite] …/높~ 높은 산 such a[a really] high mountain. が

**-으나마** be[do] … but anyway; however …/집은 작~ 자리가 좋다 The house may be small, but it's nicely located.

—でも·—としても

**으늑하다** ①(아늑하다) cozy ②be secluded ➪으슥하다. こぢんまりしている

**-으니** ①(…하니까) since it is; when [in the past] then; as/할 일이 없~ 산보나 할까요 Since we have nothing to do, shall we take a walk? ②(설명의 계속) and also/벼슬에 올랐으~ 그때 그의 나이 스물이었다 He was appointed to a government post at the age of twenty. —から

**-으니까** 《…하므로》since[as] it is [does]; so; and so (…한즉) when [in the past] then; as; and[but] then/그 소식을 듣~ 마음이 놓인다 Now that I hear the news, I feel better. —から. —ので

**으드득** ①(깨물 때) ๑~ 깨물다 munch; crunch ②(이를 갈 때) ๑이를 ~ 갈다 grind [gnash] *one's* teeth. ぼりぼり

**으드득거리다** ①(…이) crunch; be crunchy ②(…을) grit; grate; grind (*one's teeth*) /이를 ~ grind *one's* teeth.

**으드득으드득** ①(깨무는 모양) crunching; with a crunch ②(갈리는 모양) gritting; grating (이를) grinding *one's* teeth.

**으드등거리다** bicker; spat; fuss; snarl; growl; be at outs[odds] (with *one's wife*)/그 부부는 앙숙처럼 으드등거린다 Those two fight like cats and dogs.

**으드등으드등** bickering; fussing; at odds with each other.

**으뜸** (첫째) the first; the first place《두목》a chief; a leader《근본》the foundation; the basis/~으로 합격하다 pass on examination first on the list/학자로는 그가 ~이다 He is a first-rate scholar./건강은 행복의 ~이다 Health is the foundation of human happiness.

だいいち

**으등그러지다** get warped; warp; get twisted out of shape. かえりかえる

**으례** ①(물론) [as a matter] of course; to be sure; naturally; no doubt; undoubtedly; without question/그건 ~ 우리가 할 일이다 Needless to say, it is out duty to do so. ②(응당) justly; properly; naturally; [as a matter] of course ③(반드시) always; without fail; habitually/그 일에는 ~ 위험이 따른다 It is invariably attended by danger./그는 월말이면 ~ 돈을 꾸러 온다 He never fails to come to me for a loan at the end of every month./그들은 만나면 ~ 싸운다 They never meet without quarreling., They quarrel whenever they meet. いうまでもなく

**으로** by; with ▫~로/부산~ 가는 차 a train for *Busan*/맨 주먹~ with bare hands/통역~ as[in the capacity of] an interpreter/연못~ 빠지다 fall into a pond/폐병~ 죽다 die of consumption/헌 것을 새 것~ 바꾸다 change an old thing to a new one. —で. —へ. —に

**으로나** as[*with*, *etc.*] or the like; whether as[*with*, *etc.*].

**으로는** as for [its being] as[*with*, *etc.*] /보통~ 그렇게 안 한다 We usually don't do that. —では. —へは. —には

**으로서** as; by way of (자격) in the capacity of/…으로서는 [as] for; considering/한국 사람~는 영어를 잘 한다 be able to speak fluent English for a Korean. /그 여자는 여성~는 키가 크다 She is tall as women go. —として. —から

**으로써** ▫그의 세력 ~ with all his influence.

**으르다** (협박하다) threaten; menace; bluff 《무섭게 하다》intimidate; frighten; cow; scare/죽이겠다고 ~ threaten to kill (*one*). きょうはくする

**으르대다** 《딱딱거리다》snarl[snap] at《위

**으르렁거리다** ①《짐승이》 growl; snarl; roar/개가 낯선 사람에게 으르렁거린다 The dog snarls at a stranger. /사자가 사납게 으르렁거린다 Lions growl savagely ②《다투다》 wrangle[dispute, argue] with; quarrel; feud/그들은 언제나 으르렁거리고 있다 They are always bickering with each other. ほえる

협하다》 threaten; intimidate; bluff/그는 나에게 으르대면서 말했다 He spoke to me snappishly. おどしつける

**으르르** tremblingly; shiveringly/~ 떨다 tremble all over[like an aspen leaf]. ぶるぶる

**으름** 《식》 an akebi-seed/~나무 an akebi; *ARebia quinata*(학명). あけびのみ

**으름장** threat; menace; intimidation/~하다 intimidate; browbeat; threaten. きょうはく

**으리으리** ~하다 (be) magnificent; majestic; imposing; solemn/~하게 in a dignified manner; solemnly/~한 저택 a stately mansion/~한 성당 a magnificent cathedral. こうだいに

**-으면** if/날씨만 개었~ 좋을 텐데 If only the weather were finer!
—ならば, —れば

**-으면서** ①《동시에》 while; as; at the same time; between; during; over; with /생긋 웃~ with a smile ②《불구하고》 though; for all; in spite of/돈이 있~ for all *one's* wealth. —ながら

**으밀아밀** secretly; in secret/~ 속삭이다 talk in whispers. こそこそ

**으썩** 아~ 깨물다 crunch. かりかり

**으스러뜨리다** smash. ぶすらでだる. こわす

**으스러지다** be broken[smashed, be crushed] to pieces. こわれる

**으스름달밤** a hazy[misty] moonlit night. おぼろつきよ

**으스스** ①《추운 모양》 ~하다 (be) chilly; somewhat chill/그날은 ~ 추웠다 It was rather cold on that day. ②《무서운 모양》 ~하다 feel a thrill; thrill (*with*)/ ~해지는 이야기 a thrilling tale; a blood-curdling story. ひえびえ

**으쓱**¹ ~하다 (be) horrible; blood-curdling; chilling; hair-raising. ぞっと

**으쓱**² ~하다 perk *one*self up; lift *one's* head up; be proud; be elated/그는 장관이 되어서 어깨가 ~하였다 He was highly elated at becoming a member of the Cabinet. つんとすまして

**으쓱거리다** 《엔체하다》 be vain; be selfconceited; presume (*upon*); be puffed up; grow uppish 《어깨를》 perk up the shoulders/어깨를 으쓱거리며-걷다 strut along; swagger about.

**으슥하다** (be) retired and quiet/으슥한 뜰 a retired and quiet garden. さびしい

**으슬렁으슬렁** slowly; loiteringly/~ 걷다 walk slowly; loiter along; lag. のそりのそり

**으슬으슬** shivering/~하다 (be) chilly;

chill; be rather cold/오늘은 ~ 춥다 The weather is chilly today. ひえびえ

**으슴푸레하다** (be) dusky; gloomy; dim; dimly-lighted/달빛이 ~ The moon shines dimly. /복도에 등불이 으슴푸레하게 비치고 있었다 A light shone dimly in the passage. おぼろげである

**으아** mewl; mule. ああ, お—

**으악** ①《놀라게》 boo! ②《구토》 puke! [with a puke]. わっ

**으츠러지다** get crushed; get bruised; be squashed. こわれる

**욱물다** clench *one's* teeth; set[grind, gnash] *one's* teeth; compress *one's* lips /그는 이를 욱물고 죽어 있었다 He was found dead with his teeth firmly set [shut].

**욱박다** oppress; suppress; intimidate; scare; coerce; overawe. よくあつする

**욱박지르다** intimidate; threaten; face (*one*) down; browbeat; bull; scare; suppress /욱박지르기도 하고 달래기도 해서 what with threats, what with entreaties. おどかす

**-은** ①《형용사와 함께》 ... that[which] is; ... who is ②《동사와 함께》 ...that[who] has done/그 사람이 받~ 편지 the letter that the man received. —しいた

**은**(恩) ①《은공》 favo[u]r; merits ②《은덕》 beneficial influence; favo[u]r and indebtedness ③《은혜》 favo[u]rs; kindness; indebtedness; obligation ④《은택》 grace and benevolent influence. おん

**은**(銀) 《광》 silver 《화》 Ag. /~그릇 silverware/~같은 silvery/~입힌 silver-plated[·gilt]/~본위 the silver standard/~지금(地金) silver bullion/순~ pure[refined] silver; sterling/구리 그릇에 ~을 입히다 silver copperware. ぎん

**-은가** 《의문》 whether it is[did]; is it?; did it? —のか

**은감**(殷鑑) taking warning by *another's* failure; a caution; a warning; an example. いんかん

**은거**(隱居) retirement[seclusion] [from the world]; sequestration/~하다 live [dwell] in retirement; go into retirement/산중에 ~하다 retire to *one's* hermitage in the mountain. いんきょ

**은고**(恩顧) special favour; patronage/ ~를 입다 receive favours from (*one*). おんこ

**은공**(恩功) favours; merits.

**은광**(銀鑛) a silver mine 《광석》 silver ore. ぎんこう

**은군자**(隱君子) ①《군자》 a man of virtue living in seclusion; a wise man who does not seek fame; a hermit ②《은근자》 a· prostitute ③《국화》 a chrysanthemum. いんくんし

**은근**(慇懃) ①《정중》 politeness; courtesy; civility/~하다 (be) courteous; polite; civil/~히 courteously; with much courtesy/~한 태도 a courteous demeanor

/~을 다하다 pour *one's* heart into (*something*) ②《다정》intimacy; friendship /~하다 (be) intimate; be on intimate terms (*with*)/~한 우정 a close friendship. いんぎん

**은근짜** a [an unlicensed] prostitute. いんくんし
**은금**(銀金) silver and gold/~ 보배 money and valuables; treasures. ぎんときん
**은급**(恩給) a pension ⇨연금. おんきゅう
**은기**(銀器) a silver vessel; silverware. ぎんせいのきぶつ
**은니**(銀泥) silver paint. ぎんでい
**은닉**(隱匿) concealment; hiding/~하다 conceal; shelter; harbour; hide; give refuge to/범인을 ~하다 harbour a culprit/~ 물자 concealed goods/장물 ~ 죄 secretion of stolen goods. いんとく
**은딴** a chief snake charmer.
**은덕**(恩德) a favour; a benefit; an obligation; a debt of gratitude/나는 그가 베풀어 준 ~에 감사하고 있다 I am grateful for the benefits I receive from him. おんとく
**은덕**(隱德) good done by stealth; a secret act of charity[virtue]; a hidden virtue/~을 베풀다 do good by stealth. いんとく
**은도금**(銀鍍金) silver-plating; silver gilt; silvering/~하다 plate with silver/~ 한 silver-plated[-gilt].
**은둔**(隱遁) retirement [from the world]; seclusion; withdrawal from ordinary life/~하다 retire from the world; live in retirement[seclusion]; sequester[seclude] *oneself* from the world[society] /~ 생활 a life in seclusion; a retired [sequestered] life/~자 a recluse; a hermit/~주의 quietism; monasticism. いんとん
**은류**(隱流) an undercurrent; hidden flow. かくれてながれること
**은막**(銀幕) the screen; silver screen 《은막계》the moviedom. ぎんまく
**은명**(恩命) gracious words[commands] from the throne. おんめい
**은모**(隱謀) a plot; an intrigue. いんぼう
**은미**(隱微) abstruseness; mystery; occultness/~하다 (be) abstruse; occult; subtle; latent; obscure. いんび
**은밀**(隱密) privacy; secrecy/~하다 (be) secret; confidential/~히 in secret; in privacy; confidentially/~히 조사하다 make confidential inquiries/그와 ~히 이야기하다 have some private talk with him. おんみつ
**은박**(銀箔) silver leaf[foil]; beaten silver /~지 silver paper. ぎんぱく
**은반**(銀盤) ①《소반》a silver tray with legs ②《스케이트장》a skating rink/~의 녀왕 the queen on the ice. ぎんばん
**은반상**(銀飯床) silver dishes[bowls].
**은발**(銀髮) silver[-white] hair; gray[grey(영)] hair. ぎんぱつ

**은방**(銀房) a silversmith's shop.
**은방울꽃**(銀—) 【식】a lily-of-the-valley. すずらん
**은배**(銀杯) a silver cup. ぎんぱい
**은백**(銀白) silver-white; silver-gray.
**은백색**(銀白色) a silver-white color/~의 silver-white[-gray]. ぎんいろのようなしろいろ
**은벽**(隱僻) being unfrequented/~하다 (be) out-of-the-way; remote; secluded 《왕래가 드문》 unfrequented/~치 an unfrequented place[part]; a remote corner of the county; an obscure spot.
**은복**(隱伏) lying concealed[hidden]; lurking/~하다 lie concealed[hidden]; lurk. かくれふせること
**은부**(殷富) wealth; richness; opulence; affluence; prosperity/~하다 (be) wealthy; opulent; abundant. いんぷ
**은분**(銀粉) silver dust; powdered silver. ぎんふん
**은비**(隱庇) protection; coverture/~하다 conceal; cover (*up*); shield; protect/증거를 ~하다 suppress[cover up] evidence /죄상을 ~하다 cover up the traces of a crime. おおいかくすこと
**은빛**(銀—) silver ˜colour¸; silveriness/ ~의 silver ˜coloured¸; silvery. ぎんいろ
**은사**(恩賜) an Imperial[a Royal, His Majesty's] gift/~의 bestowed by His Majesty/~하다 bestow as a token of the king's bounty/~금 a king's[royal] bounty/~품 a king's[royal] gift. おんし
**은사**(恩師) *one's* [respected] teacher; a teacher to whom *one* is greatly indebted. おんし
**은사**(恩赦) 《일반》amnesty 《개인》pardon /~를 입다 be granted a general amnesty. おんしゃ
**은사**(隱事) a secret; a hidden affair; a private affair. いんじ
**은사**(隱士) a hermit; a recluse. いんじ
**은산**(銀山) a silver mine. ぎんざん
**은상**(恩賞) a gracious reward [by the king]/~을 받다 receive a reward. おんしょう
**은서**(隱栖, 隱棲) 《생활》a life in seclusion; a secluded life 《집》a hermitage/ ~하다 live in seclusion. かくれてくらすこと
**은설**(銀屑) silver dust.
**은성**(殷盛) prosperity/~하다 (be) prosperous; flourish; thriving. いんせい
**은세계**(銀世界) a silver world; the whole land scape mantled in silvery snow; a vast snowy scene/아침에 일어나 보니 온통 ~였다 I awoke to find the world turned silver. ぎんせかい
**은세공**(銀細工) silverwork/~품 silverware. ぎんざいく
**은수저**(銀—) silver spoons and chopsticks; silver. ぎんせいのさじとはし
**은시계**(銀時計) a silver watch.

은신(隱身) hiding[concealing] oneself/~하다 hide oneself 《가려서》take cover/~처 a hiding-place; a refuge; a hideaway 《범죄자의》a hide-out 《구》; a den. みをかくすこと

은애(恩愛) affection; kindness and affection; love; tender feeling. おんあい

은어(銀魚) 【어】a sweetfish; an ayu. あゆ

은어(隱語) a secret language; a cant/~로 말하다 talk in secret language. いんご

은연(隱然) latently; though not in name/~하다 (be) underlying; latent/~중 in secret; in private; tacitly/~중 한 파벌을 이루다 form a party behind the scenes(in the back room).

은옥색(銀玉色) light blue; water green. うすいたまいろ

은우(恩遇) a favourable treatment; hospitability/~하다 treat with a favour; receive heartily. おんぐう

은원(恩怨) love and hate; benefit and enmity. おんえん

은위(恩威) justice and mercy; stern but kindly justice/~ 병행(竝行)하다 temper justice with mercy. おんい

은유(隱喩) a metaphor/~적으로 metaphorical[ly]. いんゆ

은은하다(殷殷—) (be) roaring; pealing; bellowing/~은은히 with roaring sounds; rumbling/은은히 울리다 boom; roar; reverberate.

은은하다(隱隱—) (be) latent 《소리가》indistinct/은은히 covertly; secretly/종소리가 은은하게 들려 왔다 There came to my ears the distant peals of a bell. かすかであからかでない

은의(恩義, 恩誼) a favour; an obligation/~에 보답하다 repay one's kindness. おんぎ

은인(恩人) a benefactor 《남자》a patron 《여자》a benefactress; a patroness/그는 너의 생명의 ~이다 You owe him your life. おんじん

은인(隱忍) endurance; patience/~하다 (be) patient; endure; put up with; bear up. いんにん

은인(隱人) a hermit; a recluse; an anchoret.

은일(隱逸) ①《사람》a hidden[secluded] scholar ②《숨음》hiding oneself from the world/~하다 hide oneself from the world; seclude oneself from society. いんいつ

은잔(銀盞) a silver cup. ぎんぱい

은짬 secrecy; privacy.

은장도(銀粧刀) an ornamental silver knife[sword].

은재(隱才) a hidden talent.

은저울(銀—) a small steelyard[balance] for weighing silver. ぎんのはかり

은적(隱迹) abscondence; concealment of one's traces[whereabouts]/~하다 abscond (from); conceal one's whereabouts. あとかたをかくすこと

은전(恩典) grace; special favour/~을 입다 be granted a special favour/특별한 ~으로서 as a special act of grace. おんてん

은전(銀錢) a silver coin. ぎんせん

은정(恩情) favo[u]r; grace; graciousness. おんじょう

은제(銀製) 《은으로 된》made of silver 《제품》silverware. ぎんせい

은조사(銀造紗) a thin silk made in China.

은종이(銀—) silver paper 《담배 포장용》tin foil. ぎんがみ

은줄(銀—) 《줄》a silver cord.

은진(殷賑) 《가멸음》abundance; opulence 《흥성함》prosperity; flourishingness; thrivingness. いんしん

은초(銀—) a white wax candle; beautiful candlelight.

은총(恩寵) favo[u]r; grace/하느님의 ~에 의해 by the grace of God/~을 입다 be in favo[u]r with 《a person》. おんちょう

은침(銀鍼) a silver needle [used for acupuncture].

은칭(銀秤) a precious-metal scale. ぎんのはかり

은택(恩澤) favo[u]rs; benevolence/~을 입다 enjoy benevolent influence; receive favo[u]rs. おんたく

은퇴(隱退) retirement; retreat/~하다 retire from active life 《권투 선수 등》retire from ring 《배우·음악가 등》retire from the stage/정계에서 ~하다 retire from active politics/~ 경기 a farewell 《boxing》 match. いんたい

은파(銀波) the silvery waves; white waves. ぎんば

은폐(隱蔽) concealment; hiding; suppression/~하다 conceal; hide; cover up; suppress/사실을 ~하다 suppress[cover up] a fact. いんぺい

은피(隱避) refuge; shelter; concealment/~하다 take refuge[shelter] 《in, under》; conceal oneself. いんぴ

은하(銀河) the Milky Way; the Galaxy/~계(系) the galactic system/~면 the galactic plane. ぎんが

은행(銀行) a bank/~에 예금하다 deposit money in a bank/보통[특수, 시중] ~ an ordinary commercial[a chartered, a city] bank/~ 거래 bank-account/~권(券) a bank-note. ぎんこう

은행(銀杏) 【식】a gingko nut/~나무 a gingko tree. いちょう

은현(隱現) appearing and disappearing/~하다 appear and disappear; come in and out of sight. いんげん

은혈(銀穴) a silver lode; a silver mine. ぎんをさいくつするあな

은혈(隱穴) ①《구멍》an invisible hole[cave] ②《내통》secret communication. かくれあな

**은혜**(恩惠) a benefit; a favour; a boon; a grace; kindness／어버이의 ~ parental love; debt to one's parent／~를 갚다 repay[return] another's kindness／~를 입다 be put under obligation; be indebted to／~를 베풀다 bestow favours on (one)／~를 잊지 않는 grateful; sensible of kindness. おんけい

**은혼식**(銀婚式) a silver wedding [anniversary]. ぎんこんしき

**은홍색**(殷紅色) pink; pale rosecolour; rosepink.

**은화**(銀貨) a silver [coin]; white money／~ 본위제 the silver standard. ぎんか

**은화 식물**(隱花植物) a cryptogam; a flowerless plant. いんかしょくぶつ

**은휘**(隱諱) suppression; coverture; dissimulation; hiding／~하다 cover [up]; suppress; sink (a fact); draw a veil over; keep (a matter) secret[dark]; conceal; hide.

**을** 《목적격 조사》 ¶팔 ~ 잡다 seize (one) by the arm／말 ~ 타다 ride[mount] a horse／물 ~ 마시다 drink [a cup of] water／여행 ~ 떠나다 set out on a trip／달 ~ 보다 look at the moon／하늘 ~ 날다 fly (in) the sky／3시간 ~ 잠자다 sleep (for) three hours. ―を

**을**(乙) the second 《급수의》 B 《후자》 the latter／~반 class B.

**을근거리다** menace; act menacing.

**을러메다** 《고압적으로》 take a high-handed measure; act[speak] high-handedly 《위압》 coerce (one into submission, etc.); bully. おどしつける

**을망정** even if[though]; rather … than; but／죽 ~ 그 짓은 못 하겠다 I would rather die than do it. ―としても

**을밋을밋** tardily; dilatorily 《차일피일》 from day to day／빚을 ~ 미루어 가다 let the debt stand over indefinitely.

**을씨년스럽다** ①《쓸쓸하다》 (be) lonely; lonesome; desolate ②《가난하다》 (be) poor; needy; poor-looking; destitute／옷이 너절해서 ~ look wretched with shabby clothes. せきばくとしている

**을야**(乙夜) ten in the afternoon; the second watch at night. いつや

**을종**(乙種) class B; second grade. おつしゅ

**읊다** 《짓다》 write[compose] 《외다》 recite [sing] [a poem]. うそぶく

**읊조리다** recite. うそぶく

**음**(音) ①《소리》 a sound; a tone 《조음(噪音)》 a noise／~의 고저 pitch ②《자음》 the sound of a word[character]; 《한자의》 the pronunciation (of a Chinese character). おん

**음**(陰) secrecy; darkness／~으로 secretly; in secret／~으로 양으로 both openly and secretly. いん

**음가**(音價) phonetic value. おんか

**음각**(陰刻) 【미】 intaglio; impression／~하다 intaglio; engrave. いんこく

**음감**(音感) a sense of sound／~ 교육 auditory education; acoustic training. おんかん

**음건**(陰乾) drying (a thing) in the shade／~하다 dry (a thing) in the shade. かげぼし

**음경**(陰莖) 【해】 the penis／~ 숭배 phallicism. いんけい

**음계**(音階) the musical scale／~를 연습하다 do the scale／전~ the gamut; the diatonic scale. おんかい

**음계**(陰界) the world of the dead; the under[nether] world. きしんのせかい

**음곡**(音曲) music; musical perfomance／~ 중지 the suspension of musical entertainments. おんきょく

**음공**(陰功) unknown merits; hidden merits. かくれたこうろう

**음극**(陰極) the negative pole; the cathode／~선 the cathode ray. いんきょく

**음기**(陰氣) ①《음험》 trickery; craftiness ②《찬 기운》 a chill; chilliness; gloominess; dreariness. いんき

**음낭**(陰囊) 【해】 the scrotum (pl. ~es, -ta). いんのう

**음녀**(淫女) a woman of loose morals; a girl of easy virtue; a vamp. みだらなおんな

**음담**(淫談) obscene conversation; bawdy [filthy] talk. みだらなことば

**음덕**(陰德) good done by stealth; hidden virtue／~을 베풀다 do (a person) private kindness; do good in private. いんとく

**음독**(音讀) ~하다 read Chinese characters phonetically. おんどく

**음독**(飲毒) taking poison／~하다 take poison／~ 자살하다 suicide by taking poison; poison oneself to death.

**음동**(陰冬) gloomy[dreary] winter. いんきなふゆ

**음락**(淫樂) sensual pleasure.

**음란**(淫亂) lewdness; incontinence／~하다 (be) lewd; lecherous; lustful; wanton; incontinent. いんらん

**음랭**(陰冷) ~하다 (be) shady and cool; cloudy and cold.

**음량**(音量) volume (of one's voice). おんりょう

**음력**(陰曆) the lunar calendar／~을 쓰다 follow the lunar calendar／~설 the Lunar New Year's Day. いんれき

**음료**(飲料) a drink; a beverage／~를 공급하다 provide drink／~로서 적당하다 be good to drink. いんりょう

**음료수**(飲料水) drinking water; potable water. いんりょうすい

**음률**(音律) rhythm; metre／~학 rhythmics. おんりつ

**음매** 《소 울음》 moo; [with] a moo. もおー

**음모**(陰毛) pubic hair; pubes. いんもう

**음모**(陰謀) a plot; a conspiracy; an intrigue; a machination／~하다 plot; intrigue; conspire; form a conspiracy／~에 가담하다 be implicated in a plot／

~자 a plotter; an intriguer. いんぼう
**음문**(陰門) 【해】 the vulva; the vagina. いんもん
**음물**(淫物) a lewd fellow; a libertine; a satyr; a wanton. みだらなもの
**음미**(吟味) close examination 《감상》 appreciation; a test; inquiry／ ~하다 examine closely; inquire; test 《감상하다》 appreciate／시를 ~하다 relish poems. ぎんみ
**음미**(淫靡) obscenity; lasciviousness/~하다 obscene.
**음반**(音盤) a phonograph record; a disk.
**음방**(淫放) dissipation; lewdness. いんぼう
**음병**(吟病) groaning with illness. びょうきでしんぎんすること
**음보**(音譜) a musical score. おんぷ
**음복**(陰伏) lying concealed／~하다 lie concealed; lascivious; in decent. いんぷく
**음부**(音符) a [musical] note; a score; notation／~를 적다 write notes[musical scores]／2분 ~ a minim; a half note ／4분[8분, 16분, 32분] ~ a crotchet [quaver, semiquaver, desemiquaver]. おんぷ
**음부**(陰部) 【해】 the pubic region; the pubes; the private[secret, privy] parts; the secret《속》. いんぶ
**음부**(淫婦) a lewd woman. いんぶ
**음분**(淫奔) wantonness; running mad after men／~하다 be wanton; carry on with men; behave lewdly. いんぽん
**음비**(陰秘) sneakiness; treacherousness／ ~하다 (be) sneaky; snaky; treacherous. きょうあくでおろかなこと
**음사**(淫辭) obscene[improper] language; foul[nasty, dirty] talk; ribaldry. いんじ
**음사**(陰事) ①《비밀사》 a secret; private affairs ②《잠자리》 sexual intercourse [commerce, union]; coition／~하다 have sexual intercourse.
**음산**(陰散) ~하다 (be) cloudy and gloomy; cloudy and cool／~한 날씨 dismal weather.
**음색**(音色) a tone [colour]; the quality of a tone; a clang-tint. おんしょく
**음서**(淫書) a foul book 《총칭》 obscene literature; pornography. いんしょ
**음성**(音聲) ①〖언〗 the phonetics[sounds] of a language ②⇨목소리／~ 베스트 audition／~학 phonetics／~학자 a phonetician／여자 ~을 내다 assume a woman's voice.
**음성**(陰性) ~의〖의〗 atonic;〖물〗 negative ／~ 콜레라 dormant cholera／검사 결과는 ~이었다 The result of the examination was negative. いんせい
**음소**(音素)《음성》 a phoneme／~ 기호 a phonemic symbol／~ 문자 alphabetic [phonemic] writing. おんそ
**음속**(音速) the velocity[speed] of sound ／~의 sonic／초~ supersonic speed. おんそく

**음수**(陰數) 【수】 a negative number; a minus quantity; a minus. ふすう
**음순**(陰脣) 【해】 the labium(pl. -bia) ／대 [소]~ the labia majora[minora]. いんしん
**음습**(淫習) lewd manners; a habit of profligacy. みだらなしゅうかん
**음습**(陰濕) ~하다 (be) unsunny and moist; shady and damp. いんしつ
**음식**(飲食) 《먹고 마시기》 eating and drinking 《식물》 food [and drink]; diet; eatables; a meal; foodstuffs／~용 for table use／~점 an eating house; a restaurant／~을 먹다 eat and drink／~을 절제하다 eat and drink in moderation. いんしょく
**음신**(音信) news; correspondence 《편지》 a letter. おんしん
**음실**(陰室) a dark room; an unsunny[a gloomy. a shadowy] room. いんしつ
**음심**(淫心) the desire of vicious[evil] courses; lust; sensual desire. いんしん
**음악**(音樂) music; the musical art／~적인 musical; melodious／~회 《연주회》a recital; a concert／~을 연주하다 play[perform] music／~의 대가 a great musician／~가 a musician／~ 감상실 a music hall／~ 영화 a musical [film]／~ 효과 a musical effects. おんがく
**음악**(淫樂) a lewd music. いんがく
**음액**(陰液) 《섹액》 semen; sperm; spermatic[seminal] fluid.
**음약**(陰約) a secret promise[agreement] ／~하다 promise secretly. ひみつなやくそく
**음양**(陰陽) 《음과 양》 the cosmic dual forces 《남성과 여성》the male and female principles 《태양과 달》the sun and the moon 《그늘과 양지》shade and light 《소극과 적극》the positive and negative; the active and passive. いんよう
**음역**(音域) 〖음〗 compass; musical range ／~이 넓은 목소리 voice of great compass. おんいき
**음역**(音譯) transliteration／~하다 transliterate. おんやく
**음영**(吟咏) recitation of a poem／~하다 recite [a poem]. ぎんえい
**음영**(陰影) 《그림자》 shadow 《그늘》 shade ／~을 나타내다 shade (a picture). いんえい
**음예**(淫穢) indecency; obscenity; lewdness ／~하다 (be) indecent; lewd; obscene; immoral. みだらできたないこと
**음예**(陰翳) shade 《어둠》 gloom; being clouded (over). いんえい
**음욕**(淫慾) carnal desire; sensual[sexual] appetite; lust／~을 억세하다 control [restrain] one's passion; rule lust／~에 탐닉하다 indulge in sexual pleasures. いんよく
**음용**(音容) one's voice and appearance. おんよう

음용(飮用) ~의 for drinking/~에 적합한 good to drink; drinkable/~수 drinking water; water to drink 《게시》 Fit to drink. いんよう

음우(陰雨) a long spell of rainy weather. いんう

음우(霪雨) a long and nasty rain [of the rainy season]; a heavy and long-continued rain.

음운(陰雲) dark clouds. いんうん

음운(音韻) vocal sounds/~ 조직 system/~학 phonology/~학자 a phonologist. おんいん

음울(陰鬱) gloominess and dullness; dismalness/~하다 (be) gloomy; dismal; melancholy/~한 성격 a melancholy temperament[disposition]/~한 날씨 a gloomy weather. いんうつ

음위(陰痿) impotence; impotency. いんい

음으로(陰−) privately; implicitly; indirectly; secretly; in secret/~ 양으로 publicly and privately. かげで

음음하다(陰陰−) (be) thickly clouded; gloomy. うすくらくものさびしい

음의(音義) the pronunciation[sound] and meaning [of a Chinese character]. おんぎ

음일(淫佚) licentious indulgence ⇨음황(淫荒). こころいくまでみだらにあそぶこと

음자(音字) a phonetic sign; a phonogram. おんじ

음전 ~하다 (be) gentle; well-behaved; prudent; dignified 《침착》 calm/행동이 ~하다 be gentle in manner.

음전기(陰電氣) 【물】 negative electricity. いんでんき

음전자(陰電子) 【물】 a negative electron; a negatron. いんでんし

음절(音節) 【언】 a syllable; 【음】 a musical measure/~로 나누다 syllabicate; syllabize; syllabify/단~의 말 a monosyllable/~ 문자 syllabic writing; a syllabary. おんせつ

음정(音程) an[a musical] interval /전~ a tone; a [whole] step/반~ a semi-tone. おんてい

음조(音調) tune 《음색》 tone 《전조(轉調)》 modulation 《운율》 rhythm 《아름다운 음조》 euphony. おんちょう

음조(陰助) secret assistance/~하다 assist secretly; help by stealth. かげでたすけること

음주(飮酒) drinking/~하다 drink/~에 빠지다 be addicted to drinking/그는 ~가 과하다 He is too fond of drink. いんしゅ

음지(陰地) a shady spot. いんち

-음직하다 it is possible to; it is all right to; it is[seems] likely to/믿음직한 사람 a man you can trust.

음질(音質) tone quality.

음집 the vagina (of an animal).

음차(音叉) 【물】 a tuning fork. おんさ

음창(陰瘡) 【의】 an ulcer[a chancre] on the vulva.

음청(陰晴) fine and cloudy; change of weather. いんせい

음축(陰縮) atrophy[shriveling] of the penis.

음충하다 (be) cunning; artful; tricky; crafty; guileful; wily/음충한 사람 a snake in the grass; a man to be wary of. こうかつである

음치(音痴) tone-deafness/~의 deaf to music/나는 ~이다 I have no ear for music. おんち

음침하다(陰沈−) (be) gloomy; dismal; dark; sombre/음침한 날씨 gloomy weather. うっとうしい

음탐(淫貪) a taste for lewdness/~하다 (be) sensual; lewd; lustful; amorous.

음탕(淫蕩) dissipation; debauchery/~하다 (be) dissipated; voluptuous; obscene; immoral. いんとう

음택(陰宅) a tomb. はか

음통(陰通) ~하다 have one's initial sexual intercourse; lose one's innocence [virginity].

음파(音波) a sound-wave/~ 측정 phonometry/~ 탐지기 sonar. おんぱ

음표(音標) 【음】 a musical note; a musical score; notation/~를 적다 write notes[musical scores]/4분~ a quarter note 《미》; a crotchet 《영》. おんぴょう

음표 문자(音標文字) 【언】 phonetic notation[sign]; a phonogram/만국~ international phonetic sign. おんぴょうもじ

음풍(淫風) lewd[immoral] manners; loose morals; immorality. いんぷう

음풍 농월(吟風弄月) poetical enthusiasm /~하다 compose poetry.

음하다(淫−) (be) lecherous; lewd. みだらである

음해(陰害) damage done in secret/~하다 damage[hurt; injure] secretly.

음핵(陰核) 【해】 the clitoris. いんかく

음행(淫行) an obscene act; lewd[immoral, unchaste] conduct. いんこう

음향(音響) a sound 《소음》 a noise/~ 전파 sound propagation/~학 acoustics /~ 측정기 a phonometer/이 음악당은 ~ 장치가 나쁘다 This music hall has bad acoustics. おんきょう

음험(陰險) ~하다 (be) insidious; snaky; wily/~한 사람 an insidious man/~한 수작을 부리다 use subtle[treacherous measures]. いんけん

음화(陰畵) a negative [picture]. いんが

음황(淫荒) ~하다 (be) lewd; obscene. いんこう

음훈(音訓) the Korean pronunciation and translation of a Chinese character. おんくん

음흉(陰凶) wickedness; treacherousness /~하다 (be) cunning; wily; crafty; tricky/~한 사람 a tricky guy; a crafty fellow. いんけんできょうあくなこと

읍(邑) a town/~에 가다 go up to town.

**읍(揖)** a low bow[an obeisance] with *one's* hands in front.

**읍례(揖禮)** a low bow[obeisance] with *one's* hands in front／～하다 make a low[deep] bow with *one's* hands in front.

**읍민(邑民)** the townsmen; the townsfolks; the townspeople.

**읍양(揖讓)** 《예의로써 사양함》 courteous concession 《태도》 a courteous and humble attitude／～하다 yield courteously; assume[show] a courteous and humble attitude.

**읍지(邑誌)** the history of a town.

**읍청(泣請)** a sincere request (with *tears*)／～하다 entreat; implore; throw *oneself* on *another's* mercy.

**읍체(泣涕)** shedding tears; sobbing; weeping／～하다 shed tears; weep; sob.

**읍촌(邑村)** towns and villages.

**읍하다(揖—)** make a low[deep] bow with *one's* hands in front.

**응** 《긍정》 yea; yes; all right; O. K. 《부정》 no／～ 꼭 갈께 Oh yes, I will come without fail.

**응결(凝結)** congelation; condensation 《피 따위의》 coagulation／～하다 congeal; freeze; condense／～ 물 a congelation／～점 the freezing point／～제 a coagulant.

**응고(凝固)** 《응결》 congelation (얼음 따위); coagulation (피 따위); 《응축》 condensation 《고결》 solidification／～하다 congeal; solidify.

**응급(應急)** emergency; makeshift／～하다 take a temporary expedient／～의 first-aid; temporary／～책 emergency measures 《둘러 맞추기》 shift／～조치 damage control.

**응급 치료(應急治療)** first aid; first-aid dressing[treatment]／～소 a first-aid room[station]／～를 하다 give the first aid (to *one*).

**응낙(應諾)** consent; assent; compliance／～하다 consent (to); agree (to); respond (to); assent (in); accept (*a recommendation*).

**응달** the shade; the shady side／～에서 in the shade／～에 두다 keep (*a thing*) in the shade.

**응답(應答)** an answer; a response; a reply (to)／～하다 answer; reply to; report with／질의 ～ questions and answers／～자 a respondent.

**응당(應當)** for sure; without fail; necessarily.

**응대(應對)** ①《응답》 a reply; a response／～하다 reply to; answer ②《면담》 an interview; a talk／～하다 have an interview with; meet and talk with ③ 《응접》 reception／～하다 receive (*guests*); wait on (*customers*).

**응등그러지다** ①《뒤틀리다》 be[get] twisted; be awry; be distorted ②《몸이》 crouch 《무서워서》 cower.

**응등그리다** shrink; duck (*one's head*); shrug (*one's shoulders*).

**응모(應募)** 《예약》 subscription 《지원》 application 《참가》 entry 《지원병의》 enlistment 《광고의》 response; answer 《병적·회원 따위에의》 enrollment／～하다 subscribe for[to]; apply[enter] for／～ 신청 an application for subscription／～자 an applicant; a subscriber／～ 자금 a subscribed capital.

**응보(應報)** retribution; nemesis／인과 ～ As a man sows, so he shall reap.

**응분(應分)** ～의 appropriate; due; proportionate; suitable 《분에 맞는》 according to *one's* circumstances[*one's* station, *one's* ability, *one's* means]; 《미치는 한도 내의》 within *one's* power／～의 대우를 받다 be given proper treatment.

**응사(應射)** firing back／～하다 shoot[fire] back; respond to *one's* firing.

**응석** playing the baby; being a spoilt child／～부리다 play the baby (to); get spoilt／～부리듯 coaxingly.

**응석받다** give in to a child's whims; indulge; pamper; spoil.

**응성깊다** ①《도량이 크다》 (be) magnanimous; liberal; large-minded ②《야하지 않다》 (be) elegant; graceful; refined ③ 《되바라지지 않다》 (be) unobtrusive; modest ④《깊숙하다》 (be) deep; profound.

**응소(應訴)** acceptance of legal suit [standing as a defendant]; a counter-suit; contesting a suit.

**응소(應召)** ～하다 obey a summons to the colo[u]rs; obey a calling-up order／～병 a selectee／～자 a draftee／～을 draft quota.

**응수(應酬)** 《대답》 a reply; a response 《답례》 a return 《교환》 an exchange／～하다 respond; return; retort.

**응수(應數)** 《바둑 등에서》 a countermove／～하다 make a countermove.

**응시(應試)** applying for an examination／～하다 apply for an examination.

**응시(凝視)** a steady gaze; a stare／～하다 gaze at (*one*); stare at; watch intently; look hard at.

**응애응애** waw; with a mewl／～ 울다 mewl; whine.

**응어리** ①《근육의》 a stiff muscle; a knot [kink, cramp, charley horse] in a muscle ②《과일 등의》 the pith (of *fruit*); the core; the heart ③《사물의》 the gits [nub, point, substance] of a matter.

**응얼거리다** grumble; gripe; complain.

**응용(應用)** application; practice 《이용》

**응원**(應援) ①(원조) aid; assistance; help; support 《원병》 reinforcement/~하다 aid; assist; give assistance; help ②《성원》 cheering; backing; rooting/~하다 aid; support; back; reinforce; assist/~기 a rooter's pennant/~ 연설 a campaign speech; a speech in support. おうえん

**응전**(應戰) a response/~하다 accept battle[a challenge]; respond[reply] to a fire; return a fire. おうせん

**응접**(應接) reception; an interview/~하다 receive; see; interview/~실 a parlour; a drawing[reception] room/~ 시간 a callhour/손님을 ~하다 receive a visitor. おうせつ

**응종**(應從) obedience; compliance/~하다 obey; comply with.

**응징**(膺懲) chastisement; punishment/~하다 chastise; punish/~지사(之師) a punitive expedition. ようちょう

**응천 순인**(應天順人) obeying the will of heaven and following the voices of the people.

**응체**(凝滯) stoppage; impediment; delay/~하다 get stopped; be impeded; be delayed. ぎょうたい

**응축**(凝縮) condensation/~하다 condense/~기(器) a condenser. ぎょうしゅく

**응포**(應砲) returning [the] fire/~하다 return[answer] the enemy's gunfire.

**응하다**(應—) 《응답하다》 reply; answer; respond 《필요·수요에》 meet; satisfy 《승낙하다》 comply with; accept 《모집에》 apply[subscribe] (for)/…에 응해서 according to; in compliance with 《비례하여》 in response[proportion] to/쾌히 ~ comply with (one's request) gladly/수요에 ~ meet a demand/도전에 ~ accept a challenge/국력에 응하여 군비를 제한한다 limit the armament to the resources of the country. おうずる

**응혈**(凝血) a clot of blood; grume; gore; coagulated[clotted, curdled] blood/~하다 curdle; coagulate. こりかたまった ち

**응화**(應和) a response/~하다 respond.

**의** ⇒별항 참조(page 1653).

**의**(誼) 《사이》 mutual[social] relation 《교제 관계》 terms/~좋게 on good terms; like good friends; in harmony/~가 좋다 be on good[intimate] terms with; be good[great] friends with/그 부부는 ~좋게 지낸다 The couple gets along like a pair of lovebirds. ぎ

**의**(義) ①(정의) justice; loyalty; righteousness ②(의리) relationship; ties; bonds/군신의 ~ the relations of sovereign and subject. ぎ

**의**(醫) 《의술》 medicine 《의사》 a doctor; a physician/~는 인술이다 Medicine is a benevolent art.

**의가**(醫家) a medical practitioner.

**의거**(依據) dependence/~하다 depend on; be based upon/자료에 ~하여 on the basis[authority] of the data. いきょ

**의거**(義擧) a worthy[laudable, noble] undertaking 《의협적인》 a heroic[brave] deed/4. 19 ~ 기념일 April 19th Student Revolution Day. ぎきょ

**의걸이**(衣—) 《장》 a wardrobe chest.

**의견**(意見) an idea; a view; an opinion/~의 일치 coincidence of opinions/~이 같다 agree with (one); be of the same opinion; be of the same mind/~이 다르다 disagree with; be of different opinion/그는 전연 반대 ~이었다 His opinion was quite to the contrary. いけん

**의견서**(意見書) one's written opinion; one's opinion in writing. いけんしょ

**의결**(議決) 《결정》 a resolution; a decision (of a meeting); 《통과》 passing (a vote, a resolution)/~하다 decide; pass a vote (of); resolve/~ 기관 a legislative[deliberative] organ/~권 the right of voting. ぎけつ

**의고**(擬古) imitation of archaic style [form]/~하다 imitate archaism; copy after archaic style/~문 a [pseudo-]classical style/~주의 (교육상의) classicism 《예술상의》 classicalism 《조형·미술 따위의》 archaism 《사이비 고대주의》 pseudo-archaism/~ 적 pseudo-archaic; classical. ぎこ

**의곡**(歪曲) ~하다 distort; bend; curve; warp; crook 《곱새기다》strain; distort; stretch/~된 해석 a distorted view 《편견의》 a biased interpretation 《억지의》 a strained[forced] interpretation. わいきょく

**의과**(醫科) the medical department/~대학 a medical college/~생 a medical student. いか

**의관**(衣冠) clothing and head-gear/~을 갖추다 be in full uniform; be in full dress. いかん

**의관**(醫官) a medical officer. いかん

**의관 문물**(衣冠文物) civilization [of a country]. いかんぶんぶつ

**의구**(依舊) ~하다 remain[be just] as it was; remain unchanged. むかしとおなじであること

**의구**(疑懼) apprehension/~하다 doubt; suspect; apprehend; fear/~심 misgivings; apprehensions. ぎく

**의기**(意氣) spirits; heart; mind/~ 양양한 triumphant; exultant/~가 당당하다 be irresistibly high-spirited/~ 왕성하다 be in high-spirits/그 소식이 우리들의 ~를 꺾었다 That news dampened our spirits. いき

**의기**(義旗) a banner of righteousness; a

**의기(義氣)** 《의협심》 chivalrous spirit; heroism 《공공심》 public spirit /~있는 chivalrous; heroic; public-spirited /~의 사나이 a man of chivalrous spirit; a public-spirited man. ぎき

**의기(疑忌)** suspicion and abhorrence /~하다 suspect and abhor; distrust and avoid.

**의기 상투(意氣相投)** affinity; sympathy; mutual understanding /~하다 be of a mind.

**의기 양양(意氣揚揚)** ~하다 (be) triumphant; exultant; be in high spirits /~하여 triumphantly; in triumph; with elation; proudly. いきようよう

**의념(疑念)** apprehensions; misgivings. ぎねん

**의논(議論)** consultation; conference /~하다 take counsel (*with*); consult (with *one*); talk (over *a matter*); with (*one*) /~할 사람 an adviser; someone to confer with. ぎろん

**의단(疑端)** the origin of suspicion; a factor of doubt.

**의당(宜當)** properly; naturally; indisputably; necessarily /학생이 선생에게 질문하는 것은 ~한 일이다 It is quite proper that a student should ask questions of his teacher. あたりまえに

**의대(衣帶)** a dress; clothes.

**의덕(懿德)** virtuous conduct; goodness; virtue.

**의도(義徒)** a group of upright men. ぎと

**의도(意圖)** a design; an intention; an aim; a purpose /나는 그의 ~를 전연 모른다 I am in complete ignorance of his intention. いと

**의량(衣糧)** clothing and provisions.

**의량(意量)** intention and capacity of mind; motivation and ability. いしとどりょう

**의려(疑慮)** apprehensions; misgivings; fear /~하다 apprehend; fear.

**의례(依例)** following a precedent /~하다 follow precedent. れいによること

**의례(儀禮)** ceremony; courtesy /~적 ceremonial; formal /가정 ~ ritual standards; folk mores and family rituals /~적인 방문을 하다 pay a formal[courtesy, protocol] visit[call] (*to*). ぎれい

**의례건(依例件)** a matter of precedent; customary affairs[tasks] /~으로 생각하다 take (*things*) for granted. とうぜんのもの

**의례히(依例―)** as usual; in *one's* usual way 《꼭》without fail. とうぜんに

---

# 의

① 《소유·소속·동격》 -'s; -s'; of; belonging to /나~ 책 my book /형님 ~ 소유인 책 the books in my brother's possession; the books in the possession of my brother; the books [which] my brother is possessed of; the books belonging to my brother; the books which belong to my brother; the books owned by my brother; the books [which] my brother owns /돈~ 가치 the value of money 《금전적 가치》 the monetary value /인간 ~ 가치 a man's worth; the worth of man /우리들은 중학교~ 학생이다 We are students of a middle school [middle school students]. /집~ 지붕 the roof of a house; a housetop.

② 《…에 관한》 of; with respect to related to /나~ 친구 a friend of mine 동양 미술~ 책 a book on Oriental Fine Arts /고대 문학~ 권위 an authority on ancient literature /국제법 ~ 전문가 an expert in[at] international law.

③ 《…이 들어 있는, …으로 되어 있는》 ◑ 한 상자~ 사과 a box of apples /한 포대~ 밤 a bag of chestnuts /두 아름~ 나뭇단 two armfuls of fagot /유리 ~ 창문 a window of glass 《유리창》 a glass window pane /청동~ 상 a statue in bronze; a bronze statue.

④ 《장소·시간》 ◑ 강가~ 도시 a town [situated, located] on a river /오후 5시 발~ 목포행 급행 the 5 p.m. express for *Mokpo* /세계~ 나라들 the countries of [in] the world; the countries all over the world[all the world over].

⑤ 《…에 의한, …으로부터의》 ◑ 그녀~ 연애 편지 a love letter from her /극장~ 출구 an exit from the theater /김 동인 ~ 소설 a novel [written] by *Kim Dongin*; a novel of *Kim Dongin* /그는 전라도~ 사람이다 He is[comes] from the State of *Junra-Do*.

⑥ ◑문~ 열쇠 a key to the door /집~ 입구 an entrance to a house /100만원짜리~ 수표 a check[cheque] for 1,000,000 *won* /1년~ 계획을 세우다 make plans [plan] for the year.

⑦ ◑영어~ 편지 a letter [written] in English /최대~ 겸손 the greatest humility /반대~ 의견을 내세우다 form an opinion to the contrary /남~ 뺨을 때리다 slap[strike] a person across the face /남~ 팔을 잡다 take[seize] a person by the arm.

**의론(議論)** argument 《토론》 discussion 《논쟁》 dispute／~하다 argue; dispute; discuss. ぎろん

**의롭다(義―)** 《바르다》 (be) just; righteous 《의기가 있다》 (be) chivalrous; public-spirited; heroic. せいぎがある

**의롱(衣籠)** a wardrobe.

**의뢰(依賴)** ①《원》 a request; a favour 《위임》 trust; commission／~하다 request; ask 《위임》 commission; trust (one) with／~인 《변호사 등의》 a client／~장 a written request ②《의지》 reliance; dependence／~하다 rely[depend] on／~심 a spirit of dependence. いらい

**의료(醫療)** medical treatment[care]／~기관 medical institution／~ 시설 medical facilities／~품 medical supplies. いりょう

**의료(衣料)** clothing; clothes. いりょう

**의류(衣類)** clothing; dresses; clothes 《전옷가지》 one's wardrobe. いるい

**의리(義理)** ①《바른 도리》 justice; righteousness 《인도》 humanity 《덕》 morality; integrity 《의무》 duty; obligation／~가 강한 사람 a man of probity／~가 없다 have no sense of duty[justice] ②《사귀는 도리》 relationship; ties; bonds; relations／친구의 ~ the ties of friendship. ぎり

**의모(義母)** 《의붓어미》 a stepmother 《수양어머니》 a foster mother 《의로 맺은》 a sworn mother. ぎぼ

**의무(義務)** a duty; an obligation; a responsibility／~적인 obligatory; compulsory／~가 있다 ought to (pay)／관념 a sense of duty／~를 다하다[게을리하다] perform[neglect] one's duty／~이행 performance of a duty／~ 교육 compulsory education. ぎむ

**의문(疑問)** a question; a doubt／~의 doubtful／~의 죽음 a mysterious death／~점 a point in doubt／~사 an interrogative／~문 an interrogative sentence／~을 품다 have doubts. ぎもん

**의뭉스럽다, 의뭉하다** be intelligent though look foolish; be foolish-looking; be deeper than one things.

**의미(意味)** 《의의》 meaning; sense; significance 《취지》 import／~하다 mean; signify／~있는 signficant; meaningful／~없는 insignificant; meaningless／엄밀한 ~로 in a strict sense. いみ

**의범(儀範)** a pattern of manners; a model of etiqutte. ぎはん

**의법(依法)** ~하다 be pursuant[conformable] to [the] law／~ 처분 disposition according to law／~하여 according to the law. ほうによること

**의병(義兵)** 《단칭》 a loyal soldier; a volunteer 《복칭》 a loyal army／~을 일으키다 raise an army in the cause of justice[loyalty]; raise a loyal army. ぎへい

**의복(衣服)** clothes; garments 《총칭》 clothing／~ 한 벌 a suit [of clothes]／좋은 ~을 입은 사람들 well-dressed persons. いふく

**의부(義父)** 《의붓아비》 a stepfather 《수양아버지》 a sworn father 《의로 맺은》 a foster father. ぎふ

**의부(義婦)** a woman of probity; a chaste woman.

**의분(義憤)** righteous indignation／~을 느끼다 burn with righteous indignation／~을 참다 repress one's righteous indignation. ぎふん

**의불합(意不合)** incongruity of spirits; uncongeniality; disagreement／~하다 (be) uncongenial.

**의붓** step／~딸 a stepdaughter／~아들 a stepson／~아비 a stepfather／~자식 a stepchild.

**의빙(依憑)** dependence ⇨ 의거. よりどころ

**의사(意思)** 《의향》 intention 《의견》 an opinion; a view 《생각》 a mind／~ 소통하다 come to an understanding／~를 수행하다 carry out one's intentions／~를 명백히 하다 speak one's mind. いし

**의사(義士)** a righteous person; a martyr. ぎし

**의사(義死)** ~하다 die in the cause of justice[humanity]; die in a just cause. せいぎのためにしぬこと

**의사(醫師)** a doctor; a physician 《외과의》 a surgeon／단골 ~ a family doctor／~가 되다 become a doctor／~의 진찰을 받다 consult a doctor／~의 치료를 받다 commit to a doctor's care／~ 면허 a medical license〈영·미〉／돌팔이 ~ a quack [doctor]. いし

**의사(縊死)** death by hanging oneself／~하다 hang oneself. いし

**의사(議事)** proceedings; business／~당 an assembly hall／~ 진행 progress of proceedings／국회 ~당 the National Assembly building; the Capitol〈미〉; the Houses of Parliament〈영〉／~록 the minutes of proceedings. ぎじ

**의사 표시(意思表示)** declaration of intention／~하다 declare one's intention; declare oneself. いしひょうじ

**의상(衣裳)** clothes; dresses 《연극 등의》 costume／~ 도락 fondness for dress／~ 철학 "Sartor Resartus". いしょう

**의생(醫生)** a physician of the Chinese school; a herb doctor. いせい

**의서(醫書)** a medical book; a book on medicine. いし

**의석(議席)** 《의칭》 a seat (in an assembly hall); a parliamentary seat 《복칭》 the floor〈국회의〉／~에 앉다 take one's seat／~을 획득하다 《선거에서》 win seats [places]. ぎせき

**의성(擬聲)** 《음성》 onomatopoeia／~어 an onomatopoeic word／~어의 onomatopoeic; onomatopoetic. ぎせい

**의세(倚勢)** ~하다 rely on power; trust to authority. かさにきること

**의수(義手)** an artificial arm[hand]; an arm[a hand] prosthesis. ぎしゅ

**의술(醫術)** medicine; the medical art/~의 medical/~을 개업하다 commence medical practice. いじゅつ

**의식(衣食)** food and clothing; means of subsistence[livelihood]/~을 위하여 일하다 work for *one's* bread. いしょく

**의식(意識)** consciousness; senses/~하다 be conscious (*of*)/~의 흐름 stream of consciousness/~적[으로] conscious`ly/~을 잃다 lose *one's* consciousness[senses]/~을 회복하다 come to *one's* senses. いしき

**의식(儀式)** a ceremony; a ritual; a rite/~을 거행하다 perform a ceremony. ぎしき

**의식주(衣食住)** food, clothing and housing. いしょくじゅう

**의심(疑心)** 《의혹》 doubt 《혐의》 suspicion 《의문》 question/~하다 doubt; be doubtful of; suspect; call (*a matter*) in question/~스럽다 (be) doubtful/~없는 undoubted; unquestioned/~을 품다 have a doubt (*about*)/~을 풀다 dispel *one's* doubt/~할 여지가 없다 be above suspicion/~이 많은 suspicious; distrustful; incredulous. ぎしん

**의아(疑訝)** doubt; suspicion; distrust/~하다 suspect; wonder; doubt/~스러운 듯이 dubiously; suspiciously/~스러운 dubious; suspicious; doubtful.
うたがいまどうこと

**의안(義眼)** an artificial[a glass, false] eye. ぎがん

**의안(議案)** a bill/~에 찬성[반대]하다 support[oppose] a measure/~을 기초하다 draw up a bill/~을 [의회에] 제출[상정]하다 present[introduce] a bill to the Assembly. ぎあん

**의약(醫藥)** a medicine; a remedy/~분업 separation of dispensary from medical practice. いやく

**의업(醫業)** medicine; the medical profession/~에 종사하다 practice medicine. いぎょう

**의역(意譯)** free translation/~하다 translate freely; give a free translation/그의 번역은 너무 ~에 치우쳤다는 비난이 있다 His translation is criticized of being too free. いやく

**의연(義捐)** subscription/~금 a contribution/수해~금 a relief fund for flood victims. ぎえん

**의연히(依然—)** as before 《아직》 still; as it used to be; yet 《다름없이》 unchanged/그 대로 still remain unchanged.

**의연히(毅然—)** firmly; in a dauntless[an unflinching] manner; boldly/그는 ~ 불행을 견디고 있다 He bears his misfortune with fortitude.

**의열(義烈)** nobility of soul; heroism/~하다 (be) noble; heroic; gallant. ぎれつ

**의옥(疑獄)** a public scandal; a criminal case; a graft case/~ [사건]에 연루하다 be involved in a scandal. ぎごく

**의외(意外)** ~의 《뜻밖의》 unexpected; unlooked·for; unforeseen 《놀라운》 surprising 《우연한》 accidental/~의 일 a surprise; an unlooked·for event/~로 unexpectedly; contrary[beyond] to *one's* expectation/~로 여기다 be surprised (*at*). いがい

**의욕(意慾)** will; volition/생활 ~ the will to live/~이 강한 사람 a man with strong intention. いよく

**의용(義勇)** heroism; bravery for a righteous cause/~군 a volunteer army. ぎゆう

**의용(儀容)** a mien; bearing; manners; presence/~을 갖추다 tidy *one*self. ぎょう

**의원(醫院)** a medical practitioner's office; a hospital; a physician's office/~장 the head physician. いいん

**의원(依願)** [in] accordance with *one's* request/~ 면관 dismissal[retirement] at *one's* own request. いがん

**의원(醫員)** a physician 《의사》 a doctor 《조수》 a medical assistant. いいん

**의원(議員)** a member (of *an assembly*); a Member of Parliament(略: M.P.); a Member of Congress(略: M.C.)(미)/~으로 당선되다 be elected a member (*of*)/~이 되다 obtain a seat in Parliament. ぎいん

**의의(意義)** meaning; sense; significance/~ 있는 significant; meaningful/~깊은 말 a term of profound significance.
いぎ

**의인(義人)** a righteous person.

**의인법(擬人法)** personification/~을 쓰다 personify. ぎじんほう

**의자(椅子)** a chair/긴 ~ a sofa; a lounge; a couch/접는 ~ a folding chair/~에 앉다 sit on[in] a chair. いす

**의장(衣欌)** a wardrobe; a chest.

**의장(意匠)** a design/~가 a designer/~등록 registration of designs/~ 미술 the art of design. いしょう

**의장(儀仗)** implements[arms] used in the national ceremonies; a cortege/~병 a guard of honor. ぎじょう

**의장(議長)** the chairman 《영·미 하원의》 the Speaker 《호칭》 Mr. Chairman!/~대리 the deputy speaker/국회 ~ the Speaker [of the National Assembly].
ぎちょう

**의장(議場)** an assembly hall; a chamber 《의회》 the House; the floor/~은 대격론으로 수라장이 되었다 The floor was thrown tnto disorder with a great deal of discussion. ぎじょう

**의적(義賊)** a chivalrous robber; a Robin Hood; a benevolent picaroon. ぎぞく

**의전(儀典)** rituals; rites; a ceremony/~관 a master of ceremonies; a ceremonial officer. ぎてん

**의절**(義絕) 《처족과의》 legal separation/~하다 break with (*a friend*). きせつ

**의점**(疑點) a doubtful[moot] point; a doubt.

**의젓이** in a dignified[sober, serious] way.

**의젓잖다** (be) undignified; flippant; unreliable; unpleasant; be lacking in seriousness[sobriety]. かんろくがない

**의젓하다** (be) dignified; weighty/의젓하게 처신하다 behave with dignity. そうちょうだ

**의정**(議定) arrangement; agreement/~하다 confer and agree upon/~서 a protocol. ぎてい

**의제**(議題) a subject[topic] for discussion; a program⟨미⟩;《전체》an agenda/~로 하다 make (*a matter*) a subject for discussion. ぎだい

**의족**(義足) an artificial[a wooden] leg [limb]. ぎそく

**의존**(依存) dependence; reliance/~하다 depend on; be dependent upon; rely upon/상호 ~ interdependence.

**의중**(意中) one's mind[heart]; one's inner thoughts[feelings, heart]/~을 떠보다 sound (*a person's*) views. いちゅう

**의중지인**(意中之人) the choice of one's heart; one's choice. いちゅうのひと

**의증**(疑症) a suspicious nature; a distrustful temperament/그는 ~이 많다 He has a suspicious nature.

**의지** a device for wrapping a corpse used in place of a coffin.

**의지**(依支) 《도움》a support; a prop; a help; an aid; assistance; dependence 《보호》a protection/~하다 lean on; turn to; rest against/그는 벽에 몸을 ~ 한다 He leans against the wall. もたれること

**의지**(意志) intention; purpose; will; volition/~가 강한 사람 a man of strong [iron] will/~력 will power/자유 ~ free will. いし

**의지**(義肢) an artificial limb. ぎし

**의지가지 없다** be helpless[homeless]; have no one to rely upon; have nothing to lean on; have no place[one] to turn to /그는 ~ He has no one to rely upon. よりどころがない

**의처증**(疑妻症) a morbid suspicion of one's wife's chastity.

**의초** affection between brothers and sisters; fraternity; fraternal love.

**의중**(意衷) one's mind; one's heart; one's intention; one's idea. ないしんのしんい

**의취**(意趣) inclination; mind; proclivity. いしゅ

**의치**(義齒) a false[an artificial] tooth; a denture/~를 해서 끼다 have a false tooth put in/~술(術) dental prosthesis. ぎし

**의탁**(依託) reliance; dependence/~하다 rely[depend] on; turn to; entrust oneself to/~할 곳 없다 have no place to go to. いたく

**의태**(擬態) simulation; imitation; mimesis; camouflage; [protective] mimicry /~하다 simulate; mimic/~어 mimesis. ぎたい

**의표**(儀表) a mien; demeanor; bearing; presence; deportment; manners/당당한 ~ a noble mien; commanding presence. ぎひょう

**의하다**(依一) 《원인》 be due to; be owing to 《의존》 depend on; be dependent on 《근거》 be based on 《수단》 appeal to; have recourse to/관례에 의하여 according to custom/이 조약에 의하여 in virtue of this treaty/그것은 사정에 의해서 달라진다 That depends upon circumstances. よる

**의학**(醫學) medical science; medicine/~을 연구하다 study medicine/~계 the medical world/~부 the medical department; medical school⟨미⟩. いがく

**의합**(意合) ①《의가 좋음》friendly relationship; amicability/~해서 살다 get along amicably ②《뜻이 맞음》congeniality; a concordance of views/~하지 않다 disagree with each other. なかのよいこと

**의향**(意向) 《의사》an intention 《생각》an idea; a mind; an inclination; a disposition/~을 타진하다 sound *another's* opinion. いこう

**의향**(衣香) mothproof perfume.

**의협**(義俠) chivalry; heroism; gallantry /~심이 많다 be full of chivalry. ぎきょう

**의형제**(義兄弟) a sworn brother/~를 맺다 form brotherly ties; swear to be brothers. ぎけいてい

**의혹**(疑惑) doubt; suspicion; distrust/~을 풀다 clear one's doubts/~의 눈으로 보다 eye (*a person*) with suspicion. ぎわく

**의혼**(議婚) discussion[consultation] on matrimony[marriage]; negotiation of a marriage/~하다 discuss[negotiate] a marriage.

**의회**(議會) 《한국·프랑스》the National Assembly 《영국·카나다》the Parliament《미국》the Congress 《일본·스웨덴·덴마크》the Diet/~ 정치 parliamentarism. ぎかい

**이**¹ ① a tooth 《송곳니》a fang/~가 아프다 have a toothache ②《기계의》a cog; the teeth (of *a saw, a gear*) ③《사기그릇 따위의》broken[jagged] edges (of *a cup, a vase*). は

**이**² a louse (*pl.* lise);《집합적》vermin/~를 잡다 catch[hunt] lice; delouse. しらみ

**이**³ this (*pl.* these); present; current/당신의 ~ 시계 this watch of yours.

**이**(二, 貳) two 《제 2의》the second/~ 대 two generations. に

**이**(利) ①《이득》profit; gain[s]/~를 보다 make a profit; gain/이 장사는 ~가

이 748 이끼

없다 This business does not pay. ②《유익》 benefit; good; interests 《장점》 an advantage /우유는 어린애에게 ~롭다 Milk is good for children. ③《이자》 interest/6분 ~로 돈을 꾸다 borrow money at the rate of six percent interest.

이(里) ①《거리》 ri, a Korean league ②《행정 구역》 village; township; ri, the smallest administrative.

이(釐) ①《돈의 단위》 ri, the tenth of a jun ②《길이의 단위》 ri, the tenth of a boon ③《무게의 단위》 ri, the tenth of a boon.

이(浬) a nautical[sea] mile; a knot.

이(哩) a mile/~수 mileage.

이(理) ①《도리》 reason 《진리》 truth 《공정》 justice/~에 맞지 않는 말을 하다 speak against all reason ②《원칙》 a principle.

이가(離家) leaving one's home for other place/~하다 leave home.

이가 원소(二價元素) 《화》 dyad.

이까짓 this kind of; such a (trifle); so trifling[slight, little, small]/~ 것 하고 깔본 것이 잘못이었다 I did wrong in making light of the matter.

이간(離間) alienation; estrangement/~하다 alienate/그는 그 부부를 ~시켰다 He split the couple up/~책 a discord-producing intrigue.

이깔나무 a kind of larch tree.

이갈다 grind[gnash] one's teeth; grit one's teeth 《분해서》 grind one's teeth with vexation.

이강(以降) since; after; henceforth/1월 1일 ~ on and after the first of January.

이같은 such; of the kind[sort]/~ 사정으로 under such circumstances as these.

이같이 like this; thus; so; in this way [manner]; in such a manner; so much /~ 많은 돈 such a big sum of money.

이거(移去) removal; moving away/~하다 remove; move away; leave; deport from.

이거(移居) removal; moving; changing one's residence[abode]; 《외국으로》 migrate/일본으로 ~하다 migrate to Japan.

이것 ①《지시》 this; this thing; this fact /~으로 with this; now; here/네 잘못은 ~뿐이 아니다 This is not the only mistake you have made. ②《의 부를 때》 ~ 좀 봐 I say!, Say!《미ㆍ구》.

이것저것 this and that; one thing and another; something or other/~ 해 보다 try one thing or another.

이겨내다 overcome (difficulties); conquer (the enemy); get over (a disease); resist (a temptation)/유혹을 ~ overcome a temptation; put the devil behind one.

이결(已決) a matter already settled/사전 matters already decided[settled].

이겹실 double-ply thread 《여러 겹》 twine.

이경(二更) the second watch of the night (around 10 p.m.).

이골나다 become used[accustomed] to; get inured to; grow experienced in; become skil[l]ful[good] at.

이곳 here; this place/~에 here; in this place/~으로 오신 지 얼마나 되십니까 How long have you been here?

이공(理工) science and engineering/~대학 the science and engineering college.

이과(理科) 《학문》 science 《과목》 the science course 《학부》 the science department.

이관(移管) transfer of control[authority, superintendence]/~하다 transfer/국고에 ~하다 transfer to the national treasury.

이교(異敎) a foreign religion; paganism; heathenism; heresy/~의 pagan; heretical/~도 a pagan; a heathen; an idolator/~를 전파하다 propagate heresy.

이구(耳垢) earwax; cerumen.

이구 동성(異口同聲) a unanimous voice; common consent/~으로 with one mouth[voice]; by common consent/사람들은 ~으로 그를 칭찬했다 They praised him with one accord.

이국(異國) a strange land; a foreign country[land]; an alien land/~적인 exotic/~인 a foreigner; a stranger; an alien/~풍 exoticism; foreign[alien] customs.

이궁(離宮) 1《태자궁》 the Palace of the Crown Prince 2《별궁》 a detached palace; a royal villa; a secondary palace.

이권(利權) rights and interests 《광산ㆍ철도의》 concessions; vested rights/~을 포기하다 renounce one's interests/~ 추구 grafting; grabbing; hunting for concession.

이끌다 guide; lead; head/바른 길로 사람을 ~ guide[lead] a man into the right.

이끌리다 be guided; be led; be headed/이끌리어 가다 be taken away; be taken along.

이글이글 deeply flushed; (burn) lively /~하다 (be) burning; blazing; glowing《voice》 flushing/전신이 ~했다 My body was all of a glow.

이금(泥金) gold dust mixed with glue; gilt paint.

이끗(利—) the first step for profit; the beginning of making gains.

이끼 moss; a lichen; a liverwort/구르는

**돌은 이끼도 안 낀다**《속담》A rolling stone gathers no moss. こけ

**이기**(利己) self-interest; selfishness; egoism／~적인 selfish; egoistic; self-seeking／그는 ~적인 사람이다 He has an eye to the main chance.／~주의 egoism／~주의자 an egoist[egotist]. りこ

**이기**(利器) ① a convenience; a device／문명의 ~ a modern convenience; a factor of civilization ②《재능》[practical] ability; [useful] talent ③《연모》a sharp-edged tool. りき

**이끼나** Oh!, Oh my!, Oh my goodness!, My!, My eye! あっ

**이기다**[1] ①《승리하다》win (*a battle*); gain a victory (*over*); hold the field; have the best of it 《쳐부수다》defeat; beat; triumph (*over*); 《정복하다》conquer／싸움에서 ~ win a battle／시합에 ~ win the game ②《극복하다》overcome; surmount; get over／유혹을 이겨내다 overcome a temptation. かつ

**이기다**[2] ①《반죽하다》knead (*flour*); mash (*potatoes*); work (*mortar*) ②《짓찧다》mince; chop; pound into pieces／고기를 ~ mince meat ③《기타》beat; paddle (*the wash*). こねる

**이기죽거리다** make invidious[sly, insinuating] remarks; talk at; carp／이기죽이기죽 (*talk*) invidiously; with sly hints; insinuatingly; carping.
くだらぬことをなかなかとしゃべる

**이김수** a winning move.

**이나** ①《그러나》but; while; though; although [and] yet／말은 사실」 행동이 나빴다 He spoke the truth, but what he did was bad. ②《정도》as many[much, long, far] as; about; around／그는 죽은 것」 다름없다 He is as good as dead. ③《선택》or; and; either … or／어느 것」 좋은 걸로 가져라 Take whichever[whatever] you like. —か. —でも

**이나마** although (*it is*)／초라한 집」 내 집 한 채 가졌으면 좋겠다 I wish I had a house of my own however humble it might be. —でも. —なりとも

**이날** ①《오늘》today; this day／~에 이르기까지 그의 행방은 불명이다 His whereabouts is unknown to this day. ②《당일》that day; the very[same] day. このひ

**이날저날** this day and that day 《차일피일》from day to day／~ 미루어 나가다 put off from day to day. そのうち

**이남**(以南) south of (*Seoul*); South of Korea／38선 ~ south of the 38th Parallel. いなん

**이남박** a rice-washing bowl; a wooden bowl with grooves running around the inside [used for washing rice].

**이내** ①《곧》soon; presently; at once; right away; immediately; instantly; straight away／그는 ~ 왔다 He was not long in coming. ②《그후》ever since; ever afterward. すぐ

**이내**(以內) within; inside (*of*); not exceeding; less than／3일 ~에 돈을 돌려 주겠다 I will pay back the money within three days. いない

**이냥** as it is; as one is; as it stands／~ 가겠다 I will go as I am. このまま

**이네들** these people; they. このひとたち

**이념**(理念) an idea; an ideology 《교리》a doctrine／~형 a form[type] of idea. りねん

**이녕**(泥濘) a muddy place; a mudhole 진창. ていねい

**이놈** this man[fellow]; this damn] guy／~아 You rascal!, You rat!, You scoundrel! こいつ

**이뇨**(利尿) urination; excretion of urine; diuresis／~하다 urinate; pass water／~ 곤란 difficulty in urination／~제 a diuretic; a hydragogue. りにょう

**이다** ①《지정하는 말》be／그는 학생~ He is a pupil. ②《되다》come; be／이번 생일이 되면 만 열 살~ I shall be ten years old next birthday. ③《수량》number; weigh; measure; cover. —である. —だ

**이따금** from time to time; sometimes; [every] now and then; as often as not; once in a while／~ 소식을 듣다 hear from (*a person*) once in a while.
ときどき

**이따위** such; like this; of this kind[sort]; this kind[sort]／~ 짓을 다시는 않겠다 I will never do such a thing again.
このたぐい

**이다지** so much; thus; to this extent [degree]; so (*large*)／~ 눈이 많이 올 줄은 몰랐다 I did not expect so much snow here. こんなに

**이단**(異端) heresy; paganism; heathenism／~ 을 주창하다 express a heretical view[doctrine]／~자 a heretic; a heathen. いたん

**이달** this month; the current[present] month／~ 봉급 this month's pay; one's pay for this month／~ 중에 in the course of this month. このつき

**이때** at this time[moment]; now; then; on this occasion／바로 ~ 한 여자가 다방으로 들어왔다 At this point a woman came into the tearoom. このとき

**이대로** as it is; as it stands; as one is; intact; untouched／~ 두시오 Leave it as it is.／~모임에 ~ 가도 좋으냐 May I go to the meeting as I am? このまま

**이도**(吏道) the duty of officials／~ 쇄신 renovation of officialdom. りどう

**이도**(利刀) a sharp-edged knife; a sharp [trenchant] sword. りとう

**이똥** tartar; the yellow on *one*'s teeth. はくそ

**이동**(異同) difference and sameness; distinction; difference／~ 식별 identification. いどう

**이동**(移動) movement; transfer; locomotion; drift; migration／~하다 move;

**이동** transfer; migrate; travel/인구의 ~ the movement[drift] of population/~ 경찰 railway police; mobile police; highway police/~ 병원 a hospital on wheels/~ 진료소 a traveling clinic/~ 신고 a report of one's removal. いどう

**이동(異動)** a change; [an] alteration; shifting/내각의 ~ a reshuffle of the cabinet/인사 ~ changes of personnel; reshuffling of personnel.

**이동(以東)** east of (*Seoul*)/서울 ~ east of *Seoul*; *Seoul* and eastward. いとう

**이둔(利鈍)** sharpness and dullness; nimbleness and slowness; cleverness and stupidity. りどん

**이드르르** glossily; lustrously; brightly/~하다 (be) glossy; lustrous; bright 《피부 따위가》 soft and delicate; soft and shiny/~한 머리털 glossy[lustrous] hair. つやつや

**이득(利得)** gain; profit; benefit; returns; 《법》 issue/부당 ~ profiteering. いとく

**이든지** whether … or; either … or; or; no matter (*who, what, when, where, how*)/이것 ~ 그것 ~ 마음대로 가져라 You may take either this one or that.
—でも. —なりと

**이들이들하다** (be) glossy ⇨이드르르하다.

**이듬¹** 《다음》 next; the following/~해 the next[following] year. つぎ

**이듬²** 《농사의》 the second hoeing; the second weeding; the second plowing/~하다 give (*a field*) a second hoeing [weeding, plowing].

**이등(二等)** the second class; the second/~의 second; second-rate[-class]/~이 되다 finish second/~으로 졸업하다 graduate second in *one's* class. にとう

**이등변 삼각형(二等邊三角形)** 《수》 an isosceles triangle. にとうへんさんかっけい

**이등분(二等分)** bisection/~하다 divide equally[in half]; divide into two equal parts/나는 사과를 ~으로 쪼갰다 I cut an apple into two equal parts.

**이라고** 《이것은 무엇 ~ 하느냐 What do you call this?/네가 가는 곳이 어디라고 말했느냐 Where did you say it was that you are going?⇨라고.
—だと

**이락(利落)** ~의 ex dividend[interest]/~ 채권 《증권》 an ex div. bond. りおちかがく

**이란** 《이라고 하는》 that is [called]; 《이라고 하는 것은》 "as for [the one that is called]"/운명 ~ 참 야릇하다 Fate plays strange tricks. —という

**이란성(二卵性)** ~의 biovular/~ 쌍둥이 (*one of*) fraternal twins.

**-이람** do you mean to say that it is?/그런 놈도 사람~ Would you call the likes of him a human being?
—か. —というのか

**이랑¹** the ridge and furrow (*of a field*).

**이랑²** and; or; what with/기쁨 ~ 슬픔 으로 with; a mixture of joy and sadness.
—やら. —なり

**이래(以來)** ①《그후》 since; since then; after that/나는 전쟁 ~ 줄곧 여기 있었다 I have been here ever since the war. ②《금후》 in future; after this; hereafter.
いらい

**이래(邇來)** recent years. じらい

**이래라저래라** ordering (*a person*) to do this and to do that; ordering (*a person*) about. ああしろこうしろ

**이래봬도** such as I am; humble as I am; whatever you may take me for.
こうみえても

**이래저래** this or that; one thing or another; one way or another; somehow or other/~ 바쁘다 I am busy with one thing or another. ああしてこうして

**이랬다저랬다** this way and that way; (be) changeable; fickle; unreliable/그는 말을 ~한다 He says first one thing and then the opposite.
ああしたりこうしたり

**이러** 《마소를 몰 때》 Get up!, Giddap!, Haw! 《급히 몰 때》 Gee-ho!, Gee-up! どう

**이러구러** thus and thus/~ 10년의 세월을 보냈다 Thus and thus I spent ten years. あれこれ

**이러나저러나** in any way; anyhow; in either case; in either way/~ 마찬가지 이다 It is all one[the same] to me.
いずれにしても

**이러니저러니** this or that; something or other/~ 말할 것 없이 without saying this or that/지금 와서 ~해야 소용없다 It is too late now to raise any objections. とやかく

**이러이러하다** be so and so; such and such/~이러이러한 사람 such and such a person. かくかくである

**이러쿵저러쿵** this or that ⇨이러니저러니. なんかの

**이러하다** be this way; be like this; be as follows/사실인측 ~ The fact is this.
こうである

**이럭저럭** somehow or other; in one way or another/~하는 동안에 in the meantime; meanwhile/그들은 ~ 살고 있다 They are making a living by one means or another. そうしているなかに

**이런** ①《이러한》 such; like this; of this kind[sort]; this kind[sort] of/~ 재미 있는 책은 읽은 적이 없다 I have never read such an interesting book. ②《놀람》 Oh!, O dear! こんな

**이렇게** like this; thus; in this way; so/나는 일이 ~ 될 줄 몰랐다 I don't know things would come to this./~ 추운 날씨는 처음이다 I have never seen such cold weather as this.

**이렇다** be like this ⇨이러하다. こうである

**이렇다저렇다** this or that ⇨이러니저러니.
ああだこうだ

**이렇듯** thus; like this; so [like]/~ 잘 될 줄 몰랐다 I did not expect to succeed

이렇지않다 751 이리저리

**이렇지 않다** (be) not like this/내가 떠났을 때는 이렇지 않았다 It was not like this when I left. こうでない

**이레** 《날짜》 the seventh day [of the month]; 《날수》 seven days.

**이력**(履歷) one's personal history; one's career; one's antecedents; one's past; one's record; one's background/나는 그의 ~을 알고 있다 I know his antecedents. りれき

**이례**(異例) an exception; a singular[an exceptional] case; an unprecedented case 《위례》 unconventionality/그의 승진은 ~다 His promotion is exceptional.

**이로**(理路) reasoning; argument/~ 정연하다 be consistent (in one's theory); be logical.

**이로부터** ①《시간》 from now on; from this time forth; in [the] future; hereafter ②《이유·결과》 from this cause; hence; as a result of this/~ 여러 문제가 일어났다 Out of this many questions arose. これから

**이론**(異論) an objection; a dissent; a different[an opposite] opinion[view]/이 일에 대해서 하등 ~이 있을 리 없다 There can be no two opinions as to this matter. いろん

**이론**(理論) theory/~적 theoretical/~상 theoretically; in theory/~을 세우다 theorize; advance a theory/~과 실천을 일치시키다 reconcile theory and practice/~가 a theorist. りろん

**이롭다**(利—) (be) profitable; lucrative; gainful; beneficient; advantageous 《유리》 favourable 《좋다》 good 《교훈적》 instructive/소년들에게 이로운 책 a book good for youngsters. ゆうりである

**이롱**(耳聾) deafness/~증 a symptom of deafness. じろう

**이루** by any means; by no means; [cannot] possibly; utterly/~ 헤아릴 수 없는 numberless/~ 형용할 수 없다 can hardly describe it. すべて

**이루**(耳漏) 《의》 otorrhoea; discharge from the ear. じろう

**이루**(二壘) 《야구》 the second base; the middle sack/~수 a second baseman; a second baser[sacker]/~타를 치다 a two-base hit. にるい

**이루다** ①《성취하다》 accomplish; achieve; attain; effect 《실현하다》 realize 《완성하다》 complete; finish 《실행하다》 fulfill; carry out /소망을 ~ realize one's desire ②《형성하다》 make; form; constitute/사회를 ~ form society/좋은 자연 환경을 ~ form a good natural circumstances. なる

**이루어지다** ①《성취·실현되다》 get[be] accomplished[done, achieved, attained, effected, realized]/뜻이 ~ one's purpose is realized ②《형성되다》 be formed [made up, constituted]. たっせいする

**이룩하다** 《건립·주립하다》 erect; build; set up; establish; found 《성취하다》 accomplish; achieve; complete/새 살림을 ~ set up a household; establish[create] a house. たっせいする

**이류**(二流) ~의 second-class; second-rate; minor; inferior/ ~ 작가 a second-rate writer.

**이륙**(離陸) a take-off; a hop-off; taking [flying] off; leaving the ground/~하다 《비행기가》 take[hop] off; take the air; leave the ground/~과 착륙을 연습하다 practice taking-off and landing. りりく

**이륜**(彝倫) 《인문》 humane duties; morality; moral duties[principles]; 《인문·도덕》 ethics and morality. じんりん

**이륜**(二輪) 《수레의》 two wheels 《꽃의》 two flowers/~차 a two-wheeled vehicle; a cart; a two-wheeler.

**이르다**¹ 《시간이》 (be) early; premature /아직 ~ It is quite early yet./금년은 벼는 ~ The rice crop is early this year. はやい

**이르다**² ①《도착하다》 reach; arrive (at, in); get (to)/이르는 곳마다 everywhere one goes; throughout/이 길로 가면 부산에 이른다 This road leads to Busan. ②《정도·범위》 reach; extend to; come to; lead to. いたる

**이르다**³ ①《알리다》 let (a person) know; inform; report; tell 《고자질》 tell on (a person)/미리 ~ give notice beforehand ②《가라사대》 say/옛말에 이르기를 an old saying has it that. いう

**이르집다** ①《뜯어벗기다》 pull off; peel; pick/장판귀를 ~ pick at the end of the floor paper ②《날조하다》 make up; fabricate; cook up; fake up; frame up /사건을 ~ frame up an affair. かわをむく

**이른바** so-called; as it is called; what is called/저런 여자가 ~ 전후파 여성이다 Such a woman is what we call a post-war girl. いわゆる

**이를테면** so to speak; as it were; in other words 《요컨대》 in a word; in short /인생이란 ~ 아침 이슬 같은 것이다 "Our life is, so to speak, a morning dew. いうならば

**이름** ⇨별항 참조.

**이름씨** 《언》 a noun; a substantive.

**이리**¹ 《물고기의》 soft roe; milt.

**이리**² 《동》 a wolf; Canis lupus(학명)/~떼 a pack of wolves. やまいぬ

**이리**³ ①《방향》 this way; this direction; this side; here/~ 오십시오 This way, please. ②《이렇게》 in this way; like this; so/~ 많이 so many[much]. ここに

**이리이리** so and so; such and such; in this way/~ 하라고 말하다 tall (a person) to do such and such. うんぬん

**이리저리** 《이쪽저쪽으로》 this way and that; here and there 《이렇게저렇게》

**이러쿵저러쿵** like this and that 《곳곳에》 in places 《사방으로》 all about／~ 둘러보다 look this way and that／~ 돌아다니다 wander[roam, ramble] about; loaf around.

**이리쿵저리쿵** this and that; one thing and[or] another ⇨이러저러니. あれやこれや

**이리하다** say[read] like this ⇨이러하다. こうする

**이마** the forehead; the brow／~의 땀을 닦다 mop one's brow／~를 찌푸리다 knit [bend, wrinkle] one's brows. ひたい

**이마적** recently; lately; of late; these days; nowadays. さいきん

**이만** this[so] much／오늘은 ~ 합니다 So much for today. これだけ

**이만저만** 《정도》 in no small degree; not a little 《수》 in no small number 《양》 in no small quantity／~ 놀라지 않았다 be not a little surprised. ちょっとやそっと

**이만큼** this much[big, long]; so much [many]; to this extent[degree]／~ 공부 하면 합격할 것이다 If I work so hard, I shall pass the examination. これだけ

**이만하다** be this much; be as much[big, long] as this; be to this extent[degree] ／내 책상은 ~ My desk is this large. これくらいだ

**이맘때** about this time; at this time of day[night]／어제 ~ 도착했다 I came here about this time yesterday.

**이맛살** wrinkles on the brow[forehead] ／~을 찌푸리다 knit[wrinkle, bend] one's brows; frown. ひたいのしわ

**이맞다** be in gear (with); gear (into, with); mesh (with); engage (with)／이 맞추다 engage; clutch. びったりあう

**이면** 《조사》 if[when] it is; as for／여기서 한 3분~ 간다 It's about three minutes [walk] from here.

**이면(裏面)** the back; the reverse; the other side 《내부》 the inside／인생의 ~ the seamy side of life／~에서 활약하다 play an active part in the background.

**이면(二面)** ①《두 개의 면》 two faces; two sides ②《신문의》 the second page／~은 경제난이다 The second page is devoted to financial affairs. にめん

**이명(異名)** another name; a second name; an alias 《별명》 a nickname; sobriquet. いめい

**이명(耳鳴)** ringing[singing, buzzing, drumming] in the ears／~증 《의》 tinnitus. みみなり

**이모(姨母)** one's mother's sister; a maternal aunt. ははのしまい

**이모(異母)** a different mother／~ 형제 a brother by a different mother; brothers born of different mothers.

**이모부(姨母夫)** the husband of one's maternal aunt; a maternal uncle-by-marriage. ははのしまいのおっと

**이모작(二毛作)** two crops a year; two-crop farming; semiannual crops／~하 다 raise two crops (of rice) a year／~ 지대 a two-crop area. にもうさく

**이목(耳目)** 《귀와 눈》 《주의》 eye and ear 《주의》 public attention[notice]／~을 끌다 attract[arrest] public attention／~을 피 하다 avoid public notice; shun publicity. じもく

**이목구비(耳目口鼻)** ear, eye, mouth, and nose 《용모》 features; looks; a countenance／~가 반듯하다 have regular features／~가 반반하다 have good [pretty] features.

**이몽가몽** a trance; dreaminess／~하다 feel as if in a dream; be in a trance; (be) dreamlike; dreamy; dim; vague; faint; indistinct. うつらうつら

**이무기** a monster serpent; a python. うわばみ

**이문(利文)** profit; gain; returns／상당한 ~을 남기다 make a good profits. りえきのぜに

**이문(異聞)** a strange report; curious information; strange tales. いぶん

**이물** the bow; the prow; the head; the stem／~에서 고물까지 from stem to stern. へさま

**이미** ①《벌써》 already; now／~ 때가 늦다 It is now too late. ②《앞서》 previously; beforehand／~ 말한 바와 같이 as previously stated[mentioned]. すでに

**이민(移民)** 《이주》 emigration(국내로); immigration(국내로) 《이주자》 an emigrant(외국에 간); an immigrant(외국에서 온); a settler(개척지의)／~하다 emigrate (into, to)(외국으로); immigrate (into, to)(국내로); plant settlers (on)／많은 사람이 미국으로 ~한다 A large number of people emigrate to America from this country.／~법 immigration[emigration] law. いみん

**이바지** ~하다 contribute (to); be conductive to; make for; go far[do much] toward 《공급》 supply／한국의 경제 발전 에 ~하다 contribute to the economical growth of Korea.

**이박자(二拍子)** 〖음〗 binary time.

**이반(離反)** estrangement; alienation; defection (from a person); disaffection／ ~하다 be estranged (from); be disaffected (toward)／민심이 현 정부로부터 ~ 하고 있다 The public are alienated from the present Government. りはん

**이발(理髮)** 《깎음》 haircutting; a haircut 《다듬기》 hairtrimming; hairdressing／ ~하다 get[have] a haircut／~을 해야겠 다 I must have a haircut.／~ 기계 a hair-clipper. りはつ

**이밥** plain boiled rice.

**이방(異邦)** an alien country; a foreign country[land]／~인 an alien; a foreigner 《성경》 a Gentile. いほう

**이배(二倍)** double; twice; two times／~ 하다 double／이익을 ~하다 double the

이번 (금번) this time 《최근》 recently; lately 《현재의》 present; new; now 《다음번》 next time 《머지않아》 shortly; soon 《다음의》 next 《지난번의》 last; recent/~은 네가 갈 차례다 Now it is your turn to go.

이번(二番) number two; No. 2; the second.

이법(理法) a law 《과학상의》 a scientific law/자연의 ~ the order of nature; natural laws.

이변(異變) 《사고》 an accident 《재앙》 a disaster; a calamity 《변고》 an extraordinary phenomenon/그에게 무슨 ~이나 없었는지 I fear that something has happened to him.

이별(離別) parting; separation 《이혼》 divorce/~을 애석해 하다 be loath to part/아내와 ~하다 divorce one's wife/~가 a farewell song/~주(酒) a farewell drink.

이병(罹病) contracting a disease; suffering from illness/~하다 contract[take, catch, get] a disease; suffer from illness/~율 the attack rate.

이보다 than this/~ 앞서 prior to this; before this/~ 나쁘다 be worse than this.

이복(異腹) a different mother/~ 형제 brothers by a different mother; half brothers.

이봐 Hi!, Hey!, Say!, I say; Look here!, Haloo!

이부(異父) a different father/~ 형제 uterine brothers; brothers by different fathers; half brothers.

이부(二部) ①two parts 《제2의》 the second part; part two/~ 수업을 하다 adopt a double-shift school system ②《두 권》 two copies/이 사전 ~ two copies of this dictionary.

이부자리 bedding; a mattress 《요》 bed clothes 《이불》 a quilt/~를 개다 fold up[turn down] the bedding.

이북(以北) 《북》 north 《38선 이북》 north Korea.

이분(二分) dividing in two/~하다 divide (a thing) in two; halve/~의 일 one half/~ 음부 《음》 a half-note; a minim 《영》.

이분자(異分子) a heterogeneous element; an alien[a foreign] element; an outsider.

이불 《이부자리》 bedding; bedclothes 《누비 이불》 a quilt 《침대 덮개》 counterpane; coverlet 《홑이불》 a sheet/~을 뒤집어 쓰다 pull one's bedclothes over one's head.

이쁘다 (be) pretty 예쁘다.

이비(理非) the rights and wrongs; the relative merits.

이비(耳鼻) ear and nose/~인후과 otorhinolaryngology.

이사(移徙) removal; house-moving/~하다 change one's residence[abode]/내일 오정까지 ~하겠읍니다 We shall move in by tomorrow noon.

이사(二死) 《야구》 two outs.

이사(理事) a director 《공공 단체의》 trustee/~가 되다 obtain a seat on the board of directors/~관 a secretary; a councilor/상무 ~ an executive director.

# 이 름

①《명칭》 a name; a personal name; an appellation; a denomination/~을 짓다 give a name; christen; name/그는 ~만의 선생이다 He is a teacher only in name./아무개의 ~을 부르다 call a person by name/나는 정원에 있는 꽃의 ~을 죄다 별 수 있다 I can name all the flowers in the garden.

②《성명》 a name; a full name 《실명·통칭》 a given[personal, Christian] name; a first name〈미〉;《애칭》 a pet name 《성》 a surname; a family name/~을 묻다 ask (a person's) name/~을 바꾸다 change one's name/~을 속이다 assum another's[a false] name; give a wrong name/예수의 ~으로 빌다 pray in Jesus' name/나는 그 사람의 ~을 안다 I know him by name.

③《명성》 a [good] name; reputation; fame 《악명》 notoriety/~있는 사람 a man of name; a famous person/~나다 become famous[renowned]/ ~을 멸치다 get[win] a name; have one's name up; make[get, win] oneself a name; gain fame; win[obtain] distinction/~을 후세[역사]에 남기다 leaves one's name behind[in history]/부모의 ~을 더럽히다 stain one's family name; disgrace one's parents/~을 팔다 trade on one's fame; take advantage of one's popularity; prostitute one's reputation/그 작품으로 그는 ~이 났다 With that work his name was made./사람은 죽어도 ~은 남는다 Man lives but for one generation, his name for many., A man dies but his name remains./이 지역은 깡패 지대로 ~이 있다 The quarter is notorious for hoodlums.

④《구실》 a pretext; an excuse; a plea 《명목》 a cause/자선이란 ~ 아래 under the pretext[mask] of charity.

**이사이** these days; nowadays; lately; recently; of late. このあいだ

**이삭** a spike; a head; shuckings; an ear (of *grain*)/～을 줍다 glean (*a field*)/～이 나오다 be in the ear; come into ears.

**이산**(離散) dispersion; scattering; separation; break-up/일가 ～의 비운에 처해 있다 The family had the misfortune to be broken up./～ 가족 dispersed families. りさん

**이산화**(二酸化) 【화】dioxide/～ 탄소 carbon dioxide. にさんか

**이삼**(二三) two or three/～ 일 a few days; two or three days. にさん

**이상**(以上) ①《수량·정도》 more than; over; above; beyond; and upward; upward of/그 ～ 말할 것이 없다 I have nothing further[more] to say. ②《위에 말한》 above-mentioned; stated above/～은 그의 연설의 대요다 The above is the gist of his speech. ③《…한 바에는》 since; now that; seeing that/약속을 한 ～ since you have promised. いじょう

**이상**(異常) strangeness; queerness; oddity; abnormality; extraordinariness/～하다 《기이》(be) strange; queer; odd 《보통과 다름》 unusual; uncommon; abnormal 《수상》 suspicious/～하게 들리다 sound strange/그의 행동이 ～하다 His behavior is suspicious/～아(兒) an abnormal child. いじょう

**이상**(異狀) 《고장》 an accident; disorder 《변화》 change 《신체의》 indisposition/～이 있다 be abnormal 《기계에》 be out of order 《사람에》 be indisposed/그는 정신에 ～이 생겼다 He has been mentally deranged. いじょう

**이상**(理想) an ideal; the goal [of ambition]; the ultimate objection/그녀는 ～이 높다 She has a lofty ideal. りそう

**이색**(異色) ①different colour ②《색다른 것》 novelty of/～의 of a different colour; novel/～ 인종 a race of a different colour. いしょく

**이서**(以西) ～의 west of/서대문 ～의 west of West Gate. いせい

**이서**(裏書) endorsement/～하다 endorse/～인 an endorser/공동 ～ a joint endorsement. うらがき

**이설**(異說) a different view; a divergent view[opinion]; heterodoxy; a heresy/이 문제에 관하여 ～이 분분했다 Many conflicting opinions have been expressed on this subject. いせつ

**이성**(理性) reasoning power; rationality; 【철】 Logos/～에 호소하다 appeal to *one's* reason/～이 결핍되다 be devoid of reason/～ 동물 rational creatures/순수 ～ pure reason. りせい

**이성**(異姓) a different surname; a different family name. いせい

**이성**(異性) ①the other[opposite] sex/그는 ～간에 교제가 넓다 He has a large acquaintance of the opposite sex. ②《다른 성질》 different nature; 【화】isomerism. いせい

**이세**(二世) ①【종】the present and the future world ②《인명 뒤에》the Second; Junior ③《다음 세대》 a second[next] generation. にせい

**이속**(異俗) different[strange] customs. いぞく

**이송**(移送) transfer; removal; transportation/～하다 transfer; remove; transport/사건의 ～ removal[transfer, transmission] of a case. いそう

**이수**(離愁) sorrow of parting; the pain of parting.

**이수**(離水) ～하다 leave the water; take [hop] off from the water.

**이수**(里數) ①《거리》 the mileage; the distance ②《마을 수》 the number of villages. りすう

**이수**(履修) completion/～하다 complete; finish; go through/본과를 ～하다 complete[study] the regular course. りしゅう

**이쑤시개** a toothpick/～로 이를 쑤시다 pick *one's* teeth; use a toothpick.

**이순**(耳順) the sixtieth year of age 《사람》 a sexagenarian/～에 달하다 attain *one's* sixtieth year of age. じじゅん

**이슥하다** late; (be) advanced/밤이 이슥하도록 일하다 work far into the night. ふけている

**이슬** ①dew 《방울진》 dewdrops/교수대의 ～로 사라지다 end *one's* days on the gallow[gibbet] ②《눈물》 tear-drops/～지다 (*one's* eyes) become tearful. つゆ

**이슬받이** ①《때》 the time when dew begins to form; dewfall ②《도롱이》 a grass kilt worn as protection from dew; a dew-kilt ③《사람》 a person who clears the way of dewdrops for another ④《길》 a dew-laden path. つゆのおりるころ

**이슬비** a drizzle; a mizzle; a misty rain; a fog rain/종일토록 ～가 내렸다 It drizzled from morning till night.

**이승** this world; this life/～의 괴로움 the trials of this life. このせい

**이승**(二乘) square ⇨자승. にじょう

**이식**(利息) interest ⇨이자. りそく

**이식**(利殖) increase of wealth; money-making/그는 ～에 눈이 밝지 못하다 He knows little of the art of making money. りしょく

**이식**(移植) transplantation 《식물의》 naturalization 《피부의》 grafting/～하다 transplant (*a flower*); 《식물을》 naturalize 《피부를》 graft/외국의 식물을 마당에 ～하다 colonize foreign plants in a garden. いしょく

**이식**(二食) two meals of a day.

**이신 동체**(異身同體) one flesh/부부는 ～이다 Man and wife are one flesh.

**이신론**(理神論) 【철】 deism. りしんろん

**이심**(二心) double-heartedness; duplicity

/그는 ~을 품고 있지 않나 생각된다 I suspect him of duplicity. にしん

이심(異心) 《다른 마음》a different intention[mind, heart]; 《배신》 a treasonous intention[thought, idea, design]/~을 품다 play a double game. いしん

이심각(離心角) an eccentric angle. りしんかく

이심권(離心圈) an accentric orbit. りしんけん

이심률(離心率) eccentricity. りしんりつ

이심 전심(以心傳心) telepathy; mind-transference/~하다 communicate telepathically. いしんでんしん

이십(二十) twenty; a score/~대의 여자 a woman in her twenties. にじゅう

이십오시(二十五時) the twenty-fifth hour. にじゅうごじ

이아치다 《손해를 끼치다》cause damage; lead to loss; harm; injure; spoil; ruin 《방해되다》 be a hindrance; stand in one's way 《방해하다》 hinder obstruct; interfere (with). そんがいをあたえる

이악하다 (be) keen for gain; be wideawake to one's own interest; be shrewd; sharp; smart; clever/이악한 아이 a smart boy.

이앓이 toothache; odontalgia/~를 하다 have[suffer from] a toothache. しつう

이앙(移秧) rice planting; rice transplantation/~하다 plant out the rice/~에 분주하다 be busily planting the rice.

이야기 ⇨별항 참조(page 1659).

이야말로 indeed; just; the very/~ 바로 내가 찾던 책이다 This is the very book that I have been looking for. これこそ

이양(移讓) transfer; handing over; relinquishment/정권을 ~하다 turn over the reins of government. いじょう

이어, 이어서 《다음에》 next; secondly; in the second place 《그 후에》 after; then; subsequently; soon after/화가 연~ 닥쳐 온다 Disasters come treading on each other's heels. つづいて

이어(耳語) a whisper.

이어(俚語) 《비어》 vulgarity; colloquialism《속》; slang. りご

이어(移御) change of the king's residence/~하다 change the king's residence. くんしゅがいどころをうつすこと

이어차 Heave-ho! / ~ 이어차 짐을·나르다 carry a load with the cry of heave-ho. よいさ

이언정 though; although; even if.

이엉 straw thatch/지붕에 ~을 잇다 thatch a roof with straw; thatch. とま

이에 hereupon; thereupon; whereupon; on this; immediately after that; consequently. ここにおいて

이에서 than this; compared with this/~ 더한 불행은 없다 There can be no greater misfortune than this. これより

이에짬 a joint; a juncture; a connection. あわせめ

이여(爾餘) the rest; the other.

이역(異域) ①《이국》 a foreign[an alien] country[land, part] ②《먼 곳》 a remote place; a different village/~에서 죽다 die in an alien land. いいき

이역(二役) a double role; two roles[par-

# 이 야 기

①《담화》 a conversation; a talk 《잡담》 a chat; a gossip/~하다 speak (to a person); converse (with a person); talk (to a person); chatter (with a person); gossip (about a person, matter); have a talk[chat] (with a person)/~를 잘 하는 사람 a good talker[speaker]; 《수다장이》 a talkative person/~를 걸다 speak to; address oneself to/사냥 ~를 하다 talks about hunting.

②《화제》 a topic [of conversation]; the subject/~하다 talk (about, on); speak (about, of); tell/할 ~가 많다 I have many things to tell you. /이제 그 ~는 그만두라 Let us say no more about it.

③《소문》 talk; a rumo[u]r; a report; hearsay/~하다 say/~를 들어 알고 있다 I know it by hearsay. /좋은 ~가 있다 I will tell you what., Tell you what. /너의 ~는 자주 들었다 I've often heard about you.

④《사실·허구》 a story; a tale 《사실담》 an account 《전설》 a legend; a statement/~하다 tell (a story); give an account (of a matter); relate; narrate (a story)/그 ~만큼 재미있는 ~를 알고 있나요 Can you match that story?

⑤《진술》 a statement/~하다 state; tell; relate/입장을 ~하다 state one's case.

⑥《기타》 a negotiation(교섭); 《의사 소통》 understanding 《합의》an agreement 《상담》 a consultation/~하다 《상담》 talk with (a person) about (a matter); consult with (a person); discuss (a matter) with (a person)/~가 상통하다 have[keep] a good understanding with (a person)/~가 다르지 않습니까 It is against our agreement., That's not my understanding. /그와 만나 ~하려면 언제쯤이 가장 좋을까요 When is the best time to approach him? / ~ 상대가 없다 I have no one to talk to.

이역시(一亦是) this too[also, again].

이연(離緣) divorce; legal separation; the dissolution of marriage[adoption]/~하다 《아내와》 divorce 《one's wife》; renounce one's marriage vows 《양자와》 cancel adoption.

이연발(二連發) 《총》 a double-barreled gun; a double-chambered rifle.

이연식(二連式) ~의 duplex.

이열(二列) two rows; a double line; a double file[column]/~로 행진하다 march two abreast.

이염(耳炎) otitis; inflammation of the ear/중~ otitis media.

이염화물(二鹽化物) 【화】 a bichloride.

이온 【화】 an ion/양~ a cation; a positive ion/음~ an anion; a negative ion/~화하다 ionize.

이와전와(以訛傳訛) transmitting errors; perpetuating mistakes/~하다 transmit errors; perpetuate mistakes.

이완(弛緩) relaxation; laxity; slackness; 【의】 atony/~하다 slacken; relax; lax; be slackened/해방후 도덕의 ~이 심했다 After the Liberation, moral deterioration is simply remarkable among our countrymen.

이왕(已往) the past; bygones/~의 past; bygone/~에 already; now that; as long as/~에 늦었으니 천천히 가자 It is already late, so let's take our time.

이외(以外) 《제외》 except; save 《for》; but; outside 《of》; aside[apart] 《from》; beyond 《그 외에》 besides; in addition 《to》; aside[apart] 《from》〈미〉/그 ~의 일은 아무것도 모른다 I know only this./도둑질 ~는 모든 것을 다 했다 I did everything except stealing.

이외(理外) above reasoning; transcendental/ ~의 이(理) a transcendental reason[truth].

이욕(利慾) greed; avarice; love of gain [money]; covetousness; cupidity/~에 눈이 멀다 be blinded by avarice.

이용(利用) use; utilization; turning to account; improvement; economy/~하다 make use of; utilze; take advantage of/여가를 ~하다 make [good] use of one's leisure/그는 언제나 나를 ~하려고 한다 He is always trying to make a cat's paw of me./~법 how to use 《a book》/~자 a user.

이울다 wither; droop; fade 《쇠약》 weaken; be enervated; be on the wane/달이 이울어 가고 있다 The moon is waning./서 나라의 국위도 이울고 있다 The prestige of that country is on the decline.

이웃 the neighborhood 《집》 next door [house]; 《사람》 a neighbor; a neighborhcod/~의 neighboring; next; adjoining /그녀는 내 ~에 산다 She likes next door to me.

이원(梨園) ①《배밭》 a pear orchard 《연예계》 the treatrical world; the stage/~의 꽃 a star of the treatrical ②《배우학원》 an institute of acting (in former days).

이원(利源) source of gain[profit].

이원(二元) duality/~론 dualism/~ 방송 simultaneous broadcast by two stations.

이원제(二院制) a bicameral system; a two-chamber[house] system.

이월(二月) February(略: Feb.).

이월(移越) carrying forward/~하다 carry forward 《a sum, an account balance》/다음 연도로 ~하다 carry 《a sum》 forward to next year.

이유(理由) 《까닭》 a reason; a cause; a ground《근거》; 《동기》 why; motive 《구실》 a pretext; an excuse/~가 있어서 with good reason/건강상의 ~로 for reason of health.

이유(離乳) weaning; ablactation/~하다 wean 《a child》 from the breast[from it mother]; ablactate 《a baby》/~기 the weaning period.

이윤(利潤) profit; gain; a profit margin /상당한 ~을 올리다 make a good profit /~ 통제 control of corporate profits.

이율(利率) the rate of interest/법정 ~ the legal rate of interest/협정 ~ the conventional rate of interest.

이율 배반(二律背反) antinomy.

이윽고 after a while; before long; soon after; in a short time; presently; shortly/그는 ~ 왔다 It was not long before he came.

이음(異音) 《음성》 an allophone.

이의(異義) 《뜻》 a different meaning 《주의》 a different principle.

이의(異意) 《의견의》 a different opinion [view].

이의(異議) 《반대》 an objection; an exception 《항의》 a protest 《불찬성》 a dissent; 【법】 a demurrer/종업원들은 밤일에 ~를 신립했다 The workers objected to working nights.

이익(利益) ①《이윤》 profit; gain 《수익》 returns/많은 ~을 올리다 make a large profit ②《편익》 benefit; profit; good; interests; advantage/사회의 ~을 도모하다 labour for the public good/공동의 ~을 증진하다 promote their common interests.

이인(二人) two men[persons]/~승 a double seater/~ 삼각(三脚) a three-legged race.

이인(異人) ①《기재》 a genius; a wizard 《미·구》; a man of no common ability ②《다른 사람》 different people/동명~ a

**이인종(異人種)** an alien[a different] race /~간의 결혼 interracial[mixed] marriage.

**이입(移入)** introduction; importation /~하다 bring in (*from*); import; introduce /감정 ~ 『심』 empathy.

**이자** the spleen (췌장) the pancreas.

**이자(利子)** interest /~를 붙여 돈을 빌려 주다 put *one's* money out at interest.

**이자 택일(二者擇一)** alternative; selecting one alternative /~하다 choose between the two.

**이장(移葬)** exhuming and burying elsewhere /~하다 exhume and bury in another place; change the burial site.

**이장(里長)** the head of a village; a *ri* chief.

**이재(罹災)** suffering (from *a calamity*); affliction /~하다 suffer (from *a calamity*); fall victim (to *a calamity*) /~민 the sufferers.

**이제** now; this occasion / ~야말로 절호의 기회다 Now is the time, or never. / 정말 더위는 ~부터다 the hottest season is yet.

**이조(李朝)** the *yi* Dynasty.

**이쪽¹** this side[way]; our side / 은행은 ~에 있다 The bank is on this side of the street to come.

**이쪽²** a broken piece of tooth; a chip from tooth.

**이족(異族)** ① (이민족) a foreign race ② (이성) a different family.

**이족(二足)** ~의 two footed; biped (*animal*).

**이종(姨從)** cousin by a maternal aunt.

**이종(異種)** a different kind[sort] /~의 of a different kind[species].

**이종(移種)** transplantation /~하다 transplant.

**이종(二種)** the second class /~ 우편물 the second-class mail[matter].

**이주(移住)** (이사) removal (인종·동물의) migration (외국으로) emigration (외국에서) immigration /~하다 move; migrate; emigrate; immigrate / ~민 an emigrant; an immigrant.

**이주간(二週間)** two weeks; a fortnight.

**이죽거리다** make invidious remarks; carp; prattle.

**이죽거리다** prattle; chatter; tattle; rattle.

**이중(二重)** ~의 double; twofold; duplicate /~으로 doubly; twice; over again / ~ 생활 a double life /~ 인격[국적] dual personality[nationality] / ~ 인격자 a double-faced person; a Dr. Jekyll /~ 결혼 bigamy /~창 『음』 a duet /환희의 ~창 a double occasion for joy /~ 촬영 an overlap /~으로 하다 double; duplicate; put on above the other.

**이즈음** these days; lately; recently; of late /~의 사건 a recent event /~ 그녀는 어떻게 지내고 있습니까 How is she these days?

**이지(理智)** intellect; reasoning power; intelligence /~로 판단하다 judge by intellect / ~주의 intellectualism / ~적인 용모 an intellectual countenance.

**이지러지다** break off; chip (달이) wane /저 유리컵들은 모두 이지러졌다 That glasses are all chipped.

**이지렁스럽다** be unabashedly deceitful; be not so sweet as one looks; be a devil with an angel's face.

**이지마는** but; however; though.

**이직(移職)** change of occupation /~하다 change *one's* job[occupation]; take up another employment.

**이직자(離職者)** the jobless; the unemployed; a person out of work.

**이질(姨姪)** the children of *one's* wife's sister.

**이질(痢疾)** 『의』 dysentery.

**이질(異質)** heterogeneity; an unusual man /~의 heterogeneous.

**이질풀(痢疾─)** 『식』 the crane's-bill; *Geranium nepalense* (학명).

**이차(二次)** ① (두 번째) the second (부차) secondary ② 『수』 quadratic /그런 일은 ~적인 문제다 A question like that is of secondary importance. /제 ~ 세계 대전 the Second World War.

**이차어피(以此於彼)** in any case; anyhow; at any rate; after all; in the long run; at best; at all; of course /~ 그러리라고 생각했다 I thought as much.

**이착(二着)** the second place; a runner-up /~하다 finish second; come in second.

**이채(異彩)** a conspicuous color /~를 띠다 be conspicuous; show brilliance /그는 반에서 ~를 띠고 있다 He cuts[makes] a brilliant[conspicuous] figure in his class.

**이처럼** thus; like this; in this way [manner]; so much; this much /~ 아침 일찍기 at this hour of the morning /~ 재미있는 일은 없다 Nothing is more interesting than this.

**이체 동심(異體同心)** two in body but one in mind /부부는 ~이다 Man and wife are one flesh.

**이초(離礁)** ~하다 get off the rock[reef]; refloat /~시키다 A refloat (*a ship*); get (*a ship*) off the rocks.

**이촉** the root of a tooth; a fang.

**이출(移出)** ~하다 ship; ship (*out of*); export /~ 신고서 《세관의》a declaration of clearance.

**이취(泥醉)** dead-drunkenness; great intoxication; fuddle／~하다 get dead drunk; lose control of *oneself* by taking too much wine; be boozy(미). でいすい

**이층**(二層) the first[upper] storey(영); the second floor(미)／~에서 upstairs／~집 a two-storeyed house／~에 올라가다 go upstairs／그들의 아파트는 그 빌딩 ~에 있다 Their apartment is on the second floor of the building.

**이치**(理致) 《도리》 reason justice; right 《원칙》 principle／아이에게 ~를 말해도 허사다 It is no use reasoning with a child.

**이칭**(異稱) another name; a by-name; an alias; a pseudonym. いしょう

**이커서니** oof; heave; yo-heave-ho; yo-ho. よいさ

**이키나** 《놀람》 Wow!, Oh!／~ 큰일났다 Heavens!, Dear me! おゝ、お…

**이타**(利他) altruism／~적 altruistic／~주의 altruism／~주의자 an altruist. りた

**이탄**(泥炭) peat; turf／~지 a peat bog [moss]; turbary. でいたん

**이탈**(離脫) secession; separation／~하다 secede from; break away from; leave (*a party*)／직장을 ~하다 desert *one's* job; walk out on *one's* job(미). りだつ

**이탓저탓** on one excuse or another; on a hocus-pocus pretence. なんだかんだと

**이태** two years. にねん

**이토**(泥土) mud; mire／~암 clay rock; pelite／~층 a dirt bed. でいど

**이롱**(耳痛) 《의》earache; otalgia; otalgy. みみのびょうき

**이튿날** 《다음날》the next[following] day 《2일》the second day [of the month]／~ 아침 the next morning. あくるひ

**이틀**[1] ①two days ②《초 이틀》the second day [of the month].

**이틀**[2] ①《치조》 an alveolus; the sockets of teeth ②《의치》 a dental plate; a full denture. しそう

**이름** an opening[a gap] between tooth. はのすきま

**이판암**(泥板岩) 《광》 shale.

**이팔**(二八) sixteen／~ 청춘 a sixteen-year-old; sweet sixteen.

**이편** ①《자기》 I; we／~의 my; our／~의 잘못 my[our] fault; a fault on my [our] part／~으로선 for my[our] part ②《이쪽》 this side. こちらのほう

**이풍**(異風) 《모양》 novelty; strangeness 《풍속》 a strange custom; a quaint custom. いふう

**이핑계저핑계** one excuse or another; a hocus-pocus pretence.

**이하**(以下) ~의 less than;[and] under; below 《하기(下記)》 the following／평년작 ~ below the average crop／10세 ~의 어린이 children under ten years old／~ 동문 and so on; etc. いか

**이하선**(耳下腺) the parotid gland／~염 parotitis; mumps. じかせん

**이화**(理學) physical science／~의 scientific／~ 박사 a doctor of science (略: D. Sc.)／~사 a bachelor of science (略: B. Sc.). りがく

**이합**(離合) meeting and parting／정당의 ~ 집산 changing alignment of political parties. りごう

**이항**(二項) 《수》 ①~[식]의 binomial／~식 a binomial [expression]. にこう

**이항**(移項) 《수》 transposition／~하다 transpose. いこう

**이해**(利害) interests; concern; advantages and disadvantages／~를 같이하다 have common interests with others. りがい

**이해**(理解) understanding; comprehension; appreciation／~하다 understand; grasp; comprehend; appreciate; make out／~성 있는 아내 a sympathetic wife／~성 없는 남편 an unappreciative husband／음악을 ~하다 appreciate music; have an ear for music／~하기 쉽다[어렵다] be easy[difficult] to understand.

**이해력**(理解力) the comprehensive faculty; the understanding; the power to understand; sense／~을 기르다 cultivate the power of understanding.

**이행**(履行) performance; fulfilment; discharge; execution／~하다 fulfil; carry out; perform; discharge; execute; put into practice／약속을 ~하다 fulfil[make good, stand to] *one's* promise. りこう

**이행**(移行) ~하다 《풍향이》 veer to; switch over to. いこう

**이향**(異鄉) a foreign country. たきょう

**이향**(離鄉) leaving *one's* home／~하다 leave *one's* home[*one's* native place]. りきょう

**이호**(二號) No. 2; number two.

**이혼**(離婚) a divorce; the dissolution of marriage／~하다 divorce／~ 소송 a divorce suit／~ 수속 divorce procedure[formalities]. りこん

**이화**(李花) plum blossoms. りか

**이화**(梨花) pear blossoms.

**이화학**(理化學) physics and chemistry／~ 연구소 the Physico-Chemical Research Institute. りかがく

**이회**(二回) twice; two times／월(月) ~ twice a month. にかい

**이후**(以後) 《금후》 after this; from now on; in [the] future 《이래》 after; since／8월 15일 ~ on and after August 15th／그 ~ thereafter; since then. いご

**익**(翼) 《날개》a wing 《비행기의》a plane; 《군》 a flank 《항공》 a airfoil. つばさ

**익년**(翌年) the next year; the year after. よくねん

**익다** ①《과실이》 ripen; be[get] ripe; mellow 《계획 등이》 come to a head／익은 ripe; mature; mellow／익지 않은 green; unripe ②《음식이》 be boiled[cooked]／잘 익은 well-done[-cooked]／너무 ~ be overdone ③《익숙하다》 get used; become

**익명 (匿名)** anonymity; pseudonymous names/ ~의 anonymous/ ~으로 anonymously/ ~의 편지 an anonymous letter/ ~으로 기고하다 contribute to (a magazine) anonymously/ ~으로 기부하다 subscribe (to the funds) anonymously/ ~ 투고 an unsigned[anonymous] contribution/ ~ 비평 unsigned criticism/ ~ 작가 an anonym; an anonymous author[writer]. とくめい

**익모초 (益母草)** 【식】 a motherwort; Leonurus sibiricus(학명). めはじき

**익몰 (溺沒)** drowning/ ~하다 drown; be drowned. できぼつ

**익반죽** mixing dough with hot water; kneading with hot-water; hot-water dough/ ~하다 knead with hot-water.

**익사 (溺死)** [death from] drowning/ ~하다 be drowned [to death]/ ~자 a drowned person/ 그는 수영중에 ~했다 He was drowned while bathing./ ~체 the body a of drowned person/ ~할 뻔하다 be near being drowned. できし

**익살** humour; good-humoured banter; pleasantry; a joke; a jest;a wisecrack 〈미〉/ ~떨다(부리다, 피우다) crack jokes; jest; talk humorously; play the fool/ ~스럽다 be funny[waggish, facetious, comical, clownish]; droll/ ~군 a jokester; a wag; a funnyman; a humorist; a comic; a comedian/ ~스럽게 이야기하다 speak humorously. こっけい

**익수 (一手)** an old hand; a skilled person.

**익숙하다** 《능숙하다》 (be) skilled[experienced, practiced]; skillful; be good (at); be a good hand at (잘 알다》 (be) familiar; be well acquainted (with). なれている

**익애 (溺愛)** dotage/ ~하다 dote upon; love (a person) to idolatry; lavish one's love upon. できあい

**익월 (翌月)** the next[following, ensuing] month. よくげつ

**익은이** a well boiled piece of meat. にたにく

**익일 (翌日)** the next[following, succeeding] day. よくじつ

**익조 (翌朝)** the next morning; the following morning. よくちょう

**익조 (益鳥)** a beneficial[useful] bird.

**익충 (益蟲)** a useful[beneficial] insect. えきちゅう

**익히다** ①《과일을》 make ripe; ripen; mature; mellow 《술·간장을》 brew; ferment; mature; age (soysauce, wine); 《음식을》 cook; boil/ 고기를 잘 ~ get the meat well done ②《익숙하게 하다》 make oneself familiar with; acquaint oneself with; habituate oneself to; learn (by heart); practice/영화 회화를 ~ practice English conversation.

**인 (仁)** 《인자》 benevolence; humanity; virtue; selflessness; manship; goodness; benevolence; charity/자기를 희생하며 ~을 이루다 sacrifice oneself for the good of others. じん

**인 (印)**, a seal; a stamp. いん

**인 (寅)** 《십이지의》 the Tiger; the third of the twelve horary signs. いん

**인 (燐)** 【화】 phosphorus(기호: P)/ ~의 phosphorus; phossy《속》/ ~을 포함한 phosphorus/ ~과 화합시키다 phosphorate. りん

**-인 (人)** a man; a person/문화 ~ a cultured man. —にん. —じん

**인가 (人家)** a house; a dwelling-house; a human habitation/ ~가 드문 sparsely-populated/ ~가 많다 be crowded with houses; be thickly inhabited. じんか

**인가 (認可)** sanction; permission/ ~하다 sanction; authorize; give a permit/ ~를 얻다 obtain the sanction of; be authorized by. にんか

**인가 (隣家)** a neighbo[u]ring house; a neighbo[u]r's; the next door. りんか

**인가 근처 (人家近處)** the neighbourhood of a human habitation/ ~에서 떨어져 out of sight and sound of a human habitation.

**인가난 (人一)** a dearth[shortage] of qualified people.

**인각 (印刻)** engraving [a seal]/ ~하다 engrave a seal; carve. いんこく

**인간 (人間)** a human being; a man; a mortal 《인류》 mankind; humanity/ ~의 human; mortal/ ~계 the world of mortals; the terrestrial world/ ~ 고락 (苦樂) [touches of] humanity; humaneness/ ~ 사회 human society; the community of men/ ~성 human nature; humanity/ ~애 human love/ ~은 만물의 영장이다 Man is lord of creation. にんげん

**인감 (印鑑)** a seal-impression/ ~ 증명[제] a certificate[registration] of a seal impression. いんかん

**인갑 (鱗甲)** ①《비늘과 껍데기》 a scale and a shell ②《비늘 모양의 껍데기》 a scale armo[u]r; 《등》 a scutum/ ~이 있는 s-cutate; scutellate. うろことこう

**인건비 (人件費)** personal expenditure[expenses]. じんけんひ

**인걸 (人傑)** a remarkable[great] man; a hero; a great figure. じんけつ

**인격 (人格)** personality; character/ ~ 교육[양성] character building[formation] of character/ ~ 문제 a matter of personality/ ~ 상실 depersonalization/ ~자 a man of character/ ~주의 personalism/ 이중 ~ a double personality/ ~을 존중하다[무시하다] respect[disregard] (a person's) personality. じんかく

**인견**(人絹) rayon ⇨인조견. じんけん

**인견**(引見) an interview; a reception/～하다 receive (one)[in audience]; grant an interview (to)/내객을 ～하다 receive callers. いんけん

**인경** a large bell. おおきいかね

**인계**(引繼) 《사무의》 taking over (another's duties)(인수); 《인도》 handing over (one's duties); 《계승》 succession (to)/～하다 hand over (one's duties) to; take over (another's duties)/사무를 ～받다 take over the official duties. ひきつぎ

**인꼭지**(印一) the handle of a seal.

**인공**(人工) human work[skill, labour]; 《기교》 art/～의 artificial/～의 미 beauty of art/자연과 ～ nature and art/～ 호흡 artificial respiration/～으로 artificially/～ 강우 rainmaking; artificial rain/～물 an artifact/～미 man-created beauty/～ 부화 artificial incubation/～ 수정 a test-tube insemination/～ 수태 artificial conception/～ 위성 an artificial satellite; a man-made moon/～ 일광 artificial daylight[sunlight]/～ 접종 artificial infection/～ 호흡이 시행되었다 Artificial respiration was tried upon him. じんこう

**인과**(因果) causality 《원인과 결과》 cause and effect 《운명》 fate/～ 관계 causality; causal relation/～성 causality/～율 the law of causality. いんが

**인광**(燐鑛) phosphate ore[rock]. りんこう

**인광**(燐光) phosphorescence/～을 받다 emit phosphorescence. りんこう

**인교**(隣交) relations with a neighbouring country. りんこう

**인구**(人口) population; inhabitants/～가 조밀한[희박한] 곳 a thickly[sparsely]-populated district/～ 과잉 overpopulation/～ 문제 the population problem/과잉 ～ surplus population/～ 조사를 하다 take a census of the population. じんこう

**인국**(隣國) a neighbouring[an adjacent] country/～간의 우의 relations of good neighbourhood. りんごく

**인권**(人權) human[personal] rights; the rights of man/～ 문제 a question affecting human rights/～ 선언 the Declaration of Human Rights/～ 유린 an outrage upon personal rights/～을 유린하다 trample upon human rights. じんけん

**인끈**(印一) the cord attached to the handle of a seal; a seal-chain. いんじゅ

**인근**(隣近) the neighbourhood; the vicinity/～의 neighbouring; near-by. りんきん

**인기**(人氣) popularity; popular favor; public interest/～ 배우 a star; a popular actor; a stage favorite/～ 소설 a sensational[catching] novel/～ 투표 a popularity[straw] vote/～를 얻다 gain in public favor. にんき

**인기척** a sign of man's presence/～이 있다 show signs of people present/～이 났다 I heard someone approaching. ひとけ

**인날**(人一) January 7th of the lunar month.

**인내**(忍耐) patience 《견인》 perseverance 《참음》 endurance 《굳셈》 fortitude/～하다 bear[endure] patiently; be patient (with)/그것을 하는 데는 상당한 ～력이 필요하다 It requires much perseverance to do it. にんたい

**인대**(靱帶) 《해》 a ligament/～의 ligamentous/～ 관절 a syndesmosis/～ 장치 ligamentous apparatus. じんたい

**인덕**(仁德) benevolence; humanity; goodness; graciousness. じんとく

**인데** ¶그럴 리가 없을 터～ It cannot be, I believe., That's not what I expected/그는 지금 도착했을 터～ He should have arrived by this time. ―だが

**인도**(人道) ①《도덕》 humanity/～주의 humanism; humanitarianism/～ 문제 a question touching humanity ②《보도》 a pavement〈영〉; a sidewalk〈미〉; a footpath/～에 어긋나다 be contrary to humanity; be inhumane. じんどう

**인도**(引渡) delivery; turning over 《주고받기》 transfer/～하다 deliver (goods); transfer/～ 장소 a place of delivery/～증 a bill of parcels/본선 ～ free on board(略: f.o.b.)/현장 ～ spot delivery. ひきわたし

**인도**(引導) 《지도》 guidance 《선도》 introduction/～하다 guide; introduce; lead/～자 《안내자》 a guide 《선도자》 an introducer 《후원자》 a backer/그는 하녀의 ～를 받아 응접실에 들어갔다 He was guided by a maidservant into the drawing room. いんどう

**인동**(忍冬) dried honeysuckle stems and leaves [used in herbalist remedies]/～초 [Japanese] honeysuckle.

**인두** a hotiron; a small iron; a smoothing iron 《땜질하는》 a soldering iron/～판 an ironing board/～질하다 iron. やきごて

**인두**(咽頭) the pharynx/～의 pharyngeal. いんとう

**인두겁**(人一) human shape/～을 쓴 악마 a demon in human shape.

**인두세**(人頭稅) a poll-tax; capitation taxes/～를 받다 levy a poll-tax. にんとうぜい

**인물리다**(人一) feel sick from the jostling of a crowd. ひとによう

**인들** granted that it be[is]; even though it be[is].

**인력**(人力) human power[strength]; man-power 《자연에 대하여》 human agency/～으로는 할 수 없다 be beyond the power of man. じんりょく

**인력**(引力) human power[strength]; 《지구의》 attraction/～있는 attractive; magnetic/～의 법칙 the law of gravitat-

**인력거(人力車)** a ricksha[w](J)/~군 a rickshaw-man; a rikisha-puller/~ 요금 rickshaw fare/~에 타다 take[ride in] a rickshaw/~로 가다 go by rickshaw. じんりきしゃ

**인례(引例)** an example; an instance; a citation/~하다 draw[cite] an instance /일례를 여기에 ~한다 As an instance, the foll wing is here given. いんれい

**인류(人類)** the human race; human beings; mankind; man/~의 human; racial/~ 발달사 the history of human progress/~사 the history of man/~ 사회 human society/~애 love for humanity[mankind]/~ 역사 human history/~학 anthropology/~학자 an anthropologist/전 ~의 복지를 증진하다 promote the welfare of all mankind. じんるい

**인륜(人倫)** 《도덕》 morals; morality 《인도》 humanity; human/~ 도덕 ethics and morality/~에 어긋나다 transgress the moral law. じんりん

**인마(人馬)** men and horses/~가 함께 골짜기로 떨어졌다 They fell into the valley, men and horses. じんば

**인망(人望)** popularity; popular favour /~가 a popular person; a person of wide reputation/~이 높다 enjoy a high reputation/~을 잃다 lose *one's* popularity; forfeit *people's* esteem. じんぼう

**인면(人面)** a human face/~ 수심 a beast with a human face. じんめん

**인멸(湮滅)** 《자연적》 extinction 《고의적》 destruction/~하다 《자연히》 be extinct 《고의로》 destroy; make away with/증거를 ~하다 destroy the proof; stifle evidence. えんめつ

**인명(人名)** a person's name/~부 a list of names; a directory/~록 a directory 《서명》 who's who/~ 사전 a biographical dictionary. じんめい

**인명(人命)** human life; a life/~을 구조하다 save a life/위험에 빠진 ~을 구하다 rescue (*a person*) whose life is in danger. じんめい

**인몰(湮沒)** ~하다 be buried; fall into ruins; sink into oblivion. えんぼつ

**인문(人文)** civilization; culture/~의 cultural; humanistic/~ 과학 cultural sciences; the humanities/~주의 humanism /~주의자 a humanist/~ 지리 human geography/~학과 the humanists. じんぶん

**인물(人物)** 《사람》 a man; a person 《별난》 a character 《역사상의》 a figure 《인품》 character 《인격자》 personality/~ 시험 a character[personality] test/~평 personal criticism/~화 a figurepainting 《초상화》 a portrait/등장 ~ dramatis personae; [stage] characters/위험 ~ a dangerous character/훌륭한 ~이다 He has a fine personality. じんぶつ

**인민(人民)** the people; the populace; the public/~ 공화국 a people's republic/ ~당 the people's party/~ 민주주의 a people's democracy/~ 위원회 《소련의》 the Council of people's Commissars/~ 재판 a people's court/~ 정치 government by[for, of] the people/~의, ~에 의한, ~을 위한 정치 a government of the people, by the people, and for the people. じんみん

**인발(印—)** a seal impression; the stamp of a seal. なついんのあと

**인방(引枋)** a lintel and a threshold; a molding; a cornice; a baseboard/상(上) ~ the upper lintel; the crosspiece. かもい

**인방(隣邦)** a neighbouring state[country, nation]/~의 우의(友誼) [relations of] good neighbourhood. りんぼう

**인보(印譜)** a book of impressions of seals. いんぷ

**인복(人福)** the luck to have good acquaintances.

**인본(印本)** a printed book. いんぽん

**인봉(印封)** ①《봉인하기》 sealing/~하다 seal ②《관인을 봉하기》 sealing of an official seal case after the closing hour /~하다 seal up an official seal case after the closing hour.

**인부(人夫)** 《일군》 a labourer; a coolie 《운반부》 a porter; a carrier/~ 십장 a foreman; a cooliemaster/선로 ~ a trainman; a railway worker. にんぷ

**인부심(人—)** placing Indian-millet cakes at the front and back door for passersby on the seventh day after the birth of a child/~하다 celebrate the baby's 7th day.

**인분(人糞)** night soil; human excrements/~ 비료 human manure. じんぷん

**인비(人秘)** secrecy of personal affairs.

**인사(人士)** people; men; persons. じんし

**인사(人事)** ①《사람의 일》 things human; human affairs 《개인에 관한》 personnel affairs/~하다 greet; salute; make a bow; thank; acknowledge/작별 ~를 하다 say good-bye/정중히 ~하다 bow politely; bow low ②《사람이 하는 일》 human affairs; what man can do ③ 《직원 관계》 personal affairs; personnel /~과 the personnel section/~ 이동 personnel changes/~ 행정 personnel administration. じんじ

**인사 불성(人事不省)** unconsciousness; faint; loss of consciousness/~의 unconscious; insensible; senseless/~이 되다 become unconscious; pass out 《미·속》. じんじふせい

**인산(燐酸)** 《화》 phosphoric acid/~ 석회 phosphate of lime/~ 비료 phosphatic fertilizer; phosphate. りんさん

**인산(因山)** an Imperial[a king's] funeral.

**인산 인해(人山人海)** a crowd of people /집 앞에 ~를 이루고 있다 A big crowd

**인삼**(人蔘) ginseng. にんじん

**인상**(人相) a look; features; personal appearance; a cast of countenance; physiognomy/~학 physiognomy/~학자 a physiognomist/~을 보다 read [judge] one's character by the face. にんそう

**인상**(引上) (가격 따위의) raising; increase; advance 《끌어 올림》 pulling up/~하다 increase; raise/물가 ~ a raise in prices/임금 ~ a raise in wages/가격이 천원으로 ~되었다 The price was raised to 1,000 won. ひきあげ

**인상**(印象) impression/~파 the impressionist school/~주의 impressionism/~적 묘사 an impressionistic[a graphic] description/첫~ the first impression/좋은[깊은] ~을 주다 impress (a person) favorably[deeply]/~을 받다 get an impression/잊을 수 없는 ~ an unforgettable impression. いんしょう

**인상**(鱗狀) ~의 scale-like; scaly; squamous. うろこもよう

**인색**(吝嗇) stinginess; miserliness; niggardliness/~하다 (be) stingy; close-fisted; miserly/~하게 굴지 마라 Don't be so stingy.

**인생**(人生) life; human life[existence]/~의 human; life/~의 목적 the chief end of life/~관 one's view of life; an outlook on life/~ 문제 the problem of life/~ 철학 the philosophy of life/~ 행로 the tenor[path] of one's life/~을 비관하다 take a pessimistic[gloomy] view of life/~ 무상 Red at morn, dead at eve/~은 꿈이다 Life is but an empty dream. じんせい

**인석**(隣席) the next seat.

**인석**(人石) the two stone statues before a 《king's》 grave.

**인선**(人選) the choice[selection] of a [suitable] person/~하다 choose men; select a suitable person/각료의 ~ the selection of cabinet members. じんせん

**인성**(人性) human nature; humanity; 《본능》 human instinct/~론 Treatise of Human Nature. じんせい

**인성**(燐性) ~의 phosphoric.

**인세**(印稅) a royalty (on a book); the stamp duty/1할의 ~로 출판을 계약하다 contract for publication with ten percent royalties. いんぜい

**인솔**(引率) ~하다 lead; have in charge/~자 a leader; a person in charge; a guide. いんそつ

**인쇄**(印刷) printing/~하다 print/~술 [the art of] printing/~물 printed matter/~소 a printing hous[office, shop]/~ 용지 printing paper/~공 a pressman; a printer/~가 선명하다[나쁘다] It is clearly[poorly] printed. いんさつ

**인수**(人數) the number of persons; numerical strength/그들의 ~는 7명이었다 They were seven in number. にんず

**인수**(引受) 《부담·담당》 undertaking 《수락》 acceptance 《보증》 guaranty; security/~하다 undertake; take charge of; answer for; take over; accept; guarantee/~ 어음 an accepted[acceptable] bill/~인 a guarantor 《보증자》 a surety; a claimer 《시체·분실물의》 a claimant. ひきうけ

**인수**(印綬) 《관직의 표》 the seals of office/수상의 ~를 띠다 take the seals of the prime minister's office. いんじゅ

**인수**(引水) conduction of water/~하다 conduct water. いんすい

**인수**(因數) 〖수〗 a factor/소~ a prime factor/~ 분해 factorization/~ 분해하다 solve into factors. いんすう

**인순**(因循) ①《머뭇거림》 vacillation; indecision; shilly-shally/~하다 be vacillate; be irresolute ②《보수적》 conservatism/~하다 be conservative. いんじゅん

**인술**(仁術) 《의술》 a benevolent art; the healing art/의술은 ~이다 Medicine is a benevolent art. じんじゅつ

**인습**(因襲) habit; conventionality; convention; tradition/~적 conventional; traditional/~에 추종하다 follow a long usage/~을 타파하다 break [a longestablished] usage. いんしゅう

**인시류**(鱗翅類) 〖충〗 Lepidoptera 《학명》.

**인식**(認識) recognition; cognizance 《이해》 understanding/~하다 recognize; cognize; understand/~론 〖철〗 epistemology/~ 부족 lack of understanding[knowledge]/옳게 ~하다 have a correct understanding (of); show a true perception (of). にんしき

**인신**(人身) the human body; one's person/~ 매매 human traffic; the slave trade; traffic in human cargo/~ 공격 a personal attack[criticism]/~ 보호법 the Habeas Corpus Act. じんしん

**인심**(人心) men's minds; the people's hearts; the public feeling; the temper of the people 《인정》 the human heart 《기풍》 the tone/~ 소관 dependence on one's mind/~을 얻다 win the heart of the people. じんしん

**인심**(仁心) benevolence; generousity; liberality/~ 쓰다 be liberal; be generous; grant (one a favour)/남의 것으로 ~ 쓰다 rob peter to pay paul; be generous at another's expense. じんしん

**인애**(仁愛) charity; love; humanity/~ 심이 있는 benevolent; charitable. じんあい

**인양**(引揚) pulling up 《난파선의》 salvage 《시체의》 recovery/~하다 pull up; recover; salvage/~ 작업 salvage work [operation]/침몰선을 ~하다 salve a sunken ship

**인어**(人魚) 《암컷》 a mermaid 《수컷》 a merman. にんぎょ

**인연(人煙)** human habitations／～을 보기 드문 지방 a sparsely-populated corner of the country. じんえん

**인연(因緣)** 《인과》 cause and occasion 《불교》 karma; fate; destiny 《연분》 affinity; connection; relation／～을 맺다 form relations／돈과는 ～이 없다 Money and I are strangers. いんえん

**인영(人影)** 《사람 모습》 a figure; a form a sign of man 《그림자》 a shadow of a person. じんえい

**인욕(人慾)** human desires[wants]; human passions／～을 초탈하다 rise above human desires. じんよく

**인욕(忍辱)** fortitude; forbearance; endurance.

**인용(引用)** quotation; citation／～하다 quote (from); cite (an instance);《참조》 refer to／～구[문] a quotation／～부 a quotation mark／～점 inverted commas. いんよう

**인용(認容)** admission; acknowledgment ／～하다 acknowledge; admit.

**인원(人員)** 《인원수》 the number of persons[men]; 《정원》 the complement 《직원》 the staff／～ 부족이다 be understaffed [undermanned]; be short of hands. じんいん

**인위(人爲)** human work 《인공》 art; artificiality 《인력》 human power／～적 도태 〖생〗 artificial selection／～적으로 artificially. じんい

**인유(人乳)** human milk. じんにゅう

**인육(人肉)** human flesh／～ 시장 a white slave market. にんげんのにく

**인육(印肉)** stamp ink; an ink[ing] pad. いんにく

**인의(仁義)** humanity and justice; humanity／～ 충효[의孝] humanity, justice, loyalty and filial piety. じんぎ

**인자(人子)** the son of a man 《그리스도》 the Son of Man. じんし

**인자(因子)** a factor／재물이 행복의 한 ～ 일는지도 모른다 Wealth may be a factor of happiness／유전 ～ a factor; a gene. いんし

**인자(仁慈)** charity; benevolence／～하다 (be) charitable; benevolent; gracious.

**인자(仁者)** a benevolent person. じんしゃ

**인장(印章)** a seal／위조 ～ a forged seal／～을 위조하다 counterfeit a seal／～ 위조인 the counterfeiter of a seal. いんしょう

**인재(人材)** a man of parts[ability, talent]; a capable[an able] man 《총칭》 talent／～주의 the merit system／～를 등용하다 open the offices to the talented. じんざい

**인재(印材)** materials for seals. いんざい

**인적(人的)** (being) human／한국은 ～ 자원 이 풍부하다 Korea is rich in human resources.／～ 손해 the loss of man power. じんてき

**인적(人跡)** a trace of human footsteps; human traces／～이 끊어진 uninhabited; out-of-the-way; desolate. じんせき

**인절미** cake made from glutinous rice.

**인접(隣接)** adjacency; contiguity／～하다 adjoin; be adjacent to; be contiguous to／～한 adjoining; contiguous／～지 adjacent land／～한 마을 neighboring towns and villages. いんせつ

**인정(仁政)** humane government; benevolent government[rule]／～을 베풀다 rule [govern] with benevolence. じんせい

**인정(人情)** 《정》 humaneness; sympathy; kindness; tenderness 《인성》 human nature; humanity／～있는 사람 a tender-hearted person／～미 a human touch; human appeal／～이 넘치는 친절 heart-warming hospitality／～에 끌리다 be moved to pity; be prompted by pity／세상 ～은 얼음장같이 차다 The public are cold as ice to me. にんじょう

**인정(人定)** the curfew that used to be rung around 10 p. m. じんてい

**인정(認定)** 《승인》 recognition 《확인》 confirmation 《인허》 authorization; sanction／～하다 《승인》 recognize; admit; acknowledge 《확인》 confirm 《인가》 sanction 《알다》 see; find; notice／문교부 ～ 교과서 textbooks authorized by the Ministry of Education／시인으로 ～ 을 받다 be acknowledged as a poet. にんてい

**인제** 《이제》 now 《앞으로》 after this; in future／～ 도리가 없다 Nothing can be done now.／～야 그이가 왔다 He has just come at long last. いま

**인조(人造)** ～의 artificial 《모조》 imitation 《합성》 synthetic／～ 고무 synthetic gum／～ 진주 an artificial pearl／～ 인간 a robot／～견 artificial[synthetic] silk; rayon／～ 비료 artificial fertilizer[manure]／～ 섬유 staple fiber; a synthetic textile. じんぞう

**인종(人種)** a [human] race／～의 평등 racial equality／～적 편견 racial prejudice／～학 ethnology／～ 문제 the race problem／황색 ～ the yellow race[people]／흑색 ～ the black race[people]／～ 차별 racial discrim inations; segregation. じんしゅ

**인종(忍從)** self-surrender; submission; resignation／～하다 submit to; endure. にんじゅう

**인주(印朱)** vermilion inkpad; cinnabar seal-ink／～합(盒) an inkpad case. いんにく

**인줄(人一)** 〖민〗 sacred straw festoons.

**인중(人中)** the raphe[perpendicular furrow] of the upper lip. にんちゅう

**인즉** to speak of; speaking of／말 ～ 옳소 What he says is true. —なれば

**인증(引證)** a reference; a quotation 《인용》 a citation 《예증》 an illustration／～하다 quote (from); cite. いんしょう

**인증(人證)** 〖법〗 the testimony of a wit-

**인증(認證)** 〖법〗 certification/~하다 certify; authenticate; attest/~식 an attestation ceremony. にんしょう

**-인지** ᄋ~라 as it is; since it is/학교에 가는 길~라 지금 들르지 못하겠네 I'm on my way to school, so I can't stop in now. —세이카

**인지(人智)** human intelligence[knowledge, understanding]/~의 발달 the advancement of human knowledge. じんち

**인지(印紙)** a stamp/수입 ~ a revenue stamp/~세(稅) stamp duty/~를 붙이다 stamp; affix a stamp/~를 첨부하다 affix a stamp (to). いんし

**인지(認知)** recognition; acknowledg[e]ment/~하다 recognize [legally]; acknowledg[e]/사생아를 ~하다 recognize an illegitimate child (as one's own). にんち

**인지상정(人之常情)** human nature; humaneness; humanity.

**인질(人質)** a hostage; a [personal] security/~로 잡다 take[hold] (a person) as a hostage. ひとじち

**인책(引責)** ~하다 take the responsibility on oneself; assume the responsibility (for)/~ 사임하다 assume the responsibility and resign one's post. いんせき

**인척(姻戚)** a relative by marriage; affinity/~ 관계다 be related by marriage. いんせき

**인체(人體)** the human body; the system 《육체》 flesh/~ 구조 the structure of the human body/~ 모형 an anatomical model of the human body/~ 해부학 human anatomy/~에 영향을 끼치다 affect the human body. じんたい

**인촌(鄰村)** the next[neighbouring] village. りんそん

**인총중(人總中)** [among] a crowd/ ~에 among the crowd of people.

**인축(人畜)** men and[or] beasts[cattle]; humans and animals; living creatures [things]/~ 무해 No harm to man and beast. じんちく

**인치(引致)** custody/~하다 arrest; take (one) to a police station; take (one) into custody/피의자를 본서에 ~되어 문초를 받았다 The suspect was taken to the police station and questioned. いんち

**인치다(印—)** seal; put a stamp on; affix a seal to. なついんする

**인칭(人稱)** 〖언〗 person/~ 대명사 a personal pronoun/제 1[2,3] ~ the first [second, third] person. にんしょう

**인퇴(引退)** retirement 《은둔》 seclusion/ ~하다 retire (from); seclude oneself (from the world). いんたい

**인파(人波)** a surging crowd (of people); a flood of people; waves[a tide, a surge] of humanity/~를 헤치고 나아가다 jostle through a crowd/~에 휩쓸리다 be buffeted by the waves of humanity. ひとなみ

**인편(人便)** [through] the agency of a person/~으로 보내다 send (a thing) by someone. ひとのびん

**인품(人品)** 《풍채》 personal appearance; bearing 《품격》 [personal] character; personality. じんぴん

**인하(引下)** reduction; a cut; lowering/ ~하다 pull[draw] down; lower; reduce 《값을》 cut/물가 ~ the reduction of price/임금 ~ a reduction in wages; a wage cut/가격을 ~하다 cut a price down. ひきさげ

**인하다(因—)** be due to; be attributable to; be because of; be owing to; come (from)/부주의로 인한 due to carelessness/사고로 인하여 죽다 die from an accident/병으로 인해서 결석하다 be absent because of illness. よる

**인해 전술(人海戰術)** human wave tactics; infiltration tactics; the strategy of throwing waves of men into action. じんかいせんじゅつ

**인행(印行)** publication/~하다 print. いんこう

**인허(認許)** consent; recognition/~하다 recognize; consent; approve. にんきょ

**인형(人形)** a doll 《꼭두각시》 a puppet/ ~극 a doll play; a puppet show/~ 같은 doll-like. にんぎょう

**인형(仁兄)** you 《편지에서》 Dear Friend. じんけい

**인화(人和)** harmonious personal relations; (national) concord. ひとのわらく

**인화(印畵)** a print/~하다 print [a photograph]; make a print (of)/~지(紙) printing paper. いんが

**인화(引火)** ignition/~하다 catch[take] fire; ignite/~성 《인》flammability; ignitability/~점 a flashing point; the ignition point/~하기 쉽다 be inflammable.

**인화(燐化)** 〖화〗 ᄋ~물 phosphid[e]/~ 수소 hydrogen phosphate; phosphine.

**인화(燐火)** phosphorescence; phosphorous light; the glow[glimmer] of a firefly. りんか

**인회석(燐灰石)** 〖광〗 apatite. りんかいせき

**인후(仁厚)** benevolence/~하다 (be) benevolent. じんこう

**인후(咽喉)** the throat/~의 faucal; guttural/~병 a swelling[swollen] sore throat/~염 a sore throat. いんこう

**일** ⇒별항 참조(page 1664).

**일(一)** one 《제1》 the first. いち

**일가(一家)** ①《가정》 a home; a family/ ~의 family; domestic/~ 단란 a fireside circle/~ 친척 one's kin[s]folk/~를 다스리다 keep house; look after the family ②《학파》 a school 《대가》 an authority/~를 이루다 establish a school of one's own. いっか

**일가(一價)** 〖화〗 monovalence; univalence /~의 monovalent; univalent; monatomic/~ 원소 a monad. いっか

**일가견**(一家見) one's own[private] opinion; a personal view.

**일각**(一刻) a minute; a short space of time; a moment/~을 아끼다 grudge even a minute/~의 여유도 없다 There is not a moment to lose. いっこく

**일각**(一角) a corner; a section/~ 대문 a front gate with two posts and a roof/~수(獸) a unicorn. いっかく

**일간**(日刊) daily issue/~의 daily/~ 신문 a daily newspaper. にっかん

**일간**(日間) someday; one of these days/~ 가겠소 I'll come one of these days. きんじつちゅう

**일간 두옥**(一間斗屋) a small house; a humble house; a hut.

**일갈**(一喝) a thundering cry/~하다 thunder; shout at.

**일개**(一箇) one; a piece/~의 one; single/나는 ~ 가난한 학생이다 I am but a poor student. りっこ

**일깨우다** convince (a person) of; waken (a person) to; tell (a person) about/그의 잘못을 그에게 일깨워 주었다 I brought to his attention what he had done wrong. かくせいさせる

**일개인**(一個人) an individual 《사인(私人)》 a private person/~의 individual; private; personal/나 ~의 생각 my personal[private] view.

**일거**(一擧) one effort; one action/~에 일을 결정하다 decide (a matter) by one effort. いっきょ

**일거**(逸居) a quiet life; a leisurely life/~하다 lead a retired life; lead an idle life; live a leisurely life. いっきょ

**일거리** work; employment; things to do; a task/나날의 ~ one's routine work/~를 맡기다 entrust (a person) with a task. ようむ

**일거 양득**(一擧兩得) attaining two advantages at one move; killing two birds with one stone/그렇게 하면 ~이다 It serves two ends. いっきょりょうとく

**일거 일동**(一擧一動) one's every action; every movement (of a person); everything one does/남의 ~을 주시하다 watch every movement of (a person). いっきょいちどう

**일건**(一件) a matter; an affair; a case; an item/~ 서류 the papers relating to the affair. いっけん

**일껏** with [much] effort[trouble]; at great pains/~ 오라고 했는데 그는 안 왔다 He did not come, though I told him to. わざわざ

**일격**(一擊) a single blow; one stroke/~에 at a blow; with one stroke/~을 가하다 give[deal] (a person) a blow. いちげき

**일견**(一見) a sight; a glance; a look/~하다 take[have, cast, get] a glance at; have a squint at; catch a glimpse/백문이 불여 ~이다 A thousand hearings are not worth one seeing. いっけん

**일결**(一決) ~하다 be agreed; be decided; come to decision; be brought to a conclusion/중의(衆議) ~하여 on unanimous agreement. いっけつ

**일계**(一計) a plan/~를 생각해 내다 think [work] out a plan.

**일계**(日計) daily account; daily expenses/~표 〖경〗 daily trial balance. にっけい

**일고**(一考) consideration; a thought/~하다 give a thought to; take into consideration/이것은 ~를 요하는 문제다 This is a matter for consideration. いっこう

**일고**(一顧) a notice/~의 가치도 없다 be beneath notice; do not deserve even a passing note/~의 가치가 있다 It is worth our attention. いっこ

**일고동** a chief point; the point; the most important part. ようてん

**일고 삼장**(日高三丈) late morning; broad daylight; late in the day.

**일곱** seven/~ 번째 the seventh/~ 살 먹은 아이 a boy of seven. しち

**일공**(日工) ①《날품일》daily employment; a day-to-day engagement ②《날품삯》daily pay; a day's wage/~장이 a day laborer. ひやとい

**일과**(日課) a daily lesson; a daily work《매일의 일》the daily routine/~표 a daily schedule; a schedule (of lessons)/그는 매일 아침 산보하는 것을 ~로 삼고 있다 He makes a point of taking a walk every morning. にっか

**일관**(一貫) consistency/~하다 be consistent; run through (all)/~ 작업 integrated work/그는 시종 ~ 학문에 전념했다 He was constant in his devotion to learning. いっかん

**일괄**(一括) a bundle/~하다 bundle up; tie up into a bundle; lump together《개괄하다》summarize/~ 계약 a contract in bulk/~ 구입 a blanket purchase/~ 판매 sale by bulk. いっかつ

**일광**(日光) sunlight; sunshine; sunbeams; the rays of the sun/~ 소독 sterilization by sunning; disinfection by sunlight/~욕 a sunbath; sunbathing/직사 ~ direct sunlight/~에 소독하다 expose (a thing) to the sun. にっこう

**일구다** ①raise 〔topsoil〕; clear 〔land〕; bring under cultivation ②(a mole) raise a mound; burrow in. おこす

**일구 월심**(日久月深) lapse of time/~하다 days and months go by.

**일구 이언**(一口二言) double-tongue; breaking one's word/~하다 break one's word; be double-tongued. しょくげんすること

**일국**(一國) one nation/~ 일당주의 one party system. いっこく

**일군** 1《품팔이》a labourer; a workman; a worker《막일의》a navvy 2《역량 있는

**일군(一郡)** one country. いちぐん

**일군(一軍)** ①(전군) the whole army[force]; 《하나의 군》an army/~의 지휘관 a commander-in-chief ②(제1군) the First Army. いちぐん

**일근(日勤)** daily service/~하다 serve everyday; work every day. にっきん

**일급(一級)** the first class.

**일급(日給)** daily wages/~ 노동자 a day-labourer/~제 day rate plan/~으로 지불하다[고용하다] pay[hire] (a person) by the day. にっきゅう

**일기(一期)** 《기간》a term; a period 《반년》a half-year 《3개월》a quarter 《일생》one's span of life/~ 배당금 a regular[quarterly] dividend. いっき

**일기(一騎)** a single horseman/~ 당천의 용사 a match for a thousand; a matchless warrior; a man of unsurpassed prowess.

**일기(日記)** a diary; a journal/여행 ~ one's diary of a travel/학생 ~ a student-diary/~장 a diary; a daybook/나는 내 생각과 경험을 ~에 적습니다 I record my thoughts and experiences in a diary. にっき

**일기(日氣)** weather/~ 불순 (being) unseasonable; unsettled; changeable/~ 예보 a weather forecast[report]/~가 좋든 나쁘든 in fair weather or foul. てんき

**일년(一年)** a[one] year/~의 yearly; annual/~생 식물 an annual plant/~중 all the year round/~감【식】a tomato /~초 an annual [plant]/~지계(之計)는 정초에 있다 New Year's Day is the key of the year. いちねん

**일념(一念)** a single heart; a concentrated mind; an ardent wish/~으로 기도하다 pray from one's whole heart. いちねん

**일능(一能)** one merit; one accomplishment/~ 있는 사람을 원합니다 I want a man with some merit or other. いちのう

**일다¹** ①(발생하다) happen; come to pass; occur; come about ②(발흥(勃興)하다) spring up; prosper ③(일어나다) rise; go up. はっする

**일다²** 《개간하다》plow; break up (the soil); clear (the land). おこす

**일다³** 《쌀 따위를》wash (rice); scour; clean out/쌀을 ~ wash rice. とぐ

**일단(一旦)** once/~ 유사시에 in case of emergency/그 사건은 ~ 끝났다 The case was closed for the moment. いったん

**일단(一端)** 《한쪽 끝》one end 《일부》a part/그의 성격의 ~을 알게 되다 get a glimpse of his character. いったん

**일단(一團)** a body; a group; a party 《배우 등의》a troupe; a company/악당의 ~ a pack[gang] of villains/~을 조직하다 form[make, organize] a party. いちだん

**일단(一段)** 《계단의》a step of a stair-case 《등급》a gradation 《문장의》a passage; a paragraph.

**일단락(一段落)** 《쉼》a pause 《결말》a conclusion; a chapter/이제 ~지었다 With this we have completed the first stage of the work. いちだんらく

**일당(一黨)** 《동류》[fellow-]conspirators; a ring; the same party; participators 《일단》a gang/~이 체포되었다 All the fellow-conspirators were nabbed. いっとう

**일당(一堂)** ¶~에 모이다 meet together (in a hall).

**일당(日當)** daily allowance; daily pay [wages]; earnings of the day; per diem 《미》/~ 1,000원을 지불하다 pay[grant] 1,000 won a day.

**일대(一代)** a generation; one's whole life 《일생》one's lifetime/~의 영웅 the greatest hero of the day/~기(記) a life story; a life; a biography/~에 재산을 이루다 make a fortune in one's lifetime. いちだい

**일대(一隊)** a company (of soldiers); a party, a troop; a gang. いったい

**일대(一帶)** a zone; a tract; a region/ ~의 whole; throughout/~에 all over; throughout/그 지방 ~에 all over the district. いったい

**일대(一大)** one great[large]/~ 성황 a great prosperity. いちだい

**일대사(一大事)** a matter of great importance[grave concern]; a serious[grave] affair; an emergency/국가의 ~ an affair of vital importance to the State. いちだいじ

**일떠나다** leave[set out] [on one's way]. early in the morning. はやくしゅっぱつする

**일더위** early heat; early hot weather. はやめのあつさ

**일도 양단(一刀兩斷)** cutting in two with one stroke of the sword; decisiveness /~하다 cut (a thing) in two with a slash of the sword/~의 조치를 취하다 take a drastic[decisive] measure. いっとうりょうだん

**일독(一讀)** a perusal/~하다 read through /~의 가치가 있다 be worth reading; be worth while to read. いちどく

**일동(一同)** all; everyone; all (of us, them)/회원 ~ all the member/~ 모두 승낙했다 They all gave consent. いちどう

**일되다** grow early; ripen early/금년은 벼가 일된다 The rice crop are early this year. そうじゅくする

**일득(一得)** one advantage[benefit]; a merit/~ 일실 an advantage and a disadvantage; a merit and a demerit/~ 이 있으면 일실 있다 There is no rose without a thorn. いっとく

**일등**(一等) the first class; the first rank [grade]; 《한 등급》 one degree/~객 a first-class passenger/~병 a private first class《略: pfc》/~품 a first-class article 《品質》 the finest stuff/~상을 타다 win the first prize. いっとう

**일락**(逸樂) pleasure; enjoyment/~ 생활 a life given up to pleasure. いつらく

**일락 서산**(日落西山) the sun setting on the western hills/~하다 the sun set-son the western hills[in the west].

**일람**(一覽) a look; a sight; a perusal 《개요》 a summary; an epitome/~하다 take a look at; take a view of; peruse (*a book*)/~표 a table; a list; a conspectus/보고서를 ~하십시오 Please look through the report. いちらん

**일러두기** explanatory notes; introductory remarks. はんれい

**일러바치다** tell[carry] tales (*about, against*); inform; tell on 《학생이》 sneak/그가 한 일을 선생님께 ~ tell our teacher on him.

**일러주다** ①《알려주다》 let (*one*) know; tell; break the news to (*one*)/출발 시간을 일러주십시오 Please let me know the time of your departure. ②《미리 통지하다》 give notice beforehand. いってやる

**일력**(日曆) a daily pad calendar. ひめくり

**일련**(一連) ①《연속》 a series (*of*); a chain (*of*)/~의 사건 a chain of events/~의 거래 a series of transactions ②《종이의》 a ream (of *paper*). いちれん

**일련 탁생**(一蓮托生) a pledge to rise or sink together; casting *one's* lot with another; sharing the fate with another. いちれんたくしょう

**일렬**(一列) a row; a line; a rank/~로 in a row[line]; 《종렬로》 in a file/~로 줄서다 《매표소 따위에서》 stand in single file; form a queue. いちれつ

**일례**(一例) an example; an instance/~를 들면 for example; for instance; to cite[give] an instance of. いちれい

**일로**(一路) 《한 줄의 길》 a road 《곧장》 straight/~ 평안하시기를 빕니다 wish (*a person*) bon voyage. いちろ

**일루**(一壘) 《야구》 the first base/~수 the first baseman/~타(打) a[one] timer; a base hit; an ordinary. いちるい

**일루**(一縷) a blash; a gleam; a shred (of *hope*)/~의 희망 a ray[gleam] of

# 일

①work; employment; a task 《직업》 a job; an occupation 《사무》 business 《근무》 duties 《사명》 mission/~하다 work; labo[u]r/하루 ~ a day's work/쉬운 ~ an easy job[piece of work]/어려운 ~ a difficult task; a hard job/급한 ~ urgent business/큰 ~을 하다 achieves a great work[deed]/~을 하고 있다 be at work/~을 얻다 get a job; find work/오늘은 할 ~이 많다 I have many things to do today./이것은 쉬운 ~이 아니다 This is no easy task./그는 요즘 술 마시는 것이 ~이다 He does nothing but drink these days./~이 손에 잡히지 않는다 be unable to bring *one*self to work/~을 맡다 accept[take] a job/~을 시키다 put (*a person*) to work/~을 쉬다 stay away from work/우리는 관청 ~을 하고 있다 We are working for government offices.

②《사정》 circumstance 《사태》 things; matters/극히 사소한 ~로 화를 내다 get angry on the slightest provocation[for nothing]/어떤 ~이 있더라도 under any circumstances.

③《계획·사업》 a scheme; a project; a plan; a program; an undertaking/~을 진행시키다 carry a program forward/~이 척척 잘 되어 간다 The plan is on a fair way to success.

④《경험》 experience/그곳에 한번 가 본 ~이 있다 I once visited there./비행기를 타 본 ~이 없다 I have never traveled by plane./한국에서 편지를 받으신 ~이 한 번도 없읍니까 Have you never received a letter from Korea?/중국에 가 본 ~이 있느냐 Have you ever been to China?/그에게 한 번 편지를 받은 ~이 있다 I once got a letter from him.

⑤《사고》 an accident 《사건》 an incident; an event; an occurrence 《분규》 trouble/~이 생기면 in [case of] emergency/~은 그 시합에서 발단했다 The trouble originated in a game./~을 저지르다 make trouble.

⑥ a matter; a thing; a fact; an affair; a proposition; a job《속》/불쾌한 ~ an unpleasant matter; an ugly job; something unpleasant/귀찮은 ~ an awkward proposition/학교 ~에 관하여 이야기하다 speak about the school affairs/네가 참견할 ~이 아니다 That's none of your business./그 ~이라면 for that matter/내 ~은 걱정 말다 Don't trouble yourself about me./~이 복잡해지지나 않을까 I am afraid that will complicate the matter./~이 이렇게 되었으니 하는 수 없다 Now that things have come to such a pass, we can't help it./이것이 어머니께 알려지면 큰 ~이다 If it gets to mother's ears, there will be trouble.

hope; a slender hope; the last straw.

**일류(一流)** first class[rank, rate]; topnotch/~의 first-class[-rank, -rate]; top-ranking; of the first class[order]; foremost; leading/ ~ 극장 a first-class theater/~ 음악가 an A-1 muscian/ ~ 회사 leading companies.

**일륜(日輪)** the orb of day; the sun.

**일률(一律)** uniformity 《무차별》 indiscrimination/~적 uniform; indiscriminate/~적으로 in a wholesale manner 《똑같이》 uniformly 《무조건으로》 unqualifiedly; absolutely/그런 문제는 ~적으로 생각할 수는 없다 We cannot think of them in the same light.

**일리(一里)** one ri.

**일리(一理)** some reason; some truth/그의 말에도 ~는 있다 There is some truth in what he says., His view is true in a way./그것도 ~는 있다 There is something[some reason] in that.

**일리 일해(一利一害)** advantages and disadvantages; merits and demerits/모든 사물은 ~가 있다 Every good has its evil., Where there is good there is evil.

**일막(一幕)** one act/~극 a one-act play.

**일말(一抹)** a spray; a wreath 《소량》 a touch (of); a shadow (of); a tinge (of)/~의 불안 a touch[tinge, shadow] of uneasiness.

**일망 타진(一網打盡)** a round-up; a wholesale arrest/~하다 make a wholesale arrest (of); [make a] round-up.

**일매지다** (be) equal; even; uniform; be all alike.

**일맥(一脈)** a vein/양자간에는 ~ 상통하는 점이 있다 There is a thread of connections between the two./…과 ~ 상통하는 점이 있다 have something to do with.

**일면(一面)** ①《한 면》 one side 《전면》 the whole surface/~에 《전면에》 all over/시대상의 ~ a sign of the time/그의 성격에는 그런 ~이 있다 His character has such a phase./화려한 도시 생활에는 비참한 ~이 있다 The gay city-life has a seamy side to it. ②《양상》 an aspect; a phase 《신문의》 the first page.

**일면식(一面識)** a sight acquaintance; a bowing[nodding] acquaintance/~도 없는 사람 an utter stranger/~도 없는 a man whom one has never met.

**일명(一命)** one's life/~을 잃다 lose one's life.

**일명(一名)** 《한 사람》 a person 《별명》 another name/기자 ~ 名 A reporter wanted.

**일모(日暮)** 《일몰》 sunset; nightfall; sundown 《미》; 《황혼》 dusk; twilight 《저녁》 evening; before nightfall/~까지 돌아오다 come back by sunset[sundown].

**일모작(一毛作)** a single crop/~ 전답 a single-crop field.

**일목(一目)** ① a glance; a look/~ 요연하다 be obvious; be plain.

**일몰(日沒)** sunset; sundown《미》/ ~ 후[전]에 after[before] sunset.

**일무(一無)** nothing; not even one/~ 소득 no profit[gain] at all/~ 소식 no tidings[news] at all; not a single word.

**일문(一門)** ①《일족》 a family; a clan ② 《집안》 one's kinsfolk; one's folks 《대포의》(a piece of) gun.

**일문(日文)** Japanese; Japanese writing.

**일문(逸文)** a scattered and lost writing [script].

**일문(逸聞)** an unknown episode.

**일문 일답(一問一答)** the procedure of giving an immediate answer to each question; the procedure of one question and one answer/~하다 proceed one question and one answer.

**일미(一味)** relish; a good flavour; daintiness; deliciousness.

**일민(逸民)** a hermit; a retired person.

**일박(一泊)** a night's lodging/~하다 stay [stop] for the night[overnight] put up for a night; pass a night (at)/~ 여행 an overnight trip/~ 여행을 하다 make an overnight trip.

**일반(一般)** ~의 《전반의》 general 《보편의》 universal 《통례의》 common; usual 《대중의》 popular/~ 교양 과목 liberal arts /~ 투표 a popular vote; a referendum (pl. ~s, -da)/~ 회계 general account/ ~적으로 말하면 generally speaking/성적은 ~적으로 우수하다 The results are on the whole excellent.

**일방(一方)** 《한쪽》 one side 《딴쪽》 the other side 《상대의》 one party 《다른》 the other party/~ 무역 a one-way trade/~ 통행 one-way [traffic]/~에 치우치다 lean to one side.

**일배(一杯)** a cup; a glass; a glassful; a cupful.

**일번(一番)** the first; No. 1/~의 first; foremost; top/~ 타자 《체》 a lead-off man/학급에서 ~이다 be at the head [top] of the class.

**일벌** 《충》 a working[a worker] bee.

**일변(一邊)** ①《한쪽》 one side ②《일방》 one hand; the other hand/일도 해야 되고 ~ 손님도 만나야 된다 On the one hand I have to work, on the other hand I have many visitors to see.

**일변(日邊)** daily interest; interest per diem.

**일변(一變)** a complete change/~하다

**일별**(一別) parting/~하다 part from; separate from/~ 이래 since we met last; since I saw you last.　いちべつ

**일별**(一瞥) a glance; a glimpse; a look/~하다 cast[have] a look; glance (at); catch[get] a glimpse of/~할 가치도 없다 be beneath notice.　いちべつ

**일보**(一步) a step; a pace/~ 전진 a step forward/~ 물러나다 take a step back[ward]; yield a step.　いっぽ

**일보**(日步) daily interest; interest per diem/~ 10원 interest of 10 won per diem.　ひぶ

**일보**(日報) a daily report 《신문》 daily news; a daily.　にっぽう

**일보다** attend to the duties of an office [to one's business]; manage[conduct] business.　ようだしする

**일본할미꽃** 《식》 a Pulsatilla; an anemone; Pulsatilla cernua (학명).

**일봉**(一封) an endosure; an envelope/그는 금~을 받았다 He got a gift of money.　いっぷう

**일부**(一部) ①《일부분》a part/~의 partial; divisional; sectional/~의 사람은 some people/그것은 ~는 나무로 일부는 금속으로 되어 있다 It is made partly of wood, and partly of metal. ②《한 권》a copy/근저(近著) ~를 증정합니다 I will make you a present of a copy of my new book.　いちぶ

**일부**(日賦) a daily payment[installment]/~로 갚다 pay by daily installment[payment]/~금 daily installment[payment]/~ 저금 daily savings/~ 판매 sale on daily-installment terms.　ひぶ

**일부**(一夫) a husband; one man/~의 monogamous/~ 이처 bigamy; having two wives/~ 일부 monogamy/~ 다처 polygamy/~ 종사 serving but a single husband/~ 종신 having but a single husband during life.　いっぷ

**일부러** 《고의로》 intentionally; on purpose; by design 《짐짓》 knowingly; wittingly 《특히》 specially; expressly/~ 가다 take the trouble to go/그는 ~ 모른 체했다 He would not understand me./~거기 갈 것은 없다 You don't have to go there on purpose.　わざわざ

**일부분**(一部分) a part; a portion; a section; a division/~의 partial; sectional/~을 수정하다 amend partially[in part].　いちぶぶん

**일비**(日費) daily expenses[expenditure].　まいにちのひよう

**일비지력**(一臂之力) a muscle[bit] of strength; a helping hand; an assistance/~을 빌려 주다 help; give (one) a [helping] hand; do one's bit.　いっぴのちから

**일사**(一事) one thing; a single item/~ 부재리 the principle of not deliberating the same measure twice during the same session of the Assembly.　いちじ

**일사**(逸史) an unofficial history.　いっし

**일사**(逸事) a fact unknown to the world; a hidden fact; an anecdote.　いつじ

**일사반기**(一四半期) the first quarter.

**일사병**(日射病) sunstroke; heatstroke/~에 걸리다 have sunstroke; be sunstruck.　にっしゃびょう

**일사 불란**(一絲不亂) being in perfect order; being shipshape/~하다 be in perfect[strict] order; (be) shipshape/~하게 in perfect[strict] order.　いっしもみだれないこと

**일사 천리**(一瀉千里) dashing flow of torrents; rapid advance/~로 with lightning speed[rapidity]; in great haste/원안(原案)은 ~로 가결되었다 The bill was passed with great rapidity.　いっしゃせんり

**일산**(日産) 《생산고》 daily output[production]; 《일본산》 Japanese products; Japan-made.　にっさん

**일삼다** 《일로 삼다》 make it one's business to (do something); deal in 《전념하다》 devote oneself to; engage in 《탐닉하다》 give oneself up to; indulge in/술 마시는 것을 ~ do nothing but drink; be given to drink.

**일상**(日常) everyday; daily; usually; always/~의 daily; everyday; ordinary·/~ 생활 daily life; [everyday] life/~의 행실 one's everyday conduct/~ 쓰는 물건 things of daily necessity/~복 everyday dress/~사 an everyday experience[occurrence, affair].　にちじょう

**일색**(一色) ①《한 빛》one colour/~의 monochromatic; one-colour/~화 a monochrome; a monotint ②《미인》a paragon of beauty; a rare beauty; the fairest of the fair ③《비유적》¶ 그 위원회는 공산당 ~이었다 The committee seats were exclusively occupied by Republicans.　いっしき

**일생**(一生) a lifetime; one's life/~의 lifelong; for life/~의 사업 one's life-work/~의 한(恨) a lifelong regret/~의 일 one's life work/~에 한 번 once in a lifetime/~을 독신으로 지내다 live and die a bachelor/~을 바치다 devote [dedicate, consecrate, give] one's life (to a cause)/~ 일대의 좋은 기회 the chance of a life time.　いっしょう

**일서**(逸書) a scattered and lost book.

**일석 이조**(一石二鳥) killing two birds with one stone/그것은 ~다 It serves a double purpose.　いっせきにちょう

**일선**(一線) a line 《전선》 the fighting line; the front/~에 서다 take the lead.　いっせん

**일설**(一說) another opinion; one report [opinion, view, version]/~에 의하면 according to another opinion[report, view, version].　いっせつ

**일세**(一世) 《그 시대》 the age 《일생》 a life time/~의 of the age; of *one's* life/~의 호걸 the greatest hero of the day.

**일소**(一掃) a [clean] sweep; a clean-up; ~하다 sweep[wash] away; clean up; wipe out; drive off 《나쁜 것을》 deterge/다년 간의 폐습을 ~하다 clear away abuses of many year's standing/부패 분자를 ~하다 make a clean sweep of the corrupt elements/의심을 ~하다 clear away doubts.

**일소**(一笑) a laugh/~에 부치다 laugh (*a matter*) off[away]/그는 나의 기우를 ~에 부쳤다 He laughed away my fears.

**일손** ①《하고 있는 일》 the work in hand ②《일솜씨》 skill; performance/~이 오르다 improve in *one's* skill/~이 떨어지다 fall off in *one's* skill ③《일하는 사람》 a hand; a help/~이 모자라다 be short-handed; be undermanned/~을 빌다 ask (*a person*) a [helping] hand; be given a hand.

**일쑤** habitual practice/…하기가 ~다 be always doing (*something unpleasant*)/거짓말하기가 ~다 He tells a lie every time he turns around.

**일수**(日數) ①《날수》 the number of days/입원 가료의 ~ days of hospital treatment ②《날의 운수》 the day's luck/~가 좋다 The day is lucky.

**일수**(日收) money lending at daily interest; a loan collected by daily installment/~장이 a moneylender who collects by daily installment.

**일수 판매**(一手販賣) monopoly; sole agency/~를 특약하다 enter into a special contract for sole agency.

**일숙박**(一宿泊) a night's lodging/전주에 ~ 여행을 하다 make an overnight trip to *Chonju*.

**일순간**(一瞬間) an instant; a moment/~의 momentary/~에 in an instant[a moment].

**일습**(一襲) a suit/겨울옷 ~ a suit of winter clothes; a winter suit.

**일승 일패**(一勝一敗) victory and defeat/~의 승부 a ding-dong contest; a seesaw match.

**일시**(一時) 《한때》 at one time; once 《잠시》 for a time[while]; 《임시로》 provisionally 《동시에》 all together; at the same time/~적 방편 a temporary expedient[measure]/~적 분노 the anger of the moment/~적 현상 a passing phenomenon/~에 갑부가 되었다 He became a millionaire overnight./~적 충동 the impulse of the moment.

**일시**(日時) the time; the date; the date and hour (*of*).

**일시 동인**(一視同仁) universal brotherhood[benevolence]; fraternal spirit/~의 impartial; cosmopolitan.

**일식**(日蝕) 【천】 an eclipse of the sun; a solar eclipse.

**일식경**(一息耕) a good while; some time/~이 지나서 after a good while; after a long time.

**일신**(一新) ~하다 renew 《기분을》 refresh/면목을 ~하다 undergo a complete change/생활을 ~하다 begin a new life.

**일신**(日新) ~하다 be renewed day by day; undergo a change day after day.

**일신**(一身) *one*self; *one's* life/~상의 사정으로 for personal reasons/~상의 대사 a matter of great personal importance/~ 동체가 되다 become one flesh.

**일신교**(一神敎) monotheism/~의 monotheistic.

**일심**(一審) the first instance/~에서 무죄가 되다 be acquitted[free of charges] at the first trial/~ 재판소 the court of the first instance.

**일심**(日甚) daily intensification/~하다 get worse day by day; get serious from day to day; grow more severe daily.

**일심**(一心) ①《한 마음》 one mind[soul]/~ 동체 one flesh; two hearts beating as one/그들은 ~ 동체가 They were one in body and spirit. ②《전심》 a single heart; whole heartedness; concentration of mind/~으로 with all *one's* mind; heart and soul/~으로 생업에 종사하다 pursue *one's* calling with all *one's* mind.

**일야**(一夜) one night.

**일야**(日夜) night and day.

**일약**(一躍) at a [single] bound; at a jump/그는 ~ 문단에서 이름을 떨쳤다 He leaped into literary eminence.

**일어**(日語) Japanese; the Japanese language.

**일어나다** ①《기상하다》 rise; get up[out of bed]; sit up; turn out/일찍 일어나는 사람 an early-riser/자리 위에 일어나 앉다 sit up in *one's* bed ②《일어서다》 get up; pick *one*self up; regain *one's* feet 《넘어졌다가》 recover *one's* legs/간신히 ~ scramble to *one's* feet ③《자지 않고 있다》 sit up/우리들은 벌써 다섯 시 부터 일어나 있다 We have been up since five. ④《원인》 arise[spring, result] from; come of; originate in; have its origin in/말다툼은 오해에서 일어났다 The quarrel originated in a misunderstanding. ⑤《발흥하다》 spring up; rise; come into being 《융성하다》 prosper; be prosperous; flourish/새로운 산업이 일어났다 A new industry has sprung up lately. ⑥《발생하다》 occur; break out; take place; happen; come to pass; rise; arise 《생기다》 come into existence/신문은 세계에서 일어나는 일을 우리에게 알려 준다 The newspaper tells us what is going on in the world./일대 사건이 일어났다 A matter of grave concern has happened. ⑦(열・전기가) be produced/물체를 마찰하면 열과 전기가 일어난다 Friction generates heat and electricity. ⑧(불이) be kindled; be made; get lively/불이 일어났다 The fire is made.

**일어서다** stand up; rise to one's feet 《분기하다》 bestir oneself; brace oneself (up); rise (up)/간신히 ~ struggle to one's feet/벌떡 ~ spring[leap, jump] to one's feet/그는 농촌을 구제하고자 일어섰다 He set himself to save the agricultural village.

**일어 탁수**(一魚濁水) One man's mistake [error, misconduct] does damage[injury, mishief] to many.

**일언**(一言) a [single] word/~하다 speak [say] a word/남아 ~은 중천금 A word of honour is as good as a bond./~ 그 하에 거절당했다 I was met by a flat refusal.

**일언이폐지**(一言以蔽之) One sentence can cover the whole/~하면 in a word.

**일없다** (be) needless; useless/이렇게 많이는 ~ I don't need so many.

**일엽**(一葉) one leaf; one leaf[sheet] of paper/~ 지추(知秋) knowing autumn from [the fall of] a single leaf; A straw shows which way the wind blows.

**일요일**(日曜日) Sunday/~ 이외의 날 the week-days/~도 없이 일하고 있다 We are working without a day's rest./~판(版) a Sunday edition.

**일용**(日用) everyday[daily] use/~의 daily; of daily necessity/~품 daily necessities/~ 식료품 staple articles of food/~문 social[familiar] letter/~기구 ordinary utensils; utensils of daily use.

**일울다** [cocks] crow early.

**일원**(一員) a member/사회[클럽]의 ~ a member of society[club].

**일원**(一圓) 《일대》 the whole/서울 전역 ~에 걸쳐서 extending over the whole district of Seoul.

**일원**(一元) (being) unitary/~론 monism/~적 single; unitary/~화 unification/~화하다 unify.

**일원제**(一院制) the unicameral system; the single-chamber system/ ~ 회의 a unicameral legislature.

**일월**(一月) January(略: Jan.).

**일월**(日月) the sun and the moon 《시간》 time; days; years/~ 성신 the host[s] of heaven.

**일위**(一位) ①《첫째》 the first[foremost] place; the premier position; the first rank/~를 차지하다 take[hold] the foremost place; stand first; be at the top of (a class) ②《한 분》 one person ③《수》 the unit's place.

**일으키다** ①《세우다》 get up [right]; raise; help[pick] (one) up/아이를 일으켜 주다 help a child to his feet/일으켜 세우다 make (one) stand ②《창시하다》 start; initiate; commence; open; begin; bring about; give rise to 《사업 따위》 undertake 《운동・계획 따위》 set on foot 《설립》 establish 《재홍》 re-establish/사업을 ~ promote an enterprise/군사를 ~ rise in arms (against) ③《깨우다》 wake [up]; call/깊은 잠에서 ~ be aroused out of a sound sleep ④《집안・몸을》 ¶ 비천한 처지에서 몸을 ~ rise from a lowly position; spring from obscurity/그는 빈곤에서 몸을 일으켰다 He has come up from poverty. ⑤《야기하다》 cause; raise; breed; bring about[on]; give rise to 《유인・촉발하다》 provoke; invite/홍미를 ~ arouse one's interest/폭동을 ~ raise a riot/전쟁[대소동]을 ~ bring about war [great commotion] ⑥《제기하다》 ¶소송을 ~ institute[bring] an action[a suit] against; go to law ⑦《발병하다》 fall[get, be taken] ill; be attacked with/뇌빈혈을 ~ have an attack of cerebral anaemia ⑧《발생하다》 produce; generate/전기를 ~ generate electricity ⑨《불을》 make [a fire]; kindle/불을 불어 ~ blow up the fire.

**일의 대수**(一衣帶水) a narrow strait; a narrow streak of water.

**일이**(一二) one or two/~ 일[간] [in] one or two days/~삼 one・two・three.

**일익**(一翼) a role; a part/~을 담당하다 bear a part.

**일익**(日益) daily; everyday; day by[after] day; from day to day/사태가 ~ 악화하다 the situation is getting worse by the day/~ 더워집니다 It is growing hotter everyday., It is getting hotter and hotter.

**일인**(一人) one person/~당 for each [person]; per head/~ 독재 one-man[personal] dictatorship/~분 a portion for one person 《식사의》 one helping/~칭 《언》 first person.

**일인**(日人) 《단수》 a Japanese 《복수》 the Japanese.

**일일**(一日) a[one] day; the first day [of a month]/~이 천추 같다 feel as if one day were years/제 ~ the first day.

**일일이** 《하나씩》 one by one 《상세히》 in detail 《모두》 everyone of them; in everything[every case]/~ 조사하다 examine (a thing) one by one/~ 설명하다 explain in detail[point by point]/~ 보고하다 report in full/~ 트집잡다 find fault with everything (a person) does.

**일일지장**(一日之長) being one's superior/그 점에서 그는 나보다 ~이다 He is my superior[a cut above me] in that field., He is a step in advance of me there.

**일임**(一任) ~하다 leave (a matter) [entirely] to (one); commit (a matter) to one's care; trust (a person) with a matter/자네에게 ～하네 I leave it to you., I leave the matter in your hands. いちにん

**일자**(日字) ①(날짜) a date; dating/～를 정하다 fix [upon] a date; name a day (for) ②(날수) days; time/다소의 ～ some time; a certain number of days/그것을 완성하려면 꽤 ～가 걸립니다 Days are required for finishing it.

**일자리** a position; a situation (일) employment; work; a job/～를 찾다 look for a job[employment]/～를 잃다 lose one's job; be discharged. しごとば

**일자 무식**(一字無識) [utter] ignorance; illiteracy/～장이 an illiterate person; an ignoramus.

**일잠** going to bed early/～자다 go to bed early. よいね

**일장**(一場) ①(연극의) a scene/～의 희극 a comical scene ②(한바탕) a[one] time; a round/～의 연설을 하다 make[deliver] a speech; address. いちじょう

**일장 일단**(一長一短) merits and demerits.

**일재**(逸材, 逸才) superior talent. いっさい

**일전**(一戰) a fight; a battle; an engagement/적과 ～하다 fight a battle with an enemy (경기) have a game. いっせん

**일전**(一轉) ～하다 (회전) turn round (일변) make a complete change. いってん

**일전**(日前) the other day; some time[a few days] ago/～부터 for some days [time] past/～ 편지에 in one's last letter. いぜん

**일절**(一節) a section; a passage; a verse (시의) a stanza (단어의) a syllable.

**일점**(一點) (점 하나) a point (접수의) an article; one (시의) a verse; a stanza (음절) a syllable.

**일점홍**(一點紅) ①(미인) the only fair among those present ②(특출) excellence; superiority; prominence ⇒홍일점. こういってん

**일정**(日程) the day's program (의사의) the order of the day; the calendar (심의 사항) the agenda (경기의) a fixture/～에 올리다[넣다] place (a bill) on the order of the day; place on the calendar/～을 변경하다 alter a day's program. にってい

**일정**(一定) ～하다 (be) fixed (규정) set (같다) uniform (표준) standard/～하게 uniformly/～한 수입 a regular income/～한 서식 a set form/～한 일 a steady job; a regular work/～하게 하다 unify; secure a unity of; standardize/복장을 ～하게 하다 standardize the clothing. いってい

**일제**(一齊) ～히 (다 같이) altogether (동시에) all at once (이구 동성으로) in a chorus; simultaneously/～히 외치다[말하다] shout[say] in chorus[unison]/～ 사격을 하다 fire a volley (at)/～ 검거 a roundup. いっせい

**일조**(一朝) ¶ ～에 in a day/～ 유사시에 in case of [an] emergency/～ 일석에 in a day; overnight/로마는 ～ 일석에 이루어지지 않았다 Rome was not built in a day. いっちょう

**일족**(一族) (친족) relatives; kinsmen (가족) the whole family. いちぞく

**일종**(一種) a kind; a sort (변종) a variety; a species/～의 a kind[sort] of; of a kind[sort]/동물의 ～ a species of animal/그는 ～의 천재다 He is a genius of a kind[sort]./벼는 풀의 ～이다 The rice plant is a kind[variety] of grass. いっしゅ

**일좌**(一座) ①(한 자리) a seat ②(만좌) the company; the party; all those present. いちざ

**일주**(一周) a round; a turn (경기장의) a lap/～하다 go[travel] round; take a turn; sail round; make a tour (of)/세계를 ～하다 go[travel] round the world; make a tour of the world/세계 ～ 비행을 하다 make a round-the-world flight/～기(期) (천) a period/～년 the first anniversary/～ 여행 the round trip. いっしゅう

**일주기**(一周忌) the first anniversary of one's death.

**일주 운동**(日週運動) 【천】 diurnal motion. いっしゅううんどう

**일쭉알쭉** smooth and slippery; slipping easily this way and that [like fine textured cloth]/～하다 slip[slide] easily this way and that; give way easily. よろよろ

**일중**(日中) ①(오정 때) noon; midday; noontide ②(한 끼니 먹음) taking but one meal a day at noon/～하다 take but one meal a day at noon. にっちゅう

**일지**(日誌) a diary; a journal. にっし

**일찌감치** earlier ⇒일찍거니. はやめに

**일찌거니** rather early; a little early/좀 a little[bit] earlier [than]/～ 떠나다 make[get off, to] a little earlier start/물론 ～ 와 주면 더욱 좋다 Of course, if you're a bit earlier, all the better.

**일찌기** ①early/～ 일어나다 get up early/그는 ～ 부모를 여의었다 He lost his parents at an early age./～ 죽다 die young ②(전에) earlier; once; one time; formerly/이런 일은 ～ 들어 본 일이 없다 I have never heard of such a thing. とっくに

**일찍** early/좀 ～ a little[bit] earlier/～ 일어나다 rise[get up] early/～ 떠나다 make an early start/～ 피는 early flowering. とっくに

**일직**(日直) day duty/～하다 be on day duty/～ 장교 an orderly officer; an officer of the day. にっちょく

**일직선**(一直線) a straight line/～으로 in a straight line; straight; in a beeline/～으로 나아가다 advance in a straight

**line**／비행기는 도시의 상공을 ~으로 가로질렀다 The plane flew in a beeline across the city.

**일진**(日辰) (간지(干支)) the sexagenary cycle of a day 《운수》 the day's luck／오늘은 ~이 나쁘다 This is not a lucky day for me.

**일진**(一陣) q~ 청풍 a [blast of] cool breeze／창으로 ~ 광풍이 불어 들어와 촛불이 모두 꺼졌다 A gust of wind blowing at the window put out all the candles.

**일진 월보**(日進月步) rapid progress; steady advance／~하다 make rapid progress.

**일진 일퇴**(一進一退) advance and retreat; ebb and flow／~하다 advance and retreat; everchange; ebb and flow／~의 now advancing and now retreating; everchanging／~의 승부 a seesaw game／그의 병세는 ~하고 있다 Sometimes he gets a little better but then he has a relapse[gets worse].

**일차**(一次) 《수》 linear; of the first degree; one time; once; the first／~ 방정식 an equation of the first degree; a simple[linear] equation／~ 시험 a primary examination.

**일착**(一着) ①《경주의》 the first arrival／경주에서 ~이 되다 win the first place ②《옷의》 a suit ⇨벌.

**일책**(一策) a plan; an idea／~을 생각해 내다 think out a plan／~을 내놓다 suggest a plan; make a suggestion／그것도 ~이다 That's a good idea, too.／~이 떠올랐다 I hit upon a plan.

**일처 다부**(一妻多夫) polyandry／~의 polyandrous.

**일척**(一擲) casting away; squandering (*money*) all at one time／~하다 cast (*a thing*) away; squander [all at one time]; throw.

**일천**(日淺) ~하다 (be) short; not long／창립 이래 아직 ~하다 It is only a short time since the company was founded., It is but of yesterday's birth.

**일철**(一轍) ①《같은 길》 the same way [route, course] ②《한 줄의 길》 a single track.

**일체**(一體) one body; one flesh／~가 되어 in a body; as a man／부부는 ~ Man and wife are one flesh.／~ 양면론 the double aspect theory／~화 unification; integration.

**일체**(一切) all; everything; entirely 《부사적》 altogether／~의 all; every; whole／~ 관계 없다 have nothing to do with／~의 비용 the whole cost (*of*)／사건의 진상은 ~ 비밀로 되어 있다 Absolute secrecy is preserved as to the actual state of the matter.／외상 ~ 사절 Positively no credit.

**일촉 즉발**(一觸即發) a touch-and-go situation; a delicate situation／양국은 ~의 관계에 있다 The relation between the two countries is extremely delicate.

**일축**(一蹴) a kick／~하다 kick 《거절하다》 reject flatly 《이기다》 beat easily／가볍게 ~하다 brush off lightly／그의 제안을 ~했다 I spurned[turned down] his proposal.

**일출**(日出) sunrise ⇨해돋이.

**일출**(逸出) ①《탈출》 escape／~하다 flee from; escape from ②《특출》 eminence／~하다 stand out.

**일취 월장**(日就月將) rapid progress; steady advance／~의 progressive; ever-advancing／~하다 make rapid progress.

**일취지몽**(一炊之夢) an empty dream.

**일층**(一層) ①《건물의》 the ground-floor 〈영〉; the first floor〈미〉／~집 a one-storyed house ②《한결》 more; still more [further]; all the more／~의 진보 further progress／~ 더 재미있는 more interesting／~ 노력하다 make greater efforts; work harder [than ever].

**일치**(一致) 《부합》 coincidence 《동의》 agreement; unanimity; consent 《협동》 union; co-operation 《조화》 harmony／~하다 《합치하다》 coincide; agree; accord (*with*); 《협력하다》 harmonize (*with*); co-operate 《동의》 unite; consent (*to*)／~하여 in union; unitedly／~ 단결 union; solidarity; harmonious co-operation／단결하여 일하다 work in concert with／그들은 서로 의견이 ~했다 They agreed among themselves.／관민이 ~ 단결하여 일에 착수하다 undertake a thing with unanimity between the government and people／이상과 실제는 결코 ~하지 않는다 The ideal and the real never coincide.

**일컫다** ①《호칭》 call; style; name; designate／스스로 대학자라고 ~ style *one*self as a great scholar／그녀자는 미녀라고 일컬어진다 She is reputed to be a beauty. ②《칭찬하다》 praise; admire; commend; pay tribute to／모든 사람이 그의 덕을 일컬었다 Everybody extolled his supreme virtue.

**일탈**(逸脫) deviation; omission [by mistake]; departure／~하다 deviate (*form*); omit; depart (*from*)／오랜 습관에서의 ~ a radical departure[deviation] from long-standing customs.

**일터** the place where *one* works 《근무처》 *one's* place of employment 《사무소》 *one's* office 《공사장》 a site for a construction work.

**일통**(一統) unification／~치다 unify; unite／~하다 unify; unite; integrate; combine／천하를 ~하다 bring the whole country under *one's* sway.

**일파**(一派) a school; a party; a faction／~를 창설하다 create a school 《종교의》 found a new sect.

**일판**(一版) an edition 《초판》the first edition.

**일패**(一敗) a single defeat/~도지(塗地)a complete[crushing] defeat/~도지하다 meet with a complete defeat; suffer a crushing defeat/구승 ~ nine wins and one defeat.

**일편**(一片) a piece; a bit/~의 양심 a bit of conscience/~단심 a sincere heart; sincerity/~단심의 sincere; single[true, whole]-hearted. いっぺん

**일편**(一篇) a piece/~의 시 a piece of poetry.

**일평생**(一平生) all one's life; all days of one's life; till the end of one's life/~의 lifelong (friend)/~의 사업 one's lifework/~잊지 못할 never-to-be-forgotten/~독신으로 지내다 remain a bachelor[spinster] all one's life. しゅうせい

**일폭**(一幅) a scroll/~의 명화 a notable painting/동양화 ~ a scroll of Oriental painting/그 광경은 마치 ~의 그림과 같다 The scene looks like a picture scroll spread out. いっぷく

**일표**(一票) a vote; a ballot/일인. ~주의 one man one vote [principle].

**일품**(一品) an article 《요리의》a dish/~요리 one course dinner 《선택 요리》 dishes a lacarte/천하 ~ an article of peerless quality. いっぴん

**일품**(逸品) an article par excellence; a superb article; a rarity/그림의 ~ a fine piece of painting. いっぴん

**일필**(一筆) one stroke of a brush[pen]/~휘지 dashing off with one stroke of a brush/~휘지하다 write with one stroke of a brush. いっぴつ

**일하다** work; toil 《힘들여·애써》labour 《근무하다》serve (at)/일하고 있다《하는 중이다》be at work/바쁘게 ~ busy oneself/그는 처자를 위하여 뼈가 빠지게 일했다 He slaved for his family./먹고 살려고 ~ work for a livelihood; earn one's bread/일하지 않은 자는 먹지 말라 No work no pay., If any does not work, neither should he eat. しごとをする

**일한**(日限) a fixed time; an appointed day[time]; a date/~이 정해진 일 a job to be done by a fixed date/~을 연기하다 extend the time[term]/~을 어기지 않다 be punctual/~을 정하다 fix[set] the date[term]; give timelimits. にちげん

**일할**(一割) ten per cent; 10%/~할인 ten per cent discount.

**일할**(日割) 《일정표》a programme 《경기 개최일》a fixture; a schedule/~을 정하다 make a programme/시험 ~ an examination schedule/~표 a timetable; a schedule.

**일행**(一行) ①《동아리》a party; a company 《수행원》one's suite 《홍행자의》one's troupe/관광단 ~ a tourist party; a party of sightseers/~속에 들다 join a party ②《한줄》a line; a row 《시의》a line of verse/~ 띄어서 쓰다 write on every other line. いちぎょう

**일혈**(溢血) 【의】extravasation/~을 일으키다 the brain extravasates. いっけつ

**일호**(一號) number one; No. 1.

**일화**(逸話) an anecdote/그녀에게는 많은 ~가 있다 Many anecdotes are told of her./~집 a collection of anecdotes. いつわ

**일화**(日貨) 《상품》Japanese goods 《화폐》Japanese money/~배척 a boycott of Japanese goods.

**일확 천금**(一攫千金) making a fortune at a stroke; a bonanza/~하다 make one's fortune at one stroke; get rich quick/~을 꿈꾸다 dream of wealth got at a stroke. いっかくせんきん

**일환**(一環) a link/계획의 ~을 이루다 form a link in the chain of the programme. いっかん

**일회**(一回) once; a[one] time; a round; a game 《승부의》an event/~전 the first round(innings)/~《약의》a dose 《월부 따위의》an installment.

**일후**(日後) 《뒷날》another day 《나중》future/~의 future; coming/~에 in [the] future; after this; in after days. こんご

**일훈**(日暈) a ring around the sun; a halo/~하다 (the sun) have a ring around (it). にちうん

**일흔** seventy; three score and ten. しちじゅう

**일희 일비**(一喜一悲) ~하다 have joy and sorrow in quick alternation; be now glad, now sad/선거가 시작되어 후보자들은 ~의 상태다 Now that the poll[voting] is going on, candidates are agitated, now being optimistic, now pessimistic.

**읽다** 《책을》read; peruse 《암송하다》recite; chant/읽기 reading; reading lessons 《발음》pronunciation/읽고 쓰기 reading and writing/읽기 쉬운 easy to read 《필적이》readable; legible/읽기 어려운 hard to read 《필적이》illegible/한 자 한 자 음미해 가며 ~ dwell on each word; read word by word/널리 ~ ely/정신들여 ~ peruse; read carefully [with care]/다 ~ read[get] through/소리내어 ~ read out[off]; read aloud/신문에서 ~ read about (a matter) in a newspaper/책을 읽다가 잠이·들다 read oneself to sleep/이 책은 읽기에 재미있다 This book reads interesting./그는 편지를 읽지 않고 버려두었다 He left the letter unread. よむ

**읽히다** let read; have (a book) read (by one)/널리 읽히는 책 a widely-read book. よます

**잃다** ①《상실하다》lose; miss 《빼앗기다》be deprived[be bereft] of/재산을 ~ lose one's fortune/희망을 ~ lose one's hope ②《일행·길을》lose one's way; get lost;

stray[become separated] from/나는 공원에서 길을 잃었다 I was lost in the park.　うしなう

**임** 《남자》a lover 《여자》a love; a sweetheart.

**임간**(林間) ~에[서] In a wood[forest]/~ 학교 a school in the woods; an open-air school; a camping[forest] school.　りんかん

**임검**(臨檢) an official inspection 《경관의》visitation 《습격 조사》a raid 《배의》boarding/~하다 visit and inspect; raid; make a raid (on); pay a surprise visit (to); 《배를》board/~증 a certificate of inspection/현장을 ~하다 make an official inspection of the spot/~반 a raiding party 《배의》a boarding party.　りんけん

**임계**(臨界) 〖수·물〗 ~의 critical/~ 온도[압력, 각] the critical temperature[pressure, angle]/~량 critical mass.　りんかい

**임관**(任官) appointment (to an office); 《장교의》commission/~하다 be appointed (to an office); be gazetted (as); 《군인이》receive one's commission/~식 a ceremony of one's installation/~ 장교 a commissioned officer/소위로 ~하다 be commissioned a second lieutenant.　にんかん

**임균**(淋菌) 〖의〗a gonococcus(pl. -cocci).　りんきん

**임금** 《군주》a ruler; a sovereign;a monarch; an emperor; a king.　おう

**임금**(賃金) 《노임》wages; pay/최고[최저, 생활] ~ maximum[minimum, living] wages/~ 노동자 a wage earner/~ 수준 a wage level/~ 인상 a wage increase [raise]/~ 제도 the wage system/~ 투쟁 a struggle for higher wages/기준 ~ the standard[basic] wage/~을 지불하다 pay [wages].　ちんぎん

**임기**(任期) one's term[period] of office [service]; one's tenure [of office]; one's incumbency 《의원의》a term of membership 《지사의》governorship/~ 만료 completion[expiration] of one's term of office/~중 during one's term[tenure] of office/~를 마치다 wind up one's service; finish up one's tenure of office.　にんき

**임기 응변**(臨機應變) adaptation to circumstances/~의 extemporaneous; emergency/ ~하다 take such a step as the occasion demands/~할 재주가 있다 have the ability to accommodate oneself to circumstances.　りんきおうへん

**임대**(賃貸) lease; letting out on hire/~하다 hire; rent; lease; let (a thing) out on hire/~차(借) lease; letting and hiring; charter/~ 계약 a lease contract/~료 rent 《배의》charterage/~인 a leaseholder; a lessor.　ちんたい

**임독**(淋毒) 〖의〗gonorrhoeal; clap《속》/~

균 a gonococcus(pl. -cocci).　りんどく

**임립**(林立) ~하다 stand close together; bristle/항구에 돛대가 ~해 있다 The harbor bristles with masts.　りんりつ

**임면**(任免) appointments and removals [dismissals]/~하다 appoint and dismiss[remove]/~권 the power to appoint and dismiss.　にんめん

**임명**(任命) appointment 《무관의》commission/~하다 appoint (a person) to[as] /~식 a ceremony of appointment; an investiture/정부는 그를 비서관으로 ~했다 The government appointed him to the post of secretary.　にんめい

**임목**(林木) a forest tree.

**임무**(任務) duty; task; service; official duties 《사명》a mission/~를 수행하다 discharge[carry out] one's duties/~에 당하다 set about one's task.　にんむ

**임무관**(林務官) a forester; an inspector of state forests; a forestry officer.

**임박**(臨迫) pressure; urgency; imminence/~하다 draw near; impend; be on the point[brink] of/기한이 ~했다 The time draws near.　じきがせまること

**임부**(姙婦) a pregnant woman;a woman with child 《초산(初産)의》an expectant mother.　にんぷ

**임사**(臨死) ~하다 face death; stand in the presence of death; stand face to face with death.　しにのぞむこと

**임사**(臨事) ~하다 have an affair at hand; face a crisis.　ことにのぞむこと

**임산물**(林産物) forest products.　りんさんぶつ

**임산부**(姙産婦) pregnant women and nursing mothers.　にんさんぷ

**임상**(臨床) ~의 clinical/~ 의학 clinics/~ 강의 a clinical lecture[instruction]/~ 실험[실습] bedside and clinical demonstration[training]/~적 연구 a clinical study/~ 진찰하다 clinically examine.　りんしょう

**임석**(臨席) attendance; presence/~하다 attend; be present at/~ 경관 a policeman present/~하에 with (a person) in attendance.　りんせき

**임시**(臨時) ~의 extra; special; extraordinary; temporary 《일시적》transient; transitory 《급조의》improvised/ ~로 specially; extraordinarily; temporarily /~ 고용인 a temporary employee/~ 국회 an extra session of the National Assembly/~ 뉴스 news special/~ 수입[지출] extraordinary income[disbursement]/~ 열차 a special train/~ 총회 an extraordinary general meeting/~ 휴업 a special holiday 《게시》No Business Today.　りんじ

**임시 변통**(臨時變通) adaptation to circumstances; a temporary arrangement/~하다 make shift with (a thing); temporize; resort to a temporary expedient /~으로 만든 책상 an impromptu desk.

임신(姙娠) conception; pregnancy/~하다 become[be] pregnant; be in the family way; conceive/~중의 여자 a pregnant woman/~중에 during the period of maternity/~중이다 be in the family way; be with child/~ 중절 suspension of conception. にんしん

임야(林野) forests and fields; woodland. りんや

임업(林業) forestry/~ 시험장 a forestry experiment station/~ 경제 forestry economy. りんぎょう

임용(任用) employment; appointment/~하다 appoint (one)/공무원 ~령 the Official Appointment Regulations.
にんよう

임원(任員) an officer; an official; an executive〈미〉; a person in charge (총칭) the board/~ 선거 the election of officers/~ 회의 a meeting of officers; the staff meeting. やくいん

임은(賃銀) pay ⇨임금(賃金). ちんぎん

임의(任意) pleasure; discretion; option/~의 optional; free; voluntary/~로 at one's option[pleasure]; at will; as one pleases/~ 선택 option; free choice/~로 행동하다 act at one's discretion/~의 삼각형 any trianlge/~로 하게 하다 leave (a matter) to one's discretion.
にんい

임자 ①(주인) the owner; the possessor; the proprietor/~ 없는 ownerless; belonging to nobody/~ 있는 여자 a married woman/~ 없는 집 a vacant house ②(당신) you. しゅじん

임장(臨場) attendance; appearance on the scene; presence/~하다 attend visit; be present (at); appear. りんじょう

임전(臨戰) presence in a battle/~하다 go into action/~ 태세 preparations for action/~ 무퇴 knowing no retreat at a battlefield. りんせん

임정(林政) forestry administration[management]. りんせい

임정(臨政) a provisional government/~ 요인 key figures of the provisional government.

임종(臨終) ①(죽게 된 때) the dying hour; [the hour of] death; the end; one's last moment (죽음에 다다름) facing death; standing in the presence of death/~하다 face death; stand in the presence of death/~의 말 one's last [dying] words ②(임종의 배석) being at one's bedside when one dies; presence at one's death/~하다 be present at one's death; be at one's bedside when one dies/원통하게도 아버지가 돌아가실 때 ~ 못 했다 I regret I could not be present at my father's deathbed.
りんじゅう

임지(任地) one's post; the place of one's appointment/~로 향하다 proceed to [leave for] one's new post. にんち

임질(淋疾) 〖의〗 gonorrhoea/~의 gonorrhoeal/~균 a gonococcus(pl. ·cocci)/~ 환자 a gonorrheal patient/~에 걸리다 suffer from gonorrhoea. りんしつ

임차(賃借) hire; hiring (부동산의) lease /~인 a leasee; a lease-holder; a tenant (마차 따위의) a hirer/~료 rent; hire/~ 부동산 leasehold estate/~하다 lease (land); hold a lease (on land); take a lease (of a building). ちんしゃく

임천(林泉) a forest and a fountain.
りんせん

임치(任置) a deposit/~하다 deposit (in a bank, with a person); leave (a thing) with (a person)/~ 증서 a deposit certificate.

임파(淋巴) 〖생〗 lymph/~액 lymph/~ 선〔염〕 [the inflammation of] the lymphatic gland. りんし

임하다(臨─) ①(면하다) face; front (on); look down (upon)/큰 거리에 임한 집 the house standing upon the street. /바다에 임해 있다 face the sea ②(당하다) stand [be] in the presence of; face; meet/ 그때에 임하여 at that juncture[very moment]/죽음에 임하여 in the presence [at the moment] of death; on one's deathbed/출발에 임하여 한 마디 인사 말씀을 올립니다 At the moment of my departure I should like to say a few parting words. ③(임석하다) attend; be present at; present oneself at/개회식에 ~ attend[be present at] the opening ceremony. ことにあたる

임학(林學) forestry; dendrology/~자 a dendrologist. りんがく

임항(臨港) ¶~선(線) a boat-train line/ ~ 열차 a boat-train/ ~ 철도 a port [harbour] railway.

임해(臨海) the seaside; the seashore/~ 의 seaside; marine/~ 지역 littoral districts/~ 학교 a seaside school.

임행(臨幸) a visit (of the King); a Royal visit[attendance]/ ~하다 pay a visit to; attend. りんこう

입 ①(사람·동물의) the mouth; lips 〖해〗 os(pl. ·ora)/~의 oral/~속 [the interior of] the mouth/꼭 다문 ~ a firm-set mouth[lips]/~이 큰 big-mouthed/~ 을 오므리다 purse one's lips/~에 풀칠하다 earn one's living/~을 다물다 shut one's mouth/~을 크게 벌리시오 Open your mouth very wide. ②(말) speech; tongue; words/~이 무거운 of few words; taciturn/~이 가벼운 talkative/~ 밖에 내다 disclose; betray; mention; express/~을 열다 break the silence/~을 다물다 keep one's mouth shut; hold one's tongue; fall silent/그녀는 천성이 ~이 무겁다 She is slow of speech by nature. / 그는 ~이 무거우니까 비밀을 얘기해도 괜찮다 As he is a discreet man, you may let him into the secret. /~은 재앙의 근

원이다 Thoughtless speech may work great mischief. ③(미각) taste; palate/~에 맞다 suit one's taste/~에 대지도 않고 놔두다 leave untasted/술은 내 ~에 안 맞는다 Wine is not my taste. ④(사람수) the number of persons (가족수) the number of mouths to feed[of dependents] ⑤(부리) a bill(넓적한); a beak(갈구리 모양의). くち

**입가** about the mouth; at one's lips /~에 미소를 띠고 with a smile about one's mouth[lips]. くちもと

**입가심** ~하다 take off the aftertaste/약을 먹고 사과로 ~하다 eat an apple to chase the medicine taste.

**입각(入閣)** entry into a Cabinet/~하다 enter the Ministry; join the Cabinet/문교부 장관으로 ~이 확실하다 It is certain that he will enter the Cabinet as Minister of Education. にゅうかく

**입각(立脚)** ~하다 be based[grounded] on; take one's ground on; rest on the basis of/~점 a standpoint; a viewpoint (입장) a footing; a scaffold/사실에 ~하다 be based on facts. りっきゃく

**입감(入監)** imprisonment; confinement/~중이다 be in jail[prison]; be serving a term [in prison]. にゅうかん

**입경(入京)** arrival in the capital/~하다 arrive in Seoul; enter the capital city. にゅうきょう

**입고(入庫)** (상품의) warehousing (전차의) entering the car-shed/~하다 enter the car-shed/상품의 ~ warehousing of goods. にゅうこ

**입관(入棺)** encoffinment/~하다 place[put] the body in a coffin/~식 rites of placing a body in a coffin. にゅうかん

**입교(入敎)** conversion/~하다 be converted (to); become a believer (in) become a convert (to). にゅうきょう

**입구(入口)** a way in; a gateway; an entrance/공원의 ~ a park-gate/~에 서 있지 말라 Don't stand in the doorway/~를 막다 stop up the entrance. いりぐち

**입구(入寇)** invasion/~하다 invade/외적의 ~ foreign invasion.

**입국(入國)** entry[entrance] into a country/~하다 enter a country; be admitted into a country/~ 허가 formalities for entry/~ 허가 an entry permit/~이 허가되다 be admitted into[to] the country. にゅうこく

**입궁(入宮)** a visit to the palace/~하다 proceed[go] to the palace.

**입궐(入闕)** attendance at the Royal Court; a visit to the Royal Palace/~하다 proceed[go] to the Royal Court; visit the Royal Palace. きゅうでんにはいること

**입금(入金)** (수령) receipt of money (수령금) money received; receipts (받을 돈) money due; money coming in/~하다 receive/~ 전표 a receive[paying-in] slip/5,000원만 ~했다 He paid 5,000 won on account. にゅうきん

**입길** the mouth of one who speaks ill of another's fault/~에 오르내리다 be disputed by others.

**입김** breath/유리창은 사람의 ~으로 흐려져 있었다 The windowpanes were dim with the steam of breaths.

**입납(入納)** (전지에) to/~박나댁 ~ To Mr. Park.

**입내¹** (흉내) mimicry/~장이 a mimic[ker]/남의 ~를 내다 mimic another.

**입내²** (구취) mouth odo[u]r; [the smell of] one's breath/~가 나다 have a foul breath. くちくさみ

**입노릇** eating and drinking/~을 하다 have a bite; eat.

**입다** ①(옷을) put on; get into; don; slip on (입고 있다) wear; have on; be dressed in/옷을 입은 채 자다 sleep in one's clothes/옷을 잘 ~ be well dressed ②(은혜를) owe; be indebted to; be due to; enjoy (a person's) patronage; be favored (with); (손해를) suffer (a loss)/은혜를 ~ receive favor; share in the benefit/재난을 ~ meet a misfortune[calamity] ③(상을 입다) be in[go into] mourning (for). きる

**입담** eloquence; fluency; the gift of speech/~ 좋은 well-spoken; eloquent; fluent. はなしぶり

**입당(入黨)** joining a political party; accession to a party/~하다 join a political party/~자 an incoming member /민주당에 ~하다 affiliate oneself with the Democratic Party. にゅうとう

**입대(入隊)** enlistment/~하다 join[enter] the army; be enlisted (for the army)/~자 a recruit/~식 the ceremonial parade of new recruits. にゅうたい

**입덧나다** lose one's appetite due to pregnancy. つわりがおこる

**입도(入道)** conversion to Taoism/~하다 become a Taoist. にゅうどう

**입동(立冬)** the first day[beginning] of winter. りっとう

**입되다** be luxurious in diet; dine well (까다롭다) be fastidious.
しょくもつにぜいたくだ

**입뜨다** (be) slow of speech; taciturn/입뜬 사람 a man of few words.

**입락(入落)** pass and failure.
ごうかくらくだい

**입례(立禮)** a stand-up salute[bow]/~하다 bow[salute] standing. りつれい

**입론(立論)** a proposition; an argument; a position/~하다 argue; make out a case; make[put forward] an argument /확고한 ~ a well-grounded argument. りつろん

**입맛** an appetite; one's palate/~이 있다 [없다] have a good[poor] appetite/~ 떨어지다 one's appetite fails 《사람이 주어》 lose one's appetite/~을 돋우다 st-

**입맛 다시다** ①《음식을 보고》smack one's lips; lick one's chops／배고픈 소녀는 그것을 보고 입맛을 다셨다 The hungry girl licked her chops at the sight of it. ②《침을 빨다》lick one's lips ③《난처해서》lick one's lips in perplexity; smack; one's lips; tut.

**입맛쓰다** (be) perplexing; embarrassing; awkward／실패해서 입맛이 쓰다 He is chagrined at his failure.

**입맞추다** kiss; give (one) a kiss; press one's lips against; smack; give a smacking kiss／사랑의 입맞춤을 하다 kiss (her) with love. くちづけする

**입매** ①《간단한 식사》eating a small bite; a dab of food／～하다 eat just a bite ②《눈가림》scamping; camouflage／～하다 scamp[fudge, slapdish] one's work. かんたんなしょくじ

**입멸**(入滅) ①《입도》entering Nirvana／～하다 enter[pass into] Nirvana; attain Buddhahood ②《죽음》death [of a saint]／～하다 die. にゅうめつ

**입모습** shape of the mouth／～이 예쁜 소녀 a sweet-mouthed girl／그녀는 ～이 귀엽다 She has a lovely mouth.

**입목**(立木) a growing[standing] tree 《재목으로서》a standing timber. りつぼく

**입몰**(入沒) immersion; devotion; absorption／～하다 be immersed in; get oneself absorbed in.

**입묘**(入廟) transferring the mortuary tablet to the family shrine after the second anniversary of (a person's) death／～하다 transfer (the mortuary tablet) to the family shrine.

**입묵**(入墨) tattooing／～하다 tattoo／잔등에 ～하다 have one's back tattooed／오른쪽 팔에 용을 ～하다 have a dragon tattooed on one's right arm. いれずみ

**입문**(入門) entrance into a private school／～하다 enter a private school; become (a person's) pupil／～서 a guide; a manual; a primer／경제학 ～ an introduction to economics／문학 ～ an introduction to the study of literature. にゅうもん

**입바르다** (be) straightforward; plainspoken; outspoken／입바른 소리 plain speaking; a straight talk／입바른 소리를 하다 speak plainly; call a spade a spade／입바른 소리를 잘 하는 사람 a plainspoken person; an outspoken person. いうことがただしい

**입방**(立方) 《수》cube／～체 a cube／～직(積) volume／～근(根) the cube root／～체의 용적 cubic content／～으로 전개하다 extract the cube root／정～체 a regular solid. りっぽう

**입방아찧다** make complaints; find fault／입방아 찧는 사람 a shrew; a nagging [sharp-tongued] woman. しきりにつまらぬことをいう

**입버릇** a way[habit] of saying; one's cant 《말버릇》one's favourite phrase／～이 나쁜 foul-mouthed／그는 민주주의라는 말을 쓰는 것이 ～이 되어 있다 He never opens his mouth without saying "Democracy". くちぐせ

**입법**(立法) law-making; legislation／～자 a legislator／～회의 a legislative council／～기관 a legislative organ／～권을 행사하다 exercise legislative power／～의 정신에 배치되다 be contrary to the spirit of legislation. りっぽう

**입비**(立碑) erection of a monument／～하다 raise[erect] a monument. ひをたてること

**입비뚤이** a person with a wry mouth. くちのゆがんだひと

**입사**(入社) entering[joining] a company／～하다 enter[join] the company; enter the service of／～시험 an examination for service in a business company／대회사에 ～하다 join a certain big company. にゅうしゃ

**입사**(入射) 《물》incidence／～의 incident／～각 an incidence angle; an angle of incidence. にゅうしゃ

**입사**(入絲) inlaiding; damascening／～하다 inlay; damascene.

**입사**(入嗣) the investure of the heir[successor]／～하다 invest (one) with the heir[the successor].

**입싸다** be rash of speech; (be) glib[-tongued]／너는 입이 싸서 탈이야 You are too ready to speak. くちがかるい

**입산**(入山) 《불교에서의》entering the priesthood／～하다 enter[join] the priesthood; become a bonze; renounce the world. にゅうざん

**입상**(入賞) winning a prize／～하다 win a prize; win the first place／～자 a prize-winner; a winning contestant／1등으로 ～하다 win[take] the first prize. にゅうしょう

**입상**(立像) a statue 《소형의》a statuette. りつぞう

**입상**(粒狀) ～의 granular; granulous; graniform／～설탕 granular sugar／～조직 granular texture. りゅうじょう

**입선**(入選) ～하다 be accepted; be selected／～자 the winners; the winning competitors／～작 a winning piece of work／그녀의 그림은 올해의 국전에 ～했다 His painting was accepted for this year's National Art Exhibition. にゅうせん

**입성** 《옷》clothes; a dress 《총칭》clothing; costume. ころも

**입성**(入城) a triumphal entry into a castle／～하다 enter a castle; make a triumphal entry into a fortress／～식 formal[triumphal] entry. にゅうじょう

**입성수**(一星數) necromancy; divination. くちうら

**입소**(入所) entering; admission/~하다 enter the institution; be admitted to the institution/~시키다 put[cast] (a person) into prison; commit (a person) to a prison/~중이다 be in prison. にゅうしょ

**입속말** a murmur; a mutter; muttering/~하다 mutter (to oneself); grumble (at, over, about); murmur (at, against)/중얼중얼 ~하다 grumble (oneself). つぶやき

**입수**(入手) arrival; receipt; obtainment/~하다 receive; get; come to hand/~난 difficulty of procuring/~ 경로 means of acquisition. にゅうしゅ

**입수염** a moustache; a mustache(미)/~을 기르다 grow a moustache.

**입술가락** a rough[an unpolished] spoon.

**입술** a lip/~을 빨다 lick one's lips/~을 깨물다 bite one's lips/추위에 나의 ~이 터지다 My lips chap in cold weather./~이 얇은[두꺼운] thin[thick]-lipped. くちびる

**입시**(入侍) an audience (with the King, etc.); court presentation/~하다 be received in audience be His[Her] Majesty; be granted an audience.

**입시**(入試) an entrance examination.

**입씨름** bickering; [exchange of] high words; a brawl; a dispute/~하다 bicker; have high words (with); argue (with); dispute (with); quarrel.

**입신**(立身) a rise in the world; success [a rise, advancement] in life/~하다 rise (in the world); rise to eminence[distinction, greatness]; work oneself up to (a high position); have a brilliant career; better oneself/~ 양명 rising in the world and gaining fame/~ 출세 success in life; a successful career/자신의 운명을 개척하여 ~하다 carve one's way to fortune. りっしん

**입씻기다** give a sop to Cerberus; put a gold muzzle/입씻기기 위해서 내게 오만원을 내놓았다 He offered me 50,000 won to keep dumb about it. くちをふさぐ

**입아귀** the corner of the mouth.

**입안**(立案) a plan; a scheme; a design/~하다 plan [out]; frame; devise; originate; draft; form/~자 a designer; a framer/규약을 ~하다 draw up regulations. りつあん

**입양**(入養) adoption; adopting (a person) as one's child[son]; being adopted into (a person's) family. ようしになること

**입어**(入御) the Emperor's withdrawal into the inner palace/~하다 retire[enter] into the inner palace. にゅうぎょ

**입영**(入營) entering barracks; enlistment; enrollment/~하다 join the army; enter barracks/~중이다 be in the army; be serving with the colors.

**입옥**(入獄) imprisonment/~하다 be put in[into] prison; be sent to prison; be imprisoned/~시키다 commit (one) to prison. にゅうごく

**입욕**(入浴) a bath; bathing/~하다 take [have, use] a [hot] bath; have a tub; bathe. にゅうよく

**입용**(入用) want; demand; requirement; necessity/~되다 be in need[want] (of); be necessary. にゅうよう

**입원**(入院) hospitalization; admission to a hospital/~하다 enter hospital; be sent to hospital/~료 charges for hospital accommodation/~ 수속 arrangements for entering a hospital/~ 환자 an inpatient/~ 가료를 요하다 require treatment in [a] hospital. にゅういん

**입자**(粒子) 《물》 a particle/~량 particle weight. りゅうし

**입짧다** have a small[feeble, weak] appetite; eat sparingly/입짧은 사람 a spare[light, small] eater; a small feeder. すききらいする

**입장**(入場) entrance; admission; admittance/~하다 get in; enter; be admitted (into); gain entrance/~권 an admission ticket 《역의》 a platform ticket/~료 an admission fee[charge]/~무료 Admission [is] free/~세 an admission tax/~식 an entrance ceremony/~료를 받다 charge an admission/~료를 지불하다 pay admission. にゅうじょう

**입장**(立場) 《지위》 a position; a situation 《견지》 a viewpoint; a standpoint; a point of view; an angle/자기의 ~을 밝히다 make one's position clear/괴로운 ~에 있다 be in a painful position. たちば

**입장단**(一長短) beating time orally/~을 맞추다 beat time by the mouth.

**입적**(入寂) entering Nirvana; death 《입멸》(入滅). にゅうめつ

**입적**(入籍) entry in a family register/~하다 have one's name entered in the family register. にゅうせき

**입전**(入電) a telegram received/워싱턴으로부터의 ~에 의하면 according to a cablegram from Washington. にゅうでん

**입절**(立節) constancy; integrity; fidelity/~하다 keep one's integrity unsullied; stick to one's colours; keep one's principles; remain faithful to one's principles.

**입정**(入定) confining oneself to a room for enlightenment; a religious meditation; death of priest.

**입정놀리다** eat something all the time. しきりにかんしょくする

**입정사납다** (be) foul-mouthed[-spoken, -tongued]; 《욕잘하다》(be) abusive; violent-tongued/입정사납게 abusively; scurrilously; in abusive[foul] language. くちがわるい

**입주**(入住) ~하다 move in; take possession of (*a house*)/~자 an occupant of a house/~제 a living-in system.

**입증**(立證) proof; establishment (of *a fact*); substantiation (of *one's statement*)/~하다 prove; give proof; establish/~하는 사실 facts corroborative of (*a crime*)/유죄[무죄]를 ~하다 prove[establish] *one's* innocence/그 아이의 건강은 어머니의 정성을 ~하는 것이다 The child's good health attests his mother's care. りっしょう

**입지**(立地) location/~ 조건 conditions of location/~ 조건이 나쁘다 be inconveniently located. りっち

**입지**(立志) fixing *one's* aim in life; determination to make a success in life/~하다 fix *one's* aim in life; have a fixed purpose in life/~ 소설 an edifying[inspiring] novel/~전(傳) the biography of a self-made man/~ 전속의 인물 a self-made man. りっし

**입짓** a motion of a mouth; eating/~을 하다 make a mouth. くちぶり

**입찰**(入札) a tender〈영〉; a bid〈미〉/~하다 tender[bid] for; offer[submit] a tender; make a bid (*for*)/~ 가격 the price tendered; bidding price/~ 기일 time appointed for handing in tenders/~ 보증금 a security for a tender[bid]/~자 a bidder〈미〉/공사 ~ 광고 an advertisement of tender for engineering work/~을 모집하다 invite tenders/~에 부치다 sell (*a thing*) by tender/경쟁~ a public tender. にゅうさつ

**입천장**(一天障) 【해】 the palate; the roof of the mouth. こうがい

**입체**(立體) 《수》a solid [body]/~의 solid; cubic; vertical/~감 cubic effect/~ 교차 《도로의》a two[multi]-level crossing/~ 교차로[도] a freeway; a fly-over roadway/~ 묘사 cubic[solid] delineation/~ 사진 a stereo[scopic] picture/~ 영화 a three-dimension film; a cinerama 〈미〉/~ 음향 stereophonic sound/~파 《미》cubism/대도시의 ~적 팽창 the vertical expansion of great cities. りったい

**입체**(立替) payment for another 《가불》 advance 《대여》 a loan/~하다 pay (for *another*); [pay in] advance; loan/그의 여비를 충분히 ~해 주었다 I made a large advance to meet his travelling expenses.

**입초**(入超) the excess of imports over exports; the unfavourable balance of trade. にゅうちょう

**입초**(立哨) 《순경의》 point-duty; watch/~인 a guard 《파일 따위의》 a picket/~병 a sentry/~서다 stand[keep] watch[guard]; 《입초병이》 stand[be] on sentry 《순경이》 stand on pointduty. ほしょうにたつこと

**입추**(立秋) the first day[setting-in] of autumn. りっしゅう

**입추**(立錐) 【】~의 여지도 없다 be closely packed; be filled to overflowing[capacity]; be densely crowded/강당은 ~의 여지도 없을 만큼 구경군으로 차 있었다 The hall was filled with spectators leaving no standing room. りっすい

**입춘**(立春) the first day[setting-in] of spring; onset of spring [around 3, 4 February]. りっしゅん

**입태자**(立太子) ~하다 proclaim the Heir Apparent to the Throne. りったいし

**입하**(立夏) the first day [the setting-in] of summer [around 5, 6 May]. りっか

**입하**(入荷) a fresh supply of good; receipt[arrival] of goods/~ 통지 an arrival notice. にゅうか

**입학**(入學) entrance[admission] into a school/~하다 enter a school; be admitted into a school/~금 an entrance[a matriculation] fee/~기 the admission period/~생 a new student; an entering student/~ 수속 registration for admission/~ 시험 an entrance examination/~식 an entrance ceremony/~ 원서 an application for admission/~ 자격 entrance requirements/~ 지원자 a candidate for admission/~을 지원하다 apply to a school for admission. にゅうがく

**입항**(入港) arrival; docking; entry into port/~하다 enter port[harbour]; make port; dock; put into port/~선 incoming[inbound] vessels/그 배는 오늘 ~할 예정이었다 The boat was scheduled to make port today. にゅうこう

**입향 순속**(入鄕循俗) In Rome do as the Romans do.

**입헌**(立憲) constitutionalism/~국 a constitutional country/~ 군주 정체 constitutional monarachy/~ 정치 constitutional government/~주의 constitutionalism/ ~ 정치를 운용하다 conduct[work] constitutional government. りっけん

**입회**(立會) ①《동석》 presence; witnessing/~하다 be present; attend; witness/~자 a witness 《투표의》 a teller/~ 재판 a mixed court/나는 선거의 개표에 ~ 했다 I was among the witnesses at the opening of the ballot. ②《거래소의》 a session; a call/전장(前場) ~ the morning[afternoon] session. たちあい

**입회**(入會) joining; entrance; admission/~하다 join; enter (*a society*); be come a member of/~금 an entrance fee/~ 신청자 an applicant for membership/~자 an entrant; a person admitted to membership/~를 신청하다 apply for membership/누구나 ~할 수 있음 The membership is open to all. にゅうかい

**입후보**(立候補) candidacy〈미〉; candidature/~하다 stand as a candidate (for *an election*); stand for〈영〉/~자 a can-

입히다 ①(옷을) clothe; dress; put on/옷을 ~ put clothes on (*a person*) ②(도금하다) plate; coat; gild/반지에 금을 얇게 ~ plate[wash] a ring with gold ③(씌우다·올리다) cover 《베니어판을》 veneer 《당의를》 coat/사탕을 입힌 sugar-coated (*tablet*) ④(죄·손해 따위를) charge[fix] (*a guilt* on *a person*); cause (*a damage* to)/손해를 ~ inflict losses upon (*a person*).

잇¹ 〖식〗 a safflower; a bastard[dyers'] saffron.

잇² (이불 따위의) a cover/베갯 ~ a pillow-slip[-cover, -case].

잇다¹ (지붕을) roof (이엉으로) thatch (널빤지로) shingle (기와로) tile/이엉으로 이은 농가가 두어서너 채 산기슭에 있었다 A few straw-thatched cottages stood at the foot of a hill. /기와를 다시 이어야 하겠다 We must have our roof retiled.

잇다² ①(집합·연결하다) unite; join; connect; attach; link; combine/줄을 ~ link strings together/조각을 ~ join fragments together ②(계승하다) succeed (*to*); carry on; inherit/가업을 ~ succeed to the family business/왕위를 ~ accede [come] to the throne/아버지의 뜻을 ~ follow in the footsteps of *one's* father ③(생명을) maintain; sustain; preserve (*life*)/목숨을 겨우 이어가다 eke out a bare existence; keep body and soul together/그는 빵과 물로 목숨을 이었다 He sustained himself on bread and water.

있다 ⇨별항 참조(page 1672 ).

잇닿다 keep; be continuous; follow; continue/잇닿아서 continuously; successively; one after another[the other]; in rapid succession/잇달아 총회가 있었다 Then a plenary meeting followed.

잇달다 continue; go on; be continuous (*to*); be connected to/거실은 침실에 잇

## 있　다

①(존재하다) be; there is[are]; be in existence; exist/책은 책상 위에 ~ The book is on the table. /옛날에 어진 임금이 있었다 Once there lived a wise king.

②(위치하다) stand (산·건물 따위가) lie (도시·나라가); be(길·강이); run; situated/그 섬은 부산의 서남 150 마일 지점에 ~ The island lies[lies] 150 miles southwest of *Busan*. /학교는 어디에 있느냐 Where is the school situated[located]?/중국은 한국의 서쪽에 ~ China lies to the west of Korea.

③(소유하다) have; own; possess 《부여되다) be blessed with(좋은 것을); be cursed with(나쁜 것을)/그녀는 음악에 대한 재주가 ~ She is endowed with musical talents. /그는 열병이 ~ He is cursed with fever. /좋은 기억력이 ~ He is blessed with a good memory.

④(머무르다) stop; stay; remain/좀 더 있으면 a little bit later on/너 여기 있거라 You stay here. /당분간 지금 있는 곳에 있거라 Remain where you are for the present.

⑤(거행되다) be held[given]; take place; open (회의가) meet; come off/다음 회의는 언제 있게 될까 When is the next meeting to be held?/곧 시험이 ~ An examination will come off[be held] shortly.

⑥(발생하다) there is[are]; occur; happen; arise; take place; come about; break out/화재가 있었다 A fire broke out. /그들 사이에 무슨 일이 있었는지 모르겠다 I don't know what has passed between they.

⑦(포함되다) bear; contain; include/그 책에 서진 목록이 ~ The book contains a bibliography. /과목 중에 독일어가 ~ German is included in the curriculum.

⑧(달리다) have (*a thing*) attached to (*it*); be equipped[fitted, provided] (*with*)/그 집에는 목욕탕이 ~ The house is provided with a bathroom.

⑨(경험하다) have experience/그를 한 번 만난 적이 ~ I have met him once before. /학교에서 가르친 일이 있읍니까 Have you ever taught school?

⑩(재산) be rich[wealthy]/있는 사람 a well-off person.

⑪(동작의 계속) be (*doing*); 《상태의 존속》 be; remain/그녀는 일을 하고 ~ She is at work. /담이 무너져 ~ The wall is broken. /아버지는 장사를 하고 ~ My father is engaged in business.

⑫(상태) go; remain; keep/서 ~ keep standing/먹지 않고 ~ go without food /맨발로 ~ go barefoot.

⑬(…에 존재하다) consist (*in*); reside (*in*); lie (*in*)/성공은 노력하는 데 ~ Success depends on labo[u]r. /허물은 그에게 ~ The blame rests with him., It is his fault., He is to blame. /행복은 자기 본분을 다하는 데 있다 Happiness consists in trying to do *one's* duty.

**잇대다** 닿아 있다 The sitting room opens into a bedroom.

**잇대다** ①(계속하다) keep up; go[keep] on (*with*); carry on; continue/잇대서 c-ontinuously; without a break; uninterruptedly/그는 세 시간 잇대서 연설했다 He spoke for three hours at a stretch. ②(이어대다) piece on (*one thing to another*); join; put together; add to/잇댄 부분 an added part/차를 ~ link cars together.

**잇몸** a teethridge; a gum/~을 드러내고 웃다 [show one's teeth and] grin.

**잇새** an opening between teeth/~에 고기가 끼었다 I got a shred of meat stuck between my teeth. はとはとのあいだ

**잇속** (이의) a row[set] of teeth/~이 좋다[나쁘다] have a regular[an irregular] set of teeth. はのならびかた

**잇속**(利一) calculation; self-interest/~이 있는 장사 a profitable business. ださん

**잇솔** a tooth-brush. はぶらし

**잇자국** a tooth-mark; an impression of teeth. はのあと

**잇집** the socket of a tooth. しそう

**잉걸불** live charcoal.

**잉부**(孕婦) a pregnant woman; a woman with child[in pregnancy]. みもちおんな

**잉손**(仍孫) posterity of the seventh generation.

**잉아** threads used to hold up the warp while weaving; warp ties.

**잉앗대** a warp-tie stick [on a loom].

**잉어**(一魚) 〖어〗 a carp(*pl.* carps. 집합적 carp)/붉은 ~ a golden[red] carp. こい

**잉여**(剩餘) the remainder; a surplus; a balance; what is left over; a margin/~금 a surplus [fund]; balance in hand/~ 가치 surplus value/~ 정리 the remainder theorem/~액(額) an excess; a surplus.

**잉잉** a whimper; a mewl/~ 울다 mewl; whimper. いやんーいやん

**잉조**(剩條) the remainder; hawt is left over.

**잉존**(仍存) ~하다 retain[keep] as before.

**잉태**(孕胎) conception; pregnancy/~하다 conceive; become pregnant; go with child. こをはらむこと

**잊다** ①(망각하다) forget; be forgetful of/잊을 수 없는 ineffaceable (*experience*)/잊지 않고 without forgetting[fail]/이름을 ~ forget *one's* name/침식을 ~ forget *one's* sleep and food; be devoted to (*a thing*)/은혜를 ~ forget *another's* kindness; be ungrateful/제 자신을 ~ forget *oneself*/나는 사람의 얼굴을 잘 잊어버린다 I have a poor memory for faces./내가 말한 것은 잊지 말라 Don't fail to remember what I have said. ②(염두를 떠나다) dismiss (*a thing*) from *one's* mind; think no more of; put out of *one's* mind 《단념하다》give up; forget/지루함을 ~ beguile the tima; relieve tedium/술로 슬픔[고통]을 ~ drown *one's* sorrows[pain] in wine/잊을래야 잊혀질 않네 That memory always haunts me. ③(놓고 오다) leave (*a thing*) behind 《가져오는 것을》forget to bring [take] (*a thing*). わすれる

**잊히다** pass out of mind[*one's* memory]; be forgotten/잊히지 않는 일 an unforgettable event/그녀가 잊히지 않았다 She was always on my mind. わすられる

**잎** 《나무의》 a leaf(*pl.* leaves); 《칼날 모양을 한》 a' blade 《침엽》 a needle 《집합적으로》 foliage/우거진 ~ thick foliage/~이 없는 leafless; bare/~이 나오다 spring into leaf/바람에 나뭇~이 움직인다 The wind stirs the leaves. は

**잎나무** brushwood.

**잎담배** leaf tobacco. はたばこ

**잎사귀** a leaf; a leaflet. は

**잎샘** a cold spell in the early spring; lingering cold in the leafing season/~하다 get cold in leafing time.

**잎전**(一錢) a brass coin [formerly used in Korea].

**자[1]** ①(단위) a ja; a Korean foot ②(도구) a ruler; a rule; a measure; a square/~로 재다 measure with a rule/~로 재서 팔다 sell (*cloth*) by the measure/삼각~ a set square. しゃく

**자[2]** (감탄사) Come on!, Come now!, Here!/~ 한 잔 들게 Come on, have a drink. さあ. じゃあ

**-자** ①(하자마자) as soon as; no sooner than; when; on; at/그는 나를 보~ 울음을 터뜨렸다 On seeing me, he burst into cry. ②let [us]a가~ Let's go./먹~ Let's eat./마시~ Let's drink./앉~ Let's sit down.

**자(子)** ①(아들) a son; a child ②(선생) the master/공~ Confucius ③(십이지의) the Rat; the third of the twelve horary signs/~년 the Year of the Rat. し. こ. こども

**자(字)** ①(글) a character; a letter (한자 따위) an ideograph/작은 ~로 쓴 written in tiny lettering/한~(漢一) Chinese characters ②(이름의) a pseudonym; another name; an alias. じ

**자(者)** ①(사람) a person; one; a fellow; some/그~ he; that fellow/그 자리에서 죽은 ~도 있다 Some were killed on the spot. ②(것) a thing; that; this/전~와 후~ the former and the latter. しゃ. もの

**자(自)** (부터) from; on and after/근무시간, ~ 오전 9시 지 오후 5시 Business hours, from 9 a.m. to 5 p.m. から

**자가(自家)** (집) one's own house[family]; (자기) one's self; self/~ 당착 self-contradiction. じか

**자가사리** 〖어〗 a kind of catfish; *Liobagrus mediodiposalis*(학명). こうらいはげぎき

**자가용(自家用)** ①(개인용) [for] private use; personal use (가정용) family use ②(자가용차) a private car[automobile]; a car for personal use. じかよう

**자각(自覺)** consciousness; self-consciousness (각성) awakening/~하다 become conscious; awaken to; be aware of; realize/그녀는 자신의 무지를 ~하고 있다 She is conscious of her ignorance./~ 증상 a subjective symptom. じかく

**자간(子癎)** 〖의〗 eclampsia. しかん

**자갈** gravel; pebbles; shingle; ballast; macadam/~ 길 a gravel road/~밭 gravelly field. じゃり

**자강(自彊)** strenuous efforts/~하다 make strenuous efforts/~지책(之策)을 강구하다 encourage people to make strenuous efforts. じきょう

**자개** mother-of-pearl; a nacre/~ 그릇 mother-of-pearl ware/~를 박다 inlay with mother-of-pearl. かいがら

**쪼개** a piece of bean split in two.

**쪼개다** split ⇒쪼개다. わる

**자개미** the groin; the armpit.

**자객(刺客)** an assassin/그는 ~의 손에 죽었다 He fell a victim to an assassin. しかく

**자격(資格)** qualification (직책) capacity (능력) competency (회원 따위의) eligibility/~을 얻다 qualify *oneself* for/당신은 교사로서의 충분한 ~을 갖추고 있다 You are quite a competent teacher./~ 시험 a qualifying examination/~증 a certificate of qualification/입학 ~ entrance requirements. しかく

**자격지심(自激之心)** a guilty conscience; a feeling of self-accusation/그것은 그의 ~에서 나온 말이다 He said that out of self-accusation.

**자결(自決)** ①(자기 결정) self-determination/~하다 determine for[by] *oneself*/민족 ~ self-determination of races ②(자살) suicide/~하다 kill *oneself*; [commit] suicide. じけつ

**자경단(自警團)** civil militia; a vigilance committee; vigilante corps(미).

**자경마들다** hold the reins for *oneself* while riding.

**자계(自戒)** self-discipline/~하다 admonish *oneself*. じかい

**자고(慈姑)** 〖식〗 the arrowhead plant; *Sagittaria sagittifolia*(학명).

**자고(鷓鴣)** 〖조〗 a partridge. しゃこ

**자고로(自古一)** from old[ancient] times; from remote ages; from time immemorial; since the days of antiquity traditionally/~ 한국인은 흰옷을 즐겨 입었다 We Koreans traditionally have preferred to wear white clothes. むかしから

**자괴지심(自愧之心)** a sence of shame/~을 느끼다 be sensible to shame; have

a sense of shame. みずからはじるこころ

**자꾸** repeatedly; frequently; always; again and again; eagerly／그녀는 ~ 나에게 구혼됐다 She eagerly proposed me to marry her. しきりに

**자구 행위**(自救行爲) 【법】 self-help. じきゅうこうい

**자국** (흔적) marks; traces; print (움푹한) an impression (한 줄기의) a track (지나간) a trail (상처의) a scar (짐승의) a spoor／발~ footprints／눈물 ~ traces of tears／~나다 leave a mark (on). あとかた

**자국**(自國) one's [own] country; one's native land; one's father-land; one's mother[home] country／~의 native; home; domestic／~민 one's fellow countrymen. じこく

**자국눈** a snowfall barely enough to leave footprints; a light fall of snow.

**자국물** water gathered in footprints; a small puddle. あしあとにたまったみず

**자국밟다** follow; trail [after] (one); shadow (one); pursue (추적) give chase／자국밟게 하다 put (dogs) on the trail. とうぶつする

**자궁**(子宮) 【해】 the womb; the uterus／~외 임신 extrauterine pregnancy／~ 내막염 endometritis／~ 절개 hysterotomy／~암 uterine cancer. しきゅう

**자귀**¹ (연장) an adz. おの

**자귀**² (짐승의 발자국) a spoor; a trail; tracks [of wild animals].
どうぶつのあしあと

**자귀**(字句) words and phrases; wording (집합적) phraseology／~의 verbal／~를 수정하다 make some change in the wording. じく

**자귀나무** 【식】 a silk-tree; *Albizzia julibrissin*(학명). ねむのき

**자귓밥** chips from an adz. こっぱ

**자규**(子規) 【조】 the cuckoo.

**자그르르, 짜그르르** simmering ⇒지그르르, 찌그르르. じいじい

**자그마치** a few; a little; some (반의적) as much as／술 좀 ~ 마셔라 Don't drink too much.

**자그마하다** (be) rather small; be of a somewhat small size／자그마한 rather small; undersized; small statured. ちいさい

**자극**(刺戟) (물건) a stimulus; an impetus; a spur (일) stimulation (격려) encouragement／~하다 stimulate; give an impetus to; irritate (신경 따위를) excite／야심은 노력의 ~이 될 때가 많다 Ambition is often a stimulant of industry. しげき

**자극**(磁極) 【물】 a magnetic pole／~성 magnetic polarity. じきょく

**자끈** with a crack ⇒지끈. ばちん

**자근거리다** tease ⇒지근거리다. からかう

**자근먹거리다** annoy ⇒지근먹거리다.

**자글자글** with a sizzling sound ⇒지글지글.　じゅじゅ

**자금**(自今) from now on; henceforth; hereafter; in future. じこん

**자금**(資金) funds; capital; money／~ 부족으로 공사가 중지되었다 Lack of funds halted the work.／~을 조달하다 raise the capital(funds)．／~난 financial difficulty／회전 ~ a revolving fund.

**자금거리다** be gritty to the teeth ⇒지금거리다.

**자급**(自給) self-supply; self-sufficiency／~하다 support oneself; supply oneself／경제적으로 ~ 자족을 이룩하다 achieve [attain] economic self-sufficiency.／~ 경제주의 autarky. じきゅう

**자긍**(自矜) (자찬) self-praise; self-admiration (자부) self-conceit. じまん

**자기**(自己) (자신) self; oneself (자아) self; ego (나) I／~의 one's own; personal; private (명사뒤에) of mine／~ 스스로 in person (제 힘으로) for oneself (혼자) by oneself／~ 자신을 알라 know oneself／~ 경멸 self-contempt. じこ

**자기**(自棄) self-abandonment ⇒자포 자기.

**자기**(瓷器) porcelain; china[ware]; crockery. じき

**자기**(磁氣) 【물】 magnetism／~를 띤 magnetic／~ 감응 magnetic induction／~ 회로 magnetic circuits. じき

**자기**(自期) one's inner determination; a resolution in one's heart.

**자기**(自記) ①(자기가 씀) writing by oneself ②(자동 작용) self-register／~하다 write by oneself; register [automatically]／~ 온도계[우량계] a self-registering thermometer[rain gauge]. じき

**자나깨나** day and night; awake or asleep／그 여자는 ~ 그 일만 생각하고 있다 The thought is ever present in her mind.
ねてもさめても

**자낭**(子囊) 【식】 a seed bag; an ascus; a sporangium／~ 포자 an ascospore. しのう

**자네** you／~ 집 your house. きみ

**자녀**(子女) children; sons and daughters; offspring. しじょ

**자눈** scale; graduation／~을 매기다 graduate. しゃくのめもり

**자녹자녹** ~하다 (be) soft-moving; gentle; swaying. ゆらゆら

**자다** ①(잠을) [have a] sleep (잠들다) go to sleep; fall asleep (자리에 들다) go to bed; retire／잘[잘못] ~ sleep well[badly]／어젯밤에 한잠도 못 잤다 I could not sleep a wink last night. ②(풍파 따위가) go[die] down; subside; abate; fall off; sink; calm down／바람이 차츰 잔다 The wind dies down. ③(시계 따위가) run down／시계가 잔다 The clock has run down. ④(성교하다) have sexual intercourse. ねる

**짜다**¹ ①(맛이) (be) salty; briny ②(마음이) (be) unpleasant; displeased／짠맛 a salty taste.

**짜다²** ①(만들다) piece together; put (*things*) together; assemble; construct; make／책상을 ~ make a table ②(편성하다) form; organize; prepare／전율 ~ make up a party／계획을 ~ form a plan ③(한통이 되다) unite (*with*); cooperate (*with*); enter into partnership ④(실・끈으로) weave; spin; knit／털실로 양말을 ~ knit stockings out of wool ⑤(물기를) wring; compress; squeeze; press, rack／젖은 옷을 ~ wring [out] wet clothes／귤에서 즙을 ~ press the juice out of an orange ⑥(억지로) press out; squeeze; cudgel[rack] one's brains／이 문제를 풀기 위해 머리를 짜내고 있는 중이다 I am now racking brains to solve this problem. ⑦(착취하다) exploit; squeeze; extort; exact／가난한 사람들에게서 많은 세금을 짜내다 squeeze the poor with heavy taxes ⑧(눈물을) weep; cry; sob／그녀는 온종일 눈물만 짜고 지냈다 She did nothing but cry all day long.  つくる

**자단**(紫檀) 【식】 a red sandalwood.  したん

**자담**(自擔) personal charge／~하다 take charge (of *something*) in person[personally].  じこふたん

**자당**(自黨) one's [own] party／~ 사람들 members of one's party／~에 끌어 넣다 bring (*one*) over to one's own party.  じとう

**자당**(慈堂) your[his, her, *etc.*] mother.

**자당**(蔗糖) 【화】 cane sugar; saccharose.

**자도**(紫桃) 【식】 a plum／~나무 a plum tree; a damson.  すもも

**자독**(自瀆) self-pollution; masturbation; self-abuse; onanism.

**자동**(自動) automatic action[movement]／~하다 move automatically; act by itself; move[work] of its own accord／~식 automatic／~ 전화 an automatic [dial] telephone／~ 판매기 a slotmachine 《음식점의》 an automat／~ 소총 an automatic rifle.  じどう

**자동사**(自動詞) 【어】 an intransitive verb (略: vi.)／불완전 ~ an incomplete intransitive verb.  じどうし

**자동 자전거**(自動自轉車) a motorcycle; an autocycle《미・속》.  じどうしゃ

**자동차**(自動車) a [motor] car; an automobile《미》; an auto《미・속》／~로 가다 go to motoring／~에 타다 ride in a car／아버지는 ~로 일터에 가신다 Father drives to work.／~ 경주 a motor race／화물 ~ a truck〈미〉; a lorry〈영〉.  じどうしゃ

**자두** 【식】 a plum ⇒자도(紫桃).  すもも

**자드락** the decline of a hill／~길 a·hill path.

**자드락거리다** annoy (*a person*) ⇒지드럭거리다.  うるさくねだる

**자드락나다** (비밀이) be found out; get out; be exposed[disclosed]; come to light.  ばくろする

**자득**(自得) ①(만족) self-complacency; self-satisfaction ②(터득) apprehension; understanding／~하다 (be) self-complacent; feel[be] self-satisfied; apprehend; understand／자업 ~ the natural consequence of one's [mis]deed／그가 가난해진 것도 모두 자업 ~이다 His poverty is of his own making.／자업 ~이라 생각하고 단념해라 You must take the consequences of your own deeds.  じとく

**짜들다** be hardened ⇒찌들다.

**짜들름짜들름** piece by piece; little by little ⇒찌들름찌들름.

**자디잘다** (be) very small; be of a very small size; fine (사람이) (be) meticulous; overscrupulous.  びしょうだ

**자라** 【동】 a fresh-water turtle.  かめ

**자라다¹** ①(성장하다) grow (양육하다) be bred; be brought up／모유로 자란 아이 a child raised on mother's milk／봄은 만물이 자라는 계절이다 Spring is the growing season. ②(증가하다) increase／그 도시의 인구는 점점 자라고 있다 The city is rapidly increasing in its population.  せいちょうする

**자라다²** ①(충분하다) be enough; be sufficient; suffice; last [out]／이 석탄으로 겨우내 자랄 수 있을까 Will this coal last out the winter? ②(도달하다) reach; come up to／내 힘이 거기까지 자라지는 못한다 It is beyond my reach.  たりる

**자라풀** 【식】 a kind of frogbit; *Hydrocharis asiatica*(학명).

**자락** the lower edges[ends] of garments; the bottom; the train.  すそ

**자란자란** to the brim ⇒지런지런.  なみなみ

**자랑** self-praise; vanity; boast; brag; pride／~하다 be proud[boastful, vain] of; brag[boast] of; make a boast of／~스러운 얼굴 a boastful look／그녀가 아들을 ~하는 것도 당연하다 She may well be proud of her son.  ほこり

**자랑거리** a source of pride; something *one* is proud of／새로 산 코트가 그녀의 ~자 기쁨이다 The new coat is her pride and joy.  ほこるべきもの

**자력**(資力) means; resources; capital funds／~이 있는[없는] 사람 a man of [without] means／그는 집을 장만할 만한 ~이 없다 He could not afford to buy a house.  しりょく

**자력**(自力) one's own power[exertion, ability, strength]; self-effort／~으로 by one's own effort[power]／~으로 살아가다 carve out a career for *oneself*.  じりき

**자력**(磁力) 【물】 magnetism; magnetic force／~계 a magnetometer／~선(線) magnetic line of force.  じりょく

**자료**(資料) materials; data／~를 수집하다 collect material[data]／연구 ~ research materials[data]／통계 ~ statistical data.  しりょう

**자루¹** (주머니) a [gunny] sack; a bag／~에 넣다 put (*a thing*) into a bag／쌀

~ a rice bag. きふくろ

**자루²** 《손잡이》 a handle; a haft 《칼 따위의》 a hilt 《창 따위의》 a shaft/권총 ~ a revolver handle/낫에 ~를 달아 put a handle on a sickle. え

**자르다¹** cut [off]; chop; sever/둘로 ~ cut in two/도끼로 나무를 ~ chop firewood with an ax. きる

**자르다²** tie up; tighten ⇒조르다. しめる

**자르르, 짜르르** dribbling; dripping 르르, 찌르르. ざあーっ

**짜르륵** with a gurgling sound ⇒찌르륵.

**자리** ①《좌석》 a seat; one's place/~에 앉다 take one's seat/~에서 일어나다 rise up from one's seat/~를 양보하다 offer [give] one's seat to (a lady). ②《여지》 room 《공간》 space/한 사람만 더 들어갈 ~가 있다 There is room left for one more. ③《현장》 the spot/그 ~에서 on the spot/나는 그 ~에서 거절했다 I declined then and there. ④《위치》 a situation; a position; a location 《대지》 a site/그 학교는 ~가 좋다 The school stands in a good situation. ⑤《지위》 a position; a post 《관직》 an office/~에서 물러나다 resign one's post ⑥《깔개》 a mat; matt.ng ⑦《잠자리》 a bed/~에서 일어나다 get up ⑧《계수의》 a figure 《주판의》 reed 《숫자의》 unit; place/~를 틀리다 잡다 get digits wrong ⑨《흉터》 a mark; an impression/총에 맞은 ~ [the mark of] a bullet wound. させき

**자리**(自利) self-interest; one's own interests; personal gain[profit]. じり

**자리개** a straw rope; a sheaf rope.

**자리끼** drinking water placed on one's beside for night use.

**자리보전**(一保全) being confined to one's bed/~하다 be bed up with illness.
びょうしょうにつくこと

**자리옷** night clothes; a nightgown; a nightdress; pajamas. ねまき

**자리자리** ~하다 (be) asleep; numb.
ひりひり

**자리잡다** take one's place; place oneself/그 공원은 시(市)의 중심가에 자리잡고 있다 The park lies in the centre of the city. ていちゃくする

**자립**(自立) 《독립》 independence; self-reliance 《자활》 self-support; self-sustenance/~하다 establish oneself; become independent/~해서 장사를 하다 do business on his own account/~ 경제 economical independence. じりつ

**자릿내** a stale smell/~가 나다 smell stale. いろいろのかびくさい臭

**자릿자릿** ~하다 《저리다》 (be) benumbed 《쑤시다》 tingling 《마음조이다》 thrilling; suspenseful; thrilled. ひりひり

**자마구** 【식】 pollen [of cereals].
いねのしべこ

**자막**(字幕) 《영화의》 a title; a caption/설명 ~ an insert title. じまく

**자만**(白滿) self-satisfaction/~하다 be self-satisfied.

**자만**(自慢) 《자찬》 self-praise 《자부》 self-conceit; vanity 《큰소리》 boasting; brag 《자랑》 pride/~하다 be proud of; brag[boast] of; make a boast of/그녀는 자신의 용모에 관하여 은근히 ~하고 있다 She inwardly prides herself on her good looks. じまん

**자매**(姉妹) sisters/~ 기관 sister agencies/~ 학교 a sister school/~ 회사 an affiliated company. しまい

**자멸**(自滅) self-destruction; self-ruin; suicide; natural decay/~하다 destroy [ruin, kill] oneself; perish/저 회사는 현상태가 지속되었다가는 머지않아 ~할 것이다 That company will soon be ruined, if it is left as it is. じめつ

**자명**(自明) self-evidence/~하다 (be) self-evident; obvious; self-explaining; axiomatic[al]/전체가 부분보다 큼은 ~한 이치다 That a whole is greater than any of its parts is axiomatic. じめい

**자명종**(自鳴鐘) an alarm clock.

**자모**(字母) ①《음표 문자》 an alphabet; a letter; a syllabic ②《활자》 a matrix(pl. -trices); a printing type. じぼ

**자모**(慈母) a loving[an affectionate] mother/~회 a mother's meeting. じぼ

**자모음**(子母音) vowels and consonants.
しおんとぼいん

**자못** very; greatly; exceedingly; remarkably/그 일은 ~ 어렵다 It is an exceedingly hard job. とても

**자문**(諮問) a question; an inquiry consultation/~하다 inquire; put[submit] a question to; consult/~ 기관 a consultative body/~ 위원 an advisory committee. しもん

**자문**(自問) ~하다 question[ask] oneself/~ 자답 a soliloquy; a monologue. じもん

**자물쇠** a lock; a padlock 《자동》 a snaplock/~가 잠겨 있다 be locked; be on the lock/~를 열다 unlock 《열쇠 따위로》 pick a lock. じょうまえ

**자미중** a mendicant Buddhist priest.
たくはつにあるくそう

**자빠드리다** throw[tumble, bring] down.
ひっくりかえす

**자빠지다** ①《넘어지다》 fall on one's back; fall backward ②《눕다》 lie down ③《이탈하다》 fall away (from); drop away [off]. ひっくりかえる

**자박**(一광) a nugget of gold.

**자박자박** walk softly/자박자박 with soft steps. そろそろする

**자반**(佐飯) salted dry fish.

**자발**(自發) ①~적 spontaneous; voluntary/~성 spontaneity/~적으로 행동하다 act spontaneously. じはつ

**자방**(子房) an ovary. しぼう

**자배기** a large and round earthen vessel.

**자백**(自白) avowal; admission 《고백》 confession 《자인》 acknowledg[e]ment/~

**자벌레** 〖충〗 a looper; measuring worm. しゃくとりむし

**자변**(自辨) paying one's own expenses/~하다 pay one's own expenses.

**자복**(自服) confession/~하다 make a full confession (to a fault). じはくしふくじゅうすること

**자본**(資本) capital; a fund 《자산》 assets /외국 ~ foreign capital/운전 ~ working capital/독점 ~ monopolistic capital/~주(主) a financier; a capitalist /~가 계급 the capitalist class/~주의 capitalism/~주의 경제 capitalist economy/~금 capital; a share capital/금융 ~ financial capital. しほん

**자불기** being whipped[lashed] by one's wife; pettycoat government/~ 맞다 be tied to one's wife's apron strings.

**자봉침**(自縫針), **자봉틀**(自縫—) a sewing machine/~ 바늘[실] a sewing machine needle[thread]. ミシン

**자부**(子婦) a daughter-in-law. しふ

**자부**(自負) self-conceit; pride; self-admiration/~하다 be self-conceited 《자신》 be self-confident. じふ

**자부심**(自負心) self-conceit; pride/~이 강한 사람 a very self-conceited person /~을 상하게 하다 hurt[wound] one's pride. じふしん

**자비** 《탈것》 any man-carried vehicle.

**자비**(自備) one's own preparation[s]/~ 하다 prepare oneself (for).

**자비**(自費) one's own expense[charge]/ ~ 출판하다 finance the publication of one's book at one's own expense. じひ

**자비**(慈悲) 《인정》 mercy 《인애》 charity; benevolence 《관대》 clemency 《연민》 compassion; pity 《사랑》 love/~하다 (be) merciful; benevolent; kind hearted/ ~심 a merciful heart/저 친구는 ~심도 인정도 없다 He is a stranger to pity or mercy. じひ

**자산**(資産) property; a fortune; estate; means 《부채(負債)와 상대적으로》 assets /~가 a wealthy person; a man of property/~ 재평가 revaluation of property/~을 남기다 leave an estate. しさん

**자살**(自殺) suicide; self-destruction; death by one's own hand/~하다 kill oneself; commit suicide; take one's own life/~자 a suicide/~ 방조 aiding and abetting suicide/~ 방조죄 the crime of aiding self-destruction/~ 미수 attempted suicide/~음독~하다 commit suicide by taking poison. じさつ

**자살**(刺殺) stabbing (a person) to death. しさつ

**자상**(仔詳) details; particulars; minuteness/~하다 (be) detailed; minute; meticulous; be in detail/~히 in detail; minutely; in full. しさい

**자상 행위**(自傷行爲) 〖법〗 crippling oneself (to avoid military service).

**자새** a small reel/~질 reeling. ちいさいリール

**자색**(姿色) beauty (in a woman); comeliness/~이 뛰어나다 surpass (others) in beauty. ししょく

**자색**(紫色) purple; violet/~ 수정 〖광〗 amethyst. ししょく

**자생**(自生) 《우연 발생》 autogenesis; spontaneous generation; 《야생》 wild growth/~하다 grow wild/~ 식물 native [wild] plants. じせい

**자서**(自序) the author's preface/~하다 write one's own preface (to one's work). じじょ

**자서**(字書) a dictionary; a lexicon; a wordbook. じじょ

**자서**(自署) an autograph; a signature;a sign manual/~하다 affix one's signature; sign one's name/책에 ~하다 autograph a book. じしょ

**자서전**(自敍傳) an autobiography; one's life story/~을 쓰다 write the story of one's own life. じじでん

**자석**(磁石) a magnet 《나침반》 a compass /~은 철을 잡아당긴다 Magnet attracts iron./~의 인력(引力) magnetic attraction/천연 ~ a natural magnet; a lodestone. じしゃく

**자석영**(紫石英) an amethyst ⇒자수정. しせきえい

**자선**(慈善) charity; benevolence; philanthropy 《자선 행위》 almsgiving/그는 자기의 모든 재산을 ~사업에 바쳤다 He gave all he had to charity./~가 a philanthropist; a charitable person/~ 기금 a charity fund/~ 남비 a charity pot/~ 병원 a charity hospital/~ 사업 charitable work. じぜん

**자선**(自選) self-selection/~하다 《자기 선정》 elect oneself 《작품율》 make a selection from one's own work/~ 시집 a collection of poem selected by the author.

**자설**(自說) one's own view[opinion]/~ 을 주장하다 maintain one's opinion/~을 굽히다 change[switch, revise, revamp] one's thinking 《변경하다》 turn one's coat. じせつ

**자성**(自省) self-examination 《반성》 reflection 《내성》 introspection/~하다 examinate oneself; reflect; introspect/~ 을 촉구하다 ask (a person) to reconsider (the matter). じせい

**자성**(磁性) 〖물〗 magnetism/~을 띠게 하다. magnetize/~체 a magnetic substance. じせい

**자세**(仔細) minuteness; details/~하다 (be) detailed; minute; full; particular /~히 in detail; in full; minutely; closely/~한 이야기는 다음 편지로 미루겠읍니다 The particulars will be given by

자세(姿勢) a posture; an attitude; a pose《몸가짐》 a carriage/바른 ~ a correct pose of body/~가 좋다[나쁘다] carry oneself well[ill]/ ~를 바로잡다 straighten oneself/ ~를 고치다 correct one's carriage. しさい

자세(藉勢) ~하다 strut about in borrowed plumes; make use of another's influence.

자손(子孫) sons and grandsons; progeny; descendants; offspring; posterity/~에게 전하다 hand down (a thing) to posterity. しそん

자수(自手) one's own hands[efforts]/~성가하다 make one's fortune by one's own efforts.

자수(自首) self-surrender; self-denunciation; voluntary surrender/~하다 give oneself up/그는 경찰에 ~했다 He delivered himself to the police. じしゅ

자수(刺繡) embroidery/~하다 embroider; do embroidery (on)/~본 embroidery designs/~실 embroidery. ししゅう

자수(自修) self-study; self-teaching; self-culture/~하다 teach oneself; study for oneself. じしゅう

자수정(紫水晶) an amethyst.

자숙(自肅) self-discipline; self-control/~하다 exercise self-control. じしゅく

자순(諮詢) consultation; inquiry/~하다 consult; inquire; refer (a matter) to (a person). しじゅん

자습(自習) self-study; self-teaching/~하다 teach oneself; study for oneself/ ~시간 study hours/~ 문제 homework 《숙제 따위》hometesk. じしゅう

자습서(自習書) a self-teaching manual; a key; crib《영·속》; a pony《미·속》/수험생의 ~ the examinee's book. じしゅうしょ

자승(自乘) square; multiplication by itself/~하다 multiply by itself; square /3의 ~은 9다 The square of three is nine. ~근 a square root. じじょう

자승 자박(自繩自縛) falling into a trap set by oneself/~하다 fall into a trap set by oneself; be caught in one's own trap. じじょうじばく

자시(子時) the Watch of the Rat; the time between midnight and two o'clock in the morning. ねのこく

자시(自恃) self-reliance/~하다 feel[have, place] reliance upon oneself; be self-reliant; be one's own master.

자씨(姉氏) [your, his] elder sister. あね

자시다 eat ⇒먹다.

자식(子息) ①《자녀》one's children; one's sons and daughters/~이 넷 있다 have four children ②《욕》a creature; a guy; a chap; a fellow; a bloke/개~ son of a bitch. しそく

자신(自身) one's self; oneself/~의 own /나~ myself/~의 생명을 내걸다 risk  one's life/과식하는 건 너 ~에게 나쁘디 You have yourself to thank if you eat too much. じしん

자신(自信) self-confidence; confidence in oneself; assurance/~하다 be self-confident; be confident (of)/나는 다시 ~을 얻었다 I recovered my old confidence. じしん

자실(自失) losing one's wits; being dazed; abstraction; absent-mindedness/~하다 lose one's wit; be dazy/망연 ~하다 be distrait; be dazed. じしつ

자심(滋甚) getting worse; aggravation.

자아 now; come; here; well ⇒자. さあ. やあ

자아(自我) 【철】self; ego/~가 강한 egotistic; egoistic; selfish/ ~ 보존 self-preservation/~ 억제 self-repression/ ~ 의식 self-consciousness/~ 비판 self-criticism[-accusation]. じが

자아내다 ①《실을》spin ②《생각을》excite; arouse; stir up; provoke《눈물을》draw /눈물을 ~ draw tears from one's eyes. しぼりだす

자아 울리다 suck up (water). ひきあげる

자애(慈愛) affection; love; kindness; benevolence/어머니의 ~ the love of mother. じあい

자애(自愛) self-love; self-regard; taking care of oneself; looking after oneself 《이기주의》selfishness/~하다 take care of[look after] oneself. じあい

자약(自若) ~하다 (be) self-possessed; composed; calm; compose oneself/현명한 자는 ~한 태도로 고난을 참는다 A wise man bears misfortune with equanimity. じじゃく

자양(滋養) nourishment; nutrition; alimentation/밀에는 ~분이 많다 Wheat contains a great deal of nutriment./~가치 nutritive value/~분 a nutritious element. じよう

자양화(紫陽花) 【식】a hydrangea.

자업 자득(自業自得) the natural consequences of one's own deed/ ~이다 One must lie on the bed one has made

자연(自然) ①《천지 만물》nature/~ 현상 natural phenomena/~의 법칙 the law of nature/~의 미[힘] the beauty[forces] of nature/~과 친하다[벗하다] commune with nature ②《자연 상태》~의 natural; wild/~색 a natural colour/ ~으로 돌아가라 return[get back] to nature ③《당연》~하다 (be) natural ④《자연적이다》~스럽다 (be) natural 《기교가 없다》unartificial《꾸밈이 없다》unaffected ⑤《저절로 됨》~하다 (be) natural; spontaneous/그 문제는 ~히 소멸됐다 The problem was allowed to die. しぜん

자연(紫煙) tobacco-smoke. しえん

자연 과학(自然科學) natural science.

자연수(自然數) natural number.

자연주의(自然主義) naturalism/~자 nat-

uralist.
**자엽**(子葉) 〖식〗 a seed leaf; a cotyledon; a seminal leaf. しよう
**자영**(自營) 《독립적 영업》 individual[independent] business 《자급》 self-support/ ~하다 support *oneself*/~ 사업 an independent enterprise. じえい
**자예**(雌蕊) a pistil. しずい
**자오선**(子午線) 〖천〗 the meridian/ ~ 통과 《천체의》 transit. しごせん
**자오의**(子午儀) 〖천〗 a meridian transit instrument. しごぎ
**자욱하다** (be) thick; dense; heavy/방안에 연기가 ~ The room is clouded with smoke.
**자외선**(紫外線) 〖물〗 ultra-violet rays. しがいせん
**자용**(自用) ~하다 put[turn] to private use; appropriate (*a thing*) to *oneself*/ ~의 for one's own use; private; for personal use. みずからのひよう
**자우**(慈雨) a seasonable rain; a welcome [good, beneficial] rain/한천(旱天)의 ~ a looked-for rainfall during the dry season. じう
**자욱하다** (be) dense ⇨자옥하다.
**자웅**(雌雄) male and female; the sex 《승패》 victory or defeat; supremacy; mastery/~을 다투다 contend for supremacy/~ 동체(同體) hermaphrodite. しゆう
**자원**(自願) volunteering/~하다 volunteer (*for*)/종군을 ~하다 volunteer for military service. みずからねがうこと
**자원**(資源) 〖경〗 resources/천연 ~ natural resources/지하 ~ underground resources/~이 풍부하다 be full of resources/ ~을 개발하다 develop[exploit] natural resources. しげん
**자위**¹ 〖얼레〗 a large reel; a fig spool.
**자위**² 〖눈·달걀의〗 《흰 ~ 《눈의》 the white of the eye 《달걀의》 the white of an egg/노른 ~ 《달걀의》 the yolk of an egg /검은 ~ 《눈의》 the pupil of the eye.
**자위**(自慰) ①《자기 위안》 self-consolation /~하다 comfort *oneself*; flatter *oneself* ②《수음》 solitary vice; masturbation; self-abuse; onanism. じい
**자위**(自衛) self-defense[-protection, -preservation]/~의 self-protecting; self-preserving[-preservative]/~하다 protect[defend] *oneself*; console *oneself*/~책을 강구하다 take a step to protect[defend] *oneself*. じえい
**자위뜨다** ①《태아가》 cause the onset of labour pains ②《물건이》 move. たいじがうごきはじめる
**자유**(自由) ⇨별항 참조. じゆう
**자유 자재**(自由自在) ~하다 (be) free; unrestricted/~로 quite freely; at *one's* pleasure; at will; with perfect freedom. じゆうじざい
**자율**(自律) self-control; self-regulation; 〖철〗 autonomy/~적 autonomous 《생리의》 autonomic/~ 신경계 autonomic nervous system. じりつ
**자음**(字音) the sound[pronunciation] of a word[character]. じおん
**자음**(子音) 〖언〗 a consonant ⇨닿소리/~의 consonantal. しおん
**자의**(自意) *one's* own will; self-will; wilness; selfishness. みずからのいし
**자의**(字義) the meaning of a word/~대로 해석하다 interpret a word literally. じぎ
**자의**(恣意) wilfulness; self-will; waywardness/~대로 행동하다 act wilfully. ほしいままにすること
**자의식**(自意識) 〖심〗 self-consciousness; self-awareness/~이 강하다 be highly self-conscious. じいしき
**자인**(自認) admittance; self-acknowledgment/~하다 acknowledge; admit/분

## 자 유

freedom; liberty/~ 결혼 free marriage/~ 경제 free economy/~권 civil liberties/~당 the Liberal Party/~민 free people/~ 방임주의 laissez faire/~ 사상 liberal ideas[thought]/~ 세계 the free world/~시(詩) free verse/~주의 liberalism/~ 진영 the Free World; the Western Camp/~형 (수영의) free style/~ 천지 a land of freedom/신앙의 ~ freedom of worship[religion]/언론(출판)의 ~ freedom of speech[the press] /~의 나라 한국 Korea, the nurse of liberty/~를 구속하다 restrain (*a person's*) liberty/~를 옹호하다 defend *one's* liberty/~를 주다 give (*a person*) liberty/~를 부르짖다 cry for liberty/~ 재량에 맡기다 give (*a person*) a free hand; leave to the discretion of (*a person*)/ ~를 존중하다 prize freedom more than life; prize liberty above life/~롭다 be free[liberal, unrestricted]/~로이 freely; at will[liberty]; as one likes[wishes, pleases]/영어를 ~로이 구사하다 have a good command of English/~ 아니면 죽음을 달라 Give me liberty or give me death. /누구나 ~롭게 의견을 말할 수 있다 Each member will be at liberty to state his own views. /이 세상일이란 만사가 네 ~대로 되는 게 아니다 We cannot have our will[way] in everything in this world. /~ 재량에 맡기다 give (*a person*) a free hand.

**짜임** being put[pieced] together; formation; composition; structure; constitution; assembly 《부서의》 system; organization/~새 the make; structure; the way something is put together.

**자임**(自任) pretension/ ~하다 consider oneself (as); look upon oneself (as); pretend/미래의 대통령으로 ~하다 look upon oneself as a president of the future. じにん

**자자**(藉藉) ~하다 《소문 따위가》 be wide-spread; be spread abroad; create public sensation;(be) loud/그 계획에 대하여는 세간의 비난이 ~하다 The people are loud against the plan./명성이 ~하다 be highly reputed[renowned]; enjoy a high reputation.

**자자 손손**(子子孫孫) posterity; descendants; one's children's children 《대대》 generation after generation/~에 전하다 hand (a thing) down to posterity. ししそんそん

**자작**(自作) ①《자제(自製)》 one's own work[production, composition]/~의 of one's own making[writing, composing]/~하다 make[write] by oneself ②《농》 cultivation of one's own farm/~하다 cultivate one's own farm/~농 an independent[owner] farmer; an owner cultivator; a yeoman. じさく

**자작**(子爵) a viscount/~ 부인 a viscountness. ししゃく

**자작**(自酌) pouring wine for oneself; self-service/~하다 pour wine for oneself; serve oneself.

**자작거리다** walk sluggishly; walk wearily/자작자작 wearily; sluggishly. よちよちあるく

**자작나무** 《식》 the white birch; Betula platyphylla(학명). しらかば

**자장**(磁場) the magnetic field. じば

**자장가**(―歌) a lullaby; a cradle song/~를 들으며 자다 fall asleep to a lullaby.

**자장자장** hushaby[e]; rockaby[e]; sleep, sleep/~ 잘 자라 Hushaby baby, go to sleep now. ねんねよ

**자재**(資材) material; resources/인적(人的) ~ human resources/건축 ~ construction materials. しざい

**자재**(自在) 《존재》 self-existence 《자유》 unrestrictedness; freedom/~하다 (be) free; unrestricted/~로 quite freely; at will; as one pleases. じざい

**자적**(自適) self-satisfaction; complacency; self-contentment/ ~하다 be self-satisfied; be complacent/유유 ~한 생활을 하다 lead a life of ease and contentment, live free from wordly cares.

**자전**(自傳) an autobiography/ ~체의 소설 an autobiographical novel. じてん

**자전**(字典) a dictionary; a lexicon/신한 영한 ~ shin Han English Korean Dictionary. じてん

**자전**(自轉) rotation/~하다 rotate[revolve] on its own axis/지구의 ~이 밤과 낮을 생기게 한다 The revolution of the earth causes day and night. じてん

**자전거**(自轉車) a bicycle; a cycle; a bike 《속》; 《삼륜》a tricycle/~ 경기 a bicycle race/~를 타다 ride (on) a bicycle /~ 여행 a bicycle trip/~로 가다 go by bicycle; go on a bicycle. じてんしゃ

**자전기**(磁電氣) magneto-electricity.

**자정**(子正) midnight; 12 p. m. れいじ

**자정향**(紫丁香) 《식》 a lilac.

**자제**(子弟) one's son; youngsters (of one's family)/명문의 ~ sons of an illustrious family. してい

**자제**(自制) self-control[mastery, repression, restraint, command]/~하다 control[restrain] oneself; be master of oneself/현명한 자는 자기의 행위와 쾌락을 ~한다 The wise man exercises restraint in his behavior and enjoyment. /~력 the power of self-control. じせい

**자제**(自製) one's own making[manufacture]/~의 of one's own making; made by oneself; home-made. じせい

**자조**(自嘲) self-scorn. じちょう

**자조**(自助) self-help; self-dependence/~는 최선의 도움이다 Self-help is the best help. じしょ

**자족**(自足) selp-sufficiency/~하다 (be) self-sufficient/~ 경제 self-sufficient economy. じそく

**자존**(自存) self-existence/~의 self-existent/~하다 exist by[of] oneself. じそん

**자존**(自尊) self-respect 《자중》 self-esteem 《자긍》 self-importance/~의 self-respecting; self-important; self-conceited/ ~하다 respect[esteem] oneself. じそん

**자존심**(自尊心) the spirit of self-respect; pride/~이 강한 사람 a man of great self-respect/너는 ~이 강하다 You have much self-respect. じそんしん

**자주** often; frequently; repeatedly/당신들은 ~ 만납니까 Do you see much of each other?/~ 있는 일 a common[an every day] affair/~자주 repeatedly/ ~ 다니다 frequent (a place). しきりに

**자주**(自主) independence 《자립》 autonomy 《자발적》 voluntary/~국 a sovereign; an independent state/~권 autonomy; sovereign rights/~적인 independent; autocephalous; autonomous/~성 independence; sovereignty. じしゅ

**자주빛**(紫朱―) purple[violet] color.

**자주장**(自主張) self-will; having one's own way/~하다 have one's own way; be self-willed.

**자중**(自重) 《자존》 self-respect 《자애》 self-love; taking care of oneself 《신중》 prudence; circumspection; caution/~하다 respect oneself; be prudent; be cautious; be circumspect. じちゅう

자지 the penis; the cock《미·속》.

자지러뜨리다 shrink; double (up) ⇨지러뜨리다/우스워서 몸을 ~ double up with laughter. ひるませる

자지러지다 shrink; cower ⇨지러지다/놀라서 ~ shrink with fright. いんきょう

자진(自進) volunteering/~하다 volunteer/~ 입대하다 volunteer for military service. みずからすすんですること

자질 measuring/~하다 take measurement; measure.

자질(資質) nature; [natural] disposition; temperament; quality. ししつ

자질구레하다 (be) small; trifling/자질구레한 일 a trifling matter; a trifle. どれもこれもほそい

자찬(自讚) self-praise; self-admiration; self-applause/~하다 praise[admire] oneself. じさん

자책(自責) self-reproach[condemnation, accusation, reproof]/~하다 reproach [blame] oneself (for)/~하는 마음 a guilty conscience. じせき

자처(自處) ①《자살》 suicide ②《자임》 pretension; assumption/~하다 fancy oneself to be; pose as; pretend (to)/사회 개혁자로 ~하다 pose as a social reformer. じしょ

자천(自薦) self-recommendation/~하다 recommend oneself. じせん

자철광(磁鐵鑛) 【광】 magnetite. じてっこう

자청(自請) volunteering/~하다 volunteer. みずからねがうこと

자체(字體) the form of a character; a style of penmanship; type; print/정~로 명확하게 쓰다 write clearly in the square style. じたい

자체(自體) 《사람의》 oneself 《사물의》 itself /그 생각 ~가 어리석다 The idea itself is absurd. じたい

자초 지종(自初至終) the whole story[circumstances]; all the details; full particulars/나는 사건의 ~을 얘기하고 그의 의견을 청했다 I gave him the full particulars of the affair, and asked for his advice. はじめからおわりまで

자축거리다 limp ⇨저축거리다. びっこひく

자축거리다 limp slightly ⇨저축거리다. びっこひく

자축발이 a lame person; a cripple. びっこのひと

자취 《형적》 traces; vestiges; marks; signs 《증거》 evidences 《행방》 one's whereabouts/~를 감추다 conceal one's whereabouts/~도 없다 there is nothing left of (the castle). あと

자취(自炊) cooking food for oneself/~하다 cook for oneself; do one's own cooking; board oneself/그는 ~하고 있다 He cooks his own meals. じすい

자취(自取) ~하다 bring upon oneself. みずからまねくこと

자치(自治) self-government; self-administration; autonomy; home-rule/~의 self-governing; autonomous/~하다 govern oneself.

자친(慈親) one's [loving] mother. はは

자침(磁針) a magnetic needle/~ 방위 magnetic bearing. じしん

자칫 at the slightest slip; with the slightest provocation/~ 목숨을 잃을 뻔하다 come near losing one's life/~하면 미치다 get mad on the slightest provocation. ひょっと

자칭(自稱) ①〖언〗 the first person ②《자임》 self-appointed; self-styled; would-be/~하다 style[call, describe] oneself/~ 문학사 a self-styled[-appointed] Master of Arts/~ 시인 a would-be poet. じしょう

자타(自他) oneself and others; 〖철〗 subject and object; 〖언〗 transitive and intransitive verbs/그는 ~가 공인(共認)하는 위대한 학자다 He is generally admitted to be a great scholar. じた

자탄(自嘆) ~하다 feel grief for oneself; lament one's own deed[folly, etc]. みずからたんそくすること

자태(姿態) a figure; personal appearance /아름다운 ~ a beautiful figure. したい

자택(自宅) one's own house[home]; a private residence/~에서 at one's home. じたく

자토(瓷土) kaolin; crockery[china] clay. とうど

자통(自通) ~하다 master by oneself; come to understanding for oneself.

자퇴(自退) ~하다 leave (school) voluntarily. みずからひきさがること

자투리 a piece of cloth left after selling a roll of cloth by the measure. はぎれ

자파(自派) one's own party[faction].

자판(自判) 〖법〗 one's own judgement[decision]/~하다 (상급 법원에서) reverse the original decision. じはん

자판(自辦) ~하다 ①(일을) manage in person; dispose of for oneself; doing things in person ②(비용을) pay one's own expenses; pay oneself.

자포 자기(自暴自棄) desperation; despair; self-abandonment/~하다 become desperate; abandon oneself to despair/~하지 맙시다 Don't abandon yourself to despair. じぼうじき

자폭(自爆) self-destruction; blowing oneself; suicidal explosion/~하다 《배가》 scuttle oneself 《비행기가》 dash one's plane into an enemy position/~시키다 《건물 따위를》 blow up by oneself. じばく

자품(資稟) [natural] disposition; inherent character; nature. ひととなりとほんせい

자필(自筆) one's own handwriting; an autograph; 〖법〗 a holograph/~의 autograph[ic]; of[written in] one's own handwriting; written by oneself/~ 이력서 a curriculum vitae in one's own

handwriting/~로 in one's own handwriting.

**자학**(自虐) self-torment/~하다 torture oneself.

**자해**(字解) a glossary.

**자해**(自害) suicide; self-injury/~하다 kill oneself; commit suicide; injure[hurt] oneself.

**자행**(恣行) waywardness; willfulness; selfindulgence/~하다 do as one pleases; be self-indulgent.

**자형**(字形) type; print; the form of a letter.

**자형**(姉兄) an elder sister's husband; a brother-in-law.

**자혜**(慈惠) charity; benevolence; philanthropy/~ 병원 a charity hospital.

**자화**(磁化) 〖물〗magnetization/~하다 magnetize.

**자화상**(自畫像) a self-portrait/~을 그리다 paint one's own portrait.

**자화 수정**(自花受精) 〖식〗self-fertilization.

**자화 자찬**(自畫自讚) self laudation; self-praise/~하다 praise oneself; blow one's own trumpet.

**자활**(自活) self-support/~하다 support [maintain] oneself/~을 강구하다 look for means of self-support.

**자획**(字畫) [the number of] strokes in a Chinese character.

**짝**¹ one of a pair[couple]; one of a set; a partner; a counterpart/양말 한 ~ an odd sock/~을 맞추다 pair; make a pair of; match/누구에게나 ~은 있다 Every Jack must have his Jill.

**짝**² (갈비의) a side of beef[pork] ribs (곳·꼴) place; shape; look/아무 ~에도 못 쓴다 It is no good anywhere.

**짝**³ (소리) ripping; tearing (여는 모양) wide open/종이를 ~ 찢다 tear a paper.

**작**(作) (작품) a work; a production (농작) a harvest; a crop; a yield/풍~ a good harvest/흉~ a poor harvest/헤밍웨이 ~ a work by Hemingway.

**작**(爵) peerage; a degree of nobility; court rank.

**작가**(作家) a writer; an author; an artist/신진 ~ a rising [young] writer/규수 ~ an authoress; a ladywriter; a woman writer[novelist].

**작가**(作歌) song writing; versification/~하다 write a song; compose a song.

**작고**(作故) death/~하다 die; pass away; be dead/~한 the late/~한 사람들 (총칭) the deceased.

**작곡**(作曲) [musical] composition/~하다 compose the music/~가 a composer.

**짝귀** ears which are not the same size 《사람》 a person who has one ear bigger than the other.

**작금**(昨今) recently; lately; of late/~의 recent; new/~에 시작된 일이 아니다 It is of no recent date. /~ 양일(兩日) both yesterday and today.

**작년**(昨年) last year; the past year/~의 오늘 today last year/~ 봄 last spring.

**작농**(作農) farming; husbandry; cultivation of land/~하다 farm; cultivate.

**작다** 《크기가》 (be) small; little; tiny 《미세하다》 (be) minute; fine 《사소하다》 delicate 《연소하다》 (be) young; little 《사소》 (be) trifling; slight; trivial; insignificant; petty/작은 일 a trifle/작은 벌레 a tiny insect/키가 ~ be small-statured/우리집에는 작은 아이들이 셋 있읍니다 We have three little sons.

**작달막하다** (be) pudgy; dumpy; stumpy /작달막한 체격 short build.

**작달비** a downpour.

**작당**(作黨) forming a gang/~하다 band together; form a gang[group, league].

**작대**(作隊) ~하다 form ranks; stand in formation.

**작대기** a rod; a pole (지움표) a crossing off or out.

**작대기 바늘** a big needle.

**작도**(作圖) drawing figures; 〖수〗 construction/~하다 construct; draw a figure.

**작동**(昨冬) last winter.

**작두**(斫—) a fodder-chop; a straw-cutter /~질 chopping[cutting] fodder.

**작두콩** 〖식〗 a horse bean.

**작란**(作亂) ~하다 ①《난리를 일으킴》raise a war; rise in revolt ②play ⇨장난.

**작량**(酌量) consideration; allowance; extenuation/~하다 consider; take into consideration; extenuate.

**작렬**(炸裂) explosion/~하다 explode.

**짝맞다** match.

**짝맞추다** match; make a pair of 《two things》.

**작명**(作名) dubbing; naming/~하다 name; dub.

**작문**(作文) composition; writing 《문장》 a composition/봄이라는 제목으로 ~을 썼다 I wrote a composition on the spring. /영~ English composition.

**작미**(作米) ~하다 hull rice.

**작반**(作伴) going[travelling] together/~하다 go[travel] together; go in company with; accompany.

**작배**(作配) pairing off; making a match; getting married/~하다 pair off; make a match 《of》; marry.

**작벌**(斫伐) felling/~하다 fell; cut down.

**작법(作法)** composition; method; making a law[rule]/〜하다 make a law[rule]. さほう

**작변(作變)** rising in revolt; raising a rebellion/〜하다 rise in revolt; raise a rebellion. へんらんをおこすこと

**작별(作別)** farewell; parting; leave-taking/〜의 말 a farewell word/드디어 〜할 날이 왔다 At last there came a parting day./이제 〜해야겠읍니다 I must say good-bye. わかれること

**작보(昨報)** the previous[yesterday's] report/〜한 바와 같이 as stated in yesterday's report. さくほう

**작부(酌婦)** a barmaid; a waitress. しゃくふ

**짝사랑** one-sided love; unrequited love/〜하다 love in vain. へんあい

**작살** a harpoon; a fish spear/〜을 쏘다 fire a harpoon. やす

**작성(作成)** framing; drawing up/〜하다 draw up; frame/내가 그 서류를 〜하고 그가 서명하였다 I draw up the papers and he signed. さくせい

**작시(作詩)** versification; verse-making [-writing]/〜하다 versify/〜법 the art of verse-making; versification. さくし

**작심(作心)** resolution; determination/〜하다 make up one's mind/〜삼일 a resolution that lasts only three days. けっしんすること

**작야(昨夜)** last night. さくや

**작약(芍藥)** 〖식〗 a peony. しゃくやく

**작약(炸藥)** an explosive; gunpowder.

**작약(雀躍)** dancing[leaping] for joy/〜하다 jump[dance, leap] for joy; exult (over). じゃくやく

**작업(作業)** work; operations 《군대의》 fatigue duty/〜하다 work; conduct operations/〜장 a work-shop; a works/〜실 a workroom/〜복 work dress; work[ing] clothes 《군대의》 a fatigue-dress 《공장의》 overalls 《수부의》 a jumper/〜화 work shoes. さぎょう

**짝없다** 《비길 데 없다》 (be) matchless; incomparable 《주책 없다》 preposterous; incongruous/짝없는 말 preposterous remarks.

**작열(灼熱)** red heat; incandescence/〜하다 become red hot; be burning/〜하는 태양 a scorching[broiling] sun. しゃくねつ

**작용(作用)** action; effect; agency; operation; working 《기능》 a function; a process/〜하다 act[operate, work] (on); exert action (on); function/자연의 〜 natural operation/동화 〜 the process of assimilation/심리 〜 a mental process/화학 〜 chemical action[process]. さよう

**작월(昨月)** last month.

**작위(作爲)** 〖법〗《인위》 artificiality 《행위를 하는 것》 commission/〜범 a commissive crime/부〜 nonfeasance; omission/〜 동사 a factitive verb. さくい

**작위(爵位)** peerage; title and rank of nobility. しゃくい

**작은마마** 〖의〗 varicella; chicken-pox. みずぼうそう

**작은아버지** an uncle; a younger brother of one's father. おじさん

**작은어머니** an aunt; the wife of one's father's younger brother. おばさん

**작은집** ①《분가》 a branch family 《아들집》 one's son's home 《동생집》 one's younger brother's home ②《첩》 a concubine; a [secret] mistress.

**작인(作人)** a sharecropper; a tenant farmer.

**작일(昨日)** yesterday. さくじつ

**작자(作者)** ①《저작자》 an author; a writer 《각본가》 a dramatist; a playwriter ②《사람》 a person; a fellow ③《작인》 a tenant-farmer ④《살 사람》 a buyer; a purchaser. さくしゃ

**짝자꿍** a baby's hand-clapping/〜하다 clap hands.

**작작** properly; moderately; not too much /술 좀 〜 마셔라 Don't drink too much. ちゃんと

**작작(綽綽)** 〜하다 (be) free and easy; leisurely; unconstrained/여유 〜하다 be free and easy.

**짝짝거리다** smack one's lips; lick one's chops/짝짝거리며 먹다 smack one's lips while eating. べたべたする

**작잠(柞蠶)** a tussah; tusser. さくさん

**작전(作戰)** 〖군〗 [military] operations; tactics; manoeuvres; strategy/공동 〜 allied operations; combined action/〜상 tactically/〜 개시일 D-day/〜 계획 a plan of operation[campaign]/〜 계획을 세우다 map out a plan of campaign/〜 명령 an operation order/〜 비행 an operational flight/공격 〜 offensive[active] operation/방어 〜 defensive operation. さくせん

**작정(作定)** 《결정·결심》 a decision; a determination 《의향》 an intention; a thought; an idea 《목적》 a plan; a purpose /〜하다 decide; intend; purpose/나는 여행을 떠날〜이다 I am planning to make a tour. つもり

**작조(昨朝)** yesterday morning. さくちょう

**작죄(作罪)** 〜하다 commit a sin; commit a crime. はんざいをおこすこと

**작주(昨週)** last week. さくしゅう

**작주(酌酒)** filling (a glass) with wine; serving wine.

**짝짓다** pair; make a pair (of); match; make a match; mate/남녀를 짝지어 주다 mate a woman with a man.

**작차다** be filled [up]. じゅうまんする

**짝채우다** make a set; mate; match/찻잔을 하나 사서 〜 buy a teacup to match the set.

**작첩(作妾)** 〜하다 take[keep] a concubine[mistress]. めかけをかこうこと

**작추**(昨秋) last autumn. さくしゅう
**작춘**(昨春) last spring. さくしゅん
**작폐**(作弊) ~하다 cause an abuse. へいがいをかもすこと
**작품**(作品) a performance; a work; a production/예술 ~ a work of art/문예 ~ a literary work. さくひん
**작풍**(作風) a [literary] style; a style of writing/~을 모방하다 model *one's* style on (*another's*). さくふう
**작하**(昨夏) last summer. さくか
**짝하다** become a partner; partake. ともになる
**작회**(作戲) an interruption; a hindrance; a disturbance/~하다 disturb; hinder; interrupt; interfere.
**작히** how [much]. さぞ
**잔**(盞) a cup; a glass; a wine bowl 《받이 달린》 a goblet/포도주 한 ~ a glass of wine/차 한 ~ a cup of tea. さかずき
**잔가시** fine bones of fish. ちいさいとげ
**잔걸음** walking within a short distance.
**잔고**(殘高) the balance 《부기》 the remainder/~표 a balance sheet/차인 ~ balance/이월 ~ the balance carried over. ざんだか
**잔고기** tiny fish; minnows.
**잔꾀** little selfish wiles; petty guile.
**잔교**(棧橋) a [landing] pier; a landing stage/배를 ~에 대다 bring a boat alongside the pier. さんばし
**잔금** fine[thin] wrinkles; fine[small] lines. ほそかいせん
**잔금**(殘金) the rest [of the payment]; the balance/ ~은 모두 이것뿐이다 This is all the money left. ざんきん
**잔기**(殘期) the remainder of a period [term]. のこったきかん
**잔기침** successive clearing of the throat; coughing successively to clear *one's* throat.
**잔누비**[질] close quilting.
**잔다리밟다** rise to a high position step by step. ちいがだんだんしょうかくする
**잔당**(殘黨) remnants [of a defeated party]. ざんとう
**잔대**(盞臺) a saucer [for a wine cup].
**잔도**(棧道) a plank road. さんどう
**잔돈** small coin[money]; change; coppers/~이 없읍니다 I have no change./~으로 치르다 pay in small change. わずかなおかね
**잔돈푼** ①《잡비》 pocket money; spending money〈미〉; 《집안용》 running expenses ②《소액》 a small-sum of money. わずかなおかね
**잔뜩** ①《충분히》 full; fully 《많이》 plentifully; a great deal (*of*); a lot (*of*)/~ 마시다 drink *one's* fill ②《힘껏》 with all *one's* might 《외곬으로》 with a whole heart; whole-heartedly; intently. きわめて
**잔둥**[이] the back ⇒등. せ
**잔디** 〖식〗[a patch of] grass; turf; sod /~를 심다 turf; put (*a yard*) in turf/~밭 a lawn; a grassplot/~밭에 들어 가지 마시오 Keep off the grass.
**잔루**(殘壘) 《야구》 runners left on base/ ~하다 be left on the bases. ざんるい
**잔류**(殘留) remaining behind; being left behind/~하다 remain behind; stay; be left behind/~ 부대 remaining forces. ざんりゅう
**잔말** small talk; useless talk; small complaints; mutter; nag; a scolding; bitch〈속〉/~하다 complain; grumble; nag; scold; chatter/~ 말고 일이나 해라 Cut the chatter and get down to work. つまらぬことば
**짠맛** a salty taste.
**잔망**(孱妄) ~스럽다, ~하다 (be) puerile and infirm; childish and weak for *one's* age; infirm and rash.
**잔멸**(殘滅) ruin; decline; decay/ ~하다 go to ruin; perish; decline; decay. ざんめつ
**잔명**(殘命) the remainder of *one's* doomed life. のこされたいのち
**잔무**(殘務) remaining affairs[business]; unsettled affairs/~를 정리하다 arrange [wind up] the affairs. ざんむ
**짠물** salt water; brine; seawater/ ~고기 saltwater-fish. えんすい
**잔물결** ripples; rippling waves; wavelets/~이 일다[을 일으키다] ripple; ruffle.
**잔민**(殘民) impoverished people.
**잔밉다** (be) provoking; hateful; detestable. だいきらいだ
**잔병**(一病) an indisposition; minor ailments; slight illness/~꾸러기 a sickly person/그는 어렸을 때부터 늘 ~을 앓는다 He has been sickly from childhood.
**잔병**(殘兵) the remnants of a defeated army; remnant troops. ざんぺい
**잔부**(殘部) the remainder; the remnant; the rest; what is left.
**잔부끄럼** shyness; bashfulness; timidity /~을 타는 사람 a bashful person.
**잔불질** shooting small game/~하다 shoot small game.
**잔상**(殘像) 〖심〗 an after-image. ざんぞう
**잔생이** awfully; terribly; horribly; detestably; abominably 《애걸》 imploringly. しつこく
**잔서**(殘暑) the lingering summer heat. ざんしょ
**잔설**(殘雪) the remaining[unmelted] snow; snow of yester-year. ざんせつ
**잔셈** a small account. こまかいけいさん
**잔소리** 〖힐책〗 a scolding; a rebuke; a lecture; fault-finding/~하다 scold; rebuke; lecture; give[read] a lecture to 《탈잡다》 find fault with/그는 나에게 늘 ~를 한다 He is always finding fault with me. いさかい
**잔속** details; the detailed internal conditions. こまかいないよう

**잔손** elaborate care/~이 드는 일 laborious[troublesome] work/~질 a small touch; a final touch.　てまめなこと

**잔솔** a young pine/~밭 a grove of young pines.

**잔술(盞-)** liquor by the cup; draft liquor/~집 a pothouse.　いっぱいのさけ

**잔심부름** sundry errands[jobs]; odd jobs.　こまごましたつかい

**잔악(殘惡)** inhumanity; atrocity; brutality; cruelty/~하다 (be) inhuman; atrocious; brutal; cruel; fiendish.

**잔액(殘額)** the balance; the remainder/~을 지불하다 pay the balance/차입금 ~ the balance of the loan.　ざんがく

**잔업(殘業)** overtime work/~하다 work overtime; work extra hours/~ 수당 pay for overtime.

**잔여(殘餘)** the remainder; the remnant; the rest; the residue/~의 remaining; residuary/~액 the balance; the remainder/~ 재산 [법] the residue; remaining assets.　ざんよ

**잔용(-用)** (용돈) pocket money; spending money (부녀자의) pin money.

**잔월(殘月)** a waning[morning] moon.　ざんげつ

**잔인(殘忍)** cruelty; brutality; inhumanity; cold-bloodedness/~하다 (be) cruel; brutal; hard-hearted; inhuman; cold-blooded; merciless; atrocious/~성을 발휘하다 show one's brutal nature.　ざんにん

**잔일** small matters; fine details.　こまかいしごと

**잔입** the limited appetite one has on getting out of bed.　すぐち

**잔자누룩하다** (be) peaceful; calm; quiet; tranquil.　へいわだ

**잔작하다** (be) puerile for one's age; underdeveloped.

**잔잔하다** (바람 따위가) (be) gentle; soft; smooth; calm; quiet; tranquil/잔잔한 바다 a smooth[calm] sea/잔잔한 목소리로 in a quiet[gentle] voice.　しずかだ

**잔잔하다(潺潺-)** (흐름이)(be) murmuring/잔잔한 시냇물 a murmuring stream.　さらさらながれる

**잔재(殘滓)** leftovers; remnants; waste matter (액체의) dregs.　ざんさい

**잔재미** amiability; affability/~있는 amiable; affable/~를 보다 have a nice little time of it; get a subtle pleasure from it.　ちいさなたのしみ

**잔적(殘賊)** the remnant of the enemy; surviving enemy/~ 소탕 mopping up of the enemy remnants.　ざんてき

**잔적(殘賊)** remnants of a defeated group of robbers/~을 소탕하다 round up the bandits still at large.　ざんぞく

**잔전(-錢)** small change ⇨잔돈.　のこったおかね

**잔존(殘存)** survival/~하다 be still alive; be extant; survive 《잔류하다》 be left; remain/~ 기관 a vestigial[residual, rudimentary] organ/~ 생물 a relict.　ざんそん

**잔주** drunken grumbling/~하다 grumble while drunk.

**잔주름** fine wrinkles.　こじわ

**잔줄** a fine line.　こまかいせん

**짠지** radish preserved with salt.

**잔질다** (be) weak; faint-hearted.　こころがよわい

**잔짐승** little crawling creatures.

**잔채** finely sliced radish.　くいのこりのおかず

**잔챙이** the smallest one; a small variety; small potatoes

**잔치** a banquet; a feast/~가 한창일 때 그 자리에 뛰어들었다 When the feast was at its height, he rushed into the hall./생일 ~ a birthday party.

**잔칼질** mincing/~하다 mince; chop fine.　こまかにきること

**잔털** fine hairs.

**잔판머리** the last; the end; the denouement; the wind-up; the close/연극의 ~ The denouement of a play.　うぶけ

**잔풀나기** a person boastful of his first little success (이른 봄)early spring.

**잔풀 호사(-豪奢)** luxury beyond one's means.　ひじょうなうぬぼれ

**잔품(殘品)** remnants; unsold stock[goods]; the stock left (팔다 남은) the old plug.　ざんぴん

**짠하다** (be) bitterly regretful; touching; pitiful.　こうかいする

**잔학(殘虐)** cruelty; brutality; atrocity; inhumanity/~하다 (be) cruel; atrocious; brutal; inhuman/~ 행위 a brutal act.　ざんぎゃく

**잔해(殘骸)** remains 《동물의》 a carcass 《파편물》 a wreck/비행기의 ~ the wreck of an aeroplane.

**잔허리** the small of the back.

**잔혹(殘酷)** cruelty; brutality; atrocity; heartlessness/~하다 (be) cruel; brutal; heartless; atrocious; merciless/~한 짓을 하다 do a cruel thing.　ざんこく

**잘** 《충분히》 thoroughly; fully; well 《능숙하게》 skilfully; cleverly; well; ably 《성공적으로》 successfully; satisfactorily 《친절히》 kindly 《바르게》 properly; right 《주의해서》 carefully 《충실히》 faithfully 《열심히》 hard 《정확히》 exactly; closely 《보통》 usually; habitually 《가끔》 often 《많이》 much; a great deal/~ 자다 sleep well/(일이) ~ 되다 go well/~ 해결하다 solve satisfactorily/피아노를 ~ 치다 play the piano well/~ 있었니 How have you been?/~ 알다 know well/~ 듣다 listen to carefully/옷이 ~ 맞다 a dress fits nicely.　よく

**잘가닥, 짤까닥** ①with a click[snap] ②with a slap/사진을 ~ 찍다 snap a picture/자물쇠를 ~ 걸다 click the door shut.　ぺたりと

**잘가당, 짤까당** with a click／~하다 click; give a snap. かちん

**짤깍눈이** a person with sore eyes.

**잘강잘강** chewing; masticating ⇒질겅질겅. ぐじゃぐじゃ

**잘겁하다** be shocked; be startled ⇒질겁하다. びっくりする

**잘그랑, 짤그랑** with a cling; jingling; rattling／~하다 cling; jingle; rattle. がちゃん

**잘끈** firmly; fast; tightly; solidly／~ 동이다 tie fast. きゅっと

**잘금거리다, 짤금거리다** trickle; dribble ⇒질금거리다.

**잘나다** ①(사람됨이) (be) of excellent calibre; uncommon; great／잘난 사람 a great man ②(생김새가) (be) handsome; of pleasing appearance／그 녀석 잘났군 He is quite handsome. ③(반어적으로) (be) worthless; useless; good-for-nothing. すぐれている

**잘다** ①(작다) (be) small; little; of a small size; tiny; minute; fine／잘게 자르다 cut small[fine] ②(인품이) (be) small; of small calibre; fussy; stingy／그는 사람이 ~ He is a fussy man.／잘게 베다 cut (a thing) fine[small]. こまかい

**잘똑거리다** limp ⇒절뚝거리다. ちんばひく

**잘똑하다** be pinched in ⇒질뚝하다. くぼんでいる

**잘되다** go well; come out well (번영하다) prosper; thrive (진척하다) make good progress／모든 일이 잘되어 간다 Everything is going on well.／제일 잘된 사람 the most successful man. よくなる

**잘뚜마기** the slender part; the neck; the small.

**잘라매다** bind[tie] (a thing) tightly／허리끈을 ~ tie one's sash tight. きつくしばる

**잘라먹다** ①(음식을) bite off; cut and eat ②(갚을 것을) bilk; leave (a bill) unpaid; fail to pay; cheat (one) of a loan／빚을 잘라먹을 작정이냐 Do you mean to disown your debt?. ちぎってくう

**잘랑잘랑, 짤랑짤랑** clink; jingle. がらんがらん

**잘래잘래, 짤래짤래** shaking one's head. ふりふり

**잘록잘록, 짤록짤록** pinched[sloped] in／~하다 (be) pinched[sloped] in [my places]. くぼんでいる

**잘록하다, 짤록하다** (be) slender[slim, narrow] at one part[in the middle]. いちぶぶんがくぼんでいる

**잘리다** ①(절단되다) be cut; break／목이 ~ 《해고당하다》be dismissed; be discharged; be fired〈미〉 ②(먹히다) be cheated out of; have a loan uncollected ③(졸라매이다) be tied up tight. きられる

**잘못** ①(과실) a fault; an error (큰) a blunder 《오류》a mistake; an error; a slip (죄) blame／~을 깨닫다 see the error of one's ways／그것은 내 ~이다 It is my fault. ②(부사적으로) by mistake; through an error／~ 알다 mistake／~ 생각하다 misunderstand／정부에서 이런 정책을 쓰는 것은 큰 ~이다 It is a big mistake for the Government to adopt such a policy. まちがい

**잘못하다** 《그릇하다》mistake; make a mistake[an error]; do wrong; commit a fault; do amiss (실수) fail (in)／그는 자기가 잘못했다고 말했다 He acknowledged himself in the wrong. まちがう

**잘박** with a splash／~하다 splash; make a splash／~거리다 splash／잘박거리며 냇물을 건너다 splash across the stream／~잘박 with splash after splash. ばしゃっ

**잘싹** with a slap[spank, bang]／~하다 spank; make a spanking sound; slap; bang／따귀를 ~ 갈기다 slap (a person) in the face／~거리다 keep spanking[slapping]; bang and bang／~잘싹 spanking away. びしゃっ

**짤싸리** house slippers.

**잘잘, 짤짤** (끓다) bubbling; simmering; seething; boiling (치맛자락 따위가) dragging (on the ground); (쏘다니다) darting about; going around hurriedly (혼들다) shaking (윤기가) glossily／치맛자락을 ~ 끌다 drag the ends of one's skirt／물이 ~ 끓는다 The water is simmering. かっか

**잘잘못** good and[or] evil; right and[or] wrong; merits and demerits／~간에 right or wrong. せいご

**잘토시** a sable hand-muff.

**잘팍** with a squish／~하다 (진흙이) give a squish／~거리다 (진흙이) squish and squish; slosh away. びしゃびしゃ

**잘하다** be skilful; be a good hand; be expert (in)／말을 ~ be a good talker／영어를 ~ speak English well. よくやる

**짧다** ①(be) short; brief 《기간이》be of brief duration／짧은 기간 a short [period of] time／짧은 일생 a short span of life／나는 머리를 짧게 깎았다 I had my hair cut short. ②(부족하다) (be) inadequate; (be) short of／밑천이 ~ be short of funds. みじかい

**짧다랗다** (be) shortish; rather short; be on the short side.

**잠** ①(수면) sleep; slumber／깊은[얕은] ~ a deep[light] sleep／~을 자다 sleep; go to sleep／~에서 깨다 awake[start] from one's sleep ②(누에의) the dormant period of the silkworm ③(푼한 것의) pressing[smoothing] down; compression; tamping setting. ねむり

**짬** ①(겨를) leisure; time to spare; free time; spare time／~이 있다 be free; be not busy ②(틈) crack; interstice; a crevice; an opening. あいだ

**잠깐** [for] a little while; [for] a moment [minute]; [for] some time／~ 뵐 수 있

올까요 May I see you for a minute? しばらく

**잠깨다** awake [from one's sleep]; wake up. めざめる

**잠결** while asleep/~에 in *one's* sleep; while asleep/~에 듣다 hear half asleep. めざめぎわ

**잠꼬대** talking in *one's* sleep; sleep-talking (실없는 말) a silly talk; nonsense; bosh/~하다 talk in *one's* sleep; say silly things. ねごと

**잠꾸러기** a heavy sleeper; a lie-a-bed; a sleepy head; a late riser. ねぼうすけ

**잠귀** auditory sensation in sleep/~ 밝다 be quick-waking; be easily awakened; be wakeful/~가 어둡다 be unwakeful; be a sound sleeper. ねみみ

**잠그다**[1] (물에) soak; dip; immerse (*in*); moisten (*with*)/나는 손가락을 물에 잠갔다 I dipped my fingers in water. しずめる

**잠그다**[2] (자물쇠를) lock; lock up; fasten/분명히 문에 자물쇠를 잠갔느냐 Are you sure you locked the door? おろす

**잠기다**[1] ①(물에) be soaked; soak (*in*); be under (*water*); be immersed; be submerged in (*water*); (침수로) be flooded ②(탐닉하다) indulge in/악습에 ~ indulge *one*self in a bad habit ③(열중하다) be absorbed in; be sunk[lost] in; be intent on/그는 명상에 잠겼다 He was sunk[lost] in contemplation. ④(목이) get hoarse. しずむ

**잠기다**[2] (자물쇠가) lock; be locked; be fastened/이 문은 자동적으로 자물쇠가 잠긴다 This door locks automatically. かかる

**잠두**(蠶豆) 〖식〗 a broad[horse] bean. そらまめ

**잠들다** fall[be sound] asleep; sink into sleep; drop off to sleep/푹 ~ fall fast asleep/아기가 울다가 잠들었다 The baby cried itself to sleep. /술을 마시고 ~ drink *one*self to sleep. ねる

**잠란**(蠶卵) a silkworm egg[seed]/~지 (紙) a silkworm egg card. さんらん

**잠망경**(潛望鏡) a periscope. せんぼうきょう

**잠매**(潛賣) an illicit sale; black-marketing; smuggling/~하다 sell secretly; smuggle; black-market[eer]. やみうり

**잠박**(蠶箔) a silkworm feeding basket. さんばく

**잠방이** farmer's knee-breeches/얻은 ~ something got from someone else that is no great marvel. ズボンした

**잠복**(潛伏) ①(숨음) concealment; hiding; ambush/~하다 conceal *one*self; be hidden; hide; lie hidden[concealed]; lurk; go[be] in hiding/그 악학한 살인범은 현재 부산 시내에 ~중이다 The atrocious murderer is now in hiding in the city of *Busan*. ②(병의) incubation/~하다 be dormant; be latent/~기 the incubation; the latent period/그 병은 ~기가 길다 The disease has a long incubation period. せんぷく

**잠사**(蠶絲) silk yarn[thread]/~업 silk-reeling industry. さんし

**잠상**(潛商) a secret[an illicit] dealer; a smuggler (암시장의) a black-marketeer. せんしょう

**잠세력**(潛勢力) potential energy; latent force. せんせいりょく

**잠수**(潛水) diving/~하다 go under water; make a dive; submerge/~복 a diving-suit[-dress]/~병(病) submarine sickness/~부 a diver/~함 a submarine. せんすい

**잠시**(暫時) a short time[while]; a [little] while/~ 동안 for a short time; for a while[moment]/~ 기다려 주시오 Wait a little while, please. ざんじ

**잠식**(蠶食) encroachment; aggression; an inroad; invasion/~하다 encroach (*upon*); make an inroad (*upon*, *into*)/영토를 ~하다 encroach on the territory.

**잠실**(蠶室) a silkworm-rearing[-raising] room.

**잠아**(蠶蛾) 〖충〗 (누에 나방) a silkworm moth.

**잠약**(-藥) a sleeping drug[medicine] (정제) a sleeping pill[tablet].

**잠언**(箴言) an aphorism; a maxim (성서의) the proverbs. くんかいのことば

**잠업**(蠶業) sericulture; sericultural industry/~ 시험장 a sericultural laboratory.

**잠열**(潛熱) 〖물〗 (지하의) latent heat (인체의) dormant temperature. せんねつ

**잠옷** night clothes; pajamas (남자용) a night shirt (부인·어린이용) a night gown[dress]. ねまき

**잠입**(潛入) infiltration/~하다 smuggler *one*self (*into*); sneak[filter, steal] (*into*); (비행기 따위가) get through. せんにゅう

**잠자다** sleep; go to sleep; have a sleep (잠깐) take a nap/잠자는 아이 a sleeping child. ねる

**잠자리**[1] 〖충〗 a dragon-fly/고추 ~ a red dragon-fly. とんぼ

**잠자리**[2] ①(잘데) a place for sleeping; a bed (침대) a bedstead (배·기차의) a berth/~에 들다 go to[into] bed ②(성교) sexual intercourse/~하다 have sexual intercourse. しんだい

**잠자코** (말없이) without a word (허가없이) without leave/~ 있다 keep *one's* mouth shut; hold *one's* tongue[peace]/~ 있어라 I wish you would hold your tongue. だまって

**잠잠하다** (be) quiet; still; deserted/잔 잠하게 quietly/거리는 ~ All is quiet in the street. しずかにだまる

**잠재**(潛在) latency; dormancy/~하다 be [lie] latent; be dormant; lie hidden/~적 latent; dormant/~ 능력 latent faculties/~ 의식 subconsciousness/~ 수요 potential demand/~ 실업자 the po-

**잠정**(暫定) ~의 provisional; tentative/ ~안 a tentative plan/~ 조치를 취하다 take tentative measures[steps]. ざんてい

**잠종**(蠶種) a silkworm specie/~ 개량 silkworm species improvement. さんしゅ

**잠주정** sleep peevishness ⇨잠투세.

**잠투세** sleep peevishness; the habit of being fretful before or after sleeping/ ~하다 fret before falling asleep 《깨어나서》wake up crying. ねとぼけ

**잠항**(潛航) submarine voyage; navigation under water/~하다 move[navigate] under water/~정 a submarine [boat]. せんこう

**잠행**(潛行) travelling in disguise/~하다 travel in disguise. せんこう

**잡가**(雜歌) a vulgar song; a popular song; a folk-song; a ballad. ざっか

**잡거**(雜居) mixed residence[living]/~하다 live[reside, dwell] together/~지(地) a mixed-residence quarter. ざっきょ

**잡건**(雜件) miscellaneous matters; the miscellanies; sundries. ざっけん

**잡것**(雜一) 《물건》miscellaneous things; a sundries 《사람》a man of coarse fibre; a rogue. いろいろのもの

**잡곡**(雜穀) [miscellaneous] cereals; minor grains/~상 a corn chandler; a dealer in cereals/~밥 boiled-rice mixed with other cereals. ざっこく

**잡귀**(雜鬼) fiends; demons; evil spirits.

**잡기**(雜技) gambling; gaming; games of chance/~판 a gambling place; a gaming house.

**잡기**(雜記) miscellaneous notes/~장 a notebook; an exercise book. ざっき

**잡년**(雜一) a loose woman; a slattern; a slut/이 ~아 You slut! みだらなおんな

**잡념**(雜念) earthly[worldly] thoughts/ ~을 버리다 banish worldly thoughts from one's mind. ざつねん

**잡놈**(雜一) a sloven; an indecent fellow; a menial. ぞんざいなにんげん

**잡다**¹ ①《손으로》catch; get; take 《쥐다》seize; hold; take hold of; grasp; grip; clutch/공을 ~ catch a ball/팔을 ~ seize[hold] (a person) by the arm ②《체포하다》catch; arrest; seize; capture 《포획하다》catch; get; take; seize/도둑을 ~ catch a thief ③《권력·기회 따위를》take; seize; assume; wield/기회를 ~ seize upon an opportunity ④《담보로》hold (a thing) in pawn; take (a thing) on security/저당을 잡고 돈을 꾸어 주다 lend money on security ⑤《결정하다》fix; decide; settle 《선정하다》choose 《예약하다》reserve; book/골라 ~ choose[pick up, select] (a thing)/날짜를 ~ fix the date (for) ⑥《결점을》find (fault); pick [point] out (a person's defects)/사람의 흠을 ~ find fault with a person ⑦《논 따위에 물을》conduct[irrigate] water ⑧《자리를》occupy[take up] much room [space]. にぎる

**잡다**² ①《죽이다》butcher; kill (animals); slaughter/돼지를 ~ butcher a hog ②《모함하다》plot against (a person); slander/사람 잡는 소리는 그만둬라 Stop slandering me. ③《불을》put out[extinguish] [a fire]/물로 불을 ~ quench a fire with water ④《마음을》get a grip on oneself; steady (one's mind); settle down/들뜬 마음을 ~ hold the rein over one's mind. ころす

**잡다**³ 《요량하다》estimate; value; calculate/적게 잡아서 at the least; at the lowest estimate. すいていする

**잡다**⁴ ①《굽은 것을》make straight; straighten out[up]; untend/굽은 바늘을 [바로] ~ make a bent needle straight ②《주름을》crease; pleat; fold; gather in /바지에 주름을 ~ crease trousers. なおす

**잡다**(雜多) ~하다 (be) miscellaneous; sundry. ざった

**잡담**(雜談) gossip; small talk; chit-chat; tittle-tattle; empty talk/~하다 gossip; chat; tattle; have an idle talk/그녀는 그와 얼마 동안 ~을 했다 She had a chat with him for some time. ざつだん

**잡도리** supervision; management; control/~하다 superintend; oversee.

**잡동사니** mixture; odds and ends. ごちゃまぜ

**잡되다**(雜一) ①《추잡하다》(be) base; sordid; indecent; broad/잡된 소리 broad talk ②《불순하다》(be) impure; foul. ふじゅんだ

**잡록**(雜錄) a miscellany; miscellaneous records. ざつろく

**잡말**(雜一) dirty talk ⇨잡소리. みだらなことば

**잡맛**(雜一) a taste other than the original one; a mixed taste. まじったあじ

**잡목**(雜木) miscellaneous[inferior] wood / ~ 숲 a copse; a coppice. ざつぼく

**잡무**(雜務) miscellaneous business[duties, affairs]; routine work/~를 처리하다 dispose of routine business/~로 바쁘다 be busy[pressed] with this and that. ざつむ

**잡물**(雜物) 《불순물》impurities; foreign matters 《여러가지 물건》miscellaneous things; sundries; miscellany. ざつぶつ

**잡박**(雜駁) confusion; medley; disunity; looseness; incoherence/~하다 be in confusion; lack unity; (be) loose; slipshod/~한 생각 loose ideas. ざっぱく

**잡배**(雜輩) a villain; a rougue; a rascal.

**잡병**(雜病) various diseases of infectious nature.

**잡보**(雜報) general news/~란 the general news columns. ざっぽう

**잡비**(雜費) sundries; sundry expenses/

**잡샐뱅이** ~ 제정 petty expense account／~가 꽤 많이 든다 Sundries come up to a considerable amount. ざっぴ

**잡살뱅이** odds and ends; rubbish. かくしゅのこまもの

**잡살전(一廛)** a seeds store.

**잡상스럽다(雜常—)** ①《음탕하다》(be) lewd; lecherous; lustful; licentious; wanton; incontinent ②《상스럽다》(be) vulgar; low; mean; base／행동이 ~ be coarse in manners. いんとうだ

**잡색(雜色)** 《빛깔》various colors; variegation 《사람》all kinds of people; a motley crew／~의 parti-colored; variegated; motley. こんごうしき

**잡서(雜書)** miscellaneous books 《여러 가지를 적은》 a book on miscellaneous subjects. ざっしょ

**잡석(雜石)** stones of all sizes.

**잡설(雜說)** idle talk ⇒잡소리. ざっせつ

**잡성화(雜性花)** 【식】polygamous flowers.

**잡세(雜稅)** miscellaneous taxes. ざつぜい

**잡소리(雜—)** 《외설한》obscene《dirty》talk; foul《broad》talk; smut 《잠담》useless 《idle》talk; prattle; nonsense.

**잡손질(雜—)** unnecessary work《handling》／~하다 play with one's fingers.

**잡수시다** eat; take; have／과일 좀 잡수시죠 Help yourself to the fruit, please. めしあがる

**잡수입(雜收入)** miscellaneous receipts《income》; sundry receipts. ざっしゅうにゅう

**잡술(雜術)** wicked magics; witchcraft.

**잡스럽다(雜—)** (be) vulgar; low; mean; indecent. やひだ

**잡신(雜神)** evil spirits ⇒잡귀.

**잡심(雜心)** worldly thoughts ⇒잡념.

**잡아당기다** 《끌다》pull; draw; tug 《팽팽하게》stretch 《뒤로》pull back／나는 밧줄을 세게 잡아당겼다 I gave a strong pull at the rope. ひきよせる

**잡아떼다** ①《손으로》pull out of place; pull down; take off; pluck《tear》off; pick ②《모르는 척하다》feign《pretend》ignorance; play the innocent; refuse flatly. ひきはなす

**잡아먹다** ①《먹다》slaughter (a bull); butcher (a hog); 《짐승이》devour; eat ravenously ②《괴롭히다》torment; torture／날 잡아먹어라 Kill me, if you dare!

**잡역(雜役)** odd jobs 《군사》fatigue duty／~부(夫) an odd-job man; a handy man／그는 군대에서 ~을 하고 있다 He does fatigue duty in the army. ざつえき

**잡용(雜用)** ①sundry expenses; sundry uses ②⇒잡비(雜費). ざつよう

**잡을손뜨다** (be) sluggish; lazy; be slow-handed《slow-footed》. うでがたたない

**잡음(雜音)** noises; static 《반대》dissenting voices; objections; complaints／도회의 ~ city《town》noises／라디오에서 ~이 난다 The radio is affected by noises The radio program is hampered《disturbed》by noises. ざつおん

**잡인(雜人)** an outsider. かんけいのないひと

**짭짤하다** (be) nice and salty; have a good salty taste to it／짭짤한 고기 반찬 a nicely salted meat dish.

**짭짭** licking one's chops; smacking one's lips. ちぇちぇ

**잡종(雜種)** a cross; a hybrid; a mixed breed／~의 cross《half》-bred; hybrid／~의 말 a crossbred horse／~개 a mongrel [dog]. ざっしゅ

**잡죄다** ①《잡도리하다》supervise; superintend; oversee; take care of ②《독촉하다》hurry; rush; hasten.

**잡증(雜症)** secondary diseases; subsidiary ill effects.

**잡지(雜誌)** 《총칭》a magazine 《전문적》a journal 《정기 간행물》a periodical／월간 ~ a monthly magazine／문예〔종합〕~ a literary〔general〕magazine. ざっし

**잡채(雜菜)** chop suey; an olio.

**잡초(雜草)** weeds; coarse grass／~가 우거졌다 Weeds have overrun the garden.／~ 제거기 a weeder. ざっそう

**잡치다** spoil; ruin; make a mess of／이 실수로 그의 계획이 잡쳐 버렸다 This mistake he had made spiked his gun.／일생을 ~ blast one's career; be ruined for life. しっぱいする

**잡칙(雜則)** miscellaneous rules《regulations》.

**잡탕(雜湯)** ①《국》mixed soup; a hotch-potch ②《난잡》a mixture; a medley; a pell-mell／~이 되나 be mixed up／~을 만들다 jumble together; mix up. ごたまぜ

**잡풀(雜—)** weeds ⇒잡초. ざっそう

**잡품(雜品)** miscellaneous articles; sundries.

**잡혼(雜婚)** a mixed marriage; an intermarriage／~하다 intermarry／혹인종·백인종간의 ~ white and black intermarriage. ざっこん

**잡화(雜貨)** miscellaneous goods; general merchandise 《식료 잡화》grocery／~상 a dealer in miscellaneous goods／~점 a general shop《store》. ざっか

**잡히다¹** ①《손에》be caught《arrested, seized, taken up》; fall into the hands of／경관에게 ~ be caught by the police ③《담보로》put《give》(a thing) in《at》pawn ③《결점·흠을》have (a weakness) discovered ④《물이》water is held ⑤《모양이》take a form. とらえられる

**잡히다²** 《도조(賭租)를》get estimated at; be rated.

**잡히다³** ①《굽은 것이》get《be》straightened out《up》; be made straight ②《주름이》get《be》creased／주름이 잘 잡힌 바지 well creased trousers.

**잡힐손** ability; capability. さいのう

**잣** pine-nuts／~기름 pine-nuts oil／~나무 the big cone pine; *Pinus pentaphylla* 《학명》. まつのみ

**잣눈** scale; graduation

**잣다** ①《물을》pump up《out》; suck up;

draw up ②(물레를) spin; revolve 《실을》 make yarn.
**잣새** 〖조〗 a crossbill; *Loxia curvirostra* (학명).
**잣송이** a pine cone.
**잣엿** pine-nut taffy.
**잣죽**(—粥) a gruel made of rice and pinenuts.
**잣징** a tiny[small] hobnail.
**장**(長) ①《우두머리》 the head; the chief; the chieftain; the boss《미》; the director; the chairman 《사령관》 the commander /한 집안의 ~ the head of a family ②《장점》 a merit; a strong[good] point; an advantage. ちょう
**장**(帳) a curtain; a tent. とばり
**장**(將) a general; a commander 《지도자》 a leader /일군의 ~ a commander of an army /~이 되다 take command (of an army); take the leadership. しょう
**장**(張) a leaf (of *a book*); a sheet (of *paper*); a piece (of *paper*); a page /책을 한~ 넘기다 turn over the leaves of a book. まい
**장**(章) 《책의》 a chapter 《기장》 a sign; a mark; a badge; an emblem 《인장》 a seal /이 책에서 문학 비평의 ~은 특히 재미있다 The chapter of literary criticism in this book is particularly interesting. しょう
**장**(場)¹ a market 《정기적인》 a fair /~보러 가다 go to market /~에 물건을 내다 take commodities to market. しじょう
**장**(場)² 《장소》 a place; a ground; a track; a field 《공간》 room; space 《연극의》 a scene 《물리에서》 a field /제 3~ the third scene; scene Ⅲ. ばしょ
**장**(腸) the intestines; guts; the bowels /~의 병 an intestinal trouble[disorder] /~이 나쁘다 have a bowel trouble; have weak intestines. ちょう
**장**(醬) 《간장》 soy; soysauce; soybean sauce 《간장과 된장》 soy and bean paste. しょうゆ
**장**(欌) a wardrobe; a chest of drawers; a cabinet; a closet; a cage /새 ~ a bird cage /옷 ~ a wardrobe; a chest of drawers.
**장**(臟) the five vital organs of the body [heart, liver, lungs, kidney, spleen]; the vitals; the viscera; the internal organs.
**-장**(丈) 《척도》 a measure of length [10 *ja*]; 《존칭》 an esteemed elder /노인 ~ an elderly person /춘부 ~ your venerable father. —じょう
**장가** 《결혼》 a marriage; a wedding; taking wife; getting a bride 《집》 the bride's house /~들이다 marry (*a son*) to a woman.
**장가**(長歌) a long poem[song]. ちょうか
**장가처**(一妻) *one's* legal wife; *one's* first wife. ほうりつしょうのつま
**장간**(醬間) the saltiness of soysauce.

**장갑**(掌匣) [a pair of] gloves 《벙어리 장갑》 [a pair of] mittens 《권투용》 a muffle 《승마·크리켓용》 a gauntlet /~을 끼다 put on *one's* gloves /~을 벗다 put off *one's* gloves. てぶくろ
**장갑**(裝甲) armor; an armor plate /~하다 armor; arm /~한 armored; iron-clad /~ 부대 an armored corps /~ 포대 an armed[armored] battery. そうこう
**장강**(長江) a long river.
**장거**(壯擧) a great[fine] undertaking; a daring enterprise; a heroic attempt; a brilliant scheme. そうきょ
**장거리**(場—) a market place.
**장거리**(長距離) a long distance; a long range /~ 경주 a long-distance race; a cross country race /~ 전화 a long-distance call[telephone]. ちょうきょり
**장건건이**(醬—) a sauce [such as soysauce, bean paste, and hot-pepper paste].
**장검**(長劍) a long sword /~을 차다 wear a long sword (at *one's* side). ちょうけん
**장결석**(腸結石) 〖의〗 enterolite.
**장결핵**(腸結核) 〖의〗 intestinal tuberculosis.
**장골**(壯骨) a muscular man; stout-built physique. つよくおおきいこっかく
**장공**(長空) the vast sky. たかくとおいそら
**장과**(漿果) 〖식〗 a berry. しょうか
**장관**(壯觀) a grand sight; magnificent [marvelous] spectacle; a spectacular sight; grandeur; splendor; imposing spectacle /천하의 ~이다 be one of the grandest sights imaginable. そうかん
**장관**(長官) a minister; a Cabinet minister; a Cabinet member; a Secretary 〈미〉; 《우두머리》 a chief; a head; a governor /문교부 ~ the Minister of Education. ちょうかん
**장관**(將官) 《육군》 a general [officer]; 《해군》 a flag officer; an admiral. しょうかん
**장광**(長廣) length and width /~설 a long-winded talk; a mighty tongue.
**장교**(將校) an officer; a commissioned officer /~와 사병 officers and men /육군 ~ a military officer /고급 ~ a high-ranking officer. しょうこう
**장구** a double-headed drum pinched in at the middle; a drum shaped like an hourglass /~ 대가리 a long protruding head or a person with such a head. つづみ
**장구**(長久) a long period of time; a long time; eternity /~하다 (be) long[-ranged]; lasting; be of long standing /무운 ~를 빌다 wish (*a person*) good luck in war. ちょうきゅう
**장구**(葬具) articles used at funerals; a funeral outfit. そうぐ
**장구**(長驅) riding far on horseback; pursuing the enemy a great distance; a long march; a long drive /~하다 ride a great distance. ちょうく

**장구(長軀)** tall stature; towering height. ちょうく

**장구벌레**〖충〗 a mosquito larva(*pl* -vae). ぼうふら

**장구채** ①a *chang-gu* drumstick ②〖식〗*Melandrium firmum*(학명). つづみのばち

**장국(醬—)** soup flavored with soysauce /~밥 beef soup with rice in it. すまししる

**장군(場—)** marketeers; marketers; market crowds.

**장군(將軍)** a general 《장기의》"check" in chess. しょうぐん

**장군풀**〖식〗a kind of medicinal rhubarb plant; *Rheum coreanum*(학명).

**장권(獎勸)** encouragement; promotion; stimulation/~하다 encourage; promote; stimulate. しょうれいしてすすめること

**장궤양(腸潰瘍)**〖의〗intestinal ulcer.

**장귀(章句)** the chapter and verse; a passage. しょうく

**장금(場—)** the market price/~이 오르다[내리다] The market rises[drops].

**장끼**〖조〗A cock-pheasant.

**장기(長技)** special skill; *one's* strong point; *one's* favorite performance; *one's* forte/그의 ~는 무엇이냐 What is his speciality? とくぎ

**장기(臟器)** the internal organs; the viscera; the bowels ぞうき

**장기(將棋)** [the game of] chess/~를 두다 play chess; have a game of chess/~짝 a chessman/~판 a chessboard. しょうぎ

**장기(帳記, 掌記)** bookkeeping; an account. きちょうすること

**장기(長期)** a long time[period, term, date]/~의 prolonged; protracted/~계획 a long-range plan/~체류 a long [prolonged] stay/~에 걸치다 be prolonged; extend over time. ちょうき

**장김치(醬—)** vegetables[*kimchi*] pickled in soysauce.

**장나무** a long stick; a pole.

**장난** 《놀이》a game; play 《회롱·》mischief; prank; a joke 《실없는 일》trifle; fun; hobby/어린애 같은 ~ childish mischief/불~ 말아라 Don't play with fire! いたずら

**장난감** a toy; a plaything 《놀림감》a sport/~ 가게 a toy shop/~ 말 a toy horse/~이 되다 be made a plaything (*by*). おもちゃ

**장날(場—)** a market day.

**장남(長男)** the eldest son. ちょうなん

**장내(場內)** the inside of the hall[ground, premises]/~는 입추의 여지도 없다 There is no standing-room in the hall. じょうない

**장녀(長女)** the eldest daughter. ちょうじょ

**장년(壯年)** the prime of manhood[life]/~에 달하다 reach manhood; attain the prime of manhood/~기(期) (*in one's*) manhood; (*in*) the prime of the life. そうねん

**장뇌(樟腦)**〖화〗camphor/~를 넣다 camphorate/~유 camphor oil. しょうのう

**장님** a blind man; the blind/~이 되다 become[go] blind; lose *one's* sight/타고난 ~이다 be born blind. もうじん

**장다리** a flowering stalk [of radishes, cabbages]/~무우 a seed radish.

**장단(長短)** ①《길이》the long and the short; length ②《장단점》merits and demerits; advantages and disadvantages/사물에는 ~이 있다 Things have good and bad points of their own. ③《박자》rhythm; beat; time. ちょうたん

**장딴지**〖해〗the calf [of the leg]. ふくらはぎ

**장담(壯談)** assurance; a positive statement; assertion; guarantee; vouching/~하다 assure; vouch (*for*)/어떻다고 ~ 못하겠다 I cannot commit myself either way. いさましいことば

**장대(長—)** a bamboo pole/~로 하늘 재기《속담》attempting the impossible.

**장대(壯大)** ~하다 (be) big and strong; stout; sturdy; grand; magnificent/~한 건물 an imposing building/~한 사나이 a mighty man. そうだい

**장대(長大)** ~하다 (be) huge; immense. ちょうだい

**장도(壯途)** an important mission; an ambitious undertaking[course]/북극 탐험의 ~에 오르다 embark on the enterprise of an Arctic expedition. そうと

**장도(壯圖)** a grand scheme[attempt]; a great undertaking; a brilliant project; a daring enterprise. そうと

**장도(粧刀)** an encased ornamental knife.

**장도리** a hammer/~의 자루 the handle of a hammer/~로 치다 hammer/~로 못을 박다 drive in a nail with a hammer.

**장독** a crock[jar] of soysauce; a [soy] jar. しょうゆがめ

**장독대(醬—臺)** a jar stand; a terrace where soysauce crocks are placed.

**장돌림(場—)** a traveling marketeer; a roving market dealer.

**장두(檣頭)** a masthead/~등 a top-light /국기를 ~에 올리다 hoist the national flag at the masthead. しょうとう

**장두** ~하다 compare (*two routes*) to see which is shorter.

**장등(長燈)** ~하다 keep a light on all through the night; burn light till late at night.

**장래(將來)** the future; the time to come; the prospect 《부사적》in future; hereafter; some day[time]/그는 ~를 촉망받고 있다 Future greatness is expected of him. /~성 a prospect. しょうらい

**장려(壯麗)** splendor; grandeur; magnificence/~하다 (be) splendid; magnificent; grand; imposing. そうれい

장려(獎勵) encouragement; promotion; stimulation/~하다 encourage; promote; stimulate/저축을 ~하다 encourage saving/~금 a subsidy; a bounty.　しょうれい

장력(張力) 〖물〗 tension/표면 ~ surface tension.　ちょうりょく

장렬(壯烈) ~하다 (be) glorious; heroic; brave; gallant/~한 죽음을 하다 die gloriously; die a heroic death.　そうれつ

장렬(葬列) a funeral procession/~에 참가하다 join a funeral train.　そうれつ

장례(葬禮) a funeral [ceremony]; a funeral service; funeral rites/~를 거행하다 hold a funeral; perform a funeral service/~비 funeral expenses.　そうれい

장로(長老) an elder; a senior; a superior 《교회의》 an elder; a presbyter/~ 교회 the Presbyterian Church.　ちょうろう

장롱(欌籠) a wardrobe; a bureau〈미〉; a dresser.

장루(檣樓) a crow's nest.

장리(掌理) management; control; direction; supervision/~하다 manage; control; direct; administer.　しょうり

장리(長利) an annual interest of fifty percent.

장림(長霖) a long rainy season; a long spell[stretch] of rainy weather.

장마 the rainy spell in [early] summer; a spell of rainy weather/~가 지다 the rainy season sets in/~가 걷히다 the rainy season is over/~철 the rainy [wet] season.　つゆ

장막(帳幕) a tent; a curtain; a fall; a hanging/철[죽]의 ~ the iron[bamboo] curtain/신비의 ~에 싸이다 be wrapped [shrouded] in mystery.　てんまく

장만 preparation; raising/~하다 prepare; raise; get/집을 ~하다 get a house /음식을 ~하다 prepare food.
つくっておくこと

장맞이 ~하다 lie in ambush (for); ambush; waylay.

장면(場面) a scene 《연극》 a situation 《장소》 a place 《광경》 spectacle/연애 ~ a love scene/~이 바뀌다 the scene shifts; the scene changes.　ばめん

장명등(長明燈) a hanging lantern at the end of the eaves[on the gate].

장모(丈母) the wife's mother; a man's mother-in-law.　つまのはは

장목(長木) lumber; timber.　ざいもく

장목(樟木) 〖식〗 a camphor tree.

장문(長文) a lengthy piece of writing; a long article 《편지》 a long letter / ~의 전보 a long telegram.　ちょうぶん

장문(掌紋) the lines of the palm.
てのひらのもん

장물(臟物) stolen goods[articles, property]/~을 은닉하다 secrete stolen goods.
ぞうぶつ

장미(薔薇) 《꽃》 a rose 《나무》 a rose-tree /~빛의 rosy; rose-colored/가시 없는 ~ 는 없다 Every rose has its thorns./들 ~ a wild rose; a brier.　ばら

장미(壯美) sublime beauty; grandeur; sublimity; magnificence/~하다 (be) sublime; grand; magnificent.　そうび

장미계(長尾鷄) 〖조〗 a long-tailed rooster.
をながどり

장발(長髮) long hair; a long-haired person/~의 a long-haired/~족(族) a "hippie" style long-haired youth.

장방형(長方形) a rectangle; an oblong/ ~의 oblong; rectangular.　ちょうほうけい

장벽(障壁) 《벽》 a fence; a wall; a barrier/~을 쌓다 raise a barrier/~을 없애다 let down the bars/언어 ~ a language barrier.　しょうへき

장변(場邊) market interest; the rate of interest prevailing at a market place /~ 놀이하다 practice usury.

장병(長病) a long-suffered disease.
ながわずらい

장병(將兵) officers and men; soldiers; military men.　しょうへい

장보다(場一) 《사다》 buy in the market 《팔다》 sell in the market; market/장보러 가다 go to market.

장복(長服) constant use of a medicine/ ~하다 use constantly; take habitually.

장본(張本) the origin; the root; the cause.　ちょうほん

장본인(張本人) the ringleader; the prime mover; an originator; a chief; the author of a mischief/그가 음모의 ~이었다 He was the very author of the plot.　ちょうほんにん

장부 〖건〗 a tenon; a pivot; a dovetail.
ほぞ

장부(丈夫) a full-grown man; a mighty man; a manly man.　じょうぶ

장부(帳簿) an account book 《등기부》 a register/~에 기입하다 book; enter account/~계 a bookkeeper; an accountant/~ 정리 adjustment of accounts.
ちょうぼ

장부(臟腑) entrails; intestines; guts; the viscera.　はらわた

장비(葬費) funeral expenses.
そうしきのひよう

장비(裝備) equipment; outfit; fitting/ ~하다 equip (a ship) with; fit out (a ship)/우수한 ~를 갖춘 부대 well-equipped troops.　そうび

장사 trade; business; commerce; commercial pursuits/~하다 engage in business; conduct a trade/수지맞는 ~ a paying business/~를 그만두다 give up one's business.

장사(葬事) a funeral [service]; a burial /~지내다 hold a funeral; bury.

장사(壯士) a strong man; a muscular man.　そうし

장사(長蛇) a serpent; a long snake.

장사(아)치 a peddler; a trader.

**장사진**(長蛇陣) a long line[file, row]; a long queue/~을 치다 form a long line [queue]. ちょうだのじん

**장사판** trade; commercial[business] pursuits.

**장살**(長—) 〖건〗 the perpendicular strips of a lattice.

**장삼**(長衫) a Buddhist monk's robe. しい

**장삼 이사**(張三李四) some misters; the common crowd; everybody.

**장상**(長上) 《연장》 one's senior; one's elders 《지위의》 one's superior; one's betters; a handicraftman. ちょうじょう

**장색**(匠色) an artisan; a craftsman. しょうじん

**장생**(長生) long life; longevity/~하다 live long; enjoy longevity/불로 ~의 비결 the secret of perpetual youth. ながいき

**장서**(藏書) a collection of books; one's library/~가 a book-collector. ぞうしょ

**장서**(長逝) ~하다 die; pass away. ちょうせい

**장석**(長石) 〖광〗 feldspar; felspar. ちょうせき

**장석**(長席) a long straw mat.

**장선**(腸線) a gut; a catgut. ちょうせん

**장설**(壯雪) a heavy [fall of] snow. たいせつ

**장성**(將星) generals. しょうせい

**장성**(長城) a long wall. ちょうじょう

**장성**(長成) growth; maturity/~하다 grow up; grow to maturity/~해서 어른이 되다 grow into an adult. せいちょう

**장세**(場稅) a market tax. しじょうのぜいきん

**장소**(場所) 《자리》 space; room 《좌석》 a seat 《지점》 a place; a spot; a point; a section 《위치》 the position; the situation 《현장》 a scene/회합 ~ a place of meeting/사건의 ~ the scene of the accident /~가 좋아서 장사가 잘 된다 The locality brings a great deal of business. ばしょ

**장속**(裝束) dress; outfit; an attire/~하다 dress [up]; be dressed; be attired. しょうぞく

**장손**(長孫) the eldest grandson by the eldest son. うえのまご

**장송**(長松) 《나무》 a tall pine tree 《목재》 a long pine board. おおきいまつ

**장송**(葬送) escorting a funeral; attending a funeral/~하다 escort a funeral /~곡 a funeral march. そうそう

**장수** a trademan; a merchant; a dealer; a seller 《행상인》 a peddler/생선 ~ a fishmonger/술~ a wine dealer/책~ a bookseller. しょうばいにん

**장수**(長壽) long life; longevity; macrobiosis/~하다 live long; enjoy longevity/~의 비결 the secret of longevity /~약 the elixir of life. ちょうじゅ

**장수**(將帥) a general; a commander-in-chief.

**장수벌**(將帥—) 〖충〗 a queen bee. じょおうばち

**장승**(長丞) a milestone; a totem pole.

**장시간**(長時間) many long hours; long time/~에 걸쳐 for [many] hours/~회담하다 have a long talk [with]. ちょうじかん

**장시세**(場市勢) the market price[rate]; the market; quotations. しか

**장식**(裝飾) decoration; adornment; ornament[ation]; 《가게의》 dressing/~하다 decorate; adorn; ornament; dress; trim/방을 꽃으로 ~하다 decorate a room with flowers. そうしょく

**장식**(葬式) a funeral service[ceremony, rite] ⇒장례식. そうしき

**장신**(長身) a tall stature[figure].

**장신구**(裝身具) personal ornaments; accessories; trinketry. そうしんぐ

**장아찌** sliced vegetables preserved in soybean sauce.

**장악**(掌握) hold; grasp; command; seizure/~하다 hold; command; seize/정권을 ~하다 come into power; assume the reins of the government/실권을 ~하다 hold real power. しょうあく

**장안**(長安) Seoul, the capital city. ソウル

**장애**(障碍) an obstacle; a hindrance; a difficulty; an impediment; a hitch 《운동 기구》 hurdles 《병》 troubles/~를 극복하다 surmount an obstacle/~를 an obstacle; an obstruction 《경기의》 a hurdle 《경마의》 a [jumping] bar 《골프의》 a bunker. しょうがい

**장액**(漿液) serum; intestinal juice. しょうえき

**장야**(長夜) a long night; the long nights of winter. ちょうや

**장약**(裝藥) charging gunpowder; charge /~하다 charge [a gun] with powder.

**장어**(章魚) 〖어〗 《낙지》 a small octopus. うなぎ

**장엄**(莊嚴) grandeur; solemnity; sublimity; stateliness/~하다 (be) magnificent; solemn; grand; impressive/~한 장면 an impressive scene[sight]. そうごん

**장염**(腸炎) 〖의〗 enteritis.

**장원**(壯元) a person who won the first place in the higher civil service examination.

**장원**(長遠) a long period of time; a long time; permanence/~하다 (be) lasting; permanent/~한 계획 a plan for a long future; a long-range plan.

**장원**(莊園) a manor. そうえん

**장유**(長幼) old and young/~ 유서다 The younger should give precedence to the elder., Elders first. ちょうよう

**장유**(醬油) soysauce and sesame oil. しょうゆ

**장음**(長音) a prolonged sound 《음성》 a long vowel[syllable]. ちょうおん

**장음계**(長音階) 〖음〗 the gamut; the ma-

**장의(葬儀)** a funeral [service]; funeral rites; obsequies／~를 치르다 hold a funeral service／~사(師) an undertaker; a mortician〈미〉／~차 a [motor] hearse. そうぎ

**장의자(長椅子)** a sofa; a bench; a lounge; a couch.

**장인(丈人)** the wife's father; a man's father-in-law. じょうじん

**장인(匠人)** an artisan; a workman; a craftsman. しょうじん

**장일(葬日)** the day of the funeral. そうしきのにち

**장자(長子)** the eldest son／~ 상속권 the right of primogeniture／~ 상속법 primogeniture. ちょうじゃ

**장자(長者)** (어른) an elder; one's superior[senior]; (부자) a rich[wealthy] man; a millionaire (덕망가) a man of moral influence; an elder of virtue／~를 존경하다 respect one's superiors. ちょうじゃ

**장작(長斫)** firewood／~을 패다 chop[split] firewood／~을 지피다 feed a fire with firewood. ぶちきったたきぎ

**장전(裝塡)** charge (of a gun); loading／~하다 load[charge, feed] a gun. そうてん

**장전(欌廛)** a furniture store.

**장점(長點)** a merit; a good[strong] point; a forte (미덕) a virtue (이점) graces; an advantage／~과 단점 merits and demerits／남의 ~을 인정하다 see the good in others. ちょうしょ

**장정(壯丁)** an able-bodied man; a sturdy youth; an adult 《징병 적령자》 a young man of conscription age／~ 검사 a physical examination of conscripts. そうてい

**장정(裝幀)** binding (of books); book cover design／~하다 bind (표지를) design／그 책은 가죽 ~이다 The book is bound in leather.／~자 a designer／견고한 ~ durable binding. そうてい

**장정(長程)** a long way; a great distance. ちょうてい

**장조(長調)** 〔음〕a major key. ちょうちょう

**장조모(丈祖母)** the wife's grandmother. つまのそぼ

**장조부(丈祖父)** the wife's grandfather. つまのそふ

**장조카(長—)** the eldest son of one's eldest brother. ちょうけいのちょうなん

**장족(長足)** a long foot; a great stride [pace]／~의 진보를 하다 make remarkable[rapid] progress; make rapid strides. ちょうそく

**장주릅(場—)** a market broker; a middleman.

**장죽(長竹)** a long [smoking] pipe. ながいたけ

**장중(掌中)** ~에 in one's hands[possession, power]; within one's grip[power]; (지배 하에) at (a person's) mercy／~에 들어가다 fall into one's hands[possession]. しょうちゅう

**장중(莊重)** solemnity; gravity; impressiveness／~하다 (be) solemn; grave; impressive; sublime; serious／~한 어조로 in a solemn tone／~한 음악 solemn music. そうちゅう

**장지** a paper sliding door; a sliding door／~를 열다 open a paper sliding door. しょうじ

**장지(長指)** the middle finger. なかゆび

**장지(將指)** the middle finger 《발가락》 the big[great] toe. てのなかゆび

**장지(壯志)** a grand ambition; a lofty aspiration／~를 품다 entertain a great ambition. そうし

**장지(葬地)** a burial place[ground].

**장질부사(腸窒扶斯)** enteric fever〈영〉; typhoid fever〈미〉／~ 예방 주사 a typhoid inoculation. ちょうチブス

**장차(將次)** some day; in [the] future. だんだん

**장차다(長—)** (길다) (be) straight and long (멀다) far; distant; be long way off. まっすぐでながい

**장창(長槍)** a long spear; a long lance. ながいやり

**장책(長册)** an accounting book; a ledger／~을 달다 keep books／~에 달다 enter in the books[accounts, ledger].

**장처(長處)** a strong point; one's forte. ちょうしょ

**장천(長天)** the boundless[vast] sky.

**장총(長銃)** a [long-barreled] rifle.

**장취(長醉)** being drunk all the time; incessant drunkenness／~하다 be always drunk. いつもよっていること

**장취(將就)** development; progressiveness; growth／~하다 progress; develop; drive ahead／~성 possibility of future growth.

**장치(藏置)** storage／~하다 store [away]; keep in store; lay up; lay in a stock; preserve. ぞうち

**장치(裝置)** equipment; installation; contrivance; provision 《대포의》 mounting; an apparatus／~하다 equip (a ship) with; install; arrange; place／난방 ~ a heating system. そうち

**장침(長針)** a long needle 《시계의》 the long hand; the minute hand ⇒분침(分針). ちょうしん

**장침(長枕)** a long pillow that serves as an armrest; an armrest. ひじかけ

**장쾌(壯快)** ~하다 (be) stirring; lively; exciting; thrilling／~한 기도 a stirring attempt. そうかい

**장탄(裝彈)** charging／~하다 load (a revolver); charge (a gun). だんがんをこめること

**장탄식(長嘆息)** a long[heavy, deep] sigh／~하다 draw a long[deep] sigh; heave[give] a heavy sigh. ちょうたんそく

**장터(場—)** a market site[place].

**장롱(醬桶)** a soysauce cask; a soy barrel.

**장파(長波)** 〖물〗 a long wave／～ 라디오 a long-wave radio set.

**장판(場—)** a market place[square]; a crowded[thronged] place; a place swarming with people.

**장판(壯版)** a floor covered with laminated paper／～방 a room with paper-covered floor／～지(紙) papers lacquered with bean oil.

**장판(藏版)** ownership of copyright.

**장편(長篇)** a long work (of *art*); a long piece／～ 소설 a novel; a full-length novel／～ 영화 a long film.

**장편(掌篇)** a very short piece of writing [story]; *a conte*(F)／～ 소설 a short-short story.

**장폐색증(腸閉塞症)** 〖의〗enterostenosis; intestinal obstruction.

**장품(臟品)** stolen goods ⇨장물.

**장피(獐皮)** the skin of a roe deer.

**장하다(長—)** (be) excellent (*at, in*); proficient (*in*); skillful; good (*at*); adept／문장에 ～ write in a good style; be an able[a talented] writer／장한 생각 a splendid[bright] idea.

**장하다(壯—)** (훌륭하다)(be) great; splendid; glorious (용감하다)brave; admirable; praiseworthy (굉장하다)grand; magnificent (놀랍다)wonderful; surprising／장한 죽음을 하다 die an honorable death／장한 구경거리 a grand spectacle.

**장학(奬學)** encouragement[promotion]of learning[study]／～하다 encourage learning／～금 a scholarship／～금을 얻다 win[gain] a scholarship.

**장한(壯漢)** a strong man.

**장해(障害)** an obstacle; a hindrance ⇔ 장애.

**장행회(壯行會)** a farewell party; a send-off party[dinner]; a rousing send-off／～를 열다 hold a farewell party (for *a person*).

**장혈(獐血)** blood of a roe deer.

**장형(杖刑)** flogging／～하다 flog.

**장형(長兄)** the eldest brother.

**장화(長話)** a long talk.

**장화(長靴)** high boots; boots〈미〉.

**장황(張皇)** ～하다 (be) lengthy; tedious; long and boring; dull／～한 연설 a tedious discourse; a tirade.

**잦다¹** (기울다) lean backward[s].

**잦다²** (빈번하다)(be) frequent; incessant／요즈음은 화재가 잦을 때다 Fires are frequent at this time of the year.

**잦뜨리다** bend back[backwards]; throw back ⇨젖드리다.

**잦바듬하다** lean back ⇨젖버듬하다.

**잦아지다** dry up; be boiled dry; sink; go down.

**잦은 걸음** a quick pace; quick steps／～으로 with quick steps.

**잦추다** urge incessantly; press repeatedly／빚을 갚으라고 ～ press (*a person*) for the payment of a debt.

**잦혀놓다** (뒤집다)turn over[up]; turn upside down; lay (*a thing*) face down (뒤로 미루다) put[lay] aside; leave out／접시를 ～ turn over a plate／하던 일을 잦혀놓고 친구를 맞이하다 meet a friend laying aside doing.

**잦혀지다** (뒤집히다)be turned over; lie face down[upside down]／책이 잦혀져 있다 A book lies open.

**잦히다¹** (뒤집다)turn over[down]; turn upside down (몸을 뒤로)pull back; lean backwards; bend back／어깨를 ～ pull back *one's* shoulder.

**잦히다²** (밥을)stew; simmer; hang the rice over a slow fire.

**재¹** (타고 남은) ashes／타서 ～가 되다 be reduced to ashes; lie in ashes[rubble]／～떨이 an ash tray／담배 ～를 털다 shake off the ashes from *one's* cigarette.

**재²** (고개) a ridge; a [mountain] pass／～를 넘다 cross a ridge; cross over a pass; go over a hill.

**-째¹** (차례·등급) 의 첫 ～로 졸업하다 graduate at the head of *one's* class／여기에 온 것은 이번이 세 번～다 This is the third time I have been here.

**-째²** (그대로) together[along] with; as it is; inclusive of／나무를 뿌리～ 뽑다 pull up a tree by the roots.

**재(災)** a calamity; a disaster; a misfortune.

**재(齋)** (불공) the Buddhist service[mass] for the deceased／～를 올리다 have a mass read for the repose of a soul[the dead].

**재(財)** (부) wealth; riches 《금전》 money 《재산》 fortune; assets 《재물》 propertry; goods.

**재-(再)** again; re-／～심 a re-examination／～출발 a restart; a fresh start.

**재가(在家)** ～하다 stay at home; retire from public life; live in retirement／～승(僧) a married Buddhist priest.

**재가(再嫁)** a second marriage; remarriage／～하다 marry again; remarry.

**재가(裁可)** sanction; approval／～하다 sanction; approve; give sanction (*to*)／～를 얻다 obtain (*a person's*) sanction.

**재깍** with a click; with a snap.

**재깍거리다** keep clicking.

**재간(才幹)** ability; talent; capability; caliber/학식 ~이 남보다 뛰어나다 excel both in talent and attainments/손~ manual skill; dexterity. さいかん

**재간(再刊)** republication; reissue; second edition/~하다 republish; reprint; reissue. さいかん

**재갈** a bit/~물리다 bit a horse. くつわ

**재깔이다** talk garrulously; jabber ⇒지껄이다. ぺちゃぺちゃいう

**재감(在監)** 〖법〗 imprisonment; staying in prison/~하다 be in prison[jail]; be imprisoned/~자 a convict; a prison inmate. ざいかん

**재강** the sediment[lees] of fermented liquor/~장 soysauce steeped in liquor lees. さけかす

**재개(再開)** reopening; resumption/~하다 open again; reconvene; resume/무역을 ~하다 reopen foreign trade. さいかい

**재개(再改)** a second revision[amendment] /~하다 revise[amend] again. ふたたびあらためること

**재개의(再改議)** a second amendment/~하다 make a second amendment.

**재거(再擧)** a second attempt; beginning again/~하다 make another attempt; try again. さいきょ

**재건(再建)** rebuilding; reconstruction; rehabilitation/~하다 rebuild; reconstruct; rehabilitate/한국을 ~하다 reconstruct Korea/~비 rebuilding expenses. さいけん

**재검사(再檢査)** reinspection; re-examination/~하다 reinspect; re-examine; examine over again; recheck.

**재검토(再檢討)** reappraisal; re-examination; review/~하다 re-examine; reappraise; review; take a new look at. さいけんとう

**재결(裁決)** decision; judgment; arbitration 《배심원의》 verdict/~하다 give decision[judgment]; arbitrate; decide/~에 따르다 abide by decision/~권 a casting vote. さいけつ

**재경(在京)** ~하다 be[reside] in Seoul; stay in Seoul/~ 동창생 alumni in Seoul /~ 외국인 foreign residents in Seoul. ざいきょう

**재계(財界)** 《금융계》 the financial world; financial circles 《경제계》 the economic world 《실업계》 the business world/~의 불경기 a business[an economic] depression. ざいかい

**재계(齋戒)** purification/~하다 purify oneself/목욕 ~하고 기도드리다 off prayers after performing purification. さいかい

**재고(再考)** reconsideration/~하다 reconsider; think twice; think better 《of》 /사직의 건은 ~해 보십시오 I would advise you to reconsider your intended resignation. さいこう

**재고(在庫)** stock; the stockpile/~의 in store; in stock/~량 the total stock/~품 goods in store/~ 조사 stocktaking; [an] inventory. ざいこ

**재교(再校)** the second proof/~하다 read the second proofs; proofread a second time. さいこう

**재교육(再敎育)** re-education; retraining /~하다 re-educate; retrain/~을 받다 be re-educated; be retrained. さいきょういく

**재군비(再軍備)** rearmament; remilitarization/~하다 rearm; remilitarize (a country).

**재귀(再歸)** return; reflection; recurrence; relapsing; recursive/~하다 return; come[go] back/~ 대명사 a reflexive pronoun/~열 〖의〗 recurrent[relapsing] fever. さいき

**재근(在勤)** holding office; staying in office/~하다 hold office[a post]; serve; work/해외 ~ 수당 a foreign service allowance. ざいきん

**재기(才氣)** talent; a flash of wit/~가 발랄하다 be very witty[clever]; be of brilliant talent. さいき

**재기(再起)** a comeback; rising again 《회복》 recovery; restoration; rally/~하다 come back; rise again; recover; restore; rally/~ 불능이다 be beyond recovery/그는 ~ 불능이라고들 한다 His recovery is pronounced as hopeless[impossible]. さいき

**재난(災難)** 《불행》 a misfortune 《재액》 a calamity; a disaster; a fatality 《불의의 사고》 an accident; a catastrophe/~이 덮쳤다 A misfortune befell him., An accident happened to him./~의 연속 a series of accidents; a run of ill luck. さいなん

**재넘이** a mountain blast; a wind blowing down the mountain.

**재녀(才女)** a woman of talent; a gifted woman. さいじょ

**재년(災年)** a year of calamity; a year of famine. やくどし

**재능(才能)** talent; ability; capability; aptitude; capacity; faculty; gift/어학적 ~ a linguistic talent/숨은 ~ a hidden talent/타고난 ~ one's natural gift /~을 발휘하다 show[demonstrate] one's talent[ability]/~을 닦다 cultivate one's talents; improve one's ability/그녀는 뛰어난 ~을 타고났다 She is richly gifted by nature. さいのう

**재다¹** ①《자로》 measure; gauge 《측량하다》 survey 《수심을》 sound/산의 높이를 ~ measure the height of a mountain ②《헤아리다》 calculate; view; give careful consideration/일을 재서 하다 carry out one's plan with discretion ③《염탐하다》 spy upon 《a person》; search 《a person》 on a subject /형세를 ~ feel out the situation ④《탄환을》 load 《a

**재다** gun); charge; feed (*a gun*) ⑤《으시대다》be proud of; be boast of; be highbrowed／그것은 젤 만한것이 못된다 That is nothing to proud of ⑥《사람을》lodge／솜을 ~ have the cotton pressed ⑦《쟁이다》pile on[up]; put in layers; lay one thing on another. はかる

**재다²** (動作이) (be) quick; nimble; agile; alert (입이) talkative; loose-tongued／손이 잰 사람 a person with nimble fingers. はやい

**째다** ①《찢다·절개하다》tear (*up*); rip; cut open; cleave; incise／칼로 주머니를 ~ cut *one's* pocket open with knife ②《부족하다》be short of; (be) insufficient ③《작다》(be) tight; firm; too small／이 옷은 너무 뺀다 This suit is too tight for me. やぶく

**재단**(財團) 【법】a foundation 《재단 법인》a foundational juridical person／금융 ~ a syndicate. ざいだん

**재단**(裁斷) 《재결》decision; judgment 《마름질》cutting／~하다 judge; decide; rule 《마르다》cut／~을 내리다 pass judgment (*on*)／~기 a cutter. さいだん

**재담**(才談) a witticism／~하다 talk wittily. しゃれ

**재당숙**(再堂叔) *one's* father's second cousin.

**재당질**(再堂姪) a second cousin's son.

**재덕**(才德) talent and virtue／~을 겸비하다 be both talented and virtuous. さいとく

**재떨이** an ash tray. はいさら

**재도**(再度) a second time; twice; again ⇒재차. さいど

**재독**(再讀) reading again; a second reading／~하다 read again reread; reperuse. さいどく

**재동**(才童) a clever child; a child of talent; an infant prodigy.

**재래**(在來) ~의 usual; common; ordinary; traditional; conventional／~의 습관 traditional[old] customs／~종 a native kind; the natural species. ざいらい

**재래**(再來) a second coming[advent]; r-eincarnation／~하다 come again／예수의 ~ the Second Advent of Christ／예수~설 Adventism. さいらい

**재략**(才略) tact; parts; resources／~이 있다 be resourceful; be tactful; be adroit. さいりゃく

**재량**(才量) ability and magnanimity; capability and generosity／~이 있다 be resourceful and generous. さいりょう

**재량**(裁量) discretion; decision／~ 처분 discretional[discretionary] disposition. さいりょう

**재력**(才力) ability; capability; talent. さいりょく

**재력**(財力) wealth; financial power[ability, status, means]; competence／~있는 사람 a man of means[wealth]. ざいりょく

**재련**(再鍊) 《쇠의》resmelting; reforging 《목재·석재의》refinishing (*wood*); retouching／~하다 reforge; resmelt; refinish; retouch.

**재롱**(才弄) sweet performances of a child／~부리다 do something sweet; play in a lovely manner.

**재료**(材料) stuff; material 《원료》raw material 《자료》data 《성분》ingredients／이 집은 좋은 ~를 썼다 This house is built of good materials.／건축 ~ building materials. ざいりょう

**재류**(在留) residence／~하다 reside; dwell; stay／서울 ~의 외국인 foreign residents in *Seoul*. ざいりゅう

**재리**(財利) property and profit. ざいかとりえき

**재림**(再臨) a second coming[advent]; reincarnation／~하다 come again; be reincarnated. さいりん

**째마리** 《물건》rubbish; scum; trash; junk; drege 《사람》human waste[debris]; dross of mankind; a bum〈미〉; the scum of society〈미〉; a hobo.

**재명**(才名) fame for *one's* talent; talent and game. さいめい

**재명년**(再明年) year after next. さらいとし

**재명일**(再明日) the day after tomorrow. あさって

**재목**(材木) wood; timber〈영〉; lumber〈미〉《통나무》a log／~을 벌채하다 lumber／~상 the lumber business; a lumber seller; a timber dealer[trader]／~ 적재장 a timberyard. ざいもく

**째못** a peg. きくぎ

**재무**(財務) financial affairs／~ 행정 financial administration／~부 장관 The Finance Minister; the Minister of Finance／~ 감독관 a comptroller [of the treasury]. ざいむ

**재물**(財物) property; goods; means; effects; treasures; a fortune／남의 ~을 빼앗다 rob (*a person*) of his property. ざいぶつ

**재미** amusement; enjoyment; fun; interest 《만족》satisfaction 《취미》comfort; hobby／이 책을 ~있게 읽었다 I have read this book with great interest.

**재미**(在美) residing in America／~중이다 be in America／~ 교포 Korean residents in America／~ 유학생 Korean students studying in America.

**재민**(災民) the afflicted people; the sufferers; the victims of calamity[disaster]／~ 구호금 disaster relief fund／전(戰)~ war sufferers. りさいみん

**재빠르다** (be) quick; swift; nimble; agile; alert; prompt／손이 ~ have nimble fingers. すばやい

**재발**(再發) 《병의》relapse; recurrence; return; recrudescence 《재발송》a second dispatch[sending] (of *a letter*)/~하다 recur; relapse; return 《다시 보내다》 send out[dispatch] again. さいはつ

**재방송**(再放送) rebroadcast[ing]; 《녹음의 재생》 transcription/~하다 rebroadcast.

**재배**(再拜) bowing twice; a second bowing[obeisance]/~하다 bow twice. さいはい

**재배**(栽培) cultivation; culture; growth; growing/~하다 cultivate; grow; raise /그는 과실을 ~하고 있다 He is growing fruit. さいばい

**재배치**(再配置) re-location; re-assignment /~하다 re-locate; re-assign.

**재벌**(財閥) a financial clique; plutocracy; realignment; rearrangement/~의 횡포 plutocratic despotism. ざいばつ

**재범**(再犯) 《죄》 a second offense 《범인》 a second conviction; a second offender /~하다 commit a second offense. さいはん

**재변**(才辯) a clever talk; a witty remark. さいべん

**재변**(災變) a natural calamity. さいへん

**째보** 《언청이》 a harelipped person 《경망한 자》 a frivolous person; a flattering fellow. いぐち

**재보**(財寶) riches; valuables; treasures wealth; precious things. ざいほう

**재보험**(再保險) 【경】 reinsurance; reassurance/~하다 reinsure. さいほけん

**재복무**(再服務) 【군】 extension of *one's* military service; re-enlistment. さいふくむ

**재봉**(裁縫) sewing; needlework/~하다 sew; do needlework/~사 a tailor; a dress-maker/~을 배우다 take lessons in sewing/그녀는 ~을 잘 한다 She is skilful with her needle. さいほう

**재봉틀**(裁縫─) a sewing machine ⇒자봉침. ミシン

**재분배**(再分配) redistribution; reallotment/~하다 redistribute; reallot/부(富)의 ~ redistribution of wealth.

**재사**(才士) a man of talent[ability]; a man of parts; a clever person; a wit /~ 다병 Men of genius are often of delicate health. さいし

**재산**(財產) property; a fortune; an estate 《자산》 assets/~을 만들다 make[amass] a fortune/~을 몰수하다 forfeit a property/~권 property right/~가 a man of property; a man of fortune/ ~을 물려받다 in herit[succeed to, come into] a fortune/~ 관리 property management/~ 목록 a list of property; an inventory/~세 property tax. ざいさん

**재삼**(再三) two or three times 《부사적》 more than once; repeatedly; again and again; often; frequently/~ 시험하다 try again and again. さいさん

**재상**(宰相) a prime minister; the premier [under the king]. さいしょう

**재색**(才色) wit and beauty/~을 겸비하다 be beautiful and talented; have both wit and beauty. さいしょく

**재생**(再生) restoration to life; revival; rebirth; a return to life; resuscitation 《폐물의》 rejuvenation; remaking; reproduction; reclamation/~하다 revive; r-esuscitate; return to lift 《폐물을》 remake; rejuvenate; regenerate/~의 감이 있다 feel greatly relieved/~ 녹음 rere-cording. さいせい

**재생산**(再生產) reproduction/~하다 reproduce/축소 ~ reproduction of regressive scale. さいせいさん

**재선**(再選) re-election; a second selection /~하다 re-elect; select a second time. さいせん

**재설**(再說) recapitulation; a repeated explanation/~하다 explain again; recapitulate. さいせつ

**재세**(在世) being alive; living/~ 시에 during *one's* lifetime; while *one* was alive/~중에 그를 알고 있는 사람들 people who knew him in life. ざいせ

**재송**(再送) resending; reforwarding/~하다 send again; resend; reforward/~ 전보 《재송원》 a retransmitted telegram-[me]; 《재송할》 a telegram to be transmitted. さいそう

**재수**(財數) luck; fortune/~ 좋은 사람 a lucky[fortunate] person/~가 트였다 Fortune has begun to smile upon him. /~없게 unluckily; by ill luck; unfortunately. うん

**재수입**(再輸入) reimport; reimportation /~하다 reimport/~품 reimported goods; reimports/~ 면허장 《세관의》 a reimport permit; a bill of store. さいゆにゅう

**재수출**(再輸出) re-export; re-exportation /~하다 re-export/~품 re-exports; goods re-exported[for re-export].

**재승덕**(才勝德) ~하다 be more talented than virtuous. さいゆしゅつ

**재시합**(再試合) a return game[match]; rematch [of a game]. さいしあい

**재시험**(再試驗) a re-examination; a retest/~하다 re-examine; examine[test] again. さいしけん

**재식**(才識) talents and knowledge; ability and discernment[intelligence]. さいのうとけんしき

**재식**(栽植) planting [trees]/~하다 plant; set. さいしょく

**재실**(再室) a second wife. さいこんのつま

**재심**(再審) re-examination 《재판의》 re-trial; a new trial/~하다 re-examine; try over again; hear again/~을 청구하다 apply for a new trial/~ 법원 a court of review. さいしん

**재심사**(再審査) re-examination/~하다 re -examine; examine again. さいしんさ

**재앙**(災殃) 《재난》 disaster; calamity; woe 《불행》 misfortune; evil/~을 당하다 meet with a misfortune[calamity].

**재액**(災厄) a calamity; a disaster; a mishap; a misfortune. さいやく

**재야**(在野) ~의 out of power[office]; in opposition /재조 ~를 막론하고 whether in office or out of office. ざいや

**재약하다**(-藥-) load (a gun); charge. かやくをこめる

**재양**(載陽) ~하다 dry (starched silk) on a board /~를 a drying device /~판 a drying board. あたたかくなること

**째어지다** split; tear; rend; burst; rip; cleave 《금이 가다》 crack 《둘로 ~ be split in two /네 옷이 째어졌다 Your clothes are torn. われる

**재연**(再燃) recrudescence; recurrence; revival; resuscitation /~하다 revive; break up again 《붙이》 burn up again /문제가 ~됐다 The problem has come to the fore again. さいねん

**재연**(再演) a second presentation 《연극・영화 따위》 rerunning (of a movie); an encore(F) /~을 청하다 encore; call[cry] for an encore. さいえん

**재영**(在營) ~하다 be in military service; be in the army[navy]. ざいえい

**재예**(才藝) talent and accomplishments /~에 뛰어난 부인 a highly accomplished woman. さいげい

**재외**(在外) ~의 abroad; overseas /~ 공관 embassies and legations abroad /~ 대리점 an agency abroad /~ 투자 overseas investment. ざいがい

**재욕**(財慾) greediness[desire] for wealth /~이 많다 be greedy for wealth. ざいよく

**재우다**¹ 《자게 하다》 put[make] (a person) to sleep; induce sleep /자장가를 불러 아이를 ~ lullaby a child to sleep. ねかせる

**재우다**² 《재다》 load with; press down ⇒ 재다.

**재우치다** finish up quickly; dispatch (work); make a short work (of) /일을 ~ finish a job up quickly; make short work of it. すばやくする

**재원**(財源) financial[economic] resources; funds; a revenue source /~이 풍부하다 be abundant in resources /~을 고갈시키다 drain[exhaust] the resources. ざいげん

**재원**(才媛) a talented lady; an accomplished young lady. さいえん

**재위**(在位) being upon the throne; the period of one's reign /~하다 be on the throne; reign /~ 5년에 서거하시다 die in the fifth year of (one's) reign. ざいい

**재의**(再議) reconsideration; rediscussion /~하다 reconsider; discuss again /~에 붙이다 submit (a matter) for reconsideration. さいぎ

**재인**(才人) ①《재사》 a man of talent ⇒재사 ②《광대》 an acrobatic tumbler. さいじん

**재인식**(再認識) reperception; reappraisal; a new understand (of) /~하다 renew understanding; see (a matter) in a new light /정세를 ~하다 have a new understanding of the situation.
さいにんしき

**재일**(在日) residing in Japan /~ 교포 Korean residents in Japan. ざいにち

**재임**(在任) being in office /~하다 be in office; hold office; hold office[a post] /~ 시에 while in office; during one's term[tenure] of office. ざいにん

**재임**(再任) reappointment /~하다 be reappointed. さいにん

**재입국**(再入國) re-entry (into a country) /~하다 re-enter /~ 허가서 a re-entry permit.

**재자**(才子) a man of talent[ability]; a man of parts; a wit; a clever man / ~ 가인 wit and beauty. さいし

**재작년**(再昨年) the year before last. おととし

**재작일**(再昨日) the day before yesterday ⇒그저께. おとつい

**재재거리다** chatter; jabber; prattle; gibber; gable. しゃべりまくる

**재재하다** (be) garrulous; talkative; chattering. やかましい

**재적**(在籍) enrollment /~하다 be on the register[roll] /이 반은 ~ 학생 수가 52명이다 This class has 52 pupils on the register. ざいせき

**재정**(財政) economy; finances; financial affairs (of a company) /~이 풍부하다 be well off; be in abundant circumstances /~ 고문 a financial advisor /~ 곤란 financial trouble[embarrassment, straits, difficulties] /~ 문제 a financial question[problem] /흑자 ~ balanced finance. ざいせい

**재정**(再訂) revision /~하다 revise /~판 a revised edition. さいてい

**재정**(裁定) decision; arbitration; adjudication /~하다 decide; arbitrate; adjudicate /~ 거래 arbitrage; arbitration. さいてい

**재제**(再製) remanufacture; reproduction /~하다 remake; remanufacture; rework; reproduce /~ 고무 reclaimed rubber. さいせい

**재조**(在朝) ~의 now in power[office]; governmental / ~ 재야의 명사 noted people in and out of official life.
ざいちょう

**재조사**(再調査) re-examination; reinvestigation /~하다 re-examine; reinvestigate.

**재종**(再從) a second cousin /~간 a second cousinship /~손 the grandson of a cousin /~질(姪) a son of one's second cousin. またいとこ

**재주** 《재능》 ability; talent; gifts; parts 《솜씨》 skill; dexerity /~있는 talented; capable; gifted / ~ 없는 talentless;

재주(在住) residence/~하다 live; reside; be resident/부산 ~의 외국인 foreign residents in *Busan*; foreigners living in *Busan*. ざいじゅう

재주넘다 make[cut, turn] a somersault/비행기가 재주를 넘다 An airplane loops the loop. とんぼかえりをする

재줏군 a person of high talents/그는 대단한 ~이다 He is clever to fingernails [highly intelligent].

재중(在中) ~의 containing/견본 ~ (우편) Samples/사진 ~ (우편) Photographs. ざいちゅう

재지(才智) talent; tact; intelligence/~ 있는 clever; talented; intelligent/~에 찬 tactful; resourceful. さいち

재지(災地) the afflicted area; the stricken districts; the affected land. さいがいち

재직(在職) ~하다 hold office; be in office[service]/그는 본교에 ~한 지 20년이 된다 He has served this school for twenty years./~ 기간 one's tenure of office; one's period of service in a position. ざいしょく

재질(才質) natural endowment; natural gifts; talent. さいしつ

재차(再次) 《부사적》 twice; again; a second time 《두 번째로》 for the second time 《한번 더》 once more; once again/~ 시도하다 try again; make another[a second] attempt. ふたたび

재채기 a sneeze; sneezing. くしゃみ

재천(在天) existing in Heaven/인명은 ~이다 Life and death are providential. ざいてん

재청(再請) 《두 번째》 a second request; an encore(F); 《동의어에 대한》 seconding/~하다 request a second time; encore; second (a motion). ふたたびたのむこと

재촉 pressing; urging; demand/~하다 press (a person for); request; demand/그는 빚을 조금도 ~하지 않았다 He was very easy with me over the debt./식사를 ~하다 call for a meal.

재출발(再出發) a restart a fresh[new] start/~하다 make a restart; start afresh. さいしゅっぱつ

재취(再娶) a second marriage; re-marriage/~하다 marry again. ふたたびめとること

재치(才致) wit; cleverness; resources; tact/~있는 사람 a man of tact; a tactful[witty] person.

재침략(再侵略) reinvasion/~하다 reinvade. さいしんりゃく

재탄(滓炭) dust coal; [char]coal dust.

재탕(再湯) ~하다 boil again; re-infuse; make a rehash (of).

재티 dust of ashes; cinders; ashes/~가 눈에 들어가다 get cinders in one's eye. はいのごみ

재판(再版) reprint 《제2판》 a second edition[impression]/~이 되다 run into a second edition. さいはん

재판(裁判) justice 《공판》 a trial; hearing 《판결》 judgment; decision/~하다 administer justice; judge (a person, a case); decide on (a case)/~장 the chief judge/정식 ~ a formal trial/~을 열다 hold a court/~은 피고의 승소로 끝났다 The case was decided in favor of the defendant/~관 a judge 《총칭》 the bench/궐석 ~ judgment by default. さいばん

재판서(裁判書) court records; a written judgment; the document of a judgment. さいばんしょ

재판소(裁判所) a court of justice[law]; a law-court; a court-house/~에 출두하다 come into court; appear in court/~ 소장 the president of a court. さいばんしょ

재편성(再編成) reorganization; reforming; reshuffle; revamps/~하다 reorganize; reform; revamp/학급을 ~하다 rearrange classes. さいへんせい

재평가(再評價) revaluation; reappraisal; reassessment/~하다 revaluate/자산 ~ revaluation of property/자산 ~ 법 the Assets Revaluation Law. さいひょうか

째푸리다 frown; get cloudy ⇒찌푸리다. しわをよせる

재필(才筆) a brilliant pen; a clever[facile] style/~을 휘두르다 give reins to one's literary skill. さいひつ

재하(在荷) stock; goods (in stock); goods on hand; stored goods; the inventory/시장은 ~ 과잉 상태다 The market is over stocked.

재하자(在下者) a subordinate; a person who is under one's authority. めうえのひとにつかえるひと

재학(才學) ability and learning; talent and scholarship/~을 겸비하다 excel in both ability and learning. さいがく

재학(在學) being in school/~하다 be in school[college]; attend school[college]/~생은 2천 명이다 2,000 students are enrolled in the school. ざいがく

재할인(再割引) 《경》 a rediscount/~하다 rediscount (a bill)/~ 어음 a rediscount bill/~율 rediscount rate. さいわりびき

재해(災害) a calamity; a disaster; an accident/~ 방지 prevention of disasters/~를 입다 suffer from a disaster; meet with an accident/~ 구호법 the Disaster Relief Law. さいがい

재향(在鄕) the country; the countryside; rural districts/~ 군인 a veteran [soldier]〈미〉; an exsoldiers 《총칭》 soldiers on the reserve list. ざいごう

재현(再現) reappearance; a second appearance; revival; re-emergence/~하다 reappear; re-emerge; come back/~부 《음》 recapitulation. さいげん

재혼(再婚) a second marriage; a remar-

재화(才華) [a] brilliant talent. さいか

재화(災禍) (재난) a calamity; a disaster (불행) a misfortune; an evil／～를 당하다 meet with a misfortune／～를 피하다 keep off a misfortune. さいか

재화(財貨) (상품) goods; commodities (재산) property; wealth. ざいか

재확인(再確認) reaffirmation; reconfirmation／～하다 reaffirm; confirm again; reconfirm. さいかくにん

재회(再會) meeting again; reunion／～하다 meet[see] (a person) again／～를 기약하다 promise to meet again／～는 기약하기가 어렵다 We may not meet again. さいかい

재흥(再興) revival; restoration; re-establishment (부흥) rehabilitation／～하다 revive; restore; re-establish; rehabilitate／폐가를 ~하다 revive an extinct family. さいこう

짹소리 a chirp; a tweet ⇨찍소리／～하다 give a chirp[tweet]. うんともすんとも

짹짹거리다 tweet; twitter; chirp. ちゅーちゅ

잽싸다 (be) nimble; agile; quick. すばしこい

잿물¹ lye (가성소다) caustic soda. あく

잿물² (도자기용) glaze; enamel／도자기에 ~을 올리다 put glaze on pottery. うわやく

잿밥(齋—) rice offered to Buddha／부처님에게 ~을 올리다 offer rice to Buddha.

잿빛 ash color; gray〈미〉; grey〈영〉／얼굴이 ~이 되다 one's face turns ashen. かいしょく

쟁강거리다, 쟁강거리다 clank; clink／쟁강 clinking; clanking. がちゃづく

쟁개비 a small pan.

쟁권(爭權) contention for power／～하다 contend for power. けんりをあらそうこと

쟁그랍다 (be) crawly; creepy ⇨징그럽다.

쟁그리다 scowl ⇨찡그리다. しわをよせる

쟁기 a [Korean] plow; a plough〈영〉／～질 plowing[ploughing]. すき

쟁단(爭端) a cause[source] of strife[dispute, discord]. そうたん

쟁론(爭論) a dispute; a quarrel; a controversy; an altercation; an argument／～하다 dispute (with); quarrel (with); argue. そうろん

쟁반(錚盤) a tray; a salver; a server.

쟁선(爭先) contention for the first place; struggle to be foremost／～하다 contend for the first place; rival for priority.

쟁송(爭訟) a dispute (by a lawsuit)／～하다 dispute; go to law with (a person). そしょう

쟁의(爭議) a dispute; conflicts; a controversy; a trouble／～를 조정하다 adjust a dispute／～권 the right to[of] strike／노동 ~ a labor dispute. そうぎ

쟁이다 pile up; heap up; make a neat pile of (things); accumulate／고기를 ~ leave sliced meat in piles[stacks].
つみかさねる

쨍쨍 blazing[ly]; bright[ly]; glaring[ly]／～하다 (be) bright; blazing. かんかん

쨍쨍거리다 mutter; grumble ⇨ぶつぶついう

쟁쟁하다(錚錚—) (뛰어나다) (be) prominent; eminent; outstanding; leading; conspicuous; foremost; first class／당내의 쟁쟁한 인물 one of the shining lights of the party.

쟁쟁하다(琤琤—) ①(귀에 남다) linger[ring] (in one's ears)／그의 말소리가 아직도 귀에 ~ His words still linger[are still ringing] in my ears. ②(소리가) (be) clear; have a nice ring to it; (be) sonorous; resonant／쟁쟁한 목소리 a clear [ringing] voice. りんりんとなる

쟁탈(爭奪) a contest; a struggle; a competition; a scramble／～하다 struggle [scramble, fight, contest] for／우승패 ~전 a contest for the championship trophy. そうだつ

쟁투(爭鬪) a strife; a struggle; a fight; a combat／～하다 fight; struggle; strive. そうとう

쟁퉁이 (거만한) a haughty person (가난한) a grumpy person; a person who has let poverty make him mean and cross. ひがみこんじょうのひと

쟁패전(爭覇戰) a struggle[fight, contest] for supremacy (경기의) a championship game. そうはせん

저¹ ①(나) I; me ②(자기) self; oneself／～희들 We／～의 의견으로는 in according to my opinion. わたくし

저² (지칭) that (pl. those); the／~ 사람 that man／~ 집들 those houses. あの―

저³ (느낌씨) well; I say; say〈미〉／~ 최 선생님 I say, Mr. Choi. あの―. え

저(著) (저술) one's writings; [written] by／이박사 ~ [written] by Dr. Lee.

저(著) (젓가락) [a pair of] chopsticks. はし

저각(底角) 〖수〗 a base angle. ていかく

저간(邇間) that time; then; that occasion／～의 of the time; during the period. そのあいだ

저같이 so; like that; [in] that way／~ 해라 Do like that.／그 아이를 ~ 호되게 꾸짖지 않아도 될 텐데 He should not have scolded the boy so severely.
あのように

저것 that; that thing [over there]; that one／이것~ 생각한 끝에 after a great deal of thinking. あれ

저격(狙擊) shooting; sniping; sharpshooting／～하다 shoot[fire] (at)／～대 a sharpshooting squad／～병 a sniper; a sharpshooter. そげき

저고리 a coat; a Korean jacket／～를 입다 put on one's coat. うわぎ

저곡(貯穀) storing crops/~하다 store crops; have crops in store/~미 stored rice; rice held in stock.
こくもつをちょぞうすること

저공(低空) a low sky[altitude]/~으로 비행하다 fly low; fly at a low altitude/~ 비행 low flying/~ 폭격 low-altitude bombing. ていくう

저광수리 〖조〗 a goshawk.

저금(貯金) a deposit (행위) saving (돈) savings/~하다 save; lay[put] by (money); have money (in the bank)/월급 중에서 ~하다 save (a sum) out of one's salary. ちょきん

저급(低級) low grade[class]; inferiority/~하다 (be) low; low-graded; inferior; low-toned 《야비한》 vulgar/~한 노래 a vulgar song. ていきゅう

저기 that place; there/~에 there; over there; yonder/~ 있는 저 건물이 정거장입니다 That building over there is the station. あそこ

저기압(低氣壓) a low pressure; a depression/~의 중심 the center of a depression/정계의 ~ a political storm center. ていきあつ

저나마 even that/구두가 낡았지만 ~ 신을 수 밖에 없다 I have to put on that pair of shoes, worn out as they are.
あれでも

저냐 fried meat[fish].

저냥 as that; as it is/~ 두어라 Leave it as it is. あのまま

저네 those people [over there]; they[them]. あのひとら

저녁 ①evening/~이면 혼히 of an evening/~이 될 무렵에 toward evening ②《식사》 the evening meal; supper; dinner/~에 초대하다 invite to dinner.

저녁때 evening [time]; dusk; sunset; eventide/~에 귀가하다 return home towards evening.

저녁밥 supper; the evening meal/~을 먹다 take supper/~을 짓다 prepare supper; get dinner ready. ゆうはん

저놈 that damn guy; he; that damn thing.

저능(低能) low intelligence; feeble-mindedness; weak-mindedness/~하다 mentally weak; weak[feeble]·minded/~아(兒) a weak[feeble]·minded child.
ていのう

저따위 of that sort[kind]; that kind (of); that sort (of)/~는 처음 본다 I have never seen such a person in all my life. あんなやつ

저다지 so; so much; like that; to that extent[degree]/~도 완고한 사람은 일찌기 본 일이 없다 He is the most obstinate fellow I have ever seen. あんなに

저당(抵當) mortgage; security; collateral/~하다 mortgage; hypothecate; give (a thing) as security/집을 ~잡히다 mortgage one's house/~권 mortgage; hypothec. ていとう

저대로 as it is[stands]; like that/~ 두다 leave it just as it is; leave it alone.
あのまま

저돌(猪突) recklessness; foolhardiness; rashness/~하다 rash recklessly; make a reckless[wild] rush; make a headlong rush/~적으로 recklessly; foolhardily. ちょとつ

저들 those people [over there]; they [them]. あれら

저락(低落) fall; decline; depreciation/~하다 fall; go down; depreciate; decline. ていらく

저러하다 suchlike; (be) like that/저러한 사람 such a person. あのようだ

저런¹ such; so; like that; of that sort [kind]/~ 정직한 사람 such an honest man as he.

저런² 《감탄사》 Oh dear!, Oh my!, Good heavens!, Goodness!, Indeed! あんな

저렇다 be like that. 저러하다. ああだ

저력(底力) latent[potential] energy; reserve of force/경제적 ~ economic staying power/~ 있는 목소리 a deep [tone of] voice.

저렴(低廉) cheapness; moderateness; a low price/~하다 (be) cheap; lowpriced; moderate; inexpensive/~한 값 moderate prices. ていれん

저류(底流) an undercurrent/의식의 ~ subconscious current. ていりゅう

저르렁거리다, 쩌르렁거리다 clang and clang; tinkle and tinkle; jingle and jingle. がらんがらんする

저름나다 《마소가》 fall lame. ちんばになる

저리 (저렇게) so; like that; in that way; to that extent 《방향》 that way; that direction; over there; there; thither/~ 좀 비키시오 Step aside, please./이리 ~ here and there. あのように

저리(低利) low interest; a low rate of interest/~로 대부하다 put lend money at a low rate of interest/~ 금융 cheap credit. ていり

저리다 《손발이》 be[fall] asleep; be benumbed; become numbed 《쑤시다》 be [feel] sore; have a dull pain/다리가 저리고 쑤신다 I have pins and needles in my legs. しびれる

저마(苧麻) ramie; China Grass; Boehmeria nivea《학명》.

저마다 each one; everyone/~ 자기가 옳다고 한다 Every man claims that he himself is right. おのおの

저만큼 so; like that; so much; that much; to that extent/~ 영어를 하면 좋겠는데 I wish I could speak English that much. あのくらい

저만하다 be that much[so much]; be to that extent; be as much as that/저만하면 충분하다 That much is good enough for me. あれくらいだ

저맘때 about[around] that time; at that

저면(底面) the base.

저명(著名) prominence; eminence; distinction／～하다 (be) well-known; eminent; noted; prominent; celebrated; famous; notable. ちょめい

저물가(低物價) low prices／～ 정책 a low-price policy. ていぶっか

저물다 《해가》 grow[get] dark[dim]; (the sun) set; (night) fall 《끝나다》 draw to a close; end; come to an end／저물도록 till a late hour／6시에 해가 저물었다 Night fell at six. ひがくれる

저미(低迷) hanging low／～하다 hang low／암운(暗雲)이 ～한다 Dark clouds hang low. ていめい

저미다 slice; cut thin／저며내다 slice off [away]／고기를 얇게 ～ cut meat into thin slices. うすくきる

저버리다 go back on; turn one's back on; back down; forsake; desert; break 《one's promise》／은혜를 ～ go back on one's obligation／약속을 ～ back down on a promise. はいはんする

저벅거리다 tramp; trample; walk with sounding footsteps. どしんどしんする

저번(這番) last; last time; the other day; some time ago; lately; previously／～의 last; recent; previous／～에 만났을 적에 when I saw him last. このまえ

저변(底邊) the base. ていへん

저분저분 ～하다 (be) sociable; mix nicely with people. むしゃむしゃ

저상(沮喪) dejection; depression; discouragement; damp; demoralization／～하다 be dejected; be depressed; be disheartened／적군은 의기가 ～되어 있다 The enemy troops are demoralized.

저서(著書) one's writings; a book; a [literary] work／그는 ～가 많다 He has written many books. ちょしょ

저선(底線) 《수》 the base; the base line.

저성(低聲) a low voice[tone]; a subdued voice／～으로 in a low voice; in an undertone. ていせい

저속(低俗) vulgarity; baseness／～하다 (be) vulgar; base; low／그의 말씨는 ～하다 He is vulgar in his speech. ていぞく

저수(貯水) storage of water; reservoir water／～하다 keep [water] in store; build up in reservoir／～지 a [storing] reservoir. ちょすい

저수(底數) 《수》 a base 《기수》 a radix.

저술(著述) writing [of books]; authorship; literary work[pursuits]; 《저작물》 a work; a book; one's writing／～하다 write 《a book》／역사에 관해 ～하다 write on history. ちょじゅつ

저승 the world beyond; the other[next] world; the world[life] to come; a better land／～으로 가다 go to Heaven; join the majority. あのよ

저압(低壓) low pressure; low tension[voltage]／～부 a locality of low pressure／～ 전류 a low-tension current. ていあつ

저열(低熱) a slight fever; a low [bodily] temperature. ていねつ

저열(低劣) baseness; vulgarity／～하다 (be) base; vulgar low; mean／～한 사람 a mean[base] fellow. ていきゅう

저온(低溫) a low; temperature／～ 냉업 low-temperature refrigeration／～ 소독 《살균》 low-temperature pasteurization. ていおん

저울 《천칭》 a balance; [a pair of] scales 《대저울》 a weighing beam; a beam scale; a steelyard／～에 달다 weigh 《a thing》 in the balance. はかり

저육(豬肉) pork／～ 구이 roast pork. ぶたのにく

저율(低率) a low rate／～의 이자 a low interest; a low rate of interest. ていりつ

저의(底意) one's original purpose; one's real intention; one's will[motive]／～를 알 수 없다 I can't understand what you really mean to do.

저이 that person; him; she[her]／～들 those people; they[them]. あのひと

저자 ①《시장》 a market; a fair／～보러 가다 go to market 《to buy, sell》②《가게》 a market[grocery] stand. しじょう

저자(著者) a writer 《남자》 an author 《더자》 an authoress／소설의 ～ the author of a novel. ちょしゃ

저자상어 an angelfish; an angelshark.

저작(著作) 《저서》 a book; a work 《저술》 writing; authorship; literary work [production]／～하다 write a book／～가 a writer; an author. ちょさく

저작(咀嚼) chewing; mastication／～하다 chew; masticate／음식을 ～하다 masticate[chew] one's food well／～근 a muscle of mastication. そしゃく

저장(貯藏) storage; storing; keeping; preservation／～하다 store; keep; lay up; conserve／～해 둔 in store／대량의 식료를 ～하다 lay a large quantity of food in stores. ちょぞう

저적에 last time; before this; some time ago; the other day. あのときに

저절로 of itself; of its own accord; spontaneously 《자동적으로》 automatically／저 사람 앞에 나가면 ～ 머리가 수그러진다 I can't resist my impulse to bow in his presence. みずから

저조(低調) 《소리》 a low tone; an undertone 《침체》 dullness; inactiveness／～를 나타내다 show lack of enthusiasm／시황이 ～하다 The market is sluggish., The trade is dull. ていちょう

저조(低潮) 《지》 a low-tide; low water／～에 at low tide／최～ the neap [tide]. ていちょう

**저쪽** that side[direction]; over there; the other side[direction]/~에 there; over there; yonder; that way/나의 집은 ~에 있다 My home stands on that side. あっち

**저주**(詛呪) a curse; imprecation; a malediction; a backward blessing/~하다 curse; imprecate evil (*upon*)/세상을 ~하다 curse the world. のろうこと

**저지**(沮止) obstruction; hindrance; impediment; retardation; interception/~하다 obstruct; hinder; check; hamper; hold back retard; impede; block/발달을 ~하다 check the growth; arrest the development. そし

**저지**(低地) low[·lying] land; lowlands. ていち

**저지레** spoiling; ruining; marring/~하다 spoil; ruin; mar.

**저지르다** do; spoil; commit (*an error*); mar/그는 여자 관계로 곤란한 일을 저질렀다 He got into a terrible mess over a woman. ひきおこす

**저처럼** like that; so; to that extent /저같이. あのように

**저촉**(抵觸) conflict; contravention; contradiction/~하다 be contrary to; be inconsistent with/법령(法令)에 ~하다 be in conflict with laws and regulations. ていしょく

**저축**(貯蓄) saving; laying-by; hoarding 《저금》 savings/~하다 save; store up; hoard/~을 장려하다 encourage savings /~ 은행 a savings bank/~ 운동 a savings campaign. ちょちく

**저축거리다** limp; hobble/저축저축 limping; hobbling. かるくびっこひく

**저출거리다** limp; hobble ⇨저축거리다. すこしびっこをひく

**저큼** never repeating a mistake; learning from *one's* slip[error].

**저탄**(貯炭) a stock [pile] of coal/~소 a coal·yard[·depot]; a coaling station 《배의》 a bunker.

**저택**(邸宅) a mansion; a residence/훌륭한 ~ a lordly[stately] mansion; a fine house/그의 시골에는 훌륭한 ~이 있다 He has a fine home in his country. ていたく

**저통**(箸筒) a chopstick stand[holder]. はしばこ

**저편** that side[direction] ⇨저쪽. あっち

**저포**(紵布) ramie cloth ⇨모시.

**저하**(低下) a fall; a drop; lowering; decline 《가치의》 depreciation 《품질의》 deterioration/~하다 fall; drop; depreciate; deteriorate/수준의 ~ a lowering of standards/생산을 ~시키다 curtail production. ていか

**저학년**(低學年) the lower classes; lower grades. ていがくねん

**저항**(抵抗) ①《반항》 resistance 《반대》 opposition 《도전》 defiance; struggle/~하다 resist; oppose; stand against; withstand/완강히 ~하다 offer stubborn resistance/공격에 ~하다 resist an attack ② 《물》 resistance/공기의 ~을 감소시키다 dwindle[lessen] the air resistance/~력 [power of] resistance; resisting power [force]. ていこう

**저해**(沮害) obstruction; impediment; check/~하다 obstruct; check; impede; retard; stunt; block/그것은 세계 평화를 ~한다 It is an obstruction to the world peace. そがい

**저희들** we; those persons/~의 our/ ~을 us. じぶんたち

**적** (때) the time (*when*); the occasion/ 그가 왔을 ~에 내가 없었다 When he came to see me I was out. とき

**적**(賊) 《도둑》 a thief; a robber 《역적》 a rebel; an insurgent; a traitor. とうぞく

**적**(敵) an enemy; a foe 《적수》 an opponent; a rival; a match; an antagonist /~을 사랑하다 love *one's* enemy. てき

**적**(積) 《수》 the product 《면적》 the area /20은 5와 4의 ~이다 twenty is the product of five by four. せき

**적**(籍) 《호적》 the census register; a domicile 《단체의》 membership/서울에 ~이 있다 be domiciled[domiciliated] in *Seoul*.

**적**(的) ①《목표》 a target; a mark; an object; a focus/선망의 ~이 되다 become an object of envy ②《접미어》 ·ic; ·ical; ·like/가급~ so far as possible. —てき

**적가**(嫡家) the main family.

**적갈색**(赤褐色) a reddish brown color. あかかっしょく

**적개심**(敵愾心) a hostile feeling; hostility; enmity; animosity/~을 일으키게 하다 arouse[rouse] the animosity (*of*). てきがいしん

**적객**(謫客) a person in exile; an exile; a person banished.

**적거**(謫居) exile; banishment/~하다 be in exile; live in exile. はいしょにおること

**적격**(適格) conformity to the standard [qualification]; a proper qualification (*for*); competence; fitness; eligibility /~자 a qualified person. てきかく

**적꼬치**(炙—) a skewer.

**적곡**(積穀) storing of grains/~하다 store grain.

**적공**(積功) building up merit/~하다 build up merit. こうをつむこと

**적괴**(賊魁) the ringleader; the chief of a gang of robbers[rebels]. とうぞくのかしら

**적구**(赤狗) a communist; a commie; the Reds.

**적국**(敵國) the enemy[hostile] country; the enemy; a hostile power. てきこく

**적군**(赤軍) the Red Army. せきぐん

**적군**(賊軍) rebels; a rebel army; ·insurgents. ぞくぐん

**적군**(敵軍) the enemy [troops, force].

**적굴**(賊窟) a den of robbers.
**적권운**(積卷雲) an alto-cumulus.
**적극**(積極) the positive/～성 있는 사람 a man of initiative/～적으로 활동하다 work on positive lines/～적 태도로 나가다 take up a positive attitude. せっきょく
**적금**(赤金) red gold 《구리》 copper. あかがね
**적기**(敵機) an enemy[a hostile] plane. てっき
**적기**(赤旗) a red flag. せっき
**적기**(摘記) a summary; an epitome/～하다 summarize; sum up; epitomize.
**적기**(適期) ～의 timely; opportune/지금이 ～다 the present is most opportune for (doing *something*). てっき
**적나라**(赤裸裸) nakedness; nudity 《솔직》 frankness; plainness; straightforwardness/～하다 (be) nude; bare; frank; plain/～한 사실 a naked[bald] fact. せきらら
**적남**(嫡男) a legitimate son. ちゃくなん
**적녀**(嫡女) a legitimate girl. ちゃくじょ
**적년**(積年) many years; an accumulation of years/～의 공 efforts[labor] of many years/～의 폐해 an evil of long standing. せきねん
**적다**¹ 《기록하다》 write [down_]; record; put[take] down; note; make a memorandum of/영어로 ～ write in English /나는 날마다 일기를 적고 있다 I keep a diary everyday. きろくする
**적다**² 《수가》 (be) few; be of small number 《양이》 little; be of small quantity 《드물다》 rare; be few and far between/수입이 ～ have a small income. すくない
**-쩍다** feel; have[give] a feeling (*of*)/미심～ be doubtful; be suspicious/미안～ be embarrassed/겸연～ be abashed; be bashful. —そうだ. —らしい
**적다마**(赤多馬) a chestnut horse; a sorrel horse; a bay [horse].
**적당**(賊黨) a gang a thieves[rebels]; a band of robbers; bandits. ぞくとう
**적당**(適當) fitness; suitableness; propriety; appropriateness/～하다 (be) fit; suitable; proper; right; appropriate /～한 직업 a suitable calling/～한 때에 at a proper time. てきとう
**적대**(敵對) hostility; antagonism/～하다 show hostility (*toward*); oppose; be hostile (*to*)/공공연한 ～ 행위 open hostilities. てきたい
**적대시**(敵對視) regarding with hostility /～하다 (be) hostile (*to*); regard with hostility/～하는 태도 hostile attitude. てきたいし
**적도**(赤道) the equator/ ～에서의 지구의 주위 the circumference of the earth at the equator/～제(祭) the ceremony of crossing the equator. せきどう

**적도**(適度) moderation; proper degree [amount]; temperance; moderate exercise. てきど
**적도**(賊徒) a group of thieves. ぞくと
**적동**(赤銅) 【광】 red copper/～광 cuprite; red copper ore. せきどう
**적란운**(積亂雲) a cumulo-nimbus. せきらんうん
**적량**(適量) a proper quantity 《약의》 a proper dose. てきりょう
**적량**(積量) carrying capacity; tonnage/ 배의 ～ the carrying capacity of a vessel; a ship's tonnage. せきりょう
**적령**(適齡) the right[suitable] age (*for*) /～기에 이르다 reach[attain] the suitable age; be old enough (to *marry*)/결혼 ～ the marriageable age. てきれい
**적례**(適例) a good[an apposite] example; an apt[a typical] instance/다음 것이 ～다 The following is an example in point. てきれい
**적록**(摘錄) a summary; a gist; a compendium/～하다 summarize; sum up; epitomize. てきろく
**적료**(寂寥) desolateness; loneliness/～하다 (be) lonely; desolate; lonesome. ひっそり
**적리**(赤痢) dysentery; bloody flux/～는 보통 여름에 발생한다 Dysentery usually comes in summer. /～ 환자 a dysentery patient. せきり
**적립**(積立) accumulation; reserving; laying[putting] by/～하다 save up (*money*); accumulate; amass; reserve/ 그는 월급의 일부를 매달 ～한다 He saves up part of his salary every month. /～ 금 a reserve [fund]/～ 저금 installment savings. つみたて
**적마**(赤魔) a Red demon; the Red menace.
**적막**(寂寞) loneliness; desolation; solitude/～하다 (be) lonely; dreary; desolate; deserted/～한 광경 a dreary[desolate] sight. せきばく
**적멸**(寂滅) 【불】 death; annihilation/～하다 be annihilated; pass away; die; attain Nirvana.
**적모**(嫡母) one's father's legal wife. ちゃくぼ
**적목질**(赤木質) 【식】 heartwood.
**적바르다** narrowly meet the demand; be just enough.
**적바림** ～하다 make[take] a note of; jot down; note; record. じじつをきにゅうすること
**적발**(摘發) disclosure; exposure 《고발》 prosecution/～하다 disclose; expose; lay bare; prosecute; unmask/위반자를 ～하다 prosecute an offender. てきはつ
**적법**(適法) legality; lawfulness/～하다 (be) legal; lawful/～이다 be lawful/ ～이 아니다 be unlawful. てきほう
**적병**(敵兵) the enemy; the enemy soldier [troops]. てきへい

**적부**(適否) propriety; suitability; fitness /~를 판단하다 judge whether a thing is proper or not.

**적분**(積分) 【數】 integral calculus/~의 integral/~ 방정식 an integral equation/~법 integration/~학 integral calculus. せきぶん

**적분**(積忿) pent-up indignation[rancor] /~을 풀다 vent[give vent to] one's pent-up rancor (on). つもりかさなったうらみ

**적비**(賊匪) bandits; brigands; rebels. ひぞく

**적빈**(赤貧) abject[dere] poverty; indigence; destitution; penury/~하다 be in dire poverty; suffer from utter destitution/~하기 짝이 없다 He is as poor as a church mouse. せきひん

**적사**(積卸) loading and unloading/~하다 load and unload; ship and discharge /화물을 ~하다 coad and unload goods. つみおろし

**적산**(敵産) enemy property/~을 몰수하다 confiscate enemy property/~ 관리인 an enemy property administrator.

**적색**(赤色) 《빛깔》red color; red/《공산주의》communism; Red/~ 리트머스 시험지 red litmus paper; red test paper. あかいろ

**적서**(嫡庶) a legitimate children and illegitimate children; the direct line of descent and the illegitimate line of descent. ちゃくしょ

**적선**(積善) accumulation of virtuous[good] deeds/~하다 accumulate virtuous deeds; build up merits. せきぜん

**적선**(敵船) an enemy ship. てきせん

**적설**(積雪) drifted snow; deep snow; snowdrifts/~이 3피트에 달했다 The snow was 3 feet deep. せきせつ

**적설초**(積雪草) 【식】a ground ivy.

**적성**(赤誠) sincerity; singleness of heart; devotion/~을 다하다 devote one's sincerity; devote oneself (to). せきせい

**적성**(適性) aptitude/~ 검사 an aptitude test/~ 검사를 받다 undergo a quality test. てきせい

**적성**(敵性) hostility; animosity; antagonism; enemy character/~을 나타내다 manifest hostility[enemy character]/ ~ 국가 a hostile country. てきせい

**적세**(敵勢) the strength of the enemy; the morale of the foe/~를 무찌르다 shatter the enemy morale. てきせい

**적소**(謫所) a place of exile; the place that one is banished to.

**적소**(適所) the right[proper] place; a proper[suitable] position/~에 있다 be in the right place. てきしょ

**적손**(嫡孫) a legal posterity; a legitimate grandson[grandchild]. ちゃくそん

**적송**(積送) shipment 《위탁 판매를 위한》 consignment/~하다 ship; forward; consign/~인 a shipper; a forwarder.

**적송**(赤松) 【식】a [Japanese] red pine.

**적쇠** a grill; a grid ⇨석쇠.

**적수**(赤手) a bare hand; an empty hand; naked fists/~로 without the use of any weapon; barehanded/~ 공권으로 거부가 되다 make an enormous fortune starting with nothing. せきしゅ

**적수**(敵手) a rival; a match; an opponent; a competitor/그는 나의 ~가 못 된다 He is no match for me. てきしゅ

**적시**(敵視) enmity; hostility/~하다 be hostile (to); look upon (a person) as an enemy. てきし

**적시다** wet; drench; moisten; dampen; soak/옷을 ~ get one's clothes wet/눈물로 소매를 ~ wet the sleeves with tears. ひたす

**적신호**(赤信號) a red[danger] signal; a red light; a stoplight. あかしんごう

**적실**(的實) exactness; preciseness; accuracy/~하다 (be) accurate; exact; precise. めいかくなこと

**적실**(嫡室) the legal[legitimate] wife. てきしつ

**적심**(赤心) sincerity; the true heart; the faithful mind/~을 토로하다 reveal one's inmost heart. せきしん

**적십자**(赤十字) the Red Cross/~사 the Red Cross Gross Society/~ 간호원 a Red Cross nurse/~ 병원 the Red Cross Hospital. せきじゅうじ

**적악**(積惡) accumulated wickedness; a long course of evil life; a series of evil deeds/~하다 accumulated wickedness. せきあく

**적약**(適藥) effective medicine; a good remedy[cure]. てきやく

**적어도** at [the] least; at a minimum; to say the least of it/~ 5,000원은 들 것이다 It will cost you at least 5,000 won.

**적역**(適役) a fit post; a suitable office/그 일에는 그가 가장 ~이다 He is the right man for the work. てきやく

**적역**(適譯) an exact rendering; an adequate[a proper] translation/~하다 give a good translation of; translate properly.

**적연**(寂然) ~하다 (be) lonely. せきぜん

**적외선**(赤外線) infrared rays/~ 사진 infrared photography. せきがいせん

**적요**(摘要) a summary; an outline; an epitome; a synopsis; a compendium/~난 the remarks column. てきよう

**적용**(適用) application/~하다 apply (to) /~의 범위 the limit of application/일반적으로 ~되다 be universally applicable. てきよう

**적우**(積雨) a long rain; a long spell of rain.

**적운**(積雲) a cumulus. せきうん

**적울**(積鬱) deep melancholy; pent-up indignation/~하다 be congested with melancholy; smoulder. せきうつ

**적원**(積怨) pent-up rancour; a built-up

**적위**(赤緯) 〖천〗 declination. せきい

**적위군**(赤衛軍) the Red Guards; the Red Army. せきいけん

**적은집** a mistress; a kept woman; a concubine; a concubine's house／～을 두다 keep a mistress. めかけ

**적응**(適應) fitness; suitability; adaptation／～하다 fit; be fit for; be suited to; be adapted for／그녀는 환경에 잘 ～한다 She adapts herself to her environment. てきおう

**적의**(敵意) animosity; enmity; hostility; hostile feeling／～를 보이다 show hostility (*against*)／～가 있는 hostile; inimical antagonistic. てきい

**적의**(適宜) appropriateness; suitableness; suitability／～하다 (be) fit; fitting; proper; right; suitable／～한 조처를 취하다 take proper steps. てきぎ

**적의**(適意) agreement to *one's* mind[wish, will, taste, liking]／～하다 (be) agreeable; satisfactory; acceptable. てきい

**적이** somewhat; to some extent; in some measure; slightly／그 소식에 ～ 안심되오 I was slightly relieved at the news. いくらか

**적이나** at the very least; ever so little; a little at least; if at all possible／～후회하니 다행이다 I am glad he was sorry a little at least. いくらかでも

**적임**(適任) fitness (to the *post*); suitability; competence／그는 이 일에 ～자(者)다 He is well fitted for this work. てきにん

**적자**(赤子) 《아이》 a baby; an infant 《신하》 *one's* subjects; the people. あかご

**적자**(赤字) red letters [red figures; a deficit; a loss／～가 되다 show a loss ／～ 경영 deficit operation／～ 예산 an unbalanced budget. あかじ

**적자**(嫡子) a legitimate child[son]. ちゃくし

**적자**(適者) a fit person; the fit／～ 생존 the survival of the fittest／～ 생존의 법칙 the law of the survival of the fittest. てきしゃ

**적장**(敵將) the enemy's general; the enemy commander; the commander of the enemy force. てきしょう

**적재**(適材) a person fit for the post; the right man／～ 적소 a right man in a right place. てきざい

**적재**(摘載) ～하다 give a summary of; give an excerpt[extract] from; reprint an extract from. てきさい

**적재**(積載) loading; lading; carrying／～하다 load; lade; carry; take on[in]／배에 화물을 ～하다 load[lade] a ship with goods／～ 화물 cargo on board. せきさい

**적적하다**(寂寂―) (be) lonesome; lonely; solitary; desolate／적적한 곳 a lonely place／당신이 없어서 무척 적적했다 We missed you badly. さびしい

**적전**(敵前) ～의 in front[the face] of the enemy／～에 상륙하다 land in the face of the enemy; land on a hostile coast.

**적절**(適切) pertinence; appropriateness 《표현의》 felicity／～하다 (be) pertinent; fit; fitting; apt／～한 비유 a fitting comparison. てきせつ

**적정**(敵情) the movements of the enemy ／～을 살피다 reconnoiter the enemy's movements[positions]. てきじょう

**적정**(適正) propriety; appropriateness; reasonableness／～하다 (be) proper; right; reasonable; normal; fair／～한 가격 reasonable[normal] prices; just and fair prices. てきせい

**적중**(的中) a hit; a good hit／～하다 make a good hit; hit (*the mark*); 《예언 따위가》 come true; turn out true 《상상이》 guess right; make a good guess 《계략이》 take; work／～하지 않다 miss the mark; go wild／너의 예언이 ～했다 Your prophecy[prediction] came true. てきちゅう

**적지**(敵地) an enemy[the hostile] land [territory, country]／～에 침입하다 advance into the enemy's country. てきち

**적진**(敵陣) the enemy camp; the enemy line／～을 무찌르다 attack the enemy's position. てきじん

**적채**(積債) accumulated debts; a long standing obligation.

**적처**(嫡妻) a legitimate wife. ちゃくさい

**적철광**(赤鐵鑛) 〖광〗 hematite. せきてっこう

**적첩**(嫡妾) *one's* legal[legitimate] wife and *one's* concubine. ほんさいとめかけ

**적출**(積出) shipment; for warding／～하다 ship off; send off; forward／～ 통지서 an advice of shipment／～항 the port of shipment. つみだし

**적출**(摘出) extracting; an extract; picking[taking] out／상처에서 유리의 파편을 ～하다 extract the fragments of glass from a wound. てきしゅつ

**적출**(嫡出) a legitimate child. ちゃくしゅつ

**적치**(積置) ～하다 pile up and keep／석탄 ～장 a coal yard／목재 ～장 a timber-yard.

**적탄**(敵彈) the enemy's shells[bullets]／～을 무릅쓰고 in the face of enemy fire／～에 쓰러지다 fall under the enemy fire. てきだん

**적토**(赤土) red earth[soil]; clay. せきど

**적통**(嫡統) the main line of descent; the line of descent from the legal wife.

**적파**(嫡派) the main line of a family; descendants from the legal wife.

**적평**(適評) a just criticism; an apt remark; an appropriate comment. てきひょう

**적폐**(積弊) an evil of long standing; accumulated evils／～를 일소하다 clean

적포도주(赤葡萄酒) red wine.

적하(積荷) a load; a freight; a cargo (적재) loading; shipping; lading／~ 명세서 a freight list／~ 목록 a manifest／~ 비용 lading costs.

적함(敵艦) an enemy warship[vessel]; hostile craft.

적합(適合) suitability; fitness; agreement; conformity／~하다 (be) suitable; fit; compatible／목적에 ~하다 suit one's purpose.

적혈(赤血) red blood／~구 《의》 a red blood cell; a red blood corpuscle／~염《화》 potassium ferricyanide.

적화(赤化) communization; sovietization／~하다 communize; infect (a person) with Bolshevik ideas／~를 방지하다 check the spread of communism.

적화(赤禍) the Red peril; the Red scare.

적확(的確) exactness; precision; accuracy; infallibility／~하다 (be) precise; accurate; exact; infallible／~한 증거 a positive proof.

적회(積懷) pent-up emotion.

적흑색(赤黑色) a reddish black [color].

적히다 be recorded; be put on record; be written down／역사에 적혀 있다 be recorded in history.

전(田) a field; a farm.

전(前) 《앞》 the front 《사람의》 the presence 《편지 따위에서》 Dear; Sir 《부사적》 before; till; to; under; ago 《과거》 the past; the last time／~ 주소 the one's former address.

전(煎) grilled food／생선 ~을 부치다 grill fish.

전(廛) a store; a shop; a stall.

전(篆) seal characters.

전(錢) 《돈》 money; a coin 《단위》 the hundredth part of one won／동~ a copper [coin, piece].

전-(全) all; whole; entire; total; complete／~국민 the whole nation／~세계 the whole world.

-전(傳) 《전기》 a life; a biography; a chronicle／위인~ the lives of great men.

-전(殿) a hall; a palace; a sanctum／북마~ an abode of demons; pandemonium.

-전(戰) a war; a battle 《경기의》 a game; a match／근대~ modern warfare／시가~ street fighting／육박~ a hand-to-hand fight.

전가(轉嫁) 《재혼》 a second marriage; remarriage 《죄·책임의》 imputation／~하다 《재혼하다》 marry again; remarry 《책임 따위를》 impute (a crime to a person); shift (on).

전가(田家) a farm house; a rural cottage.

전가(傳家) ~하다 pass on one's house to one's son; transfer the headship of a house to one's son／~지보(之寶) an heirloom.

전각(殿閣) a royal palace.

전각(前脚) forelegs.

전간(癲癇) 《의》 epilepsy／~을 일으키다 have an epileptic fit.

전갈(全蠍) 《동》 a scorpion／~좌《천》 the Scorpion.

전갈(傳喝) a [verbal] message／~하다 give a [verbal] message; send[deliver] a [verbal] message.

전개(展開) unfolding; development; expansion 《군대의》 deployment／~하다 unfold; develop; evolve; spread out; unroll／신국면을 ~하다 take a new turn.

전거(典據) authority; source; reference／명백한 ~를 보이다 give chapter and verse.

전거(奠居) decision on one's place of residence／~하다 decide where to liver.

전거(轉居) removal; a change of abode [address]／~하다 remove; move; transfer one's residence (to)／~를 통지하다 notify change of address.

전거리(木) fagot; bunches of firewood twigs.

전격(電擊) 《충격》 an electric shock 《급습》 a lightning attack／~하다 attack rapidly／런던을 ~하다 make a lightning attack on London.

전경(全景) a complete view; a bird's-eye view; the whole view; a general view／서울의 ~을 보다 see the whole view of Seoul.

전경(前景) the front view; the foreground／그 사진의 ~에 옛다리가 있다 We see an old bridge in the foreground of the picture.

전고(典故) an authentic precedent.

전고(前古) ancient times; olden days.

전고(傳告) ~하다 tell; inform (of); report.

전곡(田穀) dry field grain[crop].

전곡(錢穀) money and grain.

전골 beef with vegetables cooked in casserole／~를 a casserole [pan].

전공(專攻) a specialty; a major; a special subject of study／~하다 study specially; make a speciality (of)／~ 과목 a subject of special study.

전공(戰功) military merit; distinguished war services／~을 세우다 distinguish oneself in war; render distinguished military services.

전공(前功) a former merit; past services.

전공(電工) an electrician; an electrical engineer.

전과(前科) a previous conviction; a criminal record／그는 ~가 있다 He has been previously convicted／~자 an ex

·convict; a former convict. ぜんか
전과(戰果) war results; military achievements／～를 확대하다 improve the fruit of [a] battle. ぜんか
전과(轉科) change of one's major study; change of one's service branch in the army／～하다 change one's course (to).
전관(前官) one's former post. ぜんかん
전관(專管) exclusive jurisdiction[management]／～하다 have exclusive jurisdiction (over); have power (over). せんかん
전광(電光) electric light; a bolt; [a flash of] lightning／～을 내다 emit electric sparks. でんこう
전광(顚狂) lunacy; madness; insanity. てんかんときちがい
전교(轉交) 《물건을》 delivery[transfer] through a person 《편지를》 sending (a letter) in care of a person／～로 편지를 보내다 address a letter in care of (a person).
전교(全校) the whole school／～생 all the students of a school; the whole student body. ぜんこう
전구(電球) an electric bulb; a light bulb ／40와트의 ～ a 40-watt bulb／끊어진 ～ a burnt-out light bulb／백열 ～ a incandescent bulb. でんきゅう
전구(前驅) a forerunner; a precursor; an outrider; the van; the vanguard. ぜんく
전국(全─) undiluted liquor[soysauce]／～의 pure; undiluted／～ 간장 pure soysauce／～ 술 raw spirit.
전국(全局) the whole aspect[field] (of affairs); the general situation; the general state (of affairs)／～을 살피다 take in the general situation. ぜんきょく
전국(全國) the whole country[nation]／～의 nation-wide; national／～에 all over the country; throughout the nation／～에서 모이다 come together from all over the country／～적으로 on a national scale; all over the country; across[throughout] the nation. ぜんこく
전국(戰國) a country at war; a country in civil war. せんこく
전국(戰局) the war situation; the state [aspect] of the war; the tide of war／～이 호전되다 the tide of war turns in one's favor. せんきょく
전군(全軍) the whole[entire] army[force]／～ 지휘관 a commander-in-chief. ぜんぐん
전권(全權) plenary[absolute] power[authority]; plenipotentiary powers／～을 장악하다 have full powers (over)／～ 대사[공사] an ambassador[a minister] plenipotentiary. ぜんけん
전권(專權) an exclusive right; supreme power; arbitrary power／～하다 exercise [wield] axclusive right. せんけん

전권(全卷) the whole book; the entire volume (영화의) the whole reel／～을 통하여 from cover to cover; throught the book. ぜんかん
전극(電極) an electrode; a pole (양극) positive 《음극》 negative. でんきょく
전근(轉勤) transference (to another office)／～하다 be[get] transferred to (another office)／부산 지점으로 ～ 명령을 받다 be transferred to the Busan branch. てんきん
전근(轉筋) a cramp. てんきん
전기(前記) ～의 above-mentioned; foregoing; said; a forementioned／～의 금액 the said sum／～의 장소에 이전하다 move to the above address. ぜんき
전기(前期) the former term; the first term; the previous term／～ 결산 settlement for the first half year／～ 국회 the last session of the Congress. ぜんき
전기(電氣) electricity／～의 electric; electrical／～를 일으키다 generate electricity／～ 공학 electrical engineering／～ 시계 an electric clock／～ 계산기 an electric calculator[computer]. でんき
전기(電機) electrical machinery and appliances／～ 공업 electrical machinery industry／～ 회사 an electrical manufacturing[supply] company. でんき
전기(傳記) a life; a biography／～ 문학 a biographical literature／～ 작가 a biographer. でんき
전기(轉機) a turning point／…을 ～로 하여 with … as a turning point. てんき
전기(轉記) posting／～하다 post (an item) ／대장에 ～하다 post (an item) in the ledger. てんき
전기(戰記) a record[an account] of war; a military history. せんき
전기(戰機) the time for battle; a war situation／～가 무르익었다 The time is ripe for a battle. せんき
전기 소설(傳奇小說) a novel; a romance. でんきしょうせつ
전나귀 《동》 a lame[limping] ass[donkey].
전나무 《식》 a fir tree. もみ
전날(前─) 《지난날》 the other day (그 전날) the preceding day／～ 말씀드린 바와 같이 as I informed you the other day. ぜんじつ
전남편(前男便) a former husband; one's ex-husband. まえのおっと
전납(前納) prepayment／～하다 pay in advance; prepay. ぜんのう
전납(全納) payment in full; full payment／～하다 pay in full.
전내기(全─) undiluted wine; unwatered [raw] sool; pure liquor.
전내기(廛─) 《팔림 물건》 cheap[coarse, poor, plain] articles[goods].
전년(前年) the previous year; the years before (작년) last year／～ 여름 in the previous summer. ぜんねん
전념(專念) close attention; concentration

of mind; undivided attention/~하다 give[devote] oneself to; be engrossed [be absorbed] in. せんねん

**전뇌(前腦)** 【해】 the forebrain; the prosencephalon.

**전능(全能)** omnipotence/~의 omnipotent; almighty; all-powerful/~의 신 the Almighty [God]; the Omnipotent. ぜんのう

**전다(煎茶)** boiling tea/~하다 boil tea.

**전단(傳單)** a leaflet; a handbill.

**전단(戰端)** the cause of war; the opening of hostilities; hostile operations/~을 열다 open hostilities. せんたん

**전단(專斷)** arbitrary decision; arbitrariness/~하다 act arbitrarily/~적 arbitrary/~적으로 arbitrarily; at one's own discretion; on one's own authority. せんだん

**전달(前一)** 《전의 달》 the previous[preceding] month 《지난 달》 last month; ultimo(略: ult). せんげつ

**전달(傳達)** delivery; transmission; conveyance/~하다 transmit; convey; communicate; deliver; notify/명령을 ~하다 serve (a person) with an order/음향의 ~ travelling of sound. でんたつ

**전담(全擔)** ~하다 take the whole responsibility/~하다 take full charge of/비용을 ~하다 be charged with the whole expenses. ぜんぶたんとうすること

**전담(專擔)** ~하다 take[be in] sole charge of. ひとりでたんとうすること

**전답(田畓)** farms; fields; dry fields and paddy fields. はたけとすいでん

**전당(典當)** pawn; pledge/~잡다 take (a thing) in pawn; hold in pledge/~잡히다 pawn; pledge; give (a thing) in pawn/~포 a pawn-shop/~표 a pawn-ticket/~물 an article in pawn; a pawned article/~물을 찾다 redeem (a thing) in pledge; take (a thing) out of pawn/~에 잡혀 있다 be in pop《영·속》 in hock《미·속》. てんとう

**전당(殿堂)** a hall 《궁성》 a palace 《신전·사당》 a tabernacle; a shrine; a temple; a sanctuary でんとう

**전대(戰隊)** a [naval] squadron; a battle corps/수뢰 ~ a torpedo boat flotilla.

**전대(纏帶)** a knapsack.

**전대(轉貸)** sublease; underlease/~하다 sublease; sublet/~인 a sublessor/집을 ~하다 sublet a house. てんたい

**전대(前代)** the predecessor [in the family line]; the former[last] generation; former ages/이것은 ~ 미문의 일이다 We have never heard of this before. ぜんだい

**전대야** a brimmed wash basin.

**전도(前途)** future; prospects; an outlook 《여정》 the journey before one; the distance to cover/우리의 ~는 다난하다 Our future is full of difficulties. ぜんと

**전도(前導)** leading the way; guidance/~하다 guide; lead. ぜんどう

**전도(傳道)** missionary work; preaching; evangelism; propagandism/~하다 preach the gospel; engage in mission work; evangelize/~사 an evangelist; a preacher; a propagandist 《선교사》 a missionary/~ 부인 a woman preacher; a missionary/기독교를 ~하다 engage in Christian mission work. でんどう

**전도(顚倒)** inversion; turning upside down; an upset; reversal; upsetting/~하다 overturn; invert; reverse; upset; turn over[upside down]; 《정신이》 lose one's head. てんとう

**전도(全圖)** a complete map[drawing]/세계 ~ the world atlas.

**전도(傳導)** 【물】 《열·전기 따위의》 conduction 《소리·빛 따위의》 transmission/~하다 conduct; transmit/~체 a conductor (of heat or electricity)/~[율] conductivity. でんどう

**전도(奠都)** the establishment of the capital city/~하다 establish[set up] the capital. てんと

**전동(箭筒)** a quiver for arrows. やづつ

**전동기(電動機)** an electromotor; an electric motor/직류 ~ a direct current motor. でんどうき

**전동자(電動子)** an armature. でんどうし

**전두(前頭)** 【해】 the sinciput/~부(部) the front/~골 the frontal bone/~엽(葉) the frontal lobe. ぜんとう

**전등(全等)** equality; identity/~하다 (be) equal; identical (with). まったくおなじ

**전등(電燈)** an electric light[lamp]/그는 ~을 켜 놓은 채 잠이 들었다 He went asleep with the light on. でんとう

**전락(轉落)** a fall; downfall; degradation 《주식》 drop; slump/~하다 fall; degrade; have a setback/400원으로 ~하다 fall[slump] to 400 won. てんらく

**전란(戰亂)** wars; hostilities; disturbances/~의 현장 the scene of war. せんらん

**전람(展覽)** exhibition; show; display/~하다 exhibit/훌륭한 그림이 ~되어 있다 Fine pictures are on show./~회 an exhibition; a show. てんらん

**전래(傳來)** transmission 《전승》; introduction 《외래》/~하다 be transmitted 《전승하다》 be handed down (from father to son); be introduced [from abroad into Korea]. でんらい

**전략(戰略)** strategy; stratagem 《전술》 tactics/~가 a strategist/~적 strategic/~상 strategically/~으로 이기다 outgeneral; outmaneuver. せんりゃく

**전략(前略)** the preceding passages omitted; the preface omitted/~하다 omit the preface. ぜんりゃく

**전량(錢糧)** money and provisions. せんこく

**전력(全力)** all one's power[strength, might]/~을 다하여 with all one's might; to the best of one's ability/~을 다

**전력**(全力) concentration of one's energies[powers]/~하다 concentrate one's energies[one's powers] on (the object); devote oneself to; throw the whole of oneself into (one's work). せんねんすること

**전력**(電力) electric power/~계 a watt-meter/~ 회사[부족] an electric power company[shortage]. でんりょく

**전력**(戰歷) war experience; a war career [record]; a battle record. せんれき

**전력**(戰力) fighting power/~ 유지[상실] the maintenance[loss] of war potential. せんりょく

**전령**(電鈴) an electric bell. でんれい

**전령**(傳令) 《사람》 a messenger; an orderly 《명령》 an official message/~하다 carry orders to/~을 보내다 send a message; send an orderly. でんれい

**전례**(典禮) a ceremony. てんれい

**전례**(前例) a precedent; a former example/~없는 unprecedented/~를 깨뜨리다 break the precedent 《관례를》 make a departure from the usual custom. ぜんれい

**전로**(前路) the way ahead. ぜんと

**전류**(電流) an electric[a voltaic] current; a flow of electricity/~의 galvanic; voltaic/~를 통하다 turn on electricity /~를 끊다 cut[shut] off the current; switch off. でんりゅう

**전리**(電離) 〖물〗 electrolytic dissociation; ionization/~하다 ionize/~층(層) ionosphere; an ionization layer. でんり

**전리품**(戰利品) a trophy 《약탈품》 booty; spoils of war. せんりひん

**전립선**(前立腺) 〖해〗 the prostate[gland]. ぜんりつせん

**전말**(顚末) 《명세》 the particulars; the details 《사실》 the facts 《설명》 an account 《사정》 the circumstances 《경과》 the course of events/~을 상세히 보고하다 report all the circumstances in detail. てんまつ

**전망**(展望) a view; a prospect; an outlook; an observation/~하다 have a view of/앞으로의 ~ the future prospect/~대 an observatory; a look out platform/~차 an observation car. てんぼう

**전매**(轉賣) resale; liquidation/~하다 resell.

**전매**(專賣) monopoly; monopolization/ ~하다 monopolize; make a monopoly of /~청 the office of Monopoly; the Monopoly Bureau/~품 monopoly goods; a patented article. せんばい

**전매 특허**(專賣特許) a patent/~를 인가하다 grant a patent/~권 patent rights /~품 a patented article/~인 a patentee. せんばいとっきょ

**전면**(前面) the front; the frontage 《전경》 the foreground/~의 front; frontal; in [the] front; fore/~을 돌로 장식하다 be fronted with stone/~ 저항 《항공》 head resistance. ぜんめん

**전면**(全面) the whole[entire] surface/~적 개정 a sweeping change[revision]/~ 파업 an overall strike/~ 전쟁 an all-out war; the global war. ぜんめん

**전멸**(全滅) annihilation; complete[total] destruction/~하다 be annihilated; be completely[totally] destroyed; be wiped out/그 도시는 ~했다 The whole town was wiped out. せんめつ

**전모**(全貌) a full portrait; the entire picture; the whole aspect; the whole affair/그것으로 사건의 ~가 밝혀졌다 It throws light upon the whole affair. ぜんぼう

**전몰**(戰沒) death on the battle field/~ 하다 die[fall] fighting; die[be killed, fall] in battle/ ~ 용사 the fallen heroes/~자 the war dead. せんぼつ

**전무**(全無) total nonexistence; total lack; total absence/~하다 be wholly lacking [wanting]. まったくないこと

**전무**(專務) special duty; principal business/여객 ~ a guard〈영〉; a conductor〈미〉. せんむ

**전무식**(全無識) ignorance; complete illiteracy/~쟁이 an ignoramus.

**전무 후무**(前無後無) ~하다 be the first and [probably] the last; be unprecedented and at the same time will not be seen/~의 대발견 an epoch-making discovery.

**전문**(全文) the full text/~을 인용하다 quote a whole sentence/조약의 ~ the full text of a treaty. ぜんぶん

**전문**(前文) the above[foregoing] sentence[statement]; the preamble(조약문 따위의). ぜんぶん

**전문**(前門) the front gate. ぜんもん

**전문**(電文) a telegram; a cablegram; the message[text] of a telegram. でんぶん

**전문**(專門) a specialty; a special subject of study; a line/~하다 specialize (in); major (in)〈미〉/~가 a specialist; a professional [man]; an expert(전체); a technical expert(개인)/~ 교육 a professional[technical] education/~ 학교 a college; a professional school/~ 지식 expert[technical] knowledge/~의 (醫) a medical specialist/~ 밖이나 be not in one's line; be off one's beat/~화하다 specialize/그것은 나의 ~이 아니다 It is out of my field. せんもん

**전문**(傳聞) ~하다 learn by hearsay; be told; hear [from others]/~한 바에 의하면 from what I hear; according to a rumour/~ 증거 hearsay evidence.

**전문**(錢文) money. おかね

**전물**(奠物) offerings [to God, to Buddha]. しんぶつにそなえるくもつ

**전반**(前半) the first half/~기 the first

전반(半年)/5회째의 ~ the first half of the fifth inning. ぜんはん
전반(全般) the whole/~의 whole; general/사회 ~ the world at large/~적 general; overall/국민 ~ the people at large. ぜんぱん
전반사(全反射) 〖물〗 total reflection. ぜんはんしゃ
전발(電髮) a permanent [wave]. でんぱつ
전방(前方) the front/~의 front; forward/~ 지휘소 a command post(略：CP)/100미터 ~에 a hundred metres ahead/~ 기지 〖군〗 an advanced base. ぜんぽう
전방(廛房) a shop; a store/미〉. てんぽ
전배(前杯) earlier[beforehand] drinking.
전번(前番) the other day; last time/~에 last time; before this; previously; sometimes ago/~에 만났을 때 when I saw him last. このまえ
전범(戰犯) 〖법죄〗 war crimes 《범죄자》 a war criminal/~ 용의자 a suspected war criminal. せんぱん
전법(戰法) tactics; strategy; a plan of campaign. せんぽう
전벽(全壁) 〖건〗 a blind[blank] wall. ぜんたいがかべのこと
전변(轉變) mutation; changefulness/~하다 change; vary; mutate/~무상한 ever-changing; evanescent; changeful. てんぺん
전별(餞別) a farewell; a send-off/~하다 give a send-off; send off; see off/~사 a farewell address[speech]. せんべつ
전병(煎餠) a fried rice-cake. せんべい
전병사(戰病死) death from a disease contracted at the front/~하다 die from a disease contracted at the front.
전보(塡補) supplement; complement; filling up; making up/~하다 supplement; complement; fill; make up (a deficiency). てんぽ
전보(戰報) war intelligence[news]; a war report.
전보(電報) a telegram; a wire; a cablegram(해외); 《무전》 a wireless [telegram]; a radiogram/~하다, 치다 telegraph; send telegram; wire; cable/~ 용지 a telegram form. でんぽう
전복(顚覆) overturning; overthrowing (a government); capsize (a boat)/~하다 overturn; overthrow 《뒤집히다》 overturn; capsize/열차를 ~시키다 overturn a train. てんぷく
전복(全鰒) 〖어〗 an ear-shell; an abalone; an ormer; a sea-ear/~쌈 a dish of sliced abalone wrapped with pinenuts. あわび
전봇대(電報─) a telegraph pole; an telectric pole. でんしんばしら
전부(全部) all; the whole 《부사적》 all; in full; in its entirety; altogether; in all; all told/대금을 ~치르다 pay purchase-money in all. ぜんぶ

전부(前部) the front part; the fore/~ 배의 ~ the forepart of a ship. ぜんぶ
전부(前夫) one's former husband/~의 자식 a child by her former husband. ぜんぶ
전분(澱粉) starch; farina; dextrin[e]/~질 starchiness. でんぷん
전비(戰費) war expenditure[funds]; the cost of war. せんぴ
전비(戰備) war[warlike] preparations; preparations for war; war preparedness/~를 갖추다 prepare for war; make warlike preparations. せんぴ
전비(前非) one's past folly[error, sin]; former evil deeds[ways]/~를 뉘우치다 see the error of one's way.
전사(戰士) a soldier; a fighter; a champion/무명~의 묘 the tomb of an unknown soldier. せんし
전사(戰死) death in battle[action]/~하다 be killed in action; die[fall] in battle; die fighting/~자 the war dead. せんし
전사(轉寫) transcription; copying/~하다 transcribe; copy from/~기 a transcriber. てんしゃ
전사(戰史) a military history. せんし
전삭(前朔) past[last] month. ぜんげつ
전상(戰傷) a war wound/~자 the[a] war wounded. せんしょう
전색맹(全色盲) total color blindness[의] achromatopsia. ぜんしきもう
전생(前生) 〖종〗 a previous state of existence; a former life/~에서부터의 약속 predestination; one's fate. ぜんせ
전생애(全生涯) one's whole life/~를 통하여 throughout[in all] one's life; from cradle to grave. ぜんしょうがい
전서(篆書) a seal character; writing in seal characters. てんしょ
전서(全書) a complete work[book, collection]/백과 ~ an encyclopedia/법령 ~ a statute book. ぜんしょ
전서구(傳書鳩) 〖조〗 a carrier[homing] pigeon. でんしょばと
전선(電線) a telegraph[wire] line; an electric wire; a cable(해저의). でんせん
전선(戰船) a warship. いくさぶね
전선(戰線) the fighting[firing] line; the front[battle] line/적의 ~을 돌파하다 break through the enemy line/적의 ~ 후방에 behind the enemy lines. せんせん
전선(全線) the whole line; all lines.
전선(前線) ①〈일선〉 the front[foremost] line/~ 기지 an advanced base; an outpost/병력을 ~으로 보내다 send troops up to the front line ②〈기상〉 a front/한랭[온난] ~ a cold[warm] front. ぜんせん
전설(傳說) a legend; a tradition/~적인 물에 불과하다 be nothing but a legendary person. でんせつ
전설(前說) one's previous view[opinion,

**전성(展性)** 《물》 malleability／～이 풍부하다 be malleable. てんせい

**전성(全盛)** the height of prosperity／～하다 attain the highest stage of prosperity; be at its full glory／～기[시대] the golden age; the palmy days; *one's* best days(사람의). ぜんせい

**전세(田稅)** a land tax; a farm tax. はたけのぜいきん

**전세(前世)** ①(전대) former time; former generations; past ages; prehistoric ages ②a former life. ぜんせ

**전세(傳貰)** a contract form of lending out something for a certain amount of money which is to be paid back at the end of the fixed term. ちんがり

**전세(戰勢)** the progress of a battle[campaign]; the war situation／～가 불리하다 The war is not going in our favour. せんそうのけいせい

**전세계(全世界)** the whole world／～에 all over[throughout] the world. ぜんせかい

**전세계(前世界)** a prehistoric age; the world before now[this]. ぜんせかい

**전세기(前世紀)** the former[last] century. ぜんせいき

**전소(全燒)** total destruction [by fire]／～하다 be totally[entirely, completely] destroyed by fire; be burnt down [to the ground]. ぜんしょう

**전속(專屬)** ～의 exclusively attached to／～하다 belong exclusively to; be under the exclusive control of／BBS ～ 악단 an orchestra attached to BBS. せんぞく

**전속(轉屬)** transference／～하다 be transferred to. てんぞく

**전속력(全速力)** full speed[steam]／자동차는 ～으로 달리기 시작했다 The car began to run at full speed. ぜんそくりょく

**전손(全損)** 《경》 a total loss／～ 담보 security for total loss only(T. L. O.). ぜんそん

**전송(餞送)** seeing (*a person*) off; a send-off／～하다 see (*a person*) off; give a send-off. せんべつをしておくること

**전송(轉送)** forwarding; transmission／～하다 forward; transmit／저에게 오는 편지는 이 주소로 ～해 주시요 Will you please forward the letters for me to this address. てんそう

**전송(電送)** electrical transmission／～하다 telegraph; wire (*a message*); transmit／사진을 ～하다 transmit a picture by wireless; radio a photo. でんそう

**전수(傳受)** receipt; acceptence／～하다 receive; accept; be given 《비결 따위를》 be instructed; be taught; be initiated. でんじゅ

**전수(傳授)** instruction; initiation／～하다 give instruction (*in*); initiate (*a person*) into. でんじゅ

**전수(全數)** the whole; the total number [figure]; unanimity. ぜんすう

**전수(專修)** specialization／～하다 specialize (*in*)／～과 a special course; major (*in*)〈미〉; specialize (*in*). せんしゅう

**전술(前述)** ～의 aforesaid; above-[previous-]mentioned; foregoing; preceding. ぜんじゅつ

**전술(戰術)** tactics; the art of war／～가 a tactician. ぜんじゅつ

**전습(傳習)** learning／～하다 learn; be instructed (*in*). でんしゅう

**전습(前習)** *one's* former habits.

**전습(傳習)** ～하다 transmit; descend.

**전승(全勝)** a complete victory／～하다 win[gain] a complete victory (경기에서) be unbeaten. ぜんしょう

**전승(傳承)** transmission; handing down／～하다 hand down; transmit from generation to generation. でんしょう

**전승(戰勝)** a victory; a triumph／～하다 win[gain] a victory; be victorious／～을 빌다[축하하다] pray for[celebrate] victory. せんしょう

**전시(全市)** the whole city. ぜんし

**전시(展示)** exhibition; display／～하다 exhibit (*a thing*); put (*a thing*) on display[view]／여러 가지 상품이 ～되어 있다 A variety of things are displayed for sale. てんじ

**전시(戰時)** war-time[-period]; time of war／～ 산업 the wartime industry／～경기(景氣) a war boom. せんじ

**전시대(前時代)** former ages[times]; past generations. ぜんじだい

**전신(全身)** the whole body／～에 all over the body; from head to foot／～의 힘 all *one's* strength／～ 사진 a full-length portrait／～ 불수 total paralysis／～이 땀투성이가 되었다 be all in a sweat／～ 운동 an exercise of the whole body. ぜんしん

**전신(前身)** *one's* former self; *one's* past life[history]; the predecessor (of *a school*). ぜんしん

**전신(電信)** telegraph 《해외》 wire cable; a cablegram／～으로 by telegraph; by cable／～국[기] a telegraph office[instrument]／～이 불통됐다 Telegraphic communication was interrupted. でんしん

**전실(前室)** *one's* former wife; *one's* divorced wife／～ 자식 a child born of *one's* former wife. ぜんさいの敬語

**전심(全心)** *one's* whole heart[soul]／～을 기울여 with *one's* whole heart[soul].

**전심(專心)** concentration of mind; undivided attention; the whole heart／～하다 devote[bend] *oneself* (*to*); put heart and soul (*into*). せんしん

**전아(典雅)** elegance／～하다 (be) graceful; refined; elegant. てんが

**전압(電壓)** voltage; electric pressure／～

전액(全額) the total[full] amount; the sum total/~보험 full insurance/~지불 payment in full; full payment/~담보 full coverage. ぜんがん

전야(田野) fields; farms. でんや

전야(前夜) the previous night; the night before; an eve (of); last night(간밤)/크리스마스 ~ Christmas Eve/결혼 ~ the night before the wedding/~제(祭) an eve. ぜんや

전약(前約) a previous engagement[appointment]. ぜんやく

전어(錢魚) 〖어〗 a gizzard[hickory] shad; Konosirus Punctatus(학명). このしろ

전언(傳言) a message; word/~하다 send (a person) word; bring (a person) word (전언을 전해 주다)/저 사람에게 ~이 있다 I have a message for him. でんごん

전언(前言) one's previous remarks[words, statement]/~을 취소하다 withdraw[take back] one's words. ぜんげん

전업(轉業) change of business[trade, occupation, employment]/~하다 change one's business; change from one employment to another. てんぎょう

전업(專業) a special[principal] occupation; speciality/…을 ~으로 하다 make a speciality of; specialize in. せんぎょう

전역(戰役) a war; a battle; a campaign. せんえき

전역(全譯) a complete translation/~하다 translate (a book) in full[completely].

전역(戰域) a war zone; a battle area; a war area; a range of [military] operations; a theater of war.

전연(全然) (아주) entirely; completely; wholly; altogether (조금도)[not] at all/나는 그 일에 대해서는 ~ 모른다 I have not the remotest[slightest] idea of it. ぜんぜん

전열(電熱) electric heat/~기 an electric heater(난방용); an electric [cooking] range[stove](요리용). でんねつ

전열(前列) the front rank[row]/~ 왼편에서 다섯 번째 the fifth from the left in the front row[rank]. ぜんれつ

전열(戰列) a battle line; a line of battle/~을 이탈하다 leave the line of battle. せんれつ

전염(傳染) (접촉에 의한) contagion; communication (간접의) infection/ ~하다 be contagious; be communicated/~성의 contagious; infectious; catching (유행성의) epidemic/ ~병 an infectious [a contagious] disease; an epidemic/~병 환자 a case of infectious disease/성홍열은 ~한다 Scarlet fever is contagious. でんせん

전염병(傳染病) an infectious[a contagious] disease; an epidemic/~ 연구소 the Infectious Diseases Research Laboratory[Institute]. でんせんびょう

전와(轉訛) corruption (of a word)/~하다 be corrupted from[into]. てんか

전용(專用) exclusive use; private use/~하다 use solely; use exclusively; be for private use/~의 private; exclusive/대통령의 ~ 비행기 a presidential plane. せんよう

전용(轉用) diversion/~하다 use for another purpose; divert to. てんよう

전우(戰友) a comrade[-at-arms]; a companion[-brother-]-in-arms. せんゆう

전운(戰雲) a war-cloud. せんうん

전원(田園) farms; fields; fields and gardens (시골) the country; rural district (교외) suburbs/~ 생활 rural life. でんえん

전원(電源) sources of [hydraulic] electricity/~ 개발 development of power resources. でんげん

전원(全院) the whole House/~ 위원회 the committee of the whole House. ぜんいん

전원(全員) all [the] members; the entire staff (배 따위의) the whole crew; all hands/ ~ 출동하다 be present in full force. ぜんいん

전월(前月) last month. ぜんげつ

전위(前衛) 〖군〗 an advance guard; a vanguard (정구의) a forward[net] player (축구의) a forward/~ 부대 the advance guards. ぜんえい

전위(傳位) abdication of the throne; demise of the crown/~하다 abdicate[demise] the throne.

전위(電位) electric potential/~계 an electrometer/양[음] ~ positive[negative] potential/~ 강하 a potential drop/ ~ 차(差) a potential difference. でんい

전유(專有) ~하다 monopolize; take sole possession of/~권 an exclusive right; monopoly. せんゆう

전유(全乳) pure milk.

전율(戰慄) ~하다 shudder (at); shiver with fright/~할 만한 horrible; shocking; bloodcurdling/~시키다 make (a person) shudder. せんりつ

전음(全音) 〖음〗 a whole tone/~정 a whole step/~계 the diatonic scale; the whole gamut. ぜんおん

전음(顫音) 〖음〗 trill.

전의(專意) concentration of mind; undivided attention/~하다 devote oneself to; put one's heart and soul into; apply oneself closely to. せんい

전의(轉義) a derivative meaning (of a word); a figurative meaning. てんぎ

전의(戰意) an intention to fight; hostile intention; a fighting spirit/~가 없다 have no fighting spirit/~를 잃다 lose one's fighting spirit. せんい

전의(銓議) (조사) inquiry; examination; investigation (심의) consideration; deliberation/~하다 inquire into; examine; investigate; consider; deliberate

**전인(前人)** a predecessor; former people (옛 사람들)／～ 미답의 삼림 a trackless [virgin] forest. ぜんじん

**전일(前日)** the preceding day; the day before／출발의 ～ the day before one's departure. ぜんじつ

**전일(專一)** the whole mind; concentration／～하다 concentrate one's whole mind (upon); devote oneself (to). せんいち

**전일제(全日制)** a full-time system. ぜんにちせい

**전임(專任)** full-time service[employment]; full service／～의 fulltime; whole-time; regular／～ 강사 a full-time instructor／～ 교사 a full-time teacher. せんにん

**전임(前任)** 《사람》 one's predecessor; a former official 《자리》 the post previously occupied; a previous appointment／～자 a predecessor in office／～지 one's former[last] post. ぜんにん

**전임(轉任)** transference／～하다 be transferred (to); be removed to another post／서울에서 뉴욕으로 ～ 명령받다 be transferred from Seoul to New York／～지 one's new post. てんにん

**전입(轉入)** moving in／～하다 move into [in]／～생 a student[pupil] transferred from another school／～ 신고 a moving-in notice. てんにゅう

**전자(前者)** the former; the first／～와 후자 the former and the latter. ぜんしゃ

**전자(篆字)** a seal character. てんじ

**전자(專恣)** ～하다 abuse; usurp; take high-handed measures.

**전자(電子)** 【물】 an electron／～ 학설 the electron theory／～가(價) [electron] valency／～ 공학 electronics／～ 현미경 an electron microscope／～ 음악 electronic [electrophonic] music. でんし

**전자(電磁)** 엑~기(氣) electromagnetism／～석[철] an electromagnet／～파 electromagnetic waves. でんじ

**전작(田作)** dry field farming 《농작물》 farm crops; dry field crops. ぜんさく

**전작(前酌)** wine previously taken; previous intoxication／나는 ～이 있다 I have already taken some [cups of] liquor.

**전장(全長)** the total length; an over-all length／～ 5피트다 have an oven-all length of five feet. ぜんちょう

**전장(田庄)** one's farmstead; fields in one's possession.

**전장(戰場)** a battlefield; a field of battle; the front; a battleground／～의 이슬로 사라지다 be killed in battle; fall on the field of battle. せんじょう

**전장(電場)** 【물】 an electric field. でんば

**전장(前檣)** the foremast (배의).

**전장(前章)** the preceding[foregoing] chapter; the last[prior] chapter; the chapter before.

**전장(前場)** 【경】《증권》 the morning stock market session; the first call. ぜんば

**전재(轉載)** reprinting; transcription; reproduction／～하다 reprint from; reproduce from; take from／미국 잡지에서 ～하다 reprint [the article] from an American magazine. てんさい

**전재(戰災)** war damage／～를 입다 suffer war damages／～ 도시 a war-ravaged city／～민(民) war refugees[victims]. せんさい

**전쟁(戰爭)** 《전란》 a war; a warfare; hostilities 《전투》 a fight; a battle／～하다 go to war with; make[wage] war against 《전투》 fight (with, against); fight a battle／～에 대비하다 prepare for defense／～ 고아 a war orphan／～에 이기다 win a war; be victorious／～에 지다 lose a war. せんそう

**전적(戰跡)** an old battlefield; the scene of a former battle; vestiges of war. せんせき

**전적(轉籍)** ～하다 transfer one's domicile; enter another's family register. てんせき

**전적(全的)** total; whole; entire／～인 지지 a full support／～으로 동의하다 give blanket consent／～인 협력 whole-hearted co-operation. ぜんてき

**전적(戰績)** military achievments; a war record 《경기상의》 results; a record; a score／빛나는 ～ brilliant achievements; a splendid record. せんせき

**전적(典籍)** books; records ⇨서적(書籍).

**전전(輾轉)** ～하다 roll about／～ 불매(不寐)하다 be sleepless rolling about in the bed. てんてん

**전전(轉戰)** ～하다 fight in one place after another; participate[take park] in various battles. てんせん

**전전(轉轉)** ～하다 《임자를 바꾸어》 pass through many hands; change hands many times 《헤매다》 wander from place to place; roam about 《구르다》 roll; go rolling／직업을 바꾸어 ～하다 change from job to job. てんてん

**전전(戰前)** ～의 prewar; ante-bellum(L); 《불교》 avant-guerre(F)／～파 the prewar generation. せんぜん

**전전 긍긍(戰戰兢兢)** ～하다 be panicstricken; be in great fear／스캔들이 폭로되지 않을까 하고 그는 ～하고 있다 He is in constant fear lest the scandal [should] come to light. せんせんきょうきょう

**전전일(前前日)** two days before 《그저께》 the day before yesterday.

**전절(前節)** the foregoing paragraph; the last[prior] paragraph.

**전정(前程)** the distance to be covered in one's travel; the way ahead; the journey before one. ぜんてい

**전정(前庭)** 《앞뜰》 a front garden; a front court[yard]. ぜんてい

**전정(前情)** old love; former affection; old friendship. きゅうじょう

**전정(剪定)** pruning; trimming／～하다 p-

**전제**(前提) 〖논〗 a premise／대〖소〗~〖논〗 a major[minor] premise／~ 조건 a precondition. ぜんてい

**전제**(專制) absolution; despotism; autocracy／~하다 be absolute; be despotic; be autocratic; be arbitrary; tyrannize; act the tyrant to[over]／~주의 absolutism; despotism. せんせい

**전조**(前兆) a sign; an omen; a symptom; a precursor.／비가 올 ~ a sign of rain／좋은[나쁜] ~ a good[bad, an evil] omen. ぜんちょう

**전조**(前條) the preceding article[paragraph]. ぜんじょう

**전조**(前朝) a former dynasty. ぜんちょう

**전조**(轉調) 〖음〗 transition; modulation. てんちょう

**전족**(纏足) foot-binding／~하다 bind one's feet; have one's feet bound. てんそく

**전죄**(前罪) a previous crime[conviction, sin]. ぜんざい

**전주**(田主) the owner of a fields.

**전주**(典主) a pawnbroker. てんしゅ

**전주**(電柱) an electric pole; telegraph[telephone] poles／~ 광고 a poster on a telegraph pole. でんしんばしら

**전주**(電鑄) 〖화〗 electrotyping／~하다 electrotype.

**전주**(錢主) a financier; a capitalist／~가 되다 finance (an enterprise). しほんぬし

**전주**(轉住) removal; migration／~하다 move to; migrate to. てんじゅう

**전주**(前週) last week(지난 주일); the preceding week(그 전주)／~의 오늘 this day [last] week.

**전주**(前奏) 〖음〗 an overture; a prelude／세계 대전의 ~ a prelude to the World War. ぜんそう

**전중**(典重) courteousness／~하다 (be) gentle; well-be-haved[-mannered].

**전지**(田地) a farm [land]; rice-field; cultivated land; fields. でんち

**전지**(全紙) the whole[uncut] paper／그 기사로 ~를 메웠다 The paper is full of accounts of this affair. ぜん

**전지**(全知) omniscience／~의 all-knowing; omniscient／~ 전능의 신 Almighty God. ぜんち

**전지**(電池) an electric cell; a battery／~가 닳았다 The battery is run down.／~ 회로 a battery circuit. でんち

**전지**(戰地) the seat[theatre] of war; the front. せんち

**전지**(轉地) a change of air; a change of climate／~하다 go (to a place) for a change of air／진해로 ~하다 go to Chinhae for a change of air. てんち

**전지**(剪枝) lopping; trimming; pruning／~하다 lop; trim; prune.

**전직**(轉職) change of employment[occupation]／~하다 change one's occupation [employment]／실업계에서 문학계로 ~하다 leave business for literary work. てんしょく

**전직**(前職) one's former occupation[job]; the office[post] held previously; one's former office／~ 장관 an ex-minister. まえのしょくぎょう

**전진**(前進) an advance; a forward movement 《호령》 Forward!／~하다 advance; go[press] forward; go[push] ahead; make headway／~ 명령을 내리다 order [troops] to advance. ぜんしん

**전진**(戰陣) a battle-field; battle formation. せんじん

**전진**(戰塵) the dust of combat／~을 씻다 wash off the dust of combat. せんじん

**전질**(全帙) a complete set [of books].

**전집**(全集) one's complete collected works; a complete collection／디킨즈 ~ Dickens's Complete works／~물 a complete works series. ぜんしゅう

**전차**(電車) an electric car; a tramcar〈영〉; a streetcar〈미〉; a trolley car; an electric train／~타기에 편리하다 be convenient for electric cars／~ 정류장 a streetcar stop／~ 운전사 a motorman. でんしゃ

**전차**(前借) an advance／~하다 borrow[obtain] in advance／~금 money-borrowed in advance. ぜんしゃく

**전차**(轉借) subletting; sublease; subtenancy／~하다 borrow at second hand; sublet; sublease／~인 a sublessee; an undertenant; a subtenant. てんしゃく

**전차**(戰車) a [war] tank／중[경]~ a heavy[light] tank／~병 a tank man／~대 a tank corps[unit]／~포 a tank gun／대~포 an antitank gun／~호 an antitank trench; a tank trap. せんしゃ

**전착**(顚錯) ~하다 invert the order; put the cart before the horse.

**전채**(戰債) 〖경〗 war debt[s]; war bonds. ぜんさい

**전처**(前妻) one's former wife 《이혼한》 one's divorced wife／~ 소생의 자식 the child by one's former wife. ぜんさい

**전철**(前轍) ⁋~을 밟다 follow one's example; follow in the wake of another; tread in another's step; repeat the same failure [as…]. ぜんてつ

**전철**(轉轍) ~하다 switch; shunt／~기 points〈영〉; a switch〈미〉. てんてつ

**전철**(電鐵) an electric railway. でんてつ

**전첩**(戰捷) a victory／~하다 win a victory. せんしょう

**전체**(全體) 《전부》the whole／~의 whole; entire; general／~ 회의 a plenary session／~주의 totalitarianism／~적으로 generally; on the whole; in general. ぜんたい

**전초**(前哨) an outpost; an advanced post／~ 부대[군무] outpost troops[duty]／~전 a [patrol] skirmish; an outpost action／총선거의 ~전 a skirmish of the

**전축**(電蓄) an electric gramophone; a record player.

**전출**(轉出) efflux (*form*); 《직원의》 transfer/~하다 move out (*of*); 《직원이》 be transferred (to *a new post*)/방계 회사로 ~하다 to be transferred to a subsidiary company.

**전충**(塡充) filling; tamping/~하다 fill up tamp 《포화(飽和)》 saturate.

**전취**(戰取) win [a war]; achieve; gain.

**전치**(全治) complete cure[recovery]; full recovery/~하다 be completely cured[recovered]/상처가 ~되었다 The wound healed completely.

**전치사**(前置詞) 【언】 a preposition/이 동사에는 어떤 ~가 필요한가 What preposition is required after this verb?/~구 a prepositional phrase.

**전칙**(典則) a law; a rule.

**전칭**(全稱) 【논】 ¶ ~ 명제 a universal [proposition]/~ 판단 a universal judgement.

**전쾌**(全快) complete recovery; complete cure(전치)/~하다 recover [completely] get well; recover from *one's* illness ⇨ 전답.

**전택**(田宅) farm and house.

**전토**(田土) cultivated lands; fields.

**전토**(全土) the whole land[country, territory]/중국 ~ the whole of China; all over China.

**전통**(傳統) 《인습》 tradition; convention 《계승》 succession/~에 구애되지 않다 be bound by no tradition/오랜 ~ a time-honored tradition/~적인 문학 conventional literature.

**전통**(全通) the opening of the whole line [of a railroad, of a telephone, of a highway]/~하다 be opened (to *traffic*) all the way.

**전통**(全統) 《부사적》 entirely; on the whole ⇨온통.

**전투**(戰鬪) fighting; a fight; a battle; an action; hostilities/~하다 fight; battle; have a fight[battle]; engage in (*a battle*)/~ 행위 an act of hostility /~ 부대 a combat unit/~기 a fighter [plane].

**전파**(電波) 【물】an electric wave/~ 탐지기 a radiolocator; a radar〈미〉/~ 방해 jamming.

**전파**(傳播) spread; propagation; circulation; diffusion; dissemination/~하다 propagate; transmit; spread; disseminate; circulate/음향의 ~ propagation of sound.

**전판**(全一) all; the whole; the entire lot /~ 거짓말이다 It is a downright lie from start to finish. あますことなくぜんぶ

**전패**(戰敗) a defeat [in war]/~국(國) a defeated nation; a vanquished country.

**전패**(全敗) a complete defeat/~하다 be completely defeated (*in*); sustain a crushing defeat.

**전편**(全篇) the whole book[volume]/~을 통해서 from cover to cover; from title page to colophon.

**전편**(前篇) the first part[volume].

**전폐**(全廢) total abolition/~하다 abolish altogether; do away with/노예 제도의 ~ the abolition of slavery/~론 abolitionism.

**전폐**(前弊) old abuses. まえからのへいがい

**전포**(廛鋪) a store〈미〉; a shop〈영〉

**전폭**(全幅) the full width [of cloth];the whole piece [of cloth]/~적으로 지지하다 give (*a person*) full[whole-hearted] support.

**전표**(傳票) a chit; a slip 《약식의》 a ticket/~를 떼다 sign[give] a chit; issue a voucher/지불[수납] ~ a paying-out [a receiving] slip.

**전표**(錢票) a check; a cheque; a bill.

**전하**(電荷) 【물】 an electric charge.

**전하**(殿下) His[Her] Imperial[Royal] Highness.

**전하다**(傳一) ①《전달하다》convey; report; deliver; communicate; transmit/출석할 뜻을 ~ notify *one's* intention to be present ②《전수하다》teach; make known /제자에게 지식을 ~ impart knowledge to *one's* disciples ③《남겨 주다》hand down; leave; transmit ④《전도하다》transmit; conduct ⑤《도입하다》introduce (*into*).

**전학**(轉學) change[transfer] to another school/~하다 change *one's* school; remove from one school to another.

**전함**(戰艦) 【군】a battleship; a warship.

**전항**(前項) the preceding clause; the foregoing paragraph; 【수】 the antecedent.

**전해**(前一) the preceding[previous] year 《작년》last year.

**전해**(電解) 【물】 electrolysis/~하다 electrolyze/~의 electrolytic/~물 an electrolyte.

**전향**(轉向) ~하다 turn[swing] to; be converted to/~자 a convert/우익으로 ~하다 swing to the right.

**전혀**(全一) quite; totally; completely; utterly; wholly; entirely 《조금도 …않다》at all; in the least 《정말》truly; really/동정심이라고는 ~ 없다 He has not a particle of sympathy.

**전형**(典型) a type; a model; a pattern; a specimen/~적 한국인 a typical Korean.

**전형**(銓衡) choice; selection/~하다 select; make choice/~에 누락되다 be left out of selection/~ 위원[회] a screeni-

전호(前號) the preceding[last] number/~에서 계속되다 be continued from the last issue. ぜんごう

전호(前胡) 【식】 a kind of carrot; Anthriscus Sylvestris(학명). のだけ

전화(電話) a [tele]phone/공중 ~ a public telephone/~ 번호 a telephone number/~기 a [tele]phone/~ 번호부 a telephone directory/~가입자 telephone subscriber/~ 교환국 an exchange office; a central⟨미⟩/~ 교환수 a telephone operator[girl]/~를 걸다 ring up; phone (불러내다) ring up (자동식의) dial/~를 끊다 ring off [the telephone]; hang up the receiver. でんわ

전화(戰禍) the evils[afflictions, the dogs] of war; the horrors[disasters, ravages] of war/~를 입다 suffer the damages of war. せんか

전화(戰火) war fire; fire and sword.

전화(電化) electrification/~하다 electrify/철도의 ~ electrification of railways. でんか

전화(轉化) change; transformation/~하다 change; be transformed. てんか

전화 위복(轉禍爲福) ~하다 turn a misfortune into a blessing.

전환(轉換) conversion; switch-over 《주의·마음의》 diversion/~하다 convert; turn; divert; ventilate/노래를 불러서 기분을 ~하다 divert oneself in singing/~기(器) an electric switch. てんかん

전황(戰況) the progress of a battle; the war situation/~을 보고하다 report on the military situation. せんきょう

전황(錢荒) money distress; shortage of money; tight money-market/~하다 (be) short of money; pressed for funds. きんゆうのわるいこと

전회(前回) the last time[occasion]; (연속물의) the last installment. ぜんかい

전회(轉回) ~하다 revolve; rotate/180도의 ~ a turn of 180 degrees.

전횡(專橫) arbitrariness; despotism 《압제》 tyranny/~하다 act arbitrarily; tyrannize over. せんおう

전후(前後) order; sequence 《앞과 뒤》 front and rear; before and behind; in front and in the rear (때) before and[or] after (대개) about; or so; thereabouts/대전 ~ before and after the Great War/~의 관계 《문장의》 the context/~ 생각도 없이 regardless of the consequence; recklessly; thoughtlessly. ぜんご

전후(戰後) ~의 after the war; postwar; post-bellum(L); après guerre(F)/~의 한국 postwar Korea/~의 문제 postbellum questions/~파의 청년들 young men of the postwar type. せんご

전훈(電訓) telegraphic instructions[order]. でんぽうのくんれい

절¹ (부처 모신 데) a temple; a monastery/~에 불공드리러 가다 go to a temple to worship [Buddha]. てら

절² (인사) a bow; an obeisance 《경례》 a salutation/~하다 bow (to one); make a bow; make an obeisance (to)/그들은 서로 ~을 하였다 They saluted each other with a bow. おじぎ

절(節) (문법) a clause; a paragraph (물리) node (절개) loyalty; chastity 《경계》 an item. せつ

-절(節) (접미어) a season; a festival day/성탄 ~ Christmas Day. —せつ

절가(折價) ①(값을 정함) ~하다 fix the price ②(값을 깎음) ~하다 beat down the price.

절간 a Buddhist temple; a temple building ⇒절. てら

절감(切感) ~하다 feel keenly[acutely, painfully, heartily, sincerely]/외국어의 필요성을 ~하다 feel keenly the necessity of linguistic knowledge.
せつじつにかんじること

절감(節減) reduction; retrenchment; curtailment/~하다 reduce; retrench; curtail; cut down/경비를 ~하다 cut down[curtail] expenses; retrench in expenditures. せつげん

절갑류(節甲類) 【동】 Entomostraca(학명).

절개(切開) incision; operation/~하다 incise; operate upon/~ 수술 an surgical operation/종기를 ~하다 incise a tumour. せっかい

절개(節概) vinginity 《정조》 chastity; constancy 《절조》 fidelity (to one's principles); honour/~를 지키다 remain faithful (to)/~가 있는 사람 a man of integrity. せつがい

절검(節儉) economy; thrift; frugality/~하다 economize; save. せっけん

절경(絶景) a superb view; a wonderful [charming, an enchanting] view; picturesque scenery. ぜっけい

절골(折骨) a broken[fracture] of bone/~하다 break a bone; suffer a fractured bone. ほねがきれること

절교(絶交) break of friendship; a rupture/~하다 break off [friendship] (with); cut[drop, sever] one's acquaintance with; break with/이게 너와는 ~다 I will no longer have anything to do with you. ぜっこう

절구 a mortar/~질 pounding in a mortar/~에 빻다 pound in a mortar/~통 the body of a mortar. つきうす

절귀(絶句) 【문】 《한시의》 a Chinese quatrain. ぜっく

절규(絶叫) a scream; an exclamation/~하다 scream; exclaim; cry out/정계의 정화를 ~하다 cry loudly[raise a cry] for the purification of the political world. ぜっきょう

절급(切急) urgency; imminence/~하다 (be) urgent; imminent.

**절기(絕棍)** abhorrence; abomination／~하다 abhor; abominate. はなはだきらうこと

**절기(絕奇)** exquisiteness; excellence／~하다 (be) exquisite; excellent. はなはだめずらしいこと

**절기(節氣)** the 24 solar terms. せっき

**절다**¹ 《소금에》 be saturated (with salt). しおにつかる

**절다**² 《발을》 walk lamp; limp／부상자는 다리를 절며 가 버렸다 The wounded man hobbled away. びっこをひく

**절단(切斷, 截斷)** ~하다 cut [off]; sever [from]; 《수족의》 amputate／~기 a cutting machine／~면 a section／~ 환자 an amputee. だんぜつ

**절대(絕大)** hugeness; immensity／~하다 (be) greatest; tremendous; immense; highest. ぜつだい

**절대(絕對)** absoluteness／~의 absolute; positive; unconditional／~로 absolutely; positively 《부정》 on no account／~적 absolute／~의 진리 an absolute truth／~다수 an absolute majority／~권〔온도, 시간, 운동〕 absolute authority [temperature, time, motion]／~자 the absolute／~주의 absolutism／~ 반대 positive opposition／~ 원리 an absolute principle. ぜったい

**절대(絕代)** distant ages ⇨절세(絕世). ぜつだい

**절도(絕倒)** ①《기절함》 a swoon; a fainting fit／~하다 fall down in a swoon ②《우스워서》 laughing oneself into convulsions／~하다 laugh oneself into convulsions.

**절도(絕島)** a desert[a lonely, an isolated] island. ぜっとう

**절도(竊盜)** theft; petty stealing 《사람》 a thief／~범 larceny. せっとう

**절뚝거리다** limp; hobble; walk lame; walk with a limp. びっこをひく

**절뚝발이, 쩔뚝발이** a cripple; a lame person. びっこ

**절렁거리다, 쩔렁거리다** clink; clank; jingle; make tinkling sound／절렁절렁〔쩔렁쩔렁〕 clinking; clanking.

**절레절레, 쩔레쩔레** shaking one's head.

**절로** ①automatically ②there. みずから

**절륜(絕倫)** ~하다 (be) peerless; matchless; unequalled; unsurpassed／정력이 ~한 사람 a man of untiring[indefatigable, unbounded] energy; a man of hustle. ぜつりん

**절망(切望)** an earnest desire／~하다 desire earnestly; be anxious for／그는 대학에 다니기를 ~했다 He was very anxious to go to a university. せつぼう

**절망(絕望)** despair; hopelessness／~하다 despair (of); lose[give up] hope (of); be driven to despair／~적 hopeless; desperate／~의 구렁텅이에 있다 be sunk in the depths of despair. ぜつぼう

**절망고(絕望顧)** ~하다 be very busy; be fully occupied (with).

**절멸(絕滅)** 《자연히》 extinction 《박멸》 extermination; eradication／~하다 《근절》 stamp out; exterminate; eradicate 《끊기다》 become extinct; die out. ぜつめつ

**절명(絕命)** the end of life／~하다 expire; die; breathe one's last. ぜつめい

**절묘(絕妙)** ~하다 (be) superb; exquisite; miraculous／~한 필치 an exquisite touch／~한 재주 a miraculous feat. ぜつみょう

**절무(絕無)** nothing; nought; nil; nothing; total absence／~하다 be none at all; (be) nil; totally absent. ぜつむ

**절미(節米)** rice saving／~하다 economize in rice／~ 운동 a movement for saving rice; a save-the-rice campaign. せつまい

**절박(切迫)** pressure; urgency／~하다 draw near; be imminent／시간이 ~하다 Time presses. せっぱく

**절반(折半)** 「a」half／~하다 halve; divide into halves 《베다》 cut in half／~의 크기〔값〕 half the size[price]. せっぱん

**절버덕** splash ⇨첨버덕. ばしゃ

**절벽(絕壁)** ①《낭떠러지》 a precipice; a precipitous cliff ②《귀머거리》 a stone-deaf person／~을 기어 오르다 scale[climb up] a cliff ぜっぺき

**절부(節婦)** a virtuous woman; a chaste woman. せっぷ

**절사(節士)** a man of principle. せっし

**절사(節死)** ~하다 die for one's principles; die with one's integrity unsullied.

**절상(折傷)** fracture; a fractured bone／~하다 break a bone; suffer a fracture; fracture. せっしょう

**절색(絕色)** a woman of matchless beauty; a paragon of beauty.

**절선(切線)** 【수】 a tangent [line]. せっせん

**절세(絕世)** ~하다 retire from the world／~의 peerless; matchless／~의 미인 a rare beauty. ぜっせい

**절손(絕孫)** ~하다 let one's family line die out; have[leave] no posterity. おとこのこがないこと

**절승(絕勝)** fine scenery／~하다 (be) superb; grand; unsurpassed. せっしょう

**절식(絕食)** 《단식》 fasting; self-starvation; abstinence from food／~하다 fast; abstain from food; go without food／~하여 죽다 starve oneself to death; die of self-starvation. ぜっしょく

**절식(節食)** temperance in eating／~하다 eat moderately[sparingly]; be temperate in eating; eat in moderation. せっしょく

**절식(絕息)** expiring／~하다 expire; breathe one's last [breath]; die.

**절실(切實)** ~하다 《긴급하다》 (be) urgent; serious 《적절하다》 proper; pertinent／~히 keenly 《간절히》 heartily／필요성을 ~히 느끼다 feel keenly the necessity of (it). せつじつ

**절약**(節約) saving; economy 《단축》 abridgement/~하다 save [on]; economize [in]; retrench [in]; práctise economy /음식을 ~하다 save on food/시간[비용] ~ economy of time[in expenditures]. せつやく

**절연**(絶緣) ①〖전〗 isolation/~하다 isolate; insulate ②《관계의》 ~하다 break with; break off relations (with *one*); sever *one's* connection (*with*); get through (*with*). ぜつえん

**절요**(絶要, 切要) importance; urgency/ ~하다 (be) important; urgent. せつよう

**절용**(節用) frugal use; frugality/~하다 use frugally; economize. せつよう

**절원**(切願) entreaty; solicitation; supplication/~하다 implore; entreat; beg; solicit. ぜつがん

**절원**(絶遠) a far distance; remoteness/ ~하다 be far away off, distant; (be) remote. ぜつえん

**절음**(絶飮) ~하다 give up drinking; abstain (*from*) drinking. きんしゅすること

**절음**(節飮) temperance in drinking/~ 하다 be temperate in drinking. さけをてきどうにのむこと

**절의**(節義) fidelity to *one's* principle/~ 를 지키다 adhere to *one's* principles. せつぎ

**절이다** pickle, salt (*vegetables*)/생선을 소금에 ~ preserve fish with salt; salt fish. しおづけにする

**절재**(絶才) great gift; matchless talent.

**절전**(節電) economy in power consumption; power saving/~하다 economize (*in*) power[electricity]/~ 운동 powersaving movement. でんりょくをせつやくすること

**절절, 쩔쩔** ①《끓는 모양》 boiling; steaming ②《흔드는 모양》 shaking slowly. ぐらぐら

**쩔쩔매다** be at *one's* wit's end; be at a loss 《*what* to do》; be bewildered; be confused; be in a tight box; do not know what to do/바빠서 ~ be pressed with business. にっちもさっちもいかない

**절절이**(節節―) each word; every word; by phrase. ふしぶしに

**절절하다**(切切―) (be) earnest; eager; fervent; urgent. ひじょうにねっしんだ

**절정**(絶頂) 《산 꼭대기》 the summit; the top 《정점》 the height; the zenith; the peak; the crest; a climax/불경기의 ~ the depth of depression. ぜっちょう

**절제**(節制) temperance; moderation/~ 하다 be temperate; be moderate 《금다》 abstain from/~가 a temperate person /음식의 ~ temperation in eating and drinking. せいよく

**절조**(節操) principles; integrity; fidelity; honour/~가 있는 사람 a man of principle/~가 없는 사람 an unprincipled man. せっそう

**절족 동물**(節足動物) 〖동〗 an arthropod; Arthropoda(학명). せっそくどうぶつ

**절지**(絶地) a most remote region.

**절차**(節次) steps of procedure; formalities; a programme/수출입 ~에 정통하다 be familiar with export-import procedure/~상 for the sake of formalities/ ~에 따라서 according to the program [procedure]. せつじ

**절찬**(絶讚) ~하다 speak in the highest terms of praise; extol/~을 받다 win great admiration; be extolled. ぜっさん

**절창**(絶唱) an excellent singing; an excellent piece of poetry. ぜっしょう

**절책**(切責) ~하다 reproach[scold] severely. ふかくせめること

**절청**(竊聽) eavesdropping; tapping/~하 다 eavesdrop; tap; listen in on; overhear. ぬすみぎきすること

**절충**(折衷) negotiation; parley/~하다 negotiate[bargain] with (*one*) about/~ 안 a compromise [plan]; a conciliatory measure/~주의(主義) eclecticism. せっちゅう

**절충**(折衝) a compromise; eclecticism/~ 하다 compromise with; make a compromise/…에 관하여 ~중이다 negotiations are going on[are in progress] about be under negotiations. せっしょう

**절취**(竊取) theft/~하다 steal; pilfer; purloin; embezzle. せっしゅ

**절치**(切齒) teeth-glindiny/~하다 grind *one's* teeth with vexation. せっし

**절친**(切親) a close friendship; intimacy /~하다 (be) intimate (*with*); close; be on the best[warmest] terms (*with*)/~ 한 사이다 be on terms (*with*).

**절통**(切痛) ~하다 (be) most regrettable; bitterly mortifying.

**절판**(絶版) ~하다 be out of print/~된 책 an out-of-print book. ぜっぱん

**절품**(絶品) a unique article; a rarity; nonpareil. ぜっぴん

**절품**(切品) absence of stock/~하다 be out of stock/~이 되다 run out of stock. しなぎれ

**절필**(絶筆) 《마지막 글》*one's* last writing 《끝음》 giving up writing. ぜっぴつ

**절핍**(切逼) pressure (for *money*); stringency; tightness (of *money*)/~하다 (be) pressing; tight; stringent. さしせまること

**절핍**(絶乏) exhaustion; drain/~하다 get [be] exhausted; be drained; give out.

**절하**(切下) 〖경〗 reduction 《평가(平價)의》 devaluation/~하다 cut down; reduce (*to*)/평가 ~하다 devaluate; devalue \미.

**절해**(絶海) the farthest seas/~의 고도 a lonely island in the distant sea; an isolated island. ぜっかい

**절호**(絶好) ~의 capital; splendid; golden (*opportunity*)/~의 기회 a golden opportunity. ぜっこう

**절후**(節候) seasons; the time of the year. きせつ

**젊다** (be) young; youthful/젊은이 young men; the young/젊어 보이다 look young; be youthful-looking/나이에 비해 ~ look young for *one's* age. わかい

**점**(占) divination; fortunetelling/~치다 《쳐주다》 tell fortune; divine; forecast 《치게 하다》 consult a fortuneteller; have *one's* fortune told. うらない

**점**(點) ① 《반점》 a spot; a speck; a speckle; a dot ② 《표기》 a point; a dot; a mark ③ 《점수》 a mark; a point 《야구》 a run 《축구》 a goal ④ 《논점》 a point; a respect; a reason; a score ⑤ 《입장》 a point of view ⑥ 《지점》 a point 《범위》 an extent ⑦ 《수효》 items; a piece/의류 백~을 도둑맞다 have ten pieces of dress stolen ⑧ 《소수점》 a decimal point ⑨ 《화》 a point ⑩ 《바둑의》 a piece《돌》; a cross 《관의 눈목》 ⑪ 《피부의》 a birthmark; a macula. てん

**점가**(漸加) a gradual increase/~하다 increase gradually/~ 속도 acceleration of velocity. だんだんふえること

**점감**(漸減) a gradual decrease/~하다 diminish [decrease] gradually; dwindle. ぜんげん

**점거**(占據) a occupation; possession/~하다 occupy/불법 ~ illegal [unlawful] occupation (*of*)/~지 an occupied territory. せんきょ

**점검**(點檢) inspection; examination 《인원의》 a roll-call/~하다 inspect; take a roll-call of (*men*); call the roll/불시 ~ a spot check [test]. てんけん

**점괘**(占卦) a divination sign/~가 좋다 [나쁘다] have a good [an ill] divination sign.

**점근**(漸近) 《수》 ~의 asymptotic[al]/~급수 《수》 asymptotic series. ぜんきん

**점대**(占-) divining-rods.

**점두**(店頭) a shop[store] front 《진열장》 a shop[show] window/~에 진열하다 display (*an article*) in the shop-window/~ 장식 window dressing. てんとう

**점둥이**(點-) 《개》a brindled dog 《사람》a person with a birthmark[mole].
はんてんのあるいぬ

**점등**(點燈) lighting/~하다 light [a lamp]/~ 시간 the lighting hour. てんとう

**점등**(漸騰) 《산》 a gradual rise/~하다 rise gradually.

**점락**(漸落) 《산》 a gradual fall (*of prices*)/~하다 sag; fall gradually.

**점령**(占領) occupation 《공략》 capture/~하다 take; occupy; capture/~지 an occupied area/~군 occupation forces. せんりょう

**점막**(店幕) an inn; a tavern.

**점막**(粘膜) 《생》 a mucous membrane; a mucosa/~선(腺) a mucous gland/~ 분비물 rheum; a mucous discharge.
ねんまく

**점멸**(點滅) flickering/~하다 switch on and off/~기 a switch. てんめつ

**점묘**(點描) a sketch; depiction; description of parts; a partial depiction; a spot[-ty] description; 《미》 painting with dots; pointillism/~하다 depict; portray; delineate. てんびょう

**점박이**(點-) 《동물》 a dapple[brindled] animal 《사람》 a person with a birthmark[mole]; 《웃음거리》 a laughingstock.
はんてんのあるいももの

**점서**(占書) a book on divination; a fortune[-telling] book.

**점선**(點線) a dotted line/~을 긋다 draw a dotted line/~으로 표시된 부분 the part shown in dotted line. てんせん

**점성**(粘性) 《물》 viscosity; cohesion.
ねんせい

**점성**(占星) horoscope; horoscopy; astrology/~가 an astrologer. せんせい

**점수**(點數) marks; the number of marks 《경기의》a score; points/좋은 ~를 따다 get good marks (*in*). てんすう

**점술**(占術) the art of divination; fortune telling. せんじゅつ

**점신세**(漸新世) 《지》 the Oligocene Age.

**점심**(點心) lunch[eon]; a noonday meal /~ 시간 the noon recess/~을 싸 가지고 다니다 bring *one's* own lunch. ひるめし

**점심나절**(點心-) the forenoon.

**점안수**(點眼水) an eye-lotion; an eye-wash[-water]. てんがんすい

**점액**(粘液) mucus; viscous fluid[liquid] /~성의 mucus; viscous; sticky/~질의 사람 a phlegmatic man/~ 분비 secretion of mucus. ねんえき

**점원**(店員) a clerk; a shop-man[-boy]; a shop-woman[-girl]; a shop-assistant 《판매원》 a salesman; a saleswoman 《여자》 a salesgirl. てんいん

**점유**(占有) occupancy; possession/~하다 occupy; possess/~자 an occupant/~권 a possessory right/~ 재산 chose in possessions. せんゆう

**점입 가경**(漸入佳境) ~하다 become more and more interesting; grow more exciting.

**점자**(點字) braille points; raised letters [print]/~로 발행하다 publish (*a book*) in raised type[braille]/~서 a book in braille [points]. てんじ

**점잔** a dignified air/~부리다 assume a dignified air; behave in a genteel way; put on airs. おとなしいこと

**점잖다** (be) gentle; well-mannered 《위엄 있다》 dignified 《존경할 만하다》 respectable 《고상》 noble/점잖은 말을 쓰다 use refined[graceful] language. おとなしい

**점장이**(占-) a fortuneteller; a diviner; a prognosticator. はっけみ

**점재**(點在) ~하다 be scattered[studded, interspersed, dotted] (*with*)/호반에는 별장들이 ~하고 있다 The lakeside is dotted with villas.

**점적**(點滴) drops; drippings. てんてき

**점점**(漸漸) increasingly 《많이》 more and

**점점이(點點─)** here and there; scattered; sporadically/물거울 ~ 세다 count articles one by one. てんてん

**점주(店主)** the proprietor [of a shop]; the head of a concern; a shopkeeper; a storekeeper《미》. てんしゅ

**점증(漸增)** a gradual increase/~하다 increase gradually.

**점진(漸進)** gradual progress; gradations; slow but steady advance/~하다 progress[advance] gradually; make gradual progress/~주의 gradual progressivism. ぜんしん

**점차(漸次)** gradually; by degrees. ぜんじ

**점착(粘着)** cohesion; adhesion/~하다 stick; cohere; adhere (to)/~력 cohesive power; cohesion;《물》viscosity/~제 adhesive; gluing agent/~성의 cohesive; sticky; gluey. ねんちゃく

**점철(點綴)** interspersion/~하다 dot; strew; be scattered with; intersperse/바다에는 뱃불이 반딧불처럼 ~ 해 있다 The sea is studded with the glow-worm lights of the shipping. てんてつ

**점토(粘土)** clay/~ 세공 claywork/~암 clay stone. ねんど

**점판암(粘板岩)**《광》clay-slate stone; argillite. ねんばんがん

**점포(店舗)** a shop《영》; a store《미》/~를 닫다 close[shut] up a store; give up one's business. てんぽ

**점하다(占─)** occupy; hold; get; take [up]/의회에서 과반수를 ~ have[command] a majority in the Assembly.

**점호(點呼)** a roll-call/~하다 call[take] the roll; muster out/인원을 ~하다 take a roll call of men. てんこ

**점화(點火)** ignition; lighting/~하다 ignite; light; fire; set off/~ 장치《발동기의》a spark[ing] plug;《전》an igniter. てんか

**접(接)**《식》a graft; grafting/~하다 graft; ingraft; engraft; put a graft into (a stock). つぎき

**접각(接角)**《수》a contiguous[an adjacent] angle. せっかく

**접객(接客)** reception; welcome/~하다 receive; welcome; entertain (a guest)/~원《호텔 따위의》a receptionist/~용의 for customers. せっきゃく

**접객업(接客業)** the service trade; a personal service occupation[trade]; entertaining business. せっきゃくぎょう

**접견(接見)** a reception; an interview/~하다 receive (one) [in audience]; give an interview. せっけん

**접경(接境)** a boundary; a border《국경》a frontier; a border [line].

**접골(接骨)** bonesetting/~하다 set a bone/~의(醫) a bone-setter/~술 the art of bonesetting. せっこつ

**접근(接近)** approach; access; contiguity; proximity; approximation/~하다 approach; draw[get] near; come[get] close《인접》be contiguous to; adjoin/~하기 쉬운 사람 an easily approachable[accessible] person. せっきん

**접다** fold [up]; wrap up; turn up[down];《구부리다》bend 《둘로》double/부채를 ~ fold[close] a fan. たたむ

**접때** the other day; a few days ago; the last time/~ 편지에 in one's late letter.

**접대(接待)** reception/~하다 welcome; receive; attend to; entertain/~부 the cateress; a service girl; a waitress/~실 a reception room. せったい

**접두어(接頭語)**《언》a prefix. せっとうご

**접목(椄木)**《농》grafting 《나무》a grafted tree/~하다 graft [trees] together; graft [a tree] on (another). つぎき

**접미어(接尾語)** a suffix. せつびご

**접본(接本)** the stock; a grafted tree.

**접빈(接賓)** reception; welcome; entertainment/~하다 receive (guests); welcome; entertain.

**접선(接線)**《수》a tangent [line]; (접촉) a contact/~하다 make contact (with); contact. せっせん

**접속(接續)** connection/~하다 join; connect; link/~역 a junction [station]/~사《언》a conjunction/~곡《음》a medley; a potpourri(F). せつぞく

**접수(接收)** requisition; requisitioning/~하다 requisition; take over[control of]/철도를 ~하다 take over a railway /~ 가옥 a requisitioned house. せっしゅう

**접수(接受)** receipt; acceptance/~하다 receive; be in receipt of 《무전을》pick up; accept; take up; open the books (for application). せつじゅ

**접시** ①《식사용의》a plate(평평한); a dish (움푹한); a platter(큰 것); a saucer(받침 접시)/굴 한 ~ a plate of oysters ②《저울의》a scale; a bowl. さら

**접시꽃**《식》a hollyhock; Althaea rosea (학명). たちあおい

**접신(接神)** ~하다 be possessed by a demon(spirit)/~론 theosophy.

**접안경(接眼鏡)**《물》an ocular [piece]; an eyepiece.

**접어들다** enter; set in 《세월의》approach /가을로 ~ the autumn [season] draws near[approaches]. ちかづいてくる

**접자(摺─)** a carpenter's rule; a jointed measuring stick; a folding ruler. おりたたみのしゃく

**접전(接戰)** a hand-to-hand fight; close fighting 《경기의》a close game[contest] /~하다 fight hand-to-hand[at close quarter];《선거・경기에서》have a close contest[game]. せっせん

**접점(接點)**《수》a point of contact. せってん

**접종(接種)**《의》inoculation; vaccination

접종(接種) ~하다 inoculate; vaccinate/병균을 ~하다 inoculate (*a person*) with [a] virus. せっしゅ

접종(接踵) ~하다 follow on the heels of; come in the wake of/크고 작은 사건들이 ~하여 일어났다 Events, great and small, occurred in [rapid] succession.

접지(摺紙) sheet-folding/~하다 fold paper [to bind a book]. おりかみ

접지(椄枝) 【식】 a branch graft[ing]; a slip.

접질리다 have[suffer] a sprain; be wricked/팔꿈치가 ~ one's elbow is sprained. すじちがいする

접첩접첩 into many folds.

접첩(摺帖) a folding album.

접촉(接觸) contact; touch 《충돌》 collision /~하다 touch; contact with/~각[면] a contact angle[surface]/~ 감염 contagion/~기《전》 a contactor/개인전 ~ a personal contact. せっしょく

접치다 fold (우산을) furl 《책상을》 collape. たたむ

접치이다 get folded; be furled. たたむ

접칼(摺—) a folding knife; a pocketknife; a grafting knife.

접피술(接皮術) skin graft[ing]; transplantation of skin.

접하다(接—) ①《접촉하다》 touch; come in contact with; be close to ②《인접하다》 adjoin; touch; border (*on*); be adjacent [be next] to ③《받다》 receive; have; get 《일이 주어》 come to hand ④《귀신이》 possess; take possession of; inspire/마귀가 ~ be possessed by a demon.
せっしょくする

접합(接合) ①《접속》 union; junction; joining 《혈관 따위》 inosculation/ ~하다 unite; join; connect ②《생식 세포》 zygosis; conjugation/~하다 conjugate/~자(子) a zygote. せつごう

접히다 ①《접어지다》 be folded ②《하수가》 take odds. おりたたまれる

젓 salted[pickled] fish/새우~ pickled shrimps/조개~ pickled clams. しおから

젓가락 a pair of chopsticks. はし

젓다 ①《배를》 row 《노를》 work at (*oars*); pull (*an oar*)/배를 ~ row[oar] a boat ②《휘젓다》 stir; churn; beat; whip/달걀을 ~ beat up an egg.

정¹ 《쇠 연장》 a chisel; a burin. のみ

정² 《정말》 really; indeed; in truth/~ 그렇다면 if you will have it so; if you insist upon it. まことに

정(情) 《감정》 feeling 《정서》 emotion 《애정》 love; affection 《정조》 sentiment 《열정》 passion 《인정》 human nature 《동정》 sympathy 《심정》 heart/아이들에 대한 어머니의 ~ a motherly affection toward children. じょう

정(疔) 【의】 a carbuncle; a furuncle.

정(正) ①《옳음》 right[eousness]; justice ②《부(副)에 대한》 the original; the text ③《자격의》 regular; ordinary ④《수》 plus; positive ⑤《정확》 just; right 《방위》 due ⑥《정미》 net; clear. せい

정(錠) a tablet; a tabloid. じょう

정가(情歌) ~하다 harp on bygones.

정가(庭苽) 【식】 a kind of pigweed[goosefoot].

정가(正價) [net] price; a normal[true, fair] price. せいか

정가(定價) a fixed[regular] price; the net price/~를 붙이다 set a price (on *a thing*)/~표(票) a price tag/~로 팔다 sell at a fixed price. ていか

정가극(正歌劇) 【음】 a grand opera; *opera seria* (It). ほんかくてきなかげき

정각(正刻) 《부사적》 just; sharp; punctually/~ 5시에 just at five; at five sharp. ちょうどそのじこく

정각(定刻) the appointed time 《기차 따위의》 scheduled time/일을 ~에 시작하여야 한다 We should always be on time at work. ていこく

정각(頂角) 【수】 a vertical angle. ちょうかく

정각(亭閣) an arbour; a bower. あずまや

정간(停刊) suspension [discontinuance] of publication/~하다 suspend publication; stop issue. ていかん

정간(井間) checks; checkers; a checkered pattern.

정갈하다 (be) neat and proper; clean; smart; trim; dapper; tidy; snug/정갈한 옷차림을 하다 be neatly dressed; tidy *one*self up. さっぱりしている

정감(情感) emotion; sentiment; feeling /~에 호소하다 apeal to (*a person's*) feelings. かんじょう

정강(政綱) a political programme[creed]; 《정당의》 a policy; a platform; a plank (조목). せいこう

정강마루 【해】 the ridge of the shin.

정강이 the shin; the shank/~뼈 the tibia; a shinbone. むこうずね

정객(政客) a politician. せいきゃく

정객(正客) the guest of honour. せいきゃく

정거(停車) stoppage; stopping; a stop/ ~하다 stop (at *a station*); 《세우다》 make a stop 《사고로》 be held up/기차는 사고 때문에 ~했다 The train was held up by an accident. ていしゃ

정거장(停車場) a [railway] station; a depot《미》; 《자동차 따위의》 a stand.
ていしゃじょう

정격(正格) regularity/~의 regular; correct; orthodox/~ 활용 a regular conjugation. せいかく

정견(定見) 《견해》 a definite view[opinion]; 《학설》 a fixed opinion 《정책》 a fixed policy 《주의》 a fixed principle 《확신》 a conviction. ていけん

정견(政見) *one's* political views 《정당의》 the platform/ ~을 발표하다 state[set forth] *one's* political views/ ~ 발표회 a campaign meeting. せいけん

정결(貞潔) chastity; faithfulness/ ~한

부인 a chaste wife.

**정결(精潔)** ~하다 (be) clean; neat/부엌을 ~히 하다 keep the kitchen clean.

**정경(情景)** a miserable condition; a sad plight.

**정경(政經)** politico-economic[s]; political economy; politics and economics.

**정계(淨界)** holy confines; an undefiled place.

**정계(正系)** a legitimate line.

**정계(政界)** the political world[circles, quarters]; the world of politics/~의 움직임 a political trend.

**정계(定界)** ①《경계》a boundary; a frontier ②《경계 획정》delimitation; demarcation/~하다 fix the boundaries; delimitate; demarcate the frontier line.

**정곡(正鵠)** the main point; the mark; the bull's-eye/~을 얻다[잃다] hit[miss] the mark.

**정곡(情曲)** one's immost feelings; one's true heart.

**정공(正攻)** a frontal attack/~하다 make a frontal attack; fight openly and squarely; play fair.

**정과(正果)** food preserved in honey; saccades/새앙 ~ preserved ginger.

**정과(正課)** a subject of the regular curriculum; a required course/~ 외의 과목 an extra-curricular subject.

**정관(定款)** 〖법〗 the articles of association [incorporation]/~으로 규정되다 be fixed by the aritcles of association.

**정관(靜觀)** serene contemplation/~하다 contemplate; wait-and-see/~주의 a wait-and-see policy.

**정관(精管)** 〖해〗 a spermaduct; a seminal duct/~ 수술 vasectomy.

**정관사(定冠詞)** 〖언〗 the definite article.

**정교(政敎)** ①《정치와 종교》 religion and politics; church and state; the temporal and spiritual powers ②《정치와 교육》 politics and education.

**정교(情交)** ①《친교》 friendship; intimacy ②《육체 관계》 illicit intercourse; intimacy; a liaison/~하다 have illicit intercourse (with); establish a liaison.

**정교(精巧)** ~하다 (be) elaborate; exquisite; delicate/~한 기계 an elaborate machine.

**정교(正敎)** 〖종〗 orthodoxy/~회 the Orthodox Church.

**정교사(正敎師)** a regular teacher; a licensed teacher.

**정구(庭球)** [lawn-]tennis/~를 하다 play tennis/~공 a tennis ball.

**정국(政局)** the political situation/~을 수습하다 save a political situation/~의 불안정 political instability/~의 위기 a political crisis.

**정권(政權)** administrative[political] power; the reins of power/~을 잃다 go out of power/~을 쥐다 take[seize] power/~ 교체(交替) a change of regime.

**정규(定規)** ①《규칙》 an established rule ②《자》 a rule; a ruler.

**정규(正規)** regularity; formality; legality/~의 교육을 받다 have regular school education/~전 regular warfare.

**정극(正劇)** a traditional[legitimate, conventional, an orthodox] drama.

**정근(精勤)** 《근면》 diligence 《무결근》 regular attendance/~하다 be diligent; be industrious/~상 a prize for good attendance.

**정금(正金)** 《금은화》 specie 《현금》 cash; hard money/~으로 지불하다 pay in cash /~ 은행 a specie bank.

**정기(正氣)** ①《바른 기풍》 fair and square spirits ②《천지의》 the spirit which animates and controls the universe.

**정기(定期)** a fixed time[term, period]; a stated period; a regular interval; 〖상〗 the option market/~의 fixed; regular; periodical/~ 간행물 a periodical/~ 항로 regular service; regular line/~선(船) a [regular] liner/~ 예금 fixed deposit[account]/~ 총회 a regular general meeting/~ 승차권 a season ticket; a commutation ticket〈미〉/~ 휴업일 a scheduled holiday.

**정기(精氣)** essence; spirit and energy.

**정나미(精—)** attachment; affection/~가 떨어지다 be disgusted (with).

**정남(正南)** due south.

**정남(貞男)** a male virgin; a sexually inexperienced man.

**정낭(精囊)** 〖해〗 a seminal vesicle; a spermatic sac.

**정낮** high noon ⇒한낮.

**정녀(貞女)** a chaste woman《처녀》a virgin; a maiden.

**정년(丁年)** full age/~자 an adult; a major/~에 달하다 attain one's majority; come[be] of age.

**정년(停年)** the age limit; retirement age /~제 the agelimit system/~ 퇴직 retirement under the age limit.

**정녕(叮嚀, 丁寧)** 《확실히》 certainly; surely; no doubt; to be sure/~ 그러냐 Are you sure?

**정다각형(正多角形)** 〖수〗 an equilateral[a regular] polygon.

**정다면체(正多面體)** 〖수〗 a regular polyhedron.

**정담(政談)** a political speech; a discussion of politics.

**정담(情談)** a tête-à-tête(F); lovers' talk.

**정담(鼎談)** a three-man talk.

**정답(正答)** correct[right] answer.

**정답다(情—)** (be) intimate; familiar; c-

**정당(正堂)** the main house[building].

**정당(正當)** ~하다 (be) just; right; proper; just and proper; lawful/~히 justly; rightly; properly/~한 사유 a just cause/~방위 〖법〗 legal defence; legitimate self-defence/~ 방위로 in self-defence; 〖법〗 *se defendendo*(L)/~한 수단에 의해 by fair means. せいとう

 lose; friendly 《화합》 harmonious/손을 정답게 맞다 receive a visitor warmly.

**정당(政黨)** a political party/~에 적을 두다 belong to[be a member of] a political party. せいとう

**정당(精糖)** sugar refining 《제품》 refined sugar.

**정대(正大)** fairness; justice/~하다 (be) fair; just; open [as the day]; fair and square. せいだい

**정떨어지다(情—)** be disgusted with; fall out of love (*with*). いやになる

**정도(正道)** the path of right[virtue, duty]; the right path; righteousness/~에서 어긋나다 stray from the right path. せいどう

**정도(定都)** establishing the capital city/~하다 set up the capital. みやこをきめること

**정도(征途)** ①《원정 길》a military expedition ②《여로》a journey; a travel/~오르다 go on an expedition; start[set out] on a journey. せいと

**정도(程度)** 《도》 grade; degree 《분량》 measure 《비율》 rate 《범위》 extent 《한도》 limit 《표준》 standard 《척도》 moderation/네 말엔 어느 ~ 진리가 있다 There is a certain degree of truth in what you say. ていど

**정독(精讀)** perusal; careful reading/~하다 peruse; read carefully[with care]. せいどく

**정돈(整頓)** order; arrangement; adjustment/~하다 put in order; put to rights; adjust; arrange/~된 orderly; in [good] order. せいとん

**정돈(停頓)** a standstill; a deadlock; a stalemate/~하다 come to a standstill; reach a deadlock; reach the end of the road/~ 상태에 빠지다 reach a stalemate; come to a standstill. ていとん

**정동(正東)** due east. まひがし

**정동(精銅)** refined copper. せいどう

**정들다(情—)** become attached (*to*); become intimate (*with*)/정든 학생들 one's beloved students. じょうがうつる

**정란(靖亂)** suppression of a rebellion/~하다 suppress a rebellion.

**정랑(情郞)** a lover; a sweetheart. じょうふ

**정략(政略)** a political game[move]; policy/~ 결혼 an expedient marriage/~적 political/~가(家) a political tactician. せいりゃく

**정량(定量)** a fixed quantity/~ 분석 quantitative analysis. ていりょう

**정려(精勵)** diligence; industry; assiduity/~하다 work hard. せいれい

**정력(精力)** energy; vigour; vitality/~왕성한 energetic/~가 a person of great energy/~의 소모 lose of energy. せいりょく

**정련(精練)** good training[drill]/~하다 drill[train] well. せいれん

**정련(精鍊)** refining 《철의》 tempering 《구리의》 smelting/~하다 refine; temper; smelt/~소 a refinery. せいれん

**정렬(貞烈)** chastity; virtue/~하다 (be) virtuous; chaste. ていれつ

**정렬(整列)** a parade; a line up/~하다 stand in a row; form a line; line up/~하여 기다리다 wait in line. せいれつ

**정령(政令)** a government ordinance[decree]; a cabinet ordinance[order].

**정령(精靈)** a soul [of the deceased]; the spirit; the ghost/~설 《철》 animism; spiritualism. せいれい

**정례(定例)** fixed rule; a usage; a custom; a precedent/~ 기자회견 a regular press conference/~에 의하여 according to usage. ていれい

**정론(正論)** sound reasoning. せいろん

**정론(定論)** a settled view; an established theory. ていろん

**정론(政論)** political arguments; politics/~을 하다 discuss current political affairs[matters]; talk politics. せいろん

**정류(停留)** a stop; stoppage/~하다 stop; halt; make[come to] a stop/~장 a stop; a depot《미》. ていりゅう

**정류(精溜)** 〖화〗 rectification; refinement/~하다 rectify; purify; refine/~ 주정(酒精) refined spirit.

**정류(整流)** 〖전〗 rectification/~하다 rectify; adjust/~기 a rectifier/~자(子) a commutator. せいりゅう

**정률(定率)** a fixed rate/~세 proportional taxation. ていりつ

**정률(定律)** 〖물〗 a fixed law. ていりつ

**정리(廷吏)** a sergeant; a court clerk. ていり

**정리(定理)** 〖수〗 a theorem. ていり

**정리(整理)** arrangement; regulation; disposal; adjustment; readjustment/~하다 regulate; arrange; dispose of; put in order; adjust; readjust/교통을 ~하다 regulate[control] traffic. せいり

**정리(情理)** reason and feeling/~를 다하여 타이르다 reason with (*a person*); expostulate (with *a person*) (*on*). じょうり

**정립(鼎立)** a triangular position/~하다 be in a triangular position; be a three-cornered contest/당시 3국은 서로 ~하고 있었다 At that time the three countries were opposed to one another. ていりつ

**정말(正—)** a true story; the truth; a fact; a reality 《부사적》 really; truly; actually; quite; indeed 《진정으로》 in real earnest. ほんとうのこと

정맥(精麥) cleaning barley 《보리》 cleaned barley. せいばく

정맥(靜脈) 【해】 a vein /~의 venous/ ~ 주사 a venous injection/ ~ 경화증 phlebosclerosis. じょうみゃく

정면(正面) the front [side]; the facade /~의 front; frontal/~에 in front of /~도(圖) a front view/~으로 공격하다 attack (the enemy) in front; attack (a person) openly. しょうめん

정명(定命) one's [predestined] span of life; the normal length of life; one's fate/~으로 죽다 die a natural death; die in one's bed. じょうみょう

정모(正帽) a full dress hat; a formal hat. せいぼう

정묘(精妙) exquisiteness; fineness/~하다 (be) exquisite; fine; subtle. せいみょう

정무(政務) affairs of state; state; state [political] affairs/~ 차관 a parliamentary vice-minister/~ 위원 a political committeeman 《총칭》 a political committee. せいむ

정문(正門) the front-gate; the main entrance/~으로 들어가다 go in at the front-gate. せいもん

정문(正文) the [official] text. せいぶん

정문(頂門) the crown of the head; the pate/~에 일침을 놓다 give an admonition to the point. ちょうもん

정물(靜物) still life; inanimate objects/ ~화 a [picture of] still life; a still-life study. せいぶつ

정미(精米) rice cleaning 《쌀》 cleaned rice /~하다 clean rice/~소 a rice [cleaning] mill. せいまい

정미(精美) supreme beauty; refinement; exquisiteness/~하다 (be) exceedingly beautiful. せいび

정미(精微) minuteness/~하다 (be) minute; fine; delicate. せいび

정미(情味) mood; warm heart; sentiment; attraction. じょうみ

정밀(精密) minuteness; precision; thoroughness/~하다 《세밀》 (be) minute; close; detailed; thorough 《정확》 (be) precise; exact; accurate 《미묘》 (be) delicate; nice; fine/~ 검사 a close examination (of)/~ 과학 the exact sciences. せいみつ

정밀(靜謐) peace; tranquility/~하다 (be) peaceful; tranquil.

정박(碇泊, 渟泊) anchorage/ ~하다 cast [come to] anchor; moor/~지[항] an anchorage[harbour]/~ 기간 lay days. ていはく

정반대(正反對) direct opposition/~의 direct opposite; reverse; conflicting/~로 in direct opposition (to). せいはんたい

정반합(正反合) 【철】 thesis-antithesis-synthesis. せいはんごう

정밤중(正-中) midnight; the dead of the night ⇒ 한밤중.

정방(精紡) spinning.

정방형(正方形) a [regular] square; a perfect[an exact] square. せいほうけい

정배(定配) exile; banishment/~하다 banish; transport; exile/~ 가다 go into exile.

정백(精白) 【 ~당(糖) refined sugar/~미 polished rice. せいはく

정벌(征伐) 《토벌》 conquest; subjugation 《원정》 an expedition; a crusade/~하다 subjugate; conquer; send an expedition to[against]; stamp out; suppress. せいばつ

정범(正犯) the principal offence 《사람》 the principal offender. せいはん

정변(政變) a political change; a change of government 《폭력·비합법의》 a coup d'etat(F). せいへん

정병(精兵) picked men[troops]; crack troops; the flower of the army. せいへい

정보(情報) information; intelligence; a report; news 《밀고》 a tip-off 《경마 따위의》 a dope/~를 누설하다 divulge [reveal] information/~를 제공하다 give information/~망 networks of intelligence[information]. じょうほう

정복(正服) uniform dress/~ 경찰관 a policeman in full uniform. せいふく

정복(征服) conquest; subjugation/~하다 conquer; subdue; subjugate/~자 a conqueror/~욕 the lust of conquest/ ~할 수 없는 unconquerable. せいふく

정본(正本) the original[legal, formal] copy; the text. せいほん

정부(正否) right or wrong. せいひ

정부(正副) principal and assistant[vice]; 《서류의》 original and copy; senior and junior/~ 2통을 제출하다 submit [an application] in duplicate. せいふく

정부(正負) 【수】 positive and negative; plus and minus. せいふ

정부(政府) the government; the administration 《내각》 the ministry/~의 government[al]; ministerial / ~ 당국 the government authorities /~신-를 수립하다 set up[establish] a new government. せいふ

정부(情夫) a sweetheart; a lover; a paramour; an adulterer. じょうふ

정부(情婦) a mistress; a paramour. じょうふ

정부(貞婦) a virtuous woman; a faithful wife. ていふ

정북(正北) due north. せいほく

정분(情分) friendly feelings; friendship /~이 있다 be on terms of intimacy. あたたかいこころ

정비(整備) complete equipment; good organization/~하다 be completely equipped; be organized well/~군 a fully equipped army/~원 《항》 a groundman[-crew]/전선을 ~하다 consolidate the front. せいび

정비례(正比例) 【수】 direct proportion[ra-

**정비례**(定比例) 【수】 constant[definite] proportion/~하다 be in direct proportion to; be directly proportional to. せいひれい

**정빈**(正賓) a guest of honour.

**정사**(正史) authentic history[records, chronicles, accounts]. せいし

**정사**(正使) a senior envoy; the chief delegate. せいし

**정사**(正邪) right and wrong; good and evil/~를 구별하다 distinguish[know] right from wrong; discriminate between right and wrong/~를 막론하다 whether right or wrong. せいじゃ

**정사**(政事) political affairs; administrative business/~를 다스리다 manage the affairs of state. せいじ

**정사**(情死) a double suicide; a love suicide/~하다 commit a double suicide; die together for love/~ an attempted double suicide/그들은 ~했다 The lovers killed themselves together. じょうし

**정사**(情事) a love affair; a romance/~를 알다 understand love/~에 눈뜨다 become sexually awakened; become adolescent/혼외 ~ extramarital intercourse. じょうじ

**정사**(情史) one's love story; a romance. じょうし

**정사**(靜思) meditation; contemplation/~하다 meditate; contemplate. せいし

**정사**(精査) careful examination; minute investigation/~하다 investigate minutely[thoroughly]; examine carefully [closely]. せいさ

**정사**(精舍) a monastery; a cloister; a private school. せいしゃ

**정사**(淨寫) a fair copy ⇨정서. じょうしゃ

**정사면체**(正四面體) a regular tetrahedron.

**정사영**(正射影) 【수】 an orthogonal projection/~법 orthography. せいしゃえい

**정사원**(正社員) a regular member; a full member of the staff

**정산**(精算) exact calculation; an accurate account 《결산》 settlement of accounts/~하다 settle accounts; keep an accurate account/~서 a settlement of accounts/~인 an average adjuster. せいさん

**정삼각형**(正三角形) 【수】 a regular[equilateral] triangle. せいさんかっけい

**정상**(正常) normality; normalcy/~하다 (be) normal/~적 normal/~ 가격 a normal price/~ 상태 normal state/~ 속도 a normal speed/~으로 돌아가다 return to normalcy[normal condition]. せいじょう

**정상**(呈上) presentation/~하다 present (one) with; make (one) a present of (a thing). ていじょう

**정상**(政商) a businessman with political affiliations; a businessman who is a party supporter/~배(輩) businessmen with party ties.

**정상**(情狀) conditions; circumstances/~을 참작하다 take the circumstances into consideration/~을 참작하여 사형을 일등 감하다 commute the penalty of death by one degree on account of extenuating circumstances. じょうじょう

**정상**(頂上) the top; the summit; the crest of a mountain 《극점》 the zenith; the highest peak/~에 on[at] the top of/~ 회담 a parley at the summit/~을 정복하다 gain[win] the summit (of a mountain). ちょうじょう

**정상**(精詳) minuteness; detail/~하다 (be) minute; detailed; circumstantial. せいみつでしょうさいなこと

**정상파**(定常波) 【물】a stationary wave. ていじょうは

**정상화**(正常化) normalization/~하다 normalize; be normalized. せいじょうか

**정색**(正色) 《얼굴》 a sober face; a serious look; a straight face/~하다 maintain a serious countenance; show one's seriousness[earnestness, sincerity]; assume a solemn air; wear a sober look. せいしょく

**정서**(正西) due west. まにし

**정서**(正書) square-hand[printed style] characters/~하다 write in the square style; write squarehand. せいしょ

**정서**(精書) ~하다 write out fair.

**정서**(情緒) emotion; feeling; heart-string /자상한 ~ tender sentiments/~가 넘쳐 흐른다 be overcome with emotions/~ 교육 culture of [aesthetic] sentiments. じょうちょ

**정서**(淨書) a fair[clean] copy/~하다 copy[write out] fair; make a fair[clean] copy of. じょうしょ

**정석**(定石) the cardinal principle 《바둑의》 formulas[rules] in the game of badook. じょうせき

**정선**(精選) careful selection/~하다 select carefully[with care]; 《골라내다》 single [pick] out/~품 choice goods; select [picked] goods. せいせん

**정선**(停船) stopping of a vessel 《검역시의》 quarantine/~하다 stop; heave to; quarantine/안개 때문에 ~하였다 The ship was brought to a stop in the fog. ていせん

**정설**(定說) 《학리상의》 an established theory 《개인의》 a settled conviction; a definite opinion/~을 뒤집어 엎다 overthrow an established theory. ていせつ

**정성**(精誠) 《성의》 sincerity 《노력》 effort; exertion; labour 《고심》 care; pains/~ 어린 선물 a gift with one's best wishes/~껏 with one's utmost sincerity; with one's whole heart; elaborately/그 여자는 온 ~을 다하여 그 일을 했다 She did it with all her heart. せいせい

**정성 분석**(定性分析) 【화】qualitative analysis. ていせいぶんせき

**정세**(情勢) 《상황》 the state of things [affairs]; the situation; conditions 《징조》 circumstance; appearances; indications; signs/세계 ~ the world situation/지금 ~로는 according to the present situation/~를 판단하다 judge [size up] the situation/~는 이미 변했다 This is no longer the case. じょうせい

**정세**(精細) detail ⇨정상(精詳). せいさい
**정수**(井水) well water. せいすい
**정수**(正數) a positive number. せいすう
**정수**(定數) ①《일정수》 a fixed number; a stated number 《의원의》 a quorum;《수》 a constant/출석자 ~에 미달시에는 unless a quorum is present/~를 넘다 exceed the fixed number/~에 달하다 make up the fixed number ②《운명》 fate; destiny. ていすう

**정수**(精粹) purity; pureness/~하다 (be) pure; genuine.
**정수**(靜水) still[stagnant] water/~[세척]법 stand washing/~학 hydrostatics. せいすい

**정수**(精髓) cream; essence; quintessence; genius; pith/동양 문화의 ~ the cream of the Eastern culture/~를 골라내다 take essence of; select. せいずい
**정수**(精水) semen; sperm; spermatic fluid.
**정수**(淨水) clean water/~지(池) a cleaning bed. じょうすい
**정수**(整數) 《수》 an integral[a whole] number; an integer/~론 number theory. せいすう

**정수리**(頂一) the crown [of the head]. ちょうもん
**정수 식물**(挺水植物) 《식》 an emerged plant. ていすいしょくぶつ
**정숙**(貞淑) chastity; feminine modesty; female virtue/~하다 (be) chaste; virtuous; modest/~하기로 이름이 높다 have a reputation for womanly virtue. ていしゅく

**정숙**(靜肅) silence; stillness; hush; quiet[ness]/~하다 (be) silent; still; quiet /~히 silently; quietly; in an orderly manner/~히 하여라 Keep quiet., Don't make a noise., Be silent. せいしゅく
**정승**(政丞) a minister [of state].
**정시**(正視) ~하다 look (one) in the face; look straight[squarely] at/사실을 ~하다 look at a fact squarely. せいし
**정시**(定時) a fixed time; regular hours 《예정시》 schedule/~의 periodical; ordinary/~ 운행하다 move on schedule; operate regularly/~에 도착하다 arrive on schedule. ていじ
**정식**(正式) due form; formality/ ~의 regular; formal; due/~으로 formally; properly; in due[proper] form/~ 결혼 legal marriage/~ 방문 a formal visit /~ 수락 formal acceptance/~ 통지 a formal notice/~으로 소개받다 be formally introduced/~으로 방문하다 make a formal call (at, on); pay a formal visit (to). せいしき

**정식**(定式) 《규정》 an established rule; an order; the usual way; convention 《공식》 a formula. ていしき
**정식**(定食) a regular meal 《요리점의》 table d'hote(F); a dinner/저녁으로 ~을 먹다 have a set supper. ていしょく
**정식**(整式) 《수》 an integral expression.
**정신**(挺身) volunteering/~하다 go ahead of others; offer oneself/~대 the volunteers/난국에 ~하다 offer oneself[volunteer] to undertake the difficult task. ていしん
**정신**(精神)⇨별항 참조(page 1701). せいしん
**정신**(艇身) a boat's length/1[반]~의 차로 이기다 win [the race] by a [boat's] length[by half a length].
**정실**(正室) a lawful wife/~의 자식 a legitimate child. せいしつ
**정실**(情實) private[personal] considerations 《두둔》 favouritism/~을 배제하다 set[put] aside all personal considerations/그는 ~에 의해서 승진되었다 He got promoted through favoritism. じょうじつ

**정애**(情愛) love; affection. じょうあい
**정액**(定額) a fixed amount[sum]; a specified amount/~ 소득 a fixed income /~ 예금 a fixed deposit; a deposit by installments/~에 달하다 come up to the specified amount. ていがく
**정액**(精液) ①《생》 semen; sperm/~관 a spermaduct/~ 사출 a seminal emission ②《진수(眞髓)》 an extract; an essence. せいえき
**정야**(靜夜) a silent night. せいや
**정양**(靜養) rest; recuperation 《요법》 a rest cure/~하다 rest quietly; recuperate; take a rest/~차 for a rest; for [the benefit of] one's health. せいよう
**정어리** 《어》 a sardine. いわし
**정언적**(定言的) 《논》 categorical/~ 명제(命題) a categorical proposition/~ 판단[명령] categorical judgement[imperative]. ていげんてき
**정업**(正業) an honest[a respectable, a legitimate] occupation/~자 an honest dealer/~을 영위하다 make an honest living; live an honest life. せいぎょう
**정업**(定業) a fixed occupation; regular employment; a profession/~을 잡다 get a regular employment/~이 없다 be out of [regular] employment. ていぎょう
**정연**(整然) ~하다 (be) orderly; regular; systematic/~히 in [good, perfect] order; in good shape; in a regular manner/~한 보조 a measured step/모든 것이 ~히 놓여졌다 All are arranged in nice order. せいぜん
**정열**(情熱) passion; enthusiasm; passionate sincerity of emotion/~적인 pass-

정예(精銳) the best; the flower; the pick 《정병》picked troops; the pick of an army; a crack unit／~하다 (be) efficient; highly trained; picked; effective. せいえい

정오(正午) [high] noon; midday／~에 at noon; at midday／~의 싸이렌 the noon siren. しょうご

정오(正誤) correction; ractification／~하다 correct[rectify] an error／~표 errata; corrigenda. せいご

정온(定溫) fixed temperature／~ 동물 a homoiothermic animal. ていおん

정온(靜穩) stillness; tranquility; silence; serenity／~하다 (be) silent; quiet; still／폭풍우 전의 ~ the hush[calm] before a storm／밤의 ~ the stillness of the night. せいおん

정욕(情慾) passion; sexual[sensual] desire; lust／~의 노예 a slave of passions／~의 억제 restraint[control] of passion／~을 만족시키다 gratify one's lust／~에 지배되다 be swayed by passion／~을 일으키게 하다 inflame (a person) with desire. じょうよく

정용(整容) ~하다 tidy oneself up.

정원(定員) a regular staff; a personnel; full number 《수용력》 capacity; the full strength 《정족수》 a quorum／버스의 ~ the seating capacity of a bus／~에 달하다 reach the regular number／~에 미달하다 lack the quorum／이 사무실의 ~은 10명이다 The regular personnel of this office is ten. ていいん

정원(庭園) a garden／옥상 ~ a roof garden／~사(師) a gardener／~술(術) [landscape-]gardening／~을 만들다 lay out a garden. ていえん

정월(正月) January. しょうがつ

정유(精油) refined oil.

정육(精肉) fresh meat; dressed meat／~상 a butcher.

정육면체(正六面體) 《수》 a regular hexahedron; a cube.

정은(正銀) pure[solid] silver. じゅんぎん

정음(正音) ①《글자의》 correct pronunciation of a letter ②⇒훈민정음. せいおん

정의(正義) justice; right; righteousness／~의 just; righteous／~의 싸움 a righteous war; fighting for a rightful cause／~는 마침내 승리한다 Right will prevail in the end. ／힘이 ~다 Might is right. せいぎ

정의(定義) a definition／~를 내리다 define (a word); give a definition／"전쟁"이란 말의 ~ a definition of a word "war". ていぎ

정의(精誼) friendship; companionship; friendly feelings／깊은 ~ deep friendship／옛 ~를 생각해서 for old acquaintance sake／~가 두텁다 be friendly; be warm-hearted. じょうぎ

정의(精義) 《뜻》 the exact meaning 《해석》 a detailed exposition; a full commentary／민법 ~ a Commentary of the Civil Law.

정의 상통(情意相通) ~하다 come to an understanding 《남녀가》 become intimate.

정인(情人) 《남녀》 a sweetheart; a lover 《남자》 a paramour 《여자》 a [lady-]love; a mistress. じょうじん

정일(定日) the fixed date[day]; the appointed day. ていじつ

정자(正字) a correct letter; an unsimplified character／~법 《언》 orthography. せいじ

정자(精子) spermatozoon (pl. -zoa); antherozoid／~ 세포 spermatid. せいし

정자(亭子) an arbour; a summerhouse; a pavilion; a bower／~나무 a big tree serving as a shady resting place in a village. あずまや

정자법(正字法) 《어》 orthography.

정자형(丁字形) T-shape; T-form; the figure "T"／~의 T-shaped／~의 자 a T-square. ていじけい

정작 a real fact; truth; actuality; reality 《부사적》 truly; really; actually; practically／~ 말하면 to tell the truth／~ 화가 난다 I am very angry with him.／~ 알아 보니 거짓말이었다 Upon actual investigation, it turned out to be a false report. まことに

정장(正裝) full uniform; full dress／~하다 be in full uniform; be in full dress; be formally attired／~을 갖추어야 할 모임 a white tie function. せいそう

정장석(正長石) 《광》 orthoclase. せいちょうせき

정재(淨財) well-earned money; offering; a subscription／~를 모으다 collect alms; take up a collection. じょうざい

정쟁(政爭) a political strife[dispute, controversy, warfare]／~의 도구로 삼다 make a political issue of (a thing). せいそう

정저와(井底蛙) a frog in the well／~의 견해 narrow[bigoted] views; a one-sided opinion.

정적(政敵) a political opponent[rival, enemy, foe, antagonist]. せいてき

정적(靜的) static[al]; 《소극적》 passive／~으로 statically. せいてき

정적(靜寂) silence; stillness; quiet／~하다 (be) still; silent; quiet／밤의 ~ perfect stillness of the night／~을 깨뜨리다 break the silence. せいじゃく

정전(政戰) political warfare; a political maneuver; a political campaign. せいせん

정전(停戰) the suspension[cessation] of hostilities; a truce／~하다 suspend hostilities; have a truce／~ 회담 a cease-fire conference[negotiation]／~을 명하다 order to suspend hostilities. ていせん

정전(停電) a stoppage of electric current; an electricity failure; the giving out of the electric power; no light 《전차의》 a tie-up/~하다 the power gives out; the [electric] current is off; be tied up/천둥으로 ~됐다 The thunderstorm caused power failure. ていでん

정전기(靜電氣) 【물】 static electricity/~ 감응 static induction. せいでんき

정절(正切) 【수】 a tangent. せいせつ

정절(貞節) faithfulness; fidelity; constancy; virtue/~한 아내 a faithful[devoted] wife/~을 지키다 lead a chaste life. ていせつ

정점(定點) 【수】 a fixed[definite] point.

정점(頂點) the height 《극치》 the climax; the apex/삼각형의 ~ the apex of triangle/영화의 ~에 있다 be at the height [zenith] of one's prosperity. ちょうてん

정접(正接) 【수】 a tangent/~면 a tangential plane/~ 전류계 a tangential galvanometer. せいせつ

정정(訂正) correction 《개정》 revision/~하다 correct; revise; rectify/~ 재판 the revised second edition/~판 a revised edition/오류를 ~하다 correct errors. ていせい

정정(政情) political conditions[affairs]/~의 안정 the stability of the political situations/~에 통달하다 be familiar[conversant] with political conditions. せいじょう

정정 당당(正正堂堂) ~하다 (be) fair and square; open and aboveboard/~히 fairly [and squarely]; openly/~한 승부 a fairly contested match/~하게 싸우다 play fair[on the square]; fight openly and squarely. せいせいどうどう

정정법(政淨法) the Political Purification Law.

정정하다(亭亭—) 《노익장하다》 (be) hale and hearty; vigorous; active 《우뚝 솟다》 be standing lofty and alone/그는 80을 넘었으나 아직도 ~ He is turned 80 and still an active man. そびえている

정제(整齊) symmetry/~하다 (be) symmetrical; regular. せいせい

정제(錠劑) a tablet; a tabloid; a pill. じょうざい

정제(精製) refining/~하다 refine /~소 a refinery/~법 refining process/~한 refined; purified/~ 소금 refined salt. せいせい

정조(正條) express provisions[stipulations]/~식 【농】 checkrowing.

정조(貞操) chastity; [feminine] virtue; [female] honour/~대 a chastity belt /~ 유린 a violation of chastity/~를 지키다 remain faithful (to one's husband)/~를 중히 여기다 prize chastity/ ~를 바치다 surrender one's chastity to; give oneself to (a man). ていそう

정조(情調) a mood; a tone; an atmosphere. じょうちょう

정조(情操) sentiment; feeling/~ 교육 culture of sentiments/고상한 ~ a noble sentiment. じょうそう

정조(正租) unhulled rice. いね

정조(正調) the orthodox[conventional] tune.

정족(鼎足) the legs of a tripod/~지세 (之勢) triangular position; three cornered situation. ていそく

정족수(定足數) a quorum; a fixed number/오늘 국회 본회의는 의원 ~ 미달로 유회되었다 Today's National Assembly plenary session was adjourned because of lack of quorum. ていそくすう

정종(正宗) refined sool. まさむね

정좌(正座) ~하다 sit straight[square]. せいざ

정좌(靜坐) quiet sitting/~하다 sit quietly. せいざ

정좌(鼎坐) ~하다 sit [together] in a tr-

---

## 정 신

《지력》 mind 《영혼》 soul; spirit 《의지》 will 《의도》 intention 《동기》 motive 《심성》 mentality 《시대 풍조·경향》 genius /~적으로 mentally; morally; spiritually/~적인 mental; moral; spiritual /~적 사랑 Platonic[spiritual] love/~ 적 타격 a mental blow[shock]/~적 피로 brain weariness; mental fatigue/ ~ 과학 mental science/~ 교육 moral education/~력 mental power/~ 박약 mental weakness; feeble-mindedness/ ~병 a mental disease[ailment]; psychosis/~ 병원 a mental hospital/~ 분열증 dementia; schizophrenia/~ 상태 a mental condition; a state of mind/~ 요법 psychotherapy; mental healing/ ~ 위생 mental hygiene/~ 이상 mental disorder; alienation/~ 장애 mental disorder/~ 착란 mental derangement/ ~ 통일 mental concentration/사랑의 ~ the spirit of love/애국의 ~ patriotic spirit; patriotism/~을 쏟다 devote one's heart and soul to (a work)/~을 발달시키다 develop the mind/~을 집중하다 concentrate one's attention on (something)/건전한 ~은 건전한 육체에 깃든다 A sound mind in a sound body./~ 일도 하사 불성 Where there is a will, there a way./~에 이상이 없다 be of sound is mind; be mentally sound.

iangle.　ていざ
**정주(定住)** domiciliation／～하다 domiciliate; settle down／～지[자] a permanent home[resident]／서울에 ～하다 settle down[make one's home] in Seoul.
　　　　　　　　　　　　　　　　ていじゅう
**정중(正中)** the middle／～선[신경, 동맥] a median line[nerve, artery].
　　　　　　　　　　　　　　　　せいちゅう
**정중(鄭重)** courtesy; civility; politeness; consideration／～하다 (be) courteous; civil; solemn／～히 courteously; politely／～한 대접 hospitable treatment; a courteous reception／～히 대하다 treat (a person) courteously; treat (a person) with consideration.　　　ていちょう
**정지(停止)** 《금지》 suspension; temporary prohibition; ban 《휴지》 standstill; stop 《정돈》 deadlock 《중절》 interruption 《세습·작위 따위의》 abeyance／～하다 stop; interrupt; suspend／발행[영업]을 ～하다 suspend publication[business]／전투 행위를 ～하다 suspend hostilities. ていし
**정지(整地)** 《건축을 위한》 land readjustment 《경작을 위한》 soil preparation／～하다 readjust the land (for *construction*); prepare the soil (for *planting*).　せいち
**정지(靜止)** rest; stillness; stationariness; standstill 《휴지》 standing still／～의 stationary／～하다 rest; stand still; be at[come to] a standstill／자연계의 어느 것이든 한시도 ～하는 일이 없다 Nothing in nature stands still for a moment.
　　　　　　　　　　　　　　　　せいし
**정직(正直)** honesty; uprightness; integrity／～하다 (be) honest; upright; square／～한 사람 an honest person／너에게 ～하게 말하겠다 I shall be quite honest with you.／～은 최선의 정책이다 Honesty is the best policy.　　　しょうじき
**정직(定職)** a regular occupation; a fixed employment; a steady job／～을 얻다 find a regular employment.
**정직(停職)** suspension from office／～을 명하다 suspend one from office; order (*an offical*) suspended／그는 ～당했다 He was suspended from office. ていしょく
**정진(精進)** close application; devotion 《금욕》 abstinence from flesh 《종교적》 religious purification／～하다 devote oneself (*to*); apply oneself (*to*); abstain from flesh; strive to／문학 연구에 ～하다 devote oneself to the study of literature.　　　　　　　　　　　しょうじん
**정차(停車)** a stop ⇒정거(停車)／～ 시간 stoppage time／～ 신호 a stop signal／비상 ～ an emergency stop.　　ていしゃ
**정착(定着)** fixation 《사진의》 fixing／～하다 fix／～물 a fixture／～액 a fixing solution／～제 a fixing agent／그는 간신히 2루에 ～했다 He finally found himself at second base.　　　　ていちゃく
**정찬(正餐)** a formal dinner.
**정찰(正札)** a price label; a price-mark [-tag]／～ 가격 a marked price; a net price／～이 붙은 상품 a plain-maked article／～제 에누리 없음 Marked price and no overcharge.　　　しょうふだ
**정찰(偵察)** reconnaissance; reconnoiter; scouting; patrol／～하다 reconnoiter; patrol; scout／～기 a scout plane／～대 a reconnoitering party; a patrol team／～병 a scout／～ 비행 a reconnaissance flight／～у 임무를 띠고 출발하다 start charged with reconnoitering duties[on scouting service].　　　　　ていさつ
**정찰(精察)** close inspection[examination]／～하다 examine closely.　せいさつ
**정채(精彩)** luster; brilliance; life; vividness／～가 없다 be lifeless; lack vividness; be lacking in vitality. せいさい
**정책(政策)** a policy; measures／외교[대외] ～ a foreign policy／～ 협정 a policy agreement／～상의 문제 a matter of policy／～을 유지하다 make no departure from one's policy／～을 협정하다 fix a policy.　　　　　　　　せいさく
**정처(正妻)** the lawful wife.　せいさい
**정처(定處)** a fixed place[abode]; a definite destination／～없이 with no definite objective in view; aimlessly／～없는 나그네 길에 오르다 set out on a journey with no definite objective in view.
　　　　　　　　　　　　　きまったところ
**정철(正鐵)** wrought iron.　せんてつ
**정철(精鐵)** refined iron.　せいてつ
**정청(政廳)** a govenment office[house].
**정체(正體)** 《본성》 true character; true colors 《원래 꼴》 a natural shape; one's original form／～ 모를 strange; mysterious; funny／～ 불명의 사람 a total stranger; a nondescript; an undeintified person／～를 감추다 wear[put on] a mask／～를 폭로하다 debunk／～를 나타내다 show oneself in true colors; show one's colors.　　　　　　しょうたい
**정체(政體)** the form[system] of government; political system; government／민주 ～ democracy／입헌[전제] ～ constitutional[dictatorial] form of government／～를 변경하다 change the form of government.　　　　　　　　せいたい
**정체(停滯)** 《정돈》 accumulation 《폭주》 congestion 《침체》 stagnation 《자금·화물의》 a tie-up 《지불의 지연》 falling into arrears／～하다 stagnate; pile up; accumulate; be tied up; fall into arrears／자금의 ～ a tie-up of funds／사무가 ～되다 business is [seriously] delayed／금융이 ～되어 있다 The money market is sluggish.　　　　　　　　ていたい
**정초(正初)** the first decade of January／～에 early in January.　　としのはじめ
**정초(定礎)** the laying of the corner[foundation]-stone／～하다 lay the cornerstone of (*a building*).
**정충(精蟲)** 《동》 a spermatozoon (*pl*.-zoa); a zoosperm; a spermatozoid／～ 형성

spermatogenesis. せいちゅう
**정충(貞忠)** loyalty; fealty; devotion.
**정취(情趣) 《기분》** mood **《느낌》《아치》** artistic effect (of *a painting*); charms; charming effect; flavor/~있는 charming; appealing; tasteful/그의 그림에는 사람을 매혹할 만한 ~가 있다 There is something in his paintings which appeals to our imagination.
　　　　　　　　　　　　　じょうしゅ
**정치(定置)** fixation; settling/~의 fixed stationary/~하다 station.
**정치(政治) 《시정》** government; administration; statecraft **《정사》** politics; political affairs; the affairs of state/~가 a politician; a professional politician; ~ 공작 political maneuvering/~ 기자 a political writer/~ 단체 a political organization[body]/~ 도덕 political morality/~ 난 a political column/~ 문제 a political issue[question]/~ 범 political offense; a political offender/~ 사상 political ideas/~ 운동 a political campaign[movement, agitation]/~ 자금 political funds/~ 조직 a political system; a body politic/~ 학 political science; politics/금권 ~ plutocracy/~적 수완 statesmanship; political ability/~상의 문제로 삼다 make a political issue (of)/~ 운동에 참가하다 take part in a political campaign[movement]. せいじ
**정치(情致)** a charming effect; a romantic touch; being artistic[appealing].
　　　　　　　　　　　　　じょうち
**정치(鼎峙)** a triangular position/~하다 take a triangular position; be in a three-cornered contest; stand in a trio.
　　　　　　　　　　　　　ていじ
**정치(精緻)** fineness **《미세》** minuteness; subtlety **《정교》** exquisitenes **《섬세》** delicacy/~하다 (be) exquisite; fine; delicate; minute. せいち
**정칙(正則)** a regular system; regularity; normality/~ 영어 correct[normal, proper, natural, good] English/~의 영어 연구 a systematic study of English.
　　　　　　　　　　　　　せいそく
**정칙(定則)** a law; an established rule.
　　　　　　　　　　　　　ていそく
**정탐(偵探)** secret investigation/~하다 spy; investigate/~군 a spy.
　　　　　　　　　　　たんさくすること
**정태(情態)** stationariness/~의 static[al]; station/~ 통계 static statistics.
　　　　　　　　　　　　　じょうたい
**정태(靜態)** flattering attitude. せいたい
**정토(征討)** conquest ⇒정벌(征伐). せいとう
**정토(淨土)** paradise; the promised[holy] land; the Buddhist Elysium; pure land/서방(西方) ~ the paradise in the west.
　　　　　　　　　　　　　じょうど
**정통(正統) 《혈통》** legitimacy; orthodoxy **《왕위》** lineal descent of royalty/~의 legitimate; orthodox/~ 정부 a de jure government/~파 the orthodox school [party]/~파의 신앙 the orthodox faith; orthodoxy. せいとう
**정통(精通)** complete knowledge/~하다 be well versed[informed] in; have a thorough knowledge of; be conversant[familiar] with; be at home in[on]/한국의 사정에 ~하다 He is well acquainted with Korean affairs./4개 국어에 ~하다 He is an expert in four languages.
　　　　　　　　　　　　　せいつう
**정퇴(停退)** deferment; postponement/~하다 postpone; defer; put off.
**정판(整版) 【인】** recomposition/~하다 recompose.
**정평(正評)** a happy hit; a pertinent criticism. ただしいひひょう
**정평(定評)** a reputation; a settled opinion; public acknowledgment/그는 대학자라는 ~이 있다 He has the reputation of being a great scholar./그것은 일반의 ~이다 That is what everybody says.
　　　　　　　　　　　　　ていひょう
**정품(精品)** choice goods; articles of the best quality
**정풍 운동(整風運動)** purification drive/경찰(警察) ~ purification drive by policemen.
**정하다(定―) 《결정하다》** decide (*on*); fix; determine **《협정하다》** arrange; agree upon **《날짜를》** set; appoint **《선정하다》** choose **《결심하다》** resolve; determine; be resolved; be determined **《규칙을》** lay down; establish/직업을 ~ choose[decide on] *one's* occupation/태도를 ~ define *one's* attitude. きめる
**정하다(呈―) ①《제출하다》** present (*a petition, a written complaint, etc.*); file; offer **②《나타내다》** show (*symptoms, appearance, etc.*); display; exhibit; present. だす
**정하다(淨―)** (be) clear; clean; pure/정한 물 clear water. すんでいる
**정학(停學)** suspension from school; rustication/1주일 간의 ~ one week's suspension from school/~을 명하다 suspend [a student] from school; send down a student; order a student to stay out from school. ていがく
**정한(定限) ①《기한》** a definite period of time; a limited time **②《한도》** a fixed limit. ていげん
**정한(精悍)** intrepidity; fierceness/~하다 (be) intrepid; dauntless; fierce; fearless. せいかん
**정해(正解)** a correct interpretation; a correct answer[solution]/~하다 interpret correctly; give a correct answer [solution]/~자(者) a correct solver; one who gives a correct answer. せいかい
**정해(精解)** precise[accurate] solution[interpretation]/~ 하다 solve[interpret] precisely. せいかい
**정향(丁香)** clove buds; *Syringa palibiniana*(학명)/~나무 a kind of clove tree;

정현(正弦) 〖수〗 a sine [of an angle]/~호 an arc-sine/~ 곡선 a sine curve. せいげん

정혈(精血) life blood. しんせんなけつえき

정형(定型) a [fixed] type; a definite form/~시 set-form verse/~화 standardization/~적 typical. ていけい

정형(整形) ¶ ~ 수술 plastic operations; orthopedic treatment/~ 외과 plastic surgery; orthopedia/~ 외과의[사] a plastic[an orthopedist] surgeon. せいけい

정형(定形) a fixed[regular] form. ていけい

정호(正號) 〖수〗 a positive sign. せいごう

정혼(定婚) betrothal; engagement/~하다 arrange a marriage; betroth. けっこんがきまること

정혼(精魂) the spirit ⇨정령(精靈). せいこん

정화(正貨) specie/~로 in specie/~ 준비 specie[gold] reserve/~ 결핍 a shortage [lack] of specie/~ 유출[유입] the outflow[inflow] of specie/~ 지불 specie payment. せいか

정화(情火) passion of love; fire of passion; flame of love/~를 붙놓다 kindle the passion; have a burning passion/~에 불타다 burn with passion[love]. じょうか

정화(情話) a love-story; a romance; lover's talk; a *tête-a-tête*(F)(애인간의). じょうわ

정화(淨化) purification; clean-up/~하다 purify; purge; clean up/~ 운동 a purge a clean up movement/~ 장치 a purification plant 《하수의》 ˚sewage disposal facilities; sewerage. じょうか

정화(精華) essence; quintessence; flower; glory/기사도의 ~ the flower of chivalry. せいか

정화수(井華水) clear well-water drawn at early dawn.

정확(正確) correctness; exactness; veracity/~하다 (be) exact; correct; authentic/~한 발음 correct pronunciation/~한 시간 correct[exact] time/보도의 ~ the veracity of information/~하게 말하자면 to be exact; correctly[precisely] speaking/~한 것은 모른다 I don't know for certain. せいかく

정확(精確) precision; accuracy; exactitude/~하다 (be) accurate; precise; exact/~히 accurately; precisely. せいかく

정황(政況) the political situation.

정황(情況) conditions; circumstances; a situation; the state of things/현(現) ~으로는 under these circumstances; as matters stand. じょうきょう

정회(情懷) heart; affectionate remembrances; fond recollection; dear memories. じょうかい

정회(停會) suspension 《의회의》 prorogation 《휴회》 adjournment/~하다 suspend; prorogue. ていかい

정회원(正會員) a regular member/~의 자격 full membership.

정훈(政訓) troop information and education.

정휴일(定休日) a regular[set] holiday. ていきゅうび

정히(正一) truly; surely; certainly; quite; just. ただしくまさに

젖 《기관》 the breast[s]; 《액체》 milk; mother's milk(모유); 《우유》 cow's milk /~빛의 milky/~을 빨다 suck *one's* breast/소의 ~을 짜다 milk the cow/~을 먹이다 suckle; nurse; give the breasts to/~을 떼다 wean [a baby from its mother]/~가슴 the breast[s]; the bosom/~꼭지 the teat[s]; the nipple[s]/~니 a milk tooth; the first set of teeth/~먹이 a new-born baby/~몸살 a disease caused by the inflammation of the breast; mastitis/~소 a milch cow. ちち

젖내 《냄새》 the smell of milk/~나다 be [still] suckling; be [still] in swaddling clothes; be babyish[childish, puerile, immature, green]. ちちのにおい

젖다 get wet; be drenched; be soaked; /젖은 wet; damp/이슬에 젖은 장미 roses washed by dew/땀에 ~ be wet with perspiration/물에 ~ get wet; be soaked/함빡 ~ be wet[soaked] to the skin; be soaking wet/네 말은 귀에 젖도록 들었다 That's enough out of you. ぬれる

젖떨어지다 be[get] weaned

젖떼기 one[a chid, an animal] that is weaned.

젖먹이 a sucking child; a suckling; a [new-born] baby. にゅうじ

젖멍울 《젖샘》 the mammary gland 《명울》 mastitis.

젖히다 turn over; turn up (*a card*); open /페이지를 ~ turn over the leaves (of *a book*); turn the pages. ひっくりかえす

제¹ 《저기》 that place; there; over there /~ 있는 건물이 우리 학교입니다 The building over there is our school. あそこ

제² 《저·자기》 self; oneself 《자기의》 *one's* own/~가 좋아서 하는 일 a self-imposed work/~ 몸 self; oneself/~ 마음대로 of *one's* own accord; of *one's* own freewill/~ 것을 만들다 make (*a thing*) *one's* own/~ 생각만 하다 be thinking only of oneself/~ 이익만 생각하다 look to *one's* own interest/~멋대로 as one pleases; at will; *ad libitum*(L). わたくし

제(題) a subject ⇨제목(題目). だい

제(祭) 《제사》 religious service 《축제》 a festival/기념 ~ a commemoration/50년 ~ a jubilee. さい

제(除) ①subtraction ⇨제법 ②exclusion ⇨제거. じょ

제(帝) an emperor.

제(弟) ①《자칭》 I ②《아우》 a younger

제 844 제대

brother. てい
제(諸) many; several; various; manifold/~비용[경비] expenses; costs; charges; overhead.
제(第) No., number/~삼국 the third power[country]/~삼자 a third party [person]; an outsider. だい
-제(制) a system; an organization; an institution/7시간~ the seven-hour system/4년~ 대학 a four-year college. —せい
-제(劑) a medicine; a drug/소화~ a digestive; a peptic. —ざい
-제(製) make; manufacture 《제본》 binding/외국~의 물건 articles of foreign manufacture[make]/영국~의 English make; made in England/강철~의 steel. —せい
제가(齊家) household management/~하다 manage *a person's* family affairs; manage a household. せいか
제가(諸家) 《여러 학자》 various[many] masters; all the schools (of *art*)/《친척들》 the whole family; all the relatives. しょか
제각기(一各其) each; severally/~ 앞을 다투어 everybody for himself/사람은 ~ 생각이 다르다 Many men, many minds. /사람은 ~ 장단점이 있다 Each man has his merits and faults. おのおのごとに
제감(除減) deduction; subtraction/~하다 deduct; take away; subtract. のぞきへらすこと
제강(製鋼) steel manufacture/~법 a steel making process/~소 steel works/~업 the steel industry. せいこう
제거(除去) removal; exclusion; eradication/~하다 get rid of; clear (*of*); remove; exclude; eliminate /생활의 낭비를 ~하다 eliminate the wastefulness of life/장애물을 ~하다 remove obstacles. じょきょ
제것 *one's* possession[belongings].
제곱 《수》 a square/~하다 square (*a number*); multiply (*a number*) by itself /~수 a square number. じじょう
제공(提供) tender; proffer; offer/~하다 make an offer; proffer/~ 가격 the price offered/정보를 ~하다 furnish information.
제공권(制空權) the mastery[command] of the air; air supremacy/~을 잡다 [잃다] win[lose] the air. せいくうけん
제과(製菓) confectionery/~하다 confection/~ 회사 a confectionery company/~업 the confectionery industry/~업자 a confectioner. せいか
제관(帝冠) a crown; a diadem; the Imperial crown.
제관(祭官) 《제사 맡은 사람》 an officiating priest 《참례자》 those who participate in sacrifices. さいかん
제관(製罐) can manufacturing; canning 〈미〉; tinning〈영〉.
제구(祭具) utensils used in religious services. さいぐ
제구(諸具) various articles[utensils, fixtures, tools]. いろいろのきぐ
제구실 *one's* duty/~을 하게 되다 become an adult(연령); become independent(독립); become a selfsupporting man(자활)/~을 못 하다 be not worth *one's* salt. じぶんのやくわり
제국(帝國) an empire/~의 Imperial/~주의 imperialism; expansionism〈미〉/반~주의 감정 anti-imperialist sentiment/~주의적 imperialistic. ていこく
제국(諸國) all[various, many] countries. しょこく
제군(諸君) gentlemen; my friends; you 《부하에게》 my lads 《연설의 경우》 Ladies and Gentlemen! しょくん
제금(提琴) a violin; a fiddle《속》 /~가 a violinist; a fiddle《속》. ていきん
제기¹ 《장난감》 a Korean shuttlecock; a *jegee*/~ 차다 play Korean shuttlecock game; play *jegee*.
제기² shucks; damn it; confound it; fie/~랄 Damn it!, Go and hang it!/~ 비싸기도 하군 그래 It's damn expensive! ちぇっ.あ—
제기(祭器) receptacles[vessels] used in religious services. さいき
제기(提起) 《요구》 presentation 《소송》 institution 《항의》 lodging 《발언》 suggestion/~하다 present; propose; institute; lodge; bring (*forward*); 《문제 따위를》 start/소송을 ~하다 institute[lodge, file] a law suit. ていき
제기다¹ ①《지르다》 kick with [the] toe; nudge with [the] elbow; toe; elbow ②《연장으로》 cut with light repeated strokes ③《물을》 pour [water] a little at a time.
제기다² ①《눈을》 have[get] a white spot in the pupil of an eye ②《살짝》 slip out; sneak away.
제단(祭壇) an altar; the seat of religious service. さいだん
제딴은 as for *one*; for *one's* part; for *one*self; in *one's* own opinion/~ 아주 열심히 공부하는 것으로 알고 있다 He fancies himself to be working very hard. じぶんのかんがえでは
제당(製糖) sugar-manufacture[-refining] /~업 the sugar-manufacturing industry/~소 a sugar-manufactory/~ 회사 a sugar-manufacturing company.
제때 an appointed[a scheduled, a proper] time.
제대(除隊) discharge from military service; disbandment/~하다 disband; demobilize/~병 a discharged[time-expired] soldier/~되다 be discharged from military service; leave the colours/만기 전에 ~가 되다 be discharged before

제대 one's time/의병 ~ 되다 be invalided out of the army. じょたい

**제대**(梯隊) 〖군〗 an echelon.

**제대로** 《제가 생긴 대로》 plainly; frankly; as it is 《정상적으로》 favourably; normally; without a hitch 《규칙적으로》 regulary 《충분히》 sufficiently; satisfactorily/~ 잘 되다 be restored to; come to a peaceful settlement; go well; be successful/~편지도 ~ 못 쓴다 He can't write a letter properly/무엇이든지 다 하는 사람은 한 가지도 ~ 못 한다 Jack of all trades and master of none. /나는 ~ 교육도 못 받았다 I have had no regular education. じぶんなりに

**제도**(制度) a system 《시설》 an order 《조직》an organization 《질서》an order /결혼 ~ the marriage institution/교육 ~ the educational system/~를 바꾸다 change the system/~를 개선하다 improve[reform] the system. せいど

**제도**(濟度) salvation 《속죄》 redemption 《교정》 eclamation/~하다 save; reclaim; redeem/~할 수 없다 be past[beyond] redemption; be incorrigible. さいど

**제도**(製圖) draughtsmanship; drafting 《지도·해도의》 cartography; 〖수〗 drawing /~하다 draw; draft/~가 a draughtsman; a drafts-man〈미〉/~ 기구 drawing instruments/~실 a drawing[drafting] room/~판 a drawing board; a trestle board. せいず

**제도**(諸島) a group of islands; an archipelago/남양 ~ The South Sea Islands.

**제독**(制毒) protection against poison/~하다 protect against poison; neutralize a poison.

**제독**(提督) a squadron commander; an admiral; a commodore〈미〉. ていとく

**제동**(制動) 〖전〗 damping/~하다 brake (a car); damp/~간 a safety lever/~수 a brakeman/~ 잔치 a damping device; an arresting gear/~ 활강 〈스키의〉 glissade/~ 회전 a stem turn. せいどう

**제동기**(制動機) a brake/동력 ~ a power brake/자동 ~ an automatic brake/자력(自力) ~ a magnetic brake/전기 ~ an electric brake/진공 ~ a vacuum brake/~를 걸다 apple[put on] the brakes. せいどうき

**제등**(提燈) a [paper-]lantern/~ 행렬 a lantern procession. ちょうちん

**제등수**(諸等數) 〖수〗 a compound number. しょとうすう

**제련**(製鍊) refining; refinement; smeeting/~하다 refine; smelt; purify/~소 a refinery; a smelting works/~업 the refining industry/ ~업자(業者) a refiner. せいれん

**제령**(制令) an institution; a regulation. せいれい

**제례**(祭禮) religious ceremonies. さいれい

**제마**(製麻) hemp-dressing/~하다 manufacture hemp (goods)/~ 회사 a hemp-dressing company. せいま

**제막**(除幕) unveiling/~하다 unveil (a bust, a statue)/~식 the ceremony of unveiling; the unveiling ceremony (of a statue, bust). じょまく

**제멋** one's own taste[way, fancy, style].

**제면**(製麵) manufacturing noodles/~하다 make noodle; make wheat vermicelli/~기(機) a noodle-making machine. せいめん

**제면**(製綿) ginning cotton/~하다 gin cotton. せいめん

**제명**(除名) expulsion; striking off a name/~하다 expel (from); oust; strike [take] a name off a list[roll]/~되다 be struck off the list; be expelled from membership/그는 그 회(會)에서 ~당했다 He was expelled from the society. じょめい

**제명**(題名) a title/…의 ~으로 출판되다 be published under the title (of). だいめい

**제모**(制帽) a regulation[uniform, school] cap/제복 ~의 학생 a student in uniform. せいぼう

**제모**(製帽) hat[cap] manufactu ぅ/~업 the hat industry; capping; hatting.

**제목**(題目) a subject; a theme 《책의》 a title; a heading[headline]; 《사진의》 caption/작문의 ~ the subject of composition/~을 붙이다 give a title to; entitle (a book) だいもく

**제문**(祭文) a funeral address; a memorial address. さいぶん

**제물** 《국물》 the water in which food was cooked; soup left after food is cooked 《순수한 것》 genuine stuff.

**제물**(祭物) an offering; a sacrificial offering; things offered in sacrifice. さいもつ

**제물에** of itself; of its own accord; naturally/상처가 ~ 나았다 The wound healed of itself./불이 ~ 꺼졌다 The fire went out of itself. しぜんに

**제반**(諸般) ~의 various; all; every/~ 정세 all circumstances/~ 준비를 갖추다 make all preparations. しょはん

**제발** kindly; [if you] please; pray; I beg 《꼭》 by all means/~ 용서하세요 Excuse me, please./~ 좀 조용히 해 주게 For goodness' sake, don't start making a noise about it. なにとぞ

**제발 덕분에**(一德分一) for the love of God; for God's[Heaven's] sake; in mercy's name/~ 살려 주십시오 Spare me [my life] for mercy's [Peter's] sake. なにとぞ

**제방**(堤防) a bank; an embankment; a dike; a dyke; a levee〈미〉/~이 무너지다 a dike breaks. ていぼう

**제백사**(除百事) laying aside everything/ ~하다 throw[put] aside everything/

제번(除煩) saving trouble; without ceremony/~하다 save trouble; be without ceremony/~하옵고 《편지 허두에》 I hasten to inform you that….

~하고 찾아 뵙겠읍니다 I'll let everything else go and visit you.

제벌(除伐) 《임업》 improvement[salvage] cutting. じょばつ

제법 pretty; fairly; passably; considerably; tolerably/~ 중대한 일 a matter of no small consequence/~이다 be better than expected/~ 시간이 걸리다 take a great deal of time/그는 ~ 문장가(家)다 He is very much of a writer. かなり

제법(製法) a method[process] of manufacture; how to make 《과자·요리의》 a recipe [for making a cake]. せいほう

제복(制服) a uniform; a regulation[uniform] dress 《고용인의》 livery 《법관 따위의》 a gown/학교에는 ~을 입고 가지 않으면 안 된다 We have to go school in uniform. せいふく

제복(除服) going out of mourning/~하다 leave off mourning; go out of mourning. じょふく

제복(祭服) garment worn in religious [memorial] services 《카톨릭교》 a pallium; a pall. さいふく

제본(製本) bookbinding/~하다 bind (a book)/~소 a bookbindery/~이 잘 되어 있도록 be well bound/이것을 ~해 주십시오 I want to have the book bound. せいほん

제분(製粉) milling/~하다 grind to flour/~기 a mill/~업 the milling industry/~소 a flour[ing]-mill/~업자 a miller. せいふん

제불이 one's kinsmen; one's relatives. じぶんのけつぞく

제비¹ 《추첨》 a lot 《뽑기》 lottery; a raffle 《한 장의》 a lottery-ticke./~ 뽑다 draw lots/~ 뽑아 결정하다 decide[choose] by lot. くじ

제비² 《조》 a swallow. つばめ

제비꽃 《식》 a violet; a pansy. すみれ

제빙(除氷) deicing/~하다 deice/~ 장치 a deicing device; a deicer.

제빙(製氷) 《제조》 ice-manufacture 《얼음의》 artificial ice/~기 an ice[-making] machine; a refrigerator/~소〔공장〕 an ice-plant〔-manufactory〕/~ 회사 an ice [-manufacturing] company. せいひょう

제사(祭祀) religious service; sacrificial rites/~를 지내다 perform a religious service. さいし

제사(製絲) spinning 《견사의》 silk-reeling [-manufacture]; filature/~하다 draw silk; make thread/~공 a silk-reel worker/~ 공장 a filature; a silk mill/~업 the silk-reeling industry/~업자 a silk manufacturer. せいし

제사(題詞) an epigraph; a prefatory motto. だいじ

제사날로 of one's own accord; of one's own free will/가만히 내버려두면 ~ 돌아올걸 Let him alone, and he will return of his own accord. みずから

제산(除算) division/~하다 divide. じょさん

제살이 self-support/~하다 support oneself; earn one's own living. じかつすること

제삼 계급(第三階級) the bourgeoisie; the third estate. だいさんかいきゅう

제삼국(第三國) the third power[country]. だいさんごく

제삼자(第三者) a third person; the disinterested party; an outsider. だいさんしゃ

제상(祭床) a table used in a religious [memorial] service; a sacrificial table.

제상(除霜) defrost; deice/~ 장치 a defroster; a deicer.

제서(題書) a prefatory motto; an epigraph ㅡ제자(題字). だいじ

제석(除夕) New Year's Eve; the watch night. おおみそか

제석(祭席) a mat used in religious[memorial] services. さいしょうのござ

제설(除雪) snow removal/~하다 remove snow/~기 a snowplow/~차 a snowplow car[locomotive]. じょせつ

제설(諸說) diverse views[opinions]; various theories 《풍설》 different rumours /이 사건에 대하여는 ~이 분분하다 Various views are expressed on this affair. しょせつ

제세(濟世) relief; salvation/~하다 save [relieve] the world/~ 안민 saving the world and relieving the people/~주 a savior. さいせい

제소(提訴) instituting/~하다 institute a suite, bring an action (against). ていそ

제수(除數) 《수》 the divisor; the number to be divided by. じょすう

제수(弟嫂) a younger brother's wife; a sister-in-law. おとうとのつま

제수(祭需) ①things used in religious services ②ㅡ제물(祭物).

제술(製述) literary composition/~하다 compose (literary works); write.

제시(提示) presentation/~하다 《법》 exhibit; present/~금 show money/~ 기간 time of presentation/~부 《음·연》 exposition/~ 어음 《상》 enfaced paper /~하는 대로 at[on] presentation. ていじ

제씨(弟氏) your[his] esteemed younger brother おとうとさん

제씨(諸氏) gentlemen; Messrs/독자 ~ my reader[s]/이·김·박 ~ Messrs, Lee, Kim, and Bark. みなさん

제시간(一時間) the appropriate[proper, scheduled] time/~에 on time.

제실(帝室) the Imperial Household[Family]/~의 of the Imperial court. ていしつ

제안(提案) a proposal; a proposition; an

**제압**(制壓) ascendancy; supremacy; control/~하다 control; gain control over; dominate. せいあつ

**제액**(題額) writing an inscription for a tablet. だいがく

**제야**(除夜) New Year's Eve; the watch night/~의 종 the watch-night bell; the bell speeding the old year/~의 종 소리를 듣고 자다 go to bed at midnight when the temple bells ring in the New Year. じょや

**제약**(製藥) (제조) medicine manufacture; pharmacy (약) a manufactured medicine/~하다 manufacture drugs[medicines]/~ 공장(회사) a pharmaceutical factory[company]/~사 a pharmacist; an apothecary/~업자 a drug manufacturer; a pharmacist/~ 화학 pharmaceutical chemistry. せいやく

**제약**(制約) (제한) condition 《속박》 a restriction/~하다 control; dominate; restrict/시간의 ~을 받다 be restricted by time/인생에는 여러 가지 ~이 있다 Life is hampered by a variety of restrictions. せいやく

**제어**(制御, 制馭) control; governing; domination; suppression; mastery; management/~하다 control; govern; dominate/~기 《전》 a controller/~봉 《원자로의》 a control rod/~하기가 쉽다 be easy to control; be controllable. せいぎょ

**제언**(堤堰) a dam; a barrage. みずだめ

**제역**(除役) exemption from [military] service/~하다 exempt (one) from military service. じょえき

**제염**(臍炎) 《의》 inflammation of the navel. さいえん

**제염**(製鹽) salt manufacture/~소 a saltern; a salt-manufactory[-works]/~업 salt[-making] industry[business]/~업자 a salter. せいえん

**제오**(第五) the number five(略: No. 5); the fifth/~의 the fifth/~열 the Fifth Column; the Fifth Columnists. だいご

**제왕**(帝王) an emperor; a sovereign; a monarch/~의 imperial; monarchic[al] /~학 a study of regal principles/~ 절개 수술 《의》 a caesarean operation. ていおう

**제외**(除外) exclusion; exception 《면제》 exemption/~하다 except; make an exception of; exclude; exempt (one) from/~례 an exception; an exemption /~ 조항 an escape clause/회원에서 ~ 하다 exclude (a person) from membership/배심 의무에서 ~하다 exempt (a person) from jury duty. じょがい

**제요**(提要) gist; a summary; a résumé (F)/~하다 summarize; epitomize/물리학 ~ elements of physics. ていよう

**제욕**(制慾) control of passions[appetites] /~하다 mortify[control] one's passions; regulate one's desires; be ascetic. せいよく

**제우**(諸友) friends. しょゆう

**제웅** a Jack[man] of straw; a straw figure.

**제위**(祭位) the enshrined deity; a deity worshipped; a deity for worship. さいしをうけるしんぶつ

**제위**(帝位) the crown; the throne/~에 오르다 ascend[accede to] the throne/ ~를 계승하다 succeed to the throne/~ 를 빼앗다 usurp the throne. ていい

**제위**(諸位) gentlemen. みなさん

**제유**(製油) oil-manufacture[-refining]/ ~하다 manufacture oil/~소 an oil factory. せいゆ

**제유법**(提喩法) 《언》 synecdoche.

**제육** pork/~ 구이 roasted thin pork chops/~전 a pork butcher[shop].

**제육감**(第六感) the sixth sense/~으로 안 다 I know that by instinct., My sixth sense tell me that. だいろっかん

**제융**(製絨) wool-weaving/~소 a woolen factory; a wool mill.

**제의**(提議) a proposal; a proposition; an offer; an overture 《제언》 a suggestion /~하다 propose; offer; make an overture; move; suggest; make a proposal/~자 a proposer; a mover/계획을 ~하다 propose a plan/~에 동의하다 agree to (a person's) proposal; accept a suggestion put forward by. ていぎ

**제이**(第二) number two (略: No. 2); the second/~의 the second (또 하나의) a second; another 《중요성이》 secondary; of second[minor] importance/~군 《체》 the second string/~당 the second largest party/~인칭 《언》 the second person/~ 주제 《음》 the subsidiary [theme] /~의 천성 a second nature/~ 고향 one's second[adopted] home. だいに

**제인**(諸人) everyone; all [the] people.

**제일**(祭日) a festival day. さいじつ

**제일**(除日) the last day of the year. じょじつ

**제일**(第一) number one(略: No. 1); the first; the best; leading (부사적으로) most; best/~의 first; initial; 《화》 primary 《주요한》 prime; principal; chief 《으뜸의》 the greatest the best/~과 the first lesson; lesson one/~기 the first term[period]; 《병의》 the first stage /~당 the leading[dominant] party/~ 심 the first trial/~인자 the first[-ranking] man; the leading person/~인칭 《언》 the first person/~ 종 우편 first class mail matter/~ 먼저 firstly; firstly; in the first place/~안전 ~ safety first/ 세계 ~의 부자 the richest man in the world/성공에는 인내가 ~이다 Persever-

ance is the first essential to success.
だいいち

**제자**(題字) a prefatory motto[inscription]. だいじ

**제자**(弟子) a disciple; a follower 《도제》 an apprentice; a student 《학생》 a pupil /~를 두다 take pupils[apprentices]/ ~가 되다 become *one's* disciple. でし

**제자**(諸子) ①《제군》you; gentlemen ②《중국의》sages; masters/~ 백가 all philosophers and literary scholars. みなさん

**제자리** the proper place; the original place/~ 걸음하다 《군대나 물가가》mark time; be at a standstill; be in a stalemate

**제작**(制作) a work; a production/~하다 produce (*a work* of *art, etc.*).

**제작**(製作) manufacture; production/~ 하다 manufacture; make; produce; turn out/~ 번호 the factory number/~비 production cast[s]/~소 a factory; a works; a workshop; a plant; a mill/ ~자 a maker; a manufacturer (영화의) a producer/~품 a manufactured article; products; output/영화 ~ the production of films/비행기를 ~하다 make [turn out] airplanes. せいさく

**제재**(製材) sawing; lumbering 《목재》 planed wood/~소 a saw[lumber]-mill. せいざい

**제재**(制裁) restraint; sanctions; punishment/~하다 restrain; take sanctions (*against*); put restraint on (*one*); place (*one*) under restraint/~국 a sanctionist country/《위반자에게 ~하다》 discipline an offender/법들의 ~를 받다 be brought under the law. せいさい

**제재**(題材) a subject-matter; a theme; a topic. だいざい

**제적**(除籍) removal (of *a name*) from the register 《국적에서의》denationalization/~하다 remove (*a person's name*) from the register; put (*a ship*) out of commission 《학적에서》 expel 《국적에서》 denationalize. じょせき

**제전**(祭典) a festival; a religious service; festivities/~을 베풀다 hold a festival. さいてん

**제절**(諸節) 《여러분》 all of you; everybody/댁내 ~이 무고하신지요 How are your people?, How is your family? みなさん

**제정**(祭政) the church and state/~ 일치 the unity of church and state 《제도》 theocracy. さいせい

**제정**(制定) enactment; establishment by law; institution/~하다 enact; lay down; establish; legislate/~자 a legislator/법률을 ~하다 enact[make] a law; legislate. せいてい

**제정**(帝政) Imperial government[rule, regime]; monarchical rule/~ 시대 the monarchical days/~ 러시아 Czarist Russia. ていせい

**제제 다사**(濟濟多士) a galaxy of brilliant men. さいさいたし

**제조**(製造) manufacture; production; preparation; construction/~하다 manufacture; make; produce; prepare/~ 능력 manufacturing capacity/~법 a manufacturing process 《비결》 a recipe (과자 따위의)/~비 manufacturing[production] cost/~소 a manufactory; a factory; a plant; a mill/~업 manufacturing industry/~지 the place of production/~품 manufactures; finished articles/펄프에서 종이를 ~하다 make paper from pulp. せいぞう

**제족**(諸族) whole family; whole clan.

**제주**(祭酒) sacred wine; wine offered before the altar; a drink-offering/~ 를 올리다 offer wine before the altar. さいしゅ

**제주**(祭主) 《상제》a chief mourner 《주하는 사람》 the master of religious rites.

**제주고지새**(濟州—) 〘조〙 a Japanese grosbeak; *Eophona personata*(학명).

**제중**(濟衆) salvation of the people[world]/~하다 save the world; work the salvation of the people.
すべてのひとをきゅうさいすること

**제지**(制止) restraint; repression; check; curb; control/~하다 restrain; put restraint upon; keep (*one*) from; check; arrest; rein/군중을 ~하다 control[keep back] the crowd/~할 수 없는 uncontrollable. せいし

**제지**(製紙) paper manufacture; paper making/~하다 make[manufacture] paper/~ 공장 a papermill[manufactory] /~ 기계 a paper-making machine/~업 the paper[manufacturing] industry/ ~업자 a paper manufacturer/~ 회사 a paper[-manufacturing] company/~ 용 펄프 paper pulp.

**제차**(第次) order ◦차례(次例). じゅんじょ

**제창**(齊唱) a unison; a homophony/~하다 sing in unison/애국가를 ~하다 sing the national anthem in unison.
せいしょう

**제창**(提唱) 《제의》 proposal 《창도》 advocacy 《논술》 a discourse/~하다 lecture (*one*); propose; advocate; discourse/~ 자 an advocate; an exponent/인류 평등을 ~하다 proclaim[advacate] the equality of men. ていしょう

**제철** a season; suitable time/~의 사과 apples of the season/~이 지나다 be out of season; the season is off.
よいじせつ

**제철**(蹄鐵) a horseshoe ◦편자. ていてつ

**제철**(製鐵) iron manufacture /~업 iron industry/~소 an iron-foundry; an iron-works[-mill]. せいてつ

**제쳐놓다** lay aside; put aside; leave out; set apart/모든 일을 다 제쳐놓고 everything else aside. よける

**제초**(除草) weeding/~하다 weed [out] (*a garden, etc.*)/~기 a weeder. じょそう

**제출**(提出) introduction; presentation 《항의의》 lodging/~하다 present; tender; send in 《서류를》 file; bring forward; introduce (*a bill*); submit/~자 an introducer; a presenter/사표를 ~하다 hand in[tender] one's resignation/원서를 ~하다 submit[send in] one's application /의견을 ~하다 advance an opinion; set forth one's views/항의를 ~하다 lodge a complaint against. ていしゅつ

**제출물로** of itself ⇒제물에. じぶんかってに

**제충**(除蟲) ~하다 worm; get rid of worms; stamp out (*noxious insects*)/~제 an insect powder; insecticide/~분(粉) insect powder. じょちゅう

**제충국**(除蟲菊) 〖식〗 a pyrethrum flower; a vermifuge-chrysanthemum/ ~ 가루 insectifuge; pyrethrum. じょちゅうぎく

**제취**(除臭) deodorization/~하다 deodorize/~제 a deodorant; a deodorizer.

**제치다** clear away ⇒젖히다. かたづける

**제칠**(第七) number seven; the seventh /~ 천국 the Seventh Heaven.

**제택**(第宅) residence and arbour. すみかとあずまや

**제판** the sole master of the stage[field]; unrivalled sphere of activity. じぶんのてんか

**제판**(製版) 〖인〗 plate making/~하다 plate; make a stereotype plate/전기 ~ electrotype process/~소 a plate-maker's shop. せいはん

**제패**(制霸) ①(정복) mastery; supremacy domination/~하다 rule; dominate; gain supremacy/세계 ~ world conquest [hegemony]/~전(戰) a struggle for supremacy/~를 다투다 contend for supremacy ②(경기의) championship/ ~하다 win[gain] a championship/우주의 ~를 다투다 fight for the supremacy of space. せいは

**제폐**(除弊) ~하다 do away with abuses. へいがいをなくすこと

**제품**(製品) manufactured goods; a [finished] manufacture/한국[국내] ~ an article of Korean make; home products /외국 ~ an article of foreign make; foreign-made goods. せいひん

**제하다**(除—) ①(제외하다) exclude; except (빼다) deduct; subduce/제하다 except; but; exclusive of; save/봉급에서 ~ deduct (*a sum*) from one's salary/일요일을 제하고 이 달에는 26일이 있다 There are twenty-six days [in] this month, exclusive of Sundays. ②(나눗셈) divide. のぞく

**제한**(制限) restriction; limitation; restraint; limit/~하다 restrict; limit; restrain; confine; keep within bounds/~ 속도 speed limit; regulation speed/시간 ~ time limit/산아 ~ birth control/생산 ~ a curtailment of output/수입 ~

import restrictions/~의 범위를 넘다 go out of bounds/~을 완화[해제]하다 relax[lift, remove] restriction. せいげん

**제한**(際限) a limit; a bound; an end/~이 없는 unlimited; limitless; boundless; endless/~없이 boundlessly; infinitely; to an unlimited extent. さいげん

**제해권**(制海權) command[mastery] of the sea/~을 잡다 rule[command] the sea; have[secure] command of the sea. せいかいけん

**제행**(諸行) all worldly things; all phenomena/~ 무상 All is vanity., Nothing is certain in this world. しょぎょう

**제향**(祭享) a festival; rituals.

**제헌**(制憲) establishment of a constitution/~하다 establish a constitution/~ 국회 the Constitutional Assembly/~절 Constitution Day; Constitution[al] Promulgation Day. せいけん

**제혁**(製革) tanning/~업 tanning/~소 a tannery. せいかく

**제현**(諸賢) [Ladies and] Gentlemen. しょけん

**제형**(梯形) 〖수〗 a trapezium; a trapezoid 〈미〉; 〖군〗 an echelon formation (진(陣)의 형상). ていけい

**제형**(諸兄) my dear friends.

**제형**(蹄形) U-shape/ ~의 hoof-shaped; U-shaped/~ 자석 a horseshoe magnet. ていけい

**제호**(題號) a title (of *a book*). だいごう

**제화**(製靴) 의 ~공 a shoemaker/~ 공장 a shoemaking factory/~업 the shoe industry.

**제회**(際會) ~하다 face; meet; confront /위기에 ~하다 face a crisis; be confronted by an emergency/그는 국가 풍운에 ~하여 공명(功名)을 세웠다 He distinguished himself in the national upheaval. さいかい

**제후**(諸侯) feudal lords. しょこう

**제휴**(提携) concert; co-operation; coalition/~하다 join hands; act in concert; co-operate (*with*); move in harmony/ 기술 ~ a technical tie-up/~하여 운동을 일으키다 join hands to start a movement. ていけい

**젠장** Hang[Damn] it!, Gosh!, How vexatious!/~ 비가 오네 Confound the rain! えいくそ

**젠체하다** be affected; put on[give oneself] airs; assume an air of importance; stand on one's dignity 《자기 도취》 look satified with oneself/그는 언제나 젠체한다 He always puts on airs. /너무 젠체하지 말아라 Don't give yourself such airs. ふりをする

**젯메**(祭—) boiled-rice offered in memorial services.

**젯밥**(祭—) boiled-rice offered in a religious service to one's ancestors.

**쟁그렁거리다, 쨍그렁거리다** jangle; clang; clank; be jangling; clangour/쟁그렁쟁

조 850 조교

그렁[쩽그렁쩽그렁] clang-clang; with a clang. がちゃんがちゃんする

조 〖식〗 millet (조알) a millet seed. あわ

조(兆) a million millions; a billion〈영〉; a thousand billion; a trillion〈미〉. ちょう

조(朝) (왕조) a dynasty (치세) a reign/명(明)~ the Myung Dynasty/영묘(英廟)~에 in the reign of the King Yongjong. ちょう

조(調) a tune (시의) a tone (시의) a meter (곡조) an air; a tune/장난~로 jokingly/시비~로 defiantly. ちょう

조(條) (조항) an article; a passage; a line; an item; a clause/제 5~ Article 5. じょう

조가(弔歌) a dirge; an elegy; a lament; a funeral song. ちょうか

조가비 a shell/~ 세공 shell work/~를 줍다 gather[pick up] shells. かいがら

조각 (쪽) a piece (갈쭉한) a slip (얇은) a slice (도려낸) a scrap (잘라낸) a cut (고기 등의) a chop (파편) a fragment/빵~ a scrap[crumb] of bread/유리 ~ a broken piece of glass; a splinters of glass/종이 ~ a piece[scrap, slip, strip] of paper/포탄 ~ [bomb]shell fragments. かけら

조각(組閣) organization[formation] of a Cabinet[Ministry]/~하다 form[organize] a cabinet[ministry]/~ 본부 the Cabinet organization headquarters.

조각(彫刻) sculpture; sculptural art; carving; engraving/~하다 sculpture (나무에) carve (금속성의 곁에) engrave/~가 an engraver; a carver; a sculptor (여자) a sculptress/~도 a graver; a burin; a carving-knife/ ~술 sculptural art; sculpture; the plastic art; engraving/나무로 상을 ~하다 carve an image in wood. ちょうこく

조각나다 (깨지다) break; be broken; be smashed (갈라지다) split; cleave (의견 따위가) have a split in opinion/두 ~ break[be broken] in two. こなごなになる

조각달 a crescent [moon]; (상현의) a waxing-moon (하현의) a waning-moon.

조각보(一褓) a crazy wrapper. はぎれをつぎあわせたふろしき

조각조각 in pieces[scraps]; disjoined; disconnected/~ 찢다 tear (a letter) to pieces/~ 부서지다 break to pieces. ばらばら

조간(朝刊) a morning paper[edition]. ちょうかん

조간(遭艱) ~하다 lose one's parent; have one's father[mother] die; go into mourning for one's parent.

조갈(燥渴) thirst/~증 a disease attended by great thirst/~이 나다 feel[get] thirsty. のどがかわくこと

조감도(鳥瞰圖) a bird's-eye-view (공중으로부터의) an aeroview. ちょうかんず

조감독(助監督) 〖연〗 an assistant director.

조갑(爪甲) a nail. そうこう

조강(糟糠) "chaff and bran"; (고생살이) a humble living/~지처(之妻) a wife married in poverty; a love-in-the cottage wife; one's good old(faithful) wife; one's old mate/~지처는 불하당(不下堂) One should not divorce an old wife married in penury. かすとぬか

조개 a shellfish/~를 잡다 dig out shellfish. かい

조개구름 a cirrocumulus cloud. けんせきせん

쪼개다 split; divide; part (a thing into); cleave; smash/나무를 ~ split wood /도끼로 장작을 ~ chop wood with an ax[e]. わける

조객(弔客) a caller for condolence/~록(錄) the list of callers for condolence/ a guest book for condolers. ちょうきゃく

조건(條件) a condition; a stipulation; a term/계약의 ~ the terms of contract /노동 ~ a labor condition/필수 ~ a precondition/~을 붙이다 attach[annex] a condition (to)/그는 유리한 ~으로 채용됐다 He was employed on favorable terms. じょうけん

조격(阻隔) separation/~하다 be separated (from); be remote from. そかく

조계(早計) a premature scheme (경솔) overhastiness; rashness; prematurity/~의 rash; hasty; premature. そうけい

조계(租界) a concession; a settlement/외국 ~ a foreign settlement[concession] /영국 ~ a British concession. そかい

조고(祖考) my deceased(late) grandfather. そこう

조고(操觚) (문필 생활) literary occupation journalism/~계 the literary world; literary circles/~자 a writer; an author; a journalist; a man of letters. そうこ

조곡(弔哭) wailing in mourning; keening/~하다 make a call of condolence and wail. ちょうこく

조곡(組曲) 〖음〗 a [musical] suite.

조공(朝貢) tribute/~하다 bring a tribute to a country/~국 a tributary state; a vassal. ちょうぐう

조공(租貢) taxes/~하다 pay taxes.

조관(朝官) a courtier (복칭) the court official. ちょうかん

조관(條款) a stipulation; a provision; a clause; an article/최혜국 ~ a most favoured nation clause. じょうかん

조광(躁狂) frenzy; a mad excitement; (의) mania. いらだちくるうこと

조교(助敎) an assistant teacher (조수) an assistant. じょきょう

조교(照校) collation/~하다 collate/~ 전보 a collated telegram.

조교(吊橋) a suspension bridge/~를 세우다 construct a suspension bridge; suspend a bridge over a river. つりばし

**조교수**(助敎授) an assistant professor. じょきょうじゅ

**조국**(祖國) the fatherland; *one's* native land/~을 방위하다 defend *one's* fatherland/~애(愛)에 불타다 burn with love for *one's* country/~을 위하여 싸우다 fight[rise in arms] for *one's* fatherland. そこく

**조국**(肇國) the founding of a nation/~하다 found a nation[state]. ちょうこく

**조규**(條規) a stipulation; articles; provisions; regulations (of *a law*)/헌법 ~에 따라 under the terms of the Constitution. じょうぶんのきてい

**쪼그랑박** a stunted gourd. ちじこまったひょう

**쪼그랑할멈** a withered old woman.

**쪼그리다** crush ⇨쭈그리다. ちじめる

**조그마하다** (be) small; of a small size; tiny 《왜소하다》 dwarfish 《사소하다》 (be) petty;trifling; trivial; insignificant 《어리다》 (be) young; little/조그마한 일 a small matter; a trifle/조그마한 가게 a petty shop/조그마한 일에 성을 내다 get angry over trifles. ややちいさい

**조고만큼** (양) just a little; in small quantities (정도) slightly; a little. すこし

**조금** ①《양》 a small quantity; a little; a dash/~ 더 just a little more/~씩 little by little; bit by bit; a little at a time/~ 사다 buy in small lots/돈이 ~ 밖에 없다 I have only a little money. ②《수》 a small number; a few/~ 더 a few more/이 작문에는 미스가 ~ 있다 There are some mistakes in this composition. ③《정도》 something 《부사적으로》 somewhat; rather; a bit; a little; in a small measure/그는 귀가 ~ 멀다 He is slightly deaf./저 친구는 ~ 모자란다 He is a little wanting. /~이라도 돈이 있으면 if (*one*) has any money/오늘은 ~ 낫다 I am a shade better today. ④《시간》 a moment; a minute; a second; a [little] while/~ 전에 a little while ago /~만 있으면 in a short time; soon/~ 있다 오너라 Call again a little later. ⑤ 《거리》 a little way; a short distance/~ 멀어져서 a little way off; at a short distance/~씩 전진하다 advance inch by inch/강을 따라 ~가다 go a little way alone the river. すこし

**조금**(潮—) the neap tide.

**조금도** [not] in the least; [not] at all/나는 ~ 놀라지 않았다 I was not a bit surprised.

**조급**(躁急) a hasty[quick] temper; impatience/~하다 (be) impatient; impetuous/~히 impetuously; hastily impatiently/~한 사람 a person of impetuous disposition; a hasty person/그렇게 ~ 굴지 말라 Don't be so impatient., There is no hurry. そうきゅう

**조기** 【어】 a yellow corvina; *Pseudosciaena manchurica*(학명)/~젓 pickled[salted] yellow corvina. いしもち

**조끼** a waistcoat(영); a vast(미). チョッキ

**조기**(弔旗) a flag at half-mast; a mourning flag; a flag draped with black/~를 달다 hang a flag draped in black; hang[hoist] a flag at half-mast. ちょうき

**조기**(早起) early rising/~하다 get up early; rise early in the morning/~하는 습관이 붙다 get the early rising habit. そうき

**조기**(早期) an early stage[period]/~ 치료[진단] early treatment[diagnosis]/~ 진단을 받다 be diagnosed in good time /~ 치료로 목숨을 건졌다 An early treatment has saved his life. そうき

**조기**(造機) engineering; engine construction.

**조난**(遭難) a disaster; an accident 《파선》 a shipwreck/~하다 meet with a disaster[an accident]; be in distress 《파선》 be wrecked/폭풍우로 ~하다 be wrecked in a storm/~선 a ship in distress; a wrecked ship/~ 현장 the scene of a disaster/~ 신호 a signal of distress; a distress signal/철도 사고의 ~자 victims of a railway accident/~자의 이야기 the account of a survivor (of *a disaster*). そうなん

**쪼다** 《모이를》 peck (*at*); pick up 《돌 따위를》 chisel/새가 콩을 ~ a bird pecks at beans/징으로 돌을 ~ cut a stone with a chisel. つつく

**조달**(早達) ①《빠른 출세》 success[advancement] in life in *one's* early age; a rapid rise/~하다 succeed in life in *one's* early age; rise rapidly in the world; attain distinction in *one's* early age ②《조숙》 precocity; early maturity; premature development/~하다 mature young; grow early.

**조달**(調達) 《공급》 supply 《관청에서》 procurement 《식량·일용품 따위의》 provision 《자금》 raising 《주문의》 execution; fulfillment/~하다 supply (*a thing*); provide (*food*); raise (*money*); execute (*an order*). ちょうたつ

**조도**(調度) proper management of matters[affairs, business]; 《살림》 making a proper living 《경비》 expenses; expenditure/~하다 manage matters properly; make[lead] a proper living; spend money. ちょうど

**조도**(照度) intensity of illumination/~계 an illuminometer. しょうど

**조독**(爪毒) an inflammation caused by scratching.

**조동사**(助動詞) 【언】 an auxiliary verb. じょどうし

**쪼들리다** be troubled[annoyed]; be oppressed; be in distressed condition; be straitened/돈에 ~ be straitened[pressed] for money/일에 ~ be pressed with business/빚에 ~ be harassed with de-

**조락(凋落)** withering 《영락》 downfall; reduced circumstances 《몰락》 decline; decay; fall/～하다 《말라죽다》 fade; wither 《영락하다》 be in reduced circumstances 《쇠퇴하다》 decay; decline; be ruined/自然主義 문학의 ～ the decay of the naturalist school in literature. ちょうらく

**조락노** a hemp string; a tow rope.

**조란(鳥卵)** a bird's egg. とりのたまご

**조랑조랑** in clusters/뜰에 있는 감나무에 감이 ～ 달렸다 The persimmon tree in my garden has borne abundant[is covered with] fruit. ずずつなぎ

**조략(粗略)** coarseness; plainness; crudeness/～하다 (be) coarse; crude; rough; plain; poor. そりゃく

**조량(照亮, 照諒)** discernment; penetration; insight/～하다 see through; discern; penetrate into; fathom (one's heart).

**조력(助力)** aid; assistance; support; help 《협력》 cooperation/～하다 help; aid; give[render] (a person) assistance (in, at); assist/당신의 ～에 의하여 with[by] your kind assistance/친구의 ～을 바라다 ask for a friend's help; turn to a friend for aid[help]/외부의 ～은 필요치 않다 I do not need assistance from outside. じょりょく

**조련(操鍊)** training; military exercise; drill/～하다 drill; train/～장 a parade ground/～을 받다 be put through a drill; be under training. くんれん

**조령 모개(朝令暮改)** an unsettled course of action; lack of principle; changeableness; unpredictability; unreliability/～하다 change an order frequently/～의 정책 a fickle[an erratic] policy; inconsistency of policy. ちょうれいぼかい

**조례(弔禮)** condolatory etiquette[manners]. ちょうもんすること

**조례(條例)** regulation; rules; law; an ordinance; an act/～를 반포[취소]하다 issue[revoke] regulations[an ordinance]/철도 ～ the railway law[regulations]/신문지 ～ a press law. じょうれい

**조례(照例)** reference to the precedents [former examples]/～하다 refer to a precedent.

**조로(朝露)** the morning dew 《무상》 transiency/인생은 ～와 같다 Men's life vanishes like the dew., Life is but a span. ちょうろ

**조로(早老)** premature old age/～한 prematurely old.

**조롱(吊籠)** a hanging cage[basket]; the gondola 《of a balloon》.

**조롱(鳥籠)** a cage for birds; a [bird] cage. とりかご

**조롱(嘲弄)** ridicule; mockery; sneer 《냉소》 banter; derision; chaff/～하다 ridicule; deride; laugh[sneer, jeer] at; make fun of; mock. ちょうろう

**조롱박** 【식】 a bottle gourd; a calabash; a water dipper made of a gourd; a cucubit.

**조루(早漏)** 【의】 premature ejaculation/～하다 ejaculate prematurely. そうろう

**조류(鳥類)** birds; fowls; the feathered tribe/～학 ornithology/～학자 an ornithologist. ちょうるい

**조류(潮流)** an ocean[a tidal] current; the tide 《추세》 a trend; a current/세상 ～에 역행하다 go against the current to the times/세상 ～에 따르다 go with the stream of the times/시대 ～란 어길 수가 없다 There is no swimming against the current of the times.
ちょうりゅう

**조류(藻類)** 【식】 seaweeds; Algae《학명》/～의 algoid. そうるい

**조르다** ①《매다》 tie [up]; 《죄다》 tighten; wring; strangle; constrict/허리띠를 졸라매다 tie[fasten] a girdle/닭의 목을 ～ wring a fowl's neck ②《요구하다》 importune; tease (for); badger (one to do)/사진기를 사 달라고 ～ badger (one's father) to buy one a camera ③《재촉하다》 press (a person) for; urge (a person to do); request; demand/빚을 빨리 갚아 달라고 ～ dun (one) for a debt; press (one) for payment of debt; urge to pay a debt. むすびつける

**조르르, 쪼르르** trickling; dribbling; running. ちょこちょこ

**조르륵, 쪼르륵** dribbling ⇒조르르, 쪼르르. ちょろちょろ

**조리(笊籬)** a bamboo ladle; a bamboo strainer/～로 쌀을 일다 rinse rice using a bamboo strainer.

**조리(條理)** logic; reason/～가 선 reasonable; logical; consistent/～에 닿지 않다 unreasonable; inconsistent; illogical; incoherent/～에 닿다 stand to reason; be reasonable. じょうり

**조리(調理)** 《조섭》 care of health; recuperation 《처리》 proper disposition; appropriate disposal[handling] of a matter 《요리》 cooking; cookery/～하다 take care of one's health; recuperate 《요리하다》 cook; prepare food 《처리하다》 deal with a matter properly[appropriately]/～대 a dresser/～실 cuisine. ちょうり

**조리개** ①《끈》 a tightening string[cord] ②《사진》 an iris.

**조리다** boil (fish) down/고기를 간장에 ～ boil beef down in soysause. にしめる

**조림** hard-boiled food/통～ canned food.

**조림(造林)** afforestation; forestation; reforestation/～하다 afforest; reforest; plant trees/～을 장려하다 encourage to afforest a mountain/～학 forestry.
ぞうりん

**조립(組立)** construction; organization; set-up 《기계의》 assembly/～하다 put together; set-up; construct/～식 가옥 a house on the knockdown plan/～ 주택

**조릿조릿** ~하다 feel uneasy; be full of anxiety. ひやひや

**조마**(調馬) horse-training[-taming]; horsebreaking/~하다 break[train, tame] a horse/~사 a horse trainer/~장 a riding ground; a paddock.

**조마조마** nervously; uneasily; anxiously; in thrilling suspense; with a beating heart/~하다 feel nervous; be kept in suspense/사람을 ~하게 하다 put (*one*) into a flutter; keep (*one*) in suspense. ひやひや

**조만간**(早晩間) sooner or later; in time; by and by; in the long run/내각은 ~ 총사직할 것이다 The general resignation of the Cabinet is only a question of time./이런 종류의 일은 ~ 폭로된다 This sort of thing is bound to come out sooner or later. おそかれはやかれ

**조망**(眺望) a view; a prospect 《전망》 a lookout/~하다 take[command] a view of; look out over[on]/그 언덕은 ~이 좋다 There is a good view from the hill./나무가 ~을 가로막다 The tree obstructs the view. ちょうぼう

**조망**(鳥網) a fowler's[fowling] net; a bird net. とりあみ

**조매**(嘲罵) a jeer; revilement; abuse; insulting remarks/~하다 jeer at; revile against; ridicule; flout at. ちょうば

**조명**(照明) lighting; illumination/직접 [간접] ~ direct[indirect] illumination /무대 ~ stage lighting[illumination] /~이 좋지 않다 It is poorly lighted [illuminated]/~ 공학 illumination engineering/~기 an illuminator/~탄 a flare bomb/~ 효과 light effect/~제 an illuminator. しょうめい

**조명**(助命) sparing *one's* life 《포로의》 quarter 《수인(囚人)의》 clemency/ ~하다 spare *one's* life; give quarter to (*a person's*)/~해 달라고 애원하다 ask for *a person's* life; appeal for mercy.

**조명나다** have a bad reputation; have an ill name; be notorious.

**조모**(祖母) a grandmother. そぼ

**조모**(朝暮) morning and evening. ちょうぼ

**조목**(條目) an article; a clause; an item /~별로 기입하다 itemize/일람표에 기입된 4가지 ~ four items on the list. じょうもく

**조몰락거리다** finger (*a toy*); fumble with [at]. しきりにもむ

**조무**(朝霧) morning mist[fog]. あさぎり

**조문**(弔問) a call of condolence/~하다 call (at *a place*) to express condolence /~객(客) callers to express condolence. ちょうもん

**조문**(弔文) a funeral address; a memorial address; a tribute to *one's* memory. ちょうぶん

**조문**(條文) 《본문》 the text (of *regulations*); 《조항》 provisions/헌법의 ~ the text of the Constitution/~에 명기되어 있다 be expressly stated in the text (of *the law*). じょうぶん

**조물주**(造物主) the Creator; the Maker [of the universe]; the Supreme Being; God. ぞうぶつしゅ

**조미**(調味) seasoning; flavor/~하다 season; give flavor to; flavor/~료 seasonings; condiments; dressing; spices; materials. ちょうみ

**조미**(造米) rice cleaning; rice-processing operations. ぞうまい

**조밀**(稠密) density/~하다 (be) dense; close; populous; crowded/인구 ~한 지방 a densely populated[a crowded] district/이 도시는 인구가 ~하다 This city is densely populated./그 근처는 인가가 ~하다 Houses are closely crowded in that neighbor. ちゅうみつ

**조바심**¹ threshing millet/~하다 thresh ears of millet.

**조바심**² worry; anxiety; uneasiness/그는 ~을 치면서 보고 있었다 He watched it with his heart in his mouth.
ひやひやするこころ

**조박**(糟粕) 《술의》 grains; brewer's grains; draff; *sool* lees 《학문의》 dregs; lees; leavings/고인의 ~을 핥다 imitate old masters; merely follow the footsteps of *one's* predecessors. そうはく

**조반**(朝飯) breakfast/~을 먹다 [take] breakfast/~은 빵과 커피로 떼웠다 I breakfasted on bread and a cup of coffee. あさめし

**조반기**(早飯器) a brass bowl with a lid.

**조발**(調髮) haircut; hairdressing ⇨이발.

**조발성 치매증**(早發性癡呆症) 《의》 dementia praecox.

**조밥** boiled millet [and rice]; cooked millet.

**조방**(助幇) pandering; pimping; procuring/~을 보다 pimp; pander.
ぼんひきすること

**조방 농업**(粗放農業) extensive agriculture. そほうのうぎょう

**조백**(早白) gray hair in youth; premature growth of gray hair/~하다 have gray hair while young.

**조법**(助法) 《법》 subsidiary laws. じょほう

**조법**(漕法) [a] form of rowing.

**조변 석개**(朝變夕改) an unsettled course of action; lack of principle/~하다 be fickle; be unsettled/~하는 정책 a fickle policy; an on-again-off-again policy; inconsistency of policy.

**조뼛조뼛** shy and hesitant/~하다 (be) shy and hesitant. もじもじ

**조병창**(造兵廠) an arms-manufactory; an arsenal; an armory《미》.
へいきをつくるところ

**조복**(朝服) a court dress; an official dress.

조부(弔賻) condolence and presents for funeral expenses.

조부(祖父) a grandfather/~모 grandparents. そふ

조분(鳥糞) bird droppings 《해조의》 guano /~석 guano [deposit]. ちょうふん

조비(祖妣) one's deceased grandmother. そひ

조사(弔詞) a funeral address; words of condolence 《영결식에서의》 a memorial address. ちょうじ

조사(助詞) an auxiliary word; a particle. じょし

조사(祖師) the founder of a sect or school. そし

조사(措辞) wording; diction; phraseology /~법 syntax. そじ

조사(早死) a premature[an early] death /~하다 die young; die an early death; die at an early age; die before one's time/술 때문에 ~했다 Wine brought him to an early death. はやじに

조사(調査) investigation; examination; inquiry 《인구 따위의》 census-taking/~하다 inquire[look] (into); investigate (into); examine (into); take a census/~한 바 upon investigation/원인을 ~하다 inquire into the cause; investigate the cause/인물을 ~하다 examine into one's character/~ 결과 그것은 단순한 소문으로 판명됐다 Upon investigation it was found to be a mere rumor./~ 결과 findings/~서 a written investigation/~ 용지 a questionnaire/~원 an investigator; an examiner/~ 자료 data for research[investigation]. ちょうさ

조사(照査) examination by reference; verification/~하다 examine by reference; verify; check (up).

조사(照射) irradiation/~하다 irradiate /뢴트겐을 ~하다 apply X-rays (to); X-ray (a person's chest).

조산(早產) premature birth/~하다 give premature birth to; bear prematurely /~아 a prematurely born infant. そうさん

조산(造山) an artificial[a miniature] hill; a rockery/~을 만들다 build an artificial hill. ぞうざん

조산원(助産員) a midwife; a maternity nurse. じょさんいん

조삼 모사(朝三暮四) swindling by a clever trick; the confidence game. ちょうさんぼし

조상(祖上) an ancestor; a forefather/~의 ancestral/~ 전래의 ancestral; hereditary/~을 숭배하다 worship ancestors /~ 숭배 ancestor worship; necrolatry.

조상(早霜) an early frost/~하다 have an early frost.

조상(彫像) a [carved] statue/대리석의 ~ a statue of marble. ちょうぞう

조상(弔喪) condolence/~ 하다 condole with (one). しをとむらうこと

조색(調色) mixing colours/~판 a [painter's] palette. ちょうしょく

조색 기구(阻塞氣球) a barrage balloon. そさいききゅう

조서(詔書) an Imperial rescript/~ 환발 (渙發) the issue[promulgation] of an Imperial rescript. しょうしょ

조서(調書) 〖법〗 a protocol; a record; writing evidence/~의 작성 drawing up of a protocol/~를 작성하다 put a deposition on record. ちょうしょ

조석(朝夕) morning and evening 《식사》 morning meal and evening meal. ちょうせき

조선(造船) shipbuilding; ship construction /~하다 build[construct] a ship/여객 선의 ~비 the cost of building a passenger boat/~술 shipwright/~ 공 a shipwright/~ 능력 shipbuilding capacity/~소 a dockyard; a shipyard/~학 naval architecture; ship building. ぞうせん

조섭(調攝) care of health ⇒조리(調理). ととのえおさめること

조성(造成) make; manufacture; production/~하다 make; manufacture; produce; build up/공포 분위기를 ~하다 produce a terror atmosphere.

조성(組成) formation; composition; constitution/~하다 compose; constitute; make up; form/~분(分) a component [part]; constituent [element]/~물 a composite; a composition. そせい

조성(助成) 《조장》 furtherance; fostering; promoting 《기여》 aid; assistance/~하다 help; further; assist; aid; promote; contribute to; subsidize.

조성(鳥聲) the song of a bird; a bird call. ちょうせい

조성(照星) 《가늠쇠》 the muzzle sight; the foresight.

조세(阻世) early[premature, untimely] death/~하다 die early[young, prematurely]. そうせい

조세(助勢) encouragement; reinforcement; help; support; assistance; backing /~하다 encourage; assist; help; support; stand by[for]. じょせい

조세(租稅) taxes; taxation; rates/~의 부담 the burden of taxation/~의 경감 a reduction in[of] taxation/~를 부과하다 impose[levy] a tax upon/~를 바치다 pay taxes/~를 면제하다 exempt (a person) from taxes/과중한 ~에 시달리다 groan under the heavy burden of taxation. そぜい

조소(嘲笑) 《웃음》 scornful[derisive] laugh 《조롱》 ridicule; derision; sneer/~하다 laugh[mock, jeer] at; ridicule; laugh scornfully/~적[으로] scornful[ly]; mocking[ly]/~당하다 be mocked and derided; be jeered[laughed] at./그는 동네 사람들의 ~거리였다 He was a laughingstock of the whole town.

조소(彫塑) 〖미〗 carving and modeling; a clay model. ちょうそ

조손(祖孫) grandfather and grandson.

조쇠(早衰) infirmity early in life／～하다 become weak early in life.

조수(助手) a helper; an assistant／운전～ an assistant driver／여자～ a coadjutress／병원～ a hospital assistant／～로 일하다 serve as an assistant. じょしゅ

조수(鳥獸) birds and beasts; fur and feather. ちょうじゅう

조수(潮水) the tides; tidal[tide] water／～표 tide table. ちょうすい

조숙(早熟) early maturity; premature growth; premature development; precocity; prematurity／～하다 mature[ripen] early; grow early／～아 a precocious child. そうじゅく

조술(祖述) exposition; propagation; commentation／～하다 expound; comment (upon *a text*); propagate／～자 an expounder; an exponent.

조습(燥濕) dryness and dampness; aridity and humidity. かんそうとしっけ

조시(肇始) origination; creation; foundation; institution／～하다 originate; create; found. ちょうし

조식(朝食) breakfast; the morning meal. ちょうしょく

조식(粗食) a plain diet; coarse[simple] food; poor[meager] fare; a frugal meal／～하다 live on plain fare[diet]; take simple meal／～에 익숙해지다 become accustomed to plain fare／～가 a man on a frugal diet.

조신(朝臣) (총칭) the court; a courtier; court officials. ちょうしん

조신(操身) carefulness of conduct[behavior]; circumspection／～하다 be careful of oneself; exercise circumspection. こうどうをつつしむこと

조실 부모(早失父母) losing *one's* parents early in life／～하다 lose parents early in life.

조심(操心) (주의) heed; carefulness; care (경계) caution; precaution; guard (신중) prudence; circumspection; discretion／～하다 take care (*of*); be careful (*about*); take precaution (*against*); look out; be watchful against (*temptation*); be prudent; be circumspect／～하여 with care; carefully; cautiously／～하고 있다 be on *one's* guard; be on the alert; be wide awake; keep *one's* eyes open／도둑을 ～하다 be on guard against thieves／불을 ～하다 mind the fire; take precaution against fire／몸을 ～하다 take care of *one*self; be careful of *one's* health／길 ～ Watch your step.／그 사람의 행동에 ～하라 Keep a sharp lookout on his behavior. ちゅういすること

조아(爪牙) claws and teeth; clutches and fangs 《고굉(股肱)》 a right-hand man. そうが

조아리다 knock *one's* forehead on the floor[ground]; kowtow; give a deep bow. くびをうなだれる

쪼아먹다 peck at and eat; pick. ほじくりたべる

조아팔다 sell separately; sell in small quantity. こうりする

조악(粗惡) coarseness; crudeness／～하다 (be) coarse; crude; be of poor[inferior] quality／～품 coarse[crude] articles; goods of poor quality／품질이 ～하다 be coarse in quality; be of coarse quality.

조암 광물(造岩鑛物) rock-forming minerals. ぞうがんこうぶつ

조앙(早秧) early seedlings of rice.

조야(粗野) rusticity; rudeness; coarseness; vulgarity; grossness／～하다 (be) coarse; rough; vulgar; rude; unpolished; rustic／～한 말씨 coarse speech [language]／～한 사람 a man of rough manners／그녀는 ～한 여성이다 She is a woman of coarse fibre. そや

조야(朝野) the whole nation; the government and the people／～의 명사 men of distinction both in and out of government／～가 일심 합력하여 the whole nation moving with one accord[as one man]; the whole nation making a united effort. ちょうや

조약(條約) a treaty; a convention; an agreement; a pact／평화 ～ a peace treaty／～ 규정 the treaty provisions [terms, stipulations]／～ 개정 treaty revision／～안(案) a treaty-draft／～의 비준 the ratification of a treaty／미국과 ～을 체결하다 conclude a treaty with the United States of America／～을 지키다[위반하다, 개정하다] observe[break, revise] a treaty／～을 폐기하다 denounce a treaty. じょうやく

조약돌 a gravel; pebbles.

조양(調養) care of health ⇒조리(調理). ととのえおさめること

조어(助語) 〖언〗 a grammatical particle; an expletive.

조어(釣魚) fishing [with a rod and line]; angling／～하다 fish with rod and line; angle (*fish in a brook*).

조언(助言) advice; a suggestion; a hint; counsel／～하다 advice; counsel; give (*a person*) advice[counsel, hint]; suggest／～을 구하다 ask advice of (*a person*); seek advice from (*a person*)／～을 받아들이다 take[listen to] (*a person's*) advice／～자 an adviser; a counsellor. じょげん

조업(操業) work; operation／～하다 operate; work／～을 정지하다 cease operations／～을 단축하다 cut down[reduce, curtail] operations／～을 개시하다 start operation／～비 operating expenses／～

일수 days operated. そうぎょう

조역(助役) 《조력자》 an assistant; a helper 《역의》 an assistant stationmaster /~군 an assistant of rough work.
　　　　　　　　　　　　　　　じょやく

조연(助演) supporting[assisting] performance/~하다 play a supporting role/~자 a supporting player; a member of the supporting cast.　じょえん

조영(造營) building; [a] construction; [an] election/~하다 build; erect.

조예(造詣) attainments; scholarship/학문에 ~가 깊은 사람 a man of great erudition/…에 ~가 깊다 have a profound [deep] knowledge of (*literature, etc.*); be [well] versed in (*history, etc.*); be at home in.　ぞうけい

조용하다 《잠잠하다》 (be) quite; silent; still 《안온하다》 (be) calm; placid; tranquil; serene; peaceful 《부드럽다》 (be) soft; gentle 《겸잠다》 (be) graceful 《한적하다》 (be) deserted/조용한 태도 graceful deportment/조용한 곳 a quiet place/조용한 목소리 a gentle voice/조용한 관중 silent audience/조용히 이야기하다 speak in a calm tone /조용해지다 become [grow] still; quiet down 《바람 따위가》 abate; subside/장내는 쥐죽은 듯이 조용해졌다 Hushed silence reigned over the room., The hall became as silent as death.　しずかだ

조우(遭遇) ①《만남》 an encounter; meeting/~하다 encounter (*a difficulty*); meet with; come across; be confronted/~전 an encounter ②《임금의 신임》 ~하다 winning royal confidence/~하다 have one's lord's confidence; enjoy the confidence of the Emperor.　ぞうぐう

조운(漕運) marine transportation; shipping; carriage by sea; freighting/~하다 transport[carry] by sea/~선 a cargo vessel; a freight [ship]; a freighter/~업 marine transportation business; shipping business[trade]/~업자 a shipping agent.　そううん

조원(造園) landscape gardening/~하다 make[lay out] a garden; landscape/~가 a landscape gardener[architect]/~술 landscape gardening[architecture].

조위(弔慰) [the expression of] condolence/~하다 condole with (*a person*); offer one's condolence to (*a person*)/~전보를 치다 telegraph one's condolence (*to*)/~금 condolence money; a solatium for bereavement.　ちょうい

조율(調律) tuning; intonation 《해음(諧律)》 harmony/~하다 tune; intonate; modulate/~사 a tuner/~기 a key; a regulator/~료 a charge for tuning/이 피아노는 ~해야겠다 This piano needs tuning.　ちょうりつ

조음(噪音) a noise; a din/거리의 ~ noisy street sounds/~ 방지 arrest of noises.　そうおん

조음(調音) 《목소리의》 articulation; modulation 《악기의》 tuning/~하다 articulate; tune.　ちょうおん

조응(照應) correspondence; agreement; accordance/~하다 agree[accord] with; correspond to.　しょうおう

조의(弔意) condolence; mourning 《고인에 대한》 a mark of respect to the dead /~를 표하다 express one's condolence /그의 유가족에게 우리들은 삼가 ~를 표하는 바 입니다 We respectfully tender his bereaved family our condolence and sympathy.　ちょうい

조인(鳥人) an airman; a birdman; an aviator.

조인(調印) signature; signing; sealing /~하다 affix[set] one's seal (*to*); put one's seal (*on*); affix[put] one's signature (*to*)/~국 a signatory power/~식 the signing ceremony/~자 a signer; a signatory/~ 장소 the place of signature.　ちょういん

조일(朝日) the morning sun.　あさひ

조작(操作) [an] operation; [a] handling; [a] manipulation/~하다 operate[work] (*a machine*); manipulate (*the market*).　そうさ

조작(造作) fabrication; manufacturing; concoction/~하다 《날조하다》 fabricate; forge; fake; invent; make up; turn up; concoct 《안출하다》 cook up[devise]; 《만들다》 construct; manufacture/ ~된 소문 a cooked-up rumor/~된 민의 fabricated public opinion/그 정보는 선동적인 신문의 ~이다 The report is an invention of sensational newspapers. /그것은 전혀 그가 ~한 이야기이다 The story is a pure invention on his part. /~설 a fabrication; a made-up story/~자 a fabricator.　ぞうさく

조잡(粗雜) coarseness; rudeness; crudeness/~하다 (be) rough; coarse; rude; crude; gross/~한 짓 a coarse act/ ~한 사람 a man of coarse brain/~한 생각 a crude idea.　そざつ

조장(弔狀) a letter of condolence.
　　　　　　　　　くやみのぶんしょう

조장(助長) promotion; furtherance/~하다 promote; foster; accelerate/…의 발달을 ~하다 promote[foster] the development[growth] of/운동은 건강을 ~한다 Exercise promotes health. /정부는 국내 산업 ~의 대책을 세웠다 The government took measures to promote domestic industry.　じょちょう

조장(組長) a head; a foreman.

조전(弔電) a telegram of condolence; telegraphic condolence/~을 치다 telegraph one's condolence (*to*)/우리는 곧 유가족에게 ~을 쳐보냈다 We lost no time in sending a telegram of condolence to the bereaved family.　ちょうでん

조전(操典) a drill book; a drill manual /보병 ~ drill regulations for the infantry; an infantry training manual.

**조절**(調節) regulation; control; adjustment 《음성의》 modulation 《라디오의》 tuning in／～하다 regulate; control; adjust; tune in／물가의 ～ the regulation [control] of prices／목소리의 ～ the modulation of one's voices／～기(器) a regulator／당신은 방의 온도를 ～하여야 합니다 You must regulate the temperature of the room. ちょうせつ

**조정**(朝廷) the [royal] court. ちょうてい

**조정**(調停) mediation; arbitration／～하다 mediate; arbitrate; settle; make up／～자 an arbitrator／～안(案) a mediation plan; an arbitration proposal／～ 세액 the tax amount settled／분쟁을 ～하다 accord[reconcile] a difference; make up a quarrel／～을 제의하다 offer[tender] one's good offices; offer mediation. ちょうてい

**조정**(調整) regulation; adjustment; co-ordination; control／～하다 regulate; co-ordinate／가격을 ～하다 adjust the price (of)／외교 문제를 ～하다 adjust diplomatic affairs／세금의 연말 ～ the year-end adjustment of taxes.

**조정**(漕艇) rowing; boating／～하다 row a boat／～ 경기 a boat race.

**조제**(粗製) crude[coarse] manufacture／～하다 manufacture coarse articles／～ 남조 mass production of inferior articles; quick and careless manufacture; sacrifice of quality to quantity／～ 설탕 raw [unrefined] sugar／～품 a crude[an inferior] article; coarse manufactures. そせい

**조제**(調劑) preparation; compounding／～하다 prepare medicine; make up a prescription 《처방에 의해》 fill a prescription／～사 a pharmacist／～실 a pharmacy／～시키다 have the prescription filled. ちょうざい

**조제**(調製) making 《조합》 preparation; manufacture 《주문품의》 execution／～하다 make; prepare; compound; execute／～법 a recipe／～품 a preparation. ちょうせい

**조조**(早朝) early morning／～에 early in the morning／내일 ～에 early tomorrow morning. そうちょう

**조조하다**(躁躁—) (be) impatient; impetuous; hasty; be in a hurry; (be) quick-tempered／조조하게 굴다 do without deliberation[due caution]. せっかちだ

**조졸**(早卒) a premature death; an early death／～하다 die young[early]; die before one's time; die an early death; die prematurely. はやじに

**조종**(弔鐘) a knell; a funeral bell.

**조종**(祖宗) ancestors[forefathers] of a king[an emperor].

**조종**(操縱) control; management; operation; manipulation／～하다 manage; controll; handle; operate; manipulate 《비행기를》 pilot 《차를》 drive 《배후에서》 pull the wires／～하기 어렵다[쉽다] be hard[easy] to manage[control]／기계를 ～하다 operate a machine／비행기를 ～하다 pilot[fly] an airplane／남편을 마음대로 ～하다 twist[turn] one's husband around one's finger／여자에게 ～당하다 be tied to a woman's apron strings／～법 operation; control／～사 a pilot; an aviator 《여자》 an aviatrix／～석 a pilot seat; a cockpit／～ 장치 steering gear; controls. そうじゅう

**조주**(助奏) 【음】 an ob[b]ligato.

**조준**(照準) aim; laying; sight／～하다 aim; lay; take aim[a sight]; sight／～ 연습 사격 a sighting shot／～이 틀리다 be faulty at aim／～을 맞추다 aim; lay; take aim[a sight]／～기(器) a sight／～망원경 a sighting telescope／～선 a line of sight／～ 폭격 precision bombing／전시(全視) ～ panoramic sight／직접 ～ direct laying.

**조지다** ①《단단히 맞추다》 fix tightly; tighten up; screw up ②《단속하다》 exercise strict control (over); make double-sure; hold (a person) to. はめこむ

**조직**(組織) 《사회·단체 등의 통일체》 organization; formation 《구조》 constitution; structure 《체계·제도》 system 《생물의》 tissue／～하다 form; organize; constitute; set up／사회[경제] ～ social [economic] structure[organization]／～자 an organizer; a constitutor／～학 histology／～력 organizing ability; systematizing talent／～적[으로] systematical[ly]; methodical[ly]／내각을 ～하다 organize[form] a cabinet／재～하다 reorganize／～적으로 연구하다 make a systematic study of; study on system／사회는 타인과 고립해서는 살아 나갈 수 없도록 ～되어 있다 Society is so constituted that no individual can subsist in isolation from others. そしき

**조짐**(兆朕) symptoms; signs; indications; a foreboding; an omen／…의 ～이 있다 show signs (of); betoken; forebode. ちょうこう

**조짚** millet straw[s].

**조차** even; too; in addition; into the bargain／너～ 그럴 줄은 몰랐다 I didn't know that even you would do that.／점심도 못 먹고 저녁～ 굶었다 I didn't eat any lunch and then skipped dinner as well. —も．—さえ

**조차**(操車) 《철도》 [railway] operation／～하다 operate (a locomotive)／～계 a train dispatcher／～장 a switchyard; a shunting yard. そうしゃ

**조차**(潮差) the range of tide; tidal range.

**조차**(租借) lease (of territory, of a house)／～하다 lease; obtain a lease on (an island) from; lease (a territory) from／～지 lease／～지 a leased territory; a holding／～하고 있다 hold a lease of

조찬(朝餐) breakfast ⇒조반(朝飯). あさめし そしゃく

조처(措處) management; conduct; arrangement; disposition; settlement/~하다 manage; conduct; arrange; settle; dispose (of)/적절한 ~ a measure suited to the occasion; a proper step[measure]/재빨리 ~하다 take prompt action (on). とりはからうこと

조첨(照尺) the backsight [of a gun]. しょうしゃく

조청(造淸) grain syrup.

조촉(弔燭) a funeral candle.

조촐하다 《아담하다》 (be) snug; trim; neat 《단정하다》 (be) refined; elegant; neat; tidy; decent/조촐한 방 a snug room/조촐한 용모 neat and elegant appearance/옷 입은 것이 ~ be dapper in dress. こざっぱりしている

조춤거리다 hesitate; wince; waver; vacillate; flinch /조춤조춤 hesitatingly; hesitantly; irresolutely; irresolutely; flinching. ためらう

조총(鳥銃) a fowling-piece; a gun; a matchlock; a firelock. ちょうじゅう

조총(弔銃) three volley of musketry/~부대 a firing party/~을 놓다 fire a volley for the dead.

조추(早秋) early autumn; early fall. しょしゅう

조춘(早春) early spring. そうしゅん

조충(條蟲) 《촌충》 a tapeworm; a taenia /~약 a taeniafuge; a taeniacide. じょうちゅう

조치 thick broth; heavy soup; thick gravy soup.

조치(措置) a measure; a step/~하다 take a measure; take action. そち

조치개 a necessary adjunct; an essential accessory.

조칙(詔勅) an Imperial edict[proclamation, rescript, message]. しょうちょく

조카 a nephew/~의 아들 a grandnephew/~뻘 the relation of nephew/그는 내 ~뻘이다 He stands to me in the relation of nephew. /~ 며느리 a nephew's wife/~ 딸 a niece/~ 사위 a niece's husband. おい

조타(操舵) steering; steerage / ~기 the steering gear/~수 a steersman / ~실 a steering house.

조탁(彫琢) 《보석의》 carving; chiselling; polishing [gems]; 《문장의》 elaboration /~하다 carve; chisel; carve and polish 《문장을》 elaborate. ちょうたく

조탄(粗炭) low-grade coal.

조탕(潮湯) a hot sea-water bath. かいすいのゆ

조퇴(早退) leaving early; leaving (office, school) earlier than usual/~하다 leave (office, school) earlier than usual/1시간 일찍 ~하다 get[take] a hours off; leave [work] a hours early. そうたい

조판(組版) typesetting; composition/ ~하다 set up type; do typesetting/~ 완성 【인】 making up/~되어 있다 be in type/~가 ~으로 짜다 set type in a galley. くみはん

조팝나무 【식】 a bridal wreath; Spiraea prunifolia(학명). しじみばな

조폐(造幣) coinage; mintage/~하다 mint; stamp coin/~ 각인 mintage mark /~국 the mint. ぞうへい

조포(弔砲) a minute-gun; a gun of condolence; an artillery salute for the dead. ちょうほう

조품(粗品) coarse products. そひん

조피 Japanese peppercorns/~나무 the Japanese pepper; the prickly ash. さんしょうのみ

조피볼락 【어】 a rockfish; a rock cod; Sebastes schlegeli(학명).

조하(早夏) early summer. しょか

조하(朝霞) the morning haze[mist]. あさがすみ

조하다(燥—) (be) dried; parched; arid (기후 등이). かんそうしている

조하다(躁—) (be) hasty; quick-tempered; impatient; impetuous. せっかちだ

조함(造艦) naval shipbuilding/~ 계획 a naval construction program.

조합(照合) comparison; collation/~하다 compare; check (with)/사본을 원고와 ~하다 check a copy with the manuscript.

조합(調合) 《약 따위의》 mixture; compounding; mixing; preparation 《조미》 seasoning; flavoring/~하다 mix; compound; prepare; make up 《조미하다》 season; dress/~를 a mixture; a preparation. ちょうごう

조합(組合) ①《단체》 an association; a league 《합자의》 a partnership 《동업의》 a guild 《노동자의》 a union/노동 ~ a trade[labour] union / ~원 a member of the association (the union, etc.); a partner/~ 규약 the articles of an association/~을 만들다 organize an association; form a partnership/~에 가입하다 join the association/~에 받아들이다 admit (a person) into the association; take (a person) into partnership/판매 ~ marketing[selling] cooperative association ②《수》 combination. くみあい

조항(條項) articles [and clauses]; items; a provision. じょうこう

조해(潮解) 【화】 deliquescence/~하다 deliquesce. ちょうかい

조행(操行) manners; behavior; deportment/~이 바른 학생 a pupil of good conduct/~이 좋다 be well conducted/~이 나쁘다 be dissolute in conduct. そうこう

조혈(造血) hematosis; hemotopoiesis; sanguification/~하다 increase[make] the blood.

조형(造形) mo[u]lding; modeling/~하다 mould; shape; model / ~ 미술 the

**조혼**(早婚) an early marriage/~하다 marry early[young]; marry at an early age/~자 an early-married person /~을 장려하다 encourage early marriage/요즘 젊은이에겐 ~이 유행하고 있다 Nowadays, early marriage prevails in the young. そうこん

**조홍**(潮紅) ①《홍조》 flush [in the face]; blushing ②《폐병 환자의》 hectic spots. かおをあからめること

**조화**(造花) an artificial flower; an imitation flower. ぞうか

**조화**(造化) creation; nature/~의 신 the Creator; the Maker of the Universe/~의 묘 the wonders of nature/~의 장난 a freak of nature/우리가 이렇게 만난 것도 하느님의 ~다 It is the providence of God that has brought us thus together. ぞうか

**조화**(調和) 《일치》 harmony; accord; agreement 《음색의》 symphony 《균형》 symmetry/~하다 harmonize with; agree with; be consistent (with)/~된 harmonious 《균형이 잡힌》 symmetrical/~ 되지 않은 inharmonious; asymmetrical; out of keeping (with); discordant/~ 되어 harmoniously; in agreement/~ 가 결핍하다 lack harmony; disagree/이 두 색은 ~가 안된다 These two colours do not agree[harmonize]. ちょうわ

**조환**(吊環) 《체조의》 flying rings.

**조회**(照會) inquiry; reference; communication/~하다 inquire (of a person, about a matter); write to; refer to; communicate with(one)/~ 전보 a telegram of inquiry/직접 ~하다 write direct to /~중이다 be in communication with/ 상세한 것은 사무소에 ~하시오 For particulars apply to the office. しょうかい

**조회**(朝會) a morning meeting; a morning get-together(미). ちょうかい

**조후**(兆候) indications. ちょうこう

**조휼**(弔恤) sympathy; pity/~하다 have sympathy (for); take pity on.
かなしみをあわれんでなぐさめること

**조흔**(爪痕) a nail-mark; a scratch; a crescent spot [made by pinching].
つめあと

**조흥**(助興) addition to the amusement[enjoyment, pleasure]/~하다 brighten things up; add to the pleasure[enjoyment, delight]; contribute to the excitement[fun, amusement].
きょうみをくわえること

**쪽**[1] 《남자의》 a chignon/~지다 do one's hair up in a chignon. ふじんのもとどり

**쪽**[2] 《조각》 a piece; a slice; a cut/빵 한 ~ a slice of bread.

**쪽**[3] 《방향》 a direction; a way; a side/동 ~ the east/오른 ~ the right side/양 ~ both sides/우리 ~ our side/위 ~ the upper side/길을 걸을 때는 왼 ~으로 가시오 Keep left side walking along the street. /길을 건널 때는 양 ~을 잘 살펴라 Look both ways carefully before crossing the street. ほう

**쪽**[4] 《늘어선 모양》 in a row; in a line/ ~ 고르다 be all of equal size; be uniform[equal]/~ 늘어서다 stand in a row.
ずらっと

**쪽**[5] 《식》 the indigo plant. あい

**족**(足) ①a foot 《동물의》 a cloven foot; a hoof 《소의》 the leg 《돼지의》 the shank 《양의》 the trotter/돼지~ pettitoes ② 《켤레》 pair (of socks). あし

**-족**(族) 《동·식물의》 a family. 《종족》 a tribe/몽고~ The Mongol tribe. —ぞく

**족당**(族黨) a family; colleagues ⇒족속.
ぞくとう

**족대** a kind of fishing net.

**족대**(足臺) a step; a stool; a footstool.

**족대기다** ①《강요하다》 compel; force; constrain; press; enforce; coerce/기부금을 내라고 ~ press (a person) to contribute ②《볶아치다》 hurry (a person) urge forward[on, onward]/~세든 사람을 족대겨서 내보내다 evict[drive out, eject] one's tenant ③《경치다》 torment; torture; inflict pain (upon); persecute (박해하다)/ 죄수를 ~ torment a prisoner. おしつける

**족도**(足蹈) a leap; a jump/~하다 leap; hop up; bound; vault.

**족두리** a black crown-like headpiece worn by women on formal occasions/민 ~ a plain jogduri/~하님 a maidservant formerly taken.

**족두리풀** 《식》 wild-ginger plant; Asiasrum heterotropoides (학명).

**쪽마루** a veranda of one or two floorboards[planks]. ながいいたのとこ

**쪽박** a small gourd; a gourd dipper.

**족발**(足—) the shank; a pork hock.

**쪽발이** a thing which has only one leg left; a one-legged thing; a cloven foot.

**족벌주의**(族閥主義) nepotism.

**족보**(族譜) genealogy; pedigree; lineage; a family-tree; a genealogical record [table]/~를 캐다 look into one's genealogy[pedigree]. ぞくふ

**족생**(族生) gregarious growth/~하다 grow gregariously[in clusters]/~. 식물 a social plant. ぞくせい

**족속**(族屬) 《가족》 a family 《일가》 kinsmen; relatives 《패》 fellows; colleagues.

**족쇄**(足鎖) fetters; shackles [for the feet]/~를 채우다 fetter; shackle; put (a person) in stock.

**족인**(族人) clansmen[kinsmen]; relatives.
ぞくじん

**족자**(簇子) a hanging picture[scroll]/~ 걸이 a pole with hooks for hanging a scroll.

**족자리** handles on both sides of a pot.

**쪽잘거리다** eat reluctantly; chew by bits.
しきりに噛る

**족장**(族丈) an elder of a clan.

**족장**(族長) the head of a family[tribe];

a patriarch/~ 시대 the patriarchal age. ぞくちょう

**족적**(足跡) a footprint; footmarks/~을 남기다 leave one's footmarks. あしあと

**족제**(族制) clanship; the system of relationship. ぞくせい

**족제**(族弟) younger distant relatives.

**족제비** 〖동〗 a weasel. いたち

**-족족** 《마다》 every[each] time; whenever; as often as/오는 ~ whenever[as aften as] one comes; each[every] time one calls/친구들을 만나는 ~ 이 말을 전해주시오 Give this information whatever time you meet your friends./여러 번 해보았으나 하는 ~ 실패했다 I made several attempts and failed as many times. まいに

**쪽지**(-紙) a slip of paper; a tag; a label/~에 몇자 적다 jot a few words down on a slip/배달 불능의 ~가 붙어서 편지가 돌아왔다 The letter came back with a tag explaining its nondelivery. はしがき

**쪽지**(足指) the toes ⇒발가락. あしのゆび

**쪽지**(足趾) the heel. かかと

**족집게** [hair-]tweezers/~로 털을 뽑다 pluck a hair out with tweezers.

**족척**(族戚) blood relatives and relatives-in-law; relatives in blood and law; kindred. ぞくせき

**족출**(簇出) ~하다 spring up like mushrooms after rain/그 시대에는 위인이 ~했다 The age was highly productive of great men. ぞくぞくとあらわれること

**족치다** ①《작게 만들다》 make small ②《줄이다》 lessen; reduce; minimize ③《깨뜨리다》 destroy; mangle/의자를 ~ break a chair ④《족대기다》 compel; press/사람을 족쳐서 일을 시키다 force (a person) to work. ちいさくする

**족편**(足-) calf's-hoot jelly.

**족하다**(足-) 《충분하다》 (be) sufficient; enough; complete 《동사적 용법》 serve; answer/한 번하면 ~ One glance at it is quite enough./그것으로 ~ That will do./자격이 ~ He is fully qualified./그와는 족히 문학을 논할 만하다 He is well worth talking literature with. まんぞくだ

**존경**(尊敬) respect; esteem; honour;; reverence; veneration/~하다 respect; honour; revere; have a [high] regard for; look up to a person/~할 honourable; estimable; respectable/~심에서 out of respect for; in deference to; out of courtesy to/나는 마음 속으로 그를 ~하고 있다 I enthrone him in my heart./우리들은 그들에 대하여 ~도 우정도 가질 수 없나 We can have no respect and no friendship for them. そんけい

**존공**(尊公) your esteemed father. そんこう

**존귀**(尊貴) nobility/~하다 (be) high and noble; exalted; princely; of royal blood/~하신 분 an august[exalted] person[age]; dignitaries. そんき

**존당**(尊堂) your[his, etc.] esteemed mother. そんどう

**존대**(尊待) treatment with respect/~하다 treat with politeness[respect]; respect; (be) polite (to); hold (a person) in [high] esteem/~받다 be esteemed[held in esteem]/~어 a term of respect; an honorific. そんだい

**존대인**(尊大人) your esteemed father.

**존득거리다, 쫀득거리다** 《존득존득하다》(be) sticky[glutinous, adhesive]; elastic [rubbery, tough].

**존립**(存立) existence; life; remaining[being] independent/~하다 exist; be in existence/국가의 ~을 위협하다 threaten the national existence/~ 기간 〖법〗 duration. そんりつ

**존망**(存亡) life and death; existence; destiny; fate/위급 ~의 때 a crisis; a critical moment/국가 지주의 ~에 있는 이 time of national crisis/국가의 ~에 관한 문제다 It is a question of life or death for the nation., The national existence is at the stake. そんぼう

**존비**(尊卑) [the] high and [the] low; the upper and the lower classes; aristocrat and plebeian; high rank and low rank/~ 귀천 noble and mean; high and low. そんぴ

**존속**(存續) continuance; continued existence; duration; continuation/~하다 continue to exist; last; continue; keep up. そんぞく

**존속**(尊屬) 〖법〗 an ascendant; an ancestor 《직계의》 a lineal ancestor/~ 살해 a parricide. そんぞく

**존숭**(尊崇) reverence; respect; veneration; adoration/~하다 honour; venerate; respect; revere/국민 ~의 대상이 되다 be an idol of the people. そんすう

**존심**(存心) bearing (something) in mind; laying (something) to one's heart/~하다 bear[keep] in mind; take (an advice) to heart. ぞんしん

**존안**(尊顏) your [esteemed] face. そんがん

**존엄**(尊嚴) dignity; majesty; augustness; sanctity/~하다 (be) dignified; majestic; august; sacred; solemn/법의 ~ the dignity of law/법의 ~을 지키다 uphold the majesty of the law/~을 손상하다 impair the dignity (of)/신의 ~을 더럽히다 be guilty of profanation; blaspheme against God. そんげん

**존영**(尊影) one's portrait. そんえい

**존의**(尊意) your esteemed opinion[view, idea]. そんい

**존장**(尊長) an elder; a senior. そんちょう

**존재**(存在) existence; subsistence; being /~하다 exist; subsist; be in existence; be present 《잔존하다》 remain/신의 ~ the existence of God/~ 이유 reason for being; raison d'etre(F)/~론 ontology

/~하지 않는 non-existent/~를 인정받다 win recognition/나의 ~는 아주 무시당하고 있다 I am completely ignored./~물 an existence; a being/~의의 the significance[meaning] of existence. そんざい

**존절** frugality; saving; thrift/~하다 economize (on); be economical[sparing] (of); be thrifty; be frugal.

**존존하다, 쫀쫀하다** (be) finely woven; be of fine weave. せいみつだ

**존중**(尊重) respect; [high, great] esteem; appreciation/~하다 respect; esteem; value; appreciate; think highly (of); hold in high respect[esteem]; set store (by); have a high regard (for)/~할 만한 respectable; estimable/친구의 의사를 ~하여 in deference to the wishes of one's friend/여론을 ~하다 have a regard for public opinion/우리는 이군의사를 ~한다 We have a regard for Mr. Lees opinion./명예를 생명 이상으로 ~하다 hold honor dearer than one's life. そんちょう

**존체**(尊體) your esteemed self[health]. そんたい

**존칭**(尊稱) an honorific title; a title [of honour]. そんしょう

**존택**(尊宅) your esteemed house. そんたく

**존폐**(存廢) maintenance or abolition; existence/~ 문제 the question of maintenance or abolition (of the institution); the problem of keeping or discarding. そんはい

**존필**(尊筆) your handwriting; handwriting of a dignitary(귀인의). そんぴつ

**존한**(尊翰) your esteemed letter. そんかん

**존함**(尊啣, 尊銜) your [honorable] name/~을 듣고 안 지 오래입니다 I have long since known you by name.

**존형**(尊兄) you. そんけい

**존호**(尊號) eulogistic posthumous title of a king[queen]. そんごう

**존후**(尊候) [the state of] your health. そんこう

**졸가리** dry bits of twig; a stripped stalk [stem] ⇨줄거리.

**졸경**(卒更) (순라) a night patrol 《밤새의 고민》 tossing about in bed.

**졸계**(拙計) a foolish plan; a poor scheme. まずいけいかく

**졸고**(拙稿) a manuscript written in my hand; my manuscript. せっこう

**졸곡**(卒哭) ① (삼우제 뒤의) a sacrificial ceremony performed following the third sacrifice after burial ② (석달 뒤의) a sacrificial ceremony performed in the third month after burial.

**졸공**(拙工) poor workmanship; a bad workman(사람). せっこう

**졸깃졸깃, 쫄깃쫄깃** ~하다 (be) sticky; chewy.

**졸년**(卒年) the year of (a person's) death/~ 월일 the date of death. しんだとし

**졸다**¹ doze; take a nap; fall into a doze 《깜박하다》 drop [off] into a doze 《앉아서》 drop asleep; drowse; snooze/책을 읽다가 ~ doze over a book/청중의 대부분은 졸고 있었다 Most of audience were asleep. まどろむ

**졸다**² (졸아들다) shrink; contract 《영기다》 condense 《끓어서》 be boiled away [down]. へる

**쫄딱** completely; wholly; altogether; utterly/~ 망하다 be completely ruined; be totally spoiled. すっかり

**졸때기** ① (작은 일) a small work; a trivial labour; a [mere] trifle; an odd job ② (사람) a nobody; a nonentity; a mere cipher; a man of straw. わずかなこと

**졸도**(卒倒) a swoon; a fainting fit; a faint; fainting; 《의》 syncope/~하다 fall down in a swoon; faint; swoon; fall unconscious; go into fits/공포 때문에 ~했다 The fright made her sink down in a swoon./아버지는 오늘 아침 뇌일혈로 ~하셨다 My father had a stroke of apoplexy this morning. そっとう

**졸다** be[get] hampered in development; be stunted; be shriveled; be withered/~든 짐승 scrubby animals/~든 나무 stunted trees. いじける

**졸라대다** badger (a person to do); tease [importune] (a person for); clamor (for)/사달라고 ~ ask (a person) to buy (a thing)/과자를 달라고 ~ clamor for candy. せがむ

**졸라매다** tighten; constrict; strangle/띠를 ~ tie[fasten] a girdle/목을 졸라매어 죽이다 strangle[throttle] (one) [to death]. むすびつける

**쫄래동이** a flippant[frivolous] child; a flippant and mischievous boy. ずうずうしいおとこのこ

**졸렬**(拙劣) clumsiness; awkwardness/~하다 (be) poor; clumsy; awkward/~한 수단 a bungling step; a clumsy means. せつれつ

**졸론**(拙論) 《자기의》 my unworthy view [treatise, comment, opinion]; (보잘것 없는) an absurd view; a silly argument. せつろん

**졸루**(拙陋) stupidity[foolishness] and meanness[baseness]/~하다 (be) mean; lowly. せつろう

**졸리다**¹ 《남에게》 be[get] teased[pestered, pressed, coaxed, annoyed, importuned] by (a person for something); be badgered by (a person to do); 《매이다》 be tightened[fastened, strangled]. うるさくせめられる

**졸리다**² feel sleepy; grow drowsy; be heavy with sleep/졸려 보이는 sleepily; drowsily; sleepy-looking/졸린듯이 sleepily; drowsily/졸려서 죽겠다 I feel dying with sleep. ねむけがえる

졸막졸막 in various small sizes/ ~하다 be motley; be a jumble; be a mixture of variety of things.

졸망졸망 ~하다 (be) small-sized; be all bumpy/~한 아이들 a bunch of small children/감나무에 감이 ~ 열려 있다 The persimmon tree is laden with persimmons.

졸문(拙文) 《졸렬한》 a poor[clumsy] writing 《자기 글》 my writing.

졸병(卒兵) a private; a common soldier ⇨병졸(兵卒).

졸보(拙甫) a good-for-nothing [fellow]; a stolid person; a thickhead; a fathead.

졸부(猝富) sudden riches; an overnight millionaire; a *nouveau riche*(F).

졸사(猝死) sudden death/~하다 die suddenly; drop[fall] dead; pop.

졸사간(猝乍間) 《갑자기》 suddenly; all of a sudden 《잠깐 동안》 in a moment; in an instant.

졸서(卒逝) passing [away]; dying; decease/~하다 pass away; depart this life; decease.

졸속주의(拙速主義) a rough-and-ready method.

졸아들다 shrink; contract 《주름지다》 wrinkle; crumple; shrivel 《엉기다》 condense; compress 《끓어서》 be boiled away/이것은 세탁해도 졸아들지 않는다 This won't shrink in the wash.

졸아붙다 《물 따위가》 get boiled dry; be boiled down.

졸아지다 be boiled away; be contracted; be reduced; shrink.

졸업(卒業) graduation/~하다 graduate [be graduated] from[at]; complete a course; finish school/~하면 after[upon] graduation/대학을 ~하다 graduate from[at] a university/수석으로 ~하다 graduate first on the list/그 여자는 우등으로 대학을 ~했다 She graduated from a college with honors./~ 논문 a graduation thesis/~ 시험 a graduation examination/~식 a graduation ceremony; the commencement [ceremony]/〈미〉/~장 a diploma; a sheepskin《속》.

졸연하다(猝然―, 卒然―) (be) sudden; abrupt; unexpected/졸연히 suddenly; abruptly; all of a sudden; unexpectedly.

졸음 drowsiness; sleepiness/~이 오다 become[feel] drowsy[sleepy]; go to the land of nod/나는 몹시 ~이 왔다 A great drowsiness grew upon me.

졸이다 ①《마음을》 be anxious about; worry[trouble] *one*self; brood over (*a matter*)/돌아오기를 마음 졸이며 기다리다 wait in anxious suspense for *one's* return/그녀는 그 사전으로 퍽 마음을 졸이고 있다 She is very much worried about it. ②《끓어서》 boil down[hard]/국을 ~ 다.

졸자(拙者) a stupid fellow 《본인》 I; me.

졸작(拙作) 《졸렬한》 a poor work; trash; rubbish 《자기의》 unworthy work of mine.

졸장부(拙丈夫) a man of small calibre; an illiberal fellow 《겁장이》 a coward; a faintheart.

졸저(拙著) 《자기 작품》 my humble work 《보잘것 없는 작품》 a poor composition; a poor book[work].

졸졸 《물이》 trickling[ly]; murmuring[ly]; 《사람을》 (follow *a person*) persistently; hanging on; sticking close; tagging along/시냇물이 ~ 흐르다 a brook murmurs along/수도물이 ~ 나오다 water trickles down from the faucet/어린아이가 어머니를 ~ 따라다닌다 The children is always tagging at his mother's heels.

졸중풍(卒中風) 《의》 apoplexy/~에 걸리다 be seized with apoplexy.

졸지(猝地) ~에 suddenly; abruptly; all of a sudden 《뜻밖에》 unexpectedly/~에 여러 가지 일이 일어나서 계획했던 것이 틀렸다 Such a multitude of unexpected incidents have baffled my plan.

졸직(拙直) ~하다 (be) narrow-minded and rigid; illiberal and unadaptable.

졸참나무 《식》 a queritron; *Quercus glandulifera*《학명》.

졸책(拙策) a poor policy[shift].

졸필(拙筆) ①《악필》 a poor[bad] hand; bad [hand] writing; a villainous scrawl/~이다 write a poor[bad] hand ②《악필가》 a bad penman ③《자기 필적》 my handwriting.

졸하다(卒―) die; pass away; decease.

졸하다(拙―) 《재주없고 용렬하다》 (be) clumsy; awkward; bungling; poor 《졸직하다》 narrow-minded; illiberal; hidebound/졸한 사람 a narrow-minded person.

졸한(猝寒) [a] sudden cold[chill]; an unexpected cold wave.

좀¹ 《충》 a moth; a bristle tail; a bookworm/~ 먹은 moth-eaten/책이 다 ~ 먹었다 The books are all worm-eaten.

좀² 《그 얼마나》 how; how much; surely; indeed; no doubt; certainly; presumably; I am sure/~ 걱정하셨겠어요 You must have felt very anxious./~ 시장하겠나 You have been hungry, I dare say./자네 얼굴을 보시면 어머니께서 ~ 기뻐하시겠나 How glad your mother will be to see you!

좀³ ①《잠깐》 just a moment[minute]; for a moment[while, few minutes, s-

**좀** hort time/~ 기다려 주십시오 Please wait a bit., Half a minute, please./나와 함께 ~ 갑시다 Go a little way with me./~ 다녀오겠다 I shall go out just a little while./신문을 ~ 보고 싶습니다 I just want to glance at the paper. ②《조금》 a bit; a little; just; slightly; somewhat/~ 피곤하다 be somewhat weary/술기가 ~ 있다 be slightly intoxicated/~ 성나는 일만 있으면 이내 폭행을 하려 든다 He is ready to use violence towards others on the slightest provocation./나는 몸이 ~ 나는 것 같다 I am inclined to be stout. ちょっと

**좀-** petty small. ちいさい

**좀것** ①《사람》 a [person with] small mind; a man of small calibre; a little soul ②《물건》 small things; trifles (잡동산이) odds and ends. ちいさいもの

**좀피** cheap tricks; petty tricks/~를 쓰다 play cheap tricks (on); resort to petty tricks; be tricky.

**좀노릇** petty job; trifling work. おおざっぱでなくこまかいこと

**좀놈** a petty person; a man of small caliber. きのちいさいひと

**좀도둑** a sneak [thief]; a filcher; a pilferer/~질 petty theft; pilfering/~질을 하다 pilfer; filch; commit petty theft/우리가 집을 비운 동안에 ~이 들었다 The house was broken into while we were away. こそとろぼう

**좀말** small talk; a narrow-minded remark. さしょうなことば

**좀먹다** ①《벌레가》 (moths) eat; be moth-eaten/좀먹은 책 a moth-eaten book ②《비유적으로》 erode; eat away; destroy/동심을 ~ spoil the childish mind. しみむしがくう

**좀생이** 《잔 물건》 small things; 《천》 the pleiades. こまかいもの

**좀스럽다** 《성질이》 (be) small-minded; petty 《규모가》 small; be on a small scale; (be) insignificant/좀스러운 사람 a petty person/좀스러운 일 petty jobs; trifles/좀스럽게 별걸 다 알려고 한다 Why are you so curious to know about such petty matters? どりょうがせまい

**좀처럼** 《쉽사리》 easily; lightly; readily 《여간해서》 [not] aften; rarely; seldom/그는 ~ 성을 내지 않는 사람이다 He is not such a man as to rage into passion readily./그런 대사업이란 ~ 성취할 수 없다 Such a great work is not to be achieved easily./그런 천재는 ~ 만날 수 없다 Such a genius is rarely to be met with./이런 기회는 ~ 오지 않는다 Such opportunities do not occur every day. ちょっとやそっとでは

**좀팽이** a small[little] man; a narrow-minded fellow. ちいさいひと

**좁다** 《폭이》 (be) narrow 《면적이》; limited 《갑갑하다》 close; tight; confined 《마음이》 narrow-minded; illiberal/좁은 소견 a small mind/마음이 좁은 사람 a narrow-minded person; a man of narrow views/좁은 안계 a narrow horizon/그는 마음이 ~ He is narrow-minded./세상은 따지고 보면 좁은 것이다 This is a small world after all. せまい

**좁다랗다** (be) narrow and close/좁다란 길 a narrow path. せまい

**좁쌀** a millet seed. あわ

**좁쌀풀** 《식》 a loosestrife; Lysimachia davurica(학명).

**좁히다** ①《좁게》 narrow; contract; reduce ②《죽대기다》 force; constrain; compel; press; urge/문제의 범위를 ~ limit the field of a problem. せまばめる

**종¹** a servant; a slave; a thrall/~의 근성 a servile spirit/~의 신분 slavery; bondage; thraldom; serfdom/~으로 삼다 make a slave (to, of)/~과 같이 일하다 work like a slave; drudge/~으로 팔리다 be sold for a slave.

**종²** 《파 따위의》 [the end of] a stalk (of scallion, garlic). はなあやめ

**종(縱)** length/~의 vertical; longitudinal/~으로 lengthwise; lengthways; vertically/~으로 자르다 cut (a thing) lengthways. たて

**종(種)** ①《종류》 a sort; a kind; a class; a variety; a category ②《분류 단위》 a species 《동물》 a breed; a stock/~의 기원 the Origin of Species/각~의 every variety of/일~ 의 귀금속 a kind of precious metals/일~의 독특한 향기 a unique aroma/이것은 장미의 일~이다 This is one variety of roses./~마 a stallion; a breeding horse/~우 a bull; breeding cow/잡~ hybrid; crossbred. しゅ

**종(終)** the end; finis(L); the finish. おわり

**종(鍾)** a bell; a buzzer 《현관의 초인종》 a door-bell 《손종》 a hand-bell/~소리 a sound of a bell/시(時)~ a time-bell/~을 치는 방망이 a wood bell hammer/~을 울리다 ring a bell/~을 치다 strike a bell. かね

**종-(從)** 《사촌》 a second-degree relative/~형 one's cousin. じゅう

**-종(宗)** a religious sect; a denomination/조계 ~ the Choge sect.

**종가(宗家)** the head[main] family; the head-[original-]house. そうけ

**종가래** a small spade[plow, shovel]. ちいさいすき

**종가세(從價稅)** a tariff ad valorem(L.)/~을 an ad valorem tariff/종가 5부의 관세 an import duty of five percent ad valorem. じゅうかぜい

**종각(鐘閣)** a bell tower; a belfry.

**종개념(種概念)** 《논》 species; specific concept(notion). しゅがいねん

**종견(種犬)** a breeding dog. たねいぬ

**종결(終結)** termination; a close; a conclusion/~하다 terminate; come[be bro-

**종경**(終境) the end; the limit; limits; [the] bounds. おわり

**종고모**(從姑母) a female cousin of one's father.

**종곡**(終曲) 《음》 a finale. しゅうきょく

**종관**(縱觀) inspection; perusal ⇒종람. おもうままにみること

**종관**(縱貫) running[penetrating] lengthwise/~하다 run through lengthwise; traverse/~ 철도 the railway running through (the land). じゅうかん

**종교** (宗敎) a faith; a religion; a creed; a cult/~적 religious; ecclesiastical; spiritual/~적 감정 religious feeling/~를 믿다 believe in a religion/~를 박해하다 persecute a religion/~에 위안을 구하다 seek solace[consolation] in religion/저 사람들은 각각 ~가 다르다 They are followers of different faiths. /~가 a religionist; a clergyman/~ 개혁 religious reformation; the Reformation /~ 교육 religious education/~ 문제 a religious question/~ 문학 religious literature/~ 철학 philosophy of religion. じゅうきょう

**종구라기, 종구락** a small gourd.

**종국**(終局) an end; a close; a conclusion; a termination 《바둑의》 the end of a game; a finale/~의 final; ultimate; eventual/~의 승리 ultimate victory /~에 가서는 after all; ultimately; in the long run/~을 고하다 end; come [be brought] to an end; be concluded [settled]/전쟁도 드디어 ~을 고했다 The war came to an end at last. /~ 판결 final judgment[decision]. しゅうきょく

**종군**(從軍) following the army; going to the front/~하다 serve in a war; take part in a campaign; go to the front; see active service/~을 지원하다 apply[petition] for permission to go to war/~의 허가를 얻다 obtain permission to join the army/~ 간호부 a war nurse /~ 기자[기장] a war correspondent [medal]. じゅうぐん

**종굴박** a small gourd.

**종극**(終極) finality; extremity; the ultimate/~의 final; ultimate; extreme. しゅうきょく

**종금**(從今) after this; henceforward; henceforth; from now on; hereafter. これから

**쫑긋거리다** move[purse] the lips; move [prick, cock] the ears. すぼめる

**종기**(腫氣) a swell[ing]; a boil; a tumor; an abscess/목에 ~가 났다 A swelling came out on the neck. はれもの

**종기**(終期) the termination; the end; the close. しゅうき

**종내**(終乃) 《마침내》 at last; at length; finally 《결국》 after all/그는 ~ 가버렸다 He went away at length. /그녀는 병상에 눕더니 ~ 일어나지 못했다 She lay on a bed of illness, never to rise again.

**종년** a servant[slave] girl.

**종놈** a servant; a slave.

**종다래끼** a small bamboo basket. ちいさいざるかご

**종다수**(從多數) following the views of t. he majority; agreeing to the views of the majority; abiding by the decision of the majority/~ 취결(取決)하다 decide by majority. たすうのいけんにしたがうこと

**종단**(縱斷) vertical section; scissure 《분할》 a split; a division/~하다 cut vertically[longitudinally]; run through; traverse/~적 vertical; longitudinal/ ~을 획책하다 attempt at dividing[splitting up] [the existing party arrangement]/~면 a longitudinal[vertical] section. じゅうだん

**종단**(宗團) the religious order.

**종달거리다** grumble; complain; mutter; murmur/종달종달 grumblingly; mutteringly. ぶつぶついう

**종달새** 《조》 a lark; a skylark. ひばり

**종답**(宗畓) paddy-fields that produce the crop used in the ancestral sacrifices of the clan.

**종당**(從當) 《필경》 after all; in the end 《꼭》 necessarily; from the very nature of things.

**종대**(縱隊) a column of troops; a file/ ~를 짓다 form a column/중대 ~ a company column/2열 ~로 행진하다 march in file. じゅうたい

**종독**(腫毒) a malignant tumo[u]r. はれもののどくけ

**종돈**(種豚) a breeding pig. たねぶた

**종두**(種痘) vaccination for smallpox; inoculation/~하다 vaccinate; inoculate with vaccine/~를 받다 be vaccinated (for smallpox)/~가 잘 되었다 The vaccination has taken. /~ 증명서 a vaccination certificate. しゅとう

**종두 지미**(從頭至尾) from head to tail; from beginning to end. はじめからおわりまで

**종람**(縱覽) inspection 《열람》 reading/~ 하다 inspect (a factory); visit; read/~ 시키다 exhibit; throw (a thing) open to public inspection/~을 환영[거절]한다 invite[decline] inspection/~권 an admission ticket; a pass/~실 an exhibition room; a reading room/~자 a visitor; a reader; a spectator. じゅうらん

**종래**(從來) 《부사적》 hitherto; up to now /~의 usual; customary; traditional/ ~의 사업 the former business/~의 관계 one's past connections/~에는 up to now[this time]; so far/~와 같이 as in the past; as usual; as before; as ever.

**종량세**(從量稅) a specific duty/~을 a specific tariff. じゅうりょうぜい

**종려**(棕櫚) 【식】a hemp palm; a palm/~수 the palm tree/~유 palm oil. しゅろ

**종렬**(縱列) a column; a file; a train/단(單)~ a single column/~ 행진하다 defile/~을 이루다 form a file.

**종론**(宗論) a dispute over a religious question. しゅうろん

**종료**(終了) an end; a close; 《완료》completion 《기간의》expiration 《임대차·연금 따위》cesser/~하다 《마치다》close; end; complete; conclude 《끝나다》come to an end; be completed [concluded]/세계 대전이 ~했다 The World War is over[comes to an end]. しゅうりょう

**종루**(鐘樓) a bell tower; a belfry. しょうろう

**종류**(種類) a kind; a sort; a class 《동·식물의》a species; a variety 《액면》a denomination/~가 다른 여러 가지의 물건 things of every description; all[various] kinds of things/~별로 나누다 classify. しゅるい

**종마**(種馬) a breeding horse; a stallion. たねうま

**종막**(終幕) the last act (of *a play*); an end; a close/~이 가까와지다 draw to a close/~이 되다 the curtain falls[drops]; come to an end. しゅうまく

**종말**(終末) an end; a close; a conclusion/~을 고하다 come to an end/전쟁도 ~에 가까와 왔다 The war is drawing to a close. しゅうまつ

**종말론**(終末論) 【종】eschatology. しゅうまつろん

**종매**(從妹) a female younger cousin. じゅうまい

**종목**(種目) an item; a line; an event/영업 ~ lines of business. しゅもく

**종묘**(種苗) 《싹을 기름》planting a seedling 《묘목》a seedling[sapling]; a young plant/~하다 plant [a seedling]/~장 field for seedling; a nursery. たねなえ

**종묘**(宗廟) the ancestral temple of the royal family. そうびょう

**종물**(從物) 【법】an accessory [thing]. じゅうぶつ

**종반**(宗班) the royal clan.

**종반전**(終盤戰) 《바둑·장기의》the end game 《선거 따위의》[get into] the last [final] stage (of *the election campaign*).

**종발**(鍾鉢) a small bowl.

**종배**(終一) an animal's last brood[litter] of the season.

**종배**(終杯) the last wine cup[glass] in drinking. おわりのさかずき

**종범**(從犯) participation in a crime; aiding and abetting; accessory/~의 accessory (*to*)/살인죄의 ~ accessory to murder/~자 an accessory (to *a crime*); an accomplice. じゅうはん

**종법**(宗法) family rules; a clan constitution. しゅうほう

**종별**(種別) classification; assortment/~하다 classify; assort. しゅべつ

**종복**(從僕) an attendant; a servant.

**종사**(宗嗣) the descendant[heir] of the main family of a clan.

**종사**(從死) killing oneself to follow (*a person*) in death 《아내의》suttee/~하다 die in attendance on (*a person*); follow to the grave. じゅうし

**종사**(從事) ~하다 engage in (*business*); pursue (*a calling*); practise (*medicine*); carry on (*trade*); employ oneself (in *writing books*); 《열심히》devote oneself to/그는 무슨 직업에 ~하고 있읍니까 What business is he engaged in?, What is he by occupation[profession]?/그는 신문 사업에 ~하고 있읍니다 He is engaged in newspaper work. じゅうじ

**종사**(縱射) a raking fire; an enfilade/~하다 rake (with *fire*); enfilade.

**종산**(宗山) a family cemetery.

**종서**(縱書) vertical writing/~하다 write vertically; write in vertical lines[columns]. たてがき

**종선**(從船) a small boat carried by a ship; a barge.

**종선**(縱線) a vertical line. じゅうせん

**종성**(終聲) 【언】a final consonant. まつおん

**종성**(鐘聲) the pealing[sound] of a bell. しょうせい

**종성**(宗姓) the royal family; the relatives of the king.

**종속**(從屬) subordination; dependency/~하다 be subordinate[subject] (*to*); be dependent on[upon]/~적인 subordinate; dependent; secondary; auxiliary/~시키다 subordinate (*a thing*) to (*a person*)/~구〔절〕a subordinate phrase [clause]/~국 a vassal state. じゅうぞく

**종손**(宗孫) the eldest son of one's son and heir. ほんけをつぐまご

**종손**(從孫) the grandson of one's brother; a grandnephew. じゅうそん

**종손녀**(從孫女) the granddaughter of one's brother; a grandniece.

**종수**(從嫂) the wife of a paternal cousin. いとこきょうだいのつま

**종수**(種樹) planting (*a tree*); tree planting/~하다 plant (*a tree*).

**종숙**(從叔) a male cousin of one's father. ちちのいとこのきょうだい

**종숙모**(從叔母) the wife of a cousin of one's father. ちちのじゅうていのつま

**종시**(終始) 《처음과 끝》the last and the beginning 《내내》all through; from beginning to end/~ 일관하여 consistently; from first to last/~ 일관하다 be consistent/~ 잠자코 그들의 토론을 듣고 있었다 He remained silent from first to last listening to their discussion

**종씨**(宗氏) a person who has the same family name with him.

**종씨**(從氏) 《자기의》 my elder cousin 《남의》 your〔his, *etc.*〕 cousin.

**종시속**(從時俗). conforming to the times; following the customs of the day／~하다 conform to the times; follow the customs of the day.

**종식**(終熄) cessation 《근절》 eradication／~하다 cease; come to an end; be brought to a close; be eradicated; be extirpated／그 병은 완전히 ~되었다 The disease was stamped out altogether. しゅうそく

**종신**(宗臣) ①《원훈》 a distinguished minister of state ②《왕족》 a minister from the royal family.

**종신**(終身) ①《한평생》 a whole life; a life ②《임종》 being at *one's* parent's death bed ③《죽음》 the end of life; *one's* death／~하다 be at *one's* parent's death bed; be with *one's* parent at his death／~ 연금 a life annuity／~ 징역 life imprisonment／~ 징역자 a lifer《속》／~형 a life sentence〔term〕; penal servitude for life／~ 회원 a life member／~ 징역을 언도받다 be sentenced to life imprisonment; be given a life sentence. しゅうしん

**종실**(宗室) an Imperial〔a Royal〕family. そうしつ

**종심**(終審) ①《최후의 심판》 the last judgement ②〖법〗 the final examination〔trial〕／~ 재판소 the court of last resort. しゅうしん

**종아리** the calf [of the leg]／~뼈〖해〗a fibula; a splint bone／~를 때리다 lash (*a person*) on the calf. ふくらはぎ

**종알거리다** murmur; mutter; grumble／혼자 ~ mutter to *one*self. ぶつぶついう

**종야**(終夜) all night; the whole night／~ 운전 《버스의》 an all-night service／~등 (燈) an all-night lamp. しゅうや

**종양**(腫瘍) 〖의〗 a tumour; an ulcer. しゅよう

**종언**(終焉) 《임종》 the end [of life]; last moments; death 《종말》 an end; a close／~하다 die; end／~을 고하다 come to an end; be brought to a close. しゅうえん

**종업**(從業) work in service; attending to *one's* work／~하다 be employed〔in the service, in employment〕; work 《쉬고 있던 사람이》 return to work; resume work／~ 시간 working hours／~원《한 사람》 an employee; an operative; a [service] worker (총칭) men. じゅうぎょう

**종업**(終業) ①《마침》 leaving of work; close of work; the end of work／~하다 close〔leave〕 work／~ 시간 the closing hour ②《끝냄》 completion of a work／~하다 complete〔finish〕. じゅうぎょう

**종연**(終演) the end of a show.

**종열차**(終列車) the last train.

**종요로이** importantly; momentously; necessarily; indispensably.

**종요롭다** (be) important; indispensable; pivotal.

**종용**(慫慂) suggestion; persuasion; instance; advice／~하다 advice; urge; suggest; persuade; induce／자수를 ~했다 I advised him to surrender himself to police officers. しょうよう

**종용하다**(從容—) (be) calm; serene; composed; undisturbed ⇒조용하다. おだやかだ

**종우**(種牛) a seed bull. たねうし

**종유**(種油) seed[vegetable] oil ⇒채유(菜油).

**종유동**(鐘乳洞) a stalactite grotto〔cave, cavern〕. しょうにゅうどう

**종유석**(鐘乳石) 〖광〗 stalactite. しょうにゅうせき

**종이** paper／~ 접기 paper work／~표 a paper cover／색 ~ colored paper／~ 한 장의 차이 a very slight difference／이 ~에 주소를 쓰시오 Write your address on this paper. かみ

**종인**(宗人) a person of the same clan; a distant relative.

**종인**(從因) a secondary〔an incidental〕cause; a by-cause.

**종일**(終日) all day [long]; all the day; the whole day／~토록 공부하다 study all day long／~ 독서하고 지냈다 I spent the whole day in reading. しゅうじつ

**종자**(宗子) the eldest son of the patriarch of the head family. ほんけのちょうなん

**종자**(從者) a follower; a vassal; an attendant; a servant 《수행자》 a retinue [suite]／~를 데리고 with an attendant. じゅうしゃ

**종자**(種子) 《식물의》 a seed 《동물의》 a breed; a stock; a strain／~가 좋다 be of a good stock／~를 받고자 기르다 keep for breeding [purposes]. しゅし

**종자**(鍾子) a small bowl. ちいさいつぼ

**종자매**(從姉妹) female cousins. じゅうしまい

**종작** the gist; the rough idea; the point. よさん

**종작없다** (be) fickle; inconstant; without any fixed principle／종작없는 말 senseless remarks; nonsense. つかみどころがない

**종잘거리다** prattle; ; mutter; jabber ⇒종알거리다. たわいなくしゃべる

**종잡다** get the gist〔point〕; get a rough idea; roughly understand／당신의 말은 종잡을 수가 없다 I have not the remotest idea of what you mean／그의 설명을 들었으나 종잡을 수 없었다 I was none the wiser for his explanation. つもる

종장(終章) the last of the 3 verses of a (*sijo*) poem; the last part of a song.

종적(蹤跡) one's traces; one's whereabouts/～을 감추다 disappear; cover one's trail; leave no trace behind.

종전(從前) ～의 previous; former; old; usual/～과 같이 as usual; as before; as in the past/～에와 같음을 be same as before. しゅうぜん

종전(終戰) the end of the war; the termination[cessation] of hostilities/～하다 the war ends[comes to an end]/～후의 postwar. しゅうせん

종점(終點) the end; the terminus; the terminal〈미〉/마포 ～ the end[terminus] of the *Mapo* line. しゅうてん

종제(從弟) a younger cousin of paternal side. じゅうてい

종조(宗祖) the founder (of *a sect*); the father; the originator. そふのいとこ

종조모(從祖母) a grandaunt; the wife of *one's* granduncle. そふのいとこのつま

종조부(從祖父) a granduncle; a great uncle. そふのことこ

종족(宗族) a clan; a family; kindred. そうぞく

종족(種族) 《인류의》 a race; a tribe 《동식물의》 a family/～ 보존 preservation of the species/～ 본능 racial instinct/～학 speciology.

종졸(從卒) a soldier servant; an officer's servant; an orderly〈미〉. じゅうそつ

종종(種種) ①《가지가지》 a variety (of *articles*); different kinds ②《가끔》 now and then; occasionally/～ 친구를 찾아가다 visit a friend every now and then. しゅじゅ

종종걸음 short and quick steps; mincing steps/～으로 걷다 walk with short, quick paces[mincing steps]. ちょこちょこあるき

종주(宗主) a suzerain/～국 a suzerain state/～권을 요구하다 claim the suzerainty on (*a country*). そうしゅ

종중(宗中) the families of the same clan /～답 the paddy fields owned by a clan.

종지 a small cut[bowl]. ちいさいつぼ

종지(宗支) main family line and branch.

종지(宗旨) the main meaning; the point.

종지(終止) stop; termination; end; cessation/～하다 terminate; end; stop; come to an end; cease/～부 a period; a full stop/…에 ～부를 찍다 put an end to…. しゅうし

종지뼈 the kneecap; the patella. ひざざら

종진(縱陣) a column; a line ahead/～을 치다 form a column. じゅじん

종질 slavery; bondage/～하다 serve as a servant[slave]; be a slave.

종질(從姪) a cousin's son. いとこのこ

종질녀(從姪女) a cousin's daughter.

종차(從此) after this; hence [forth]; hereafter; in [the] future. これから

종착역(終着驛) a terminal station; a terminus/인생의 ～ the terminus of one's life/부산은 경부선의 ～이다 The *Gyeongbu* line terminates in *Busan*. しゅうちゃくえき

종처(腫處) a boil; an abscess. はれものができたところ

종척(宗戚) the paternal and maternal relatives of the king.

종첩(一妾) a slave concubine.

종축(種畜) breeding stock. しゅちく

종친(宗親) the royal family; kindred of the king. そうしん

종타(縱舵) 〖공〗 a vertical rudder.

종탑(鐘塔) a bell tower; a belfry.

종파(宗派) 《종교의》 a sect; a denomination 《가족의》 the lineage of the eldest son/～적 sectarian/～ 싸움 a sectarian strife. しゅうは

종파(種播) sowing; seeding.

종피(種皮) 〖식〗 the testa (*pl.* -tal); the spermoderm; the episperm. しゅひ

종합(綜合) synthesis; generalization; 〖철〗 colligation/～하다 synthesize; integrate; put together/～ 대학 a university/～ 병원 a general hospital/～ 예술 a synthetic[composite] art/～주의 synthesism/～ 철학 synthetic philosophy/각종 보고를 ～하다 put various reports together/～해서 생각하다 think of collectively/이것을 ～하면 아마 이렇게 될 것이다 Summing up, this will come to the following result. そうごう

종항(終航) the last voyage[trip].

종헌(終獻) the last[third] libation in a sacrifice.

종형(從兄) an elder cousin. じゅうけい

종형제(從兄弟) [male] cousins.

종회(宗會) a family council/～를 열다 hold a family council.

종횡(縱橫) length and breadth 《직물의》 angles/～ 무진으로 freely; at will; ri-warp and woof/～으로 뻗은 철도망 a network of railroads/～ 무진의 재치 a wealth of wit/문제를 ～ 무진으로 논하다 discuss[deal with] a problem from all angles. じゅうおう

좆 the penis ⇒자지. いんきょう

쫓기다 be chased[run after, pursued]; be driven[ousted, expelled, removed]; 《일에》 be pressed (with *business*); have a pressure of business/일에 ～ be pressed with work[business]. おわれる

쫓다 ①《뒤를》 follow; run after 《동반하다》 accompany ②《따르다》 follow (*a precedent*) ③《복종하다》 obey; submit to; conform; act upon; abide by; accept/명령을 쫓아 in obedience to *one's* order/관습을 쫓아서 according to custom/충고를 ～ act upon *one's* order. したがう

쫓다 ①《쫓아 버리다》 drive away; drive (*a person*) out of/파리 떼를 ～ drive away flies/거지를 쫓아내다 turn away a beggar from *one's* door ②《뒤쫓다》 run after (*a person*); chase; pursue; give chase to/후퇴하는 적을 ～ follow a retreating enemy ③(따르다) follow; follow suit/유행을 ～ follow[run after] the fashion ④(따라가다) catch up with; keep up with; compete with/앞서 가는 사람을 쫓아가다 catch up with a person ahead.

**좋다**[1] ⇨별항 참조 (page 1716).

**좋다**[2] 《느낌》 Good!, Well!, All right!, O.K.! 《환성》 Whee!/～ 하자 Very well [All right O.K.], I'll do it.

**좋아지다** ①(상태가) become[grow] better (아름다와지다) become finer[more beautiful]/날씨가 ～ The weather clears up., The weather becomes better[improves]/경기가 ～ Business is improving [picking up, looking up]./건강이 작년보다 좋아졌다 He become better than last year. ②(좋아하게 되다) get[come, learn] to like (*a thing*); become[grow] fond of/점점 ～ develop a liking (*for*) /나는 이 집이 좋아졌읍니다 I have become fond of this house.

**좋아하다** ①(유쾌해 하다) be pleased; be amused; be delighted; be glad/그 소식에 모두들 좋아했다 All were delighted at the news. ②(사랑하다) love (기호) like (선택하다) prefer/그들은 서로 좋아하는 사이다 They are in love with each other./그는 스포츠를 무엇보다도 좋아한다 He is partial to sports. /나는 술을 좋아했다 I had a weakness for wine. /나는 그녀보다는 그를 더 좋아한다 I love him more than her./그 여자는 음악을 대단히 좋아했다 She had a passion for music.

**좋이** well; nicely; fully; properly; suitably; rightly; rather/그는 60세는 ～ 넘었을 것이다 He must be well over [past] sixty.

**좌**(左) 《속칭》 the left; the left side (사상) a liftist/～와 같다 be as follows; be as mentioned below/～에 속하다 belong to the left.

**좌**(座) a seat; throne; base (성좌) a constellation (극단) a theatrical company; a troupe/스칼라～ La Scala.

**좌각**(左脚) the left leg.

**좌객**(座客) the guests [who are] present.

**좌경**(左傾) an inclination to the left; communistic leanings; Bolshevization ～하다 incline to the left; become leftish/～ 분자 radical[leftist] elements; the left; the radicals/～ 사상 leftist thinking; radical thoughts/～ 운동 a left movement/～파 left[radical] elements; the left/～ 색채를 띤 잡지 a journal of leftist coloring.

**좌고**(坐高) one's height when seated; one's sitting height.

**좌고 우면**(左顧右眄) 《주저》 irresolution; looking around; vacillation/～하다 look to right and left; look around nervously 《주저》 be irresolute; vacillate; waver/～ 갈 바를 모르다 look this and that way; waver in *one's* attitude.

**좌골**(坐骨) the hipbone[huckelbone]; the ischium/～ 신경 the sciatic nerves/～ 신경통 hip-gout; sciatica.

**좌기**(左記) ¶～의 undermentioned; the following/～ 사람 the following person /～와 같이 as undermentioned[underwritten, follows].

**좌단**(左袒) support; taking sides with/ ～하다 support; take sides with; side with/～자 a supporter.

**좌담**(座談) a table-talk; conversation; a colloquy/～하다 converse with; exchange a table-talk/～회 a round-table talk/～에 능하다 be a good talker[conversationalist]/～ 회를 가지다 hold a symposium (*on*); have a discussion meeting.

**좌르륵** with a great rush; with a splash /～ 흐르다 pour[run] down; rush[gush] out.

**좌불안석**(坐不安席) ～하다 feel out of place; cannot stay quiety; be ill at ease; have a birdlike restlessness/나는 걱정이 되어서 ～했다 Fear kept me restless.

**좌상**(坐像) a seated[sitting, sedentary] figure[image, statue].

**좌상**(坐商) keeping a shop (사람) a shopkeeper [as contrasted with a hawker].

**좌서**(左書) a letter which is written with left hand.

**좌석**(座席) 《자리》 a seat 《비행기의》 a cockpit 《교회의》 a pew [앉을 장소] [sitting] room/～을 잡다 get[take, secure] a seat (in *a bus*)/[열차] ～은 전부 예약됐음 All seats are taken.

**좌선**(坐禪) religious meditation; umbilical contemplation/～하다 sit in contemplation[meditation].

**좌선**(左旋) levorotation/～하다 turn to the left.

**좌선회**(左旋回) rotation to the left; levorotation; levorotatory/～하다 rotate [turn] to the left.

**좌수우봉**(左授右捧) giving and taking[exchanging] on the spot/～하다 exchange on the spot.

**좌시**(坐視) ～하다 stand idly (*by*); look (*on*) with indifference/차마 ～할 수 없다 I cannot sit idle watching it.

**좌시**(坐市) a marketplace.

**좌식**(坐食) eating the bread of idleness/ ～하다 live in idleness.

**좌안**(左岸) the left bank (of *a river*).

**좌약**(坐藥) 《의》 a suppository.

**좌업**(坐業) a sedentary occupation[work]; a sitting-down job/～자 a sedentary worker.

**좌욕**(坐浴) a sitz[hip] bath.

**좌우**(左右) right and left/～하다 command; control; gain control of (*a market*); dominate; sway; carry off／~로 흔들리다 roll from side to side／운명을 ~하다 decide *one's* destiny. ひだりとみぎ

**좌우**(座右) *one's* [right] side／~에 비치다 keep (*a book*) at *one's* elbow. ざゆう

**좌우간**(左右間) anyhow; anyway; in any circumstance; in any case; in any event; at any rate／~ 준비만은 해 두자 In any case[At all events], I will make preparations for it. とにかく

**좌우명**(座右銘) a favourite maxim[motto]. ざゆうのめい

**좌우익**(左右翼) 《군대의》the left and right wings of the army; the left and right column 《주의의》the left and right wing[er].

**좌익**(左翼) 《대형》the left wing[flank]; 《주의》the left wing 《사람》the leftist; the left winger 《야구》the left field／~ 단체 a leftist organization; a group of radicals／~ 분자 the leftwing element; leftist faction／~ 사상 leftism; radicalism／~수《체》a left fielder／~ 운동 a left[radical] movement／~ 사상에 물들다 be tinctured with radicalism. さよく

**좌장**(座長) the chairman; the president 《흥행의》the proprietor; the boss. ざちょう

**좌전**(座前) 《좌하》addressed to the presence (*of*); to …. ざぜん

**좌절**(挫折) a setback; a breakdown; a collapse; frustration; a reverse (*of one's fortune*); an eclipse; ruin 《용기의》discouragement／~하다 《계획이》get ruined; be upset; breakdown; collapse; fall through; suffer a setback 《용기·기력 따위가》get discouraged[disheartened, daunted]／계획이 ~되다 a plan is ruined[upset]. ざせつ

**좌정**(坐定) ~하다 sit; be seated; take a seat. すわること

**좌종**(坐鍾) a table clock.

**좌지우지**(左之右之) ~하다 command; control ⇨좌우하다.

**좌천**(左遷) relegation／~하다 relegate; consign (*one*) to an inferior position 《좌천되다》be relegated／그의 이번 발령은 ~이다 His new appointment is a demotion[change for the worse]. させん

**좌초**(坐礁) running aground; stranding ／~하다 run aground[ashore, on a rock]; strand; strike a rock; go on a reef／폭풍우로 배는 ~하였다 The tempest drove the ship on the rocks. ざしょう

**좌측**(左側) the left [side]／~에 on the left／~ 통행 "Keep to the left". さそく

**좌파**(左派) the left wing; the left faction [of a party]; 《사람》the left wingers; the leftists／~ 사회당 the leftist socialists; the left faction of the Socialist Party. さは

**좌판**(坐板) a low bench; a board to sit on.

**좌편**(左便) the left side; the left. さそく

**좌표**(座標) 《수》co-ordinates／각[직각, 사각, 곡선, 구면] ~ angular[rectangular, oblique, curvilinear, spherical] co-ordinates／~ 기하학 co-ordinate geometry. ざひょう

**좌하**(座下) Mister(略: Mr.); Esquire(略: Esq.)

**좌향**(左向) ~좌 《구령》Left turn[face]!／~앞으로 가《구령》Left wheel!

**좌현**(左舷) port; port side／~에 on the port side／방향을 ~으로 잡다 give (*the vessel*) port helm. さげん

**좌회전**(左回轉) turning left／~하다 turn to the left.

**좍** ①broadly; extensively／소문이 ~ 퍼졌다 The rumor has got abroad.; The rumor spread in a flash. ②widely ③pouring down／비가 ~ 퍼붓는다 It rains heavily[hard, in showers]. ばっと

**좍좍** ①《비가》in torrents; in showers; heavily／비가 ~ 온다 It rains in torrents. ②《글을》with facility; fluently. ちゃあちゃあ

**좔좔** with a gush[rush]; gushing; flowing freely／~거리다 gush; pour down. ちゃあちゃあ

**좽이**《투망》a casting-net. とあみ

**죄**(罪) 《법률상의》a crime 《정신적인》a sin 《반칙》an offence 《과실·허물》blame; fault 《벌》punishment 《유죄》guilt／~를 범하다 commit a crime 《정신적인》commit a sin／~를 자복(自服)하다 submit to a sentence; plead guilty／스스로 ~를 뒤집어 쓰다 take the guilt upon *oneself*／~를 자백하다 confess oneself to be guilty／나에게는 ~가 없다 I am not to blame. つみ

**죄갚음** atonement for sins; expiation 《고행》penance／~하다 make amends for *one's* offenses; redeem *one's* faults; pay the penalty for sin; do penance.

**죄과**(罪過) an offense 《죄악》sin 《과오》a fault[an error]／~없는 사람을 벌하다 punish (*a person*) for nothing. ざいか

**죄과**(罪科) an offense; a crime; guilt／~를 묻다 make inquire into a crime.

**죄다**¹ ①tighten (*up*); stiffen; strain; stretch; string／나사를 ~ tighten (*up*) a screw ②《마음을》feel anxious[nervous, uneasy, tense]; tense up／마음을 ~ be fidgety[edgy]; be held in suspense. ひきしめる

**죄다**² 《모두》all; entirely; altogether／도서관의 책을 ~ 읽었다 I have read every book in the library. みんな

**죄다** ①《볕에 비치다》[the sun] shine ②《볕·불에》expose to the sun; put over the fire／이불을 햇볕에 ~ expose bedding to the sun; air bedclothes. さす

**죄명**(罪名) the name of a crime; charge／사기의 ~으로 on the charge of fraud; charged with fraud. ざいめい

**죄목**(罪目) the name of a crime.

**죄밀** a guilty conscience; a sense of guilt; remorse for *one's* crime/~을 느끼다 have qualms of conscience.

**죄받다(罪-)** be punished; be condemned /죄받을 짓 a sinful act. ばつをうける

**죄벌(罪罰)** punishment[a penalty] for a crime. ざいせき

**죄범(罪犯)** a crime ⇨죄(罪). つみ

**죄상(罪狀)** the nature of a crime; the circumstances of a crime; criminality; guilt; charge/~ 인부(認否) arraignment/~ 항목서 a bill of particulars/~이 명백해지다 be proved guilty. ざいじょう

**죄송(罪悚)** regret; feeling sorry/~하다 (be) sorry/~합니다 I beg your pardon., I am sorry. おそれおおいこと

**죄수(罪囚)** a prisoner; a convict; a jailbird. ざいしゅう

**죄악(罪惡)** 《종교상》 a sin 《벌률상》 a crime 《도덕상》 a vice/~감 a sense of guilt/~을 범하다 commit a sin[crime]. ざいあく

**죄어들다** become tight; become narrower; shrink. たるみがなくなる

**죄어치다** ①《죄다》 tighten; strain ②《몰다》 urge; press. ひきしめる

**죄업(罪業)** 【불】 act that will lead to sin; an iniquity/~을 쌓다 commit many sins; live a sinful life. ざいごう

**죄이다** 《물건이》 get tightened; be drawn up 《마음이》 feel anxious[uneasy, nervous]; be tense. ひきしめられる

**죄인(罪人)** a criminal; an offender; a culprit 《종교상》 a sinner. ざいにん

**죄임성(-性)** suspense; fidget[s]; eager expectation. しんちゅうにきたいすること

**죄장(罪障)** 【불】 sins/~의 소멸을 위하여 in expiation of *one's* sins.

**죄적(罪跡)** evidence[traces] of a crime/~을 들추다 trace out a crime. ざいせき

**죄주다(罪-)** punish; condemn. ばつする

**죄증(罪證)** proofs[evidence] of guilt; witness/~을 인멸하다 destroy all the proofs of *one's* guilt. ざいしょう

**죄짓다(罪-)** commit a crime 《종교상의》 do sinful things. つみをおかす

**죄책(罪責)** ①《죄의 책임》 liability for a crime/~을 묻다 charge with a crime ②⇨죄벌(罪罰). ざいせき

**죔틀** a vise. はさみき

**주(主)** 《주인》 *one's* master; *one's* employer 《수령》 a chief 《신》 the Lord 《주요 부분》 primary importance; the first consideration/인격 양성은 ~로 하다 make character-building the prime object/청중은 ~로 여성들이었다 The audience consisted mainly of women. ぬし

**주(周)** 《둘레》 a circumference; a circuit.

# 좋 다

①《모양·상태·성질 따위가》 (be) fine; nice; good/좋은 집[책, 그림] a good house[book, picture]/마음씨가 ~ be good-natured[-humored]/그것이 그녀의 좋은 점이다 That's one good thing about her./날씨가 ~ It is a lovely day./좋은 소식 good news/그는 머리가 ~ He is bright[smart, clever]./좋든 나쁘든 for better or for worse.

②《알맞다》 (be) right; proper; suitable; good/좋을 대로 하시오 do as *one* pleases; suit *one*self/그 직위에 좋은 사람 a good man for the post/이곳은 휴식하기에 좋지 않다 This is not a good place to rest in.

③《유익하다》 (be) beneficial; good; favo[u]rable/건강에 ~ be good for [the] health/치통에 ~ be good for toothache/우유는 어린아이의 건강에 ~ Milk is good for [the] health of children.

④《기호》 like 《기교》 (be) good; able; skilled 《비교》 (be) better; preferable 《선택》 [had] better; like better; prefer/필적이 ~ write a good hand/사과보다 배가 좋더라 I like pears better than apples./너는 여름과 겨울 중 어느 쪽이 좋으냐 Which do you like better, summer or winter?/곧 병원에 가 보는 게 ~ You had better go to a doctor at once./너는 화술이 ~ You are a good talker./어디로 가는 게 좋을까 Where'd I better go?/더 이상 이곳에 있지 않는 게 ~ We had better not remain here any longer./그는 말솜씨가 ~ He has great conversational power.

⑤《소원》 wish; desire; hope/그래, 내가 죽으면 좋겠니 So, do you wish me dead?/내게 100만 원이 있다면 좋겠다 I wish I had ten million *won.*/하지 않는 편이 좋겠다 You [had] better not try.

⑥《[…해도] 상관 없다》 may; do not care (*if*); do not mind (*doing*)/정원에 들어가도 좋습니까 May I go into the garden?/예, 좋습니다 Yes, you may./그녀가 없어도 ~ I can do very well without her./어떻게 되어도 ~ I don't care what happens./남들이 뭐라 해도 ~ I don't care[mind] what others say about me.

⑦《[…하지 않아도] 좋다》 need not (*do*); do not have to/내일은 오지 않아도 ~ You don't need to come tomorrow./일부러 설명하지 않아도 ~ You need not trouble yourself to explain./좋은 것이 아니라도 ~ It doesn't have to be good.

**주(州)** 《행정 구획》 a province 《미국의》 a state/뉴욕~ the State of New York.

**주(洲)** ①《퇴적》 a sandbank /삼각~ [river] delta ②《대륙》a continent /아시아~ the Continent of Asia.

**주(註)** an annotation; foot notes; comments; explanatory notes; commentary /~를 달다 annotate; make note on; comment on.

**주(株)** ①《주식》 a share; a stock〈미〉; an interest (in *a business*) /~가의 상승[하락] a rise[fall] in share /~를 모집하다 offer stocks for subscription ②《그루》 나무 한 ~ a tree /은행 ~ bank stocks.

**주(週)** a week /금[전, 내]~ this[last, next] week.

**주(朱)** vermilion; Chinese red; 《광》 cinnabar.

**주(酒)** alcoholic beverages; liquors.

**주가(酒家)** a tavern ⇒술집.

**주가(株價)** the price[value] of a stock.

**주가(住家)** a dwelling; a house; a residence; an abode.

**주간(主幹)** the manager; the superintendent /~하다 manage; edit /편집 ~ the chief editor.

**주간(週刊)** a weekly; weekly publication /~ 잡지 a weekly magazine.

**주간(晝間)** daytime; day /~에 in the daytime; during the day; by day /별은 ~에는 안 보인다 Stars are invisible in the daytime.

**주간(週間)** a week /교통 안전 ~ Traffic Safety Week /인권 강조 ~ Human Rights Week.

**주강(鑄鋼)** cast steel /~업 steel casting.

**주객(主客)** 《사람》 host and guest 《사물》 principal and auxiliary /~이 전도됐다 The relations are turned.

**주객(酒客)** a drinker; a tippler; a thirsty soul.

**주거(住居)** a dwelling; a habitation; a residence; an abode /~하다 dwell; reside; live (*in*); inhabit /~인 an occupant of a house; resident.

**주걱** a large wooden spoon; a rice scoop.

**주검** 《시체》 remains; a corpse; a dead body /~을 묻다 bury a body.

**주격(主格)** 《언》 the nominative[subjective] case.

**주견(主見)** *one's* own opinion[view]; an independent idea; a firm conviction; a fixed view.

**주경 야독(晝耕夜讀)** farm by day and study by night.

**주고도(走高跳)** the running high jump.

**주고받기** ~하다 give and take; exchange; reciprocate /편지를 주고 받다 correspond [exchange] letters with.

**주공(奏功)** success; efficacy /~하다 succeed; be successful 《주효하다》 be effective; take effect.

**주공(鑄工)** a caster; a cast-iron worker.

**주관(主管)** superintendence; supervision 《사람》 a supervisor /~하다 superintend; supervise; manage; have charge of /~ 사항 matters in *one's* charge.

**주관(主觀)** subjectivity; subjectiveness 《자아》 the subject; ego /~적 비평 subjective criticism /~에 치우치다 be too subjective.

**주광(酒狂)** drunken frenzy; delirium tremens.

**주광도(走廣跳)** the running broad jump.

**주교(主敎)** ①《교직》 a prelate; a primate; a bishop 《대주교》 an archbishop ②《주요 종교》 the principal religion; a dominant religion.

**주교(舟橋)** a pontoon bridge.

**주구(走狗)** ①《앞잡이》 a tool; a cat's paw; a puppet /남의 ~가 되다 be made a cat's paw of (*one*) ②《사냥개》 a hound; a hunting dog.

**주구(誅求)** exaction; extortion /~하다 exact; extort; squeeze.

**주군(主君)** *one's* [liege] lord; *one's* master.

**주군(駐軍)** stationing troops /~하다 station troops.

**주권(株券)** a share certificate; a stock certificate; a share /가~ a script /기명 ~ a registered share /~을 현금으로 바꾸다 cash shares.

**주권(主權)** sovereignty; sovereign[supreme] power[rights]; supremacy /~자 the sovereign; the ruler; the chief of a state /~ 재민설 the theory of sovereignty residing in the people /~을 잡다 rule[reign] supreme.

**쭈그러뜨리다** press[squeeze] out of shape; crush; crumple /모자를 납작하게 ~ crumple a hat flat.

**쭈그러지다** be crushed; be crumpled; be [get] pressed[squeezed] out of shape 《살기가》 be withered; grow gaunt; shrivel /쭈그러진 손 a shriveled hand.

**쭈그렁이** 《물건》 a thing crushed out of shape 《사람》 a withered old person.

**쭈그리다** 《쭈그러뜨리다》 crush 《몸을》 crouch; squat; bend low; stoop /불을 쬐려고 ~ stoop over the fire /쭈그리고 걷다 walk with a stoop.

**주근깨** freckles; flecks; 《의》 lentigo(*pl.* -tigines) /얼굴에 ~가 있다 have a freckled face.

**쭈글쭈글** ~하다 (be) crumpled; rumpled; wrinkled; withered /~한 바지 crumpled trousers.

**주금(株金)** a share 《투자금 총액》 a stock / ~ 계정 capital account(略 : a/c) /~

**주금** 을 붙입하다 pay up one's shares. かぶきん

**주금**(鑄金) casting／~가 a metal worker.

**주금류**(走禽類) 【鳥】 runners; cursorial birds; Cursores(학명). そうきんるい

**주급**(週給) weekly wages[pay, salary]. しゅうきゅう

**주기**(酒氣) the influence of alcohol; intoxication. しゅき

**주기**(週期) a periodic time; a period 《주기성》 periodicity／~을 the law of periodicity／~적 periodic[al]／~적으로 periodically／~ 운동 a periodic movement／~적으로 순환하다 move in a cycle; circulate periodically. しゅうき

**주기도문**(主祈禱文) the Lord's Prayer.

**주낙** a [fishing] reel and line with multiple hooks.

**주년**(周年) an anniversary; a whole year／5~ the fifth anniversary. しゅうねん

**주뇌**(主腦) the leaders ⇒수뇌(首腦).

**주눅들다** feel small; be self-conscious. きがちいさくなる

**주눅좋다** (be) shameless; unabashed; unblushing; impudent; cheeky. はれんちだ

**주다**¹ ①《증여하다》 give 《수여하다》 bestow; award 《급여하다》 provide[supply] (one) with 《백분하다》 share with 《임히다》 inflict on／일거리를 ~ provide work (for one)／암시를 ~ drop a hint／타격을 ~ give a blow to ②《해 주다》 do (a thing) for a person／저고리를 입혀 ~ help a person on with his coat. やる

**주다**² 《조동사》 do for (a person)／문을 열어 ~ open the door for (a person)／아내에게 외투를 입혀 ~ help one's wife on with her coat. ―(して)あげる

**주단**(紬緞) silks and satins; silk goods.

**주달**(奏達) ~하다 report (a matter) to the Emperor. そうたつ

**주당**(酒黨) a drinker. さけのみ

**주대** a rod and line. いととたけ

**주도**(周到) thoroughness／~하다 (be) careful; thorough; complete; elaborate／용의~한 계획 an alert and cautious plan; the plan prepared to the minutest details. しゅうとう

**주도**(主導) leading; taking the initiative／~하다 lead; assume leadership of／~자 a leader; a prime mover／~권을 잡다 take the leadership; take the leading part. しゅどう

**주독**(酒毒) alcoholic poisoning; alcoholism. しゅどく

**주동**(主動) leadership; motive power／~하다 take the lead[initiative]／~자가 되다 take the leading part. しゅどう

**주되다**(主―) be the head of; take the lead of; lead others (in some work)／그가 주되어서 일을 했다 He played most active part in it. しゅになる

**주두**(柱頭) ①【건】 a capital ②【식】 a stigma. ちゅうとう

**주둔**(駐屯) stationing; staying; posting／~하다 be stationed; station; post; stay／~군 stationary troops; occupation army 《수비대》 a garrison. ちゅうとん

**주둥이** 《입》 the mouth; lips 《말》 tongue 《부리》 a bill(편편한); 《매의 부리 따위》 a beak 《물건의》 a mouth[piece]／~를 놀리다 wag one's tongue／~가 싸다 be glib tongued. くち

**주란**(酒亂) drunken frenzy.

**주란사**(―紗) cloth woven from gassed cotton thread.

**주람**(周覽) a tour; a round trip／~하다 make a tour. しゅうらん

**주량**(酒量) one's drinking capacity／~이 늘다 gain drinking capacity／~이 크다 be a heavy drinker. しゅりょう

**주럽** ①《피로》 fatigue; weariness; exhaustion／~멸다 rest oneself; rest from one's fatigue ②~:주접. ひろう

**주렁주렁** in abundance; in clusters／마당의 감나무에 감이 ~ 달렸다 The persimmon tree in my garden has borne abundant with fruits. ぶらぶら

**주력**(注力) putting forth strength; concentrating one's effort／~하다 concentrate (one's effort) on something; exert oneself for.

**주력**(主力) the main force[strength, body]／~전 a major engagement; the clash of the main forces／~함 a capital ship／~ 함대 the main fleet／~을 결집하다 concentrate the main forces. しゅりょく

**주력**(酒力) Dutch courage.

**주련**(柱聯) a verse couplet carved or written on a plank which is put on a pillar. ちゅうれん

**주렴**(珠簾) a beaded hanging screen.

**주례**(主禮) ①officiating at[presiding over] a ceremony ②《사회자》 an officiator; a master of ceremonies; the one in charge of a ceremony／~ 목사 a presiding minister. しゅれい

**주로**(主―) mainly; chiefly; principally; in the main 《대개》 generally; mostly; for the most part／그것은 ~ 너의 책임이다 You are mainly responsible for it. しゅとして

**주로**(走路) a track; a course. そうろ

**주루**(酒樓) a drinking shop. しゅろう

**주룩주룩, 쭈룩쭈룩** ①《주름이》 with wrinkles[rumples, folds] ②《비가》 pouring hard; in sudden down pours／비가 ~ 온다 The rain keeps pouring down. くちゃくちゃ

**주류**(主流) the main current[stream]／사회 불안의 ~ the main current of social unrest. しゅりゅう

**주류**(酒類) alcoholic liquors／~의 판매 liquor selling. しゅるい

**주륙**(誅戮) death punishment; execution／~하다 punish (a person) with death; execute. ちゅうりく

**주르르, 쭈르르** trickling; dribbling／그녀의 뺨으로 눈물이 ~ 흘렀다 Tears streamed down her cheeks／ ~ 흐르다 flow out. すうっと

**주름** (피부의) wrinkles; furrows (물건의) creases; rumples; folds (옷의) a plait; a fold／~잡다 plait; fold／~잡히다 become wrinkled[crumpled, rumpled]／~을 펴다 smooth out; unrumple. しわ

**주름살** (구김살) wrinkles (접은 줄) pleats; folds; creases.

**주름잡다** ①plait; crease ②(지배하다) manage; control; take the lead (in)／금융계를 ~ have a firm grip on the banking business.

**주름통** bellows [on a camera].

**주릅** (거간) a broker; a commission-merchant[agent]; a go-between; an intermediary; a middleman；집~ a real-estate agent; a rental agent／~듣다 act as a broker. ブローカー

**주리다** be[go] hungry; starve; famish; be famished (갈망하다) be hungry after; hanker after; hunger[thirst] for[after]／돈[사랑]에 ~ hanker after money [love]. うえる

**주리틀다** impose leg-screw torture; torture a suspect by twisting his legs with two sticks inserted between them.

**주립**(州立) state[-established]; province [-established]; provincial／~ 대학 a state university.

**주마**(走馬) running a horse (닫는 말) a running horse／~하다 drive [a horse]. うまをはしらせること

**주마등**(走馬燈) (등) a revolving lantern; a kaleidoscope (광경) a shifting[moving] panorama／~처럼 변하는 역사 a hundred changing turns of the historical kaleidoscope.

**주막**(酒幕) an inn; a tavern／~장이 an innkeeper. さかば

**주말**(週末) the week-end／~ 여행 a week-end trip／~경(頃)에 over the week-end. しゅうまつ

**주맥**(主脈) the main range (of *mountains*). しゅみゃく

**주머니** a moneybag; a pocketbook; a bag; a sack (작은) a pouch (호주머니) a pocket／뒷~ a hip pocket／속~ an inside pocket／~가 든든하다 have a long[heavy, plump, well-filled, well-lined, fat] purse[pocket]／~를 털다 empty *one's* purse to the last penny.
ふくろ

**주머니밑천** ready money in *one's* pocket.
**주머니칼** a knife; a pocketknife.
**주먹** a fist; the bunch of fives／~으로 탁자를 치다 bang the table with *one's* fist／~만한 돌 a fist-sized rock[stone]. こぶし

**주먹구구**(一九九) (셈) counting on *one's* fingers (어림) a rough calculation.

**주먹다짐** fisticuff; striking with the fists (강제) compulsion／~하다 fist; strike with *one's* fist; use *one's* fist (*on*)／그는 그 노인에게 ~했다 He rained blows on the old guy.

**주먹밥** a rice-ball. にぎりめし

**주먹질** [a bout of] fisticuff; fistfighting; an exchange of blows (권투에서) rally／~하다 strike[beat] (*a person*) with *one's* fist; give (*a person*) a good punch／마침내 그들은 ~까지 하게 됐다 They finally came to blows.
こぶしをふるうこと

**주멸**(誅滅) extermination; extirpation; eradication／~하다 exterminate; extirpate; eradicate. ちゅうめつ

**주명곡**(奏鳴曲) 〖음〗 a sonata.
そうめいきょく

**주모**(酒母) yeast; ferment. しゅぼ

**주모**(主謀) heading a conspiracy[scheme, plot]; taking the lead in conspiracy／~하다 lead a conspiracy[scheme, plot]; stir up; organize／~자 a ringleader; the author (of *a plot*); a prime mover; a leader／이 반란의 ~자는 누구야 Who led the mutiny? しゅぼう

**주목**(朱木) 〖식〗 a yew [tree]; *Taxus cuspidata*(학명).

**주목**(注目) attention; notice; note; observation; remark／~하다 pay attention to; watch; observe; keep an eye on; take notice of／~할 만하다 be worth noticing／~을 끌다 attract attention.
ちゅうもく

**주무**(主務) management; chief control of an affair; the official[person] in charge; a manager／~하다 have chief control; be in charge of (*an affair*)／~ 장관[관청] the competent Minister[authorities, office]. しゅむ

**주무르다** ①(물건을) finger; fumble with (비비다) rub (몸을) massage／어깨를 ~ massage (*a person's*) shoulder ②(농락하다) inveigle; entice; take in hand; cajole; take in. てなずける

**주무자**(主務者) the person in charge; a manager. しゅむしゃ

**주묵**(朱墨) a cinnabar-stick; red ink.
しゅぼく

**주문**(呪文) a magic formula[chanting]; an incantation; a conjuration; a spell; a charm; a curse／~을 외우다 make an incantation. じゅもん

**주문**(注文) (마춤) an order; ordering (주문서) an indent (요구) a request; a wish／~하다 order (*a thing*) from; give (*a person*) an order for (*a thing*)／~서 an order sheet (외국에서의) an indent／재~ repeat order／견본 ~ sample order／우편 ~ 거래 orders by post; mail order business／~을 받다 take [book] orders／~을 취소하다 cancel[revoke, withdraw] an order／그것은 어려운 ~이다 It is a difficult bill to fill.

**주문**(奏聞) ~하다 report (*a matter*) to the

**주문**(主文) the text; 《언》 the principal [main] clause.　しゅぶん

**주물**(鑄物) cast-iron ware; a cast-iron product／~공장 a foundry.　いもの

**주물럭거리다** finger; fumble with／주물럭주물럭 fingering; fumbling.

**주미**(駐美) ~의 stationed[resident] in America／~ 한국 대사 the Korean Ambassador to[in] the United States of America.

**주민**(住民) inhabitants; residents; dwellers／~ 등록 resident registration／~없는 deserted; unsettled.　じゅうみん

**주밀**(周密) completeness; cautiousness; prudence; thoroughgoing preparation／~하다 (be) scrupulous; cautious; prudent; exhaustive; careful／~한 설계 thoroughgoing design.

**주반**(酒飯) 《술과 밥》 sool[wine] and boiled-rice 《양조용》 boiled-rice for brewing.　しゅはん

**주반**(酒盤) the table laden with sool [wine] and some eatables.

**주발**(周鉢) a brass rice-bowl／~ 뚜껑 the lid of a brass rice-bowl.　しょっき

**주방**(廚房) a kitchen; a cookroom 《호텔 따위의》 a cuisine.

**주배**(酒杯) a [wine-]cup; a wine-glass ⇒ 술잔.　しゅはい

**주번**(週番) weekly duty／~ 사관 the officer of the week.　しゅうばん

**주벌**(誅罰) punishment; chastisement／~하다 punish; chastise.

**주벌**(誅伐) a punitive expedition／~하다 send a punitive expedition (against *rebels*).　ちゅうばつ

**주범**(主犯) the principal offence 《사람》 the principal offender.　しゅはん

**주법**(主法) the main law.　しゅほう

**주법**(走法) [a] form of running／~이 틀리다 run in a wrong form.

**주벽**(酒癖) one's behavior under the influence of alcohol; a drinking habit／~이 나쁘다 be quarrelsome in one's cups.　しゅへき

**주변** adaptability; resourcefulness; tactfulness; flexibility; versatility; shiftiness／그는 말~이 좋다 He has the gift of gab.　あしらい

**주변**(周邊) a circumference; 《수》《명면도의》 a perimeter 《토지의》 environs; outskirts／서울 및 그 ~에 in and around Seoul; in Seoul and its suburbs[outskirts].　しゅうへん

**쭈뼛** ~하다 ①《솟다》 stand on end; stand up; stand erect; bristle up ②《주저하다》 (be) shy and hesitant; timid／머리끝이 ~하다 have one's hair stand (up) on end (at *a sight*).　おじおじ

**주병**(酒餠) sool[wine] and rice-cake.　さけともち

**주병**(駐兵) stationing troops 《주둔병》 stationary troops／~하다 station[keep] troops／~권 the right of stationing troops.　ちゅうへい

**주보**(週報) 《신문》 a weekly [periodical]; 《보고》 a weekly bulletin.　しゅうほう

**주보**(酒甫) a drunkard; a heavy drinker; an alcoholic.　さけのみ

**주보**(酒保) 《군》 a canteen; a post of exchange; a PX.　しゅほ

**주복**(主僕) master and servant; lord and retainer; employer and employee.　しゅぼく

**주봉**(主峰) the highest[main] peak [of the mountain].　しゅほう

**주부**(主部) the main[a principal] part; 《언》 a subject.　しゅぶ

**주부**(主婦) the mistress[lady] of a house; a housewife 《하숙집의》 the landlady.　しゅふ

**주부코** a red bulbous nose; a whisky nose.　あかいはな

**주붕**(酒朋) a boon[pot, drinking] companion.　のみともだち

**주빈**(主賓) the guest of honour; honour guest; the chief guest.　しゅひん

**주사**(主事) a junior official 《총칭》 the clerical staff.　しゅじ

**주사**(主辭) 《논》 the subject [of a sentence].　しゅじ

**주사**(注射) injection 《접종》 inoculation／~하다 inject; inoculate (*a person*) with; syrings; give a injection (*of*)／~기 an injector; a syringe／~약 an injection; a vaccine／~침 an injection syringe; a needle／예방 ~ preventive injection／피하 ~를 놓다 inject [medicines] hypodermically[under the skin].　ちゅうしゃ

**주사**(朱砂) 《광》 cinnabar.　しゅしゃ

**주사**(走査) 《텔레비전의》 scanning／~하다 scan.

**주사**(酒邪) drunken frenzy／~가 있는 사람 a vicious drinker; a person who loses his temper over his cups.　わるいさけくせ

**주사**(酒肆) a drinking shop; a tavern.

**주사**(紬絲) silk thread.　きぬいと

**주사위** a die(*pl.* dice)／~의 눈 the spot on a die; a pip／~ 놀이를 하다 play (*at*) backgammon／~를 던지다 cast a die.　さい

**주사위뼈** small bones; a tiny bone.　さいころをつくるほね

**주사 청루**(酒肆青樓) the gay quarters; bars and brothels.

**주산**(主山) a guardian mountain [located to the north of a town or a grave].

**주산**(珠算) abacus calculation; calculation on the abacus／~하다 count[figure] on an abacus.　しゅざん

**주산물**(主產物) principal[major, prime] products.　しゅさんぶつ

**주산지**(主產地) a chief[main] producing district[place] (*of*).

**주살** an arrow with a string attached to its nock／~질 shooting a string-attac-

주상(主上) the Sovereign; the King; His [Your] Majesty. しゅじょう
주상(主喪) the master of funeral rites; the chief mourner.
주상(酒商) 《장사》 liquor selling 《장수》 a liquor dealer.
주상(酒傷) illness from drinking alcohol.
주색(朱色) vermilion. しゅしょく
주색(酒色) wine and woman; dissipation and debauchery; sensual pleasures/~ 잠기 wine, woman and gambling games/~에 빠지다 give oneself up to wine and sex. しゅしょく
주서(朱書) rubrication; writing in red/~하다 write in red ink; rubricate; mark[color] with red. しゅしょ
주석(主席) the head; the chief/국민 정부 ~ the President of the National Government. しゅせき
주석(柱石) a pillar 《주추》 a foundation-stone; a mainstay; a main prop/국가의 ~ the pillar of a state. ちゅうせき
주석(朱錫) tin; 〖화〗 Sn/~ 그릇 tinware/~을 입히다 tin. しんちゅう
주석(註釋) an annotation; notes; comments; a commentary/~하다 annotate; comment (on); expound/~자 an annotator/~을 달다 annotate; append notes (to a book). ちゅうしゃく
주석(酒席) a banquet; a feast/~을 베풀다 give a banquet. しゅせき
주석(酒石) 〖화〗 crude tartar/~산 tartaric acid. しゅせきさん
주선(周旋) 《알선》 good offices; kind offices 《추천》 recommendation 《중개》 agency; [inter]mediation/~하다 recommend; use one's influence[good offices]/~료 brokerage; commission/~업 brokerage 《고용인의》 employment agency/~인 an agent 《중매인》 a ge-between; a broker 《토지 가옥의》 a realestate agent. しゅうせん
주선(酒仙) a son of Bacchus; a hard drinker.
주섬주섬 one by one/옷을 ~ 입다 put on clothes one piece after another. ひとつひとつ
주성(酒性) one's behavior under the influence of liquor. さけくせ
주성분(主成分) the chief ingredient; the principal element. しゅせいぶん
주세(酒稅) a tax on liquor; liquor-tax. しゅぜい
주소(住所) a dwelling [place]; a residence; an abode; an address; 〖법〗 a domicile/~록 an address book; a directory/~ 불명 address unknown/~ 성명 one's name and address/현~ the present address/~가 부정하다 have no fixed abode; be a floater〈미〉/~ 성명을 말하다 give one's name and address. じゅうしょ
주속(紬屬) silks.
주술(呪術) incantation; sorcery.
じゅじゅつ
주시(注視) a steady gaze; close observation/~하다 gaze steadily; fix one's eyes on; observe (one) closely; watch [look at] (a thing) carefully; scrutinize/~은 세계의 ~의 대상이 되다 become the cynosure of the world. ちゅうし
주식(株式) shares〈영〉; stocks〈미〉/~ 발행액 the issue prices of shares/~ 배당 a stock dividend/~ 시장[거래소] a stock market[exchange]; 《유럽에서》 a bourse/~ 시세 stock quotations/~ 중매업 stockbroking/~ 중매인 a stock broker 《투기자》 a stock speculator/~ 합자 회사 a joint-stock limited partnership/~ 회사 a [joint-]stock company; corporation/~ 할당 allotment of shares/~의 양도 transfer of shares/~을 매매하다 deal in stocks[shares]. かぶしき
주식(酒食) food and drink. しゅしょく
주식(晝食) lunch; luncheon. ひるめし
주식(主食) the principal[staple] food; a staple article of food/쌀은 동양 제국의 ~이다 Rice is the principal[staple] food of Oriental nations./쌀을 ~으로 하다 live on rice. しゅしょく
주심(主心) firmness of mind; iron will; backbone. ほんしん
주심(主審) the chief; umpire; the umpire-in-chief. しゅしん
주아(主我) 〖철〗 ego; self egocentrism/~주의 egoism. しゅが
주아(珠芽) 〖식〗 a bulbil; a bublet.
しゅが
주악(奏樂) playing music; a musical performance/~하다 play[perform] music/~자 a performer; a player/악대의 ~ band music. そうがく
주안(主眼) the principal object[aim]; the chief end[aim]; the principal point; the object in view/~점 the essential [main] point; the keynote/인격 양성을 ~으로 하여 with an eye to character-building. しゅがん
주안(酒案) 《술상》 a liquor table.
주야(晝夜) day and night/~ 평분선 equinoctial line/~ 교대로 in day and night shifts/~ 골몰하다 be busy day and night. ちゅうや
주어(主語) 〖언〗 the subject. しゅご
주어(齟齬) ①《안 맞음》 discordance; discrepancy; disagreement; variance/~하다 be discrepant; disagree; be at variance/사실과 ~하다 be contrary to the fact ②《일 진행의》 ~하다 suffer a setback; go wrong; miscarry.
주역(主役) the leading part[role]; the lead 《배우》 the leading actor[actress]; the star; hero[heroine]/~을 맡다 take the leading part[role] in; play the lead; star (in a play). しゅやく
주역(周易) 《역경》 the Book of Changes; Yi-king (Chin). しゅうえき
주연(主演) starring; playing the leading

**주연** /~하다 play the leading part[role] in; star (in *a play*); ~자 a leading actor[actress]; a star; the star player; a leading man[lady]/그 여자는 많은 영화에 ~해 왔다 She has starred in many pictures.

**주연**(酒宴) a feast; a drinking bout[party]; a carousal; a revel/~을 열다 revel; carouse; give a banquet. しゅえん

**주연**(酒筵) a drinking bout[party]. しゅえん

**주연**(周延) 〖논〗 distribution/~하다 distribute/~칙(則) the rule of distribution/~적인 distributive. しゅうえん

**주옥**(珠玉) 〖보석〗 a jewel; a gem 〖집합적〗 jewelery/~ 같은 글 a beautiful composition; a writing of rare beauty/~을 박다 adorn with jewels.

**주요**(主要) importance/~하다 (be) important; chief; leading; principal; staple; main/~ 산물 staple products/~ 도시 principal cities/~ 수출품 chief[principal] exports/~ 수입품 the staple for import/~ 인물 《극의》 the leading character/~한 역할을 맡아하다 play a prominent part. しゅよう

**주워내다** take out; pick out; select/나쁜 것들을 주워냈다 He took out those of worse ones.

**주워담다** pick and put in. ひろっていれる

**주워대다** quote this and that; use quibbles; equivocate/거짓말을 ~ make up lies. あれこれといんようする

**주워듣다** learn of; get wind of/남한테 주워들은 지식 knowledge picked up from others. あれこれとききおぼえる

**주워먹다** pick up and eat; grab a bite to eat/돌아다니며 ~ go around pecking.

**주워 모으다** gather; collect/주워 모은 것 a collection 〖혼합물〗 a mixture; odds and ends; pickings; waifs and strays.

**주워섬기다** chatter[rattle on, spiel, shoot off *one's* mouth, carry tales] about all sorts of things. ならべたてる

**주위**(主位) the main position; the premier[first] place. しゅい

**주위**(周圍) 〖언저리〗 the circumference; the girth 〖환경〗 the surroundings; environments 〖부근〗 the environs; the vicinity; the neighbourhood/~의 surrounding; attendant/~의 사람들 *one's* surroundings/~의 사정 circumstances; surroundings 《환경》 environment/그는 집 ~를 달렸다 He ran all round the house.

**주유**(周遊) a tour; a round trip/~하다 tour; make a round trip; go on a tour; take a pleasure trip/세계를 ~하다 make a trip around the world. しゅうゆう

**주유**(侏儒) a dwarf; a pygmy. しゅじゅ

**주유**(注油) oiling; lubrication 《급유》 oil supply/~하다 oil; lubricate 《급유》 fill; feed/~기(器) a lubricator/~소 an oil [a gasoline] station; a filling station. ちゅうゆ

**주육**(酒肉) wine and meat. しゅにく

**주은**(主恩) 《임금의》 the benevolence of the Emperor 《주인의》 *one's* master's favour 《천주의》 divine grace. しゅおん

**주음**(主音) 〖음〗 prime; keynote. しゅおん

**주의**(主意) 〖요지〗 the point; a gist; a tenor 《목적》 an object; a purpose 《의미》 the main meaning[purport]; the effect/~론 〖철〗 voluntarism/~적 volitional. しゅい

**주의**(主義) a principle; a doctrine; an ism; a cause 《방침》 a policy; a rule; a basis/~를 관철하다[굽히다] carry out [deviate from] *one's* principle/~를 지키다[버리다] stick to[desert] *one's* principle. しゅぎ

**주의**(注意) ①《주목》 attention; notice; heed/~하다 pay attention[heed] to; notice; heed; attend to; take note of 《귀를 기울이다》 listen to/~를 끌다 attract[draw, engage] (*a person's*) attention ②《조심》 [a] care; watchfulness; caution 《경고》 [a] warning/~하다 take care; have a care; be watchful (*of, against*); look out for 《경고하다》 warn (*a person*) against/~가 부족한 careless; negligent /건강에 ~하십시오 Take care[Be careful] of your health./한마디 ~하고 싶다 I should like to give you a word of caution./기차에 ~《게시》 Beware of the train ③《충고》 advice; suggestion / ~하다 advise; counsel; suggest/잠깐 ~ 말씀 드리겠읍니다 Let me give you a piece of advice. ④《흥미》 interest/~하다 be interested in/~력 attentiveness/~ 사항 suggestions; hints/~ 산만 distraction/~를 끌다 arouse interest. ちゅうい

**주의**(周衣) a Korean-styled overcoat.

**주의**(主翼) the main planes (of *an airplane*). しゅよく

**주인**(主人) 《가장》 the head[master] of a family 《남편》 *one's* man; *one's* husband 《손님에 대하여》 the host(남자); the hostess(여자); 《여관·음식점 따위의》 the landlord; the landlady(여자); the proprietor 《고용주》 an employer; the master 《물건의 주인》 the owner (of *goods*)/상점 ~ a shop keeper/~을 섬기다 serve *one's* master/~인 체하다 assume a proprietary air. しゅじん

**주인**(主因) a principal[primary, leading] cause; the prime factor; the main reason/너의 실패의 ~은 태만에 있다 Your failure is mainly due to your negligence. しゅいん

**주인공**(主人公) 《가장》 the head (of *a family*); the master (of *a house*); 《소설·영화 따위의》 a hero; a heroine(여자). しゅじんこう

주일(週日) a week／오늘부터 일주일째에 this day week／다음 ~ next week; the following week.　しゅじつ

주일(主日) a holiday; the Lord's day; Sunday.　にちようび

주일(駐日) ~의 stationed[resident] in Japan／~ 미국 대사 the United States Ambassador to Japan／~ 한국 대사관 the Embassy of the Republic of Korea to Japan.

주임(主任) the person in charge; the head; the chief; the manager／~ 교사 the teacher in charge (of *a class*)／영업부 ~ a business manager／편집 ~ the managing editor／회계 ~ a chief treasurer／~을 명하다 put *a person* in full charge of a department.　しゅにん

주입(注入) ①《부어넣기・고취》 injection; influx 《신 사상 따위의》 infusion／~하다 《부어넣다》 pour[put] into 《고취하다》 infuse into／사상을 ~하다 infuse an idea into *one* ②《공부 따위》 cramming／~하다 cram／~식 교육 cramming education／~식 교육은 백해무익이다 Cramming edication does more harm than good.　ちゅうにゅう

주자(鑄字) type casting[founding];《활자》 a metal movable[printing] type／~하다 cast[found] (*metal types*)／~소 a type foundry.

주자(走者) 〖체〗 a runner.　そうしゃ

주작(做作) fabrication; invention; falsehood.　でっちあげ

주장(主張) assertion; contention; maintenance 《고집》 insistence; persistence 《주창》 advocacy 《권리로서》 a claim 《견해》 one's opinion; one's doctrine／~하다 assert; maintain; contend; claim; persist (*in*); insist (*on*); 《창도하다》 advocate／권리를 ~하다 assert *one's* rights; insist on *one's* rights／무죄를 ~하다 insist on *one's* innocence 《변호사가》 plead (*a person's*) innocence／~을 굽히다 compromise.　しゅちょう

주장(主將) 《군의》 the commander-in-chief 《경기단의》 the captain.　しゅしょう

주장(主掌) 《관장》 charge; management 《주재》 presiding; supervision／~하다 take charge of; have (*a matter*) in charge; preside (*at, over*)／사무를 ~하다 take charge of[supervise] business affairs.

주재(駐在) residence; stay／~하다 reside (*at, in*); be stationed (*at*); stay／~국 the country of residence／~관 a resident officer[official]／~소 a police sub-station.　ちゅうざい

주재(主宰) superintendence; supervision; presidency／~하다 superintend; supervise; take charge (*of*); 《편집에서》 edit／~자 the head; the chairman; the presiding officer／회의를 ~하다 preside over a meeting.　しゅさい

주저(躊躇) hesitation; indecision; vacillation／~하다 hesitate; waver; vacillate; have scruples about／~하면서 hesitatingly; falteringly／그것을 인정하는데 ~하지 않는다 I make no bones about admitting that.　ちゅうちょ

주저롭다 be hard up; be destitute[pressed, pinched, strained] (*for*)／돈에 ~ be hard up for money.　とぼしい

주저앉다 sit down [on the heels]; plant *oneself* down 《함몰하다》 fall into; sink; become indented 《벽・지붕 따위가》 cave in／땅바닥에 털썩 ~ plump[flop] down on the ground.　そのばにすわる

주저앉히다 《의자 따위에》 force (*a person*) to sit down 《못 떠나게》 make (*a person*) stay on.　そのばにすわらせる

주적거리다 《아는 체하다》 show off piddling knowledge; parade[make a display of] *one's* ignorance; be pedantic 《어린 아이가》 toddle.　ひょろひょろする

주전(主戰) advocating war; pro-war／~하다 advocate war／~론 a pro-war argument; advocacy of war; jingoism／~론자 a war advocate; a jingoist; a warmonger.　しゅせん

주전(鑄錢) mintage; coinage／~하다 mint (*coins, money*); coin; strike coin.

주전부리 snacking between meals／~하다 take a snack between meals.

주전자(酒煎子) a [copper, brass] kettle／~ 주둥이[뚜껑] the spout[lid] of a kettle／~에 물을 끓이다 boil water in a kettle.　やかん

주절(主節) 〖연〗 the principal clause.　しゅせつ

주점(主點) the principal[main] point; an important point.

주점(酒店) a wine[sool] shop; a grog shop; a boozer; a pub《영・속》.　さかば

주접들다 be depauperate; be undergrown／주접든 식물 a depauperated plant.　しおれる

주접스럽다 《음식에 대하여》 (be) avaricious; greedy (in *eating*); gluttonous.　どんよくだ

주정(酒酊) misconduct affected by liquor; drunken frenzy; drunken rowdiness／~하다 act in a drunken and disorderly way／~군[장이] a drunken brawler; a bad drunk.　さけくせのわるいこと

주정(酒精) alcohol; spirits; a hard liquor〈미〉／~ 음료 alcoholic beverages[drinks]／~ 중독 alcoholic poisoning; alcoholism／~ 중독자 an alcoholic.　しゅせい

주정(舟艇) a boat; a craft／상륙용 ~ a landing craft.　しゅうてい

주정설(主情說) 〖철〗 emotionalism.　しゅじょうせつ

주제 《몰골》 seedy appearance; shabby looks 《비유적》 be impertinent[cheeky, smart-alecky].

주제(主題) 《주제목》 the main[principal] subject; the subject matter 《작품의》 the theme; the motif／~가 a theme

**주제곡** song／～의 《주제목의》 subjective 《작품의》 thematic／～의 전개 thematic development. しゅだい

**주제꼴** poor[plain, mean, humble] dress; mean attire; coarse appearance.

**주제넘다** (be) forward; cheeky; smartalecky; saucy; conceited; impudent; impertinent; put (oneself) forward／주제넘게 impertinently; impudently; presumptuously／주제넘는 말을 하다 talk fresh[saucy]; have a saucy tongue; give cheek／주제넘는 소리 마라 Don't say such saucy things.

**주조**(主調) 〖음〗 the keynote; the dominant note. しゅちょう

**주조**(酒造) 《약주 따위》 brewing 《소주》 distilling. しゅぞう

**주조**(鑄造) casting; founding 《화폐의》 minting; mintage／～하다 cast (metal types); found (a bell); mint[coin] (money); strike (a coin)／～소 a foundry／～인 a founder; a caster／～ 화폐 a metalic coin. ちゅうぞう

**주조**(主潮) the main current／구주 문예의 ～ the main current of European literature. しゅちょう

**주종**(主從) employer and employee; master and servant; lord and retainer [vassal]; the principal and subordinate／～ 공생 〖생〗 helotism／ ～관계 the relation between master and servant. しゅじゅう

**주주**(株主) a shareholder〈영〉; a stockholder〈미〉／～ 결의권 the voting right of stockholders／～ 총회 a general meeting of stockholders. かぶぬし

**주줍다** ①《어줍다》(be) dull; inanimate ②《수줍다》(be) shy; bashful; timid.

**주즙**(舟楫) shipping; craft.

**주지**(主旨) the general purport; the main meaning; the gist; the point. しゅし

**주지**(主持) the resident[head] priest [of a Buddhist temple]. じゅうじ

**주지**(周知) common[universal] knowledge／～의 well[widely] known; established; universally known／～의 사실 a matter of common knowledge; a wellknown fact／그것은 ～의 사실이다 It is a wellknown fact. しゅうち

**주지**(周紙) a roll [of paper]; a scroll [of paper].

**주지**(主知) ～의 intellectual／～설[주의] intellectualism／～주의자 an intellectualist. しゅち

**주지 육림**(酒池肉林) a sumptuous repast [feast, banquet]. しゅちにくりん

**주지주의**(主知主義) intellectualism. しゅちしゅぎ

**주차**(駐箚) residence; stay／～하다 reside (in, at); be stationed (at)／～의 주재인 resident; residing; stationed／～관 a resident (at)／동경 ~ 한국 공사 the Korean Minister at Tokyo ⇨주재(駐在).

**주차**(駐車) parking／～하다 park [a car]／～ 금지 《게시》 "No Parking [Here]."／～ 위반 parking violation／～장 a parking place[lot]〈미〉; a car park〈영〉. ちゅうしゃ

**주착**(主著) a definite view; a fixed opinion／～ 망나니[바가지] a wishy-washy [indecisive, injudicious, indiscreet] person／～이 없다 have no definite opinion of one's own. ていけん

**주찬**(酒饌) food and drink; viands and beverage; wine and food. さけとさかな

**주찬**(晝餐) lunch; luncheon. ごさん

**주창**(主唱) advocacy; instance; promotion／～하다 advocate; promote; advance／～자 an advocate; a promoter; a prime mover／평화를 ～하다 advocate peace. しゅしょう

**주책**(誅責) a severe reprimand／～하다 severely reprimand.

**주책**(籌策) a trick; an artifice; a stratagem; a scheme. ちゅうさく

**주철**(鑄鐵) cast-iron 《주철하기》 iron casting／～소 an iron-foundry[works]. ちゅうてつ

**주청**(州廳) the [State] capital; the Statehouse.

**주청**(奏請) petitioning the king／～하다 petition the king (for). そうせい

**주체**(主體) the subject 《중심》 the core; the nucleus／～성《性》 subjectivity; independence／권리의 ～ the subject of rights. しゅたい

**주체**(酒滯) indigestion from[caused by] drinking.

**주체못하다** be unable to take care of (one's trouble); be hard to deal with; have too many[much]; (be) superabundant／그는 주체 못할 만큼 돈이 많다 He has more money than enough[than he knows what to do with].

**주체스럽다** (be) troublesome; hard[difficult] to deal with.

**주쳇덩어리** a thing[person] that is hard to handle[manage]; "a real problem [on one's hands]".

**주최**(主催) auspices; sponsorship／ ～하다 sponsor／～자 the sponsor; the promotor／그 자선 바자는 A신문사 ～였다 The charity bazaar was held under the sponsorship of[sponsored by] the A press. しゅさい

**주추**(柱一) the footing[base] stone of a pillar; the pedestal of a column.

**주축**(主軸) the principal axis. しゅじく

**주출거리다** ①《당황하여》do not know what to do; be at a loss; be indecisive; be thrown into a confusion ②《주저하다》 hesitate; be scrupulous (at); waver; falter. ためらう

**주춧돌**(柱一) a foundation stone; a footstone; a cornerstone. そせき

**주치**(主治) having a patient in 'charge／～하다 treat (a patient) in charge／～의 a physician in charge; an attendant physician/~ 효능 the chief virtues.

**주택**(住宅) a [dwelling-]house; a residence 《총칭》 housing/~ 공사 the Housing Corporation/한국 ~ 은행 the Korea Housing Bank/~난 a housing shortage/~ 문제 the housing problem/~지 a residendential section[quarter] (of *a town, .city*)/간이[조립] ~ a prefabricated house; a prefab〈미〉/그 건물은 ~으로는 부적당하다 The building is not fit to live in.

**주토**(朱土) red clay[earth].

**주파**(走破) ~하다 run; cover/1마일 10분으로 ~하다 cover[run] one mile in ten minutes.

**주파**(周波) a cycle; a wave; periodicity /~계 a frequency meter/~수(數) frequency/장[단, 전]~ a long[short, all] wave.

**주판**(籌板, 珠板) an abacus 《수지 계산》 account/~알 a counter/~질하다 use the abacus 《타산적》 be calculating/~을 잘 놓다 be clever with *one's* abacus.

**주포**(主砲) the principal battery; the main armament.

**주필**(主筆) the chief editor; the editor in chief/부~ a subeditor〈영〉; an associate editor〈미〉.

**주필**(朱筆) a vermilion-brush/~을 가하다 correct; revise.

**주학**(晝學) study in the daytime/~하다 study in the daytime.

**주항**(周航) circumnavigation; sailing round/~하다 sail round; circumnavigate /세계 ~ a voyage round the world; a round-the-world trip/세계를 ~하다 circumnavigate[sail around] the globe.

**주항라**(紬亢羅) sheer silk.

**주해**(註解) a note; an explanatory note; an annotation; a commentary; a comment; an exposition/~하다 comment upon; make notes upon; annotate/~자 an annotator; a commentator/~를 단 책 an annotated edition/~가 붙은 annotated; with notes.

**주행**(舟行) navigation; sailing/~하다 navigate; sail/이 강은 ~할 수 있다 This river is navigable.

**주행 기중기**(走行起重機) a travelling crane.

**주향**(酒香) the odour of wine[sool].

**주형**(主刑) the principal penalty.

**주형**(鑄型) a mold; a cast /주형 matrix[die]/~을 뜨다 cast (*a mold*)/ ~에 붓다 pour into a mold.

**주호**(酒豪) a hard[heavy] drinker; a sot; a toper.

**주혼**(主婚) officiating at a marriage.

**주홍**(朱紅) scarlet; bright orange color.

**주화**(鑄貨) coinage; mintage; minting/ ~하다 coin; mint; strike coins/~ 능력 minting capacity.

**주화론**(主和論) advocacy of peace; pacifism/~자 an advocate of peace; a pacifist.

**주황**(朱黃) light[lemon] chrome yellow; reddish-yellow; yellow-brown.

**주효**(酒肴) food and wine[beverages].

**주효**(奏効) 《성공》 fruition; success 《유효》 efficacy/~하다 succeed; take effect; bear fruit; prove effective; be effectual[fruitful, successful]; tell; work well/그의 시도는 ~하지 않았다 His attempt proved in effectual.

**주휴**(週休) a weekly holiday.

**주흥**(酒興) merrymaking over wine; conviviality/~을 깨드리다 wetblanket [dampen] conviviality.

**죽**¹ ten pieces/접시 한 ~ [a set of] ten plates.

**죽**² ①《늘어선 모양》 in a row[line]/자동차가 ~ 늘어서 있었다 There was an array of motorcars. ②《계속하여》 all through; all the time; throughout; consecutively; all during/지금까지 ~ 기다렸읍니다 I have been waiting for you all this while. ③《대강 빨리》 ~보다 run through; look over ④《피륙을 찢는 소리》 ⑴손수건을 ~ 찢어 상처에 감았다 He tore off his handkerchief and bandaged the wounded part. ⑤《처진 모양》 droopingly/~ 처지다 droop; limp ⑥《물에 빠지는 모양》 ⑴물이 ~ 빠지다 《홍수의》 The water sinks[goes down, subsides] very fast. ⑦《거리가 멀리 떨어진 모양》 far; away/~ 멀어지다 stand well back.

**죽**(粥) [rice-]gruel; porridge; hot cereal; pap/~을 먹다 eat gruel/~을 끓이다 cook hot cereal.

**죽**(竹) bamboo.

**죽견**(竹筧) a bamboo water pipe.

**죽기**(竹器) bamboo-ware.

**죽는소리** ①《불평·우는 소리》 a complaint; a grievance; a plaintive[feeble] protestation/~하다 make complaints; complain (*about*); whine ②《비명》 a shriek; a scream; a screech/아파서 ~를 지르다 give a cry of pain; shriek with pain.

**죽단** ⇨별항 참조( page 1722)

**죽담** a stone wall.

**죽대** 〖식〗 a Solomon's-seal; *Polygonatum lasianthum*(학명).

**죽더끼** a plank[board] sawn out of the outside of a log.

**죽도**(竹刀) a fencing-stick; a bamboo-stick[-sword].

**죽도화나무** 〖식〗 a yellow rose; *Kerria japonica*(학명).

**죽력**(竹瀝) 〖한〗 tabasheer [juice from h-

**죽렴(竹簾)** a bamboo blind; a bamboo hanging-screen. ちくれん

**죽롱(竹籠)** a bamboo basket. たけかご

**죽림(竹林)** a bamboo grove. ちくりん

**죽마(竹馬)** a child's hobbyhorse; stilts /~지우(之友) a childhood friend; a friend from childhood; an old chum; an old playmate. ちくば

**죽물(粥—)** thin porridge[gruel]; thin and watery gruel. かゆのしる

**죽바디** in side shank.

**죽방울** 《장난감》 a diabolo /~ 받다 play with a diabolo.

**죽백(竹帛)** annals; a history[-book]; historical records /~지공(之功)이 있다 one's name goes down in history. ちくはく

**죽비(竹扉)** 《사립문》 a bamboo door.

**죽사리** [a matter of] life and death /~치다 make desperate[frantic] efforts.

**죽순(竹筍)** a bamboo shoot[sprout] /우후 ~처럼 나온다 spring up like mushrooms after rain. たけのこ

**죽솔(粥—)** a few spoonfuls of porridge ⇨죽(粥). しょうりょうのかゆ

**죽어지내다** ①《눌리어》 live under other's oppression /그는 아버지 앞에서 죽어지낸다 He lives under his father's thumb. ②《가난하여》 suffer from dire poverty; be hard pressed (for *living*). よくあつされたせいかつをする

**죽여버리다** do away with (*a person*); do (*a person*) to death.

**죽엽(竹葉)** a bamboo leaf. ちくよう

**죽은목숨** ①《살 길 없는》 a life as good as dead; a person beyond the realm of hope[help] [such as a sick person]; a hopeless case; a person as good as dead /너는 인제 ~이다 You are a dead [marked] man now. ②《자유를 잃은》 a person living at another's mercy; an enslaved life.

**죽을둥살둥** desperately; frantically; to oth and nail /~ 싸우다 fight against (*enemy*) tooth and nail. むちゃくちゃ

**죽을뻔살뻔** across the death line /~ 내빼다 escape with bare life; escape life and limb; escape by the skin of one's teeth; have a narrow escape.

**죽을병(一病)** a fatal[mortal] disease /~에 걸리다 suffer from a mortal disease.

**죽을상(一相)** an agonized look; a frantic [desperate] look.

**죽을힘** the last effort; a frantic[desperate] effort /~을 다해서 frantically; desperately; for one's life / ~을 다해서 헤엄치다 swim for one's life /~을 다해서 싸우다 fight a desperate fight; fight to the death.

**죽음** death; decease 《높은 사람의》 demise /~의 공포 the fear of death /~을 면하다 escape death /비열한 ~을 하다 die an ignoble death.

**죽의장막(竹—帳幕)** the Bamboo Curtain.

**죽이다** ①《살해하다》 kill; slay 《모살하다》 murder; slaughter 《도살하다》 butcher; put (*a person*) to death; take (*a person's*) life /목졸라 ~ strangle (*a person*) to death /사람을 ~ kill[slay, murder] a man /죽인다고 협박하다 threaten (*a person's*) life ②《억제하다》 hold[keep] back; restrain; suppress; repress /숨을 ~ hold one's breath /발소리를 ~ muffle one's steps ③《잃다》 suffer the death[loss] of /전쟁에 아이를 ~ lose a son in the war ④《멈추다》 stop; let go out /불을 ~ put out a fire[light]. ころす

**죽일놈** Rascal!, Wretch!, S.O.B.! /이 ~아 Damn you!, Be damned to you. /그놈 ~이군 He is a rascal, indeed.

**죽자꾸나하고** with great endurance; with utmost perseverance; with great fortitude; firmly; resolutely. いのちをかけて

**죽장(竹杖)** a bamboo stick. ちくじょう

**죽장구(竹—)** a drum with a bamboo body.

**죽장기(一將棋)** a poor chess player; a poor hand at chess /~를 두다 play a poor hand of chess. へぼしょうぎ

**죽젓개(粥—)** a porridge-stirrer; a ladle.

**죽젓개질** hindrance; obstruction; impeding; blocking; interrupting /~하다 obstruct; hinder; get in the way; block interrupt. かゆをわくときかきまぜること

**쭉정이** empty heads of grain; blasted [blighted] ears. しいな

**죽죽, 쭉쭉** ①《줄줄이》 in rows[lines]; row after row; in streaks /줄을 ~ 긋다 draw line after line ②《거침없이》 briskly; directly; rapidly; in sheets; in showers /~ 나아가다 push on; advance rapidly /비가 ~ 내린다 The rain comes down in sheets. ③《갈기갈기》 into shreds; in[to] pieces /~ 찢다 tear to pieces. ずっと

**죽지** ①《팔의》 a shoulder ②《날개의》 a wing joint.

**죽지떼다** ①《활을 쏘고》 lower one's shoulder after shooting an arrow ②《배후를 믿고》 act overbearing; be imperious; be stuck-up; put on airs.

**죽창(竹窓)** a bamboo window. ちくそう

**죽창(竹槍)** a bamboo spear. ちくそう

**죽책(竹柵)** a bamboo palisade[stockade, fence]. ちくさく

**죽총(竹叢)** a bamboo bush[thicket].

**죽치기** wholesale trade.

**죽치다** live in seclusion; shut oneself up in; confine oneself to (one's house); remain indoors /집안에 죽치고 있다 remain [stay, be] indoors; keep[be shut up in] the house. ちっきょする

**죽침(竹針)** a bamboo[knitting] needle. たけばり

**죽통(竹筒)** a bamboo tube. ちくとう

죽통(粥筒) 《구유》 a feeding trough; a manger.

죽피(竹皮) bamboo sheath.

준(準) 《교정을 봄》 correcting [proof]; correction／~보다 make correction in proof.

준-(準) quasi-; semi-; associate／~동사 【언】 verbals／~회원 an associate member.

준거(峻拒) strict refusal; strong denial; harsh rejection.

준거(準據) 《따름》 conformity 《전거(典據)》 authority 《표준》 a standard／~하다 be based upon; conform to; be in conformity with／법률에 ~하다 comply with the law／~할 규정이 없다 We have no rule to go by.

준걸(俊傑) a great man[figure]; a master spirit; a hero.

준결승전(準決勝戰) a semi-final game／~에 진출하다 go on[play in] the semi-finals.

준골(俊骨) an eminent physique; a man of eminent physique[ability].

준공(竣工) completion／~하다 be completed; be finished／~식 the ceremony for the completion of (a house, etc.)／~에 가깝다 be nearing completion／새 교사가 ~되었다 The new school house has been completed.

준교사(準敎師) an assistant teacher (of a primary school, etc.).

준금치산(準禁治産) quasi-incompetence／~자 a quasi-incompetent person.

준급(峻急) steepness／~하다 (be) steep and dangerous; precipitous.

준급(準急) a semi-express [train]; a local express《미》.

준돈 《돈치기의》 the given coin to hit.

준동(蠢動) wriggling; squirming／~하다 《벌레가》crawl; wriggle 《활동》 be active 《출몰》 infest 《무리가》 be active; stir; infest.

준득준득 ①《차져서》 ~하다 (be) resilient and glutinous ②《질겨서》 ~하다 (be) tough and tenacious.

준령(峻嶺) a high and steep peak; a dangerous high range.

준례(準例) a precedent; a model case [example].

준론(峻論) a sharp[stern] discourse.

준마(駿馬) a swift[gallant] horse[steed]; an excellent horse.

준말 a shortened word; an abbreviation; an abbreviated word.

준물(俊物) a man of eminent ability[personality]; a great character.

준법(峻法) stringent law.

준법(遵法) law-abiding／~정신 the spirit of obeying laws／~정신을 앙양하다 promote law-abiding spirit／~ 투쟁 a law-abiding struggle.

준봉(峻峰) a steep peak; a lofty mountain.

준봉(遵奉) observance／~하다 observe; obey; follow; adhere to; conform to ／국법을 ~하다 obey[abide by] the laws of the country.

준비(準備) preparation; arrangements; readiness 《예비》 provision／~하다 prepare; arrange; make preparation[arrangement]; get leady (for)／~의 preparatory; preparative; preliminary 《예비의》 reserve／~ 단계 a preparatory stage／ ~ 운동 warming up／~위원 a committee of arrangements／~금 a reserve fund／식사 ~를 하다 provide [for] a dinner; get a dinner ready.

준사(俊士) a man of eminent ability; a great man; a talented man; a boy wonder《미》／그 학교는 수 많은 ~를 배출했다 The school has turned out many men of talent.

준사관(準士官) 《육군의》 a non-commissioned officer; a sub-officer 《해군의》 a warrant-officer.

준사원(準社員) 《회사의》 a junior employee 《회의》 an associate member.

준설(浚渫) dredging／~하다 dredge (a river)／~기 a dredger; a dredging machine; a dredge／~ 인부 a dredger／~작업 dredging work[operations].

준수(遵守) observance; compliance／~하다 observe; conform to; follow; obey ／법률[규칙]을 ~하다 observe the law [rules].

준수(俊秀) superior talent and elegance／~하다 excel in talent and elegance; (be) superior and refined.

준순(逡巡) hesitation; irresolution; indecision／~하다 hesitate; vacillate; be hesitant; be irresolute; shrink back.

준승(準繩) ①《수준기와 먹줄》 a level and an inked string ②《법식》 a rule; a standard; a norm.

준시(蹲柿) a flat dried persimmon.

준어(鱒魚) ①【어】 Squaliot urbus curriculus(학명) ②【어】 ⇨송어(松魚).

준엄(峻嚴) strictness; sternness; rigidity ／~하다 (be) severe; rigorous; strict; stern; stringent; relentless／~한 얼굴을 하다 look stern.

준열(峻烈) severity; rigor; sternness／~하다 (be) rigorous; stern; severe; relentless; ruthless; scathing／~한 비판 sharp criticism.

준예(俊乂) a great man; a great genius; a man of talent.

준용(準用) applying correspondingly／~하다 apply correspondingly (to); apply with necessary changes／이 경우에는 ‥에 관한 본조(本條)의 규정을 ~한다 The provision of this article with respect

**준우승**(準優勝) a victory in the semifinals/～자 a winner of the semifinals.

**준위**(准尉) a sub-officer; a warrant officer(略：W.O.).

**준장**(准將) 《육군》a brigadier general 《해군》a commodore 《공군》an air-commodore.

**준재**(俊才) a brilliant[talented] man; a man of talent. しゅんさい

**준절**(峻截, 峻切) 《높고 험함》precipitousness; steepness 《위엄》sternness; strictness; rigidity; dignity/～하다《높고 험하다》(be) steep; precipitous 《위엄》stern; strict; rigid; dignified. たかくけわしいこと

**준족**(駿足) ①《말》a swift horse ②《사람》a talented man/～의 swift[light]-footed.

**준좌**(蹲坐) 《주저앉음》squatting on the heels; crouching 《중지》discontinuance; suspension/～하다 squat down; stop half-way; hold up; discontinue. うずくまること

**준주**(準州) a territory/하와이 ～ the territory of Hawaii.

**준준결승전**(準準決勝戰) a quarter-final [game]. じゅんじゅんけっしょうせん

**준지**(準紙) 《교정쇄》corrected pageproof. こうせいしたかみ

**준치** 《어》a kind of shad fish; *Ilisha elongata*《학명》. ひら

**준칙**(準則) a standing[working] rule; a guide; a standard 《기준》a criterion/법률은 행위의 ～이다 Law is the rule of conduct. じゅんそく

**준평원**(準平原) a peneplain. じゅんへいげん

**준하다**(準一) 《비례하다》be proportionate to; be in proportion to 《준용하다》apply correspondingly (*to*); 《기준하다》follow; conform to; correspond to/…에 준해서 correspondingly in proportion. ならう

**준행**(遵行) following in accordance with an order[the rule]; observance/～하다 follow in accordance with an order [the rule]. じゅんこう

**준행**(準行) following in accordance with the rule/～하다 follow[put into effect] in accordance with the rule. じゅんこう

**준험**(峻險) steepness; precipitousness/～하다 (be) steep; rugged; precipitous/～한 산 a rugged mountain.

**준회원**(準會員) an associate member.

**줄**[1] 《끈》a rope; a cord 《연·악기 따위의》a string 《전화·낚시 따위의》a line 《선》a line; a stripe 《수준》level 《열》a row; a line/전기～ electric cord; power line/전화～ a telephone wire/～을 긋다 draw a line/～에 걸리다 be caught in a line. せん

**줄**[2] 《쇠를 깎는》a file 《굵은》a rasp/～ 질을 하다 file. やすり

**줄**[3] 《식》the water-oat; the Indian rice; *Zizania latifolia*《학명》. まこも

---

# 죽 다

①《사망하다》die; be gone; pass away; leave the world 《아어》join the majority; sink into the grave; go to one's long home; return to Mother Earth 《숨이 끊어지다》expire; breathe *one's* last 《목숨을 잃다》be killed 《전쟁·사고 따위로》lose *one's* life; suffer death; meet *one's* death 《목숨을 버리다》lay down *one's* life; throw away *one's* life; give up *one's* life; yield *one's* life 《자살하다》kill *oneself*; take *one's* own life; commit suicide; do away with *oneself*/죽은 사람 the deceased; a dead person; dead persons/죽은 동생 the deceased brother/죽은 친구 a dead friend/죽느냐 사느냐의 문제 a matter of life and death/죽을 각오로 at the risk of *one's* life/물에 빠져 ～ be drowned/타 ～ be burned to death/목을 매어 ～ die by hanging/굶어 ～ be starved to death/철도 사고로 죽다 be killed in a railway accident/약을 먹고 ～ kill *oneself* by taking poison/나이 50에 ～ die at [the age of] fiftly[fiftly years of age when he was fiftly]/거지가 되어 ～ die a beggar/편안히 ～ die an easy death/무참히 ～ die[meet with] a violent death/죽을 지경이다 be in a tight position; be in a corner/그는 죽은 듯이 그 곳에 누워 있었다 He lay there like one dead./그녀가 보고 싶어 죽겠다 I am dying to see her./아이구 죽겠다 My, it's murder!/그 노인의 친구는 이미 많이 죽어 버렸다 The old man outlasted many of his friends.

②《멎다》run down; stop 《꺼지다》die out; go out/시계가 죽었다 The clock has run down[stopped]./～어 가는 불 a dying fire

③《기(氣)가》be dejected[dispirited, crestfallen]; be out of spirits; have no life; be lifeless 《풀기가》be thin of starch/그는 풀이 죽어 있었다 He was in low spirits.

④《초목이》wither; perish; die 《서리 따위로》be blasted/그 나무는 죽었다 The tree is dead./죽은 잎 withered[dead, dried] leaves.

⑤《야구에서》be [put] out 《장기·바둑에서》be captured[lost].

**줄⁴** ①《방법》 how to do／그는 돈을 쓸 ~ 모른다 He doesn't understand the value of money. ②《예상》 여기서 너와 만날 ~ 은 몰랐다 This is the last place where I expected to meet you.／비가 올 ~ 알았으면 그는 떠나지 않았을 텐데 He would not have gone if he had known it was going to rain. ―こと

**줄거리** 《가지》 a stalk; a stem; a leafstalk 《골자》 outline; a plot.

**줄걷다** 《줄타다》 walk (on) a tightrope. あみわたりすぐ

**줄곧** all the time; all along; all the way; from start to finish／저 사람에게는 ~ 의사가 붙어 있다 The doctor is in constant attendance upon him.

**줄글** a long article.

**줄긋다** draw a line; line[rule] paper; line through; run a line through; underline. せんをひく

**줄기** ①《식물의》 a trunk 《화초의》 a stem 《벼·보리 따위의》 a stalk 《대·등 따위의》 a cane ②《줄》 a line; a stripe／한 ~의 광선 a ray[streak] of light ③《물 따위의》 a stream; a current 《혈관의》 a vein ④《산의》 a range ⑤《비 따위의》 a drop of rain. みき

**줄기차다** (be) strong; vigorous; be bursting with vitality 《계속하다》 incessant; constant; continuous／시냇물이 줄기차게 흘러간다 The stream rushes along exuberantly.

**줄깃줄깃, 쫄깃쫄깃** ~하다 (be) chewy; sticky. しなしな

**줄넘기** rope-skipping; rope-jumping／~ 하다 skip[jump] rope; turn a skipping rope. なわとび

**줄다** ①《감소되다》 decrease; lessen; run low; diminish; fall off; abate; sink／체중이 ~ lose weight ②《축소되다》 contract; diminish in size; be shortened; shrink; dwindle／줄지 않다 《빨아도》 be unshrinkable. へる

**줄다리기** a tug of war／~하다 play at a tug of war. あみひき

**줄달다** follow one after another; continue in unbroken succession／줄달아 생기다 spring up like so many mushrooms. れつをなす

**줄달음질** running at a lightning speed／~하다 hurry to; fly in great haste; run like a shot. つっぱしる

**줄대다** continue; go on; keep on; go [come, appear] in succession. れんぞくする

**줄드리다** 《줄을 걸다》 hang a rope 《줄을 꼬다》 make[twist, strand] a rope.

**줄먹줄먹** in various small sizes[quantities] ⇨줄막줄막. いろいろ

**줄멍줄멍** small things in a group; all bumpy ⇨줄망줄망. でこぼこ

**줄모** rice-plants planted in a straight line.

**줄목** a chief[main, turning] point.

**줄무늬** stripes／~의 striped／세로[가로] ~ vertical[lateral] stripes／~천 striped cloth.

**줄더더기** a medley; a motley (of colors); a patchwork.

**줄밑걷다** trace[find out] (the source of a rumor). こんぽんをさぐる

**줄바둑** a poor [game of] badook／~ 두는 사람 a poor badook player.

**줄방귀** a succession of breaking wind; breaking wind time after time.

**줄방석**(一方席) a rush seat-mat.

**줄버들** a row of willow trees.

**줄불** a string of fire crackers.

**줄사다리** a rope ladder. なわばしご

**줄삼치** 《어》 a bonito.

**줄어들다** dwindle away; grow smaller; shrink; diminish; decrease／점점 줄어 들어 없어지다 dwindle away into nothing. へる

**줄이다** 《감소하다》 decrease; reduce; diminish; lessen 《단축·축소하다》 shorten; cut down; condense; boil down; shrink 《생략하다》 abbreviate; abridge 《간단히》 simplify 《절감하다》 curtail／경비를 ~ cut down the expenses／긴 문장을 ~ condense a long composition (into five pages). へらす

**줄자** a tape measure; a tapeline／~로 재다 tape measure. まきじゃく

**줄잡다** make a conservative[moderate, low] estimate (of); estimate conservatively; underestimate／줄잡아서 at a moderate estimate／비용을 ~ make a rock-bottom estimate of the expenses.

**줄줄** trickling; in a stream ⇨졸졸. ざあざあ

**줄줄이** in row after row; all in rows; all rows.

**줄참외** the striped cantaloup.

**줄치다** draw a line; mark with lines 《빨랫줄 따위를》 stretch a rope. せんをひく

**줄타다** walking on the tightrope; rope-dancing／~하다 walk on a tightrope; balance on a rope／~ 광대 a tightrope walker[dancer]; a funambulist.

**줄타다** walk on a tightrope. あみわたりをする

**줄팔매** a sling [of a stone].

**줄행랑**(一行廊) ①《행랑》 a line of servants' quarters ②《도망》 abscondence; flight／~치다 abscond; run away; make off.

**줌** ①《분량》 a handful; a fistful; a grip; a grasp／한 ~의 모래 a handful of sand ②《활의 줌통》 the handle of a bow. にぎり

**줌밖** ~의 out of one's grasp; out of the clutches.

**줌벌다** be beyond one's grasp; be too big to hold in the hand.

**줍다** pick up; gather (shells); 《거두다》 collect; find (a purse)／이삭을 ~ glean; gather ears of corn. ひろう

**줏대** the metal rim of a wheel.

**줏대**(主一) a fixed principle; a definite

opinion; a settled conviction/ ~있는 사람 a man of principle; a man of steady characton. こころのちゅうすう

중 a priest; a monk; a bonze/ ~이 되다 become a priest; enter the priesthood. ぼうず

중(中) ①《중앙》the center; the middle 《중위》medium; average/~키의 사람 a man of medium height ②《동안》during; through; within; in the course of; while/부재~에 during[in] one's absence ③《진행중》under; at; in course [process] of/식사~이다 be at table; 통화~이다 Line is busy[engaged]. /근무~이다 He is on duty. ④《중에서》among; in; out of; of ⑤《내내》all over; throughout/오전~ all through the morning. なか

중(重) 《겹》fold 《무게》weight 《중요》heavy; important/ ~폭격기 a heavy bomber/이 반지는 2돈 ~이다 This ring weighs 2 don.

중가(重價) a great[high, dear] price. じゅうか

중간(重刊) republication; reprint; reissue/~하다 republish; reprint; reissue. じゅうかん

중간(中間) the middle; midways; halfway 《중간의》midterm/~ 계급 the middle class/~ 고사 a midterm examination/~ 노선 neutrality/~ 상인 a middle man; a broker/~ 선거 off-year election(미)/~ 역 an intermediate station/~ 착취 intermediary exploitation; kickback〈미〉. ちゅうかん

중간자(中間子) 《물》a mes[otr]on/중(重)~ a heavy meson. ちゅうかんし

중간치(中間一) 《물건》an average article 《크기의》an article of medium size. ちゅうかんのもの

중간파(中間派) a neutral party; the neutrals; the independents; the middle ·of·the roaders. ちゅうかんは

중갑판(中甲板) the middle deck.

중값(重一) a great[high, dear] price. 증가(重價). じゅうか

중개(仲介) intermediation 《조정》mediation/ ~하다 mediate; intermediate (between two parties); act as go·between; intercede/ ~국 a mediating power/ ~자 a go·between; an intermediary; an agent/…의 ~로 through the intermediation (of)/~ 역을 하다 act as a go·between[an intermediary]. ちゅうかい

중개업(仲介業) a brokerage; the brokerage business 《주선업》agency/ ~자 a broker; a middleman; a jobber; a commission merchant. ちゅうかいぎょう

중거리(中距離) a medium distance[range]. ちゅきょり

중견(中堅) the backbone; the mainstay; 《군》the main body; the centrer [field] /~ 인물 a leader; leading figures/~ 작가 a writer of medium standing/회사의 ~이 되다 form[prove oneself] the backbone of a company. ちゅうけん

중경상(重輕傷) serious and slight injuries/ ~자 seriously and slightly injured persons. じゅうけいしょう

중계(中繼) relay; hook up〈미〉/ ~하다 relay/ ~국 a relay station/ ~ 방송 relay; hook·up〈미〉/실황 ~ relay of actual conditions/현장 ~ relay from the spot. ちゅうけい

중계 무역(中繼貿易) entrepôt[transit] trade. ちゅうけいぼうえき

중계항(中繼港) a transit port; an intermediate port. ちゅうけいこう

중고(中古) 《시대의》the middle age; medieval times/ ~의 medieval/ ~ 문학 medieval literature/~품 a slightly used article. ちゅうこ

중고연령자(中高年齡者) persons of middle or advanced age.

중공업(重工業) heavy industry/ ~자 a heavy industrialist. じゅうこうぎょう

중과(衆寡) odds; disparity in numbers /~ 부적이다 We are outnumbered[overcome by numbers]. しゅうか

중구(衆口) mouth of the multitude/~ 난방이라 It is difficult to stop the voice of the people. しゅうこう

중궁(中宮) an empress; a queen. ちゅうぐう

중권(中卷) the middle[second] volume of a set of three.

쫑그리다 prick up ears; cock[raise, move] the ears. みみをたてる

중금고(重禁錮) major imprisonment; close arrest labour; close confinement. じゅうきんこ

중금속(重金屬) 《화》a heavy metal. じゅうきんぞく

중급(中級) an intermediate grade/ ~품 fair average quality. ちゅうきゅう

중기(中期) the middle [years] (of an era); 《세포 분열의》the metaphase. ちゅうき

중기관총(重機關銃) a heavy machine gun. じゅうきかんじゅう

중기병(重騎兵) heavy cavalry.

중길(中一) 《물건》an article of medium quality; medium goods; average·grade goods; middlings. なかほどのもの

중난(重難) ~하다 (be) exceedingly difficult; serious. じゅうだいにしてこんなんなこと

중년(中年) middle[mature] age; early manhood 《일생의》middle/ ~의 middle ·aged/그는 ~ 고개를 넘어섰다 He is past his middle age.

중노동(重勞動) heavy labo[u]r.

중농(中農) a middle·class farmer/ ~제 (制) medium scale farming. ちゅうのう

중농주의(重農主義) physiocracy/ ~자 a physiocrat. じゅうのうしゅぎ

중뇌(中腦) the midbrain; mesencepha-

**중늙은이**(中一) a middle-aged person; an elderly man. ちゅうねんのろうじん

**중다**(衆多) a great number; numbers/～하다 (be) many; numerous. たすう

**중단**(中斷) discontinuance; suspension; interruption; abatement/～하다 discontinue; interrupt; suspend; break continuity. ちゅうだん

**중단**(中段) 《계단의》the landing 《중앙부》the middle 《상단·하단에 대하여》the middle tier/～의 침대 a middle berth. ちゅうだん

**중대**(重大) importance; gravity; seriousness/ ～하다 (be) important; serious; weighty; grave; of great importance/ ～한 책임 grave responsibility/～한 사건 a serious[grave] affair/～하여지다 become serious; aggravate. じゅうだい

**중대**(中隊) 《보병·공병》a company 《포병》battery 《기병》a squadron/ ～장 a company commander; a captain/보병 ～ an infantry company. ちゅうたい

**중대가리** ①《머리》a shaven head; a tonsure 《짧게 깎은 머리》a close-cropped hair ②《사람》a person with a close-cropped head. ぼうずあたま

**중대화**(重大化) aggravation/ ～하다 become serious; aggravate; assume serious proportions. じゅうだいか

**중떨거리다** grumble (at, about); complain (of). ふへいをいう

**중도**(中途) halfway; midway; midcourse/～에서 돌아서다 turn back halfway 중도 퇴학하다 give up school. ちゅうと

**중도**(中道) the middle of the road/ ～ 정책 the middle-of-the-road policy. ちゅうどう

**중도위** a broker; a middleman.

**중독**(中毒) poisoning; toxication; toxic effect/～ 증상 toxic symptoms/식～ poisoning from eating; food poisoning/아편 ～ opiumism/알코올 ～ alcoholism /그는 연탄 가스 ～으로 죽었다 He was poisoned to death by the gas of a bricket. ちゅうどく

**중돈**(重噸) a long ton; a gross ton.

**중동**(中一) the middle part [of a thing]. まんなかのぶぶん

**중동**(中東) the Middle East/～ 조약 기구 the Middle East Treaty Organization (略: M. E. T. O.).

**중동**(仲冬) December of the lunar; the mid-winter. ちゅうとう

**중동끈**(中一) a sash; a girdle.

**중동무이**(中一) leaving something halfdone[unfinished]; stopping halfway/～하다 leave (things) half-done[unfinished]; give up halfway; go half way. ちゅうとでとめること

**중등**(中等) 《급》the middle[second] class [grade]; 《질》medium quality 《위》the average; mediocrity/～ 교육 secondary education/～ 교원 a secondary school teacher/～ 학교 a secondary school/～ 품 medium-grade articles; middlings. ちゅうとう

**중략**(中略) an ellipsis; an omission [of interior parts]; 《주(註)로서》 "omitted" /～하다 omit the interior parts; skip. ちゅうりゃく

**중량**(重量) weight 《파운드의》poundage/총～ gross weight/～톤 weight ton; deadweight tonnage/～ 화물 a weight cargo; a deadweight/～ 부준[초과] short[over] weight/항공 우편의 ～ air mail poundage. じゅうりょう

**중량급**(中量級) the middle weight class.

**중력**(衆力) the force of numbers; force of the masses. しゅうりょく

**중력**(重力) 《물》gravity; gravitation/～ 가속도 acceleration of gravity/～ 단위 a gravitational unit/～ 중심 the center of gravity/～의 법칙 the law of gravity. じゅうりょく

**중령**(中領) 《해군》a commander 《육군》lieutenant-colonel.

**중로**(中路) halfway; mid-course; midway /～에서 halfway; midway. ちゅうと

**중로**(中老) middle age/～의 middle-aged; elderly.

**중론**(衆論) public opinion; the voice of the people/～에 의하여 결정하다 refer (a matter) to public opinion. しゅうろん

**중류**(中流) ①《시내의》the middle of the river; mid-stream ②《사회》the middle class/～ 가정 the middle-class family/ ～ 계급의 인사 middleclass people. ちゅうりゅう

**중리**(重利) ①《복리》compound interest ②《큰 이익》a big profit. ふくり

**중립**(中立) neutrality; neutralization/～하다 stand neutral; sit on the fence/ ～국 a neutral power[state]; a neutral / ～ 선언 declaration of neutrality/～ 성 neutrality/～주의 neutralism/～파 a neutral faction[party]/～을 지키다 adhere to neutrality. ちゅうりつ

**중망**(衆望) 《기대》popular expectation 《신망》public confidence/～을 받다 be the centre of popular hopes. しゅうぼう

**중매**(仲媒) 《결혼》matchmaking; matchmaker; a go-between/～하다 serve as a matchmaker; act as go-between/～ 결혼 a marriage arranged by a go-between/～인(人) a matchmaker. ちゅうばい

**중매**(仲買) brokerage/～하다 act as broker/～인(人) a broker/～점 a brokerage house[firm]/매매 및 ～업 a general merchant and commission agent.

**중명**(重名) fame; honour; glory.

**중목**(衆目) public attention; all the eyes /～을 모으다 become the focus of public attention.

**중문**(重門) an inner gate.

**중문**(重文) 《문법》a compound sentence.

**중미**(中米) moderately polished rice.
**중바닥** the centre of the town; the busiest quarters; the principal street.
**중바랑** a monk's knapsack.
**중반전**(中盤戰) 《바둑 등의》 the middle game 《선거전 등의》 the middle phase.
**중발**(中鉢) a small rice-bowl made of brass. ちゅうがたのさら
**중배**(中─) 《물건의》 the thickest part《짐승의》 a second litter [of an animal]／~부르다 be bulged out in the middle; be pot-bellied.
まんなかのほうがふくれたもの
**중벌**(重罰) severe punishment; heavy penalty／~에 처하다 sentence 《a person》 to a severe punishment. じゅうばつ
**중범**(重犯) ①《중대범》 felony 《중범인》 a felon ②《거듭 저지름》 repetition of crimes 《사람》 a perpetrator of several crimes; an old offender／~의 경우에는 in the case of a repeated offence.
じゅうはん
**중변**(重邊) high interest; a high rate of interest.
**중병**(重病) a serious[severe] illness／~환자 a serious case／~에 걸리다 get [fall, be taken] seriously ill; be attacked by a serious illness. じゅうびょう
**중보**(重寶) a treasure of great value; a priceless treasure. きちゅうなたから
**중복**(中伏) the middle of the dog-days.
ちゅうふく
**중복**(中腹) 《산의 중턱》 the mountain's breast; the mid-slope of a mountain 《중배》 a bulged-out middle／~에 halfway up[down] a hill／그 산의 ~ 위는 눈에 쌓여 있다 The upper helf of the mountain is enveloped[blanketed] in snow.
ちゅうふく
**중복**(重複) overlapping; repetition; duplication; redundancy／~하다 overlap; duplicate; be repeated; be redundant／~한 superfluous《소용없는》; 《어귀 따위의》 tautological／~을 피하다 avoid overlapping[duplication]. じゅうふく
**중부**(中部) the central[middle] part[portion]; the center[middle]; the heart／~ 지방 the central districts; the Middle West《미》／~ 태평양 mid-Pacific.
ちゅうぶ
**중부**(仲父) an uncle; one's father's elder brother. ちちのすぐしたのおとうと
**중분**(中分) ①《등분》 bisection; division into two equal parts／~하다 bisect; divide into two equal parts ②《중년의 운수》 fate of one's middle life.
**중뿔나다**(中─) intrude; intermeddle; be officious[middlesome, impertinent, presumptuous]／중뿔난 사람 a meddler; an officious person; a busybody.
かいにゅうする
**중사**(中士) a sergeant.
**중산 계급**(中産階級) the middle class《사람들》 the middle classes; middle class people. ちゅうさんかいきゅう
**중산모**(中山帽) a bowler《영》; a derby《미》.
**중상**(中傷) slander; aspersion; calumny; defamation／~하다 slander; defame; calumniate; throw[fling] mud at 《a person》; asperse／~적 sanderous; calumnious／~적 보도 a slanderous report／~자 a slanderer; a scandal-monger／그는 남을 ~하기 좋아한다 He is a scandal-monger. ちゅうしょう
**중상**(重賞) high prize; a liberal reward.
じゅうしょう
**중상**(重傷) a serious[severe] wound[injury]／~자 a seriously wounded[injured] person／~을 입다 receive[sustain] a serious wound; be seriously wounded／~을 입히다 inflict a severe injury [wound]《upon》. じゅうしょう
**중상**(中商) a broker; a middleman.
なかがいにん
**중상주의**(重商主義) mercantilism; the mercantile system. じゅうしょうしゅぎ
**중생**(衆生) mankind; human beings; the world; living things／~의 제도를 위하여 in order to save mankind.
しゅうせい
**중생**(重生) 《기독교》 second birth; rebirth／~하다 be born again; be reborn.
**중생대**(中生代) the Mesozoic[Era, Age].
ちゅうせいだい
**중석**(重石) tungsten; scheelite.
タングステン
**중석기 시대**(中石器時代)《고고학》 the Mesolithic era. ちゅうせっきじだい
**중선거구**(中選擧區) a medium electoral district／~제 the medium constituency [electorate] system.
**중설**(重說) repetition; reiteration; repeated explanation／~하다 reiterate; repeat the same thing. じゅうせつ
**중설**(衆說) public opinion. しゅうせつ
**중성**(中性) ①《언》 the neuter gender／~의 neuter ②《화》 neutrality／~의 neutral／~ 반응 neutral action. ちゅうせい
**중성화**(中性化) neutralization／~하다 neutralize. ちゅうせいか
**중세**(中世) the middle ages; medieval times／~의 medieval／~기 the Middle Ages／~사(史)《역》 medieval history.
ちゅうせい
**중세**(重稅) a heavy tax; heave[excessive] taxation／~를 부과하다 impose a heavy tax《on》／~에 시달리다 groan[labor] under the heavy burden[load] of taxation／~를 부담하다 bear a heavy duty. じゅうぜい
**중소기업**(中小企業) small and medium enterprises.
**중수**(重修) repair; improvement; remodeling／~하다 repair; improve; remodel.
**중수**(重囚) a felon.
つみのおもいしゅうじん
**중수**(重數) weight／~가 무겁다[가볍다] be

**중수**(重水) 〖화〗 heavy water. じゅうすい
**중수소**(重水素) heavy hydrogen.　じゅうすいそ
**중순**(中旬) the second[middle] ten days of a month/5월 ~에 about the middle of May; in mid-May/내월 ~에 about the middle of next month. ちゅうじゅん
**중시**(重視) serious consideration/~하다 attach importance to; take a serious view of; lay stress on (*a point*); value [think] much/~되다 be much accounted of/정부는 이 사건을 ~하고 있다 The Government is taking serious view of this incident.　じゅうし
**중신**(重臣) a senior statesman; a chief [key] retainer.　じゅうしん
**중심**(中心) 《복판》 the center[heart, middle]; 《촛점》 the focus 《중핵》 the nucleus; the core 《중추》 the pivot 《중점》 stress; emphasis; importance 《평형》 balance/도시의 ~ the center[hub] of a city/공업의 ~ an industrial center/문제의 ~ the crux of a problem/~을 벗어난 out of center[focus]; eccentric/흥미의 ~ 인물 a centre of interest/그는 일행 중의 ~ 인물이다 He is the life and soul of the party.　ちゅうしん
**중심**(重心) the centre of gravity/~을 잡다 maintain the equilibrium; balance *one*self [on one leg]/~을 잃다 lose balance[the equilibrium]/~이 잡히지 않다 be unable to poise.　じゅうしん
**중심**(衆心) the public feeling[opinion]; the public mind; the popular sentiments.　しゅうしん
**중압**(重壓) [heavy] pressure; heavy burden/~하다 press hard/~감(感) an oppressive feeling/~을 가하다 bring pressure upon; put the screw on (*a person*).　じゅうあつ
**중앙**(中央) the center; the middle; the heart/~의 central; middle; mid/~에서 in the middle[center]/도시의 ~ the center of the city/~ 문단 literary circles in the metropolis/~ 정부 the central government/~ 집행 위원회 a central executive committee.　ちゅうおう
**중앙 집권**(中央集權) centralized authoritarian rule/~화 centralization of power /~화되다 be centralized/~제 centralism.　ちゅうおうしゅうけん
**중야**(中夜) midnight.　まよなか
**중언**(重言) repetition; reiteration/~하다 repeat; reiterate.　じゅうげん
**중얼거리다** mutter; grumble; murmur/중얼중얼 muttering/혼자서 ~ mutter to *one*self/대우가 나쁘다고 ~ grumble at the poor treatment.　つぶやく
**중역**(重譯) a translation from a translation; a retranslation/~하다 retranslate.　じゅうやく
**중역**(重役) a director; the directorate/ ~ 회의 a meeting of directors/~ 회

board of directors; the directorate/~이 되다 obtain a seat on a board of directors.　じゅうやく
**중엽**(中葉) the middle part [of a period] /16세기 ~ the mid-sixteenth century /고려 ~에 about the middle of the time of *Koryo* Dynasty.　ちゅうよう
**중외**(中外) ~의 domestic and foreign; internal and external/~에 at home and abroad; in all parts of the world /~에 선명하다 declare[announce] the world.　ちゅうがい
**중요**(重要) importance; consequence/~하다 (be) important; momentous; weighty; essential; be of importance[consequence, moment]/~한 사람 a person of importance[consequence]/~한 지위 an important position/~한 상품 staple commodities[products]/~한 사항 an important matter[affair]/~한 문제 a serious[an important] question/오늘 신문의 ~ 기사 the highlights[highlighted news] in today's paper/~성 importance; gravity/그것은 문제로서는 ~성이 없다 It cuts a small figure in the matter.　じゅうよう
**중요시**(重要視) ~하다 attach great importance to; make[think] much of; take a serious view of/대단히 ~되다 《사람이》 be held in high repute; carry great prestige.　じゅうようし
**중용**(中庸) moderation; a middle course; the happy[golden] mean; medium/~의 moderate/~을 취하다 take the golden mean; hit[strike] the happy mean /~을 벗어나다 be immoderate/언동에 ~을 취함은 미덕이다 It's virtuous to practice temperance in *one's* conduct and speech.　ちゅうよう
**중용**(重用) promotion to a responsible post/~하다 promote (*a person*) to a responsible post; appoint (*a person*) to a position of trust/~되다 be taken into confidence (by *one's* superior).
**중우**(衆愚) the vulgar crowd; the mob; the blind populace/~ 정치 mobocracy; ochlocracy.
**중원**(中元) July 15th of the lunar month.　ちゅうげん
**중원**(中原) 《들판의》 the center of a field 《나라의》 the midlands 《경쟁장》 the field of contest/~에서 패권을 다투다 compete for the supremacy in a country.　ちゅうげん
**중위**(中位) ~의 medium; middle; average; middle/~수 《수》 the median.　ちゅうい
**중위**(中尉) 《육군의》 the first lieutenant 《영국 해군의》 a sub-lieutenant 《미국 해군의》 a lieutenant junior grade. ちゅうい
**중위**(重圍) a close investment; a close siege/~에 빠지다 be closely surounded (*by*); be closely be sieged/~를 탈출하다 break through a siege.　じゅうい

**중유**(重油) heavy oil; crude petroleum [oil]; Diesel oil. じゅうゆう

**중은**(重恩) great favour[obligation]／~을 입다 be under great obligation; receive great favours. じゅうおん

**중음**(中音) 【음】 alto 《여성의》 contral to 《남성의》 baritone. ちゅうおん

**중음**(重音) 《음성》 a double sound. ふくおん

**중의**(衆意) public[popular, general] opinion／그가 적임자라는 점에 ~가 일치했다 It is universally admitted that he is suitable for the post. しゅうい

**중의**(衆議) a general consultation[deliberation]／~에 의하여 결정하다 decide by majority of votes[public opinion]／이것은 ~에 의하여 결정함이 타당하다 It is proper that this should be decided by majority of votes. しゅうぎ

**중이**(中耳) the mid-ear; the tympanum (pl. ·na)／~염 tympanitis; otitis media. ちゅうじ

**중이층**(中二層) the mezzanine [floor].

**중인**(重因) a major cause (for). おもなげんいん

**중인**(衆人) many people; the people; the multitude; the public／~ 앞에서 in public[company]; before all the people／~ 환시중에 모욕하다 insult (a person) in public. しゅうじん

**중임**(重任) ①《중한 책임》 a heavy responsibility; an important duty[mission]; 《중요 위치》 a responsible post; a position of trust／~을 맡다 take a heavy trust[responsibility]; take upon oneself an important task／~을 메고 있다 be entrusted with an important mission ② 《재임》 reappointment 《재선》 re-election／~하다 be reappointed; be re-elected／그의 ~을 반대하지 않는다 I have no objection to his reappointment. じゅうにん

**중장**(中將) 《육군》 a lieutenant general 《해군》 a vice admiral. ちゅうしょう

**중장비**(重裝備) heavy equipment.

**중재**(仲裁) mediation; intermediation; arbitration; peacemaking／~하다 mediate; arbitrate (between); make up／~인 a mediator; an arbitrator／싸움의 ~를 하다 mend[arbitrate, mediate] a quarrel; make peace between two quarreling parties／~를 제의하다 offer mediation／~ 결정 an award／~ 재판 arbitration／~ 조약 an arbitration treaty／강제[임의] ~ compulsory[voluntary] arbitration. ちゅうさい

**중전**(中殿) the queen／~마마 Her Majesty the Queen. ちゅうでん

**중전기**(重電氣) heavy electric equipment.

**중전차**(重戰車) 【군】 a heavy tank.

**중절**(中絶) interruption; stoppage; discontinuance; intermission／~하다 be interrupted; be stopped; be suspended. ちゅうぜつ

**중절거리다** mutter 〓중얼거리다. ぐずぐずいう

**중절모**(中折帽) a soft hat; a felt hat; a wide-awake [hat]. なかおれぼうし

**중점**(中點) the middle[central] point; the median [point]; the center.

**중점**(重點) 《중심점》 the pivotal point 《강조》 emphasis; stress／~주의[생산] priority policy[production]／~적으로 in priority; preponderantly／~을 두다 lay emphasis[stress] on; emphasize; give [place] priority to／~으로 조사[연구]를 배급 concentrate upon the subject／~ 배급 priority rationing; rationing on priority basis／~주의 priority policy. じゅうてん

**중정**(重訂) the second revision; a re-revision／~하다 revise twice. じゅうてい

**중정**(中正) impartiality; fairness／~하다 (be) fair; impartial; mean／~한 의견 an unbiased opinion／~한 impartial; fair; unbiased. ちゅうせい

**중정**(中庭) a courtyard; quadrangle.

**중조**(重曹) 【화】 bicarbonate of soda; baking soda《속》. じゅうそう

**중죄**(重罪) felony; a grave[capital, serious] offence[crime]／~의 felonious／~를 범하다 commit a grave[serious] offence／~범 a felon. じゅうざい

**중중거리다** grumble; complain; mutter; murmur in a reproachful tone 〓중얼거리다. ぐずぐずいう

**중증**(重症) a serious[severe] illness／~환자 a serious case／그는 ~으로 생명이 위독하다 He is seriously ill and has no hope of recovery. じゅうしょう

**중지**(中止) stoppage; suspension; interruption 《금지》 suppression／~하다 stop; suspend; suppress; call off (a game, a strike); put the lid on《속》／~되다 be suspended; be stopped; come[be brought] to a standstill／연설을 ~시키다 stop the speaker／공사를 ~하다 discontinue the work／회의는 ~되었다 The meeting was broken off.／나는 그의 행동을 ~시키겠다 I will pull up his action. ちゅうし

**중지**(中指) the middle finger. なかゆび

**중지**(衆智) wisdom of the many／~를 모으다 seek the counsel of many people. しゅうち

**중직**(重職) an important[a weighty] office; a responsible post[position]; a position of trust／~을 맡다 hold[occupy] a responsible[an important] post. じゅうしょく

**중진**(重鎭) 《사람》 a leader; a leading man; a pillar 《학계의》 an authority／저작계의 ~ an outstanding figure in the book-writing world／그는 정계의 ~이다 He is one of the leading figures in our political circles. じゅうちん

**중진국**(中進國) a semi-developed country [nation].

중창(中—) the middle layer of a shoe sole.

중창(重刱) renewal; repair／ ～하다 renew; repair. たてものをしゅうりすること

중책(重責) a heavy responsibility／ ～을 맡다 assume a heavy responsibility. じゅうせき

중천(中天) midair; the mid-heaven; the zenith ／달이 ～에 걸려 있다 The moon hangs high in the sky. ちゅうてん

중첩(重疊) ～하다 be piled up; be placed one upon another; rise one above another／ 산악이 ～하여 하늘을 찌르고 있다 Mountain upon mountain soars into the blue. かさねること

중추(仲秋) mid-autumn; the eighth lunar month／ ～ 명월 the harvest moon. ちゅうしゅう

중추(中樞) the centre; the pivot; the backbone; the brain 《촛점》the focus ／ ～의 central; leading／ 상업의 ～ an artery of trade／～ 신경(神經) the central nerve／～적 인물 a central[pivotal] figure／ 서울은 한국의 정치 ～다 Seoul is the political hub of Korea.
ちゅうすう

중축(中軸) the axis. ちゅうじく

중춘(仲春) February of the lunar month.
ちゅうしゅん

중층(中層) the middle storey[stratum, layer, class, floor].

중치(中—) 《품질》an article of medium [average] quality; middlings; medium [quality] goods 《값》medium-prized one 《크기》medium-sized one.
なかほどのもの

중침(中針) a medium-sized needle.

중키(中—) middle height; medium stature[size]／ ～의 미남자였다 He was a handsome man of medium height.

중탄산(重炭酸) 【화】bicarbonate／ ～ 소다 bicarbonate of soda; sodium bicarbonate／～염 bicarbonate／～ 칼리 bicarbonate of potassium.

중탕(中湯) a hot spring of moderate temperature.

중탕(重湯) cooking[warming up] in a double boiler／～하다 cook[warm up] in a double boiler.

중태(重態) a serious[grave, critical] condition／～에 빠지다 fall into a critical condition; take a serious turn(병을 주어로)／환자는 ～다 The patient is in a serious condition.／그의 병은 ～에 빠졌다 His illness assumed a very grave character. じゅうたい

중턱(中—) ①《산의》the mountain's breast; the mid-slope of a mountain／ ～ 에 halfway up[down] (a hill, a mountain)／산의 ～에 오두막이 있었다 A shed stood halfway up the mountain. ②《입체물의》the middle part. ちゅうふく

중토(重土) 【화】baryta. じゅうど

중톱(中—) a medium-sized saw.

ちゅうがたのこぎり
중퇴(中退) leaving school in mid-course; dropping out of school／ ～하다 leave school in mid-course; leave school without finishing complete course 《대학을》 leave a university without graduating. ちゅうたい

중파(中波) 《전파》a medium wave.
ちゅうは

중판(中判) 《사진》medium size／ ～형(型) 의 사진 a photo of cabinet size.

중판(重版) a double valve／～의 double; double-valved. じゅうはん

중편(中篇) 《제2권》the second part [of three parts]; the second[middle] volume 《중편의 글》a medium length story, ／～ 소설 a medium-length story.
ちゅうへん

중평(衆評) popular[public] opinion 《평판》common talk／이 문제에 관한 ～은 각색이다 Public opinion is divided as to this question. しゅうひょう

중포(重砲) a heavy gun／ ～병 a heavy artillery; a heavy artillery man／～ 대 a heavy artillery regiment.
じゅうほう

중포격(重砲擊) heavy bombardment／ ～하다 bombard heavily.

중폭격(重爆擊) heavy bombing／ ～하다 bomb heavily／～기(機) a heavy bomber.

중품(中品) medium quality.

중풍(中風) 《의》palsy; paralysis／ ～의 paralytic; palsied／～에 걸리다 have a stroke of paralysis. ちゅうぶ

중하(仲夏) the fifth lunar month; mid-summer. ちゅうか

중하(重荷) 《짐》heavy burden 《부담》heavy responsibility. じゅうか

중하다(重—) 《무겁다》(be) heavy 《병이》serious; critical (일이) grave; important／중한 죄 a grave charge／중한 벌 a heavy punishment／중한 책임 a heavy responsibility／병이 ～ be seriously ill.
おもい

중학교(中學校) a lower secondary[middle] school; a junior high school(미)／～ 학생 a middle-school student／～의 과정 a middle-school course／ ～에 다니다 attent a middle school／～를 졸업하다 finish[leave] middle school; complete the middle-school course.
ちゅうがっこう

중합(重合) polymerization. じゅうごう

중항(中項) 【수】the mean／ 비례 ～ the mean proportional.

중형(重刑) a heavy penalty; a severe punishment／～에 처하다 sentence (a person) to a severe punishment／～을 과하다 inflict heavy penalty upon (a person); punish severely. じゅうけい

중형(仲兄) one's second eldest brother.
ちゅうけい

중형(中型) a medium[middle] size／ ～의

**중혼**(重婚) double marriage; bigamy/~하다 commit bigamy; marry (*a person*) bigamously/~의 bigamous/~죄를 범하다 commit bigamy; be guilty of bigamy/~자 a bigamist.

**중화**(中和) 《화학적》 neutralization; counteraction 《평형》 equability / ~하다 neutralize; counteract/~성의 counteractive/산을 염기로 ~시키다 neutralize acid with a base/둘은 서로 ~한다 One neutralizes the other. / ~점 the neutral point.

**중화기**(重火器) heavy firearms.

**중환**(重患) a serious illness/~자 a serious case; one who is seriously ill.

**중후**(重厚) courtesy and sincerity; gentlehood and honesty/~하다 (be) courteous and sincere; gentle and honest/그는 ~한 사람이다 His personality is gentle and sincere.

**중흥**(中興) restoration; revival; rehabilitation/~하다 revive; restore; rehabilitate/쇠퇴한 가운(家運)을 ~하다 revive a declined trend of the family.

**중히**(重一) with care; with caution; with respect/~ 여기다 《소중히》 value; hold dear; make[think] much of; set a high value on 《주의》 respect; honor/사람을 ~ 쓰다 appoint (*a person*) to a post of trust; give (*a person*) a important position/건강을 무엇보다 ~ 여기다 set health before everything else/부모를 ~ 여기다 be filial[devoted] to one's parents.

**쥐**¹ 《동》 a rat; a mouse(*pl.* mice)/ ~약 rat poison; ratsbane / ~꼬리만큼 a mere particle / 독안에 든 ~와 같다 be like a rat in a trap/~잡기 운동 an anti-rat drive. ねずみ

**쥐**² 《경련》 convulsions; a cramp /~가 나다 convulse; have a cramp; be seized with a cramp. こむらがえり

**쥐구멍** a rat-hole; a mousehole/~을 찾다 seek a loophole[hiding place] / 부끄러워서 ~이라도 있으면 들어가 숨고 싶었다 I felt inclined to sink into the ground with shame., I was so overwhelmed with shame that I wished the floor would open and engulf me. /~에도 볕들 날이 있다《속담》 It is a long lane that has no turning., Fortune knocks at our door by turns.

ねずみのしゅつにゅうするあな

**쥐나다** ①《부끄러워서》 blush, (with *shame*) ②《경련하다》 convulse; have a cramp.

こむらがえりがする

**쥐눈이콩** 《식》 a kind of small bean; *Rhynchosia Volubilis*(학명).

**쥐다** take in *one's* hand; hole 《잡다》 grasp; clasp; seize; grip/남의 손을 ~ grasp another's hand/주먹을 ~ clench [double, close] *one's* fist / 권력을 ~ have power/정권을 ~ come into[be in] power/돈을 ~ come into money. にぎる

**쥐대기** a clumsy craftsman.

**쥐덫** a mousetrap; rattrap/~을 놓다 set a trap for rats. ねずみとりき

**쥐똥나무** 《식》 a privet. いぼたのき

**쥐머리** a kind of short ribs.

うしのあばらにく

**쥐며느리** 《충》 a sow bug. わらじむし

**쥐방울** 《식》 a Dutchman's pipe.

**쥐뿔같다** (be) trifling; trivial; insignificant; nonsensical; worthless.

くらない

**쥐색**(一色) dark gray.

**쥐숨듯이** without leaving any trace.

なんのけいせきものこさずに

**쥐알봉수** a smart fellow; a shrewd guy; a sly dog. はしっこいひと

**쥐어뜯다** tear; rend/머리털을 ~ rend[tear] *one's* hair/그 말을 들으니 가슴 속이 쥐어 뜯기는 것 같은 느낌이다 My heart bleeds to hear it. むしる

**쥐어박다** fist; strike with *one's* fist; deal a blow. こぶしでうつ

**쥐어주다** put (*a thing*) in *a person's* hand; let (*a person*) have; hand over 《뇌물을》 bribe (*a person*).

**쥐어지르다** deal a blow; hit; punch.

こぶしでうつ

**쥐어흔들다** grab and shake; brandish; sway; wave; swing/정계를 ~ hold sway over the political world/어깨를 ~ shake (*a person*) by the shoulder.

てでゆさぶる

**쥐엄질** 《젖먹이의 재롱》 the way a baby opens and closes its hands.

**쥐여지내다** be placed under (*a person's*) control; live in the grips of (*a person*); live under (*a person's*) thumb/그는 아내에게 쥐여지낸다 He is dominated by his wife., He is kept under his wife's thumb.

**쥐잡듯이** 《모조리》 [one and] all; to the last man 《샅샅이》 one by one/한 집 한 집 ~ 수색했다 They went the rounds of inquiry from door to door.

ひとつひとつぜんぶ

**쥐정신**(一精神) amnesia; a weak memory; a short memory; forgetfulness.

よくわすれること

**쥐젖** a [small] wart. いぼ

**쥐죽은 듯하다** be still as a stone; be silent as the grave; (be) hushed and still; be in a deathly silence/쥐죽은 듯이 고요한 한밤중 the dead hours of the night/교실 안은 쥐죽은 듯이 조용했다 The class was as silent as the grave.

きゅうにしずかになる

**쥐참외** 《식》 a snake-gourd; *Trichosanthes cucumeoides*(학명). きからすうり

**쥐치** 《어》 a filefish; a foolfish; leather-

fish.  かわはぎ
**쥐코밥상**(一床) a frugal meal; a poor [humble] table.
**쥐코조리** a man of no calibre.
**쥐포육장수**(一脯肉一) a miser; a close-fisted fellow.
**쥔** the master ⇨주인(主人).  あるじ
**쥘부채** a [folding] fan / ~꼴의 fanshaped.
**쥘쌈지** a [small] pouch; a tobacco pouch.
**즈런즈런** in affluence; in abundance; plentifully/~하다 (be) affluent; opulent; abundant; plentiful /살림이 ~하다 be well off; lead an abundant life; live in clover.  ふくぶく
**즈음** an occasion; the time; a period /이~은 nowadays; lately; now /그~ at that time; on that occasion/ ~하여 when; at the time; in case; on the occasion (of).  とき
**즉** if; when; then; on/알아 본 ~ 거짓 이었다 On inquiry, the report proved false./네 말을 들은 ~ 참 안됐다 I am sorry to hear that.
**즉**(即) ①(곧) namely; that is [to say]; so to speak ②(바로) just; precisely; exactly; nothing but; neither more nor less/당신의 출세가 ~ 나의 출세다 Your success means my success./이것 이 ~ 내가 원했던 것이다 This is just a thing I wanted.  すなわち
**즉각**(即刻) on the spot; at once; right away; immediately; in a moment/ ~ 승낙하다 give a ready consent; accept immediately/~ 대답하다 give a ready answer; make an immediate reply /~ 거절하다 I declined then and there.  そっこく
**즉결**(即決) an immediate[a prompt, a quick] decision; 〖법〗 summary judgment[dealing, action]; snap judgment〈미〉 /~하다 decide on the spot[immediately]; 〖법〗try[deal with] summarily/ ~ 재판 a summary decision[judgment] /~ 처분 summary conviction. そっけつ
**즉낙**(即諾) a ready consent /~하다 readily consent to; give a ready consent [nod].  そくだく
**즉납**(即納) immediate payment / ~하다 pay immediately[on the spot]. そくのう
**즉단**(即斷) immediate decision / ~하다 decide immediately.  そくだん
**즉답**(即答) a prompt[an immediate, ready] answer; an early reply[answer] /~하다 reply at once[promptly]; give an immediate answer / ~을 요구하다 ask for a prompt reply.  そくとう
**즉매**(即賣) spot sale; stock sale/ ~하다 sell on the spot.  そくばい
**즉사**(即死) instantaneous death/~하다 die on the spot; be killed instantly / 어린애가 자동차에 치어 ~했다 A child was run over by a car and killed on the spot.  そくし

**즉살**(即殺) killing promptly; killing outright/~하다 kill on the spot; kill outright.
**즉석**(即席) ~의 immediate; ready; instant; extemporaneous; impromptu; offhand/~에서 offhand; extempore; impromptu; on the spot; immediately/ ~ 연설 an offhand speech; an extemporaneous oration/~ 연설을 하다 speak extempore; make an impromptu speech /시를 ~에서 짓다 extemporize a poem.  そくせき
**즉시**(即時) at once; immediately; instantly; right away[off]; without delay; directly/그는 ~ 허락했다 He gave me a ready consent./이 문제는 ~ 해결해야 한다 This question calls for immediate solution. /~ 거래 direct[spot] transaction/~불 spot[immediate, down] payment/~ 인도 spot delivery/~ 통고 an immediate notice/~ 항고 an immediate complaint.  そくじ
**즉위**(即位) accession to the throne/~하 다 come[accede] to the throne; ascend the throne/ ~식 an enthronement[a coronation] ceremony/~식을 행하다 perform the ceremony of accession to the throne.  そくい
**즉음**(即吟) an improvised poem; improvisation/~하다 improvise a poem.
**즉응**(即應) adaptation; agreement; conformity/~하다 adapt[accommodate] oneself to; conform to 《응낙》 agree with 《대처》 meet; cope with/시대 요구에 ~ 한 교육 education adapted to the times /신정세에 ~하다 meet a new situation.  そくおう
**즉일**(即日) a same[very] day/~로 on the same[very] day/~로 돌아오다 return on the same day.  そくじつ
**즉전**(即錢) cash down; spot[ready] cash.
**즉전 즉결**(即戰即決) a lightning war plan.
**즉조**(即祚) enthronement ⇨즉위.  そくい
**즉좌**(即座) [on] the spot ⇨즉석.  そのば
**즉치다** give a hard blow instantly.
**즉행**(即行) prompt execution; immediate operation/~하다 carry into immediate execution[operation]; carry out promptly[immediately]/민주화 ~ the immediate adoption of democracy/즉일 ~ 이다 It is to be carried into effect promptly on this very day.  そっこう
**즉향**(即向) ~하다 leave promptly for (a place); start at once for (a place).
  そのばにむかっていくこと
**즉효**(即效) immediate effect (of medicine) /~하다 produce[have, take] immediate effect 《고통이 없어지다》 give immediate relief; afford instantaneous relief/~약 a quick[an instant [aneous]] remedy; a quick cure.
**즉흥**(即興) improvised amusement/~의 impromptu; extemporary; extempore /~시 an impromptu [poem]; an exte-

mpore verse／~ 시인 an improviser／~곡[음] an impromptu. そっきょう

**즐거움** joy; delight; gladness; happiness. たのしみ

**즐겁다** (be) pleasant; happy; merry; cheerful; delightful; joyful／즐겁게 pleasantly; joyfully; cheerfully／즐거운 추억 a pleasant memory／즐거운 옛날 the good old days. たのしい

**즐기다** enjoy (oneself); amuse oneself; take pleasure[delight] in; make merry 《좋아하다》like; be fond of／자연[인생]을 ~ enjoy nature[life]／담배를 ~ be fond of tobacco. たのしむ

**즐비**(櫛比) ~하다 stand closely together; stand in a continuous row; form line.

**즐풍 목우**(櫛風沐雨) the storms of life. しっぷうもくう

**쯤** about; some; roughly; almost／지금~ by now; by this time／4시~에 at about four o'clock. くらい

**즙**(汁) 《과실의》juice 《초목의》sap／~내 다 express[press out] the juice (of the grape); squeeze[extract] juice (from a lemon)／~이 많은 juicy; succulent. しる

**즙나다**(汁一) attain proficiency; become skilful. しごとになれる

**즙내다**(汁一) extract[squeeze, press] juice. しるをしぼりだす

**즙액**(汁液) juice／~이 많은[없는] juicy [juiceless].

**즙철**(緝綴) ~하다 collect and edit.

**증**(症) 《징후》symptoms 《병세》the condition of illness／무서움~이 나다 show signs of fear. しょう

**증**(證) 《증거》proof; evidence; testimony 《증서》a certificate; a warrant. しょう

**증가**(增加) an increase; a rise; a gain 《인구 따위》growth／ ~하다 increase (in); grow; rise／인구가 ~하다 go on increasing in population／~율 the rate of increase. ぞうか

**증간**(增刊) a special[an extra] number／ ~호 a special issue. ぞうかん

**증감**(增減) increase and[or] decrease; rise and[or] fall／ ~하다 increase and decrease; rise and fall. ぞうげん

**증강**(增强) reinforcement; increase／ ~ 하다 reinforce; increase／병력을 ~하다 reinforce one's troop. ぞうきょう

**증거**(證據) evidence; proof; testimony 《근거》authority／ ~ 능력 admissibility of evidence／물적 ~ material evidence ／충분한 ~ abundant[sufficient] evidence; ample proof／~물 evidence; vouchers; an exhibit／~ 인멸 suppression and destruction of proofs of guilt／~ 를 내세우다 adduce[give] evidence／~ 를 제공하다 afford[furnish] proof／~ 자료 corroborative facts. しょうこ

**증결하다**(增結一) add a [passenger] car (to a train).

**증권**(證券) a bill; a document 《공사채(公社債)》a security; a debenture; a bond ／유가 ~ securities／~ 매매 dealing in bonds and securities／ ~ 시장 the securities market／정부 발행 ~ government securities. しょうけん

**증급**(增給) a raise of wages; increased pay[wages]／~하다 increase[raise] (a person's) pay; give (a person) a pay raise.

**증기**(蒸氣) vapour 《수증기》steam 《총칭》exhalation ／ ~ 기관 a steam-engine／ ~ 펌프 a steam-pump／ ~ 선 a steam-ship／ ~ 난방 steam heating／ ~ 압력 steam pressure. じょうき

**증나다**(症一) get disgusted; get angry. はらだたしさやいやきがさす

**증답**(贈答) present-giving; an exchange of presents[gifts]／ ~하다 exchange gifts[presents]; give presents to each other／ ~품 a gift; a present. ぞうとう

**증대**(增大) enlargement／~하다 enlarge; augment; increase／ ~판 an enlarged edition. ぞうだい

**증류**(蒸溜) distillation／ ~하다 distill／ ~주(酒) spirituous liquors; spirits／~ 기(器) a distiller. じょうりゅう

**증명**(證明) 《증거》proof; evidence 《논증》 demonstration 《증언》testimony; attestation 《확증》authentication／~하다 《실증하다》prove; bear out; show 《증언하다》testify (to); bear witness to 《신원을》identify 《입증하다》verify; demonstrate; authenticate／~서 a physician's certificate／학설을 ~하다 demonstrate a theory. しょうめい

**증모**(增募) ~하다 《병정 등을》recruit larger enlistment 《학생 등을》receive larger enrollment. ぞうぼ

**증문**(證文) a deed ⇒증서(證書). しょうもん

**증발**(蒸發) evaporation; vaporization／ ~하다 vaporize; evaporate 《물이》steam ／ ~성의 vaporable; vaporific／ ~하기 쉬운 volatile. じょうはつ

**증발**(增發) 《통화의》an increased issue (of notes); 《열차의》operation of an extra train／ ~하다 issue additional (paper money); increase the railway service. ぞうはつ

**증배**(增配) 《배당의》an increased dividend 《배급의》an increase of rations／ ~ 하다 《배당을》declare an increased dividend 《배급물을》increase the rations. ぞうはい

**증병**(增兵) reinforcement／ ~하다 reinforce; reinforcements; dispatch. ぞうへい

**증보**(增補) an enlargement 《보유(補遺)》 a supplement／~하다 enlarge; supplement／ ~판 a revised and enlarged edition. ぞうほ

**증봉**(增俸) a salary increase; an increase in salary／ ~하다 increase[raise] the salary. ぞうほう

**증빙**(證憑) evidence; witness; proof 《근거》authority. しょうひょう

**증산**(增產) increased production[output] ／~하다 increase[boost, step up] prod-

증서(證書) a deed; a note 《채무의》 a bond 《영수증 따위의》 a voucher 《증명서》 a certificate 《졸업 증서》 a diploma 《차용~》 an IOU; a bond of debt／~를 작성하다 execute a deed. しょうしょ

증설(增設) an increase／~하다 increase; establish more (schools, parks, etc.) ぞうせつ

증세(症勢) symptoms 《병상》 the condition of a patient／…의 ~를 나타내다 develop symptoms of. びょうきのようす

증세(增稅) increased taxes／~하다 increase taxes[taxation]. ぞうぜい

증손(增孫) a great-grandson. そうそん

증쇄(增刷) an additional printing／~하다 print in addition.

증수(增水) ~하다 rise; swell; be swollen／~기 the annual flooding period. ぞうすい

증수(增收) flooding; increased revenue [receipts]; 《농산물》 an increased yield／~하다 increase in receipts. ぞうしゅう

증수(增修) enlargement of a book.

증수회(贈收賄) corruption; bribery／~사건 a bribery case.

증습(蒸濕) sultriness; mugginess／~하다 (be) steaming hot; muggy; sultry.

증식(增殖) increase; propogation／~하다 increase; multiply. ぞうしょく

증애(憎愛) hatred and affection; love and hatred. ぞうあい

증액(增額) an increase; an additional sum／~하다 increase; raise. ぞうがく

증언(證言) testimony; evidence; witness／~하다 testify to[that]; bear witness to[that]; arrest [to]／무죄를 ~하다 testify to (a person's) innocence／~서 a written testimony／~대에 서다 [take] the witness stand. しょうげん

증여(贈與) donation; presentation／~하다 give; present (a thing) to (a person)／~자 a giver; a presenter; a donor. ぞうよ

증오(憎惡) hatred; detestation／~하다 hate; detest; abhor; loathe. ぞうお

증원(增員) increase of the staff／~하다 increase the staff[personnel]. ぞういん

증원(增援) reinforcement／~하다 reinforce／~대 reinforcements. ぞうえん

증유(贈遺) bequest／~하다 bequeath／~물 a bequest. ぞうい

증음기(增音器) a sound amplifier 《오르간의》 a knee swell.

증인(證人) a witness; an attestor 《보증인》 a surety／~이 되다 testify (to a fact); 《법정에서》 give evidence／~석 the witness box[stand]. しょうにん

증인(證印) a seal affixed to a document. しょういん

증자(增資) an increase of capital／~하다 increase the capital. ぞうし

증적(證跡) 《증거》 evidence 《흔적》 traces; marks／~을 남기다 leave traces; leave marks. しょうせき

증정(贈呈) presentation／~하다 present; donate／~본(本) a presentation; a complimentary[free] copy／~자 a giver; a presenter／~품 a present; a gift. ぞうてい

증정(增訂) revision and enlargement／~하다 revise and enlarge／~판 a new edition; a revised and enlarged edition. ぞうてい

증조고(曾祖考) 《돌아간》 the deceased great-grandfather. しんだいひいおじいさん

증조모(曾祖母) a [paternal] great-grandmother. そうそぼ

증조부(曾祖父) a [paternal] great-grandfather. そうそふ

증조비(曾祖妣) 《돌아간》 the deceased great-grandmother. しんだいひいおばあさん

증좌(證左) proof 《증거(證據)》. しょうさ

증주(增註) additional notes／~하다 make additional notes; enlarge annotations. ぞうちゅう

증지(證紙) a certificate stamp.

증진(增進) ~하다 promote; increase; advance; further／건강을 ~하다 promote[build up] health; conduce[be conducive] to health. ぞうしん

증축(增築) an extension; an addition／~하다 extend[enlarge, add to] a building. ぞうちく

증파(增派) reinforcement／~하다 dispatch additional (troops, ships).

증편(蒸─) steamed rice-cake with yeast.

증폭(增幅) amplification／~하다 amplify／~기 an amplifier. ぞうふく

증표(證票) ①《증거》 evidence; a proof ②《표》 a voucher. しょうひょう

증험(證驗) a test; an attempt／~하다 try; have a try; attempt. しょうけん

증회(贈賄) bribery; graft／~하다 bribe; offer a bribe to (a person); corrupt／~사건 a bribery[graft] case／~자 a briber. ぞうわい

증후(症候) symptoms. しょうこう

지 《동안》 since; after; from／그들이 결혼한 ~ 10년이 되다 It is ten years since they are married. ─(して)から

-지 ①《의문》 예그가 올는~ 안 올는~ 모르겠다 I don't know whether he will come or not. ②《말끝》 예내일은 누가 오겠~ Someone may come to see me tomorrow. ③《부정》 예나는 가고 싶~ 않다 I do not want to go.

지(至) to…; till／자 오전 8시 ~ 오후 5시 from 8 a.m. to 5 p.m. ─まで

지(肢) the limbs. し

지(知) intelligence; intellect. ち

지(智) wisdom. ち

지가(地價) land prices; the price of land 《가치》 the value of land. ちか

지각(知覺) ①《심》 perception; sensation／~하다 feel; perceive／~ 기관 the organs of perception／~ 신경 sensory

**지각** ②(분별) discretion; good sense; judg[e]ment/ ~하다 reach the age of reson; cut one's wisdom teeth/ ~없는 insensible; sleepy. ちこく

**지각**(遲刻) being late/ ~하다 be[come] late; be behind time/학교에 ~하다 be late for[at] school/ ~계 a report for being late; a late report/ ~ 일수 the number of days late. ちこく

**지각**(地殼) the [earth's] crust; the lithosphere/ ~ 구조학 tectonic geology/ ~이동설 diastrophism. ちかく

**지간**(枝幹) the trunk and branches. しかん

**지갑**(紙匣) ①(종이갑) a box made with paper; a carton ②(돈지갑) a purse; a pocketbook. かみのはこ

**찌개** dish served in the pot; a pot stew /생선 ~ a fish pot-stew.

**지개**(志槪) spirit ⇨지기(志氣). しき

**찌꺼기** ①(앙금) dregs; lees; grounds; sediment; residuum/차 ~ tea grounds ②(불용물) refuse; leavings; remains; remnants/먹다 남긴 ~ leftovers (of food). のこりもの

**찌꺼분하다** ①(눈이) (be) dirty; gummy ②(어수선하다) (be) disorderly; untidy; scattered. どんよりしている

**지껄이다** talk; chatter; chat/ (빨리) gabble/잘 지껄이는 사람 a chatter-box; a great talker. べちゃべちゃいう

**지게** an A-frame; a chigeh/ ~을 지다 carry the A-frame on one's back.

**지게미** ①(술의) sool lees; brewer's grains ②(눈꼽) gum in the corner of the eye ③(비듬) dandruff. さけかす

**지겟군** an A-frame-man; a burden carrier.

**지견**(知見) knowledge; insight. ちけん

**지견**(智見) wisdom and knowledge. ちけん

**지겹다** (be) very tired of; fed up with; sick of/일이 ~ I am sick of this work. ながたらしい

**지경**(枝莖) the branches[sprigs] and stalks. しけい

**지경**(地境) ①(경계) a boundary; a border; bounds ②(형편) situation; circumstances/파멸할 ~이다 stand on the brink of ruin. ちかい

**지계**(地階) 〖전〗〖지하실〗 the basement (1층) the groundfloor. ちかい

**지계**(持戒) 〖종〗 observing the Buddhist commandments. じかい

**지고**(至高) sublimity; supremacy/ ~하다 (be) highest; supreme; most sublime; loftiest. しこ

**지골**(指骨) 〖해〗 a phalanx; phalange. しこつ

**지골**(肢骨) bones of the extremities. しこつ

**지공**(至恭) supreme courtesy; the utmost politeness/ ~하다 (be) supremely courteous; very polite.

**지공 무사**(至公無私) supreme[perfect] fairness and impartiality.

**지관**(地官) a geomancer/ ~을 찾아가서 묏자리를 물어 봤다 I went to a geomancer and asked him for a lucky site for burials.

**지교**(至交) eternal[close] friendship; friendship in need. しこう

**지교**(智巧) wisdom; sense; wits/ ~하다 (be) wise; sensible; intelligent. さいちにたけてこうみょうちなこと

**지구**(地球) the earth; the globe/ ~ 물리학 geophysics/ ~ 중심적 geocentric/ ~의(儀)〔본〕 a [terrestrial] globe/ ~ 구조학 geognosy. ちきゅう

**지구**(地溝) 〖지〗 rift [in the earth]; a graben. ちこう

**지구**(地區) 〔지역〕 a district; a region; a zone; an area; a section(미);〔대지〕 a lot. ちく

**지구**(知舊) an appreciative friend; an old acquaintance; an old friend.

**지구**(持久) persistence; perseverance; endurance/ ~하다 stay; endure; persevere/ ~책 dilatory tactics/ ~력 endurance; staying power; tenacity/ ~전 an endurance contest. じきゅう

**지국**(支局) a branch [office]/신문사 ~ a branch office of a newspaper. しきょく

**지궐련** a cigarette.

**찌그러뜨리다** crush; batter; squash. まげる

**찌그러지다** be battered; be crushed; be withered. ゆがむ

**지그리다** shut[close] a door softly[lightly]; shut loosely. おしつぶす

**지그시** ①(참는 모양) patiently; perseveringly; persistently; without letup/고생을 ~ 견디다 endure one's hardship stoically ②(누르거나 당기는 모양) gently; softly; quietly/여자의 손을 ~ 당기다 pull a girl's hand stealthily. そっと

**지극**(至極) the height; the extreme; the utmost/ ~하다 (be) extreme; utmost/ ~히 very; exceedingly; extremely. しごく

**지끈** with a snap[crack, crash]/ ~하다 give a snap. ぽきっと

**지근**(支根) rootlets; radicles. しこん

**지근**(떡)거리다 ①annoy (a person); tease; bother; pester ②(씹다) chew softly ③(골치가) have a shooting pain [in one's head]. うるさくねだる

**지글거리다** sizzle; bubble up; simmer; seethe/지글지글 sizzling; bubbling; simmering; seething/미움으로 속이 지글 타다 one's mind seethes with hatred. ぐつぐつにえる

**지금**(只今) ①(현재) the present; the present day[time]; now/ ~부터 from now [on]; after this; hence/ ~까지 till now; hither to; up to the present/ ~에 와서는 now that things have come to such a pass; at this juncture/ ~도 still; even now[to this day] ②(지금막) just; only[but] just; but now; a moment ago ③(지금 곧) soon; at once; immediately; [just] in a moment／～갑니다 I will come at once., I am coming. ただいま

지금(地金) a metal; ore (토대가 되는) ground metal 《화폐의》 bullion. じがね

지금껏 till now; so far; all this while／～ 알려지지 않은 비밀 a secret hitherto unknown to the world. いままで

지급(支給) ～하다 give; allow; grant; furnish[supply, provide] (a person) with／～품 articles supplied; supplies／의식을 ～하다 supply (a person) with food and clothing. しきゅう

지급(至急) ～하다 (be) urgent; pressing; express／～히 urgently; immediately; promptly; at once／～한 용무 urgent[pressing] business. しきゅう

찌긋거리다 《눈을》 wink (at a person); 《옷을 당기다》 pull (a person) by the sleeve. まばたきする

지긋이 slowly; gently; tenderly; calmly; lightly.

지긋지긋하다 ①(불쾌하다) (be) disgustful; offensive; repulsive ②(잔인하다) (be) cruel; outrageous; merciless; horrible／지긋지긋한 광경 a horrible sight. あいそうがつきる

지긋하다 (be) advanced in years; well up in years／나이가 지긋한 사람 a man well advanced in years. こうれいである

찌끼 lees; dregs ⇨찌꺼기. のこりもの

-지기 ①(논밭의) an area of land; a measure of land／밭 두 마～ two majiki of fields ②(사람) a keeper; a guard／문～ a gatekeeper／산～ a forest ranger. —まき

지기(地氣) exhalation from the earth; vapor; fertility of soil. ちき

지기(志氣) spirit; sentiment／～ 상합 mutual understanding; affinity／애국의 ～ spirit of patriotism; patriotic sentiment. しき

지기(紙器) a paper container(봉기); a papermade article (지제품). 

지기(知己) a bosom friend; congenial friends. ちき

지나가다 ①(통과하다) pass [by]; go past; pass through／숲을 ～ pass through a wood／문 앞을 ～ pass one's door ②(경과하다) pass; elapse; go by; go on／지나간 일 the past; a past event; bygones ③(한도를 지나) go too far; go beyond; go past. つうかする

지나다 ①(기한이) expire; be out; terminate／기한이 지났다 The time limit has expired. ②(통과하다) go past; pass [by]; pass through ③(경과하다) pass; go on; go by; elapse／지난 일 bygones; a thing of the past. すぎる

지나새나 always; all the time; night and day. いつも

지나오다 pass; come along[through]／지나온 일을 생각하다 remember things gone by. とおってくる

지나치다 《과도하다》 go too far; do too much; carry (a joke) too far; go to excessive lengths／지나친 excessive; immoderate／지나치게 too; immoderately; excessively／지나친 요구 inordinate demands. どをすぎる

지난(至難) extreme difficulty／～하다 (be) most difficult; very hard. しなん

지난번(-番) last time; some time ago; the other day／～에 받은 편지 the last letter received. このまえ

지날걸 on one's way (to)／～에 by one's way; while passing. とおるついで

지남(指南) teaching; instructions; guidance／～하다 teach; instruct; give lessons (in a thing). しなん

지남철(指南鐵) a magnet. じしゃく

지남침(指南針) a magnetic needle／～ 방위 a compass bearing. じしゃくのはり

지낭(智囊) a wise man; a witty person; the brain. ちのう

지내다 ①(세월을) spend[pass] one's time; get along 《생활하다》 live; make a living／독서로 ～ spend one's time in reading ②(치르다) hold; observe／장사를 ～ hold a funeral ③(겪다) go through; experience. すごす

지내듣다 take no notice of; pay no attention (to)／남의 말을 ～ pay little attention to what others have to say. うわのそらできく

지내보다 have relations; associate with; get on with; mix with／사람은 지내보아야 안다 It takes time to know a person really. こうさいしてみる

지네 《동》 a centipede. むかで

지노(紙-) a paper-string／～를 꼬다 twist paper into a string. かみひも

지느러미 a fin／등(가슴, 꼬리)～ a dorsal [pectoral, caudal] fin. ひれ

지능(知能) intelligence; intellect; mental faculties／～적 intellectual; mental／～을 계발하다 develop one's intellectual powers／～ 검사 a intelligence test; an I. Q. test／～범 an intellectual offense[crime]／～ 지수 intelligence quotient(略: I.Q.)／～ 연령 the I.Q. age. ちのう

지니다 《보전하다》 keep; preserve; retain 《가지다》 carry; have 《품다》 hold; cherish; entertain／몸에 ～ take with; bring; carry 《무기를》 be armed／병독을 ～ carry a poisonous virus. ほじする

지닐재주 a splendid[marvelous] memory. よくきおくしているのうりょく

지다¹ ①(패배하다) be defeated; be beaten; suffer a defeat／경쟁에 ～ lose in a contest／논쟁에 ～ be argued down ②(굴복하다) be overcome with; submit to; give in; yield to／유혹에 ～ yield to temptation. まける

지다² ①(등에) bear (a burden); carry (something) on one's back ②(빚을) run [get, fall] into (debt); incur (debts);

**owe**/빚을 ~ run[get, fall] into debt; incur debts ③《책임을》 hold; bear; assume (*a responsibility*) ④《신세 따위를》 receive (*favours*); be placed under obligation

**지다³** ①《해·달이》 sink; set; go down ②《잎·꽃이》 fall; be gone; be strewn (to *the ground*)/지기 시작하다 begin to fall ③《때·얼룩이》 come off[out]; be taken out; be removed ④《숨이》 breathe *one's* last [breath]; die. しずむ

**-지다¹**《되다》 become; grow; get/좋아[나빠]~ get better grow cold[er]. なる

**-지다²**《생기다》 ㉠그늘~ be shady; be shaded/장마~ The rainy season has set in/얼룩~ become stained. なる

**찌다¹**《살이》 grow fat; gain[put on] weight/살찐 fat; plump; stout. こえる

**찌다²**《날씨가》 be sultry; be humid; get steaming hot/찌는 듯이 덥다 It is boiling[steaming] hot. むしむしする

**찌다³**《김으로》 steam; heat with steam/감자를 ~ steam potatoes. むす

**찌다⁴**《베다》 cut; mow. きる

**지다위** ①~하다《의지》 depend[rely] on ② ~하다《전가》 lay[throw] [the blame on one]; impute [a crime to one].

**지당(至當)** propriety; justice; reasonableness/~하다 (be) proper; right; just; reasonable; fair/~한 조처 a proper measure/그렇게 하는 것이 ~하다 It is right of you to do so., You ought to do so., It is proper that you should do so. しとう

**지대(地帶)** a zone; a belt; a region/비무장 ~ demilitarized zone(略: D. M. Z.)/중립 ~ a neutral zone/구름 ~ hilly districts. ちたい

**지대(至大)** ~하다 (be) [very] great; considerable; vast; immense/~한 관심사 a matter of great interest. しだい

**지대(址臺)** a foundation.

**지대(地代)** [ground-]rent/~를 받다 collect ground-rents. ちだい

**지대(支隊)** a detached force. したい

**지더리다** (be) mean; vile; gross; low; vulgar; dirty. いやしい

**지덕(知德)** wisdom and virtue/그는 ~을 겸비한 사람이다 He combines knowledge and virtue. ちとく

**지도(地圖)** a map《도시의》 a plan《해도》 a chart《지도책》 an atlas/~를 그리다[보다] draw[consult] a map/윤곽[접는] ~ an outline[a folding] map/~책 an atlas. ちず

**지도(指導)** guidance; directions; leadership/~하다 guide; direct; coach; lead /~자 a leader; a coacher; a director /~법 a method of guidance/~원 an instructor; an advisor/연극을 ~하다 coach a play. しどう

**지도리** a hinge; hook-and-eye hinges.

**지독(至毒)** ~하다 (be) severe; intense; terrible《엄청나다》 unreasonable《가혹》 cruel/~한 추위 the severe cold/~한 구두쇠 an awful miser/~한 모욕 a gross insult. きわめてひどいこと

**지동(地動)** ①《지자전》 rotation《지구의 공전》 revolution/~설 the Copernican theory ②《지진》 terrestrial movement; earth tremor. ちどう

**지두(枝頭)** the tip of a branch.

**지두(指頭)** the finger-top; the tip of a finger. しとう

**지둔(遲鈍)** ~하다 (be) dull-witted; stupid; thick-headed. ちどん

**지둔(至鈍)** great stupidity/~하다 (be) very stupid; dull-witted; thick-headed. きわめてにぶいこと

**지동** rotation ⇨지동(地動). ちとう

**지드럭거리다, 찌드럭거리다** annoy; pester; pick on; tease. うるさくする

**찌득찌득하다** (be) tough; hard [to crack]; sticky. かたい

**찌들다** ①《때가 끼다》 get dirty; be smudged ②《고생으로》 get thin (*from*); be worn out; be careworn.

**지등롱(紙燈籠)** a paper lantern.

**지라**《해》 the spleen. すいぞう

**지랄** ①~하다《행위》 be mad; riot; rage; act violently《발버둥질》 struggle [and kick] ②~하다《지랄병》 have an epileptic fit/~장이 an epileptic. きょうき

**지랄병(一病)** epilepsy《발작》 an epileptic fit. てんかん

**지략(智略)**《슬기》 cleverness; strategy; resourcefulness/~이 풍부하다 be resourceful; be full of resources. ちりゃく

**지러지다** be stunted.

**지렁이**《동》 an earthworm/~도 밟으면 꿈틀거린다《속담》 Even a worm will turn., Even a fly has it's anger. みみず

**지례¹**《미리》 in advance; beforehand; previously. まえもって

**지례²**《움직이는 물건》 a lever《목재》 a hand-spike/~질 levering/~질하다 lever; raise with a lever. てこ

**지레짐작** forejudging; prejudgement《조급한》 hasty conclusion《추측》 guess《기대》 anticipation/~하다 forejudge; form a hasty conclusion. よそく

**지레채다** know beforehand; forejudge; foreknow; foresee/남의 이야기를 ~ guess the point of another's story in advance. よそくする

**지려(智慮)** prudence; wisdom/~있는 prudent; long-headed; wise.

**지력(地力)** fertility of soil/~ 체감(遞減) decreasing fertility. ちりょく

**지력(智力)** mental power[faculty]; intellect; intellectual power. ちりょく

**지력(地歷)** geography and history.

**지력선(指力線)** a magnetic curve; lines of force.

**지령(指令)** an order; a notice; an instruction/~하다 order; give instructions; direct; notify/~을 내리다[기다리다] g-

**ive**[wait for] instructions. しれい

**지령**(指令) the issue number of a periodical.

**지로**(指路) guidance／～하다 guide; show (*a person*) the way しろ

**지론**(至論) a most reasonable opinion. しろん

**지론**(持論) a cherished opinion; a stock argument; *one's* pet theory. じろん

**지뢰**(地雷) a [ground] mine／～를 밟다 strike a mine／～ 지대 a mine field／～ 화약 blasting powder. じらい

**지루하다** (be) tedious; boresome; tiresome; dull. ながたらしい

**지류**(支流) a tributary; a branch stream; an affluent. しりゅう

**지르다**[1] ①(발로) kick; give (*a person*) a kick (손으로) strike; knock; give (*a person*) a blow ②(집에 꽂다) return ③(건너 지르다) draw across; cross ④(속으로) strike into; pierce; thrust ⑤(나무의 순을) trim; nip; clip ⑥(길을) take a short cut; take a short way; cut across (*a field*) ⑦(돈을) bet; stake. つく

**지르다**[2] (소리를) raise; utter; set up／고함을 ～ yell; shout; holler／비명을 ～ shriek; scream; let out a shriek. はりあげる

**찌르다** ①(칼 따위로) pierce; stab; prick; thrust ②(자극하다) assail (*one's nostrils*) ③(비밀을) inform (*against*); report ④(공격하다) attack ⑤(투자하다) invest 《노름에서》 stake; bet ⑥(냄새가) stink; smell nasty. さす

**지르되다** be slow in growth; grow slowly. せいちょうがおくれる

**지르디디다** 《서다》 stand on tiptoe 《걷다》 [walk on] tiptoe.

**지르르, 찌르르** ①～하다 《물기·기름기가》 (be) slimy; wet; dripping; dribbing; slippery ②～하다 《뼈마디가》 (be) benumbed; numb. すべすべ

**지르잡다** wash out a stain／지르잡아 빨다 wash off a spot／얼룩을 ～ wash the stain out; wash out the stain.

**지르퉁하다** (be) sulky; morose; ill-humored／무엇 때문에 지르퉁하느냐 What makes you so sulky? むっとしている

**-지를** ①도리어 결과가 좋～ 못했다 On the contrary the results were no good at all.

**지름** a diameter／반～ a radius; semidiameter. ちょっけい

**지름길** a short cut[way]; a shorter road ／～로 가다 take a short cut[shorter way]. しょうけい

**지릅뜨다** strain *one's* eyes; glare／성이 나서 눈을 ～ glare at (*a person*) with anger. めをみはる

**지리**(地利) ①(편리·잇점) a geographical advantage; advantages of ground[position] ②(생산) profits from land; production; produce. ちり

**지리**(地理) 《지세》 geographical features; topography 《지리학》 geography／～[학] 상의 geographical／～학자 a geographer ／동물～학 zoogeography. ちり

**지리다**[1] 《냄새가》 (be) smelling of urine ／지린내 smell of urine.

**지리다**[2] (오줌·똥을) evacuate[let out] against *oneself*. ちびる

**지리멸렬**(支離滅裂) discontinuity; incoherence／～하다 (be) incoherent; chaotic; disjointed. しりめつれつ

**지리하다**(支離—) (be) tedious; dull; tiresome／지리한 이야기 a tedious[dull] talk／지리한 여행 a monotonous journey. ながたらしい

**-지마는** but; however; yet; notwithstanding／그녀는 나이가 어리～ 분별이 있다 Though she is young, she is discreet. —であるが

**지망**(志望) wish; desire; aspiration 《선택》 choice／～ 학교 wish; desire; aspire (*to*); prefer; choose／～ 학교 the school of *one's* choice／～대로 as *one* wishes. しぼう

**지망지망** carelessly; neglectfully; heedlessly; rashly／일을 ～하다 do a slipshod [slapdash] job. うっかり

**지맥**(支脈) a spur; an offset 《광산의》 a feeder. しみゃく

**지면**(地面) 《지표》 the surface [of land, the earth]; 《지상》 the ground. じめん

**지면**(紙面) 《신문의》 paper, a sheet 《여백》 space／～이 허락하면 if space permits. しめん

**지면**(誌面) a sheet of a magazine／～을 통해 through a magazine. しじょう

**지명**(地名) the name of a place; a geographical designation[name]. ちめい

**지명**(知名) a wide reputation／～ 인사 a man of fame; a well-known person／～ 작가 an eminent writer. ちめい

**지명**(知命) ①～하다 《명을 앎》 know *one's* own destiny ②(나이) the age of fifty years. ちめい

**지명**(指名) naming; nomination／～하다 name; nominate／～ 수배 arrangements for the search (of *an identified criminal*)／～순으로 in the order of the persons called[mentioned]. しめい

**지모**(智謀) practical ingenuity; resourcefulness. ちぼう

**지목**(地目) the classification of land; land category. ちもく

**지목**(指目) spotting; pointing out; judging／～하다 spot; point out; judge／범인으로 ～하다 spot (*a person*) as the culprit. しもく

**지묘**(至妙) superbness／～하다 (be) excellent／～한 작전 the superb execution of a stratagem. しみょう

**지묵**(紙墨) paper and ink[-stick]. かみとすみ

**지문**(指紋) a fingerprint／～을 남기다 leave *one's* fingerprints (*on*) ／ ～법 the finger-print expert. しもん

**지문**(地文) the physical features and changes of the earth. ちもん
**지물**(紙物) paper; various kinds of paper／~포 a paper goods store. かみ
**지미**(至微) minuteness; fineness／~하다 (be) minute; infinitesimal; fine. きわめてさいびなこと
**지미**(至美) superb beauty／~하다 (be) very beautiful. きわめてうつくしいこと
**지미**(地味) the [nature of] soil. ちみ
**지반**(地盤) ①(토대) the base; the foundation 《땅바닥》 the ground ②(기반) footing; foothold／~을 닦다 establish one's foothold／확고한 ~을 얻다 gain a firm foothold; get a strong footing ③(세력 범위) a sphere of influence 《선거구》 a constituency／~을 구축하다 lay the foundation 《정당이》 nurse one's constituency. じばん
**지반**(池畔) a pond side; the shores of a pond. ちはん
**지방**(脂肪) fat; grease 《돼지의》 lard 《고래 따위의》 speck／~ 과다 excess fat; obesity／~이 많은 음식물 fatty food／~분 fat. しぼう
**지방**(地方) 《한 지방》 a locality; a region; a district; a part [of the country]; an area 《수도 이외의》 the provinces 《시골》 the country 《부근》 neighbourhood; vicinity／~ 공무원 a local public service employee[worker]／~ 단체 a local body／~ 순회 a provincial tour／~ 자치 local self-government／~ 장관 a provincial [prefectural] governor／~ 행정 loca-administration. ちほう
**지배**(支配) 《관리》 control; superintendence 《지휘》 direction 《처리》 management 《통치》 rule; government／~하다 control; govern; rule; direct; dominate／~자 a ruler; a dominator／~계급 the ruling[governing] class／~를 받다 be [put] under the control[rule] of; be subject to (laws, etc.)／~권 control; supremacy; management／ 감정에 ~ 되다 be influenced by a passion.
しはい
**지배인**(支配人) a manager; a superintendent; an executive／총~ a general manager. しはいにん
**지벅거리다, 찌뻑거리다** stumble along; walk with difficulty／지벅지벅[찌뻑찌뻑] wits difficulty. ふらつきながらあるく
**지번**(地番) a lot number.
**지벌**(地閥) social standing and [noble] lineage. ちいともんばつ
**지범거리다** pick up one by one[piece by piece].
**지변**(地變) an extraordinary geographical phenomenon; a natural calamity; a terrestrial upheaval. ちへん
**지병**(持病) a chronic disease; an old complaint／두통이 나의 ~이다 Headache is a chronic disease with me. じびょう
**지보**(至寶) a most valuable treasure／음악계의 ~ the pride of musical circles. しほう
**지복**(至福) the highest good; the supreme bliss; beatitude.
**지부**(支部) a branch[-office]; a chapter／~장 the manager of a branch. しぶ
**지뿌드드하다** (be) uncomfortable; be out of sorts; (be) indisposed.
ぞくぞくかんきがする
**찌부러뜨리다** deflate; crumple; crush.
**찌부러지다** get[be] deflated[crushed, crumpled]; collapse; be ruined.
**지부럭거리다 찌부럭거리다** play[trifle] with; tease／지부럭지부럭 teasingly.
からかう
**지부지기** 《식》 a roof-tile moss. つめれんげ
**지분**(脂粉) paint[rouge] and powder.
しふん
**지분거리다** tease; trouble; annoy／지분지분 teasingly; annoyingly. からかう
**지불**(支拂) payment; discharge; defrayment／~하다 pay; defray 《빚을》 discharge 《어음을》 honour 《계산서를》 meet／~액 the amount payable[due, paid]／~기일 the date of payment／~명령 an order for payment／~을 거절하다 refuse payment／~기한이 차다 《어음의》 fall due; mature／~ 방법[조건] the terms of payment／~을 정지하다 stop[suspend] payment. しはらい
**지붕** a roof; covering; roofing; the housetop／~ 마루 the ridge of a roof／~을 잇다 roof; cover with a roof／용마루~ a ridge[saddle] roof／둥근~ a dome. やね
**지빈**(至貧) extreme poverty／~하다 (be) extremely poor; as poor as a church-mouse. ひどくひんこんなこと
**지사**(支社) a branch [office]. ししゃ
**지사**(志士) a patriot; a public-spirited man／애국 ~ a patriot. しし
**지사**(知事) a [provincial] governor／~의 gubernatorial. ちじ
**지상**(地上) ~의 terrestrial; subastral 《현세의》 earthy／~에 낙원 a heaven on earth; a paradise on earth／~부대 a ground unit／~권 superficies; lease [hold]; surface rights. ちじょう
**지상**(紙上) paper／~에서[으로] 《편지로》 by letter 《인쇄로》 in print 《신문으로》 through the press. しじょう
**지상**(誌上) ~에 in a magazine[journal]／~다음호~에 발표함 To be made public in the next number. しじょう
**지상**(至上) ~의 highest; supreme; utmost／예술~주의 the art-for-art principle／~권 supremacy; sovereignty; supreme power／~ 명령 a supreme order; 《철》 a categorical imperative. しじょう
**지상**(地相) a land aspect／~학 physiography.
**지상선**(地上仙) a prosperous person; one greatly blessed.
**지상자**(紙箱子) a carton; a handbox; a

**지새는달** the moon at dawn; the moon in the morning sky.

**지새다** the day breaks; it dawns.

**지새우다** awake[stay up] all night; see the night out. よるをあかす

**지서**(支署) a branch office; a [police] substation; a police box. ししょ

**지선**(支線) a branch line; a local line; a feeder line. しせん

**지선**(至善) supreme good / ～하다 (be) extremely good; very kind and dutiful. じぜん

**지설**(紙屑) paper scraps; waste paper.

**지성**(至誠) [absolute] sincerity / ～껏 sincerely; with one's whole heart and soul. しせい

**지성**(知性) intelligence; intellect; mentality/그의 학설은 ～에 호소하고 있다 His theory appeals to our intelligence. ちせい

**지세**(地貰) ground[land] rent; rent.

**지세**(地勢) terrain; geographical feature; topography. ちせい

**지세**(地稅) a land tax. ちぜい

**지소**(至小) minuteness / ～하다 minute; microscopic.

**지소**(支所) a branch [office]; a substation.

**지속**(持續) duration / ～하다 《계속하다》 continue; last; remain 《견디다》 endure; stand out; hold out 《버티다》 keep up; sustain; maintain; support/～성(性) durability/～ 기간 duration/～적 lasting; continuous/～전(戰) a retaining action. じぞく

**지속**(遲速) speed; velocity; progress/일의 ～ the speed of one's work. ちそく

**지수**(止水) still water. しすい

**지수**(指數) an index [number]; an exponent/생활비 ～ the index figure of the cost of living/물가 ～ the index number of prices; a price index. しすう

**지숙**(止宿) lodging/～하다 lodge at; put up at (a place). ししゅく

**지순**(至順) ～하다 be as meek as a lamb. きわめてじゅうじゅんなこと

**지스러기** remnants; refuse. かす

**지시**(指示) direction; orders; indication; instructions/～하다 direct; give directions; show; indicate; point out/～약 《화》an indicator /～하에 under one's directions[instructions]/～에 따라서 in accordance with one's directions/～서 directions; an order/～ 대명사[형용사] 《언》a demonstrative pronoun[adjective]. しじ

**지식**(知識) knowledge; acquaintance; knowhow〈미〉; 《전문》information 《학문》learning 《소양》attainments 《이해》understanding/일반적 ～ general knowledge[information]/초보 ～ an elementary knowledge/해박한 ～ an extensive knowledge/예비 ～ preliminary knowledge/～인 an intellectual/변변찮은 ～ a little knowledge; a smattering knowledge (of English)/전문적 ～ an expert [a professional] knowledge[information]/기초 ～ basic[foundation] knowledge. ちしき

**지식욕**(知識慾) a thirst for knowledge; intellectual appetite; a desire for learning; love for learning / ～에 불타다 have a voracious appetite for knowledge; thirst[hunger] for knowledge. ちしきよく

**지신**(地神) earthly deities; the God of the earth. ちじん

**지실**(知悉) complete knowledge[information] / ～하다 know everything[all] about; be well aware of; be fully informed of. ちしつ

**지심**(地心) the centre of the earth. ちしん

**지싯거리다** badger (one to do); press; tease; importune; ask for persistemly /지싯지싯 importunately; irksomely; persistently. からかう

**지아비** my husband[spouse, consort].

**지악**(至惡) ①《극악》～한 heinous; most wicked; atrocious ②《악착》～스럽다 (be) fussy; sedulous; hard /～스럽게 fussily; hard; sedulously. しあく

**지압 요법**(指壓療法) finger-pressure therapy[cure]. しあつりょうほう

**지애**(至愛) deep love. しあい

**지양**(止揚) 《철·논》 aufheben(G); sublation/～하다 sublate; aufheben. しよう

**지어내다** make up; invent; manufacture; fabricate/지어낸 얘기 a made-up[an invented] story; an invention/새 말을 ～ create[make up] a new word. ねつぞうする

**지어미** one's wife.

**지어차**(至於此) ～하다 (things) come to such a pass.

**지언**(至言) a good[wise] saying; a maxim. しげん

**지엄**(至嚴) extreme strinctness[sternness].

**지에밥** steamed [glutinous] rice.

**지역**(地域) an area; a zone; a region; a tract of land/～별로 by regional groups/～ 대표 local union delegates/～ 사회 a [local] community. ちいき

**지역권**(地役權) 《법》easement; [real] servitude/～자 a servitude holder. ちえきけん

**지연**(紙鳶) a kite. たこ

**지연**(遲延) delay; postponement; tardiness; lateness/～하다 delay; be put off; be late / 출발이 ～되다 be delayed in one's departure/오래 ～된 long-deferred. ちえん

**지열**(地熱) terrestrial heat; the heat of the earth. ちねつ

**지열**(止熱) ～하다 the temperature falls [goes down]; break a fever.

**지엽**(枝葉) ①《가지와 잎》 branches and leaves; branch and leaf ②《중요하지 않은 일》 unessentials; minor details／~문제 an off[a side] issue／~적인 unessential; minor.

**지옥**(地獄) hell; Hades; the inferno／~에 떨어지다 go to Hell／~ 같은 infernal; hellish／~과 극락 heaven and hell; Hades and Paradise.

**지완**(遲緩) slowness; dilatoriness; tardiness／~하다 (be) slow; slack; tardy.

**지용**(智勇) wisdom and courage; sagacity and valor／그는 ~을 겸비한 명장이다 He is a great general who combines wisdom with valor.

**지우**(知友) an intimate [friend]; an acquaintance.

**지우**(知遇) warm friendship; favour／~에 보답하다 requite *one's* patronage／~를 입다 enjoy the favour of *one's* acquaintance.

**지우개** an eraser; a wiper; a cleaner.

**지우다**¹ ①《등에》 put (*something*) on *a person's* back; saddle (*a person*) with; make *a person's* bear[carry] ②《부담시키다》 charge (*a person*) with (*a duty*); lay a burden upon (*a person*); lay (*a duty* upon *a person*); entrust (*a person* with *a task*)／책임을 ~ 《책임 전가》 shift the responsibility on to (*a person*).

**지우다**² 《없어지게 하다》 erase; wipe out; rub out; strike out／칠판의 글씨를 ~ erase[wipe out] the words on a blackboard.

**지우다**³ ①《형성하다》 form／그늘을 ~ cast shade upon; shade ②《눈물 따위》 shed; spill; drop ③《꽃 따위》 scatter; strew 《숨을》 expire; breathe *one's* last.

**지우다**⁴ 《이기다》 beat; get the better of; defeat; put (*a person*) to the worse／씨름에서 상대방을 ~ overmatch (*a person*) in wrestling.

**지우산**(紙雨傘) an oil-paper umbrella.

**지원**(支援) support; aid; backing／~하다 support; back up; bolster up／~을 청하다 ask (*a person's*) support; ask (*a person*) to support／~자 a supporter; a patron; a sponsor.

**지원**(志願) 《지망》 desire; application 《자진》 volunteering／~하다 desire for; volunteer for; apply for; volunteer *one's* service／입학을 ~하다 apply for admission[enrollment] to a school／~자 a written application／~자 an applicant; a volunteer; a candidate／~병 a volunteer.

**지위** a carpenter =목수(木手).

**지위**(地位) 《신분》 position; standing; station in life; status 《계급》 a rank 《직업》 a position; a post; a situation／사회적 ~가 높은 사람 a man of high social standing／~ 있는 사람 a man of position[rank].

**지위지다** ①《병으로》 get[become] thin[emaciated, weak, haggard] (from *illness*); lose flesh; be worn out／병으로 매우 ~ become worn out from illness ②《살림이 줄다》 decline; sink; be reduced; wane／가운이 지위지기 시작한다 One begins to sink in fortune.

**지유삼**(紙油衫) a raincoat made of oiled paper; a waterproof[coat].

**지육**(知育) intellectual training; mental culture／~에 치우치다 over-emphasize mental training.

**지은**(知恩) being grateful[thankful] to (*one for favour*).

**지은**(至恩) a great favour; an unforgettable debt of gratitude.

**지의**(地衣) 【식】 a lichen.

**지이**(地異) a convulsion of nature; a natural disaster.

**지인**(知人) an acquaintance／~ 관계 acquaintanceship.

**지일**(至日) 《동지》 the winter solstice 《하지》 the summer solstice.

**지자**(智者) a wise man; a man of wisdom; a sage 《총칭》 the wise／~ 불혹이다 A wise man knows his own mind.

**지자**(知者) a man of intelligence; a man of knowledge and experience.

**지자기**(地磁氣) terrestrial magnetism.

**지장**(支障) 《장애》 hindrance; impediment; obstacle 《불편》 inconvenience／~이 없으면 if it is convenient to you／~이 있다 be hindered; be prevented; be interrupted.

**지장**(指章) a thumb-print／~을 찍다 seal (*a document*) with the thumb.

**지저귀다** sing; chirrup; chirp; twitter／새가 지저귀는 소리 a bird's twitterings [chirpings].

**지저분하다** (be) dirty; slovenly; filthy 《난잡하다》 (be) untidy; disorderly／지저분한 거리 a dirty street／지저분한 방 a room in a mess.

**지적**(地積) acreage; the acreage of a lot.

**지적**(地籍) a land register／~도 a land registration map.

**지적**(指摘) pointing out; indication／~하다 point out; indicate／잘못을 ~하다 point out mistakes.

**지적**(知的) intellectual; mental／~ 생활 intellectual life／~ 감정 intellectual feelings.

**지전**(紙廛) a paper goods shop.

**지전**(紙錢) a note; a bill《미》 《지폐》 paper money; currency notes.

**지전류**(地電流) 【물】 an earth current.

**지절**(志節) principle and faith; integrity.

**지절**(肢節) a joint; an articulation.
**지절거리다** chatter; gabble; talk glibly〔volubly〕; rattle on; wag one's tongue.
**지점**(支點) ①《지레의》a fulcrum ②《건》a bearing.
**지점**(地點) a spot; a place; a position; a point／유리한 ~ a vantage point／예정한 ~ the intended spot.
**지점**(支店) a branch 〔office, shop〕／~을 내다〔설치하다〕 open〔establish〕 a branch office (in, at).
**지정**(知情) understanding〔knowing〕 a person's plight〔situation, position〕.
**지정**(指定) appointment; designation; assignment／~하다 designate; appoint; assign; name／~한 시간에 at the appointed hour／~ 상인 an authorized merchant; a purveyor／~일〔자〕 a specified date.
**지정**(至情) 《충정》 sincere feelings; deep affection 《정분》 deep friendship／~에 감동되다 be moved〔touched〕 by a person's sincerity.
**지정거리다** stop just a moment; loiter on the way; delay.
**지정 지미**(至精至微) utmost minuteness／~하다 (be) extremely minute〔fine, detailed〕.
**지정 지밀**(至情至密) utmost precision〔minuteness〕／~하다 (be) extremely minute〔precise, exact, detailed〕.
**지정학**(地政學) geopolitics／~상의 geopolitic; goepolitical／~자 geopolitician; geopolitist.
**지제**(紙製) ~의 paper〔-made〕; made of paper／~ 인형 a paper doll.
**지조**(志操) constancy; purpose; principles; fidelity／~가 굳다 have a firm purpose; be firm of purpose／~를 굳게 지키다 be true to one's principles／~가 약하다 be weak of purpose.
**지조**(地租) a land tax; the tax on land.
**지족**(知足) ~하다 be content〔ed〕 with; be satisfied with.
**지존**(至尊) His majesty 〔the Emperor〕; the King.
**지주**(支柱) a pillar; a prop; a stay; a support／~를 세우다 prop up; support; stay.
**지주**(地主) a landowner; a landholder／~ 계급 the landed class／대〔소〕~ a large〔small〕 landowner.
**지주**(蜘蛛) 《충》 a spider (거미).
**지중**(地中) ~의 underground; subterranean／~에 in〔under〕 the ground〔earth〕／~에 묻히다 be buried in the earth／~ 송전선 an underground transmission line.

**지중**(至重) ~하다 (be) very precious; very important.
**지지**(支持) support; maintenance; backing／~하다 support; uphold; stand by; hold; prop up／~자 a supporter; an upholder.
**지지**(地誌) a topography; a geographical description.
**지지**(遲遲) slowness; tardiness／~하다 (be) slow; lagging; tardy／~하게 slowly; languidly; tardily.
**지지난달** the month before last.
**지지난밤** the night before last.
**지지난번**(一番) the time before last.
**지지난해** the year before last／~에 two years ago.
**지지다** 《지짐질》 fry; frizzle 《머리를》 curl one's hair with heated tongs; singe one's hair.
**지지랑물** eavesdrops; the raindrop from the eaves.
**지지러지다** ①《움츠리다》 shrink 〔up〕; be quite unmanned (by); quail (before, at); wince under; cower ②《생물이》 weaken; grow weak〔feeble〕; be enfeebled.
**지지르다** ①《내리누르다》 press; weight ②《남의 의견을》 keep〔hold, pin〕 down; check; get under.
**지지리** very; awfully; exceedingly; terribly／~ 못 생기다 be very ugly.
**지지하다** (be) trifling; insignificant; trivial; worthless／지지한 일로 걱정하다 worry about trifles.
**지진**(地震) an earthquake; a shock 〔of earthquake〕／~의 중심 the epicentre; the seismic centre／~계 a seismograph; a seismometer.
**지질**(地質) the nature of the soil; the geology／~학 geology／~학상의 geological／~학자 a geologist.
**지질**(紙質) the quality of paper.
**지질리다** 《내리눌리다》 be weighted (by a stone); 《억눌리다》 be kept〔bepinned〕 down.
**지질지질** ~하다 (be) trifling; boring.
**지질펀펀하다** (be) even; flat.
**지질하다** ①《지루하다》 (be) boring; tedious; sickening ②《변변찮다》 (be) insignificant; trivial 《무가치하다》 (be) rubbish; worthless.
**지짐거리다** be rainy; rain off and on; be wet.
**지짐이** a stew／고기 ~ meat stew.
**지짐질** frying／~하다 fry.
**지참**(遲參) late attendance／~하다 come〔arrive〕 late; be behind time／~자 a late comer.
**지참**(持參) bringing／~하다 bring〔take〕 (a thing) with one; carry; fetch.

**지척**(咫尺) a very short distance; an inch/~지간(之間)이다 be very close; be within a foot.

**지척거리다** stagger; reel; wobble; shamble along/지척지척 tottering; reelingly.

**지천**(至賤) ~하다 ①(천하다) very humble[low] ②(많음) superabundant; superfluous.

**지청**(支廳) a branch office.

**지청구** ~하다 scold; rebuke.

**지체** lineage; family stock; pedigree; birth/~가 of good lineage/~가 낮은 of humble birth.

**지체**(肢體) the limbs and the body/~가 부자유한 lame; crippled.

**지체**(遲滯) delay; retardation arrear/~하다 delay; hold off; be overdue/마을 사람들은 세금을 ~없이 납부했다 The villagers paid their taxes without delay.

**지초**(芝草) a kind of iris; *Formes japonicus*〈학명〉.

**지촉**(紙燭) paper and candles.

**지총**(紙銃) popgun.

**지축**(地軸) the axis of the earth.

**지출**(支出) expenditure; expenses/~하다 pay; disburse; expend; defray/수입과 ~ revenue and expenditure; incomings and outgoings/~액 expenditure.

**지충**(地蟲) 【충】a grub; a ground beetle.

**지취**(志趣) aim; purpose.

**지층**(地層) a stratum(*pl.* strata); a layer.

**지치**(智齒) a wisdom-tooth.

**지치다**[1] (피로하다) be[get] tired; be exhausted/몹시 ~ be tired[worn] out; be used up; be dead tired/일에 ~ be tired from *one's* work.

**지치다**[2] (미끄름을) skate; glide; slide/얼음지치기 skating; sliding/얼음 지치러 가다 go skating.

**지치다**[3] 《소나 말이》 have a watery stool (지ril이다).

**지치다**[4] 《문을》 shut; close.

**지친**(至親) a very near relative 《관계》 near relationship.

**지침**(指針) 《자석의》a compass needle 《시계의》 a hand 《기계의》 an index; an indicator 《인도물》 a guide/생활의 ~ a guiding principle in *one's* life/~면(面) a dial.

**지침거리다** walk at a quick pace; mince *one's* steps.

**지칭**(指稱) designation/~하다 designate.

**지키다** ①(수호하다) guard; defend from [against]; protect; hold/나라를 ~ defend *one's* country/자기를 ~ defend *oneself* ②(고수하다)/③(감시하다) watch; keep watch on[over]/문을 ~ guard the door ④(이행하다) keep; abide by 《복종하다》 observe; follow (*to*); keep/약속을 ~ keep *one's* word; be faithful to *one's* promise ⑤(보존하다) preserve; keep/《유지》maintain/~체면을 ~ preserve[keep up] appearances.

**지탄**(指彈) ~하다 《손가락을 튀기다》fillip; flip; make a fillip 《배척하다》shun; send (*a person*) coventry; ostracize.

**지탱**(支撑) maintenance; support; preservation/~하다 keep [up]; maintain; preserve; support.

**지통**(止痛) ~하다 stop[relieve] the pain.

**지파**(支派) a sect; a branch; an offshoot.

**지팡이** a stick; a walking-stick; a cane/~에 의지하다 hang on[lean upon] *one's* stick.

**지편**(紙片) a piece[slip] of paper; a strip of paper.

**지평**(地平) ground level/~면[각] a horizontal plane[angle]/~선(線) the horizon; a horizontal line/~선상에 above the horizon.

**지폐**(紙幣) paper money; a [bank] note; a bill.

**지폭**(紙幅) the width of paper.

**지표**(指標) an index; 【수】a characteristic; 【의】an indication.

**지푸라기** a piece of straw.

**찌푸리다** 《날씨가》cloud over; get[be] cloudy 《얼굴을》frown; make a face; scowl/찌푸린 날씨 cloudy weather/눈살을 ~ knit *one's* brow.

**지피다** burn; make a fire; kindle/석탄 [장작]을 ~ burn coal[wood]/난로에 불을 ~ make a fire in the stove.

**지필**(紙筆) paper and pens[writing brushes].

**지하**(地下) ①(땅의 아래) ~의 underground; subterranean/~에 below ground/~도(道) an underground passage; a subway〈미〉/~ 운동 an underground movement[campaign]〈미〉/~ 자원 underground resources ②(저승) Hades; the nether world.

**지하철**(地下鐵) the snbway〈미〉; the underground railway〈영〉/~로 가다 go by subway/~역 a subway station.

**지학**(地學) physical geography.

**지함**(紙函) a carton; cardboard box.

**지함**(地陷) subsidence; depression; a cave-in; sinking/~하다 sink; be depressed; cave in.

**지핵**(地核) the nucleus[core] of the earth; the centrosphere.

**지행**(知行) knowledge and behaviour/~ 합일설 the principle that "to know and act are one and the same".

**지향**(指向) pointing/~하다 point to/~전파 beam.

**지향**(志向) intention; aim/~없이 aimlessly.

**지헌**(至賢) supreme sagacity ~하다 (be) very wise. きわめてかしこいこと

**지혈**(止血) stopping of bleeding; stanching/~제(劑) a hemostatic; a styptic/~대(帶) a tourniquet. しけつ

**지협**(地峽) an isthmus; a neck of land/~의 isthmian. ちきょう

**지형**(地形) topography; the lay of the land; natural[geographical] features. ちけい

**지형**(紙型) a paper mould; a *papier mâche* mould(F)/~을 뜨다 take a *papier-mâché* mould. しけい

**지혜**(智慧, 知慧) wisdom; sense; intelligence; sagacity/~있는 wise; resourceful; wise; sagacious/~가 나다 grow in wisdom/~를 짜내다 rack one's brains. ちえ

**지호**(指呼) beckoning/~하다 beckon (to a person)/~지간(之間)에 있다 be near at hand; be within call[hail]. しこ

**지화자** corresponding to hand clapping; a shout to mark time in accompanying singing or dancing. こりゃこりゃ

**지환**(指環) a ring ⇨반지. ゆびわ

**지황**(地黃) 〖식〗 the foxglove.

**지효**(知曉) thorough knowledge; conversance/~하다 have a thorough knowledge of.

**지효**(至孝) the utmost filial piety.

**지휘**(指揮) command; direction; orders; instructions/~하다 command; order; lead; direct 《악단을》 conduct/~관 a commander; a commanding officer/~자 a director; a leader 《음악의》a conductor 《응원단의》 a cheer leader/~봉 a baton.

**직**(職) 《일자리》 employment; work; a position; a job 《직업》 a calling; a trade; an occupation 《직무》 duties 《관공직》 an office; a post. しょく

**직**(直) ①《당번》 duty; watch; guard ② 《곧은》 straight; perpendicular; upright; direct. とうばん

**직각**(直角) a right angle/~의 rectangular; right-angled/~ 삼각형 a right-angled triangle / ~을 이루다 be at right angles (to). ちょっかく

**직각**(直覺) intuition; direct perception/~하다 intuit; know intuitively/~적으로 알다 know by intuition. ちょっかく

**직간**(直諫) personal admonition[remonstrance, reproof]/하다 reprove (a person) face to face. ちょっかん

**직감**(直感) intuition/~하다 perceive immediately/~적으로 intuitively; by intuition. ちょっかん

**직격**(直擊) direct hit/~탄 a directly hit ·/~탄에 맞다 be directly hit by a bomb.

**직결**(直結) direct connection; 《물》 direct coupling/~하다 connect directly with; link directly with/~ 발전기 a direct coupling generator. ちょっけつ

**직경**(直徑) 〖수〗 a diameter ⇨지름. ちょっけい

**직계**(直系) a direct line/~ 가족 family members in a direct line/~ 혈족 a lineal relation/~ 회사 a directly affiliated concern. ちょっけい

**직계**(職階) position-class/~ 제도 the job classification system.

**직고**(直告) ~하다 tell[reveal] the truth 《고백하다》 frankly confess.

**직공**(職工) a worker 《공장의》 an operative; a [factory, mill] hand/~장 a foreman. しょっこう

**직관**(直觀) intuition/~하다 intuit; know intuitively/~적으로 intuitively; by intuition. ちょっかん

**직구**(直球) 〖체〗 《야구》 a straight ball/~를 던지다 drive. ちょっきゅう

**직권**(職權) authority; official power/~ 외의 outside one's authority / ~을 행사하다[남용하다] exercise[abuse] one's authority. しょっけん

**직기**(織機) a loom; a weaving machine.

**직녀**(織女) ①《사람》 a woman weaver ② ⇨직녀성(織女星). しょくじょ

**직녀성**(織女星) 〖천〗 Vega; the Weaving Girl [Star]. しょくじょせい

**직능**(職能) function/~ 검사 performance test/~ 대표[제] vocational representation [system]/~ 조합 a craft union. しょくのう

**찍다** ①《도장을》 stamp; seal; set a seal (to); impress ②《인쇄하다》 print; put into print ③《점을》 mark (with a dot); point; dot ④《도끼 따위로》 cut; hew ⑤《구멍을》 punch ⑥《사진을》 [take a] photograph《자기가》: have one's photograph taken《남으로 하여금》 ⑦《액체를》 dip (a pen in). おす

**직답**(直答) a prompt[ready] answer [reply]; 《직접 답변》 direct[personal] answer /~하다 give a ready answer; answer offhand/나는 너의 ~을 들어야 하겠다 I would have your ready answer. ちょくとう

**직력**(職歷) one's business experience[career].

**직렬**(直列) 〖물〗 a series/~ 회로 a series circuit.

**직로**(直路) a straight road; a direct route. ちょくろ

**직류**(直流) ①〖물〗 direct current(略: D. C.); continuous current; series flow/~ 전동기 a direct current motor ②《물줄기》 a straight stream. ちょくりゅう

**직류**(直溜) straight distillation.

**직립**(直立) standing straight/~하다 stand erect[straight, upright]; 《높이》 rise perpendicularly. ちょくりつ

**직매**(直賣) direct sales/~하다 sell directly/~소 a direct sale depot[shop].

**직면**(直面) ~하다 face; be confronted by [with]; confront/지금 ~하고 있는 문제 problems that are now being faced

**직명(職名)** 《직업명》 [the name of] an occupation 《관공서의》 an official title. しょくめい

**직무(職務)** [a] duty; a function/~의 수행 performance of one's duty/~ 방해 interference with one's duty/~상의 official. しょくむ

**직물(織物)** cloth; a textile [fabrics]; woven stuff/~ 공업 textile industry/~류 drapery; soft goods. おりもの

**직봉(職蜂)** a working bee; a worker bee.

**직부(織婦)** a woman weaver. しょくふ

**직분(職分)** duty 《본분》 a sphere/~을 다하다 do one's best duty/교사의 ~ duties of a teacher. しょくぶん

**직사(直射)** 《포화의》 direct[frontal] fire 《일광의》 direct rays/~하다 fire direct (upon); shine directly upon/~포 a direct-firing gun. ちょくしゃ

**직사각(直四角)** a regular square.

**직사주의(直寫主義)** 《미·문》 literalism/~적인 literalistic/~자 a literalist.

**직삼(直蔘)** ginseng dried in its original shape.

**직상(直上)** ①《바로 위》 ~에 just[right] above ②《올라감》 ~하다 rise straight upward. ちょくじょう

**직석(直席)** impromptu. そくせき

**직선(直線)** a straight line; a beeline/~의 rectilineal; straight/~으로 in a straight line; straight/~을 긋다 draw a straight line/~ 거리 a lineal distance. ちょくせん

**직설(直說)** plain speaking; frankness/~하다 talk frankly; speak without reserve/~법 【언】 the indicative mood. ありのままのはなし

**직세(直稅)** a direct tax. ちょくぜい

**직소(直訴)** [make] a direct appeal/~하다 appeal directly. じきそ

**직소(直所)** a watchhouse; a guard box. しゅくちょくするところ

**직소(職所)** the place of one's work; one's office; one's post. しょくむにつとめること

**찍소리** a chirp; a tweet 《한마디》 a word; a single word; a syllable/~없이 without a word; without complaining; in silence.

**직속(直屬)** ~하다 be under direct control (of)/~의 under immediate[direct] control (of). ちょくぞく

**직손(直孫)** direct descendants. ちょっけいのしそん

**직수굿하다** obedient. くっぷくする

**직수입(直輸入)** direct importation/~하다 import (goods); direct/~ 무역 direct import trade/~품 direct imports. ちょくゆにゅう

**직수출(直輸出)** direct exportation/~하다 export (goods) direct. ちょくゆしゅつ

**직시(直視)** ①《바로 봄》 ~하다 look (a person) in the face; look squarely at (one) ②《의》 ~의 orthoptic. ちょくし

**직시류(直翅類)** 【충】 Orthoptera(학명).

**직신(稷神)** the god of agriculture.

**직신거리다** tease persistently for; importune. ねちねちとねだる

**직심(直心)** honesty; uprightness; straightforwardness. じきしん

**찍어당기다** hook and pull; hook in.

**찍어매다** stitch up; sew[patch] together.

**직언(直言)** direct speech; outspoken advice/~하다 speak plainly[bluntly, directly] to; speak out/~가 a plain-spoken[an outspoken] man. ちょくげん

**직업(職業)** an occupation; a job; a profession; a calling; a trade/~적 professional; vocational/~ 소개소 an employment agency[exchange]; a placement bureau/~ 학교 a vocational[trade] school/~ 의식 occupational consciousness /~ 여성 a professional[career] woman [girl]/~ 교육 vocational education[training]/~에 종사하다 follow an occupation[a calling); take up a career/~병 an occuptional disease. しょくぎょう

**직역(職域)** one's occupation[post]/~별로 by occupation group. しょくいき

**직역(直譯)** a literal[word-for-word] translation/~하다 translate literally[word for word]/~적 metaphrastic. ちょくやく

**직영(直營)** direct management[control] /~하다 manage[control, operate] directly. ちょくえい

**직원(職員)** the personnel; the staff 《한 사람》 a member of the staff/~ 명부 a staff register; a roster/~의 이동 a personnel change; a change in the staff/~록 a list of government personnel[officials]/~실 a faculty room. しょくいん

**직원주(直圓柱)** 【수】 a right cylinder. ちょくえんちゅう

**직원추(直圓錐)** 【수】 a right circular cone. ちょくえんすい

**직유(直喩)** 【언】 a simile. ちょくゆ

**직인(職印)** an official seal 《정부의》 a government seal. しょくいん

**직임(職任)** a function; a duty; a vocation.

**직장(直腸)** 【해】 the rectum/~의 rectal /~염 《의》 procititis. ちょくちょう

**직장(職長)** a foreman. しょくちょう

**직장(職掌)** the division of official duties; functions; duties/~상의 official; functional. しょくむのぶんしょう

**직장(織匠)** a weaver.

**직재(直裁)** a direct[prompt] decision/~하다 decide personally[immediately]. ちょくさい

**직전(直前)** ~에 just[immediately] before; just prior to/시험 ~에 just before the examination; on the eve of the examination. ちょくぜん

**직절(直節)** fidelity; integrity; loyalty.

**직접**(直接) direct[ly]; at first hand; straight; in person／〜적 direct; first hand; immediate 《자신의》 personal. ごうちょくなせつがい　ちょくせつ

**직제**(職制) office organization; service regulations／〜를 개정하다 revise the office regulations. しょくせい

**직조**(織造) weaving／〜하다 weave／〜소 a weaving shop; a textile mill.

**직종**(職種) a type of occupation. おりものをおること

**직직거리다, 찍찍거리다** keep dragging[scuffing] one's shoes. ずるずる

**직진**(直進) 〜하다 go right on; make straight for; make a straight drive[advance] on; go straight ahead.

**직차**(職次) position; the order of official ranks. しょくせきのじゅんばん

**직책**(職責) duty; functions／〜을 다하다 discharge one's duties／그는 〜을 완수하기 위해서는 어떠한 위험도 두려워하지 않는다 He was ready to face any danger to fulfill his responsibility. しょくせき

**직토**(直吐) 〜하다 tell the truth[fact].

**직통**(直通) through traffic; through[direct] service; direct communication／〜하다 communicate directly with; have a through[direct] service／〜 전화 a trunk call. ちょくつう

**직품**(職品) a position; the grades of official ranks. かんしょくのかいきゅう

**직필**(直筆) unbiassed writing／〜하다 write plainly (on matter); write in frank language. ちょくひつ

**직하**(直下) ①《아래》〜에 directly[just, right] under／적도 〜 right on the equator [line] ②《떨어짐》〜하다 fall perpendicularly; fall plumb down／급전 〜하다 make a rapid[swift] movement; take a rapid turn. ちょっか

**직하다**(直—) ①《바르다》(be) right; up right ②《고지식하다》(be) simple and honest; simple-minded; stupidly honest. どうりがただしい

**직할**(直轄) direct control[jurisdiction]; immediate supervision. ちょっかつ

**직함**(職銜) one's official title. かんしょくのな

**직항**(直航) a direct voyage 《비행기의》 a nonstop flight／〜하다 sail[fly] direct [straight] to[for].

**직행**(直行) going straight[direct]; 《바꾸어 타지 않고》 running straight through 《무정차》 going non-stop／사고 현장에 〜하다 rush right[straight] to the scene of the accident. ちょっこう

**직후**(直後) 〜에 immediately[directly, right] after／〜 직후 directly after the termination of the war. ちょくご

**진**(辰) the Dragon; the fifth of the 12 horary signs. たつ

**진**(津) 《나무의》 resin; gum 《담배의》 nicotine; tar／〜이 나오다 excrete resin／〜이 많은 gummy.

**진**(陣) 《진형》 a battle array; battle formation 《진지》 a position 《진영》 a [military] camp 《대열》 lines; ranks／〜을 치다 pitch a camp; encamp; camp; occupy a position. じん

**진**(眞) 《진리》 truth; reality; true; real 《진짜》 genuine. しん

**진가**(眞價) true[real] worth; true[intrinsic] value; true merit／〜를 발휘하다 prove one's worth／〜를 인정하다 appreciate (a person) as his true worth. しんか

**진가**(眞假) truth or falsehood; genuineness or spuriousness／〜를 조사하다 examine the genuineness of (an article). しんぎ

**진간장**(陳艮醬) thick soy.

**진갈이** tillage of fields right after a rainfall／〜하다 till fields right after a rainfall.

**진감**(震撼) a shock; alarm; fright／〜하다 shake; shock. しんかん

**진갑**(進甲) the 61st birthday; the sixty-first anniversary of one's birth.

**진강**(進講) a lecture in the Royal presence／〜하다 give a lecture in the Royal presence. しんこう

**진개**(塵芥) dust and dirt; rubbish; refuse. じんかい

**진객**(珍客) a rare guest; a welcome visitor. ちんきゃく

**진걸레** a wet scrub cloth; a wet mop; a wet floorcloth[house cloth].

**진격**(進擊) an attack; a drive; a charge／〜하다 attack; advance. しんげき

**진경**(眞境) the actual state of things; the actual facts of a case; the real condition[state]; 《경계》 the real borderline.

**진계**(塵界) the dusty world; this world. じんかい

**진공**(進攻) an attack ⇨진격(進擊). しんこう

**진공**(眞空) a vacuum／〜의 vacuous; hollow; empty／〜 방전 vacuum discharge／〜으로 하다 make (a thing) vacuous／〜 소제기 a vacuum cleaner. しんくう

**진공**(進供) presenting to the king.

**진과**(珍果) rare fruit. ちんか

**진과**(珍菓) rare sweets.

**진구렁** a mire; a muddy place; swampy ground／〜속에 빠지다 get stuck in the mud. ぬかるみのくぼち

**진국**(眞—) ①《국물》 undiluted liquor; genuine liquid ②《사람》 a man of sincerity.

**진군**(進軍) march; onset; advance／〜하다 march[advance] (on a place)／〜을 명하다 order the advance／〜 중이다 be on the march. しんぐん

**진권**(進勸) recommendation／〜하다 recommend; propose.

**진귀**(珍貴) 〜하다 valuable; highly-prized; precious. ちんき

**진금(珍禽)** a rare bird; an uncommon game.
**진급(進級)** promotion. しんきゅう
**진기(珍奇)** rarity; curiosity／~하다 (신기하다) new; novel (이상하다) uncommon (희귀하다) rare (기이하다) strange; queer; wonderful; quaint. ちんき
**진기(珍器)** a curious vessel. ちんき
**진기(振起)** ~하다 stimulate; stir up.
**진기(津氣)** stickiness; viscosity.
**진날** a wet day／~ 개 사귀기 meeting with an unpleasant and troublesome affair.
**진념(軫念)** Imperial solicitude[anxiety]. しんねん
**진노(震怒)** rage; violent anger; wrath／~하다 rage; fury into a violent anger. しんど
**진눈¹** sleet; wet snow. あめまじりのゆき
**진눈²** bleary eyes.
**진눈깨비** sleet／~가 내린다 It sleets. みぞれ
**진단(診斷)** diagnosis／~하다 make a diagnosis of; diagnose (as)／~서 a medical certificate／의사의 ~을 받다 consult a doctor; undergo a medical examination／건강 ~ a medical examination [checkup]. しんだん
**진달(進達)** delivery; forwarding; transmission／~하다 deliver; forward; pass on. しんたつ
**진달래** 《식》 the azalea. つつじ
**진땀(津—)** greasy sweat 《찬땀》 cold sweat. あぶらあせ
**진담(珍談)** an amusing story; news 《일화》 an anecdote. ちんだん
**진담(眞談)** serious talk／농담을 ~으로 듣다 take a joke seriously. まことのことば
**진답(陳畓)** deserted rice fields.
**진대** parasitism; sponging／~ 붙이다 parasitize; sponge. うるさくねだること
**진도(進度)** [the rate of] progress／학과의 ~ progress of classwork／~표 (학과의) a teaching schedule for the term; a progress chart. しんと
**진동(振動)** vibration; swing; oscillation／~하다 vibrate; oscillate; swing／~기(器) a vibrator; an oscillator／~수 the number of vibrations. しんどう
**진동(震動)** (지진 따위의) a shock; a tremor; a quake (폭발 따위의) concussion／~하다 shake; vibrate; quiver; quake／~을 느끼다 feel a shock. しんどう
**진두(陣頭)** the head of an army／~에 서다 be in the forefront (of)／~ 지휘하다 command at the head of (an army). じんとう
**진둥한둥** fussily; sedulously; busily. あたふた
**진드기** 《충》 a [dog] tick; a mite／~같이 달라붙다 fasten on (a person) like a tick. だに
**진득이** patiently; calmly; sedately 《위엄있게》 with dignity.
**진득진득** ~하다 (be) sticky; gluey; adhesive (먹같이) viscous (와나스처럼) tacky. ねばねば
**진득찰** 《식》 Siegesbeckia glabrescens (학명). こめなもみ
**진득하다** (be) quiet and serious; staid; dignified; sedate; calm／진득한 사람 a man of dignified presence. おちついている
**진디** 《충》 a plant louse; an aphid. だに
**진디등에** 《충》 a black fly; a buffalo gnat.
**진딧물** (부엌 같은 곳의) a cockroach. ありまき
**진력(盡力)** endeavour[s]; exertions; services; labours (알선) good offices／~하다 make an effort; endeavour; exert oneself (남을 위해) render (one) a service; use one's influence. じんりょく
**진로(進路)** a course; a way (태풍 따위의) a path. しんろ
**진료(診療)** medical examination and treatment／~소 a clinic／~하다 diagnose and treat／~를 받다 receive [medical] treatment; be treated. しんりょう
**진리(眞理)** [a] truth; a fact／~를 탐구하다 seek after [the] truth／보편적 ~ a universal truth／만고 불변의 ~ an eternal[a permanent] truth. しんり
**진맥(診脈)** examination of pulse／~하다 feel[take, examine] the pulse. みゃくをとること
**진면목(眞面目)** one's true character／~을 발휘하다 reveal[show] one's true character. しんめんぼく
**진멸(殄滅)** ~하다 annihilate; wipe out.
**진묘(珍妙)** ~하다 queer; funny; odd.
**진무(鎭撫)** pacification／~하다 pacify; placate; quiet. ちんぶ
**진묵(眞墨)** superior Chinese ink-stick.
**진문(珍聞)** (새로운) news (기담) a strange [curious] story (새로운 사실) a revelation. ちんぶん
**진문(陣門)** a camp gate. じんもん
**진물** [watery] secretions from a sore; discharge. できものからでるしる
**진물진물** ~하다 (be) sore; inflamed; ulcerated; septic (눈이) bleared. ぶよぶよ
**진미(珍味)** [a food of] delicate flavour; a dainty; a rich diet／해륙의 ~ the spoils of chase and net; all sorts of delicacies. ちんみ
**진미(眞味)** true taste. ほんとうのあじ
**진미(陳米)** old rice; long-stored rice.
**진발** muddy[dirty] feet[shoes].
**진배 없다** (be) as good as／새것이나 ~ be as good as new. かわりない
**진버짐** serpigo; ringworm／~이 난 얼굴 a serpiginous face.
**진범(眞犯)** the true culprit. しんはんにん
**진범인(眞犯人)** a real criminal[culprit]. しんはんにん
**진법(陣法)** disposition [of troops]; battle formation[array]. じんほう
**진보(珍寶)** a treasured article; a treasu-

re 《여러 가지의》 valuables.　ちんほう
**진보**(進步) progress; improvement; advance／ ～하다 progress; improvement; advance; make progress ／ ～적 의견 advanced views.　しんぽ
**진본**(珍本) a rare book.　ちんぽん
**진본**(眞本) 《책의》 the original copy 《서화의》 a genuine writing[painting].　しんぽん
**진부**(津夫) a ferrymaster; a ferryman.
**진부**(眞否) 《진상》 truth or falsehood; the real facts (of);《확실성》 accuracy／ ～를 확인하다 ascertain the reality; ascertain whether it is true or not.　しんぴ
**진부**(陳腐) platitude; commonplaceness; triteness ／ ～하다 (be) old-fashioned; commonplace; stale; worn-out／ ～한 생각 an old-fashioned idea.　ちんぶ
**진사** an one-eyed person ⇨애꾸눈이.　めっかち
**진사**(珍事) a rare incident; an odd event; a marvel.　ちんじ
**진사**(眞絲) silk thread.
**진사**(陳謝) an apology／ ～하다 apologize to (one) for; tender one's apology.　ちんしゃ
**진사**(塵事) worldly affairs.　けがたこと
**진사**(震死) death by lightning／ ～하다 be struck dead by lightning.　しんし
**진사**(進士) a person who has only passed the first examination for office.　しんし
**진사건**(珍事件) a mystery case; a rare event.　ちんじけん
**진사고**(珍事故) a rare accident; a [strange] mishap.　ちんじこ
**진산**(鎭山) a guardian mountain.
**진상**(眞相) the truth (of a matter); the actual facts／ ～을 말하다 lay bare the truth of a matter／ ～을 구명하다 inquire into the real state of affairs; get down to bed-rock.　しんそう
**진상**(進上) presentation／ ～하다 present (a thing) to (one); make[send] (one) a present.　しんじょう
**진서**(珍書) a rare book[volume]; a treasured book.　ちんしょ
**진선**(津船) a ferryboat; a ferry.　わたしぶね
**진선미**(眞善美) truth, goodness and beauty; the true, the good and the beautiful.　しんぜんび
**진설**(陳設) ～하다 prepare a table of eatables.
**진성**(眞性) 《처부 자질》 one's true character 《진짜》 genuineness ／ ～의 genuine (cholera).　しんせい
**진성**(眞誠) sincerity; single-minded devotion.
**진세**(塵世) this dirty world; the world; this carnal world.　じんせい
**진소위**(眞所謂) really; indeed; truly; in truth.　それこそ
**진속**(塵俗) the world; this earthly life;

this world.　じんぞく
**진출** ①《새옷》 clothes that have not been washed ②《모시옷》 ramie-cloth garments made in spring or fall.
**진솔**(眞率) sincerity; frankness; honesty／ ～한 simple.　しんそつ
**진수**(珍羞) a [choice] delicacy／ ～ 성찬 spoils of chase and net; all sorts of delicacies.　ちんきなしょくもつ
**진수**(眞髓) the essence; the quintessence; the soul; the gist.　しんずい
**진수**(進水) launching／ ～하다 be launched 《배가》 leave the ways 《배를》 launch a ship／ ～식 the launching ceremony／ ～대(臺) the launching platform[ways].　しんすい
**진숙**(振肅) strict enforcement[maintenance]／ ～하다 enforce strictly; regulate.　しんしゅく
**진술**(陳述) a statement; a declaration 《증언》 a testimony／ ～하다 state; give an account of; set forth; declare／ ～서 a [written] statement; a declaration／ 의견을 ～하다 set forth one's views.　ちんじゅつ
**진시**(趁時) at once ⇨진작.　まえもって
**진시**(眞是) truly; in reality; really.
**진신**(搢紳) court nobles; high officials; gentry; gentlefolks.
**진실**(眞實) truth; reality; fact 《성실》 sincerity／ ～한 true; sincere; real; faithful; honest／ ～하게[로, 히] truly; really; in reality; sincerely.　しんじつ
**진실성**(眞實性) fidelity; the authority (of a report); credibility ／ ～을 의심하다 doubt the truth[veracity] of (a report).　しんじつせい
**진심**(眞心) one's heart; one's true mind 《성심》 sincerity／ ～으로 from the bottom of one's heart; heartily; sincerely／ ～을 토로하다 speak out of one's heart; lay one's heart open to.　しんしん
**진심**(盡心) one's whole heart／ ～하다 give one's whole mind to; devote oneself to.　じんしん
**진알**(進謁) ～하다 be granted an audience.　こうきなひとにあうこと
**진압**(鎭壓) repression; subjugation／ ～하다 repress; subjugate; put down; quell／ 폭동을 ～하다 put down a riot.　ちんあつ
**진앙**(震央) the seismic centre.　しんおう
**진애**(塵埃) 《먼지》 dust; dirt 《쓰레기》 rubbish; garbage.　じんあい
**진액**(津液) juice 《나무의》 sap.　しんえき
**진언**(進言) advice; counsel 《제의》 a memorial; a suggestion ／ ～하다 advice; suggest.　しんげん
**진언**(眞言) sayings of Buddha.　しんごん
**진역**(震域) 《한국》 Korea.　しんいき
**진연**(塵煙) a cloud of dust; dust rising like a cloud.
**진연**(塵緣) worldly[earthly] connections [ties].　じんえん

**진열(陳列)** show; exhibition; display/~하다 place (*things*) on exhibition; display; exhibit 《배열》 arrange/~관[소] 《회화의》 a museum; gallery /~품 an exhibit/~중이다 be on view[display] /~장[실] a show-case[-room]. ちんれつ

**진영(陣營)** a camp; quarters/민주~ the democratic camp/전체주의 ~ the totalitarian camp. じんえい

**진영(眞影)** a portrait; a picture; a likeness. しんえい

**진옴** 《한의학》 watery itch; watery scabies.

**진완(珍玩)** a curious and valuable[a highly-prized] thing.

**진외가(陳外家)** one's grandmother's old home.

**진용(陣容)** battle array[formation]; 《인원》 personnel 《운동 경기단·내각 따위의》 a line-up.

**진운(進運)** progress; advance[ment]/세상의 ~에 따르다 keep pace[abreast] with the times; move with the times. しんうん

**진원지(震源地)** the seismic centre; the epicentre. しんげんち

**진위(眞僞)** truth or falsehood; authenticity; truth. しんぎ

**진의(眞意)** the ultimate purpose; one's real intention. しんい

**진의(眞義)** the true meaning[sense, significance]. しんぎ

**진인(眞因)** the real cause[motive, reason]/죽음의 ~ the real cause of a person's death.

**진일** scrubbing and washing; kitchen work.

**진일(盡日)** all day [long].

**진입(進入)** ~하다 enter; march into; make one's way into. しんにゅう

**진잎** vegetable leaves.

**진짜** a genuine[real, sterling] article; a real thing/~의 true; real; genuine 《인공에 대하여》 natural/~ 진주 a natural peal. ほんもの

**진자(振子)** 《물》 a pendulum. しんし

**진자리** ①《그자리》 the place; the spot/~에서 then and there; on that occasion; on the spot ②⇒진작. げんば

**진작** 《곧》 at once; immediately; directly 《더 빨리》 earlier/~ 말씀을 못 드려 죄송합니다 I apologize for not having said this before. まえもって

**진작(振作)** stimulation; rousing/~하다 promote; brace up. しんさく

**진작(眞斫)** oak firewood.

**진장(珍藏)** treasuring/~하다 treasure [up]. だいじにほぞんすること

**진상(陳醬)** aged soy-sauce.

**진장(振張)** 《증진》 promotion 《환기》 awakening 《진기》 enhancement 《고무》 rousing/~하다 awaken; promote; enhance; arouse. しんちょう

**진재(陳材)** long-stored dried medicinal herbs.

**진재(震災)** an earthquake disaster 《지진》 an earthquake/~로 전멸하다 be wiped out by an earthquake. しんさい

**진저리** 《떨림》 shivering; quivering; shuddering 《싫증》 detest; abhorrence; disgust/~나다 become [thoroughly] disgusted with[at]; detest; get sick of; be fed up with 《싫어하다》 abhor/~치다 shiver (with *cold*); tremble (for *fear*).

**진적(珍籍)** a rare book ⇒진서. ちんしょ

**진적(眞蹟)** the real relics[remains, ruins, vestiges]. しんせき

**진적(陳跡)** remains; ruins; relics.

**진전(進展)** development; progress/~하다 develop; [make] progress/연구에~을 보다 advance in one's studies/~이 빠르다 proceed rapidly; make a rapid progress. しんてん

**진절머리** disgust;dislike; aversion; repugnance/~나다 be sick of; be disgusted with; feel a repugnance to. おののき

**진정(眞正)** genuineness/~한 true; real; genuine/~한 사랑 true love/~한 학자 a scholar in the true sense of the word. しんせい

**진정(眞情)** ①《진의》 true mind[heart]; 《진실》 earnestness 《성심》 sincerity/~으로 true; earnest;sane; sincere/~으로 truly; in earnest; from one's heart; seriously/~을 털어놓고 이야기하다 have a heart-to-heart talk (with *a person*) ② 《참된 사정》 the real situation (*of*); the real state (*of*); the true picture (*of*). しんじょう

**진정(陳情)** a petition; an appeal/~하다 state the whole circumstances; petition; make representations/~자 a petitioner/~서 a [written] petition; a representation; a memorial. ちんじょう

**진정(鎭靜)** ~하다 calm down; be soothed; subside; be calmed/~제 a sedative; a tranquilizer. ちんせい

**진정(進呈)** presentation/~하다 give; present/~자 a presenter/경품 ~ premiums offered/무료 ~ a free gift. しんてい

**진종일(盡終日)** all day [long]; all through the day; from morning till night; throughout the day/어제는 ~비가 왔다 It rained yesterday from morning till night.

**진주(眞珠)** a pearl/양식 ~ a cultured pearl/인조 ~ an artificial pearl/~조개 a pearl oyster. しんじゅ

**진주(進駐)** advance; march/~하다 advance[march] into; be stationed; make an entry into/~군 the occupation forces[army]. しんちゅう

**진중(珍重)** ~하다 (be) valuable; precious; treasured/~히 여기다 highly esteem[value]; prize; treasure. ちんちょう

**진중(陣中)** ~에서 at the front; in camp

/~ 생활 camp life. じんちゅう

**진중**(鎭重) ~하다 (be) sedate; gentle; grave; reserved; imposing; dignified. しんちょうなこと

**진지** meal; rice/~ 잡수셨읍니까 Have you take your meal? ごはん

**진지**(陣地) a position; quarters; an encampment/~를 펴다 take up a position /~전 position warfare; position-war [operations]. じんち

**진지**(眞摯) seriousness; sincerity; earnestness/~한 serious; sober; sincere earnest/~하게 in earnest; seriously; earnestly. しんし

**진지러지다** 《움츠리다》 shrink [up]; quail (before, at); flinch; shudder (at the sight of). ちぢむ

**진진**(津津) ~하다 (be) full of (interests); tasteful/흥미가 ~하다 be full of interest. しんしん

**진집** an opening; a gap; a chink; an aperture; a crack. ほころび

**진찰**(診察) medical examination (진단) diagnosis/~하다 see (a patient); examine/~권 a consultation ticket/~시간 consultation hours/~실 a consultation room; an examining room/무료 ~ consultation free. しんさつ

**진참**(進參) attending (a banquet)/~하다 attend (a banquet); participate in; be present.

**진창** mud; mire/~길 a muddy road/ ~에 내던지다 throw (something) into the mud. ぬかるみ

**진척**(進陟) advance; improvement; progress/~하다 progress; headway; proceed; make good progress; advance. しんちょく

**진천 동지**(震天動地) ~하다 shake the sphere[earth and sky]; make the whole world wonder 《음향이》rend the air. てんちをゆりうごかすこと

**진체**(振替) change; transfer/~ 계정 a transfer/~ 저금 transfer savings. ふりかえ

**진출**(振出) drawing (a check); issue/~ 하다 draw; issue (a check, a bill)/~일 the date of issue. ふりだし

**진출**(進出) ~하다 advance; find one's way into; push[enter] into. しんしゅつ

**진췌**(盡悴, 盡瘁) the utmost exertion/ ~하다 devote all one's energies to; devote oneself to.

**진취**(進取) ~하다 progressive; pushing; enterprising/~의 기상 a progressive spirit; a spirit of enterprise. しんしゅ

**진취**(進就) making gradual progress[development]/~하다 progress gradually (in). だんだんとじょうじゅしていくこと

**진치다**(陣一) encamp; take up a position; pitch[form] a camp. じんをはる

**진칠**(進漆) varnishing the royal coffin/ ~하다 lacquer[varnish] the royal coffin.

**진탕**(一宕) to one's heart's content; freely; as one likes/~ 마시다 drink one's fill. あきるほど

**진탕**(震盪) shock; concussion/~하다 shake; give a shock/뇌~ 《의》concussion of the brain. しんとう

**진통**(鎭痛) alleviation[soothing] of pain /~하다 relieve the pain/~제 an anodyne; a pain-killer. ちんつう

**진통**(陣痛) labour pains; throes; travail /~을 느끼다 suffer throes (of childbed); feel pains. じんつう

**진퇴**(進退) advance or retreat 《처신》 one's course of action 《사임여부》 resignation or remaining in office/~를 결정하다 decide on one's course of action. しんたい

**진티** the cause (of a trouble); the start; the beginning. はたんのきんいん

**진펄** a bog; a marsh; a swamp.

**진폭**(振幅) 『물』 the amplitude [of vibration]. しんぷく

**진품**(珍品) a rare[priceless] article; a rarity. ちんぴん

**진피** pertinacity; persistence.

**진필**(眞筆) one's own handwriting; an autograph; a genuine writing/이것은 위필이냐 ~이냐 Is this writing forged or genuine? しんぴつ

**진하다**(津一) 《빛깔이》 (be) dark; deep 《국물 따위가》 thick; strong; heavy; rich/진한 차[커피] strong tea[coffee]. こい

**진하다**(盡一) 《없어지다》 be used up; become exhausted. つくす

**진학**(進學) entrance into a school of higher grade/~하다 enter a school of higher grade/~을 지망하다 apply for admission to a school of higher grade/ 대학에 ~하다 go on to university.

**진합 태산**(塵合泰山) Many a little makes a muckle., Many drops make a shower.

**진항**(進航) ~하다 steam [ahead]; proceed; head (toward); sail. しんこう

**진해**(震駭) fright; alarm/~하다 be greatly alarmed; be frightened; be startled. しんがい

**진해제**(鎭咳劑) a cough remedy[medicine]. ちんがいざい

**진행**(進行) progress; an advance/~하다 [make] progress; advance; make headway; go on 《기차 따위가》 move; run /~이 빠르다[느리다] make rapid[slow] progress. しんこう

**진헌**(進獻) presenting gifts to the king /~하다 present (gifts) to the king.

**진현**(進見) ~하다 be received in audience.

**진형**(陣形) [battle] formation; battle array/공격 ~ offense disposition.

**진호**(鎭護) safeguard/~하다 protect; guard; safeguard. ちんご

**진혼**(鎭魂) repose of soul/~곡 requiem.

**진홍**(眞紅) crimson; scarlet.

진화(進化) 《생물의》 evolution 《발달》 development/～하다 develop; evolve/～론 the theory of evolution; Darwinism/～적 evolutionary.
진화(鎭火) ～하다 extinguish; get under control; put out/불은 이윽고 ～되었다 The fire was soon put out[brought under control].
진황지(陳荒地) waste land; wilds.
진흙 《질척질척한》 mud; mire; dirt 《차진》 clay/～의 muddy; dirty/그의 옷은 ～ 투성이였다 His clothes were covered with dirt.
진흥(振興) promotion; development; encouragement; advancement/～하다 develop; grow 《조성하다》 promote; advance; forward; encourage/～책 measures for the promotion (of)/산업의 ～을 피하다 promote the development of industry.
질(帙) ①《책갑》 a folding case for books; a book-wrapper ②《한 벌》 a set of books /이 책은 다섯 권이 한 ～이다 This book is complete in five volumes.
질(膣) the vagina; the vaginal canal/～구[벽, 부] the vaginal opening[wall, region].
질(質) 《성질》 nature; character 《본질》 property 《품질》 quality 《기질》 temper; temperament; disposition 《종류》 kind; sort 《성분》 matter 《경향》 aptitude; propensity/～이 나쁜 bad; vicious; of bad nature/신경～ a nervous temperament/～로 말하면 in [point of its] quality/～을 향상시키다 raise the quality.
질겁하다 be appalled; be astounded; be frightened; be scared; start; take fright; be surprised; be startled/질겁해서 소리를 지르다 cry out in consternation.
질경질경 ～ 씹다 chew; masticate.
질경이 【식】 a [greater] plantain; a white man's foot-print.
질고(疾苦) suffering from illness; the pain of sickness; affliction; distress.
질고(疾故) sickness; illness; a disease.
질곡(桎梏) bonds; fetters; shackles/인습의 ～에서 벗어나다 free oneself from the fetters of convention.
질권(質權) the right of pledge/～ 설정자 a pledger[pledgor]; a mortgager/～자 a mortgage creditor; a pledgee/～을 설정하다 establish the right of pledge.
질그릇 unglazed earthenware; unglazed pottery/～의 unglazed.
질끈 tying tight; firmly/수건을 머리에 ～ 동여매다 wear[tie] a towel around one's head tightly.
질근질근 ①《꼬는 모양》 새끼를 ～ 꼬다 twist[make] a rope loosely ②《씹는 모양》 chewing; gnawing.
질금거리다, 찔금거리다 trickle; dribble; fall[run down] off and on/비가 ～ rain off and on.
찔끔하다 be startled; be alarmed; be intimidated; get struck with fear/나는 그의 말에 찔금했다 His words came home to me.
질급(窒急) ～하다 be greatly astonished ⇨질겁하다.
질굿이 ①《참는 모양》 patiently; forbearingly; with patience[forbearance]/모욕을 ～ 참다 bear firmly[suffer patiently] an insult ②《슬그머니》 [pulling] gently; softly/소매를 ～ 잡아당기다 tug gently at (a person's) sleeve.
질기(窒氣) suffocation/～하다 be suffocated ⇨질식(窒息).
질기다 (be) tough; stiff; rigid; stark 《씹기에》 hard to masticate/질긴 고기 tough meat.
질기둥이 《물건》 tough stuff 《사람》 man of tenacity; a tough fellow.
질기와 an unglazed roof tile.
질깃질깃, 찔깃찔깃 ～하다 (be) pertinacious; tough; tenacious.
질깃하다 (be) somewhat tough; stiff; rigid; stark; stubborn.
질나팔(一喇叭) an earthen trumpet.
질남비 an earthen pot.
질녀(姪女) a niece.
질다 《반죽·밥이》 (be) soft; watery 《땅이》 muddy; slushy; wet/밥이 너무 ～ The rice has come out too soft./진 길 a muddy road.
질동이 a clay[an earthen] jar.
질뚝배기 a large earthen[clay] bowl.
질둔(質鈍) clumsiness; stolidity/～하다 (be) stolid; dull; witted; slow-witted.
질량(質量) 【물】 mass; quantity of matter /～ 단위 a mass unit/～ 불변의 법칙 the law of the constancy of mass.
질러가다 take a shorter way; take a short cut; cut across (a field); 《모퉁이를 돌지 않고》 cut off a corner/질러가는 길 a shorter road.
질름거리다, 찔름거리다 brim over; flow over the brim 《조금씩 주다》 give bit by bit[little by little]/찔름찔름[찔름찔름] little by little; bit by bit; (by) piecemeal.
질리다¹ 《채이다》 be[get] kicked; get hit; be struck/엉구리를 ～ get a kick on the side.
질리다² ①《질력나다》 become disgusted with; get sick of/이 일에는 질렸다 I am fed up with this work. ②《파랗게》 turn pale; lose[change] color/무서워서 ～ be white with fear ③《기가》 cower; be

쬘리다 cowed; be overawed ④(물감이) dye unevenly／옷감에 물이 ~ A cloth get dysed unevenly. ⑤(값이 먹히다) take; cost／이 책은 200원이 찔렸다 This book cost me 200 won.　あきる

찔리다 be stuck; be pricked; be pierced／손을 가시에 ~ get a hand pricked by a thorn／스스로 돌이켜서 양심에 찔리는 바 없다 As I look into my heart, I have nothing to be ashamed of.　さされる

질문(質問) a question; an interrogation 《의회의》 an interpellation／~하다 question; quiz〈미〉; put a question to; ask (one) a question; interrogate／~자 a questioner; an interrogator／~서 a written inquiry; a questionaire／~에 대답하다[응하다] answer a question／연달아 ~하다 shoot question after question.　しつもん

질박(質樸, 質朴) simplicity ／ ~하다 (be) simple; simple and honest ／ ~한 풍습 simple manners.　しつぼく

질빵 a sling 《총의》 a shoulder belt ／ ~을 지다 have a backsack strapped across one's chest.

질벅거리다 (be) wet and soft; muddy／길이 매우 질벅거렸다 It was a very muddy walk.　どろどろする

질번질번하다 《살림이 넉넉하다》(be) wealthy; abundant; affluent.　ふくぶくしい

질병(一甁) an earthen bottle.

질병(疾病) a disease; a disorder; a malady／~의 예방 prevention of a disease.　しっぺい

질부(姪婦) the wife of a nephew.　おいのつま

질사(窒死) death from[by] suffocation／~하다 die from[by] suffocation; be suffocated[choked] to death.

질산(窒酸)【화】 nitric acid／~은 caustic silver; nitrate of silver／~염 a nitrate／아~ nitrous acid.　ちっさん

질색(窒塞)《몹시 싫음》disgust; detestation; abomination; abhorrence; dismay; shock／~하다 disgust; detest; loathe; abhor; be appalled; be shocked ／그런 짓은 ~이다 Such an act is abhorrent to my feelings.　ちっそく

질서(姪壻) the husband of a niece.　めいのおっと

질서(秩序) [public] order 《규율》 discipline《순차》system; method／~ 정연하게 in good order; in an orderly manner／사회의 ~를 문란케 하다 disturb public order／~가 어지럽다 be in disorder; be out of order.　ちつじょ

질소(質素) simplicity; plainness; homeliness／~하다 (be) simple; plain; frugal ／ ~하게 살다 live simply[plainly, frugally].　しっそ

질소(窒素) nitrogen／~ 비료 nitrogeneous fertilizer[manure]／산화~ nitric oxide ／석회 ~ nitrolime[calcium cyanamide].　ちっそ

질솥 an earthenware kettle.

질시(嫉視) jealousy; regarding with jealousy[dislike]／~하다 regard (a person) with jealousy; look on (a person) with jealous eyes／ ~를 받다 be regarded with ealousy.　しっし

질식(窒息) suffocation; asphyxiation; asphyxia／~하다 be suffocated; be choked; be asphyxiated／~시키다 suffocate; asphyxiate; choke ／ ~하여 죽다 be suffocated to death.　ちっそく

질실(質實) simplicity and sincerity ／ ~하다 (be) simple and sincere[honest].　しつじつ

질역(疾疫) 《유행병》 an epidemic 《페스트 따위》 a pestilence; a plague.　しつえき

질욕(叱辱) reproof; reproach; rebuke; reprimand／~하다 reprove; rebuke; reproach; rebuke; reprimand.　しかりののしること

질의(質疑) a question; an interrogation; an inquiry／ ~하다 question; inquire of; interrogate／~ 응답난 "Answers to Questions" column.　しつぎ

질의(質議) discussion; argument: debate／~하다 discuss; argue; debate.　しつぎ

질적(質的) qualitative ／~으로 양적으로 quantitatively as well as qualitatively; both in quality and in quantity.　しつてき

질주(疾走) a scamper; a scud; a scuttle; speeding／~하다 scuttle; scamper; scud; run at full speed; run like a shot; speed [away]／~하는 자동차 a speeding motorcar.　しっそう

질직(質直) simplicity and honesty／~하다 (be) simple[plain] and honest.　しっちょく

질질 ①(끄는 모양) trailingly; draggingly ②(흐르는 모양) dribbling; oozing／~ 끌다 drag; draggle 《미루다》 prolong; protract; drag on／오줌을 ~ 싸다 dribble urine／기름이 ~ 흐르다 ooze oil.

질질거리다 gad about; roam around; tramp.

질책(叱責) rebuke; reproof; reprimand; reproach／~하다 reprove; rebuke; reprimand; call (one) to task; scold／~을 받다 be reproved; be reprimanded; be called to task／그를 몹시 ~했다 I pitched into him《속》.　しっせき

질척하다 (be) wet and soft; muddy／반죽이 ~ dough is too wet and soft; dough is too gooey.　どろどろだ

질컥하다 (be) muddy; sloppy; (be) gooey; sticky.　どろどろだ

질타(叱咤) scolding ／ ~하다 scold; give (a person) a scolding.　しった

질탕관(一湯罐) an earthen kettle; an earthenware pot.

질투(嫉妬) jealousy／~하다 be jealous; regard (a person) with jealousy／~심 jealousy／~심을 일으키다 become jealous of (one)／그녀는 ~를 느꼈다 She felt

**질펀거리다** be sloppy; de muddy; slosh away; squish and squash. どろどろだ

**질펀하다** ①(넓편하다) be wide and flat ②(게으르다) (be) idle; indolent; lazy /질펀히 idly; indolently/질펀히 앉아서 이야기하다 talk while lolling in a chair.

**질풍(疾風)** a rushing wind; a gust; a gale; a hurricane; a violent wind; a squall/~같이 달아나다 flee on the wings of the wind. しっぷう

**질항아리** a clay [water-]jar.

**질호(疾呼)** shout; calling out / ~하다 shout; call out; yell/대성 ~하다 call out in a loud voice; vociferate. しっこう

**질환(疾患)** a disease; an ailment; trouble; a disorder; malady; a complaint.

**질흙** (진흙) mud (차진 흙) clay; potter's clay; unglazed clay. とうど

**짊어지다** ①(짐을) bear; carry[have] (something) on one's back (어깨에) shoulder ②(빚을) get[run] into (debt); incur (debts)/빚을 많이 ~ be heavily in debt ③(책임을) bear; assume; take upon oneself/책임을 ~ shoulder[assume] the responsibility. おう

**짐** ①(하물) a load; a burden (뱃짐) a cargo (기차의) goods; freight(미); (수하물) luggage; baggage(미); (부담) a burden; a charge/~을 싣다 load (a cart) /~을 풀다 unpack (a package) /~이 과중하다 be overloaded/~을 가볍게 하다 lighten the load ②(마음의) a burden / ~이 되다 be a burden to (one) /~을 든 기분이 나다 feel relieved. にもつ

**찜** a steamed[boiled] dish; hard-boiled food 《찜질》 fomentation/닭~ steamed chicken/삼치~ hardboiled bonitos. につめためもの

**짐(朕)** I; We/~의 Our. ちん

**짐구루마** a cart/~삯 cartage/~를 끌다 draw a cart/~군 a cart-puller[-man]. 

**짐군** a porter; a luggage porter (역의) a red cap(미). にもつをはこぶひと

**짐마차(一馬車)** a wagon; a cart; a dray.

**짐바리** a load on the packsaddle; a pack on a pack animal.

**찜부럭** petulance; ill humor; peevishness; fretfulness/ ~내다 be fretful; be touchy; be irritable; get cross. いらだつこと

**짐승** 《네발짐승》 a beast 《맹수》 a brute 《동물》 an animal/그 녀석은 ~만도 못한 놈이다 He is worse than a brute. けだもの

**짐자동차(一自動車)** a [motor-]lorry〈영〉; a truck; a van.

**짐작** guess; conjecture; inference; estimation 《판단》 judgment; discretion/~하다 guess; conjecture; infer; gather (from); judge/눈~ eye measure/손~ measuring roughly with one's hands/~이 가다 come to form an idea of. しんしゃく

**짐짝** a package; pack; a parcel; an item of freight[baggage]/~ 세 개가 있다 There are three pieces of luggage.

**찜질** fomentation; applying a poultice /~하다 foment; poultice; apply a hot [cold] pack to/얼음 ~ apply an ice pack. につめること

**짐짐하다** ①(맛이) (be) salty and untasty; tasteless; unsavoury; insipid ②(마음에) (be) weighing on one's mind; nervous. しょっぱい

**찜찜하다** feel constrained[embarrassed, awkward]; feel ill at ease; (be) uncomfortable. ちゅうちょする

**짐짓** on purpose; intentionally; deliberately/그는 ~ 모르는 체했다 He affected ignorance. わざと

**짐차(一車)** 《기차》 a goods wagon《van》; a freight car 《자동차》 a truck. かもつしゃ

**집¹** ①(사람의) a house; residence; a dwelling[-house]; a home/석조 ~ a stone house; a house built[made] of stone/쓰러져 가는 ~ a house ready to tumble down/~ 없는 사람들 houseless [homeless] people/~을 짓다 (남으로 하여금) have a house built ②(가족·가정) a home; a family; a household/ ~ 생각이 나다 get homesick; think of home/~에 안 일을 처리하다 manage one's family affairs ③(동물의) a nest; a home; a lie / 거미~ a cobweb / 개~ a kennel/벌~ a beehive ④(물건의) a case; a box; a protector/두꺼비~ a fuse box/칼~ a sheath; a scabbard ⑤(바둑의) a cross.

**집²** ①(아내) one's wife ②(정부·첩) a mistress/적은~ one's concubine. つま

**집³** juice =즙(汁). じゅ. しる

**-집(集)** collections (of writings)/단편 ~ collected short stories/수필~ a collection of essays. しゅう

**집게** [a pair of] tongs 《소형의》 pincers; nippers ⇒《펜치》pliers. やっとこ

**집게발** claws; chelae / ~로 집다 《게가》 nip with its claws. かになどのはさみのようなあし

**집게뼘** the length between extended thumb and index finger.

**집게손가락** the index finger; the forefinger; the first finger. しょくし

**집결(集結)** concentration; collection; assembly; building up/~하다 concentrate; mass; collect/~점 a concentration /대군을 ~하다 concentrate a large army. しゅうけつ

**집계(集計)** a total / ~하다 add[sum] up; total / ~표 a tabulation / ~를 내다 find the total of. しゅうけい

**집괭이** a domestic[pet, house] cat.

**집구석** within[around] the house; indoors/~에 박혀 있다 stay[keep] indoors; keep to the house; be stuck indoors. いえのなか

**집권(執權)** seizure of political power; coming into power／~하다 come into power; seize political power; take power. しっけん

**집권(集權)** centralization of power[authority]／~하다 centralize the power／중앙~ centralization of power; centralized authoritarian rule. しゅうけん

**집금(集金)** collection of money 《회계의》 bill collecting／~하다 collect money; collect bills／~다니다 go round bill collecting. しゅうきん

**집나다** ①a house is put on sale ②《바둑》 a nest is formed; a square is made.

**집념(執念)** concentration of one's attention; tenacity of purpose／~하다 concentrate one's mind; keep one's mind on; be intent upon. しゅうねん

**집다** ①《쥐다》 pick [up]; pinch／손으로 집어 먹다 eat with fingers ②《사이에 끼다》 pinch; nip; hold between ③《주워 가지다》 find; pick. つまむ

**집단(集團)** a group; a mass; a body／~이민 collective emigration／~폭행 mob violence／~수용소 a concentration camp／~으로 조직하다 collectivize. しゅうだん

**집달리(執達吏)** 《법》 a bailiff; a process-server. しったつり

**집대성(集大成)** achieving a synthesis; integration into a greater whole; summation／~하다 make a synthesis of; be comprehensive of; embrace; sum up; integrate. しゅうたいせい

**집도(執刀)** performance of an operation／~하다 operate; perform a surgical operation／~자 an operator／수술은〔해 부는〕김박사 ~로 행하여졌다 The operation was performed by Dr. Kim. しっとう

**집돼지** a [barnyard] pig.

**집뒤짐** a domiciliary search[visit]／~하다 search a house; make a domiciliary visit on (one) いえさがし

**집례(執禮)** an officiant; a master of ceremony.

**집메주** homemade soybean malt.

**집무(執務)** the performance of one's official duties; execution of one's business／~하다 work; attend to one's business; conduct business; beat one's desk／~요령 a guide to office routine／~시간 후 out of[after] office hours／~의 경험 experience in office routine／~시간중 면회 사절 "All visits declined during office hours". しつむ

**집문서(一文書)** a house deed; deed papers; a title deed／~를 잡히고 돈을 빌리다 loan money with the deed for security. いえのけんりしょ

**집물(什物)** household furniture and utensils; miscellaneous household goods.

**집배(集配)** collection and delivery／~하다 collect and deliver／편지 ~인 a postman; a mailman. しゅうはい

**집비둘기** a dove; a house[domestic] pigeon.

**집사(執事)** a steward; a manager 《교회의》 a deacon 《여자》 a deaconess. しつじ

**집산(集散)** reception and distribution／~하다 receive[collect] and distribute／~지 a collecting and distributing centre; a primary point. しゅうさん

**집산주의(集産主義)** collectivism／~의 collectivistic／~자 a collectivist／~화(化) collectivization／~화하다 collectivize. しゅうさんしゅぎ

**집성(集成)** gathering together into a systematic whole; collection; compilation／~하다 gather and form into; compile; collect. しゅうせい

**집세(一貰)** a rent; a house-rent; a rental／비싼〔싼〕 ~ a high[low] rent／밀린 ~ back rent; arrears of rent／~를 내다 pay (a sum) in rent; pay for the house／~를 올리다〔내리다〕 raise[lower] the rent.

**집속** the inside of the gate／~으로 들어가다 go into the house. いえのなか

**집심(執心)** steadfastness[tenacity] of purpose; devotion (to one's work)／~해서 공부하다 devote oneself to one's study. しゅうしん

**집안** ①《가족·친척》 a family; a household; a home; one's relatives[kin]; a clan／온 ~ the whole family; all the family／~싸움 a domestic quarrel; a family squabble[trouble]／~의 큰일 a matter of concern to the family／~의 수치를 밖에 드러내지 마라 Wash your dirty linen at home.／~식구 members of a household; a family ②《집 속》 the inside[interior] of a house／~일 a house work／~의 공기 the indoor air／~을 치우다 clean the house up／~에 들어박이다 remain indoors. かぞく

**집안사람** ①《아내》 my wife／~으로부터 안부를 전해 달라고 합니다 My wife asks to be remembered to you. ②《살붙이》 one's folks／우리 ~들 my folks. つま

**집안심부름** odd jobs for a family; domestic chores／~하다 do odd jobs for a family[in one's home]; do domestic chores; aid domestic affairs.

**집알이** a courtesy visit to a newly-moved family／~하다 make the first visit on (a person's) new house; visit (a person's) new house for the first time.

**집약(集約)** ~하다 integrate; be intensive／~적 intensive／~적 방법 an intensive method／~ 농업[어업] intensive agriculture[fishery]. しゅうやく

**집어먹다** ①《음식을》 eat with one's fingers ②《착복하다》 pocket; embezzle／대금을 ~ pocket[peculate] a large sum／공금을 ~ embezzle public money; divert public money into one's own pocket.

**집어삼키다** 《먹다》 pick up and swallow; drink in 《가로채다》 usurp; make off with; swipe; embezzle; seize upon／한 입에 꿀꺽 ~ gulp down; swallow at one gulp／공금을 ~ embezzle public funds／남의 재산을 ~ seize upon, (a person's) property disposess (a person) of his property. つまみくいする

**집어세다** ①《막 먹다》 eat greedily; eat ravenously; eat away with a savage appetite ②《닥달하다》 urge; reproach severely; give a good scolding; carp at. たいしょくする

**집어치우다** 《중지하다》 stop (doing); cease (to do, doing); discontinue; leave off; bring a matter to an end 《단념하다》 give up; abandon 《사직하다》 resign; quit／일을 ~ lay aside one's work; leave off one's work／이야기를 ~ leave off talking; drop the subject／공부를 ~ give up one's studies／회사를 ~ leave (the service of) the company; resign from office. とちゅうでやめてしまう

**집오리** 〖조〗《총칭 또는 암컷》 a [domestic] duck 《수컷》 a drake／~가 운다 A duck quacks.

**집요**(執拗) obstinacy; persistence; pertinacity; tenacity／~하다 (be) obstinate; stubborn; persistent; tenacious／~하게 stubbornly; obstinately; tenaciously; persistently／~한 반항 stubborn resistance／~한 질문 inveterate[tenacious] questions. しつよう

**집임자** the owner of a house; a landlord; a house owner. おおや

**집적**(集積) accumulation; pile／~하다 accumulate; conglomerate.

**집적거리다** 《참견하다》 meddle (with); dabble; have a finger (in); poke one's nose (into); 《건드리다》 tease; make a nuisance of oneself; provoke／남의 일에 ~ meddle with (a person's) business; poke one's nose into (a person's) affairs／사람을 ~ needle[provoke] a person／자신없는 일은 직접거리지 않는다 I do not attempt a task I don't feel equal to.／집적집적 《건드림》 teasingly; needling; razzing 《참견》 meddling; dabbling. なんでもかんでもてをつける

**집정**(執政) administration／~자 an administrator; a dictator／~하다 hold the power of state; govern; administrate. しっせい

**집주**(集注) concentration; converging; focusing; riveting／~하다 concentrate; focus; converge／목적에 전력을 ~하다 bring all one's energies to bear on one's object. しゅうちゅう

**집주**(集註) a variorum adition.

**집주름** a house broker; a house agent. いえのちゅうかいにん

**집주인**(一主人) 《임자》 the owner of a house; a landlord[landlady]; 《가장》 the head of a family; the master of a house. おおや

**집중**(集中) concentration／~하다 concentrate; centralize; centre／정력의 ~ concentration of energy／주의를 ~하다 concentrate one's attention (on)／나는 공부에 전력을 ~한다 I focus[concentrate] all my energies on the study.／논의는 한 점으로 ~됐다 The discussion centred round one point.／~ 포화 a concentrated fire／~ 폭격 saturation bombing. しゅうちゅう

**집진기**(集塵器) a dust collector.

**집찔하다** (be) saltish 《못마땅하다》 unsatisfactory; disagreeable. しょっぱい

**집집** every door; each and every house; house after house／~이 from door to door; in every house; at every door; ~마다 at every door; from door to door. いえごと

**집착**(執着) 《애착》 attachment 《고집》 tenacity; persistence／~하다 cling[stick, hold fast] to; be excessively attached to; yearn after／~력 stickiness; adhesiveness／~심 tenacity of purpose; attachment／그는 일을 시작하면 완성할 때까지 ~하는 성질이다 He will stick to his task until it is finished. しゅうちゃく

**집찰계**(集札係) a ticket collector.

**집채** a house; a building／~같다 be as large as a house; be of great size [bulk]／~ 같은 파도 a billow; a big[giant] wave. いえ

**집치장**(一治粧) the interior decoration of a house／~하다 decorate [the interior of] a house; do the interior decorating／~이 좋다 be nicely decorated.

**집탈**(執頃) fault-finding; picking flaws／~하다 find fault (with); pick holes[a hole] (in); cavil at another's faults.

**집터** a house site; a lot／~를 닦다 level a site for a house／~를 사다 buy a lot for a building／~ 서리 the spare space around a house[building]. いえのしきち

**집필**(執筆) writing／~하다 write; pen／잡지에 ~하다 write for a magazine／~료 payment for writing／~자 the author; the writer. しっぴつ

**집하**(集荷) gathering of goods／~하다 gather goods; collect cargos.

**집합**(集合) a gathering; a meeting; an assembly; a group／~하다 gather; collect; assemble; congregate／군대를 ~시키다 gather an army／우리는 정거장에 집합하기로 되어 있다 We are to meet at the station.／~ 나팔 a muster call／~ 명사 〖언〗 a collective noun／~ 시간 a meeting hour of meeting／~ 장소 a meeting place; a rendezvous. しゅうごう

**집해**(集解) a collection of commentaries; a variorum edition.

**집행**(執行) execution; enforcement; performance; conduct／~하다 execute; enforce; carry out; carry into effect 《거

**집행하다)** hold/직무를 ~ perform[discharge] one's duties/형을 ~하다 execute a sentence/장례를 ~하다 hold a funeral/~ 기간 the term of execution/~ 기관 an executive organ[body]/~ 수속 execution formalities/~ 영장[명령] a write[an order] of execution/~자 an executor/~ 처분 an execution measure.　しっこう

**집행 유예(執行猶豫)** probation 《일시적 연기》 a stay of [an] execution; respite 《판결》 a suspended sentence/ ~하다 place (a person) on probation; allow (a person) to go on probation 《일시적으로》 grant (a person) a stay of execution.　しっこうゆうよ

**집형(執刑)** the execution of a sentence/~하다 execute a sentence.
　けいをしっこうすること

**집회(集會)** a meeting; an assembly; a gathering/~하다 meet together; gather; assemble/~소 a meeting place; an assembly-hall/~의 자유 freedom [liberty] of assembly/불법 ~ an unlawful assembly.　しゅうかい

**집히다** get picked up; be held between one's fingers; can be held in one's hand /바늘이 잘 집히지 않는다 The needle is hard to pick up. /손에 집히는 대로 먹다 eat anything one can put his hands on.　はさまれる

**짓** 《행위》 doing; an act (of behavior); conduct; a motion/눈~ a sign with the eyes; a look/이건 누가 한 ~이냐 Who has done it?, Who is the author of the mischief?　こうい

**짓거리** 《흥에 겨운》 an act[a gesture] out of merriment 《짓》 an act; a deed; a doing.

**짓궂다** (be) annoying; harassing; troublesome/짓궂게 조르다 insist on [having] importune.　あくしつだ

**짓다**¹ ⇨별항 참조.

**짓다**² 《유산하다》 miscarry; abort/아기를 ~ have a miscarriage.こをりゅうざんする

**짓둥이** behaviour; deportment; demeanour; conduct.　まねるさま

**짓마다** break to pieces; beat hard; smash/그릇을 ~ smash plates to pieces.　こなごなにこわす

**짓먹다** eat [have] one's fill; eat stomach full 《과식하다》 over-eat (oneself); have the bellyful of.　やたらにたべる

**짓무찌르다** 《치다》 defeat; beat; rout; smash; crush down 《죽이다》 slaughter; massacre.　おしつぶす

**짓밟다** trample down; tread upon 《유린하다》 ravage/인권을 ~ infringe upon human rights/민의를 ~ override the wishes of the people.　やたらにふむ

**짓씹다** chew thoroughly; masticate; crush with the teeth.　がりがりとかむ

**짓이기다** ①《반죽하다》 knead (flour); mix up ②《칼로》 mince; chop up; hash/감자를 ~ mash potatoes.　よくなれさせる

**짓적다** be ashamed (of oneself).
　はずかしい

**짓찧다** 《곡식 따위를》 pound (rice); pulverize; crush down 《이마 따위를》 strike; hit; bump (one's head) against (the wall)/고추를 절구에 ~ pulverize red pepper in a mortar.

**징**¹ 《악기》 a gong.　どら

**징**² 《구두의》 a hobnail; a clout nail/구두에 ~을 박다 put[get] heel and toe plates on one's shoes.

**징거두다** ①《꿰매다》 tack; baste; stitch slightly ②《준비하다》 prepare; make arrangements (for); get ready (for); provide for[against].

**징건하다** feel heavy on the stomach/음식이 너무 기름져서 속이 좀 ~ The dinner was so rich that I feel stuffy.
　しょうかしないではらがはる

**징걸이** a shoemaker's jack.

**징검다리** stepping-stones/실패를 성공에의 ~로 하여라 Make your failure a stepping-stone to success.　とびいし

**징검징검** 《꿰매는 모양》 sewing loosely 《걷는 모양》 striding; with long stride/~ 꿰매다 sew loosely/~ 걷다 stride; stalk; walk with long steps.
　ぽつんぽつんと

**징경이** 《조》 the osprey; the fish hawk.

**징계(懲戒)** a disciplinary punishment; discipline/~하다 punish for delinquency/~ 파면 a disciplinary dismissal/~ 처분 a disciplinary measure/~ 위원 a disciplinary committee.　ちょうかい

**징그다** tack; baste; sew loosely[with long stitches].

**징그럽다** (be) crawly; creepy; repulsive hideous/징그러운 광경 a repulsive sight.　むごい

**찡그리다** make a wry face; frown; scowl; make a grimace/그는 말을 하지 않고 얼굴만 찡그렸다 He made no reply, but simply scowled.　かおをしかめる

**찡긋거리다** wink at; warn by knitting brows; twist[wrinkle] one's face at (a person).　かおやめであいずする

**찡기다** be crumpled; be rumpled; be wrinkled; be creased.　もみくちゃになる

**징두리** the foundation[lower part] of a house.　かべのかぶ

**징모(徵募)** enlistment; recruiting/~하다 recruit; raise/강제 ~대(隊) a pressgang.　ちょうぼ

**징발(徵發)** levy; requisition; commandeering 《말꼬이 따위의》 forage/~하다 commandeer; press into service/~대 a foraging party/~되다 be placed under requisition.　ちょうはつ

**징벌(懲罰)** discipline; punishment; chastisement/~을 동의하다 make a motion for disciplinary measures (against a person)/~ 위원회 a disciplinary committee.　ちょばつ

**징병(徵兵)** conscription; draft; [compulsory] military service; enlistment/사람) a conscript/~ 검사 a physical examination for conscrpition/~ 기피 evasion of conscripiton/~을 면제받다 be exempted from military service. ちょうへい

**징세(徵稅)** the levy of taxes; tax collection/~하다 collect taxes; levy[impose] taxes upon/~리(吏) a revenue official; a tax-collector.

**징수(徵收)** collection; levy/~하다 collect; levy; charge; assess; impose (on)/세금을 ~하다 collect taxes/부가 ~하다 levy additional [taxes]; collect additional dues[fees]/~제 a collection unit. ちょうしゅう

**징악(懲惡)** reproval of vice; chastisement for evil-doing/~하다 chastise vice; punish the wicked. ちょうあく

**찡얼거리다** (불평하다) grumble; murmur; complain (어린아이가) whimper; whine; be fretful. むずかる

**징역(懲役)** penal servitude; imprisonment with[at] hard labour/~하다 serve time[a prison term]/무기 ~ penal servitude for life/유기 ~ penal servitude for a term. ちょうえき

**징역살이(懲役—)** a life behind bars; a prison life/~하다 serve time; be doing penal servitude. ちょうえきぐらし

**징용(徵用)** drafting; commandeering/~하다 draft; commandeer/~령 the Personal Service Drafting Law/~자 draftees. ちょうよう

**징장구** a gong and a drum. どらとたいこ

**징조(徵兆)** symptoms; an indication; a foreboding/뇌염이 만연할 ~가 보인다 The sleeping sickness shows signs of spreading./열이 있는 것은 병의 ~다 Fever indicates illness. ちょうちょう

**징집(徵集)** ①(징모) levy; enlistment; recruitment/~하다 levy; enlist; recruit; call up[out]; muster/~연기 postponement of enlistment ②(수집) collection; gathering. ちょうしゅう

**찡찡거리다** (불평하다) grumble (at); complain (of); murmur (at, against); whimper/대우가 나쁘다고 ~ complain of ill treatment. ぐずぐずいう

**찡찡이** a person who sounds odd because of a nasal polyp. はなのかけたひと

**찡찡하다** (겸연쩍다) (be) awkward; uncomfortable (코가 막혀) stuffy; blocked; clogged. ふあんにおもう

**징청(澄淸)** clearness; limpidity; lucidity/~하다 (be) clear; limpid; lucid; serene. すんできれいなこと

**징치(懲治)** correction; castigation; chastisement; discipline/~하다 correct; chastise. ちょうじ

**징후(徵候)** 《병의》 a symptom 《일반적》 a sign; an indication; a foretoken; an omen/구름은 비의 ~다 Clouds are signs of rain. ちょうこう

**찢기다** get[be] torn/갈기갈기 ~ be to-

---

## 짓 다

①《만들다》 make; manufacture/옷을 ~ have a suit made/구두를 ~ (자기가) make shoes (시켜서) have one's shoes made.

②《건조하다》 build; construct; make/벽돌로 지은 집 a brick house; a house built of brick/집을 ~ build (oneself) a house/새가 집을 지었다 The bird build a nest.

③《작성하다》 write; compose; make/시를 ~ compose a poem/작문을 ~ write a composition/그는 여덟 살 때 시를 짓기 시작했다 He began to compose a poem when he was eight years old.

④《열을》 form; make; constitute/원을 지어 in a circle/열을 지어 in line/열을 짓다 form a line[queue]; line up; draw up.

⑤《재배·경작》 cultivate; grow; raise; farm; rear/벼농사를 ~ grow[raise] rice; till a rice-field/이 곳에서는 밀농사를 많이 짓는다 Here much wheat is grown.

⑥《죄를》 commit; be guilty (of)/죄를 ~ commit a crime 《도덕상의 죄》 commit a sin/그는 죄를 지었다 He is guilty of the crime./벌이 무서워서 죄를 짓지 않는 자가 많다 The fear of punishment deters many people from crime.

⑦《표정 따위를》 show; express; look (glad, sad)/미소를 ~ smile; wear[put forth] a smile/슬픈 표정을 ~ take on a sad look.

⑧《밥을》 boil 《약을》 prepare; compound (medicines); 《처방에 의해서》 fill a prescription/밥을 ~ boil rice; cook rice/저녁을 ~ prepare[cook] supper/약을 ~ prepare medicine; make up[fill] a prescription.

⑨《허구》 make up; invent; fabricate/지어낸 이야기 a made-up[an invented] story; story; an invention

⑩《결말 따위》 settle; solve 《사물이 주어》 come to a settlement/양국간의 국경 문제는 원만히 해결지어졌다 The problem about the boundary between the two countries has come to a peaceful settlement.

rn to ribbons/그 여자의 마음은 슬픔으로 갈기갈기 찢겼다 Her heart was rent with grief. やぶられる

**짖다** ①**(개가)** bark **(늑대가)** howl/짖는 소리 **(개의)** a bark **(늑대의)** a howl/그 놈은 모르는 사람만 보면 짖는다 He barks at a stranger. ②**(까막까치가)** caw; croak/까마귀가 짖는다 A crow caws[croaks]. ほえる

**찢다** tear; rend; split; cleave/편지를 갈기갈기 ~ tear a letter to pieces. やぶる

**찢뜨리다** **(무심히)** tear apart (by *accident*); rip up; leave in ribbons; shred. やぶる

**찢어발기다** tear to threads[pieces]. ひきさく

**찢어지다** be rent; be torn/가슴이 찢어지는 듯한 heart-rending[-aching]/잘 ~ tear easily. さける

**질다** **(빛깔이)** (be) dark; deep **(초목이)** thick/짙은 안개 a dense fog/짙게 화장하다 powder *one's* face thick. こい

**질푸르다** (be) deep blue.

**짚** straw/밀~ wheat straw/밀~ 모자 a straw hat/~을 묶다 tie up straw in sheaves わら

**짚가리** a rick; a stack of straw.

**짚나라미** shredded bits of straw.

**짚다** ①**(맥 따위를)** feel; take; examine/열이 있나 이마를 짚어 보다 feel *one's* forehead to see if *one* has fever ②**(지팡이를)** use; carry/지팡이를 짚고 걷다 walk with a cane[stick] ③**(짐작하다)** figure (*out*); guess; count on the fingers/달수를 ~ count the months on *one's* fingers ④**(손을 받치다)** put; rest/책상 위에 팔꿈치를 ~ rest *one's* elbows on the desk. はかる

**짚동우리** a straw basket.

**짚뭇** a bundle of straw. わらたば

**짚북더기** a scattered heap of straw. わらのかたまり

**짚불** straw fire/~을 피우다 make fire with straw.

**짚수세미** a straw scrubbing-brush; a scrub brush made of straw. わらのたわし

**짚신** straw-shoes[-sandals]/~을 삼다 make straw sandals. わらじ

**짚자리** straw mat/~를 짜다 weave a straw mat. わらのござ

**짚재** straw-ashes; ashes from burnt straw. わらばい

**찧다** **(곡식을)** pound (*rice*); hull; husk; ram/절구에 쌀을 ~ pound rice in a mortar/엉덩방아를 ~ come down flop on *one's* buttock. つく

**차**(茶) 《음료》 tea 《녹차》 green tea 《홍차》 black tea 《커피》 coffee 《나무》 a tea plant 《잎》 tea-leaves／~를 끓이다 make[prepare, fix] tea／~를 따르다 pour tea into a cup／~를 한 잔 마시다 take [drink] a cup of tea／진한[엷은] ~를 좋아한다 He likes his tea strong[weak].／~ 그릇 a tea set／찻숟가락 a teaspoon／~·주전자 a teapot [stand]. ちゃ

**차**(車) 《일반적으로》 a vehicle 《자동차》 a [motor-]car; an automobile; a truck 《차량》 a [railway] carriage 《화차》 a freight car／자가용~ a car of one's own／~로 가다 go by car[train]／~로 나르다 carry (goods) in a car[truck]／~ 사고 vehicular accidents／~삯 fare; hire／화~ a freight car／자, ~를 탑시다 Well, let's get into the car. くるま

**차**(此) 《이것》 this; these; present／~제 (際)에 now; on this occasion／~로써 보면 in view of these facts.

**차**(差) 《차이》 difference 《불일치》 disparity; inequality 《변화》 variation 《차별》 discrimination 《잉여》 the remainder 《간격의》 balance／품질의 ~ difference in quality／연령의 ~ disparity in[of] age／임금의 ~ wage differentials／~가 있다 differ from; there is a difference from／빈부의 ~가 심하다 There is a big gulf between the rich and the poor.／그들 간에는 천양지~가 있다 They are as like as chalk and cheese. さ

**차**(次) ①《계제》 on the point[verge] of (doing); by the way／시장에 갔던 ~에 아주머니 집에 들렀다 I called at my aunt's on my way to the market. ②《다음의》 next; the following; below／~기 next term／~장 a vice-chief; a deputy chief／~석 the next seat 《관리 따위》 an official next in rank; an assistant 《수상자》 the runner-up ③《목적》 for the purpose of; with the intention of; so that／인사 ~ 내방하다 pay a courtesy call[visit]; come to pay one's respects／사업 ~ 홍콩에 갔다 He went to Hong Kong for his business. ④《순서》 order; sequence 《수학의》 degree／1~ 방정식 a simple equation; an equation of the first degree／수삼 ~ 읽다 read several times／1~ 시험에 합격했다 He passed the primary examination. ついでに

**차가**(借家) ①《빌어든 집》 a rented[hired] house ②《빌어들기》 renting／~하다 rent a house／~인 a tenant／~료(料) a house-rent. しゃくや

**차가다** carry off; snatch away; run away with 《유괴하다》 kidnap／매가 병아리를 차갔다 An eagle swooped down upon a chicken and snatched it away.／날치기는 부인의 손에서 지갑을 차갔다 The thief snatched away the purse in a lady's hand. つかみさる

**차간**(車間) a train[streetcar] compartment.

**차깔하다** 《문을 ~ close[shut] a door securely.

**차감**(差減) ~하다 strike a balance; balance／~을 계산하다 balance [an account]; offset; strike a balance／~ 잔액 a balance／손익을 ~하다 balance the profit and loss.

**차갑다** (be) cold; chilly／차가운 날씨 cold [chilly] weather／얼음처럼 ~ be as cold as ice; be ice-cold. つめたい

**차꼬** a foot-cangue; shackles; fetters／~를 채우다 put (a person) in fetters／그는 ~를 차고 있다 He has fetters on.

**차고**(車庫) 《자동차의》 a garage 《전차의》 a car shed[barn]; 《기차의》 a train depot／전차를 ~에 넣다 house tram cars／자동차를 ~에 넣다 put a car into a garage; garage [a car]. しゃこ

**차고음**(次高音) 《음》 mezzo-soprano. じこうおん

**차곡차곡** in orderly fashion; neatly squarely; one after another／옷을 ~ 개다 fold [up] clothes neatly／~ 문제를 풀다 solve a problem step by step[systematically]. きちんきちんと

**차관**(次官) a vice-minister; an undersecretary〈영〉; an assistant secretary〈미〉／문교부 ~ the Vice-Minister[Deputy Minister] of Education／사무 ~ a permanent vice-minister. じかん

**차관**(借款) a loan／~을 신청하다 apply [ask] for a loan／~을 체결하다 contract a loan／~ 협정 a loan agreement／공공[재정] ~ a public[financial] loan／장기[단기] ~ a long[short]-term loan. しゃっかん

**차광**(遮光) ~하다 shade[shield] the light; hinder[intercept] the light/~기 a flash suppresser [on a gun]/~막 a shade/~ 장치 a shutter 《사진기의》 an iris shutter/~판 a glare shield [on aircraft]. しゃこう

차근차근 compactly; in detail; minutely; attentively/ ~하다 (be) minute; attentive/몹시 ~하다 be overscrupulous/성질이 ~한 사람 a scrupulously careful person/일을 ~ 처리하다 dispose of a matter methodically[systematically]/그는 ~ 자기의 소신을 말했다 He dwelt at full length on his conviction. きちんきちん

차금(借金) a debt; borrowings ⇒빚. しゃっきん

차기(次期) the next term[period]/~ 국회 the next session of the National Assembly/~ 대통령 the President for the next term.

차남(次男) one's second son. じなん

차내(車內) the inside[interior] of a car [train]/~에서 in the car; on the train /~ 금연 No smoking in the car!/~ 회견 an interview in the train. しゃない

차녀(次女) one's second daughter. じじょ

차다[1] 《한랭하다》(be) cold; chilly/찬 바람 a chilly[cold] wind/찬물 cold water /차디찬 사람 a cold-hearted[an icy] person/차지다 become[get] cold[chill] /얼음장같이 ~ be ice-cold; be as cold as ice. つめたい

차다[2] 《충만하다》be full of; be filled with 《달이》(be) full; be at the full; wax 《조수가》rise; flow 《기한이》expire; fall[become] due; run out/가득 ~ fill; brim '/마음에 ~ be satisfied (with); meet with satisfaction; prove[be] satisfactory/마음에 안~ prove[be] unsatisfactory; leave something[much] to be desired/강당은 청중으로 차 있었다 The auditorium was crowded to the limit./ 전도가 희망에 ~ one's future is full of hope/앞길은 위험에 차 있다 Our way [ahead] is full of danger./달도 차면 기운다 A flow will have an ebb., Every flood[tide] hath its ebb. みちる

차다[3] ①《발로》kick; give (one) a kick/ 개를 ~ kick a dog; give a kick at a dog/문을 차서 열다 kick the door open ②《혀를》clack; cluck/혀를 ~ clack the tongue (over). ける

차다[4] 《패용하다》put on; fasten on; carry; wear/칼을 ~ wear a sword at one's side; gird on a sword/패물을 ~ wear trinkets/시계를 ~ strap on[wear] a watch/물건을 허리에 ~ carry[wear] a thing by one's side. つるす

차닥거리다 pat; tap; beat lightly 《바르다》paste haphazardly; slap together /차닥차닥 patteringly; pit-a-pat.
べたべたうつ

차단(遮斷) interception; isolation 《검역》quarantine/~하다 cut[shut] (a person) off from; intercept; isolate/~기 a circuit breaker 《건널목의》a crossing[lifting] gate/~ 장치 a cut-off/적의 퇴로를 ~하다 intercept the enemy's retreat. しゃだん

차대(車臺) a car-body; a car-truck 《전차 따위의》a platform.

차도(差度) improvement [of sickness]; recovery; convalescence/~가 있다 be getting better; convalesce; progress favorably; take a turn for the better/그의 병은 ~가 있다 He is recovering from his illness., He is getting better.

차도(車道) a road[carriage] way; a car lane; a traffic lane; a drive-way《미》. しゃどう

차돌 quartz; silicates/~ 같은 사람 a man of firm[steady] character/~ 모래 silica sand; glass silica.

차등(差等) grade; gradation; graduation; discrimination/~이 있다 be different in grade[s]/~을 매기다 grade; graduate; discriminate/~ 세율 a graded tariff; a graduated tax scale.
つぎのとうきゅう

차디차다 be ever so cold; icy; be as cold as ice; be cold as can be.
きわめてつめたい

차라리 rather; preferably/이런 고통 속에서 사느니 ~ 죽는 것이 낫다 I would rather die than live in this agony./이쪽이 ~ 낫다 This would be better./그렇게 하려면 ~ 안 하는 것이 낫다 It would be better not to do it at all than to do it that way. むしろ

차란차란 《차다》completely filling [it] up 《드리우다》drooping[hanging] low/~한 머리채 long braid of hair; a long pigtail[queue]/물이 독에 ~ 차다 A jar is brimful of water. みちみちて

차랑거리다 《움직이다》swing gently 《소리나다》tinkle; jingle; ting/차랑차랑 《움직임》with a gentle sway 《소리》ting-a-ling, ting-ting/긴 머리채가 차랑거린다 Her long pigtail sways on her back.
ちゃりんちゃりんとなる

차량(車輛) vehicles; cars; a [railway] carriage 《객차・화차의 총칭》rolling stock /한 ~분의 화물 a carload/~ 회사 a rolling stock company/철도 ~ railroad cars. しゃりょう

차력(借力) ~하다 culture one's physical strength by virtue of medicine.

차렵 《이불》a thin quilt; a lightly padded quilt.

차례(次例) ①《번》order; sequence; arrangement; precedence/~로 in [good] order; one by one; one after another [the other]; in turn; by turns/~를 따라 according to the order[program]; in regular order/~를 바꾸다 change the order; follow the wrong order ②《회수》time; round/한 ~ once/두 ~ twice/ 여러 ~ several times/한 ~ 이기다 win

one round of a game. しだい
**차례(茶禮)** ancestor-memorial services; a brief family-memorial service.
**차례걸음(次例一)** proceeding in due order; orderly procession.
**차례차례(次例次例)** one by one; one after another 《순서로》 in turn 《이어서》 in succession/~로 in order; one by one; one after another[the other]/선착순으로 ~ 받다 be accepted in order of application/카드를 번호대로 ~ 놓다 arrange the cards in numerical order.
**차로(遮路)** interception[blocking] of the road 《방역(防疫)을 위한》 quarantine/~하다 bar[obstruct] the passage.
**차로(叉路)** a branch-road; a forked road 《십자로》 a crossroads.
**차륜(車輪)** a rundle; a wheel/~ 제동기 a wheel brake/착륙 ~ a landing wheel. しゃりん
**차리다** ①《외관을》 equip oneself (with); dress up/외모를 ~ show up; make a show/웃음 차려입다 dress up ②《준비하다》 make ready; prepare for/살림을 ~ establish a home/점포를 ~ set up a shop /차려 놓다 set[put] up; put[place] in position ③《정신을》 pull oneself together; concentrate one's mind/정신을 차려 일하라 devote one's attention to the task at hand; do the job carefully[attentively] ④《간직하다》 maintain; preserve/인사를 ~ observe decorum/체면을 ~ keep up appearances/제 욕심을 ~ seek a personal profit[personal advantage, selfish end]. ととのえる
**차림새** 《복색》 attire; array 《몸차림》 outfit; equipment 《단장》 toilet; make-up /~만 봐도 그 여자의 성격을 알 수 있었다 Her appearance betrayed her character. みなり
**차마** too … to; for [all] the world/ ~ 견딜수 없는 모욕 an intolerable[unpardonable] insult/~ 볼 수 없는 비참한 광경 a most pitiful sight/그의 농담은 ~ 들을 수 없다 I can't stand his jokes./그에게 ~ 화를 낼수 없었다 I cannot have the heart to be angry at him. まさか
**차마(車馬)** horses and vehicles/~의 통행 vehicular traffic/~ 통행 금지 "No Thoroughfare for Horses and Vehicles."
**차멀미** car sickness/~하다 get[be] carsick; have car sickness.
**차면(遮面)** hiding one's face; putting a wall[screen] between people/~하다 hide one's face. かおをかくすこと
**차반** a capital dinner; a sumptuous repast; splendid dishes.
**차반(茶盤)** a tea tray; a tea board; tea serving tray. ちゃばん
**차변(借邊)** the debtor(略: Dr.); 《부기의》 the debit side/~에 기입하다 debit (a sum) against[to] (a person); enter (a sum) to the debit of (a person)/~ 계정 [잔고] debtor account[balance]/~ 기입

a debit entry/~ 난 a debit side. かりかた
**차별(差別)** discrimination; distinction; partiality 《차이》 difference/~하다 be partial; discriminate (between, against) /~없이 without distinction; fairly; impartially/~하는 discriminative; discriminatory/선악의 ~쯤은 알고 있다 I know right from wrong/~ 관세 differential duties 《세율》 a discriminative tariff/~ 대우 discriminative treatment /~ 대우를 하다 treat (a person) with discrimination; discriminate against (a person)/~ 임금 differential wages/인종 ~ racial discrimination 《흑인에 대한》 [racial] segregation/인종 ~ 철폐 abolition of racial discrimination. さべつ
**차부(車夫)** a cartman; a cart-drawer. しゃふ
**차분하다** (be) calm; composed; quiet; self-possessed/차분한 태도 a quiet attitude; a calm manner/마음을 차분히 가라앉히다 calm[compose] oneself; keep cool; gather one's wits. ちんちゃくだ
**차붓소(車夫一)** a cart-ox; an ox pulling a cart. にぐるまひきのうし
**차비(車費)** 《운임》 carfare; train[railway, bus] fare; charges 《운반료》 carriage/서울까지의 왕복 ~는 얼마입니까 What is the fare to Seoul and back? うんちん
**차비(差備)** 《준비》 preparations; [preliminary] arrangements; equipment 《예비》 provision/~하다 prepare; make preparations[arrangements]; get[make] ready 《치장을 하다》 equip oneself (for)/아무 ~도 없이 without any preparation.
じゅんびすること
**차서(次序)** order ⇒차례(次例). じじょ
**차석(次席)** the next seat[position]; 《관리》 an official next in rank; an assistant (manager, director); 《경기》 the second winner/~에 앉다 sit next to; rank next to/~ 검사 an associate prosecutor /~ 서기 a subhead clerk. じせき
**차수(差數)** disparity; balance; difference [in number].
**차수(次數)** 【수】 degree. じすう
**차시(此時)** this time; this day; this occasion.
**차압(差押)** attachment; distraint; sequestration/~하다 attach; seize; distrain (upon)/재산을 ~하다 attach[seize] (a person's) property. さしおさえ
**차액(差額)** difference; balance; margin /큰[적은] ~ a wide[narrow] margin /무역의 ~ the balance of trade/ ~을 지불하다 pay the balance/~의 증감은 사업의 성과를 말한다 The loss or gain of the balance shows the outcome of business. さがく
**차양(遮陽)** 《모자의》 a brim; a peak 《집의》 the eaves 《창의》 a blind; shutter /~이 넓은 모자 a broad-brimmed hat. ひさし

**차용**(借用) borrowing; loan/~하다 borrow; have[get] a loan (*of*)/~증 a bond of debt[loan]/돈의 ~을 부탁하다 ask (*a person*) for a loan of money; apply to (*a person*) for an advance of money/~ 증서 an I.O.U. a bond of debt[loan]. しゃくよう

**차원**(次元) 【수】 a dimension/~이 다르다 be entirely different/제 3~의 three-dimensional. じげん

**차월**(借越) an outstanding debt; debit balance 《수표의》 an overdraft; overdrawing/~하다 overdraw; let a debt stand over; leave a debt outstanding/~로 되어 있다 remain outstanding.

**차위**(次位) the second rank[place]; 《경기의》 a runner-up/~를 차지하다 hold the second place. じい

**차이**(差異) difference 《구별》 distinction 《불균형》 disparity 《부동》 dissimilarity/신분의 ~ disparity in social standing[status]/능력의 ~ discrepancy in ability/현저한 ~ a striking[remarkable, sharp]/소문과 실제로 보는 것과는 큰 ~ 있다 There is all the difference between seeing and hearing./빈부의 ~ a gulf between the rich and the poor. さい.

**차익**(差益) marginal profit[s]. さえき

**차일**(遮日) 《햇볕가리개》 a sun-shade 《창문의》 a [sun-]blind 《장막》 an awning/~로 가리다 shade (*a thing*) from the sun/~을 내리다 《창의》 pull the blinds down.

**차일 피일**(此日彼日) ~하다 put off from day to day; let delay; delay day by day; procrastinate/그는 ~하고 숙제를 끝었다 He put off writing his home task from day to day.

**차입**(差入) ~하다 《감옥에》 make a present to a prisoner; send (*a thing*) in to a prisoner/~물 a present to a prisoner/~ 식사 a lunch sent into a prisoner. さしいれ

**차자**(次子) *one's* second son. じし

**차장**(次長) a vice-chief[director]; a deputy[assistant]-chief/편집 ~ a senior editor; an associate editor. じちょう

**차장**(車掌) a conductor〈미〉; a guard〈영〉/~실 the conductor's compartment/버스 ~ a bus girl[conductress]/~대(臺) the conductor's platform. しゃしょう

**차전병**(一煎餅) glutinous rice-biscuit[cake].

**차점**(次點) the second highest mark[number of points]; the next[second] score 《경기》 the second winner; the runner-up 《선거》 the second largest number [of votes]/~으로 당선되다 be stood second on the list of successful candidates. じてん

**차제**(次弟) order ⇨차례(次例). しだい

**차제**(此際) on this occasion; at this junction[time]; now; under these circumstances/~에 여러분에게 감사의 인사를 드립니다 I will take this opportunity of thanking you for helping me. /~의 최선책은 이것이다 This is the best policy to cope with the situation. このさい

**차조** 【식】 glutinous millet. もちあわ

**차조기** 【식】 a purple perilla plant; *Perilla nankinensis*(학명). しそ

**차조밥** boiled glutinous millet.

**차종**(茶鐘) a teacup; a tea bowl/~에 차를 따르다 serve[pour] tea into a cup.

**차주**(借主) 《일반적》 a borrower; a hirer 《부동산의》 a renter; a tenant; a lessee. かりぬし

**차주**(車主) the owner of a car[vehicle]. くるまのぬし

**차중**(車中) 《찻속》 in the car[train]; 《차 탄 동안》 while aboard [the train]; while in the car. しゃちゅう

**차중음**(次中音) 【음】 tenor/~ 가수 a tenor; a tenorist.

**차지** ~하다 hold; occupy; take; have 《가지다》 capture; take possession (*of*); make (*a thing*) *one's* own; keep (*a thing*) as *one's* own/최후의 승리를 ~하다 win the final victory/중요한 자리를 ~하다 occupy an important position/독~하다 monopolize; have solely to *one*self. じこのぶん

**차지**(借地) leased land; rented ground 《빌림》 lease of land/~권 lease; leasehold/~인 a tenant; a leaseholder/조(租)~ the lease of a foreign territory. しゃくち

**차지다** (be) sticky; glutinous; heavy/이 떡은 대단히 ~ This rice-cake is very glutinous. ねばい

**차질**(蹉跌) a failure; a miscarriage; a setback; fiasco/~하다 fail; miscarry; end in a failure[fiasco]/일생의 ~ a shipwreck of life/~을 가져오다 bring about a failure/사업에 ~이 생겼다 The business struck a snag. さてつ

**차차**(次次) 〖점점〗 step by step; gradually; little by little; more and more 《그 동안에》 by and by; in〖with the lapse of〗 time; afterwards/~ 추워진다 be getting colder/~ 좋은 일도 있겠지 Something will turn up in due course of time. /~ 자세한 것을 알 수 있을 것이오 All the details will be known in time. おいおい

**차창**(車窓) a car[train] window/~ 밖을 내다보다 look out of the carriage window/~으로 내다보이는 풍경 the scenery seen from a car window. しゃそう

**차처**(此處) here; this place. ここ

**차체**(車體) a frame; a [car-]body; a chassis. しゃたい

**차축**(車軸) an axle [shaft]. しゃじく

**차츰차츰** gradually; by degrees; step by step; little by little; inch by inch; by and by; more and more. だんだん

**차치**(且置) leaving (*it*) unmentioned[untouched]; putting aside/~하다 let alone; set aside[apart]/～하고 exclusive of; apart from/모든 것을 ～하고 before everything else; first of all.

**차탄(嗟歎)** ①《개탄》 lamentation; deploration/～하다 lament; deplore; sigh/읽고 ～하여 마지않다 sigh after reading ②《감탄》 admiration/～하다 admire. ひどいなげき

**차탈 피탈(此頉彼頉)** one excuse or another; all sorts of excuse; a hocuspocus/～하다 make one excuse or another; make all sorts of excuses/～ 일을 자꾸 미루다 keep putting the matter off with some pretext or other.

**차폐(遮蔽)** cover; shelter; shielding; 《군》 difilade/～하다 cover; shelter; defilade; shield (from *radioactivity*)/～을 cover; shelter/～ 진지 a covered position. しゃへい

**차표(車票)** a ticket; a pass/～ 파는 곳 a box office; a booking office/～ 판매계 a ticket agent〈미〉; a booking clerk〈영〉/～를 조사하다 examine tickets/편도 ～ a oneway ticket〈미〉; a single ticket. じょうしゃけん

**차항(次項)** the following clause/～ 참조 confer(略 : cf.) the next item[clause].

**차호(次號)** the next number[issue]; the forthcoming issue/～ 계속 [to be] continued [in the next issue]/～ 완결 [to be] concluded [in the forthcoming issue]. じごう

**차흡다(嗟—)** 《문》 Alas!, Oh, how sad I am!, Woe is me.

**차회(次回)** next time/～의 next/～에 next time; another time/～로 미루다 postpone to[till] next time. このかい

**차회(次會)** the next meeting[session].

**차후(此後)** after this; henceforth; hereafter; from now on 《장래》 in [the] future/～에는 더 조심해라 Be more careful in future. こののち

**착** closely; tightly; sticking fast; low; deep/～ 들러붙다 stick fast to/～ 가라앉은 목소리 a subdued[deep, low] voice. きちっと

**착(着)** ①《도착》 arrival; reaching; getting to/～4시 서울역 ～의 기차 the train due at *Seoul* station on four o'clock ②《경주》 order of arrival/2～이다 be a runner-up. ちゃく

**착각(錯角)** 《수》 alternate angles. さっかく

**착각(錯覺)** an [optical] illusion; a hallucination/～하다 have[be under] an illusion (*that*); become the victim of an illusion/～의 illusory; illusive/～적 halluciuatory/～을 일으키다 be under a hallucination; have an illusion/～하고 있다 cherish[be possessed with] the illusion (*that*)/눈은 ～에 빠지기 쉽다 The eye is deceived by the illusion. さっかく

**착검(着劍)** 《호령》 Fix bayonets!/～하다 fix a bayonet; carry a sword; wear a sword.

**착고(着錮)** shackles; fetters ⇨차꼬.

**착공(着工)** starting [construction] work /～하다 start[begin] work/～ 일자 the date of the start[commencement, embarkment] of construction work/본 철도 공사는 내주에 ～한다 Construction work on this railway line begins next week. ちゃっこう

**착근(着根)** ～하다 take[strike] root; root.

**착란(錯亂)** distraction; derangement; aberration 《무질서》 disarrangement; confusion/～하다 be distracted; get confused; be deranged/정신 ～ distraction; dementation; mental derangement[aberration]/정신을 ～시키다 drive (*a person*) distracted; derange *a person* mind/～ 상태 a state of dementia. さくらん

**착륙(着陸)** landing; alighting/～하다 land; alight; make a landing; reach the ground/도중 ～하다 make a stop en route[on the way]; stop off[over] (*at*) /～장 a landing field[ground]; an airstrip/불시 ～하다 make a forced[an emergency] landing/무～ 비행 a non -stop flight. ちゃくりく

**착목(着目)** observation; giving *one*'s mind to ⇨착안.

**착발(着發)** 《발착》 arrival and departure 《폭발》 percussion/～ 신관(信管) a percussion-fuse/～탄(彈) a percussion-shell. ちゃくはつ

**착복(着服)** ①《착의》 getting dressed ②《횡령》 embezzlement; peculation/～하다 embezzle; divert to *one*'s private use; pocket/그는 거액의 공금을 ～했다 He embezzled a large sum of public money./그는 이익을 전부 ～했다 He pocketed all the profits. ちゃくふく

**착살맞다, 착살스럽다** ①《인색하다》 (be) stingy; niggardly; pinch and scrape ②《다랍다》 (be) narrow-minded; small/착살맞은 사람[짓] a niggardly person[thing to do]. けちだ

**착상(着想)** [hitting on] an idea; a conception; a turn of thought/～하다 conceive an idea; hit on an idea/좋은[독창적] ～ a clever[an original] idea/～이 좋다 be cleverly conceived; be a clever conception[idea]/그의 문장의 ～은 기발하다 His writings are marked by originality of ideas. ちゃくそう

**착색(着色)** colouring; colouration; painting/～하다 colour; paint/～ 사진 a coloured photograph/～화 a coloured picture; a coloured print/～ 유리 stained glass. ちゃくしょく

**착석(着席)** taking a seat/～하다 take a seat; take a chair sit down/～하고 다 be seated; be in *one*'s seat/～시키다 seat (*a person*); induce (*a person*) to take a seat. ちゃくせき

**착수(着手)** start; commencement; setting about; outset/~하다 start; commence; under take 《일을》 set one's hands to; embark on (an enterprise)/새 사업에 ~하다 embark[start] on a new enterprise/그 일[조사]에 ~하다 set about the work[making inquiries]/~자 a starter. ちゃくしゅ

**착수**(着水) alighting on the water/~하다 alight[land] on the water 《우주선의》splash down. ちゃくすい

**착수금**(着手金) a retaining fee; a deposit 《약조금》 bargain money 《시작하는》 money paid to initiate work.
ちゃくしゅきん

**착실**(着實) ~하다 (be) steady [and honest]; sound; steady-going 《믿을 만하다》 trustworthy 《충실》 faithful/~한 부자 quite a rich person; a well-heeled person/~한 사람 a reliable[trustworthy] person/~한 생각 a solid[sober] view.
ちゃくじつ

**착심**(着心) giving one's mind to; setting one's thoughts on; concentration.

**착안**(着眼) one's view; one's aim/~하다 pay attention to; take note of; have an eye on; fix one's eyes upon/~이 좋다 be right in one's way of looking at the matter/~점 the point aimed at 《견지》one's view point/그는 우리보다 ~점이 한층 더 높다 He aims much loftier than we do. ちゃくがん

**착암기**(鑿岩機) a rock-drill. さくがんき

**착염**(錯鹽) a complex salt. さくえん

**착오**(錯誤) a mistake; an error/시각의 ~ an optical illusion; hallucination/시대 ~ anachronism/~에 빠지다 fall[drift] into an error; commit a mistake.
さくご

**착용**(着用) putting on; wearing/~하다 wear; put on; have on/제복을 ~하고 있다 be in uniform/참석자는 예복 ~을 바람 Full dress to be worn[is in order] to the occasion. ちゃくよう

**착유**(搾乳) milking/~하다 milk (a cow, a goat)/~장 a dairy; a dairy farm/~기 a milker/~하는 여자 a milkmaid; a dairymaid. さくにゅう

**착유기**(搾油機) an oil-press.

**착의**(着衣) getting dressed; one's clothes; clothing/~하다 get dressed; put on clothes. ちゃくい

**착임**(着任) arrival at one's post/~하다 arrive at one's post. ちゃくにん

**착잡**(錯雜) confusion; intricacy; tangled; disorder/~하다 (be) confused; tangled; mixed together; complicated/~한 사건 a complicated affair/~한 얘기[문장] an involved story[construction]/그 여자의 표정은 ~한 심정을 나타내고 있었다 Her face betrayed a mixture of emotions within. さくざつ

**착전**(着電) the arrival of a telegram; a telegram[cablegram] received/런던으로부터의 ~에 의하면 according to the cablegram [received] from London.

**착정**(鑿井) well-drilling[sinking]/~하다 sink[bore] a well.

**착종**(錯綜) complication; intricacy/~하다 be complicated; be involved; be knotty/~된 complicated; knotty; intricate. さくそう

**착착**(着着) steadily; step by step; rapidly/~ 진척하다 make steady progress; progress steadily/공사는 ~ 진척하고 있다 The construction is making steady progress. きちんきちん

**착취**(搾取) ①extortion; exploitation/~하다 exploit; extort; sweat (one's workers)/자본가의 ~ capitalist exploitation/식민지를 ~하다 exploit a colony/돈을 ~하다 screw (a person) out of his money ②《과즙》squeezing out; extraction/~하다 squeeze out; extract/오렌지에서 즙을 ~하다 squeeze[press] juice from[out of] oranges/~ 계급 the exploiting class/~ 노동 sweated labor; sweat shop labor. さくしゅ

**착탄거리**(着彈距離) the range of a gun; shooting[firing] distance/~ 내[외]에 있다 be within[out of] range.
ちゃくだんきょり

**착탄지점**(着彈地點) an impact area.
ちゃくだんちてん

**착하**(着荷) arrivals; arrival[receipt] of goods/~ 인도[지불] delivery[payment] on arrival.

**착하다**(着-) (be) gentle; good 《친절》kind 《온순》 meek 《순종》 obedient 《고분고분하다》docile/착한 사람 a man of sincerity; a good man/착한 아이 a meek[docile, good] child/착하게 nicely; gently/마음이 ~ be kindhearted; be of good[nice] disposition; have a sweet temper/부모의 말씀을 어기지 않아야 착한 사람이다 Only those who respect the advice of their parents are to be praised.

**찬**(贊, 讚) praise; eulogy; panegyric/그림에 ~을 쓰다 write a panegyric over [under] a painting; write a sentence [poem] on a painting in praise of it.
さん

**찬**(饌) a side-dish; subsidiary articles of diet/~이 많다 have many side dishes/~거리 side-dish makings; groceries.
せん

**찬가**(讚歌) a hymn; a doxology. さんか

**찬간**(饌間) a kitchen; a pantry.

**찬광**(饌—) a cellar; a store room for food supplies; a pantry; a kitchen cupboard.

**찬기**(-氣) cold air[draft]/~가 돌다 be chill with cold air.

**찬김** cold air; chilly atmosphere/~이 가시다 warm slightly.

**찬동**(贊同) approval; approbation; support; endorsement/~하다 approve (of); support; give one's approval; endorse/~을 얻어서 with (a person's) approval[support]／～의 뜻을 표하다 express one's approval.　さんどう

**찬란(燦爛)** brilliancy; brightness; radiancy; glitter／～하다 (be) brilliant; shining; bright; glittering; radiant／～한 보석 a brilliant[radiant] jewel／～한 별 glittering stars／～히 빛나다 glitter.　さんらん

**찬모(饌母)** a woman cook [in charge of making side dishes].

**찬무대** a cold current; the Arctic Current.　かんりゅう

**찬물** cold water／～을 한 잔 마시다 drink a cup of cold water／～을 끼얹다 pour cold water (over).　みず

**찬미(讚美)** praise; glorification; extolment; admiration／～하다 praise; glorify; extol; eulogize; admire; adore／～자 an admirer; an adorer／신을 ～하다 praise God[the Lord]; give praise[glory] to God／인생을 ～하다 sing praise of life.　さんび

**찬미가(讚美歌)** a hymn; a psalm／～집 a hymn-book; a hymnal／～를 부르다 chant a psalm.　さんびか

**찬바람** cold wind.　れいふう

**찬반(贊反)** pros and cons.

**찬밥** cold boiled-rice.　ひやめし

**찬방(饌房)** a pantry.

**찬부(贊否)** approval or disapproval; yes or no; for and against; pros and cons／～를 결정하다 approve or disapprove 《투표로》 vote on (a matter)／～를 묻다 put (a matter) to a vote.　さんぴ

**찬비** cold rain.

**찬사(讚辭)** a eulogy; a [tribute of] praise; a panegyric; an encomium; a compliment; kind remarks／～를 아끼지 않다 be unsparing of[in] one's praise.　さんじ

**찬상(讚賞)** admiration; praise; applause／～하다 admire; praise; extol; laud.

**찬성(贊成)** approval; agreement; seconding; support; endorsement／～하다 《동의》 approve of (a plan); give a person's approval (to); agree (to a person's opinion); 《의안 따위에》 support; second; stand by; vote for; favour 《학설 따위에》 endorse; advocate 《계획에》 take interest in (a project)／～자 an approver; a supporter 《주의 동의》 an advocate 《찬조원》 a patron／～ 투표 a vote in favour of (a motion)／～파 the consenting party／～을 구하다 ask one's approval／～을 얻다 be supported by (a person)／만장의 ～을 얻다 meet with unanimous approbation／의안에 ～하다 support a bill; vote for a measure／나는 너의 말에 ～ 할 수 없다 I can't go with you in what you say.　さんせい

**찬송(讚頌)** praise; glorification; extolment; admiration; a eulogy; an encomium／～하다 praise; glorify; chant hymns of praise to／～가 a hymn; a psa-

lm／하느님을 ～하다 give glory to God; praise God.　さんび

**찬술** cold sool[wine].

**찬술(撰述)** writing; composing／～하다 write; compose.　せんじゅつ

**찬술(纂述)** editing; compilation／～하다. edit; compile.　さんじゅつ

**찬양(讚揚)** commendation; praise; admiration／～하다 praise; admire; commend／～높이 ～하다 admire highly; speak in high terms／그들은 소리 높이 그를 ～했다 They were loud in his praise.　さんよう

**찬연(燦然)** brilliancy; radiancy; resplendence／～하다 (be) brilliant; resplendent; radiant／～히 빛나다 shine[glitter] brilliantly.　さんぜん

**찬위(簒位)** usurpation; taking the throne／～하다 usurp a throne.　さんい

**찬의(贊意)** approval; approbation／～를 표하다 express one's approval.　さんい

**찬이슬** cold dew.　つめたいつゆ

**찬장(饌欌)** a cupboard; a sideboard.

**찬조(贊助)** support; backing; advocacy; patronage; approval 《후원》 sponsorship; auspices; endorsement; approval 《장려》 encouragement／～하다 support; patronize; render assistance; advocate／～금 a contribution／～ 연설 a supporting speech／～자 a supporter; an assistant／～ 출연하다 appear as a guest star／～을 얻다 obtain[have] (a person's) patronage[endorsement].　さんじょ

**찬찬** fast; hard; tightly／～ 동이다 tie fast; bind hard.　くるくると

**찬찬하다** 《꼼꼼하다》 (be) attentive; considerate; punctilious; scrupulous; cautious 《침착하다》 (be) calm; quiet; self-possessed; placid／그녀는 성격이 아주 ～ She is very calm and attentive.　ちんちゃくだ

**찬칼(饌—)** a small kitchen-knife; a carving knife 《식탁용》 a table-knife.

**찬탄(讚嘆)** admiration; praise; applause; laudation／～하다 admire; praise [highly]; extol; speak highly of／～하여 마지 않다 be lost in admiration (for).　さんたん

**찬탈(簒奪)** usurpation／～하다 usurp; seize／～자 a usurper／왕위를 ～하다 usurp a throne.　さんだつ

**찬평(贊評)** praising and criticizing; a favorable criticism[comment]／ ～하다 comment[criticize] favorably.

**찬합(饌盒)** a nest[tier] of [lacquered] boxes; a picnic box／팥밥을 ～에 담다 fill a nest of boxes with red boiled rice.

**찰** 《곡식》 sticky; glutinous 《형편》 persistent; extreme／～거머리 a sticky leech／～밥 glutinous rice.

**찰가난** extreme[abject, dire] poverty; destitution; indigence; beggary／～뱅

이 a very poor man.

**찰깍** 《붙는》 sticking tight[close, fast]; 《소리》 with a slap[snap]/~ 잠그다 fasten (*a lock*) with a snap/~찰깍 with slap; after slap; snapping and snapping.

**찰깍정이** a nasty[mean] miser.

**찰거머리** (거머리)a leech (사람)a nuisance; a sticky person/~처럼 달라붙다 stick like a leech.

**찰것** glutinous food; heavy eatables[stuff].

**찰과상**(擦過傷) an obrasion; a scratch/~을 입다 have[sustain] a scratch.

**찰교인**(一敎人) a devout[pious] man.

**찰나**(刹那) a moment; an instant; a juncture; the very moment/~주의 impulsiveness; momentalism/~적 쾌락 momentary pleasure/그 ~에 at that very moment; at that juncture/…하려는 ~에 on the point of (*doing*); impulsively.

**찰딱거리다** cling (*to*); stick (*to*).

**찰떡** rice cake made of glutinous rice; glutinous rice cake.

**찰락거리다** trickle/찰락찰락 trickling.

**찰랑거리다** ①(쇠붙이가) jingle; clink; tinkle/찰랑찰랑 tinkling; ding-dong; clinking ②(물이) splash/찰랑찰랑 full to the brim 《넘칠듯》 brimfully; splashing.

**찰바닥거리다** splash; slop; dabble (*one's legs in the water*)/찰바닥찰바닥 splashing/아이들은 웅덩이 속에서 찰바닥거리기를 좋아한다 Some children love slopping about in puddles.

**찰밥** boiled glutinous rice; cooked dish of glutinous rice.

**찰방** splash[ingly]; splatter[ingly]; dabbling[ly].

**찰벼** unhulled grains of glutinous rice.

**찰싹** with a slap[spank]; splashingly/~ 매리다 spank; slap (*a person* on *the face*)/~ 매질하다 whip with a crack.

**찰상**(擦傷) a scratch; a graze.

**찰짜** an overscrupulous person.

**찰찰** spilling; overflowing/~ 넘치다 overflow; run over; inundate; be filled [full] to overflowing.

**찰찰**(察察) exact; punctilious; meticulous/~한 사람 a meticulous[careful] person.

**찰흙** clay.

**참¹** 《참으로》 really; truly; in truth; indeed; in fact; actually; surely 《감탄》 oh; well; ugh; now/~ 춥다 It is awfully[terribly] cold today./~ 재미있었다 I had such a good time, indeed./~ 별꼴이야 Fiddlesticks!, How odd it is!

**참²** 《진실》 truth; reality; actuality 《성실》 sincerity; fidelity 《사실》 a fact 《진정》 genuineness.

**참-** true; real; genuine/~말 truth; reality; a fact/~사랑 a true man; an honest man/~사랑 a true love.

**참**(站) 《장소》 a post town; a post station; a stage; a stop; a resting place 《시간》 a rest period; a break; a recess 《계단》 the landing (of *the stairs*)/내가 나가려는 ~이었다 I was just about to leave home.

**참가**(參加) participation; joining; adherence; entry/~하다 participate; take part (*in*); join (경기 따위에) enter for; start/~자 a participator; a participant; an entrant 《경기의》 an entry/~국 a participating nation/경기에 ~하다 take part[participate] in a game/조약에 ~하다 become a party to[adhere to] a treaty/~에 신청하다 send an entry.

**참깨** 《식》 a sesame/~씨 a sesame seed/~를 찧다 grind sesame seeds.

**참견**(參見) interference; meddling; participation; taking part; association/~하다 interfere (in *a matter*, with *a person*); meddle (*in*); step (*in*)/~ 잘 하는 officious; busy; meddlesome/남의 일에 ~하다 meddle in other's affairs; poke *one's* nose into another's business/쓸데없는 ~ 말라 Mind[Attend to] your own business.

**참경**(慘景) a terrible[horrible] sight; a frightful scene; a disastrous spectacle.

**참고**(參考) reference; consultation 《비교》 comparison/~하다 refer to consult (*a book*); compare with/~서 a reference book 《책끝 따위의》 a book of reference/~ 서류 reference documents/~인 a reference 《증인》 a witness/~ 자료 reference materials/~가 되다 be of [great] value; be a good guide/주석을 ~하다 consult[refer to] the notes/…을 ~로 하여 with reference (*to*); in the light (*of*).

**참관**(參觀) a visit 《시찰》 inspection/~하다 visit; inspect/~일 a visiting-day/~인 a visitor 《선거 따위의》 a witness/수업을 ~하다 see[visit] a class at work/개표를 ~하다 witness the opening of the ballot.

**참괴**(慙愧) humiliation; shame; mortification 《후회》 remorsefulness/~에 못 견디다 be overwhelmed[overcome] with shame.

**참극**(慘劇) a tragedy; a catastrophe; a tragic event/~의 현장 the scene of a tragedy/~을 연출하다 enact a tragedy.

**참기름** sesame oil/~을 치다 season (*food*) with sesame oil.

**참나무** a kind of oak; *Quercus serrata*

(학명). くぬぎ
**참녀**(參一) participation ⇒참여. さんよ
**참다** bear; endure 《관용》 tolerate; stand; put up with 《억누르다》 control; suppress; keep[hold] back; choke[gulp] down /참을 수 없는 unbearable; intolerable /웃음을 꾹 ~ stifle *one's* laughter/꾹 ~ possess *one's* soul in patience/치통을 ~ endure toothache/노여움을 ~ suppress *one's* anger; restrain *one's* wrath/배고픔을 ~ bear[stand] *one's* hunger/이 이상 참을 수 없다 I can't bear[stand] this any longer./싫어도 참아야 한다 If you don't like it, you may lump it. こらえる
**참담**(慘憺) ①《비탄》 grief; sorrow; anguish; lamentation/~하다 abandon *oneself* to grief; break *one's* heart (*from*) ②《비참》 misery; wretchedness; pitiableness; distress/~하다 (be) miserable; wretched; pitiable/~한 생활 a wretched[miserable] life/~한 죽음을 하다 die a miserable death. さんたん
**참대** 《식》 a long-jointed bamboo; *Phyllostachys bambusoides*(학명). まだけ
**참돔** 《어》 a red sea-bream; *Chrysophrys major*(학명).
**참되다** (be) honest; faithful; sincere; right-minded/참된 사람 a genuine[sincere, an honest] person/참된 친구 a faithful friend. まことらしい
**참뜻** true meaning; sincere intention. しんい
**참람**(僭濫) presumptuousness; presumption; arrogation; audacity/~하다 (be) presumptuous; arrogant; audacious; insolent/~한 말을 하다 talk saucy; say pert things. ふそん
**참렬**(參列) attendance; presence; participation/~하다 attend (*a ceremony*); take part (*in*); go to/~자 those present; attendance 《개인》 an attendant/의식에 ~하다 sit at a ceremony. さんれつ
**참례**(參禮) attending a ceremony; attendance; presence; participation/~하다 attend (*a ceremony*); take part (*in*); share (*in*). さんれい
**참말** a true story; a fact; a real fact; an authentic story[account]/~로 very; really; indeed 《확실히》 certainly/~로 놀라다 be really surprised/그게 ~일까 Can that be true?/너 ~로 말 잘 했다 You have said well, indeed. しんじつのことば
**참망**(僭妄) audacity; assumption; presumption; recklessness; unreasonableness/~하다 (be) audacious; assumptive; presumptuous; reckless. ふそん
**참먹** an ink-stick of good quality; Chinese ink of superior quality.
**참모**(參謀) 《총칭》 the staff 《개인》 a staff officer 《상담역》 an adviser; a braintruster/~부 the General Staff [office]/~장 the chief of staff/~ 총장[차장] the Chief[Vice-Chief] of the General Staff/연합 ~ 본부 the Joint Chiefs of Staff. さんぼう
**참바** a rope/~로 [마소를] 매놓다 tether.
**참밥**(站一) a snack; a workbreak snack.
**참배**(參拜) worship; a visit/~하다 [go and] worship at, pray before, pay homage to, visit (*a shrine*). さんぱい
**참빗** a fine-tooth[ed] bamboo comb. めのつんだたけぐし
**참사**(慘死) a tragic death/~하다 meet with a tragic death; be killed (in *an accident*)/교통 사고로 ~하다 be killed in a traffic accident. ざんし
**참사**(慘事) a disaster; a disastrous accident; a catastrophe; a tragedy/~를 야기하다 cause a terrible accident. さんじ
**참사**(參事) a secretary; an advisor; a councilor/~관 a councilor; an adviser /~회 a council. さんじ
**참사람** a true[an honest] man/~이 되다 reform *oneself*; turn over a new leaf.
**참살**(斬殺) beheading; decapitation/~하다 behead; decapitate/~당하다 have *one's* head cut off; be beheaded; be decapitated. ざんさつ
**참살**(慘殺) murder; slaughter; butchery 《다수의》 massacre/~하다 murder cruelly; murder in cold-blood; butcher/~ 사건 an atrocious murder case. ざんさつ
**참상**(慘狀) a terrible[dreadful] sight[scene]; a wretched spectacle; a pitiable [miserable] state of affairs/~을 빚어내다 present a terrible sight[spectacle] /이재민의 ~은 가슴 아프다 The condition of the sufferers is most pitiable. さんじょう
**참새** 《조》 a sparrow/~떼 a flock of sparrows/~같이 재잘거리다 chatter like a sparrow. すずめ
**참서**(讖書) a prophetic book.
**참석**(參席) attendance; presence; participation/~하다 be present (*at*); present *oneself* (*at*); attend; take part (*in*) /회의에 ~하다 attend[be present at] the meeting[conference]/~자가 많다 [적다] have[there is] a large[small, poor] attendance. さんせき
**참선**(參禪) study and practice of the doctrine of the *Sun* cult[sect]/~하다 study and practise the *Sun* cult/~자 a *Sun* votary. さんぜん
**참섭**(參涉) meddling; interference; tampering/~하다 meddle[interfere] (*in, with*); intervene (*in*). かんけいすること
**참소**(讒訴) false charge; slander; traducement/~하다 calumniate; slander; traduce; make a false charge against (*one*). ざんそ
**참수**(斬首) beheading; decapitation/~하다 behead; decapitate. ざんしゅ
**참숯** hardwood charcoal; charcoal made

of oak wood. かたすみ

**참신**(斬新) novelty; `originality/~하다 (be) novel; original; up-to-date; new and striking/~한 교수법 an up-to-date method of teaching/~한 의장(意匠) a novel design. ざんしん

**참언**(讒言) a false charge[representation]; a slander; a calumny; a defamation/~하다 slander; calumniate; defame; make a false representation/~자 slanderer; a calumniator. ざんけん

**참언**(讖言) a prophecy; à prediction. よげんすることば

**참여**(參與) participation (in public affairs)/~하다 participate in; take part in; join in; have a share[hand] in; have anything to do; concern oneself in [with]/~자 a participant/국정에 ~하다 take part in the conduct of state affairs/분배에 ~하다 come in for a share/네가 ~할 바 아니다 You have nothing to do with this., This dose not concern you. さんよ

**참예**(參詣) worship; a visit to a temple [shrine]; a pilgrimage/~하다 visit[worship at] a temple[shrine]; make[go on] a pilgrimage (to)/~자 a visitor; a worshiper 《순례자》 a pilgrim. さんけい

**참외** 《식》 a melon/~밭 a melon field [patch]/~ 덩굴 a melon vine. まっかうり

**참으로** really; truly; indeed;how/그 소식을 들으니 ~ 기쁘다 I am really very pleased to hear the news./그는 ~ 똑똑한 아이다 He is really a bright boy. まことに

**참을성** 《인내》 patience; endurance; perseverance; forbearance/~있는 patient; persevering/~있게 patiently; with patience/~있게 기다리다 wait with patience[forbearance]. にんたいせい

**참의원**(參議院) the Senate; the Upper House; the House of Councilors/~ 의원 [의장] a member[the President] of the House of Councilors[Upper House]. さんぎいん

**참작**(參酌) consideration; allowance; qualification/~하다 take into consideration[account]; allow for (damages); make allowances for; consult; refer to/사정을 ~하다 allow for circumstances. さんしゃく

**참전**(參戰) participation in[entry into] a war/~하다 participate in[enter, join] a war/연합국측으로 ~하다 enter the war on the Allied side. さんせん

**참정**(參政) ·participation in government /~하다 participate in government. さんせい

**참정권**(參政權) suffrage; franchise; political rights; voting right; right to vote; votes/여성 ~ woman suffrage/~ 획득 the acquisition of the franchise/ ~을 부여하다 give[grant] the suffrage (to); enfranchise. さんせいけん

**참조**(參照) reference; comparison/~하다 refer (to); compare (with)/~하라 see; confer(略:cf.); vide(略:v.)/전 항 ~ quod vide(略:q.v.). さんしょう

**참조기** 《어》 a yellow corvenia; Pseudosciaena manchuria(학명). いしもち

**참주**(僭主) a tyrant; a despot.

**참죽나무** 《식》 Cedrela sinensis(학명). ちゃんちんのき

**참참**(站站) a rest; a recess; repeated stops[breaks]; every relay station/~이 at intervals; leisurely. ときどき

**참척**(慘慽) the loss of one's child[grandchild]/~당하다 be bereaved of a child [grandchild].

**참칭**(僭稱) pretension; assumption of a title; an unjustified title/~하다 pretend (to a throne); claim the title to; assume the title of. せんしょう

**참패**(慘敗) a miserable defeat; a crushing[serious, an overwhelming] defeat 《경기의》a skunk《미·속》;《야구의》a shut-out/~하다 suffer[sustain] a crushing defeat; be routed;《경기에서》be beaten utterly[all hollow] 《야구에서》be shut out(영패)/원정군은 ~당했다 The visiting team was badly hammered. さんぱい

**참하다** ①(얌전하다) (be) mild; quiet; meek; modest; reserved 《선량하다》good [-tempered]/참한 아이 a lamb of a boy ②(말쑥하다) (be) trim; tidy; neat; fair; smart. ちょうどあう

**참하다**(斬一) cut off (a person's) head; behead. おとなしい

**참학**(慘虐) cruelty; brutality; atrocity; inhumanity; savagery/~하다 (be) cruel; savage; brutal; atrocious/~한 행위 a brutal act; brutalities; atrocities. きわめてざんこくなこと

**참해**(慘害) heavy damage; havoc; disaster; ravage/전쟁의 ~ the horrors of war/~를 입다 suffer severely from (a storm). さんがい

**참형**(慘刑) a cruel[brutal] punishment; a merciless penalty. さんけい

**참호**(僭號) a self-assumed title. せんけい

**참호**(塹壕) a trench; a dugout; a foxhole; an entrenchment/~ 생활 life in the trenches/~ 작업 trench-digging operations/~열 trench fever/~를 파다 dig [make] a trench[foxhole]; throw up [open] trenches. ざんごう

**참혹**(慘酷) misery; wretchedness; pitiableness; distress/~하다 (be) miserable; wretched; tragic[al]; sad; pitiable; pathetic; sorrowful/~한 얘기 a tragic tale/~한 생활 a wretched life/ ~한 죽음을 당하다 die in great misery. ざんこく

**참화**(慘禍) evil; calamity; a terrible effect/전쟁의 ~ the horrors[ravages] of war. さんか

**참회(參會)** attendance (at *a meeting*)/~하다 attend (*a meeting*); be present at (*a meeting*)/다수의 ~자가 있었다 There were a large number of attendants. さんかい

**참회(懺悔)** 《고백》 confession 《회오》 repentance; penitence/~하다 confess; make a confession; be penitent; repent of/~록 a confession 《책이름》 The Confessions/~자 confessant; a penitent/~의 눈물 penitential tears/죄를 ~하다 confess *one's* sins/고백은 ~의 표시이다 Confession is *one* mark of repentance. ざんげ

**찹쌀** glutinous rice. もちごめ

**찻물(茶—)** tea 《녹차》 green tea 《홍차》 black tea 《커피》 coffee. おちゃ

**찻삯** the fare (on *train, streetcar*).

**찻집(茶—)** a tea-house[stall]; 《다방》 a tearoom; a resting[wayside] booth; a refreshment/길가의 ~에서 다과를 먹었다 I took some refreshments at a wayside tea-house. きっさてん

**창¹ (구멍)** a hole [made in paper or cloth] a tear; a rent/저고리에 난 ~ a tear in the coat.

**창² (구두의)** the sole (*of shoes*)/~밑 an outer sole/~을 갈다 resole (*shoes*).

**창(槍)** a spear 《던지는》 a javelin 《기병의》 a lance/~던지기 javelin throw[throwing]/~으로 찌르다 spear (*a person*); thrust a spear. やり

**창(瘡)** syphilis ⇨창병(瘡病). そう

**창(窓)** a window 《배의》 a port/~유리 window-pane/~틀 a window frame/유리 ~ a glass window/~을 열다[닫다] open[close, shut] a window/~에서 밖을 내다보다 look out of a window/~에서 얼굴을 내밀다 stick *one's* head out of the window/~을 열어 주시겠읍니까 Will you please open the window? まど

**창가(娼家)** the house of a prostitute; a bawdy house; a whore-house; a brothel; a house of ill fame; a cathouse 《미·속》. しょうか

**창가(唱歌)** 《노래함》 singing 《노래》 a song; vocal music/~대 a choir/~집 a collection of songs/~를 잘 하다[못 하다] be good[bad] at singing. しょうか

**창간(創刊)** the first edition[publication]; foundation (of *a journal, periodical*)/~하다 found; start/~호 the initial [first] number[issue] of (*a magazine*)/~ 기념호 a special number in commemoration of the foundation (of *the journal*)/~호를 발행하다 issue its first number; publish the first edition. そうかん

**창건(創建)** establishment; founding; foundation; organization; inauguration; creation/~하다 establish; found; organize; start; inaugurate; create/그 회사는 ~된 지 오래지 않다 It is not very long since the company was established. そうけん

**창견(創見)** an original view; originality/~이 풍부하다 be original; be fertile; have a creative mind. そうけん

**창게 【動】** a horseshoe[-crab]; a king-crab.

**창고(倉庫)** a warehouse; a storehouse 《동양의》 a go-down 《군수품의》 a magazine/~ 계원 a warehouse keeper; a storekeeper/~업 warehousing [business]/~인도 exwarehouse; ex-store/~ 회사 warehouse[storage] company/보세 ~ a bonded warehouse/~에 맡기다 warehouse; store (*goods*). そうこ

**창공(蒼空)** the blue sky; the azure; the blue expanse of heaven; the firmament. そうくう

**창구(創口)** the lips of a wound; a cut; a wound; a gash.

**창구(窓口)** a window; a wicket/~의 서비스[를 개선하다] [give better] service at the window. まどぐち

**창궁(蒼穹)** the blue sky; the vault of heaven; the dome of the sky; welkin. あおぞら

**창궐(猖獗)** fury; rage; rampancy/~하다 rage; be virulent; be rampant; be rife/콜레라가 전국적으로 ~하다 The cholera is prevalent throughout the country. しょうけつ

**창극(唱劇)** the *Chang*-play; a Korean classical opera.

**창끝(槍—)** a spear-head; the point of a spear/~으로 찌르다 stab (*one*) with a spear (*one*).

**창기(娼妓)** a prostitute; a harlot; a streetgirl; a whore; a white slave 《미》/가난 때문에 ~로 팔리다 be driven by poverty to white slavery. しょうぎ

**창기병(槍騎兵)** a lancer.

**창녀(娼女)** a prostitute; a whore; a harlot; a street-girl. しょうじょ

**창달(暢達)** a fluency; activity; liveliness; briskness/언론의 ~ the promotion of the freedom of speech. すくすくとそだつこと

**창당(創黨)** formation of a political party/~하다 form[organize] a political party/~ 정신 the spirit underlying the formation of the party.

**창대(槍—)** a spear-handle[-shaft].

**창도(唱導)** advocacy/~하다 advocate; advance; preach; uphold/~자 an advocate; an exponent; a proponent/자유를 ~하다 espouse the cause of liberty.

**창독(瘡毒)** virus of the boil.

**창립(創立)** founding; foundation; establishment; creation; formation/~하다 found; establish; form; organize; set up/~ 위원[사무실] the organizing committee[office]/~자 the founder/~ 취지서 the prospectus/~ 30주년을 축하하다 celebrate the 30th anniversary of the foundation. そうりつ

창망(蒼茫) the boundless expanse of water; the blue sea/~하다 (be) vast; boundless. そうぼう
창문(窓門) a window 《배의》 a port. まど
창받다 《구두의》 put a sole on a shoe 《양말의》 put a patch on a sock.
ぎゅうひなどをあてる
창백(蒼白) pallor; paleness; pallidness; whiteness/~하다 (be) pale; pallid; white; livid/~해지다 turn pale[white]/너는 안색이 몹시 ~하다 you are looking awfully washed out. そうはく
창병(瘡病) syphillis; pox《속》. ばいどく
창부(倡夫) an actor.
창부(娼婦) a prostitute; a whore; a harlot; a street-girl/~ 생활을 하다 prostitute oneself; live[go] on the streets.
しょうふ
창살(窓—) 《문의》 a lattice; a grating; a grille 《감옥의》 iron bars/~문 a latticed door.
창상(創傷) a cut; a wound by an edged weapon; a gash; an injury. そうしょう
창설(創設) foundation; establishment; creation/~하다 found; establish; create/~자 the founder/학교를 ~하다 found a school. そうせつ
창성(昌盛) prosperity; flourishing; thriving/~하다 prosper; thrive; flourish.
しょうせい
창세(創世) the creation of the world/~기(記) 【성】 the Genesis. そうせい
창술(槍術) [the art of] using the spear; spear exercise/~가 an expert spearman; a lancer.
창시(創始) origination; commencement; initiation; foundation/~하다 initiate; originate; found; create/~자 an originator; a founder; an initiator. そうし
창안(創案) 《생각》 an original idea[plan]; an originality 《입안》 origination/이 기계는 조박사의 ~에서 나온 것이다 This machine has originated from[is originally designed by] Dr. Cho. そうあん
창업(創業) the commencement of an enterprise; establishment; foundation; inauguration 《건국》 founding a nation [dynasty]/~하다 start (a new enterprise); start business; begin operations; establish; found/~비 initial[starting] expenses/~은 쉬우나 끝까지 유지하기가 어렵다 The difficulty is not to start an enterprise but to carry it to final success. そうぎょう
창연(蒼然) ~하다 (be) blue; bluish 《어두컴컴하다》 dim; gloomy; gray; shady; somber 《고색》 antiquated/고색이 ~하다 be black with age; antique; hoary with antiquity. そうぜん
창연(悵然) dejection; gloom[iness]; depression/~하다 (be) dejected; gloomy; depressed; dispirited; downcast.
しついしたさま
창연(蒼鉛) bismuth; 【화】 Bi. そうえん

창의(創意) an original idea 《독창》 originality/~력 an initiative spirit; initiativeness/~가 풍부한 original; inventive/~력이 없다 lack originality. そうい
창이(創痍) a wound; a bruise/만신~가 되다 be covered with wounds; be thoroughly hurt[injured]. そうい
창일(漲溢) overflow; innundation; exuberance/~하다 overflow; innundate; exuberate. ちょういつ
창자 【해】 intestines; bowels 《내장》 the entrails; guts/~의 intestinal; enteric/~가 끊어질 듯이 아프다 have a splitting stomach-ache 《옆배가》 have stitches in the side. はらわた
창작(創作) creation; origination 《작품》 original[creative] work 《저작》 creative writing/~하다 create; write an original work/~가 a creative writer 《저자》 an author 《소설가》 a novelist/~욕 an appetite for writing; the will to write/~품 a creation 《제작》 an original production; a literary work/~에 종사하다 engage in writing a creative work/~ 분야에서 활약하다 《문학에서》 play an active part in the field of creative literature. そうさく
창제(創製) invention; discovery; origination/~하다 invent; originate; discover. そうせい
창조(創造) creation/~하다 create/~적 creative; original/~력 creative power; originality/~자 a creator/~물 a creatrue 《총칭》 creation/천지 ~ the creation of the universe/신은 만물을 ~하셨다. God created all things. そうぞう
창졸(倉卒) suddenness; unexpectedness; precipitation; hurry. またたくま
창졸간(倉卒間) ¶ ~ in the midst of great hurry; at a moment of precipitation[rush, haste]. またたくま
창증(脹症) dropsy of the peritonium; ascites; abdominal dropsy.
はらのふくれるびょうき

창창하다(蒼蒼—) ①《빛이》 (be) blue; azure; green/창창한 대해 the blue sea; the deep ②《장래가》 (be) long; wide; broad; bright; prosperous; rosy/앞길이 ~ be still young; have a long future before one. あおあおとしている
창천(蒼天) the blue sky; the [vault of] heaven; the firmament. そうてん
창파(滄波) big waves; billows; big rollers/만경 ~ the ocean; the vast expanse of waters.
창포(菖蒲) 【식】 a sweet flag; a calamus/~꽃 an iris flower/~원 a garden of irises. しょうぶ
창피(猖披) disgrace; shame; dishonour/~하다 (be) ashamed; shameful/~ 당하다 be put to shame; be put out of countenance/~를 주다 shame; expose [put] (a person) to shame; make (a person) blush[ashamed]/~를 무릅쓰다 d-

**창하** isgrace *oneself*; humiliate *oneself*. はじ
**창하(倉荷)** warehouse goods／~ 증권 a warrant; a warehouse certificate.
**창해(滄海)** the vast blue sea; the ocean; the deep; the vast expanse of waters／~ 일속(一粟) a mere drop in the bucket[ocean]. そうかい
**창호(窓戶)** windows and doors. まどとかと
**창호지(窓戶紙)** sliding screen paper; paper for sliding doors／~를 바르다 paper a sliding door[screen].
**창황(倉皇)** ~하게 hastily; in a great hurry; in a rush／~하게 떠나다 leave hastily[in great haste]. そうこう
**찾다** ①《추구》 seek; search; hunt; trace; look[seek, search] for; follow; grope／셋집을 ~ hunt[look] for a house to let／진리를 ~ seek for truth／분실물을 ~ search for a lost article ②《저금을》 draw (*one's savings*)／은행 예금을 ~ draw on *one's* bank account ③《전당물 따위를》 redeem; take out／전당포에서 반지를 ~ redeem *one's* ring from the pawn shop ④《방문》 call at (*a place*); call on (*a person*); visit 《들르다》 drop in／그는 나를 찾아왔다 He paid me a visit. ⑤《더 달라고》 ask[inquire] for／아무를 ~ ask [inquire] for a person ⑥《사전을》 consult (*a dictionary*); look up (*a word* in *a dictionary*)／사전에서 단어를 ~ look up a word in a dictionary. さがす
**찾아내다** find out; discover; detect; locate; look[hunt] for; seek／사망 원인을 ~ trace the cause of (*a person's*) death／내 책을 찾아내시오 Please find me my book.
**찾을모** 《장점》 a merit; a good[strong] point 《가치》 value; worth／그 여자에게는 하등 ~가 없다 There is nothing in her. ちょうしょ

**채¹** 《북·장구의》 a drumstick 《새찍》 a whip／말 ~ a whip; a switch／총 ~ a horsehair duster／파리 ~ a fly swatter. むち
**채²** a bearing poles 《수레의》 shafts／가마 ~ a palanquin pole／상여 ~ the pallbearers' poles on a funeral bier. ながえ
**채³** 《집》 the numeral designating the number of houses or buildings／본 ~ the main house[building, wing]／사랑 ~ a detached building[the detached wing of a house] used for a reception／집 ~ 같은 바위 a rock as big as a house.
**채⁴** the length of a long and slender object 《머리채》 a tress of hair.
**채⁵** 《반찬의》 a cold dish of sliced vegetables dressed with seasonings and vinegar／무우 [오이] ~ a cold dish of sliced radishes[cucumbers].
**채⁶** 《아직》 yet; as yet; so far 《겨우》 only／~ 완성되지 못했다 It is not yet completed.／그의 소설 작품은 ~ 완성되지 못했다 He has not yet finished his novel.

**채⁷** just as it is; intact; as it stands; with no change／뼈 ~로 다 먹다 eat[devour] bones and all／통 ~로 삼키다 swallow (*a thing*) without chewing it／나는 옷을 입은 ~ 잠들어 버렸다 I fell asleep with my clothes on.／앉으신 ~로 계십시오 Please keep your seats. まま
**채(菜)** vegetable salad. やさい
**채결(採決)** a division; a vote; an adoption; a roll·call《미》／~하다 divide; take a vote (*on a question*); put to the vote／긴급 ~ a snap division／~을 요구하다 call for a division[roll·call] (*on a measure*). さいけつ
**채광(採鑛)** mining／~하다 mine; dig for minerals／~권 mining rights／~ 야금학 [the science of] mining and metallurgy／~학자 a mining expert. さいこう
**채광(採光)** lighting／~하다 take in light; admit the light／~창(窓) a skylight／~을 좋게 하다 better lighting／이 방의 ~은 좋지 않다 The light in this room is poor. さいこう
**채굴(採掘)** mining; digging; exploitation／~하다 mine (*gold, silver, coal*); dig; exploit; work (*a mine*); 《경영》 operate／~권 mining[mineral] rights; a mineral concession／~량 the output (*of a gold mine*)／~장 a stope／~지 diggings／석탄[금]을 ~하다 mine coal[gold]. さいくつ
**채권(債券)** a debenture; a [loan] bond; a note／기명(記名) ~ a registered bond／국고 ~ exchequer[treasury] bonds／장기[단기] ~ a long[short] term bond／~ 소유자 a bond·holder／~을 발행하다 issue bonds. さいけん
**채권(債權)** credit; claim; an obligatory right／~ 제출 기간 the period for reporting obligations／~ 담보 security for an obligation／~법 the law of obligations／~ 양도 cession[assignment, transfer] of an obligation／~자 a creditor; an obligee／그에 대하여 나는 ~이 있다 I am his creditor. さいけん
**채귀(債鬼)** a creditor; a dun／~에 시달리다 be duned; be tormented by creditors. さいき
**채그릇** a wicker; a piece of wickerwork; a wickerware.
**채근(採根)** 《식물》 digging[pulling] roots out 《원인》 finding out[tracing back] the origin 《채무》 pressing; urging; hounding (*for the repayment*); dunning／~하다 《식물》 dig (*roots*) out; pull out 《원인》 find out; trace back 《채무》 press[urge] [the payment of a debt] dun.
**채금(採金)** gold mining; exploitation／~하다 mine gold. きんをさいくつすること
**채다¹** ①get[be] kicked／말에 ~ get kicked by a horse ②《도난》 get snatched [seized, robbed].
**채다²** 《눈치 따위를》 perceive; recognize;

채다³ notice; find (out); smell out; get wind of/사람이 싫어하는 것을 눈치 ~ sense (a person's) dislike. しる
채다³ 《훔치다》 snatch; seize; filch; pilfer 《잡아당기다》 pull with a jerk 《정도》 accelerate/날치기가 돈지갑을 ~ A pickpocket walks[makes] off with the purse. ぬすむ
채다⁴ fasten; complete; satisfy ⇨채우다. つるさす
채독(菜毒) vegetable poison/~에 걸리다 suffer from a vegetable-born disease.
채료(彩料) the colored pigment; the water paint/~붓 a color-paint brush/ ~ 상자 a paint box/~ 접시 《한 벌의》 a paint palette/~를 칠하다 paint.
채마(菜麻) garden vegetables.
채마밭(菜麻一) a green farm; a kitchen garden; a truck farm; a garden for vegetables/~에 거름을 주다 fertilize [manure] the green farm.
채무(債務) a debt; an obligation; liabilities; indebtedness/~자 a debtor; an obligor/~국(國) a debtor power[country, nation]/~증서 a bond; an obligation/~ 불이행 default[non-fulfilment] of obligations/~를 이행하다 pay[settle] one's debt; meet one's obligation [liabilities]. さいむ
채반(一盤) a wicker tray/~상 a big round flat face; a moon face.
채벌(採伐) felling; deforestation; lumbering/미/~하다 cut down; fell; hew; chop down; lumber/미/~ 시기 the felling season; the cutting period/~지(地) a cut-over area/~자 a feller; a wood-cutter. さいばつ
채비(一備) preparations ⇨차비. じゅんび
채산(採算) doing accounts; [commercial] profit/~점 break-even point/독립 self-support; self-sustenance/~이 맞다 pay; be profitable[paying]; be remunerative/~에 맞추어 사다 buy on a yield basis. さいさん
채색(彩色) painting; colouring; colouration; variegation 《배합》 a colour scheme /~하다 colour; paint; decorate; variegate/~판 chromatic printing; a coloured print/~화 a coloured picture; a painting/들은 가지가지 꽃으로 ~되어 있다 The field is variegated with all kinds of flowering plants. さいしき
채석(採石) stone-cutting; quarrying/~ 하다 quarry[cut] stones/~권[자] [an owner of] the stone quarrying rights / ~기 a quarrying machine/~장 a quarry; a stone pit/~장이 a quarry man. さいせき
채소(菜蔬) vegetables; greens; green stuff/~ 가게 a greengrocer's [shop]; a vegetable shop/ ~업 greengrocery. さいそ
채송화(採松花) 《식》 a garden portulaca; a rose moss; Portulaca grandiflora(학명). まつばぼたん
채식(菜食) living on vegetables; a vegetarian diet; vegetable diet[food]/~하다 live on vegetables/~ 동물 a herbivorous[grass-eating] animal/~주의 vegetarianism/~주의자 a vegetarian. さいしょく
채약(採藥) digging medical plants/ ~ 하다 dig medical plants; gather medical herbs. さいやく
채용(採用) 《採擇》 adoption; acceptance; introduction; use 《임용》 engagement; appointment; employment/ ~하다 adopt (a plan); accept (a proposal); introduce (a system); use 《임용》 employ; engage; appoint/ ~ 시험 an examination for service/ ~ 조건 hiring specifications[qualification, requirements]/ ~ 후보자 a prospective employee/임시로 ~하다 appoint (a person) on probation/ 서기로 ~하다 employ (a person) as a clerk. さいよう
채우다¹ ①《자물쇠를》 lock; fasten/문에 쇠를 ~ lock the door ②《단추 따위를》 button on [up];《훅크를》 hook/단추를 ~ button [up] one's coat; fasten a button. かける
채우다² 《물에》 soak (in water); 《얼음에》 ice 《냉동》 refrigerate/과일을 얼음에 채워 보존하다 preserve fruits by iceing. さます
채우다³ 《기한을》 complete (a term) fulfill 《욕심을》 satisfy; gratify; look after only 《중만하다》 fill [up]; 《수효를》 make up for/가득 ~ fill; brim/욕심을 ~ satisfy[gratify] one's desire/술잔을 ~ fill a wine glass; fill a glass with wine/ 배를 ~ fill up one's stomach. `おぎなう
채우다⁴ make[let] (a person) wear (something).
채유(採油) drilling for oil/ ~하다 drill for oil; extract oil (from olives) / ~권 oil concessions[rights]; drilling right. さいゆ
채유(菜油) rapeseed oil; colza oil. さいゆ
채자(採字) type-picking/~하다 pick type; set type. ぶんせん
채잡다 take the lead; lead a party/일을 ~ take charge of matters; take things in hand.
채전(菜田) a kitchen garden; a vegetable garden.
채전에 a long time[while] ago. ずっとまえ
채점(採點) marking; grading; rating; scoring/ ~하다 mark; give marks; grade; score/ ~부 a grade-[score-]book/ ~자 a marker; a scorer/ ~표 a list of marks; a grade list/시험지를 ~하다 grade examination papers/~이 박하다[후하다] be a bad[good] marker. さいてん
채주(債主) a creditor; an obligee. さいしゅ
채지다 be uneven; be irregular; be dyed

채찍 a whip; a lash; a rod; a cane/ ~질하다 whip; lash; spur[urge] on; encourage/ ~을 휘두르다[울리다] wield [crack, swish] a whip.　むち

채질 whipping; lashing; flogging.

채집(採集) collection; collecting; gathering/ ~하다 collect; gather; make a collection of/ ~가 a collector/곤충 ~ insect collecting; bugging; bug hunting/나비를 ~하다 collect[catch] butterflies for specimens.　さいしゅう

채취(採取) picking; gathering; extraction; gleaning/ ~하다 collect; gather; fish (*pearl*); extract (*alcohol, radium*); mine (*coal*)/ ~기 the picking season/ ~자 a picker; a gatherer; a collector/진주 ~장 pearl fisheries.　さいしゅう

채치다¹ (속도·가격이) advance (in *price*); speed; quicken; accelerate; rise; go up/값이 갑자기 ~ prices jump.

채치다² ①(채찍질) whip;. lash; flog ②(독촉) urge; spur on; lash/사람을 ~ urge a person.　むちでつよくうつ

채치다³ (당기다) jerk; pull violently/사람의 팔을 ~ jerk at (*a person's*) arm.　せいきゅうにひっぱる

채치다⁴ mince; slice; chop up/무우를 ~ shred a raddish.　しみになる

채칼(菜―) a vegetable-grater.

채탄(採炭) coal-mining/ ~하다 mine coal/ ~량 the output of coal/ ~부 a coal miner; a pitman.　さいたん

채택(採擇) adoption; choice; selection/ ~하다 adopt; select/ ~ 여부를 결정하다 vote upon (*a bill*); decide upon (*a matter*).　さいたく

채필(彩筆) a paintbrush.

채화(彩畵) a painting; a colored picture/수~ a watercolor [painting].

채화(菜花) flowers on vegetables; vegetable flowers.

책(册) a book; a volume 《작품》a work/ ~값 the price of a book; a book price/ ~장 a sheet[leaf] of the book/ ~ 뚜껑 a cover; a binding/~을 출판하다 publish[bring out] a book/한 ~으로 묶다 bind up in one volume/그는 ~을 많이 읽었다 He is wellread.　さつ

책(責) ①(책임)responsibility; liability 《책임자》one who is in charge of ②(책망)blame; reproof; censure/ ~하다 condemn; blame; censure; reproach.　せき

책(策) a scheme; a plan; means; measures/대응~ countermeasures/선후~을 강구하다 take measures; devise some means.

책가위(册―) (책의 커버)a jacket; a book cover.　さつのひょうしカバー

책꽂이 a bookshelf; a bookcase.

책권(册卷) a volume; a book/그는 많은 ~을 가지고 있다 He has quite a lot of books., He has a large library.

책동(策動) maneuvers; activities; mischief-making/ ~하다 manoeuvre; be active; be at work/ ~가 a mischief-maker/배후에서 ~하다 maneuver behind the scene.　さくどう

책략(策略) a stratagem; a trick; tactics; strategy; manoeuvres/ ~가 a tactician; a schemer; a strategist/여러 가지 ~을 쓰다 use every artifice.　さくりゃく

책력(册曆) an almanac; a book-calendar.

책망(責望) (비난) blame; censure; charge/ ~하다 charge[lay, put, throw, cast] the blame on (*another*); rebuke (*a person*) for; take (*a person*) to task; condemn; reproach 《비난》find fault with 《힐문》demand 《문책》question, call to account/ ~을 받다 be scolded; get a scolding/행실을 ~하다 reproach (*a person*)/자신을 ~하다 blame[reproach] oneself.　ひなん

책무(責務) 《의무》duty; obligation 《책임》responsibility/ ~를 다하다 discharge *one's* obligation, do *one's* duty.　せきむ

책받침(册―) a pad inserted under a note-book sheet; an underlay.

책방(册房) a bookstore; a bookshop; a bookseller's.　しょてん

책벌(責罰) punishment 《법률상의》penalty; visitation; retribution/ ~하다 punish; inflict penalty on (*a culprit*).　せきばつ

책보(册褓) a book wrapper 《보자기》a [cloth] wrapper; a wrapping cloth; a kerchief/ ~ 꾸러미 a bundle; a parcel in a wrapper/~에 싸다 wrap in a kerchief.　ほんをつつむふろしき

책사(册肆) a bookshop; a bookstore/그는 ~를 한다 He keeps a bookshop.　しょてん

책사(策士) a schemer; a man of resources; a tactician; a machinator.　さくし

책상(册床) a desk; a 〔writing〕 table/ ~보 a desk-cover/ ~에 앉다 sit at *one's* desk/ ~을 두드리다 bang the table; rap on the table.　つくえ

책상다리(册床―) sitting on cross-legged; sitting with *one's* legs crossed/그는 ~를 하고 앉아 있었다 He was sitting cross-legged.

책상물림(册床―) a naive academic; a novice from the ivory tower; an inexperienced person/그는 정말 ~이다 He is green to his job.　よのなかにうといこと

책상보(册床褓) a desk-cover; a table cloth.　つくえのカバー

책임(責任) ⇨별항 참조( page 1749).

책자(册子) a booklet; a leaflet; a pamphlet.　ほん

책잡다(責―) find faults with; take to task for; blame (*a person*)/직구 태만을 책잡히다 be taken to task for neglecting *one's* duty.　せめる

책장(册欌) a bookcase; a bookchest.

책장(册張) a leaf of a book; the pages

/ ~을 넘기다 turn over the pages[leaves] of a book.

**책점**(冊店) a bookstore; a bookshop; a bookseller's.　しょてん

**챗열** a whiplash; a whipcord.
　むちのようななかいひも

**챙** a visor; an eave awning.　いえのひさし

**챙기다** 《모으다》 gather [all together]; collect 《짐 꾸리다》 pack 《정리하다》 get in order／서류를 ~ get papers in order／소지품을 ~ pack[collect] one's belongings.　せいとんする

**처**(處) a place 《기구》 an office／과학 기술 ~ the Ministry of Science and Technology／근무 ~ one's place of employment; one's office／총무 ~ the Ministry of General Affairs.　—しょ

**처**(妻) a wife 《해학적》 one's better-half 《배우자》 a spouse／조강지 ~ a good old wife; a wife who has shared one's difficulties／ 그 여자를 ~로 삼다 make her one's wife.　つま

**처가**(妻家) one's wife's old home; the house of one's wife's parents／ ~ 살이 living at one's wife's house.つまのじっか

**처깔하다** keep the door tightly shut; shut the door fast.

**처결**(處決) decision; resolution／ ~하다 settle; decide; dispose of; arrange.　しょけつ

**처남**(妻男) a brother-in-law; a brother of one's wife.　つまのおとこきょうだい

**처넣다** 《밀어넣다》 push[shove] into; stuff; cram; eat 《투자하다》 put into; invest[sink] in／가방에 책들을 ~ pack a bag with books.

**처네** 《이불》 a thin quilt; a coverlet 《아이 없는》 a quilt for carring a baby.

**처녀**(處女) a virgin; a maiden; a maid 《처녀성》 virginity／ ~궁〖天〗 the virgo／ ~막〖解〗 the hymen; the maidenhead／ ~성 virginity; virginhood; maidenhood／ ~작[품] one's maiden[first] work／ ~지 virgin soil; virgin earth／ ~다운 maidenly; maidenlike; virginal／ ~성을 빼앗기다 be deflowered; be deprived of her virginity[virgin, purity].　しょじょ

**처단**(處斷) judgment; decision; arbitrament／ ~하다 《결정》 decide 《처분》 deal with; punish.　しょだん

**처덕**(妻德) the virtue of a wife; one's wife's help.　つまのとく

**처덕거리다** slap; flap [washings with a bar]／처덕처덕 flapping; slapping.
　らんだする

**처뜨리다** make say; let droop／어깨를 ~ droop one's shoulders.　しきりにたれさす

**처량**(凄凉) ~하다 《황량하다》 (be) desolate; bleak; dreary; deserted 《구슬프다》 plaintive; lonely; lonesome; melancholy; solitary; mournful; sad／ ~한 노래 a plaintive song／ ~한 모습 a lonesome[wretched] look／ ~한 심사 melancholy[pensive] mood.　せいりょう

**처럼** as; like; as … as; so … as／평상시 ~ as usual／그는 원숭이 ~ 나무에 올라갔다 He climbed the tree like a monkey.／눈 ~ 희다 be as white as snow／거지 ~ 보이다 look like a beggar.　ように

**처렁거리다** clang; jingle／처렁처렁 clanging; jingling.　ちゃりんちゃりん

**처리**(處理) handling; treatment; disposal; transaction; dealing; administration; management; arrangement; settlement; discretion／ ~하다 handle; treat; manage; take care of; dispose of (a thing); transact; deal with; settle (a matter); get rid of; bring (a matter) to a conclusion／사무를 ~하다 conduct[transact] business／가사를 ~하다 run a household; manage household affairs／문제를 ~하다 deal with a problem.　しょり

**처마** the eaves／ ~밑에서 비를 잠시 피하다 take short shelter from rain under the eaves.　のき

**처매다** bandage up thoroughly.
　きつくしばる

**처먹다** shovel into one's mouth; tuck in; eat greedily／처먹어라 Dig in!, Tuck in!　むさぼりくう

**처방**(處方) a prescription; a receipt／ ~하다 prescribe／ ~전 a prescription／ ~조제소 a dispensary／ ~을 쓰다 write a prescription／ ~에 의해서 조제하다 make up[dispense, prepare] a prescription; fill a prescription.　しょほう

**처벌**(處罰) punishment／ ~하다 punish; discipline; inflict punishment on／ ~받다 be[get] punished; receive[bear, suffer] punishment／엄중히 ~하다 punish severely; deal severely with (a person)／ ~을 면하다 escape punishment.　しょばつ

**처부모**(妻父母) one's wife's parents; one's father and mother-in-law.　つまのふぼ

**처분**(處分) disposal; disposition; dealing; management; proceeding; action; ameasure 《처벌》 punishment／ ~하다 dispose of; deal[do] with; take action; manage 《처벌》 punish／ ~품 clearance goods[articles]／공매 ~ disposition by public sale／체납 ~ disposition for failure in [tax] payment／재산을 ~하다 dispose of one's property／위반자를 엄중히 ~하다 deal with an offender severely.　しょぶん

**처사**(處士) a retired gentleman; a scholar in retirement.　しょし

**처사**(處事) management (of an affair); transaction; disposal; conduct; handling a matter; an action／ ~를 잘 하다 take a proper step; deal with (a matter) properly.　ことをしょりすること

**처삼촌**(妻三寸) an uncle of one's wife.
　つまのしゅくふ

**처상**(妻喪) one's wife's death; mourning

**처서**(處暑) one of the 24 seasonal divisions occurring about the end of August. しょしょ

**처세**(處世) conduct of life; ~하다 go [walk] through the world; get on in the world/~법[술] the secret of success in life; worldly[practical] wisdom; prudence/~훈(訓) instructions in worldly[practical] wisdom/~술이 능란하다 be worldly wise; be skilled in worldly matters/그는 ~할 줄 모른다 He is lacking in worldly wisdom. しょせい

**처소**(處所) 《장소》 location; a place 《거처》 a living place; a residence 《행방》 whereabouts/~ 불명 an unidentified location/임시 ~ a temporary residence [abode]/~를 숨기다 cover one's traces / ~를 찾아내다 locate; follow up (a person's) residence. しょしょ

**처시하**(妻侍下) a man tied to his wife's apron-strings; a wife-ridden man; a henpecked husband/저 집은 ~판이야 The wife is the ruler of that house.
かかてんかのおとこ

**처신**(處身) one's conduct; behavior; deportment; demeanor/~하다 behave[manage] oneself; carry oneself/~이 단정하다 be well-behaved; be of good behaviour/점잖게 ~하다 play a noble part.
みのふりかた

**처신 사납다**(處身—) (be) slovenly; untidy; irregular; loose in morals; ill-conducted/처신 사나운 남자 a sloven; a loose fish/ 그는 상처 이후로 처신 사나운 생활을 한다 Ever since he lost his wife, he has been living a disreputable life.
たらしない

**처신없다**(處身—) (be) flippant; light; undignified; cheap/처신없이 굴다 make oneself cheap/처신없는 일 an undignified act[behavior]. いげんがない

**처연**(悽然) sadly; plaintively/~하다 (be) pathetic; sad; sorrowful/~한 음조 a plaintive melody. せいぜん

**처음** the first; the beginning; the start; the opening; the outset 《기원》 the origin 《초기》 the early stage/생전 ~으로 for the first time in one's life/맨 ~ the very beginning/~이 중요하다 A good beginning is half the battle./이것이 ~이자 마지막이다 This is the first and the last./그 회사는 ~에는 아주 작은 규모였다 The company began in a small way. はじめ

**처자**(處子) a virgin; a maiden ⇒처녀(處女). しょし

**처자**(妻子) one's wife and children; one's dearest ones 《가족》 one's family/~를 부양하다 support[provide for] one's family. さいし

**처장**(妻葬) the funeral [ceremony] of one's wife.

**처절**(悽絶) extreme sadness; ghastliness; gruesomeness/ ~하다 (be) ghastly; gruesome; lurid; extremely weird; ominous/~한 광경 a gruesome scene[picture]. せいぜつ

**처제**(妻弟) a sister-in-law; a younger sister of one's wife. つまのいもうと

**처조모**(妻祖母) the grandmother of one's wife. つまのそぼ

**처조부**(妻祖父) the grandfather of one's wife. つまのそふ

**처조카**(妻—) a nephew of one's wife.
つまのおい

**처족**(妻族) the relatives[family] of one's wife. つまのしんせき

**처지**(處地) a situation; a condition; circumstances 《형편》 one's standing[status]; one's means[lots]/비참한 ~ a miserable[pathetic, wretched] situation/어색한 ~에 놓여 있다 be [placed] in an awkward situation; be in a fix/그의 ~가 되어 봐라 Try to put yourself in his place. たちば

**처지다** ①《침강》 subside; sink 《지층 따위가》 dip 《용해물이》 precipitate ②《늘어지다》 hang; droop/버드나무의 처진 가지 the pendent branches of a willow ③《뒤떨어지다》 fall behind 《낙오》 draggle 《남다》 remain; stay; stop; linger/혼자 뒤~ remain behind all alone. しずむ

**처지르다** stuff; pack; cram; squeeze/불을 ~ make a big[huge] fire/난로에 석탄을 ~ shovel coal into a stove.
しきりにつきさす

**처질**(妻姪) one's wife's niece ⇒처조카.
つまのおいめい

**처참**(處斬) decapitation; beheading/~하다 decapitate; behead/ ~을 당하다 be beheaded; be decapitated.

**처참**(悽慘) ghastliness; wretchedness; gruesomeness/~하다 (be) ghastly; gruesome; lurid; grim; appalling; wretched/현장은 몹시 ~했다 The scene presented a ghastly sight./~한 싸움이었다 It was a bloody battle/~한 최후를 마치다 meet with a tragic end[death]; die a miserable death. せいさん

**처창**(悽愴) desolateness; dreariness/~하다 (be) desolate; dreary/~히 drearily; desolately. せいそう

**처처**(處處) various[several] places/~에 in several places; in places; here and there. しょしょ

**처첩**(妻妾) wife and concubine.
ほんさいとめかけ

**처치**(處置) 《처리》 disposition; dealing; management; disposal 《방책》 action; proceeding; a measure; a step/~하다 deal with; dispose of; take measures[steps, action]; get rid of; do away with /단호한 ~를 하다 take strong measures [a decisive step]/~ 곤란이다 do not know what to do with/일을 신속히 ~하다 deal summarily with; take prompt

처하다 935 척주

action on. しょち
처하다(處—) ①《행동하다》 conduct oneself; behave; act 《처리하다》 deal[cope] with; conduct; manage/역경에 처하여 있다 be in a fix; be in adversity ②《처벌하다》 condemn; sentence/사형에 ~ sentence (a person) to death; punish (a person) with death/구류에 ~ order detention for (a person). しょする
처형(妻兄) a sister-in-law; an elder sister of one's wife. つまのあね
처형(處刑) punishment 《형의 집행》 execution/~하다 punish; execute/~대 a scaffold; the gallows/~장 an execution-ground/가스 ~을 받다 be executed in a gas[lethal] chamber. しょけい
척[1] pretense ⇨척[2]. —するふり
척[2] ①《달라붙는 모양》 closely; fast; tight/~ 달라붙다 stick fast ②《선뜻》 instantly 《이내·곧》 immediately 《서슴치 않고》 without hesitation 《술술》 with dispatch, off the reel. べたっと
척(隻) the numerals designating the numbers of ships/배 한 ~ a vessel; a ship/군함 한 ~을 출동시키다 dispatch a warship.
척(尺) a Korean foot/ ~수로 재서 팔다 sell (cloth, etc.) by the measure/~수가 모자라다 be short of measure. しゃく
척각(隻脚) one leg/~의 one-legged/~의 사람 a one-legged person.
척결(剔抉) hollowing out; putting out; gouging out/~하다 gouge; scoop out. てっけつ
척골(蹠骨) 〚해〛 metatarsus(pl. -si). せっこつ
척골(脊骨) the backbone; the spine; the spinal column ⇨척추골. せっこつ
척도(尺度) a [linear] measure; an index; a barometer/문명의 ~ an index of civilization/~가 되다 be[constitute] a measure (of). しゃくど
척량(脊梁) the spinal column; the ridge of the spine; the line of the backbone ⇨등성마루. せきりょう
척박(瘠薄) barrenness; sterility/ ~하다 (be) barren; sterile; lean/~한 땅 barren[sterile, unproductive] land.
척사(擲柶) the yoot ⇨윷.
척살(刺殺) ①《죽임》 assassination(암살); stabbing one to death/~하다 assassinate; stab one to death ②《체》 touching out/~하다 put[touch] out (a runner). しさつ
척수(尺數) 'number of feet ⇨척(尺).
척수(隻手) one hand; a single hand/ ~로 single-handed[ly]; all alone/~의 사람 a one-armed person. せきしゅ
척수(脊髓) 〚해〛 the spinal cord[marrow]; Medulla spinalis(학명)/~ 마비 spinal paralysis/~막염 cerebrospinal meningitis/~병 a spinal complaint[trouble]/~ 신경 spinal nerves/~주사 a spinal injection/~ 회백질염 poliomyelitis. せきずい
척식(拓殖) colonization; exploitation/~의 colonial/~하다 colonize; settle/~자 a colonist/~ 은행 a colonial bank. たくしょく
척신(隻身) single life; celibacy/~으로 alone; by oneself; unaided; without a companion. ひとりみ
척주(脊柱) 〚해〛 the spinal column; the

---

**책 임**

responsibility 《의무》 duty 《부담》 obligation; liability 《죄의》 blame/~감 a sense of duty/연대 ~ collective responsibility/유한[무한] ~ limited[unlimited] liability/공동 ~ collective responsibility/중대한 ~ heavy[high] responsibility/일가족 부양의 ~ a family responsibility/사고에 대한 ~ liability for an accident/~있는 a responsible post; a position of trust/~을 지다 bear [assume, shoulder] the responsibility (for, of); hold oneself responsible for / ~이 있다 be responsible for; be answerable[accountable] for (a person) / ~을 떠맡다 undertake[accept] the responsibility (for); take the responsibility for (the matter); charge oneself with/~을 지우다 hold (a person) responsible (for); pass the buck to《미·구》 / ~을 완수하다 fulfill[serve] one's responsibility; do[discharge] one's duty/ ~을 회피하다 avoid[evade, shirk] one's responsibility/ ~을 묻다 call (a person) to account/ ~을 같이 하다 share the responsibility (with)/이 방의 청소는 네 ~이다 You are responsible for the sweeping of this room., It is your duty to sweep this room./모든 ~은 내게 있다 The sole responsibility is mine./미성년자는 자기 행동에 대한 ~이 없다 An infant is unaccountable[not accountable] for his actions./버스 운전수와 차장은 손님의 안전에 대해 ~이 있다 The driver and the conductress of a bus are responsible for the safety of the passengers./~은 네게 있다 You are responsible[answerable] for it./가족을 부양한다는 것은 큰 ~이다 Supporting a family is a great responsibility.

**척지**(脊~) 만곡《의》 scoliosis. せきちゅう

**척지**(尺地) 《작은 땅》a foot of land 《가까움》 a foot away; a stone's throw. せきち

**척지다**(隻—) come to hate each other/그 사람과 척진 일은 없다 I have no grudge against him.

**척척** ①《잘 되는》 quickly; rapidly; steadily; promptly; with dispatch; readily/질문에~ 대답하다 answer questions readily ②《달라붙는》 stick to[on]; adhere to/옷이 몸에 ~ 달라붙는다 My clothing clings to my body. ③《쌓는》 heap by heap; high/서류가 책상 위에 ~ 쌓여 있다 Papers are piled high on the desk. ④《감기는》 coil by coil; twining; clinging/~ 감기다 twine[coil] itself round; twist about; cling to ⑤《개키는》 fold by fold; in orderly fashion/이불을 ~ 개키다 fold up the bedding. きちんきちん

**척척하다** (be) wet; damp/비에 척척하게 젖다 get wet in the rain; be wet from the rain. じめじめする

**척촉**(躑躅) a rhododendron ⇒철쭉. つつじ

**척촌**(尺寸) [Korean] foot and inch/~의 땅 a small piece of land. しゃくすん

**척추**(脊椎)《해》 the backbone; the spinal column; the vertebra(*pl.* -brae)/~염《의》 spinitis/~ 만곡 spinal curvature/~ 동물 *Vertebrata*(학명)/무~ 동물 *Invertebrata*(학명). せきつい

**척추골**(脊椎骨) the vertebra. せきついこつ

**척출**(斥黜) ousting/~하다 oust; dismiss [remove] from office.

**척탄**(擲彈) 《군》 a [hand] grenade/~병 a grenadier/~통(筒) a grenade-thrower. てきだん

**척토**(尺土) an inch of land[ground, territory]; a foot of territory. せきど

**척후**(斥候) 《군》《임무》 reconnaissance; patrol duty 《사람》a scout; a patrol; a reconnoitering soldier/~대 a reconnoitering party/~전 skirmishes of scouts; a patrol encounter; an affair of outposts/정찰 ~ a reconnoitering patrol/추적 ~ a contact patrol/~를 내보내다 send out a scouts. せっこう

**천** (피륙) cloth; stuff; material/~ 조각 a piece of cloth/양복~ suiting; cloth; stuff/~을 짜다 weave cloth.

**천** (千) a thousand/~분의 일 a[one] thousandth/수~의 thousands of (*people*)/~ 배로 하다 increase thousand fold/~에 하나 one in a thousand.

**천**(薦) recommendation ⇒천거. せん

**천개**(天蓋) the lid of a coffin; a coffin lid. てんがい

**천거**(薦擧) recommendation; support/~하다 recommend; put in a good word for (*one*); 《추거》 choose/~하다 recommend (*a person*)/의장으로 ~되다 be chosen president. せんきょ

**천격**(賤格) mean style; mean character 《사람》 a person of low birth/~스럽다 be mean[low, base]. いやしいこっそう

**천견**(淺見) a shallow view; a superficial idea/~ 박식(薄識) superficial learning and a shallow view. せんけん

**천계**(天界) the heaven; the sky. てんかい

**천계**(天啓) a divine revelation; a sign from heaven. てんけい

**천고**(千古) remote antiquity 《영원》 eternity/~ 불멸의 eternal; everlasting; immortal/~의 명언 an eternal truth; an unchangeable maxim. せんこ

**천골**(賤骨) a humble[low] person; a mean look.

**천공**(天空) the sky; the firmament; the heaven/~에 높이 오르다 shoot up skywards. てんくう

**천공**(天功) Nature's work; wonders of Nature. てんこう

**천공**(穿孔) boring; perforation; punching; drilling/~하다 bore; punch/~기 a perforator; a punch. せんこう

**천구**(天球) the celestial sphere/~도(圖) a celestial map/~의(儀) a celestial globe. てんきゅう

**천국**(天國) Heaven; Paradise; the Kingdom of Heaven; Zion/~의 heavenly; celestial/지상의 ~ an earthly heaven/~에 가다 go to Heaven. てんごく

**천군 만마**(千軍萬馬) [many] thousands of troops and horses/~의 사이를 왕래하다 fight a hundred battles/그는 ~의 용장이다 He is a brilliant veteran.

**천극**(天極) the celestial poles. てんきょく

**천금**(千金) a thousand pieces of gold; a lot of money; fortune/일확 ~ making a big fortune with one swoop[at one stroke]/남아 일언은 중~이다 A word of honor is as good as a bond. せんきん

**천기**(天氣) weather/~도 a weather map. てんき

**천기**(天機) the profound secrets of Nature 《기밀》 a deep secret; a precious secret/~를 누설 말라 The secret should not be divulged. てんき

**천기**(喘氣) a light case of asthma. かるいぜんそく

**천녀**(賤女) a lowly[humble] woman; a woman of low birth; a woman of the people. みぶんのいやしいおんな

**천년**(千年) a thousand years; a millennium.

**천단**(淺短) shallowness; superficiality/~하다 (be) shallow and short. せんたん

**천단**(擅斷) arbitrary decision; arbitrariness/~하다 decide arbitrarily[at *one's* discretion]; decide on *one's* own authority[responsibility]. せんだん

**천당**(天堂) Heaven; Paradise; the Kingdom of Heaven; Zion/~에 가다 go to Heaven 《죽다》 die. てんどう

**천대**(賤待) contemptuous[scornful, disdainful] treatment; inhospitable[cold] reception/~하다 contempt; scorn; treat (*one*) coldly; be inhospitable to; give[show, turn] the cold shoulder／ ～받다 be treated contemptuously; get disdainful treatment／ ～받을 짓을 하다 incur the contempt of others. れいぐう

천더기(賤一) a despised person; a child of scorn／ ～ 노릇하다 be treated as a child of scorn. れいぐうされるひと

천도(天桃) a heavenly peach.

천도(天道) ①〖천〗 the orbits of heavenly bodies ②(섭리) [Divine] Providence. てんどう

천도(遷都) transfer of the capital; moving the seat of government／ ～하다 transfer the capital; move the seat of government. せんと

천도교(天道敎) the religion of *Chondokyo*; the *Chondokyo* religion. てんどうきょう

천동(天動) thunder ⇨천둥. かみなり

천동설(天動說) 〖천〗 the Ptolemaic[geocentric] theory. てんどうせつ

천둥 thunder／～ 소리 a peal of thunder／멀리서 ～ 소리가 울려 왔다 The thunder rolled in the distance. かみなり

천둥벌거숭이 a man of reckless valour; a reckless simpleton.

천둥지기(天一) a rice-field that has no irrigation system and depends solely upon the rainfall. うすいにたよるはたけ

천람(天覽) the inspection of the Emperor 《연예(演藝)의》an Imperial Command; a Royal Command／～에 공하다 submit (*a thing*) to His Majesty's inspection. てんらん

천랑성(天狼星) 〖천〗 Sirius. てんろうせい

천량 money and food; possessions／～이 다 떨어지다 have run out of money and food. ざいさん

천려(淺慮) lack of prudence; indiscretion; thoughtlessness. せんりょ

천려 일실(千慮一失) a slip of a wise man. せんりょのいっしつ

천렵(川獵) fishing [in a river]／～하다 fish in a river. かわりょう

천로 역정(天路歷程) The Pilgrim's Progress.

천루(賤陋) meanness; baseness／～하다 (be) mean; base; dirty; low; vile; nasty; despicable. いやしくきたないこと

천륜(天倫) morals; moral laws／～에 어그러지다 violate[transgress] moral laws. てんりん

천리(千里) one thousand *ri*; a far-away place／～길도 한 걸음부터 시작된다 A journey of a thousand miles must begin with the first step. せんり

천리(天理) a natural law[principle]; a law of nature／～에 어긋나다 go[be] against nature. てんり

천리마(千里馬) a horse so swift that it can make a thousand *ri* a day; an excellent horse. せんりのこま

천리안(千里眼) 《투시》 clairvoyance; the second sight 《안식》 insight; penetration／～을 가진 사람 《남자》 a clairvoyant 《여자》 a clairvoyante. せんりがん

천마(天馬) a flying horse; Pegasus. てんば

천막(天幕) a tent 《큰것》 a pavilion 《작은》 a dog-tent 《원추형의》 a bell-tent 《배의》 an awning／～ 생활 camping／～을 치다 〔걷다〕 pitch[strike] a tent. てんまく

천만(千萬) 《수효》 ten million 《무수》 a myriad 《부사적》 very much; exceedingly; extremely／～ 장자 a billionaire; a multi-millionaire／유감 ～이다 It is really regrettable (*that*)., It is quite deplorable (*that*)／～의 말씀입니다 Not at all., Don't mention it. せんまん

천만고(千萬古) remote antiquity 《영원》 eternity. せんまんこ

천만년(千萬年) countless years; hundreds of millions of years; eternity. せんまんねん

천만 다행(千萬多幸) being extremely fortunate; being very lucky; a piece of colossal good fortune; capital luck／～하다 (be) extremely fortunate; very lucky／～으로 다치지 않았다 By a lucky chance, I escaped unhurt.

천만번(千萬番) tens of thousands of times; over and over again; repeatedly／～ 죽어 마땅하다 The likes of you cannot die too often.

천만 부당(千萬不當) absolute injustice[impropriety, unreasonableness]／～하다 (be) utterly unjust; absolutely; unfair; exceedingly unreasonable／～한 말 absolutely unreasonable remark.

천만사(千萬事) all things; all kinds of affairs; everything; all matters; all／～ 다 뜻대로 되지 않는다 All things go wrong. いろいろのこと

천만세(千萬世) all ages; countless generations／～에 걸쳐 for all ages to come; throughout ages; forever. せんまんせい

천만세(千萬歲) eternity. せんまんねん

천만 의외(千萬意外) a great surprise; being entirely beyond *one's* expectation／～로 quite unexpectedly; much to *one's* surprise; all of a sudden. まったくいがい

천만인(千萬人) tens of millions of people; countless numbers of people. せんまんにん

천만층(千萬層) all levels; innumerable [various] ranks[classes, grades]／물건도 ～이다 There is an endless variety of articles in the world.

천망(薦望) recommendation; nomination／～하다 recommend (*to*); nominate／이씨의 ～으로 on the recommendation of Mr. *Lee*. かんりをすいせんすること

천명(天命) ①《수명》 *one's* life／～이 끊이다 come to *one's* journey's end ②《하늘의 명령》 God's will; Heaven's decree; the appointment of heaven 《운명》 fate; destiny; kismet; karma／～을 알다[에

**좇다]** submit to Heaven's will; take life philosophically／ ～에 따르다 resign *one*self to fate. てんめい

**천명(闡明)** clarification; elucidation／～하다 make clear; elucidate; declare; throw light (*on*)／그는 정치에 관심이 없다고 ～했다 He proclaimed that he was indifferent to politics. せんめい

**천문(天文)** astronomy 《현상》 astronomical phenomena／～ 단위 astronomical chronology／～대 an astronomical observatory／ ～도 an astronomical chart／～시[일] astronomical time[day]／ ～학 astronomy／～학자 an astronomer／～학상의 astronomical／～학적 숫자에 달하다 reach astronomical figures. てんもん

**천문동(天門冬)** 【식】 a kind of asparagus; *Asparagus cochincinensis*(학명).
おにやがらのね

**천민(賤民)** a man of humble[lowly] birth; the poor; the underprivileged.
せんみん

**천박(淺薄)** shallowness; superficiality／～하다 (be) shallow; superficial; crude／～한 사람 a shallow-witted[-hearted] person／～한 지식 superficial knowledge／～한 생각 a half-baked idea; a superficial view／～한 비평가 a shallow critic.
せんぱく

**천방 지축(天方地軸)** ①《명사적으로》recklessness; foolhardiness 《급함》 rashness; precipitation ②《부사적으로》headlong; recklessly; foolhardily; rashly; blindly 《황급히》 hurry-scurry／ ～으로 날뛰다 rush recklessly; make a headlong rush.
てんぼうちちく

**천백번(千百番)** ever so many times.

**천벌(天罰)** the wrath of God; Heaven's judgment[justice]; divine punishment [vengeance]; Nemesis／～을 받다 be punished by Heaven; be visited with Heaven's judgment. てんばつ

**천변(川邊)** riverside; a bank of a river; an edge of a stream／～의[에] along a river／～의 풍경 river[side] scenery／～에 살다 live along a river. かわべ

**천변(天變)** a natural disaster[calamity]／～ 지이(地異) the disturbances of the elements; a convulsion of nature.
てんぺん

**천변 만화(千變萬化)** innumerable[incalculable] changes; kaleidoscopic changes; immense[infinite] variety／～하다 change endlessly; make kaleidoscopic changes／～하는 경치 shifting scenes.

**천병 만마(千兵萬馬)** vast numbers[hordes] of infantry and cavalry; a big army.

**천보(賤—)** vulgarity; meanness; baseness; coarseness; grossness.
いやしいほんせい

**천복(天福)** a heavenly blessing; benediction／～을 빌다 ask a blessing [of Heaven]. てんぷく

**천부(天賦)** innateness; inherence 《천품》 gift; endowment; inheritance／～의 natural; gifted; inborn; inherent; endowed／～의 재능 an inherent[a native] talent／그는 ～의 재능을 가지고 있다 He is a gifted man. てんぷ

**천부(賤夫)** a man of low[humble] birth.
せんぷ

**천부당 만부당(千不當萬不當)** being utterly unreasonable ⇨천만 부당.

**천분(天分)** 《천성》 nature 《특질》 sphere; province 《천부의 재능》a natural gift; talents; endowments／～이 있는 사람 a talented[gifted] man／ ～을 발휘하다 display *one's* talent. てんぶん

**천사(天使)** an angel／대～ a seraph(*pl.* ～s, -phim)／소～ a cherub(*pl.* ～s,-bim)／～ 같은 목소리 an angelic voice／～ 같은 angelic; seraphic; cherubic. てんし

**천사 만고(千思萬考)** mature consideration; careful deliberation; deep meditation／～하다 ponder carefully on.
せんしばんこう

**천산(天産)** natural production[products]／～물 natural products[produce].
てんさん

**천상(天上)** heaven; paradise／～의 heavenly; celestial／～ 천하 heaven and earth; the whole world; under the sun／～의 음악 heavenly music. てんじょう

**천상바라기(天上—)** one who has the habit of looking upwards.

**천상의(天象儀)** a planetarium.

**천생(天生)** what is destined[preordained] by Heaven; what is natural 《부사적》 by nature／～ 배필 a predestined marriage; a well-matched couple／ ～ 연분 marriage ties preordained by Providence／그는 ～의 음악가이다 He is a musician by nature. てんせい

**천석(泉石)** water and stones ⇨수석(水石). せんせき

**천석군(千石君)** a large[great] land owner.

**천성(天性)** nature; natural disposition 《기질》 a temperament 《본능》 an instinct／～의 natural; constitutional; instinctive／ ～이 정직하다 be honest by nature／ ～이 온순하다 have a gentle disposition／습관은 제 2의 ～이다 Habit is a second nature. てんせい

**천세(千歲), eternity; a thousand years; distant future. せんざい

**천세력(千歲曆)** a one hundred year almanac; a century almanac; a perpetual calendar. せんざいれき

**천수(天數)** ①《천명》 the natural span of life／ ～를 누리다 live out the alloted span of life; die full of years ②《천운》 fate; fortune; lot. てんすう

**천시(天時)** a good[golden, favorable] opportunity; a good time／～를 포착하다 seize an opportunity; take the tide as it offers. てんじ

천시(賤視) contempt; disregard; disdain ⇨멸시. ないがしろにみること

천식(喘息) 〖의〗 asthma／~ 환자 an asthmatic [patient].

천신(天神) the gods of heaven／~ 지기(地祇) the gods of heaven and earth. てんしん

천신(薦新) offering[presenting] a new product to the gods／~하다 offer[present] a new fruits to the gods.

천신 만고(千辛萬苦) difficulties and privations; all sorts of hardships; severe trials／~하다 undergo[go through] all sorts of hardships; have a tough time／~하여 아이를 기르다 manage to bring up one's child under difficulties.
せんしんばんく

천심(天心) the will of Heaven; the divine will; providence 《하늘의 중심》 the zenith／~은 헤아릴 수 없다 Inscrutable are the ways of Heaven.／인심은 ~이다 The voice of people [is] the voice of God. てんしん

천안(天顔) the Imperial[Emperor's] countenance／~을 배알하다 be received in audience by His Majesty. てんがん

천앙(天殃) Heaven's punishment; divine retribution; the wrath of God／~을 받다 be punished by Heaven. てんばつ

천애(天涯) ①《하늘 끝》 the skyline; the horizon ②《인격한 땅》 a far-off country; a distant land／~의 고아 a stranger in a strange land; an exile. てんがい

천양(天壤) Heaven and Earth／~ 간(之間) the whole universe; the space between heaven and earth／~지간(之列) extreme opposition; miles of difference; all the difference in the world／그들의 사고나 관념에는 ~지관이 있다 In thought and ideas they're poles asunder.
てんじょう

천언 만어(千言萬語) innumerable[countless] words; endless arguments.

천업(賤業) a mean occupation 《고된 일》 drudgery. せんぎょう

천여(天與) a godsend; Heaven's gift／~의 heaven-sent; providential. てんよ

천역(賤役) a mean task[job]. せんえき

천연(天然) nature; natural state; being natural 《자발》 spontaneity／~ 가스 natural gas／~ 기념물 a natural monument／~물 a natural substance[object]; the natural form[of a thing]／~색 natural color; technicolor／~색 사진 color photograph 《영화》 a technicolor film／~자원 natural resources／~의 미 natural beauty. てんねん

천연(遷延) delay; procrastination postponement／~하다 delay; procrastinate; be delayed; be put off／~책(策) a dilatory policy[motion]; a delaying move／~할 수 없다 It admits of no delay.
せんえん

천연덕스럽다 be natural[unaffected]; be unmoved ⇨천연스럽다.

천연두(天然痘) smallpox／~ 환자 a case of smallpox／~에 걸리다 be infected with smallpox; contract smallpox.
てんねんとう

천연스럽다(天然—) (be) natural; unartificial; unaffected; calm; quiet; cool 《태연》 composed／천연스럽게 calmly; coolly 《침착하게》 as if nothing had happend; boldly; fearlessly; without flinching 《태연히》 undauntedly; nonchalantly 《무관심하게》 with utter indifference／천연스런 안색 a natural expression of face／천연스러운 목소리로 얘기하다 speak in a natural voice. てんねんだ

천엽(千葉) the reticulum of a ruminant; the tripe of an ox's stomach／~수선(水仙) a double daffodil／~의 double-petalled; double-flowered.

천왕성(天王星) 〖천〗 Uranus. てんのうせい

천왕지팡이(天王—) a tall fellow; a lamp-post《속》; a gangling fellow《미》.

천우(天宇) the universe; the cosmos.

천우 신조(天佑神助) the divine care; the grace of Heaven; Providence／~로 어려움을 피하다 escape providentially.
てんゆうしんじょ

천운(天運) destiny; fate; fortune; one's lot; one's star. てんうん

천은(天恩) the blessing of Heaven; the grace of God. てんおん

천의(天意) the divine will; the will of heaven; God's will; Providence. てんい

천인(天人) heaven[God] and man; heavenly phenomena and human affairs; a man of talent[s]; a beautiful woman／~이 공노할 죄다 It is an offense against God and man. てんじん

천인(賤人) a man of humble origin; a lowly man. せんじん

천일(天日) ①《하늘과 해》 the sky and the sun ②《햇빛》 sunlight; sunshine／~ 제염 salt manufacture by spontaneous evaporation. てんじつ

천일 야화(千一夜話) the Arabian Nights' Entertainments; The Thousand and One Nights.

천일홍(千日紅) 〖식〗 a globe amaranth.

천입(擅入) intrusion; trespassing; forcing entrance (to)／~하다 break into; force an entrance to; enter by force.
とびこんでいくこと

천자(天子) an emperor; a sovereign 《하늘의 아들》 the Son of the God[Heaven].
てんし

천자(千字) the Thousand [Chinese] Characters／~문 the Thousand Characters Text; a primer of Chinese characters.

천자 만홍(千紫萬紅) the resplendency of floral display; variegated display of flowers; a riot of colours.
せんしばんこう

천잠(天蠶) a wild silkworm／~사 silk

**천장**(天障) the ceiling／둥근 ~ a dome; a cupola／~동(燈) a ceiling light／~ 속에 매달려 있다 hang from the ceiling. てんじょう

**천장**(遷葬) reburial; reinterment／~하다 rebury somewhere else; reinter.
はかをうつすこと

**천재**(天才) 《재능》genius; natural gift 《사람》a [man of] genius; a prodigy／뛰어난 ~ transcendent genius／~ 기질을 발휘하다 display one's genius[natural talent]; give fullplay to one's genius／~ 기질의 사람 He is something of a genius. てんさい

**천재**(天災) a natural calamity; a natural disaster／~를 만나다 be visited by a natural calamity; meet with disaster.
てんさい

**천재**(千載) a thousand years／~ 일우(一遇)의 기회 a rare opportunity; the chance of one's lifetime／~ 일우(一遇)의 호기를 놓치다 miss a golden[rare] opportunity. せんざい

**천재 지변**(天災地變) extraordinary phenomena in heaven and earth; a natural disaster[calamity]／일본은 ~이 많다 Japan is subject to natural disasters.
てんさいちへん

**천정**(天井) the ceiling ⇨천장／~ 부지로 올라가는 물가 skyrocketing living costs.
てんじょう

**천정**(天頂) the zenith; the height／~의 (儀) a zenith telescope／~점(點) the zenith. てんちょう

**천정**(天定) what has been preordained by Heaven; Providence／~ 배필 a predestined marriage; a wellmatched couple／~ 연분 marriage ties preordained by Providence.

**천제**(天帝) God; Heaven; the Creator; Providence. てんてい

**천조**(天助) providential[Heaven's] help; special Providence. てんじょ

**천조**(踐祚) accession (to the throne)／~ 하다 ascend[accede to] the throne.

**천주**(天主) the Lord of Heaven; God; the Creator. てんしゅ

**천주교**(天主教) Roman Catholicism／~ 신부 a Roman catholic father／~ 신자 a Roman catholic／~[教]회 the Roman catholic church. てんしゅきょう

**천지**(天地) ①《하늘과 땅》heaven and earth; earth and sky 《우주》the universe 《세계》the world／~ 만물 creation／~를 진동시키다 《위업 따위로》make the whole world shake ②《사회》a world; a sphere／자유의 ~ a free land／신 ~ a new heaven and a new earth／별 ~ a world by itself[of its own]. てんち

**천지**(天池) the crater lake on Mt. paektoo.

**천지개벽**(天地開闢) the beginning of the world; the Creation／~하다 create Heaven and Earth／~이래 since the world began; from time immemorial.
てんちがはじめてあくこと

**천지 신명**(天地神明) gods of heaven and earth／~에 맹세하다 swear by the gods of heaven and earth; call Heaven to witness. てんちしんめい

**천지판**(天地板) the cover and bottom boards of a coffin.

**천직**(天職) a mission [in life]; a calling; a [real] vocation／~을 다하다[자각하다] fulfill[find out] one's mission／나는 이 일을 ~으로 알고 있다 I feel a call to this work. てんしょく

**천진 난만**(天眞爛漫) innocence; naivete; naiveness; spontaneity／~하다 (be) simple and innocent; naive; artless; unaffected; open-hearted／~한 어린이 a simple and innocent child／그의 행동에는 ~한 데가 있다 He had a sort of naivet naivety and openness of behaveanor. てんしんらんまん

**천질**(天質) one's innate nature; natural disposition 《기질》a temperament.
てんしつ

**천질**(賤質) 《자기를 낮춘 말》I.
じぶんのせいしつの卑稱

**천징어**(一魚) 《어》a bullhead.

**천차 만별**(千差萬別) infinite variety／~하다 (be) multifarious; motley; of various; kinds／~의 multifarious; motley; an infinite／사람의 마음은 ~이다 So many men, so many minds.
せんさばんべつ

**천착**(穿鑿) boring; excavation; search; in quiry; exploration; investigation／~하다 bore; excavate; search; seek for; explore; investigate／남의 사삿일을 ~하다 dig[pry] into a person's private affairs.

**천착**(舛錯) ①《심정》ill nature; cross temper; surliness／~스럽다[하다] (be) ill-natured; mean-spirited／~스러운 사람 a vixenish person ②《얼굴》meanness; humbleness; ugliness／~스럽다[하다](be) mean-looking; ill-looking; vulgar; ugly／~스러운 사람 a vixenish person.

**천참 만륙**(千斬萬戮) cutting[hacking] (a person) to pieces／~하다 hack (a person) to pieces.

**천창**(天窓) a skylight; a scuttle. てんまど

**천천히** slowly; without haste; leisurely; gradually／~ 말하다[걷다] speak[walk] slowly／~ 하시오 Take your time about it., Take it easy. ゆっくりに

**천첩**(賤妾) ①《첩》a concubine; a [secret] mistress ②《낮추는 말》I.

**천체**(天體) a heavenly body; a celestial sphere; an orb／~ 관측 astronomical observation／~ 망원경 an astronomical telescope／~ 역학 gravitational astronomy／~학 uranography／~의 운동

**천추**(千秋) 《천년》a thousand years 《오랜 세월》many years／〜의 한이 되는 일 a matter of great regret／하루를 〜같이 기다리다 wait impatiently for (*a person*). せんしゅう

**천축**(天竺) India. てんじく

**천출**(賤出) an illegitimate child; a bastard.

**천층 만층**(千層萬層) countless classes; all levels.

**천치**(天癡) an idiot; an imbecile. あほう

**천칭**(賤稱) cálling (*a thing, one*) scornfully／ 〜하다 call (*a thing, one*) scornfully[with contempt]. せんしょう

**천태 만상**(千態萬象) all kinds of forms and figures; a great diversity. せんたいばんじょう

**천트다**(薦一) ①《천거받다》be recommended (*for, to*) ②《경험없는 일을》embark on (*an inexperienced enterprise*).

**천편 일률**(千篇一律) monotony; grooviness; lack in variety／그의 말은 〜적이다 He always harps on the same string. せんぺんいちりつ

**천평칭**(天平秤) a balance／ 〜에 달다 weigh (*a thing*) in the balance. はかりのひとつ

**천품**(天禀) natural disposition; temperament; innateness 《천질》natural gifts [endowments]／그는 뛰어난 〜을 가지고 있다 He is a gifted man. てんびん

**천품**(賤品) low-grade articles. じぶんのせいしつ

**천하**(天下) the universe; the earth; the world; the whole country; the whole land; the public／〜의 영웅 the greatest hero of the world／〜없이도 whatever happens; under any circumstances／〜에 [둘도] 없는 unique; unequaled; unparalleled; matchless／〜에 이름을 날리다 spread *one's* name around the world／ 〜를 정복하다 conquer the world. てんか

**천하다**(賤一) ①《비열》(be) base; mean; despicable 《창피》(be) shameful; ignoble／천한 짓 a mean act／천하게 죽다 die an ignoble death ②《비천》(be) humble; low 《야비》(be) vulgar mean／천한 신분 a humble position／그녀는 천한 집안에서 태어난 사람이었다 She was a woman of humble birth. いやしい

**천하 만국**(天下萬國) all nations; all countries on earth; the whole world.

**천하 명창**(天下名唱) an excellent singer [vocalist]; a world famous singer.

**천하 일색**(天下一色) a woman of matchless beauty. ぜっせいのびじん

**천하 일품**(天下一品) a unique article; the best specimen in existence／〜이다 be peerless; be unique／그의 영어 실력은 〜이다 He stands unchallenged in his knowledge of English.

**천하 장사**(天下壯士) a matchless warrior; a titan／기운이 〜다 He is a pillar of strength.

**천학**(淺學) superficial learning[knowledge]; shallow learning／〜 배재(非才)를 돌보지 않고 in spite of my lock knowledge and adility. せんがく

**천행**(天幸) Heaven's favour; God's blessing; [good] luck; good fortune; a boon／〜으로 살아나다 have a narrow escape dy good luck. てんこう

**천험**(天險) a natural stronghold; a natural barrier for defense／〜을 의지하다 take to a natural stronghold. てんけん

**천형병**(天刑病) leprosy／〜자 a lepra. らいびょう

**천혜**(天惠) Heaven's blessing; the grace of God; a gift of nature. てんけい

**천화**(天禍) Heaven's vengeance; divine punishment; the wrath of God; divine wrath／ 〜를 입다 incur the wrath of Heaven.

**철**[1] 《계절》a season; the time／사〜 four seasons 《부사적》all the year round; always／여름〜 summer; the summer season／계〜의 옷 the clothes of the season／계〜을 만나다 be in *one's* heyday[prime]; have *one's* best days／〜이 른[늦은] 사과 early[late] apples／경치는 〜따라 바뀐다 The scenery varies from season toseasen. きせつ

**철**[2] 《분별》discretion; prudence; wisdom; good sense; reasonableness／나이를 먹으면 〜이 든다 Years bring wisdom.／〜이 없다 have no sense[discretion]. ぶんべつ

**철**(鐵) iron 《강철》steel. てつ

**철**(綴) binding; filing／ 〜하다 bind; file／책을 〜하다 bind a book／서류〜 a file [of documents, papers]／신문〜 a newspaper file.

**철갑**(鐵甲) an iron covering 《더께》a coating; a crust／ 〜하다 form a coating; coat／ 〜선 an ironclad ship／먹〜 a coating of ink. てつでつくったよろい

**철거**(撤去) 《퇴거》withdrawal 《제거》removal 《명도》evacuation; clearing away／〜하다 remove; withdraw; evacuate; clear away／장애물을 〜하다 remove the obstacles. てっきょ

**철꺽** sticking tight; with a slap[snap]／〜 잠그다 fasten a lock with a clap／ 〜 달라붙다 stick fast[tight]; cling tight. べたっと

**철겹다** be behind the season; be out of season; unseasonable／철겨운 꽃 a flower late for the season; late flowers. きせつにおくれる

**철골**(鐵骨) a steel skeleton; an iron [steel] frame／ 〜 건물 a steel-frame building／〜 구조 steel frame construction. てっこつ

**철공**(鐵工) an ironworker; an iron-smith; a blacksmith／ 〜소 an ironworks; an iron foundry. てっこう

철관(鐵管) an iron pipe[tube]/ ~을 묻다 lay iron pipes [underground]/수도~ an iron water pipe; a water main. てっかん

철광(鐵鑛) an iron mine 《광석》iron ore. てっこう

철교(鐵橋) an iron bridge; a railway bridge/ ~를 놓다 build[construct] an iron bridge. てっきょう

철권(鐵拳) a strong fist/~ 세례를 퍼붓다 rain blows upon (a person). てっけん

철궤(鐵櫃) a steel safe; an iron box.

철그렁 clinking; with a clink/~ 소리나다 clink; clank. がちゃん

철근(鐵筋) steel reinforcing/~ 콘크리트 steel[ferro] concrete; reinforced concrete/ ~ 콘크리트 건물 a steel-concrete building. てっきん

철기(鐵器) ironware; hardware《미》/ ~ 시대 the Iron Age. てっき

철기(鐵騎) an armored horseman; brave cavalry. てっき

철나다 become sensible[wise]; attain the age of discretion; cut one's wisdom teeth/철날 나이 an age of discretion.
ぶんべつがつく

철떡 ~거리다 slop from side to side; splash; keep lapping[slopping]; drag; trail/젖은 옷이 ~거리다 one's wet clothing slings to one's body. べたっと

철도(鐵道) a railway〈미〉; a railway; rail/ ~ 편에 부치다 send by rail/ ~를 부설하다 build[construct] a railroad/~ 사고 a railroad accident/고속 ~ a high-speed railroad. てつどう

철두 철미(徹頭徹尾) being thorough[exhaustive]; thoroughness 《부사적》from beginning to end; from start to finish; in every way/나는 너를 ~ 싫어한다 I hate you out and out. てつどうてつび

철들다 become sensible[wise] ⇨철나다.
ぶんべつがつく

철렁거리다 keep jingling; clink; tinkle; keep lapping[slopping] ⇨찰랑거리다.

철렌즈(凸─) a convex lens.

철로(鐵路) a railroad ⇨철도. てつろ

철록어미 a heavy smoker; a chain smoker.

철리(哲理) the philosophy; the philosophical principles [of anything]/ ~를 실천하다 put one's philosophy into practice. てつり

철망(鐵網) a wire-gauge[cage]; 《난롯가의》 a fire-guard; a wire-screen 《총칭》 a wire netting. てつもう

철매 soot ⇨검댕. けむりのやに

철면(凸面) a convex surface/ ~ 렌즈 a convex lens. とつめん

철면피(鐵面皮) a brazen face; a brazenfacedness; impudence; cheek《속》/그는 ~한 놈이다 He is a cheeky[brazen-faced, audacious] fellow. てつめんぴ

철모(鐵帽) a helmet; a steel[iron] cap;
a head-piece. ヘルメット

철모르다 have no sense[discretion]; lack judgment; be thoughtless; be simple minded[innocent]/철모르는 아이 an innocent child; a thoughtless child.
ぶんべつがつかない

철문(鐵門) an iron gate. てつもん

철물(鐵物) metal fittings; ironmongery; ironwork; ironware; hardware〈미〉/~ 장수 an ironmonger; a hardwareman.

철벅 with a splash. どぶんと

철벽(鐵壁) an iron wall; an impregnable fortress/ ~의 impregnable/~ 같은 진 an impregnable position. てつぺき

철병(撤兵) withdrawal[evacuation] of troops/ ~하다 withdraw troops; evacuate/~을 요구하다 demand evacuation /월남에서 ~하다 withdraw troops from Vietnam. てっぺい

철복(─服) clothes of[for] the season; seasonal attire/ ~을 갈아입다 change to the clothes of the season.

철봉(鐵棒) an iron rod[bar]; a crowbar 《체조용》an exercise bar; a horizontal bar/ ~을 하다 exercise on the horizontal bar. てつぼう

철부지(─不知) ①《어린아이》a mere child; just a child ②《지각없는》a person who has no sense; a person of immature judgment; a stupid[foolish] child/ ~ 노릇을 하다 behave like a mere child.

철분(鐵分) iron content/ ~이 있다 contain iron; (be) ferric/ ~을 함유한 물 chalybeate water. てつのせいぶん

철비(鐵扉) an iron door. てつび

철빈(鐵貧) extreme[dire] poverty; destitution; beggary. ごくひん

철사(鐵絲) a wire; wiring/ ~를 뽑다 draw a wire; draw metal into wire/ ~ 그물 a wire net/~ 세공 wirework/ 가시 ~ barbed wire. はりがね

철삭(鐵索) a cable; a wire rope 《화물 운반용》a cable way.

철상(撤床) clearing the offertory table / ~하다 clear [the offertory table].

철새 a seasonal[migratory] bird.
こうちょう

철색(鐵色) iron blue; steel blue. てついろ

철썩 with a splash; with a thud[slam, slap]; plump; heavily/~ 주저앉다 sit down heavily (on a chair)/머리를 ~ 때리다 slap (a person) on the head.
ばしゃっと

철석(鐵石) iron and stone 《굳음》adamant; firmness; solidity/~ 같은 마음 an iron[adamantine] will. てっせき

철석 간장(鐵石肝腸) a hard heart; a firm mind; an adamant resolution/ ~을 녹이다 disarm one's hardheartedness; make one's firm purpose waver; captivate [a man].

철석영(鐵石英) 《광》 ferruginous quartz.

철설(鐵屑) scrap-iron; ferrous scrap 《쇠의 줄밥》iron filings. てつくず

철성(鐵聲) a metallic sound[voice]. てつのおん

철수(撤收) evacuation; withdrawal／~하다 withdraw; evacuate／군대를 ~시키다 withdraw the troops／~자 an evacuee. てっしゅう

철시(撤市) closing up shop; suspension of business／~하다 close up shop; close market place; suspend business／~하여 파업하다 go on strike closing all the stores.

철심(鐵心) a firm mind; an iron will《기계의》an iron core; a metal supporting frame. てっしん

철야(徹夜) an all-night vigil; sitting up all night; an all-night sitting／~하다 sit[be] up all night; keep vigil／~하여 시험 공부하다 cram for the examination throughout the night／~ 작업 all-night work. てつや

철없다 have no sense[discretion]; (be) indiscreet; lack judgment; (be) thoughtless[foolish]／~한 없는 짓을 하다 act thoughtlessly[foolishly]. ふんべつがない

철요(凸凹) convexity and concavity; convex and concave; unevenness; irregularity. とつおう

철음(綴音) the sound of a syllable. てつおん

철인(哲人) a man of wisdom; a sage; a philosopher. てつじん

철자(綴字) spelling; orthography／~하다 spell／단어를 ~하다 spell a word／~가 틀리다 be misspelled; misspell a word／~법 a spelling system; the rules of orthography. てつじ

철재(鐵材) iron [material]; an iron frame／~로 집을 짓다 build a house with iron frames. てつざい

철저(徹底) thoroughness; exhaustiveness／~하다 (be) thorough; thoroughgoing; exhaustive／~한 thorough; thoroughgoing／그의 검역은 ~하다 His thrift is thoroughgoing. てってい

철정(鐵釘) a [an iron] nail. てくぎ

철제(鐵製) steel; iron make; [made of] iron《철제품》an iron; iron-work; iron ware; hardware／건물용 ~품 ironwork for building. てつせい

철제(鐵蹄) 《편자》a horseshoe《말》a strong[swift] horse; a sturdy and gallant steed／~에 유린되다 be overrun by the cavalry. てってい

철조망(鐵條網) wire-entanglements; barbed-wire entanglements／~을 뚫고 가다 break through wire-entanglements. てつじょうもう

철주(掣肘) interference; restriction／~하다 restrict; interfere with; check; curb／행동에 ~를 받다 have *one's* freedom of action curbed. せいちゅう

철주자(鐵鑄字) [a] metal type [for printing]. きんぞくのかつじ

철쭉 a royal azalea; rhododendron [schl-ippenbachii]《학명》／~꽃 a royal azalea blossom. しろふねつつじ

철창(鐵窓)《창》a steel-barred window《감옥》prison bars; a prison; a jail／~에서 신음하다 pine behind the iron bars／~ 생활 life behind the bars. てっそう

철찾다 suit the season; be seasonable.

철책(鐵柵) an iron fence; an iron railings[impalement]. てっさく

철천지원(徹天之冤) a lasting regret; an inveterate grudge; deep-rooted rancor／~을 풀다 vent *one's* inveterate grudge／~을 품다 have[nurse] a deep-rooted ranco (against). ふかいうらみ

철철 overflowing; brimming over／~ 넘치다 brim over; run over; overflow／~ 넘도록 붓다 fill to overflowing[brim over] the pot. じゃーじゃ

철철이 each and every season; at each season; around the calendar.

철총이(－驄－) a horse with bluish-gray hair spotted with white.

철추(鐵椎) an iron hammer／~를 가하다 deal a hard blow (to). かなづち

철칙(鐵則) an iron rule; a strict regulation. てっそく

철통(鐵桶) a steel tub; an iron pail／~같은 경계망 a strict police cardon／우리는 ~같이 경계하고 있었다 We were on strict watch.

철퇴(撤退) withdrawal; evacuation／~하다 evacuate; withdraw from; clear out of／~ 명령 an evacuation order／도시 ~를 명령받다 be ordered out of the city. てったい

철퇴(鐵槌) an iron hammer／~를 가하다 deal a hard[heavy] blow (to). てっつい

철판(凸版) a relief《인쇄》relief printing／~ 인쇄 relief[anastatic] printing／아연 ~ a zinc relief. とっぱん

철판(鐵板) an iron[a steel] plate; a sheet of iron. てっぱん

철편(鐵鞭) an iron rod[cane]. てつべん
편(鐵片) a piece[scrap] of iron. てっぺん

철폐(撤廢) abolition; removal／~하다 abolish; remove; do away with／이민 제한을 ~하다 let down [their] immigration barriers. てっぱい

철폐(鐵肺) an iron lung. てつはい

철필(鐵筆) a pen; a stencil pen; a metallic pencil; a stylus (pl. ~es, styli)／~대 a penholder／~촉 a pen point. てっぴつ

철하다(綴－) file; bind／서류를 ~ file papers／서류를 철해 놓다 keep papers on file.

철학(哲學) philosophy／~을 공부하다 study philosophy／~ 개론 an introduction to philosophy; an outline of philosophy／인생 ~ the philosophy of life. てつがく

철혈(鐵血) blood and iron／~ 정책 a blood-and-iron policy. てっけつ

**철형**(凸形) convex; convexity／~의 convex. とっけい

**철회**(撤回) recall; repeal; withdrawal; retraction／~하다 withdraw; recall; repeal; retract／사표를 ~하다 withdraw one's resignation. てっかい

**첨가**(添加) adding; annexing; [an] addition／~하다 add; annex; append; affix／원금에 이자를 ~하다 add the interest to the principal／~물 an addition; an annex. てんか

**첨계**(檐階) terrace stones; stone steps／~돌 individual terrace stones; a [stepping] stone.

**첨단** (尖端) a fine point; the spearhead; a [pointed] tip[end, head]／유행의 ~을 걷다 set the fashion／시대의 ~을 걷다 be in the van of the new era. せんたん

**첨대**(籤—) a bamboo slip; a bamboo lay／~를 꽂다 put the bamboo slip between (the leaves of a book).

**첨망**(瞻望) looking up; lifting one's face upwards／~하다 look up at; lift one's face upwards to. せんぼう

**첨벙** with a splash／~ 뛰어 들다 jump into (water) with a splash. どぼんと

**첨병**(尖兵) a [military] spearhead. せんぺい

**첨부**(添付) appending; annexing／~하다 append; annex; accompany (a thing) with／원서에 이력서를 ~하여 제출하다 submit an application with one's personal history. てんぷ

**첨삭**(添削) correction; revision／~하다 correct; look over; revise／작문을 ~하다 correct a composition. てんさく

**첨서**(添書) an addition [of a note]; an added note; a postscript; a supplementary note／~하다 add [as a note]; insert; append. てんしょ

**첨예**(尖銳) sharpness; acuteness; being radical／~하다 (be) sharp 《심각하다》 acute／노동 쟁의는 점점 ~화했다 The labour dispute has become acute. せんえい

**첨위**(僉位) gentlemen; my friends; all of you. せんい

**첨유**(諂諛) flattery 더러운 아첨. へつらうこと

**첨작**(添酌) pouring additional wine into an offertory cup; putting more (wine) in／술을 두 번 ~하다 add more wine to the cup twice.

**첨지**(籤紙) a piece of paper used as a marker; a tag; a card.

**첨첨** pile after pile; heap upon heap; on and on; layer on layer／책을 ~ 쌓다 pile up books. だんだん

**첨탑**(尖塔) a spire; a pinnacle; a steeple.

**첩**(妾) a concubine; a [secret] mistress／~을 두다 keep a secret mistress／~살림 living with a concubine. めかけ

**첩**(貼) a park [of herb-medicine]; a package [of prepared herbs]／약 두 ~ two packages of prepared herbs.

**첩**(帖) an album; a [note] book／사진~ a photo album／일기~ a diary.

**첩경**(捷徑) ①《지름길》 a nearer way; a shortcut 《쉬운 길》 a short[quick, easy] way; a royal road; a simplified method／학문에는 ~이 없다 There is no royal road to learning. ②《부사적》 be liable to; be prone to; easily; be apt to [tending to]／돈을 꾸어 주면 ~ 잃기 쉽다 If you lend money, you are liable to lose it. しょうけい

**첩로**(捷路) a shortcut; a shorter way. しょうろ

**첩며느리**(妾—) the concubine of one's son. むすこのめかけ

**첩박다** lock the door[gate]; board up／문을 ~ board a door up.

**첩보**(捷報) news of a victory. しょうほう

**첩보**(牒報) a written report to a superior official／~하다 report to a superior official.

**첩보**(諜報) intelligence; secret information／~ 기관 an intelligence organization[agency]; a secret service／~망 an intelligence network. ちょうほう

**첩부**(貼付) pasting[sticking]; affixing／~하다 paste; stick; apply (a plaster); put (a stamp) on／편지에 우표를 ~하다 put[stick] a stamp on a letter; stamp a letter. てんぷ

**첩실**(妾室) a concubine. たにんのめかけ

**첩약**(貼藥) a pack of prepared herb medicine; medical herbs in package.

**첩자**(諜者) a spy; a secret agent; a stool pigeon 《미·속》／~ 노릇하다 engage in espionage. ちょうじゃ

**첩장가**(妾—) ¶ ~들다 take a concubine [with due ceremony].

**첩첩**(牒牒) fold upon fold; layer upon layer; pile upon pile; in piles／산이 ~이 쌓이다 have mountains lie range after ranger／~ 산중 the heart of mountains rising one above another. じょうじょう

**첩첩**(喋喋) glibly; volubly; eloquently／~ 이구(利口)이다 He talks very glibly. ちょうちょう

**첫-** the first; new; maiden; starting; beginning. はじめ

**첫가을** early autumn; the beginning of autumn.

**첫걸음** 《걸음》 the first step; a start 《초보·기본》 elements; rudiments; the first steps／성공에의 ~ the first step to success. しょほ

**첫겨울** early winter; the beginning of winter. はつふゆ

**첫고등** the first chance[opportunity]; the very start／~에 실패하다 make an unsuccessful start; fail at the outset.

**첫공연**(—公演) the première[first public] performance 초연.

**첫국밥** the first meal after childbirth.

**첫기제**(—忌祭) the first anniversary of

**첫길** 《초행길》 an unaccustomed course [route]; one's first trip [to a place]. はじめてのみち

**첫나들이** 《아이의》 going out for the first time after its birth 《신부의》 the first visit to a bride to her native home after marriage.

**첫날** the first day[night]; the opening day[night]/회의의 ~ the opening session.

**첫날밤** the bridal night; the night of one's wedding; the first night of a married couple. しょや

**첫낯** an unfamiliar face; a stranger; a first meeting/~에 그런 요구를 할 수 없다 I can't make such a request of him on our first meeting. はじめてあうこと

**첫눈**[1] 《일견》 the first sight[look, glance, glimpse]/~에 at first look[glance] /~에 들다 be attracted at first sight /나는 ~에 그녀한테 반했다 I fell in love with her at first sight. いっけん

**첫눈**[2] the first snow of the season. はつゆき

**첫딸** a female firstborn; one's first[-born] daughter.

**첫대**(一臺) first [of all]; in the first place ᠀첫째로. はじめのところ

**첫더위** the first heat of the year; the first spell of hot weather/~가 시작되다 the first hot weather sets in.

**첫돌** 《아기의》 the first anniversary of a baby's birthday 《행사의》 the first anniversary. まんいちねんめのたんじょうび

**첫마디** the first word; an initial remark; an opening remark[word]/~를 시작하다 open one's word; open the conversation. はじめのことば

**첫말** the first word; the first remark ᠀첫마디. はじめのことば

**첫머리** 《시작》 the beginning; the start; the outset; the first 〔part〕/책을 ~부터 읽다 read a book from the beginning. しょっぱな

**첫무대**(一舞臺) one's first appearance [on the stage]; one's début(F)/~를 밟다 make one's début. はつぶたい

**첫물** 《옷》 new clothes worn for the first time; a first wear; a first wearing.

**첫밭** the start; the outset/~에 at the outset. まずさいしょのきょくめん

**첫배** the first hat[litter]/~ 돼지 the first litter of pigs. はじめてこをはらむこと

**첫번**(一番) the first time; a first time/ ~부터 from the first[start]/~ 보고 서로 사랑하게 됐다 They fell in love at first sight./~ 경험 the first experience. たいいちばんめ

**첫봄** early spring; the beginning of spring. しょしゅん

**첫사랑** one's first love 《어릴 때의》 calf love 《사람》 one's first lover[sweetheart] /~에 실패하다 lose one's first love/ ~의 맛도 모르다 have never experienced calf love. はつこい

**첫새벽** the grey of the morning; early dawn/~같이 일어나다 get up very early in the morning. あかつき

**첫서리** the first frost [of the season]. はつしも

**첫소리** 《초성》 an initial sound 《첫마디》 the first word[remark].

**첫솜씨** a first try of one's skill; the first attempt[performance]; a green hand / ~치고는 잘 되었다 You have done pretty well for a greenhorn.

**첫술** the first spoonful of food [at meals]/~에 배부를 수 없다 You must not expect too much at your first attempt. いちばんめのさし

**첫아들** one's first son/ ~을 얻다 get a boy as one's first child.

**첫얼음** the first freeze [of the season]. はつこうり

**첫여름** early summer; the beginning of summer. しょか

**첫이레** the seventh day after the birth of a baby. なぬか

**첫인상**(一印象) one's first impression/~ 이 좋다 give a good[favorable] first impression/~을 말하다 give one's first impression (of Korea). はついんしょう

**첫잠** a sleep one has just fallen into; the first stage of sleep/~을 달게 자다 fall into a good sleep.

**첫째** the first; the foremost; number one / ~로 시간을 지켜라 Above all, you should be punctual./그는 학급에서 ~ 다 He tops his class. いちばんめ

**첫정**(一情) a first affection[love, attachment]/서로 ~이 들다 fall in love with each other for the first time. はじめのなさけ

**첫추위** the first cold of the winter; the first spell of cold weather.

**첫출전**(一出戰) one's first campaign; a maiden battle/ ~하다 make[set out upon] one's first campaign. はじめのしゅっせん

**첫판**(一番) the first round; the beginning/~ 씨름에 지다 get beaten in the first round of wrestling. たいいっかいせん

**첫판**(一版) the first editior[printing]/ 책의 ~을 발간하다 publish the first edition of a book. しょはん

**첫해** the first year/미국 생활의 ~ the first year of my life in America. しょねん

**첫해산**(一解産) a woman's first delivery [of a child]/2개월이면 ~을 할 것이다 She is going to be a mother in a couple of months.

**첫행보**(一行步) one's first errand[visit]; 《장사》one's first venture at peddling [hawking]/~에 상당한 이(利)를 보았다 He made a considerable profit on

**첫혼인(-婚姻)** a first marriage／～하다 get married for the first time.

**첨** a membrane／갈대～ the white membrane inside a reed.

**청(靑)** blue [color]／하늘은 ～색이다 The sky is blue. あお

**청(請)** a request; a favor; one's wishes／～하다 ask; beg; request; appeal; solicit; make a request／～을 들어 주다 grant a request／～을 들어 주지 않다 turn down[refuse] a request. せい

**청(廳)** a hall; a building **(대청)** the main floored room／～사 an office[government] building／구～ a ward office／시～ the City Hall／중앙～ the Capitol building. ちょう

**청가(請暇)** 《요청》 application for leave 《휴가》 leave of absence; furlough／2주의 ～원을 내다 apply for two weeks' leave of absence. せいか

**청가뢰(靑-)** 〖충〗 a green Spanish fly; a blister beetle; a cantharides.

**청각(聽覺)** the sense of hearing; auditory[acoustic] sense／～을 날카롭게 하다 keep one's ears wide open／～ 신경 auditory nerves. ちょうかく

**청각채(靑角菜)** 〖식〗 a kind of seaweed used to flavor *kimchi*; *Gloiopeltis furcata*(학명). みる

**청강(聽講)** attending a lecture; attendance at a lecture／～하다 listen to[attend] a lecture; audit a course; sit in on a class／～료 an admission fee／～생 a student. ちょうこう

**청개구리(靑-)** 〖동〗 a tree frog; a green frog; a tree toad.

**청객(請客)** inviting guests.

**청검(淸儉)** probity; frugality and uprightness.

**청결(淸潔)** cleanness; cleanliness; neatness; purity 《개인의》 personal cleanliness／～하다 (be) clean; neat; sanitary／몸과 마음이 ～하다 be pure in body and mind. せいけつ

**청계(淸溪)** a clear[limpid, pellucid] stream.

**청고(淸高)** integrity and loftiness; uprightness and purity／～하다 (be) upright and lofty; pure and cleanhanded. きよらかでこうしょうなこと

**청공(靑空)** the blue[azure] sky ⇒청천(靑天). あおぞら

**청과(靑果)** vegetables and fruits; fruits; greens; green stuff／～ 시장 a vegetable and fruit market; a produce market／～점 a green grocery. せいか

**청관(聽官)** the organ of hearing; the auditory organ[s]. ちょうかん

**청교도(淸敎徒)** a Puritan／～의 Puritanical／～주의 Puritanism. せいきょうと

**청구(請求)** 《요구》 demand 《청원》 request 《신청》 application 《변상 따위》 claim／～하다 request; demand; claim／지불을 ～하다 demand payment／～서 a bill; a written claim. せいきゅう

**청구(靑丘)** green hills; another name for Korea.

**청기(靑旗)** a blue flag. あおいろのはた

**청기와(靑-)** green tiles[slates]／～ 장수 a man who makes a trade secret of his special technique. あおいかわら

**청널(廳-)** the floorboards of a main hall.

**청년(靑年)** a young man; a youth 《총칭》 a young people; the youth; the younger[rising] generation／그는 유망한 ～이다 He is a promising young man. せいねん

**청녹색(靑綠色)** bluish green.

**청따구리** 〖조〗 a Korean black-napped green woodpecker; *Picus canus jessoensis*(학명).

**청담(淸淡)** purity and honesty; integrity; uprightness; disinterestedness; simplicity／～하다 (be) honest; disinterested; upright; plain／～한 사람 a man of integrity. せいたん

**청담(晴曇)** relative clearness[cloudiness] of the sky. せいどん

**청대(靑-)** 〖식〗 green[unripe] bamboo. あおだけ

**청대콩(靑-)** green[unripe] bean; roasted unripe beans with their shells on. あおまめ

**청동(靑銅)** bronze／～기(器) bronze ware／～ 시대 the Bronze Age／～ 화로 a bronze brazier／～ 세공 bronze work. せいどう

**청동호박** a fully-ripened pumpkin.

**청등롱(靑燈籠)** a lantern made of blue silk ⇒청사 등롱.

**청등 홍가(靑燈紅街)** a red-light[brothel] district; gay quarters.

**청람(晴嵐)** heat haze; heat waves [in the air].

**청랑(晴朗)** [weather] clearness; serenity; pleasantness／～하다 (be) clear; fair; serene. せいろう

**청량(淸凉)** coolness; being cool and refreshing／～하다 (be) clear and cool; crisp; refreshing／～ 음료수 a refreshing[cooling] drink; mineral water. せいりょう

**청력(聽力)** the hearing ability; the power[sense] of hearing／～이 좋다 have a keen sense of hearing. ちょうりょく

**청렴(淸廉)** integrity; uprightness／～하다 (be) honest; upright; cleanhanded; incorruptible／～한 사람 a man of integrity. せいれん

**청령(蜻蛉)** a dragonfly ⇒잠자리. せいれい

**청료(靑蓼)** 〖식〗 a kind of smartweed.

**청룡도(靑龍刀)** a broad Chinese sword; a scimitar with a blue-dragon figure on it. せいりょうとう

**청루(靑樓)** a brothel; a house of an ill fame; a whorehouse. せいろう

**청루 주사**(靑樓酒肆) brothels and bars; gay quarters.

**청류**(淸流) a clear[limpid] stream. せいりゅう

**청매**(靑梅) a green plum. あおうめ

**청맹과니**(靑盲—) an amaurotic eye[person]; an eye that is blind though it looks perfect. あきめくら

**청명**(淸明) serenity; brightness; fineness; fairness/~하다 (be) fine; fair; bright; clear/~한 일기 a bright weather/~한 하늘 a clear sky. せいめい

**청밀**(淸密) honey. はちみつ

**청백**(淸白) uprightness; integrity; innocence; purity/~하다 (be) upright; honest; clean-handed; incorruptible/~한 사람 a man of spotless integrity. せいはく

**청병**(請兵) asking for a dispatch of troops/~하다 request [a dispatch of] troops.

**청부**(請負) a contract (for *work*); contracted work/ ~맡다 have a contract (*for*)/~를 맡기다 put out to contract; have a work done by contract/ ~업 the contracting business. うけおい

**청빈**(淸貧) honest[honorable, noble] poverty/~에 만족하다 be satisfied to be poor but honest. せいひん

**청사**(靑史) history; the annals/ ~에 이름을 남기다 leave *one's* name in history /이름이 ~에 빛나다 be famous in history. せいし

**청사**(靑絲) blue yarn[thread]. せいし

**청사**(廳舍) government[office] buildings. ちょうしゃ

**청사 등롱**(靑紗燈籠) a lantern covered with blue silk in the middle and with red silk at both ends.

**청사진**(靑寫眞) a blueprint 《구상》 conception/ ~을 뜨다 make a blue print of /~ 지도 a blueprint map. あおじゃしん

**청산**(靑山) green[blue] mountains/인간도처유(人間到處有)~ To a brave man every soil is his country., Opportunity awaits a man everywhere. せいざん

**청산**(靑酸) [hydro]cyanic acid / ~가리 potassium cyanide. せいさん

**청산**(淸算) 《정리》liquidation 《셈의》 settling[squaring, clearing up] accounts; paying off; clearing/ ~하다 pay off; clear; go into liquidation/빚을 ~하다 pay off *one's* debt. せいさん

**청산 유수**(靑山流水) fluency; eloquency; a fluent tongue/~로 이야기하다 speak very fluently; be a fluent speaker.

**청상 과부**(靑孀寡婦) a young widow.

**청상**(淸爽) being fresh and cooling; refreshingness; crispness/~하다 (be) refreshing; fresh and cheerful; bracing; crisp. せいそう

**청색**(靑色) blue[green] color; blue/~ 사진 a blueprint. あおいろ

**청서**(淸書) a fair[clean] copy: making a fair copy/ ~하다 make a fair copy (*of*); copy out neatly. せいしょ

**청석**(靑石) a blue stone.

**청설**(淸雪) vindication of *one's* honor/ ~하다 clear *one's* name; vindicate *one's* honor. うらみをきれいにはらすこと

**청소**(淸掃) cleaning; sweeping; du:ting /~하다 clean; sweep/오물을 ~하다 collect[clear away] the night soil/ ~부 a cleaner; a sweeper. せいそう

**청소년**(靑少年) young boys and girls; teenagers; youth; the younger generation /~기 an adolescent period/~단 a teenager group/~ 범죄 juvenile delinquency. せいしょうねん

**청송**(靑松) a green pine [tree]. せいしょう

**청수**(淸秀) handsomeness/ ~하다 (be) handsome; fair. せいしゅう

**청수**(淸水) clear[pure] water. せいすい

**청승꾸러기** a jinx; a person with bad luck written on his face; a sad-looking person; a loser.

**청승맞다** [one's face or manner] be suggestive of ill luck; wretched; miserable/청승맞게 울다 wail in an ominously sorrowful manner.

**청신**(淸新) freshness; novelty/ ~하다 (be) fresh; new/ ~미가 있는 문장 a style marked by freshness. せいしん

**청신경**(聽神經) the auditory[acoustic] nerve. ちょうしんけい

**청신남**(淸信男) a male Buddhist believer [follower]. うばそく

**청신녀**(淸信女) a female Buddhist believer[follower]. うばい

**청실**(靑—) blue yarn[thread]. せいし

**청심제**(淸心劑) cordials; sweetener; invigorating liquor.

**청아**(淸雅) grace; refinement; elegance /~하다 (be) elegant; graceful; refined/~한 음악 elegant music/~한 목소리 a clear ringing voice. せいが

**청알**(請謁) ~하다 beg for an audience (with *a king*). せいえつ

**청야**(淸夜) a clear[bright] night. せいや

**청어**(靑魚) 《어》a herring/ ~알 herring roe/~회 raw herring. にしん

**청옥**(靑玉) sapphire. せいぎょく

**청울치** dried inner bark of arrowroot; a string made of the inner bark of arrowroot.

**청와**(靑蛙) a green frog ⇒청개구리. あおいかわら

**청요리**(淸料理) a Chinese dish; Chinese cookery; Chinese food/~집 a Chinese restaurant.

**청우**(晴雨) fair or rainy weather; rain or shine/~에 불구하다 in spite of rain or shine. せいう

**청우계**(晴雨計) a barometer; a weatherglass; a rainglass/ ~가 올라가다 The barometer rises. せいうけい

**청운**(靑雲) 《구름》blue clouds 《고위》high

**청원** ranks[offices] / ~의 뜻을 품다 aspire after greatness[distinction] / ~객 an ambitious man.

**청원(請援)** asking for assistance[help]; calling for aid[rescue] / ~하다 ask (a person) for assistance[help].
じょりょくをねがうこと

**청원(請願)** a petition; an application; a request / ~하다 petition; make petition; ask; request; apply for / 정부에 보호를 ~하다 petition the government for protection.
せいがん

**청유(淸遊)** a picnic; a pleasant outing; a pleasure excursion[trip] / 하루의 ~ a one-day pleasure trip; a day's outing.
せいゆう

**청음(淸音)** 〖문〗 《닿소리》 a voiceless sound[consonant] a sured sound 《목소리》 a clear[silvery] voice.
せいおん

**청음기(聽音機)** a sound detector; an audiphone.
ちょうおんき

**청의(靑衣)** 《푸른 옷》 a blue dress[suit]; 《천한 사람》 a man of lowly condition; a person of humble birth.

**청이불문(聽而不聞)** turning deaf ears (to); hearing and yet paying no attention (to) / ~하다 turn a deaf ear (to).
きいてもきかぬふりをすること

**청자(靑瓷)** celadon; *Koryo* celadon. せいじ

**청장(請狀)** a letter of invitation; a formal invitation; an invitation [card] / ~을 받다 get an invitation; be invited.

**청재(淸齋)** purification.
みをきれいにさいかいすること

**청전(靑田)** green rice-fields; paddy-fields under crop; unripe rice fields 《입도》 the standing rice / ~ 선매 selling rice before the harvest.
あおた

**청절(淸節)** pure chastity; integrity; fidelity.
せいせつ

**청정(淸淨)** purity; cleanness; cleanliness / ~하다 (be) pure; clean; stainless / ~순박한 처녀 a pure and innocent girl.
せいじょう

**청정(蜻蜓)** a dragonfly ⇒잠자리.

**청조(靑鳥)** 《새》 a grosbeak; a blue bird 《사자》 a messenger 《편지》 a letter.
せいちょう

**청종(聽從)** obeying; following; listening (to) / ~하다 obey; follow; listen (to) / 부모의 명을 ~하다 obey one's parents.
ちょうじゅう

**청주(淸酒)** clear strained rice wine.
せいしゅ

**청죽(靑竹)** a green bamboo 《마르지 않은》 a newly-cut bamboo; unseasoned bamboo.
あおだけ

**청중(聽衆)** an audience; hearers; auditors / 많은 ~ a large audience[attendance] / ~을 열광시키다 arouse[move] one's audience to enthusiasm.
ちょうしゅう

**청지기(廳—)** a steward; a manager of the household of a high official.

**청직(淸直)** serenity; integrity; honesty; uprightness / ~하다 (be) honest; upright; just; clean-handed / ~한 사람 a man of integrity; an upright man.
せいれんでしょうじきなこと

**청진(聽診)** auscultation; stethoscopy / ~하다 auscultate; stethoscope; examine with a stethoscope / ~기 a stethoscope / ~로 진찰하다 examine with a stethoscope.
ちょうしん

**청참외(靑—)** a green melon.

**청처짐하다** (be) slow; sluggish; slowmoving / 청처짐한 걸음 a slow pace; a snail's pace.
だらしない

**청천(靑天)** the blue sky[heaven]; a clear[cloudless] sky; the vault of heaven.
せいてん

**청천(淸泉)** a clear[crystal] spring; a clean spring.
せいせん

**청천(晴天)** fine[fair] weather; an unclouded[a cloudless] sky / ~이 계속되다 have a spell of fine weather. せいてん

**청천 백일(靑天白日)** clear[fair, fine] weather; a clear day; a blue sky / ~의 몸이 되다 be proven innocent.
せいてんはくじつ

**청천 벽력(靑天霹靂)** a bolt from the blue; a thunderbolt from a clear sky / ~으로 out of the blue. せいてんへきれき

**청첩장(請牒狀)** an invitation card; a letter of invitation / ~을 내다 send an invitation [card] / ~을 받다 get an invitation; be invited.

**청청하다(靑靑—)** (be) bright green; blue; verdant / 산에 나무가 ~ A hill is nicely wooded.
あおあおとしている

**청초(靑草)** green grass 《담배》 green tobacco / 썬 ~ cut[shredded] green tobacco.
せいそう

**청초(淸楚)** neatness; tidiness; smartness / ~하다 (be) neat and tidy; smart; nice / ~한 옷 neat[smart] clothes / ~하게 차리고 있다 be neatly dressed. せいそ

**청촉(請囑)** asking; begging; a request.
せいたく

**청추(淸秋)** fine autumn weather; a bright autumn 《음력 8월》 the 8th month by the lunar calendar.
せいしゅう

**청춘(靑春)** youth; springtime of life; bloom of youth; the heyday of youth / ~의 youthful; young / ~의 정열에 불타다 burn with youthful ardor.
せいしゅん

**청춘 소년(靑春少年)** a young man[boy]; a lad; a young in the bloom of youth.
せいしゅんしょうねん

**청출어남(靑出於藍)** Blue comes from indigo … [but is bluer]., A pupil excels his master.

**청취(聽取)** hearing; listening; receiving; picking up[catching] a sound signal / ~하다 listen to; give a hearing (to); catch; listen in[to]. ちょうしゅ

**청칠(靑漆)** green[blue] paint[lacquer].
あおいうるし

**청컨대(請─)** we earnestly desire that …; it is my earnest hope that …; it is to be hoped that ….

**청탁(淸濁)** purity and impurity; good and bad; likes and dislikes. せいだく

**청탁(請託)** solicitation; entreaty; supplication / ~하다 entreat[beseech] (one to do); solicit (for); supplicate (one for) / 취직 자리를 ~하다 ask (a person) to get a job for one.

**청태(靑苔)** 《이끼》 green moss[lichen]; 《김》 seaweed; laver. せいたい

**청파(靑─)** an autumn-sown stone-leek. あおねぎ

**청편지(請便紙)** a letter of solicitation; a letter of earnest request; a letter of favour. こいがうてがみ

**청포(靑布)** blue hemp cloth. あおいろのぬの

**청포(淸泡)** green-lentil jelly.

**청풍(淸風)** a cool[refreshing] breeze; pure cool air / ~명월 a fresh wind and a bright moon. せいふう

**청하다(請─)** 《부탁하다》 ask; request; desire; beg 《간청하다》 entreat 《청원하다》 apply 《초빙하다》 invite; ask / 면회를 ~ ask for an interview / 그는 음식을 청했다 He begged for a meal. こう

**청향(淸香)** noble fragrance[odour]. せいこう

**청허(聽許)** sanction; approval; grant / ~하다 give assent to; grant (one's request); sanction; approve. ちょうきょ

**청혼(請婚)** a proposal[an offer] of marriage / ~하다 propose [a marriage] to; ask for[seek] a marriage; ask one's hand in marriage.

**청홍(靑紅)** 《청홍색》 blue and red.

**체¹** a sieve; a bolter 《선광용》 a jig / ~로 치다 sieve; sift; screen; weed out. とうし

**체²** pretense; pretending; false show / ~하다 pretend (illness, to be ill); affect / 그는 벙어리인 ~ 하였다 He pretend to be dumb.

**체³** pshow!, For shame!, Tsk! ちぇっ

**체(體)** 《몸·형체》 an object; a body; physique; constitution; frame; build 《본보기·서체》 a style. たい

**체(滯)** indigestion ⇒체증(滯症). くいもたれ

**체가(遞加)** acceleration; successive increase; increase in order / ~하다 increase in order[successively]; accelerate. ていか

**체감(遞減)** successive diminution; decrease in order / ~하다 decrease in order; diminish successively / 보수 ~의 법칙 the law of diminishing returns. ていげん

**체격(體格)** physique; structure of body; build; frame; make; setup; construction / ~ 검사를 받다[에서 떨어지다] undergo[fail in] a physical examination. たいかく

**체결(締結)** conclusion / ~하다 conclude; enter into (a contract, etc.) / 평화 조약을 ~하다 conclude a peace treaty (with). ていけつ

**체경(體鏡)** a large looking glass.

**체경(滯京)** staying in the capital city / ~하다 stay in Seoul[in the capital]. たいきょう

**체계(體系)** a system; an organization / ~적[으로] systematic[ally] / ~를 세우다 systematize; organize; formulate a system. たいけい

**체계(遞計)** moneylending; usury / ~돈 money for lease at interest / ~집 a loan agency[office].

**체공(滯空)** remaining in the air / ~하다 stay in the air / ~기록 a duration[flight] record / ~ 비행 an endurance flight.

**체관(諦觀)** seeing clearly; a philosophic view 《체념》 resignation / ~하다 see clearly; take a philosophic view. ていかん

**체구(體軀)** the body; stature; physical constitution / ~가 건장한 사나이 a man of magnificent[strong] physique / ~가 장대[왜소]하다 have a gigantic[small] frame. たいく

**체기(滯氣)** the symptoms[an indication] dyspepsia suffer from indigestion.

**체납(滯納)** delinquency in payment [of taxes or duties]; non-payment; arrearage / ~하다 fail to pay; lie over; default; be remiss in one's payment / 세금을 ~하다 fail to pay one's taxes; get behind on one's taxes / ~액 an amount in arrear[s] / ~자 a defaulter; a delinquent [taxpayer] / ~ 처분 delinquency disposition. たいのう

**체내(體內)** the interior of the body / ~의 in the body; in the system / ~ 기생충 an endoparasite; an entozoon / ~ 당분 body sugar / ~ 수정 entosomatic fertilization. たいない

**체념(諦念)** ①《체관》 clear vision / ~하다 see clearly ②《단념》 resignation / ~하다 resign. ていねん

**체능(體能)** physical fitness[aptitude] / ~ 검사 a physical placement test. しんたいののうりょく

**체득(體得)** 《체험》 realization 《이해》 comprehension 《숙련》 mastery / ~하다 get [learn, realize] by experience; realize; comprehend / 요령을 ~하다 learn the knack of (a trade) / 학설의 깊은 이치를 ~하다 realize the true meaning of a theory; learn the underlying meaning of a theory by experience. たいとく

**체량(體量)** weight ⇒체중. たいりょう

**체력(體力)** physical strength / ~ 검정 an examination of physical strength; a strength test / ~이 강한 사람 a man of great physical strength / 우리들은 ~에 있어서 서양 사람보다 못하다 We are inferior to Westerners in bodily strength. たいりょく

**체루(涕淚)** falling tears. ているい

**체류(滯留)** a stay; a visit; sojourn／～하다 stay; stop (at *a hotel, with a person's*); make a stay; sojourn／～일수 the length of *one's* visit／～지 the temporary place of residence／호텔에 ～하다 stay[put up] at a hotel; be a guest at a hotel.

**체맹(締盟)** conclusion of a treaty[an alliance]／～하다 conclude a treaty／～국 a treaty power 《조약 조인국》a signatory.

**체머리** shaking *one's* head to and fro; a shaky head／～ 흔들다 have a shaky head.

**체면(體面)** *one's* face; prestige; dignity; a good name／～상 for honor's sake; to save *one's* face／～을 유지하다 keep up[maintain] *one's* dignity[prestige]／국가의 ～을 손상시킨 자 a disgrace to *one's* country／사람이 ～이 있어야지 You should have some sense of honor.

**체모(體貌)** dignity ⇨체면.

**체미(滯美)** stay[ing] in America／～하다 stay in America／～중에 during *one's* stay in America.

**체발(剃髮)** tonsure／～하다 [take the] tonsure; shave *one's* head 《삭발 위승》 enter the [Buddhist] priesthood.

**체벌(體罰)** corporal punishment／～을 가하다 inflict corporal punishment on (*a person*).

**체법(體法)** the style and penmanship of written characters.

**체병(滯病)** digestive disorders.

**체부(遞夫)** a mailman; postman.

**체소(體小)** small stature; short build／～하다 (be) [rather] small; smallish; short in stature／～한 사나이 short-statured man; a little[short] man.

**체송(遞送)** conveyance; forwarding／～하다 convey; send by post; mail; forward.

**체신(遞信)** communications／～부 the Ministry of Communications／～ 사무 post and telegraphic service[s].

**체액(體液)** body fluids; humors／～병리학 humoral pathology.

**체약(締約)** 《협약》a convention; a treaty; an agreement 《체맹》the conclusion of a convention.

**체언(體言)** 《언》an uninflected word; a noun; a substantive.

**체온(體溫)** [body] temperature; the body heat／～계 a [clinical] thermometer／～을 재다 take *one's* temperature／～을 유지하다 maintain the body heat.

**체위(體位)** the level of physical fitness; a physical standard; physical condition／국민의 ～ 향상 the improvement of the physical condition of a nation／～를 향상하다 improve physical condition; elevate the physical standard.

**체육(體育)** physical education[training]; 《과목》physical exercise; gymnastics; athletics／～을 장려하다 encourage physical training／～가 a physical culturist[educator].

**체읍(涕泣)** crying; weeping／～하다 cry; weep; shed tears.

**체재(體裁)** 《생김새》style 《외형》form; appearance; show 《꾸밈새》make-up; format／책의 ～ the format[get up] of a book／～를 갖추고 있다 have proper from[style]／이 책은 ～가 아담하다 This book is of elegant format.

**체재(滯在)** staying; [a] stay ⇨체류.

**체적(體積)** volume; cubic volume[measure]; capacity／～계 a volumenometer; a stereometer／～측정 volumenometry／～학 stereometry.

**체전부(遞傳夫)** a letter-carrier; a mail-man〈미〉; a postman〈영〉⇨우체부.

**체제(體制)** setup; formation; constitution; a system; a structure／사회의 ～ the structure[fabric] of a society／군대의 편성 ～ the organization of an army／산업의 전시 ～ wartime industrial mobilization.

**체조(體操)** physical[gymnastic, athletic] exercises·physical training／～하다 practice gymnastics; have[do] physical [gymnastic, athletic] exercises／～ 기구 gymnastic apparatus[devices]／기계 ～ heavy gymnastics／미용 ～ callisthenics.

**체중(體重)** [body] weight／～을 달다 weigh[measure] *oneself*／～이 늘다[줄다] gain[lose] in weight.

**체증(滯症)** indigestion; digestive disorders／～에 걸리다 suffer from indigestion／～ 환자 a dyspeptic patient[case].

**체지(體肢)** the body and the limbs; *one's* trunk and limbs／～ 크다 be huge-limbed; have a large body.

**체질** sieving; screening; sifting／～하다 sieve; pass (*something*) through a sieve; screen; sift.

**체질(體質)** constitution; habitude／～의 constitutional／～상의 결함 constitutional defects／그는 대단히 튼튼한 ～이다 He has a very healthy constitution.

**체취(體臭)** body odour[s]; *one's* personal smell／그의 작품에는 그의 ～가 풍긴다 His work reveals his idiosyncrasy.

**체통(體統)** dignity; an official's decency; honor; prestige ⇨체면.

**체팽창(體膨脹)** cubical expansion.

**체포(逮捕)** arrest; arrestment; capture

/ ~하다 capture; seize; take into custody/그는 혐의를 받고 ~되었다 He was placed under arrest upon suspicion. /~장 a warrant of arrest. たいほ

체하다 pretend (to *do*, to *have done*); make believe; feign/안 들리는 ~ pretend not to hear/모르는 ~ affect ignorance. ふりをする

체하다(滯—) sit[lie] heavy on the stomach; digest ill/아침 먹은 것이 체했다 What took for breakfast lies heavy on my stomach. くいもたれする

체한(滯韓) staying in Korea/ ~하다 stay in Korea.

체험(體驗) experience/~하다 experience; go through/ ~담 the story of *one's* experience/어려운 고난을 ~하다 go through many hardships/노동 생활을 ~하다 experience a life of labor. たいけん

체현(體現) embodiment; impersonation; personification/~하다 embody; personify; impersonate.

체형(體刑) a jail sentence; penal servitude (처벌) corporal punishment/ ~을 과하다 impose a jail sentence; sentence (*a person*) to penal servitude. たいけい

체화(滯貨) 《화물의》 the accumulation of freight 《상품의》 the accumulation of stocks[hoods]; stockpiles of goods/ ~하다 accumulate; be held up/~를 일소하다 clear out the accumulated goods.
たいか

체후(體候) health /기~ 만강하시나이까 May I have the pleasure to know that you are enjoying good health?, How are you these days?

쳇바퀴 the rim of a sieve[bolter]; the frame of a sieve/ ~에 체를 매달다 fix a sieve net on its frame.

쳇불 the meshes of a sieve; a sieve net.

쳐가다 carry away; sweep away[off]; 《분뇨 따위를》 dig up/쓰레기를 ~ clear away garbage[rubbish]/소 외양간의 두엄을 ~ clean a cow-shed of manure.

쳐내다 clean; remove; sweep out[up].
はこびだす

쳐넣다 push[shove, thrust, throw] into; eat; shove down (*food*)/책을 상자에 ~ pack books in a box.

쳐다보다 ①《위로 치보다》 look up; turn up the eyes; cast an upward glance/사람 얼굴을 ~ look up at *one's* face ②《우러러보다》 look up to; respect; esteem/공부만 잘 해 봐라 친구들도 자연히 너를 쳐다볼 게다 Distinguish yourself with good results, and all your classmates will respect you. みあげる

쳐들다 ①《올리다》 lift; raise; hold up/손을 ~ raise a hand ②《유리한 조건을》 cite; quote; mention; refer to/선생의 말씀으로 쳐들면 citing what the teacher told him ③《결점을》 point out; indicate; refer to (*the fault* of *others*) /님의 결점을 ~ mention another's faults; refer to another's weakness. もちあげる

쳐들어가다 raid; make a raid on; invade; penetrate into. おしこんでいく

쳐버리다 sweep[take] away; clear; remove; clean up/쓰레기를 ~ clean up garbage; cart rubbish off.
せいとんしてしまう

쳐올리다 《머리를 짧게》 have *one's* hair trim[cut] short.

쳐주다 ①《셈하다》 count; reckon; calculate/돈을 ~ pay the bill ②《인정하다》 acknowledge; treat (*as*); look upon (*as*)/나는 그의 지력과 수완을 높이 쳐준다 I have a high opinion of his intelligence and ability ③《치어 주다》 clean [remove] (*something*) for one. みてやる

쳐죽이다 beat[strike, knock] (*a person*) to death; strike dead. なぐりころす

초 a candle; a taper/ ~심지 the wick of a candle; a candlewick/양~ a candle. ろうそく

초(秒) a second/ ~침 a second-hand.
びょう

초(草) ①a draft; drafting/~하다 draft; make a draft/편지의 ~를 잡다 draft a letter; write a draft of *one's* letter ②⇨초서(草書). そう

초(醋) vinegar/ ~를 치다 vinegar; add [use] vinegar/ ~간장 soysauce mixed with vinegar/ ~에 절이다 pickle in vinegar.

초(初) the beginning; the commencement; the first/내월 ~ early next month. はじめ

초(抄) an extract[excerpt]; a selection /괴테 시 ~ selected poems of Goethe.
しょう

초-(超) super-; ultra-; sur-/ ~경험적 transcendental; metempirical/~현대적 ultramodern/ ~자연적 supernatural/ ~인간적 superhuman/ ~현실주의 surrealism. ちょう

초가(草家) a straw-[grass-]roofed house; a house with strawthatched roof/ ~ 삼간 a small cottage; a three room thatched house. わらぶきのいえ

초가(樵歌) a woodcutter's song. しょうか

초가을(初—) early autumn [fall]; the beginning of autumn. はつあき

초개(草芥) bits of straw[grass]; a worthless thing/~ 같나 be worthless [as bits of straw]/~ 같은 인생 a worthless life; a humble life. そうかい

초겨울(初—) early winter; the beginning of winter. はつふゆ

초경(初經) 《첫 월경》 menarche.

초경(初更) the first watch [of the night]; early evening.

초계(哨戒) patrolling/ ~하다 patrol/~정(艇) a patrol-boat/~중에 on patrol.
しょうかい

초고(草稿) a rough copy; a draft; a manuscript/~를 만들다 prepare[make] a draft/~를 보고 연설하다 make a speech

**초꽂이** a sconce [for candlestick].　ろうそくたて

**초과**(超過) excess; surplus/~하다 exceed; be in excess (of)/수입 ~ excess of imports over exports/인구의 ~ a surplus population/인플레는 공급에 대한 수요의 ~다 Inflation is an excess of demand over supply.　ちょうか

**초교**(初校) the first proof-reading; the first proof[-sheet]/~를 보다 read the first proof.　しょこう

**초국가주의**(超國家主義) ultranationalism/~자 an ultranationalist.
　　　ちょうこっかしゅぎ

**초군**(樵軍) a woodcutter; a woodman.　きこり

**초근 목피**(草根木皮) coarse and miserable food; roots of herbs and barks of trees/~로 연명하다 barely manage to stay alive with the aid of[eating] herbroots and treebarks.　そうこんぼくひ

**초금**(草琴) a reed; a grass harp/~을 불다 blow on a grass harp.　くさぶえ

**초급**(初級) a primary grade[class]; the lowest[beginner's] class/~ 영문법 English Grammar for Beginners/~ 학교 a primary school.　しょきゅう

**초급**(初給) a starting[initial, beginning] salary/~은 만 원이었다 I began[started] with a salary of ten thousand won.　しょきゅう

**초기**(初期) 《시대》 the early days[period]; 《병의》 the first[initial, incipient] stage/~의 early; initial/~의 결핵 incipient consumption.　しょき

**초년**(初年) ①《첫해》 the first year 《초기》 early years/ ~급(級) the beginners' class ②《인생의》 young age; earlier years.　しょねん

**초념**(初念) one's original intention (purpose) 《초지(初志)》.

**초단**(初段) the first grade/바둑 ~자 a first-grade player of Badook.　しょだん

**초단파**(超短波) 『물』 ultra-short waves microwaves.　ちょうたんぱ

**초당**(草堂) a thatched hut.

**초당파**(超黨派) super[supra]-partisan; bipartisan.

**초대**(初一) a green hand; a greenhorn; a novice/골프에 있어서는 그는 아직 ~다 He is still a beginner[greenhorn] in golf.　しろうと

**초대**(招待) invitation/~하다 invite [ask] one (to); be host to/~권 a courtesy card.　しょうたい

**초대**(初代) 《제 1 대》 the first generation; the founder/~의 the first/~ 회장 the first president of the association.
　　　しょだい

**초동**(樵童) a woodcutter; a wood-boy; a young woodsman.　しょうどう

**초동**(初冬) early winter.　はつふゆ

**초두**(初頭) the beginning; the outset; the first/사업 ~에 실패하다 fail at the very beginning of an undertaking.

**초들다** mention; refer to; cite/남의 결점을 ~ mention[bring up] a person's shortcomings.　しょとう

**초등**(初等) ~의 elementary; primary/~ 교육 elementary[primary] education.
　　　しょとう

**초라떼다** be snubbed; be taken down a peg or two; meet with a rebuff because of one's obtrusiveness.
　　　はじをかく

**초라하다** (be) shabby; miserable; wretched[poor]-looking; seedy/초라한 옷 shabby clothes.　みすぼらしい

**초래**(招來) ~하다 bring about[on]; cause; incur; lead; give rise to; court/위험을 ~하다 invite[bring on] danger.
　　　しょうらい

**초략**(抄略) 《약탈》 pillage; plunder; spoliation/~하다 plunder; pillage; loot.

**초련** an early crop to be used until the regular harvest time.

**초련**(初鍊) a rough-planed[hewn] board; preliminary arrangements.
　　　あらましすること

**초례**(醮禮) the nuptials; a marriage[wedding] ceremony.

**초로**(草路) the pass across the grass field.　くさむらのなかのどうろ

**초로**(草露) dew on the grass blade/~와 같은 목숨 transient life　そうろ

**초로**(初老) the age of forty years; the beginning of middle age/~의 신사 an elderly gentleman.

**초록**(抄錄) an abstract; an extract; a summary; an excerpt/ ~하다 excerpt; extract/시사 ~ a summary of current affairs.　しょうろく

**초록**(草綠) green; grass-green/~빛 green color.　きみどりいろ

**초롱** a tinplate container; a tin〈영〉; a can〈미〉; 《용량》 a can[bucket]-ful [of liquid]/물 두 ~ two pails of water.
　　　せきゆかん

**초롱**(一籠) a silk-covered lantern; a lantern of gauze; a hand-lantern.

**초롱꽃** 『식』 a [dotted] bellflower.
　　　ほたるぶくろ

**초름하다** ①《못이 적다》 (be) dissatisfying (in amount, quantity); less than due amount[quantity] ②《넉넉치 못하다》 (be) not abundant[rich]; scarce ③《모자라다》 (be) wanting; short of.
　　　すこしすくない

**초립**(草笠) a straw hat [worn by a young married man of below twenty].

**초립동**(草笠童) a lad [wearing a straw hat]; a young adult.

**초막**(草幕) a straw-thatched hut.

**초만원**(超滿員) being filled to overflowing/~의 filled to overflowing/~을 이루다 be overly filled-up.　ちょうまんいん

**초망**(草莽) ~하다 (be) boorish[rustic, uncouth]; be unfamiliar with the ways of the world; (be) naive／~한 야인 a boor.　そうぼう

**초매**(草昧) ①《태고》 primitive state; primitiveness／태고의 ~ 시대 the remote unenlightened[uncivilized] ages ②《혼란》 confusion; disorder; disorganization; chaos.　そうまい

**초면**(初面) the first meeting[interview]; seeing[meeting] for the first time／~의 인상 one's first impression／~ 친구 a stranger.　はじめてあうこと

**초멸**(剿滅) extirpation; extermination／~하다 《일소》 clean (a place) of (the enemy); 《전멸》 exterminate; root out.

**초목**(草木) trees and grass; plants; vegetation／~이 우거지다 have lush vegetation.　そうもく

**초문**(初聞) the latest[last] news; hot news／금시 ~이다 That's quite news to me, I have never heard of it before.

**초미**(焦眉) emergency; urgency; imminence／~의 urgent; pressing; imminent; burning.　しょうび

**초민**(焦悶) impatience; worry; trouble／~하다 be worried (about); be impatient; be sad at heart.　はがゆいこと

**초밥**(酢—) vinegared rice and fish[seaweed].

**초배**(初褙) the first coat of wallpaper; the underpapering of a wall／~하다 underpaper; paste the first coat of wallpaper on.

**초벌**(初—) the first; the primary; a rough job ⇨애벌／~김 the first weeding.　まっさいしょ

**초범**(初犯) the first offence／~자 a first offender.　しょはん

**초범**(超凡) extraordinariness; being out of the common／~하다 be extraordinary; be uncommon.
ふつうのものよりすぐれていること

**초벽**(初壁) the inner first coat of clay of a wall ⇨맞벽.

**초병**(哨兵) a sentinel; a sentry; a military guard／~선 a sentry line／~ 근무 sentry-duty.　しょうへい

**초보**(初步) ①《시작》 the beginning; the start; the outset; the first step／~를 잘못 디디다 take a false step ②《첫걸음》 first steps; the ABC (of)／수학의 ~ the rudiments of arithmetic.　しょほ

**초복**(初伏) the first day of dog days; the beginning of the hottest period.
しょふく

**초본**(抄本) an extract; an abstract／호적 ~ an abstract of[an extract copied from] the census register.

**초본**(草本) 《식》 herbs; a ceous plants／~의 herbal／~경(莖) a herbaceous system.　そうほん

**초봄**(初—) early spring; the beginning of spring／~부터 from early spring.

**초부**(樵夫) a woodcutter.　しょうふ

**초빙**(招聘) invitation[employment]／~하다 extend a call to (a person); engage; employ／전문가를 ~하다 call in a specialist.　しょうへい

**초사**(焦思) worry／~하다 worry about; be anxious (for).　しょうし

**초산**(初産) one's first childbirth／~부 a woman born her first child.　しょさん

**초산**(硝酸) nitric acid ⇨질산.　しょうさん

**초산**(醋酸) acetic acid.　さくさん

**초상**(肖像) a portrait; a likeness／~화가 a portrait-painter／~화를 그리게 하다 sit for one's portrait.　しょうぞう

**초상**(初霜) the first frost of the season.
はつしも

**초상**(初喪) 《장례》 a death; a mourning; funeral services[rites]／~집 a house of mourning[death]／~ ~을 치르다 hold a funeral.　にんげんがしぬこと

**초상화**(肖像畵) a portrait／유화의 ~ a portrait in oil／~를 그리게 하다 sit for one's portrait.　しょうぞうが

**초색**(草色) [dark] green.　そうしょく

**초생**(初生) the beginning of a month／~달 a new[young] moon.　しょせい

**초서**(草書) the cursive[running] style of penmanship 《글씨》 cursive characters／~체 활자 script type／~체로 쓰다 write in a cursive hand.　そうしょ

**초석**(硝石) [potassium] nitrate／칠레 ~ nitrate of soda.　しょうせき

**초석**(礎石) a foundation stone; a cornerstone; a foundation／원자학의 ~을 놓다 lay the foundation of atomic science.
そせき

**초석**(草席) a straw mat.

**초석**(礁石) a reef; a submerged[sunken] rock.　しょうせき

**초설**(初雪) the first snow [of the season].　はつゆき

**초성**(初聲) an initial sound.

**초속**(初速) 《물》 initial velocity 《탄환의》 muzzle velocity.

**초속**(秒速) a velocity per second／~ 20미터 a speed of 20 meters a second.

**초속도**(超速度) super[ultra]-high speed／~ 윤전기 a super-high speed rotary press.　ちょうそくど

**초순**(初旬) the first third[ten days] of a month／~에 early in [January]; at the beginning of a month.　しょじゅん

**초승** first days [of the month].　しょせい

**초시류**(鞘翅類) 《충》 Coleoptera(학명)／~의 곤충 the coleopteron.

**초식**(草食) grass-eating; living on grass; eating vegetables／~하다 eat grass; live on grass[vegetables]／~ 동물 a grasseating animal.　そうしょく

**초심**(初心) ①《처음 마음》 one's original intention[purpose, aim] ②《미숙》 greenness／~의 uninitiated; inexpert; green ③《초심자》 a beginner; a greenh-

**초심(焦心)** impatience; restlessness; worry; trouble/～하다 be worried about; be concerned about; be impatient; be anxious (*for*). しょうしん

**초심(初審)** the first trial[hearing]/～ 재판소 a court of first instance. しょしん

**초안(草案)** a [rough] draft/헌법 ～ the draft of a constitution/～을 기초하다 draft[frame] a bill; prepare a draft. そうあん

**초야(草野)** an out-of-the-way place; the boondocks; the backwoods; a remote corner of the country/～에 묻혀 살다 live in seclusion; remain in private life; live in absolute privacy. へきそん

**초야(初夜)** the first half part of a night 《첫날밤》the first night; the bridal night; a wedding night. しょや

**초역(抄譯)** an abridged translation; translation of selected passages; a selected translation/ ～하다 translate selected passages (*from*). しょうやく

**초연(超然)** detachment; transcendence; aloofness/～하다 stand[keep] aloof from (*a matter*); be unconcerned; be above/～히 대중에 섞이지 않다 keep aloof from the crowd. ちょうぜん

**초연(初演)** the first performance 《배우의》one's debut on the stage; *a première*(F)/이 나라에서의 ～ the first performance of a play in this country.

**초연(硝煙)** gunsmoke; the smoke of battle/～ 탄우 속에 in the thick of the fight[ing]; in the midst of the gunsmoke and bullets. しょうえん

**초연(悄然)** ～히 dispiritedly; with a heavy heart; in a low spirit; dejectedly; crestfallenly. しょうぜん

**초열 지옥(焦熱地獄)**《불교》an inferno. しょうねつじごく

**초엽(初葉)** the early years[days]; the beginning; the initial phase/건국 ～에 in the opening years of the establishment of a state. しょよう

**초옥(草屋)** a grass-roofed house; a straw-thatched hut. くさや

**초원(草原)** a plain; a grassland 《북미의》 a prairie 《남미의》a pampas 《러시아・중아시아의》a steppe. そうげん

**초월(超越)**《탁월》superiority; [super-]excellence; transcendence/～하다 transcend; excel; surpass; be superior to/인력을 ～하다 transcend human power. ちょうえつ

**초유(初有)** ～의 first; initial; original/이것은 우리나라 ～의 일이다 This is really unexampled[unprecedented] in the history of this country. さいしょ

**초음(超音)** supersonic/ ～파 supersonic waves/～속 supersonic speed.

**초음속(超音速)**【물】supersonic speed.

**초인(超人)** a superman/～적 superhuman /～적인 노력 superhuman efforts[Herculean]/～주의 supermanism; overmanism. ちょうじん

**초인종(招人鐘)** a call-bell; a buzzer; a [door-]bell/ ～ 소리가 난다 There is the door bell ringing.

**초일(初日)** the first[opening] day; an opening; the opening night of a show 《연극의》the *première*(F). しょじつ

**초임(初任)** the first appointment/ ～ 인사를 하다 make an inaugural address /～ 교원 a newly appointed teacher/ ～급 2만 원이었다 I started off[began] with a salary of twenty thousand *won*. しょにん

**초입(初入)**《어귀》an entrance; an entry an approach; a way in; the mouth《처음 들어감》the first entrance/～에서 of the entrance/～객 the first customer of the day. はじめてはいるいりぐち

**초자연적(超自然的)** supernatural/～ 현상 supernatural phenomena/ ～주의 supernaturalism. ちょうしぜんてき

**초잡다(草—)** draft; make a draft (*of*)/ 연설을 ～ draft a speech. したがきする

**초장(初章)**【음】the first movement 《글》 the first chapter; the first of the verses of a Korean *shijo* poem.

**초장(醋醬)** soysauce mixed with vinegar and pine-nut meal.

**초재(草材)** native medicinal herbs. そうやく

**초저녁(初—)** early [in the] evening; the early hours of evening/아직 ～이었다 The night was still young.

**초절(超絶)** transcendence; supremacy《탁월》excellence/ ～하다 transcend; excel; surpass/ ～주의 transcendentalism/～주의자 a transcendentalist. ちょうぜつ

**초점(焦點)** a focus(*pl.* ～es, -ci);a focal point/ ～을 맞추다 focus; bring to a focus; adjust the focus (*of*)/공격의 ～ 이 되다 bear the brunt to an attack. しょうてん

**초조(焦燥)** anxiousness; impatience; irritation/～하다 (be) impatient; irritated; anxious/～한 기분으로 in an impatient mood/귀환을 ～하게 기다리다 wait impatiently for (*a person's*) return. しょうそう

**초조(初潮)** the first menstruation; the first menses ⇨초경(初經).

**초주검되다** be half dead; get half killed /맞아서 ～ be beaten half to death/그 녀석을 초주검되게 해 줄 테다 I will beat him within an inch of his life. しちにおちいる

**초지(初志)** *one's* original intention[purpose]/ ～를 관철하다 accomplish *one's* purpose/나는 ～를 관철하련다 I will carry out my original intention. しょし

**초지(草紙)** paper used in preparing a

초진(初診) the first medical examination／ ～의 환자 a new patient／ ～료 fee for the first medical examination.
초집(草—) a straw-thatched house.
초집(抄輯) [a collection of] excerpts[abstracts]／ ～하다 excerpt (*from*); extract (*from*); make an abstract (*of*)／법안 extracts of bills; a copy of extracted bills. ぬきがきしたきろく
초창(草創) origination; beginning; the start; an early stage／사업의 ～ the beginning of a business／～기 infancy; an early stage.
초청(招請) invitation／ ～하다 invite (*a person*) to; ask (*a person*) to／～에 응하다 accept an invitation／강사를 ～하다 invite[call in] a lecturer／ ～장 an invitation [card]. しょうせい
초체(草體) the cursive[running] style of brushmanship 《글자》 a cursive character／～로 쓰다 write in a cursive hand [style]／ ～ 활자 script type. そうたい
초추(初秋) early autumn[fall]; the beginning of autumn. しょしゅう
초춘(初春) early spring; the beginning of spring. しょしゅん
초출(抄出) extraction; excerption; selection／ ～하다 make an extract (*from*); extract (*from*); excerpt (*from*); single out. しょうしゅつ
초출(初出) appearing for the first time; the first [of the season]／ ～ 참외 the first melon of the season. はつで
초출(超出) excellence; remarkableness; outstandingness; eminence.
ぬきんでること
초췌(憔悴) haggardness; emaciation／ ～하다 (be) haggard; thin; emaciated; gaunt; worn out／그는 모습이 ～하다 He looks haggard. しょうすい
초취(初娶) one's first wife. しょこんのつま
초치(招致) a summons; [an] invitation ／ ～하다 summon; invite／외국 대사를 회담에 ～하다 summon an ambassador for a conference. しょうち
초친놈 a worthless playboy; a rake of no promise; a hopeless *roué*(F).
초침(秒針) a second-hand [of a watch].
びょうしん
초탈(超脫) transcendence; detachment; aloofness／～하다 transcend; rise above the ways of the world／속세를 ～하다 keep aloof from the world; rise above the ways of the world.
초토(焦土) scorched[parched] earth; burnt ground／ ～화하다 be burnt to the ground; be reduced to the ashes／아름다운 거리는 전쟁으로 ～화되었다 War turned the beautiful streets into ruins.
しょうど
초특급(超特急) a super-express [train] ／ ～으로 by a super-express [train].
ちょうとっきゅう

초특작품(超特作品) a super-film[-production]; a special feature.
초판(初—) the first round[period, bout, scene]／ ～에는 실패했다 I failed [in it] at first. しょ
초판(初版) the first edition／～ 1만 부 the first printing of 10,000 copies. しょはん
초피(貂皮) sable; marten. てんのかわ
초하(初夏) the beginning of summer; early [in the] summer. しょか
초하다(草—) draft; make a draft; draw [write] up／법안을 ～ draft a bill／편지를 ～ draft a letter. したがきする
초하다(抄—) 《베끼다》 transcribe; copy 《엮다》 abstract; make an abstract[extract] of／시선집(詩選集)을 ～ make a selection of poems. うつしとる
초하룻날(初—) the first [day] of the month. そのつきのついたちのひ
초학(初學) 《처음 배움》 first learning; start of studies 《초학의 학문》 the rudiments; elements; a beginner's course／～자 a beginner; a novice; a tyro. しょがく
초학(初瘧) the first attack of malaria.
초한(初寒) the first cold of the season; the first spell of cold weather. しょかん
초한(峭寒) severe[intense] cold.
초행(初行) a first trip[journey]／일본은 ～입니다 This is my first visit to Japan. ／ ～ 길 a road new to one; one's first trip. はじめておこなうこと
초현실주의(超現實主義) surrealism／～자 a surrealist ちょうげんじつしゅぎ
초혜(草鞋) straw sandals. わらじ
초호(初號) the first number (of *a magazine*).
초혼(初婚) one's first marriage／그녀는 45세의 ～이었다 She married for the first time at forty-five. しょこん
초혼(招魂) invocation of the spirit of a deceased／ ～하다 invoke the spirit of the deceased [calling his name three times]／ ～제(祭) a memorial service for the war dead; Decoration Day.
しょうこん
초화(硝化) nitrification.
초화(草花) a flowering plant. そうか
초환(招還) recall; summons／～하다 recall; summon[order] home.
まねきかえすこと
초회(初回) the first time[round]／ ～전 the first round (of *boxing*); the first inning (of *baseball*). しょかい
촉(鏃) a point; a pointed part 《살촉》 an arrow-head; a steel point 《펜촉》 the pen; the nib of a pen／만년필 ～ the tip of the fountain pen. やじり
촉(燭) candlelight; candlepower ／ 60～ 짜리 전구 a 60 candlepower bulb. しょく
촉각(觸角) 《충》 a feeler; an antenna(*pl.* -nae); a tentacle／달팽이의 ～ a horn of a snail. しょっかく
촉각(觸覺) a sense of touch; tactile[tactual] sense. しょっかく

**촉감**(觸感) tactile sensation[impression]; [the sense of] touch; feel／그것은 나무 같은 ~이 있다 It feels like wood. しょっかん

**촉관**(觸官) the touch[tactile] organ; the sense of touch.

**촉광**(燭光) candlelight 《강도》 candlepower／30 ~의 전구 a thirty candlepower bulb. しょっこう

**촉구**(促求) stimulating; giving impetus (to); 《요구》 insisting; pressing; urging 《격려》 spurring／~하다 urge; press／맹성을 ~하다 demand (a person's) serious reflection.

**촉규화**(蜀葵花) a rose mallow; a hollyhock; Althaea rosea(학명).

**촉급**(促急) pressure; urgency; imminence; impendence／~하다 (be) pressing; impending／~한 용무로 on urgent business. そっきゅう

**촉노**(觸怒) ~하다 incur the displeasure of (one's superior); touch off the anger of an elder; provoke (a person) to anger. いかりにふれること

**촉대**(燭臺) a candle-stick. しょくだい

**촉력**(燭力) candle power. しょっこう

**촉뢰**(觸雷) a conact minel／~하다 touch [strike] a torpedo[mine].

**촉루**(燭淚) guttered candlewax ⇒촛농. しょくるい

**촉루**(髑髏) a skull; a cranium; a skeleton. どくろ

**촉망**(囑望) hope; expectation／~하다 expect[hope] much from (a person); hold expectations (for)／가장 ~되는 학생 the most likely student to succeed. しょくぼう

**촉매**(觸媒) 【화】 a catalyst; a catalyzer／~ 반응 catalysis. しょくばい

**촉모**(觸毛) a feeler; tentacle; an antenna(pl. -nae).

**촉박**(促迫) urgency; imminence; tensity／~하다 (be) imminent; urgent; pressing／시일이 ~하다 a set-date is near at hand. そくはく

**촉발**(觸發) ′contact detonation／~ 장치 contact-detonating device／~ 수뢰 a contact mine. しょくはつ

**촉새** 〖조〗 a black-faced bunting／~ 부리 a thing with the shape of a beak; a person with a beak-shaped mouth. からあおじ

**촉성**(促成) promotion of growth／~하다 promote[hasten] the growth (of); stimulate[foster] the realization (of)／야채의 ~ 재배 intensive cultivation of vegetables. そくせい

**촉수**(觸手) 【동】 a feeler; a tentacle／~를 뻗치다 extend its tentacles／~ 엄금 Hands off. しょくしゅ

**촉수**(觸鬚) a feeler; a tentacle; a palp; a barbel; a palpus.

**촉심**(燭心) a wick. ろうそくのしん

**촉진**(促進) promotion; speeding up; furtherance; acceleration; facilitation; hastening; hurrying up／~하다 promote; press for; hasten; speed up; expedite／평화를 ~하다 promote peace／회복을 ~하다 hasten its recovery. そくしん

**촉촉하다** damp; (be) moist. しめっぽい、

**촉탁**(囑託) entrusting[charging] (a person) with an affair; commissioning; part-time engagement 《사람》 a part-time employee; a non-regular staff／~하다 entrust[commission] (a person) with (a matter); give (a person) charge of／~ 교사 a part-time instructor／~ 관리 a part-time employee of a government office. しょくたく

**촌**(寸) ①《단위》 a Korean inch(치); a unite of linear measurement ②《촌수》 a degree of kinship [especially on the father's side]／삼~ an uncle／사~ a cousin. すん

**촌**(村) a village; a rural community; the country side; a rural district／~에서 살다 live in the country／~장 the village chief[head]. むら

**촌가**(寸暇) a little[moment's] leisure; a little spare moment／~라도 헛되이 해서는 안 된다 You must make use every available time. すんか

**촌가**(村家) a country house; a village house. そんか

**촌각**(寸刻) a moment ⇒촌음. すんこく

**촌공**(寸功) a bit of merit; a small service. すんこう

**촌극**(寸劇) a short dramatical performance; a dramatic sketch; a little piece of a side-show; a skit.

**촌극**(寸隙) a spare moment; just a little while. すんか

**촌길**(村-) a country lane[road]. いなかみち

**촌내**(寸內) a near relatives.

**촌놈**(村-) a country fellow; a country cousin; a rustic; a rube; a boor; a backwoodsman; a country bumpkin／~티가 나다 have the earmarks of a peasant. いなかもの

**촌뜨기**(村-) a countryman; a peasant; a hillbilly; a hayseed; a rustic／~짓을 하다 commit untraveled men's blunders. いなかもの

**촌락**(村落) a village; a hamlet. そんらく

**촌로**(村老) the village seniors. ·そんろう

**촌명**(村名) the name of a village; a village name. そんめい

**촌민**(村民) villagers; village folk[people]; inhabitants of a village. そんみん

**촌백충**(寸白蟲) a tapeworm; a taenia ~촌음. さなだむし

**촌보**(寸步) a few steps／피로해서 ~도 옮길 수 없다 I am so tired I can't move an inch. すんぽ

**촌부**(村婦) a country woman. そんぷ

**촌사람**(村-) a countryman; a rural dweller; a rustic; a plowman; a peas-

**촌샌님**(村―) an aged countryman; a country gentleman.

**촌수**(寸數) the degree of kinship[consanguinity]; the distance of blood relationship/ ~를 캐다 trace the degree of kinship.

**촌스럽다**(村―) (be) countrified; rustic; boorish; farmlike; farmerly/촌스럽게 in country fashion.　いなかくさい

**촌시**(寸時) a moment; an instant; a second.　しばらくのあいだ

**촌음**(寸陰) a moment; an instant; the slightest space of time/ ~을 아끼다 improve every minute[moment]; value each instant.　すんいん

**촌전척토**(寸田尺土) a small farm[field, lot].

**촌지**(寸地) a smallest piece of land; an inch of land[territory].

**촌지**(寸志) a token of good will; a trifle present; a slight token of gratitude/ ~이니 받아 주십시오 This is just a token of my gratitude, please accept it.　すんし

**촌철**(寸鐵) a small weapon 《경귀》 a pithy saying[remark]; an epigram; a bit of wit/ ~ 살인의 경귀 a witty remark piercing home.　すんてつ

**촌촌**(村村) from village to village/ ~걸식 begging around from village to village/ ~이 돌아다니다 go around all the villages.　どのむらでも

**촌충**(寸蟲) a tapeworm; a taenia/ ~ 구제약 a taeniacide; a taenifuge/ ~류 tapeworms.　さなだむし

**촌탁**(忖度) ~하다 guess what is in (*a person's*) mind; conjecture; sense (*a person's*) feelings/자기 마음으로 남을 ~하다 judge others in terms of *oneself*.　そんたく

**촌토**(寸土) the smallest piece of land; an inch of ground[territory]/ ~도 양보하지 않다 cede not an inch of ground [territory]; won't yield.　すんど

**촌티**(村―) a smack[taste, air] of the country (about *a person*)/ ~나다 have a touch[air] of the country about one; have hayseed in *one's* hair.

**출랑거리다** ①《행동을》 act frivolous; be irresponsible; be flippant; be slopping/출랑거리며 돌아다니다 gad about; flit [flitter] about ②《물이》 toss about; splash; lap; slop.

**출랑이** a rash person; a frivolous character.　けいそつなひと

**출싹거리다** frolic; act[be] frivolous 《부추기다》 agitate; stir up; make (*a person*) restless.　ふざけまわる

**출출** with an empty stomach; without eating anything at all/ ~하다 be somewhat hungry; feel a bit empty/~하니 요기나 합시다 Let's drop in somewhere to fill up our empty stomach, will you?　ちょろちょろ

**촘촘하다** (be) close; dense; thick/모를 촘촘하게 심다 plant rice seedlings close together.　めがこまかい

**촛농**(―膿) drops of wax; guttered candle[wax]/ ~이 흐르다 [a candle] gutters down.　しょくるい

**촛대**(―臺) a candlestick; a candlestand; a candle holder/ ~에 초를 꽂다 fix a candle in a candlestick.　ろうそくたい

**촛병**(醋甁) a vinegar bottle.

**촛불** candle-light/ ~을 켜다 light up a candle/ ~로 책을 읽다 read by candle-light.　ろうそくのひ

**총** 《말의》 the hairs of a horse's mane [tail].

**총** (總) all; whole; entire; total; general; gross; overall/~수입 gross receipts; the gross revenue; the gross income/ ~파업 a general strike.

**총**(銃) a gun; a rifle; firearms/ ~을 쏘다 fire[shoot] a gun/자동 ~ an automatic rifle.　じゅう

**총가**(銃架) a rifle-stand; a gun-rest[mount].　じゅうをかけておくささえ

**총각**(總角) a bachelor; an unmarried man.　みこんのおとこ

**총감**(總監) an inspector general; a superintendent general; a commissioner.

**총검**(銃劍) rifles and swords 《무기》 arms 《총에 꽂는 칼》 a bayonet; side-arms/ ~으로 찌르다 bayonet/ ~술 bayonet exercises.　じゅうけん

**총격**(銃擊) [rifle] shooting.　じゅうげき

**총결산**(總決算) total[final] settlement of accounts; total liquidation; final balancing of books/ ~하다 settle[balance] an account totally; liquidate all/과거를 ~하다 liquidate the past.

**총경**(總警) a police superintendent.

**총계**(總計) a total; the total[whole] amount; the sum[grand] total; the aggregate; the gross 《부사적》 in all[total]; all told; all together/ ~하다 total; totalize/ ~는 약 5만 원이나 the total amounts to about 50,000 *won*.　そうけい

**총공격**(總攻擊) a general[all-about] attack[offensive]/ ~하다 make a general attack (*on*)/모든 전선에 걸쳐 ~을 하다 launch an all-about offensive along the entire front.　そうこうげき

**총괄**(總括) generalization; summarization; summing up; a summary; bracketing [lumping] together/ ~하다 generalize; sum up/대체적인 ~ a sweeping generalization.　そうかつ

**총구**(銃口) the muzzle of a gun[rifle]/ ~ 뚜껑 a muzzle cap/ ~ 마개 a plug.　じゅうこう

**총군**(銃―) a gunner; a hunter; a gunman.

**총급**(悤急) being very busy; a big hurry/ ~하다 be in a hurry; (be) very

busy. あわただしくきゅうなこと
**총기**(聰氣) brightness; intelligence; sagacity; sense; wit; a good memory; retentiveness／그는 ~라고는 전혀 없다 He has not a lick of sense about him. めいびんなこと
**총기**(銃器) small arms. じゅうき
**총대**(銃—) a gun-stock; the barrel-mounting of a gun. じゅうしょう
**총대**(總代) a deputy; a representative 《대변자》a spokesman／회사의 ~가 되다 represent the company／졸업생 ~ the representative of the graduates／~가 되다 represent.
**총독**(總督) a governor-general; a viceroy ／~부 the government-general. そうとく
**총동원**(總動員) a general mobilization／~하다 make[effect] a general mobilization (of)／전학교가 ~되어 식목했다 All the teachers and students took part in planting trees. そうどういん
**총득점**(總得點) the total score; total points[runs, goals] made／~ 100점을 얻다 score 100 in all.
**총람**(總攬) general control; superintendence／ ~하다 oversee; superintend; preside over; control; supervise. そうらん
**총량**(總量) 《액》the total amount 《양》the total weight.
**총력**(總力) total strength; the aggregate power; all one's energy; one's might and main／ ~을 다하여 with all one's might／ ~전 a total[totalitarian] war.
**총렵**(銃獵) shooting〈미〉; hunting〈영〉; sporting／ ~하다 hunt [with a gun]; shoot／ ~을 금하다 prohibit hunting／ ~가 a hunter; a sportsman／ ~법 a game law. じゅうりょう
**총론**(總論) an outline; an introduction; general remarks; a general summary ／ ~에서 각론으로 들어가다 descend from the general to the particulars. そうろん
**총론**(叢論) a collection of treatises[essays]. そうろん
**총리**(總理) ①general overseeing[control]; presiding over; superintendence／ ~하다 preside over; oversee; control／ 국무를 ~하다 preside over[run] affair of state ②《국무 총리》a premier; a prime minister. そうり
**총림**(叢林) a dense wood; a bush; a grove; a jungle; a thicket. そうりん
**총망**(忽忙) hurry; being very busy; precipitation／ ~하다 be in a hurry; be in haste; flurried／ ~히 in a great hurry; hurriedly／ ~중에 그것을 잊어버렸다 I forgot it in my hurry. そうぼう
**총명**(聰明) brightness; intelligence; sagacity; wisdom; a good memory／ ~하다 be bright[intelligent, wise, sagacious]. そうめい
**총목록**(總目錄) the table of contents; a full list; a [general] catalog. そうもく
**총무**(總務) 《일》general affairs[business]; 《사람》a manager; a director; an executive／학우회 ~ a manager of the students' association／~ 부장 a general-manager[director]. そうむ
**총미**(銃尾) the breech[butt] of a gun.
**총민**(聰敏) cleverness; keenness; smartness and quickness／~하다 (be) clever [and keen]; sharp; smart and quick. そうびんえいめいなこと
**총보**(總譜) a score／연주를 들으며 ~를 보다 follow the score while listening to the music.
**총본산**(總本山) the head temple [of a Buddhist sect]. そうほんさん
**총부리**(銃—) the muzzle [of a rifle]／~를 겨누다 point[aim at] a gun. じゅうこう
**총사**(叢祠) a [wayside] shrine. そうし
**총사냥**(銃—) shooting；총렵. じゅうりょう
**총사령관**(總司令官) the supreme commander; the commander-in-chief(略: C.-in -C., C. inc., C.I.C.). そうしれいかん
**총사직**(總辭職) general resignation; resignation in a body／ ~하다 resign in a body／내각 ~ the resignation of the Cabinet. そうじしょく
**총살**(銃殺) execution by shooting; shooting (a person) to death／ ~하다 shoot (a person) to death／ ~당하다 be shot dead[to death]. じゅうさつ
**총상**(銃床) a barrel of a gun ➾총대. じゅうしょう
**총상**(銃傷) a bullet[gunshot] wound／~으로 죽다 die from a bullet wound. じゅうしょう
**총생**(叢生) fasciculation; dense[thick] growth; fascicle／ ~하다 grow dense [thick]; cluster／ ~한 fasciculate; fasciated; fascicled. そうせい
**총서**(叢書) a collection of books; a library; a series [of books]／~로 출판되다 be published in a series／가정 ~ a home library. そうしょ
**총선거**(總選擧) a general election／~하다 hold a general election; appeal[go] to the country. そうせんきょ
**총설**(總說) introduction; general remarks ➾총론(總論). そうせつ
**총성**(銃聲) the report of a gun; a gun shot ➾총소리. じゅうせい
**총소리**(銃—) the report of a gun; a gun report; a gun shot／~를 듣다 hear the report of a gun; hear a shot. じゅうせい
**총수**(總帥) the supreme leader; the commander-in-chief.
**총수**(總數) the aggregate; the total [number]. そうすう
**총수**(銃手) a gunman; a gunner; a hunter; a rifleman.
**총신**(銃身) [the bore of] the barrel of a

총아(寵兒) a favorite[pet] child; a favorite; a darling／운명의 ～ a fortune's favorite; a pampered child of fortune.

총안(銃眼) a loophole; an eyelet; a crenel; an embrasure／～을 내다 crenellate.

총알(銃—) a bullet; a shot／～을 잰 총 a loaded gun／～을 재우다 load[charge] a gun／～이 벽을 꿰뚫었다 A bullet went through a wall.／～구멍 a shot hole; a bullet hole.

총애(寵愛) favor; good graces; love; patronage; affection／～하다 love tenderly; pet／～를 받다 win one's favor.

총액(總額) the total[sum] amount; the sum[grand] total 《부사적》in all; in total; in the aggregate.

총열(銃—) the barrel of a gun／～ 소제기 a jag.

총우(寵遇) patronage; a special grace [favor]／～하다 patronize; show special grace／～를 받다 enjoy (a person's) favor.

총원(總員) the whole[total] number (of persons); all members 《배의》all hands 《부사적》in all; all told／～ 기상 All hands turn out!

총의(總意) a common will; general opinion[sentiment]; consensus [of opinion]／～는 개정에 반대다 The consensus is against revision.

총장(總長) ①《학교》the president; the chancellor《영》②《사무 총장》the secretary-[director-] general ③《군대의》the chief-of-staff／참모 ～ the chief of the general staff.

총재(總裁) a president; a governor／한국 은행의 the Governor of the Bank of Korea／～가 되다 assume the presidency of／한국 적십자사 ～ the president of the Korean Red Cross Society.

총좌(銃座) a machine-gun emplacement.

총중(叢中) ～에 amidst a crowd[multitude, throng]／만록 ～ 홍일점 a woman in a men's party.

총질(銃—) shooting; firing／～하다 shoot[fire] [a gun].

총집(叢集) ～하다 crowd; throng 《새가》flock together 《벌레가》swarm.

총창(銃創) a bullet[gunshot] wound／다리에 ～을 입다 receive a bullet wound in the leg／팔의 ～에 붕대를 감다 dress a bullet wound in one's arm.

총채 a horsehair duster／～질하다 dust (a thing).

총첩(寵妾) one's favorite mistress.

총체(總體) all; the whole／～적으로 generally; in general; generally speaking; on the whole.

총총(怱怱) hastily; in haste; hurriedly; in a hurry; quickly／～하다 (be) hasty; rushed; hurried／～히 가버리다 beat a hurry retreat; hurry away[off].

총총(蔥蔥) thickly; dense[ly]／나무가 ～히 심다 be planted close together; be densely wooded.

총총(叢叢) densely; numerously／～하다 (be) dense; crowded; numerous／하늘에 별이 ～히 박혀 있다 The sky is studded[strewn] with stars.

총총걸음 a quick pace; quick steps; hurried walking／그녀는 ～으로 사라졌다 She hurried away with mincing steps.

총총들이(蔥蔥—) close; tight[ly]／나무를 ～ 심다 plant trees close to each other.

총출동(總出動) general mobilization／～하다 be all mobilized; be all called out／군대의 ～ the general mobilization of troops.

총칙(總則) general rules[provisions]／민법 ～ general provisions of the civil code.

총칭(總稱) a general name; a generic term; an overall designation／～하다 give a general name to; call[name] collectively.

총칼(銃—) a gun and sword; fire arms.

총탄(銃彈) a bullet; a shot.

총통(總統) a president; a chancellor; generalissimo.

총평(總評) a general survey[review, critique]／스포츠계의 ～ a general review of the sporting circles.

총포(銃砲) guns; fire-arms／～ 상점 a gunshop; a dealer in fire-arms.

총할(總轄) a general control[supervision]; superintendence／～하다 superintend; preside over; have general control (over).

총합(總合) gathering together; generalization; synthesis／～하다 synthesize; gather together; coordinate; integrate／～하여 생각하다 think collectively.

총화(銃火) rifle-fire; gun-fire／～를 무릅쓰고 under fire; defying[braving] the enemy's gun-fire.

총화(總和) a total-amount; a sum[grand] total／～하다 sum up; count up.

총회(總會) a general meeting; a plenary session[sitting]; 《종교의》a synod／결의를 ～에 붙이다 leave the decision up to a general meeting／주주 ～ a general meeting of stock holders.

총희(寵姬) one's favorite mistress.

총히(總—) all; wholly; entirely; altog-

**좌절**(挫折) a setback; a breakdown; rust; collapse; a frustration 《기력의》 discouragement / ~좌절.　くじけおれること

**촬영**(撮影) photographing; picture-taking 《영화》 filming / ~하다 take a photograph[picture] of; photograph; photo; make a film of / ~이 금지되어 있다 photographing is prohibited[forbidden].　さつえい

**최-**(最) the most; the extreme; ultra / ~남단 the southernmost / ~첨단 the spearhead.　さい

**최경례**(最敬禮) the deepest bow; the most respectful salutation / ~하다 make a deepest bow; salute[greet] with the most respect.　さいけいれい

**최고**(最高) maximum / ~의 the highest; supreme; maximum; superlative / 물가지수가 ~에 달했다 The price index hit [reached] a new high. / ~ 가격 the highest[top] price / 최고로 아름다운 여인 The most beautiful woman.　さいこう

**최고**(催告) notification; demanding 《지불의》 call / ~하다 notify; press (*a person*) for (*payment*).　さいこく

**최귀**(最貴) being most valuable.

**최근**(最近) 《때의》 the latest; the nearest; the most recent; the latest date 《거리의》 the nearest[shortest] 《부사》 lately; in recent years / ~까지 아주 더웠다 It was very hot until recently.　さいきん

**최근세**(最近世) recent times; the modern period / 한국 ~사(史) a History of Modern Korea.

**최근친자**(最近親者) the next of kin; the most-close relative; the nearest relative.

**최긴**(最緊) ~하다 (be) most important; essential; indispensable; vital / ~한 문제 the most important question[problem].　もっともきんようなこと

**최다**(最多) being most numerous; the maximum; the greatest in number[quantity] / ~의 군중 the largest crowd [mob].　さいた

**최다수**(最多數) the maximum; the greatest number; the largest majority / ~의 최대 행복 the greatest happiness of the greatest number.

**최단**(最短) the shortest; the nearest [distance] / ~ 거리를 가다 go the nearest way; take the shortest course / ~ 시일 the shortest time.　さいたん

**최대**(最大) the greatest; the biggest; the largest; the maximum / ~의 the greatest; maximum / ~의 노력을 기울이다 exert every effort (*in*); make every possible effort / ~ 압력 the maximum pressure.　さいだい

**최대 한도**(最大限度) the maximum / ~의 비용 the maximum expense[allowance] / ~의 속력을 내다 run with the maximum speed.　さいだいげんど

**최량**(最良) the best; the most excellent; the supreme; the ideal / 품질 ~이다 be [stand] supreme in quality; be top in quality.　さいりょう

**최루**(催淚) causing[producing] tears / ~탄(彈) a tear bomb; a lachrymatory bomb.　さいるい

**최면**(催眠) somnolency; hypnosis; hypnogenesis; hypnotic[induced] sleep / ~상태에 빠지다 be hypnotized / ~ 상태에서 깨우다 dehypnotize; break the hypnotic spell.　さいみん

**최면술**(催眠術) hypnotism; mesmerism / ~을 걸다 mesmerize; excercise a mesmeric power over / ~사 a hypnotist; a mesmerist.　さいみんじゅつ

**최면제**(催眠劑) a sleeping pill[drug]; a soporific / 자살하기 위하여 ~를 과량으로 먹다 take over-doses of sleeping pills to take *one's* own life.　さいみんざい

**최상**(最上) the best; the finest; the highest / ~의 the best; the finest / ~의 행복 the supreme happiness; bliss / ~급 《계급》 the upper crust; the high society.　さいじょう

**최선**(最善) the highest good 《노력》 the best; *one's* [level] best / 그로서는 ~을 다했다 He did the best that was in him.　さいぜん

**최선**(最先) the first; the foremost; the head; out in front / ~으로 도착하다 arrive first; arrive ahead of others / ~으로 달리다 run at the head; run ahead.　まっさき

**최성기**(最盛期) the golden age[days]; the height of prosperity; the zenith; the prime; the season / 사과는 지금이 ~다 Apples are in seasons now.

**최소**(最小, 最少) the smallest; the fewest; the minimum; the least 《부사적》 at the least; at the minimum / 비용을 ~한으로 줄이다 reduce expenses to the minimum / ~한도 the minimum; the bottom limit.　さいしょう

**최신**(最新) the newest; the latest; up-to-date / ~식(式) the newest[latest] type[style] / ~식 유행 the latest fashion.　さいしん

**최악**(最惡) the worst / ~의 경우에는 at the worst; if things come to the worst / ~의 경우에 대비하다 prepare *one*self for the worst.　さいあく

**최우등**(最優等) being most excellent; superiority; the highest class / ~으로 졸업하다 graduate with top honors[the greatest distinction] / ~생 a top student; a top-honors man.

**최음제**(催淫劑) an aphrodisiac [medicine].

**최장**(最長) the longest; the oldest / ~ 다섯 자를 넘지 못한다 do not exceed five feet at the longest / ~거리 the longest distance.　さいちょう

**최저**(最低) the lowest / ~의 the lowest; lowermost; minimum / ~ 생활비 the

**최적(最適)** (being) the best suited; best fitted; most suitable; most agreeable/~규모 the optimum size;~조건 the optimum [condition]. さいてき

**최전선(最前線)** the foremost front; the advance[first] line; the line of battle; the frontmost line[s].

**최종(最終)** ~의 last; final; terminal/~까지 to the last[end]/~에 가서 in the end/~목적 ultimate object/~역 a terminal station. さいしゅう

**최초(最初)** the very first; the very beginning; the start; the outset/~의 first; original; initial/~에는 그럴 계획이 아니었다 It was not the original plan to do so. さいしょ

**최촉(催促)** pressing; urging ⇨재촉. さいそく

**최하(最下)** the lowest; the most inferior; the worst/~의 the lowest; the worst/~가격 the minimum[lowest] price/~급 the lowest grade[class]/~층 the lowest class. さいか

**최혜국(最惠國)** the most favored nation/~대우 most-favored-nation treatment/~조관 the most-favored-nation clause. さいけいこく

**최후(最後)** ①(맨 뒤) the last; the end; the conclusion/~의 the last; final; closing; ultimate ②(죽음) one's death[end]; one's fate/~의 승리를 얻다 win an ultimate victory. さいご

**추(錘)** 《저울의》a weight; a poise 《낚싯줄의》a bob; a sinker 《먹줄의》a plumb; a plummet 《시계의》a pendulum weight/낚시~를 닮다 weight a line. すい

**추(醜)** ugliness 《더러움》dirtiness. しゅう

**추가(追加)** an addition 《추가물》an addendum(pl. -da); supplement/예산에 ~하다 supplement a budget/~시험을 보다 take a make-up test. ついか

**추거(推擧)** recommendation ⇨추천/~하다 recommend (a person) for. すいきょ

**추격(追擊)** pursuit; chase; a follow-up attack/~하다 pursue; give chase (to)/맹렬히 적을 ~하고 있다 be in hot pursuit of the enemy; be pressing hard on the enemy. ついげき

**추경(秋耕)** autumn plowing. しゅうこう

**추경(秋景)** autumn scene; autumnal scenery. しゅうけい

**추계(秋季)** autumn ⇨추기(秋期).しゅうき

**추계(推計)** estimation/~학 stochastics; the theory of statistical inference. すいけい

**추고(推敲)** polish; improvement; choice of diction/~하다 polish; improve/~의 여지가 있다 admit of further polish. すいこう

**추고(推考)** inference; deduction; deliberation/~하다 infer; deduce; deliberate; investigate. すいこう

**추고 마비(秋高馬肥)** an autumn when the sky is clear and horses are growing stout.

**추곡(秋穀)** the harvested[an autumn] grain[rice]/~수납 a purchase of autumnal harvest grain by the government.

**추공(秋空)** the autumn sky. あきぞら

**추광(秋光)** a sign of autumn ⇨추색(秋色). しゅうしょく

**추피(醜怪)** ugliness; scandalousness/~하다 ugly; grotesque. しゅうかい

**추교(醜交)** an illicit connection; an evil relation; an improper relation; a liaison/~의 소문 a rumor of a scandalous relation. しゅうこう

**추구(追求)** pursuit; chase; running after; going into thoroughly/~하다 pursue; run after; go into thoroughly; press hard/죄상을 ~하다 press (a person) to confess his crime. ついきゅう

**추구(追究)** thoroughgoing study; close inquiry; thorough investigation/~하다 cross-examine; inquire into (a matter) closely/진리를 ~하다 seek truth. ついきゅう

**추구(推究)** thinking thorough (a matter); inference/~하다 infer; inquire into (a matter) thoroughly. すいきゅう

**추궁(追窮)** close inquiry; pressing hard; thorough investigation/~하다 go after; probe to the bottom/책임을 ~하다 call (a person) to account. ついきゅう

**추근추근** tenaciously; persistently; doggedly; demandingly/~하다 (be) dogged; tenacious; persistent; importunate; demanding/여자를 ~쫓아다니다 keep after[pester] a girl.

**추급(追給)** supplementary pay; additional grant[allowance]/~하다 provide as supplementary pay; supply additional grant[allowance]. ついきゅう

**추기(秋氣)** a sign of autumn; the early chill of autumn; an indication of autumn [in the air]. しゅうき

**추기(秋期)** autumn; fall《미》. しゅうき

**추기(追記)** an additional note; an addendum; an epilog[ue]. ついき

**추기(樞機)** the most important affairs [of state]; the helm of the state; the vital part [of a thing]/~에 참여하다 take part in the deliberation of the most important state affairs. すうき

**추기다** (꾀다) instigate; stimulate; entice; seduce; tempt 《선동하다》incite (a person) to do; stir up/추겨서 싸우게 하다 egg (a person) on to fight. おだてる

**추남(醜男)** an ugly [looking] man; an ill-favored man.

**추납(追納)** supplementary pay[ment]; a follow-up payment.

**추녀** the eaves; the protruding corners of Korean eaves/~끝에 매달린 고드름 icicles hanging from the eaves. のき

**추녀(醜女)** an ugly woman; an unlovely

woman.　しゅうじょ
**추념**(追念) commemoration; remembrance/～식 a commemoration ceremony.
　ついねん
**추다**¹ 《찾아내다》 find out; recover; get back; rummage out 《비밀 따위》 worm out 《추리다》 arrange[put] in order; set rights; square [up]; 《올리다》 pull up; lift/몸을 ～ lift oneself up
**추다**² praise; speak highly of/공부를 잘 한다고 ～ praise 《a student》 for his good marks.　おべっかをいう
**추다**³ dance/춤을 ～ perform a dance/장단에 맞추어 춤을 ～ dance to the music [a melody].　まう
**추단**(推斷) 《판단》 inference; deduction 《처단》 judg[e]ment; decision; punishment/～하다 infer[deduce, gather] [from evidence]; 《처단하다》 render judg[e]ment on; mete out punishment for.　すいだん
**추담**(醜談) filthy[indecent, nasty, foul] talk; a dirty story; a smutty story/～을 하다 tell an obscene story; talk filth[smut].　みにくいことば
**추대**(推戴) ～하다 have 《a person》 as head[president, director]; be under [the presidency of]/신 박사를 학장으로 ～하다 have Dr. Shin for[as] the director of a college.　すいたい
**추도**(追悼) mourning; lamentation/～하다 mourn for[over] 《a person》; lament 《a person's》 death/ ～사 a memorial address[tribute]/～식 a memorial ceremony.　ついとう
**추라치** 《어》 a kind of large minnow; a big kind of killifish〈미〉.　おおきいめだか
**추락**(墜落) a fall; a crash; a plunge/～하다 fall; drop; crash; plunge/거꾸로 ～하다 fall headlong to the ground/권위가 ～되다 lose one's prestige[authority].　ついらく
**추량**(推量) guess; conjecture ⇒추측(推測).　すいりょう
**추레하다** poor-looking; (be) shabby/차림새가 ～ be in seedy clothes.
　みすぼらしい
**추렴** collection of money; raising of money 《각자 부담》 sharing the expenses; going to Dutch; a Dutch treat/～하다 make up a purse; pass a hat around.
**추렴새** collecting together; contributing jointly; a share; a contribution/ ～가 많다 A share is large.
**추록**(追錄) a supplement; an addition; a postscript/～하다 supplement; add.
　ついろく
**추론**(推論) reasoning; inference; deduction/～하다 reason; infer; deduce; draw deduction from/～식 〖논〗 syllogism.
**추리**(推理) reasoning; inference; deduction/～하다 reason; infer; deduce; figure out/～ 소설 a detective story/～력 reasoning power; the power[faculty] of reasoning/간접적 ～ indirect inference.　すいり

**추리다** choose; select; pick out/추려 내다 select; pick out; single out/짚을 ～ pick straw [weeding out the short].
　よりだす
**추명**(醜名) a bad reputation; a scandal; notoriety/～을 사다 make oneself notorious; make a bad name for oneself.
　しゅうめい
**추모**(追慕) ～하다 cherish the memory of a deceased person/선친을 ～하다 look back upon the memory of one's late father with reverence and affection.
　ついぼ
**추문**(醜聞) a scandal; ill fame; a scandalous report; ignominy/그에게는 ～이 붙어 다닌다 He is the object of continual[frequent] scandal.　しゅうぶん
**추물**(醜物) 《물건》 an ugly[dirt, filthy, foul] object 《사람》 an ugly person; a dirty[filthy] fellow.　みにくいもの
**추미**(追尾) ～하다 follow; pursue; shadow; tail.　ついび
**추밀**(樞密) important secret; affairs of state/～원 the Privy Council〈영〉/～원 고문관 a Privy Councillor〈영〉; a member of the Privy Council.　すうみつ
**추방**(追放) expulsion; banishment; deportation; driving out; exile; purge/～하다 expel; banish; deport; purge; exile/국외로 ～당하다 be exiled from the country.　ついほう
**추백**(追白) a postscript ⇒추신(追伸).
**추분**(秋分) the autumnal equinox/ ～날 the Autumnal Equinox Day. しゅうぶん
**추비**(追肥) [applying of] additional fertilizer.　ついひ
**추사**(秋思) autumnal sentiment[thoughts].　しゅうし
**추사**(墜死) a death caused by a fall[crash].
**추산**(推算) calculation; computation; estimate/～하다 put; estimate (at); calculate/그 이득은 백만불로 ～된다 The gain is estimated at one million dollars.　すいさん
**추상**(推想) guess; conjecture; imagination; surmise; inference/ ～하다 guess; conjecture; imagine/그것은 ～에 불과하다 It is mere guesswork./도저히 ～할 수가 없다 It is past all conjecture.
　おしはかっておもうこと
**추상**(抽象) abstract; abstraction/ ～적 abstract; nonobjective/시간의 개념을 ～하다 abstract the notion of time/～ 명사 an abstract noun.　ちゅうしょう
**추상**(秋霜) ①《서리》 frost of autumn ②《비유적》 severity; sternness/～ 같은 severe; rigorous; relentless.　しゅうそう
**추상**(追想) retrospection; recollection; reminiscence/험난했던 과거를 ～하다 look back on one's wretched past/～록 reminiscences.　ついそう
**추색**(秋色) autumnal scenery; a sign of

**추서**(追書) a postscript(略 : P. S.).

**추석**(秋夕) the harvest[moon] festival [on the 15th of August by the lunar calendar]. しゅうせき

**추썩거리다** 《어깨를》keep shrugging 《옷》 rock up; pull up/어깨를 ~ shrug one's shoulders from time to time/웃을 ~ keep pulling up one's cost. かたをすくめる

**추세**(趨勢) tendency; trend; drift; current; tide/일반적 ~ a general tendency; the trend of events; the current of the world/세상의 ~에 따르다 swim with the current. すうせい

**추소**(追訴) a supplementary legal suit/ ~하다 bring a supplementary suit (against).

**추속**(醜俗) unseemly customs;ugly[foul] manners. みにくくみだらなふうぞく

**추수**(秋收) [autumn] harvesting; a harvest; gathering a harvest/~하다 harvest/ ~기 a harvest time/~ 감사절 Thanksgiving Day. しゅうしゅう

**추스르다** pick and trim; set in order; put into shape; take good care of 《구스르다》cajole; coax; fawn upon/백성을 잘 추슬러 다스리다 get the people under complete control. おだてる

**추습**(醜習) a vice; indecent practices. みにくいしゅうかん

**추시**(趨時) keeping pace with the times; keeping abreast of the times. じぞくにしたがうこと

**추신**(追伸) an added note; a postscript.

**추심**(追尋) ~하다 take[get, receive] back what is one's own/은행에서 돈을 ~하다 draw one's money from one's bank; receive payment.

**추악**(醜惡) 《행위가》abominableness; foulness; scandalousness; vileness 《모습이》 ugliness; unsightliness/~하다 (be) vile; foul; abominable; ugly; dirty/~ 한 짓 a dirty trick/~한 소문 a scandalous rumor/~한 녀석 an abominable person; a viper; a loathsome creature. しゅうあく

**추앙**(推仰) reverence; adoration;respect; worship/~하다 adore; worship; respect; revere; look up to. あがめたてまつること

**추야**(秋夜) an autumn night/~장 긴긴밤 the live-long autumn night. あきのよる

**추어**(鰍魚) a mudfish; a loach ⇒미구라지 /~탕 loach soup. どじょう

**추어내다** expose; disclose; uncover; reveal; dig out[up]; find out; seek out ⇒ 들추어 내다. さぐりだす

**추어올리다** ①pull up; lift up; hoist / 치마를 ~ pull up one's skirt ②《사람을》 praise; speak highly of; cry up to the skies/친구를 ~ rave about[of] one's friend. おだてあげる

**추어주다** praise; laud; extol; compliment; flatter; cajole; wheedle/일을 잘 했다고 ~ praise (a person) for doing a good job. おだてる

**추억**(追憶) recollection; memory; remembrance; retrospection/ ~하다 recall; recollect; go over in one's mind/영원히 ~할 만한 가치가 있다 deserve permanent remembrance. ついおく

**추업**(醜業) a life of shame; a shameful life[trade]; prostitution; shameful occupation/~에 종사하다 live a life of shame. しゅうぎょう

**추요**(樞要) importance; vitality/ ~하다 (be) important; vital; critical/ 군사상 ~ 지점 a point of strategical importance. すうよう

**추위하다** be susceptible to the cold; complain of the cold/그는 곧잘 추위한다 He is terribly susceptible to the cold.

**추월**(秋月) the autumn moon. さむげつ

**추위** the cold; coldness; cold weather; a chill; chilliness/~에 견디다 bear the cold/~에 떨다 shiver with cold/ ~가 심하다 It is very cold. さむさ

**추이**(推移) transition; shift; change/~ 하다 change; undergo a change[transition]; shift; move/계절의 ~ the change of the seasons. すいい

**추인**(追認) confirmation; ratification/ ~하다 confirm; ratify. ついにん

**추자**(楸子) pondweed; a walnut. おにぐるみ

**추잠**(秋蠶) autumn silkworms/~을 놓다 raise silkworms in autumn. しゅうさん

**추잡**(醜雜) filthiness; obscenity/ ~하다 (be) dirty; indecent; obscene; nasty; foul; filthy; loathsome/~한 이야기 filthy[indecent] talk/~한 사람 an indecent person. げんこうのきたないこと

**추장**(推奬) commendation; recommendation/~하다 commend; recommend/~ 할 만하다 be worthy of commendation. すいしょう

**추장**(酋長) a chief[tain]. しゅうちょう

**추저분하다**(醜—) (be) dirty and messy; filthy; slovenly/추저분한 방 a messy room/추저분한 누옥 a drab little hut. きたない

**추적**(追跡) chase; pursuit; tracing; following (after)/~하다 pursue; give chase (to); follow (after)/도둑을 맹렬히 ~하다 follow the thief in hot pursuit. ついせき

**추절**(秋節) the autumnal season; autumnal days; autumn; fall〈미〉. あきのきせつ

**추접**(醜—) ~하다 (be) nasty; filth/; foul; indecent; obscene; low-down; sordid/~스러운 놈 a dirty fellow; a mean-spirited fellow. きたないこと

**추접지근하다** unclean; filthy; (be) rather dirty. きたならしい

**추정**(推定) deduction; presumption; assumption; inference／～하다 presume; assume; infer／～을 내리다 draw a deduction／～ 범죄 a constructive crime. すいてい

**추종**(追從) obeying; servile following 《모방》imitation／～하다 follow; be servile to; wait on hand and foot／그는 누구의 말이든지 ～한다 He is at everyone's beck and call. ついじゅう

**추증**(追贈) posthumous conferment of honors.

**추지**(推知) inference; conjecture; deduction／～하다 conjecture; guess; surmise; infer. すいち

**추지다** (be) wet; damp; moist; humid.

**추진**(推進) drive; propulsion／～하다 propel; drive forward 《사업을》promote／이 운동의 ～ 세력 the driving force of this movement／～기 a propeller; a screw propeller／～력이 강하다 have a positive drive. すいしん

**추징**(追徵) additional charge; supplementary collection／～하다 make an additional charge; collect in addition; collect as a supplement／～금 money collected in addition. ついちょう

**추찰**(推察) guess; conjecture; inference; surmise 《동정》sympathy; consideration／～하다 guess; gather; conjecture; surmise／～이 맞다 guess right. すいさつ

**추천**(推薦) recommendation 《지명》nomination／～하다 recommend ( for, to); say a good word ( for); put in a good opinion (of)／《지명하다》nominate／당신이라면 쾌히 ～하겠소 I will gladly recommend you. すいせん

**추천**(鞦韆) a [rope] swing ‥그네. しゅうせん

**추첨**(抽籤) drawing lots; a drawing; a lottery／～하다 draw[cast] lots; hold a lottery／～에 당선되다 draw a lot; have got a lucky number. ちゅうせん

**추축**(樞軸) a pivot; an axle; an axis; a pivotal point; a cardinal point; the center [of point]／～국 an Axis power. すうじく

**추출**(抽出) abstraction;《화》extraction／～하다 draw; abstract; extract／～물 an extract. ちゅうしゅつ

**추측**(推測) guess; conjecture; supposition; presumption／～하다 guess; suppose; surmise; conjecture／～에 지나지 않다 be mere guesswork. すいそく

**추켜들다** raise; hold up／사람을 ～ hold (a person) up／어린이를 ～ raise[lift] a boy aloft.

**추켜잡다** lift up; hold up／치맛자락을 ～ hold up one's skirt to keep it from dragging. まくりあげる

**추탕**(鰍湯) loach soup. どじょうしる

**추태**(醜態) a shameful conduct; disgraceful behavior 《상태》an unseemly sight; an offensive appearance; a scandalous condition／～를 폭로하다 reveal its scandalous condition. しゅうたい

**추파**(秋波) an amorous glance; an ogling look／～를 던지다 cast an amorous glance (at). しゅうは

**추풍**(秋風) the autumn wind／～ 낙엽 falling leaves in autumn winds. しゅうふう

**추풍**(醜風) unseemly customs. みにくいふうぞく

**추하다**(醜—) ①《불결하다》(be) dirty; filthy; foul; unclean; squalid; shabby ②《비루하다》(be) mean; base; disgusting; abominable; loathsome／추한 사람 a filthy person. みにくい

**추한**(醜漢) an ugly fellow[guy]; a low-down type. しゅうかん

**추해당**(秋海棠) 【식】a begonia; an elephant's-ear. しゅうかいどう

**추행**(醜行) an indecent act; disgraceful [scandalous] conduct; misconduct／～을 적발하다 bring a scandal to light; expose a scandal／여자에게 ～하다 assault a girl; rape a girl[woman].

**추호**(秋毫) a bit; a hair／～도 의심치 않는다 I have not the slightest doubt.／그것을 훔칠 생각은 ～도 없었다 I had not the slightest intention to steal it.／그에게는 양심따위는 ～도 없다 He has not a spark[an atom] of conscience. しゅうごう

**추화**(秋花) autumn flowers.

**추회**(追懷) recollection; reminiscence; retrospection／옛날을 ～하다 look back upon the old days; recollect the past. ついかい

**추후**(追後) ～에 later on; afterwards; by and by／～ 통고가 있을 때까지 until further notice／～에 전화하겠읍니다 I will [tele]phone you later on. のち

**축**[1] the group[bunch] of people[thing]／～에 끼지 못하다 cannot associate with others on an equal footing／그녀는 똑똑한 ～에 낀다 She is one of the clever ones. なかま

**축**[2] droopingly; sluggishly; loosely; languidly／어깨가 ～ 늘어지다 one's shoulders droop; have drooping shoulders. だらっと

**축**(祝) ① a written prayer ⇨축문 ② celebration; congratulation ⇨경축. しゅく

**축**(丑) the Sign of the Ox 《축방》the Direction of the Ox 《축시》the Watch of the Ox. ちゅう

**축**(軸)《굴대》an axis; an axle《기계의》a shaft; a pivot《두루마리의》a spindle; a roller; rolls of paper; a roll／종이 두 ～ two rolls of paper／지(地) ～ the axis of the earth. じく

**축가**(祝歌) a festive song 《크리스마스의》a carol 《결혼식의》an epithalamium.

**축가다**(縮—) be lacking; be deficient; shrink; be reduced／몸이 ～ loose weight; run down weight. すいじゃくする

**축감**(縮減) reduction; decrease／～하다 be decreased[reduced]. しゅくげん

**축견세(畜犬稅)** a dog tax.

**축구(蹴球)** football/~를 하다 play football[soccer]/~ 선수 a football player; a footballer/미식 ~ American football. しゅうきゅう

**축나다(縮—)** decrease; run low; lack; be deficient; fall[become] short of. すいじゃくする

**축년(逐年)** year after year; from year to year. ちくねん

**축농증(蓄膿症)** 『의』ozena; empyema. ちくのうしょう

**축다** become wet; get damp; become moist. じめじめする

**축대(築臺)** a terrace; an elevation; stone embankment/~를 쌓다 build around high up with stone enforcement.

**축도(縮圖)** a reduced drawing[copy]; a miniature copy; a tabloid edition; a pantography/~를 그리다 make a miniature copy (of)/인생의 ~ an epitome of human life. しゅくず

**축도(祝禱)** benediction/~를 하다 pronounce a benediction. しゅくとう

**축록(逐鹿)** running for a high position; competition for a high office 《정권 다툼》 a scramble for political power/ ~ 전 competition for a position; an election campaign. ちくろく

**축류(畜類)** livestock; domestic animals.

**축문(祝文)** a written prayer (for *the deceased*); a memorial address [offered at memorial services of *one's* ancestors]. しゅくぶん

**축배(祝杯)** a toast; a drink in celebration/~를 들다 drink a toast; drink (to *a person's*) success or health/서로 ~를 들다 toast each other. しゅくはい

**축복(祝福)** blessing; benediction; blessedness/~하다 bless; call a blessing upon/~받은 blessed/목사가 교인을 위해 ~하였다 The pastor blessed the congregation. しゅくふく

**축사(縮寫)** drawing on a smaller scale; scaling down/ ~하다 draw[copy] on a smaller scale; make a reduced copy /~ 지도 a scale map. しゅくしゃ

**축사(祝辭)** greetings; congratulations; a congratulatory address[speech, message]/~를 하다 deliver a congratulatory address/결혼 ~ wedding congratulations. しゅくじ

**축사(畜舍)** a stall; a stable; a cattle shed.

**축산(畜産)** livestock farming; stock raising[breeding, farming]/~업자 a livestock raiser; a rancher. ちくさん

**축생(畜生)** 《금수》 animals; beasts; a brute/~만도 못한 놈 a man no better than a brute. ちくしょう

**축성(築城)** fortification; construction of a castle/~하다 build[construct] a castle; fortify/~학 [the science of] fortification. ちくじょう

**축성(祝聖)** benediction. しゅくせい

**축소(縮小)** abridgment; reduction; curtailment; retrenchment/~하다 reduce; cut down; retrench; curtail/사업을 ~하다 reduce business. しゅくしょう

**축쇄(縮刷)** printing in smaller type/~하다 print a reduced-size edition/~판 a reduced-size edition. しゅくさつ

**축수(祝手)** invocation by prayer; imploration; supplication/~하다 invoke by prayer.

**축수(祝壽)** wishing (*a person*) a long life /~하다 wish (*a person*) a long life; congratulate (*a person*) on his long life.

**축승(祝勝)** celebration of a victory; rejoicing over a victory. しゅくしょう

**축시(丑時)** the Watch of the Ox; the period between 1 and 3 a.m. うしみつ

**축어(逐語)** verbalism/~적 word for word; verbatim/~ 번역 a word-for-word [literal] translation.

**축연(祝宴)** a feast; a banquet/~을 열다 hold a banquet[feast] in celebration of (*the event*). しゅくえん

**축우(畜牛)** cattle; a domestic cow[ox].

**축원(祝願)** praying; a prayer; supplication; invocation/~하다 pray; supplicate; say[utter] a prayer/세계 평화를 ~하다 pray for the peace of the world. しゅくがん

**축음기(蓄音器)** a phonograph〈미〉; a record player; a gramophone〈영〉/ ~를 틀다 play a record; turn the phonograph on/~판 a record; a disk. ちくおんき

**축의(祝意)** 《사물》 celebration 《사람에 대한》 congratulation/모든 기관은 그날 ~를 표하고 휴업한다 All firms will be closed in honor of the occasion[event]. しゅくい

**축의(祝儀)** a festival; a celebration ⇒축전(祝典). しゅくぎ

**축이다** wet; moisten; dampen; dip/목을 ~ wet *one's* whistle/수건을 ~ wet a towel. しめらす

**축일(祝日)** a festival [day]; a gala day; a flag[red-letter] day/전승 ~ a V-Day. しゅくじつ

**축일(逐一)** 《상세히》 in full [detail]; minutely 《하나하나》 one after another; one by one; from point to point; in order; item by item. ちくいち

**축일(逐日)** day after day; day by day; daily; every day/~ 증가하다 increase by the day. まいにち

**축재(蓄財)** the accumulation of wealth [riches]; money-grubbing; accumulated wealth; amassed wealth/ ~하다 amass; make money/~자 a moneymaker. ちくざい

**축적(蓄積)** accumulation; storing up; stockpiling; amassment/~하다 accumulate; amass; pile up; stockpile/지식을 ~하다 accumulate a store of knowledge. ちくせき

**축전(祝典)** a festival; festivities; a celebration; a commemoration; festive celebration／~ 행사 festive activities／~ 기분 a festive mood.

**축전(祝電)** a congratulatory telegram [message]; a telegram of good wishes／~을 치다 send a congratulatory telegram to (*a person*).

**축전기(蓄電器)**【전】an electric condenser／가변 ~ a variable condenser／결합 ~ a coupling condenser／용량 ~ a capacity condenser.

**축전지(蓄電池)**【전】a storage battery.

**축제(築堤)** banking[embanking] a river／~하다 dike; embank [a river]／~ 공사 embanking; embankment works.

**축제일(祝祭日)** a public[national] holiday; a gala day.

**축조(逐條)** article by article; clause by clause; item by item; point by point; seriatim／의안을 ~ 심의하다 consider the bill clause by clause.

**축조(築造)** building; construction／~하다 build; construct; erect／~ 중이다 be under[in course of] construction.

**축지다(縮—)** (사람의 가치가) discredit *oneself*; fall into discredit (몸이) grow weak; be run down; lose weight; fail in health／앓아서 몸이 ~ lose some weight due to illness.

**축지법(縮地法)** a magic method of contracting space.

**축짓다(軸—)** make a pivot; fix an axle／종이로 ~ roll paper into a roll.

**축차(逐次)** successively; one after another; in due order.

**축척(縮尺)** a reduced scale／~도 a map on a reduced scale.

**축첩(蓄妾)** keeping a concubine[mistress]; concubinage／~하다 keep a concubine.

**축축** all drooping[sagging, hanging down] low; drooping all the time／나뭇가지가 ~ 늘어진다 The branches all droop low.

**축축하다** (be) slightly[moderately] wet; moist; damp; humid; clammy; sticky; dampish／빨래가 이슬에 ~ The laundry is moist with dew.

**축출(逐出)** driving out; expulsion; deporation／~하다 drive[turn, send, put] out; kick out; eject; expel／그는 학교에서 ~당할 것이다 He will be sent down from the school.

**축포(祝砲)** a salute [of guns]; a cannon salute; a *feu de joie*(F)／~를 놓다 fire a salute.

**축하(祝賀)** congratulation; celebration; felicitation; rejoicing／~하다 greet; congratulate[felicitate] (*a person*) on (*일을*) celebrate; keep [a festival]／전승을 ~하다 celebrate a war victory.

**축하다(縮—)** (be) wilted; languid.

**축항(築港)** harbor construction／~하다 construct a harbor／~ 공사를 시작하다 start harbor construction; begin to improve the harbor.

**춘경(春耕)** spring plowing.

**춘경(春景)** spring scenery.

**춘계(春季)** spring ⇒춘기.

**춘곤(春困)** fatigue in the spring tide.

**춘광(春光)** spring scenes ⇒춘색.

**춘궁(春宮)** the Crown Prince; the Prince Imperial.

**춘궁기(春窮期)** the farm hardship period; the season of spring poverty[shortage]; the spring austerity.

**춘기(春期)** spring; the spring season; springtime／~ 방학 the spring vacation／~ 운동회 a spring athletic meet.

**춘기 발동기(春機發動期)** the age of puberty[adolescence]; the period of sexual awakening／~에 달하다 arrive at puberty; become adolescent.

**춘난(春暖)** spring warmth; the warmth of spring／~지절(之節) warm spring weather.

**춘맥(春麥)** early[spring-sown] barley.

**춘면(春眠)** sleep on a spring morning; drowsiness[fatigue] in the spring.

**춘몽(春夢)** spring dreams; a spring fantasy; an empty dream／그의 계획은 일장의 ~으로 돌아갔다 All his ideas came to naught.

**춘복(春服)** clothes for spring wear; spring wear.

**춘부장(春府丈, 椿府杖)** your [honored] father.

**춘분(春分)** the vernal[spring] equinox／~날 the Spring[Vernal] Equinox Day.

**춘사(春思)** spring sentiments[musings]; feeling of spring; spring fever; a surge of lust; thoughts of sex.

**춘사(椿事)** an accident; a mishap (대춘사) a disaster (비극) a tragedy／공장에 ~가 발생했다 An unexpected accident happened[occurred] at the factory.

**춘산(春山)** mountains in springtime.

**춘삼월(春三月)** March of the lunar month／~ 호시절 the spring season; the mild weather of spring.

**춘색(春色)** spring scenery; vernal air; nature in spring.

**춘설(春雪)** spring snow.

**춘소(春宵)** a spring evening[night].

**춘수**(春水) spring water. しゅんしょう

**춘수**(春愁) spring sadness; melancholy aroused in springtime. しゅんしゅう

**춘신**(春信) tidings of spring; signs[tokens] of spring 《화신》 news of flowers. しゅんしん

**춘심**(春心) lustful desires; spring sentiment[s]. しゅんしん

**춘야**(春夜) spring night. しゅんや

**춘약**(春藥) a sexual stimulant; an aphrodisiac [dose]. せいよくをたかめるくすり

**춘양**(春陽) spring sunshine; the spring sun 《철》 the spring season; spring tide. しゅんよう

**춘우**(春雨) a spring rain; a spring drizzle. しゅんう

**춘일**(春日) a spring day. しゅんじつ

**춘잠**(春蠶) spring silkworms; a spring breed of silkworms/~을 치다 raise silkworms in spring. しゅんさん

**춘절**(春節) the spring season; the springtime. しゅんき

**춘정**(春情) sexual[carnal] desire; sexual urge; lust; passion/~을 돋우다 excite sexual desire; be suggestive; be provocative. しゅんじょう

**춘초**(春初) early spring; the beginning of spring. はるさき

**춘추**(春秋) spring and autumn 《세월》 years 《연령》 age; years/ ~가 기울다 decline in age[one's years]/~복 spring and autumn wear; between season wear. しゅんじゅう

**춘추 필법**(春秋筆法) the guiding principle of Confucius in writing the Annals.

**춘풍**(春風) the spring breeze[wind]/ ~에 돛단 듯하다 Everything goes all right[smoothly]./ ~ 추우(秋雨) the spring wind and the autumn rain. しゅんぷう

**춘하 추동**(春夏秋冬) the four seasons; all the year round; always.

**춘화**(春花) spring flowers. しゅんか

**춘화**(春畵) a pornography; an obscene [licentious, dirty, filthy] picture. しゅんが

**춘흥**(春興) the lure of spring; the spring fever; the charms[pleasures] of spring / ~에 겨워하다 be overjoyed with the charms of springs.

**출가**(出家) leaving home; entering the Buddhist priesthood/ ~하다 leave home; renounce the world. しゅっけ

**출가**(出嫁) marriage; wedding; a woman's being married/ ~하다 [a woman] be married to/ ~시키다 marry one's daughter off.

**출간**(出刊) publication; issue ⇒출판(出版) /~하다 publish; issue. しゅっぱん

**출강**(出講) ~하다 lecture; give lectures (at a school).

**출격**(出擊) a sally; a sortie; going out to attack[raid]/ ~하다 sally forth; make a sortie; set out to make an assault.

**출경**(出京) leaving the capital 《상경》 going to the Seoul/ ~하다 leave[go to] the capital; go to the capital from the country. しゅつげき

**출고**(出庫) delivery; taking goods out of the warehouse/ ~세 the delivery tax /~ 지시서 a delivery order. しゅっこ

**출구**(出口) an exit; a way out; a gateway; an outlet/그는 둘러보며 ~를 찾았다 He looked around for a way out. /비상 ~ fire escape[exit]. でぐち

**출구**(出柩) taking a coffin out of the house/~하다 carry a coffin out of the house. しゅっかん

**출근**(出勤) attendance (at office)/~하다 go[come] to the office; show up at [for] work; attend the office; report /회사에 ~하다 show up at one's desk in the "company" office/8시에 ~하다 come[go] to the office at eight/~부 (簿) an attendance book[record]; a time book. しゅっき

**출금**(出金) payment; defrayment 《예금의》 drawing 《기부의》 contribution 《출자》 investment/ ~하다 pay; draw out; contribute (to); invest money (in)/~액 the amount of contribution. しゅっきん

**출납**(出納) 《금전》 receipts and payments [disbursements, expenses]; revenue and expenditure; incomings and outgoings/현금 ~을 하다 handle the cash/ ~부 a cash-book. すいとう

**출동**(出動) going[moving] out 《군대·경관의》 mobilization 《함선》 sailing / ~하다 be mobilized; be caved out; set out; sail/~ 준비를 하다 get ready to move / ~ 명령 an order for action. しゅつどう

**출두**(出頭) appearance; presence; attendance/ ~하다 appear; attend; report oneself (at); present oneself (at)/법정 ~의 통지를 받다 be ordered to appear in court. しゅっとう

**출람**(出藍) excelling[surpassing] one's master[teacher]/ ~지재(之才) a person who excels his teacher.

**출렁거리다** lap; slop; slash; roll; swell /물이 독 안에서 ~ The water in a jar is slopping from side to side. ゆれる

**출력**(出力) generating power[capacity]; output of power/~이 작다 have a small output.

**출렵**(出獵) ~하다 go out hunting.

**출마**(出馬) running for office; coming forward as a candidate/~하다 run for office/선거에 ~하다 run[stand] for election. しゅっぱ

**출몰**(出沒) appearing and disappearing / ~하다 make frequent appearances; come and go; frequent; pop in and out; haunt/호랑이가 ~한다 Tigers lurk there. しゅつぼつ

**출발**(出發) departure; leaving; starting /~하다 leave; start; set out (from a

**출범** *place*); 《배가》 embark 《비행기가》 take [hop] off/여행에 ~하다 start on a journey.

**출범**(出帆) departure; sailing [away]/~하다 sail; put off; put to sea; leave/기선의 뱃고동 소리는 ~을 알린다 The steam-whistle signals the time of departure.

**출병**(出兵) the dispatch of troops/~하다 send[dispatch] troops; send a military expedition/한국군의 월남 ~ the dispatch of Korean troops to Vietnam.

**출분**(出奔) abscondence; decampment 《사랑의 도피》 elopement/~하다 run away; abscond; decamp; bolt/~자 a runaway; an absconder.

**출비**(出費) expenses; expenditure; outgo; outlay/~를 절약하다 cut down on expenses; curtail expenses/이 계획은 많은 ~가 필요하다 This projects require very heavy expenditure.

**출사**(出仕) going into government service[office]/40에 처음 ~하다 enter government service for the first time at forty.

**출사**(出師) the dispatch of troops; an expedition/~하다 dispatch the troops; send an expedition.

**출산**(出産) child birth; delivery; parturition/~하다 give birth to; be delivered of/~율 a birth rate.

**출상**(出喪) carrying the coffin out of the house/~하다 carry the coffin out of the house.

**출생**(出生) birth; childbirth/~하다 《낳아지다》 be born 《낳다》 give birth to; be delivered of/둘째 아들로 ~하다 be born the second son.

**출석**(出席) attendance; presence/~하다 be present (at); present oneself at/회의에 ~하다 attend[be present at] a meeting/~표 a table of attendance.

**출세**(出世) success in life; rising in the world; [career] advancement/~하다 have great success in life; rise in the world/~할 기회를 놓치다 miss a chance to get ahead in life.

**출신**(出身) 《태생》 a native 《졸업》 a graduate 《가문》 origin; birth; affiliation/그는 대학 ~이다 He is a college graduate./~[학]교 one's alma mate(L).

**출어**(出漁) going out fishing/~하다 go out fishing; sail out for fishing.

**출어**(出御) the going out of the king; the appearance of the king.

**출연**(出演) one's appearance on stage; one's performance 《첫 출연》 debut.

**출영**(出迎) meeting 《영접》 reception/~하다 receive; greet; meet; go[come] [out] to meet (a person) on arrival/많은 친지의 ~을 받다 be met[received] by many friends at (a place).

**출옥**(出獄) discharge[release] from prison/~하다 be discharged from prison; be set free; come out of prison; leave prison/만기 ~하다 be discharged upon expiration of one's term.

**출원**(出願) application; submitting application/ ~하다 apply for; make an application for/전매 특허 ~증 "Patent Applied for".

**출입**(出入) 《들어오고 나감》 coming and going; going in and out; entrance and exit 《모임》 attendance 《요청》 indentation/~하다 visit; frequent; go in and out; enter and leave 《배가》 enter and clear/자유로 ~할 수 있다 have[be allowed] free access to (a house).

**출자**(出資) financing; investment; contribution/ ~하다 invest[put] money into/~액 the amount of contribution [investment].

**출장**(出張) 《관리의》 an official tour[trip]; 《회사 등의》 a business trip/~하다 take a business[an official] trip/~ 명령을 받다 receive an order to go to (a place).

**출장**(出場) 《참가》 appearance; participation/~하다 appear; be present at 《참가하다》 take part in; enter/경기에 ~하다 enter a race.

**출전**(出典) a source; a source book; the origin; the provenance/~을 밝히다 give [indicate] the source; give authorities (for a statement).

**출전**(出戰) 《출정》 departure for the front 《참가》 participation/ ~하다 《출정하다》 depart for the front; go to the war; serve in the war/선수권을 쟁취하기 위하여 ~하다 enter for an event to win the championship.

**출정**(出廷) appearance in court; a court appearance/ ~하다 appear in court; attend court; be in court.

**출정**(出征) departure for the front/~하다 depart for the front; go to the front; go to war; take part in a war 《종군하다》 serve in the war/의용군으로 ~하다 go to war as a volunteer/~ 군인 a soldier at the front.

**출제**(出題) setting[giving] questions (for examination); presenting problems 《문제》 the questions[problems] in the examination/ ~하다 set[give] questions (for examination).

**출중**(出衆) pre-eminence/~하다 (be) uncommon; extraordinary; pre-eminent/그는 ~한 재간을 가졌다 He was endowed with extraordinary talents.

**출진**(出陣) going to war/ ~하다 go to battle; take the field.

출찰(出札) issue of a ticket/ ~계 a ticket clerk〈미〉; a booking clerk〈영〉/~구 a booking-office〈영〉; a ticketoffice〈미〉. しゅっさつ

출처(出處) source; origin; provenance/소문의 ~를 밝히다 trace [the source of] a report/뉴스의 ~ the source of [the] news. しゅっしょ

출초(出超) an excess of exports [over imports]/10월에는 1억원의 ~였다 We had a favorable trade balance of one hundred million *won* in October. しゅっちょう

출출하다 feel hungry; be somewhat hungry. ひもじい

출타(出他) absence; being away from home/~하다 go[be] out/~하고 안 계시다 He has gone out and is not back yet. がいしゅつ

출판(出版) publication; publishing; issue/~하다 publish; put[bring] out;issue; print/그는 ~ 사업을 시작했다 He has started in the publishing business. しゅっぱん

출판권(出版權) the right of publication; publication rights; copyright ⇨판권(版權). しゅっぱんけん

출품(出品) exhibition; display/ ~하다 exhibit; display; put on exhibition[display]/그림을 전람회에 ~하다 exhibit *one's* pictures at a public show/~물 an exhibit. しゅっぴん

출하(出荷) shipment; forwarding/ ~하다 forward (*goods*); ship make a shipment (*to*)/화물을 ~하다 ship goods from (*Seoul station*). しゅっか

출항(出港) departure (of *a ship* from *a port*)/~하다 leave port; sail from (*a port*); set sail; clear/~을 정지하다 lay an embargo on a ship. しゅっこう

출항(出航) a take-off; departure/~하다 leave; sail from; take off.

출현(出現) appearance; apparition; advent/~하다 appear; make *one's* appearance. しゅつげん

출혈(出血) bleeding; loss of blood; hemorrhage; sacrifice/~하다 bleed; lose blood/다량의 ~을 보다 bleed badly[freely]. しゅっけつ

출화(出火) a fire; an outbreak of fire/~하다 a fire breaks out/~의 원인 the origin[cause] of a fire. しゅっか

출회(出廻) 《상》movement; arrivals on the market/~하다 arrive on the market; be moving/보리의 ~기 the season for movements of barley. でまわること

춤¹ 《분량》 a grip; a grasp; a handful. にぎり

춤² height of a rim/병의 ~이 높다 The vase is tall.

춤³ trouser[waist] tops /허리에 손을 넣다 put *one's* hands in *one's* trouser tops. こしまわり

춤⁴ 《무용》dancing; a dance; a step/~추다 dance; tread a [dainty] measure; step[foot] it; shake a leg〈속〉/《나비 따위가》flutter about 《새가》circle; wheel/남의 장단에 ~을 추다 dance to (*a person's*) tune; be manipulated; be made a puppet (*of*). おどり

춥다 《날씨·기후 따위가》(be) cold; chilly 《춥게 느끼다》 feel chilly; catch[take] a chill/지난 겨울은 몹시 추웠다 We have had a severe winter. さむい

충(蟲) an insect; a bug; a worm; a moth. むし

충격(衝擊) impact; shock; collision/ ~하다 shock; strike; against/그의 죽음은 그녀에게 큰 ~을 주었다 His death was a great shock to her. しょうげき

충고(忠告) 《조언》advice; counsel; suggestion 《간언》admonition; remonstrance; exhortation 《경고》warning/~하다 advise; warn; give warning; admonish; counsel; remonstrate to/ ~를 무시하다 disregard[ignore, take no heed of] (*a person's*) advice; do against (*a person's*) counsel. ちゅうこく

충군(忠君) loyalty[devotion] to *one's* sovereign[king]. ちゅうくん

충근(忠勤) devotion; faithfulness; loyalty; faithful service; faithful discharge of *one's* duties. ちゅうきん

충나다(蟲—) get infested with (*worms*).

충노(忠奴) a faithful servant. ちゅうぼく

충당(充當) appropriation; assignment; devotion/~하다 allot; assign (*for, to*); appropriate (*to, for*); apply (*to*); set aside (*for*)/생활비에 ~할 돈 money to meet *one's* living expenses. じゅうとう

충돌(衝突) a collision; a clash 《불일치》a conflict; a discord 《전투》an encounter/~하다 collide with[against]; come into collision with; run[strike] against [into]/어제 여기서 큰 열차 ~ 사고가 있었다 There was a horrible smash on the railway here yesterday. しょうとつ

충동(衝動) ①《의식》impulse; impetus; shock; urge/일시적 ~에 못 이기다 give in to the impulse of the moment ②《교사·선동》instigation; incitement/~하다 instigate; set (*a person*) on; egg[spur] on. しょうどう

충량(忠良) loyalty/~하다 (be) loyal. ちゅうりょう

충렬(忠烈) unswerving loyalty/ ~하다 (be) loyal and true; devoted and faithful. ちゅうれつ

충류(蟲類) the insect family; worms; insects. ちゅうるい

충만(充滿) abundance; fullness; repletion/~하다 be full (*of*); be filled[crowded] (*with*); (be) abundant/그 안내서는 유익한 기사로 ~하다 The guidebook is replete with useful information. じゅうまん

충매(蟲媒) 《식》entomophily/ ~화 an

entomophilous flower. ちゅうばい

**충복**(忠僕) a faithful[dutiful] servant; a henchman. ちゅうぼく

**충분**(充分) ~하다 (be) sufficient; enough; ample; good; thorough; satisfactory/상상력[실력]을 ~히 발휘하다 give full play to one's imagination[ability]. じゅうぶん

**충사**(忠死) loyal death/ ~하다 die[lay down one's life, give [up] one's life] for one's loyalty. ちゅうし

**충색**(充塞) filling up; congestion/~하다 fill up; congest.

**충성**(忠誠) loyalty; devotion; allegiance; integrity; patriotism/~스럽다 (be) loyal; patriotic; devoted; true/ ~을 다하다 be loyal[faithful, devoted] (to). ちゅうせい

**충순**(忠純) faithfulness; honesty/~하다 (be) faithful; honest; true. ちゅうじゅん

**충순**(忠順) loyalty; fidelity; devotion/ ~하다 (be) dutiful; obedient.

**충신**(忠臣) a loyal subject; a faithful retainer/~은 두 임금을 섬기지 않는다 A faithful retainer will not serve two masters. ちゅうしん

**충실**(忠實) faithfulness; devotion; loyalty; honesty; fidelity/~하다 (be) faithful; honest; devoted; true; loyal; conscientious/내용이 ~한 저술 a substantial work. ちゅうじつ

**충실**(充實) 《실질》substantiality; fullness 《충족》repletion; replenishment (완비) completeness; perfection/ ~하다 (be) full; replete; complete; rich; substantial/~한 생활 a full life. じゅうじつ

**충심**(衷心) one's true heart; one's inmost feelings[heart]/~으로부터 환영 a hearty[cordial] welcome/ ~에서 우러나오는 동정 heartfelt[hearty] sympathy. ちゅうしん

**충심**(忠心) loyalty; fidelity; allegiance; integrity/~이 지극하다 (be) loyal; true; faithful; devoted.

**충양돌기**(蟲樣突起) 《해》 the vermiform appendix/~염 appendicitis/ ~ 절제수술 appendectomy. ちゅうようとっき

**충언**(忠言) honest[good] advice; counsel /~하다 give good counsel; advise/~은 역이다 Unpleasant advice is a good medicine. ちゅうげん

**충욕**(充慾) gratification of one's desire/ ~하다 gratify one's desire; satisfy one's want.

**충용**(忠勇) loyalty and courage[valor]/ ~하다 (be) loyal and courageous[brave]. ちゅうゆう

**충용**(充用) appropriation/~히다 appropriate (to, for); apply (to). じゅうよう

**충원**(充員) supplement of the personnel; 《군》《보충 인원》the reserves; recruits 《인원 보충》drafts; recruitment; levying; draft/~하다 supplement the personnel; levy; recruit.

**충의**(忠義) loyalty; devotion; faithfulness; fidelity; allegiance/~를 다하다 be faithful; be devoted. ちゅうぎ

**충이다** shake; swing; joggle; sway/쌀자루를 ~ shake a rice bag from side to side; joggle rice in the bag. ゆれる

**충일**(充溢) overflow; exuberance; abundance; adequacy; sufficiency/ ~하다 overflow; be full (of); be overflowing (with); be affluent; be abundant; be exuberant. じゅういつ

**충재**(蟲災) damage from insects.

**충적**(沖積) 《지》 ~의 alluvial/ ~기《층》 the alluvial age[formation]/~토 alluvial soil. ちゅうせき

**충전**(充電) charging; electrification/ ~하다 charge; electrify/축전지에 ~하다 charge an accumulator[a storage battery] with electricity. じゅうでん

**충절**(忠節) faithfulness; loyalty; fidelity; allegiance; devotion. ちゅうせつ

**충정**(衷情) one's true feeling[heart]/ ~을 털어 놓다 open one's heart to (another). ちゅうじょう

**충족**(充足) sufficiency; adequacy; satisfaction; fullness; being enough/ ~하다 (be) sufficient; adequate; satisfactory; full; enough/ ~ 이유의 원리 《철》 principle of sufficient reason. じゅうそく

**충직**(忠直) uprightness; faithfulness; honesty/ ~하다 (be) faithful; honest; upright; true/그는 주인에게 ~한 머슴이다 He is a servant true to his master. ちゅうちょく

**충천**(衝天) ~하다 rise high; shoot up; soar/의기가 ~하다 one's spirit soars to the skies; be in high spirits. しょうてん

**충충** 1.《걸음을》walking fast; hastily; briskly; with a brisk step 2.《물의 모양》deep; deeply/~하다 (be) deep; profound 3.《어둠 침침》gloomily; somberly; dimly/~하다 (be) gloomy; somber; dimly-lit. せかせか

**충충하다** 1.《빛깔이》(be) dark; gloomy; shady; dim 2.《물이》(be) full and deep /우물에 물이 ~ A well has plenty of water in it. さえない

**충치**(蟲齒) a decayed tooth; decay of teeth; 《의》 caries/~를 예방하다 prevent tooth-decay; prevent teeth from decaying. むしば

**충해**(蟲害) a plague of vermin; insect pests; fly; damage from insects; vermin damage; a blight/콩에 ~가 많았다 There has been a great deal of fly on the beans. ちゅうがい

**충혈**(充血) congestion/~하다 be congested 《눈이》be bloodshot/~한 눈 bloodshot eyes/~시키다 congest; engorge. じゅうけつ

**충혼**(忠魂) 《전사자의 넋》the loyal dead; the war dead 《충의심》a loyal soul[spi-

**충효**(忠孝) loyalty and filial piety／～쌍전(雙全)되다 be at once a loyal subject and a filial son. ちゅうこう

**췌담**(贅談) redundant words. むだくち

**췌론**(贅論) a pleonasm; a redundant expression.

**췌액**(膵液) pancreation; pancreatic juice／～소 pancreatin. すいえき

**췌언**(贅言) superfluous[redundant] words; verbiage; pleonasm; tautology／교육의 중요성은 ～할 필요가 없다 There is no need of a pleonasm on the importance of education. ぜいげん

**췌육**(贅肉) superfluous flesh. ぜいにく

**췌장**(膵臟) the pancreas／～액 pancreation／～염 《의》 pancreatitis. すいぞう

**취객**(醉客) a drunkard; a drink-sodden fellow; a drunken man. すいかく

**취관**(吹管) a blowpipe／～분석 blowpipe analysis.

**취광**(醉狂) drunken frenzy; delirium tremens 《사람》 a drunken man; a drunk; a drunkard; a boozer;" a lush[souse] 《속》. すいきょう

**취급**(取扱) 《사람의》 treatment 《사무·물건의》 dealing; handling; use 《교묘한》 manipulation 《관리》 management／～하다 《사람을》 treat; deal with 《사무·물건을》 handle; manage／사회 문제를 ～한 소설 a novel that treats of social problems／전보를 ～하다 accept[take in] telegram. とりあつかい

**취기**(醉氣) effects of drink; tipsiness; intoxication; inebriation／～가 만면하다 one's face glows with the wine. すいき

**취담**(醉談) a talk[speech] under the influence of liquor／～이 진담이다 In wine there is truth.
さけによってすることば

**취득**(取得) acquisition／～하다 acquire; obtain／～물 an acquisition／소유권을 ～하다 acquire the ownership (of)／～자 an acquisitor. しゅとく

**취락**(聚落) a community; communal society. しゅうらく

**취리**(取利) moneylending.

**취면**(就眠) ～하다 go to bed[sleep]; retire; turn in 《잠자리에 들다》 go to bed; retire to bed. すいみん

**취미**(趣味) taste; interest; relish／문학 ～ literary taste／～가 서로 다르다 have quite different tastes／우리는 같은 ～를 가지고 있다 We have congenial tastes. しゅみ

**취사**(取捨) selection or rejection; choice／～하다 choose; select／마음대로 ～하다 take or leave as one likes／～ 선택하다 choose; take or leave (a thing). しゅしゃ

**취사**(炊事) cooking; cookery／～하다 cook; do [the] cooking／～장 a kitchen／～ 도구 cooking[kitchen] utensils／～ 당번 the cook's duty 《병사의》 a kitchen police. すいじ

**취색**(翠色) verdure; jade colo[u]r.

**취생 몽사**(醉生夢死) living like a drunkard and dying like a dreamer; dreaming one's life away／～하다 dream[slumber] one's life away; pass through life in a dreamy state; drone one's life away; live to no purpose／～하는 사람 a happy-go-lucky fellow. すいしょく

**취석**(臭石) 《광》 stinkstone.

**취소**(臭素) bromine; 《화》 Br／～지 bromide paper／～칼리 bromide of potash; potassium bromide. しゅうそ

**취소**(取消) cancellation; retraction 《무효》 annulment／～하다 retract; rescind; withdraw; revoke; recall; take back; 《법》 reverse／약속을 ～하다 retract[withdraw] from an engagement.
とりけし

**취안**(醉眼) drunken eyes; eyes dim with drink. すいがん

**취안**(醉顔) the face of an intoxicated person; a drunken face[look]. すいがん

**취약**(脆弱) fragility; frailty; brittleness; flimsiness／～하다 (be) weak; fragile; frail; delicate; tender; brittle.
やわらかくよわいこと

**취언**(醉言) drunken words; talking under the influence of drink.
さけによってすることば

**취업**(就業) employment; commencement of work／～하다 go[begin] to work／～시간 the working hour／～중이다 be at work／내년 봄부터 ～할 예정이다 plan to operate [the business] from next spring. しゅうぎょう

**취역**(就役) ～하다 go into commission; be placed in commission.

**취연**(炊煙) kitchen smoke. すいえん

**취옥**(翠玉) 《광》 nephrite. すいぎょく

**취용**(取用) borrowing／～하다 borrow.

**취우**(驟雨) a shower. しゅうう

**취음**(取音) borrow the sounds (from Chinese characters) in transcribing.

**취의**(趣意) 《의미》 purport; meaning 《목적》 an object; a purpose 《요지》 the point; the drift／방문의 ～ the object of one's visit／～서 a prospectus. しゅい

**취인**(取人) selection; choice／～하다 select; choose.

**취임**(就任) inauguration; installation／～하다 take office (as); be installed; be inaugurated／～식 an inauguration; an inaugural ceremony／～ 인사 an inaugural address／교수로 ～하다 take up a professorship. しゅうにん

**취입**(吹込) ～하다 have (one's speech, etc.) recorded; make a record (of); put on a record[disk, tape]; speak[sing] into a gramophone／그 녀자는 바이얼린 독주를 ～했다 She recorded her violin solo on the gramophone.

**취장**(膵臟) pancreas.

**취재**(取材) subject selection; choice of subject; selection of material/ ~하다 collect[gather] data (on *the case*); 《신문 기자가》 cover (*a fire*)/신문은 온통 월남전에 관하여 ~되어 있다 The paper is all covered with the news which is derived from the Vietnam War/ ~기자 a news reporter. しゅざい

**취조**(取調) investigation; inquiry; examination; research/ ~하다 investigate; inquire (*into*); examine/경찰의 ~를 받다 be examined by the police. とりしらべ

**취주**(吹奏) flute[trumpet]-blowing; music-playing/ ~하다 play; sound; blow /트럼펫을 ~하다 blow[play] a trumpet /~ 악대 a brass band. すいそう

**취중**(醉中) ~에 in drink; under the influence of liquor; when drunk/~에 실수하다 make a drunken slip; make a mistake while in *one's* cups.
さけによっているあいだ

**취중**(就中) ①《무엇보다도》above all; before everything[anything else]; most of all ②《특별히》particularly; in particular; especially. なかんずく

**취지**(趣旨) 《생각》an opinion; an idea 《목적》an object; a purpose; an aim; a gist 《의의·요지》a sense; a meaning; a tenor; a purport; an import; effect/본회의 설립 ~는 빈민 구제에 있다 The society has been organized with the relief of the poor for its main object.

**취직**(就職) finding employment/ ~하다 get a position[job, place]; find work[employment]; obtain work; get employment/무역 회사에 ~하다 be employed in the trading company/~난 a job shortage. しゅうしょく

**취진**(驟進) rapid elevation in the official world/ ~하다 go up by leaps and bounds; rise rapidly in the official world.

**취처**(娶妻) marriage; taking a woman to[as] wife/ ~하다 get married to a woman; take a woman[girl] in marriage; marry (*a woman*).
つまをめとること

**취체**(取締) 《통제》control 《단속》regulation; supervision 《관리》management/ ~하다 control; supervise; oversee; keep control over; manage/ ~를 엄중히 하다 keep strict order; maintain strict control of[supervision over]; make stringent regulations (*on*). とりしまり

**취침**(就寢) going to bed/ ~하다 go to bed; retire/~ 전에 before retiring/~ 시각 bed time. しゅうしん

**취태**(醉態) drunkenness; intoxication/ ~를 부리다 put on a drunken display; hit the booze and become wild《미·속》.
すいたい

**취하**(取下) withdrawal/ ~하다 withdraw; drop/신청을 ~하다 withdraw *one's* application. とりさげ

**취하다**(取―) ①《채용하다》adopt; take ②《선택하다》prefer; choose; pick; take/많은 가운데서 하나를 ~ choose[pick] one out of many ③《섭취하다》take; have/자양물을 ~ take nourishing food.
とる

**취하다**(醉―) ①《술에》get drunk; become intoxicated; get tipsy; be in *one's* cups /취한 체하고 pretending to be drunk ②《배·차 따위에》get[feel] sick; be nauseated ③《중독되다》get poisoned/담배에 ~ get sick from smoking; smoke *one*self sick ④《열중하다》be elated; be exalted; be intoxicated; get fascinated/환희에 ~ be in an ecstacy of happiness; be beside *one*self with happiness. よう

**취학**(就學) ~하다 enter[attend] a school / ~ 아동 schoolchildren/~ 연령 the school age/~시키다 send to school.
しゅうがく

**취한**(醉漢) a drunken fellow; a drunkard. すいかん

**취한**(取汗) ~하다 sweat out [a cold].

**취항**(就航) commission; service/ ~하다 put out to sea; set sail; start on a voyage; enter service 《새 배가》go into commission; be put on (*the line, route*)/샌프란시스코 항로에 ~하다 be put on the San Francisco line[route].
しゅうこう

**취화**(臭化) 《화》bromination/ ~하다 brominate. しゅうか

**취흥**(醉興) conviviality; joviality[merriment, hilarity] over *one's* cups; the fun of being drunk/그 바람에 모처럼 올랐던 ~이 깨져 버렸다 That brought a chill over the merrymaking party.

**-측**(側) the side/주주~에서는 아무 이의도 없었다 There was no objection on the part of the shareholders. そく. がわ

**측근**(側近) the surroundings; around (*a person*)/ ~에 모시다 stand by (*a person's*) side/~에 아무도 없다 have nobody around. そっきん

**측근자**(側近者) persons close to (*the premier, ect.*); *one's* staff members; the immediate members of *one's* staff; close associates; brain trusters; close attendants; *entourage*(F)/대통령의 ~ persons close to the President. そっきんしゃ

**측도**(測度) measurement [of degree]; gauging/ ~하다 measure; gauge. そくど

**측량**(測量) measurement 《토지의》surveying; a survey 《물 깊이의》sounding / ~하다 measure; survey; sound/ ~ 술 surveying/~ 기사 a surveyor/ ~ 기계 surveying instruments/ ~도 a survey map; a plan of survey/ ~ 대(隊) a surveying corps; a survey party /토지를 ~하다 survey land. そくりょう

**측면**(側面) the side; the flank; 《수》the lateral face/~에서 원조하다 give indirect aid (*to*); aid (*a person*) indirectly /적의 ~을 찌르다 attack the enemy

**측문** in the flank. そくめん
**측문(仄聞)** ~하다 hear casually; learn by hearsay/~한바에 의하면, from what I heard by chance …. そくぶん
**측백나무(側柏一)** 《식》 an Oriental arbor vitae; a thuja; *Biota Orientalis*(학명). このてがしわのき
**측보기(測步器)** a pedometer.
**측사(側射)** a flanking fire.
**측사기(測斜器)** a clinometer. そくしゃき
**측선(側線)** 《철도의》 a sidetrack; a siding /~에 넣다 sidetrack (*a train*). そくせん
**측수(測水)** sounding; plumbing/~하다 sound the depth; strike[take] soundings. すいしんのはかること
**측심(測深)** sounding the depth/~하다 sound (*the sea*); plumb; take sounding /~기 a sounder; a depth finder.
**측연(惻然)** ~하다 be compassionate; sympathetic/. そくぜん
**측연(測鉛)** a plumb; a sounding-lead; a plummet; a lead/~을 던져 넣다 cast the lead. そくえん
**측열기(測熱器)** a calorimeter.
**측우기(測雨器)** a rain gauge; a pluviometer; a udometer; a hyetometer; an ombrometer. そくりき
**측원기(測遠器)** a range finder; a telemeter. そくえんき
**측은(側隱)** compassion; commiseration; pity; mercy/~하다 (be) pitiable; pitiful; piteous 《감동하다》 touching/~지심(之心) compassion; pity; mercy. そくいん
**측전기(測電器)** an electrometer.
**측점(測點)** 《측량의》 a station; a measuring point. そくてん
**측정(測定)** 《토지의》 measurement; survey; sounding; fathoming 《수심의》 plumbing 《구경 따위의》 calibration/~하다 measure; gauge; survey; sound; calibrate/정확히 ~하다 take an accurate measurement (*of*). そくてい
**측정(測程)** a log/~선 a log line/~기 a log/~판 《해양》 a chip log.
**측지(測地)** land surveying/~하다 survey land/~학 geodesy. そくち
**측추(測錘)** a plumb; a sounding lead.
**측표(測標)** a [depth] mark.
**측후(測候)** meteorological observation/ ~하다 make a meteorological observation/~소 a meteorological station [observatory]; a weather bureau. そっこう
**츱츱하다** (be) mean; servile; shameless; impudent/츱츱하게 남의 물건을 자꾸 달라다 He keeps asking me for things shamelessly. ずうずうしい
**층(層)** 《건물의》 a storey; a story 《미》; a floor 《계단》 stairs; a staircase; a flight of stairs 《지층》 a layer; a stratum (*pl.* -ta); 《석탄 등의》 a bed/2-층 a two story[two storied] house/사무실은 6-에 있다 The office is on the sixth floor. かさなり

**층각(層閣)** a many-storied building. そうかく
**층계(層階)** 《층층다리》 steps; stairs; a flight of stairs; a staircase; a footboard 《입구의》 doorsteps/~를 오르내리다 go up and down the stairs.
**층나다(層一)** show[have] [a structure of] layers; be terraced; become differentiated[uneven]; (be) differential; be graded; uneven. さがでる
**층대(層臺)** stairs; a flight of stairs; a staircase.
**층돌(層一)** a touchstone; a Lydian stone; a stone for assaying gold.
**층루(層樓)** a many-storeyed building[turret]. たかどの
**층면(層面)** the surface of the stratum; the stratification plane. そうめん
**층상(層狀)** ~의 stratiform; stratified/ ~운(雲) a stratiform cloud. そうじょう
**층새(層一)** the quality of gold.
**층생첩출(層生疊出)** ~하다 appear in succession; crop up; mushroom.
**층암 절벽(層岩絕壁)** an overhanging[an impending, a precipitous] cliff.
**층애(層崖)** a stratal precipice[cliff].
**층운(層雲)** 《기상》 a stratus(*pl.* -ti). そううん
**층적운(層積雲)** 《기상》 roll cumulus; stratocumulus(*pl.* -li). そうせきうん
**층지다(層一)** have layers; be terraced; become differentiated; be graded; uneven. てこぼこになる
**층집(層一)** a house of two-or-more storeys; a many-storeyed building/우리 사무실은 2-에 있다 Our office is on the two storied floor.
**층층(層層)** layer upon layer; pile after pile; all stories[storeys].
**층층대(層層臺)** a staircase; stairs; a flight of stairs.
**층층 시하(層層侍下)** having both parents and grandparents alive.
**층하(層下)** ~하다 discriminate against /~없이 impartially; without discrimination.
**치¹** 《길이의 단위》 a Korean inch; a *chi* (3.03030cm). すん
**치²** ①《몫》 a share; a part; a portion/ 하루~의 식량 food for one day ②《사람》 a fellow; a guy《미·비》/그 ~ that fellow; he.
**치(値)** 《수》 numerical value/~를 구하다 seek[find] the value. ち
**치(齒)** a tooth.
**치가(治家)** home management/~하다 put *one's* house in order; manage a home [well]; look after *one's* family affairs [excellently]. いえをおさめること
**치가떨리다(齒一)** gnash[grind] *one's* teeth with indignation[vexation]; be tense with indignation. ふんがいにたえずみぶるいする
**치감(齒疳)** 《의》 Riggs' disease; pyorrhea

**치경(齒莖)** a gum; a teethridge. はぐき

**치고** as for; when it comes to; be that as it may/그것 그렇다~ be that as it may/양복은 이것이 최고다 This is a suit of finest quality. ―として

**치골(恥骨)** the pubis; the pubic bones.

**치골(癡骨)** a simpleton; a fool; a dunce. おろかしゃ

**치골(齒骨)** 《의》 the dentine [of a tooth]. しこつ

**치과(齒科)** dental surgery; dentistry; dental service/~ 병원 a dental clinic; a dental hospital. しか

**치관(齒冠)** the crown [of a tooth]. しかん

**치국(治國)** statecraft; government/ ~책(策) statecraft. ちこく

**치근(齒根)** the root of a tooth. しこん

**치근거리다** tease; plague; bother/치근거리는 사람 a dogged person; a nuisance/치근치근 teasingly. うるさくいう

**치기(稚氣)** senselessness; foolishness; childishness/ ~에 가득 찬 childish; puerile.

**치다**[1] ①《때리다》 strike; beat; thrash/되~ strike back/치고 받고 하다 fight; come to blows ②《두드리다》 beat(북을); ring(종을); play [on](풍금 따위를); drive [hammer] in(못을); flap(손뼉을) ③《던지어 맞히다》 [make a good] hit; strike/공을 ~ hit a ball ④《떡을》 bounce (boiled rice into rice-cake) ⑤《벼락 따위》 fall; strike/산에는 눈보라가 몹시 쳤다 A blizzard raged over the mountains.

**치다**[2] ①《공격・토벌》 attack; assault; subjugate; overcome; conquer ②《베어 내다》 cut; prune; trim; lop off[away]/머리를 짧게 ~ clip[cut] one's hair close ③《껍질을》 peel; rind; pare. こうげきする

**치다**[3] 《깨끗이하다》 clean [out]; remove; carry[take] away; get rid of; dredge/우물을 ~ clean a well/똥을 ~ remove the human waste[dung]. かたづける

**치다**[4] ①《체 따위로》 sieve; sift; bolt ②《장난을》 do; play ③《소리를》 shout; utter; cry. ふるう

**치다**[5] ①《사육하다》 raise; keep; rear/그 여자는 닭을 치고 있다 She keeps chickens. ②《새끼를》 breed/새는 봄에 새끼를 친다 Birds breed in the spring. ③shoot out; spread ④keep/하숙을 ~ keep a lodger[roomer]. くわえる

**치다**[6] 《양념을》 put[pour] into; mix with; season with /나물에 참기름을 ~ season vegetables with sesame oil. ふるう

**치다**[7] 《휘장・천막 따위를》 put up; hang; draw; attach; fasten/창에 커튼을 ~ hang a window with a curtain. はる

**치다**[8] weave/허리끈을 ~ braid a belt.

**치다**[9] 《화투를》 shuffle(섞다); play(놀다)/화투를 ~ play cards.

**치다**[10] ①《셈을》 value; appraise; estimate; calculate/총 경비를 100만 원으로 ~ estimate the total expenditures at one million won ②《여기다》 consider. かかる

**치다**[11] 《수레바퀴가》 run over; knock[turn] down/치고 도망친 자동차 a hit-and-run car.

**치다**[12] ①《전보를》 telegraph to (a person) ②《시험을》 take; sit for; try (an examination)/시험칠 준비를 하다 prepare[read, study] for an examination. うつ

**-치다** do hard/넘~ overflow; flow [over]; brim over.

**치다꺼리** ①《일처리》 management; conduct; disposition; disposal/ ~하다 manage; conduct; dispose of (a matter) ②《조력》 assistance; help/ ~하다 help; assist (one in doing).

**치달다** run up; go up; rush up 《언덕을》 run uphill 《계단을》 run upstairs/새가 하늘 높이 ~ A bird soars sky high. はしりあがる

**치대다** 《문지르다》 rub; knead 《위에 대다》 put on the upper side/빨래를 ~ rub laundry. こすりつける

**치도곤(治盜棍)** a club for flogging a criminal.

**치독(治毒)** anti-toxic remedy; counterpoison/ ~하다 counteract[neutralize] poison 《해독제를 써서》 mithridatize. どくけをなくさせること

**치둔(癡鈍)** stupidity; dumbness; dullness/ ~하다 (be) stupid; dumb; knucklehead; dull-witted. むちでにぶいこと

**치뜨다** raise[lift] (one's eyes)/눈을 ~ lift up one's eyes; look up. にらみあげる

**치뜨리다** toss (a thing) up; throw up; fling up.

**치들다** (be) mean; dirty; ugly. やることがきたない

**치란(治亂)** 《평화와 전란》 peace and[or] war; vicissitudes of fortune 《난의 평정》 suppression of a revolt[rebellion]/ ~하다 put down a revolt; suppress a rebellion. ちらん

**치런치런** ①《넘칠락말락》 full to the brim; brimfully; to the full; overflowingly; affluently ②《스칠락말락》 close to. なみなみと

**치렁거리다** drag; trail; hang down; droop; drag on 《날짜》 be prolonged[protracted]; drag it out/커튼이 바람에 치렁거린다 The curtain blows in the wind. ぶらんぶらんする

**치련(治鍊)** refining 《쇠의》 tempering 《구리의》 smelting/ ~하다 refine; temper; smelt.

**치례** make-up; dressing/ ~하다 dress [smarten] oneself up; be dressed up/옷 ~하다 dress up; be in full feather. そうしょく

**치료(治療)** medical treatment[attention]; medical cure; remedy/ ~하다 cure; heal; treat (a disease, a person for); cure (a patient of, a disease); give medical treatment; attend to/ ~법 a

치루 method[course] of medical treatment; a remedy／~비 doctor's bills; a medical[doctor's] fee／물리 ~ physical therapy／전기 ~ electrotherapy／응급 ~ 하다 give first aid／그 환자는 ~를 받지 않으면 안 된다 The sick man must be cared for. ちりょう

치루(痔瘻) 〖의〗 piles; hemorrhoids.
치루(痔瘻) 〖의〗 anal fistula. じろう
치룽 a basket; a crate.
치룽구니 a fool; a simpleton; an ass; a dunce.
치르다 《돈을》 pay (off); make payment; pay one's bill; square[settle] one's accounts 《경험》 experience; undergo; carry out; go through／물건 값을 ~ pay for an article. しはらう
치를떨다(齒一) 《인색하여》 grudge; spare 《분해서》 grind one's teeth with vexation. けちけちする
치마 a skirt. スカート
치마분(齒磨粉) tooth powder. はみがきこな
치매(癡呆) 〖의〗 dementia; imbecility／~증 dementia praecox. あほう
치면하다 (be) almost full to the brim; nearly brimful.
치명(致命) ~의 fatal; mortal; deadly／그것은 그 산업에 ~적인 타격이다 It is a deathblow to the industry.／~상 a fatal[mortal, death] wound. ちめい
치민(治民) rule; reign; government／~하다 reign[rule] over; govern／~의 도를 깨닫다 learn[be awake to] the ways of governing the people of one's country. ちみん
치밀(緻密) minuteness; delicacy; accuracy; precision／~하다 《정밀하다》(be) precise; minute; fine; close 《정교하다》(be) elaborate; delicate 《정확하다》(be) exact; accurate／~하게 조사하다 investigate minutely[closely]／~한 두뇌 a fine brain. ちみつ
치밀다 《위로 밀다》 push[throw, force] up; boost 《감정이》 rise; well up; rage／눈물이 치밀어오른다 Tears spring[well] in one's eyes. したからつきあげる
치받다 butt up; push up counter (to); push up against. おしあげる
치받이 a slope; an incline; an ascent; a climb; an upgrade; 〖건〗 mud plastered on the ceiling.
치받치다 《불길·연기 따위가》 rise 《분출》 belch; shoot up 《감정이》 rise; well 《밑을》 prop; bolster[shore] ⋯p／분노가 ~ flare up in anger.
치부(致富) acquisition of wealth; making money／~하다 become rich; amass a fortune. ふうしゃにすること
치부(置簿) 《직접 기입》 register; an entry; booking 《전기(轉記)》 posting／~하다 register; make an entry; enter in an account[a day]-book／~책 a ledger; a waste-book. きろくすること
치분(齒粉) tooth powder. はみがきこな

치사(致死) ~의 causing death; fatal／~량 《약의》 a fatal[lethal] dose／과실 ~죄 accidental homicide. ちし
치사(致謝) thank; gratitude; appreciation／~하다 thank (a person) for; express one's thanks[gratitude].
치사(恥事) ~하다 (be) shameful; dishonorable; disgraceful; ignominious 《비열하다》 mean; dirty／~스러운 줄을 모르다 be shameless; be brazen-faced; be lost to all sense of shame／~스러운 짓 a shameful conduct. はずかしいこと
치산(治産) ①《살림》 living; livelihood／~하다 get one's living; gain one's livelihood ②《재산 관리》 management of one's property[estate]／~하다 manage one's property[estate]. ちさん
치산(治山) forestry conservancy[conservation, protection]; antiflood[flood control] afforestation／~하다 reserve[protect] forest; afforest (a mountain)／~치수(治水) anti-flood afforestation ちさん
치살리다 praise[extol] (a person) to the skies; speak highly of; sing the praises of; flatter. べたほめする
치상(齒狀) ~의 dentiform.
치석(齒石) tartar; discolouration on teeth／~제거 scaling. しせき
치석(治石) trimming stone [for building purposes]; stonecutting／~하다 cut[dress] stone; trim stone.
치성(致誠) devotion; loyal[faithful] service 《신명·부처에게》 sacrificial service [to spirits]. じょうじゅするようにすること
치세(治世) a reign; a regime 《태평한 세상》 peaceful times. ちせい
치소(嗤笑) a despising[scornful] laugh; a sneer; derision／~하다 deride; laugh [jeer, mock] at; sneer at. ちょうしょう
치소(癡笑) idiotic laughter. あほうわらい
치수(-數) measure; size; dimensions／옷의 ~를 재다 take (a person's) measurements for new clothes／~를 잘못재다 take wrong measurements.
치수(治水) the control of water; flood control; river improvement[conservancy]／~하다 embank a river; execute levee[flood prevention, conservancy] works／~ 공사 embankment[levee] works; water conservation works／~ 공학 hydraulic engineering. ちすい
치수(齒髓) the dental pulp; the pulp [of a tooth]／~염 〖의〗 pulpitis. しずい
치수금 a rule; a scale; measurement 《기준》 a standard.
치수대다(-數-) take the measurements of; measure [the length of]／광목을 ~ measure the length of a piece of cotton.
치술(治術) administrative ability[capacity, skill]. ちじゅつ
치신경(齒神經) 〖해〗 dental nerves.
치신사납다 (be) slovenly; indecent; be deadly ashamed[mortified]; (be) sha-

**치심**(侈心) a luxurious[an extravagant] mind.

**치아**(齒牙) a tooth. しが

**치아**(穉兒) an infant; a child.

**치안**(治安) [the] public peace[order]／경찰 the peace police／～국 the Headquarters of National Police／～을 유지하다 maintain[keep] public peace. ちあん

**치약**(齒藥) 《가루》 tooth-powder; tooth-paste 《크림 모양의》 dental cream.

**치열**(齒列) a set[row] of teeth／～이 고르다[고르지 않다] have a regular[an irregular] set of teeth. はならび

**치열**(熾烈) ～하다 (be) severe; keen; intense／～한 전투 a fierce battle; a sharp fighting. しれつ

**치열**(治熱) controlling a fever／이열(以熱) ～ Set a thief to catch a thief.

**치올리다** lift up; push up. おしあげる

**치외 법권**(治外法權) extraterritoriality; extraterritorial rights 《영사 재판권》 consular jurisdiction. ちがいほうけん

**치욕**(恥辱) [a] disgrace; [a] shame; dishonor; humiliation; [an] insult／～을 참다 pocket an insult. ちじょく

**치우다** ①《정리하다》 put (things) in order; put (things) straight《없애다》 clear away; remove 《몰아 넣다》 put away 《옆에》 lay aside／책을 책장에 ～ replace a book in the bookcase ②《딸을》 give in marriage; marry; marry off (one's daughter). かたづける

**치우치다** 《기울다》 lean; incline (to, toward); slant (toward); 《편파적》 be biased; be partial (to); have a partiality (for); be prejudiced; be unfair／사치에 ～ be inclined to luxury. かたよる

**치유**(治癒) healing; cure／～하다 (고치다) cure; heal 《낫다》 get over; recover／그 여자는 병원에 입원해서 곧 ～되었다 She recovered herself quickly in the hospital. ちゆ

**치음**(齒音) 《음성》 a sibilant; a dental sound[consonant]. しおん

**치이다**¹ ①《그물 등에》 be trapped[caught] (in a net) ②《피룩의 올이》 wear out; be worn off. もつれる

**치이다**² get hit; be crushed; be squeezed; get run over; get trapped[entrapped]／기차에 치여 죽다 be run over and killed by a train.

**치이다**³ 《값이》 take; cost; require／그가 산 집은 비싸게 치였다 The house he bought cost him dear. かかる

**치인**(癡人) an idiot; a fool; a dunce／～의 꿈 a fool's dream. あほうなひと

**치자**(治者) 《통치자》 the sovereign; the ruler 《권력자》 a man of power; a man of influence／～와 피～ the ruler and the ruled.

**치자**(梔子) gardenia seeds／～나무 a gardenia; a cape jasmine; *Gardenia jasminoides*(학명). くちなしのみ

**치장**(治粧) embellishment; decoration; adornment 《얼굴의》 make-up／～하다 embellish; decorate; adorn; smarten[spruce] up; dress[deck, doll] up; beautify; ornament[adorn] oneself (with)／웃음～하다 dress[roll] up／얼굴을 ～하다 paint[powder] one's face; make one's toilet.

**치적**(治績) merits of administration; administrative achievements／그의 ～은 훌륭했다 His administration was a great success. ちせき

**치정**(癡情) blind[foolish] love 《불의》 illicit love 《투심》 jealousy／～ 살인 사건 a scandalous murder[homicide] case／～에 빠지다 be blinded by passion.

**치조**(齒槽) 《해》 an alveolus; a socket for a tooth／～ 농루《의》 pyorrhoea alveolaris／～염 alveolitis. しそう

**치졸**(稚拙) ～하다 (be) childish; crude／～한 필치로 with uncertain childish strokes. ちせつ

**치죄**(治罪) punishment; penalty; retribution／～하다 punish; bring (a person) to punishment; penalize. ちざい

**치주**(馳走) a lope; a gallop／～하다 lope [gallop] along; run away. ちそう

**치중**(置重) ～하다 lay stress upon; attach importance to; emphasize／너무 ～하다 give undue value[stress] (to)／이 학교에서는 체육에 ～하고 있다 Special importance[emphasis] is attaching of physical culture in this school.

**치중**(輜重) 《병참》 military supplies 《짐》 a pack[load] on a horse. しちょう

**치지**(置之) ～하다 leave (a thing, a matter) to itself; lay aside. すておくこと

**치질**(痔疾) 《의》 hemorrhoids; piles／～을 절개하다 excise a hemorrhoid tumour／～ 수술 hemorrhoidectomy／～환자 a sufferer from piles; a victim of piles. じしつ

**치천하**(治天下) dictatorship to the world／～하다 dictate to the world.

**치치다** (획을) stroke[draw a line] upwards; make an upward stroke 《치올리다》 raise; lift; toss[throw] up.

**치켜세우다** extol (one) to the skies; sing the praises of (a person); be loud in one's praise[s]; speak highly of／치켜세워 격려하다 encourage (a person) with high praise. ほめちぎる

**치키다** raise; lift; heave; pull up; draw up／눈썹을 ～ raise one's eyebrows. うえにひきあげる

**치타**(齒朶) 《식》 the fern.

**치태**(癡態) foolery; silliness／～부리다 make a fool of oneself (over a woman); cut a ridiculous figure. ばかようす

**치통**(齒痛) [a] toothache; dentalgia／～이 나다 have [a] toothache; suffer from a toothache. しつう

**치패**(致敗) insolvency; bankruptcy; failure／～하다 become insolvent[bankrupt]; fail; be brought to ruin; be ruin;

be ruined; come to smash; get broke 《속》.

**치평**(治平) governing so as to secure peace/~하다 govern so as to secure peace. ちへい

**치하**(治下) under the rule (*of*); under the regime[reign] (*of*)/영국 ~에 들어가다 come[fall] under British rule[yoke]. ちか

**치하**(致賀) congratulation; compliments/~하다 (사람을) congratulate (*a person*) on (일을) celebrate; keep; observe.

**치한**(癡漢) ① (못난이) a fool; an idiot ② (호색한) a lewd man; a sex maniac. あほうなひと

**치행**(癡行) folly; silliness; a foolish move[act]; an idiotic thing to do.

**치행**(治行) preparations for a journey/~하다 make preparations for a journey. かざること

**치환**(置換) ~하다 replace 《대용하다》 substitute for 《옮기다》 transport; displace; rearrange/C와 D를 ~하다 replace C with D. ちかん

**칙령**(勅令) an Imperial ordinance[order]; a royal decree[edict]/~을 내리다 issue an Imperial decree. ちょくれい

**칙명**(勅命) an Imperial command[order]/~을 따라 in accordance with an Imperial command. ちょくめい

**칙사**(勅使) an Imperial messenger. ちょくし

**칙살스럽다** (be) miserly; stingy; be low[base]; be niggardly[petty] (*of*)/칙살스럽게 살면서 돈을 모으다 save up money by living close[stingy]. けちくさい

**칙선**(勅選) Imperial[Royal] nomination. ちょくせん

**칙어**(勅語) an Imperial message[rescript]; a message from the Throne. ちょくご

**칙유**(勅諭) Imperial instructions; an Imperial mandate. ちょくゆ

**칙임**(勅任) Imperial[royal] appointment. ちょくにん

**칙재**(勅裁) Imperial decision/~를 바라다 submit to Imperial decision. ちょくさい

**칙지**(勅旨) Imperial order[will]. ちょくし

**칙칙하다** (be) gaudy; glaring; loud/칙칙한 색 a gaudy colour. どすぐろい

**칙필**(勅筆) a royal autograph; the king's own handwriting. ちょくひつ

**칙허**(勅許) Imperial sanction[grant, permission]. ちょっきょ

**친**-(親) parental; *one's* blood; real; pro-; favoring/~형제 *one's* blood[real] brothers. しん

**친가**(親家) *one's* maiden home. じっか

**친고**(親告) a personal accusation/~하다 accuse[complain] personally. しんこく

**친교**(親交) [close] friendship; friendly relation[terms]; intimacy/~를 맺다 form a close friendship with. しんこう

**친구**(親舊) 《동무》 a friend; a companion; 《총칭》 company; a pal《속》; 《놈》 a fellow; a hap; a guy《미·비》/일생의 ~ a lifelong friend/사람은 그가 사귀는 ~로 알아볼 수 있다 You can judge a man by the company he keeps. しんゆう

**친권**(親權) parental authority[prerogatives]/~자 a person in parental authority/ ~을 행사하다 exercise parental rights. しんけん

**친근**(親近) intimacy; familiarity; friendship; cordiality 《애정》 affection/~하다 (be) intimate with; well acquainted with; familiar with/~감을 느끼다 feel friendly towards (*a person*); *one's* heart goes toward (*another*); take kindly to. しんきん

**친기**(親忌) a religious service held on the anniversary of *one's* parent's death. ふぼのさいし

**친남매**(親男妹) *one's* real[blood] brothers and sisters.

**친누이**(親—) *one's* real[blood] sister. じつまい

**친동기**(親同氣) *one's* real[blood] brother [sister].

**친등**(親等) the degree of kinship[consanguinity]/제4~의 친척 a relation in the fourth degree.

**친명**(親命) an order[the instructions] of *one's* parents. ふぼのめいれい

**친모**(親母) *one's* real[blood] mother. しんぼ

**친목**(親睦) friendship; friendliness; intimacy; amity/회원의 ~을 도모하다 promote[cultivate, foster] friendship[fraternity] among the members/ ~회 a social meeting. しんぼく

**친미**(親美) ~의 pro-American/ ~ 정책 pro-American policy.

**친밀**(親密) intimacy; close friendship[relationship]; amity/~하다 (be) intimate; friendly; close; chummy/~하게 되다 become intimate with; make friends with. しんみつ

**친부**(親父) *one's* real[own] father. しんぷ

**친부모**(親父母) *one's* real[own] parents/~처럼 나를 돌보아 주고 있다 He looks after me with parental affection. しんふぼ

**친분**(親分) friendship; intimacy; acquaintance; closeness of friendship/~이 두터워지다 get more closely acquainted. じょうぎがあること

**친불**(親佛) (being) pro-French.

**친불친**(親不親) whether intimate or not; friends or not friends.

**친사돈**(親査頓) the parents of *one's* son [daughter]-in-law.

**친산**(親山) a parent's grave. ふぼのはか

**친상**(親喪) mourning for *one's* parents/~을 당하다 be bereaved of *one's* parents; have a parent die; be bereaved of a parent. ふぼのそうしき

**친서**(親書) an autograph letter／국왕의 an autograph letter〔a personal message〕 from the King. しんしょ

**친선**(親善) friendly relations; friendship; goodwill; close relationship 《외교상의》 *rapprochement*(F)／ ~의 close; friendly; intimate／ ~ 시합을 하다 have a friendly game. しんぜん

**친소**(親疎) the relative degree of intimacy〔familiarity〕; intimacy and estrangement／ ~를 가리지 않고 사귀다 associate〔mix〕 with people whether they are intimate with one or not; mix with anybody without discrimination. しんそ

**친소**(親蘇) pro-Soviet.

**친속**(親屬) kinsfolk; relatives ⇨친족(親族). しんぞく

**친손자**(親孫子) *one's* own grandchild.

**친솔**(率率) all the members of a family. おなじうちのかぞく

**친수**(親受) receiving (*something*) in person／ ~하다 receive (*something*) in person. しんじゅ

**친수**(親授) giving〔bestowing〕 (*something*) in person／ ~하다 give〔bestow〕 (*something*) in person. しんじゅ

**친숙**(親熟) ~하다 (be) well acquainted with／그와는 ~한 사이다 He is my close acquaintance.

**친심**(親審) investigation in person／ ~하다 investigate in person〔personally〕. みずからしんさすること

**친아버지**(親—) *one's* real〔own〕 father／ ~ 같은 사랑 fatherly love. じっぷ

**친아우**(親—) *one's* real〔own〕 younger brother〔sister〕.

**친애**(親愛) dear; love; affection／ ~하는 신사 숙녀 여러분 Dear ladies and gentlemen. しんあい

**친어머니**(親—) *one's* real〔own〕 mother. じつぼ

**친언니**(親—) *one's* real〔own〕 elder brother 〔sister〕. じつし

**친열**(親閱) a personal inspection〔review〕／ ~하다 inspect in person; make a personal inspection of (*troops*).

**친영**(親英) pro-British／ ~ 정책 a pro-British policy／ ~주의 Anglophilism.

**친우**(親友) an intimate〔a bosom, a close, a dear, a choice〕 friend; a chum; a crony／그는 나의 ~다 He is one of my best friends. しんゆう

**친위대**(親衛隊) the bodyguards.

**친의**(親誼) intimacy. じょうぎがあること

**친일**(親日) pro-Japanese／ ~ 분자 a Japanophile; a Japanese sympathizer.

**친임**(親任) direct Imperial appointment／ ~하다 appoint directly／ ~식을 거행하다 hold an investiture.

**친자식**(親子息) *one's* real〔own〕 children. じつのこ

**친재**(親裁) Imperial decision／ ~하다 (*the king*) decide in person. しんさい

**친전**(親展) "Personal"; "Confidential".

**친절**(親切) kindness; friendliness 《호의》 goodwill／ ~하다 (be) kind; good; kind 〔warm〕-hearted; obliging; friendly／남의 ~을 이용하다 take advantage of another's kindness; abuse (*a person's*) kindness. しんせつ

**친정**(親政) direct Imperial rule. しんせい

**친정**(親庭) the house of *one's* wife's parents; the parents family of a married woman; *one's* old home／처를 ~에 보내다 send *one's* wife back to the home of her birth. じっか

**친제**(親弟) *one's* real〔own〕 younger brother.

**친족**(親族) a relative〈영〉; a relation〈미〉; kinsfolk／ ~이라고는 씨도 없다 have no relatives or in-laws (in *this town*)／ ~ 결혼 intermarriage; consanguinity marriage. しんぞく

**친지**(親知) a close acquaintance; an intimate friend／ ~간에 싸우다 quarrel among〔between〕 friends. しんち

**친척**(親戚) a relative〈영〉; a relation 〈미〉; a connection; a kinsman 《복수》 kinsfolk／그와는 ~이다 He is a relation of mine. しんせき

**친친** round and round tight; winding tight; coil upon coil／ ~ 감다 tie〔wind〕 many times round (*something*). くるくる

**친친하다** (be) damp; dampish; moist; wet; humid. じめじめする

**친탁**(親—) ~하다 《용모나 성격이》 take after〔resemble〕 *one's* father's side.

**친필**(親筆) *one's* own handwriting; an autograph; a personal note／ ~의 서한 a letter in *one's* own hand. しんぴつ

**친하다**(親—) ①《가깝다》 (be) intimate; friendly; familiar; close／친한 친구 an intimate friend ②《사귀다》 become intimate〔make friend, strike friendship〕 with. したしい

**친할머니**(親—) *one's* own〔real〕 grandmother.

**친할아버지**(親—) *one's* own〔real〕 grandfather.

**친형**(親兄) *one's* own〔real〕 elder brother; a woman's own〔real〕 elder sister.

**친형제**(親兄弟) *one's* own brothers／ ~ 같은 교제 a close friendship.

**친화**(親和) harmony; fellowship; 《화》 affinity. しんわ

**친환**(親患) illness of *one's* parents. ふぼのびょうき

**친히**(親—) ①《친하게》 intimately; familiarly ②《몸소》 personally; in (*one's* own) person／ ~ 방문하다 pay a personal visit (*to*); make a personal call (on *a person*, at *a person's house*); give a visit personally. みずから

**칠**(七) seven; the seventh. しち

**칠**(漆) 《재료》paints(뻬끼); lacquer(옻); 《칠하기》 coating varnishing(니스); lacquering(옻); painting(뻬끼)／잉크~ an ink stain; a spot of ink. うるし

**칠기**(漆器) lacquer ware; lacquered ware; lacquer. しっき

**칠떡거리다** draggle; trail; drag/칠떡칠떡 dragging. ずるずるひきずる

**칠독**(漆毒) lacquer poison[ing]. うるしのどくけ

**칠뜨기**(七—) ①《칠삭동이》a person born prematurely at the 7th month of pregnancy ②《바보》a fool; a dunce; a moron; an idiot. つきだらけのこ

**칠럼거리다** overflow; run over/칠럼칠럼 overflowing; running over. あふれる

**칠렁칠렁** [full] to the brim; to the full; brimfully; overflowingly; affluently/~하다 be full to the brim; be overflowing; keep splashing water. なみなみ

**칠령 팔락**(七零八落) unevenness; irregularity; lack of uniformity/ ~하다 (be) uneven; unsymmetrical; irregular.

**칠면조**(七面鳥) ①《조》a turkey 《수컷》a turkey cock 《암컷》a turkey hen ②《줏대 없는 사람》a temperamental[an unpredictable] person; a whimsical[capricious] person; a timeserver. しちめんちょう

**칠목기**(漆木器) lacquered woodenware.

**칠변형**(七邊形) a heptagon; a septangle.

**칠보**(七寶) the Seven Treasures [gold, silver, lapis, crystal, coral, agate, pearl]. しちほう

**칠분 도미**(七分搗米) 70-percent polished rice. しちぶずきのこめ

**칠붓**(漆—) a lacquering brush; a paintbrush.

**칠삭동이**(七朔童—) ①(*a person*) born prematurely at the 7th month of pregnancy ②《바보》a fool; a dunce; a moron; an idiot.

**칠색**(七色) the prismatic[primary] colo[u]rs; the seven colo[u]rs. しちしょく

**칠색**(漆色) lacquer colo[u]r; lacquer sheen. うるしいろ

**칠생**(七生) 【종】the seven lives/ ~까지 even to the seventh life; through eternity.

**칠석**(七夕) the seventh [night] of July of the lunar month; the Vega festival /~물 the rainfall on the seventh of July of the lunar calendar. しちせき

**칠성**(七星) 《북두칠성》the Great Bear〈미〉; the Plough〈영〉; the Plow〈미〉; the Great[Big] Dipper〈미〉; the seven stars [of the Big Dipper]. しちしょう

**칠소반**(—小盤) a small lacquered dining table.

**칠순**(七旬) ①《70일》seventy days ②《연령》seventy years of age/~ 노인 a person of seventy years old; a seventy years old man[woman]. しちじゅうにち

**칠실**(漆室) a dark room. うるしむろ

**칠십**(七十) seventy/제 70의 the seventieth. しちじゅう

**칠야**(漆夜) a pitch-dark[-black] night.

まっくらなよ

**칠언 절귀**(七言絶句) a quatrain with seven Chinese characters in each line[with seven-word lines]. しちごんぜっく

**칠요**(七曜) the seven days of the week. しちよう

**칠월**(七月) July《略: Jul., Jy.》/ ~혁명 《프랑스의》the July Revolution. しちがつ

**칠일**(漆—) lacquering; painting; varnishing; daubing/ ~하다 lacquer; paint; daub; varnish; do lacquering[lacquer work]; do painting[paint work]. うるしをぬるしごと

**칠일**(七日) the seventh of the month; seven days/~장 a funeral held seven days after the death. しちにち

**칠장**(漆欌) a lacquered chest of drawers.

**칠장이**(漆匠—) a lacquerer; a painter. うるしぬびをするこると

**칠전 팔기**(七顚八起) an undaunted struggle with adverse circumstances; ups and downs of life/~의 노력 an undaunted struggle with adverse circumstances. しちてんはっき

**칠전 팔도**(七顚八倒) ~하다 undergo various difficulties[hardships]; writhe in agony; toss *one*self about in excessive pain; be schooled in adversity; go through many hardships.

**칠정**(七情) the seven passions [of joy, anger, sorrow, fear, love, hate and lust]. しちじょう

**칠지**(漆紙) lacquered paper.

**칠창**(漆瘡) inflammation of skin caused by lacquer poison; boils caused by lacquer poison.

**칠칠하다** ①《길차다》(be) well-grown; exuberant; fresh and crisp ②《청결하다》(be) neat; clean ③《민첩하다》(be) smart; deft; bright; quick; nimble/그렇게 칠칠 않은 사람은 성공 못 한다 Such a sluggard will not succeed in anything. こぎれいだ

**칠판**(漆板) 《흑판》a blackboard/ ~닦이 a blackboard[chalk] eraser. こくばん

**칠포**(漆布) ①lacquered cloth ②(관에 씌우는) a piece of lacquered cloth pasted over a coffin to be lacquered.

**칠하다**(漆—) 《뻥끼를》paint 《니스를》varnish 《벽을》plaster 《옷을》lacquer/기름을 ~ oil; lubricate; plaster (*something*) with oil. ぬる

**칠함**(漆函) a lacquered box[case, chest].

**칠현**(七賢) the Seven Sages [of ancient China].

**칠현금**(七絃琴) a heptachord; a seven stringed harp. しちげんきん

**칠화**(漆畵) a lacquer painting. うるしえ

**칠흑**(漆黑) pitch-black; coal-black; jetblack/~ 같은 검은 머리 jet-black hair; raven hair.

**칡**¹ 【식】an arrowroot; *Pueraria hirsuta*(학명). くず

**칡**² striped/~소 a striped cow[ox].

**침** spittle; sputum 《타액》saliva spit/남

**침** 의 얼굴에 ~을 뱉다 spit on another's face/~을 흘리다 run saliva. つば

**침**(針) 《가시》 a thorn; a spine; a prickle 《바늘》 a needle; a stylus 《시계의》 a hand 《곤충의》 a sting. しん

**침**(鍼) 〖의〗 《도구》 a needle 《침술》 acupuncture/~술(術) acupuncture/~술사 〔장이〕 an acupuncturist. はり

**침감** a persimmon sweetened in salt water. しぶぬき

**침강**(沈降) sedimentation; precipitation; sinking/~하다 precipitate; sink/~ 속도 《적혈구의》 blood sedimentation rate/~ 수갱(堅坑) a dropshaft. ちんこう

**침골**(枕骨) the rear part of a skull.

**침공**(侵攻) attack; assault; invade; onset; onslaught/~하다 attack; assault; assail; set upon.

**침구**(鍼灸) acupuncture and moxibustion/~술사 a practitioner in acupuncture and moxibustion; an acupuncturist. しんきゅう

**침구**(寢具) bedding; bedclothes/~를 펴다 prepare a bed; make the bed; make up a bed. しんぐ

**침노하다** invade; encroach on[upon]; conquer; plunder/남의 권리를 ~ encroach upon another's right. うばいとる

**침담그다**(沈一) soak (a persimmon) in salt water to remove the astringency (of it); sweeten (an astringent persimmon) in salt water.

**침대**(寢臺) a bed; a bedstead 《휴식용》a couch 《기차의》 a berth 《기선의》 a bunk 《간이 침대》 a cot/~권 a berth ticket; a pullman ticket/ ~를 예약하다 book a sleeping berth/ ~차 a sleeping car; a sleeper. しんだい

**침독**(鍼毒) poison from acupuncture; poisoning caused by improper practice of acupuncture. はりのどくけ

**침략**(侵掠) plunder; pillage; despoilment/~하다 plunder; pillage; despoil. しんりゃく

**침략**(侵略) aggression; invasion; encroachment; raid/~하다 invade; encroach against/~자 an aggressor; an invader/ ~주의 a policy of aggression; an aggressive policy. しんりゃく

**침례**(浸禮) 〖종〗 baptism by immersion/~ 교회 the Baptist Church/~를 받다 receive baptism by immersion.しんれい

**침로**(針路) a ship's course/우리들은 섬 쪽으로 ~를 돌렸다 We directed our course towards the island. しんろ

**침맞다**(鍼一) 《침구》 be treated with acupuncture; get acupunctured 《도난당하다》 get (something) pilfered; be filched. はりをしてもらう

**침모**(針母) a seamstress; a needlewoman/난~ a live-out[part-time] seamstress.

**침목**(枕木) a sleeper 《영》; a cross-tie 《미》; a block; a rail tie. まくらぎ

**침몰**(沈沒) sinking 《침수에 의한》 foundering; submersion 《파선》 shipwreck/~하다 ship; go down; founder; go to the bottom/배는 승무원을 태운 채 ~했다 The ship went down with her crew./~선 구조 작업 salvage. ちんぼつ

**침묵**(沈默) silence; reticence; taciturnity/~하다 hold one's tongue; become silent; be reticent/~을 깨다 break [the] silence. ちんもく

**침방**(寢房) a bedroom ⇒침실. しんぼう

**침뱉다** spit; expectorate/자기 얼굴에 침을 뱉다 disgrace oneself.

**침범**(侵犯) 《영토의》 invasion 《권리의》 violation; infringement/~하다 《침입하다》 invade; break into; make a raid upon 《침해하다》 violate; trespass[encroach, infringe] on 《병의》 attack; affect; visit 《관권 따위를》 visit; trample upon/인권을 ~하다 violate personal rights/병이 ~하다 be attacked with a disease/국적 불명의 항공기가 우리편 영공(領空)을 ~하였다 An unidentified aircraft violated out territorial air. しんぱん

**침불안석**(寢不安席) ~하다 cannot get an easy sleep because of worry; cannot sleep well due to anxiety.

**침사**(沈思) contemplation; meditation; deep thought; profound reflection; rumination/ ~하다 be lost in thoughts; contemplate; meditate; ponder; muse (on, upon, over, of). ちんし

**침삼키다** ①《먹고 싶어하다》 gulp; swallow ②《먹고 싶어하다》 lick one's lips; with to eat ③《부러워하다》 lust (for); gloat (on, over); be envious (of). つばをのみこむ

**침상**(針狀) ~의 needle-shaped; pointed/~엽(葉) a needle leaf.

**침상**(寢狀) a bed; a bedstead; a berth ⇒침대(寢臺). しんだい

**침선**(針線) needle and thread; sewing ⇒ 바느질. しんせん

**침소**(寢所) a bedchamber; a bedroom; a sleeping place. しんじょ

**침소 봉대**(針小棒大) exaggeration; overstatement; grandiloquence; magnification/~하다 exaggerate; magnify; overstate; overdraw; make a mountain out of a molehill. しんしょうぼうだい

**침수**(浸水) ①《물이 들어옴》 flooding; inundation; submersion/~하다 be flooded; be inundated; be submerged; be under water 《배에》 make[take in] water; spring a leak ②《물에 잠김》 soaking; steeping/~하다 be soaked/~ 지구 flooded districts. しんすい

**침술**(鍼術) acupuncture. しんじゅつ

**침습**(浸濕) taking moisture/ ~하다 get wet[moist]; become damp.

**침식**(寢食) 《먹고 잠》 eating and sleeping 《생활》 life/~을 잊고 공부하다 be absorbed in one's studies. しんしょく

**침식**(浸蝕) corrosion; erosion/~하다 erode; sculpture; wear out; bite (on)/강이 바위를 ~해서 깊은 곳을 이루고 있다

The river has won deep channels through the soft rock. しんしょく

**침실**(寢室) a bedroom; a bedchamber; a sleeping room. しんしつ

**침염**(浸染) ~하다 《물감에》dye[be dyed] gradually[little by little]; 《악습에》be addicted; be infected with. しんせん

**침엽**(針葉) 【식】a needle [leaf]; a needle-shaped leap/ ~수 a needle-leaf tree; an acerose tree. しんよう

**침요**(寢—) a mattress; bedclothes.

**침울**(沈鬱) melancholy; gloom; dejection/ ~하다 《음울하다》(be) melancholy; gloomy; dismal; cheerless 《흐리다》(be) dull; gloomy/~한 얼굴 a dismal look; a gloomy face. ちんうつ

**침월**(侵越) ~하다 invade; intrude; enter into [forcibly]; make an inroad (into) break into.

**침윤**(浸潤) saturation; permeation/~하다 《액체가 물체에》be saturated (with); be soaked 《일이》permeate/공산주의의 ~을 방지하다 prevent the infiltration of communism. しんじゅん

**침음**(沈吟) meditation; pondering/ ~하다 meditate; ponder (on). ちんぎん

**침의**(寢衣) night dress ⇨자리옷. しんい

**침의**(鍼醫) an acupuncturist; a needle-doctor; a practitioner in acupuncture. はりのいし

**침입**(侵入) an invasion; a raid; an irruption; an inroad; an incursion; an aggression; trespass; intrusion/ ~하다 invade; raid into; encroach on 《인가 따위에》force one's way into 《해수 따위가》rush into flood (a ship)/저택에 ~하다 force one's way into one's residence. しんにゅう

**침장이**(鍼—) a needle doctor; an acupuncturist 《아편 중독자》an opium[a dope] addict[fiend]. はりをするひと

**침재**(針才) skill[talent] in needlework.

**침전**(沈澱) precipitation; sedimentation; deposition/ ~하다 settle; precipitate; be deposited/바닥에 무엇인가 ~되어 있다 Something is deposited at the bottom. ちんでん

**침전지**(沈澱池) a settling pond[basin]; a depositing reservoir. ちんでんち

**침점**(侵占) capturing[occupying] by invasion; capture; encroaching/~하다 encroach on; occupy [after invasion]; capture.

**침정**(沈靜) presence of mind/~하다 (be) calm; serene. ちんせい

**침정**(沈正) composure and honesty/~하다 (be) calm and honest; sedate and true. ちんちゃくでしょうじきなこと

**침주다**(鍼—) treat with acupuncture; a-cupuncture; apply acupuncture. はりをする

**침중**(沈重) ①《성질의》composure; serenity; calmness; presence of mind/ ~하다 (be) calm; self-possessed; keep cool ②《병이 중함》~하다 (be) very[seriously, dangerously] ill. ちんちょう

**침징지**(沈澄池) a settling basin. ちんでんち

**침착**(沈着) self-possession; calmness; coolness; composure; repose; harmony/~하다 (be) self-possessed; calm; composed; well-balanced; quiet; cool; serene; sedate; placid; staid; dispassionate/그의 ~한 태도에 일동은 경복(敬服)했다 All of them were struck with admiration of his self-possession. ちんちゃく

**침체**(沈滯) stagnation; dullness; slackness; inactivity/~하다 (be) dull; stagnant; slack; depressed; inactive/경제계는 요즘 ~ 상태에 있다 The latest economical status shows a downward trend. ちんたい

**침취**(沈醉) dead drunkenness/~하다 get dead drunk; be beastly drunk. ちんすい

**침침**(駸駸) rapidity; quickness; swiftness/ ~하다 (be) rapid; swift; quick; speedy/~한 성장 rapid growth. しんしん

**침침하다**(沈沈—) ①《어둡다》(be) gloomy; somber; dim/전등이 ~ The electric lamp gives a bad light. ②《흐리다》(be) dimmed; blurred. うすくらい

**침탈**(侵奪) pillage; plunder; spoliation; despoliation; loot; despoilment; depredation; 【법】disseizin; disseisin/~하다 plunder; pillage; depredate; despoil; sack. しんだつ

**침통**(沈痛) ~하다 (be) grave; sad; dismal; disconsolate; touching; pathetic; serious/그는 ~한 얼굴을 하고 그 자리에 임하였다 He was present at the meeting with a very grave countenance. ちんつう

**침투**(浸透) infiltration; penetration; permeation; saturation; osmosis/ ~하다 infiltrate; permeate; penetrate; saturate; pass into/물은 모래에 ~한다 Water percolates through sand. しみとおること

**침하**(沈下) sinking 《수중으로》submersion/~하다 sink; subside; settle; submerge; sink to the bottom.

**침해**(侵害) infringement; violation; encroachment; trespass 《권리의》disturbance/~하다 infringe[encroach, trespass] on (another's right); violate; damnify; disturb/권리를 ~하다 infringe upon one's rights. しんがい

**침향**(沈香) 【식】an aloeswood; an agila-wood; Aquilaria agallocha(학명).

**침흘리개** one who has the habit of drivelling[slavering]; a slobberer; a drooler. よだれをながすひと

**칩거**(蟄居) keeping the house; domiciliary confinement; seclusion; sticking [close] to home/~하다 keep[stay] indoors; keep the house/방안에 ~하다 shut oneself up in one's room; remain indoors. ちっきょ

**칩룡**(蟄龍) ①《숨어 있는 용기》 a dragon in concealment[hiding] ②《숨어 있는 영웅》 an incognito[a hidden] hero; a great man in hiding[concealment].

**칩복**(蟄伏) lying in concealment; seclusion; confinement／～하다 lie dormant; hide[conceal] *one*self; live in seclusion. ちっぷく

**칫솔**(齒―) a toothbrush.

**칭**(稱) ①《이름》 a name; a title; an appellation ②《문법의》 person／3인～ 단수 the third person singular [number].

**칭병**(稱病) malingery; counterfeit illness／～하다 malinger; pretend to be ill; sham illness. しっぺいにかこつけること

**칭사**(稱辭) [words of] praise; a eulogy; a compliment／～를 보내다 eulogize; pay *one's* tribute of praise; speak of (*something*) in terms of high praise. ほめることば

**칭송**(稱頌) eulogy; praise; admiration; applause／～하다 praise highly; loud; applaud; admire; eulogize; pay a tribute to／모든 사람의 ～을 받다 command universal admiration.

**칭양**(稱揚) admiration; praise; commendation／～하다 admire; praise highly; speak highly of; pay a tribute to. しょうよう

**칭얼거리다** whimper; whine; fret; be peevish／어린애가 ～ a baby cries peevishly. だだをこねる

**칭찬**(稱讚) praise; applause; admiration／～하다 praise; admire; speak highly [well] of; compliment; commend; extol／～받을 가치가 있다 deserve admiration; merit praise／극구 ～하다 extol (*a person*) to the skies. しょうさん

**칭탁**(稱託) a pretext; an excuse; a pretence／…을 ～하여 on[under] the pretext[pretence] of …. かこつけること

**칭탄**(稱歎) ～하다 admire; applaud; praise; laud. しょうたん

**칭탈**(稱頉) a pretext; an excuse; a clock; a feint／～하다 pretend [to have other things to do]; make an excuse[a pretext]. ことにかこつけること

**칭하다**(稱―) ①《일컫다》 call; name; designate 《주장하다》 claim／스스로 대교육가라 ～ style *one*self as a great educator ②《속이다》 represent *one*self as; pretend; feign／신문 기자라고 ～ representing *one*self as a reporter. いう

**칭호**(稱號) a title; an appellation; a designation 《학위》 a degree／～를 부여하다 confer a title *on*. しょうごう

**카** 《냄새가 코를 찌를 때》 Phew [what a strong smell]!

**카랑카랑** ~하다 [the weather, a voice] be clear and crisp.

**칵칵** disgorging; hawking; with repeated coughs [to clear one's throat]/~하다 keep coughing away.

**칵칵거리다** disgorge; hawk; keep coughing [to clear one's throat].

**칼**[1] a knife; a blade 《군도》a saber 《검》a sword/ ~끝 the point of a sword/ ~날 an edge; the edge of a sword/ ~등 the back of a sword/ ~집 a sheath/부엌~ a kitchen knife/주머니~ a pocket knife/펜은 ~보다 강하다 The pen is mightier than the sword.

**칼**[2] 《형구》a cangue; a pillory/ ~을 쓰다 wear a cangue; be put in pillory/ ~을 씌우다 put (a person) in pillory.

**칼국수** knife-cut noodles.

**칼금** a scratch.

**칼깃** long and stiff feathers of a bird; a flight feathers; a plume.

**칼날** the edge of a sword/~이 서다 the edge of a sword is sharp.

**칼락거리다** cough; hack; keep coughing [hacking].

**칼맞다** be stabbed; be cut.

**칼부림** employing a sword 《유혈극》bloodshed/~하다 employ a sword [to hurt (one)]; shed blood/싸움 끝에 ~까지 하다 go so far as to stab at each other in a fight.

**칼새** 〖조〗 [chimney] swift; salangane.

**칼자국** a scar from a knife[sword].

**칼자루** a handle; a grip 《단도》a haft 《검》a hilt.

**칼잡이** a butcher.

**칼질** cutting 《칼부림》wielding a knife/ ~하다 cut; wield a knife.

**칼집** a sheath; a scabbard/칼을 ~에 넣다 sheath[scabbard] a knife[sword].

**칼춤** a sword dance/ ~을 추다 perform a sword dance.

**칼치** 〖어〗a hair tail; a scabbard fish.

**칼칼하다** 《목이》(be) thirsty; dry《미·속》.

**칼판** a block; a chopping board; a kitchen board; a trencher.

**캄캄하다** (be) dark; pitch-black; somber; murky; gloomy.

**캐내다** dig ~캐내다.

**캐다** ①《파내다》dig out; unearth ②《규명하다》inquire into; dig into; probe; explore/사실 여부를 ~ inquire into the truth of the matter.

**캐묻다** ask inquisitively; be inquisitive (about); make a searching inquiry.

**캑** coughing.

**캥캥** with yelp after yelp/ ~거리다 (a fox) keep yelping.

**캥캥하다** (be) lean; thin; emaciated.

**커녕** 《도리어》far from; anything but; in no wise; not at all (…뿐만 아니라 또…) not to mention; not to speak of; to say nothing of; not only… but [also] / 이 책은 이롭기는 ~ 아주 해롭다 So far from doing any good, this book does a good deal of harm./그는 불어는 ~ 영어도 못 한다 He knows no English, to say nothing of French. —(는)커녕 —(은)새에두고

**커다랗다** (be) very big; very large; huge /집을 커다랗게 짓다 build an enormous house.

**커다래지다** grow very big; become very large/키가 ~ become taller; acquire height/사건이 ~ a matter grows serious.

**-컨대** ¶ 요~ in short/생각~ come to think of it. —을진대

**컬럭거리다** cough; hawk.

**컬컬하다** 《목이》(be) thirsty; dry《미·속》.

**컴컴하다** 《어둠다》(be) dark 《침침하다》dim 《마음이》(be) shady; black-hearted; under-hand /컴컴해지다 darken; grow dark/날이 컴컴해지다 It is getting dark.

**컴컴거리다** (a dog) keep barking.

**켕기다** ①《당기다》strain ②《버티다》hold out against ③《꺼리다》be discouraged; be cowed; be scared/줄이 ~ a rope is stretched tautly.

**켜** a layer; a ply/여러 ~로 쌓다 heap up in several layers.

**켜다** ①《불을》light; kindle; turn[switch]

on; strike (*a match*)/전등을 ~ turn [switch] on the electric lamp/촛불을 ~ light a candle ②(마시다) drink; drain; empty ③(톱으로) saw off; saw (*timber*) into (*boards*) ④(실을) reel off /누에고치에서 실을 ~ reel off raw silk from cocoons ⑤(기지개를) straighten (*one's back*)/기지개를 ~ stretch *oneself* ⑥(악기를) play on/바이얼린을 ~ play the violin. つける

**켤레** a pair/양말〔구두〕한 ~ a pair of socks[shoes].

**케케묵다** (낡다) (be) old; antiquated; stale (구식이다) (be) old-fashioned; out of date 《진부하다》 (be) hackneyed; time-worn; trite/케케묵은 얘기를 하다 tell on old story/무척 케케묵은 친구로군 What a mouldy sort of fellow he is! とてもふるい

**코¹** ①(동물의) a nose (코끼리의) a trunk 《개·말 따위의》 a muzzle (돼지의) a snout/콧수염 a moustache/감기 a cold in the head/담배 snuff/~카타르 《의》 nasal catarrh ~가 막히다 *one's* nose is stopped up ②(콧물) nasal mucus; snivel; watery mucus of the nose /~를 흘리다 snivel/~를 풀다 blow *one's* nose. はな

**코²** 《뜨개옷 따위의》 a stitch.

**코걸이** a nose pendant.

**코골다** snore/코고는 사람 a snorer/코를 골기 시작하다 fall to snoring. いびきかく

**코끝** the tip[end] of *one's* nose. はなのさき

**코끼리** an elephant /수~ a bull elephant/암~ a cow elephant. ぞう

**코납작이** ①a person with a flat nose ②(기가 꺾인 사람) a person frustrated by shame. はなぺちゃ

**코딱지** nose-dirty; nasal mucus/~를 후비다 pick *one's* nose. はなくそ

**코대답**(一對答) an answer through the nose (시원찮은 대답) a cold answer/~하다 answer indifferently[nonchalantly].

**코떼다** 《편잔맞다》 have *one's* nose bitten off 《거절당하다》 be rebuffed 《창피당하다》 be put to shame 《야단맞다》 get it hot/돈을 꾸어달랬다가 ~ get turned down cold when one tries to borrow money.

**코똥** pooh-poohing ⇨코방귀. はなあらし

**코뚜레** a nose-ring; a cow's nose-ring. はなかい

**코랑코랑** ~하다 be not full; be partly empty. ごそごそ

**코맹녕이** a snuffling person; a snuffler; a whinner; a person who speaks through the nose. はなつまりのひと

**코머거리** a person with a stopped-up [congested] nose.

**코문돈** children's pocket money.

**코밑** the joint where the nose meets the upper lip. はなのした

**코방귀** a pooh-pooh; a snort; pooh-poohing; snorting/ ~뀌다 pooh-pooh; snort at; sniff at. はなあらし

**코방아찧다** fall flat on *one's* face. はなをつく

**코싸쥐다** cover *one's* face for shame; hang *one's* head in shame. はじをかく

**코세다** (be) self-assertive; stiffnecked; stubborn/코센 사람 a stubborn person. がんこだ

**코숭이** the end of a mountain range.

**코앞** under *one's* nose; in front of *one's* nose/~에 있는 것도 못 보다 fail to see what is right under *one's* nose. めのまえ

**코웃음** a sneer; sneering/~치다 sneer. あざわらうこと

**코찡찡이** a person with a broken nose; a person who twangs because of a nasal disease. はなづまりのひと

**코침주다** tickle the nose through a nostril to induce sneezing.

**코털** vibrissa; the hairs in the nostril/ ~을 뽑다 pull out the hairs of the nostril. はなげ

**코푸렁이** a simpleton; an idiot; a fool. ぐしゃ

**코풀다** blow *one's* nose. はなをかむ

**코피** a nosebleed; nasal hemorrhage; blood from the nose/~가 흐르다 have a nosebleed. はなぢ

**콕** with a rap; with a thrust/닭이 ~ 쪼다 a hen peck at (*a thing*). ぐっと

**콜록거리다** cough; have a fit of coughing. ごほんごほんする

**콜록쟁이** a person with a hacking cough.

**콜콜** snoring (물이) gurgling / ~거리다 snore; keep snoring/~ 자다 sleep snoring/물이 ~ 흘러 나오다 flow out steadily. ぐうぐう

**콧구멍** the nostrils. はなのあな

**콧김** breathing through the nose; snorting. はないき

**콧날** the line of the nose; the nose bridge/~이 우뚝 선 미녀 a beautiful woman with a shapely nose. はなすじ

**콧노래** humming; a hum/~하다 hum; croon. はなうた

**콧대** the bridge[ridge] of the nose/ ~가 세다 be haughty/~ 센 사람 a self assertive person. はなすじ

**콧물** nasal mucus; snivel; nose drippings/ ~을 흘리다 snivel; drivel; run at the nose. はなみず

**콧방울** the rounded sides of the nose.

**콧병**(一病) nose trouble/ ~을 앓다 have nose trouble.

**콧살** wrinkles around the nose. はなしわ

**콧소리** a nasal voice[tone]; a twang/ ~로 말하다 speak through *one's* nose. はなごえ

**콧숨** breathing through the nose. はないき

**콩¹** 《식》 a bean 《완두》 a pea (대두) a soybean/ ~깻묵 a bean cake. まめ

**콩²** 《소리》 with a rap[thud]. こん

**콩가루** bean flour. まめのこな

**콩깍지** a hull; a shuck.
**콩꼬투리** a [bean] pod; a legume. まめのさや
**콩나물** sprouting beans; bean sprouts／~국 bean-sprout soup.
**콩노굿** bean blossoms[flowers]. まめのはな
**콩댐** ~하다 polish the floor paper with ground beans.
**콩떡** a bean-rice cake.
**콩밥** bean-mixed rice／~먹다 eat bean-mixed rice 《징역살다》 serve a penal servitude; be put to prison.
**콩버무리** a bean-mixed rice cake.
**콩볶듯** ~하다 crack; crackle; rattle; snap／콩볶듯하는 기관총 소리 the cracking [rattle] of machine guns. あめあられと
**콩새** 〔조〕a Korean hawfinch; Coccothraustes coccothraustes japonicus(학명). しめ
**콩설기** a rice cake with thin layers of beans.
**콩엿** wheat gluten mixed with popped beans in it.
**콩잎** bean leaves. まめのは
**콩자반**(一佐飯) beans cooked with soy.
**콩죽**(一粥) mixed gruel of rice and beans.
**콩칠팔칠** gibbering ⇒콩팔칠팔.
**콩케팔케** a pell-mell; a hotchpotch; a jumble; a muddle. ごじゃごじゃ
**콩콩** whining; bowwow／~거리다 whine; keep barking. きゃんきゃん
**콩튀듯팥튀듯** ~하다 be hopping mad; jump up with anger. いかりくるって
**콩팔칠팔** gibbering; jabbering; chattering／~하다 gibber; jabber; chatter. べちゃくちゃ
**콩팥** 〔해〕the kidney. じんぞう
**콱** with a thrust; thrusting[poking, sticking] hard／칼로 ~ 찌르다 thrust a dagger home. ぶすっと
**콸콸** in a rush; in a torrent／냇물이 ~ 흐르고 있다 The stream is rushing along. どくどく
**쾅** with a bang; with a boom; with a thud／~하는 소리 a thud／주먹으로 테이블을 ~ 치다 bang one's fist on the table.
**쾌** a string [of twenty dried pollacks].
**쾌감**(快感) a pleasant sensation; an agreeable feeling／~을 느끼다 feel fine [pleasant]. かいかん
**쾌거**(快擧) an inspiring[a gallant, a heroic] deed. かいきょ
**쾌남아**(快男兒) a fine[jolly] fellow; a brick; a regular guy〈미〉. かいだんじ
**쾌담**(快談) a pleasant talk; a lively talk; a hearty chat／~하다 talk pleasantly (with); enjoy a pleasant chat (with). かいだん
**쾌도**(快刀) a sharp blade[sword]／~ 난마 하다 cut the Gordian knot; take a drastic measure. かいとう
**쾌락**(快諾) a ready consent; a willing assent／~하다 give a ready consent; consent readily. かいだく
**쾌락**(快樂) pleasure; enjoyment; amenities／~하다 (be) pleasant; delightful／육체적인 ~ carnal pleasure／인생의 ~ pleasure of life／~을 추구하다 seek [pursue] pleasure／그는 현세의 ~을 향유했다 He had his share of worldly pleasure. かいらく
**쾌론**(快論) a pleasant talk 쾌담. かいだん
**쾌마**(快馬) a swift horse; a fleet steed.
**쾌미**(快味) a pleasant taste; an agreeable sensation. ここちよいかんじ
**쾌변**(快辯) fluency of speech; eloquence; oratory／~을 토하다 make an eloquent address[speech].
**쾌보**(快報) good[welcome, cheerful, encouraging] news; glad tidings; a joyful report. こころよいしらせ
**쾌복**(快復) complete recovery ⇨쾌차(快差).
**쾌사**(快事) a pleasant matter[event]; a joyful event; a delight. かいじ
**쾌설**(快雪) vindication of one's honour／~하다 vindicate of one's honour.
**쾌속**(快速) high[great] speed; celerity／~하다 (be) speedy; swift／~의 high-speed; fast; swift; speedy／~으로 at a high speed／~ 열차 a fast train／~조《음》allegro. かいそく
**쾌승**(快勝) a signal[decisive] victory／~하다 win a signal victory; come off with flying colours. かいしょう
**쾌유**(快癒) complete recovery. かいゆ
**쾌의**(快意) a good[an agreeable] intention; a pleasure; a delight.
**쾌적**(快適) agreeableness; pleasantness; delightfulness／~하다 (be) agreeable; delightful; pleasant. かいてき
**쾌전**(快戰) a good fight[play].
**쾌주**(快走) fast sailing／~하다 sail run [fast]; scud／~선 a clipper.
**쾌차**(快差) restoration to health; recovery (from illness)／~하다 recover／병이 ~하다 recover from illness. かいゆ
**쾌척**(快擲) ~하다 give a ready donation; make a generous contribution; give willingly. ここちよくなげること
**쾌청**(快晴) fine weather; fair[bright] and clear weather／일기가 ~하다 The weather[day] is as fine as can be. かいせい
**쾌쾌하다**(快快一) (be) pleasant; refreshing; bright 《활발하다》 brisk. ゆうかんでここちよい
**쾌하다**(快一)《몸이》(be) well; healthy 《유쾌하다》 (be) pleasant; agreeable／쾌히 willingly; readily. びょうきがよくなっている
**쾌활**(快活) ~하다 (be) cheerful; merry; lively; jolly; jovial; gay; light-hearted; sprightly／~하게 cheerfully; merrily; lively; light-heartedly／~한 사람 a jolly fellow. かいかつ

**쾌활**(快闊) ~하다(be) extensive; pleasantly wide open. かいかつ

**쾌히**(快一) 《유쾌히》pleasantly; agreeably; cheerfully 《기꺼이》gladly; readily; willingly; with [good] grace/ ~ 돈을 빌려주다 lend money with a good grace.

**쾨쾨묵다** (be) old; antiquated; wormeaten; hackneyed 《뒤떨어진》outdated 《진부한》trite/그 따위 쾨쾨묵은 소리는 하지 마라 Don't say such a trite thing.

**쾨쾨하다** (be) bad-smelling; stinking; offensive/생선이 썩어서 ~ The fish is rotten and stinking. くさい

**쿡** stinging hard ぐっと

**쿨링거리다** wave noisily/물통의 물이 혼들려 쿨렁거렸다 The water in the pail waved noisily. ぼちゃんぼちゃん

**쿨렁쿨렁** ~하다 be not full; be partly empty.

**쿨룩거리다** give coughs; hack. ごほん

**쿨쿨** snoring/ ~거리다 snore; sleep audibly. こぼこぼ

**쿵** plump; heavily; with a thud /무엇 인지 마루에 ~ 떨어졌다 Something fell heavily on the floor. どんと

**쿵쿵** with bangs[bumps]/마루 위를 ~ 달리다 scamper around on the floor noisily. どんどん

**퀄퀄** gurgling; spouting/ ~거리다 gurgle; spout/샘물이 ~ 쏟아지다 a spring spouts. どくどく

**큄하다** be big and fishy; have big and lacklustre eyes.

**퀴퀴하다** (be) stinking; bad-smelling/생선이 썩어서 냄새가 ~ The fish is rotten and stinking. くさい

**크기** size; dimensions; magnitude 《덩치》bulk 《용적》volume/상당한 ~의 of fairly large size/ ~가 같다[다르다] be[be not] equal in size.

**크나크다** (be) very big; huge; great; gigantic/크나큰 집 a very big[large] house. きわめておおきい

**크다**[1] 《모양이》(be) big; large 《덩치가》(be) bulky; massive; voluminous 《소리가》(be) loud 《위대하다》(be) great; grand 《강대하다》(be) mighty; powerful 《거대하다》(be) gigantic; huge; colossal; enormous 《광대하다》(be) vast; extensive; spacious 《심대하다》(be) severe; heavy/큰 인물 a great man/큰 손해 heavy loss/큰 나라 a powerful country/큰 기대를 가지다 expect great things from (a person)/그는 나이에 비해 키가 ~ He is taller than other for his age. おおきい

**크다**[2] 《자라다》grow [up]/다 큰 아이 a grown-up child. せいちょうする

**크디크다** (be) very big; huge; great. きわめておおきい

**크렁크렁** ~하다 be almost full (to the brim). なみなみ

**큰갓** a broad-brimmed Korean hat.

**큰계집** 《첩에 대하여》one's wife.

**큰기침** a cough; clearing one's throat/ ~하다 clear one's throat; hem.

**큰길** a main[principal] street; a high road; a [leading] thoroughfare. おおとおり

**큰누이** the eldest sister.

**큰달** an odd month; a long month 《만월》a full moon. おおきなつき

**큰딸** the eldest daughter.

**큰댁**(一宅) the house of one's eldest brother; the head family[house]; the main stock. ほんけ

**큰돈** a large sum [of money]; a lot of money 《경비》a great cost/ ~을 벌다 make a lot of money; realize a large profit. たがくのおかね

**큰마누라** 《첩에 대하여》a legal wife; one's wedded wife. ほんさい

**큰마음** resolution; boldness; daring/ ~ 먹고 resolutely; boldly; daringly.

**큰말** ①《큰소리로》big talk; bragging ②《언》a heavy isotope of a word.

**큰매부**(一妹夫) the husband of one's eldest sister.

**큰머리** a woman's formal hairdo.

**큰물** a flood; an inundation 《대홍수》a deluge/ ~나다 be flooded; be inundated; be in flood. こうずい

**큰방**(一房) a large[main] room; the inner room; the living room of the lady of the house.

**큰불** a great fire 《화재》a conflagration; big fire. おおきいひ

**큰비** a heavy rain; a downpour; a big rainfall/ ~가 온다 It rains heavily. ごうう

**큰사람** ①《키가》a tall man; giant ②《위대한 사람》a great man; an eminent person; a big gun. おおきいひと

**큰사랑**(一廊) ①《크게 지은》a large detached room (for receiving guests) ②《어른의》a detached room used as the private quarters of the head of a family.

**큰사위** the husband of one's eldest daughter; a son-in-law of one's eldest daughter. ちょうじょのむこ

**큰살림** high living / ~하다 live high.

**큰상**(一床) ①《성대한 음식》a capital dinner; a bountiful table offered to the central figure of the day ②《큰상》a large dinner table.

**큰소리** ①《큰》a loud[big, stentorian] voice; a yell; a shout/ ~로 부르다 call in a loud voice ②《치는》a growl; a snarl; brawling ③《과장하는》tall talk; high-sounding words; a loud boasting; bragging; magnilquence/ ~치다 talk big; brag; talk in grandiose style/ 또 ~ 치는군 There goes his bragging talk again. どなりごえ

**큰손가락** the thumb.

**큰손녀**(一孫女) the eldest granddaughter.

**큰손님** a distinguished[an important] guest; a guest of honor.
**큰손자**(一孫子) the eldest grandson.
**큰솥** a cauldron; the biggest cooking-pot in a kitchen range.
**큰아가씨** 《하인이》 the eldest married daughter or the wife of the eldest son.
**큰아기** 《딸》 the eldest daughter 《계집애》 a girl; a young lady. ちょうじょ
**큰아들** the eldest son. ちょうなん
**큰아버지** an uncle; the elder brother of *one's* father.
**큰아이** the eldest child.
**큰어머니** an aunt; the wife of the elder brother of *one's* father. はくぼ
**큰언니** the eldest brother[sister].
**큰오빠** a girl's eldest brother. ちょうけい
**큰옷** ceremonial robes. れいふく
**큰일** ①《대업》 a great thing ②《중대사》 a matter of grave concern; a serious matter ③《위기》 a crisis ④《예식·잔치》 a big ceremony[banquet]; a wedding; a funeral／ ~을 치르다 go through[carry out] a wedding[funeral]: だいじ
**큰절** a deep bow／ ~하다 make a deep bow; bow low.
**큰조카** *one's* eldest brother's eldest son.
**큰집** ①《넓은》 a large house ②《종가》 the head family[house]; the main stock.
**큰처남**(一妻男) the eldest of *one's* wife's brothers.
**큰체하다** hold *one's* head high; mount the high horse; wear a high hat.

**큰춤** dancing in gala dress.
**큰치마** a long trailing skirt.
**큰칼** a large sword[knife]; 《형구》 a big cangue; a large pillory.
**큰코다치다** have a bitter experience; have a hard time of it; pay dealy (*for*)／믿지 못할 사람을 믿었다가 큰코다쳤다 I made the bitter mistake of putting my faith in someone who could not be trusted. ひどいめにあう
**큼직이** big; large; greatly／글자를 ~ 쓰다 write in large characters[letters].
**큼직큼직** all quite big[large]／~하다 (be) all quite big[large].
**큼직하다** (be) pretty[fairly] big.
**키**[1] 《신장》 stature; height／~가 큰[작은] 사람 a tall[short] person／~순으로 in order of[according to] stature／그는 나보다 5인치 가량 ~가 크다[작다] He is five inches taller[shorter] than I. しんちょう
**키**[2] 《까부는》 a winnow／~질하다 winnow.
**키**[3] 《배의》 a rudder 《키자루》 a helm 《타륜(舵輪)》 a [steering] wheel／~잡이 a steersman／~를 잡다 steer. かじ
**키다** ①《불을》 kindle; light ②《마시다》 drink down ③《톱질》 saw. ともす
**키다리** a tall man[fellow]; a gangling fellow〈미〉. せいたか
**키우다** 《아이를》 bring up; rear; raise; nurse 《동·식물을》 breed; raise. そだてる
**킥킥** ~거리다 giggle; titter. くつくつ
**킬킬** ~거리다 giggle; cackle. げらげら
**킹킹** ~거리다 groan; whimper.

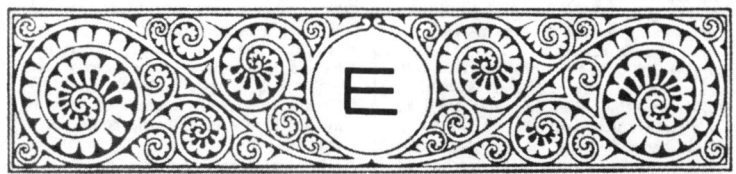

타(打) a dozen／연필 두 ~ 주시오 I will take two dozens of pencil. ダース
타(他) the other[rest]; others／~의 추종을 불허하다 be peerless[unrivalled]. ほか
타개(打開) a break; a breakthrough; a development; a new turn／~하다 break; tide over a difficult situation; break through; effect a breakthrough／~책(策) a way out. だかい
타격(打擊) a [hard] blow; a shock (야구) batting; hitting; slugging (경구) a stroke／치명적인 ~ a fatal blow／~을 주다 deal a blow on／~왕 (야구) a champion batter. だげき
타계(他界) ①(다른 세계) another world; the other world ②(죽음) death; demise／~하다 depart [from] this life; pass away; die. にかい
타고나다 be endowed with／타고난 born; inborn; natural; native／타고난 재능 natural faculty. うまれつく
타고올(他一) another[strange] country.
타고장(他一) another place. たきょう
타관(他關) a strange land; a strange country ⇨타향. たきょう
타구(唾具) a spittoon; a cuspidor; a spit-box. たんつぼ
타구(打毬) a kind of polo. だきゅう
타구(打球) (야구) batting (친 공) a batted ball／~봉(棒) a bat; a club.
타국(他國) a foreign country; a strange [an alien] land; another country／~어 a foreign language／~인 a foreigner; a stranger; an alien. たこく
타기(唾棄) casting away with hate[contempt]; throwing away in disgust; rejection／~하다 throw away in disgust; detest; hate; reject／~할 detestable.

타기(惰氣) indolence; inactivity; sluggishness; dullness; slackness. だき
타기(舵機) a rudder; a helm; a steering gear／~실 the steering room.
타내다 get; receive; be allowed／그는 어머니한테서 용돈을 타냈다 He got pocket money from his mother. もらいうける
타년(他年) another year; in future year.
타념(他念) another thought; some one thought. ほかのかんがえ
타다¹ ①(불에) burn; be burnt; blaze／잘 타는 easy to burn／그 불로 많은 집들이 탔다 Many houses were destroyed in the fire. ②(눋다) be scorched; be charred／밥이 탔다 The rice has got scorched. ③(볕에) be sunburnt; be tanned with the sun／볕에 탄 얼굴 a sunburned face ④(격정으로) burn; blaze (근심 따위로) be worried; be nervous. もえる
타다² (섞다) mix; mingle; adulterate (with). まぜる
타다³ ①(탈것에) take; get on[in, into]; ride in[on]; take[have] a ride in (배에) go[get] aboard (a ship); go on board; embark in[on]; sail on／기차를 타고 가다 go[travel] by train／자전거 탈 줄 아니 Can you ride a bicycle? ②(물건 위에) get[step] on; get up; mount ③(틈타서) take advantage of; avail oneself of (기회를) seize; take. のる
타다⁴ (받다) get; receive; gain; take; accept; be given (상 따위를) be awarded／십만원 월급을 ~ receive a salary of 100,000 won. うける
타다⁵ ①(맷돌로) grind／탄 보리 ground [cracked] barley ②(가르다) divide; part／머리를 한 가운데서 ~ part one's hair in the middle. わける
타다⁶ ①(부끄럼 따위) feel; be aware of; be sensitive to／부끄럼을 ~ be abashed; ②be shy (영향) be influenced by; affect; suffer from; be poisoned (by)／추위를 ~ be sensitive to the cold. かぶれる
타다⁷ ①(연주하다) play [on]; perform on／풍금을 ~ play [on] the organ ②(솜을) whip; beat; willow (cotton).
타닥거리다 ①(걸음을) plod along; walk wearily／타닥타닥 길을 걷다 plod one's way ②(살림을) make a bare living; eke out a scanty livelihood ③(두드리는 모양) beat pat-pat. とぼとぼとあるく
타달거리다 trudge along; hobble along／타달타달 trudgingly. とぼとぼとあるく
타당(妥當) propriety; appropriateness／~하다 (be) right; apposite; appropriate; reasonable; fit／네가 그렇게 하는 것은 ~하다 It is right that you should do so.／~성 propriety／보편~성 《철》 universal validity. だとう
타도(打倒) overthrow; knocking down／~하다 overthrow; knock down; strike down／공산주의 ~ Down with com-

**타도**(他道) another province.
**타동**(他動) 〖언〗 transitivity／~의 transitive／~사 〖언〗 a transitive verb.  たどう
**타드랑** clattering; rattling／~타드랑 with a clattering noise.  がちゃん
**타락**(墮落) degradation; corruption (사람의) fall (여자의) ruin／ ~하다 fall; degenerate; be ruined; go to the dogs; be corrupted; go astray; go to the bad 〈미〉/예술의 ~ decadence of art／~한 학생 a depraved student.  だらく
**타락**(駝酪) cow's milk.  ぎゅうにゅう
**타락줄** a hair-rope.
**타래** 《실 따위의》 a coil／실 한 ~ a coil of thread.  まき
**타래박** a dipper; a ladle／ ~으로 물을 푸다 dip up water.
**타래버선** embroidered Korean socks.
**타래송곳** a corkscrew.
**타래쇠** a spiral; a volute; a coil.
**타래타래** spirally; round and round.  くるくる
**타려**(他慮) other worries[cares]; another anxiety.
**타력**(他力) external power (남의 조력) outside help (종교의) salvation from without.  たりき
**타력**(打力) 〖야구〗 batting[hitting] power.
**타력**(惰力) 〖물〗 inertia; momentum; force of habit／~으로 달리다 run by inertia.  だりょく
**타륜**(舵輪) a steering wheel; the wheel.
**타마**(一油) coal tar.
**타매**(唾罵) an abuse; a slander; an insult／ ~하다 call (one) names; abuse.  つばをはきののしること
**타맥**(打麥) harvest of barley／ ~하다 thresh the barley.
**타면**(打綿) cotton beating／~기 a cotton gin.
**타면**(他面) the other side[hand, phase, aspect]; [on] the other hand.
**타문**(他聞) publicity; reaching others' ears／~을 꺼리다 fear publicity／ ~을 꺼리는 일 a confidential matter.  たぶん
**타박** faultfinding; objection; grumbling ／ ~하다 find fault with; object (to); grumble (at)／음식을 ~하다 grumble at the food／ ~할 메가 없다 I have no fault to find with it.
**타박**(打撲) knocking; a stroke; a contusion; a blow／ ~하다 knock; beat; give a blow／ ~상 a bruise／ ~상을 입히다 bruise.  だぼく
**타박거리다** trudge[trod] along plod.  とぼとぼとあるく
**타박타박** 《음식이》 being dry; not moist ／ ~하다 (be) dry; be not moist／먹이 ~해서 먹기 힘들다 The rice cake is so dry it is hard to eat.  ぱさぱさ
**타방**(他方) 《다른 곳》 another place[side, quarter]; a different direction (일방) the other side[hand].  たほう
**타분하다** ①(냄새가) (be) bad-smelling; offensive; stinking ②(행동이) (be) inanimate; spiritless (인색하다) (be) stingy; niggardly; stint.
**타사**(他事) other matters／ ~를 돌볼 겨를이 없다 have no time to think about other things.  だじ
**타산**(打算) calculation; self-interest／ ~하다 calculate; reckon; count／ ~적 calculating; selfish; mercenary／ ~적인 생각 a mercenary spirit／그는 언제나 ~적이다 He is always consulting his own interests.  ださん
**타산지석**(他山之石) an object lesson; any example one may profit by.  たざんのいし
**타살**(他殺) murder; foul play／아무래도 ~ 같다 There is every reason to believe that it is a murder.  たさつ
**타살**(打殺) clubbing (a person) to death／ ~하다 kill by a blow; strike[club] (a person) dead.  なぐりころすこと
**타색**(他色) another color.
**타석**(他席) another seat.  よそのせき
**타선**(唾線) 〖해〗 salivary glands.  だせん
**타성**(惰性) nertia; momentum; force of habit; the course of least resistance／ ~으로 담배를 피우다 smoke from force of habit.  だせい
**타성**(他姓) another surname[family name].  たせい
**타성**(他性) 〖철〗 otherness; differentness.
**타수**(舵手) a helmsman; a steersman; a cox; a coxswain.
**타수**(打手) a hitter (야구) a batter (크리켓) a bowler.  だしゃ
**타악기**(打樂器) a percussion instrument.  だがっき
**타액**(唾液) saliva (뱉은) spittle (가래) sputum／ ~을 분비하다 salivate; secrete saliva／ ~ 분비 salivation; a flow of saliva／ ~선 the salivary glands.  つば
**타용**(他用) diversion／~하다 use for another purpose; divert.  だよう
**타울거리다** strive; struggle; be overeager.  じたばたする
**타원**(楕圓) an elliptical; ~의 elliptic[al]; oval／~체 an ellipsoid; an ovoid／ ~ 운동 elliptic motion／ ~을 elliptically.  だえん
**타율**(他律) heteronomy／ ~의 heteronomous.  たりつ
**타의**(他意) another intention; an ulterior motive; a secret purpose; malice; ill-will／별로 ~가 있어 한 것은 아니다 I have done it meaning no harm whatever.  たい
**타이르다** reason (with); prevail upon; admonish; advise; persuade; give (a person) instructions／잘못을 ~ reason with (a person) on his mistake.  いいきかせる
**타인**(他人) 《다른 사람》 another person; others (미지의 사람) a stranger (국외자)

**타일**(他日) some day; another day / ~을 기약하고 헤어지다 part from (a person, meeting) deferring the matter to some future occasion. たじつ

**타자**(打者) 《야구》 a batter; a batsman; a hitter / 2번 ~ the second hitter. だしゃ

**타자기**(打字機) a typewriter; a machine 《미·속》. タイプライター

**타자수**(打字手) a typist; / 양성소 a typing school / 국문 ~ a typist in Korean. タイピスト

**타작**(打作) 《마당질》threshing / ~하다 thresh / 벼 100석을 ~하다 harvest 100 bushels of rice.

**타짯군** a sharper; a card cheat. いんちき

**타전**(打電) sending a telegraph; telegraphing / ~하다 telegraph; wire; send a telegraph (to); 《해저 전신》cable 《무전》wireless. だでん

**타점**(打點) (붓으로) dotting; marking with a dot (마음으로) singling out; making a choice in one's heart / ~하다 mark with a dot; single out[choose] in one's heart. だてん

**타조**(駝鳥) 《조》 an ostrich. だちょう

**타종**(他宗) (다른 종교) another religion (다른 종파) another sect. たしゅう

**타진**(打診) ① 《의》 percussion; tapping ② (떠봄) sounding; tapping / ~하다 percuss; tap; sound; sound out; put[throw] out a feeler / 정세를 ~하다 float a trial balloon. だしん

**타처**(他處) another place / ~에서 온 사람들 people from other places; out-of-town[-village] people / ~ 지불 어음 a domiciled bill. たしょ

**타척**(打擲) striking; beating; knocking down / ~하다 strike; beat; knock down.

**타태**(墮胎) feticide; wilful abortion / ~하다 commit feticide; cause abortion / ~아 an abortive [offspring] / ~시키다 cause[induce] abortion. だたい

**타파**(他派) another party[school, sect].

**타파**(打破) breaking; destruction; defeat; conquest; overthrow / ~하다 break down (evil customs); overthrow (bureaucracy); explode (a fallacy) / 봉건적인 풍습을 ~하다 break down feudalistic customs. だは

**타합**(打合) a previous arrangement; preliminaries / ~하다 make [previous] arrangements; prearrange / 그 전에 관해서는 미리 ~이 돼 있다 Arrangements have been made on that matter.

**타향**(他鄕) another countryside; a place away from home; a foreign land; foreign parts / ~에서 떠돌아다니다 wander in a strange land. たきょう

**타협**(妥協) a compromise; mutual concession; give-and-take; understanding; agreement / ~하다 compromise; make a compromise; give and take; split the difference; meet (a person) halfway; come to terms[an understanding] / ~적인 태도를 취하다 take a compromising[conciliatory] attitude. だきょう

**타화 수정**(他花受精) 《식》 cross-fertilization.

**탁** with a bang; with a thud / 마음이 ~ 놓이다 be[feel] quite relieved. ばんと

**탁견**(卓見) (의견) a fine idea; distinguished[excellent] views (식견) lofty outlook; foresight; far-sightedness; clear-sightedness; penetration. すぐれたいけん

**탁구**(卓球) ping-pong; table-tennis / ~시합 a. table-tennis game. たっきゅう

**탁랑**(濁浪) muddy waves. だくろう

**탁론**(卓論) a lofty[sound] argument; an exalted view. たくろん

**탁류**(濁流) a muddy stream; a turbid current / ~가 휩쓸고 있다 The muddy water rushes on in a vast expanse. だくりゅう

**탁립**(卓立) towering; mounting; rising / ~하다 soar; rise; tower. たくりつ

**탁마**(琢磨) (옥석을) polishing (학덕을) cultivating; close application of oneself (to) / ~하다 polish (a gem); cultivate (oneself); apply oneself to (one's study). たくま

**탁목조**(啄木鳥) 《조》a woodpecker. たくぼくちょう

**탁발**(卓拔) excellence; superiority; eminence; prominence / ~하다 (be) excellent; eminent; distinguished; lofty. たくばつ

**탁발**(托鉢) 《종》 religious mendicancy; friarhood / ~하다 [a Buddhist priest] beg around; go about as a begging priest. たくはつ

**탁본**(拓本) a rubbed copy; a rubbing / ~하다 take a rubbing (of). たくほん

**탁상**(卓上) ~의 on the table[desk]; (이론만의) theoretical; academic 《실행 불능의》 impracticable / ~ 연설 an afterdinner speech.

**탁선**(託宣) an oracle; a divine message.

**탁설**(卓說) an excellent opinion; distinguished[excellent] views / 명론 ~ sound arguments and excellent views. たくせつ

**탁성**(濁聲) a thick[hoarse, graff] voice. だくせい

**탁송**(託送) consignment / ~하다 consign; send (by, through, under the care of) / ~품 a consignment. たくそう

**탁아소**(託兒所) a day[public] nursery; a nursery school; a pre-kindergarten.

**탁엽**(托葉) 《식》 a stipule. たくよう

**탁용**(擢用) selection / ~하다 select; employ. たくよう

**탁월**(卓越) excellence; eminence; superiority; prominence; pre-eminence / ~하다 (be) excellent; eminent; prominent; distinguished / 인물 재질이 모두 ~하다 surpass others both in character

**탁월풍**(卓越風) 《기상》 the prevailing wind.

**탁음**(濁音) 《음성의》 a sonant; a voiced sound 《심장의》 cardiac dullness／~의 sonant.

**탁이**(卓異) striking difference; conspicuousness; being outstanding; prominency; uniqueness; singularity／~하다 (be) strikingly different; conspicuous; prominent; unique.

**탁자**(卓子) a table; a desk／~에 둘러앉다 sit round the table.

**탁자손**(卓子—) a support under a shelf or table.

**탁절**(卓絕) excellence ⇒탁월.

**탁절**(卓節) lofty virtues; noble character.

**탁주**(濁酒) coarse liquor; unrefined [raw] *sool*.

**탁지**(度地) land surveying; a geodetic survey／~하다 survey the land.

**탁출**(卓出) excellence ⇒탁월.

**탁탁** ①《절도 있게》 in a business-like way; quickly; promptly; with-despatch ②《쓰러짐》 ¶ ~ 쓰러지다 fall one after another ③《숨이》 ¶ ~ 숨이 막히다 be choky; be stuffy; be short of breath ④《침을》 spit-spit／ 침을 ~ 뱉다 spit and spit again.

**탁탁거리다** keep crackng[popping, snapping, banging].

**탁탁하다** (be) fine; close (in *weave*)／살림이 ~ be well[comfortably] off.

**탁하다**(濁—) (be) muddy turbid; thick 《술 따위》 cloudy 《피 따위》 impure／마음이 탁한 사람 a person with dark designs.

**탄강**(誕降) birth; nativity; advent; incarnation／~하다 get born; be incarnated.

**탄갱**(炭坑) a coal pit; a coal-mine.

**탄고**(炭庫) a coal cellar; a coal bin.

**탄공**(彈孔) a shot hole.

**탄광**(炭鑛) a coal-mine; a colliery／~회사 a coal-mine company.

**탄금**(彈琴) playing [on] the *Kayakeum*／~하다 play [on] the *Kayakeum*.

**탄내**(炭—) a scorched smell／그 과자는 ~가 난다 The cake tastes scorched.

**탄대**(彈帶) a cartridge belt 《주머니로 된》 a cartridge bag.

**탄도**(彈道) a trajectory; the path of a projectile／~탄(彈) a ballistic missile／~학 ballistics.

**탄띠**(彈—) a cartridge belt.

**탄력**(彈力) elasticity; flexibility; elastic force; resilience; spring／어린 나무에 ~ 있는 가지 the resilient bough of a young tree.

**탄로**(坦路) a broad and level highway.

**탄로**(綻露) discovery; detection; exposure; divulgence; disclosure／ ~나다 be detected; be found [out]; be discovered; come to light; be laid bare; be exposed; be divulged; transpire; come out／비밀 결사의 조직이 ~났다 The system of the secret society was disclosed.

**탄막**(彈幕) a barrage／고정 ~ a standing barrage／~ 포화 covering fire.

**탄말**(炭末) charcoal dust.

**탄망**(誕妄) falsehood; absurdity／~하다 (be) false; absurd.

**탄미**(歎美) admiration; adoration; appreciation／~하다 admire; appreciate; adore; praise; laud; extol／한국의 풍경을 ~하다 admire the beautiful scenery of Korea.

**탄산**(炭酸) 《화》 carbonic acid／~가리 potassium carbonate; corbonate potash／~ 가스 carbonic acid gas; carbon dioxide／~염 a carbonate.

**탄산**(炭山) a coal mine.

**탄상**(歎賞) admiration; praise; applause／~하다 admire; praise; extol; aplaud; speak highly of／보는 사람 모두가 ~해 마지 않았다 All those who saw it were filled with[lost in] admiration.

**탄생**(誕生) birth; ~하다 be[get] born; come into the world; first see the light of day／~을 축하하다 celebrate *one's* birthday／~일 a birthday.

**탄성**(歎聲) a sigh; a groan／~을 발하다 sigh; heave[breathe, utter] a sigh of despair[grief]; draw a long breath.

**탄성**(彈性) 《탄신》 elasticity／~계 an elastometer／~ 고무 elastic gum／~체 an elasntic body.

**탄소**(炭素) carbon; 《화》 C／~봉 a carbon rod／~지 carbon paper.

**탄수**(炭水) coal and water; 《화》 carbon and hydrogen／ ~선 a supply-ship／~차 a tender.

**탄수화물**(炭水化物) 《화》 a carbohydrate.

**탄식**(歎息) a sigh; lamentation; deploring; grief／~하다 sigh; heave[draw, fetch] a sigh; lament (*for*)／자식의 불운을 ~하다 lament [over] *one's* misfortune.

**탄신**(誕辰) a birthday; the king's birthday.

**탄알**(彈—) a shot; a ball 《소총탄》 a bullet 《포탄》 a shellet／~이 비오듯 하다 bullets fall thick and fast.

**탄압**(彈壓) suppression; crushing; pressure／~하다 suppress; crush; bring pressure upon (*a person*); use an iron hand／~을 받다 be pressed; be subjected to great pressure.

**탄약**(彈藥) ammunition／ ~고 a powder magazine 《임시의》 a powder dump; shot locker／~차 an ammunition car／~통

a cartridge; rounds of ammunition; a cartouche. だんやく

**탄우**(彈雨) a shower[rain, hail] of bullets[shells]. だんう

**탄원**(歎願) entreaty; supplication; appeal 《정부 따위에의》 petition/ ~하다 entreat; supplicate; solicit; petition; implore/~하는 표정으로 with an imploring look. たんがん

**탄일**(誕日) one's birthday; one's natal day. たんじょうび

**탄자** a blanket; a rug.

**탄저병**(炭疽病) 《의》 anthrax. たんそびょう

**탄전**(炭田) a coalfield. たんでん

**탄주**(彈奏) play; performance/ ~하다 play [on]; perform; pluck/~법 touch/ ~자 a player. だんそう

**탄지** embers of tobacco ashes. たばこのすいさし

**탄질**(炭質) the quality of coal. たんしつ

**탄착**(彈着) hit; impact/~ 관측 spotting; range-finding/ ~점 a shooting objective だんちゃく

**탄창**(彈倉) 《군》 a magazine. だんそう

**탄층**(炭層) a coal seam; a coal bed. たんそう

**탄탄**(坦坦) ~하다 (be) level; even; flat; smooth/~대로 a broad and level highway.

**탄탄하다** (be) solid; compact; strong; hard; adamant; stable. かたい

**탄평**(坦平) evenness; flatness/ ~하다 (be) even; flat; level; smooth.

**탄하**(呑下) swallowing/~하다 swallow; down; gulp down. のみくだすこと

**탄하다** ①《간섭하다》meddle; interfere (in, with); poke one's nose into ②《대꾸하다》 retort; gainsay. おせっかいする

**탄핵**(彈劾) impeachment; denunciation; accusation; censure/ ~하다 impeach (a person of a crime); denounce; censure; arraign/야당은 정부 ~안을 제출했다 The opposition introduced a motion of impeachment against the government./~자 an impeacher; a denunciator. だんがい

**탄화**(彈火) gun-fire; artillery fire.

**탄화**(炭化) 【화】 carbonization/~하다 carbonize; char/~물 a carbide/ ~ 수소 hydrocarbon. すみび

**탄환**(彈丸) a projectile; a shot; a bullet; a ball; a cannon ball 《파열탄》 a shell /빗발치는 ~ 속을 나아가다 advance under a hail of bullets. だんがん

**탄회**(坦懷) openheartedness; candidness; frankness/ ~하다 (be) openhearted; candid/허심 ~ frankness; candidness; openmindedness. たんかい

**탈** 《가면》 a mask/ ~을 벗다 unmask; throw off a mask (of). かめん

**탈**(頉) ①《변고》a hitch; a trouble; a snag; a mishap; something wrong; breakdown/ ~없이 도착하다 arrive safely ②《병》 sickness; illness ③《흠》 a fault; a defect; a flaw 《핑계》 an excuse; a pretext. さしさわり

**탈각**(脫却) riddance; cleaning out/ ~하다 get rid[clear] of; free oneself from. だっきゃく

**탈각**(脫殼) ~하다 cast off [the shell]; shed; exuviate. だっこく

**탈거**(脫去) ①《탈각》 tearing[stripping, taking] off; casting off ②《탈출》 extrication; escape. だっきょ

**탈것** 《교통 기관》 a vehicle; a conveyance 《마차》 a carriage 《자동차》 an automobile 《가마》 a palanquin 《배》 a craft. のりもの

**탈고**(脫稿) the completion of one's writing/ ~하다 finish writing; complete the manuscript/그가 집필중인 소설은 곧 ~된다 The novel he is writing is near completion. だっこう

**탈곡**(脫穀) threshing; thrashing/ ~하다 thresh; thrash/ ~기 a threshing machine; a thresher. だっこく

**탈구**(脫臼) dislocation/~하다 be dislocated; be put out of joint. だっきゅう

**탈놀음** a masque/ ~하다 put on a masque play. かめんげき

**탈당**(脫黨) secession; withdrawal from a party; bolting《미》/ ~하다 secede [bolt] from the party; leave the party /그는 자유당을 ~했다 He resigned his membership of the Liberal Party. だっとう

**탈락**(脫落) falling off/ ~하다 fall off; shed; slough away (off)/ ~하다 be omitted; be left out; be excluded; be missing; fall off/공천에서 ~되다 be left out of the public nomination. だつらく

**탈락거리다** keep slapping[slupping, slipping, jogging, jerking, jolting, clattering]. ぶらんぶらんする

**탈략**(奪略) plunder; pillage; despoilment / ~하다 pillage; plunder; despoil; strip (a person) of (a thing). だつりゃく

**탈루**(脫漏) omission; being left out; missing/~하다 get omitted; be left out; be missing. だつろう

**탈리**(脫離) drop off ⇨이탈. だつり

**탈모**(脫毛) 《자연의》 falling-out of the hair; loss of hair 《고의적》 depilation/ ~하다 lose hair 《빠지다》 fall out/이 세척제는 ~를 방지한다 This lotion stops the hair from falling out. だつもう

**탈모**(脫帽) doffing one's hat[cap]/ ~하다 take off[remove, doff] one's hat; uncover; expose one's head; raise[tip] one's hat. だつぼう

**탈바가지** a mask made of calabash [gourd].

**탈바닥** splashing; spattering/ ~거리다 splash 《물을》 be spatter. ぽちゃ

**탈발**(脫髮) loss of hair ⇨탈모. だつもう

**탈방** plop; splashing; sloppping. どぶん

**탈법 행위**(脫法行爲) an evasion of the law;

a slip from the grip of the law. だっぽうこうい

**탈싹** with a plop[thud]. ちょこん

**탈산**(脫酸) 【화】 deoxidization; deoxidation／～하다 deoxidize. だっさん

**탈상**(脫喪) expiration of the period of mourning／～하다 come out of[finish] mourning; leave off[get over] mourning.

**탈색**(脫色) decolorization; discharge／～하다 decolorize; discharge. だっしょく

**탈선**(脫線) ①《기차 따위가》derailment／～하다 get[be] derailed; derail; run off the line[rails]; leave the rails; leave the metals〈영〉; jump[leave] the track 〈미〉; be ditched ②《행동 따위》deviate from the right path; get of compass; go astray／논의가 ～하다 argue beside the point. だっせん

**탈선**(脫船) desertion[running away] from a ship／～하다 desert from a ship; run away from a ship.

**탈세**(脫稅) an evasion of taxes; tax dodging／～하다 evade[dodge] a tax／저 상점은 ～의 혐의가 있다 That firm has fallen under suspicion of tax dodging. だつぜい

**탈속**(脫俗) unworldliness; unconventionality; freedom [from social conventions]; absence of vulgarity／～하다 be above worldly things; die to the world; rise above the world. だっぞく

**탈수**(脫水) 【화】 dehydration／～하다 dehydrate／～제 a dehydrating agent; a desiccant. だっすい

**탈신 도주**(脫身逃走) desertion; escape／～하다 desert; a run away soldier.

**탈영**(脫營) desertion from the barracks [encampment]; being AWOL／～하다 desert; go over the hill; go AWOL／～병 a deserter; a runaway soldier. だつえい

**탈옥**(脫獄) prison-breaking／～하다 break[out of] prison[jail]; escape from prison／～을 기도하다 plan an escape from jail. だつごく

**탈의**(脫衣) taking off one's clothes undressing／～하다 omit[leave out] a word ／～실 a locker room. だつい

**탈자**(脫字) an omitted word[letter]; a missing word[letter]; an omission／～하다 omit[leave out] a word／～가 많 다 Many words are left out. だつじ

**탈장**(脫腸) rupture; hernia. だっちょう

**탈저**(脫疽) gangrene; sphacelus 《장자 등 의》 mortification.

**탈적**(脫籍) cancellation of one's name in the register ⇨제적. だっせき

**탈죄**(脫罪) evasion of punishment／～하 다 evade[escape] punishment. だつざい

**탈주**(脫走) escape; flight; desertion; abscondence; decampment; leg bail／～하다 desert; run away; escape; flee／～병 a deserter／～자 an absconder.

だっそう

**탈지**(脫脂) removal of fat[grease]; fatremoved; non-fat／～하다 remove the fat[grease]／～하지 않은 양모 wool in the grease. だっし

**탈출**(脫出) ①《빠져나감》escape; extrication／～하다 escape from; get out of; extricate oneself from (danger) ②《의》 《직장(直腸) 따위의》prolapse 《눈 따위의》 proptosis／～하다 fall down; prolapse／ 적국을 ～하다 escape from the enemy land. だっしゅつ

**탈춤** a masque[masked] dance／～을 추 다 play a masque dance.

**탈취**(脫臭) deodorization／～하다 deodorize／～제 a deodorizing agent; a deodorant; a deodorizer. だっしゅう

**탈취**(奪取) capture; seizure; wresting／ ～하다 capture; carry off; seize; wrest (a thing) from／요새를 ～하다 carry a fortress. だっしゅ

**탈타리** a penniless ⇨빈털터리.

**탈탈** totteringly; trudgingly／～거리다 trudge along (one's way); trudge on／ 달구지가 ～ 굴러가다 a cart clatters along. ばたばた

**탈퇴**(脫退) withdrawal; secession／～하 다 secede[withdraw, break away] (from); leave; disconnect oneself／나는 그 단체에서 ～하기로 작정했다 I have decided to secede[withdraw] from the association. だったい

**탈피**(脫皮) ecdysis; moulting; casting off 《허물》 slough／～하다 cast (off) the skin／구태를 ～하다 break from the convention. だつび

**탈하다**(頉—) plead; make a pretext of; make an excuse of; make a plea of／할 일이 있다고 ～ plead that one has business to attend to.

**탈함**(脫艦) desertion from a warship／ ～하다 desert[run away] from a warship.

**탈항**(脫肛) 【의】 proctocele; prolapse of the anus／～하다 suffer from prolapse of the anus. だっこう

**탈화**(脫化) ①《탈피》casting off; exuviation／～하다 exuviate; cast off a skin; slough ②《비유》emergence／～하다 emerge from. だっか

**탈환**(奪還) recapture; retaking; recovery; forcible recovery／～하다 take back by force; win back; retake; recapture; recover; regain; reconquer. だっかん

**탈회**(脫會) withdrawal from (a society) ／～하다 withdraw from (a society); leave; secede from (an association); give up one's membership.

**탐**(貪) avarice; greed; covetousness／ ～하다 be covetous (of); be greedy (for); devour／음식을 ～하다 devour[eat] greedily. どん

**탐검**(探檢) inquiry; investigation; prob-

**탐관 오리**(貪官汚吏) a covetous[corrupt] official.

**탐광**(探鑛) prospecting / ~하다 prospect [a region for gold]. たんこう

**탐구**(探究) search; research; investigation; inquiry; quest; study / ~하다 investigate; make researches in; inquire into; search for; explore / 진리를 ~하다 investigate truth; research for truth / ~자 an investigator. たんきゅう

**탐나다**(貪一) be covetous for (a thing); be appetizing; want; wish [care, long] for / 나는 저 책이 탐난다 I want[wish to have] that book.

**탐내다**(貪一) want; desire; covet; lust (for, after); have a desire[lust, yen] for; be greedy for; be mad after; be dying for / 남의 것을 ~ covet what belongs to others.

**탐닉**(耽溺) (빠짐) indulgence; addiction (방탕) dissipation; prodigality; debauchery / ~하다 be indulged; abandon oneself to; be addicted to; be immersed in; dissipate; take to loose living; be dissipated / 주색에 ~하다 be addicted to sensual pleasures; indulge in wine and woman. たんでき

**탐독**(耽讀) reading with avidity / ~하다 read with avidity; be absorbed in reading; steep oneself (in); pore over; devour books / 소설을 ~하다 pore over a novel; devour a novel. たんどく

**탐락**(耽樂) indulgence in pleasure / ~하다 indulge in pleasures. たんらく

**탐련**(耽戀) giving oneself up wholly for love; indulgence in love; falling madly in love; falling madly in love / ~하다 give oneself up wholly for love; indulge in love.

**탐리**(貪吏) a covetous[corrupt] official; a greedy official. たんり

**탐리**(貪利) greed; avarice; covetousness; cupidity; love of gain / ~하다 be greedy[avaricious, covetous, grasping]. たんり

**탐문**(探問) detection / ~하다 detect; learn by inquiry; search out; trace out; smell out / ~한 바에 의하면 according to what we have learned. たんもん

**탐미**(耽美) love of beauty / ~주의 aestheticism / ~주의자 an aesthete. たんび

**탐방** with a splash[plop] / ~거리다 splash about. どぶん

**탐방**(探訪) [private] inquiry / ~하다 inquire (into); make inquiry of; have an interview (with) / ~기사를 쓰다 report (for a newspaper). たんぼう

**탐사**(探査) inquiry; investigation / ~하다 inquire into; investigate (into); look into; spy out. たんさ

**탐상**(探賞) sightseeing; exploration of beauties; excursion / ~하다 sightsee; see[do] the sights; explore the sight.

**탐색**(探索) (수색) a search (취조) an inquiry; investigation / ~하다 inquire into; investigate (into); look into; research (for, after); espy / 엄중한 ~을 명하다 order a rigid search (of). たんさく

**탐스럽다** (be) desirable; appetizing; attractive; very nice; charming; beautiful; lovely / 이게 제일 ~ This suits my taste best. ほれぼれする

**탐승**(探勝) a sightseeing / ~하다 do sights; visit scenic spots. たんしょう

**탐식**(貪食) gluttony; voracity; ravenousness; edacity / ~하다 eat greedily; wolf one's food; be gluttonous; make a pig of oneself. たんしょく

**탐심**(貪心) avarice; an acquisitive mind; covetousness; greediness; selfishness. むさぼるこころ

**탐욕**(貪慾) greed; avarice; rapacity; covetousness; cupidity / 그는 ~의 덩어리 다 He is avarice itself. どんよく

**탐장**(貪贓) graft; bribes / ~하다 indulge in graft; get by graft / ~질 graft; corrupt practice.

**탐재**(貪財) coveting for property / ~하다 covet for[thirst after] property; be a varicious. さいぶつをむさぼること

**탐정**(探偵) (일) detective service[work]; secret investigation; detection (군사상 의) espionage (사람) a detective; a criminal[detective] agent; a spy; a sleuth ⟨미⟩ / ~하다 investigate[inquire into] (a matter) secretly; do detective work / ~에게 뒤밟히다 be shadowed by a detective / ~소설 a detective story. たんてい

**탐정**(探情) sounding / ~하다 feel out; sound; fly a kite. いこうをさぐること

**탐조**(探照) throwing[beaming] a searchlight / ~하다 beam, turn) a searchlight (on) / ~등 a searchlight. たんしょう

**탐지**(探知) detection / ~하다 find out; detect; get wind of; ferret out; spy out / 전파 ~기 a radar / 비밀을 ~하다 smell out a secret. たんち

**탐탁하다** (be) satisfactory; gratifying; be to one's satisfaction / 탐탁하지 않은 손님 an unlooked-for guest. まんぞくだ

**탐탐히**(耽耽一) with vigilant hostility; gloatingly / ~ 기다리다 be prepared for; look forward to. たんだん

**탐해등**(探海燈) a searchlight [that sweeps the sea]; a flashlight / ~으로 해면을 살피다 sweep the sea with a searchlight. たんかいとう

**탐험**(探險) exploration; expedition / ~하다 explore; make an exploration (of) / ~가 an explorer / ~선 a research ship / 북극을 ~하러 가다 go on an Arctic expedition. たんけん

**탐호**(貪好) fanatic love; devotion; indulgence／～하다 indulge in; be fond of; be a fanatic lover of; be devoted to; take much delight in.

**탐혹**(耽惑) indulgence; infatuation 《여자에게》 spooniness／～하다 indulge oneself in; be infatuated with 《여자에게》 be spoony／여자에게 ～하다 be infatuated with a woman.

**탑**(塔) a tower; a pagoda; a steeple (of *a church*)/기념 a monument／5층～ a five-storied pagoda. とう

**탑본**(搨本) a rubbed copy; a folio of rubbed copies／～하다 take a rubbing of.

**탑비**(塔碑) a tower and a monument [at a tomb]. とうとせきひ

**탑삭** with a dash; violently; quickly; all of a sudden. ばくっと

**탑삭나룻** a shaggy beard. ふさふさしたひげ

**탑삭부리** a man with a shaggy beard. ふさふさしたひげのひと

**탑새기주다** interfere with[in]; obstruct; disturb; get in way of; hinder／남의 일에 ～ throw a monkey wrench into someone else's project; upset (*a person's*) apple cart.

**탑소록하다** (be) thick; shaggy ⇒덥수룩하다. ふさふさしている

**탑승**(搭乘) riding; boarding／～하다 《기차 따위의》 ride (*in*); board 《배에》 [be on, go on] board／～객 a passenger／비행기에 ～하다 ride in an airplane. とうじょう

**탑재**(搭載) loading; embarkation; entrainment／～하다 load; embark; entrain; take in／그 배는 무거운 대포를 ～하고 있었다 The ship had heavy guns on board. とうさい

**탑파**(塔婆) *a stupa*(Sans)／～를 세우다 set up *a stupa*. とうば

**탓** 《원인》 reason 《영향》 influence; effect／나이 ～으로 because of[owing to] one's age／그의 죽음은 절제가 없었던 ～이다 His death was due to intemperance.

**탓** ～하다 put[lay] blame upon; lay the fault to; attatch blame to; blame; impugn; charge; accuse／세상의 무정을 ～하다 accuse the hardness of the world.

**탕** ①《문 따위》 a bang; boom／존은 책을 ～ 내던졌다 John threw his book down with a slam. ②《총소리 따위》 a bang ③《빈 모양》 《가구가 없어서 방이 ～ 비어 있다 The room looks bare without furniture. がらんと

**탕**(湯)¹ ①《국》 soup; broth 《제사용》 soup offered at ancestor memorial service ②《한약》 medicine in draught [as opposed to pills or powder]. とう

**탕**(湯)² 《목욕탕》 a hotbath; a [public] bath-house／～하다 take a [hot]bath／～에 가다 go to the bath-house; go to take a bath. とう

**탕감**(蕩減) writing off (*debts*); remission; cancellation／～하다 write off (*a debt*); remit; cancel; forgive.

**탕개** 《동차》 take-up 《장치》 a take-up／～목 a piece of wood used for tightening up a fastening rope／～줄 a fastening rope.

**탕객**(蕩客) a libertine; a debauchee; a fast liver; a prodigal. ほうとうなひと

**탕거리**(湯一) soup[broth] stuff; material to prepare soup with. しるをたくざいりょう

**탕관**(湯罐) a kettle; a pot [used for preparing soup or a medical decoction].

**탕그랑거리다** clang; jingle; tingle; rattle.

**탕기**(湯器) a soup bowl[dish].

**탕메**(湯一) boiled-rice and soup offered to the deceased souls.

**탕면**(湯麪) noodle soup; noodles in broth.

**탕반**(湯飯) boiled rice served in soup.

**탕부**(蕩婦) a woman of loose morals; a woman of easy virtue; a lewd[wanton] woman; a libertine; a demimondaine; a slut. ほうとうなふじょ

**탕산**(蕩産) ～하다 squander *one's* fortune. とうさん

**탕솥**(湯一) a soup kettle. しるをにるかま

**탕수**(湯水) hot-water; hot-spring water／～통 a hot-water tank. ゆみず

**탕심**(蕩心) a dissipated[prodigal, profligate, riotous] mind. とうしん

**탕약**(湯藥) a medicinal decoction; an infusion. とうやく

**탕일**(蕩逸) dissipation; misconduct／～하다 (be) misbehaving; loose; dissolute; profligate.

**탕자**(蕩子) a prodigal; a libertine; a debauchee. とうし

**탕전**(帑錢) the privy purse.

**탕진**(蕩盡) waste; squandering; dissipation; dilapidation／～하다 squander; run through; dissipate; waste; exhaust; dilapidate／가산을 ～하다 squander [dissipate, exhaust, run through] *one's* fortune.

**탕치**(湯治) hot-spring cure; taking the baths／～하다 take the baths[waters]／～요양 spa treatment; hot spring cure. とうじ

**탕치다**(蕩一) ①《재산을 탕진하다》 run through *one's* fortune ②《탕감하다》 forgive (*one*) a debt; cancel a debt.

**탕탕** 《소리가》 bang-bang ②《호언을》big; with big words; with hot air／거짓말을 ～하다 lie through *one's* teeth. でかでか

**탕탕평평**(蕩蕩平平) impartiality; fairness; unbiasedness; equitableness／～하다 (be) fair; impartial; unbiased; equitable.

**태**¹ 《그릇의》 a crack ／ ～가다[먹다] crack; be crack; be cracked. ひび

태² 《새쫓는》 a cracking whip [to scare birds away from crops].
태(胎) the placenta; the womb/ ~를 가르다 cut the umbilical cord. こぶくろ
태(態) form; figure ⇨맵시. すがた
태가(駄價) portage; carriage; freight; freightage.
태깔(態一) ①《태와 빛깔》 figure[form] and color ②《거만한 태도》 a haughty attitude. ありさまといろ
태깔스럽다(態一) (be) haughty; arrogant.
태고(太古) ancient times; remote antiquity[ages]; early ages/~의 ancient/~적 사람을 ancient people. たいこ
태공(太公) a grand duke; a prince/ ~국 a grand duchy; an archduchy/~비 a grand duchess.
태교(胎敎) prenatal care; antenatal training. たいきょう
태극기(太極旗) the national flag of Korea; the *Tai-geuk* flag. たいきょくき
태극선(太極扇) a fan with a mark of *T-ai-geuk*.
태기(胎氣) indications of pregnancy; feeling of conception.
태나다 be born ⇨태어나다. うまれる
태내(胎內) the interior of the womb/ ~의 아이 a child in the mother's womb.
태다수(太多數) a large[great] number; a multitude; a multiplicity.
きわめておおきいこと
태도(態度) an attitude; manner; behavior; an air; bearing; a posture; carriage; deportment; demeanor/ 거만한 ~를 취하다 assume an overbearing[arrogant] attitude. たいど
태독(胎毒) 【의】 congenital boils[syphilis]. だいどく
태동(胎動) ①《태아의》 quickening; fetal movement; signs of forthcoming activity/~하다 quicken ②《비유적》 fomentation/민주화의 ~이 보인다 There is a quickening of democratization. たいどう
태두(泰斗) an[a great] authority; a leading light 《전문가》 an expert; a luminary; a star; a savant/한국 의학계의 ~ a luminary in the medical profession of Korea.
태람(台覽) inspection by (*one's superiors*)/~하다 be honoured with an inspection by (*one's superiors*).
태령(太嶺, 泰嶺) a steep[precipitous] and high pass; a sharp divide.
태만(怠慢) negligence; neglect; inattention; remissness; slackness/~하다 (be) neglectful; inattentive; negligent; remiss; careless/직무에 ~하다 be negligent[remiss] in *one's* duties; neglect *one's* duties. たいまん
태모(胎母) a pregnant woman. にんぷ
태몽(胎夢) a dream of conception.
태무(殆無) ~하다 (be) very scarce; virtually nonexistent; very few/성공의 가능성이 ~하다 There is not the remotest chance of success.

태반(太半) the greater[better] part; the majority; the most part/인생의 ~을 외국에서 보내다 spend the greater part of *one's* life abroad. だいぶぶん
태반(胎盤) 【의】 the placenta; the afterbirth/~ 형성 placentation; placentization
태백성(太白星) the evening star; Venus. きんせいの別稱
태벌(笞罰) flogging ⇨태형.
태부족(太不足) great want/ ~하다 (be) in great want (*of*).
태산(泰山) a high mountain; a tremendous thing/~같이 동하지 않다 be firm [as steady] as a rock. たいざん
태산 북두(泰山北斗) an authority ⇨태두. たいざんほくと
태산 준령(泰山峻嶺) high mountains and steep passes.
태상왕(太上王) the abdicated king.
태생(胎生) ①《출생》 birth; origin 《출생지》 *one's* birth place/서울 ~ a person born in *Seoul* ②《생》 viviparity; viviparousness/~학 embryology; ontogenesis. たいせい
태서(泰西) the Occident; the West; the Western countries. たいせい
태선(苔蘚) 【의】 lichen. こけ
태세(態勢) an attitude; setup; preparations; arrangements/전투 ~를 취하다 hold battle position. たいせい
태수(太守) a governor general; a viceroy.
태아(胎兒) a fetus; an embryo; an unborn baby/~의 embryonic. たいが
태안젓(太眼—) pickled pollack's eyes.
태양(太陽) the sun/ ~의 solar/ ~ 광선 the sun's ray; the sunlight; the rays of the sun; sunbeams/ ~신 the sun god/ 평균 ~일 the mean solar day/ ~은 열을 방사한다 The sun radiates heat. たいよう
태어나다 be born; come into being[existence]/가난한 집에 ~ be born of a poor family. うまれる
태업(怠業) sabotage; loafing on the job / ~하다 go on sabotage[a go-slow strike]; loaf on the job. たいぎょう
태없다 (be) modest; unassuming; unaffected/태없는 사람 a democratic person; a man of plebeian habits. きどらない
태연(泰然) coolness; calmness; composure/ ~하다 (be) cool; calm; composed; self-possessed; unshaken/그는 그 소식을 듣고도 ~하였다 He did not turn a hair at the news. たいぜん
태연 자약(泰然自若) imperturbability; composure; self-possession; presence of mind/ ~하다 (be) perfectly calm; cool and collected; calm and self-possessed. たいぜんじじゃく
태엽 a spring; a [mechanical] spring/ ~을 감다 wind a spring.
태우다¹ ①《연소하다》 burn; commit to the

**태우다** flames; put in the fire; incinerate; lay in ashes／나는 부주의로 새 양복을 태워 구멍을 내었다 I was careless enough to burn a hole in my new coat. ②《그을리다》scorch; burn; singe 《까맣게》char／밥을 ~ burn the rice ③《가슴·속을》burn 《걱정하다》worry／사람의 속을 ~ make (*a person*) worry; make (*a person*) awfully anxious. もやす

**태우다²** 《탈것에》carry; accommodate; let ride; take (*a person* on *board*); give a ride; pick up (*a person* on *foot*)／자동차가 손님을 태우려고 섰다 The car stopped to pick up passengers. のせる

**태우다³** 《분배하다》divide; share; distribute 《골을》have [one's hair] parted in the middle 《쪼개게 하다》have something divided. わける

**태위**(胎位) 《醫》presentation.
**태음**(太陰) the moon／~력 the lunar calendar. たいいん
**태자**(太子) the Crown Prince; the Prince Imperial／~궁 the Crown Prince's palace. たいし
**태작**(駄作) a poor work; trash; rubbish／저 사람이 쓰는 글은 모두가 ~이다 All that comes out of his pen is poor stuff.
**태장**(笞杖) a bamboo paddle (*an instrument for punishment*); beating [on the buttocks]; flogging; flagellation.
**태주** the spirit[ghost] of a little girl who died of smallpox／~할미 a woman who manages the girl spirit.
**태중**(胎中) the period of maternity／그 여자는 ~이다 She is pregnant[with child]. たいちゅう
**태질치다** ①《메어치다》throw down; hurl; fling ②《타작하다》thresh. なげつける
**태치다** thresh (*grain*). なげつける
**태타**(怠惰) laziness; idleness; sloth; indolence; sluggishness／~하다 (be) idle; lazy; indolent; slothful; sluggish. たいだ
**태탕**(駘蕩) ~하다 (be) mild; pleasant; genial; serene／춘풍 ~ a genial spring breeze[weather]. たいとう
**태평**(泰平, 太平) ①《국가·가정의》peace; tranquillity; perfect[profound] peace; quiet／~하다 (be) peaceful; tranquil; quiet／~을 구가하다 enjoy the blessing of peace ②~하다《마음이》(be) easy [-going]; carefree／~한 사람 an easygoing person; a happy-go-lucky person. たいへい
**태평양**(太平洋) the Pacific [Ocean]／~ 동맹 the Pacific Alliance／~ 전쟁 the Pacific War／~ 지역 the Pacific area. たいへいよう
**태풍**(颱風) a typhoon. たいふう
**태형**(笞刑) whipping; flogging; the lash／~을 가하다 flog; lash (*a person*) on the buttocks.
**태환**(兌換) conversion／~하다 convert／~ 은행 a bank of issue／~ 제도 the c-onversion system. だかん
**태후**(太后) the Empress Dowager.
**택사**(澤瀉) 《植》*Alisma canaliculatum*(학명). へらおもだか
**택일**(擇日) choice of[choosing] an auspicious day／~하다 choose an auspicious day; fix upon the day; fix a date. きつじつをえらぶこと
**택지**(擇地) selecting land; the selection of site／~하다 select as good land; select a site (*for*). よいとちをえらぶこと
**택지**(宅地) a site for a house[-building]. たくち
**택출**(擇出) selection; choice／~하다 select; pick up. えらびだすこと
**택칠**(澤漆) 《植》a surge; *Euphorbia helioscopia*(학명).
**택하다**(擇一) choose; select; make a choice of; prefer 《선거하다》select／치욕보다 차라리 죽음을 ~ prefer death to dishonor; would rather die than live in disgrace. えらぶ
**댄덩이**(胎一) a blockhead; a fathead; a dumbbell; a simpleton.
**댄자리개** a straw rope used for binding rice[barley] in sheaves.
**탯줄**(胎一) the umbilical cord; the navel-string. へそのお
**탱알** 《植》a Tatarian aster.
**탱자** 《植》a trifoliate orange／~나무 a hardy-orange tree; *Citrus trifoliata*(학명). からたちのみ
**탱탱** ~하다 (be) taut; tight; tightly stretched; distended／줄을 ~히 당기다 tighten a rope; stretch a rope tight.

**터¹** ①《땅》a site; a place; building land; a building lot[site]／~를 닦다 level the ground ②《기초》the foundation; the ground; footing; foothold; groundwork／이제 장사~가 잡혔다 He has his business well on its way. とち
**터²** ①《처지》one's status[lot, livelihood, social standing]; family circumstances ②《관계》relationship; friendship; terms.
**터³** 《예정》intention; expectation／…할 ~이다 intend; have the intention of (*doing*); expect; think of (*doing*)／내가 직접 갈 ~이다 I intend to go in person. つもり
**터놓다** release; unstop; undam; clear; open (*it*) up／터놓고 without reserve; unreservedly; frankly; freely／터놓고 이야기하다 open *one's* heart (*to*). かいほうする
**터다지다** consolidate [the foundation of a building]; roll[level] the ground (*for*)／집터를 ~ consolidate the foundation of a building. とちがためにする
**터닦다** ①《땅을》build up[prepare] a site for a building; clear the foundation of a building; bulldoze ②《기초를》consolidate a foundation; prepare the ground (*for*). せいちする

**터덕거리다** ①《걸음을》 walk wearily; plod (on, along); trudge (along)/터덕터덕 barely ②《가난하여》 eke out a scanty livelihood; make a bare living《일을》 struggle. とぼとぼとあるく

**터덜거리다** ①《걸음을》 walk wearily; plod; trudge ②《소리를》 sound cracked; clink dully. あしをひきずってあるく

**터드렁거리다** sound cracked. がらんがらん

**터뜨리다** explode; detonate; blow up; blast; burst/증기를 ~ break one's boil /울분을 ~ let loose one's indignation. はれつさせる

**터득(攄得)** understanding; comprehension; apprehension; realization; grasping/~하다 understand; comprehend; grasp; see; learn/진리를 ~하다 understand[perceive] a truth. しこうしておぼえること

**터럭** hair; feathers/동정심이라고는 ~ 끝만큼도 없다 He has not a particle of tender feeling. かみ

**터무니없다** (be) unfounded; groundless; unreasonable; absurd; preposterous; exorbitant; excessive; wild; fabulous; have no foundation/터무니 없는 말을 하다 say an extravagant thing. こんきょがない

**터밭** a field attached to a home site; a kitchen garden.

**터벅터벅** 《걸음걸이가》 trudgingly; totteringly; walking with difficulty; trudgingly/~ 걸어가다 plod[trudge] along; plod one's way. てくてく

**터분하다** (be) ill-smelling; foul; offensive; fetid; ransid; rank. うっとうしい

**터세다** 《집터가》 (be) unlucky; haunted; jinxed; ill-boding.

**터수** status; relationship 《가제》 family circumstances; living; household.

**터알** the field[vegetable garden] adjoining one's house; a kitchen garden.

**터울** the disparity of age among one's children [which is regarded as indicating the frequency of childbirth of the mother]/~이 잦다 be frequent in conceiving a baby. としちがい

**터울거리다** make desperate[frantic] efforts; struggle hard (with). もがく

**터전** the site; the grounds/넓은 ~ a large lot. きち

**터주(−主)** a house guardian deity[god]. ちじん

**터주다** permit; allow; leave (it) open; give leave; lift[remove] the ban/입학할 길을 ~ leave a way open for entering a school. かいほうしてやる

**터지다** ①《폭발하다》 explode; burst; erupt; blow up/중대 사건이 ~ a serious matter pops up ②《트더지다》 rip; tear 《금가다》 crack; be cracked 《피부가》 get chapped hands/입술이 ~ one's lips crack ③《탄로나다》 come to light; be exposed; be divulged. ばくはつする

**턱**¹ a jaw; a chin/~으로 사람을 부리다 have (a person) at one's back [and call]. あご

**턱**² 《높은 데》 a raised part; a raise; an elevated place/고개 ~ the top of a pass[slope].

**턱**³ 《대접》 a treat; a feast; a good meal; an entertainment/오늘은 내가 한 ~ 낼 차례다 It is my treat now. おごり

**턱**⁴ ①《풀어지는 끝》¶ 마음이 ~ 놓이다 be relieved; feel reassured ②《잡는 모양》 ¶ 손을 ~ 잡다 hold (a person's) hand passionately ③《태연히》 ¶ 그 사람이 ~ 우리 앞에 나타났다 He composedly appeared in front of us. ぎゅっと

**턱**⁵ ①《까닭》 reason; grounds/그럴 ~이 없다 There is no reason for that. ②《정도》 extent; degree/아직 그 ~이다 That's all the further we've gotten. わけ

**턱걸이** 《운동》 chinning/ ~하다 do chinning exercises 《의존》 parasitism; sponging off others《미·구》/~하다 chin oneself; do a chin-up. けんすい

**턱밑** ①《턱의 밑》 the tip of the chin ② 《가까운》 beneath one's chin/~에 두고도 보지 못한다 can't see[fail to find] what is right under one's nose. あごのした

**턱받기** a pinafore; a bib. よだれかけ

**턱살** the lower jaw; the chin. あご

**턱없다** (be) unreasonable; exorbitant; immoderate/턱없이 돈을 쓰다 spend one's money away unreasonably. りゆうがない

**턱자가미** the joint of the upper jaw and the lower jaw.

**턱주가리** the lower jaw; the tip of the chin. したあご

**턱찌끼** left-over food; leavings (at the table); remnants of food. ざんぱん

**턱짓** moving one's chin as a gesture; pointing with one's chin/~하다 express by the movement of the chin.

**턱턱** ①《일을》¶ 일을 ~ 처리하다 do things with dispatch; use dispatch ②《침을》 ¶침을 아무데나 ~ 뱉다 spit on everywhere ③《숨이》¶이 방은 숨이 ~ 막힌다 This room is very stuffy. てきぱき

**털** ①《머리털》 hair 《솜털》 down/ ~이 없는 bald; smooth; hairless ②《짐승의》 fur 《거친》 a skin 《토끼 따위의》 a flix 《양모》 wool /안에 ~을 댄 외투 a furlined overcoat ③《깃》 feather bird/새~ bird feathers/닭~을 뽑다 pluck a chicken. かみ

**털갈다** 《새가》 moult 《짐승이》 shed hair/ 털가는 시절 the moulting season; the moult.

**털끝** the end of a hair; the tips of hair; hair tips 《근소》 a bit; a jot; a whit/ 그렇게 할 생각은 ~만큼도 없다 I haven't the slightest intention to do so. けのさき

**털다** ①《떨다》 shake off; throw off 《먼지를》 dust 《솔로》 brush up/담뱃재를 ~

**털럭거리다** flick the ashes from cigar[cigarette] ②(내다) lay out 《투자하다》 invest 《기부하다》 contribute/그는 가산을 톡톡 다 털어 먹었다 He ran through his fortunes. ③(가져가다) take away; make off (with).

**털럭거리다** keep slapping[jogging, jerking, jolting, clattering]/털럭털럭 with slaps[jolt]; clatteringly.

**털목**(--木) coarse cotton [cloth].

**털방석**(--方席) a fur cushion.

**털배자**(--褙子) a fur waistcoat[vest]; a fur-lined Korean vest[waistcoat].

**털버덕** ~거리다 splash; make splashing/~털버덕 with a splash.

**털버선** woolen [Korean] socks.

**털벙** with a plop; with a splash.

**털보** a hairy[shaggy, hirsute] person.

**털복숭아** 《식》 a downy peach; a fuzzy peach.

**털북숭이** a hairy[shaggy, hirsute] person[object].

**털붓** a writing-brush.

**털붙이** ①(모피) furs; fur pieces; fur goods; a skin ②(털옷) fur clothes; wollen goods[stuff].

**털썩** flop; with a thud/ ~거리다 flop/그릇을 ~ 떨어뜨리다 drop a plate with a thud.

**털썩이잡다** ruin; spoil; fail; blast; wreck.

**털수세** a thick bristling beard.

**털실** woolen yarn; worsted; knitting wool/~로 스웨터를 짜다 knit a sweater with wool.

**털어놓다** ①(물건을) empty out; shake out; spill; throw out ②(마음을) open one's heart; unbosom oneself; tell frankly/그는 나에게 고민을 털어놓고 얘기했다 He confided his trouble to me.

**털어먹다** spend the last cent.

**털집** a fast liver; a libertine; a prodigal; a debauchee.

**털터리** ①(빈털터리) a man who is broke; a man without ready money ②(낡은 차) a rattling thing ③(오토바이) a motorcycle.

**털털** ploddingly; clinkingly; clatteringly.

**털털하다** (be) easy; free and easy.

**털토시** fur-lined wristlets.

**텀벙** with a plump[splash, plop, flop] ~ 강으로 뛰어들다 plunge[jump] into the river with a splash.

**텁석** all of a sudden; suddenly; greedily; abruptly 《세게》 firmly /~ 덤비다 jump at; make a sudden spring at.

**텁석나룻** bushy whiskers; shaggy whiskers.

**텁석부리** a man with bushy whiskers.

**텁수룩하다** (be) unkempt; untrimmed; shaggy; bushy/구레나룻이 텁수룩하게 나다 have a shaggy growth of whiskers.

**텁텁이** a sloppy person; an easy person.

**텁텁하다** ①(음식이) (be) thick and tasteless 《입속이》 (be) unpleasant; disagreeable ②(눈이) (be) vague; dim; obscure ③(성미가) (be) easy; broad-minded/성미가 텁텁해서 누구하고도 잘 사귀다 be so broad-minded as to associate with men of all shades.

**텃세**(-貰) rent for a house site; the site tax.

**텃세**(-勢) ~하다 lord it over a newcomer taking advantage of the fact that one has been longer in the doing; disregard a newcomer.

**텅** hollow/가구가 없어 방안이 ~ 빈 것 같다 The room looks bare without furniture.

**텅텅** ①(빈 모양) all hollow ②(총소리) bang, bang.

**테** ①(둘린 언저리) a frame(틀의); a brim (모자의); a rim(안경 따위의); a hoop (기물 따위의); a frill(장식한); margin; border(주변)/금~ 안경 goldrimmed spectacles/~가 넓은 모자 a broad-brimmed hat ②⇒테두리.

**테두리** ①(둘레) girth; circumference; caliber ②(테) a hoop; a rim ③(윤곽) an outline 《범위》 a limit; a framework/법규의 ~안에서 정치 활동을 하다 engage in a political movement within the legal limit.

**테밖** being outside the circle[sphere]/정치의 ~ outside the sphere of politics.

**테안** within the limit (of); within the circle[bound, sphere]/성적이 입학자 ~에 들다 one's record [of grades] meets the standard for admission to the school.

**템** as much as; as long as/그는 하루에 한 되 ~이나 먹는다 He eats as much as a doe a day.

**토** a grammatical particle; a postposition.

**토건업**(土建業) engineering and construction enterprise/~자 a civil engineering and building constructor.

**토관**(土管) an earthen pipe.

**토피**(土塊) a lump of earth[dirt].

**토구**(土寇) local rebels.

**토구**(討究) study; research; investigation/ ~하다 study; research; investigate.

**토굴**(土窟) a cave; a den/ ~에서 사는 사람 a cave dweller.

**토끝** the end piece of a roll of fabric; a fag-end.

**토끼** 《집토끼》 a rabbit 《들토끼》 a hare/

**~굴** a rabbit burrow／**~** 사육장 a rabbit warren. うさぎ

**토기**(土器) earthenware; an earthen vessel. どき

**토기**(吐氣) nausea; a sickly feeling; qualm. はきけ

**토농**(土農) a native farmer; an indigenous farmer. どちゃくののうみん

**토닥거리다** tap; pat; beat lightly.

**토단**(土壇) an earthen platform; a terrace. つちでつくっただん

**토담**(土一) a dirt-wall; a mud-wall; a plaster-well.

**토대**(土臺) ①《건축의》a foundation; a stereobate; a ground sill ②《일의》a foundation; a base; ground work; a cornerstone／성공할 **~**를 쌓다 pave the way for *one's* success. どだい

**토라지다** pout; get sulky／그녀는 왜 토라졌나 What makes her sulky?

**토란**(土卵) 《식》an elephants'-ear.

**토렴** **~하다** warm up (*boiled rice, etc.*) by applying hot water or soup repeatedly.

**토로**(吐露) **~하다** express set forth; lay bare／의견을 **~하다** express *one's* opinion.

**토론**(討論) a debate; a discussion; an oratorical contest; argumentation／**~하다** debate; discuss; argue／**~회** a debating society. とうろん

**토롱**(土壟) a grave mound.

**토리** a spool of thread／**~**실 balled string[thread]. いとのまるくまいたもの

**토리**(土理) fertility of soil; the nature of soil.

**토마루**(土一) a mud floor.

**토막** a piece; a bit; a cut; a fragment／**~치다** sever; cut in pieces／나무 **~** a piece of wood／생선 **~** a cut of fish／**~내다** cut[chop] into pieces. きれ

**토막**(土幕) a mud hut; a cellar-hovel; an underground shack. つちこや

**토멸**(討滅) conquest; annihilation; extermination／**~하다** conquer; annihilate; exterminate. とうめつ

**토목**(土木) engineering works 《토목 공사》 public works／**~** 건축 the engineering and construction industry／**~** 공사 public works／**~** 공학 civil engineering. どぼく

**토목공이**(土木一) a fool; an ass; a boor; a dunce. おろかもの

**토민**(土民) the natives; the aborigines. どみん

**토반**(土班) the native gentry.

**토벌**(討伐) subjugation; suppression／**~하다** subjugate; suppress; put down; subdue／공비(共匪)를 **~하다** liquidate[subdue] red guerrillas／**~**군 a punitive force. とうばつ

**토벽**(土壁) a mud wall; a dirt wall; the earthen wall; a plaster wall. つちかべ

**토병**(土兵) the native[local] troops.

どへい
**토비**(土匪) native insurgents; rebellious natives; local rebels. どひ

**토비**(討匪) suppression of rebels[insurgents]／**~하다** suppress redels.

**토사**(土砂) earth and sand. どしゃ

**토사**(吐瀉) vomiting and diarrhea／**~하다** vomit and run off at the bowels.

**토사 곽란**(吐瀉癨亂) vomiting and diarrhea; acute gastroenteritis.

**토산**(土山) an earthy mountain. つちやま

**토산**(土産) ¶ **~물**(物) local products; native produce. どさん

**토색**(土色) earth color. つちいろ

**토색**(討索) exaction; extortion; blackmail／**~하다** extort; blackmail (*a person*) for; practice extortion.

**토성**(土星) 《천》 Saturn. どせい

**토성**(土城) mud fortification; a mud[an earthen] castle. どじょう

**토속**(土俗) folkways; local customs／**~**학 folklore. どぞく

**토시** wristlets.

**토신**(土神) 《민》 an earth god; a deity of earth. どじん

**토실**(吐實) confessing／**~하다** tell the truth; confess; own up to.

**토실토실** **~하다** (be) plump; chubby／**~한** 볼 chubby cheeks／**~한** 아이 a plump child. まるまる

**토심스럽다**(吐心一) feel bad; unpleasant; (be) disgusting. ふゆかいにおもう

**토악질**(吐一) 《구토》 an attack of vomiting 《부정 이득을》 disgorgement／**~하다** vomit; disgorge; throw up／먹었던 돈을 **~하다** repay[disgorge] what one has embezzled.

**토약**(吐藥) an emetic.

**토양**(土壤) soil; earth／비옥한 **~** fertile[sterile] soil／**~** 조사 agronomical survey／**~**학 soil science. どじょう

**토어**(土語) the native[local] language; the vernacular tongue[language]. どご

**토역**(土役) mud work; earthwork／**~하다** do mud work[earthwork]／**~**군 a navvy; a construction laborer.

**토연**(土煙) a cloud of dust.

**토옥**(土屋) a mud hut. つちかべのいえ

**토옥**(土沃) the fertility[richness] of soil／**~하다** (be) rich; fertile; productive. とちがこえていること

**토요일**(土曜日) Saturday. どようび

**토욕**(土浴) wallowing in mud[dirt]／**~하다** wallow in mud[dirt].

**토우**(土雨) a dust storm; a rain of dust.

**토우**(土偶) a clay doll[icon].

**토의**(討議) discussion; debate; deliberation／**~하다** discuss; debate[deliberate] (*upon*)／**~**에 붙이다 submit (*a subject*) to debate／**~** 사항 items on the agenda. とうぎ

**토인**(土人) a native; an aboriginal 《총칭》 aborigines. どじん

**토장**(土葬) interment; burial; inhumat-

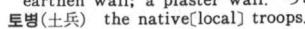

**토장**(土醬) bean paste ⇨된장.
**토적**(土賊) local bandits; local rebels [insurgents]. どぞく
**토적**(討賊) suppression of a rebellion/~하다 subdue a rebellion.
**토정**(吐精) seminal emission ⇨사정. しゃせい
**토정**(吐情) ~하다 speak *one's* mind; open [unlock] *one's* heart; unbosom *oneself*.
**토제**(吐劑) a vomit; an emetic.
**토지**(土地) ①(땅·흙) land; a piece[tract] of land; a lot[plot]; soil/~를 경작하다 cultivate land; till the soil ②(소유지) an estate; real estate ③(영지) territory/~ 개혁 land reform. とち
**토찌끼** dregs of soysauce.
**토질**(土質) the nature of the soil; the soil. どしつ
**토질**(土疾) an endemic disease; a local [vernaculr] disease.
**토착**(土着) settling; aboriginality/~하다 settle [in a new territory]; become native/~민 aborigines; natives; original settlers. どちゃく
**토척**(土瘠) barrenness [of land]/~하다 (be) barren; sterile; unproductive. とちがやせていること
**토탄**(土炭) peat; turf. どろすみ
**토파**(吐破) speaking *one's* mind freely; talking frankly/~하다 tell[say] frankly; disclose freely; talk without reserve. とろ
**토풍**(土風) local[native] customs; the manners of a place. とちのふうぞく
**토하다**(吐一) ①(게우다) vomit; throw[fetch] up (뱉다) spew; spit (뿜다) emit; eject; belch; send forth[out, up]/먹은 것을 ~ throw up what *one* has eaten ②(토로) speak (*one's* mind); disclose; express; confess/본심은 ~ tell what is in mind. はく
**토현삼**(土玄蔘) 〖식〗 a figwort; *Scrophularia koraiensis*(학명). ちょうせんごまのはぐさ
**토혈**(吐血) spitting[vomiting] blood; hemoptysis/~하다 spit[vomit] blood.
**톡** ①(소리) with a pat[rap, thud, snap] /어깨를 ~ 치다 give (*a person*) a pat on the shoulder ②(모양) protrudingly; bulgingly/배가 ~ 나오다 have a bulging belly. ぶくり
**톡배다** (be) close woven.
**톡탁** with a tap[rap] ⇨툭탁. とんとん
**톡톡** with a pat ⇨톡. ぶくりぶくり
**톡톡이** ①(많이) much; a lot; a great deal/돈을 ~ 벌다 make quite a lot of money ②(심하게) hard; severely; soundly; heavily/~ 얻어맞다 be beaten soundly; get a good beating. ひどく
**톡톡하다** ①(액체가) (be) thick; rich; heavy ②(피륙이) (be) thick; close; close -woven. しるがこい
**톨** a grain; a nut/한~의 쌀 a grain of rice. つぶ
**톰방** plop; with a splash/~톰방 with splashes[plops]; splashing[plopping] repeatedly/~거리다 keep splashing [plopping]; splash about. どぼん
**톱** a saw/~으로 켜다 cut with a saw; saw (*of*)/~날 a saw blade; a saw tooth/~밥 sawdust/~질 sawing. のこ
**톱니바퀴** a toothed wheel; a cogwheel; a pitch[gear] wheel; a saw-toothed [serrated]/~ 장치 a gear; toothed gearing.
**톱상어** 〖어〗 a saw-shark; *Pristiophorus japonicus*(학명). のこぎりざめ
**톱톱하다** (be) thick; heavy; coarse. しるがこい
**톳** a bundle (of *laver*).
**톳나무** a big tree; a gigantic[towering] tree. おおきいき
**통**¹ ①(배추 따위) the bulk; the body/배추 ~이 크다 The cabbage has a large head ②(광목 따위) a roll/광목 한 ~ a roll of cotton cloth.
**통**² ①(사이에·때문에) consequence; result; influence [of something disturbing] /난리~에 죽었다 He died in the ravage of war. ②(무리) a gang; a group; a party. あいだ
**통**³ (전혀) all; the whole; entirely; utterly; wholly; in all; collectively/그녀는 동정이라고는 ~ 없다 She has not a particle of sympathy. すべて
**통**(桶) a cask; a tub; a kit; a barrel; a pail; a bucket; a keg/성냥 한 ~ a box of matches/~조림 canned food. おけ
**통**(筒) a tube; a pipe; a gun barrel; a tin; a can (역량) caliber/소매~이 좁다 a sleeve is tight/그는 ~이 큰 사람이다 He is a man of big caliber. つつ
**통**(統) (동네의) a neighborhood unit; a small section of a city; a *tong*/ ~장 the head of a *tong*.
**통**(通) ①(사람) an authority; an expert (*on*); a well-informed person; a person in the know/그는 재정~이다 He is conversant with financial affairs. ②(서류의) a copy; letters/소식~ informed sources. つう
**통가리** a rick[stack] of corn. いなむら
**통각**(痛覺) sense[sensation] of pain/~제 an algometer/~ 과민증 hyperalgesia. つうかく
**통각**(洞角) a hollow horn. どうかく
**통각**(統覺) 《심·철》 apperception/~하다 apperceive. とうかく
**통간**(通姦) adultery ⇨간통(姦通). かんつう
**통감**(統監) supervision; superintendence; command; [Resident] General/~하다 supervise: take supreme command (*of*). とうかん
**통감**(痛感) ~하다 fully realize; feel keenly[acutely]/상호 협조의 필요성을 ~하

다 feel[realize] keenly the necessity of mutual cooperation. つうかん

**통거리** completely; all; entirely; wholly /땅을 ~로 사다 buy up the whole lot of land (at). まるまる

**통겨주다** disclose; reveal; tip off; expose; let out (a secret). しらしてやる

**통겨지다** ①《드러나다》get[be] disclosed; come to light; be brought to light; be exposed; come out/비밀이 ~ a secret is disclosed ②《어긋나다》come apart [off]; be put out of joint. ばれる

**통격**(痛擊) severe[savage] attack; a severe[hard] blow/ ~하다 strike a hard blow. つうげき

**통견**(洞見) insight; penetration; divination; acumen; discernment/ ~하다 have insight into; see through; discern. どうけん

**통계**(統計) statistics; statistical data; figures; a numerical statement/ ~하다 gather statistics (of)/ ~를 작성하다 compile statistics/~표 a statistical table[chart]. とうけい

**통고**(通告) notice; notification; announcement/ ~하다 notify (a person) of; give notice of/사전에 ~하다 give (a person) previous notice/~서 a notice; a written notice. つうこく

**통곡**(痛哭) wailing; lamentation; keening; loud weeping/~하다 weep loudly; wail; keen; lament; mourn[weep] bitterly. つうこく

**통과**(通過) passage; transit; carriage; passing/ ~하다 pass (by, through, over, off)/세관을 ~하다 pass a custom house/의안을 ~시키다 carry a bill; put a measure through. つうか

**통관**(通款) treachery; secret communication with the enemy/ ~하다 communicate secretly with the enemy. つうかん

**통관**(通關) entry; clearance; customs clearance/~하다 enter[clear] (a ship) /~ 수속 때문에 for customs procedure /~ 수속을 하다 clear; pass customs entry/ ~세 a clearance[customs] fee. つうかん

**통관**(通觀) a general view[survey]/ ~하다 survey; take a general view[survey] (of). つうかん

**통관**(通貫) piercing ⇒관통. かんつう

**통괄**(統括) generalization; summarization; recapitulation; synthesis/ ~하다 summarize; generalize; epitomize. とうかつ

**통규**(通規) general[common] principles; general rules[provisions]. つうき

**통근**(通勤) attending office; going to work; commuting; commutation/ ~하다 attend[go to] office; go to work; commute/나는 인천에서 ~한다 I commute from Inchun/~자 commuter/~ time to attend office. つうきん

**통기**(通寄) notification ⇒통지. つうち

**통기공**(通氣孔) a vent; a spile-hole 《광산의》 an air pit.

**통기다** loosen ⇒퉁기다. はじけさせる

**통김치** pickles made of whole cabbages / ~쌈 pickled cabbage leaves stuffed with rice.

**통나무** a pole; a log; unsplit wood.

**통단** a large sheaf. おおきくくくったたば

**통달**(通達) mastery; conversance; expertise/ ~하다 be conversant (with); be well versed (in); be at home (in)/영어에 ~하다 be versed[well up] in English. つうたつ

**통닭** a chicken cooked whole.

**통대구** a dried whole codfish.

**통독**(通讀) reading [a book] from beginning to end/ ~하다 peruse; read through; read [a book] from cover to cover. つうどく

**통람**(通覽) a general survey[view]; a perusal/ ~하다 survey; look over; glance over; read through. つうらん

**통렬**(痛烈) severity; fierceness; sharpness/ ~하다 (be) severe; fierce; sharp; bitter; cutting; scathing/나는 그를 ~히 비난했다 I called him down like anything. つうれつ

**통령**(統領) leadership; command; generalship/ ~하다 lead; command; assume the leadership of; take the lead of. とうりょう

**통례**(通例) the custom; the rule; a common[an ordinary] practice/그렇게 하는 것이 ~다 It is the custom to do so. つうれい

**통로**(通路) a passage; a passageway; a way; a pathway; a path; a roadway; an approach; an aisle; an avenue/ ~를 막다 obstruct[block] the passage. つうろ

**통론**(通論) an outline; an introduction /문학 ~ an introduction to literature /법학 ~ an outline of law. つうろん

**통론**(痛論) a heated discussion; a vehement argument/~하다 criticize severely; argue[discuss] vehemently[earnestly]. つうろん

**통마늘** a whole bulb of garlic.

**통말**(桶一) a round-measure.

**통매**(痛罵) condemnation; denunciation; an invective; a diatribe; harsh criticism/ ~하다 condemn; denounce; criticize severely; abuse grossly. つうば

**통메다**(桶一) ①hoop a tub ②be closely packed; be crowded; be jammed; be packed like sardines. たがをはめる

**통메장이**(桶一) a hooper; a cooper.

**통명**(通明) brilliantness; intelligence; smartness; brightness/ ~하다 (be) intelligent; bright; smart; brilliant; wise. そのことにあかからなこと

**통밀다** average/통밀어 on the average /손님은 통밀어 하루에 50명 끌이다 The number of guests is fifty on an/aver-

**통발**¹ a fishtrap; a fishweir made of willow or bamboo.

**통발**² 〖식〗 a bladderwort.

**통법**(通法) ①〖법〗 general[common] rules [provisions] ②〖수〗 a principle[rate] of conversion[exchange] (of *measures*).

**통변**(通辯) interpretation.

**통보**(通報) information; a report; a bulletin; a dispatch/ ~하다 report; send information (to)/기상 ~ a weather news; a weather forecast〈미〉.

**통보**(通寶) currency; coin.

**통부**(通訃) information of *one's* death/ ~하다 send a letter announcing a death; announce[inform of] death.

**통분**(痛忿) great indignation/ ~하다 be greatly indignant.

**통분**(通分) 〖수〗 reduction of fractions to a common denominator/ ~하다 reduce (*fractions*) to a common denominator.

**통사**(通士) a man of the world.

**통사정**(通事情) a frank[confidential] talk/ ~하다 open *one's* heart; confide in.

**통산**(通算) summing up; the sum total/ ~하다 sum up; add up; aggregate; total; include/미결 일수를 ~하다 include the number of the days in the detention house.

**통상**(通常) ordinarily; normally; usually; generally; commonly/ ~의 ordinary; common; usual; regular/ ~복 everyday dress; morning dress; a business suit.

**통상**(通商) commerce; trade; commercial relations[intercourse]/ ~하다 trade (with *a country*)/일본과 ~을 시작하다 open trade with Japan/ ~ 조약 a commercial treaty.

**통상**(筒狀) cylinder-shape/ ~의 cylindrical; tubiform; tubular.

**통석**(痛惜) lamentation; deep regret; great sorrow/ ~하다 regret deeply; lament; be deeply grieved/ ~해 마지않다 I cannot but feel the deepest regret.

**통설**(通說) a popular view; a common opinion.

**통성**(通性) a common trait.

**통성명**(通姓名) exchanging names/ ~하다 exchange names; introduce themselves to each other.

**통소**(洞簫) a bamboo flute.

**통속** (무리) a gang; confederates (밀약) a secret agreement; a cabal/무슨 ~인지 알 수 없다 I can't guess what secret agreement they have made.

**통속**(通俗) popularity; conventionality/ ~적인 common; popular; conventional/이 문제는 ~적으로 다루어지고 있다 The subject is treated in a popular vein. / ~ 문학 a popular literature.

**통솔**(統率) leadership; command; control; generalship/ ~하다 command; control; lead; assume the leadership (*of*) / ~하에 있다 be under the command of/ ~자 a leader.

**통솟곳** an awl; a drill with a crescent blade.

**통수**(統帥) supreme[high] command; leadership/ ~하다 lead; take command / ~권 the prerogative of supreme command/ ~자 a leader; a supreme commander.

**통신**(通信) (서면상의) correspondence (서신) communication (보도) news (정보) intelligence; information; a letter; a report/ ~하다 correspond with (*a person*); communicate (*a matter*) to (*a person*); report (for *a paper*)/소식을 정부에 ~하다 communicate [the] information to the government/ ~강의 a correspondence course/ ~망 a communications network.

**통심정**(通心情) rapport; cordial understanding; shared sympathy/ ~ 하다 open *one's* heart; have a rapport; confide in.

**통약**(通約) reduction to a common measure;〖수〗commensuration/ ~하다 reduce to a common measure; commensurate / ~수 commensurate number.

**통양**(痛痒) pain and itch (영향) concern; interest/조금도 ~을 느끼지 않다 be quite indifferent to; do not matter at all to (*one*).

**통어**(統御) (통치) rule reign (제어) control (관리) management/ ~하다 rule; govern; control; manage; assume control of/학생을 잘 ~한다 have the students well in hand.

**통역**(通譯) interpreting; oral translation; interpretation (사람) an interpreter/ ~하다 interpret; translate orally/ ~관 a secretary interpreter; an [official] interpreter.

**통용**(通用) common[popular] use; circulation; currency/ ~ 하다 be in common use; be current; pass (차표 따위) be available/이 화폐는 어디서나 ~됩니다 This coin passes goes every where. / ~어 a current word[language].

**통운**(通運)¹ a good luck; the better fortune; a stroke of good luck; a break / ~하다 get lucky; come into luck; be in luck's way/대 ~ a splendid stroke of luck.

**통운**(通運)² transportation; forwarding; shipping; express/ ~하다 transport; forward; ship; carry; convey/ ~ 회사 a transport company; an express company.

**통유**(通有) commonness; a common trait / ~하다 be common (*to*); be a common characteristic (*of*)/ ~성 (성격)

a common trait **(물질)** common properties of matter. つうゆう

**통으로** wholly; all together; in the lump; in the gross/~ 삼키다 swallow (*a thing*) whole/~ 팔다 sell by the lump; sell wholesale. ぜんぶ

**통음**(痛飮) hard[heavy] drinking; a carousal/ ~하다 imbibe[drink] heavily; carouse; go on a binge. つういん

**통일**(統一) unity; unification; coordination; consolidation; uniformity; concentration **(표준화)** standardization **(통어)** rule/ ~하다 unify; consolidate; standardize/~이 없다 lack unity; be without coordination/나라를 ~하다 unify a nation; bring a country under a single authority/~성 unity/남북 ~ unification of North and South [Korea].
とういつ

**통일 천하**(統一天下) domination of the whole world; unification [of a country] /~하다 unify a country; bring the whole country under one's rule; domineer over the land.

**통짜다** ①**(맞추다)** put[fit, piece] together; frame; assemble ②**(동아리가 되다)** form a gang[group]/통짜고 음모하다 form a gang to plot/통짜고 남을 속이려 하다 conspire together to cheat (*a person*). くみたてる

**통짜로** all; wholly ⇨통째. かたまりで

**통장**(通帳) **(은행의)** a passbook; a bank-book **(외상거래의)** a chit-book/~에 치부하다 enter into a chit-book/저금 ~ a savings passbook/예금 ~ bankbook; a deposit passbook. つうちょう

**통장수**(桶—) ① a tub[pail] dealer; a cooper ② a peddler of pickled seafood carried in a tub. おけや

**통장이**(桶—) a hooper; a cooper.

**통장작**(—長斫) log firewood; unsplit firewood.

**통째** whole; all [together]/~로 구운 것 a barbecue/~로 먹다 eat (*something*) whole/닭을 ~로 먹다 eat up the whole chicken. ぜんぶのままで

**통절**(痛切) ~하다 (be) severe; keen; poignant/ ~히 keenly; severely; earnestly/ ~히 느끼다 feel keenly[vividly] /그 필요는 ~히 느껴졌다 The necessity was keenly felt. つうせつ

**통점**(痛點) a pain-spot. つうてん

**통정**(通情) ①having frank talk ②rapport ③adultery ④**(세상 인정)** the way of the world.

**통젖** the handles of a tub; the bail of a pail.

**통제**(統制) control; regulation; management/ ~하다 control; exercise control over; regulate; hold under control; regulate; govern/~를 해제하다 remove the control (*from*). とうせい

**통제부**(統制府) a naval station[yard]; an admiralty port.

**통조림**(桶—) canned goods; tinned provisions/ ~하다 can; tin. かんづめ

**통지**(通知) notice; notification; communication; report; information **(상업상의)** advice/ ~하다 notify (*a person*) of; inform; advise; let (*a person*) know/추후 ~가 있을 때까지 till further notice. つうち

**통지기** an adulterous female slave or servant; a housemaid of easy virtue.

**통찰**(洞察) penetration; insight; discernment/~하다 penetrate into; see through; discern/예언자는 미래를 ~한다 The prophet reads the future. どうさつ

**통처**(痛處) a pain-spot. ひどくいたむところ

**통천하**(通天下) ~하다 pervade[permeate] all over the world; reach every part of the world.

**통철**(通徹) penetration; interpenetration / ~하다 penetrate; pierce; interpenetrate. つうてつ

**통철**(洞徹) mastery ⇨통달. どうてつ

**통첩**(通牒) a note; a notification; a circular; an instruction/~하다 notify (*a person*) of; give notice to; communicate/ ~을 발하다 send[issue] a natification/최후 ~ an ultimatum. つうちょう

**통촉**(洞燭) seeing; judgment; discernment; [sympathetic] understanding/ ~하다 see; realize; understand; judge; discern. りょうさつ

**통치**(統治) rule; reign; government/ ~하다 rule over (*a country, a people*); hold sway over; administer/영국의 ~하에 있다 be under British rule/신탁 ~ trusteeship. とうち

**통치**(通治) ~하다 cure all kinds of diseases; be [medically] effective on a broad spectrum/만병 ~약 a cure-all; a panacea.

**통치마** a seamless one-piece skirt.

**통칙**(通則) **(원칙)** a principles; general rules[provisions]. つうそく

**통칭**(通稱) a popular name; an alias; a common designation. つうしょう

**통쾌**(痛快) a keen pleasure; a thrill/~하다 (be) most[awfully] pleasant; extremely delightful; incisive; merciless /~하게 느끼다 be highly delighted.
つうかい

**통탄**(痛歎) bitter lamentation; deep regret; bitter grief/ ~하다 lament bitterly; regret deeply; grieve; deplore/ ~할 deplorable; lamentable. つうたん

**통탕** **(총소리)** bang-bang **(구르는 소리)** with stamps; with repeated poundings/ 총소리가 ~거리다 a gun is [guns are] banging away. びしゃん

**통터지다** burst out; pour out; explode/ 울음이 ~ burst into tears; burst out crying. そそぎでる

**통통** stamping/~거리다 stamp/~ 걸음 a stamp/~거리며 계단을 오르다 stamp upstairs. まるまる

**통통하다** (be) plump; chubby; full; portly; corpulent／통통하게 살찐 여자 a plump woman／통통한 볼 chuddy cheeks.

**통틀다** take out all; empty completely／전 생애를 통틀어 throughout one's whole life.

**통팥** whole[unsplit] red beans.

**통폐(通弊)** a common abuse[evil]／이것들은 현대 사회의 ～다 These are evils common to all the classes in society.

**통풍(通風)** ventilation; airing／～하다 let air in; circulate air／～이 잘 되다 be well ventilated／～ 장치 the ventilation arrangement.

**통풍(痛風)** gout; arthritis／～에 걸리다 be afflicted with gout.

**통-(通一)** ⇨별항 참조(page 1786).

**통학(通學)** attending school／～하다 go to [attend] school／걸어서 ～하다 go to [attend] school on foot／～ 구역 a school district／～생 a day student; a day boy.

**통한(痛恨)** bitter grief[sorrow, woe]; deep regret; mortification／～하다 grieve bitterly; regret deeply／～지사 a matter of great regret.

**통할(統轄)** supervision; control／～하다 supervise; preside over; control／～ 구역 the area under the direct control／～자 one in charge; one who assumes control (of).

**통합(統合)** unity; unification; synthesis; combination; coordination／～하다 unify; unite; combine; coordinate／～적 synthetic; unified.

**통항(通航)** navigation; sailing; communication by sea／～하다 《항행》 navigate; sail 《내왕》 ply／이 강은 어디까지 배가 ～할 수 있습니까 How far is this river navigable?

**통행(通行)** passing; passage; transit; traffic／～하다 pass; go [through, along]／～을 방해하다 obstruct traffic; obstruct the passage／～ 금지 《게시》 "No thoroughfare"; suspension of traffic／～ 금지 시간 curfew hour.

**통혈(通穴)** a vent; a ventilation opening; a funnel 《광산의》 an air-shaft 《터널의》 an air-pit／～하다 open ventilation.

**통혼(通婚)** proposal of marriage; intermarriage／～하다 marry [with].

**통화(通貨)** currency; current coins; the medium of circulation／～의 팽창의 경향이 현저히 저지되었다 The inflational trend has been considerably checked.

**통화(通話)** conversation by telephone; a telephone call／～하다 talk over the telephone; speak by telephone (with)／～ 중입니다 The line is busy.／～ 수 the number of telephone calls.

**통효(通曉)** conversance; thorough knowledge／～하다 be conversant (with); be well acquainted with／그는 그 일에 ～했다 He has the business at his finger tips.

**퇴각(退却)** ①《후퇴》 retreat; withdrawal; retirement; falling back／～하다 retreat; beat[make] a retreat; withdraw; rctire; fall back; abandon; give up／평양으로 ～하다 retreat[fall back] on *Pyungyang* ②《거절》 rejection; refusal to accept／～하다 reject; refuse to accept／～ 명령 an order[a signal] to retreat.

**퇴거(退去)** leaving; quitting; withdrawal; evacuation; going away; exodus／～하다 leave; withdraw; evacuate; retire／～시키다 expel (*a person*) from.

**퇴경(退京)** leaving the capital／～하다 leave *Seoul*[the capital].

**퇴골(腿骨)** a leg bone; the thigh bone.

**퇴관(退官)** retirement from office[the government service]; resignation of one's post[commission]／～하다 retire from office[the government service]; resign.

**퇴교(退校)** leaving school; expulsion[dismissal] from school; withdrawal from school／～하다 leave[give up] school／～ 처분을 받다 be dismissed[expelled] from the school.

**퇴군(退軍)** retreat ⇨퇴각.

**퇴근(退勤)** leaving one's office[one's desk, one's work]; coming[going] home from work／～하다 leave the office／～ 시간 the closing hour; the close of the office hours.

**퇴기(退妓)** a retired *kisaeng*; an ex-*kisaeng*.

**퇴기다** ①flip; snap; fillip／옷의 먼지를 ～ flip a little dust from one's coat ②repel; reject; turn down; splash／기름종이가 물방울을 ～ oil paper repels water ③spring; let off ⇨튀기다.

**퇴락(頹落)** ruin; decay; dilapidation; downfall／～하다 dilapidate; go to ruin; fall into decay; decay; decline.

**퇴렴** heating up (*rice, noodles*) by pouring; hot water.

**퇴로(退路)** the [path of] retreat; a withdrawal route／～를 차단하다 cut off[intercept] the retreat.

**퇴물(退物)** ①《남은 음식》 a reception table after it has been removed; leftover food; leavings ②《써서 낡은》 a used thing; a retired person; a hand-me-down／그는 아버지의 ～을 입었다 He wore a hand-me-down from his father. ③《거절당한》 a reject; a thing rejected [refused, declined, sent back].

**퇴물림**(退—) a hand-me-down ⇒퇴물. さがりもの

**퇴박맞다** get rejected; be refused[repelled, rebuffed]; be sent back; be turned down/나의 면회 신청은 퇴박맞았다 My request for an interview was refused.

**퇴박하다** reject; decline; refuse; turn down.

**퇴보**(退步) retrogression; retrocession; retrogradation; a setback/ ~하다 go [fall] backward; retrograde; retrocede; be set back/병으로 쉬었더니 ~했다 My absence owing to illness has set me back. たいほ

**퇴비**(堆肥) a vegetable manure heap a compost. たいひ

**퇴사**(退社) ①(퇴직) retirement from a company/ ~하다 retire[withdraw] from a company; leave a company ② (퇴근) leaving the office [for the day] / ~하다 go home from[leave] the office. たいしゃ

**퇴산**(退散) dispersal/ ~하다 disperse 《해산》 break up/ ~시키다 disperse; break up/적을 ~시키다 put the enemy to flight. たいさん

**퇴색**(退色, 褪色) fading; discoloration; decolorization/ ~하다 get discolored; discolor; fade; lose color/ ~하지 않는 색 a fast[lasting, an unfading] color. たいしょく

**퇴석**(退席) leaving one's seat/ ~하다 leave one's seat; retire from. たいせき

**퇴석**(堆石) ① a pile of stones ②(지) moraine; an apron. たいせき

**퇴세**(頹勢) a decay; a decline; the downward tendency; a deteriorating situation/ ~를 만회하다 check one's decline; turn the tide of war. たいせい

**퇴속**(退俗) ~하다 retire from the Buddhist priesthood; return to the laity.

**퇴속**(頹俗) corrupt customs; degenerate morals; decadence. すたれたふうぞく

**퇴송**(退送) sending back/ ~하다 send back; reject; decline[refuse] to accept.

**퇴신**(退身) retirement; resignation/ ~하다 retire; resign; withdraw.

## 통 하 다

①**(길이)** run; be open for traffic; lead to/그 길은 숲 속으로 통한다 The road runs through the forest./모든 길은 로마로 통한다 All roads lead to Rome.

②**(뜻이)** make sense 《의사가》 enjoy understanding; understand [each other]; be congenial (to, with); 《언어가》 be understood; be spoken; be the medium of communication/이 글은 뜻이 통하지 않는다 This sentence doesn't make sense./서로 의사가 ~ understand each other's sentiments/사무실에는 그와 통하는 사람이 적었다 In the office he found few persons congenial to him./국민의 뜻이 고위층에 ~ the conditions of the people are appreciated by the government.

③**(혈액·공기가)** go[pass] through; be circulated/피가 잘 통하지 않는다 have a poor circulation of the blood/공기가 잘 ~ have good ventilation.

④**(전화가)** go through; be put through; (a line) be on; be on the line; (the phone) be working/전화가 통하지 않는다 the line[telephone service] is interrupted; a call fails to go[get] through/김씨에게 전화했으나 통하지 않았다 I could not get Mr. Kim on the telephone., I could not get through to Mr. Kim [by phone].

⑤**(통달하다)** be well versed (in); be an expert (in, on); be a master (of); be well informed (on); be familiar (with); be well acquainted (with); be conversant (with); be at home (in)/불어에 ~ be proficient in French; know one's French /오랫 동안 이곳에 있었기 때문에 나는 그 사정에 통한다 My long sojourn in this place familiarized me with its condition./천문에 ~ know a lot about astronomy.

⑥**(통용하다)** pass; hold good; be good; circulate; be valid/그 증명서는 이미 통하지 않는다 The certification is no longer valid.

⑦**(인정받다)** pass (for, as); be known (as); go by the name of /권위자로 ~ be acknowledged as an authority/S란 이름으로 ~ pass under the name of S; go by the name of S.

⑧**(내통하다)** communicate secretly with; betray/누구와 통하고 있다 be in secret communication with somebody /적과 비밀을 ~ betray a secret to the enemy; let the enemy in on a secret.

⑨**(정을)** become intimate with; share intimacy with; commit adultery with; form a liaison with; misconduct oneself with; have illicit intercourse with/그 여자는 누구와 정을 통했다 She had immoral relations with a someone.

⑩**(통과·경유하다)** pass through; get through; via/라디오를 통해서 via radio.

**퇴역(退役)** retirement from service; a [military] discharge／ ～하다 retire from service; be discharged from military service／～시키다 decommission／～연금 a retiring pension／～ 장교 a retired officer. たいえき

**퇴염(退染)** ①〖탈색〗 bleaching ②⇒토렴. せんしょくをあらうこと

**퇴영(退嬰)** retrogression; conservatism／～하다 retrograde; retrogress／～적인 conservative; retrogressive／～ 정책 a conservative policy／～주의 conservatism. たいえい

**퇴원(退院)** leaving the hospital 《감화원에서의》 discharge from a reformatory／그는 곧 ～할 것이다 He will soon be out of hospital. たいいん

**퇴위(退位)** abdication／～하다 abdicate [the throne]／～시키다 depose; dethrone.

**퇴은(退隱)** retirement; seclusion／～하다 retise (from); seclude oneself. たいいん

**퇴임(退任)** retirement from office; vacation (of an office)／～하다 retire from office; resign one's post. たいにん

**퇴짜(退―)** turning down; rejection; refusal; rebuff; a reject; a thing refused／～놓다 refuse; reject; turn down／～맞다 get rejected; be turned down.

**퇴장(退場)** leaving 《무대에서》 exit withdrawal／～하다 exit; make one's exit; go away; withdraw／아이들을 ～시키다 send the children out of the room. たいじょう

**퇴적(堆積)** accumulation; a heap; a pile／～하다 accumulate; be piled／책상에 보고서가 ～해 있었다 I found the table heaped with bulletins.／～물 a deposit. たいせき

**퇴정(退廷)** leaving the court／～하다 leave the royal court; leave the courtroom. たいてい

**퇴직(退職)** retirement; resignation／～하다 retire[withdraw] from office; go out of office; go on the retired list／그는 무능하다는 이유로 강제 ～당했다 He was compulsorily retired as incompetent.／～금 retirement grants[allowance, pay, emoluments]／～자 a retired employee／～ 연령 retirement age; age limits. たいしょく

**퇴진(退陣)** decampment; disengagement; withdrawal／～하다 break camp; break encampment／야당은 내각의 ～을 요구했다 the Opposition requested the Cabinet to resign en bloc. たいじん

**퇴청(退廳)** leaving office [for the day]／～하다 leave the office／～시간 the closing hour; closing time／～ 시간은 5시다 The office closes at five. たいちょう

**퇴치(退治)** 〖정벌〗 conquest; subjugation 《박멸》 wiping out; elimination; clean-up; extermination／ ～하다 conquer; subdue; subjugate／문맹 ～ a crusade against illiteracy／쥐를 ～하다 rid (a house) of rats. たいじ

**퇴침(退枕)** a wooden pillow.

**퇴폐(頹廢)** corruption; degeneration; decay; decline; decadence; deterioration／～하다 get corrupted; degenerate／도의의 ～ moral decadence; the corruption of morals. たいはい

**퇴하다(退―)** turn down; thrust[send] back; reject; spurn／뇌물을 ～ reject [spurn] the bribe. しりぞく

**퇴학(退學)** withdrawal from the school／～하다 leave school; give up school／～시키다 take a person out of school／병 때문에 나는 ～해야 했다 Because of illness I had to leave school. たいがく

**퇴혼(退婚)** a breach of promise of marriage／～하다 break off an engagement; break off one's marriage.

**퇴화(退化)** degeneration; retrogression; devolution／～하다 degenerate; retrograde／～시키다 degenerate／사용하지 않는 기관은 ～한다 An unused organ will atrophy. たいか

**퇴회(退會)** secession; withdrawal [from a party, association]; withdrawal from membership／ ～하다 withdraw (from); drop out; secede／～자 a seceder; a withdrawing[seceding] member. たいかい

**뒷마루** the floor of a Korean verandah.

**투(套)** ①〖법식〗 a [set] form; a style／편지～ the forms of letter writing; letter writing ②〖버릇〗 a way; a habitual way; a habit; a manner／말～ one's way of talking.

**투강(投江)** throwing (a thing, oneself) into a river／～하다 throw (a thing, oneself) into a river.

**투견(鬪犬)** a dogfight; a fighting dog. とうけん

**투계(鬪鷄)** a fighting cock; a gamecock; a gamefowl; cockfighting; a cockfight／～하다 have[stage] a cockfight／～장 a cockpit; a pit. とうけい

**투고(投稿)** a contribution／～하다 contribute (to); write (for)／그는 자주 이 잡지에 ～한다 He is a frequent contributor to this magazine.／～란 the readers' column／ ～자 a contributor. とうこう

**투광기(投光器)** a light projector; a footlight; a floodlight. とうこうき

**투구** a helmet; a headpiece／ ～를 쓰다 wear a helmet／～끈 a helmet cord. かぶと

**투구(投球)** throwing a ball; pitching／～하다 throw a ball; pitch.

**투구풍뎅이** 〖충〗 a beetle; Allomyrina dichotomus (학명).

**투그리다** snarl ready to fight.

**투기(妬忌)** jealousy; envy; jaundice; heartburnings／ ～하다 be jealous; feel envy; regard with jealousy; be green with envy/ ~에 눈이 뒤집혀 in a fit of jealous rage; blinded by jealousy. ねたみきらうこと

**투기(投機)** a venture; speculation; adventure/ ~하다 gamble; speculate (on)/ ~에 손을 대다 dabble in speculation/ ~적으로 사다 buy on spec/ ~ 사업 a speculative business. とうき

**투기(投棄)** abandonment; casting away; throwing out/ ~하다 cast[fling] away; throw out[away]; abandon. とうき

**투기(鬪技)** a contest; a match; a competition/ ~장 an arena; a ring. とうぎ

**투덕거리다** pat; tap; beat lightly. とんとんとたたく

**투덜거리다** grumble; complain; nag; mutter[mumble] (something) to oneself/ 대우에 대해 ~ complain of one's treatment. ふへいをならす

**투망(投網)** a casting-net; a cast-net/ ~을 던지다 cast a net; throw a cast-net. なげあみ

**투매(投賣)** a bargain sale; a sacrifice sale; dumping; a slaughter sale/ ~하다 dump; sell (goods) at a sacrifice [loss]/ ~ 상품 distress merchandise. なげうり

**투명(透明)** limpidness; transparency; clearness; clarity; pellucidity/ ~하다 (be) transparent; limpid; clear/무색 ~한 colorless and transparent/ ~체 a transparent body. とうめい

**투묘(投錨)** anchoring; mooring; anchorage/ ~하다 anchor; moor; cast[drop, let fall] anchor/ ~지 an anchorage [ground]. とうびょう

**투미하다** stupid; stolid; silly; (be) dull; heavy[thick]-headed. ぼんやりしている

**투박하다** (be) crude; coarse; uncouth; ungainly; unshapely/투박한 옷감 thick coarse fabric; muslin; gunny.

**투병(鬪病)** struggle against a disease/ ~ 생활 10년 ten years' struggle against a disease; life under medical treatment for ten years.

**투사(投射)** 《수》 projection; projecting; 《물》 incidence/ ~하다 project (on)/ ~각 an angle of incidence/ ~선 an incident ray. とうしゃ

**투사(鬪士)** a fighter; a combatant; a champion/자유의 ~ a fighter for freedom/그는 ~형의 얼굴이다 He is a man of the athletic type. とうし

**투사(透寫)** tracing/~하다 trace (a writing, drawing); make a tracing/ ~지 tracing paper. とうしゃ

**투상스럽다** (be) uncouth ⇨ 몹상스럽다.

**투서(投書)** ① an anonymous note[notice]; an anonymous communication[letter]/ ~하다 send (a note) anonymously ②(투고) contribution; correspondence/~하다 contribute (an article to); write a letter to. とうしょ

**투석(投石)** stone-throwing[-hurling]/ ~하다 throw[cast, hurl] a stone (at).

**-투성이** covered[smeared] with; full of; filled with/너의 옷이 흙~다 Your clothes are bespattered [all over] with mud. —まみれ

**투수(投手)** 《야구의》 a pitcher; a hurler; a twirler; a moundman (크리켓의》 a bowler/그는 ~로서 잘 싸웠다 He did well on the box./ ~전 a pitching duel/왼손잡이 ~ a southpaw. とうしゅ

**투숙(投宿)** staying[stopping] at (a hotel)/ ~하다 stay[stop] at (a hotel); lodge (in)/ ~자 a guest; a lodger. とうしゅく

**투시(透視)** ①《뚫어봄》 seeing; through ②《알아차림》 second sight; clairvoyance/ ~하다 see through; divine; sense; see/ ~화 perspective drawing/ ~화법 perspective. とうし

**투신(投身)** ①《자살》 suicide by drowning; death by drowning/~하다 drown oneself (in a river)/그녀는 ~ 자살했다 She drowned herself in the river. ②《종사》 ~하다 be engaged (in); attend to; carry on. とうしん

**투실투실** chubby ⇨ 토실토실. まるまる

**투심(妬心)** envy; jealously. ねたむこころ

**투안(偸安)** snatching a moment of ease / ~하다 dicker for time. とうあん

**투약(投藥)** medication; dosage; administration [of medicine]; [medical] prescription/ ~하다 prescribe medicine; medicate/환자에게 ~하다 prescribe for a patient; dose a patient. とうやく

**투어(套語)** a cliche; an old-cliche; a hackneyed expression[phrase]. とうご

**투열(透熱)** 《물》 diathermancy/ ~계 a diathermometer/ ~ 요법 diathermic treatment; diathermy.

**투영(投影)** ①《그림자》 a cast shadow/ ~ 하다 reflect; cast a reflection; throw an image on ②《수》 projection/~하다 project/ ~도 a projection chart. とうえい

**투옥(投獄)** imprisonment; confinement / ~하다 cast (a person) into prison; imprison; throw (a person) into prison/ ~당하다 be sent[taken] to jail. とうごく

**투우(鬪牛)** a fighting bull; a bullfight / ~하다 fight a bull; have a bullfight / ~사 a bullfighter; a matador; a toreador. とうぎゅう

**투원반(投圓盤)** the discus throw; discus throwing.

**투입(投入)** throwing[putting] in; put in; investment; 《심》 introjection/ ~하다 throw[put] (a thing) in; invest/ ~ 자본 investment. とうにゅう

**투자(投資)** investment/ ~하다 invest (in); put[sink] (money) in; lay out (one's money)/광산에 ~하다 invest in a mine/ ~액 an amount invested. とうし

**투쟁(鬪爭)** fighting; a fight; a combat; a struggle; a conflict; strife; a campaign/ ~하다 fight; combat; struggle;

**투**(鬪)strive (with)/~ 위원회 a struggle committee. とうそう
**투전**(投錢) a kind of money-throwing [coin-tossing] game. とうせん
**투전**(鬪牋) a game of cards; gambling card; Korean playing cards/ ~하다 play cards; gamble with cards/ ~군 a card player; a gambler.
**투정** grumbling; growling/ ~하다 grumble (for); growl; fret; be peevish/나의 동생은 밥먹을 때 ~한다 My brother grumbles over his food./잠~ growling when one wakes up. ねだること
**투조**(透彫) open work (in sculpture). すかしぼり
**투지**(鬪志) a fighting spirit/~ 만만하다 be full of a fighting spirit/~에 불타다 burn with combativeness. とうし
**투창**(投槍) a dart; javelin throw[ing]/ ~하다 throw the javelin/~ 선수 a javelin thrower. やりなげ
**투척**(投擲) throwing; a throw/~하다 throw/~ 경기 throwing event; weight throwing; shot-putting. とうてき
**투철**(透徹) penetration; thoroughness; clearness; transparency/ ~하다 (be) penetrating; lucid; clear; pure; thorough/ ~한 두뇌 clear brains. とうてつ
**투포수**(投捕手) the battery; the pitcher and catcher.
**투포환**(投砲丸) the shot-put/ ~하다 put the shot/ ~ 선수 a shot-putter.
**투표**(投票) (채결) vote; suffrage (투표하기)poll; ballot (표찰)a vote (무기명의)a ballot/~로 결정하다 decide[settle] by vote/~권 voting right/ ~ 용지 ballot paper. とうひょ
**투하**(投下) (아래로) throwing down; dropping/~하다 throw down; drop; airdrop/역에 폭탄을 ~하다 drop[release] bombs upon a station/~탄 a dropped bomb. とうか
**투하**(投荷) jettison; jetsam/ ~하다 jettison. なげに
**투함**(投函) mailing; posting/~하다 mail (a letter); post (a letter); drop (a letter) into the letter box. とうかん
**투항**(投降) surrender (투항 조건) capitulation/ ~하다 surrender; capitulate; give up[lay down] one's arms/ ~자 a surrenderer/ ~ 조약 a treaty of surrender[capitulation]. とうこう
**툭** ①(소리) with a bang[thud, pop]; with a pat[rap, snap]··탁, 톡 ②(모양) protrudingly⇒툭. ぶくり
**툭수리차다** be reduced to beggary; be brought to begging.
**툭탁** with a tap[rap]; rat-tat/ ~하다 beat each other; fight each other/ ~거리기 시작하다 come to blow; take to one's fists. とんとん
**툭툭** with bangs[pats, snaps]; protrudingly.
**툭툭하다** ①(국물이) (be) thick; rich; heavy ②(천이) (be) thick; close; closewoven.
**툭하면** at the slightest provocation; at the drop of a hat; without any reason; de apt to; be ready to/그녀는 ~ 운다 She is apt[liable] to cry. ややもすれば
**툴툴거리다** growl; complain; grumble; mutter/봉급이 적다고 ~ complain about the salary; complain that one is not paid well. ふへいをならす
**툼벙** with a plump ⇒텀벙. どぶん
**툽상스럽다** uncouth; vulgar; (be) clumsy; boorish; crude; coarse/툽상스럽게 대답하다 answer bluntly[brusquely].
**툽툽하다** thick and heavy. にごっている
**퉁** ①(소리) with a boom; booming/~ 울리다 boom a drum; beat a drum ②(저질의 놋쇠) brass of inferior quality. どん
**퉁겨지다** come apart··퉁겨지다. みつかる
**퉁기다** ①(받친 것을) spring; snap; slip/기둥받침을 ~ slip a pillar stay ②(뼈를) put out of joint; dislocate ③(기회를) miss[lose, fling away] chance; let a chance slip. はじけさせる
**퉁명스럽다** (be) abrupt; brusque; curt; blunt; unaffable/퉁명스럽게 curtly; brusquely; bluntly/퉁명스러운 대답 a blunt answer/~ 퉁명스럽게 말하다 talk bluntly; speak stiffly. ぶっきらぼうに
**퉁방울** (방울) a brass bell.
**퉁방울이** a pop-eyed[goggle-eyed] person; a popeye/~ 금붕어 a pop-eyed goldfish.
**퉁소** a bamboo flute.
**퉁어리적다** (무분별) (be) indiscreet; senseless; impudent; thoughtless (경솔) rash. むふんべつだ
**퉁탕** beating; pounding; pattering; stamping; with a bang. どんどん
**퉁탕거리다** keep beating[pounding, pattering]/어린애가 퉁탕거리며 마루 위를 돌아다닌다 A child is scampering around on the floor.
**퉁퉁** with a stamp; stamping. まるまる
**퉁퉁걸음** a stamp; walking with pounding[quick] steps. いそぎあし
**퉁퉁하다** (be) plump ⇒통통하다.
**튀각** fried tangle flake of kelp oiled and toasted.
**튀기다**¹ ①(물 따위를) send (a thing) flying; send (a thing) off; splash; spatter; dabble/손가락으로 물을 ~ splash the water with one's finger ②flip; fillip; snap; jerk. はじく
**튀기다**² (기름에) fry; pop/기름에 생선을 ~ fry fish in oil. あげる
**튀다** ①(오르다) spring; bound; jump; hop; rebound; leap; bounce; sputter; splash; splatter/흙물이 ~ muddy water splashes ②(달아나다) run away; fly [away]; flee; take to flight/사슴이 튀었다 a deer ran away. はねる

**튀어나다** bound; bounce off; rebound; resile; recoil; spring back/공이 잘 튀어난다 The rubber ball bounds well. とびでる

**튀하다** scald/닭을 튀하서 털을 뽑다 scald a chicken and remove the feather. ゆかく

**트기** ①(사람) a half-breed; a half-blood; a cross; a crossbreed/백인과 흑인의 ~ a mulatto/백인과 황색인과의 ~ a Eurasian ②(동물) a hybrid [between a male donkey and a cow]. あいのこ

**트다**¹ ①(싹이) sprout; bud out; spring [come] up; peep from the ground/싹이 ~ come into bud; bud out ②(피부가) crack; open up; be[get] chapped/손이 ~ one's hands get chapped ③(먼동이) break open; dawn; grow light; turn gray; (the east) break/동이 ~ It dawns., The day breaks. はつめいする

**트다**² (길하다) open; clear the way; make way (for another)/성공의 길이 ~ pave way for success. ひらく

**트더지다** be unsewn; be rent; be ripped/봉투가 ~ an envelope gets ripped/옷이 ~ one's clothes are unsewn.

**트레머리** a chignon; hairdo in coil/ ~하다 wear a chignon; do one's hair into a chignon.

**트레트레** round and round; in coils; in spirals/ ~하다 warped; twisted; whirled; be in coils[spirals]. くるくる

**트림** belching; eructation; a belch; a burp/ ~하다 belch; burp; eruct. げっぷ

**트릿하다** ①(가슴·배가) (be) dyspeptic; have an indigestion; feel heavy on the stomach/속이 ~ feel helchy ②(흐릿하다) (be) shady; underhand; indistinct/트릿한 사나이 a fellow of shady character. いがもたれる

**트이다** ①(길·장래가) get cleared; be opened; open; spread [out]/터널이 ~ a tunnel is opened ②(생각이) be liberal [openhearted]; become sensible/트인 사람 a sensible person; a man of the world ③(운이) become better/운이 트이는 것을 바라고 살다 live in hopes of better fortune ④(구멍이) be pierced with a hole; a hole is made.

**트적지근하다** be[feel] uncomfortable in the stomach; (be) belchy/너무 먹어서 속이 ~ I have eaten too much and feel uncomfortable in the stomach.
いがもたれてうっとうしい

**트집** ①(틈) a split; a gap; an opening; a difference; a crack; a trouble/찻잔에 ~이 생겼다 The teacup cracked ②(결점) a fault (말썽) roublet a blemish. さけめ

**트집나다** have a split; have a hitch; get cracked.

**트집잡다** find fault with pick flaws with/그들은 무엇이든 트집잡아 싸움을 건다 They will pick a quarrel with you on some pretext or other. けちをつける

**트집장이** a faultfinder; a nagger; a nit-picker. けちばかりつけるひと

**특가**(特價) a special price[offer]; a bargain price; a specially reduced price/ ~ 제공 a special offer. とっか

**특공**(特功) special merit; a great achievement; distinguished service. とっこう

**특과**(特科) a special course; 《군》 an arm of the army other than infantry/ ~병 a technical soldier/ ~생 a student of a special course. とっか

**특권**(特權) special rights; a privilege; a prerogative/ ~ 계급 the privileged classes/ ~을 행사하다 exercise the privilege[prerogative] (of)/ ~ 침해 breach of privilege. とっけん

**특근**(特勤) working overtime; special service; special duty; extra work/ ~하다 do extra work; work overtime/ ~ 수당 overtime allowance.

**특급**(特急) a limited[special] express/ ~을 타다 take a limited express. とっきゅう

**특급**(特給) special distribution/ ~하다 distribute specially. とっきゅう

**특기**(特技) special ability; one's special art; speciality. とくぎ

**특대**(特待) special treatment/ ~하다 treat specially; give a special treatment/ ~생 a scholarship student/ ~생이 되다 get[gain] a scholarship. とくたい

**특대**(特大) extra-large; outsized; king-sized/ ~호 잡지 an enlarged special edition.

**특등**(特等) special class[grade]; top[premium] grade/ ~석 a special[reserved] seat/ ~실 a special class room. とくとう

**특례**(特例) (특별한 예) a special case[example]; (예외) an exception; a particular instance[case]/ ~를 만들다 make an exception. とくれい

**특매**(特賣) a special[bargain] sale; a sale at a special price/ ~하다 sell at a special price; offer as a bargain. とくばい

**특면**(特免) a special pardon; a free pardon; dispensation; special exemption/ ~하다 exempt specially; give a special pardon; dispense. とくめん

**특명**(特命) special command[order]; special appointment/ ~하다 order[appoint] specially/ ~을 띠고 on a special mission. とくめい

**특무**(特務) special duty[service]/ ~기관 the Special Service Agency; the secret military agency/ ~병 a special service man. とくむ

**특배**(特配) special distribution; a bonus; special delivery/ ~하다 distribute[ration] exceptionally[specially].

**특별**(特別) 《특수》 speciality 《예외》 exception; beings pecial/~하다 (be) special; extraordinary; especial; peculiar; exceptional; extra; uncommon/ ~히 주의하다 pay special attention (to)/그 사람만은 ~이다 He is an exception[a special case]/~ 급행 a special[limited] express; a super express/~석 a reserved[special] seat. とくべつ

**특보**(特報) a flash; special news; a special report/ ~하다 flash; give a special report (on)/뉴우스 ~ news flash/전과를 ~하다 flash the military achievements. とくほう

**특사**(特赦) (일반)amnesty (개인)a special pardon; a free pardon; dispensation; an act of grace/~하다 give as a special grant; grant specially/~에 의해 출국하다 be released from prison on a general amnesty. とくしゃ

**특사**(特使) a special envoy[messenger]; an ambassador at large/대통령의 ~ a presidential personal envoy/~를 파견하다 dispatch a special envoy. とくし

**특사**(特賜) a special grant (from King)/ ~하다 give as a special grant; grant specially.

**특산물**(特産物) a special product; an indigenous product; a local speciality /인삼은 개성의 ~이다 Ginseng is a speciality of *Kaesung*. とくさんぶつ

**특상**(特上) ~의 the finest; the best; the choicest/~품 an extra fine brand; choice goods[articles].

**특상**(特賞) a special prize; a special reward. とくしょう

**특색**(特色) a characteristic; a distinction; a specific character; a [specific] feature; a color/이것이 현대의 ~이다 This is a unique feature of our time. とくしょく

**특선**(特選) special selection[choice, approval/~이 되다 be specially selected / ~품 choice goods. とくせん

**특설**(特設) special establishment[installation, accommodation]/~하다 set up [establish, organize] specially/~ 전화 a specially installed telephone; an unlisted telephone. とくせつ

**특성**(特性) a special[distinctive] quality; a characteristic; a peculiarity; a property; an individuality; a feature/인간의 ~ a characteristic man. とくせい

**특수**(特秀) excellence; superiority; preeminence; prominence/~하다 (be) prominent; striking; outstanding; distinguished.

**특수**(特殊) speciality; peculiarity; characteristic; particularity/~하다 (be) special; specific; particular; distinct; unique/ ~한 예 a special example/~ 학급 a special class.

**특약**(特約) a special contract; a special agreement[arrangement]; contract specially/ ~점 a special agent; an agency. とくやく

**특용**(特用) special use/~하다 use specially; have the special use of. とくよう

**특우**(特遇) special treatment[courtesy] / ~하다 give special treatment; treat (*a person*) with distinction. とくたい

**특유**(特有) special quality/ ~하다 (be) peculiar; characteristic (*of*); proper; specific; particular/한국 ~의 풍습 a custom peculiar to Korea/ ~성 peculiarity. とくゆう

**특이**(特異) ~하다 (be) peculiar; particular; special; unique; unusual;singular /그녀는 ~한 복장을 하고 있었다 She was dressed in singular fashion. とくい

**특작**(特作) a special production[make] /~품 a feature (*film*); 《영화의》 a special film.

**특장**(特長) a strong point; a special feature; a forte; a merit. とくちょう

**특전**(特典) a privilege; a special favor; an advantage/세금 면제의 ~ the privilege of exemption from taxation/ ~을 취소하다 revoke the privilege (*of*). とくてん

**특전**(特電) a special telegram[dispatch] /로이타 ~ Reuter's special [service]. とくでん

**특점**(特點) a distinctive[distinguishing, characteristic] mark; a characteristic; a special feature; peculiarity. とくてん

**특정**(特定) specification/ ~하다 specify / ~의 specially fixed; specified; specific/~ 계약 a specified contract/ ~ 상속인 a singular successor/~ 자본 special capital. とくてい

**특제**(特製) special make[manufacture]/ ~하다 make[manufacture] specially/ ~의 specially-made; of special make; specially bound/ ~품 a specially-made article. とくせい

**특종**(特種) ①《종류》 a special kind ②《기사》 a scoop; a news beat; exclusive news/ ~을 싣다 publish the exclusive news; scoop. とくしゅ

**특지**(特旨) special consideration[order, grace]; a special Royal order. とくし

**특지**(特志) ①《뜻》 special intention; special interest ②《사람》 a volunteer; a person interested. とくべつのこころざし

**특진**(特進) a special promotion of rank / 2 계급 ~ a double promotion of rank. とくしん

**특질**(特質) a property; a characteristic; a special quality 《특성》 a specific character. とくしつ

**특집**(特輯) a special edition/~하다 prepare as a special edition; make up a special edition/뉴우스 ~ a special news program/~ 기사 feature articles.

**특징**(特徵) a special[distinctive] feature; a distinguishing mark; a characteristic; a stamp 《인상의》 identifying marks

**특징** 《개인의》 individuality 《생물의》 diagnosis／～있는 얼굴 a face with a noticeable feature／그는 어딘가 ～이 있다 There is something about him which distinguishes him from others. とくちょう

**특청(特請)** a special request／～하다 request specially; make special request. とくべつにねがうこと

**특출(特出)** distinction; prominence; preeminence／～하다 stand out; find prominence; attain distinction; prominent; superior; especially outstanding. とくしゅつ

**특칭(特稱)** special designation; a special name;《논》a particular／～하다 give a special name (to); particularize／～명제 a particular proposition. とくしょう

**특파(特派)** special assignment; dispatch／～하다 dispatch specially; send on special assignment／～대사 an ambassador extraordinary／～원 a special correspondent. とくは

**특품(特品)** premium goods; an article of special quality; an extra fine brand.

**특필(特筆)** special writing; a special article; special mention; a feature／～하다 write[mention] specially; feature; give prominence (to)／대서 ～하다 write in golden letters. とくひつ

**특허(特許)** ① special permission; a license; a permit ② charter ③《전매》patent／～하다 give a special permission for; charter; patent／～를 얻다 get a patent[special permit]／～국 a Patent Bureau／～권 a patent right; the right to patent／～ 소유자 a patentee／～품 a patented article. とっきょ

**특혜(特惠)** a special favor[benefit]; a privilege／～를 받다 receive preferential treatment／～ 관세 preferential tariff[duties]. とっけい

**특효(特效)** special efficacy[virtue, power]／～약 a special remedy; a specific [medicine]. とっこう

**특히(特一)** expressly; specially; especially; particularly; in particular; in special measure／～ 주의하다 pay special attention／오늘 아침은 ～ 춥다 It is especially cold this morning. とくに

**튼튼하다** compact; firm; (be) solid; strong; sturdy; healthy; hardy／몸이 ～ have a strong body. じょうぶだ

**틀** ①《테》a frame; framework ②《모형》a mold; a matrix／～에 넣고 붓다 cast into a mold ③《공식》formality ④《기계》a machine; a device; a gadget ⑤《도량》caliber; capacity; degree of ability《풍모》presence; stateliness／그 애는 장군~이다 The child has the dignified presence of a future general.／재봉~ a sewing machine. かた

**거지** dignity; stateliness; an imposing manner[attitude]／～가 없다 lack dignity.

**틀누비** machine-quilting; quilting by a sewing machine.

**틀다** ①《돌리다》turn; twist; distort; wring／핸들을 오른쪽으로 ～ turn a handle to the right／나사못을 ～ turn a screw／고동을 ～ turn a cock／라디오를 ～ turn on a radio ②《일을》oppose; cause to be reversed ③《솜을》whip／튼 솜 whipped cotton／솜을 ～ whip[willow] cotton. ねじる

**틀리다** ①《잘못되다》go wrong[amiss, awry]; become wrong／틀린 생각 a wrong opinion／맞춤법이 ～ the spelling is wrong; be misspeled／틀리지 않고 하다 go through without stumbling／당신 생각이 틀렸네 You are wrong[in error]．／그에 대한 자네의 생각은 틀렸네 You are mistaken about him.／일기 예보가 또 틀렸다 The weather forecast was wrong again. ②《꼬이다》get[be] turned[wound]; get[be] distorted／넥타이가 ～ one's tie gets twisted.

**틀림** ①《잘못》an error; being wrong; a mistake; a fault; slip／내 기억에 ～이 없다면 if I remember right[ly][correctly]／～없이 비가 온다 It is sure to rain.／계산에 ～ 있다 There is mistaken in the calculation[bill]／그녀는 ～이 없다 She is quite a reliable person.／그의 말은 ～없다 What he says is right.／《다름·》being not the same; being different／～없도록 to make sure [of it]; for caution's sake／당신 말하는 사람이 내 친구임에 ～이 없다 The man that you are talking about is none other than my friend., There is no doubt about it, the man that you are talking about must be my friend.／값에는 ～이 없으나 질에는 틀림이 있다 There is not any difference in the quality. まちがい

**틀어넣다** push[thrust] (in); squeeze (into); stuff[crowd, jam, tuck] (a thing) into／가방에 책을 ～ pack books into one's bag. ねじいれる

**틀어막다** ①《구멍을》fill; plug; stuff; stop [up]／쥐구멍을 ～ stop up a rathole ②《행동·말을》curb; put a stop to; restrain; contain／입을 ～ put a gag on; gag; bind (a person) to secrecy. つめこむ

**틀어박다** cram; stuff; fill; pack (in); charge; plug. おしこむ

**틀어박히다** confine oneself to; be isolated [from society]／집에 ～ hold up at home／방에만 틀어박혀 있지 말고 산책이라도 해라 You shut yourself up in your room too much, go for a walk. おしこまれる

**틀어지다** ①《빗나가다》sheer; turn aside; deviate; go astray; swerve／이야기가 옆으로 ～ wander from the subject ②《꼬이다》kink; go[be] awry; be distorted; get[be] twisted／넥타이가 틀어져 있다 have one's tie twisted ③《사이가》be [become] estranged from; fall out with; be alienated from/저 두 형제는 요즈음 사이가 틀어졌다 The two brothers have lately become estranged. ④《일이》 go wrong; break down; end in failure/교섭이 ~ negotiations break down/일이 ~ a plan goes wrong[is a fiasco, fails]/계약이 ~ a contract goes wrong[doesn't work out the way it should]/그것 때문에 예정이 틀어졌다 That upset the arrangement. /만사가 모두 틀어졌다 Everything went athwart [awary]. くいちがう

틈 ①《벌어진 사이》 a crack; a gap; an opening; a rift; a chink/~이 나다 be cracked/구름의 ~ 사이로 through a rift in the clouds ②《겨를》 spare[leisure] time; time to spare; leisure/ ~이 없다 have no time; be busy; be pressed for time/오후에는 ~이 좀 있읍니다 I have some leisure from my work in the afternoon. /~보아 놀러 오시오 Come and visit when you see your way clear. /그는 ~있는 대로 공부를 한다 He spends every free moment studying ③《간격》 room; spare; time/빈~ 없이 들어차다 be packed full; be filled to capacity ④《기회》 an opportunity; a chance/ ~을 타다 make the most of a chance/그녀는 ~을 타서 문 있는 쪽으로 도망했다 She saw her opportunity and made for the door ⑤《불화》 friction; estrangement; alienation/둘 사이에 ~이 생기다 grow friction between the two.
すきま

틈바구니 a crack ⇨틈. すきま
틈새기 gap; narrow space.
ひじょうにせまいすきま
틈서리 the edge of an opening[gap, crevice]. すまえ

틈입(闖入) intrusion; forced entry; trespass; inroad/~하다 trespass on; intrude into; force into; rush in; burst into/~자 an intruder; a trespasser.
틈틈이 ①《틈마다》 at each gap; in every opening ②《기회마다》 at each moment of leisure; at odd moments; in *one's* spare moments/~ 돼지를 기르다 raise pigs in *one's* spare moments.
티¹ 《먼지》 a mote; dust; a grit; a particle; a foreign element/눈에 ~가 들다 have a mote in *one's* eye. ちり
티² 《결점》 a flaw; a speck; a spot; a defect; a blemish/옥에 ~ a fly in the ointment; a flaw in a gem.
티³ 《모양》 manner; way; a style[touch, smack, an air] (*of*)/부자 ~를 내다 give *one*self the air of a millionaire; act the lord/군인 ~가 나는 soldierly/시골 ~가 나다 have a bit of the country about *one*; be countryfied; have hayseed in *one's* hair/그는 학자 ~가 있다 He has something of a scholar about him. もよう
티격나다 break up with; fall out with; split; quarrel with.
티끌 dust; a mote/~ 모아 태산이다 《속담》 Many a mickle makes a mickle. /~을 털다 shake off the dust. ほこり
티눈 a corn/발에 ~이 박히다 have a corn on the sole of *one's* foot/ ~약 a corn plaster.
티뜯다 ①《흠을 찾다》 find fault with; pick a hole[flaw] in; pick on; nag/글을 ~ pick a hole in what *one* has written ②《티를 뜯다》 scrape off dirt; clean.
あらをさがす
티보다 pick on ⇨티뜯다. あらさがしする
티티새 〖조〗 a dusky thrush; *Turdus fuscada*(학명).

**파** 〖식〗 a stone-leek; a Welsh onion; *Allium fistulosum*(학명). ねぎ

**파(派)** 〖학파·유파〗 a school 《당》 a party 《당파》 a faction 《분파》 a group 《종파》 a sect／두 ~로 갈라지다 be divided into two parties[factions]. は

**파(破)** ①〖물건의〗 damage; breakage／~나다 break; spoil; mar ②〖사람의〗 a defect; a weak point; a fault. は

**파격(破格)** an exception; 〖언〗 a solecism／~의 special; unprecedented; exceptional 《변칙의》 broken／ ~적 special; a flaw; exceptional; unexampled; unprecedented; abnormal 《변칙의》irregular. はかく

**파견(派遣)** dispatch／~하다 dispatch; send／~대 a detachment; a contingent／ ~군 an expeditionary army. はけん

**파경(破鏡)** ①〖거울〗 a broken mirror ②〖달〗 a half moon; a crescent[new] moon ③〖이혼〗 divorce. はきょう

**파계(破戒)** transgression[violation] of a commandment; apostasy／~하다 break [violate] commandment／ ~승(僧) an apostate; a sinful priest. はかい

**파고(波高)** the height of the wave.

**파곡(波谷)** the trough of the sea.

**파과(破瓜)** puberty／~기(期) age of[arrival at] puberty. はか

**파괴(破壞)** destruction; demolition／~하다 destroy; wreck; demolish; be broken (*down*)／~적 destructive／ ~주의자 a destructionist／ ~행위(분자) subversive activities[elements]. はかい

**파구(波丘)** the crest of the wave; the ridge of a wave. なみのいただき

**파국(破局)** ①〖약국〗 ~하다 shut up *one's* drug-store ②〖판국의〗 catastrophe; cataclysm. はきょく

**파근하다** feel languid; feel heavy; (be) soft; lithe; flexible.

**파급(波及)** spreading; extending／~하다 spread; extend 〖영향〗 influence; affect／전국에 ~하다 extend all over the country. きゅう

**파기(破棄)** ~하다 destroy; repudiate abrogate; breach 《계약 동의》 annul 《판결 동의》 reverse. はき

**파김치** ①〖김치〗 stone-leek pickles ②〖느른해짐〗 ~가 되다 be exhausted; get dead tired; be ready to drop.

**파나다(破—)** get broken[cracked, damaged]; become defective; have a flaw／파난 물건 a broken[damaged] article; defective goods. こわれる

**파내다** dig out; unearth. ほじくりだす

**파니** idly; lazily. ぶらぶら

**파다** ①〖땅·구멍을〗 dig (*a hole*); drive (*a tunnel*); 〖뚫다〗 excavate; sink〖우물을〗; cave (*a rock*)〖바위를〗; 〖동물이〗 burrow ②〖문제 따위를〗 probe (*a matter*) to the bottom; investigate ③〖새기다〗 engrave; carve(*in, on*); cut (*a seal*). ほる

**파다하다(播多—)** (be) wide-spread; widely rumored. ひろくひろまっている

**파다하다(頗多—)** (be) numerous; abundant; have a good many. おびただしい

**파닥거리다** (ᆞᆞᆞ가) flap the wings; flutter; beat the air ②〖물고기가〗 leap; splash; beat the water／파닥파닥 splashing; leaping. はたはたする

**파도(波濤)** surges; waves 《큰 물결》 a billow 《밀려오는》 a surf／~ 소리 the sound[roar] of the waves／~가 높다 have a rough sea; the sea runs high. はとう

**파동(波動)** a wave [motion]; fluctuation; [an] undulation／~하다 wave; fluctuate; undulate／~설 the wave theory／정치 ~ political upheaval. はどう

**파두(巴豆)** a croton [plant]. はず

**파뜩** in a flash／~하다 flash. はっと

**파라문(婆羅門)** 〖승족〗 Brahmana 《승려》 a Brahman; a Brahmin／~교 Brahmanism. ばらもん

**파라밀다(婆羅蜜多)** *Paramita*(Sans); entrance into *Nirvana*. はらみった

**파란** 《법랑》 enamel／~을 입히다 enamel; cover with enamel. ほうろう

**파란(波瀾)** ①〖파도〗 waves ②〖분요(紛擾)〗 troubles; disturbance; storm 〖성쇠〗 ups and downs. はらん

**파랑** blue 〖초록〗 green／ ~새 the "Blue Bird" 《행복》 happiness. あおいろ

**파랑(波浪)** waves; a billow. はろう

**파랗다** 〖초록〗 (be) blue; green 《창백하다》 pale; pallid; white／파랗게 칠하다〖물들이다〗 paint[dye] blue／파란 하늘 a blue sky／파랗게 질렸다 turned pale [in the face]. あおい

**파래** a green laver; a sea lettuce. あおさ

**파래박** gourd-shell used for scooping water out of a boat.

**파래지다** become green[blue, pale];《안색이》go white. あおくなる

**파렴치(破廉恥)** shamelessness; infamy／～하다 (be) shameless; infamous／～한(漢) a shameless dog. はれんち

**파르르** ①《떠는 모양》shiveringly／～ 떨다 tremble ②《끓는 모양》hissing; sizzling／～ 끓다 be hissing hot ③《화내는 모양》simmering／～ 화를 내다 simmer. ぷりぷり

**파르스름하다** (be) bluish; greeny; somewhat blue; greenish.

**파릇파릇** ～하다 (be) freshly green; vardant; fresh and green.

**파리** 【충】a fly／～약 flypoison《물약》fly water／～를 쫓다《부채로》fan flies away／～채 a flyflap. はえ

**파리모(玻璃母)** a lump of glass.

**파리목숨** an ephemeral life; a cheap life; insignificant existence.

**파리하다** (be) emaciated; exhausted; worn[-out]／파리해지다 become emaciated [haggard]; be worn out.

**파립(破笠)** a worn-out[torn] bamboo hat. やぶれがさ

**파먹다** ①《음식을》eat into《벌레가》bore into ②《도식하다》eat the bread of idleness. ほってたべる

**파면(罷免)** dismissal; discharge／～하다 be ruined; go to ruin; remove (a person from office／～되다 be dismissed; be discharged. ひめん

**파멸(破滅)** ruin; destruction; downfall; wreck／～하다 be ruined; go to ruin; be wrecked. はめつ

**파문(波紋)** a ripple; a water-ring／～을 일으키다 start a water-ring《영향을 주다》create a stir. はもん

**파문(破門)**《종교상의》excommunication《일반의》expulsion／～하다 excommunicate; expel; strike (a person) out of (a list of students)／～되다 be excommunicated; be expelled. はもん

**파묻다**¹《땅 속에》bury《매장하다》lay (a person) to rest; inter／시체를 ～ bury a dead body／눈에 파묻히다 be buried under snow. うめる

**파묻다**²《물어 보다》inquire searchingly.

**파물(破物)** a defective[damaged] article; a broken stuff. はそんしたもの

**파발(擺撥)** a post-town; a stage／～마(馬) a post horse.

**파방치다(罷榜—)** shut up (one's house); wind up (one's family affairs). くらしをかたづける

**파방판(罷榜—)** the end; the finish; the close. ついていたことがおわったところ

**파벌(派閥)** a clique; a faction／～ 다툼 factional strife; faction.

**파병(派兵)** dispatch of troops／～하다 send an army (against).

**파삭파삭** ～하다 (be) fragile; brittle; easily broken[breakable]; frail. ばさばさ

**파산(破産)** bankruptcy; failure／～하다 fail; go bankrupt／～ 관리인 a bankruptcy administrator／～ 선고를 하다 adjudicate (a person) insolvent.

**파상(波狀)** wave; undulation／～의 wavy; undulating; wave-like／～ 공격 a repeated attack; an attack in waves. はじょう

**파상풍(破傷風)** 【의】tetanus. はしょうふう

**파생(派生)** derivation／～하다 derive; be derived (from);《사건이》give rise to／～적 derivative《이차(부차)적》secondary／～어(語) a derivative. はせい

**파선(破船)** shipwreck; wreck／～하다 be shipwrecked. はせん

**파선(波線)** a wave-line; a wave; a wavy line; an undulating line. はせん

**파손(破損)** damage; breakage; wreckage; injury／～하다 be damaged; be broken (down)／～된 damaged; broken. はそん

**파송(派送)** dispatch ⇨파견(派遣). はけん

**파쇄(破碎)** ～하다 smash; crush. はさい

**파쇠(破—)** scrap iron.

**파수(把守)** watch; guard《순경의》point-duty／～하다 guard; [keep] watch; be on guard[the watch]／～보다 stand[keep] watch; stand upon one's guard《파수병이》stand on sentry／～병 a sentry; a guard; a sentinel／～군 a guard; a watch.

**파악(把握)** grasp; mental[intellectual] hold; understanding; seizing／정세를 ～ 하다 grasp the situation. はあく

**파안 대소(破顏大笑)** a broad smile (on one's face)／～하다 give[show] a broad smile; break into a smile.

**파약(破約)** a breach of promise[contract]／～하다 break an agreement; infringe a promise[contract]. はやく

**파업(罷業)** a strike; a walk out《미·속》／～하다 walk out; [go on] strike／～권 the right to strike／～ 파괴자 a strikebreaker／～중이다 be on strike. ひぎょう

**파열(破裂)** explosion; bursting《화산의》ruption／～하다 explode; erupt; burst; be broken off／심장[혈관]의 ～ rupture of the heart[a blood vessel]. はれつ

**파옥(破獄)** prison[jail]-breaking／～하다 break out of jail; break [from a] prison. はごく

**파의(罷議)** ～하다 cancel; call off; break off; drop. そうだんをとめること

**파일** Buddha's birthday[festival]; April 8th by the old calendar.

**파장(波長)** wave length／～이 같다 be equal in wave length; be of the same wave length／～계 a cymometer. はちょう

**파장(罷場)**《과거의》the conclusion of state examinations《시장의》close of a marketplace／～하다 close a market.

**파적(破寂)** ～하다 kill time; divert ones-

**파종(播種)** sowing; seeding/～하다 sow; seed. はしゅ

**파죽지세(破竹之勢)** irresistible force/～로 나아가다 carry everything before one. はちくのいきおい

**파지(破紙)** waste paper; useless paper. やぶれたかみ

**파직(罷職)** dismissal[removal] from office; discharge/～하다 dismiss[remove] (*a person*) from office; fire(미). ひしょく

**파천황(破天荒)** unprecedentedness/～의 record-breaking; unprecedented; unheard-of/～의 사건 a most sensational event. はてんこう

**파철(破鐵)** scrap iron ⇒파쇠.

**파초(芭蕉)** 【식】 a banana; a plantain/～꽃 a plantain flower/～ 열매 a banana. ばしょう

**파출(派出)** dispatch; despatch; sending out (군대 등의) detachment; sending out/～하다 send out; despatch; detach/～소 a branch office (경찰관의) a police-box[-stand].

**파충(爬蟲)** 【동】 a reptile/～류 reptiles.

**파치(破一)** (제조품 중의) a waster (못among 된) unsalable goods. はそんしたもの

**파탄(破綻)** ①(실패·불성립) failure; rupture; ruin; disagreement (교섭 등의 결렬) a break-off (파산) bankruptcy/～하다 fail; be ruined ②(터짐) breaking/～하다 break (*up, down*). はたん

**파탈(擺脫)** freedom from restraint/～하다 (be) free and wild; unrestrained.

**파편(破片)** a [broken] piece; a fragment; a bit; a splinter. はへん

**파하다(破一)** (격파하다) beat; smash; defeat (파쇄하다) crush; destroy. うちやぶる

**파하다(罷一)** (마치다) close; finish; end 《학교 수업이》 be over[out]; (그만두다) put an end to; cut short/일을 ～ stop work; leave off work/혼담을 ～ break off marriage talks. おわる

**파행(爬行)** creeping/～하다 crawl; creep/～ 동물 a reptile. はこう

**파행(跛行)** limping/～하다 limp/～ 경기 (景氣) spotty prosperity; a limping boom. はこう

**파혼(破婚)** a breach of promise of marriage/～하다 break off a betrothal[an engagement] (*with*). はこん

**파훼(破毀)** ①destruction ②【법】reversal; recall (판결·계약의) revocation 《무효화》 annulment/～하다 annul; reverse; recall. はき

**파흥(破興)** ～하다 spoil *one's* pleasure; kill joy; dampen; cast a chill over (*the company*). きょうしゅをそこなうこと

**팍** (세게) violently (맥없이) flop/～ 쓸어지다 fall flop. ぶすっと

**팍삭** (주저앉는 모양) flop (깨지는 모양) fragilely. だらりと

**팍신하다** (be) soft; flossy; spongy/팍신한 솜 flossy cotton. ふわっとしている

**팍팍하다** ①(물기가 없어) (be) dry and hard to masticate ②(다리가) Q 다리가 ～ I have leaden feet. ばさばさする

**판** ①(일이 일어나는 곳) a place; a spot/싸움～ a battle field ②(판국) [the] state of affairs; the situation/이러한 ～에 in this juncture ③(때) the moment (경우) the case; the occasion/막～에 at the last moment/…할 ～이다 be going to (*do*); be about to (*do*); be on the point of (*doing*) ④(횟수) a game; a bout; a round; a match/한 ～ 겨루다 have a match[game, bout, tournament]; have a turn (at *wrestling*). ば

**판(板)** (판자) a board; boarding (두꺼운) a plank (집합적으로) planking (금속판) a plate (얇은) a sheet/장기～ a chessboard.

**판(版)** ①(판목) a [printing] block (인쇄판) a plate (거푸집) a cast ②(인쇄) print[ing]; an edition; an impression/개정 증보～ a revised and enlarged edition ③(비유적으로) Q ～에 박은 듯한 stereotyped; trite. はん

**판(判)** (책 따위의) the size; getup; format. ばん

**판(瓣)** (꽃잎) a petal (악기의) a ventil (기계의) a valve. べん

**판가름** ～하다 contend as to which is right; inquire into the rights and wrongs of a case.

**판각(板刻)** wood engraving; engraving on wood; wood cutting/～하다 make a print from a wood block; engrave (*letters*) on wood/～자(字) a block letter/～사(師) a wood-cutter; a block-cutter. はんこく

**판검사(判檢事)** judges and public prosecutors; judicial officers. はんけんじ

**판결(判決)** ①(시비 결정) judg[e]ment 【법】 [judicial] decision; finding; adjudication (선고) sentence/～하다 decide; pass judgement; sentence (*a person*) to; give [a] decision (on *a case*)/～에 복종하다 accept the decision/～문 the decision/～에 불복하다 protest against a judgement; demur to a judgement/～례(例) a judicial precedent; a leading case/～을 내리다 give a decision (*upon*); find. はんけつ

**판교(板橋)** a board bridge ⇒널다리.

**판국(版局)** a situation; the state of affairs/이런 ～에 under these circumstances; in this situation. きょくめん

**판권(版權)** copyright/～ 소유 ownership of copyright; copyright reserved/～ 침해 an infringement of the copyright/～ 소유자 a copyright holder. はんけん

**판금(板金)** metal plate; sheet metal. ばんきん

**판나다** ①(끝나다) end; close; be over ②(없어지다) run out; be exhausted be

**판다르다** (be) entirely different (*from*). おもめんがちがう

**판단(判斷)** judgement; adjudication 《단정》 decision 《결론》 conclusion 《추단》estimation／～하다 judge; decide; conclude;〔해석하다〕interpret／나의 ～으로는 in my [own] judgement／잘못 ～하다 misjudge; judge erroneously. はんだん

**판도(版圖)** territory; domain; dominion／～를 넓히다 extend the territory [of a country]. はんと

**판독(判讀)** reading ⇒해독(解讀). はんどく

**판돈** stakes; a bet／～을 떼다 divide up stakes[the money on the board].

**판동거리다** drone; loaf around; lead an idle life; live in idleness／판듯판듯 idly; lazily; sluggishly. なまける

**판들다** go bankrupt; get broke《속》; be ruined; go bankrupt.

**판례(判例)**〔법〕a [judicial] precedent; a leading case／～를 인용하다 cite a precedent／～법 case law. はんれい

**판로(販路)** a market (for *goods*); an outlet; a *débouché*(F)／～를 개척하다 find [open] a market (*for*). はんろ

**판리(辦理)** management; conduct／～하다 manage; conduct. しょりすること

**판막(瓣膜)**〔해〕a valve／심장 ～증(症) mitral disease. べんまく

**판막다** bring (*a game*) to an end by winning decisively. しょうりにおわる

**판막음** winning so decisively as to cause a game to an end. さいごのしょうり

**판매(販賣)** sale; selling／～하다 sell; market; deal in／현금 ～ a sale for cash [money]; a cash sale／～ 가격 a sale [selling] price／～ 수익 the margin／총～점 a selling agent／～원 a seller; a salesman; an agent 《여자》 a saleswoman／～점 a shop; a store〈미〉／～중이다 be on the market; be on sale. はんばい

**판명(判明)** becoming clear／～하다 become clear[plain]; prove[turn out] to be 《알려지다》 known 《신원 등이》 be identified as. はんめい

**판목(版木)** a printing[an engraving] block; a woodcut. はんぎ

**판몰이** a sweep; sweepstakes／～하다 sweep the board; take the pool.

**판무(判無)** total absence; none at all; nil／～하다 there is none…; de nil…. まったくないこと

**판무(辦務)** management／～하다 manage／～관 a commissioner. べんむ

**판무식(判無識)** utter ignorance; dense illiteracy／～쟁이 an utterly ignorant person. まったくちしきのないこと

**판문(板門)** a board door[gate]; a door made of boards. いたのもん

**판박이** ①《책》a printed book ②《모양》a set form; a cast; a stereotyped; a conventional thing. いんさつしたもの

**판별(判別)** distinction; discernment／～하다 distinguish (between *A* and *B*); tell (*A*) from (*B*); judge. はんべつ

**판본(板本)** a book printed from wood block; a printed book. はんぽん

**판사(判事)** a judge; justice／부장 ～ a chief judge／예심 ～ an examining[a preliminary] judge／～석 a judgment seat; a judge's bench; the bench. はんじ

**판상(一上)** the best[finest] of all. すべてのなかでじょうとう

**판상(辨償)** compensation ⇒변상. べんしょう

**판상놈(一常一)** a very humble person; a very vulgar fellow. かりゅうなひと

**판새류(瓣鰓類)**〔동〕bivalve mollusc; *Lamellibranchiata* 《학명》.

**판세(版勢)** ①《도박》 the drift of a game ②《형세》 the situation; the state of affairs[the things] ③《전망》 the prospect; outlook 《징조》 signs; indications／～가 일변했다 The tide is turned. あるばめんのじょうせい

**판셈** apportionment[distribution] of a debtor's property among creditors／～하다 distribute[apportion] a debtor's property between[among] creditors.

**판소리** the song[reciting] of a drama by the *chang* reciter.

**판수** ①《점장이》a blind fortune-teller ② a blind person ⇒소경.

**판시(判示)** presenting[showing] the judgement of a case／～하다 present[show] the judgement of a case.

**판시세(販時勢)** current market prices ⇒ 판세(版勢). あるばめんのじょうせい

**판연(判然)** ～하다 (be) clear; distinct; explicit; evident／～히 distinctly; clearly; plainly; palpably. はんぜん

**판유리(板琉璃)** sheet glass; plate glass 《창의》 pane. ょたガラス

**판이(判異)** ～하다 (be) entirely different (*from*)／～한 의견 entirely different opinion[view]. おおきいにことなること

**판자(板子)** a board 《두꺼운》a plank／～집 a board-framed house; a barrack; a makeshift hut／～로 막다 board up. いた

**판장(板墻)** a boarding; a board fence[wall]／～이 되다 get old and infirm.

**판장원(一壯元)** the most talented person among them.

**판재(板材)** boards for a coffin ⇒관재.

**판정(判定)** judgement; finding; adjudication 《배심관의》 verdict／～하다 judge; decide; adjudge; find; verdict／～으로 이기다 win on decision ／ ～승 《권투》 a win[victory] on a decision; decision. はんてい

**판주다** pick out one as the best of all.

**판중(一中)** ～에서 among (*a group* of).

**판치다** be the master of the situation; be the sole figure in the scene; stand unchallenged.

**판판이** every time; every game. まったく

**판판하다** (be) even; level; flat. たいらだ

**판화(版畵)** a print; a woodcut; an engraving. はんが
**판히(判―)** clearly; distinctly; obviously; patently; plainly.
**팔** ①(손) an arm/~을 끼고 with one's arm's folded; with folded arms/~없는 armless/가는 ~ a thin arm ②(고굉(股肱)) a right-hand [man]/그는 나의 한 ~이 되어서 일해 왔다 He has worked as my right-hand man. うで
**팔(八)** eight (여덟째) the eighth. はち
**팔각(八角)** an octagon/~의 octagonal. はっかく
**팔걸이** an elbow rest. ひじかけ
**팔괘(八卦)** the Eight Trigrams for divination. はっけ
**팔구(八九)** eight or nine. はちく
**팔꿈치** an elbow; 〖해〗 a cubitus/…에 ~를 얹다 rest one's elbow upon …. ひじさき
**팔난봉** a libertine; a lecher; a Lothario; a debauchee. どうらくしゃ
**팔다** ①(판매하다) sell; offer for sale (처분하다) dispose of/팔 수 있는 salable/~다 ~ leave out; exhaust one's stock; clear out; sell out/파는 사람 a seller/팔 물건 an article for sale/비싸게[싸게] ~ sell dear[cheap]/정조를 ~ sell[prostitute] one's chastity/손해 보고[이익을 보고] ~ sell (goods) at a loss[profit]/팔아 치우다 sell (off, out); dispose of ②(배반하다) betray; play (a person) false; deceive/나라를 ~ betray one's country/친구를 ~ betray[sell] one's friend ③(돌리다) turn; direct/한눈 ~ look to right or left; look aside ④(곡식을) buy[purchase] cereal ⑤(이름을) take advantage of; trade on (another's name)/…의 이름을 팔아서 under the pretext of…; trading on…. うる
**팔다리** the legs and arms; the limbs. うでとあし
**팔딱거리다** ①(가슴이) go pitapat; throb; pulsate/맥이 ~ the pulse beats[pulsates] [quick] ②(물고기·개구리가) struggle; leap; hop; jump.
**팔딱팔딱** ①(가슴이) pitapat; pulsating ②(물고기·개구리가) struggling; leaping.
**팔도(八道)** [the eight provinces of] Korea. はちどう
**팔도 음정(八度音程)** 〖음〗 an octave; a diatonic octave; an octachord.
**팔뚝** 〖해〗 the forearm. うで
**팔뚝 시계(―時計)** a wrist-watch. うでどけい
**팔랑개비** a paper windmill. ふうしゃ
**팔랑거리다** flap; fly; flutter; wave.
**팔랑팔랑** flapping; waving; fluttering/~하다 fly ⇒팔랑거리다. ひらひら
**팔리다** ①(물건 따위가) sell; be sold/잘 ~ [팔리지 않다] have a good[poor] sale/잘 팔리는 물건 a good[quick] seller/잘 안 팔리는 물건 a poor seller ②(마음이) be engrossed[absorbed] in; be given up to; lose one's head over/눈이 딴 데 ~ one's eyes go stray; look at something else/여자에게 마음이 ~ be fascinated by a woman. うばられる
**팔림새** sale; demand/~가 좋다 sell well; have a large sale; command a good sale/~가 나쁘다 be in poor demand; be unsalable.
**팔만 장안(八萬長安)** Seoul.
**팔매** throwing; hurling/~치다 throw; hurl. いしなげをすること
**팔매질** throwing/ ~하다 throw; hurl/돌~ stone-throwing. いしなげをすること
**팔면(八面)** all sides; every side; 〖수〗 eight faces/~의 octahedral/~체 an octahedron. はちめん
**팔모(八―)** eight angles. はっかく
**팔목** the wrist; 〖해〗 carpus/~을 잡다 grasp[grab, grip] (a person) by the wrist/~ 시계 a wrist watch. うでくび
**팔방(八方)** every direction; all directions [sides]; every side/~에 in all directions; on every side. はっぽう
**팔방 미인(八方美人)** everybody's friend; a flunkey. はっぽうびじん
**팔베개** 팩 ~를 베다 rest one's head on one's elbow. うでまくら
**팔변형(八邊形)** an octagon/ ~의 octagonal.
**팔분 쉼표(八分―標)** a quaver rest.
**팔분 음표(八分音標)** a quaver; an eight note. はちぶおんぷ
**팔 분의(八分儀)** an octant.
**팔불용(八不用)** a good-for-nothing [fellow]. おろかもの
**팔싹** ①(연기·먼지가) suddenly; lightly ②(갑자기 앉는 모양) suddenly. ばっと
**팔삭동이(八朔童―)** ①(여덟 달 만에 낳은 아이) a child born in the eighth month of pregnancy ②(달이 차기도 전에 낳은 아이) a prematurely-born infant ③(모자라는 사람) a half-witted person; a stupid.
**팔씨름** arm-wrestling; an arm strength contest/~을 하다 have an arm strength contest (with). うでずもう
**팔심** the muscular strength of one's arm.
**팔십(八十)** eighty; a forescore (제80) the eightieth. はちじゅう
**팔오금** the crook of the arm.
**팔월(八月)** August. はちがつ
**팔월한가위(八月―)** August 15th of the lunar calendar.
**팔인교(八人轎)** a palanquin[letter] carried by eight bearers.
**팔자(八字)** destiny; fate; one's lot/~ 좋은 fortuna…; lucky; happy/~ 좋게 fortunately; happily/~ 좋은 사람 a lucky man[fellow]. うん
**팔자걸음(八字―)** walking out-toed/~으로 걷다 toe out.
**팔자땜** a compensation for one's doom [evil destiny]/~하다 go through hell.
**팔짝** jumping up suddenly. ばっと

팔짱 folding *one's* arms/~끼다 fold *one's* arms/~을 끼고 with arms across; with folded arms. うでぐみ

팔재간(—才幹) (씨름의) skill with *one's* arms.

팔절판(八折版) octavo size/~의 책 a book printed in octavo.

팔찌 a bracelet; an armlet《영》. うでわ

팔짓 ~하다 swing *one's* arms; motion with arms. うでをふること

팔척 장신(八尺長身) a man of great stature; a big fellow; a giant.

팔촌(八寸) ①(촌수) third cousin; first cousin twice removed ②(치수) 8 *chon* [inches]. はっすん

팔팔 ①(끓는 모양) with a sizzling sound; steaming; bubblingly ②(재온이) burningly/몸이 ~ 끓다 have a high[violent] fever; burn with fever ③(뛰는 모양) ¶ ~ 뛰다 leap; jump. ぐらぐら

팔팔하다 (be) bilious; violent; hasty; quick-tempered; impatient. せっかちだ

팔풍받이(八風—) a wind-blown[-swept] place; a place exposed to the wind.

팔회목 the wrist; the small of the arm.

팡파지다 (be) well-developed[-rounded] ⇒ 펑퍼지다 ひらべったい

팡파짐하다 (be) stocky built; stumpy; pudgy/팡파짐한 사람 a pudge; a stocky man. ひらべったくひろい

팡팡 (물이) copiously (눈이) heavily (소리가) pop pop/(눈이) ~ 내린다 It is snowing heavily ⇒펑펑. どくどく

팥 a red-bean; an Indian bean; *Phaseolus angularis*(학명). あずき

팥꼬투리 a red-bean pod. あずきのさや

팥꽃 the red-bean blossom. あずきのはな

팥닭 【조】 a water-rail; *Rallus aquaticus* (학명).

팥떡 rice-cake coated with ground red-beans. あずきもち

팥밥 rice boiled together with red beans. あずきめし

팥소 bean-paste [jam]; bean jam. あずきあん

팥죽 rice gruel boiled together with red beans. あずきがゆ

패(牌) ①(나무패) a wooden ticket[tag, tally, check]; (상패) a medal (문패) a door-plate/나무~를 붙이다 fasten[tie] [a package] with a wooden tag (동아리) a party; a set; a company; a group (단체) circles; a troop (악당의) a gang (도당) a body of *one's* troops; *one's* men/한~가 되다 join (in); take part in/문인~ the literary set; the *literati*(F). はい

패가(敗家) ~하다 become bankrupt; be brought to ruin; be ruined/~ 망신 ruining both *oneself* and *one's* family.

패각(貝殼) a shell; (~상(狀)의) conchoidal /~ 추방 ostracism. かいがら

패검(佩劍) 《차는 칼》 side arms 《칼을 참》 wearing a sword/~하다 wear[carry] a sword. つるぎをみにつるすこと

패군(敗軍) a defeated army/~지장(之將)은 병법을 말하지 않는다 A defeated general should not talk tactics., A general who has lost his day has lost his say. はいぐん

패권(覇權) supremacy; rulership; mastery; leadership; hegemony/ ~을 잡다 hold[bear] sway (over); have the hegemony (of *the land*)/~을 다투다 strive [contest] for supremacy. はけん

패기(覇氣) ambition; spirit/~ 만만한 ambitious; spirited. はき

패다¹ ①(장작을) chop; split/장작을 ~ chop wood ②(때리다) ③(이삭이) be in the ear; come into ears; come out/며칠 후면 벼이삭이 필 것이다 The rice plants will come out in a few days. ぶったきる

패다² ①(파게 하다) have[let] (*a person*) dig (*the ground*) ②(패이다) be dug; be cut; become hollow; fall in; sink/비에 땅이 ~ The ground is hollowed out by the rain. ほられる

패담(悖談) improper talk; perverse remarks.

패덕(悖德) immorality; moral depravity /~ 행위 immoral conduct; an immoral act. はいとく

패도(佩刀) a sword worn ⇒패검. はいとう

패도(覇道) military rule[government]; the rule of might; ruling by force/~ 정책 the plans for world aggression. はどう

패랭이 a bamboo-hat worn by a mourner or a humble person.

패랭이꽃 【식】 a China[an Indian] pink; *Dianthus sinensis*(학명). せきちく

패려(悖戾) crabbedness; perversity/ ~하다 (be) crabbed; perverse; cross-grained. ねじけたこと

패류(貝類) shellfish/ ~학 conchology/ ~학자 a conchologist. かいるい

패륜(悖倫) immorality; immoral conduct; impropriety/~의 immoral; sinful; illicit/ ~아 an immoral[a depraved] person.

패리(悖理) irrationality; unnaturalness /~하다 (by) unreasonable; irrational.

패망(敗亡) defeat; reversal/ ~하다 be defeated; be beaten; be routed. はいぼう

패멸(敗滅) destruction; ruin; annihilation; demolition/~하다 get destroyed [ruined, annihilated]. はいめつ

패모(貝母) 【식】 a checkered lily; a guinea-hen flower; *Fritillaria verticillata* (학명). あみがさゆり

패물(佩物) personal ornaments[outfit-things]; trimmings; trinkery; trinkets. みにつけるもの

패배(敗北) defeat; loss 《궤주(潰走)》 rout / ~하다 be defeated; be routed; be beaten/~주의 defeatism/완전히 ~하다 be completely defeated; suffer a severe

**패병**(敗兵) routed soldiers[troops].

**패보**(敗報) the news of defeat; the information of defeat. はいほう

**패사**(稗史) an unofficial history; a private narrative history. はいし

**패산**(敗散) rout; a crushing defeat/~하다 be routed.

**패석**(貝石) a fossil shell. かいいし

**패설**(悖說) an unreasonable remark.

**패설**(稗說) ①《항담》 talk[gossip] of the town ②《설화》 a romantic story; a folktale.

**패세**(敗勢) the reverse tide of a war; a losing situation; signs of defeat; a backing situation. はいせい

**패소**(敗訴) a lost case; losing a[one's] suit/~하다 lose one's suit[case]. はいそ

**패습**(悖習) a bad[vicious] habit 《악폐》 a vice; an abuse; an evil habit; an evil custom/~을 없애다 《개인의》 break oneself of a bad habit 《사회의》 get rid of a bad custom. よくないしゅうかん

**패악**(悖惡) moral deterioration; depravity; corruption/~하다 (be) corrupt; depraved; deteriorate; vicious.

**패역**(悖逆) rebelliousness; rebellion; treason/~하다 (be) rebellious; traitorous.
　　　　　　　　　　　　　いぎゃく

**패연**(沛然) ~히 heavily/~히 내리는 비 a heavy rain[fall]/비가 ~히 내린다 It rains heavily[cats and dogs].

**패옥**(佩玉) court-dress jewels[gems].
　　　　　　　　　　　　　はいぎょく

**패용**(佩用) wearing/~하다 wear (one's medal, tag); bear. はいよう

**패운**(敗運) a declining fortune; ruinous luck; being fated to lose.

**패이다** be dug ⇒패다². ほられる

**패인**(敗因) the cause of defeat/군의 사기 저하가 ~이 되었다 Demoralization of the soldiers resulted in the defeat.
　　　　　　　　　　　　　はいいん

**패자**(覇者) a supreme ruler 《경기의》 a champion [of a game]. はしゃ

**패자**(敗者) a loser 《복수》 the defeated [conquered, vanquished]. はいしゃ

**패잔**(敗殘) survival after defeat/~병[군] remants [of a defeated troop]; stragglers. はいざん

**패잡다** back[finance] a gambler.

**패장**(敗將) a defeated general; a defeated person. はいしょう

**패적**(敗敵) a defeated enemy; a vanquished enemy; a fleeing enemy.

**패전**(敗戰) a defeat; a reverse; a lost battle/~하다 be defeated; lose a battle[war]/~국 a defeated nation/~주의 defeatism. はいせん

**패주**(敗走) rout/~하다 be routed; take to flight. はいそう

**패차다**(牌-) be nicknamed; be dubbed; earn oneself the nickname (of).

**패총**(貝塚) a shell mound[heap]; a kitchen midden. かいづか

**패퇴**(敗退) defeat/~하다 retreat (경기에서) lose a game. はいたい

**패하다**(敗一) be defeated[beaten]; suffer a defeat/군대는 싸움에 패했다 The army was defeated. まける

**패향**(悖郷) the filthy-infested country [vicinity]; a district of moral decadence.

**패혈증**(敗血症) 【의】 septicaemia; blood poisoning. はいけつしょう

**팩** weakly ⇒픽. どんと

**팬둥거리다** drone; lead an idle life; loaf around. なまけてばかりいる

**팬들거리다** lead an idle life; idle[loaf] one's time away/팬들팬들 idly; indolently. なまけてばかりいる

**팽**¹ 【식】 a hackberry [fruit]; a [Chinese] nettle tree nut.

**팽**² ①(도는 모양) round; around; quickly; circling/~ 돌다 go clear round ②《머리가》 reelingly/머리가 ~ 돈다 reel; swim. ぐるっと

**팽개치다** ①(먼지다) throw; cast; toss; fling ②(버리다) throw up; give up (내버려 두다) lay aside; neglect; leave[let] (something) alone/그런 일을 그냥 팽개쳐 두어서는 안 된다 You must not leave the matter unsettled. なげすててしまう

**팽그르르** round and round (spinning, whirling, revolving, turning) around rapidly/팽이가 ~ 돈다 A top spins.
　　　　　　　　　　　　　くるくる

**팽글팽글** round and round about/팽이가 ~ 돈다 A top spins round and round.

**팽나무** 【식】 a [Chinese] nettle tree; a hackberry; Celtis sinensis(학명). えのき

**팽대**(膨大) swelling; expansion/~하다 swell; expand. ぼうだい

**팽배**(澎湃) surging/~하다 surge/~하는 파도 surging waves. ほうはい

**팽이** a top/~를 돌리다[치다] spin a top /~치기 top spinning.

**팽창**(膨脹) distention; 【물】《기체 따위의》 expansion (통화 따위) inflation 《증대》 increase/~하다 swell; expand; increase; inflate/~성 expansibility/~력 expansive power; tension/도시의 ~ the growth of a town/통화의 ~ inflation of currency/~계수 the coefficient of expansion/~률 the rate of expansion.
　　　　　　　　　　　　　ぼうちょう

**팽팽롭다** (be) hard to please; fastidious; cross.

**팽팽** round and round/~ 돌다 turn round and round; circle fast.

**팽팽하다** ①《맞줄·돛 따위가》 (be) taut; tight/팽팽히 tight[ly]; tensely; full/새끼를 팽팽히 치다 tighten a rope; stretch a rope tight ②《융통성없다》 (be) hidebound 《면협하다》 (be) illiberal 《박하다》 (be) peevish. きっぱりしている

**팽팽하다**(膨膨一) (be) bursting (with); be filled to breaking point.

**팽하다** (be) neither more nor less; (be) moderate(적당하다); temperate; just right. ちょうどよい

**퍅퍅** impetuously/~ 쏘다 say a cutting thing; make a cutting remark 《입바른 소리》 speak plainly; speak out; intolerant(편벽하다). ばさっと

**퍅하다(愎-)** (be) peevish; touchy. おこりっぽい

**퍼내다** bail[dip, ladle] out; dip[scoop] up/물을 ~ bail[scoop, ladle] out water.

**퍼니** aimlessly; indolently; idly; aimlessly/~ 놀다 loaf away one's days; take one's ease; lead an idle life. ぶらぶら

**퍼더버리고 앉다** sit comfortably with one's feet stretched out; sit comfortably.

**퍼덕거리다** ①《새가》 flap[beat] the wings; flutter ②《물고기가》 leap; splash; jump. ばたばたする

**퍼뜨리다** spread; circulate; diffuse 《종교 따위를》 propagate/소문을 ~ spread a rumor/세상에 ~ spread abroad. まきちらす

**퍼뜩** suddenly; in a flash/좋은 생각이 ~ 떠올랐다 A good idea struck me suddenly., A happy idea flashed across my mind. きゅうに

**퍼렁** blue; green. あおいろ

**퍼렇다** (be) deep[fresh] blue[green]; 《안색이》 deadly[ghastly] pale 《실색해서》 white. あおい

**퍼르르** bubbling; seething; in a burst of flame; trembling ⇒파르르. かっと

**퍼먹다** ①《퍼서》 scoop and eat; spoon out[up] ②《많이》 eat greedily/음식을 ~ shovel up[down] food; shovel food into one's mouth. がつがつく う

**퍼범하다** neglect one's appearance; be careless about one's appearance.

**퍼붓다** ①《물 따위를》 pour[shower] 《water》 upon 《one》; 《포탄을》 rain 《shells》 upon 《육설을》 heap; hurl ②《비가》 rain in torrents; pour down/비가 억수같이 ~ It rains cats and dogs., It pours down. そそぐ

**퍼석퍼석** crumbly; being fragile/ ~하다 (be) fragile; crumbly; frail; crisp. ばさばさ

**퍼지다** ①《널리》 come into fashion(유행); spread 《보급》 be diffused 《유포》 be circulated ②《삶은 것이》 be properly steamed; swell ③《넓어지다》 widen; extend; stretch; spread/전염병은 삽시간에 마을에 퍼졌다 The epidemic prevailed quickly in the village. ひろくなる

**퍽¹** 《매우》 very [much]; highly; remarkably; greatly/오늘은 ~ 춥다 It is so cold today./우리는 ~ 재미있었다 We were highly delighted. きわめて

**퍽²** ①《힘있게》 forcefully; ǀ with an effort ②《넘어지는 모양》 like a dead weight; with a thud/~ 쓰러지다 fall with a thud; fall down all of heap. きゅっと

**퍽석** 《앉는 모양》 plump; heavily/~ 의자에 주저앉다 drop heavily into a chair; plump on a chair. どさっと

**퍽신하다** (be) soft; fluffy; spongy; cushiony. べたべたしている

**퍽퍽** ①《찌르는 모양》 repeatedly; forcefully ②《쓰러지는 모양》 in rapid succession/~ 쓰러지다 fall down one after another ③《쏟아지는 모양》 thick and fast; in torrents ④《깎이는 모양》 easily; yielding. とじんと

**퍽퍽하다** ①(be) dry and stuffy/이 빵은 ~ This bread is dry and stuffy. ②(be) leaden/다리가 ~ I have leaden legs. ばさばさだ

**편더기** a wide plain; an open field; flatlands. へいげん

**펀둥거리다** loaf away; lead an idle life; idle away/펀둥펀둥 idly; lazily. ぶらぶらする

**펀뜻** in an instant; in a flash; quickly; instantly/그의 이름이 ~ 생각나지 않는다 His name does not occur to me instantly. はったと

**편편하다** flat; (be) even ⇒판판하다.

**펀하다** (be) vast; boundless; wide/펀한 바다 a vast sea. こうだいだ

**펄군** a person who is indifferent to his appearance; a dowdy person. きどらないひと

**펄떡거리다** ①《가슴이》 go pitapat; throb; palpitate/펄떡펄떡 pitapat ②《물고기 따위가》 leap; jump.

**펄럭거리다, 펄렁거리다** flutter; flap; flicker 《기 따위》 waver/펄럭펄럭[펄렁펄렁] fluttering; flapping; flickering/태극기가 바람에 ~ A Korean national flag flutters in the wind.

**펄썩** ①《주저앉는 모양》 plump; suddenly/그는 ~ 주저앉았다 He sat down plump. ②《연기나 먼지가》 puffily/바람이 불 때마다 먼지가 ~ 났다 Every gust of wind stirred up the dust. ぽんと

**펄쩍** suddenly; fast; lightly/~ 뛰다 jump; start; leap/~ 뛰며 좋아하다 jump for joy. ぽんと

**펄쩍거리다** 《뛰다》 leap; jump; flounce 《날다》 flutter; flap/펄쩍펄쩍 leaping; fluttering; flapping; jumping.

**펄펄** ①《끓는 모양》 boiling; seethingly; bubbling/~ 끓다 boil up; seethe ②《나는 모양》 fluttering; flapping/~ 날리다 flutter about; flap ③《뛰는 모양》 jumping; leaping/좋아서 ~ 뛰다 jump for joy. ぐらぐら

**펄펄하다** ①《성질이》 (be) quick-tempered; hasty ②《생기있다》 (be) active; full of life; lively. げんきがいい

**펑** pop /~하다 pop/~하고 with a pop; with an explosion/나는 ~하는 소리를 들었다 I heard it go pop. ぽん

**펑덩** in a plop; in a splash ⇒풍당

**펑퍼지다** get well-developed.

**펑퍼짐하다** (be) pudgy; stocky built; plump/펑퍼짐한 사람 a thick-set man; a pudge; a stocky man; a humpty-dumpty. ひろびろとひろがっている

**펑펑** (쏟아지는 모양) profusely; copiously /땀을 ~ 흘리다 all in a sweat; weltering in sweat/~ 흐르다 flow in streams; stream down/눈이 ~ 내린다 The snow falls thick and fast. どうどう

**펴놓다** ①(펴다) keep[leave] (a book) open ②(마음을) disclose; confide; reveal; take (a person) into one's confidence. ひろげておく

**펴다** ①(벌리다) spread out; open; expand ②(구긴 것을) smooth out [creases]; (접힌 것을) unfold (굽은 것을) straighten (말린 것을) uncoil (오므라진 것을) stretch/책을 ~ open a book/자리를 ~ spread[prepare, make] a bed/몸을 ~ straighten oneself; pull[draw] oneself up ②(기를) feel relieved; be animated; feel at ease ③(광포하다) spread; propagate; popularize; diffuse (발행하다) publish; bring out; issue ④(경영하다) keep; run (개시하다) open ⑤(넉넉하게 하다) relieve[free] from (poverty) ⑥(세력을) establish (one's influence); extend (one's power). ひろげる

**편** (떡) rice cake. もち

**편(便)** ①(한쪽) side; part (방향) direction; way /왼~에 (좌측)on the left hand[side]/(좌방) to the left/동~에 in the direction of to the east; toward ②(기회) chance; opportunity /철도[배] ~으로 by rail[ship] ③(한패) a side; one's own side; a party/ ~들The take part[sides] with; stand by (one); one's own side/제~으로 끌다 make friends of people. べん

**편(編)** (편집) compilation; editing/김박사~ compiled[edited] by Dr. Kim. へん

**편(篇)** (권)a volume; a book (시의)a canto (장·절)a chapter; a section; a part/상[중·하]~ the first[second, third] volume. へん

**편가르다(便—)** divide into (two) parties [sides, teams]/편갈라 일을 하다 work in teams[groups].

**편각(偏角)** [지] declination; angle of deviation; [수] amplitude. へんかく

**편갈리다(便—)** be[get] divided into [two] teams[parties].

**편강(片薑)** sliced dried ginger.

**편견(偏見)** prejudice; a bias/~을 가지다 be prejudiced[have a prejudice] against/~을 버리다 cast away all prejudices/~없는 unprejudiced; fair. へんけん

**편곡(編曲)** [음] arrangement/~하다 arrange/이 바이올린곡은 피아노곡으로는 되어 있다 This music for the violin is also arranged for the piano.

**편광(偏光)** [물] polarized light/~ 프리즘 a polarizer/~ 현미경 a polarization microscope. へんこう

**편기(偏嗜)** ~하다 like unbalancedly/ ~하는 음식 one's special favourite dish [food]. かたよったしこう

**편기(偏忌)** jealousy/~하다 be jealous.

**편년(編年)** ¶~사 a chronicle; annals/ ~체(體) a chronological form[order]. へんねん

**편달(鞭撻)** (격려) encouragement; urging; whipping (채찍질) lashing; whipping/~하다 urge; whip; encourage; spur on/가일층 ~해 주십시요 I must seek your further advice and encouragement. べんたつ

**편답(遍踏)** travels ⇒편력(遍歷). へんれき

**편당(偏黨)** partiality for[to] a party/~하다 be partial to a party; side with a party/~을 짓다 form a faction.

**편대(編隊)** formation; forming ranks/ ~ 비행 a formation flight; flying in formation/~장(長) a flight leader/~를 짓다 form ranks; make a formation; get in line. へんたい

**편도(扁桃)** [식] an almond; the almond tree; Prunus amygdalus (학명). へんとう

**편도선(扁桃腺)** the tonsils/~염 tonsillitis; quinsy/~ 비대(肥大) an enlarged tonsil. へんとうせん

**편두통(偏頭痛)** [의] megrim; migraine; hemicrania; sick headache.

**편들다(便—)** side with; stand in with; take one's part; back/그는 언제나 우리에게 편든다 He is always on our side. / 신은 정의에 편들어 주신다 God is on the side of justice. かたをもつ

**편람(便覽)** a handbook; a manual/영어 ~ a handbook of English. びんらん

**편람표(便覽表)** a chart; a table/계산 ~ a ready reckoner.

**편력(遍歷)** travels; pilgrimage/ ~하다 travel[tour] about/~자 a pilgrim/전국을 ~하다 make a tour of the country. へんれき

**편리(便利)** convenience (알맞음) handiness (이익) advantage (설비의) facilities /~하다 (be) convenient; handy; expedient/~상 for the sake of convenience/~한 장소 a convenient place/ ~하지 못한 inconvenient/교통이 ~하다 be convenient for transportation. べんり

**편린(片鱗)** a part; a glimpse/그것으로 그의 성격의 ~을 알아볼 수 있다 It enables us to get a glimpse of his personality.

**편마암(片麻岩)** [광] gneiss. へんまがん

**편만(遍滿)** pervation; diffusion; spread / ~하다 pervade; permeate; spread [about]; pervasive. へんまん

**편모(偏母)** one's lone mother; one's widowed mother/~ 시하에 있다 be under one's lone mother's roof.

**편모(鞭毛)** a flagellum(pl. -la, ~s)/ ~충 a flagellate. べんもう

**편무(片務)** [법] ~적 unilateral/~ 계약 a

**편물**(編物) 〖만들기〗 knitting; a knit-work 〖갈쿠리 바늘의〗 crochet 〖만든 것〗 knitted goods/～하다 knit; crochet.

**편발**(編髮, 辮髮) a pigtail; the Chinese queue[cue].

**편법**(便法) an easier[a handy] method; an expedient; a convenient mode; an expediential policy; a short cut[way] /일시적 ～ a temporary expedient.

**편벽**(偏僻) an eccentricity; crankiness/ ～하다 (be) eccentric; crotchety; cranky.

**편복**(便服) home wear; weekday clothes; everyday clothes[wear]; undress.

**편복**(蝙蝠) a bat ⇨박쥐.

**편쌈**(便―) a fight between two groups / ～하다 fight between two groups; have a gang fight/ ～군 a gang fighter.

**편상화**(編上靴) lace-shoes; boots⟨영⟩; high shoes⟨미⟩.

**편성**(偏性) one-sidedness; prejudice; bias; bigotry; partiality/～이 eccentric; crotchety.

**편성**(編成) formation; organization; composition; footing/～하다 form; organize; compose; compile/추경 예산을 ～ 하다 make up[draw up] a revised supplementary budget.

**편수** a head artisan[craftsman].

**편수**(編修) editing; compilation/ ～하다 edit; compile; prepare for the press/ ～관 an editorial officer/～국 the Text Book Compilation Bureau.

**편술**(編述) editing; compilation/ ～하다 edit; compile; write.

**편승**(便乘) 〖승차·승선〗 take (a car, a ship); get aboard (a car)⟨미⟩; 〖기회 이용〗 avail oneself of; take advantage of.

**편시**(片時) an instant; a [single] moment; a little while.

**편식**(偏食) an unbalanced diet/ ～하다 have an unbalanced diet.

**편심**(偏心) a one-sided mind; a partial disposition 〖기계〗 eccentricity/～륜 an eccentric [wheel]/ ～봉 an eccentric rod.

**편안**(便安) 〖무사〗 being well; peace; tranquility 〖편한〗 ease; comfort; coziness/～하다 (be) well; peaceful; comfortable/～한 생활 a quiet[peaceful] life /～히 앉으십시오 Please sit comfortably.

**편암**(片岩) 〖광〗 schist [rock].

**편애**(偏愛) partiality; favoritism/ ～하다 love with partiality; show favoritism; be partial to.

**편액**(扁額) a tablet; a framed picture; a plaque.

**편역들다** side with; support ⇨편들다.

**편영**(片影) a sign; a speck (of *cloud*); a shadow/적의 ～도 볼 수가 없었다 Not a sign of the enemy was to be found.

**편육**(片肉) slices of boiled meat.

**편의**(便宜) convenience; facility 〖이익〗 advantage 〖득책〗 expedience/～주의〔주의자〕 opportunism[an opportunist]/～ 상 for convenience sake; from personal convenience/～를 도모하다 consult (*a person's*) convenience.

**편의대**(便衣隊) plain-clothes soldiers; snipers; irregular troops; a partisan.

**편이**(便易) handiness; convenience; facility/～하다 (be) convenient; easy; handy.

**편익**(便益) benefit 〖편리〗 convenience 〖이익〗 advantage/～을 얻다 be benefited; benefit/상호 ～을 위해서 for mutual benefit.

**편입**(編入) entry; incorporation (*in*); admission 〖전입〗 transfer 〖군에〗 enrollment (*in*); enlistment/그는 시험을 거쳐 4학년에 ～되었다 He has been admitted through examination into the fourth year class.

**편자** a horseshoe/말에 ～를 박다 shoe a horse.

**편자**(編者) an editor; a compiler; an author.

**편짜다**(便―) make up parties; separate into groups/편짜서 화투놀이를 하다 play cards in teams.

**편짝**(便―) a side/이 ～ this side/한～ 으로 기울다 lean to one side.

**편재**(遍在) ubiquity; omnipresence/～하 다 be ubiquitous; be omnipresent.

**편재**(偏在) maldistribution/ ～하다 be maldistributed/물자가 ～하고 있다 Materials are maldistributed.

**편재**(騙財) swindle; defraudation/～하다 swindle; defraud.

**편전**(便殿) the Imperial resting house; a side room of a palace.

**편제**(編制) formation; footing; organization/～하다 form; compose; organize /전시[평시] ～ a war[peace] footing.

**편주**(扁舟) a small boat; a skiff/일엽 ～ a tiny boat.

**편죽**(片竹) a bamboo piece; a chip of bamboo.

**편중**(偏重) preponderance/～하다 attach too much importance (*to*); lean upon/ 지능 교육의 ～ too much intellectual training.

**편지**(便紙, 片紙) a letter; an epistle 《간략 한》 a billet; a note 《상업용》 a favor/ ～하다 write[send] a letter/～를 부치다 mail[post] a letter/나는 영숙에게 사랑

**편집(編執)** bias; obstinacy; bigotry/ ～광(狂) monomania 《사람》 a monomaniac. へんしゅう

**편집(編輯, 編集)** editing; compilation/ ～하다 edit; compile/～장(長) a managing editor; an editor-in-chief/잡지를 ～하다 edit a magazine/～ 회의를 열다 hold an editorial conference. へんしゅう

**편차(偏差)** declination; variation; deflection; 《수》 deviation 《항로의》 drift/표준 ～ standard deviation. へんさ

**편찬(編纂)** compilation; editing/ ～하다 compile; edit/～물 a compilation/～자 a compiler; an editor/이 책은 잘 ～되어 있다 This book is excellently got up. へんさん

**편찮다(便—)** 《불편하다》 (be) uncomfortable 《병으로》 (be) unwell; indisposed/몸이 ～ feel[be] unwell. やすらかでない

**편철(片鐵)** a piece of metal. てつのかけら

**편충(鞭蟲)** *Trichocephalus* (학명).

**편취(騙取)** defraudation; swindle/ ～하다 cheat; swindle; deceive; defraud/돈을 ～하다 swindle money (out, of). へんしゅ

**편친(偏親)** a parent; an only parent/～시하 having only one parent to serve. かたおや

**편침의(偏針儀)** a deflector.

**편토(片土)** a small piece of land; a small plot of ground. ちいさいとち

**편파(偏頗)** 《편역 듦》 partiality; favouritism 《불공평》 unfairness 《치우침》 one-sidedness/사람을 ～적으로 냉대하다 discriminate against[in favor of] (*a person*). へんば

**편편(片片)** 《조각》 pieces; scraps 《얇은》 flakes/～이 in pieces; in flakes. へんべん

**편편 옥토(片片沃土)** fertile land.

**편편이(便便—)** by each messenger; with each mail. たより毎に

**편편하다(便便—)** ①《아무 일 없다》 (be) free; have nothing to do ②《편안하가》 be free from care; peaceful; ③《편》 comfortable/편편히 지나다 lead a comfortable life. なごやかだ

**편평(扁平)** ～하다 (be) flat; level; even /～ 족(足)a flat foot/도로 표면을 ～하게 고르다 make the surface of a road level. へんべん

**편하다(便—)** (be) comfortable 《용이하다》 easy 《걱정없다》 free from cares/편히 c̅omfortably; easily/편한 일 an easy task/편히 살다 live in comfort; lead an easy life/마음이 ～ be free from care. やすらかだ

**편향(偏向)** propensity; inclination; tendency; 《물》 deflection.

**편협(偏狹, 編狹)** narrow-mindedness; illiberality/～하다 (be) narrow-minded; illiberal; intolerant. へんきょう

**편형 동물(扁形動物)** 《동》 *Platyhelminthes* (학명).

**펼치다** open; outstretch; spread; extend; expand; unfold; unroll/우산을 ～ unfurl[open] *one's* umbrella/넓은 평야가 시야에 펼쳐졌다 A broad plain spreads before us. ひろげる

**폄(貶)** ～하다 disparage; speak ill of; depreciate; belittle. けなすこと

**폄강(貶降)** degradation; downgrading; degrading/～하다 degrade; reduce to a lower rank; demote. へんこう

**폄척(貶斥)** degradation; demotion〈미〉/～하다 degrade; reduce (*to*).

**평(評)** criticism; a comment 《명성》 reputation/ ～하다 comment (*on*); speake of (*a person*); criticize/～이 좋은[나쁜] popular[unpopular]. ひょう

**평(坪)** a *pyong*/～수 an area; acreage 《건평》 floor space/～수가 넓다 be spacious. つぼ

**평-(平)** 《보통의》 common; plain; ordinary 《단순한》 mere/～사원 a mere clerk /～당원 the rank-and-file member.

**평가(評價)** valuation; appraisal; assessment 《인물 등의》 estimation/～하다 value; estimate; appraise; appreciate; judge/ ～액 an appraised value. ひょうか

**평가(平價)** 《경》 par; parity/～절하 devaluation.

**평각(平角)** 《수》 a straight angle. へいかく

**평결(評決)** decision 《배심원 등의》 a verdict/～하다 decide/원고에 유리한 ～ a verdict for the plaintiff. ひょうけつ

**평경(平鏡)** clear glasses [with unrefracted lenses].

**평교(平交)** friends in the same age bracket; friends of about the same age.

**평균(平均)** ①《보통》 an average/～의 average; mean/～하다 average/일인 ～ per head/ ～ 이상[이하]이다 be above [below] the average/ ～을 잡다 take the average ②《균형》 balance; equilibrium/ ～하다 balance; equilibrate/ ～이 잡힌 well balanced. へいきん

**평년(平年)** 《윤년이 아닌》 the common year 《예년》a normal[an average] year/ ～작 이상 above the normal[average] crop. へいねん

**평다리치다** sit at *one's* ease with legs stretched out. くつろぐ

**평등(平等)** equality; parity/～하다 (be) equal; even; equable/～주의 [the principle of] equality/～하게 분배하다 divide equally/～한 권리 an equal right. びょうどう

**평란(平亂)** suppression of rebellion/ ～하다 suppress a rebellion. へいてい

**평론(評論)** comment; criticism 《저작물의》 a review/ ～하다 criticize; comment (*on*); review/문예 ～ literary criticism /시국을 ～하다 comment on the current situation/～가 a critic; a publicist. ひょうろん

**평맥(平脈)** normal pulse. へいみゃく

**평면**(平面) a plane／~의 plane; flat; level／~ 기하 plane geometry／~각 a plane angle. へいめん

**평미레** a strickle; a striker／~질하다 level with a grain leveler. とがき

**평미리치다** make equal[uniform]／밭이랑을 ~ level down the ridges of the field. ならす

**평민**(平民) common people; a commoner／~주의 democratism; democracy／~적 democratic. へいみん

**평방**(平方) a square／ ~을 전개하다 find the root (*of*)／~근(根) a square root (of *a number*)／~형 a square／~일 마일 one square mile. へいほう

**평범**(平凡) commonness; mediocrity／~하다 be common; ordinary 《무특색하다》(be) featureless 《범용하다》(be) mediocre 《별일 없다》(be) uneventful／~한 생활을 하다 live a humdrum life／~한 사람 a mediocrity. へいぼん

**평복**(平服) an ordinary dress; plain clothes 《사복》civilian clothes. へいふく

**평상**(平床) a flat wooden bed.

**평상**(平常) normal [times]／ ~시의 normal; usual; ordinary; everyday／철도는 ~시대로 복구되었다 The railroad service has been restored to normal[normalcy]. へいじょう

**평상시**(平常時) ordinary times／~의 normal; usual; ordinary／~에는 normally; usually. へいじょうじ

**평생**(平生) one's [whole] life; a lifetime／~의 한 a lifelong regret／~ 소원 one's lifelong desire; a desire cherished for life／그는 ~ 독신으로 지냈다 He remained single all his life. しょうがい

**평석**(評釋) critical notes; annotation; commentary／~하다 annotate. ひょうしゃく

**평소**(平素) ①ordinary times ⇒평상시(平常時) ②《지난날》~에 in the past; from long ago. へいそ

**평시**(平時) ①《평화시》time of peace; peacetime／~의 in peace time; peacetime／~ 편제 peace organization／~ 정원 (定員) peace establishment ②《평상시》ordinary times／~에는 ordinarily; usually. へいじ

**평안**(平安) peace; welfare; tranquility／~하다 (be) in peace; peaceful／항해의 ~함을 기원합니다 I wish you a happy voyage[bon voyage]. へいあん

**평야**(平野) a [level] plain; an open field 《대평원》a prairie〈미〉／호남 ~ the plains of Honam. へいや

**평온**(平溫) ①《평균 온도》an average temperature ②《평상시의》a normal temperature／인체의 ~은 36.9도이다 The normal temperature of the human body is 36.9 degrees. へいおん

**평온**(平穩) quiet[ness]; peace; serenity／~하다 (be) quiet; serene／ ~해지다 become quiet; quiet down／~ 무사히 in peace and quiet／동부 전선은 극히 ~하다 Everything is quite on the eastern front. へいおん

**평원**(平原) a plain; a prairie〈미〉／~ 광야(廣野) a vast plain; a prairie. へいげん

**평유**(平癒) recovery [from illness]; restoration to health／~하다 recover health; get well; recover (*from*). へいゆ

**평의**(評議) conference; consultation 《토의》discussion／~하다 confer; discuss; consult (*with*)／~원(員) a councilor; a trustee／~회 a council; a conference. ひょうぎ

**평이**(平易) 《평탄》plainness 《단순》simplicity 《용이》easiness／ ~하다 (be) easy; simple; plain／ ~하게 easily; simply; plainly／~한 문체 a sinple style／~하게 설명하다 explain simply. へいい

**평일**(平日) ①⇒평상시(平常時) ②⇒평소(平素) ③《일요일에 대하여》a weekday／~에 on weekdays. へいじつ

**평작**(平作) a normal[an average] crop／벼는 ~이 예상된다 The rice is expected to be an average crop. へいさく

**평전**(評傳) a critical biography.

**평점**(評點) a mark; examination[grade] marks; grades. ひょうてん

**평정**(平靜) calm; composure 《침착》serenity／~하다 (be) calm; composed; serene／마음의 ~ presence[peace, serenity] of mind. へいせい

**평정**(平定) suppression; repression; subdual／ ~하다 suppress; quell; subdue; put down／반란을 ~ put down rebels. へいてい

**평정**(評定) rating; valuation; evaluation／~하다 rate (*a person's merit*)／근무 ~ the efficiency rating system. ひょうてい

**평좌**(平坐) sitting at one's ease／~하다 sit at *one's* ease. あぐらをかくこと

**평준**(平準) ①《수준》level ②《평균》equality／~ 점 a level point. へいじゅん

**평지** 《식》a rape; a coleseed. あぶらな

**평지**(平地) level land[ground]; 《평원》a plain／~에 풍파를 일으키다 create a disturbance where everything is in peace. へいち

**평직**(平織) plain fabrics. ひらおり

**평치**(平治) ~하다 govern a country peacefully; rule over the people peacefully. へいち

**평탄**(平坦) evenness; flatness／~하다 (be) even; smooth; flat; level／그 여자의 일생은 ~했다 Her life ran in a groove. へいたん

**평판**(評判) 《명성》reputation; fame 《악명》notoriety 《인망》popularity／~이 난 reputed; notorious; famed／~이 나쁜 《나쁘다》be well[ill] spoken of; have a good[bad] reputation／~을 얻다 get [win] a reputation 《인기를》win popularity.

**평판**(平版) lithograph; offset／~ 인쇄 [술] lithography; offset printing. へいげん

**평평하다**(平平—) ①**(평탄하다)** (be) flat; even; level; horizontal ②**(평범하다)** (be) ordinary; commonplace.

**평풍**(屛風) a folding screen ⇨병풍.

**평행**(平行) parallelism; parallel/~의 parallel/~하다 parallel; be parallelled to[with]/~선과 ~하여[하게] parallel to line/~선 parallel lines. へいこう

**평형**(平衡) balance; equilibrium/~하다 (be) balanced/~을 유지하다 balance; equilibrate/~을 잃다 lose the balance; overbalance. へいこう

**평화**(平和) peace **(화합)** harmony/~하다 (be) peaceful; harmonious/~적으로 peacefully; harmoniously; in peace/~조약 a peace treaty/~적 공존 peaceful coexistence/~공세 a peace offensive. へいわ

**평활**(平滑) ~하다 (be) smooth; flat; level; even/~하게 하다 smooth; make smooth/~근 a smooth muscle. へいかつ

**평활**(平闊) ~하다 (be) flat and wide; level and broad. へいかつ

**폐**(肺) 【해】 the lungs/~의 pulmonary; pneumonic/~가 나쁘다 have a weak chest. はい

**폐**(弊) ①**(폐단)** an evil/음주의 ~ the evil of drink/관습의 ~ the evil of convention ②**(괴로움)** trouble; cumberance; inconvenience/~를 끼치다 trouble *a person*; bother; cause inconvenience to *a person*. へい

**폐가**(弊家) my place; my humble house.

**폐가**(廢家) ①**(집)** a deserted house ②**(무후)** an extinct family/~하다 the house comes to an end/그 집은 ~가 되었다 The family has become extinct[has died out]. はいか

**폐간**(廢刊) discontinuance (of *a publication*)/~하다 cease to publish; go out of existence/그 잡지는 ~되었다 The magazine has gone out of existence. はいかん

**폐결핵**(肺結核) 【의】 phthisis; pulmonary tuberculosis; consumption/~환자 a consumptive [patient]. はいげっかく

**폐과**(閉果) 【식】 an indehiscent fruit.

**폐관**(閉館) close (*its doors*)/~하다 be closed. はいかん

**폐관**(閉管) **(악기의)** a closed pipe **(취관 분석용의)** a matrass.

**폐관**(廢官) abolition of an office[a post].

**폐광**(廢鑛) a dead mine; an abandoned pit/~하다 abandon a mine. はいこう

**폐교**(廢校) abolition of a school/~하다 abolish[close] a school. はいこう

**폐기**(廢棄) **(풍속·제도)** disuse; abandonment; abolition **(조약)** abrogation **(법률)** repeal; denunciation/~하다 disuse; abolish; abandon/조약을 ~하다 abrogate a treaty. はいき

**폐기종**(肺氣腫) 【의】 emphysema of the lungs; vesicular emphysema. はいきしゅ

**폐낭**(肺囊) a lung sac.

**폐농**(廢農) giving up farming/~하다 fail in farming; give up[stop] farming. のうごうをやめること

**폐단**(弊端) an evil; an abuse; a vice; evil practices/~을 고치다 remedy[correct] an abuse. へいがい

**폐려**(敝廬, 弊廬) my humble house.

**폐렴** pneumonia ⇨폐렴. はいえん

**폐롭다**(幣—) ①**(귀찮다)** (be) troublesome; inconvenient; bothersome ②**(성질이)** (be) moody; fastidious; overnice; particular. わずらわしい

**폐륜**(廢倫) failing to marry; remaining single/~하다 remain single; do not marry. けっこんしないこと

**폐리**(弊履) worn-out sandals. へいり

**폐립**(廢立) enthronement and dethronement/~하다 enthrone and dethrone [a king]. はいりつ

**폐막**(閉幕) the falling of the curtain/~하다 end; come to a close; close. へいまく

**폐문**(肺門) the hilum of a lung; the pulmonary hilum. はいもん

**폐문**(閉門) closing a gate/~하다 close a gate; shut a door/~시간 the closing time. へいもん

**폐물**(廢物) a useless article[thing]; waste [material]; **(찌끼·쓰레기)** refuse **(오물)** dirt/~이 되다 become useless/~이용 the utilization of waste materials [products]. はいぶつ

**폐방**(廢房) a deserted room; a disused room/~하다 desert a room.

**폐방**(弊邦, 敞邦) my[our] [humble] country.

**폐백**(幣帛) ①**(신부의)** gifts offered to the parents of the bridegroom by the bride ②**(신랑의)** silks offered to the bride by the bridegroom ③**(일반의)** a gift; a present.

**폐병**(廢兵) a disabled[crippled, an invalid] soldier. はいへい

**폐병**(肺病) consumption; a lung[chest] trouble; a lung[pulmonary] disease[complaints]/~환자 a consumptive [patient]; a lunger(속)·속(俗)/~으로 죽다 die of consumption. はいびょう

**폐부**(肺腑) ①**(폐)** the lungs ②**(마음 속)** the bottom[depths] of *one's* heart; *one's* inmost heart ③**(급소)** a vital point; a critical area/그의 말은 ~에서 우러 나온 것이다 His speech was a true expression of his heart. はいふ

**폐비**(廢妃) deposal of a queen **(왕비)** a deposed queen/~하다 depose a queen.

**폐사**(弊社) our company[firm]. へいしゃ

**폐색**(閉塞) blockade; stoppage/~하다 blockade; block [up]; bottle up/~선 a blockader/~을 occlusive/~전선 an occluded front/항구를 ~하다 block up

**폐선** [bottle up] a port. へいそく
**폐선(廢船)** a scrapped[retired] ship; an abandoned ship. はいせん
**폐쇄(閉鎖)** closing; closure 《공장 폐쇄》a lockout/~하다 close; shut; lock; wind up; lock out/~기 breech mechanism/~ 기관 closed institutions/우리는 내일로 이 사업을 ~한다 We will wind up this business tomorrow. へいさ
**폐습(弊習)** a bad habit; an evil practice [custom]; abuses/~을 없애다 break down[do away with] evil customs/~을 시정하다 remedy abuses. へいしゅう
**폐시키다(弊─)** annoy; bother; cause trouble to (a person); trouble (a person).
**폐어(廢語)** an absolete[a disused] word. はいご
**폐어(肺魚)** 〖어〗 a lungfish; a dipnoan [fish]/~류(類) Dipnoi(학명).
**폐업(廢業)** quitting of one's business/~하다 give up[close, quit] one's business 《폐점》shut up one's shop 《의사업·변호사업 따위의》give up one's practice/~계 a report of cessation of business/~하게 되다 be driven out of business.
はいぎょう
**폐염(肺炎)** 〖의〗 pneumonia/급성 ~ acute pneumonia/그 환자는 ~으로 죽었다 The patient died of pneumonia. はいえん
**폐엽(肺葉)** 〖해〗 a lobe of the lung; a lunglobe. はいよう
**폐원(閉院)** the closing[recess] of the Assembly[Parliament]/~하다 close; recess [the Assembly, the Parliament]/~식 the closing ceremony of the Assembly. へいいん
**폐위(廢位)** dethronement/~하다 dethrone; depose (a sovereign). はいい
**폐인(廢人)** 《불구자》a crippled person 《병자》an invalid. はいじん
**폐일언(蔽一言)** ~하고 in a word; in short; to sum up. 一言でいうこと
**폐장(肺臟)** 〖해〗 the lungs ⇨폐. はいぞう
**폐장(閉場)** closing (of a place)/ ~하다
**폐절(廢絶)** extinction/~하다 become extinct/~가 an extinct family. はいぜつ
**폐절제(肺切除)** 〖의〗 pneumonectomy; pneumectomy.
**폐점(弊店)** our shop; we. へいてん
**폐점(閉店)** closing of business[a shop]; close of operations/ ~하다 close out; close[wind up] business/~ 방매 a closing sale. へいてん
**폐정(閉廷)** dismissing the court/~하다 dismiss the court/~되다 the court adjourns. へいてい
**폐정(弊政)** misgovernment; maladministration/~을 일신하다 renovate the maladministration. へいせい
**폐제(廢帝)** a deposed[dethroned] emperor; an ex-emperor. はいてい
**폐제(幣制)** a monetary system.
**폐지(廢止)** abolition; disuse/~하다 abolish; do away with; discontinue 《법률 따위를》abrogate/그 법률은 ~되었다 The law has fallen into desuetude. はいし
**폐질(廢疾)** an incurable[a fatal] disease.
はいしつ
**폐차(廢車)** a scrapped car[train]; a car [train] out of commission; a car[train] retired from service. はいしゃ
**폐첨(肺尖)** 〖의〗 the apex of a lung/~카타르 the catarrh of the apex [of the lungs]; capillary bronchitis. はいせん
**폐출혈(肺出血)** 〖의〗 hemorrhage of the lungs; a lung hemorrhage.
**폐침윤(肺浸潤)** [amyloid] infiltration of the lungs.
**폐품(廢品)** waste articles[materials]; useless[cast-away] articles/~ 회수 collection of waste articles; recovery of scrap.
**폐풍(弊風)** evil customs; bad habits ⇨폐습(弊習). へいふう
**폐하(陛下)** 《삼인칭》His[Her] Majesty 《이인칭》Your Majesty/황제 ~ His Majesty; H. M. the Emperor/왕후 ~ Her Majesty; H. M. the Empress. へいか
**폐하다(廢─)** 《그만두다》give up; discontinue 《철폐하다》abolish 《군주를》dethrone; depose/학업을 ~ give up one's studies/임금을 ~ depose a king; take the crown from a king. はいする
**폐학(廢學)** giving up one's studies/~하다 discontinue[give up, abandon] one's studies; leave school.
**폐함(廢艦)** a scrapped warship; a ship placed out of commission; a decommissioned warship/~ 처분하다 put (a warship) out of commission; strike (a warship) off the list. はいかん
**폐합(廢合)** abolition and amalgamation/~하다 abolish and amalgamate/~ 정리 reorganization; rearrangement.
はいごう
**폐해(弊害)** an evil; evil practices; abuses 《악영향》an ill[a bad] effect; an evil influence/~를 가져오다 be attended by evils/~를 끼치다 exert an evil influence upon; have an injurious effect upon. へいがい
**폐허(廢墟)** the ruins/그 도시는 ~가 되어 있다 The city is now in ruins. はいきょ
**폐환(肺患)** lung trouble ⇨폐병. はいかん
**폐활량(肺活量)** the capacity of the lungs; breathing capacity/~계(計) a spirometer; a pneumatometer. はいかつりょう
**폐회(閉會)** closing of a meeting; a close; adjournment/~하다 close (a meeting); adjourn/~사 a closing address; ~식 a closing ceremony/~를 선언하다 declare the meeting closed/ ~되다 be closed. へいかい
**폐흉막(肺胸膜)** 〖해〗 the pulmonary pleura.
**-포** period/달〖해〗~ a period of about a month[year].
**포(脯)** slices of dried meat seasoned w-

**포** 1028 **포물선**

ith spices／육～ slices of dried beef／～를 뜨다 slice meat. ほ

**포(砲)** ①〖대포〗a gun; a cannon; a piece; a battery 《총칭》gunnery ordnance; artillery ②〖옛 무기의〗a bombard／～를 쏘다 fire a gun. ほう

**포(苞)** 〖식〗a bract. ほう

**포가(砲架)** a gun carriage／～를 설치하다 set a gun carriage. ほうか

**포개다** pile up; heap up; put one upon another; lay one on top of the other／장작을 ～ stack firewood.

**포갬포갬** one on top of the other／이부자리를 ～ 쌓다 pile bedclothes one upon another. かさねがさね

**포격(砲擊)** bombardment; cannonade; shelling／～하다 bombard; cannonade; shell; fire on／～을 받다 be bombarded. ほうばき

**포경(捕鯨)** whaling; whale fishing／～선 a whaler; a whaleboat; a whaling vessel／～업 whale fishing[fishery]; the whaling industry／～ 회사 a whaling company. ほげい

**포경(包莖)** 〖의〗phimosis／～ 수술 an operation for phimosis. ほうけい

**포고(布告)** proclamation; promulgation; announcement; notification 《포고문》a decree／～하다 proclaim; announce; declare; decreep; promulgate; notify／선전 ～하다 declare war against[upon]／프랑스는 이탈리아에 대해 선전 ～했다 France declared war against[on] Italy. ふいく

**포곡조(布穀鳥)** a cuckoo ⇒뻐꾸기.

**포공영(蒲公英)** odandelion⇒민들레.たんぽぽ

**포괄(包括)** inclusion; comprehension／～하다 include; comprehend; comprise; contain; embrace; cover／～ 계승인 a general successor／～적으로 inclusive[ly]; general[ly]／협정의 ～ 범위 the coverage of an agreement. ほうかつ

**포교(布敎)** missionary work; propagation／～하다 propagate; propagandize; preach／～사(師) a missionary 《군목》a chaplain／～에 종사하다 be engaged in missionary work. ふきょう

**포구(浦口)** a port; a harbour; an inlet.

**포구(砲口)** the muzzle 《구경》the caliber.

**포군(暴君)** a tyrant ⇒폭군. ぼうくん

**포군(砲軍)** a gunner. ほうへい

**포근하다** ①(be) soft and comfortable; downy; fluffy ②(be) mild; warm／겨울 날씨가 ～ It is mild for the winter. ふくよかだ

**포기** a root; a plant／배추 한 ～ a cabbage／～ 가름 a division; multiplication of a plant by separating the roots.

**포기(抛棄)** abandonment; resignation 《권리 따위의》surrender; waiver 《요구 따위의》relinquishment／～하다 give up; abandon; throw up 《요구·권리 따위를》renounce; surrender; waive; forfeit 《방치하다》lay aside／지위를 ～하다 throw up one's position／계획을 ～하다 abandon [give up] one's attempt[plan]. ほうき

**포달** abusive[offensive, foul] language; insulting remarks; abuse; an insult／～부리다 call all sorts of names; curse and swear. むじひなこと

**포대(布袋)** a burlap bag ⇒부대. ふくろ

**포대(砲臺)** a battery 《요새》a fort; a fortress; a casemate／～를 구축하다 construct[erect] a battery; build a fort. ほうだい

**포대기** a baby's quilt; a blanket for baby's use; baby's bedding.

**포도(葡萄)** 〖식〗grapes 《나무》a grape vine／～당 grape sugar; dextrose; glucose／～산〖화〗racemic acid／～색 dark purple／～송이 a bunch of grapes／～원 a vineyard; a vinery; a grapery／～주 [grape] wine; port [wine]; vinous liquor／～즙 grape juice／건～ raisins／～주는 ～로 만든다 Wine is made from grapes. ぶどう

**포도(鋪道, 舖道)** a paved street; a pavement. ほどう

**포도(暴徒)** a mob ⇒폭도. ぼうと

**포도둥** with a flitter; fluttering／～하다 flutter; flap rapidly (the wings). はたはた

**포동포동** ～하다 (be) plump; full 《여자가》buxom／～한 얼굴 a full face／～하게 살찐 소녀 a plump girl.

**포드닥** with a flap; fluttering／～하다 flap (the wings); beat the air. ばたばた

**포란(抱卵)** incubation／～하다 incubate; brood 《eggs》／～기 sitting.

**포렴(布廉)** a shop[sign] curtain. めののれん

**포로(捕虜)** a prisoner [of war]《略：P.O.W.》; a war prisoner; a captive／～ 송환 the repatriation of prisoners of war／～ 수용소 a prisoners' camp; a concentration camp／～가 되다 be taken prisoner[s]. ほりょ

**포르르** 《끓다》seething; bubbling 《타다》in a burst of flame; ablaze 《떨다》trembling; fitting／～하다 bubble; burn aflame; seethe; boil; tremble. ばたばた

**포만(飽滿)** a full stomach; satiety／～하다 eat one's fill[to one's heart's content]; be satisfied with. ほうまん

**포말(泡沫)** a bubble; a foam／～ 몽환(夢幻)의 세상 a transient life. ほうまつ

**포목(布木)** linen and cotton; dry goods 〈미〉; drapery〈영〉／～전 a linen shop; a dry goods store〈미〉; a draper's〈영〉.

**포문(砲門)** 《포안》a porthole 《군함의》a gunport 《성채의》an embrasure 《포구》the muzzle／일제히 ～을 열었다 All the guns opened fire simultaneously. ほうもん

**포물선(抛物線)** 〖수〗a parabola／～경(鏡) a parabolic reflector／～ 운동 a parabolic motion／～체 a paraboloid／～을 그

리다 describe a parabola. ほうぶつせん

**포미**(砲尾) the gun breech; the breech [of a cannon].

**포박**(捕縛) arrest; apprehension／ ～하다 arrest; apprehend; catch; seize; place *a person* under arrest. ほばく

**포백**(布帛) linen and silk; hemp and silk.

**포백**(曝白) bleaching in the sun／ ～하다 bleach in the sun. めのきさらすこと

**포병**(砲兵) artillery; an artilleryman; a gunner／～ 대대 an artillery battalion／ ～ 사령관 an artillery commander. ほうへい

**포복**(匍匐) creeping ／～하다 creep; crawl; grovel; go on all fours／～ 식물 a groundling. ほふく

**포복 절도**(抱腹絶倒) ～하다 split[shake, hold] *one's* sides with laughter; be convulsed with laughter／ ～케 하다 set in an uproar; throw (*a person*) into convulsions. ほうふくぜっとう

**포부**(抱負) ambition; aspiration／～를 말하다 express *one's* hopes[wishes]; speak of *one's* aspiration. ほうふ

**포삭포삭** ～하다 (be) brittle; fragile; crumbly. ぼろぼろ

**포살**(砲殺) shooting to death／～하다 shoot (*a person*) to death; execute by shooting. じゅうさつ

**포상**(砲床) a gun platform; a gun emplacement.

**포상**(褒賞) a reward; a prize／～하다 give a prize (*to*)／～을 주다[받다] award [receive, win] a prize／ ～ 수여 prize giving. ほうしょう

**포석**(鋪石) a paving-stone.

**포석**(布石) strategic arrangement of *badook* stones／ ～하다 arrange stones in strategic position [in the game of *badook*]. ふせき

**포섭**(包攝) winning over to *one's* side; bringing round （가입）enlist; 〖논〗connotation／～하다 win (*a person*) over; bring round (*someone*) to *one's* side; enlist; connote／～ 공작을 하다 contrive to win (*a person*) over. ほうせつ

**포성**(砲聲) the sound of firing; the boom[roaring] of a gun[cannon]; cannonade／～이 천지를 진동했다 The roar of guns shook heaven and earth. ほうせい

**포수**(砲手) （사냥군）a hunter; a huntsman 《대포수》an artilleryman 《해군》a gunner. ほうしゅ

**포수**(捕手) 《야구》a catcher.

**포술**(砲術) artillery; gunnery／～ 연습 a gunnery practice.

**포승**(捕繩) a policeman's rope. ほじょう

**포식**(飽食) gluttony; satiation／～하다 be fed up; glut[satiate] *oneself* (*with*); eat *one's* fill／난의(暖衣) ～하다 be well-fed and well-clad; live in clover. ほうしょく

**포신**(砲身) a gun barrel; the barrel of a gun[cannon]. ほうしん

**포실하다** (be) well-off; rich; wealthy／포실한 생활을 하다 live comfortably. ゆたかだ

**포악**(暴惡) atrocity; violence; outrageousness; tyranny; savagery／～하다 (be) atrocious;outrageous; brutal／～ 무도한 살인범 a ruthless murderer. ほうあく

**포안**(砲眼) an embrasure; a gun hole.

**포연**(砲煙) the smoke of cannon; powder-smoke／ ～ 탄우(彈雨) 속을 under a rain[shower] of shells; in the thick of the battle. ほうえん

**포열**(砲列) a train of artillery;a battery ／～을 치다 arrange[lay] a field battery; place guns in position. ほうれつ

**포영**(泡影) ①《거품과 그림자》foam and shadow ②《덧없음》uncertainty; transiency. ほうえい

**포옹**(抱擁) a hug; an embrace／ ～하다 hug; embrace; cuddle; hold (*a person*) to *one's* breast／서로 ～하다 embrace[hug] each other. ほうよう

**포용**(包容) 《포괄》comprehension; implication 《관용》tolerance／～하다 comprehend; embrace; include 《사람을》tolerate／～력 capacity／～성이 크다 possess a capacious mind／그는 사람을 ～할 아량이 있다 He has a capacity for tolerance. ほうよう

**포위**(包圍) a siege; an investment／～하다 《둘러싸다》surround 《군대 따위가》invest 《포위 따위가》throw a cordon round／～망 an encircling net／군대가 시를 ～했다 The soldiers invested the city. ほうい

**포유**(包有) containing; holding／ ～하다 contain; hold; have (*in*). ほうゆう

**포유**(哺乳) lactation; nursing／ ～하다 suckle; nurse／～ 동물 a mammal／～류 〖동〗the *Mammalia* 《학명》. ほにゅう

**포육**(脯肉) slices of dried meat. ほしじし

**포의**(布衣) a scholar without a government office／～ 한사(寒士) a poor scholar without a government office. ふい

**포의**(胞衣) 〖해〗the placenta; the afterbirth. えな

**포자**(胞子) 〖식〗a spore; 〖동〗a cyst／～ 생식 spore reproduction. ほうし

**포장**(布帳) a curtain 《인력거 따위의》a [folding] top[hood]／～ 마차 a covered carriage[wagon《미》]／～을 씌우다[걷다] pull up[let down] the top. カーテン

**포장**(包裝) packing／ ～하다 pack; wrap (*a thing*) up／～지 packing[wrapping] paper／종이로 ～하다 wrap (*it*) up in paper. ほうそう

**포장**(包藏) wrapping and putting away; storing up; concealment [of a thing] ／～하다 wrap up; wrap and put away; store up. ほうぞう

**포장**(褒獎) stimulation; incitement／～하다 incite; give an encouragement (*to*). ほうしょう

**포장**(鋪裝) pavement; concrete facing／

**포장** ~하다 pave; cover with cement／도로를 아스팔트로 ~하다 pave a street with asphalt. ほそう

**포장(袁章)** a medal [of merit].

**포전(圃田)** a kitchen[vegetable] garden. やさいばたけ

**포전(浦田)** a riverside field.

**포전(砲戰)** an artillery duel[engagement]; a mutual bombardment[cannonade].

**포좌(砲座)** 【군】 a gun platform 《성의》 a barbette 《포가》 a gun carriage; a gun mount; a cage. ほうざ

**포주(抱主)** the employer 《남자》 the master 《여자》 the mistress of a brothel; a pimp. かかえぬし

**포주(庖廚)** a butcher shop ⇒푸주.

**포진(布陣)** the line up／ ~하다 line up; take one's position. ふじん

**포집다** ①(잡다) hold[lay hand on] (a thing) again ②(그릇을) lay (a vessel) over[upon] another[the other].

**포착(捕捉)** capture; 《동》 prehension／ ~하다 grasp; seize; catch; understand; 의미를 ~하기 곤란하다 The meaning is beyond my grasp., I can't get at the expact meaning. ほそく

**포척(布尺)** a linen measuring tape.

**포촌(浦村)** a seaside village. ぎょそん

**포충망(捕蟲網)** an butterfly net; an insect net. ほちゅうあみ

**포충엽(捕蟲葉)** an insectivorous leaf. ほちゅうよう

**포탄(砲彈)** a cannon ball 《유탄》 a shell 《실탄》 a shot 《일반의》 a projectile／적에게 ~을 퍼붓다 rain[hail] shells upon the enemy. ほうだん

**포탈(逋脫)** tax evasion[avoidance]; evasion of taxes／ ~하다 evade[dodge] a tax; defraud the revenue. ほだい

**포탑(砲塔)** a [gun] turret 《군함의》 a cupola. ほうとう

**포태(胞胎)** conception; pregnancy／ ~하다 conceive; get[become] pregnant; go with child. ほうたい

**포펌(襃貶)** praise and censure; criticism／ ~하다 criticize. ほうへん

**포피(包皮)** 【해】 the foreskin; the prepuce／ ~ 절단 circumcision.

**포학(暴虐)** tyranny; despotism; cruelty; outrage／ ~하다 (be) tyrannical; despotic／갖은 ~ 무도한 짓을 다하다 perpetrate all possible atrocities. ぼうぎゃく

**포함(包含)** inclusion; implication／ ~하다 《속에》 contain; hold; comprise; include; comprehend; embrace; cover 《의미를》 imply／이 책은 많은 문제를 ~하고 있다 This book embrace many subjects. ほうがん

**포함(砲艦)** a gunboat. ほうがん

**포합(抱合)** ①(껴안음) embracing each other ②【화】 combination; affinity／ ~하다 embrace each other. ほうごう

**포합어(抱合語)** an incorporating language. ほうごうご

**포항(浦港)** a port; a harbour.

**포화(砲火)** gun-fire; artillery fire／서로 ~을 퍼붓다 exchange fire／아군은 적을 향하여 포화를 열었다 Our forces opened fire on the enemy. ほうか

**포화(布靴)** cloth shoes; canvas shoes; tennis shoes. ぬのぐつ

**포화(飽和)** 【화】 saturation／ ~하다 be[become] saturated／ ~기 a saturator／ ~ 용액《화합물》 a saturated solution[compound]. ほうわ

**포환(砲丸)** a cannonball; a slug; 《체》 a shot. ほうがん

**포환 던지기(砲丸—)** shot-put[ting]／ ~하다 put the shot／ ~ 선수 a shot-putter; a weight putter.

**포획(捕獲)** capture; seizure／ ~하다 capture; seize; catch; make a prize of (a thing)／ ~물 a prize; a booty. にかく

**포효(咆哮)** 《맹수의》 a roar; a howl／ ~하다 roar; howl／ ~하는 파도 소리를 듣다 hear the roar of the sea. ほうこう

**폭** ①(깊게) deeply; soundly; completely／ ~ 잠들었다 fall asleep soundly ②(힘있게) thrusting hard ③(꼭 덮거나 싸다) wrapping carefully[tightly]／담요로 몸을 ~ 싸다 wrap oneself in a blanket ④(함빡 곯다) boil／ ~ 삶다 boil to pulp ⑤(남김없이) with nothing left; exhaustively ⑥(꺼지다) sink; hollow／발 밑의 땅이 ~ 꺼졌다 The ground under his feet sank all of a sudden. すっぽり

**폭(幅)** 《넓이》 width; breadth／ ~이 좁은 [넓은] narrow[wide]／그 길은 ~이 100 피트다 The road is 100 feet wide. はば

**폭거(暴擧)** [an act of] violence; an outrage 《폭동》 a riot 《무모한 짓》 a reckless attempt／ ~로 나오다 resort to violence／ ~를 경고하다 warn (a person) against recklessness. ぼうきょ

**폭격(爆擊)** an aerial bombing[bombardment]; a bombing [raid]／ ~하다 bomb; make a bombing raid／ ~으로 집을 잃은 사람들 people bombed out; bombed-out people. ばくげき

**폭군(暴君)** a tyrant 《전제 군주》 a despot; an autocrat. ぼうくん

**폭도(暴徒)** a mob; rioters; insurgents／ ~를 진압하다 put down a mob. ぼうと

**폭동(暴動)** a riot; a disturbance; rioting; an uprising; a seditious act of violence 《반란》 an insurrection; a rebellion 《군대의》 a mutiny／ ~을 선동하다 instigate a riot／ ~죄 a charge of sedition[rioting]. ぼうどう

**폭등(暴騰)** an abnormal[a sudden] rise; a jump; soaring／ ~하다 jump; soar; rise; abnormally; boom／주식(主食) 및 연료 값이 ~했다 Prices of staple food and fuel have skyrocketed. ぼうとう

**폭락(暴落)** a sudden[heavy] fall; a slump 《붕락》 a crash／ ~하다 decline; heavily; slump; fall suddenly／생사의

**폭력(暴力)** violence; force／~단 a toughgang／~에는 ~으로 대한다 meet violence with violence; give measure for measure／~으로 무리하게 by main force. ぼうりょく

**폭렬(爆裂)** blasting／~하다 blow (*a thing*) up to pieces; blast (*a thing*) to bits. ばくれつ

**폭로(暴露)** exposure; discovery; disclosure／~하다 (드러내다) expose; disclose; reveal; divulge (*a secret*); betray; lay bare; bring (*a matter*) to light (드러나다) be discovered; be revealed; be laid bare; be brought to light／비밀을 ~하다 lay bare (*a person's*) secret／~ 전술 exposure[mudslinging] tactics. ばくろ

**폭뢰(爆雷)** a depth bomb[charge]. ばくらい

**폭리(暴利)** excessive profits (부당한) profiteering (고리) exorbitant interest; usury／~를 단속하다 control profiteering. ぼうり

**폭명(爆鳴)** detonation／~ 가스 detonating gas. ばくめい

**폭민(暴民)** a mob; rioters／~ 정치 mobrule; ochlocracy; mobocracy.

**폭발(爆發)** explosion; detonation; blow up; blasting; bursting; blowing up (화산의) eruption／~하다 explode; burst (*up*); blow up; detonate (화산이) erupt; go into eruption／가스 ~로 파괴되다 be wrecked by a gas explosion. ばくはつ

**폭사(爆死)** death resulting from bombing／~하다 be killed by a bomb; be bombed to death. ばくし

**폭사(暴死)** sudden death／~하다 die suddenly; drop[fall] death. ぼうし

**폭삭** all; wholly; entirely; completely／그 건물이 ~ 주저앉았다 The building collapsed completely. すっかり

**폭서(暴暑)** intense[severe, torrid] heat. ぼうしょ

**폭설(暴雪)** a heavy snow; a storm of snow.

**폭소(爆笑)** a burst[roar] of laughter; an explosive laugh／~하다 burst out laughing; burst forth into a roar of laughter／~를 터뜨렸다 There was a burst into laughter. ばくしょう

**폭식(暴食)** voracious eating; gluttony／~하다 eat to excess[too much]; overeat *oneself*／그는 ~하여 병이 났다 He overeat himself into sickness.／~가 a gourmand; a glutton. ぼうしょく

**폭신하다** (be) soft; cushiony ⇒폭신하다. ふれふわだ

**폭압(暴壓)** oppression; coercion; repression／~하다 oppress; coerce; repress; curb[check] by force. ぼうあつ

**폭약(爆藥)** an explosive [compound]; blasting powder; detonator／고성능 ~ a high explosive／~에 점화하다 set off the blasting powder. ばくやく

**폭양(曝陽)** the burning[scorching] sun; the blazing sunlight.

**폭언(暴言)** violent[harsh] language; wild[strong] words／~을 토하다 use violent language. ぼうげん

**폭우(暴雨)** a pouring[heavy, violent] rain; a downpour [of rain]; a torrential rain. ぼうう

**폭원(幅員, 幅圓)** the width; breadth／~ 5피트 five feet in width.

**폭위(暴威)** tyranny; abuse of power; great violence／~를 떨치다 be rampant; be furious; be violent.

**폭음(暴飮)** excessive[heavy] drinking; intemperance／~하다 drink too much [to excess]; drink hard[heavily]／~ 폭식하다 eat and drink immoderately. ぼういん

**폭음(爆音)** an explosive[a bursting] sound; an explosion (기관의) roaring (비행기의) the drumming[whirr] of a propeller／~을 내며 날다 fly with a whirr; thunder over head. ばくおん

**폭정(暴政)** despotic government; tyranny; misrule／~을 펴다 tyrannize over a country. ぼうせい

**폭주(輻輳)** congestion; overcrowding; concourse; pressure／~하다 be congested; be [over]crowded／~를 완화하다 relieve the congestion (*of*). ふくそう

**폭주(暴注)** downpour [of rain]／~하다 rain hard[heavily]; rain in torrents.

**폭죽(爆竹)** a firecracker; a petard; a squib／~을 터뜨리다 set off[shoot] firecrs. ばんちく

**폭취(暴醉)** ~하다 get[be] dead-drunk. ひどくようこと

**폭침(爆沈)** sinking by explosion; blowing up／~하다 (가라앉히다) blow up; explode and sink (가라앉다) be sunk; be blown up and sunk. ばくちん

**폭탄(爆彈)** a bomb; a bomb shell／수소 ~ a hydrogen bomb; an H-bomb／시한 ~ a time bomb. ばくだん

**폭파(爆破)** explosion; blowing up／~하다 blast; demolish; explode／암석을 ~하다 blast a rock [with dynamite]. ばくは

**폭포(瀑布)** a waterfall; falls (작은) a cascade (큰) a cataract／나이아가라 ~ Niagara Falls. ばくふ

**폭폭** ①(찌르다) piercing repeatedly ②(썩다) rotting rapidly ③(삶다) boiling completely[well] ④(욕) abusing roundly ⑤(쏟다) pouring violently ⇒폭폭. なみなみ

**폭풍(暴風)** a storm; a wild[violent, stormy] wind／~권(圈) a storm zone[area]／~ 신호[경보] a storm signal[warning]／~이 일어난다 A storm arises.／그 배는 심한 ~으로 난파했다 The ship was wrecked in a terrible storm.

**폭풍(爆風)** a bombshell[detonation] blast. ばくふう

**폭풍우(暴風雨)** a rainstorm; a storm; a tempest; a hurricane **(태풍)** a typhoon /~가 일다 a storm rises[breaks, comes on]. ぼうふうう

**폭한(暴寒)** severe[intense] cold. こくかん

**폭한(暴漢)** a rough; a ruffian; a rowdy; a tough《미·속》 ~에게 습격을 당하다 be assaulted by a ruffian. ぼうかん

**폭행(暴行)** [an act of] violence; an outrage; violation; riotous conduct; an attack; an assault/~하다 behave violently; assault; attack; act outrageously/~을 가하다 do violence (to); commit an outrage[act of violence] (against). ぼうこう

**폴딱** palpitate; throb; jump ⇒팔딱. ぴょん

**폴락** flutter ⇒팔락. ひらりと

**폴싹** rising dust or smoke; collapsing; flopping. ばっと

**폴짝** opening[closing] the door suddenly. ぴょんと

**폴폴** in a rage; flapping; seething. ぐらぐら

**폿소리(砲—)** the boom[roar] of a gun ⇒포성(砲聲). ほうせい

**퐁당** with a plop[splash]/물에 ~ 빠지다 fall plop into the water. どぶん

**표(表)** **(통계표)** a table **(목록)** a list **(예정표)** a schedule/**정가~** a price list/시간~ a time-table. ひょう

**표(標)** **(부호)** a sign; a mark **(표현)** a token; a mark **(휘장)** a badge **(증거)** proof; evidence **(상표)** a brand; trademark/가슴에 ~를 달다 wear a badge on one's breast. しるし

**표(票)** a ticket; a pass **(투표의)** a vote/ 이름~ a name-card/번호~ number-check/무료~ a free pass/왕복~ a return [ticket]; a round-trip ticket〈미〉/~파는 곳 a booking office〈영〉/**(기차의)** a ticket office〈미〉/**(극장의)** a box office/~파는 창구 a ticket-window/~찍는 가위 a ticket puncher/배급~ a ration-coupon/깨끗한 한 ~를 던지다 cast a clean [an honest] vote (for)/~를 지참한 사람만 입장을 허가함 Admission by ticket only.

**표결(表決)** a vote; division/~하다 take a vote; divide; take division (on); determine by vote/~권(權) a vote. ひょうけつ

**표고** 〖식〗 a kind of mushroom; Cortinellus shiitake(학명). しいたけ

**표구(表具)** mounting / ~하다 mount (a picture)/~사 a paper hanger; a mounter; a paperer. ひょう

**표기(表記)** ①**(겉에 쓰기)** inscription on the face/~의 mentioned[inscribed] on the face[outside]/~ 금액 the sun inscribed on the face ②**(내용 표시)** declaration/~의 declared; insured/~ 가격 declared[insured] value. ひょうき

**표기(標記)** a mark; a sign/~하다 mark (a thing); put a mark on (a thing). ひょうき

**표나다(表—)** be characteristic (of); be conspicuous; stand out **(흔적)** make a mark; show signs; give evidence (of); leave traces/표나게 굴다 act conspicuous/회색은 먼지 묻은 표가 안 난다 Gray does not show the dust. めにつく

**표독(慓毒)** brutality; cold-bloodedness; atrocity/~하다 (be) cruel; brutal; cold-hearted; merciless; ruthless. ざんにんなこと

**표등(標燈)** signal-lamp; a target-lamp. ひょうとう

**표류(漂流)** drifting/~하다 drift [about] be adrift / ~자 a person adrift on the sea; a castaway/~선 a drifting ship. ひょうりゅう

**표리(表裏)** **(겉과 속)** inside and outside; obverse and reverse **(양면)** both sides **(언동의)** double-dealing/~ 부동한 double-hearted[-faced]/그는 ~ 부동한 사람이다 He has two faces. ひょうり

**표말(標抹)** a signpost/길가에 ~을 세우다 set up a signpost by the road-side.
めじるしのくい

**표면(表面)** **(윗면)** the surface; the face **(외면)** the exterior; the outside **(외관)** appearance; show/~의 external; outside; outward; apparent; seeming/~장력 〖물〗 surface tension/일의 진상이란 결코 ~만을 보고 알 수는 없는 법이다 The true condition of affairs is not to be known by external appearances.
ひょうめん

**표면화(表面化)** ~하다 come to the fore [front]; come into the open; come to the surface; become an issue; break **(공표)** come to light/그 사전으로 그들의 의도가 ~되었다 The events have disclosed their designs. ひょうめんか

**표명(表明)** expression; demonstration; manifestation/ ~하다 express; make an expression (of); demonstrate/반대 의사를 ~하다 express oneself against (a matter); declare against. ひょうめい

**표모(漂母)** an old washerman.

**표목(標木)** a mark post; a signpost.
めじるしのくい

**표묘(縹緲)** **(멀고 아득함)** haziness; indistinctness **(넓고 끝없음)** vastness; limitlessness/~하다 (be) distant and hazy; vast and dim/~한 태평양 the vast expanse of the Pacific. ひょうびょう

**표박(漂泊)** wandering; roaming; vagabondage/~하다 wander about; tramp; drift/~ 인종 a nomadic race[tribe].
ひょうはく

**표방(標榜)** advocacy; espousal/ ~하다 **《내세우다》** profess (oneself to be); **《주장하다》** stand for; advocate; espouse (the

**표백**(表白) expression; manifestation; exhibition 《자백》confession／～하다 express; manifest; confess. ひょうはく

**표백**(漂白) bleaching／～하다 bleach／～분(粉) bleaching power／～액 a bleaching solution; a bleach; a decolorant. ひょうはく

**표범**(豹―) 〖동〗a leopard; a panther／～나비 a fritillary／암～ a leopardess; a pantheress. ひょう

**표변**(豹變) sudden change; volte-face／～하다 change suddenly; switch; undergo a change of heart 《변절》turn *one's* coat／～ 잘하는 changeable; fickle. ひょうへん

**표본**(標本) 《박물의》a specimen 《견본》sample 《전형》an example; a type／식물[동물] ～ a botanical[zoological] specimen. ひょうほん

**표상**(表象) ①《상징》a symbol; an emblem／～하다 symbolize; be emblematic *(of)*／평화의 ～ emblem of peace ②〖철〗an idea; 〖심〗a [re]presentation *(of)*／～의 중심 the center of ideas. ひょうしょう

**표석**(表石) a grave marker; a tombstone ⇨묘표. ひょうせき

**표석**(標石) a boundary stone; a stone post[landmark]; a milestone. ひょうせき

**표석**(漂石) 〖지〗an erratic block[boulder]. ひょうせき

**표시**(表示) indication; expression; manifestation／～하다 indicate; express; show; manifest／그는 사랑의 ～로 그 여자에게 꽃을 보냈다 He send her flowers as a sign of his love for her. ひょうじ

**표어**(標語) a motto; a slogan; a catchword; a watchword／선거의 ～ an election slogan. ひょうご

**표연**(飄然) ～하다 (be) airy; aimless 《목적없이》aimlessly／그녀는 ～히 집을 나다 She left home aimlessly. ひらひら

**표음**(表音) phonetic representation／～문자 phonetic symbols; phonetics. ひょうおん

**표의**(表意) semantic[ideographic] representation／～문자 semantic symbols; pictographs; ideographs. ひょうい

**표장**(表裝) 《표구》mounting 《서적 등의》binding／～하다 mount *(a picture)* with; bind *(a book)* in. ひょうそう

**표장**(標章) a mark; a sign; an emblem; a badge. ひょうしょう

**표적**(表迹) 《부호》a sign; a mark 《흔적》traces; marks 《표시》a token; a sign; a manifestation 《증거》a certificate; a proof *(of)*; evidence *(of)*; 《기념품》a memento; a souvenir／감사의 ～으로 in token of *one's* gratitude.

**표적**(標的) a target 《목표물》a mark; an object; a butt／～에 빗맞다 miss the mark. ひょうてき

**표절**(剽竊) crib; piracy; plagiarism; abstraction／～하다 crib; pirate; plagiarize; abstract／～자 a pirate; a plagiarist. ひょうせつ

**표정**(表情) [facial] expression; a look; a countenance／무～한 얼굴 a blank look／슬픈 ～ a sad expression[countenance]. ひょうじょう

**표제**(表題, 標題) 《책의》a title 《신문의》a heading; a head[-line]; a caption 〈미〉; 《주제》a subject／～어 a lemma *(pl. -ta)*／～ 음악 program music. ひょうだい

**표주**(標註) a top note; a marginal note／～하다 add a note *(to)*; note in the margin. ひょうちゅう

**표주**(標柱) a signpost; a marking post. ひょうちゅう

**표주박**(瓢―) a gourd dipper; a calabash. ふくべ

**표준**(標準) a standard; a norm; a cannon; a level 《비판의》a criterion／～형 a standard type／～을 정하다 set [up] a standard. ひょうじゅん

**표지**(表紙) a cover; binding／～의 도안 a cover design. ひょうし

**표지**(標紙) a paper; a bill; a certificate; a mark; a note. ひょうし

**표지**(標識) 《기준》a criterion 《안표》a [land] mark; a sign; a signal; a beacon／항로 ～ channel marks. ひょうしき

**표징**(表徵) a mark; a sign; a symbol; an indication. ひょうちょう

**표착**(漂着) drifting ashore／～하다 be cast[thrown] ashore; be washed ashore; drift[float] ashore／섬에 ～하다 be cast away by the waves upon the shore of an island. ひょうちゃく

**표창**(表彰) commendation; awarding; honouring; public acknowledgment of *a person's* meritorious services／～하다 commend [officially]; honour *(a person)*; give recognition *(for)*／～식 a commendation ceremony／～받다 win official commendation. ひょうしょう

**표토**(表土) 〖지〗top soil; regolith. ひょうど

**표표**(飄飄) floatingly; buoyantly; airily. ひょうひょう

**표피**(表皮) 〖해〗the cuticle; the epidermis; the outer skin. ひょうひ

**표하다**(表―) express; show; manifest; demonstrate; offer; pay／경의를 ～ pay respects *(to)*; do *(a person)* honour. ひょうする

**표하다**(標―) mark; put a mark *(on)*／읽은 곳을 ～ mark the place that *one* has read. しるす

**표한**(剽悍) fierceness; ferocity; savageness／～하다 (be) fierce; ferocious; savage. ひょうかん

**표현**(表現) expression; [re]presentation; manifestation／～하다 express; represent; manifest／～예술적 ～ artistic present.

푯대(標—) a sign[mark, signal] post. ひょうげん
푯돌(標—) a stone post/～을 세우다 set up a landmark stone.
푯말(標—) a signpost. ひょうしきのくい
푯수(標數) the number of chits[votes].
푸근푸근 ～하다 (be) soft; cushony; spongy; fluffy/～하여 따뜻해 보이는 이불 a bulging and warm-looking quilt.
푸근하다 ①(겨울 날씨가) (be) mild; soft; genial; warm/겨울 날씨로서는 아주 ～ It is an unusually warm day in winter. ②(넉넉하여) (be) comfortably [well] off; better off《충분하여》plentiful. ふくよかだ
푸나무 plants and trees; vegetation. そうもく
푸네기 a near[blood] relative; a kin.
푸념 ①(불평) a grievance; a complaint; grumbling/～하다 make a complaint (of); complain (of) ②(무당의) the ravings of a soceress/～하다 rave.
푸다 ①(물을) dip out; bail out; draw; pump/우물물을 ～ draw water from a well ②(곡식·밥을) scoop out; take out/솥에서 밥을 ～ scoop rice out of a pot.
푸닥거리 an exorcism; an exorcising service with prayers and offerings/～하다 perform an exorcism; profuse.
푸닥지다 profuse; (be) abundant. ありあまるほどだ
푸대접(—待接) cold[icy] treatment; frigid reception; inhospitality/～하다 treat (a person) coldly[with coldness, unkindly, in a cold way]; receive (a person) with indifference; give (a person) a cold reception/나는 ～을 받았다 I was given cold reception. れいぐう
푸덕 with a flap [of the wings]. ばたばた
푸두둥 fluttering. ばたばた
푸드덕 with a flap ⇒푸덕. ばたばた
푸드득 with a gush.
푸둑푸둑 often; frequently; from time to time; frequently; often. ちらばら
푸렁이 blue (one); blue thing. あおいもの
푸르께하다 (be) bluish; greenish.
푸르다 ①(청색) (be) blue; azure《초록》green; verdant/푸른 하늘 the blue sky ②(서슬이) (be) sharp/서슬이 ～《칼날이》have a sharp edge《세력이》be high and mighty. あおい
푸르데데하다《푸르다》(be) bluish; greenish《창백하다》rather pale[pallid]. いやしいほどあおいろがかっている
푸르디푸르다 (be) very green[blue]; fresh-coloured green[blue]. まっあおい
푸릇푸릇 all spotted green or blue; green [blue] here and there/～하다 be all spotted green or blue; be green[blue] here and there/풀이 ～ 돋아나다 grass sprouts out all green here and there.
푸새¹ grasses; plants. ざっそう

푸새² starching/～하다 starch (a shirt).
푸서 a ravel; a frayed end. ほどけくち
푸서기 ①(물건) a brittle[fragile] stuff ②(사람) a fragile[delicate] person. なんじゃくなもの
푸석돌 a crumbly stone; a soft stone. もろいいし
푸석푸석 ～하다 (be) fragile; brittle; breakable/～ 부서지다 crumble; break into crumbs.
푸성귀 vegetables; greens; greenstuff.
푸접없다 (be) unfriendly; cold and distant; cool. つめたい
푸주(—廚) a butcher's[shop]; a meat-shop.
푸지다 plentiful; copious; (be) abundant/푸지게 먹다 eat plenty; eat freely. たくさんだ
푸푸 with puffs[whiffs] of breath/～하다 breathe out; be puffy; blow in puffs[whiffs].
푸하다 (be) swollen; bulged; inflated; puffy/푸한 머리 untidy hair/푸한 짐 a loose bundle. ふっくらしている
푹 ①(빈틈없이) with no gaps; (wrapping) carefully/이불을 ～ 덮다 tuck the bedding up snug ②(느긋하게) fast; sound[ly]/잠을 ～ 자다 sleep soundly ③(흠뻑) completely; entirely/～ 삶다 boil hard[well] ④(죄다) completely; exhaustively. すっぽり
푹석푹석 ～하다 (be) crisp; crumbly; friable; brittle. ぼこぼこ
푹신하다 (be) soft; spongy; cushiony; elastic; bouncy; springy; soft and fluffy; downy/푹신한 침대 a comfortable bed. ふかぶかしている
푹푹 ①(힘있게) with repeated force/바늘로 ～ 쑤시다 prick (one's body) with a needle repeatedly ②(따끔따끔하게) prickly; prickingly; tinglingly/손가락이 ～ 쑤신다 My finger is pricking[tingling]. ③(아낌없이) freely; carelessly; lavishly; unsparingly/돈을 ～ 쓰다 spend money freely[carelessly] ④(썩는 모양) completely; perfectly/～ 썩다 grow rotten fast ⑤(흠뻑) hard; well/～ 삶다 boil hard[well] ⑥(찌는 듯이) sultry; muggy/～ 찌는 날씨 sultry weather ⑦(깊이) deeply/발이 ～ 빠지다 one's feet sink deep. ずけずけ
푹하다 (be) warm ⇒푸근하다.
푼 ①(화폐) a poon; a penny; a cent《무게》a poon; one tenth of a chi/돈~이나 모으다 make a pretty penny ②(백분율) percentage; per cent/5 ～ 이자를 지불하다 pay 5% interest. もん
푼거리 buying[selling] firewood by the bundle; dealing in a small way/～하다 buy[sell] firewood by the bundle; deal in a small way/～나무 firewood sold by the bundle. こうり
푼거리질 buying a small faggot; a small bundle of firewood.

**푼끌** a small chisel. ちいさいのみ
**푼나무** firewood sold by the bundle. こうりのたきぎ
**푼내기** ①(도박) penny gambling; penny ante ②⇒푼거리 ③홍정 small-time business; small dealings.
**푼더분하다** ①(얼굴이) (be) full; plump／푼더분한 얼굴 a full face ②(넉넉하다) (be) ample; plentiful／푼더분한 보수 rich payment／푼더분한 대접 a liberal reception. ふくよかだ
**푼돈** small [amount of] money; loose money; broken money. わずかなおかね
**푼리(分厘)** ①(화폐) a *poon* and a *ri*; pennies and farthings ②(길이・무게) a very small measure in length[weight]; a smidgen／~을 다투다 quarrel over a fraction of a cent; watch every farthing. ぶりん
**푼사** floss [silk]; filoselle.
**푼주** a rather shallow porcelain bowl.
**푼치** a little difference; a small gap. わずかなちがい
**푼푼이** penny by penny; little by little／~ 모은 돈 money saved penny by penny; a pretty money saved little by little. こまごまと
**푼푼하다** ①(넉넉하다) (be) enough; sufficient; plentiful ②(너굴너굴하다) (be) liberal; magnanimous; broad-minded. ほうふだ
**풀¹** (식물) grass (잡초) a weed (약초) a herb (총칭) herbage (목초) pasture／한 포기의 ~ a root of grass／~을 뜯어 먹다 feed on grass (마소가) graze／정원의 ~을 뽑다 weed a garden; pull up weed in the garden. くさ
**풀²** (밀가루의) paste (녹말의) starch (갖풀) glue (공업용) size／~을 먹이다 starch (*one's shirt*)／~을 쑤다 make paste [starch]／고무~ gum [arabic]; mucilage. のり
**풀가사리** 〖식〗 a glue plant; *Gloiopeltis furcata* (학명). ふくろ
**풀기** ①(옷의) starch[iness]／~가 있는 starchy; starched／~가 센 샤쓰 a stiffly starched shirt ②(활기) liveliness; animation; activity; vitality／~가 있다 be full of spirit[life]; be vigorous[animated]／~가 없다 be spiritless[dull, inert]; be in low spirits.
**풀다** ①(짐・끈 따위를) untie (*a string*); undo (*a bundle*); loosen (*one's hair*); unfasten (*a rope*); unlace (*one's shoes*); (천의 가장자리를) fray (딴 것을) unweave (끈 것을) untwist／머리를 ~ let down *one's* hair; loosen *one's* hair ②(문제를) slove; answer; work out; explain (해석) interpret (해명) elucidate／뜻을 ~ explain the meaning／학리를 ~ expound a doctrine ③(의심을) resolve; dispel; satisfy; clear away[up] (*one's doubts*); (오해를) remove (*a misunderstanding*)／모든 의혹이 풀렸다 All doubts were resolved. ④(원한을) vent; satisfy; revenge; pay off (*old scores*); (울적을) dispel; dissipate (*gloom*); (소원을) realize (*one's desire*); gratify (*one's wishes*); have (*one's wish*) fulfilled／기분을 ~ divert *one*self; recreate[refresh] *one*self ⑤(타다) dissolve (*salt in water*); melt／물감을 ~ dissolve dye[color] ⑥(해제하다) remove (*a prohibition, the embargo*); dissolve; free; acquit／금령을 ~ lift the ban; remove a prohibition／봉쇄를 ~ remove[raise, lift] a blockade／포위를 ~ raise a siege ⑦(코를) blow (*one's nose*) ⑧(몸을) warm up(경기에 앞서); (해산하다) deliver (*a baby*); give birth to a child ⑨(꿈 따위를) read; interpret; expound (*one's dream*)／점괘를 ~ interpret[expound] *one's* divination sign／성명을 ~ interpret[expound] divination by the letters[characters] of a name ⑩(논으로 만들다) turn[convert] land into (*a paddy*). とく
**풀떡거리다** spring[leap] up repeatedly／풀떡풀떡 leaping. さっと
**풀떼기** thick gruel of grain flour.
**풀등** a grassy sandbank.
**풀럭거리다** flap; flutter; waver (*in the wind*)／풀럭풀럭 fluttering; flapping; flickering. ひらりと
**풀리다** ①(매였던 것이) come loose; get untied; be frayed (천 따위) ravel (머리칼 따위) stray／풀린 머리칼을 빗어 올리다 comb up loose hair／끈이 풀렸다 The string came untied.／네 구두끈이 풀렸다 Your shoelace has come untied. ②(누그러지다) relent (toward *one*); grow gentle (노엽이) soften in temper／노엽이 ~ *one's* anger is gone[appeased]; *one's* anger has melted away ③(문제 등이) be solved (의심 등이) thaw; melt (열이) be dispelled; break (피로가) abate; be relieved of (*one's fatigue*); (추위가) abate; moderate／풀리지 않는 문제 an unsolved[insoluble] problem／산책으로 갑갑한 마음이 풀렸다 I feel refreshed after a walk., A walk cheered me up.／열이 좀 풀린 것 같습니다 There is a slight abatement in the temperature. ③(해제되다) be removed; be lifted; be dissolved; be absolved; be freed／금령이 ~ a ban is lifted; a prohibition is removed／봉쇄가 ~ a blockade is lifted [raised, removed]／포위가 ~ a siege is raised ④(타지다) dissolve; melt／밀가루가 잘 ~ flour dissolves well ⑤(돈이) be[get] circulated; be released; go into circulation／은행 돈이 ~ money in the bank is released ⑥(피로가) recover from (*one's fatigue*); (힘이) (*one's strength*) be gone. とける
**풀막(―幕)** a grass-roofed hut[shed].
**풀매** a small quern[stone].
**풀머리** loosened[let-down] hair／~하다 let[wear] *one's* hair down.

**풀먹이다** starch (*clothes*). のりづけする
**풀무** [a pair of] bellows 《야로》 a forge. ふいご
**풀무질** blowing with the bellows; ~하다 blow with the bellows; work[blow] the bellows.
**풀뭇간(一間)** 《대장간》 a blacksmith's shop; a smithy.
**풀밭** a grass field; a meadow; a grass plot; pasture land 《잔디밭》 a lawn/~에서 놀다 play on the grass.
**풀비** a [straw] starch brush; a [straw] paste brush.
**풀썩** suddenly; in a cloud/연기가 ~ 났다 A cloud of smoke rose suddenly. /자동차가 지날 때 먼지가 ~ 났다 A motorcar raised a cloud of dust as it passed. ふわっと
**풀솜** 《명주의》 silk-wadding; floss [silk]/~ 나물 cottonweed; *Gnaphalium japonicum*(학명)/~ 할머니 a maternal grandmother.
**풀쐐기** 《충》 a caterpillar. てんぐちょうの幼虫
**풀쑤다** ①《풀을》 make paste; make[prepare] starch ②《재산을》 squander; dissipate] (*a fortune*). のりをたく
**풀숲** a cluster of grass; a grassy place; a bush.
**풀어 내다** ①《얽힌 것을》 unravel; disentangle (*tangled thread*)/짐을 ~ undo a bundle ②《문제를》 solve[workout, unravel] (*a difficult problem*)/수수께끼를 ~ solve[interpret, find out, guess] a riddle; answer[solve, figure out] a puzzle ③《오해를》 remove (*a misunderstanding*). ときほぐす
**풀어 놓다** 《맨 것을》 undo; untie; unpack; unfasten 《방면》 [set] free; release; loosen/보따리를 ~ undo a package/개를 풀어 놓아라 Let the dog loose.
**풀어지다** ①《국수가》 (*noodles*) turn soft ②《눈이》 become bleared; go[get] bleary. とける
**풀잎** a leaf of grass; a blade/~ 피리 a reed [pipe]. くさのは
**풀쩍** ~거리다 keep opening and closing (*the door*); come in and go out all the time; keep coming in and going out. ぼん
**풀쩍풀쩍** opening and closing (*the door*) repeatedly; coming in and going out all the time; leaping[jumping] repeatedly.
**풀젓개** a paste-stirrer.
**풀죽다** ①《옷이》 lose its starch; come unstarched/옷이 ~ clothes lose their starch ②《기세가 죽다》 lose *one's* starch; be dejected[disheartened, discouraged]; be in low spirit/풀이 죽어서 다 니다 go around down in[at] the mouth.
**풀질** pasting; applying paste/ ~하다 paste; apply paste (*to*). のりづけ
**풀집** a starch[paste]-seller's shop.
**풀쳐생각** relaxing; unburdening *one's* mind, putting *one's* mind at ease/~하다 unburden *one's* mind (*of*); take it easy. だんねんしじいすること
**풀치** 《어》 a young hairtail[scabbard fish].
**풀칠** ①《종이 따위에》 applying paste (*to*) ②《생계》 bare livelihood; a hand-to-mouth existence/~하다 paste; apply paste (입에) gain a bare livelihood; live from hand to mouth; maintain a hand-to-mouth existence/뼈빠지게 일해서 겨우 입에 ~하다 work hard merely to keep the wolf from the door. のりづけ
**풀풀** ①《새가》 flapping; fluttering/새가 ~ 날다 a bird flies flapping its wings ②《끓는 모양》 boiling hard; seething/물이 ~ 끓는다 Water is boiling up. こんこん
**풀풀하다** (be) easily angry; short-tempered; irascible; petulant. ふへいをならす
**품¹** ①《옷의》 width (of *a coat*)/ ~이 넓다[좁다] be of broad[narrow] width ②《가슴》 the bosom; the breast/손을 ~에 끼다 with *one's* hands in *one's* bosom/~속에 넣다 put[tuck] (*a thing*) in *one's* bosom/~에 안다 hold[carry] (*a baby*) in *one's* bosom; embrace; hug; embosom/앞 ~ the breast width/뒷 ~ the width between armpits.
**품²** 《노고》 labour 《수고》 trouble/ ~삯 wages; pay/~이 들다 require [much] labor; be troublesome/ ~을 덜다 save (*one*) trouble; save labour. ろろく
**품³** 《동작·됨됨이》 appearance; looks 《모양》 shape; form/사람된 ~ *one's* character[nature]/걷는 ~ the way *one* walks /그는 생긴 ~은 거칠거칠하지만 마음은 좋은 사람이다 He is a good man with a rough exterior./몸 놀리는 ~이 신사답다 He bears himself like a gentleman.
**품(品)** ①《품질》 quality 《품등》 grade ②《품물》 an article; goods; stuff; wares ③《품격》 elegance; grace; refinement; nobility ④《품직》 degree[grade] of official rank. ひん
**품값** wages; pay; cost of labor. ろうちん
**품갚음** ~하다 return work for work; work in return; exchange labor.
**품격(品格)** elegance; refinement; dignity; character; nobility/ ~이 있다 be elegant[refined, dignified]/ ~을 높이다 ennoble (*a person*); dignify[elevate] *one's* character/ ~을 멸어드리다 lose *one's* dignity; degrade *one*self/학문은 사람의 ~을 높인다 Learning ennobles a man. ひんかく
**품계(品階)** grade; rank; degree of official rank/~가 높은 사람 a person of high rank.

**품고**(稟告) a statement (to *a superior*)／~하다 report[tell, inform, state] (*a superior*) (*of*).　ひんこく

**품군** a day laborer; a[wageworker.　やといひと

**품다** ①(안다) hold (*a baby*) to *one's* bosom; put (*a thing*) in *one's* bosom; embrace; hug; sit on (*eggs*)／비수를 가슴에 ~ carry[put, conceal] a dagger in *one's* bosom／애기를 품에 ~ hold a baby in *one's* bosom ②(마음에) hold; entertain (의심·악의 따위를) harbour／불안을 품고 있다 in trembling uncertainty／희망을 ~ entertain a hope／원한을 ~ harbour hatred／그들은 사회에 대하여 분노의 감정을 품고 있다 They harbour a feeling of anger against society.　いだく

**품달**(稟達) a report (to *a superior*).　ひんこく

**품돈** wages; pay for *one's* labour.　ろうちん

**품등**(品等) (품질) quality (등급) grade.　ひんとう

**품목**(品目) the name of an article; a list of articles (한 품목) an item／~별로 by item／주요 수출 ~ the chief items of export／~별로 나누다 itemize; divide by[in] items.　ひんもく

**품사**(品詞) (언) a part of speech／~론 accidence／팔~ the eight parts of speech.　ひんし

**품삯** cost of labour; hire; wages; pay.　ろうちん

**품성**(品性) character／~이 훌륭한[천한] 사람 a man of fine[low] character／~을 도야하다 form[build] character.　ひんせい

**품성**(稟性) nature; natural disposition.　ひんせい

**품속** the bosom／~에 in *one's* bosom／~에 간직하다 keep in *one's* bosom／자연의 ~에 안기다 be [nestled] in the bosom of nature.　むねのうち

**품앗이** exchange of work; working in turn for one another／~하다 exchange work; work in turn for one another.

**품위**(品位) ①(품격) elegance; grace; dignity; refinement／~있는 refined; elegant; graceful／~없는 언사 vulgar language／~를 높이다 ennoble (*a person*); dignify[elevate] *one's* character／~를 지키다 keep[maintain] *one's* dignity ②(품직·직위) rank; position ③(품등) grade (품질) fineness (금의) carat／~가 낮은 광석 low-grade ore／~가 낮다 be low in quality[grade].　ひんい

**품의**(稟議) consultation (with *a superior*)／~하다 consult (with *a superior*).　ひんぎ

**품절**(品切) absence[out] of stock／~이 되다 run out of stock.　しなぎれ

**품종**(品種) (종류) a kind; a description (상품 따위) a grade (변종) a variety (가축의) breed／~ 개량 (가축의) improvement of breed (식물의) plant breeding.　ひんしゅ

**품질**(品質) quality／~이 좋다[나쁘다] be of good[inferior] quality／~을 개량하다 improve (*a thing*) in quality／…에 비해 ~이 낮다 be inferior to (*a thing*) in quality.　ひんしつ

**품팔다** work[labour] for a wage; earn *one's* wage.

**품팔이** being a wage worker; hiring oneself out as a day laborer; doing day labor／~하다 work for wages; hire oneself out as a day laborer／~군 a day laborer; a wageworker; a farm hand[laborer].

**품평**(品評) criticism; evaluation; comment／~하다 criticize; evaluate; comment (on).　ひんぴょう

**품평회**(品評會) a competitive show[exhibition); a fair／농산물 ~ an agricultural show[fair].　ひんぴょうかい

**품하다**(稟─) tell; say; propose; request; mention; relate／…할 것을 품하나이다 I beg to propose[request] you (*that*).　じょうしんする

**품행**(品行) conduct; behavior (학생의) deportment; demeanor; moral character; morals／~이 단정한[나쁜] 사람 a man of good[loose] conduct／~이 단정하다 be well-conducted[-behaved]; be of good conduct／그 여자는 ~이 단정하다 Her conduct is perfect[good]., She has a clean character.

**풋-** (덜 익은) green; unripe (새로운) new; fresh; young; unexperienced; early.

**풋감** a green[an unripe] persimmon.

**풋것** the first product of the season; freshly harvested fruit[vegetables, grain] of the year.

**풋고추** unripe[green] red pepper.

**풋곡식**(─穀─) new grain[cereals]; unripe grain[cereals].　しんこく

**풋과실**(─果實) green[unripe] fruits.　みじゅくのくだもの

**풋김치** Kimchi prepared with young vegetables.

**풋나기** a raw stripling; a greenhorn／~의 green; raw; inexperienced; unfledged; callow.　しろうと

**풋나물** seasoned vegetables prepared with the first of the season.

**풋내** the smell of new greens／~나다 have a smell of fresh young greens; sound like a greenhorn.

**풋담배** green tobacco.

**풋대추** (덜 익은) green[unripe] jujubes (말리지 않은) fresh[undried] jujubes.　あおいなつめのみ

**풋돈냥** a small amount of money which has casually come into *one's* hand; a petty fortune.

**풋바심** ~하다 harvest grain before it is ripe.

**풋밤** unripe chestnuts.
**풋배** green[unripe] pears.
**풋벼** green[unripe] rice/~바심 harvesting unripe rice. みじゅくのいね
**풋사랑** calf love; puppy love.
**풋잠** a light sleep just begun.
**풋장** branch fuel cut and dried in autumn.
**풋장기**(一將棋) unskilled chess; a green hand at chess.
**풍** with poop/ ~하고 방귀를 뀌다 break wind "poop". ほん
**풍**(風)¹ wind/남~ the south wind.
**풍**(風)² (허풍) a boast; a brag; exaggeration; tall[big] talk/ ~을 떨다[치다] brag; exaggerate; talk big[tall, gas]; blow one's own trumpet; draw a long bow; be full of hot air. ほらふき
**풍**(風)³ palsy ⇨풍병(風病). ふうびょう
**-풍**(風) ①(양식) a style; a mode; a fashion; a type/ 미국~의 건물 an American style building ②(풍습) manners [and customs]; a custom; way /~에 ~을 지키다 keep to the good old ways/도시~ town[urbane] manners; urbanity/시골~ rural manners; rurality. —ふう
**풍각쟁이**(風角—) a street singer[musician]; a strolling singer.
**풍간**(諷諫) insinuative exhortation/~하다 exhort by innuendo[insinuation]. ふうかん
**풍격**(風格) character; personality (풍채) appearance/~있는 사람 a man of dignified[noble] presence. ふうかく
**풍경**(風景) (경치) a landscape; scenery (전망) a view; a prostpect/바다의 ~ a seascape/~이 수려한 곳 a beauty spot; a place of scenic beauty/~화 a landscape (painting, picture)/가두 ~ a street scene; a scene on the street/전원 ~ a rural landscape; a scene of the countryside. ふうけい
**풍경**(風磬) a wind-bell with a "fish" clapper.
**풍경치다**(風磬—) keep going in and out busily; frequent.
**풍광**(風光) scenery; view/ ~이 명미하다 have beautiful scenery; have great scenic[natural] beauty. ふうこう
**풍교**(風敎) education of public morals / ~를 해치다 corrupt[be injurious to] public morals. ふうきょう
**풍구**(風—) ①a winnower; a winnowing machine ②(풀무) bellows. ふうしゃ
**풍금**(風琴) an organ/~을 치다 play (on) the organ / ~을 배우다 take lessons in playing the organ[organ lessons]; learn on the organ/~ 연주자 an organist; an organ grinder. ふうきん
**풍기**(風紀) (기율) discipline (사회의) public morals[decency]; (풍속) manners/~ 문란 demoralization; the corruption[decay, relaxation] of public morals/~

를 단속하다 enforce discipline; control public morals/요즈음 학생의 ~가 퇴폐했다 Students of today have deteriorated in their morals. ふうき
**풍기다** ①(냄새를) give out (an odor); send forth; scent (악취를) stink/좋은 냄새를 ~ shed[give out, send forth] a sweet scent[fragrance]/술 냄새가 ~ smell[stink] of wine ②(겨·검불을) winnow[fan] (grain)/겨를 ~ winnow[fan] away chaff ③(새를) scatter (birds); start (birds). におわす
**풍년**(豊年) a year of abundance; a fruitful[an abundant, a rich, a bumper] year (풍작) a good harvest/금년은 ~이 될 것 같다 We shall probably have a good harvest this year./~ 축제 the celebration of a good harvest; a harvest festival. ほうねん
**풍덩** with a splash; with a plop/~ 떨어지다 fall plop into (the water); drop with a plop/그는 물속에 ~ 뛰어 들어갔다 He plunged plop into the water. どぶん
**풍뎅이** a gold bug; a May beetle; a May bug.
**풍도**(風度) one's appearance and attitude /대인의 ~ the attitude[bearing] of a gentleman. ふうさいとたいど
**풍랑**(風浪) wind and waves; heavy seas /~과 싸우다 battle with[struggle against] the wind and waves/~이 심하다 The waves are high. ふうろう
**풍력**(風力) the force[velocity] of the wind/~계 an anemometer; an anemograph/~은 한 시간에 60마일에 달했다 The wind attained a velocity of sixty miles an hour. ふうりょく
**풍로**(風爐) a small kitchen-range[furnace]; a small portable range. ふうろ
**풍로**(風露) wind and dew. ふうろ
**풍류**(風流) ①(멋) refinement; elegance; taste/~를 아는 tasteful; elegant; graceful/~를 모르는 사람 a prosaic person; a matter-of-fact man/~적인 생활을 하다 live a poetical[an idyllic] life ②(음악) music/~가 a man of refined taste; a person of a romantic turn of mind/ ~장 elegant society. ふうりゅう
**풍마 우세**(風磨雨洗) getting weather-beaten/~하다 get weather-beaten.
ふうにさらされること
**풍만**(豊滿) ~하다 (be) plump; corpulent; buxom/~한 미인 a plump, voluptuous beauty. ほうまん
**풍매**(風媒) wind-fertilization; anemophily/ ~의 wind-fertilized/ ~화(花) an anemophilous flower/~ 식물 an anemophilous plant. ふうばい
**풍모**(風貌) features; countenance; appearance/ ~에 접하다 get into personal touch with (one)/그는 당당한 ~를 가지고 있었다 He possessed a commanding presence. ふうぼう

**풍문(風聞)** a rumor; a report; hearsay; a [town] talk／～에 의하면 'Rumor has it[says] (that)., It is rumored (that)／～을 퍼드리다 spread[start, circulate]. ふうぶん

**풍물(風物)** scenery; natural features[objects]; 《풍속·사물》 scenes and manners;／～시(詩) a poem concerning a landscape; natural poetry／한국의 ～ things Korean; the country and the people of Korea. ふうぶつ

**풍미(風味)** flavour; taste; savor／～있는 dainty; savory; delicious; tasty; of fine flavor／독특한 ～ a racy flavor. ふうみ

**풍미(風靡)** ～하다 overwhelm; dominate; sway; make a clean sweep (of)／인심을 ～하다 sway the minds of men. ふうび

**풍백(風伯)** the god of winds; Aeolus. ふうはく

**풍범선(風帆船)** a sailing ship[boat, vessel]; a sailer.

**풍병(風病)** ①nervous disorders; paralysis; palsy ②leprosy. ふうびょう

**풍부(豊富)** abundance; affluence; plenty; wealth; opulence; richness／～하다 (be) rich; abundant／～하게 richly; abundantly／～한 자원 [an] abundance of resources／～한 지식 a wealth of knowledge／내용을 ～히 하다 enrich the contents／그는 학문이 ～하다 He has a great store of learning. ほうふ

**풍비 박산(風飛雹散)** ～하다 be all scattered; scatter in all directions. ふうひほうさん

**풍상(風霜)** wind and frost 《고생》 hardships／～을 겪다 suffer hardships. ふうそう

**풍선(風扇)** ①《선풍기》 a fan; an electric fan; a punka[h] ②《농기구》 a winnower.

**풍선(風船)** a balloon／～을 날리다 fly[send up] a balloon／～껌 bubble gum 《낱개》 a piece of bubble gum／고무 ～ a toy balloon. ふうせん

**풍설(風雪)** wind and snow; a snowstorm; a blizzard／수색대는 맹렬한 ～에도 출발했다 The search party started[set out] in defiance of a furious blizzard. ふうせつ

**풍설(風說)** a rumor; an unfounded report; hearsay; a talk／～이 유포되다 a rumor gets afloat[abroad]. ふうせつ

**풍성(風聲)** ①《바람 소리》 the sound of wind ②《명성》 fame; reputation. かぜのおと

**풍성(豊盛)** abundance; plentitude; richness; affluence; opulence／～하다 (be) abundant; plenteous; affluent; rich; exuberant.

**풍속(風俗)** manners; customs; popular [public] morals／～을 해하다 be injurious to public morals／～ 소설 a novel of manners. ふうぞく

**풍속(風速)** the velocity of the wind; wind velocity／한 시간 20킬로의 ～으로 at a speed of twenty kilometers an hour／～계 an anemometer; a wind gauge. ふうそく

**풍수(風水)** divination by configuration of the ground／～설 the theory of configuration of the ground. ふうすい

**풍수해(風水害)** damage from storms and floods／～는 극심하다 Serious[Great] damage has been caused by the storms and floods. ふうすいがい

**풍습(風習)** customs 《풍속》 manners 《관례》 practice. ふうしゅう

**풍식(風蝕)** wind erosion; weathering. ふうしょく

**풍신(風神)** ①《풍백》 the god of wind ②《풍채》 appearance; presence; mien／～이 좋다 have a fine appearance[presence]. かぜのかみ

**풍아(風雅)** elegance; grace; refinement; daintiness／～하다 (be) elegant; graceful; refined; tasteful／～한 마음 a poetical turn of mind. ふうが

**풍악(風樂)** classic music.

**풍안(風眼)** goggles. ふうがん

**풍압(風壓)** wind-pressure／～계(計) a pressure-anemometer. ふうあつ

**풍어(風漁)** a big haul; a big[good] catch／연어의 ～ a big catch of salmon. ほうりょう

**풍염(豊艶)** voluptuousness／～하다 (be) voluptuous; plump and beautiful. ほうえん

**풍요(豊饒)** richness; wealth; abundance／～하다 (be) rich; abundant; plentiful; bountiful; opulent. ほうじょう

**풍우(風雨)** wind and rain; a storm; a rainstorm／～를 무릅쓰고 in spite[the teeth] of the storm. ふうう

**풍운(風雲)** ①wind cloud ②《형세》 the state of affairs; the situation／～을 일으키다 bring about a crisis. ふううん

**풍운아(風雲兒)** a lucky adventurer; a free lance; a soldier of fortune. ふううんじ

**풍월(風月)** ① wind and moon; beauties of nature／～을 즐기다 enjoy [the beautiful of] nature ②《시가》 poetry／～하다 dabble in poetry; write poetry／～객 a person who dabbles in poetry; a poet. ふうげつ

**풍유(諷諭)** a hidden meaning 《수사》 an allegory／～하다 exhort by insinuation／～ 소설 an allegory. ふうゆ

**풍의(風儀)** appearance ⇨풍채. ふうさい

**풍자(諷刺)** a satire; a sarcasm; an irony; an innuendo／～하다 satirize; lampoon／사회에 대한 ～ a satire on society／～가 a satirist; a lampooner／～ 소설 a satirical novel. ふうし

**풍작(豊作)** a good[rich, an abundant] harvest; a bumper[heavy] crop／벼의 대～ an extremely bountiful rice harv-

**풍재(風災)** damage from wind; a disaster caused by wind. かぜのさいがい

**풍전 등화(風前燈火)** a light before the wind; a candle flickering in the wind /그 소년의 생명은 ~와 같다 The life of the boy hangs by a hair. ふうぜんのともしび

**풍정(風情)** elegance; refinement; tasteful appearance; an artistic air. ふぜい

**풍조(風鳥)** a bird of paradise. ふうちょう

**풍조(風潮)** ①《바닷물》 the lee tide ②《추세》 a tendency; a trend; a drift; the tide; stream; fashion/세상 ~ the trend[drift] of the world; the tone of society. ふうちょう

**풍족(豊足)** abundance; plenty; ampleness; opulence/~하다 (be) abundant; plentiful; ample/수산물이 ~하다 be rich in marine products. ほうふ

**풍진(風疹)** 〖의〗 rubella; German measles.

**풍진(風塵)** ①《티끌》 wind-blown dust ②《속세》 worldly affairs; cares of life; ~을 피하다 live in seclusion; lead a sequestered life. ふうじん

**풍질(風疾)** nervous disorders ⇒풍병. ふうしつ

**풍차(風車)** a windmill/~간 a windmill shed. ふうしゃ

**풍채(風采)** appearance; air; mien; presence; bearing/~가 좋다 have a fine presence. ふうさい

**풍치(風致)** artistic effect; taste; [scenic] beauty/정원은 ~가 있다 This garden is tastefully arranged./~림 an ornamental plantation[forest]. ふうち

**풍침(風枕)** an air cushion; a pneumatic pillow.

**풍토(風土)** natural features (of *a region*); climate/~에 순화하다 acclimatize/~병 an endemic disease/~학 climatology. ふうど

**풍파(風波)** ① wind and waves; a storm; a tempest; rough seas/해상은 ~가 거칠다 The sea is rough. ②《분쟁》 a trouble; a disturbance; a quarrel ③《고생》 a storm; hardships. ふうは

**풍편(風便)** rumor; hearsay/~에 듣다 know by hearsay. かぜのたより

**풍해(風害)** damage from[done by] a storm ⇒풍재. ふうがい

**풍향(風向)** the direction of the wind; the wind/~이 바뀌다 shift[veer] (*round to the east*). ふうこう

**풍화(風化)** 〖지〗 weathering;〖화〗 efflorescence/~하다 weather; effloresce/~하는 efflorescent/~물 efflorescence/~작용 weathering; the action of the elements. ふうか

**풍후(豊厚)** ①《얼굴이》 plumpness; chubbiness/~하다 (be) plump; chubby ②《풍족》 abundance; richness/~하다 (be) abundant; rich.

**풍흉(豊凶)** a good and bad harvest; a rich or poor harvest. ほうきょう

**피¹** ①《혈액》 blood;《핏덩이》 gore/~투성이가 되다 be covered with blood all over ②《혈연》 blood; blood relation 《혈족》 consanguinity/~를 나눈 형제 a blood brother/~는 물보다 진하다 Blood is thicker than water. ち

**피²** 〖식〗 barnyard millet; *Echinochloa frumentacea*(학명). ひえ

**피³** 《경멸》 pshaw; with a sneer/~하다 sneer. ペ. へへん

**피가수(被加數)** 〖수〗 a summand. ひかすう

**피감수(被減數)** 〖수〗 a minuend. ひげんすう

**피검(被檢)** being arrested/~되다 be arrested; be rounded up/~자 the arrested; a person in custody. けんきょされること

**피격(被擊)** being fired at; suffering attack/~당하다 be attacked (*by*); be assaulted[raided]. こうげきをうけること

**피고(被告)** (민사의) a defendant (형사의) the accused/~ 변호인 the counsel for the defense/~석 the dock; the bar. ひこく

**피고름** bloody pus. ちうみ

**피곤(疲困)** fatigue; weariness; tiredness; exhaustion/~하다 (be) tired; fatigued; wearied; exhausted. ひろう

**피골(皮骨)** skin and bones/~이 상접하다 be reduced to a skeleton; be all skin and bones. かわとほね

**피근피근** refusing to listen; stubbornly; obstinately/~하다 (be) stubborn; obstinate; perverse.

**피나무** 〖식〗 a linden tree; a lime tree; a bass [wood]; *Tilid amurensis japonica*(학명). ひえ

**피난(避難)** refuge; shelter; harborage; evacuation/~하다 take[seek] refuge; take[find] shelter; retire to a safe place; get under cover; escape/~자 a refugee; an evacuee. ひなん

**피낭(被囊)** 〖동·식〗 a cyst.

**피눈물** tears of blood; bitter tears/~을 흘리다 weep tears of blood; shed bitter tears. けつるい

**피다** ①《꽃이》 come[be] out; (*trees*) blossom; flower; open/피어 있다 be in bloom[flower] (*a fire*)/향을 피우다 burn incense ③《기타》 얼굴 빛이 ~ one's complexion blooms; look better. めぐむ

**피딱지** a clot of blood; a blood clot. こりかたまったち

**피땀** greasy sweat/~흘리며 일하다 toil and moil. ちのあせ

**피대(皮俗)** a leather bag. てさげカバン

**피대(皮帶)** a belt; a band.

**피똥** bloody stools; excrement mixed with blood. けつべん

**피동**(被動) passivity; passiveness / ~적으로 passively. ひどう

**피둥피둥** ①(몸이) fat; plump; corpulent ②(말을) refusing to listen; stubborn / ~하다 (be) fat; plump; corpulent; heedless / ~ 살찌다 be fat[corpulent]. びんびん

**피뜩** suddenly; all of a sudden; quickly.

**피라미**〖어〗a dace; Zacco platypus(학명). こうらいばす

**피란**(避亂) refuge ⇒피난. ひなん

**피력**(披瀝) stating frankly[openly] / ~하다 state (one's view) frankly; express; open; confess; reveal / 의견을 ~하다 express one's view; voice one's opinion. ひれき

**피로**(披露) 〖발표〗announcement 〖소개〗introduction 〖광고〗advertisement / ~하다 announce; introduce; advertise / 결혼 ~연 a wedding reception[feast]; a wedding dinner〈미〉. ひろう

**피로**(疲勞) fatigue; weariness; exhaustion / ~하다 (be) tired; fatigued; exhausted / ~가 풀리다 be relieved of one's fatigue. ひろう

**피뢰침**(避雷針) a lightning rod[conductor]. ひらいしん

**피륙** cloth; woven good; a fabric; piece goods (여자·어린이용) dress goods / ~ 장수 a draper.

**피리** a pipe; a flute; a recorder; a fife / ~를 불다 play a flute; pipe; play (a tune) on the flute. ふえ

**피마**(一馬)〖동〗a [grown-up] mare. めうま

**피마자**(萞麻子)〖식〗a castor-oil plant; a castorbean; Ricinus communis(학명) / ~유 castor oil. ひまし

**피막**(被膜)〖동·해〗a tunic / ~있는 tunicate; tunicated. ひまく

**피막이풀**〖식〗a marsh pennywort; Hydrocotyle sibthorpioides(학명).

**피맺히다** be bruised. ちがにじむ

**피명**(被命) ~하다 be ordered[appointed]; receive an [official] order[appointment]. めいれいをうけること

**피물**(皮物) skins; hides; leather goods.

**피병원**(避病院) an isolation hospital; a quarantine hospital; a detention hospital. ひびょういん

**피보험자**(被保險者) an insured person (총칭) the insured. ひほけんしゃ

**피보호자**(被保護者) a ward (남자) a protégé(F); (여자) a protégée(F).

**피복**(被服) clothing; clothes / ~대[비] clothing allowance[expense] / ~상 a clothier. ひふく

**피복**(被覆) covering; a mantle / ~선 covered[coated] wire / ~ 재료 covering material.

**피봉**(皮封) an envelope ⇒걸봉. うわふう

**피부**(皮膚)〖해〗the skin / ~가 거칠다 have a rough skin / ~ 감각 skin[cutaneous] sensation / ~병 a skin disease. ひふ

**피비린내** bloody stink; bloodiness / ~ 나는 싸움 a bloody fight[battle]. ちなまぐささ

**피살**(被殺) being killed / ~하다 be killed [murdered]. ころされること

**피상**(皮相)〖외관〗an outward look (천박) superficiality / ~자네 관찰은 ~적이다 You take a superficial view of the matter. ひそう

**피상속인**(被相續人)〖법〗an ancestor; a predecessor; an inheritee.

**피새나다** come to light; be discovered. ばれる

**피새내다** lose one's temper easily. おこる

**피서**(避暑) summering / ~하다 summer; pass[spend] the summer (at, in) / ~를 가다 go to a summer resort. ひしょ

**피선**(被選) ~하다 be chosen; be[get] elected.

**피선거권**(被選擧權) eligibility for election; qualification for election; electoral eligibility / ~이 있다 be eligible for (an M.P.).

**피선거인**(被選擧人) an eligible person; the elect.

**피습**(被襲) ~하다 be attacked; be set upon; be assaulted. しゅうげきされること

**피승수**(被乘數)〖수〗a multiplicand. ひじょうすう

**피신**(避身) [secret] escape; refuge; shelter; concealing oneself / ~하다 escape secretly; beat a safe retreat; conceal oneself. みをさけること

**피아**(彼我) self and others; both sides; he and I; they and we; this and that / ~ 국정이 다르다 The conditions of the two countries are different. ひが

**피안**(彼岸) ①〖종〗Paramita (San); 〖열반〗Nirvana(San); (맞은 편) the other side[shore] / 태평양의 ~ (on) the other shore[side] of the Pacific. ひがん

**피어나다** ①(불이) burn up again; rekindle (itself) / 숯불이 ~ the charcoal fire glows again ②(소생) come back to life; come to oneself; be brought to life come to one's senses ③(생활이) (it) ease up; recover ④(꽃이) bloom; come into bloom; (a flower) come out. よくなる

**피우다** ①(불을) burn; kindle; make[build] (a fire) / 난로에 불을 ~ make[start] a fire in a stove ②(담배를) have a smoke ③(냄새를) give off[send out] (an odor); scent / 꽃이 냄새를 피웠다 The flowers scented[perfumed] the air. ④(먼지를) raise[make, kick up] (dust) ⑤(재주를) do; play; display; perform / 익살을 ~ play the fool; jest. おこす

**피육**(皮肉) skin and flesh. ひにく

**피의자**(被疑者) a suspect; a suspected person / 살인 사건의 ~ a suspect in a murder. ひぎしゃ

**피임**(被任) appointment to an office / ~하다 be appointed / 교수로 ~되다 be appointed professor. にんめいされること

**피임**(避妊) contraception; prevention of conception[maternity]/～하다 prevent conception/～기구 a contraceptive appliance/～ 수술 a contraceptive operation. ひにん

**피자 식물**(被子植物) angiosperm. ひししょくぶつ

**피장파장** a tie; evenness; [both] the same; no difference between (*us*); a draw/～이다 That makes us no difference. しょうはいゆうれつのないこと

**피제수**(被除數) 〖수〗 a dividend; the number to be divided. ひじょすう

**피죽**(一粥) gruel made of barnyard millet.

**피죽**(皮竹) bamboo sheath. たけのひょうひ

**피지급**(被支給) receiving payment/～인 a payee.

**피지샘**(皮脂—) 〖해〗 a sebaceous gland; *Glandula sebadcea*(학명).

**피진**(皮疹) 〖의〗 efflorescence; exanthema.

**피질**(皮質) 〖생〗 cortex. ひしつ

**피차**(彼此) (이것과 저것) this and that (서로) you and I; both sides; each other/～간에 좋아한다 They are fond of each other. ひし

**피천** petty money/～ 한 잎 없다 be penniless. びたせん

**피천**(被薦) ～하다 be[get] recommended. すいせんされること

**피체**(被逮) ～하다 be arrested; get caught. とらえられること

**피층**(皮層) 〖식〗 cortex. ひそう

**피치자**(被治者) the governed; the ruled /치자와 ～ the ruler and the ruled.

**피침**(被侵) being raided; being violated /～하다 (침략하다) be invaded (침범하다) be violated. しんぱんされること

**피탈**(被奪) suffering robbery; having (*something*) taken away/～하다 be robbed of (*a thing*). うばわれること

**피탈**(避脫) escape/～하다 escape; avoid; get away (*from*).

**피톨** a globule; blood corpuscle. けっきゅう

**피통치**(被統治) being subject (*to*); being governed[ruled] (*by*)/～국 a subject state.

**피폐**(疲弊) poverty; impoverishment; exhaustion/～하다 become poor; become impoverished/～해 있다 be in an exhausted condition.

**피하**(皮下) under the skin/～ 주사를 놓다 inject (*medicine*) under the skin/～ 주사 hypodermic injection/～ 출혈 hypodermal bleeding. ひか

**피하다**(避—) ①(비키다) avoid (*the heat*); avert[ward off] (*danger*); keep off (*evil*); escape (*danger, death, disaster*) /날아오는 돌을 ～ duck a stone thrown at one ②(피신) take refuge ⇒피신하다 ③(책임·의무를) shirk; evade; sidestep; duck/정병을 ～ evade military service/책임을 ～ shirk *one's* responsibility. さける

**피한**(避寒) wintering; hibernation/～하다 winter (*at, in*); pass[spend] the winter (*at, in*); go to (*a place*) during [for] the winter; hibernate. ひかん

**피해**(被害) damage; injury; casualties/ ～ 망상 persecution mania/～지 the stricken[damaged] district/우리집은 큰 ～를 입었다 Much damage was done to our house. ひがい

**피핵**(被劾) ～하다 be impeached; be denounced; be censured. だんがいされること

**피혁**(皮革) hides [and skins]; leather/～ 상 a dealer in hides and skins; a pelterer. ひかく

**피화**(避禍) ～하다 escape disaster[calamity]; keep out of harm's way. わざわいをさけること

**픽** ①(쓰러지는 모양)〖마루 위에 ～ 쓰러지다 sink to the floor in a faint; fall senseless to the floor ②(웃는 모양)〖～ 웃다 smile aimlessly ③(새는 모양)〖～ 소리내며 타이어의 바람이 빠졌다 Air hissed to escape from the tire. どしん

**핀잔** personal reproof; snubbing/～주다 reprove (*a person*) to his face; cast a reproach in *one's* face; upbraid; snub; rebuff/～먹다 be snubbed; meet with a rebuff

**필**(匹) (마소) a head/소 두 ～ two head of cows. ひき

**필**(疋) a roll (of *cloth*)/～로 사다 buy a whole roll of (*cloth*). ひき

**필**(畢) finished; done; completed/ ～하다 finish; end; complete/학업을 ～하다 complete[finish] a school course. あめふり

**필가**(筆家) a calligrapher; a calligraphist; a penman.

**필가**(筆架) a writing-brush rack; a penrack. ひっか

**필갑**(筆匣) (붓집) a writing-brush rack. ふでばこ

**필경**(筆耕) copying/～하다 copy/～료 copying-fee. ひっこう

**필경**(畢竟) after all; finally; in the end; in the long run/～에 가서는 그 여자와 결혼할 것이다 He will marry her after all. ひっきょう

**필공**(筆工) a brush-maker; a writing-brush maker. ひっこう

**필관**(筆管) the stem of a writing brush. ひっかん

**필기**(筆記) taking notes; note/ ～하다 take notes; write[note] down/연설을 ～하다 take down a speech/～ 시험 a written examination. ひっき

**필낭**(筆囊) a bag for writing brushes. ふでいれ

**필단**(筆端) ①(붓끝) the tip of the pen [brush] ②(필세(筆勢)) manipulation of *one's* pen; a stroke of the pen.

**필담(筆談)** conversation by writing/~하다 talk by means of writing; chat by letter. ひったん

**필답(筆答)** a written answer[reply]/~하다 answer in writing/~시험 a written examination. ひっだん

**필독(必讀)** required reading; indispensable[must] reading/~서 a must book/학생~의 서 a book which must necessarily be read by students; a student's companion. ひつどく

**필두(筆頭)** ①(붓끝) the tip[head] of a writing brush ②(연명의 첫째) the first on the list[in a roll]/그의 이름이 ~에 올라 있다 His name tops the list. ひっとう

**필력(筆力)** the power of the pen[brush]. ひつりょく

**필마(匹馬)** a single horse/~단기 a solitary ride without servant. ひつば

**필멸(必滅)** being doomed to perish/~의 perishable; mortal; doomed to decay/생자 ~ All living things must die.

**필명(筆名)** a pen name; *a nom do plume* (F); pseudonym/~이 높다 be a famous calligrapher[writer]. ひつめい

**필묵(筆墨)** brush and Chinese ink; pen and ink. ひつぼく

**필방(筆房)** a writing-brush maker's [shop]; a stationery store.

**필법(筆法)** (운필법) a style of penmanship; the technique of calligraphy; how to use the brush 《문체》 a style of writing/춘추의 ~ the style of the Confucian Annals, the *Chunchu*. ひっぽう

**필봉(筆鋒)** the force of *one's* pen.

**필부(匹婦)** 《한 여자》 a woman; an individual woman 《신분이 낮은 여자》 an ordinary[a common] woman; a woman of lowly birth. ひっぷ

**필부(匹夫)** a common man; a lowly man 《신분이 낮은 남자》 an ordinary man/~ 필부 humble men and women. ひっぷ

**필사(必死)** 《꼭 죽음》 inevitable death 《생명을 걺》 desperation/~적으로 노력하다 make desperate efforts. ひっし

**필사(筆寫)** copying; transcription/~하다 copy; transcribe. ひっしゃ

**필산(筆算)** ciphering; calculation with figures/~하다 cipher; calculate [with figures]. ひっざん

**필상(筆商)** a writing-brush dealer[peddler]. ひつのぎょうしょうにん

**필생(畢生)** coexistence with life/~의 lifelong/~의 역작[걸작] *one's* magnum opus[masterpiece]. ひっせい

**필생(筆生)** 《등사판의》 a stenciler a copyist.

**필석(筆石)** 《고생물》 a graptolite.

**필설(筆舌)** brush and tongue; writing and speech/나이아가라 폭포의 장관은 이루 ~로 표현할 수 없다 The grandeur of the Niagara Falls transcends words.

**필세(筆勢)** a stroke of the brush[pen]; 《필법》 the style of penmanship 《필력》 the power of the pen. ひっせい

**필수(必須)** indispensability/~의 indispensable; required; necessary/~과목 a required subject/~ 조건 an indispensable[essential] condition. ひっすう

**필수품(必需品)** a necessary; a necessity; a requisite; an essential. ひつじゅひん

**필승(必勝)** certain victory/~을 기하다 《자신》 be sure[certain] of victory 《각오》 resolve to secure[win, gain] a victory at any cost. ひっしょう

**필시(必是)** certainly; surely; no doubt. きっと

**필업(畢業)** completion (of *one's* school course)/~하다 complete (*one's* school course). しごとをかんりょうすること

**필연(必然)** certainly; surely; infallibly; without fail/~적 결과로서 as an inevitable consequence/~성 inevitability; necessity. ひつぜん

**필요(必要)** ⇒별항 참조.

**필유 곡절(必有曲折)** There must be some reason for it., There must be something in it.

**필자(筆者)** the writer; the author/~의 잘못 a clerical error. ひっしゃ

**필적(筆蹟)** handwriting; a hand; penmanship/~이 좋다[나쁘다] write a good [poor, bad] hand/~을 판단하다 analyze *one's* handwriting. ひっせき

**필적(匹敵)** a rival; a match; an equal/~하다 equal; rival; be as good as; be a match for; can match; be equal to; compare with/~할 만한 자가 없다 have no equal[match]. ひってき

**필전(筆戰)** a paper battle; the war of the pen. ひっせん

**필주(筆誅)** denunciation in writing/~를 가하다 denounce (*a person*) in writing; openly attack (in *a paper*).

**필지(必至)** inevitability/~하다 be in evitable[unavoidable]; be sure to come. ひっし

**필지(必知)** a must to know; indispensable information.

**필지(筆紙)** pen and paper/~로 다할 수 없다 It is indescribable. ひっし

**필진(筆陣)** 《포진》 a maneuver in a battle by pen 《진용》 the writing staff; a line-up of the writers. ひつじん

**필치(筆致)** 《문체》 style 《필세》 a stroke of the pen[brush]; 《일필》 a touch/그의 ~는 훌륭하다 The strokes of his brushes are fine. ひっち

**필통(筆筒)** ①(붓갑) a writing-brush case 《붓통》 a writing-brush stand ②(연필갑) a pencil case. ひっとう

**필하다(畢一)** finish; complete; end; be[get] through; make an end of/일을 ~ finish[complete] *one's* work. おわる

**필화(筆禍)** a serious slip of the pen/~

**필 임다** be indicted for *one's* article (in *a magazine*). ひっか

**필흥(筆興)** delight in practicing calligraphy.

**핍박(逼迫)** (궁핍) pressure; tightness (금융) stringency/ ~하다 become tight; get stringent; be urgent; persecute; molest/ 금융계가 ~하다 The money market is stringent. ひっぱく

**핍진(乏盡)** exhaustion; running out/ ~하다 get exhausted; run out.
ぜんぶなくなること

**핍진(逼眞)** verisimilitude; truthfulness to life/ ~하다 (be) true to life; lifelike; vivid.

**핏골집** a kind of sausage.

**핏기(一氣)** the color of the skin[face]; complexion/ 그의 얼굴은 ~가 없어졌다 The colour had fled from his cheeks/ 그녀는 몸이 아파서 얼굴에 ~가 없다 Her cheeks are pale with sickness.
けっき

**핏대** ①(혈관) the vein/ ~를 올리다 have *one's* blood up ②(피의 줄기) the stalk of a barnyard grass. けっかん

**핏덩어리** ① a clot of blood; a blood clot ②(갓난아이) a newborn baby.

**핏발** being bloodshot; a bloodshot condition/ ~이 삭다 congestion/ ~서다 be bloodshot; be congested (with *blood*)/ ~선 눈 bloodshot[red and inflamed] eyes.
じゅうけつ

**핏줄** ①(혈관) a vein; a blood vessel ②(혈족) blood; blood relation; stock; lineage; a family line/ ~은 속일 수 없다 Blood is thicker than water/ ~이 같다 be related (to *a person*) by blood; be of the same blood/ 그들은 ~을 나눈 형제다 They are of the same blood., They are blood brothers. けっかん

**핑** ①(도는 꼴) round; circling/ ~ 돌다 turn round; circle/ 학교를 한 바퀴 ~ 돌다 walk all round the school/ 술이 ~ 돌다 the alcohol goes to *one's* head ②(둘러싸는 꼴) around〈미〉; round ③(어질한 꼴) dizzily/ 머리가 ~ 돌다 get dizzy[giddy]. ぐるりと

**핑계** a pretext; an excuse; a pretence; a quibble; a dodge/ ~하다 make a pretext[pretence] of; pretend; use (*a thing*) as an excuse for; quibble/ 그것은 ~에 불과하다 That is only pretext., That's a mere excuse /아프다는 ~로 on the pretext[with a plea] of illness/ 병을 ~하다 plea illness; find a excuse in *one's* illness/ 그는 요리조리 ~삼아 일을 게을리한다 He shirks his work on some pretext or other./ ~ 말고 모임에 출석하라 Come to the meeting without making any excuses. かこつけ

**핑구** a toy top with a small knob at the top.

**핑그르르** round and round; around smoothly/ 팽이가 ~ 돌다 a top spins/ 공을 ~ 돌리다 spin a ball round. くるくる

## 필 요

necessity; need; requirement; indispensability/ ~하다 (be) necessary; needed; needful; essential; indispensable; requisite/ ~성 necessity / ~악 a necessary evil/ ~품 a necessity; a necessary; a requisite/ ~에 따라 as occasion demands[arises, calls]/ ~없는 unnecessary; needless; uncalled-for / ~할 경우 in case of need[necessity]; if [when] necessary 《시에서》if need be/ …가[이] ~하다 need; require; be in need of; (*a thing*) be needed[required]/ … 할 ~가 있다 have got to (*do*)《구》; have to (*do*)《구》; must (*do*); need (to *do*) /두말할 ~가 없었다 It was not necessary to tell him twice., He didn't need to be told twice./서두를 ~가 있을까 Is there any need to hurry?/내가 그렇게 해야만 할 ~가 어디 있단 말인가 What need have I to do so?/~에는 법이 없다 Necessity knows[has] no law. /~는 발명의 어머니 Necessity is the mother of invention./그 병은 즉시 수술을 해야 할 ~가 있다 The disease demands [calls for] an immediate operation. /책을 빌리려면 열람 카드가 ~하다 A library card is a requisite for taking out a book. /그에게 ~ 이상의 돈을 주지 마십시오 Don't give him more money than is necessary[he needs]./그 일을 완성하는 데는 얼마의 돈이 ~한가 How much [money] is it necessary[required] to complete the work?/너는 좀 쉴 ~가 있다 You have need of[to take] a rest. / 어린이에게는 충분한 수면이 ~하다 Children must have plenty of sleep./가르치는 데는 인내가 ~하다 Patience is a requirement in teaching./이 구두는 수선할 ~가 있다 These shoes want repairing[need repairs]./할 ~가 없는데 했다 I needn't have done it./할 ~가 없어서 안 했다 I did not need to do it /이런 일에는 용기가 ~하다 It takes courage to do this kind of work./아무래도 5000원은 ~하다 I must have five thousand *won*., I am awfully in need of 5,000 *won*.

**하¹** (하도) much; very; excessively; greatly／~ 졸라대다 tease hard for (*something*)／~ 비싸다 be very expensive.

**하²** (입김) with a hot wet breath／~다 breathe on (*something*) to dampen [wet] it. は—. は—

**하³** (감탄·웃음) Ha!, Aha! ほう!は!

**하**(下) ①(하등) the low class[grade]; inferiority ②(아래) lower part／~와 같다 be as follows ③(하권) the last volume. した

**하가**(下嫁) the marriage of a royal princess to a subject.

**하감**(下疳) 【의】 chancre／연성[경성] ~ soft[hard] chancre.

**하감**(下瞰) ~하다 look down (*upon*); take a bird's-eye view (*of*). かかん

**하강**(下降) descent; a fall; descension (가라 앉음) subsidence／~하다 descend; go[come] down; fall. かこう

**하객**(賀客) a congratulator; a well wisher.

**하게하다** (말을 놓다) use familiar style speech forms (*with*).

**하계**(夏季) summer ⇨하기(夏期). かき

**하계**(下界) (현세) this world; the lower world (지상) the earth (낮은 곳) a lower place[region]. げかい

**하고** (및) and (대해서) against (함께) with; along with／너~ 나 you and I／적 ~ 싸우다 fight against the enemy.—と

**하고많다** (be) numerous; very many; innumerable／하고 많은 중에 among the many／하고 많은 재산을 당대에 다 탕진했다 He squandered a tremendous fortune in his lifetime. ひじょうにおおい

**하곡**(夏穀) a summer crop; wheat and barley／~ 수매가(收買價) the barley purchasing price.

**하관**(下官) a lower[subordinate] official; a petty[junior] official (자칭) I. げかん

**하관**(下棺) ~하다 lower a coffin into the grave. ひつぎをまいそうすること

**하교**(下敎) ①(명령) orders; an instruction [an order] from a superior ②(교시) instruction; teaching／~하다 deign to instruct[order] ③(전교) an order from the king; a royal command／~를 충실히 지키다 be obedient to the orders of.

**하구**(河口) the mouth of a river. かこう

**하국**(夏菊) 【식】 an elecampane; *Inula britanica*(학명).

**하권**(下卷) the last volume (두권 중의) the second volume (세권 중의) the third volume. げかん

**하극상**(下剋上) a revolt (against *senior officers*); a mutiny.

**하급**(下級) a low[er] class[grade]／~ 의 low-class; junior; lower; inferior／ ~ 관청 a subordinate office／~ 관리 a petty[minor, low ranking, subordinate] official. かきゅう

**하급생**(下級生) a lower-grade student; a lower class boy[girl]; freshies and sophs《미·속》. かきゅうせい

**하기**(下記) [what is] stated below; the following／~ 사항 the following items／~와 같이 as follows; as in the following.

**하기**(夏期) summer; the summer season; summertime／~ 휴가 a summer vacation／~ 방학 the summer vacation／~ 학교[강습회] a summer school[institute, lecture class]. かき

**하기는** ①(…하는 것은) as for doing[being]／~ 하지만 do all right but; be all right but ②(실상은) in fact; indeed／~ 네말이 옳다 Indeed, you are right.／~ 그것이 틀림없다 Really it must be so. ③(그러나) but; however; though; only／~ 예외도 있지 There are indeed some exceptions. じつは

**하기야** indeed; definitely／~ 돈만 있으면 좋은 사업이지 It would definitely be a good business if one just had the money.

**하나¹** one; a unit (유일) [the] only one／~의 (한개의) one; a [single]; (동일한) identical; the same／~도 남김없이 without exception; to the very last／단 ~ a single; only one／~로 만들다 unite[make] into one／~씩 one by one; separately／~ 둘 one or two; a few／~걸러 alternately. ひとつ

**하나²** however; yet; but (하지만) do[*say, think, be, etc.*] but. しかしながら

**하나님** God ⇨하느님. キリスト

**하나하나** one after another; one by one; piece by piece (개별적으로) individually;

하녀(下女) a maid[-servant]; a domestic[-servant]. げじょ

하념(下念) gracious consideration; care; patronage; concern／～하다 be concerned for; be solicitous for; care for. ごけねん

하눌타리 《식》a snake-gourd; Trichosanthes quadricirrha(학명).

하느님 [the Lord of] Heaven; God; the Creator; the Divinity; the supreme Being／～의 가호 divine protection／～의 말씀 the world of God／～의 은혜 the grace of God／～을 믿다[공경하다] believe in [revere] God／～께 맹세하다 swear by God／～ 맙소사 Heaven forbid!／～만이 안다 God only knows. キリスト

하늘 ①(천공) the sky; the air (땅에 대해) the heavens／맑은 ～ a clear[bright, serene] sky／～을 날다 fly through the sky／～빛 sky-blue [-colour]／～을 찌르는 sky-scraping／～의 용사 an air hero／푸른 ～ the blue sky ②(천당) Heaven／～에 계신 아버지 our Father which art in Heaven ③(섭리) Heaven; Providence (하느님) Heaven; God／～은 스스로 돕는 자를 돕는다 Heaven helps those who helf themselves.／～ 무서운 말 a blasphemous remark. そら

하늘소 《충》a long-horned beetle.

하늬, 하늬바람 a west wind. にしかぜ

하니 (그러하니) so; therefore; consequently; on that ground; that is why. そうだから

하다¹ ①(행하다) do (하고 놀다) play (a game); (해 보다) attempt; try (행동) act (실행) carry on; practise (착수) go in for; set about／하고 있는 the work in hand／할 일이 많다[없다] have much [nothing] to do／해 보다 try to do; have a try／문학을 ～ go in for literature／～ 말고 두다 leave a thing half-done[unfinished] ②(배우다) study; prosecute (a study); learn (알다) know ③(연출하다) perform; act; play ④(만들다) make; make (something) of (one) ⑤(음식) take; have; eat; drink; smoke; help oneself to ⑥(종사하다) act as; serve as; do duty as／하녀 노릇을 ～ serve as [a] maid ⑦(값이) cost; be valued; be worth／얼마나 하느냐 How much is it? する

하다² (매우) be quite; be indeed／좋기도 ～ be quite nice／빠르기도 ～ be speedy indeed.

-하다 (접미사) ¶공부～ study／결혼～ get married／기뻐～ be glad; be pleased (with)／분주～ be busy (with one's work).

하다못해 at least; at best; at most; just／～ 그만두고 말았다 It ended in my giving it up. しょうがなくて

하단(下段) ①(글의) a lower column ②(계단의) a lower step[tier]; 《침대차의》 the lower berth; the latter[lower] part. げだん

하달(下達) a command; a mandate; orders／～하다 notify [to] an inferior; convey to the people／상정(上程)을 ～하다 convey the will and ideas of those who governing to those who are governed.

하답(下答) an answer; a reply／～하다 answer; reply.

하대(下待) contemptuous[scornful] treatment; inhospitable[cold] reception／～하다 treat contemptuously; give a cold reception.

하도 too much; excessively; to excess; very much indeed; ever so hard／～ 바쁘다 be ever so busy／세월이 ～ 빨리 가다 time flies ever so fast. とても

하돈(河豚) 《어》a swellfish; a puffer; a globe fish.

하등(下等) (열등) inferiority (조야(粗野)) coarseness (하급) a lower class; low grade／～의 low; coarse; inferior; in bad taste; vulgar／～ 동물[식물] the lower animals[plants]／～ 사회 the lower classes; the lower order of society. かとう

하등(何等) 《부사》[not] in the slightest degree; [not] at all; least／～의 no; any; not at all; least／～의 이유도 없이 without any reason; for naught. なんら

하락(下落) 《가격의》a fall[drop, decline] (in price); depreciation (품질의) deterioration; degradation; sink; degrade／～하다 fall [off]; drop; come down／～ 경향 a downward movement; a falling tendency. げらく

하략(下略) the rest is omitted; the concluding[the last] part omitted. げりゃく

하량(下諒) sympathetic understanding [consideration]／～하다 take into consideration; consider／곤란한 사정을 ～하다 appreciate the difficulties an inferior is having.

하려(下慮) gracious consideration ⇒하념(下念). ごけねん

하례(下隷) a male slave[servant]. げにん

하례(賀禮) congratulation; celebration／～하다 celebrate; congratulate.

하롱거리다 go off at half cock; act rashly[hastily]／하롱하롱 hastily; rashly; flippantly; lightly.

하루 ①(초하루) the first day [of a month] ②(낮수) a[one] day／～일 a day's work／～에 per day; a day／～ 종일 all day [long]; from morning to[till] night／～ 걸러 every other[second] day; on alternate days ③(어느날) ～ 는 one day; someday. いちにち

하루갈이 the size of field or paddy that

**하루거리** 〖의〗 a tertain malarial fever/ ~에 걸리다 be taken with tertian ague.

**하루바삐** as soon as possible 《하루라도 빨리》 to make sooner even a day/ ~하다 lose no time in doing (*something*)/ ~ 회복되기를 빕니다 I pray for your earliest possible recovery. いちにちもはやく

**하루살이** 〖충〗 a dayfly./~ 같은 short-lived; fugitive; ephemeral/~ 같은 존재 an ephemeral existence/~ 같은 인생 this ephemeral life. かがんぼ

**하루아침** ●ne morning/~에 in a [single] day; in a brief interval[space of time]/~에 부자가 되다 wake up to find *oneself* suddenly rich/로마는~에 이루어진 것이 아니다 Rome was not built in a day. たんじかん

**하루하루** from day to day; day after day; day by day/~ 연기하다 put off (*a matter*) from day to day; put (*anything*) off and off/~ 나아가다 get better day by day/~ 추워진다 It is growing colder day by day. まいにち

**하룻날** the first day [of a month]. ついたち

**하룻밤** one[a] night/~ 사이에 in a single night/~을 보내다 《잠들어》 pass a night (*in, at*)/~을 뜬눈으로 새다 sit up all night. いちや

**하류**(下流) ①(하천의) the lower course of a stream; the downstream ②(하류 사회) the lower classes; the lower order[stratum] of society. かりゅう

**하륙**(下陸) landing; unloading / ~하다 land; disembark. じょうりく

**하르르** ~하다 (be) thin; flimsy.

**하리다**¹ 《사치하다》be addicted to extravagance; indulge in luxury 《옷차림을》 be in gala dress; be resplendently dressed; be in full feather/음식에 ~ luxuriate[wallow] in food.

**하리다**² 《우둔하다》 (be) stupid; silly. ぼんやりしている

**하리망당하다** (be) vague (*in memory*) ⇒ 흐리멍덩하다. ぼんやりしている

**하릴없다** (be) not to be helped/하릴없이 helplessly; as there in no help 《부득이하여》against *one's* will. どうすることもできない

**하마**(下馬) dismounting/~하다 dismount [from a horse]; get off[alight from] a horse/~비(碑) a notice stone requiring riders to dismount. うまからおりること

**하마**(河馬) 〖동〗 a hippopotamus(*pl,* -ni, ~es); a riverhorse; a hippo《속》. かば

**하마터면** 《거의》 nearly; almost 《간신히》 barely; narrowly/~ 차에 칠 뻔했다 I narrowly missed being run over./그는 교통 사고로 ~ 죽을 뻔했다 He was very close to death in the traffic accident. ややもすれば

**하명**(下命) 〖명령〗 an order from above; a command 〖주문〗 an order/~하다 order; command; give orders/~을 바랍니다 We solicit your orders. かめい

**하묘**(下錨) anchoring/~하다 drop[cast] anchor; anchor/~ 중이다 be at anchor / ~지 an anchorage

**하문**(下門) the vulva; the vagina. いんもん

**하물**(荷物) a load; a burden 《화물》 goods 《수하물》 luggage; baggage/~ 취급소 a luggage [and parcel] office/~ 임시 보관소 a baggage checking bureau/ ~선 a cargo ship; a freighter. にもつ

**하물며** (긍정) much[still] more (부정) much[still] less/ ~ …에 있어서는 더욱 그렇다 much more is it the case with /영어조차 모르거늘 ~ 불어(佛語)를 알 수 있으랴 He knows no English, not to speak of French. そのうえ

**하미**(下米) rice of inferior quality; low-grade rice.

**하민**(下民) ordinary persons; common people; lower orders. かみん

**하박**(下膊) 〖해〗 forearm; the antebrachium/ ~골(骨) the bones of the forearm; the radius and the ulna. かはく

**하반**(下半) the latter half [of the two portion]/ ~기(期) the latter[second] half of the year/~신(身) the lower half of *one's* body. かはん

**하백**(河伯) the God of water. すいじん

**하번**(下番) ~하다 come off[be relieved of] guard[duty]. かばん

**하복**(下腹) the abdomen; the abdominal region. したばら

**하복**(夏服) clothes for summer wear; summer clothes[uniform]. なつふく

**하부**(下付) ~하다 grant; give; issue/~금 a grant; a subsidy;a bounty. かふ

**하부**(下部) the lower part/~ 조직 a subordinate organization. かぶ

**하뿔싸** O my! ●뿔사. ああ!

**하불하**(下不下) at least. すくなくとも

**하사**(下賜) an Imperial grant[donation] /~ 하다 give; confer; grant; bestow (on *one*);《금전을》donate/~품 an Imperial gift/ ~금 an Imperial donation [bounty]. かし

**하사**(何事) what; something; everything; anything; what matter. なにごと

**하사**(下司) a subordinate agency[office]; a lower post.

**하사**(下士) 《육공군·해병》 a staff sergeant 《해군》 a petty officer second class. かし

**하사관**(下士官) 《육군》 a non-commissioned officer 《해군》 a warrant officer; a petty officer. かしかん

**하산**(下山) ①《산에서 내림》a descent from a mountain/~하다 descend[go down, climb down] a mountain; go[come] downhill ②《절에서》leaving a temple/ ~하다 leave a temple. げざん

**하상**(河床) a river bed. かしょう
**하서**(下書) a letter [from a superior].
**하선**(下船) leaving a ship/ ～하다 leave a ship; go ashore; disembark. げせん
**하선**(下線) an underline/ ～친 부분 the underlined part.
**하선**(荷船) a freight vessel; a cargo boat; a tramp. にもつせん
**하세**(下世) 《별세》death; demise/ ～하다 die; pass away. しぬこと
**하소연** an appeal; a complaint; a petition/～하다 appeal to (one); complain of; supplicate. うったえること
**하수**(下水) foul water; drainage; sewage /～구(口) a sink-hole/～도 a drainage[sewerage] system; a drain/ ～도 공사 drainage works/～도를 치다 clean[scour] a drain. げすい
**하수**(下手) ①《솜씨가 못함》unskillfulness; being clumsy; a poor hand ②《살인》 ～하다 murder; lay (murderous) hands on ③《착수》～하다 start[set] to work; lay hold of/ ～인(人) the perpetrator of (a crime); the slayer. へた
**하숙**(下宿) lodging; board and lodging; board and room《미》/ ～하다 lodge; take up one's quarters[lodgins]; board / ～을 치다 take in lodgers/～ 생활을 하다 live in lodgings/～비 board charge/～집[을 하다] [run] a boarding [rooming〈미〉, lodging〈영〉] house/～ 방 a rented room; a room for rent. げしゅく
**하순**(下旬) the last[closing] ten days (of a month); the last decade/5월 ～에 toward the end of May. げじゅん
**하시**(下視) ①《아래를 봄》looking down [from a height]/ ～하다 overlook; look down ②《경멸》contempt; negligence / ～하다 make light of; look down upon; hold (one) in contempt. かし
**하야**(下野) ～하다 retire to private life [from public life]; go out of office.
**하야말갛다** (one's complexion) be clean and fair ⇒허여멀겋다. しろくてきれいだ
**하야말쑥하다** (one's complexion) be clean and fair ⇒허여멀쑥하다.
しろくてすきとっとしてきれいだ
**하얗다** (be) pure[perfectly] white; snow [virgin]-white; immaculate/그녀의 머리가 ～ Her hair is snow white. /일어나 보니 눈이 하얗게 쌓여 있었다 I awoke to find the ground silvery white with snow. とてもしろい
**하얘지다** whiten; turn white; turn grey; become snow[pure]-white/머리가 ～ one's hair turns white[gray]/얼굴이 ～ one's face goes pale.
**하여간**(何如間) anyhow; at any rate; in any case; anyway/그것은 ～ be that as it may. とにかく
**하여튼**(何如—) anyhow; anyway; somehow or other; in either case; generally speaking. とにかく

**하역**(荷役) loading and unloading; cargo -working/ ～하다 load and unload; do the cargo-working/ ～ 인부 a stevedore; a longshoreman.
**하연**(賀宴) a banquet in celebration; festivities; a feast in congratulation/ ～을 베풀다 hold[give] a banquet (in honour of the occasion). がえん
**하열**(下劣) ～하다 (be) base; mean; sordid; vulgar. げれつ
**하염없다** · be bemused with worries; be lost in thought; (be) absentminded; blank; idle; have a dull time/하염없는 나날 idle days. ぼさっとしている
**하염없이** with troubled mind; deep in thought; blankly; idly/～ 세월을 보내다 pass time doing nothing; idle away one's time; time hangs heavy on one's hand/ ～ 생각에 잠기다 be lost in thought.
**하오**(下午) afternoon; post meridiem(L) (略 : p.m.)/～ 4시에 at four o'clock in the afternoon; at 4 p.m. ごご
**하옥**(下獄) imprisonment/ ～하다 throw into[put in] prison; imprison.
**하우 불이**(下愚不移) Born unwise, die unwise.
**하원**(下院) the Lower House[Chamber]; 《영국》the House of Commons 《한·일·미》the House of Representatives. かいん
**하위**(下位) a subordinate position; a low- [er] rank; a low grade/ ～의 subordinate; low-ranking/～다 be below (a persons) in rank; occupy a subordinate position (to). かい
**하의**(夏衣) summer clothes[wear]. なつふく
**하의**(下衣) [a pair of] trousers; pants 《미·구》. したぎ
**하인**(下人) a servant; a menial; a maid servant/ ～을 두다 keep a servant. げにん
**하인**(何人) who; what[whatever] person; anyone; anybody/ ～을 막론하고 whoever it may be/ ～이든지 anybody; everybody. なにびと
**하인방**(下引枋) 《전》 the lower lintel (of a door, window); the baseboard (of a room); skirting.
**하인배**(下人輩) servants; menials. げにんたち
**하일**(夏日) summer days. なつのひ
**하자마자** as soon as; no sooner than; hardly[scarcely] … when[before]; immediately (on); the moment; the minute /그는 대학을 졸업～ 실업계에 투신하였다 Immediately on graduating from the university, he went into business.
**하잘것 없다** (be) little; tiny; insignificant; trivial/하잘것 없는 일로 시간을 낭비했다 I have spent time [in] · doing a trivial task[poor job]. つまらない
**하장**(賀狀) a greeting card a complimentary[congratulatory] letter[card]/연(

하저(河底) a river-bed; the bottom of a river.
하전(荷電) electric charge.
하절(夏節) the summer [season]; summer. なつのきせつ
하정(下情) ①(심정) my humble mind[intention]; my situation ②(민정) the condition of the people. かじょう
하정(賀正) New Year's congratulations [greetings]; (연하장에) a Happy New Year! がせい
하제(下劑) (약) a purgative; a laxative; an aperient. げざい
하주(荷主) (적출(積出)인) a shipper 《하송 (荷送)인》 a consignor 《소유자》 a goods-holder. にぬし
하지(夏至) the summer solstice/ ~선 the Tropic of Cancer. げし
하지(下肢) the lower limbs. かし
하지만 but; however; though; notwithstanding/다 그럴 듯~ 나는 찬성할 수 없다 That's all very well, but I do not agree. しかしながら
하지하(下之下) the lowest of its kind; the poorest[worst] of all/~의 the lowest; the worst. げのげ
하직(下直) leave-taking; farewell; good-by[e]/~하다 say good-by[e]; take leave of (one's superior); bid farewell [adieu] (to); make one's.
하차(下車) getting off (a train, etc.)/~하다 leave alight (from); get off (the train, etc.)/~구(口) the way out/그는 목포에서 ~했다 He alighted [from the train] at Mokpo. げしゃ
하찮다 (be) worthless ⇨하지않다. たいしたことはない
하처(何處) what place; where; wherever ⇨어디.
하천(河川) rivers; waterways/~ 개수(改修) river-improvement/~학 potamology/~ 부지 a dry river-bed/~ 오염 the river contamination. かせん
하천인(下賤人) a man of humble origin [position]; a man ignobly born. げせんにん
하청(下請) a subcontract/~하다 subcontract/~을 주다 sublet; underlet/~ 공장 a subcontract factory[plant].
하체(下體) the lower part of one's body 《음부》 privy parts; privates. かたい
하측(下側) the under[down] side.
하층(下層) a lower layer; a substratum (pl. -ta); (아래층) down stairs/~ 사회 the lower classes; lower class society /~ 계급 the lower classes. かいか
하치(下一) an article of inferior quality; lowgrade goods/이 물건은 ~다 This article is of inferior quality. げひん
하치않다 (be) trivial; insignificant; of little importance; good-for-nothing; of no account; worthless/하치않은 일 a matter of no importance[weight]; a trifle/하치않은 녀석 a worthless fellow; a small fry; a nobody /하치않은 일로 싸웠다 We quarreled over a trifle. たいしたことは
하퇴(下腿) the lower leg; the crus/ ~골 the fibula and the tibia; the leg bones/~ 동맥 the crural artery. かたい
하편(下篇) the last[second, third] volume of a book ⇨하권. げへん
하표(賀表) a congratulatory[complimentary] address 《일국의 원수에게 하는》 an address of loyalty. がひょう
하품 a yawn; a gape/ ~하다 [give a] yawn/남이 ~하는 것을 보자 자기도 하품이 난다 Yawning is catching[is infectious]. あくび
하품(下品) ①(상스러움) vulgarity; coarseness; grossness; bad taste ②(하치) poor quality; low grade. げひん
하필(何必) why necessarily?, why of all thing?/ ~이면 of all occasion[places, person]/~ 그가 올 줄은 몰랐다 He was the last person of all that I expected to come.
하하 Ha! Ha!/~ 웃다 laugh "Ha! Ha!, laugh loudly. はは!
하학(下學) dismissal of a class school/ ~하다 school is over/~후에 after school [hours]; out of school hours/~ 시간 dismissal time.
하항(河港) a river port. かこう
하해(河海) rivers and seas/~ 같은 은혜 great favor; unlimited grace.
하행(下行) going away from the capital; going down/~ 열차 a down-train.
하향(下向) looking[facing, bending] downward/~세[경향] a downward[declining] tendency; downtrend. げこう
하향(下鄕) going to one's country home / ~하다 go to one's country home.
하현(下弦) the last phase[quarter] of the moon/ ~의 달 the waning moon. かげん
하혈(下血) a bloody flux/~하다 discharge[pass] blood; flux; haemorrhage; bleed.
하환어음(荷換―) a documentary bill [drabt]/ ~을 작성하다 draw a documentary bill (on)/~ 신용장 a documentary (letter of) credit.
하회(下廻) falling short/~하다 fall short of; be below/금년의 수출액은 작년보다 ~한다 This years exports fall short of last year's.
하회(下回) the next time[chapter]; the reply (to a letter)/~를 기다리다 await (a person's) reply. じかい
학(學) 《학문》 learning 《연구》 study 《학업》 studies 《학술》 science 《학식》 erudition 《지식》 knowledge/사회 ~ sociology. がくもん
학(鶴) 〚조〛 a crane.
학감(學監) a school superintendent[overseer]; 《단과 대학의》 a dean. がっかん

**학계(學界)** academic circles[world]; learned circles/그는 ~에 연구를 발표했다 He laid his studies before the academic world. がっかい

**학과(學科)** 《과목》a subject of study 《과정》a course of study; a curriculum/~ 시험 an examination in subjects of study; an achievement test/~ 증설[을 허가하다] [permit] establishment of new departments. がっか

**학과(學課)** a lesson; school work/~ 시간표 a table (of lessons); a schedule 〈미〉/~를 복습[예습] 하다 review[prepare] one's lesson. がっか

**학관(學館)** an educational institute; an academy; a private educational institution/영어 ~ an English-language institute. がっかん

**학교(學校)** a school; a college 《총칭》 an educational establishment[institution]/ ~에서 in[at] school/~를 졸업하다 graduate from school/~ 교육 school education/~ 생활 school life/~ 성적 one's school record/국민 ~ a primary [an elementary] school/중~ a middle school/고등 ~ a high school/대~ a college; a university/음악 ~ a school [an academy] of music/~에서 제적하다 strike *a person's* name off the school register/~에 무단 결석하다[를 빼먹다] play truant[hooky《미·속》]/~ 급식 a school lunch/~ 방송(T. V · 라디오의) the school hour/~ 성적 one's school record/~ 신문 a school paper. がっこう

**학구(學究)** ①《학문 탐구》study; learning 《사람》 a vilage-school teacher; a student; a scholar/~적 scholastic; academic/~적 저작 a scholarly work ②《학도》 a student; a scholar/~ 생활 an academic[a scholarly] life; a life of learning. がっきゅう

**학구(學區)** a school district/~제 the school district system. がっく

**학급(學級)** a [school] class; a grade〈미〉; a form〈영〉/~을 편성하다 organize a class〈영〉/~회 a class meeting. がっきゅう

**학기(學期)** a [school] term/~말 시험 a terminal examination/~말 휴가 term-end holidays/신~ a fresh[new] term. がっき

**학내(學內)** 예 ~의 in the university; on campus; intramural. がくない

**학년(學年)** a school year a grade/1[2, 3]~생 a first[second, third] year student; a freshman[sophomore, junior]〈미〉/~말 시험 an annual examination/그는 3~이다 He is in the third grade. がくねん

**학당(學堂)** a school; a village school. がくどう

**학대(虐待)** cruelty; ill-treatment; maltreatment/~하다 treat (a person) cruelly[badly]/약자를 ~하다 oppress[bully] the weak/당신이 ~받는 걸 보고 가만 둘 수 없다 I can't allow you to be ill-treated/동물 ~ 방지회 the Society for the Prevention of Cruelty to Animals(略: S. P. C. A.). ぎゃくたい

**학덕(學德)** learning and virtue/~을 겸비한 사람 a man with both learning and virtue/~을 겸비하다 be eminent in both learning and virtue. がくとく

**학도(學徒)** a student; a scholar/사회 과학의 ~ a student of social science/~병 a student soldier. がくと

**학동(學童)** a school-child(boy, girl). がくどう

**학력(學力)** scholarship; scholastic ability/~ 검사 a scholarship achievement test/~이 뛰어난 사람 a person excellent in scholarship. がくりょく

**학력(學歷)** a school career; an academic background; [formal] schooling/~을 불문하고 regardless[irrespective] of one's school career/~이 없는 사람 a person without school education. がくれき

**학령(學齡)** school age/~ 미달의 아이 a pre-school child/~ 아동 children of school age. がくれい

**학리(學理)** a theory; a scientific principle/~의 응용 application of scientific principles/~적 theoretical. がくり

**학명(學名)** a scientific name; a technical term/식물 ~ a botanical name/동물 ~ a zoological name. がくめい

**학무(學務)** school[educational] affairs/~과 a section of school[educational] affairs; the school-board. がくむ

**학문(學問)** learning 《학업》study 《학술》a science 《지식》knowledge/~이 있는[없는] 사람 a learned[an uneducated] man/~에는 왕도(王道)가 없다 There is no royal road to learning./~이 깊다 be erudite; be a man of deep learning. がくもん

**학벌(學閥)** an academic clique/~을 타파하다 break down[do away with] academic cliquism/~ 싸움 rivalry between school factions. がくばつ

**학병(學兵)** a student soldier. がくとへい

**학부(學府)** a seat[centre] of learning/대학은 최고 ~다 A university is the highest seat of learning./최고 ~ the highest seat of learning; the highest educational institution. がくふ

**학부(學部)** a department; a faculty 《예과(豫科)에 대하여》 the university course/문(공·이·의·법)~ the Faculty of Literature[Engineering, Physical Science, Medicine, Law]. がくぶ

**학부형(學父兄)** parents of students/~회 a parents association.

**학비(學費)** school expenses/~를 대주다 supply a student with his school expenses/~를 벌다 earn one's school expenses/~는 아저씨가 대고 있다 I depend upon my uncle for my school expen-

**학사**(學士) a college graduate; a bachelor; a university/ 문[법・이・의・경제] Bachelor of Arts[Law, Science, Medicine, Economy]/~ 학위 a bachelor's degree/~ 등록제 the bachelor registration system. がくし

**학살**(虐殺) slaughter 《대대적》 massacre; carnage/ ~하다 slaughter; massacre; butcher/ ~자 a slaughterer; a slayer/ 대량 ~ a large-scale massacre; a holocaust. ぎゃくさつ

**학생**(學生) a student; a pupil; a schoolboy; a schoolgirl; a scholar/ ~복 a school uniform/~증 a student's identification card/ ~간에 인기가 있다 be popular with[among] the students/~다운 태도 bearing like a student; manner proper to a student/ ~회 a students association. がくせい

**학생감**(學生監) the dean of students; a censor; a proctor. がくせいかん

**학설**(學說) a theory; a doctrine/신 ~을 세우다 set up[formulate, advance] a new theory. がくせつ

**학수고대**(鶴首苦待) ~하다 wait with a craned neck/우리는 당신이 와주기를 ~하고 있다 We are eagerly looking forward to your visit.

**학술**(學術) 《과학》 science 《학문》 learning; scholarship 《학문과 예술》 art[s] and science[s]/ ~ 강연 a scientific lecture/ ~이 발달한 나라 a Country whose scienific is greatly advanced. がくじゅつ

**학술원**(學術院) the [Korean] Academy of Arts and Sciences. がくじゅついん

**학습**(學習) learning; study/ ~하다 study; learn/ ~장 a workbook/ ~을 지도하다 coach *a person's* study. がくしゅう

**학식**(學識) scholarship; learning; scholarly attainments; knowledge/ ~이 없다 lack scholarship; be uneducated; be unlettered. がくしき

**학업**(學業) studies; schoolwork 《성적》 scholarship/~ 성적이 우수하다 be a good scholar; do well at school/~에 태만하다 neglect *one's* school work. がくぎょう

**학예**(學藝) art[s] and science[s]; liberal arts; literary accomplishments 《문화・교양》 culture/~부 a department of art and science/~회 a class day; an exhibition of student works; literary exercises. がくげい

**학용품**(學用品) school things[supplies]. がくようひん

**학우**(學友) a classmate; a schoolmate; a fellowstudent/ ~회 a students' society [association]. がくゆう

**학원**(學園) a campus; a school/ ~의 자유 academic[campus] freedom/~ 생활 school life; student life. がくえん

**학원**(學院) an [educational] institute; an academy; a school; a seminary. がくいん

**학위**(學位) a [university] degree; a doctorate/ ~ 논문 a thesis for a degree; a doctoral dissertation/박사 ~ a doctor's degree/ ~를 수여하다 confer a degree (on *a person's*); grant a degree (*to*)/~를 받다 be granted a degree; receive a degree. がくい

**학자**(學者) a scholar; a learned man; a man of learning; an erudite; a savant 《학구》 an academical person/저 사람은 정말로 ~답다 He looks[like] a scholar, indeed./ ~ 고문단 《대통령의》 a brain trust《미》. がくしゃ

**학자**(學資) school expenses 《자금》 an education fund/~ 보험 educational endowment insurance. がくし

**학장**(學長) a dean; a president; a rector. がくちょう

**학적**(學籍) a school register 《대학 따위의》 a college register/~부 school register; a college register/~에서 빼 버리다 strike (*a person's*) name off the school register. がくせき

**학점**(學點) a unit; a point; a credit/ 4 ~의 불어 강의를 수강하다 take a French course for four credits[points]/ ~ 교환제 cross registration system. がくてん

**학정**(虐政) oppressive[tyrannical] government; [grinding] tyranny; despotism /~에 신음을 하다 groan under tyranny. ぎゃくせい

**학제**(學制) an educational system; a school system/ ~ 개혁안 the proposed educational system reform/ ~를 고치다 reform the system of education. がくせい

**학질**(瘧疾) malaria; malarial fever/ ~ 모기 《충》 an anopheles [mosquito]/ ~에 걸리다 be ill[taken] with malaria. マラリヤ

**학창**(學窓) a school; a compus; an educational institute/ ~ 생활 school[student] life/ ~을 떠나다 leave school. がくそう

**학칙**(學則) school regulations/ ~을 지키다[어기다] observe[break] school[college] regulations. がくそく

**학통**(學統) a scholastic mantle.

**학파**(學派) a school; a sect; a doctrinal faction/두 ~로 갈리다 be divided into two different schools. がくは

**학풍**(學風) 《특징》 academic traditions[features]; 《연구법》 a method of study 《학과》 a school 《학교의 기풍》 school character/두 사람은 ~이 다르다 They belong to different schools. / ~을 세우다 set up the character of a school; establish a school tradition. がくふう

**학해**(學海) the world of knowledge[literature and science]; the vast field of learning/ ~의 지침 a guiding star of the world of knowledge. がっかい

**학행**(學行) learning and virture. がくぎょう

**학형(學兄)** Mr …; you.

**학회(學會)** a learned society; an institute; an academy/한글 ~ the Korean Language [Research] Society. がつかい

**한** ①(하나)a; one/~ 사람 a[one] man/~ 마디 a[one] word ②(같은)the same/~들은 ~집에서 산다 The two live in the same house. ③(온·전)the whole; the entire/~여름을 낚시질로 보내다 spend all the summer in fishing ④(가장·한창)the peak; the extreme; the most; the very/~겨울 midwinter/~가운데 the very middle ⑤(대략)about; approximately/~ 열흘 about ten days. ひとつの

**한(恨)** (원한)a grudge; regret; rancor 《한탄》lamentation; grief; deploration/천추의 ~ a lasting regret/~을 풀다 revenge oneself (on a person); wreak one's grudge (on a person). うらむこと

**한(限)** ①(한계)a limit; limits; bounds/욕망에는 ~이 없는 것 같다 There seems to be no end to avarice. ②(기한)a time limt; a term; a period /열흘을 ~하고 돈을 꾸어 주다 lend money on the condition that it be returned within ten days ③(범위)as [so] far as/내가 알고 있는 ~ 그는 정직한 사람이다 So far as I know, he is an honest man. /따로 규정이 없는 ~ unless otherwise provided/네가 가지 않는 ~ 나도 가지 않겠다 Unless you go, I won't go either. かぎり

**한가(閑暇)** spare[leisure] time /~하다 [돕다] (be) free; leisure[d]; not busy; unoccupied (한산) (be) dull; slack; inactive/돈 있고 ~한 사람들 wealthy leisured people/~ 할 때 할 일이다 This is for leisure hours. ひま

**한가닥** ⓐ ~의 희망 a ray[gleam] of hope/~의 희망마저 잃다 lose one's last hope.

**한가운데** the very middle; the center; the midst; the heart/태평양 ~ in the midst of the pacific/방 ~ 눕다 lie right in the middle of the room/과녁 ~ 를 맞히다 hit the target right in the center. まんなか

**한가위** August 15th of the lunar month the Harvest Moon festival.

**한가을** late autumn; harvest season;(수확기) the busy harvesting season; the whole autumn[fall]; all autumn long / ~ 아무것도 않고 놀다 idle away the whole fall.

**한가지** ①(일종)a kind; a sort; a variety 《한가지 일》one thing; another kind ②(동일)the same/이것은 나에게는 사형 선고나 ~다 This is as much as a death sentence to me./영(靈)과 혼(魂)은 요컨대 ~다 The spirit and the soul are one and the same after all. おなじもの

**한각(閑却)** negligence; neglect; oversight/~하다 neglect; slight; ignore; disregard. かんきゃく

**한간(一間)** a[one] kan/~ 방 a room one kan in area.

**한갓** simply; merely only; alone/그것은 ~ 핑계에 불과하다 That is simply an excuse, and nothing more./~ 시간의 문제 merely a question of time/계으른 것이 ~ 결점이다 The only draw-back is that he is lazy. ただ

**한갓지다** (be) quiet; lonely; desolate; deserted; out-of-the-way; secluded; remote/한갓진 촌에 살다 live in an out-of-the-way village. かんせいだ

**한 개(一箇)** one 《단위》a unit/비누 ~ a cake[bar] of soap/이 사과는 ~ 20원입니다 These apples cost twenty won each[apiece].

**한거(閑居)** a quiet[secluded, retired] life; a leisurely life; an idle life / ~하다 lead a retired life; lead an idle life; live a leisurely life/소인이 ~하면 나쁜 짓을 한다 The devil makes work for idle hands. かんきょ

**한꺼번에** ①at a time; at a stretch[breath, sitting, stroke]/과자를 ~ 다 먹어 버리다 eat all the cakes up at one sitting ②(동시에)at the same time; all together; simultaneously/사람이 ~ 밀어닥치다 people crowd in all at the same time. いっぺんに

**한걱정** a great anxiety; a big worry/~ 생기다 have a great headache/~ 놓다 be relieved of a great anxiety. おおきなゆうりょ

**한걸음** a step; a pace/피로하여 ~도 더 못 걷겠다 I am too tired to walk another step. / ~ 안걸음 step by step/천리길도 ~으로부터 A journey of a thousand miles begins with one step. ひとあし

**한(限)―)** ①(한도까지)to the limit; to the utmost; to one's satisfaction/~ 즐기다 enjoy oneself to one's heart's content/~ 먹다 eat one's fill ②(최선을 다해)to the best of one's ability; with all one's might/~ 일하다 work to the best of one's ability; work as hard as one can.

**한겨울** the depth of winter; the midwinter. げんとう

**한결** (눈에 띄게)conspicuously; remarkably (한층)much more; still more 《특히》especially/비를 맞은 단풍이 ~ 아름답다 Rain adds a special charm to the red-tinted autumnal leaves./고독감이 ~ 더해졌다 My sense of isolation becomes doubly acute./고치니까 ~ 보기가 낫다 The change makes it look much nicer.

**한결같다** (be) uniform; equal; similar; identical 《변함없다》(be) unchangeable; constant/한결같은 사랑 constant love/한결같은 태도 a consistent attitude. ひたすらである

**한결같이** constantly; consistently; invariably; as ever/차별 철폐를 ~ 주장하다

consistently advocate abolishing discrimination/ ~ 사랑하다 love (*a person*) as ever. はじめからおわりまで
**한겻** a quarter of a day/ ~ 일 a job that will take several hours; a guarter-day's work.
**한겻지다** (be) secluded; out-of-the-way ⇨한갓지다.
**한계(限界)** a limit; a bound; limitations; a margin/ ~ 가격 a ceiling price/ ~ 능률 marginal efficiency/ ~ 온도 a critical temperature/ ~를 넘다 pass [exceed, overstep] the limit/인간 능력의 ~ the limitations of human faculty [power]/ ~ 개념 a concept of limitation. げんかい
**한계(韓系)** of Korean ancestry/ ~ 미국인 a Korean-American.
**한고비** the most serious moment; the most painful hour[moment] climax/ 그 외교 문제도 이제는 ~를 넘었다 The diplomatic question has now passed its critical point./병의 ~ the crucial stage of an illness/~ 넘다 the crisis is over; the worst is over. やまば
**한교(韓僑)** Korean [national] abroad; overseas Korean merchants.
**한구석** a corner; a nook; a secluded place/방 ~에 놓다 put (*a thing*) in a corner of a room/ ~에 앉다 sit in a corner/마을 ~에 살다 live in an obscure nook of a town[village]. かたすみ
**한국(寒國)** a cold country[region]. さむいくに
**한국(韓國)** Korea; the Republic Of Korea(略: R.O.K.)/ ~ 사정에 밝다 be well informed on Korean affairs/ ~화하다 Koreanize/ ~ 국민 the Korean [people]/ ~ 동란[전쟁] the Korean War/ ~ 말 Korean/ ~ 사람 a Korean/ ~ 식 Korean-style/ ~ 머리 hair-dressing of Korean style/ ~ 요리 Korean dishes. かんこく
**한국(寒菊)** a winter chrysanthemum.
**한군데** ①(한곳) a[one] place/ 그 책 파는 데가 ~ 있다 There is one store where the book is sold. ②(같은 장소) the same place/그들은 모두 ~서 왔다 All of them came from the same part of the country.
**한근심** a big worry; a great anxiety/ ~놓다 be relieved of a great anxiety.
**한글** Korean; the Korean alphabet(syllabary); the *Hangeul*/ ~ 맞춤법 the rules[system] of spelling of Korean/ ~ 날 *Hangeul* Proclamation Day.
**한끝** 《일단》 one end; one edge 《극한》 the last extremity; a bound; a limit/끈의 ~을 잡다 hold one end of a rope. いったん
**한끼** one[a] meal/ ~에 세 그릇 먹다 eat three bowls at a meal.
**한기(寒氣)** the cold; a cold wave; the cold weather 《급격한 온도 저하》 a cold snap〈미〉; chill; chilliness. かんき

**한길** 《큰길》 a [main] street; a highway; a thoroughfare/ ~을 막다 block the road/집이 없어 ~에 나서게 되다 be about to be driven out on the street with no house.
**한나절** half a day/ ~ 일 half-a-day's work/ ~이나 잠자다 sleep for the whole morning[afternoon]. はんにち
**한난(寒暖)** temperature; heat and cold. かんだん
**한낮** high noon; noonday; noontide; midday; broad daylight. しょうご
**한낱** ①(하나) one [item] ②(하잘것 없는) only; mere[ly]; nothing but/ ~ 서생(書生) a mere student/나는 ~ 고학생에 불과하다 I am nothing but[no more than] a self-supporting student. ただの
**한눈팔다** look away[aside, off]; take one's eyes off (*a thing*); avert one's eyes 《공부하다가》 look away from one's book/한눈 팔면서 걷다 walk along gazing around/책을 보지 않고 ~ take one's eyes off[look away from] one's book. めをそらす
**한다하는** respectable; prominent; influential/ ~ 학자 an eminent scholar/ ~ 사람 a somebody /그는 스스로 ~ 사람으로 생각하고 있다 He thinks himself somebody. めだった
**한닥거리다** sway; move; shake; wobble /한닥한닥 moving[swaying, shaking, wobbling] repeatedly/한닥한닥하는 의자 a rickety[an unsteady] chair/책상 다리가 한닥한닥 놀다 the legs of a table are wobbly[rickety]. ゆるむ
**한달음에** straight through; without a pause for breath; at run/ ~ 갔다 오다 take a run to (*the town*).
**한담(閑談)** a quiet talk; a chat; idle talk; gossip/ ~하다 talk quietly; gossip; [have a] chat; have an idle talk (*with*)/ ~으로 시간 가는 줄 몰랐다 While chatting we took no note of time.
かんだん
**한때** a time; once; [at] one time; for a time[while]; temporarily; provisionally/ 그 모자는 ~ 유행했다 The hat was once in fashion. しばらくのあいだ
**한대(寒帶)** 《지》 the frigid zone; the arctic regions/ ~ 동물·[식물] a polar[an arctic] animal[plant]. かんたい
**한댕거리다** shake[swing] lightly/한댕한댕 shaking; swinging.
ぶらぶらとかるくゆれる
**한더위** the extreme[intense] heat; great heat; the hot season/ ~가 물러가다 the hot season gets over. こくしょ
**한데¹** a place ⇨한군데. ひとところ
**한데²** ①(노천) the open air; outdoors/ ~서 자다 sleep under the open sky ②《규정 지역 밖》 outside [of a fixed area] the wrong place/자동차가 ~로 달리다 a car runs off the road. そと
**한뎃뒷간** an out-side privy[latrine]

**한뎃부엌** an outdoors kitchen.

**한뎃솥** an outdoors oven; an oven set up outside the kitchen.

**한도**(限度) a limit; bounds/인내에도 ~가 있다 Human patience has its limits. /~를 넘는 행동을 취해서는 안 된다 You should refrain from going too far. /~를 넘다 go beyond[exceed] the limit (of); go too far/ ~에 이르다 reach the limit. げんど

**한독**(悍毒) fierceness; ferocity/ ~하다 (be) fierce; ferocious; savage; truculent. どうもう

**한독**(韓獨) Korea and Germany/ ~의 Korean and German; Korean-German.

**한돌림** one[a] round; one circumference /술이 ~ 돌다 the liquor is passed a round once; have a round of drinks.

**한동생** a brother[sister]-german; fullbrothers and sisters/ ~끼리 싸우다 brothers quarrel [among themselves]. ひとまわり

**한동안** for a good while; for a long time /~ 머물다 stay quite a while. しばらくのあいだ

**한동자** cooking some more rice [after a meal].

**한되다**(限—) be regrettable; be deplorable; be sorry for/자식의 무지함이 ~ regret one's child's ignorance/젊어서 공부 못 한 것이 ~ regret that one couldn't study while young. いかんである

**한두** one or two; a couple/ ~ 번 once or twice/ ~ 사람 one or two persons / ~ 가지 일 a thing or two; one or two things. いちにの

**한둔**(—屯) camping-out; bivouac/ ~하다 sleep[pass the night] in the open; sleep under the open sky[stars].

**한둘** one or two/사과 ~ one or two apples. いちに

**한드랑거리다** swing ⇨한들거리다. ぶらぶらはせまくゆれる

**한드작거리다** swing ⇨한들거리다.

**한들거리다** swing; sway; dangle; shake; tremble; waver; flicker/한들거리는 등불 a flickering light/치마가 바람에 ~ a skirt sways in the wind/나뭇잎이 바람에 ~ leaves are trembling in the wind. かるくゆらゆらゆれる

**한란**(寒暖) heat and cold; temperature. かんだん

**한란계**(寒暖計) a thermometer; the mercury/ ~는 실내에서 30도를 나타내고 있다 The thermometer reads[stands at, indicates, registers, records] 30°C in the room. かんだんけい

**한랭**(寒冷) chill; cold; coldness/ ~하다 (be) cold; chilly / ~ 전선 (기상) a cold front. かんれい

**한량**(閑良) a prodigal; a profligate; a debauchee (옛 제도) one of the military officer class who has not passed the State Examination.

**한량**(限量) a limited quantity; a limit; a limits; bounds/위를 보면 ~이 없다 Do not compare yourself with those above you. /욕심엔 ~이 없다 Greed knows no bounds. げんりょう

**한량하다**(寒涼—) (be) thin and languid; pale and wan.

**한련**(旱蓮) 【식】 a tropaeolum; a [garden] nasturtium; *Tropaeolaceae*(학명)/~초 (草) a kind of same.

**한류**(寒流) a cold current. かんりゅう

**한마**(悍馬) an unruly horse; a vicious horse; a spirited horse. かんば

**한마디** a [single] word/ ~하다 speak a word about; make a remark[comment] on/말 ~ 하지 않고 가버리다 leave without a word; take French leave. いちげん

**한마음** [the whole world as] one mind the same mind; like-mindedness; accord/그들은 ~이다 They have one mind between[among] than. /~ 한뜻 everyone being of the same mind[being in accord, having the same idea]/ ~으로 with one accord. いっしん

**한만**(韓滿) Korea and Manchuria/ ~ 국경 the frontier of Korea and Manchuria; the Korean-Manchurian border.

**한매**(寒梅) early plum blossoms.

**한명**(限命) the appointed limit of life; the destined duration of life.

**한모금** a draft; a draught (극소량) a drop/ ~의 물 a draught of water/ ~에 at one draft.

**한목** all together; all at one time/물건을 ~ 보내다 send things together/1년 치 봉급을 ~ 타다 receive a year's pay in a lump. ぜんぶ

**한몫** a share; a portion; a quota; a whack《속》; a rake-off; a split;a divvy /이익을 ~ 단단히 보다 get a good share of the profit/ ~ 들다 have a share [take one's share] (in).

**한문**(漢文) Chinese composition 《한문학》 Chinese classics. かんぶん

**한물** the best season; the peak; the height/창경원에 벚꽃이 ~이다 The cherry blossoms at *Changkyong* Palace are at their best[in full bloom]/꽃이 ~지다 flowers are at their best/ ~지나다[가다] be past its season.

**한미 경제 협력 위원회**(韓美經濟協力委員會) the Korea-U.S. Economic Cooperation Committee(略: ECC.)

**한미 관계**(韓美關係) Korean-American relations.

**한미 상호 방위 협정**(韓美相互防衛協定) the ROK-U.S. Mutual Defense Agreement.

**한미 원자력 협정**(韓美原子力協定) the ROK-U.S. Atomic Energy Agreement.

**한미 재단**(韓美財團) the American-Korean Foundation(略: A.K.F.).

**한미 행정 협정**(韓美行政協定) the ROK-U.S. Agreement on Status-of-Forces in Korea.

**한미 협회**(韓美協會) the Korean-American Association.
**한밑천** a sizable amount of capital; competent fortune; sufficient means/~ 장만하다 amass a sizable fortune.
**한바닥** the busiest quarters.
**한바퀴** a round; a turn/연못을 ~ 돌다 go round a pond.
**한바탕** a scene; a round; a bout; an event 《씨름》 a fall/~ 연설을 하다 make a speech/~ 야단을 치다 give (a person) a good scolding/~ 부는 사나운 바람 a sudden puff[a gust] of wind.
**한발** a step/~ 한 발 step by step 《서서히》 gradually; bit by bit/~ 늦다 fall a step behind (a person)/~ 먼저 떠나다 start a little before (a person)/~ 늦어 기차를 놓치다 miss the train by a second.
**한발**(旱魃) a drought; a spell of dry weather; want of rain/~로 인해 곡물이 흉작이 되었다 The drought has ruined the crops./~ 대책 measures against drought; counter drought measures/~ 피해 drought damage.
**한발짝** a step/~ 앞으로 나서다[뒤로 물러서다] take a step forward[backward]/지쳐서 이제 ~도 움직일 수 없다 I am too tired to walk another step.
**한밤중** midnight; the middle[dead] of the night/~에 in the middle of [the] night; at midnight; at [the] dead of night/~까지 far into [the] night; at midnight/모두 잠든 ~에 at dead of night when all is silent.
**한방**(漢方) Chinese [herb] medicine/~ 약 a Chinese [herb] medicine/~의 herb doctor; a doctor[physician] of the Chinese school.
**한방울** a drop ⇒방울.
**한배** ①《동물》 a litter/돼지 새끼 ~ a litter of pigs ②《사람》 a womb; a venter; a belly/~의 형제 brothers of the same venter.
**한번** once; one time 《어디》 just/~ 그 얘기를 들으면 결코 잊지 않을 것이다 Once you hear the story, you will never be able to forget it./~에 《단번에》 at once; at a time/다시 ~ once more/~ 만 once only; once [and] for all; for once/내가 ~ 해 보죠 Let me have a try.

**한 벌** a suit; a set/가구 ~을 갖추다 collect a complete set of household articles.
**한복**(韓服) Korean clothes[costume, attire]/한국 부인은 가정에서 대개 ~을 입는다 Most Korean woman wear Korean clothes at home.
**한복판** the very middle; the center; the heart/~의 middle; central/과녁 ~을 맞히다 hit the target right in the center/그는 길 ~에 쓰러졌다 He fell on the middle of the road.

**한부**(悍婦) a shrew; a termagant; a virago; a spitfire; a vixen.
**한불**(韓佛) Korea and France/~의 Franch-Korean.
**한사**(寒士) a penniless[poor] scholar.
**한 사람** one person/~씩 one at a time; one by one 《잇따라》 one after another 《개별적으로》 individually/~ 한 사람씩 방을 나갔다 They left the room one by one[one after another].
**한사리** the flood[spring] tide.
**한사코**(限死―) at the risk of one's life; with[for] all one's life; to the last; desperately; doggedly; persistently; relentlessly/~ 조르다 tease (a person for something) persistently/~ 싸우다 fight at the risk of one's life/~ 반대하다 persist in one's opposition; be dead set against; oppose stoutly.
**한사하다**(限死―) risk one's neck; stake one's life; be desperate[frantic].
**한산**(閑散) ①《한가》 leisure/~하다 (be) at leisure; leisurely; disengaged/거리가 이 시간에는 ~하다 The traffic is light about this time. ②《불경기》 dullness; inactivity; slackness; flatness/~하다 (be) dull; inactive; slack; stagnant/~한 시장 a dull[flat] market/~기 a slack season; an off season.
**한 살** ①《나이》 one year of age ②《한몸·결합》 one flesh; the same flesh/~이 되다 they stick together [and become one].
**한삼덩굴** Japanese hop; Humulus japonicus(학명).
**한색**(寒色) 《미》 a cold colour.
**한서**(寒暑) cold and heat; temperature winter and summer/~의 차가 적다 The heat and cold are moderate./이곳은 ~의 차가 심하다 The temperatures here vary greatly with the seasons.
**한서**(漢書) 《중국 서적》 Chinese books[classics]; Chinese literature.
**한선**(汗腺) 《해》 a sweat-gland; Glandula sudorifera(학명).
**한세상**(一世上) ①《일평생》 one's[whole] life; a lifetime/독신으로 ~을 보내다 remain single all one's life[to the end of one's life] ②《한창 때》 one's palmy days; heyday; the golden age; one's best day.
**한세월**(閑歲月) spare time; leisure/~을 보내다 live a retired[quiet] life.
**한소**(韓蘇) Korean-Soviet/~ 관계 Korean-Soviet relations.
**한속** (같은 뜻) the same, mind 《공모》 conspiracy; confederacy/~이 되어서 속이다 conspire together to cheat (a person).
**한손** one[a single] hand/~의 one-handed; single-handed/~에는 우산 한 손에는 보통이를 들고 with an umbrella in

one hand and a package in the other.
**한손놓다** 《일이》come to an end for the moment 《한 장면이》be completed/일은 이것으로 한손놓았다 With this I've got the hard part of the work done. いちだんらくする
**한손잡이** a one-handed person.
**한수**(一手) a trick; a move; a skill; a game; a means/ ~ 높다 be a cut above (one).
**한순**(一巡) one round of shooting five arrows/우리들은 활을 ~씩 쏘았다 Each of us had a round of shooting five arrows.
**한순배**(一巡杯) one round of drink/ ~ 돌리다 pass [the liquor] around once; have a round of drinks.
**한술** a spoonful of food 《적은 음식》a small quantity (of food)/나는 떠나기 전에 점심을 ~떴다 I had a mouthful of luncheon before I started.
**한숨** ①《잠》a [wink of] sleep; a snatch of sleep; a doze/그날 밤은 ~도 자지 못했다 I had a sleepless night. ②《탄식》a [deep]˜sigh; a deep[heavy] breath 《연인들의》an amorous sigh; a sigh of relief/모두들 안도의 ~을 쉬었다 Every one gave a sigh of relief. ③《호흡·휴식》a breath; a rest; pause; relief; a wink of sleep; a nap/ ~에 at[in] a breath; at a heat/ ~ 쉬다 take breath/물 한 그릇을 ~에 들이켜다 down a bowl of water at one draft.
**한시**(漢詩) a Chinese poem 《총칭》Chinese poetry. かんし
**한시도**(一時─) even for a moment/ ~ 잊지 않다 keep[bear] (something) in mind all the time; never forget even for a moment/ ~ 몸에서 떼지 않다 always carry (a thing) about[on] one.
**한식**(韓式) Korean [style]/~집 a Korean-style house.
**한심**(寒心) a pity; a regret; disappointment; hopelessness/ ~하다 (be) pitiful; pitiable; miserable; sorry; lamentable; grievous/~하기 짝이 없다 be extremely deplorable/그의 장래가 심히 ~스럽다 I am rather doubtful about his future. かんしん
**한아**(閑雅) elegance; gracefulness; daintiness (of a scene)/ ~하다 (be) graceful; elegant; dainty; refined. かんが
**한아름** an armful/~의 책 an armful of books.
**한악**(悍惡) ferocity; fierceness/ ~하다 (be) ferocious; fierce; savage; cruel. ざんにん
**한약**(漢藥) a Chinese medicine; a herb remedy; herbs/ ~국 a dispensary of Chinese medicine; a herb shop. かんやく
**한어**(韓語) Korean [language]; a Korean word. かんこくご
**한어**(漢語) Chinese [language]; 《어귀》a Chinese word. かんご

**한없다**(恨─) be gratified; have nothing to be regretted[desired]; be perfectly happy/내 집이라고 한번 쓰고 살아 봤으면 한없겠다 I should be very happy if I could ever own a house of my own.
**한없다**(限─) (de) unlimited; boundless; endless; unmeasurable; infinite 《영원하다》eternal/한없는 생명 eternal life/아들을 한없이 사랑하다 love one's son no end[ever so much]/욕심은 ~. Avarice [Desire] knows no bounds. はてしない
**한여름** ①《한창》midsummer; the middle of summer ②《한철》the whole summer; all summer long/ ~ 밤의 꿈 "A Midsummer Night's Dream"/ ~도 잠깐 가다 the summer passes away quickly.
せいか
**한역**(韓譯) translation into Korean; a Korean translation/ ~하다 translate into Korean; put into Korean/영문 ~ translation from English into Korean; English-[to]-Korean translation.
**한역**(漢譯) a Chinese translation/~하다 translate[put] into Chinese. かんやく
**한염**(旱炎) tropical[torrid, intense] heat.
**한영**(韓英) Korea and England/ ~의 Korean-British; Anglo-Korean; Korean-English/ ~ 사전 a Korean-English dictionary.
**한옆** one side[flank]/ ~으로 비켜서다 step aside.
**한외**(限外) out of bounds; beyond the limit/ ~ 원심기 an ultracentrifuge/ ~ 현미경 an ultramicroscope/ ~ 발행 an excessive issuance[overissue] [of paper currency]. げんがい
**한용**(悍勇) intrepidity; dauntlessness; daring; valour/ ~하다 (be) intrepid; daring; dauntless; plucky; valiant; lion-hearted.
**한우**(寒雨) winter rain 《찬비》a cold rain.
かんう
**한운**(閑雲) floating clouds; wandering clouds/~ 야학(野鶴) wandering clouds and wild cranes/~ 야학을 벗삼다 lead a leisurely life. かんうん
**한움큼** a handful; a grasp/ ~의 소금 a handful of salt/ ~ 쥐다 make one grip of.
**한월**(寒月) a winter[wintry] moon.
かんげつ
**한유**(閑遊) idling; loafing ~하다 amuse oneself; take a holiday; idle away the time. ぶらぶらあそぶこと
**한음**(漢音) the classical Chinese pronunciation of Chinese characters; the original pronunciation of Chinese characters. かんおん
**한의**(漢醫) a physician of the Chinese[the old] school; a herb doctor. かんぽうい
**한이**(韓伊) Korea and Italy/~의 Korean Italian.
**한인**(韓印) Korea and India/ ~의 Korean-Indian.

한인(漢人) a Chinese. ちゅうごくじん
한인(閑人) a leisured person; an idle person; a man of leisure; a loafer/물입(勿入) No admittance except on business. かんじん
한인(韓人) a Korean; a *Coréen*(F). かんこくじん
한일 각료 회담(韓日閣僚會談) the Korea-Japan Ministerial Conference.
한일 회담(韓日會談) the Korean-Japanese Conference; the Korea-Japan talks.
한입 (음식물의) a mouthful; a bite/가득 먹다 cram (*something*) in *one's* mouth/~에 at a mouthful.
한자(漢字) a Chinese character[ideograph]/~어 a word written in Chinese characters/~ 제한 limitation in[restriction on] the use of Chinese characters/~ 철폐 abolition of Chinese characters/상용 ~ the Chinese characters for common use. かんじ
한자리 ①(장소) a place (방) a room (경우) an occasion ②(한몫) position; rank/~에 모이다 meet at a place.
おなじところ
한짝 one odd; one[a] direction; one side.
한잔(一盞) ①(분량) a cup (of *tea*); a glass (of *beer*); a cupful; a glassful ②(음주) a drink/~하다 have a drink; take a drop/~ 눈치다 have a drop in (*a person's*) eye/오늘밤 ~하게 Let's have a drink tonight./맥주 ~ 더 하시겠 읍니까 Would you like another glass of beer?
한잠 a sleep; a nap; a deep[sound] sleep/어젯밤은 ~도 못 잤다 I could not get a wink of sleep last night./~ 푹 자다 have a sound sleep. じゅくすい
한 장(一帳) a sheet; a piece [of]; (솥) a lap (유리) a pane/페이지를 ~씩 넘기다 turn over[go through] the pages[leaves].
한재(旱災) damage from a drought; a drought disaster/ ~ 지구 the drought-stricken district/ ~를 입다 suffer from a drought. かんがい
한적(閑寂) quiet[ness]; tranquility/ ~하다 (be) quiet; secluded; sequestered; restful/ ~한 곳 live a retired life / ~한 곳 a retired[quiet] place; a secluded spot. かんじゃく
한적(漢籍) Chinese classics[literature]/그는 ~에 밝다 He is well posted in Chinese literature. かんせき
한절(寒節) the cold season; midwinter. かんてん
한 점(一點) a point (바둑) a stone; a speck (작은) a dot/하늘에는 구름 ~ 없다 There is not a speck of cloud in the sky. / ~을 놓다 put a stone in advance.
한정(限定) limitation; qualification;〖논〗 determination (뜻의) definition/ ~하다 limit (뜻을) define; restrict; place limit upon; set limits to; qualify/ ~ 가격 the ceiling price; the [price] ceiling/ ~된 지면 limited space/ ~ 상속 qualified acceptance of inheritance.
げんてい
한정(閑靜) quietness; quiet; tranquility / ~하다 (be) quiet; restful; retired. かんせい
한제(韓製) [of] Korean make[manufacture]; made in Korea 《국산의》 home-made.
한제(寒劑) a freezing mixture; a cryogen. かんざい
한조각 a piece [of]; a bit; a fragment / ~의 동정 a particle[bit] of sympathy/ ~의 양심 a bit of conscience.
한족(韓族) the Korean race.
한족(漢族) the Han race. かんぞく
한종신(限終身) all life long; for life; throughout *one's* life; till death.
しぬまで
한종일(一終日) all day [long].
ひがくれるまで
한 줄 (가로) a[one] line; a row; a rank (세로) a[one] file/~씩 걸러 쓰십시오 Write on every other line.
한 줄기 ①(한 가닥) a streak; a ray/~의 연기 a streak of smoke/ ~의 희망 a ray[gleam] of hope ②(한바탕) a spell /소나기가 ~ 오다 have a [spell of] shower.
한 줌 a handful (of *rice*); (길이의) a hand /~의 토지 a small lot (of *land*) /~의 쌀 a handful of rice. ていっぱい
한중(韓中) Korea and China/~의 무역 Korean-Chinese trade.
한중(寒中) midwinter; the cold season; the depth of winter/~ 훈련 midwinter training; winter exercise/~ 수영 midwinter swimming.
한즉 if so; then/ ~ 인제 어떻게 하는 것이 좋을까 Then, what should we do now?. そうだから
한증(汗蒸) a sudatorium; a sudatory; a sweating bath/~하다 take a sweating [steam] bath/~막 a sweating bathroom/~막 같다 be sweltering[ly] hot.
むしぶろ
한지(韓紙) Korean paper.
한직(閑職) a sinecure [office]; an easy post[office]/~에 있는 사람 a sinecurist/~이 아니다 be hardly a sinecure; be no[not a] sinecure. かんしょく
한집안 a family; *one's* folk; members of a family; *one's* family people 《친척》 relatives; a clan; *one's* kinsfolk/~이나 다름없다 be in close relation with each other/~ 식구처럼 대우하다 treat (*a person*) as a member of *one's* family; give (*a person*) family comforts.
おなじぞく
한차례 one round; a turn; once; a time / ~ 씨름을 하다 have a round of wrestling.

**한참** ①(한동안) for some time; for time [a while]; for a spell/~만에 after a good while/소나기가 ~ 퍼부었다 There was a shower for some time. ②(휴식) a rest; a break; a spell/~의 일 a spell of work/~에 열개 먹다 eat ten of them at one sitting[without stopping]. しばらくのあいだ

**한창** ①(절정) the height; the summit; the zenith; the peak; the climax (꽃의) (in) full bloom; (at it's) best (인생의) prime; flower; bloom/ 요사이는 딸기가 ~이다 Strawberries are in [season] now. ②(사람의) prime; flower; bloom/그 여자는 지금이 ~이다 She is in the prime of youth. ③(부사적으로) ¶ ~일 때 in the midst (of)/~ 연주회가 진행중입니다 The Concert is in full swing. /폭풍이 ~일 때 in the midst of a storm. まっさかり

**한천**(旱天) dry weather; a [spell of] drought (염천) hot[broiling] weather/~의 자우(慈雨) a rainfall eagerly longed for. ひでりのそら

**한천**(寒天) (추운 철) cold weather; a bleak wintry sky (식품) Bengal isinglass; [vegetable] gelatine; gelidium jelly. かんてん

**한촌**(寒村) a poor village; a remote[forlorn, an out-of-the-way] hamlet; a deserted village. かんそん

**한추위** severe[intense] cold; a spell of cold weather; a cold snap. きびしいさむさ

**한층**(一層) ①(더욱) more; still[much] more; the more; all the more/ 8월이 되면 ~ 더 더워진다 It gets hotter in August. ②(층계) a step; the first step[flight, story, level, floor]. いっそう

**한카랫군** a team of three plowmen.

**한칼** ①a single stroke [of a sword]/~로 베다 cut down at a blow ②(고기) a slice of meat.

**한탄**(恨歎) sigh; lamentation; grief; deploration; woe/~하다 sigh [for grief] /덧없는 인생을 ~하다 mourn for the frailty of life/ ~할 노릇이다 It is to be regretted (that).

**한턱** an entertainment; a treat/ ~하다 stand treat for (a person); give (a person) a treat; treat (a person) to (something)/저녁을 ~ 내다 give a dinner (for a person)/그는 우리에게 술을 ~ 냈다 He treated us to a drink. おごること

**한테** at; for; by (a person)/ 영국 사람~ 배우다 be taught by an Englishman/ 개~ 돌을 던지다 throw a stone at a dog/ 동생~ 돈을 주었다 I gave some money to my brother. ーに

**한테서** from; of; through/ 멀리 친구~ 온 편지 a letter from a friend far away/자네 이야기는 김군~ 들었네 I heard of you through Mr. Kim. ーから

**한통속** a party; a company; a set; a group; one and the same group/ 음모의 ~ a party to a plot/~이 되어 in conspiracy[collusion, cahoots] (with).

**한통치다** put[add, join] together; sum up; combine; unite; mix/한통쳐서 as a group; in the gross; in one lot/모두 한통쳐서 도둑놈으로 생각하다 regard all of them as robbers. とうごうする

**한파**(寒波) a cold wave/~가 전국을 엄습했다 A cold wave swept[hit] [over] the country. かんぱ

**한판** (승부의 일 회) a game; a round (씨름 따위의) a bout/장기를 ~ 두다 play[have] a bout[game] of chess/씨름을 ~ 하다 have a round of wrestling.

**한패**(一牌) one of the [same] party[group, set]; fellows; a confederate/그도 ~임에 틀림없다 He must be one of the party.

**한편**(一便) (한쪽) one side; one hand; the other side; one way; in the mean time; meanwhile; in addition to/그에게 사실을 말해 주고 싶지만 ~으로는 그의 감정을 상하고 싶지 않다 I feel like telling him the truth, but on the other hand I'd hate to hurt his feelings./ 길의 ~을 걷다 keep to one side of the road. いっぽう

**한평생**(一平生) one's whole life (부사적) all[throughout] one's life; as long as one lives/그는 ~ 독신으로 지냈다 He lived and died a bachelor. /그는 ~ 한 번도 성공할 수 없었다 He could never get on well in the world all his life [until the end of his life]. しょうがい

**한푼** a small coin; a farthing; a penny; a copper; a red cent(미)/ ~도 없는 빈털터리가 되다 become penniless; be reduced to the last penny/~의 가치도 없다 be not worth a [brass] farthing.

**한풀꺾이다** be discouraged; be disheartened; be crushed/밀려오는 대병력을 보고 그들은 한풀꺾였다 They flinched before the great force marching against them./첫 번에 실패하자 그의 열의는 한풀꺾였다 The initial failure daunted[chilled] his ardor. はきがなくなる

**한풀다**(恨ー) realize one's heart's desire; attain one's long-cherished object; accomplish the object one has so much at heart/나는 오랫 동안 뱃힌 한을 풀었다 What I had long hoped for came true.

**한풀이**(恨ー) ~하다 vent one's spite; satisfy one's grudge; revenge oneself on; pay off old scores; take out (one's anger).

**한풍**(寒風) a cold[an icy, a chilly] wind /살을 에이는 듯한 ~ a cutting[biting, piercing, bleak] wind. かんぷう

**한하다**(限ー) limit; restrict; place limit (on)/사원에 한하여 입장을 허가하다 Admission to employees only./일요일에 한해서 무료 입장이다 Admission is free on Sundays only. かぎる

**한학(漢學)** Chinese literature; Chinese classics; sinology/ ～자 a scholar of Chinese classics/～의 대가 an authority on Chinese classics. かんがく

**한해(旱害)** damage from drought; drought disaster/ ～를 입다 suffer from a drought/～ 지구 a drought-stricken area. かんがい

**한해(寒害)** damage from cold weather/ 서북지방에 ～가 있었다 In the Northwestern districts the crops suffered damage due to cold weather. かんがい

**한해살이** 〖식〗 an annual plant; annuals.

**한호(韓濠)** Korea and Australia/ ～의 Korean-Australian.

**한화(閑話)** idle[small] talk; gossip; a chat/～하다 talk idly; chat; have chitchat; gossip. かんわ

**한화(韓貨)** 〖화폐〗 Korean money[currency]; 〖화물〗 Korean goods.

**한훤(寒暄)** compliments of the season. かんけん

**할(割)** percentage; percent; rate; proportion/정가의 2～을 할인해서 팔다 sell at twenty percent discount. わり

**할갑다** (be) loose 헐겁다. さしこみのあながおおきい

**할거(割據)** ～하다 maintain one's independence free from the central authority; hold one's own ground/군웅(群雄) ～ rivalry of powerful leaders[lords, chiefs]/군웅 ～하다 each of the several lords holds his own ground. かっきょ

**할근거리다** gasp [for breath]; pant; wheeze; puff [and blow]; breathe hard [heavily]/숨을 할근거리면서 말하다 gasp out; puff out; speak while panting/ 할근할근 gasping[ly]. あえぎ

**할날** one day; a day. いちにち

**할딱거리다** pant; puff; breathe heavily; be out of breath/숨이 차서 ～ be panting for breath. あえぎ

**할딱할딱** panting; puffing; breathing heavily/ ～ 달리다 run along panting. ぜいぜい

**할당(割當)** allotment; quota; rationing; assignment/～하다 assign; allot; allocate; apportion; give a quota; divide among; distribute among; assess/일을 ～하다 assign (a person) for a task/～금 allotment/ ～ 배급 quota delivery; rationing/ ～제 the quota system. わりあて

**할똥말똥** not ready to do/ ～하다 be not inclined to do; seem not likely to do. いいかげんに

**할듯할듯** be ready to do; be about[going] to do; nearly/ ～하다 look as if one is going to do. ―しそうで

**할랑거리다** ①(물건이) be loose, be loose-fitting ②(행동이) be rash; be hasty; be precipitate; be careless; be heedless; be thoughtless. ぐすい

**할랑하다** (be) loose; loose-fitting. ぐすい

**할례(割禮)** 〖종〗 circumcision/ ～하다 circumcise; perform the circumcision. かつれい

**할말** ①(하고 싶은) one's say; a claim/이 제 내가 ～이 있다 It is now my say./네 게 ～이 있다 I have something to tell you. ②(해야 할) what one ought[has] to say; one's say/ ～은 해야 한다 You should say what you have to say. ③ (불평) a complaint/뭐 ～이 있는가 Have you anything to complain of?

**할머니** (조모) a grandmother; a grandma (노파) an old lady[woman]; a granny (친척의) a related woman of one's grandmother's generation. おばあさま

**할미꽃** 〖식〗 a pasqueflower; Pulsatilla Koreana(학명). おきなぐさ

**할미새** 〖조〗 a wagtail; Motacillidae(학명).

**할복(割腹)** self-disembowelment/ ～하다 disembowel oneself; rip up one's own abdomen[belly]/～ 자살 suicide by disembowelment. かっぷく

**할선(割線)** 〖수〗 a secant. わりせん

**할쑥하다** (be) haggard; worn out/병으로 할쑥해지다 become worn out from illness.

**할아버지** ①(조부) a grandfather; a grandpa (소아·애칭) a grand[d]ad ②(노인) an old man ③(친척의) a related man of one's grandfather's generation. おそうふさま

**할애(割愛)** ～하다 part with (something); share (something) with (a person); spare (something)/[기사를] 다음호로 ～하다 keep for the next issue/지면 관계로 부득이 ～했다 Space did not permit us to insert. かつあい

**할양(割讓)** cession; alienation/ ～하다 cede; alienate/토지의 ～ the cession of territory. かつじょう

**할인(割引)** discount; reduction; an allowance; price-cutting/ ～하다 discount; reduce; cut off/ ～권 (승차권) a discount ticket/ ～ 요금 a discoun* [charge, commission]/ ～해서 팔다 sell at a discount[reduced price]/ ～ 시간 the term of discount; reduced fare hours/ 단체 ～ a party-trip reduction/은행 ～ bank[banker's] discount/수표를 은행에서 ～하다 get a bill discounted at a bank. わりびき

**할인(割印)** a tally impression/～을 찍다 imprint a seal; affix a seal over two edges[at the joining of two papers]/ ～을 찍은 서류 documents with a tally impression. わりいん

**할일** things to do/ ～이 많다 have lots to do; be busy.

**할짝거리다** lick lightly [with the tip of the tongue]; lap/개가 우유를 할짝거리고 있다 The dog is lapping milk. かるくなめる

**할주(割註)** an inserted note. わりちゅう

**할쭉거리다** lick lightly ☞할짝거리다.

**할쭉하다** (be) haggard.

**할증**(割增) (임금 따위) an extra [fare, charge]; (주식 따위의) a premium; a bonus/ ～하다 increase proportionally/～요금 an extra charge/ ～배당금 an extra dividend; a bonus/ ～ 임금 extra[premium] wages.

**할퀴다** ①(손톱으로) scratch; claw; maul/얼굴을 할퀴다 be scratched on the face/고양이가 사람을 ～ a cat claws a person ②(훔치다) filch; pilfer; swipe.

**핥다** lick; lap [up]/우유를 깨끗이 ～ lap up milk/개가 사람의 손을 ～ a dog licks a person's hand.

**핥아먹다** ①(혓바닥으로) lick up; lap up ②(남의 물건을) swindle; defraud; cheat; wheedle; fleece; acquire (a person's things) by fraud.

**함**(函) a box; a case; a chest /우편～ a mail-box /사서～ a post-office box (略: P. O. B.).

**함께** together (with, along); in company with; in unison/나도 아이들과 ～ 놀았다 I joined the children's sports.

**함교**(艦橋) 〖군〗 the bridge [of a warship]; the navigating platform/ ～에 서다 stand on the bridge of a warship/ ～ 갑판 the bridge deck.

**함구**(緘口) ～하다 hold one's tongue; keep one's mouth shut; keep one's lips tight; keep[be] silent/ ～령 a gag law; a muzzle law/ ～ 불언하다 keep one's mouth shut [and remain silent]/그는 ～ 무언이었다 He would not open his mouth.

**함기**(艦旗) an ensign.

**함닉**(陷溺) ～하다 ①(물 속에) fall[sink] into; drown ②(주색에) be addicted; give oneself up (to); indulge in; abandon oneself (to).

**함대**(艦隊) (대함대) a fleet (소함대) a squadron/유격 ～ a flying squadron; a task force/ ～ 기지 a fleet base/연합 ～ a combined fleet/주력 ～ the main fleet.

**함락**(陷落) ①(적진의) fall; reduction/～하다 fall; surrender; be reduced ②(토지의) fall; subsidence; sinking; caving in; collapse/ ～호(湖) a cave-in lake /～ 지진 a fallen[cave-in] earthquake.

**함량**(含量) content; contained quantity.

**함령**(艦齡) the age[life] of a warship.

**함루**(含淚) ～하다 be moved to tears; one's eyes swim with tears; tears come to one's eyes; (one's eyes) swim[dim, glisten] with tears.

**함몰**(陷沒) (땅등의) depression; caving in (멸망) total destruction/ ～하다 sink; cave in/ ～해(海) an ingression sea.

**함묵**(緘默) ～하다 keep one's mouth shut; keep silent; hold one's tongue.

**함미**(鹹味) a salt taste; saltiness; a flavor[touch] of salt.

**함미**(艦尾) the stern of a warship/ ～ 포 a stern gun[chaser].

**함빡** all [in all]; thoroughly; completely/비에 ～ 젖다 one's clothes are all wet with rain.

**함박꽃** 〖식〗 a peony [flower].

**함박꽃나무** 〖식〗 a magnolia; *Magnolia parviflora*(학명).

**함박눈** large flakes of snow/ ～이 오다 It snows in large flakes.

**함봉**(緘封) seal; closing/ ～하다 seal.

**함부로** indiscriminately 《마구》 at random; thoughtlessly; disorderly; recklessly; without permission[good reason]; rudely; as one pleases[likes, chooses]; at will/말을 ～ 하다 talk at random/일을 ～ 하다 do a job in a rough[slap-dash] fashion/돈을 ～ 쓰다 spend money recklessly.

**함분**(含憤) ～하다 bear resentment (toward); have a rancour (against); hold a grudge (against).

**함상**(艦上) ～의(에) ~board; on board.

**함석** zinc; galvanized iron sheet; sheetzinc/～집 a house with zinc roof[with galvanized iron roofing]/ ～을 입히다 zinc/～판 sheet zinc.

**함선**(艦船) warships and other vessels (선박) vessels; naval vessels.

**함성**(喊聲) a war cry; a battle cry; a great outcry/ ～을 지르다 give a battle cry; raise a great war whoop.

**함소**(含笑) ～하다 wear a smile; hold a laugh in one's mouth; have[wear] a smile about one's mouth.

**함수**(含水) 〖화〗 hydrous; hydrated/ ～량 the amount of contained water/ ～ 탄소 a carbohydrate/ ～ 화합물 a hydrated compound.

**함수**(函數) 〖수〗 a function/ ～론 the theory of function/ ～식 a functional formula/ ～ 관계 functional relation.

**함수**(鹹水) salt-water; sea water; brine /～어 salt water fish/ ～호 a salt-water lake; a lagoon.

**함수**(艦首) the bow [of a warship]/ ～ 포 a bow gun [chaser].

**함수초**(含羞草) 〖식〗 a sensitive plant; *Mimosa pudica*(학명).

**함씨**(咸氏) your[his, etc.] nephew.

**함양**(涵養) cultivation; culture; fostering/ ～하다 cultivate; foster; develop; build [up]; train; promote/그것은 국민의 도의심을 ～했다 It cultivated the moral sense of the people./덕성을 ～하

다 cultivate moral character. かんよう

함열(艦列) a column; a line ahead.

함원(含怨) ～하다 bear (a peron) a grudge; have a rancour (against); bear[cherish, nurse] ill will. うらみをいだくこと

함유(含有) ～하다 contain; have (in); hold; include／～ 성분 a component／알코올의 ～량 alcohol content／위스키는 알코올 ～량이 많다 Whisky contains a large percentage of alcohol. がんゆう

함입(陷入) depression; subsidence. かんにゅう

함자(銜字) your[his, etc.] name／선생님의 ～가 어떻게 되십니까 What is your name, sir?

함장(艦長) a captain [of a warship]; the commander of a warship／～실 the captain's cabin. かんちょう

함재(艦載) carrying aboard a warship; loading on a warship／～하다 carry [load] aboard a warship／～기 a deck plane／～ 수뢰정 a torpedo launch.
かんさい

함적(艦籍) the navy list／～에서 빼다 strike (a ship) off the navy list.

함정(陷穽) a pit; a pit fall; a trap／자신이 만든 ～에 빠지다 be caught in one's own snare; be hoist with one's own petard／～을 놓다 lay[set] a trap (for).
かんせい

함정(艦艇) a naval vessel; a war vessel.
かんてい

함지 ①《나무 그릇》 a large scooped wooden bowl ②《함지박》 a scooped wooden dish ③《금 잡는》 a pan for gold panning.

함지(陷地) sunken land; a hollow. かんち

함체(艦體) the hull of a warship.

함축(含蓄) implication; significance; pregnancy／～하다 imply; comprehend; suggest／그가 말하는 것은 ～이 있다 What he says is full of suggestions[significance]／～성 있는 significant; suggestive. がんちく

함치르르 ～하다 (be) sleek; slick; glossy; bright ⇨함치르르.

함포(艦砲) 《군》 the guns of a warship／～ 사격 bombardment from a warship[naval guns]; shelling from a warship. かんぼう

함함하다 (be) soft and gleaming.

함해(陷害) ～하다 land (one) in a misfortune; entrap (one).

함혐(含嫌) harboring suspicion[enmity]／～하다 be suspicious of; feel enmity toward.

함호(鹹湖) a salt lake ⇨함수호.

함흥차사(咸興差使) a lost[burnt] messenger／그는 한번 가디니 ～다 He has gone and never returned.

합(合) ①《합계》 the sum total; grand total／～이 400만원이다 The sum total is four million wan; amount up to a million won ②《논》 synthesis ③《천》 [astronomical] conjunction ④ 홉.
あわせること

합(盒) a small round brass vessel; a brass bowl with a lid. ふたつきのさら

합격(合格) ①《적합》 coming up to the standard[mark]; standing the test; making the grade／～하다 come up to the standard[mark]; stand the test ②《급제》 passing[success in] [an examination]; eligibility [for an office]／～하다 pass[succeed in] [an examination]; 《채용되다》 be found eligible[qualified] [for a post]／～ 여부 success or failure／～자 a successful applicant／～품 goods found acceptable／～점 a passing mark. ごうかく

합계(合計) the sum total; the total [amount, sum]; the aggregate／～하다 add [sum] up; total; in the aggregate; altogether; put together; in all; all told／～ 10,000원이 되다 amount to 10,000 won in all. ごうけい

합금(合金) 《화》 all alloy; ～하다 alloy; make an alloy (of). ごうきん

합내(閤內) your family; an hono[u]red family／～ 제절 all [members of] your family.

합당(合當) ～하다 (be) adequate; suitable; proper; apt／～한 예 an example appropriate to the case. だとう

합당(合黨) a party merger／～하다 [parties] merge; merge the [parties].

합동(合同) ①《합병》 combination; union／～의 joint; united; combined／～하다 combine; unite／～ 관리 joint control[management]／～ 신문 syndicated [chain] papers ②《수》 congruence／～결혼[식] a mass[group, joint] wedding [ceremony]／～ 관리 joint control[management]／～ 사업 joint undertaking; a combine／~기업 ～ a trust; a cartel／～ 위원회 a joint committee／～ 위령제 a joint service for the [war] dead. ごうどう

합뜨리다 unite ⇨합치다. へいごうする

합력(合力) ①《물》 a resultant [force] ②《협력》 joint efforts; co-operation／～하다 join forces; co-operate with; work together; unite one's efforts with.
ごうりょく

합류(合流) ①《냇물》 confluence; conflux／～하다 join; flow together ②《합동》 joining; linking; union／～하다 join; unite[link up] (with); be merged (into); incorporate (with)／자유당에 ～하다 join the Liberals／～점 the confluence [of rivers]. ごうりゅう

합리(合理) rationality／～하다 (be) rational; reasonable; logical／～성 rationality／정부는 산업의 ～화를 단행해야 한다 The Government should decidedly carry out industrial rationalization／산업의 ～화 the rationalization of industry. ごうり

**합명회사(合名會社)** an unlimited partnership. ごうめいがいしゃ

**합방(合邦)** annexation of a State to another; unification of two countries/한일 ~ the Japanese annexation of Korea/ ~하다 annex a state (to).

**합배뚜리** a jar with a lid.

**합법(合法)** legality; lawfulness; legitimacy/ ~적 lawful; legal; legitimate/ ~성 lawfulness/~적 수단으로 by lawful[legal, legitimate] means. ごうほう

**합병(合併)** combination; union; annexation/ ~하다 amalgamate; combine[unite] with; annex/두 회사를 ~하다 merge[amalgamate] two companies/~ 선거 a combined election. がっぺい

**합보시기** a cup with a lid ふたつきのつぼ

**합본(合本)** ①(책) copies bound together in book form[in a volume]/ ~하다 bind (copies) together[in one volume] ② joint stock. がっぽん

**합사(合祀)** enshrining together/ ~하다 dedicate to several deities; enshrine together.

**합사(合絲)** a braid; a plaited thread/ ~하다 plait threads; twist threads together. よりいと

**합삭(合朔)** the conjunction of moon and sun.

**합산(合算)** adding up; footing/ ~하다 add up; add[put] together; sum up; aggregate; total; foot up. がっさん

**합석(合席)** sitting[meeting, consulting] together/~하다 sit[meet, consult] together; sit in company(with a person) /나도 ~했다 I was among the company.

**합설(合設)** consolidation; setting up together/~하다 consolidate; set up together.

**합성(合成)** composition/~의 component; synthetic/ ~하다 compose/~ 고무[연료, 염료, 섬유, 석유, 수지] synthetic rubber[fuel, dyestuff, oil, fiber, resin]/ ~물 a compound/~ 비료 compound fertilizer/물은 수소와 산소의 ~체다 Water is a compound of hydrogen and oxygen. / ~주 compound[synthetic] liquor. ごうせい

**합세(合勢)** joining forces; forming an alliance/ ~하다 join forces; form an alliance. ごうりょく

**합수(合水)** confluence[junction, joining, meeting] of two streams/ ~하다 flow together; join; meet/ 세 강이 이 지점에서 ~한다 Three rivers meet one another at this point. ごうりゅう

**합숙(合宿)** joint billet/ ~하다 lodge together (운동 선수가)stay in a camp for training/ ~소 a boarding house/ ~ 훈련 camp training. がっしゅく

**합승(合乘)** riding together; sharing a vehicle/ ~하다 ride together/ ~차 a jitney [cab]; an omnibus/택시를 ~하다 share a taxi (with a person).のりあい

**합심(合心)** unison; accord/ ~하다 be united; act in accordance with/서로 ~해서 하자 Let's work in unison.

**합의(合意)** mutual agreement; mutual consent; concurrence/ ~하다 consult [counsel] together; confer (with); hold the conference; take[go into] counsel /쌍방의 ~에 의해 by mutual consent/ ~ 결혼 a consensual marriage. ごうい

**합의(合議)** consultation; conference; counsel/ ~하다 consult together (about); confer/ ~ 재판 collegial[collegiate] judgment/ ~ 사항 items of understanding. ごうぎ

**합일(合一)** union; oneness; unity/ ~하다 unite; be united; consolidate. ごういつ

**합자(合資)** joint stock; partnership/ ~하다 join stocks; enter[go] into partnership (with)/~ 회사 a limited partnership; a joint stock company. ごうし

**합작(合作)** collaboration; a joint (합작물을) work (합력) co-operation/ ~하다 collaborate (with a person); produce conjointly; work together; cooperation (with a person)/화가 수명의 ~ the joint performance of several artists/ ~자 a collaborator; a joint author/~ 회사 a joint-venture company. がっさく

**합장(合掌)** ~하다 (손을 접어서) one's clasp[hold] hands (손을 펴서) put[press] one's open hands together; join the hands[palms]/~ 배례 worshipping with the palms of the hands together/~하고 with one's hands pressed in prayer.

**합장(合葬)** burying together/~하다 bury[inter] together/처를 남편과 ~하다 bury the wife together with her husband.

**합재떨이** an ashtray with a lid.

**합저(合著)** collaboration ⇒공저.きょうちょ

**합주(合奏)** [a] concert; [an] ensemble/ ~하다 play in concert/ ~곡 an ensemble/2부 ~ a duet[te]. がっそう

**합죽거리다** mumble with a toothless mouth. もぐもぐいう

**합죽선(合竹扇)** a fan with spokes made of double slips of bamboo.

**합죽이** a person who looks toothless; a person with hollow cheeks and lips.

**합죽하다** a toothless mouth (be) puckered; pursed; look toothless.

**합죽할미** a toothless old hag.

**합죽합죽** mumbling; toothlessly mouthing.

**합중국(合衆國)** a federation; a united states/미~ the United States of America. がっしゅうこく

**합창(合唱)** singing together; choral singing; chorus/ ~하다 sing in chorus/ ~곡 a chorus; a part song/혼성[남녀] ~ a mixed chorus/다 같이 크리스마스 캐롤을 ~했다 We all joined in singing the Christmas carols. がっしょう

**합창(合唱)** healing up [of a boil]/ ~하다 heal up [of a boil].
できもののきずがなおること

**합체(合體)** union; combination; incorporation/ ~하다 unite; be united; incorporate; combine (*with*); be combined; consolidate; amalgamate; merge.
がったい

**합치(合致)** agreement; accord; concurrence 《부합》coincidence; tally/ ~하다 agree (*with*); concur/당신의 말은 사실과 ~하지 않는다 Your statement does not agree[check, tally] with the facts.
がっち

**합치다(合―)** ①《하나로》put together; unite; combine 《병합》amalgamate 《총합》add up/힘을 ~ join efforts ②《합계하다》sum up; add up; total ③《섞다》mix; compound/물과 술을 ~ mix liquor with water ④《겹치다》put (*things*) together; put[lay] (*a thing*) upon (*another*).
あわせる

**합판(合版)** joint publication/ ~하다 publish jointly.

**합판(合板)** a veneer board; plywood.

**합판(合辦)** joint management; a pool 《미》/ ~의 joint.
ごうべん

**합판화(合瓣花)** 《식》a compound[gamopetalous] flower.
ごうべんか

**합평(合評)** commentary; a joint review/ ~하다 jointly criticize/~회 a meeting for joint review; a panel discussion.
がっぴょう

**합하다(合―)** ①《여럿이》unite ⇒합치다 ②《마음에》fit; suit; agree; harmonize with; be in accord with; be in tune with/취미에 ~ suit *one's* taste ③《만나다》meet; join; gather; come together ④《합쳐지다》be united; be made into one; combine; be combined.
あう

**합헌(合憲)** ~의 constitutional/~성 constitutionality.

**합환주(合歡酒)** nuptial cups/~를 주고 받다 exchange nuptial cups.

**핫-** ①《솜옷》padded with cotton wool ②《배우자 있는》having a spouse/ ~아비 a man with a wife; a married man/~어미 a married woman.

**핫것** cotton-padded clothes[bedding].

**핫길** 《품질》inferior quality 《물건》an article of inferior quality; the lowest grade.

**핫바지** ①《솜바지》cotton-padded trousers ②《촌뜨기》a bumpkin; a clodhopper.
わたいれのズボン

**핫반** double sheets of cotton wool.

**핫옷** cotton-wadded[padded] clothes.
わたいれのちゃんちゃんこ

**핫이불** cotton-padded bedclothes.
わたいれのふとん

**핫퉁이** ①《솜많이 둔 옷》well-wadded clothes ②《철 지난 옷》wadded clothes worn beyond the season.

**항(項)** 《조항》a clause 《문장의》a paragraph 《항목》an item 《수학의》a term/재정의 ~을 참고하시오 See under "Finance".
こう

**-항(港)** a harbour; a port/군산 ~ *Kunsan* harbour.
みなと

**항간(巷間)** the world; the street; (*about*) the town/ ~에 떠도는 이야기 a topic widely talked about/ ~에 소문이 돌다 a rumor is going around town. こうかん

**항거(抗拒)** resistance; disobeyance; rebellion/ ~하다 resist (*to*); oppose; disobey/ ~죄 an offense of resisting lawful order.
こうきょ

**항고(抗告)** 《법》a complaint; an appeal; a protest/ ~하다 complain (against *a decision*); appeal (from *a decision*); file a protest (*against*)/ ~심 hearing of a complaint/~장 a bill[memorandum] of complaint/즉시 ~하다 lodge an immediate appeal (*against*). こうこく

**항공(航空)** aviation; flight; aerial navigation; air voyage[travel]/~기 aircraft; flyng machine/ ~ 모함 an aircraft carrier/ ~ 우편 airmail/ ~ 우표 an airmail stamp/~ 회사 an aviation [airline] company/~ 시대 an aerial age/~ 시설 air service; airline facilities/ ~학 aeronautics.
こうくう

**항구(恒久)** permanency; perpetuity/ ~하다 (be) permanent; perpetual; lasting; eternal/ ~적 평화를 확립하다 establish permanent peace/ ~성 permanency.
こうきゅう

**항구(港口)** a harbour 《육지를 포함한》a port; a haven/ ~를 나가다 clear a port; leave a port/ ~에 들르다 call at[touch] a port/ ~ 도시 a port city [town].
こうこう

**항구(桁構)** a girder.

**항기(降旗)** a flag of surrender; a white flag.
こうき

**항내(港內)** the inside of a harbor/~ 시설 harbor facilities.

**항다반(恒茶飯)** a matter of common[everyday] occurrence.
にちじょうありふれたこと

**항도(港都)** a port town. みなとまち

**항독소(抗毒素)** an anti-toxine; an antivenom/~ 치료법 an antitoxin treatment.
こうどくそ

**항등식(恒等式)** 《수》an identical equation; an identity.
こうとうしき

**항라(亢羅)** a kind of silk gauze; sheer silk.

**항렬(行列)** the degree of relationship.

**항례(恒例)** an established custom; a usual practice/ ~의 usual; customary; annual.
こうれい

**항로(航路)** a sea-route; a ship's course; a steamship line[service]/ ~ 변경 a deviation of route/비행 ~ an air line; an air route/정기 ~ a regular service line/~를 바꾸다 change cour-

**항론(抗論)** refutation; contradiction/~하다 refute; confute; contradict. こうろん

**항만(港灣)** harbors; harbors and bays/~공사 harbor construction work/시설 habor facilities/~개량 harbor improvement/~운송 transportaion service in harbors/~하역(荷役) harbor loading and unloading. こうわん

**항명(抗命)** disobedience/~하다 disobey (a person's) order/하극상 장교를 ~죄로 다스리다 investigate a mutinous[rebellious] officer for disobedient conduct. こうめい

**항목(項目)** a head; a heading; an item; a clause; a provision/그것은 이 ~에 들어 있다 It is included under this head. こうもく

**항무(港務)** harbor affairs; port business. こうむ

**항문(肛門)** 《해》 the anus; the fundament/~의 anal/~병 an anal[a rectal] ailment 《치질》 piles/~부 the anal region. こうもん

**항변(抗辯)** 《피고의》 a plea; defense 《항론》 a protest; refutation; confutation/~하다 make a plea; demur; refute; confute; contradict; argue (with)/상관에게 ~하다 remonstrate with one's superior/사실 부인의 ~ a plea of the general issue. こうべん

**항병(降兵)** a surrendered soldier[army]. こうへい

**항복(降伏, 降服)** 《복종》 surrender; submission 《조건부의》 capitulation/~하다 surrender; capitulate; yield; give in (to); strike one's flag; hang the white flag; submit; yield (to)/~을 권고하다 invite (the enemy) to surrender. こうふく

**항산(恒産)** property; an estate; ample means/~이 없으면 항심도 없다 A real property, a real purpose., Competency is the first requisite for constancy of the mind. こうさん

**항산균(抗酸菌)** an acid-fast bacterium.

**항상(恒常)** always; at all times; incessantly; habitually; as a rule; incessantly; ordinarily/그는 부모님께 ~ 걱정만 끼친다 He is constant source of anxiety to his parents. いつも

**항생 물질(抗生物質)** 《의》 an antibiotic/~학 antibiotics. こうせいぶっしつ

**항서(降書)** a capitulatory letter; a written surrender.

**항설(巷說)** gossip rumor in the street; town talk/~이 분분하다 Wild rumors are abroad. こうせつ

**항성(恒星)** 《천》 a fixed[permanent] star; a sun/~의 sidereal/~ 주기 a sidereal revolution. こうせい

**항세(港稅)** port duty; harbor dues.

**항소(抗訴)** 《법》 the appeal suit; an appeal (to a higher court)/~하다 appeal enter lodge an appeal (against)/~를 기각하다 dismiss turn down an appeal; /~권 the right of appeal/~심(審) a trial on an appeal case/~ 이유 the grounds of an appeal.

**항속(航續)** flight; flying; cruising/~거리 a cruising flying radius range/~력 a cruising flying power capacity/~ 시간 the duration of cruise [flight].

**항쇄 족쇄(項鎖足鎖)** a pillory and shackles. くびかせとてかせ

**항습(恒習)** a usual regular, steady, customary habit.

**항시(恒時)** always 항상. いつも

**항심(恒心)** a stable mind; stability of mind; constancy; steadfastness. こうしん

**항아리(缸一)** a jar; a pot/꿀~ a honey jar/물~ a water jar. つぼ

**항어(抗禦)** defense; resistance/~하다 resist; defend (against). ていこうしてふせぐこと

**항언(抗言)** protestation; a protest; a retort; a rejoinder/~하다 protest; rejoinder; a retort; oppose. こうげん

**항업(恒業)** a fixed occupation; a steady job.

**항오(行伍)** ranks; files; an array; a formation/~ 정연하다 be in regular rank; be in perfect order. こうご

**항외(港外)** outside the port[harbor]/배가 ~ 나가서 sail out of a harbor/~에 정박하다 lie at anchor off the harbor.

**항용(恒用)** ordinariness; a commonplace (부사적) always; at all times. いつも

**항원(抗元, 抗原)** 《생》 antigen.

**항의(抗議)** a protest; a remonstrance; an objection; an exception/~하다 protest; make a protest; offer[raise] an objection (to)/~를 제출하다 enter[file] a protest (against)/엄중 ~ a strong protest. こうぎ

**항일(抗日)** resistance to Japan; anti-Japan; anti-Japanese/~ 운동 an anti-Japanese movement/~ 사상 anti-Japanese sentiments.

**항쟁(抗爭)** contention; opposition; dispute; wrangle; struggle; resistance/~하다 contend; dispute; wrangle; resist; oppose. こうそう

**항적(抗敵)** resistance. こうてき

**항적(航跡)** a wake; a furrow; a track/다른 배의 ~을 따라가다 steer in the wake of another vessel. こうせき

**항전(抗戰)** fighting (against); armed resistance/~하다 resist; fight (against); offer armed resistance/철저한 ~ do-or-die resistance/대일 ~ resistance to Japan. こうせん

**항정(航程)** 1.《배의》 the run[passage] of a ship; the distance covered by a ship; a sailing distance/1일 간의 ~ a day's

**sail** 2**(비행기의)** a lap; a leg／전 ~을 난다 fly[cover] the whole distance.

**항주(航走)** sailing; run／~하다 sail;run／~력(力) cruising speed.

**항진(亢進)** rise; acceleration **(병세 따위의)** exacerbation／~하다 rise; accelerate. こうしん

**항차** much[still] more or less ⇨하물며. いわんや

**항체(抗體)** 【생】 an antibody. こうたい

**항풍(恒風)** a constant wind. こうふう

**항해(航海)** voyage; a navigation; a crossing; a cruise; a [sea] trip／~하다 sail; make a voyage (to); navigate; cruise; take a passage (for)／태평양을 ~하다 sail the Pacific／원양 ~ an ocean voyage. こうかい

**항행(航行)** sailing; navigation; a cruise／~하다 navigate; sail; steam; cruise／이 강은 ~이 허용되어 있다 This river is open to navigation／~권 the right of navigation. こうこう

**해**¹ the sun／~가 저물다 it gets dark／~가 자다 the sun sets[goes down, sinks]／방에 ~가 비친다 The sun shines into the room. ひ

**해**² ①**(1년)** a year／~마다 year after year; every year／~가 바뀌다 the year changes ②**(낮)** the daytime／~가 점점 짧아진다 The days are getting shorter／이 ~ this year／지난 ~ last year. とし

**해**³ with a light giggle／~ 웃다 give a light giggle. へえ

**해(害)** harm; injury; damage **(손상)** detriment **(해독)** evil; an injurious influence／~하다 injure; damage; harm; hurt; spoil; impair; mar／건강을 ~치다 injure one's health／작물에는 거의 ~가 없었다 The crops suffered little harm.／음주 흡연의 ~ the bad[ill] effects of drinking and smoking. がい

**해-(該)** that; the said; the (person, matter) in question／~교 that school; the side school. がい

**해감** water sediment; fur／~내가 나다 smell of mud／~이 끼다 fur forms. みずあか

**해거(駭擧)** strange[scandalous] behavior [action]. きかいなきょどう

**해거름** sunset; sundown; dusk; nightfall／~에 at sunset[nightfall]. ひぐれ

**해껏** all day long; until sunset; till dark／~일하다 work till dark. ひぐれまで

**해결(解決)** settlement; solution; fixing (up)／~하다 solve (a question); effect a settlement; bring (a matter) to a settlement／문제를 평화적으로 ~하다 bring a matter to a peaceful settlement. かいけつ

**해고(解雇)** discharge; dismissal; lay-off／~하다 discharge; dismiss; fire (out); lay off; turn off／그는 태만 때문에 ~될 것이다 He will be dismissed[fired] for idleness／~ 통지 a dismissal notice. かいこ

**해골(骸骨)** bones; a skeleton; a skull; the cranium. がいこつ

**해골바가지(骸骨-)** a skeleton ⇨해골. がいこつ

**해공전(海空戰)** air-sea operations; a battle between aircraft and warships. かいくうせん

**해관(海關)** the maritime customs／~세 customs duties; import duties／~ 세율 customs tariff. かいかん

**해괴(駭怪)** strangeness; eccentricity; oddity; scandalousness; monstrousness／~하다 (be) strange; eccentric; scandalous; odd; monstrous／~ 망측하다 be extremely scandalous[disgraceful]／~ 한 처사 an improper management; an extraordinary measure. あやしいこと

**해구(海口)** the entrance to a harbor; the mouth of a harbor; the approach to a bay.

**해구(海狗)** 【동】 a seal; a sea bear; a sea cat; an eared seal／~신 the penis of a sea bear. おっとせい

**해구(海寇)** pirates; sea marauders. かいこう

**해국(海國)** an island country; a maritime country; a seagirt country／~민 a maritime nation／~주의 navalism.

**해국(海菊)** 【식】 a kind of aster.

**해군(海軍)** the navy; the naval service; the fleet; naval forces／~을 확장하다 expand[increase] the Navy／~ 기지 a naval base／~ 사관 학교 the naval Academy. かいぐん

**해굴성(-性)** 【식】 positive heliotropism. こうじつせい

**해꼬무레하다** (be) fair and whitish／해꼬무레한 얼굴 a fair and whitish face. うすしろい

**해금(奚琴)** 【음】 a Korean fiddle.

**해금(解禁)** removal of the embargo; lifting of the ban／~하다 remove the embargo; lift the ban; cancel a ban／~기 **(수렵의)** the open season; the opening of the shooting season. かいきん

**해끔하다** (be) whitish. いろがきれいでややしろい

**해기(海氣)** sea air; a smell of the sea; a sea breeze; the oceanic atmosphere／~욕 sea-air bathing. かいき

**해낙낙하다** (be) satisfied; content[ed]; pleased. まんぞくにかんじる

**해난(海難)** a disaster at sea; a shipwreck; perils of the sea; a shipping casualty／~을 당하다 meet with a disaster at sea／~ 구조선 a salvage boat／~ 구조 salvage／~ 작업 salvage work. かいなん

**해납작하다** (be) white and broad. しろくてひらたい

**해내(海內)** (within) a seagirt land.

**해내다** ①**(완수하다)** accomplish; achieve;

**해넘이** [the] sunset/ ~ 때에 at sunset time. ひのいり

**해녀(海女)** a woman diver/진주잡이 ~ a woman diver for pearls/제주도는 ~로 유명하다 *Jeju-do* is famous for woman divers. あま

**해단(解團)** disbanding/ ~하다 disband (*an athletic team*)/ ~식 the ceremony of disbanding.

**해달(海獺)** 〖동〗 a sea otter. らっこ

**해답(解答)** a solution (to *a problem*); answer (to *a question*)/ ~하다 solve (*a problem*); answer (*a question*)/바른 ~을 하다 give a correct answer; answer correctly/~자 a solver; an answerer. かいとう

**해당(解黨)** dissolution [of a party]/ ~하다 dissolve [a party].

**해당(該當)** ~하다 come[fall] under; come[fall] within the purview of; correspond to; be applicable to/~ 항목을 보다 turn to the appropriate heading/ ~ 사항 pertinent[relevant] data. がいとう

**해당화(海棠花)** 〖식〗 a wild rose; a sweet brier[briar]; *Rosa rugosa*(학명). かいどうのはな

**해대다** attack; go at; lick; abuse; beat /그는 싸움에서 두 사람을 해낼 수 있다 He can lick two persons in a fight./아무 개를 ~ go at[light into] a person. やっつける

**해도** even though *one* does[thinks, says]; even though [it] is.

**해도(海島)** an island in the sea. うみのなかのしま

**해도(海圖)** a [maritime] chart; a hydrographic chart/ ~에 기재되어 있지 않은 uncharted; not marked on the chart/ 그 섬은 ~에 실려 있지 않다 That island is not charted. かいず

**해도(海濤)** sea waves; billow.

**해독(害毒)** evil; harm; mischief; virus; poison; taint; canker/이런 종류의 책은 사회에 ~을 끼친다 Books of this kind work mischief to society. どく

**해독(解毒)** counteracting[neutralizing] poison/ ~하다 counteract[neutralize] the poisonous effects; mithridatize/~ 제 an antidote; a counterpoison; a toxicide. げどく

**해독(解讀)** decoding; deciphering; making out (*the meaning, etc.*)/ ~하다 decipher; decode/~하기 어려운 indecipherable. かいどく

**해돈(海豚)** a porpoise; a dolphin ⇒돌고래.

**해돋이** [the] sunrise; [the] sunup〈미〉/ ~에 at sunrise.

**해동(解凍)** thawing; a thaw/~하다 thaws/ ~으로 길이 질퍽거린다 The roads are bad[muddy] because of the thaw. とけること

**해동갑(一同甲)** until sunset; all day long; coinciding with the sunset/ ~하다 coincide with the sunset/ ~해서 일 하다 work till sunset/ ~길을 걷다 go *one's* way until sunset.

**해동청(海東靑)** a peregrine falcon; a duck hawk ⇒송골매.

**해뜨리다** wear away[out, down] ⇒해어 뜨리다. しだいにすりへらす

**해득(解得)** comprehension; apprehension; understanding; grasp/ ~하다 understand; comprehend; grasp; apprehend/ ~력이 둔한 사람 a man of feeble apprehension.

**해득해득** ~하다 be spotted with white.

**해라하다** use the plain style of speech.

**해람(解纜)** unmooring; sailing off; leaving; weighing anchor/ ~하다 weigh anchor; unmoor; setsail; leave (*a port*); sail (*from*). かいらん

**해로(海路)** a sea route; a seaway/ ~로 가다 go by sea[water]. かいろ

**해로(偕老)** growing old together in wedded life/~하다 grow old together in wedded life/백년 ~하다 (*husband and wife*) share the happily married years together/백년 ~의 가약을 맺다 be united as a man and wife for weal or woe.

**해로동혈(偕老同穴)** ①〖부부의〗 growing old together and sharing a common grave / ~하다 grow old together and are buried in the same grave ②〖동〗 Venus's flower-basket.

**해롭다(害—)** (be) harmful; injurious; detrimental; have an injurious effect (*on*) /술은 건강에 ~ Drinking is injurious to *one's* health. /심신에 ~ be harmful both to mind and body. ゆうがいだ

**해롱거리다** behave like a spoilt child.

**해류(海流)** an ocean current; a current /~도 a current chart/ ~병 an ocean current bottle. かいりゅう

**해륙(海陸)** land and sea; sea and air/ ~ 양면 작전 amphibious operations/~ 양서 동물 an amphibious animal; an amphibian. かいりく

**해리(海里)** a knot; a nautical[sea] mile. かいり

**해리(海狸)** 〖동〗 a beaver; a castor/ ~향 (香) castor [the secretion from a beaver's groin]. かいり

**해리(解離)** 〖화〗 dissociation/ ~하다 dissociate.

**해마(海馬)** 〖어〗 a sea horse (하마) a hippocampus (해상) a walrus; 〖동〗 a walrus.

**해마다** every year; each year; year after year; annually. としごと

**해만(海灣)** ①〖만〗 a bay; a gulf ②〖바다와

해말갛다 (be) fair; fair-skinned. いろがしろくてさっぱりしている
해말쑥하다 (be) clear and fair; fair skinned.
해맑다 (be) white and clean. しろくてあおい
해망적다 silly; stupid; (be) dull; unenlightened. おろかだ
해먹다 do something bad(bothersome]; "do the damn thing"; take unjust possession of something／일이 힘들어 해먹을 수가 없다 The work is too damn much trouble to do. こしらえてたべる
해면(海面) the surface of the sea; the sea level／~에 떠오르다 float up to the surface of the sea. かいめん
해면(海綿) a sponge／~ 고무 sponge rubber／목욕용 ~ a bath sponge／~으로 빨아 내다 sponge up／~ 동물 the Porifera／~ 조직 spongy tissue. かいめん
해면(海免) release; exoneration [from duty, obligation]; discharge; acquittal; firing [from a job]／~하다 release; exonerate; discharge; acquit. めんしょく
해명(解明) explanation; elucidation／~하다 elucidate; explain; make clear／~을 요구하다 demand an explanation (of a person)／발언 내용을 ~하다 clarify the statement [one made on the assembly floor]. かいめい
해몽(解夢) interpretation of a dream／~하다 interpret[read] a dream.
해무(海務) maritime[marine, sea] affairs／~ 협회 the marine association.
해무(海霧) a sea fog; a fog on the sea／~는 오후에야 겼다 The sea fog lifted in the afternoon. かいむ
해묵다 (물건이) get a year old; age a year (일이) drag on for a year [without getting finished]. としをすごす
해물(海物) marine products／~상 a dealer in marine products.
해미 a thick sea fog; a heavy fog on the sea／바다에 ~가 끼다 the sea is covered with heavy fog.
해미(海味) tasty dishes from the sea; sea food. うみからとれたしょくもつ
해바라기 《식》 a sunflower; *Helianthus annuus*(학명). ひまわり
해바라지다 too large; (be) unduly wide／해바라진 사람 a swallow person／해바라진 생각 a superficial idea. ぶかっこうにふちがひろい
해박(該博) profundity; erudition／~하다 (be) erudite; profound; extensive／그는 ~한 학식의 소유자다 He is a man of great learning[erudition]. がいはく
해반닥거리다 goggle; turn *one's* eyes up and down／눈을 해반닥거리며 피로하다 turn *one's* eyes up and down in agony. しろめをぎょろぎょろさせる
해반드르르하다 (be) fair and charming.

해반주그레하다 (be) fair-complexioned. しろくてつつがある
해반지르르하다 (be) fair-complexioned; neat and fair. せいそでつやつやしている
해발(海拔) above the sea; above [the] sea level／그 산은 ~ 3,000 미터이다 The mountain is[rises] 3,000 meters above the sea level. かいばつ
해방(解放) liberation; emancipation; deliverance／~하다 liberate; set free; emancipate／노예를 ~하다 emancipate slaves; set slaves free／여성 ~ 운동 a movement for the emancipation of women／~자 a liberator; an emancipator. かいほう
해방(海防) coast[coastal] defense; maritime defense／~함 a coast guard ship; a coastal defense ship. かいぼう
해법(海法) sea laws; maritime law. かいほう
해법(解法) a solution; a key[clue] to solution.
해변(海邊) the beach; the seashore; the seaside; the coast／~에 살다 live by the seashore／~을 산책하다 take a walk along the beach; stroll about the beach. かいへん
해병(海兵) a marine／~대 the marine corps〈미〉; the Marine Amphibious Force／~대원 a marine; a leatherneck《미·속》. かいへい
해보다 ①(시험해 보다) try; have a try (at); attempt; make an attempt[a trial] (at)／누가 제일 빠른가 해 보자 Let's try and see who can the fastest. ②(경험해 보다) experience; know; try／사랑을 ~ experience love ③(싸움) pit *one's* strength; fight; stand against／그놈과는 끝까지 해 보겠다 I will fight him to the bitter end. してみる
해부(解剖) 〖의〗 ①(의학상의) dissection; postmortem; autopsy ②(분석) an analysis／~하다 dissect; hold a post-mortem; analyze／~의 결과 타살로 판명되었다 The post-mortem examination showed that it was a case of murder.／~학 [the study or science of] anatomy／시체 ~ autopsy; a post-mortem. かいぼう
해빈(海濱) the seacoat; the seashore; the seaside; the beach. はまべ
해빙(解氷) a thaw; thawing [of ice]／~하다 thaw; break up／한강이 ~되었다 The Han river is now free from ice.／~기 the thawing season／~기가 되었다 The thawing season has set in. かいひょう
해사(海事) maritime affairs[matters]／~ 금융 shipping finance／~ 법규 sea laws／~ 협회 the Maritime Association. かいじ
해사(海蛇) 〖동〗 a sea snake／~과 〖천〗 Hydra; the Water Snake.
해사하다 fair; (be) fair-complexioned;

**해산(海産)** marine products／～동물 marine animals／～업 the marine products industry.

**해산(解散)** ①(흩어짐) break-up; dispersion ②(해체) dissolution; disorganization; disbandment; liquidation／～하다 break up; disperse; dissolve; disband; wind up／회의를 ～하다 break up a meeting／강제 compulsory winding-up／임의 ～ voluntary winding-up. かいさん

**해산(解産)** childbirth; delivery; parturition; confinement; *accouchement*(F)／～을 돕다 assist at a childbirth／～기 period[term] of delivery／～ 촉진제 an oxytocic／～ 어미 a woman just out of childbirth. ぶんべん

**해산물(海産物)** marine products／～이 풍부하다 be rich in marine products.

**해삼(海蔘)** 【동】a sea slug; a sea cucumber. なまこ

**해상(海上)** on the sea; sea; maritime; marine／～에서 폭풍을 만나다 be overtaken by a storm at sea／～ 경비대 coast guards／～ 무역 sea-borne[floating] trade; overseas trade. かいじょう

**해상(海床)** 【지】the bottom[bed] of the sea; the ocean[sea] floor. かいしょう

**해상(海商)** ①(해상업) marine commerce ②(업자) a sea trader. かいしょう

**해상(海象)** 【동】a morse; a walrus.

**해상(解喪)** ～하다 come out of[finish] mourning; leave off[get over] mourning.

**해서(楷書)** the printed style of writing; the square style of Chinese handwriting. かいしょ

**해석(解析)** analysis; analytical research／～하다 analyze／～기하학【수】analytical geometry／～학 analytics. かいせき

**해석(解釋)** (판단) interpretation (추정) construction (번역) translation (정의) definition (설명) explanation (해설) exposition (주석) comment; at explanatory note; a commentary／～하다 interpret; construe; put a construction (on); translate; define; explain; expound／좋을 대로 ～하라 Put your own construction on it.／～의 차이 discrepancies of interpretation／여러 가지로 ～되다 admit of various interpretations. かいしゃく

**해설(解說)** explanation; elucidation; commentary; interpretation; exposition／～하다 explain; comment on (*the text*); interpret; elucidate／～자 a commentator; an expounder／뉴스 ～ news comment[ary]. かいせつ

**해성단계(海成段階)**【지】a sea terrace.

**해성층(海成層)** the sea layer [of the earth]. かいせいそう

**해소(咳嗽)** a cough ⇒해수. せき

**해소(海嘯)** ① the sound of ebbing waves／～하다 [ebbing waves] resound ② (해일) tidal waves; a sea-quake; a seismic wave. かいしょう

**해소(解消)** ①(해산) dissolution; disorganization; liquidation／～하다 be dissolved; be disorganized; be liquidated ②(해약) annulment; cancellation／～하다 cancel (*a contract*); annul; break off ③(해결) solution; settlement／～하다 be solved; be settled／정계의 불안은 ～되었다 The political unrest died down.／난문제의 ～ clearing up a difficult problem. かいしょう

**해소(解訴)** withdrawal[discontinuance] of a case; dropping a lawsuit／～하다 drop a lawsuit; withdraw[discontinue, abandon] a case.

**해소수** a little over a year. いちねんあまりのあいだ

**해소일(一消日)** waste the time; idle away *one's* day; leading an idle life／～하다 idle[loaf, dawdle] away the days of *one's* years.

**해손(海損)** sea damage; average [loss]／～ 공탁금 an average deposit／공동 ～ general average／화물 ～ sea damaged goods／～ 조항 an average clause／～ 계약 an average bond. かいそん

**해송(海松)** 【식】a species of pine; *Pinus Thunbergii*(학명); (잣나무) Big Cone Pine.

**해수(咳嗽)**【의】a cough; a tussis; a coughing／～약 cough medicine; a cough remedy; cough drops; cough syrup. せき

**해수(海水)** sea water; salt water; brine／～욕 sea-bathing; a sea bath／～욕을 하다 bathe in the sea／～욕장 a swimming beach; a [sea] bathing resort. かいすい

**해수(海獸)** a sea[marine] animal. かいじゅう

**해쓱하다** (be) pale; wan; pallid／그녀의 얼굴은 해쓱해 보였다 She looked pale.

**해시계(一時計)** a dial; a sundial.

**해식(海蝕)**【지】erosion of the sea.

**해신(海神)** the sea god; the god of the sea (로마의) Neptune (희랍의) Poseidon.

**해심(海深)** the depth of the sea／～을 재다 plumb[sound] the sea.

**해안(海岸)** the seashore; the [sea]coast; the seaside; the seaboard; the waterfront; the beach; the strand／～에서 on the shore／～을 산보하다 take a walk along the beach／～ 경비 coast[al] defense／～선 a costline／～지방 a seaside district. かいがん

**해야** only if *one* does[says, thinks]; only if it is／～하다 must; have[got] to.

**해약(解約)** cancellation[annulment] of a contract／～하다 cancel[rescind, annul] a contract; call off (보험을) surrender (*one's* insurance policy). かいやく

**해양(海洋)** the ocean; the sea[s]／～의 자유 the freedom of the sea／～성 기후

oceanic climate／~ 식물 an ocean ophyte／~ 소설 a sea story／~ 문학 sea literature／~형 oceanography. かいようがく
**해어**(海魚) sea fish. かいぎょ
**해어**(海語) nautical terms; sea-terms／~ 사전 a dictionary of nautical terms. かいご
**해어뜨리다** wear away[down]／옷을 ~ wear out one's clothes／구두를 ~ wear one's shoes out[into holes]. すりへらしてしまう
**해어지다** get tattered; get[be] worn out [away, down]／해어진 ragged; worn out; fraged／옷이 누덕누덕 ~ one's clothes are worn to rags. すりへる
**해엄**(解嚴) removal[lifting, withdrawal] of martial law／~하다 remove[lift, withdraw] martial law. けいかいをかいじょすること
**해연**(海淵) the lowest depth of an ocean. かいえん
**해연**(海燕) ①〘동〙 a kind of sea urchin; Clypeaster japonicus〔학명〕②〘바다제비〙 〘조〙 a [stormy] petrel.
**해연풍**(海軟風) a sea breeze.
**해열**(解熱) removal[alleviation] of fever／~하다 alleviate a fever／~제 a fever remedy; an antifebrile; afebrifuge; an antipyretic. げねつ
**해오라기** 〘조〙 the white[snowy] heron. しらさぎ
**해오라기난초** 〘식〙 a kind of orchis.
**해왕성**(海王星) 〘천〙 Neptune.
**해외**(海外) foreign countries; overseas／ ~로 abroad; across the ocean／~로 가다 go abroad／그는 ~ 사정에 대해서 정통하다 He has a thorough knowledge of foreign affairs.／다녀간 그는 ~에서 생활했다 For many years he lived beyond the seas.／~ 공관 a diplomatic office in the foreign country／~ 무역 foreign[overseas] trade／~ 문학 foreign literature／~ 여행 a trip abroad／ ~ 홍보 활동 an overseas information activity／한국 ~ 개발 공사 The Korea Overseas Development Corporation. かいがい
**해우**(海牛) 〘동〙 a sea cow; a manatee; a dugong／~류 Sirenia. かいぎゅう
**해운**(海運) shipping; marine[sea, ocean] transportation; maritime[sea-born] traffic／~계 the shipping world[circles] ／~업 the shipping industry[trade]; marine transportation business／~ 정책 a shipping policy／대한 ~ 공사 the Korea Shipping Corporation(略: KSC). かいうん
**해웃값** a charge for a prostitute[kisaeng]; a prostitute's fee. はなだい
**해원**(海員) a seaman; a mariner; a sailor 《총칭》 a crew／~ 생활 a seafaring life; a sailor's life／~ 용어 a nautical term／~ 양성소 a seamen's training school. かいいん

**해원**(解寃) ~하다 satisfy one's grudge; vent one's spite; pay off old scores; revenge oneself on (a person). うらみをなくすこと
**해음**(諧音) 〘음〙 harmony; consonance; melody; concord.
**해읍스름하다** (be) whitish; not quite white enough. しろっぽい
**해의**(海衣) 〘식〙 layer; sloke.
**해이**(解弛) relaxation; slackening; looseness／~하다 relax; get[become] loose; slacken; flag; become remiss; be off one's guard／마음이 ~하다 one's attention relaxes／기강이 ~하다 discipline slackens[grows lax]. ゆるみ
**해일**(海溢) tidal[storm] waves; overflowing of the sea; a sea-quake; a seismic wave／~하다 [the sea] overflow; have tidal wave／~이 덮치다 be struck [hit] by a tidal wave／~에 휩쓸리다 be washed away by a tidal wave／~ 경보 a tidal wave warning. つなみ
**해임**(解任) release from office; dismissal; discharge; displacement／~하다 release (a person) from office; dismiss; discharge; recall／~장 a letter of dismissal [discharge]; walking paper／~제 the recall system. かいにん
**해자**(垓字) a moat／~를 파다 dig a moat.
**해자**(楷字) the square style of Chinese handwriting; a clearly written character.
**해작질** toying with one's food[drink]／~ 하다 toy with one's food[drink]. ほじくりだすこと
**해장** drinking to relieve a hangover／~ 하다 chase a hangover with a drink before breakfast／~국 a broth to chase a hangover／~술 alcohol used as a hangover-chaser／~술을 마시다 take a hair of the dog that bit one. むかえざけ
**해저**(海底) the bottom[bed] of the sea; the sea-bottom; the sea-bed; the floor of the ocean／~ 터널 an undersea tunnel; a submarine tunnel／~ 유전 a submarine oil field／~ 전선 a submarine cable [line]. かいてい
**해적**(海賊) a pirate; a sea robber／~이 출몰하는 바다 pirate infested waters／ ~선 a pirate ship; a sea rover／~ 행위 piracy. かいぞく
**해전**(一前) before sunset. ひぐれのまえ
**해전**(海戰) a sea fight; a naval battle [engagement, action]. かいせん
**해정**(解酲) drinking to relieve a hangover ⇨해장. むかえざけ
**해제**(解除) ①〘취소〙 cancellation; removal; revocation; dissolution; rescission ②〘해방〙 release; discharge; absolution; exoneration／~하다 cancel; revoke; dissolve; rescind; remove; lift; relieve; acquit／계약을 ~하다 cancel[rescind] a contract／무장 ~ disarming; disarmament／폭풍경보 ~ lifting of a storm

warning; all clear／계약 ~ revocation of a contract.

해제(解題) a bibliographical introduction／~하다 give a bibliographical explanation (of).

해조(害鳥) an injurious bird; a harmful bird 《총칭》 vermin.

해조(海鳥) a seabird; a seafowl／~분(糞) kelp meal／~회(灰) kelp.

해조(海藻) seaweeds; marine plants; algae (비료용) seaware.

해 주다 do as a favor; do (something) for (a person) help with／편지 번역을 ~ translate a letter for (a person). してやる

해죽 grinning; smiling／~거리다 give a broad grin.

해중(海中) the middle[bottom] of the sea／~에 뛰어들다 jump[plunge] into the sea (배에서) jump overboard.

해지다 go worn out ⇒해어지다.

해직(解職) release from office; dismissal／~하다 release (a person) from his office[position]／~되다 be dismissed from the office／~ 수당 a dismissal[severance] pay; a discharge allowance.

해질녘 (일몰) sunset; nightfall; sundown 《황혼》 dusk; twilight 《저녁》 evening／~에 toward nightfall[evening]; at sunset.

해찰스럽다 (be) rash; rough; imprudent; indiscreet; careless; unmannerly; inconsiderate 《경망하다》(be) flippant; unserious.

해척(解尺) selling (cloth) by the measure; retailing cloth／~하다 sell by the measure; retail cloth.

해체(解體) ①(분해) taking to pieces; dismantling; dismantlement ②(해산) dissolution; disorganization ③(해부) dissection／~하다 disjoint (a machine); demount; dissolve; disorganize; disband; dissect／정당을 ~하다 disband[dissolve] a party／공장을 ~하다 dismantle a factory.

해초(海草) seaweeds; sea plants; algae.

해초류(海鞘類) (동) Ascidiacea (학명).

해춘(解春) thawing; the beginning of spring; the spring thaw／~하다 it thaws; spring begins; the spring thaw sets in.

해충(害蟲) a noxious[harmful] insect; a blight 《총칭》 vermin／~을 박멸하다 exterminate vermin[noxious insects]／~ 구제 extermination of vermin.

해치다(害ー) injure; harm; hurt; impair; spoil; mar; damage／감정을 ~ hurt (a person's) feelings; offend (a person)／미관을 ~ spoil the beauty (of)／과로하여 건강을 ~ damage one's health with overwork.

해타(懈惰) laziness ⇒해태(懈怠).

해탈(解脫) deliverance [of one's soul]; [Buddhistic] emancipation; salvation／~하다 be delivered from (sin, passions, attachments)／사바를 ~하다 be delivered from worldly existence; get freed from the ties of this world.

해태(海苔) lavar; sloke.

해태(懈怠) idleness; laziness; indolence; sloth; sluggishness／~하다 (be) lazy; idle; indolent; slothful; sluggish.

해토(解土) thawing of the ground／~하다 [the ground] thaw (out)／~머리 the beginning of the thaw.

해파리 《동》 a jellyfish; a medusa.

해판(解版) 《인》 distribution of printing type／~하다 distribute type; decompose／~공 a type distributor.

해포 a couple of years; some years.

해포석(海泡石) meerschaum; sepiolite.

해표(海豹) 《동》 a sea leopard; a seal.

해풍(海風) a sea wind[breeze].

해하다(害ー) injure (one's health); damage; do harm (to); hurt (one's feelings); impair／건강을 ~ injure one's health／감정을 ~ hurt a person's feelings.

해학(諧謔) humor; a jest; a joke; good humored banter; pleasantry; fun; a wisecrack 〈미〉／~적인 humorous; witty／~가 a humorist; a wit; a joker／그는 ~을 모른다 He has no sense of humor.／~ 소설(小說) a humorous story.

해항(海港) a seaport.

해해거리다 giggle; titter; cackle.

해행(蟹行) walking sideways／~하다 walk[go] sideways.

해협(海峽) 《지》 a channel; a sound; straits／대한 ~ the Straits of Korea／~을 건너다 cross the channel.

해화석(海花石) 《동》 star coral.

해후(邂逅) a chance[causal] meeting; an encounter; a fortuitous meeting／~하다 meet by chance; happen[chance] to meet; come[fall] across (a person); encounter.

핵(核) (세포의) a nucleus (pl. -lei); (과실의) a kernel; a core／~ 분열 nuclear fission／원자~ the nucleus of an atom／~공격 a nuclear attack／~탄두 a nuclear warhead.

핵과(核果) 《식》 a stone-fruit; a drupe; a putamen.

핵막(核膜) 《생》 nuclear membrane.

핵무기(核武器) nuclear weapons／~의 개발 nuclear weapons' development／~ 보유국 a nuclear power／전술[전략] ~ a tactical[strategic] nuclear weapon.

**핵무장**(核武裝) nuclear armaments/ ~하다 be armed with nuclear weapons/ ~을 금지하다 denuclearize (*a country*)/ ~ 철폐 nuclear disarmaments. かくぶそう

**핵물질**(核物質) nuclear materials. かくぶっしつ

**핵반응**(核反應) nuclear reaction. かくはんのう

**핵분열**(核分裂) nuclear fission/ ~ 물질 fissionable materials[minerals]/ ~ 폭탄 a fission acid. かくぶんれつ

**핵산**(核酸) nucleic acid.

**핵시대**(核時代) the atomic[nuclear] age; the nuclear age. かくじだい

**핵실험**(核實驗) a nuclear test[experiment]; nuclear testing/ ~의 금지 a nuclear test ban/ ~ 경쟁 nuclear testing competition/ 대기권 ~ an atmospheric nuclear test/ 지하 ~ an underground nuclear test. かくじっけん

**핵심**(核心) a kernel; the core/문제의 ~ the kernel[heart] of a question/ ~을 찌르다 touch the core/ ~에 언급하다 touch the core (*of*)/문제의 ~을 파악하다 get at the heart. かくしん

**핵융합**(核融合) 〖물〗 nuclear fusion/ ~ 폭탄 a [nuclear] fusion bomb. かくゆうごう

**핵전쟁**(核戰爭) [a] nuclear war[warfare]. かくせんそう

**핵질**(核質) nuclear substance; nucleoplasm. かくしつ

**힐기죽** glancing ⇨힐기죽.

**햅쌀** new rice; the year's new crop of rice/ ~밥 rice cooked from the new crop. しんまい

**햇-** new; the first product of the year.

**햇것** a new crop; the year's crop.

**햇곡식**(一穀一) a new crop grain; of the year's harvest. はつもの しんこく

**햇무리** a halo; a ring around the sun/ ~하다 the sun has a ring around it. ひがさ

**햇발** sunbeams ⇨햇살.

**햇볕** sunlight; sunbeams/ ~을 쬐다 bask in the sun; sunbathe/ ~에 타다 get sunburnt[brown]; get a tan. ひのひかり

**햇빛** sunshine; sunlight/ ~에 쬐다 sun; expose to the sun/ ~에 말리다 dry in the sun/ ~을 들이다 let the sun in. にっこう

**햇살** sunbeams; sunlight the rays of the sun/ ~을 받다 be in the sun/부드러운 ~ soft sunlight; soft[gentle] rays of the sun/ ~이 퍼지다 the sun spreads its beams.

**햇수**(一數) the number of years/온 지 ~로 3년이다 It is my third year here.

**햇콩** new beans; the year's crop of beans. はつまめ

**햇팥** new red beans; the year's crop of red beans.

**행**(行) ①a line; a row ②(시의) a line [of verse]; a verse; a line [of verse]. ぎょう

**행**(幸) good luck; happiness; fortune/ ~인지 불행인지 for good or for evil; luckily or unluckily. さいわい

**-행**(行) (가는 곳) bound for; destination/그 배는 부산~이다 The ship is bound for *Busan*. 一ゆき

**행각**(行脚) travelling on foot; a walking-tour (순례) a pilgrimage/ ~하다 go on a walking-tour[pilgrimage]/강연 ~에 나서다 go on a lecture tour. あんぎゃ

**행간**(行姦) committing adultery/ ~하다 commit adultery[fornication]; fornicate (*with*).

**행간**(行間) space between lines/ ~을 띄다 leave space between lines; space out. ぎょうかん

**행객**(行客) a traveler; a tourist; a wayfarer; a stranger. こうかく

**행구**(行具) traveling gear[suit, outfit]. こうそく

**행군**(行軍) marching; a march/ ~하다 march/4열 종대로 시내를 ~하다 parade a street in four columns/ ~ 대형 march formation/강~ a forced march/설중(雪中) ~ a march through the snow/ ~로 a route. こうぐん

**행길** a main road ⇨한길.

**행낭**(行囊) a pouch; a mail-bag(미); a postbag(영).

**행내기** an ordinary person; a common being; a mediocrity/그는 ~가 아니다 He is no ordinary type., He is no pushover. めだたないふつうのひと

**행년**(行年) *one's* age[years]. こうねん

**행동**(行動) action; conduct; movement; behaviour/ ~하다 act; behave (*oneself*); conduct; move/그의 ~은 신사적이었다 He behaved like a gentleman./단체 ~ group[united] action/ ~주의 〖심〗 behaviorism/신중히 ~하다 take a cautious action; play safe. こうどう

**행동 거지**(行動擧止) bearing; manners; all *one's* actions. こうどう

**행락**(行樂) enjoyment; amusement; pleasure; a good time/ ~하다 have a good time; enjoy[amuse] *one*self/ ~객 a holiday-maker; a hiker. こうらく

**행랑**(行廊) rooms on both sides of the main gate where servants live; servants quarters/ ~살이 living the life of a resident servant.

**행려**(行旅) travel/ ~ 병사자 a person who died unidentified on the road/ ~병자 an ill way farer; a charity patient.

**행렬**(行列) (행진) a procession;a parade; a queue; 〖수〗 matrix/ ~을 짓다 stand in line; form a queue/ ~에 끼어들다 break into a line [of waiting people]

**행로**(行路) a path; a road; a course; a career/인생 ～는 다난하다 Life is full of troubles[rubs]./인생 ～ the path of life; life's journey[pilgrimage]. こうろ

**행림**(杏林) medical men; physicians/～제 medical circles. きょうりん

**행망적다** (be) careless; negligent; inattentive. むとんじゃくだ

**행매**(行賣) 《팔기 시작함》starting to sell 《행상》peddling/～하다 start selling; begin to sell; peddle. うりはじめること

**행방**(行方) one's whereabouts; one's traces; the place [where] one has gone/그는 ～불명이다 He is missing./～불명자 a missing person/～을 감추다 cover one's traces; conceal one's whereabouts; hide out. ゆくえ

**행보**(行步) walking; going on foot/～하다 walk; go on foot. ほこう

**행복**(幸福) happiness; felicity; well-being; bliss; blessedness 《행운》good fortune/～하다 (be) happy; blessed; blissful; fortunate; lucky; felicitous/～하게 살다 live a happy life; live happily/～감 euphoria, a feeling of well-being. こうふく

**행불행**(幸不幸) happiness or misery; good or bad luck; weal or woe; good or ill fortune; lights and shadows/인생의 ～ the lights and shadows of life. たこうとふこう

**행사**(行使) use; exercise/～하다 use; employ; exercise/특권을 ～하다 employ one's privilege/실력을 ～하다 resort to forced measures/위조 지폐를 ～하다 pass[utter, circulate] counterfeit bank notes. こうし

**행사**(行事) an event; a function; an observance/연중 ～ annual functions[events, observances]; the year's regular events. ぎょうじ

**행상**(行商) 《일》peddling; hawking 《행상인》a hawker; a peddler〈미〉/～하다 peddle; hawk. ぎょうしょう

**행상**(行賞) awarding (a person) a prize; bestowal of rewards/～하다 give a reward; award a prize to (a person); reward (a person or his services). こうしょう

**행색**(行色) ①《차림새》appearance; externals ②《행동》demeanor; attitude; behavior/～이 초라하다 look shabby.

**행서**(行書) the semi-cursive style of writing. ぎょうしょ

**행선**(行船) sailing/～하다 sail. でぶね

**행선지**(行先地) one's destination; the place where one is going.

**행성**(行星) a planet ⇒유성. こうせい

**행세**(行勢) seizing[assuming] political power/～하다 wield[exercise] power.

**행세**(行世) conduct; manners; behavior/～하다 conduct oneself; behave well/～를 잘못하다 misconduct oneself; misbehave/～하는 집안 a distinguished [noble] family. しょせい

**행수**(行首) the head[leader] of a group; a boss. おやかた

**행수**(行數) the number of lines. ぎょうのかず

**행습**(行習) habit; practice/～이 사납다 have a bad habit. しゅうかん

**행신**(行身) manners; deportment; behavior ⇒처신. よわたり

**행실**(行實) manners; conduct; behavior; demeanor/그는 ～이 나쁜 사람이다 He is a man of loose conduct[morals]/～을 고치다 turn over a new leaf; mend one's way.

**행심**(幸甚) ～하다 (be) extremely happy [glad]; be much obliged. こうじん

**행악**(行惡) violence; wickedness/～하다 do violence[evil, wrong]; practice wickedness. あくじをなすこと

**행여**(幸—) by chance; possibly/～ 올까 하여 기다렸다 I have waited in case you might drop by. さいわいに

**행여나**(幸—) by chance ⇒행여. さいわいにも

**행운**(幸運) good luck; good fortune; a lucky[good] break〈미〉/～을 빕니다 I wish you the best of luck./～의 절정에 있다 be at the top of fortune's wheel. こううん

**행운 유수**(行雲流水) smooth; going smoothly[swimmingly]; being free and easy. こううんりゅうすい

**행원**(行員) a bank employee; a bank clerk. ぎんこういん

**행위**(行爲) an action; an act; a deed; conduct; behavior; a work; doings/그의 ～는 꼭 미친 사람 같다 He behaves himself exactly like a madman./～능력 legal capacity/도덕[적] ～ a moral act. こうい

**행음**(行淫) committing adultery/～하다 commit adultery; have illicit intercourse (with).

**행인**(行人) a passer-by; a foot passenger; a wayfarer; a pedestrian/～의 발길이 끊어졌다 The street is deserted. つうこうにん

**행자**(行者) a pilgrim; an ascetic.

**행장**(行狀) ①《품행》behavior; deportment; conduct; demeanor; doings; manners ②《사후 기록》records of a deceased person's life; a necrology; a history of the deceased. ぎょうじょう

**행장**(行裝) travel gear; a traveler's equipment; a traveling outfit[equip, outfit] oneself for a journey/～을 갖추다 equip oneself for a journey/～을 풀다 take off one's traveling attire. こうそう

**행적**(行績) the achievements of one's lifetime; one's work[contributions]. ぎょうせき

**행전**(行錢) being the banker at a gamb-

**행전**(行纏) leggings; putties[puttees]/ ~을 치다 wrap one's legs with putties. きゃはん

**행정**(行政) administration/ ~적 executive; administrative/ ~적 수완이 있다 have administrative ability[capacity] / ~ 개혁 a reform of the administrative structure/ ~학 political science. ぎょうせい

**행정**(行程) ①《거리》road distance; a distance to cover; a journey/하루의 ~ a day's journey ②《기계》a travel; an excusion. こうてい

**행주** a dish cloth[towel]/ ~질하다 wipe with a dish cloth/ ~치마 an apron. さらぶきん

**행중**(行中) a company; a party/ ~에 끼다 join a party; join the company [group]. どうはんしゃ

**행진**(行進) a march; a parade/ ~하다 march; proceed; parade/의기 양양하게 ~하다 march off in triumph/ ~곡 a march; field music/결혼 ~곡 a wedding march. こうしん

**행차**(行次) an honored going[coming]; a visit; a trip; traveling/ ~하다 go; come; visit; go on a trip.

**행티** ill-willed behaviou[u]r/ ~사납다 be peevish[mean, malicious]/ ~부리다 show ill will; do mean things. ちゃめ

**행패**(行悖) ~하다 do violence; misbehave (oneself)/ ~를 부리다 behave badly; commit an outrage (on).

**행포**(行暴) violence; lawless acts/ ~하 다 do violence; commit lawless acts; perpetrate an outrage. らんぼう

**행하**(行下) a tip; a gratuity; a gift of money from a master to his servant/ ~를 주다 tip; give a gratuity (to).

**행하다**(行一) ①《행위》do; act; behave; conduct oneself 《실행하다》carry out; perform; practice; execute; fulfill; enforce; commit/선을 ~ do good; do what is good ②《거행하다》hold; observe; celebrate; keep/의식을 ~ hold a ceremony/결혼식을 ~ have a wedding ceremony. おこなう

**행형**(行刑) 《법》the execution of a sentence/ ~하다 execute a sentence; execute. ぎょうけい

**행화**(杏花) 《식》an apricot blossom. あんずのはな

**행흉**(行凶) murder; assassination/ ~하 다 commit murder.

**향**(向) 《방향》direction 《방위》situation 《집의》exposure; aspect/남~ 집 a house facing south.

**향**(香) perfume; incense/ ~을 피우다 burn incense. こう

**향가**(鄕歌) native songs; old Korean folksongs. きょうか

**향곡**(鄕曲) the country; rural districts.

**향관**(鄕貫) the birthplace of one's first ancestor ⇨관향. かんきょう

**향관**(鄕關) one's native place; one's [ancestral] home.

**향교**(鄕校) a Confucian temple and a school belonging to it. きょうこう

**향국**(鄕國) one's native place; one's home [land].

**향긋하다** (be) fragrant; have a faint sweet scent.

**향기**(香氣) fragrance; perfume; aroma; a sweet smell[odor]; a scent/꽃~ the scent of a flower/ ~가 떠돌다 be fragrant with the scent. こうき

**향기롭다**(香氣一) (be) fragrant; aromatic; sweet-smelling; sweet-scented; odoriferous/향기로운 향수 an aromatic perfume/향기로운 냄새 a sweet[fragrant] smell. かんばしい

**향나무**(香一) 《식》aromatic trees[plants]; a Chinese juniper. かおりのよいき

**향남**(向南) facing south/ ~하다 face south. みなみにむかうこと

**향내**(香一) fragrance ⇨향기(香氣).かおり

**향년**(享年) one's age at death/향년 70 He died at the age of 70; He died at seventy. きょうねん

**향당**(鄕黨) a village community; villagers; townspeople.

**향도**(嚮導) a guide 《군대의》a fugleman; guidance; conduct; leading; leadership / ~하다 guide; conduct; lead; fugle.

**향동**(向東) facing east/ ~하다 face east. ひがしにむかうこと

**향락**(享樂) pleasure; enjoyment/ ~하다 enjoy/인생을 ~하다 enjoy one's life/ ~ 생활 a gay life; dissipation/ ~주의자 a hedonist; an epicurean/ ~적인 pleasureseeking; merry-making. きょうらく

**향로**(香爐) a bronze censor; an incense ·burner/ ~석(石) the stone before a tomb that the incense burner is put on. こうろ

**향료**(香料) ①《식품의》spices; spicery ② 《화장품의》materials for making perfume[incense]; perfume; perfumery; aromatic essence[oils]/ ~류 perfumery/ ~ 식물 aromatic plants. こうりょう

**향리**(鄕里) one's home town[native village]. きょうり

**향목**(香木) aromatic trees[plants] ⇨향나 무. こうぼく

**향미**(香味) flavor; smack/ ~료 flavorings; seasonings; spices. こうみ

**향방**(向方) 《방위》a direction 《길》a course; a line 《목적지》one's destination/ ~을 모르다 do not know the direction; have no sense at all; don't know which way is up. ゆきさき

**향배**(向背) attitude; for or against; where one stands or leans (on an issue) / ~를 정하다 define[clarify] one's attitude (toward). こうはい

**향복**(享福) enjoying happiness ~하다 en-

joy happiness; live a happy life.
**향북**(向北) facing north／～하다 face north.
**향불**(香—) an incense fire; burning incense／～을 피우다 burn incense.
**향사**(向斜) 【지】 a syncline.
**향상**(向上) elevation; rise 《개선》 improvement; betterment 《진보》 progress; advancement／～하다 rise; be elevated; become higher; improve／여성 지위의 ～ the rise in wonen's social status／생활 수준을 ～시키다 elevate the standard of living／～심(心) aspiration; ambition.
**향속**(鄕俗) country[rural] ways[manners, customs].
**향수**(享受) enjoyment; fruition／～하다 enjoy.
**향수**(享壽) enjoying the longevity／～하다 enjoy old age; live to a ripe old age／100세를 ～하다 be blessed with a longevity of a hundred [years].
**향수**(香水) a perfume; a scent; perfumed[scented] water; liquid scents 《인공의》 a synthetic[an artificial] perfume 《꽃의》 a floral perfume 《총칭》 perfumery／～를 바르다 use perfume; perfume.
**향수**(鄕愁) homesickess; nostalgia; thoughts of home 《병적인》 nostomania／～를 느끼다 feel homesick; long very much for one's home.
**향습성**(向濕性) 【식】 positive hydrotropism.
**향악**(鄕樂) Korean music.
**향연**(香煙) ①《향의》 the smoke of incense burning ②《담배》 fragrant tobacco [cigarettes].
**향연**(饗宴) a banquet; a dinner; a feast; an entertainment／～을 베풀다 hold[give] a banquet[dinner].
**향유**(享有) enjoyment; possession／～하다 enjoy; possess; participate in (benefit)／인권의 ～ the enjoyment of personal rights.
**향유**(香油) ①《참기름》 sesame oil ②《머리 기름》 perfumed hair-oil.
**향유고래** 《동》 a sperm whale; a cachalot.
**향응**(饗應) an entertainment; a treat; a dainty repast; a banquet; a dinner; a feast／～하다 entertain (a person at dinner); treat; give a party; hold a banquet.
**향의**(向意) intention; inclination; thought／～하다 intend to; be inclined to; have a mind to (do).
**향일성**(向日性) 【식】 [positive] heliotropism.
**향자**(向者) the other day.
**향점**(向點) 【천】 the apex／태양 ～ the solar apex.
**향지성**(向地性) 【식】 [positive] geotropism.

**향초**(香草) ①《풀》 fragrant grass ②《담배》 fragrant tobacco.
**향촉**(香燭) incense and candles [used in sacrifices].
**향촌**(鄕村) the country; a country village; country districts.
**향취**(香臭) fragrance ⇨향기.
**향탕**(香湯) fragrant water with which a corpse is washed.
**향토**(鄕土) one's native place[province, land]; one's home; one's birthplace; the country／～ 문학 fork literature／～색 local color／～ 예비군 the local defense force／～ 예술 local crafts; provincial art.
**향포**(香蒲) a bulrush ⇨부들.
**향하다**(向—) ①《대하다》 face; front; look out on; turn towards／바다를 ～ look out on the sea ②《가다》 proceed to; go to[towards] start for; be off to／육지를 향해 항해하다 sail towards the land ③《쏠리다》 lean towards; tend towards／마음이 고향을 ～ one's mind go off to one's home; yearn for home.
**향학심**(向學心) desire[love] for learning; intellectual appetite; a scholarly bent／～에 불타다 burn with the desire for learning; aspire after further knowledge.
**향학열**(向學熱) enthusiasm for[an ardent love of] learning.
**향합**(香盒) an incense box[jar].
**향화**(香火) ①《향불》 incense fire; burning incense ②《제사》 an ancestor-memorial service.
**향후**(向後) hereafter; henceforth; from new on.
**허** Ah!, Oh!, Alas!, Dear me!／～, 이거 실수 했군 Oh dear, I have made a mistake.
**허**(虛) an unguarded position.
**허가**(許可) permission; leave 《승인》 approval; sanction; grant 《면허》 license; a permit; a certificate 《입학》 admission 《인정》 authorization; authority 《특허》 concession／～를 신청하다 apply for a license／～증 a permit; a license; a charter／건축 ～ permission to build／입학 ～ admission to a school.
**허갈**(虛喝) bluffing; a bluff／～하다 bluff (a person).
**허깨비** a spook; a ghost; a goblin; a phantom; a hallucination／～를 보다 see a phantom.
**허겁지겁** confusedly; in a flurry; flustered; hurry-scurry／～하다 be flustered; fluster; scurry; be all in a fluster.
**허공**(虛空) the empty sky[air]; the empty space; an empty void 《공중》 the air; the sky／～에 사라. ~ vanish into thin air／～을 응시하다 stare into space.
**허구**(虛構) a lie; a fabrication; a ficti-

on; a falsehood; a concoction an invention; a made-up thing／그의 이야기는 전혀 ~였다 His story was an entire fabrication. きょこう

**허구렁**(虛—) an empty hollow[depression]／~에 빠지다 fall into a pit. ほらあな

**허구리** the waist; the small of the back. わきばら

**허기**(虛飢) hunger／~지다 be[go] hungry; be pressed by hunger; be famished (욕망) be hungry for[after]; thirst for／~증 a hungry feeling; a gnawing hunger. ひもじさ

**허다**(許多) many; much; great[vast] numbers／~하다 (be) numerous; frequent; common; many／그런 예가 ~하다 we have a number or examples of that sort. きょた

**허덕거리다** (숨이 차서) pant; gasp for breath; be exhausted; be tired out (애쓰다) struggle; make frantic efforts; work madly／무거운 짐을 지고 ~ pant under a heavy load. もがく

**허덕지덕** panting; gasping for breath; dog-tired; striving; madly; frantically. あくせくと

**허두**(虛頭) opening words[remarks]／~를 꺼내다 begin to say; open words[remarks].

**허둥거리다** be flurried[fluttered, flustered]; be thrown into confusion; rush about madly／어쩔 줄 몰라 ~ be so flustered that one doesn't know what to do. あわてふためく

**허둥지둥** all flustered; in a hurry; hurriedly／~하다 get[be] all flustered／~ 도망치다 flee helter-skelter; run away with bare life. じたばた

**허드레** trash; odds and ends／허드레일 odd jobs; a trifing job／허드렛물 water for sundry uses.

**허드재비** an object of no importance; a trash; odd bits[jobs].

**허락**(許諾) (승인) consent; assent; approval; sanction (허가) permission; permit; leave; grant／~하다 consent to; give consent to; permit; allow／그는 딸 의 결혼을 ~하지 않았다 He forbade his daughter to marry. きょだく

**허랑**(虛浪) dissoluteness; frivolity; looseness／~하다 (be) loose; sloppy; frivolous; dissolute; be not serious. うわついていること

**허례**(虛禮) empty forms; formalities; formal courtesy; artificial manners／~를 폐하다 dispense with empty forms; do away with mere formalities／~ 허식 vanity. きょれい

**허론**(虛論) empty theory ⇒공론.

**허룩하다** (be) more or less empty; almost empty／쌀자루가 ~ a rice bag is almost empty.

**허룽거리다** play fast and loose; act frivolously; behave lightly. せかせかする

**허름하다** (be) shabby; mean; seedy; poorlooking (싸다) cheap; low／그는 주제 가 허름했다 He looked seedy; He was poorly dressed.

**허름숭이** an unreliable person; a careless[reckless] fellow. ぎぜんしゃ

**허리** ①(신체의) the waist; the small of the back; the loin (짐승의) the haunch; the pelvic region／~가 구부러졌다 one's body has become bent ②(옷의) the [of clothes]. こし

**허리띠** a belt (여자용의) a sash; a girdle; a band (총칭) belting／~를 풀다 untie[undo] a belt; ungirdle oneself. こしおび

**허리질러** across the middle. まっなかに

**허리춤** inside the waist of one's trousers ／ ~에 손을 넣다 put one's hand into the waist of one's trousers.

**허리통** the measure of one's waist; measure／~을 재다 measure one's waist. こしまわり

**허릿매** the shape of one's waist; the waistline／~가 곱다 have a shapely waist. こしのせん

**허망**(虛妄) salsehood; falsity; untruth／ ~하다 (be) vain; untrue; false; unreliable; groundless／~지설 a groundless [an reliable] view. きょぼう

**허명**(虛名) an empty name; a false reputation; notoriety; publicity／ ~ 무실 하다 be vain; be false; be empty; be unsubstantial. きょめい

**허무**(虛無) nothingness; nihility; nihil／ ~하다 (be) nonexistent; nil; null; futile; vain; empty; nihilistic／~ 사상 nihilistic thoughts[ideas]／ ~주의 nihilism／~주의자 a nihilist. きょむ

**허문**(虛聞) a false[groundless] rumor; an unfounded report. きょぶん

**허물**[1] a skin; a shell; a covering; a scar ／뱀이 ~을 벗다 a snake casts off its skin. ぬけがら

**허물**[2] (과실) a fault; an error; a mistake; a misdeed; a blame (결점) a fault; a defect; a flaw; a weak point／ ~을 감추다 conceal a defect. かしつ

**허물다** demolish; destroy; pull[tear, break, take] down／벽[집]을 ~ take[break] down a well[house]; flatten out a wall[house]. こわす

**허물벗다**[1] ①(뱀 따위가) cast off the skin; slough; exuviate ②(피부) [the skin] peel off; be scraped. かわむける

**허물벗다**[2] clear oneself of a false charge; exculpate oneself.

**허물어지다** crumble down; collaps; fall down; be destroyed／건물이 요란한 소리를 내며 허물어졌다 The building fell down with a crash. こわされる

**허물없다** frank; be on familiar[friendly] terms; be unceremonious／허물없는 사

이 be on familiar terms with each other. あけすけだ

**허방** a hollow; a sunken[hollow] place; a depression／～을 디디다 step in a hollow. くぼち

**허방짚다** miscalculate; fall because of a miscalculation; be frustrated; miss. ごさんする

**허방치다** miscalculate ⇒허방짚다. しっぱいする

**허벅다리** the thigh.

**허벅살** the flesh of the thigh.

**허벅지** the fleshy inside of the thigh.

**허벅허벅** very soft; all flabby／～하다 be very soft; be all flabby.

**허보**(虛報) a false report; false news／～를 전하다 circulate a false report.

**허분허분** soft and juicy／～하다 (be) soft and juicy.

**허비**(虛費) waste; useless expenses／～하다 waste (money); cast[throw] away／쓸데없는 일에 돈을 ～하다 waste one's money on useless things. むだづかい

**허비다** scratch 《맹수가》 maul 《귀를》 pick／손톱으로 귀를 ～ pick one's ears with one's fingernail. ひっかく

**허비적거리다** scratch; keep picking[digging out] (with a fingernail). しきりにひっかく

**허사**(虛事) a vain attempt; a failure／～로 돌아가다 come to naught[nothing]; end in failure; be in vain; prove futile. うわごと

**허상**(虛像) 【물】 a virtual image.

**허설**(虛說) a false[groundless] report[story].

**허세**(虛勢) a bluff; a bluster; a fanfaronade; a false show of power[influence, strength, courage]; a bold front／～부리다 bluff; make a show of power. きょせい

**허송**(虛送) wasting time ⇒허송 세월.

**허송 세월**(虛送歲月) wasting[killing] time; passing time aimlessly[idly]／～하다 waste[kill] time; pass time aimlessly [idly]; idle one's time away. さいげつをむだに過ごすこと

**허수**(虛數) 【수】 an imaginary quantity [number]. きょすう

**허수룩하다** (be) almost empty ⇒허룩하다. すたれている

**허수아비** a scarecrow 《무능자》 a dummy 《괴뢰》 a puppet; a figurehead／～를 세우다 set up scarecrows (in a paddy field)／～ 사장 a dummy boss. かかし

**허수하다** feel a certain emptiness ⇒허전하다. わびしい

**허술하다** (be) shabby; humble; poor; worn-out／허술한 집 a shabby[humble] cottage. すたれている

**허식**(虛飾) affectation; ostentation; show; foppery; false[glittering] display; dandism／～하다 affect; show off／～을 좋아하다 be fond of[care for] demonstration[display]. きょしょく

**허실**(虛實) truth and falsehood; fact and fiction／～을 확인하다 ascertain the truth. きょじつ

**허심**(虛心) disinterestedness; dispassionateness; freedom from prejudice; an open mind. きょしん

**허심 탄회**(虛心坦懷) frankness; candidness; open-mindedness／～하다 be open-minded; frank; candid／～하게 이야기하다 speak frankly. きょしんたんかい

**허약**(虛弱) weakness; infirmity; feebleness; debility 《정신의》 imbecility; 【의】 adynamia; asthenia／～하다 (be) weak; feeble; infirm; frail; delicate; decrepit／신체가 ～하다 have a weak[delicate] constitution; be in delicate health. きょじゃく

**허언**(虛言) a lie; a falsehood; an untruth／～하다 lie; fabricate. きょげん

**허여멀쑥다** (be) nice and fair; have a fair complexion. しろくてきれいだ

**허여멀쑥하다** (be) nice and fair. しろくてきれいだ

**허영**(虛榮) vanity; vainglory; empty fame／여자의 ～ feminine vanity／～심 [a sense of] vanity／～에 차다 be full of[filled with] vanity. きょえい

**허영거리다** totter; falter; be shaky; stagger／허영거리는 걸음 faltering[tottering] steps／허영허영 totteringly; falteringly; staggeringly. よろめく

**허옇다** (be) very white; snow-white; pure white; quite pale／얼굴이 ～ look [quite] pale. まっしろい

**허예지다** get[become] pure white. しらむ

**허욕**(虛慾) vain ambitions; avarice; greed／～ 많은 사람 a grasping person. むさぼり

**허용**(許容) permission; allowance; approval; sanction; admission 《용서》 pardon; forgiveness; toleration／～하다 permit; approve; grant; allow; admit; pardon; forgive／관용상 ～되어 있다 It is sanctioned by usage. きょよう

**허우룩하다** feel a certain emptiness; be lonely; feel the miss (of)／자네가 없어서 퍽 허우룩했네 We missed you badly. こころさびしい

**허울** show; look; appearance／～이 좋다 have a good-looking appearance. うわべ

**허위**(虛威) bluff; Dutch courage. きょい

**허위**(虛僞) fiction; falsehood; 《논》 fallacy／～ 진술을 하다 make a false statement／～ 고발 a false accusation／～ 신고 a false return[report]／～ 진술 misrepresentation／～ 행위 a fraud act. きょぎ

**허위넘다** struggle up[over]／고개를 ～ go over a pass panting and heaving.

**허위단심** struggling with all one's might; laboriously／아들을 보려고 ～ 먼 곳을 찾아왔다 struggle a long distance to see

**허위대** a [fine] tall figure[build] / ～가 좋다 have a fine figure. たいかく

**허위적거리다** struggle; paw (*the air*); flounder / 물 밖으로 나오려고 ～ paw the air to get out of the water. しきりにもがく

**허장 성세**(虛張聲勢) an empty boast; bluff; boaster; bravado / ～하다 bluff; bluster; swagger. かけおどし

**허적거리다** ransack; rummage; scatter / 닭들이 건초 더미를 ～ chickens scatter a bunch of hay. ひっかきまわす

**허전**(虛傳) a false report; a false rumor / ～하다 inform a false report.

**허전거리다** totter; falter; stagger / 허전거리며 걸어가다 totter along. あしがふらふらだ

**허전하다** feel empty; miss (*something*); feel lonesome / 네가 없어서 ～ We miss you very much. こころぼそい

**허점**(虛點) a blind point[spot] / 법의 ～을 찌르다 make an illicit use of law.

**허정** ～하다 (be) empty; hollow; vacant; vacuous. みかけだおし

**허정거리다** lose *one's* legs. ふらふらだ

**허족**(虛足) 〖동〗 a pseudopodium (*pl.* -dia).

**허출하다** feel hungry; (be) hungry / 배가 ～ be hungry; have an empty stomach. ひもじい

**허탄**(虛誕) untruth ⇨허망(虛妄). きょたん

**허탈**(虛脫) collapse; prostration; atrophy marasmus; blankness of [mind]; despondency / ～하다 collapse; atrophy; be prostrated; be despondent / ～ 상태에 있다 be thoroughly absent-minded. きょだつ

**허탕** vain effort; lost[fruitless] labor / 모든 노력이 ～이 되었다 All our efforts were in vain. / 나의 일은 결국 ～으로 끝났다 My work have been for nothing after all. とろう

**허탕**(虛蕩) dissoluteness; profligacy.

**허투**(虛套) sham; pretense; simulation; feigning / 그것은 ～로 하는 동정이다 It is only mock sympathy. ごまかし

**허투루** carelessly; roughly; negligently; in a slovenly way / 일을 ～하다 do a rough job / 물건을 ～ 다루다 handle things roughly. ぞんざいに

**허튼계집** a loose[an unchaste] woman; a slut; a slattern; a wanton; a woman of loose morals.

**허튼맹세**(一盟誓) an irresponsible[a unreliable] oath / ～를 하다 make an idle vow. むせきにんなちかい

**허튼소리** irresponsible utterance; idle talk; an unreliable[a baseless] talk / ～가 아니다 be no joke. むだばなし

**허튼수작**(一酬酌) an unreliable talk; idle talk ⇨허튼소리. むだこと

**허파** the lungs 《소·양·돼지의》 lights. はいぞう

**허풍**(虛風) boasting; bragging; a big talk; exaggeration; a fanfaronade / 그는 좀 ～이 있다 His statement is rather exaggerated. / ～선이 a boaster; a braggart; a gasbag. ほらふき

**허풍선**(虛風扇) a bellows; a blower. ふいご

**허하다**(虛一) 《속이》(be) hollow; empty; vacant; void 《기력이》 weak; feeble; delicate; frail.

**허하다**(許一) 《허가》 permit; allow; give permission for 《허락》 grant; approve; accept. ゆるす

**허한**(虛汗) cold sweat. ねあせ

**허행**(虛行) a trip in vain; a fruitless; journey; a disappointing trip / ～하다 make a trip in vain; make a fruitless trip.

**허허** ha-ha; with a laugh / ～ 웃다 laugh loudly. は！は！

**허허바다** a vast expanse of ocean; the vast expanse of water; a vast empty sea. おおうなばら

**허허벌판** a vast expanse of plain; a prairie. こうや

**허허실실**(虛虛實實) taking things as they come; leaving a matter to take its course. きょきょじつじつ

**허혼**(許婚) approval of marriage[engagement]; consent to a marriage; accepting *one's* hand in marriage / ～하다 approve of[consent to] *one's* marriage. けっこんをきょだくすること

**허화**(虛華) ostentation; empty[outward] show / ～하다 (be) showy; be full of glitter, glamorous.

**허황**(虛荒) ～하다 (be) false; ungrounded; unreliable; unbelievable. きまぐれ

**헌** ①《낡은》 old; shabby; second-hand; worn-out / ～옷 old[worn-out] clothes ②《부스럼》 with a boil on it / 헌데 a boil.

**헌거**(軒擧) elation; high spirits; exuberance; euphoria 《풍채가》 be imposing; be portly / ～롭다 be high-spirited; be triumphant. けんしう

**헌걸스럽다** (be) elated; high-spirited. りりいい

**헌걸차다** be full of elation; (be) elated. ひじょうにつよい

**헌것** old[worn-out, second-hand, used] things. ふるいもの

**헌계집** a once married woman; a woman who has lost her man. けっこんしたことのあるおんな

**헌금**(獻金) a gift of money; contribution; a donation; a subscription 《교회에서》 a collection 《불전에서》 an offering / ～하다 contribute; donate; subscribe / ～자 a contributor; a donor.

**헌납**(獻納) contribution; presentation; donation / ～ 하다 present; contribute; donate / ～품 an offering; a gift / ～자 a contributor; a donor. けんのう

**헌데** a swelling; a boil.

**헌등**(獻燈) a votive lantern. けんとう

**헌법(憲法)** the constitution; a constitutional law／～상의 권리 one's constitutional rights／～을 개정하다 revise the constitution／～ 기관 a constitutional institution. けんぽう

**헌병(憲兵)** a gendarme 《총칭》gendarmerie; a military policeman (略：M.P.)／～사령관 a provost marshal. けんぺい

**헌상(獻上)** an offering to a superior; presentation／～하다 present (a thing to a superior)／～품 an offering; a present. けんじょう

**헌쇠** scrap-iron; ferrous scraps. ふるいてつ

**헌신(獻身)** devotion; self-sacrifice／～하다 devote[dedicate] oneself (to)／ sacrifice oneself (to)／～적으로 일하다 work devotedly; work in dead earnest. けんしん

**헌신짝** a worn-out shoe; an old shoe／～같이 버리다 throw it away like an old shoe. ふるくなったはきもの

**헌앙(軒昂)** elation ⇒헌거. けんこう

**헌옷** old[worn-out] clothes.

**헌장(憲章)** a constitution; a charter of constitution／국제 연합 ～ The Charter of the United Nations／어린이 ～ the Children's Charter. けんしょう

**헌정(憲政)** constitutional government; constitutionalism／～을 실시하다 adopt constitutional government.

**헌정(獻呈)** offering; perstantation／～하다 offer; persent.

**헌책(獻策)** suggestion; recommendation; advice; counsel／～하다 suggest a plan; advance[make] suggestions; lay one's program (before); make recommendations. けんさく

**헌칠하다** have a well-proportioned figure; have a smart[dashing] figure.

**헐가(歇價)** a low price ⇒헐값. やすね

**헐값(歇一)** a low price; a low price than ever or other place／～에 사다 bun[have] a dead bargain; get (a thing) dog-cheap. やすね

**헐객(歇客)** a loose man; a libertine; a dissolute person. だらしないひと

**헐겁다** (be) loose; loose-fitting／장갑이 손에 ～ gloves are loose[loose-fitting] on the hand. すかすかだ

**헐근거리다** gasp; pant; wheeze; breathe-hard. ぜいぜいいう

**헐다¹** ①《피부가》be sore; get[have] a tumor on it／얼굴에 ～ have a swelling on one's face ②《옷이》get old; become shabby; wear out／옷이 ～ one's clothes wear out. ただれる

**헐다²** ①《쌓은 것을》destroy; demolish; pull[break, take, tear] down／집을 ～ pull down a house ②《험담하다》slander; speak ill of (a person); cnsure ③《돈을》break; change. こわす

**헐떡거리다** pant; gasp; breathe hard[heavily]; puff／헐떡거리며 말하다 speak panting; gasp out. あえぐ

**헐떡이다** gasp ⇒헐떡거리다. あえぐ

**헐떡하다** 《얼굴이》(be) pale; wan; worn 《눈이》hollow; sunken. あおざめている

**헐뜯다** slander; defame; disparage; speak ill of; pick on／사람을 ～ pick on (a person); speak ill of (a person). そしる

**헐렁거리다** ①《물건이》be loose; fit loose／신이 ～ one's shoes fit loose ②《행동이》act[behave] rashly[imprudently]; be light[frivolous]. ぐずだ

**헐렁이** an imprudent person; a frivolous person. うわつきもの

**헐렁하다** loose-fitting; (be) [fit] loose. ゆるい

**헐레벌떡** panting and puffing; helter-skelter／～ 달려가다 run along panting and puffing.

**헐벗다** be poorly[shabbily] clothed; be in rages／헐벗은 사람 a person in rags. ぼろをきている

**헐쑥하다** (be) thin and pale; drawn; lean; emaciated. あおざめている

**헐어지다** ①《낡아지다》get old; become shabby; wear out ②《무너지다》collapse; crumble; fall down. つぶれる

**헐하다(歇一)** ①《값이》(be) cheap; inexpensive; low [in price]／헐하게 사다 buy cheap ②《쉽다》(be) easy; light; simple ③《벌이》(be) light; lenient／헐한 벌이 light[lenient] punishment.

**험객(險客)** ①《성질이 험악한》a roughneck; a tough[sinister, dangerous] character ②《험구가》a slanderer; a foul-mouthed person. ずるいひと

**험구(險口)** abuse; slander 《사람》a foul mouthed person; a slanderous person／～하다 abuse; slander; defame; speak ill of (a person). あっこう

**험난(險難)** difficulty; roughness; danger; toughness／～하다 (be) rough and difficult; perilous; be full of danger. けんなん

**험담(險談)** slander; abuse; calumny; backbiting／～하다 slander; speak ill of (a person); talk scandal about; backbite. あっこう

**험로(險路)** a steep path; a rough[rugged] road; a breakneck road. けんろ

**험산(驗算)** 【수】verification of accounts; checking; proof／～하다 verify accounts; prove; check figures. けんざん

**험상(險狀)** ruggedness; roughness; grimness; sinisterness／험상스러운 얼굴 a grim face; a sinister look.

**험악(險惡)** ～하다 (be) dangerous; perilous; treatening; stormy 《사태가》grave; critical; ugly; gloomy 《험준하다》(be) rugged／형세는 날로 ～해진다 The situation is getting uglier every day. けんあく

**험조(險阻)** ruggedness. けんそ

**험준(險峻)** steepness; precipitousness／

~하다 (be) steep; rugged; precipitous / ~한 산 a rugged mountain. けんしゅん

험하다(險一) ①(험준하다)(be) steep; rugged; precipitous ②(날씨가)(be) foul; stormy; rough ③(험상하다)(be) sinister; grim; savage-looking/험한 얼굴 a grim[sinister] face ④(험악하다)(be) serious; grave; critical. けわしい

험화 【化】 saponification/ ~하다 saponity.

헙수룩하다 (머리털이)(be) shaggy; unkempt; dishevelled 《차림새가》(be) shabby; poor-looking; seedy/헙수룩한 옷 shabby clothes. ぼうぼうとしている

헙헙하다 ①(사람됨이)(be) easy-going; be not firm ②(손 쓰는 품이)(be) liberal. けちでない

헛 false; vain; fruitless; empty/ ~수고 vain effort; lost labor. むなしい

헛가게 a stall; a booth. ほしみせ

헛간 an open shed; a barn. なや

헛걸음 a trip[call] in vain; a fruitless [disappointing] journey/ ~하다 make a trip in vain; go in vain; make a fruitless call. むだあし

헛구역(一嘔逆) queasiness; a queasy feeling/ ~ 나다 be queasy. からはきけ

헛글 fruitless learning.

헛기운 a show of courage 《술 취한 때의》 Dutch courage.

헛기침 clearing one's throat; ahem/ ~하다 clear one's throat. からせき

헛김 an air leak/ ~나다 get a leak; spring a leak 《맥빠짐》 get frustrated; lose heart; be dispirited.

헛노릇 a fruitless[vain] effort; lost labor/ ~하다 labor in vain; do useless work.

헛돌다 (바퀴가) skid 《기계가》 run idle.

헛되다 (be) vain; futile; fruitless; empty; unavailing; unreliable; untrue; false; groundless/시간을 헛되이 보내다 pass one's time idly. むだだ

헛듣다 mishear; hear amiss; misunderstand.

헛디디다 miss one's footing[step]; take a false step; lose one's stepping/계단을 ~ miss one's footing on the steps. ふみそこなう

헛말 《거짓말》 a lie; a falsehood 《빈말》 empty talk; idle words.

헛맹세(一盟誓) an idle[a false, an empty] pledge[vow]/~하다 make an idle [a false, an empty] pledge[vow].

헛물키다 labor in vain; make vain[fruitless] efforts. しつぼうする

헛방(一放) 《헛총질》 a miss shot; a wrong hit; 《공탄》 a blank shot 《헛된말》 empty talk/~놓다 miss one's aim; fail to hit. くうほう

헛배 《실속없이》 a bloated up; a false sense of satiety 《가스로》 get bloated up [with gas]/ ~가 부르다 《먹지 않아도》 have a false sense of satiety.

헛보다 get the wrong view (of); fail to see [properly]; mistake. みあやまる

헛보이다 get improperly seen; be misviewed; get mistaken. ごかいされる

헛부엌 an open-air kitchen.

헛불 a random shot; a poor shot/ ~놓다 misshoot; miss a shot. むだうち

헛소리 《헛말》 gibberish; empty talk; nonsense; silly talk 《정신없는 말》 talking in delirium/ ~하다 talk delirium 《당치 않은》 talk nonsense. そらごと

헛소문(一所聞) a groundless[false] rumor; idle gossip.

헛손질 pawing the air/ ~하다 paw the air.

헛수 《바둑・장기》 a useless[wrong] move / ~를 두다 make a useless[wrong] move. むだなて

헛수고 vain error; lost[fruitless] labor / ~하다 make vain efforts; work in vain; lose one's labor/ ~로 돌아가다 one's labor comes to nothing. とろう

헛웃음 a smirk; a [conscious] simper; a forced[feigned, an affected] laugh/ ~을 웃다 force a laugh; smirk; smile a forced smile. つくりわらい

헛일 vain[fruitless] effort; lost labour / ~하다[되다] make vain efforts; exert oneself to no purpose. むだなこと

헛잠 a feigned[pretended] sleep; playing possum. そらね

헛잡다 《잘못 쥐다》 fail to grip[cluth, grasp]; let slip through one's fingers 《잘못 고르다》 pick up wrongly; fail to pick up the right one 《도둑을》 arrest by mistake/찻잔을 헛잡아 떨어드리다 let a cup slip and drop. あやまってつかむ

헛장 a brag; big[tall] talk; a bulff / ~치다 bluff; burl pretended defiance (at a person).

헛짚다 make a false[wrong] stop ⇨헛다리짚다.

헛총(一銃) a blank catridge; a blank shot/~을 놓다 fire blank shots/~질하다 fire a blank. くうほう

헛턱 《빈턱》 an unrealized entertainment; a Barmecide's feast.

헛헛증(一症) hungriness; a chronic hunger/ ~이 있다 suffer from chronic hunger.

헛헛하다 feel hungry; be [very] hungry. ひもじい

헝겁지겁 leaping with joy; dancing for joy; in raptures. よろこびまくって

헝겊 a small piece of cloth/ ~ 조각 a scrap of cloth.

헝클다 tangle; entangle; dishevel; kink; disarrange/실을 ~ tangle thread. もつれさせる

헝클어지다 be tangled; be entangled; be in a tangle; kink/헝클어진 실 tangled thread. からまる

헤 agape; wide open/~하고 웃다 laugh

with *one's* mouth wide open. はあん

**헤근거리다** be shaky; be rickety; wobble /헤근헤근 shaking; loose/사개가 헤근거리며 놀다 dovetails wobble. ぐらぐらする

**헤다**¹ 《헤엄치다》 swim; take[have] a swim. およぐ

**헤다**² count ⇨세다. けいさんする

**헤다**³ 《멋대로 하다》 act[behave] as *one* likes; have *one's* own way.

**헤대다** bustle about; busy *oneself* about. かけまわる

**헤덤비다** rush about. せかせかする

**헤뜨리다** scatter[about]; strew; disperse /방안에 종이 조각을 ~ litter a room with scraps of paper. ばらまく

**헤매다** ①《돌아다니다》 wander[roam] about; rove; walk around; search around (*for*)/거리를 ~ wander about in the street ②《갈피못하나》 be at a loss; be perplexed; have a bard time; grope/어쩔 줄 몰라 ~ be at a loss what to do. さまよう

**헤먹다** (be) loose[-fitting]; (*a hole*) get loose. ゆるい

**헤무르다** (be) feeble; flaccid; unstrung; falling apart/헤무른 사람 a feeble[sapless] person. ぐにゃぐにゃだ

**헤룸다** (be) weak and watery; flabby and pale.

**헤벌어지다** be very wide; get shallow/헤벌어진 그릇 an open shallow dish.

**헤벌쭉** wide open/~하다 (be) wide open /~ 웃다 smile a broad smile.

**헤살** 《훼방》 slander; an obstacle /공연히 ~놓지 마라 Don't intrude where are not wanted. ぼうがい

**헤식다** fragile; frail; soft; flabby; infirm; (be) brittle/헤식은 쌀 soft rice. もろい

**헤실헤실** frittering away; inadvertently running out of/돈을 ~ 다 써 버리다 fritter away all the money *one* has. しらずしらず

**헤심헤심하다** (be) loose; slack. こころぼそい

**헤아리다** ①《고려하다》 consider; weigh; ponder; deliberate/일을 잘 헤아려서 하다 undertake a plan with due consideration ②《추측하다》 fathom; sound; conjecture; surmise/두 사람의 마음을 ~ fathom a person ③《수를》 count; calculate; compute; estimate/헤아릴 수 없다 be incalculable[innumerable]. こうりょうする

**헤어나다** get out of; get over; find *one's* way out of; extricate *oneself* from/헤어날 길이 없다 have no way out. まぬがれる

**헤어지다** ①《이별》 part from; part company (*with*); separate; divorce *oneself* (*from*); bid farewell 《분산》 break up/아내와 ~ divorce *one's* wife ②《흩어지다》 get scattered[strewn, dispersed]/ 졸업생이 각처로 ~ The graduates are scattered in all directions ③《갈라지다》 become chapped. すりむける

**헤엄** swimming; a swim/~치다 swim; have a swim/나는 ~을 조금도 못 친다 I can't swim a stroke. およぎ

**헤적이다** ransack; rummage/공을 찾느라 수풀을 ~ rummage the thicket to search a ball.

**헤죽거리다** walk briskly swinging *one's* arms/헤죽헤죽 walking briskly swinging *one's* arms.

**헤집다** tear up; dig up; turn up/닭이 흙을 ~ a chicken scratches the dirt up. ほりかきちらす

**헤치다** ①《파다》 dig up; turn up/흙을 파~ dig up earth ②《흩드리다》 disperse; scatter; break up/군중을 ~ disperse a crowd ③《좌우로》 push aside; pull a part; make *one's* way through.

**헤프다** ①《물건이》 be not durable; be soon used up; be eay to wear out/이 비누는 ~ This soap doesn't last long. ② 《돈이》 (be) wasteful; uneconomical/돈을 헤프게 쓰다 spend money lavishly ③ 《입이》 (be) verbose; voluble; talkative; wordy/그는 입이 ~ He talks too much; He is a verbose speaker ④《몸가짐이》 (be) loose; dissipated; dissolute/~이 헤픈 여자 a loose woman.

**헤피** wastefully; lavishly; extravagantly/돈을 ~ 쓰다 waste[squander] money. むだに

**헤하다** beam with joy; grin.

**헷갈리다** ①《마음이》 be confused; *one's* attention is distracted ②《뜻이》 be confused[tangled]; be hard to distinguish 《길 따위가》 be hard to find[see, make out]. ろうばいする

**헹가래** tossing; hoisting (*one*) shoulder-high/~치다 toss[hoist] (*a person*) shoulder-high. どうあげ

**헹구다** wash out; rinse away/빨래를 ~ rinse laundry in fresh water after washing. ゆすぐ

**헹글헹글** loose-fitting; baggy/~하다 (be) loose-fitting; baggy. だぶだぶ

**혀** ①《사람의》 a tongue 《동물의》 a lingua /~가 잘 돌아가다 have a glib tongue/~를 깨물다 bite *one's* tongue ②《악기의》 the clapper [of a bell]. した

**혀꼬부랑이** a person with a speech impediment. したもつれるひと

**혀끝** the tip of the tongue. ぜったん

**혀짤배기** a tongue-tied person. したたらずのひと

**혀차다** ①《혀를 참》 click *one's* tongue; tut; be wonder-struck ②《놀라와서》 admire; marvel; be astounded. したをうつ

**혁대(革帶)** a leather belt/~장식 a buckle. かわおび

**혁명(革命)** a revolution; a revolutionary upheaval/~하다 make a revolution; revolutionize/~을 일으키다 raise a re-

혁신(革新) reform; renovation; innovation/~하다 reform; renorate; innovate/정체의 ~ a political reform/ ~과 a reformist group/~ 세력 the progressive force/~ 운동 a revolution movement/ ~자 a reformer. かくしん

혁혁(赫赫) ~하다 (be) bright; brilliant; radiant; glorious; distinguished/명성이 ~하다 have a brilliant reputation. かっかく

현(弦) ①(활의 시위)a bowstring ②(악기의)a string; a chord; gut ③(기하)a chord 《사건》a subtence 《직각 삼각형의 사변》a hypotenuse ④(달의)a quarter. げん

현(現) the present; the existence; the actuality/~ 대통령 the President in office. げん

현(絃) (줄)a string; a chord; catgut 《바이올린의》gut. げん

현가(現價) the present[current] price. げんか

현거(現居) dwelling at present; one's present residence[address].

현격(懸隔) a difference; a disparity; a discrepancy; a gulf; a chasm/~하다 be different; be wide apart from each other/~한 차이 a wide difference. けんかく

현관(玄關) the porch; the entrance; the front door. げんかん

현관(顯官) (고관)a high official; a [government] dignitary. けんかん

현교(懸橋) a suspended[suspension] bridge; a bridge (over a gorge).

현군(賢君) a wise[good] king. けんくん

현금(現今) now; today; at present; in these days; a modern days; the present day[time]/~에 이르기까지 until[up to] the persent. げんこん

현금(玄琴) (악기의)a kind of harp.

현금(現金) cash; actual[ready] money 《맞돈》cash down; prompt[spot] cash; ready funds/~으로 지불하다 pay in cash/ ~ 수입 a cash income/~ 출납부 a cash book/~ 거래 a cash transaction. げんきん

현기(眩氣) dizziness; giddiness; vertigo /~증 vertigo; dizziness; giddiness/~증을 느끼다 be[feel] dizzy; get[feel] giddy. めまい

현념(懸念) concern; anxiety; misgivings; uneasiness; apprehension/ ~하다 be anxious (about, for); feel uneasy; be concerned about. けねん

현달(顯達) attaining eminence and acquiring fame; eminence/ ~하다 attain eminence and acquire fame; win fame and eminence; become famous and successful. けんたつ

현대(現代) modern time; today; our time; the present age[day, generation]/ ~의 modern; of today; present-day/~화 하다 modernize; be modernized/ ~ 교육 modern education/~문 《문체》current style/~ 문학 current literature/ ~ 사상 modern ideas; contemporary thought/~ 생활 present-day life/ ~식 modern style/~어 living language[idiom]/~인 a modern/~ 작가 a contemporary writer. げんだい

현등(舷燈) 《선박의》a side light 《항공기》 a position light.

현란(眩亂) dizziness; the whirl of the brain/~하다 (be) dizzy; dazed; confused. せいしんがくらむみだれること

현란(絢爛) brilliancy; floweriness; gaudiness; splendor; gorgeousness/ ~하다 (be) gorgeous; brilliant. げんらん

현량(賢良) wisdom and virtue/ ~하다 (be) wise and good[virtuous]. けんりょう

현명(賢明) intelligence; wisdom; sagacity 《분별》prudence 《양식》good sense 《상책》advisability/ ~하다 (be) wise; sage; prudent; discreet/~한 판단 sound judgment/~한 사람 a wise man/~한 조치를 취하다 adopt[takeup] a wise policy; act wisely. けんめい

현명(懸命) staking[risking] one's life/ ~하다 stake[risk] one's life.

현명(顯名) winning a name[fame]/~하다 win a name; gain fame; become famous[prominent].

현모(賢母) a wise mother/~ 양처 a wise mother [to her children] and a good wife [to her husband]. けんぼ

현목(玄木) unbleached cotton cloth[muslin].

현몽(現夢) ~하다 appear[come to a person] in a dream; appear in a person's dream.

현묘(玄妙) mystery; abstruseness; occultness; mysteriousness/ ~하다 (be) abstruse; occult; recondite; deep; mysterious/~한 사상 a profound idea.

현무암(玄武岩) 《광》basalt; whinstone. げんぶがん

현물(現物) the actual thing[article]; 《주식의》spot goods; spot; actual shares 〈영〉; stocks〈미〉/~ 가격 spot prices[quotation]/~ 급여 an allowance in kind /~ 거래[매매] spot trading[transaction]/~ 소득 income in kind/~ 시장 the spot market/~점 a spot firm. げんぶつ

현미(玄米) uncleaned[unhulled] rice; brown rice. げんまい

현미경(顯微鏡) a microscope/ ~으로 보다 look at (a thing) through a microscope /~ 사진 a microphotograph/전자 ~ an electron microscope/~ 검사 a microscopic examination/~ 관찰 fractography /~의 촛점을 맞추다 focus a microscope

**현부**(賢婦) a wise[virtuous] woman; a virtuous daughter-in-law. げんぷ

**현부인**(賢夫人) a wise woman; a lady of wisdom; your [honored] wife. けんぷじん

**현사**(賢士) a sage; wise scholar. げんし

**현삼**(玄蔘) 〖식〗 a kind of figwort; *Scrophularia buergeriana*(학명).

**현상**(現狀) the present situation[state]; the actual state[condition]; the existing state of things[affairs]/~ 유지 maintenance of the status quo/~을 유지하다 maintain the status quo. げんじょう

**현상**(現象) an appearance; a happening; a phenomenon(*pl.* -mena)/일시적 ~ a passing phase/~계 〖철〗 the phenomenal world/사회 ~ a social phenomenon /자연 ~ natural phenomena/물리 ~ physical development. げんしょう

**현상**(現像) 《사진의》 developing; development/~하다 develop (*a film*)/~액(液) a developing solution; a developer /~지(紙) a developing-out paper(略: D.O.P.). げんしょう

**현상**(賢相) a wise minister of state; a wise premier. けんしょう

**현상**(懸賞) offer of a prize[reward]; a prize; a reward/~하다 offer a prize [reward]; set a price on (*an offender's head*)/~금 a prize [money]/~ 모집 a prize contest/~ 당선자 a prize winner /~ 문제 a problem for the prize contest /~을 타다 win a prize. けんしょう

**현상태**(現狀態) the present circumstances [situation]/~로는 judging by the present situation.

**현세**(現世) this world; this life; the present age/~주의 secularism. げんせい

**현손**(玄孫) descendants of the fourth generation; a great-great-grandson. げんそん

**현송**(現送) cash sending; shipment of gold; specie shipment/ ~하다 send in cash; send the [actual] goods/금을 ~ 하다 ship gold (*to*); make a gold shipment (*to*). げんそう

**현수**(懸垂) suspension/~ 운동 exercising on a horizontal bar/ ~막 a hanging [suspended] banner[placard]/ ~선(線) 〖수〗 a catenary. けんすい

**현숙**(賢淑) fidelity; womanly[feminine] wisdom and virtue/ ~하다 (be) wise and virtuous; fidel; graceful.

**현시**(現時) today; now; the present time. げんじ

**현시**(顯示) revelation; show; display/ ~하다 show; display; unfold; reveal; uncover.

**현시대**(現時代) the present age ⇒현대(現代). げんじだい

**현신**(賢臣) a loyal vassal; a wise retainer.

**현신**(現身) ~하다 present *one*self before a superior; put in *one's* appearance. げんしん

**현실**(現實) the actual; reality; actuality; the realities of life 《공론에 대한》 a hard fact/~을 무시하다 ignore realities/~론 realism; a bread-and-butter theory/~ 도피 escapism/~성 a bread-and-butter theory/~성 reality/~주의 actualism; realism げんじつ

**현실화**(現實化) actualization; realization; materialzation/~하다 actualize; realize 《금리 환율 따위의》 readjust to a realistic level.

**현악**(絃樂) 〖음〗 string music / ~기 a string[ed] instrument; the strings/~ 사중주 a string quartet[te]/~ 합주 a string orchestra.

**현안**(懸案) an outstanding question; a pending question[problem]/~으로 남겨 두다 leave (*a matter*) in abeyance. けんあん

**현애**(懸崖) an overhanging cliff; a precipice; an escrap. けんがい

**현양**(顯揚) exaltation; extolment/~하다 gain fame; become famous; exalt; extol. けんよう

**현역**(現役) active service 《휴직에 대한》 service on full pay/~에 복무중이다 be in active service; be on service/~ 군인 a soldier on service; a serviceman on active duty/~ 장교 an officer on the active list. げんえき

**현연하다**(泫然─) tears are dropping copiously; tears stream down ceaselessly. げんぜん

**현연하다**(現然─) (be) palpable; visible; clear; plain; distinct. まのあたりにはっきしている

**현연하다**(顯然─) (be) clear; manifest. はっきあらわれている

**현연하다**(眩然─) dazed; (be) dazzled. めがくらんでいる

**현우**(賢友) a wise[an intelligent] friend.

**현우**(賢愚) wisdom or folly; cleverness or foolishness; the wise and the foolish. けんぐ

**현월**(玄月) September of the lunar month.

**현유**(現有) actuality; the actual[existing] being/~의 existent; in being; on hand/~ 금액 cash on hand/~ 물품 goods in stock.

**현인**(賢人) a sage; a wise man. けんじん

**현임**(現任) the present office[post]/~자 the present holder of the office. げんしょく

**현장**(現場) the [actual] spot; the scene [ot action]; 《작업의》 the scene of labor / ~을 목격하다 be an eyewitness of the disaster[accident]/ ~ 감독 a site [field] overseer/ ~ 검증 an on-the-spot inspection (of *the scene* of *a murder*)/ ~ 보고 a field report/ ~ 시찰

a spot inspection／～ 조사 an on-the-spot probe.  げんば

**현재(現在)** ①now; at present; the present [time]／나는 ～의 지위에 만족한다 I am contented where I am. ②《문법》the present tense／그 동사는 ～다 The verb is in the present. ③《실제》actuality／～의 회원수 the actual membership.  げんざい

**현재(賢才)** distinguished ability[talent]; a man of talent[ability]; a wise man.  けんさい

**현저(顯著)** ～하다《두드러지다》(be) notable; remarkable; marked; conspicuous; salient; striking; distinguished; considerable; evident《명백하다》(be) obvious; eminent; prominent; outstanding／～하게 발달하다 make a remarkable [conspicuous] progress.  けんちょ

**현정부(現政府)** the present Government; the present Administration.  げんせいふ

**현제(舷梯)** an accommodation ladder; a gangway ladder (of *a vessel*).

**현존(現存)** living; extant《형용사적》existing／ ～하다 exist; be in existence; be extant; subsist; remain subsisting／～의 existing; living; actual;extant／ ～ 작가 living writers.  げんそん

**현지(現地)** the actual place; the field; the [very] spot／ ～ 방송 on-the-spot broadcast／～ 조사하다 a field investigation party／～ 시찰 여행 a fact-finding tour／～ 특파원 a correspondent on the scene[in the field].  げんち

**현직(現職)** the present office[post]; the office now occupied[held]／ ～ 대통령 the incumbent president／～에 머물다 remain in *one's* present post. げんしょく

**현직(顯職)** high office; an eminent[prominent] post.  けんしょく

**현찰(現札)** cash; actual[ready] money.

**현처(賢妻)** an intelligent wife; a wise[virtuous] wife; a good housewife.  けんさい

**현철(賢哲)** a sage 《총칭》the wise; sagacity; wisdom／～하다 (be) wise; intelligent; sagacious.  けんてつ

**현칭(現稱)** the present name.  げんざいのめいしょう

**현탁액(懸濁液)**《물·화》suspension.

**현품(現品)** the actual article[goods]; stock in hand; goods in stock; stocks／～을 보지 않고는 뭐라 말할 수 없다 I cannot say either way before I inspect the article.  げんぴん

**현하(現下)** the present time ⋮ 현금.げんか

**현하 구변(懸河口辯)** fluency in speech; eloquence; an eloquent speech.  けんがのくちさき

**현행(現行)**《형용사적》existing; current;" prevailing／～의 existing; present; current; in operation／～중에 체포되다 be arrested in the very act; be caught red-handed／ ～ 규정 the regulations in force／ 맞춤법 the current spelling system／～범(범죄)a flagrant delict[offense];《사람》a criminal caught red-handed[in the act]／ ～법 the existing[operative] law.  げんこう

**현현(顯現)** a manifestation; an expression; evidence／～하다 manifest; express; evidence.

**현혹(眩惑)** a daze; bewilderment; dazzlement／ ～하다 dazzle; daze; blind; ～시켜 …하게 하다 dazzle[mislead] (*a person*) into doing.  げんわく

**현화 식물(顯花植物)** a phanerogamous plant; a phanerogam.

**현황(現況)** the present position; the present condition[status, situation].  げんきょう

**현훈(眩暈)** dizziness; giddiness; vertigo／ ～증 vertigo.  めまい

**혈(穴)**《구멍》a hole 《풍수지리의》a spot where influences to *one's* fortune converge 《침의》a region for acupuncture.

**혈거(穴居)** cave dwelling; troglodytism／～하다 live[dwell] in a cave／ ～인 a cave-man; a cave-dweller; a troglodyte／ ～ 시대 the cave age. けっきょ

**혈관(血管)**《해》a blood vessel; a vein; an artery／ ～ 압축 thlipsis／ ～ 압축기 a compressor／ ～ 파열 rupture[bursting, laceration] of the blood vessels.  けっかん

**혈괴(血塊)** clotted blood; a clot of blood; gore／옷에 ～가 붙어 있었다 The clothing was stained with clots of blood.

**혈구(血球)** a blood corpuscle; a globule／～ 계수 the blood count／백～ a leucocyte; a migratory cell; a white blood cell／적～ a red blood corpuscle; a hematocyte.  けっきゅう

**혈기(血氣)** ①《체력》vitality; strength; stamina ②《의기》animal spirits; hot blood; youthful vigor[ardor]／～가 왕성하다 be full of youthful vigor; be in the prime of health.  けっき

**혈뇨(血尿)**《의》haematuria.

**혈담(血痰)** bloody phlegm.  けったん

**혈로(血路)** a perilous way out; a difficult escape-route／～를 열다 find a perilous way out; cut[carve out] a way through (*the enemy*).  けつろ

**혈루(血淚)** tears of blood; bitter tears ～를 흘리다 shed[cry] bitter tears.  けつるい

**혈맥(血脈)**《혈관》a blood vessel《정맥》a vein《동맥》an artery《혈연》blood relationship; consanguinity／ ～ 상통(相通) consanguinity; blood relationship.  けつみゃく

**혈맹(血盟)** a blood pledge.

**혈반(血斑)**《의》a blood spot.  けっぱん

**혈변(血便)** bloody excrement.  けつべん

**혈병(血餠)** a blood clot; a cruor.

**혈상(血相)** the color of *one's* face; a threatening[menacing] look.

**혈색**(血色) color of the face; complexion／~이 좋지 않다 look pale; have a bad complexion; look sallow. けっしょく

**혈색소**(血色素) hemoglobin.

**혈서**(血書) writing in blood; something written in blood／~하다 write in blood／~로 맹서하다 write a pledge with [in] one's blood. けつしょ

**혈석**(血石) 〖광〗 bloodstone; heliotrope.

**혈성**(血誠) devotion; sincerity; loyalty.

**혈속**(血屬) a blood-relation; a relative [connection] by blood 《남자》 a kinsman 《여자》 a kinswoman; kinsfolk; kinship. げぞく

**혈손**(血孫) 《자손》 direct descendants; one's own flesh and blood.

**혈안**(血眼) a bloodshot eye／~이 되어 찾다 make a desperate effort to find; look for (a thing) with eager eyes. じゅうけつしため

**혈압**(血壓) blood pressure／고[저] ~ high [low] blood pressure／~계 a sphygmomanometer／~을 재다 measure one's blood pressure. けつあつ

**혈액**(血液) blood／~형 blood group; a type of blood／~검사 a blood test／~ 금고[은행] a blood bank／~ 순환 circulation (of blood)／운동을 하면 ~의 순환이 좋아진다 Exercise whips up the circulation [of the blood]. けつえき

**혈연**(血緣) blood-relation; family ties [connections]／~ 관계 blood-relationship; kinship; consanguinity／~ 단체 a kinship society. けつえん

**혈온**(血溫) 〖의〗 blood-heat; the temperature of the blood／~점(點) the blood-heat point. ちのおんど

**혈육**(血肉) ①《피와 살》 blood and flesh ②《자녀》 one's own children; kinsmen; blood relations／~ 상쟁 domestic discord[trouble]／슬하에 ~이 없다 be childless. けつにく

**혈장**(血漿) 〖해〗 blood plasma／~ 공장 plasma plant. けっしょう

**혈전**(血栓) a thrombus／~증(症) 〖의〗 thrombosis.

**혈전**(血戰) a bloody[sanguinary] battle; a desperate[bloody] fight; a murderous battle; a war to the knife[death]／~하다 fight a bloody battle; fight desperately. けっせん

**혈족**(血族) 〖관계〗 kinship; blood-relationship; ties of blood 《사람》 one's flesh and blood; a blood-relation／~ 결혼 a consanguineous marriage; an intermarriage／~ 관계 blood relationship; kinship. けつぞく

**혈청**(血淸) 〖의〗 serum (pl. sera)／~ 주사 a serum injection／~ 요법 serum treatment[therapy]; serotherapy／~학 serology. けっせい

**혈충**(血忠) utmost loyalty.

**혈침**(血沈) 〖의〗 precipitation of blood／~을 재다 measure the precipitation of blood.

**혈통**(血統) blood; descent; lineage; pedigree; stock; a family line／~주의《국적 취득의》 jus sanguinis(L)／~이 끊어지다 The line has died out.／~이 좋다 come of a good stock. けっとう

**혈투**(血鬪) a bloody fight ⇨혈전(血戰).

**혈판**(血判) sealing with blood／~하다 seal with one's blood／~서 a petition sealed with blood／연판장에 ~하다 seal a compact with blood.

**혈한**(血汗) ①〖의〗 a blood sweat ②《피와 땀》 blood and sweat.

**혈행**(血行) circulation of the blood／~계 a tachometer／~ 기관 circulatory organs／~ 장해 interruption in blood circulation／~을 돕다 quicken the circulation of the blood. けっこう

**혈혈**(子子) solitary; alone／~하다 (be) solitary; lonely／~ 단신 all alone in the world; have neither friends nor relatives／~ 무의(無依)하다 have no one to turn to for help. けつけつ

**혈흔**(血痕) a blood-stain／~이 묻은 blood-stained. けっこん

**혐기**(嫌忌) dislike; aversion; abhorrence／~하다 dislike; detest; avert／~성 식물 an anaerobe. けんき

**혐염**(嫌厭) dislike; loathing; disgust; hate; detestation／~하다 dislike; loathe; hate; be disgusted (with). けんえん

**혐오**(嫌惡) hatred; disgust; aversion; repugnance; abomination; abhorrence; antipathy／~하다 hate dislike; detest; be averse to; abominate; loathe／~의 정을 품다 feel hatred (toward); feel repugnance to revolt at; nurse hatred (against). きらいにくむこと

**혐의**(嫌疑) ①〖의심〗 suspicion; charge／~하다 suspect; be suspicious of／~자 a suspected person; a suspect (범죄의) a criminal suspect／~를 받다 fall[come] under suspicion／~를 두다 suspect (one) of／그는 절도의 ~로 잡혔다 He was arrested on the suspicion of theft. ②《미움》 aversion; detestation／~하다 dislike; feel an aversion to. けんぎ

**혐점**(嫌點) a cause of suspicion; a suspicious aspect; a questionable point. いみきらわれるてん

**협**(峽) a gorge; a ravine; a defile. はざま

**협각**(夾角) 〖수〗 an included angle. きょうかく

**협객**(俠客) a man of chivalrous spirit; a chivalrous person; a street knight／그는 ~나은 데가 있으므로 흔히 두목이라고 불리운다 He is often called a boss, having a dash of chivalry in his composition. きょうかく

**협격**(挾擊) attack on both sides[flanks]; pincer attack／~하다 attack (the enemy) from both sides[flanks]; 《포위로》 catch (the enemy) in a cross-fire.

협곡(峽谷) a gorge; a ravine; a glen; a canyon; a gulch〈미〉. きょうこく

협골(頰骨) 《해》 the cheekbone; the zygomatic bone. ほおぼね

협공(挾攻) an attack from both flanks / ~하다 an attack (the enemy) from both sides/~ 작전 a pincer operation / ~을 받다 be attacked on both sides; find oneself between two fires. きょうこう

협궤(狹軌) a narrow gauge/ ~ 철도 a narrow gauge railway. きょうき

협기(俠氣) a chivalrous spirit; chivalry / ~ 있는 사람 a chivalrous[a gallant] man. きょうき

협동(協同) cooperation; collaboration; common action; concert; union/ ~하다 cooperate; collaborate; work together; unite; act in concert[union]; join forces with/~ 조합 a cooperative union/ ~ 정신 cooperative spirit; esprit de corps(F); the spirit of teamwork/~ 기업 a cooperative[joint] enterprise/ ~ 일치하여 행동하다 act in concert. きょうどう

협량(狹量) narrow-mindedness/ ~하다 (be) narrow-minded; ungenerous; intolerant. きょうりょう

협력(協力) cooperation; combined efforts / ~하다 unite; act in concert with; work together; cooperate with (one)/ ~자 a collaborator; a co-worker/상호 ~ mutual cooperation/새 사업에 ~해 주시기를 바랍니다 I must beg you to cooperate with me in the new attempt. きょうりょく

협로(狹路) a narrow road 《큰 길의》 a branch road 《산속의》 a mountain road. きょうろ

협문(夾門)・ a side-gate[-door].

협박(脅迫) 《공갈》threat; menace; 《법》intimidation/~하다 threaten dislike; detest; be averse to/~장 a threatening [an intimidation] letter/ ~죄 [a crime of] intimidation / ~하여 자백시키다 intimidate one into confession/권총으로 ~하다 threaten (a person) with a revolver. きょうはく

협사(俠士) a chivalrous person ⇒협객 (俠客). おとこだてのひと

협살(挾殺) 《야구》run-down.

협상(協商) 《교섭》 negotiations; conversations 《협약》 an entente(F); 《불교》 an agreement/~하다 negotiate/ ~ 조약 an entente [cordiale](F); an agreement; an understanding/ ~국 the Entente Power; the Allies/~을 맺다 conlude an entente (with). きょうしょう

협성(協成) collaboration/ ~하다 collaborate; work out together; accomplish in concert[cooperation]. きょうりょくしてなしとげること

협소(狹小) narrowness; smallness/ ~하다 (be) narrow; confined; limited; small-sized/ ~한 방 a small room/지역이 ~하다 be small in area. きょうしょう

협실(夾室) a side room. わきへや

협심(協心) cooperation; unison; accord; concert/ ~하다 act in unison/~해서 일하다 work in unison. きょうしん

협심증(狹心症) stricture of the heart; angina pectoris; stenocardia.

협애(狹隘) narrowness; tightness; limitedness/ ~하다 (be) narrow; limited; confined. きょうあい

협약(協約) an agreement; a convention; a pact 《정치》 an entente(F)/~하다 conclude an agreement/~노동 ~ a labor agreement/단체 ~ a collective agreement/~국 Entente Powers. きょうやく

협의(協議) conference; consultation; discussion/ ~하다 confer (with); consult (with); deliberate (on a matter); discuss (a matter); talk over; hold conference/ ~ 사항 subjects[topics] of discussion; the program; a matter for consultation/ ~ 이혼 a divorce by agreement/ ~회 a conference; a council/충분히 ~하다 deliberate fully (over a matter)/ ~가 잘 되다 come to an agreement. きょうぎ

협의(狹義) a narrow sense/ ~의 교육 education in a narrow sense/ ~로 해석하다 construe in a limited[restricted] sense of the term. きょうぎ

협잡(挾雜) trickery; swindle; imposture; fraudulence; deception/ ~하다 cheat; swindle; embezzle; commit fraud; impose/~군 a swindler; a imposter; a cheat; a trickster/~물(物) a spurious [bogus] article; a fake; a sham/~질 fraudulent practices /도박에서 ~하다 cheat in gambling.

협장(脇杖) crutches/~을 짚고 걷다 walk on crutches. ささえ

협정(協定) agreement; arrangement; convention; pact/ ~하다 agree upon (the price); arrange (with); stipulate (with); make arrangements (for)/ ~ 가격 an agreed[a stipulated] price/ ~서 a protocol/~ 세율 a conventional tariff / ~ 임금 wages agreed (upon); agreed wages/~ 조항 agreed terms; stipulations/휴전 ~ an armistice agreement/ 상호 ~ a bilateral agreement/ ~이 성립하다 reach an agreement/ ~을 맺다 conclude a convention. きょうてい

협조(協調) 《협력》cooperation; concerted action 《조화》 harmony 《타협》 conciliation/ ~하다 cooperate; act in concert (with)/ ~심 a spirit of harmony/ 국제간의 ~ international cooperation/ ~적 정신으로 in a spirit of cooperation. きょうじょ

협주곡(協奏曲) 《음》 a concerto. きょうそうきょく

협죽도(夾竹桃) 《식》 a sweet oleander; a rosebay; a garden phlox.

협착(狹窄) **(**좁음**)** narrowness; 〖의〗 stricture; constriction; strangulation; stenosis; contraction／～하다 (be) narrow; small; limited; strangulated; constricted／요도(尿道) ～ 〖의〗 stricture of the urethra／～ 골반 a contracted pelvis／～탄 a miniature cartridge; miniature munition. ひじょうにせまいこと

협찬(協贊) consent; assent; approval; sanction／～하다 approve; consent[assent] to／의회의 ～을 얻다 be approved by the assembly. きょうさん

협촌(峽村) a mountain[an isolated] village; a remote hamlet.

협하다(狹一) (be) narrow-minded; illberal; intolerant. せまい

협화(協和) harmony; concert; concert; 〖음〗 consonance／～하다 be in harmony [concord] with; act in concert; be consonant (with)／～음 〖음〗 a consonance; a concord; euphony. きょうわ

협회(協會) a society; an associatoin; a league (학술적) an institution／농구 ～ the Basket League／아시아 ～ the Asiatic Society. きょうかい

혓바늘 an eruption on the tongue／～이 돋다 have a rough tongue[a cat's tongue].

혓바닥 the flat of the tongue／～으로 핥다 lap with the tongue.

혓소리 〖언〗 a lingual [sound]. ぜつおん

형(兄) **(**남자끼리의**)** an elder brother **(**선배**)** a senior **(**여자끼리의**)** an elder[older] sister **(**친구가**)** you／～만한 아우 없다《속담》 The younger sibling is never the equal of the older. あに

형(刑) a punishment; a penalty (선고) a sentence／～을 받다 be sentenced to; be convicted／～을 언도하빠 pass[pronounce] a sentence on. けい

형(形) form; shape; format／대～ large size／소～ small size. かたち

형(型) **(**원형**)** a model; a mold; a matrix **(**양식**)** style; type; pattern／최신～ the latest models (of)／신～ 자동차 a new model car. かた

형강(形鋼) section[shape] steel／～ 압연기 a rolling mill for section steel.

형광(螢光) 〖물〗 fluorescent light／～등 a fluorescent lamp／～체 a fluorescent substance／～성 fluorescence; fluorescent／～ 조명 fluorescent lighting／～ 표백 fluorescent bleaching／～을 발하다 fluoresce. けいこう

형구(刑具) an implement of punishment . [torture]. けいぐ

형국(形局) appearance; phase **(**형세**)** a situation **(**관상・풍수지리의**)** aspect.

형극(荊棘) thorns; brambles／～의 길 a thorny path; a brambly way **(**수난의 길**)** the way of the Cross. とげ

형기(刑期) the term of imprisonment; a prison term; the term of penal servitude; one's time／～가 만료되어 출옥하다 leave prison[be set free] at the expiration of one's term. けいき

형륙(刑戮) **(**형벌**)** a punishment; a penalty **(**사형**)** capital punishment; execution／～하다 send to the scaffold; condemn (a person) to capital punishment.

형률(刑律) penal code; criminal law. けいりつ

형명(刑名) charge; the name of a penalty[crime]. けいめい

형무소(刑務所) a prison; a jail; a penitentiary. けいむしょ

형벌(刑罰) a punishment; a penalty／～하다 punish; inflict[impose] a punishment[penalty] on／～을 면하다 escape punishment[justice]. けいばつ

형법(刑法) 〖법〗 criminal law; jus criminal; crown law〈영〉／～에 비추어 처분하다 deal with (a person) according to the provisions of the criminal code／국제 ～ international criminal law. けいほう

형부(兄夫) a brother-in-law; the husband of a girl's elder sister.

형사(刑事) ①**(**사건**)** a criminal[penal] case／～상의 책임 penal responsibility ②**(**사람**)** a police investigator; a hound of the law; a [police] detective／～ 재판 a criminal trial／～ 문제 a criminal case／～범 a criminal[penal] offense／～ 사건 a criminal case; a penal offence／～ 소송 criminal action[prosecution]. けいじ

형상(形狀) form; shape; configuration. けいじょう

형상(形象) ①**(**물건**)** shape; form ②**(**상상의**)** a shape; a figure; an appearance; a phenomenon(pl. -mena). けいしょう

형색(形色) form and color; general looks; appearance.

형석(螢石) 〖광〗 fluorspar; fluorite. けいせき

형설(螢雪) diligent study／～지공(之功) diligent study; fruits of diligent study／～의 공을 쌓다 prosecute one's studies for years. けいせつ

형성(形成) formation／～하다 form; make; constitute; mold; take shape; build up／～소 formative stuff; plastic element／～질 〖동〗 formative substance／～기(期) a formative period／～층 〖식〗 cambium／인간 ～ character building／～되다 be formed[built up, constituted].

형세(形勢) ①**(**사물의**)** the situation; the position[state] of affairs; the state of things (전망) the prospects; the outlook (징후) signs; indications; appearance／～가 불리하다 The situation is unfavorable. ②**(**살림의**)** circumstances／～가 어렵다 be in difficult circumstances. けいせい

형소법(刑訴法) the Criminal Procedure Code.

형수(兄嫂) **(**형의 아내**)** the wife of one's

형승지지(形勝之地) a scenic[beauty] spot; a place of natural beauty; picturesque lands[regions].

형식(形式) a formality; a form 《철학》a mode／정당한 ～을 밟다 go through due formalities／～ 논리 formal logic／～론 formalism／～미 the beauty of form／～주의자 a formalist.  けいしき

형안(炯眼) a quick[sharp, keen] eye; a penetration eye; perspicacity; acuteness; keen insight; farsightedness／～지사(之士) a man of acute discernment[keen insight].  けいがん

형언(形言) expression; description／～하다 describe; express／～할 수 없다 It is beyond description. けいようしていうこと

형옥(刑獄) ①《형벌》a penalty; a punishment; imprisonment ②《감옥》a prison.  けいごく

형용(形容) ①《형상》form; figure; appearance ②《서술》description 《비유》a metaphore; a figure of speech; a figurative expression／～하다 qualify; modify; describe; put into words／～사 an adjective／～어 an epithet／～할 수 없다 beyond expression.  けいよう

형이상(形而上) ～의 metapyvsical; abstract; immaterial; incorporeal／～학 metaphysics; metaphysical philosophy／～학자 a metaphysician.  けいじじょう

형이하(形而下) ～의 physical; concrete; corporeal; material／～학 a concrete [physical] science.  けいじか

형장(刑場) an execution-ground; a place of execution／～의 이슬로 사라지다 die on the execution-ground[scaffold].  けいじょう

형장(兄丈) you.

형적(形迹) 《흔적》traces; vestiges; marks; signs; evidence; indications／고대 문명의 ～ vestiges of ancient civilization／～이 있다 There is an indication (that).  けいせき

형정(刑政) penal administration／～국 Bureau of Penal Administration.  けいせい

형제(兄弟) 《남자》brothers 《여자》sisters 《동포》brothren／피를 나눈 ～ a brother by blood／～애 brotherly affection／사촌 ～ cousins／이복 ～ half brothers[sisters]／～ 싸움 a quarrel[trouble] between brothers／의～ plighted brothers／친～ full brothers[sisters]. きょうだい

형제 자매(兄弟姉妹) brothers and sisters; brothren.

형지(型紙) a paper pattern (for a dress).

형질(形質) ①《형태와 성질》form and nature[quality] ②《생》characteristics／유전 ～ an inherited character.

형찰(詗察) a secret investigation／～하다 investigate secretly.  けいさつ

형처(荊妻) my wife.  じぶんのつま

형체(刑體) form; shape; the body／～를 갖추다 be given a form; be embodied／～미 physical beauty; the beauty of form.  けいたい

형태(形態) form; shape; 【심】configuration／～를 바꾸다 transform; transfigure／～미 physical beauty; the beauty of form／～학 morphology.  けいたい

형통(亨通) ～하다 go well; turn out well; prove successful／만사가 ～하다 everything goes well.

형틀(刑─) a chair in which a criminal is fastened to be interrogated.  けいぐ

형편(形便) ①《일의 경로·결과》the situation; the state [of things]; the aspect [of affairs]／일을 ～에 맡기다 allow the situation to develop in its own way ②《살림의》one's family circumstances[fortune]; one's family situation／～이 어렵다 be badly off ③《형세》a condition; a state; convenience; circumstances／적의 ～을 살피다 watch the movements of the enemy ④《지세(地勢)》the geographical aspect[features]; the lay of the land; the topography／재정 ～ financial conditions.  なりゆき

형편없다 be beyond description; be terrible／형편없이 고생하다 suffer terribly [miserably] (form)／형편없이 지다 be beaten all hollow.

형평(衡平) balance; equilibrium; equipoise／～ 운동 the social equality movement; the leveling movement.

형해(形骸) 《떠데》the body; a frame; a skeleton; framework 《잔해》a ruin; a wreck／그 절은 ～마저 남기지 않았다 Nothing remains of the temple now.  けいがい

형형(炯炯) glaring; piercing; penetrating／～하다 (be) glaring; piercing; sharp; gleaming／안광이 ～하다 be eagle-eyed; have glittering eyes.  けいけい

형형색색(形形色色) all sorts and kinds; various diverse; sundry／～으로 variously; in various[many] ways. いろいろ

형화(螢火) the light of a glowworm; the glow of a firefly.  けいか

혜고(惠顧) 《왕림》a gracious your[his] visit 《돌봐줌》your[his] kind regards [attention]／～하다 kindly visit; regard with kindness.  けいこ

혜람(惠覽) gracious perusal (of a letter)／～하다 deign to read; kindly read.

혜림(惠臨) your[his] gracious visit／～하다 graciously visit; kindly come.

혜민(慧敏) ～하다 (be) clever; sagacious; shrewd; astute.  けいびん

혜사(惠賜) ～하다 bestow; graciously give; kindly grant.  けいし

혜서(惠書) your letter／～는 받아 보았음니다 Your letter has been noted with thanks.

혜성(彗星) a comet／～ 같은 meteoric; comet-like; meteor-like／～년(年) comet year.  けいせい

혜시(惠施) almsgiving; charity/ ~하다 kindly give; bestow; give [money] in charity[alms]. けいし

혜안(慧眼) a quick[sharp] eye/ ~을 갖다 have an eye for (art, etc.). けいがん

혜여(惠與) ~하다 bestow; kindly grant; graciously give. けいよ

혜존(惠存) (증정본에) with compliments (of the author); (사진 따위에) "To[Presented to] Mr … with best wishes from m …". けいそん

혜증(惠贈) ~하다 bestow. けいぞう

혜찰(惠札) your kind[gracious] letter.

혜택(惠澤) a favour; a boon; benefit/ ~을 받다 receive a favour from; enjoy benevolent influence; share in the benefit. けいたく

혜한(惠翰) your kind[gracious] letter.

혜함(惠函) your kind[gracious] letter.

호 with a blow[puff]/ ~하다 blow. ふう

호(戶) a house; a door. こ

호(湖) a lake ⇒호수(湖水). みずうみ

호(號) (번호) a number; (명칭) an issue/ a title (아호) a pen name (크기) a size /제 2~ number two(略: No. 2) /제 1 ~ number one. ごう

호-(好) good/~기회 a fine opportunity /~인상 a good impression. こう-

호가(呼價) the price named[asked]; a bid; a price offered/~하다 (살 사람이) name a price; bid; make a bid (팔 사람이) demand[ask] a price. いいね

호각(號角) a whistle/ ~을 불다 blow a whistle. ホイッスル

호감(好感) good feeling; a favourable [good] impression; good will/사람에 ~을 가지다 be favourably disposed towards a person. こうかん

호강 living in extravagance; luxury/ ~하다 enjoy luxury; live in extravagance; live luxuriously/~스럽다 (be) easy and comfortable; cozy/~스러운 살림 a luxurious life.

호깨나무 a raisin tree; Hovenia dulcis(학명).

호걸(豪傑) a hero; a mighty warrior/~스럽다 (be) heroic; gallant; intrepid; brave/~남자 a heroic man/~같은 태도 a heroic[gallant] air. ごうけつ

호격(呼格) 〖언〗 the vocative case. こかく

호경기(好景氣) good times; prosperity; a boom/~ 시대 prosperous days; a boom period/~ good times/시장은 ~다 The market is quite lively[booming].

호곡(號哭) wailing; [wild] lamentation /~하다 weep[cry] bitterly; wail; lament aloud; moan; bewail. ごうこく

호과(胡瓜) (오이) a cucumber.

호광(弧光) an arc light/ ~등 an arc lamp/~ 전압 arcing voltage. ここう

호구(戶口) census; number of houses/~ 조사 census taking/~ 조사원 a census taker/~ 조사하다 take the census.

호구(好球) (야구) a nice ball/~를 놓치다 miss a nice ball.

호구(虎口) ①(위험) a tiger's mouth; danger/ ~에서 빠져 나오다 escape from the jaws of death; get out of danger ②(바둑의) an area on the badug checkerboard that is surrounded by three opponent pieces. ここう

호구(糊口) living; subsistence; livelihood (겨우 살) bare livelihood/ ~하다 make one's living; live from hand to mouth; keep the pot boiling /~지책 (之策) a means of livelihood. ここう

호기(好期) a good season; a good[right] time (of one's life). こうき

호기(好機) a good[golden] opportunity; a good time; a favourable chance/~를 놓치다 miss a golden opportunity. こうき

호기(豪氣) a heroic temper; a stout heart; a sturdy spirit/~부리다 give oneself the airs of a great man; play the hero; pose as a hero/ ~스럽다 (be) of a heroic temper; gallant; intrepid. ごうき

호기심(好奇心) curiosity/ ~에서 out of curiosity; prompted[impelled] by curiosity/~이 많은[강한] curious; inquisitive/~을 만족시키다 satisfy one's curiosity. こうきしん

호농(豪農) a rich[wealthy] farmer. ごうのう

호다 sew[stitch] together/호아 넣다 tuck in; sew (a thing) in[into].

호담(豪膽) boldness; a stout heart; iron nerves; dauntlessness/~하다 (be) stout[iron]-hearted; dauntless/그는 ~하다 He has iron nerves. ごうたん

호도(胡桃) a walnut ⇒호두. くるみ

도(糊塗) ~하다 gloss over; varnish; temporize; patch up/~지책 an expedient. こと

호도깝스럽다 (be) rash; reckless; unstable. せっかちだ

호도애 〖조〗 an eastern turtledove.

호되다 (be) severe; cruel; violent; harsh/호되게 severely; roughly; roundly /호된 비평 a severe criticism /호되게 때리다 beat (one) soundly. ひどい

호두(胡-) 〖식〗 a walnut /~를 까다 crack a walnut/~나무 a walnut tree. くるみ

호드기 a reed pipe/~를 불다 whistle at a reed.

호드득거리다 ①(튀는 소리) make a cracking sound; crackle ②(방정떨다) act rashly; be frivolous; be imprudent.

호드득호드득 ①(소리) popping; crackling; snapping/옥수수가 ~ 튀다 corn keeps popping ②(방정) rashly; imprudently.

호들갑떨다 be extrangant[over-excited] in speech; be bubbing over; be exuberant.

호들갑스럽다 (be) 9rupt and frivolous; flippant; rash; imprudent /호들갑스럽게 굴다 act hastily; take a rash step.

**호등**(孤燈) an arc lamp[light]. かるはずみだ
**호떡**(胡―) a Chinese stuffed pancake. ことう
**호락질** single-handed farming/ ~하다 farm single-handed.
**호락호락** (수월하게) easily; readily (성격이) yielding/~하다 (be) ready; easily manageable; tractable. やすやす
**호랑**(虎狼) (맹수) tigers and wolves; wild beasts (사람) a cruel man/~지심(之心) a cruel mind[heart]. ころう
**호랑나비** (범나비)a large spotted butterfly. こちょう
**호랑이** ①(호랑) a tiger (암컷) tigress/~도 제말하면 온다(속담) Talk of the devil, and he is sure to appear. /~에게 고기 달라다 ask when one should espect to be asked of ②(사람) a fierce person. とら
**호래아들** a boor; a barbarian; a rude person.
**호렴**(胡―) roughly processed salt.
**호령**(號令) ①(명령)a [word of] command; an order/~하다 command; [give an] order ②(꾸짖음) rating; a bluster /~하다 hurl words of thunder at; storm at. ごうれい
**호르르** whistling ⇒후루루. ぴいぴい
**호로병**(葫蘆瓶) a calabash. ひさご
**호롱** a kerosene lamp.
**호루루기** a whistle. ホイッスル
**호로로** ①(새 따위가) flapping; fluttering /~ 날아가다 fly with a flap of the wings ②(타는 모양) lightly; rapidly ③(호각을) piping; whistling/~불다 whistle; pipe. ばたばた
**호리** 【농】 a one-ox plow/ ~하다 plow with a one-ox plow/~질 one-ox plowing/~질하다 plow with a one-ox plow.
**호리**(毫釐) a whit; a bit; the slightest amount/~지차(之差) the slightest difference[deviation]/~불차(不差) exact; lacking any difference. ごうり
**호리다** ①(홀리다) fascinate; charm; bewitch; captivate ②(빼앗다) seduce ⇒후리다. うっとりさせる
**호리병**(葫―瓶) a gourd; a calabash/~박 【식】 a bottle gourd. ひさご
**호리호리하다** (be) [tall and] willowy slender; slim ⇒후리후리하다/호리호리한 여자 a slim woman. すらとしている
**호마**(胡馬) a Manchurian horse.
**호마**(胡麻) 【식】 sesame; a gingili [plant]; *Sesamum orientale*(학명); (씨)a sesame seed/~유 sesame oil gingili. こま
**호말**(毫末) a minute particle; the least thing (부사적) [not] in the least; [not] a bit. ごうまつ
**호매**(豪邁) dauntlessness; valor; intrepidity; indomitableness/~하다 (be) undaunted; daunted; dauntless /~한 기상 an indomitable[intrepid] spit. ごうまい
**호면**(胡麵) Chinese noodles ⇒당면.

**호명**(呼名) calling (*a person*) by name; [a] roll call; [a] call-over/~하다 call (*a person*) by name; call the roll; call [over] the names.
**호무하다**(毫無―) be not the slightest; not at all/나를 미워할 리 ~ He hasn't the slightest reason to hate me.
**호미** 【농】 a weeding hoe.
**호밀**(胡―) 【식】 rye. はたむぎ
**호박** 【식】 a pumpkin; a squash/ ~씨 a pumpkin seed/ ~ 같은 얼굴 a fat old pumpkin face. カボチャ
**호박**(琥珀) 【광】 amber/~의 succinic/~산(酸) succinic acid/~잠(簪) an amber hairpin. こはく
**호박벌** 【충】 a carpenter bee. くまばち
**호반**(湖畔) the shores of a lake; a lake side/ ~ 의 lake-side; on the lake/ ~ 시인 the Lake Poets/~의 집 a lakeside cottage. こはん
**호반**(虎班) (옛 제도) a military family[stock].
**호반새**(湖畔―) 【조】 a Korean ruddy kingfisher.
**호발**(毫髮) the tiniest[most minute] hair (비유적) a single iota (부사적) [not] a bit[jot, whit]/~ 부동(不動)하다 don't move at all; be immovable. ごうはつ
**호방**(豪放) (be) large[broad]-minded; unaffected/~한 필치 a vigorous[soul-packed] touch[penmanship]. ごうほう
**호배추**(胡―) 【식】 a Chinese cabbage.
**호법**(護法) (헌법의) the defense/ of the constitution (종교의) the defense of a religion. ごほう
**호변**(好辯) eloquence; oratory; fluency / ~가 an eloquent speaker. こうべん
**호별**(戶別) (집집마다) each house/ ~ 방문하다 make a house-to-house visit/~세 a house rate[tax]/ ~ 조사 a house-to-house investigation[census]. こべつ
**호복**(胡服) Chinese clothes.
**호봉**(號俸) serial step; salary step.
**호부**(豪富) a rich[wealthy] person.
**호부**(好否) likes and[or] dislikes (호불호) good and[or] bad/ ~ 간에 whether *one* likes it or not. すききらい
**호비다** ①(오비다) scoop[scrape] out (끌로) gouge ②(후비다) dig up; grub (귀·이를) pick/귀를 ~ pick *one's* ear.
**호비작거리다** keep gouging[picking] ⇒후비적거리다. しきりにえぐる
**호비칼** a gouge; a router. まるのみ
**호사**(好事) a good thing; a happy[an auspicious] event/ ~ 다마(多魔) Lights are usually followed by shadows/ ~가 a busybody; a hustler. こうじ
**호사**(豪奢) extravagance; luxury (차림의) dandyism; foppery/ ~스럽다 (be) luxurious; extravagant; sumptuous/ ~하다 live in extravagance; live in great splendor (옷차림을) primp; dress up; be in gala dress/그는 큰 저택에서 ~스런 생활을 하고 있다 He lives in ext-

**호산(呼算)** **(주판의)** addition [and subtraction] of figures read [out] aloud.

**호상(互相)** mutual ⇒상호.

**호상(豪商)** a wealthy merchant[businessman].

**호상(護喪)** ①**(사람)** the funeral director ②**(일)** taking charge of[directing] a funeral/ ～하다 take charge of[direct] a funeral.

**호상(好喪)** a propitious mourning [of a person dying old and rich].

**호색(好色)** lust; lewdness; sensuality/ ～하다 be fond of sex; be sensual[lascivious, lewd]/ ～군 a lewd[lascivious] man; a sensualist; a Don Juan/ ～ 문학 obscene[pornographic, erotic] literature/ ～의 lustful; lewd; sensual; lecherous/ ～가 a lewd man; a sensualist.

**호생(互生)** 【식】growing in alternation / ～의 alternate/ ～엽(葉) alternate leaves [on a plant].

**호선(互先)** **(바둑)** alternative moving/ ～으로 두다 alternate black and[with] white.

**호선(互選)** co-optation; mutual election / ～하다 elect by mutual vote; elect upon a mutual basis; elect from among themselves/ ～ 의원 a member elected by mutual vote/ ～ 투표 mutual vote.

**호선(弧線)** an arc [of a circle].

**호소(呼訴)** an appeal; a petition/ ～하다 appeal[resort] to; have recourse to **(불평 따위를)** complain of/ 여론에 ～하다 appeal to the public.

**호소(湖沼)** lakes and marshes.

**호송(護送)** escort; convoy/ ～하다 escort; convoy (*transports*); **(범인을)** send (*a person*) under guard/ ～차 a prison [motor-]van; a patrol waggon.

**호수(湖水)** a lake/ 호숫가에 on [the shore of] a lake-side.

**호수(戶數)** the number of houses[families].

**호수(好手)** **(바둑·장기의)** a good move.

**호수(號數)** number; a register[serial] number/ 집 ～ the number of a house.

**호시절(好時節)** a good season.

**호시 탐탐(虎視眈眈)** ～하다 watch for an opportunity[a chance] (to *prey* upon *one's opponent*); keep a vigilant eye (*on*).

**호신(護身)** self-protection/ ～하다 protect *oneself*; defend *oneself*/ ～용으로 for self-protection/ ～술 the art of self-protection.

**호심(湖心)** the centre of a lake.

**호심경(護心鏡)** a breast-plate.

**호안(好顏)** a happy face.

**호안(護岸)** protecting the banks; an embankment **(해안의)** a sea wall[bank]/ ～ 공사 embankment work.

**호양(互讓)** mutual concession; give-and-take; compromise/ ～하다 make a mutual concession; compromise/ ～ 정신으로 문제를 해결하다 settle a matter by mutual concessions.

**호언(豪言)** big talking[words]; boasting; a rant/ ～하다 talk big; boast and brag; speak boastfully[bombastically].

**호언(好言)** kind words; nice words.

**호연(好演)** an excellent[a good] acting / ～하다 act[perform] we'll; put up a good show.

**호연(皓然)** ①pure[snow] white/ ～하다 be snow white ②clearly; patently/ ～하다 (be) clear; patent

**호연(浩然)** great; magnanimous; vast/ ～하다 (be) vast; magnanimous/ ～지기를 기르다 cultivate a magnanimous spirit.

**호열자(虎列刺)** 【의】cholera/ ～균 a cholera germ[bacterium, bacillus]/ ～가 발생[만연·유행]하다 an epidemic of cholera breaks out[spreads, prevails].

**호염(胡鹽)** crude salt ⇒호렴.

**호외(戶外)** the open [air]/ ～의 open-air; out-door/ ～ 운동 out-door[open-air, field] exercise.

**호외(號外)** **(신문·잡지의)** an extra **(일정 수 밖의)** an extra number; a supernumerary/ ～를 발행하다 issue an extra.

**호우(豪雨)** a heavy rain; downpour/ ～가 쏟아졌다 It rained heavily[cats and dogs, in torrents]/ ～ 주의보 torrential[heavy] rain warning/ 집중 ～ a local downpour.

**호운(好運)** good fortune ⇒행운(幸運).

**호위(護衛)** guard; escort **(함대의 호송)** convoy/ ～하다 guard; convoy; escort / ～병 a guard; an escort; a bodyguard/ 경찰의 ～ 아래 under police escort.

**호유(豪遊)** an extravagant pleasure/ ～하다 have a great spree.

**호음(豪飮)** heavy drinking/ ～하다 drink heavily[deep, hard]; drink spree.

**호읍(號泣)** wailing/ ～하다 weep bitterly; be wail; wail.

**호응(呼應)** ①**(기맥 상통)** response; acting in concert/ ～하다 act in concert; respond to; be in sympathy (*with*) ②【문】 concord ③**(부름에 응함)** hailing each other.

**호의(好意)** goodwill; friendliness; favour; kindness/ ～의 kind; well-meaning; kindly; friendly/ ～를 가지고 with good intentions/ ～에 감사합니다 I thank you warmly for your kindness.

**호의(狐疑)** 《의심》 doubt 《주저》 hesitation / ~하다 《의심》 doubt 《주저》 be hesitant; hesitate; waver. こぎ

**호의(好誼)** deep friendship. こうぎ

**호의호식(好衣好食)** dressing well and faring richly; living in clover / ~하다 dress well and fare richly; live well [in clover] / ~하는 사람들 well-fed and well-clad people. こういこうしょく

**호인(好人)** a good natured man; a soft-headed person 《무골 호인》 a good[nice] fellow. こころのよいひと

**호인(胡人)** a Manchurian.

**호장(豪壯)** ①《호화》 magnificence; splendour / ~하다 (be) splendid; magnificent; grand ②《호담》 vigorousness; bravery; boldness / ~하다 (be) grand; bold; brave. ごうそう

**호저(豪豬)** 〖동〗 a porcupine.

**호적(戶籍)** census registration 《장부》 a [census] register / ~ 등본[초본] a copy of a person census register / ~에 올리다 have a person name entered in the census register / ~을 조사하다 check up one's family register. こせき

**호적(胡笛)** kind of clarinet ⇒날라리.

**호적(號笛)** a whistle; a horn; a hooter; a siren / ~을 불다 hoot; whistle. ごうてき

**호적(好適)** ~하다 (be) pleasant; agreeable; comfortable / ~지(地) an ideal [the-best] place / 피서지로 ~하다 be ideal for a summer resort. こうてき

**호적수(好敵手)** a good rival[match]; one's closet match; a good[worthy] opponen / ~를 만나다 meet one's match / 틀림없이 그는 나의 ~다 I certainly find a match in him.

**호전(好戰)** bellicosity; jingoism / ~적 warlike; bellicose / ~국 a warlike country / ~적 민족 a warlike race.

**호전(好轉)** a favourable turn[move]; improvement; a change for the better / ~하다 improve; change[take a turn] for the better / 경기가 ~하고 있다 Business is looking up[picking up]. こうてん

**호접(蝴蝶)** 〖충〗 a butterfly. こちょう

**호젓하다** (be) lonesome; dreary; lonely; desolate / 호젓한 산길 a lonely mountain path. ひっそりしている

**호정(糊精)** 〖화〗 dextrine.

**호정(戶庭)** a front yard / ~ 출입 《노인·환자의》 moving around in the yard / ~ 출입을 못하다 be confined to bed.

**호조(好調)** satisfactoriness; a favourable tone[trend, tendency]; favourableness / ~를 보이다 take a favorable turn; show a favorable tendency.

**호졸근하다** 《옷 따위가》 (be) limp; (be) droop; be wet enough to lose starch 《몸이》 (be) tired; droop; (be) limp with exhaustion.

**호종(扈從)** attendance / ~하다 attend on (a king) be in attendance on (a king).

**호주(戶主)** the head of a family; the master of a house; a householder / ~ 상속권 the right of succeeding (a person) as the head of a family / ~ 상속인 the heir[ess] / ~와의 관계 relation to the head of a family. こしゅ

**호주(好酒)** love of liquor / ~하다 be fond of drink / ~객 a drinker; a thirsty soul; a sot. さけをこのむこと

**호주머니** a pocket 《지갑》 a purse / 조끼 ~ a vest pocket / ~에 넣다 put (a thing) in one's pocket. ポケット

**호초(胡椒)** black pepper ⇒후추.

**호출(呼出)** a call 《소환》 a summons / ~하다 call (one) to[before]; summon / ~장 a summons. よびだし

**호치(皓齒)** pearly teeth. こうし

**호칭(互稱)** the name[title] that each calls the other; mutual designations.

**호칭(呼稱)** a name; a title; a designation; an appellation / ~하다 call; name; designate. こしょう

**호콩(胡一)** a monkey-nut〈영〉; a peanut〈미〉. らっかせい

**호타자(好打者)** 《야구》 a good[nice] hitter 《강타자》 a slugger

**호탕(豪宕)** dauntlessness; indomitableness; intrepidity / ~하다 (be) dauntless; intrepid; valorous; indomitable. ごうとう

**호탕(浩蕩)** being vast[boundless, broad-minded]. こうとう

**호통** a yell; a shout / ~치다 yell; shout / ~ 바람 (at the instigation of) the yell or shout / 일을 빨리 하라고 ~치다 yell (for someone) to get the job done fast. どなること

**호투(好投)** 《야구》 clean[fine] pitching[delivery] / ~하다 pitch well[a good pitch].

**호평(好評)** popularity; favorable criticism; public favor; a favorable comment / ~하다 criticize[comment on] favorably; receive well[favorably] / ~을 받다 be favorably commented upon / ~대 ~ great public favor. こうひょう

**호포(砲砲)** a signal gun / ~를 쏘다 fire a signal gun. ごうほう

**호풍(胡風)** ①《풍속》 Manchurian[barbarous] customs ②《바람》 the north wind.

**호피(虎皮)** a tiger skin[fur] / ~ 방석 a tigerskin cushion. とらのかわ

**호학(好學)** love of learning / ~하다 be fond of learning; be studious / ~지사 a lover of learning. こうがく

**호한(好漢)** a regular guy《미·속》; a fine [nice] fellow. こうかん

**호한(浩瀚)** extensiveness; voluminousness; bulkiness; magnitude / ~하다 (be) voluminous; bulky. こうかん

**호해(湖海)** lakes and seas. こかい

**호혈**(虎穴) a tiger's den/ ～을 벗어나다 escape from the jaws of death. けけつ

**호협**(豪俠) chivalrousness; gallantry; bravery/ ～하다 (be) gallant; chivalrous; heroic. ごうきょう

**호형**(弧形) an arc/ ～을 그리다 draw an arc.

**호형 호제**(呼兄呼弟) close friendship/ ～하다 call each other brother. こけい

**호혜**(互惠) reciprocity; mutual benefits/ ～ 조약 a reciprocal treaty/ ～ 통상 reciprocal trading/ ～ 관세율 a reciprocal[bargaining] tariff/ ～ 무역 reciprocal trading/ ～주의 reciprocity.
ごけい
**호호**¹ ho! ho!/ ～ 웃다 laugh gently; smile/ ～거리다 giggle and giggle. ほほ

**호호**² 《입김을》 blowing and blowing; puff-puff/ ～하다 blow and blow; puff and puff/추위서 손을 ～불다 warm one's hands with one's breath. ほほ

**호호**(戶戶) house after house; every house[door, family]; door-to-door. ここ

**호호**(浩浩) [being] vast; boundless/ ～하다 (be) vast; boundless. こうこう

**호호**(皓皓) white; clean; bright/ ～하다 (be) white; clean; bright. こうこう

**호호 백발**(皓皓白髮) hoary hair.

**호화**(豪華) splendor; gorgeousness; extravagance; magnificence; pomp/～스럽다, 하다 (be) splendid; gorgeous; most luxurious; sumptuous/ ～스러운 저택 a palatial mansion/ ～선(船) a de luxe liner; a luxury ship/～판 [a] de luxe edition; an edition de luxe/ ～롭게 살다 be lapped in luxury. ごうか

**호환**(虎患) a disaster caused by tigers; the ravages of tigers.

**호황**(好況) a prosperous condition;a boom; prosperity/～의 prosperous; favourable/～을 보이다 show signs of prosperity; be prosperous/～이다 be prosperous; be in a prosperous condition; boom〈미〉.

**호흡**(呼吸) ①《숨》breath; respire/ ～하다 breathe; respire ②《일의 장단》time; rhythm; tune/코로 ～하다 breathe through the nose/ ～이 맞다 be in rhythm; tune (with)/인공 ～ artificial respiration/～기 the respiratory organs/ ～ 곤란 difficulty[oppression] of breathing; difficult breathing. こきゅう

**혹**¹ ①《군살》a wen; a protuberance; an outgrowth 《약대의》a hump/ ～을 떼다 cut a wen/ ～ 떼러 갔다가 혹 붙이고 온다 Many go out for wool and come back shorn. ②《나무마디》a knot. こぶ

**혹**² 《입김 소리》with a whiff[puff]/ ～하다 puff (마시는 모양)at a draught [gulp]/～하다 gulp/단숨에 ～ 들이마시다 drink (it) down at a gulp. ごくり

**혹**(或) ①《혹시》maybe; possibly; by chance; perhaps ②《혹간》sometimes; at times; rarely ③《또는》or; or else; either… or ④《혹자》some [people]/ ～은 그렇게 말한다 Some people say so.
あるいは
**혹간**(或間) sometimes ⇒잔혹. あるいは

**혹독**(酷毒) 《모짊》severity; harshness; cruelty 《혹렬》intensity/ ～하다 (be) severe; harsh; cruel; stern; intense; relentless/ ～한 추위 intense[severe] cold. あまりひどいこと

**혹란**(惑亂) bewilderment; confusion/ ～하다 (be) bewildered; confused.
わくらん
**혹렬**(酷烈) 《혹독》severity; intensity/～하다 (be) severe; rigorous; intense.
こくれつ
**혹부리** a wenny man.
かおにこぶがあるひと
**혹사**(酷使) driving (a person) hard; working (a person) hard; enslaving/～하다 work[drive] (one) hard; keep another's nose to the grindstone/～ 당하는 노동자 down-trodden workers.

**혹사**(酷似) a striking resemblance; a strong likeness/～하다 resemble closely; be the very image of; bear a close resemblance to. こくじ

**혹살**《쇠고기》aitchbone; beef round.

**혹서**(酷暑) intense[scorching, torrid] heat/～의 very hot; sweltering; burning/～에 견디다 stand the heat of summer. こくしょ

**혹설**(或說) a view;an opinion [given by a certain man].

**혹성**(惑星) ①《천》a planet ②《비유적》정계의 ～ a dark horse in politics; a mystery[an enigmatic] man in political circles/～ 운동 planetary motion[circulation]. わくせい

**혹세 무민**(惑世誣民) ～하다 seduce the public.

**혹시**(或是) ①《만일》by any chance; if; provided[supposing] that; in case (of) ②《아마》may; maybe/ ～ 그럴는지도 모른다 It may be so., It is not impossible.
あるとき
**혹신**(惑信) misguided[fatuous] belief/～하다 believe blindly.

**혹심**(酷甚) (being) extreme[severe]/～하다 (be) extreme; severe/～한 피해를 입다 suffer heavy losses.

**혹애**(惑愛) infatuation; dotage/～하다 love blindly[violently to death]. できあい

**혹열**(酷熱) brutal heat ⇒혹서(酷暑).
こくねつ
**혹염**(酷炎) intense heat ⇒혹서(酷暑).
こくしょ
**혹왈**(或曰) some say;… others say; it is said. あるひとがいうには

**혹운**(或云) some say ⇒혹왈(或曰).

**혹위**(一胃) 《소 따위의》a paunch; a rumen.

**혹자**(或者) ①《사람》some one; a certain person ②《혹시》maybe; perhaps/～는 그렇게들 말한다 Some people say so.

**혹평(酷評)** severe[sharp, bitter, harsh] criticism; strictures/ ~하다 criticize severely; speak bitterly/~한 a severe critic; a hypercritic.

**혹하다(惑─)** ①《반하다》be fascinated; be charmed; be bewitched; be possessed/아름다움에 ~ be smitten with (*a person's*) charms ②《…에 빠짐》indulge (*in*); be addicted (*to*)/장기에 ~ be much taken with chess ③《미혹됨》get deluded[misled, led into error, trapped].

**혹한(酷寒)** severe[intense] cold/~에 견디다 endure[stand] the intense cold.

**혹형(酷刑)** a severe punishment[penalty]/~하다 punish severely; inflict a severe punishment (*on*).

**혼(魂)** 《영》the soul 《정신》the spirit/~이 없는 soulless.

**혼가(婚家)** a house in which there is a marriage.

**혼가(婚嫁)** marriage ⇒혼인(婚姻).

**혼겁(魂怯)** extreme astonishment.

**혼구(婚具)** a wedding outfit.

**혼기(婚期)** marriageable age/~의 marriageable/~에 달하다 reach a marriageable age/~를 잃다 lose[miss] a chance of marriage.

**혼나다(魂─)** ①《놀라다》be frightened ②《곤란을 겪다》have be startled a hard time of it; have bitter experiences/시험치르느라 ~ sweat out an exam.

**혼내다(魂─)** ①《놀래다》surprise; frighten; startle ②《해대다》handle (*a person*) roughly; treat (*a person*) badly 《징계》teach (*a person*) a lesson/이 너석을 단단히 혼내 줘야지 I'll bring him to cry mercy., He shall smart for this.

**혼담(婚談)** a proposal of marriage; marriage talk[s]/~이 있다[을 거절하다] have[decline] an offer[a proposal] of marriage.

**혼담(魂膽)** soul; mind.

**혼도(昏倒)** falling into a swoon/~하다 swoon; faint away; fall from dizziness; be stunned.

**혼돈(混沌)** chaos; confusion; nebulosity/~하다 (be) chaotic; confused; disorderly/~ 상태에 빠지다 be reduced to a chaotic state; be thrown into confusion.

**혼동(混同)** confusion; mixing/~하다 confuse; [mis]take (*one*/thing) for; mix up/공사를 ~하다 mix up public and private affairs.

**혼뜨다(魂─)** be frightened ⇒혼나다.

**혼란(混亂)** confusion; chaos; disorder; pell-mell/~하다 (be) confused; disorderly; chaotic; be a mess/~ 상태에 있다 be in [a state of] disorder/~을 초래하다 lead to[result in] confusion.

**혼란(昏亂)** [mental] derangement; confusion; muddle/~하다 be muddled; be deranged; be dazed.

**혼령(魂靈)** a spirit; a soul ⇒영혼.

**혼례(婚禮)** a marriage ceremony; nuptials; a wedding/~에 참석 하다 attend [be present at] a wedding.

**혼매(昏昧)** stupidity; ignorance; idiocy/~하다 (be) stupid; ignorant; silly.

**혼미(昏迷)** stupidity; bewilderment; uncousciousness/~하다 be stupefied; lose *one's* consciousness; be muddle-headed/~ 상태에 있다 be in confusion.

**혼방(混紡)** mixed[blended] spinning/~사 mixed[blended] yarn.

**혼백(魂魄)** the soul; the ghost; the spirit.

**혼백(魂帛)** a silk spirit-tablet/~상자 a case in which the spirit-tablet is kept.

**혼비 백산(魂飛魄散)** ~하다 be scared out of *one's* wits; become astonished; be terrified.

**혼사(婚事)** nuptials; marriage ceremony.

**혼상(婚喪)** marriage[s] and funeral[s].

**혼색(混色)** a compound colour; a hue.

**혼선(混線)** entanglement of wires 《혼란》confusion/~하다 get entangled 《뒤엉이》get mixed up 《전화가》get crossed; be crossed/전화가 ~되어 있다 The wires[lines] are mixed.

**혼성(混成)** composition; mixture/~의 mixed; composite/ ~하다 mix[blend; combine/ ~물 a mixture; a medley/~어 a hybrid word/ ~팀 a combine team.

**혼성(混聲)** 【음】a mixed voice/~ 사부 합창 a mixed quartette.

**혼솔(渾率)** whole family.

**혼수(昏睡)** coma; trance; lethargy/~상태에 빠지다 fall into a coma.

**혼수(婚需)** articles used in a marriage 《신부의》a trousseau.

**혼식(混食)** mixed food/~하다 eat mixed food.

**혼신(渾身)** the whole body; all the body/~의 힘을 다하여 with all *one's* might.

**혼야(昏夜)** a dark midnight.

**혼약(婚約)** engagement; a promise of marriage; a marriage promise; affiance/~하다 make an engagement; engage *one*self to.

**혼연(渾然)** wholly; in perfect harmony/~하다 (be) entire; harmonious/~히 wholly; in perfect harmony; entirely/~ 일체가 되다 be joined together; form a complete whole.

혼욕(混浴) promiscuous[mixed] bathing／~하다 bathe promiscuously.

혼용(混用) ~하다 use (a thing) together with (another); mix. こんよう

혼인(婚姻) a marriage; a wedding／~하다 marry; be man and wife; be married／~을 취소하다 annul one's marriage／~신고 a report of marriage; a marriage registration. こんいん

혼일(混一) unification; amalgamation; consolidation／~하다 consolidate; unify. こんいつ

혼일(婚日) the wedding day; the marriage day. けっこんにち

혼입(混入) mixing; mingling; mixture／~하다 mix; mingle; intermix. こんにゅう

혼자 alone 《단독》by oneself 《혼자 힘으로》 single-handed／~ 앉아 있다 sit all alone／나는 이 세상에서 나 ~다 I am all alone in the world. ひとり

혼작(混作) 〖농〗 mixed cultivation[crops]／~하다 grow[cultivate] together. こんさく

혼잡(混雜) confusion; disorder／ ~하다 (be) confused; disordered 《복잡하다》 complicated 《붐비다》 (be) crowded; bustling／아침[저녁]의 ~한 시간 the morning[evening] rush hours／~속에 휩쓸리다 be lost in the crowd.

혼잣말 soliloquy; monologue／~하다 soliloquize; talk to oneself; think loud. ひとりごと

혼잣손 single-handedness; a single hand／~으로 일하다 work singlehanded. ひとりだち

혼재(婚材) a marriageable person.

혼전(混戰) a confused fight; a mixed fight; a scuffle; a free [for all] fight; a rough-and-tumble／ ~하다 fight in confusion. こんせん

혼절(昏絶) fainting; a swoon／ ~하다 faint [away]; go faint; swoon; become insensible. こんぜつ

혼쭐나다(魂一) 《혼나다》get scared; be struck dumb; astound (a person); 《황홀하다》be transported with delight. ひどいめにあう

혼처(婚處) a marriageable person; a suitable clan with which to unite in marriage.

혼천의(渾天儀) 〖천〗 a celestial globe. こんてんぎ

혼취(昏醉) [dead] drunkenness; intoxication／~하다 get dead drunk; be boozy. こんすい

혼탁(混濁) muddiness; impurity; turbidity／~하다 (be) turbid; cloudy; dull; muddy; thick／ ~한 세상 the corrupt world. こんだく

혼합(混合) mingling; mixture; intermixture／~하다 mix; mingle; blend; compound; intermix／~ 경기 a mixed competition／~ 교육 mixed education／~

물 a mixture／ ~법 〖수〗 alligation／~비례 a mixed proportion／물과 술을 ~하다 mingle wines and water. こんごう

혼행(婚行) a marriage procession.

혼혈(混血) mixed blood[breed]; racial mixture／~아 a half-blood[breed]／《흑백인의》 a mulatto 《서양인과 동양인의》 a Eurasian／저 사람은 ~아 같다 He seems to be a half-blood. こんけつ

혼혼(昏昏) ~하다 (be) confused; muddled. くらいさま

혼화(混和) mixture; mingling／~하다 mix; mingle／~제 a compound／ ~기 a mixer; crutcher. こんわ

혼화(混化) compound; blend／ ~하다 be made into a compound; compound (with).

혼효(混淆) confusion; mixture; a jumble; a mess; a tangle／ ~하다 mix up; (be) confused; jumbled; tangled; be messed up／공사(公私)를 ~하다 mix up public and private affairs. こんこう

홀- 《짝 없음》 single.

홀(笏) a mace; a baton. こつ

홀가분하다 (be) light; easy; nimble／홀가분한 행장 a light traveling outfit／터놓고 이야기 해 버리면 홀가분할 것이다 Make a clean breast of it and you will feel relieved.

홀딱 ①《벗는 모양》[removing it] completely; quickly 《뒤집는 모양》[turning it] inside out 《뛰어넘는 모양》 with a jump; in a bound; easily／옷을 ~ 벗다 slip off one's clothes／윗옷을 ~ 뒤집다 turn one's coat inside out ②《반하는 모양》 deeply [in love with]; madly ③《속는 모양》 (be) nicely [taken in]／그는 그녀에게 ~ 반했다 He is awfully struck on her.／~ 속아 넘어가다 be completely taken in. さっと

홀딱거리다 be apt to slip out; slip all the time. すかすかする

홀랑 all naked／옷을 ~ 벗다 strip oneself all naked. すってんてん

홀로 alone; single-handed／~ 살다 live alone; remain single／ ~ 싸우다 fight alone. ひとりで

홀리다 ①《매혹되다》 be charmed; be fascinated; be bewitched／청중은 그의 웅변에 홀렸다 The audience was under the spell of his eloquence. ②《여우·귀신에》 be possessed; be obsessed／여우에 ~ be possessed by a fox ③《유혹》 get tempted; be deluded／돈에 홀려 나쁜 짓을 하다 be tempted by money to do wrong. みわくされる

홀림길 a maze; a labyrinth／~에 빠지다 be lost in a maze; beat a loss.

홀맺다 tie[knot] (a thing) securely. かたくむすぶ

홀몸 a single[an unmarried] person; a person without a spouse／평생을 ~으로 지내다 remain single all one's life. どくしん

**홀보드르르하다** (be) nice and soft.
**홀소리** 〖어〗 a vowel ⇒모음.
**홀수(-數)** an odd〔uneven〕number.
**홀씨** 〖생〗 a spore.
**홀시(忽視)** contempt; neglect; disregard /~하다 despise; hold (a person) in contempt; look down on; make light of.
**홀아비** a widower/~ 살림 the life of w-idower.
**홀알** a wind egg.
**홀어미** a widow.
**홀연(忽然)** suddenly; all of a sudden; on a sudden; abruptly; unexpectedly; in an instant; in a flash/~히 사라지다 vanish as if by magic/그녀는 ~히 안개 속으로 사라졌다 She faded in a flash into the fog.
**홀짝** ①《지나가다》quickly; rapidly /그해도 ~ 지나갔다 The year spen on. ②《코를》with a sniff/~거리다 sniff; snuff ③《액체를》with a sip; sipping /~거리다 sip; suck; sup/ ~ 차를 마시다 sip tea.
**홀쭉하다** ①《날씬함·야윔》(be) long and slender/허리가 ~ have a slim waist ② 《뾰족하다》(be) pointed/꼬리가 ~ have a pointed tail.
**홀쳐매다** tie up/자루를 ~ tie up the top of a bag.
**홀치기** 《염색》variegation; dapple 《천》variegated cloth.
**홀태**¹ a threshing machine; a thresher ⇒벼훑이.
**홀태**² 《생선》a slim fish without spawn 《물건》a slim thing.
**홀태바지** tight trousers.
**홀태질** hackling; threshing; thrashing/ ~하다 hackle; thresh; thrash.
**홀하다(忽-)** ①《경솔·소홀하다》(be) careless; inconsiderate; negligent; hasty; rash ②《대수롭지 않다》be of little importance.
**훌훌** 《불이》in flames 《뛰는 모양》with leaps and bounds 《나는 모양》flying/ 새가 ~ 날아가다 a bird flutters away 《마시는 모양》with slurps 《던지는 모양》 tossing and tossing ⇒훌훌.
**훌훌하다** (be) soft ⇒훌훌하다.
**홈** a groove 《기둥의》a flute 《쇠시리》a quirk/~을 따라 cat〔hollow out〕a groove.
**홈빡** all/~ 젖은 옷 dripping-wet clothes /비에 ~ 젖다 be soaked with rain.
**홈질** broad stitching/ ~하다 broad-stitch.
**홈착거리다** 《더듬다》search; fumble 《눈물을》wipe away/주머니를 ~ search〔fumble in〕 one's pocket/눈물을 ~ keep wiping tears from one's eyes.
**홈착작거리다** search〔fumble〕 leisurely/ 주머니를 ~ search〔fumble around in〕 one's pocket leisurely.
**홈타기** a fork; a crotch/나무 ~ the crotch of a tree.
**홈통(-桶)** ①《물이 흘러내리는》a water 〔rain〕-pipe; a gutter/집에 ~을 달다 gutter a house ②《문지방의》a groove.
**홈파다** groove; cut〔hollow out〕a groove (in)/책상 가장자리에 홈을 파다 cut a groove along the edges of a table.
**홈패다** get grooved; be dug out/길이 비에 ~ a road is dug out by the rain.
**홈홈하다** wear a look of satisfaction.
**홉** a hob; a Korean measure of capacity (=0.048 standard gallon).
**흡뜨다** look daggers at (one).
**홋홋하다** (be) of small members/살림이 ~ have a small family.
**홍(紅)** red; a red colo〔u〕r.
**홍꽉지(紅-)** a kite with a round piece of red paper at its top.
**홍당무(紅唐-)** a carrot; a red radish/ 얼굴이 ~가 되다 turn as red as a turkeycock.
**홍대(鴻大, 洪大)** hugeness; enormity; immensity; tremendousness/~하다 (be) immense; vast; stupendous; tremendous; enormous.
**홍도(紅桃)** 〖식〗《나무》a peach tree which puts out red blossoms 《꽃》a red peach blossom.
**홍두깨** ①《다듬이질의》a long-and-round wooden instrument for fulling cloths ②《농》soil which an inexpert plowman 〔ploughman〈영〉〕has neglected/~살 a kind of beef jowl/그것은 마치 아닌 밤중에 ~ 같았다 It was, as it were, a bolt from the blue.
**홍등가(紅燈街)** a red-light district; a brothel area; gay quarters.
**홍련(紅蓮)** a red lotus/ ~ 지옥 the hell of ice.
**홍로 점설(紅爐點雪)** a drop in the bucket.
**홍루(紅淚)** 《미인의 눈물》a woman's tear 《피눈물》bloody tears.
**홍매(紅梅)** red plum blossoms.
**홍모(鴻毛)** wild-goose down/목숨을 ~같이 가볍게 여기다 make nothing of one's life.
**백(紅白)** red and white/~전 a contest between red and white teams.
**보(弘報)** public information; publicity /~과(課) the Public Information Section/~ 조사 연구소 the Office of Information Research/~ 활동 public relations(略: P. R.).
**홍보석(紅寶石)** a ruby.
**홍살문(紅-門)** a red gate with spiked top.
**홍삼(紅蔘)** ginseng steamed red.

**홍색**(紅色) red 《진홍》crimson. こうしょく

**홍소**(哄笑) a roar of laughter; loud laughter 《천한》a guffaw; a horse laugh／～하다 roar with laughter; laugh loud[ly]; burst out laughing. こうしょう

**홍수**(洪水) a flood; an inundation; a deluge／노아의～ Noah's flood／～가 나다 have a flood／～ 예보 flood warnings／～ 지역 a flooded area[district]. こうずい

**홍수**(紅樹) a mangrove tree／～림 a mangrove forest.

**홍수막이** 《민》an exorcism held at the beginning of the year to dispel evils for the year. やくはらい

**홍순**(紅脣) 《입술》red lips; rouged lips 《꽃송이》a flower half in bloom.

**홍시**(紅柿) a red-ripe persimmon.

**홍안**(紅顔) a rosy[ruddy] face／～의 rosy cheeked; ruddy-faced／～의 미소년 a handsome[fair] youth. こうがん

**홍어**(洪魚) 《어》a skate; a thorn back. えい

**홍업**(鴻業) a great undertalking; a great exploit. こうぎょう

**홍역**(紅疫) 《의》the measles／～에 걸리다 catch[have, get] the measles. まし

**홍염**(紅焰) 《불꽃》red blazes of flame; 《천》a solar prominence. こうえん

**홍엽**(紅葉) 《단풍든 잎》t(i)nged autumnal leaves; red[scarlet-tinged] leaves 《단풍나무의》scarlet maple leaves. こうよう

**홍예**(虹蜺) a rainbow; an arch／～문 the arch of a gate; an arched gate／～틀다 build as an arch; arch (a gate). にじ

**홍옥**(紅玉) 《루비》ruby; carbuncle·《사과》a Jonathan. こうぎょく

**홍은**(鴻恩) great favor[benevolence]／～을 입다 receive great favors. こうおん

**홍인종**(紅人種) the red race; American Indian; the Red Indian.

**홍일점**(紅一點) 《여자》the only female among those present 《이채로움》standing out; surpassing. こういってん

**홍적세**(洪積世) 《지》the diluvial epoch. こうせきせい

**홍조**(紅潮) 《얼굴의》flush 《월경》menses／그의 얼굴은 기쁨으로 ～를 띠었다 His face was flushed with joy. こうちょう

**홍진**(紅塵) dust in the air／～ 세계 the dusty world／～ 만장 a cloud of dust.

**홍차**(紅茶) [black] tea／～한 잔 주시오 Give me a cup of tea.／설탕을 넣은 ～ tea with sugar. こうちゃ

**홍채**(虹彩) 《해》the iris of the eye／～염(炎) iritis. こうさい

**홍초**(紅─) 《초》a red candle 《연》a paper knite that is all red except for the tail. あかいろうそく

**홍치마**(紅─) a red skirt.
あかいろのスカート

**홍하**(紅蝦) 《물고기》a [spiny] lobster.

**홍합**(紅蛤) 《어》a sea mussel. あかがい

**홀-** 《한 겹》single; one-ply; single layer／～으로 되다 be made of a single sheet／～이다 be one sheet.

**홀겹** a single layer.

**홀눈** 《동》a stemma; an ocellus (pl. -lli). かため

**홀몸** ①《배우자 없는》a single[an unmarried] person; a bachelor 《여자》a spinster／～으로 살다 live single ②《임신하지 않은》a woman who is not pregnant 《홋홋한》a person without encumbrances 《혼자서》single-handedness; alone／～으로 여행하다 travel alone.
ひとりみ

**홀벌** 《단벌》a single one; the only one 《한 겹》single-ply／～ 옷 the only clothes one has.

**홀벌사람** a shallow-minded person.

**홀벽**(一壁) a single partition; a thin wall.

**홀소리** a single sound; a monosyllabic sound. たんおん

**홀실** single-ply thread.

**홀옷** unlined clothes; summer clothes.

**홀이불** a sheet.

**홀지다** be simplified. たんじゅんになる

**홀집** 《전》a house without an annexe.

**홀창**(一窓) 《전》a sliding window without an inner window.

**홀치마** ①《한 겹의》an unlined skirt ②《속치마 없이 입은》a skirt worn without an underskirt.

**화**(火) ①《불》fire ②《성》anger; wrath; rage; resentment; indignation／그는 걸핏하면 ～를 낸다 He gets angry on the slightest provocation／아내에게 ～를 터트렸다 He vented his anger on his wife.／홧김에 남편에게 대들었다 In a fit of anger[rage], she flewout at her husband. ③《오행의》"Fire"-one of the five primary element ④《화요일》Tuesday. ひ

**화**(禍) 《재난》disaster; calamity; woe 《불행》misfortune; evil lamity／～를 당하다 meet wiht a calam ity; get killed／～를 피하다 keep off a misfortune. わざわい

**화**(和) the sum; the total [amount]. わ

**화**(化) conversion; -ization／～하다 "-ize"／합리～ rationalization／기계～하다 mechanize.

**화가**(畵家) an artist; a painter／인물～ a portrait painter／풍경～ a landscape painter／～가 되다 enter upon a painting career. がか

**화가**(畵架) 《미》an easel. がか

**화간**(和姦) 《법》fornication; collusion in adultery adultery with consent. ／～하다 fornicate (with a woman). わかん

**화강석**(花崗石) granite. かこうせき

**화강암**(花崗岩) granite. かこうがん

**화객선**(貨客船) a cargo-passenger ship.

**화격**(畵格) 《화법》art of drawing 《화품》artistic merit; style. がほう

**화경**(火耕) 《농》kaingin[firefield] farm-

**화경(火鏡)** a burning lens[glass].

**화경(花梗)** 〖식〗 a flower stalk; a peduncle; a stem. かこう

**화고(畫稿)** a study; a sketch; dessin(F).

**화공(火攻)** attacting with fire／～하다 attact with fire. かこう

**화공(畫工)** a painter; an artist.

**화공(靴工)** a shoemaker. かこう

**화관(花冠)** 〖관〗 a woman's ceremonial coronet 《꽃의》 the corolla. かかん

**화광(火光)** a light; a flicker; the light of fire／～이 충천 하다 flames light up the sky. ひのひかり

**화교(華僑)** Chinese merchants; Chinese emigrants; Chinese resident abroad. かきょう

**화구(火口)** ①〖지〗 a crater ②《아궁이》 a fuel hole／～곡(谷) a crater valley／～구(丘) a volcanic cone／～호(湖) a crater lake. かこう

**화끈** ～거리다 burn; glow; flush; fell

**화근(禍根)** the source[root] of evil(calamity]／～을 제거하다 lay the axe to the root of evil／～이 되다 be one's ruin. hot; throb with heat／귀가 ～거린다 My ears tingle[burn]. ほかほか

**화끈달다** 《격앙하다》 be[get] excited; be agitated 《격분하다》 be enraged; be infuriated／화끈 달아 말도 안 나왔다 I got too excited for words.

**화급(火急)** urgency; emergency／～하다 (be) urgent; pressing; exigent／그 돈 은 ～하게 쓸 데가 있다 The money is urgently needed. かきゅう

**화기(火氣)** 《불기》 heat of fire 〖노기〗 anger; ire 《답답한 기운》 a stifling sensation in the chest／～ 엄금 No Fire., Inflammable. ひのき

**화기(火器)** 〖군〗 fire-arms 《불담는》 a fire container／소(小) ～ a rifle; small arms／중(重) ～ heavy weapons／자동 ～ a automatic firearm[weapon]. かき

**화기(和氣)** harmony; concord 《기색》 peacefulness／～ 애애한 in peace and harmony／～ 애애한 가정 a home in peace and happiness. わき

**화기(花期)** the flower season. かき

**화나다(火一)** get[become] angry; get into rage; be indignant; flare up／화나게 하다 enrage; exasperate; provoke; rouse [stir] the gorge. きをもむ

**화난(禍難)** a disaster; a misfortune; a mishap; a calamity. かなん

**화내다(火一)** fly into a passion; get into a rage; lose one's temper; be fired up／그는 아내에게 화를 냈다 He flew into a passion with his wife.

**화냥년** a wanton[dissolute] woman; a woman of loose morals. うわきおんな

**화농(化膿)** 〖의〗 maturation; suppuration; purulence／～하다 mature; suppurate; come to a head; gather [head]; be ripe／～균 a suppurative germ／～ 작

용 pyogenesis. かのう

**화닥닥** hurry-scurry; with a start; madly／～거리다 start; fluster. あわてふためて

**화단(花壇)** a flower-bed 《꽃밭》 a flower garden. かだん

**화단(畫壇)** painting circles. がだん

**화답(和答)** a response／～하다 respond (in singing, reciting or verse).

**화대(花代)** 《기생의》 a charge for a kisaeng. はなだい

**화대(花臺)** a flowerpot stand. かだい

**화덕(火一)** 《솥거는》 a cooking stove; a stove 《화로》 a live charcoal pot. ひばち

**화도(畫圖)** pictures; paintings.

**화독(火毒)** inflammation caused by a burn／～내 the smell of burnt food. ひのどくけ

**화동(化同)** harmony; unison／～하다 be in harmony; get in unison. わごう

**화두(話頭)** topic[subject] of conversation／～를 바꾸다 change the topic. わとう

**화드득** ～거리다 keep going slosh crack; crackle／화드득화드득 crack[l]ing away. ばちばち

**화라지** long branches [for fuel].

**화락(和樂)** harmony; unity; peace／～하다 get alone amicably／그 집은 온 집안이 ～하다 They live in perfect harmony., Perfect peace regins in his family. わらく

**화랑(畫廊)** a picture gallery. がろう

**화려(華麗)** splendor; magnificence; gorgeousness; sumptuousness; brilliance／～하다 (be) splendid; magnificent; gorgeous; sumptuous; brilliant; florid; spectacular. かれい

**화력(火力)** heating power; 〖군〗 fire power／～ 발전 power electric generation／～ 전기 a thermal[steam] power electricity. かりょく

**화로(火爐)** a brazier; a fire pot[box]／～를 둘러싸고 앉다 sit around a brazier. ひばち

**화로수(花露水)** 《향수》 a floral perfume. はなのこうすい

**화룡 점청(畫龍點睛)** the finishing touch (on a thing); final achievement. がりょうてんせい

**화류(花柳)** ①《꽃과 버들》 blossoms and willows ②《노는 계집》 a woman of the gay world／～병(病) a social disease. かりゅう

**화류(樺榴)** red sandalwood／～장(欌) a chest made of red sandalwood.

**화류계(花柳界)** a frivolous community; the gay quarters／～ 여자 a woman of the gay world. かりゅうかい

**화면(畫面)** a scene; the look of a picture; 〖수〗 a picture plane／～ 구성 the composition of a picture. がめん

**화목(火木)** firewood.

**화목(花木)** a flowering tree. かぼく

**화목(和睦)** harmony; intimacy; peace;

화문(花紋) flower patterns; figures of flowers/ ~석(席) a mat woven with flower designs.

화물(貨物) goods 《운송 화물》freight〈미〉; 《뱃짐》cargo/~ 열차 a freight train〈미〉; a goods train〈영〉/~ 자동차 a truck; a [motor-]lorry〈영〉/~ 선 a cargo boat; freight vessel; a freighter/~ 운송 goods transport; freight/~차 a freight car〈미〉; a luggage van〈영〉/~철도 ~ rail freight.

화미(華美) pomp; splendour; gorgeousness/ ~하다 (be) splendid; pompous; showy.

화반(花盤) ①〖건〗a board put on top of the *chobang* (=first cornice on a pilla) to hold the *jany-yeo* (=beam support) ②《꽃 담는》a kind of flowerpot shaped like a flower.

화반석(花斑石) red marble.

화방(花房) a flower shop.

화방(畵房) 《화실》a studio; an *atelier*(F); 《화랑》a gallery.

화방(畵舫) a decorated pleasure boat.

화방수(一水) a whirel [pool]; an eddy.

화백(畵伯) an artist; a [noted, master] painter.

화벌(華閥) a distinguished family; a titled family.

화법(畵法) the art of drawing; the canons of painting/ ~에. 맞다[안맞다] be in[out of] drawing.

화법(話法) 〖문〗narration/직접[간접] ~ direct[indirect] narration.

화변(禍變) a great disaster[calamity].

화병(花甁) a [flower-]vase/~에 꽃을 꽂다 put a flower in a vase.

화보(花譜) a catalogue of flowers.

화보(畵報) a pictorial; a graphic; pictorial news 《보도를 겸한》a picture report /시사 ~ news in pictures.

화보(畵譜) a picture album.

화복(禍福) fortune and misfortune; good or[and] evil/인생의 ~ the ups and downs of life.

화본(畵本) a canvas; a drawing paper.

화본과(禾本科) 〖식〗*Graminaceae*(학명)/ ~ 식물 grasses.

화부(火夫) a stoker; a fireman〈미〉;《화장터의》a cremator; a burmer at a crematory.

화분(花盆) a flowerpot.

화분(花粉) pollen; anther dust/~열 hay fever.

화불 단행(禍不單行) Misfortunes never come singly.

화사(花蛇) a striped snake.

화사(畵師) an artist; a painter.

화사(華奢) luxury; extravagance/~하다 (be) luxurious; extravagant; sumptuous; pompous.

화산(火山) a volcano/~의 volcanic/~ 대(帶) a volcanic zone/~회(灰) volcanic ashes/~국 a volcanic country/~ 분출물 ejecta/~암(岩) volcanic rocks/ ~ 열도(列島) achain of volcanic islands /활[사, 휴]~ an active[an extinct, a dormant] volcano/일본은 ~ 지대에 있다 Japan lie in the volcanic zone.

화살 an arrow 《굵은》a bolt/~대 the shaft of an arrow/~촉 an arrowhead /~표 an arrow/~을 먹이다 fix an arrow in *one's* bow.

화상(火床) a [fire-]grate.

화상(火傷) burn 《끓는 물로》a scald/~ 을 입다 get[be] burnt; have a burn/ 손에 ~을 입었다 I got burnt in the hand.

화상(和尙) 《불교》a bonze; a Buddhist priest.

화상(畵像) a portrait; a likeness; a picture/~ 면적 《텔레비전의》a picture area.

화상(華商) a Chinese merchant.

화상(畵商) a picture dealer; a dealer in paintings.

화색(和色) a congenial look; a soft look; a genial expression.

화생(化生) transformation/ ~하다 transform/~ 방전(放戰) 〖군〗chemical; biological and radiological warfare.

화서(花序) inflorescence; anthotaxy/유한〖원심〗~ definite(centrifugal) inflorescence.

화서지몽(華胥之夢) a [midday] nap; a siesta.

화석(火石) a flint ⇒부싯돌.

화석(化石) 《작용》petrifaction; fossilization 《돌》a fossi/ ~화(化)하다 petrify; fossilize/동물〖물고기〗의 ~ a fossil animal[fish]/~층(層) a fossil bed.

화선지(畵仙紙) Chinese drawing paper.

화성(火星) Mars/ ~인(人) a Martian; an inhabitant of Mars.

화성(化成) transformation; metamorphosis/ ~하다 transform; metamorphose / ~ 공업 the chemical and synthetic industry.

화성(和聲) 〖악〗harmony/ ~적 harmonic/ ~학 harmonics.

화성암(火成岩) igneous rocks.

화세(火勢) the force of the fire[flames]; 《화력》caloric force.

화속(火速) 《신속》quickness; fastness; rapidity 《긴급》urgency; an emergency / ~하다 (be) quick; fast; rapid; urgent.

화수(花樹) a flowering tree.

화수분 inexhaustible wealth.

화수회(花樹會) a convivial meeting of

**화순(和順)** submissiveness; docility; meekness; gentleness/~하다 (be) submissive; obedient; docile; meek; gentle.
**화술(話術)** the art of conversation[telling a story]/ ~에 능한 사람 a good conversationalist[storyteller, talker].
**화승(火繩)** a match-cord/~총 a matchlock; a firelock.
**화시(花時)** the flower season.
**화씨(華氏)** Fahrenheit/ ~ 40도 40°F/ ~ 한란계 a Fahrenheit thermometer.
**화식(火食)** cooked food; eating of cooked food/ ~하다 eat cooked food; eat cooked.
**화식도(花式圖)** a [botanical] diagram of a flower.
**화신(化身)** incarnation; personification /그 악한은 악마의 ~이었다 The villain was a fiend incarnate.
**화신(花信)** tidings of flowers; information about flowers for viewing/ ~풍(風) the spring breeze.
**화신(火燼)** ashes.
**화실(畵室)** a studio; an *atlier*(F).
**화심(花心)** ①《꽃의 중심》the central part of a flower ②《미인의 마음》a beauty's heart.
**화심(禍心)** treachery; treacherous designs; an ulterior motive; an evil intention.
**화안(花顔)** a face as fair as May rose; a beautiful face.
**화압(花押)** a signature.
**화약(火藥)** gunpowder/ ~고 a powder magazine/ 대포에 ~을 재다 load a gun /~을 폭발시키다 blow up[explode] gunpowder.
**화연(花宴)** a banquet celebrating *one's* sixtieth birthday.
**화열(和悅)** peace and joy/ ~하다 (be) peaceful and happy.
**화염(火焰)** flames; a blaze/ ~ 방사기 a flame-thrower/ ~에 싸이다 be enveloped[wrapped] in flames.
**화엽(花葉)** ①《꽃잎》a petal ②《꽃과 잎》flowers[blossoms] and leaves.
**화예(花蕊)** a stamen; a pistil.
**화요일(火曜日)** Tuesday《略: Tues》.
**화용(花容)** a lovely face; a blooming beauty/ ~ 월태(月態)의 as fair as a May rose.
**화원(花園)** a flower-garden.
**화월(花月)** ①《꽃과 달》blossoms and the moon ②《꽃에 비치는》the moonlight shining on blossoms.
**화유(花遊)** flower viewing[enjoyment] ⇒ 꽃놀이.
**화음(和音)** 《악》 a chord; an accord/~의 chordal/기초 ~ the primitive chord /5도 ~ the fifth.

**화음(華音)** Chinese pronunciation; the modern Chinese readings of Chinese characters.
**화응(和應)** response; agreement/ ~하다 respond to; agree with.
**화의(和議)** ①《강화》negotiations for peace《명의》peace conference《중재》arbitration《화해》reconciliation/~하다 make peace; conclude peace; be reconciled with ②《법》composition/ ~하다 make a composition (*with*)/ ~법 the Composition Law; the Law of Composition/ ~ 사건 a composition matter.
**화인(火印)** 《표》a brand; a brand-iron / ~을 찍다 brand.
**화인(火因)** the origin[cause] of a fire/ ~ 불명의 화재 a fire of unknown origin.
**화잠(花簪)** a floral hair-pin.
**화장(火葬)** cremation/ ~하다 cremate/ 전기 ~ electric cremation/ ~ 인부 a cremator; burner at a crematory/~ 터 a crematorium; a crematory; a cremation ground.
**화장(化粧)** toilet[te]; make-up 《옷 매무새》 dressing; beauty care/~하다 make *one's* toilet; paint[powder] *one's* face; dress *one*self 《배우가》 make up *one's* face/눈물로 ~이 지워졌다 Her tears washed away the paint from her face. / ~대 a dressing table; a toilet stand / ~ 비누 a toilet soap/ ~ 상자 a vanity case/~품 toilet articles.
**화장걸음(一長一)** leisurely steps; a gentlemanly gait.
**화재(火災)** a fire 《큰 화재》 a conflagration/ ~ 경보[기] a fire-alarm/ ~ 보험 fire insurance/ ~ 경보 장치 fire-warning facilities/ ~ 방지 주간 Fire Prevention Week/ ~를 일으키다 cause[start] a fire/ ~가 나다 a fire breaks out[starts].
**화재(畵才)** talent for art/그는 ~가 있다 He is a bit of painter.
**화저(火著)** [a pair of] tongs; a set of fire irons.
**화전(火田)** fields burnt away for cultivation/~민(民) firefield farmers; brand-tillers.
**화전(花煎)** ①《꽃전》a cake made in the shape of a flower ②《부꾸미》fried flower cookies.
**화전(火箭)** an incendiary arrow; a fiery dart; a flare; a rocket [signal].
**화전(和戰)** 《전쟁과 평화》 peace and[or] war 《강화》 making[concluding] peace (*with*)/ ~ 조약 a peace treaty.
**화전지(花箋紙)** paper for writing letters [poems].
**화젓가락(火一)** fire tongs ⇒부젓가락.
**화제(話題)** a subject; a topic; a theme [of conversation]/ ~가 풍부한 사람 a person of ample stock of topics/야구 가 학생들 사이의 중요한 ~였다 Baseball

was the chief topic of conversation among the students. わだい

**화제**(畵題) 〖그림 제목〗 the title[subject, theme] of a picture[painting]; 〖그림 위의〗 a composition written on a picture to explain it. がだい

**화조**(花鳥) 〖꽃과 새〗 flowers and birds; 〖새〗 birds that visit flowers 〖그림·조각〗 a painting[sculpture] of flowers and birds/ ~ 화첩(畵帖) an album of flowers and birds. かちょう

**화족**(華族) 〖사람〗 a peer; a noble[man]; 〖전체〗 the nobility; the peerage; the aristocracy.

**화주**(火酒) 〖주정〗 alcohol 〖독한 술〗 strong liquor; firewater《미·속》.

**화주**(花主) the style [of a flower].

**화주**(貨主) a goods-holder; the owner of goods.

**화중군자**(花中君子) the lotus flower. かちゅうのくんし

**화중왕**(花中王) the peony. かちゅうのおう

**화중지병**(畵中之餠) pie in the sky; something not available. えのなかのもち

**화증**(火症) anger; ire; passion/ ~이 나다 get angry[mad]; fly into temper[a rage].

**화차**(火車) a train ⇨기차.

**화차**(貨車) a goods waggon[van]〈영〉; a freight car〈미〉 ~ 인도 〖상〗 free on rail(略: f.o.r.)〈영〉; free on board(略: f.o.b.)〈미〉. かしゃ

**화창**(和暢) balminess; brightness [of weather]; placidity/ ~하다 〖날씨가〗 (be) balmy; bright; sunny; genial 〖마음이〗 (be) content[ed] and peaceful; placid and happy/ ~한 봄날 a balmy spring day. てんきがさわやかなこと

**화채**(花菜) juice mixed with fruits as a punch.

**화첩**(畵帖) a picture book[album]. がちょう

**화초**(花草) a flowe; rflowering plants / ~ 재배 floriculture/ ~밭 a flower garden/ ~ 전시회 a flower show.

**화촉**(華燭) 〖결혼식〗 a wedding; a marriage ceremony 〖초〗 painted candles/ ~을 밝히다 celebrate a wedding; solemnize a marriage. かしょく

**화치다** (a ship) roll; (a boat) rock.

**화친**(和親) friendship; friendly relations; amity/ ~하다 〖…과 ~을 맺다〗 enter into friendly relations with/ ~ 조약 a peace treaty / ~ 협상(協商) an entente cordiale(F). わしん

**화침**(火針) a red-hot needle [used in breaking a boil]/ ~질하다 break[open, lance] a boil with a red-hot needle.

**화탁**(花托) 〖식〗 the receptacle; the torus; the thalamus. かたく

**화태**(禍胎) the root of evil ⇨화근.

**화톳불** a bonfire; an outdoor fire/ ~을 놓다 make a bonfire. おおかがりひ

**화통**(火筒) a funnel.

**화투**(花鬪) Korean playing cards; "flower cards"/ ~치다 play cards. はなふだ

**화판**(花瓣) 〖식〗 a petal ⇨꽃잎. かべん

**화판**(畵板) a drawing board. がばん

**화편**(花片) fallen petals of flowers.

**화평**(和平) peace; harmony; placidity/ ~하다 (be) peaceful; harmonious; placid/ ~을 제창하다 make an overture of peace/ ~ 교섭 peace negotiations/ ~ 문제 the issue of peace/ ~ 조건 terms of peace.

**화폐**(貨幣) 〖경화〗 a coin; money 〖집합적〗 coinage 〖통화〗 currency/보조 ~ subsidiary coins/~ 제도 a monetary system/ ~ 가치 value in money/ ~ 개혁 currency reform 〖명가 절하〗 devaluation/~ 단위 a monetary unit/ ~ 본위 the monetary standard/ ~ 위조 counterfeiting/ ~ 표준 standard money/위조 ~ a counterfeit coin[piece of currency]/ ~를 주조하다 mint coins. かへい

**화포**(花苞) 〖식〗 a bract.

**화포**(火砲) a gun; a firearm.

**화포**(花砲) 〖장난감〗 a firecracker.

**화포**(畵布) a convas.

**화포**(花布) 〖미〗 figured cotton cloth; fancy cotton cloth.

**화폭**(畵幅) a picture; a drawing. がふく

**화풀이** satisfying resentment; letting off -steam; venting one's wrath/ ~하다 satisfy one's resentment; let off steam; vent one's wrath (on)/나한테 ~할 것 없다 You shouldn't take your anger out on me.

**화품**(畵品) artistic merit of a picture; a style of a picture. がひん

**화풍**(畵風) a style of painting. がふう

**화풍**(和風) a gentle breeze; a balmy wind. わふう

**화피**(花被) 〖식〗 the perianth; of a flower the floral envelope.

**화필**(畵筆) a painting brush; a painter's [an artist's] brush. がひつ

**화하다**(化—) 〖변화하다〗 change[turn, reduce] into[to]; be turned[reduced] into 〖변형시키다〗 transform (into, to); be transformed/한국~ be Koreanized.
へんかする

**화하다**(和—) ①〖섞다〗 mix; mingle; blend ②〖온화하다〗 be mild; be genial; be congenial. こんごうする

**화학**(化學) chemistry/ ~적으로 chemical[ly]/ ~자 a chemist/유기[무기] ~ organic[inorganic] chemistry/ ~ 약품 chemicals/ ~ 비료 a chemical fertilizer/ ~ 공업 chemical industry/~ 작용·[변화] chemical action[change]/ ~ 선(線) actinic rays/ ~ 결합 chemical combination/ ~ 기계 chemical instruments[appliances, implements]/ ~ 기호 chemical signs[symbols]/ ~ 반응 a chemical reaction/ ~ 방정식 a chemical equation/~ 변화 a chemical change/~ 섬유 a synthetic[chemical] fiber / ~ 실험실 a chemical laboratory/~ 용법 chemotherapy/ ~ 제품 chemical goods[products]; chemicals/물리 ~ physical chemistry/열~ thermal chemistry/유기 ~ organic chemistry/응용 ~ applied chemistry. かがく

**화합**(化合) 〖화〗 chemical combination/ ~하다 combine (*with*)/ ~물 a chemical compound/수소와 산소는 ~해서 물이 된다 Hydrogen combines with oxygen to form water. かごう

**화합**(和合) 《평화》 peace 《조화》 harmony 《결합》 unity/ ~하다 be harmonious; be in harmony; live in peace; be in full accord/~하여 살다 live in perfect harmony/ ~ 일치 unity; unanimity.

**화해**(火海) a sea of flames; a wide expanse of fire.

**화해**(和解) reconciliation; an amicable settlement; accommodation; composition 《타협》 compromise/ ~하다 be reconciled; make peace; come to terms 《소송을 하지 않고 당사자끼리》 settle out of court/서로 ~해서 다시 친구가 되자 Let us become reconciled and be friends again. わかい

**화현**(和絃) 〖악〗 a chord; a concord. わおん

**화협**(和協) harmonious co-operation/ ~하다 be in harmony with/ ~하여 일하다 work in harmony. わきょう

**화형**(火刑) burning at the stake; the stake/~을 당하다 suffer at the stake.

**화환**(花環) a wreath; a garland 《헌화》 a floral tribute/ ~을 바치다 place[lay] a wreath (at[on] *the tomb*). はなわ

**화훼**(花卉) flowering grass[plants]/ ~ 재배 floriculture; cultivation of flowers/ ~ 재배가 a floriculturist. かき

**확**¹ (절구의) the hollow of a grain mortar/절구 ~이 넓다 a mortar has a large bowl. うす

**확**² (빨리) rapidly; in a flash 《돌연》 suddenly 《세게》 violently 《불이》 flaring up; with a burst/불이 별안간 ~ 타올랐다 The fire sprang into a blaze. さっと

**확견**(確見) a definite idea[view].

**확고**(確固) firmness; fixedness/ ~하다 (be) firm; fixed; determined; resolute / ~한 결심 a firm determination/ ~한 신념 a firm belief. かっこ

**확답**(確答) a definite answer[reply]/ ~하다 answer[reply] definitely; give a definite answer[reply]/ ~을 주지 않다 give no definite answer. かくとう

**확대**(擴大) magnification; magnifying 《사진의》 enlarging/ ~하다 《넓히다》 magnify 《넓어지다》 spread; expand 《사전 따위가》 assume serious proportions 《사진을》 enlarge/두 배로 ~된 사진 a twice enlarged photo/ ~경 a magnifying glass[lens]; a magnifier/ ~ 재생산 expansive reproduction / ~기(器) an enlarger/ ~율(率) magnification [power]; lens power. かくだい

**확론**(確論) an infallible[a solid] argument; an indisputable opinion/ ~하다 discuss[argue] definitely.

**확률**(確率) probability/~ 곡선 a probability curve/~ 오차 a probable error. かくりつ

**확립**(確立) establishment/~하다 establish; settle; fix/지위를 ~하다 establish *one's* position. かくりつ

**확보**(確報) a definite[reliable] report; authentic news/~하다 give a definite report. かくほう

**확보**(確保) security; insurance; guarantee/~하다 secure; insure; guarantee; ensure; maintain/식량을 ~하다 secure foodstuffs. かくほう

**확산**(擴散) 〖물〗 diffusion/~하다 diffuse /빛의 ~ diffusion of light/핵 ~ 금지 조약 nonproliferation treaty. かくさん

**확성기**(擴聲器) a loud speaker; a [sound] magnifier; a megaphone; a speech trumpet/~로 말하다 speak over a loudspeaker. かくせいき

**확수**(確守) adhesion/~하다 adhere to; stick to; cling to; hold fast to.

**확신**(確信) conviction; assurance; confidence; firm belief/~하다 be convinced (*of*); be confident (*of*); believe firmly /나는 우리편이 이긴다고 ~한다 I feel confident that our team will win. かくしん

**확실**(確實) certainty; reliability; authenticity/~하다 《틀림없다》 (be) sure; certain; secure 《믿을 만하다》 (be) reliable; trustworthy; valid 《견실하다》 (be) sound; solid; substantial/ ~성이 있다 wear an aspect of certainty/~히 certainly; surely; reliably; to a certainty/~한 사실 a certain fact/~한 대답 a definite answer/ ~성 certainty; reliability; validity/그가 성공할 것은 ~하다 He is sure to succeed./비가 올 것만은 ~하다 I can assure you of one thing. かくじつ

**확약**(確約) a definite promise/ ~하다 give *one's* word (*to*); commit *one*self (*to*); guarantee/ ~은 할 수 없다 I can not make a definite promise. かくやく

**확언**(確言) assertion; affirmation; definite statement/ ~하다 say positively; assert; affirm/그 점은 ~하기 어렵다 I am not positive about the point. かくげん

**확연**(確然) definitely; positively; certainly; surely/~하다 (be) definite; positive; certain; sure.

**확인**(確認) confirmation; certification; validation; affirmation/ ~하다 confirm; affirm; validate; certify; ascertain/~ 사항 items confirmed/ ~ 통지서 a confimation note/ ~ 판결 a declaratory judgment/진상을 ~하다 get at the truth/…의 사실을 ~하다 ascertain the

**확장**(擴張) extension; enlargement; expansion／～하다 expand; extend; enlarge／점포를 ～하다 enlarge the store／업무를 ～하다 expand[extend] the business／군비 ～ an increase in armaments; an armaments boost／영토 ～ territorial expansion.

**확적하다**(確的—) (be) certain; postive; sure.

**확정**(確定) 《결정》decision; settlement 《귀결》conclusion 《확인》confirmation; ascertainment／～하다 decide; fix; settle; confirm／～된 settled; decided; certain; definite／～ 판결 an irrevocable[a final and conclusive] judgement／～안(案) a final draft／～일자 a fixed date; an inconvertible date／이것은 ～된 사실이다 This is an established fact.

**확증**(確證) corroboration; confirmation 《증거》conclusive[strong] evidence; a positive[decisive, convincing] proof／～하다 prove positively; give positive proof of／～을 잡다 secure positive evidence (of).

**확지**(確知) definite knowledge／～하다 know definitely; know for a fact.

**확집**(確執) 《불화》discord; dissension; strife; feud 《고집》adhesion／～하다 be at feud with; adhere to.

**확청**(廓淸) a purge; expurgation; a clean-up／～하다 purge; clean up; purify.

**확충**(擴充) expansion; amplification 《논》distribution／～하다 amplify; expand; generalize／생산력 ～ an expansion of productive capacity.

**확호**(確乎) firmly; determinedly／～하다 (be) firm; resolute; definite; fixed; steady／～부동한 firm; unyielding; steady; steadfast.

**확확** 《불이》all ablaze; in flames 《세게》violently 《바람이》with great puffs; with gusts／～ 타오르는 fiery; blazing; flaming.

**환**¹ 《줄》a kind of file[rasp]／～ 쓸다 file; rasp.

**환**² 《그림》a rough drawing; a sketch; a painting／ ～을 치다 draw[make] a sketch.

**환**(丸) a pill ⇒환약(丸藥).

**환**(換) 《경》a money order; exchange／외국 ～ foreign exchange／우편 ～ postal money order／～을 발행하다 draw a bill of exchange／～시세 the rate of exchange; exchange rates／전보 ～ telegraphic remittance／～거래 exchange dealing／소액 ～ a postal note.

**환가**(換價) conversion [into money]; realization／～하다 convert into money; cash; sell; realize／～성 marketability; market value／ ～율 a conversion rate ／재산을 ～하다 realize property.

**환각**(還却) return／～하다 return; give back.

**환각**(幻覺) 《심》a hallucination; a illusion／～병 hallucinosis／～제 a hallucinoyen／～를 일으키다 hallucinate; have hallucinations.

**환갑**(還甲) one's 60th birthday anniversary／～ 노인 a sexagenarian／～ 잔치를 베풀다 give a banquet on one's 60th birthday.

**환거**(還去) returning; going back.／ ～하다 return.

**환경**(環境) environment; circumstances; surroundings／ ～에 좌우되다 be influenced by one's surroundings／좋은 ～에서 자란 아이 a child raised in a good neighborhood／～위생 environment[al] sanitation[hygiene]／가정[사회적] ～ home[social] environment／～생활 ～ life environment; living conditions.

**환곡**(換穀) exchanging grain／～하다 exchange grain.

**환골 탈퇴**(換骨奪胎) adaptation; recast; modification／～하다 adapt; remodel; modify; recast.

**환관**(宦官) a eunuch.

**환국**(還國) return to one's country ⇒귀국(歸國).

**환군**(還軍) the withdrawl of an army／～하다 withdraw an army.

**환궁**(還宮) return[ing] to the palace／～하다 return to the palace.

**환권**(換券) changing old deeds[documents] for new one's／～하다 change (deeds, documents).

**환금**(換金) 《경》exchange／～하다 exchange／～ 수수료 a commission[charge] for exchange.

**환급**(還給) return restoration／～하다 give back; return.

**환기**(喚起) awakening／～하다 arouse; awaken／주의를 ～시키다 call (a person's) attention to (a fact)／여론을 ～시키다 rouse[arouse, stir up] public opinion.

**환기**(換氣) ventilation／～하다 ventilate／～가 잘[안] 되다 be well[ill] ventilated／～ 장치 ventilation facilities[equipment, arrangement]／～창 a vent; a window for ventilation.

**환난**(患難) a misfortune; troubles; a mishap.

**환납**(還納) return; restoration／ ～하다 return [public goods].

**환담**(歡談) a pleasant talk／ ～하다 have a pleasant chat[talk]; hobnob with (a person).

**환대**(歡待) a warm reception; hospital treatment; welcome; hospitality／～하다 give a warm reception; receive cordially; entertain warmly／～를 받다 be received cordially.

**환도**(環刀) a service-sword; a saber／～

**뼈 〖해〗** the hip bone. ぐんとう
**환도(還都)** returning to the former capital／～하다 return to the former capital.
**환등(幻燈)** a magic lantern／～기(器) a magic lantern apparatus. げんとう
**환락(歡樂)** pleasure; enjoyment; amusement／～하다 enjoy *oneself*; have fun／인생의 ～ the pleasure of life／～가(街) an amusement centre／～에 빠지다 give *oneself* up to pleasure. かんらく
**환롱(幻弄)** trickery; imposture; cajolement／～하다 play a trick upon (*one*); impose upon; cajole. ぺてん
**환류(還流)** reflux 《전기·해류의》 a return current／～하다 flow back (*to*); current returns; return (*to*). かんりゅう
**환매(還買)** barter／～하다 barter.
**환멸(幻滅)** disillusion／～의 비애를 느끼다 feel the sorrow of disillusion[a sad disillusionment]／크게 ～을 느끼다 be greatly disillusioned.
**환명(換名)** ～하다 assume *another's* name.
**환몽(幻夢)** an empty dream. げんむ
**환문(喚問)** summons／～하다 summon (*a person*) for examination.
**환발(渙發)** promulgation; proclaimation／～하다 promulgate; proclaim. かんぱつ
**환본(還本)** ～하다 be restored to the original condition. ほんにかえること
**환부(患部)** an affected part／～를 치료하다 dress an affected part. かんぷ
**환부(還付)** return; restitution; retrocession／～하다 return; give back; retrocede. かんぷ
**환산(換算)** change; conversion／～하다 change (*into*); convert (*into*)／～율 exchange rates／～표 an exchange table／미터로 ～하여 calculated in terms of meters. かんさん
**환상(幻想)** an illusion; a vision／～적 visionary／～곡(曲) 《음》 fantasia／～가 a dreamer; a visionary. げんそか
**환상(幻像)** a phantasm; a phantom; an illusion; a vision／～을 쫓다 pursue phantoms.
**환상(環狀)** annulation／～의 ring-shaped; loop／～ 도로 a loop[circular] road／～선 a loop[belt] line. かんじょう
**환생(還生)** new birth; rebirth 《화신》 reincarnation／～하다 be reincarnated; be born again. さいせい
**환성(喚醒)** awakening; disillusion／～하다 wake up; disillusion. かんき
**환성(歡聲)** a shout of joy[jubilation]; a cheer; cheers; a hurrah／～을 울리다 set up a shont of joy. かんせい
**환세(幻世)** the transient world; the mutable world. げんせい
**환세(喚歲)** change of the year. としがあらたまること
**환속(還俗)** return to secular life; secularization／～하다 leave the priesthood; return to secular life.

**환송(還送)** sending back; returning／하다 send back; return. かんそう
**환송(歡送)** a send-off; farewell／～하다 give *a person* a hearty send-off／～회 a farewell meeting[party]／성대한 ～을 받다 be given[receive] a good send-off.
**환술(幻術)** magic [arts]; the black art; witchcraft· sorcery. げんじゅつ
**환시(環視)** concentration [of attention／～하다 watch; concentrate attention on／중인 ～리에 in the full view of the public; in public. かんし
**환심(歡心)** favor; good graces／～을 사다 curry favor with (*a person*); win (*a person's*) favor; ingratiate *oneself* (with *a person*). かんしん
**환약(丸藥)** a pill; a bolus; a globule; a pellet. じょうざい
**환언(換言)** ～하다 say in other words; put (*it*) in another way; change an expression／～하면 in other words; namely; to wit; or; that is [to say]. かんげん
**환영(幻影)** a vision; a phantom／～을 쫓다 be lured by[under] an illusion. げんえい
**환영(歡迎)** welcome; reception／ ～하다 welcome; receive warmly; give a welcome to *a person*／～사 an address of welcome／～을 받다 be warmly welcomed; be given a warm reception; be liked／독자 투고 ～ Contributions from readers are cordially invited／～ 만찬회 a reception dinner／～사를 하다 give an address of welcome／～회(會) a welcome meeting[party]. かんげい
**환우기(換羽期)** the moulting season. かんうき
**환원(還元)** ①《원상 복귀》 restoration／～하다 restore; be restored to [the former condition] ②〖화〗 reduction 《산화물의》 deoxi[di]zation 《분해》 resolution／～하다 reduce; deoxidize 《환원되다》 be reduced／～ 작용 a reducing process／～시키다 《원상태로》 vivify／～제 a reducing agent. かんげん
**환자(患者)** a patient; a case (of *cholera*); a sufferer／무료 ～ a free patient; a charity patient／입원 ～ an inpatient／명부 a sick list／절망적인 ～ a hopeless case. かんじゃ
**환장(換腸)** a complete change of heart [personality]／～하다 become a changed man; be out of *one's* mind; go crazy. きょうきのさた
**환전(換錢)** 《경》 a money order／ ～하다 change [a 10,000 *won* note]／～ 수수료 a commission [charge] for exchange.
**환절(換節)** a change of seasons／～기 a change of season. きせつがかわること
**환절(環節)** 〖동〗 a segment; a somite; a metamere; a ring. かんせつ
**환지(一紙)** sketching paper.
**환초(環礁)** a lagoon; island; an atoll.

환치다 sketch; paint; daub／대를 ~ sketch a bamboo.

환택(還宅) returning to one's honored home; going home.

환퇴(還退) refunding a purchase／~하다 have (a purchase) returned; refund; (a purchase).

환표(換票) ①〖경〗 a money order ②〖선거의〗 replacement of the contents of a ballot box with fake votes 《부정 투표》 forgery of votes／~하다 replace the contents of a ballot box with fake votes.

환품(換品) exchange of goods[articles]／~하다 exchange (goods).

환하다 ①《밝다》(be) bright; light／환하게 하다 brighten; lighten ②《앞이》(be) open; unobstructed ③《얼굴이》(be) fine; bright; handsome ④《통달하다》(be) familiar (with); conversant (with); well acquainted (with) ⑤《명백하다》(be) clear; distinct; plain; evident; patent／시세(市勢)에 ~ be conversant with the market prices.

환향(還鄉) returning to one's native soil [hometown]／~하다 come[go] home／금의(錦衣) ~ returning home loaded with honors; returning home in glory.

환형(環形) a ring shape／~의 ringshaped; looped／~ 동물 Annelida.

환호(歡呼) a cheer; an ovation; an acclamation／~하다 cheer; give cheers／~속에 amidst hearty cheers／~성을 올리다 set up a shout of joy.

환후(患候) the sicknes [illness] of a person hono[u]red.

환희(歡喜) joy; delight／~하다 be delighted; rejoice; be glad.

활 a bow 《궁술》 archery／~의 명수 an expert archer 《현악기의》 the bow／~을 쏘다 shoot an arrow／~을 메우다 make a bow.

활강(滑降) 《스키의》 descent／~ 경기 a downhill race.

활개 ①《사람의》 arms／~치다 swing one's arms ②《새의》 wings／~차다 flap the wings; flutter.

활개똥 a runny discharge from diarrhea.

활갯짓 swinging of the arms in walking／~하다 swing one's arms.

활계(活計) living 《생계(生計)》 livelihood.

활공(滑空) gliding; a glide; volplane／~하다 glide; volplane／~거리 gliding distance.

활극(活劇) a stormy[riotous] scene 《영화》 an action film[picture]／서부 ~ a horse open《미·속》; a western [film]／~을 연출하다 make a scene; have a nice scene.

활기(活氣) activity; viogour; spirit; energy／~있는 active; full of life; lively／~를 띠다 be animated; be spurred; become lively／온 거리는 ~를 띠고 있었다 All the town was up.

활달(豁達) generosity; broad-mindedness; magnanimity／~하다 (be) generous; broadminded; magnanimous／~한 태도 mag-nanimity.

활대 a [sail] yard; a stick; a boom.

활동(活動) activity; motion; operation; working; action／~하다 be active; lead an active life; play[take] an active part (in);《운동》 canvass; campaign 《작용》 function; work／~력 activity／~적인 active; energetic／정신 ~ mental activity／~가 a man of action／~ 범위 the scope[sphere] of activity／정치 ~ political activities.

활등 the back of a bow／~코 a highbridged nose.

활량 an archer; a bowman 《무위 도식자》 an idler; a drone.

활력(活力) vital power[force, energies]; vitality／~소(素) a tonic; a vitamin.

활로(活路) ways[means] of living; a way out (of a difficulty); a means of escape／~를 열다[찾다] find a way out [of the difficulty]; cut one's way through [the enemy].

활무대(活舞臺) a living stage; the arena／~에 나오다 come upon the stage of action.

활물(活物) a living being 《종합적》 life／~ 기생 a parasitism on living things.

활발(活潑) liveliness; briskness; vivacity; vigo[u]r／~하다 (be) active; vivacious; brisk; vigorous 《쾌활하다》 (be) cheerful／~히 activity; briskly／~한 동작 a vigorous action; a sprightly manner／~한 사람 an active person.

활변(滑便) loose feces; lax stools.

활보(闊步) striding; strutting／~하다 stalk; stride; walk with a swinging gait; strut／거리를 ~하다 stalk [along] the streets.

활불(活佛) "a living Buddha"; a merciful person.

활비비 a bow drill.

활빈당(活貧黨) [a band of] Robin Hoods outlaws who rob in order to help the poor.

활빙(滑氷) [ice-]skating／~하다 skate／~ 장 a skating rink.

활살(活殺) life and[or] death.

활색(活塞) 〖공〗 a piston.

활석(滑石) talc; steatite／~분 talcum powder.

활성(活性) 〖화〗 (being) active; activated／~의 active; activated／~화하다 activate.

**활수**(滑手) liberality/ ~하다 (be) free [generous] with one's money; liberal.

**활시위** a bow-string/ ~를 메우다[풀다] string[unstring] a bow.

**활안**(活眼) penetrating eyes; insight; penetration.

**활액**(滑液) 〖해〗 synovia.

**활약**(活躍) activity; action/ ~하다 be active (in); take[play] an active part (in)/정계에서 ~하다 play an active part in politics.

**활연**(豁然) 《돌연》 all of a sudden 《널리》 far and wide; extensively/~하다 (be) wide; open/ ~히 깨닫다 a truth bursts upon one.

**활엽수**(闊葉樹) a broad-leaved tree.

**활용**(活用) ①《응용》 practical use; application/ ~하다 utilize; apply 《이용》 make the most of ②〖문〗《어미의》 inflection《격의》 declension《동사의》 conjugation/ ~하다 inflect; conjugate; decline/ ~어 inflected[inflective] words/ ~형 an inflectional form; an inflected form.

**활유어**(蛞蝓魚) 〖어〗 a lancelet.

**활인화**(活人畵) a living picture; a tableau vivant(pl. tableau vivants)(F).

**활자**(活字) 〖인〗 a printing[movable] type 《총칭》 type/ ~ 주조 type founding[casting]/ ~ 인쇄 type-printing/ ~체 print/ ~판 a printed edition/ ~를 짜다 set (up) type.

**활짝** 《넓게》 extensively; widely 《완전히》 completely; entirely/창문을 ~ 열다 throw open the window/날씨가 ~ 개었다 The weather has cleared up.

**활짱** the body of a bow.

**활전**(活栓) a [stop] cock.

**활주**(滑走) sliding; gliding《비행기의》 planing《공중》 taxi《지상》《빙상의》 skating/ ~하다 glide 《수상·육상의》 taxi《스키에서》 slide/ ~로 a runway; an air strip; a taxiway; a landing strip / ~장 a gliding range.

**활죽** a boom.

**활집** a bow case.

**활차**(滑車) a pulley; a block/고정[동(動)] ~ a fixed[movable] pulley.

**활촉**(一鏃) an arrowhead; the barb [of an arrow].

**활터** an archery ground.

**활판**(活版) 〖인〗[movable] type printing; typography; printing/ ~ 인쇄 type printing; typography/ ~소 a printing house/ ~을 짜다 set type; compose.

**활하다**(滑—) ①《미끄럽다》(be) smooth; slippery; sleek ②《헐겁다》(be) loose-fitting ③《더변이》 (be) loose.

**활화**(活畵) a picturesque scene.

**활화산**(活火山) a buring mountain; an active volcano.

**활활** ①《불이》 [burn] furiously; in flames/장작이 ~ 타다 firewood burns vigorously ②《부채질》[fan] briskly/ ~ 부치다 fan briskly.

**활황**(活況) activity/~을 띠다 show [signs of] activity《상점 따위가》 do brisk business.

**홧김**(火—) ~에 in a fit of anger; in the heat of passion/ ~에 치다 strike (a person) in anger.

**홧홧하다** (be)[feel] hot; feverish; fiery /방안이 ~ The room is hot and stuffy. /홧홧한 더위 sweltering[broiling] heat.

**황**(黃) ① yellow ⇒황색(黃色) ② ⇒석류황(石硫黃).

**황갈색**(黃褐色) yellowish brown/ ~의 yellowish brown.

**황감**(黃柑) a mellow mandarin orange.

**황감**(惶感) deep[reverent] gratitude/ ~하다 (be) filled with awe and gratitude.

**황겁**(惶怯) awe; fear/ ~하다 (be) awestricken; filled with fear.

**황계**(黃鷄) a yellow cock[hen].

**황고**(皇考) one's deceased father.

**황고집**(黃固執) stubbornness; obduracy; obstinacy《사람》 a hard-headed[a full-headed, an obstinate] person.

**황공**(惶恐) being awe-stricken; fear[fulness]/ ~하다 (be) awe-stricken; be afraid; overwhelmed with awe/ ~ 무지하다 be extremely awe-stricken.

**황구**(黃口) ①《새의 새끼》 a chicken; a young bird ②《어린이》 a child; an infant.

**황구**(黃狗) a yellow dog.

**황국**(皇國) the Empire.

**황국**(黃菊) a yellow chrysanthemum.

**황궁**(皇宮) the Imperial Palace.

**황금**(黃金) 《금》 gold《금전》 money《재물》 wealth/ ~의 gold; golden/ ~은 만능이다 A golden key will open most locks., money makes the mare [to] go. / ~ 숭배 money-worship/~ 세계 a Utopia/ ~색 a golden colour/ ~ 만능 시대 a mammonish age/ ~ 시대 the golden age.

**황급**(遑急) precipitation; hurry/ ~하다 (be) in precipitation; in a great hurry / ~히 hastily; in haste.

**황기**(黃旗) a yellow flag.

**황기**(皇旗) the Imperial ensign[standard].

**황기끼다**(惶氣—) be struck with awe; be fear-stricken.

**황녀**(皇女) a[an Imperial] princess.

황달(黃疸) 〖의〗 jaundice.　おうだん
황답(荒畓) a barren paddyfield.
　　あれはてたはたけ
황당(荒唐) absurdity; nonsense／ ~하다 (be) absurd; preposterous; wild; nonsensical／ ~한 absurd; wild; nonsensical／ ~한 풍설을 퍼뜨리다 set wild rumours afloat.　こうとう
황당 무계(荒唐無稽) absurdity; claptrap; nonsense／ ~하다 (be) absurd; wild; nonsensical; fabulous／ ~한 이야기 an absurd story; a cock-and-bull story.
　　こうとうむけい
황도(黃道) 〖천〗 the ecliptic ／ ~대 the zodiac.　こうどう
황도(皇都) the capital of an empire.
　　こうじょう
황동(黃銅) brass／ ~색 brass yellow／~광(鑛) copper pyrites; chalcopyrite.
　　こうどう
황락(荒落) desolation; desertion; bleakness／ ~하다 (be) desolate; bleak; deserted.　こうりょう
황랍(黃蠟) yellow wax; yellow beeswax.
　　みつろう
황량(荒凉) desolateness; dreariness／ ~하다 (be) desolate; deserted; wild; dreary; ruined／ ~한 벌판 a desolate plain; a wilderness.　こうりょう
황련(黃連) 〖깽깽이 뿌리〗 barberry root.
황례포(皇禮砲) an Imperial salute.
황로(荒路) a deserted road; a rough road.　わるいみち
황로(黃櫨) 〖식〗 a wax-tree.
황록색(黃綠色) yellowish green.
황룡(黃龍) a yellow dragon／ ~수(鬚) a variety of chrysanthemum.
황릉(皇陵) an Imperial sepulchre; an Emperor's tomb.　こうりょう
황린(黃燐) 〖화〗 yellow phosphor／ ~ 성냥 locofoco.
황림(荒林) a denuded forest.
황마(黃麻) 〖식〗 a jute; yellow hemp／~부대 a jute[gunny] bag.　おうま
황막(荒漠) wildness; vastness／ ~하다 (be) extensive and devastated; vast and desolate／ ~한 평야 a vast wilderness.　こうばく
황망(慌忙) being in a flurry; being in haste／ ~하다 (be) in hot haste; flurried／ ~히 in a flurry; helter-skelter.
　　あわてること
황망(惶忙) busyness／ ~하다 (be) very busy.　あわていそぐこと
황매(黃梅) a yellow plum [tree].
황명(皇命) an Imperial command; an Imperial mandate.
황모(黃毛) hair from a weasel's tail／ ~필 a writing brush made of weaseltail hair.　いたちのけ
무(荒蕪) wilderness; desolation; barrenness／ ~하다 (be) wild; waste; barren ／ ~의 desolate; waste; wild／ ~지(地) a barren tract; a wilderness; waste land.　こうぶ
황민(荒民) famine-stricken people; famine sufferers.
황밤(黃-) dried chestnuts.
황비(皇妃) an empress.　こうひ
황사(皇嗣) the Crown Prince; the Imperial heir.　こうし
황사(黃絲) yellow thread.　きいろいいと
황산(黃酸) 〖화〗 the oil of vitriol; sulphuric acid／ ~염 a sulphate／ ~동 copper sulphate／ ~지 parchment-paper／ ~ 암모늄 ammonium sulfate／ ~ 아연 sulfate of zinc.　りゅうさん
황상(皇上) the present Emperor; His Majesty.
황새 〖조〗 a stork／뱁새가 ~를 따라가려 하다 try to do what is beyond one's capacity.　こうのとり
황새걸음 long strides; the gait of a stork／ ~으로 걷다 stalk; take long steps; stride.
황색(黃色) yellow／ ~ 인종 the yellow race／ ~ 신문 a yellow paper[journal]; yellow press.　きいろ
황석(黃石) 〖광〗 yellow calcite.
황설(荒說) an absurd[a groundless] argument; a baseless opinion.
황성(皇城) ①〖궁성〗 the Imperial Palace ②〖수도〗 the capital.　こうじょう
황소 a bull／ ~처럼 일하다 work like a horse.
황소걸음 (느린 걸음) a slow step; a leisurely pace／ ~하다 walk slowly[leisurely].　のろいあゆみ
황소바람 a draught; a draft.
손(皇孫) an Imperial grandchild.
　　こうそん
황송(惶悚) ~하다 (be) gracious; awful; awe-inspiring; august／ ~하게 graciously.　おそれかしこむこと
황숙(黃熟) ~하다 ripen yellow.
황실(皇室) the Imperial Household[House, Family]／ ~ 재산 the Imperial estate.　こうしつ
황아(荒一) sundries; variety goods／ ~ 장수 a peddler of sundries.　ざっか
황야(荒野) a wilderness; a desert land; a waste; the wilds.　こうや
황양목(黃楊木) 〖식〗 the boxwood tree.
황어(黃魚) 〖어〗 a dace.
황연(晃然) brightly; clearly／ ~하다 (be) bright; clear.　あかるいさま
황열(黃熱) 〖의〗 yellow fever.　おうねつ
황옥(黃玉) 〖광〗 topaz; yellow jade.
　　おうぎょく
황운(皇運) the fortunes of an Emperor.
　　こううん
황위(皇位) the Imperial Throne／ ~를 잇다[에 오르다] succeed to[ascend] the Throne.　こうい
황위(皇威) Imperial prestige[power].
　　こうい
황은(皇恩) Imperial favour[benevolence].
황음(荒淫) sexual indulgence; carnal ex-

cesses／ ～ 무도하다 be dissipated and depraved.　こういん
황의(黃衣) 《옷》 yellow clothes.　おうい
황인종(黃人種) the yellow race.
황자(皇子) a[an Imperial] prince; a prince of the Blood.　おうじ
황작(黃雀) ①《꾀꼬리》a golden oriole ②《참새》a sparrow.　うぐいす
황잡(荒雜) incoherence; desultoriness／～하다 (be) loose; desultory; incoherent; slipshod／～한 생각 loose ideas／～한 지식 unsystematic knowledge.
황저(皇儲) the Crown prince; the heir apparent to the throne.
황전(荒田) barren land; a waste; a waste field.　こうでん
황제(皇帝) a crowned head; an emperor／～의 Imperial／～ 폐하 His Majesty the Emperor.　こうてい
황조(皇祖) 《황제의》 Imperial ancestors 《할아버지》 one's own revered dead grandfather.　おうちょう
황조(皇祚) the Imperial Throne／～를 잇다 ascend the Throne.　こうそ
황조(黃鳥) 【조】 a golden oriole.　うぐいす
황조롱이 【조】 a kestrel.
황족(皇族) the Imperial[Royal] family 《개인》 an Imperial[a Royal] prince[princess]; a prince[princess] of the Blood／～ 회의 an Imperial Family Council.　こうぞく
황지(荒地) a waste; waste[barren] land.　こうち
황지(黃紙) yellow paper.　きいろいかみ
황진(黃塵) 《흙먼지》dust in the air／만장(萬丈)의 ～ a cloud of dust.　こうじん
황차(況且) much more; much less ⇒하물며.　いわんや
황천(黃泉) Hades; the land of the dead／～ 길 a journey to the other world [one's last home]／～객 a dead person／～객(客)이 되다 die; turn up one's toes.　こうせん
황천(皇天) ①《하늘》High Heaven; Heaven on High; God's Heaven ②《하나님》God／～ 후토 the gods of heaven and earth.
황철광(黃鐵鑛) 【광】 iron pyrites.　おうてっこう
황촌(荒村) a deserted[desolated] village.　こうそん
황칠(黃漆) a yellow dye from Jeju Island／～ 나무 Textoria morbifera《학명》.　きいろいうるし
황탄(荒誕) absurdity; fallacy／～하다 (be) absurd; fantastic; utter nonsense; wild; fabulous／～ 무계(無稽)하다 be absurd through and through.　こうたん
황태손(皇太孫) the eldest grandson of an Emperor [in the direct line].　こうたいそん
황태자(皇太子) the Crown Prince; the Prince Imperial／～를 책봉하다 proclaim the Heir Apparent to the Throne／～비(妃) the Crown Princess.　こうたいし
황태후(皇太后) the Queen Mother; the Empress Dowager.　こうたいごう
황토(黃土) loess; yellow soil.　おうど
황통(皇統) the Imperial line／～을 잇다 accede to the Throne.　こうとう
황파(荒波) rough seas; high waves; heavy seas; the open sea／～가 일다 be rough; be high.
황폐(荒廢) desolation; dilapidation; waste; ruin／～하다 be devastated; go to ruin; be laid waste／～케 하다 lay waste; devastate／～지 waste land／산림 ～ forest denudation.　こうはい
황포(黃袍) the Imperial robe.
황하다(荒—) (be) rough; careless; sloppy; slipshod.　あらい
황해(黃海) the Yellow Sea.
황혼(黃昏) dusk; [evening] twilight; gloaming／～에 at dusk[sundown]; in the gathering darkness／～이 지다[깃들다] dusk falls.／나무가 여러 그루 ～ 속에 흐릿하게 보였다 Trees loomed in the twilight.　たそがれ
황홀(恍惚) 《무아경》rapture; trance; ecstasy／～하다 (be) charming; enchanting; fascinating／～한 광경 a charming spectacle／～하여지다 be enraptured; be enchanted; be lost in admiration／～하여 in raptures.　こうこつ
황화(荒貨) variety goods; small items; notions; fancy goods; haberdashery〈영〉／～방 a haberdasher〈영〉; a fancy goods store〈미〉.　ざっか
황화(黃禍) the yellow peril.
황화(黃化) 【화】 sulfuration[sulphuration〈영〉]; sulfurization／～하다 sulfurate; sulfurize／～ 암모늄[은, 수소, 철, 동] ammonium[silver, hydrogen, iron, copper] sulfide.
황후(皇后) an Empress; an Imperial consort; a Queen／～폐하 Her Majesty the Empress.　こうご
홰¹ 《새장의》 a perch; a roost 《새벽 닭 우는》 cockcrow.　とりのとまりぎ
홰² 《햇불의》 a [pine] torch; a link; a flambeau; a firebrand／～에 불을 붙이다 kindle[light] a torch.　たいまつ
홰나무 【식】 the pagoda-tree.
홰치다 flap[clap, beat] the wings; flutter／닭이 ～ a hen flaps its wings.　はねばたく
홰홰 round and round／～ 휘두르다 brandish 《a stick》／～ 감기다 coil[twine] around 《a pole》.　びゅうびゅう
핵 ① ⇒책핵 ②《갑자기》suddenly; with a jerk; quickly 《힘있게》 violently／～ 던지다 jerk／～ 잡아당기다 pull with a jerk.　さっと
핵핵 ①《날쎄게》snap-snap; with dispatch; quickly ②《갑자기》swish-swish; speedily; fast／자동차가 ～ 지나가다 Cars zoom by. ③《던지다》flinging repeated-

ly **(부리치다)** with shove after shove; with jerk after jerk ④**(때리다)** with whack after whack/채찍으로 ~ 갈기다 keep whacking with a whip. さっとさっと

**횃대** a clothes-rack[hanger]. えもんかけ

**횃불** a torch; a link; a firebrand **(군호의)** a signal fire; a beacon **(노영(露營)의)** a bonfire; a campfire/ ~을 들다 carry a torch in *one's* hand/ ~을 켜다 light[kindle] a torch. たいまつのあかり

**횃줄** a clothesline.

**횅뎅그렇하다** (be) empty and desolate; unduly wide and hollow **(빈 것 같다)** appear empty[bare, vacant]; look hollow. がらんとしている

**횅하다** ①**(정통하다)** (be) well versed in; conversant *(with, in)* ②**(공허하다)** (be) empty; hollow; vacant/집이 ~ a house is empty ③⇨횅뎅그렇하다.

**회(灰)** ①⇨석회(石灰) ②**(벽토)** mortar; plaster **(백토의)** stucco/~를 바르다 plaster; stucco.

**회(蛔)** a roundworm; an ascarid; a mawworm. かいちゅう

**회(會)** **(회합)** a meeting; a gathering **(사교상의)** a party **(단체)** a society; an association; a club/~를 열다 give a party; hold[open] a meeting/~를 조직하다 form[organize] a society. あつまり

**회(膾)** [slices of] raw fish[meat]/ ~를 치다 slice raw fish[meat]/생선~ sliced [slices] raw fish. さしみ

**회(回)** **(횟수)** a time **(경기의)** a round; a bout **(야구의)** an inning[innings〈영〉]; **(연재물의)** an instalment **(트럼프·권투·골프 따위의)** a round; a bout; a game **(권투 따위의)** the first round/ ~을 거듭하다 do[hold] it several times. かい

**회갑(回甲)** *one's* 60sh birthday; full anniversary 60 years of age.

**회개(悔改)** repentance; penitence/~하다 be penitent; repent *(of)*.

**회견(會見)** an interview; a meeting/ ~하다 interview; meet; have an interview with/단독 ~ a single interview; an exclusive interview *(with)*/비공식 ~ an informal interview/ ~을 거절하다 refuse to be interviewed by newsmen. かいけん

**회계(會計)** **(계산)** accounts; accounting **(재정)** finance/~하다 keep accounts **(지불)** pay a bill/~과 the accounting section; an accounts section/~ 연도 a fiscal[financial] year/~학 accountancy /~ 장부 an account-book/~ 서류 financialdouments. かいけい

**회고(回顧)** reflection; recollection; retrospection/~하다 look back on; reflect [upon]/~담(談) recollections/~록(錄) reminiscences memoirs. かいこ

**회고(懷古)** retrospection; reminiscence/ ~하다 retrospect; look back upon the past; recall the past to *one's* mind/ ~적인 retrospective/ ~담 reminiscences /~시 a reminiscent poem. かいこ

**회공** being hollow[empty] inside/~하다 become hollowed; be sunk; get empty. むなしいこと

**회과(悔過)** repentance; remorce; penitence; regret/~하다 repent of; be penitent for/~ 자책(自責) self-reproach[-condemnation, reproof, accusation]. あやまちをこうかいすること

**회관(會館)** a hall; an assembly-hall/기독교 청년 ~ the Y. M. C. A. [Hall]/학생 ~ the student's hall. かいかん

**회교(回敎)** 【종】 Mohammedanism; Islamism; Islam/~국 a Mohammedan country/~도 a Mohammedan; a Moslem/~ 사원 a mosque.

**회구(懷舊)** recollection ⇨회고(懷古).
かいきゅう

**회구(繪具)** pigment; paint ⇨채료(彩料).

**회군(回軍)** the withdrawal of an army[of troops]; a troop withdrawal/~하다 withdraw the army. ぐんをいをもどすこと

**회귀(回歸)** recurrence; *(one)* complete revolution/~하다 revolve; recur/~선 (線) the tropic/~ 무풍대 the calm zone of the tropics/~적 periodic/~ 곡선 a regression curve/태양의 주위를 ~하다 revolve round the sun. かいき

**회규(會規)** the rules[regulations] of a society; the bylaw of an assembly.
かいき

**회기(回期)** date of return.

**회기(會期)** **(회의의)** a session; a sitting **(기간)** a term/ ~ 연장 the extension of a session/국회 ~중 during the Assembly Session/~를 연장하다 extend the session. かいき

**회나무** 【식】 a Korean spindle tree.

**회담(會談)** a conversation; a talk **(회견)** an interview/ ~하다 talk together; meet for discussion; interview/장시간 ~하다 have a long talk (with *a person*) /본~ full-dress[main] talks/비공식 ~ an off-the-record conference /예비 ~ preliminary talks. かいだん

**회답(回答)** a reply; a response; an answer/~하다 [make an] answer; [give a] reply **(응답)** respond/…의 ~으로 in answer[reply] to/편지로 ~하다 answer[reply to] a letter. かいとう

**회당(會堂)** **(예배당)** a chapel; a church **(공회당)** an assembly hall; a hall.

**회독(回讀)** reading *(a book)* in turn/~하다 read *(a book)* in turn/잡지 ~회 a circulating magazine library/ ~료 a fee for the circulating library. かいどく

**회똑거리다** wobble; jitter ⇨휘똑거리다.
よろめく

**회똘회똘** winding ⇨휘둘휘똘. くねくね

**회동(會同)** meeting[gathering] together / ~하다 meet [together]; assemble; have a meeting; get together. かいどう

**회동그라지다** **(눈이)** open wide 《놀다가》

**회동그랗다** ①(가든하다) be completely finished; be completed ②(눈이) (be) wide-opened／남은 일을 회동그랗게 해치우다 clean up unfinished work.

**회두리** the end[finish]; the last round／～ 씨름 the last round of a wrestling match／～판 the last scene[state]. びり

**회람(回覽)** circulation／～하다 circulate／～판 a circulating bulletin; a notification board／～ 잡지 a circulating magazine／～판을 돌리다 pass on a circular notice. かいらん

**회랑(回廊)** a corridor; a passage; a gallery; a veranda; a cloister／공중 ～ an air corridor (to). かいろう

**회례(回禮)** (선물) a return present (답례) a return call／～하다 make a present in return (답례하다) make a return present; return a call／～로 in acknowledgment (of); on return for.

**회례(廻禮)** a round of complimentary visits[calls]／～하다 pay social visits／신년의 ～를 하다 make the New Year's calls. かいれい

**회로(回路)** ①(물) a circuit ②(the way back 《돌아오는 길》) the return way／～차단기 a circuit breaker／～에 on one's way back／직렬[병렬] ～ a series[parallel] circuit. かいろ

**회로(懷爐)** a bosom-warmer; a pocket heater. かいろ

**회뢰(賄賂)** bribery (물건) a bribe／～사건 a graft case; a bribery case／～를 주다 bribe (a person)／～를 받다 take[accept, receive] a bribe (from); be bribed; graft 《미·구》. わいろ

**회류(會流)** confluence (회류하는 강) junction; a confluent／～하다 flow[run] together; merge (into); join／～점 a junction. かいりゅう

**회리바람** a whirlwind; an eddywind; a cyclone; a tornado／～꽃 a kind of anemone; *Anemone reflexa*(학명). つむじかぜ

**회마(回馬)** a return horse; turning *a person's* horse round.

**회매하다** feel neat and tidy[light]; (be) neat and tidy; light／회매한 몸차림 a light outfit (for *a journey*).

**회맹(會盟)** a league; a covenant／～하다 league[band] together; form a league; enter into a covenant. かいめい

**회명(會名)** the name of a society[an association].

**회명(晦冥)** darkness／～하다 (be) dark. かいめい

**회모(懷慕)** longing; yearning／～하다 long[yearn] for／어머니를 ～하며 울다 cry for *one's* deceased mother.

**회목** the wrist or the ankle. あしくび

**회목(檜木)** 《식》 a kind of cypress; the Chinese juniper.

**회무(會務)** affairs of a society／～는 시급히 처리해 주기를 바란다 We want to have the affairs of the society administered with all speed. かいむ

**회문(回文)** (회장) a circular [letter]; a round-robin (한 시체의) a palindrome／～을 돌리다 send a circular; circulate a letter.

**회백색(灰白色)** light gray; light ash color. かいはくしょく

**회벽(灰壁)** a wall plastered with lime.

**회보(回報)** a report (답보) a reply; an answer (돌아와서 내는) bringing back a report／～하다 reply (to); answer; respond to; give a reply; send an answer. かいほう

**회보(會報)** a bulletin; a report; the transactions of a society／동창회 ～ an alumni bulletin. かいほう

**회복(回復)** recovery (복구) restoration (명예 따위) retrieval (건강) recuperation (재건) rehabilitation (부활) revival／～하다 (병자가) recover (from *illness*); be restored to [good] health (다시 찾다) recover; regain; retrieve／～기 [period of] convalescence／명예를 ～하다 regain *one's* good reputation／건강을 ～하다 regain[recover] *one's* health; be restored to health／원기를 하다 recover strength; be refreshed／의식을 ～하다 recover consciousness. かいふく

**회복(恢復)** restoration; rehabilitation; reestablishment／～하다 restore; rehabilitate／국토를 ～하다 regain a lost country; rehabilitate a country. かいふく

**회부(回附)** transmission／～하다 transmit; refer; send [over]; forward; pass on (to)／그 사건은 하급 재판소에 ～되었다 The case was remitted to a lower court.

**회비(會費)** (일시적인) a fee (회원의) a membership fee (클럽, 학회 등의) the subscription／～ 미납자 a member [dues]delinquent／～를 거두다 collect dues／～는 당일 납부할 것 The subscription to be paid at the meeting. かいひ

**회사(回謝)** a present in token of *one's* gratitude／～하다 express *one's* gratitude／～ 선물 a return present.

**회사(會社)** a company (略：Co.); a corporation(미); (상사(商社)) a firm／～법 the corporation law; the company law／～원 a company employee／～에 근무하다 be employed in a company／～ 업무 company affairs／～ 중역 a member of the directory. かいしゃ

**회상(回想)** recollection; retrospection; reminiscence／ ～하다 look back upon; recollect; retrospect／～록 reminiscences; memoirs. かいそう

**회상(會商)** a conference; a negotiation; talks; a parley／～하다 negotiate (*with*); hold conference (*with*).

**회색(灰色)** gray; ash color; drab color／～ 분자 a wobbler／그 여자는 ～ 옷을 입고

있었다 She dressed in grey. かいしょく

**회생**(回生) restoration to life; revival; resuscitation/~하다 revive; be restored to life again/기사(起死)~의 신약(神藥) a wonder drug to restore the dead to life. かいせい

**회서**(回書) a letter of reply. かいしょ

**회석**(會席) a place of meeting; a meeting. かいせき

**회선**(回船) 《돌아가는 배》a return boat; the boat back 《배를 돌림》turning a boat around/~하다 turn back a ship. かいせん

**회선**(回線) a circuit; an electrical circuit /전화 ~ a telephone circuit.

**회선**(回旋) rotation; revolution/ ~하다 revolve; rotate; turn[spin] round 《기계가》run/~곡 a rondo/~ 기중기 a rotary crane/~ 운동 rotary[spinal] motion/~ 포대 a [rotating] turret. かいせん

**회송**(回送) sending back; returning/ ~하다 forward; send on/~점 a forwarding agency/~차 an out-of-service [train]/편지를 이사한 주소로 ~하다 forward a letter to one's new address. かいそう

**회수**(回收) 《수금》collection 《철회》withdrawal/~하다 collect; withdraw; recover/통화 ~ the withdrawal of notes in circulation/폐품 ~ the recovery of waste materials/대금을 ~하다 collect loans. かいしゅう

**회수**(回數) the number of times; the frequency[oftenness]/~를 거듭하다 repeat so many times. かいすう

**회수권**(回數券) a coupon ticket; a [railway] coupon ticket 《승차권》a commutation ticket/~ 사용자 a commuter/철도 ~ a railroad commuter's ticket/10회의 ~ a ticket of ten coupons. かいすうけん

**회시**(回示) ①《회답》a reply; an answer [from the other party] ②《죄인을》taking a criminal around for exhibition.

**회식**(會食) dining together/ ~하다 dine together; dine with (a person). かいしょく

**회신**(灰燼) ashes; embers/ ~으로 화하다 be reduced to ashes 《건물 따위》be burnt to the ground 《도시·건물 따위》be razed to the ground. かいじん

**회심**(悔心) repentance; penitence; remorse. こうかいするこころ

**회심**(回心) a change of heart; conversion; regeneration/ ~하다 change one's heart; convert; repent/~시키다 convert (one). かいしん

**회심**(會心) congeniality; complacency/ ~지우(之友) a congenial friend/~ 작품 a work aften one's heart/~의 미소를 짓다 smile a complacent[self-satisfied] smile. かいしん

**회양목**(一楊木) 【식】a box-tree 《재목》boxwood.

**회연**(會宴) a banquet; a dinner party ⇒ 연회(宴會). えんかい

**회오**(悔悟) repentance; remorse; penitence; regret/~하다 repent (of); feel remorse (for); regret/~의 penitential /~자 a penitent/ ~의 눈물 tears of remorse. かいご

**회오리바람** a whirlwind; a cyclone; a twister. つむじかぜ

**회오리봉**(一峰) a conical peak.

**회원**(會員) a member (of a society, of an association);《총칭》membership/~국 a member nation/~ 명부 a membership list/~증 a membership card/ ~의 자격 qualifications for membership/~을 모집하다 collect[raise, seek] members. かいいん

**회유**(懷柔) appeasement; conciliation; pacification 《매수(買收)》winning over/ ~하다 conciliate; pacify; appease; placate/~책 a conciliatory[an appeasement] measure[policy]. かいじゅう

**회유**(回遊) an excursion; a tour; a cruise/ ~하다 make[go on] an excursion; make a cruise[tour]. かいゆう

**회음**(會飲) compotation/ ~하다 drink together[in company]/~자 a compotator. かいいん

**회의**(會議) a meeting; a council; a conference 《협의》a consultation 《회기중의》a session/ ~하다 confer; sit/ ~록 assembly[conference] records; minutes /~실 a conference[council, assembly] room/국제 ~ an international convention/국무 ~ the Cabinet council/비밀 ~ a meeting behind closed doors/~에 참석하다 attend a meeting[conference]. かいぎ

**회의**(懷疑) doubt; scepticism; incredulity/ ~파 the sceptic school/ ~설 scepticism/ ~론자 a sceptic/그는 10대에 인생에 대한 ~에 시달렸다 He was tormented by his doubts about life in his teen age. かいぎ

**회임**(懷孕) pregnancy; conception/ ~하다 become[be] pregnant; conceive. みもち

**회자**(膾炙) 《회와 구운 고기》raw meat and roast meat 《인구에》[what is found] in everyone's mouth/ ~하다 be in everybody's mouth; be on every man's lips; be a household word. かいしゃ

**회자 정리**(會者定離) Those who meet must part., We never meet but we part.

**회장**(回腸) 【생】the ileum/ ~염 ileitis. かいちょう

**회장**(會長) the president; the chairman / ~석(席) the chair/ ~이 되다 take the chair; preside over (at) a meeting. かいちょう

**회장**(會場) 《회합 장소》a meeting-place; an assembly hall 《건물》a building 《회장지(地)》the grounds. かいじょう

**회장**(會葬) attending a funeral/ ~하다

**회장(會葬)** attend a funeral/ ~자 persons who attend a funeral; mourners/그의 장례식에는 다수의 ~자가 있었다 There was a large attendance at his funeral. かいそう

**회장(回章)** a circular [letter]/~을 돌리다 send a circular[letter]. かいしょう

**회전(回電)** a reply telegram[by wire]/~하다 answer a telegram; wire back.

**회전(回轉)** revolution; rotation/~하다 revolve; rotate; turn[go] round/~의 자 a pivot[swivel] chair/~ 무대 a revolving stage/~ 목마 a merry-go-round/~축 the axis of rotation; a pivot/~ 운동 rotary motion/지구는 태양의 주위를 ~한다 The earth moves [revoles] around the sun. かいてん

**회전(會戰)** a battle; a fight; an engagement; an encounter/~하다 fight (a battle); encounter; meet.

**회전(回戰)** 【체】 an innings/제2~ the second inning.

**회절(廻折)** 【물】 diffraction/~하다 diffract/~ 격자(格子) a diffraction grating.

**회조(回漕)** shipping; transportation by ship/~하다 forward[transport] by sea; ship/~점(店) a shipping/~업 shipping business[trade]. かいそう

**회죄(悔罪)** repenting one's sin.

**회중(會衆)** an audience; an attendance; attendants (교회의) a congregation; a gathering/~은 그의 웅변에 깊이 감동했다 The audience were deeply moved by his eloquence. かいしゅう

**회중(懷中)** one's pocket; the bosom/~시계 a watch/~전등 an electric torch; a flash-light(미)/~물에 조심하시라 Beware of pickpockets. かいちゅう

**회진(回診)** [a doctor's] round of visits /~하다 visit one's patients; make a round of visits to one's patients. かいしん

**회집(會集)** [a] gathering; an assemblage; a crowd/~하다 gather; assemble; meet. かいしゅう

**회창거리다** totter ⇒휘청거리다. ひょろひょろする

**회천(回天)** restoration of the national prestige/~하다 rehabilitate [a nation]/~ 지업(之業) a Herculean labour; an epoch-making deed.

**회초리** a whip; a switch; a rod; a cane; a lash/~로 때리다 whip (a person) with a switch.

**회춘(回春)** recovery; restoration to health/~하다 recover from a serious illness; regain one's health/~제 a rejuvenator [tonic]; an aphrodisiac. かいしゅん

**회충(蛔蟲)** a roundworm; a belly-worm /~이 생기다 get roundworms. かいちゅう

**회치다(膾—)** slice raw fish[meat]/생선을 ~ prepare a raw fish dish. さしみをつくる

**회칙(會則)** the rules[regulations] of a society; the articles of an association/우리 클럽에는 ~과 부칙이 있다 Our club has a constitution and bylaws. かいそく

**회태(懷胎)** pregnancy. みもち

**회편(回便)** a return courier; a return messenger; return post[mail].

**회포(懷抱)** one's bosom; one's heart; one's thoughts/슬픈 ~ sad thoughts.

**회피(回避)** shirking; evasion/~하다 evade; shirk; dodge/~ 전술 dodging[evasive] tactics/책임을 ~하다 evade[shirk] one's responsibility. かいひ

**회한(悔恨)** remorse; repentance; regret; contrition/~하다 regret; repent; be penitent of/~의 정에 사로잡히다 be smitten with remorse. かいこん

**회합(會合)** a meeting; a gathering; a congregation/~하다 meet; assemble; gather together/~ 장소 a place of meeting/~의 약속을 하다 make an appointment. かいごう

**회항(回航)** (순항) cruising; sailing about; a cruise (귀항) a return cruise; sailing back/~하다 cruise; navigate/배를 ~시키다 bring[take] (a ship) home. かいこう

**회향(回向)** 【종】 a memorial (for the dead); a mass [for the reponse of one's soul]/~하다 turn one's face (불교에서) hold a memorial service.

**회향(懷鄕)** longing[yearning] for home; homesickness/~하다 long[yearn] for home; be homesick/~병 homesickness; nostalgia/~병에 걸리다 get[feel] homesick. かいきょう

**회향(茴香)** 【식】 a fennel/~풀 the fennel plant. かいきょう

**회혼(回婚)** the 60th wedding anniversary; the diamond wedding.

**회화(會話)** conversation (대화) a dialogue/~하다 talk with; have a conversation (with)/~ 실력 one's speaking ability/영어 ~ a conversation in English/그녀는 영어 ~를 잘 한다 She speaks English well., She is a good speaker of English. かいわ

**회화(繪畫)** pictures (유화) paintings (선화) drawings/~관 a picture-gallery/~ 전람회 an art exhibition; an exhibition [a showing] of pictures. かいひ

**회환(回還)** return; coming back/~하다 return; come back.

**회회교(回回敎)** Mohammedanism; Islam /~도 a Mohammedan; a Moslem/~ 연맹 the Moslem League. かいきょう

**회회하다(恢恢—)** (be) bast; immense; roomy.

**회훈(回訓)** government instructions [sent in response to request]/~하다 give [send] return instructions; reply with instructions.

**획** ①(돌다) with a swerve; with a whirl /시계 바늘을 ~ 돌리다 whirl the clock hands around ②(불다) with a whiff in a gust/바람이 ~ 불다 have a gust of wind. さっと

**획(畫)** a stroke; a dash/~을 내려[가로] 긋다 make a vertical[horizontal] stroke.

**획기적(畫期的)** epoch-making; epochal/ ~인 사건[발견] an epoch-making event [discovery]/그것은 한국 역사에 ~인 일이다 It marks an epoch in Korean history. かっきてき

**획득(獲得)** acquisition; possession (점유) occupation/ ~하다 acquire; obtain; get; get possession of/~룰 an acquisition/~ 된 성격 an acquired character/ 그 팀은 축구에서 1점을 ~했다 The team scored a goal in football. かくとく

**획법(畫法)** ihe canons of brushing strokes; a style of penmanship.

**획수(畫數)** the number of strokes [in a Chinese character]; the stroke count.

**획순(畫順)** the stroke order [in writing a character].

**획일(畫一)** uniformity; standardization / ~의 uniform; standardized/ ~주의 [the principle of] standardization/ ~적 교육 uniform education. かくいつ

**획정(畫定)** demarcation; delimitation/ ~하다 demarcate; mark out/국경을 ~ 하다 demarcate the frontiers.

**획책(畫策)** a plan; a project; a scheme / ~하다 plan; form a plan (책동하다) maneuver. かくさく

**획획** with swerve after swerve ⇒획. さっと

**횟가루(灰—)** lime powder; powdered lime. せっかいのこな

**횟돌(灰—)** limestone. せっかいせき

**횟반** a lump of solidified lime. せっかい.のかたまり

**횟배** stomach trouble caused by worms.

**횡(橫)** width; crossways ⇒가로. よこ

**횡격막(橫隔膜)** 【생】 the diaphragm. おうかくまく

**횡관(橫貫)** running[cutting] across/ ~ 철도 a railroad running across [the country]. おうかん

**횡단(橫斷)** crossing; crosscutting; intersection; traversing/ ~하다 cross; get [go] across; traverse; intersect; divide crosswise/ ~면 a transverse[cross] section; a transection/ ~로 a crosscut / ~선 a transversal [line]; a traverse/~ 보도 a pedestrian crossing/ 태평양 ~ 비행 a transpacific flight/여러 개의 철도가 국내를 ~하고 있다 The country is traversed by several railways. おうだん

**횡대(橫隊)** a rank; a line/ 2열 ~ a double line/ ~로 in line[flank]/ ~가 되다 form 진 marching in a line/ ~가 되다 form in line. おうだい

**횡도(橫道)** (부정) unrighteous ways; injustice (옆길) a side road; a by-road; a byway. よこみち

**횡듣다(橫—)** hear amiss; mishear/사람의 말을 ~ mishear a person. ききまちがい

**횡렬(橫列)** a line; a line abreast. よこにならぶこと

**횡령(橫領)** usurpation; unlawful possession; disposition (탈취) seizure/ ~하다 seize upon; usurp/~자 an embezzler; a usurper/ ~죄 embezzlement; disseizin[disseisin]/재산을 ~하다 seize one's property. おうりょう

**횡문근(橫紋筋)** 【생】 a striated muscle.

**횡보다(橫—)** mistake; see wrongly/신호를 ~ mistake a signal; misread a signal. みまちがう

**횡사(橫死)** a violent[tragic] death; an accidental death/ ~하다 come to a tragic death; die an unnatural death. おうし

**횡서(橫書)** writing in a lateral line; writing from left to right (글씨) letters written sideways/ ~하다 write horizontally[in a lateral line, sideways]; write from left to right. よこがき

**횡선(橫線)** a horizontal[cross] line; 【수】 (횡좌표) an abscissa/ ~ 수표 a crossed check/ ~을 긋다 cross. よこせん

**횡설 수설(橫說竪說)** a contradictory speech; a jargon; nonsense/~하다 talk at random; talk wild[ly]/네 말은 ~이라 이해할 수 없다 What you say is all Greek to me.

**횡수(橫數)** a chance[an accidental] hit; a lucky shot/ ~로 돈을 모으다 make money by sheer good luck. いがいなうん

**횡액(橫厄)** an [unexpected] accident; an unforeseen disaster[calamity]/~에 걸리다 have an accident. いがいなさいやく

**횡와(橫臥)** ~하다 lie on one's side.

**횡일(橫溢)** ~하다 overflow; be filled [full] to overflowing; be replte with. おういつ

**횡재(橫財)** a windfall; an unexpected financial gain/~하다 come into unexpected fortune; have a windfall. おうざい

**횡전(橫轉)** a lateral turning (비행기의) a [barrel] roll/ ~하다 turn sideways [laterally]; make a barrel roll.

**횡진(橫震)** a horizontal shock.

**횡진(橫陣)** a line abreast; a rank.

**횡철(橫綴)** spelling sideways; sidewise spelling.

**횡탈(橫奪)** unlawful seizure/ ~하다 usurp; seize upon. おうだつ

**횡파(橫波)** 【물】 transverse wave. よこなみ

**횡포(橫暴)** (포학) tyranny (탄압) oppression (폭력) violence (고압) high-handedness/ ~하다 (be) arbitrary; tyrannical; oppressive; violent; unreasonable /경찰의 ~ the arrogance of the police.

**횡행**(橫行) rampancy; prevalence; prevalency／ ～하다 (옆으로 가다)go sidewise; walk sideways (발호)be rampant; overrun (활보)swagger; strut; stalk／밤거리에 도적이 ～한다 The streets are infested with robbers at night.

**효**(孝) filial piety[duty]／부모에게 ～를 다하다 tend one's parents with filial piety.

**효**(効) efficacy; properties ⇨효능(效能).

**효경**(孝經) the Book of Filial Duty.

**효과**(効果) effect; effectiveness (능률)efficiency (결과)fruit／무대 ～ a stage effect／ ～가 있다 be effective[effectual, fruitful]; prove fruitful／나의 노력 도 ～가 없었다 My efforts were of no avail.

**효녀**(孝女) a filial[dutiful] daughter.

**효능**(效能) effect; virtue; efficacy／ ～ 서 a statement of virtues／약의 ～ the virtue[effect] of medicine／ ～이 나타나 다 take effect.

**효도**(孝道) filial piety[duty]／ ～를 다하 다 be dutiful to one's parents; discharge one's filial duties.

**효득**(曉得) understanding; grasping／ ～ 하다 understand; grasp.

**효력**(效力) effect (효능)virtue (법률의)validity; efficacy／ ～을 발생하다 become effective; come into effect[force, operation, validity]／ ～이 있다 be effective[efficacious, valid]／법적 ～을 갖 다 have legal force.

**효모**(酵母) yeast; leaven; barm／ ～균 (菌) yeast fungus.

**효부**(孝婦) a filial[dutiful, obedient, devoted] daughter-in-law.

**효성**(孝誠) filial piety／ ～스럽다 (be) dutiful; filial／ ～이 지극한 사람 a person who loves one's parents／부모에게 ～을 다하다 discharge one's duties to one's parents.

**효성**(曉星) (금성)Venus (샛별)the morning star／문단(文壇)의 ～ the [shining] star of the literary world.

**효소**(酵素) ferment; enzyme／ ～원(原)(생화학)zymogen.

**효수**(梟首) ～하다 gibbet[pillory] a head ／ ～대 a gibbet; a stock／ ～ 경중하다 display the criminals' heads as a warning to the people.

**효순**(孝順) dutifulness; obedience; filial piety／ ～하다 (be) dutiful; obedient.

**효시**(嚆矢) (최초)the beginning; the first; the first person (to do); the pioneer (in); (선례)the first instance (of)／ 미국 유학은 그를 ～로 한다 He was the first one to go to America for study.

**효심**(孝心) filial piety[duty, affection] ／ ～이 있는 dutiful; filial; devoted.

**효양**(孝養) dutiful service to one's parents; the discharge of filial duties[piety, devotion]／그는 양친에게 ～을 다하고 있 다 He is dutiful to his parents.

**효용**(効用) (유용성)utility; usefulness (효험)effect; good; virtue／ ～ 가치 effective value／ ～ 체감 법칙 the law of diminishing utility[returns]／한계 ～ marginal utility／ ～이 있다[없다] be useful[be of no use].

**효용**(驍勇) bravery; valiancy; valor; prowess／ ～하다 (be) valiant; valorous; brave.

**효유**(曉諭) instruction; inculcation admonition／ ～하다 instruct; inculcate.

**효율**(効率) 【물】efficiency ／ ～ 곡선 an efficiency／ ～ 평가 merit rating／열～ thermal efficiency／높은 ～ a high degree of efficiency.

**효자**(孝子) a dutiful[good, an obedient] son.

**효장**(驍將) a valiant[veteran] general; a leader／문단의 ～ a master[veteran] writer; a literary star.

**효제**(孝悌) filial piety and brotherly love ／ ～ 충신(忠信) filial piety and brotherly.

**효종**(曉鐘) the morning bell.

**효천**(曉天) dawn; the morning sky／ ～ 의 별 fading stars at dawn.

**효행**(孝行) filial piety[devotion]; filial ／그는 ～이 지극하다 He shows great devotion to his parents.

**효험**(效驗) efficacy; effect; virtue (of a medicine)／ ～이 없다 be ineffective[inefficacious]; have no effect／이 약은 위 병에 아주 ～이 있다 This is a good remedy for stomach trouble.

**후** blowing; with a puff／촛불을 ～ 불어 끄다 blow out a candlelight with a puff.

**후**(後) ①(시간·순서)after; afterward[s]; later (…이래)since; hence (…다음) next to; following (위치)behind／그～ after that; then; afterward／그～ 내내 ever since／조반 ～ after breakfast／한 이틀 ～에 a couple of days after[later] ／～에 또 뵙겠읍니다 See you later., So long.／그～로는 그를 만나지 못했다 I haven't seen him since. ②(추후)later; after; farther[further]／ ～고구려 later Koguryo.

**후**(后) an Empress.

**후**(侯) (후작)a marquis.

**후가**(後嫁) a woman's second marriage.

**후각**(嗅覺) the sense of smell／ ～ 기관 the organ of smell／ ～ 신경 the olfactory nerve／ ～이 예민하다 have a keen nose[sense of smell].

**후감**(嗅感) the olfactory sensation ⇨후각

**후갑판(後甲板)** the quarter-deck.

**후거리(後—)** a crupper; a saddle breeching.

**후견(後見)** 〖법〗 guardianship; wardship; prompting/ ～하다 guard; act as guardian/ ～인 a guardian; a tutor; a curator/피～인 a ward/ ～을 받다 be placed under the guardianship (of); be under[in] ward.

**후계(後繼)** succession/ ～하다 succeed to (another's office); succeed (a person) in his office/ ～자 a successor an inheritor (후사) an heir(남자); an heiress (여자)/김씨의 ～자로 선출되다 be elected[chosen, picked out] as a successor to Mr. Kim.

**후고(後顧)** (뒤를 돌아봄) looking back (후환) future troubles (후일의 은고) future favors/ ～하다 look back/ ～의 근심 anxiety[solicitude] about one's future; anxiety about one's home/ ～의 근심을 없애다 free (a person) from family cares; free (a person) from anxiety about the future.

**후골(喉骨)** the Adam's apple.

**후관(嗅官)** the olfactory organ; the organ of smell.

**후광(後光)** (윤광) a halo (원광) a nimbus; an aureola[aureole]; a glory (태양의) a corona/ ～이 비치다 a halo[nimbus] envelopes one's head.

**후군(後軍)** the rearguard/ ～이 되다 close[bring up] the rear.

**후굴(後屈)** 〖의〗 retroflexion (of the uterus)/자궁 ～증 the retroflexion of the uterus.

**후궁(後宮)** (궁) a royal harem (사람) a royal concubine[harem].

**후끈** ～하다 (be) hot; flushed; be in a glow; be all of a glow.

**후끈거리다** feel hot[warm]; burn; flush; glow/후끈후끈 hotly; warmly/술을 마시니 얼굴이 후끈거리다 My cheeks are flushed with wine.

**후기(後期)** the latter term; the second half-year; 〖생〗(핵분열의)the anaphase/～ 시험 the second-term[final] examination/～ 인상파 the later impressionists; the postimpressionists/ ～ 환자 a late case/전쟁의 ～ the late period[stage] of a war.

**후기(後記)** a postscript (略: p. s.)/편집 ～ a postscript by the editor.

**후년(後年)** (내내년) year after next (훗날에.) later years; later/내～ three years from now/ ～에 가서 in future years; in later[after] years.

**후념(後念)** a [musical] refrain ⇨후렴(後斂).

**후뇌(後腦)** 〖해〗 the hindbrain.

**후딱** quickly; speedily; at once; promptly; immediately; in an instant[a moment, a jiffy]/일을 ～ 해치우다 get a job done in a jiffy/～ 자리에서 일어나다 leave one's seat promptly.

**후닥닥** in a hurry; in haste; hurriedly /～ 놀라다 be suddenly startled/～ 계단을 뛰어내리다(뛰어오르다) hurry downstairs[upstairs].

**후닥닥거리다** scamper; keep jumping (급히 서두르다) hurry; rush; make haste /후닥닥후닥닥 in a great hurry; with all haste; hurry-scurry; with a start/ 닭이 기적 소리에 놀라서 ～ chickens scamper at the sound of a train whistle.

**후단(後段)** (이야기 따위의) the latter part (of a tale)/(연극 따위의) the latter scene[act].

**후당(後堂)** a separate house in the rear.

**후대(後代)** future[coming] generations; after[later] ages/～에 이름을 전하다 hand one's name down to posterity.

**후대(後隊)** the rear ranks[line].

**후대(厚待)** a warm[hearty, cordial] reception; kind treatment; hospitality/ ～하다 give a warm[cordial] reception; entertain warmly; receive treat hospitably[liberally]/ ～를 받다 be kindly treated[received].

**후더침(後—)** complications arising from childbirth[illness]; afterpains.

**후덕(厚德)** liberality; generosity; liberal favor; great virtue/ ～ 군자 a man of virtue.

**후동이(後童—)** the later born of two twins; the younger, twin.

**후두(喉頭)** 〖해〗 the larynx/～의 laryngeal/～ 염 laryngitis/～음 laryngeal voice[sound]/～ 결핵 laryngeal tuberculosis/～ 카타르 laryngeal catarrh.

**후두(後頭)** 〖의〗 the occiput; the back of the head/～ 골 the occipital bone/～ 부 the occipital region.

**후드득거리다** ①(방정떨다) act rashly; be imprudent; be frivolous ②(튀는 소리) crackle; make a cracking sound/후드득후드득 cracking.

**후들거리다** tremble; shake; shiver/～후 후들 tremblingly; shiveringly/후들후들 멸리는 손으로 with trembling hands /다리가 ～ one's legs are trembling.

**후등(後燈)** (자동차 따위의)a rear-light; a taillight.

**후락(朽落)** ～하다 (노후하다) be worn out; decay (퇴색하다) fade; discolor.

**후래삼배(後來三杯)** three glasses of wine offered to a late comer.

**후략(後略)** omission of what follows; the rest omitted.

**후레아들** a boor; a lout; an ill-bred[ill-mannered] fellow.

**후려(後慮)** anxiety about one's future/ ～를 없애다 free (a person) from solicitude[anxiety] about the future.

**후려치다** flog; lash; whip／채찍으로 사람을 ~ lash (*a person*) with a whip; whip (*a person*). ぶんなぐる

**후련하다** (상태)feel refreshed[cool]; (안심)feel relieved／빚을 다 갚아서 ~ The load is off my mind now that I have cleared off my debts.／토하고 나니 속이 ~ feel better after throwing up. さっぱりする

**후렴**(後斂) a [musical] refrain; a burden.

**후록**(厚祿) a generous stipend; a liberal salary; rich emoluments. こうきゅう

**후루루** (불다)whistling; blowing 《타는 모양》flickeringly; in a flame／~ (호각을) whistle. ぴりぴり

**후루룩** (날다)with a flutter 《마시다》with a slurp[gulb, gurgle]／새가 ~ 날아가다 a bird flutters away／~ 마시다 sip; sup. ばたばた

**후리다** ①(깎아 내다)shave 《대패로》plane; scrape／낫으로 풀을 ~ mow[cut] down grass with a sickle ②(채가다)carry off; run away with; snatch away (피어서)kidnap; spirit away／도둑놈은 부인의 손에서 지갑을 후려갔다 The thief snatched away the purse in a lady's hand. ③(혹하다)captivate; charm; bewitch; seduce ④(그물로)round up; net; bag; catch (with *a net*)／그물로 고기를 ~ chase[catch] fish with a net.

**후리질** fishing with a net; seining／~하다 fish with a [large] net; seine.

**후리후리하다** (키)high in stature; tall and thin／후리후리한 몸매 a willowy[slender, graceful] figure. すらりとしている

**후림** a trick; a wile; an artifice／~ 비둘기 a decoy pigeon／~에 넘어가다 be caught by a trick. たくらみ

**후림대** the poles at both ends of a fishing net (후림) seduction; conquest; trick; wile.

**후림불** a by-blow; entanglement; involvement／~을 만나 싸우다 suffer a by-blow in a quarrel involving others.

**후릿고삐** lashing rein[halter].

**후릿그물** a seine; a dragnet. ひきあみ

**후머리**(後一) the end; the tail end [of a process or column]. さいご

**후면**(後面) the back side; the reverse side; the rear／학교의 ~에 in the rear [at the back] of the school. こうめん

**후무리다** appropriate; embezzle; pocket; possess *one*self of. ちゃくふくする

**후문**(後門) a back[rear] gate ⇒뒷문. こうもん

**후물거리다** mumble; gum; chew[mouth] with toothless gums.

**후물림**(後一) a hand-me-down (의복)used clothes／이 양복은 형의 ~이다 This coat is my brother's cast-off coat. うけついだもの

**후물후물** mumbling; gumming; chewing [mouthing] with toothless gums／~하다 mumble ⇒후물거리다.

**후미** a bay; an inlet; an arm of the sea; an embayment.

**후미**(後尾) the rear 《배의 고물》the stern／~의 rear; back／~ 경호 the rear guard／~등(燈) a tail light／ ~에 at the rear[back] (*of*).

**후미**(後味) aftertaste／~가 좋다 have[leave] a pleasant aftertaste; leave a pleasing[clean] taste in *one's* mouth. あとあじ

**후미지다** ①(해변아)form an inlet; [an arm of the sea] runs deep into the land ②(장소가)(be) sequestered; secluded; retired／후미진 곳 a recess; a nook.

**후박**(厚薄) thick and[or] thin; (being) liberal and[or] stingy; much and[or] little 《불공평》partiality／~이 없이 impartially; without partiality／상여에 ~이 있다 be partial in giving rewards [bonuses]. こうはく

**후박나무**(厚朴—) 【식】① *Magnolia hypoleuca*(학명) ②*Machilus Thunbergii*(학명). こうぼく

**후반**(後半) the latter[second] half／~기 the latter[second] half of the year／~전 the second half of the game 《야구》the latter half of the ninth innings／시합이 ~전에 들어가다 advance into latter half of a game. こうはん

**후방**(後方) the rear 《일선에 대한》the home[domestic] front／~의 rear; back [ward]; 《일선에 대한》behind the gun[s]; on the home front／~ 근무 rear service [at the base]／~ 부대 troops in rear／ ~으로 물러나다 step backward; recede／ ~에 배속되다 be assigned to the base. こうほう

**후배**(後輩) *one's* junior 《젊은이들》younger men; the younger generation／학교의 ~ *one's* junior in school／~를 돌봐주다 patronize *one's* juniors. こうはい

**후보**(後報) a later report; further news ／~를 기다리고 있다 The report remains to be confirmed. こうほう

**후보**(厚報) generous compensation[remuneration]; rich payment.

**후보**(候補) (입후보)candidature; candidacy(미); (후보자)a candidate／~생 a cadet／~자 명부 an eligible list; an elective list; a slate[ticket]〈미〉／공천 ~ an offical[adopted, authorized] candidate; a party candidate／당선 ~ a suceessful candidate／그는 명년에 대통령 ~로 나설 것이다 He will run for presidency next year. こうほ

**후부**(後夫) *one's* second husband; *one's* remarried man. のちぞいのおっと

**후부**(後部) the rear; the back part 《선박의》the stern／~의 back; rear; hind／~에 at the rear[back]. こうぶ

**후분**(後分) *one's* luck[fortune] in *one's* later years[life]／~이 좋다 be lucky in

**후비**(後備) the second reserve／～병 a second reservist／～역으로 편입되다 be transferred to the second reserve.

**후비**(后妃) a queen; an empress.

**후비다** 《귀·이 등을》 dig up; pick／후비어 파다 dig up 《파내다》 grub; examine closely; ferret out; pry into 《캐내다》 peck[pick] at／귀를 ～ pick *one's* ears.

**후비적거리다** keep scooping[scraping] out; keep gouging 《귀·코를》 keep picking／귀[코]를 ～ keep picking *one's* ears [nose].

**후사**(後事) ①《죽은 뒤의 일》 affairs after *one's* death ②《장래의 일》 future affairs／～를 부탁하다 entrust (*another*) with future affairs; ask (*another*) to look after *one's* affairs.

**후사**(後嗣) 《남자》 an heir 《여자》 an heiress 《후계자》 a successor.

**후사**(厚賜) a liberal grant; a generous gift.

**후사**(厚謝) a generous[handsome] reward; a handsome remuneration[recompense]／～하다 reward warmly; thank heartily.

**후산**(後産) the afterbirth／～하다 bear the afterbirth.

**후살이**(後―) remarriage; a second marriage [for a woman]; 《사람》 a woman who marries again／～하다 marry again; remarry.

**후생**(後生) 《후진》 juniors; younger students[scholars]; 《내생》 the future life; the life after death 《후세대》 future generations.

**후생**(厚生) social[public] of people; improvement of living 《건강의 증진》 promotion of health／～ 사업 public welfare enterprises; social work／～ 시설 welfare facilities.

**후세**(後世) 《장래》 coming age; future 《후대 사람》 future generations; posterity／～에 이름을 남기다 retain *one's* name in history; earn *one's* place in history.

**후속**(後續) succession; succeeding; following／～의 succeeding; following／～ 부대 reinforcements／～차(車) the car behind.

**후손**(朽損) decay; rot／～하다 decay; fall into ruin[decay]; perish; be ruined.

**후손**(後孫) descendants; an offspring; a scion 《총칭》 posterity／…의 ～이다 be descended from; be a descendant of.

**후송**(後送) evacuation; sending back (to *the rear*)／～하다 send (*a person*) back (to *the rear*); evacuate／～ 병원 an evacuation hospital.

**후수**(厚酬) generous compensation.

**후신**(後身) 《후계자》 the successor; *one's* future being; *one's* future state of existence; *one's* later self／국제 경제 협조처는 대외 활동 본부의 ～이다 The International Cooperation Administration has succeeded to the Foreign Operations Administration.

**후실**(後室) *one's* second wife／～ 자식 a child born of *one's* second wife.

**후안**(厚顔) impudence; effrontery; shamelessness; cheek《속》／～ 무치한 사람 a shameless[brazen-faced] fellow; a saucy [cheeky, brazen-faced] person／～ 무치하다 be brazen-faced; be impudent; be shameless.

**후열**(後列) the back[rear] row.

**후예**(後裔) descendants ⇒후손(後孫).

**후원**(後苑, 後園) a back garden[in a palace].

**후원**(後援) support; backing; patronage; help; assistance; aid／～하다 support; give[lend] support to; be[stand] behind (*a movement*); give backing (*to*); back up; aid; favour; second; stand by／～자 a supporter; a helper; a sponsor／…의 ～하에 under the auspices of／～ 부대 troops stationed in support of the front line／～회 a supporters' association／당신의 ～을 부탁합니다 I hope to have your support.

**후위**(後衛) 《정구》 a back-player 《축구》 a back; 『군』 the rear [guard]／～가 되다 bring up the rear.

**후유증**(後遺症) ①《의》 a sequela (*pl.* -e) ②《비유적》 aftermath／선거의 ～ the aftermath of elections.

**후은**(厚恩) great favor; great obligations; indebtedness; deep kindness／～을 입다 receive[meet with] great kindness; owe (*a person*) great obligations; lie under the obligations (*to*).

**후음**(喉音) a guttural sound; gutturals.

**후의**(厚意) 《호의》 kindness; goodwill; good wishes; kind intentions／～를 거절하다 decline (*another's*) kind offer／～에 감사하다 thank (*a person*) for his kindness.

**후의**(厚誼) kindness; kind intentions; good wishes／～에 보답하다 repay (*a person*) for his kindness; do something for (*a person's*) favor／～에 감격하다 be deeply affected by (*a person's*) generous act.

**후인**(後人) posterity; future generations.

**후일**(後日) some [other] day; later days; the future／～ 에 in [the] future; one of these days／～담(譚) reminiscences; remembrance／～ 또 만나자 I'll see you again.

**후임**(後任) 《사람》 a successor (to *a post*)／…의 ～으로 in succession to …; as a successor to …; in place of／그가 사임하

면 자비를 ~으로 하겠다 You shall take his place when he resigns.

**후자**(後者) the latter; the other one／전자가 ~보다 낫다 The one is better than the other. こうしゃ

**후작**(侯爵) a marquis; a marquess／~ 부인 a marchioness. こうしゃく

**후장**(後裝) breechloading／~총 a breechloading rifle[gun]. こうそう

**후정**(後庭) a back garden[yard].

**후정**(厚情) good wishes; kindness; hospitality; favor. こうじょう

**후제**(後—) [at] some later time. そのうちいつか

**후조**(候鳥) a migratory bird; a bird of passage／ ~의 이동 the migration of birds. こうちょう

**후주곡**(後奏曲) 〖음〗 a postlude.

**후줄근하다** (be) limp; wilted; droop; be a little soggy; be wet enough to lose starch／옷이 이슬에 젖어 ~ one's clothes get wet with dew and lose their starch.

**후중** a quality coffin made of pine board.

**후중**(後重) being constipated[costive]／~하다 (be) constipated; costive.

**후지**(厚志) kindness; good wishes; intention[thought]／ ~에 감사합니다 Many thanks for your kindness. こうじ

**후진**(後陣) a rear guard. こうじん

**후진**(後進) ①(후배) a junior; a younger man ②(후진성) backwardness; underdevelopment／ ~의 backward; underdeveloped／ ~국 a backward nation／ ~에게 길을 열어주다 make room for the younger generation. こうしん

**후진**(後震) an after-quake; an aftershock.

**후차**(後車) a rear car; the vehicle that follows 《뒷바퀴》 a hind[rear] wheel.

**후처**(後妻) a second wife／~를 얻다 marry a second wife. ごさい

**후천**(後天) a posterior; postnatal nature／성격은 ~적으로 형성된다 You can form Your own personal character in the course of your lifetime. こうてん

**후추** pepper／ ~를 치다 pepper (a disk). こしょう

**후춧가루** ground pepper; pepper grounds. こしょうのふんまつ

**후충**(候蟲) seasonal insects. こうちゅう

**후취**(後娶) a second marriage; remarriage 《사람》 one's second wife／ ~를 얻다 take a second wife; remarry. ごさい

**후치사**(後置詞) a postposition.

**후탈**(後頉) ①(병후·산후의) an afterbirth trouble; a physical trouble after a sickness ②(사건 처리 후의) an after-effect; an aftermath; a trouble succeeding a matter settled／ ~없게 일을 잘 처리하다 handle things so that there will be no trouble later on.

**후터분하다** (be) a bit sultry[muggy]; stuffy／후터분한 날씨 rather sultry weather. むんむんする

**후텁지근하다** (be) sultry; sticky; stuffy. むんむんする

**후퇴**(後退) 《퇴각》 retrogression; retrocession; degradation 《퇴각》 retreat; recession／ ~하다 retrocede; retrograde; go [move, fall] back; back; recede／자동차를 ~시키다 back a car. こうたい

**후편**(後便) a later messenger; a later mail 《뒤쪽》 the back side.

**후편**(後篇) the second volume; the latter part; the concluding part. こうへん

**후하다**(厚—) ①(인심이) (be) cordial; hospitable; warm[kind]-hearted／후한 대접 a cordial reception ②(인색하지 않다) (be) lenient; generous; liberal; open[free]-handed／후하게 generously; free-handedly／금전에 ~ be generous with one's money. あつい

**후학**(後學) a junior. こうがく

**후항**(後項) the succeeding[following] clause; a later item;〖수〗 the consequent; the latter term. こうこう

**후행**(後行) 《동반》 escorting a bride[bridegroom];《사람》 an escort of a bride[bridegroom]／ ~하다 escort[accompany] [a bride, a bridegroom]

**후형질**(後形質) 〖생〗 metaplasm.

**후환**(後患) the consequences; future troubles; an evil consequence／ ~을 남기다 sow seeds of trouble／ ~을 두려워하여 for fear of future troubles. こうかん

**후회**(後悔) repentance; penitence; regret; remorse／ ~하다 repent of; be penitent for; be sorry for／나중에 ~하다 be sorry for (it) afterwards／~ 막급 There is no use crying over spilt milk. こうかい

**후후** with puff after puff; blowing and blowing／촛불을 ~ 불어 끄다 blow out the candles one after another／ ~ 불다 keep puffing.

**후후년**(後後年) three years from now.

**훅** quickly; with a sip[slurp]; with a gulp／국을 ~ 들이마시다 slurp up soup; glup soup down. ぐっ

**훅훅** sucking away; with sip after sip [slurp after slurp]. ぐっぐっ

**훈**(訓) the Korean rendering[reading] of a Chinese character. くん

**훈**(勳) 《공훈》merit 《훈위》the order of merit／ ~ 일등 the First Order of Merit. いさお

**훈**(暈) ①(해·달의 무리) a halo(pl -s, -es); a ring; a corona; a burr ②(퍼진 자리) blurred fringes of strokes drawn with Chinese ink. かさ

**훈감하다** (be) rich and savo[u]ry; tasteful; delicious／평판이 과히 훈감하지 못하다 have not a very savory reputation. ふうがである

**훈계**(訓戒) counsel; admonition 《경고》 a lecture; caution; warning／ ~하다 counsel; admonish; exhort (one to do *something*); caution, warn (*one against errors*)/과도의 흡연을 삼갈 것을 ~하다 caution (*a person*) against excessive smoking. くんかい

**훈고**(訓告) admonishment; exhortation; a gentle reproof/ ~하다 admonish; exhort (*one to do*); reprove gently. くんこく

**훈고**(訓詁) exposition 《성경의》exegesis; interpretation; annotation; scholia [of a Chinese classic]/ ~학자 a scholiast. くんこ

**훈공**(勳功) distinguished services; meritorious deeds; merits; exploits/ ~을 세우다 distinguish *oneself*; render distinguished services. くんこう

**훈기**(勳記) a patent of decoration; a diploma [of merit]/~를 수여하다 diploma a patent of decoration. くんき

**훈기**(薰氣) warmth/몸의 ~ the body heat; human warmth.

**훈김**(薰—) ①《훈기》warmth ②《세력》the influence of a powerful man/아버지 ~으로 출세하다 rise in the world through *one's* father's influence.

**훈도**(訓導) 《가르침》instruction 《교사》a primary-school teacher.

**훈도**(薰陶) discipline; training; education; instruction; tuition/~하다 discipline; drill; train; instruct; educate/김선생의 ~를 받다 study under[receive instruction from] Mr. *Kim*. くんとう

**훈독**(訓讀) the Korean reading[rendering, translation] of a Chinese character; rendering Chinese writings into Korean. くんどく

**훈등**(勳等) an order of merit. くんとう

**훈련**(訓練) drill; training; discipline; schooling/~하다 drill; train; discipline; exercise/~ 교관 a drill-master/병정들이 ~을 받고 있다 The troops are being drilled. くんれん

**훈련 교본**(訓練敎本) a drill-book[-manual]; drill regulations/보병 ~ drill regulations for the infantry.

**훈련소**(訓練所) a training school[station, institute]/육군 신병 ~ an army training camp for recruits. くんれんじょ

**훈령**(訓令) instructions; an [official] order; a directive/ ~하다 instruct; give [issue] an order[instructions]/다음 ~이 있을 때까지 대기하다 await[wait for] further instructions. くんれい

**훈록**(馴鹿) 《순록》a reindeer.

**훈륜**(暈輪) a halo; a ring; a corona. うんい

**훈민정음**(訓民正音) 《한글》the Korean script.

**훈사**(訓辭) instructions; an admonitory /졸업식에서의 교장 선생님의 ~ the principal's address on a commencement day. くんじ

**훈색**(暈色) iridescence/ ~의 iridescent.

**훈수**(訓手) teaching; instruction/ ~하다 teach; instruct. さしず

**훈시**(訓示) an instruction; an address/ ~하다 address/학생들에게 ~하다 deliver an address to the students. くんじ

**훈신**(勳臣) a statesman of merit; a meritorious subject[retainer]. くんしん

**훈영**(暈影) 《사진》a halation. ハレーション

**훈위**(勳位) court rank and honors; an order of merit. くんい

**훈유**(訓諭) admonition; exhortation/ ~하다 admonish; exhort. くんゆ

**훈육**(訓育) training; instruction; education; discipline/~하다 train; instruct; educate; discipline/~주임 선생 a teacher in charge of discipline. くんいく

**훈장**(勳章) a medal; a decoration; an order; a mark of honor/ ~을 수여하다 decorate; confer a decoration[an order] (*upon*)/~을 달다 wear a decoration. くんしょう

**훈장**(訓長) a teacher of a private school for the study of Chinese classics.

**훈전**(訓電) telegraphic instructions/ ~하다 instruct telegraphically; send telegraphic instructions/정부의 ~을 바라다 ask for telegraphic instructions from the government.

**훈제**(燻製, 薰製) smoking/ ~의 smoked; smoke-dried/~ 연어 smoked salmon. くんせい

**훈증**(薰蒸) 《더위》mugginess; sultriness 《소독》fumigation/ ~하다 (be) sultry; muggy; fumigate/~ 소독기 a fumigator. むしあつさ

**훈풍**(薰風) a warm breeze; a balmy wind. くんぷう

**훈학**(訓學) instruction (in *a village school*); teaching.

**훈화**(訓話) an apologue; a moral tale [story]; a fable; a lesson/오늘 아침 교장 선생님의 ~가 있었다 The principal spoke to us this morning. んんわ

**훈훈하다**(薰薰—) (be) comfortably warm /방이 ~ A room is comfortably warm. ぽかぽかする

**훈훈하다**(醺醺—) (be) slightly intoxicated; tipsy.

**훌떡** ①《벗는 꼴》quick; nimbly 《죄다》completely; absolutely/ ~ 벗다 strip *oneself* of *one's* clothes ②《뒤집히는 모양》entirely; perfectly /저고리를 ~ 뒤집다 turn a coat inside out [entirely] ③《뛰어넘는 모양》quickly; nimbly/담을 ~ 뛰어넘다 jump[leap] over a fence nimbly ④《덮는 꼴》/머리부터 ~ 이불을 뒤집어 쓰다 pull *one's* bedclothes over *one's* head ⑤《벗어지는 꼴》Q 가죽이 ~ 벗어졌다 The skin peeled off. さっと

**훌렁** quickly; nimbly ⇨훌떡. すってんてん

**훌렁거리다** (be) loose/옷이 훌렁거린다 The clothes hang loose on me.

**훌렁하다** (be) loose/바지의 무릎이 ~ The trousers are baggy at the knee. すかすかしている

**훌륭하다** ①《좋다》(be) fine; nice; excellent; splendid; grand／훌륭히 finely; nicely; excellently; splendidly／훌륭한 성과 excellent results ②《존경할 만하다》(be) honourable; respectable《가치있다》(be) worthy／훌륭한 직업[인물] a respectable occupation[person] ③《감탄할 만하다》(be) admirable (writing); creditable; commendable／훌륭한 저작 an admirable writing ④《고상》(be) noble (spirit); lofty; high／자네 동기는 참 훌륭하네 You have acted from noble motives. ⑤《위대》(be) great (scholar); prominent／훌륭한 학자 a great scholar ⑥《충분》(be) sufficient／이런 것을 팔아도 훌륭히 장사가 됩니다 It pays well enough to sell these things. ほめるべきだ

**홀부들하다** (be) nice and soft. ふわふわしている

**홀뿌리다** 《몸을》shake oneself free from (the grasp, etc.); tear oneself away (from);《요구 따위를》refuse (one's request) point-blank; give a flat denial.

**홀부시다** ①《깨끗이》rinse out; wash clean／병을 ~ rinse out a bottle ②《음식을》eat up; dispose of; dispatch; make short work of／떡 한 그릇을 잠깐 동안에 ~ dispose of a dish of rice cakes in no time at all.

**홀쩍** 《날쌔게》quickly; with a jump; nimbly《마시는 모양》at a gulp; at a draught／~ 날아가다 fly off. ぐいっと

**홀쩍거리다** ①《액체를》sip; sup; sack (up)／차를 홀쩍거리며 마시다 sip a cup of tea ②《콧물을》snivel[sniff] repeatedly／훌쩍훌쩍 snivelling ③《울다》sob; snivel; blubber; weep silently／훌쩍거리며 곤란한 사정을 이야기하다 sob out one's tale of distress.

**홀쭉하다** 《몸이》(be) slender; slim; lanky《끝이》long and sharp[pointed]. やつれている

**훌훌** ①《나는 모양》gently; lightly ②《뛰는 모양》lightly; nimbly ③《타는 모양》오 불이 ~ 타오르다 burst into flames. たちまち

**훌훌하다** (be) watery; washy; thin; weak; wishy-washy. きはくである

**훑다** thresh; hackle; strip《씻거하다》remove; scrub out／버들가지의 껍질을 ~ scrub away the bark of a willow twig. しごく

**훑어보다** give a searching glance at; look carefully at; scrutinize／그 책을 찾아 고서점을 훑어보았다 I looked around all the second-hand book store for the book. ひとめかおをじろじろみる

**훑이다** be thrashed; be hackled; be stripped (off)／벼가 잘 훑이지 않다 the rice is hard to thresh.

**훔척거리다** 《뒤지다》search; fumble; rummage; ransack《눈물을 》wipe one's tears. あさりまわる

**훔쳐내다** wipe out[up, off]; mop; swab／걸레로 물을 훔쳐내다 wipe up the water with a cloth.

**훔쳐때리다** deal (one) a hard blow.

**훔쳐먹다** embezzle; steal; swipe／훔쳐먹는 맛이 그만이다 Stolen fruit tastes sweet. ぬすみとる

**훔치개질** ①《후무리기》theft; stealing; pilfering／~하다 steal; pilfer; sneak; snitch《미·속》②《닦기》wiping out[up, off]; moping; swabbing／~하다 wipe out[up, off]; mop; swab. ぬすむこと

**훔치다** ①《절도》steal; pilfer《채어 가지다》make free with another's possessions; sneak; snitch《미·속》／…을 훔치어 도망치다 run away[make off] with … ②《닦다》wipe; mop; rub; scrub／그는 얼굴의 땀을 훔쳐냈다 He wiped the sweat from his face. ぬすむ

**훔치적거리다** 《뒤지다》search《one's bosom》for (something);《눈물을》wipe one's tear's now and then.

**훔켜잡다** grasp fast; clutch／멱살을 ~ grab (a person) by the neck.

**훔파다** dig in deep[ly]. ほじくる

**훔훔하다** wear a look of satisfaction.

**훗날**(後—) later days; some [other] day／~에 some [other] day; later on／~을 위해《참고》for future reference《증거》as a future proof. こじつ

**훗달**(後—) next month.

**훗배앓이**(後—) afterpains; complications; following childbirth. あとばら

**훗번**(後—) next game; next time.

**훗보름**(後—) the latter half of a month.

**훗서방**(後書房) a second husband／~을 얻다 marry again. あとのおっと

**훗일**(後—) the future／~을 계획하다 lay plans for the future; map out one's future course.

**훗훗하다** (be) hot; uncomfortably warm. ほかほかしている

**훙서**(薨逝) death; decease; demise／~하다 die; demise; pass away.

**훤뇨**(喧閙)《떠듦》uproar; tumult《소음》noise; clamour; a hubbub／~하다 raise a clamour; be uproarious. かまびすくさわがしいこと

**훤당**(萱堂) your [honored] mother. けんどう

**훤소**(喧騷) noise; din; uproar; tumult; clamor／~하다 (be) noisy; tumultuous. けんそう

**훤전**(喧傳) ~하다 noise about[abroad] (one's fame, etc.)／세상에 ~되다《유명지다》make a noise in the world. けんでん

**훤조**(喧噪) uproar ⇒훤소. けんそう

**훤칠하다** have a full well-developed figure; (be) strapping／훤칠한 여자 a strapping girl. すらりとしている

**훤하다** ①《앞이》(be) open; unobstructed《얼굴이》bright; sunny《통달》familiar (with) ②《흐릿하게 밝다》(be) dimly white; gray; light／훤하게 동이 튼다 The dawn begins to whiten the sky.

훤화(喧譁) clamour; noise/~하게 clamorously;noisily; loudly. けんか

월떡 quickly ⇨훌떡. すっかり

월썩 be far; far more; far and away; beyond expectation[s]/예상보다 ~ 낫다 be better than [was] expected.

월씬 ①(정도) be far; by a long way;far and away/이것이 ~ 낫다 This is far[much] better. ②(공간적으로) far [away, off]; in the distance; a long way off/ ~ 뒤떨어져 있다 be a long way behind ③(시간적으로) ¶~ 이전에 a long time ago. はるかに

월쩍 wide; broad 《정도》 very; exceedingly ⇨활짝. ぱっと

월월 ①(나는 모양) with a flapping; gently; lightly/ ~ 날아가버리다 flutter away ②(불이) in great flames; vigorously ③(부채질) briskly; vigorously.
ばたばた

훼기(毁棄) demage; destruction; [법] wilful injury/ ~하다 destroy; damage.
こわしてすてること

훼단(毁短) picking flaws; faultfinding / ~하다 find fault (with); pick flaws [holes] (in). きたん

훼방(毁謗) 《비방》 slander; calumny; defamation; vilification 《방해》 interference; interruption/~하다 slander; defame; vilify; traduce 《방해》 interfere with/남의 출세를 ~하다 stand in the way of a person's promotion/ ~하지 말라 Don't put a spoke in my wheel!
きぼう

훼사(毁事) ~하다 throw cold water[a wet blanket] on (a scheme); put a spike in one's wheel.

훼살 interference; obstruction/ ~하다 interfere; obstruct; throw a monkey wrench (in).

훼상(毁傷) injury; wound; bodily; harm; damage/~하다 injure; wound.
きしょう

훼손(毁損) damage; injury/~하다 damage; injure; impair; 명예에 ~ defamation /공공물을 ~하다 destroy public property. きそん

훼언(毁言) slander; calumny/ ~하다 slander; calumniate; speak ill of.
ちゅうしょうすることば

훼예(毁譽) praise and censure; [성평] praise and blame/그는 세인의 ~ 포평 개의치 않는다 He is deaf to either praise or blame of the world. きよ

휑뎅그럼하다 (be) hollow; empty 《휑하다. がらんとしている

휑하다 (be) empty; vacant; hollow 《통달하다》 be familiar with/그 집은 휑했다 The house looked very bare.
がらんとしている

휘 ①(바람 소리) whistling; soughing; with a whistle; whizzing/바람이 온종일 ~ 불었다 The wind whistled all day long ②(한숨 소리) with a sigh/한숨을 ~ 쉬다 sigh; give[heave] a sigh (of regret). ひゅう

휘(諱) ①(이름) a tabooed name; the name of a king[one's ancestor] ②(죽은 뒤의) a posthumous designation[name, title]. き

휘감기다 coil[wind, twine] round/덩굴풀은 살대에 휘감긴다 The vine winds round a pole. くるっとまかれる

휘감다 wind[twist, twine] around; coil /밧줄을 둘둘 ~ round a rope in a coil.
ぐるぐるまく

휘갑치다 ①(마감하다) dispose of (a matter); fix (up); bring (a matter) to a conclusion ②(변두리를) border; hem; stitch up/멍석 가장자리를 ~ hem the edges of a straw mat.

휘기(諱忌) ~하다 conceal; keep (a matter) secret; hush (up). きき

휘날리다 《바람에》 fly; flap; flutter; wave (in the wind)/기폭이 바람에 ~ The flag flaps[waves] in the wind.

휘늘어지다 hang down; droop/버들가지가 ~ the branches of a willow droop.

휘다 bend; curve; warp; be bent/위로 올라감에 따라 가지가 휘기 시작했다 The branch began to bend as I climbed along it. まげる

휘달리다 ①(분주하게 지내다) be always in a whirl; live a very busy life ②(달아나다) rush away; run at full speed/자동차가 ~ A car speeds along.

휘돌다 trun [round]; revolve/사람을 끌고시내를 휘돌아 다니다 take (a person) all over the city. ぐるぐるまわる

휘돌리다 whirl; turn; spin; remove; rotate/손으로 바퀴를 ~ spin a wheel by hand. ぐるぐるまわす

휘두르다 ①(붙잡고) whirl[swing] (a thing) round; brandish; flourish/지팡이를 ~ flourish one's stick ②(얼을 빼다) confuse; bewilder 《제 뜻대로》 make a puppet (of a person); twist (a person) round one's little finger/그는 아내한테 휘둘려 지낸다 He is under apron strings.

휘뚝거리다 ①be unsteady; totter; wobble /굽높은 구두를 신고 ~ totter on high heels ②(조바심) feel nervous[jittery]; be worried; upset.
ぐらぐらとどうようする

휘뚤휘뚤 windingly; meanderingly/ ~하다 (be) winding; meandering/길이 ~ 하다 A road is winding. くねくね

휘둥그러지다 become wide-eyed; get surprised; be startled/놀라서 눈이 ~ stare[open one's eyes] in wonder[astonishment].

휘둥그렇다 (be) wide-opened.

휘말다 ①(적셔서 더럽히다) make wet and dirty; spoil/옷을 ~ get one's clothes wet and dirty ②(마구 휘감다) wind around carelessly. ぐるぐるまく

휘몰다 hurry; drive;urge on; speed up

/가축을 휘몰아 들이다 drive in the cattle. せきたてる
**휘몰이** chasing (into *a place*); rounding up; corralling; driving/ ~하다 chase (into *a place*); round up. せきたてること
**휘발(揮發)** volatilization/~하다 volatilize/~성 volatility/ ~유 benzine 《가솔린》 gasoline. きはつ
**휘보(彙報)** an itemized collection of reports 《잡지》 a magazine. いほう
**휘석(輝石)** 《광》 pyroxene.
**휘선(輝線)** 《의》 the bright line of a gaseous element in spectrum/ ~ 스펙트럼 a line spectrum.
**휘어대다** force[squeeze, push] in. きせん
**휘어박다** ①《넘어뜨리다》 throw down; overthrow ②《굴복시키다》 make (*a person*) give in; bring (*a person*) to one's knees.
**휘어박히다** get brought down; be thrown down 《굴복하다》 yield; give in; submit.
**휘어잡다** ①hold something supple[bent, doubled up] in *one's* hand; grasp/버들가지를 ~ hold willow branches in *one's* hand ②《사람을》 control; have (*a person*) under *one's* control[in *one's* grasp]/휘어잡히다 be under (*a person's*) control[thumb].
**휘어지다** bend; curve 《재목 따위》 warp/판자가 ~ a board warps. まがる
**휘우뚱** ~하다 shake; totter; reel; (be) rickety/한쪽으로 ~하다 be leaning to one side. ひょろひょろ
**휘우듬하다** (be) slightly crooked; somewhat bent[curved]. ややまがっている
**휘장(揮帳)** a curtain; a hanging; a bunting/ ~을 치다 draw[stretch] a curtain. カーテン
**휘장(徽章)** a badge; an insignia/~을 달다《달고 있다》put on[bear, wear] a badge. きしょう
**휘적거리다** swing (*one's arms*)/팔을 휘적거리며 걷다 walk with a swagger. いばってあるく
**휘적휘적** swinging *one's arms*/ ~ 걷다 swagger.
**휘젓다** ①《젓다》 stir [up]; churn; beat up/달걀을 잘 휘저어야 한다 You must beat[whip] up an egg. ②《팔 따위를》 flourish; wave out; swing ③《어지럽게》 disturb; upset/편안한 마음을 휘저어 놓다 disturb the peace of mind.
**휘정거리다** stir up [the sediments in water]; muddle.
**휘주근하다** ①《지쳐서》 (be) languid; dull /휘주근해서 땅바닥에 철썩 앉다 sink exhausted on the ground ②《늘어지다》 (be) limp; flabby; flaccid/이 풀먹인 칼라는 더운 날에는 금방 휘주근해진다 This starched collar soon gets limp in hot weather. ぐにゃぐにゃだ
**휘지다** get worn out; be exhausted; be fagged out.
**휘지르다** spoil; stain; soil (*one's clothes*) /바지를 온통 휘질렀다 I have got my pants all dirty.
**휘지비지(諱之秘之)** ~하다 hush up (*a matter*); smother[suppress]/조사가 ~ 끝났다 The investigations resulted in fade-out. ぼやかすこと
**휘집(彙集)** collection 《유취》 assortment/ ~하다 collect; assort.
**휘청거리다** yield; (be) flexible; pliant; stagger/회초리가 ~ a switch is flexible. ひょろひょろする
**휘청휘청** yielding; flexibly; pliantly; resiliently.
**휘추리** a twig; a spray; a sprig.
**휘파람** a whistle/~ 불다 [give a] whistle.
**휘필(揮筆)** writing ⇨휘호.
**휘하(麾下)** troops under *one's* command /~의 under *one's* command/~에 모이다 rally round (*a person*). きか
**휘호(揮毫)** 《서예》 writing; 《미》 painting; drawing/ ~하다 write; paint/ ~료 a fee for a painting. きごう
**휘황찬란하다(輝煌燦爛—)** (be) resplendent; brilliant; iridescent/불빛이 휘황찬란한 무대 a high-lighted stage. きらきらしている
**휘휘** round and round/단장을 ~ 휘두르다 flourish *one's* stick. くるくる
**휘휘하다** (be) dreary; desolate; forlorn /휘휘한 황야 a desolate wilderness. こうはいしている
**휙** ①《돌아가는 꼴》 swiftly; suddenly; with a jerk/문이 ~ 열렸다 The door flew open. ②《던지는 꼴》 light and nimbly/사자를 향해서 창을 ~던지다 dart a spear at the lion. ばっと
**휩싸다** wrap up; surround 《비호하다》 protect; shield/머리를 붕대로 ~ bind round *one's* head. とりまく
**휩싸이다** get wrapped up 《비호하다》 get protected; be shielded/비밀에 ~ be shrouded in mystery. おおわれる
**휩쓸다** sweep over; make a clean sweep (*of*)/유럽 전토를 ~ sweep over the whole of Europe.
**휫손** skill of control[management]; 《경영수완》 executive skill. せいぎょりょく
**휴가(休暇)** holidays; a vacation 《사가》 leave of absence 《장기 휴가》 furlough /~를 얻다 take a holiday[vacation]/ 여름 ~ the summer holidays. きゅうか
**휴간(休刊)** discontinuation; suspension of publication/~하다 suspend[discontinue] publication/연중 무~입니다 be issued all the year round. きゅうかん
**휴강(休講)** no lecture [for the day]/ ~하다 give no lecture [for the day];《교사가》 absent *oneself* from school/김교수 금일 ~ Prof. *Kim* is absent today., No lecture given today by Prof. *Kim*. きゅうこう
**휴게(休憩, 休憩)** a rest; a recess 《막간의》 a respite/~하다 rest (*oneself*); ta-

ke breath [a rest] / 10분간 ~ ten minutes recess / ~실[소] a rest-room[house] きゅうけい

**휴관**(休館) ~하다 close (*a theater*) / 금일 ~ 《게시》 closed for today.

**휴교**(休校) temporary closure of a school; temporary cessation of study / ~하다 close [school] temporarily / 1개월 간 ~한다 School is closed for a month. きゅうこう

**휴대**(携帶) carrying along (with *one*) / ~하다 carry (*something*) with one / ~용 라디오 a portable radio / 총기는 ~금지이다 The carrying of firearms is prohibited. けいたい

**휴등**(休燈) ~하다 suspend[stop] the use of an electric light.

**휴면**(休眠) 및 ~기 a resting stage[period]. きゅうみん

**휴식**(休息) rest; a respite; repose; recess; relief; relaxation / ~하다 rest; take a rest; repose / ~ 시간 a recess; a breathing time / 잠깐 ~하다 rest a while; take a little rest. きゅうそく

**휴양**(休養) a rest; repose; relaxation; recreation; recuperation / ~하다 rest; take a rest; relax; repose 《병후에》 recruit (*oneself*) / ~하러 온천에 가다 go to hot springs for relaxation. きゅうよう

**휴업**(休業) closing 《영업의》 suspension of business[trading]; 《공장의》 a shutdown 《학교의》 holidays[vacation]; 《극장의》 no performance / ~하다 《상점 따위가》 close *one's* doors; be closed; suspend business[operation]; 《노동자가》 rest from labor; take *one's* day off[take a holiday] 〈미〉 / ~일 a holiday; a business holiday / 저 공장은 아직도 ~중이다 The factory still remains idle. きゅうぎょう

**휴연**(休演) suspension of performance; canceling a performance[appearance] / ~하다 cancel a performance 《극장이》 suspend the performance 《사람이》 absent *one*self from the stage / 금일 ~함 "Today's performance canceled".

**휴일**(休日) a holiday 《고용인의》 an off-day / 매주 일 회 ~을 주다 give an off-day every week / 우리는 멋진 ~을 보냈다 We had a splendid holiday. きゅうじつ

**휴장**(休場) 《사람의》 [an] absence 《극장 따위의》 closure / ~하다 close[shut] (*a theater*).

**휴재**(休載) non-appearance / ~하다 be not published; do not appear. きゅうさい

**휴전**(休戰) a suspension of hostilities; a truce; an armistice / ~하다 suspend hostilities; make a truce / ~ 조약 an agreement of armistice[truce] / ~ 협정을 맺다 conclude a truce (*with*). きゅうせん

**휴정**(休廷) recess[adjournment] of court; holding no court / ~하다 court is recessed[adjourned] / ~일 a non-judicial day / 토요일은 ~이다 No court will be held on Saturday. きゅうてい

**휴지**(休止) cessation; pause; suspension; stoppage; standstill; discontinuance; a deadlock / 차량의 운행이 ~ 상태에 있다 Traffic is tied up. きゅうし

**휴지**(休紙) waste paper; toilet paper; paper scraps / ~통 a waste[-paper] basket. ちらがみ

**휴직**(休職) suspension from office[service]; temporary rest[retirement] from office / ~하다 temporarily rest[retire] from *one's* office / ~ 장교 a suspended officer. きゅうしょく

**휴진**(休診) suspension of medical examination / ~하다 accept no patients 《의사가》 suspend examination / 금일 ~ "No consultation to be held for the day." きゅうしん

**휴학**(休學) temporary absence from school / ~하다 withdraw from school temporarily / 오랫 동안 ~하고 있다 be long absent from school. きゅうがく

**휴한**(休閑) fallow / ~지(地) land in fallow; idle land. きゅうかん

**휴항**(休航) suspension of sailing / ~하다 suspend sailing 《배가》 be laid up.

**휴행**(携行) ~하다 take[carry] with *one*; take along. けいこう

**휴화산**(休火山) a dormant[an inative, sleeping] volcano / 그것은 ~이다 The volcano lies dormant[asleep]. きゅうかざん

**휴회**(休會) adjournment; recess / ~하다 adjourn; recess; suspend the session / ~를 선언하다 declare adjournment; call a recess. きゅうかい

**휼계**(譎計) a trick; a wile; a deceitful scheme / ~에 넘어가다 fall for a scheme.

**휼금**(恤金) relief money; a relief fund / 이재민에게 ~ 40만 원을 희사했다 He donated[contributed] 400,000 *won* in aid of the sufferers.

**휼미**(恤米) the relief rice[grain].

**휼민**(恤民) the relief[aid] of the sufferers[indigent] / ~하다 relieve[aid] the sufferers[indigent].

**휼병**(恤兵) the relief of soldiers / ~ 사업 war relief work.

**휼전**(恤典) charity relief from the government.

**흉** ①《부스럼·상처의》 a scar; a cicatrice / 이마에 ~이 있다 have a scar on the forehead ②《결점》 a fault; a defect 《흠》 a flaw / 남의 ~을 보지 말라 One who lives in a glass house should not throw stones. あやまり

**흉가**(凶家) a haunted house.

**흉강**(胸腔) the thoracic cavity; the thorax. きょうこう

**흉격**(胸膈) the lower chest. きょうかく

**흉계**(凶計) an evil scheme; a sinister[wicked] design; a plot / ~를 꾸미다 revolve[devise] wicked designs; concoct

흉골(胸骨) 【해】 the breast bone; the sternum. tricks. じゃあくなたくらみ

흉골(胸骨) 【해】 the breast bone; the sternum. きょうこつ

흉곽(胸廓) 【해】 the thorax(*pl.* ~es, -races)/~ 성형술【의】 thoracoplasty. きょうかく

흉금(胸襟) the inner mind; the heart; the bosom/~을 털어 놓고 이야기하다 have a heart-to-heart talk (*with*). きょうきん

흉기(凶器) a deadly weapon; a murderous[lethal, destructive] weapon; arms; weapons/~를 휴대하다 carry a [deadly] weapon.

흉내 imitation (태도 따위) mimicry (말소리의) impersonation/ ~내다 imitate; mimic; monkey (모방) ape/남의 말을 ~내다 mimic one's way of talking. まね

흉년(凶年) a lean year; a year of famine[of bad harvest]/~ 거지 a beggar in a lean year. きょうねん

흉당(凶黨) rebels; traitors.

흉도(凶徒) (악당) a gang of scoundrels; rascals; villains; rogues; blackguards (폭도) rioters; outlaws.

흉막(胸膜) 【해】 the pleura(*pl.* -rae)/ ~염【의】 pleurisy. きょうまく

흉몽(凶夢) an evil dream; a bad dream; a nightmare/ ~에서 깨다 start (*up*) from a nightmare.

흉문(凶聞) bad news; news of death; tragic news. きょうほう

흉물(凶物) a snake; a villain; a crafty person/ ~스럽다 (be) villainous; infamous; wicked. きょうあくなひと

흉배(胸背) ①(가슴과 등) breast and back ②(관복의) embroidered patches on the breast and on the back of official uniforms.

흉벽(胸壁) ①(가슴의 외벽) walls of the chest ②【군】 a breastwork; a parapet. きょうへき

흉변(凶變) a calamity; a disaster; a catastrophe (암살) assassination/ ~을 당하다 get assassinated. きょうへん

흉보(凶報) bad[ill, sad] news; evil tidings/유족에게 ~를 전하다 break sad news to the family. きょうほう

흉보다 speak ill of; say nasty things about.

흉복(胸腹) the chest[breast] and the abdomen[belly]/ ~통 a pain in the midriff.

흉부(胸部) the chest; the breast/그 장교는 ~에 관통상을 입었다 The officer was shot through the breast. きょうぶ

흉사(凶事) an event of ill omen; a disaster; an evil; a misfortune. きょうじ

흉상(凶相) ①(외모) an ugly face; an unseemly appearance; a vicious look/ ~이다 be evil-favored[-faced]; be evil-looking ②(상격) an evil physiognomy. ふきつなそう

흉상(胸像) a bust/ ~을 만들다 set up [erect] the bust (of *a person*). きょうぞう

흉악(凶惡) ~하다 (be) wicked; villainous; atrocious; diabolical; malignant/ ~ 망측하다 be most wicked[malignant] / ~범 a brutal criminal. きょうあく

흉어(凶漁) a poor catch[haul]/잇달은 ~로 어부들은 죽을 지경이다 Fishermen are hard hit by the prolonged scarcity of fish.

흉위(胸圍) the circumference[girth] of the chest/ ~가 90센치다 I measure ninety centimeter round the chest.

흉인(凶刃) an assassin's dagger[knife, blade]/대통령은 아슬아슬하게 ~을 모면했다 The President narrowly escaped assassination.

흉일(凶日) a bad day; a black[blackletter] day; an ill-starred day; an unlucky day. きょうじつ

흉작(凶作) a bad[poor, lean] crop[harvest]; a failure of crops/금년은 벼가 ~이다 The rice crop is short this year. きょうさく

흉잡다 find fault with (*a person*); carp [cavil] at [faults]; pick at; criticize.

흉잡히다 be talked of; be found fault with/나는 결코 남에게 흉잡힐 일은 하지 않겠다 I shall never do anything which will bring contempt upon me.

흉장(胸墻) a breast-high wall; a breastwork; a parapet.

흉조(凶兆) an ill[evil] omen; a foreboding/ ~의 ill-boding; ominous; portentous. きょうちょう

흉중(胸中) one's heart[mind, bosom]; feeling/그는 비밀을 ~에 품고 있다 He kept the secret to himself. きょうちゅう

흉증(凶證) ①an ill[evil] omen ⇒흉조 ② (음흉함) slyness; snakiness; insidiousness/ ~스러운 사람 an insidious man; a snake. きょうちょう

흉추(胸椎) 【해】 the thoracic vertebrae.

흉측(凶測) ~하다 (be) terribly wicked [evil, villainous].

흉탄(兇彈) an assassin's bullet[shell]/ ~에 쓰러지다 fall a victim to an assassin's bullet; fall by a murderer's hands.

흉터 a scar/ ~가 아직 남아 있다 The scar still remains.

흉통(胸痛) a pain in the chest/ ~을 느끼다 have a pain in the chest. きょうつう

흉포(凶暴) ferocity; atrocity; brutality; outrage; barbarity/ ~하다 (be) ferocious; atrocious/ ~성을 발휘하다 show [display] one's brutality. きょうぼう

흉풍(凶豊) rich and poor harvest; famine and plenty/ ~이 없다 usually have a good steady harvest.

흉하다(凶—) ①(사악하다) (be) bad; evil; wicked; ill-natured; malicious; villai-

흉하적 faultfinding; carping; picking flaws／～하다 find fault with; look for defects.

흉한(兇漢) a ruffian; a villain; a rascal 《하수인》an assassin; a murderer／～은 그 자리에서 잡혔다 The villain was arrested then and there. きょうかん

흉행(兇行) a felon deed. きょうこう

흉허물 ～없다 friendly; (be) intimate; close／～없는 사이다 be on intimate terms with. あやまち

흉험(凶險) wiliness; slyness; snakiness／～하다 (be) sly; wily; snaky; underhand／～한 수단을 쓰다 use subtle tricks[underhand measures].

흉헙다(凶—) (be) ugly; awful; terrible／보기 ～ be awful to look at.

흉화(凶禍) an evil[a terrible] disaster／～를 입다 get murdered; meet with evil. きょうあくなさいか

흉흉하다(洶洶—) be panic-stricken; be filled with alarm／인심이 ～ People are less haunted with fear.
きょうきょうとしている

흐너뜨리다 pull[break] down; demolish; destroy. こわす

흐너지다 crumble; callapse; break down; fall [down]; give way. こわれる

흐늘다 yearn for[after]; long[thirst] for／고향을 ～ long for home. あこがれる

흐느끼다 be moved to tears／흐느껴 울며 말하다 sob out (a thing); say (a thing) between sobs. すすりなく

흐느적흐느적 ～하다 get loose; get shaky; get wobbly; become rickety／책상다리가 ～ 놀다 The leg of a table is rickety.
ゆらゆら

흐느거리다 ①《놓고 지내다》be idle; loiter; loaf ②《흔들리다》swing; sway; rock 《매달린 것이》hang loosely／버들가지가 바람에 ～ The willow branches are swaying gently in the breeze. のらくらする

흐늘어지다 dangle ⇒휘늘어지다.

흐늘썩거리다 act slowly; behave sluggishly.

흐늘흐늘 ～하다 (be) soft; pulpy; mushy; flabby; limp／～해지다 become pulpy; limp. どろどろ

흐들갑스럽다 be extravagant[overexcited] in speech. はなざきだ

흐려지다 ①《날이》get cloudy[overexcited]; cloud (up, over) ②《눈이》get bleary; grow dim／나이 먹는 데 따라 눈이 ～ one's eyes grow dim as one gets old.

흐르다¹ ①《유동하다》flow; stream; run 《쫄쫄》trickle 《스며나오다》ooze 《흘러내리다》run down／물은 항상 낮은 곳으로 흐른다 Water always flows downword. ②《부동하다》float; drift／꽃잎이 냇물 위로 흐른다 Petals float down the stream. ③《넘치다》overflow; run over; brim over; drop／너무 많이 부으면 흐른다 Never fill the cup too full, or it will brim over ④《쏠리다》lapse[fall] into; run [incline] to; be carried away by; be swayed by／감정에 ～ be swayed by sentiment ⑤《세월이》elapse; pass (away); flow by 《어느새》slip by／몇 해가 흘렀다 Several years elapsed[passed away, flowed away]. ⑥《새다》leak／파이프에서 물이 흐른다 Water is leaking from the pipe. ⑦《퍼지다》prevail／얼마 동안 무거운 침묵이 흘렀다 An awkward silence hung between them for a time.
ながれる

흐르다² 《홀레하다》(animals) copulate; couple; mate 《새가》tread (a hen); pair 《짐승이》cover. こうびする

흐르르 ～하다 (be) soft; flabby; flimsy; squashy; flaccid; limp／종이가 얇고 ～ 하다 the paper is thin and flimsy.
ぐにゃぐにゃ

흐리다¹ ①《혼탁하다》(be) muddy; impure; thick; cloudy 《술이》／비가 와서 강물이 흐렸다 The rain has made the river muddy., The river looks thick after the rain. ②《하늘이》(be) cloudy 《동사적으로》cloud [over]; become covered with cloud／하늘이 아주 흐렸다 The sky is overcast., The sky has clouded up. ③《희미하다》(be) dim; vague; obscure; indistinct; gloomy; dusky／흐린 램프 밑에서 독서하다 read in the dim light of lamp ④《눈이》be purblind; grow dim; be blurred／나이먹으면 눈이 흐려진다 Our sight grows dim[misty] with age. ⑤⇨흐리터분하다. ぼんやりしている

흐리다² ①《지우다》efface; rub[wipe] out; erase／한 자 흐려 버리다 cross out a word 《지우개로》erase a word ②《물을》make (water) muddy[cloudy]; make unclean ③《명예 따위를》bring disgrace upon／집안의 명예를 ～ bring disgrace on one's family.

흐리마리 ～하다 (be) vague; indefinite; ambiguous; doubtful; obscure／대답이 ～하다 give an evasive reply; be vague in one's answer. ぼんやり

흐리멍덩하다 (be) vague; dim; confused; muddled; faint; hazy; dubious／너의 이야기는 ～ Your statement is too hazy.
ぼんやりしている

흐리터분하다 ①《사물이》(be) indistinct; obscure; not clear; vague ②《마음씨가》(be) shady; underhand; suspicious／흐리터분한 짓 underhand dealing.

흐릿하다 (be) rather cloudy[dim, dull, vague, hazy, blurred; indistinct]／안개 속에 등불 빛이 ～ Lights are burning dimly in the fog. うすぼんやりしている

흐무러지다 ①《너무 익다》be overripe ②

**흐물흐물** 《물에 불어서》 get very soft[too soft]/ 쌀이 물에 불어서 ~ rice gets very soft soaking up water. ふやけている

**흐물흐물** ~하다 (be) soft; flabby; pulpy; limp; flaccid/ ~하도록 삶다 boil to pulp. どろどろ

**흐뭇하다** (be) delighted; satisfied/보기에 흐뭇한 광경이었다 It was a lovely sight to see./흐뭇해 웃다 smile with satisfaction. まんぞくだ

**흐슬부슬** ~하다 (be) crumbling; (be) not viscous; be not sticky/과자가 ~하다 cakes crumble. ぼろぼろ

**흐지부지** ①wasting; to no purpose/돈을 ~ 써 버리다 waste[throw away] all the money ②《흐리멍덩》 hushing up; in secret/결말이 ~되다 an issue ends in smoke. ぼやけて

**흐트러뜨리다** 《꽃 따위를》 scatter 《군중 따위를》 strew 《구름 따위를》 disperse/방을 ~ have the room in disorder. ばらまく

**흐트러지다** 《정신이》 straggle 《산란하다》 disperse; scattered; be dispersed 《퇴산하다》 break up; disperse/사방으로 ~ scatter about in all directions. ちる

**흐흐** pshaw; pooh; humph. ふふ

**흑** 《호느낌》 with a sob.

**흑(黑)** ①a black color; black ⇨흑색 ②《바둑돌》 a black *badook* stone[piece]. くろ

**흑귀자(黑鬼子)** a nigger; a darky.

**흑기(黑旗)** a black flag. くろいはた

**흑내장(黑內障)** 〖의〗 black cataract; amaurosis.

**흑노(黑奴)** a negro slave.

**흑단(黑檀)** ebony; black wood/ ~의 ebony.

**흑대두(黑大豆)** black soybeans.

**흑두재상(黑頭宰相)** a young minister.

**흑막(黑幕)** a black curtain 《내막》 concealed circumstances; the inside/틀림없이 무슨 ~이 있을 게다 Some one is certainly pulling the wire. くろまく

**흑맥주(黑麥酒)** black[dark] beer; porter; bock beer. くろビール

**흑반(黑斑)** a black spot; melasma. くろいはんてん

**흑발(黑髮)** black hair/윤기가 흐르는 ~ glossy black hair. くろかみ

**흑빵(黑—)** dark bread; brown bread.

**흑백(黑白)** black and white 《시비》 right and wrong; good and bad/ ~ 영화 a black and white film/금명간에 ~을 가려달라 I must have justice done in a day or so. こくびゃく

**흑보기** a cross-eyed person; a squinter. やぶにらみのひと

**흑사병(黑死病)** 〖의〗 the [black] plague; black death; the pest. こくしびょう

**흑사탕(黑砂糖)** muscovado; raw[unrefined] sugar.

**흑색(黑色)** a black colour/ ~의 black/ ~ 인종 the black race. くろいろ

**흑선(黑線)** a black line. こくせん

**흑수(黑手)** a trick; an artifice; a ruse; wiles; an evil design/ ~단 the Black Hand.

**흑수(黑穗)** black; smut/ ~병 a smut disease; stinking. くろほ

**흑수정(黑水晶)** morion; dark cairngorm.

**흑숙학숙** 《되는 대로》 at random; carelessly 《어름어름》 in an obscure way/결말을 ~ 내다 obscure the issue.

**흑심(黑心)** evil intentions; a black heart / ~이 있는 evil-disposed[-minded]; black-hearted.

**흑암(黑暗)** darkness.

**흑야(黑夜)** a dark night. まっくらいよる

**흑연(黑鉛)** 〖광〗 black lead; graphite. こくえん

**흑연(黑煙)** black[murky] smoke/자욱한 ~ a dense cloud of black smoke. こくえん

**흑요석(黑曜石)** 〖광〗 obsidian.

**흑운(黑雲)** dark[black] clouds. こくうん

**흑운모(黑雲母)** 〖광〗 biotite.

**흑의(黑衣)** a black dress; black clothes / ~를 입은 사람 a person in black. こくい

**흑인(黑人)** a Negro; coloured man; a darky; a nigger/ ~ 영가(靈歌) a [Negro] spiritual/ ~ 차별 대우 segregation 〈미〉. こくじん

**흑자(黑子)** black checkers 《사마귀》 a mole. ほくろ

**흑자(黑字)** black letters; black figures /[재정 상태가] ~이다 be in the black. くろじ

**흑점(黑點)** a black spot; a macula/태양의 ~ a sunspot; a spot on the sun. こくてん

**흑조(黑潮)** 〖지〗 the Black[Japan] Current; the Black Stream.

**흑죽학죽** ①《어름어름 넘김》 settling (*a matter*) in the dark ②《엉터리로》 desultorily; perfunctorily; hit-or-miss/일을 ~ 해치우다 do a hit-or-miss job of it.

**흑지(黑—)** black checkers; black stones used in *badook*.

**흑책질** interruption; obstruction; disturbance/ ~하다 hinder; obstruct. じゃま

**흑칠(黑漆)** black lacquer. くろいろのうるし

**흑탄(黑炭)** black coal. こくたん

**흑토(黑土)** black soil[earth] / ~대(帶) the black earth zone[district]. こくど

**흑판(黑板)** a blackboard/ ~ 지우개 an eraser; a chalk eraser; a wiper. こくばん

**흑흑** with sobs; sobbing/ ~ 느껴울다 sob; weep convulsively. しくしく

**흔감(欣感)** rejoicing/ ~하다 rejoice; be rejoiced (*at*).

**흔극(釁隙)** alienation; rift; schism/ ~이 생기다[나다] be alienated; a rift develops. きんげき

**흔단(釁端)** the apple of discord; the seed of alienation. あらそいのいとぐち

**흔덕거리다** swing; sway; rock; be shaky.

**흔덕이다** be loose; be unsteady; be shaky; totter. がたがたする

**흔드렁거리다** sway; swing. ぶらぶらする

**흔드적거리다** swing; sway.

**흔들거리다** swing; sway; shake; be swayed. ゆれる

**흔들다** swing; sway; shake; wave; wag/손을 흔들어 작별하다 wave a farewell/손수건을 ~ wave[flutter] one's handkerchief/사람의 마음을 흔들어 놓다 disturb (a person). ゆすぶる

**흔들리다** sway; rock; shake; tremble; joggle 《차가》 jolt 《매달린 것이》 swing 《마음이》 waver/좌우로 ~ rock from side to side. ゆさぶられる

**흔들비쭉이** a cross-grained[cranky] person; a peevish fellow.

**흔들의자(一椅子)** a rocking chair; a rocker.

**흔들흔들** swayingly; swingingly; wavingly; rockingly/~하다 sway; swing; rock.

**흔연하다(欣然—)** (be) joyous; joyful; cheerful/흔연히 joyfully; cheerfully; gladly 《쾌히》 with a good grace; willingly. うれしい

**흔적(痕迹)** traces; marks; evidences; signs/시체에 타살의 ~이 있었다 The body bore marks of violence. こんせき

**흔전거리다** live in easy circumstances; be well off; live in luxury.

**흔전만전** plentifully; in plenty; copiously/~ 쓸 돈이 있다 have money enough and to spare.

**흔전하다** (be) plentiful; abundant; profuse; copious. じゅんたくだ

**흔쾌(欣快)** pleasure; joy; delight/~하다 (be) pleasant; happy; delightful. きんかい

**흔하다** (be) plentiful; rife; common; commonplace; be met with everywhere/흔한 것이 여자다 If there's one thing we have enough of, it's woman. ありふれている

**흔흔히(欣欣—)** gladly; joyously.

**흔희(欣喜)** delight; joy; gladness; rejoicing/~하다 rejoice; be glad; be delighted (with)/~ 작약하다 jump[dance] for joy. きんき

**흔히** commonly 《주로》 usually; mostly 《대개》 mainly; generally/이런 일은 ~ 있는 일이다 Such things are apt to happen.

**흘게늦다** (be) loose; loose-jointed; loose-hinged/저 사람은 ~ He wants screwing up. ゆるんでいる

**흘겨보다** glance sidelong; give a sharp sidelong glance at. よこめでみつめる

**흘근거리다** walk slowly[lazily]; proceed at reduced speed. ぶらぶらあるく

**흘금거리다** look askance[sidewise] at a person frequently; cast a sidelong glance[look] (at). ちらっとみる

**흘끗** at a glance/~ 보다 catch a glimpse of; steal a glance at. ちらっと

**흘굿거리다** keep looking sideways. しきりににらむ

**흘기다** glare fiercely at; give a sharp sidelong glance (at)/그녀는 나를 무섭게 흘겼다 She gave me a fierce sidelong scowl. にらむ

**흘기죽죽** with a displeased look from the corner of one's eyes/~하다 look displeased[discontented].

**흘깃** with a [sharp] glance/~ 보다 [cast a glance at a person. ちらっと

**흘깃거리다** keep glaring[scowling] (at). しきりににらむ

**흘깃흘깃** glaring and glaring; scowling and scowling/~ 보다 keep glaring. ちらっと

**흘러보다** sound (out); tap; feel (a person's) pulse/사람의 의견을 ~ sound (a person's) views; seek (a person's) opinion. あたってみる

**흘레** copulation; coition/~하다 copulate; couple; tread (a hen); 《새 따위가》 pair/말을 ~ 붙이다 serve a horse. こうび

**흘리다** ①《흐르게 하다》 spill; slop; shed; drop/눈물을 ~ shed[drop] tears ②《빠뜨리다》 drop; lose/돈을 ~ lose one's money ③《글씨를》 write in a cursive hand; scribble/편지를 흘려 쓰다 scribble a letter. こぼす

**흙구덩이** a hole[hollow, cavity] in the ground. じめんのくぼみ

**흙내** the smell of the soil[dirt]/~나다 smell of the soil[dirt]. つちのにおい

**흙다리** an earthen bridge. どばし

**흙담** a mud-wall; a plaster wall.

**흙더미** a heap of earth.

**흙덩이** a clod; a lump of earth. つちくれ

**흙메 (土山)** a mountain of earth.

**흙무더기** a heap[pile] of earth.

**흙뭉치** a lump[ball] of kneaded clay. こねたつちのかたまり

**흙뭉텅이** a big lump[ball] of kneaded clay. こねたおおきいつちのかたまり

**흙받기** ①《자동차의》 a mudguard; a splashboard ②《미장이의》 a mixing board. つちはらい

**흙빨래** soiled clothes with muddy water; a dress which is stained with muddy water.

**흙방(一房)** a mud-plastered room. どしつ

**흙벽(一壁)** a mud-plastered wall.

**흙비** a dust storm; a sandstorm.

**흙빛** earth colour/~의 bluish-black 《안색이》 pale; ashy/얼굴이 ~이 되다 turn pale as ashes. つちいろ

**흙손** a trowel 《마무리하는》 a float. こて

**흘림** the cursive[running] style of penmanship; writing in a cursive hand/~으로 쓰다 write in a cursive hand.

**흘림흘림** by[in] driblets; little by little; by piecemeal/돈을 ~ 갚다 return mon-

흘립(屹立) ~하다 tower high; soar/벼랑이 강물 위에 ~하고 있다 The cliff overhangs the stream. きつりつ

흘수(吃水) draft; water drawn (by a vessel); sea gauge/~표 the draft mark/~이 깊은[얕은] 배 a deep[light, shallow]-draft vessel. きっすい

흘쩍거리다 prolong[protract, drag out, delay] (a plan) on purpose.

흘쩍흘쩍 dawdling; loafing; idling; delaying. ぐずぐずする

흙 《토양》earth 《지면》soil 《진흙》the ground; clay/~을 파다 dig in the ground/사람은 한 줌의 ~에 지나지 않는다 Man is but a lump of clay. つち

흙감태기 being covered all over with mud/~가 되다 be covered all over with mud.

흙손질 troweling; plastering with a trowel/~하다 trowel; level with a float.

흙일 earthwork/~하는 사람 a coolie 《토역군》a navvy. つちしごと

흙주머니 a sandbag.

흙질 mud-plastering/~하다 plaster with mud; stucco; trowel.

흙칠 ~하다 soil[smear] with mud; be stained with mud.

흙탕물 muddy water.

흙투성이 covering with mud/·~가 되다 be covered with mud. どろだらけ

흠 Hum!, Hm!, Hmph! ふん

흠(欠) ①《상처 자국》a scar; a cicatrice/그는 얼굴에 ~이 있다 He has[bears] a scar on his face. ②《물건의》a flaw; a scratch[crack, speck]; 《과일의》a bruise/그 금강석에는 ~이 있다 There is a flaw in the diamond. ③《결점》a defect; a flaw; a blemish; a drawback/그의 ~이라면 단지 술 마시는 것뿐이다 Drinking is one flaw in his otherwise perfect character. きず

흠결(欠缺) shortage; deficiency; deficit. かけること

흠구덕(欠—) slander 《비난》disparagement; backbiting/~하다 slander; speak ill of; cry down; disparage. ちゅうしょう

흠내다(欠—) scar; crack; flaw (a tea cup)/얼굴에 ~ scar one's face. きずをつける

흠뜯다(欠—) speak ill of others; backbite; behind their backs; whisper against/그는 남을 잘 흠뜯는 사람이다 He is a scandalmonger[scandalbearer]. ちゅうしょうする

흠모(欽慕) admiration; adoration/~하다 admire; adore; make an idol of/그는 여전히 동향인의 ~를 받고 있다 He is still the idol of his countrymen. きんぼ

흠빨다 suck hard/흠빨며 감빨다 suck (it) up greedily.

흠뻑 fully; thoroughly; completely/~ 젖은 옷 dripping clothes/~ 젖다 be soaked to the skin; be soaked with rain/~ 기뻐하다 be greatly pleased; be much delighted/땀에 ~ 젖다 《사람이》be all in sweat 《옷이》be wringing wet with sweat. たっぷり

흠신(欠身) ~하다 make a bow; bow. あくびとのび

흠실흠실 to pulp; to jelly; yielding to the touch/~하다 be boiled soft/~하게 삶다 reduce to jelly[pulp]/고기를 ~ 삶다 boil meat tender. ぐにゃぐにゃ

흠앙(欽仰) admiration; adoration; reverence; high regard/~하다 admire; adore; esteem; entertain a high regard (for);《숭배하다》make an idol of. きんぎょう

흠잡다(欠—) find fault with; pick flaws; look for defects; carp[cavil] at/흠잡을 데가 없다 be faultless; leave nothing to be desired/게으른 것을 ~ criticize (a person's) laziness/그는 남의 흠잡기를 좋아한다 He is fond of finding fault with others.

흠정(欽定) ~하다 authorize; establish/~의 authorized[established] by the king; compiled by royal order/~ 시인 a poet laureate/~ 헌법 a constitution granted by the king. きんてい

흠지다(欠—) get scarred; get marred[cracked]; be scratched; have a flaw[scratch, crack, speck]. きずができる

흠집(欠—) a scar; a cicatrice/이마에 ~이 있다 have a scar on one's forehead.

흠축(欠縮) shortage; deficiency; want; deficit/~내다 cause a shortage (of); make a deficit (of). けつぼう

흠치르르 sleek; glossy/~하다 (be) sleek; glossy/~ 윤이 흐르다 be sleek; be smooth and glossy. つやつや

흠칫 recoiling[shrinking] with a fright [surprise]/~하다 recoil; shrink.

흡기(吸氣) breathing in; inspiration/~하다 breathe in; inspire; inhale/~기 (器) an aspirator. きゅうき

흡력(吸力) absorptivity; absorption power. きゅうりょく

흡반(吸盤) a sucker; a sucking disk; an acetabulum. きゅうばん

흡사(恰似) 《명사적》close resemblance 《부사적》just as; as if[though]; as it were/~하다 closely resemble; be much [about] the same; (be) alike; be just as/아주 ~하다 be as like as two peas [eggs]; be exactly alike; be a copy (of)/~ 죽은 것 같다 look as if dead; be more dead than alive/~ 달이 뜬 것같이 훤하다 It is as bright as if the moon had risen.

흡상(吸上) suction; sucking/~하다 suck [draw, pump] up; draw up. すいあげ

흡수(吸收) absorption; suction; assimilation 《열의》decalescence 《빛의》extinction/~하다 absorb; assimilate; suck in/~성의 absorbent; absorptive/~력

흡수(吸水) suction [of water]; water suction/~ 펌프 a suction pump.

흡습성(吸濕性) ~의 hygroscopic.

흡연(吸煙) smoking [tobacco]/~하다 smoke [tobacco, a cigarette, a pipe]; have a smoke; have a pipe/~자 a smoker/~실 a smoking room/~ 금지 No smoking [is allowed here]/과도하게 ~은 몸에 해롭다 It is bad for the health to smoke like a chimney.

흡연(洽然) ~하다 (be) satisfying; gratifying/~히 to one's satisfaction; gratifyingly.

흡연(翕然) with one accord; spontaneously; unanimously/학급의 동정은 ~히 그 가난한 소년에게로 쏠렸다 The sympathy of the whole class was centered upon the poor boy.

흡열 반응(吸熱反應) 『화』 endothermic reaction.

흡인(吸引) ①《흡입》 absorption; suction/~하다 absorb; suck up/~력 absorption force 《자기의》 attractive force ②《끌어들임》 attraction/~하다 attract; draw/의자를 ~하다 attract[absorb] foreign capital.

흡입(吸入) inhalation; inspiration/~하다 inhale; inspire; suck in/ ~관 an induction pipe/ ~기 an inhaler; an inspirator; a nebulizer.

흡족(洽足) ~하다 (be) sufficient; ample; satisfactory; enough/~히 to one's heart's content; sufficiently; enough; fully/ ~히 먹다 eat one's fill; do full justice to (the dinner)/그만하면 그에게 ~하게 해 준거다 You have done enough for him.

흡착(吸着) adhesion; absorption/ ~제 an absorbent.

흡출(吸出) sucking out; drawing out/ ~하다 suck out; draw out.

흡혈(吸血) blood-sucking/~귀(鬼) a vampire; a bloodsucker.

흥 Hum!, Hm!, Hmph!, Pish!

흥(興) fun; pleasure; mirth; joy; excitement/ ~에 겨워 in the excess of mirth/ ~이 나다 get merry[excited] (over something); become interested (in); warm up (to one's work)/~을 깨치다 spoil pleasure[fun]; kill joy; put [throw] a wet blanket on/~을 돋구다 add to the amusement.

흥감 exaggeration; grandiosity; bombast; a tall[big] talk/ ~하다 be give to exaggeration; (be) bombastic; pompous/~스럽게 exaggeratedly; pompously; with much ado/ ~부리다 exaggerate; stretch; blow one's own trumpet[horn]; talk big[tall]/ ~스럽게 떠들어 대다 make a fuss too much/그는 사소한 일에도 ~스럽게 떠들어 댄다 He makes trouble over a mere trifle.

흥건하다 be full to the brim; be full of water 《음식이》 have too much liquid in/웅덩이에 빗물이 흥건히 괴었다 A puddle is full of rainwater./국이 ~ Soup is watery.

흥겹다(興—) be full of fun; (be) gay; joyful; interesting/흥겹게 gaily; merrily; joyously; pleasantly/흥겨운 김에 in the excess of mirth/한참 흥겨운 판에 in the midst of one's merriment/ 흥겹게 놀다 be absorbed in play.

흥글방망이놀다 disturb; stir up troubles; give rise to complications; frustrate.

흥기(興起) rise; ascendancy/~하다 rise; ascend; be in the ascendant.

흥김(興—) (in) the midst of merriment; (under) the influence of excitement/ ~에 큰 소리로 노래 부르다 have such a good time that one sings in a loud voice.

흥나다(興—) get merry; grow excited; have fun/흥나서 노래부르다 sing with much mirth/흥나면 시를 읊는다 When I am in the mood, I recite poems.

흥덩흥덩 having too much water in it/ ~하다 have too much water in it/~ 국물 뿐이구나 The soup is all water with no meat in!

흥뚱새 『조』 a Chinese tree pipit; Anthus hodgsoni(학명).

흥뚱흥뚱 half-heartedly; inattentively; carelessly; heedlessly/~ 듣다 pay little [no] attention to; listen to (a person) in an absent sort of way/일을 ~하다 do a job carelessly.

흥망(興亡) rise and fall; ups and downs 《운명》 destinies; vicissitudes/로마의 ~ the rise and fall of Rome; the destinies of Rome/민족의 ~ the varied fortunes of races/국가의 ~에 관한 문제 a problem affecting the destinies of the nation.

흥미(興味) interest; zest; taste; gusto/ ~있다 be interesting; be amusing; be entertaining/ ~없다 be uninteresting; be dull; be of no interest/깊은 ~를 가지고 with keen[deep] interest/~ 위주로 for the sake of arousing the interest (of)/~를 잃다 lose interest in/문학에 비상한 ~를 가지다 take a great interest in literature/그는 새로운 ~를 가지고 그 책의 연구를 시작했다 He began to study the book with new interest.

흥분(興奮) excitement; stimulation; agitation; excitation/~하다 be[grow, get]

**excited; excite** *oneself*; **be stimulated; work** *oneself* **up; get a kick[thrill]**《속》／～하여 **excitedly; in excitement; in a sweat**／～시키다 **excite; work** (*a person*) **up; stimulate; arouse** (*a person's*) **feelings**／매우 ～하고 있다 **be on a tiptoe of excitement**／～하지 말라 **Don't get excited.**, **Don't be upset.**／～하여 심장마비로 죽었다 **Excited, he collapsed with a heart attack.**／환자를 ～시키면 안 된다 **The patient must not be excited.**／～ 상태 **excited condition[state]**／～제 **a stimulant; an excitant; an invigorator.** こうふん

**흥산**(興産) **industrial developement[enterprise]**／～하다 **undertake an industrial enterprise; develop industry; promote industries.** さんぎょうをおこすこと

**흥성흥성**(興盛興盛) **prosperously; flourishingly; thrivingly**／～하다 **(be) prosperous; thriving; flourishing; booming**／장사가 ～하다 **one's business is booming[thriving].**

**흥신소**(興信所) **a credit bureau[association]; an inquiry office[agency]**／상업 ～ **a commercial inquiry agency.** こうしんじょ

**흥얼거리다 hum; croon; sing to** *oneself*. ふんえい

**흥얼흥얼 humming; crooning**／～ 혼자 노래하다 **croon to** *oneself*. ふんふん

**흥업**(興業) **an industrial enterprise; promotion of industries**／～하다 **promote industries; under-take an industrial enterprise.** こうぎょう

**흥에 띄다**(興—) **be in the excess of mirth; be driven by inspiration; be all wrapped up in** *one's* **enjoyment.**

**흥이야항이야 meddlingly; interferingly;**／～하다 **thrust[poke]** *one's* **nose into; intermeddle; obtrude** *oneself* **to**／남의 일에 ～하다 **thrust[poke, stick]** *one's* **nose into another** *person's* **business.**

**흥정** 《매매》 **buying and[or] selling; marketing** 《거래》 **dealing**／～하다 **strike a bargain; haggle over terms** 《거래》 **do business; deal** 《매매》 **buy and sell**／～ 붙이다 **act as [a] broker; help strike a bargain**／～은 붙이고 싸움은 말리란다 **One should help bargaining and stop quarrels.**／～거리 **merchandise**／～군 **a broker; a dealer; a trader; parties to a bargain.**

**흥진 비래**(興盡悲來) **After joy come tears.**, **Upon the full tide of pleasure steals sadness.**, **Good and ill luck are closely interwoven.**

**흥청거리다 exult; be highly elated; indulge in revelry**／그는 성공해서 흥청거리고 있다 **He is transported with his success.**

**흥청망청 gaily; merrily; jollily** ⇨흥청흥청.

**흥청흥청 with elation; exultantly; merr-**

**ily; gaily**／～ 놀고 마시다 **go on a racket; hold high junks; drink the cup of pleasure to the dregs.**

**흥취**(興趣) **interest; gusto; taste**／ ～가 있다 **be interesting; be fun** ⇨흥미(興味). きょうしゅ

**흥치**(興致) 《흥미》**delight; pleasure; interest; amusement** 《풍치》 **taste** 《아치》 **elegance.** おもしろみとおもむき

**흥타령**(―打令) **a kind of folksong with a "hum" at the end of each line.**

**흥패**(興敗) **rise and fall; destiny**／국가의 ～에 관한 중대한 문제 **a great question affecting the destinies of the nation**／일국의 ～가 달려 있는 싸움 **a battle on which the fate of a country depends.** こうはい

**흥하다**(興—) **rise** 《번영하다》 **prosper; boom; be prosperous[flourishing, thriving]**／흥하는 집안 **a prosperous[thriving] family**／장사가 ～ **business prospers[flourishes, thrives, booms]; do good[prosperous] business**／흥하든 망하든 해 보겠다 **I will try, sink or swim.**, **I will ma' ke a spoon or spoil a horn.** おこる

**흥행**(興行) 《사업》 **the entertainment industry; a show enterprise** 《연예》 **a show; a run; a performance**／ ～하다 **give a performance; perform; run** (*a show*); **produce** (*a play*); **exhibit**／～ 가치 **box-office value**／～권 **right of performance[production]**; 《연극의》 **dramatic[stage] rights**／～물 **a performance; a production; an exhibition**／ ～ 가치가 있는 영화 **a picture of proven box-office power; a film with audience appeal**／주간 ～ **a matinee.** こうぎょう

**흥흥 hum hum; hmph hmph.** ふんふん

**흥흥거리다** ①《콧노래》 **hum; sing to** *oneself*; **croon** ②《울다》 **whine; whimper.** ふんふんいう

**흩날리다 scatter; blow off[away]**／낙엽이 바람에 흩날리고 있다 **The dead leaves have blown away.**

**흩다 scatter; strew** 《군중을》 **disperse** 《머리털 따위를》 **dishevel**／머리털을 흩다 **with** *one's* **disheveled hair**／휴지 조각을 ～ **scatter bits of waste paper**／적을 ～ **rout the enemy; put the enemy to rout.** ちらす

**흩뜨리다 scatter[strew]** (*about*); **disperse.**

**흩어지다 be scattered; be dispersed; scatter; be littered; break up**／소문이 ～ **rumor gets abroad**／유태 민족은 전 세계에 흩어져 살고 있다 **The Jewish race is spread all over the world.**／공원에는 쓰레기가 흩어져 있다 **The parks are scattered with rubbish.** ちらばる

**흩이다 be scattered; be dispersed**／꽃이 바람에 흩인다 **Blossoms are scattered by the wind.** ちらされる

**희가**(戱歌) **a limerick; a comic song.**

**희가극**(喜歌劇) **a comic opera.** きかげき

**희곡**(戱曲) **a drama; a play**／ ～적 dra-

**희구(希求)** 《희망》 hope; desire 《요구》 request 《기대》 expectation/ ~하다 beg; request; entreat; desire; hope. きき ゅう

**희귀(稀貴)** rareness; rarity/ ~한 rare; curious; phenomenal/ ~한 물건 a rarity; a curiousity; rare articles/ ~한 일 a rarity/~한 사건 a rare[an uncommon] occurrence[event]/~한 책 a rare book. けう

**희끄무레하다** (be) whitish; rather fair/ 희끄무레한 얼굴 a rather fair face. しろみがかっている

**희극(喜劇)** a comedy 《광대극》 a farce; a funny show〈미〉/ ~적 comic; farcical / ~을 상연하다 play a comedy/ ~ 배우 a comic actor(남자); actress(여자)/ ~ 작가 a comic dramatist; a comedy writer; a comedian/한바탕 ~이 벌어졌 다 A comic scene was enacted on the spot. きげき

**희끈거리다** get[feel] dizzy[giddy]; one's head turns[swins]/희끈희끈 reelingly; dizzily. めまいがする

**희끔하다** (be) whitish.

**희끗거리다** get dizzy ⇒희끈거리다. めがくらむようだ

**희끗희끗** spotted[speckled] with white; grizzled; grizzly/ ~하다 (be) grizzled; grizzly/~한 사람 a grizzle-haired man/높은 산에는 ~ 눈이 남아 있 다 Patches of snow remain on the lofty mountains.

**희기(喜氣)** a happy frame of mind;good humour; a mood of cheerfulness; happy feeling; gay spirit.

**희나리** green firewood; wet firewood. なまのたきぎ

**희넓적하다** (be) white and broad[flat].

**희년(稀年)** seventy years of age.

**희노(喜怒)** joy and anger ⇒희로(喜怒). きど

**희다** (be) white 《피부가》 fair 《머리가》 grey 《쓰지 않다》 blank/얼굴이 ~ 하 ve a fair[white] face/머리가 ~ have gray hair/눈같이 ~ be snow-white/ 살결이 ~ have a fair complexion; be of light complexion/흰 구름이 창공에 떠 있었다 Fleecy clouds floated in the blue sky. しろい

**희담(戲談)** 《농담》a joke; a jest; a pleasantry; a banter. しゃれ

**희대(稀代)** uncommonness; rarity/ ~의 uncommon; rare; extraordinary; unique; unhead-of/ ~의 악한 a notorious [double-dyed] villain/~의 영웅 a unique hero. きだい

**희떱다** ①《허영》(be) very showy; vainglorious; pretentious ②《손크다》(be) open-handed; liberal ③《반지빠르다》(be) conceited; presumptuous; saucy; impudent.

**희똑거리다** reel; swim; be dizzy; get giddy. めまいがする

**희뚝희뚝 ~하다** (be) dotted with white 《머리가》grizzly/머리가 ~한 gray-haired; grizzled; grizzle-haired.

**희디희다** (be) snow-white; pure white; as white as snow. いろがひじょうにしろい

**희락(喜樂)** joy and pleasure; felicity; happiness. きらく

**희로(喜怒)** joy and anger 《감정》emotion feelings/ ~ 애락의 정 feelings of joy and anger/ ~ 애락을 겉으로 나타내다 betray[show, give vent to] one's feelings/~ 애락의 감정을 드러내지 않다 disguise one's feelings. きど

**희롱(戲弄)** ridiculing; jesting; a joke/ ~하다 joke with; poke fun at; make fun[sport] of; ridicule; tease; toy[sport] with/ ~조로 in mocking tone/운 명의 ~ a trick of fate/ ~조로 말하다 say a thing in[for] sport.
たわむれてもてあそぶこと

**희롱거리다** joke; jest; play pranks 《술 마 시고》 rollick 《조롱하다》 make fun[sport] of. ふざける

**희맑다** (be) white and clean.

**희망(希望)** 《소망》hope; wish; desire 《포 부》aspiration 《기대》ambition; prospect; expectation 《요구》request/ ~하다 hope for; be hopeful of; wish; desire; be desirous of; anticipate/~적 관측 wishful thinking/오래 품어 온 ~ one's long-cherished desire; one's dearest ambition/일루의 ~ a ray of hope/ ~을 가지고 in hopes of; in the hope that/ ~에 살다 live in hope/헛된 ~을 가지 다 hope against hope/그의 눈은 ~에 빛 나고 있었다 His eyes gleamed with hope. きぼう

**희멀겋다** (be) white and glossy; nice and fair. しろくてつやつやしている

**희멀쑥하다** (be) white and clean; clean and fair.

**희묵(戲墨)** my [humble] writing; my [unworthy] drawing.

**희롭다** (be) white and flabby; wan.

**희미(稀微)** dimness; mistiness; vagueness/~하다 (be) faint; dim; vague; indistinct; misty; hazy/ ~하게 faintly; dimly; vaguely/ ~한 빛 a glimmer/ ~해지다 become faint[dim]/ ~하게 기억하다 have a dim recollection (of) /종소리가 ~하게 들렸다 The faint sound of a bell fell on my ears./날이 밝 아지면서 별빛이 차차 ~해졌다 The stars faded before the encroaching day.
かすかなこと

**희박(稀薄)** thinness; rarity; rarefaction /~하다 (be) thin; weak 《희소하다》(be) thin; dilute; sparse/~한 공기 a rarefied [thin] air/인구가 ~한 지역 a sparsely [thinly] populated district. きはく

**희번덕거리다** turn one's eyes up and do-

**희번드르르하다** wn; keep goggling *one's* eyes/눈을 희번덕거리면서 피로와하다. turn *one's* eyes up and down in agony/성이 나서 눈을 ~ let *one's* eyes pop out with anger. きょろきょろする

**희번드르르하다** (be) snow-white and glossy.

**희번지르르하다** (be) neat and fair.

**희번하다** (be) dimly white; dawn gray; faintly light/동녘 하늘이 희번해졌다 The dawn whitened the eastern sky.

**희보**(喜報) good [favourable] news; joyful [glad] tidings.

**희불그레하다** (be) pinkish.

**희붐하다** (be) faintly light; white/희붐해지다 grow light; turn gray.

**희비**(喜悲) joy and sorrow/~극 a tragicomedy/ ~ 쌍곡선 mingled feelings of joy and sorrow/~가 교차하다 have mingled feelings of joy and sorrow.

**희사**(喜捨) almsgiving; alms; charity; voluntary; contribution/ ~하다 give alms; give in charity (*to*); give a donation of; offer/ ~를 청하다 make a collection (*for*); pass[send] the hat round (*for*)/ ~금 alms; a gift of money; donations/ ~함 an offertory chest [box]. きしゃ

**희사**(喜事) a joyful event; a happy accident; a matter for congratulation.

**희색**(喜色) a glad countenance; a happy [pleased] look; a joyful look/ ~ 만연하다 look joyful[happy]; be all smiles beam/그의 얼굴에 ~이 떠올랐다 A look of pleasure came to his face. きしょく

**희생**(犠牲) 【헌신】 sacrifice 【자기 희생】 self-sacrifice[immolation]/~하다 sacrifice; make a victim of (*a person*)/~적 정신 a self-sacrificing spirit/어떤 ~을 치르더라도 at all costs[any cost]/자기를 ~하다 sacrifice oneself; make a martyr of oneself/그는 가족을 위해 자신을 ~했다 He sacrificed himself for the sake of his family./~심 a spirit of [self]-sacrifice/어머니는 자식들을 위하여 생명까지라도 ~할 것입니다 A mother will sacrifice even her life for her children. ぎせい

**희세**(稀世) uncommonness; uniqueness; /~의 rarity rare; uncommon; extraordinary; unique/ ~의 영웅 a hero for the century; an extraordinary hero / ~지재(之才) a phenomenal talent; a genius of extraordinary caliber. きだい

**희소**(稀少) scarcity; rarity/ ~하다 (be) sparse; scarce; rare/ ~ 물자 scarce materials/ ~ 가치 scarcity value. きしょう

**희소**(喜笑) ~하다 laugh with joy[delight]. きしょう

**희소식**(喜消息) good news; glad tidings /무소식이 ~이다 No news is good news./ ~을 듣고 그는 좋아 날뛰었다 At the glad tidings he was beside himself with joy.

**희수**(稀壽) *one's* seventieth birthday.

**희수**(喜壽) seventy seven years of age. きじゅ

**희열**(喜悅) joy; delight; gladness; rapture; glee. きえつ

**희염산**(稀塩酸) 【화】 diluted hydrochloric acid. きえんさん

**희오**(戲娛) fun; frolic; lark/ ~하다 [make] fun; frolic; play pranks; make merry. たわむれ

**희우**(喜雨) a welcome rain; a beneficial rain; a rain after drought. じう

**희원**(希願) hope; desire ⇨희망(希望). きぼう

**희유**(稀有) (being) rare; uncommon/ ~하다 (be) rare; uncommon; phenomenal /~한 사건 a rare[an uncommon] occurrence/ ~한 물건 a black swan; a blue dahlia; a white crow/이런 일은 ~하다 Such a thing rarely happens./이 계절치고서는 ~의 날씨다 This is phenomenal weather for the time of the year. けう

**희유**(嬉遊) ~하다 play merrily; have a good time; have fun; make merry. きゆう

**희읍스름하다** (be) whitish; be not white [clean] enough.

**희작**(戲作) 【소설】 a story; a novel 《총칭》 fiction 【희곡】 a drama; a play. げさく

**희종**(稀種) a rere variety.

**희초산**(稀硝酸) 【화】 dilute nitric acid.

**희치희치** 【피륙·종이가】 worn out here and there; out of shape here and there 【벗어지다】 peeling[coming] off here and there/책상의 칠이 ~ 벗어지다 varnish comes off a table here and there.

**희타**(犠打) 【야구에서】 sacrifice [hit].

**희학**(戲謔) joking; jesting; kidding; a sport; a prank; a banter/~하다 joke; jest; play (*with*); make fun (*of*)/그는 ~을 잘 한다 He is a man of wit and humor. /~질 joking; jesting; kidding. ぎぎゃく

**희한**(稀罕) rarity; scarcity/ ~하다 (be) rare; uncommon; curious/ ~한 물건 a rarity/ ~한 사람 a rare person/저런 학자는 ~하다 Such scholars are rarely met with. ひじょうにまれなこと

**희화**(戲畫) a comic picture; a caricature. ぎが

**희황산**(稀黃酸) 【화】 dilute sulphuric acid.

**희희** laughing idiotically; simpering/~웃다 simper; laugh like an idiot. ひひ

**희희 낙락**(喜喜樂樂) rejoicing; jubilation / ~하다 rejoice; be in delight; be glad; jubilate/ ~하여 merrily; joyfully; cheerfully; mirthfully.

**흰개미** 【충】 a white ant; a termite.

**흰떡** bar-shaped [white] rice cake.

**흰머리** 《머리털》 white[gray] hair 《머리》 a gray head. しらが

**흰무리** [white] race-cake; rice cakes steamed without shaping.
**흰밥** plain white rice [cooked with nothing mixed in]; boiled rice.
**흰소리** a snobbish[pretentious] remark; a loud boast; bluffing; bragging／ ~치다 talk big[tall]; brag (*of*); boast (*of* that …). からいばり
**흰옷** white clothes. はくい
**흰자** 《달걀의》 the white of an egg; glair; albumen.
**흰자위** ①《눈의》 the white of the eye ② ⇨흰자.
**흰죽** rice-gruel／ ~을 끓이다 boil rice down into gruel ／어린애에게 ~을 먹이다 feed gruel to a little child [with a spoon].
**흰줄** a white stripe.
**흿하다** be abstracted; be absent-minded 《당황하여》 be dazed 《놀라서》 be aghast 《술 따위를 마시고》 feel *one's* brains muddled／너무 술을 마시면 머리가 횟해진다 Excessive drinking muddles *one's* brains.／정신이 ~ be stupefied[stunned].
**횟허케** fast; swiftly; sipeedily／ ~ 걷다 walk fast.
**히죽** ~거리다 give one sweet smile after another. にこっと
**히죽이** smilingly; beamingly／ ~ 웃다 smile sweetly; beam with a smile; smile a sweet smile／그는 자기도 모르게 ~ 웃었다 An unconscious smile beamed over his countenance.
**힐기죽거리다** sway *one's* body[hips] [in walking].
**힐난(詰難)** criticism; censure; reproach／ ~하다 criticize; censure; denounce ／실패를 ~하다 needle (*a person*) over the failure of〈미〉. なじりひなんすること
**힐문(詰問)** cross-examination[question]; rigid inquiry／ ~하다 question[examine] closely; cross-examine; put (*a person*) through close examination; grill; press (*a person*) hard with questions／ …의 실패를 ~하다 needle (*a person*) over the failure of〈미〉. きつもん
**힐책(詰責)** reproof; rebuke; reproack; reprimand／ ~하다 reproach; reprove; censure; rebuke／부주의를 ~하다 reproach[reprove] (*a person*) for his careles-

# 힘

①**power; energy; vigor** 《내적인》 [physical] strength 《외적인》 [main] force 《특히 강력한》 might／ ~이 센 strong; powerful; mighty／ ~없이 feebly; dejectedly; disappointedly／ ~을 겨루다 have a strength contest; try[measure, match] *one's* strength against another's／ ~을 쓰다 put forth *one's* strength／그는 ~이 장사다 He is a Hercules ／ ~이 빠지다 *one's* strength is gone; weaken; be enervated.

②《능력》 ability; power; prowess; capacity; faculty; capability／ ~이 미치는 한 as far as *one* can; to the best [utmost] of *one's* ability; for all *one* is worth／그런 일을 할 ~이 없다 It is beyond my power to do so.／ ~이 미치지 않는 일을 하다 bite off more than *one* can chew／ ~이 모자라는 in capable; incompetent.

③《노력》 effort[s]; exertion; endeavor; labo[u]r／ ~을 다하다 make every effort[endeavor] exert *oneself* for (*a thing*)／ ~이 모자라다 be beyond *one's* power; be more than *one* can do／ ~을 합하다 unite their efforts; co-operate／ ~을 들이다 devote *one's* energies to; put labo[u]r[work, effort] into; put *one's* back to; put *one's* shoulder to the wheel; devote *oneself* (*to*); put *one's* heart and soul (*into*).

④《물리적인》 force; energy; power／증기의 ~ the power of steam／열의 ~ the energy of heat／자연의 ~ natural forces.

⑤《효력》 power; influence; efficacy／ …의 ~으로 by force of; by dint of; by [in] virtue of; on the strength of through.

⑥《위력》 influence; sway; power; authority; weight; might／돈의 ~ the power of money／경찰의 ~ the power [authority] of the police／ ~을 내다 pluck[muster] up *one's* courage[spirits] ／아버지의 ~으로 취직하다 get a job through the influence of *one's* father.

⑦《정신적인》 courage; spirit; heart; ginger; nerve; pep／정계에서 ~을 부리다 exercise[wield] much powerin politics.／ ~을 얻다 be encouraged; gain courage; be emboldened; be cheered up ／ ~을 내다 pluck[muster] up *one's* spirits[courage].

⑧《강조》 emphasis; stress; force; power／ ~을 주어 emphatically; forcibly／ ~있는 문장 forceful[powerful] sentences.

⑨《조력》 help; support; aid; assistance; good offices; service; contribution／ ~을 빌다 enlist the help (*of*)／ ~을 빌리다 help; aid; lend a helping hand to; give assistance[aid] to; entend help／ ~이 되다 help; be helpful; stand by.

힘 ⇨별항 참조(page 1851).

**힘껏** with all *one's* might; with might and main; a shard as *one* can; to the best of *one's* ability／ ～ 일하다 work hard as *one* can; work with all *one's* might／ ～ 돕다 do *one's* best[utmost] to help／ ～ 싸우다 fight for all *one* is worth.

**힘겨룸** measuring *one's* strength with *another's*; a strength contest／ ～하다 have a strength contest; measure[try] *one's* strength against (*another*)／ ～해보자 Let us see who is the stronger, you or I.

**힘꼴** muscle; brawn／ ～이나 쓰는 남자 a strong man; a man of great strength.

**힘들다** 《힘이 들다》(be) heavy; tough; laborious; toilsome; painful 《어렵다》(be) hard; difficult 《수고가 되다》(be) troublesome／힘드는 일 an arduous[a strenuous] job／힘드는 문제 a difficult problem／농사가 잘 안 되어서 살기 ～ be pinched [economically] because of a bad harvest.

**힘들이다** ①《정성껏》make efforts; exert *one*self; use *one's* endeavour; show a zeal for ②《힘을 내다》put forth[out] *one's* strength／힘들여 운반하다 carry the load laboriously.

**힘빼물다** boast of *one's* strength; assume [put on] an air of a strong man.

**힘부치다** be not strong[capable] enough to; be beyond *one's* power[ability]; be too much for *one*／나에게는 힘부치는 일이다 The task is beyond[out of] my power., The task exceeds my strength.

**힘세다** (be) strong; powerful／그는 대단히 ～ He is of Herculean strength., He is strong as a horse.

**힘쓰다** ①《노력하다》exert *one*self; make efforts; try hard／목적을 달성하려고 ～ strive after *one's* object／문제를 해결하려고 ～ set *one*self to solve a problem ②《열중하다》be assiduous; be diligent (*in*); be industrious／학업에 ～ attend to *one's* studies with diligence ③《고심하다》take pains; be at great pains／범인을 잡으려고 대단히 힘썼다 I have had hard work to hunt up the culprit.／힘써 모은 돈이다 The money has been saved by the sweat of my brow. ④《조력하다》helf; aid; assist; give (*a person*) assistance (*in*, *on*)／친구의 취직을 위해서 ～ help a friend land a job.

**힘없이** feebly; droopingly; dejectedly／그는 질문에 ～ 대답했다 He answered the question helplessly[weakly].

**힘입다** owe; be indebted to (*a person*) for (*a matter*); enjoy (*a person's*) favor／나의 성공은 그의 조력에 힘입은 바 크다 My success is chiefly due to his help.／그는 부친에게 힘입은 바 크다 He owes much to his father., He is much indebted to his father.／아버지의 교육에 힘입어 성공하다 owe *one's* success to *one's* father's education.

**힘있다** ①《힘세다》(be) strong; have strength ②《문장·어조가》(be) forceful; powerful; heavy／힘있는 어조 a heavy accent ③《지위·권력으로 보아》(be) influential; carry weight; have power／일을 이루게 하는 데 힘이 있다 carry enough weight to see a plan trough.

**힘주다** devote *one's* strengh (*to*); concentrate (*upon*); put stress (*on*).

**힘줄** ①《근육》a tendon; a sinew; a muscle ②《섬유》a fiber; a string ③《혈관》a vein／～이 당기다 have a strain in a muscle／～이 굵은 팔 a sinewy arm／～이 많다 be stringly; be fibrous.

**힘줌말** an intensive[emphatic] word.

**힘차다** (be) forcible; powerful; (be) full of strength; (be) energetic 《벅차다》hard; difficult; tough; laborious／힘차게 forcibly; strongly; powerfully; vigorously／힘찬 일 a tough job; a laborious task／힘찬 표현 a forcible expression／힘찬 연설 a powerful speech／힘차게 잡아당기다 give a strong pull.

**힝** clearing *one's* nose.

# 불규칙 변화표

## 1. 형용사 · 부사

| 원 급 | 비 교 급 | 최 상 급 |
|---|---|---|
| bad 나쁜 | worse | worst |
| badly 나쁘게 | worse | worst |
| evil 사악한 | worse | worst |
| far 먼 ((거리) | farther | farthest |
| ((정도) | further | furthest |
| good 좋은 | better | best |
| ill 나쁜 | worse | worst |
| late 늦은 ((시간) | later | latest |
| ((순서) | latter | last |
| little 적은 | less | least |
|  | lesser (적은 쪽의) |  |
| many 수가 많은 | more | most |
| much 양이 많은 | more | most |
| old 늙은 ((노약·신구) | older | oldest |
| ((형제·자매) | elder, older 《미》 | eldest, oldest 《미》 |
| well 잘 | better | best |

## 2. 동 사

(현대 미국어 용법에 의한 변화를 주체로 보였다. 고닥은 중요한 단어. 뭘기체는 드물게 쓰는 단어. 현재형이 2음절 이상인 단어에는 특히 액센트의 위치를 표시하였다.)

| 현 재 | 과 거 | 과 거 분 사 | 현재분사 |
|---|---|---|---|
| **A** abide 머물다, 살다 | abode, abided | abode, abided |  |
| **arise** 일어나다, 생기다 | **arose** | **arisen** [ərízn] |  |
| **awake** 눈을 뜨다 | **awoke, awaked** | **awaked, awoke** |  |
| **B** backbite 험구를 하다 | backbit | backbitten, backbit |  |
| backslide 뒷걸음질 치다 | backslid | backslidden, backslid |  |
| **be (am, is, are)** …이다 | **was, were** | **been** |  |
| **bear**¹ 견디다, 나르다 | **bore** | **borne** |  |
| **bear**² 낳다 | **bore** | **borne**, 《수동》 **be born**, |  |
| **beat** 치다 | **beat** | **beaten** ⌊be **borne** by |  |
| **become** …이 되다 | **became** | **become** |  |
| befall 일어나다, 생기다 | befell | befallen |  |
| beget 생기게 하다, 초래하다 | begot | begotten, begot | -tting |
| **begin** 시작하다, 시작되다 | **began** | **begun** | **-nning** |
| begird 둘러싸다, 에두르다 | begirt, begirded | begirt, begirded |  |
| behold 보다, 바라보다 | beheld | beheld |  |
| **bend** 구부리다, 구부러지다 | **bent** | **bent** |  |
| bereave 빼앗다, 잃게 하다 | bereaved, bereft | bereaved, bereft |  |
| beseech 청하다, 구하다 | besought | besought |  |
| beset 포위하다, 둘러싸다 | beset | beset | -tting |
| bespeak 미리 요구하다 | bespoke | bespoken, bespoke |  |
| bespread 전면에 퍼지게 하다 | bespread | bespread |  |
| bestrew 흩뿌리다 | bestrewed | bestrewed, bestrewn |  |
| bestride 걸터 타다 | bestrode | bestridden, 《+영》 |  |
|  |  | bestrid, bestrode |  |
| bet 걸다, 내기를 하다 | bet, betted | bet, betted | -tting |
| betake …로 향하다, 가다, 의 | betook | betaken |  |
| bethink 숙고하다 ⌊지하다 | bethought | bethought |  |
| **bid** 명하다 | **bade, bid, bad**《+영》 | **badden, bid** | **-dding** |
| **bind** 묶다, 동이다 | **bound** | **bound** |  |
| **bite** 물다, 물어 뜯다 | **bit** | **bitten, bit** |  |
| bleed 피가 나오다 | bled | bled |  |
| blend 혼합하다 | blended, blent | blended, blent |  |

| 현재 | 과거 | 과거분사 | 현재분사 |
|---|---|---|---|
| **bless** 은총을 내리다 | blessed, blest [blest] | blessed, blest [blest] | |
| **blow** 바람이 불다, 꽃이 피다 | blew | blown | |
| **break** 깨뜨리다, 부서지다 | broke | broken, broke (+영) | |
| **breed** 새끼를 낳다 | bred | bred | |
| **bring** 갖고 오다 | brought | brought | |
| **broadcast** 방송하다 | -casted | -casted, broadcast (영) | |
| **build** 세우다, 조립하다 | built | built | |
| **burn** 타다, 태우다 | burnt, burned | burnt, burned | |
| **burst** 터지다, 터지게 하다 | burst | burst | |
| **buy** 사다 | bought | bought | |
| C **can** …할 수 있다 | could [kud] | —— | |
| **cast** 던지다 | cast | cast | |
| **catch** 잡다 | caught [kɔ:t] | caught [kɔ:t] | |
| **chide** 꾸짖다 | chided, chid | chided, chid, chidden | |
| **choose** 가리다, 선택하다 | chose | chosen | |
| **cleave** 쪼개(지)다, 갈라지다 | cleft, cleaved, clove | cleft, cleaved, cloven | |
| **cling** 달라붙다 | clung | clung | |
| **clothe** 옷을 입다 | clothed, clad | clothed, clad | |
| **come** 오다 | came | come | |
| **cost** 비용이 들다 | cost | cost | |
| **creep** 기다 | crept | crept | |
| **crow** (수탉이) 울다 | crowed, crew | crowed | |
| **curse** 저주하다 | cursed, curst | cursed, curst | |
| **cut** 자르다, 베다 | cut | cut | -tting |
| D **dare** 감히 …하다 | dared, (+영) durst | dared | |
| **deal** 다루다, 관계하다 | dealt | dealt | |
| **dig** 파다 | dug | dug | -gging |
| **do, does** 하다, 행하다 | did | done | |
| **draw** 긋다, 그리다 | drew | drawn | |
| **dream** 꿈꾸다 | dreamed, dreamt [dremt] | dreamed, dreamt [dremt] | |
| **drink** 마시다 | drank | drunk | |
| **drive** 쫓다, 차를 몰다 | drove | driven [drívn] | |
| **dwell** 살다 | dwelt, dwelled | dwelt, dwelled | |
| E **eat** 먹다 | ate [미 eit / 영 et] | eaten | |
| F **fall** 떨어지다 | fell | fallen | |
| **feed** 음식을 주다 | fed | fed | |
| **feel** 느끼다 | felt | felt | |
| **fight** 싸우다 | fought | fought | |
| **find** 발견하다 | found | found | |
| **flee** 도망치다 | fled | fled | |
| **fling** 내던지다 | flung | flung | |
| **fly** 날다 | flew | flown | |
| **forbear** 억제하다, 삼가다 | forbore | forborne | |
| **forbid** 금하다 | forbade, forbad | forbidden | -dding |
| **forecast** 예측하다 | forecast, forecasted | forecast, forecasted | |
| **forego** 버리다, 그만두다 | forewent | foregone | |
| **foreknow** 미리 알다 | foreknew | foreknown | |
| **foresee** 예견하다 | foresaw | foreseen | |
| **foretell** 예고하다 | foretold | foretold | |
| **forget** 잊다 | forgot | forgotten, forgot | -tting |
| **forgive** 용서하다 | forgave | forgiven | |
| **forsake** 저버리다 | forsook | forsaken | |
| **forswear** 맹세코 그만두다 | forswore | forsworn | |
| **freeze** 얼다, 얼리다 | froze | frozen | |
| G **gainsay** 반박하다 | gainsaid | gainsaid | |
| **get** 얻다 | got | got, gotten | -tting |
| **gild** 금박을 입히다 | gilded, gilt | gilded, gilt | |
| **gird** 허리를 띠 따위로 두르다 | girt, girded | girt, girded | |

| 현　　　　재 | 과　　거 | 과　거　분　사 | 현재분사 |
|---|---|---|---|
| give 주다 | gave | given | |
| go 가다 | went | gone | |
| grave (모양을) 새기다 | graved | graven, graved | |
| grind (갈아서) 가루로 만들다 | ground | ground | |
| grow 성장하다 | grew | grown | |
| H hamstring 절름발이를 만들다 | -strung, 《+영》 | -strung,《+영》-stringed | |
| hang 걸다, 매달다 | hung　　　└-stringed | hung | |
| have, has 갖다 | had | had | |
| hear 듣다 | heard | heard | |
| heave 〖항해〗 감아 올리다, 던 | hove | hove | |
| hew 베어 넘기다　　　└지다 | hewed | hewn, hewed | |
| hide 숨기다, 숨다 | hid | hidden, hid | |
| hit 맞히다, 때리다 | hit | hit | -tting |
| hold 잡다, 유지하다 | held | held | |
| hurt 상처내다 | hurt | hurt | |
| I inlay 박아 넣다 | inlaid | inlaid | |
| inset 끼워넣다 | inset, 《+영》 insetted | inset, 《+영》 insetted | -tting |
| K keep 유지하다 | kept | kept | |
| kneel [ni:l] 무릎을 꿇다 | knelt [nelt], kneeled | knelt [nelt], kneeled | |
| knit 짜다 | knitted, knit | knitted, knit | -tting |
| know 알다 | knew | known | |
| L lade 짐을 싣다 | laded | laden, laded | |
| lay 놓다, 눕히다 | laid | laid | |
| lead 이끌다 | led | led | |
| lean 기대다 | leaned, leant [lent] | leaned, leant [lent] | |
| leap (껑충) 뛰다 | leaped, leapt [《미》 li:pt / 《영》 lept] | leaped, leapt [《미》 li:pt / lept] | |
| learn 배우다, 알다 | learned, learnt | learned, learnt | |
| leave 떠나다 | left | left | |
| lend 빌리다 | lent | lent | |
| let …시키다 | let | let | -tting |
| lie 드러눕다, 가로놓이다 | lay | lain | lying |
| light 빛나다, 내리다 | lighted, lit | lighted, lit | |
| lose 잃다 | lost | lost | |
| M make 만들다 | made | made | |
| may …일지도 모르다 | might | —— | |
| mean 의미를 갖다 | meant [ment] | meant [ment] | |
| meet 만나다 | met | met | |
| methinks …라 생각되다 | methought | —— | |
| misgive 염려케 하다 | misgave | misgiven | |
| mislay 잘못 놓다 | mislaid | mislaid | |
| mislead 그릇 판단케 하다 | misled | misled | |
| misread 잘못 읽다 | misread [misréd] | misread [misréd] | |
| misspell 잘못 쓰다 | misspelled, misspelt | misspelled, misspelt | |
| mistake 틀리다 | mistook | mistaken | |
| misunderstand 오해하다 | misunderstood | misunderstood | |
| mow 베다 | mowed | mowed, mown | |
| must¹ …하지 않으면 안 되다 | had to, must | have had to | |
| must² …에 틀림없다 | must have+*p.p.* | —— | |
| O ought to …하여야 하다 | ought to have+*p.p.* | —— | |
| outbid 비싼 값을 매기다 | outbade, outbid | outbidden, outbid | -dding |
| outdo …보다 낫다 | outdid | outdone | |
| outgo …보다 빨리 가다 | outwent | ontgone | |
| outgrow …보다 크게 되다 | outgrew | outgrown | |
| outlay 소비하다, 쓰다 | outlaid | outlaid | |
| outride …보다 빨리 타고 가 다, 앞지르다 | outrode | outridden | |
| outrun …보다 빨리 달리다 | outran | outrun | -nning |
| outshine 보다 빛나다 | outshone | outshone | |

불규칙 변화표 1138

| 현재 | 과거 | 과거분사 | 현재분사 |
|---|---|---|---|
| outspread 펼치다, 퍼지다 | outspread | outspread | |
| outwear …보다 오래 가다 [견 | outwore | outworn | |
| overbear 압도하다   ㄴ디다] | overbore | overborne | |
| overblow 날려 버리다 | overblew | overblown | |
| overcast 어둡게 하다 | overcast | overcast | |
| overcome 정복하다 | overcame | overcome | |
| overdo 도를 지나치다 | overdid | overdone | |
| overdraw 과장하여 말하다 | overdrew | overdrawn | |
| overdrink 과음하다 | overdrank | overdrunk | |
| overeat 과식하다 | overate | overeaten | |
| overgrow 전면에 자라다 《잡초 따위가》 | overgrew | overgrown | |
| overhang …위에 걸치다 | overhung | overhung | |
| overhear 언뜻[귓결에] 듣다 | overheard | overheard | |
| overlay 들씌우다 | overlaid | overlaid | |
| overleap 뛰어 넘다 | overleaped, overleapt | overleaped, overleapt | |
| overlie …위에 눕다 | overlay | overlain | -lying |
| overpay 더 많이 지불하다 | overpaid | overpaid | |
| override 짓밟다 | overrode | overridden | |
| overrun 침략하다 | overran | overrun | -nning |
| oversee 감독하다 | oversaw | overseen | |
| oversell 너무 팔다 | oversold | oversold | |
| overset …을 뒤엎다 | overset | overset | -tting |
| overshoot 지나치다 | overshot | overshot | |
| oversleep 너무 오래 자다 | overslept | overslept | |
| overspend 낭비하다 | overspent | overspent | |
| overspread 온면에 덮다 | overspread | overspread | |
| overtake 따라 붙다 | overtook | overtaken | |
| overthrow 뒤집어 엎다 | overthrew | overthrown | |
| overwork 지나치게 일하다 | -worked, overwrought | -worked, overwrought | |
| overwrite 너무 쓰다 | overwrote | overwritten | |
| P partake (얼마큼) 마시다, 먹다 | partook | partaken | |
| pass 통과하다, 통과시키다 | passed | passed, *past* | |
| pay 지불하다 | paid | paid | |
| pen 가두다 | penned, pent | penned, pent | -nning |
| prove 증명하다 | proved | proved, proven | |
| put 놓다 | put | put | -tting |
| Q quit 포기하다, 그만두다 | quitted, quit | quitted, quit | -tting |
| R radiocast 라디오로 방송하다 | radiocast, radiocasted | radiocast, radiocasted | |
| read [ri:d] 읽다 | read [red] | read [red] | |
| reave 약탈하다 | reaved, reft | reaved, reft | |
| rebuild [ribíld] 재건하다 | rebuilt | rebuilt | |
| recast [riká:st] 고쳐 만들다 | recast | recast | |
| relay 교체시키다 | relaid | relaid | |
| rend 찢다, 분열시키다 | rent | rent | |
| repay 환불하다, 보답하다 | repaid | repaid | |
| reread [riri:d] 다시 읽다 | reread [-réd] | reread [-réd] | |
| resell [risél] 전매하다 | resold | resold | |
| retake [ritéik] 회복하다 | retook | retaken | |
| rewrite [riráit] 다시 쓰다 | rewrote | rewritten | |
| rid 면하게 하다 | rid, ridded | rid, ridded | -dding |
| ride 말 따위를 타다 | rode | ridden | |
| ring 울리다 | rang [ræŋ] | rung [rʌŋ] | |
| rise 올리다, 올라가다 | rose | risen [rizn] | |
| rive [raiv] 잡아 뜯다 | rived | rived, riven [rívn] | |
| roughcast [rʌ́f-] 초벽을 치다, …의 대강 줄거리를 세우다 | roughcast | roughcast | |
| run [rʌn] 달리다 | ran [ræn] | run [rʌn] | -nning |
| S saw 톱으로 썰다 | sawed | sawed, sawn | |

# 불규칙 변화표

| 현재 | 과거 | 과거분사 | 현재분사 |
|---|---|---|---|
| say 말하다 | said [sed] | said [sed] | |
| see 보다 | saw | seen | |
| seek …을 구하다 | sought [sɔːt] | sought [sɔːt] | |
| sell 팔다 | sold | sold | |
| send 보내다 | sent | sent | |
| set 배치하다, 설치하다 | set | set | -tting |
| sew [sou] 꿰매다 | sewed | sewed, sewn | |
| shake 떨다, 흔들다 | shook [ʃuk] | shaken | |
| shall …일 것이다 | should [ʃud] | —— | |
| shave 면도하다 | shaved | shaved, *shaven* | |
| shear 양 따위의 털을 깎다 | sheared | sheared, shorn | |
| shed 흘리다 | shed | shed | -dding |
| shine 반짝이다 | shone | shone | |
| shoe 말에 편자를 박다 | shod | shod, shodden | |
| shoot 쏘다, 발사하다 | shot | shot | |
| show 보이다, 증명하다 | showed | shown, showed | |
| shred 조각을 내다 | shredded, shred | shredded, shred | -dding |
| shrink 오그라들다, 움츠리다 | shrank, shrunk | shrunk, shrunken | |
| shut 닫다 | shut | shut | -tting |
| sing 노래하다 | sang, sung [sæŋ, sʌŋ] | sung [sʌŋ] | |
| sink 가라앉다, 가라앉히다 | sank, sunk | sunk, *sunken* | |
| sit 앉다 | sat | sat | -tting |
| slay 죽이다, 살해하다 | slew | slain | |
| sleep 자다 | slept | slept | |
| slide 미끄러지다[뜨리다] | slid | slid, slidden | |
| sling 던지다 | slung | slung | |
| slink 살금살금 걷다 | slunk | slunk | |
| slit 가늘게 베다, 찢다 | slit | slit | -tting |
| smell 냄새를 맡다, 냄새 나다 | smelled, smelt | smelled, smelt | |
| smite 세게 치다 | smote | smitten, smit, smote | |
| sow 종자를 뿌리다 | sowed | sown, sowed | |
| speak 말하다 | spoke | spoken | |
| speed 급히 가다, 서둘게 하다 | sped, speeded | sped, speeded | |
| spell 철자하다 | spelled, spelt | spelled, spelt | |
| spellbind 주박(呪縛)하다 | spellbound | spellbound | |
| spend 소비하다, 쓰다 | spent | spent | |
| spill 흘리다, 흐르다 | spilled, spilt | spilled, spilt | |
| spin 실을 잣다 | spun | spun | -nning |
| spit 침을 뱉다 | spat, spit | spat, spit | -tting |
| split 찢다, 갈라지다 | split | split | -tting |
| spoil 망쳐놓다, 망치다 | spoiled, spoilt | spoild, spoilt | |
| spread 펴다, 펼치다 | spread | spread | |
| spring 뛰다, 뛰게 하다 | sprang, sprung | sprung | |
| squat 웅크리다 | squatted, squat | squatted, squat | -tting |
| stand 서다, 세우다 | stood | stood | |
| stave 통널을 떼내다 | staved, stove | staved, stove | |
| steal 훔치다 | stole | stolen | |
| stick 찌르다, 고집하다 | stuck | stuck | |
| sting 찌르다, 자극하다 | stung | stung | |
| stink 악취를 풍기다 | stank, stunk | stunk | |
| strew 흩뿌리다, 뿌리다 | strewed | strewed, strewn | |
| stride 활보하다 | strode | stridden, strid | |
| strike 치다 | struck | struck, *stricken* | |
| string 실로 꿰다 | strung | strung | |
| strive 노력하다 | strove | striven [strívn] | |
| sunburn 볕에 태우다 | sunburned, sunburnt | sunburned, sunburnt | |
| swear 신명에게 맹세하다 | swore | sworn | |
| sweat [swet] 땀을 흘리다 | sweat, sweated | sweat, sweated | |
| sweep 쓸다, 청소하다 | swept | swept | |

| 현재 | 과거 | 과거분사 | 현재분사 |
|---|---|---|---|
| swell 부풀다, 부풀리다 | swelled | swelled, swollen | |
| swim 수영하다 | swam | swum | -mming |
| swing 흔들리다, 흔들다 | swung | swung | |
| T take 취하다, 타다, 먹다, 마시다 | took | taken | |
| teach 가르치다, 교육하다 | taught | taught | |
| tear [tɛər] 찢다, 잡아찢다 | tore | torn | |
| telecast 텔레비전 방송을 하다 | telecast, telecasted | telecast, telecasted | |
| tell 말하다, 알리다 | told | told | |
| think 생각하다, …라 여기다 | thought | thought | |
| thrive 번창하다, 무성하다 | throve, thrived | thrived, thriven | |
| throw 던지다 | threw | thrown [θrívn] | |
| thrust 밀다 | thrust | thrust | |
| tread 걷다, 밟다 | trod | trodden, trod | |
| U unbend 똑바로 펴다 | unbent | unbent | |
| unbind (매듭을) 풀다 | unbound | unbound | |
| underbid …보다 싸게 하다 | underbid | underbid, underbidden | |
| undergo 경험하다 | underwent | undergone | |
| underlay …의 밑에 깔다 | underlaid | underlaid | |
| underlie …의 밑에 있다, 눕다 | underlay | underlain | -lying |
| undersell …보다 싼 값에 팔다 | undersold | undersold | |
| understand 이해하다 | understood | understood | |
| undertake 인수하다, 떠맡다 | undertook | undertaken | |
| underwrite 밑에 기명하다 | underwrote | underwritten | |
| undo 원상대로 하다 | undid | undone | |
| ungird …의 띠를 끄르다 | ungirt, ungirded | ungirt, ungirded | |
| unlay 꼬인 것을 바로잡다 | unlaid | unlaid | |
| upset 뒤집어 엎다 | upset | upset | -tting |
| W wake (잠을) 깨다, 깨우다 | waked, woke | waked, woken, (+영) woke | |
| waylay 매복하다 | waylaid | waylaid | |
| wear 몸에 지니고[입고] 있다 | wore | worn | |
| weave 베를 짜다, 엮다 | wove | woven, wove | |
| wed …와 결혼하다 | wedded | wedded, wed | -dding |
| weep 울다 | wept | wept | |
| will …할 것이다 | would [wud] | —— | |
| win 이기다, 얻다 | won [wʌn] | won [wʌn] | -nning |
| wind [waind] 감다 | wound [waund] | wound [waund] | |
| withdraw 움츠리다 | withdrew | withdrawn | |
| withhold 보류하다 | withheld | withheld | |
| withstand 저항하다, 반항하다 | withstood | withstood | |
| work 일하다, 공부하다 | worked, wrought[rɔːt] | worked, wrought[rɔːt] | |
| wrap 싸다, 감싸다 | wrapped, wrapt | wrapped, wrapt | -pping |
| wring 짜다, 짜내다 | wrung | wrung | |
| write 쓰다 | wrote | written | |

## 영문 전보 쓰는 법

영어 전보를 칠 때 가장 주의하여야 할 점은 「간결 명료」하여야 하는 것이다. 특히 해외 전보에서는 한 낱말이라도 비싼 요금을 지불해야 되므로 용건에 불필요한 단어는 생략한다. 그러므로 쓸 때나 읽을 때나 착오를 일으키지 않도록 많은 주의를 해야 한다.

다음에 보통 생략되는 단어 및 주의를 요하는 점 등을 언급하겠다.

① **경칭(敬稱)·의례적인 자구(字句)는 생략.**
② **주어 1인칭은 생략. 2인칭도 때로는 생략.**
  I LEAVE FOR BUSAN TOMORROW
  (내일 부산으로 출발)⇒LEAVING FOR BUSAN TOMORROW
  【주의】현재분사는 「가까운 미래」를, 원형은 「명령」을 나타낸다. cf. TELEGRAPH FIVE THOUSAND [WON] (5천원 전신환 보내라)
③ **관사·전치사·형용사·관계 대명사 따위라도 뜻이 통하기만 하면 생략된다.**
  MOTHER LEFT [BY THE] SIX FIVE TRAIN(모친 6시 5분 기차로 출발)
④ **구문·어구는 가장 간결한 것을 고르며, 긴 절이나 구는 피한다.**
  IF YOU DO NOT DECIDE AT ONCE YOT MAY SUFFER A GREAT LOSS(만일 곧 결정하지 않으면 큰 손실을 받을지 모름)⇒ HESITATION MAY CAUSE YOU GREAT LOSS

⑤ 그 외에 약속으로, 피어리드는 STOP, 코머는 COMMA, 의문 부호는 /Q/, 「"」는 QUOTE, 「"」는 UNQUOTE라 한다.

이상 설명한 것은 Plain language (보통어)의 경우이며, 그 외에 Code telegram(암호 전보)가 있다. 앞서 말한 보통의 전보는 우리말처럼 될수록 간단하고 알기 쉽게 작성해야 한다. 상용(商用) 또는 특수 분야의 전보에서는 편의에 따라 보통 영어 외에 숫자·약어·약호 따위를 만들어 사용한다.

〈상용 약어의 보기〉
**KAL** Korean Air Lines
**SMC** Shinjin Motor Company
**B/L** Bill of Lading
**COD** Cash on Delivery
**L/C** Letter of Credit

또 Comma(,)나 Period(.) 따위의 Punctuation이나 Underline(밑줄), Parenthesis(괄호) 따위도 한 단어로 계산된다는 것을 알아두어야 한다.

〈보통어 전보의 보기〉
1. RETURNED SAFE THANKS KINDNESS THERE
   (무사히 도착 신세 많았음 감사드림)
2. CONGRATULATE MARRIAGE
   (결혼 축하함)
3. LEAVE KIMPO 7:30 MONDAY MORNING MEET FRISCO
   (월요일 오전 7시 반 김포 출발 프리스코 (San Francisco) 마중 바람)
4. MOTHER SERIOUSLY ILL COME IMMEDIATELY
   (모친 위독 곧 오라)
5. EARTHQUAKE NO DAMAGE
   (지진 피해 없음)
6. HEAVY DEMAND SHIP IMMEDIATELY
   (원매자 많음 곧 보내라)
7. STOP SHIPPING DEMAND SMALL
   (원매자 적음 선적 중지 바람)
8. CABLE LOWEST PRICE PROMT SHIPMENT
   (선적의 최저 가격 타전 급요망)
9. GOODS ORDERED OUT WITHIN WEEK NEW GOODS ARRIVE
   (주문품 현재 품절 1주내 신품 도착 예정)
10. CABLE STOCK
    (재고품 수량 전보로 송신 요망)

## 게시·간판·광고문 실례

| | |
|---|---|
| 갈고리 사용을 금함 | Use no hooks. |
| 갈아타지 못함 | No transfer. |
| 강매(强賣) 사절 | |
| | No sale to be forced on any at this door./No hawkers. |
| 개인 교수합니다 | Private lessons given. |
| 개인용, 사실(私室) | Private. |
| 개 조심 | Beware of the dog. |
| 깨지는 물건, 취급 주의 | |
| | Fragile-Handle with care. |
| 건조한 데 보관할 것 | Keep dry. |
| 경적 | Sound horn. |
| 경품 증정 | Premiums offered. |
| 고장 | Out of order. |
| 공사중 | Under construction. |
| 공중 전화 | Public telephone. / Call box. |
| 금연 | No smoking. |
| 금일 개점 | Opened today. |
| 금일 매진 | All sold out today. |
| 금일] 휴업 | Closed (today). |
| 금일 휴진 | No consultation today. |
| 기중(忌中) | In mourning. |
| 담배 꽁초[버리는 곳] | Cigaret butts. |
| 마시지 못함 | Unfit for drinking. |
| 막혔음, 통과 못함 | |
| | No trespassing. /Dead End. |
| 매품(賣品) | For sale. |
| 면회 사절 | Interview declined. |
| 무용자 출입 금지 | |
| | No admittance except on business. |

|  |  |
|---|---|
| 문을 닫으시오 | Shut the door after you. |
| 바겐 세일, 염가 특매 | Bargain sale day. |
| 발 밑 조심 | Watch your step. |
| 반문 사절 | No visitors allowed. |
| 벽보 첨부 금지 | Post no bills. |
| 변소 | Toilet 《공중 변소》 Lavatory./W.C./ Comfort station; Rest room 〈미〉/ 《여자용 변소》 Ladies. |
| 보행자 통행 금지 | Closed to pedestrians. |
| 불조심 | Beware of fire. |
| 비매품(非賣品) | Not for sale. |
| 비상구 | Fire escape./ Emergency exit. |
| 음료수 | Fit for drinking. |
| 일방 통행 | One side only./ One way only. |
| 임시 휴업 | Closed temporarily. |
| 입구 | Entrance./Way in. |
| 입장 개방 | Open to public. |
| 입장 무료 | Admission free. |
| 입장 환영 | Welcome to all visitors. |
| 작업중, 운전중(공장 따위) | In operation. |
| 잔디에 들어가지 마시오 | Keep off the grass. |
| 재고 정리 염가 판매 | Clearance sale. |
| 접수계[원] | Receptionist. |
| 정지선 | Stop line. |
| 정지, 앞에 커브 있음 | Stop, curve ahead. |
| 정찰제, 에누리 없음 | No reduction allowed. |
| 제차 통행 금지 | Closed to all vehicles. |
| 조용히 | Quiet. |
| [좌석] 만원 | Room for standing only. |
| 주의 | Caution. |
| 주차 금지 | No parking. |
| 주차장 | Parking area. |
| 천천히, 서행 | Go slow. |
| 초심자 환영 | Welcome to beginners. |
| 추월 금지 | No passing. |
| 출구 | Exit [égzit, éksit]./Way out. |
| 출입 금지 | Off limits. |
| 출입 자유 | On limits. |
| 침을 뱉지 마시오 | No spitting. |
| X마스 세일 | X-mas sale. |
| 탈모 | Please remove your hats. |
| 통행 금지 | No thoroughfare. |
| 특매품 | Bargain special. |
| 팔린 물건 | Sold. |
| 페인트 주의 | Wet[Fresh] paint. |
| 피아노 교수 | Piano lessons given. |
| 학교 앞, 서행 | School, go slow. |
| 화재 경보기 | Fire alarm. |
| 회의중 | Now in session. |
| 회전 금지 | No turn./ No U turn. |
| 횡단 금지 | No crossing. |
| 횡단 보도 | Pedestrians' crossing. |
| 휴지 버리지 마시오 | No dumping. |
| 빈 차 | For hire. |
| 사용 금지 | Not in use. |
| [상품] 목록 무료 증정 | Catalog offered free. |
| 셋집 | house for rent./House to let. |
| 셋집 원함 | Wanted to rent. |
| 소매치기 조심 | Beware of pickpockets. |
| 소변 엄금 | No nuisance. |
| 소화전 | Fire hydrant [háidrənt]. |
| 속도 제한(시속 40킬로) | Speed limit; 40 k.p.h. |
| 손 대지 말 것 | Hands off. |
| 수리중 | Under repairs. |
| 수송부 | Motor pool. |
| 수예・편물 | Handicraft, embroidery & knitting. |
| 수하물 보관소 | Parcel room./ Cloakroom. |
| 습기 주의 | Guard against damp. |
| 승무원 외 출입 금지 | The train crew only. |
| 신을 벗으시오 | Shoes off. |
| 안내 | Inquiry. |
| 안내소 | Information. |
| 안전 지대 | Safety zone. |
| 야간 영업 | Staying open. |
| 야간 영업함 | To stay open [till ten]. |
| 연말 대매출 | Year-end sale. |
| 영어 교수 | Instruction given in English. |
| 영업 시간 | Business hours. |
| 영업중 | In operation. |
| 옆문을 이용하시압 | side entrance. |
| 예약 필(豫約畢) | Reserved. |
| 요금 선불 | Fare forward. |
| 우측 통행 | Keep to the right. |
| 우회하시오 | Detour. |
| 운임 선불 | Freight forward. |
| 운전석 출입 금지 | Keep out from driver's seat. |
| 위험 | Danger. |
| 위험, 고압 전류 | Warning, high voltage. |
| 위험물 지입 엄금 | Inflammables and explosives strictly prohibited to be brought in. |

## 새 스탠다드 韓英辭典

| | | | |
|---|---|---|---|
| 重版 印刷●2000年 | 10月 | 1日 | |
| 重版 發行●2000年 | 10月 | 5日 | |

編著者●明文堂 辭書部
發行者●金　　東　　求
發行處●明　　文　　堂
　　　　서울특별시 종로구 안국동 17~8
　　　　대체　010041-31-0516013
　　　　전화　(영) 733-3039, 734-4798
　　　　　　　(편) 733-4748
　　　　FAX 734-9209
　　　　등록　1977. 11. 19. 제1~148호

● 낙장 및 파본은 교환해 드립니다.
● 불허복제 · 판권 본사 소유.

값 20,000원
ISBN 89-7270-619-1　11740